The STUDENT BIBLE

Notes by Philip Yancey and Tim Stafford

New International Version

Zondervan Publishing House
Grand Rapids, Michigan 49530, USA

The Student Bible, New International Version®
Copyright © 1986, 1992, 1996 by Zondervan Publishing House
All rights reserved

Requests for information should be addressed to
The Zondervan Corporation
Grand Rapids, Michigan, 49530

The Holy Bible, New International Version
Copyright © 1973, 1978, 1984 by International Bible Society

Library of Congress Catalog Card Number 86-50028

Published by Zondervan Publishing House
Grand Rapids, Michigan 49530, U.S.A.
http://www.zondervan.com

Printed in the United States of America
All rights reserved

96 97 98 99 00 01 02 8 7 6 5 4 3 2   Q

Contents

The Books of the Old Testament

The Books of the New Testament

Alphabetical Order
OF THE BOOKS OF THE BIBLE

The books of the New Testament are indicated by *italics*.

Why the Student Bible?

THE BIBLE IS THE MOST important book ever written—a gift to us from God himself. Styles and tastes change, but people all through history have recognized the Bible's uniqueness. They have treated it with special reverence, yet, strangely, even people who value the Bible often fail to read it. Most Americans believe the Bible to be from God. But Gallop polls reveal that only a small percentage of them can name basic Biblical facts, such as four of the Ten Commandments. Their Bibles sit somewhere on a shelf or coffee table, impressive to look at, but unread.

Christians we meet mention repeatedly their guilt about not reading the Bible consistently. They believe in the Bible. They expect to find help there. But they do not read the Bible nearly as often as they think they should.

Troubled by this reality, we began work on *The Student Bible*. Our aim: to produce an edition of the New International Version of the Bible that ordinary people could—and would—read on a regular, sustained basis. We used modern research techniques to try to find an answer to the question, "What keeps you from reading the Bible?" We discovered three main reasons. In developing this edition of the Bible, we worked hard to address those three reasons.

"I Get Discouraged"

Simple discouragement was the most common reason we heard for not reading the Bible. Many people we surveyed had tried to read the Bible regularly, but such experiments usually ended in failure.

The Bible is a big book—about 1,000 pages long. People who plan to read through the whole Bible starting with Genesis often get bogged down somewhere around Numbers or Deuteronomy. Fatigue sets in.

Other people never even start a reading plan. With busy schedules and limited confidence, they feel sure they'll fail such a project. Instead, they occasionally turn to familiar passages from the Gospel of John or the Psalms. They wouldn't know where to start venturing out into unfamiliar books.

We spent much time and research trying to find an answer to the discouragement problem. The result: the **3-Track Reading Plan**, which recognizes that people approach the Bible at different levels. All three "tracks" suggest reading one chapter a day—just 5 or 10 minutes, for most readers.

Track 1 requires a commitment of two weeks at a time, reading one chapter a day. By following it, a reader can encounter some of the most fundamental parts of the Bible. Pages 7-8 present two-week selections on Jesus and Paul, and a two-week sampling of the Old Testament. Pages 15-16 list a variety of further options depending on your personal interests. Just a few hours of investment can yield a solid introduction into the best of books.

Track 2 represents the next level of commitment. It takes six months, reading about one chapter a day. In Track 2 you will read at least one chapter from every book in the Bible. When you finish, you will have read the best-known, most-quoted, easiest-to-understand portions of the Bible. (The Zondervan book *Discovering God* offers a more detailed overview of the Bible based on Track 2.)

Track 3 includes every word of the Bible. Reading about one chapter a day, you devote three years to reading the entire Bible.

We believe the 3-track plan offers a handy, realistic method for approaching the Bible. It builds in several levels of success to combat the discouragement that afflicts Bible readers. A complete description for the 3-track plan follows on the next pages. In addition, the How to Read section in the Introduction to each Bible book uses the icon above and describes how the 3-track plan fits into that book.

"I Can't Understand It"

Many readers grow up with very little exposure to the Bible. They may never have heard of Goliath or Abraham. Often they ask, "What is the point of reading about spears and chariots a' village wells and leprosy?"

Because it was written several thousand years ago, the Bible presents a culture gap. It mentions hard-to-pronounce names and refers to many outdated customs. For most readers, the Bible is the most ancient book in their library.

Most of us need some coaching on how to jump the 2,000-year gap back to when the Bible was written. *The Student Bible* addresses this problem with hundreds of additional notes scattered throughout the book. Each of these features is marked with a distinctive design element or icon.

Introductions: Each of the 66 books of the Bible is preceded by an Introduction that gives crucial background on the book and tells why it was written. By reading these Introductions, you'll gain a sense of how one particular book is different from, and yet fits together with, every other book in the Bible. In addition, you'll get clues to each book's contemporary relevance.

Insights: Throughout *The Student Bible,* you'll find short articles marked with this "Insight" icon. Written in the style of a modern magazine article, Insights include important background information right in the Bible, near the passage they shed light on. They condense the material that, in our judgment, will most help you understand and find meaning in the Bible. At the end of each Insight, **Life Questions** help relate the passage to practical life situations.

Profiles: We have selected "100 People You Should Know" in the Bible. Profiles marked with this icon give background material to help introduce these people. In a few cases these Profiles are combined with Insights or are found in a book's Introduction; these, too, are marked with the Profiles icon. Each of these Profiles also features a **Life Question**.

Highlights: Much shorter notes, marked off from the text in this manner, appear frequently in *The Student Bible.* These explain confusing verses, point out interesting facts, and, in effect, highlight something in the passage that might get easily overlooked. They're designed to catch your attention and draw you to read the Bible more closely.

"I Can't Find It"

"I spend a lot of time just flipping through the Bible, looking for something," we were told again and again. Many Bible readers are searching for help on specific issues—but they don't know where to find it.

Everybody has heard of something in the Bible—the Ten Commandments, the Golden Rule, the story of Daniel in the lions' den. But how do you know where to look for them? The Bible is too large just to flip through on a random search.

To aid in such a search, this edition of *The Student Bible* has greatly expanded a section called "**Where to Find It**." It appears at the back of this book, just before the maps section. You'll notice that the side of the book is marked with a colored tab that indicates this section's location. We hope this becomes the first place you turn when you want to find something in the Bible. The "Where to Find It" section includes the following features: a glossary of the proper names mentioned in the Bible notes; a list of miracles, parables, and other important Bible events and teachings; a guide to familiar psalms; a capsule history of the Old Testament kings and prophets. This is also where you'll find an index of the "100 People You Should Know" Profiles.

In addition to all these features, "Where to Find It" includes a Subject Guide. The Guide concentrates on major passages, not single verses. Whether you are looking for information about a familiar passage or are searching for help with a crucial life question, the Subject Guide should eliminate the "I can't find it" problem.

We hope these notes and features will help you learn some of the basic facts about the background and message of each book in the Bible. *The Student Bible* does not, of course, take the place of a Bible commentary or concordance. It is primarily a *reading* Bible. We believe that the habit of regular Bible reading is the best way for ordinary Christians to become familiar with the full breadth of God's Word.

In publishing *The Student Bible,* we are not trying to add to the Bible or to enliven it. The Bible speaks for itself. It is the most powerful book ever written, and it needs no help. We, its readers, are the ones who need help, and *The Student Bible* merely offers practical aids for the average reader. A good measure of our success will be whether this book helps you to read the Bible for yourself. That, after all, is our ultimate goal.

—Philip Yancey and Tim Stafford

3-Track Plan for Reading the Bible

Of all the reasons people mention for not reading the Bible, simple discouragement ranks highest. The Bible's length alone, about 1,000 pages, is imposing. More like a self-contained library than a book, it includes 66 different books, by several dozen authors. Little wonder people get confused and discouraged.

The following 3-Track Reading Plan helps break the Bible into more manageable portions. If you're new to the Bible, begin with Track 1, then proceed to Track 2, and finally—if you're ambitious—tackle Track 3. Your understanding and appreciation for the Bible should gradually increase.

All three tracks share one thing in common: They each assign usually one chapter a day. Reading an average Bible chapter should take only 5-10 minutes.

Note that the 3-track plan for each book is included within the Introduction to the book (see, for example, "How to Read Genesis," page 24). You can record your progress by checking off the boxes here or within each individual book.

TRACK 1: Introduction to the Bible

TIME COMMITMENT:
Two Weeks

GOAL:
To survey basic biblical foundations

Track 1 is a place to begin reading the Bible. Three two-week reading courses take you quickly into passages of the Bible every Christian should know. These were selected with two concerns in mind: first, they are frequently quoted or referred to. Second, they are relatively easy to read and understand. Track 1 is a sampler, designed to whet your appetite for more.

If you like Track 1, but feel unready to tackle Track 2, you can find more Track 1 courses on pages 15-16.

1. Two Weeks on the Life and Teachings of Jesus

☐ Day 1. LUKE 1: Preparing for Jesus' arrival

☐ Day 2. LUKE 2: The story of Jesus' birth

☐ Day 3. MARK 1: The beginning of Jesus' ministry

☐ Day 4. MARK 9: A day in the life of Jesus

☐ Day 5. MATTHEW 5: The Sermon on the Mount

☐ Day 6. MATTHEW 6: The Sermon on the Mount

☐ Day 7. LUKE 15: Parables of Jesus

☐ Day 8. JOHN 3: A conversation with Jesus

☐ Day 9. JOHN 14: Jesus' final instructions

☐ Day 10. JOHN 17: Jesus' prayer for his disciples

☐ Day 11. MATTHEW 26: Betrayal and arrest

☐ Day 12. MATTHEW 27: Jesus' execution on a cross

☐ Day 13. JOHN 20: Resurrection

☐ Day 14. LUKE 24: Jesus' appearance after resurrection

2. Two Weeks on the Life and Teachings of Paul

☐ Day 1. ACTS 9: The conversion of Saul
☐ Day 2. ACTS 16: Paul's Macedonian call and a jailbreak
☐ Day 3. ACTS 17: Scenes from Paul's missionary journey
☐ Day 4. ACTS 26: Paul tells his life story to a king
☐ Day 5. ACTS 27: Shipwreck on the way to Rome
☐ Day 6. ACTS 28: Paul's arrival in Rome
☐ Day 7. ROMANS 3: Paul's theology in a nutshell
☐ Day 8. ROMANS 7: Struggle with sin
☐ Day 9. ROMANS 8: Life in the Spirit
☐ Day 10. 1 CORINTHIANS 13: Paul's description of love
☐ Day 11. 1 CORINTHIANS 15: Thoughts on the afterlife
☐ Day 12. GALATIANS 5: Freedom in Christ
☐ Day 13. EPHESIANS 3: Paul's summary of his mission
☐ Day 14. PHILIPPIANS 2: Imitating Christ

3. Two Weeks on the Old Testament

☐ Day 1. GENESIS 1: The story of creation
☐ Day 2. GENESIS 3: The origin of sin
☐ Day 3. GENESIS 22: Abraham and Isaac
☐ Day 4. EXODUS 3: Moses' encounter with God
☐ Day 5. EXODUS 20: The gift of the Ten Commandments
☐ Day 6. 1 SAMUEL 17: David and Goliath
☐ Day 7. 2 SAMUEL 11: David and Bathsheba
☐ Day 8. 2 SAMUEL 12: Nathan's rebuke of the king
☐ Day 9. 1 KINGS 18: Elijah and the prophets of Baal
☐ Day 10. JOB 38: God's answer to Job
☐ Day 11. PSALM 51: A classic confession
☐ Day 12. ISAIAH 40: Words of comfort from God
☐ Day 13. DANIEL 6: Daniel and the lions
☐ Day 14. AMOS 4: A prophet's stern warning

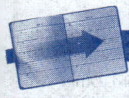
TIME COMMITMENT:
Six Months

GOAL:
To gain an overview of the entire Bible

rack 2 includes 186 of the 1,189 chapters in the Bible. Many well-known parts of the Bible are not represented, and from some books (Leviticus, for example), you will read only a single chapter. These 186 chapters have been selected because they are understandable to the average reader without commentary. Taken together, they provide a good foundation of Bible understanding.

If you miss a few days, don't worry. Just resume reading when you can, about a chapter a day. In 180 total days, you will get an overview that includes something from every book in the Bible.

Track 2 recommends reading the Introduction to each book. You may also find it helpful to read the Insights that appear next to the assigned chapters.

GENESIS	☐ 1	☐ 2	☐ 3	☐ 4
	☐ 7	☐ 8	☐ 15	☐ 19
	☐ 22	☐ 27	☐ 28	☐ 37
	☐ 41	☐ 45		
EXODUS	☐ 3	☐ 10-11	☐ 14	☐ 20
	☐ 32			
LEVITICUS	☐ 26			
NUMBERS	☐ 11	☐ 14		
DEUTERONOMY	☐ 4	☐ 8	☐ 28	
JOSHUA	☐ 2	☐ 6	☐ 7	☐ 24
JUDGES	☐ 6	☐ 7	☐ 16	
RUTH	☐ 1			
1 SAMUEL	☐ 3	☐ 16	☐ 17	☐ 20
2 SAMUEL	☐ 6	☐ 11	☐ 12	
1 KINGS	☐ 3	☐ 8	☐ 17	☐ 18
2 KINGS	☐ 5	☐ 17	☐ 22	
1 CHRONICLES	☐ 17			
2 CHRONICLES	☐ 20	☐ 30	☐ 32	
EZRA	☐ 3			
NEHEMIAH	☐ 2	☐ 8		
ESTHER	☐ 4			
JOB	☐ 1-2	☐ 38	☐ 42	
PSALMS	☐ 19	☐ 23	☐ 27	☐ 51
	☐ 84	☐ 103	☐ 139	
PROVERBS	☐ 4	☐ 10	☐ The proverbs listed in "Verbal Dynamite" (page 676)	
ECCLESIASTES	☐ 3			
SONG OF SONGS	☐ 2			
ISAIAH	☐ 6	☐ 25	☐ 40	☐ 52
	☐ 53	☐ 55		
JEREMIAH	☐ 2	☐ 15	☐ 31	☐ 38
LAMENTATIONS	☐ 3			
EZEKIEL	☐ 1	☐ 2-3	☐ 4	☐ 37
DANIEL	☐ 1	☐ 3	☐ 5	☐ 6
HOSEA	☐ 2-3	☐ 11		
JOEL	☐ 2			
AMOS	☐ 4			
OBADIAH	☐ Obadiah			
JONAH	☐ 3-4			
MICAH	☐ 6			

NAHUM	☐ 1			
HABAKKUK	☐ 1			
ZEPHANIAH	☐ 3			
HAGGAI	☐ 1			
ZECHARIAH	☐ 8			
MALACHI	☐ 3			
MATTHEW	☐ 5	☐ 6	☐ 13	☐ 19
	☐ 26	☐ 27	☐ 28	
MARK	☐ 1	☐ 2	☐ 3	☐ 4
	☐ 5	☐ 6	☐ 7	☐ 8
	☐ 9	☐ 10	☐ 11	☐ 12
	☐ 13	☐ 14	☐ 15-16	
LUKE	☐ 1	☐ 2	☐ 10	☐ 12
	☐ 15	☐ 16	☐ 18	☐ 24
JOHN	☐ 3	☐ 6	☐ 10	☐ 14
	☐ 15	☐ 16	☐ 17	☐ 20
ACTS	☐ 1	☐ 2	☐ 5	☐ 9
	☐ 16	☐ 17	☐ 26	☐ 27
	☐ 28			
ROMANS	☐ 3	☐ 7	☐ 8	☐ 12
1 CORINTHIANS	☐ 13	☐ 15		
2 CORINTHIANS	☐ 4	☐ 12		
GALATIANS	☐ 3			
EPHESIANS	☐ 2	☐ 3		
PHILIPPIANS	☐ 2			
COLOSSIANS	☐ 1			
1 THESSALONIANS	☐ 3-4			
2 THESSALONIANS	☐ 2			
1 TIMOTHY	☐ 1			
2 TIMOTHY	☐ 2			
TITUS	☐ 2			
PHILEMON	☐ Philemon			
HEBREWS	☐ 2	☐ 11	☐ 12	
JAMES	☐ 1			
1 PETER	☐ 1			
2 PETER	☐ 1			
1 JOHN	☐ 3			
2 and 3 JOHN	☐ 2, 3 John			
JUDE	☐ Jude			
REVELATION	☐ 1	☐ 12	☐ 21	

TIME COMMITMENT:
Three Years

GOAL:
To read all the way through the Bible with understanding

Track 3 takes you completely through the Bible, reading every word. Other Bible-reading plans allot only a year for this project, requiring that at least 3 chapters be read each day. But many readers find such a pace to be unrealistic and discouraging. For this reason, Track 3 assigns usually only one chapter a day. (Some short chapters have been combined, so occasionally you will read two brief chapters in a day.) In all, the reading plan works out evenly to a three-year total.

The Track 3 plan alternates between the Old Testament and New Testament. This mixing provides variety and reduces the fatigue that may set in from reading long sections of the Old Testament.

GENESIS

☐ 1	☐ 2	☐ 3	☐ 4
☐ 5	☐ 6	☐ 7	☐ 8
☐ 9	☐ 10-11	☐ 12	☐ 13
☐ 14	☐ 15	☐ 16	☐ 17
☐ 18	☐ 19	☐ 20	☐ 21
☐ 22	☐ 23	☐ 24	☐ 25
☐ 26	☐ 27	☐ 28	☐ 29
☐ 30	☐ 31	☐ 32	☐ 33
☐ 34	☐ 35	☐ 36	☐ 37
☐ 38	☐ 39	☐ 40	☐ 41
☐ 42	☐ 43	☐ 44	☐ 45
☐ 46	☐ 47	☐ 48	☐ 49
☐ 50			

MATTHEW 1-9

☐ 1	☐ 2	☐ 3	☐ 4
☐ 5	☐ 6	☐ 7	☐ 8
☐ 9			

EXODUS

☐ 1	☐ 2	☐ 3	☐ 4
☐ 5	☐ 6	☐ 7	☐ 8
☐ 9	☐ 10-11	☐ 12	☐ 13
☐ 14	☐ 15	☐ 16	☐ 17
☐ 18	☐ 19	☐ 20	☐ 21
☐ 22	☐ 23	☐ 24	☐ 25
☐ 26	☐ 27	☐ 28	☐ 29
☐ 30	☐ 31	☐ 32	☐ 33
☐ 34	☐ 35	☐ 36	☐ 37
☐ 38	☐ 39	☐ 40	

MATTHEW 10-20

☐ 10	☐ 11	☐ 12	☐ 13
☐ 14	☐ 15	☐ 16	☐ 17
☐ 18	☐ 19	☐ 20	

LEVITICUS 1-14

☐ 1	☐ 2	☐ 3	☐ 4
☐ 5	☐ 6	☐ 7	☐ 8
☐ 9	☐ 10	☐ 11-12	☐ 13
☐ 14			

MATTHEW 21-28

☐ 21	☐ 22	☐ 23	☐ 24
☐ 25	☐ 26	☐ 27	☐ 28

LEVITICUS 15-27

☐ 15	☐ 16	☐ 17	☐ 18
☐ 19	☐ 20	☐ 21	☐ 22
☐ 23	☐ 24	☐ 25	☐ 26
☐ 27			

MARK 1-8

☐ 1	☐ 2	☐ 3	☐ 4
☐ 5	☐ 6	☐ 7	☐ 8

NUMBERS

☐ 1-2	☐ 3	☐ 4	☐ 5
☐ 6	☐ 7	☐ 8	☐ 9
☐ 10	☐ 11	☐ 12	☐ 13
☐ 14	☐ 15	☐ 16	☐ 17
☐ 18	☐ 19	☐ 20	☐ 21
☐ 22	☐ 23	☐ 24	☐ 25
☐ 26	☐ 27	☐ 28	☐ 29
☐ 30	☐ 31	☐ 32	☐ 33
☐ 34	☐ 35	☐ 36	

MARK 9-16

☐ 9	☐ 10	☐ 11	☐ 12
☐ 13	☐ 14	☐ 15-16	

DEUTERONOMY 1-17

☐ 1	☐ 2	☐ 3	☐ 4
☐ 5	☐ 6	☐ 7	☐ 8
☐ 9	☐ 10	☐ 11	☐ 12
☐ 13	☐ 14	☐ 15	☐ 16
☐ 17			

LUKE 1-8

☐ 1	☐ 2	☐ 3	☐ 4
☐ 5	☐ 6	☐ 7	☐ 8

DEUTERONOMY 18-34

☐ 18	☐ 19	☐ 20	☐ 21
☐ 22	☐ 23	☐ 24	☐ 25

□ 26	□ 27	□ 28	□ 29
□ 30	□ 31	□ 32	□ 33
□ 34			

LUKE 9-16

□ 9	□ 10	□ 11	□ 12
□ 13	□ 14	□ 15	□ 16

JOSHUA

□ 1	□ 2	□ 3	□ 4
□ 5	□ 6	□ 7	□ 8
□ 9	□ 10	□ 11	□ 12-13
□ 14-15	□ 16-17	□ 18	□ 19
□ 20	□ 21	□ 22	□ 23
□ 24			

LUKE 17-24

□ 17	□ 18	□ 19	□ 20
□ 21	□ 22	□ 23	□ 24

JUDGES

□ 1	□ 2	□ 3	□ 4
□ 5	□ 6	□ 7	□ 8
□ 9	□ 10	□ 11	□ 12
□ 13	□ 14	□ 15	□ 16
□ 17	□ 18	□ 19	□ 20
□ 21			

JOHN 1-7

□ 1	□ 2	□ 3	□ 4
□ 5	□ 6	□ 7	

RUTH

□ 1	□ 2	□ 3	□ 4

1 SAMUEL 1-15

□ 1	□ 2	□ 3	□ 4
□ 5	□ 6	□ 7	□ 8
□ 9	□ 10	□ 11	□ 12
□ 13	□ 14	□ 15	

JOHN 8-14

□ 8	□ 9	□ 10	□ 11
□ 12	□ 13	□ 14	

1 SAMUEL 16-31

□ 16	□ 17	□ 18	□ 19
□ 20	□ 21	□ 22	□ 23
□ 24	□ 25	□ 26	□ 27
□ 28	□ 29	□ 30	□ 31

JOHN 15-21

□ 15	□ 16	□ 17	□ 18
□ 19	□ 20	□ 21	

2 SAMUEL

□ 1	□ 2	□ 3	□ 4
□ 5	□ 6	□ 7	□ 8
□ 9	□ 10	□ 11	□ 12
□ 13	□ 14	□ 15	□ 16
□ 17	□ 18	□ 19	□ 20
□ 21	□ 22	□ 23	□ 24

ACTS 1-7

□ 1	□ 2	□ 3	□ 4
□ 5	□ 6	□ 7	

1 KINGS 1-11

□ 1	□ 2	□ 3	□ 4-5
□ 6	□ 7	□ 8	□ 9
□ 10	□ 11		

ACTS 8-14

□ 8	□ 9	□ 10	□ 11
□ 12	□ 13	□ 14	

1 KINGS 12-22

□ 12	□ 13	□ 14	□ 15
□ 16	□ 17	□ 18	□ 19
□ 20	□ 21	□ 22	

ACTS 15-21

□ 15	□ 16	□ 17	□ 18
□ 19	□ 20	□ 21	

2 KINGS

□ 1	□ 2	□ 3	□ 4
□ 5	□ 6	□ 7	□ 8
□ 9	□ 10	□ 11	□ 12
□ 13	□ 14	□ 15	□ 16
□ 17	□ 18	□ 19	□ 20
□ 21	□ 22	□ 23	□ 24
□ 25			

ACTS 22-28

□ 22	□ 23	□ 24	□ 25
□ 26	□ 27	□ 28	

1 CHRONICLES 1-14

□ 1-9	□ 10	□ 11	□ 12
□ 13	□ 14		

ROMANS 1-8

☐ 1	☐ 2	☐ 3	☐ 4
☐ 5	☐ 6	☐ 7	☐ 8

1 CHRONICLES 15-29

☐ 15	☐ 16	☐ 17	☐ 18
☐ 19	☐ 20	☐ 21	☐ 22
☐ 23-27	☐ 28	☐ 29	

ROMANS 9-16

☐ 9	☐ 10	☐ 11	☐ 12-13
☐ 14	☐ 15-16		

2 CHRONICLES 1-18

☐ 1	☐ 2	☐ 3	☐ 4
☐ 5	☐ 6	☐ 7	☐ 8
☐ 9	☐ 10	☐ 11	☐ 12
☐ 13	☐ 14	☐ 15	☐ 16-17
☐ 18			

1 CORINTHIANS 1-9

☐ 1	☐ 2	☐ 3	☐ 4-5
☐ 6	☐ 7	☐ 8-9	

2 CHRONICLES 19-36

☐ 19	☐ 20	☐ 21	☐ 22
☐ 23	☐ 24	☐ 25	☐ 26-27
☐ 28	☐ 29	☐ 30	☐ 31
☐ 32	☐ 33	☐ 34	☐ 35
☐ 36			

1 CORINTHIANS 10-16

☐ 10	☐ 11	☐ 12	☐ 13
☐ 14	☐ 15	☐ 16	

EZRA

☐ 1-2	☐ 3	☐ 4	☐ 5
☐ 6	☐ 7	☐ 8	☐ 9
☐ 10			

NEHEMIAH

☐ 1	☐ 2-3	☐ 4	☐ 5
☐ 6	☐ 7	☐ 8	☐ 9
☐ 10	☐ 11	☐ 12	☐ 13

2 CORINTHIANS

☐ 1	☐ 2-3	☐ 4	☐ 5
☐ 6	☐ 7	☐ 8-9	☐ 10
☐ 11	☐ 12-13		

ESTHER

☐ 1	☐ 2	☐ 3	☐ 4
☐ 5	☐ 6-7	☐ 8	☐ 9-10

JOB 1-21

☐ 1	☐ 2	☐ 3	☐ 4
☐ 5	☐ 6	☐ 7	☐ 8
☐ 9	☐ 10	☐ 11	☐ 12
☐ 13	☐ 14	☐ 15	☐ 16
☐ 17	☐ 18	☐ 19	☐ 20
☐ 21			

GALATIANS

☐ 1	☐ 2	☐ 3	☐ 4
☐ 5-6			

JOB 22-42

☐ 22	☐ 23	☐ 24	☐ 25-26
☐ 27	☐ 28	☐ 29	☐ 30
☐ 31	☐ 32	☐ 33	☐ 34
☐ 35	☐ 36	☐ 37	☐ 38
☐ 39	☐ 40	☐ 41	☐ 42

EPHESIANS

☐ 1	☐ 2	☐ 3	☐ 4
☐ 5	☐ 6		

PSALMS 1-40

☐ 1-2	☐ 3-4	☐ 5	☐ 6
☐ 7	☐ 8	☐ 9	☐ 10
☐ 11-12	☐ 13-14	☐ 15-16	☐ 17
☐ 18	☐ 19	☐ 20-21	☐ 22
☐ 23-24	☐ 25	☐ 26	☐ 27
☐ 28-29	☐ 30	☐ 31	☐ 32
☐ 33	☐ 34	☐ 35	☐ 36
☐ 37	☐ 38	☐ 39	☐ 40

PHILIPPIANS

☐ 1	☐ 2	☐ 3	☐ 4

PSALMS 41-80

☐ 41	☐ 42-43	☐ 44	☐ 45
☐ 46-47	☐ 48	☐ 49	☐ 50
☐ 51	☐ 52	☐ 53-54	☐ 55
☐ 56	☐ 57	☐ 58	☐ 59
☐ 60-61	☐ 62	☐ 63-64	☐ 65
☐ 66	☐ 67	☐ 68	☐ 69
☐ 70	☐ 71	☐ 72	☐ 73
☐ 74	☐ 75	☐ 76	☐ 77
☐ 78	☐ 79	☐ 80	

COLOSSIANS

☐ 1	☐ 2	☐ 3	☐ 4

PSALMS 81-121

☐ 81	☐ 82	☐ 83	☐ 84
☐ 85	☐ 86	☐ 87	☐ 88
☐ 89	☐ 90	☐ 91	☐ 92-93
☐ 94	☐ 95	☐ 96	☐ 97
☐ 98-99	☐ 100-101	☐ 102	☐ 103
☐ 104	☐ 105	☐ 106	☐ 107
☐ 108	☐ 109	☐ 110-111	☐ 112
☐ 113	☐ 114	☐ 115	☐ 116-117
☐ 118	☐ 119:1-48	☐ 119:49-96	☐ 119:97-144
☐ 119:145-176		☐ 120-121	

1 THESSALONIANS

☐ 1-2	☐ 3-4	☐ 5

2 THESSALONIANS

☐ 1-2	☐ 3

PSALMS 122-150

☐ 122-123	☐ 124-125	☐ 126-128	☐ 129-130
☐ 131-132	☐ 133-134	☐ 135	☐ 136
☐ 137-138	☐ 139	☐ 140	☐ 141-142
☐ 143	☐ 144	☐ 145	☐ 146
☐ 147	☐ 148	☐ 149-150	

PROVERBS

☐ 1	☐ 2	☐ 3	☐ 4
☐ 5	☐ 6	☐ 7	☐ 8
☐ 9	☐ 10	☐ 11	☐ 12
☐ 13	☐ 14	☐ 15	☐ 16
☐ 17	☐ 18	☐ 19	☐ 20
☐ 21	☐ 22	☐ 23	☐ 24
☐ 25	☐ 26	☐ 27	☐ 28
☐ 29	☐ 30	☐ 31	

1 TIMOTHY

☐ 1-2	☐ 3-4	☐ 5	☐ 6

ECCLESIASTES

☐ 1	☐ 2	☐ 3	☐ 4
☐ 5	☐ 6	☐ 7	☐ 8
☐ 9	☐ 10	☐ 11	☐ 12

SONG OF SONGS

☐ 1	☐ 2	☐ 3	☐ 4
☐ 5	☐ 6	☐ 7	☐ 8

2 TIMOTHY

☐ 1	☐ 2	☐ 3	☐ 4

ISAIAH 1-36

☐ 1	☐ 2	☐ 3	☐ 4-5
☐ 6	☐ 7	☐ 8	☐ 9
☐ 10	☐ 11	☐ 12	☐ 13
☐ 14	☐ 15	☐ 16	☐ 17
☐ 18	☐ 19-20	☐ 21	☐ 22
☐ 23	☐ 24	☐ 25	☐ 26
☐ 27	☐ 28	☐ 29	☐ 30
☐ 31	☐ 32	☐ 33	☐ 34
☐ 35	☐ 36		

TITUS

☐ 1	☐ 2-3

ISAIAH 37-66

☐ 37	☐ 38-39	☐ 40	☐ 41
☐ 42	☐ 43	☐ 44	☐ 45
☐ 46	☐ 47	☐ 48	☐ 49
☐ 50	☐ 51	☐ 52	☐ 53
☐ 54	☐ 55	☐ 56	☐ 57
☐ 58	☐ 59	☐ 60	☐ 61
☐ 62	☐ 63	☐ 64	☐ 65
☐ 66			

PHILEMON

☐ Philemon

JEREMIAH 1-26

☐ 1	☐ 2	☐ 3	☐ 4
☐ 5	☐ 6	☐ 7	☐ 8
☐ 9	☐ 10	☐ 11	☐ 12
☐ 13	☐ 14	☐ 15	☐ 16
☐ 17	☐ 18	☐ 19	☐ 20
☐ 21	☐ 22	☐ 23	☐ 24
☐ 25	☐ 26		

HEBREWS 1-7

☐ 1	☐ 2	☐ 3-4	☐ 5-6
☐ 7			

JEREMIAH 27-52

☐ 27	☐ 28	☐ 29	☐ 30
☐ 31	☐ 32	☐ 33	☐ 34
☐ 35	☐ 36	☐ 37	☐ 38
☐ 39	☐ 40	☐ 41	☐ 42
☐ 43	☐ 44-45	☐ 46	☐ 47
☐ 48	☐ 49	☐ 50	☐ 51
☐ 52			

HEBREWS 8-13

☐ 8	☐ 9	☐ 10	☐ 11
☐ 12	☐ 13		

LAMENTATIONS

☐ 1	☐ 2	☐ 3	☐ 4
☐ 5			

EZEKIEL 1–24

☐ 1	☐ 2-3	☐ 4	☐ 5
☐ 6	☐ 7	☐ 8	☐ 9
☐ 10	☐ 11	☐ 12	☐ 13
☐ 14	☐ 15	☐ 16	☐ 17
☐ 18	☐ 19	☐ 20	☐ 21
☐ 22	☐ 23	☐ 24	

JAMES

☐ 1	☐ 2	☐ 3-4	☐ 5

EZEKIEL 25–48

☐ 25	☐ 26	☐ 27	☐ 28
☐ 29	☐ 30	☐ 31	☐ 32
☐ 33	☐ 34	☐ 35	☐ 36
☐ 37	☐ 38	☐ 39	☐ 40
☐ 41	☐ 42	☐ 43	☐ 44
☐ 45	☐ 46	☐ 47	☐ 48

1 PETER

☐ 1	☐ 2	☐ 3	☐ 4-5

DANIEL

☐ 1	☐ 2	☐ 3	☐ 4
☐ 5	☐ 6	☐ 7	☐ 8
☐ 9	☐ 10	☐ 11	☐ 12

2 PETER

☐ 1	☐ 2	☐ 3

HOSEA

☐ 1	☐ 2-3	☐ 4	☐ 5
☐ 6-7	☐ 8	☐ 9	☐ 10
☐ 11-12	☐ 13-14		

1 JOHN

☐ 1-2	☐ 3	☐ 4	☐ 5

JOEL

☐ 1	☐ 2	☐ 3

AMOS

☐ 1	☐ 2	☐ 3	☐ 4

☐ 5	☐ 6	☐ 7	☐ 8
☐ 9			

OBADIAH

☐ Obadiah

JONAH

☐ 1-2	☐ 3-4

2 and 3 JOHN

☐ 2 John, 3 John

MICAH

☐ 1	☐ 2	☐ 3	☐ 4
☐ 5	☐ 6	☐ 7	

NAHUM

☐ 1	☐ 2	☐ 3

JUDE

☐ Jude

HABAKKUK

☐ 1	☐ 2	☐ 3

ZEPHANIAH

☐ 1	☐ 2	☐ 3

REVELATION 1–7

☐ 1	☐ 2	☐ 3	☐ 4-5
☐ 6	☐ 7		

HAGGAI

☐ 1	☐ 2

REVELATION 8–14

☐ 8	☐ 9	☐ 10-11	☐ 12
☐ 13	☐ 14		

ZECHARIAH

☐ 1	☐ 2-3	☐ 4-5	☐ 6
☐ 7	☐ 8	☐ 9	☐ 10
☐ 11	☐ 12-13	☐ 14	

MALACHI

☐ 1	☐ 2	☐ 3-4

REVELATION 15–22

☐ 15-16	☐ 17	☐ 18	☐ 19
☐ 20	☐ 21	☐ 22	

TWO WEEKS ON BECOMING A CHRISTIAN

- ☐ Day 1. Genesis 3: The first sin creates a need.
- ☐ Day 2. Isaiah 52: Salvation prophesied.
- ☐ Day 3. Isaiah 53: The role of the suffering servant.
- ☐ Day 4. Luke 15: Three stories about God's love.
- ☐ Day 5. John 3: Jesus explains "born again."
- ☐ Day 6. John 10: The good shepherd.
- ☐ Day 7. Acts 8: Conversions spread outside the Jews.
- ☐ Day 8. Acts 26: Paul testifies of his conversion before a king.
- ☐ Day 9. Romans 3: God's provision for sin.
- ☐ Day 10. Romans 5: Peace with God.
- ☐ Day 11. Galatians 3: Salvation unavailable by obeying the law.
- ☐ Day 12. Ephesians 2: New life in Christ.
- ☐ Day 13. 1 Peter 1: Future rewards of salvation.
- ☐ Day 14. 2 Peter 1: Making your salvation sure.

TWO WEEKS ON PRAYERS OF THE BIBLE

- ☐ Day 1. Genesis 18: Abraham's plea for Sodom.
- ☐ Day 2. Exodus 15: Moses' song to the Lord.
- ☐ Day 3. Exodus 33: Moses meets with God.
- ☐ Day 4. 2 Samuel 7: David's response to God's promises.
- ☐ Day 5. 1 Kings 8: Solomon's dedication of the temple.
- ☐ Day 6. 2 Chronicles 20: Jehoshaphat prays for victory.
- ☐ Day 7. Ezra 9: Ezra's prayer for the people's sins.
- ☐ Day 8. Psalm 22: A cry to God for help.
- ☐ Day 9. Psalm 104: A prayer of praise.
- ☐ Day 10. Daniel 9: Daniel's prayer for the salvation of Jerusalem.
- ☐ Day 11. Habakkuk 3: A prophet's prayer of acceptance.
- ☐ Day 12. Matthew 6: The Lord's prayer.
- ☐ Day 13. John 17: Jesus' prayer for his disciples.
- ☐ Day 14. Colossians 1: Paul's prayer of thanksgiving.

TWO WEEKS ON THE HOLY SPIRIT

- ☐ Day 1. Judges 14: The Spirit gives Samson strength.
- ☐ Day 2. 1 Samuel 10: King Saul's experience.
- ☐ Day 3. Matthew 3:1–4:10: Role in Jesus' baptism and temptation.
- ☐ Day 4. John 14: Jesus promises the Spirit.
- ☐ Day 5. John 16: The work of the Spirit.
- ☐ Day 6. Acts 2: The Spirit comes at Pentecost.
- ☐ Day 7. Acts 10: The Spirit guides Peter to accept Gentiles.
- ☐ Day 8. Romans 8: Christians' victory in the Spirit.
- ☐ Day 9. 1 Corinthians 2: Wisdom from the Spirit.
- ☐ Day 10. 1 Corinthians 12: Gifts of the Spirit.
- ☐ Day 11. 1 Corinthians 14: Gifts of tongues and prophecy.
- ☐ Day 12. Galatians 5: Life in the Spirit.
- ☐ Day 13. Ephesians 4: Unity and gifts.
- ☐ Day 14. 1 John 4: Signs of the Spirit.

TWO WEEKS ON WOMEN OF THE BIBLE

- ☐ Day 1. Genesis 2: Eve, the first woman.
- ☐ Day 2. Genesis 18: Sarah laughs at God's promise.
- ☐ Day 3. Genesis 24: Rebekah's marriage to Isaac.
- ☐ Day 4. Genesis 27: Rebekah, the manipulative mother
- ☐ Day 5. Judges 4: Deborah's leadership frees her people.
- ☐ Day 6. Ruth 1: Ruth and Naomi's deep friendship.
- ☐ Day 7. 1 Samuel 1: Hannah prays for a son.
- ☐ Day 8. 1 Kings 17: A poor widow and the prophet Elijah.
- ☐ Day 9. 1 Kings 21: Jezebel, an emblem of wickedness.
- ☐ Day 10. Esther 2: Esther is chosen as queen.
- ☐ Day 11. Esther 4: Esther's courage at the risk of death.

☐ Day 12. Luke 1: Mary and Elizabeth receive great news.
☐ Day 13. Luke 2: Mary gives birth to Jesus.
☐ Day 14. John 11: Mary and Martha and their brother's death.

TWO WEEKS ON MEN OF THE OLD TESTAMENT

☐ Day 1. Judges 6: God calls Gideon to rescue his people.
☐ Day 2. Judges 7: Gideon conquers his fears—and his enemies.
☐ Day 3. 1 Samuel 3: God calls young Samuel.
☐ Day 4. 1 Kings 3: Solomon is given wisdom.
☐ Day 5. 1 Kings 19: Elijah runs for his life.
☐ Day 6. 2 Kings 5: Elisha heals a powerful foreign general.
☐ Day 7. Isaiah 6: God calls the prophet Isaiah.
☐ Day 8. 2 Kings 18: King Hezekiah under military siege.
☐ Day 9. 2 Kings 19: Isaiah speaks God's word to King Hezekiah.
☐ Day 10. 2 Chronicles 34: Josiah sets his nation back on course.
☐ Day 11. Nehemiah 2: Nehemiah courageously begins rebuilding a wall.
☐ Day 12. Jeremiah 38: Jeremiah, in prison, refuses to change his message.
☐ Day 13. Daniel 1: Daniel risks his life in captivity.
☐ Day 14. Daniel 5: Daniel's word to a royal orgy.

TWO WEEKS ON SOCIAL JUSTICE

☐ Day 1. Exodus 3: God hears the cries of the slaves.
☐ Day 2. Leviticus 25: The year of jubilee, a time of economic revolution.
☐ Day 3. Ruth 2: A poor woman finds help.
☐ Day 4. 1 Kings 21: Elijah speaks to a land-grabbing, murderous king.
☐ Day 5. Nehemiah 5: Nehemiah demands justice for the poor.
☐ Day 6. Isaiah 5: Warning to fun-loving materialists.
☐ Day 7. Isaiah 58: Worship that God appreciates.
☐ Day 8. Jeremiah 34: Freedom for slaves.
☐ Day 9. Amos 2: Sins against God by his own people.
☐ Day 10. Amos 6: Warning to the complacent.
☐ Day 11. Micah 6: What the Lord requires.
☐ Day 12. Luke 3: John the Baptist tells how to prepare for Jesus.
☐ Day 13. Matthew 6: Jesus speaks on material things.
☐ Day 14. James 2: How to treat the rich and the poor.

TWO WEEKS ON GOD AND NATURE

☐ Day 1. Genesis 1: God creates the earth.
☐ Day 2. Genesis 2: God creates human beings.
☐ Day 3. Proverbs 8: Wisdom's view of creation.
☐ Day 4. Genesis 7: God preserves the species.
☐ Day 5. Job 38: The greatness of nature.
☐ Day 6. Job 39: The wildness of nature.
☐ Day 7. Job 40: God's mastery of nature.
☐ Day 8. Psalm 8: Praise for the Creator.
☐ Day 9. Psalm 98: Nature joins in the praise.
☐ Day 10. Psalm 104: God sustains the earth.
☐ Day 11. Isaiah 40: The ruler of all creation.
☐ Day 12. Romans 8: The "groanings" of our present state.
☐ Day 13. Isaiah 65: Preview of a restored earth.
☐ Day 14. Revelation 22: The end of history.

FURTHER TWO-WEEK COURSES FOR PERSONAL STUDY

Two weeks on Abraham, Isaac, and Jacob:
Genesis 12, 13, 15, 17, 18, 19, 22, 24, 27, 28, 29, 31, 32, 33.
Two weeks on Moses and the exodus:
Exodus 2, 3, 4, 7, 12, 14, 16, 19, 32; Numbers 14; Deuteronomy 1, 2, 4, 31.
Two weeks on David:
1 Samuel 16, 17, 18, 20, 21, 22, 24; 2 Samuel 6, 7, 11, 12, 13, 15, 18.

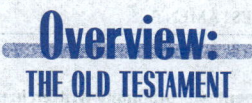

Overview:
THE OLD TESTAMENT

The Five Books

The first five books of the Bible tell the origins of the Jewish race and culture.

GENESIS: The book of beginnings describes creation, the first rebellions against God, and God's choosing of Abraham and his offspring.

EXODUS: God rescued the Israelites from slavery in Egypt and led them to the Desert of Sinai. There, he gave Moses the laws to govern the new nation.

LEVITICUS: God set up laws for the Israelites, mostly regarding holiness and worship.

NUMBERS: Because of their rebellion and disobedience, the Israelites had to wander in a wilderness for 40 years before entering the promised land.

DEUTERONOMY: Just before his death, Moses made three emotional farewell speeches, recapping history and warning the Israelites against further mistakes.

History Books

The next 12 books continue the history of the Israelites. They moved into the land of Canaan and established a kingdom that lasted almost 500 years.

JOSHUA: After Moses' death, Joshua commanded the armies that conquered much of the territory in the promised land.

JUDGES: The new nation fell into a series of dismal failures. God raised up leaders called "judges."

RUTH: This story of love and loyalty between two widows shines out brightly in an otherwise dark period.

1 SAMUEL: Samuel became a transition leader between the time of the judges and that of the kings. He appointed Israel's first king, Saul. After his own failure, Saul tried violently to prevent God's king-elect David from taking the throne.

2 SAMUEL: David, a man after God's own heart, brought the nation together. But after committing adultery and murder, he was haunted by family and national crises.

1 KINGS: Solomon succeeded David, with mixed success. At his death, a civil war tore apart the nation. Successive kings were mostly bad, and the prophet Elijah had dramatic confrontations with King Ahab.

2 KINGS: This book continues the record of the rulers of the divided kingdom. None of the northern kings followed God consistently, and so Israel was finally destroyed by an invader. The South, Judah, lasted much longer, but finally Babylon conquered Judah and deported its citizens.

1 CHRONICLES: The book opens with the most complete genealogical record in the Bible, then adds many incidents from the life of David (often the same as those in 2 Samuel).

2 CHRONICLES: Often paralleling the books of Kings, this book records the history of the rulers of Judah, emphasizing the good kings.

EZRA: After being held captive in Babylon for decades, the Jews were allowed to return to their homeland. Ezra, a priest, emerged from one of the first waves of refugees.

NEHEMIAH: Nehemiah returned from the Babylonian captivity after the temple had been rebuilt. He concentrated on restoring the protective wall around Jerusalem and joined Ezra in leading a religious revival.

ESTHER: This story is set among captive Jews in Persia. A courageous Jewish queen foiled a plan to exterminate her people.

Books of Poetry

Almost one-third of the Old Testament was originally written in poetry. These books concentrate on questions about pain, God, life, and love.

JOB: The best man of his day suffers the greatest personal tragedy. The entire book deals with the question, "Why?"

PSALMS: These prayers and hymns cover the full range of human emotion; together, they represent a personal journal of how to relate to God. Some were also used in public worship services.

PROVERBS: The proverbs offer advice on every imaginable area of life. The style of wise living described here leads to a fulfilled life.

ECCLESIASTES: A life without God, "under the sun," leads to meaninglessness and despair, says the Teacher in a strikingly modern book.

SONG OF SONGS: This beautiful poem celebrates romantic and physical love.

Books of the Prophets

During the years when kings ruled Israel and Judah, God spoke through prophets. Though some prophets did predict future events, their primary role was to call God's people back to him.

ISAIAH: The most eloquent of the prophets, Isaiah analyzed the failures of all the nations around him and pointed to a future Messiah who would bring peace.

JEREMIAH: Jeremiah led an emotionally tortured life, yet held to his stern message. He spoke to Judah in the last decades before Babylon destroyed the nation.

LAMENTATIONS: All Jeremiah's warnings about Jerusalem came true, and Lamentations records five poems of sorrow for the fallen city.

EZEKIEL: Ezekiel spoke to the Jews who were captive in Babylon. He often used dramatic stories and "enacted parables" to make his points.

DANIEL: A captive in Babylon, Daniel rose to the office of prime minister. Despite intense political pressure, he lived a model life of integrity and left highly symbolic prophecies about the future.

HOSEA: By marrying a loose-living wife, Hosea lived out his message: that Israel had committed spiritual adultery against God.

JOEL: Beginning with a recent catastrophe in Judah (a locust plague), Joel foretold God's judgment on Judah.

AMOS: A country boy, Amos preached to Israel at the height of its prosperity. His grim warnings focused on materialism.

OBADIAH: Obadiah warned Edom, a nation bordering Judah.

JONAH: Jonah reluctantly went to Nineveh and found Israel's enemies responsive to God's message.

MICAH: Micah exposed corruption in every level of society, but closed with a promise of forgiveness and restoration.

NAHUM: Long after Jonah had stirred Nineveh to repentance, Nahum foretold the mighty city's total destruction.

HABAKKUK: Habakkuk addressed his book to God, not people. In a frank dialogue with God, he discussed problems of suffering and justice.

ZEPHANIAH: Zephaniah focused on the coming day of the Lord, which would purge Judah, resulting in a remnant used to bless the entire world.

HAGGAI: After returning from the Babylonian captivity, the Jews began rebuilding the temple of God. But before long they set aside that task to work on their own homes. Haggai reminded them to put God first.

ZECHARIAH: Writing around the same time as Haggai, Zechariah also urged the Jews to work on the temple. He used a more uplifting approach, describing how the temple would point to the coming Messiah.

MALACHI: The last Old Testament prophet, Malachi faced a nation that had grown indifferent. He sought to stir them from apathy.

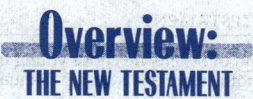

Overview:
THE NEW TESTAMENT

History Books

The word *gospel* means "good news." Almost half of the New Testament consists of four accounts of the life of Jesus and the good news he brought to earth. Each of these four books, or Gospels, has a different focus and a different audience; taken together, they give a complete picture of Jesus' life and teaching. About a third of their pages are devoted to the events of his last week on earth, including the crucifixion and resurrection.

Acts continues the history into the period after Jesus left earth.

MATTHEW: Written to a Jewish audience, this Gospel links the Old and New Testaments. It presents Jesus as the Messiah and King promised in the Old Testament. Matthew emphasizes Jesus' authority and power.

MARK: Mark probably had pragmatic Roman readers in mind. His Gospel stresses action and gives a straightforward, blow-by-blow account of Jesus' work on earth.

LUKE: A doctor, Luke was also a fine writer. His Gospel provides many details of human interest, especially in Jesus' treatment of the poor and needy. A joyful tone characterizes Luke's book.

JOHN: John has a different, more reflective style than the other Gospels. Its author selected seven signs that pointed to Jesus as the Son of God and wove together everything else to underscore that point.

ACTS: Acts tells what happened to Jesus' followers after he left them. Peter and Paul soon emerged as leaders of the rapidly spreading church.

The Letters

The young church was nourished spiritually by apostles who set down their beliefs and messages in a series of letters. The first 13 such letters (Romans through Philemon) were written by the apostle Paul, who led the advance of Christianity to non-Jewish people.

Paul's Letters:

ROMANS: Written for a sophisticated audience, Romans sets forth theology in a logical, organized form.

1 CORINTHIANS: A very practical book, 1 Corinthians takes up the problems of a tumultuous church in Corinth: marriage, factions, immorality, public worship, and lawsuits.

2 CORINTHIANS: Paul wrote this follow-up letter to defend himself against a rebellion led by certain false apostles.

GALATIANS: A short version of the message of Romans, this book addresses legalism. It shows how Christ came to bring freedom, not bondage to a set of laws.

EPHESIANS: Although written in jail, this letter is Paul's most optimistic and encouraging. It tells of the advantages a believer has in Christ.

PHILIPPIANS: The church at Philippi ranked among Paul's favorites. This friendly letter stresses that joy can be found in any situation.

COLOSSIANS: Written to oppose certain cults, Colossians tells how faith in Christ is complete. Nothing needs to be added to what Christ did.

1 THESSALONIANS: Composed early in Paul's ministry, this letter gives a capsule history of one church, as well as Paul's direct advice about specific problems.

2 THESSALONIANS: Stronger in tone than his first letter to the Thessalonians, the sequel goes over the same topics, especially the church's questions about Christ's second coming.

1 TIMOTHY: As Paul neared the end of his life, he chose young men such as Timothy to carry on his work. His two letters to Timothy form a leadership manual for a young pastor.

2 TIMOTHY: Written just before Paul's death, 2 Timothy offers Paul's final words to his young assistant.

TITUS: Titus was left in Crete, a notoriously difficult place to nurture a church. Paul's letter gave practical advice on how to go about it.

PHILEMON: Paul urged Philemon, owner of runaway slave Onesimus, to forgive his slave and accept him as a brother in Christ.

Other Letters:

HEBREWS: No one knows who wrote Hebrews, but it probably first went to Christians in danger of slipping back into Judaism. It interprets the Old Testament, explaining many Jewish practices as symbols that prepared the way for Christ.

JAMES: James, a man of action, emphasized the right kind of behavior for a believer. Someone who calls himself or herself a Christian ought to act like it, James believed, and his letter spells out the specifics.

1 PETER: Early Christians often met violent opposition, and Peter's letter comforted and encouraged Christians who were being persecuted for their faith.

2 PETER: In contrast to Peter's first letter, this one focused on problems that sprang up from the inside. It warns against false teachers.

1 JOHN: John could fill simple words—*light, love, life*—with deep meaning, and in this letter, he elegantly explains basic truths about the Christian life.

2 JOHN: Warning against false teachers, John counseled churches on how to respond to them.

3 JOHN: Balancing 2 John, this companion letter mentions the need to be hospitable to true teachers.

JUDE: Jude gave a brief but fiery exposé of heretics.

REVELATION: A book of visions and symbols, Revelation is the only New Testament book that concentrates on prophecy. It completes the story, begun in Genesis, of the cosmic battle between good and evil being waged on earth. It ends with a picture of a new heaven and new earth.

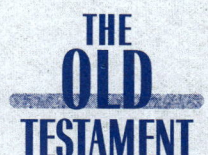

THE
OLD
TESTAMENT

GENESIS

God at Work
Everything—literally everything—begins here

THE BIBLE BEGINS WITH WORDS that have become famous, "In the beginning God created." God, like an artist, fashioned a universe. How can we grasp the grandeur of this?

Michelangelo, perhaps the greatest artist in history, may help us to understand. He painted Rome's famous Sistine Chapel to retell Genesis' story of creation. His experience proves one thing: Creativity is work.

> *And God blessed the seventh day and made it holy, because on it he rested from all the work of creating that he had done.*
> *2:3*

An Exhausting Effort

Michelangelo had 6,000 square feet of ceiling to cover—the size of four average house roofs. Anyone who has painted a ceiling with a paint roller has caught a hint of the physical difficulty of such a task. But Michelangelo's plan called for 300 separate, detailed portraits of men and women. For more than three years the 5'4" artist devoted all his labors to the exhausting strain of painting the vast overhead space with his tiny brushes.

Sometimes he painted standing on a huge scaffold, a paintbrush high over his head. Sometimes he sat, his nose inches from the ceiling. Sometimes he painted while lying on his back. His back, shoulders, neck, and arms cramped painfully.

In the long days of summer, he had light to paint 17 hours a day, taking food and a chamber pot with him on the 60-foot scaffold. For 30 days at a stretch he slept in his clothes, not even taking off his boots. Paint dribbled into his eyes so he could barely see. Freezing in the winter, sweating in the summer, he painted until at last the ceiling looked like a ceiling no more. He had transformed it into the creation drama, with creatures so real they seemed to breathe. Never before or since have paint and plaster been so changed.

The Miracle of Life

But, as Michelangelo knew very well, his work was a poor, dim image of what God had created. Over the plaster vault of the Sistine Chapel rose the immense dome of God's sky, breathtaking in its simple beauty. Mountains, seas, the continents—all these, and much more, are the creative work of God, the Master Artist.

God's world, so much bigger and more beautiful than Michelangelo's masterpiece, is the product of incomparably greater energy. As author Eugene Peterson has written, "The Bible begins with the announcement, 'In the beginning God created,' not 'sat majestic in the heavens' and not 'was filled with beauty and love.' He created. He did something." In the beginning, God went to work.

Genesis focuses attention on this creative, hardworking God. The word *God* appears 30 times in the 31 verses of chapter 1. He grabs our attention in action. Genesis is an account of his deeds, ringing splendidly with the magnificent effort of creation.

Mending Broken Pieces

Genesis also talks about the work of humankind—but the tone changes abruptly. God had barely finished creating the universe when human rebellion marred it, like a delinquent spraying graffiti on the Sistine Chapel. Chapters 3—11 of Genesis portray a series of disasters: Adam and Eve's rebellion, Cain's calculated murder of his brother, the worldwide wickedness leading to the great flood, and human arrogance at Babel.

God immediately began to mend the pieces his creatures had broken. He narrowed his scope from the whole universe to a single man—not a king or wealthy landowner, but a childless nomad, Abraham. Abraham, Sarah, Isaac, Rebekah, Jacob, Rachel, Joseph—the upward thrust from chapter 12 on came through God's work in these startlingly human individuals. They were far from perfect, yet God picked them up where they were and carried them forward. He promised them great things. He moved through them to restore his art. His creative activity did not stop on the seventh day.

Genesis and Revelation

Many people read the Old Testament as though it portrayed the "bad old days" before Jesus. But that's not an accurate picture. Actually, the first three chapters of Genesis link to the last book of the Bible, Revelation. They are like brackets of perfection around the sadness of life marred by sin, death, suffering, and hatred. In Genesis we learn that life didn't start out that way. In Revelation we find out it won't end that way either. But the Old and New Testaments take place between those brackets. Through Abraham, through Moses, ultimately in Jesus, God is hard at work to make things right.

How to Read Genesis

Genesis is one of the most enjoyable Old Testament books, full of memorable stories of people and events. It is a crucial book to know, for the rest of the Bible often refers back to it.

Genesis tells the story of many beginnings—the beginning of the universe, the beginning of sin, and perhaps most important, the beginning of God's work to restore a sinful humanity.

The book breaks into two major sections. The first 11 chapters take a big view. They give the origins of human society, including the familiar stories of Adam and Eve, Cain and Abel, Noah's ark, and the tower of Babel. Here, a few words carry great significance. You need to read slowly and reflectively, for what happens in a single line may echo off events for centuries to come. For instance, Adam and Eve's sin, because it was the first sin, became an emblem of disobedience against God.

Beginning at chapter 12, Genesis tells a different kind of story—that of a single family. The pace of the story slows to develop the personalities of Abraham, Isaac, Jacob, and Joseph. These fathers and sons are full of human faults and oddities. Do you recognize any of their traits in people you know?

Seeing their fully human personalities, try to understand what God's plans were for them as individuals—and through them, for the restoration of a whole world marred by sin.

PEOPLE YOU'LL MEET IN GENESIS

ADAM AND EVE (p. 26)
CAIN AND ABEL (p. 30)
NOAH (p. 32)
ABRAHAM (p. 36)
LOT (p. 38)

ISHMAEL (p. 40)
SARAH (p. 42)
ISAAC (p. 45)
REBEKAH (p. 48)
JACOB (p. 53)

LABAN (p. 57)
RACHEL (p. 60)
ESAU (p. 63)
JOSEPH (p. 78)

3-TRACK READING PLAN

For an explanation and complete listing of the 3-track reading plan, turn to page 7.

TRACK 1: **Two-Week Courses on the Bible**
The Track 1 reading program on the Old Testament includes three chapters from Genesis. See page 8 for a complete listing of this course.

TRACK 2: **An Overview of Genesis in 14 Days**
☐ Day 1. Read the Introduction to Genesis and chapter 1, the story of creation.
☐ Day 2. Read chapter 2, the story of Adam and Eve.
☐ Day 3. Read chapter 3, where sin enters a perfect world.
☐ Day 4. Read chapter 4, the story of Cain and Abel.
☐ Day 5. Read chapter 7, the story of Noah and the great flood.
☐ Day 6. Read chapter 8, the end of the great flood.
☐ Day 7. Read chapter 15, God's covenant with Abraham.
☐ Day 8. Read chapter 19, the destruction of Sodom and Gomorrah.
☐ Day 9. Read chapter 22, God's testing of Abraham.
☐ Day 10. Read chapter 27, in which Jacob cheats his brother Esau.
☐ Day 11. Read chapter 28, when Jacob, fleeing Esau, dreams about God.
☐ Day 12. Read chapter 37, the story of Joseph sold into slavery.

☐ Day 13. Read chapter 41, in which Joseph is raised to the highest position in Egypt.
☐ Day 14. Read chapter 45, in which Joseph reveals his identity to his brothers.
Now turn to page 9 for your next Track 2 reading project.

TRACK 3: **All of Genesis in 49 Days**
After you have read through Genesis, turn to pages 10–14 for your next Track 3 reading project.

☐1 ☐2 ☐3 ☐4 ☐5 ☐6 ☐7 ☐8
☐9 ☐10–11 ☐12 ☐13 ☐14 ☐15 ☐16 ☐17
☐18 ☐19 ☐20 ☐21 ☐22 ☐23 ☐24 ☐25
☐26 ☐27 ☐28 ☐29 ☐30 ☐31 ☐32 ☐33
☐34 ☐35 ☐36 ☐37 ☐38 ☐39 ☐40 ☐41
☐42 ☐43 ☐44 ☐45 ☐46 ☐47 ☐48 ☐49
☐50

The Beginning

1 In the beginning God created the heavens and the earth. ²Now the earth was*ᵃ* formless and empty, darkness was over the surface of the deep, and the Spirit of God was hovering over the waters.

³And God said, "Let there be light," and there was light. ⁴God saw that the light was good, and he separated the light from the darkness. ⁵God called the light "day," and the darkness he called "night." And there was evening, and there was morning—the first day.

⁶And God said, "Let there be an expanse between the waters to separate water from water." ⁷So God made the expanse and separated the water under the expanse from the water above it. And it was so. ⁸God called the expanse "sky." And there was evening, and there was morning—the second day.

⁹And God said, "Let the water under the sky be gathered to one place, and let dry ground appear." And it was so. ¹⁰God called the dry ground "land," and the gathered waters he called "seas." And God saw that it was good.

¹¹Then God said, "Let the land produce vegetation: seed-bearing plants and trees on the land that bear fruit with seed in it, according to their various kinds." And it was so. ¹²The land produced vegetation: plants bearing seed according to their kinds and trees bearing fruit with seed in it according to their kinds. And God saw that it was good. ¹³And there was evening, and there was morning—the third day.

¹⁴And God said, "Let there be lights in the expanse of the sky to separate the day from the night, and let them serve as signs to mark seasons and days and years, ¹⁵and let them be lights in the expanse of the sky to give light on the earth." And it was so. ¹⁶God made two great lights—the greater light to govern the day and the lesser light to govern the night. He also made the stars. ¹⁷God set them in the expanse of the sky to give light on the earth, ¹⁸to govern the day and the night, and to separate light from darkness. And God saw that it was good. ¹⁹And there was evening, and there was morning—the fourth day.

²⁰And God said, "Let the water teem with living creatures, and let birds fly above the earth across the expanse of the sky." ²¹So God created the great creatures of the sea and every living and moving thing with which the water teems, according to their kinds, and every winged bird according to its kind. And God saw that it was good. ²²God blessed them and said, "Be fruitful and increase in number and fill the water in the seas, and let the birds increase on the earth." ²³And there was evening, and there was morning—the fifth day.

²⁴And God said, "Let the land produce living creatures according to their kinds: livestock, creatures that move along the ground, and wild animals, each according to its kind." And it was so. ²⁵God made the wild animals according to their kinds, the livestock according to their kinds, and all the creatures that move along the ground according to their kinds. And God saw that it was good.

²⁶Then God said, "Let us make man in our image, in our likeness, and let them rule over the fish of the sea and the birds of the air, over the livestock, over all the earth,*ᵇ* and over all the creatures that move along the ground."

²⁷So God created man in his own image,
in the image of God he created him;
male and female he created them.

ᵃ2 Or possibly became   *ᵇ26 Hebrew; Syriac all the wild animals*

28God blessed them and said to them, "Be fruitful and increase in number; fill the earth and subdue it. Rule over the fish of the sea and the birds of the air and over every living creature that moves on the ground."

29Then God said, "I give you every seed-bearing plant on the face of the whole earth and every tree that has fruit with seed in it. They will be yours for food. 30And to all the beasts of the earth and all the birds of the air and all the creatures that move on the ground—everything that has the breath of life in it—I give every green plant for food." And it was so.

31God saw all that he had made, and it was very good. And there was evening, and there was morning—the sixth day.

2 Thus the heavens and the earth were completed in all their vast array.

2By the seventh day God had finished the work he had been doing; so on the seventh day he rested*a* from all his work. 3And God blessed the seventh day and made it holy, because on it he rested from all the work of creating that he had done.

Adam and Eve

4This is the account of the heavens and the earth when they were created.

When the LORD God made the earth and the heavens— 5and no shrub of the field had yet appeared on the earth*b* and no plant of the field had yet sprung up, for the LORD God had not sent rain on the earth*b* and there was no man to

---

> ### 1:31 God Takes Time
>
> *Why did God take "six days" to create? Why not make it all instantaneously—as he certainly could have? Genesis introduces God's normal way of working: through a process. Work that begins with a word may take time to complete. Similarly, Israel was freed from slavery overnight, but required forty years to reach the promised land. Christians are born anew in an instant, and, in a process that lasts a lifetime, God makes them new. The new heaven and new earth have been a long time coming, but God is in the process of making all things new.*

---

work the ground, 6but streams*c* came up from the earth and watered the whole surface of the ground— 7the LORD God formed the man*d* from the dust of the ground and breathed into his nostrils the breath of life, and the man became a living being.

8Now the LORD God had planted a garden in the east, in Eden; and there he put the man he had formed. 9And the LORD God made all kinds of trees grow out of the ground—trees that were pleasing to the eye and good for food. In the

---

a2 Or ceased; also in verse 3   b5 Or land; also in verse 6   c6 Or mist   d7 The Hebrew for man (adam) sounds like and may be related to the Hebrew for ground (adamah); it is also the name Adam (see Gen. 2:20).

ADAM AND EVE *First in Everything*

THEY WERE THE FIRST HUMAN beings on earth, part of God's original creation. As such, Adam and Eve set the standard for everything that followed. Their lives illustrate what God expects and loves from human beings—as well as what he loathes.

First ecologists. They were the first to name animals, the first to tend a garden, the first to be placed in charge of all the creatures. They took on the huge task of caring for earth and guiding its proper use.

First to form a relationship with God. Adam and Eve were made in God's image. He conversed with them and gave them responsibilities. When they failed God they felt ashamed and feared meeting him.

First married couple. God himself made the introductions and gave the first couple the delight of each other, body and soul. They also became the first parents, though their very first child (Cain) brought much pain as well as joy.

First to sin against God. They had only to follow directions, but they failed. In response they hid from God and blamed each other. "Think of all the squabbles Adam and Eve must have had in the course of their nine hundred years," wrote Martin Luther. "Eve would say, 'You ate the apple,' and Adam would retort, 'You gave it to me.'"

In the end, the first two human beings were banished from Eden and driven out into a world full of problems God had never intended for them to confront. In that, as in everything, these two led the way for all of us.

Life Questions: Are you ever in a position to set an example for others? What can you learn from Adam and Eve's experience?

middle of the garden were the tree of life and the tree of the knowledge of good and evil.

¹⁰A river watering the garden flowed from Eden; from there it was separated into four headwaters. ¹¹The name of the first is the Pishon; it winds through the entire land of Havilah, where there is gold. ¹²(The gold of that land is good; aromatic resin*a* and onyx are also there.) ¹³The name of the second river is the Gihon; it winds through the entire land of Cush.*b* ¹⁴The name of the third river is the Tigris; it runs along the east side of Asshur. And the fourth river is the Euphrates.

¹⁵The LORD God took the man and put him in the Garden of Eden to work it and take care of it. ¹⁶And the LORD God commanded the man, "You are free to eat from any tree in the garden; ¹⁷but you must not eat from the tree of the knowledge of good and evil, for when you eat of it you will surely die."

¹⁸The LORD God said, "It is not good for the man to be alone. I will make a helper suitable for him."

¹⁹Now the LORD God had formed out of the ground all the beasts of the field and all the birds of the air. He brought them to the man to see what he would name them; and whatever the man called each living creature, that was its name. ²⁰So the man gave names to all the livestock, the birds of the air and all the beasts of the field.

But for Adam*c* no suitable helper was found. ²¹So the LORD God caused the man to fall into a deep sleep; and while he was sleeping, he took one of the man's ribs*d* and closed up the place with flesh. ²²Then the LORD God made a woman from the rib*e* he had taken out of the man, and he brought her to the man.

²³The man said,

"This is now bone of my bones
    and flesh of my flesh;
she shall be called 'woman,'*f*
    for she was taken out of man."

²⁴For this reason a man will leave his father and mother and be united to his wife, and they will become one flesh.

²⁵The man and his wife were both naked, and they felt no shame.

The Fall of Man

3 Now the serpent was more crafty than any of the wild animals the LORD God had made. He said to the woman, "Did God really say, 'You must not eat from any tree in the garden'?"

²The woman said to the serpent, "We may eat fruit from the trees in the garden, ³but God did say, 'You must not eat fruit from the tree that is in the middle of the garden, and you must not touch it, or you will die.'"

⁴"You will not surely die," the serpent said to

2:23–25 The First Marriage

Adam joyfully recognized that he and Eve belonged together. As verse 24 suggests, this suitability is the basis for all marriages. This passage was quoted by Jesus (Matthew 19:5; Mark 10:7–8) and Paul (1 Corinthians 6:16; Ephesians 5:31) in their comments on sex and marriage.

the woman. ⁵"For God knows that when you eat of it your eyes will be opened, and you will be like God, knowing good and evil."

⁶When the woman saw that the fruit of the tree was good for food and pleasing to the eye, and also desirable for gaining wisdom, she took some and ate it. She also gave some to her husband, who was with her, and he ate it. ⁷Then the eyes of both of them were opened, and they realized they were naked; so they sewed fig leaves together and made coverings for themselves.

3:7 Sin and Shame

When Adam and Eve disobeyed God, they immediately became ashamed of their bodies and wanted to hide. Ever since, sinful human beings have been "hiding" from each other and from God.

God asked Adam and Eve three questions, typical of the questions he puts to anyone "in hiding": 1) Where are you? (And why are you hiding from me?) 2) Who told you that you were naked? (And why did you believe somebody else, not me?) 3) What is this you have done? (And are you ready to take responsibility for it?)

⁸Then the man and his wife heard the sound of the LORD God as he was walking in the garden in the cool of the day, and they hid from the LORD God among the trees of the garden. ⁹But the LORD God called to the man, "Where are you?"

¹⁰He answered, "I heard you in the garden, and I was afraid because I was naked; so I hid."

¹¹And he said, "Who told you that you were naked? Have you eaten from the tree that I commanded you not to eat from?"

¹²The man said, "The woman you put here

---

*a 12 Or good; pearls   *b 13 Possibly southeast Mesopotamia   *c 20 Or the man   *d 21 Or took part of the man's side   *e 22 Or part   *f 23 The Hebrew for woman sounds like the Hebrew for man.

with me—she gave me some fruit from the tree, and I ate it."

¹³Then the LORD God said to the woman, "What is this you have done?"

The woman said, "The serpent deceived me, and I ate."

¹⁴So the LORD God said to the serpent, "Because you have done this,

"Cursed are you above all the livestock
    and all the wild animals!
You will crawl on your belly
    and you will eat dust
    all the days of your life.
¹⁵And I will put enmity
    between you and the woman,
    and between your offspring*a* and hers;
he will crush*b* your head,
    and you will strike his heel."

a 15 Or *seed*   *b 15* Or *strike*

¹⁶To the woman he said,

"I will greatly increase your pains in
        childbearing;
    with pain you will give birth to children.
Your desire will be for your husband,
    and he will rule over you."

¹⁷To Adam he said, "Because you listened to your wife and ate from the tree about which I commanded you, 'You must not eat of it,'

"Cursed is the ground because of you;
    through painful toil you will eat of it
    all the days of your life.
¹⁸It will produce thorns and thistles for you,
    and you will eat the plants of the field.
¹⁹By the sweat of your brow
    you will eat your food
until you return to the ground,

Where We Came From
Above all else, Genesis says this: God did it

THE BIOLOGY TEACHER DISPLAYS A chart showing six animals. At one end is an ape standing upright, its hands swinging below its knees. At the other end, a rather hairy, stooped man in skins. "These are the stages of human evolution," the teacher declares, "over a period of several million years."

One agonized student shoots up his hand. "I believe in the Bible," he stammers, "that God made the earth and that the first man was Adam."

The teacher lets him finish, then dismisses his view. "Everybody is free to have his own religious beliefs. But science has proven that evolution is a fact."

Scenes like this have thrown confusion over the first three chapters of the Bible. It's impossible to read about Adam and Eve without wondering how they fit in with the bones scientists proclaim as "earliest man."

> The LORD God formed the man from the dust of the ground and breathed into his nostrils the breath of life, and the man became a living being. 2:7

The Main Point

These differences stir up controversy, even court cases. Certainly they are important issues. It's unfortunate, though, that the debate over process diverts attention from the main truth Genesis teaches.

Above everything else, it proclaims this: God did it. We are not here by accident, nor are we here merely to please ourselves. We owe our very existence to God. Every helium atom, every spiral galaxy, every living creature exists because God wants it to. Genesis 1–3 is the artist's signature on the painting, saying, "This is mine."

God Made Us Good

Genesis 1–3 pays humanity its highest compliment. After making all the glories of the world, God topped off his work with man and woman. He put them in charge. Unlike the animals, they were like him, "in his image." "Very good," he said to himself when he had finished. With humans he quit, satisfied.

Nobody, including God, has been satisfied with human beings since then. We were made good, but we disobeyed God right from the beginning. We've been suffering the consequences ever since. Genesis helps us understand why the universe is so flagrantly lovely, and yet so tragic. It is lovely because God made it. But it is tragic because he entrusted it to us—and we failed.

Life Questions: People say they can see God reflected in stars, forests, sunsets. What about people? How can you see God's artistry in them?

since from it you were taken;
for dust you are
and to dust you will return."

[20]Adam[a] named his wife Eve,[b] because she would become the mother of all the living.

[21]The LORD God made garments of skin for Adam and his wife and clothed them. [22]And the LORD God said, "The man has now become like one of us, knowing good and evil. He must not be allowed to reach out his hand and take also from the tree of life and eat, and live forever." [23]So the LORD God banished him from the Garden of Eden to work the ground from which he had been taken. [24]After he drove the man out, he placed on the east side[c] of the Garden of Eden cherubim and a flaming sword flashing back and forth to guard the way to the tree of life.

Cain and Abel

4 Adam[a] lay with his wife Eve, and she became pregnant and gave birth to Cain.[d] She said, "With the help of the LORD I have brought forth[e] a man." [2]Later she gave birth to his brother Abel.

Now Abel kept flocks, and Cain worked the soil. [3]In the course of time Cain brought some of the fruits of the soil as an offering to the LORD. [4]But Abel brought fat portions from some of the firstborn of his flock. The LORD looked with favor

> ### 4:4 Improper Offerings
> *Why God preferred Abel's offering to Cain's is uncertain; later in the Old Testament both animal and agricultural offerings were accepted by God. Quite possibly, Cain's problem was his attitude. Cain certainly became instantly angry with God when things did not go his way.*

on Abel and his offering, [5]but on Cain and his offering he did not look with favor. So Cain was very angry, and his face was downcast.

[6]Then the LORD said to Cain, "Why are you angry? Why is your face downcast? [7]If you do what is right, will you not be accepted? But if you do not do what is right, sin is crouching at your door; it desires to have you, but you must master it."

[8]Now Cain said to his brother Abel, "Let's go out to the field."[f] And while they were in the field, Cain attacked his brother Abel and killed him.

[9]Then the LORD said to Cain, "Where is your brother Abel?"

"I don't know," he replied. "Am I my brother's keeper?"

[10]The LORD said, "What have you done? Listen! Your brother's blood cries out to me from the ground. [11]Now you are under a curse and driven from the ground, which opened its mouth to receive your brother's blood from your hand. [12]When you work the ground, it will no longer yield its crops for you. You will be a restless wanderer on the earth."

[13]Cain said to the LORD, "My punishment is more than I can bear. [14]Today you are driving me from the land, and I will be hidden from your presence; I will be a restless wanderer on the earth, and whoever finds me will kill me."

[15]But the LORD said to him, "Not so[g]; if anyone kills Cain, he will suffer vengeance seven times over." Then the LORD put a mark on Cain so that no one who found him would kill him. [16]So Cain went out from the LORD's presence and lived in the land of Nod,[h] east of Eden.

[17]Cain lay with his wife, and she became pregnant and gave birth to Enoch. Cain was then building a city, and he named it after his son Enoch. [18]To Enoch was born Irad, and Irad was the father of Mehujael, and Mehujael was the father of Methushael, and Methushael was the father of Lamech.

[19]Lamech married two women, one named Adah and the other Zillah. [20]Adah gave birth to Jabal; he was the father of those who live in tents and raise livestock. [21]His brother's name was Jubal; he was the father of all who play the harp and flute. [22]Zillah also had a son, Tubal-Cain, who forged all kinds of tools out of[i] bronze and iron. Tubal-Cain's sister was Naamah.

[23]Lamech said to his wives,

"Adah and Zillah, listen to me;
  wives of Lamech, hear my words.
I have killed[j] a man for wounding me,
  a young man for injuring me.
[24]If Cain is avenged seven times,
  then Lamech seventy-seven times."

[25]Adam lay with his wife again, and she gave birth to a son and named him Seth,[k] saying, "God has granted me another child in place of Abel, since Cain killed him." [26]Seth also had a son, and he named him Enosh.

At that time men began to call on[l] the name of the LORD.

---

[a]20,1 Or *The man*   [b]20 *Eve* probably means *living.*
for *brought forth* or *acquired.*   [e]1 Or *have acquired*   [c]24 Or *placed in front*   [d]1 *Cain* sounds like the Hebrew
Masoretic Text does not have *"Let's go out to the field."*   [f]8 Samaritan Pentateuch, Septuagint, Vulgate and Syriac;
means *wandering* (see verses 12 and 14).   [i]22 Or *who instructed all who work in*   [g]15 Septuagint, Vulgate and Syriac; Hebrew *Very well*   [h]16 *Nod*
probably means *granted.*   [l]26 Or *to proclaim*   [j]23 Or *I will kill*   [k]25 *Seth*

From Adam to Noah

5 This is the written account of Adam's line.

When God created man, he made him in the likeness of God. ²He created them male and female and blessed them. And when they were created, he called them "man.ᵃ"

³When Adam had lived 130 years, he had a son in his own likeness, in his own image; and he named him Seth. ⁴After Seth was born, Adam lived 800 years and had other sons and daughters. ⁵Altogether, Adam lived 930 years, and then he died.

⁶When Seth had lived 105 years, he became the fatherᵇ of Enosh. ⁷And after he became the father of Enosh, Seth lived 807 years and had other sons and daughters. ⁸Altogether, Seth lived 912 years, and then he died.

⁹When Enosh had lived 90 years, he became the father of Kenan. ¹⁰And after he became the father of Kenan, Enosh lived 815 years and had other sons and daughters. ¹¹Altogether, Enosh lived 905 years, and then he died.

¹²When Kenan had lived 70 years, he became the father of Mahalalel. ¹³And after he became the father of Mahalalel, Kenan lived 840 years and had other sons and daughters. ¹⁴Altogether, Kenan lived 910 years, and then he died.

¹⁵When Mahalalel had lived 65 years, he became the father of Jared. ¹⁶And after he became the father of Jared, Mahalalel lived 830 years and had other sons and daughters. ¹⁷Altogether, Mahalalel lived 895 years, and then he died.

¹⁸When Jared had lived 162 years, he became the father of Enoch. ¹⁹And after he became the father of Enoch, Jared lived 800 years and had other sons and daughters. ²⁰Altogether, Jared lived 962 years, and then he died.

²¹When Enoch had lived 65 years, he became the father of Methuselah. ²²And after he became the father of Methuselah, Enoch walked with God 300 years and had other sons and daughters. ²³Altogether, Enoch lived 365 years. ²⁴Enoch walked with God; then he was no more, because God took him away.

5:24 The Man Who Did Not Die

All but one of the brief biographies in chapter 5 end with the words "and then he died." We know very little about the exception, Enoch, except that he walked with God. Enoch did not die; he "was no more, because God took him away." Based on this evidence, Hebrews 11:5–6 commends Enoch as a man of faith, since "without faith it is impossible to please God."

²⁵When Methuselah had lived 187 years, he became the father of Lamech. ²⁶And after he became the father of Lamech, Methuselah lived 782 years and had other sons and daughters. ²⁷Altogether, Methuselah lived 969 years, and then he died.

²⁸When Lamech had lived 182 years, he had a son. ²⁹He named him Noahᶜ and said, "He will comfort us in the labor and painful toil of our hands caused by the ground the LORD has cursed." ³⁰After Noah was born, Lamech lived 595 years and had other sons and daughters. ³¹Altogether, Lamech lived 777 years, and then he died.

ᵃ2 Hebrew *adam*   ᵇ6 *Father* may mean *ancestor*; also in verses 7-26.   ᶜ29 *Noah* sounds like the Hebrew for *comfort*.

CAIN AND ABEL *Blood Brothers*

THEIR PARENTS HAD STARTED THE rebellion against God. Not much time passed before Cain took sin to its logical conclusion. The first child on earth became the first murderer.

Cain and Abel were the first of many feuding siblings. After them came Isaac and Ishmael, Jacob and Esau, Rachel and Leah, Joseph and his brothers. It's a theme song in Genesis (and in life): Blood kin have a hard time getting along. They can make bitter rivals.

The Bible tells us little about Abel and a good deal about Cain. That makes sad sense because as sinful humans we see more of ourselves in Cain than in Abel. Cain wears his emotions on his sleeve: first murderous anger, then defensiveness and finally shame and fear. In response to Cain's great crime, God both punishes and protects him. He must leave home to wander all his life, yet God also provides him with a measure of protection, "the mark of Cain" (4:15).

Cain's children set the pattern for humanity as it has lived ever since, a mixture of good and bad. On the one hand, as musicians, metalworkers and farmers, they helped civilize the earth. On the other hand, Cain's problems got passed down to future generations. Where Cain felt shame for his crime and punishment, his descendant Lamech would boast about his own murderous deed (Genesis 4:23–24).

Life Questions: Which of Cain's responses to God—anger, defensiveness, fear, shame—do you identify with most easily?

[32]After Noah was 500 years old, he became the father of Shem, Ham and Japheth.

The Flood

6 When men began to increase in number on the earth and daughters were born to them, [2]the sons of God saw that the daughters of men were beautiful, and they married any of them

> ### 6:2 The Sons of God
>
> *This mysterious description may refer to the "sons of Seth," the line of God's people from Adam to Noah, or it may refer to angels, often called "sons of God" in the Old Testament. However you interpret it, the point is that evil behavior increased in the world, a fact that led to punishment by a flood.*

they chose. [3]Then the LORD said, "My Spirit will not contend with[a] man forever, for he is mortal[b]; his days will be a hundred and twenty years."

[4]The Nephilim were on the earth in those days—and also afterward—when the sons of God went to the daughters of men and had children by them. They were the heroes of old, men of renown.

[5]The LORD saw how great man's wickedness on the earth had become, and that every inclination of the thoughts of his heart was only evil all the time. [6]The LORD was grieved that he had made man on the earth, and his heart was filled with pain. [7]So the LORD said, "I will wipe mankind, whom I have created, from the face of the earth—men and animals, and creatures that move along the ground, and birds of the air—for I am grieved that I have made them." [8]But Noah found favor in the eyes of the LORD.

[9]This is the account of Noah.

Noah was a righteous man, blameless among the people of his time, and he walked with God. [10]Noah had three sons: Shem, Ham and Japheth.

[11]Now the earth was corrupt in God's sight and was full of violence. [12]God saw how corrupt the earth had become, for all the people on earth had corrupted their ways. [13]So God said to Noah, "I am going to put an end to all people, for the earth is filled with violence because of them. I am surely going to destroy both them and the earth. [14]So make yourself an ark of cypress[c] wood; make rooms in it and coat it with pitch inside and out. [15]This is how you are to build it: The ark is to be 450 feet long, 75 feet wide and 45 feet

high.[d] [16]Make a roof for it and finish[e] the ark to within 18 inches[f] of the top. Put a door in the side of the ark and make lower, middle and upper decks. [17]I am going to bring floodwaters on the earth to destroy all life under the heavens, every creature that has the breath of life in it. Everything on earth will perish. [18]But I will establish my covenant with you, and you will enter the ark—you and your sons and your wife and your sons' wives with you. [19]You are to bring into the ark two of all living creatures, male and female, to keep them alive with you. [20]Two of every kind of bird, of every kind of animal and of every kind of creature that moves along the ground will come to you to be kept alive. [21]You are to take every kind of food that is to be eaten and store it away as food for you and for them."

[22]Noah did everything just as God commanded him.

7 The LORD then said to Noah, "Go into the ark, you and your whole family, because I have found you righteous in this generation. [2]Take with you seven[g] of every kind of clean animal, a male and its mate, and two of every kind of unclean animal, a male and its mate, [3]and also seven of every kind of bird, male and female, to keep their various kinds alive throughout the earth. [4]Seven days from now I will send rain on the earth for forty days and forty nights, and I will wipe from the face of the earth every living creature I have made."

[5]And Noah did all that the LORD commanded him.

[6]Noah was six hundred years old when the floodwaters came on the earth. [7]And Noah and his sons and his wife and his sons' wives entered the ark to escape the waters of the flood. [8]Pairs of clean and unclean animals, of birds and of all creatures that move along the ground, [9]male and female, came to Noah and entered the ark, as God had commanded Noah. [10]And after the seven days the floodwaters came on the earth.

[11]In the six hundredth year of Noah's life, on the seventeenth day of the second month—on that day all the springs of the great deep burst forth, and the floodgates of the heavens were opened. [12]And rain fell on the earth forty days and forty nights.

[13]On that very day Noah and his sons, Shem, Ham and Japheth, together with his wife and the wives of his three sons, entered the ark. [14]They had with them every wild animal according to its kind, all livestock according to their kinds, every creature that moves along the ground according to its kind and every bird according to its kind, everything with wings. [15]Pairs of all creatures that

---

[a]3 Or *My spirit will not remain in*   [b]3 Or *corrupt*   [c]14 The meaning of the Hebrew for this word is uncertain.   [d]15 Hebrew *300 cubits long, 50 cubits wide and 30 cubits high* (about 140 meters long, 23 meters wide and 13.5 meters high)   [e]16 Or *Make an opening for light by finishing*   [f]16 Hebrew *a cubit* (about 0.5 meter)   [g]2 Or *seven pairs*; also in verse 3

have the breath of life in them came to Noah and entered the ark. [16]The animals going in were male and female of every living thing, as God had commanded Noah. Then the LORD shut him in.

[17]For forty days the flood kept coming on the earth, and as the waters increased they lifted the ark high above the earth. [18]The waters rose and increased greatly on the earth, and the ark floated on the surface of the water. [19]They rose greatly on the earth, and all the high mountains under the entire heavens were covered. [20]The waters rose and covered the mountains to a depth of more than twenty feet.[a,b] [21]Every living thing that moved on the earth perished—birds, livestock, wild animals, all the creatures that swarm over the earth, and all mankind. [22]Everything on dry land that had the breath of life in its nostrils died. [23]Every living thing on the face of the earth was wiped out; men and animals and the creatures that move along the ground and the birds of the air were wiped from the earth. Only Noah was left, and those with him in the ark.

[24]The waters flooded the earth for a hundred and fifty days.

8 But God remembered Noah and all the wild animals and the livestock that were with him in the ark, and he sent a wind over the earth, and the waters receded. [2]Now the springs of the deep and the floodgates of the heavens had been closed, and the rain had stopped falling from the sky. [3]The water receded steadily from the earth. At the end of the hundred and fifty days the water had gone down, [4]and on the seventeenth day of the seventh month the ark came to rest on the mountains of Ararat. [5]The waters continued to recede until the tenth month, and on the first day of the tenth month the tops of the mountains became visible.

[6]After forty days Noah opened the window he had made in the ark [7]and sent out a raven, and it kept flying back and forth until the water had dried up from the earth. [8]Then he sent out a dove to see if the water had receded from the surface of the ground. [9]But the dove could find no place to set its feet because there was water over all the surface of the earth; so it returned to Noah in the ark. He reached out his hand and took the dove and brought it back to himself in the ark. [10]He waited seven more days and again sent out the dove from the ark. [11]When the dove returned to him in the evening, there in its beak was a freshly plucked olive leaf! Then Noah knew that the

8:11 Peace Symbol

The dove with an olive branch stands as a symbol for peace, and the origin of that symbol traces back to this account of restored peace between God and his creation. The olive leaf carried by the dove told Noah that lower elevations (where olives grow) were above water and had sprouted new life.

water had receded from the earth. [12]He waited seven more days and sent the dove out again, but this time it did not return to him.

[13]By the first day of the first month of Noah's six hundred and first year, the water had dried up from the earth. Noah then removed the covering from the ark and saw that the surface of the ground was dry. [14]By the twenty-seventh day of the second month the earth was completely dry.

---

[a]20 Hebrew *fifteen cubits* (about 6.9 meters)   [b]20 Or *rose more than twenty feet, and the mountains were covered*

NOAH *Starting Over*

THE PROBLEM WITH THE PLANET God made was not its geology, biology or meteorology. The problem centered, rather, in a single species: *Homo sapiens.* Sin, spreading like a disease, had taken over human thought and action. As a result God chose to blot out much of his creation and start all over again, using Noah for this new beginning.

Characteristically, Noah obeyed right away when God announced his plans. Noah "walked with God," says Genesis (6:9). He worked hard, building a gigantic, seaworthy structure and storing up food for hundreds of animals. Repeatedly the Bible says that Noah did everything "just as God commanded him."

Noah and his family spent more than a year confined in the ark. When they emerged at last to step out on muddy ground, their first action was to worship God. Impressed, God made a new covenant with Noah, promising never again to destroy the earth. He urged Noah and his family to be fruitful and multiply, just as he had urged Adam and Eve in the beginning.

Did this new beginning work? The last we hear of Noah shows that sin had not been remedied. Noah got drunk, shamed himself in front of his sons, and cursed one of his grandsons (9:20–24). Not even a flood could solve the problem of sin, for it lived on inside the best of people, even Noah.

Life Questions: If you were given an assignment like Noah's, how would you respond?

¹⁵Then God said to Noah, ¹⁶"Come out of the ark, you and your wife and your sons and their wives. ¹⁷Bring out every kind of living creature that is with you—the birds, the animals, and all the creatures that move along the ground—so they can multiply on the earth and be fruitful and increase in number upon it."

¹⁸So Noah came out, together with his sons and his wife and his sons' wives. ¹⁹All the animals and all the creatures that move along the ground and all the birds—everything that moves on the earth—came out of the ark, one kind after another.

²⁰Then Noah built an altar to the LORD and, taking some of all the clean animals and clean birds, he sacrificed burnt offerings on it. ²¹The LORD smelled the pleasing aroma and said in his heart: "Never again will I curse the ground because of man, even though[a] every inclination of his heart is evil from childhood. And never again will I destroy all living creatures, as I have done.

²²"As long as the earth endures,
    seedtime and harvest,
    cold and heat,
    summer and winter,
    day and night
    will never cease."

God's Covenant With Noah

9 Then God blessed Noah and his sons, saying to them, "Be fruitful and increase in number and fill the earth. ²The fear and dread of you will fall upon all the beasts of the earth and all the birds of the air, upon every creature that moves along the ground, and upon all the fish of the sea; they are given into your hands. ³Everything that lives and moves will be food for you. Just as I gave you the green plants, I now give you everything.

⁴"But you must not eat meat that has its lifeblood still in it. ⁵And for your lifeblood I will surely demand an accounting. I will demand an accounting from every animal. And from each man, too, I will demand an accounting for the life of his fellow man.

⁶"Whoever sheds the blood of man,
    by man shall his blood be shed;
    for in the image of God
    has God made man.

⁷As for you, be fruitful and increase in number; multiply on the earth and increase upon it."

⁸Then God said to Noah and to his sons with him: ⁹"I now establish my covenant with you and with your descendants after you ¹⁰and with every living creature that was with you—the birds, the livestock and all the wild animals, all those that came out of the ark with you—every living creature on earth. ¹¹I establish my covenant with you: Never again will all life be cut off by the waters of a flood; never again will there be a flood to destroy the earth."

9:4 Reverence for Life

In the Garden of Eden God had provided plants for humanity's food. Here, for the first time, he gave permission to add meat to their diet. Still, an animal was not to be eaten with "its lifeblood still in it." Kosher dietary requirements kept by Orthodox Jews today derive partly from this statement. Leviticus 17:10–14 gives more detail.

The intent, many commentators believe, was to remind God's people to reverence life, including animal life. This passage makes clear, however, that human life has a special significance. Ironically, capital punishment derives its legitimacy from this. Murderers who destroy human life actually attack the image of God. Therefore God demands an accounting.

¹²And God said, "This is the sign of the covenant I am making between me and you and every living creature with you, a covenant for all generations to come: ¹³I have set my rainbow in the clouds, and it will be the sign of the covenant between me and the earth. ¹⁴Whenever I bring clouds over the earth and the rainbow appears in the clouds, ¹⁵I will remember my covenant between me and you and all living creatures of every kind. Never again will the waters become a flood to destroy all life. ¹⁶Whenever the rainbow appears in the clouds, I will see it and remember the everlasting covenant between God and all living creatures of every kind on the earth."

9:12 The Reason for Rainbows

Throughout the Bible, God makes covenant agreements with the people he loves. This first recorded covenant was marked by an appropriate symbol—the rainbow. While later covenants applied specifically to the Israelites, this one extended—and still extends—to every living creature.

¹⁷So God said to Noah, "This is the sign of the covenant I have established between me and all life on the earth."

The Sons of Noah

¹⁸The sons of Noah who came out of the ark were Shem, Ham and Japheth. (Ham was the

---

[a] 21 Or *man, for*

father of Canaan.) [19]These were the three sons of Noah, and from them came the people who were scattered over the earth.

[20]Noah, a man of the soil, proceeded[a] to plant a vineyard. [21]When he drank some of its wine, he became drunk and lay uncovered inside his tent. [22]Ham, the father of Canaan, saw his father's nakedness and told his two brothers outside. [23]But Shem and Japheth took a garment and laid it across their shoulders; then they walked in backward and covered their father's nakedness. Their faces were turned the other way so that they would not see their father's nakedness.

[24]When Noah awoke from his wine and found out what his youngest son had done to him, [25]he said,

"Cursed be Canaan!
    The lowest of slaves
    will he be to his brothers."

[26]He also said,

"Blessed be the LORD, the God of Shem!
    May Canaan be the slave of Shem.[b]
[27]May God extend the territory of Japheth[c];
    may Japheth live in the tents of Shem,
    and may Canaan be his[d] slave."

[28]After the flood Noah lived 350 years. [29]Altogether, Noah lived 950 years, and then he died.

The Table of Nations

10 This is the account of Shem, Ham and Japheth, Noah's sons, who themselves had sons after the flood.

The Japhethites

[2]The sons[e] of Japheth:
    Gomer, Magog, Madai, Javan, Tubal, Meshech and Tiras.
[3]The sons of Gomer:
    Ashkenaz, Riphath and Togarmah.
[4]The sons of Javan:
    Elishah, Tarshish, the Kittim and the Rodanim.[f] [5](From these the maritime peoples spread out into their territories by their clans within their nations, each with its own language.)

The Hamites

[6]The sons of Ham:
    Cush, Mizraim,[g] Put and Canaan.
[7]The sons of Cush:
    Seba, Havilah, Sabtah, Raamah and Sabteca.
The sons of Raamah:
    Sheba and Dedan.

[8]Cush was the father[h] of Nimrod, who grew to be a mighty warrior on the earth. [9]He was a mighty hunter before the LORD; that is why it is said, "Like Nimrod, a mighty hunter before the LORD." [10]The first centers of his kingdom were Babylon, Erech, Akkad and Calneh, in[i] Shinar.[j] [11]From that land he went to Assyria, where he built Nineveh, Rehoboth Ir,[k] Calah [12]and Resen, which is between Nineveh and Calah; that is the great city.

[13]Mizraim was the father of
    the Ludites, Anamites, Lehabites, Naphtuhites, [14]Pathrusites, Casluhites (from whom the Philistines came) and Caphtorites.
[15]Canaan was the father of
    Sidon his firstborn,[l] and of the Hittites, [16]Jebusites, Amorites, Girgashites, [17]Hivites, Arkites, Sinites, [18]Arvadites, Zemarites and Hamathites.

Later the Canaanite clans scattered [19]and the borders of Canaan reached from Sidon toward Gerar as far as Gaza, and then toward Sodom, Gomorrah, Admah and Zeboiim, as far as Lasha. [20]These are the sons of Ham by their clans and languages, in their territories and nations.

The Semites

[21]Sons were also born to Shem, whose older brother was[m] Japheth; Shem was the ancestor of all the sons of Eber.

[22]The sons of Shem:
    Elam, Asshur, Arphaxad, Lud and Aram.
[23]The sons of Aram:
    Uz, Hul, Gether and Meshech.[n]
[24]Arphaxad was the father of[o] Shelah, and Shelah the father of Eber.
[25]Two sons were born to Eber:
    One was named Peleg,[p] because in his time the earth was divided; his brother was named Joktan.
[26]Joktan was the father of
    Almodad, Sheleph, Hazarmaveth, Jerah, [27]Hadoram, Uzal, Diklah, [28]Obal, Abimael, Sheba, [29]Ophir, Havilah and Jobab. All these were sons of Joktan.

a20 Or soil, was the first   b26 Or be his slave   c27 Japheth sounds like the Hebrew for extend.   d27 Or their
e2 Sons may mean descendants or successors or nations; also in verses 3, 4, 6, 7, 20-23, 29 and 31.   f4 Some
manuscripts of the Masoretic Text and Samaritan Pentateuch (see also Septuagint and 1 Chron. 1:7); most manuscripts of
the Masoretic Text Dodanim   g6 That is, Egypt; also in verse 13   h8 Father may mean ancestor or predecessor or
founder; also in verses 13, 15, 24 and 26.   i10 Or Erech and Akkad—all of them in   j10 That is, Babylonia
k11 Or Nineveh with its city squares   l15 Or of the Sidonians, the foremost   m21 Or Shem, the older brother of
n23 See Septuagint and 1 Chron. 1:17; Hebrew Mash   o24 Hebrew; Septuagint father of Cainan, and Cainan was the
father of   p25 Peleg means division.

[30]The region where they lived stretched from Mesha toward Sephar, in the eastern hill country.

[31]These are the sons of Shem by their clans and languages, in their territories and nations.

[32]These are the clans of Noah's sons, according to their lines of descent, within their nations. From these the nations spread out over the earth after the flood.

The Tower of Babel

11 Now the whole world had one language and a common speech. [2]As men moved eastward,[a] they found a plain in Shinar[b] and settled there.

[3]They said to each other, "Come, let's make bricks and bake them thoroughly." They used brick instead of stone, and tar for mortar. [4]Then they said, "Come, let us build ourselves a city, with a tower that reaches to the heavens, so that we may make a name for ourselves and not be scattered over the face of the whole earth."

[5]But the LORD came down to see the city and the tower that the men were building. [6]The LORD said, "If as one people speaking the same language they have begun to do this, then nothing they plan to do will be impossible for them.

11:6 Human Ambition

People are ambitious—they want to succeed. Genesis portrays humans as so ambitious that they try to compete with, rather than serve, God. This was Adam and Eve's sin (3:5,22), and at Babel people were at it again, in a citywide effort. God frustrated their plans by confusing their language.

[7]Come, let us go down and confuse their language so they will not understand each other."

[8]So the LORD scattered them from there over all the earth, and they stopped building the city. [9]That is why it was called Babel[c]—because there the LORD confused the language of the whole world. From there the LORD scattered them over the face of the whole earth.

From Shem to Abram

[10]This is the account of Shem.

Two years after the flood, when Shem was 100 years old, he became the father[d] of Arphaxad. [11]And after he became the father of Arphaxad, Shem lived 500 years and had other sons and daughters.

[12]When Arphaxad had lived 35 years, he became the father of Shelah. [13]And after he became the father of Shelah, Arphaxad lived 403 years and had other sons and daughters.[e]

[14]When Shelah had lived 30 years, he became the father of Eber. [15]And after he became the father of Eber, Shelah lived 403 years and had other sons and daughters.

[16]When Eber had lived 34 years, he became the father of Peleg. [17]And after he became the father of Peleg, Eber lived 430 years and had other sons and daughters.

[18]When Peleg had lived 30 years, he became the father of Reu. [19]And after he became the father of Reu, Peleg lived 209 years and had other sons and daughters.

[20]When Reu had lived 32 years, he became the father of Serug. [21]And after he became the father of Serug, Reu lived 207 years and had other sons and daughters.

[22]When Serug had lived 30 years, he became the father of Nahor. [23]And after he became the father of Nahor, Serug lived 200 years and had other sons and daughters.

[24]When Nahor had lived 29 years, he became the father of Terah. [25]And after he became the father of Terah, Nahor lived 119 years and had other sons and daughters.

[26]After Terah had lived 70 years, he became the father of Abram, Nahor and Haran.

[27]This is the account of Terah.

Terah became the father of Abram, Nahor and Haran. And Haran became the father of Lot. [28]While his father Terah was still alive, Haran died in Ur of the Chaldeans, in the land of his birth. [29]Abram and Nahor both married. The name of Abram's wife was Sarai, and the name of Nahor's wife was Milcah; she was the daughter of Haran, the father of both Milcah and Iscah. [30]Now Sarai was barren; she had no children.

[31]Terah took his son Abram, his grandson Lot son of Haran, and his daughter-in-law Sarai, the wife of his son Abram, and together they set out from Ur of the Chaldeans to go to Canaan. But when they came to Haran, they settled there.

[32]Terah lived 205 years, and he died in Haran.

The Call of Abram

12 The LORD had said to Abram, "Leave your country, your people and your father's household and go to the land I will show you.

[2]"I will make you into a great nation
    and I will bless you;
I will make your name great,

---

[a]2 Or *from the east;* or *in the east*   [b]2 That is, Babylonia   [c]9 That is, Babylon; *Babel* sounds like the Hebrew for *confused.*   [d]10 *Father* may mean *ancestor;* also in verses 11-25.   [e]12,13 Hebrew; Septuagint (see also Luke 3:35, 36 and note at Gen. 10:24) *35 years, he became the father of Cainan.* [13]*And after he became the father of Cainan, Arphaxad lived 430 years and had other sons and daughters, and then he died. When Cainan had lived 130 years, he became the father of Shelah. And after he became the father of Shelah, Cainan lived 330 years and had other sons and daughters*

and you will be a blessing.
³I will bless those who bless you,
    and whoever curses you I will curse;
and all peoples on earth
    will be blessed through you."

⁴So Abram left, as the LORD had told him; and Lot went with him. Abram was seventy-five years old when he set out from Haran. ⁵He took his wife Sarai, his nephew Lot, all the possessions they had accumulated and the people they had acquired in Haran, and they set out for the land of Canaan, and they arrived there.

⁶Abram traveled through the land as far as the site of the great tree of Moreh at Shechem. At that time the Canaanites were in the land. ⁷The LORD appeared to Abram and said, "To your off-spring*ᵃ* I will give this land." So he built an altar there to the LORD, who had appeared to him.

⁸From there he went on toward the hills east of Bethel and pitched his tent, with Bethel on the west and Ai on the east. There he built an altar to the LORD and called on the name of the LORD. ⁹Then Abram set out and continued toward the Negev.

Abram in Egypt

¹⁰Now there was a famine in the land, and

ᵃ7 Or *seed*

Abraham
God begins to rebuild

AFTER SCANNING CENTURIES, GENESIS CHANGES dramatically at chapter 12. Leaving the big picture of world history, it settles on one lonely individual—not a great king or a wealthy landowner, but a childless nomad, Abraham.

At God's call, Abraham had uprooted himself from civilization and begun wandering in the wilderness. With a few changes (cattle substituted for sheep, Conestoga wagons for tents), you could make a cowboy movie out of his life. Moving his flocks from place to place, fighting skirmishes and pitched battles with hostile local people, Abraham had to be tough to survive. But this hardly made him unique; lots of tough nomads wandered the Middle East. What made this particular wanderer so important?

> "I will make you into a great nation and I will bless you . . . and all peoples on earth will be blessed through you."
> 12:2–3

God's New Way of Working

Abraham was important, first of all, simply because God chose him. Shortly after the destruction caused by the great flood, God picked Abraham as the foundation of a new humanity. On several remarkable occasions God spoke directly to him, promising to make his family great in the land he roamed. The promises were hard to believe: Abraham's wife was barren, Abraham was getting too old to have children, he owned no land and had no prospect of any. Nonetheless, God asked Abraham to trust him.

The second reason why Abraham matters follows from the first: When God spoke to him, Abraham listened. He was far from perfect. Sometimes he strayed from the path God put him on, lying and trying to make the promises work out in his own way. Yet in the decisive moments of life, he listened to God and obeyed. He was willing to sacrifice anything for God—even his only son. God put his brand on Abraham, the mark of circumcision. His descendants were to be forever known as "God's people."

Uncensored Truth

The life of Abraham is a fascinating story, true to life, full of bad moments as well as good. He was hardly a theologian; a more comprehensive understanding of God would have to wait for Moses. But Abraham's faith is the root of Judaism and, thus, of Christianity. In his encounters with God we get raw, uncensored truth; not religion invented by a philosopher, but religion as it really happens when God meets man.

No wonder the New Testament cites Abraham more than 80 times, and Paul tells Christians they are the true descendants of Abraham (Galatians 3:6–9). Abraham's life began to unfold the story of God's long-range plans. Two thousand years later, Abraham's descendant Jesus came to fulfill the promises made to Abraham and his descendants.

Life Questions: God asked Abraham to leave his home and family and go to a far-off foreign country. If you were in his place, how would you have responded? Has God ever asked anything hard or risky of you?

Abram went down to Egypt to live there for a while because the famine was severe. [11]As he was about to enter Egypt, he said to his wife Sarai, "I know what a beautiful woman you are. [12]When the Egyptians see you, they will say, 'This is his wife.' Then they will kill me but will let you live. [13]Say you are my sister, so that I will be treated well for your sake and my life will be spared because of you."

12:13 Abraham's Half-Truth

"A lie is an attempt to deceive," according to one definition, and by that standard Abraham was lying when he claimed Sarai was his sister. Yet he was telling half the truth, for she was his half sister (20:12). Abraham pulled this same trick years later and got caught again (chapter 20). On both occasions he had feared for his life, a situation in which half-truths are particularly appealing.

[14]When Abram came to Egypt, the Egyptians saw that she was a very beautiful woman. [15]And when Pharaoh's officials saw her, they praised her to Pharaoh, and she was taken into his palace. [16]He treated Abram well for her sake, and Abram acquired sheep and cattle, male and female donkeys, menservants and maidservants, and camels.

[17]But the LORD inflicted serious diseases on Pharaoh and his household because of Abram's wife Sarai. [18]So Pharaoh summoned Abram. "What have you done to me?" he said. "Why didn't you tell me she was your wife? [19]Why did you say, 'She is my sister,' so that I took her to be my wife? Now then, here is your wife. Take her and go!" [20]Then Pharaoh gave orders about Abram to his men, and they sent him on his way, with his wife and everything he had.

Abram and Lot Separate

13 So Abram went up from Egypt to the Negev, with his wife and everything he had, and Lot went with him. [2]Abram had become very wealthy in livestock and in silver and gold.

[3]From the Negev he went from place to place until he came to Bethel, to the place between Bethel and Ai where his tent had been earlier [4]and where he had first built an altar. There Abram called on the name of the LORD.

[5]Now Lot, who was moving about with Abram, also had flocks and herds and tents. [6]But the land could not support them while they stayed together, for their possessions were so great that they were not able to stay together. [7]And quarreling arose between Abram's herdsmen and the herdsmen of Lot. The Canaanites

and Perizzites were also living in the land at that time.

[8]So Abram said to Lot, "Let's not have any quarreling between you and me, or between your herdsmen and mine, for we are brothers. [9]Is not the whole land before you? Let's part company. If you go to the left, I'll go to the right; if you go to the right, I'll go to the left."

[10]Lot looked up and saw that the whole plain of the Jordan was well watered, like the garden of the LORD, like the land of Egypt, toward Zoar. (This was before the LORD destroyed Sodom and Gomorrah.) [11]So Lot chose for himself the whole plain of the Jordan and set out toward the east. The two men parted company: [12]Abram lived in the land of Canaan, while Lot lived among the cities of the plain and pitched his tents near Sodom. [13]Now the men of Sodom were wicked and were sinning greatly against the LORD.

13:3 On the Road

The main trade route through Canaan passed north to south through Shechem, Bethel, Hebron, and Beersheba. As Abraham and his children traveled, they naturally stopped in those places. These place-names crop up again and again in the story of God's work.

[14]The LORD said to Abram after Lot had parted from him, "Lift up your eyes from where you are and look north and south, east and west. [15]All the land that you see I will give to you and your offspring[a] forever. [16]I will make your offspring like the dust of the earth, so that if anyone could count the dust, then your offspring could be counted. [17]Go, walk through the length and breadth of the land, for I am giving it to you."

[18]So Abram moved his tents and went to live near the great trees of Mamre at Hebron, where he built an altar to the LORD.

Abram Rescues Lot

14 At this time Amraphel king of Shinar,[b] Arioch king of Ellasar, Kedorlaomer king of Elam and Tidal king of Goiim [2]went to war against Bera king of Sodom, Birsha king of Gomorrah, Shinab king of Admah, Shemeber king of Zeboiim, and the king of Bela (that is, Zoar). [3]All these latter kings joined forces in the Valley of Siddim (the Salt Sea[c]). [4]For twelve years they had been subject to Kedorlaomer, but in the thirteenth year they rebelled.

[5]In the fourteenth year, Kedorlaomer and the kings allied with him went out and defeated the Rephaites in Ashteroth Karnaim, the Zuzites in Ham, the Emites in Shaveh Kiriathaim [6]and the

---

[a]15 Or *seed*; also in verse 16   [b]1 That is, Babylonia; also in verse 9   [c]3 That is, the Dead Sea

Horites in the hill country of Seir, as far as El Paran near the desert. [7]Then they turned back and went to En Mishpat (that is, Kadesh), and they conquered the whole territory of the Amalekites, as well as the Amorites who were living in Hazazon Tamar.

[8]Then the king of Sodom, the king of Gomorrah, the king of Admah, the king of Zeboiim and the king of Bela (that is, Zoar) marched out and drew up their battle lines in the Valley of Siddim [9]against Kedorlaomer king of Elam, Tidal king of Goiim, Amraphel king of Shinar and Arioch king of Ellasar—four kings against five. [10]Now the Valley of Siddim was full of tar pits, and when the kings of Sodom and Gomorrah fled, some of the men fell into them and the rest fled to the hills. [11]The four kings seized all the goods of Sodom and Gomorrah and all their food; then they went away. [12]They also carried off Abram's nephew Lot and his possessions, since he was living in Sodom.

[13]One who had escaped came and reported this to Abram the Hebrew. Now Abram was living near the great trees of Mamre the Amorite, a brother[a] of Eshcol and Aner, all of whom were allied with Abram. [14]When Abram heard that his relative had been taken captive, he called out the 318 trained men born in his household and went in pursuit as far as Dan. [15]During the night Abram divided his men to attack them and he routed them, pursuing them as far as Hobah, north of Damascus. [16]He recovered all the goods and brought back his relative Lot and his possessions, together with the women and the other people.

[17]After Abram returned from defeating Kedorlaomer and the kings allied with him, the king of Sodom came out to meet him in the Valley of Shaveh (that is, the King's Valley).

[18]Then Melchizedek king of Salem[b] brought out bread and wine. He was priest of God Most High, [19]and he blessed Abram, saying,

"Blessed be Abram by God Most High,
  Creator[c] of heaven and earth.
[20]And blessed be[d] God Most High,
  who delivered your enemies into your
    hand."

14:20 Mystery Man

Melchizedek appeared to Abraham without warning, received tremendous honor, and then disappeared. Yet hundreds of years later he earned mention in Psalm 110, and hundreds of years after that in Hebrews 7:11–17. Melchizedek remains a mysterious figure, but he does set an important precedent for the Messiah: The same man can serve as both priest and king. (Jewish priests came from one tribe, and kings from another, different tribe.) Though Melchizedek did not have the proper family lineage, his spiritual power impressed Abraham, the father of Judaism.

Then Abram gave him a tenth of everything.
[21]The king of Sodom said to Abram, "Give me the people and keep the goods for yourself."
[22]But Abram said to the king of Sodom, "I

[a]13 Or *a relative*; or *an ally*   [b]18 That is, Jerusalem   [c]19 Or *Possessor*; also in verse 22   [d]20 Or *And praise be to*

LOT *Different Pathways*

PEOPLE WHO GROW UP CLOSE together—neighbors, friends, cousins, even siblings—sometimes end up in very different places in life. Looking back, one wonders what made the difference.

Take Lot as an example. Abraham's nephew, he apparently latched on to his uncle after losing his own father. When God called Abraham to leave home and strike out for unknown territory, Lot packed up and joined Abraham on the long trip.

Abraham reciprocated with love. Even after the two men had separated to make better use of grazing lands, Abraham cared enough about his nephew to stage a daring raid to rescue Lot from kidnappers. Later, when God announced he would destroy Lot's adopted town of Sodom, Abraham pleaded with God to save it.

Though Lot started out close to Abraham, he ultimately chose a very different pathway. Abraham remained a nomad, following God all his days. Lot preferred the cushy surroundings of the city—despite Sodom's reputation as a center of immorality. Soon Lot grew attached.

Even when God sent angels warning him to escape the coming judgment, Lot had a hard time tearing himself away. He lost everything and ended up in a cave, engaged in drunken incest with his own daughters. In contrast, the more faithful Abraham became the father of God's chosen people and one of the great patriarchs of the Old Testament.

Life Questions: If someone offered you a comfortable, successful position in a morally questionable situation, would you accept? Why or why not?

have raised my hand to the LORD, God Most High, Creator of heaven and earth, and have taken an oath ²³that I will accept nothing belonging to you, not even a thread or the thong of a sandal, so that you will never be able to say, 'I made Abram rich.' ²⁴I will accept nothing but what my men have eaten and the share that belongs to the men who went with me—to Aner, Eshcol and Mamre. Let them have their share."

God's Covenant With Abram

15 After this, the word of the LORD came to Abram in a vision:

"Do not be afraid, Abram.
I am your shield,ᵃ
your very great reward.ᵇ"

²But Abram said, "O Sovereign LORD, what can you give me since I remain childless and the one who will inheritᶜ my estate is Eliezer of Damascus?" ³And Abram said, "You have given me no children; so a servant in my household will be my heir."

⁴Then the word of the LORD came to him: "This man will not be your heir, but a son coming from your own body will be your heir." ⁵He took him outside and said, "Look up at the heavens and count the stars—if indeed you can count them." Then he said to him, "So shall your offspring be."

⁶Abram believed the LORD, and he credited it to him as righteousness.

15:6 What God Looks For

God accepted Abraham not because he led a perfect life but because of his responsiveness to God's promises. This verse was quoted three times in the New Testament to demonstrate that salvation by faith was nothing new (Romans 4:3; Galatians 3:6; James 2:23). Even in the Old Testament, God looked for faith, not moral perfection.

⁷He also said to him, "I am the LORD, who brought you out of Ur of the Chaldeans to give you this land to take possession of it."

⁸But Abram said, "O Sovereign LORD, how can I know that I will gain possession of it?"

⁹So the LORD said to him, "Bring me a heifer, a goat and a ram, each three years old, along with a dove and a young pigeon."

¹⁰Abram brought all these to him, cut them in two and arranged the halves opposite each other; the birds, however, he did not cut in half. ¹¹Then birds of prey came down on the carcasses, but Abram drove them away.

¹²As the sun was setting, Abram fell into a deep sleep, and a thick and dreadful darkness came over him. ¹³Then the LORD said to him, "Know for certain that your descendants will be strangers in a country not their own, and they will be enslaved and mistreated four hundred years. ¹⁴But I will punish the nation they serve as slaves, and afterward they will come out with great possessions. ¹⁵You, however, will go to your fathers in peace and be buried at a good old age. ¹⁶In the fourth generation your descendants will come back here, for the sin of the Amorites has not yet reached its full measure."

¹⁷When the sun had set and darkness had fallen, a smoking firepot with a blazing torch appeared and passed between the pieces. ¹⁸On that day the LORD made a covenant with Abram and said, "To your descendants I give this land, from the riverᵈ of Egypt to the great river, the Euphrates— ¹⁹the land of the Kenites, Kenizzites, Kadmonites, ²⁰Hittites, Perizzites, Rephaites, ²¹Amorites, Canaanites, Girgashites and Jebusites."

Hagar and Ishmael

16 Now Sarai, Abram's wife, had borne him no children. But she had an Egyptian maidservant named Hagar; ²so she said to Abram, "The LORD has kept me from having children. Go, sleep with my maidservant; perhaps I can build a family through her."

Abram agreed to what Sarai said. ³So after Abram had been living in Canaan ten years, Sarai his wife took her Egyptian maidservant Hagar and gave her to her husband to be his wife. ⁴He slept with Hagar, and she conceived.

16:2 A Substitute Wife

According to custom, a man could sleep with a servant and include her children in his household. Abraham was trying to get the children he and his wife longed for and to "help God out" in fulfilling his promise of a son. Abraham's way was not God's way, however, and Abraham's attempt led to considerable jealousy and sorrow. The same practice also led to trouble for Jacob's family (chapter 30).

When she knew she was pregnant, she began to despise her mistress. ⁵Then Sarai said to Abram, "You are responsible for the wrong I am suffering. I put my servant in your arms, and now that she knows she is pregnant, she despises

---

ᵃ1 Or sovereign   ᵇ1 Or shield; / your reward will be very great   ᶜ2 The meaning of the Hebrew for this phrase is uncertain.   ᵈ18 Or Wadi

me. May the LORD judge between you and me."

[6] "Your servant is in your hands," Abram said. "Do with her whatever you think best." Then Sarai mistreated Hagar; so she fled from her.

[7] The angel of the LORD found Hagar near a spring in the desert; it was the spring that is beside the road to Shur. [8] And he said, "Hagar, servant of Sarai, where have you come from, and where are you going?"

"I'm running away from my mistress Sarai," she answered.

[9] Then the angel of the LORD told her, "Go back to your mistress and submit to her." [10] The angel added, "I will so increase your descendants that they will be too numerous to count."

[11] The angel of the LORD also said to her:

"You are now with child
    and you will have a son.
You shall name him Ishmael,[a]
    for the LORD has heard of your misery.
[12] He will be a wild donkey of a man;
    his hand will be against everyone
    and everyone's hand against him,
and he will live in hostility
    toward[b] all his brothers."

[13] She gave this name to the LORD who spoke to her: "You are the God who sees me," for she said, "I have now seen[c] the One who sees me." [14] That is why the well was called Beer Lahai Roi[d]; it is still there, between Kadesh and Bered.

[15] So Hagar bore Abram a son, and Abram gave the name Ishmael to the son she had borne. [16] Abram was eighty-six years old when Hagar bore him Ishmael.

The Covenant of Circumcision

17 When Abram was ninety-nine years old, the LORD appeared to him and said, "I am God Almighty[e]; walk before me and be blameless. [2] I will confirm my covenant between me and you and will greatly increase your numbers."

[3] Abram fell facedown, and God said to him, [4] "As for me, this is my covenant with you: You will be the father of many nations. [5] No longer will you be called Abram[f]; your name will be Abraham,[g] for I have made you a father of many nations. [6] I will make you very fruitful; I will make nations of you, and kings will come from you. [7] I will establish my covenant as an everlasting covenant between me and you and your descendants after you for the generations to come, to be your God and the God of your descendants after you. [8] The whole land of Canaan, where you are now an alien, I will give as an everlasting possession to you and your descendants after you; and I will be their God."

[9] Then God said to Abraham, "As for you, you must keep my covenant, you and your descendants after you for the generations to come. [10] This is my covenant with you and your descendants after you, the covenant you are to keep: Every male among you shall be circumcised. [11] You are to undergo circumcision, and it will be the sign of the covenant between me and you. [12] For the generations to come every male among you who is eight days old must be circumcised, including those born in your household or bought with money from a foreigner—those who are not your offspring. [13] Whether born in your household or bought with your money, they

---

[a]11 *Ishmael* means *God hears.*   [b]12 Or *live to the east / of*
means *well of the Living One who sees me.*   [e]1 Hebrew *El-Shaddai*
[g]5 *Abraham* means *father of many.*   [c]13 Or *seen the back of*   [d]14 *Beer Lahai Roi*
[f]5 *Abram* means *exalted father.*

ISHMAEL *Second Best*

YOU MIGHT CALL ISHMAEL A mistake. His birth came about when Sarah and Abraham doubted God's promise to provide them a child in their old age. The two conspired to "help God out" by using an Egyptian servant, Hagar, as a substitute wife for Abraham. Then, when God fulfilled his promise and Sarah bore a son of her own, she cruelly drove the servant and her son out into the desert. Ishmael, the innocent victim of this scheming, suffered the consequences.

Yet God also blessed Ishmael. He "heard the boy crying" when Ishmael was nearly dying of thirst in the desert (21:17). God promised that Ishmael's descendants would comprise a great nation. The Bible records that Ishmael had twelve sons, and that "the Ishmaelites" were Israel's neighbors for centuries. In fact, Arabs today traditionally trace their lineage to Ishmael.

Ishmael apparently kept in contact with his original family; he attended Abraham's funeral, and his daughter would marry Abraham's grandson Esau. Yet his place in Abraham's "covenant" with God was lost. In a similar way, Ishmael's son-in-law Esau would enjoy the earthly blessings of success, even though God's greatest blessing was reserved for his brother Jacob. In the Bible's accounting, God's "covenant blessing" always matters more than earthly success.

Life Questions: Have you ever tried to "help God out" when you thought he couldn't possibly help you in the way you wanted? What was the result?

must be circumcised. My covenant in your flesh is to be an everlasting covenant. 14Any uncircumcised male, who has not been circumcised in the flesh, will be cut off from his people; he has broken my covenant."

15God also said to Abraham, "As for Sarai your wife, you are no longer to call her Sarai; her name will be Sarah. 16I will bless her and will surely give you a son by her. I will bless her so that she will be the mother of nations; kings of peoples will come from her."

17Abraham fell facedown; he laughed and said to himself, "Will a son be born to a man a hundred years old? Will Sarah bear a child at the age

17:17 Laughing at God

Abraham was a man of faith, but his faith was less than 100 percent. Here, nearing the age of 100, he laughed heartily at God's promise that he would father a son, and he demonstrated his lack of belief by suggesting that God accept Ishmael as an adequate substitute. Some time later Sarah, his wife, shared in the "joke" (18:12).

of ninety?" 18And Abraham said to God, "If only Ishmael might live under your blessing!"

19Then God said, "Yes, but your wife Sarah will bear you a son, and you will call him Isaac.a I will establish my covenant with him as an everlasting covenant for his descendants after him. 20And as for Ishmael, I have heard you: I will surely bless him; I will make him fruitful and will greatly increase his numbers. He will be the father of twelve rulers, and I will make him into a great nation. 21But my covenant I will establish with Isaac, whom Sarah will bear to you by this time next year." 22When he had finished speaking with Abraham, God went up from him.

23On that very day Abraham took his son Ishmael and all those born in his household or bought with his money, every male in his household, and circumcised them, as God told him. 24Abraham was ninety-nine years old when he was circumcised, 25and his son Ishmael was thirteen; 26Abraham and his son Ishmael were both circumcised on that same day. 27And every male in Abraham's household, including those born in his household or bought from a foreigner, was circumcised with him.

The Three Visitors

18 The LORD appeared to Abraham near the great trees of Mamre while he was sitting at the entrance to his tent in the heat of the day. 2Abraham looked up and saw three men standing nearby. When he saw them, he hurried from the entrance of his tent to meet them and bowed low to the ground.

3He said, "If I have found favor in your eyes, my lord,b do not pass your servant by. 4Let a little water be brought, and then you may all wash your feet and rest under this tree. 5Let me get you something to eat, so you can be refreshed and then go on your way—now that you have come to your servant."

"Very well," they answered, "do as you say."

6So Abraham hurried into the tent to Sarah. "Quick," he said, "get three seahsc of fine flour and knead it and bake some bread."

7Then he ran to the herd and selected a choice, tender calf and gave it to a servant, who hurried to prepare it. 8He then brought some curds and milk and the calf that had been prepared, and set these before them. While they ate, he stood near them under a tree.

9"Where is your wife Sarah?" they asked him.

"There, in the tent," he said.

10Then the LORDd said, "I will surely return to you about this time next year, and Sarah your wife will have a son."

Now Sarah was listening at the entrance to the tent, which was behind him. 11Abraham and Sarah were already old and well advanced in years, and Sarah was past the age of childbearing. 12So Sarah laughed to herself as she thought, "After I am worn out and my mastere is old, will I now have this pleasure?"

13Then the LORD said to Abraham, "Why did Sarah laugh and say, 'Will I really have a child, now that I am old?' 14Is anything too hard for the LORD? I will return to you at the appointed time next year and Sarah will have a son."

15Sarah was afraid, so she lied and said, "I did not laugh."

But he said, "Yes, you did laugh."

Abraham Pleads for Sodom

16When the men got up to leave, they looked down toward Sodom, and Abraham walked along with them to see them on their way. 17Then the LORD said, "Shall I hide from Abraham what I am about to do? 18Abraham will surely become a great and powerful nation, and all nations on earth will be blessed through him. 19For I have chosen him, so that he will direct his children and his household after him to keep the way of the LORD by doing what is right and just, so that the LORD will bring about for Abraham what he has promised him."

20Then the LORD said, "The outcry against Sodom and Gomorrah is so great and their sin so

---

a19 *Isaac* means *he laughs.*   b3 Or *O Lord*   c6 That is, probably about 20 quarts (about 22 liters)
d10 Hebrew *Then he*   e12 Or *husband*

grievous [21]that I will go down and see if what they have done is as bad as the outcry that has reached me. If not, I will know."

[22]The men turned away and went toward Sod-

om, but Abraham remained standing before the LORD.[a] [23]Then Abraham approached him and said: "Will you sweep away the righteous with the wicked? [24]What if there are fifty righteous people in the city? Will you really sweep it away and not spare[b] the place for the sake of the fifty righteous people in it? [25]Far be it from you to do such a thing—to kill the righteous with the wicked, treating the righteous and the wicked alike. Far be it from you! Will not the Judge[c] of all the earth do right?"

[26]The LORD said, "If I find fifty righteous people in the city of Sodom, I will spare the whole place for their sake."

[27]Then Abraham spoke up again: "Now that I have been so bold as to speak to the Lord, though I am nothing but dust and ashes, [28]what if the number of the righteous is five less than fifty?

Will you destroy the whole city because of five people?"

"If I find forty-five there," he said, "I will not destroy it."

[29]Once again he spoke to him, "What if only forty are found there?"

He said, "For the sake of forty, I will not do it."

[30]Then he said, "May the Lord not be angry, but let me speak. What if only thirty can be found there?"

He answered, "I will not do it if I find thirty there."

[31]Abraham said, "Now that I have been so bold as to speak to the Lord, what if only twenty can be found there?"

He said, "For the sake of twenty, I will not destroy it."

[32]Then he said, "May the Lord not be angry, but let me speak just once more. What if only ten can be found there?"

He answered, "For the sake of ten, I will not destroy it."

[33]When the LORD had finished speaking with Abraham, he left, and Abraham returned home.

Sodom and Gomorrah Destroyed

19 The two angels arrived at Sodom in the evening, and Lot was sitting in the gateway of the city. When he saw them, he got up to meet them and bowed down with his face to the ground. [2]"My lords," he said, "please turn aside to your servant's house. You can wash your feet and spend the night and then go on your way early in the morning."

[a]22 Masoretic Text; an ancient Hebrew scribal tradition *but the LORD remained standing before Abraham*   [b]24 Or *forgive*; also in verse 26   [c]25 Or *Ruler*

SARAH *Who's Laughing?*

SHE WAS BEAUTIFUL. SHE HAD a wonderful, wealthy husband. Sarah should have been content. Instead her life revolved around the one thing she lacked—a child. Although God had promised that her husband Abraham would father a great nation, as the decades passed Sarah remained childless. The odds of giving birth gradually dwindled. More descendants than the stars in the sky? God's promise seemed laughable as Sarah celebrated her ninetieth birthday.

A resourceful woman, Sarah came up with an alternate plan. She would use her servant Hagar as a surrogate mother. Obviously Sarah felt deep inner conflict about this decision, for when Abraham got Hagar pregnant, Sarah mistreated her and sent her away. Hagar returned, but Sarah's inner conflict persisted. She would ultimately drive both mother and son into the desert.

Meanwhile, God kept repeating the amazing promise that Sarah would become the mother of a nation. Once, Abraham fell face down and laughed incredulously at the notion. Sarah cackled too. But the joke turned on them both when old Sarah finally got pregnant. After all her years of waiting, her longings were fulfilled.

"God has brought me laughter," Sarah said when her son was born (21:6). It was a wonderful pun; in obedience to God (17:19), Abraham named his son Isaac, which means "he laughs" in Hebrew.

Life Questions: When a person has deep longings that seem impossible to fulfill, what should he or she do?

"No," they answered, "we will spend the night in the square."

³But he insisted so strongly that they did go with him and entered his house. He prepared a

19:1 A Man of Substance

The angels found Lot in the gateway to Sodom—a fact loaded with significance. Traditionally, city fathers gathered in the gateway to make important decisions. Lot's presence suggests that he had become "one of them" during his time in Sodom, which may explain why he struggled against leaving.

meal for them, baking bread without yeast, and they ate. ⁴Before they had gone to bed, all the men from every part of the city of Sodom—both young and old—surrounded the house. ⁵They called to Lot, "Where are the men who came to you tonight? Bring them out to us so that we can have sex with them."

⁶Lot went outside to meet them and shut the door behind him ⁷and said, "No, my friends. Don't do this wicked thing. ⁸Look, I have two daughters who have never slept with a man. Let me bring them out to you, and you can do what you like with them. But don't do anything to these men, for they have come under the protection of my roof."

⁹"Get out of our way," they replied. And they said, "This fellow came here as an alien, and now he wants to play the judge! We'll treat you worse than them." They kept bringing pressure on Lot and moved forward to break down the door.

¹⁰But the men inside reached out and pulled Lot back into the house and shut the door. ¹¹Then they struck the men who were at the door of the house, young and old, with blindness so that they could not find the door.

A Catastrophe Sent from God
Sodom: a city that earned destruction

SHOULD A CATASTROPHE BE READ as a punishment from God? Do floods, famines, earthquakes come because God is angry? The Bible's answer is, "Sometimes, and sometimes not." In Genesis, several catastrophes seemed to "just happen"—they were not a punishment or a warning, though God used them to advance his plans. These included several famines such as the one that brought Joseph to power (chapter 41), a war (chapter 14), a rape (chapter 34).

But a few catastrophes God took full credit for—like the one at Sodom and Gomorrah. As usual, the Bible shows little or no interest in telling us the scientific facts about the destruction. Was it a volcanic eruption? The Bible doesn't say, and the area, now apparently at the bottom of the Dead Sea, cannot easily be investigated. The Bible stresses not how it happened, but why.

> "Do you have anyone else here—sons-in-law, sons or daughters, or anyone else in the city who belongs to you? Get them out of here, because we are going to destroy this place."
> 19:12–13

Gang Rape

Sodom was a wretched place. The whole town saw the coming of strangers as a chance for homosexual gang rape. Sexual violence was not the town's only problem. Ezekiel 16:49 says that Sodom was "arrogant, overfed and unconcerned; they did not help the poor and needy." God would have let the city stand if Abraham could have located just ten righteous people. Apparently, ten such people did not exist. God's great patience finally ran out.

Years earlier, Abraham had refused to accept even a well-earned reward from the government of Sodom (14:21–24). He wanted nothing to do with such a society. But Lot had chosen the path of prosperity, the easy and successful life on the fertile plain near Sodom.

Lot had become a somebody there, a civic heavy who made important decisions in the city gateway. He was so entangled with life in Sodom he hesitated to leave until it was nearly too late. When Sodom went up in smoke, his hard-earned importance disappeared too. The shock was too great for him. Unable to start over, he ended up in a cave, too drunk to know that his two daughters were having sex with him. He is the perfect example of a man who, excessively tangled in a corrupt system, cannot bear to leave it behind.

Jesus did not let his followers think of Sodom simply as "those terrible people." He warned them that God would be even harder on those who saw Jesus' miracles, but ignored them (Matthew 11:24). God's patience has a limit.

Life Questions: Are any catastrophes of our time punishments from God? How would you know?

[12]The two men said to Lot, "Do you have anyone else here—sons-in-law, sons or daughters, or anyone else in the city who belongs to you? Get them out of here, [13]because we are going to destroy this place. The outcry to the LORD against its people is so great that he has sent us to destroy it."

[14]So Lot went out and spoke to his sons-in-law, who were pledged to marry[a] his daughters. He said, "Hurry and get out of this place, because the LORD is about to destroy the city!" But his sons-in-law thought he was joking.

[15]With the coming of dawn, the angels urged Lot, saying, "Hurry! Take your wife and your two daughters who are here, or you will be swept away when the city is punished."

[16]When he hesitated, the men grasped his hand and the hands of his wife and of his two daughters and led them safely out of the city, for the LORD was merciful to them. [17]As soon as they had brought them out, one of them said, "Flee for your lives! Don't look back, and don't stop anywhere in the plain! Flee to the mountains or you will be swept away!"

[18]But Lot said to them, "No, my lords,[b] please! [19]Your[c] servant has found favor in your[c] eyes, and you[c] have shown great kindness to me in sparing my life. But I can't flee to the mountains; this disaster will overtake me, and I'll die. [20]Look, here is a town near enough to run to, and it is small. Let me flee to it—it is very small, isn't it? Then my life will be spared."

[21]He said to him, "Very well, I will grant this request too; I will not overthrow the town you speak of. [22]But flee there quickly, because I cannot do anything until you reach it." (That is why the town was called Zoar.[d])

[23]By the time Lot reached Zoar, the sun had risen over the land. [24]Then the LORD rained down burning sulfur on Sodom and Gomorrah—from the LORD out of the heavens. [25]Thus he overthrew those cities and the entire plain, including all those living in the cities—and also the vegetation in the land. [26]But Lot's wife looked back, and she became a pillar of salt.

[27]Early the next morning Abraham got up and returned to the place where he had stood before the LORD. [28]He looked down toward Sodom and Gomorrah, toward all the land of the plain, and he saw dense smoke rising from the land, like smoke from a furnace.

[29]So when God destroyed the cities of the plain, he remembered Abraham, and he brought Lot out of the catastrophe that overthrew the cities where Lot had lived.

Lot and His Daughters

[30]Lot and his two daughters left Zoar and settled in the mountains, for he was afraid to stay in Zoar. He and his two daughters lived in a cave. [31]One day the older daughter said to the younger, "Our father is old, and there is no man around

19:26 Don't Look Back

Lot and his family found it hard to leave their adopted home of Sodom, despite its immorality. Angel messengers warned them to hurry, not even stopping to look back. When Lot's wife disobeyed, she turned into a pillar of salt—perhaps caught in volcanic explosions that engulfed Sodom. For this she became a symbol of indecision. Jesus urged his followers to remember her example when their time of trouble came (Luke 17:32).

here to lie with us, as is the custom all over the earth. [32]Let's get our father to drink wine and then lie with him and preserve our family line through our father."

[33]That night they got their father to drink wine, and the older daughter went in and lay with him. He was not aware of it when she lay down or when she got up.

[34]The next day the older daughter said to the younger, "Last night I lay with my father. Let's get him to drink wine again tonight, and you go in and lie with him so we can preserve our family line through our father." [35]So they got their father to drink wine that night also, and the younger daughter went and lay with him. Again he was not aware of it when she lay down or when she got up.

[36]So both of Lot's daughters became pregnant by their father. [37]The older daughter had a son, and she named him Moab[e]; he is the father of

19:37 Family Quarrels

Lot's determination to enjoy life in Sodom ended tragically here, in drunken incest. The resulting sons founded the family-nations of Moab and Ammon, which for centuries fought with their distant relatives in Israel and tempted them to sin.

the Moabites of today. [38]The younger daughter also had a son, and she named him Ben-Ammi[f]; he is the father of the Ammonites of today.

---

[a]14 Or *were married to*   [b]18 Or *No, Lord*; or *No, my lord*
small.   [e]37 *Moab* sounds like the Hebrew for *from father.*

[c]19 The Hebrew is singular.   [d]22 *Zoar* means
[f]38 *Ben-Ammi* means *son of my people.*

Abraham and Abimelech

20 Now Abraham moved on from there into the region of the Negev and lived between Kadesh and Shur. For a while he stayed in Gerar, ²and there Abraham said of his wife Sarah, "She is my sister." Then Abimelech king of Gerar sent for Sarah and took her.

³But God came to Abimelech in a dream one night and said to him, "You are as good as dead because of the woman you have taken; she is a married woman."

⁴Now Abimelech had not gone near her, so he said, "Lord, will you destroy an innocent nation? ⁵Did he not say to me, 'She is my sister,' and didn't she also say, 'He is my brother'? I have done this with a clear conscience and clean hands."

⁶Then God said to him in the dream, "Yes, I know you did this with a clear conscience, and so I have kept you from sinning against me. That is why I did not let you touch her. ⁷Now return the man's wife, for he is a prophet, and he will pray for you and you will live. But if you do not return her, you may be sure that you and all yours will die."

⁸Early the next morning Abimelech summoned all his officials, and when he told them all that had happened, they were very much afraid. ⁹Then Abimelech called Abraham in and said, "What have you done to us? How have I wronged you that you have brought such great guilt upon me and my kingdom? You have done things to me that should not be done." ¹⁰And Abimelech asked Abraham, "What was your reason for doing this?"

¹¹Abraham replied, "I said to myself, 'There is surely no fear of God in this place, and they will kill me because of my wife.' ¹²Besides, she really is my sister, the daughter of my father though not of my mother; and she became my wife. ¹³And when God had me wander from my father's household, I said to her, 'This is how you can show your love to me: Everywhere we go, say of me, "He is my brother." '"

¹⁴Then Abimelech brought sheep and cattle and male and female slaves and gave them to Abraham, and he returned Sarah his wife to him. ¹⁵And Abimelech said, "My land is before you; live wherever you like."

¹⁶To Sarah he said, "I am giving your brother a thousand shekels*a* of silver. This is to cover the offense against you before all who are with you; you are completely vindicated."

¹⁷Then Abraham prayed to God, and God healed Abimelech, his wife and his slave girls so they could have children again, ¹⁸for the LORD had closed up every womb in Abimelech's household because of Abraham's wife Sarah.

The Birth of Isaac

21 Now the LORD was gracious to Sarah as he had said, and the LORD did for Sarah what he had promised. ²Sarah became pregnant and bore a son to Abraham in his old age, at the very time God had promised him. ³Abraham gave the name Isaac*b* to the son Sarah bore him. ⁴When

---

a 16 That is, about 25 pounds (about 11.5 kilograms)   *b 3 Isaac* means *he laughs.*

ISAAC *Ordinary People*

ISAAC SPENT HIS LIFE SURROUNDED by strong people. His father Abraham was a giant of faith who uprooted his family at God's call and moved to unknown territory. Isaac married a strong-willed woman, Rebekah, who dominated him and sometimes manipulated him to get her way. One of Isaac's sons, Jacob, grew up to become a major figure of the Old Testament, father of the twelve tribes of Israel.

For all that strength around him, Isaac was a rather ordinary, almost passive person. Maybe it was because his parents had dreamed of his birth for so long that they sheltered him, their only child. Maybe his personality formed in reaction to all those other, powerful figures. Regardless, the Bible portrays Isaac as a person who fit into other people's plans. Even when his father led him up a mountain to sacrifice him to God, Isaac did not protest or rebel (Genesis 22).

When famine drove Isaac to a foreign land, he lied about his relationship with Rebekah rather than risk a conflict with the local king. When his herdsmen bickered with other shepherds over water rights, Isaac simply moved on, avoiding a fight. In Isaac's old age, when his grown sons Jacob and Esau quarreled, Isaac seemed powerless to stop them. Instead of sorting out the details and resolving the feud, he sent Jacob away.

Despite his weaknesses, Isaac is counted among the three famous patriarchs of Old Testament faith: Abraham, Isaac and Jacob. In bringing blessings to the entire world, God uses all kinds—even quiet, ordinary people.

Life Questions: Think of an organization or cause you consider important. How many of those involved could be described as "ordinary people"? What do they contribute?

his son Isaac was eight days old, Abraham circumcised him, as God commanded him. 5Abraham was a hundred years old when his son Isaac was born to him.

6Sarah said, "God has brought me laughter, and everyone who hears about this will laugh with me." 7And she added, "Who would have said to Abraham that Sarah would nurse children? Yet I have borne him a son in his old age."

Hagar and Ishmael Sent Away

8The child grew and was weaned, and on the day Isaac was weaned Abraham held a great feast. 9But Sarah saw that the son whom Hagar the Egyptian had borne to Abraham was mocking, 10and she said to Abraham, "Get rid of that slave woman and her son, for that slave woman's son will never share in the inheritance with my son Isaac."

11The matter distressed Abraham greatly because it concerned his son. 12But God said to him, "Do not be so distressed about the boy and your maidservant. Listen to whatever Sarah tells you, because it is through Isaac that your offspring*a* will be reckoned. 13I will make the son of the maidservant into a nation also, because he is your offspring."

14Early the next morning Abraham took some food and a skin of water and gave them to Hagar. He set them on her shoulders and then sent her off with the boy. She went on her way and wandered in the desert of Beersheba.

15When the water in the skin was gone, she put the boy under one of the bushes. 16Then she went off and sat down nearby, about a bowshot away, for she thought, "I cannot watch the boy die." And as she sat there nearby, she*b* began to sob.

17God heard the boy crying, and the angel of God called to Hagar from heaven and said to her, "What is the matter, Hagar? Do not be afraid; God has heard the boy crying as he lies there. 18Lift the boy up and take him by the hand, for I will make him into a great nation."

19Then God opened her eyes and she saw a well of water. So she went and filled the skin with water and gave the boy a drink. 20God was with the boy as he grew up. He lived in the desert and became an archer. 21While he was living in the Desert of Paran, his mother got a wife for him from Egypt.

The Treaty at Beersheba

22At that time Abimelech and Phicol the commander of his forces said to Abraham, "God is with you in everything you do. 23Now swear to me here before God that you will not deal falsely with me or my children or my descendants. Show to me and the country where you are living as an alien the same kindness I have shown to you."

24Abraham said, "I swear it."

25Then Abraham complained to Abimelech about a well of water that Abimelech's servants had seized. 26But Abimelech said, "I don't know who has done this. You did not tell me, and I heard about it only today."

27So Abraham brought sheep and cattle and gave them to Abimelech, and the two men made a treaty. 28Abraham set apart seven ewe lambs from the flock, 29and Abimelech asked Abraham, "What is the meaning of these seven ewe lambs you have set apart by themselves?"

30He replied, "Accept these seven lambs from my hand as a witness that I dug this well."

31So that place was called Beersheba,*c* because the two men swore an oath there.

32After the treaty had been made at Beersheba, Abimelech and Phicol the commander of his forces returned to the land of the Philistines. 33Abraham planted a tamarisk tree in Beersheba, and there he called upon the name of the LORD, the Eternal God. 34And Abraham stayed in the land of the Philistines for a long time.

Abraham Tested

22 Some time later God tested Abraham. He said to him, "Abraham!"

"Here I am," he replied.

2Then God said, "Take your son, your only son, Isaac, whom you love, and go to the region of Moriah. Sacrifice him there as a burnt offering on one of the mountains I will tell you about."

3Early the next morning Abraham got up and saddled his donkey. He took with him two of his servants and his son Isaac. When he had cut enough wood for the burnt offering, he set out for the place God had told him about. 4On the third day Abraham looked up and saw the place in the distance. 5He said to his servants, "Stay here with the donkey while I and the boy go over there. We will worship and then we will come back to you."

6Abraham took the wood for the burnt offering and placed it on his son Isaac, and he himself carried the fire and the knife. As the two of them went on together, 7Isaac spoke up and said to his father Abraham, "Father?"

"Yes, my son?" Abraham replied.

"The fire and wood are here," Isaac said, "but where is the lamb for the burnt offering?"

8Abraham answered, "God himself will provide the lamb for the burnt offering, my son." And the two of them went on together.

9When they reached the place God had told him about, Abraham built an altar there and arranged the wood on it. He bound his son Isaac

---

a 12 Or seed   *b 16 Hebrew; Septuagint the child*   *c 31 Beersheba can mean well of seven or well of the oath.*

and laid him on the altar, on top of the wood. [10]Then he reached out his hand and took the knife to slay his son. [11]But the angel of the LORD called out to him from heaven, "Abraham! Abraham!"

"Here I am," he replied.

[12]"Do not lay a hand on the boy," he said. "Do not do anything to him. Now I know that you fear God, because you have not withheld from me your son, your only son."

[13]Abraham looked up and there in a thicket he saw a ram[a] caught by its horns. He went over and took the ram and sacrificed it as a burnt offering instead of his son. [14]So Abraham called that place The LORD Will Provide. And to this day it is said, "On the mountain of the LORD it will be provided."

[15]The angel of the LORD called to Abraham from heaven a second time [16]and said, "I swear by myself, declares the LORD, that because you have done this and have not withheld your son,

your only son, [17]I will surely bless you and make your descendants as numerous as the stars in the sky and as the sand on the seashore. Your descendants will take possession of the cities of their enemies, [18]and through your offspring[b] all nations on earth will be blessed, because you have obeyed me."

[19]Then Abraham returned to his servants, and they set off together for Beersheba. And Abraham stayed in Beersheba.

Nahor's Sons

[20]Some time later Abraham was told, "Milcah is also a mother; she has borne sons to your brother Nahor: [21]Uz the firstborn, Buz his brother, Kemuel (the father of Aram), [22]Kesed, Hazo, Pildash, Jidlaph and Bethuel." [23]Bethuel became the father of Rebekah. Milcah bore these eight sons to Abraham's brother Nahor. [24]His concubine, whose name was Reumah, also had sons: Tebah, Gaham, Tahash and Maacah.

---

[a]13 Many manuscripts of the Masoretic Text, Samaritan Pentateuch, Septuagint and Syriac; most manuscripts of the Masoretic Text *a ram behind him*   [b]18 Or *seed*

Promises, Promises
God promised to give Abraham all that he longed for . . . and more

> "Through your offspring all nations on earth will be blessed, because you have obeyed me." 22:18

HUMAN BEINGS HAVEN'T CHANGED MUCH in 4,000 years. The longing for children and the desire for land still surge up with surprising emotional power.

Consider the estimated six million American couples—one in seven would-be parents—who are unable to have children. For most of them, this brings deep anguish. Or think about the people who work double shifts, sacrificing their free time in order to own a home rather than rent.

Abraham would have understood. When God wanted his attention, he promised him land and more sons than he could count. To a Babylonian emigrant, 75 years old and childless, owning nothing but his tents and animals, the promises sounded wonderful. In fact, they sounded impossible. Yet, because God himself was making the promise, Abraham "believed the LORD, and he credited it to him as righteousness" (15:6).

For the God who had created the heavens and the earth, making good on the promises ought to have been a snap. But God did not make it easy for Abraham. Not until 25 years later, when Abraham was 100, did the promise of a son come true. Then, incredibly, God told Abraham to make a human sacrifice of his little boy. It was really asking too much.

Astonishingly, Abraham followed God's orders. And God gave him back his son.

Far from Fulfilled

When Abraham died, God's promises were far from fully realized. Abraham had only that one son to cling to. His only land was a burial plot. He still lived in a tent, and his only permanent structures were altars erected to worship the God who had made all those promises.

God, having promised him everything a man of that time could want, apparently wanted Abraham to think even bigger thoughts. He had slipped some words in along with the promises of offspring and land: "All peoples on earth will be blessed through you" (12:3). God wanted to bless, not just Abraham, but the whole world. Thousands of years later, in the time of Jesus, the full meaning of those words became clear (see Galatians 3:6–9,16–18).

Life Questions: What kind of promises does God make today? What longings does he fulfill?

The Death of Sarah

23 Sarah lived to be a hundred and twenty-seven years old. [2]She died at Kiriath Arba (that is, Hebron) in the land of Canaan, and Abraham went to mourn for Sarah and to weep over her.

[3]Then Abraham rose from beside his dead wife and spoke to the Hittites.[a] He said, [4]"I am an alien and a stranger among you. Sell me some property for a burial site here so I can bury my dead."

[5]The Hittites replied to Abraham, [6]"Sir, listen to us. You are a mighty prince among us. Bury your dead in the choicest of our tombs. None of us will refuse you his tomb for burying your dead."

[7]Then Abraham rose and bowed down before the people of the land, the Hittites. [8]He said to them, "If you are willing to let me bury my dead, then listen to me and intercede with Ephron son of Zohar on my behalf [9]so he will sell me the cave of Machpelah, which belongs to him and is at the end of his field. Ask him to sell it to me for the full price as a burial site among you."

[10]Ephron the Hittite was sitting among his people and he replied to Abraham in the hearing of all the Hittites who had come to the gate of his city. [11]"No, my lord," he said. "Listen to me; I give[b] you the field, and I give[b] you the cave that is in it. I give[b] it to you in the presence of my people. Bury your dead."

[12]Again Abraham bowed down before the people of the land [13]and he said to Ephron in

their hearing, "Listen to me, if you will. I will pay the price of the field. Accept it from me so I can bury my dead there."

[14]Ephron answered Abraham, [15]"Listen to me, my lord; the land is worth four hundred shekels[c] of silver, but what is that between me and you? Bury your dead."

23:15 Let's Make a Deal

This may be the oldest recorded business deal. The elaborate politeness sounds very much like bargaining in the Middle East today. Underneath the smooth words, shrewd negotiating is going on. The Hittites were probably reluctant to allow Abraham, an alien, to own property of any kind lest he gain a legal foothold in their country. Abraham zeroed in on Ephron, who stood to gain financially from the sale.

[16]Abraham agreed to Ephron's terms and weighed out for him the price he had named in the hearing of the Hittites: four hundred shekels of silver, according to the weight current among the merchants.

[17]So Ephron's field in Machpelah near Mamre—both the field and the cave in it, and all the trees within the borders of the field—was deeded [18]to Abraham as his property in the presence of all the Hittites who had come to the gate of the city. [19]Afterward Abraham buried his wife Sarah in the cave in the field of Machpelah near Mamre

a3 Or the sons of Heth; *also in verses 5, 7, 10, 16, 18 and 20 4.5 kilograms*   *b11 Or sell*   *c15 That is, about 10 pounds (about*

REBEKAH *Forceful Woman*

"I'D RATHER BE A HAMMER than a nail," sang Paul Simon, meaning it's better to be an active force than to let others drive you. Rebekah followed that philosophy. When Abraham's servant asked for a drink of water, she took the initiative. "I'll draw water for your camels too, until they have finished drinking," she said (24:19). And although camels require a lot of water, Rebekah didn't just walk to the well to draw it—she ran (v. 20).

When offered marriage to an unknown relative hundreds of miles' journey across dangerous wilderness, Rebekah grabbed the chance. Her family wanted time to adjust to the idea, but she got ready to leave the next day, never to see her home again.

Initiative is admirable, but an overdose can lead to trouble. Rebekah waited twenty years to have a child and then gave birth to twins. God told her that Jacob, the younger, would be God's chosen. In an attempt to manage Jacob's success, Rebekah pushed him into deceiving his father and stealing his brother's blessing. "Just do what I say," she told him (27:13). Rebekah thought she could control everything, regardless of whether her actions pleased God.

The ploy worked as she predicted, but Rebekah had not foreseen the fury of Esau, Jacob's outwitted brother. Fearing for Jacob's life, she arranged to send him back to her childhood home. "When your brother is no longer angry . . . I'll send word for you to come back from there," she told Jacob (27:45). For Rebekah, that time never came—she died without seeing her favorite child again.

Life Questions: When can initiative like Rebekah's be helpful? Under what conditions can it lead to trouble?

(which is at Hebron) in the land of Canaan. ²⁰So the field and the cave in it were deeded to Abraham by the Hittites as a burial site.

Isaac and Rebekah

24 Abraham was now old and well advanced in years, and the LORD had blessed him in every way. ²He said to the chief*ᵃ* servant in his household, the one in charge of all that he had, "Put your hand under my thigh. ³I want you to swear by the LORD, the God of heaven and the God of earth, that you will not get a wife for my son from the daughters of the Canaanites, among

whom I am living, ⁴but will go to my country and my own relatives and get a wife for my son Isaac."

⁵The servant asked him, "What if the woman is unwilling to come back with me to this land? Shall I then take your son back to the country you came from?"

⁶"Make sure that you do not take my son back there," Abraham said. ⁷"The LORD, the God of heaven, who brought me out of my father's household and my native land and who spoke to me and promised me on oath, saying, 'To your offspring*ᵇ* I will give this land'—he will send his angel before you so that you can get a wife for my son from there. ⁸If the woman is unwilling to come back with you, then you will be released from this oath of mine. Only do not take my son back there." ⁹So the servant put his hand under the thigh of his master Abraham and swore an oath to him concerning this matter.

¹⁰Then the servant took ten of his master's camels and left, taking with him all kinds of good things from his master. He set out for Aram Naharaim*ᶜ* and made his way to the town of Nahor. ¹¹He had the camels kneel down near the well outside the town; it was toward evening, the time the women go out to draw water.

¹²Then he prayed, "O LORD, God of my master Abraham, give me success today, and show kindness to my master Abraham. ¹³See, I am standing beside this spring, and the daughters of the townspeople are coming out to draw water.

¹⁴May it be that when I say to a girl, 'Please let down your jar that I may have a drink,' and she says, 'Drink, and I'll water your camels too'—let her be the one you have chosen for your servant Isaac. By this I will know that you have shown kindness to my master."

¹⁵Before he had finished praying, Rebekah came out with her jar on her shoulder. She was the daughter of Bethuel son of Milcah, who was the wife of Abraham's brother Nahor. ¹⁶The girl was very beautiful, a virgin; no man had ever lain with her. She went down to the spring, filled her jar and came up again.

¹⁷The servant hurried to meet her and said, "Please give me a little water from your jar."

¹⁸"Drink, my lord," she said, and quickly lowered the jar to her hands and gave him a drink.

¹⁹After she had given him a drink, she said, "I'll draw water for your camels too, until they have finished drinking." ²⁰So she quickly emptied her jar into the trough, ran back to the well to draw more water, and drew enough for all his camels. ²¹Without saying a word, the man watched her closely to learn whether or not the LORD had made his journey successful.

²²When the camels had finished drinking, the man took out a gold nose ring weighing a beka*ᵈ* and two gold bracelets weighing ten shekels.*ᵉ* ²³Then he asked, "Whose daughter are you? Please tell me, is there room in your father's house for us to spend the night?"

²⁴She answered him, "I am the daughter of Bethuel, the son that Milcah bore to Nahor." ²⁵And she added, "We have plenty of straw and fodder, as well as room for you to spend the night."

²⁶Then the man bowed down and worshiped the LORD, ²⁷saying, "Praise be to the LORD, the God of my master Abraham, who has not abandoned his kindness and faithfulness to my master. As for me, the LORD has led me on the journey to the house of my master's relatives."

²⁸The girl ran and told her mother's household about these things. ²⁹Now Rebekah had a brother named Laban, and he hurried out to the man at the spring. ³⁰As soon as he had seen the nose ring, and the bracelets on his sister's arms, and had heard Rebekah tell what the man said to her, he went out to the man and found him standing by the camels near the spring. ³¹"Come, you who are blessed by the LORD," he said. "Why are you standing out here? I have prepared the house and a place for the camels."

³²So the man went to the house, and the camels were unloaded. Straw and fodder were brought for the camels, and water for him and his men to wash their feet. ³³Then food was set be-

ᵃ2 Or *oldest*   *ᵇ7* Or *seed*   *ᶜ10* That is, Northwest Mesopotamia   *ᵈ22* That is, about 1/5 ounce (about 5.5 grams)   *ᵉ22* That is, about 4 ounces (about 110 grams)

fore him, but he said, "I will not eat until I have told you what I have to say."

"Then tell us," ˌLabanˌ said.

³⁴So he said, "I am Abraham's servant. ³⁵The LORD has blessed my master abundantly, and he has become wealthy. He has given him sheep and cattle, silver and gold, menservants and maidservants, and camels and donkeys. ³⁶My master's wife Sarah has borne him a son in her*a* old age, and he has given him everything he owns. ³⁷And my master made me swear an oath, and said, 'You must not get a wife for my son from the daughters of the Canaanites, in whose land I live, ³⁸but go to my father's family and to my own clan, and get a wife for my son.'

³⁹"Then I asked my master, 'What if the woman will not come back with me?'

⁴⁰"He replied, 'The LORD, before whom I have walked, will send his angel with you and make your journey a success, so that you can get a wife for my son from my own clan and from my father's family. ⁴¹Then, when you go to my clan, you will be released from my oath even if they refuse to give her to you—you will be released from my oath.'

⁴²"When I came to the spring today, I said, 'O LORD, God of my master Abraham, if you will, please grant success to the journey on which I have come. ⁴³See, I am standing beside this spring; if a maiden comes out to draw water and I say to her, "Please let me drink a little water from your jar," ⁴⁴and if she says to me, "Drink, and I'll draw water for your camels too," let her be the one the LORD has chosen for my master's son.'

⁴⁵"Before I finished praying in my heart, Rebekah came out, with her jar on her shoulder. She went down to the spring and drew water, and I said to her, 'Please give me a drink.'

⁴⁶"She quickly lowered her jar from her shoulder and said, 'Drink, and I'll water your camels too.' So I drank, and she watered the camels also.

⁴⁷"I asked her, 'Whose daughter are you?'

"She said, 'The daughter of Bethuel son of Nahor, whom Milcah bore to him.'

"Then I put the ring in her nose and the bracelets on her arms, ⁴⁸and I bowed down and worshiped the LORD. I praised the LORD, the God of my master Abraham, who had led me on the right road to get the granddaughter of my master's brother for his son. ⁴⁹Now if you will show kindness and faithfulness to my master, tell me; and if not, tell me, so I may know which way to turn."

⁵⁰Laban and Bethuel answered, "This is from the LORD; we can say nothing to you one way or the other. ⁵¹Here is Rebekah; take her and go,

and let her become the wife of your master's son, as the LORD has directed."

⁵²When Abraham's servant heard what they said, he bowed down to the ground before the LORD. ⁵³Then the servant brought out gold and silver jewelry and articles of clothing and gave them to Rebekah; he also gave costly gifts to her brother and to her mother. ⁵⁴Then he and the men who were with him ate and drank and spent the night there.

When they got up the next morning, he said, "Send me on my way to my master."

⁵⁵But her brother and her mother replied, "Let the girl remain with us ten days or so; then you*b* may go."

⁵⁶But he said to them, "Do not detain me, now that the LORD has granted success to my journey. Send me on my way so I may go to my master."

⁵⁷Then they said, "Let's call the girl and ask her about it." ⁵⁸So they called Rebekah and asked her, "Will you go with this man?"

"I will go," she said.

⁵⁹So they sent their sister Rebekah on her way, along with her nurse and Abraham's servant and his men. ⁶⁰And they blessed Rebekah and said to her,

"Our sister, may you increase
    to thousands upon thousands;
may your offspring possess
    the gates of their enemies."

⁶¹Then Rebekah and her maids got ready and mounted their camels and went back with the man. So the servant took Rebekah and left.

⁶²Now Isaac had come from Beer Lahai Roi, for he was living in the Negev. ⁶³He went out to the field one evening to meditate,*c* and as he looked up, he saw camels approaching. ⁶⁴Rebekah also looked up and saw Isaac. She got down from her camel ⁶⁵and asked the servant, "Who is that man in the field coming to meet us?"

"He is my master," the servant answered. So she took her veil and covered herself.

⁶⁶Then the servant told Isaac all he had done. ⁶⁷Isaac brought her into the tent of his mother Sarah, and he married Rebekah. So she became his wife, and he loved her; and Isaac was comforted after his mother's death.

The Death of Abraham

25 Abraham took*d* another wife, whose name was Keturah. ²She bore him Zimran, Jokshan, Medan, Midian, Ishbak and Shuah. ³Jokshan was the father of Sheba and Dedan; the descendants of Dedan were the Asshurites, the Letushites and the Leummites. ⁴The sons of Midian were Ephah, Epher, Hanoch, Abida and Eldaah. All these were descendants of Keturah.

---

a 36 Or *his*   *b 55* Or *she*   *c 63* The meaning of the Hebrew for this word is uncertain.   *d 1* Or *had taken*

[5]Abraham left everything he owned to Isaac. [6]But while he was still living, he gave gifts to the sons of his concubines and sent them away from his son Isaac to the land of the east.

[7]Altogether, Abraham lived a hundred and seventy-five years. [8]Then Abraham breathed his last and died at a good old age, an old man and full of years; and he was gathered to his people. [9]His sons Isaac and Ishmael buried him in the cave of Machpelah near Mamre, in the field of Ephron son of Zohar the Hittite, [10]the field Abraham had bought from the Hittites.[a] There Abraham was buried with his wife Sarah. [11]After Abraham's death, God blessed his son Isaac, who then lived near Beer Lahai Roi.

Ishmael's Sons

[12]This is the account of Abraham's son Ishmael, whom Sarah's maidservant, Hagar the Egyptian, bore to Abraham.

[13]These are the names of the sons of Ishmael, listed in the order of their birth: Nebaioth the firstborn of Ishmael, Kedar, Adbeel, Mibsam, [14]Mishma, Dumah, Massa, [15]Hadad, Tema, Jetur, Naphish and Kedemah. [16]These were the sons of Ishmael, and these are the names of the twelve tribal rulers according to their settlements and camps. [17]Altogether, Ishmael lived a hundred and thirty-seven years. He breathed his last and died, and he was gathered to his people. [18]His descendants settled in the area from Havilah to Shur, near the border of Egypt, as you go toward Asshur. And they lived in hostility toward[b] all their brothers.

Jacob and Esau

[19]This is the account of Abraham's son Isaac.

Abraham became the father of Isaac, [20]and Isaac was forty years old when he married Rebekah daughter of Bethuel the Aramean from Paddan Aram[c] and sister of Laban the Aramean. [21]Isaac prayed to the LORD on behalf of his wife, because she was barren. The LORD answered his prayer, and his wife Rebekah became pregnant. [22]The babies jostled each other within her, and she said, "Why is this happening to me?" So she went to inquire of the LORD.

[23]The LORD said to her,

"Two nations are in your womb,
    and two peoples from within you will be
        separated;
one people will be stronger than the other,
    and the older will serve the younger."

[24]When the time came for her to give birth, there were twin boys in her womb. [25]The first to come out was red, and his whole body was like a hairy garment; so they named him Esau.[d] [26]After this, his brother came out, with his hand grasping Esau's heel; so he was named Jacob.[e] Isaac was sixty years old when Rebekah gave birth to them.

[27]The boys grew up, and Esau became a skillful hunter, a man of the open country, while Jacob was a quiet man, staying among the tents. [28]Isaac, who had a taste for wild game, loved Esau, but Rebekah loved Jacob.

[29]Once when Jacob was cooking some stew, Esau came in from the open country, famished. [30]He said to Jacob, "Quick, let me have some of that red stew! I'm famished!" (That is why he was also called Edom.[f])

[31]Jacob replied, "First sell me your birthright."

[32]"Look, I am about to die," Esau said. "What good is the birthright to me?"

[33]But Jacob said, "Swear to me first." So he swore an oath to him, selling his birthright to Jacob.

25:33 No Sympathy for Esau

Esau's birthright, which he sold for a meal, was his inheritance as the firstborn son. He stood to be head of a large extended family and its property. Though his brother Jacob took advantage of him, the Bible gives Esau little sympathy for his role as victim: he "despised his birthright" (verse 34) by letting his hunger overwhelm his concern for things of lasting value. Because of this, he was later labeled "godless" (Hebrews 12:16).

[34]Then Jacob gave Esau some bread and some lentil stew. He ate and drank, and then got up and left.

So Esau despised his birthright.

Isaac and Abimelech

26 Now there was a famine in the land—besides the earlier famine of Abraham's time—and Isaac went to Abimelech king of the Philistines in Gerar. [2]The LORD appeared to Isaac and said, "Do not go down to Egypt; live in the land where I tell you to live. [3]Stay in this land for a while, and I will be with you and will bless you. For to you and your descendants I will give all these lands and will confirm the oath I swore to your father Abraham. [4]I will make your descendants as numerous as the stars in the sky and will give them all these lands, and through your offspring[g] all nations on earth will be blessed, [5]because Abraham obeyed me and kept my require-

---

[a]10 Or *the sons of Heth*   [b]18 Or *lived to the east of*
mean *hairy*; he was also called Edom, which means *red*.   [c]20 That is, Northwest Mesopotamia   [d]25 *Esau* may
[f]30 *Edom* means *red*.   [g]4 Or *seed*   [e]26 *Jacob* means *he grasps the heel* (figuratively, *he deceives*).

ments, my commands, my decrees and my laws." ⁶So Isaac stayed in Gerar.

⁷When the men of that place asked him about his wife, he said, "She is my sister," because he was afraid to say, "She is my wife." He thought, "The men of this place might kill me on account of Rebekah, because she is beautiful."

⁸When Isaac had been there a long time, Abimelech king of the Philistines looked down from a window and saw Isaac caressing his wife Rebekah. ⁹So Abimelech summoned Isaac and said, "She is really your wife! Why did you say, 'She is my sister'?"

Isaac answered him, "Because I thought I might lose my life on account of her."

¹⁰Then Abimelech said, "What is this you have done to us? One of the men might well have slept with your wife, and you would have brought guilt upon us."

¹¹So Abimelech gave orders to all the people: "Anyone who molests this man or his wife shall surely be put to death."

¹²Isaac planted crops in that land and the same year reaped a hundredfold, because the LORD blessed him. ¹³The man became rich, and his wealth continued to grow until he became very wealthy. ¹⁴He had so many flocks and herds and servants that the Philistines envied him. ¹⁵So all the wells that his father's servants had dug in the time of his father Abraham, the Philistines stopped up, filling them with earth.

¹⁶Then Abimelech said to Isaac, "Move away from us; you have become too powerful for us."

¹⁷So Isaac moved away from there and encamped in the Valley of Gerar and settled there. ¹⁸Isaac reopened the wells that had been dug in the time of his father Abraham, which the Philistines had stopped up after Abraham died, and he gave them the same names his father had given them.

¹⁹Isaac's servants dug in the valley and discovered a well of fresh water there. ²⁰But the herdsmen of Gerar quarreled with Isaac's herdsmen and said, "The water is ours!" So he named the well Esek,ᵃ because they disputed with him. ²¹Then they dug another well, but they quarreled over that one also; so he named it Sitnah.ᵇ ²²He moved on from there and dug another well, and no one quarreled over it. He named it Rehoboth,ᶜ saying, "Now the LORD has given us room and we will flourish in the land."

²³From there he went up to Beersheba. ²⁴That night the LORD appeared to him and said, "I am the God of your father Abraham. Do not be afraid, for I am with you; I will bless you and will increase the number of your descendants for the sake of my servant Abraham."

²⁵Isaac built an altar there and called on the name of the LORD. There he pitched his tent, and there his servants dug a well.

²⁶Meanwhile, Abimelech had come to him from Gerar, with Ahuzzath his personal adviser and Phicol the commander of his forces. ²⁷Isaac asked them, "Why have you come to me, since you were hostile to me and sent me away?"

²⁸They answered, "We saw clearly that the LORD was with you; so we said, 'There ought to be a sworn agreement between us'—between us and you. Let us make a treaty with you ²⁹that you will do us no harm, just as we did not molest you but always treated you well and sent you away in peace. And now you are blessed by the LORD."

³⁰Isaac then made a feast for them, and they ate and drank. ³¹Early the next morning the men swore an oath to each other. Then Isaac sent them on their way, and they left him in peace.

³²That day Isaac's servants came and told him about the well they had dug. They said, "We've found water!" ³³He called it Shibah,ᵈ and to this day the name of the town has been Beersheba.ᵉ

³⁴When Esau was forty years old, he married Judith daughter of Beeri the Hittite, and also Basemath daughter of Elon the Hittite. ³⁵They were a source of grief to Isaac and Rebekah.

Jacob Gets Isaac's Blessing

27 When Isaac was old and his eyes were so weak that he could no longer see, he called for Esau his older son and said to him, "My son."

"Here I am," he answered.

²Isaac said, "I am now an old man and don't know the day of my death. ³Now then, get your weapons—your quiver and bow—and go out to the open country to hunt some wild game for me. ⁴Prepare me the kind of tasty food I like and bring it to me to eat, so that I may give you my blessing before I die."

⁵Now Rebekah was listening as Isaac spoke to his son Esau. When Esau left for the open country to hunt game and bring it back, ⁶Rebekah said to her son Jacob, "Look, I overheard your father say to your brother Esau, ⁷'Bring me some game and prepare me some tasty food to eat, so that I may give you my blessing in the presence of the LORD before I die.' ⁸Now, my son, listen carefully and do what I tell you: ⁹Go out to the flock and bring me two choice young goats, so I can prepare some tasty food for your father, just the way he likes it. ¹⁰Then take it to your father to eat, so that he may give you his blessing before he dies."

¹¹Jacob said to Rebekah his mother, "But my brother Esau is a hairy man, and I'm a man with smooth skin. ¹²What if my father touches me? I would appear to be tricking him and would bring

---

ᵃ20 *Esek* means *dispute.*   ᵇ21 *Sitnah* means *opposition.*   ᶜ22 *Rehoboth* means *room.*   ᵈ33 *Shibah* can mean *oath* or *seven.*   ᵉ33 *Beersheba* can mean *well of the oath* or *well of seven.*

Con Man in God's Family?

The Bible doesn't cover up Jacob's scheming

> *"He has deceived me these two times: He took my birthright, and now he's taken my blessing!"*
> *27:36*

ASK PEOPLE WHY THEY DON'T go to church, and you'll often hear this answer: "There are too many hypocrites." It may be an excuse, but there's a troubling reality behind it. How can a religion with such high standards include so many people with such low standards?

Jacob's life poses the same question. The Bible does not mince words in describing his grasping, con-man character. He took advantage of his twin brother's impulsiveness to switch places with him in the family (25:29–34). Later, seeing that his father Isaac still favored Esau, Jacob (with his mother) tricked the old man into blessing him in place of his brother. (A father's blessing was not merely symbolic. It had a permanent significance, like a swearing-in ceremony.)

The Tricks Backfire

Dressed up in Esau's clothes and some fresh goatskins, Jacob flatly lied to his father and took the Lord's name in vain. Isaac, trusting his nose over his ears, fell for it (27:1–40). Yet the trick backfired. Jacob had to run for his life, and he spent 20 years in exile with his uncle. Uncle Laban gave Jacob a dose of his own medicine, planting an unwanted sister in his wedding bed and repeatedly changing his wages as head shepherd.

You might think Jacob would learn that tricks aren't nice. Yet Jacob didn't noticeably improve his ways. He made a poor husband, neglecting one of his wives and creating rivalry. He favored two sons, so that the neglected ones grew jealous to the point of murder. He certainly doesn't seem like choice material for a religious leader.

God Makes the Choice

But God chose Jacob. He was always making those kinds of choices, sometimes with no apparent reason at all. Often he went against the time-honored practice of letting the firstborn son be number one, as he did in choosing number-two sons Abel, Jacob, and Ephraim. In fact, an inspired prophecy marked Jacob as God's choice before he was even born—before he had done a single thing to merit the choice.

So God's choice did not necessarily depend on how a person behaved. God chose the one he wanted—it was as simple as that.

Is this fair? That's what the apostle Paul asked in Romans 9. He concluded that we have no right to find fault with God's choices, knowing as little as we do compared to his infinite understanding. And while we may never understand God's choices, we should note that all the "rejected" brothers of Genesis—Cain, Canaan, Ishmael, Reuben, Esau, and Manasseh—were treated more than fairly. Their offspring multiplied into nations under God's protection.

No One Excluded

For his chosen people, God had a much greater honor. Good or bad, they would be made a channel of blessing for the whole world. He told Abraham, right from the beginning, "All peoples on earth will be blessed through you" (12:3). By selecting a few, God planned to extend his blessings to all. And that is how it worked out: Abraham's small, fault-ridden family grew into a sizable, fault-ridden nation that brought forth, in the fullness of time, a faultless Jesus.

No wonder Paul wrote that we have no business questioning the wisdom of God. We may not see why he chose people like Jacob. But unquestionably, those choices worked for good—and the whole world became eligible to join the "chosen people." As Paul wrote, "You are all sons of God through faith in Christ Jesus. . . . There is neither Jew nor Greek, slave nor free, male nor female, for you are all one in Christ Jesus. If you belong to Christ, then you are Abraham's seed" (Galatians 3:26–29). God has a habit of choosing flawed people to achieve great good. Who can say what he is doing with the hypocrites of our day?

Life Questions: Why do you think God chooses imperfect people like Jacob? Why did he choose you?

down a curse on myself rather than a blessing."

[13]His mother said to him, "My son, let the curse fall on me. Just do what I say; go and get them for me."

[14]So he went and got them and brought them to his mother, and she prepared some tasty food, just the way his father liked it. [15]Then Rebekah took the best clothes of Esau her older son, which she had in the house, and put them on her younger son Jacob. [16]She also covered his hands and the smooth part of his neck with the goatskins. [17]Then she handed to her son Jacob the tasty food and the bread she had made.

[18]He went to his father and said, "My father." "Yes, my son," he answered. "Who is it?"

[19]Jacob said to his father, "I am Esau your firstborn. I have done as you told me. Please sit up and eat some of my game so that you may give me your blessing."

[20]Isaac asked his son, "How did you find it so quickly, my son?"

"The LORD your God gave me success," he replied.

[21]Then Isaac said to Jacob, "Come near so I can touch you, my son, to know whether you really are my son Esau or not."

[22]Jacob went close to his father Isaac, who touched him and said, "The voice is the voice of Jacob, but the hands are the hands of Esau." [23]He did not recognize him, for his hands were hairy like those of his brother Esau; so he blessed him. [24]"Are you really my son Esau?" he asked.

"I am," he replied.

[25]Then he said, "My son, bring me some of your game to eat, so that I may give you my blessing."

Jacob brought it to him and he ate; and he brought some wine and he drank. [26]Then his father Isaac said to him, "Come here, my son, and kiss me."

[27]So he went to him and kissed him. When Isaac caught the smell of his clothes, he blessed him and said,

"Ah, the smell of my son
    is like the smell of a field
    that the LORD has blessed.

27:27 Sense of Smell

An old man, Isaac had lost his eyesight and apparently much of his sense of touch. He could still smell though, and thought he recognized his son by the scent of his clothes. In an age before deodorants and frequent laundering, people had distinctive scents.

[28]May God give you of heaven's dew
    and of earth's richness—
    an abundance of grain and new wine.
[29]May nations serve you
    and peoples bow down to you.
Be lord over your brothers,
    and may the sons of your mother bow
        down to you.
May those who curse you be cursed
    and those who bless you be blessed."

[30]After Isaac finished blessing him and Jacob had scarcely left his father's presence, his brother Esau came in from hunting. [31]He too prepared some tasty food and brought it to his father. Then he said to him, "My father, sit up and eat some of my game, so that you may give me your blessing."

[32]His father Isaac asked him, "Who are you?"

"I am your son," he answered, "your firstborn, Esau."

[33]Isaac trembled violently and said, "Who was it, then, that hunted game and brought it to me? I ate it just before you came and I blessed him— and indeed he will be blessed!"

[34]When Esau heard his father's words, he burst out with a loud and bitter cry and said to his father, "Bless me—me too, my father!"

[35]But he said, "Your brother came deceitfully and took your blessing."

[36]Esau said, "Isn't he rightly named Jacob[a]? He has deceived me these two times: He took my birthright, and now he's taken my blessing!" Then he asked, "Haven't you reserved any blessing for me?"

[37]Isaac answered Esau, "I have made him lord over you and have made all his relatives his servants, and I have sustained him with grain and new wine. So what can I possibly do for you, my son?"

[38]Esau said to his father, "Do you have only one blessing, my father? Bless me too, my father!" Then Esau wept aloud.

[39]His father Isaac answered him,

"Your dwelling will be
    away from the earth's richness,
    away from the dew of heaven above.
[40]You will live by the sword
    and you will serve your brother.
But when you grow restless,
    you will throw his yoke
    from off your neck."

Jacob Flees to Laban

[41]Esau held a grudge against Jacob because of the blessing his father had given him. He said to himself, "The days of mourning for my father are near; then I will kill my brother Jacob."

---

[a]36 *Jacob* means *he grasps the heel* (figuratively, *he deceives*).

The Women of Genesis

Despite their low status, they were anyone's equal

> The man said, "This is now bone of my bones and flesh of my flesh; she shall be called 'woman,' for she was taken out of man." 2:23

PARTNER SOUGHT FOR VAST CREATIVE endeavor. Global plans. Unlimited compensation. Immediate responsibilities include maintenance of large property, care and authority over all kinds of creatures—flying, walking, creeping, crawling. Object: teamwork and companionship. Female only. Contact Adam.

No woman after Eve got such an opportunity. After sin came into the picture, the original idea of marriage got twisted. " 'To love and to cherish' became 'to desire and to dominate,' " as author Derek Kidner put it. Throughout the Old Testament you catch only glimpses of the original spontaneous joy with which man greeted woman and regarded her as a partner. Granted, the people of God had a higher view of women than did their pagan neighbors. Still, women had value chiefly as seconds to men, whose children they bore, whose desires they fulfilled.

Yet the women of Genesis were no pushovers. They had strong characters, minds of their own. They exerted all the influence they were allowed, and then some.

The Joke Was on Her

Sarah, Abraham's partner, was caught laughing at God's astonishing promise (18:12–15). She thought she knew better than to expect babies at the age of 90. She later had the grace to admit the joke was on her (21:6). Though the New Testament commends her as an ideal submissive wife (1 Peter 3:5–6), she certainly expressed her views strongly to Abraham. Twice she had her rival Hagar driven out of their home and into the desert.

Hagar, though only a servant girl, showed backbone too. After her first expulsion from Abraham and Sarah's home she met God himself, who comforted her and sent her back to Abraham with promises of a great future. Later she showed strength of character by bringing up her son alone in the desert.

A Scheme that Backfired

Rebekah shows up in Chapter 24 as a young girl drawing water for a stranger's camels. By the next day you know she has a mind of her own—and enough courage to set off with a stranger for marriage in unknown territory. Her husband Isaac loved her, and so did her son Jacob. From her, it seems, Jacob got his strong, scheming personality. She initiated the plan to install him in family leadership, against the custom of firstborn sons—and against his father's will. Sadly for Rebekah, her scheme partly backfired, and she never saw Jacob again.

Rachel and Leah, sisters, fought for years over Jacob. Rachel had the looks, as well as a corner on her husband's love. Jacob neglected Leah, whom he hadn't wanted to marry in the first place. But to make up for that slight, God gave Leah children—four sons in a row. Rachel took each one like a fist to the face, which is probably what Leah intended. After a while, Jacob seemed to be just a tool in the struggle for dominance between two sisters, especially when Leah cooly informed him that she had hired his services for the night (30:16).

Who won? It's hard to say. Rachel held the love of Jacob to the end, her two sons most favored by him though last in line. But Leah's sons gained prominence of their own, especially Judah, who became the ancestor of kings—and Jesus. Leah would have enjoyed knowing that she, not Rachel, was great-great-great-grandmother to the King of kings.

Hardly Delicate Violets

In short, the women in Genesis were not delicate violets, but tough, pioneer women. One cannot approve of everything they did, by a long shot. But their toughness and courage demolish any theory that women are, by nature, weak. They used every advantage they had, fairly or unfairly—and did it skillfully. For instance, Rachel displayed classic chutzpah in facing down her father as he searched for some idols she had stolen. She sweetly claimed she couldn't stand up because she was having her period. In truth, she was sitting on the goods, knowing perfectly well even Laban lacked the nerve to try moving a woman in that condition (31:25–35).

They were a match for their men: in courage, in character, in independence, in determination, in orneriness. In that culture they were second-class citizens. But in real life these women were, as God intended, the equal of anybody.

Life Questions: Creative people often find ways to transcend the limits put on them. What do you feel hemmed in by? How can you achieve God's will despite obstacles?

[42]When Rebekah was told what her older son Esau had said, she sent for her younger son Jacob and said to him, "Your brother Esau is consoling himself with the thought of killing you. [43]Now then, my son, do what I say: Flee at once to my brother Laban in Haran. [44]Stay with him for a while until your brother's fury subsides. [45]When your brother is no longer angry with you and forgets what you did to him, I'll send word for you to come back from there. Why should I lose both of you in one day?"

[46]Then Rebekah said to Isaac, "I'm disgusted with living because of these Hittite women. If Jacob takes a wife from among the women of this land, from Hittite women like these, my life will not be worth living."

28 So Isaac called for Jacob and blessed[a] him and commanded him: "Do not marry a Canaanite woman. [2]Go at once to Paddan Aram,[b] to the house of your mother's father Bethuel. Take a wife for yourself there, from among the daughters of Laban, your mother's brother. [3]May God Almighty[c] bless you and make you fruitful and increase your numbers until you become a community of peoples. [4]May he give you and your descendants the blessing given to Abraham, so that you may take possession of the land where you now live as an alien, the land God gave to Abraham." [5]Then Isaac sent Jacob on his way, and he went to Paddan Aram, to Laban son of Bethuel the Aramean, the brother of Rebekah, who was the mother of Jacob and Esau.

[6]Now Esau learned that Isaac had blessed Jacob and had sent him to Paddan Aram to take a wife from there, and that when he blessed him he commanded him, "Do not marry a Canaanite woman," [7]and that Jacob had obeyed his father and mother and had gone to Paddan Aram. [8]Esau then realized how displeasing the Canaanite women were to his father Isaac; [9]so he went to Ishmael and married Mahalath, the sister of Nebaioth and daughter of Ishmael son of Abraham, in addition to the wives he already had.

Jacob's Dream at Bethel

[10]Jacob left Beersheba and set out for Haran. [11]When he reached a certain place, he stopped for the night because the sun had set. Taking one of the stones there, he put it under his head and lay down to sleep. [12]He had a dream in which he saw a stairway[d] resting on the earth, with its top reaching to heaven, and the angels of God were ascending and descending on it. [13]There above it[e] stood the LORD, and he said: "I am the LORD, the God of your father Abraham and the God of Isaac. I will give you and your descendants the

land on which you are lying. [14]Your descendants will be like the dust of the earth, and you will spread out to the west and to the east, to the north and to the south. All peoples on earth will be blessed through you and your offspring. [15]I am with you and will watch over you wherever you go, and I will bring you back to this land. I will not leave you until I have done what I have promised you."

[16]When Jacob awoke from his sleep, he thought, "Surely the LORD is in this place, and I was not aware of it." [17]He was afraid and said, "How awesome is this place! This is none other than the house of God; this is the gate of heaven."

[18]Early the next morning Jacob took the stone he had placed under his head and set it up as a pillar and poured oil on top of it. [19]He called that place Bethel,[f] though the city used to be called Luz.

[20]Then Jacob made a vow, saying, "If God will be with me and will watch over me on this journey I am taking and will give me food to eat and clothes to wear [21]so that I return safely to my father's house, then the LORD[g] will be my God [22]and[h] this stone that I have set up as a pillar will be God's house, and of all that you give me I will give you a tenth."

Jacob Arrives in Paddan Aram

29 Then Jacob continued on his journey and came to the land of the eastern peoples. [2]There he saw a well in the field, with three flocks of sheep lying near it because the flocks were watered from that well. The stone over the mouth of the well was large. [3]When all the flocks were gathered there, the shepherds would roll the stone away from the well's mouth and water the sheep. Then they would return the stone to its place over the mouth of the well.

[4]Jacob asked the shepherds, "My brothers, where are you from?"

"We're from Haran," they replied.

28:12 A Stairway to Heaven

God's grace: this is what Jacob found while traveling alone in the desert. Through his own greedy scheming he had won the family birthright and then, ironically, had had to run away from the family. Yet God came to him full of promises, not the reproaches he deserved. Jacob had not looked for God, but God looked for him. Jacob's vision of a stairway to heaven looked forward to Jesus, who himself is the bridge between heaven and earth (John 1:51).

---

[a]1 Or *greeted*   [b]2 That is, Northwest Mesopotamia; also in verses 5, 6 and 7   [c]3 Hebrew *El-Shaddai*   [d]12 Or *ladder*   [e]13 Or *There beside him*   [f]19 *Bethel* means *house of God*.   [g]20,21 Or *Since God . . . father's house, the LORD*   [h]21,22 Or *house, and the LORD will be my God,* [22]*then*

⁵He said to them, "Do you know Laban, Nahor's grandson?"

"Yes, we know him," they answered.

⁶Then Jacob asked them, "Is he well?"

"Yes, he is," they said, "and here comes his daughter Rachel with the sheep."

⁷"Look," he said, "the sun is still high; it is not time for the flocks to be gathered. Water the sheep and take them back to pasture."

⁸"We can't," they replied, "until all the flocks are gathered and the stone has been rolled away from the mouth of the well. Then we will water the sheep."

⁹While he was still talking with them, Rachel came with her father's sheep, for she was a shepherdess. ¹⁰When Jacob saw Rachel daughter of Laban, his mother's brother, and Laban's sheep, he went over and rolled the stone away from the mouth of the well and watered his uncle's sheep. ¹¹Then Jacob kissed Rachel and began to weep aloud. ¹²He had told Rachel that he was a relative of her father and a son of Rebekah. So she ran and told her father.

¹³As soon as Laban heard the news about Jacob, his sister's son, he hurried to meet him. He embraced him and kissed him and brought him to his home, and there Jacob told him all these things. ¹⁴Then Laban said to him, "You are my own flesh and blood."

Jacob Marries Leah and Rachel

After Jacob had stayed with him for a whole month, ¹⁵Laban said to him, "Just because you are a relative of mine, should you work for me for nothing? Tell me what your wages should be."

¹⁶Now Laban had two daughters; the name of the older was Leah, and the name of the younger was Rachel. ¹⁷Leah had weak*a* eyes, but Rachel was lovely in form, and beautiful. ¹⁸Jacob was in love with Rachel and said, "I'll work for you seven years in return for your younger daughter Rachel."

¹⁹Laban said, "It's better that I give her to you than to some other man. Stay here with me." ²⁰So Jacob served seven years to get Rachel, but they seemed like only a few days to him because of his love for her.

²¹Then Jacob said to Laban, "Give me my wife. My time is completed, and I want to lie with her."

²²So Laban brought together all the people of the place and gave a feast. ²³But when evening came, he took his daughter Leah and gave her to Jacob, and Jacob lay with her. ²⁴And Laban gave his servant girl Zilpah to his daughter as her maidservant.

²⁵When morning came, there was Leah! So Jacob said to Laban, "What is this you have done to me? I served you for Rachel, didn't I? Why have you deceived me?"

²⁶Laban replied, "It is not our custom here to give the younger daughter in marriage before the older one. ²⁷Finish this daughter's bridal week; then we will give you the younger one also, in return for another seven years of work."

²⁸And Jacob did so. He finished the week with Leah, and then Laban gave him his daughter Rachel to be his wife. ²⁹Laban gave his servant girl Bilhah to his daughter Rachel as her maidservant. ³⁰Jacob lay with Rachel also, and he loved Rachel more than Leah. And he worked for Laban another seven years.

Jacob's Children

³¹When the LORD saw that Leah was not loved,

a 17 Or *delicate*

LABAN *Cheater*

HOW FITTING THAT JACOB, WHO had cheated his brother at least twice, fell into the hands of his uncle Laban, a notorious double-crosser. Deceit must have run in the family: Laban was brother to Rebekah, who had helped her son Jacob dupe his own father. Now Jacob learned how it felt to have the joke turned on him.

Laban won the first match by palming off his older daughter Leah on Jacob, who had just worked seven years to earn the beautiful Rachel. Throughout the rest of their working relationship, Jacob and Laban competed to outwit each other. Time and again Jacob accused Laban of changing his wages. Meanwhile Jacob schemed to get the biggest and best flock while tending Laban's animals.

Caught up in their wiles, neither man seemed to notice the obvious: Each trick damaged relationships. For example, deceit enabled Leah to share Rachel's husband, yet what did she really gain? For the rest of their lives the two quarreled miserably over Jacob's favor.

Jacob's flocks increased due to his cunning, but in the process Laban's sons grew hostile. Laban got cheap labor from Jacob, but Jacob so resented it that one day he left without warning, taking Laban's daughters with him. Laban never learned that, though cheating may get you what you want, it usually involves a heavy cost.

Life Questions: What is the best way to respond when someone tries to cheat you?

he opened her womb, but Rachel was barren. **32**Leah became pregnant and gave birth to a son. She named him Reuben,[a] for she said, "It is because the LORD has seen my misery. Surely my husband will love me now."

29:30 Playing Favorites

Throughout his life, Jacob's favoritism would cause problems in his family. He must have learned the habit from his own parents (see 25:28). Here, he favors one wife over the other. Later, he spoiled his son Joseph with favors, making his other sons so jealous they wanted to kill Joseph (see 37:4,18).

33She conceived again, and when she gave birth to a son she said, "Because the LORD heard that I am not loved, he gave me this one too." So she named him Simeon.[b]

34Again she conceived, and when she gave birth to a son she said, "Now at last my husband will become attached to me, because I have borne him three sons." So he was named Levi.[c]

35She conceived again, and when she gave birth to a son she said, "This time I will praise the LORD." So she named him Judah.[d] Then she stopped having children.

30 When Rachel saw that she was not bearing Jacob any children, she became jealous of her sister. So she said to Jacob, "Give me children, or I'll die!"

2Jacob became angry with her and said, "Am I in the place of God, who has kept you from having children?"

3Then she said, "Here is Bilhah, my maidservant. Sleep with her so that she can bear children for me and that through her I too can build a family."

4So she gave him her servant Bilhah as a wife. Jacob slept with her, **5**and she became pregnant and bore him a son. **6**Then Rachel said, "God has vindicated me; he has listened to my plea and given me a son." Because of this she named him Dan.[e]

7Rachel's servant Bilhah conceived again and bore Jacob a second son. **8**Then Rachel said, "I have had a great struggle with my sister, and I have won." So she named him Naphtali.[f]

9When Leah saw that she had stopped having children, she took her maidservant Zilpah and gave her to Jacob as a wife. **10**Leah's servant Zil-

pah bore Jacob a son. **11**Then Leah said, "What good fortune!"[g] So she named him Gad.[h]

12Leah's servant Zilpah bore Jacob a second son. **13**Then Leah said, "How happy I am! The women will call me happy." So she named him Asher.[i]

14During wheat harvest, Reuben went out into the fields and found some mandrake plants, which he brought to his mother Leah. Rachel said to Leah, "Please give me some of your son's mandrakes."

15But she said to her, "Wasn't it enough that you took away my husband? Will you take my son's mandrakes too?"

"Very well," Rachel said, "he can sleep with you tonight in return for your son's mandrakes."

16So when Jacob came in from the fields that evening, Leah went out to meet him. "You must sleep with me," she said. "I have hired you with my son's mandrakes." So he slept with her that night.

17God listened to Leah, and she became pregnant and bore Jacob a fifth son. **18**Then Leah said, "God has rewarded me for giving my maidservant to my husband." So she named him Issachar.[j]

19Leah conceived again and bore Jacob a sixth son. **20**Then Leah said, "God has presented me with a precious gift. This time my husband will treat me with honor, because I have borne him six sons." So she named him Zebulun.[k]

21Some time later she gave birth to a daughter and named her Dinah.

22Then God remembered Rachel; he listened to her and opened her womb. **23**She became pregnant and gave birth to a son and said, "God has taken away my disgrace." **24**She named him Joseph,[l] and said, "May the LORD add to me another son."

Jacob's Flocks Increase

25After Rachel gave birth to Joseph, Jacob said to Laban, "Send me on my way so I can go back to my own homeland. **26**Give me my wives and children, for whom I have served you, and I will be on my way. You know how much work I've done for you."

27But Laban said to him, "If I have found favor in your eyes, please stay. I have learned by divination that[m] the LORD has blessed me because of you." **28**He added, "Name your wages, and I will pay them."

29Jacob said to him, "You know how I have worked for you and how your livestock has fared

---

a32 Reuben sounds like the Hebrew for he has seen my misery; the name means see, a son.   *b33 Simeon probably means one who hears.*   *c34 Levi sounds like and may be derived from the Hebrew for attached.*   *d35 Judah sounds like and may be derived from the Hebrew for praise.*   *e6 Dan here means he has vindicated.*   *f8 Naphtali means my struggle.*   *g11 Or "A troop is coming!"*   *h11 Gad can mean good fortune or a troop.*   *i13 Asher means happy.*   *j18 Issachar sounds like the Hebrew for reward.*   *k20 Zebulun probably means honor.*   *l24 Joseph means may he add.*   *m27 Or possibly have become rich and*

under my care. **30**The little you had before I came has increased greatly, and the LORD has blessed you wherever I have been. But now, when may I do something for my own household?"

31"What shall I give you?" he asked.

"Don't give me anything," Jacob replied. "But if you will do this one thing for me, I will go on tending your flocks and watching over them: **32**Let me go through all your flocks today and remove from them every speckled or spotted sheep, every dark-colored lamb and every spotted or speckled goat. They will be my wages. **33**And my honesty will testify for me in the future, whenever you check on the wages you have paid me. Any goat in my possession that is not speckled or spotted, or any lamb that is not dark-colored, will be considered stolen."

30:33 Misplaced Faith

In this classic encounter between two schemers, each trying to take advantage of the other, Jacob placed considerable faith in an animal-breeding trick. Many people have believed in similar methods over the centuries. Modern genetics indicates that Jacob's results had nothing to do with such techniques. God's intervening power increased Jacob's flocks, as Jacob himself acknowledged (31:7–9).

34"Agreed," said Laban. "Let it be as you have said." **35**That same day he removed all the male goats that were streaked or spotted, and all the speckled or spotted female goats (all that had white on them) and all the dark-colored lambs, and he placed them in the care of his sons. **36**Then he put a three-day journey between himself and Jacob, while Jacob continued to tend the rest of Laban's flocks.

37Jacob, however, took fresh-cut branches from poplar, almond and plane trees and made white stripes on them by peeling the bark and exposing the white inner wood of the branches. **38**Then he placed the peeled branches in all the watering troughs, so that they would be directly in front of the flocks when they came to drink. When the flocks were in heat and came to drink, **39**they mated in front of the branches. And they bore young that were streaked or speckled or spotted. **40**Jacob set apart the young of the flock by themselves, but made the rest face the streaked and dark-colored animals that belonged to Laban. Thus he made separate flocks for himself and did not put them with Laban's animals. **41**Whenever the stronger females were in heat, Jacob would place the branches in the troughs in front of the animals so they would mate near the branches, **42**but if the animals were weak, he would not place them there. So the weak animals went to Laban and the strong ones to Jacob. **43**In this way the man grew exceedingly prosperous and came to own large flocks, and maidservants and menservants, and camels and donkeys.

Jacob Flees From Laban

31 Jacob heard that Laban's sons were saying, "Jacob has taken everything our father owned and has gained all this wealth from what belonged to our father." **2**And Jacob noticed that Laban's attitude toward him was not what it had been.

3Then the LORD said to Jacob, "Go back to the land of your fathers and to your relatives, and I will be with you."

4So Jacob sent word to Rachel and Leah to come out to the fields where his flocks were. **5**He said to them, "I see that your father's attitude toward me is not what it was before, but the God of my father has been with me. **6**You know that I've worked for your father with all my strength, **7**yet your father has cheated me by changing my wages ten times. However, God has not allowed him to harm me. **8**If he said, 'The speckled ones will be your wages,' then all the flocks gave birth to speckled young; and if he said, 'The streaked ones will be your wages,' then all the flocks bore streaked young. **9**So God has taken away your father's livestock and has given them to me.

10"In breeding season I once had a dream in which I looked up and saw that the male goats mating with the flock were streaked, speckled or spotted. **11**The angel of God said to me in the dream, 'Jacob.' I answered, 'Here I am.' **12**And he said, 'Look up and see that all the male goats mating with the flock are streaked, speckled or spotted, for I have seen all that Laban has been doing to you. **13**I am the God of Bethel, where you anointed a pillar and where you made a vow to me. Now leave this land at once and go back to your native land.'"

14Then Rachel and Leah replied, "Do we still have any share in the inheritance of our father's estate? **15**Does he not regard us as foreigners? Not only has he sold us, but he has used up what was paid for us. **16**Surely all the wealth that God took away from our father belongs to us and our children. So do whatever God has told you."

17Then Jacob put his children and his wives on camels, **18**and he drove all his livestock ahead of him, along with all the goods he had accumulated in Paddan Aram,[a] to go to his father Isaac in the land of Canaan.

19When Laban had gone to shear his sheep, Rachel stole her father's household gods. **20**Moreover, Jacob deceived Laban the Aramean by not

*a*18 That is, Northwest Mesopotamia

telling him he was running away. ²¹So he fled with all he had, and crossing the River,ᵃ he headed for the hill country of Gilead.

Laban Pursues Jacob

²²On the third day Laban was told that Jacob had fled. ²³Taking his relatives with him, he pursued Jacob for seven days and caught up with him in the hill country of Gilead. ²⁴Then God came to Laban the Aramean in a dream at night and said to him, "Be careful not to say anything to Jacob, either good or bad."

²⁵Jacob had pitched his tent in the hill country of Gilead when Laban overtook him, and Laban and his relatives camped there too. ²⁶Then Laban said to Jacob, "What have you done? You've deceived me, and you've carried off my daughters like captives in war. ²⁷Why did you run off secretly and deceive me? Why didn't you tell me, so I could send you away with joy and singing to the music of tambourines and harps? ²⁸You didn't even let me kiss my grandchildren and my daughters good-by. You have done a foolish thing. ²⁹I have the power to harm you; but last night the God of your father said to me, 'Be careful not to say anything to Jacob, either good or bad.' ³⁰Now you have gone off because you

longed to return to your father's house. But why did you steal my gods?"

³¹Jacob answered Laban, "I was afraid, because I thought you would take your daughters away from me by force. ³²But if you find anyone who has your gods, he shall not live. In the presence of our relatives, see for yourself whether there is anything of yours here with me; and if so, take it." Now Jacob did not know that Rachel had stolen the gods.

³³So Laban went into Jacob's tent and into Leah's tent and into the tent of the two maidservants, but he found nothing. After he came out of Leah's tent, he entered Rachel's tent. ³⁴Now Rachel had taken the household gods and put them inside her camel's saddle and was sitting on them. Laban searched through everything in the tent but found nothing.

³⁵Rachel said to her father, "Don't be angry, my lord, that I cannot stand up in your presence; I'm having my period." So he searched but could not find the household gods.

³⁶Jacob was angry and took Laban to task. "What is my crime?" he asked Laban. "What sin have I committed that you hunt me down? ³⁷Now that you have searched through all my goods, what have you found that belongs to your

ᵃ21 That is, the Euphrates

RACHEL *Love and Grief*

JACOB ARRIVED PENNILESS AT HIS cousin Rachel's home, having traveled hundreds of miles on foot. To some he might appear a poor catch—a fugitive from his family, his character tainted with the grasping, scheming qualities that had created the problem. Rachel, however, could grasp and scheme quite well herself. In strength and cunning, Jacob had met his match.

In an age not known for romance, when young people often waited for their parents to arrange their marriages, Jacob fell profoundly in love with Rachel. He worked fourteen years to gain her (after being tricked into marrying her sister along the way). Clearly, to him, beautiful Rachel was worth the labor. He loved her from first sight to last breath.

Rachel knew what it was to be deeply loved, but she also knew piercing sorrow. More than anything she wanted children, and while her sister produced six sons for Jacob and two servants also bore him children, Rachel remained childless. Her rivalry with her sister Leah, told in Genesis 29 and 30, was profound and bitter. Finally Rachel gave birth to Joseph, her first son. Some years later she died in childbirth bearing Benjamin, her second. (Showing love even after her death, Jacob counted these two sons as his favorites.)

Rachel's fierce love for her children became an emblem for Israel. More than a thousand years after she lived, the prophet Jeremiah, mulling over the destruction of Israel, heard "mourning and great weeping, Rachel weeping for her children and refusing to be comforted, because her children are no more" (Jeremiah 31:15). The same haunting poetry is quoted in Matthew 2:18 regarding the slaughter of babies by King Herod. Even today the phrase "Rachel weeping" serves as shorthand for the sufferings of the Jewish people.

Rachel was a strong woman whose loyalty to her husband and desire for children outweighed everything else. She and her sister became part of a traditional Jewish wedding blessing: "May the LORD make the woman who is coming into your home like Rachel and Leah, who together built up the house of Israel" (Ruth 4:11).

Life Questions: Jacob longed for a wife. Rachel longed for children. What do you want more than anything else?

household? Put it here in front of your relatives and mine, and let them judge between the two of us.

³⁸"I have been with you for twenty years now.

Your sheep and goats have not miscarried, nor have I eaten rams from your flocks. ³⁹I did not bring you animals torn by wild beasts; I bore the loss myself. And you demanded payment from me for whatever was stolen by day or night. ⁴⁰This was my situation: The heat consumed me in the daytime and the cold at night, and sleep fled from my eyes. ⁴¹It was like this for the twenty years I was in your household. I worked for you fourteen years for your two daughters and six years for your flocks, and you changed my wages ten times. ⁴²If the God of my father, the God of Abraham and the Fear of Isaac, had not been with me, you would surely have sent me away empty-handed. But God has seen my hardship and the toil of my hands, and last night he rebuked you."

⁴³Laban answered Jacob, "The women are my daughters, the children are my children, and the flocks are my flocks. All you see is mine. Yet what can I do today about these daughters of mine, or about the children they have borne? ⁴⁴Come now, let's make a covenant, you and I, and let it serve as a witness between us."

⁴⁵So Jacob took a stone and set it up as a pillar. ⁴⁶He said to his relatives, "Gather some stones." So they took stones and piled them in a heap, and they ate there by the heap. ⁴⁷Laban called it Jegar Sahadutha,[a] and Jacob called it Galeed.[b]

⁴⁸Laban said, "This heap is a witness between you and me today." That is why it was called Galeed. ⁴⁹It was also called Mizpah,[c] because he said, "May the LORD keep watch between you and me when we are away from each other. ⁵⁰If you mistreat my daughters or if you take any wives besides my daughters, even though no one is with us, remember that God is a witness between you and me."

⁵¹Laban also said to Jacob, "Here is this heap, and here is this pillar I have set up between you and me. ⁵²This heap is a witness, and this pillar is a witness, that I will not go past this heap to your side to harm you and that you will not go past this heap and pillar to my side to harm me. ⁵³May the God of Abraham and the God of Nahor, the God of their father, judge between us."

So Jacob took an oath in the name of the Fear of his father Isaac. ⁵⁴He offered a sacrifice there in the hill country and invited his relatives to a meal. After they had eaten, they spent the night there.

⁵⁵Early the next morning Laban kissed his grandchildren and his daughters and blessed them. Then he left and returned home.

Jacob Prepares to Meet Esau

32 Jacob also went on his way, and the angels of God met him. ²When Jacob saw them, he said, "This is the camp of God!" So he named that place Mahanaim.[d]

³Jacob sent messengers ahead of him to his brother Esau in the land of Seir, the country of Edom. ⁴He instructed them: "This is what you are to say to my master Esau: 'Your servant Jacob says, I have been staying with Laban and have remained there till now. ⁵I have cattle and donkeys, sheep and goats, menservants and maidservants. Now I am sending this message to my lord, that I may find favor in your eyes.'"

⁶When the messengers returned to Jacob, they said, "We went to your brother Esau, and now he is coming to meet you, and four hundred men are with him."

⁷In great fear and distress Jacob divided the people who were with him into two groups,[e] and the flocks and herds and camels as well. ⁸He thought, "If Esau comes and attacks one group,[f] the group[f] that is left may escape."

⁹Then Jacob prayed, "O God of my father Abraham, God of my father Isaac, O LORD, who said to me, 'Go back to your country and your relatives, and I will make you prosper,' ¹⁰I am unworthy of all the kindness and faithfulness you have shown your servant. I had only my staff when I crossed this Jordan, but now I have become two groups. ¹¹Save me, I pray, from the hand of my brother Esau, for I am afraid he will come and attack me, and also the mothers with their children. ¹²But you have said, 'I will surely make you prosper and will make your descendants like the sand of the sea, which cannot be counted.'"

¹³He spent the night there, and from what he had with him he selected a gift for his brother Esau: ¹⁴two hundred female goats and twenty male goats, two hundred ewes and twenty rams, ¹⁵thirty female camels with their young, forty cows and ten bulls, and twenty female donkeys

---

^a47 The Aramaic *Jegar Sahadutha* means *witness heap.*
^b47 The Hebrew *Galeed* means *witness heap.* ^c49 *Mizpah* means *watchtower.* ^d2 *Mahanaim* means *two camps.* ^e7 Or *camps;* also in verse 10 ^f8 Or *camp*

and ten male donkeys. [16]He put them in the care of his servants, each herd by itself, and said to his servants, "Go ahead of me, and keep some space between the herds."

[17]He instructed the one in the lead: "When my brother Esau meets you and asks, 'To whom do you belong, and where are you going, and who owns all these animals in front of you?' [18]then you are to say, 'They belong to your servant Jacob. They are a gift sent to my lord Esau, and he is coming behind us.'"

[19]He also instructed the second, the third and all the others who followed the herds: "You are to say the same thing to Esau when you meet him. [20]And be sure to say, 'Your servant Jacob is coming behind us.'" For he thought, "I will pacify him with these gifts I am sending on ahead; later, when I see him, perhaps he will receive me." [21]So Jacob's gifts went on ahead of him, but he himself spent the night in the camp.

Jacob Wrestles With God

[22]That night Jacob got up and took his two wives, his two maidservants and his eleven sons and crossed the ford of the Jabbok. [23]After he had sent them across the stream, he sent over all his possessions. [24]So Jacob was left alone, and a man

32:24 Wrestling with God

This nighttime encounter, as strange as any in the Bible, sounds somewhat similar to Jacob's previous on-the-road encounter with God (28:12) in a dream. But this time God left Jacob evidence of his physical presence—a limp.

wrestled with him till daybreak. [25]When the man saw that he could not overpower him, he touched the socket of Jacob's hip so that his hip was wrenched as he wrestled with the man. [26]Then the man said, "Let me go, for it is daybreak."

But Jacob replied, "I will not let you go unless you bless me."

[27]The man asked him, "What is your name?"

"Jacob," he answered.

[28]Then the man said, "Your name will no longer be Jacob, but Israel,[a] because you have struggled with God and with men and have overcome."

[29]Jacob said, "Please tell me your name."

But he replied, "Why do you ask my name?" Then he blessed him there.

[30]So Jacob called the place Peniel,[b] saying, "It is because I saw God face to face, and yet my life was spared."

[31]The sun rose above him as he passed Peniel,[c] and he was limping because of his hip. [32]Therefore to this day the Israelites do not eat the tendon attached to the socket of the hip, because the socket of Jacob's hip was touched near the tendon.

Jacob Meets Esau

33 Jacob looked up and there was Esau, coming with his four hundred men; so he divided the children among Leah, Rachel and the two maidservants. [2]He put the maidservants and their children in front, Leah and her children next, and Rachel and Joseph in the rear. [3]He himself went on ahead and bowed down to the ground seven times as he approached his brother.

[4]But Esau ran to meet Jacob and embraced him; he threw his arms around his neck and kissed him. And they wept. [5]Then Esau looked up and saw the women and children. "Who are these with you?" he asked.

Jacob answered, "They are the children God has graciously given your servant."

[6]Then the maidservants and their children approached and bowed down. [7]Next, Leah and her children came and bowed down. Last of all came Joseph and Rachel, and they too bowed down.

[8]Esau asked, "What do you mean by all these droves I met?"

"To find favor in your eyes, my lord," he said.

[9]But Esau said, "I already have plenty, my brother. Keep what you have for yourself."

[10]"No, please!" said Jacob. "If I have found favor in your eyes, accept this gift from me. For to see your face is like seeing the face of God, now that you have received me favorably. [11]Please accept the present that was brought to you, for God has been gracious to me and I have all I need." And because Jacob insisted, Esau accepted it.

[12]Then Esau said, "Let us be on our way; I'll accompany you."

[13]But Jacob said to him, "My lord knows that the children are tender and that I must care for the ewes and cows that are nursing their young. If they are driven hard just one day, all the animals will die. [14]So let my lord go on ahead of his servant, while I move along slowly at the pace of the droves before me and that of the children, until I come to my lord in Seir."

[15]Esau said, "Then let me leave some of my men with you."

"But why do that?" Jacob asked. "Just let me find favor in the eyes of my lord."

[16]So that day Esau started on his way back to

---

[a]28 *Israel* means *he struggles with God.*　　[b]30 *Peniel* means *face of God.*　　[c]31 Hebrew *Penuel,* a variant of *Peniel*

Seir. [17]Jacob, however, went to Succoth, where he built a place for himself and made shelters for his livestock. That is why the place is called Succoth.[a]

[18]After Jacob came from Paddan Aram,[b] he arrived safely at the[c] city of Shechem in Canaan

33:15 Surface Reconciliation

On the surface, Jacob and Esau had reconciled. Underneath the niceties, however, mistrust continued, at least on Jacob's part. He did not want Esau to accompany him on his way, nor did he wish Esau to leave some of his men for "protection." He let his brother think he was on his way to Seir (verse 14), but turned north to Succoth as soon as Esau was out of sight.

and camped within sight of the city. [19]For a hundred pieces of silver,[d] he bought from the sons of Hamor, the father of Shechem, the plot of ground where he pitched his tent. [20]There he set up an altar and called it El Elohe Israel.[e]

Dinah and the Shechemites

34 Now Dinah, the daughter Leah had borne to Jacob, went out to visit the women

of the land. [2]When Shechem son of Hamor the Hivite, the ruler of that area, saw her, he took her and violated her. [3]His heart was drawn to Dinah daughter of Jacob, and he loved the girl and spoke tenderly to her. [4]And Shechem said to his father Hamor, "Get me this girl as my wife."

[5]When Jacob heard that his daughter Dinah had been defiled, his sons were in the fields with his livestock; so he kept quiet about it until they came home.

[6]Then Shechem's father Hamor went out to talk with Jacob. [7]Now Jacob's sons had come in from the fields as soon as they heard what had happened. They were filled with grief and fury, because Shechem had done a disgraceful thing in[f] Israel by lying with Jacob's daughter—a thing that should not be done.

[8]But Hamor said to them, "My son Shechem has his heart set on your daughter. Please give her to him as his wife. [9]Intermarry with us; give us your daughters and take our daughters for yourselves. [10]You can settle among us; the land is open to you. Live in it, trade[g] in it, and acquire property in it."

[11]Then Shechem said to Dinah's father and brothers, "Let me find favor in your eyes, and I will give you whatever you ask. [12]Make the price for the bride and the gift I am to bring as great

---

a17 Succoth means shelters.   *b18 That is, Northwest Mesopotamia*   *c18 Or arrived at Shalem, a*   *d19 Hebrew hundred kesitahs; a kesitah was a unit of money of unknown weight and value.*   *e20 El Elohe Israel can mean God, the God of Israel or mighty is the God of Israel.*   *f7 Or against*   *g10 Or move about freely; also in verse 21*

ESAU *Surprising Choice*

MANY PEOPLE FIND ESAU MORE attractive than his brother Jacob. Esau was an outdoorsman—rugged, impulsive, simple and unaffected. Jacob was the stay-at-home mama's boy who angled deceitfully for any personal advantage. He virtually stole his brother's inheritance from him.

Anyone can understand Esau's murderous feelings toward Jacob. As the oldest brother, Esau stood next in line to lead the family. Instead he became the lost brother, holding no significant place in God's plan.

Why God's surprising choice of the younger brother? The apostle Paul reflects on this question in Romans 9:10–18, pointing out that God's preference for Jacob began even before his birth. Again and again in history, God narrowed his focus to a single person in order to carry out his plan to save the world. God couldn't choose everyone—moreover, those individuals God did choose were not always the ones we admire. God makes his own judgments, Paul says, and God's people must bow before him even when they do not understand.

Yet in the stories recorded here, the reasons behind God's unexpected choice become clearer. Esau had major character flaws. At every crossroads he consistently followed his own desires, showing little spiritual sensitivity and no long-term vision. Jacob the grasper at least recognized that the family inheritance was precious; to Esau, momentary hunger mattered more (Genesis 27). And when it came to marriage, Esau chose the local women, even though they came from the wrong heritage and displeased his parents.

God seemed to hold no place in Esau's thinking. Jacob, however unattractively, set his sights higher. God channeled Jacob's passion and strong ambition toward divine purposes.

Life Questions: Do ordinary desires—for food, romance, peer approval, success—conflict with spiritual ambitions in your life? How can you deal with such conflicts?

as you like, and I'll pay whatever you ask me. Only give me the girl as my wife."

[13]Because their sister Dinah had been defiled, Jacob's sons replied deceitfully as they spoke to Shechem and his father Hamor. [14]They said to them, "We can't do such a thing; we can't give our sister to a man who is not circumcised. That would be a disgrace to us. [15]We will give our consent to you on one condition only: that you become like us by circumcising all your males. [16]Then we will give you our daughters and take your daughters for ourselves. We'll settle among you and become one people with you. [17]But if you will not agree to be circumcised, we'll take our sister[a] and go."

[18]Their proposal seemed good to Hamor and his son Shechem. [19]The young man, who was the most honored of all his father's household, lost no time in doing what they said, because he was delighted with Jacob's daughter. [20]So Hamor and his son Shechem went to the gate of their city to speak to their fellow townsmen. [21]"These men are friendly toward us," they said. "Let them live in our land and trade in it; the land has plenty of room for them. We can marry their daughters and they can marry ours. [22]But the men will consent to live with us as one people only on the condition that our males be circumcised, as they themselves are. [23]Won't their livestock, their property and all their other animals become ours? So let us give our consent to them, and they will settle among us."

[24]All the men who went out of the city gate agreed with Hamor and his son Shechem, and every male in the city was circumcised.

[25]Three days later, while all of them were still in pain, two of Jacob's sons, Simeon and Levi, Dinah's brothers, took their swords and attacked the unsuspecting city, killing every male. [26]They put Hamor and his son Shechem to the sword and took Dinah from Shechem's house and left. [27]The sons of Jacob came upon the dead bodies and looted the city where[b] their sister had been defiled. [28]They seized their flocks and herds and donkeys and everything else of theirs in the city and out in the fields. [29]They carried off all their wealth and all their women and children, taking as plunder everything in the houses.

[30]Then Jacob said to Simeon and Levi, "You have brought trouble on me by making me a stench to the Canaanites and Perizzites, the people living in this land. We are few in number, and if they join forces against me and attack me, I and my household will be destroyed."

[31]But they replied, "Should he have treated our sister like a prostitute?"

Jacob Returns to Bethel

35 Then God said to Jacob, "Go up to Bethel and settle there, and build an altar there to God, who appeared to you when you were fleeing from your brother Esau."

[2]So Jacob said to his household and to all who were with him, "Get rid of the foreign gods you have with you, and purify yourselves and change your clothes. [3]Then come, let us go up to Bethel, where I will build an altar to God, who answered me in the day of my distress and who has been with me wherever I have gone." [4]So they gave Jacob all the foreign gods they had and the rings in their ears, and Jacob buried them under the oak at Shechem. [5]Then they set out, and the terror of God fell upon the towns all around them so that no one pursued them.

[6]Jacob and all the people with him came to Luz (that is, Bethel) in the land of Canaan. [7]There he built an altar, and he called the place El Bethel,[c] because it was there that God revealed himself to him when he was fleeing from his brother.

[8]Now Deborah, Rebekah's nurse, died and was buried under the oak below Bethel. So it was named Allon Bacuth.[d]

[9]After Jacob returned from Paddan Aram,[e] God appeared to him again and blessed him. [10]God said to him, "Your name is Jacob,[f] but you will no longer be called Jacob; your name will be Israel.[g]" So he named him Israel.

[11]And God said to him, "I am God Almighty[h]; be fruitful and increase in number. A nation and a community of nations will come from you, and kings will come from your body. [12]The land I gave to Abraham and Isaac I also give to you, and I will give this land to your descendants after you." [13]Then God went up from him at the place where he had talked with him.

[14]Jacob set up a stone pillar at the place where God had talked with him, and he poured out a drink offering on it; he also poured oil on it. [15]Jacob called the place where God had talked with him Bethel.[i]

The Deaths of Rachel and Isaac

[16]Then they moved on from Bethel. While they were still some distance from Ephrath, Rachel began to give birth and had great difficulty. [17]And as she was having great difficulty in childbirth, the midwife said to her, "Don't be afraid, for you have another son." [18]As she breathed her last—for she was dying—she named her son Ben-Oni.[j] But his father named him Benjamin.[k]

---

[a]17 Hebrew *daughter*   [b]27 Or *because*   [c]7 *El Bethel* means *God of Bethel.*   [d]8 *Allon Bacuth* means *oak of weeping.*   [e]9 That is, Northwest Mesopotamia; also in verse 26   [f]10 *Jacob* means *he grasps the heel* (figuratively, *he deceives*).   [g]10 *Israel* means *he struggles with God.*   [h]11 Hebrew *El-Shaddai*   [i]15 *Bethel* means *house of God.*   [j]18 *Ben-Oni* means *son of my trouble.*   [k]18 *Benjamin* means *son of my right hand.*

[19]So Rachel died and was buried on the way to Ephrath (that is, Bethlehem). [20]Over her tomb Jacob set up a pillar, and to this day that pillar marks Rachel's tomb.

[21]Israel moved on again and pitched his tent beyond Migdal Eder. [22]While Israel was living in that region, Reuben went in and slept with his father's concubine Bilhah, and Israel heard of it.

35:22 A Sin that Lies Sleeping

This passage offers no indication that what Reuben did was wrong, let alone subject to punishment. Yet his deed was not forgotten. Decades later, when Jacob called his sons in for a final blessing, he brought up this sin (49:4) and predicted that leadership would pass from Reuben, the firstborn.

Jacob had twelve sons:

[23]The sons of Leah:

Reuben the firstborn of Jacob,
Simeon, Levi, Judah, Issachar and Zebulun.

[24]The sons of Rachel:

Joseph and Benjamin.

[25]The sons of Rachel's maidservant Bilhah:

Dan and Naphtali.

[26]The sons of Leah's maidservant Zilpah:

Gad and Asher.

These were the sons of Jacob, who were born to him in Paddan Aram.

[27]Jacob came home to his father Isaac in Mamre, near Kiriath Arba (that is, Hebron), where Abraham and Isaac had stayed. [28]Isaac lived a hundred and eighty years. [29]Then he breathed his last and died and was gathered to his people, old and full of years. And his sons Esau and Jacob buried him.

Esau's Descendants

36 This is the account of Esau (that is, Edom).

[2]Esau took his wives from the women of Canaan: Adah daughter of Elon the Hittite, and Oholibamah daughter of Anah and granddaughter of Zibeon the Hivite— [3]also Basemath daughter of Ishmael and sister of Nebaioth.

[4]Adah bore Eliphaz to Esau, Basemath bore Reuel, [5]and Oholibamah bore Jeush, Jalam and Korah. These were the sons of Esau, who were born to him in Canaan.

[6]Esau took his wives and sons and daughters and all the members of his household, as well as his livestock and all his other animals and all the goods he had acquired in Canaan, and moved to a land some distance from his brother Jacob. [7]Their possessions were too great for them to remain together; the land where they were staying could not support them both because of their livestock. [8]So Esau (that is, Edom) settled in the hill country of Seir.

[9]This is the account of Esau the father of the Edomites in the hill country of Seir.

[10]These are the names of Esau's sons:

Eliphaz, the son of Esau's wife Adah, and Reuel, the son of Esau's wife Basemath.

[11]The sons of Eliphaz:

Teman, Omar, Zepho, Gatam and Kenaz.

[12]Esau's son Eliphaz also had a concubine named Timna, who bore him Amalek. These were grandsons of Esau's wife Adah.

[13]The sons of Reuel:

Nahath, Zerah, Shammah and Mizzah. These were grandsons of Esau's wife Basemath.

[14]The sons of Esau's wife Oholibamah daughter of Anah and granddaughter of Zibeon, whom she bore to Esau:

Jeush, Jalam and Korah.

[15]These were the chiefs among Esau's descendants:

The sons of Eliphaz the firstborn of Esau:

Chiefs Teman, Omar, Zepho, Kenaz, [16]Korah,[a] Gatam and Amalek. These were the chiefs descended from Eliphaz in Edom; they were grandsons of Adah.

[17]The sons of Esau's son Reuel:

Chiefs Nahath, Zerah, Shammah and Mizzah. These were the chiefs descended from Reuel in Edom; they were grandsons of Esau's wife Basemath.

[18]The sons of Esau's wife Oholibamah:

Chiefs Jeush, Jalam and Korah. These were the chiefs descended from Esau's wife Oholibamah daughter of Anah.

[19]These were the sons of Esau (that is, Edom), and these were their chiefs.

[20]These were the sons of Seir the Horite, who were living in the region:

Lotan, Shobal, Zibeon, Anah, [21]Dishon, Ezer and Dishan. These sons of Seir in Edom were Horite chiefs.

[22]The sons of Lotan:

---

[a] 16 Masoretic Text; Samaritan Pentateuch (see also Gen. 36:11 and 1 Chron. 1:36) does not have *Korah*.

Hori and Homam.[a] Timna was Lotan's sister.

[23]The sons of Shobal:

Alvan, Manahath, Ebal, Shepho and Onam.

[24]The sons of Zibeon:

Aiah and Anah. This is the Anah who discovered the hot springs[b] in the desert while he was grazing the donkeys of his father Zibeon.

[25]The children of Anah:

Dishon and Oholibamah daughter of Anah.

[26]The sons of Dishon[c]:

Hemdan, Eshban, Ithran and Keran.

[27]The sons of Ezer:

Bilhan, Zaavan and Akan.

[28]The sons of Dishan:

Uz and Aran.

[29]These were the Horite chiefs:

Lotan, Shobal, Zibeon, Anah, [30]Dishon, Ezer and Dishan. These were the Horite chiefs, according to their divisions, in the land of Seir.

The Rulers of Edom

[31]These were the kings who reigned in Edom before any Israelite king reigned[d]:

[32]Bela son of Beor became king of Edom. His city was named Dinhabah.

[33]When Bela died, Jobab son of Zerah from Bozrah succeeded him as king.

[34]When Jobab died, Husham from the land of the Temanites succeeded him as king.

[35]When Husham died, Hadad son of Bedad, who defeated Midian in the country of Moab, succeeded him as king. His city was named Avith.

[36]When Hadad died, Samlah from Masrekah succeeded him as king.

[37]When Samlah died, Shaul from Rehoboth on the river[e] succeeded him as king.

[38]When Shaul died, Baal-Hanan son of Acbor succeeded him as king.

[39]When Baal-Hanan son of Acbor died, Hadad[f] succeeded him as king. His city was named Pau, and his wife's name was Mehetabel daughter of Matred, the daughter of Me-Zahab.

[40]These were the chiefs descended from Esau, by name, according to their clans and regions:

Timna, Alvah, Jetheth, [41]Oholibamah, Elah, Pinon, [42]Kenaz, Teman, Mibzar, [43]Magdiel and Iram. These were the

chiefs of Edom, according to their settlements in the land they occupied.

This was Esau the father of the Edomites.

Joseph's Dreams

37 Jacob lived in the land where his father had stayed, the land of Canaan.

[2]This is the account of Jacob.

Joseph, a young man of seventeen, was tending the flocks with his brothers, the sons of Bilhah and the sons of Zilpah, his father's wives, and he brought their father a bad report about them.

[3]Now Israel loved Joseph more than any of his other sons, because he had been born to him in his old age; and he made a richly ornamented[g] robe for him. [4]When his brothers saw that their father loved him more than any of them, they hated him and could not speak a kind word to him.

[5]Joseph had a dream, and when he told it to his brothers, they hated him all the more. [6]He said to them, "Listen to this dream I had: [7]We were binding sheaves of grain out in the field when suddenly my sheaf rose and stood upright, while your sheaves gathered around mine and bowed down to it."

[8]His brothers said to him, "Do you intend to reign over us? Will you actually rule us?" And they hated him all the more because of his dream and what he had said.

37:8 Big Mouth

God revealed Joseph's future by way of two dreams. Foolishly, Joseph told everything to his brothers, who hated him all the more. The spoiled, naïve Joseph we meet here is a different character from the careful, prudent leader who would emerge from prison years later to lead Egypt.

[9]Then he had another dream, and he told it to his brothers. "Listen," he said, "I had another dream, and this time the sun and moon and eleven stars were bowing down to me."

[10]When he told his father as well as his brothers, his father rebuked him and said, "What is this dream you had? Will your mother and I and your brothers actually come and bow down to the ground before you?" [11]His brothers were jealous of him, but his father kept the matter in mind.

---

[a]22 Hebrew *Hemam,* a variant of *Homam* (see 1 Chron. 1:39) the Hebrew for this word is uncertain. [c]26 Hebrew *Dishan,* a variant of *Dishon* [e]37 Possibly the Euphrates [f]39 Many manuscripts of the Masoretic Text, Samaritan Pentateuch and Syriac (see also 1 Chron. 1:50); most manuscripts of the Masoretic Text *Hadar* [b]24 Vulgate; Syriac *discovered water;* the meaning of [d]31 Or *before an Israelite king reigned over them* [g]3 The meaning of the Hebrew for *richly ornamented* is uncertain; also in verses 23 and 32.

Joseph Sold by His Brothers

¹²Now his brothers had gone to graze their father's flocks near Shechem, ¹³and Israel said to Joseph, "As you know, your brothers are grazing the flocks near Shechem. Come, I am going to send you to them."

"Very well," he replied.

¹⁴So he said to him, "Go and see if all is well with your brothers and with the flocks, and bring word back to me." Then he sent him off from the Valley of Hebron.

When Joseph arrived at Shechem, ¹⁵a man found him wandering around in the fields and asked him, "What are you looking for?"

¹⁶He replied, "I'm looking for my brothers. Can you tell me where they are grazing their flocks?"

¹⁷"They have moved on from here," the man answered. "I heard them say, 'Let's go to Dothan.'"

So Joseph went after his brothers and found them near Dothan. ¹⁸But they saw him in the distance, and before he reached them, they plotted to kill him.

¹⁹"Here comes that dreamer!" they said to each other. ²⁰"Come now, let's kill him and throw him into one of these cisterns and say that a ferocious animal devoured him. Then we'll see what comes of his dreams."

²¹When Reuben heard this, he tried to rescue him from their hands. "Let's not take his life," he said. ²²"Don't shed any blood. Throw him into this cistern here in the desert, but don't lay a hand on him." Reuben said this to rescue him from them and take him back to his father.

²³So when Joseph came to his brothers, they stripped him of his robe—the richly ornamented robe he was wearing— ²⁴and they took him and threw him into the cistern. Now the cistern was empty; there was no water in it.

²⁵As they sat down to eat their meal, they looked up and saw a caravan of Ishmaelites coming from Gilead. Their camels were loaded with spices, balm and myrrh, and they were on their way to take them down to Egypt.

²⁶Judah said to his brothers, "What will we gain if we kill our brother and cover up his blood? ²⁷Come, let's sell him to the Ishmaelites and not lay our hands on him; after all, he is our brother, our own flesh and blood." His brothers agreed.

²⁸So when the Midianite merchants came by, his brothers pulled Joseph up out of the cistern and sold him for twenty shekels[a] of silver to the Ishmaelites, who took him to Egypt.

²⁹When Reuben returned to the cistern and saw that Joseph was not there, he tore his clothes.

³⁰He went back to his brothers and said, "The boy isn't there! Where can I turn now?"

³¹Then they got Joseph's robe, slaughtered a goat and dipped the robe in the blood. ³²They took the ornamented robe back to their father and said, "We found this. Examine it to see whether it is your son's robe."

³³He recognized it and said, "It is my son's robe! Some ferocious animal has devoured him. Joseph has surely been torn to pieces."

³⁴Then Jacob tore his clothes, put on sackcloth and mourned for his son many days. ³⁵All his sons and daughters came to comfort him, but he refused to be comforted. "No," he said, "in mourning will I go down to the grave[b] to my son." So his father wept for him.

³⁶Meanwhile, the Midianites[c] sold Joseph in Egypt to Potiphar, one of Pharaoh's officials, the captain of the guard.

Judah and Tamar

38 At that time, Judah left his brothers and went down to stay with a man of Adullam named Hirah. ²There Judah met the daughter of a Canaanite man named Shua. He married her and lay with her; ³she became pregnant and gave birth to a son, who was named Er. ⁴She conceived again and gave birth to a son and named him Onan. ⁵She gave birth to still another son and named him Shelah. It was at Kezib that she gave birth to him.

⁶Judah got a wife for Er, his firstborn, and her name was Tamar. ⁷But Er, Judah's firstborn, was wicked in the LORD's sight; so the LORD put him to death.

⁸Then Judah said to Onan, "Lie with your brother's wife and fulfill your duty to her as a brother-in-law to produce offspring for your

38:8 A Brother's Duty

Having children was so important in Old Testament times that if a man died childless, his brother was required to sleep with his widow in order to produce a family for him. (The regulations are found in Deuteronomy 25:5–10.)

Onan's sin was a deliberate refusal to treat his brother's widow fairly by giving her children. Family quarrels had split Jacob and Esau and had sent Jacob's son Joseph into slavery; now the next generation was carrying on in the same way.

brother." ⁹But Onan knew that the offspring would not be his; so whenever he lay with his brother's wife, he spilled his semen on the

---

a28 That is, about 8 ounces (about 0.2 kilogram) *b35* Hebrew *Sheol* *c36* Samaritan Pentateuch, Septuagint, Vulgate and Syriac (see also verse 28); Masoretic Text *Medanites*

ground to keep from producing offspring for his brother. ¹⁰What he did was wicked in the LORD's sight; so he put him to death also.

¹¹Judah then said to his daughter-in-law Tamar, "Live as a widow in your father's house until my son Shelah grows up." For he thought, "He may die too, just like his brothers." So Tamar went to live in her father's house.

¹²After a long time Judah's wife, the daughter of Shua, died. When Judah had recovered from his grief, he went up to Timnah, to the men who were shearing his sheep, and his friend Hirah the Adullamite went with him.

¹³When Tamar was told, "Your father-in-law is on his way to Timnah to shear his sheep," ¹⁴she took off her widow's clothes, covered herself with a veil to disguise herself, and then sat down at the

entrance to Enaim, which is on the road to Timnah. For she saw that, though Shelah had now grown up, she had not been given to him as his wife.

¹⁵When Judah saw her, he thought she was a prostitute, for she had covered her face. ¹⁶Not realizing that she was his daughter-in-law, he went over to her by the roadside and said, "Come now, let me sleep with you."

"And what will you give me to sleep with you?" she asked.

¹⁷"I'll send you a young goat from my flock," he said.

"Will you give me something as a pledge until you send it?" she asked.

¹⁸He said, "What pledge should I give you?"

"Your seal and its cord, and the staff in your

Family Battles
The closer they are, the harder they fight

JOSEPH AND HIS BROTHERS FOUGHT bitterly—almost to the death. Nobody, it seems, can fight like brothers and sisters. Their very closeness seems to rub salt in their wounds.

Take a contemporary example: Esther Pauline Friedman came into this world 17 minutes before her sister Pauline Esther Friedman. The identical twins dressed alike, took the same classes, even shared the same purse, with one set of keys, one comb, one lipstick. They slept in the same twin bed. The first time they were separated, in fact, was after their double wedding.

> "Here comes that dreamer!" they said to each other. "Come now, let's kill him." 37:19–20

The middle-aged Esther Pauline hooked a job replacing the original Ann Landers at the *Chicago Sun Times.* Two months later Pauline Esther started her own column with the *San Francisco Chronicle,* calling herself Abigail Van Buren. Ann sniffed to *Time* that her sister Abby's column was "very imitative." The feud was on. For eight years the two women who had dispensed advice to thousands could not resolve a petty family squabble.

Finally, the two were partially reconciled. They told journalists they were "very close." Yet bitter feelings lived on. Seventeen years after making up, Abby said about Ann, "If she looked old, if she needed a face-lift, believe me, it's because she needed it. I'm quite opposed to chopping myself up, but it was her right. Why not? When you cry a lot, it's got to show."

A Father's Favorite

Joseph's story is the last of the brotherly battles of Genesis. Cain and Abel, Isaac and Ishmael, Jacob and Esau all quarreled. Joseph set his 11 brothers against him by telling his dream of their bowing down to him. He was his father's favorite and perhaps flaunted it. So when his brothers got a chance, they paid him back. They sold him as a slave to traveling merchants, who took him to Egypt. Never expecting to see him again, they cooked up a story that he had been killed by wild animals.

God had other plans. In Egypt, he gave Joseph the interpretation to several dreams. It was a ticket to prominence. Egyptians of that day were fascinated by dreams: Archaeologists have uncovered lengthy textbooks on dream interpretation. Joseph soon found himself at the top of Pharaoh's government.

But success was not enough. The Bible story goes on from there, for God wanted forgiveness within the family. A famine forced Joseph's brothers out of Palestine; they came to Egypt looking for food. Kneeling before Joseph—so Egyptian by now that they did not recognize him—they begged for the right to buy food.

A Strange Struggle

So began one of the strangest struggles of the Bible. Joseph could have made up with his brothers on the spot, welcoming them with open arms. Or he could have taken revenge, putting them to death. He did neither. He began a series of elaborate tests, demanding things from them, playing tricks on

hand," she answered. So he gave them to her and slept with her, and she became pregnant by him. [19]After she left, she took off her veil and put on her widow's clothes again.

[20]Meanwhile Judah sent the young goat by his friend the Adullamite in order to get his pledge back from the woman, but he did not find her. [21]He asked the men who lived there, "Where is the shrine prostitute who was beside the road at Enaim?"

"There hasn't been any shrine prostitute here," they said.

[22]So he went back to Judah and said, "I didn't find her. Besides, the men who lived there said, 'There hasn't been any shrine prostitute here.'"

[23]Then Judah said, "Let her keep what she has, or we will become a laughingstock. After all, I did send her this young goat, but you didn't find her."

[24]About three months later Judah was told, "Your daughter-in-law Tamar is guilty of prostitution, and as a result she is now pregnant."

Judah said, "Bring her out and have her burned to death!"

[25]As she was being brought out, she sent a message to her father-in-law. "I am pregnant by the man who owns these," she said. And she added, "See if you recognize whose seal and cord and staff these are."

[26]Judah recognized them and said, "She is more righteous than I, since I wouldn't give her to my son Shelah." And he did not sleep with her again.

[27]When the time came for her to give birth, there were twin boys in her womb. [28]As she was giving birth, one of them put out his hand; so the midwife took a scarlet thread and tied it on his wrist and said, "This one came out first." [29]But when he drew back his hand, his brother came out, and she said, "So this is how you have broken out!" And he was named Perez.[a] [30]Then his brother, who had the scarlet thread on his wrist, came out and he was given the name Zerah.[b]

Joseph and Potiphar's Wife

39 Now Joseph had been taken down to Egypt. Potiphar, an Egyptian who was one of Pharaoh's officials, the captain of the guard, bought him from the Ishmaelites who had taken him there.

---

[a]29 *Perez* means *breaking out.*   [b]30 *Zerah* can mean *scarlet* or *brightness.*

---

them, accusing them. For nearly two years he played these games. They brought confusion and fear to his brothers—and an admission of guilt.

Twenty years had not erased the brothers' memory of Joseph. The moment their troubles began, their guilt surfaced. "They said to one another, 'Surely we are being punished because of our brother. We saw how distressed he was when he pleaded with us for his life, but we would not listen'" (42:21). For Joseph, the drama brought tremendous emotional strain. Five times Genesis records that he broke into tears, once weeping so loudly that people in the next room heard him.

Joseph felt the strain of forgiveness. He wanted to reconcile with his brothers, whom he loved, but it was not easy. And until they had been pushed to the point of admitting and accepting their guilt, reconciliation could not occur. Their sins had planted deep-rooted bitterness, and only an emotionally wrenching struggle could pull it out.

Seeds of Bitterness

In this sense Joseph's story is the story of God and his people—the struggle to root out the sin that began in Genesis 3. Victory over sin does not happen automatically or easily. Ultimately, it demanded the death of God's Son.

Joseph's story points toward Jesus—a man God sent to save his people, one who was hated and betrayed by them just as Joseph was. But God's will to save conquers all. As Joseph told his brothers, "You intended to harm me, but God intended it for good to accomplish . . . the saving of many lives" (50:20).

The Birth of a Nation

Joseph closes one chapter in the story of Israel. The children of Abraham were transformed from a chain of individuals to a nation. God did not choose Joseph over his brothers, as he did Abraham over Lot, Isaac over Ishmael, Jacob over Esau. The brothers' reconciliation opened the way for them to become one family of 12 tribes—a single nation.

But the story leads on. Prosperous and numerous though the 12 were to become, they still had no land. And so Genesis ends happily, but on a note of suspense: When will Joseph's bones go back to the land God promised? When will God's promises be fulfilled?

Life Questions: Have you ever fought hard with a person close to you, and then experienced reconciliation? What process did you go through?

²The LORD was with Joseph and he prospered, and he lived in the house of his Egyptian master. ³When his master saw that the LORD was with him and that the LORD gave him success in everything he did, ⁴Joseph found favor in his eyes and became his attendant. Potiphar put him in charge of his household, and he entrusted to his care everything he owned. ⁵From the time he put him in charge of his household and of all that he owned, the LORD blessed the household of the Egyptian because of Joseph. The blessing of the LORD was on everything Potiphar had, both in the house and in the field. ⁶So he left in Joseph's care everything he had; with Joseph in charge, he did not concern himself with anything except the food he ate.

Now Joseph was well-built and handsome, ⁷and after a while his master's wife took notice of Joseph and said, "Come to bed with me!"

⁸But he refused. "With me in charge," he told her, "my master does not concern himself with anything in the house; everything he owns he has entrusted to my care. ⁹No one is greater in this house than I am. My master has withheld nothing from me except you, because you are his wife. How then could I do such a wicked thing and sin against God?" ¹⁰And though she spoke to Joseph day after day, he refused to go to bed with her or even be with her.

¹¹One day he went into the house to attend to his duties, and none of the household servants was inside. ¹²She caught him by his cloak and said, "Come to bed with me!" But he left his cloak in her hand and ran out of the house.

¹³When she saw that he had left his cloak in her hand and had run out of the house, ¹⁴she called her household servants. "Look," she said to them, "this Hebrew has been brought to us to make sport of us! He came in here to sleep with me, but I screamed. ¹⁵When he heard me scream for help, he left his cloak beside me and ran out of the house."

¹⁶She kept his cloak beside her until his master came home. ¹⁷Then she told him this story: "That Hebrew slave you brought us came to me to make sport of me. ¹⁸But as soon as I screamed for help, he left his cloak beside me and ran out of the house."

¹⁹When his master heard the story his wife told him, saying, "This is how your slave treated me," he burned with anger. ²⁰Joseph's master took him and put him in prison, the place where the king's prisoners were confined.

But while Joseph was there in the prison, ²¹the LORD was with him; he showed him kindness and granted him favor in the eyes of the prison warden. ²²So the warden put Joseph in charge of all those held in the prison, and he was made responsible for all that was done there. ²³The warden paid no attention to anything under Joseph's care, because the LORD was with Joseph and gave him success in whatever he did.

The Cupbearer and the Baker

40 Some time later, the cupbearer and the baker of the king of Egypt offended their master, the king of Egypt. ²Pharaoh was angry with his two officials, the chief cupbearer and the

40:2 Important Officials

When Joseph was thrown into prison on a false charge, his future seemed to vanish. Yet in prison he came into contact with men who would eventually help raise him to the highest post in the nation. The "chief baker" and "chief cupbearer" were important officials in Pharaoh's court.

chief baker, ³and put them in custody in the house of the captain of the guard, in the same prison where Joseph was confined. ⁴The captain of the guard assigned them to Joseph, and he attended them.

After they had been in custody for some time, ⁵each of the two men—the cupbearer and the baker of the king of Egypt, who were being held in prison—had a dream the same night, and each dream had a meaning of its own.

⁶When Joseph came to them the next morning, he saw that they were dejected. ⁷So he asked Pharaoh's officials who were in custody with him in his master's house, "Why are your faces so sad today?"

⁸"We both had dreams," they answered, "but there is no one to interpret them."

Then Joseph said to them, "Do not interpretations belong to God? Tell me your dreams."

⁹So the chief cupbearer told Joseph his dream. He said to him, "In my dream I saw a vine in front of me, ¹⁰and on the vine were three branches. As soon as it budded, it blossomed, and its clusters ripened into grapes. ¹¹Pharaoh's cup was in my hand, and I took the grapes, squeezed them into Pharaoh's cup and put the cup in his hand."

¹²"This is what it means," Joseph said to him. "The three branches are three days. ¹³Within three days Pharaoh will lift up your head and restore you to your position, and you will put Pharaoh's cup in his hand, just as you used to do when you were his cupbearer. ¹⁴But when all goes well with you, remember me and show me kindness; mention me to Pharaoh and get me out of this prison. ¹⁵For I was forcibly carried off from the land of the Hebrews, and even here I have done nothing to deserve being put in a dungeon."

¹⁶When the chief baker saw that Joseph had

given a favorable interpretation, he said to Joseph, "I too had a dream: On my head were three baskets of bread.ᵃ ¹⁷In the top basket were all kinds of baked goods for Pharaoh, but the birds were eating them out of the basket on my head."

¹⁸"This is what it means," Joseph said. "The three baskets are three days. ¹⁹Within three days Pharaoh will lift off your head and hang you on a tree.ᵇ And the birds will eat away your flesh."

²⁰Now the third day was Pharaoh's birthday, and he gave a feast for all his officials. He lifted up the heads of the chief cupbearer and the chief baker in the presence of his officials: ²¹He restored the chief cupbearer to his position, so that he once again put the cup into Pharaoh's hand, ²²but he hangedᶜ the chief baker, just as Joseph had said to them in his interpretation.

²³The chief cupbearer, however, did not remember Joseph; he forgot him.

40:23—41:13 A Forgotten Man

Joseph had carefully prepared the way for his release from prison (verses 14–15). Everything worked according to plan except for one detail: the chief cupbearer forgot all about Joseph. Humanly speaking, Joseph was a forgotten man, stuck in prison with no hope of ever getting out. God alone remembered his existence.

Pharaoh's Dreams

41 When two full years had passed, Pharaoh had a dream: He was standing by the Nile, ²when out of the river there came up seven cows, sleek and fat, and they grazed among the reeds. ³After them, seven other cows, ugly and gaunt, came up out of the Nile and stood beside those on the riverbank. ⁴And the cows that were ugly and gaunt ate up the seven sleek, fat cows. Then Pharaoh woke up.

⁵He fell asleep again and had a second dream: Seven heads of grain, healthy and good, were growing on a single stalk. ⁶After them, seven other heads of grain sprouted—thin and scorched by the east wind. ⁷The thin heads of grain swallowed up the seven healthy, full heads. Then Pharaoh woke up; it had been a dream.

⁸In the morning his mind was troubled, so he sent for all the magicians and wise men of Egypt. Pharaoh told them his dreams, but no one could interpret them for him.

⁹Then the chief cupbearer said to Pharaoh, "Today I am reminded of my shortcomings. ¹⁰Pharaoh was once angry with his servants, and he imprisoned me and the chief baker in the house of the captain of the guard. ¹¹Each of us had a dream the same night, and each dream had a meaning of its own. ¹²Now a young Hebrew was there with us, a servant of the captain of the guard. We told him our dreams, and he interpreted them for us, giving each man the interpretation of his dream. ¹³And things turned out exactly as he interpreted them to us: I was restored to my position, and the other man was hanged.ᶜ"

¹⁴So Pharaoh sent for Joseph, and he was quickly brought from the dungeon. When he had shaved and changed his clothes, he came before Pharaoh.

¹⁵Pharaoh said to Joseph, "I had a dream, and no one can interpret it. But I have heard it said of you that when you hear a dream you can interpret it."

¹⁶"I cannot do it," Joseph replied to Pharaoh, "but God will give Pharaoh the answer he desires."

¹⁷Then Pharaoh said to Joseph, "In my dream I was standing on the bank of the Nile, ¹⁸when out of the river there came up seven cows, fat and sleek, and they grazed among the reeds. ¹⁹After them, seven other cows came up—scrawny and very ugly and lean. I had never seen such ugly cows in all the land of Egypt. ²⁰The lean, ugly cows ate up the seven fat cows that came up first. ²¹But even after they ate them, no one could tell that they had done so; they looked just as ugly as before. Then I woke up.

²²"In my dreams I also saw seven heads of grain, full and good, growing on a single stalk. ²³After them, seven other heads sprouted—withered and thin and scorched by the east wind. ²⁴The thin heads of grain swallowed up the seven good heads. I told this to the magicians, but none could explain it to me."

²⁵Then Joseph said to Pharaoh, "The dreams of Pharaoh are one and the same. God has revealed to Pharaoh what he is about to do. ²⁶The seven good cows are seven years, and the seven good heads of grain are seven years; it is one and the same dream. ²⁷The seven lean, ugly cows that came up afterward are seven years, and so are the seven worthless heads of grain scorched by the east wind: They are seven years of famine.

²⁸"It is just as I said to Pharaoh: God has shown Pharaoh what he is about to do. ²⁹Seven years of great abundance are coming throughout the land of Egypt, ³⁰but seven years of famine will follow them. Then all the abundance in Egypt will be forgotten, and the famine will ravage the land. ³¹The abundance in the land will not be remembered, because the famine that follows it will be so severe. ³²The reason the dream was given to Pharaoh in two forms is that the matter

---

ᵃ 16 Or *three wicker baskets*   ᵇ 19 Or *and impale you on a pole*   ᶜ 22,13 Or *impaled*

has been firmly decided by God, and God will do it soon.

[33]"And now let Pharaoh look for a discerning and wise man and put him in charge of the land of Egypt. [34]Let Pharaoh appoint commissioners over the land to take a fifth of the harvest of Egypt during the seven years of abundance. [35]They should collect all the food of these good years that are coming and store up the grain under the authority of Pharaoh, to be kept in the cities for food. [36]This food should be held in reserve for the country, to be used during the seven years of famine that will come upon Egypt, so that the country may not be ruined by the famine."

[37]The plan seemed good to Pharaoh and to all his officials. [38]So Pharaoh asked them, "Can we find anyone like this man, one in whom is the spirit of God[a]?"

[39]Then Pharaoh said to Joseph, "Since God has made all this known to you, there is no one so discerning and wise as you. [40]You shall be in charge of my palace, and all my people are to submit to your orders. Only with respect to the throne will I be greater than you."

Joseph in Charge of Egypt

[41]So Pharaoh said to Joseph, "I hereby put you in charge of the whole land of Egypt." [42]Then Pharaoh took his signet ring from his finger and put it on Joseph's finger. He dressed him in robes of fine linen and put a gold chain around his neck. [43]He had him ride in a chariot as his second-in-command,[b] and men shouted before him, "Make way[c]!" Thus he put him in charge of the whole land of Egypt.

[44]Then Pharaoh said to Joseph, "I am Pharaoh, but without your word no one will lift hand or foot in all Egypt." [45]Pharaoh gave Joseph the name Zaphenath-Paneah and gave him Asenath daughter of Potiphera, priest of On,[d] to be his wife. And Joseph went throughout the land of Egypt.

[46]Joseph was thirty years old when he entered

41:45 Erasing Joseph's Past

Proud Egyptians did not care for Hebrews. In order that Joseph's ethnic past be erased as quickly as possible, Pharaoh gave Joseph an Egyptian name and married him into a prominent Egyptian family. Joseph gave his own sons Hebrew names, however, a practice that suggests he maintained his own identity.

the service of Pharaoh king of Egypt. And Joseph went out from Pharaoh's presence and traveled throughout Egypt. [47]During the seven years of abundance the land produced plentifully. [48]Joseph collected all the food produced in those seven years of abundance in Egypt and stored it in the cities. In each city he put the food grown in the fields surrounding it. [49]Joseph stored up huge quantities of grain, like the sand of the sea; it was so much that he stopped keeping records because it was beyond measure.

[50]Before the years of famine came, two sons were born to Joseph by Asenath daughter of Potiphera, priest of On. [51]Joseph named his first-born Manasseh[e] and said, "It is because God has made me forget all my trouble and all my father's household." [52]The second son he named Ephraim[f] and said, "It is because God has made me fruitful in the land of my suffering."

[53]The seven years of abundance in Egypt came to an end, [54]and the seven years of famine began, just as Joseph had said. There was famine in all the other lands, but in the whole land of Egypt there was food. [55]When all Egypt began to feel the famine, the people cried to Pharaoh for food. Then Pharaoh told all the Egyptians, "Go to Joseph and do what he tells you."

[56]When the famine had spread over the whole country, Joseph opened the storehouses and sold grain to the Egyptians, for the famine was severe

41:56 An Unusual Famine

Famine is common in the Middle East. There are records of two Egyptian famines so severe that starving people killed and ate each other. But it was rare for famine to affect both Egypt and Palestine at the same time, for they depended on totally different sources of water— Egypt on the Nile and Palestine on local rainfall.

throughout Egypt. [57]And all the countries came to Egypt to buy grain from Joseph, because the famine was severe in all the world.

Joseph's Brothers Go to Egypt

42 When Jacob learned that there was grain in Egypt, he said to his sons, "Why do you just keep looking at each other?" [2]He continued, "I have heard that there is grain in Egypt. Go down there and buy some for us, so that we may live and not die."

[3]Then ten of Joseph's brothers went down to buy grain from Egypt. [4]But Jacob did not send

---

[a]38 Or *of the gods*   [b]43 Or *in the chariot of his second-in-command*; or *in his second chariot*   [c]43 Or *Bow down*
[d]45 That is, Heliopolis; also in verse 50   [e]51 *Manasseh* sounds like and may be derived from the Hebrew for *forget*.
[f]52 *Ephraim* sounds like the Hebrew for *twice fruitful*.

Benjamin, Joseph's brother, with the others, because he was afraid that harm might come to him. ⁵So Israel's sons were among those who went to buy grain, for the famine was in the land of Canaan also.

⁶Now Joseph was the governor of the land, the one who sold grain to all its people. So when Joseph's brothers arrived, they bowed down to him with their faces to the ground. ⁷As soon as Joseph saw his brothers, he recognized them, but he pretended to be a stranger and spoke harshly to them. "Where do you come from?" he asked.

"From the land of Canaan," they replied, "to buy food."

⁸Although Joseph recognized his brothers, they did not recognize him. ⁹Then he remembered his dreams about them and said to them, "You are spies! You have come to see where our land is unprotected."

¹⁰"No, my lord," they answered. "Your servants have come to buy food. ¹¹We are all the sons of one man. Your servants are honest men, not spies."

¹²"No!" he said to them. "You have come to see where our land is unprotected."

¹³But they replied, "Your servants were twelve brothers, the sons of one man, who lives in the land of Canaan. The youngest is now with our father, and one is no more."

¹⁴Joseph said to them, "It is just as I told you: You are spies! ¹⁵And this is how you will be tested: As surely as Pharaoh lives, you will not leave this place unless your youngest brother comes here. ¹⁶Send one of your number to get your brother; the rest of you will be kept in prison, so that your words may be tested to see if you are telling the truth. If you are not, then as surely as Pharaoh lives, you are spies!" ¹⁷And he put them all in custody for three days.

¹⁸On the third day, Joseph said to them, "Do this and you will live, for I fear God: ¹⁹If you are honest men, let one of your brothers stay here in prison, while the rest of you go and take grain back for your starving households. ²⁰But you must bring your youngest brother to me, so that your words may be verified and that you may not die." This they proceeded to do.

²¹They said to one another, "Surely we are being punished because of our brother. We saw how distressed he was when he pleaded with us for his life, but we would not listen; that's why this distress has come upon us."

²²Reuben replied, "Didn't I tell you not to sin against the boy? But you wouldn't listen! Now we must give an accounting for his blood." ²³They did not realize that Joseph could understand them, since he was using an interpreter.

²⁴He turned away from them and began to weep, but then turned back and spoke to them again. He had Simeon taken from them and bound before their eyes.

42:24 Joseph in Tears

Five times Genesis tells about Joseph weeping as he dealt with his brothers (43:30; 45:2,14–15; 50:17). They had sold him into slavery, and all those years had not erased his hurt and anger. Yet he loved his brothers, and wanted to be reconciled. He felt his conflicting emotions intensely: love versus anger, forgiveness versus bitterness.

²⁵Joseph gave orders to fill their bags with grain, to put each man's silver back in his sack, and to give them provisions for their journey. After this was done for them, ²⁶they loaded their grain on their donkeys and left.

²⁷At the place where they stopped for the night one of them opened his sack to get feed for his donkey, and he saw his silver in the mouth of his sack. ²⁸"My silver has been returned," he said to his brothers. "Here it is in my sack."

Their hearts sank and they turned to each other trembling and said, "What is this that God has done to us?"

²⁹When they came to their father Jacob in the land of Canaan, they told him all that had happened to them. They said, ³⁰"The man who is lord over the land spoke harshly to us and treated us as though we were spying on the land. ³¹But we said to him, 'We are honest men; we are not spies. ³²We were twelve brothers, sons of one father. One is no more, and the youngest is now with our father in Canaan.'

³³"Then the man who is lord over the land said to us, 'This is how I will know whether you are honest men: Leave one of your brothers here with me, and take food for your starving households and go. ³⁴But bring your youngest brother to me so I will know that you are not spies but honest men. Then I will give your brother back to you, and you can trade*ᵃ* in the land.' "

³⁵As they were emptying their sacks, there in each man's sack was his pouch of silver! When they and their father saw the money pouches, they were frightened. ³⁶Their father Jacob said to them, "You have deprived me of my children. Joseph is no more and Simeon is no more, and now you want to take Benjamin. Everything is against me!"

³⁷Then Reuben said to his father, "You may put both of my sons to death if I do not bring him back to you. Entrust him to my care, and I will bring him back."

ᵃ 34 Or move about freely

38But Jacob said, "My son will not go down there with you; his brother is dead and he is the only one left. If harm comes to him on the journey you are taking, you will bring my gray head down to the grave*a* in sorrow."

The Second Journey to Egypt

43 Now the famine was still severe in the land. 2So when they had eaten all the grain they had brought from Egypt, their father said to them, "Go back and buy us a little more food."

3But Judah said to him, "The man warned us solemnly, 'You will not see my face again unless your brother is with you.' 4If you will send our brother along with us, we will go down and buy food for you. 5But if you will not send him, we will not go down, because the man said to us, 'You will not see my face again unless your brother is with you.' "

6Israel asked, "Why did you bring this trouble on me by telling the man you had another brother?"

7They replied, "The man questioned us closely about ourselves and our family. 'Is your father still living?' he asked us. 'Do you have another brother?' We simply answered his questions. How were we to know he would say, 'Bring your brother down here'?"

8Then Judah said to Israel his father, "Send the boy along with me and we will go at once, so that we and you and our children may live and not die. 9I myself will guarantee his safety; you can hold me personally responsible for him. If I do not bring him back to you and set him here before you, I will bear the blame before you all my life. 10As it is, if we had not delayed, we could have gone and returned twice."

11Then their father Israel said to them, "If it must be, then do this: Put some of the best products of the land in your bags and take them down to the man as a gift—a little balm and a little honey, some spices and myrrh, some pistachio

43:11 The Perfect Gift

What kind of gift can you send to a man who has everything? Egypt was among the richest and most sophisticated countries in the world, and Israel (Jacob), a desert nomad. He wisely chose simple gifts of local produce—things that might not be available in Egypt.

nuts and almonds. 12Take double the amount of silver with you, for you must return the silver that was put back into the mouths of your sacks. Perhaps it was a mistake. 13Take your brother also and go back to the man at once. 14And may

God Almighty*b* grant you mercy before the man so that he will let your other brother and Benjamin come back with you. As for me, if I am bereaved, I am bereaved."

15So the men took the gifts and double the amount of silver, and Benjamin also. They hurried down to Egypt and presented themselves to Joseph. 16When Joseph saw Benjamin with them, he said to the steward of his house, "Take these men to my house, slaughter an animal and prepare dinner; they are to eat with me at noon."

17The man did as Joseph told him and took the men to Joseph's house. 18Now the men were frightened when they were taken to his house. They thought, "We were brought here because of the silver that was put back into our sacks the first time. He wants to attack us and overpower us and seize us as slaves and take our donkeys."

19So they went up to Joseph's steward and spoke to him at the entrance to the house. 20"Please, sir," they said, "we came down here the first time to buy food. 21But at the place where we stopped for the night we opened our sacks and each of us found his silver—the exact weight—in the mouth of his sack. So we have brought it back with us. 22We have also brought additional silver with us to buy food. We don't know who put our silver in our sacks."

23"It's all right," he said. "Don't be afraid. Your God, the God of your father, has given you treasure in your sacks; I received your silver." Then he brought Simeon out to them.

24The steward took the men into Joseph's house, gave them water to wash their feet and provided fodder for their donkeys. 25They prepared their gifts for Joseph's arrival at noon, because they had heard that they were to eat there.

26When Joseph came home, they presented to him the gifts they had brought into the house, and they bowed down before him to the ground. 27He asked them how they were, and then he said, "How is your aged father you told me about? Is he still living?"

28They replied, "Your servant our father is still alive and well." And they bowed low to pay him honor.

29As he looked about and saw his brother Benjamin, his own mother's son, he asked, "Is this your youngest brother, the one you told me about?" And he said, "God be gracious to you, my son." 30Deeply moved at the sight of his brother, Joseph hurried out and looked for a place to weep. He went into his private room and wept there.

31After he had washed his face, he came out and, controlling himself, said, "Serve the food."

32They served him by himself, the brothers by themselves, and the Egyptians who ate with him

a38 Hebrew *Sheol*   *b14* Hebrew *El-Shaddai*

by themselves, because Egyptians could not eat with Hebrews, for that is detestable to Egyptians. [33]The men had been seated before him in the order of their ages, from the firstborn to the

43:32 Prejudice

Despite his high rank, Joseph still fell victim to Egyptian prejudice: they would not eat at the same table with a Hebrew. Chapter 46 (verses 33–34) adds that Egyptians detested shepherds—and Hebrews herded sheep.

youngest; and they looked at each other in astonishment. [34]When portions were served to them from Joseph's table, Benjamin's portion was five times as much as anyone else's. So they feasted and drank freely with him.

A Silver Cup in a Sack

44 Now Joseph gave these instructions to the steward of his house: "Fill the men's sacks with as much food as they can carry, and put each man's silver in the mouth of his sack. [2]Then put my cup, the silver one, in the mouth of the youngest one's sack, along with the silver for his grain." And he did as Joseph said.

[3]As morning dawned, the men were sent on their way with their donkeys. [4]They had not gone far from the city when Joseph said to his steward, "Go after those men at once, and when you catch up with them, say to them, 'Why have you repaid good with evil? [5]Isn't this the cup my master drinks from and also uses for divination? This is a wicked thing you have done.'"

[6]When he caught up with them, he repeated these words to them. [7]But they said to him, "Why does my lord say such things? Far be it from your servants to do anything like that! [8]We even brought back to you from the land of Canaan the silver we found inside the mouths of our sacks. So why would we steal silver or gold from your master's house? [9]If any of your servants is found to have it, he will die; and the rest of us will become my lord's slaves."

[10]"Very well, then," he said, "let it be as you say. Whoever is found to have it will become my slave; the rest of you will be free from blame."

[11]Each of them quickly lowered his sack to the ground and opened it. [12]Then the steward proceeded to search, beginning with the oldest and ending with the youngest. And the cup was found in Benjamin's sack. [13]At this, they tore their clothes. Then they all loaded their donkeys and returned to the city.

[14]Joseph was still in the house when Judah and his brothers came in, and they threw themselves to the ground before him. [15]Joseph said to them, "What is this you have done? Don't you know that a man like me can find things out by divination?"

[16]"What can we say to my lord?" Judah replied. "What can we say? How can we prove our innocence? God has uncovered your servants' guilt. We are now my lord's slaves—we ourselves and the one who was found to have the cup."

[17]But Joseph said, "Far be it from me to do such a thing! Only the man who was found to have the cup will become my slave. The rest of you, go back to your father in peace."

[18]Then Judah went up to him and said: "Please, my lord, let your servant speak a word to my lord. Do not be angry with your servant, though you are equal to Pharaoh himself. [19]My lord asked his servants, 'Do you have a father or a brother?' [20]And we answered, 'We have an aged father, and there is a young son born to him in his old age. His brother is dead, and he is the only one of his mother's sons left, and his father loves him.'

[21]"Then you said to your servants, 'Bring him down to me so I can see him for myself.' [22]And we said to my lord, 'The boy cannot leave his father; if he leaves him, his father will die.' [23]But you told your servants, 'Unless your youngest brother comes down with you, you will not see my face again.' [24]When we went back to your servant my father, we told him what my lord had said.

[25]"Then our father said, 'Go back and buy a little more food.' [26]But we said, 'We cannot go down. Only if our youngest brother is with us will we go. We cannot see the man's face unless our youngest brother is with us.'

[27]"Your servant my father said to us, 'You know that my wife bore me two sons. [28]One of them went away from me, and I said, "He has surely been torn to pieces." And I have not seen him since. [29]If you take this one from me too and harm comes to him, you will bring my gray head down to the grave[a] in misery.'

[30]"So now, if the boy is not with us when I go back to your servant my father and if my father, whose life is closely bound up with the boy's life, [31]sees that the boy isn't there, he will die. Your servants will bring the gray head of our father down to the grave in sorrow. [32]Your servant guaranteed the boy's safety to my father. I said, 'If I do not bring him back to you, I will bear the blame before you, my father, all my life!'

[33]"Now then, please let your servant remain here as my lord's slave in place of the boy, and let the boy return with his brothers. [34]How can I go back to my father if the boy is not with me? No!

---

[a]29 Hebrew *Sheol*; also in verse 31

Do not let me see the misery that would come upon my father."

Joseph Makes Himself Known

45 Then Joseph could no longer control himself before all his attendants, and he cried out, "Have everyone leave my presence!" So there was no one with Joseph when he made himself known to his brothers. ²And he wept so loudly that the Egyptians heard him, and Pharaoh's household heard about it.

45:2 Weeping and Terror

This is one of the Bible's most intensely emotional scenes: it shows Joseph weeping so loudly people heard it in the next room, and Joseph's brothers speechless with terror and guilt. Though the moment ended with embraces and kissing (verses 14–15), years later the brothers were still afraid of revenge (50:15).

³Joseph said to his brothers, "I am Joseph! Is my father still living?" But his brothers were not able to answer him, because they were terrified at his presence.

⁴Then Joseph said to his brothers, "Come close to me." When they had done so, he said, "I am your brother Joseph, the one you sold into Egypt! ⁵And now, do not be distressed and do not be angry with yourselves for selling me here, because it was to save lives that God sent me ahead of you. ⁶For two years now there has been famine in the land, and for the next five years there will be no plowing and reaping. ⁷But God sent me ahead of you to preserve for you a remnant on earth and to save your lives by a great deliverance.ᵃ

⁸"So then, it was not you who sent me here, but God. He made me father to Pharaoh, lord of his entire household and ruler of all Egypt. ⁹Now hurry back to my father and say to him, 'This is what your son Joseph says: God has made me lord of all Egypt. Come down to me; don't delay. ¹⁰You shall live in the region of Goshen and be near me—you, your children and grandchildren, your flocks and herds, and all you have. ¹¹I will provide for you there, because five years of famine are still to come. Otherwise you and your household and all who belong to you will become destitute.'

¹²"You can see for yourselves, and so can my brother Benjamin, that it is really I who am speaking to you. ¹³Tell my father about all the honor accorded me in Egypt and about every-

thing you have seen. And bring my father down here quickly."

¹⁴Then he threw his arms around his brother Benjamin and wept, and Benjamin embraced him, weeping. ¹⁵And he kissed all his brothers and wept over them. Afterward his brothers talked with him.

¹⁶When the news reached Pharaoh's palace that Joseph's brothers had come, Pharaoh and all his officials were pleased. ¹⁷Pharaoh said to Joseph, "Tell your brothers, 'Do this: Load your animals and return to the land of Canaan, ¹⁸and bring your father and your families back to me. I will give you the best of the land of Egypt and you can enjoy the fat of the land.'

¹⁹"You are also directed to tell them, 'Do this: Take some carts from Egypt for your children and your wives, and get your father and come. ²⁰Never mind about your belongings, because the best of all Egypt will be yours.'"

²¹So the sons of Israel did this. Joseph gave them carts, as Pharaoh had commanded, and he also gave them provisions for their journey. ²²To each of them he gave new clothing, but to Benjamin he gave three hundred shekelsᵇ of silver and five sets of clothes. ²³And this is what he sent to his father: ten donkeys loaded with the best things of Egypt, and ten female donkeys loaded with grain and bread and other provisions for his journey. ²⁴He then sent his brothers away, and as they were leaving he said to them, "Don't quarrel on the way!"

²⁵So they went up out of Egypt and came to their father Jacob in the land of Canaan. ²⁶They told him, "Joseph is still alive! In fact, he is ruler of all Egypt." Jacob was stunned; he did not believe them. ²⁷But when they told him everything Joseph had said to them, and when he saw the carts Joseph had sent to carry him back, the spirit of their father Jacob revived. ²⁸And Israel said, "I'm convinced! My son Joseph is still alive. I will go and see him before I die."

Jacob Goes to Egypt

46 So Israel set out with all that was his, and when he reached Beersheba, he offered sacrifices to the God of his father Isaac.

²And God spoke to Israel in a vision at night and said, "Jacob! Jacob!"

"Here I am," he replied.

³"I am God, the God of your father," he said. "Do not be afraid to go down to Egypt, for I will make you into a great nation there. ⁴I will go down to Egypt with you, and I will surely bring you back again. And Joseph's own hand will close your eyes."

⁵Then Jacob left Beersheba, and Israel's sons took their father Jacob and their children and

---

ᵃ7 Or *save you as a great band of survivors*   ᵇ22 That is, about 7 1/2 pounds (about 3.5 kilograms)

their wives in the carts that Pharaoh had sent to transport him. ⁶They also took with them their livestock and the possessions they had acquired in Canaan, and Jacob and all his offspring went to Egypt. ⁷He took with him to Egypt his sons and grandsons and his daughters and grand-daughters—all his offspring.

⁸These are the names of the sons of Israel (Jacob and his descendants) who went to Egypt:

Reuben the firstborn of Jacob.
⁹The sons of Reuben:
Hanoch, Pallu, Hezron and Carmi.
¹⁰The sons of Simeon:
Jemuel, Jamin, Ohad, Jakin, Zohar and Shaul the son of a Canaanite woman.
¹¹The sons of Levi:
Gershon, Kohath and Merari.
¹²The sons of Judah:
Er, Onan, Shelah, Perez and Zerah (but Er and Onan had died in the land of Canaan).
The sons of Perez:
Hezron and Hamul.
¹³The sons of Issachar:
Tola, Puah,ᵃ Jashubᵇ and Shimron.
¹⁴The sons of Zebulun:
Sered, Elon and Jahleel.
¹⁵These were the sons Leah bore to Jacob in Paddan Aram,ᶜ besides his daughter Dinah. These sons and daughters of his were thirty-three in all.

¹⁶The sons of Gad:
Zephon,ᵈ Haggi, Shuni, Ezbon, Eri, Arodi and Areli.
¹⁷The sons of Asher:
Imnah, Ishvah, Ishvi and Beriah.
Their sister was Serah.
The sons of Beriah:
Heber and Malkiel.
¹⁸These were the children born to Jacob by Zilpah, whom Laban had given to his daughter Leah—sixteen in all.

¹⁹The sons of Jacob's wife Rachel:
Joseph and Benjamin. ²⁰In Egypt, Manasseh and Ephraim were born to Joseph by Asenath daughter of Potiphera, priest of On.ᵉ
²¹The sons of Benjamin:
Bela, Beker, Ashbel, Gera, Naaman, Ehi, Rosh, Muppim, Huppim and Ard.
²²These were the sons of Rachel who were born to Jacob—fourteen in all.

²³The son of Dan:

Hushim.
²⁴The sons of Naphtali:
Jahziel, Guni, Jezer and Shillem.
²⁵These were the sons born to Jacob by Bilhah, whom Laban had given to his daughter Rachel—seven in all.

²⁶All those who went to Egypt with Jacob—those who were his direct descendants, not counting his sons' wives—numbered sixty-six persons. ²⁷With the two sonsᶠ who had been born to Joseph in Egypt, the members of Jacob's family, which went to Egypt, were seventyᵍ in all.

²⁸Now Jacob sent Judah ahead of him to Joseph to get directions to Goshen. When they arrived in the region of Goshen, ²⁹Joseph had his chariot made ready and went to Goshen to meet his father Israel. As soon as Joseph appeared before him, he threw his arms around his fatherʰ and wept for a long time.

³⁰Israel said to Joseph, "Now I am ready to die, since I have seen for myself that you are still alive."

³¹Then Joseph said to his brothers and to his father's household, "I will go up and speak to Pharaoh and will say to him, 'My brothers and my father's household, who were living in the land of Canaan, have come to me. ³²The men are shepherds; they tend livestock, and they have brought along their flocks and herds and everything they own.' ³³When Pharaoh calls you in and asks, 'What is your occupation?' ³⁴you should answer, 'Your servants have tended livestock from our boyhood on, just as our fathers did.' Then you will be allowed to settle in the region of Goshen, for all shepherds are detestable to the Egyptians."

47 Joseph went and told Pharaoh, "My father and brothers, with their flocks and herds and everything they own, have come from the land of Canaan and are now in Goshen." ²He chose five of his brothers and presented them before Pharaoh.

³Pharaoh asked the brothers, "What is your occupation?"

"Your servants are shepherds," they replied to Pharaoh, "just as our fathers were." ⁴They also said to him, "We have come to live here awhile, because the famine is severe in Canaan and your servants' flocks have no pasture. So now, please let your servants settle in Goshen."

⁵Pharaoh said to Joseph, "Your father and your brothers have come to you, ⁶and the land of Egypt is before you; settle your father and your

ᵃ13 Samaritan Pentateuch and Syriac (see also 1 Chron. 7:1); Masoretic Text *Puvah*   ᵇ13 Samaritan Pentateuch and some Septuagint manuscripts (see also Num. 26:24 and 1 Chron. 7:1); Masoretic Text *Iob*   ᶜ15 That is, Northwest Mesopotamia   ᵈ16 Samaritan Pentateuch and Septuagint (see also Num. 26:15); Masoretic Text *Ziphion*   ᵉ20 That is, Heliopolis   ᶠ27 Hebrew; Septuagint *the nine children*   ᵍ27 Hebrew (see also Exodus 1:5 and footnote); Septuagint (see also Acts 7:14) *seventy-five*   ʰ29 Hebrew *around him*

brothers in the best part of the land. Let them live in Goshen. And if you know of any among them with special ability, put them in charge of my own livestock."

[7]Then Joseph brought his father Jacob in and presented him before Pharaoh. After Jacob blessed[a] Pharaoh, [8]Pharaoh asked him, "How old are you?"

[9]And Jacob said to Pharaoh, "The years of my pilgrimage are a hundred and thirty. My years have been few and difficult, and they do not equal the years of the pilgrimage of my fathers." [10]Then Jacob blessed[b] Pharaoh and went out from his presence.

[11]So Joseph settled his father and his brothers in Egypt and gave them property in the best part of the land, the district of Rameses, as Pharaoh directed. [12]Joseph also provided his father and his brothers and all his father's household with food, according to the number of their children.

Joseph and the Famine

[13]There was no food, however, in the whole region because the famine was severe; both Egypt and Canaan wasted away because of the famine. [14]Joseph collected all the money that was to be found in Egypt and Canaan in payment for the grain they were buying, and he brought it to Pharaoh's palace. [15]When the money of the people of Egypt and Canaan was gone, all Egypt came to Joseph and said, "Give us food. Why should we die before your eyes? Our money is used up."

[16]"Then bring your livestock," said Joseph. "I will sell you food in exchange for your livestock, since your money is gone." [17]So they brought their livestock to Joseph, and he gave them food in exchange for their horses, their sheep and goats, their cattle and donkeys. And he brought them through that year with food in exchange for all their livestock.

[18]When that year was over, they came to him the following year and said, "We cannot hide from our lord the fact that since our money is gone and our livestock belongs to you, there is nothing left for our lord except our bodies and our land. [19]Why should we perish before your eyes—we and our land as well? Buy us and our land in exchange for food, and we with our land will be in bondage to Pharaoh. Give us seed so that we may live and not die, and that the land may not become desolate."

[20]So Joseph bought all the land in Egypt for Pharaoh. The Egyptians, one and all, sold their fields, because the famine was too severe for them. The land became Pharaoh's, [21]and Joseph reduced the people to servitude,[c] from one end of Egypt to the other. [22]However, he did not buy the land of the priests, because they received a regular allotment from Pharaoh and had food enough from the allotment Pharaoh gave them. That is why they did not sell their land.

[23]Joseph said to the people, "Now that I have bought you and your land today for Pharaoh, here is seed for you so you can plant the ground. [24]But when the crop comes in, give a fifth of it to

---

a7 Or *greeted*   *b10* Or *said farewell to*   *c21* Samaritan Pentateuch and Septuagint (see also Vulgate); Masoretic Text *and he moved the people into the cities*

JOSEPH *School of Hard Knocks*

JOSEPH WAS A SPOILED BRAT, favored by his father over ten older brothers. He got the fancy clothes and preferential treatment and apparently thought he deserved them. When he had a dream of his brothers bowing down to him, he had the gall to tell them all about it.

What could make such a boy grow up? In Joseph's case, maturity came only through calamity. His resentful brothers threatened to kill him, then sold him to slave-traders. As a slave he resisted sexual temptation, and for his troubles was accused of rape and thrown into prison. Basically, the bottom fell out of Joseph's life.

Yet the man emerged with a wholly different character than the boy. Summoned before Pharaoh on a whim, Joseph the prisoner behaved with confidence and tact. Pharaoh gave him a huge government program to administer, and he carried out his tasks with tremendous skill.

Most remarkably, Joseph resisted the chance to get even. When his brothers fell into his hands, he struggled to forgive them rather than paying them back for their actions. In a time of famine, he saved his brothers—and his entire extended family—by bringing them down to Egypt to live with him.

Joseph's story shows how struggles and disappointments can turn out for good. They resulted in good for Joseph's family, who was able to escape a terrible famine. And they resulted in good for Joseph, who gained a whole new perspective on life. Looking back, he could see God at work even in all the trials he had experienced.

Life Questions: What struggles have you gone through? Can you see some positive effects on your personality as a result of these struggles?

Pharaoh. The other four-fifths you may keep as seed for the fields and as food for yourselves and your households and your children."

²⁵"You have saved our lives," they said. "May we find favor in the eyes of our lord; we will be in bondage to Pharaoh."

²⁶So Joseph established it as a law concerning land in Egypt—still in force today—that a fifth of the produce belongs to Pharaoh. It was only the land of the priests that did not become Pharaoh's.

²⁷Now the Israelites settled in Egypt in the region of Goshen. They acquired property there and were fruitful and increased greatly in number.

²⁸Jacob lived in Egypt seventeen years, and the years of his life were a hundred and forty-seven. ²⁹When the time drew near for Israel to die, he called for his son Joseph and said to him, "If I have found favor in your eyes, put your hand under my thigh and promise that you will show me kindness and faithfulness. Do not bury me in Egypt, ³⁰but when I rest with my fathers, carry me out of Egypt and bury me where they are buried."

"I will do as you say," he said.

³¹"Swear to me," he said. Then Joseph swore to him, and Israel worshiped as he leaned on the top of his staff.ᵃ

Manasseh and Ephraim

48 Some time later Joseph was told, "Your father is ill." So he took his two sons Manasseh and Ephraim along with him. ²When Jacob was told, "Your son Joseph has come to you," Israel rallied his strength and sat up on the bed.

³Jacob said to Joseph, "God Almightyᵇ appeared to me at Luz in the land of Canaan, and there he blessed me ⁴and said to me, 'I am going to make you fruitful and will increase your numbers. I will make you a community of peoples, and I will give this land as an everlasting possession to your descendants after you.'

⁵"Now then, your two sons born to you in Egypt before I came to you here will be reckoned as mine; Ephraim and Manasseh will be mine, just as Reuben and Simeon are mine. ⁶Any children born to you after them will be yours; in the territory they inherit they will be reckoned under the names of their brothers. ⁷As I was returning from Paddan,ᶜ to my sorrow Rachel died in the land of Canaan while we were still on the way, a little distance from Ephrath. So I buried her there beside the road to Ephrath" (that is, Bethlehem).

⁸When Israel saw the sons of Joseph, he asked, "Who are these?"

⁹"They are the sons God has given me here," Joseph said to his father.

Then Israel said, "Bring them to me so I may bless them."

¹⁰Now Israel's eyes were failing because of old age, and he could hardly see. So Joseph brought his sons close to him, and his father kissed them and embraced them.

¹¹Israel said to Joseph, "I never expected to see your face again, and now God has allowed me to see your children too."

¹²Then Joseph removed them from Israel's knees and bowed down with his face to the ground. ¹³And Joseph took both of them, Ephraim on his right toward Israel's left hand and Manasseh on his left toward Israel's right hand, and brought them close to him. ¹⁴But Israel reached out his right hand and put it on Ephraim's head, though he was the younger, and crossing his arms, he put his left hand on Manasseh's head, even though Manasseh was the firstborn.

48:14–20 The Younger Brother

Jacob gave his firstborn blessings to the younger of Joseph's boys, just as had been done for Isaac over Ishmael, for Jacob over Esau, and for Joseph over Reuben. In adopting both Manasseh and Ephraim as his own sons, Jacob was also giving Joseph's family a double share in the inheritance—these two grandsons would each receive a full share along with Jacob's other 11 sons. The "12 tribes" of Israel were the offspring of Jacob's 12 sons; substituting Manasseh and Ephraim for Joseph made a total of 13.

¹⁵Then he blessed Joseph and said,

"May the God before whom my fathers
    Abraham and Isaac walked,
the God who has been my shepherd
    all my life to this day,
¹⁶the Angel who has delivered me from all
      harm
    —may he bless these boys.
May they be called by my name
    and the names of my fathers Abraham
     . and Isaac,
and may they increase greatly
    upon the earth."

¹⁷When Joseph saw his father placing his right hand on Ephraim's head he was displeased; so he took hold of his father's hand to move it from Ephraim's head to Manasseh's head. ¹⁸Joseph said to him, "No, my father, this one is the firstborn; put your right hand on his head."

ᵃ31 Or *Israel bowed down at the head of his bed*   ᵇ3 Hebrew *El-Shaddai*   ᶜ7 That is, Northwest Mesopotamia

[19]But his father refused and said, "I know, my son, I know. He too will become a people, and he too will become great. Nevertheless, his younger brother will be greater than he, and his descendants will become a group of nations." [20]He blessed them that day and said,

"In your[a] name will Israel pronounce this blessing:
  'May God make you like Ephraim and Manasseh.'"

So he put Ephraim ahead of Manasseh.

[21]Then Israel said to Joseph, "I am about to die, but God will be with you[b] and take you[b] back to the land of your[b] fathers. [22]And to you, as one who is over your brothers, I give the ridge of land[c] I took from the Amorites with my sword and my bow."

Jacob Blesses His Sons

49 Then Jacob called for his sons and said: "Gather around so I can tell you what will happen to you in days to come.

[2]"Assemble and listen, sons of Jacob;
  listen to your father Israel.

[3]"Reuben, you are my firstborn,
  my might, the first sign of my strength,
  excelling in honor, excelling in power.
[4]Turbulent as the waters, you will no longer excel,
  for you went up onto your father's bed,
  onto my couch and defiled it.

[5]"Simeon and Levi are brothers—
  their swords[d] are weapons of violence.
[6]Let me not enter their council,
  let me not join their assembly,
  for they have killed men in their anger
  and hamstrung oxen as they pleased.
[7]Cursed be their anger, so fierce,
  and their fury, so cruel!
  I will scatter them in Jacob
  and disperse them in Israel.

[8]"Judah,[e] your brothers will praise you;
  your hand will be on the neck of your enemies;
  your father's sons will bow down to you.
[9]You are a lion's cub, O Judah;
  you return from the prey, my son.
  Like a lion he crouches and lies down,
  like a lioness—who dares to rouse him?
[10]The scepter will not depart from Judah,

  nor the ruler's staff from between his feet,
  until he comes to whom it belongs[f]
  and the obedience of the nations is his.
[11]He will tether his donkey to a vine,
  his colt to the choicest branch;
  he will wash his garments in wine,
  his robes in the blood of grapes.
[12]His eyes will be darker than wine,
  his teeth whiter than milk.[g]

[13]"Zebulun will live by the seashore
  and become a haven for ships;
  his border will extend toward Sidon.

[14]"Issachar is a rawboned[h] donkey
  lying down between two saddlebags.[i]
[15]When he sees how good is his resting place
  and how pleasant is his land,
  he will bend his shoulder to the burden
  and submit to forced labor.

[16]"Dan[j] will provide justice for his people
  as one of the tribes of Israel.
[17]Dan will be a serpent by the roadside,
  a viper along the path,
  that bites the horse's heels
  so that its rider tumbles backward.

[18]"I look for your deliverance, O LORD.

[19]"Gad[k] will be attacked by a band of raiders,
  but he will attack them at their heels.

[20]"Asher's food will be rich;
  he will provide delicacies fit for a king.

[21]"Naphtali is a doe set free
  that bears beautiful fawns.[l]

[22]"Joseph is a fruitful vine,
  a fruitful vine near a spring,
  whose branches climb over a wall.[m]
[23]With bitterness archers attacked him;
  they shot at him with hostility.
[24]But his bow remained steady,
  his strong arms stayed[n] limber,
  because of the hand of the Mighty One of Jacob,
  because of the Shepherd, the Rock of Israel,
[25]because of your father's God, who helps you,
  because of the Almighty,[o] who blesses you
  with blessings of the heavens above,
  blessings of the deep that lies below,
  blessings of the breast and womb.

---

[a]20 The Hebrew is singular.   [b]21 The Hebrew is plural.   [c]22 Or And to you I give one portion more than to your brothers—the portion   [d]5 The meaning of the Hebrew for this word is uncertain.   [e]8 Judah sounds like and may be derived from the Hebrew for praise.   [f]10 Or until Shiloh comes; or until he comes to whom tribute belongs   [g]12 Or will be dull from wine, / his teeth white from milk   [h]14 Or strong   [i]14 Or campfires   [j]16 Dan here means he provides justice.   [k]19 Gad can mean attack and band of raiders.   [l]21 Or free; / he utters beautiful words   [m]22 Or Joseph is a wild colt, / a wild colt near a spring, / a wild donkey on a terraced hill   [n]23,24 Or archers will attack . . . will shoot . . . will remain . . . will stay   [o]25 Hebrew Shaddai

26Your father's blessings are greater
    than the blessings of the ancient
        mountains,
    than*a* the bounty of the age-old hills.
Let all these rest on the head of Joseph,
    on the brow of the prince among*b* his
        brothers.

27"Benjamin is a ravenous wolf;
    in the morning he devours the prey,
    in the evening he divides the plunder."

28All these are the twelve tribes of Israel, and
this is what their father said to them when he
blessed them, giving each the blessing appropriate to him.

The Death of Jacob

29Then he gave them these instructions: "I am
about to be gathered to my people. Bury me with
my fathers in the cave in the field of Ephron the
Hittite, 30the cave in the field of Machpelah, near
Mamre in Canaan, which Abraham bought as a
burial place from Ephron the Hittite, along with
the field. 31There Abraham and his wife Sarah
were buried, there Isaac and his wife Rebekah
were buried, and there I buried Leah. 32The field
and the cave in it were bought from the Hittites.*c*"

33When Jacob had finished giving instructions
to his sons, he drew his feet up into the bed,
breathed his last and was gathered to his people.

50 Joseph threw himself upon his father and
wept over him and kissed him. 2Then Joseph directed the physicians in his service to embalm his father Israel. So the physicians embalmed him, 3taking a full forty days, for that was
the time required for embalming. And the Egyptians mourned for him seventy days.

50:3 An Egyptian Funeral

*Joseph's political importance is underlined by
this elaborate mummification procedure for his
father. Jacob's mourning period was only two
days shorter than that given for a pharaoh. All
the court dignitaries went along for the funeral,
a substantial journey (verse 7).*

4When the days of mourning had passed, Joseph said to Pharaoh's court, "If I have found
favor in your eyes, speak to Pharaoh for me. Tell
him, 5'My father made me swear an oath and
said, "I am about to die; bury me in the tomb I
dug for myself in the land of Canaan." Now let
me go up and bury my father; then I will return.'"

6Pharaoh said, "Go up and bury your father,
as he made you swear to do."

7So Joseph went up to bury his father. All
Pharaoh's officials accompanied him—the dignitaries of his court and all the dignitaries of
Egypt— 8besides all the members of Joseph's
household and his brothers and those belonging
to his father's household. Only their children and
their flocks and herds were left in Goshen. 9Chariots and horsemen*d* also went up with him. It
was a very large company.

10When they reached the threshing floor of
Atad, near the Jordan, they lamented loudly and
bitterly; and there Joseph observed a seven-day
period of mourning for his father. 11When the
Canaanites who lived there saw the mourning at
the threshing floor of Atad, they said, "The Egyptians are holding a solemn ceremony of mourning." That is why that place near the Jordan is
called Abel Mizraim.*e*

12So Jacob's sons did as he had commanded
them: 13They carried him to the land of Canaan
and buried him in the cave in the field of Machpelah, near Mamre, which Abraham had bought
as a burial place from Ephron the Hittite, along
with the field. 14After burying his father, Joseph
returned to Egypt, together with his brothers and
all the others who had gone with him to bury his
father.

Joseph Reassures His Brothers

15When Joseph's brothers saw that their father
was dead, they said, "What if Joseph holds a
grudge against us and pays us back for all the
wrongs we did to him?" 16So they sent word to
Joseph, saying, "Your father left these instructions before he died: 17'This is what you are to say
to Joseph: I ask you to forgive your brothers the
sins and the wrongs they committed in treating
you so badly.' Now please forgive the sins of the
servants of the God of your father." When their
message came to him, Joseph wept.

18His brothers then came and threw them-

50:19 You Intended Evil

*Joseph's summation of his experience might
apply to many human situations: You intended
evil, but God intended good. Joseph's trust that
God can bring good out of bad intentions
enabled him finally to forgive his brothers,
leaving judgment to God.*

---

*a*26 Or *of my progenitors, / as great as*   *b*26 Or *the one separated from*   *c*32 Or *the sons of Heth*
*d*9 Or *charioteers*   *e*11 Abel Mizraim means *mourning of the Egyptians.*

selves down before him. "We are your slaves," they said.

[19]But Joseph said to them, "Don't be afraid. Am I in the place of God? [20]You intended to harm me, but God intended it for good to accomplish what is now being done, the saving of many lives. [21]So then, don't be afraid. I will provide for you and your children." And he reassured them and spoke kindly to them.

The Death of Joseph

[22]Joseph stayed in Egypt, along with all his father's family. He lived a hundred and ten years [23]and saw the third generation of Ephraim's children. Also the children of Makir son of Manasseh were placed at birth on Joseph's knees.[a]

[24]Then Joseph said to his brothers, "I am about to die. But God will surely come to your aid and take you up out of this land to the land he promised on oath to Abraham, Isaac and Jacob." [25]And Joseph made the sons of Israel swear an oath and said, "God will surely come to your aid, and then you must carry my bones up from this place."

[26]So Joseph died at the age of a hundred and ten. And after they embalmed him, he was placed in a coffin in Egypt.

---

[a]23 That is, were counted as his

EXODUS

Free at Last
The slaves in Egypt get a liberator

NOTHING STIRS A NATION'S BLOOD like a liberator. The United States remembers two especially: Washington and Lincoln. George Washington led the original fight for independence. A century later Abraham Lincoln set three million people free when he signed the Emancipation Proclamation.

Other places, too, have liberators. India called a scrawny little man named Gandhi "Mahatma" (or "the great one") for leading his people to freedom. Poles honored Lech Walesa, the first freely elected head of state, for liberating Poland from Soviet communism. For the Israelites, one liberator named Moses accomplished what all these did—and more.

The Bible devotes one-eighth of its pages to the story of Moses' time (a bulk of material two-thirds the length of the entire New Testament). And when Jesus came as the great Liberator who set all humanity free, the New Testament reached back to Moses for a comparison (Hebrews 3:1–6).

Bondage in Egypt

The time was ripe for a liberator. Genesis closed with Jacob's family of 70 moving to Egypt. But in the opening scene of Exodus, 350 years later, hundreds of thousands of their ancestors were toiling on Pharaoh's huge construction projects—not as guests but as slaves.

One particularly ruthless pharaoh ordered the murder of all male Israelite babies, unwittingly setting the stage for one of the great ironies of history. Moses' parents hid him in a watertight basket among the grasses of a swamp. There, the tiny baby caught the eye of the pharaoh's daughter. The very edict intended to destroy the Israelites led to their deliverance.

Adopted into the palace, Moses got the benefit of a superb classical education. His Egyptian upbringing was balanced by Israelite nurture: In another striking irony, the pharaoh's daughter paid Moses' own mother to nurse him. The son of slaves, yet brought up in the seat of power, Moses prepared for his eventual goal of forging a nation out of a ragtag band of captives.

His career had to wait, though, for a period of humbling in the desert. Moses fled Egypt as a brash, self-confident man who liked to take matters into his own hands. Forty years later he reluctantly returned, with little besides a stick and a donkey.

Free at Last

The Israelites had endured nearly four centuries of oppression—almost twice as long as the history of America as a nation—before liberation. So far as we know, during those years they received no direct communication from heaven. Surely God must have seemed silent.

Moses faced a formidable challenge. Somehow he had to earn the trust of the slaves and inspire hope in them so that they could indeed throw off their chains. He had to prove that God had not forgotten them. When the time was right, God unleashed a spectacle of might and power that brought a cruel pharaoh to his knees—and convinced the Israelites that God really did care for them.

God used Moses in remarkable ways. He was the first person recorded in the Bible to work miracles. He met God in intimate ways granted no other human. He had a hand in the authorship of a good portion of the Old Testament. But in Jewish history he earned a place primarily as a liberator. He led the march from slavery to freedom, from Egypt to the promised land.

How to Read Exodus

Exodus divides neatly into two parts. The first 20 chapters, on the Israelites' flight from Egypt, read like an exciting novel. Movies based on the action here have strained Hollywood special-effects crews. Everything else in the Old Testament flows out of the events of the exodus—these 20 chapters simply cannot be missed.

As you read Exodus, look for important lessons that apply to your life. For example, study the life of Moses, one of a handful of truly great leaders in history. Chapter 18 shows Moses learning an important leadership principle, and chapters 32—35 include encounters and conversations with God that have no equal in the Bible.

Exodus contains much material about the nature of God. Search for each place where God makes an appearance. Exodus shows a greater proportion of miracles—direct supernatural acts of God—than any part of the Bible except the Gospels. Why were these miracles done? Can you see a pattern? What should the Israelites have learned from them? Did they?

The last 20 chapters mainly consist of laws and regulations, given at Mount Sinai, to govern the life of the nation. Read them to note the concerns and priorities important to God as he designs an entire culture.

The instructions are usually clustered in groups, encompassing every area of life:

1. Moral rules, such as the Ten Commandments
2. Civil and social rules, much like a criminal code
3. Religious and ceremonial rules for the Israelites.

See "A National Law Library," page 149, for more information on these laws.

The religious rituals with their many sacrifices and feasts seem strange to modern Westerners, but they were not at all unusual then. Also, they prepared the way for a Redeemer who was greater than Moses: Jesus Christ. You will need study books and commentaries to find all the symbols that apply to Jesus' life, as shown, for example, in the Passover. Fortunately, the Bible includes a brief but powerful commentary in Hebrews (see especially Hebrews 7—10). This book should be read alongside Exodus and the three books that follow.

PEOPLE YOU'LL MEET IN EXODUS

MOSES *(p. 83)*
JETHRO *(p. 102)*

3-TRACK READING PLAN

For an explanation and complete listing of the 3-track reading plan, turn to page 7.

TRACK 1: *Two-Week Courses on the Bible*
The Track 1 reading program on the Old Testament includes two chapters from Exodus. See page 8 for a complete listing of this course.

TRACK 2: *An Overview of Exodus in 5 Days*
☐ Day 1. Read the Introduction to Exodus and then chapter 3, God's call of Moses.
☐ Day 2. Read chapter 10 and the very brief chapter 11; they record three of the ten plagues against Egypt.
☐ Day 3. Read chapter 14, which contains the exciting story of crossing the Red Sea.
☐ Day 4. Read the Ten Commandments as recorded in chapter 20. (If you have time, chapter 19 gives the dramatic setting for these laws.)
☐ Day 5. Read chapter 32. It records the most striking example of what was to become a characteristic of the Israelites: mass rebellion.

Now turn to page 9 for your next Track 2 reading project.

TRACK 3: *All of Exodus in 39 Days*
After you have read through Exodus, turn to pages 10—14 for your next Track 3 reading project.

☐1	☐2	☐3	☐4	☐5	☐6	☐7	☐8
☐9	☐10–11	☐12	☐13	☐14	☐15	☐16	☐17
☐18	☐19	☐20	☐21	☐22	☐23	☐24	☐25
☐26	☐27	☐28	☐29	☐30	☐31	☐32	☐33
☐34	☐35	☐36	☐37	☐38	☐39	☐40	

The Israelites Oppressed

1 These are the names of the sons of Israel who went to Egypt with Jacob, each with his family: ²Reuben, Simeon, Levi and Judah; ³Issachar, Zebulun and Benjamin; ⁴Dan and Naphtali; Gad and Asher. ⁵The descendants of Jacob numbered seventy[a] in all; Joseph was already in Egypt.

⁶Now Joseph and all his brothers and all that generation died, ⁷but the Israelites were fruitful and multiplied greatly and became exceedingly numerous, so that the land was filled with them.

⁸Then a new king, who did not know about Joseph, came to power in Egypt. ⁹"Look," he said to his people, "the Israelites have become much too numerous for us. ¹⁰Come, we must deal shrewdly with them or they will become even more numerous and, if war breaks out, will join our enemies, fight against us and leave the country."

¹¹So they put slave masters over them to oppress them with forced labor, and they built Pithom and Rameses as store cities for Pharaoh. ¹²But the more they were oppressed, the more they multiplied and spread; so the Egyptians came to dread the Israelites ¹³and worked them ruthlessly. ¹⁴They made their lives bitter with hard labor in brick and mortar and with all kinds of work in the fields; in all their hard labor the Egyptians used them ruthlessly.

¹⁵The king of Egypt said to the Hebrew midwives, whose names were Shiphrah and Puah, ¹⁶"When you help the Hebrew women in childbirth and observe them on the delivery stool, if it is a boy, kill him; but if it is a girl, let her live."

1:16 New Tyrant in Town

Dictators often take out their wrath on a helpless minority: witness Hitler and the Jews or Saddam Hussein and the Kurds. At first pharaohs welcomed their Hebrew guests, and God used the peace and quiet of Egypt, far from the squabbling tribes of Canaan, to "grow" the people of Israel. But now the Israelites' very size and strength threatened the new pharaoh, who ruthlessly clamped down on them.

¹⁷The midwives, however, feared God and did not do what the king of Egypt had told them to do; they let the boys live. ¹⁸Then the king of Egypt summoned the midwives and asked them, "Why have you done this? Why have you let the boys live?"

¹⁹The midwives answered Pharaoh, "Hebrew women are not like Egyptian women; they are vigorous and give birth before the midwives arrive."

²⁰So God was kind to the midwives and the people increased and became even more numerous. ²¹And because the midwives feared God, he gave them families of their own.

²²Then Pharaoh gave this order to all his people: "Every boy that is born[b] you must throw into the Nile, but let every girl live."

The Birth of Moses

2 Now a man of the house of Levi married a Levite woman, ²and she became pregnant and gave birth to a son. When she saw that he was a fine child, she hid him for three months. ³But when she could hide him no longer, she got a papyrus basket for him and coated it with tar and pitch. Then she placed the child in it and put it among the reeds along the bank of the Nile. ⁴His sister stood at a distance to see what would happen to him.

⁵Then Pharaoh's daughter went down to the Nile to bathe, and her attendants were walking along the river bank. She saw the basket among the reeds and sent her slave girl to get it. ⁶She opened it and saw the baby. He was crying, and she felt sorry for him. "This is one of the Hebrew babies," she said.

⁷Then his sister asked Pharaoh's daughter, "Shall I go and get one of the Hebrew women to nurse the baby for you?"

⁸"Yes, go," she answered. And the girl went and got the baby's mother. ⁹Pharaoh's daughter said to her, "Take this baby and nurse him for me, and I will pay you." So the woman took the baby and nursed him. ¹⁰When the child grew older, she took him to Pharaoh's daughter and he became her son. She named him Moses,[c] saying, "I drew him out of the water."

2:10 Selective History

Exodus illustrates how selective the Bible's history is. The first chapter, for example, skips over the name of the Egyptian pharaoh (leaving a riddle for scholars to argue over ever since), and yet identifies by name two Hebrew midwives (1:15). After compressing three-and-a-half centuries into a few verses, Exodus devotes chapters 3–40 to the events of a single year. In contrast to Genesis's large cast of characters, Exodus focuses on one main character, Moses.

---

[a]5 Masoretic Text (see also Gen. 46:27); Dead Sea Scrolls and Septuagint (see also Acts 7:14 and note at Gen. 46:27) *seventy-five*   [b]22 Masoretic Text; Samaritan Pentateuch, Septuagint and Targums *born to the Hebrews*   [c]10 *Moses* sounds like the Hebrew for *draw out.*

Moses Flees to Midian

¹¹One day, after Moses had grown up, he went out to where his own people were and watched them at their hard labor. He saw an Egyptian beating a Hebrew, one of his own people. ¹²Glancing this way and that and seeing no one, he killed the Egyptian and hid him in the sand. ¹³The next day he went out and saw two Hebrews fighting. He asked the one in the wrong, "Why are you hitting your fellow Hebrew?"

¹⁴The man said, "Who made you ruler and judge over us? Are you thinking of killing me as you killed the Egyptian?" Then Moses was afraid and thought, "What I did must have become known."

¹⁵When Pharaoh heard of this, he tried to kill Moses, but Moses fled from Pharaoh and went to live in Midian, where he sat down by a well. ¹⁶Now a priest of Midian had seven daughters, and they came to draw water and fill the troughs to water their father's flock. ¹⁷Some shepherds came along and drove them away, but Moses got up and came to their rescue and watered their flock.

¹⁸When the girls returned to Reuel their father, he asked them, "Why have you returned so early today?"

¹⁹They answered, "An Egyptian rescued us from the shepherds. He even drew water for us and watered the flock."

²⁰"And where is he?" he asked his daughters. "Why did you leave him? Invite him to have something to eat."

²¹Moses agreed to stay with the man, who gave his daughter Zipporah to Moses in marriage. ²²Zipporah gave birth to a son, and Moses named him Gershom,ᵃ saying, "I have become an alien in a foreign land."

²³During that long period, the king of Egypt died. The Israelites groaned in their slavery and cried out, and their cry for help because of their slavery went up to God. ²⁴God heard their groaning and he remembered his covenant with Abraham, with Isaac and with Jacob. ²⁵So God looked on the Israelites and was concerned about them.

Moses and the Burning Bush

3 Now Moses was tending the flock of Jethro his father-in-law, the priest of Midian, and he led the flock to the far side of the desert and came to Horeb, the mountain of God. ²There the angel of the LORD appeared to him in flames of fire from within a bush. Moses saw that though the bush was on fire it did not burn up. ³So Moses thought, "I will go over and see this strange sight—why the bush does not burn up."

⁴When the LORD saw that he had gone over to look, God called to him from within the bush, "Moses! Moses!"

And Moses said, "Here I am."

⁵"Do not come any closer," God said. "Take off your sandals, for the place where you are standing is holy ground." ⁶Then he said, "I am the God of your father, the God of Abraham, the God of Isaac and the God of Jacob." At this, Moses hid his face, because he was afraid to look at God.

⁷The LORD said, "I have indeed seen the misery of my people in Egypt. I have heard them crying out because of their slave drivers, and I am concerned about their suffering. ⁸So I have come down to rescue them from the hand of the Egyptians and to bring them up out of that land into a good and spacious land, a land flowing with milk and honey—the home of the Canaanites, Hittites, Amorites, Perizzites, Hivites and Jebusites. ⁹And now the cry of the Israelites has reached me, and I have seen the way the Egyptians are oppressing them. ¹⁰So now, go. I am sending you to Pharaoh to bring my people the Israelites out of Egypt."

¹¹But Moses said to God, "Who am I, that I should go to Pharaoh and bring the Israelites out of Egypt?"

3:11–13 Who, Me?

Moses had big doubts about his ability to lead. He resisted God, bringing up his unworthiness (here) and lack of authority (verse 13), his fear of the people's distrust (4:1), his speech difficulties (4:10), and his sheer cowardice (4:13). The remainder of Exodus should give people with similar self-doubts great hope, for it traces Moses' personal development from this fumbling start to his emergence as one of history's most decisive and powerful leaders.

¹²And God said, "I will be with you. And this will be the sign to you that it is I who have sent you: When you have brought the people out of Egypt, youᵇ will worship God on this mountain."

¹³Moses said to God, "Suppose I go to the Israelites and say to them, 'The God of your fathers has sent me to you,' and they ask me, 'What is his name?' Then what shall I tell them?"

¹⁴God said to Moses, "I AM WHO I AM.ᶜ This is what you are to say to the Israelites: 'I AM has sent me to you.'"

¹⁵God also said to Moses, "Say to the Israelites, 'The LORD,ᵈ the God of your fathers—the God of Abraham, the God of Isaac and the God of

---

ᵃ22 *Gershom* sounds like the Hebrew for *an alien there.*   ᵇ12 The Hebrew is plural.   ᶜ14 Or *I WILL BE WHAT I WILL BE*   ᵈ15 The Hebrew for LORD sounds like and may be derived from the Hebrew for *I AM* in verse 14.

Jacob—has sent me to you.' This is my name forever, the name by which I am to be remembered from generation to generation.

16"Go, assemble the elders of Israel and say to them, 'The LORD, the God of your fathers—the God of Abraham, Isaac and Jacob—appeared to me and said: I have watched over you and have seen what has been done to you in Egypt. 17And I have promised to bring you up out of your misery in Egypt into the land of the Canaanites, Hittites, Amorites, Perizzites, Hivites and Jebusites—a land flowing with milk and honey.'

18"The elders of Israel will listen to you. Then you and the elders are to go to the king of Egypt and say to him, 'The LORD, the God of the Hebrews, has met with us. Let us take a three-day journey into the desert to offer sacrifices to the LORD our God.' 19But I know that the king of Egypt will not let you go unless a mighty hand compels him. 20So I will stretch out my hand and strike the Egyptians with all the wonders that I will perform among them. After that, he will let you go.

21"And I will make the Egyptians favorably disposed toward this people, so that when you leave you will not go empty-handed. 22Every woman is to ask her neighbor and any woman living in her house for articles of silver and gold and for clothing, which you will put on your sons and daughters. And so you will plunder the Egyptians."

Signs for Moses

4 Moses answered, "What if they do not believe me or listen to me and say, 'The LORD did not appear to you'?"

2Then the LORD said to him, "What is that in your hand?"

"A staff," he replied.

3The LORD said, "Throw it on the ground."

Moses threw it on the ground and it became a snake, and he ran from it. 4Then the LORD said to him, "Reach out your hand and take it by the tail." So Moses reached out and took hold of the snake and it turned back into a staff in his hand. 5"This," said the LORD, "is so that they may believe that the LORD, the God of their fathers—the God of Abraham, the God of Isaac and the God of Jacob—has appeared to you."

6Then the LORD said, "Put your hand inside your cloak." So Moses put his hand into his cloak, and when he took it out, it was leprous,[a] like snow.

7"Now put it back into your cloak," he said. So Moses put his hand back into his cloak, and when he took it out, it was restored, like the rest of his flesh.

8Then the LORD said, "If they do not believe you or pay attention to the first miraculous sign, they may believe the second. 9But if they do not believe these two signs or listen to you, take some water from the Nile and pour it on the dry ground. The water you take from the river will become blood on the ground."

10Moses said to the LORD, "O Lord, I have never been eloquent, neither in the past nor since you have spoken to your servant. I am slow of speech and tongue."

11The LORD said to him, "Who gave man his mouth? Who makes him deaf or mute? Who gives him sight or makes him blind? Is it not I, the LORD? 12Now go; I will help you speak and will teach you what to say."

13But Moses said, "O Lord, please send someone else to do it."

14Then the LORD's anger burned against Moses and he said, "What about your brother, Aaron the Levite? I know he can speak well. He is already on his way to meet you, and his heart will be glad when he sees you. 15You shall speak to him and put words in his mouth; I will help both of you speak and will teach you what to do. 16He will speak to the people for you, and it will be as if he were your mouth and as if you were God to him. 17But take this staff in your hand so you can perform miraculous signs with it."

Moses Returns to Egypt

18Then Moses went back to Jethro his father-in-law and said to him, "Let me go back to my own people in Egypt to see if any of them are still alive."

Jethro said, "Go, and I wish you well."

19Now the LORD had said to Moses in Midian, "Go back to Egypt, for all the men who wanted to kill you are dead." 20So Moses took his wife and sons, put them on a donkey and started back to Egypt. And he took the staff of God in his hand.

21The LORD said to Moses, "When you return to Egypt, see that you perform before Pharaoh all the wonders I have given you the power to do. But I will harden his heart so that he will not let the people go. 22Then say to Pharaoh, 'This is what the LORD says: Israel is my firstborn son, 23and I told you, "Let my son go, so he may worship me." But you refused to let him go; so I will kill your firstborn son.'"

24At a lodging place on the way, the LORD met ˌMoses,[b] and was about to kill him. 25But Zipporah took a flint knife, cut off her son's foreskin and touched ˌMoses'ˌ feet with it.[c] "Surely you are a bridegroom of blood to me," she said. 26So the LORD let him alone. (At that time she said

---

[a]6 The Hebrew word was used for various diseases affecting the skin—not necessarily leprosy.   [b]24 Or ˌMoses' sonˌ; Hebrew *him*   [c]25 Or *and drew near ˌMoses'ˌ feet*

"bridegroom of blood," referring to circumcision.)

27The LORD said to Aaron, "Go into the desert to meet Moses." So he met Moses at the mountain of God and kissed him. 28Then Moses told Aaron everything the LORD had sent him to say, and also about all the miraculous signs he had commanded him to perform.

29Moses and Aaron brought together all the elders of the Israelites, 30and Aaron told them everything the LORD had said to Moses. He also performed the signs before the people, 31and they believed. And when they heard that the LORD was concerned about them and had seen their misery, they bowed down and worshiped.

Bricks Without Straw

5 Afterward Moses and Aaron went to Pharaoh and said, "This is what the LORD, the God of Israel, says: 'Let my people go, so that they may hold a festival to me in the desert.'"

2Pharaoh said, "Who is the LORD, that I should obey him and let Israel go? I do not know the LORD and I will not let Israel go."

3Then they said, "The God of the Hebrews has met with us. Now let us take a three-day journey into the desert to offer sacrifices to the LORD our God, or he may strike us with plagues or with the sword."

4But the king of Egypt said, "Moses and Aaron, why are you taking the people away from their labor? Get back to your work!" 5Then Pharaoh said, "Look, the people of the land are now numerous, and you are stopping them from working."

6That same day Pharaoh gave this order to the slave drivers and foremen in charge of the people: 7"You are no longer to supply the people with straw for making bricks; let them go and gather their own straw. 8But require them to make the same number of bricks as before; don't reduce the quota. They are lazy; that is why they are crying out, 'Let us go and sacrifice to our God.' 9Make the work harder for the men so that they keep working and pay no attention to lies."

10Then the slave drivers and the foremen went out and said to the people, "This is what Pharaoh says: 'I will not give you any more straw. 11Go and get your own straw wherever you can find it, but your work will not be reduced at all.'" 12So the people scattered all over Egypt to gather stubble to use for straw. 13The slave drivers kept pressing them, saying, "Complete the work required of you for each day, just as when you had straw." 14The Israelite foremen appointed by Pharaoh's slave drivers were beaten and were

asked, "Why didn't you meet your quota of bricks yesterday or today, as before?"

15Then the Israelite foremen went and appealed to Pharaoh: "Why have you treated your servants this way? 16Your servants are given no straw, yet we are told, 'Make bricks!' Your servants are being beaten, but the fault is with your own people."

5:10 Three Kinds of Bricks

Archaeologists digging up settlements from ancient Egypt have unearthed three kinds of sun-dried bricks—some made of good straw, some containing mere roots and bits of straw, and some with no straw—confirming this account of slave labor.

17Pharaoh said, "Lazy, that's what you are—lazy! That is why you keep saying, 'Let us go and sacrifice to the LORD.' 18Now get to work. You will not be given any straw, yet you must produce your full quota of bricks."

19The Israelite foremen realized they were in trouble when they were told, "You are not to reduce the number of bricks required of you for each day." 20When they left Pharaoh, they found Moses and Aaron waiting to meet them, 21and they said, "May the LORD look upon you and judge you! You have made us a stench to Pharaoh and his officials and have put a sword in their hand to kill us."

God Promises Deliverance

22Moses returned to the LORD and said, "O Lord, why have you brought trouble upon this people? Is this why you sent me? 23Ever since I went to Pharaoh to speak in your name, he has brought trouble upon this people, and you have not rescued your people at all."

6 Then the LORD said to Moses, "Now you will see what I will do to Pharaoh: Because of my mighty hand he will let them go; because of my mighty hand he will drive them out of his country."

2God also said to Moses, "I am the LORD. 3I appeared to Abraham, to Isaac and to Jacob as God Almighty,[a] but by my name the LORD[b] I did not make myself known to them.[c] 4I also established my covenant with them to give them the land of Canaan, where they lived as aliens. 5Moreover, I have heard the groaning of the Israelites, whom the Egyptians are enslaving, and I have remembered my covenant.

6"Therefore, say to the Israelites: 'I am the LORD, and I will bring you out from under the

a3 Hebrew El-Shaddai   b3 See note at Exodus 3:15.   c3 Or Almighty, and by my name the LORD did I not let myself be known to them?

yoke of the Egyptians. I will free you from being slaves to them, and I will redeem you with an outstretched arm and with mighty acts of judgment. [7]I will take you as my own people, and I

will be your God. Then you will know that I am the LORD your God, who brought you out from under the yoke of the Egyptians. [8]And I will bring you to the land I swore with uplifted hand to give to Abraham, to Isaac and to Jacob. I will give it to you as a possession. I am the LORD.'"

[9]Moses reported this to the Israelites, but they did not listen to him because of their discouragement and cruel bondage.

[10]Then the LORD said to Moses, [11]"Go, tell Pharaoh king of Egypt to let the Israelites go out of his country."

[12]But Moses said to the LORD, "If the Israelites will not listen to me, why would Pharaoh listen to me, since I speak with faltering lips[a]?"

Family Record of Moses and Aaron

[13]Now the LORD spoke to Moses and Aaron about the Israelites and Pharaoh king of Egypt, and he commanded them to bring the Israelites out of Egypt.

[14]These were the heads of their families[b]:

The sons of Reuben the firstborn son of Israel were Hanoch and Pallu, Hezron and Carmi. These were the clans of Reuben.

[15]The sons of Simeon were Jemuel, Jamin, Ohad, Jakin, Zohar and Shaul the son of a Canaanite woman. These were the clans of Simeon.

[16]These were the names of the sons of Levi according to their records: Gershon, Kohath and Merari. Levi lived 137 years.

[17]The sons of Gershon, by clans, were Libni and Shimei.

[18]The sons of Kohath were Amram, Iz-

har, Hebron and Uzziel. Kohath lived 133 years.

[19]The sons of Merari were Mahli and Mushi.

These were the clans of Levi according to their records.

[20]Amram married his father's sister Jochebed, who bore him Aaron and Moses. Amram lived 137 years.

[21]The sons of Izhar were Korah, Nepheg and Zicri.

[22]The sons of Uzziel were Mishael, Elzaphan and Sithri.

[23]Aaron married Elisheba, daughter of Amminadab and sister of Nahshon, and she bore him Nadab and Abihu, Eleazar and Ithamar.

[24]The sons of Korah were Assir, Elkanah and Abiasaph. These were the Korahite clans.

[25]Eleazar son of Aaron married one of the daughters of Putiel, and she bore him Phinehas.

These were the heads of the Levite families, clan by clan.

[26]It was this same Aaron and Moses to whom the LORD said, "Bring the Israelites out of Egypt by their divisions." [27]They were the ones who spoke to Pharaoh king of Egypt about bringing the Israelites out of Egypt. It was the same Moses and Aaron.

Aaron to Speak for Moses

[28]Now when the LORD spoke to Moses in Egypt, [29]he said to him, "I am the LORD. Tell Pharaoh king of Egypt everything I tell you."

[30]But Moses said to the LORD, "Since I speak with faltering lips, why would Pharaoh listen to me?"

7 Then the LORD said to Moses, "See, I have made you like God to Pharaoh, and your brother Aaron will be your prophet. [2]You are to say everything I command you, and your brother Aaron is to tell Pharaoh to let the Israelites go out of his country. [3]But I will harden Pharaoh's heart, and though I multiply my miraculous signs and wonders in Egypt, [4]he will not listen to you. Then I will lay my hand on Egypt and with mighty acts of judgment I will bring out my divisions, my people the Israelites. [5]And the Egyptians will know that I am the LORD when I stretch out my hand against Egypt and bring the Israelites out of it."

[6]Moses and Aaron did just as the LORD commanded them. [7]Moses was eighty years old and Aaron eighty-three when they spoke to Pharaoh.

---

[a]12 Hebrew *I am uncircumcised of lips*; also in verse 30 units larger than clans.

[b]14 The Hebrew for *families* here and in verse 25 refers to

Aaron's Staff Becomes a Snake

⁸The LORD said to Moses and Aaron, ⁹"When Pharaoh says to you, 'Perform a miracle,' then say to Aaron, 'Take your staff and throw it down before Pharaoh,' and it will become a snake."

¹⁰So Moses and Aaron went to Pharaoh and did just as the LORD commanded. Aaron threw his staff down in front of Pharaoh and his officials, and it became a snake. ¹¹Pharaoh then summoned wise men and sorcerers, and the Egyptian magicians also did the same things by their secret arts: ¹²Each one threw down his staff and it became a snake. But Aaron's staff swallowed up their staffs. ¹³Yet Pharaoh's heart became hard and he would not listen to them, just as the LORD had said.

The Plague of Blood

¹⁴Then the LORD said to Moses, "Pharaoh's heart is unyielding; he refuses to let the people go. ¹⁵Go to Pharaoh in the morning as he goes out to the water. Wait on the bank of the Nile to meet him, and take in your hand the staff that was changed into a snake. ¹⁶Then say to him, 'The LORD, the God of the Hebrews, has sent me to say to you: Let my people go, so that they may worship me in the desert. But until now you have not listened. ¹⁷This is what the LORD says: By this you will know that I am the LORD: With the staff

Day of the Locusts

The ten plagues proved a point for both Jews and Egyptians

> "And the Egyptians will know that I am the LORD when I stretch out my hand against Egypt and bring the Israelites out of it." 7:5

LOCUSTS, OR GRASSHOPPERS, NORMALLY LIVE a solitary life, hopping from stalk to stalk and placidly munching on leaves and flowers. Then something happens—whether in response to climate, food supply, or crowded conditions—that triggers a change. The locusts grow restive, flush an ominous pink color, and begin to seek other locusts.

They become a plague. Great clattering hordes of them, millions strong, blacken the sky, shutting out sunlight. Groups of them fall to the ground like cluster bombs and disperse to destroy every sign of vegetation. Pesticide spraying may kill a few million, but the migratory swarm will barely notice such losses.

A single swarm crossing the Red Sea was once measured at 15 miles wide, three miles deep, and 100 miles long. Upon landing, the locusts consumed crops, leather, fences, and even tool handles, leaving behind total devastation over 2,000 square miles.

Why the Ten Plagues?

Exodus (7–12) depicts ten cataclysmic plagues on Egypt—including a locust swarm—in brief but graphic detail. The Bible does not concern itself with the question of how these natural phenomena occurred; it merely affirms that something supernatural took place. The miracles were an unprecedented display of God's power.

A nation was about to be born, and the Israelites' uprooting from Egypt called for such power. They had, after all, lived for centuries in Egypt. It would take a strong incentive indeed to motivate a massive, abrupt departure. And Egypt would not easily let thousands of valuable slaves walk away free.

Two Reputations at Stake

The ten plagues convincingly established Moses' authority. He had hesitated to accept a leadership role, doubting whether the other Israelites would trust him (4:1). But Moses' dramatic confrontations with Pharaoh dispelled all doubts. He and he alone could lead them to freedom.

Someone else's credibility was also at stake: that of God himself. In Egypt, religion centered around idolatry, with scores of gods—including even snakes and dung beetles—held up as objects of worship. Against that background, the plagues appear as God's open warfare against the false gods of Egypt. He said as much: "I will bring judgment on all the gods of Egypt" (12:12).

Exodus asserts more than a dozen times that the plagues were given so that Israel and Egypt would know the power of Israel's God. Evidently they worked. Egyptians became so convinced of God's power that they let thousands of slaves leave, with the wealth of Egypt showered upon them as farewell presents. The Israelites were so convinced that they left their home and history and marched out behind a single man toward a desert and a new life.

Life Questions: Do you know of any modern countries that treat minorities cruelly, like the Egyptians treated the Israelites? What would make such a government change its ways?

that is in my hand I will strike the water of the Nile, and it will be changed into blood. [18]The fish in the Nile will die, and the river will stink; the Egyptians will not be able to drink its water."

[19]The LORD said to Moses, "Tell Aaron, 'Take your staff and stretch out your hand over the waters of Egypt—over the streams and canals, over the ponds and all the reservoirs'—and they will turn to blood. Blood will be everywhere in Egypt, even in the wooden buckets and stone jars."

[20]Moses and Aaron did just as the LORD had commanded. He raised his staff in the presence of Pharaoh and his officials and struck the water of the Nile, and all the water was changed into blood. [21]The fish in the Nile died, and the river smelled so bad that the Egyptians could not drink its water. Blood was everywhere in Egypt.

[22]But the Egyptian magicians did the same things by their secret arts, and Pharaoh's heart became hard; he would not listen to Moses and Aaron, just as the LORD had said. [23]Instead, he turned and went into his palace, and did not take even this to heart. [24]And all the Egyptians dug along the Nile to get drinking water, because they could not drink the water of the river.

The Plague of Frogs

[25]Seven days passed after the LORD struck the Nile. [1]Then the LORD said to Moses, "Go to **8** Pharaoh and say to him, 'This is what the LORD says: Let my people go, so that they may worship me. [2]If you refuse to let them go, I will plague your whole country with frogs. [3]The Nile will teem with frogs. They will come up into your palace and your bedroom and onto your bed, into the houses of your officials and on your people, and into your ovens and kneading troughs. [4]The frogs will go up on you and your people and all your officials.'"

[5]Then the LORD said to Moses, "Tell Aaron, 'Stretch out your hand with your staff over the streams and canals and ponds, and make frogs come up on the land of Egypt.'"

[6]So Aaron stretched out his hand over the waters of Egypt, and the frogs came up and covered the land. [7]But the magicians did the same things by their secret arts; they also made frogs come up on the land of Egypt.

[8]Pharaoh summoned Moses and Aaron and said, "Pray to the LORD to take the frogs away from me and my people, and I will let your people go to offer sacrifices to the LORD."

[9]Moses said to Pharaoh, "I leave to you the honor of setting the time for me to pray for you and your officials and your people that you and your houses may be rid of the frogs, except for those that remain in the Nile."

[10]"Tomorrow," Pharaoh said.

Moses replied, "It will be as you say, so that you may know there is no one like the LORD our God. [11]The frogs will leave you and your houses, your officials and your people; they will remain only in the Nile."

[12]After Moses and Aaron left Pharaoh, Moses cried out to the LORD about the frogs he had brought on Pharaoh. [13]And the LORD did what Moses asked. The frogs died in the houses, in the courtyards and in the fields. [14]They were piled into heaps, and the land reeked of them. [15]But when Pharaoh saw that there was relief, he hardened his heart and would not listen to Moses and Aaron, just as the LORD had said.

8:15 Pharaoh's Hard Heart

The Bible describes Pharaoh's stubbornness in three ways. Sometimes, as here, it says Pharaoh "hardened his heart," sometimes, God "hardened his heart" (10:1), and also, "Pharaoh's heart became hard" (7:13). This is consistent with the Old Testament view: all of history was an act of God. Beyond that, the writers did not normally make clear distinctions on questions of who caused what.

The Plague of Gnats

[16]Then the LORD said to Moses, "Tell Aaron, 'Stretch out your staff and strike the dust of the ground,' and throughout the land of Egypt the dust will become gnats." [17]They did this, and when Aaron stretched out his hand with the staff and struck the dust of the ground, gnats came upon men and animals. All the dust throughout the land of Egypt became gnats. [18]But when the magicians tried to produce gnats by their secret arts, they could not. And the gnats were on men and animals.

[19]The magicians said to Pharaoh, "This is the finger of God." But Pharaoh's heart was hard and he would not listen, just as the LORD had said.

The Plague of Flies

[20]Then the LORD said to Moses, "Get up early in the morning and confront Pharaoh as he goes to the water and say to him, 'This is what the LORD says: Let my people go, so that they may worship me. [21]If you do not let my people go, I will send swarms of flies on you and your officials, on your people and into your houses. The houses of the Egyptians will be full of flies, and even the ground where they are.

[22]"'But on that day I will deal differently with the land of Goshen, where my people live; no swarms of flies will be there, so that you will know that I, the LORD, am in this land. [23]I will

make a distinction[a] between my people and your people. This miraculous sign will occur tomorrow.'"

24And the LORD did this. Dense swarms of flies poured into Pharaoh's palace and into the houses of his officials, and throughout Egypt the land was ruined by the flies.

25Then Pharaoh summoned Moses and Aaron and said, "Go, sacrifice to your God here in the land."

26But Moses said, "That would not be right. The sacrifices we offer the LORD our God would be detestable to the Egyptians. And if we offer sacrifices that are detestable in their eyes, will they not stone us? 27We must take a three-day journey into the desert to offer sacrifices to the LORD our God, as he commands us."

8:27 Oriental Bargaining

Those who have lived in the Middle East recognize in Moses' encounters with Pharaoh an example of high-level Oriental bargaining. As the pressure increased, Pharaoh kept raising his offers: from allowing sacrifices within Egypt (verse 25), to permitting sacrifices nearby in the desert (verse 28), to letting only the adult males go (10:11), to releasing all people but no flocks (10:24). Finally, with the tenth and final plague Pharaoh agreed to all Moses' demands (12:32).

28Pharaoh said, "I will let you go to offer sacrifices to the LORD your God in the desert, but you must not go very far. Now pray for me."

29Moses answered, "As soon as I leave you, I will pray to the LORD, and tomorrow the flies will leave Pharaoh and his officials and his people. Only be sure that Pharaoh does not act deceitfully again by not letting the people go to offer sacrifices to the LORD."

30Then Moses left Pharaoh and prayed to the LORD, 31and the LORD did what Moses asked: The flies left Pharaoh and his officials and his people; not a fly remained. 32But this time also Pharaoh hardened his heart and would not let the people go.

The Plague on Livestock

9 Then the LORD said to Moses, "Go to Pharaoh and say to him, 'This is what the LORD, the God of the Hebrews, says: "Let my people go, so that they may worship me." 2If you refuse to let them go and continue to hold them back, 3the hand of the LORD will bring a terrible plague on your livestock in the field—on your horses and donkeys and camels and on your cattle and sheep

and goats. 4But the LORD will make a distinction between the livestock of Israel and that of Egypt, so that no animal belonging to the Israelites will die.'"

5The LORD set a time and said, "Tomorrow the LORD will do this in the land." 6And the next day the LORD did it: All the livestock of the Egyptians died, but not one animal belonging to the Israelites died. 7Pharaoh sent men to investigate and found that not even one of the animals of the Israelites had died. Yet his heart was unyielding and he would not let the people go.

9:7 "Smart" Plagues

Like "smart bombs," targeted precisely, most of the plagues affected the Egyptians but not the Israelites—a miracle in itself. This fact should have convinced Pharaoh that he was contending against supernatural force, not just the caprice of nature. But it took ten plagues in all to persuade him to allow his main supply of cheap labor to walk away, and even then he had second thoughts and chased after them (14:5).

The Plague of Boils

8Then the LORD said to Moses and Aaron, "Take handfuls of soot from a furnace and have Moses toss it into the air in the presence of Pharaoh. 9It will become fine dust over the whole land of Egypt, and festering boils will break out on men and animals throughout the land."

10So they took soot from a furnace and stood before Pharaoh. Moses tossed it into the air, and festering boils broke out on men and animals. 11The magicians could not stand before Moses because of the boils that were on them and on all the Egyptians. 12But the LORD hardened Pharaoh's heart and he would not listen to Moses and Aaron, just as the LORD had said to Moses.

The Plague of Hail

13Then the LORD said to Moses, "Get up early in the morning, confront Pharaoh and say to him, 'This is what the LORD, the God of the Hebrews, says: Let my people go, so that they may worship me, 14or this time I will send the full force of my plagues against you and against your officials and your people, so you may know that there is no one like me in all the earth. 15For by now I could have stretched out my hand and struck you and your people with a plague that would have wiped you off the earth. 16But I have raised you up[b] for this very purpose, that I might show you my power and that my name might be proclaimed in all the earth. 17You still

---

[a]23 Septuagint and Vulgate; Hebrew *will put a deliverance*   [b]16 Or *have spared you*

set yourself against my people and will not let them go. ¹⁸Therefore, at this time tomorrow I will send the worst hailstorm that has ever fallen on Egypt, from the day it was founded till now. ¹⁹Give an order now to bring your livestock and everything you have in the field to a place of shelter, because the hail will fall on every man and animal that has not been brought in and is still out in the field, and they will die.'"

²⁰Those officials of Pharaoh who feared the word of the LORD hurried to bring their slaves and their livestock inside. ²¹But those who ignored the word of the LORD left their slaves and livestock in the field.

²²Then the LORD said to Moses, "Stretch out your hand toward the sky so that hail will fall all over Egypt—on men and animals and on everything growing in the fields of Egypt." ²³When Moses stretched out his staff toward the sky, the LORD sent thunder and hail, and lightning flashed down to the ground. So the LORD rained hail on the land of Egypt; ²⁴hail fell and lightning flashed back and forth. It was the worst storm in all the land of Egypt since it had become a nation. ²⁵Throughout Egypt hail struck everything in the fields—both men and animals; it beat down everything growing in the fields and stripped every tree. ²⁶The only place it did not hail was the land of Goshen, where the Israelites were.

²⁷Then Pharaoh summoned Moses and Aaron. "This time I have sinned," he said to them. "The LORD is in the right, and I and my people are in the wrong. ²⁸Pray to the LORD, for we have had enough thunder and hail. I will let you go; you don't have to stay any longer."

²⁹Moses replied, "When I have gone out of the city, I will spread out my hands in prayer to the LORD. The thunder will stop and there will be no more hail, so you may know that the earth is the LORD's. ³⁰But I know that you and your officials still do not fear the LORD God."

³¹(The flax and barley were destroyed, since the barley had headed and the flax was in bloom. ³²The wheat and spelt, however, were not destroyed, because they ripen later.)

³³Then Moses left Pharaoh and went out of the city. He spread out his hands toward the LORD; the thunder and hail stopped, and the rain no longer poured down on the land. ³⁴When Pharaoh saw that the rain and hail and thunder had stopped, he sinned again: He and his officials hardened their hearts. ³⁵So Pharaoh's heart was hard and he would not let the Israelites go, just as the LORD had said through Moses.

The Plague of Locusts

10 Then the LORD said to Moses, "Go to Pharaoh, for I have hardened his heart and the hearts of his officials so that I may perform these miraculous signs of mine among them ²that you may tell your children and grandchildren how I dealt harshly with the Egyptians and how I performed my signs among them, and that you may know that I am the LORD."

³So Moses and Aaron went to Pharaoh and said to him, "This is what the LORD, the God of the Hebrews, says: 'How long will you refuse to humble yourself before me? Let my people go, so that they may worship me. ⁴If you refuse to let them go, I will bring locusts into your country tomorrow. ⁵They will cover the face of the ground so that it cannot be seen. They will devour what little you have left after the hail, including every tree that is growing in your fields. ⁶They will fill your houses and those of all your officials and all the Egyptians—something neither your fathers nor your forefathers have ever seen from the day they settled in this land till now.'" Then Moses turned and left Pharaoh.

⁷Pharaoh's officials said to him, "How long will this man be a snare to us? Let the people go, so that they may worship the LORD their God. Do you not yet realize that Egypt is ruined?"

⁸Then Moses and Aaron were brought back to Pharaoh. "Go, worship the LORD your God," he said. "But just who will be going?"

⁹Moses answered, "We will go with our young and old, with our sons and daughters, and with our flocks and herds, because we are to celebrate a festival to the LORD."

¹⁰Pharaoh said, "The LORD be with you—if I let you go, along with your women and children! Clearly you are bent on evil.*ᵃ* ¹¹No! Have only the men go; and worship the LORD, since that's what you have been asking for." Then Moses and Aaron were driven out of Pharaoh's presence.

¹²And the LORD said to Moses, "Stretch out your hand over Egypt so that locusts will swarm over the land and devour everything growing in the fields, everything left by the hail."

¹³So Moses stretched out his staff over Egypt, and the LORD made an east wind blow across the land all that day and all that night. By morning the wind had brought the locusts; ¹⁴they invaded all Egypt and settled down in every area of the country in great numbers. Never before had there been such a plague of locusts, nor will there ever be again. ¹⁵They covered all the ground until it was black. They devoured all that was left after the hail—everything growing in the fields and the fruit on the trees. Nothing green remained on tree or plant in all the land of Egypt.

¹⁶Pharaoh quickly summoned Moses and Aaron and said, "I have sinned against the LORD your God and against you. ¹⁷Now forgive my sin once

---

ᵃ 10 Or *Be careful, trouble is in store for you!*

more and pray to the LORD your God to take this deadly plague away from me."

[18]Moses then left Pharaoh and prayed to the LORD. [19]And the LORD changed the wind to a very strong west wind, which caught up the locusts and carried them into the Red Sea.[a] Not a locust was left anywhere in Egypt. [20]But the LORD hardened Pharaoh's heart, and he would not let the Israelites go.

The Plague of Darkness

[21]Then the LORD said to Moses, "Stretch out your hand toward the sky so that darkness will spread over Egypt—darkness that can be felt."

10:21 Attack on False Gods

God used ten plagues as a form of warfare against the gods of Egypt (12:12). Some scholars see in each individual punishment an attack against a specific Egyptian idol. Thus they believe the plague on the Nile River opposed the Egyptians' river god, the plague of flies flouted worship of the sacred fly, the plague of darkness attacked the sun-god Ra, and the plague on livestock countered the sacred bull.

[22]So Moses stretched out his hand toward the sky, and total darkness covered all Egypt for three days. [23]No one could see anyone else or leave his place for three days. Yet all the Israelites had light in the places where they lived.

[24]Then Pharaoh summoned Moses and said, "Go, worship the LORD. Even your women and children may go with you; only leave your flocks and herds behind."

[25]But Moses said, "You must allow us to have sacrifices and burnt offerings to present to the LORD our God. [26]Our livestock too must go with us; not a hoof is to be left behind. We have to use some of them in worshiping the LORD our God, and until we get there we will not know what we are to use to worship the LORD."

[27]But the LORD hardened Pharaoh's heart, and he was not willing to let them go. [28]Pharaoh said to Moses, "Get out of my sight! Make sure you do not appear before me again! The day you see my face you will die."

[29]"Just as you say," Moses replied, "I will never appear before you again."

The Plague on the Firstborn

11 Now the LORD had said to Moses, "I will bring one more plague on Pharaoh and on Egypt. After that, he will let you go from here, and when he does, he will drive you out com-

pletely. [2]Tell the people that men and women alike are to ask their neighbors for articles of silver and gold." [3](The LORD made the Egyptians favorably disposed toward the people, and Moses himself was highly regarded in Egypt by Pharaoh's officials and by the people.)

[4]So Moses said, "This is what the LORD says: 'About midnight I will go throughout Egypt. [5]Every firstborn son in Egypt will die, from the firstborn son of Pharaoh, who sits on the throne, to the firstborn son of the slave girl, who is at her hand mill, and all the firstborn of the cattle as well. [6]There will be loud wailing throughout Egypt—worse than there has ever been or ever will be again. [7]But among the Israelites not a dog will bark at any man or animal.' Then you will know that the LORD makes a distinction between Egypt and Israel. [8]All these officials of yours will come to me, bowing down before me and saying, 'Go, you and all the people who follow you!' After that I will leave." Then Moses, hot with anger, left Pharaoh.

[9]The LORD had said to Moses, "Pharaoh will refuse to listen to you—so that my wonders may be multiplied in Egypt." [10]Moses and Aaron performed all these wonders before Pharaoh, but the LORD hardened Pharaoh's heart, and he would not let the Israelites go out of his country.

The Passover

12 The LORD said to Moses and Aaron in Egypt, [2]"This month is to be for you the first month, the first month of your year. [3]Tell the whole community of Israel that on the tenth day of this month each man is to take a lamb[b] for his family, one for each household. [4]If any household is too small for a whole lamb, they must share one with their nearest neighbor, having taken into account the number of people there are. You are to determine the amount of lamb needed in accordance with what each person will eat. [5]The animals you choose must be year-old males without defect, and you may take them from the sheep or the goats. [6]Take care of them until the fourteenth day of the month, when all the people of the community of Israel must slaughter them at twilight. [7]Then they are to take some of the blood and put it on the sides and tops of the doorframes of the houses where they eat the lambs. [8]That same night they are to eat the meat roasted over the fire, along with bitter herbs, and bread made without yeast. [9]Do not eat the meat raw or cooked in water, but roast it over the fire—head, legs and inner parts. [10]Do not leave any of it till morning; if some is left till morning, you must burn it. [11]This is how you are to eat it: with your cloak tucked into your

---

[a]19 Hebrew *Yam Suph*; that is, Sea of Reeds   [b]3 The Hebrew word can mean *lamb* or *kid*; also in verse 4.

belt, your sandals on your feet and your staff in your hand. Eat it in haste; it is the LORD's Passover.

¹²"On that same night I will pass through Egypt and strike down every firstborn—both men and animals—and I will bring judgment on all the gods of Egypt. I am the LORD. ¹³The blood will be a sign for you on the houses where you are; and when I see the blood, I will pass over

you. No destructive plague will touch you when I strike Egypt.

¹⁴"This is a day you are to commemorate; for the generations to come you shall celebrate it as a festival to the LORD—a lasting ordinance. ¹⁵For seven days you are to eat bread made without yeast. On the first day remove the yeast from your houses, for whoever eats anything with yeast in it from the first day through the seventh

Independence Day
An unusual style of celebrating freedom

THE UNITED STATES CELEBRATES JULY 4 like no other day. The parades, the picnics, and the fireworks boisterously express national pride. We showed 'em, say the politicians in their speeches. With our own sweat and blood we created a nation. We're proud to be Americans.

> "There will be loud wailing throughout Egypt—worse than there has ever been or ever will be again." 11:6

A Different Mood for the Jews

Our style of celebration—noisy and flag-waving and proud—captures something of the original spirit that led a young nation to declare independence. A similar spirit surges up in France on Bastille Day and in many other nations on their birthdays. But these celebrations bear a striking *unlikeness* to the Jewish independence day, a day called Passover.

The Jews trace their cultural birthday back to a dark, foreboding night—the Israelites' last in Egypt (Exodus 12). There are no blaring bands nor balloons nor fireworks to commemorate this event. Everything takes place inside a home, with a family or cluster of families gathered around a table. Participants taste morsels of food, pausing before each portion to hear Old Testament accounts of the history they are reliving. Their independence day resembles a worship service, not a party.

A Work of God Alone

More than anything else, the Jewish independence day expresses this one fact: God did it. No Israelite armies stood against the mighty Egyptians. Freedom came in the blackest night while Israelite families huddled around the Passover table, their bags packed, waiting for deliverance.

When God's time came, the Egyptian captors not only released the Israelites, but begged them to go and showered them with gold and riches. The Jews remember that event with humility and praise; there is no room for pride. Later, when Pharaoh changed his mind and set his chariots loose upon the fleeing tribes, God came through again. Israelites stood trembling like cowards, already second-guessing their freedom. But God destroyed the great Egyptian army.

For the children of Israel, independence from Egypt meant dependence on God. In fact, God came back to this event throughout the Bible as a way of describing himself: "I am the LORD your God, who brought you out of Egypt."

The pattern of dependence was to continue all through Exodus. When the wilderness wanderers ran out of water, God provided. When food supplies failed, God provided. When raiders attacked, God provided. Independence day merely set the tone for a national history that was an active movement of God.

Passover's New Meaning

Much later, Passover night would take on an even broader significance. During one particular Passover feast, as thousands of Jews were bringing their choice lambs to Jerusalem, one man was selected as the Passover Lamb for all humanity (1 Corinthians 5:7). The words "When I see the blood, I will pass over you" (12:13) came to convey a whole new meaning.

Today, though Jewish people still celebrate Passover, most Christians do not. Rather, that ceremony has been incorporated into a new one called the Eucharist, or the Lord's Supper, with Christ representing the Passover lamb. Although much of the ceremony's content has changed, one thing has not. The Lord's Supper, too, memorializes a time of pain and of bloodshed, a time of freedom and deliverance. It, too, was God's act alone. He gets the credit.

Life Questions: Does your church's celebration of the Eucharist, or Lord's Supper, resemble the Jewish Passover described here? How are they similar or different?

must be cut off from Israel. ¹⁶On the first day hold a sacred assembly, and another one on the seventh day. Do no work at all on these days, except to prepare food for everyone to eat — that is all you may do.

12:8–11 Fast Food

God's instructions for the Passover stress the need for haste. Roasting over fire cooks meat faster than boiling, and (unlike frying or baking) requires no pan or oven. Likewise, bread without yeast doesn't need time to rise. The emphasis on speed indicated to the Israelites how terrible this plague would be, and how swiftly they had to flee from Egypt.

¹⁷"Celebrate the Feast of Unleavened Bread, because it was on this very day that I brought your divisions out of Egypt. Celebrate this day as a lasting ordinance for the generations to come. ¹⁸In the first month you are to eat bread made without yeast, from the evening of the fourteenth day until the evening of the twenty-first day. ¹⁹For seven days no yeast is to be found in your houses. And whoever eats anything with yeast in it must be cut off from the community of Israel, whether he is an alien or native-born. ²⁰Eat nothing made with yeast. Wherever you live, you must eat unleavened bread."

²¹Then Moses summoned all the elders of Israel and said to them, "Go at once and select the animals for your families and slaughter the Passover lamb. ²²Take a bunch of hyssop, dip it into the blood in the basin and put some of the blood on the top and on both sides of the doorframe. Not one of you shall go out the door of his house until morning. ²³When the LORD goes through the land to strike down the Egyptians, he will see the blood on the top and sides of the doorframe and will pass over that doorway, and he will not permit the destroyer to enter your houses and strike you down.

²⁴"Obey these instructions as a lasting ordinance for you and your descendants. ²⁵When you enter the land that the LORD will give you as he promised, observe this ceremony. ²⁶And when your children ask you, 'What does this ceremony mean to you?' ²⁷then tell them, 'It is the Passover sacrifice to the LORD, who passed over the houses of the Israelites in Egypt and spared our homes when he struck down the Egyptians.'" Then the people bowed down and worshiped. ²⁸The Israelites did just what the LORD commanded Moses and Aaron.

²⁹At midnight the LORD struck down all the firstborn in Egypt, from the firstborn of Pharaoh, who sat on the throne, to the firstborn of the prisoner, who was in the dungeon, and the firstborn of all the livestock as well. ³⁰Pharaoh and all his officials and all the Egyptians got up during the night, and there was loud wailing in Egypt, for there was not a house without someone dead.

The Exodus

³¹During the night Pharaoh summoned Moses and Aaron and said, "Up! Leave my people, you and the Israelites! Go, worship the LORD as you have requested. ³²Take your flocks and herds, as you have said, and go. And also bless me."

³³The Egyptians urged the people to hurry and leave the country. "For otherwise," they said, "we will all die!" ³⁴So the people took their dough before the yeast was added, and carried it on their shoulders in kneading troughs wrapped in clothing. ³⁵The Israelites did as Moses instructed and asked the Egyptians for articles of silver and gold and for clothing. ³⁶The LORD had made the Egyptians favorably disposed toward the people, and they gave them what they asked for; so they plundered the Egyptians.

³⁷The Israelites journeyed from Rameses to Succoth. There were about six hundred thousand men on foot, besides women and children. ³⁸Many other people went up with them, as well as large droves of livestock, both flocks and herds. ³⁹With the dough they had brought from Egypt, they baked cakes of unleavened bread. The dough was without yeast because they had been driven out of Egypt and did not have time to prepare food for themselves.

⁴⁰Now the length of time the Israelite people lived in Egypt[a] was 430 years. ⁴¹At the end of the 430 years, to the very day, all the LORD's divisions left Egypt. ⁴²Because the LORD kept vigil that night to bring them out of Egypt, on this night all the Israelites are to keep vigil to honor the LORD for the generations to come.

Passover Restrictions

⁴³The LORD said to Moses and Aaron, "These are the regulations for the Passover:

"No foreigner is to eat of it. ⁴⁴Any slave you have bought may eat of it after you have circumcised him, ⁴⁵but a temporary resident and a hired worker may not eat of it.

⁴⁶"It must be eaten inside one house; take none of the meat outside the house. Do not break any of the bones. ⁴⁷The whole community of Israel must celebrate it.

⁴⁸"An alien living among you who wants to celebrate the LORD's Passover must have all the males in his household circumcised; then he may take part like one born in the land. No uncircumcised male may eat of it. ⁴⁹The same law applies

---

a 40 Masoretic Text; Samaritan Pentateuch and Septuagint *Egypt and Canaan*

to the native-born and to the alien living among you."

⁵⁰All the Israelites did just what the LORD had commanded Moses and Aaron. ⁵¹And on that very day the LORD brought the Israelites out of Egypt by their divisions.

Consecration of the Firstborn

13 The LORD said to Moses, ²"Consecrate to me every firstborn male. The first offspring

---

13:1 The Firstborn Principle

At the time of the Passover and the exodus from Egypt, God introduced an important principle: every firstborn male, including animals, was to be dedicated to him. Later, the Levites were established as a symbolic firstborn for all the people, with very precise accounting (Numbers 3:40–51).

---

of every womb among the Israelites belongs to me, whether man or animal."

³Then Moses said to the people, "Commemorate this day, the day you came out of Egypt, out of the land of slavery, because the LORD brought you out of it with a mighty hand. Eat nothing containing yeast. ⁴Today, in the month of Abib, you are leaving. ⁵When the LORD brings you into the land of the Canaanites, Hittites, Amorites, Hivites and Jebusites—the land he swore to your forefathers to give you, a land flowing with milk and honey—you are to observe this ceremony in this month: ⁶For seven days eat bread made without yeast and on the seventh day hold a festival to the LORD. ⁷Eat unleavened bread during those seven days; nothing with yeast in it is to be seen among you, nor shall any yeast be seen anywhere within your borders. ⁸On that day tell your son, 'I do this because of what the LORD did for me when I came out of Egypt.' ⁹This observance will be for you like a sign on your hand and a reminder on your forehead that the law of the LORD is to be on your lips. For the LORD brought you out of Egypt with his mighty hand. ¹⁰You must keep this ordinance at the appointed time year after year.

¹¹"After the LORD brings you into the land of the Canaanites and gives it to you, as he promised on oath to you and your forefathers, ¹²you are to give over to the LORD the first offspring of every womb. All the firstborn males of your livestock belong to the LORD. ¹³Redeem with a lamb every firstborn donkey, but if you do not redeem it, break its neck. Redeem every firstborn among your sons.

¹⁴"In days to come, when your son asks you, 'What does this mean?' say to him, 'With a mighty hand the LORD brought us out of Egypt, out of the land of slavery. ¹⁵When Pharaoh stubbornly refused to let us go, the LORD killed every firstborn in Egypt, both man and animal. This is why I sacrifice to the LORD the first male offspring of every womb and redeem each of my firstborn sons.' ¹⁶And it will be like a sign on your hand and a symbol on your forehead that the LORD brought us out of Egypt with his mighty hand."

Crossing the Sea

¹⁷When Pharaoh let the people go, God did not lead them on the road through the Philistine country, though that was shorter. For God said, "If they face war, they might change their minds and return to Egypt." ¹⁸So God led the people around by the desert road toward the Red Sea.ᵃ The Israelites went up out of Egypt armed for battle.

¹⁹Moses took the bones of Joseph with him because Joseph had made the sons of Israel swear an oath. He had said, "God will surely come to your aid, and then you must carry my bones up with you from this place."ᵇ

²⁰After leaving Succoth they camped at Etham on the edge of the desert. ²¹By day the LORD went ahead of them in a pillar of cloud to guide them on their way and by night in a pillar of fire to give them light, so that they could travel by day or night. ²²Neither the pillar of cloud by day nor the pillar of fire by night left its place in front of the people.

14 Then the LORD said to Moses, ²"Tell the Israelites to turn back and encamp near Pi Hahiroth, between Migdol and the sea. They are to encamp by the sea, directly opposite Baal Zephon. ³Pharaoh will think, 'The Israelites are wandering around the land in confusion, hemmed in by the desert.' ⁴And I will harden Pharaoh's heart, and he will pursue them. But I will gain glory for myself through Pharaoh and all his army, and the Egyptians will know that I am the LORD." So the Israelites did this.

⁵When the king of Egypt was told that the people had fled, Pharaoh and his officials changed their minds about them and said, "What have we done? We have let the Israelites go and have lost their services!" ⁶So he had his chariot made ready and took his army with him. ⁷He took six hundred of the best chariots, along with all the other chariots of Egypt, with officers over all of them. ⁸The LORD hardened the heart of Pharaoh king of Egypt, so that he pursued the Israelites, who were marching out boldly. ⁹The Egyptians—all Pharaoh's horses and chariots,

---

ᵃ18 Hebrew *Yam Suph*; that is, Sea of Reeds   ᵇ19 See Gen. 50:25.

horsemen[a] and troops—pursued the Israelites and overtook them as they camped by the sea near Pi Hahiroth, opposite Baal Zephon.

[10]As Pharaoh approached, the Israelites looked up, and there were the Egyptians, marching after them. They were terrified and cried out to the LORD. [11]They said to Moses, "Was it because there were no graves in Egypt that you brought us to the desert to die? What have you done to us by bringing us out of Egypt? [12]Didn't we say to you in Egypt, 'Leave us alone; let us serve the Egyptians'? It would have been better for us to serve the Egyptians than to die in the desert!"

[13]Moses answered the people, "Do not be afraid. Stand firm and you will see the deliverance the LORD will bring you today. The Egyptians you see today you will never see again. [14]The LORD will fight for you; you need only to be still."

[15]Then the LORD said to Moses, "Why are you crying out to me? Tell the Israelites to move on. [16]Raise your staff and stretch out your hand over the sea to divide the water so that the Israelites can go through the sea on dry ground. [17]I will harden the hearts of the Egyptians so that they will go in after them. And I will gain glory through Pharaoh and all his army, through his chariots and his horsemen. [18]The Egyptians will know that I am the LORD when I gain glory through Pharaoh, his chariots and his horsemen."

[19]Then the angel of God, who had been traveling in front of Israel's army, withdrew and went behind them. The pillar of cloud also moved from in front and stood behind them, [20]coming between the armies of Egypt and Israel. Throughout the night the cloud brought darkness to the one side and light to the other side; so neither went near the other all night long.

[21]Then Moses stretched out his hand over the sea, and all that night the LORD drove the sea back with a strong east wind and turned it into dry land. The waters were divided, [22]and the Israelites went through the sea on dry ground, with a wall of water on their right and on their left.

[23]The Egyptians pursued them, and all Pharaoh's horses and chariots and horsemen followed them into the sea. [24]During the last watch of the night the LORD looked down from the pillar of fire and cloud at the Egyptian army and threw it into confusion. [25]He made the wheels of their chariots come off[b] so that they had difficulty driving. And the Egyptians said, "Let's get away from the Israelites! The LORD is fighting for them against Egypt."

[26]Then the LORD said to Moses, "Stretch out your hand over the sea so that the waters may flow back over the Egyptians and their chariots and horsemen." [27]Moses stretched out his hand over the sea, and at daybreak the sea went back to its place. The Egyptians were fleeing toward[c] it, and the LORD swept them into the sea. [28]The water flowed back and covered the chariots and horsemen—the entire army of Pharaoh that had followed the Israelites into the sea. Not one of them survived.

[29]But the Israelites went through the sea on dry ground, with a wall of water on their right and on their left. [30]That day the LORD saved Israel from the hands of the Egyptians, and Israel saw the Egyptians lying dead on the shore. [31]And when the Israelites saw the great power the LORD displayed against the Egyptians, the people feared the LORD and put their trust in him and in Moses his servant.

The Song of Moses and Miriam

15 Then Moses and the Israelites sang this song to the LORD:

"I will sing to the LORD,
  for he is highly exalted.
The horse and its rider
  he has hurled into the sea.
[2]The LORD is my strength and my song;
  he has become my salvation.
He is my God, and I will praise him,
  my father's God, and I will exalt him.
[3]The LORD is a warrior;
  the LORD is his name.
[4]Pharaoh's chariots and his army
  he has hurled into the sea.
The best of Pharaoh's officers
  are drowned in the Red Sea.[d]
[5]The deep waters have covered them;
  they sank to the depths like a stone.

[6]"Your right hand, O LORD,
  was majestic in power.
Your right hand, O LORD,
  shattered the enemy.

14:21 Final Escape

Hemmed in by mountains, the sea, and the Egyptian army, the Israelites seemed doomed until God opened a highway through the sea. This miracle closed an important chapter in the Israelites' history. Never again would the powerful Egyptian empire rule over them; most of their future enemies swept in from the north and east.

---

[a]9 Or *charioteers*; also in verses 17, 18, 23, 26 and 28 Pentateuch, Septuagint and Syriac) [c]27 Or *from*

[b]25 Or *He jammed the wheels of their chariots* (see Samaritan [d]4 Hebrew *Yam Suph*; that is, Sea of Reeds; also in verse 22

[7]In the greatness of your majesty
  you threw down those who opposed you.
You unleashed your burning anger;
  it consumed them like stubble.
[8]By the blast of your nostrils
  the waters piled up.
The surging waters stood firm like a wall;
  the deep waters congealed in the heart of
    the sea.

[9]"The enemy boasted,
  'I will pursue, I will overtake them.
I will divide the spoils;
  I will gorge myself on them.
I will draw my sword
  and my hand will destroy them.'
[10]But you blew with your breath,
  and the sea covered them.
They sank like lead
  in the mighty waters.

[11]"Who among the gods is like you, O LORD?
  Who is like you—
    majestic in holiness,
    awesome in glory,
    working wonders?
[12]You stretched out your right hand
  and the earth swallowed them.

[13]"In your unfailing love you will lead
  the people you have redeemed.
In your strength you will guide them
  to your holy dwelling.
[14]The nations will hear and tremble;
  anguish will grip the people of Philistia.
[15]The chiefs of Edom will be terrified,
  the leaders of Moab will be seized with
    trembling,
the people[a] of Canaan will melt away;
[16] terror and dread will fall upon them.
By the power of your arm
  they will be as still as a stone—
until your people pass by, O LORD,
  until the people you bought[b] pass by.
[17]You will bring them in and plant them
  on the mountain of your inheritance—
the place, O LORD, you made for your
    dwelling,
the sanctuary, O Lord, your hands
    established.
[18]The LORD will reign
  for ever and ever."

[19]When Pharaoh's horses, chariots and horse-men[c] went into the sea, the LORD brought the waters of the sea back over them, but the Israelites walked through the sea on dry ground. [20]Then Miriam the prophetess, Aaron's sister, took a tambourine in her hand, and all the wom-en followed her, with tambourines and dancing. [21]Miriam sang to them:

  "Sing to the LORD,
    for he is highly exalted.
  The horse and its rider
    he has hurled into the sea."

The Waters of Marah and Elim

[22]Then Moses led Israel from the Red Sea and they went into the Desert of Shur. For three days they traveled in the desert without finding water. [23]When they came to Marah, they could not drink its water because it was bitter. (That is why the place is called Marah.[d]) [24]So the people grumbled against Moses, saying, "What are we to drink?"

[25]Then Moses cried out to the LORD, and the LORD showed him a piece of wood. He threw it into the water, and the water became sweet.

15:18 A Story for All Time

Moses' song celebrates the event from which this book gets its name: "the exodus" from Egypt, when a band of slaves escaped from the most powerful civilization on earth. The psalmists never tired of celebrating that event in song (see, for example, Psalms 78 and 105), and the prophets later harked back to the days of the exodus to stir the conscience of their nation. The Israelites' liberation gave inspiration to the slaves of the American South, who often memorialized the exodus in their spirituals.

There the LORD made a decree and a law for them, and there he tested them. [26]He said, "If you listen carefully to the voice of the LORD your God and do what is right in his eyes, if you pay attention to his commands and keep all his decrees, I will not bring on you any of the diseases I brought on the Egyptians, for I am the LORD, who heals you."

[27]Then they came to Elim, where there were twelve springs and seventy palm trees, and they camped there near the water.

Manna and Quail

16 The whole Israelite community set out from Elim and came to the Desert of Sin, which is between Elim and Sinai, on the fifteenth day of the second month after they had come out of Egypt. [2]In the desert the whole community grumbled against Moses and Aaron. [3]The Israelites said to them, "If only we had died by the LORD's hand in Egypt! There we sat around pots of meat and ate all the food we wanted, but you

---

[a] 15 Or *rulers*   [b] 16 Or *created*   [c] 19 Or *charioteers*   [d] 23 *Marah* means *bitter.*

have brought us out into this desert to starve this entire assembly to death."

⁴Then the LORD said to Moses, "I will rain down bread from heaven for you. The people are to go out each day and gather enough for that day. In this way I will test them and see whether they will follow my instructions. ⁵On the sixth day they are to prepare what they bring in, and that is to be twice as much as they gather on the other days."

⁶So Moses and Aaron said to all the Israelites, "In the evening you will know that it was the LORD who brought you out of Egypt, ⁷and in the morning you will see the glory of the LORD, because he has heard your grumbling against him. Who are we, that you should grumble against us?" ⁸Moses also said, "You will know that it was the LORD when he gives you meat to eat in the evening and all the bread you want in the morning, because he has heard your grumbling against him. Who are we? You are not grumbling against us, but against the LORD."

⁹Then Moses told Aaron, "Say to the entire Israelite community, 'Come before the LORD, for he has heard your grumbling.'"

¹⁰While Aaron was speaking to the whole Israelite community, they looked toward the desert, and there was the glory of the LORD appearing in the cloud.

¹¹The LORD said to Moses, ¹²"I have heard the grumbling of the Israelites. Tell them, 'At twilight you will eat meat, and in the morning you will be filled with bread. Then you will know that I am the LORD your God.'"

16:12–15 Food Supply

The word manna means literally, "What is it?" recalling the Israelites' first reaction to it (verse 15). Manna is a clear example of the Israelites' enforced dependence on God; they had to rely on him every day for 40 years, just to survive. God's provision of manna made greed impossible: it could not be hoarded and was distributed with precise equity (verses 17–21).

Quail, referred to here and in Numbers 11, still migrate across the Sinai peninsula, flying in great flocks between Europe and Arabia. Exhausted by their long flight, they roost on the ground or in low bushes at night, making capture easy.

¹³That evening quail came and covered the camp, and in the morning there was a layer of dew around the camp. ¹⁴When the dew was gone, thin flakes like frost on the ground appeared on the desert floor. ¹⁵When the Israelites saw it, they said to each other, "What is it?" For they did not know what it was.

Moses said to them, "It is the bread the LORD has given you to eat. ¹⁶This is what the LORD has commanded: 'Each one is to gather as much as he needs. Take an omer*ᵃ* for each person you have in your tent.'"

¹⁷The Israelites did as they were told; some gathered much, some little. ¹⁸And when they measured it by the omer, he who gathered much did not have too much, and he who gathered little did not have too little. Each one gathered as much as he needed.

¹⁹Then Moses said to them, "No one is to keep any of it until morning."

²⁰However, some of them paid no attention to Moses; they kept part of it until morning, but it was full of maggots and began to smell. So Moses was angry with them.

²¹Each morning everyone gathered as much as he needed, and when the sun grew hot, it melted away. ²²On the sixth day, they gathered twice as much—two omers*ᵇ* for each person—and the leaders of the community came and reported this to Moses. ²³He said to them, "This is what the LORD commanded: 'Tomorrow is to be a day of rest, a holy Sabbath to the LORD. So bake what you want to bake and boil what you want to boil. Save whatever is left and keep it until morning.'"

²⁴So they saved it until morning, as Moses commanded, and it did not stink or get maggots in it. ²⁵"Eat it today," Moses said, "because today is a Sabbath to the LORD. You will not find any of it on the ground today. ²⁶Six days you are to gather it, but on the seventh day, the Sabbath, there will not be any."

²⁷Nevertheless, some of the people went out on the seventh day to gather it, but they found none. ²⁸Then the LORD said to Moses, "How long will you*ᶜ* refuse to keep my commands and my instructions? ²⁹Bear in mind that the LORD has given you the Sabbath; that is why on the sixth day he gives you bread for two days. Everyone is to stay where he is on the seventh day; no one is to go out." ³⁰So the people rested on the seventh day.

³¹The people of Israel called the bread manna.*ᵈ* It was white like coriander seed and tasted like wafers made with honey. ³²Moses said, "This is what the LORD has commanded: 'Take an omer of manna and keep it for the generations to come, so they can see the bread I gave you to eat in the desert when I brought you out of Egypt.'"

³³So Moses said to Aaron, "Take a jar and put an omer of manna in it. Then place it before the LORD to be kept for the generations to come."

³⁴As the LORD commanded Moses, Aaron put

ᵃ16 That is, probably about 2 quarts (about 2 liters); also in verses 18, 32, 33 and 36   *ᵇ22* That is, probably about 4 quarts (about 4.5 liters)   *ᶜ28* The Hebrew is plural.   *ᵈ31 Manna* means *What is it?* (see verse 15).

the manna in front of the Testimony, that it might be kept. 35The Israelites ate manna forty years, until they came to a land that was settled; they ate manna until they reached the border of Canaan.

36(An omer is one tenth of an ephah.)

Water From the Rock

17 The whole Israelite community set out from the Desert of Sin, traveling from place to place as the LORD commanded. They camped at Rephidim, but there was no water for the

> ### 17:1 Change of Scenery
>
> *Unlike the Sahara and Saudi Arabian deserts, the Sinai peninsula is no dry, sandy wasteland. A high plateau in the north gives way to a broad belt of sandstone and sand, and then a tumbled mass of mountains (some reaching 9,000 feet) in the south. Herbs and acacia trees grow, and widely scattered springs permit some farming, although the Sinai cannot support a large population. Moses' 40-year stint as a shepherd here would have taught him much about wilderness survival.*

people to drink. 2So they quarreled with Moses and said, "Give us water to drink."

Moses replied, "Why do you quarrel with me? Why do you put the LORD to the test?"

3But the people were thirsty for water there, and they grumbled against Moses. They said, "Why did you bring us up out of Egypt to make us and our children and livestock die of thirst?"

4Then Moses cried out to the LORD, "What am I to do with these people? They are almost ready to stone me."

5The LORD answered Moses, "Walk on ahead of the people. Take with you some of the elders of Israel and take in your hand the staff with which you struck the Nile, and go. 6I will stand there before you by the rock at Horeb. Strike the rock, and water will come out of it for the people to drink." So Moses did this in the sight of the elders of Israel. 7And he called the place Massah*a* and Meribah*b* because the Israelites quarreled and because they tested the LORD saying, "Is the LORD among us or not?"

The Amalekites Defeated

8The Amalekites came and attacked the Israelites at Rephidim. 9Moses said to Joshua, "Choose some of our men and go out to fight the Amalekites. Tomorrow I will stand on top of the hill with the staff of God in my hands."

10So Joshua fought the Amalekites as Moses had ordered, and Moses, Aaron and Hur went to the top of the hill. 11As long as Moses held up his hands, the Israelites were winning, but whenever he lowered his hands, the Amalekites were winning. 12When Moses' hands grew tired, they took a stone and put it under him and he sat on it. Aaron and Hur held his hands up—one on one side, one on the other—so that his hands remained steady till sunset. 13So Joshua overcame the Amalekite army with the sword.

14Then the LORD said to Moses, "Write this on a scroll as something to be remembered and make sure that Joshua hears it, because I will completely blot out the memory of Amalek from under heaven."

15Moses built an altar and called it The LORD is my Banner. 16He said, "For hands were lifted up to the throne of the LORD. The*c* LORD will be at war against the Amalekites from generation to generation."

> ### 17:14 First Writing
>
> *Civilization mastered the skill of writing at least as early as 3400 B.C., when a society near present-day Iraq introduced it, but this is the Bible's first mention of the practice. Moses' training in Egypt would have included writing on "paper" made from pulpy reeds of the papyrus plant. A basket fashioned out of such reeds had helped save Moses' life as an infant (2:3).*

Jethro Visits Moses

18 Now Jethro, the priest of Midian and father-in-law of Moses, heard of everything God had done for Moses and for his people Israel, and how the LORD had brought Israel out of Egypt.

2After Moses had sent away his wife Zipporah, his father-in-law Jethro received her 3and her two sons. One son was named Gershom,*d* for Moses said, "I have become an alien in a foreign land"; 4and the other was named Eliezer,*e* for he said, "My father's God was my helper; he saved me from the sword of Pharaoh."

5Jethro, Moses' father-in-law, together with Moses' sons and wife, came to him in the desert, where he was camped near the mountain of God. 6Jethro had sent word to him, "I, your father-in-law Jethro, am coming to you with your wife and her two sons."

7So Moses went out to meet his father-in-law and bowed down and kissed him. They greeted

---

*a*7 *Massah* means *testing.*   *b*7 *Meribah* means *quarreling.*
LORD, the   *d*3 *Gershom* sounds like the Hebrew for *an alien there.*   *c*16 Or *"Because a hand was against the throne of the*   *e*4 *Eliezer* means *my God is helper.*

each other and then went into the tent. [8]Moses told his father-in-law about everything the LORD had done to Pharaoh and the Egyptians for Israel's sake and about all the hardships they had met along the way and how the LORD had saved them.

[9]Jethro was delighted to hear about all the good things the LORD had done for Israel in rescuing them from the hand of the Egyptians. [10]He said, "Praise be to the LORD, who rescued you from the hand of the Egyptians and of Pharaoh, and who rescued the people from the hand of the Egyptians. [11]Now I know that the LORD is greater than all other gods, for he did this to those who had treated Israel arrogantly." [12]Then Jethro, Moses' father-in-law, brought a burnt offering and other sacrifices to God, and Aaron came with all the elders of Israel to eat bread with Moses' father-in-law in the presence of God.

[13]The next day Moses took his seat to serve as judge for the people, and they stood around him from morning till evening. [14]When his father-in-law saw all that Moses was doing for the people, he said, "What is this you are doing for the people? Why do you alone sit as judge, while all these people stand around you from morning till evening?"

[15]Moses answered him, "Because the people come to me to seek God's will. [16]Whenever they have a dispute, it is brought to me, and I decide between the parties and inform them of God's decrees and laws."

[17]Moses' father-in-law replied, "What you are doing is not good. [18]You and these people who come to you will only wear yourselves out. The work is too heavy for you; you cannot handle it alone. [19]Listen now to me and I will give you some advice, and may God be with you. You must be the people's representative before God and bring their disputes to him. [20]Teach them the decrees and laws, and show them the way to live and the duties they are to perform. [21]But select capable men from all the people—men who fear God, trustworthy men who hate dishonest gain—and appoint them as officials over thousands, hundreds, fifties and tens. [22]Have them serve as judges for the people at all times, but have them bring every difficult case to you; the simple cases they can decide themselves. That will make your load lighter, because they will share it with you. [23]If you do this and God so commands, you will be able to stand the strain, and all these people will go home satisfied."

[24]Moses listened to his father-in-law and did everything he said. [25]He chose capable men from all Israel and made them leaders of the people, officials over thousands, hundreds, fifties and tens. [26]They served as judges for the people at all times. The difficult cases they brought to Moses, but the simple ones they decided themselves.

[27]Then Moses sent his father-in-law on his way, and Jethro returned to his own country.

At Mount Sinai

19 In the third month after the Israelites left Egypt—on the very day—they came to the

JETHRO *Advice from an In-Law*

A NEWLYWED HUSBAND CAN COUNT on one thing from his father-in-law: advice. He has, after all, married the woman his father-in-law has cared for from birth. And his father-in-law is older and more experienced than he. Under such conditions, advice is virtually inevitable.

After Moses led Israel out of Egypt, his father-in-law Jethro brought Moses' wife and children to join the rest of the Israelites. The old man stayed for a visit and observed Moses at work. Quickly he saw that the sheer volume of the work was overwhelming Moses. Jethro suggested that Moses appoint sub-officials to settle disputes, reserving only the most difficult cases for himself. Moses recognized this good advice, and acted on it.

Moses apparently liked and respected his father-in-law, and with good reason—Jethro took him in when he was running for his life after killing an Egyptian. And in addition to letting Moses marry his daughter, Jethro gave him a job. These men lived and worked together for forty years before God called Moses back to his people.

Jethro was, furthermore, a "priest of Midian." We don't know exactly how much of the true God Jethro knew before Moses came. Midianites, descended from Abraham, may have remembered "the God of Abraham, Isaac and Jacob." Surely Jethro and Moses talked often of their faith. After the Exodus, when Moses told Jethro how God had liberated the slaves from Pharaoh, Jethro acknowledged Moses' God as greater than all other gods.

Even so, Jethro did not accompany the Israelites on their journey to the promised land. He returned to his home, a believer in God remaining apart from God's chosen people.

Life Questions: Can you think of advice that proved especially helpful to you? What was it, and why was it beneficial?

Desert of Sinai. [2]After they set out from Rephidim, they entered the Desert of Sinai, and Israel camped there in the desert in front of the mountain.

[3]Then Moses went up to God, and the LORD called to him from the mountain and said, "This is what you are to say to the house of Jacob and what you are to tell the people of Israel: [4]'You yourselves have seen what I did to Egypt, and how I carried you on eagles' wings and brought you to myself. [5]Now if you obey me fully and keep my covenant, then out of all nations you will be my treasured possession. Although the

19:5 Book of the Covenant

The word covenant *appears throughout the next portion of Exodus. Chapter 19 gives the dramatic setting, and chapters 20–23 contain the actual covenant, a treaty between God and the Israelites. Chapter 24 shows the covenant being confirmed. Another word for covenant is* testament, *and, in fact, the rest of the Old Testament builds on what took place in these six chapters. Centuries later, biblical writers would dust off the old word* covenant *and apply it to Jesus Christ (as in 1 Corinthians 11:25). He fulfilled and completed the reconciliation with God begun at Sinai.*

whole earth is mine, [6]you[a] will be for me a kingdom of priests and a holy nation.' These are the words you are to speak to the Israelites."

[7]So Moses went back and summoned the elders of the people and set before them all the words the LORD had commanded him to speak. [8]The people all responded together, "We will do everything the LORD has said." So Moses brought their answer back to the LORD.

[9]The LORD said to Moses, "I am going to come to you in a dense cloud, so that the people will hear me speaking with you and will always put their trust in you." Then Moses told the LORD what the people had said.

[10]And the LORD said to Moses, "Go to the people and consecrate them today and tomorrow. Have them wash their clothes [11]and be ready by the third day, because on that day the LORD will come down on Mount Sinai in the sight of all the people. [12]Put limits for the people around the mountain and tell them, 'Be careful that you do not go up the mountain or touch the foot of it. Whoever touches the mountain shall surely be put to death. [13]He shall surely be stoned or shot with arrows; not a hand is to be laid on him. Whether man or animal, he shall not be permitted to live.' Only when the ram's horn

sounds a long blast may they go up to the mountain."

[14]After Moses had gone down the mountain to the people, he consecrated them, and they washed their clothes. [15]Then he said to the people, "Prepare yourselves for the third day. Abstain from sexual relations."

[16]On the morning of the third day there was thunder and lightning, with a thick cloud over the mountain, and a very loud trumpet blast. Everyone in the camp trembled. [17]Then Moses led the people out of the camp to meet with God, and they stood at the foot of the mountain. [18]Mount Sinai was covered with smoke, because the LORD descended on it in fire. The smoke billowed up from it like smoke from a furnace, the whole mountain[b] trembled violently, [19]and the sound of the trumpet grew louder and louder. Then Moses spoke and the voice of God answered him.[c]

[20]The LORD descended to the top of Mount Sinai and called Moses to the top of the mountain. So Moses went up [21]and the LORD said to him, "Go down and warn the people so they do not force their way through to see the LORD and many of them perish. [22]Even the priests, who approach the LORD, must consecrate themselves, or the LORD will break out against them."

[23]Moses said to the LORD, "The people cannot come up Mount Sinai, because you yourself warned us, 'Put limits around the mountain and set it apart as holy.'"

[24]The LORD replied, "Go down and bring Aaron up with you. But the priests and the people must not force their way through to come up to the LORD, or he will break out against them."

[25]So Moses went down to the people and told them.

The Ten Commandments

20 And God spoke all these words:

[2]"I am the LORD your God, who brought you out of Egypt, out of the land of slavery.

20:1–17 Long-lasting Laws

The Ten Commandments given here and in Deuteronomy 5 form a central core of morality, a major advance from other legal codes of the day. The phrase "Judeo-Christian ethics," heard often in U.S. courtrooms and legislative chambers, refers to the broad moral principles derived from laws outlined here and in the next three books.

---

[a]5,6 Or *possession, for the whole earth is mine.* [6]*You*   [b]18 Most Hebrew manuscripts; a few Hebrew manuscripts and Septuagint *all the people*   [c]19 Or *and God answered him with thunder*

³"You shall have no other gods before*
me.
⁴"You shall not make for yourself an idol
in the form of anything in heaven
above or on the earth beneath or in
the waters below. ⁵You shall not bow
down to them or worship them; for
I, the LORD your God, am a jealous
God, punishing the children for the
sin of the fathers to the third and
fourth generation of those who hate
me, ⁶but showing love to a thousand
˪generations˩ of those who love me
and keep my commandments.
⁷"You shall not misuse the name of the
LORD your God, for the LORD will not
hold anyone guiltless who misuses
his name.
⁸"Remember the Sabbath day by keeping it
holy. ⁹Six days you shall labor and do
all your work, ¹⁰but the seventh day
is a Sabbath to the LORD your God.
On it you shall not do any work, neither you, nor your son or daughter,

*3 Or *besides*

The Covenant
What difference does a stone tablet make?

MANY SCHOLARS CALL THE NEXT few chapters the most piv-
otal section of the Old Testament. The Israelites, called before a trembling and smoking mountain by loud trumpet blasts, were about to receive
something unique in all history: a stone document to be deposited in the
most valuable piece of furniture in the nation, the ark of the covenant. What
made a stone tablet so valuable? The "covenant" it summarized was sacred,
signed by the finger of God himself.

> *"Now if you obey me fully and keep my covenant, then out of all nations you will be my trea-sured possession." 19:5*

And yet someone who simply turned to Exodus and started reading the
contents of the covenant might have trouble understanding all the fuss. The covenant begins with the
familiar Ten Commandments. It proceeds from there to rules on cursing parents and knocking out
teeth, oddly mixed in with rules on interest rates and cooking young goats in their mothers' milk. What
is so special, after all, about the laws and instructions described here?

Since we don't normally communicate on stone tablets today, the question "What made a stone
tablet so valuable?" might better be rephrased, "What makes a piece of paper valuable?" Seen in that
light, our society, like the Israelites', stakes an awful lot on certain pieces of paper. Take just three
examples: a constitution, a birth certificate, and a marriage certificate.

Constitution

Resting in a helium-filled bronze case in the Library of Congress, the United States Constitution is
arguably the most valuable single piece of paper in the entire country. At a moment's notice it can be
lowered into a fireproof, shockproof safe. But dollars alone barely hint at the Constitution's value; its
real importance comes to light in a marble building down the street, where the Supreme Court hears
hundreds of legal cases.

Each case has climbed up from lower courts through an arduous, expensive process, and now
only one decision remains. Whatever the Supreme Court decides will rule as the law of the land. The
Supreme Court bases its decision on one final authority: the Constitution. If the nine members judge a
law "constitutional," the law will stand. If not, it will be overturned.

For Israel, the covenant became their Constitution. Details of the law came out in three main
places: here at Sinai (Exodus and Leviticus), during the wilderness wanderings (Numbers), and on the
plains of Moab (Deuteronomy). The complete legal code, far longer than the U.S. Constitution,
extended from the grand sweep of national policy to petty disputes of living together. God was shaping an entire culture for a group of homeless pilgrims. In all, 613 separate commands ordered their
political, social, and spiritual lives. Other nations were haunted by the unpredictability of their gods.
Who could tell what would anger or please them? But because of the covenant, Israelites knew exactly
what God required and where they stood before him. They had a basis for trust and security as a
nation.

Birth Certificate

This piece of paper, with its smudged baby footprint and fancy script, sits in a file drawer 99 percent of the time. But when you need it, you really need it. It can prove that a young-looking person

nor your manservant or maidservant, nor your animals, nor the alien within your gates. [11]For in six days the LORD made the heavens and the earth, the sea, and all that is in them, but he rested on the seventh day. Therefore the LORD blessed the Sabbath day and made it holy.

[12]"Honor your father and your mother, so that you may live long in the land the LORD your God is giving you.

[13]"You shall not murder.

[14]"You shall not commit adultery.

[15]"You shall not steal.

[16]"You shall not give false testimony against your neighbor.

[17]"You shall not covet your neighbor's house. You shall not covet your neighbor's wife, or his manservant or maidservant, his ox or donkey, or anything that belongs to your neighbor."

[18]When the people saw the thunder and lightning and heard the trumpet and saw the mountain in smoke, they trembled with fear. They stayed at a distance [19]and said to Moses, "Speak to us yourself and we will listen. But do not have God speak to us or we will die."

[20]Moses said to the people, "Do not be afraid. God has come to test you, so that the fear of God will be with you to keep you from sinning."

[21]The people remained at a distance, while Moses approached the thick darkness where God was.

Idols and Altars

[22]Then the LORD said to Moses, "Tell the Israelites this: 'You have seen for yourselves that I have spoken to you from heaven: [23]Do not make any gods to be alongside me; do not make for yourselves gods of silver or gods of gold.

[24]"'Make an altar of earth for me and sacrifice on it your burnt offerings and fellowship offerings,[a] your sheep and goats and your cattle. Wherever I cause my name to be honored, I will come to you and bless you. [25]If you make an altar of stones for me, do not build it with dressed stones, for you will defile it if you use a tool on it. [26]And do not go up to my altar on steps, lest your nakedness be exposed on it.'

[a]24 Traditionally *peace offerings*

---

deserves a driver's license or that an older person qualifies for Social Security payments. It establishes your rights as a United States citizen. A birth certificate is valuable indeed.

For Israel, the covenant established its birth as a nation. God said he had chosen the children of Israel as a treasured possession (19:5–6). He wanted a nation unlike any other, a model society centered around a commitment to him. He needed a pure people, kept separate.

The next few books of the Bible spell out the obligations, but also the rewards, of being God's chosen people, his "family." If they obeyed, the Israelites would live free from diseases, their crops would grow bountifully, their women would give birth to many children, their armies would prove victorious—in short, they would enjoy unprecedented national wealth and ecurity (23:20–28). The covenant defined those benefits—all part of being born as the children of God.

Marriage Certificate

Marriage is far more than a piece of paper, surely. It involves love and trust, sexuality, the thousand details involved in two people sharing life together. But in the eyes of the law, marriage requires a piece of paper. The document makes formal and legal the most intimate, personal relationship human beings ever have.

Later, the prophets Hosea, Jeremiah, and Ezekiel would poignantly compare the covenant to marriage. They pointed out that Israel's treatment of God amounted to adultery, and they called the nation back to its original covenant. The laws listed in numbing detail are merely the formal expression of a love relationship between God and his people.

Pieces of paper define the boundaries of a relationship, but in no way can they express it adequately. You cannot get an adequate picture of life in the United States by reading the Constitution's dry prose, nor can you understand the mystery of marriage by studying a certificate in a county courthouse. In the same way, the laws and rules in the Book of the Covenant surely do not yield a complete picture of life in a nation bound to God. But the covenant, and the context in which it came, show much about what God desired from his followers.

Life Questions: Do you own any valuable papers that express a kind of "covenant"? If you drew up a covenant between yourself and God, what would it say?

21

"These are the laws you are to set before them:

Hebrew Servants

2"If you buy a Hebrew servant, he is to serve you for six years. But in the seventh year, he shall

21:2 Slave Rights

Many of these laws set a new standard of morality: societies of that day oppressed aliens, mistreated slaves, exploited the poor, and awarded lost animals to their finder. The Israelites' rules governing slavery, for example, were enlightened for their time. Other ancient societies treated slaves as things rather than persons; Israelites were the first to honor them with formal rights. By beginning with laws protecting the lowest on the social scale, God was teaching the value of every human being.

go free, without paying anything. 3If he comes alone, he is to go free alone; but if he has a wife when he comes, she is to go with him. 4If his master gives him a wife and she bears him sons or daughters, the woman and her children shall belong to her master, and only the man shall go free.

5"But if the servant declares, 'I love my master and my wife and children and do not want to go free,' 6then his master must take him before the judges.a He shall take him to the door or the doorpost and pierce his ear with an awl. Then he will be his servant for life.

7"If a man sells his daughter as a servant, she is not to go free as menservants do. 8If she does not please the master who has selected her for himself,b he must let her be redeemed. He has no right to sell her to foreigners, because he has broken faith with her. 9If he selects her for his son, he must grant her the rights of a daughter. 10If he marries another woman, he must not deprive the first one of her food, clothing and marital rights. 11If he does not provide her with these three things, she is to go free, without any payment of money.

Personal Injuries

12"Anyone who strikes a man and kills him shall surely be put to death. 13However, if he does not do it intentionally, but God lets it happen, he is to flee to a place I will designate. 14But if a man schemes and kills another man deliberately, take him away from my altar and put him to death.

15"Anyone who attacksc his father or his mother must be put to death.

16"Anyone who kidnaps another and either sells him or still has him when he is caught must be put to death.

17"Anyone who curses his father or mother must be put to death.

18"If men quarrel and one hits the other with a stone or with his fistd and he does not die but is confined to bed, 19the one who struck the blow will not be held responsible if the other gets up and walks around outside with his staff; however, he must pay the injured man for the loss of his time and see that he is completely healed.

20"If a man beats his male or female slave with a rod and the slave dies as a direct result, he must be punished, 21but he is not to be punished if the slave gets up after a day or two, since the slave is his property.

22"If men who are fighting hit a pregnant woman and she gives birth prematurelye but there is no serious injury, the offender must be fined whatever the woman's husband demands and the court allows. 23But if there is serious injury, you are to take life for life, 24eye for eye, tooth for tooth, hand for hand, foot for foot, 25burn for burn, wound for wound, bruise for bruise.

26"If a man hits a manservant or maidservant in the eye and destroys it, he must let the servant go free to compensate for the eye. 27And if he knocks out the tooth of a manservant or maidservant, he must let the servant go free to compensate for the tooth.

28"If a bull gores a man or a woman to death, the bull must be stoned to death, and its meat must not be eaten. But the owner of the bull will not be held responsible. 29If, however, the bull has had the habit of goring and the owner has been warned but has not kept it penned up and it kills a man or woman, the bull must be stoned and the owner also must be put to death. 30However, if payment is demanded of him, he may redeem his life by paying whatever is demanded. 31This law also applies if the bull gores a son or daughter. 32If the bull gores a male or female slave, the owner must pay thirty shekelsf of silver to the master of the slave, and the bull must be stoned.

33"If a man uncovers a pit or digs one and fails to cover it and an ox or a donkey falls into it, 34the owner of the pit must pay for the loss; he must pay its owner, and the dead animal will be his.

35"If a man's bull injures the bull of another and it dies, they are to sell the live one and divide both the money and the dead animal equally. 36However, if it was known that the bull had the habit of goring, yet the owner did not keep it

---

a6 Or *before God*   b8 Or *master so that he does not choose her*   c15 Or *kills*   d18 Or *with a tool*
e22 Or *she has a miscarriage*   f32 That is, about 12 ounces (about 0.3 kilogram)

penned up, the owner must pay, animal for animal, and the dead animal will be his.

Protection of Property

22 "If a man steals an ox or a sheep and slaughters it or sells it, he must pay back five head of cattle for the ox and four sheep for the sheep.

[2]"If a thief is caught breaking in and is struck so that he dies, the defender is not guilty of bloodshed; [3]but if it happens[a] after sunrise, he is guilty of bloodshed.

"A thief must certainly make restitution, but if he has nothing, he must be sold to pay for his theft.

[4]"If the stolen animal is found alive in his possession—whether ox or donkey or sheep—he must pay back double.

[5]"If a man grazes his livestock in a field or vineyard and lets them stray and they graze in another man's field, he must make restitution from the best of his own field or vineyard.

[6]"If a fire breaks out and spreads into thornbushes so that it burns shocks of grain or standing grain or the whole field, the one who started the fire must make restitution.

[7]"If a man gives his neighbor silver or goods for safekeeping and they are stolen from the neighbor's house, the thief, if he is caught, must pay back double. [8]But if the thief is not found, the owner of the house must appear before the judges[b] to determine whether he has laid his hands on the other man's property. [9]In all cases of illegal possession of an ox, a donkey, a sheep, a garment, or any other lost property about which somebody says, 'This is mine,' both parties are to bring their cases before the judges. The one whom the judges declare[c] guilty must pay back double to his neighbor.

22:9 Punishment by Restitution

In contrast to the punishments of other contemporary codes (such as Sumer and Babylonia), the penalties for wrongdoing described in the next few chapters emphasize punishments fitted to the crime. They stress restitution rather than vengeance. Modern courtrooms are once again practicing restitution—making the criminal serve society or "make good" to the victim.

[10]"If a man gives a donkey, an ox, a sheep or any other animal to his neighbor for safekeeping and it dies or is injured or is taken away while no one is looking, [11]the issue between them will be settled by the taking of an oath before the LORD that the neighbor did not lay hands on the other person's property. The owner is to accept this, and no restitution is required. [12]But if the animal was stolen from the neighbor, he must make restitution to the owner. [13]If it was torn to pieces by a wild animal, he shall bring in the remains as evidence and he will not be required to pay for the torn animal.

[14]"If a man borrows an animal from his neighbor and it is injured or dies while the owner is not present, he must make restitution. [15]But if the owner is with the animal, the borrower will not have to pay. If the animal was hired, the money paid for the hire covers the loss.

Social Responsibility

[16]"If a man seduces a virgin who is not pledged to be married and sleeps with her, he must pay the bride-price, and she shall be his wife. [17]If her father absolutely refuses to give her to him, he must still pay the bride-price for virgins.

[18]"Do not allow a sorceress to live.

[19]"Anyone who has sexual relations with an animal must be put to death.

[20]"Whoever sacrifices to any god other than the LORD must be destroyed.[d]

[21]"Do not mistreat an alien or oppress him, for you were aliens in Egypt.

[22]"Do not take advantage of a widow or an orphan. [23]If you do and they cry out to me, I will certainly hear their cry. [24]My anger will be aroused, and I will kill you with the sword; your wives will become widows and your children fatherless.

[25]"If you lend money to one of my people among you who is needy, do not be like a moneylender; charge him no interest.[e] [26]If you take your neighbor's cloak as a pledge, return it to him by sunset, [27]because his cloak is the only covering he has for his body. What else will he sleep in? When he cries out to me, I will hear, for I am compassionate.

[28]"Do not blaspheme God[f] or curse the ruler of your people.

[29]"Do not hold back offerings from your granaries or your vats.[g]

"You must give me the firstborn of your sons. [30]Do the same with your cattle and your sheep. Let them stay with their mothers for seven days, but give them to me on the eighth day.

[31]"You are to be my holy people. So do not eat the meat of an animal torn by wild beasts; throw it to the dogs.

---

[a]3 Or *if he strikes him*   [b]8 Or *before God*; also in verse 9   [c]9 Or *whom God declares*   [d]20 The Hebrew term refers to the irrevocable giving over of things or persons to the LORD, often by totally destroying them.   [e]25 Or *excessive interest*   [f]28 Or *Do not revile the judges*   [g]29 The meaning of the Hebrew for this phrase is uncertain.

Laws of Justice and Mercy

23 "Do not spread false reports. Do not help a wicked man by being a malicious witness.

²"Do not follow the crowd in doing wrong. When you give testimony in a lawsuit, do not pervert justice by siding with the crowd, ³and do not show favoritism to a poor man in his lawsuit.

⁴"If you come across your enemy's ox or donkey wandering off, be sure to take it back to him. ⁵If you see the donkey of someone who hates you fallen down under its load, do not leave it there; be sure you help him with it.

⁶"Do not deny justice to your poor people in their lawsuits. ⁷Have nothing to do with a false charge and do not put an innocent or honest person to death, for I will not acquit the guilty.

⁸"Do not accept a bribe, for a bribe blinds those who see and twists the words of the righteous.

⁹"Do not oppress an alien; you yourselves know how it feels to be aliens, because you were aliens in Egypt.

Sabbath Laws

¹⁰"For six years you are to sow your fields and harvest the crops, ¹¹but during the seventh year let the land lie unplowed and unused. Then the poor among your people may get food from it, and the wild animals may eat what they leave. Do the same with your vineyard and your olive grove.

¹²"Six days do your work, but on the seventh day do not work, so that your ox and your donkey may rest and the slave born in your household, and the alien as well, may be refreshed.

¹³"Be careful to do everything I have said to you. Do not invoke the names of other gods; do not let them be heard on your lips.

The Three Annual Festivals

¹⁴"Three times a year you are to celebrate a festival to me.

¹⁵"Celebrate the Feast of Unleavened Bread; for seven days eat bread made without yeast, as I commanded you. Do this at the appointed time in the month of Abib, for in that month you came out of Egypt.

"No one is to appear before me empty-handed.

¹⁶"Celebrate the Feast of Harvest with the firstfruits of the crops you sow in your field.

"Celebrate the Feast of Ingathering at the end of the year, when you gather in your crops from the field.

¹⁷"Three times a year all the men are to appear before the Sovereign LORD.

¹⁸"Do not offer the blood of a sacrifice to me along with anything containing yeast.

"The fat of my festival offerings must not be kept until morning.

¹⁹"Bring the best of the firstfruits of your soil to the house of the LORD your God.

"Do not cook a young goat in its mother's milk.

God's Angel to Prepare the Way

²⁰"See, I am sending an angel ahead of you to guard you along the way and to bring you to the place I have prepared. ²¹Pay attention to him and listen to what he says. Do not rebel against him; he will not forgive your rebellion, since my Name is in him. ²²If you listen carefully to what he says and do all that I say, I will be an enemy to your enemies and will oppose those who oppose you. ²³My angel will go ahead of you and bring you into the land of the Amorites, Hittites, Perizzites, Canaanites, Hivites and Jebusites, and I will wipe them out. ²⁴Do not bow down before their gods or worship them or follow their practices. You must demolish them and break their sacred stones to pieces. ²⁵Worship the LORD your God, and his blessing will be on your food and water. I will take away sickness from among you, ²⁶and none will miscarry or be barren in your land. I will give you a full life span.

²⁷"I will send my terror ahead of you and throw into confusion every nation you encounter. I will make all your enemies turn their backs and run. ²⁸I will send the hornet ahead of you to drive the Hivites, Canaanites and Hittites out of your way. ²⁹But I will not drive them out in a single year, because the land would become desolate and the wild animals too numerous for you. ³⁰Little by little I will drive them out before you, until you have increased enough to take possession of the land.

³¹"I will establish your borders from the Red Sea*a* to the Sea of the Philistines,*b* and from the desert to the River.*c* I will hand over to you the people who live in the land and you will drive them out before you. ³²Do not make a covenant with them or with their gods. ³³Do not let them live in your land, or they will cause you to sin against me, because the worship of their gods will certainly be a snare to you."

The Covenant Confirmed

24 Then he said to Moses, "Come up to the LORD, you and Aaron, Nadab and Abihu, and seventy of the elders of Israel. You are to worship at a distance, ²but Moses alone is to approach the LORD; the others must not come near. And the people may not come up with him."

---

a31 Hebrew *Yam Suph;* that is, Sea of Reeds   *b31* That is, the Mediterranean   *c31* That is, the Euphrates

³When Moses went and told the people all the LORD's words and laws, they responded with one voice, "Everything the LORD has said we will do." ⁴Moses then wrote down everything the LORD had said.

He got up early the next morning and built an altar at the foot of the mountain and set up twelve stone pillars representing the twelve tribes of Israel. ⁵Then he sent young Israelite men, and they offered burnt offerings and sacrificed young bulls as fellowship offerings*a* to the LORD. ⁶Moses took half of the blood and put it in bowls, and the other half he sprinkled on the altar. ⁷Then he took the Book of the Covenant and read it to the people. They responded, "We will do everything the LORD has said; we will obey."

⁸Moses then took the blood, sprinkled it on the people and said, "This is the blood of the covenant that the LORD has made with you in accordance with all these words."

a5 Traditionally *peace offerings*

When God Was Obvious
Few atheists, but many rebels

WHY DOESN'T GOD INTERVENE MORE? Why doesn't he directly feed the hungry, heal all the sick, and stop all wars? If God really exists, at the least why doesn't he make himself more obvious?

People who ask such questions often assume that if God ever did spectacularly reveal himself, all doubts would vanish. Everyone would line up to believe in him.

> To the Israelites the glory of the LORD looked like a consuming fire on top of the mountain. 24:17

Astonishing Reactions

Exodus tells of a time when God made himself perfectly obvious. The plagues on Egypt revealed his mighty power. An enormous miracle at the Red Sea provided sensational deliverance. A recurring miracle supplied food for the Israelites every morning. And, if questions about God's existence arose, doubters needed only to look to the ever-present glory cloud or pillar of fire. It must have been hard to be an atheist in those days.

Yet every instance of God's faithfulness seemed to summon up astonishing human *un*faithfulness. The same Israelites who had watched God crush a pharaoh quaked at the first sign of Egyptian chariots. Three days after a miraculous escape across the Red Sea they were grumbling to Moses and God about water supplies.

A month or so later, when hunger pangs began to gnaw at them, they bitterly complained, "If only we had died by the LORD's hand in Egypt! There we sat around pots of meat and ate all the food we wanted, but you have brought us out into this desert to starve this entire assembly to death" (16:3). God responded with a provision of manna (that would continue for 40 years) and quail, but the Israelites were soon grousing about the water supplies again.

The Great Rebellion

Exodus 32 shows the Israelites at their worst. People who had eaten manna for breakfast, who had just solemnly agreed to keep every word of the covenant, who were at that moment standing beside a mountain stormy with the Lord's presence—those very people proceeded to melt down their gold jewelry and flagrantly flout the first commandment.

"Stiff-necked," God called the Israelites as he burned in anger against them. Only Moses' eloquent appeal saved their lives.

The history of the Israelites should nail a coffin lid on the notion that impressive displays of God's power will guarantee faith. (Jesus would later say, "If they do not listen to Moses and the Prophets, they will not be convinced even if someone rises from the dead," Luke 16:31.) People who had everyday proof of God demonstrated only one thing: the monotonous consistency of human nature.

The offenders would pay for their acts by wandering 40 years in a desolate wilderness while a new, untainted generation grew up to replace them. But a pattern was beginning to emerge: If the Israelites failed God in the shadow of Mount Sinai, how would they possibly withstand the seduction of new cultures in the promised land? The next generation, too, would fail God, as would all their descendants. The old covenant, as Paul would so convincingly argue in the book of Galatians, succeeded mainly by proving undeniably the need for a new one.

Life Questions: Do you ever have doubts about God's existence? What would it take to completely convince you?

9Moses and Aaron, Nadab and Abihu, and the seventy elders of Israel went up 10and saw the God of Israel. Under his feet was something like a pavement made of sapphire,[a] clear as the sky

itself. 11But God did not raise his hand against these leaders of the Israelites; they saw God, and they ate and drank.

12The LORD said to Moses, "Come up to me on the mountain and stay here, and I will give you the tablets of stone, with the law and commands I have written for their instruction."

13Then Moses set out with Joshua his aide, and Moses went up on the mountain of God. 14He said to the elders, "Wait here for us until we come back to you. Aaron and Hur are with you, and anyone involved in a dispute can go to them."

15When Moses went up on the mountain, the cloud covered it, 16and the glory of the LORD settled on Mount Sinai. For six days the cloud covered the mountain, and on the seventh day the LORD called to Moses from within the cloud. 17To the Israelites the glory of the LORD looked like a consuming fire on top of the mountain. 18Then Moses entered the cloud as he went on up the mountain. And he stayed on the mountain forty days and forty nights.

Offerings for the Tabernacle

25 The LORD said to Moses, 2"Tell the Israelites to bring me an offering. You are to receive the offering for me from each man whose heart prompts him to give. 3These are the offerings you are to receive from them: gold, silver and bronze; 4blue, purple and scarlet yarn and fine linen; goat hair; 5ram skins dyed red and hides of sea cows[b]; acacia wood; 6olive oil for the light; spices for the anointing oil and for the fragrant incense; 7and onyx stones and other gems to be mounted on the ephod and breastpiece.

8"Then have them make a sanctuary for me,

and I will dwell among them. 9Make this tabernacle and all its furnishings exactly like the pattern I will show you.

The Ark

10"Have them make a chest of acacia wood—two and a half cubits long, a cubit and a half wide, and a cubit and a half high.[c] 11Overlay it with pure gold, both inside and out, and make a gold molding around it. 12Cast four gold rings for it and fasten them to its four feet, with two rings on one side and two rings on the other. 13Then make poles of acacia wood and overlay them with gold. 14Insert the poles into the rings on the sides of the chest to carry it. 15The poles are to remain in the rings of this ark; they are not to be removed. 16Then put in the ark the Testimony, which I will give you.

17"Make an atonement cover[d] of pure gold—two and a half cubits long and a cubit and a half wide.[e] 18And make two cherubim out of hammered gold at the ends of the cover. 19Make one cherub on one end and the second cherub on the other; make the cherubim of one piece with the cover, at the two ends. 20The cherubim are to have their wings spread upward, overshadowing the cover with them. The cherubim are to face each other, looking toward the cover. 21Place the cover on top of the ark and put in the ark the Testimony, which I will give you. 22There, above the cover between the two cherubim that are over the ark of the Testimony, I will meet with you and give you all my commands for the Israelites.

The Table

23"Make a table of acacia wood—two cubits

---

[a]10 Or *lapis lazuli*   [b]5 That is, dugongs   [c]10 That is, about 3 3/4 feet (about 1.1 meters) long and 2 1/4 feet (about 0.7 meter) wide and high   [d]17 Traditionally *a mercy seat*   [e]17 That is, about 3 3/4 feet (about 1.1 meters) long and 2 1/4 feet (about 0.7 meter) wide

long, a cubit wide and a cubit and a half high.[a] [24]Overlay it with pure gold and make a gold molding around it. [25]Also make around it a rim a handbreadth[b] wide and put a gold molding on the rim. [26]Make four gold rings for the table and fasten them to the four corners, where the four legs are. [27]The rings are to be close to the rim to hold the poles used in carrying the table. [28]Make the poles of acacia wood, overlay them with gold and carry the table with them. [29]And make its plates and dishes of pure gold, as well as its pitchers and bowls for the pouring out of offerings. [30]Put the bread of the Presence on this table to be before me at all times.

The Lampstand

[31]"Make a lampstand of pure gold and hammer it out, base and shaft; its flowerlike cups, buds and blossoms shall be of one piece with it. [32]Six branches are to extend from the sides of the lampstand—three on one side and three on the other. [33]Three cups shaped like almond flowers with buds and blossoms are to be on one branch, three on the next branch, and the same for all six branches extending from the lampstand. [34]And on the lampstand there are to be four cups shaped like almond flowers with buds and blossoms. [35]One bud shall be under the first pair of branches extending from the lampstand, a second bud under the second pair, and a third bud under the third pair—six branches in all. [36]The buds and branches shall all be of one piece with the lampstand, hammered out of pure gold.

[37]"Then make its seven lamps and set them up on it so that they light the space in front of it. [38]Its wick trimmers and trays are to be of pure gold. [39]A talent[c] of pure gold is to be used for the lampstand and all these accessories. [40]See that you make them according to the pattern shown you on the mountain.

The Tabernacle

26 "Make the tabernacle with ten curtains of finely twisted linen and blue, purple and scarlet yarn, with cherubim worked into them by a skilled craftsman. [2]All the curtains are to be the same size—twenty-eight cubits long and four cubits wide.[d] [3]Join five of the curtains together, and do the same with the other five. [4]Make loops of blue material along the edge of the end curtain in one set, and do the same with the end curtain in the other set. [5]Make fifty loops on one curtain and fifty loops on the end curtain of the other set, with the loops opposite each other. [6]Then make fifty gold clasps and use them to

fasten the curtains together so that the tabernacle is a unit.

[7]"Make curtains of goat hair for the tent over the tabernacle—eleven altogether. [8]All eleven curtains are to be the same size—thirty cubits long and four cubits wide.[e] [9]Join five of the curtains together into one set and the other six into another set. Fold the sixth curtain double at the front of the tent. [10]Make fifty loops along the edge of the end curtain in one set and also along the edge of the end curtain in the other set. [11]Then make fifty bronze clasps and put them in the loops to fasten the tent together as a unit. [12]As for the additional length of the tent curtains, the half curtain that is left over is to hang down at the rear of the tabernacle. [13]The tent curtains will be a cubit[f] longer on both sides; what is left will hang over the sides of the tabernacle so as to cover it. [14]Make for the tent a covering of ram skins dyed red, and over that a covering of hides of sea cows.[g]

[15]"Make upright frames of acacia wood for the tabernacle. [16]Each frame is to be ten cubits long and a cubit and a half wide,[h] [17]with two projections set parallel to each other. Make all the frames of the tabernacle in this way. [18]Make twenty frames for the south side of the tabernacle [19]and make forty silver bases to go under them—two bases for each frame, one under each projection. [20]For the other side, the north side of the tabernacle, make twenty frames [21]and forty silver bases—two under each frame. [22]Make six frames for the far end, that is, the west end of the tabernacle, [23]and make two frames for the corners at the far end. [24]At these two corners they must be double from the bottom all the way to the top, and fitted into a single ring; both shall be like that. [25]So there will be eight frames and sixteen silver bases—two under each frame.

[26]"Also make crossbars of acacia wood: five for the frames on one side of the tabernacle, [27]five for those on the other side, and five for the frames on the west, at the far end of the tabernacle. [28]The center crossbar is to extend from end to end at the middle of the frames. [29]Overlay the frames with gold and make gold rings to hold the crossbars. Also overlay the crossbars with gold.

[30]"Set up the tabernacle according to the plan shown you on the mountain.

[31]"Make a curtain of blue, purple and scarlet yarn and finely twisted linen, with cherubim worked into it by a skilled craftsman. [32]Hang it with gold hooks on four posts of acacia wood overlaid with gold and standing on four silver bases. [33]Hang the curtain from the clasps and

---

[a]23 That is, about 3 feet (about 0.9 meter) long and 1 1/2 feet (about 0.5 meter) wide and 2 1/4 feet (about 0.7 meter) high   [b]25 That is, about 3 inches (about 8 centimeters)   [c]39 That is, about 75 pounds (about 34 kilograms)
[d]2 That is, about 42 feet (about 12.5 meters) long and 6 feet (about 1.8 meters) wide   [e]8 That is, about 45 feet (about 13.5 meters) long and 6 feet (about 1.8 meters) wide   [f]13 That is, about 1 1/2 feet (about 0.5 meter)   [g]14 That is, dugongs   [h]16 That is, about 15 feet (about 4.5 meters) long and 2 1/4 feet (about 0.7 meter) wide

place the ark of the Testimony behind the curtain. The curtain will separate the Holy Place from the Most Holy Place. ³⁴Put the atonement cover on the ark of the Testimony in the Most Holy Place. ³⁵Place the table outside the curtain on the north side of the tabernacle and put the lampstand opposite it on the south side.

26:33 A Torn Curtain

The thick curtain described here separated the Holy Place from the Most Holy Place. Anyone who ventured beyond that curtain would die. The New Testament, however, records that at Jesus' crucifixion the curtain tore in two, from top to bottom. The tearing symbolized what Christ had accomplished: he broke down the separation between God and humanity (Matthew 27:51; Hebrews 10:20).

³⁶"For the entrance to the tent make a curtain of blue, purple and scarlet yarn and finely twisted linen—the work of an embroiderer. ³⁷Make gold hooks for this curtain and five posts of acacia wood overlaid with gold. And cast five bronze bases for them.

The Altar of Burnt Offering

27 "Build an altar of acacia wood, three cubits*ᵃ* high; it is to be square, five cubits long and five cubits wide.*ᵇ* ²Make a horn at each of the four corners, so that the horns and the altar are of one piece, and overlay the altar with bronze. ³Make all its utensils of bronze—its pots to remove the ashes, and its shovels, sprinkling bowls, meat forks and firepans. ⁴Make a grating for it, a bronze network, and make a bronze ring at each of the four corners of the network. ⁵Put it under the ledge of the altar so that it is halfway up the altar. ⁶Make poles of acacia wood for the altar and overlay them with bronze. ⁷The poles are to be inserted into the rings so they will be on two sides of the altar when it is carried. ⁸Make the altar hollow, out of boards. It is to be made just as you were shown on the mountain.

The Courtyard

⁹"Make a courtyard for the tabernacle. The south side shall be a hundred cubits*ᶜ* long and is to have curtains of finely twisted linen, ¹⁰with twenty posts and twenty bronze bases and with silver hooks and bands on the posts. ¹¹The north side shall also be a hundred cubits long and is to have curtains, with twenty posts and twenty bronze bases and with silver hooks and bands on the posts.

¹²"The west end of the courtyard shall be fifty cubits*ᵈ* wide and have curtains, with ten posts and ten bases. ¹³On the east end, toward the sunrise, the courtyard shall also be fifty cubits wide. ¹⁴Curtains fifteen cubits*ᵉ* long are to be on one side of the entrance, with three posts and three bases, ¹⁵and curtains fifteen cubits long are to be on the other side, with three posts and three bases.

¹⁶"For the entrance to the courtyard, provide a curtain twenty cubits*ᶠ* long, of blue, purple and scarlet yarn and finely twisted linen—the work of an embroiderer—with four posts and four bases. ¹⁷All the posts around the courtyard are to have silver bands and hooks, and bronze bases. ¹⁸The courtyard shall be a hundred cubits long and fifty cubits wide,*ᵍ* with curtains of finely twisted linen five cubits*ʰ* high, and with bronze bases. ¹⁹All the other articles used in the service of the tabernacle, whatever their function, including all the tent pegs for it and those for the courtyard, are to be of bronze.

Oil for the Lampstand

²⁰"Command the Israelites to bring you clear oil of pressed olives for the light so that the lamps may be kept burning. ²¹In the Tent of Meeting, outside the curtain that is in front of the Testimony, Aaron and his sons are to keep the lamps burning before the LORD from evening till morning. This is to be a lasting ordinance among the Israelites for the generations to come.

The Priestly Garments

28 "Have Aaron your brother brought to you from among the Israelites, along with his sons Nadab and Abihu, Eleazar and Ithamar, so they may serve me as priests. ²Make sacred garments for your brother Aaron, to give him dignity and honor. ³Tell all the skilled men to whom I have given wisdom in such matters that they are to make garments for Aaron, for his consecration, so he may serve me as priest. ⁴These are the garments they are to make: a breastpiece, an ephod, a robe, a woven tunic, a turban and a sash. They are to make these sacred garments for your brother Aaron and his sons, so they may serve me as priests. ⁵Have them use gold, and blue, purple and scarlet yarn, and fine linen.

The Ephod

⁶"Make the ephod of gold, and of blue, purple and scarlet yarn, and of finely twisted linen—the

---

ᵃ1 That is, about 4 1/2 feet (about 1.3 meters)   *ᵇ1* That is, about 7 1/2 feet (about 2.3 meters) long and wide
ᶜ9 That is, about 150 feet (about 46 meters); also in verse 11   *ᵈ12* That is, about 75 feet (about 23 meters); also in verse 13   *ᵉ14* That is, about 22 1/2 feet (about 6.9 meters); also in verse 15   *ᶠ16* That is, about 30 feet (about 9 meters)   *ᵍ18* That is, about 150 feet (about 46 meters) long and 75 feet (about 23 meters) wide   *ʰ18* That is, about 7 1/2 feet (about 2.3 meters)

work of a skilled craftsman. [7]It is to have two shoulder pieces attached to two of its corners, so it can be fastened. [8]Its skillfully woven waistband is to be like it—of one piece with the ephod and made with gold, and with blue, purple and scarlet yarn, and with finely twisted linen.

[9]"Take two onyx stones and engrave on them the names of the sons of Israel [10]in the order of their birth—six names on one stone and the remaining six on the other. [11]Engrave the names of the sons of Israel on the two stones the way a gem cutter engraves a seal. Then mount the stones in gold filigree settings [12]and fasten them on the shoulder pieces of the ephod as memorial stones for the sons of Israel. Aaron is to bear the names on his shoulders as a memorial before the LORD. [13]Make gold filigree settings [14]and two braided chains of pure gold, like a rope, and attach the chains to the settings.

The Breastpiece

[15]"Fashion a breastpiece for making decisions—the work of a skilled craftsman. Make it like the ephod: of gold, and of blue, purple and scarlet yarn, and of finely twisted linen. [16]It is to be square—a span[a] long and a span wide—and folded double. [17]Then mount four rows of precious stones on it. In the first row there shall be a ruby, a topaz and a beryl; [18]in the second row a turquoise, a sapphire[b] and an emerald; [19]in the third row a jacinth, an agate and an amethyst; [20]in the fourth row a chrysolite, an onyx and a jasper.[c] Mount them in gold filigree settings. [21]There are to be twelve stones, one for each of the names of the sons of Israel, each engraved like a seal with the name of one of the twelve tribes.

[22]"For the breastpiece make braided chains of pure gold, like a rope. [23]Make two gold rings for it and fasten them to two corners of the breastpiece. [24]Fasten the two gold chains to the rings at the corners of the breastpiece, [25]and the other ends of the chains to the two settings, attaching them to the shoulder pieces of the ephod at the front. [26]Make two gold rings and attach them to the other two corners of the breastpiece on the inside edge next to the ephod. [27]Make two more gold rings and attach them to the bottom of the shoulder pieces on the front of the ephod, close to the seam just above the waistband of the ephod. [28]The rings of the breastpiece are to be tied to the rings of the ephod with blue cord, connecting it to the waistband, so that the breastpiece will not swing out from the ephod.

[29]"Whenever Aaron enters the Holy Place, he will bear the names of the sons of Israel over his heart on the breastpiece of decision as a continu-

ing memorial before the LORD. [30]Also put the Urim and the Thummim in the breastpiece, so they may be over Aaron's heart whenever he enters the presence of the LORD. Thus Aaron will always bear the means of making decisions for the Israelites over his heart before the LORD.

Other Priestly Garments

[31]"Make the robe of the ephod entirely of blue cloth, [32]with an opening for the head in its center. There shall be a woven edge like a collar[d] around this opening, so that it will not tear. [33]Make pomegranates of blue, purple and scarlet yarn around the hem of the robe, with gold bells between them. [34]The gold bells and the pomegranates are to alternate around the hem of the robe. [35]Aaron must wear it when he ministers. The sound of the bells will be heard when he enters the Holy Place before the LORD and when he comes out, so that he will not die.

[36]"Make a plate of pure gold and engrave on it as on a seal: HOLY TO THE LORD. [37]Fasten a blue cord to it to attach it to the turban; it is to be on the front of the turban. [38]It will be on Aaron's forehead, and he will bear the guilt involved in the sacred gifts the Israelites consecrate, whatever their gifts may be. It will be on Aaron's forehead continually so that they will be acceptable to the LORD.

[39]"Weave the tunic of fine linen and make the turban of fine linen. The sash is to be the work of an embroiderer. [40]Make tunics, sashes and headbands for Aaron's sons, to give them dignity and honor. [41]After you put these clothes on your brother Aaron and his sons, anoint and ordain them. Consecrate them so they may serve me as priests.

[42]"Make linen undergarments as a covering for the body, reaching from the waist to the thigh. [43]Aaron and his sons must wear them whenever they enter the Tent of Meeting or approach the altar to minister in the Holy Place, so that they will not incur guilt and die.

"This is to be a lasting ordinance for Aaron and his descendants.

Consecration of the Priests

29 "This is what you are to do to consecrate them, so they may serve me as priests: Take a young bull and two rams without defect. [2]And from fine wheat flour, without yeast, make bread, and cakes mixed with oil, and wafers spread with oil. [3]Put them in a basket and present them in it—along with the bull and the two rams. [4]Then bring Aaron and his sons to the entrance to the Tent of Meeting and wash them with water. [5]Take the garments and dress Aaron with the tunic, the robe of the ephod, the ephod

---

[a]16 That is, about 9 inches (about 22 centimeters)   [b]18 Or *lapis lazuli*   [c]20 The precise identification of some of these precious stones is uncertain.   [d]32 The meaning of the Hebrew for this word is uncertain.

itself and the breastpiece. Fasten the ephod on him by its skillfully woven waistband. 6Put the turban on his head and attach the sacred diadem to the turban. 7Take the anointing oil and anoint him by pouring it on his head. 8Bring his sons and dress them in tunics 9and put headbands on them. Then tie sashes on Aaron and his sons.*a* The priesthood is theirs by a lasting ordinance. In this way you shall ordain Aaron and his sons.

10"Bring the bull to the front of the Tent of Meeting, and Aaron and his sons shall lay their hands on its head. 11Slaughter it in the LORD's presence at the entrance to the Tent of Meeting. 12Take some of the bull's blood and put it on the horns of the altar with your finger, and pour out the rest of it at the base of the altar. 13Then take all the fat around the inner parts, the covering of the liver, and both kidneys with the fat on them, and burn them on the altar. 14But burn the bull's flesh and its hide and its offal outside the camp. It is a sin offering.

15"Take one of the rams, and Aaron and his sons shall lay their hands on its head. 16Slaughter it and take the blood and sprinkle it against the altar on all sides. 17Cut the ram into pieces and wash the inner parts and the legs, putting them with the head and the other pieces. 18Then burn the entire ram on the altar. It is a burnt offering to the LORD, a pleasing aroma, an offering made to the LORD by fire.

19"Take the other ram, and Aaron and his sons shall lay their hands on its head. 20Slaughter it, take some of its blood and put it on the lobes of the right ears of Aaron and his sons, on the thumbs of their right hands, and on the big toes of their right feet. Then sprinkle blood against

29:20 The Whole Body

As part of their purification, the priests daubed blood on their ears (which hear God's laws), their hands (which do his will), and their toes (which were prepared to follow in his steps).

the altar on all sides. 21And take some of the blood on the altar and some of the anointing oil and sprinkle it on Aaron and his garments and on his sons and their garments. Then he and his sons and their garments will be consecrated.

22"Take from this ram the fat, the fat tail, the fat around the inner parts, the covering of the liver, both kidneys with the fat on them, and the right thigh. (This is the ram for the ordination.) 23From the basket of bread made without yeast, which is before the LORD, take a loaf, and a cake made with oil, and a wafer. 24Put all these

in the hands of Aaron and his sons and wave them before the LORD as a wave offering. 25Then take them from their hands and burn them on the altar along with the burnt offering for a pleasing aroma to the LORD, an offering made to the LORD by fire. 26After you take the breast of the ram for Aaron's ordination, wave it before the LORD as a wave offering, and it will be your share.

27"Consecrate those parts of the ordination ram that belong to Aaron and his sons: the breast that was waved and the thigh that was presented. 28This is always to be the regular share from the Israelites for Aaron and his sons. It is the contribution the Israelites are to make to the LORD from their fellowship offerings.*b*

29"Aaron's sacred garments will belong to his descendants so that they can be anointed and ordained in them. 30The son who succeeds him as priest and comes to the Tent of Meeting to minister in the Holy Place is to wear them seven days.

31"Take the ram for the ordination and cook the meat in a sacred place. 32At the entrance to the Tent of Meeting, Aaron and his sons are to eat the meat of the ram and the bread that is in the basket. 33They are to eat these offerings by which atonement was made for their ordination and consecration. But no one else may eat them, because they are sacred. 34And if any of the meat of the ordination ram or any bread is left over till morning, burn it up. It must not be eaten, because it is sacred.

35"Do for Aaron and his sons everything I have commanded you, taking seven days to ordain them. 36Sacrifice a bull each day as a sin offering to make atonement. Purify the altar by making atonement for it, and anoint it to consecrate it. 37For seven days make atonement for the altar and consecrate it. Then the altar will be most holy, and whatever touches it will be holy.

38"This is what you are to offer on the altar regularly each day: two lambs a year old. 39Offer one in the morning and the other at twilight. 40With the first lamb offer a tenth of an ephah*c* of fine flour mixed with a quarter of a hin*d* of oil from pressed olives, and a quarter of a hin of wine as a drink offering. 41Sacrifice the other lamb at twilight with the same grain offering and its drink offering as in the morning—a pleasing aroma, an offering made to the LORD by fire.

42"For the generations to come this burnt offering is to be made regularly at the entrance to the Tent of Meeting before the LORD. There I will meet you and speak to you; 43there also I will meet with the Israelites, and the place will be consecrated by my glory.

---

a9 Hebrew; Septuagint *on them*   *b28* Traditionally *peace offerings*   *c40* That is, probably about 2 quarts (about 2 liters)   *d40* That is, probably about 1 quart (about 1 liter)

44"So I will consecrate the Tent of Meeting and the altar and will consecrate Aaron and his sons to serve me as priests. 45Then I will dwell among the Israelites and be their God. 46They will know that I am the LORD their God, who brought them out of Egypt so that I might dwell among them. I am the LORD their God.

The Altar of Incense

30 "Make an altar of acacia wood for burning incense. 2It is to be square, a cubit long and a cubit wide, and two cubits high*a*—its horns of one piece with it. 3Overlay the top and all the sides and the horns with pure gold, and make a gold molding around it. 4Make two gold rings for the altar below the molding—two on opposite sides—to hold the poles used to carry it. 5Make the poles of acacia wood and overlay them with gold. 6Put the altar in front of the curtain that is before the ark of the Testimony—before the atonement cover that is over the Testimony—where I will meet with you.

7"Aaron must burn fragrant incense on the altar every morning when he tends the lamps. 8He must burn incense again when he lights the lamps at twilight so incense will burn regularly before the LORD for the generations to come. 9Do not offer on this altar any other incense or any burnt offering or grain offering, and do not pour a drink offering on it. 10Once a year Aaron shall make atonement on its horns. This annual atonement must be made with the blood of the atoning sin offering for the generations to come. It is most holy to the LORD."

30:10 Jewish Holy Days

Orthodox Jews still faithfully honor the Day of Atonement described here, the holy day of Yom Kippur. But the New Testament book of Hebrews reinterprets this period of time as a copy, or shadow, of the real thing to come in Jesus Christ. What a high priest accomplished, through elaborate ceremony, once a year on the Day of Atonement, Christ did once for all (Hebrews 8–9). As a consequence, all of us—not just a purified priest—can confidently "enter the Most Holy Place."

Atonement Money

11Then the LORD said to Moses, 12"When you take a census of the Israelites to count them, each one must pay the LORD a ransom for his life at the time he is counted. Then no plague will come on them when you number them. 13Each one who crosses over to those already counted is to give a half shekel,*b* according to the sanctuary shekel, which weighs twenty gerahs. This half shekel is an offering to the LORD. 14All who cross over, those twenty years old or more, are to give an offering to the LORD. 15The rich are not to give more than a half shekel and the poor are not to give less when you make the offering to the LORD to atone for your lives. 16Receive the atonement money from the Israelites and use it for the service of the Tent of Meeting. It will be a memorial for the Israelites before the LORD, making atonement for your lives."

Basin for Washing

17Then the LORD said to Moses, 18"Make a bronze basin, with its bronze stand, for washing. Place it between the Tent of Meeting and the altar, and put water in it. 19Aaron and his sons are to wash their hands and feet with water from it. 20Whenever they enter the Tent of Meeting, they shall wash with water so that they will not die. Also, when they approach the altar to minister by presenting an offering made to the LORD by fire, 21they shall wash their hands and feet so that they will not die. This is to be a lasting ordinance for Aaron and his descendants for the generations to come."

Anointing Oil

22Then the LORD said to Moses, 23"Take the following fine spices: 500 shekels*c* of liquid myrrh, half as much (that is, 250 shekels) of fragrant cinnamon, 250 shekels of fragrant cane, 24500 shekels of cassia—all according to the sanctuary shekel—and a hin*d* of olive oil. 25Make these into a sacred anointing oil, a fragrant blend, the work of a perfumer. It will be the sacred anointing oil. 26Then use it to anoint the Tent of Meeting, the ark of the Testimony, 27the table and all its articles, the lampstand and its accessories, the altar of incense, 28the altar of burnt offering and all its utensils, and the basin with its stand. 29You shall consecrate them so they will be most holy, and whatever touches them will be holy.

30"Anoint Aaron and his sons and consecrate them so they may serve me as priests. 31Say to the Israelites, 'This is to be my sacred anointing oil for the generations to come. 32Do not pour it on men's bodies and do not make any oil with the same formula. It is sacred, and you are to consider it sacred. 33Whoever makes perfume like it and whoever puts it on anyone other than a priest must be cut off from his people.'"

---

a2 That is, about 1 1/2 feet (about 0.5 meter) long and wide and about 3 feet (about 0.9 meter) high   *b13* That is, about 1/5 ounce (about 6 grams); also in verse 15   *c23* That is, about 12 1/2 pounds (about 6 kilograms)   *d24* That is, probably about 4 quarts (about 4 liters)

Incense

34Then the LORD said to Moses, "Take fragrant spices—gum resin, onycha and galbanum—and pure frankincense, all in equal amounts, 35and make a fragrant blend of incense, the work of a perfumer. It is to be salted and pure and sacred. 36Grind some of it to powder and place it in front of the Testimony in the Tent of Meeting, where I will meet with you. It shall be most holy to you. 37Do not make any incense with this formula for yourselves; consider it holy to the LORD. 38Whoever makes any like it to enjoy its fragrance must be cut off from his people."

Bezalel and Oholiab

31 Then the LORD said to Moses, 2"See, I have chosen Bezalel son of Uri, the son of Hur, of the tribe of Judah, 3and I have filled him with the Spirit of God, with skill, ability and knowledge in all kinds of crafts— 4to make artistic designs for work in gold, silver and bronze, 5to cut and set stones, to work in wood, and to engage in all kinds of craftsmanship. 6Moreover, I have appointed Oholiab son of Ahisamach, of the tribe of Dan, to help him. Also I have given skill to all the craftsmen to make everything I have commanded you: 7the Tent of Meeting, the ark of the Testimony with the atonement cover on it, and all the other furnishings of the tent— 8the table and its articles, the pure gold lampstand and all its accessories, the altar of incense, 9the altar of burnt offering and all its utensils, the basin with its stand— 10and also the woven garments, both the sacred garments for Aaron the priest and the garments for his sons when they serve as priests, 11and the anointing oil and fragrant incense for the Holy Place. They are to make them just as I commanded you."

The Sabbath

12Then the LORD said to Moses, 13"Say to the Israelites, 'You must observe my Sabbaths. This will be a sign between me and you for the generations to come, so you may know that I am the LORD, who makes you holy.a

14"'Observe the Sabbath, because it is holy to you. Anyone who desecrates it must be put to death; whoever does any work on that day must be cut off from his people. 15For six days, work is to be done, but the seventh day is a Sabbath of rest, holy to the LORD. Whoever does any work on the Sabbath day must be put to death. 16The Israelites are to observe the Sabbath, celebrating it for the generations to come as a lasting covenant. 17It will be a sign between me and the Israelites forever, for in six days the LORD made the heavens and the earth, and on the seventh day he abstained from work and rested.'"

18When the LORD finished speaking to Moses on Mount Sinai, he gave him the two tablets of the Testimony, the tablets of stone inscribed by the finger of God.

The Golden Calf

32 When the people saw that Moses was so long in coming down from the mountain, they gathered around Aaron and said, "Come, make us godsb who will go before us. As for this fellow Moses who brought him up out of Egypt, we don't know what has happened to him."

2Aaron answered them, "Take off the gold earrings that your wives, your sons and your daughters are wearing, and bring them to me." 3So all the people took off their earrings and brought them to Aaron. 4He took what they handed him and made it into an idol cast in the shape of a calf, fashioning it with a tool. Then they said, "These are your gods,c O Israel, who brought you up out of Egypt."

32:4–8 Recent Discovery

Not until 1990 did archaeologists unearth the first golden calf in Palestine, and, to their surprise, it stood only a few inches tall. Contrary to popular depictions in movies and historical books, Aaron's solid gold calf too may have been very small, but elevated on a pedestal for visual emphasis. Undoubtedly the Israelites knew of the bull-god Apis, one of Egypt's important gods.

Moses stayed on Mount Sinai for nearly six weeks (24:18), which helps explain the Israelites' panicky behavior. Had Moses died or run away? Would he ever come back? Nevertheless, by flagrantly breaking the second commandment they failed their first test under the new covenant with God.

5When Aaron saw this, he built an altar in front of the calf and announced, "Tomorrow there will be a festival to the LORD." 6So the next day the people rose early and sacrificed burnt offerings and presented fellowship offerings.d Afterward they sat down to eat and drink and got up to indulge in revelry.

7Then the LORD said to Moses, "Go down, because your people, whom you brought up out of Egypt, have become corrupt. 8They have been quick to turn away from what I commanded them and have made themselves an idol cast in the shape of a calf. They have bowed down to it and sacrificed to it and have said, 'These are your

---

a13 Or *who sanctifies you*; or *who sets you apart as holy your god*; also in verse 8   b1 Or *a god*; also in verses 23 and 31   c4 Or *This is*   d6 Traditionally *peace offerings*

gods, O Israel, who brought you up out of Egypt.'

[9]"I have seen these people," the LORD said to Moses, "and they are a stiff-necked people. [10]Now leave me alone so that my anger may burn against them and that I may destroy them. Then I will make you into a great nation."

[11]But Moses sought the favor of the LORD his God. "O LORD," he said, "why should your anger burn against your people, whom you brought out of Egypt with great power and a mighty hand? [12]Why should the Egyptians say, 'It was with evil intent that he brought them out, to kill them in the mountains and to wipe them off the face of the earth'? Turn from your fierce anger; relent and do not bring disaster on your people. [13]Remember your servants Abraham, Isaac and Israel, to whom you swore by your own self: 'I will make your descendants as numerous as the stars in the sky and I will give your descendants all this land I promised them, and it will be their inheritance forever.'" [14]Then the LORD relented and did not bring on his people the disaster he had threatened.

[15]Moses turned and went down the mountain with the two tablets of the Testimony in his hands. They were inscribed on both sides, front and back. [16]The tablets were the work of God; the writing was the writing of God, engraved on the tablets.

[17]When Joshua heard the noise of the people shouting, he said to Moses, "There is the sound of war in the camp."

[18]Moses replied:

"It is not the sound of victory,
    it is not the sound of defeat;
    it is the sound of singing that I hear."

[19]When Moses approached the camp and saw the calf and the dancing, his anger burned and he threw the tablets out of his hands, breaking them to pieces at the foot of the mountain. [20]And he took the calf they had made and burned it in the fire; then he ground it to powder, scattered it on the water and made the Israelites drink it.

[21]He said to Aaron, "What did these people do to you, that you led them into such great sin?"

[22]"Do not be angry, my lord," Aaron answered. "You know how prone these people are to evil. [23]They said to me, 'Make us gods who will go before us. As for this fellow Moses who brought us up out of Egypt, we don't know what has happened to him.' [24]So I told them, 'Whoever has any gold jewelry, take it off.' Then they gave me the gold, and I threw it into the fire, and out came this calf!"

[25]Moses saw that the people were running wild and that Aaron had let them get out of control and so become a laughingstock to their enemies. [26]So he stood at the entrance to the camp and said, "Whoever is for the LORD, come to me." And all the Levites rallied to him.

[27]Then he said to them, "This is what the LORD, the God of Israel, says: 'Each man strap a sword to his side. Go back and forth through the camp from one end to the other, each killing his brother and friend and neighbor.'" [28]The Levites did as Moses commanded, and that day about three thousand of the people died. [29]Then Moses said, "You have been set apart to the LORD today, for you were against your own sons and brothers, and he has blessed you this day."

[30]The next day Moses said to the people, "You have committed a great sin. But now I will go up to the LORD; perhaps I can make atonement for your sin."

[31]So Moses went back to the LORD and said, "Oh, what a great sin these people have committed! They have made themselves gods of gold. [32]But now, please forgive their sin—but if not, then blot me out of the book you have written."

[33]The LORD replied to Moses, "Whoever has sinned against me I will blot out of my book. [34]Now go, lead the people to the place I spoke of, and my angel will go before you. However, when the time comes for me to punish, I will punish them for their sin."

[35]And the LORD struck the people with a plague because of what they did with the calf Aaron had made.

33 Then the LORD said to Moses, "Leave this place, you and the people you brought up out of Egypt, and go up to the land I promised on oath to Abraham, Isaac and Jacob, saying, 'I will give it to your descendants.' [2]I will send an angel before you and drive out the Canaanites, Amorites, Hittites, Perizzites, Hivites and Jebusites. [3]Go up to the land flowing with milk and honey. But I will not go with you, because you are a stiff-necked people and I might destroy you on the way."

33:3 Why the Israelites?

This remarkable scene shows Moses pleading with God not to abandon the Israelites, his chosen people. Eventually, God did agree to lead them on (verse 17). Why were the children of Israel chosen? Why not some other race? When the Bible touches on the question at all, it gives no comprehensive answer. Usually, the reply boils down to something like this, "I will have mercy on whom I will have mercy" (verse 19). God reserves the right to choose whomever he wants. But Exodus makes one thing clear. Israelites were not chosen because of their bravery or impressiveness or even faithfulness. Their selection was an act of God's pure grace; no one else can take the credit.

4When the people heard these distressing words, they began to mourn and no one put on any ornaments. 5For the LORD had said to Moses, "Tell the Israelites, 'You are a stiff-necked people. If I were to go with you even for a moment, I might destroy you. Now take off your ornaments and I will decide what to do with you.'" 6So the Israelites stripped off their ornaments at Mount Horeb.

The Tent of Meeting

7Now Moses used to take a tent and pitch it outside the camp some distance away, calling it the "tent of meeting." Anyone inquiring of the LORD would go to the tent of meeting outside the camp. 8And whenever Moses went out to the tent, all the people rose and stood at the entrances to their tents, watching Moses until he entered the tent. 9As Moses went into the tent, the pillar of cloud would come down and stay at the entrance, while the LORD spoke with Moses. 10Whenever the people saw the pillar of cloud standing at the entrance to the tent, they all stood and worshiped, each at the entrance to his tent. 11The LORD would speak to Moses face to face, as a man speaks with his friend. Then Moses would return to the camp, but his young aide Joshua son of Nun did not leave the tent.

Moses and the Glory of the LORD

12Moses said to the LORD, "You have been telling me, 'Lead these people,' but you have not let me know whom you will send with me. You have said, 'I know you by name and you have found favor with me.' 13If you are pleased with me, teach me your ways so I may know you and continue to find favor with you. Remember that this nation is your people." 14The LORD replied, "My Presence will go with you, and I will give you rest."

15Then Moses said to him, "If your Presence does not go with us, do not send us up from here. 16How will anyone know that you are pleased with me and with your people unless you go with us? What else will distinguish me and your people from all the other people on the face of the earth?"

17And the LORD said to Moses, "I will do the very thing you have asked, because I am pleased with you and I know you by name."

18Then Moses said, "Now show me your glory."

19And the LORD said, "I will cause all my goodness to pass in front of you, and I will proclaim my name, the LORD, in your presence. I will have mercy on whom I will have mercy, and I will have compassion on whom I will have compassion. 20But," he said, "you cannot see my face, for no one may see me and live."

21Then the LORD said, "There is a place near me where you may stand on a rock. 22When my glory passes by, I will put you in a cleft in the rock and cover you with my hand until I have passed by. 23Then I will remove my hand and you will see my back; but my face must not be seen."

The New Stone Tablets

34 The LORD said to Moses, "Chisel out two stone tablets like the first ones, and I will write on them the words that were on the first tablets, which you broke. 2Be ready in the morning, and then come up on Mount Sinai. Present yourself to me there on top of the mountain. 3No one is to come with you or be seen anywhere on the mountain; not even the flocks and herds may graze in front of the mountain."

4So Moses chiseled out two stone tablets like the first ones and went up Mount Sinai early in the morning, as the LORD had commanded him; and he carried the two stone tablets in his hands. 5Then the LORD came down in the cloud and stood there with him and proclaimed his name, the LORD. 6And he passed in front of Moses, proclaiming, "The LORD, the LORD, the compassionate and gracious God, slow to anger, abounding

34:6–7 Capsule Description

The self-description of God found in these two verses became for the Jews a profound summary of God's nature. The Old Testament quotes or alludes to this passage more than any other.

in love and faithfulness, 7maintaining love to thousands, and forgiving wickedness, rebellion and sin. Yet he does not leave the guilty unpunished; he punishes the children and their children for the sin of the fathers to the third and fourth generation."

8Moses bowed to the ground at once and worshiped. 9"O Lord, if I have found favor in your eyes," he said, "then let the Lord go with us. Although this is a stiff-necked people, forgive our wickedness and our sin, and take us as your inheritance."

10Then the LORD said: "I am making a covenant with you. Before all your people I will do wonders never before done in any nation in all the world. The people you live among will see how awesome is the work that I, the LORD, will do for you. 11Obey what I command you today. I will drive out before you the Amorites, Canaanites, Hittites, Perizzites, Hivites and Jebusites. 12Be careful not to make a treaty with those who live in the land where you are going, or they will be a snare among you. 13Break down their altars, smash their sacred stones and cut down their

Asherah poles.[a] [14]Do not worship any other god, for the LORD, whose name is Jealous, is a jealous God.

[15]"Be careful not to make a treaty with those who live in the land; for when they prostitute themselves to their gods and sacrifice to them, they will invite you and you will eat their sacrifices. [16]And when you choose some of their daughters as wives for your sons and those daughters prostitute themselves to their gods, they will lead your sons to do the same.

[17]"Do not make cast idols.

[18]"Celebrate the Feast of Unleavened Bread. For seven days eat bread made without yeast, as I commanded you. Do this at the appointed time in the month of Abib, for in that month you came out of Egypt.

[19]"The first offspring of every womb belongs to me, including all the firstborn males of your livestock, whether from herd or flock. [20]Redeem the firstborn donkey with a lamb, but if you do not redeem it, break its neck. Redeem all your firstborn sons.

"No one is to appear before me empty-handed.

[21]"Six days you shall labor, but on the seventh day you shall rest; even during the plowing season and harvest you must rest.

[22]"Celebrate the Feast of Weeks with the first-fruits of the wheat harvest, and the Feast of Ingathering at the turn of the year.[b] [23]Three times a year all your men are to appear before the Sovereign LORD, the God of Israel. [24]I will drive out nations before you and enlarge your territory, and no one will covet your land when you go up three times each year to appear before the LORD your God.

[25]"Do not offer the blood of a sacrifice to me along with anything containing yeast, and do not let any of the sacrifice from the Passover Feast remain until morning.

[26]"Bring the best of the firstfruits of your soil to the house of the LORD your God.

"Do not cook a young goat in its mother's milk."

[27]Then the LORD said to Moses, "Write down these words, for in accordance with these words I have made a covenant with you and with Israel." [28]Moses was there with the LORD forty days and forty nights without eating bread or drinking water. And he wrote on the tablets the words of the covenant—the Ten Commandments.

The Radiant Face of Moses

[29]When Moses came down from Mount Sinai with the two tablets of the Testimony in his hands, he was not aware that his face was radiant because he had spoken with the LORD. [30]When Aaron and all the Israelites saw Moses, his face was radiant, and they were afraid to come near him. [31]But Moses called to them; so Aaron and all the leaders of the community came back to him, and he spoke to them. [32]Afterward all the Israelites came near him, and he gave them all the commands the LORD had given him on Mount Sinai.

[33]When Moses finished speaking to them, he put a veil over his face. [34]But whenever he entered the LORD's presence to speak with him, he removed the veil until he came out. And when he came out and told the Israelites what he had been commanded, [35]they saw that his face was radiant. Then Moses would put the veil back over his face until he went in to speak with the LORD.

Sabbath Regulations

35 Moses assembled the whole Israelite community and said to them, "These are the things the LORD has commanded you to do: [2]For six days, work is to be done, but the seventh day shall be your holy day, a Sabbath of rest to the LORD. Whoever does any work on it must be put to death. [3]Do not light a fire in any of your dwellings on the Sabbath day."

Materials for the Tabernacle

[4]Moses said to the whole Israelite community, "This is what the LORD has commanded: [5]From what you have, take an offering for the LORD. Everyone who is willing is to bring to the LORD an offering of gold, silver and bronze; [6]blue, purple and scarlet yarn and fine linen; goat hair; [7]ram skins dyed red and hides of sea cows[c]; acacia wood; [8]olive oil for the light; spices for the anointing oil and for the fragrant incense; [9]and onyx stones and other gems to be mounted on the ephod and breastpiece.

[10]"All who are skilled among you are to come and make everything the LORD has commanded: [11]the tabernacle with its tent and its covering, clasps, frames, crossbars, posts and bases; [12]the ark with its poles and the atonement cover and the curtain that shields it; [13]the table with its poles and all its articles and the bread of the Presence; [14]the lampstand that is for light with its accessories, lamps and oil for the light; [15]the altar of incense with its poles, the anointing oil and the fragrant incense; the curtain for the doorway at the entrance to the tabernacle; [16]the altar of burnt offering with its bronze grating, its poles and all its utensils; the bronze basin with its stand; [17]the curtains of the courtyard with its posts and bases, and the curtain for the entrance to the courtyard; [18]the tent pegs for the tabernacle and for the courtyard, and their ropes; [19]the woven garments worn for ministering in the sanctuary—both the

---

[a] 13 That is, symbols of the goddess Asherah   [b] 22 That is, in the fall   [c] 7 That is, dugongs; also in verse 23

sacred garments for Aaron the priest and the garments for his sons when they serve as priests."

²⁰Then the whole Israelite community withdrew from Moses' presence, ²¹and everyone who was willing and whose heart moved him came and brought an offering to the LORD for the work on the Tent of Meeting, for all its service, and for the sacred garments. ²²All who were willing, men

and women alike, came and brought gold jewelry of all kinds: brooches, earrings, rings and ornaments. They all presented their gold as a wave offering to the LORD. ²³Everyone who had blue, purple or scarlet yarn or fine linen, or goat hair, ram skins dyed red or hides of sea cows brought them. ²⁴Those presenting an offering of silver or bronze brought it as an offering to the LORD, and

A Portable Cathedral
An unlikely sight in the desert

IN A.D. 1144 A GREAT building began to take shape in a village in northwest France. Enthusiasm for the project soon spread across the entire country, and volunteer workers streamed to the site. Working together, the people managed to construct one of the most beautiful buildings in the world, the magnificent cathedral at Chartres.

Fifty years later, after a terrible fire, the villagers of France rebuilt their cathedral from scratch. Today, tourists throng to marvel at what was splendidly fashioned to the glory of God so long ago.

> *And everyone who was willing and whose heart moved him came and brought an offering to the LORD for the work on the Tent of Meeting.   35:21*

Inspired Builders

A work of art took shape in similar fashion thousands of years earlier than Chartres, and the last chapters of Exodus provide a wealth of details. In a hostile desert landscape, a tribe of just-liberated slaves built something of exquisite beauty: a portable cathedral, or tabernacle.

God directed the project personally, specially endowing the craftsmen with skill (31:1–6) and elaborating right down to the color choice of woven yarns, the precise length of curtains and wooden frames, and the design of gold filigree. The people of Israel joined together in a flurry of activity, carefully following God's pattern. A ton of gold went into the project, as well as nearly four tons of silver and stockpiles of precious gems and rare woods.

God Moves In

After describing the tabernacle construction in great detail, the Bible devotes just five verses, the last five in Exodus, to its culmination. In a matter-of-fact tone, those sentences record a remarkable event.

Throughout the book of Exodus God had been progressively revealing himself to Moses: once in a burning bush, once in a mysterious appearance beside a rock, once on a trembling mountain, and often in a cloud-covered Tent of Meeting. God's presence caused such fear and awe that the people of Israel begged that he not speak to them directly (20:19). When Moses had come down from Mount Sinai after meeting with God, he glowed as if radioactive, and everyone was too frightened to go near him (34:30).

Yet, on the day the tabernacle was completed, this same God moved in. His glory filled the new tabernacle. God took up residence with his people.

A Visible Reminder

From then on, whenever the Israelites marched or camped, their portable cathedral stayed in the exact center of the camp, with their tents and personal belongings radiating out from the Most Holy Place and ark of the covenant. The tabernacle gave them a visible reminder of God's central place. Each day priests performed functions of sacrifice and worship there.

The story of the tabernacle, which takes up one-third of Exodus, reveals much about the character of God. He can never be taken lightly—the rituals here and in the next three books show that God must be approached with care and reverence. He cannot be experienced directly, in his fullness, by ordinary people; a holy God is simply too overwhelming. Even Moses, Exodus says, could not look on God's face and live (33:20).

And yet, amazingly, that same God who seemed so distant came near. Despite the huge gulf separating God and humanity—a gulf that all the rules on holiness and purification only hint at—God allowed personal access to himself. He made himself available.

Life Questions: Where does God "live" now?

everyone who had acacia wood for any part of the work brought it. [25]Every skilled woman spun with her hands and brought what she had spun—blue, purple or scarlet yarn or fine linen. [26]And all the women who were willing and had the skill spun the goat hair. [27]The leaders brought onyx stones and other gems to be mounted on the ephod and breastpiece. [28]They also brought spices and olive oil for the light and for the anointing oil and for the fragrant incense. [29]All the Israelite men and women who were willing brought to the LORD freewill offerings for all the work the LORD through Moses had commanded them to do.

Bezalel and Oholiab

[30]Then Moses said to the Israelites, "See, the LORD has chosen Bezalel son of Uri, the son of Hur, of the tribe of Judah, [31]and he has filled him with the Spirit of God, with skill, ability and knowledge in all kinds of crafts— [32]to make artistic designs for work in gold, silver and bronze, [33]to cut and set stones, to work in wood and to engage in all kinds of artistic craftsmanship. [34]And he has given both him and Oholiab son of Ahisamach, of the tribe of Dan, the ability to teach others. [35]He has filled them with skill to do all kinds of work as craftsmen, designers, embroiderers in blue, purple and scarlet yarn and fine linen, and weavers—all of them master

36 craftsmen and designers. [1]So Bezalel, Oholiab and every skilled person to whom the LORD has given skill and ability to know how to carry out all the work of constructing the sanctuary are to do the work just as the Lord has commanded."

[2]Then Moses summoned Bezalel and Oholiab and every skilled person to whom the LORD had given ability and who was willing to come and do the work. [3]They received from Moses all the offerings the Israelites had brought to carry out the work of constructing the sanctuary. And the people continued to bring freewill offerings morning after morning. [4]So all the skilled craftsmen who were doing all the work on the sanctuary left their work [5]and said to Moses, "The people are bringing more than enough for doing the work the LORD commanded to be done."

[6]Then Moses gave an order and they sent this word throughout the camp: "No man or woman is to make anything else as an offering for the sanctuary." And so the people were restrained from bringing more, [7]because what they already had was more than enough to do all the work.

The Tabernacle

[8]All the skilled men among the workmen made the tabernacle with ten curtains of finely twisted linen and blue, purple and scarlet yarn, with cherubim worked into them by a skilled craftsman. [9]All the curtains were the same size—twenty-eight cubits long and four cubits wide.[a] [10]They joined five of the curtains together and did the same with the other five. [11]Then they

made loops of blue material along the edge of the end curtain in one set, and the same was done with the end curtain in the other set. [12]They also made fifty loops on one curtain and fifty loops on the end curtain of the other set, with the loops opposite each other. [13]Then they made fifty gold clasps and used them to fasten the two sets of curtains together so that the tabernacle was a unit.

[14]They made curtains of goat hair for the tent over the tabernacle—eleven altogether. [15]All eleven curtains were the same size—thirty cubits long and four cubits wide.[b] [16]They joined five of the curtains into one set and the other six into another set. [17]Then they made fifty loops along the edge of the end curtain in one set and also along the edge of the end curtain in the other set. [18]They made fifty bronze clasps to fasten the tent together as a unit. [19]Then they made for the tent a covering of ram skins dyed red, and over that a covering of hides of sea cows.[c]

[20]They made upright frames of acacia wood for the tabernacle. [21]Each frame was ten cubits long and a cubit and a half wide,[d] [22]with two projections set parallel to each other. They made all the frames of the tabernacle in this way. [23]They made twenty frames for the south side of the tabernacle [24]and made forty silver bases to go under them—two bases for each frame, one under each projection. [25]For the other side, the north side of the tabernacle, they made twenty frames [26]and forty silver bases—two under each frame. [27]They made six frames for the far end, that is, the west end of the tabernacle, [28]and two frames were made for the corners of the tabernacle at the far end. [29]At these two corners the

---

[a]9 That is, about 42 feet (about 12.5 meters) long and 6 feet (about 1.8 meters) wide (about 13.5 meters) long and 6 feet (about 1.8 meters) wide (about 4.5 meters) long and 2 1/4 feet (about 0.7 meter) wide   [b]15 That is, about 45 feet   [c]19 That is, dugongs   [d]21 That is, about 15 feet

frames were double from the bottom all the way to the top and fitted into a single ring; both were made alike. ³⁰So there were eight frames and sixteen silver bases—two under each frame.

³¹They also made crossbars of acacia wood: five for the frames on one side of the tabernacle, ³²five for those on the other side, and five for the frames on the west, at the far end of the tabernacle. ³³They made the center crossbar so that it extended from end to end at the middle of the frames. ³⁴They overlaid the frames with gold and made gold rings to hold the crossbars. They also overlaid the crossbars with gold.

³⁵They made the curtain of blue, purple and scarlet yarn and finely twisted linen, with cherubim worked into it by a skilled craftsman. ³⁶They made four posts of acacia wood for it and overlaid them with gold. They made gold hooks for them and cast their four silver bases. ³⁷For the entrance to the tent they made a curtain of blue, purple and scarlet yarn and finely twisted linen—the work of an embroiderer; ³⁸and they made five posts with hooks for them. They overlaid the tops of the posts and their bands with gold and made their five bases of bronze.

The Ark

37 Bezalel made the ark of acacia wood—two and a half cubits long, a cubit and a half

37:1 Sacred Furniture

In contrast to the elaborate worship sites of the pagans, the Hebrews' tabernacle was sparsely furnished and decorated. Obviously God did not need a place to live. Rather, the furnishings mentioned in this passage—only six pieces— had a specific purpose in showing the proper way for human beings to approach God.

wide, and a cubit and a half high.ᵃ ²He overlaid it with pure gold, both inside and out, and made a gold molding around it. ³He cast four gold rings for it and fastened them to its four feet, with two rings on one side and two rings on the other. ⁴Then he made poles of acacia wood and overlaid them with gold. ⁵And he inserted the poles into the rings on the sides of the ark to carry it.

⁶He made the atonement cover of pure gold— two and a half cubits long and a cubit and a half wide.ᵇ ⁷Then he made two cherubim out of hammered gold at the ends of the cover. ⁸He made one cherub on one end and the second cherub on the other; at the two ends he made

them of one piece with the cover. ⁹The cherubim had their wings spread upward, overshadowing the cover with them. The cherubim faced each other, looking toward the cover.

The Table

¹⁰Theyᶜ made the table of acacia wood—two cubits long, a cubit wide, and a cubit and a half high.ᵈ ¹¹Then they overlaid it with pure gold and made a gold molding around it. ¹²They also made around it a rim a handbreadthᵉ wide and put a gold molding on the rim. ¹³They cast four gold rings for the table and fastened them to the four corners, where the four legs were. ¹⁴The rings were put close to the rim to hold the poles used in carrying the table. ¹⁵The poles for carrying the table were made of acacia wood and were overlaid with gold. ¹⁶And they made from pure gold the articles for the table—its plates and dishes and bowls and its pitchers for the pouring out of drink offerings.

The Lampstand

¹⁷They made the lampstand of pure gold and hammered it out, base and shaft; its flowerlike cups, buds and blossoms were of one piece with it. ¹⁸Six branches extended from the sides of the lampstand—three on one side and three on the other. ¹⁹Three cups shaped like almond flowers with buds and blossoms were on one branch, three on the next branch and the same for all six branches extending from the lampstand. ²⁰And on the lampstand were four cups shaped like almond flowers with buds and blossoms. ²¹One bud was under the first pair of branches extending from the lampstand, a second bud under the second pair, and a third bud under the third pair—six branches in all. ²²The buds and the branches were all of one piece with the lampstand, hammered out of pure gold.

²³They made its seven lamps, as well as its wick trimmers and trays, of pure gold. ²⁴They made the lampstand and all its accessories from one talentᶠ of pure gold.

The Altar of Incense

²⁵They made the altar of incense out of acacia wood. It was square, a cubit long and a cubit wide, and two cubits highᵍ—its horns of one piece with it. ²⁶They overlaid the top and all the sides and the horns with pure gold, and made a gold molding around it. ²⁷They made two gold rings below the molding—two on opposite sides—to hold the poles used to carry it. ²⁸They

---

ᵃ1 That is, about 3 3/4 feet (about 1.1 meters) long and 2 1/4 feet (about 0.7 meter) wide and high   ᵇ6 That is, about 3 3/4 feet (about 1.1 meters) long and 2 1/4 feet (about 0.7 meter) wide   ᶜ10 Or *He*; also in verses 11-29   ᵈ10 That is, about 3 feet (about 0.9 meter) long, 1 1/2 feet (about 0.5 meter) wide, and 2 1/4 feet (about 0.7 meter) high   ᵉ12 That is, about 3 inches (about 8 centimeters)   ᶠ24 That is, about 75 pounds (about 34 kilograms)   ᵍ25 That is, about 1 1/2 feet (about 0.5 meter) long and wide, and about 3 feet (about 0.9 meter) high

made the poles of acacia wood and overlaid them with gold.

²⁹They also made the sacred anointing oil and the pure, fragrant incense—the work of a perfumer.

The Altar of Burnt Offering

38 They[a] built the altar of burnt offering of acacia wood, three cubits[b] high; it was square, five cubits long and five cubits wide.[c] ²They made a horn at each of the four corners, so that the horns and the altar were of one piece, and they overlaid the altar with bronze. ³They made all its utensils of bronze—its pots, shovels, sprinkling bowls, meat forks and firepans. ⁴They made a grating for the altar, a bronze network, to be under its ledge, halfway up the altar. ⁵They cast bronze rings to hold the poles for the four corners of the bronze grating. ⁶They made the poles of acacia wood and overlaid them with bronze. ⁷They inserted the poles into the rings so they would be on the sides of the altar for carrying it. They made it hollow, out of boards.

Basin for Washing

⁸They made the bronze basin and its bronze stand from the mirrors of the women who served at the entrance to the Tent of Meeting.

The Courtyard

⁹Next they made the courtyard. The south side was a hundred cubits[d] long and had curtains

> ### 38:9–13 Tabernacle Layout
>
> *Unlike a church or synagogue, neither the tabernacle nor temple functioned as a gathering place for public meetings. Worshipers entered a large, open courtyard area to present their offerings and sacrifices. After receiving the offerings, the priests approached the Holy Place, which contained some of the sacred furniture. Only the high priest could go further, into the Most Holy Place where the ark of the covenant stayed, and he did so only once a year, on the Day of Atonement.*

of finely twisted linen, ¹⁰with twenty posts and twenty bronze bases, and with silver hooks and bands on the posts. ¹¹The north side was also a hundred cubits long and had twenty posts and twenty bronze bases, with silver hooks and bands on the posts.

¹²The west end was fifty cubits[e] wide and had curtains, with ten posts and ten bases, with silver hooks and bands on the posts. ¹³The east end, toward the sunrise, was also fifty cubits wide. ¹⁴Curtains fifteen cubits[f] long were on one side of the entrance, with three posts and three bases, ¹⁵and curtains fifteen cubits long were on the other side of the entrance to the courtyard, with three posts and three bases. ¹⁶All the curtains around the courtyard were of finely twisted linen. ¹⁷The bases for the posts were bronze. The hooks and bands on the posts were silver, and their tops were overlaid with silver; so all the posts of the courtyard had silver bands.

¹⁸The curtain for the entrance to the courtyard was of blue, purple and scarlet yarn and finely twisted linen—the work of an embroiderer. It was twenty cubits[g] long and, like the curtains of the courtyard, five cubits[h] high, ¹⁹with four posts and four bronze bases. Their hooks and bands were silver, and their tops were overlaid with silver. ²⁰All the tent pegs of the tabernacle and of the surrounding courtyard were bronze.

The Materials Used

²¹These are the amounts of the materials used for the tabernacle, the tabernacle of the Testimony, which were recorded at Moses' command by the Levites under the direction of Ithamar son of Aaron, the priest. ²²(Bezalel son of Uri, the son of Hur, of the tribe of Judah, made everything the LORD commanded Moses; ²³with him was Oholiab son of Ahisamach, of the tribe of Dan—a craftsman and designer, and an embroiderer in blue, purple and scarlet yarn and fine linen.) ²⁴The total amount of the gold from the wave offering used for all the work on the sanctuary was 29 talents and 730 shekels,[i] according to the sanctuary shekel.

²⁵The silver obtained from those of the community who were counted in the census was 100 talents and 1,775 shekels,[j] according to the sanctuary shekel— ²⁶one beka per person, that is, half a shekel,[k] according to the sanctuary shekel, from everyone who had crossed over to those counted, twenty years old or more, a total of 603,550 men. ²⁷The 100 talents[l] of silver were used to cast the bases for the sanctuary and for the curtain—100 bases from the 100 talents, one talent for each base. ²⁸They used the 1,775 shekels[m] to make the hooks for the posts, to overlay

---

a 1 Or *He*; also in verses 2-9   *b 1* That is, about 4 1/2 feet (about 1.3 meters)   *c 1* That is, about 7 1/2 feet (about 2.3 meters) long and wide   *d 9* That is, about 150 feet (about 46 meters)   *e 12* That is, about 75 feet (about 23 meters)   *f 14* That is, about 22 1/2 feet (about 6.9 meters)   *g 18* That is, about 30 feet (about 9 meters)
h 18 That is, about 7 1/2 feet (about 2.3 meters)   *i 24* The weight of the gold was a little over one ton (about 1 metric ton).   *j 25* The weight of the silver was a little over 3 3/4 tons (about 3.4 metric tons).   *k 26* That is, about 1/5 ounce (about 5.5 grams)   *l 27* That is, about 3 3/4 tons (about 3.4 metric tons)   *m 28* That is, about 45 pounds (about 20 kilograms)

the tops of the posts, and to make their bands.

²⁹The bronze from the wave offering was 70 talents and 2,400 shekels.ᵃ ³⁰They used it to make the bases for the entrance to the Tent of Meeting, the bronze altar with its bronze grating and all its utensils, ³¹the bases for the surrounding courtyard and those for its entrance and all the tent pegs for the tabernacle and those for the surrounding courtyard.

The Priestly Garments

39 From the blue, purple and scarlet yarn they made woven garments for ministering in the sanctuary. They also made sacred garments for Aaron, as the LORD commanded Moses.

The Ephod

²Theyᵇ made the ephod of gold, and of blue, purple and scarlet yarn, and of finely twisted linen. ³They hammered out thin sheets of gold and cut strands to be worked into the blue, purple and scarlet yarn and fine linen—the work of a skilled craftsman. ⁴They made shoulder pieces for the ephod, which were attached to two of its corners, so it could be fastened. ⁵Its skillfully woven waistband was like it—of one piece with the ephod and made with gold, and with blue, purple and scarlet yarn, and with finely twisted linen, as the LORD commanded Moses.

⁶They mounted the onyx stones in gold filigree settings and engraved them like a seal with the names of the sons of Israel. ⁷Then they fastened them on the shoulder pieces of the ephod as memorial stones for the sons of Israel, as the LORD commanded Moses.

The Breastpiece

⁸They fashioned the breastpiece—the work of a skilled craftsman. They made it like the ephod: of gold, and of blue, purple and scarlet yarn, and of finely twisted linen. ⁹It was square—a spanᶜ long and a span wide—and folded double. ¹⁰Then they mounted four rows of precious stones on it. In the first row there was a ruby, a topaz and a beryl; ¹¹in the second row a turquoise, a sapphireᵈ and an emerald; ¹²in the third row a jacinth, an agate and an amethyst; ¹³in the fourth row a chrysolite, an onyx and a jasper.ᵉ They were mounted in gold filigree settings. ¹⁴There were twelve stones, one for each of the names of the sons of Israel, each engraved like a seal with the name of one of the twelve tribes.

¹⁵For the breastpiece they made braided chains of pure gold, like a rope. ¹⁶They made two gold filigree settings and two gold rings, and fastened the rings to two of the corners of the breastpiece. ¹⁷They fastened the two gold chains to the rings at the corners of the breastpiece, ¹⁸and the other ends of the chains to the two settings, attaching them to the shoulder pieces of the ephod at the front. ¹⁹They made two gold rings and attached them to the other two corners of the breastpiece on the inside edge next to the ephod. ²⁰Then they made two more gold rings and attached them to the bottom of the shoulder pieces on the front of the ephod, close to the seam just above the waistband of the ephod. ²¹They tied the rings of the breastpiece to the rings of the ephod with blue cord, connecting it to the waistband so that the breastpiece would not swing out from the ephod—as the LORD commanded Moses.

Other Priestly Garments

²²They made the robe of the ephod entirely of blue cloth—the work of a weaver— ²³with an opening in the center of the robe like the opening of a collar,ᶠ and a band around this opening, so that it would not tear. ²⁴They made pomegranates of blue, purple and scarlet yarn and finely twisted linen around the hem of the robe. ²⁵And they made bells of pure gold and attached them around the hem between the pomegranates. ²⁶The bells and pomegranates alternated around the hem of the robe to be worn for ministering, as the LORD commanded Moses.

²⁷For Aaron and his sons, they made tunics of fine linen—the work of a weaver— ²⁸and the turban of fine linen, the linen headbands and the undergarments of finely twisted linen. ²⁹The sash was of finely twisted linen and blue, purple and scarlet yarn—the work of an embroiderer—as the LORD commanded Moses.

³⁰They made the plate, the sacred diadem, out of pure gold and engraved on it, like an inscription on a seal: HOLY TO THE LORD. ³¹Then they fastened a blue cord to it to attach it to the turban, as the LORD commanded Moses.

Moses Inspects the Tabernacle

³²So all the work on the tabernacle, the Tent of Meeting, was completed. The Israelites did everything just as the LORD commanded Moses. ³³Then they brought the tabernacle to Moses: the tent and all its furnishings, its clasps, frames, crossbars, posts and bases; ³⁴the covering of ram skins dyed red, the covering of hides of sea cowsᵍ and the shielding curtain; ³⁵the ark of the Testimony with its poles and the atonement cover; ³⁶the table with all its articles and the bread of

ᵃ29 The weight of the bronze was about 2 1/2 tons (about 2.4 metric tons).   ᵇ2 Or *He*; also in verses 7, 8 and 22   ᶜ9 That is, about 9 inches (about 22 centimeters)   ᵈ11 Or *lapis lazuli*   ᵉ13 The precise identification of some of these precious stones is uncertain.   ᶠ23 The meaning of the Hebrew for this word is uncertain.   ᵍ34 That is, dugongs

the Presence; [37]the pure gold lampstand with its row of lamps and all its accessories, and the oil for the light; [38]the gold altar, the anointing oil, the fragrant incense, and the curtain for the

39:32 Following Orders

The last few chapters of Exodus repeat almost verbatim what has gone before; they simply record that the Israelites followed all of God's prior instructions for building the tabernacle. The phrase "as the LORD commanded" resonates like a drumbeat through this section. A people not known for following orders took the tabernacle project very seriously. It became for them not just a symbol, but the actual reality of God living in their midst. The tabernacle was the focal point of worship for 300 years, until the temple was built. Later, the apostle Paul used this imagery when he called believers God's "temple," or dwelling place.

entrance to the tent; [39]the bronze altar with its bronze grating, its poles and all its utensils; the basin with its stand; [40]the curtains of the courtyard with its posts and bases, and the curtain for the entrance to the courtyard; the ropes and tent pegs for the courtyard; all the furnishings for the tabernacle, the Tent of Meeting; [41]and the woven garments worn for ministering in the sanctuary, both the sacred garments for Aaron the priest and the garments for his sons when serving as priests.

[42]The Israelites had done all the work just as the LORD had commanded Moses. [43]Moses inspected the work and saw that they had done it just as the LORD had commanded. So Moses blessed them.

Setting Up the Tabernacle

40 Then the LORD said to Moses: [2]"Set up the tabernacle, the Tent of Meeting, on the first day of the first month. [3]Place the ark of the Testimony in it and shield the ark with the curtain. [4]Bring in the table and set out what belongs on it. Then bring in the lampstand and set up its lamps. [5]Place the gold altar of incense in front of the ark of the Testimony and put the curtain at the entrance to the tabernacle.

[6]"Place the altar of burnt offering in front of the entrance to the tabernacle, the Tent of Meeting; [7]place the basin between the Tent of Meeting and the altar and put water in it. [8]Set up the courtyard around it and put the curtain at the entrance to the courtyard.

[9]"Take the anointing oil and anoint the tabernacle and everything in it; consecrate it and all its furnishings, and it will be holy. [10]Then anoint the altar of burnt offering and all its utensils; consecrate the altar, and it will be most holy. [11]Anoint the basin and its stand and consecrate them.

[12]"Bring Aaron and his sons to the entrance to the Tent of Meeting and wash them with water. [13]Then dress Aaron in the sacred garments, anoint him and consecrate him so he may serve me as priest. [14]Bring his sons and dress them in tunics. [15]Anoint them just as you anointed their father, so they may serve me as priests. Their anointing will be to a priesthood that will continue for all generations to come." [16]Moses did everything just as the LORD commanded him.

[17]So the tabernacle was set up on the first day of the first month in the second year. [18]When Moses set up the tabernacle, he put the bases in place, erected the frames, inserted the crossbars and set up the posts. [19]Then he spread the tent over the tabernacle and put the covering over the tent, as the LORD commanded him.

[20]He took the Testimony and placed it in the ark, attached the poles to the ark and put the atonement cover over it. [21]Then he brought the ark into the tabernacle and hung the shielding curtain and shielded the ark of the Testimony, as the LORD commanded him.

[22]Moses placed the table in the Tent of Meeting on the north side of the tabernacle outside the curtain [23]and set out the bread on it before the LORD, as the LORD commanded him.

[24]He placed the lampstand in the Tent of Meeting opposite the table on the south side of the tabernacle [25]and set up the lamps before the LORD, as the LORD commanded him.

[26]Moses placed the gold altar in the Tent of Meeting in front of the curtain [27]and burned fragrant incense on it, as the LORD commanded him. [28]Then he put up the curtain at the entrance to the tabernacle.

[29]He set the altar of burnt offering near the entrance to the tabernacle, the Tent of Meeting, and offered on it burnt offerings and grain offerings, as the LORD commanded him.

[30]He placed the basin between the Tent of Meeting and the altar and put water in it for washing, [31]and Moses and Aaron and his sons used it to wash their hands and feet. [32]They washed whenever they entered the Tent of Meeting or approached the altar, as the LORD commanded Moses.

[33]Then Moses set up the courtyard around the tabernacle and altar and put up the curtain at the entrance to the courtyard. And so Moses finished the work.

The Glory of the LORD

[34]Then the cloud covered the Tent of Meeting, and the glory of the LORD filled the tabernacle.

[35]Moses could not enter the Tent of Meeting because the cloud had settled upon it, and the glory of the LORD filled the tabernacle.

[36]In all the travels of the Israelites, whenever the cloud lifted from above the tabernacle, they would set out; [37]but if the cloud did not lift, they did not set out—until the day it lifted. [38]So the cloud of the LORD was over the tabernacle by day, and fire was in the cloud by night, in the sight of all the house of Israel during all their travels.

LEVITICUS

Living with Fire
Dangerous material more powerful than the atom

L EVITICUS SEEMS MIGHTY STRANGE TO the modern world. Unlike most of the Bible, it has few personalities and stories, and no poetry. Instead, it is crammed full of detailed rules and procedures.

Its painstaking ritual is, however, strikingly similar to the procedures surrounding nuclear technology. The specialized clothing, the concern for purification, the precise handling of crucial materials—both nuclear workers and Old Testament priests share these. This similarity gives an important clue to understanding Leviticus.

> "'I will put my dwelling place among you, and I will not abhor you. I will walk among you and be your God, and you will be my people.'"
> 26:11–12

Cleaning Up a Nuclear Spill

At the Hanford plutonium separation plant in eastern Washington, plutonium and U-235 are kept in a special high-security vault, in brass cans wrapped three times in plastic. To move the radioactive material, specially trained handlers don white protection overalls and special breather masks. They never touch the materials except through a sealed "glove box."

If an accident occurs, such as a small fire ignited by the "hot" material, the entire area must be cleansed through laborious scrubbing with soap and water. Carefully trained workers dispose of the dirty water in a specially protected toxic waste area. Anyone contaminated must also be "cleansed" from the exposure. In extreme cases, she or he must stay away from other people for months.

These rigid rules grew out of hard experience. For decades no one knew the dangers of radioactivity. Workers who used radioactive materials to hand-paint the first "glow in the dark" watches licked their paintbrushes to get a fine tip; their supervisors said they would gain sex appeal. Instead, they got cancer. The introduction of nuclear weapons and nuclear power plants increased the amount of radioactive material being handled. Gradually scientists realized: If you are going to use the atom, you must adopt procedures to fit its power.

The Intimate Presence of God

Leviticus reads something like a training manual for atomic plant workers. Its "dangerous material," however, is more powerful than the atom. Leviticus gives exhaustive detail on how to live with God.

A pamphlet on "how to survive a nuclear accident" may be dull if read on vacation, but it's gripping if read in a vibrating nuclear reactor. Similarly, Leviticus is dull if you do not realize the wonderful news behind it: God, the Creator of the universe, has entered the life of a small and insignificant tribe. The Israelites could not merely fit this God into their lives. They needed to restructure their lives—food, sex, economics—to fit with his. It was essential not just for priests, but for everyone.

Ignoring the operations manual could be deadly. It was for Aaron's two sons (chapter 10).

Free from Contamination

Today, because of Jesus Christ, we don't live in the world of Leviticus. Jesus' perfect self-sacrifice made the daily sacrifice of animals unnecessary. He replaced the high priest as our representative before God. Jesus cleanses the real source of contamination, our sinful nature. Leviticus was meant to teach people some basic truths about God, and when their lessons were complete, they could go on to bigger and better things. (The New Testament book of Hebrews spells out this graduation.)

Yet we need to be reminded of the principles Leviticus taught. It tells us that God was then, as he is today, "a consuming fire" (Hebrews 12:29). He has taught us how to live with that fire, not because we deserved to know, but because he wanted our company. We dare not treat him lightly.

How to Read Leviticus

Many well-intentioned readers, determined to read the Bible from beginning to end, bog down in Leviticus. It's a lawbook, a procedural manual for getting along with a holy and powerful God. Sheer detail can bore you, especially if you miss the point behind it.

When you read the Bible, careful attention to detail is usually a key to understanding. In Leviticus, however, you will get more from looking at the big picture than from studying the details. Some laws we simply don't understand. But Leviticus as a whole shows what kind of people God wanted the Israelites to be. As you read, keep your mind on the big picture. Pay special attention to the explanatory notes. Try to imagine how these laws affected everyday life. Keep asking yourself: How would these laws make the Israelites different from other people—and why were those differences important to God?

3-TRACK READING PLAN

For an explanation and complete listing of the 3-track reading plan, turn to page 7.

TRACK 1: **Two-Week Courses on the Bible**
See page 7 for information on these courses.

TRACK 2: **An Overview of Leviticus in 1 Day**
☐ Day 1. Read the Introduction to Leviticus and chapter 26, which summarizes the purpose of God's laws. Scan through the sectional headings of the book to get an idea of what subjects it covers.

Now turn to page 9 for your next Track 2 reading project.

TRACK 3: **All of Leviticus in 26 Days**
After you have read through Leviticus, turn to pages 10–14 for your next Track 3 reading project.

☐1 ☐2 ☐3 ☐4 ☐5 ☐6 ☐7 ☐8
☐9 ☐10 ☐11–12 ☐13 ☐14 ☐15 ☐16 ☐17
☐18 ☐19 ☐20 ☐21 ☐22 ☐23 ☐24 ☐25
☐26 ☐27

The Burnt Offering

1 The LORD called to Moses and spoke to him from the Tent of Meeting. He said, ²"Speak to the Israelites and say to them: 'When any of you brings an offering to the LORD, bring as your offering an animal from either the herd or the flock.

³"'If the offering is a burnt offering from the herd, he is to offer a male without defect. He must present it at the entrance to the Tent of Meeting so that it*ᵃ* will be acceptable to the LORD. ⁴He is to lay his hand on the head of the burnt offering, and it will be accepted on his behalf to make atonement for him. ⁵He is to slaughter the young bull before the LORD, and then Aaron's sons the priests shall bring the blood and sprinkle it against the altar on all sides at the entrance to the Tent of Meeting. ⁶He is to skin the burnt offering and cut it into pieces. ⁷The sons of Aaron the priest are to put fire on the altar and arrange wood on the fire. ⁸Then Aaron's sons the priests shall arrange the pieces, including the head and the fat, on the burning wood that is on the altar. ⁹He is to wash the inner parts and the legs with water, and the priest is to burn all of it on the altar. It is a burnt offering, an offering made by fire, an aroma pleasing to the LORD.

¹⁰"'If the offering is a burnt offering from the flock, from either the sheep or the goats, he is to offer a male without defect. ¹¹He is to slaughter it at the north side of the altar before the LORD, and Aaron's sons the priests shall sprinkle its blood against the altar on all sides. ¹²He is to cut it into pieces, and the priest shall arrange them, including the head and the fat, on the burning wood that is on the altar. ¹³He is to wash the inner parts and the legs with water, and the priest is to bring all of it and burn it on the altar. It is a burnt offering, an offering made by fire, an aroma pleasing to the LORD.

¹⁴"'If the offering to the LORD is a burnt offering of birds, he is to offer a dove or a young pigeon. ¹⁵The priest shall bring it to the altar,

ᵃ3 Or he

wring off the head and burn it on the altar; its blood shall be drained out on the side of the altar. [16]He is to remove the crop with its contents[a] and throw it to the east side of the altar, where

the ashes are. [17]He shall tear it open by the wings, not severing it completely, and then the priest shall burn it on the wood that is on the fire on the altar. It is a burnt offering, an offering made by fire, an aroma pleasing to the LORD.

The Grain Offering

2 "'When someone brings a grain offering to the LORD, his offering is to be of fine flour. He is to pour oil on it, put incense on it [2]and take it to Aaron's sons the priests. The priest shall take a handful of the fine flour and oil, together with all the incense, and burn this as a memorial portion on the altar, an offering made by fire, an aroma pleasing to the LORD. [3]The rest of the grain offering belongs to Aaron and his sons; it is a most holy part of the offerings made to the LORD by fire.

[4]"'If you bring a grain offering baked in an oven, it is to consist of fine flour: cakes made without yeast and mixed with oil, or[b] wafers made without yeast and spread with oil. [5]If your grain offering is prepared on a griddle, it is to be made of fine flour mixed with oil, and without yeast. [6]Crumble it and pour oil on it; it is a grain offering. [7]If your grain offering is cooked in a pan, it is to be made of fine flour and oil. [8]Bring the grain offering made of these things to the LORD; present it to the priest, who shall take it to the altar. [9]He shall take out the memorial portion from the grain offering and burn it on the altar as an offering made by fire, an aroma pleasing to the LORD. [10]The rest of the grain offering belongs to Aaron and his sons; it is a most holy part of the offerings made to the LORD by fire.

[11]"'Every grain offering you bring to the LORD must be made without yeast, for you are not to burn any yeast or honey in an offering made to the LORD by fire. [12]You may bring them to the

LORD as an offering of the firstfruits, but they are not to be offered on the altar as a pleasing aroma. [13]Season all your grain offerings with salt. Do not leave the salt of the covenant of your God out of your grain offerings; add salt to all your offerings.

[14]"'If you bring a grain offering of firstfruits to the LORD, offer crushed heads of new grain roasted in the fire. [15]Put oil and incense on it; it is a grain offering. [16]The priest shall burn the memorial portion of the crushed grain and the oil, together with all the incense, as an offering made to the LORD by fire.

The Fellowship Offering

3 "'If someone's offering is a fellowship offering,[c] and he offers an animal from the herd, whether male or female, he is to present before the LORD an animal without defect. [2]He is to lay his hand on the head of his offering and slaughter it at the entrance to the Tent of Meeting. Then Aaron's sons the priests shall sprinkle the blood against the altar on all sides. [3]From the fellowship offering he is to bring a sacrifice made to the LORD by fire: all the fat that covers the inner parts or is connected to them, [4]both kidneys with the fat on them near the loins, and the covering of the liver, which he will remove with the kidneys. [5]Then Aaron's sons are to burn it on the altar on top of the burnt offering that is on the burning wood, as an offering made by fire, an aroma pleasing to the LORD.

[6]"'If he offers an animal from the flock as a fellowship offering to the LORD, he is to offer a male or female without defect. [7]If he offers a lamb, he is to present it before the LORD. [8]He is to lay his hand on the head of his offering and slaughter it in front of the Tent of Meeting. Then Aaron's sons shall sprinkle its blood against the altar on all sides. [9]From the fellowship offering he is to bring a sacrifice made to the LORD by fire: its fat, the entire fat tail cut off close to the backbone, all the fat that covers the inner parts or is connected to them, [10]both kidneys with the fat on them near the loins, and the covering of the liver, which he will remove with the kidneys. [11]The priest shall burn them on the altar as food, an offering made to the LORD by fire.

[12]"'If his offering is a goat, he is to present it before the LORD. [13]He is to lay his hand on its head and slaughter it in front of the Tent of Meeting. Then Aaron's sons shall sprinkle its blood against the altar on all sides. [14]From what he offers he is to make this offering to the LORD by fire: all the fat that covers the inner parts or is connected to them, [15]both kidneys with the fat on them near the loins, and the covering of the liver, which he will remove with the kidneys. [16]The

---

[a]16 Or *crop and the feathers*; the meaning of the Hebrew for this word is uncertain.   [b]4 Or *and*   [c]1 Traditionally *peace offering*; also in verses 3, 6 and 9

priest shall burn them on the altar as food, an offering made by fire, a pleasing aroma. All the fat is the LORD's.

[17] "This is a lasting ordinance for the generations to come, wherever you live: You must not eat any fat or any blood.'"

The Sin Offering

4 The LORD said to Moses, [2]"Say to the Israelites: 'When anyone sins unintentionally and does what is forbidden in any of the LORD's commands—

[3] "'If the anointed priest sins, bringing guilt on the people, he must bring to the LORD a young bull without defect as a sin offering for the sin he

4:3 The One for the Many

For his sin, a priest had to sacrifice one bull—the same sacrifice required for a sin by the whole community (verses 13–14). The two sins were, in a sense, equal, for the high priest represented the whole community before God. The belief that a single purified individual can stand up for a nation prepared the way for Jesus, whose sinless obedience stands before God in our place.

has committed. [4]He is to present the bull at the entrance to the Tent of Meeting before the LORD. He is to lay his hand on its head and slaughter it before the LORD. [5]Then the anointed priest shall take some of the bull's blood and carry it into the Tent of Meeting. [6]He is to dip his finger into the blood and sprinkle some of it seven times before the LORD, in front of the curtain of the sanctuary. [7]The priest shall then put some of the blood on the horns of the altar of fragrant incense that is before the LORD in the Tent of Meeting. The rest of the bull's blood he shall pour out at the base of the altar of burnt offering at the entrance to the Tent of Meeting. [8]He shall remove all the fat from the bull of the sin offering—the fat that covers the inner parts or is connected to them, [9]both kidneys with the fat on them near the loins, and the covering of the liver, which he will remove with the kidneys— [10]just as the fat is removed from the ox[a] sacrificed as a fellowship offering.[b] Then the priest shall burn them on the altar of burnt offering. [11]But the hide of the bull and all its flesh, as well as the head and legs, the inner parts and offal— [12]that is, all the rest of the bull—he must take outside the camp to a place ceremonially clean, where the ashes are thrown, and burn it in a wood fire on the ash heap.

[13] "'If the whole Israelite community sins unintentionally and does what is forbidden in any of the LORD's commands, even though the community is unaware of the matter, they are guilty.

4:13 Ignorance Isn't Bliss

"I didn't know the speed limit had dropped to 30, officer. How can you give me a ticket?" Under the law, ignorance provides no excuse. This chapter and the next cover many instances of unintentional sin. Although held accountable for such wrongdoing, the Israelites could overcome their guilt by offering the prescribed sacrifices.

[14]When they become aware of the sin they committed, the assembly must bring a young bull as a sin offering and present it before the Tent of Meeting. [15]The elders of the community are to lay their hands on the bull's head before the LORD, and the bull shall be slaughtered before the LORD. [16]Then the anointed priest is to take some of the bull's blood into the Tent of Meeting. [17]He shall dip his finger into the blood and sprinkle it before the LORD seven times in front of the curtain. [18]He is to put some of the blood on the horns of the altar that is before the LORD in the Tent of Meeting. The rest of the blood he shall pour out at the base of the altar of burnt offering at the entrance to the Tent of Meeting. [19]He shall remove all the fat from it and burn it on the altar, [20]and do with this bull just as he did with the bull for the sin offering. In this way the priest will make atonement for them, and they will be forgiven. [21]Then he shall take the bull outside the camp and burn it as he burned the first bull. This is the sin offering for the community.

[22] "'When a leader sins unintentionally and does what is forbidden in any of the commands of the LORD his God, he is guilty. [23]When he is made aware of the sin he committed, he must bring as his offering a male goat without defect. [24]He is to lay his hand on the goat's head and slaughter it at the place where the burnt offering is slaughtered before the LORD. It is a sin offering. [25]Then the priest shall take some of the blood of the sin offering with his finger and put it on the horns of the altar of burnt offering and pour out the rest of the blood at the base of the altar. [26]He shall burn all the fat on the altar as he burned the fat of the fellowship offering. In this way the priest will make atonement for the man's sin, and he will be forgiven.

[27] "'If a member of the community sins unin-

---

[a]10 The Hebrew word can include both male and female. and 35   [b]10 Traditionally *peace offering*; also in verses 26, 31

tentionally and does what is forbidden in any of the LORD's commands, he is guilty. 28When he is made aware of the sin he committed, he must bring as his offering for the sin he committed a female goat without defect. 29He is to lay his hand on the head of the sin offering and slaughter it at the place of the burnt offering. 30Then the priest is to take some of the blood with his finger and put it on the horns of the altar of burnt offering and pour out the rest of the blood at the base of the altar. 31He shall remove all the fat, just as the fat is removed from the fellowship offering, and the priest shall burn it on the altar as an aroma pleasing to the LORD. In this way the priest will make atonement for him, and he will be forgiven.

32" 'If he brings a lamb as his sin offering, he is to bring a female without defect. 33He is to lay his hand on its head and slaughter it for a sin offering at the place where the burnt offering is slaughtered. 34Then the priest shall take some of the blood of the sin offering with his finger and put it on the horns of the altar of burnt offering and pour out the rest of the blood at the base of the altar. 35He shall remove all the fat, just as the fat is removed from the lamb of the fellowship offering, and the priest shall burn it on the altar on top of the offerings made to the LORD by fire. In this way the priest will make atonement for him for the sin he has committed, and he will be forgiven.

5 " 'If a person sins because he does not speak up when he hears a public charge to testify regarding something he has seen or learned about, he will be held responsible.

2" 'Or if a person touches anything ceremonially unclean—whether the carcasses of unclean wild animals or of unclean livestock or of unclean creatures that move along the ground—even though he is unaware of it, he has become unclean and is guilty.

3" 'Or if he touches human uncleanness—anything that would make him unclean—even though he is unaware of it, when he learns of it he will be guilty.

4" 'Or if a person thoughtlessly takes an oath to do anything, whether good or evil—in any matter one might carelessly swear about—even though he is unaware of it, in any case when he learns of it he will be guilty.

5" 'When anyone is guilty in any of these ways, he must confess in what way he has sinned 6and, as a penalty for the sin he has committed, he must bring to the LORD a female lamb or goat from the flock as a sin offering; and the priest shall make atonement for him for his sin.

7" 'If he cannot afford a lamb, he is to bring two doves or two young pigeons to the LORD as

a penalty for his sin—one for a sin offering and the other for a burnt offering. 8He is to bring them to the priest, who shall first offer the one for the sin offering. He is to wring its head from its neck, not severing it completely, 9and is to sprinkle some of the blood of the sin offering against the side of the altar; the rest of the blood must be drained out at the base of the altar. It is a sin offering. 10The priest shall then offer the other as a burnt offering in the prescribed way and make atonement for him for the sin he has committed, and he will be forgiven.

11" 'If, however, he cannot afford two doves or two young pigeons, he is to bring as an offering for his sin a tenth of an ephah*a* of fine flour for a sin offering. He must not put oil or incense on it, because it is a sin offering. 12He is to bring it to the priest, who shall take a handful of it as a memorial portion and burn it on the altar on top of the offerings made to the LORD by fire. It is a sin offering. 13In this way the priest will make atonement for him for any of these sins he has committed, and he will be forgiven. The rest of the offering will belong to the priest, as in the case of the grain offering.' "

The Guilt Offering

14The LORD said to Moses: 15"When a person commits a violation and sins unintentionally in regard to any of the LORD's holy things, he is to bring to the LORD as a penalty a ram from the flock, one without defect and of the proper value in silver, according to the sanctuary shekel.*b* It is a guilt offering. 16He must make restitution for what he has failed to do in regard to the holy things, add a fifth of the value to that and give it all to the priest, who will make atonement for him with the ram as a guilt offering, and he will be forgiven.

17"If a person sins and does what is forbidden in any of the LORD's commands, even though he does not know it, he is guilty and will be held responsible. 18He is to bring to the priest as a guilt offering a ram from the flock, one without defect and of the proper value. In this way the priest will make atonement for him for the wrong he has committed unintentionally, and he will be forgiven. 19It is a guilt offering; he has been guilty of*c* wrongdoing against the LORD."

6 The LORD said to Moses: 2"If anyone sins and is unfaithful to the LORD by deceiving his neighbor about something entrusted to him or left in his care or stolen, or if he cheats him, 3or if he finds lost property and lies about it, or if he swears falsely, or if he commits any such sin that people may do— 4when he thus sins and becomes guilty, he must return what he has stolen

---

a 11 That is, probably about 2 quarts (about 2 liters) *b 15* That is, about 2/5 ounce (about 11.5 grams)
c 19 Or *has made full expiation for his*

or taken by extortion, or what was entrusted to him, or the lost property he found, [5]or whatever it was he swore falsely about. He must make restitution in full, add a fifth of the value to it and give it all to the owner on the day he presents his guilt offering. [6]And as a penalty he must bring to the priest, that is, to the LORD, his guilt offering, a ram from the flock, one without defect and of the proper value. [7]In this way the priest will make atonement for him before the LORD, and he will be forgiven for any of these things he did that made him guilty."

The Burnt Offering

[8]The LORD said to Moses: [9]"Give Aaron and his sons this command: 'These are the regulations for the burnt offering: The burnt offering is to remain on the altar hearth throughout the night, till morning, and the fire must be kept burning on the altar. [10]The priest shall then put on his linen clothes, with linen undergarments next to his body, and shall remove the ashes of the burnt offering that the fire has consumed on the altar and place them beside the altar. [11]Then he is to take off these clothes and put on others,

The Reason for Sacrifice

Justice: Someone has to pay

WHEN YOU COMMIT A CRIME, you don't get off in court just by saying "Sorry, I'll try not to do it again." Justice requires that you pay for what you did.

The Israelites, therefore, could not just march into God's presence to fellowship with him. They had to bring sacrifices to pay, or "atone," for their inadequacies.

These sacrifices cost dearly. To subsistence farmers, a bull or goat represented a sizable contribution. Very poor people could give less—a pair of doves, or some flour. But, in all cases, a person would feel the cost, cost in terms of something he had worked for, something grown on his own farm.

> *"In this way the priest will make atonement for him for the sin he has committed, and he will be forgiven."*
> *4:35*

Up in Smoke

A good portion of the national economy went up in smoke each year: hundreds of animals and a lot of manpower to gather wood, keep the fire lit, and offer sacrifices. Since the Tent of Meeting stood at the center of the camp, the smell of the two-a-day sacrifices always hung over the Israelites. They rarely could afford meat, but every day they smelled the aroma of barbecue dedicated to God.

Offerings fell into three broad types. The guilt and sin offerings were usually offered first: they cleansed people from sin. Then came the burnt offerings, in which whole animals were burnt to ashes. Made at least twice a day, these sacrifices evidently expressed complete dedication to God. The final sacrifice was the fellowship offering, essentially a family meal shared in the presence of God. (The grain offerings were usually given along with one of the other offerings.)

The sequence of the offerings—forgiveness of sins, then total dedication, then fellowship—shows that their goal was fellowship with God. To reach that goal, forgiveness of sin and complete dedication to God were necessary.

Leviticus, however, does not explain this underlying philosophy; it reads more like an instruction manual on how to make sacrifices exactly the way God wanted. The exactness helped produce a proper attitude. You couldn't approach God carelessly. You had to be very careful to do just what he said, to obey him in every detail.

Can an Animal Really Pay?

The whole scene—with its concern for blood, priests, ritual—is strange to modern people. Just how can killing a goat make things right between God and people? Is the sacrifice of an animal really enough to "pay for" our mistakes? We may forget that throughout history, people have intuitively felt that sacrifice was needed to satisfy God. Many religions around the world still sacrifice today.

For us these sacrifices seem outmoded primarily because one great sacrifice—that of God's own Son—outdid them all. The animal sacrifices were not enough, ultimately, to pay for human sin. They prepared the way for a sacrifice that was.

The cost of an animal was substantial, but the true cost, even for us, is infinitely greater. Yet we don't have to pay the cost. Jesus paid it all.

Life Questions: Do you think of God as requiring sacrifice? How does the picture of God in Leviticus fit with your ideas about God?

and carry the ashes outside the camp to a place that is ceremonially clean. [12]The fire on the altar must be kept burning; it must not go out. Every morning the priest is to add firewood and

> ### 6:5–7 Double Jeopardy
>
> *An Israelite who committed a crime against another person (such as stealing) had two parties to reckon with. First, the offender had to make full restitution, along with a 20 percent penalty, to the person cheated. Second, he or she had to bring a special offering to God. A crime against another person also counted as a sin against God.*

arrange the burnt offering on the fire and burn the fat of the fellowship offerings[a] on it. [13]The fire must be kept burning on the altar continuously; it must not go out.

The Grain Offering

[14]" 'These are the regulations for the grain offering: Aaron's sons are to bring it before the LORD, in front of the altar. [15]The priest is to take a handful of fine flour and oil, together with all the incense on the grain offering, and burn the memorial portion on the altar as an aroma pleasing to the LORD. [16]Aaron and his sons shall eat the rest of it, but it is to be eaten without yeast in a holy place; they are to eat it in the courtyard of the Tent of Meeting. [17]It must not be baked with yeast; I have given it as their share of the offerings made to me by fire. Like the sin offering and the guilt offering, it is most holy. [18]Any male descendant of Aaron may eat it. It is his regular share of the offerings made to the LORD by fire for the generations to come. Whatever touches them will become holy.[b]' "

[19]The LORD also said to Moses, [20]"This is the offering Aaron and his sons are to bring to the LORD on the day he[c] is anointed: a tenth of an ephah[d] of fine flour as a regular grain offering, half of it in the morning and half in the evening. [21]Prepare it with oil on a griddle; bring it well-mixed and present the grain offering broken[e] in pieces as an aroma pleasing to the LORD. [22]The son who is to succeed him as anointed priest shall prepare it. It is the LORD's regular share and is to be burned completely. [23]Every grain offering of a priest shall be burned completely; it must not be eaten."

The Sin Offering

[24]The LORD said to Moses, [25]"Say to Aaron and his sons: 'These are the regulations for the sin offering: The sin offering is to be slaughtered before the LORD in the place the burnt offering is slaughtered; it is most holy. [26]The priest who offers it shall eat it; it is to be eaten in a holy place, in the courtyard of the Tent of Meeting. [27]Whatever touches any of the flesh will become holy, and if any of the blood is spattered on a garment, you must wash it in a holy place. [28]The clay pot the meat is cooked in must be broken; but if it is cooked in a bronze pot, the pot is to be scoured and rinsed with water. [29]Any male in a priest's family may eat it; it is most holy. [30]But any sin offering whose blood is brought into the Tent of Meeting to make atonement in the Holy Place must not be eaten; it must be burned.

The Guilt Offering

7 " 'These are the regulations for the guilt offering, which is most holy: [2]The guilt offering is to be slaughtered in the place where the burnt offering is slaughtered, and its blood is to be sprinkled against the altar on all sides. [3]All its fat shall be offered: the fat tail and the fat that covers the inner parts, [4]both kidneys with the fat on them near the loins, and the covering of the liver, which is to be removed with the kidneys. [5]The priest shall burn them on the altar as an offering made to the LORD by fire. It is a guilt offering. [6]Any male in a priest's family may eat it, but it must be eaten in a holy place; it is most holy.

[7]" 'The same law applies to both the sin offering and the guilt offering: They belong to the priest who makes atonement with them. [8]The priest who offers a burnt offering for anyone may keep its hide for himself. [9]Every grain offering baked in an oven or cooked in a pan or on a griddle belongs to the priest who offers it, [10]and every grain offering, whether mixed with oil or dry, belongs equally to all the sons of Aaron.

The Fellowship Offering

[11]" 'These are the regulations for the fellowship offering[f] a person may present to the LORD:

[12]" 'If he offers it as an expression of thankfulness, then along with this thank offering he is to offer cakes of bread made without yeast and mixed with oil, wafers made without yeast and spread with oil, and cakes of fine flour well-kneaded and mixed with oil. [13]Along with his fellowship offering of thanksgiving he is to present an offering with cakes of bread made with yeast. [14]He is to bring one of each kind as an offering, a contribution to the LORD; it belongs to the priest who sprinkles the blood of the fellowship offerings. [15]The meat of his fellowship offering of thanksgiving must be eaten on the day it

---

a12 Traditionally *peace offerings*   *b18* Or *Whoever touches them must be holy*; similarly in verse 27   *c20* Or *each*
d20 That is, probably about 2 quarts (about 2 liters)   *e21* The meaning of the Hebrew for this word is uncertain.
f11 Traditionally *peace offering*; also in verses 13-37

is offered; he must leave none of it till morning. ¹⁶"'If, however, his offering is the result of a vow or is a freewill offering, the sacrifice shall be eaten on the day he offers it, but anything left over may be eaten on the next day. ¹⁷Any meat of the sacrifice left over till the third day must be burned up. ¹⁸If any meat of the fellowship offering is eaten on the third day, it will not be accepted. It will not be credited to the one who offered it, for it is impure; the person who eats any of it will be held responsible.

¹⁹"'Meat that touches anything ceremonially unclean must not be eaten; it must be burned up. As for other meat, anyone ceremonially clean may eat it. ²⁰But if anyone who is unclean eats any meat of the fellowship offering belonging to the LORD, that person must be cut off from his people. ²¹If anyone touches something unclean—whether human uncleanness or an unclean animal or any unclean, detestable thing—and then eats any of the meat of the fellowship offering belonging to the LORD, that person must be cut off from his people.'"

Eating Fat and Blood Forbidden

²²The LORD said to Moses, ²³"Say to the Israelites: 'Do not eat any of the fat of cattle, sheep or goats. ²⁴The fat of an animal found dead or torn by wild animals may be used for any other purpose, but you must not eat it. ²⁵Anyone who eats the fat of an animal from which an offering by fire may be^a made to the LORD must be cut off from his people. ²⁶And wherever you live, you must not eat the blood of any bird or animal. ²⁷If anyone eats blood, that person must be cut off from his people.'"

The Priests' Share

²⁸The LORD said to Moses, ²⁹"Say to the Israelites: 'Anyone who brings a fellowship offering to the LORD is to bring part of it as his sacrifice to the LORD. ³⁰With his own hands he is to bring the offering made to the LORD by fire; he is to bring the fat, together with the breast, and wave the breast before the LORD as a wave offering. ³¹The priest shall burn the fat on the altar, but the breast belongs to Aaron and his sons. ³²You are to give the right thigh of your fellowship offerings to the priest as a contribution. ³³The son of Aaron who offers the blood and the fat of the fellowship offering shall have the right thigh as his share. ³⁴From the fellowship offerings of the Israelites, I have taken the breast that is waved and the thigh that is presented and have given them to Aaron the priest and his sons as their regular share from the Israelites.'"

³⁵This is the portion of the offerings made to the LORD by fire that were allotted to Aaron and his sons on the day they were presented to serve the LORD as priests. ³⁶On the day they were anointed, the LORD commanded that the Israelites give this to them as their regular share for the generations to come.

7:34 Priestly Privileges

Priests enjoyed certain privileges, such as exemption from military duty and the right to keep portions of the offerings as food. Yet the priests were not "holier than thou." They had to offer regular sacrifices for their own sins as well as for the sins of the people (9:7–12). The New Testament book of Hebrews uses this fact to underscore Christ's superiority: sinless, he offered a perfect, once-for-all sacrifice for the sake of others.

³⁷These, then, are the regulations for the burnt offering, the grain offering, the sin offering, the guilt offering, the ordination offering and the fellowship offering, ³⁸which the LORD gave Moses on Mount Sinai on the day he commanded the Israelites to bring their offerings to the LORD, in the Desert of Sinai.

The Ordination of Aaron and His Sons

8 The LORD said to Moses, ²"Bring Aaron and his sons, their garments, the anointing oil, the bull for the sin offering, the two rams and the basket containing bread made without yeast,

8:2 The First High Priest

God had set apart the tribe of Levi to perform religious duties for the entire nation. In this scene Moses' brother Aaron assumed the new office of high priest. The impressive public ceremony lasted eight days in all and culminated in a dramatic display of God's approval (9:24). From then on, the priesthood remained in Aaron's family.

³and gather the entire assembly at the entrance to the Tent of Meeting." ⁴Moses did as the LORD commanded him, and the assembly gathered at the entrance to the Tent of Meeting.

⁵Moses said to the assembly, "This is what the LORD has commanded to be done." ⁶Then Moses brought Aaron and his sons forward and washed them with water. ⁷He put the tunic on Aaron, tied the sash around him, clothed him with the robe and put the ephod on him. He also tied the ephod to him by its skillfully woven waistband; so it was fastened on him. ⁸He placed the breast-

^a25 Or *fire is*

piece on him and put the Urim and Thummim in the breastpiece. [9]Then he placed the turban on Aaron's head and set the gold plate, the sacred diadem, on the front of it, as the LORD commanded Moses.

[10]Then Moses took the anointing oil and anointed the tabernacle and everything in it, and so consecrated them. [11]He sprinkled some of the oil on the altar seven times, anointing the altar and all its utensils and the basin with its stand, to consecrate them. [12]He poured some of the anointing oil on Aaron's head and anointed him to consecrate him. [13]Then he brought Aaron's sons forward, put tunics on them, tied sashes around them and put headbands on them, as the LORD commanded Moses.

[14]He then presented the bull for the sin offering, and Aaron and his sons laid their hands on its head. [15]Moses slaughtered the bull and took some of the blood, and with his finger he put it on all the horns of the altar to purify the altar. He poured out the rest of the blood at the base of the altar. So he consecrated it to make atonement for it. [16]Moses also took all the fat around the inner parts, the covering of the liver, and both kidneys and their fat, and burned it on the altar. [17]But the bull with its hide and its flesh and its offal he burned up outside the camp, as the LORD commanded Moses.

[18]He then presented the ram for the burnt offering, and Aaron and his sons laid their hands on its head. [19]Then Moses slaughtered the ram and sprinkled the blood against the altar on all sides. [20]He cut the ram into pieces and burned the head, the pieces and the fat. [21]He washed the inner parts and the legs with water and burned the whole ram on the altar as a burnt offering, a pleasing aroma, an offering made to the LORD by fire, as the LORD commanded Moses.

[22]He then presented the other ram, the ram for the ordination, and Aaron and his sons laid their hands on its head. [23]Moses slaughtered the ram and took some of its blood and put it on the lobe of Aaron's right ear, on the thumb of his right hand and on the big toe of his right foot. [24]Moses also brought Aaron's sons forward and put some of the blood on the lobes of their right ears, on the thumbs of their right hands and on the big toes of their right feet. Then he sprinkled blood against the altar on all sides. [25]He took the fat, the fat tail, all the fat around the inner parts, the covering of the liver, both kidneys and their fat and the right thigh. [26]Then from the basket of bread made without yeast, which was before the LORD, he took a cake of bread, and one made with oil, and a wafer; he put these on the fat portions and on the right thigh. [27]He put all these

in the hands of Aaron and his sons and waved them before the LORD as a wave offering. [28]Then Moses took them from their hands and burned them on the altar on top of the burnt offering as an ordination offering, a pleasing aroma, an offering made to the LORD by fire. [29]He also took the breast—Moses' share of the ordination ram—and waved it before the LORD as a wave offering, as the LORD commanded Moses.

[30]Then Moses took some of the anointing oil and some of the blood from the altar and sprinkled them on Aaron and his garments and on his sons and their garments. So he consecrated Aaron and his garments and his sons and their garments.

[31]Moses then said to Aaron and his sons, "Cook the meat at the entrance to the Tent of Meeting and eat it there with the bread from the basket of ordination offerings, as I commanded, saying,[a] 'Aaron and his sons are to eat it.' [32]Then burn up the rest of the meat and the bread. [33]Do not leave the entrance to the Tent of Meeting for seven days, until the days of your ordination are completed, for your ordination will last seven days. [34]What has been done today was commanded by the LORD to make atonement for you. [35]You must stay at the entrance to the Tent of Meeting day and night for seven days and do what the LORD requires, so you will not die; for that is what I have been commanded." [36]So Aaron and his sons did everything the LORD commanded through Moses.

The Priests Begin Their Ministry

9 On the eighth day Moses summoned Aaron and his sons and the elders of Israel. [2]He said to Aaron, "Take a bull calf for your sin offering and a ram for your burnt offering, both without defect, and present them before the LORD. [3]Then say to the Israelites: 'Take a male goat for a sin offering, a calf and a lamb—both a year old and without defect—for a burnt offering, [4]and an ox[b] and a ram for a fellowship offering[c] to sacrifice before the LORD, together with a grain offering mixed with oil. For today the LORD will appear to you.'"

[5]They took the things Moses commanded to the front of the Tent of Meeting, and the entire assembly came near and stood before the LORD. [6]Then Moses said, "This is what the LORD has commanded you to do, so that the glory of the LORD may appear to you."

[7]Moses said to Aaron, "Come to the altar and sacrifice your sin offering and your burnt offering and make atonement for yourself and the people; sacrifice the offering that is for the people

[a]31 Or *I was commanded:*   [b]4 The Hebrew word can include both male and female; also in verses 18 and 19.
[c]4 Traditionally *peace offering*; also in verses 18 and 22

and make atonement for them, as the LORD has commanded."

⁸So Aaron came to the altar and slaughtered the calf as a sin offering for himself. ⁹His sons brought the blood to him, and he dipped his finger into the blood and put it on the horns of the altar; the rest of the blood he poured out at the base of the altar. ¹⁰On the altar he burned the fat, the kidneys and the covering of the liver from the sin offering, as the LORD commanded Moses; ¹¹the flesh and the hide he burned up outside the camp.

¹²Then he slaughtered the burnt offering. His sons handed him the blood, and he sprinkled it against the altar on all sides. ¹³They handed him the burnt offering piece by piece, including the head, and he burned them on the altar. ¹⁴He washed the inner parts and the legs and burned them on top of the burnt offering on the altar.

¹⁵Aaron then brought the offering that was for the people. He took the goat for the people's sin offering and slaughtered it and offered it for a sin offering as he did with the first one.

¹⁶He brought the burnt offering and offered it in the prescribed way. ¹⁷He also brought the grain offering, took a handful of it and burned it on the altar in addition to the morning's burnt offering.

¹⁸He slaughtered the ox and the ram as the fellowship offering for the people. His sons handed him the blood, and he sprinkled it against the altar on all sides. ¹⁹But the fat portions of the ox and the ram—the fat tail, the layer of fat, the kidneys and the covering of the liver— ²⁰these they laid on the breasts, and then Aaron burned the fat on the altar. ²¹Aaron waved the breasts and the right thigh before the LORD as a wave offering, as Moses commanded.

²²Then Aaron lifted his hands toward the people and blessed them. And having sacrificed the sin offering, the burnt offering and the fellowship offering, he stepped down.

²³Moses and Aaron then went into the Tent of Meeting. When they came out, they blessed the people; and the glory of the LORD appeared to all the people. ²⁴Fire came out from the presence of

the LORD and consumed the burnt offering and the fat portions on the altar. And when all the people saw it, they shouted for joy and fell face-down.

The Death of Nadab and Abihu

10 Aaron's sons Nadab and Abihu took their censers, put fire in them and added incense; and they offered unauthorized fire before the LORD, contrary to his command. ²So fire came out from the presence of the LORD and consumed them, and they died before the LORD.

10:2 Fatal Error

At first Aaron and his sons did everything according to God's instructions, and God honored them (8:36; 9:24). But in very short order some of the first official priests got careless about following God's explicit orders. The severe punishment sent out a strong message to other priests: they were there to carry out God's plan, not their own.

³Moses then said to Aaron, "This is what the LORD spoke of when he said:

"'Among those who approach me
  I will show myself holy;
in the sight of all the people
  I will be honored.'"

Aaron remained silent.

⁴Moses summoned Mishael and Elzaphan, sons of Aaron's uncle Uzziel, and said to them, "Come here; carry your cousins outside the camp, away from the front of the sanctuary." ⁵So they came and carried them, still in their tunics, outside the camp, as Moses ordered.

⁶Then Moses said to Aaron and his sons Eleazar and Ithamar, "Do not let your hair become unkempt,ᵃ and do not tear your clothes, or you will die and the LORD will be angry with the whole community. But your relatives, all the house of Israel, may mourn for those the LORD has destroyed by fire. ⁷Do not leave the entrance to the Tent of Meeting or you will die, because the LORD's anointing oil is on you." So they did as Moses said.

⁸Then the LORD said to Aaron, ⁹"You and your sons are not to drink wine or other fermented drink whenever you go into the Tent of Meeting, or you will die. This is a lasting ordinance for the generations to come. ¹⁰You must distinguish between the holy and the common, between the unclean and the clean, ¹¹and you must teach the Israelites all the decrees the LORD has given them through Moses."

9:23 The Glory of the Lord

Israelites were familiar with the brilliant glory of the Lord, but they had seen it only from a distance, on Mount Sinai. Even from that distance it had frightened them (Exodus 19:16–22). Now this glory had come to the Tent of Meeting itself, in the camp's center. They were indeed "close to God."

ᵃ6 Or *Do not uncover your heads*

¹²Moses said to Aaron and his remaining sons, Eleazar and Ithamar, "Take the grain offering left over from the offerings made to the LORD by fire and eat it prepared without yeast beside the altar, for it is most holy. ¹³Eat it in a holy place, because it is your share and your sons' share of the offerings made to the LORD by fire; for so I have been commanded. ¹⁴But you and your sons and your daughters may eat the breast that was waved and the thigh that was presented. Eat them in a ceremonially clean place; they have been given to you and your children as your share of the Israelites' fellowship offerings.ᵃ ¹⁵The thigh that was presented and the breast that was waved must be brought with the fat portions of the offerings made to the LORD by fire, to be waved before the LORD as a wave offering. This will be the regular share for you and your children, as the LORD has commanded."

¹⁶When Moses inquired about the goat of the sin offering and found that it had been burned up, he was angry with Eleazar and Ithamar, Aaron's remaining sons, and asked, ¹⁷"Why didn't you eat the sin offering in the sanctuary area? It is most holy; it was given to you to take away the guilt of the community by making atonement for them before the LORD. ¹⁸Since its blood was not taken into the Holy Place, you should have eaten the goat in the sanctuary area, as I commanded."

¹⁹Aaron replied to Moses, "Today they sacrificed their sin offering and their burnt offering before the LORD, but such things as this have happened to me. Would the LORD have been pleased if I had eaten the sin offering today?" ²⁰When Moses heard this, he was satisfied.

Clean and Unclean Food

11 The LORD said to Moses and Aaron, ²"Say to the Israelites: 'Of all the animals that live on land, these are the ones you may eat: ³You may eat any animal that has a split hoof completely divided and that chews the cud.

⁴"'There are some that only chew the cud or only have a split hoof, but you must not eat them. The camel, though it chews the cud, does not have a split hoof; it is ceremonially unclean for you. ⁵The coney,ᵇ though it chews the cud, does not have a split hoof; it is unclean for you. ⁶The rabbit, though it chews the cud, does not have a split hoof; it is unclean for you. ⁷And the pig, though it has a split hoof completely divided, does not chew the cud; it is unclean for you. ⁸You must not eat their meat or touch their carcasses; they are unclean for you.

⁹"'Of all the creatures living in the water of the seas and the streams, you may eat any that have fins and scales. ¹⁰But all creatures in the seas or streams that do not have fins and scales—whether among all the swarming things or among all the other living creatures in the water—you are to detest. ¹¹And since you are to detest them, you must not eat their meat and you must detest their carcasses. ¹²Anything living in the water that does not have fins and scales is to be detestable to you.

¹³"'These are the birds you are to detest and not eat because they are detestable: the eagle, the vulture, the black vulture, ¹⁴the red kite, any kind of black kite, ¹⁵any kind of raven, ¹⁶the horned owl, the screech owl, the gull, any kind of hawk, ¹⁷the little owl, the cormorant, the great owl, ¹⁸the white owl, the desert owl, the osprey, ¹⁹the stork, any kind of heron, the hoopoe and the bat.ᶜ

²⁰"'All flying insects that walk on all fours are to be detestable to you. ²¹There are, however, some winged creatures that walk on all fours that you may eat: those that have jointed legs for hopping on the ground. ²²Of these you may eat any kind of locust, katydid, cricket or grasshopper. ²³But all other winged creatures that have four legs you are to detest.

²⁴"'You will make yourselves unclean by these; whoever touches their carcasses will be unclean till evening. ²⁵Whoever picks up one of their carcasses must wash his clothes, and he will be unclean till evening.

²⁶"'Every animal that has a split hoof not completely divided or that does not chew the cud is unclean for you; whoever touches ₍the carcass of₎ any of them will be unclean. ²⁷Of all the animals that walk on all fours, those that walk on their paws are unclean for you; whoever touches their carcasses will be unclean till evening. ²⁸Anyone who picks up their carcasses must wash his clothes, and he will be unclean till evening. They are unclean for you.

²⁹"'Of the animals that move about on the ground, these are unclean for you: the weasel, the rat, any kind of great lizard, ³⁰the gecko, the monitor lizard, the wall lizard, the skink and the chameleon. ³¹Of all those that move along the ground, these are unclean for you. Whoever touches them when they are dead will be unclean till evening. ³²When one of them dies and falls on something, that article, whatever its use, will be unclean, whether it is made of wood, cloth, hide or sackcloth. Put it in water; it will be unclean till evening, and then it will be clean. ³³If one of them falls into a clay pot, everything in it will be unclean, and you must break the pot. ³⁴Any food that could be eaten but has water on it from such a pot is unclean, and any liquid that could be drunk from it is unclean. ³⁵Anything that one of their carcasses falls on becomes unclean; an oven or cooking pot must be broken up. They are

---

ᵃ14 Traditionally *peace offerings*   ᵇ5 That is, the hyrax or rock badger   ᶜ19 The precise identification of some of the birds, insects and animals in this chapter is uncertain.

unclean, and you are to regard them as unclean. [36]A spring, however, or a cistern for collecting water remains clean, but anyone who touches one of these carcasses is unclean. [37]If a carcass falls on any seeds that are to be planted, they remain clean. [38]But if water has been put on the seed and a carcass falls on it, it is unclean for you.

[39]"'If an animal that you are allowed to eat dies, anyone who touches the carcass will be unclean till evening. [40]Anyone who eats some of the carcass must wash his clothes, and he will be unclean till evening. Anyone who picks up the carcass must wash his clothes, and he will be unclean till evening.

[41]"'Every creature that moves about on the ground is detestable; it is not to be eaten. [42]You are not to eat any creature that moves about on the ground, whether it moves on its belly or walks on all fours or on many feet; it is detestable. [43]Do not defile yourselves by any of these creatures. Do not make yourselves unclean by means of them or be made unclean by them. [44]I am the LORD your God; consecrate yourselves and be holy, because I am holy. Do not make yourselves unclean by any creature that moves about on the ground. [45]I am the LORD who brought you up out of Egypt to be your God; therefore be holy, because I am holy.

[46]"'These are the regulations concerning animals, birds, every living thing that moves in the water and every creature that moves about on the ground. [47]You must distinguish between the unclean and the clean, between living creatures that may be eaten and those that may not be eaten.'"

An Invisible Danger
Taking precautions: like a surgeon preparing to operate

> *"You must distinguish between the unclean and the clean.'" 11:47*

FOR MANY YEARS SURGERY REMAINED a desperate last resort for the hopelessly ill. Surgeons knew nothing about germs. Without washing, they would don operating garb, usually an old coat caked with blood and pus from numerous operations. They would pick up the scalpel, wiped clean with an old rag after the last operation, and go to work. Half of those operated on died.

One pioneer after another stumbled on the correct sterile techniques. But each was scorned and humiliated by fellow doctors. Professor Ignaz Semmelweis, for one, discovered that making doctors wash their hands could dramatically cut the death rate in maternity wards. Yet his colleagues opposed Semmelweis strenuously, and though he argued for handwashing throughout his life, he died without seeing his ideas take hold.

Why So Slow?

Why were doctors so slow to adopt sterile techniques? The answer is simple: Germs had not yet been discovered. Doctors could not see—and reformers like Semmelweis could not give them—any reason why washing hands should make a difference.

Then Louis Pasteur discovered micro-organisms under his microscope. Sterile procedures began to make sense: they made war on germs. Even so, each reform, from rubber gloves to gauze masks, was accepted only grudgingly and with considerable opposition. It was as though doctors had a hard time remembering that something invisible could be so devastating. Fifty years of constant education and reform were necessary before "sterile technique" became a routine part of surgery, and germs became "real" to most medical minds.

Why All the Rules?

As germs are to a surgeon, "uncleanness" is to Leviticus. Chapters 11–15 describe elaborate precautions—what animals to avoid and how to treat "unclean" skin disease, mildewed clothing or walls, and bodily emissions.

Scholars point out that many clean and unclean rules have good health habits behind them, such as the rule to quarantine a person with an infectious disease or the rule against eating pork (which carries many parasites).

Others say that dietary laws were meant to keep the Israelites apart from their neighbors. Pigs were prominent in Canaanite worship; therefore the Israelites were not to eat pigs. A different dietary standard would keep the two groups from mixing socially, for a meal was always part of Middle Eastern hospitality.

Still other scholars suggest that the uncleanness rules simply fit into what Israelites intuitively thought proper. God was reinforcing a natural sense of repulsion toward creeping insects, scavenger birds, bodily emissions, and skin diseases.

Purification After Childbirth

12 The LORD said to Moses, ²"Say to the Israelites: 'A woman who becomes pregnant and gives birth to a son will be ceremonially unclean for seven days, just as she is unclean during her monthly period. ³On the eighth day the boy is to be circumcised. ⁴Then the woman must wait thirty-three days to be purified from her bleeding. She must not touch anything sacred or go to the sanctuary until the days of her purification are over. ⁵If she gives birth to a daughter, for two weeks the woman will be unclean, as during her period. Then she must wait sixty-six days to be purified from her bleeding.

⁶"'When the days of her purification for a son or daughter are over, she is to bring to the priest at the entrance to the Tent of Meeting a year-old lamb for a burnt offering and a young pigeon or a dove for a sin offering. ⁷He shall offer them before the LORD to make atonement for her, and then she will be ceremonially clean from her flow of blood.

⁸"'These are the regulations for the woman who gives birth to a boy or a girl. ⁸If she cannot afford a lamb, she is to bring two doves or two young pigeons, one for a burnt offering and the other for a sin offering. In this way the priest will make atonement for her, and she will be clean.'"

Regulations About Infectious Skin Diseases

13 The LORD said to Moses and Aaron, ²"When anyone has a swelling or a rash or a bright spot on his skin that may become an

---

11:47 Of Scallops and Rabbits

Scholars have long puzzled over the seemingly arbitrary division between "clean" and "unclean" foods. Why permit the eating of certain fish but not shrimp, and cows but not pigs? "An Invisible Danger," below, discusses some of the theories that have been proposed. Probably the best explanation is that God was indeed being arbitrary, in order to form a nation different from any other (see 20:26). In Acts 10 God shows there is nothing intrinsically wrong with the animals labeled "unclean" in Leviticus.

The Habit of Carefulness

All these explanations have merit, but the underlying basis of clean and unclean was religious. Being unclean was not dangerous or wrong. In fact, you could hardly avoid it. Practically everyone became "unclean" from time to time. But you could not worship God in the Tent of Meeting while you were unclean, nor bring anything unclean into the presence of God. His holiness would destroy it—and you (Leviticus 15:31).

So Leviticus trains God's people to watch their lives as carefully as surgeons watch their sterile techniques. They must develop the habit of carefulness, even about something they cannot see or feel. They must think about preparing themselves for God, not just do whatever "feels right."

It was not a question of how they felt about God, any more than a surgeon's concern is how he "feels" about germs. Clear, absolute standards laid out what could be acceptable to a God who is perfectly clean, absolute, unchanging. Just as surgeons had to struggle to take germs seriously, so God's people must learn to "purify themselves" for God.

Touching the Unclean

The uncleanness rules of Leviticus are outmoded because of Jesus' declaration that all things are clean (Mark 7:19; see also Acts 10:9–16). But the lessons behind these rules remain valid. God still may not be approached carelessly. Each person must examine his or her life, to be certain that God's purity is not violated.

Until Jesus' day, the slow spread of uncleanness seemed irreversible. You could avoid it, but you could not get rid of it. Contact with anything unclean made you unclean yourself. Naturally, certain diseases, notably leprosy, were twice cursed: they were both dangerous and unclean. You kept away from leprosy, absolutely.

Then Jesus touched a man with leprosy, and he became clean. Jesus touched a woman suffering from internal bleeding, and she was healed. For the first time, cleanness rather than uncleanness spread. The rules of Leviticus tell how to avoid uncleanness. Contact with Jesus, however, changes the unclean to clean.

Life Questions: Suppose sin were visible—small green spots that break out on the skin. Do you think it would help people to take sin more seriously?

infectious skin disease,[a] he must be brought to Aaron the priest or to one of his sons[b] who is a priest. [3]The priest is to examine the sore on his skin, and if the hair in the sore has turned white

---

12:8 For Poor People

This alternate offering enabled poor women to live up to their duty to God. Mary offered such a sacrifice after Jesus' birth (see Luke 2:24)—an indication that Jesus' family was not well-off.

---

and the sore appears to be more than skin deep,[c] it is an infectious skin disease. When the priest examines him, he shall pronounce him ceremonially unclean. [4]If the spot on his skin is white but does not appear to be more than skin deep and the hair in it has not turned white, the priest is to put the infected person in isolation for seven days. [5]On the seventh day the priest is to examine him, and if he sees that the sore is unchanged and has not spread in the skin, he is to keep him in isolation another seven days. [6]On the seventh day the priest is to examine him again, and if the sore has faded and has not spread in the skin, the priest shall pronounce him clean; it is only a rash. The man must wash his clothes, and he will be clean. [7]But if the rash does spread in his skin after he has shown himself to the priest to be pronounced clean, he must appear before the priest again. [8]The priest is to examine him, and if the rash has spread in the skin, he shall pronounce him unclean; it is an infectious disease.

[9]"When anyone has an infectious skin disease, he must be brought to the priest. [10]The priest is to examine him, and if there is a white swelling in the skin that has turned the hair white and if there is raw flesh in the swelling, [11]it is a chronic skin disease and the priest shall pronounce him unclean. He is not to put him in isolation, because he is already unclean.

[12]"If the disease breaks out all over his skin and, so far as the priest can see, it covers all the skin of the infected person from head to foot, [13]the priest is to examine him, and if the disease has covered his whole body, he shall pronounce that person clean. Since it has all turned white, he is clean. [14]But whenever raw flesh appears on him, he will be unclean. [15]When the priest sees the raw flesh, he shall pronounce him unclean. The raw flesh is unclean; he has an infectious disease. [16]Should the raw flesh change and turn white, he must go to the priest. [17]The priest is to examine him, and if the sores have turned white,

the priest shall pronounce the infected person clean; then he will be clean.

[18]"When someone has a boil on his skin and it heals, [19]and in the place where the boil was, a

---

13:17 Misidentification

Victims of leprosy, or Hansen's disease, have endured untold suffering because earlier versions of the Bible translated as "leprosy" the Hebrew word for "infectious skin disease" mentioned in this chapter. The symptoms described here have little to do with leprosy, a disease of the nerves—not skin—which is barely contagious.

---

white swelling or reddish-white spot appears, he must present himself to the priest. [20]The priest is to examine it, and if it appears to be more than skin deep and the hair in it has turned white, the priest shall pronounce him unclean. It is an infectious skin disease that has broken out where the boil was. [21]But if, when the priest examines it, there is no white hair in it and it is not more than skin deep and has faded, then the priest is to put him in isolation for seven days. [22]If it is spreading in the skin, the priest shall pronounce him unclean; it is infectious. [23]But if the spot is unchanged and has not spread, it is only a scar from the boil, and the priest shall pronounce him clean.

[24]"When someone has a burn on his skin and a reddish-white or white spot appears in the raw flesh of the burn, [25]the priest is to examine the spot, and if the hair in it has turned white, and it appears to be more than skin deep, it is an infectious disease that has broken out in the burn. The priest shall pronounce him unclean; it is an infectious skin disease. [26]But if the priest examines it and there is no white hair in the spot and if it is not more than skin deep and has faded, then the priest is to put him in isolation for seven days. [27]On the seventh day the priest is to examine him, and if it is spreading in the skin, the priest shall pronounce him unclean; it is an infectious skin disease. [28]If, however, the spot is unchanged and has not spread in the skin but has faded, it is a swelling from the burn, and the priest shall pronounce him clean; it is only a scar from the burn.

[29]"If a man or woman has a sore on the head or on the chin, [30]the priest is to examine the sore, and if it appears to be more than skin deep and the hair in it is yellow and thin, the priest shall pronounce that person unclean; it is an itch, an

---

[a]2 Traditionally *leprosy*; the Hebrew word was used for various diseases affecting the skin—not necessarily leprosy; also elsewhere in this chapter.   [b]2 Or *descendants*   [c]3 Or *be lower than the rest of the skin*; also elsewhere in this chapter

infectious disease of the head or chin. ³¹But if, when the priest examines this kind of sore, it does not seem to be more than skin deep and there is no black hair in it, then the priest is to put the infected person in isolation for seven days. ³²On the seventh day the priest is to examine the sore, and if the itch has not spread and there is no yellow hair in it and it does not appear to be more than skin deep, ³³he must be shaved except for the diseased area, and the priest is to keep him in isolation another seven days. ³⁴On the seventh day the priest is to examine the itch, and if it has not spread in the skin and appears to be no more than skin deep, the priest shall pronounce him clean. He must wash his clothes, and he will be clean. ³⁵But if the itch does spread in the skin after he is pronounced clean, ³⁶the priest is to examine him, and if the itch has spread in the skin, the priest does not need to look for yellow hair; the person is unclean. ³⁷If, however, in his judgment it is unchanged and black hair has grown in it, the itch is healed. He is clean, and the priest shall pronounce him clean.

³⁸"When a man or woman has white spots on the skin, ³⁹the priest is to examine them, and if the spots are dull white, it is a harmless rash that has broken out on the skin; that person is clean.

⁴⁰"When a man has lost his hair and is bald, he is clean. ⁴¹If he has lost his hair from the front of his scalp and has a bald forehead, he is clean. ⁴²But if he has a reddish-white sore on his bald head or forehead, it is an infectious disease breaking out on his head or forehead. ⁴³The priest is to examine him, and if the swollen sore on his head or forehead is reddish-white like an infectious skin disease, ⁴⁴the man is diseased and is unclean. The priest shall pronounce him unclean because of the sore on his head.

⁴⁵"The person with such an infectious disease must wear torn clothes, let his hair be unkempt,ᵃ cover the lower part of his face and cry out, 'Unclean! Unclean!' ⁴⁶As long as he has the infection he remains unclean. He must live alone; he must live outside the camp.

Regulations About Mildew

⁴⁷"If any clothing is contaminated with mildew—any woolen or linen clothing, ⁴⁸any woven or knitted material of linen or wool, any leather or anything made of leather— ⁴⁹and if the contamination in the clothing, or leather, or woven or knitted material, or any leather article, is greenish or reddish, it is a spreading mildew and must be shown to the priest. ⁵⁰The priest is to examine the mildew and isolate the affected article for seven days. ⁵¹On the seventh day he is to

examine it, and if the mildew has spread in the clothing, or the woven or knitted material, or the leather, whatever its use, it is a destructive mildew; the article is unclean. ⁵²He must burn up the clothing, or the woven or knitted material of wool or linen, or any leather article that has the contamination in it, because the mildew is destructive; the article must be burned up.

⁵³"But if, when the priest examines it, the mildew has not spread in the clothing, or the woven or knitted material, or the leather article, ⁵⁴he shall order that the contaminated article be washed. Then he is to isolate it for another seven days. ⁵⁵After the affected article has been washed, the priest is to examine it, and if the mildew has not changed its appearance, even though it has not spread, it is unclean. Burn it with fire, whether the mildew has affected one side or the other. ⁵⁶If, when the priest examines it, the mildew has faded after the article has been washed, he is to tear the contaminated part out of the clothing, or the leather, or the woven or knitted material. ⁵⁷But if it reappears in the clothing, or in the woven or knitted material, or in the leather article, it is spreading, and whatever has the mildew must be burned with fire. ⁵⁸The clothing, or the woven or knitted material, or any leather article that has been washed and is rid of the mildew, must be washed again, and it will be clean."

⁵⁹These are the regulations concerning contamination by mildew in woolen or linen clothing, woven or knitted material, or any leather article, for pronouncing them clean or unclean.

Cleansing From Infectious Skin Diseases

14 The LORD said to Moses, ²"These are the regulations for the diseased person at the time of his ceremonial cleansing, when he is brought to the priest: ³The priest is to go outside the camp and examine him. If the person has been healed of his infectious skin disease,ᵇ ⁴the priest shall order that two live clean birds and some cedar wood, scarlet yarn and hyssop be brought for the one to be cleansed. ⁵Then the priest shall order that one of the birds be killed over fresh water in a clay pot. ⁶He is then to take the live bird and dip it, together with the cedar wood, the scarlet yarn and the hyssop, into the blood of the bird that was killed over the fresh water. ⁷Seven times he shall sprinkle the one to be cleansed of the infectious disease and pronounce him clean. Then he is to release the live bird in the open fields.

⁸"The person to be cleansed must wash his clothes, shave off all his hair and bathe with water; then he will be ceremonially clean. After this he may come into the camp, but he must stay

---

ᵃ45 Or clothes, uncover his head   ᵇ3 Traditionally leprosy; the Hebrew word was used for various diseases affecting the skin—not necessarily leprosy; also elsewhere in this chapter.

outside his tent for seven days. ⁹On the seventh day he must shave off all his hair; he must shave his head, his beard, his eyebrows and the rest of his hair. He must wash his clothes and bathe himself with water, and he will be clean.

14:7 A Bird Set Free

It is difficult to assign definite symbolic meaning to all the details in this ceremony for the cleansing of skin diseases. Many scholars suggest that the bird that was killed represented purification by sacrifice, while the bird set free represented new liberty after a long quarantine. When Jesus healed a man with leprosy (Matthew 8:4), he told him to follow these instructions.

¹⁰"On the eighth day he must bring two male lambs and one ewe lamb a year old, each without defect, along with three-tenths of an ephah*a* of fine flour mixed with oil for a grain offering, and one log*b* of oil. ¹¹The priest who pronounces him clean shall present both the one to be cleansed and his offerings before the LORD at the entrance to the Tent of Meeting.

¹²"Then the priest is to take one of the male lambs and offer it as a guilt offering, along with the log of oil; he shall wave them before the LORD as a wave offering. ¹³He is to slaughter the lamb in the holy place where the sin offering and the burnt offering are slaughtered. Like the sin offering, the guilt offering belongs to the priest; it is most holy. ¹⁴The priest is to take some of the blood of the guilt offering and put it on the lobe of the right ear of the one to be cleansed, on the thumb of his right hand and on the big toe of his right foot. ¹⁵Take some of the log of oil, pour it in the palm of his own left hand, ¹⁶dip his right forefinger into the oil in his palm, and with his finger sprinkle some of it before the LORD seven times. ¹⁷The priest is to put some of the oil remaining in his palm on the lobe of the right ear of the one to be cleansed, on the thumb of his right hand and on the big toe of his right foot, on top of the blood of the guilt offering. ¹⁸The rest of the oil in his palm the priest shall put on the head of the one to be cleansed and make atonement for him before the LORD.

¹⁹"Then the priest is to sacrifice the sin offering and make atonement for the one to be cleansed from his uncleanness. After that, the priest shall slaughter the burnt offering ²⁰and offer it on the altar, together with the grain offering, and make atonement for him, and he will be clean.

²¹"If, however, he is poor and cannot afford these, he must take one male lamb as a guilt offering to be waved to make atonement for him, together with a tenth of an ephah*c* of fine flour mixed with oil for a grain offering, a log of oil, ²²and two doves or two young pigeons, which he can afford, one for a sin offering and the other for a burnt offering.

²³"On the eighth day he must bring them for his cleansing to the priest at the entrance to the Tent of Meeting, before the LORD. ²⁴The priest is to take the lamb for the guilt offering, together with the log of oil, and wave them before the LORD as a wave offering. ²⁵He shall slaughter the lamb for the guilt offering and take some of its blood and put it on the lobe of the right ear of the one to be cleansed, on the thumb of his right hand and on the big toe of his right foot. ²⁶The priest is to pour some of the oil into the palm of his own left hand, ²⁷and with his right forefinger sprinkle some of the oil from his palm seven times before the LORD. ²⁸Some of the oil in his palm he is to put on the same places he put the blood of the guilt offering—on the lobe of the right ear of the one to be cleansed, on the thumb of his right hand and on the big toe of his right foot. ²⁹The rest of the oil in his palm the priest shall put on the head of the one to be cleansed, to make atonement for him before the LORD. ³⁰Then he shall sacrifice the doves or the young pigeons, which the person can afford, ³¹one*d* as a sin offering and the other as a burnt offering, together with the grain offering. In this way the priest will make atonement before the LORD on behalf of the one to be cleansed."

³²These are the regulations for anyone who has an infectious skin disease and who cannot afford the regular offerings for his cleansing.

Cleansing From Mildew

³³The LORD said to Moses and Aaron, ³⁴"When you enter the land of Canaan, which I am giving you as your possession, and I put a spreading mildew in a house in that land, ³⁵the owner of the house must go and tell the priest, 'I have seen something that looks like mildew in my house.' ³⁶The priest is to order the house to be emptied before he goes in to examine the mildew, so that nothing in the house will be pronounced unclean. After this the priest is to go in and inspect the house. ³⁷He is to examine the mildew on the walls, and if it has greenish or reddish depressions that appear to be deeper than the surface of the wall, ³⁸the priest shall go out the doorway of the house and close it up for

a10 That is, probably about 6 quarts (about 6.5 liters)   *b10* That is, probably about 2/3 pint (about 0.3 liter); also in verses 12, 15, 21 and 24   *c21* That is, probably about 2 quarts (about 2 liters)   *d31* Septuagint and Syriac; Hebrew *31such as the person can afford, one*

seven days. ³⁹On the seventh day the priest shall return to inspect the house. If the mildew has spread on the walls, ⁴⁰he is to order that the contaminated stones be torn out and thrown into an unclean place outside the town. ⁴¹He must have all the inside walls of the house scraped and the material that is scraped off dumped into an unclean place outside the town. ⁴²Then they are to take other stones to replace these and take new clay and plaster the house.

⁴³"If the mildew reappears in the house after the stones have been torn out and the house scraped and plastered, ⁴⁴the priest is to go and examine it and, if the mildew has spread in the house, it is a destructive mildew; the house is unclean. ⁴⁵It must be torn down—its stones, timbers and all the plaster—and taken out of the town to an unclean place.

⁴⁶"Anyone who goes into the house while it is closed up will be unclean till evening. ⁴⁷Anyone who sleeps or eats in the house must wash his clothes.

⁴⁸"But if the priest comes to examine it and the mildew has not spread after the house has been plastered, he shall pronounce the house clean, because the mildew is gone. ⁴⁹To purify the house he is to take two birds and some cedar wood, scarlet yarn and hyssop. ⁵⁰He shall kill one of the birds over fresh water in a clay pot. ⁵¹Then he is to take the cedar wood, the hyssop, the scarlet yarn and the live bird, dip them into the blood of the dead bird and the fresh water, and sprinkle the house seven times. ⁵²He shall purify the house with the bird's blood, the fresh water, the live bird, the cedar wood, the hyssop and the scarlet yarn. ⁵³Then he is to release the live bird in the open fields outside the town. In this way he will make atonement for the house, and it will be clean."

⁵⁴These are the regulations for any infectious skin disease, for an itch, ⁵⁵for mildew in clothing or in a house, ⁵⁶and for a swelling, a rash or a bright spot, ⁵⁷to determine when something is clean or unclean.

These are the regulations for infectious skin diseases and mildew.

Discharges Causing Uncleanness

15 The LORD said to Moses and Aaron, ²"Speak to the Israelites and say to them: 'When any man has a bodily discharge, the discharge is unclean. ³Whether it continues flowing from his body or is blocked, it will make him unclean. This is how his discharge will bring about uncleanness:

⁴"'Any bed the man with a discharge lies on will be unclean, and anything he sits on will be unclean. ⁵Anyone who touches his bed must wash his clothes and bathe with water, and he will be unclean till evening. ⁶Whoever sits on any-

thing that the man with a discharge sat on must wash his clothes and bathe with water, and he will be unclean till evening.

⁷"'Whoever touches the man who has a dis-

charge must wash his clothes and bathe with water, and he will be unclean till evening.

⁸"'If the man with the discharge spits on someone who is clean, that person must wash his clothes and bathe with water, and he will be unclean till evening.

⁹"'Everything the man sits on when riding will be unclean, ¹⁰and whoever touches any of the things that were under him will be unclean till evening; whoever picks up those things must wash his clothes and bathe with water, and he will be unclean till evening.

¹¹"'Anyone the man with a discharge touches without rinsing his hands with water must wash his clothes and bathe with water, and he will be unclean till evening.

¹²"'A clay pot that the man touches must be broken, and any wooden article is to be rinsed with water.

¹³"'When a man is cleansed from his discharge, he is to count off seven days for his ceremonial cleansing; he must wash his clothes and bathe himself with fresh water, and he will be clean. ¹⁴On the eighth day he must take two doves or two young pigeons and come before the LORD to the entrance to the Tent of Meeting and give them to the priest. ¹⁵The priest is to sacrifice them, the one for a sin offering and the other for a burnt offering. In this way he will make atonement before the LORD for the man because of his discharge.

¹⁶"'When a man has an emission of semen, he must bathe his whole body with water, and he will be unclean till evening. ¹⁷Any clothing or leather that has semen on it must be washed with water, and it will be unclean till evening. ¹⁸When a man lies with a woman and there is an emission of semen, both must bathe with water, and they will be unclean till evening.

¹⁹"'When a woman has her regular flow of blood, the impurity of her monthly period will last seven days, and anyone who touches her will be unclean till evening.

²⁰"'Anything she lies on during her period will be unclean, and anything she sits on will be unclean. ²¹Whoever touches her bed must wash his clothes and bathe with water, and he will be unclean till evening. ²²Whoever touches anything she sits on must wash his clothes and bathe with water, and he will be unclean till evening. ²³Whether it is the bed or anything she was sitting on, when anyone touches it, he will be unclean till evening.

²⁴"'If a man lies with her and her monthly flow touches him, he will be unclean for seven days; any bed he lies on will be unclean.

²⁵"'When a woman has a discharge of blood for many days at a time other than her monthly period or has a discharge that continues beyond her period, she will be unclean as long as she has the discharge, just as in the days of her period. ²⁶Any bed she lies on while her discharge continues will be unclean, as is her bed during her monthly period, and anything she sits on will be unclean, as during her period. ²⁷Whoever touches them will be unclean; he must wash his clothes and bathe with water, and he will be unclean till evening.

²⁸"'When she is cleansed from her discharge, she must count off seven days, and after that she will be ceremonially clean. ²⁹On the eighth day she must take two doves or two young pigeons and bring them to the priest at the entrance to the Tent of Meeting. ³⁰The priest is to sacrifice one for a sin offering and the other for a burnt offering. In this way he will make atonement for her before the LORD for the uncleanness of her discharge.

³¹"'You must keep the Israelites separate from things that make them unclean, so they will not die in their uncleanness for defiling my dwelling place,ᵃ which is among them.'"

³²These are the regulations for a man with a discharge, for anyone made unclean by an emission of semen, ³³for a woman in her monthly period, for a man or a woman with a discharge, and for a man who lies with a woman who is ceremonially unclean.

The Day of Atonement

16 The LORD spoke to Moses after the death of the two sons of Aaron who died when they approached the LORD. ²The LORD said to Moses: "Tell your brother Aaron not to come whenever he chooses into the Most Holy Place behind the curtain in front of the atonement cover on the ark, or else he will die, because I appear in the cloud over the atonement cover.

³"This is how Aaron is to enter the sanctuary area: with a young bull for a sin offering and a ram for a burnt offering. ⁴He is to put on the sacred linen tunic, with linen undergarments next to his body; he is to tie the linen sash around him and put on the linen turban. These are sacred garments; so he must bathe himself with water before he puts them on. ⁵From the Israelite community he is to take two male goats for a sin offering and a ram for a burnt offering.

⁶"Aaron is to offer the bull for his own sin offering to make atonement for himself and his household. ⁷Then he is to take the two goats and present them before the LORD at the entrance to the Tent of Meeting. ⁸He is to cast lots for the two goats—one lot for the LORD and the other for the scapegoat.ᵇ ⁹Aaron shall bring the goat whose lot falls to the LORD and sacrifice it for a sin offering. ¹⁰But the goat chosen by lot as the scapegoat shall be presented alive before the LORD to be used for making atonement by sending it into the desert as a scapegoat.

¹¹"Aaron shall bring the bull for his own sin offering to make atonement for himself and his household, and he is to slaughter the bull for his own sin offering. ¹²He is to take a censer full of burning coals from the altar before the LORD and two handfuls of finely ground fragrant incense and take them behind the curtain. ¹³He is to put the incense on the fire before the LORD, and the smoke of the incense will conceal the atonement cover above the Testimony, so that he will not die. ¹⁴He is to take some of the bull's blood and with his finger sprinkle it on the front of the atonement cover; then he shall sprinkle some of it with his finger seven times before the atonement cover.

¹⁵"He shall then slaughter the goat for the sin offering for the people and take its blood behind the curtain and do with it as he did with the bull's blood: He shall sprinkle it on the atonement cover and in front of it. ¹⁶In this way he will make atonement for the Most Holy Place because of the uncleanness and rebellion of the Israelites, whatever their sins have been. He is to do the same for the Tent of Meeting, which is among them in the midst of their uncleanness. ¹⁷No one is to be in the Tent of Meeting from the time Aaron goes in to make atonement in the Most Holy Place until he comes out, having made atonement for himself, his household and the whole community of Israel.

¹⁸"Then he shall come out to the altar that is before the LORD and make atonement for it. He shall take some of the bull's blood and some of the goat's blood and put it on all the horns of the

---

ᵃ31 Or my tabernacle   ᵇ8 That is, the goat of removal; Hebrew azazel; also in verses 10 and 26

altar. ¹⁹He shall sprinkle some of the blood on it with his finger seven times to cleanse it and to consecrate it from the uncleanness of the Israelites.

²⁰"When Aaron has finished making atonement for the Most Holy Place, the Tent of Meeting and the altar, he shall bring forward the live

16:20 Scapegoat

The English word scapegoat (escape goat) was formed to capture the essence of this crucial ceremony in which a goat symbolically carried all the sins of Israel into the desert. Today the word is applied to anyone who takes the blame for something other people did.

goat. ²¹He is to lay both hands on the head of the live goat and confess over it all the wickedness and rebellion of the Israelites—all their sins—and put them on the goat's head. He shall send the goat away into the desert in the care of a man appointed for the task. ²²The goat will carry on itself all their sins to a solitary place; and the man shall release it in the desert.

²³"Then Aaron is to go into the Tent of Meeting and take off the linen garments he put on before he entered the Most Holy Place, and he is to leave them there. ²⁴He shall bathe himself with water in a holy place and put on his regular garments. Then he shall come out and sacrifice the burnt offering for himself and the burnt offering for the people, to make atonement for himself and for the people. ²⁵He shall also burn the fat of the sin offering on the altar.

²⁶"The man who releases the goat as a scapegoat must wash his clothes and bathe himself with water; afterward he may come into the camp. ²⁷The bull and the goat for the sin offerings, whose blood was brought into the Most Holy Place to make atonement, must be taken outside the camp; their hides, flesh and offal are to be burned up. ²⁸The man who burns them must wash his clothes and bathe himself with water; afterward he may come into the camp.

²⁹"This is to be a lasting ordinance for you: On the tenth day of the seventh month you must deny yourselves[a] and not do any work—whether native-born or an alien living among you—³⁰because on this day atonement will be made for you, to cleanse you. Then, before the LORD, you will be clean from all your sins. ³¹It is a sabbath of rest, and you must deny yourselves; it is a lasting ordinance. ³²The priest who is anointed and ordained to succeed his father as high priest is to make atonement. He is to put on the sacred

linen garments ³³and make atonement for the Most Holy Place, for the Tent of Meeting and the altar, and for the priests and all the people of the community.

³⁴"This is to be a lasting ordinance for you: Atonement is to be made once a year for all the sins of the Israelites."

And it was done, as the LORD commanded Moses.

Eating Blood Forbidden

17 The LORD said to Moses, ²"Speak to Aaron and his sons and to all the Israelites and say to them: 'This is what the LORD has commanded: ³Any Israelite who sacrifices an ox,[b] a lamb or a goat in the camp or outside of it ⁴instead of bringing it to the entrance to the Tent of Meeting to present it as an offering to the LORD in front of the tabernacle of the LORD—that man shall be considered guilty of bloodshed; he has shed blood and must be cut off from his people. ⁵This is so the Israelites will bring to the LORD the sacrifices they are now making in the open fields. They must bring them to the priest, that is, to the LORD, at the entrance to the Tent of Meeting and sacrifice them as fellowship offerings.[c] ⁶The priest is to sprinkle the blood against the altar of the LORD at the entrance to the Tent of Meeting and burn the fat as an aroma pleasing to the LORD. ⁷They must no longer offer any of their sacrifices to the goat idols[d] to whom they prostitute themselves. This is to be a lasting ordinance for them and for the generations to come.'

⁸"Say to them: 'Any Israelite or any alien living among them who offers a burnt offering or sacrifice ⁹and does not bring it to the entrance to the Tent of Meeting to sacrifice it to the LORD—that man must be cut off from his people.

¹⁰"'Any Israelite or any alien living among them who eats any blood—I will set my face against that person who eats blood and will cut

17:10 Kosher

To this day many Jews avoid meat unless it has been carefully drained of blood. Blood, which represented the life of living creatures, was to make atonement for, or to "cover up," sins. Thus Jesus' blood, signifying his death, has special significance to Christians. It is the blood of the ultimate sacrifice for sin.

The first Christians debated how much of the law should be required of non-Jews who became Christians (Acts 15). Of the four requirements they settled on, two were "kosher."

---

[a]29 Or *must fast*; also in verse 31   [b]3 The Hebrew word can include both male and female.   [c]5 Traditionally
peace offerings   [d]7 Or *demons*

him off from his people. [11]For the life of a creature is in the blood, and I have given it to you to make atonement for yourselves on the altar; it is the blood that makes atonement for one's life. [12]Therefore I say to the Israelites, "None of you may eat blood, nor may an alien living among you eat blood."

[13]"Any Israelite or any alien living among you who hunts any animal or bird that may be eaten must drain out the blood and cover it with earth, [14]because the life of every creature is its blood. That is why I have said to the Israelites, "You must not eat the blood of any creature, because the life of every creature is its blood; anyone who eats it must be cut off."

[15]"Anyone, whether native-born or alien, who eats anything found dead or torn by wild animals must wash his clothes and bathe with water, and he will be ceremonially unclean till evening; then he will be clean. [16]But if he does not wash his clothes and bathe himself, he will be held responsible.'"

Unlawful Sexual Relations

18 The LORD said to Moses, [2]"Speak to the Israelites and say to them: 'I am the LORD your God. [3]You must not do as they do in Egypt, where you used to live, and you must not do as they do in the land of Canaan, where I am bringing you. Do not follow their practices. [4]You must obey my laws and be careful to follow my decrees. I am the LORD your God. [5]Keep my decrees and laws, for the man who obeys them will live by them. I am the LORD.

[6]"No one is to approach any close relative to have sexual relations. I am the LORD.

[7]"Do not dishonor your father by having sexual relations with your mother. She is your mother; do not have relations with her.

[8]"Do not have sexual relations with your father's wife; that would dishonor your father.

[9]"Do not have sexual relations with your sister, either your father's daughter or your mother's daughter, whether she was born in the same home or elsewhere.

[10]"Do not have sexual relations with your son's daughter or your daughter's daughter; that would dishonor you.

[11]"Do not have sexual relations with the daughter of your father's wife, born to your father; she is your sister.

[12]"Do not have sexual relations with your father's sister; she is your father's close relative.

[13]"Do not have sexual relations with your mother's sister, because she is your mother's close relative.

[14]"Do not dishonor your father's brother by approaching his wife to have sexual relations; she is your aunt.

[15]"Do not have sexual relations with your daughter-in-law. She is your son's wife; do not have relations with her.

[16]"Do not have sexual relations with your brother's wife; that would dishonor your brother.

[17]"Do not have sexual relations with both a woman and her daughter. Do not have sexual relations with either her son's daughter or her daughter's daughter; they are her close relatives. That is wickedness.

[18]"Do not take your wife's sister as a rival wife and have sexual relations with her while your wife is living.

[19]"Do not approach a woman to have sexual relations during the uncleanness of her monthly period.

[20]"Do not have sexual relations with your neighbor's wife and defile yourself with her.

[21]"Do not give any of your children to be sacrificed[a] to Molech, for you must not profane the name of your God. I am the LORD.

18:21 Child Sacrifice and Sex

This warning against child sacrifice (repeated and expanded in 20:1–5) seems out of place in the middle of a chapter on rules about sex. Yet, for the Israelites, there was a connection. Their neighbors, who sacrificed their children as a part of their religion, also practiced temple prostitution as a way of worship. To them, sex was a way to get in touch with their gods. God's warnings against various sexual practices begin and end with warnings to behave differently from these neighbors (verses 3,24).

[22]"Do not lie with a man as one lies with a woman; that is detestable.

[23]"Do not have sexual relations with an animal and defile yourself with it. A woman must not present herself to an animal to have sexual relations with it; that is a perversion.

[24]"Do not defile yourselves in any of these ways, because this is how the nations that I am going to drive out before you became defiled. [25]Even the land was defiled; so I punished it for its sin, and the land vomited out its inhabitants. [26]But you must keep my decrees and my laws. The native-born and the aliens living among you must not do any of these detestable things, [27]for all these things were done by the people who lived in the land before you, and the land became defiled. [28]And if you defile the land, it will vomit

[a]21 Or *to be passed through ⌊the fire⌋*

you out as it vomited out the nations that were before you.

[29] "Everyone who does any of these detestable things—such persons must be cut off from their people. [30]Keep my requirements and do not follow any of the detestable customs that were practiced before you came and do not defile yourselves with them. I am the LORD your God.'"

Various Laws

19 The LORD said to Moses, [2]"Speak to the entire assembly of Israel and say to them: 'Be holy because I, the LORD your God, am holy.

[3] "Each of you must respect his mother and father, and you must observe my Sabbaths. I am the LORD your God.

[4] "Do not turn to idols or make gods of cast metal for yourselves. I am the LORD your God.

[5] "When you sacrifice a fellowship offering[a] to the LORD, sacrifice it in such a way that it will be accepted on your behalf. [6]It shall be eaten on the day you sacrifice it or on the next day; anything left over until the third day must be burned up. [7]If any of it is eaten on the third day, it is impure and will not be accepted. [8]Whoever eats it will be held responsible because he has desecrated what is holy to the LORD; that person must be cut off from his people.

[9] "When you reap the harvest of your land, do not reap to the very edges of your field or gather

---

19:9 A Form of Welfare

God's law was persistently concerned with the welfare of the poor. Everyday farming was to be done in such a way that poor and foreign people could fend for themselves. The reasons for such care are given: we are to imitate the holy character of God (verse 2), who cares for the poor, and to love our neighbor as ourselves (verse 18).

---

the gleanings of your harvest. [10]Do not go over your vineyard a second time or pick up the grapes that have fallen. Leave them for the poor and the alien. I am the LORD your God.

[11] "Do not steal.

" 'Do not lie.

" 'Do not deceive one another.

[12] "Do not swear falsely by my name and so profane the name of your God. I am the LORD.

[13] "Do not defraud your neighbor or rob him.

" 'Do not hold back the wages of a hired man overnight.

[14] "Do not curse the deaf or put a stumbling block in front of the blind, but fear your God. I am the LORD.

[15] "Do not pervert justice; do not show partiality to the poor or favoritism to the great, but judge your neighbor fairly.

[16] "Do not go about spreading slander among your people.

" 'Do not do anything that endangers your neighbor's life. I am the LORD.

[17] "Do not hate your brother in your heart. Rebuke your neighbor frankly so you will not share in his guilt.

[18] "Do not seek revenge or bear a grudge against one of your people, but love your neighbor as yourself. I am the LORD.

[19] "Keep my decrees.

" 'Do not mate different kinds of animals.

" 'Do not plant your field with two kinds of seed.

" 'Do not wear clothing woven of two kinds of material.

[20] "If a man sleeps with a woman who is a slave girl promised to another man but who has not been ransomed or given her freedom, there must be due punishment. Yet they are not to be put to death, because she had not been freed. [21]The man, however, must bring a ram to the entrance to the Tent of Meeting for a guilt offering to the LORD. [22]With the ram of the guilt offering the priest is to make atonement for him before the LORD for the sin he has committed, and his sin will be forgiven.

[23] "When you enter the land and plant any kind of fruit tree, regard its fruit as forbidden.[b] For three years you are to consider it forbidden[b]; it must not be eaten. [24]In the fourth year all its fruit will be holy, an offering of praise to the LORD. [25]But in the fifth year you may eat its fruit. In this way your harvest will be increased. I am the LORD your God.

[26] "Do not eat any meat with the blood still in it.

" 'Do not practice divination or sorcery.

[27] "Do not cut the hair at the sides of your head or clip off the edges of your beard.

[28] "Do not cut your bodies for the dead or put tattoo marks on yourselves. I am the LORD.

[29] "Do not degrade your daughter by making her a prostitute, or the land will turn to prostitution and be filled with wickedness.

[30] "Observe my Sabbaths and have reverence for my sanctuary. I am the LORD.

[31] "Do not turn to mediums or seek out spiritists, for you will be defiled by them. I am the LORD your God.

[32] "Rise in the presence of the aged, show respect for the elderly and revere your God. I am the LORD.

[33] "When an alien lives with you in your land, do not mistreat him. [34]The alien living with you

---

[a]5 Traditionally *peace offering*   [b]23 Hebrew *uncircumcised*

must be treated as one of your native-born. Love him as yourself, for you were aliens in Egypt. I am the LORD your God.

35 " 'Do not use dishonest standards when measuring length, weight or quantity. 36 Use honest scales and honest weights, an honest ephah[a] and an honest hin.[b] I am the LORD your God, who brought you out of Egypt.

37 " 'Keep all my decrees and all my laws and follow them. I am the LORD.' "

Punishments for Sin

20 The LORD said to Moses, 2 "Say to the Israelites: 'Any Israelite or any alien living in Israel who gives[c] any of his children to Molech must be put to death. The people of the community are to stone him. 3 I will set my face against that man and I will cut him off from his people; for by giving his children to Molech, he has defiled my sanctuary and profaned my holy name. 4 If the people of the community close their eyes when that man gives one of his children to Molech and they fail to put him to death, 5 I will set my face against that man and his family and will cut off from their people both him and all who follow him in prostituting themselves to Molech.

6 " 'I will set my face against the person who turns to mediums and spiritists to prostitute himself by following them, and I will cut him off from his people.

7 " 'Consecrate yourselves and be holy, because

20:7–8 The Bottom Line

These verses, along with verse 26, sum up the underlying reason for many of the laws outlined in Leviticus: God wanted the Israelites to be different. The New Testament makes clear that some of these regulations—eating forbidden animals, touching unclean persons—do not apply for all time. But at this moment, as God's people entered their new land, God wanted them to stand out from the nations around them (verses 22–24). Sadly, before long the Israelites were mimicking almost all the practices of their pagan neighbors.

I am the LORD your God. 8 Keep my decrees and follow them. I am the LORD, who makes you holy.[d]

9 " 'If anyone curses his father or mother, he must be put to death. He has cursed his father or his mother, and his blood will be on his own head.

10 " 'If a man commits adultery with another man's wife—with the wife of his neighbor—

both the adulterer and the adulteress must be put to death.

11 " 'If a man sleeps with his father's wife, he has dishonored his father. Both the man and the woman must be put to death; their blood will be on their own heads.

12 " 'If a man sleeps with his daughter-in-law, both of them must be put to death. What they have done is a perversion; their blood will be on their own heads.

13 " 'If a man lies with a man as one lies with a woman, both of them have done what is detestable. They must be put to death; their blood will be on their own heads.

14 " 'If a man marries both a woman and her mother, it is wicked. Both he and they must be burned in the fire, so that no wickedness will be among you.

15 " 'If a man has sexual relations with an animal, he must be put to death, and you must kill the animal.

16 " 'If a woman approaches an animal to have sexual relations with it, kill both the woman and the animal. They must be put to death; their blood will be on their own heads.

17 " 'If a man marries his sister, the daughter of either his father or his mother, and they have sexual relations, it is a disgrace. They must be cut off before the eyes of their people. He has dishonored his sister and will be held responsible.

18 " 'If a man lies with a woman during her monthly period and has sexual relations with her, he has exposed the source of her flow, and she has also uncovered it. Both of them must be cut off from their people.

19 " 'Do not have sexual relations with the sister of either your mother or your father, for that would dishonor a close relative; both of you would be held responsible.

20 " 'If a man sleeps with his aunt, he has dishonored his uncle. They will be held responsible; they will die childless.

21 " 'If a man marries his brother's wife, it is an act of impurity; he has dishonored his brother. They will be childless.

22 " 'Keep all my decrees and laws and follow them, so that the land where I am bringing you to live may not vomit you out. 23 You must not live according to the customs of the nations I am going to drive out before you. Because they did all these things, I abhorred them. 24 But I said to you, "You will possess their land; I will give it to you as an inheritance, a land flowing with milk and honey." I am the LORD your God, who has set you apart from the nations.

25 " 'You must therefore make a distinction between clean and unclean animals and between

---

[a] 36 An ephah was a dry measure.   [b] 36 A hin was a liquid measure.   [c] 2 Or *sacrifices*; also in verses 3 and 4
[d] 8 Or *who sanctifies you*; or *who sets you apart as holy*

unclean and clean birds. Do not defile yourselves by any animal or bird or anything that moves along the ground—those which I have set apart as unclean for you. 26You are to be holy to me*

*26 Or be my holy ones

because I, the LORD, am holy, and I have set you apart from the nations to be my own.

27"'A man or woman who is a medium or spiritist among you must be put to death. You

A National Law Library
Setting Israel apart from its neighbors

THE LAWS OF THE UNITED States would fill a library. Elaborate indexes guide lawyers where to look when dealing with a particular issue. No one person can know even a fraction of all the federal, state, and local laws.

If the Old Testament laws recorded in Leviticus (and Exodus, Numbers, and Deuteronomy) seem dull and long-winded, keep them in perspective. These—just over 600 in all—were the entire set of laws for a nation, as far as we know. Their most striking feature, to a lawyer, is brevity and simplicity. You don't have to go to law school to understand them.

The laws are listed in no particular order. A law against witchcraft is followed by a law against improper haircuts, which is followed by a law against tattoos, which in turn is followed by a law against making your daughter into a prostitute. This mixing reveals an important feature of Old Testament thinking. Life is not analyzed in separate components, but seen as a whole.

For the Israelites, separation of church and state did not exist. Every aspect of life—politics, family life, diet, economics—concerned God. Even the Ten Commandments (in Exodus 20) show this, for they include laws regarding our relationship to both God and our neighbor. The two cannot be separated.

> *"'You are to be holy to me because I, the LORD, am holy, and I have set you apart from the nations to be my own.'"*
> *20:26*

Remarkable Features

In comparison with laws from other countries at that time, the Old Testament made a considerable advance. (Indeed, these laws have greatly influenced laws for our day.) Some of the remarkable features:

People were more important than property. For instance, there was never a death penalty for a crime against someone's property. Also, slaves were treated as human beings, not property. This was not true of many other legal codes of that time.

There was no class system. In many ancient countries, a noble was treated far differently from a commoner. Not so in Israel: Everybody stood on the same level before the law. Even a foreigner had clearly defined rights.

The punishment fit the crime. No "cruel and unusual punishment" was allowed. "Eye for eye" (Leviticus 24:20) ensured that no privileged character was "let off" for a crime, while at the same time it limited revenge.

Sexuality mattered. In most countries, the law cared little whether you slept with your neighbor's wife. In Israel, sexual immorality got stern treatment.

The poor and weak had protection. Specific provisions protected their rights from the powerful and wealthy. "Welfare" offered them a way to stay alive, such as the right to "glean the fields." In 19:9,13–14,32–33, God gave protection to various groups that could not defend themselves.

Attitudes, as well as actions, mattered. For instance, Leviticus 19:18 contains the famous law to "love your neighbor as yourself." Living up to the letter of the law was not enough. The law aimed to develop loving relationships.

Designed to Be Different

While we do not understand the reasons for some of the laws (many may have been designed simply to keep the Israelites "different" from their pagan neighbors), their overall impact is clear. These rules were intended to form a nation of compassionate, consistent, fair-minded people. They insisted that each person act positively and lovingly toward his or her neighbor—and particularly toward those in need. The reason? God lived with them. Since he is both just and merciful, his people must be too.

Life Questions: Everybody has a code to live by. Does your personal rulebook show as much concern for the poor and defenseless as Leviticus's?

are to stone them; their blood will be on their own heads.'"

Rules for Priests

21 The LORD said to Moses, "Speak to the priests, the sons of Aaron, and say to them: 'A priest must not make himself ceremonially unclean for any of his people who die, ²except for a close relative, such as his mother or father, his son or daughter, his brother, ³or an unmarried sister who is dependent on him since she has no husband—for her he may make himself unclean. ⁴He must not make himself unclean for people related to him by marriage,ᵃ and so defile himself.

⁵" 'Priests must not shave their heads or shave off the edges of their beards or cut their bodies. ⁶They must be holy to their God and must not profane the name of their God. Because they present the offerings made to the LORD by fire, the food of their God, they are to be holy.

⁷" 'They must not marry women defiled by prostitution or divorced from their husbands, because priests are holy to their God. ⁸Regard them as holy, because they offer up the food of your God. Consider them holy, because I the LORD am holy—I who make you holy.ᵇ

⁹" 'If a priest's daughter defiles herself by becoming a prostitute, she disgraces her father; she must be burned in the fire.

¹⁰" 'The high priest, the one among his brothers who has had the anointing oil poured on his head and who has been ordained to wear the priestly garments, must not let his hair become unkemptᶜ or tear his clothes. ¹¹He must not enter a place where there is a dead body. He must not make himself unclean, even for his father or mother, ¹²nor leave the sanctuary of his God or desecrate it, because he has been dedicated by the anointing oil of his God. I am the LORD.

¹³" 'The woman he marries must be a virgin. ¹⁴He must not marry a widow, a divorced woman, or a woman defiled by prostitution, but only a virgin from his own people, ¹⁵so he will not defile his offspring among his people. I am the LORD, who makes him holy.ᵈ' "

¹⁶The LORD said to Moses, ¹⁷"Say to Aaron: 'For the generations to come none of your descendants who has a defect may come near to offer the food of his God. ¹⁸No man who has any defect may come near: no man who is blind or lame, disfigured or deformed; ¹⁹no man with a crippled foot or hand, ²⁰or who is hunchbacked or dwarfed, or who has any eye defect, or who has festering or running sores or damaged testicles. ²¹No descendant of Aaron the priest who

has any defect is to come near to present the offerings made to the LORD by fire. He has a defect; he must not come near to offer the food of his God. ²²He may eat the most holy food of his God, as well as the holy food; ²³yet because of his defect, he must not go near the curtain or approach the altar, and so desecrate my sanctuary. I am the LORD, who makes them holy.ᵉ' "

²⁴So Moses told this to Aaron and his sons and to all the Israelites.

22 The LORD said to Moses, ²"Tell Aaron and his sons to treat with respect the sacred offerings the Israelites consecrate to me, so they will not profane my holy name. I am the LORD.

³"Say to them: 'For the generations to come, if any of your descendants is ceremonially unclean and yet comes near the sacred offerings that the Israelites consecrate to the LORD, that person must be cut off from my presence. I am the LORD.

⁴" 'If a descendant of Aaron has an infectious skin diseaseᶠ or a bodily discharge, he may not eat the sacred offerings until he is cleansed. He will also be unclean if he touches something defiled by a corpse or by anyone who has an emission of semen, ⁵or if he touches any crawling thing that makes him unclean, or any person who makes him unclean, whatever the uncleanness may be. ⁶The one who touches any such thing will be unclean till evening. He must not eat any of the sacred offerings unless he has bathed himself with water. ⁷When the sun goes down, he will be clean, and after that he may eat the sacred offerings, for they are his food. ⁸He must not eat anything found dead or torn by wild animals, and so become unclean through it. I am the LORD.

⁹" 'The priests are to keep my requirements so that they do not become guilty and die for treating them with contempt. I am the LORD, who makes them holy.ᵍ

¹⁰" 'No one outside a priest's family may eat the sacred offering, nor may the guest of a priest or his hired worker eat it. ¹¹But if a priest buys a slave with money, or if a slave is born in his household, that slave may eat his food. ¹²If a priest's daughter marries anyone other than a priest, she may not eat any of the sacred contributions. ¹³But if a priest's daughter becomes a widow or is divorced, yet has no children, and she returns to live in her father's house as in her youth, she may eat of her father's food. No unauthorized person, however, may eat any of it.

¹⁴" 'If anyone eats a sacred offering by mistake, he must make restitution to the priest for the offering and add a fifth of the value to it. ¹⁵The priests must not desecrate the sacred offerings

---

ᵃ4 Or *unclean as a leader among his people*   ᵇ8 Or *who sanctify you*; or *who set you apart as holy*   ᶜ10 Or *not uncover his head*   ᵈ15 Or *who sanctifies him*; or *who sets him apart as holy*   ᵉ23 Or *who sanctifies them*; or *who sets them apart as holy*   ᶠ4 Traditionally *leprosy*; the Hebrew word was used for various diseases affecting the skin—not necessarily leprosy.   ᵍ9 Or *who sanctifies them*; or *who sets them apart as holy*; also in verse 16

the Israelites present to the LORD [16]by allowing them to eat the sacred offerings and so bring upon them guilt requiring payment. I am the LORD, who makes them holy.'"

Unacceptable Sacrifices

[17]The LORD said to Moses, [18]"Speak to Aaron and his sons and to all the Israelites and say to them: 'If any of you—either an Israelite or an alien living in Israel—presents a gift for a burnt offering to the LORD, either to fulfill a vow or as a freewill offering, [19]you must present a male without defect from the cattle, sheep or goats in order that it may be accepted on your behalf.

> ### 22:19 The Very Best for God
>
> *For the Israelite farmers, a farm animal represented a considerable contribution. It would have been tempting to cull out their weakest animals. Instead, they were commanded to give their very best. Similarly, at every harvest they were to bring their very first grain to the Lord (23:10). These practices reminded them again and again of God's place in their lives.*

[20]Do not bring anything with a defect, because it will not be accepted on your behalf. [21]When anyone brings from the herd or flock a fellowship offering[a] to the LORD to fulfill a special vow or as a freewill offering, it must be without defect or blemish to be acceptable. [22]Do not offer to the LORD the blind, the injured or the maimed, or anything with warts or festering or running sores. Do not place any of these on the altar as an offering made to the LORD by fire. [23]You may, however, present as a freewill offering an ox[b] or a sheep that is deformed or stunted, but it will not be accepted in fulfillment of a vow. [24]You must not offer to the LORD an animal whose testicles are bruised, crushed, torn or cut. You must not do this in your own land, [25]and you must not accept such animals from the hand of a foreigner and offer them as the food of your God. They will not be accepted on your behalf, because they are deformed and have defects.'"

[26]The LORD said to Moses, [27]"When a calf, a lamb or a goat is born, it is to remain with its mother for seven days. From the eighth day on, it will be acceptable as an offering made to the LORD by fire. [28]Do not slaughter a cow or a sheep and its young on the same day.

[29]"When you sacrifice a thank offering to the LORD, sacrifice it in such a way that it will be accepted on your behalf. [30]It must be eaten that same day; leave none of it till morning. I am the LORD.

[31]"Keep my commands and follow them. I am the LORD. [32]Do not profane my holy name. I must be acknowledged as holy by the Israelites. I am the LORD, who makes[c] you holy[d] [33]and who brought you out of Egypt to be your God. I am the LORD."

23 The LORD said to Moses, [2]"Speak to the Israelites and say to them: 'These are my appointed feasts, the appointed feasts of the LORD, which you are to proclaim as sacred assemblies.

The Sabbath

[3]"'There are six days when you may work, but the seventh day is a Sabbath of rest, a day of sacred assembly. You are not to do any work; wherever you live, it is a Sabbath to the LORD.

The Passover and Unleavened Bread

[4]"'These are the LORD's appointed feasts, the sacred assemblies you are to proclaim at their appointed times: [5]The LORD's Passover begins at twilight on the fourteenth day of the first month. [6]On the fifteenth day of that month the LORD's Feast of Unleavened Bread begins; for seven days you must eat bread made without yeast. [7]On the first day hold a sacred assembly and do no regular work. [8]For seven days present an offering made to the LORD by fire. And on the seventh day hold a sacred assembly and do no regular work.'"

Firstfruits

[9]The LORD said to Moses, [10]"Speak to the Israelites and say to them: 'When you enter the land I am going to give you and you reap its harvest, bring to the priest a sheaf of the first grain you harvest. [11]He is to wave the sheaf before the LORD so it will be accepted on your behalf; the priest is to wave it on the day after the Sabbath. [12]On the day you wave the sheaf, you must sacrifice as a burnt offering to the LORD a lamb a year old without defect, [13]together with its grain offering of two-tenths of an ephah[e] of fine flour mixed with oil—an offering made to the LORD by fire, a pleasing aroma—and its drink offering of a quarter of a hin[f] of wine. [14]You must not eat any bread, or roasted or new grain, until the very day you bring this offering to your God. This is to be a lasting ordinance for the generations to come, wherever you live.

---

[a]21 Traditionally *peace offering*   [b]23 The Hebrew word can include both male and female.   [c]32 Or *made*
[d]32 Or *who sanctifies you;* or *who sets you apart as holy*   [e]13 That is, probably about 4 quarts (about 4.5 liters); also in verse 17   [f]13 That is, probably about 1 quart (about 1 liter)

Feat of Weeks

15 " 'From the day after the Sabbath, the day you brought the sheaf of the wave offering, count off seven full weeks. **16**Count off fifty days up to the day after the seventh Sabbath, and then present an offering of new grain to the LORD. **17**From wherever you live, bring two loaves made of two-tenths of an ephah of fine flour, baked with yeast, as a wave offering of firstfruits to the LORD. **18**Present with this bread seven male lambs, each a year old and without defect, one young bull and two rams. They will be a burnt offering to the LORD, together with their grain offerings and drink offerings—an offering made by fire, an aroma pleasing to the LORD. **19**Then sacrifice one male goat for a sin offering and two lambs, each a year old, for a fellowship offering.[a] **20**The priest is to wave the two lambs before the LORD as a wave offering, together with the bread of the firstfruits. They are a sacred offering to the LORD for the priest. **21**On that same day you are to proclaim a sacred assembly and do no regular work. This is to be a lasting ordinance for the generations to come, wherever you live.

22 " 'When you reap the harvest of your land, do not reap to the very edges of your field or gather the gleanings of your harvest. Leave them

[a] *19 Traditionally peace offering*

In Celebration of God
Jewish holidays focused on one thing

> " 'Rejoice before the LORD your God for seven days.' "
> 23:40

ANTHROPOLOGISTS STUDYING REMOTE TRIBES ROUTINELY describe their feast days, for these show the people's common values. What would stand out to an anthropologist studying the United States? Undoubtedly he would notice that our celebration of Christmas, Thanksgiving, and the Fourth of July emphasize family, food, and gifts—the more the better.

What about the Israelites? Leviticus describes five feasts, all focusing on God. Each was marked by special sacrifices to God and a sacred assembly where God had "pitched his tent." Rather than giving gifts to each other, the Israelites gave gifts to God.

Sometimes they rejoiced: During the Feast of Tabernacles everyone camped out to "rejoice before the LORD" for a solid week (23:40). On other occasions, such as the Day of Atonement, they were sober and solemn (chapter 16, 23:26–32). But always their orientation was God-directed.

God over Money

Nobody worked on Israelite feast days, but their "days off" had a different motive than ours. An Israelite farmer never got a paid holiday. In fact, a holiday could cost him—it might fall on a day perfect for harvesting. But God took priority over work. The weekly Sabbath day reinforced the same idea. You had to stop working to worship.

God mattered more than wealth. This fundamental belief showed itself even more in the sabbath year and in the Year of Jubilee (chapter 25). Every seventh year, people did not farm at all. They lived off whatever the land produced by itself, and dedicated themselves to God. This would be like our closing all businesses and factories for a year.

After 49 years—seven sabbath years—the Year of Jubilee came. This time, people went for two years straight without planting. All land bought or sold during the previous 49 years went back to its original family ownership. Since the land had originally been equally distributed, this meant that no family would ever become either totally destitute or overwhelmingly rich. Any Israelites who had sold themselves as slaves would also be freed in that year.

Prosperity Came from God

Hard work and the resulting abundance were never scorned in Israel. But prosperity always came ultimately from God, not from hard work or clever dealings alone. The feasts and Sabbaths, set aside as special days, helped people remember and praise the God who had given them so much.

So far as we know, no Year of Jubilee was ever actually practiced. Some of the feasts were forgotten for long periods of time. But such failure is not surprising. After all, think what we have done to the holy day of Christmas! The feast days described in Leviticus give us a good idea of what God wanted Israel to be. Sadly, reality did not often match the ideal.

Life Questions: If someone examined the way you spend your holidays and weekends, what would he or she conclude about your priorities?

for the poor and the alien. I am the LORD your God.'"

Feast of Trumpets

[23]The LORD said to Moses, [24]"Say to the Israelites: 'On the first day of the seventh month you are to have a day of rest, a sacred assembly commemorated with trumpet blasts. [25]Do no regular work, but present an offering made to the LORD by fire.'"

Day of Atonement

[26]The LORD said to Moses, [27]"The tenth day of this seventh month is the Day of Atonement. Hold a sacred assembly and deny yourselves,[a] and present an offering made to the LORD by fire. [28]Do no work on that day, because it is the Day of Atonement, when atonement is made for you before the LORD your God. [29]Anyone who does not deny himself on that day must be cut off from his people. [30]I will destroy from among his people anyone who does any work on that day. [31]You shall do no work at all. This is to be a lasting ordinance for the generations to come, wherever you live. [32]It is a sabbath of rest for you, and you must deny yourselves. From the evening of the ninth day of the month until the following evening you are to observe your sabbath."

Feast of Tabernacles

[33]The LORD said to Moses, [34]"Say to the Israelites: 'On the fifteenth day of the seventh month the LORD's Feast of Tabernacles begins, and it lasts for seven days. [35]The first day is a sacred assembly; do no regular work. [36]For seven days present offerings made to the LORD by fire, and on the eighth day hold a sacred assembly and present an offering made to the LORD by fire. It is the closing assembly; do no regular work.

[37]("'These are the LORD's appointed feasts, which you are to proclaim as sacred assemblies for bringing offerings made to the LORD by fire— the burnt offerings and grain offerings, sacrifices and drink offerings required for each day. [38]These offerings are in addition to those for the LORD's Sabbaths and[b] in addition to your gifts and whatever you have vowed and all the freewill offerings you give to the LORD.)

[39]"'So beginning with the fifteenth day of the seventh month, after you have gathered the crops of the land, celebrate the festival to the LORD for seven days; the first day is a day of rest, and the eighth day also is a day of rest. [40]On the first day you are to take choice fruit from the trees, and palm fronds, leafy branches and poplars, and rejoice before the LORD your God for seven days. [41]Celebrate this as a festival to the LORD for seven days each year. This is to be a lasting ordinance

for the generations to come; celebrate it in the seventh month. [42]Live in booths for seven days: All native-born Israelites are to live in booths [43]so your descendants will know that I had the

23:40 Seven Days of Rejoicing

Though the worship of God was a serious business, it was also joyful. Every year, for instance, the Israelites were to hold this week-long campout and celebration, filled with rejoicing.

Israelites live in booths when I brought them out of Egypt. I am the LORD your God.'"

[44]So Moses announced to the Israelites the appointed feasts of the LORD.

Oil and Bread Set Before the LORD

24 The LORD said to Moses, [2]"Command the Israelites to bring you clear oil of pressed olives for the light so that the lamps may be kept burning continually. [3]Outside the curtain of the Testimony in the Tent of Meeting, Aaron is to tend the lamps before the LORD from evening till morning, continually. This is to be a lasting ordinance for the generations to come. [4]The lamps on the pure gold lampstand before the LORD must be tended continually.

[5]"Take fine flour and bake twelve loaves of bread, using two-tenths of an ephah[c] for each loaf. [6]Set them in two rows, six in each row, on the table of pure gold before the LORD. [7]Along each row put some pure incense as a memorial portion to represent the bread and to be an offering made to the LORD by fire. [8]This bread is to be set out before the LORD regularly, Sabbath after Sabbath, on behalf of the Israelites, as a lasting covenant. [9]It belongs to Aaron and his sons, who are to eat it in a holy place, because it is a most holy part of their regular share of the offerings made to the LORD by fire."

A Blasphemer Stoned

[10]Now the son of an Israelite mother and an Egyptian father went out among the Israelites, and a fight broke out in the camp between him and an Israelite. [11]The son of the Israelite woman blasphemed the Name with a curse; so they brought him to Moses. (His mother's name was Shelomith, the daughter of Dibri the Danite.) [12]They put him in custody until the will of the LORD should be made clear to them.

[13]Then the LORD said to Moses: [14]"Take the blasphemer outside the camp. All those who heard him are to lay their hands on his head, and

---

[a]27 Or *and fast*; also in verses 29 and 32   [b]38 Or *These feasts are in addition to the LORD's Sabbaths, and these offerings are*   [c]5 That is, probably about 4 quarts (about 4.5 liters)

the entire assembly is to stone him. ¹⁵Say to the Israelites: 'If anyone curses his God, he will be held responsible; ¹⁶anyone who blasphemes the name of the LORD must be put to death. The entire assembly must stone him. Whether an alien or native-born, when he blasphemes the Name, he must be put to death.

¹⁷"'If anyone takes the life of a human being, he must be put to death. ¹⁸Anyone who takes the life of someone's animal must make restitution—life for life. ¹⁹If anyone injures his neighbor, whatever he has done must be done to him: ²⁰fracture for fracture, eye for eye, tooth for tooth. As he has injured the other, so he is to be

24:20 An Eye for an Eye

Jesus, speaking of this law in Matthew 5:38, told his followers not to resist evil people. Apparently people had been taking "eye for eye" as a basis for private vengeance—as some do today. The law's original intent, however, was to set a standard for punishment in court. It limited vengeance and made certain that both rich and poor, native and foreigner, would pay the same price for their crimes.

injured. ²¹Whoever kills an animal must make restitution, but whoever kills a man must be put to death. ²²You are to have the same law for the alien and the native-born. I am the LORD your God.'"

²³Then Moses spoke to the Israelites, and they took the blasphemer outside the camp and stoned him. The Israelites did as the LORD commanded Moses.

The Sabbath Year

25 The LORD said to Moses on Mount Sinai, ²"Speak to the Israelites and say to them: 'When you enter the land I am going to give you, the land itself must observe a sabbath to the LORD. ³For six years sow your fields, and for six years prune your vineyards and gather their crops. ⁴But in the seventh year the land is to have a sabbath of rest, a sabbath to the LORD. Do not sow your fields or prune your vineyards. ⁵Do not reap what grows of itself or harvest the grapes of your untended vines. The land is to have a year of rest. ⁶Whatever the land yields during the sabbath year will be food for you—for yourself, your manservant and maidservant, and the hired worker and temporary resident who live among you, ⁷as well as for your livestock and the wild animals in your land. Whatever the land produces may be eaten.

The Year of Jubilee

⁸"'Count off seven sabbaths of years—seven times seven years—so that the seven sabbaths of years amount to a period of forty-nine years. ⁹Then have the trumpet sounded everywhere on the tenth day of the seventh month; on the Day of Atonement sound the trumpet throughout your land. ¹⁰Consecrate the fiftieth year and proclaim liberty throughout the land to all its inhabitants. It shall be a jubilee for you; each one of you is to return to his family property and each to his own clan. ¹¹The fiftieth year shall be a jubilee for you; do not sow and do not reap what grows of itself or harvest the untended vines. ¹²For it is a jubilee and is to be holy for you; eat only what is taken directly from the fields.

¹³"'In this Year of Jubilee everyone is to return to his own property.

¹⁴"'If you sell land to one of your countrymen or buy any from him, do not take advantage of each other. ¹⁵You are to buy from your countryman on the basis of the number of years since the Jubilee. And he is to sell to you on the basis of the number of years left for harvesting crops. ¹⁶When the years are many, you are to increase the price, and when the years are few, you are to decrease the price, because what he is really selling you is the number of crops. ¹⁷Do not take advantage of each other, but fear your God. I am the LORD your God.

¹⁸"'Follow my decrees and be careful to obey my laws, and you will live safely in the land. ¹⁹Then the land will yield its fruit, and you will eat your fill and live there in safety. ²⁰You may ask, "What will we eat in the seventh year if we do not plant or harvest our crops?" ²¹I will send you such a blessing in the sixth year that the land will yield enough for three years. ²²While you plant during the eighth year, you will eat from the old crop and will continue to eat from it until the harvest of the ninth year comes in.

²³"'The land must not be sold permanently, because the land is mine and you are but aliens and my tenants. ²⁴Throughout the country that you hold as a possession, you must provide for the redemption of the land.

²⁵"'If one of your countrymen becomes poor and sells some of his property, his nearest relative is to come and redeem what his countryman has sold. ²⁶If, however, a man has no one to redeem it for him but he himself prospers and acquires sufficient means to redeem it, ²⁷he is to determine the value for the years since he sold it and refund the balance to the man to whom he sold it; he can then go back to his own property. ²⁸But if he does not acquire the means to repay him, what he sold will remain in the possession of the buyer until the Year of Jubilee. It will be returned in the Jubilee, and he can then go back to his property.

²⁹"'If a man sells a house in a walled city, he retains the right of redemption a full year after its

sale. During that time he may redeem it. [30]If it is not redeemed before a full year has passed, the house in the walled city shall belong permanently to the buyer and his descendants. It is not to be

25:28 Property Rights

God's law provided for a kind of redistribution of wealth every 50 years, when all land would revert to its original owners. The tendency for the rich to buy up all the property (which originally had been divided equally among families) was reversed in the Year of Jubilee. In essence, you could not sell your land—only lease it out.

returned in the Jubilee. [31]But houses in villages without walls around them are to be considered as open country. They can be redeemed, and they are to be returned in the Jubilee.

[32]"The Levites always have the right to redeem their houses in the Levitical towns, which they possess. [33]So the property of the Levites is redeemable—that is, a house sold in any town they hold—and is to be returned in the Jubilee, because the houses in the towns of the Levites are their property among the Israelites. [34]But the pastureland belonging to their towns must not be sold; it is their permanent possession.

[35]"If one of your countrymen becomes poor and is unable to support himself among you, help him as you would an alien or a temporary resident, so he can continue to live among you. [36]Do not take interest of any kind[a] from him, but fear your God, so that your countryman may continue to live among you. [37]You must not lend him money at interest or sell him food at a profit. [38]I am the LORD your God, who brought you out of Egypt to give you the land of Canaan and to be your God.

[39]"If one of your countrymen becomes poor among you and sells himself to you, do not make him work as a slave. [40]He is to be treated as a hired worker or a temporary resident among you; he is to work for you until the Year of Jubilee. [41]Then he and his children are to be released, and he will go back to his own clan and to the property of his forefathers. [42]Because the Israelites are my servants, whom I brought out of Egypt, they must not be sold as slaves. [43]Do not rule over them ruthlessly, but fear your God.

[44]"Your male and female slaves are to come from the nations around you; from them you may buy slaves. [45]You may also buy some of the temporary residents living among you and members of their clans born in your country, and they will become your property. [46]You can will them

to your children as inherited property and can make them slaves for life, but you must not rule over your fellow Israelites ruthlessly.

[47]"If an alien or a temporary resident among you becomes rich and one of your countrymen becomes poor and sells himself to the alien living among you or to a member of the alien's clan, [48]he retains the right of redemption after he has sold himself. One of his relatives may redeem him: [49]An uncle or a cousin or any blood relative in his clan may redeem him. Or if he prospers, he may redeem himself. [50]He and his buyer are to count the time from the year he sold himself up to the Year of Jubilee. The price for his release is to be based on the rate paid to a hired man for that number of years. [51]If many years remain, he must pay for his redemption a larger share of the price paid for him. [52]If only a few years remain until the Year of Jubilee, he is to compute that and pay for his redemption accordingly. [53]He is to be treated as a man hired from year to year; you must see to it that his owner does not rule over him ruthlessly.

[54]"Even if he is not redeemed in any of these ways, he and his children are to be released in the Year of Jubilee, [55]for the Israelites belong to me as servants. They are my servants, whom I brought out of Egypt. I am the LORD your God.

Reward for Obedience

26 "'Do not make idols or set up an image or a sacred stone for yourselves, and do not place a carved stone in your land to bow down before it. I am the LORD your God.

[2]"'Observe my Sabbaths and have reverence for my sanctuary. I am the LORD.

[3]"'If you follow my decrees and are careful to obey my commands, [4]I will send you rain in its season, and the ground will yield its crops and the trees of the field their fruit. [5]Your threshing will continue until grape harvest and the grape harvest will continue until planting, and you will eat all the food you want and live in safety in your land.

[6]"'I will grant peace in the land, and you will lie down and no one will make you afraid. I will remove savage beasts from the land, and the sword will not pass through your country. [7]You will pursue your enemies, and they will fall by the sword before you. [8]Five of you will chase a hundred, and a hundred of you will chase ten thousand, and your enemies will fall by the sword before you.

[9]"'I will look on you with favor and make you fruitful and increase your numbers, and I will keep my covenant with you. [10]You will still be eating last year's harvest when you will have to move it out to make room for the new. [11]I will

---

[a]36 Or *take excessive interest*; similarly in verse 37

put my dwelling place[a] among you, and I will not abhor you. ¹²I will walk among you and be your God, and you will be my people. ¹³I am the LORD your God, who brought you out of Egypt so that you would no longer be slaves to the Egyptians; I broke the bars of your yoke and enabled you to walk with heads held high.

Punishment for Disobedience

¹⁴"'But if you will not listen to me and carry out all these commands, ¹⁵and if you reject my decrees and abhor my laws and fail to carry out all my commands and so violate my covenant, ¹⁶then I will do this to you: I will bring upon you sudden terror, wasting diseases and fever that will destroy your sight and drain away your life. You will plant seed in vain, because your enemies will eat it. ¹⁷I will set my face against you so that you will be defeated by your enemies; those who hate you will rule over you, and you will flee even when no one is pursuing you.

¹⁸"'If after all this you will not listen to me, I will punish you for your sins seven times over. ¹⁹I will break down your stubborn pride and make the sky above you like iron and the ground beneath you like bronze. ²⁰Your strength will be spent in vain, because your soil will not yield its crops, nor will the trees of the land yield their fruit.

²¹"'If you remain hostile toward me and refuse to listen to me, I will multiply your afflictions seven times over, as your sins deserve. ²²I will send wild animals against you, and they will rob you of your children, destroy your cattle and make you so few in number that your roads will be deserted.

²³"'If in spite of these things you do not accept my correction but continue to be hostile toward me, ²⁴I myself will be hostile toward you and will afflict you for your sins seven times over. ²⁵And I will bring the sword upon you to avenge the breaking of the covenant. When you withdraw into your cities, I will send a plague among you, and you will be given into enemy hands. ²⁶When I cut off your supply of bread, ten women will be able to bake your bread in one oven, and they will dole out the bread by weight. You will eat, but you will not be satisfied.

²⁷"'If in spite of this you still do not listen to me but continue to be hostile toward me, ²⁸then in my anger I will be hostile toward you, and I myself will punish you for your sins seven times over. ²⁹You will eat the flesh of your sons and the flesh of your daughters. ³⁰I will destroy your high places, cut down your incense altars and pile your dead bodies on the lifeless forms of your idols, and I will abhor you. ³¹I will turn your

cities into ruins and lay waste your sanctuaries, and I will take no delight in the pleasing aroma of your offerings. ³²I will lay waste the land, so that your enemies who live there will be appalled. ³³I will scatter you among the nations and will draw out my sword and pursue you. Your land will be laid waste, and your cities will lie in ruins. ³⁴Then the land will enjoy its sabbath years all the time that it lies desolate and you are in the country of your enemies; then the land will rest and

26:34 Revenge of the Land

There is little evidence that the Israelites ever followed the rules on sabbath years and Jubilee. Nevertheless, as ominously foretold here, the land eventually did get its rest. For 70 years the Babylonians held the Israelites hostage, far away from their homeland. And the land had rest.

enjoy its sabbaths. ³⁵All the time that it lies desolate, the land will have the rest it did not have during the sabbaths you lived in it.

³⁶"'As for those of you who are left, I will make their hearts so fearful in the lands of their enemies that the sound of a windblown leaf will put them to flight. They will run as though fleeing from the sword, and they will fall, even though no one is pursuing them. ³⁷They will stumble over one another as though fleeing from the sword, even though no one is pursuing them. So you will not be able to stand before your enemies. ³⁸You will perish among the nations; the land of your enemies will devour you. ³⁹Those of you who are left will waste away in the lands of their enemies because of their sins; also because of their fathers' sins they will waste away.

⁴⁰"'But if they will confess their sins and the sins of their fathers—their treachery against me and their hostility toward me, ⁴¹which made me hostile toward them so that I sent them into the land of their enemies—then when their uncircumcised hearts are humbled and they pay for their sin, ⁴²I will remember my covenant with Jacob and my covenant with Isaac and my covenant with Abraham, and I will remember the land. ⁴³For the land will be deserted by them and will enjoy its sabbaths while it lies desolate without them. They will pay for their sins because they rejected my laws and abhorred my decrees. ⁴⁴Yet in spite of this, when they are in the land of their enemies, I will not reject them or abhor them so as to destroy them completely, breaking my covenant with them. I am the LORD their

---

*a*11 Or *my tabernacle*

God. **45**But for their sake I will remember the covenant with their ancestors whom I brought out of Egypt in the sight of the nations to be their God. I am the LORD.'"

46These are the decrees, the laws and the regulations that the LORD established on Mount Sinai between himself and the Israelites through Moses.

> ### 26:41 Uncircumcised Hearts
> *Circumcision was the ritual that made a man into a Jew, so to speak. But this reference to uncircumcised hearts shows that, right from the beginning, the inward attitude, as well as the physical operation, was crucial. Six hundred years later Jeremiah accused the Israelites of being uncircumcised in heart (Jeremiah 9:26); another 600 years after him Stephen made the same complaint (Acts 7:51). On this basis Paul wrote, "A man is not a Jew if he is only one outwardly . . . No, a man is a Jew if he is one inwardly; and circumcision is a circumcision of the heart, by the Spirit" (Romans 2:28–29). Leviticus offered more than a legal system; these laws appealed to a person's relationship with God.*

Redeeming What Is the LORD's

27 The LORD said to Moses, **2**"Speak to the Israelites and say to them: 'If anyone makes a special vow to dedicate persons to the LORD by giving equivalent values, **3**set the value of a male between the ages of twenty and sixty at fifty shekels*a* of silver, according to the sanctuary shekel*b*; **4**and if it is a female, set her value at thirty shekels.*c* **5**If it is a person between the ages of five and twenty, set the value of a male at twenty shekels*d* and of a female at ten shekels.*e* **6**If it is a person between one month and five years, set the value of a male at five shekels*f* of silver and that of a female at three shekels*g* of silver. **7**If it is a person sixty years old or more, set the value of a male at fifteen shekels*h* and of a female at ten shekels. **8**If anyone making the vow is too poor to pay the specified amount, he is to present the person to the priest, who will set the value for him according to what the man making the vow can afford.

9"'If what he vowed is an animal that is acceptable as an offering to the LORD, such an animal given to the LORD becomes holy. **10**He must not exchange it or substitute a good one for a bad

one, or a bad one for a good one; if he should substitute one animal for another, both it and the substitute become holy. **11**If what he vowed is a ceremonially unclean animal—one that is not acceptable as an offering to the LORD—the animal must be presented to the priest, **12**who will judge its quality as good or bad. Whatever value the priest then sets, that is what it will be. **13**If the owner wishes to redeem the animal, he must add a fifth to its value.

14"'If a man dedicates his house as something holy to the LORD, the priest will judge its quality as good or bad. Whatever value the priest then sets, so it will remain. **15**If the man who dedicates his house redeems it, he must add a fifth to its value, and the house will again become his.

16"'If a man dedicates to the LORD part of his family land, its value is to be set according to the amount of seed required for it—fifty shekels of silver to a homer*i* of barley seed. **17**If he dedicates his field during the Year of Jubilee, the value that has been set remains. **18**But if he dedicates his field after the Jubilee, the priest will determine the value according to the number of years that remain until the next Year of Jubilee, and its set value will be reduced. **19**If the man who dedicates the field wishes to redeem it, he must add a fifth to its value, and the field will again become his. **20**If, however, he does not redeem the field, or if he has sold it to someone else, it can never be redeemed. **21**When the field is released in the Jubilee, it will become holy, like a field devoted to the LORD; it will become the property of the priests.*j*

22"'If a man dedicates to the LORD a field he has bought, which is not part of his family land, **23**the priest will determine its value up to the Year of Jubilee, and the man must pay its value on that day as something holy to the LORD. **24**In the Year of Jubilee the field will revert to the person from whom he bought it, the one whose land it was. **25**Every value is to be set according to the sanctuary shekel, twenty gerahs to the shekel.

26"'No one, however, may dedicate the firstborn of an animal, since the firstborn already belongs to the LORD; whether an ox*k* or a sheep, it is the LORD's. **27**If it is one of the unclean animals, he may buy it back at its set value, adding a fifth of the value to it. If he does not redeem it, it is to be sold at its set value.

28"'But nothing that a man owns and devotes*l* to the LORD—whether man or animal or family land—may be sold or redeemed; everything so devoted is most holy to the LORD.

---

a3 That is, about 1 1/4 pounds (about 0.6 kilogram); also in verse 16 also in verse 25   *c4* That is, about 12 ounces (about 0.3 kilogram)   *b3* That is, about 2/5 ounce (about 11.5 grams); *d5* That is, about 8 ounces (about 0.2 kilogram)   *e5* That is, about 4 ounces (about 110 grams); also in verse 7   *f6* That is, about 2 ounces (about 55 grams)   *g6* That is, about 1 1/4 ounces (about 35 grams)   *h7* That is, about 6 ounces (about 170 grams) *i16* That is, probably about 6 bushels (about 220 liters)   *j21* Or *priest*   *k26* The Hebrew word can include both male and female.   *l28* The Hebrew term refers to the irrevocable giving over of things or persons to the LORD.

29"'No person devoted to destruction[a] may be ransomed; he must be put to death.

30"'A tithe of everything from the land, whether grain from the soil or fruit from the trees, belongs to the LORD; it is holy to the LORD. 31If a man redeems any of his tithe, he must add a fifth of the value to it. 32The entire tithe of the herd and flock—every tenth animal that passes under the shepherd's rod—will be holy to the LORD. 33He must not pick out the good from the bad or make any substitution. If he does make a substitution, both the animal and its substitute become holy and cannot be redeemed.'"

34These are the commands the LORD gave Moses on Mount Sinai for the Israelites.

---

[a]29 The Hebrew term refers to the irrevocable giving over of things or persons to the LORD, often by totally destroying them.

NUMBERS

Forty Years of Misery
A joyous adventure comes to a tragic end

A S NUMBERS OPENS, THE ISRAELITES are gearing up for a great adventure. Free at last from the chains of slavery, they are headed for the promised land. Yet the book that begins with a bang ends with a whimper. Weeks, months, and then years in a hostile desert have seemed to melt the spirit of adventure. The Israelites act like people who have lost their moorings. In relentless detail, Numbers records a whole sequence of grumblings and rebellions.

Now the people complained about their hardships in the hearing of the Lord, and when he heard them his anger was aroused.
11:1

Forty-Year Detour

Stomachs complained first, as the Israelites began to long for the spices of Egypt. Soon, the great mob of people simply unraveled. At least ten times they lashed out in despair or rose up in open rebellion. They plotted against their leaders and denounced God. Revolt spread to the priests, to the top military scouts, to Moses' family, and finally to Moses himself.

The original Hebrew title of this book was not "Numbers" but rather "In the desert," and this cryptic phrase expresses a little of the Israelites' futility. Surrounded by hostile nations, they had to march under the broiling sun in a desert plagued by snakes, scorpions, and drought. Even today, visitors to the Sinai Desert marvel that an entire nation wandered that ground for so long.

A march through the desert should have taken about two weeks. Instead, it took almost 40 years. Numbers spans the years of wandering and ends where the trek began: at the very spot (Kadesh) where the Israelites' faith had failed. Of the many thousands who left Egypt, only two adults, Joshua and Caleb, would make it into the promised land.

A Different Kind of History

Most ancient histories sound very different from this book. They tell of heroic exploits by mighty warriors and unblemished leaders. With an almost numbing monotony, Numbers presents a far more realistic picture. It shows the early symptoms, the full progression, and the tragic end of grumbling and unbelief.

The Israelites lost faith not only in themselves, but in their God. Because of that, a whole generation of them lies buried in the peninsula known as Sinai.

References to the "desert wanderings" crop up again and again in the Bible. The period of rebellion left an indelible mark on the Jewish people. Exactly what went wrong? The book of Numbers is given to tell us. The apostle Paul points out that these failures "happened to them as examples and were written down as warnings for us, on whom the fulfillment of the ages has come. So, if you think you are standing firm, be careful that you don't fall!" (1 Corinthians 10:11–12).

How to Read Numbers

People who read straight through Numbers very often come away confused or discouraged. The book begins with a long description of a census and proceeds into lists of laws and rituals. These were the official records of a nation, and each word had great significance for the Israelites. (Imagine how our Yellow Pages or Congressional Record would appear to people 3,000 years from now.)

Yet, unlike Leviticus, Numbers does not consist mainly of these long descriptions. Rather, it focuses on stories, with laws and rituals sprinkled in at various points. The stories are exciting, and some, such as the story of Balaam, are quite remarkable.

The action in Numbers takes place in three different settings: (1) Chapters 1—14 begin in the same place Exodus ended: at the foot of Mount Sinai. (2) Chapters 15—19 cover a period of 37 years, the time of the desert wanderings. Moses' summary in chapter 33 lists 42 stops in the desert, but Numbers details very few of them. (3) Chapters 20—36 concern a whole new generation of Israelites, who were making final preparations before the invasion.

As you read Numbers, it will help to have a major theme in mind, such as grumbling and rebellion. Work through the book, looking at examples of this problem. Major outbreaks occur in chapters 11, 12, 13, 14, 16, 20, and 21—at least ten incidents in all. Notice the cause of each rebellion, and also God's response. Can you see parallels to the Israelites' experience in your own life?

Numbers also offers insight into the leadership of Moses by showing his response to each crisis. One illustration of his prominence: Over 80 times the book says that "the LORD said to Moses." Look for the qualities, both positive and negative, that made him an effective leader.

Other parts of the Bible often refer to Numbers. Some of the historical psalms, such as Psalms 78, 105, and 136, recast these events in poetry.

PEOPLE YOU'LL MEET IN NUMBERS

MIRIAM (p. 175)
AARON (p. 176)
BALAAM (p. 187)

3-TRACK READING PLAN

For an explanation and complete listing of the 3-track reading plan, turn to page 7.

TRACK 1:   *Two-Week Courses on the Bible*
See page 7 for information on these courses.

TRACK 2:   *An Overview of Numbers in 2 Days*
☐ Day 1. Read the Introduction to Numbers and then chapter 11, which shows a typical Israelite response to hardship.
☐ Day 2. Read chapter 14, the hinge chapter of Numbers.
Now turn to page 9 for your next Track 2 reading project.

TRACK 3:   *All of Numbers in 35 Days*
After you have read through Numbers, turn to pages 10—14 for your next Track 3 reading project.

☐1—2	☐3	☐4	☐5	☐6	☐7	☐8	☐9
☐10	☐11	☐12	☐13	☐14	☐15	☐16	☐17
☐18	☐19	☐20	☐21	☐22	☐23	☐24	☐25
☐26	☐27	☐28	☐29	☐30	☐31	☐32	☐33
☐34	☐35	☐36					

The Census

1 The LORD spoke to Moses in the Tent of Meeting in the Desert of Sinai on the first day of the second month of the second year after the Israelites came out of Egypt. He said: 2"Take a census of the whole Israelite community by their clans and families, listing every man by name, one by one. 3You and Aaron are to number by their divisions all the men in Israel twenty years old or more who are able to serve in the army. 4One man from each tribe, each the head of his family, is to help you. 5These are the names of the men who are to assist you:

from Reuben, Elizur son of Shedeur;
6from Simeon, Shelumiel son of Zurishaddai;
7from Judah, Nahshon son of Amminadab;
8from Issachar, Nethanel son of Zuar;
9from Zebulun, Eliab son of Helon;
10from the sons of Joseph:
from Ephraim, Elishama son of Ammihud;
from Manasseh, Gamaliel son of Pedahzur;
11from Benjamin, Abidan son of Gideoni;
12from Dan, Ahiezer son of Ammishaddai;
13from Asher, Pagiel son of Ocran;
14from Gad, Eliasaph son of Deuel;
15from Naphtali, Ahira son of Enan."

16These were the men appointed from the community, the leaders of their ancestral tribes. They were the heads of the clans of Israel.

17Moses and Aaron took these men whose names had been given, 18and they called the whole community together on the first day of the second month. The people indicated their ancestry by their clans and families, and the men twenty years or more were listed by name, one by one, 19as the LORD commanded Moses. And so he counted them in the Desert of Sinai:

20From the descendants of Reuben the firstborn son of Israel:
All the men twenty years old or more who were able to serve in the army were listed by name, one by one, according to the records of their clans and families. 21The number from the tribe of Reuben was 46,500.

22From the descendants of Simeon:
All the men twenty years old or more who were able to serve in the army were counted and listed by name, one by one, according to the records of their clans and families. 23The number from the tribe of Simeon was 59,300.

24From the descendants of Gad:
All the men twenty years old or more who were able to serve in the army were listed by name, according to the records of their clans and families. 25The number from the tribe of Gad was 45,650.

26From the descendants of Judah:
All the men twenty years old or more who were able to serve in the army were listed by name, according to the records of their clans and families. 27The number from the tribe of Judah was 74,600.

28From the descendants of Issachar:
All the men twenty years old or more who were able to serve in the army were listed by name, according to the records of their clans and families. 29The number from the tribe of Issachar was 54,400.

30From the descendants of Zebulun:
All the men twenty years old or more who were able to serve in the army were listed by name, according to the records of their clans and families. 31The number from the tribe of Zebulun was 57,400.

32From the sons of Joseph:
From the descendants of Ephraim:
All the men twenty years old or more who were able to serve in the army were listed by name, according to the records

1:32 Two for One

Although Joseph was only one of the twelve brothers who formed the tribes of Israel, his father Israel (Jacob) had adopted Joseph's two sons, Ephraim and Manasseh, as his own (see Genesis 48:5–6). Thus Joseph got a double share of the family inheritance, and there are really thirteen tribes of Israel.

The tribe of Levi were often treated separately, however, because of their special role in worship. This census, for example, taken primarily to prepare a roster for military purposes, excluded the tribe of Levi. As caretakers of God's tabernacle, Levites were ineligible for the draft.

of their clans and families. 33The number from the tribe of Ephraim was 40,500.
34From the descendants of Manasseh:
All the men twenty years old or more who were able to serve in the army were listed by name, according to the records of their clans and families. 35The number from the tribe of Manasseh was 32,200.

[36]From the descendants of Benjamin:

All the men twenty years old or more who were able to serve in the army were listed by name, according to the records of their clans and families. [37]The number from the tribe of Benjamin was 35,400.

[38]From the descendants of Dan:

All the men twenty years old or more who were able to serve in the army were listed by name, according to the records of their clans and families. [39]The number from the tribe of Dan was 62,700.

[40]From the descendants of Asher:

All the men twenty years old or more who were able to serve in the army were listed by name, according to the records of their clans and families. [41]The number from the tribe of Asher was 41,500.

[42]From the descendants of Naphtali:

All the men twenty years old or more who were able to serve in the army were listed by name, according to the records of their clans and families. [43]The number from the tribe of Naphtali was 53,400.

[44]These were the men counted by Moses and Aaron and the twelve leaders of Israel, each one representing his family. [45]All the Israelites twenty years old or more who were able to serve in Israel's army were counted according to their families. [46]The total number was 603,550.

[47]The families of the tribe of Levi, however, were not counted along with the others. [48]The LORD had said to Moses: [49]"You must not count the tribe of Levi or include them in the census of the other Israelites. [50]Instead, appoint the Levites to be in charge of the tabernacle of the Testimony—over all its furnishings and everything belonging to it. They are to carry the tabernacle and all its furnishings; they are to take care of it and encamp around it. [51]Whenever the tabernacle is to move, the Levites are to take it down, and whenever the tabernacle is to be set up, the Levites shall do it. Anyone else who goes near it shall be put to death. [52]The Israelites are to set up their tents by divisions, each man in his own camp under his own standard. [53]The Levites, however, are to set up their tents around the tabernacle of the Testimony so that wrath will not fall on the Israelite community. The Levites are to be responsible for the care of the tabernacle of the Testimony."

[54]The Israelites did all this just as the LORD commanded Moses.

The Arrangement of the Tribal Camps

2 The LORD said to Moses and Aaron: [2]"The Israelites are to camp around the Tent of Meeting some distance from it, each man under his standard with the banners of his family."

2:2 A Place for Everyone

The Israelites did not wander through the desert as an undisciplined mob. On the contrary, each tribe had an assigned place to camp. At the center of their camp was the Tent of Meeting (the tabernacle)—a visual reminder, each time they pitched their tents, of what should be at the center of their lives.

[3]On the east, toward the sunrise, the divisions of the camp of Judah are to encamp under their standard. The leader of the people of Judah is Nahshon son of Amminadab. [4]His division numbers 74,600.

[5]The tribe of Issachar will camp next to them. The leader of the people of Issachar is Nethanel son of Zuar. [6]His division numbers 54,400.

[7]The tribe of Zebulun will be next. The leader of the people of Zebulun is Eliab son of Helon. [8]His division numbers 57,400.

[9]All the men assigned to the camp of Judah, according to their divisions, number 186,400. They will set out first.

[10]On the south will be the divisions of the camp of Reuben under their standard. The leader of the people of Reuben is Elizur son of Shedeur. [11]His division numbers 46,500.

[12]The tribe of Simeon will camp next to them. The leader of the people of Simeon is Shelumiel son of Zurishaddai. [13]His division numbers 59,300.

[14]The tribe of Gad will be next. The leader of the people of Gad is Eliasaph son of Deuel.[a] [15]His division numbers 45,650.

[16]All the men assigned to the camp of Reuben, according to their divisions, number 151,450. They will set out second.

[17]Then the Tent of Meeting and the camp of the Levites will set out in the middle of the camps. They will set out in the same order as they encamp, each in his own place under his standard.

[18]On the west will be the divisions of the camp of Ephraim under their standard. The leader of the people of Ephraim is Elishama

---

[a]14 Many manuscripts of the Masoretic Text, Samaritan Pentateuch and Vulgate (see also Num. 1:14); most manuscripts of the Masoretic Text *Reuel*

son of Ammihud. ¹⁹His division numbers 40,500.

²⁰The tribe of Manasseh will be next to them. The leader of the people of Manasseh is Gamaliel son of Pedahzur. ²¹His division numbers 32,200.

²²The tribe of Benjamin will be next. The leader of the people of Benjamin is Abidan son of Gideoni. ²³His division numbers 35,400.

²⁴All the men assigned to the camp of Ephraim, according to their divisions, number 108,100. They will set out third.

²⁵On the north will be the divisions of the camp of Dan, under their standard. The leader of the people of Dan is Ahiezer son of Ammishaddai. ²⁶His division numbers 62,700.

²⁷The tribe of Asher will camp next to them. The leader of the people of Asher is Pagiel son of Ocran. ²⁸His division numbers 41,500.

²⁹The tribe of Naphtali will be next. The leader of the people of Naphtali is Ahira son of Enan. ³⁰His division numbers 53,400.

³¹All the men assigned to the camp of Dan number 157,600. They will set out last, under their standards.

³²These are the Israelites, counted according to their families. All those in the camps, by their divisions, number 603,550. ³³The Levites, however, were not counted

2:32 How Many Israelites?

Debate has raged among scholars about the vast numbers of Israelites reported in the censuses of Numbers. Could two-and-a-half million people (counting women and children) have left Egypt in one day and then survived for 40 years in a desolate desert? Those who defend the large numbers point out that climatic conditions might have been very different in those days when, for example, Egypt was the granary of the world. (Also, the Bible gives many indications of God's miraculous supply of food and water.) Opposing scholars note that the Hebrews had different means of counting, and that the word translated "thousand" could have other meanings, resulting in much smaller figures. Regardless, both positions admit to a very large band of people wandering around a desert for a very long time.

along with the other Israelites, as the LORD commanded Moses.

³⁴So the Israelites did everything the LORD commanded Moses; that is the way they encamped under their standards, and that is the way they set out, each with his clan and family.

The Levites

3 This is the account of the family of Aaron and Moses at the time the LORD talked with Moses on Mount Sinai.

²The names of the sons of Aaron were Nadab the firstborn and Abihu, Eleazar and Ithamar. ³Those were the names of Aaron's sons, the anointed priests, who were ordained to serve as priests. ⁴Nadab and Abihu, however, fell dead before the LORD when they made an offering with unauthorized fire before him in the Desert of Sinai. They had no sons; so only Eleazar and Ithamar served as priests during the lifetime of their father Aaron.

⁵The LORD said to Moses, ⁶"Bring the tribe of Levi and present them to Aaron the priest to assist him. ⁷They are to perform duties for him and for the whole community at the Tent of Meeting by doing the work of the tabernacle. ⁸They are to take care of all the furnishings of the Tent of Meeting, fulfilling the obligations of the Israelites by doing the work of the tabernacle. ⁹Give the Levites to Aaron and his sons; they are the Israelites who are to be given wholly to him.ᵃ ¹⁰Appoint Aaron and his sons to serve as priests; anyone else who approaches the sanctuary must be put to death."

¹¹The LORD also said to Moses, ¹²"I have taken the Levites from among the Israelites in place of the first male offspring of every Israelite woman. The Levites are mine, ¹³for all the firstborn are mine. When I struck down all the firstborn in Egypt, I set apart for myself every firstborn in Israel, whether man or animal. They are to be mine. I am the LORD."

¹⁴The LORD said to Moses in the Desert of Sinai, ¹⁵"Count the Levites by their families and clans. Count every male a month old or more." ¹⁶So Moses counted them, as he was commanded by the word of the LORD.

¹⁷These were the names of the sons of Levi:
Gershon, Kohath and Merari.
¹⁸These were the names of the Gershonite clans:
Libni and Shimei.
¹⁹The Kohathite clans:
Amram, Izhar, Hebron and Uzziel.
²⁰The Merarite clans:
Mahli and Mushi.

ᵃ9 Most manuscripts of the Masoretic Text; some manuscripts of the Masoretic Text, Samaritan Pentateuch and Septuagint (see also Num. 8:16) *to me*

These were the Levite clans, according to their families.

²¹To Gershon belonged the clans of the Libnites and Shimeites; these were the Gershonite clans. ²²The number of all the males a month old or more who were counted was 7,500. ²³The Gershonite clans were to camp on the west, behind the tabernacle. ²⁴The leader of the families of the Gershonites was Eliasaph son of Lael. ²⁵At the Tent of Meeting the Gershonites were responsible for the care of the tabernacle and tent, its coverings, the curtain at the entrance to the Tent of Meeting, ²⁶the curtains of the courtyard, the curtain at the entrance to the courtyard surrounding the tabernacle and altar, and the ropes—and everything related to their use.

²⁷To Kohath belonged the clans of the Amramites, Izharites, Hebronites and Uzzielites; these were the Kohathite clans. ²⁸The number of all the males a month old or more was 8,600.ᵃ The Kohathites were responsible for the care of the sanctuary. ²⁹The Kohathite clans were to camp on the south side of the tabernacle. ³⁰The leader of the families of the Kohathite clans was Elizaphan son of Uzziel. ³¹They were responsible for the care of the ark, the table, the lampstand, the altars, the articles of the sanctuary used in ministering, the curtain, and everything related to their use. ³²The chief leader of the Levites was Eleazar son of Aaron, the priest. He was appointed over those who were responsible for the care of the sanctuary.

³³To Merari belonged the clans of the Mahlites and the Mushites; these were the Merarite clans. ³⁴The number of all the males a month old or more who were counted was 6,200. ³⁵The leader of the families of the Merarite clans was Zuriel son of Abihail; they were to camp on the north side of the tabernacle. ³⁶The Merarites were appointed to take care of the frames of the tabernacle, its crossbars, posts, bases, all its equipment, and everything related to their use, ³⁷as well as the posts of the surrounding courtyard with their bases, tent pegs and ropes.

³⁸Moses and Aaron and his sons were to camp to the east of the tabernacle, toward the sunrise, in front of the Tent of Meeting. They were responsible for the care of the sanctuary on behalf of the Israelites. Anyone else who approached the sanctuary was to be put to death.

³⁹The total number of Levites counted at the LORD's command by Moses and Aaron according to their clans, including every male a month old or more, was 22,000.

⁴⁰The LORD said to Moses, "Count all the firstborn Israelite males who are a month old or more and make a list of their names. ⁴¹Take the Levites for me in place of all the firstborn of the Israelites, and the livestock of the Levites in place of all the firstborn of the livestock of the Israelites. I am the LORD."

⁴²So Moses counted all the firstborn of the Israelites, as the LORD commanded him. ⁴³The total number of firstborn males a month old or more, listed by name, was 22,273.

3:45 Designated Firstborn

At the first Passover (Exodus 13:2) God established the firstborn principle, which held that every firstborn male, human or animal, must be dedicated to him. Here, in careful accounting, the Levites are accepted as "designated firstborn" offerings to God. Just as a "designated hitter" in baseball is appointed to bat in place of the pitcher, so here a whole tribe is named to take the place of firstborn members from every family.

⁴⁴The LORD also said to Moses, ⁴⁵"Take the Levites in place of all the firstborn of Israel, and the livestock of the Levites in place of their livestock. The Levites are to be mine. I am the LORD. ⁴⁶To redeem the 273 firstborn Israelites who exceed the number of the Levites, ⁴⁷collect five shekelsᵇ for each one, according to the sanctuary shekel, which weighs twenty gerahs. ⁴⁸Give the money for the redemption of the additional Israelites to Aaron and his sons."

⁴⁹So Moses collected the redemption money from those who exceeded the number redeemed by the Levites. ⁵⁰From the firstborn of the Israelites he collected silver weighing 1,365 shekels,ᶜ according to the sanctuary shekel. ⁵¹Moses gave the redemption money to Aaron and his sons, as he was commanded by the word of the LORD.

The Kohathites

4 The LORD said to Moses and Aaron: ²"Take a census of the Kohathite branch of the Levites by their clans and families. ³Count all the men from thirty to fifty years of age who come to serve in the work in the Tent of Meeting.

⁴"This is the work of the Kohathites in the Tent of Meeting: the care of the most holy things. ⁵When the camp is to move, Aaron and his sons are to go in and take down the shielding curtain

---

ᵃ28 Hebrew; some Septuagint manuscripts *8,300* about 35 pounds (about 15.5 kilograms)   ᵇ47 That is, about 2 ounces (about 55 grams)   ᶜ50 That is,

and cover the ark of the Testimony with it. [6]Then they are to cover this with hides of sea cows,[a] spread a cloth of solid blue over that and put the poles in place.

[7]"Over the table of the Presence they are to spread a blue cloth and put on it the plates, dishes and bowls, and the jars for drink offerings; the bread that is continually there is to remain on it. [8]Over these they are to spread a scarlet cloth, cover that with hides of sea cows and put its poles in place.

[9]"They are to take a blue cloth and cover the lampstand that is for light, together with its lamps, its wick trimmers and trays, and all its jars for the oil used to supply it. [10]Then they are to wrap it and all its accessories in a covering of hides of sea cows and put it on a carrying frame.

[11]"Over the gold altar they are to spread a blue cloth and cover that with hides of sea cows and put its poles in place.

[12]"They are to take all the articles used for ministering in the sanctuary, wrap them in a blue cloth, cover that with hides of sea cows and put them on a carrying frame.

[13]"They are to remove the ashes from the bronze altar and spread a purple cloth over it. [14]Then they are to place on it all the utensils used for ministering at the altar, including the firepans, meat forks, shovels and sprinkling bowls. Over it they are to spread a covering of hides of sea cows and put its poles in place.

[15]"After Aaron and his sons have finished covering the holy furnishings and all the holy articles, and when the camp is ready to move, the Kohathites are to come to do the carrying. But they must not touch the holy things or they will die. The Kohathites are to carry those things that are in the Tent of Meeting.

[16]"Eleazar son of Aaron, the priest, is to have charge of the oil for the light, the fragrant incense, the regular grain offering and the anointing oil. He is to be in charge of the entire tabernacle and everything in it, including its holy furnishings and articles."

[17]The LORD said to Moses and Aaron, [18]"See that the Kohathite tribal clans are not cut off from the Levites. [19]So that they may live and not die when they come near the most holy things, do this for them: Aaron and his sons are to go into the sanctuary and assign to each man his work and what he is to carry. [20]But the Kohathites must not go in to look at the holy things, even for a moment, or they will die."

The Gershonites

[21]The LORD said to Moses, [22]"Take a census also of the Gershonites by their families and clans. [23]Count all the men from thirty to fifty

years of age who come to serve in the work at the Tent of Meeting.

[24]"This is the service of the Gershonite clans as they work and carry burdens: [25]They are to carry

4:15 Touch and Die

The precise instructions for moving the holy things reflected the awe and respect that were due God alone. Years later, King David's men flagrantly ignored these instructions and one man, Uzzah, died as a result (see "Why Did Uzzah Die?" page 446). Earlier in Numbers, two of Aaron's sons had died while trying out their own version of worship, ignoring God's directions (3:4, also Leviticus 10:1–5). In the Bible, these drastic punishments tend to occur as God's people enter a new phase of their history (see Joshua 7; 2 Samuel 6:7; Acts 5:1–11). There is no compromising God's holiness.

the curtains of the tabernacle, the Tent of Meeting, its covering and the outer covering of hides of sea cows, the curtains for the entrance to the Tent of Meeting, [26]the curtains of the courtyard surrounding the tabernacle and altar, the curtain for the entrance, the ropes and all the equipment used in its service. The Gershonites are to do all that needs to be done with these things. [27]All their service, whether carrying or doing other work, is to be done under the direction of Aaron and his sons. You shall assign to them as their responsibility all they are to carry. [28]This is the service of the Gershonite clans at the Tent of Meeting. Their duties are to be under the direction of Ithamar son of Aaron, the priest.

The Merarites

[29]"Count the Merarites by their clans and families. [30]Count all the men from thirty to fifty years of age who come to serve in the work at the Tent of Meeting. [31]This is their duty as they perform service at the Tent of Meeting: to carry the frames of the tabernacle, its crossbars, posts and bases, [32]as well as the posts of the surrounding courtyard with their bases, tent pegs, ropes, all their equipment and everything related to their use. Assign to each man the specific things he is to carry. [33]This is the service of the Merarite clans as they work at the Tent of Meeting under the direction of Ithamar son of Aaron, the priest."

The Numbering of the Levite Clans

[34]Moses, Aaron and the leaders of the community counted the Kohathites by their clans and families. [35]All the men from thirty to fifty years of age who came to serve in the work in the Tent of

---

[a]6 That is, dugongs; also in verses 8, 10, 11, 12, 14 and 25

Meeting, [36]counted by clans, were 2,750. [37]This was the total of all those in the Kohathite clans who served in the Tent of Meeting. Moses and Aaron counted them according to the LORD's command through Moses.

[38]The Gershonites were counted by their clans and families. [39]All the men from thirty to fifty years of age who came to serve in the work at the Tent of Meeting, [40]counted by their clans and families, were 2,630. [41]This was the total of those in the Gershonite clans who served at the Tent of Meeting. Moses and Aaron counted them according to the LORD's command.

[42]The Merarites were counted by their clans and families. [43]All the men from thirty to fifty years of age who came to serve in the work at the Tent of Meeting, [44]counted by their clans, were 3,200. [45]This was the total of those in the Merarite clans. Moses and Aaron counted them according to the LORD's command through Moses.

[46]So Moses, Aaron and the leaders of Israel counted all the Levites by their clans and families. [47]All the men from thirty to fifty years of age who came to do the work of serving and carrying the Tent of Meeting [48]numbered 8,580. [49]At the LORD's command through Moses, each was assigned his work and told what to carry.

Thus they were counted, as the LORD commanded Moses.

The Purity of the Camp

5 The LORD said to Moses, [2]"Command the Israelites to send away from the camp anyone who has an infectious skin disease[a] or a discharge of any kind, or who is ceremonially unclean because of a dead body. [3]Send away male and female alike; send them outside the camp so they will not defile their camp, where I dwell among them." [4]The Israelites did this; they sent them outside the camp. They did just as the LORD had instructed Moses.

Restitution for Wrongs

[5]The LORD said to Moses, [6]"Say to the Israelites: 'When a man or woman wrongs another in any way[b] and so is unfaithful to the LORD, that person is guilty [7]and must confess the sin he has committed. He must make full restitution for his wrong, add one fifth to it and give it all to the person he has wronged. [8]But if that person has no close relative to whom restitution can be made for the wrong, the restitution belongs to the LORD and must be given to the priest, along with the ram with which atonement is made for him. [9]All the sacred contributions the Israelites bring to a priest will belong to him. [10]Each man's

sacred gifts are his own, but what he gives to the priest will belong to the priest.'"

The Test for an Unfaithful Wife

[11]Then the LORD said to Moses, [12]"Speak to the Israelites and say to them: 'If a man's wife goes astray and is unfaithful to him [13]by sleeping with another man, and this is hidden from her husband and her impurity is undetected (since there is no witness against her and she has not been caught in the act), [14]and if feelings of jealousy come over her husband and he suspects his wife and she is impure—or if he is jealous and suspects her even though she is not impure—[15]then he is to take his wife to the priest. He must also take an offering of a tenth of an ephah[c] of barley flour on her behalf. He must not pour oil on it or put incense on it, because it is a grain offering for jealousy, a reminder offering to draw attention to guilt.

[16]"'The priest shall bring her and have her

5:16 Test for Adultery

The strange test for adultery described here resembles other "trials by ordeal" common then in the Middle East. Presumably, either the emotional reactions of the guilty woman would give her away physiologically (much as a lie detector may), or God would reveal test results through the outcome of the ordeal. The public trial may have helped to clear the reputation of wives who had been falsely accused by their husbands. There is no biblical record of the procedure actually being used, and the trial described is the only one like it in the Bible.

stand before the LORD. [17]Then he shall take some holy water in a clay jar and put some dust from the tabernacle floor into the water. [18]After the priest has had the woman stand before the LORD, he shall loosen her hair and place in her hands the reminder offering, the grain offering for jealousy, while he himself holds the bitter water that brings a curse. [19]Then the priest shall put the woman under oath and say to her, "If no other man has slept with you and you have not gone astray and become impure while married to your husband, may this bitter water that brings a curse not harm you. [20]But if you have gone astray while married to your husband and you have defiled yourself by sleeping with a man other than your husband"— [21]here the priest is to put the woman under this curse of the oath—"may the LORD cause your people to curse and denounce you when he causes your thigh to waste away and

---

[a]2 Traditionally *leprosy*; the Hebrew word was used for various diseases affecting the skin—not necessarily leprosy.
[b]6 Or *woman commits any wrong common to mankind*   [c]15 That is, probably about 2 quarts (about 2 liters)

your abdomen to swell.[a] 22May this water that brings a curse enter your body so that your abdomen swells and your thigh wastes away.[b]"

"'Then the woman is to say, "Amen. So be it."

23"'The priest is to write these curses on a scroll and then wash them off into the bitter water. 24He shall have the woman drink the bitter water that brings a curse, and this water will enter her and cause bitter suffering. 25The priest is to take from her hands the grain offering for jealousy, wave it before the LORD and bring it to the altar. 26The priest is then to take a handful of the grain offering as a memorial offering and burn it on the altar; after that, he is to have the woman drink the water. 27If she has defiled herself and been unfaithful to her husband, then when she is made to drink the water that brings a curse, it will go into her and cause bitter suffering; her abdomen will swell and her thigh waste away,[c] and she will become accursed among her people. 28If, however, the woman has not defiled herself and is free from impurity, she will be cleared of guilt and will be able to have children.

29"'This, then, is the law of jealousy when a woman goes astray and defiles herself while married to her husband, 30or when feelings of jealousy come over a man because he suspects his wife. The priest is to have her stand before the LORD and is to apply this entire law to her. 31The husband will be innocent of any wrongdoing, but the woman will bear the consequences of her sin.'"

The Nazirite

6 The LORD said to Moses, 2"Speak to the Israelites and say to them: 'If a man or woman wants to make a special vow, a vow of separation to the LORD as a Nazirite, 3he must abstain from wine and other fermented drink and must not drink vinegar made from wine or from other fermented drink. He must not drink grape juice or eat grapes or raisins. 4As long as he is a Nazirite, he must not eat anything that comes from the grapevine, not even the seeds or skins.

5"'During the entire period of his vow of separation no razor may be used on his head. He must be holy until the period of his separation to the LORD is over; he must let the hair of his head grow long. 6Throughout the period of his separation to the LORD he must not go near a dead body. 7Even if his own father or mother or brother or sister dies, he must not make himself ceremonially unclean on account of them, because the symbol of his separation to God is on his head. 8Throughout the period of his separation he is consecrated to the LORD.

9"'If someone dies suddenly in his presence, thus defiling the hair he has dedicated, he must shave his head on the day of his cleansing—the seventh day. 10Then on the eighth day he must bring two doves or two young pigeons to the priest at the entrance to the Tent of Meeting.

6:6 Types of Uncleanness

In its emphasis on purity, Numbers lists three types of unclean persons: victims of certain diseases, people with "a discharge of any kind" (including sexual ones), and those in contact with dead bodies. Besides offering obvious health benefits, these rules served to draw a sharp contrast between the Israelites and those who practiced other religions: Egyptians who virtually worshiped the dead, and Phoenicians and others who made sex an important part of religious rites.

An unclean person went into a period of quarantine (5:1–4). When Miriam got leprosy, she was kept away from camp for seven days (12:15). Soldiers, too, went through the same cleansing ritual if they had killed anyone or touched anyone who had died (31:19).

11The priest is to offer one as a sin offering and the other as a burnt offering to make atonement for him because he sinned by being in the presence of the dead body. That same day he is to consecrate his head. 12He must dedicate himself to the LORD for the period of his separation and must bring a year-old male lamb as a guilt offering. The previous days do not count, because he became defiled during his separation.

13"'Now this is the law for the Nazirite when the period of his separation is over. He is to be brought to the entrance to the Tent of Meeting. 14There he is to present his offerings to the LORD: a year-old male lamb without defect for a burnt offering, a year-old ewe lamb without defect for a sin offering, a ram without defect for a fellowship offering,[d] 15together with their grain offerings and drink offerings, and a basket of bread made without yeast—cakes made of fine flour mixed with oil, and wafers spread with oil.

16"'The priest is to present them before the LORD and make the sin offering and the burnt offering. 17He is to present the basket of unleavened bread and is to sacrifice the ram as a fellowship offering to the LORD, together with its grain offering and drink offering.

18"'Then at the entrance to the Tent of Meeting, the Nazirite must shave off the hair that he dedicated. He is to take the hair and put it in the fire that is under the sacrifice of the fellowship offering.

[a]21 Or *causes you to have a miscarrying womb and barrenness miscarrying womb* [c]27 Or *suffering; she will have barrenness and a miscarrying womb* [b]22 Or *body and cause you to be barren and have a miscarrying womb offering;* also in verses 17 and 18 [d]14 Traditionally *peace*

19" 'After the Nazirite has shaved off the hair of his dedication, the priest is to place in his hands a boiled shoulder of the ram, and a cake and a wafer from the basket, both made without yeast.

6:18 Well-known Nazirites

Samson and John the Baptist are two of the most famous Nazirites in the Bible. The apostle Paul took a Nazirite vow in Jerusalem (Acts 21:21–29) to demonstrate his conformity to Jewish law.

20The priest shall then wave them before the LORD as a wave offering; they are holy and belong to the priest, together with the breast that was waved and the thigh that was presented. After that, the Nazirite may drink wine.

21" 'This is the law of the Nazirite who vows his offering to the LORD in accordance with his separation, in addition to whatever else he can afford. He must fulfill the vow he has made, according to the law of the Nazirite.' "

The Priestly Blessing

22The LORD said to Moses, 23"Tell Aaron and his sons, 'This is how you are to bless the Israelites. Say to them:

24" "The LORD bless you
    and keep you;
25the LORD make his face shine upon you
    and be gracious to you;
26the LORD turn his face toward you
    and give you peace." '

27"So they will put my name on the Israelites, and I will bless them."

Offerings at the Dedication of the Tabernacle

7 When Moses finished setting up the tabernacle, he anointed it and consecrated it and all its furnishings. He also anointed and consecrated the altar and all its utensils. 2Then the leaders of Israel, the heads of families who were the tribal leaders in charge of those who were counted, made offerings. 3They brought as their gifts before the LORD six covered carts and twelve oxen—an ox from each leader and a cart from every two. These they presented before the tabernacle.

4The LORD said to Moses, 5"Accept these from them, that they may be used in the work at the Tent of Meeting. Give them to the Levites as each man's work requires."

6So Moses took the carts and oxen and gave them to the Levites. 7He gave two carts and four oxen to the Gershonites, as their work required, 8and he gave four carts and eight oxen to the Merarites, as their work required. They were all under the direction of Ithamar son of Aaron, the priest. 9But Moses did not give any to the Kohathites, because they were to carry on their shoulders the holy things, for which they were responsible.

10When the altar was anointed, the leaders brought their offerings for its dedication and presented them before the altar. 11For the LORD had said to Moses, "Each day one leader is to bring his offering for the dedication of the altar."

12The one who brought his offering on the first day was Nahshon son of Amminadab of the tribe of Judah.

13His offering was one silver plate weighing a hundred and thirty shekels,[a] and one silver sprinkling bowl weighing seventy shekels,[b] both according to the sanctuary shekel, each filled with fine flour mixed with oil as a grain offering; 14one gold dish weighing ten shekels,[c] filled with incense; 15one young bull, one ram and one male lamb a year old, for a burnt offering; 16one male goat for a sin offering; 17and two oxen, five rams, five male goats and five male lambs a year old, to be sacrificed as a fellowship offering.[d] This was the offering of Nahshon son of Amminadab.

18On the second day Nethanel son of Zuar, the leader of Issachar, brought his offering.

19The offering he brought was one silver plate weighing a hundred and thirty shekels, and one silver sprinkling bowl weighing seventy shekels, both according to the sanctuary shekel, each filled with fine flour mixed with oil as a grain offering; 20one gold dish weighing ten shekels, filled with incense; 21one young bull, one ram and one male lamb a year old, for a burnt offering; 22one male goat for a sin offering; 23and two oxen, five rams, five male goats and five male lambs a year old, to be sacrificed as a fellowship offering. This was the offering of Nethanel son of Zuar.

24On the third day, Eliab son of Helon, the leader of the people of Zebulun, brought his offering.

25His offering was one silver plate weighing a hundred and thirty shekels, and one silver sprinkling bowl weighing seventy shekels, both according to the sanctuary shekel, each filled with fine flour mixed with oil as

---

a 13 That is, about 3 1/4 pounds (about 1.5 kilograms); also elsewhere in this chapter   *b 13 That is, about 1 3/4 pounds (about 0.8 kilogram); also elsewhere in this chapter*   *c 14 That is, about 4 ounces (about 110 grams); also elsewhere in this chapter*   *d 17 Traditionally peace offering; also elsewhere in this chapter*

a grain offering; 26one gold dish weighing ten shekels, filled with incense; 27one young bull, one ram and one male lamb a year old, for a burnt offering; 28one male goat for a sin offering; 29and two oxen, five rams, five male goats and five male lambs a year old, to be sacrificed as a fellowship offering. This was the offering of Eliab son of Helon.

30On the fourth day Elizur son of Shedeur, the leader of the people of Reuben, brought his offering.

31His offering was one silver plate weighing a hundred and thirty shekels, and one silver sprinkling bowl weighing seventy shekels, both according to the sanctuary shekel, each filled with fine flour mixed with oil as a grain offering; 32one gold dish weighing ten shekels, filled with incense; 33one young bull, one ram and one male lamb a year old, for a burnt offering; 34one male goat for a sin offering; 35and two oxen, five rams, five male goats and five male lambs a year old, to be sacrificed as a fellowship offering. This was the offering of Elizur son of Shedeur.

36On the fifth day Shelumiel son of Zurishaddai, the leader of the people of Simeon, brought his offering.

37His offering was one silver plate weighing a hundred and thirty shekels, and one silver sprinkling bowl weighing seventy shekels, both according to the sanctuary shekel, each filled with fine flour mixed with oil as a grain offering; 38one gold dish weighing ten shekels, filled with incense; 39one young bull, one ram and one male lamb a year old, for a burnt offering; 40one male goat for a sin offering; 41and two oxen, five rams, five male goats and five male lambs a year old, to be sacrificed as a fellowship offering. This was the offering of Shelumiel son of Zurishaddai.

42On the sixth day Eliasaph son of Deuel, the leader of the people of Gad, brought his offering.

43His offering was one silver plate weighing a hundred and thirty shekels, and one silver sprinkling bowl weighing seventy shekels, both according to the sanctuary shekel, each filled with fine flour mixed with oil as a grain offering; 44one gold dish weighing ten shekels, filled with incense; 45one young bull, one ram and one male lamb a year old, for a burnt offering; 46one male goat for a sin offering; 47and two oxen, five rams, five male goats and five male lambs a year old, to be sacrificed as a fellowship offering. This was the offering of Eliasaph son of Deuel.

48On the seventh day Elishama son of Ammihud, the leader of the people of Ephraim, brought his offering.

49His offering was one silver plate weighing a hundred and thirty shekels, and one silver sprinkling bowl weighing seventy shekels, both according to the sanctuary shekel, each filled with fine flour mixed with oil as a grain offering; 50one gold dish weighing ten shekels, filled with incense; 51one young bull, one ram and one male lamb a year old, for a burnt offering; 52one male goat for a sin offering; 53and two oxen, five rams, five male goats and five male lambs a year old, to be sacrificed as a fellowship offering. This was the offering of Elishama son of Ammihud.

54On the eighth day Gamaliel son of Pedahzur, the leader of the people of Manasseh, brought his offering.

55His offering was one silver plate weighing a hundred and thirty shekels, and one silver sprinkling bowl weighing seventy shekels, both according to the sanctuary shekel, each filled with fine flour mixed with oil as

7:55 Gold and Silver Dishes

The plates and bowls used in Israelite worship have a history of their own. Some of these originals, perhaps all, were lost during the dark years of the judges. David produced more, which his son Solomon installed in the temple (2 Chronicles 5:1); all were taken as captured goods when the Babylonians destroyed Jerusalem (2 Kings 25:15). At last they were returned to Jerusalem when the Persian king Cyrus let the Jews return (Ezra 1:9–10).

a grain offering; 56one gold dish weighing ten shekels, filled with incense; 57one young bull, one ram and one male lamb a year old, for a burnt offering; 58one male goat for a sin offering; 59and two oxen, five rams, five male goats and five male lambs a year old, to be sacrificed as a fellowship offering. This was the offering of Gamaliel son of Pedahzur.

60On the ninth day Abidan son of Gideoni, the leader of the people of Benjamin, brought his offering.

61His offering was one silver plate weighing a hundred and thirty shekels, and one silver sprinkling bowl weighing seventy shekels, both according to the sanctuary shekel, each filled with fine flour mixed with oil as a grain offering; 62one gold dish weighing ten shekels, filled with incense; 63one young bull, one ram and one male lamb a year old, for a burnt offering; ⁶⁴one male goat for a sin offering; ⁶⁵and two oxen, five rams, five male goats and five male lambs a year old, to be sacrificed as a fellowship offering. This was the offering of Abidan son of Gideoni.

⁶⁶On the tenth day Ahiezer son of Ammishaddai, the leader of the people of Dan, brought his offering.

⁶⁷His offering was one silver plate weighing a hundred and thirty shekels, and one silver sprinkling bowl weighing seventy shekels, both according to the sanctuary shekel, each filled with fine flour mixed with oil as a grain offering; ⁶⁸one gold dish weighing ten shekels, filled with incense; ⁶⁹one young bull, one ram and one male lamb a year old, for a burnt offering; ⁷⁰one male goat for a sin offering; ⁷¹and two oxen, five rams, five male goats and five male lambs a year old, to be sacrificed as a fellowship offering. This was the offering of Ahiezer son of Ammishaddai.

⁷²On the eleventh day Pagiel son of Ocran, the leader of the people of Asher, brought his offering.

⁷³His offering was one silver plate weighing a hundred and thirty shekels, and one silver sprinkling bowl weighing seventy shekels, both according to the sanctuary shekel, each filled with fine flour mixed with oil as a grain offering; ⁷⁴one gold dish weighing ten shekels, filled with incense; ⁷⁵one young bull, one ram and one male lamb a year old, for a burnt offering; ⁷⁶one male goat for a sin offering; ⁷⁷and two oxen, five rams, five male goats and five male lambs a year old, to be sacrificed as a fellowship offering. This was the offering of Pagiel son of Ocran.

⁷⁸On the twelfth day Ahira son of Enan, the leader of the people of Naphtali, brought his offering.

⁷⁹His offering was one silver plate weighing a hundred and thirty shekels, and one silver sprinkling bowl weighing seventy shekels, both according to the sanctuary shekel, each filled with fine flour mixed with oil as a grain offering; ⁸⁰one gold dish weighing ten shekels, filled with incense; ⁸¹one young bull, one ram and one male lamb a year old, for a burnt offering; ⁸²one male goat for a sin offering; ⁸³and two oxen, five rams, five male goats and five male lambs a year old, to be sacrificed as a fellowship offering. This was the offering of Ahira son of Enan.

⁸⁴These were the offerings of the Israelite leaders for the dedication of the altar when it was anointed: twelve silver plates, twelve silver sprinkling bowls and twelve gold dishes. ⁸⁵Each silver plate weighed a hundred and thirty shekels, and each sprinkling bowl seventy shekels. Altogether, the silver dishes weighed two thousand four hundred shekels,^a according to the sanctuary shekel. ⁸⁶The twelve gold dishes filled with incense weighed ten shekels each, according to the sanctuary shekel. Altogether, the gold dishes weighed a hundred and twenty shekels.^b ⁸⁷The total number of animals for the burnt offering came to twelve young bulls, twelve rams and twelve male lambs a year old, together with their grain offering. Twelve male goats were used for the sin offering. ⁸⁸The total number of animals for the sacrifice of the fellowship offering came to twenty-four oxen, sixty rams, sixty male goats and sixty male lambs a year old. These were the offerings for the dedication of the altar after it was anointed.

⁸⁹When Moses entered the Tent of Meeting to speak with the LORD, he heard the voice speaking to him from between the two cherubim above the atonement cover on the ark of the Testimony. And he spoke with him.

Setting Up the Lamps

8 The LORD said to Moses, ²"Speak to Aaron and say to him, 'When you set up the seven

8:1 The Lord said to Moses . . .

Numbers emphasizes time and again—over 150 times—that God spoke directly to Moses, and through him to the people of Israel. When Moses' leadership was challenged, God insisted that his communication with Moses was unique (12:6–8).

lamps, they are to light the area in front of the lampstand.'"

³Aaron did so; he set up the lamps so that they faced forward on the lampstand, just as the LORD commanded Moses. ⁴This is how the lampstand was made: It was made of hammered gold—from its base to its blossoms. The lampstand was made exactly like the pattern the LORD had shown Moses.

The Setting Apart of the Levites

⁵The LORD said to Moses: ⁶"Take the Levites from among the other Israelites and make them ceremonially clean. ⁷To purify them, do this: Sprinkle the water of cleansing on them; then have them shave their whole bodies and wash

^a85 That is, about 60 pounds (about 28 kilograms) ^b86 That is, about 3 pounds (about 1.4 kilograms)

their clothes, and so purify themselves. [8]Have them take a young bull with its grain offering of fine flour mixed with oil; then you are to take a second young bull for a sin offering. [9]Bring the Levites to the front of the Tent of Meeting and assemble the whole Israelite community. [10]You are to bring the Levites before the LORD, and the Israelites are to lay their hands on them. [11]Aaron is to present the Levites before the LORD as a wave offering from the Israelites, so that they may be ready to do the work of the LORD.

[12]"After the Levites lay their hands on the heads of the bulls, use the one for a sin offering to the LORD and the other for a burnt offering, to make atonement for the Levites. [13]Have the Levites stand in front of Aaron and his sons and then present them as a wave offering to the LORD. [14]In this way you are to set the Levites apart from the other Israelites, and the Levites will be mine.

[15]"After you have purified the Levites and presented them as a wave offering, they are to come to do their work at the Tent of Meeting. [16]They are the Israelites who are to be given wholly to me. I have taken them as my own in place of the firstborn, the first male offspring from every Israelite woman. [17]Every firstborn male in Israel, whether man or animal, is mine. When I struck down all the firstborn in Egypt, I set them apart for myself. [18]And I have taken the Levites in place of all the firstborn sons in Israel. [19]Of all the Israelites, I have given the Levites as gifts to Aaron and his sons to do the work at the Tent of Meeting on behalf of the Israelites and to make atonement for them so that no plague will strike the Israelites when they go near the sanctuary."

[20]Moses, Aaron and the whole Israelite community did with the Levites just as the LORD commanded Moses. [21]The Levites purified themselves and washed their clothes. Then Aaron presented them as a wave offering before the LORD and made atonement for them to purify them. [22]After that, the Levites came to do their work at the Tent of Meeting under the supervision of Aaron and his sons. They did with the Levites just as the LORD commanded Moses.

[23]The LORD said to Moses, [24]"This applies to

National Reminders
Built-in object lessons for the Israelites

ALTHOUGH PARTS OF NUMBERS MAY seem strange to a modern reader, it clearly expresses two of the Israelites' chief values: purity and holiness. They had to become pure before they could approach God. And they were called to demonstrate God's holiness before other nations. The need for purity and holiness was reflected in what the Israelites ate and wore, and how they acted each day.

> "Aaron is to present the Levites before the LORD as a wave offering from the Israelites, so that they may be ready to do the work of the LORD." 8:11

Visual Reminders

God set aside certain groups of people as a visual reminder of purity and holiness. The Levites, who somewhat parallel the full-time clergy of our day, took care of formal religious duties (chapters 3, 4, 8). One of their clans packed up the holy objects for moving, while other clans carried the tabernacle curtains and covers and structural parts.

Numbers describes a second group: the Nazirites (chapter 6). These ordinary laypeople dedicated themselves to an extra regimen of purity. They drank no wine and let their hair grow long. Much as Amish people do today, they stood out from the majority in their dress and style.

Holiness was not left to special groups, though. Every Israelite participated in the daily offerings, sacrifices, and occasional festivals. When a family brought a whole bull and saw it skinned, butchered, and then burned on the altar, they were forced to reflect. Sin was serious, and a great gulf was fixed between them and God. In some way, either through story, ritual, or visual symbol, Numbers expresses that separateness on almost every page. In approaching God, the Israelites had to use great care.

Bridging the Gulf

The style of life described in this book differs from our own era of casual dress, informal worship, and talk of "friendship" with God. Later, the New Testament would spell out a God who is our Father, who can be approached at any time, who is interested in the personal details of our individual lives. But Numbers serves as an important background to that kind of relationship. It shows graphically just how great was the gulf between people and God, and helps us fully appreciate all that Jesus Christ did in providing a way across that gulf.

Life Questions: Words like *holiness* and *purity* are not heard in many churches today. Do you think we take God for granted and approach him too casually?

the Levites: Men twenty-five years old or more shall come to take part in the work at the Tent of Meeting, ²⁵but at the age of fifty, they must retire from their regular service and work no longer. ²⁶They may assist their brothers in performing their duties at the Tent of Meeting, but they themselves must not do the work. This, then, is how you are to assign the responsibilities of the Levites."

The Passover

9 The LORD spoke to Moses in the Desert of Sinai in the first month of the second year after they came out of Egypt. He said, ²"Have the Israelites celebrate the Passover at the appointed time. ³Celebrate it at the appointed time, at twilight on the fourteenth day of this month, in accordance with all its rules and regulations."

⁴So Moses told the Israelites to celebrate the Passover, ⁵and they did so in the Desert of Sinai at twilight on the fourteenth day of the first month. The Israelites did everything just as the LORD commanded Moses.

⁶But some of them could not celebrate the Passover on that day because they were ceremonially unclean on account of a dead body. So they came to Moses and Aaron that same day ⁷and said to Moses, "We have become unclean because of a dead body, but why should we be kept from presenting the LORD's offering with the other Israelites at the appointed time?"

⁸Moses answered them, "Wait until I find out what the LORD commands concerning you."

⁹Then the LORD said to Moses, ¹⁰"Tell the Israelites: 'When any of you or your descendants are unclean because of a dead body or are away on a journey, they may still celebrate the LORD's Passover. ¹¹They are to celebrate it on the fourteenth day of the second month at twilight. They are to eat the lamb, together with unleavened bread and bitter herbs. ¹²They must not leave any of it till morning or break any of its bones. When they celebrate the Passover, they must follow all the regulations. ¹³But if a man who is ceremonially clean and not on a journey fails to celebrate the Passover, that person must be cut off from his people because he did not present the LORD's offering at the appointed time. That man will bear the consequences of his sin.

¹⁴"'An alien living among you who wants to celebrate the LORD's Passover must do so in accordance with its rules and regulations. You must have the same regulations for the alien and the native-born.'"

The Cloud Above the Tabernacle

¹⁵On the day the tabernacle, the Tent of the Testimony, was set up, the cloud covered it. From evening till morning the cloud above the tabernacle looked like fire. ¹⁶That is how it con-

tinued to be; the cloud covered it, and at night it looked like fire. ¹⁷Whenever the cloud lifted from above the Tent, the Israelites set out; wherever the cloud settled, the Israelites encamped. ¹⁸At the LORD's command the Israelites set out, and at his command they encamped. As long as the cloud stayed over the tabernacle, they remained in camp. ¹⁹When the cloud remained over the tabernacle a long time, the Israelites obeyed the LORD's order and did not set out. ²⁰Sometimes the cloud was over the tabernacle only a few days; at the LORD's command they would encamp, and then at his command they would set out. ²¹Sometimes the cloud stayed only from evening till morning, and when it lifted in the morning, they set out. Whether by day or by night, whenever the cloud lifted, they set out. ²²Whether the cloud stayed over the tabernacle for two days or a month or a year, the Israelites would remain in camp and not set out; but when it lifted, they

9:22 Unmistakable Guidance

This passage describes a remarkable fact of the desert experience: the Israelites knew exactly whether and how far God wanted them to move each day. Although they disobeyed God in almost every other way, they usually followed his specific guidance on location.

would set out. ²³At the LORD's command they encamped, and at the LORD's command they set out. They obeyed the LORD's order, in accordance with his command through Moses.

The Silver Trumpets

10 The LORD said to Moses: ²"Make two trumpets of hammered silver, and use them for calling the community together and for having the camps set out. ³When both are sounded, the whole community is to assemble before you at the entrance to the Tent of Meeting. ⁴If only one is sounded, the leaders—the heads of the clans of Israel—are to assemble before you. ⁵When a trumpet blast is sounded, the tribes camping on the east are to set out. ⁶At the sounding of a second blast, the camps on the south are to set out. The blast will be the signal for setting out. ⁷To gather the assembly, blow the trumpets, but not with the same signal.

⁸"The sons of Aaron, the priests, are to blow the trumpets. This is to be a lasting ordinance for you and the generations to come. ⁹When you go into battle in your own land against an enemy who is oppressing you, sound a blast on the trumpets. Then you will be remembered by the LORD your God and rescued from your enemies. ¹⁰Also at your times of rejoicing—your appointed feasts and New Moon festivals—you are to

sound the trumpets over your burnt offerings and fellowship offerings,[a] and they will be a memorial for you before your God. I am the LORD your God."

The Israelites Leave Sinai

[11]On the twentieth day of the second month of the second year, the cloud lifted from above the tabernacle of the Testimony. [12]Then the Israelites set out from the Desert of Sinai and traveled from place to place until the cloud came to rest in the Desert of Paran. [13]They set out, this first time, at the LORD's command through Moses.

[14]The divisions of the camp of Judah went first, under their standard. Nahshon son of Amminadab was in command. [15]Nethanel son of Zuar was over the division of the tribe of Issachar, [16]and Eliab son of Helon was over the division of the tribe of Zebulun. [17]Then the tabernacle was taken down, and the Gershonites and Merarites, who carried it, set out.

[18]The divisions of the camp of Reuben went next, under their standard. Elizur son of Shedeur was in command. [19]Shelumiel son of Zurishaddai was over the division of the tribe of Simeon, [20]and Eliasaph son of Deuel was over the division of the tribe of Gad. [21]Then the Kohathites set out, carrying the holy things. The tabernacle was to be set up before they arrived.

[22]The divisions of the camp of Ephraim went next, under their standard. Elishama son of Ammihud was in command. [23]Gamaliel son of Pedahzur was over the division of the tribe of Manasseh, [24]and Abidan son of Gideoni was over the division of the tribe of Benjamin.

[25]Finally, as the rear guard for all the units, the divisions of the camp of Dan set out, under their standard. Ahiezer son of Ammishaddai was in command. [26]Pagiel son of Ocran was over the division of the tribe of Asher, [27]and Ahira son of Enan was over the division of the tribe of Naphtali. [28]This was the order of march for the Israelite divisions as they set out.

[29]Now Moses said to Hobab son of Reuel the Midianite, Moses' father-in-law, "We are setting out for the place about which the LORD said, 'I will give it to you.' Come with us and we will treat you well, for the LORD has promised good things to Israel."

[30]He answered, "No, I will not go; I am going back to my own land and my own people."

[31]But Moses said, "Please do not leave us. You know where we should camp in the desert, and you can be our eyes. [32]If you come with us, we will share with you whatever good things the LORD gives us."

[33]So they set out from the mountain of the LORD and traveled for three days. The ark of the covenant of the LORD went before them during those three days to find them a place to rest. [34]The cloud of the LORD was over them by day when they set out from the camp.

[35]Whenever the ark set out, Moses said,

"Rise up, O LORD!
May your enemies be scattered;
may your foes flee before you."

[36]Whenever it came to rest, he said,

"Return, O LORD,
to the countless thousands of Israel."

10:36 Famous Prayers

Moses' prayer is still repeated in Jewish services when the scroll of the law is removed from its container. Another prayer from Numbers, the blessing of 6:24–26, is quoted both in Jewish and Christian services. In ancient thought, a person's name stood for his character, including all his virtues and powers, and the benediction in 6:27 showed God "putting his name on" the Israelites.

Fire From the LORD

11 Now the people complained about their hardships in the hearing of the LORD, and when he heard them his anger was aroused. Then fire from the LORD burned among them and consumed some of the outskirts of the camp. [2]When the people cried out to Moses, he prayed to the LORD and the fire died down. [3]So that place was called Taberah,[b] because fire from the LORD had burned among them.

Quail From the LORD

[4]The rabble with them began to crave other food, and again the Israelites started wailing and said, "If only we had meat to eat! [5]We remember the fish we ate in Egypt at no cost—also the cucumbers, melons, leeks, onions and garlic. [6]But now we have lost our appetite; we never see anything but this manna!"

[7]The manna was like coriander seed and looked like resin. [8]The people went around gathering it, and then ground it in a handmill or crushed it in a mortar. They cooked it in a pot or made it into cakes. And it tasted like something made with olive oil. [9]When the dew settled on the camp at night, the manna also came down.

[10]Moses heard the people of every family wailing, each at the entrance to his tent. The LORD became exceedingly angry, and Moses was troubled. [11]He asked the LORD, "Why have you brought this trouble on your servant? What have

---

[a]10 Traditionally *peace offerings*   [b]3 *Taberah* means *burning.*

I done to displease you that you put the burden of all these people on me? ¹²Did I conceive all these people? Did I give them birth? Why do you tell me to carry them in my arms, as a nurse carries an infant, to the land you promised on oath to their forefathers? ¹³Where can I get meat for all these people? They keep wailing to me, 'Give us meat to eat!' ¹⁴I cannot carry all these people by myself; the burden is too heavy for me. ¹⁵If this is how you are going to treat me, put me to death right now—if I have found favor in your eyes—and do not let me face my own ruin."

¹⁶The LORD said to Moses: "Bring me seventy of Israel's elders who are known to you as leaders and officials among the people. Have them come to the Tent of Meeting, that they may stand there with you. ¹⁷I will come down and speak with you there, and I will take of the Spirit that is on you and put the Spirit on them. They will help you carry the burden of the people so that you will not have to carry it alone.

¹⁸"Tell the people: 'Consecrate yourselves in preparation for tomorrow, when you will eat meat. The LORD heard you when you wailed, "If only we had meat to eat! We were better off in Egypt!" Now the LORD will give you meat, and you will eat it. ¹⁹You will not eat it for just one day, or two days, or five, ten or twenty days, ²⁰but for a whole month—until it comes out of your nostrils and you loathe it—because you have rejected the LORD, who is among you, and have wailed before him, saying, "Why did we ever leave Egypt?" ' "

²¹But Moses said, "Here I am among six hundred thousand men on foot, and you say, 'I will give them meat to eat for a whole month!' ²²Would they have enough if flocks and herds were slaughtered for them? Would they have enough if all the fish in the sea were caught for them?"

²³The LORD answered Moses, "Is the LORD's arm too short? You will now see whether or not what I say will come true for you."

²⁴So Moses went out and told the people what the LORD had said. He brought together seventy of their elders and had them stand around the Tent. ²⁵Then the LORD came down in the cloud and spoke with him, and he took of the Spirit that was on him and put the Spirit on the seventy elders. When the Spirit rested on them, they prophesied, but they did not do so again.ᵃ

²⁶However, two men, whose names were Eldad and Medad, had remained in the camp. They were listed among the elders, but did not go out to the Tent. Yet the Spirit also rested on them, and they prophesied in the camp. ²⁷A young man

ran and told Moses, "Eldad and Medad are prophesying in the camp."

²⁸Joshua son of Nun, who had been Moses' aide since youth, spoke up and said, "Moses, my lord, stop them!"

²⁹But Moses replied, "Are you jealous for my sake? I wish that all the LORD's people were prophets and that the LORD would put his Spirit

11:29 Burdens of Leadership

In this striking conversation with God, Moses confessed the terrible burden involved in leading a whining, complaining band of "rabble." Although his patience neared the breaking point, he still showed mercy toward rivals. His response to other prophets here resembles Jesus' attitude toward other workers (Mark 9:38–41), as well as Paul's (Philippians 1:18).

on them!" ³⁰Then Moses and the elders of Israel returned to the camp.

³¹Now a wind went out from the LORD and drove quail in from the sea. It brought themᵇ down all around the camp to about three feetᶜ above the ground, as far as a day's walk in any direction. ³²All that day and night and all the next day the people went out and gathered quail. No one gathered less than ten homers.ᵈ Then they spread them out all around the camp. ³³But while the meat was still between their teeth and before it could be consumed, the anger of the LORD burned against the people, and he struck them with a severe plague. ³⁴Therefore the place was named Kibroth Hattaavah,ᵉ because there they buried the people who had craved other food.

³⁵From Kibroth Hattaavah the people traveled to Hazeroth and stayed there.

Miriam and Aaron Oppose Moses

12 Miriam and Aaron began to talk against Moses because of his Cushite wife, for he had married a Cushite. ²"Has the LORD spoken only through Moses?" they asked. "Hasn't he also spoken through us?" And the LORD heard this.

³(Now Moses was a very humble man, more humble than anyone else on the face of the earth.)

⁴At once the LORD said to Moses, Aaron and Miriam, "Come out to the Tent of Meeting, all three of you." So the three of them came out. ⁵Then the LORD came down in a pillar of cloud; he stood at the entrance to the Tent and summoned Aaron and Miriam. When both of them stepped forward, ⁶he said, "Listen to my words:

ᵃ25 Or prophesied and continued to do so   ᵇ31 Or They flew   ᶜ31 Hebrew two cubits (about 1 meter)
ᵈ32 That is, probably about 60 bushels (about 2.2 kiloliters)   ᵉ34 Kibroth Hattaavah means graves of craving.

"When a prophet of the LORD is among you,
   I reveal myself to him in visions,
   I speak to him in dreams.
7But this is not true of my servant Moses;

12:2 Family Jealousy

Miriam, Moses' older sister, had helped save his life when he was a baby (Exodus 2:7). But she and her brother Aaron felt some sibling rivalry for their kid brother. Irked by his foreign wife, they began undercutting his leadership by asking whether he had a monopoly on God's will.

Moses apparently did not defend himself, but God came to his defense with scathing words that made clear their special relationship. Hebrews 3:1–6 refers to God's homage to Moses, showing that as close as Moses was to God, Jesus deserved even more honor.

he is faithful in all my house.
8With him I speak face to face,
   clearly and not in riddles;
   he sees the form of the LORD.
Why then were you not afraid
   to speak against my servant Moses?"

9The anger of the LORD burned against them, and he left them.

10When the cloud lifted from above the Tent, there stood Miriam—leprous,*a* like snow. Aaron turned toward her and saw that she had leprosy; 11and he said to Moses, "Please, my lord, do not hold against us the sin we have so foolishly committed. 12Do not let her be like a stillborn infant coming from its mother's womb with its flesh half eaten away."

13So Moses cried out to the LORD, "O God, please heal her!"

14The LORD replied to Moses, "If her father had spit in her face, would she not have been in disgrace for seven days? Confine her outside the camp for seven days; after that she can be brought back." 15So Miriam was confined outside the camp for seven days, and the people did not move on till she was brought back.

16After that, the people left Hazeroth and encamped in the Desert of Paran.

Exploring Canaan

13 The LORD said to Moses, 2"Send some men to explore the land of Canaan, which I am giving to the Israelites. From each ancestral tribe send one of its leaders."

3So at the LORD's command Moses sent them out from the Desert of Paran. All of them were leaders of the Israelites. 4These are their names:

from the tribe of Reuben, Shammua son of Zaccur;
5from the tribe of Simeon, Shaphat son of Hori;
6from the tribe of Judah, Caleb son of Jephunneh;
7from the tribe of Issachar, Igal son of Joseph;
8from the tribe of Ephraim, Hoshea son of Nun;
9from the tribe of Benjamin, Palti son of Raphu;
10from the tribe of Zebulun, Gaddiel son of Sodi;
11from the tribe of Manasseh (a tribe of Joseph), Gaddi son of Susi;
12from the tribe of Dan, Ammiel son of Gemalli;

a 10 The Hebrew word was used for various diseases affecting the skin—not necessarily leprosy.

MIRIAM *Jealous Sister*

AMONG LIFE'S MOST DIFFICULT TASKS is enjoying the success of a brother or sister who outdoes you. Certainly Moses' sister Miriam found it difficult.

At Moses' birth she was the hero, watching over her baby brother and cleverly jumping in to outwit Pharaoh's daughter (Exodus 2:7). She took the spotlight again when the Israelites crossed the Red Sea, leading the women in a wild song of triumph (Exodus 15:20). As a prophetess, she played an important leadership role alongside Moses, who carried the chief responsibilities.

Then jealousy crept in. Miriam and her brother Aaron, another strong leader, began to grumble. They objected to Moses' wife, a foreigner, and they felt they ought to have equal spiritual status with Moses. "Has the LORD spoken only through Moses?" they asked. "Hasn't he also spoken through us?" (12:2).

In essence, God responded with a fierce "How dare you?" He singled out Miriam, apparently the leader of the two, for punishment. He would not tolerate jealousy among the leaders of his people—especially jealousy aimed at the humble man whom he had chosen.

Life Questions: What makes you jealous? How can you best handle those feelings?

¹³from the tribe of Asher, Sethur son of Michael;

¹⁴from the tribe of Naphtali, Nahbi son of Vophsi;

¹⁵from the tribe of Gad, Geuel son of Maki.

¹⁶These are the names of the men Moses sent to explore the land. (Moses gave Hoshea son of Nun the name Joshua.)

¹⁷When Moses sent them to explore Canaan, he said, "Go up through the Negev and on into the hill country. ¹⁸See what the land is like and whether the people who live there are strong or weak, few or many. ¹⁹What kind of land do they live in? Is it good or bad? What kind of towns do they live in? Are they unwalled or fortified? ²⁰How is the soil? Is it fertile or poor? Are there trees on it or not? Do your best to bring back some of the fruit of the land." (It was the season for the first ripe grapes.)

²¹So they went up and explored the land from the Desert of Zin as far as Rehob, toward Lebo^a Hamath. ²²They went up through the Negev and came to Hebron, where Ahiman, Sheshai and Talmai, the descendants of Anak, lived. (Hebron had been built seven years before Zoan in Egypt.) ²³When they reached the Valley of Eshcol,^b they cut off a branch bearing a single cluster of grapes. Two of them carried it on a pole between them, along with some pomegranates and figs. ²⁴That place was called the Valley of Eshcol because of the cluster of grapes the Israelites cut off there. ²⁵At the end of forty days they returned from exploring the land.

Report on the Exploration

²⁶They came back to Moses and Aaron and the whole Israelite community at Kadesh in the Desert of Paran. There they reported to them and to the whole assembly and showed them the fruit of the land. ²⁷They gave Moses this account: "We went into the land to which you sent us, and it does flow with milk and honey! Here is its fruit. ²⁸But the people who live there are powerful, and the cities are fortified and very large. We even saw descendants of Anak there. ²⁹The Amalekites live in the Negev; the Hittites, Jebusites and Amorites live in the hill country; and the Canaanites live near the sea and along the Jordan."

³⁰Then Caleb silenced the people before Moses and said, "We should go up and take possession of the land, for we can certainly do it."

³¹But the men who had gone up with him said, "We can't attack those people; they are stronger than we are." ³²And they spread among the Israelites a bad report about the land they had explored. They said, "The land we explored devours those living in it. All the people we saw there are of great size. ³³We saw the Nephilim there (the descendants of Anak come from the Nephilim). We seemed like grasshoppers in our own eyes, and we looked the same to them."

The People Rebel

14 That night all the people of the community raised their voices and wept aloud. ²All the Israelites grumbled against Moses and Aaron, and the whole assembly said to them, "If only we

---

^a21 Or *toward the entrance to*   ^b23 *Eshcol* means *cluster*; also in verse 24.

AARON *Working Together . . . and Apart*

EXODUS 1 INTRODUCES US TO one of the Bible's most famous families: Two devout parents from the tribe of Levi and their children Aaron, Miriam and Moses. Surprisingly it was Moses, the younger brother, who got the Bible's star assignments, while the elder Aaron gained fame mainly as a substitute. For example, when God called Moses to free Israel from slavery, Moses shook like a coward. In response, God proposed teamwork. Moses' older brother Aaron would join Moses and make up for his weaknesses (Exodus 4:10–16).

The two worked side by side confronting Pharaoh, leading the Israelites out of Egypt, and calming the ornery people they were supposed to lead. Aaron's gifts in public speaking made up for Moses' stumbling speech, and so Aaron often accompanied Moses to meetings and did the talking. When God gave Moses the Law governing the new nation of Israel, Aaron and his sons were appointed priests. They and only they could lead in worship at the newly built tabernacle in the center of the camp (28:1).

Twice, however, Aaron thwarted teamwork, with disastrous results. While Moses was meeting with God on Mount Sinai, the people grew restless. Aaron came up with the idea of fashioning a golden idol for them to worship (chapter 32). On another occasion, Aaron and his sister openly carped about Moses' foreign-born wife and conspired to challenge his leadership (Numbers 12). Each time, God grew very angry at Aaron.

Aaron was an effective team player, but when he tried to go out on his own he got into trouble.

Life Questions: On what "teams" do you participate? What role do you usually play—starring or substitute?

had died in Egypt! Or in this desert! [3]Why is the LORD bringing us to this land only to let us fall by the sword? Our wives and children will be taken as plunder. Wouldn't it be better for us to go

14:1 The Worst Rebellion

Chapter 14 records the tragic watershed of Numbers. Despite numerous proofs of God's power on their behalf, the Israelites cowered at the spies' report from Canaan. Fear led to open rebellion, and the nation plotted mutiny against Moses. At the very border of the promised land, theirs for the taking, they lost faith and turned away. In the face of such rebellion, God decided to wait for a whole new generation of Israelites; the original slaves would not cross into the promised land. All of them over the age of 20—except for Caleb and Joshua—were destined to fall as carcasses in the desert.

back to Egypt?" [4]And they said to each other, "We should choose a leader and go back to Egypt."

[5]Then Moses and Aaron fell facedown in front of the whole Israelite assembly gathered there. [6]Joshua son of Nun and Caleb son of Jephunneh, who were among those who had explored the land, tore their clothes [7]and said to the entire Israelite assembly, "The land we passed through and explored is exceedingly good. [8]If the LORD is pleased with us, he will lead us into that land, a land flowing with milk and honey, and will give it to us. [9]Only do not rebel against the LORD. And do not be afraid of the people of the land, because we will swallow them up. Their protection is gone, but the LORD is with us. Do not be afraid of them."

[10]But the whole assembly talked about stoning them. Then the glory of the LORD appeared at the Tent of Meeting to all the Israelites. [11]The LORD said to Moses, "How long will these people treat me with contempt? How long will they refuse to believe in me, in spite of all the miraculous signs I have performed among them? [12]I will strike them down with a plague and destroy them, but I will make you into a nation greater and stronger than they."

[13]Moses said to the LORD, "Then the Egyptians will hear about it! By your power you brought these people up from among them. [14]And they will tell the inhabitants of this land about it. They have already heard that you, O LORD, are with these people and that you, O LORD, have been seen face to face, that your cloud stays over them, and that you go before them in a pillar of cloud by day and a pillar of fire by night. [15]If you put

these people to death all at one time, the nations who have heard this report about you will say, [16]'The LORD was not able to bring these people into the land he promised them on oath; so he slaughtered them in the desert.'

[17]"Now may the Lord's strength be displayed, just as you have declared: [18]'The LORD is slow to anger, abounding in love and forgiving sin and rebellion. Yet he does not leave the guilty unpunished; he punishes the children for the sin of the fathers to the third and fourth generation.' [19]In accordance with your great love, forgive the sin of these people, just as you have pardoned them from the time they left Egypt until now."

[20]The LORD replied, "I have forgiven them, as you asked. [21]Nevertheless, as surely as I live and as surely as the glory of the LORD fills the whole earth, [22]not one of the men who saw my glory and the miraculous signs I performed in Egypt and in the desert but who disobeyed me and tested me ten times— [23]not one of them will ever see the land I promised on oath to their forefathers. No one who has treated me with contempt will ever see it. [24]But because my servant Caleb has a different spirit and follows me wholeheartedly, I will bring him into the land he went to, and his descendants will inherit it. [25]Since the Amalekites and Canaanites are living in the valleys, turn back tomorrow and set out toward the desert along the route to the Red Sea.[a]"

[26]The LORD said to Moses and Aaron: [27]"How long will this wicked community grumble against me? I have heard the complaints of these grumbling Israelites. [28]So tell them, 'As surely as I live, declares the LORD, I will do to you the very things I heard you say: [29]In this desert your bodies will fall—every one of you twenty years old or more who was counted in the census and who has grumbled against me. [30]Not one of you will enter the land I swore with uplifted hand to make your home, except Caleb son of Jephunneh and Joshua son of Nun. [31]As for your children that you said would be taken as plunder, I will bring them in to enjoy the land you have rejected. [32]But you—your bodies will fall in this desert. [33]Your children will be shepherds here for forty years, suffering for your unfaithfulness, until the last of your bodies lies in the desert. [34]For forty years—one year for each of the forty days you explored the land—you will suffer for your sins and know what it is like to have me against you.' [35]I, the LORD, have spoken, and I will surely do these things to this whole wicked community, which has banded together against me. They will meet their end in this desert; here they will die."

[36]So the men Moses had sent to explore the land, who returned and made the whole community grumble against him by spreading a bad re-

port about it— [37]these men responsible for spreading the bad report about the land were struck down and died of a plague before the LORD. [38]Of the men who went to explore the land, only Joshua son of Nun and Caleb son of Jephunneh survived.

[39]When Moses reported this to all the Israel-

ites, they mourned bitterly. [40]Early the next morning they went up toward the high hill country. "We have sinned," they said. "We will go up to the place the LORD promised."

[41]But Moses said, "Why are you disobeying the LORD's command? This will not succeed! [42]Do not go up, because the LORD is not with you. You will be defeated by your enemies, [43]for the Amalekites and Canaanites will face you there. Because you have turned away from the LORD, he will not be with you and you will fall by the sword."

[44]Nevertheless, in their presumption they went up toward the high hill country, though neither Moses nor the ark of the LORD's covenant moved from the camp. [45]Then the Amalekites and Canaanites who lived in that hill country came down and attacked them and beat them down all the way to Hormah.

Supplementary Offerings

15 The LORD said to Moses, [2]"Speak to the Israelites and say to them: 'After you enter the land I am giving you as a home [3]and you present to the LORD offerings made by fire, from the herd or the flock, as an aroma pleasing to the LORD—whether burnt offerings or sacrifices, for special vows or freewill offerings or festival offerings— [4]then the one who brings his offering shall present to the LORD a grain offering of a tenth of an ephah[a] of fine flour mixed with a quarter of a hin[b] of oil. [5]With each lamb for the burnt offering or the sacrifice, prepare a quarter of a hin of wine as a drink offering.

[6]"'With a ram prepare a grain offering of two-

tenths of an ephah[c] of fine flour mixed with a third of a hin[d] of oil, [7]and a third of a hin of wine as a drink offering. Offer it as an aroma pleasing to the LORD.

[8]"'When you prepare a young bull as a burnt offering or sacrifice, for a special vow or a fellowship offering[e] to the LORD, [9]bring with the bull a grain offering of three-tenths of an ephah[f] of fine flour mixed with half a hin[g] of oil. [10]Also bring half a hin of wine as a drink offering. It will be an offering made by fire, an aroma pleasing to the LORD. [11]Each bull or ram, each lamb or young goat, is to be prepared in this manner. [12]Do this for each one, for as many as you prepare.

[13]"'Everyone who is native-born must do these things in this way when he brings an offering made by fire as an aroma pleasing to the LORD. [14]For the generations to come, whenever an alien or anyone else living among you presents an offering made by fire as an aroma pleasing to the LORD, he must do exactly as you do. [15]The community is to have the same rules for you and for the alien living among you; this is a lasting ordinance for the generations to come. You and the alien shall be the same before the LORD: [16]The same laws and regulations will apply both to you and to the alien living among you.'"

[17]The LORD said to Moses, [18]"Speak to the Israelites and say to them: 'When you enter the land to which I am taking you [19]and you eat the food of the land, present a portion as an offering to the LORD. [20]Present a cake from the first of your ground meal and present it as an offering from the threshing floor. [21]Throughout the generations to come you are to give this offering to the LORD from the first of your ground meal.

Offerings for Unintentional Sins

[22]"'Now if you unintentionally fail to keep any of these commands the LORD gave Moses— [23]any of the LORD's commands to you through him, from the day the LORD gave them and continuing through the generations to come— [24]and if this is done unintentionally without the community being aware of it, then the whole community is to offer a young bull for a burnt offering as an aroma pleasing to the LORD, along with its prescribed grain offering and drink offering, and a male goat for a sin offering. [25]The priest is to make atonement for the whole Israelite community, and they will be forgiven, for it was not intentional and they have brought to the LORD for their wrong an offering made by fire and a sin offering. [26]The whole Israelite community and the aliens living among them will be forgiven,

---

a4 That is, probably about 2 quarts (about 2 liters)   *b4 That is, probably about 1 quart (about 1 liter); also in verse 5*   *c6 That is, probably about 4 quarts (about 4.5 liters)*   *d6 That is, probably about 1 1/4 quarts (about 1.2 liters); also in verse 7*   *e8 Traditionally peace offering*   *f9 That is, probably about 6 quarts (about 6.5 liters)*   *g9 That is, probably about 2 quarts (about 2 liters); also in verse 10*

because all the people were involved in the unintentional wrong.

27 "'But if just one person sins unintentionally, he must bring a year-old female goat for a sin offering. 28The priest is to make atonement before the LORD for the one who erred by sinning unintentionally, and when atonement has been made for him, he will be forgiven. 29One and the same law applies to everyone who sins unintentionally, whether he is a native-born Israelite or an alien.

30 "'But anyone who sins defiantly, whether native-born or alien, blasphemes the LORD, and that person must be cut off from his people. 31Because he has despised the LORD's word and broken his commands, that person must surely be cut off; his guilt remains on him.'"

The Sabbath-Breaker Put to Death

32While the Israelites were in the desert, a man was found gathering wood on the Sabbath day. 33Those who found him gathering wood brought him to Moses and Aaron and the whole assembly, 34and they kept him in custody, because it was not clear what should be done to him. 35Then the LORD said to Moses, "The man must die. The whole assembly must stone him outside the camp." 36So the assembly took him outside the camp and stoned him to death, as the LORD commanded Moses.

Tassels on Garments

37The LORD said to Moses, 38"Speak to the Israelites and say to them: 'Throughout the generations to come you are to make tassels on the corners of your garments, with a blue cord on

15:38 A Safeguard Against Lust

The Israelites had large reminders of God—such as the pillar of fire—and small ones: they wore tassels and blue cords on the corners of clothing to remind them of the Lord's commands. God specifically mentions this practice as a safeguard against lust—a reminder impossible to avoid for one tempted to adultery.

each tassel. 39You will have these tassels to look at and so you will remember all the commands of the LORD, that you may obey them and not prostitute yourselves by going after the lusts of your own hearts and eyes. 40Then you will remember to obey all my commands and will be consecrated to your God. 41I am the LORD your God, who brought you out of Egypt to be your God. I am the LORD your God.'"

Korah, Dathan and Abiram

16 Korah son of Izhar, the son of Kohath, the son of Levi, and certain Reubenites—Dathan and Abiram, sons of Eliab, and On son of Peleth—became insolent[a] 2and rose up against Moses. With them were 250 Israelite men, well-known community leaders who had been appointed members of the council. 3They came as a group to oppose Moses and Aaron and said to them, "You have gone too far! The whole community is holy, every one of them, and the LORD is with them. Why then do you set yourselves above the LORD's assembly?"

16:3 Open Revolt

Two hundred and fifty well-known council members, led by Korah, Dathan, and Abiram, rebelled against Moses' leadership. They apparently wanted more people recognized as priests. But in a dramatic test, Moses showed that he was the leader God had chosen.

This rebellion and a second one immediately afterwards (verse 41) are the only two major events that the Bible mentions during the Israelites' 37 years of wandering in the desert. Deuteronomy, however (2:7; 8:4; 29:5–6), indicates the people were well cared for.

4When Moses heard this, he fell facedown. 5Then he said to Korah and all his followers: "In the morning the LORD will show who belongs to him and who is holy, and he will have that person come near him. The man he chooses he will cause to come near him. 6You, Korah, and all your followers are to do this: Take censers 7and tomorrow put fire and incense in them before the LORD. The man the LORD chooses will be the one who is holy. You Levites have gone too far!"

8Moses also said to Korah, "Now listen, you Levites! 9Isn't it enough for you that the God of Israel has separated you from the rest of the Israelite community and brought you near himself to do the work at the LORD's tabernacle and to stand before the community and minister to them? 10He has brought you and all your fellow Levites near himself, but now you are trying to get the priesthood too. 11It is against the LORD that you and all your followers have banded together. Who is Aaron that you should grumble against him?"

12Then Moses summoned Dathan and Abiram, the sons of Eliab. But they said, "We will not come! 13Isn't it enough that you have brought us up out of a land flowing with milk and honey to kill us in the desert? And now you also want to lord it over us? 14Moreover, you haven't brought us into a land flowing with milk and honey or given us an inheritance of fields and vineyards. Will you gouge out the eyes of[a] these men? No, we will not come!"

[15]Then Moses became very angry and said to the LORD, "Do not accept their offering. I have not taken so much as a donkey from them, nor have I wronged any of them."

[16]Moses said to Korah, "You and all your followers are to appear before the LORD tomorrow—you and they and Aaron. [17]Each man is to take his censer and put incense in it—250 censers in all—and present it before the LORD. You and Aaron are to present your censers also." [18]So each man took his censer, put fire and incense in it, and stood with Moses and Aaron at the entrance to the Tent of Meeting. [19]When Korah had gathered all his followers in opposition to them at the entrance to the Tent of Meeting, the glory of the LORD appeared to the entire assembly. [20]The LORD said to Moses and Aaron, [21]"Separate yourselves from this assembly so I can put an end to them at once."

[22]But Moses and Aaron fell facedown and cried out, "O God, God of the spirits of all mankind, will you be angry with the entire assembly when only one man sins?"

[23]Then the LORD said to Moses, [24]"Say to the assembly, 'Move away from the tents of Korah, Dathan and Abiram.'"

[25]Moses got up and went to Dathan and Abiram, and the elders of Israel followed him. [26]He warned the assembly, "Move back from the tents of these wicked men! Do not touch anything belonging to them, or you will be swept away because of all their sins." [27]So they moved away from the tents of Korah, Dathan and Abiram. Dathan and Abiram had come out and were standing with their wives, children and little ones at the entrances to their tents.

[28]Then Moses said, "This is how you will know that the LORD has sent me to do all these things and that it was not my idea: [29]If these men die a natural death and experience only what usually happens to men, then the LORD has not sent me. [30]But if the LORD brings about something totally new, and the earth opens its mouth and swallows them, with everything that belongs to them, and they go down alive into the grave,[b] then you will know that these men have treated the LORD with contempt."

[31]As soon as he finished saying all this, the ground under them split apart [32]and the earth opened its mouth and swallowed them, with their households and all Korah's men and all their possessions. [33]They went down alive into the grave, with everything they owned; the earth closed over them, and they perished and were gone from the community. [34]At their cries, all the Israelites around them fled, shouting, "The earth is going to swallow us too!"

[35]And fire came out from the LORD and consumed the 250 men who were offering the incense.

[36]The LORD said to Moses, [37]"Tell Eleazar son of Aaron, the priest, to take the censers out of the smoldering remains and scatter the coals some distance away, for the censers are holy— [38]the censers of the men who sinned at the cost of their lives. Hammer the censers into sheets to overlay the altar, for they were presented before the LORD and have become holy. Let them be a sign to the Israelites."

[39]So Eleazar the priest collected the bronze censers brought by those who had been burned up, and he had them hammered out to overlay the altar, [40]as the LORD directed him through Moses. This was to remind the Israelites that no one except a descendant of Aaron should come to burn incense before the LORD, or he would become like Korah and his followers.

[41]The next day the whole Israelite community grumbled against Moses and Aaron. "You have killed the LORD's people," they said.

[42]But when the assembly gathered in opposition to Moses and Aaron and turned toward the Tent of Meeting, suddenly the cloud covered it and the glory of the LORD appeared. [43]Then Moses and Aaron went to the front of the Tent of Meeting, [44]and the LORD said to Moses, [45]"Get away from this assembly so I can put an end to them at once." And they fell facedown.

[46]Then Moses said to Aaron, "Take your censer and put incense in it, along with fire from the altar, and hurry to the assembly to make atonement for them. Wrath has come out from the LORD; the plague has started." [47]So Aaron did as Moses said, and ran into the midst of the assembly. The plague had already started among the people, but Aaron offered the incense and made atonement for them. [48]He stood between the living and the dead, and the plague stopped. [49]But 14,700 people died from the plague, in addition to those who had died because of Korah. [50]Then Aaron returned to Moses at the entrance to the Tent of Meeting, for the plague had stopped.

The Budding of Aaron's Staff

17 The LORD said to Moses, [2]"Speak to the Israelites and get twelve staffs from them, one from the leader of each of their ancestral tribes. Write the name of each man on his staff. [3]On the staff of Levi write Aaron's name, for there must be one staff for the head of each ancestral tribe. [4]Place them in the Tent of Meeting in front of the Testimony, where I meet with you.

---

[a]14 Or *you make slaves of*; or *you deceive*   [b]30 Hebrew *Sheol*; also in verse 33

⁵The staff belonging to the man I choose will sprout, and I will rid myself of this constant grumbling against you by the Israelites."

⁶So Moses spoke to the Israelites, and their leaders gave him twelve staffs, one for the leader of each of their ancestral tribes, and Aaron's staff was among them. ⁷Moses placed the staffs before the LORD in the Tent of the Testimony.

⁸The next day Moses entered the Tent of the Testimony and saw that Aaron's staff, which represented the house of Levi, had not only sprouted but had budded, blossomed and produced almonds. ⁹Then Moses brought out all the staffs from the LORD's presence to all the Israelites. They looked at them, and each man took his own staff.

¹⁰The LORD said to Moses, "Put back Aaron's staff in front of the Testimony, to be kept as a sign to the rebellious. This will put an end to their grumbling against me, so that they will not die."

17:10 What's In the Ark

The ark of the covenant was the holiest sign of God's presence. In or near it were placed a few highly significant mementos of the journey to the promised land: the stone tablets of the Law of Moses (Exodus 25:16), a jar of the miraculous manna (Exodus 16:33–34), and Aaron's sprouted staff. As a visible proof that God had chosen Aaron to be priest, the miraculous staff could help deter future rebellions.

¹¹Moses did just as the LORD commanded him.

¹²The Israelites said to Moses, "We will die! We are lost, we are all lost! ¹³Anyone who even comes near the tabernacle of the LORD will die. Are we all going to die?"

Duties of Priests and Levites

18 The LORD said to Aaron, "You, your sons and your father's family are to bear the responsibility for offenses against the sanctuary, and you and your sons alone are to bear the responsibility for offenses against the priesthood. ²Bring your fellow Levites from your ancestral tribe to join you and assist you when you and your sons minister before the Tent of the Testimony. ³They are to be responsible to you and are to perform all the duties of the Tent, but they must not go near the furnishings of the sanctuary or the altar, or both they and you will die. ⁴They are to join you and be responsible for the care of the Tent of Meeting—all the work at the Tent—and no one else may come near where you are.

⁵"You are to be responsible for the care of the sanctuary and the altar, so that wrath will not fall on the Israelites again. ⁶I myself have selected your fellow Levites from among the Israelites as a gift to you, dedicated to the LORD to do the work at the Tent of Meeting. ⁷But only you and your sons may serve as priests in connection with everything at the altar and inside the curtain. I am giving you the service of the priesthood as a gift. Anyone else who comes near the sanctuary must be put to death."

Offerings for Priests and Levites

⁸Then the LORD said to Aaron, "I myself have put you in charge of the offerings presented to me; all the holy offerings the Israelites give me I give to you and your sons as your portion and regular share. ⁹You are to have the part of the most holy offerings that is kept from the fire. From all the gifts they bring me as most holy offerings, whether grain or sin or guilt offerings, that part belongs to you and your sons. ¹⁰Eat it as something most holy; every male shall eat it. You must regard it as holy.

¹¹"This also is yours: whatever is set aside from the gifts of all the wave offerings of the Israelites. I give this to you and your sons and daughters as your regular share. Everyone in your household who is ceremonially clean may eat it.

¹²"I give you all the finest olive oil and all the finest new wine and grain they give the LORD as the firstfruits of their harvest. ¹³All the land's firstfruits that they bring to the LORD will be yours. Everyone in your household who is ceremonially clean may eat it.

¹⁴"Everything in Israel that is devoted[a] to the LORD is yours. ¹⁵The first offspring of every womb, both man and animal, that is offered to the LORD is yours. But you must redeem every firstborn son and every firstborn male of unclean animals. ¹⁶When they are a month old, you must redeem them at the redemption price set at five shekels[b] of silver, according to the sanctuary shekel, which weighs twenty gerahs.

¹⁷"But you must not redeem the firstborn of an ox, a sheep or a goat; they are holy. Sprinkle their blood on the altar and burn their fat as an offering made by fire, an aroma pleasing to the LORD. ¹⁸Their meat is to be yours, just as the breast of the wave offering and the right thigh are yours. ¹⁹Whatever is set aside from the holy offerings the Israelites present to the LORD I give to you and your sons and daughters as your regular share. It is an everlasting covenant of salt before the LORD for both you and your offspring."

²⁰The LORD said to Aaron, "You will have no

a 14 The Hebrew term refers to the irrevocable giving over of things or persons to the LORD.   b 16 That is, about 2 ounces (about 55 grams)

inheritance in their land, nor will you have any share among them; I am your share and your inheritance among the Israelites.

21"I give to the Levites all the tithes in Israel as

18:20 No Land for Levites

The tribe of Levites got special privileges, but in contrast to the wealthy priestly caste of, say, Egypt, they received no land. God himself was their share and inheritance. For food, they relied largely on offerings from other tribes. Thus the physical survival of "full-time ministers" depended on how faithful the other Israelites were.

their inheritance in return for the work they do while serving at the Tent of Meeting. 22From now on the Israelites must not go near the Tent of Meeting, or they will bear the consequences of their sin and will die. 23It is the Levites who are to do the work at the Tent of Meeting and bear the responsibility for offenses against it. This is a lasting ordinance for the generations to come. They will receive no inheritance among the Israelites. 24Instead, I give to the Levites as their inheritance the tithes that the Israelites present as an offering to the LORD. That is why I said concerning them: 'They will have no inheritance among the Israelites.'"

25The LORD said to Moses, 26"Speak to the Levites and say to them: 'When you receive from the Israelites the tithe I give you as your inheritance, you must present a tenth of that tithe as the LORD's offering. 27Your offering will be reckoned to you as grain from the threshing floor or juice from the winepress. 28In this way you also will present an offering to the LORD from all the tithes you receive from the Israelites. From these tithes you must give the LORD's portion to Aaron the priest. 29You must present as the LORD's portion the best and holiest part of everything given to you.'

30"Say to the Levites: 'When you present the best part, it will be reckoned to you as the product of the threshing floor or the winepress. 31You and your households may eat the rest of it anywhere, for it is your wages for your work at the Tent of Meeting. 32By presenting the best part of it you will not be guilty in this matter; then you will not defile the holy offerings of the Israelites, and you will not die.'"

The Water of Cleansing

19 The LORD said to Moses and Aaron: 2"This is a requirement of the law that the LORD has commanded: Tell the Israelites to bring you a red heifer without defect or blemish and that has never been under a yoke. 3Give it to Eleazar

the priest; it is to be taken outside the camp and slaughtered in his presence. 4Then Eleazar the priest is to take some of its blood on his finger and sprinkle it seven times toward the front of the Tent of Meeting. 5While he watches, the heifer is to be burned—its hide, flesh, blood and offal. 6The priest is to take some cedar wood, hyssop and scarlet wool and throw them onto the burning heifer. 7After that, the priest must wash his clothes and bathe himself with water. He may then come into the camp, but he will be ceremonially unclean till evening. 8The man who burns it must also wash his clothes and bathe with water, and he too will be unclean till evening.

9"A man who is clean shall gather up the ashes of the heifer and put them in a ceremonially clean place outside the camp. They shall be kept by the Israelite community for use in the water of cleansing; it is for purification from sin. 10The man who gathers up the ashes of the heifer must also wash his clothes, and he too will be unclean till evening. This will be a lasting ordinance both for the Israelites and for the aliens living among them.

11"Whoever touches the dead body of anyone will be unclean for seven days. 12He must purify himself with the water on the third day and on the seventh day; then he will be clean. But if he does not purify himself on the third and seventh days, he will not be clean. 13Whoever touches the dead body of anyone and fails to purify himself defiles the LORD's tabernacle. That person must be cut off from Israel. Because the water of cleansing has not been sprinkled on him, he is unclean; his uncleanness remains on him.

14"This is the law that applies when a person dies in a tent: Anyone who enters the tent and anyone who is in it will be unclean for seven days, 15and every open container without a lid fastened on it will be unclean.

16"Anyone out in the open who touches someone who has been killed with a sword or someone who has died a natural death, or anyone who touches a human bone or a grave, will be unclean for seven days.

17"For the unclean person, put some ashes from the burned purification offering into a jar and pour fresh water over them. 18Then a man who is ceremonially clean is to take some hyssop, dip it in the water and sprinkle the tent and all the furnishings and the people who were there. He must also sprinkle anyone who has touched a human bone or a grave or someone who has been killed or someone who has died a natural death. 19The man who is clean is to sprinkle the unclean person on the third and seventh days, and on the seventh day he is to purify him. The person being cleansed must wash his clothes and bathe with water, and that evening he will be clean. ²⁰But if a person who is unclean does not purify himself, he must be cut off from the community, because he has defiled the sanctuary of the LORD. The water of cleansing has not been sprinkled on him, and he is unclean. ²¹This is a lasting ordinance for them.

"The man who sprinkles the water of cleansing must also wash his clothes, and anyone who touches the water of cleansing will be unclean till evening. ²²Anything that an unclean person touches becomes unclean, and anyone who touches it becomes unclean till evening."

Water From the Rock

20 In the first month the whole Israelite community arrived at the Desert of Zin, and they stayed at Kadesh. There Miriam died and was buried.

²Now there was no water for the community, and the people gathered in opposition to Moses and Aaron. ³They quarreled with Moses and said, "If only we had died when our brothers fell dead before the LORD! ⁴Why did you bring the LORD's community into this desert, that we and our livestock should die here? ⁵Why did you bring us up out of Egypt to this terrible place? It has no grain or figs, grapevines or pomegranates. And there is no water to drink!"

⁶Moses and Aaron went from the assembly to the entrance to the Tent of Meeting and fell facedown, and the glory of the LORD appeared to them. ⁷The LORD said to Moses, ⁸"Take the staff, and you and your brother Aaron gather the assembly together. Speak to that rock before their eyes and it will pour out its water. You will bring water out of the rock for the community so they and their livestock can drink."

⁹So Moses took the staff from the LORD's presence, just as he commanded him. ¹⁰He and Aaron gathered the assembly together in front of the rock and Moses said to them, "Listen, you rebels, must we bring you water out of this rock?" ¹¹Then Moses raised his arm and struck the rock twice with his staff. Water gushed out, and the community and their livestock drank.

¹²But the LORD said to Moses and Aaron, "Because you did not trust in me enough to honor me as holy in the sight of the Israelites, you will not bring this community into the land I give them."

¹³These were the waters of Meribah,ᵃ where the Israelites quarreled with the LORD and where he showed himself holy among them.

Edom Denies Israel Passage

¹⁴Moses sent messengers from Kadesh to the king of Edom, saying:

"This is what your brother Israel says:

You know about all the hardships that have come upon us. ¹⁵Our forefathers went down into Egypt, and we lived there many years. The Egyptians mistreated us and our

20:12 Moses' Sin

After so many displays of loyalty and courage, Moses faltered. Numbers does not specify exactly what Moses did that upset God. Was it striking the rock rather than speaking to it as God commanded? Regardless, Moses lashed out angrily against the Israelites and was faulted for his lack of trust in God. In Deuteronomy, God describes the sin as "breaking faith" with him and tells Moses that he "did not uphold my holiness among the Israelites" (32:51).

The scene at Meribah brought a tragic end to a great man's career: Moses, footsore and weary, was told he too would die in the desert, before the Israelites crossed into the promised land. Deuteronomy 3:23–27 adds a postscript: Moses pleaded with God to reverse the punishment, and, when that failed, he threw the blame back on the Israelites.

fathers, ¹⁶but when we cried out to the LORD, he heard our cry and sent an angel and brought us out of Egypt.

"Now we are here at Kadesh, a town on the edge of your territory. ¹⁷Please let us pass through your country. We will not go through any field or vineyard, or drink water from any well. We will travel along the king's highway and not turn to the right or to the left until we have passed through your territory."

¹⁸But Edom answered:

"You may not pass through here; if you try, we will march out and attack you with the sword."

¹⁹The Israelites replied:

"We will go along the main road, and if we or our livestock drink any of your water, we will pay for it. We only want to pass through on foot—nothing else."

²⁰Again they answered:

"You may not pass through."

Then Edom came out against them with a large and powerful army. ²¹Since Edom refused to let them go through their territory, Israel turned away from them.

ᵃ13 *Meribah* means *quarreling*.

The Death of Aaron

²²The whole Israelite community set out from Kadesh and came to Mount Hor. ²³At Mount Hor, near the border of Edom, the LORD said to

20:21 Blood Feud

Israel asked politely for the right to pass through Edom, offering to pay for water rights. Since the Edomites were distant relatives, descendants of Jacob's brother Esau, Israel expected a favorable response. Instead, Edom's refusal meant a long, hard detour. Moses warned the Israelites not to hate the Edomites, their kin (Deuteronomy 23:7–8). But for the rest of biblical history, there were wars and hatred between the two nations.

Moses and Aaron, ²⁴"Aaron will be gathered to his people. He will not enter the land I give the Israelites, because both of you rebelled against my command at the waters of Meribah. ²⁵Get Aaron and his son Eleazar and take them up Mount Hor. ²⁶Remove Aaron's garments and put them on his son Eleazar, for Aaron will be gathered to his people; he will die there."

²⁷Moses did as the LORD commanded: They went up Mount Hor in the sight of the whole community. ²⁸Moses removed Aaron's garments and put them on his son Eleazar. And Aaron died there on top of the mountain. Then Moses and Eleazar came down from the mountain, ²⁹and when the whole community learned that Aaron had died, the entire house of Israel mourned for him thirty days.

Arad Destroyed

21 When the Canaanite king of Arad, who lived in the Negev, heard that Israel was coming along the road to Atharim, he attacked the Israelites and captured some of them. ²Then Israel made this vow to the LORD: "If you will deliver these people into our hands, we will totally destroy[a] their cities." ³The LORD listened to Israel's plea and gave the Canaanites over to them. They completely destroyed them and their towns; so the place was named Hormah.[b]

The Bronze Snake

⁴They traveled from Mount Hor along the route to the Red Sea,[c] to go around Edom. But the people grew impatient on the way; ⁵they spoke against God and against Moses, and said, "Why have you brought us up out of Egypt to die

in the desert? There is no bread! There is no water! And we detest this miserable food!"

⁶Then the LORD sent venomous snakes among them; they bit the people and many Israelites died. ⁷The people came to Moses and said, "We sinned when we spoke against the LORD and against you. Pray that the LORD will take the snakes away from us." So Moses prayed for the people.

⁸The LORD said to Moses, "Make a snake and put it up on a pole; anyone who is bitten can look at it and live." ⁹So Moses made a bronze snake and put it up on a pole. Then when anyone was bitten by a snake and looked at the bronze snake, he lived.

21:9 Bronze Snake

Jesus chose this incident as one of the examples from Old Testament history that illustrates his own person and work (John 3:14). Through the snake and through Jesus, God provided a way of escape that required only faith from the people. In typical style, the Israelites corrupted the meaning by keeping the bronze snake as an idol to worship. Centuries later, King Hezekiah destroyed this image (2 Kings 18:4).

The Journey to Moab

¹⁰The Israelites moved on and camped at Oboth. ¹¹Then they set out from Oboth and camped in Iye Abarim, in the desert that faces Moab toward the sunrise. ¹²From there they moved on and camped in the Zered Valley. ¹³They set out from there and camped alongside the Arnon, which is in the desert extending into Amorite territory. The Arnon is the border of Moab, between Moab and the Amorites. ¹⁴That is why the Book of the Wars of the LORD says:

"... Waheb in Suphah[d] and the ravines,
the Arnon ¹⁵and[e] the slopes of the ravines
that lead to the site of Ar
and lie along the border of Moab."

¹⁶From there they continued on to Beer, the well where the LORD said to Moses, "Gather the people together and I will give them water."

¹⁷Then Israel sang this song:

"Spring up, O well!
Sing about it,
¹⁸about the well that the princes dug,

---

[a]2 The Hebrew term refers to the irrevocable giving over of things or persons to the LORD, often by totally destroying them; also in verse 3.   [b]3 *Hormah* means *destruction.*   [c]4 Hebrew *Yam Suph*; that is, Sea of Reeds   [d]14 The meaning of the Hebrew for this phrase is uncertain.   [e]14,15 Or *"I have been given from Suphah and the ravines / of the Arnon ¹⁵to"*

that the nobles of the people sank—
the nobles with scepters and staffs."

Then they went from the desert to Mattanah, [19]from Mattanah to Nahaliel, from Nahaliel to

---

21:14 Out of Print

This quotation comes from a book no longer in existence. The Bible makes many mentions of such vanished books. Joshua 10:13 and 2 Samuel 1:18, for example, name the Book of Jashar. There are references to the works of various prophets or seers (Gad, Ahijah, Shemaiah) and many references to royal annals such as the book of the kings of Israel (1 Chronicles 9:1). Israel must have had a sizable library.

Bamoth, [20]and from Bamoth to the valley in Moab where the top of Pisgah overlooks the wasteland.

Defeat of Sihon and Og

[21]Israel sent messengers to say to Sihon king of the Amorites:

[22]"Let us pass through your country. We will not turn aside into any field or vineyard, or drink water from any well. We will travel along the king's highway until we have passed through your territory."

[23]But Sihon would not let Israel pass through his territory. He mustered his entire army and marched out into the desert against Israel. When he reached Jahaz, he fought with Israel. [24]Israel, however, put him to the sword and took over his land from the Arnon to the Jabbok, but only as far as the Ammonites, because their border was fortified. [25]Israel captured all the cities of the Amorites and occupied them, including Heshbon and all its surrounding settlements. [26]Heshbon was the city of Sihon king of the Amorites, who had fought against the former king of Moab and had taken from him all his land as far as the Arnon.

[27]That is why the poets say:

"Come to Heshbon and let it be rebuilt;
let Sihon's city be restored.

[28]"Fire went out from Heshbon,
a blaze from the city of Sihon.
It consumed Ar of Moab,
the citizens of Arnon's heights.
[29]Woe to you, O Moab!
You are destroyed, O people of Chemosh!
He has given up his sons as fugitives

and his daughters as captives
to Sihon king of the Amorites.

[30]"But we have overthrown them;
Heshbon is destroyed all the way to
Dibon.
We have demolished them as far as Nophah,
which extends to Medeba."

[31]So Israel settled in the land of the Amorites. [32]After Moses had sent spies to Jazer, the Israelites captured its surrounding settlements and drove out the Amorites who were there. [33]Then they turned and went up along the road toward Bashan, and Og king of Bashan and his whole army marched out to meet them in battle at Edrei.

[34]The LORD said to Moses, "Do not be afraid of him, for I have handed him over to you, with his whole army and his land. Do to him what you did to Sihon king of the Amorites, who reigned in Heshbon."

[35]So they struck him down, together with his sons and his whole army, leaving them no survivors. And they took possession of his land.

Balak Summons Balaam

22 Then the Israelites traveled to the plains of Moab and camped along the Jordan across from Jericho.[a]

[2]Now Balak son of Zippor saw all that Israel had done to the Amorites, [3]and Moab was terrified because there were so many people. Indeed, Moab was filled with dread because of the Israelites.

[4]The Moabites said to the elders of Midian, "This horde is going to lick up everything around us, as an ox licks up the grass of the field."

So Balak son of Zippor, who was king of Moab at that time, [5]sent messengers to summon Balaam son of Beor, who was at Pethor, near the River,[b] in his native land. Balak said:

"A people has come out of Egypt; they cover the face of the land and have settled next to me. [6]Now come and put a curse on these people, because they are too powerful for me. Perhaps then I will be able to defeat them and drive them out of the country. For I know that those you bless are blessed, and those you curse are cursed."

[7]The elders of Moab and Midian left, taking with them the fee for divination. When they came to Balaam, they told him what Balak had said.

[8]"Spend the night here," Balaam said to them, "and I will bring you back the answer the LORD gives me." So the Moabite princes stayed with him.

---

[a]1 Hebrew *Jordan of Jericho*; possibly an ancient name for the Jordan River   [b]5 That is, the Euphrates

⁹God came to Balaam and asked, "Who are these men with you?"

¹⁰Balaam said to God, "Balak son of Zippor, king of Moab, sent me this message: ¹¹'A people that has come out of Egypt covers the face of the land. Now come and put a curse on them for me. Perhaps then I will be able to fight them and drive them away.'"

¹²But God said to Balaam, "Do not go with them. You must not put a curse on those people, because they are blessed."

¹³The next morning Balaam got up and said to Balak's princes, "Go back to your own country, for the LORD has refused to let me go with you."

¹⁴So the Moabite princes returned to Balak and said, "Balaam refused to come with us."

¹⁵Then Balak sent other princes, more numerous and more distinguished than the first. ¹⁶They came to Balaam and said:

"This is what Balak son of Zippor says:
Do not let anything keep you from coming to me, ¹⁷because I will reward you handsomely and do whatever you say. Come and put a curse on these people for me."

¹⁸But Balaam answered them, "Even if Balak gave me his palace filled with silver and gold, I could not do anything great or small to go beyond the command of the LORD my God. ¹⁹Now stay here tonight as the others did, and I will find out what else the LORD will tell me."

²⁰That night God came to Balaam and said, "Since these men have come to summon you, go with them, but do only what I tell you."

Balaam's Donkey

²¹Balaam got up in the morning, saddled his donkey and went with the princes of Moab. ²²But God was very angry when he went, and the angel of the LORD stood in the road to oppose him. Balaam was riding on his donkey, and his two servants were with him. ²³When the donkey saw the angel of the LORD standing in the road with a drawn sword in his hand, she turned off the road into a field. Balaam beat her to get her back on the road.

²⁴Then the angel of the LORD stood in a narrow path between two vineyards, with walls on both sides. ²⁵When the donkey saw the angel of the LORD, she pressed close to the wall, crushing Balaam's foot against it. So he beat her again.

²⁶Then the angel of the LORD moved on ahead and stood in a narrow place where there was no room to turn, either to the right or to the left. ²⁷When the donkey saw the angel of the LORD, she lay down under Balaam, and he was angry and beat her with his staff. ²⁸Then the LORD opened the donkey's mouth, and she said to Balaam, "What have I done to you to make you beat me these three times?"

²⁹Balaam answered the donkey, "You have made a fool of me! If I had a sword in my hand, I would kill you right now."

³⁰The donkey said to Balaam, "Am I not your own donkey, which you have always ridden, to this day? Have I been in the habit of doing this to you?"

"No," he said.

³¹Then the LORD opened Balaam's eyes, and he saw the angel of the LORD standing in the road with his sword drawn. So he bowed low and fell facedown.

³²The angel of the LORD asked him, "Why have you beaten your donkey these three times? I have come here to oppose you because your path is a reckless one before me.ᵃ ³³The donkey saw me and turned away from me these three times. If she had not turned away, I would certainly have killed you by now, but I would have spared her."

³⁴Balaam said to the angel of the LORD, "I have sinned. I did not realize you were standing in the road to oppose me. Now if you are displeased, I will go back."

³⁵The angel of the LORD said to Balaam, "Go with the men, but speak only what I tell you." So Balaam went with the princes of Balak.

³⁶When Balak heard that Balaam was coming, he went out to meet him at the Moabite town on the Arnon border, at the edge of his territory. ³⁷Balak said to Balaam, "Did I not send you an urgent summons? Why didn't you come to me? Am I really not able to reward you?"

³⁸"Well, I have come to you now," Balaam replied. "But can I say just anything? I must speak only what God puts in my mouth."

³⁹Then Balaam went with Balak to Kiriath Huzoth. ⁴⁰Balak sacrificed cattle and sheep, and gave some to Balaam and the princes who were with him. ⁴¹The next morning Balak took Balaam up to Bamoth Baal, and from there he saw part of the people.

Balaam's First Oracle

23 Balaam said, "Build me seven altars here, and prepare seven bulls and seven rams for me." ²Balak did as Balaam said, and the two of them offered a bull and a ram on each altar.

³Then Balaam said to Balak, "Stay here beside your offering while I go aside. Perhaps the LORD will come to meet with me. Whatever he reveals to me I will tell you." Then he went off to a barren height.

⁴God met with him, and Balaam said, "I have prepared seven altars, and on each altar I have offered a bull and a ram."

⁵The LORD put a message in Balaam's mouth

ᵃ32 The meaning of the Hebrew for this clause is uncertain.

and said, "Go back to Balak and give him this message."

⁶So he went back to him and found him standing beside his offering, with all the princes of Moab. ⁷Then Balaam uttered his oracle:

"Balak brought me from Aram,
    the king of Moab from the eastern
        mountains.
'Come,' he said, 'curse Jacob for me;
    come, denounce Israel.'
⁸How can I curse
    those whom God has not cursed?
How can I denounce

those whom the LORD has not denounced?
⁹From the rocky peaks I see them,
    from the heights I view them.
I see a people who live apart
    and do not consider themselves one of the
        nations.
¹⁰Who can count the dust of Jacob
    or number the fourth part of Israel?
Let me die the death of the righteous,
    and may my end be like theirs!"

¹¹Balak said to Balaam, "What have you done to me? I brought you to curse my enemies, but you have done nothing but bless them!"

Whose Side Is Balaam On?
A balky prophet, a talking donkey, and a furious king

> Balak said to Balaam, "What have you done to me? I brought you to curse my enemies, but you have done nothing but bless them!" 23:11

NUMBERS 22–24 CONTAINS ONE OF the most bizarre stories in the entire Bible. It features a donkey speaking fluent Hebrew and showing more insight than a prophet. One man is at the center of the story, the mysterious character named Balaam.

Balaam was evidently a professional magician of a nomadic clan somewhat like the gypsies. He had an impressive reputation: Nearby kings alarmed by the Israelites hired him to work magic and get the gods on their side.

Prophet for Hire

Numbers gives enough detail to paint a colorful, dramatic story, but even so, Balaam is cloaked in a fog of mystery. Clearly, God chose to speak through him—he communicated directly to Balaam seven times. Just as clearly, Balaam proved a reluctant prophet, subject to ambition and a handsome bribe. Even his own donkey rebuked him, in the only biblical account of an animal speaking. An angel gave not Balaam, but the donkey, high praise.

Balaam appeared at a solemn occasion designed to curse the Israelites, but instead he pronounced blessings on them and curses on their enemies. He gave four stirring messages, far different in content from what his employer wanted to hear.

"How can I curse those whom God has not cursed?" Balaam asked (23:8). His magnificent prophecies shine out from scenes of comic irony. Balaam grew bolder and bolder, changing from a sorcerer into a prophet with backbone.

Prophet or Traitor?

Numbers 22–24 presents Balaam as an apparent convert. Tragically, the changes in him were only temporary. Balaam next appears in Numbers 31:8, the slain victim of an Israelite raid. Outright condemnations in 2 Peter 2:15, Jude 11, and Revelation 2:14 indicate that Balaam quickly returned to his treacherous ways. Having failed to manipulate the Israelites' God for his purposes, he resorted to manipulating the Israelites themselves. He convinced other nations to seduce them with sex and the worship of false gods. His actions led to the deaths of 24,000 people (25:9).

Some have called Balaam the Judas of the Old Testament, and certain parallels do emerge. Both men came close enough to truth to appear sincere and faithful. For a time, both seemed to serve the true God. But, motivated by ambition and greed, they renounced God and turned against him, with catastrophic results.

Part of a Bigger Battle

Seven books of the Bible refer to Balaam. The importance given to his story implies that it stood as a key event in the Israelites' relationship to pagan cultures. The Israelites were about to enter a land where magic and sorcery were used as national weapons. In a stroke of irony, God selected a spokesman who was both magician and pagan. Through him God rebuked those nations and their false gods.

Life Questions: Have you ever been used by God despite your own reluctance?

¹²He answered, "Must I not speak what the LORD puts in my mouth?"

Balaam's Second Oracle

¹³Then Balak said to him, "Come with me to another place where you can see them; you will see only a part but not all of them. And from there, curse them for me." ¹⁴So he took him to the field of Zophim on the top of Pisgah, and there he built seven altars and offered a bull and a ram on each altar.

¹⁵Balaam said to Balak, "Stay here beside your offering while I meet with him over there."

¹⁶The LORD met with Balaam and put a message in his mouth and said, "Go back to Balak and give him this message."

¹⁷So he went to him and found him standing beside his offering, with the princes of Moab. Balak asked him, "What did the LORD say?"

¹⁸Then he uttered his oracle:

"Arise, Balak, and listen;
    hear me, son of Zippor.
¹⁹God is not a man, that he should lie,
    nor a son of man, that he should change
        his mind.
Does he speak and then not act?
Does he promise and not fulfill?
²⁰I have received a command to bless;
    he has blessed, and I cannot change it.

²¹"No misfortune is seen in Jacob,
    no misery observed in Israel.ᵃ
The LORD their God is with them;
    the shout of the King is among them.
²²God brought them out of Egypt;
    they have the strength of a wild ox.
²³There is no sorcery against Jacob,
    no divination against Israel.
It will now be said of Jacob
    and of Israel, 'See what God has done!'
²⁴The people rise like a lioness;
    they rouse themselves like a lion
that does not rest till he devours his prey
    and drinks the blood of his victims."

²⁵Then Balak said to Balaam, "Neither curse them at all nor bless them at all!"

²⁶Balaam answered, "Did I not tell you I must do whatever the LORD says?"

Balaam's Third Oracle

²⁷Then Balak said to Balaam, "Come, let me take you to another place. Perhaps it will please God to let you curse them for me from there." ²⁸And Balak took Balaam to the top of Peor, overlooking the wasteland.

²⁹Balaam said, "Build me seven altars here, and prepare seven bulls and seven rams for me."

³⁰Balak did as Balaam had said, and offered a bull and a ram on each altar.

24 Now when Balaam saw that it pleased the LORD to bless Israel, he did not resort to sorcery as at other times, but turned his face toward the desert. ²When Balaam looked out and saw Israel encamped tribe by tribe, the Spirit of God came upon him ³and he uttered his oracle:

"The oracle of Balaam son of Beor,
    the oracle of one whose eye sees clearly,
⁴the oracle of one who hears the words of
        God,
    who sees a vision from the Almighty,ᵇ
    who falls prostrate, and whose eyes are
        opened:

⁵"How beautiful are your tents, O Jacob,
    your dwelling places, O Israel!

⁶"Like valleys they spread out,
    like gardens beside a river,
like aloes planted by the LORD,
    like cedars beside the waters.
⁷Water will flow from their buckets;
    their seed will have abundant water.

"Their king will be greater than Agag;
    their kingdom will be exalted.

⁸"God brought them out of Egypt;
    they have the strength of a wild ox.
They devour hostile nations
    and break their bones in pieces;
    with their arrows they pierce them.
⁹Like a lion they crouch and lie down,
    like a lioness—who dares to rouse them?

"May those who bless you be blessed
    and those who curse you be cursed!"

¹⁰Then Balak's anger burned against Balaam. He struck his hands together and said to him, "I summoned you to curse my enemies, but you have blessed them these three times. ¹¹Now leave at once and go home! I said I would reward you handsomely, but the LORD has kept you from being rewarded."

¹²Balaam answered Balak, "Did I not tell the messengers you sent me, ¹³'Even if Balak gave me his palace filled with silver and gold, I could not do anything of my own accord, good or bad, to go beyond the command of the LORD—and I must say only what the LORD says'? ¹⁴Now I am going back to my people, but come, let me warn you of what this people will do to your people in days to come."

Balaam's Fourth Oracle

¹⁵Then he uttered his oracle:

"The oracle of Balaam son of Beor,

ᵃ21 Or He has not looked on Jacob's offenses / or on the wrongs found in Israel.   ᵇ4 Hebrew Shaddai; also in verse 16

the oracle of one whose eye sees clearly,
16the oracle of one who hears the words of
God,
who has knowledge from the Most High,
who sees a vision from the Almighty,
who falls prostrate, and whose eyes are
opened:

17"I see him, but not now;
I behold him, but not near.
A star will come out of Jacob;
a scepter will rise out of Israel.
He will crush the foreheads of Moab,
the skulls*a* of*b* all the sons of Sheth.*c*

24:17 Balaam's Prophecy

This prediction delivered by Balaam came true during the reign of King David, who crushed the nations of Moab and Edom (2 Samuel 8:2,14).

18Edom will be conquered;
Seir, his enemy, will be conquered,
but Israel will grow strong.
19A ruler will come out of Jacob
and destroy the survivors of the city."

Balaam's Final Oracles

20Then Balaam saw Amalek and uttered his oracle:

"Amalek was first among the nations,
but he will come to ruin at last."

21Then he saw the Kenites and uttered his oracle:

"Your dwelling place is secure,
your nest is set in a rock;
22yet you Kenites will be destroyed
when Asshur takes you captive."

23Then he uttered his oracle:

"Ah, who can live when God does this?*d*
24 Ships will come from the shores of Kittim;
they will subdue Asshur and Eber,
but they too will come to ruin."

25Then Balaam got up and returned home and Balak went his own way.

Moab Seduces Israel

25 While Israel was staying in Shittim, the men began to indulge in sexual immorality with Moabite women, 2who invited them to the sacrifices to their gods. The people ate and bowed down before these gods. 3So Israel joined

in worshiping the Baal of Peor. And the LORD's anger burned against them.

4The LORD said to Moses, "Take all the leaders of these people, kill them and expose them in

25:1 Sexual Seduction

Militarily, Israel was doing well. Their enemies were terrified (22:3), and the man summoned to put a curse on Israel had instead spoken God's blessing (24:8–9). But the Israelites were vulnerable to sexual temptation. Moabite women offered sexual favors, then invited the foreigners to local religious services. (Numbers 31:16 reports that Balaam suggested the tactic.) It is an old method of subverting God's people, and it still works.

broad daylight before the LORD, so that the LORD's fierce anger may turn away from Israel."

5So Moses said to Israel's judges, "Each of you must put to death those of your men who have joined in worshiping the Baal of Peor."

6Then an Israelite man brought to his family a Midianite woman right before the eyes of Moses and the whole assembly of Israel while they were weeping at the entrance to the Tent of Meeting. 7When Phinehas son of Eleazar, the son of Aaron, the priest, saw this, he left the assembly, took a spear in his hand 8and followed the Israelite into the tent. He drove the spear through both of them—through the Israelite and into the woman's body. Then the plague against the Israelites was stopped; 9but those who died in the plague numbered 24,000.

10The LORD said to Moses, 11"Phinehas son of Eleazar, the son of Aaron, the priest, has turned my anger away from the Israelites; for he was as zealous as I am for my honor among them, so that in my zeal I did not put an end to them. 12Therefore tell him I am making my covenant of peace with him. 13He and his descendants will have a covenant of a lasting priesthood, because he was zealous for the honor of his God and made atonement for the Israelites."

14The name of the Israelite who was killed with the Midianite woman was Zimri son of Salu, the leader of a Simeonite family. 15And the name of the Midianite woman who was put to death was Cozbi daughter of Zur, a tribal chief of a Midianite family.

16The LORD said to Moses, 17"Treat the Midianites as enemies and kill them, 18because they treated you as enemies when they deceived you in the affair of Peor and their sister Cozbi, the daughter of a Midianite leader, the woman who

---

a 17 Samaritan Pentateuch (see also Jer. 48:45); the meaning of the word in the Masoretic Text is uncertain.   *b 17* Or possibly *Moab,* / *batter*   *c 17* Or *all the noisy boasters*   *d 23* Masoretic Text; with a different word division of the Hebrew *A people will gather from the north.*

was killed when the plague came as a result of Peor."

The Second Census

26 After the plague the LORD said to Moses and Eleazar son of Aaron, the priest, [2]"Take a census of the whole Israelite community by families—all those twenty years old or more who are able to serve in the army of Israel." [3]So on the plains of Moab by the Jordan across from Jericho,[a] Moses and Eleazar the priest spoke with them and said, [4]"Take a census of the men twenty years old or more, as the LORD commanded Moses."

These were the Israelites who came out of Egypt:

[5]The descendants of Reuben, the firstborn son of Israel, were:

through Hanoch, the Hanochite clan;

through Pallu, the Palluite clan;

[6]through Hezron, the Hezronite clan;

through Carmi, the Carmite clan.

[7]These were the clans of Reuben; those numbered were 43,730.

[8]The son of Pallu was Eliab, [9]and the sons of Eliab were Nemuel, Dathan and Abiram. The same Dathan and Abiram were the community officials who rebelled against Moses and Aaron and were among Korah's followers when they rebelled against the LORD. [10]The earth opened its mouth and swallowed them along with Korah, whose followers died when the fire devoured the 250 men. And they served as a warning sign. [11]The line of Korah, however, did not die out.

[12]The descendants of Simeon by their clans were:

through Nemuel, the Nemuelite clan;

through Jamin, the Jaminite clan;

through Jakin, the Jakinite clan;

[13]through Zerah, the Zerahite clan;

through Shaul, the Shaulite clan.

[14]These were the clans of Simeon; there were 22,200 men.

[15]The descendants of Gad by their clans were:

through Zephon, the Zephonite clan;

through Haggi, the Haggite clan;

through Shuni, the Shunite clan;

[16]through Ozni, the Oznite clan;

through Eri, the Erite clan;

[17]through Arodi,[b] the Arodite clan;

through Areli, the Arelite clan.

[18]These were the clans of Gad; those numbered were 40,500.

[19]Er and Onan were sons of Judah, but they died in Canaan.

[20]The descendants of Judah by their clans were:

through Shelah, the Shelanite clan;

through Perez, the Perezite clan;

through Zerah, the Zerahite clan.

[21]The descendants of Perez were:

through Hezron, the Hezronite clan;

through Hamul, the Hamulite clan.

[22]These were the clans of Judah; those numbered were 76,500.

[23]The descendants of Issachar by their clans were:

through Tola, the Tolaite clan;

through Puah, the Puite[c] clan;

[24]through Jashub, the Jashubite clan;

through Shimron, the Shimronite clan.

[25]These were the clans of Issachar; those numbered were 64,300.

[26]The descendants of Zebulun by their clans were:

through Sered, the Seredite clan;

through Elon, the Elonite clan;

through Jahleel, the Jahleelite clan.

[27]These were the clans of Zebulun; those numbered were 60,500.

[28]The descendants of Joseph by their clans through Manasseh and Ephraim were:

[29]The descendants of Manasseh:

through Makir, the Makirite clan (Makir was the father of Gilead);

through Gilead, the Gileadite clan.

[30]These were the descendants of Gilead:

through Iezer, the Iezerite clan;

through Helek, the Helekite clan;

[31]through Asriel, the Asrielite clan;

through Shechem, the Shechemite clan;

[32]through Shemida, the Shemidaite clan;

through Hepher, the Hepherite clan.

[33](Zelophehad son of Hepher had no sons; he had only daughters, whose names were Mahlah, Noah, Hoglah, Milcah and Tirzah.)

[34]These were the clans of Manasseh; those numbered were 52,700.

[35]These were the descendants of Ephraim by their clans:

through Shuthelah, the Shuthelahite clan;

through Beker, the Bekerite clan;

through Tahan, the Tahanite clan.

[36]These were the descendants of Shuthelah:

through Eran, the Eranite clan.

[37]These were the clans of Ephraim; those numbered were 32,500.

These were the descendants of Joseph by their clans.

---

a3 Hebrew *Jordan of Jericho*; possibly an ancient name for the Jordan River; also in verse 63   *b17* Samaritan Pentateuch and Syriac (see also Gen. 46:16); Masoretic Text *Arod*   *c23* Samaritan Pentateuch, Septuagint, Vulgate and Syriac (see also 1 Chron. 7:1); Masoretic Text *through Puvah, the Punite*

[38]The descendants of Benjamin by their clans were:

through Bela, the Belaite clan;
through Ashbel, the Ashbelite clan;
through Ahiram, the Ahiramite clan;
[39]through Shupham,[a] the Shuphamite clan;
through Hupham, the Huphamite clan.
[40]The descendants of Bela through Ard and Naaman were:
through Ard,[b] the Ardite clan;
through Naaman, the Naamite clan.
[41]These were the clans of Benjamin; those numbered were 45,600.

[42]These were the descendants of Dan by their clans:

through Shuham, the Shuhamite clan.
These were the clans of Dan: [43]All of them were Shuhamite clans; and those numbered were 64,400.

[44]The descendants of Asher by their clans were:

through Imnah, the Imnite clan;
through Ishvi, the Ishvite clan;
through Beriah, the Beriite clan;
[45]and through the descendants of Beriah:
through Heber, the Heberite clan;
through Malkiel, the Malkielite clan.
[46](Asher had a daughter named Serah.)
[47]These were the clans of Asher; those numbered were 53,400.

[48]The descendants of Naphtali by their clans were:

through Jahzeel, the Jahzeelite clan;
through Guni, the Gunite clan;
[49]through Jezer, the Jezerite clan;
through Shillem, the Shillemite clan.
[50]These were the clans of Naphtali; those numbered were 45,400.

[51]The total number of the men of Israel was 601,730.

[52]The LORD said to Moses, [53]"The land is to be allotted to them as an inheritance based on the number of names. [54]To a larger group give a larger inheritance, and to a smaller group a smaller one; each is to receive its inheritance according to the number of those listed. [55]Be sure that the land is distributed by lot. What each group inherits will be according to the names for its ancestral tribe. [56]Each inheritance is to be distributed by lot among the larger and smaller groups."

[57]These were the Levites who were counted by their clans:

through Gershon, the Gershonite clan;

through Kohath, the Kohathite clan;
through Merari, the Merarite clan.
[58]These also were Levite clans:
the Libnite clan,

26:51 Recount

The two censuses in Numbers (chapter 1 and here) stand like bookends, marking the hopeful beginning and tragic end of the vast numbers of Israelites heading toward freedom. After 40 years, the totals were nearly the same—600,000 men—but only two of the original pilgrims would cross the Jordan River. The nation renewed itself like a human body, which looks the same but replaces all its cells every few years.

---

the Hebronite clan,
the Mahlite clan,
the Mushite clan,
the Korahite clan.
(Kohath was the forefather of Amram; [59]the name of Amram's wife was Jochebed, a descendant of Levi, who was born to the Levites[c] in Egypt. To Amram she bore Aaron, Moses and their sister Miriam. [60]Aaron was the father of Nadab and Abihu, Eleazar and Ithamar. [61]But Nadab and Abihu died when they made an offering before the LORD with unauthorized fire.)

[62]All the male Levites a month old or more numbered 23,000. They were not counted along with the other Israelites because they received no inheritance among them.

[63]These are the ones counted by Moses and Eleazar the priest when they counted the Israelites on the plains of Moab by the Jordan across from Jericho. [64]Not one of them was among those counted by Moses and Aaron the priest when they counted the Israelites in the Desert of Sinai. [65]For the LORD had told those Israelites they would surely die in the desert, and not one of them was left except Caleb son of Jephunneh and Joshua son of Nun.

Zelophehad's Daughters

27 The daughters of Zelophehad son of Hepher, the son of Gilead, the son of Makir, the son of Manasseh, belonged to the clans of Manasseh son of Joseph. The names of the daughters were Mahlah, Noah, Hoglah, Milcah and Tirzah. [2]They approached the entrance to the Tent of Meeting and stood before Moses, Eleazar the priest, the leaders and the whole as-

---

[a]39 A few manuscripts of the Masoretic Text, Samaritan Pentateuch, Vulgate and Syriac (see also Septuagint); most manuscripts of the Masoretic Text *Shephupham*   [b]40 Samaritan Pentateuch and Vulgate (see also Septuagint); Masoretic Text does not have *through Ard*.   [c]59 Or *Jochebed, a daughter of Levi, who was born to Levi*

sembly, and said, [3]"Our father died in the desert. He was not among Korah's followers, who banded together against the LORD, but he died for his own sin and left no sons. [4]Why should our father's name disappear from his clan because he had no son? Give us property among our father's relatives."

[5]So Moses brought their case before the LORD [6]and the LORD said to him, [7]"What Zelophehad's daughters are saying is right. You must certainly give them property as an inheritance among their father's relatives and turn their father's inheritance over to them.

[8]"Say to the Israelites, 'If a man dies and leaves no son, turn his inheritance over to his daughter. [9]If he has no daughter, give his inheritance to his brothers. [10]If he has no brothers, give his inheritance to his father's brothers. [11]If his father had no brothers, give his inheritance to the nearest relative in his clan, that he may possess it. This is to be a legal requirement for the Israelites, as the LORD commanded Moses.'"

Joshua to Succeed Moses

[12]Then the LORD said to Moses, "Go up this mountain in the Abarim range and see the land I have given the Israelites. [13]After you have seen it, you too will be gathered to your people, as your brother Aaron was, [14]for when the community rebelled at the waters in the Desert of Zin, both of you disobeyed my command to honor me as holy before their eyes." (These were the waters of Meribah Kadesh, in the Desert of Zin.)

27:14 Moses Stayed Out

Because Moses had disobeyed God (the scene is described in 20:1–13), he was not allowed to enter the promised land. In this account he seems to accept his punishment without complaint, quietly turning over his leadership to Joshua. But in his great final speech, recorded in Deuteronomy, he bitterly raised the topic three times (Deuteronomy 1:37, 3:23–27, 4:21–24). The punishment was not forever; Moses did "get in" hundreds of years after his death, in the company of Jesus (Mark 9:4).

[15]Moses said to the LORD, [16]"May the LORD, the God of the spirits of all mankind, appoint a man over this community [17]to go out and come in before them, one who will lead them out and bring them in, so the LORD's people will not be like sheep without a shepherd."

[18]So the LORD said to Moses, "Take Joshua son of Nun, a man in whom is the spirit,[a] and lay

your hand on him. [19]Have him stand before Eleazar the priest and the entire assembly and commission him in their presence. [20]Give him some of your authority so the whole Israelite community will obey him. [21]He is to stand before Eleazar the priest, who will obtain decisions for him by inquiring of the Urim before the LORD. At his command he and the entire community of the Israelites will go out, and at his command they will come in."

[22]Moses did as the LORD commanded him. He took Joshua and had him stand before Eleazar the priest and the whole assembly. [23]Then he laid his hands on him and commissioned him, as the LORD instructed through Moses.

Daily Offerings

28 The LORD said to Moses, [2]"Give this command to the Israelites and say to them: 'See that you present to me at the appointed time the food for my offerings made by fire, as an aroma pleasing to me.' [3]Say to them: 'This is the offering made by fire that you are to present to the LORD: two lambs a year old without defect, as a regular burnt offering each day. [4]Prepare one lamb in the morning and the other at twilight, [5]together with a grain offering of a tenth of an ephah[b] of fine flour mixed with a quarter of a hin[c] of oil from pressed olives. [6]This is the regular burnt offering instituted at Mount Sinai as a pleasing aroma, an offering made to the LORD by fire. [7]The accompanying drink offering is to be a quarter of a hin of fermented drink with each lamb. Pour out the drink offering to the LORD at the sanctuary. [8]Prepare the second lamb at twilight, along with the same kind of grain offering and drink offering that you prepare in the morning. This is an offering made by fire, an aroma pleasing to the LORD.

Sabbath Offerings

[9]"'On the Sabbath day, make an offering of two lambs a year old without defect, together with its drink offering and a grain offering of two-tenths of an ephah[d] of fine flour mixed with oil. [10]This is the burnt offering for every Sabbath, in addition to the regular burnt offering and its drink offering.

Monthly Offerings

[11]"'On the first of every month, present to the LORD a burnt offering of two young bulls, one ram and seven male lambs a year old, all without defect. [12]With each bull there is to be a grain offering of three-tenths of an ephah[e] of fine flour mixed with oil; with the ram, a grain offering of two-tenths of an ephah of fine flour mixed

---

a 18 Or Spirit   *b 5 That is, probably about 2 quarts (about 2 liters); also in verses 13, 21 and 29*   *c 5 That is, probably about 1 quart (about 1 liter); also in verses 7 and 14*   *d 9 That is, probably about 4 quarts (about 4.5 liters); also in verses 12, 20 and 28*   *e 12 That is, probably about 6 quarts (about 6.5 liters); also in verses 20 and 28*

with oil; [13]and with each lamb, a grain offering of a tenth of an ephah of fine flour mixed with oil. This is for a burnt offering, a pleasing aroma, an offering made to the LORD by fire. [14]With each bull there is to be a drink offering of half a hin[a] of wine; with the ram, a third of a hin[b]; and with each lamb, a quarter of a hin. This is the monthly burnt offering to be made at each new moon during the year. [15]Besides the regular burnt offering with its drink offering, one male goat is to be presented to the LORD as a sin offering.

The Passover

[16]"'On the fourteenth day of the first month the LORD's Passover is to be held. [17]On the fifteenth day of this month there is to be a festival; for seven days eat bread made without yeast. [18]On the first day hold a sacred assembly and do no regular work. [19]Present to the LORD an offering made by fire, a burnt offering of two young bulls, one ram and seven male lambs a year old, all without defect. [20]With each bull prepare a grain offering of three-tenths of an ephah of fine flour mixed with oil; with the ram, two-tenths; [21]and with each of the seven lambs, one-tenth. [22]Include one male goat as a sin offering to make atonement for you. [23]Prepare these in addition to the regular morning burnt offering. [24]In this way prepare the food for the offering made by fire every day for seven days as an aroma pleasing to the LORD; it is to be prepared in addition to the regular burnt offering and its drink offering. [25]On the seventh day hold a sacred assembly and do no regular work.

Feast of Weeks

[26]"'On the day of firstfruits, when you present to the LORD an offering of new grain during the Feast of Weeks, hold a sacred assembly and do no regular work. [27]Present a burnt offering of two young bulls, one ram and seven male lambs a year old as an aroma pleasing to the LORD. [28]With each bull there is to be a grain offering of three-tenths of an ephah of fine flour mixed with oil; with the ram, two-tenths; [29]and with each of the seven lambs, one-tenth. [30]Include one male goat to make atonement for you. [31]Prepare these together with their drink offerings, in addition to the regular burnt offering and its grain offering. Be sure the animals are without defect.

Feast of Trumpets

29 "'On the first day of the seventh month hold a sacred assembly and do no regular work. It is a day for you to sound the trumpets. [2]As an aroma pleasing to the LORD, prepare a

burnt offering of one young bull, one ram and seven male lambs a year old, all without defect. [3]With the bull prepare a grain offering of three-tenths of an ephah[c] of fine flour mixed with oil; with the ram, two-tenths[d]; [4]and with each of the seven lambs, one-tenth.[e] [5]Include one male

29:1 Interruptions of the Story

Numbers periodically interrupts its history with lists of rules or rituals, such as in this section, chapters 28–30. Usually, they relate to what appears just before or afterward. The instructions here were not new, but God saw a need to review them just as the nation was about to enter the promised land.

goat as a sin offering to make atonement for you. [6]These are in addition to the monthly and daily burnt offerings with their grain offerings and drink offerings as specified. They are offerings made to the LORD by fire—a pleasing aroma.

Day of Atonement

[7]"'On the tenth day of this seventh month hold a sacred assembly. You must deny yourselves[f] and do no work. [8]Present as an aroma pleasing to the LORD a burnt offering of one young bull, one ram and seven male lambs a year old, all without defect. [9]With the bull prepare a grain offering of three-tenths of an ephah of fine flour mixed with oil; with the ram, two-tenths; [10]and with each of the seven lambs, one-tenth. [11]Include one male goat as a sin offering, in addition to the sin offering for atonement and the regular burnt offering with its grain offering, and their drink offerings.

Feast of Tabernacles

[12]"'On the fifteenth day of the seventh month, hold a sacred assembly and do no regular work. Celebrate a festival to the LORD for seven days. [13]Present an offering made by fire as an aroma pleasing to the LORD, a burnt offering of thirteen young bulls, two rams and fourteen male lambs a year old, all without defect. [14]With each of the thirteen bulls prepare a grain offering of three-tenths of an ephah of fine flour mixed with oil; with each of the two rams, two-tenths; [15]and with each of the fourteen lambs, one-tenth. [16]Include one male goat as a sin offering, in addition to the regular burnt offering with its grain offering and drink offering.

[17]"'On the second day prepare twelve young bulls, two rams and fourteen male lambs a year

---

[a]14 That is, probably about 2 quarts (about 2 liters)   [b]14 That is, probably about 1 1/4 quarts (about 1.2 liters)
[c]3 That is, probably about 6 quarts (about 6.5 liters); also in verses 9 and 14   [d]3 That is, probably about 4 quarts (about 4.5 liters); also in verses 9 and 14   [e]4 That is, probably about 2 quarts (about 2 liters); also in verses 10 and 15
[f]7 Or *must fast*

old, all without defect. [18]With the bulls, rams and lambs, prepare their grain offerings and drink offerings according to the number specified. [19]Include one male goat as a sin offering, in addition to the regular burnt offering with its grain offering, and their drink offerings.

[20]"'On the third day prepare eleven bulls, two rams and fourteen male lambs a year old, all without defect. [21]With the bulls, rams and lambs, prepare their grain offerings and drink offerings according to the number specified. [22]Include one male goat as a sin offering, in addition to the regular burnt offering with its grain offering and drink offering.

[23]"'On the fourth day prepare ten bulls, two rams and fourteen male lambs a year old, all without defect. [24]With the bulls, rams and lambs, prepare their grain offerings and drink offerings according to the number specified. [25]Include one male goat as a sin offering, in addition to the regular burnt offering with its grain offering and drink offering.

[26]"'On the fifth day prepare nine bulls, two rams and fourteen male lambs a year old, all without defect. [27]With the bulls, rams and lambs, prepare their grain offerings and drink offerings according to the number specified. [28]Include one male goat as a sin offering, in addition to the regular burnt offering with its grain offering and drink offering.

[29]"'On the sixth day prepare eight bulls, two rams and fourteen male lambs a year old, all without defect. [30]With the bulls, rams and lambs, prepare their grain offerings and drink offerings according to the number specified. [31]Include one male goat as a sin offering, in addition to the regular burnt offering with its grain offering and drink offering.

[32]"'On the seventh day prepare seven bulls, two rams and fourteen male lambs a year old, all without defect. [33]With the bulls, rams and lambs, prepare their grain offerings and drink offerings according to the number specified. [34]Include one male goat as a sin offering, in addition to the regular burnt offering with its grain offering and drink offering.

[35]"'On the eighth day hold an assembly and do no regular work. [36]Present an offering made by fire as an aroma pleasing to the LORD, a burnt offering of one bull, one ram and seven male lambs a year old, all without defect. [37]With the bull, the ram and the lambs, prepare their grain offerings and drink offerings according to the number specified. [38]Include one male goat as a sin offering, in addition to the regular burnt offering with its grain offering and drink offering.

[39]"'In addition to what you vow and your freewill offerings, prepare these for the LORD at your appointed feasts: your burnt offerings, grain offerings, drink offerings and fellowship offerings.[a]'"

[40]Moses told the Israelites all that the LORD commanded him.

Vows

30 Moses said to the heads of the tribes of Israel: "This is what the LORD commands: [2]When a man makes a vow to the LORD or takes an oath to obligate himself by a pledge, he must not break his word but must do everything he said.

[3]"When a young woman still living in her father's house makes a vow to the LORD or obligates herself by a pledge [4]and her father hears about her vow or pledge but says nothing to her, then all her vows and every pledge by which she obligated herself will stand. [5]But if her father forbids her when he hears about it, none of her vows or the pledges by which she obligated herself will stand; the LORD will release her because her father has forbidden her.

[6]"If she marries after she makes a vow or after her lips utter a rash promise by which she obligates herself [7]and her husband hears about it but says nothing to her, then her vows or the pledges by which she obligated herself will stand. [8]But if her husband forbids her when he hears about it, he nullifies the vow that obligates her or the rash promise by which she obligates herself, and the LORD will release her.

[9]"Any vow or obligation taken by a widow or divorced woman will be binding on her.

[10]"If a woman living with her husband makes a vow or obligates herself by a pledge under oath [11]and her husband hears about it but says nothing to her and does not forbid her, then all her vows or the pledges by which she obligated herself will stand. [12]But if her husband nullifies them when he hears about them, then none of the vows or pledges that came from her lips will stand. Her husband has nullified them, and the LORD will release her. [13]Her husband may confirm or nullify any vow she makes or any sworn pledge to deny herself. [14]But if her husband says nothing to her about it from day to day, then he confirms all her vows or the pledges binding on her. He confirms them by saying nothing to her when he hears about them. [15]If, however, he nullifies them some time after he hears about them, then he is responsible for her guilt."

[16]These are the regulations the LORD gave Moses concerning relationships between a man and his wife, and between a father and his young daughter still living in his house.

[a]39 Traditionally *peace offerings*

Vengeance on the Midianites

31 The LORD said to Moses, ²"Take vengeance on the Midianites for the Israelites. After that, you will be gathered to your people."

³So Moses said to the people, "Arm some of your men to go to war against the Midianites and to carry out the LORD's vengeance on them. ⁴Send into battle a thousand men from each of the tribes of Israel." ⁵So twelve thousand men armed for battle, a thousand from each tribe, were supplied from the clans of Israel. ⁶Moses sent them into battle, a thousand from each tribe, along with Phinehas son of Eleazar, the priest, who took with him articles from the sanctuary and the trumpets for signaling.

⁷They fought against Midian, as the LORD commanded Moses, and killed every man. ⁸Among their victims were Evi, Rekem, Zur, Hur and Reba—the five kings of Midian. They also killed Balaam son of Beor with the sword. ⁹The Israelites captured the Midianite women and children and took all the Midianite herds, flocks and goods as plunder. ¹⁰They burned all the towns where the Midianites had settled, as well as all their camps. ¹¹They took all the plunder and spoils, including the people and animals, ¹²and brought the captives, spoils and plunder to Moses and Eleazar the priest and the Israelite assembly at their camp on the plains of Moab, by the Jordan across from Jericho.ᵃ

¹³Moses, Eleazar the priest and all the leaders of the community went to meet them outside the camp. ¹⁴Moses was angry with the officers of the army—the commanders of thousands and commanders of hundreds—who returned from battle.

¹⁵"Have you allowed all the women to live?" he asked them. ¹⁶"They were the ones who followed Balaam's advice and were the means of turning the Israelites away from the LORD in what happened at Peor, so that a plague struck the LORD's people. ¹⁷Now kill all the boys. And kill every woman who has slept with a man, ¹⁸but save for yourselves every girl who has never slept with a man.

¹⁹"All of you who have killed anyone or touched anyone who was killed must stay outside the camp seven days. On the third and seventh days you must purify yourselves and your captives. ²⁰Purify every garment as well as everything made of leather, goat hair or wood."

²¹Then Eleazar the priest said to the soldiers who had gone into battle, "This is the requirement of the law that the LORD gave Moses: ²²Gold, silver, bronze, iron, tin, lead ²³and anything else that can withstand fire must be put through the fire, and then it will be clean. But it must also be purified with the water of cleansing.

And whatever cannot withstand fire must be put through that water. ²⁴On the seventh day wash your clothes and you will be clean. Then you may come into the camp."

> ### 31:19–24 Acts of War
>
> *Many readers struggle with the harsh warfare policies God demanded of the Israelites. Numbers 35:34 summarizes one basic reason why policies were so strict: so that the land itself, set apart by God, would not become defiled (see "Is a War Ever Holy?" page 248). Even so, this passage shows that killing was not taken lightly—even war heroes had to go through the process of purification.*

Dividing the Spoils

²⁵The LORD said to Moses, ²⁶"You and Eleazar the priest and the family heads of the community are to count all the people and animals that were captured. ²⁷Divide the spoils between the soldiers who took part in the battle and the rest of the community. ²⁸From the soldiers who fought in the battle, set apart as tribute for the LORD one out of every five hundred, whether persons, cattle, donkeys, sheep or goats. ²⁹Take this tribute from their half share and give it to Eleazar the priest as the LORD's part. ³⁰From the Israelites' half, select one out of every fifty, whether persons, cattle, donkeys, sheep, goats or other animals. Give them to the Levites, who are responsible for the care of the LORD's tabernacle." ³¹So Moses and Eleazar the priest did as the LORD commanded Moses.

³²The plunder remaining from the spoils that the soldiers took was 675,000 sheep, ³³72,000 cattle, ³⁴61,000 donkeys ³⁵and 32,000 women who had never slept with a man. ³⁶The half share of those who fought in the battle was:

337,500 sheep, ³⁷of which the tribute for the LORD was 675;

³⁸36,000 cattle, of which the tribute for the LORD was 72;

³⁹30,500 donkeys, of which the tribute for the LORD was 61;

⁴⁰16,000 people, of which the tribute for the LORD was 32.

⁴¹Moses gave the tribute to Eleazar the priest as the LORD's part, as the LORD commanded Moses.

⁴²The half belonging to the Israelites, which Moses set apart from that of the fighting men— ⁴³the community's half—was 337,500 sheep, ⁴⁴36,000 cattle, ⁴⁵30,500 donkeys ⁴⁶and 16,000

ᵃ12 Hebrew *Jordan of Jericho*; possibly an ancient name for the Jordan River people. 47From the Israelites' half, Moses selected one out of every fifty persons and animals, as the LORD commanded him, and gave them to the Levites, who were responsible for the care of the LORD's tabernacle.

48Then the officers who were over the units of the army—the commanders of thousands and commanders of hundreds—went to Moses 49and said to him, "Your servants have counted the soldiers under our command, and not one is missing. 50So we have brought as an offering to the LORD the gold articles each of us acquired—armlets, bracelets, signet rings, earrings and necklaces—to make atonement for ourselves before the LORD."

51Moses and Eleazar the priest accepted from them the gold—all the crafted articles. 52All the gold from the commanders of thousands and commanders of hundreds that Moses and Eleazar presented as a gift to the LORD weighed 16,750 shekels.a 53Each soldier had taken plunder for himself. 54Moses and Eleazar the priest accepted the gold from the commanders of thousands and commanders of hundreds and brought it into the Tent of Meeting as a memorial for the Israelites before the LORD.

The Transjordan Tribes

32 The Reubenites and Gadites, who had very large herds and flocks, saw that the lands of Jazer and Gilead were suitable for livestock. 2So they came to Moses and Eleazar the priest and to the leaders of the community, and said, 3"Ataroth, Dibon, Jazer, Nimrah, Heshbon, Elealeh, Sebam, Nebo and Beon— 4the land the LORD subdued before the people of Israel—are suitable for livestock, and your servants have livestock. 5If we have found favor in your eyes," they said, "let this land be given to your servants as our possession. Do not make us cross the Jordan."

6Moses said to the Gadites and Reubenites, "Shall your countrymen go to war while you sit here? 7Why do you discourage the Israelites from going over into the land the LORD has given them? 8This is what your fathers did when I sent them from Kadesh Barnea to look over the land. 9After they went up to the Valley of Eshcol and viewed the land, they discouraged the Israelites from entering the land the LORD had given them. 10The LORD's anger was aroused that day and he swore this oath: 11'Because they have not followed me wholeheartedly, not one of the men twenty years old or more who came up out of Egypt will see the land I promised on oath to Abraham, Isaac and Jacob— 12not one except Caleb son of Jephunneh the Kenizzite and Joshua son of Nun, for they followed the LORD wholeheartedly.' 13The LORD's anger burned against Is-

rael and he made them wander in the desert forty years, until the whole generation of those who had done evil in his sight was gone.

14"And here you are, a brood of sinners, standing in the place of your fathers and making the LORD even more angry with Israel. 15If you turn away from following him, he will again leave all this people in the desert, and you will be the cause of their destruction."

16Then they came up to him and said, "We would like to build pens here for our livestock and cities for our women and children. 17But we are ready to arm ourselves and go ahead of the Israelites until we have brought them to their place. Meanwhile our women and children will live in fortified cities, for protection from the inhabitants of the land. 18We will not return to our homes until every Israelite has received his inheritance. 19We will not receive any inheritance with them on the other side of the Jordan, because our inheritance has come to us on the east side of the Jordan."

20Then Moses said to them, "If you will do this—if you will arm yourselves before the LORD for battle, 21and if all of you will go armed over the Jordan before the LORD until he has driven his enemies out before him— 22then when the land is subdued before the LORD, you may return and be free from your obligation to the LORD and to Israel. And this land will be your possession before the LORD.

32:22 Trouble Ahead

According to Joshua 22:1–6, the two and a half tribes did keep their promise to fight with the others. The land they chose was appealing, with parklike scenery, wide pastures, and lush forests. However, their settlement proved troublesome. With no natural borders, the land was open to enemy attack and easy infiltration.

23"But if you fail to do this, you will be sinning against the LORD; and you may be sure that your sin will find you out. 24Build cities for your women and children, and pens for your flocks, but do what you have promised."

25The Gadites and Reubenites said to Moses, "We your servants will do as our lord commands. 26Our children and wives, our flocks and herds will remain here in the cities of Gilead. 27But your servants, every man armed for battle, will cross over to fight before the LORD, just as our lord says."

28Then Moses gave orders about them to Eleazar the priest and Joshua son of Nun and to the

a52 That is, about 420 pounds (about 190 kilograms)

family heads of the Israelite tribes. ²⁹He said to them, "If the Gadites and Reubenites, every man armed for battle, cross over the Jordan with you before the LORD, then when the land is subdued before the LORD, give them the land of Gilead as their possession. ³⁰But if they do not cross over with you armed, they must accept their possession with you in Canaan."

³¹The Gadites and Reubenites answered, "Your servants will do what the LORD has said. ³²We will cross over before the LORD into Canaan armed, but the property we inherit will be on this side of the Jordan."

³³Then Moses gave to the Gadites, the Reubenites and the half-tribe of Manasseh son of Joseph the kingdom of Sihon king of the Amorites and the kingdom of Og king of Bashan—the whole land with its cities and the territory around them.

³⁴The Gadites built up Dibon, Ataroth, Aroer, ³⁵Atroth Shophan, Jazer, Jogbehah, ³⁶Beth Nimrah and Beth Haran as fortified cities, and built pens for their flocks. ³⁷And the Reubenites rebuilt Heshbon, Elealeh and Kiriathaim, ³⁸as well as Nebo and Baal Meon (these names were changed) and Sibmah. They gave names to the cities they rebuilt.

³⁹The descendants of Makir son of Manasseh went to Gilead, captured it and drove out the Amorites who were there. ⁴⁰So Moses gave Gilead to the Makirites, the descendants of Manasseh, and they settled there. ⁴¹Jair, a descendant of Manasseh, captured their settlements and called them Havvoth Jair.[a] ⁴²And Nobah captured Kenath and its surrounding settlements and called it Nobah after himself.

Stages in Israel's Journey

33 Here are the stages in the journey of the Israelites when they came out of Egypt by divisions under the leadership of Moses and Aaron. ²At the LORD's command Moses recorded the stages in their journey. This is their journey by stages:

³The Israelites set out from Rameses on the fifteenth day of the first month, the day after the Passover. They marched out boldly in full view of all the Egyptians, ⁴who were burying all their firstborn, whom the LORD had struck down among them; for the LORD had brought judgment on their gods.

⁵The Israelites left Rameses and camped at Succoth.

⁶They left Succoth and camped at Etham, on the edge of the desert.

⁷They left Etham, turned back to Pi Hahiroth, to the east of Baal Zephon, and camped near Migdol.

⁸They left Pi Hahiroth[b] and passed through the sea into the desert, and when they had traveled for three days in the Desert of Etham, they camped at Marah.

⁹They left Marah and went to Elim, where there were twelve springs and seventy palm trees, and they camped there.

¹⁰They left Elim and camped by the Red Sea.[c]

¹¹They left the Red Sea and camped in the Desert of Sin.

¹²They left the Desert of Sin and camped at Dophkah.

¹³They left Dophkah and camped at Alush.

¹⁴They left Alush and camped at Rephidim, where there was no water for the people to drink.

¹⁵They left Rephidim and camped in the Desert of Sinai.

¹⁶They left the Desert of Sinai and camped at Kibroth Hattaavah.

¹⁷They left Kibroth Hattaavah and camped at Hazeroth.

¹⁸They left Hazeroth and camped at Rithmah.

¹⁹They left Rithmah and camped at Rimmon Perez.

²⁰They left Rimmon Perez and camped at Libnah.

²¹They left Libnah and camped at Rissah.

²²They left Rissah and camped at Kehelathah.

²³They left Kehelathah and camped at Mount Shepher.

²⁴They left Mount Shepher and camped at Haradah.

²⁵They left Haradah and camped at Makheloth.

²⁶They left Makheloth and camped at Tahath.

²⁷They left Tahath and camped at Terah.

²⁸They left Terah and camped at Mithcah.

²⁹They left Mithcah and camped at Hashmonah.

³⁰They left Hashmonah and camped at Moseroth.

³¹They left Moseroth and camped at Bene Jaakan.

³²They left Bene Jaakan and camped at Hor Haggidgad.

³³They left Hor Haggidgad and camped at Jotbathah.

---

[a] 41 Or *them the settlements of Jair*　[b] 8 Many manuscripts of the Masoretic Text, Samaritan Pentateuch and Vulgate; most manuscripts of the Masoretic Text *left from before Hahiroth*　[c] 10 Hebrew *Yam Suph*; that is, Sea of Reeds; also in verse 11

34They left Jotbathah and camped at Abronah.

35They left Abronah and camped at Ezion Geber.

36They left Ezion Geber and camped at Kadesh, in the Desert of Zin.

37They left Kadesh and camped at Mount Hor, on the border of Edom. 38At the LORD's command Aaron the priest went up Mount Hor, where he died on the first day of the fifth month of the fortieth year after the Israelites came out of Egypt. 39Aaron was a hundred and twenty-three years old when he died on Mount Hor.

40The Canaanite king of Arad, who lived in the Negev of Canaan, heard that the Israelites were coming.

41They left Mount Hor and camped at Zalmonah.

42They left Zalmonah and camped at Punon.

43They left Punon and camped at Oboth.

44They left Oboth and camped at Iye Abarim, on the border of Moab.

45They left Iyim[a] and camped at Dibon Gad.

46They left Dibon Gad and camped at Almon Diblathaim.

47They left Almon Diblathaim and camped in the mountains of Abarim, near Nebo.

48They left the mountains of Abarim and camped on the plains of Moab by the Jordan across from Jericho.[b] 49There on the plains of Moab they camped along the Jordan from Beth Jeshimoth to Abel Shittim.

50On the plains of Moab by the Jordan across

33:50–56 Final Warnings

Just before the dramatic crossing into the promised land, God gave a clear statement of his priorities and a warning of what would happen if the Israelites failed to obey. His words would one day come back to haunt them, for they failed to carry out fully any of his orders.

from Jericho the LORD said to Moses, 51"Speak to the Israelites and say to them: 'When you cross the Jordan into Canaan, 52drive out all the inhabitants of the land before you. Destroy all their carved images and their cast idols, and demolish all their high places. 53Take possession of the land

and settle in it, for I have given you the land to possess. 54Distribute the land by lot, according to your clans. To a larger group give a larger inheritance, and to a smaller group a smaller one. Whatever falls to them by lot will be theirs. Distribute it according to your ancestral tribes.

55"But if you do not drive out the inhabitants of the land, those you allow to remain will become barbs in your eyes and thorns in your sides. They will give you trouble in the land where you will live. 56And then I will do to you what I plan to do to them.'"

Boundaries of Canaan

34 The LORD said to Moses, 2"Command the Israelites and say to them: 'When you enter Canaan, the land that will be allotted to you as an inheritance will have these boundaries:

3"'Your southern side will include some of the Desert of Zin along the border of Edom. On the east, your southern boundary will start from the end of the Salt Sea,[c] 4cross south of Scorpion[d] Pass, continue on to Zin and go south of Kadesh Barnea. Then it will go to Hazar Addar and over to Azmon, 5where it will turn, join the Wadi of Egypt and end at the Sea.[e]

6"'Your western boundary will be the coast of the Great Sea. This will be your boundary on the west.

7"'For your northern boundary, run a line from the Great Sea to Mount Hor 8and from Mount Hor to Lebo[f] Hamath. Then the boundary will go to Zedad, 9continue to Ziphron and end at Hazar Enan. This will be your boundary on the north.

10"'For your eastern boundary, run a line from Hazar Enan to Shepham. 11The boundary will go down from Shepham to Riblah on the east side of Ain and continue along the slopes east of the Sea of Kinnereth.[g] 12Then the boundary will go down along the Jordan and end at the Salt Sea.

"'This will be your land, with its boundaries on every side.'"

13Moses commanded the Israelites: "Assign this land by lot as an inheritance. The LORD has ordered that it be given to the nine and a half tribes, 14because the families of the tribe of Reuben, the tribe of Gad and the half-tribe of Manasseh have received their inheritance. 15These two and a half tribes have received their inheritance on the east side of the Jordan of Jericho,[h] toward the sunrise."

16The LORD said to Moses, 17"These are the names of the men who are to assign the land for you as an inheritance: Eleazar the priest and

---

a45 That is, Iye Abarim   *b48* Hebrew *Jordan of Jericho;* possibly an ancient name for the Jordan River; also in verse 50   *c3* That is, the Dead Sea; also in verse 12   *d4* Hebrew *Akrabbim*   *e5* That is, the Mediterranean; also in verses 6 and 7   *f8* Or *to the entrance to*   *g11* That is, Galilee   *h15* *Jordan of Jericho* was possibly an ancient name for the Jordan River.

Joshua son of Nun. ¹⁸And appoint one leader from each tribe to help assign the land. ¹⁹These are their names:

Caleb son of Jephunneh,
 from the tribe of Judah;
²⁰Shemuel son of Ammihud,
 from the tribe of Simeon;
²¹Elidad son of Kislon,
 from the tribe of Benjamin;
²²Bukki son of Jogli,
 the leader from the tribe of Dan;
²³Hanniel son of Ephod,
 the leader from the tribe of Manasseh
 son of Joseph;
²⁴Kemuel son of Shiphtan,
 the leader from the tribe of Ephraim
 son of Joseph;
²⁵Elizaphan son of Parnach,
 the leader from the tribe of Zebulun;
²⁶Paltiel son of Azzan,
 the leader from the tribe of Issachar;
²⁷Ahihud son of Shelomi,
 the leader from the tribe of Asher;
²⁸Pedahel son of Ammihud,
 the leader from the tribe of Naphtali."

²⁹These are the men the LORD commanded to assign the inheritance to the Israelites in the land of Canaan.

Towns for the Levites

35 On the plains of Moab by the Jordan across from Jericho,^a the LORD said to Moses, ²"Command the Israelites to give the Levites towns to live in from the inheritance the Israelites will possess. And give them pasturelands around the towns. ³Then they will have towns to live in and pasturelands for their cattle, flocks and all their other livestock.

⁴"The pasturelands around the towns that you give the Levites will extend out fifteen hundred feet^b from the town wall. ⁵Outside the town, measure three thousand feet^c on the east side, three thousand on the south side, three thousand on the west and three thousand on the north, with the town in the center. They will have this area as pastureland for the towns.

Cities of Refuge

⁶"Six of the towns you give the Levites will be cities of refuge, to which a person who has killed someone may flee. In addition, give them forty-two other towns. ⁷In all you must give the Levites forty-eight towns, together with their pasturelands. ⁸The towns you give the Levites from the land the Israelites possess are to be given in proportion to the inheritance of each tribe: Take

many towns from a tribe that has many, but few from one that has few."

⁹Then the LORD said to Moses: ¹⁰"Speak to the Israelites and say to them: 'When you cross the

35:6 Controlling Blood Feuds

Even today some nomadic tribes still follow the principles of blood feuds. If a person is responsible, even accidentally, for another's death, a relative of the victim can in turn kill either the murderer or, as a substitute, one of the murderer's relatives. The cities of refuge put a control on this practice, making allowance for "involuntary manslaughter." The assembly judged whether the killing was accidental or intentional (verse 24).

Jordan into Canaan, ¹¹select some towns to be your cities of refuge, to which a person who has killed someone accidentally may flee. ¹²They will be places of refuge from the avenger, so that a person accused of murder may not die before he stands trial before the assembly. ¹³These six towns you give will be your cities of refuge. ¹⁴Give three on this side of the Jordan and three in Canaan as cities of refuge. ¹⁵These six towns will be a place of refuge for Israelites, aliens and any other people living among them, so that anyone who has killed another accidentally can flee there.

¹⁶"If a man strikes someone with an iron object so that he dies, he is a murderer; the murderer shall be put to death. ¹⁷Or if anyone has a stone in his hand that could kill, and he strikes someone so that he dies, he is a murderer; the murderer shall be put to death. ¹⁸Or if anyone has a wooden object in his hand that could kill, and he hits someone so that he dies, he is a murderer; the murderer shall be put to death. ¹⁹The avenger of blood shall put the murderer to death; when he meets him, he shall put him to death. ²⁰If anyone with malice aforethought shoves another or throws something at him intentionally so that he dies ²¹or if in hostility he hits him with his fist so that he dies, that person shall be put to death; he is a murderer. The avenger of blood shall put the murderer to death when he meets him.

²²"But if without hostility someone suddenly shoves another or throws something at him unintentionally ²³or, without seeing him, drops a stone on him that could kill him, and he dies, then since he was not his enemy and he did not intend to harm him, ²⁴the assembly must judge between him and the avenger of blood according

^a1 Hebrew *Jordan of Jericho*; possibly an ancient name for the Jordan River   ^b4 Hebrew *a thousand cubits* (about 450 meters)   ^c5 Hebrew *two thousand cubits* (about 900 meters)

to these regulations. 25The assembly must protect the one accused of murder from the avenger of blood and send him back to the city of refuge to which he fled. He must stay there until the death of the high priest, who was anointed with the holy oil.

26"But if the accused ever goes outside the limits of the city of refuge to which he has fled 27and the avenger of blood finds him outside the city, the avenger of blood may kill the accused without being guilty of murder. 28The accused must stay in his city of refuge until the death of the high priest; only after the death of the high priest may he return to his own property.

29"These are to be legal requirements for you throughout the generations to come, wherever you live.

30"Anyone who kills a person is to be put to death as a murderer only on the testimony of witnesses. But no one is to be put to death on the testimony of only one witness.

31"Do not accept a ransom for the life of a murderer, who deserves to die. He must surely be put to death.

32"Do not accept a ransom for anyone who has fled to a city of refuge and so allow him to go back and live on his own land before the death of the high priest.

33"Do not pollute the land where you are. Bloodshed pollutes the land, and atonement cannot be made for the land on which blood has been shed, except by the blood of the one who shed it. 34Do not defile the land where you live and where I dwell, for I, the LORD, dwell among the Israelites.'"

Inheritance of Zelophehad's Daughters

36 The family heads of the clan of Gilead son of Makir, the son of Manasseh, who were from the clans of the descendants of Joseph, came and spoke before Moses and the leaders, the heads of the Israelite families. 2They said, "When the LORD commanded my lord to give the land as an inheritance to the Israelites by lot, he ordered you to give the inheritance of our brother Zelophehad to his daughters. 3Now suppose they marry men from other Israelite tribes; then their inheritance will be taken from our ancestral inheritance and added to that of the tribe they marry into. And so part of the inheritance allotted to us will be taken away. 4When the Year of Jubilee for the Israelites comes, their inheritance will be added to that of the tribe into which they marry, and their property will be taken from the tribal inheritance of our forefathers."

5Then at the LORD's command Moses gave this order to the Israelites: "What the tribe of the descendants of Joseph is saying is right. 6This is what the LORD commands for Zelophehad's daughters: They may marry anyone they please as long as they marry within the tribal clan of their father. 7No inheritance in Israel is to pass from tribe to tribe, for every Israelite shall keep the tribal land inherited from his forefathers. 8Every daughter who inherits land in any Israelite tribe must marry someone in her father's tribal clan, so that every Israelite will possess the inheritance of his fathers. 9No inheritance may pass from tribe to tribe, for each Israelite tribe is to keep the land it inherits."

10So Zelophehad's daughters did as the LORD commanded Moses. 11Zelophehad's daughters— Mahlah, Tirzah, Hoglah, Milcah and Noah— married their cousins on their father's side. 12They married within the clans of the descendants of Manasseh son of Joseph, and their inheritance remained in their father's clan and tribe.

13These are the commands and regulations the LORD gave through Moses to the Israelites on the plains of Moab by the Jordan across from Jericho.[a]

---

[a] 13 Hebrew Jordan of Jericho; possibly an ancient name for the Jordan River

DEUTERONOMY

A Personal Plea
Moses' last chance with the people he loved

> But if from there you seek the LORD your God, you will find him if you look for him with all your heart and with all your soul. *4:29*

POLITICIANS GET THIS ADVICE: "WHEN you deliver a speech, make it seem as if you're having a personal talk in a small room with each one of your listeners." No one took that advice better than Franklin Delano Roosevelt—unless, perhaps, you consider Moses' speeches in Deuteronomy.

When Roosevelt became president of the United States in 1932, he faced a national crisis greater than any since the Civil War. Fifteen million people were unemployed in the Great Depression (a 25 percent unemployment rate), and two million of those wandered around the country, homeless, searching for work and food. In addition, war in Europe was not far away.

Fireside Chats

To combat the mood of despair, Roosevelt turned to a powerful new communications weapon: radio. The very first week of his presidency he gave his first "fireside chat" from a homey setting in the White House, and a series of such chats helped him pull the nation through its hard times.

Warm and personal in tone, the book of Deuteronomy resembles just such a fireside chat, delivered by the great leader Moses to his people, the Israelites. He, too, led a nation through dangerous times, and at the end of his life he had many parting words. This book is Moses' State of the Union address, personal diary, and tearful swan song all combined into one.

Poised on the Edge

For their length and emotional power, these speeches have no equal in the Bible. Moses passionately went over and over the same ground, occasionally lashing out, but more often showing the anguish and love of a doting parent. An undercurrent of sadness runs through the speeches: Moses knew he would not join in the triumph of entering Canaan. God had revealed that Moses would die before then.

In Exodus, Moses was marked by a quick temper and a reluctance to speak. His humility and eloquence as seen in Deuteronomy show how far he had come in 40 years.

Deep in his soul, Moses felt that the entire history of the Israelites depended on what happened next. Poised on the banks of the Jordan River, they were about to enter the promised land and face the most crucial test of their lives. How would they react to the new land? Would they keep their covenant with God or reject it for the more immediate pleasures around them?

Desert-bred, the Israelites knew little about the seductions of other cultures: the sensuality, the exotic religions, the glittering wealth. They had spent their lives in near-isolation, sheltered from civilization. Now they were marching into a land full of enticements.

Three Speeches

Moses' first great speech, in chapters 1–3, reviewed God's dealings with Israel. Moses recalled Israel's history through his own eyes, mentioning such details as the irrigation system in Egypt, the abrupt departure, the fearsome desert with its snakes and scorpions, and the amazing miracles of God. He filled the account with personal reflections, like an aging father telling his children what to remember after he is gone.

The longest speech, chapters 4–26, went over the moral and civil code the Israelites had agreed to keep. Even here, a personal tone came through. Moses did not list laws as in a textbook; he discussed and amplified and preached them. Along with the laws, he included reminders, object lessons, personal outbursts. In chapters 27–33 Moses gave a final summing up, a farewell charge from an old man facing certain death. As clearly as he could, he presented the choices facing the Israelites. He would not be with them as they chose their future. They were on their own; they held their destiny in their own hands.

How to Read Deuteronomy

Early in this century archaeologists began turning up samples of Near Eastern treaties. These "suzerainty treaties" set down in official form the relationship between a powerful king (suzerain) and the people he ruled over. Such treaties shed new light on the book of Deuteronomy, which seems to follow very closely the pattern of such a treaty. Typically, a treaty with a powerful king consisted of the following elements:

1. *A preamble identifying the parties of the treaty*, such as a king and a small cluster of tribes who want his protection.

2. *A capsule history describing previous relations between the two parties.*

3. *Rules defining each party's obligations.* The king may swear to defend some tribes with his armies in return for allegiance, taxes, and a percentage of produce.

4. *Witnesses to the treaties,* including, in many cases, a list of gods.

5. *Curses and blessings specifying what will take place if one of the parties breaks the treaty.* The king may promise the people prosperity and peace if they keep the terms, but invasion, deportation, or death if they break them.

Read Deuteronomy as an example of a treaty between a king and his people. *Treaty* is another word for the one we have been using—*covenant*—to describe the formal agreement between God and the Israelites. With a little work, you can identify various portions of Deuteronomy that parallel the five elements above.

Chapters 1—11 and 27—34 contain the best summary of Moses' speeches to the Israelites. He holds back no emotion as he retells the story of his life. Almost all the action he describes repeats what we've heard before (see Exodus 12—20; 32—34; Numbers 11—17; 20—24), but Deuteronomy provides a much more personal account.

Unlike other ancient books, the Bible gives major emphasis to "nobodies"—poor people, aliens, widows, orphans, the sick. Many of the laws relating to them repeat laws from the three preceding books. But Deuteronomy gives hidden insights into why God has such special concern for nobodies and why the Israelites should also. It also gives intriguing ideas on how such concern can be translated into actual political and economic policies. As you go through the book, mark each passage that relates to such people.

The New Testament quotes Deuteronomy more often than almost any other Old Testament book. Twenty-one of the 27 New Testament books allude to Deuteronomy; some scholars count 90 different citations. Jesus himself drew from it during his temptation (Matthew 4).

3-TRACK READING PLAN

For an explanation and complete listing of the 3-track reading plan, turn to page 7.

TRACK 1: ***Two-Week Courses on the Bible***
See page 7 for information on these courses.

TRACK 2: ***An Overview of Deuteronomy in 3 Days***
☐ Day 1. Read the Introduction to Deuteronomy and then chapter 4, part of Moses' first emotional speech.
☐ Day 2. Read chapter 8; here, Moses reveals his fears about how success may have a harmful effect on the Israelites.
☐ Day 3. Read chapter 28, which, in vivid, shocking language, sets out before the Israelites the choice between obedience and disobedience.

Now turn to page 9 for your next Track 2 reading project.

TRACK 3: ***All of Deuteronomy in 34 Days***
After you have read through Deuteronomy, turn to pages 10—14 for your next Track 3 reading project.

☐1	☐2	☐3	☐4	☐5	☐6	☐7	☐8
☐9	☐10	☐11	☐12	☐13	☐14	☐15	☐16
☐17	☐18	☐19	☐20	☐21	☐22	☐23	☐24
☐25	☐26	☐27	☐28	☐29	☐30	☐31	☐32
☐33	☐34						

The Command to Leave Horeb

1 These are the words Moses spoke to all Israel in the desert east of the Jordan — that is, in the Arabah — opposite Suph, between Paran and Tophel, Laban, Hazeroth and Dizahab. ²(It takes eleven days to go from Horeb to Kadesh Barnea by the Mount Seir road.)

³In the fortieth year, on the first day of the eleventh month, Moses proclaimed to the Israelites all that the LORD had commanded him concerning them. ⁴This was after he had defeated Sihon king of the Amorites, who reigned in Heshbon, and at Edrei had defeated Og king of Bashan, who reigned in Ashtaroth.

⁵East of the Jordan in the territory of Moab, Moses began to expound this law, saying:

⁶The LORD our God said to us at Horeb, "You have stayed long enough at this mountain. ⁷Break camp and advance into the hill country of the Amorites; go to all the neighboring peoples in the Arabah, in the mountains, in the western foothills, in the Negev and along the coast, to the land of the Canaanites and to Lebanon, as far as the great river, the Euphrates. ⁸See, I have given you this land. Go in and take possession of the land that the LORD swore he would give to your fathers — to Abraham, Isaac and Jacob — and to their descendants after them."

The Appointment of Leaders

⁹At that time I said to you, "You are too heavy a burden for me to carry alone. ¹⁰The LORD your God has increased your numbers so that today you are as many as the stars in the sky. ¹¹May the LORD, the God of your fathers, increase you a thousand times and bless you as he has promised! ¹²But how can I bear your problems and your burdens and your disputes all by myself? ¹³Choose some wise, understanding and respected men from each of your tribes, and I will set them over you."

¹⁴You answered me, "What you propose to do is good."

¹⁵So I took the leading men of your tribes, wise and respected men, and appointed them to have authority over you — as commanders of thousands, of hundreds, of fifties and of tens and as tribal officials. ¹⁶And I charged your judges at that time: Hear the disputes between your brothers and judge fairly, whether the case is between brother Israelites or between one of them and an alien. ¹⁷Do not show partiality in judging; hear both small and great alike. Do not be afraid of any man, for judgment belongs to God. Bring me any case too hard for you, and I will hear it. ¹⁸And at that time I told you everything you were to do.

Spies Sent Out

¹⁹Then, as the LORD our God commanded us, we set out from Horeb and went toward the hill country of the Amorites through all that vast and dreadful desert that you have seen, and so we reached Kadesh Barnea. ²⁰Then I said to you, "You have reached the hill country of the Amorites, which the LORD our God is giving us. ²¹See, the LORD your God has given you the land. Go up and take possession of it as the LORD, the God of your fathers, told you. Do not be afraid; do not be discouraged."

²²Then all of you came to me and said, "Let us send men ahead to spy out the land for us and bring back a report about the route we are to take and the towns we will come to."

²³The idea seemed good to me; so I selected twelve of you, one man from each tribe. ²⁴They left and went up into the hill country, and came to the Valley of Eshcol and explored it. ²⁵Taking with them some of the fruit of the land, they brought it down to us and reported, "It is a good land that the LORD our God is giving us."

Rebellion Against the LORD

²⁶But you were unwilling to go up; you rebelled against the command of the LORD your God. ²⁷You grumbled in your tents and said, "The LORD hates us; so he brought us out of Egypt to deliver us into the hands of the Amorites to destroy us. ²⁸Where can we go? Our brothers have made us lose heart. They say, 'The people are stronger and taller than we are; the cities are large, with walls up to the sky. We even saw the Anakites there.'"

²⁹Then I said to you, "Do not be terrified; do not be afraid of them. ³⁰The LORD your God, who is going before you, will fight for you, as he did for you in Egypt, before your very eyes, ³¹and in the desert. There you saw how the LORD your God carried you, as a father carries his son, all the way you went until you reached this place."

³²In spite of this, you did not trust in the LORD your God, ³³who went ahead of you on your journey, in fire by night and in a cloud by day, to search out places for you to camp and to show you the way you should go.

³⁴When the LORD heard what you said, he was angry and solemnly swore: ³⁵"Not a man of this evil generation shall see the good land I swore to give your forefathers, ³⁶except Caleb son of Jephunneh. He will see it, and I will give him and his descendants the land he set his feet on, because he followed the LORD wholeheartedly."

³⁷Because of you the LORD became angry with me also and said, "You shall not enter it, either. ³⁸But your assistant, Joshua son of Nun, will enter it. Encourage him, because he will lead Israel to inherit it. ³⁹And the little ones that you said would be taken captive, your children who do

not yet know good from bad—they will enter the land. I will give it to them and they will take possession of it. [40]But as for you, turn around and set out toward the desert along the route to the Red Sea.[a]"

1:37 Distributing Blame

God forbade Moses to enter the promised land because of the incident reported in Numbers 20. In his farewell speech, Moses could not resist expressing his own resentment at the Israelites' part in provoking his punishment. In this verse and in 3:26 and 4:21, he turned the blame back on his countrymen.

[41]Then you replied, "We have sinned against the LORD. We will go up and fight, as the LORD our God commanded us." So every one of you put on his weapons, thinking it easy to go up into the hill country.

[42]But the LORD said to me, "Tell them, 'Do not go up and fight, because I will not be with you. You will be defeated by your enemies.'"

[43]So I told you, but you would not listen. You rebelled against the LORD's command and in your arrogance you marched up into the hill country. [44]The Amorites who lived in those hills came out against you; they chased you like a swarm of bees and beat you down from Seir all the way to Hormah. [45]You came back and wept before the LORD, but he paid no attention to your weeping and turned a deaf ear to you. [46]And so you stayed in Kadesh many days—all the time you spent there.

Wanderings in the Desert

2 Then we turned back and set out toward the desert along the route to the Red Sea,[a] as the LORD had directed me. For a long time we made our way around the hill country of Seir.

[2]Then the LORD said to me, [3]"You have made your way around this hill country long enough; now turn north. [4]Give the people these orders: 'You are about to pass through the territory of your brothers the descendants of Esau, who live in Seir. They will be afraid of you, but be very careful. [5]Do not provoke them to war, for I will not give you any of their land, not even enough to put your foot on. I have given Esau the hill country of Seir as his own. [6]You are to pay them in silver for the food you eat and the water you drink.'"

[7]The LORD your God has blessed you in all the work of your hands. He has watched over your journey through this vast desert. These forty years the LORD your God has been with you, and you have not lacked anything.

[8]So we went on past our brothers the descendants of Esau, who live in Seir. We turned from the Arabah road, which comes up from Elath and Ezion Geber, and traveled along the desert road of Moab.

[9]Then the LORD said to me, "Do not harass the Moabites or provoke them to war, for I will not give you any part of their land. I have given Ar to the descendants of Lot as a possession."

[10](The Emites used to live there—a people strong and numerous, and as tall as the Anakites. [11]Like the Anakites, they too were considered Rephaites, but the Moabites called them Emites. [12]Horites used to live in Seir, but the descendants of Esau drove them out. They destroyed the Horites from before them and settled in their place, just as Israel did in the land the LORD gave them as their possession.)

[13]And the LORD said, "Now get up and cross the Zered Valley." So we crossed the valley.

[14]Thirty-eight years passed from the time we left Kadesh Barnea until we crossed the Zered Valley. By then, that entire generation of fighting men had perished from the camp, as the LORD

2:14 Children of the Desert

As he reviewed the Israelites' history, Moses recalled with bitterness the series of rebellions leading to the 40-year punishment in "that vast and dreadful desert" (1:19). Actually, of course, the people listening to him had been mere children when the decisive rebellions occurred (1:39); their parents were the ones forbidden to enter the promised land. Except for Joshua, Caleb, and Moses' own family, all those listening to Moses had grown up in the desert.

had sworn to them. [15]The LORD's hand was against them until he had completely eliminated them from the camp.

[16]Now when the last of these fighting men among the people had died, [17]the LORD said to me, [18]"Today you are to pass by the region of Moab at Ar. [19]When you come to the Ammonites, do not harass them or provoke them to war, for I will not give you possession of any land belonging to the Ammonites. I have given it as a possession to the descendants of Lot."

[20](That too was considered a land of the Rephaites, who used to live there; but the Ammonites called them Zamzummites. [21]They were a people strong and numerous, and as tall as the Anakites. The LORD destroyed them from before the Am-

[a]40,1 Hebrew *Yam Suph*; that is, Sea of Reeds

monites, who drove them out and settled in their place. ²²The LORD had done the same for the descendants of Esau, who lived in Seir, when he destroyed the Horites from before them. They drove them out and have lived in their place to this day. ²³And as for the Avvites who lived in villages as far as Gaza, the Caphtorites coming out from Caphtor*ᵃ* destroyed them and settled in their place.)

Defeat of Sihon King of Heshbon

²⁴"Set out now and cross the Arnon Gorge. See, I have given into your hand Sihon the Amorite, king of Heshbon, and his country. Begin to take possession of it and engage him in battle. ²⁵This very day I will begin to put the terror and fear of you on all the nations under heaven. They will hear reports of you and will tremble and be in anguish because of you."

²⁶From the desert of Kedemoth I sent messengers to Sihon king of Heshbon offering peace and saying, ²⁷"Let us pass through your country. We will stay on the main road; we will not turn aside to the right or to the left. ²⁸Sell us food to eat and water to drink for their price in silver. Only let us pass through on foot— ²⁹as the descendants of Esau, who live in Seir, and the Moabites, who live in Ar, did for us—until we cross the Jordan into the land the LORD our God is giving us." ³⁰But Sihon king of Heshbon refused to let us pass through. For the LORD your God had made his spirit stubborn and his heart obstinate in order to give him into your hands, as he has now done.

³¹The LORD said to me, "See, I have begun to deliver Sihon and his country over to you. Now begin to conquer and possess his land."

³²When Sihon and all his army came out to meet us in battle at Jahaz, ³³the LORD our God delivered him over to us and we struck him down, together with his sons and his whole army. ³⁴At that time we took all his towns and completely destroyed*ᵇ* them—men, women and children. We left no survivors. ³⁵But the livestock and the plunder from the towns we had captured we carried off for ourselves. ³⁶From Aroer on the rim of the Arnon Gorge, and from the town in the gorge, even as far as Gilead, not one town was too strong for us. The LORD our God gave us all of them. ³⁷But in accordance with the command of the LORD our God, you did not encroach on any of the land of the Ammonites, neither the land along the course of the Jabbok nor that around the towns in the hills.

Defeat of Og King of Bashan

3 Next we turned and went up along the road toward Bashan, and Og king of Bashan with his whole army marched out to meet us in battle at Edrei. ²The LORD said to me, "Do not be afraid of him, for I have handed him over to you with his whole army and his land. Do to him what you did to Sihon king of the Amorites, who reigned in Heshbon."

³So the LORD our God also gave into our hands Og king of Bashan and all his army. We struck them down, leaving no survivors. ⁴At that time we took all his cities. There was not one of the sixty cities that we did not take from them— the whole region of Argob, Og's kingdom in Bashan. ⁵All these cities were fortified with high walls and with gates and bars, and there were also a great many unwalled villages. ⁶We completely destroyed*ᵇ* them, as we had done with Sihon king of Heshbon, destroying*ᵇ* every city—men, women and children. ⁷But all the livestock and the plunder from their cities we carried off for ourselves.

⁸So at that time we took from these two kings of the Amorites the territory east of the Jordan, from the Arnon Gorge as far as Mount Hermon. ⁹(Hermon is called Sirion by the Sidonians; the Amorites call it Senir.) ¹⁰We took all the towns on the plateau, and all Gilead, and all Bashan as far as Salecah and Edrei, towns of Og's kingdom in Bashan. ¹¹(Only Og king of Bashan was left of the remnant of the Rephaites. His bed*ᶜ* was made of iron and was more than thirteen feet long and six feet wide.*ᵈ* It is still in Rabbah of the Ammonites.)

Division of the Land

¹²Of the land that we took over at that time, I gave the Reubenites and the Gadites the territory north of Aroer by the Arnon Gorge, including half the hill country of Gilead, together with its towns. ¹³The rest of Gilead and also all of Bashan, the kingdom of Og, I gave to the half tribe of Manasseh. (The whole region of Argob in Bashan used to be known as a land of the Rephaites. ¹⁴Jair, a descendant of Manasseh, took the whole region of Argob as far as the border of the Geshurites and the Maacathites; it was named after him, so that to this day Bashan is called Havvoth Jair.*ᵉ*) ¹⁵And I gave Gilead to Makir. ¹⁶But to the Reubenites and the Gadites I gave the territory extending from Gilead down to the Arnon Gorge (the middle of the gorge being the border) and out to the Jabbok River, which is the border of the Ammonites. ¹⁷Its western border was the Jordan in the Arabah, from Kinnereth to the Sea of the Arabah (the Salt Sea*ᶠ*), below the slopes of Pisgah.

¹⁸I commanded you at that time: "The LORD your God has given you this land to take posses-

---

ᵃ23 That is, Crete   *ᵇ34,6* The Hebrew term refers to the irrevocable giving over of things or persons to the LORD, often by totally destroying them.   *ᶜ11* Or sarcophagus   *ᵈ11* Hebrew nine cubits long and four cubits wide (about 4 meters long and 1.8 meters wide)   *ᵉ14* Or called the settlements of Jair   *ᶠ17* That is, the Dead Sea

sion of it. But all your able-bodied men, armed for battle, must cross over ahead of your brother Israelites. 19However, your wives, your children and your livestock (I know you have much livestock) may stay in the towns I have given you, 20until the LORD gives rest to your brothers as he has to you, and they too have taken over the land that the LORD your God is giving them, across the Jordan. After that, each of you may go back to the possession I have given you."

Moses Forbidden to Cross the Jordan

21At that time I commanded Joshua: "You have seen with your own eyes all that the LORD your God has done to these two kings. The LORD will do the same to all the kingdoms over there where you are going. 22Do not be afraid of them; the LORD your God himself will fight for you."

23At that time I pleaded with the LORD: 24"O Sovereign LORD, you have begun to show to your servant your greatness and your strong hand. For what god is there in heaven or on earth who can do the deeds and mighty works you do? 25Let me go over and see the good land beyond the Jordan—that fine hill country and Lebanon."

26But because of you the LORD was angry with me and would not listen to me. "That is enough," the LORD said. "Do not speak to me anymore about this matter. 27Go up to the top of Pisgah and look west and north and south and east. Look at the land with your own eyes, since you are not going to cross this Jordan. 28But commission Joshua, and encourage and strengthen him, for he will lead this people across and will cause them to inherit the land that you will see." 29So we stayed in the valley near Beth Peor.

Obedience Commanded

4 Hear now, O Israel, the decrees and laws I am about to teach you. Follow them so that you may live and may go in and take possession of the land that the LORD, the God of your fathers, is giving you. 2Do not add to what I command you and do not subtract from it, but keep the commands of the LORD your God that I give you.

3You saw with your own eyes what the LORD did at Baal Peor. The LORD your God destroyed from among you everyone who followed the Baal

---

4:2 Do Not Add

People usually remember they are not supposed to "drop" one of God's commands, but it is more subtly tempting to add commands. Religious people of Jesus' time, for example, invented elaborate rules on how far you could walk on the Sabbath. Such "legalism" may seem holy, but goes against God's directions.

---

of Peor, 4but all of you who held fast to the LORD your God are still alive today.

5See, I have taught you decrees and laws as the LORD my God commanded me, so that you may follow them in the land you are entering to take possession of it. 6Observe them carefully, for this will show your wisdom and understanding to the nations, who will hear about all these decrees and say, "Surely this great nation is a wise and understanding people." 7What other nation is so great

---

4:6 Old Testament Evangelism

As he explained various laws to the Israelites, Moses often appealed to their unique calling as a nation. God had chosen them as a "kingdom of priests" and a "treasured possession." This passage describes yet another benefit to keeping the law: what today we would call evangelism. The purity of the Israelites would serve as an example to the nations around them, who would then be attracted to the true God.

---

as to have their gods near them the way the LORD our God is near us whenever we pray to him? 8And what other nation is so great as to have such righteous decrees and laws as this body of laws I am setting before you today?

9Only be careful, and watch yourselves closely so that you do not forget the things your eyes have seen or let them slip from your heart as long as you live. Teach them to your children and to their children after them. 10Remember the day you stood before the LORD your God at Horeb, when he said to me, "Assemble the people before me to hear my words so that they may learn to revere me as long as they live in the land and may teach them to their children." 11You came near and stood at the foot of the mountain while it blazed with fire to the very heavens, with black clouds and deep darkness. 12Then the LORD spoke to you out of the fire. You heard the sound of words but saw no form; there was only a voice. 13He declared to you his covenant, the Ten Commandments, which he commanded you to follow and then wrote them on two stone tablets. 14And the LORD directed me at that time to teach you the decrees and laws you are to follow in the land that you are crossing the Jordan to possess.

Idolatry Forbidden

15You saw no form of any kind the day the LORD spoke to you at Horeb out of the fire. Therefore watch yourselves very carefully, 16so that you do not become corrupt and make for yourselves an idol, an image of any shape, whether formed like a man or a woman, 17or like any animal on earth or any bird that flies in the air,

18or like any creature that moves along the ground or any fish in the waters below. 19And when you look up to the sky and see the sun, the moon and the stars—all the heavenly array—do not be enticed into bowing down to them and worshiping things the LORD your God has apportioned to all the nations under heaven. 20But as for you, the LORD took you and brought you out of the iron-smelting furnace, out of Egypt, to be the people of his inheritance, as you now are.

21The LORD was angry with me because of you, and he solemnly swore that I would not cross the Jordan and enter the good land the LORD your God is giving you as your inheritance. 22I will die in this land; I will not cross the Jordan; but you are about to cross over and take possession of that good land. 23Be careful not to forget the covenant of the LORD your God that he made with you; do not make for yourselves an idol in the form of anything the LORD your God has forbidden. 24For the LORD your God is a consuming fire, a jealous God.

25After you have had children and grandchildren and have lived in the land a long time—if you then become corrupt and make any kind of idol, doing evil in the eyes of the LORD your God and provoking him to anger, 26I call heaven and earth as witnesses against you this day that you will quickly perish from the land that you are crossing the Jordan to possess. You will not live there long but will certainly be destroyed. 27The LORD will scatter you among the peoples, and only a few of you will survive among the nations to which the LORD will drive you. 28There you will worship man-made gods of wood and stone, which cannot see or hear or eat or smell. 29But if from there you seek the LORD your God, you will find him if you look for him with all your heart and with all your soul. 30When you are in distress and all these things have happened to you, then in later days you will return to the LORD your God and obey him. 31For the LORD your God is a merciful God; he will not abandon or destroy you or forget the covenant with your forefathers, which he confirmed to them by oath.

The LORD Is God

32Ask now about the former days, long before your time, from the day God created man on the earth; ask from one end of the heavens to the other. Has anything so great as this ever happened, or has anything like it ever been heard of? 33Has any other people heard the voice of God*a* speaking out of fire, as you have, and lived? 34Has any god ever tried to take for himself one nation out of another nation, by testings, by miraculous signs and wonders, by war, by a mighty hand and an outstretched arm, or by great and awesome

deeds, like all the things the LORD your God did for you in Egypt before your very eyes? 35You were shown these things so that you might know that the LORD is God; besides him

there is no other. 36From heaven he made you hear his voice to discipline you. On earth he showed you his great fire, and you heard his words from out of the fire. 37Because he loved your forefathers and chose their descendants after them, he brought you out of Egypt by his Presence and his great strength, 38to drive out before you nations greater and stronger than you and to bring you into their land to give it to you for your inheritance, as it is today.

39Acknowledge and take to heart this day that the LORD is God in heaven above and on the earth below. There is no other. 40Keep his decrees and commands, which I am giving you today, so that it may go well with you and your children after you and that you may live long in the land the LORD your God gives you for all time.

Cities of Refuge

41Then Moses set aside three cities east of the Jordan, 42to which anyone who had killed a person could flee if he had unintentionally killed his neighbor without malice aforethought. He could flee into one of these cities and save his life. 43The cities were these: Bezer in the desert plateau, for the Reubenites; Ramoth in Gilead, for the Gadites; and Golan in Bashan, for the Manassites.

Introduction to the Law

44This is the law Moses set before the Israelites. 45These are the stipulations, decrees and laws Moses gave them when they came out of Egypt 46and were in the valley near Beth Peor east of the Jordan, in the land of Sihon king of the Amorites, who reigned in Heshbon and was defeated by Moses and the Israelites as they came out of

a 33 Or of a god

Egypt. **47**They took possession of his land and the land of Og king of Bashan, the two Amorite kings east of the Jordan. **48**This land extended from Aroer on the rim of the Arnon Gorge to Mount Siyon*a* (that is, Hermon), **49**and included all the Arabah east of the Jordan, as far as the Sea of the Arabah,*b* below the slopes of Pisgah.

The Ten Commandments

5 Moses summoned all Israel and said:
Hear, O Israel, the decrees and laws I declare in your hearing today. Learn them and be sure to follow them. **2**The LORD our God made a covenant with us at Horeb. **3**It was not with our fathers that the LORD made this covenant, but with us, with all of us who are alive here today. **4**The LORD spoke to you face to face out of the fire on the mountain. **5**(At that time I stood between the LORD and you to declare to you the word of the LORD, because you were afraid of the fire and did not go up the mountain.) And he said:

> **6**"I am the LORD your God, who brought you out of Egypt, out of the land of slavery.
>
> **7**"You shall have no other gods before*c* me.
>
> **8**"You shall not make for yourself an idol in the form of anything in heaven above or on the earth beneath or in the waters below. **9**You shall not bow down to them or worship them; for I, the LORD your God, am a jealous God, punishing the children for the sin of the fathers to the third and fourth generation of those who hate me, **10**but showing love to a thousand ⌊generations⌋ of those who love me and keep my commandments.
>
> **11**"You shall not misuse the name of the LORD your God, for the LORD will not hold anyone guiltless who misuses his name.
>
> **12**"Observe the Sabbath day by keeping it holy, as the LORD your God has commanded you. **13**Six days you shall labor and do all your work, **14**but the seventh day is a Sabbath to the LORD your God. On it you shall not do any work, neither you, nor your son or daughter, nor your manservant or maidservant, nor your ox, your donkey or any of your animals, nor the alien within your gates, so that your manservant and maidservant may rest, as you do. **15**Remember that you were slaves in Egypt and that the LORD your God brought you out of

there with a mighty hand and an outstretched arm. Therefore the LORD your God has commanded you to observe the Sabbath day.

> **16**"Honor your father and your mother, as the LORD your God has commanded you, so that you may live long and that it may go well with you in the land the LORD your God is giving you.
>
> **17**"You shall not murder.
>
> **18**"You shall not commit adultery.
>
> **19**"You shall not steal.
>
> **20**"You shall not give false testimony against your neighbor.
>
> **21**"You shall not covet your neighbor's wife. You shall not set your desire on your neighbor's house or land, his manservant or maidservant, his ox or donkey, or anything that belongs to your neighbor."

22These are the commandments the LORD proclaimed in a loud voice to your whole assembly there on the mountain from out of the fire, the cloud and the deep darkness; and he added nothing more. Then he wrote them on two stone tablets and gave them to me.

23When you heard the voice out of the darkness, while the mountain was ablaze with fire, all the leading men of your tribes and your elders came to me. **24**And you said, "The LORD our God has shown us his glory and his majesty, and we have heard his voice from the fire. Today we have seen that a man can live even if God speaks with him. **25**But now, why should we die? This great fire will consume us, and we will die if we hear the voice of the LORD our God any longer. **26**For what mortal man has ever heard the voice of the living God speaking out of fire, as we have, and survived? **27**Go near and listen to all that the LORD our God says. Then tell us whatever the LORD our God tells us. We will listen and obey."

28The LORD heard you when you spoke to me and the LORD said to me, "I have heard what this people said to you. Everything they said was good. **29**Oh, that their hearts would be inclined to fear me and keep all my commands always, so that it might go well with them and their children forever!

30"Go, tell them to return to their tents. **31**But you stay here with me so that I may give you all the commands, decrees and laws you are to teach them to follow in the land I am giving them to possess."

32So be careful to do what the LORD your God has commanded you; do not turn aside to the right or to the left. **33**Walk in all the way that the LORD your God has commanded you, so that you

---

*a*48 Hebrew; Syriac (see also Deut. 3:9) *Sirion*   *b*49 That is, the Dead Sea   *c*7 Or *besides*

may live and prosper and prolong your days in the land that you will possess.

Love the LORD Your God

6 These are the commands, decrees and laws the LORD your God directed me to teach you to observe in the land that you are crossing the Jordan to possess, ²so that you, your children and their children after them may fear the LORD your God as long as you live by keeping all his decrees and commands that I give you, and so that you may enjoy long life. ³Hear, O Israel, and be careful to obey so that it may go well with you and that you may increase greatly in a land flowing with milk and honey, just as the LORD, the God of your fathers, promised you.

⁴Hear, O Israel: The LORD our God, the LORD is one.ᵃ ⁵Love the LORD your God with all your heart and with all your soul and with all your strength. ⁶These commandments that I give you today are to be upon your hearts. ⁷Impress them on your children. Talk about them when you sit at home and when you walk along the road, when you lie down and when you get up. ⁸Tie them as symbols on your hands and bind them on your foreheads. ⁹Write them on the doorframes of your houses and on your gates.

6:4 Most Quoted Verses

These six verses (4–9) may well be the most quoted portion in the entire Bible. Known as the Shema, they are recited every morning and every evening by orthodox Jews—and have been for hundreds of years. They graphically emphasize the importance of God's laws to the Israelites.

¹⁰When the LORD your God brings you into the land he swore to your fathers, to Abraham, Isaac and Jacob, to give you—a land with large, flourishing cities you did not build, ¹¹houses filled with all kinds of good things you did not provide, wells you did not dig, and vineyards and olive groves you did not plant—then when you eat and are satisfied, ¹²be careful that you do not forget the LORD, who brought you out of Egypt, out of the land of slavery.

¹³Fear the LORD your God, serve him only and take your oaths in his name. ¹⁴Do not follow other gods, the gods of the peoples around you; ¹⁵for the LORD your God, who is among you, is a jealous God and his anger will burn against you, and he will destroy you from the face of the land. ¹⁶Do not test the LORD your God as you did at Massah. ¹⁷Be sure to keep the commands of the LORD your God and the stipulations and decrees he has given you. ¹⁸Do what is right and good in the LORD's sight, so that it may go well with you and you may go in and take over the good land that the LORD promised on oath to your forefathers, ¹⁹thrusting out all your enemies before you, as the LORD said.

²⁰In the future, when your son asks you, "What is the meaning of the stipulations, decrees and laws the LORD our God has commanded you?" ²¹tell him: "We were slaves of Pharaoh in Egypt, but the LORD brought us out of Egypt with a mighty hand. ²²Before our eyes the LORD sent miraculous signs and wonders—great and terrible—upon Egypt and Pharaoh and his whole household. ²³But he brought us out from there to bring us in and give us the land that he promised on oath to our forefathers. ²⁴The LORD commanded us to obey all these decrees and to fear the LORD our God, so that we might always prosper and be kept alive, as is the case today. ²⁵And if we are careful to obey all this law before the LORD our God, as he has commanded us, that will be our righteousness."

Driving Out the Nations

7 When the LORD your God brings you into the land you are entering to possess and drives out before you many nations—the Hittites, Girgashites, Amorites, Canaanites, Perizzites, Hivites and Jebusites, seven nations larger and stronger than you— ²and when the LORD your God has delivered them over to you and you have defeated them, then you must destroy them totally.ᵇ Make no treaty with them, and show them no mercy. ³Do not intermarry with them. Do not give your daughters to their sons or take their daughters for your sons, ⁴for they will turn your sons away from following me to serve other gods, and the LORD's anger will burn against you and will quickly destroy you. ⁵This is what you are to do to them: Break down their altars, smash their sacred stones, cut down their Asherah polesᶜ and burn their idols in the fire. ⁶For you are a people holy to the LORD your God. The LORD your God has chosen you out of all the peoples on the face of the earth to be his people, his treasured possession.

⁷The LORD did not set his affection on you and choose you because you were more numerous than other peoples, for you were the fewest of all peoples. ⁸But it was because the LORD loved you and kept the oath he swore to your forefathers that he brought you out with a mighty hand and redeemed you from the land of slavery, from the power of Pharaoh king of Egypt. ⁹Know there-

---

ᵃ4 Or *The LORD our God is one LORD;* or *The LORD is our God, the LORD is one;* or *The LORD is our God, the LORD alone*
ᵇ2 The Hebrew term refers to the irrevocable giving over of things or persons to the LORD, often by totally destroying them; also in verse 26.   ᶜ5 That is, symbols of the goddess Asherah; here and elsewhere in Deuteronomy

fore that the LORD your God is God; he is the faithful God, keeping his covenant of love to a thousand generations of those who love him and keep his commands. ¹⁰But

those who hate him he will repay to their
    face by destruction;
he will not be slow to repay to their face
    those who hate him.

¹¹Therefore, take care to follow the commands, decrees and laws I give you today.

7:7 Why the Israelites?

Deuteronomy makes clear that God chose Israel out of pure grace. He did not select them for their impressiveness (this verse), their goodness (9:5), or their faithfulness (9:24). Rather, he chose them because he loved them, and he had made absolute promises to their ancestors. Deuteronomy promises the new land to the Israelites 69 times.

¹²If you pay attention to these laws and are careful to follow them, then the LORD your God will keep his covenant of love with you, as he swore to your forefathers. ¹³He will love you and bless you and increase your numbers. He will bless the fruit of your womb, the crops of your land—your grain, new wine and oil—the calves of your herds and the lambs of your flocks in the land that he swore to your forefathers to give you. ¹⁴You will be blessed more than any other people; none of your men or women will be childless, nor any of your livestock without young. ¹⁵The LORD will keep you free from every disease. He will not inflict on you the horrible diseases you knew in Egypt, but he will inflict them on all who hate you. ¹⁶You must destroy all the peoples the LORD your God gives over to you. Do not look on them with pity and do not serve their gods, for that will be a snare to you.

¹⁷You may say to yourselves, "These nations are stronger than we are. How can we drive them out?" ¹⁸But do not be afraid of them; remember well what the LORD your God did to Pharaoh and to all Egypt. ¹⁹You saw with your own eyes the great trials, the miraculous signs and wonders, the mighty hand and outstretched arm, with which the LORD your God brought you out. The LORD your God will do the same to all the peoples you now fear. ²⁰Moreover, the LORD your God will send the hornet among them until even the survivors who hide from you have perished. ²¹Do not be terrified by them, for the LORD your God, who is among you, is a great and awesome God. ²²The LORD your God will drive out those nations before you, little by little. You will not be allowed

to eliminate them all at once, or the wild animals will multiply around you. ²³But the LORD your God will deliver them over to you, throwing them into great confusion until they are destroyed. ²⁴He will give their kings into your hand, and you will wipe out their names from under heaven. No one will be able to stand up against you; you will destroy them. ²⁵The images of their gods you are to burn in the fire. Do not covet the silver and gold on them, and do not take it for yourselves, or you will be ensnared by it, for it is detestable to the LORD your God. ²⁶Do not bring a detestable thing into your house or you, like it, will be set apart for destruction. Utterly abhor and detest it, for it is set apart for destruction.

Do Not Forget the LORD

8 Be careful to follow every command I am giving you today, so that you may live and increase and may enter and possess the land that the LORD promised on oath to your forefathers. ²Remember how the LORD your God led you all the way in the desert these forty years, to humble you and to test you in order to know what was in your heart, whether or not you would keep his commands. ³He humbled you, causing you to hunger and then feeding you with manna, which neither you nor your fathers had known, to teach you that man does not live on bread alone but on every word that comes from the mouth of the

8:3 Words for the Devil

When tempted by Satan (Luke 4:1–13), Jesus responded with three separate quotations from Deuteronomy: this verse, and Deuteronomy 6:13,16. In the desert, Israelites had learned that God would provide all they needed. Jesus, also in the desert, quoted Scripture to forcefully remind Satan of that lesson.

LORD. ⁴Your clothes did not wear out and your feet did not swell during these forty years. ⁵Know then in your heart that as a man disciplines his son, so the LORD your God disciplines you.

⁶Observe the commands of the LORD your God, walking in his ways and revering him. ⁷For the LORD your God is bringing you into a good land—a land with streams and pools of water, with springs flowing in the valleys and hills; ⁸a land with wheat and barley, vines and fig trees, pomegranates, olive oil and honey; ⁹a land where bread will not be scarce and you will lack nothing; a land where the rocks are iron and you can dig copper out of the hills.

¹⁰When you have eaten and are satisfied, praise the LORD your God for the good land he has given you. ¹¹Be careful that you do not forget

the LORD your God, failing to observe his commands, his laws and his decrees that I am giving you this day. 12Otherwise, when you eat and are satisfied, when you build fine houses and settle down, 13and when your herds and flocks grow large and your silver and gold increase and all you have is multiplied, 14then your heart will become proud and you will forget the LORD your God, who brought you out of Egypt, out of the land of slavery. 15He led you through the vast and dreadful desert, that thirsty and waterless land, with its venomous snakes and scorpions. He brought you water out of hard rock. 16He gave you manna to eat in the desert, something your fathers had never known, to humble and to test you so that in the end it might go well with you. 17You may say to yourself, "My power and the strength of my hands have produced this wealth for me." 18But remember the LORD your God, for it is he who gives you the ability to produce wealth, and so confirms his covenant, which he swore to your forefathers, as it is today.

19If you ever forget the LORD your God and follow other gods and worship and bow down to them, I testify against you today that you will surely be destroyed. 20Like the nations the LORD destroyed before you, so you will be destroyed for not obeying the LORD your God.

Not Because of Israel's Righteousness

9 Hear, O Israel. You are now about to cross the Jordan to go in and dispossess nations greater and stronger than you, with large cities that have walls up to the sky. 2The people are strong and tall—Anakites! You know about them and have heard it said: "Who can stand up against the Anakites?" 3But be assured today that the LORD your God is the one who goes across ahead of you like a devouring fire. He will destroy them; he will subdue them before you. And you will drive them out and annihilate them quickly, as the LORD has promised you.

4After the LORD your God has driven them out before you, do not say to yourself, "The LORD has brought me here to take possession of this land because of my righteousness." No, it is on account of the wickedness of these nations that the LORD is going to drive them out before you. 5It is not because of your righteousness or your integrity that you are going in to take possession of their land; but on account of the wickedness of these nations, the LORD your God will drive them out before you, to accomplish what he swore to your fathers, to Abraham, Isaac and Jacob. 6Understand, then, that it is not because of your righteousness that the LORD your God is giving you this good land to possess, for you are a stiff-necked people.

The Golden Calf

7Remember this and never forget how you provoked the LORD your God to anger in the desert. From the day you left Egypt until you arrived here, you have been rebellious against the LORD. 8At Horeb you aroused the LORD's wrath so that he was angry enough to destroy you.

9:4 Reasons for Warfare

Commands for the Israelites to utterly destroy other nations have caused modern readers of the Old Testament much concern. This passage reveals that God was acting not because of the Israelites' superior moral character, but because of the inhabitants' own wickedness. Chapter 20:16–18 gives yet another rationale for the wars: to keep Israel free from contamination by other nations. The Israelites never followed these commands completely, and their nation was ultimately weakened and destroyed precisely because of such contamination. (See "Is a War Ever Holy?" page 248, for further details.)

9When I went up on the mountain to receive the tablets of stone, the tablets of the covenant that the LORD had made with you, I stayed on the mountain forty days and forty nights; I ate no bread and drank no water. 10The LORD gave me two stone tablets inscribed by the finger of God. On them were all the commandments the LORD proclaimed to you on the mountain out of the fire, on the day of the assembly.

11At the end of the forty days and forty nights, the LORD gave me the two stone tablets, the tablets of the covenant. 12Then the LORD told me, "Go down from here at once, because your people whom you brought out of Egypt have become corrupt. They have turned away quickly from what I commanded them and have made a cast idol for themselves."

13And the LORD said to me, "I have seen this people, and they are a stiff-necked people indeed! 14Let me alone, so that I may destroy them and blot out their name from under heaven. And I will make you into a nation stronger and more numerous than they."

15So I turned and went down from the mountain while it was ablaze with fire. And the two tablets of the covenant were in my hands.a 16When I looked, I saw that you had sinned against the LORD your God; you had made for yourselves an idol cast in the shape of a calf. You had turned aside quickly from the way that the LORD had commanded you. 17So I took the two

---

a15 Or *And I had the two tablets of the covenant with me, one in each hand*

tablets and threw them out of my hands, breaking them to pieces before your eyes.

[18]Then once again I fell prostrate before the LORD for forty days and forty nights; I ate no bread and drank no water, because of all the sin you had committed, doing what was evil in the LORD's sight and so provoking him to anger. [19]I feared the anger and wrath of the LORD, for he was angry enough with you to destroy you. But again the LORD listened to me. [20]And the LORD was angry enough with Aaron to destroy him, but at that time I prayed for Aaron too. [21]Also I took that sinful thing of yours, the calf you had made, and burned it in the fire. Then I crushed it and ground it to powder as fine as dust and threw the dust into a stream that flowed down the mountain.

[22]You also made the LORD angry at Taberah, at Massah and at Kibroth Hattaavah.

[23]And when the LORD sent you out from Kadesh Barnea, he said, "Go up and take possession of the land I have given you." But you rebelled against the command of the LORD your God. You did not trust him or obey him. [24]You have been rebellious against the LORD ever since I have known you.

[25]I lay prostrate before the LORD those forty days and forty nights because the LORD had said he would destroy you. [26]I prayed to the LORD and said, "O Sovereign LORD, do not destroy your

Healthier, Wealthier, and Wiser
Do only good things happen to good people?

DO CHRISTIANS HAVE CAR ACCIDENTS? Do they get cancer? Are they ever fired from their jobs? The answer to all three questions is, of course, yes. But that answer causes big problems for some new Christians. Doesn't the Bible promise that God will look out for and protect his followers? How can such bad things occur?

People puzzled by such questions often refer to Old Testament books where God clearly promised success and protection to the Israelites. In Deuteronomy, Moses spelled out God's promises in complete detail. Israelite wives would have many babies. All the crops—grain, grapes, olive trees—would produce bountifully. Cattle and sheep would multiply. And Moses even included this extraordinary promise: "The LORD will keep you free from every disease" (7:15).

A Special Arrangement

For the Israelites to receive these benefits, God asked only one thing in return: follow the covenant agreement first set forth in the book of Exodus. Deuteronomy repeats much of the covenant and affirms, "It was not with our fathers that the LORD made this covenant, but with us, with all of us who are alive here today" (5:3).

God had a unique relationship with the band of refugees who had been roaming the Sinai for 40 years (10:15; 14:2). Moses, for one, could not seem to get over the arrangement. "Ask from one end of the heavens to the other," he said. "Has anything so great as this ever happened, or has anything like it ever been heard of? Has any god ever tried to take for himself one nation out of another nation . . . like . . . the LORD your God did for you in Egypt before your very eyes?" (4:32,34).

Moses promised that good things would come the Israelites' way if they merely held up their end of the covenant. *If*, he said—underscoring that small but very crucial word. Threads of doubt and anxiety run all through the book. Will the Israelites stick to the terms of the covenant? Will they obey?

Dangers of Success

Moses seemed to fear the coming prosperity even more than the rigors of the desert, and he voiced those fears in chapter 8. In the promised land, a lush country of streams and fruit trees and valuable resources, the Israelites might forget God and begin to take credit for their own success. That, at least, was the danger, and the reason Moses kept urging, "Remember!" Remember the days of slavery in Egypt, and God's acts in liberating you. Remember the trials of the vast and desolate desert, and God's faithfulness there. Remember your special calling as a treasured possession of God. Do not forget, as a prosperous nation, what you learned as refugees in the Sinai.

God predicted bluntly, "When I have brought them into the land flowing with milk and honey, the land I promised on oath to their forefathers, and when they eat their fill and thrive, they will turn to other gods and worship them, rejecting me and breaking my covenant" (31:20).

> *When your herds and flocks grow large and your silver and gold increase and all you have is multiplied, then your heart will become proud and you will forget the LORD your God, who brought you out of Egypt, out of the land of slavery.*
> *8:13–14*

people, your own inheritance that you redeemed by your great power and brought out of Egypt with a mighty hand. 27Remember your servants Abraham, Isaac and Jacob. Overlook the stubbornness of this people, their wickedness and their sin. 28Otherwise, the country from which you brought us will say, 'Because the LORD was not able to take them into the land he had promised them, and because he hated them, he brought them out to put them to death in the desert.' 29But they are your people, your inheritance that you brought out by your great power and your outstretched arm."

Tablets Like the First Ones

10 At that time the LORD said to me, "Chisel out two stone tablets like the first ones and come up to me on the mountain. Also make a wooden chest.*a* 2I will write on the tablets the words that were on the first tablets, which you broke. Then you are to put them in the chest."

3So I made the ark out of acacia wood and chiseled out two stone tablets like the first ones, and I went up on the mountain with the two tablets in my hands. 4The LORD wrote on these tablets what he had written before, the Ten Commandments he had proclaimed to you on the mountain, out of the fire, on the day of the assembly. And the LORD gave them to me. 5Then I came back down the mountain and put the tablets in the ark I had made, as the LORD commanded me, and they are there now.

6(The Israelites traveled from the wells of the Jaakanites to Moserah. There Aaron died and

was buried, and Eleazar his son succeeded him as priest. 7From there they traveled to Gudgodah and on to Jotbathah, a land with streams of water. 8At that time the LORD set apart the tribe of Levi to carry the ark of the covenant of the LORD, to stand before the LORD to minister and to pronounce blessings in his name, as they still do today. 9That is why the Levites have no share or inheritance among their brothers; the LORD is their inheritance, as the LORD your God told them.)

10Now I had stayed on the mountain forty days and nights, as I did the first time, and the LORD listened to me at this time also. It was not his will to destroy you. 11"Go," the LORD said to me, "and lead the people on their way, so that they may enter and possess the land that I swore to their fathers to give them."

Fear the LORD

12And now, O Israel, what does the LORD your God ask of you but to fear the LORD your God, to walk in all his ways, to love him, to serve the LORD your God with all your heart and with all your soul, 13and to observe the LORD's commands and decrees that I am giving you today for your own good?

14To the LORD your God belong the heavens, even the highest heavens, the earth and everything in it. 15Yet the LORD set his affection on your forefathers and loved them, and he chose you, their descendants, above all the nations, as it is today. 16Circumcise your hearts, therefore, and do not be stiff-necked any longer. 17For the

---

a1 That is, an ark

As the books following Deuteronomy record, all that God and Moses feared came true. The covenant was irreparably broken. Ultimately, the Israelites received not wealth and happiness but slavery and suffering.

A Message for Us Today

The promises of Deuteronomy were given to a particular people, the Israelites, in a special covenant relationship—a covenant that God prophesied would be broken. The formula was simple: "Do good, get rewarded; do evil, get punished." But Christians of today cannot simply turn to those flagrant promises of wealth and prosperity and apply them directly. Rather, we must look at this book in light of the new covenant introduced by Jesus Christ and spelled out in the New Testament.

When Jesus came, he promised certain rewards for Christians, but he also predicted poverty, rejection, and even persecution. Rewards on this earth cannot be reduced to such a simple "Do good, get rewarded; do evil, get punished" formula. (See Hebrews 11 and "What Is True Faith?" page 1285.) Jesus' disciples proved faithful to him, and yet most of them lived through poverty and persecution and died martyrs' deaths. For them, full rewards had to wait until heaven.

Deuteronomy may offer a clue to why God does not exempt his followers from every bad thing in life. Ironically, prosperity and health may make it harder to depend on God. Moses' fears came true: The Israelites proved least faithful to God after they moved into the prosperity of the promised land. In the desert, at least, they had been forced to lean on God just for daily survival. But after a very short time in Canaan, they forgot about him. There is a grave danger in finally getting what you want.

Life Questions: When do you think most about God: when things are going well or when you are in trouble?

LORD your God is God of gods and Lord of lords, the great God, mighty and awesome, who shows no partiality and accepts no bribes. [18]He defends the cause of the fatherless and the widow, and

---

10:12 More Than a Feeling

Twelve times Deuteronomy says we are to love God. In fact, Jesus was quoting Deuteronomy 6:5 when he gave the most important commandment as "Love the Lord your God with all your heart" (Mark 12:30). How can we love when we don't feel loving? In the Bible, love is more than a feeling; it is a decision to serve another person's interest. Only through God's help can this decision be made with "all your heart."

---

loves the alien, giving him food and clothing. [19]And you are to love those who are aliens, for you yourselves were aliens in Egypt. [20]Fear the LORD your God and serve him. Hold fast to him and take your oaths in his name. [21]He is your praise; he is your God, who performed for you those great and awesome wonders you saw with your own eyes. [22]Your forefathers who went down into Egypt were seventy in all, and now the LORD your God has made you as numerous as the stars in the sky.

Love and Obey the LORD

11 Love the LORD your God and keep his requirements, his decrees, his laws and his commands always. [2]Remember today that your children were not the ones who saw and experienced the discipline of the LORD your God: his majesty, his mighty hand, his outstretched arm; [3]the signs he performed and the things he did in the heart of Egypt, both to Pharaoh king of Egypt and to his whole country; [4]what he did to the Egyptian army, to its horses and chariots, how he overwhelmed them with the waters of the Red Sea[a] as they were pursuing you, and how the LORD brought lasting ruin on them. [5]It was not your children who saw what he did for you in the desert until you arrived at this place, [6]and what he did to Dathan and Abiram, sons of Eliab the Reubenite, when the earth opened its mouth right in the middle of all Israel and swallowed them up with their households, their tents and every living thing that belonged to them. [7]But it was your own eyes that saw all these great things the LORD has done.

[8]Observe therefore all the commands I am giving you today, so that you may have the strength to go in and take over the land that you are crossing the Jordan to possess, [9]and so that

you may live long in the land that the LORD swore to your forefathers to give to them and their descendants, a land flowing with milk and honey. [10]The land you are entering to take over is not like the land of Egypt, from which you have come, where you planted your seed and irrigated it by foot as in a vegetable garden. [11]But the land you are crossing the Jordan to take possession of is a land of mountains and valleys that drinks rain from heaven. [12]It is a land the LORD your God cares for; the eyes of the LORD your God are continually on it from the beginning of the year to its end.

[13]So if you faithfully obey the commands I am giving you today—to love the LORD your God and to serve him with all your heart and with all your soul— [14]then I will send rain on your land in its season, both autumn and spring rains, so that you may gather in your grain, new wine and oil. [15]I will provide grass in the fields for your cattle, and you will eat and be satisfied.

[16]Be careful, or you will be enticed to turn away and worship other gods and bow down to them. [17]Then the LORD's anger will burn against you, and he will shut the heavens so that it will not rain and the ground will yield no produce, and you will soon perish from the good land the LORD is giving you. [18]Fix these words of mine in your hearts and minds; tie them as symbols on your hands and bind them on your foreheads.

11:18 Laws on the Head

Many commentators, both Jewish and Christian, read these sentences figuratively. But strict Jews take them literally. They wear handwritten portions of the Old Testament (including Deuteronomy 6:4–9 and 11:18–20) in a small box strapped to their foreheads, and they also mount them in a box beside the door to their homes. The boxes are called "phylacteries." Jesus referred to the practice (Matthew 23:5), commenting that it could become a showy way of expressing spiritual pride.

---

[19]Teach them to your children, talking about them when you sit at home and when you walk along the road, when you lie down and when you get up. [20]Write them on the doorframes of your houses and on your gates, [21]so that your days and the days of your children may be many in the land that the LORD swore to give your forefathers, as many as the days that the heavens are above the earth.

[22]If you carefully observe all these commands I am giving you to follow—to love the LORD your

---

[a]4 Hebrew *Yam Suph*; that is, Sea of Reeds

God, to walk in all his ways and to hold fast to him— [23]then the LORD will drive out all these nations before you, and you will dispossess nations larger and stronger than you. [24]Every place where you set your foot will be yours: Your territory will extend from the desert to Lebanon, and from the Euphrates River to the western sea.[a] [25]No man will be able to stand against you. The LORD your God, as he promised you, will put the terror and fear of you on the whole land, wherever you go.

[26]See, I am setting before you today a blessing and a curse— [27]the blessing if you obey the commands of the LORD your God that I am giving you today; [28]the curse if you disobey the commands of the LORD your God and turn from the way that I command you today by following other gods, which you have not known. [29]When the LORD your God has brought you into the land you are entering to possess, you are to proclaim on Mount Gerizim the blessings, and on Mount Ebal the curses. [30]As you know, these mountains are across the Jordan, west of the road,[b] toward the setting sun, near the great trees of Moreh, in the territory of those Canaanites living in the Arabah in the vicinity of Gilgal. [31]You are about to cross the Jordan to enter and take possession of the land the LORD your God is giving you. When you have taken it over and are living there, [32]be sure that you obey all the decrees and laws I am setting before you today.

The One Place of Worship

12 These are the decrees and laws you must be careful to follow in the land that the LORD, the God of your fathers, has given you to possess—as long as you live in the land. [2]Destroy completely all the places on the high mountains and on the hills and under every spreading tree where the nations you are dispossessing worship their gods. [3]Break down their altars, smash their sacred stones and burn their Asherah poles in the fire; cut down the idols of their gods and wipe out their names from those places.

[4]You must not worship the LORD your God in their way. [5]But you are to seek the place the LORD your God will choose from among all your tribes to put his Name there for his dwelling. To that place you must go; [6]there bring your burnt offerings and sacrifices, your tithes and special gifts, what you have vowed to give and your freewill offerings, and the firstborn of your herds and flocks. [7]There, in the presence of the LORD your God, you and your families shall eat and shall rejoice in everything you have put your hand to, because the LORD your God has blessed you.

[8]You are not to do as we do here today, everyone as he sees fit, [9]since you have not yet reached the resting place and the inheritance the LORD your God is giving you. [10]But you will cross the Jordan and settle in the land the LORD your God is giving you as an inheritance, and he will give

12:2 Historic Discovery

The Israelites did not fully follow these instructions on destroying the "high places," which were centers of idol worship. But hundreds of years after this scene with Moses, a dramatic event took place. In the midst of a temple renovation, workers came across an old scroll containing the Book of the Law. Discovery of the book had an electrifying effect on the nation. When King Josiah heard it read, he wept and tore his robes, then called for all the elders to hear the words. The event ushered in a sweeping spiritual revival that included a campaign against idolatry and the "high places." Many scholars believe Deuteronomy was the book that stirred a kingdom (see 2 Kings 22–23 for the full account).

you rest from all your enemies around you so that you will live in safety. [11]Then to the place the LORD your God will choose as a dwelling for his Name—there you are to bring everything I command you: your burnt offerings and sacrifices, your tithes and special gifts, and all the choice possessions you have vowed to the LORD. [12]And there rejoice before the LORD your God, you, your sons and daughters, your menservants and maidservants, and the Levites from your towns, who have no allotment or inheritance of their own. [13]Be careful not to sacrifice your burnt offerings anywhere you please. [14]Offer them only at the place the LORD will choose in one of your tribes, and there observe everything I command you.

[15]Nevertheless, you may slaughter your animals in any of your towns and eat as much of the meat as you want, as if it were gazelle or deer, according to the blessing the LORD your God gives you. Both the ceremonially unclean and the clean may eat it. [16]But you must not eat the blood; pour it out on the ground like water. [17]You must not eat in your own towns the tithe of your grain and new wine and oil, or the firstborn of your herds and flocks, or whatever you have vowed to give, or your freewill offerings or special gifts. [18]Instead, you are to eat them in the presence of the LORD your God at the place the LORD your God will choose—you, your sons and daughters, your menservants and maidservants, and the Levites from your towns—and you are to rejoice before the LORD your God in everything you put your hand to. [19]Be careful not to

neglect the Levites as long as you live in your land.

²⁰When the LORD your God has enlarged your territory as he promised you, and you crave meat and say, "I would like some meat," then you may eat as much of it as you want. ²¹If the place where the LORD your God chooses to put his Name is too far away from you, you may slaughter animals from the herds and flocks the LORD has given you, as I have commanded you, and in your own towns you may eat as much of them as you want. ²²Eat them as you would gazelle or deer. Both the ceremonially unclean and the clean may eat. ²³But be sure you do not eat the blood, because the blood is the life, and you must not eat the life with the meat. ²⁴You must not eat the blood; pour it out on the ground like water. ²⁵Do not eat it, so that it may go well with you and your children after you, because you will be doing what is right in the eyes of the LORD.

Who Needs Laws?
Love makes the difference in this rulebook

DEUTERONOMY REPEATS VERBATIM MANY OF the laws given in Exodus, Leviticus, and Numbers. Yet it is far from a rulebook. A different spirit pervades it: the spirit of love. The rules in Deuteronomy read more like a guide on "How to Have a Successful Family" than, say, an automobile maintenance manual. To keep up a car you need only follow the rules. To maintain a close personal relationship you need more—you need love.

What Makes Deuteronomy Different

Deuteronomy focuses on motives: *why* people should obey laws. The preceding three books barely mentioned the love of God for his people, but Deuteronomy again and again refers to it (see 4:37; 7:7–8; 10:15; 23:5). The author portrays God as a father with his children, as a mother who gives them life, as an eagle hovering over its young.

In return, God asks for obedience based on love, not on a sense of duty. At least 15 times in the book Moses tells the Israelites to love God and cling to him. God wants not just an outward conformity, but an obedience that comes from the heart. (Later, in summing up the Old Testament, Jesus quoted the first and greatest commandment from Deuteronomy: "Love the Lord your God with all your heart and with all your soul and with all your mind" [Matthew 22:37; Deuteronomy 6:5].)

Restating the Negatives

Deuteronomy also hints at why laws are needed in the first place. Moses stated the principle directly, "The LORD commanded us to obey all these decrees and to fear the LORD our God, so that we might always prosper and be kept alive, as is the case today" (6:24). In other words, the laws were given for the Israelites' own good.

Most of the Ten Commandments were given in a negative form, "You shall not." But each of these negative statements protects a privileged relationship between two people or a person and God. For example, "Do not murder" could be restated, "Human life is sacred and has enormous worth. Respect such life as the image of God, and defend it." Other commandments protect marriage, private property, honesty, and the day set aside to worship God.

Never Forget

Moses could not have emphasized the laws more strongly. "These commandments that I give you today are to be upon your hearts," he said. "Impress them on your children. Talk about them when you sit at home and when you walk along the road, when you lie down and when you get up" (6:6–7).

Moses wanted to make sure the Israelites would not possibly forget the laws. He instructed the priests to gather the whole nation together to hear them read aloud every seven years (31:9–13). Any king of Israel was required, as one of his first acts, to write out the laws by hand (17:18–19).

One last visual reminder served to impress the laws on the Israelites' minds. The priests wrote them in bold letters on stones covered with plaster. As the tribes marched across the Jordan River into the new land, they passed between the writing-covered stones (27:1–8).

No one in Israel could plead ignorance of what God required of them—his rules were carved in stone. As history would prove, obeying the rules was another matter.

Life Questions: Read over the Ten Commandments in Deuteronomy 5. How do they help us? What "rights" are they protecting?

> Be careful to obey all these regulations I am giving you, so that it may always go well with you and your children after you, because you will be doing what is good and right in the eyes of the LORD your God.
> 12:28

26But take your consecrated things and whatever you have vowed to give, and go to the place the LORD will choose. 27Present your burnt offerings on the altar of the LORD your God, both the meat and the blood. The blood of your sacrifices must be poured beside the altar of the LORD your God, but you may eat the meat. 28Be careful to obey all these regulations I am giving you, so that it may always go well with you and your children after you, because you will be doing what is good and right in the eyes of the LORD your God.

29The LORD your God will cut off before you the nations you are about to invade and dispossess. But when you have driven them out and settled in their land, 30and after they have been destroyed before you, be careful not to be ensnared by inquiring about their gods, saying, "How do these nations serve their gods? We will do the same." 31You must not worship the LORD your God in their way, because in worshiping their gods, they do all kinds of detestable things the LORD hates. They even burn their sons and daughters in the fire as sacrifices to their gods.

32See that you do all I command you; do not add to it or take away from it.

Worshiping Other Gods

13 If a prophet, or one who foretells by dreams, appears among you and announces to you a miraculous sign or wonder, 2and

13:1–5 Testing Prophets

Lots of people—cult members as well as Christians—claim that God has spoken to them. How do you evaluate those claims? Deuteronomy offers two tests. First, a prediction made in God's name must in fact come true (18:21–22). The second test, given here, matters just as much. If a prediction does come true, but the prophet tries to lead people to worship some other god, that prophet should be rejected.

if the sign or wonder of which he has spoken takes place, and he says, "Let us follow other gods" (gods you have not known) "and let us worship them," 3you must not listen to the words of that prophet or dreamer. The LORD your God is testing you to find out whether you love him with all your heart and with all your soul. 4It is the LORD your God you must follow, and him you must revere. Keep his commands and obey him; serve him and hold fast to him. 5That prophet or dreamer must be put to death, because he preached rebellion against the LORD

your God, who brought you out of Egypt and redeemed you from the land of slavery; he has tried to turn you from the way the LORD your God commanded you to follow. You must purge the evil from among you.

6If your very own brother, or your son or daughter, or the wife you love, or your closest friend secretly entices you, saying, "Let us go and worship other gods" (gods that neither you nor your fathers have known, 7gods of the peoples around you, whether near or far, from one end of the land to the other), 8do not yield to him or listen to him. Show him no pity. Do not spare him or shield him. 9You must certainly put him to death. Your hand must be the first in putting him to death, and then the hands of all the people. 10Stone him to death, because he tried to turn you away from the LORD your God, who brought you out of Egypt, out of the land of slavery. 11Then all Israel will hear and be afraid, and no one among you will do such an evil thing again.

12If you hear it said about one of the towns the LORD your God is giving you to live in 13that wicked men have arisen among you and have led the people of their town astray, saying, "Let us go and worship other gods" (gods you have not known), 14then you must inquire, probe and investigate it thoroughly. And if it is true and it has been proved that this detestable thing has been done among you, 15you must certainly put to the sword all who live in that town. Destroy it completely,*a* both its people and its livestock. 16Gather all the plunder of the town into the middle of the public square and completely burn the town and all its plunder as a whole burnt offering to the LORD your God. It is to remain a ruin forever, never to be rebuilt. 17None of those condemned things*a* shall be found in your hands, so that the LORD will turn from his fierce anger; he will show you mercy, have compassion on you, and increase your numbers, as he promised on oath to your forefathers, 18because you obey the LORD your God, keeping all his commands that I am giving you today and doing what is right in his eyes.

Clean and Unclean Food

14 You are the children of the LORD your God. Do not cut yourselves or shave the front of your heads for the dead, 2for you are a people holy to the LORD your God. Out of all the peoples on the face of the earth, the LORD has chosen you to be his treasured possession.

3Do not eat any detestable thing. 4These are the animals you may eat: the ox, the sheep, the goat, 5the deer, the gazelle, the roe deer, the wild goat, the ibex, the antelope and the mountain

---

a 15,17 The Hebrew term refers to the irrevocable giving over of things or persons to the LORD, often by totally destroying them.

sheep.[a] 6You may eat any animal that has a split hoof divided in two and that chews the cud. 7However, of those that chew the cud or that have a split hoof completely divided you may not eat the camel, the rabbit or the coney.[b] Although they chew the cud, they do not have a split hoof; they are ceremonially unclean for you. 8The pig is also unclean; although it has a split hoof, it does not chew the cud. You are not to eat their meat or touch their carcasses.

9Of all the creatures living in the water, you may eat any that has fins and scales. 10But anything that does not have fins and scales you may not eat; for it is unclean.

11You may eat any clean bird. 12But these you may not eat: the eagle, the vulture, the black vulture, 13the red kite, the black kite, any kind of falcon, 14any kind of raven, 15the horned owl, the screech owl, the gull, any kind of hawk, 16the little owl, the great owl, the white owl, 17the desert owl, the osprey, the cormorant, 18the stork, any kind of heron, the hoopoe and the bat.

19All flying insects that swarm are unclean to you; do not eat them. 20But any winged creature that is clean you may eat.

21Do not eat anything you find already dead. You may give it to an alien living in any of your towns, and he may eat it, or you may sell it to a foreigner. But you are a people holy to the LORD your God.

Do not cook a young goat in its mother's milk.

Tithes

22Be sure to set aside a tenth of all that your fields produce each year. 23Eat the tithe of your grain, new wine and oil, and the firstborn of your herds and flocks in the presence of the LORD your God at the place he will choose as a dwelling for his Name, so that you may learn to revere the LORD your God always. 24But if that place is too distant and you have been blessed by the LORD your God and cannot carry your tithe (because the place where the LORD will choose to put his Name is so far away), 25then exchange your tithe for silver, and take the silver with you and go to the place the LORD your God will choose. 26Use the silver to buy whatever you like: cattle, sheep, wine or other fermented drink, or anything you wish. Then you and your household shall eat there in the presence of the LORD your God and rejoice. 27And do not neglect the Levites living in your towns, for they have no allotment or inheritance of their own.

28At the end of every three years, bring all the tithes of that year's produce and store it in your towns, 29so that the Levites (who have no allotment or inheritance of their own) and the aliens,

the fatherless and the widows who live in your towns may come and eat and be satisfied, and so that the LORD your God may bless you in all the work of your hands.

14:28–29 Tithe to the Poor

Each year the Israelites presented a tithe of produce as an offering to God. Every third year the tithe would be distributed to needy people. God accepted the gifts to these people as an offering to himself. The principle behind this practice was later powerfully expressed in a parable by Jesus (Matthew 25:31–46), who said, "I tell you the truth, whatever you did for one of the least of these brothers of mine, you did for me."

The Year for Canceling Debts

15 At the end of every seven years you must cancel debts. 2This is how it is to be done: Every creditor shall cancel the loan he has made to his fellow Israelite. He shall not require payment from his fellow Israelite or brother, because the LORD's time for canceling debts has been proclaimed. 3You may require payment from a foreigner, but you must cancel any debt your brother owes you. 4However, there should be no poor among you, for in the land the LORD your God is giving you to possess as your inheritance, he will richly bless you, 5if only you fully obey the LORD your God and are careful to follow all these commands I am giving you today. 6For the LORD your God will bless you as he has promised, and you will lend to many nations but will borrow from none. You will rule over many nations but none will rule over you.

7If there is a poor man among your brothers in any of the towns of the land that the LORD your God is giving you, do not be hardhearted or tightfisted toward your poor brother. 8Rather be openhanded and freely lend him whatever he needs. 9Be careful not to harbor this wicked thought: "The seventh year, the year for canceling debts, is near," so that you do not show ill will toward your needy brother and give him nothing. He may then appeal to the LORD against you, and you will be found guilty of sin. 10Give generously to him and do so without a grudging heart; then because of this the LORD your God will bless you in all your work and in everything you put your hand to. 11There will always be poor people in the land. Therefore I command you to be openhanded toward your brothers and toward the poor and needy in your land.

---

[a]5 The precise identification of some of the birds and animals in this chapter is uncertain.   [b]7 That is, the hyrax or rock badger

Freeing Servants

[12]If a fellow Hebrew, a man or a woman, sells himself to you and serves you six years, in the seventh year you must let him go free. [13]And

when you release him, do not send him away empty-handed. [14]Supply him liberally from your flock, your threshing floor and your winepress. Give to him as the LORD your God has blessed you. [15]Remember that you were slaves in Egypt and the LORD your God redeemed you. That is why I give you this command today.

[16]But if your servant says to you, "I do not want to leave you," because he loves you and your family and is well off with you, [17]then take an awl and push it through his ear lobe into the door, and he will become your servant for life. Do the same for your maidservant.

[18]Do not consider it a hardship to set your servant free, because his service to you these six years has been worth twice as much as that of a hired hand. And the LORD your God will bless you in everything you do.

The Firstborn Animals

[19]Set apart for the LORD your God every firstborn male of your herds and flocks. Do not put the firstborn of your oxen to work, and do not shear the firstborn of your sheep. [20]Each year you and your family are to eat them in the presence of the LORD your God at the place he will choose. [21]If an animal has a defect, is lame or blind, or has any serious flaw, you must not sacrifice it to the LORD your God. [22]You are to eat it in your own towns. Both the ceremonially unclean and the clean may eat it, as if it were gazelle or deer. [23]But you must not eat the blood; pour it out on the ground like water.

Passover

16 Observe the month of Abib and celebrate the Passover of the LORD your God, because in the month of Abib he brought you out of Egypt by night. [2]Sacrifice as the Passover to the LORD your God an animal from your flock or herd at the place the LORD will choose as a dwelling for his Name. [3]Do not eat it with bread made with yeast, but for seven days eat unleavened bread, the bread of affliction, because you left Egypt in haste—so that all the days of your life you may remember the time of your departure from Egypt. [4]Let no yeast be found in your possession in all your land for seven days. Do not let any of the meat you sacrifice on the evening of the first day remain until morning.

[5]You must not sacrifice the Passover in any town the LORD your God gives you [6]except in the place he will choose as a dwelling for his Name. There you must sacrifice the Passover in the evening, when the sun goes down, on the anniversary[a] of your departure from Egypt. [7]Roast it and eat it at the place the LORD your God will choose. Then in the morning return to your tents. [8]For six days eat unleavened bread and on the seventh day hold an assembly to the LORD your God and do no work.

Feast of Weeks

[9]Count off seven weeks from the time you begin to put the sickle to the standing grain. [10]Then celebrate the Feast of Weeks to the LORD your God by giving a freewill offering in proportion to the blessings the LORD your God has given you. [11]And rejoice before the LORD your God at the place he will choose as a dwelling for his Name—you, your sons and daughters, your menservants and maidservants, the Levites in your towns, and the aliens, the fatherless and the widows living among you. [12]Remember that you were slaves in Egypt, and follow carefully these decrees.

Feast of Tabernacles

[13]Celebrate the Feast of Tabernacles for seven days after you have gathered the produce of your threshing floor and your winepress. [14]Be joyful at your Feast—you, your sons and daughters, your menservants and maidservants, and the Levites, the aliens, the fatherless and the widows who live in your towns. [15]For seven days celebrate the Feast to the LORD your God at the place the LORD will choose. For the LORD your God will bless you in all your harvest and in all the work of your hands, and your joy will be complete.

[16]Three times a year all your men must appear before the LORD your God at the place he will choose: at the Feast of Unleavened Bread, the Feast of Weeks and the Feast of Tabernacles. No man should appear before the LORD empty-handed: [17]Each of you must bring a gift in

---

[a]6 Or *down, at the time of day*

proportion to the way the LORD your God has blessed you.

Judges

[18]Appoint judges and officials for each of your tribes in every town the LORD your God is giving you, and they shall judge the people fairly. [19]Do not pervert justice or show partiality. Do not accept a bribe, for a bribe blinds the eyes of the wise and twists the words of the righteous. [20]Follow justice and justice alone, so that you may live and possess the land the LORD your God is giving you.

Worshiping Other Gods

[21]Do not set up any wooden Asherah pole[a] beside the altar you build to the LORD your God, [22]and do not erect a sacred stone, for these the LORD your God hates.

17 Do not sacrifice to the LORD your God an ox or a sheep that has any defect or flaw in it, for that would be detestable to him.

[2]If a man or woman living among you in one of the towns the LORD gives you is found doing evil in the eyes of the LORD your God in violation of his covenant, [3]and contrary to my command has worshiped other gods, bowing down to them or to the sun or the moon or the stars of the sky, [4]and this has been brought to your attention, then you must investigate it thoroughly. If it is true and it has been proved that this detestable thing has been done in Israel, [5]take the man or woman who has done this evil deed to your city gate and stone that person to death. [6]On the testimony of two or three witnesses a man shall be put to death, but no one shall be put to death on the testimony of only one witness. [7]The hands of the witnesses must be the first in putting him to death, and then the hands of all the people. You must purge the evil from among you.

Law Courts

[8]If cases come before your courts that are too difficult for you to judge—whether bloodshed, lawsuits or assaults—take them to the place the LORD your God will choose. [9]Go to the priests, who are Levites, and to the judge who is in office at that time. Inquire of them and they will give you the verdict. [10]You must act according to the decisions they give you at the place the LORD will choose. Be careful to do everything they direct you to do. [11]Act according to the law they teach you and the decisions they give you. Do not turn aside from what they tell you, to the right or to the left. [12]The man who shows contempt for the judge or for the priest who stands ministering there to the LORD your God must be put to death. You must purge the evil from Israel. [13]All the

people will hear and be afraid, and will not be contemptuous again.

The King

[14]When you enter the land the LORD your God is giving you and have taken possession of it and settled in it, and you say, "Let us set a king over us like all the nations around us," [15]be sure to appoint over you the king the LORD your God chooses. He must be from among your own brothers. Do not place a foreigner over you, one

17:15 Prescription for a King

Until now, the Bible has not mentioned the possibility of an Israelite king. But here, long before the nation actually got a king, God lays down his prescription for a good one. The list of qualities hardly fits the normal image of a king—or the kind of person the Israelites' descendants usually got.

who is not a brother Israelite. [16]The king, moreover, must not acquire great numbers of horses for himself or make the people return to Egypt to get more of them, for the LORD has told you, "You are not to go back that way again." [17]He must not take many wives, or his heart will be led astray. He must not accumulate large amounts of silver and gold.

[18]When he takes the throne of his kingdom, he is to write for himself on a scroll a copy of this law, taken from that of the priests, who are Levites. [19]It is to be with him, and he is to read it all the days of his life so that he may learn to revere the LORD his God and follow carefully all the words of this law and these decrees [20]and not consider himself better than his brothers and turn from the law to the right or to the left. Then he and his descendants will reign a long time over his kingdom in Israel.

Offerings for Priests and Levites

18 The priests, who are Levites—indeed the whole tribe of Levi—are to have no allotment or inheritance with Israel. They shall live on the offerings made to the LORD by fire, for that is their inheritance. [2]They shall have no inheritance among their brothers; the LORD is their inheritance, as he promised them.

[3]This is the share due the priests from the people who sacrifice a bull or a sheep: the shoulder, the jowls and the inner parts. [4]You are to give them the firstfruits of your grain, new wine and oil, and the first wool from the shearing of your sheep, [5]for the LORD your God has chosen them and their descendants out of all your tribes

---

[a]21 Or *Do not plant any tree dedicated to Asherah*

to stand and minister in the LORD's name always.

⁶If a Levite moves from one of your towns anywhere in Israel where he is living, and comes in all earnestness to the place the LORD will choose, ⁷he may minister in the name of the LORD his God like all his fellow Levites who serve there in the presence of the LORD. ⁸He is to share equally in their benefits, even though he has received money from the sale of family possessions.

Detestable Practices

⁹When you enter the land the LORD your God is giving you, do not learn to imitate the detestable ways of the nations there. ¹⁰Let no one be

18:9–13 "Detestable Ways"

This brief paragraph gives a preview of some of the "detestable ways" the Israelites would encounter in the promised land. Child sacrifice was a common part of worship in Canaan. God had already stated that the Israelites' invasion was a form of punishment on the Canaanites for these kinds of practices (9:4).

found among you who sacrifices his son or daughter in*ᵃ* the fire, who practices divination or sorcery, interprets omens, engages in witchcraft, ¹¹or casts spells, or who is a medium or spiritist or who consults the dead. ¹²Anyone who does these things is detestable to the LORD, and because of these detestable practices the LORD your God will drive out those nations before you. ¹³You must be blameless before the LORD your God.

The Prophet

¹⁴The nations you will dispossess listen to those who practice sorcery or divination. But as for you, the LORD your God has not permitted you to do so. ¹⁵The LORD your God will raise up for you a prophet like me from among your own brothers. You must listen to him. ¹⁶For this is what you asked of the LORD your God at Horeb on the day of the assembly when you said, "Let us not hear the voice of the LORD our God nor see this great fire anymore, or we will die."

¹⁷The LORD said to me: "What they say is good. ¹⁸I will raise up for them a prophet like you from among their brothers; I will put my words in his mouth, and he will tell them everything I command him. ¹⁹If anyone does not listen to my words that the prophet speaks in my name, I myself will call him to account. ²⁰But a prophet who presumes to speak in my name anything I have not commanded him to say, or a prophet

who speaks in the name of other gods, must be put to death."

²¹You may say to yourselves, "How can we know when a message has not been spoken by the LORD?" ²²If what a prophet proclaims in the name of the LORD does not take place or come true, that is a message the LORD has not spoken. That prophet has spoken presumptuously. Do not be afraid of him.

Cities of Refuge

19 When the LORD your God has destroyed the nations whose land he is giving you, and when you have driven them out and settled in their towns and houses, ²then set aside for yourselves three cities centrally located in the land the LORD your God is giving you to possess. ³Build roads to them and divide into three parts the land the LORD your God is giving you as an inheritance, so that anyone who kills a man may flee there.

⁴This is the rule concerning the man who kills another and flees there to save his life—one who kills his neighbor unintentionally, without malice aforethought. ⁵For instance, a man may go into the forest with his neighbor to cut wood, and as he swings his ax to fell a tree, the head may fly off and hit his neighbor and kill him. That man may flee to one of these cities and save his life. ⁶Otherwise, the avenger of blood might pursue him in a rage, overtake him if the distance is too great, and kill him even though he is not deserving of death, since he did it to his neighbor without malice aforethought. ⁷This is why I command you to set aside for yourselves three cities.

⁸If the LORD your God enlarges your territory, as he promised on oath to your forefathers, and gives you the whole land he promised them, ⁹because you carefully follow all these laws I command you today—to love the LORD your God and to walk always in his ways—then you are to set aside three more cities. ¹⁰Do this so that innocent blood will not be shed in your land, which the LORD your God is giving you as your inheritance, and so that you will not be guilty of bloodshed.

¹¹But if a man hates his neighbor and lies in wait for him, assaults and kills him, and then flees to one of these cities, ¹²the elders of his town shall send for him, bring him back from the city, and hand him over to the avenger of blood to die. ¹³Show him no pity. You must purge from Israel the guilt of shedding innocent blood, so that it may go well with you.

¹⁴Do not move your neighbor's boundary stone set up by your predecessors in the inheritance you receive in the land the LORD your God is giving you to possess.

ᵃ 10 Or who makes his son or daughter pass through

Witnesses

15One witness is not enough to convict a man accused of any crime or offense he may have committed. A matter must be established by the testimony of two or three witnesses.

16If a malicious witness takes the stand to accuse a man of a crime, **17**the two men involved in the dispute must stand in the presence of the LORD before the priests and the judges who are in office at the time. **18**The judges must make a thorough investigation, and if the witness proves to be a liar, giving false testimony against his brother, **19**then do to him as he intended to do to his brother. You must purge the evil from among you. **20**The rest of the people will hear of this and be afraid, and never again will such an evil thing be done among you. **21**Show no pity: life for life, eye for eye, tooth for tooth, hand for hand, foot for foot.

Going to War

20 When you go to war against your enemies and see horses and chariots and an army greater than yours, do not be afraid of them, because the LORD your God, who brought you up out of Egypt, will be with you. **2**When you are about to go into battle, the priest shall come forward and address the army. **3**He shall say: "Hear, O Israel, today you are going into battle against your enemies. Do not be fainthearted or afraid; do not be terrified or give way to panic before them. **4**For the LORD your God is the one who goes with you to fight for you against your enemies to give you victory."

5The officers shall say to the army: "Has anyone built a new house and not dedicated it? Let him go home, or he may die in battle and someone else may dedicate it. **6**Has anyone planted a

20:5 Uncommon Military Rules

The Israelites gained a reputation as fierce and bloody fighters. Yet Moses' instructions in this chapter defied normal military practice. Soldiers with new homes, new vineyards, and new fiancées—or even just plain scared soldiers—got exemptions from fighting. And before attacking any city, the army was to make a peace offer.

vineyard and not begun to enjoy it? Let him go home, or he may die in battle and someone else enjoy it. **7**Has anyone become pledged to a woman and not married her? Let him go home, or he may die in battle and someone else marry her." **8**Then the officers shall add, "Is any man afraid

or fainthearted? Let him go home so that his brothers will not become disheartened too." **9**When the officers have finished speaking to the army, they shall appoint commanders over it.

10When you march up to attack a city, make its people an offer of peace. **11**If they accept and open their gates, all the people in it shall be subject to forced labor and shall work for you. **12**If they refuse to make peace and they engage you in battle, lay siege to that city. **13**When the LORD your God delivers it into your hand, put to the sword all the men in it. **14**As for the women, the children, the livestock and everything else in the city, you may take these as plunder for yourselves. And you may use the plunder the LORD your God gives you from your enemies. **15**This is how you are to treat all the cities that are at a distance from you and do not belong to the nations nearby.

16However, in the cities of the nations the LORD your God is giving you as an inheritance, do not leave alive anything that breathes. **17**Completely destroy[a] them—the Hittites, Amorites, Canaanites, Perizzites, Hivites and Jebusites—as the LORD your God has commanded you. **18**Otherwise, they will teach you to follow all the detestable things they do in worshiping their gods, and you will sin against the LORD your God.

19When you lay siege to a city for a long time, fighting against it to capture it, do not destroy its trees by putting an ax to them, because you can eat their fruit. Do not cut them down. Are the trees of the field people, that you should besiege them?[b] **20**However, you may cut down trees that you know are not fruit trees and use them to build siege works until the city at war with you falls.

Atonement for an Unsolved Murder

21 If a man is found slain, lying in a field in the land the LORD your God is giving you to possess, and it is not known who killed him, **2**your elders and judges shall go out and measure the distance from the body to the neighboring towns. **3**Then the elders of the town nearest the body shall take a heifer that has never been worked and has never worn a yoke **4**and lead her down to a valley that has not been plowed or planted and where there is a flowing stream. There in the valley they are to break the heifer's neck. **5**The priests, the sons of Levi, shall step forward, for the LORD your God has chosen them to minister and to pronounce blessings in the name of the LORD and to decide all cases of dispute and assault. **6**Then all the elders of the town nearest the body shall wash their hands over the heifer whose neck was broken in the valley, **7**and

---

[a]17 The Hebrew term refers to the irrevocable giving over of things or persons to the LORD, often by totally destroying them.   [b]19 Or *down to use in the siege, for the fruit trees are for the benefit of man.*

they shall declare: "Our hands did not shed this blood, nor did our eyes see it done. ⁸Accept this atonement for your people Israel, whom you have redeemed, O LORD, and do not hold your people guilty of the blood of an innocent man." And the bloodshed will be atoned for. ⁹So you will purge from yourselves the guilt of shedding innocent blood, since you have done what is right in the eyes of the LORD.

Marrying a Captive Woman

¹⁰When you go to war against your enemies and the LORD your God delivers them into your hands and you take captives, ¹¹if you notice among the captives a beautiful woman and are attracted to her, you may take her as your wife. ¹²Bring her into your home and have her shave her head, trim her nails ¹³and put aside the clothes she was wearing when captured. After she has lived in your house and mourned her father and mother for a full month, then you may go to her and be her husband and she shall be your wife. ¹⁴If you are not pleased with her, let her go wherever she wishes. You must not sell her or treat her as a slave, since you have dishonored her.

The Right of the Firstborn

¹⁵If a man has two wives, and he loves one but not the other, and both bear him sons but the firstborn is the son of the wife he does not love, ¹⁶when he wills his property to his sons, he must not give the rights of the firstborn to the son of the wife he loves in preference to his actual firstborn, the son of the wife he does not love. ¹⁷He must acknowledge the son of his unloved wife as the firstborn by giving him a double share of all he has. That son is the first sign of his father's strength. The right of the firstborn belongs to him.

A Rebellious Son

¹⁸If a man has a stubborn and rebellious son who does not obey his father and mother and will not listen to them when they discipline him, ¹⁹his father and mother shall take hold of him and bring him to the elders at the gate of his town. ²⁰They shall say to the elders, "This son of ours is stubborn and rebellious. He will not obey us. He is a profligate and a drunkard." ²¹Then all the men of his town shall stone him to death. You must purge the evil from among you. All Israel will hear of it and be afraid.

Various Laws

²²If a man guilty of a capital offense is put to death and his body is hung on a tree, ²³you must not leave his body on the tree overnight. Be sure

to bury him that same day, because anyone who is hung on a tree is under God's curse. You must not desecrate the land the LORD your God is giving you as an inheritance.

22 If you see your brother's ox or sheep straying, do not ignore it but be sure to take it

22:1–7 Respect for Nature

The laws in Deuteronomy demonstrate God's concern that nature be treated with respect. In his instructions on war, Moses ordered those who laid siege to a city to choose carefully which trees to cut down (20:19). God's concern for the weak and helpless extended into the animal kingdom, for the law protected oxen, donkeys, and even birds (22:1–7).

back to him. ²If the brother does not live near you or if you do not know who he is, take it home with you and keep it until he comes looking for it. Then give it back to him. ³Do the same if you find your brother's donkey or his cloak or anything he loses. Do not ignore it.

⁴If you see your brother's donkey or his ox fallen on the road, do not ignore it. Help him get it to its feet.

⁵A woman must not wear men's clothing, nor a man wear women's clothing, for the LORD your God detests anyone who does this.

⁶If you come across a bird's nest beside the road, either in a tree or on the ground, and the mother is sitting on the young or on the eggs, do not take the mother with the young. ⁷You may take the young, but be sure to let the mother go, so that it may go well with you and you may have a long life.

⁸When you build a new house, make a parapet around your roof so that you may not bring the guilt of bloodshed on your house if someone falls from the roof.

⁹Do not plant two kinds of seed in your vineyard; if you do, not only the crops you plant but also the fruit of the vineyard will be defiled.ᵃ

¹⁰Do not plow with an ox and a donkey yoked together.

¹¹Do not wear clothes of wool and linen woven together.

¹²Make tassels on the four corners of the cloak you wear.

Marriage Violations

¹³If a man takes a wife and, after lying with her, dislikes her ¹⁴and slanders her and gives her a bad name, saying, "I married this woman, but when I approached her, I did not find proof of her virginity," ¹⁵then the girl's father and mother

ᵃ9 Or *be forfeited to the sanctuary*

shall bring proof that she was a virgin to the town elders at the gate. [16]The girl's father will say to the elders, "I gave my daughter in marriage to this man, but he dislikes her. [17]Now he has slandered her and said, 'I did not find your daughter to be a virgin.' But here is the proof of my daughter's virginity." Then her parents shall display the cloth before the elders of the town, [18]and the elders shall take the man and punish him. [19]They shall fine him a hundred shekels of silver[a] and give them to the girl's father, because this man has given an Israelite virgin a bad name. She shall continue to be his wife; he must not divorce her as long as he lives.

[20]If, however, the charge is true and no proof of the girl's virginity can be found, [21]she shall be brought to the door of her father's house and there the men of her town shall stone her to death. She has done a disgraceful thing in Israel by being promiscuous while still in her father's house. You must purge the evil from among you.

[22]If a man is found sleeping with another man's wife, both the man who slept with her and the woman must die. You must purge the evil from Israel.

[23]If a man happens to meet in a town a virgin pledged to be married and he sleeps with her, [24]you shall take both of them to the gate of that town and stone them to death—the girl because she was in a town and did not scream for help, and the man because he violated another man's wife. You must purge the evil from among you.

[25]But if out in the country a man happens to meet a girl pledged to be married and rapes her, only the man who has done this shall die. [26]Do nothing to the girl; she has committed no sin deserving death. This case is like that of someone who attacks and murders his neighbor, [27]for the man found the girl out in the country, and though the betrothed girl screamed, there was no one to rescue her.

[28]If a man happens to meet a virgin who is not pledged to be married and rapes her and they are discovered, [29]he shall pay the girl's father fifty shekels of silver.[b] He must marry the girl, for he has violated her. He can never divorce her as long as he lives.

[30]A man is not to marry his father's wife; he must not dishonor his father's bed.

Exclusion From the Assembly

23 No one who has been emasculated by crushing or cutting may enter the assembly of the LORD.

[2]No one born of a forbidden marriage[c] nor any of his descendants may enter the assembly of the LORD, even down to the tenth generation.

[3]No Ammonite or Moabite or any of his descendants may enter the assembly of the LORD, even down to the tenth generation. [4]For they did not come to meet you with bread and water on your way when you came out of Egypt, and they hired Balaam son of Beor from Pethor in Aram Naharaim[d] to pronounce a curse on you. [5]However, the LORD your God would not listen to Balaam but turned the curse into a blessing for you, because the LORD your God loves you. [6]Do not seek a treaty of friendship with them as long as you live.

[7]Do not abhor an Edomite, for he is your brother. Do not abhor an Egyptian, because you lived as an alien in his country. [8]The third generation of children born to them may enter the assembly of the LORD.

Uncleanness in the Camp

[9]When you are encamped against your enemies, keep away from everything impure. [10]If one of your men is unclean because of a nocturnal emission, he is to go outside the camp and stay there. [11]But as evening approaches he is to wash himself, and at sunset he may return to the camp.

[12]Designate a place outside the camp where you can go to relieve yourself. [13]As part of your equipment have something to dig with, and when you relieve yourself, dig a hole and cover up your excrement. [14]For the LORD your God moves about in your camp to protect you and to deliver your enemies to you. Your camp must be holy, so that he will not see among you anything indecent and turn away from you.

Miscellaneous Laws

[15]If a slave has taken refuge with you, do not hand him over to his master. [16]Let him live among you wherever he likes and in whatever town he chooses. Do not oppress him.

[17]No Israelite man or woman is to become a shrine prostitute. [18]You must not bring the earnings of a female prostitute or of a male prostitute[e] into the house of the LORD your God to pay any vow, because the LORD your God detests them both.

[19]Do not charge your brother interest, whether on money or food or anything else that may earn interest. [20]You may charge a foreigner interest, but not a brother Israelite, so that the LORD your God may bless you in everything you put your hand to in the land you are entering to possess.

[21]If you make a vow to the LORD your God, do not be slow to pay it, for the LORD your God will certainly demand it of you and you will be guilty of sin. [22]But if you refrain from making a vow, you will not be guilty. [23]Whatever your lips utter you must be sure to do, because you made your

---

[a]19 That is, about 2 1/2 pounds (about 1 kilogram)   [b]29 That is, about 1 1/4 pounds (about 0.6 kilogram)   [c]2 Or *one of illegitimate birth*   [d]4 That is, Northwest Mesopotamia   [e]18 Hebrew *of a dog*

vow freely to the LORD your God with your own mouth.

²⁴If you enter your neighbor's vineyard, you may eat all the grapes you want, but do not put any in your basket. ²⁵If you enter your neighbor's grainfield, you may pick kernels with your hands, but you must not put a sickle to his standing grain.

24 If a man marries a woman who becomes displeasing to him because he finds something indecent about her, and he writes her a certificate of divorce, gives it to her and sends her from his house, ²and if after she leaves his house she becomes the wife of another man, ³and her second husband dislikes her and writes her a certificate of divorce, gives it to her and sends her from his house, or if he dies, ⁴then her first husband, who divorced her, is not allowed to marry her again after she has been defiled. That would be detestable in the eyes of the LORD. Do not bring sin upon the land the LORD your God is giving you as an inheritance.

⁵If a man has recently married, he must not be sent to war or have any other duty laid on him. For one year he is to be free to stay at home and bring happiness to the wife he has married.

⁶Do not take a pair of millstones—not even the upper one—as security for a debt, because that would be taking a man's livelihood as security.

24:6 Respect People, Not Money

Old Testament laws contained many provisions to protect people from exploitation. Israelites could not charge each other interest for loans (Exodus 22:25). And Deuteronomy set limits on the "collateral," or pledge, that secured a loan. Here, the lender could not accept a millstone, for that would threaten the debtor's livelihood. Verses 10–13 show further safeguards. The debtor was allowed to keep everything necessary for living. And the lender could not even enter the debtor's house to get his pledge.

⁷If a man is caught kidnapping one of his brother Israelites and treats him as a slave or sells him, the kidnapper must die. You must purge the evil from among you.

⁸In cases of leprous[a] diseases be very careful to do exactly as the priests, who are Levites, instruct you. You must follow carefully what I have commanded them. ⁹Remember what the LORD your God did to Miriam along the way after you came out of Egypt.

¹⁰When you make a loan of any kind to your neighbor, do not go into his house to get what he is offering as a pledge. ¹¹Stay outside and let the man to whom you are making the loan bring the pledge out to you. ¹²If the man is poor, do not go to sleep with his pledge in your possession. ¹³Return his cloak to him by sunset so that he may sleep in it. Then he will thank you, and it will be regarded as a righteous act in the sight of the LORD your God.

¹⁴Do not take advantage of a hired man who is poor and needy, whether he is a brother Israelite or an alien living in one of your towns. ¹⁵Pay him his wages each day before sunset, because he is poor and is counting on it. Otherwise he may cry to the LORD against you, and you will be guilty of sin.

¹⁶Fathers shall not be put to death for their children, nor children put to death for their fathers; each is to die for his own sin.

¹⁷Do not deprive the alien or the fatherless of justice, or take the cloak of the widow as a pledge. ¹⁸Remember that you were slaves in Egypt and the LORD your God redeemed you from there. That is why I command you to do this.

¹⁹When you are harvesting in your field and you overlook a sheaf, do not go back to get it. Leave it for the alien, the fatherless and the widow, so that the LORD your God may bless you in

24:19 Don't Forget the Poor

Chapter 24 contains some of the regulations expressly designed to protect the poor. One, called gleaning, is still practiced today in a modern form. Certain religious organizations in America contract with farmers to harvest their "wasted" or abandoned crops in order to feed the poor. God's laws built a concern for the poor into the Israelites' daily routine.

all the work of your hands. ²⁰When you beat the olives from your trees, do not go over the branches a second time. Leave what remains for the alien, the fatherless and the widow. ²¹When you harvest the grapes in your vineyard, do not go over the vines again. Leave what remains for the alien, the fatherless and the widow. ²²Remember that you were slaves in Egypt. That is why I command you to do this.

25 When men have a dispute, they are to take it to court and the judges will decide the case, acquitting the innocent and condemning the guilty. ²If the guilty man deserves to be beaten, the judge shall make him lie down and have him flogged in his presence with the number of lashes his crime deserves, ³but he must not give him more than forty lashes. If he is flogged more

---

*a8 The Hebrew word was used for various diseases affecting the skin—not necessarily leprosy.

than that, your brother will be degraded in your eyes.

⁴Do not muzzle an ox while it is treading out the grain.

⁵If brothers are living together and one of them dies without a son, his widow must not marry outside the family. Her husband's brother shall take her and marry her and fulfill the duty of a brother-in-law to her. ⁶The first son she bears shall carry on the name of the dead brother so that his name will not be blotted out from Israel.

⁷However, if a man does not want to marry his brother's wife, she shall go to the elders at the town gate and say, "My husband's brother refuses to carry on his brother's name in Israel. He will not fulfill the duty of a brother-in-law to me." ⁸Then the elders of his town shall summon him and talk to him. If he persists in saying, "I do not want to marry her," ⁹his brother's widow shall go up to him in the presence of the elders, take off one of his sandals, spit in his face and say, "This is what is done to the man who will not build up his brother's family line." ¹⁰That man's line shall be known in Israel as The Family of the Unsandaled.

¹¹If two men are fighting and the wife of one of them comes to rescue her husband from his assailant, and she reaches out and seizes him by his private parts, ¹²you shall cut off her hand. Show her no pity.

¹³Do not have two differing weights in your bag—one heavy, one light. ¹⁴Do not have two differing measures in your house—one large, one small. ¹⁵You must have accurate and honest weights and measures, so that you may live long in the land the LORD your God is giving you. ¹⁶For the LORD your God detests anyone who does these things, anyone who deals dishonestly.

¹⁷Remember what the Amalekites did to you along the way when you came out of Egypt. ¹⁸When you were weary and worn out, they met you on your journey and cut off all who were lagging behind; they had no fear of God. ¹⁹When the LORD your God gives you rest from all the enemies around you in the land he is giving you to possess as an inheritance, you shall blot out the memory of Amalek from under heaven. Do not forget!

Firstfruits and Tithes

26 When you have entered the land the LORD your God is giving you as an inheritance and have taken possession of it and settled in it, ²take some of the firstfruits of all that you produce from the soil of the land the LORD your God is giving you and put them in a basket. Then go to the place the LORD your God will choose as a dwelling for his Name ³and say to the priest in office at the time, "I declare today to the LORD

your God that I have come to the land the LORD swore to our forefathers to give us." ⁴The priest shall take the basket from your hands and set it down in front of the altar of the LORD your God. ⁵Then you shall declare before the LORD your God: "My father was a wandering Aramean, and he went down into Egypt with a few people and lived there and became a great nation, powerful and numerous. ⁶But the Egyptians mistreated us and made us suffer, putting us to hard labor. ⁷Then we cried out to the LORD, the God of our fathers, and the LORD heard our voice and saw our misery, toil and oppression. ⁸So the LORD brought us out of Egypt with a mighty hand and an outstretched arm, with great terror and with miraculous signs and wonders. ⁹He brought us to this place and gave us this land, a land flowing with milk and honey; ¹⁰and now I bring the firstfruits of the soil that you, O LORD, have given me." Place the basket before the LORD your God and bow down before him. ¹¹And you and the Levites and the aliens among you shall rejoice in all the good things the LORD your God has given to you and your household.

¹²When you have finished setting aside a tenth of all your produce in the third year, the year of the tithe, you shall give it to the Levite, the alien, the fatherless and the widow, so that they may eat in your towns and be satisfied. ¹³Then say to the LORD your God: "I have removed from my house the sacred portion and have given it to the Levite, the alien, the fatherless and the widow, according to all you commanded. I have not turned aside from your commands nor have I forgotten any of them. ¹⁴I have not eaten any of the sacred portion while I was in mourning, nor have I removed any of it while I was unclean, nor have I offered any of it to the dead. I have obeyed the LORD my God; I have done everything you commanded me. ¹⁵Look down from heaven, your holy dwelling place, and bless your people Israel and the land you have given us as you promised on oath to our forefathers, a land flowing with milk and honey."

Follow the LORD's Commands

¹⁶The LORD your God commands you this day to follow these decrees and laws; carefully observe them with all your heart and with all your

26:16 Law of the Heart

The Old Testament gives many rules and regulations. Deuteronomy makes clear, however, that the law was meant to penetrate a person's heart. Unless the law becomes part of a person's inner attitudes, it will probably make no difference.

soul. [17]You have declared this day that the LORD is your God and that you will walk in his ways, that you will keep his decrees, commands and laws, and that you will obey him. [18]And the LORD has declared this day that you are his people, his treasured possession as he promised, and that you are to keep all his commands. [19]He has declared that he will set you in praise, fame and honor high above all the nations he has made and that you will be a people holy to the LORD your God, as he promised.

The Altar on Mount Ebal

27 Moses and the elders of Israel commanded the people: "Keep all these commands that I give you today. [2]When you have crossed the Jordan into the land the LORD your God is giving you, set up some large stones and coat them with plaster. [3]Write on them all the words of this law when you have crossed over to enter the land the LORD your God is giving you, a land flowing with milk and honey, just as the LORD, the God of your fathers, promised you. [4]And when you have crossed the Jordan, set up these stones on Mount Ebal, as I command you today, and coat them with plaster. [5]Build there an altar to the LORD your God, an altar of stones. Do not use any iron tool upon them. [6]Build the altar of the LORD your God with fieldstones and offer burnt offerings on it to the LORD your God. [7]Sacrifice fellowship offerings[a] there, eating them and rejoicing in the presence of the LORD your God. [8]And you shall write very clearly all the words of this law on these stones you have set up."

Curses From Mount Ebal

[9]Then Moses and the priests, who are Levites, said to all Israel, "Be silent, O Israel, and listen! You have now become the people of the LORD your God. [10]Obey the LORD your God and follow his commands and decrees that I give you today."

[11]On the same day Moses commanded the people:

[12]When you have crossed the Jordan, these tribes shall stand on Mount Gerizim to bless the people: Simeon, Levi, Judah, Issachar, Joseph and Benjamin. [13]And these tribes shall stand on Mount Ebal to pronounce curses: Reuben, Gad, Asher, Zebulun, Dan and Naphtali.

[14]The Levites shall recite to all the people of Israel in a loud voice:

[15]"Cursed is the man who carves an image or casts an idol—a thing detestable to the LORD, the work of the craftsman's hands—and sets it up in secret."

Then all the people shall say, "Amen!"

[16]"Cursed is the man who dishonors his father or his mother."

Then all the people shall say, "Amen!"

[17]"Cursed is the man who moves his neighbor's boundary stone."

27:12–26 A Task for Joshua

Joshua carried out Moses' instructions for these blessings and curses, as recorded in Joshua 8:31–35. Mount Ebal had special significance for the Israelites, who believed that Abraham first worshiped God near here after receiving the original promise of the land (Genesis 15).

Then all the people shall say, "Amen!"

[18]"Cursed is the man who leads the blind astray on the road."

Then all the people shall say, "Amen!"

[19]"Cursed is the man who withholds justice from the alien, the fatherless or the widow."

Then all the people shall say, "Amen!"

[20]"Cursed is the man who sleeps with his father's wife, for he dishonors his father's bed."

Then all the people shall say, "Amen!"

[21]"Cursed is the man who has sexual relations with any animal."

Then all the people shall say, "Amen!"

[22]"Cursed is the man who sleeps with his sister, the daughter of his father or the daughter of his mother."

Then all the people shall say, "Amen!"

[23]"Cursed is the man who sleeps with his mother-in-law."

Then all the people shall say, "Amen!"

[24]"Cursed is the man who kills his neighbor secretly."

Then all the people shall say, "Amen!"

[25]"Cursed is the man who accepts a bribe to kill an innocent person."

Then all the people shall say, "Amen!"

[26]"Cursed is the man who does not uphold the words of this law by carrying them out."

Then all the people shall say, "Amen!"

Blessings for Obedience

28 If you fully obey the LORD your God and carefully follow all his commands I give you today, the LORD your God will set you high above all the nations on earth. [2]All these blessings will come upon you and accompany you if you obey the LORD your God:

---

[a]7 Traditionally *peace offerings*

³You will be blessed in the city and blessed in the country.

⁴The fruit of your womb will be blessed, and the crops of your land and the young of your livestock—the calves of your herds and the lambs of your flocks.

⁵Your basket and your kneading trough will be blessed.

⁶You will be blessed when you come in and blessed when you go out.

⁷The LORD will grant that the enemies who rise up against you will be defeated before you. They will come at you from one direction but flee from you in seven.

⁸The LORD will send a blessing on your barns and on everything you put your hand to. The LORD your God will bless you in the land he is giving you.

⁹The LORD will establish you as his holy people, as he promised you on oath, if you keep the commands of the LORD your God and walk in his ways. ¹⁰Then all the peoples on earth will see that you are called by the name of the LORD, and they will fear you. ¹¹The LORD will grant you abundant prosperity—in the fruit of your womb, the young of your livestock and the crops of your ground—in the land he swore to your forefathers to give you.

¹²The LORD will open the heavens, the storehouse of his bounty, to send rain on your land in season and to bless all the work of your hands. You will lend to many nations but will borrow from none. ¹³The LORD will make you the head, not the tail. If you pay attention to the commands of the LORD your God that I give you this day and carefully follow them, you will always be at the top, never at the bottom. ¹⁴Do not turn aside from any of the commands I give you today, to the right or to the left, following other gods and serving them.

Curses for Disobedience

¹⁵However, if you do not obey the LORD your God and do not carefully follow all his commands and decrees I am giving you today, all these curses will come upon you and overtake you:

¹⁶You will be cursed in the city and cursed in the country.

¹⁷Your basket and your kneading trough will be cursed.

¹⁸The fruit of your womb will be cursed, and the crops of your land, and the calves of your herds and the lambs of your flocks.

¹⁹You will be cursed when you come in and cursed when you go out.

²⁰The LORD will send on you curses, confusion and rebuke in everything you put your hand to, until you are destroyed and come to sudden ruin because of the evil you have done in forsaking him.ᵃ ²¹The LORD will plague you with diseases until he has destroyed you from the land you are entering to possess. ²²The LORD will strike you with wasting disease, with fever and inflammation, with scorching heat and drought, with blight and mildew, which will plague you until you perish. ²³The sky over your head will be bronze, the ground beneath you iron. ²⁴The LORD will turn the rain of your country into dust and powder; it will come down from the skies until you are destroyed.

²⁵The LORD will cause you to be defeated before your enemies. You will come at them from one direction but flee from them in seven, and you will become a thing of horror to all the kingdoms on earth. ²⁶Your carcasses will be food for all the birds of the air and the beasts of the earth, and there will be no one to frighten them away. ²⁷The LORD will afflict you with the boils of Egypt and with tumors, festering sores and the itch, from which you cannot be cured. ²⁸The LORD will afflict you with madness, blindness and confusion of mind. ²⁹At midday you will grope about like a blind man in the dark. You will be unsuccessful in everything you do; day after day you will be oppressed and robbed, with no one to rescue you.

³⁰You will be pledged to be married to a woman, but another will take her and ravish her. You will build a house, but you will not live in it. You will plant a vineyard, but you will not even begin to enjoy its fruit. ³¹Your ox will be slaughtered before your eyes, but you will eat none of it. Your donkey will be forcibly taken from you and will not be returned. Your sheep will be given to your enemies, and no one will rescue them. ³²Your sons and daughters will be given to another nation, and you will wear out your eyes watching for them day after day, powerless to lift a hand. ³³A people that you do not know will eat what your land and labor produce, and you will have nothing but cruel oppression all your days. ³⁴The sights you see will drive you mad. ³⁵The LORD will afflict your knees and legs with painful boils that cannot be cured, spreading from the soles of your feet to the top of your head.

³⁶The LORD will drive you and the king you set over you to a nation unknown to you or your fathers. There you will worship other gods, gods of wood and stone. ³⁷You will become a thing of horror and an object of scorn and ridicule to all the nations where the LORD will drive you.

³⁸You will sow much seed in the field but you will harvest little, because locusts will devour it. ³⁹You will plant vineyards and cultivate them but

you will not drink the wine or gather the grapes, because worms will eat them. [40]You will have olive trees throughout your country but you will not use the oil, because the olives will drop off.

[41]You will have sons and daughters but you will not keep them, because they will go into captivity. [42]Swarms of locusts will take over all your trees and the crops of your land.

[43]The alien who lives among you will rise above you higher and higher, but you will sink lower and lower. [44]He will lend to you, but you will not lend to him. He will be the head, but you will be the tail.

[45]All these curses will come upon you. They will pursue you and overtake you until you are destroyed, because you did not obey the LORD your God and observe the commands and decrees he gave you. [46]They will be a sign and a wonder to you and your descendants forever. [47]Because you did not serve the LORD your God joyfully and gladly in the time of prosperity, [48]therefore in hunger and thirst, in nakedness and dire poverty, you will serve the enemies the LORD sends against you. He will put an iron yoke on your neck until he has destroyed you.

[49]The LORD will bring a nation against you from far away, from the ends of the earth, like an eagle swooping down, a nation whose language you will not understand, [50]a fierce-looking nation without respect for the old or pity for the young. [51]They will devour the young of your livestock and the crops of your land until you are destroyed. They will leave you no grain, new wine or oil, nor any calves of your herds or lambs of your flocks until you are ruined. [52]They will lay siege to all the cities throughout your land until the high fortified walls in which you trust fall down. They will besiege all the cities throughout the land the LORD your God is giving you.

[53]Because of the suffering that your enemy will inflict on you during the siege, you will eat the fruit of the womb, the flesh of the sons and daughters the LORD your God has given you. [54]Even the most gentle and sensitive man among you will have no compassion on his own brother or the wife he loves or his surviving children, [55]and he will not give to one of them any of the flesh of his children that he is eating. It will be all he has left because of the suffering your enemy will inflict on you during the siege of all your cities. [56]The most gentle and sensitive woman among you—so sensitive and gentle that she would not venture to touch the ground with the sole of her foot—will begrudge the husband she loves and her own son or daughter [57]the afterbirth from her womb and the children she bears. For she intends to eat them secretly during the siege and in the distress that your enemy will inflict on you in your cities.

[58]If you do not carefully follow all the words of this law, which are written in this book, and do not revere this glorious and awesome name—the LORD your God— [59]the LORD will send fearful plagues on you and your descendants, harsh and prolonged disasters, and severe and lingering illnesses. [60]He will bring upon you all the diseases of Egypt that you dreaded, and they will cling to you. [61]The LORD will also bring on you every kind of sickness and disaster not recorded in this Book of the Law, until you are destroyed. [62]You who were as numerous as the stars in the sky will be left but few in number, because you did not obey the LORD your God. [63]Just as it pleased the LORD to make you prosper and increase in number, so it will please him to ruin and destroy you. You will be uprooted from the land you are entering to possess.

[64]Then the LORD will scatter you among all nations, from one end of the earth to the other. There you will worship other gods—gods of wood and stone, which neither you nor your fathers have known. [65]Among those nations you will find no repose, no resting place for the sole of your foot. There the LORD will give you an anxious mind, eyes weary with longing, and a despairing heart. [66]You will live in constant suspense, filled with dread both night and day, never sure of your life. [67]In the morning you will say, "If only it were evening!" and in the evening, "If only it were morning!"—because of the terror that will fill your hearts and the sights that your eyes will see. [68]The LORD will send you back in ships to Egypt on a journey I said you should never make again. There you will offer yourselves for sale to your enemies as male and female slaves, but no one will buy you.

Renewal of the Covenant

29 These are the terms of the covenant the LORD commanded Moses to make with the Israelites in Moab, in addition to the covenant he had made with them at Horeb.

[2]Moses summoned all the Israelites and said to them:

Your eyes have seen all that the LORD did in Egypt to Pharaoh, to all his officials and to all his land. [3]With your own eyes you saw those great trials, those miraculous signs and great wonders. [4]But to this day the LORD has not given you a mind that understands or eyes that see or ears that hear. [5]During the forty years that I led you through the desert, your clothes did not wear out, nor did the sandals on your feet. [6]You ate no bread and drank no wine or other fermented drink. I did this so that you might know that I am the LORD your God.

[7]When you reached this place, Sihon king of Heshbon and Og king of Bashan came out to fight against us, but we defeated them. [8]We took their land and gave it as an inheritance to the Reubenites, the Gadites and the half-tribe of Manasseh.

[9]Carefully follow the terms of this covenant, so that you may prosper in everything you do. [10]All of you are standing today in the presence of the LORD your God—your leaders and chief men, your elders and officials, and all the other men of Israel, [11]together with your children and your wives, and the aliens living in your camps who chop your wood and carry your water. [12]You are standing here in order to enter into a covenant with the LORD your God, a covenant the LORD is making with you this day and sealing with an oath, [13]to confirm you this day as his people, that

A Scent of Doom
All were jubilant, except one man

OLD HABITS DIE HARD. DEUTERONOMY underscores that lesson, and a more contemporary character shows that people have not changed much. In 1901 Bill Miner got out of San Quentin Prison, where he had served 33 years in all. It was his third stint, and both previous times he had barely sniffed free air before landing in jail again.

Miner was a Wild West legend. He had robbed his first stagecoach at 16. He is credited with first using the line that has played on thousands of Westerns: "Hands up!" Stagecoach passengers called him the Gentleman Bandit because he never shot anyone and he spoke respectfully, using "Sir" and "Ma'am."

When Bill Miner emerged from prison at age 58, his long hair had turned grey and most of his friends had either died or disappeared. Stepping into a new century, he had a new lease on life. No stagecoaches were left to rob: The Wells Fargo company had sold their horses and invested in something he had never seen, steam trains.

> Because you did not serve the LORD your God joyfully and gladly in the time of prosperity, therefore in hunger and thirst, in nakedness and dire poverty, you will serve the enemies the LORD sends against you.
> 28:47–48

A Hint of Doom

Miner tried various odd jobs, but most work seemed degrading and boring to a former stagecoach robber. The old restlessness returned. One afternoon, in a Seattle theatre, he watched the movie *The Great Train Robbery*, and discovered a new career, or at least a new twist on an old one. The Gentleman Bandit, at age 60, became The Grey Fox. He went on to mastermind six train robberies, and probably more, until the Mounties tracked him down in British Columbia.

Three separate times Bill Miner had a chance for a new start. The last time, he had entered a new city, in a new century, with no one around to remind him of his reputation. Yet inevitably he went back to the familiar ways of crime. His life had the scent of doom about it.

The last chapters of Deuteronomy show the Israelites facing a situation much like that met by Bill Miner or any prisoner who emerges into freedom after many years. Four decades in the Desert of Sinai had served as a kind of imprisonment, or probation period. And then the long-awaited day of freedom arrived.

Everyone in the Israelite camp was jubilant—all but one man, Moses. He could see past the joy. When he spoke to the crowd, he spoke with an air of doom. He knew his people too well to think that geography would change their old ways.

Moses Pulls out the Stops

For 40 years Moses had led the cranky assortment of tribes. He had listened to their grumbling, endured their gossip, and survived their insurrections. Now he had one last chance to warn them not to repeat their ways.

You cannot read the last chapters of Deuteronomy without detecting a doleful sense of fatalism in Moses' words. The Israelites' settling down into a life of quiet obedience was about as likely as Bill Miner's becoming a banker. They had failed far too often; they were doomed to fail again.

he may be your God as he promised you and as he swore to your fathers, Abraham, Isaac and Jacob. [14]I am making this covenant, with its oath, not only with you [15]who are standing here with

29:5-6 Miracles in the Desert

The Sinai peninsula was a harsh place, and the Bible records the Israelites' problems with food and water supplies. But, as these two verses show, God cared for his people there, giving them daily food and drink and even making sure their clothes did not wear out.

us today in the presence of the LORD our God but also with those who are not here today.

[16]You yourselves know how we lived in Egypt and how we passed through the countries on the way here. [17]You saw among them their detestable images and idols of wood and stone, of silver and gold. [18]Make sure there is no man or woman, clan or tribe among you today whose heart turns away from the LORD our God to go and worship the gods of those nations; make sure there is no root among you that produces such bitter poison.

[19]When such a person hears the words of this oath, he invokes a blessing on himself and therefore thinks, "I will be safe, even though I persist

[a]*19 Or way, in order to add drunkenness to thirst.*

in going my own way." This will bring disaster on the watered land as well as the dry. [a] [20]The LORD will never be willing to forgive him; his wrath and zeal will burn against that man. All the curses written in this book will fall upon him, and the LORD will blot out his name from under heaven. [21]The LORD will single him out from all the tribes of Israel for disaster, according to all the curses of the covenant written in this Book of the Law.

[22]Your children who follow you in later generations and foreigners who come from distant lands will see the calamities that have fallen on the land and the diseases with which the LORD has afflicted it. [23]The whole land will be a burning waste of salt and sulfur—nothing planted, nothing sprouting, no vegetation growing on it. It will be like the destruction of Sodom and Gomorrah, Admah and Zeboiim, which the LORD overthrew in fierce anger. [24]All the nations will ask: "Why has the LORD done this to this land? Why this fierce, burning anger?"

[25]And the answer will be: "It is because this people abandoned the covenant of the LORD, the God of their fathers, the covenant he made with them when he brought them out of Egypt. [26]They went off and worshiped other gods and bowed down to them, gods they did not know, gods he had not given them. [27]Therefore the LORD's anger burned against this land, so that he brought on it all the curses written in this book. [28]In furious

Moses pulled out all the stops. He orchestrated a dramatic object lesson that would live in their memories forever. It actually took place after Moses' death, as recorded in Joshua 8:30–35. Representatives from all the tribes climbed two mountains, with a narrow valley in between. These designated speakers shouted out curses and blessings on the Israelites (see 11:26–32; 27–28). As they entered the new land, their ears rang with the dissonance of wonderful blessings and horrific curses.

Future Terrors

Moses starkly summarized the future of the Jewish race. They would, he said, have "an anxious mind, eyes weary with longing, and a despairing heart. You will live in constant suspense, filled with dread both night and day, never sure of your life. In the morning you will say, 'If only it were evening!' and in the evening, 'If only it were morning!'—because of the terror that will fill your hearts and the sights that your eyes will see" (28:65–67). His descriptions of their future are unmatched for their horror.

Just in case the Israelites didn't get the message, Moses taught them a song given him by God (chapter 32). It became a kind of national anthem, memorized by everyone and sung as they marched into Canaan. But the song is like no other national anthem. It has virtually no words of encouragement or hope, only doom.

Moses knew that even the promised land would not change his people's ingrained habits of disobeying God. They would fail in the promised land, just as they had failed in the desert. He concluded his farewell speech to the people with these words, "They are not just idle words for you—they are your life" (32:47). And then on that same day he ascended a mountain to die. He had been forbidden by God to cross into Canaan because of his own disobedience.

This sad final scene may have made the strongest impression of all. No one could get away with rebellion against God—not even Moses, "whom the LORD knew face to face" (34:10).

Life Questions: Why do you think the Bible includes accounts of big failures like this? Have you ever experienced a repeated failure: a sin or problem that keeps returning, no matter what you do?

anger and in great wrath the LORD uprooted them from their land and thrust them into another land, as it is now."

²⁹The secret things belong to the LORD our

29:24–29 God's Secrets

"I don't understand why God is doing this," people say. But God hasn't told us everything. Our finite minds could not possibly grasp some things, and other information is simply unnecessary or unhelpful for us to know. What God has told us (in his law, for instance) he intends for us to obey.

God, but the things revealed belong to us and to our children forever, that we may follow all the words of this law.

Prosperity After Turning to the LORD

30 When all these blessings and curses I have set before you come upon you and you take them to heart wherever the LORD your God disperses you among the nations, ²and when you and your children return to the LORD your God and obey him with all your heart and with all your soul according to everything I command you today, ³then the LORD your God will restore your fortunes*ᵃ* and have compassion on you and gather you again from all the nations where he scattered you. ⁴Even if you have been banished to the most distant land under the heavens, from there the LORD your God will gather you and bring you back. ⁵He will bring you to the land that belonged to your fathers, and you will take possession of it. He will make you more prosperous and numerous than your fathers. ⁶The LORD your God will circumcise your hearts and the hearts of your descendants, so that you may love him with all your heart and with all your soul, and live. ⁷The LORD your God will put all these curses on your enemies who hate and persecute you. ⁸You will again obey the LORD and follow all his commands I am giving you today. ⁹Then the LORD your God will make you most prosperous in all the work of your hands and in the fruit of your womb, the young of your livestock and the crops of your land. The LORD will again delight in you and make you prosperous, just as he delighted in your fathers, ¹⁰if you obey the LORD your God and keep his commands and decrees that are written in this Book of the Law and turn to the LORD your God with all your heart and with all your soul.

The Offer of Life or Death

¹¹Now what I am commanding you today is not too difficult for you or beyond your reach. ¹²It is not up in heaven, so that you have to ask, "Who will ascend into heaven to get it and proclaim it to us so we may obey it?" ¹³Nor is it beyond the sea, so that you have to ask, "Who will cross the sea to get it and proclaim it to us so we may obey it?" ¹⁴No, the word is very near you; it is in your mouth and in your heart so you may obey it.

30:14 Keep It Simple

Sometimes people make a relationship with God sound impossibly difficult. Moses emphasizes its simplicity. You don't have to swim oceans or ascend into heaven; you just have to understand, believe, and obey the word God has given. In a famous New Testament passage, the apostle Paul applied this lesson to confessing faith in Jesus Christ (Romans 10:6–10).

¹⁵See, I set before you today life and prosperity, death and destruction. ¹⁶For I command you today to love the LORD your God, to walk in his ways, and to keep his commands, decrees and laws; then you will live and increase, and the LORD your God will bless you in the land you are entering to possess.

¹⁷But if your heart turns away and you are not obedient, and if you are drawn away to bow down to other gods and worship them, ¹⁸I declare to you this day that you will certainly be destroyed. You will not live long in the land you are crossing the Jordan to enter and possess.

¹⁹This day I call heaven and earth as witnesses against you that I have set before you life and death, blessings and curses. Now choose life, so that you and your children may live ²⁰and that you may love the LORD your God, listen to his voice, and hold fast to him. For the LORD is your life, and he will give you many years in the land he swore to give to your fathers, Abraham, Isaac and Jacob.

Joshua to Succeed Moses

31 Then Moses went out and spoke these words to all Israel: ²"I am now a hundred and twenty years old and I am no longer able to lead you. The LORD has said to me, 'You shall not cross the Jordan.' ³The LORD your God himself will cross over ahead of you. He will destroy these nations before you, and you will take possession of their land. Joshua also will cross over ahead of you, as the LORD said. ⁴And the LORD will do to them what he did to Sihon and Og, the kings of the Amorites, whom he destroyed along with

ᵃ3 Or will bring you back from captivity

their land. ⁵The LORD will deliver them to you, and you must do to them all that I have commanded you. ⁶Be strong and courageous. Do not be afraid or terrified because of them, for the LORD your God goes with you; he will never leave you nor forsake you."

⁷Then Moses summoned Joshua and said to him in the presence of all Israel, "Be strong and courageous, for you must go with this people into the land that the LORD swore to their forefathers to give them, and you must divide it among them as their inheritance. ⁸The LORD himself goes before you and will be with you; he will never leave you nor forsake you. Do not be afraid; do not be discouraged."

The Reading of the Law

⁹So Moses wrote down this law and gave it to the priests, the sons of Levi, who carried the ark of the covenant of the LORD, and to all the elders of Israel. ¹⁰Then Moses commanded them: "At the end of every seven years, in the year for canceling debts, during the Feast of Tabernacles, ¹¹when all Israel comes to appear before the LORD your God at the place he will choose, you shall read this law before them in their hearing. ¹²Assemble the people—men, women and children, and the aliens living in your towns—so they can listen and learn to fear the LORD your God and follow carefully all the words of this law. ¹³Their children, who do not know this law, must hear it and learn to fear the LORD your God as long as you live in the land you are crossing the Jordan to possess."

Israel's Rebellion Predicted

¹⁴The LORD said to Moses, "Now the day of your death is near. Call Joshua and present yourselves at the Tent of Meeting, where I will commission him." So Moses and Joshua came and presented themselves at the Tent of Meeting.

¹⁵Then the LORD appeared at the Tent in a pillar of cloud, and the cloud stood over the entrance to the Tent. ¹⁶And the LORD said to Moses: "You are going to rest with your fathers, and these people will soon prostitute themselves to the foreign gods of the land they are entering. They will forsake me and break the covenant I made with them. ¹⁷On that day I will become angry with them and forsake them; I will hide my face from them, and they will be destroyed. Many disasters and difficulties will come upon them, and on that day they will ask, 'Have not these disasters come upon us because our God is not with us?' ¹⁸And I will certainly hide my face on that day because of all their wickedness in turning to other gods.

¹⁹"Now write down for yourselves this song and teach it to the Israelites and have them sing it, so that it may be a witness for me against them. ²⁰When I have brought them into the land flowing with milk and honey, the land I promised on oath to their forefathers, and when they eat their fill and thrive, they will turn to other gods and worship them, rejecting me and breaking my covenant. ²¹And when many disasters and difficulties come upon them, this song will testify against them, because it will not be forgotten by their descendants. I know what they are disposed to do, even before I bring them into the land I promised on oath." ²²So Moses wrote down this song that day and taught it to the Israelites.

²³The LORD gave this command to Joshua son of Nun: "Be strong and courageous, for you will bring the Israelites into the land I promised them on oath, and I myself will be with you."

²⁴After Moses finished writing in a book the words of this law from beginning to end, ²⁵he gave this command to the Levites who carried the ark of the covenant of the LORD: ²⁶"Take this Book of the Law and place it beside the ark of the covenant of the LORD your God. There it will remain as a witness against you. ²⁷For I know how rebellious and stiff-necked you are. If you have been rebellious against the LORD while I am still alive and with you, how much more will you rebel after I die! ²⁸Assemble before me all the elders of your tribes and all your officials, so that I can speak these words in their hearing and call heaven and earth to testify against them. ²⁹For I know that after my death you are sure to become utterly corrupt and to turn from the way I have commanded you. In days to come, disaster will fall upon you because you will do evil in the sight of the LORD and provoke him to anger by what your hands have made."

The Song of Moses

³⁰And Moses recited the words of this song from beginning to end in the hearing of the whole assembly of Israel:

32 Listen, O heavens, and I will speak;
　　hear, O earth, the words of my mouth.
²Let my teaching fall like rain
　　and my words descend like dew,
like showers on new grass,
　　like abundant rain on tender plants.

³I will proclaim the name of the LORD.
　　Oh, praise the greatness of our God!
⁴He is the Rock, his works are perfect,
　　and all his ways are just.
A faithful God who does no wrong,
　　upright and just is he.

⁵They have acted corruptly toward him;
　　to their shame they are no longer his
　　　children,

but a warped and crooked generation.[a]
[6]Is this the way you repay the LORD,
  O foolish and unwise people?
Is he not your Father, your Creator,[b]
  who made you and formed you?

[7]Remember the days of old;
  consider the generations long past.
Ask your father and he will tell you,
  your elders, and they will explain to you.
[8]When the Most High gave the nations their
    inheritance,
  when he divided all mankind,
he set up boundaries for the peoples
  according to the number of the sons of
    Israel.[c]
[9]For the LORD's portion is his people,
  Jacob his allotted inheritance.

[10]In a desert land he found him,
  in a barren and howling waste.
He shielded him and cared for him;
  he guarded him as the apple of his eye,
[11]like an eagle that stirs up its nest
  and hovers over its young,
that spreads its wings to catch them
  and carries them on its pinions.

32:11 Mixed Emotions

*The tender words of the song in this chapter
express God's true love for Israel. And yet the
song contains words of dreadful realism as
well. God knew the Israelites would fail him,
and this song would "testify against them"
when they turned away from him (31:21).
Indeed, the apostle Paul quoted from this in his
agonizing account of Jewish rejection of Jesus
(Romans 10:19).*

[12]The LORD alone led him;
  no foreign god was with him.

[13]He made him ride on the heights of the land
  and fed him with the fruit of the fields.
He nourished him with honey from the rock,
  and with oil from the flinty crag,
[14]with curds and milk from herd and flock
  and with fattened lambs and goats,
with choice rams of Bashan
  and the finest kernels of wheat.
You drank the foaming blood of the grape.

[15]Jeshurun[d] grew fat and kicked;
  filled with food, he became heavy and
    sleek.
He abandoned the God who made him

and rejected the Rock his Savior.
[16]They made him jealous with their foreign
    gods
  and angered him with their detestable
    idols.
[17]They sacrificed to demons, which are not
    God—
  gods they had not known,
  gods that recently appeared,
  gods your fathers did not fear.
[18]You deserted the Rock, who fathered you;
  you forgot the God who gave you birth.

[19]The LORD saw this and rejected them
  because he was angered by his sons and
    daughters.
[20]"I will hide my face from them," he said,
  "and see what their end will be;
for they are a perverse generation,
  children who are unfaithful.
[21]They made me jealous by what is no god
  and angered me with their worthless idols.
I will make them envious by those who are
    not a people;
  I will make them angry by a nation that
    has no understanding.
[22]For a fire has been kindled by my wrath,
  one that burns to the realm of death[e]
    below.
It will devour the earth and its harvests
  and set afire the foundations of the
    mountains.

[23]"I will heap calamities upon them
  and spend my arrows against them.
[24]I will send wasting famine against them,
  consuming pestilence and deadly plague;
I will send against them the fangs of wild
    beasts,
  the venom of vipers that glide in the dust.
[25]In the street the sword will make them
    childless;
  in their homes terror will reign.
Young men and young women will perish,
  infants and gray-haired men.
[26]I said I would scatter them
  and blot out their memory from mankind,
[27]but I dreaded the taunt of the enemy,
  lest the adversary misunderstand
and say, 'Our hand has triumphed;
  the LORD has not done all this.'"

[28]They are a nation without sense,
  there is no discernment in them.
[29]If only they were wise and would understand
    this
  and discern what their end will be!
[30]How could one man chase a thousand,

---

[a]5 Or *Corrupt are they and not his children, / a generation warped and twisted to their shame*   [b]6 Or *Father, who bought you*   [c]8 Masoretic Text; Dead Sea Scrolls (see also Septuagint) *sons of God*   [d]15 *Jeshurun* means *the upright one,* that is, Israel.   [e]22 Hebrew *to Sheol*

or two put ten thousand to flight,
unless their Rock had sold them,
    unless the LORD had given them up?
[31]For their rock is not like our Rock,
    as even our enemies concede.
[32]Their vine comes from the vine of Sodom
    and from the fields of Gomorrah.
Their grapes are filled with poison,
    and their clusters with bitterness.
[33]Their wine is the venom of serpents,
    the deadly poison of cobras.

[34]"Have I not kept this in reserve
    and sealed it in my vaults?
[35]It is mine to avenge; I will repay.
    In due time their foot will slip;
their day of disaster is near
    and their doom rushes upon them."

> ### 32:35 God's Vengeance
> *The New Testament quotes this verse twice, in two very different ways. The apostle Paul emphasized that because vengeance is God's business, not ours, we should never seek revenge (Romans 12:19). But the author of Hebrews also cited these words to highlight the seriousness of rejecting God, who will certainly judge his people (Hebrews 10:30).*

[36]The LORD will judge his people
    and have compassion on his servants
when he sees their strength is gone
    and no one is left, slave or free.
[37]He will say: "Now where are their gods,
    the rock they took refuge in,
[38]the gods who ate the fat of their sacrifices
    and drank the wine of their drink
        offerings?
Let them rise up to help you!
    Let them give you shelter!

[39]"See now that I myself am He!
    There is no god besides me.
I put to death and I bring to life,
    I have wounded and I will heal,
    and no one can deliver out of my hand.
[40]I lift my hand to heaven and declare:
    As surely as I live forever,
[41]when I sharpen my flashing sword
    and my hand grasps it in judgment,
I will take vengeance on my adversaries
    and repay those who hate me.
[42]I will make my arrows drunk with blood,
    while my sword devours flesh:
the blood of the slain and the captives,
    the heads of the enemy leaders."

[43]Rejoice, O nations, with his people,[a,b]
    for he will avenge the blood of his
        servants;
he will take vengeance on his enemies
    and make atonement for his land and
        people.

[44]Moses came with Joshua[c] son of Nun and spoke all the words of this song in the hearing of the people. [45]When Moses finished reciting all these words to all Israel, [46]he said to them, "Take to heart all the words I have solemnly declared to you this day, so that you may command your children to obey carefully all the words of this law. [47]They are not just idle words for you—they are your life. By them you will live long in the land you are crossing the Jordan to possess."

Moses to Die on Mount Nebo

[48]On that same day the LORD told Moses, [49]"Go up into the Abarim Range to Mount Nebo in Moab, across from Jericho, and view Canaan, the land I am giving the Israelites as their own possession. [50]There on the mountain that you have climbed you will die and be gathered to your people, just as your brother Aaron died on Mount Hor and was gathered to his people. [51]This is because both of you broke faith with me in the presence of the Israelites at the waters of Meribah Kadesh in the Desert of Zin and because you did not uphold my holiness among the Israelites. [52]Therefore, you will see the land only from a distance; you will not enter the land I am giving to the people of Israel."

Moses Blesses the Tribes

33 This is the blessing that Moses the man of God pronounced on the Israelites before his death. [2]He said:

"The LORD came from Sinai
    and dawned over them from Seir;
    he shone forth from Mount Paran.
He came with[d] myriads of holy ones

> ### 33:1–29 Dying Words
> *Just before he died, Moses gave a final word to the Israelites, most of whom had lived their entire adult lives under his leadership. Now they would no longer have him to lean on. As they prepared to enter the promised land without him, he bequeathed to them something more valuable than money, stronger than power, deeper than learning: a blessing. Tribe by tribe, Moses spoke of God's personal care and salvation for the people of Israel.*

---

[a]43 Or *Make his people rejoice, O nations*   [b]43 Masoretic Text; Dead Sea Scrolls (see also Septuagint) *people, / and let all the angels worship him /*   [c]44 Hebrew *Hoshea*, a variant of *Joshua*   [d]2 Or *from*

from the south, from his mountain
slopes.[a]
[3]Surely it is you who love the people;
all the holy ones are in your hand.
At your feet they all bow down,
and from you receive instruction,
[4]the law that Moses gave us,
the possession of the assembly of Jacob.
[5]He was king over Jeshurun[b]
when the leaders of the people assembled,
along with the tribes of Israel.

[6]"Let Reuben live and not die,
nor[c] his men be few."

[7]And this he said about Judah:

"Hear, O LORD, the cry of Judah;
bring him to his people.
With his own hands he defends his cause.
Oh, be his help against his foes!"

[8]About Levi he said:

"Your Thummim and Urim belong
to the man you favored.
You tested him at Massah;
you contended with him at the waters of
Meribah.
[9]He said of his father and mother,
'I have no regard for them.'
He did not recognize his brothers
or acknowledge his own children,
but he watched over your word
and guarded your covenant.
[10]He teaches your precepts to Jacob
and your law to Israel.
He offers incense before you
and whole burnt offerings on your altar.
[11]Bless all his skills, O LORD,
and be pleased with the work of his
hands.
Smite the loins of those who rise up against
him;
strike his foes till they rise no more."

[12]About Benjamin he said:

"Let the beloved of the LORD rest secure in
him,
for he shields him all day long,
and the one the LORD loves rests between
his shoulders."

[13]About Joseph he said:

"May the LORD bless his land
with the precious dew from heaven above
and with the deep waters that lie below;
[14]with the best the sun brings forth
and the finest the moon can yield;

[15]with the choicest gifts of the ancient
mountains
and the fruitfulness of the everlasting hills;
[16]with the best gifts of the earth and its
fullness
and the favor of him who dwelt in the
burning bush.
Let all these rest on the head of Joseph,
on the brow of the prince among[d] his
brothers.
[17]In majesty he is like a firstborn bull;
his horns are the horns of a wild ox.
With them he will gore the nations,
even those at the ends of the earth.
Such are the ten thousands of Ephraim;
such are the thousands of Manasseh."

[18]About Zebulun he said:

"Rejoice, Zebulun, in your going out,
and you, Issachar, in your tents.
[19]They will summon peoples to the mountain
and there offer sacrifices of righteousness;
they will feast on the abundance of the seas,
on the treasures hidden in the sand."

[20]About Gad he said:

"Blessed is he who enlarges Gad's domain!
Gad lives there like a lion,
tearing at arm or head.
[21]He chose the best land for himself;
the leader's portion was kept for him.
When the heads of the people assembled,
he carried out the LORD's righteous will,
and his judgments concerning Israel."

[22]About Dan he said:

"Dan is a lion's cub,
springing out of Bashan."

[23]About Naphtali he said:

"Naphtali is abounding with the favor of the
LORD
and is full of his blessing;
he will inherit southward to the lake."

[24]About Asher he said:

"Most blessed of sons is Asher;
let him be favored by his brothers,
and let him bathe his feet in oil.
[25]The bolts of your gates will be iron and
bronze,
and your strength will equal your days.

[26]"There is no one like the God of Jeshurun,
who rides on the heavens to help you
and on the clouds in his majesty.
[27]The eternal God is your refuge,
and underneath are the everlasting arms.

---

[a]2 The meaning of the Hebrew for this phrase is uncertain.
verse 26.   [c]6 Or but let   [d]16 Or of the one separated from

[b]5 Jeshurun means the upright one, that is, Israel; also in

He will drive out your enemy before you,
    saying, 'Destroy him!'
²⁸So Israel will live in safety alone;
    Jacob's spring is secure
in a land of grain and new wine,
    where the heavens drop dew.
²⁹Blessed are you, O Israel!
    Who is like you,
    a people saved by the LORD?
He is your shield and helper
    and your glorious sword.
Your enemies will cower before you,
    and you will trample down their high
        places.ᵃ"

The Death of Moses

34 Then Moses climbed Mount Nebo from the plains of Moab to the top of Pisgah, across from Jericho. There the LORD showed him the whole land—from Gilead to Dan, ²all of Naphtali, the territory of Ephraim and Manasseh, all the land of Judah as far as the western sea,ᵇ ³the Negev and the whole region from the Valley of Jericho, the City of Palms, as far as Zoar. ⁴Then the LORD said to him, "This is the land I promised on oath to Abraham, Isaac and Jacob when I said, 'I will give it to your descendants.' I have let you see it with your eyes, but you will not cross over into it."

⁵And Moses the servant of the LORD died there in Moab, as the LORD had said. ⁶He buried himᶜ in Moab, in the valley opposite Beth Peor, but to this day no one knows where his grave is. ⁷Moses was a hundred and twenty years old when he died, yet his eyes were not weak nor his strength gone. ⁸The Israelites grieved for Moses in the plains of Moab thirty days, until the time of weeping and mourning was over.

34:5 Moses Gets a Preview

To his great disappointment, Moses could not lead his people into the new land, for reasons mentioned in 32:48–52. But God allowed him a final look over all the promised land. And, in a very unexpected way, Moses did realize his dream of setting foot in the promised land. Over a thousand years later, he returned with the prophet Elijah and visited with Jesus on the Mount of Transfiguration (Matthew 17; Mark 9; Luke 9).

⁹Now Joshua son of Nun was filled with the spiritᵈ of wisdom because Moses had laid his hands on him. So the Israelites listened to him and did what the LORD had commanded Moses. ¹⁰Since then, no prophet has risen in Israel like Moses, whom the LORD knew face to face, ¹¹who did all those miraculous signs and wonders the LORD sent him to do in Egypt—to Pharaoh and to all his officials and to his whole land. ¹²For no one has ever shown the mighty power or performed the awesome deeds that Moses did in the sight of all Israel.

ᵃ29 Or *will tread upon their bodies*   ᵇ2 That is, the Mediterranean   ᶜ6 Or *He was buried*   ᵈ9 Or *Spirit*

JOSHUA

The Difference 40 Years Can Make
They faced overwhelming odds with renewed hope

"Do not be terrified; do not be discouraged, for the LORD your God will be with you wherever you go." 1:9

ON THE SURFACE, NOT MUCH had changed in 40 years. The band of refugees amassing beside the Jordan River greatly resembled a similar horde from four decades before. They had panicked once. Would they again?

The Israelites still faced overwhelming odds. They had no chariots or even horses. They had only primitive arms, an untested new leader, and long-delayed marching orders from God.

A New Spirit, a New Leader

Yet, in another sense, everything had changed. Older Israelites with fearful, slave mentalities had died off in the desert—all the older generation except Joshua and Caleb, two legendary warriors. The new generation had decided to trust God, no matter what. In stark contrast to the spies in Numbers (13:31–33), Joshua's scouts brought back this report, "The LORD has surely given the whole land into our hands; all the people are melting in fear because of us" (2:24).

The book of Joshua contains not a word about rebellion against a leader or grumbling against God. It is a good news book, a welcome relief from the discouraging tone of Numbers and the fatalism of Deuteronomy. What a difference 40 years had made!

As newly appointed leader of the Israelites, Joshua took on two main tasks. First, he was to direct a military campaign to take control of the land God had promised. Then, he would parcel out the conquered land among all the tribes.

Learning to Follow Instructions

Once inside Canaan, the Israelites followed God's instructions precisely, even when doing so must have strained their faith to new limits. The residents of Jericho had shut themselves behind stone walls, awaiting the onslaught of the feared Israelites. But how did the Israelites spend their first week in Canaan? They built a stone monument to God, performed circumcision rituals, and held a Passover celebration. No conquering army had ever behaved in such a manner.

Everything in Joshua seems handpicked to strike home the point that God was really in charge. Covering a period of approximately seven years, Joshua's 24 chapters devote only a few sentences to some extensive military campaigns (see chapters 10—11). But key events, such as the fall of Jericho, get detailed coverage, underscoring that the Israelites succeeded when they relied on God, not on military might. The few negative stories (such as the battle of Ai and the trick of the Gibeonites) show what happened when the Israelites did not seek God's will.

A Book of Hope

The Bible does not give history for its own sake. Rather, it presents practical and spiritual lessons. Fortunately, Joshua's lessons are overwhelmingly positive ones. Guided by God, the nation of Israel met with unprecedented success. In fact, the book concludes that "not one of all the LORD's good promises to the house of Israel failed; every one was fulfilled" (21:45).

The book of Joshua gives a fresh breeze of hope. Writers of hymns and spirituals have often gone back to it to try to recapture the spirit of success that swept over God's people those first few years in the new land. It *can* work: people can follow God. Joshua shows how.

How to Read Joshua

P hrases in the first two paragraphs of Joshua hint at the tone to follow. "I will never leave you nor forsake you," God promised. "I will give you every place where you set your foot." "Be careful to obey all the law my servant Moses gave you . . . that you may be successful wherever you go."

Often the Israelites offer examples of what *not* to do. Already the books of Exodus, Numbers, and Deuteronomy have given negative examples, and the historical books to follow will describe further failures in lurid detail. But the Old Testament does offer a few bright spots of hope, the book of Joshua being one of the brightest.

(The "good news" character of Joshua causes some people to compare it to the New Testament books of Ephesians and Philippians, which share its success-and-triumph tone. You may want to read one of those New Testament books along with Joshua.)

Fast-paced battle action appears in chapters 1–11, "the book of war." The latter chapters, "the book of distribution," mostly concern the parceling out of the land.

You can casually read about the military campaigns of Joshua, but to truly appreciate them you must study a map or Bible atlas. Joshua is a very geographical book. Place-names appear in every chapter, describing the military progress and also the division of the land among the tribes of Israel.

As you read Joshua, keep two major themes in mind: Joshua's leadership and God's direct involvement in history. Study Joshua's life as an example of leadership. What were the reasons behind his few failures, such as those recorded in chapters 7 and 9? You may also want to refer to the background passages on his life in Exodus (17,24,32,33) and Numbers (11,13,26). What lesson did Joshua learn at each of these key moments?

PEOPLE YOU'LL MEET IN JOSHUA

RAHAB *(p. 244)*
JOSHUA *(p. 263)*

3-TRACK READING PLAN

For an explanation and complete listing of the 3-track reading plan, turn to page 7.

TRACK 1: *Two-Week Courses on the Bible*
See page 7 for information on these courses.

TRACK 2: *An Overview of Joshua in 4 Days*
☐ Day 1. Read the Introduction to Joshua and then chapter 2, the story of Rahab and the spies.
☐ Day 2. Read the story of Jericho in chapter 6; the Israelites practiced very unorthodox military tactics, but learned to rely on God.
☐ Day 3. Success at Jericho immediately preceded a great failure; read about it in chapter 7.
☐ Day 4. Read chapter 24, part of Joshua's stirring farewell speech to the nation he led so well.

Now turn to page 9 for your next Track 2 reading project.

TRACK 3: *All of Joshua in 21 Days*
After you have read through Joshua, turn to pages 10–14 for your next Track 3 reading project.

☐1	☐2	☐3	☐4	☐5	☐6	☐7	☐8
☐9	☐10	☐11	☐12–13	☐14–15	☐16–17	☐18	☐19
☐20	☐21	☐22	☐23	☐24			

The LORD Commands Joshua

1 After the death of Moses the servant of the LORD, the LORD said to Joshua son of Nun, Moses' aide: ²"Moses my servant is dead. Now then, you and all these people, get ready to cross the Jordan River into the land I am about to give to them—to the Israelites. ³I will give you every place where you set your foot, as I promised Moses. ⁴Your territory will extend from the desert to Lebanon, and from the great river, the Euphrates—all the Hittite country—to the Great Sea*ᵃ* on the west. ⁵No one will be able to stand up against you all the days of your life. As I was with Moses, so I will be with you; I will never leave you nor forsake you.

⁶"Be strong and courageous, because you will lead these people to inherit the land I swore to their forefathers to give them. ⁷Be strong and very courageous. Be careful to obey all the law my servant Moses gave you; do not turn from it to the right or to the left, that you may be successful wherever you go. ⁸Do not let this Book of the Law depart from your mouth; meditate on it day and night, so that you may be careful to do everything written in it. Then you will be pros-

1:8 Secret of Success

Three times in this short speech God urged Joshua to "be strong and courageous." Joshua must have quaked at the prospect of taking over for a great man like Moses. But God promised him the resources he needed: God's own presence (verse 5) and the Book of the Law, which Joshua was to lean on every day.

perous and successful. ⁹Have I not commanded you? Be strong and courageous. Do not be terrified; do not be discouraged, for the LORD your God will be with you wherever you go."

¹⁰So Joshua ordered the officers of the people: ¹¹"Go through the camp and tell the people, 'Get your supplies ready. Three days from now you will cross the Jordan here to go in and take possession of the land the LORD your God is giving you for your own.'"

¹²But to the Reubenites, the Gadites and the half-tribe of Manasseh, Joshua said, ¹³"Remember the command that Moses the servant of the LORD gave you: 'The LORD your God is giving you rest and has granted you this land.' ¹⁴Your wives, your children and your livestock may stay in the land that Moses gave you east of the Jordan, but all your fighting men, fully armed, must cross over ahead of your brothers. You are to help your

brothers ¹⁵until the LORD gives them rest, as he has done for you, and until they too have taken possession of the land that the LORD your God is giving them. After that, you may go back and occupy your own land, which Moses the servant of the LORD gave you east of the Jordan toward the sunrise."

¹⁶Then they answered Joshua, "Whatever you have commanded us we will do, and wherever you send us we will go. ¹⁷Just as we fully obeyed Moses, so we will obey you. Only may the LORD your God be with you as he was with Moses. ¹⁸Whoever rebels against your word and does not obey your words, whatever you may command them, will be put to death. Only be strong and courageous!"

Rahab and the Spies

2 Then Joshua son of Nun secretly sent two spies from Shittim. "Go, look over the land," he said, "especially Jericho." So they went and entered the house of a prostitute*ᵇ* named Rahab and stayed there.

²The king of Jericho was told, "Look! Some of the Israelites have come here tonight to spy out the land." ³So the king of Jericho sent this message to Rahab: "Bring out the men who came to you and entered your house, because they have come to spy out the whole land."

⁴But the woman had taken the two men and hidden them. She said, "Yes, the men came to me, but I did not know where they had come from. ⁵At dusk, when it was time to close the city gate, the men left. I don't know which way they went. Go after them quickly. You may catch up with them." ⁶(But she had taken them up to the roof and hidden them under the stalks of flax she had laid out on the roof.) ⁷So the men set out in pursuit of the spies on the road that leads to the fords of the Jordan, and as soon as the pursuers had gone out, the gate was shut.

⁸Before the spies lay down for the night, she went up on the roof ⁹and said to them, "I know that the LORD has given this land to you and that a great fear of you has fallen on us, so that all who live in this country are melting in fear because of you. ¹⁰We have heard how the LORD dried up the water of the Red Sea*ᶜ* for you when you came out of Egypt, and what you did to Sihon and Og, the two kings of the Amorites east of the Jordan, whom you completely destroyed.*ᵈ* ¹¹When we heard of it, our hearts melted and everyone's courage failed because of you, for the LORD your God is God in heaven above and on the earth below. ¹²Now then, please swear to me by the LORD that you will show kindness to my family, because I have shown kindness to you. Give me

---

ᵃ4 That is, the Mediterranean   *ᵇ1* Or possibly *an innkeeper*   *ᶜ10* Hebrew *Yam Suph*; that is, Sea of Reeds
ᵈ10 The Hebrew term refers to the irrevocable giving over of things or persons to the LORD, often by totally destroying them.

a sure sign [13]that you will spare the lives of my father and mother, my brothers and sisters, and all who belong to them, and that you will save us from death."

[14]"Our lives for your lives!" the men assured her. "If you don't tell what we are doing, we will treat you kindly and faithfully when the LORD gives us the land."

[15]So she let them down by a rope through the window, for the house she lived in was part of the city wall. [16]Now she had said to them, "Go to the hills so the pursuers will not find you. Hide yourselves there three days until they return, and then go on your way."

[17]The men said to her, "This oath you made us swear will not be binding on us [18]unless, when we enter the land, you have tied this scarlet cord in the window through which you let us down, and unless you have brought your father and mother, your brothers and all your family into your house. [19]If anyone goes outside your house into the street, his blood will be on his own head; we will not be responsible. As for anyone who is in the house with you, his blood will be on our head if a hand is laid on him. [20]But if you tell what we are doing, we will be released from the oath you made us swear."

[21]"Agreed," she replied. "Let it be as you say." So she sent them away and they departed. And she tied the scarlet cord in the window.

[22]When they left, they went into the hills and stayed there three days, until the pursuers had searched all along the road and returned without finding them. [23]Then the two men started back. They went down out of the hills, forded the river and came to Joshua son of Nun and told him everything that had happened to them. [24]They said to Joshua, "The LORD has surely given the whole land into our hands; all the people are melting in fear because of us."

Crossing the Jordan

3 Early in the morning Joshua and all the Israelites set out from Shittim and went to the Jordan, where they camped before crossing over. [2]After three days the officers went throughout the camp, [3]giving orders to the people: "When you see the ark of the covenant of the LORD your God, and the priests, who are Levites, carrying it, you are to move out from your positions and follow it. [4]Then you will know which way to go, since you have never been this way before. But keep a distance of about a thousand yards[a] between you and the ark; do not go near it."

[5]Joshua told the people, "Consecrate yourselves, for tomorrow the LORD will do amazing things among you."

[6]Joshua said to the priests, "Take up the ark of the covenant and pass on ahead of the people." So they took it up and went ahead of them.

[7]And the LORD said to Joshua, "Today I will begin to exalt you in the eyes of all Israel, so they may know that I am with you as I was with Moses. [8]Tell the priests who carry the ark of the covenant: 'When you reach the edge of the Jordan's waters, go and stand in the river.'"

[9]Joshua said to the Israelites, "Come here and listen to the words of the LORD your God. [10]This is how you will know that the living God is among you and that he will certainly drive out before you the Canaanites, Hittites, Hivites, Perizzites, Girgashites, Amorites and Jebusites. [11]See, the ark of the covenant of the Lord of all the earth will go into the Jordan ahead of you. [12]Now then, choose twelve men from the tribes of Israel, one from each tribe. [13]And as soon as the priests who carry the ark of the LORD—the Lord of all the earth—set foot in the Jordan, its waters flowing downstream will be cut off and stand up in a heap."

[14]So when the people broke camp to cross the Jordan, the priests carrying the ark of the covenant went ahead of them. [15]Now the Jordan is at flood stage all during harvest. Yet as soon as the priests who carried the ark reached the Jordan and their feet touched the water's edge, [16]the water from upstream stopped flowing. It piled up in a heap a great distance away, at a town called Adam in the vicinity of Zarethan, while the water flowing down to the Sea of the Arabah (the Salt Sea [b]) was completely cut off. So the people crossed over opposite Jericho. [17]The priests who carried the ark of the covenant of the LORD stood firm on dry ground in the middle of the Jordan, while all Israel passed by until the whole nation had completed the crossing on dry ground.

4 When the whole nation had finished crossing the Jordan, the LORD said to Joshua, [2]"Choose twelve men from among the people, one from each tribe, [3]and tell them to take up twelve stones from the middle of the Jordan from right where the priests stood and to carry them

---

[a]4 Hebrew *about two thousand cubits* (about 900 meters)   [b]16 That is, the Dead Sea

over with you and put them down at the place where you stay tonight."

4So Joshua called together the twelve men he had appointed from the Israelites, one from each

---

3:16 Stopping the Jordan River

A 1927 earthquake caused the 40-foot clay banks of the Jordan River to collapse, totally damming the Jordan for 21 hours. Whatever means God used to allow the Israelites to cross, this miracle in Joshua achieved a similar result during the river's swollen flood stage. The miracle echoed the crossing of the Red Sea 40 years before, helping to establish Joshua as a worthy successor to Moses. Joshua and the Israelites crossed at a location very close to where Jesus was later baptized.

---

tribe, 5and said to them, "Go over before the ark of the LORD your God into the middle of the Jordan. Each of you is to take up a stone on his shoulder, according to the number of the tribes of the Israelites, 6to serve as a sign among you. In the future, when your children ask you, 'What do these stones mean?' 7tell them that the flow of the Jordan was cut off before the ark of the covenant of the LORD. When it crossed the Jordan, the waters of the Jordan were cut off. These stones are to be a memorial to the people of Israel forever."

8So the Israelites did as Joshua commanded them. They took twelve stones from the middle of the Jordan, according to the number of the tribes of the Israelites, as the LORD had told Joshua; and they carried them over with them to their camp, where they put them down. 9Joshua set up the twelve stones that had been[a] in the middle of the Jordan at the spot where the priests who carried the ark of the covenant had stood. And they are there to this day.

10Now the priests who carried the ark remained standing in the middle of the Jordan until everything the LORD had commanded Joshua was done by the people, just as Moses had directed Joshua. The people hurried over, 11and as soon as all of them had crossed, the ark of the LORD and the priests came to the other side while the people watched. 12The men of Reuben, Gad and the half-tribe of Manasseh crossed over, armed, in front of the Israelites, as Moses had directed them. 13About forty thousand armed for battle crossed over before the LORD to the plains of Jericho for war.

14That day the LORD exalted Joshua in the sight

of all Israel; and they revered him all the days of his life, just as they had revered Moses.

15Then the LORD said to Joshua, 16"Command the priests carrying the ark of the Testimony to come up out of the Jordan."

17So Joshua commanded the priests, "Come up out of the Jordan."

18And the priests came up out of the river carrying the ark of the covenant of the LORD. No sooner had they set their feet on the dry ground than the waters of the Jordan returned to their place and ran at flood stage as before.

19On the tenth day of the first month the people went up from the Jordan and camped at Gilgal on the eastern border of Jericho. 20And Joshua set up at Gilgal the twelve stones they had taken out of the Jordan. 21He said to the Israelites, "In the future when your descendants ask their fathers, 'What do these stones mean?' 22tell them, 'Israel crossed the Jordan on dry ground.' 23For the LORD your God dried up the Jordan before you until you had crossed over. The LORD your God did to the Jordan just what he had done to the Red Sea[b] when he dried it up before us until we had crossed over. 24He did this so that all the peoples of the earth might know that the hand of the LORD is powerful and so that you might always fear the LORD your God."

Circumcision at Gilgal

5 Now when all the Amorite kings west of the Jordan and all the Canaanite kings along the coast heard how the LORD had dried up the Jordan before the Israelites until we had crossed over, their hearts melted and they no longer had the courage to face the Israelites.

2At that time the LORD said to Joshua, "Make flint knives and circumcise the Israelites again." 3So Joshua made flint knives and circumcised the Israelites at Gibeath Haaraloth.[c]

4Now this is why he did so: All those who came out of Egypt—all the men of military age—died in the desert on the way after leaving Egypt. 5All the people that came out had been circumcised, but all the people born in the desert during the journey from Egypt had not. 6The Israelites had moved about in the desert forty years until all the men who were of military age when they left Egypt had died, since they had not obeyed the LORD. For the LORD had sworn to them that they would not see the land that he had solemnly promised their fathers to give us, a land flowing with milk and honey. 7So he raised up their sons in their place, and these were the ones Joshua circumcised. They were still uncircumcised because they had not been circumcised on the way. 8And after the whole nation had been

---

[a]9 Or *Joshua also set up twelve stones*   [b]23 Hebrew *Yam Suph*; that is, Sea of Reeds   [c]3 *Gibeath Haaraloth* means *hill of foreskins.*

circumcised, they remained where they were in camp until they were healed.

[9]Then the LORD said to Joshua, "Today I have rolled away the reproach of Egypt from you." So the place has been called Gilgal[a] to this day.

[10]On the evening of the fourteenth day of the month, while camped at Gilgal on the plains of Jericho, the Israelites celebrated the Passover. [11]The day after the Passover, that very day, they ate some of the produce of the land: unleavened bread and roasted grain. [12]The manna stopped the day after[b] they ate this food from the land; there was no longer any manna for the Israelites, but that year they ate of the produce of Canaan.

5:12 No More Free Lunch

For 40 years God had provided manna, a miraculous food that appeared like dew on the ground every night. In the desert, manna had been necessary for survival. In Palestine, however, the free food stopped. Israelites would be able to grow or gather adequate food for themselves.

The Fall of Jericho

[13]Now when Joshua was near Jericho, he looked up and saw a man standing in front of him with a drawn sword in his hand. Joshua went up to him and asked, "Are you for us or for our enemies?"

[14]"Neither," he replied, "but as commander of the army of the LORD I have now come." Then Joshua fell facedown to the ground in reverence, and asked him, "What message does my Lord[c] have for his servant?"

[15]The commander of the LORD's army replied, "Take off your sandals, for the place where you are standing is holy." And Joshua did so.

6 Now Jericho was tightly shut up because of the Israelites. No one went out and no one came in.

[2]Then the LORD said to Joshua, "See, I have delivered Jericho into your hands, along with its king and its fighting men. [3]March around the city once with all the armed men. Do this for six days. [4]Have seven priests carry trumpets of rams' horns in front of the ark. On the seventh day, march around the city seven times, with the priests blowing the trumpets. [5]When you hear them sound a long blast on the trumpets, have all the people give a loud shout; then the wall of the city will collapse and the people will go up, every man straight in."

[6]So Joshua son of Nun called the priests and said to them, "Take up the ark of the covenant of the LORD and have seven priests carry trumpets in front of it." [7]And he ordered the people, "Advance! March around the city, with the armed guard going ahead of the ark of the LORD."

[8]When Joshua had spoken to the people, the seven priests carrying the seven trumpets before the LORD went forward, blowing their trumpets, and the ark of the LORD's covenant followed them. [9]The armed guard marched ahead of the priests who blew the trumpets, and the rear guard followed the ark. All this time the trumpets were sounding. [10]But Joshua had commanded the people, "Do not give a war cry, do not raise your voices, do not say a word until the day I tell you to shout. Then shout!" [11]So he had the ark of the LORD carried around the city, circling it once. Then the people returned to camp and spent the night there.

[12]Joshua got up early the next morning and the priests took up the ark of the LORD. [13]The seven priests carrying the seven trumpets went forward, marching before the ark of the LORD and blowing the trumpets. The armed men went ahead of them and the rear guard followed the ark of the LORD, while the trumpets kept sounding. [14]So on the second day they marched around the city once and returned to the camp. They did this for six days.

[15]On the seventh day, they got up at daybreak and marched around the city seven times in the same manner, except that on that day they circled the city seven times. [16]The seventh time around, when the priests sounded the trumpet blast, Joshua commanded the people, "Shout! For the LORD has given you the city! [17]The city and all that is in it are to be devoted[d] to the LORD. Only Rahab the prostitute[e] and all who are with her in her house shall be spared, because she hid the spies we sent. [18]But keep away from the devoted things, so that you will not bring about your own destruction by taking any of them. Otherwise you will make the camp of Israel liable to destruction and bring trouble on it. [19]All the silver and gold and the articles of bronze and iron are sacred to the LORD and must go into his treasury."

[20]When the trumpets sounded, the people shouted, and at the sound of the trumpet, when the people gave a loud shout, the wall collapsed; so every man charged straight in, and they took the city. [21]They devoted the city to the LORD and destroyed with the sword every living thing in it—men and women, young and old, cattle, sheep and donkeys.

[22]Joshua said to the two men who had spied out the land, "Go into the prostitute's house and

---

[a]9 *Gilgal* sounds like the Hebrew for *roll.*   [b]12 Or *the day*   [c]14 Or *lord*   [d]17 The Hebrew term refers to the irrevocable giving over of things or persons to the LORD, often by totally destroying them; also in verses 18 and 21.   [e]17 Or possibly *innkeeper*; also in verses 22 and 25

bring her out and all who belong to her, in accordance with your oath to her." ²³So the young men who had done the spying went in and brought out Rahab, her father and mother and brothers and all who belonged to her. They brought out her entire family and put them in a place outside the camp of Israel.

²⁴Then they burned the whole city and everything in it, but they put the silver and gold and the articles of bronze and iron into the treasury of the LORD's house. ²⁵But Joshua spared Rahab the prostitute, with her family and all who belonged to her, because she hid the men Joshua had sent as spies to Jericho—and she lives among the Israelites to this day.

²⁶At that time Joshua pronounced this solemn oath: "Cursed before the LORD is the man who undertakes to rebuild this city, Jericho:

"At the cost of his firstborn son
    will he lay its foundations;
at the cost of his youngest
    will he set up its gates."

6:26 Cursed City

Joshua's curse was fulfilled literally when a man attempted to rebuild the city of Jericho in the days of King Ahab (see 1 Kings 16:34).

²⁷So the LORD was with Joshua, and his fame spread throughout the land.

Achan's Sin

7 But the Israelites acted unfaithfully in regard to the devoted things*a*; Achan son of Carmi, the son of Zimri,*b* the son of Zerah, of the tribe of Judah, took some of them. So the LORD's anger burned against Israel.

²Now Joshua sent men from Jericho to Ai, which is near Beth Aven to the east of Bethel, and told them, "Go up and spy out the region." So the men went up and spied out Ai.

³When they returned to Joshua, they said, "Not all the people will have to go up against Ai. Send two or three thousand men to take it and do not weary all the people, for only a few men are there." ⁴So about three thousand men went up; but they were routed by the men of Ai, ⁵who killed about thirty-six of them. They chased the Israelites from the city gate as far as the stone quarries*c* and struck them down on the slopes. At this the hearts of the people melted and became like water.

⁶Then Joshua tore his clothes and fell facedown to the ground before the ark of the LORD, remaining there till evening. The elders of Israel did the same, and sprinkled dust on their heads. ⁷And Joshua said, "Ah, Sovereign LORD, why did you ever bring this people across the Jordan to deliver us into the hands of the Amorites to destroy us? If only we had been content to stay on the other side of the Jordan! ⁸O Lord, what can I say, now that Israel has been routed by its enemies? ⁹The Canaanites and the other people of the country will hear about this and they will surround us and wipe out our name from the earth. What then will you do for your own great name?"

¹⁰The LORD said to Joshua, "Stand up! What are you doing down on your face? ¹¹Israel has sinned; they have violated my covenant, which I commanded them to keep. They have taken

*a1 The Hebrew term refers to the irrevocable giving over of things or persons to the LORD, often by totally destroying them; also in verses 11, 12, 13 and 15.   *b1 See Septuagint and 1 Chron. 2:6; Hebrew Zabdi; also in verses 17 and 18.
c5 Or as far as Shebarim

RAHAB   *A Prostitute's Faith*

PEOPLE WHO STUDY THE BIBLE are often surprised to find a prostitute held up as an example of faith. In two separate places the New Testament commends the prostitute named Rahab. The writers pass over both her profession and the lie that she told the king of Jericho (2:4–5). Her vision is what they admire. Rahab saw things differently than every one else in her community, and she gambled her future on that vision.

Word of the Israelites' amazing successes had spread. According to Rahab, the residents of Jericho were "melting in fear" at the news of Israel's triumphs over Egypt and other nations. Yet the people of Jericho determined all the more to dig in and fight. Rahab took the opposite course: She decided to join the opposition. Concluding that Israel's God was the real God, she chose to switch to his side.

Perhaps her social position—a prostitute living on the margins of society—made it easier for Rahab to take a stand against her own people. (Centuries later people on the margins of respectability often accepted Jesus, too.) Regardless, because she risked her neck to save the Israelite spies, they made sure that she and her entire family survived the assault.

Life Questions: Do you know anyone with real vision? If so, what do they see that others don't?

some of the devoted things; they have stolen, they have lied, they have put them with their own possessions. [12]That is why the Israelites cannot stand against their enemies; they turn their backs

and run because they have been made liable to destruction. I will not be with you anymore unless you destroy whatever among you is devoted to destruction.

[13]"Go, consecrate the people. Tell them, 'Consecrate yourselves in preparation for tomorrow; for this is what the LORD, the God of Israel, says: That which is devoted is among you, O Israel. You cannot stand against your enemies until you remove it.

[14]"'In the morning, present yourselves tribe by tribe. The tribe that the LORD takes shall come forward clan by clan; the clan that the LORD takes shall come forward family by family; and the family that the LORD takes shall come forward man by man. [15]He who is caught with the devoted things shall be destroyed by fire, along with all that belongs to him. He has violated the covenant of the LORD and has done a disgraceful thing in Israel!'"

[16]Early the next morning Joshua had Israel come forward by tribes, and Judah was taken. [17]The clans of Judah came forward, and he took the Zerahites. He had the clan of the Zerahites come forward by families, and Zimri was taken. [18]Joshua had his family come forward man by man, and Achan son of Carmi, the son of Zimri, the son of Zerah, of the tribe of Judah, was taken.

[19]Then Joshua said to Achan, "My son, give glory to the LORD,[a] the God of Israel, and give him the praise.[b] Tell me what you have done; do not hide it from me."

[20]Achan replied, "It is true! I have sinned against the LORD, the God of Israel. This is what I have done: [21]When I saw in the plunder a beautiful robe from Babylonia,[c] two hundred shekels[d] of silver and a wedge of gold weighing fifty shekels,[e] I coveted them and took them. They are hidden in the ground inside my tent, with the silver underneath."

[22]So Joshua sent messengers, and they ran to the tent, and there it was, hidden in his tent, with the silver underneath. [23]They took the things from the tent, brought them to Joshua and all the Israelites and spread them out before the LORD.

[24]Then Joshua, together with all Israel, took Achan son of Zerah, the silver, the robe, the gold wedge, his sons and daughters, his cattle, donkeys and sheep, his tent and all that he had, to the Valley of Achor. [25]Joshua said, "Why have you brought this trouble on us? The LORD will bring trouble on you today."

Then all Israel stoned him, and after they had stoned the rest, they burned them. [26]Over Achan they heaped up a large pile of rocks, which remains to this day. Then the LORD turned from his fierce anger. Therefore that place has been called the Valley of Achor[f] ever since.

Ai Destroyed

8 Then the LORD said to Joshua, "Do not be afraid; do not be discouraged. Take the whole army with you, and go up and attack Ai. For I have delivered into your hands the king of Ai, his people, his city and his land. [2]You shall do to Ai and its king as you did to Jericho and its king, except that you may carry off their plunder and livestock for yourselves. Set an ambush behind the city."

[3]So Joshua and the whole army moved out to attack Ai. He chose thirty thousand of his best fighting men and sent them out at night [4]with these orders: "Listen carefully. You are to set an ambush behind the city. Don't go very far from

[a]19 A solemn charge to tell the truth   [b]19 Or *and confess to him*   [c]21 Hebrew *Shinar*   [d]21 That is, about 5 pounds (about 2.3 kilograms)   [e]21 That is, about 1 1/4 pounds (about 0.6 kilogram)   [f]26 *Achor* means *trouble.*

it. All of you be on the alert. [5]I and all those with me will advance on the city, and when the men come out against us, as they did before, we will flee from them. [6]They will pursue us until we have lured them away from the city, for they will say, 'They are running away from us as they did before.' So when we flee from them, [7]you are to rise up from ambush and take the city. The LORD your God will give it into your hand. [8]When you have taken the city, set it on fire. Do what the LORD has commanded. See to it; you have my orders."

[9]Then Joshua sent them off, and they went to the place of ambush and lay in wait between Bethel and Ai, to the west of Ai—but Joshua spent that night with the people.

[10]Early the next morning Joshua mustered his men, and he and the leaders of Israel marched before them to Ai. [11]The entire force that was with him marched up and approached the city and arrived in front of it. They set up camp north of Ai, with the valley between them and the city. [12]Joshua had taken about five thousand men and set them in ambush between Bethel and Ai, to the west of the city. [13]They had the soldiers take up their positions—all those in the camp to the north of the city and the ambush to the west of it. That night Joshua went into the valley.

[14]When the king of Ai saw this, he and all the men of the city hurried out early in the morning to meet Israel in battle at a certain place overlooking the Arabah. But he did not know that an ambush had been set against him behind the city. [15]Joshua and all Israel let themselves be driven back before them, and they fled toward the desert. [16]All the men of Ai were called to pursue them, and they pursued Joshua and were lured away from the city. [17]Not a man remained in Ai or Bethel who did not go after Israel. They left the city open and went in pursuit of Israel.

[18]Then the LORD said to Joshua, "Hold out toward Ai the javelin that is in your hand, for into your hand I will deliver the city." So Joshua held out his javelin toward Ai. [19]As soon as he did this, the men in the ambush rose quickly from their position and rushed forward. They entered the city and captured it and quickly set it on fire.

[20]The men of Ai looked back and saw the smoke of the city rising against the sky, but they had no chance to escape in any direction, for the Israelites who had been fleeing toward the desert had turned back against their pursuers. [21]For when Joshua and all Israel saw that the ambush had taken the city and that smoke was going up from the city, they turned around and attacked the men of Ai. [22]The men of the ambush also came out of the city against them, so that they were caught in the middle, with Israelites on both sides. Israel cut them down, leaving them neither survivors nor fugitives. [23]But they took the king of Ai alive and brought him to Joshua.

[24]When Israel had finished killing all the men of Ai in the fields and in the desert where they had chased them, and when every one of them had been put to the sword, all the Israelites returned to Ai and killed those who were in it. [25]Twelve thousand men and women fell that day—all the people of Ai. [26]For Joshua did not draw back the hand that held out his javelin until he had destroyed[a] all who lived in Ai. [27]But Israel did carry off for themselves the livestock and plunder of this city, as the LORD had instructed Joshua.

[28]So Joshua burned Ai and made it a permanent heap of ruins, a desolate place to this day. [29]He hung the king of Ai on a tree and left him there until evening. At sunset, Joshua ordered them to take his body from the tree and throw it down at the entrance of the city gate. And they raised a large pile of rocks over it, which remains to this day.

The Covenant Renewed at Mount Ebal

[30]Then Joshua built on Mount Ebal an altar to

8:30–34 Blessings and Curses

The scene in this section, which describes the carrying out of Moses' instructions in Deuteronomy 27–28, was a profoundly symbolic event in the history of the Israelites. It elaborately portrayed what would happen if they obeyed the covenant, and if they disobeyed. The two mountains, Ebal and Gerizim, formed a natural amphitheater ideal for such a public ceremony. From their peaks much of the promised land could be seen. (Mount Gerizim eventually became the seat of worship for the Samaritans, which helps explain Jesus' conversation in John 4.)

the LORD, the God of Israel, [31]as Moses the servant of the LORD had commanded the Israelites. He built it according to what is written in the Book of the Law of Moses—an altar of uncut stones, on which no iron tool had been used. On it they offered to the LORD burnt offerings and sacrificed fellowship offerings.[b] [32]There, in the presence of the Israelites, Joshua copied on stones the law of Moses, which he had written. [33]All Israel, aliens and citizens alike, with their elders, officials and judges, were standing on both sides of the ark of the covenant of the LORD,

---

[a]26 The Hebrew term refers to the irrevocable giving over of things or persons to the LORD, often by totally destroying them.   [b]31 Traditionally *peace offerings*

facing those who carried it—the priests, who were Levites. Half of the people stood in front of Mount Gerizim and half of them in front of Mount Ebal, as Moses the servant of the LORD had formerly commanded when he gave instructions to bless the people of Israel.

34Afterward, Joshua read all the words of the law—the blessings and the curses—just as it is written in the Book of the Law. **35**There was not a word of all that Moses had commanded that Joshua did not read to the whole assembly of Israel, including the women and children, and the aliens who lived among them.

The Gibeonite Deception

9 Now when all the kings west of the Jordan heard about these things—those in the hill country, in the western foothills, and along the entire coast of the Great Sea*a* as far as Lebanon (the kings of the Hittites, Amorites, Canaanites, Perizzites, Hivites and Jebusites)— **2**they came together to make war against Joshua and Israel.

3However, when the people of Gibeon heard what Joshua had done to Jericho and Ai, **4**they resorted to a ruse: They went as a delegation whose donkeys were loaded*b* with worn-out sacks and old wineskins, cracked and mended. **5**The men put worn and patched sandals on their feet and wore old clothes. All the bread of their food supply was dry and moldy. **6**Then they went to Joshua in the camp at Gilgal and said to him and the men of Israel, "We have come from a distant country; make a treaty with us."

7The men of Israel said to the Hivites, "But perhaps you live near us. How then can we make a treaty with you?"

8"We are your servants," they said to Joshua. But Joshua asked, "Who are you and where do you come from?"

9They answered: "Your servants have come from a very distant country because of the fame of the LORD your God. For we have heard reports of him: all that he did in Egypt, **10**and all that he did to the two kings of the Amorites east of the Jordan—Sihon king of Heshbon, and Og king of Bashan, who reigned in Ashtaroth. **11**And our elders and all those living in our country said to us, 'Take provisions for your journey; go and meet them and say to them, "We are your servants; make a treaty with us." ' **12**This bread of ours was warm when we packed it at home on the day we left to come to you. But now see how dry and moldy it is. **13**And these wineskins that we filled were new, but see how cracked they are. And our clothes and sandals are worn out by the very long journey."

14The men of Israel sampled their provisions but did not inquire of the LORD. **15**Then Joshua made a treaty of peace with them to let them live, and the leaders of the assembly ratified it by oath.

16Three days after they made the treaty with

9:14 Tricked!

The Gibeonites saved themselves by performing an elaborate deception on the Israelite soldiers, acting as if they had come from far away. The Israelites tried to check their story, but neglected the most important test of all: they "did not inquire of the LORD." Throughout Joshua, God shows that he is in charge and that following him is the only way to victory.

The Gibeonites' trick saved their lives, but they were forced to become servants. Some of them later converted to Judaism. The book of Nehemiah includes Gibeonites (sometimes called Hivites) among those who helped rebuild the walls of Jerusalem. And at least one of King David's "mighty men" was a Gibeonite. (See also the incident recorded in 2 Samuel 21:1–14.) Even so, the Gibeonites often caused trouble for Israel.

---

the Gibeonites, the Israelites heard that they were neighbors, living near them. **17**So the Israelites set out and on the third day came to their cities: Gibeon, Kephirah, Beeroth and Kiriath Jearim. **18**But the Israelites did not attack them, because the leaders of the assembly had sworn an oath to them by the LORD, the God of Israel.

The whole assembly grumbled against the leaders, **19**but all the leaders answered, "We have given them our oath by the LORD, the God of Israel, and we cannot touch them now. **20**This is what we will do to them: We will let them live, so that wrath will not fall on us for breaking the oath we swore to them." **21**They continued, "Let them live, but let them be woodcutters and water carriers for the entire community." So the leaders' promise to them was kept.

22Then Joshua summoned the Gibeonites and said, "Why did you deceive us by saying, 'We live a long way from you,' while actually you live near us? **23**You are now under a curse: You will never cease to serve as woodcutters and water carriers for the house of my God."

24They answered Joshua, "Your servants were clearly told how the LORD your God had commanded his servant Moses to give you the whole

---

a 1 That is, the Mediterranean   *b 4* Most Hebrew manuscripts; some Hebrew manuscripts, Vulgate and Syriac (see also Septuagint) *They prepared provisions and loaded their donkeys*

land and to wipe out all its inhabitants from before you. So we feared for our lives because of you, and that is why we did this. ²⁵We are now in your hands. Do to us whatever seems good and right to you."

²⁶So Joshua saved them from the Israelites, and they did not kill them. ²⁷That day he made the Gibeonites woodcutters and water carriers for the community and for the altar of the LORD at the place the LORD would choose. And that is what they are to this day.

The Sun Stands Still

10 Now Adoni-Zedek king of Jerusalem heard that Joshua had taken Ai and totally de-

Is a War Ever Holy?

Why did God order a ruthless military campaign?

HOLY WAR. IRONICALLY, THE TERM applies to the most vicious, bloody wars. And often, far too often, Christians have been at the heart of such holy wars.

There is something irrational and even repulsive about a holy war. It harnesses all the best energies of religion for one of the ugliest acts of human nature. And yet anyone who reads the Bible cannot ignore the holy wars in the Old Testament.

Whole books have been written about the problem, and no brief article can begin to cover the issues. But modern readers need some background to help understand why a fierce holy war is presented in such a good light.

> The LORD said to Joshua, "Do not be afraid of them, because by this time tomorrow I will hand all of them over to Israel, slain." 11:6

A Land Promised to the Israelites

The Israelites' fighting style fit the harsh pattern of warfare in that day. Contemporary Egyptian and Assyrian reports boasted of mass executions, torture, and the systematic razing of cities. But God's involvement raises unique questions. He personally ordered the destruction of seven Canaanite nations, with no survivors. Why?

The Old Testament makes clear that the Canaanites were not being uprooted on a sudden whim. God had promised the land to the Israelites over 400 years before Joshua. He had called one man, Abraham, to found a nation of chosen people. He repeated those promises often (Genesis 12:1–3; 15:5–18; 17:2–8; 26:3,23–24; 28:13–14) and finally called the Israelites out of Egypt to take over the promised land. Almost from the beginning Canaan was a vital part of God's plan.

Delayed Punishment

Israel's inheritance, however, meant kicking out the Canaanites. How could innocent people simply be pushed aside, or killed? In answer to this question, the Bible makes clear that the Canaanites were *not* "innocent." Through their long history of sin, they had forfeited their right to the land.

Four hundred years before Joshua, God had told Abraham that his descendants would not occupy the land until the sin of its inhabitants had "reached its full measure" (Genesis 15:16). Later, just days before the onset of Joshua's campaign, Moses stated, "It is not because of your righteousness or your integrity that you are going in to take possession of their land; but on account of the wickedness of these nations, the LORD your God will drive them out before you" (Deuteronomy 9:5).

Historians have uncovered plenty of evidence of this wickedness. Canaanite temples featured prostitutes, orgies, and human sacrifice. Relics and plaques of exaggerated sex organs hint at the morality that characterized Canaan.

Canaanite gods, such as Baal and his wife Anath, delighted in butchery and sadism. Archaeologists have found great numbers of jars containing the tiny bones of children sacrificed to Baal. Families seeking good luck in a new home practiced "foundation sacrifice." They would kill one of their children and seal the body in the mortar of the wall. In many ways, Canaan had become like Sodom and Gomorrah. The Bible records that God has patience with decadent societies for a time, but judgment inevitably follows. For Sodom and Gomorrah it took the form of fire and brimstone. For Canaan it came through Joshua's conquering armies. Later, God let his own chosen people be ravaged by invaders as punishment for their sins. The judgment pronounced on Canaan seems severe, but no more severe than what was later inflicted on Israel itself.

The Contamination Problem

The Israelites could not simply settle down as new neighbors among existing Canaanite cities.

stroyed[a] it, doing to Ai and its king as he had done to Jericho and its king, and that the people of Gibeon had made a treaty of peace with Israel and were living near them. ²He and his people were very much alarmed at this, because Gibeon was an important city, like one of the royal cities; it was larger than Ai, and all its men were good fighters. ³So Adoni-Zedek king of Jerusalem appealed to Hoham king of Hebron, Piram king of Jarmuth, Japhia king of Lachish and Debir king of Eglon. ⁴"Come up and help me attack Gibeon," he said, "because it has made peace with Joshua and the Israelites."

⁵Then the five kings of the Amorites—the kings of Jerusalem, Hebron, Jarmuth, Lachish and Eglon—joined forces. They moved up with all their troops and took up positions against Gibeon and attacked it.

⁶The Gibeonites then sent word to Joshua in the camp at Gilgal: "Do not abandon your servants. Come up to us quickly and save us! Help us, because all the Amorite kings from the hill country have joined forces against us."

⁷So Joshua marched up from Gilgal with his entire army, including all the best fighting men. ⁸The LORD said to Joshua, "Do not be afraid of them; I have given them into your hand. Not one of them will be able to withstand you."

⁹After an all-night march from Gilgal, Joshua took them by surprise. ¹⁰The LORD threw them into confusion before Israel, who defeated them in a great victory at Gibeon. Israel pursued them along the road going up to Beth Horon and cut them down all the way to Azekah and Makkedah. ¹¹As they fled before Israel on the road down from Beth Horon to Azekah, the LORD hurled large hailstones down on them from the sky, and more of them died from the hailstones

---

[a] 1 The Hebrew term refers to the irrevocable giving over of things or persons to the LORD, often by totally destroying them; also in verses 28, 35, 37, 39 and 40.

From the time when the tribes had made a golden calf while Moses was receiving the Ten Commandments (Exodus 32), Israelites had shown a fatal weakness to infection from outside. They seemed particularly susceptible to sins of sex and idolatry, Canaan's national specialties.

Israel's later history offers a negative proof of why God commanded utter destruction of Canaanites. The damning phrase in Joshua, "the Israelites did not drive out the people," hints at trouble to come, and the very next book, Judges, tells of the devastating results. The Israelites slid to one of their lowest levels because they had not fulfilled the original mission of cleansing the land of impure elements.

A Struggle beyond Nations

Looking back at this period of time, we tend to see the battles of Joshua as national or racial struggles: the Israelites versus the people of Canaan. But the Bible presents the warfare as a wider struggle: one between those who followed God and those who opposed him.

When God judged groups, as he judged the world in Noah's day or as he judged Sodom and Gomorrah, those few who remained faithful to him found a way of escape. And in Joshua one bright story shines out: the story of Rahab, a non-Israelite. A typical Canaanite who worked as a professional prostitute, she nevertheless learned to fear and then trust the God of Israel. She escaped the fall of Jericho. Furthermore, she went on to marry a leading Israelite and become one of the ancestors of the Messiah himself, Jesus.

Rahab claimed that others in her city of Jericho had quaked in fear for 40 years, waiting for the judgment of the God of Israel (2:9–11). Yet only she took the further step of seeking help. If others in Canaan had repented and turned to God, they might well have escaped punishment, as Rahab did.

Holy Wars Today

One fact about "holy war" is very clear. We cannot argue from a war specifically commanded by God in Joshua to any national situation today. In the Old Testament, God was dealing primarily with one particular nation, the Israelites, for a stated purpose. When the Messiah finally emerged out of that nation, everything changed.

Jesus' followers all lived in the same territory captured by Joshua, the "promised land." But four times, in his very last words, Jesus commanded his disciples to go out, away from Jerusalem, into all the world. Go, he told them, not as conquering armies but rather as bearers of the good news that applies to all people, all races, all nations.

Anyone who looks to the book of Joshua for a rationalization of a holy war must also look ahead to Jesus. Although on a holy crusade, he chose against violent means. In fact, he chose suffering and death. Nothing in the New Testament gives consolation to a religious warrior.

(For a longer discussion of this topic, see *The Goodness of God*, by John Wenham.)

Life Questions: What arguments have you heard Christians use for or against wars?

than were killed by the swords of the Israelites.
12On the day the LORD gave the Amorites over
to Israel, Joshua said to the LORD in the presence
of Israel:

"O sun, stand still over Gibeon,
  O moon, over the Valley of Aijalon."
13So the sun stood still,
  and the moon stopped,
  till the nation avenged itself on[a] its
    enemies,

as it is written in the Book of Jashar.

The sun stopped in the middle of the sky and
delayed going down about a full day. 14There has
never been a day like it before or since, a day
when the LORD listened to a man. Surely the LORD
was fighting for Israel!

15Then Joshua returned with all Israel to the
camp at Gilgal.

Five Amorite Kings Killed

16Now the five kings had fled and hidden in
the cave at Makkedah. 17When Joshua was told
that the five kings had been found hiding in the
cave at Makkedah, 18he said, "Roll large rocks up
to the mouth of the cave, and post some men
there to guard it. 19But don't stop! Pursue your
enemies, attack them from the rear and don't let
them reach their cities, for the LORD your God
has given them into your hand."

20So Joshua and the Israelites destroyed them
completely—almost to a man—but the few who
were left reached their fortified cities. 21The
whole army then returned safely to Joshua in the
camp at Makkedah, and no one uttered a word
against the Israelites.

22Joshua said, "Open the mouth of the cave
and bring those five kings out to me." 23So they
brought the five kings out of the cave—the kings
of Jerusalem, Hebron, Jarmuth, Lachish and Eglon. 24When they had brought these kings to
Joshua, he summoned all the men of Israel and
said to the army commanders who had come
with him, "Come here and put your feet on the
necks of these kings." So they came forward and
placed their feet on their necks.

10:24 Act of Humiliation

*This act—stepping on a neck—was the ultimate
way to humiliate a king. It expressed utter,
enforced submission. Egyptian and Assyrian
sculptures frequently portrayed this custom.*

25Joshua said to them, "Do not be afraid; do
not be discouraged. Be strong and courageous.
This is what the LORD will do to all the enemies

you are going to fight." 26Then Joshua struck and
killed the kings and hung them on five trees, and
they were left hanging on the trees until evening.

27At sunset Joshua gave the order and they
took them down from the trees and threw them
into the cave where they had been hiding. At the
mouth of the cave they placed large rocks, which
are there to this day.

28That day Joshua took Makkedah. He put the
city and its king to the sword and totally destroyed everyone in it. He left no survivors. And
he did to the king of Makkedah as he had done
to the king of Jericho.

Southern Cities Conquered

29Then Joshua and all Israel with him moved
on from Makkedah to Libnah and attacked it.
30The LORD also gave that city and its king into
Israel's hand. The city and everyone in it Joshua
put to the sword. He left no survivors there. And
he did to its king as he had done to the king of
Jericho.

31Then Joshua and all Israel with him moved
on from Libnah to Lachish; he took up positions
against it and attacked it. 32The LORD handed
Lachish over to Israel, and Joshua took it on the
second day. The city and everyone in it he put
to the sword, just as he had done to Libnah.
33Meanwhile, Horam king of Gezer had come up
to help Lachish, but Joshua defeated him and his
army—until no survivors were left.

34Then Joshua and all Israel with him moved
on from Lachish to Eglon; they took up positions
against it and attacked it. 35They captured it that
same day and put it to the sword and totally
destroyed everyone in it, just as they had done to
Lachish.

36Then Joshua and all Israel with him went up
from Eglon to Hebron and attacked it. 37They
took the city and put it to the sword, together
with its king, its villages and everyone in it. They
left no survivors. Just as at Eglon, they totally
destroyed it and everyone in it.

38Then Joshua and all Israel with him turned
around and attacked Debir. 39They took the city,
its king and its villages, and put them to the
sword. Everyone in it they totally destroyed. They
left no survivors. They did to Debir and its king
as they had done to Libnah and its king and to
Hebron.

40So Joshua subdued the whole region, including the hill country, the Negev, the western foothills and the mountain slopes, together with all
their kings. He left no survivors. He totally destroyed all who breathed, just as the LORD, the
God of Israel, had commanded. 41Joshua subdued them from Kadesh Barnea to Gaza and
from the whole region of Goshen to Gibeon. 42All

---

[a]13 Or *nation triumphed over*

these kings and their lands Joshua conquered in one campaign, because the LORD, the God of Israel, fought for Israel.

⁴³Then Joshua returned with all Israel to the camp at Gilgal.

Northern Kings Defeated

11 When Jabin king of Hazor heard of this, he sent word to Jobab king of Madon, to the kings of Shimron and Acshaph, ²and to the northern kings who were in the mountains, in the Arabah south of Kinnereth, in the western foothills and in Naphoth Dor*a* on the west; ³to the Canaanites in the east and west; to the Amorites, Hittites, Perizzites and Jebusites in the hill country; and to the Hivites below Hermon in the region of Mizpah. ⁴They came out with all their troops and a large number of horses and chariots—a huge army, as numerous as the sand on the seashore. ⁵All these kings joined forces and made camp together at the Waters of Merom, to fight against Israel.

⁶The LORD said to Joshua, "Do not be afraid of them, because by this time tomorrow I will hand all of them over to Israel, slain. You are to hamstring their horses and burn their chariots."

⁷So Joshua and his whole army came against them suddenly at the Waters of Merom and attacked them, ⁸and the LORD gave them into the hand of Israel. They defeated them and pursued them all the way to Greater Sidon, to Misrephoth Maim, and to the Valley of Mizpah on the east, until no survivors were left. ⁹Joshua did to them as the LORD had directed: He hamstrung their horses and burned their chariots.

11:9 Advanced Weaponry

If a guerrilla band in Central America captured an F-16 fighter, what could they do with it? Probably nothing, unless they had trained pilots. The Israelites faced a similar situation. War-horses and chariots were advanced weapons of war that the Israelites would not master for hundreds more years. Joshua probably crippled the captured horses to ensure they would not fall into enemy hands again. Militarily and economically, the Israelites were up against people more sophisticated than they.

¹⁰At that time Joshua turned back and captured Hazor and put its king to the sword. (Hazor had been the head of all these kingdoms.) ¹¹Everyone in it they put to the sword. They to-

tally destroyed*b* them, not sparing anything that breathed, and he burned up Hazor itself.

¹²Joshua took all these royal cities and their kings and put them to the sword. He totally destroyed them, as Moses the servant of the LORD had commanded. ¹³Yet Israel did not burn any of the cities built on their mounds—except Hazor, which Joshua burned. ¹⁴The Israelites carried off for themselves all the plunder and livestock of these cities, but all the people they put to the sword until they completely destroyed them, not sparing anyone that breathed. ¹⁵As the LORD commanded his servant Moses, so Moses commanded Joshua, and Joshua did it; he left nothing undone of all that the LORD commanded Moses.

¹⁶So Joshua took this entire land: the hill country, all the Negev, the whole region of Goshen, the western foothills, the Arabah and the mountains of Israel with their foothills, ¹⁷from Mount Halak, which rises toward Seir, to Baal Gad in the Valley of Lebanon below Mount Hermon. He captured all their kings and struck them down, putting them to death. ¹⁸Joshua waged war against all these kings for a long time. ¹⁹Except for the Hivites living in Gibeon, not one city made a treaty of peace with the Israelites, who took them all in battle. ²⁰For it was the LORD himself who hardened their hearts to wage war against Israel, so that he might destroy them totally, exterminating them without mercy, as the LORD had commanded Moses.

²¹At that time Joshua went and destroyed the Anakites from the hill country: from Hebron, Debir and Anab, from all the hill country of Judah, and from all the hill country of Israel. Joshua totally destroyed them and their towns. ²²No Anakites were left in Israelite territory; only in Gaza, Gath and Ashdod did any survive. ²³So Joshua took the entire land, just as the LORD had directed Moses, and he gave it as an inheritance to Israel according to their tribal divisions.

Then the land had rest from war.

11:23 Two Accounts of Warfare

Judges 1 summarizes the incidents recorded in Joshua, but from a different point of view. Joshua presents the campaign as highly successful; Judges shows that many military goals were never achieved. One possible explanation: Joshua presented the wars as a series of raids on territory and did not include the "mopping up" and settlement process. Judges shows that, after they divided up the land, the Israelites proved far less successful in the second phase of conquest.

---

*a*2 Or *in the heights of Dor*   *b*11 The Hebrew term refers to the irrevocable giving over of things or persons to the LORD, often by totally destroying them; also in verses 12, 20 and 21.

List of Defeated Kings

12 These are the kings of the land whom the Israelites had defeated and whose territory they took over east of the Jordan, from the Arnon Gorge to Mount Hermon, including all the eastern side of the Arabah:

²Sihon king of the Amorites,
who reigned in Heshbon. He ruled from Aroer on the rim of the Arnon Gorge— from the middle of the gorge—to the Jabbok River, which is the border of the Ammonites. This included half of Gilead. ³He also ruled over the eastern Arabah from the Sea of Kinnereth[a] to the Sea of the Arabah (the Salt Sea[b]), to Beth Jeshimoth, and then southward below the slopes of Pisgah.

⁴And the territory of Og king of Bashan,
one of the last of the Rephaites, who reigned in Ashtaroth and Edrei. ⁵He ruled over Mount Hermon, Salecah, all of Bashan to the border of the people of Geshur and Maacah, and half of Gilead to the border of Sihon king of Heshbon.

⁶Moses, the servant of the LORD, and the Israelites conquered them. And Moses the servant of the LORD gave their land to the Reubenites, the Gadites and the half-tribe of Manasseh to be their possession.

⁷These are the kings of the land that Joshua and the Israelites conquered on the west side of the Jordan, from Baal Gad in the Valley of Lebanon to Mount Halak, which rises toward Seir (their lands Joshua gave as an inheritance to the tribes of Israel according to their tribal divisions— ⁸the hill country, the western foothills, the Arabah, the mountain slopes, the desert and the Negev—the lands of the Hittites, Amorites, Canaanites, Perizzites, Hivites and Jebusites):

⁹the king of Jericho	one
the king of Ai (near Bethel)	one
¹⁰the king of Jerusalem	one
the king of Hebron	one
¹¹the king of Jarmuth	one
the king of Lachish	one
¹²the king of Eglon	one
the king of Gezer	one
¹³the king of Debir	one
the king of Geder	one
¹⁴the king of Hormah	one
the king of Arad	one
¹⁵the king of Libnah	one
the king of Adullam	one
¹⁶the king of Makkedah	one
the king of Bethel	one
¹⁷the king of Tappuah	one
the king of Hepher	one
¹⁸the king of Aphek	one
the king of Lasharon	one
¹⁹the king of Madon	one
the king of Hazor	one
²⁰the king of Shimron Meron	one
the king of Acshaph	one
²¹the king of Taanach	one
the king of Megiddo	one
²²the king of Kedesh	one
the king of Jokneam in Carmel	one
²³the king of Dor	
(in Naphoth Dor[c])	one
the king of Goyim in Gilgal	one
²⁴the king of Tirzah	one

thirty-one kings in all.

Land Still to Be Taken

13 When Joshua was old and well advanced in years, the LORD said to him, "You are very old, and there are still very large areas of land to be taken over.

13:1 Dividing Up the Land

Chapter 13 introduces an abrupt transition. The rest of Joshua tells about what happened five to seven years after the crossing of the Jordan. Chapters 13–22 give a kind of land-title record for the new nation. Genesis 48–49 and Deuteronomy 33 provide background material. For example, Reuben's tribe forfeited the right to first choice because of a sexual sin, and Simeon and Levi lost their rights because of their violent past.

---

²"This is the land that remains: all the regions of the Philistines and Geshurites: ³from the Shihor River on the east of Egypt to the territory of Ekron on the north, all of it counted as Canaanite (the territory of the five Philistine rulers in Gaza, Ashdod, Ashkelon, Gath and Ekron—that of the Avvites); ⁴from the south, all the land of the Canaanites, from Arah of the Sidonians as far as Aphek, the region of the Amorites, ⁵the area of the Gebalites[d]; and all Lebanon to the east, from Baal Gad below Mount Hermon to Lebo[e] Hamath.

⁶"As for all the inhabitants of the mountain regions from Lebanon to Misrephoth Maim, that is, all the Sidonians, I myself will drive them out before the Israelites. Be sure to allocate this land to Israel for an inheritance, as I have instructed you, ⁷and divide it as an inheritance among the nine tribes and half of the tribe of Manasseh."

---

a3 That is, Galilee   *b3* That is, the Dead Sea   *c23* Or *in the heights of Dor*   *d5* That is, the area of Byblos
e5 Or *to the entrance to*

Division of the Land East of the Jordan

[8]The other half of Manasseh,[a] the Reubenites and the Gadites had received the inheritance that Moses had given them east of the Jordan, as he, the servant of the LORD, had assigned it to them.

[9]It extended from Aroer on the rim of the Arnon Gorge, and from the town in the middle of the gorge, and included the whole plateau of Medeba as far as Dibon, [10]and all the towns of Sihon king of the Amorites, who ruled in Heshbon, out to the border of the Ammonites. [11]It also included Gilead, the territory of the people of Geshur and Maacah, all of Mount Hermon and all Bashan as far as Salecah— [12]that is, the whole kingdom of Og in Bashan, who had reigned in Ashtaroth and Edrei and had survived as one of the last of the Rephaites. Moses had defeated them and taken over their land. [13]But the Israelites did not drive out the people of Geshur and Maacah, so they continue to live among the Israelites to this day.

[14]But to the tribe of Levi he gave no inheritance, since the offerings made by fire to the LORD, the God of Israel, are their inheritance, as he promised them.

[15]This is what Moses had given to the tribe of Reuben, clan by clan:

[16]The territory from Aroer on the rim of the Arnon Gorge, and from the town in the middle of the gorge, and the whole plateau past Medeba [17]to Heshbon and all its towns on the plateau, including Dibon, Bamoth Baal, Beth Baal Meon, [18]Jahaz, Kedemoth, Mephaath, [19]Kiriathaim, Sibmah, Zereth Shahar on the hill in the valley, [20]Beth Peor, the slopes of Pisgah, and Beth Jeshimoth [21]—all the towns on the plateau and the entire realm of Sihon king of the Amorites, who ruled at Heshbon. Moses had defeated him and the Midianite chiefs, Evi, Rekem, Zur, Hur and Reba—princes allied with Sihon—who lived in that country. [22]In addition to those slain in battle, the Israelites had put to the sword Balaam son of Beor, who practiced divination. [23]The boundary of the Reubenites was the bank of the Jordan. These towns and their villages were the inheritance of the Reubenites, clan by clan.

[24]This is what Moses had given to the tribe of Gad, clan by clan:

[25]The territory of Jazer, all the towns of Gilead and half the Ammonite country as far as Aroer, near Rabbah; [26]and from Heshbon to Ramath Mizpah and Betonim, and from Mahanaim to the territory of Debir; [27]and in the valley, Beth Haram, Beth Nimrah, Succoth and Zaphon with the rest of the realm of Sihon king of Heshbon (the east side of the Jordan, the territory up to the end of the Sea of Kinnereth[b]). [28]These towns and their villages were the inheritance of the Gadites, clan by clan.

[29]This is what Moses had given to the half-tribe of Manasseh, that is, to half the family of the descendants of Manasseh, clan by clan:

[30]The territory extending from Mahanaim and including all of Bashan, the entire realm of Og king of Bashan—all the settlements of Jair in Bashan, sixty towns, [31]half of Gilead, and Ashtaroth and Edrei (the royal cities of Og in Bashan). This was for the descendants of Makir son of Manasseh—for half of the sons of Makir, clan by clan.

[32]This is the inheritance Moses had given when he was in the plains of Moab across the Jordan east of Jericho. [33]But to the tribe of Levi, Moses had given no inheritance; the LORD, the God of Israel, is their inheritance, as he promised them.

Division of the Land West of the Jordan

14 Now these are the areas the Israelites received as an inheritance in the land of Canaan, which Eleazar the priest, Joshua son of Nun and the heads of the tribal clans of Israel allotted to them. [2]Their inheritances were assigned by lot to the nine-and-a-half tribes, as the LORD had commanded through Moses. [3]Moses had granted the two-and-a-half tribes their inheritance east of the Jordan but had not granted the Levites an inheritance among the rest, [4]for the sons of Joseph had become two tribes—Manasseh and Ephraim. The Levites received no share of the land but only towns to live in, with pasturelands for their flocks and herds. [5]So the Israelites divided the land, just as the LORD had commanded Moses.

Hebron Given to Caleb

[6]Now the men of Judah approached Joshua at Gilgal, and Caleb son of Jephunneh the Kenizzite said to him, "You know what the LORD said to Moses the man of God at Kadesh Barnea about you and me. [7]I was forty years old when Moses the servant of the LORD sent me from Kadesh Barnea to explore the land. And I brought him back a report according to my convictions, [8]but my brothers who went up with me made the hearts of the people melt with fear. I, however,

[a]8 Hebrew *With it* (that is, with the other half of Manasseh)   [b]27 That is, Galilee

followed the LORD my God wholeheartedly. ⁹So on that day Moses swore to me, 'The land on which your feet have walked will be your inheritance and that of your children forever, because you have followed the LORD my God wholeheartedly.'ᵃ

¹⁰"Now then, just as the LORD promised, he has kept me alive for forty-five years since the time he said this to Moses, while Israel moved about in the desert. So here I am today, eighty-

14:10 Seven-Year Fight

Just how long did the capture of Palestine take? The book of Joshua doesn't say, but a little arithmetic shows that the fighting had been going on for about seven years. Caleb was 40 when Moses first sent him to explore the land (verse 7). Israel spent 38 years in the desert after that (Deuteronomy 2:14), making Caleb 78 when they finally invaded. Since he had now reached 85, the last seven years of Caleb's life must have been spent fighting. He was one of the two oldest Israelites; all others of his generation had died in the desert.

five years old! ¹¹I am still as strong today as the day Moses sent me out; I'm just as vigorous to go out to battle now as I was then. ¹²Now give me this hill country that the LORD promised me that day. You yourself heard then that the Anakites were there and their cities were large and fortified, but, the LORD helping me, I will drive them out just as he said."

¹³Then Joshua blessed Caleb son of Jephunneh and gave him Hebron as his inheritance. ¹⁴So Hebron has belonged to Caleb son of Jephunneh the Kenizzite ever since, because he followed the LORD, the God of Israel, wholeheartedly. ¹⁵(Hebron used to be called Kiriath Arba after Arba, who was the greatest man among the Anakites.)

Then the land had rest from war.

Allotment for Judah

15 The allotment for the tribe of Judah, clan by clan, extended down to the territory of Edom, to the Desert of Zin in the extreme south. ²Their southern boundary started from the bay at the southern end of the Salt Sea,ᵇ ³crossed south of Scorpionᶜ Pass, continued on to Zin and went over to the south of Kadesh Barnea. Then it ran past Hezron up to Addar and curved around to Karka. ⁴It then passed along to Azmon and joined the Wadi of Egypt, ending at the sea. This is theirᵈ southern boundary.

⁵The eastern boundary is the Salt Sea as far as the mouth of the Jordan.

The northern boundary started from the bay of the sea at the mouth of the Jordan, ⁶went up to Beth Hoglah and continued north of Beth Arabah to the Stone of Bohan son of Reuben. ⁷The boundary then went up to Debir from the Valley of Achor and turned north to Gilgal, which faces the Pass of Adummim south of the gorge. It continued along to the waters of En Shemesh and came out at En Rogel. ⁸Then it ran up the Valley of Ben Hinnom along the southern slope of the Jebusite city (that is, Jerusalem). From there it climbed to the top of the hill west of the Hinnom Valley at the northern end of the Valley of Rephaim. ⁹From the hilltop the boundary headed toward the spring of the waters of Nephtoah, came out at the towns of Mount Ephron and went down toward Baalah (that is, Kiriath Jearim). ¹⁰Then it curved westward from Baalah to Mount Seir, ran along the northern slope of Mount Jearim (that is, Kesalon), continued down to Beth Shemesh and crossed to Timnah. ¹¹It went to the northern slope of Ekron, turned toward Shikkeron, passed along to Mount Baalah and reached Jabneel. The boundary ended at the sea.

¹²The western boundary is the coastline of the Great Sea.ᵉ

These are the boundaries around the people of Judah by their clans.

¹³In accordance with the LORD's command to him, Joshua gave to Caleb son of Jephunneh a portion in Judah—Kiriath Arba, that is, Hebron. (Arba was the forefather of Anak.) ¹⁴From Hebron Caleb drove out the three Anakites—Sheshai, Ahiman and Talmai—descendants of Anak. ¹⁵From there he marched against the people living in Debir (formerly called Kiriath Sepher). ¹⁶And Caleb said, "I will give my daughter Acsah in marriage to the man who attacks and captures Kiriath Sepher." ¹⁷Othniel son of Kenaz, Caleb's brother, took it; so Caleb gave his daughter Acsah to him in marriage.

¹⁸One day when she came to Othniel, she urged himᶠ to ask her father for a field. When she got off her donkey, Caleb asked her, "What can I do for you?"

¹⁹She replied, "Do me a special favor. Since you have given me land in the Negev, give me also springs of water." So Caleb gave her the upper and lower springs.

ᵃ9 Deut. 1:36   ᵇ2 That is, the Dead Sea; also in verse 5   ᶜ3 Hebrew *Akrabbim*   ᵈ4 Hebrew *your*
ᵉ12 That is, the Mediterranean; also in verse 47   ᶠ18 Hebrew and some Septuagint manuscripts; other Septuagint manuscripts (see also note at Judges 1:14) *Othniel, he urged her*

20This is the inheritance of the tribe of Judah, clan by clan:

21The southernmost towns of the tribe of Judah in the Negev toward the boundary of Edom were:

Kabzeel, Eder, Jagur, 22Kinah, Dimonah, Adadah, 23Kedesh, Hazor, Ithnan, 24Ziph, Telem, Bealoth, 25Hazor Hadattah, Kerioth Hezron (that is, Hazor), 26Amam, Shema, Moladah, 27Hazar Gaddah, Heshmon, Beth Pelet, 28Hazar Shual, Beersheba, Biziothiah, 29Baalah, Iim, Ezem, 30Eltolad, Kesil, Hormah, 31Ziklag, Madmannah, Sansannah, 32Lebaoth, Shilhim, Ain and Rimmon—a total of twenty-nine towns and their villages.

33In the western foothills:

Eshtaol, Zorah, Ashnah, 34Zanoah, En Gannim, Tappuah, Enam, 35Jarmuth, Adullam, Socoh, Azekah, 36Shaaraim, Adithaim and Gederah (or Gederothaim)a—fourteen towns and their villages.

37Zenan, Hadashah, Migdal Gad, 38Dilean, Mizpah, Joktheel, 39Lachish, Bozkath, Eglon, 40Cabbon, Lahmas, Kitlish, 41Gederoth, Beth Dagon, Naamah and Makkedah—sixteen towns and their villages.

42Libnah, Ether, Ashan, 43Iphtah, Ashnah, Nezib, 44Keilah, Aczib and Mareshah—nine towns and their villages.

45Ekron, with its surrounding settlements and villages; 46west of Ekron, all that were in the vicinity of Ashdod, together with their villages; 47Ashdod, its surrounding settlements and villages; and Gaza, its settlements and villages, as far as the Wadi of Egypt and the coastline of the Great Sea.

48In the hill country:

Shamir, Jattir, Socoh, 49Dannah, Kiriath Sannah (that is, Debir), 50Anab, Eshtemoh, Anim, 51Goshen, Holon and Giloh—eleven towns and their villages.

52Arab, Dumah, Eshan, 53Janim, Beth Tappuah, Aphekah, 54Humtah, Kiriath Arba (that is, Hebron) and Zior—nine towns and their villages.

55Maon, Carmel, Ziph, Juttah, 56Jezreel, Jokdeam, Zanoah, 57Kain, Gibeah and Timnah—ten towns and their villages.

58Halhul, Beth Zur, Gedor, 59Maarath, Beth Anoth and Eltekon—six towns and their villages.

60Kiriath Baal (that is, Kiriath Jearim) and Rabbah—two towns and their villages.

61In the desert:

Beth Arabah, Middin, Secacah, 62Nib-

shan, the City of Salt and En Gedi—six towns and their villages.

63Judah could not dislodge the Jebusites, who were living in Jerusalem; to this day the Jebusites live there with the people of Judah.

15:63 Hints of Failure

In several key places (13:2–7; 16:10; 23:4) and in Judges 1, the Bible indicates that pockets of Canaanites remained in the land. The Israelites "could not dislodge" them, or did not "drive them out." The unconquered tribes became thorns in Israel's side.

Allotment for Ephraim and Manasseh

16 The allotment for Joseph began at the Jordan of Jericho,b east of the waters of Jericho, and went up from there through the desert into the hill country of Bethel. 2It went on from Bethel (that is, Luz),c crossed over to the territory of the Arkites in Ataroth, 3descended westward to the territory of the Japhletites as far as the region of Lower Beth Horon and on to Gezer, ending at the sea.

4So Manasseh and Ephraim, the descendants of Joseph, received their inheritance.

5This was the territory of Ephraim, clan by clan:

The boundary of their inheritance went from Ataroth Addar in the east to Upper Beth Horon 6and continued to the sea. From Micmethath on the north it curved eastward to Taanath Shiloh, passing by it to Janoah on the east. 7Then it went down from Janoah to Ataroth and Naarah, touched Jericho and came out at the Jordan. 8From Tappuah the border went west to the Kanah Ravine and ended at the sea. This was the inheritance of the tribe of the Ephraimites, clan by clan. 9It also included all the towns and their villages that were set aside for the Ephraimites within the inheritance of the Manassites.

10They did not dislodge the Canaanites living in Gezer; to this day the Canaanites live among the people of Ephraim but are required to do forced labor.

17 This was the allotment for the tribe of Manasseh as Joseph's firstborn, that is, for Makir, Manasseh's firstborn. Makir was the ancestor of the Gileadites, who had received Gilead and Bashan because the Makirites were great soldiers. 2So this allotment was for the rest of the people of Manasseh—the clans of Abiezer, Helek, Asri-

---

a 36 Or *Gederah and Gederothaim*   b 1 *Jordan of Jericho* was possibly an ancient name for the Jordan River.
c 2 Septuagint; Hebrew *Bethel to Luz*

el, Shechem, Hepher and Shemida. These are the other male descendants of Manasseh son of Joseph by their clans.

³Now Zelophehad son of Hepher, the son of Gilead, the son of Makir, the son of Manasseh, had no sons but only daughters, whose names were Mahlah, Noah, Hoglah, Milcah and Tirzah. ⁴They went to Eleazar the priest, Joshua son of Nun, and the leaders and said, "The LORD commanded Moses to give us an inheritance among our brothers." So Joshua gave them an inheritance along with the brothers of their father,

17:4 Daughters' Rights

See Numbers 27:1–11 and Numbers 36 for the historical context to these women's appeal.

according to the LORD's command. ⁵Manasseh's share consisted of ten tracts of land besides Gilead and Bashan east of the Jordan, ⁶because the daughters of the tribe of Manasseh received an inheritance among the sons. The land of Gilead belonged to the rest of the descendants of Manasseh.

⁷The territory of Manasseh extended from Asher to Micmethath east of Shechem. The boundary ran southward from there to include the people living at En Tappuah. ⁸(Manasseh had the land of Tappuah, but Tappuah itself, on the boundary of Manasseh, belonged to the Ephraimites.) ⁹Then the boundary continued south to the Kanah Ravine. There were towns belonging to Ephraim lying among the towns of Manasseh, but the boundary of Manasseh was the northern side of the ravine and ended at the sea. ¹⁰On the south the land belonged to Ephraim, on the north to Manasseh. The territory of Manasseh reached the sea and bordered Asher on the north and Issachar on the east.

¹¹Within Issachar and Asher, Manasseh also had Beth Shan, Ibleam and the people of Dor, Endor, Taanach and Megiddo, together with their surrounding settlements (the third in the list is Naphoth[a]).

¹²Yet the Manassites were not able to occupy these towns, for the Canaanites were determined to live in that region. ¹³However, when the Israelites grew stronger, they subjected the Canaanites to forced labor but did not drive them out completely.

¹⁴The people of Joseph said to Joshua, "Why have you given us only one allotment and one portion for an inheritance? We are a numerous people and the LORD has blessed us abundantly."

¹⁵"If you are so numerous," Joshua answered, "and if the hill country of Ephraim is too small for you, go up into the forest and clear land for yourselves there in the land of the Perizzites and Rephaites."

¹⁶The people of Joseph replied, "The hill country is not enough for us, and all the Canaanites who live in the plain have iron chariots, both those in Beth Shan and its settlements and those in the Valley of Jezreel."

¹⁷But Joshua said to the house of Joseph—to Ephraim and Manasseh—"You are numerous and very powerful. You will have not only one allotment ¹⁸but the forested hill country as well. Clear it, and its farthest limits will be yours; though the Canaanites have iron chariots and though they are strong, you can drive them out."

Division of the Rest of the Land

18 The whole assembly of the Israelites gathered at Shiloh and set up the Tent of Meeting there. The country was brought under their control, ²but there were still seven Israelite tribes who had not yet received their inheritance.

³So Joshua said to the Israelites: "How long will you wait before you begin to take possession of the land that the LORD, the God of your

18:3 Missing an Opportunity

Such verses as 17:13 and 18:3 imply that the Israelites could have driven out the Canaanites, but chose not to. They were using the Canaanites for forced labor and demanding tribute from them—perhaps they learned to rely too comfortably on these services. Also, some tribes balked at campaigns simply because of fear (17:16).

fathers, has given you? ⁴Appoint three men from each tribe. I will send them out to make a survey of the land and to write a description of it, according to the inheritance of each. Then they will return to me. ⁵You are to divide the land into seven parts. Judah is to remain in its territory on the south and the house of Joseph in its territory on the north. ⁶After you have written descriptions of the seven parts of the land, bring them here to me and I will cast lots for you in the presence of the LORD our God. ⁷The Levites, however, do not get a portion among you, because the priestly service of the LORD is their inheritance. And Gad, Reuben and the half-tribe of Manasseh have already received their inheritance on the east side of the Jordan. Moses the servant of the LORD gave it to them."

⁸As the men started on their way to map out

ᵃ11 That is, Naphoth Dor

the land, Joshua instructed them, "Go and make a survey of the land and write a description of it. Then return to me, and I will cast lots for you here at Shiloh in the presence of the LORD." ⁹So the men left and went through the land. They wrote its description on a scroll, town by town, in seven parts, and returned to Joshua in the camp at Shiloh. ¹⁰Joshua then cast lots for them in Shiloh in the presence of the LORD, and there he distributed the land to the Israelites according to their tribal divisions.

Allotment for Benjamin

¹¹The lot came up for the tribe of Benjamin, clan by clan. Their allotted territory lay between the tribes of Judah and Joseph:

¹²On the north side their boundary began at the Jordan, passed the northern slope of Jericho and headed west into the hill country, coming out at the desert of Beth Aven. ¹³From there it crossed to the south slope of Luz (that is, Bethel) and went down to Ataroth Addar on the hill south of Lower Beth Horon.

¹⁴From the hill facing Beth Horon on the south the boundary turned south along the western side and came out at Kiriath Baal (that is, Kiriath Jearim), a town of the people of Judah. This was the western side.

¹⁵The southern side began at the outskirts of Kiriath Jearim on the west, and the boundary came out at the spring of the waters of Nephtoah. ¹⁶The boundary went down to the foot of the hill facing the Valley of Ben Hinnom, north of the Valley of Rephaim. It continued down the Hinnom Valley along the southern slope of the Jebusite city and so to En Rogel. ¹⁷It then curved north, went to En Shemesh, continued to Geliloth, which faces the Pass of Adummim, and ran down to the Stone of Bohan son of Reuben. ¹⁸It continued to the northern slope of Beth Arabah[a] and on down into the Arabah. ¹⁹It then went to the northern slope of Beth Hoglah and came out at the northern bay of the Salt Sea,[b] at the mouth of the Jordan in the south. This was the southern boundary.

²⁰The Jordan formed the boundary on the eastern side.

These were the boundaries that marked out the inheritance of the clans of Benjamin on all sides.

²¹The tribe of Benjamin, clan by clan, had the following cities:

Jericho, Beth Hoglah, Emek Keziz, ²²Beth Arabah, Zemaraim, Bethel, ²³Avvim, Parah, Ophrah, ²⁴Kephar Ammoni, Ophni

and Geba—twelve towns and their villages.

²⁵Gibeon, Ramah, Beeroth, ²⁶Mizpah, Kephirah, Mozah, ²⁷Rekem, Irpeel, Taralah, ²⁸Zelah, Haeleph, the Jebusite city (that is, Jerusalem), Gibeah and Kiriath—fourteen towns and their villages.

This was the inheritance of Benjamin for its clans.

Allotment for Simeon

19 The second lot came out for the tribe of Simeon, clan by clan. Their inheritance lay within the territory of Judah. ²It included:

Beersheba (or Sheba),[c] Moladah, ³Hazar Shual, Balah, Ezem, ⁴Eltolad, Bethul, Hormah, ⁵Ziklag, Beth Marcaboth, Hazar Susah, ⁶Beth Lebaoth and Sharuhen—thirteen towns and their villages;

⁷Ain, Rimmon, Ether and Ashan—four towns and their villages— ⁸and all the villages around these towns as far as Baalath Beer (Ramah in the Negev).

This was the inheritance of the tribe of the Simeonites, clan by clan. ⁹The inheritance of the Simeonites was taken from the share of Judah, because Judah's portion was more than they needed. So the Simeonites received their inheritance within the territory of Judah.

Allotment for Zebulun

¹⁰The third lot came up for Zebulun, clan by clan:

The boundary of their inheritance went as far as Sarid. ¹¹Going west it ran to Maralah, touched Dabbesheth, and extended to the ravine near Jokneam. ¹²It turned east from Sarid toward the sunrise to the territory of Kisloth Tabor and went on to Daberath and up to Japhia. ¹³Then it continued eastward to Gath Hepher and Eth Kazin; it came out at Rimmon and turned toward Neah. ¹⁴There the boundary went around on the north to Hannathon and ended at the Valley of Iphtah El. ¹⁵Included were Kattath, Nahalal, Shimron, Idalah and Bethlehem. There were twelve towns and their villages.

¹⁶These towns and their villages were the inheritance of Zebulun, clan by clan.

Allotment for Issachar

¹⁷The fourth lot came out for Issachar, clan by clan. ¹⁸Their territory included:

Jezreel, Kesulloth, Shunem, ¹⁹Hapharaim, Shion, Anaharath, ²⁰Rabbith, Kishion, Ebez, ²¹Remeth, En Gannim, En Haddah and Beth Pazzez. ²²The boundary touched Tabor, Shahazumah and Beth Shemesh,

---

a 18 Septuagint; Hebrew *slope facing the Arabah* does not have *Sheba.*　　*b 19* That is, the Dead Sea　　*c 2* Or *Beersheba, Sheba*; 1 Chron. 4:28

and ended at the Jordan. There were sixteen towns and their villages. 23These towns and their villages were the inheritance of the tribe of Issachar, clan by clan.

Allotment for Asher

24The fifth lot came out for the tribe of Asher, clan by clan. 25Their territory included:

Helkath, Hali, Beten, Acshaph, 26Allammelech, Amad and Mishal. On the west the boundary touched Carmel and Shihor Libnath. 27It then turned east toward Beth Dagon, touched Zebulun and the Valley of Iphtah El, and went north to Beth Emek and Neiel, passing Cabul on the left. 28It went to Abdon,*a* Rehob, Hammon and Kanah, as far as Greater Sidon. 29The boundary then turned back toward Ramah and went to the fortified city of Tyre, turned toward Hosah and came out at the sea in the region of Aczib, 30Ummah, Aphek and Rehob. There were twenty-two towns and their villages.

31These towns and their villages were the inheritance of the tribe of Asher, clan by clan.

Allotment for Naphtali

32The sixth lot came out for Naphtali, clan by clan:

33Their boundary went from Heleph and the large tree in Zaanannim, passing Adami Nekeb and Jabneel to Lakkum and ending at the Jordan. 34The boundary ran west through Aznoth Tabor and came out at Hukkok. It touched Zebulun on the south, Asher on the west and the Jordan*b* on the east. 35The fortified cities were Ziddim, Zer, Hammath, Rakkath, Kinnereth, 36Adamah, Ramah, Hazor, 37Kedesh, Edrei, En Hazor, 38Iron, Migdal El, Horem, Beth Anath and Beth Shemesh. There were nineteen towns and their villages.

39These towns and their villages were the inheritance of the tribe of Naphtali, clan by clan.

Allotment for Dan

40The seventh lot came out for the tribe of Dan, clan by clan. 41The territory of their inheritance included:

Zorah, Eshtaol, Ir Shemesh, 42Shaalabbin, Aijalon, Ithlah, 43Elon, Timnah, Ekron, 44Eltekeh, Gibbethon, Baalath, 45Jehud, Bene Berak, Gath Rimmon, 46Me Jarkon and Rakkon, with the area facing Joppa.

47(But the Danites had difficulty taking possession of their territory, so they went up and attacked Leshem, took it, put it to the sword and occupied it. They settled in Leshem and named it Dan after their forefather.)

48These towns and their villages were the inheritance of the tribe of Dan, clan by clan.

Allotment for Joshua

49When they had finished dividing the land into its allotted portions, the Israelites gave Joshua son of Nun an inheritance among them, 50as the LORD had commanded. They gave him the town he asked for—Timnath Serah*c* in the hill country of Ephraim. And he built up the town and settled there.

51These are the territories that Eleazar the priest, Joshua son of Nun and the heads of the tribal clans of Israel assigned by lot at Shiloh in the presence of the LORD at the entrance to the Tent of Meeting. And so they finished dividing the land.

Cities of Refuge

20 Then the LORD said to Joshua: 2"Tell the Israelites to designate the cities of refuge,

20:2 Cities of Refuge

The cities of refuge were designed to aid a person who caused an accidental death or "involuntary manslaughter." They provided a sanctuary from revenge. They did not, however, shelter a person who had committed a premeditated, intentional murder. (See Numbers 35:6 and Deuteronomy 4:41–43; 19:1–21.)

as I instructed you through Moses, 3so that anyone who kills a person accidentally and unintentionally may flee there and find protection from the avenger of blood.

4"When he flees to one of these cities, he is to stand in the entrance of the city gate and state his case before the elders of that city. Then they are to admit him into their city and give him a place to live with them. 5If the avenger of blood pursues him, they must not surrender the one accused, because he killed his neighbor unintentionally and without malice aforethought. 6He is to stay in that city until he has stood trial before the assembly and until the death of the high priest who is serving at that time. Then he may go back to his own home in the town from which he fled."

7So they set apart Kedesh in Galilee in the hill country of Naphtali, Shechem in the hill country of Ephraim, and Kiriath Arba (that is, Hebron) in the hill country of Judah. 8On the east side of the

---

a28 Some Hebrew manuscripts (see also Joshua 21:30); most Hebrew manuscripts *Ebron west, and Judah, the Jordan,*   *c50* Also known as *Timnath Heres* (see Judges 2:9)   *b34* Septuagint; Hebrew

Jordan of Jericho[a] they designated Bezer in the desert on the plateau in the tribe of Reuben, Ramoth in Gilead in the tribe of Gad, and Golan in Bashan in the tribe of Manasseh. ⁹Any of the Israelites or any alien living among them who killed someone accidentally could flee to these designated cities and not be killed by the avenger of blood prior to standing trial before the assembly.

Towns for the Levites

21 Now the family heads of the Levites approached Eleazar the priest, Joshua son of Nun, and the heads of the other tribal families of Israel ²at Shiloh in Canaan and said to them, "The LORD commanded through Moses that you give us towns to live in, with pasturelands for our livestock." ³So, as the LORD had commanded, the Israelites gave the Levites the following towns and pasturelands out of their own inheritance:

⁴The first lot came out for the Kohathites, clan by clan. The Levites who were descendants of Aaron the priest were allotted thirteen towns from the tribes of Judah, Simeon and Benjamin. ⁵The rest of Kohath's descendants were allotted ten towns from the clans of the tribes of Ephraim, Dan and half of Manasseh.

⁶The descendants of Gershon were allotted thirteen towns from the clans of the tribes of Issachar, Asher, Naphtali and the half-tribe of Manasseh in Bashan.

⁷The descendants of Merari, clan by clan, received twelve towns from the tribes of Reuben, Gad and Zebulun.

⁸So the Israelites allotted to the Levites these towns and their pasturelands, as the LORD had commanded through Moses.

21:8 Towns for the Levites

As part of their calling to serve God, the Levites got no land in Canaan. Rather, they received 48 towns scattered in the other tribes' lands—four towns from each tribe. This forced them to depend not on their inheritance of the land, but on God (see Numbers 18:20). It dispersed the priests among all the people and enabled them to instruct the tribes in the law and to lead worship.

⁹From the tribes of Judah and Simeon they allotted the following towns by name ¹⁰(these towns were assigned to the descendants of Aaron who were from the Kohathite clans of the Levites, because the first lot fell to them):

¹¹They gave them Kiriath Arba (that is, Hebron), with its surrounding pastureland,

in the hill country of Judah. (Arba was the forefather of Anak.) ¹²But the fields and villages around the city they had given to Caleb son of Jephunneh as his possession.

¹³So to the descendants of Aaron the priest they gave Hebron (a city of refuge for one accused of murder), Libnah, ¹⁴Jattir, Eshtemoa, ¹⁵Holon, Debir, ¹⁶Ain, Juttah and Beth Shemesh, together with their pasturelands—nine towns from these two tribes.

¹⁷And from the tribe of Benjamin they gave them Gibeon, Geba, ¹⁸Anathoth and Almon, together with their pasturelands—four towns.

¹⁹All the towns for the priests, the descendants of Aaron, were thirteen, together with their pasturelands.

²⁰The rest of the Kohathite clans of the Levites were allotted towns from the tribe of Ephraim:

²¹In the hill country of Ephraim they were given Shechem (a city of refuge for one accused of murder) and Gezer, ²²Kibzaim and Beth Horon, together with their pasturelands—four towns.

²³Also from the tribe of Dan they received Eltekeh, Gibbethon, ²⁴Aijalon and Gath Rimmon, together with their pasturelands—four towns.

²⁵From half the tribe of Manasseh they received Taanach and Gath Rimmon, together with their pasturelands—two towns.

²⁶All these ten towns and their pasturelands were given to the rest of the Kohathite clans.

²⁷The Levite clans of the Gershonites were given:

from the half-tribe of Manasseh,

Golan in Bashan (a city of refuge for one accused of murder) and Be Eshtarah, together with their pasturelands—two towns;

²⁸from the tribe of Issachar,

Kishion, Daberath, ²⁹Jarmuth and En Gannim, together with their pasturelands—four towns;

³⁰from the tribe of Asher,

Mishal, Abdon, ³¹Helkath and Rehob, together with their pasturelands—four towns;

³²from the tribe of Naphtali,

Kedesh in Galilee (a city of refuge for one accused of murder), Hammoth Dor and Kartan, together with their pasturelands—three towns.

³³All the towns of the Gershonite clans were thirteen, together with their pasturelands.

³⁴The Merarite clans (the rest of the Levites) were given:

from the tribe of Zebulun,

---

[a]8 *Jordan of Jericho* was possibly an ancient name for the Jordan River.

Jokneam, Kartah, 35Dimnah and Nahalal, together with their pasturelands—four towns;

36from the tribe of Reuben,

Bezer, Jahaz, 37Kedemoth and Mephaath, together with their pasturelands—four towns;

38from the tribe of Gad,

Ramoth in Gilead (a city of refuge for one accused of murder), Mahanaim, 39Heshbon and Jazer, together with their pasturelands—four towns in all.

40All the towns allotted to the Merarite clans, who were the rest of the Levites, were twelve.

41The towns of the Levites in the territory held by the Israelites were forty-eight in all, together with their pasturelands. 42Each of these towns had pasturelands surrounding it; this was true for all these towns.

43So the LORD gave Israel all the land he had sworn to give their forefathers, and they took possession of it and settled there. 44The LORD gave them rest on every side, just as he had sworn to their forefathers. Not one of their enemies withstood them; the LORD handed all their enemies over to them. 45Not one of all the LORD's good promises to the house of Israel failed; every one was fulfilled.

Eastern Tribes Return Home

22 Then Joshua summoned the Reubenites, the Gadites and the half-tribe of Manasseh 2and said to them, "You have done all that Moses the servant of the LORD commanded, and you have obeyed me in everything I commanded. 3For a long time now—to this very day—you have not deserted your brothers but have carried out the mission the LORD your God gave you. 4Now that the LORD your God has given your brothers rest as he promised, return to your homes in the land that Moses the servant of the LORD gave you on the other side of the Jordan. 5But be very careful to keep the commandment and the law that Moses the servant of the LORD gave you: to love the LORD your God, to walk in all his ways, to obey his commands, to hold fast to him and to serve him with all your heart and all your soul."

6Then Joshua blessed them and sent them away, and they went to their homes. 7(To the half-tribe of Manasseh Moses had given land in Bashan, and to the other half of the tribe Joshua gave land on the west side of the Jordan with their brothers.) When Joshua sent them home, he blessed them, 8saying, "Return to your homes with your great wealth—with large herds of livestock, with silver, gold, bronze and iron, and a great quantity of clothing—and divide with your brothers the plunder from your enemies."

9So the Reubenites, the Gadites and the half-tribe of Manasseh left the Israelites at Shiloh in Canaan to return to Gilead, their own land, which they had acquired in accordance with the command of the LORD through Moses.

10When they came to Geliloth near the Jordan in the land of Canaan, the Reubenites, the Gadites and the half-tribe of Manasseh built an imposing altar there by the Jordan. 11And when the

22:10–30 Explosive Quarrel

Chapter 22 records a misunderstanding that could have led to civil war. Several Israelite tribes built a large altar. This inflamed the other tribes. Weren't the builders grossly violating God's law by erecting an altar, a function only priests should perform? Were these tribes so soon abandoning the rules of worship Moses and Joshua had laid down? Or, perhaps, had they provocatively built their altar on the western side of the Jordan River to stake a claim to others' land? The western tribes soon learned the truth: the easterners had built not an altar, but a monument to commemorate their national unity with the western tribes. A civil war was averted after some heated exchanges. The incident reveals the intensity of religious feeling in the new nation.

Israelites heard that they had built the altar on the border of Canaan at Geliloth near the Jordan on the Israelite side, 12the whole assembly of Israel gathered at Shiloh to go to war against them.

13So the Israelites sent Phinehas son of Eleazar, the priest, to the land of Gilead—to Reuben, Gad and the half-tribe of Manasseh. 14With him they sent ten of the chief men, one for each of the tribes of Israel, each the head of a family division among the Israelite clans.

15When they went to Gilead—to Reuben, Gad and the half-tribe of Manasseh—they said to them: 16"The whole assembly of the LORD says: 'How could you break faith with the God of Israel like this? How could you turn away from the LORD and build yourselves an altar in rebellion against him now? 17Was not the sin of Peor enough for us? Up to this very day we have not cleansed ourselves from that sin, even though a plague fell on the community of the LORD! 18And are you now turning away from the LORD?

19"'If you rebel against the LORD today, tomorrow he will be angry with the whole community of Israel. 19If the land you possess is defiled, come over to the LORD's land, where the LORD's tabernacle stands, and share the land with us. But do not rebel against the LORD or against us by building an altar for yourselves, other than the altar of the LORD our God. 20When Achan son of Zerah acted unfaithfully regarding the devoted things,[a] did not wrath come upon the whole community of Israel? He was not the only one who died for his sin.'"

²¹Then Reuben, Gad and the half-tribe of Manasseh replied to the heads of the clans of Israel: ²²"The Mighty One, God, the LORD! The Mighty One, God, the LORD! He knows! And let Israel know! If this has been in rebellion or disobedience to the LORD, do not spare us this day. ²³If we have built our own altar to turn away from the LORD and to offer burnt offerings and grain offerings, or to sacrifice fellowship offerings[b] on it, may the LORD himself call us to account.

²⁴"No! We did it for fear that some day your descendants might say to ours, 'What do you have to do with the LORD, the God of Israel? ²⁵The LORD has made the Jordan a boundary between us and you—you Reubenites and Gadites! You have no share in the LORD.' So your descendants might cause ours to stop fearing the LORD.

²⁶"That is why we said, 'Let us get ready and build an altar—but not for burnt offerings or sacrifices.' ²⁷On the contrary, it is to be a witness between us and you and the generations that follow, that we will worship the LORD at his sanctuary with our burnt offerings, sacrifices and fellowship offerings. Then in the future your descendants will not be able to say to ours, 'You have no share in the LORD.'

²⁸"And we said, 'If they ever say this to us, or to our descendants, we will answer: Look at the replica of the LORD's altar, which our fathers built, not for burnt offerings or sacrifices, but as a witness between us and you.'

²⁹"Far be it from us to rebel against the LORD and turn away from him today by building an altar for burnt offerings, grain offerings and sacrifices, other than the altar of the LORD our God that stands before his tabernacle."

³⁰When Phinehas the priest and the leaders of the community—the heads of the clans of the Israelites—heard what Reuben, Gad and Manasseh had to say, they were pleased. ³¹And Phinehas son of Eleazar, the priest, said to Reuben, Gad and Manasseh, "Today we know that the LORD is with us, because you have not acted unfaithfully toward the LORD in this matter. Now you have rescued the Israelites from the LORD's hand."

³²Then Phinehas son of Eleazar, the priest, and the leaders returned to Canaan from their meeting with the Reubenites and Gadites in Gilead and reported to the Israelites. ³³They were glad to hear the report and praised God. And they talked no more about going to war against them to devastate the country where the Reubenites and the Gadites lived.

³⁴And the Reubenites and the Gadites gave the altar this name: A Witness Between Us that the LORD is God.

Joshua's Farewell to the Leaders

23 After a long time had passed and the LORD had given Israel rest from all their enemies around them, Joshua, by then old and well advanced in years, ²summoned all Israel—their elders, leaders, judges and officials—and said to them: "I am old and well advanced in years. ³You yourselves have seen everything the LORD your God has done to all these nations for your sake; it was the LORD your God who fought for you. ⁴Remember how I have allotted as an inheritance for your tribes all the land of the nations that remain—the nations I conquered—between the Jordan and the Great Sea[c] in the west. ⁵The LORD your God himself will drive them out of your way. He will push them out before you, and you will take possession of their land, as the LORD your God promised you.

⁶"Be very strong; be careful to obey all that is written in the Book of the Law of Moses, without turning aside to the right or to the left. ⁷Do not associate with these nations that remain among you; do not invoke the names of their gods or swear by them. You must not serve them or bow down to them. ⁸But you are to hold fast to the LORD your God, as you have until now.

⁹"The LORD has driven out before you great and powerful nations; to this day no one has been able to withstand you. ¹⁰One of you routs a thousand, because the LORD your God fights for you, just as he promised. ¹¹So be very careful to love the LORD your God.

¹²"But if you turn away and ally yourselves with the survivors of these nations that remain among you and if you intermarry with them and associate with them, ¹³then you may be sure that the LORD your God will no longer drive out these nations before you. Instead, they will become snares and traps for you, whips on your backs and thorns in your eyes, until you perish from this good land, which the LORD your God has given you.

¹⁴"Now I am about to go the way of all the earth. You know with all your heart and soul that not one of all the good promises the LORD your God gave you has failed. Every promise has been fulfilled; not one has failed. ¹⁵But just as every good promise of the LORD your God has come true, so the LORD will bring on you all the evil he has threatened, until he has destroyed you from this good land he has given you. ¹⁶If you violate the covenant of the LORD your God, which he commanded you, and go and serve other gods

---

[a]20 The Hebrew term refers to the irrevocable giving over of things or persons to the LORD, often by totally destroying them.   [b]23 Traditionally *peace offerings*; also in verse 27   [c]4 That is, the Mediterranean

and bow down to them, the LORD's anger will burn against you, and you will quickly perish from the good land he has given you."

The Covenant Renewed at Shechem

24 Then Joshua assembled all the tribes of Israel at Shechem. He summoned the elders, leaders, judges and officials of Israel, and they presented themselves before God.

²Joshua said to all the people, "This is what the LORD, the God of Israel, says: 'Long ago your forefathers, including Terah the father of Abraham and Nahor, lived beyond the River*a* and worshiped other gods. ³But I took your father Abraham from the land beyond the River and led him throughout Canaan and gave him many descendants. I gave him Isaac, ⁴and to Isaac I gave Jacob and Esau. I assigned the hill country of Seir to Esau, but Jacob and his sons went down to Egypt.

⁵"'Then I sent Moses and Aaron, and I afflicted the Egyptians by what I did there, and I brought you out. ⁶When I brought your fathers out of Egypt, you came to the sea, and the Egyptians pursued them with chariots and horsemen*b* as far as the Red Sea.*c* ⁷But they cried to the LORD for help, and he put darkness between you and the Egyptians; he brought the sea over them and covered them. You saw with your own eyes what I did to the Egyptians. Then you lived in the desert for a long time.

⁸"'I brought you to the land of the Amorites who lived east of the Jordan. They fought against you, but I gave them into your hands. I destroyed them from before you, and you took possession of their land. ⁹When Balak son of Zippor, the king of Moab, prepared to fight against Israel, he sent for Balaam son of Beor to put a curse on you. ¹⁰But I would not listen to Balaam, so he blessed you again and again, and I delivered you out of his hand.

¹¹"'Then you crossed the Jordan and came to Jericho. The citizens of Jericho fought against

you, as did also the Amorites, Perizzites, Canaanites, Hittites, Girgashites, Hivites and Jebusites, but I gave them into your hands. ¹²I sent the hornet ahead of you, which drove them out before you—also the two Amorite kings. You did not do it with your own sword and bow. ¹³So I gave you a land on which you did not toil and cities you did not build; and you live in them and eat from vineyards and olive groves that you did not plant.'

¹⁴"Now fear the LORD and serve him with all faithfulness. Throw away the gods your forefathers worshiped beyond the River and in Egypt, and serve the LORD. ¹⁵But if serving the LORD seems undesirable to you, then choose for yourselves this day whom you will serve, whether the gods your forefathers served beyond the River, or the gods of the Amorites, in whose land you are living. But as for me and my household, we will serve the LORD."

¹⁶Then the people answered, "Far be it from us to forsake the LORD to serve other gods! ¹⁷It was the LORD our God himself who brought us and our fathers up out of Egypt, from that land of slavery, and performed those great signs before our eyes. He protected us on our entire journey and among all the nations through which we traveled. ¹⁸And the LORD drove out before us all the nations, including the Amorites, who lived in the land. We too will serve the LORD, because he is our God."

¹⁹Joshua said to the people, "You are not able to serve the LORD. He is a holy God; he is a jealous God. He will not forgive your rebellion and your sins. ²⁰If you forsake the LORD and serve foreign gods, he will turn and bring disaster on you and make an end of you, after he has been good to you."

²¹But the people said to Joshua, "No! We will serve the LORD."

²²Then Joshua said, "You are witnesses against

---

a2 That is, the Euphrates; also in verses 3, 14 and 15   *b6* Or *charioteers*   *c6* Hebrew *Yam Suph*; that is, Sea of Reeds

Filling Moses' Shoes
Joshua could follow orders as well as give them

Israel served the Lord throughout the lifetime of Joshua.
24:31

LIKE ALL THE ISRAELITES, JOSHUA began in humble surroundings. He was born a slave in Egypt and followed Moses across the Red Sea to freedom. He first appears in the Bible as a military commander. Soon after escaping from Egypt, the Israelites confronted a new enemy, and Moses turned to Joshua to lead their very first battle (Exodus 17:9–15).

A month later, when Moses climbed craggy Mount Sinai to meet with God, Joshua was at his side. He first reported to Moses the strange sounds coming from the camp, sounds that turned out to be the Israelites' great spiritual rebellion (Exodus 32:17). Joshua rose to become Moses' trusted number-two man, an aide who served him at almost every major crisis. Moses changed his name from Hoshea, which meant "help," or "salvation," to Joshua, meaning "The Lord saves." (The Greek form of Joshua is *Jesus*.)

Becoming Number One

On the verge of entering Canaan, Moses turned to Joshua again, choosing him as one of 12 spies sent to collect information about the land. Ten came back frightened, with predictions of doom. Only Joshua and Caleb had faith that God would keep his promises to the Israelites despite the military odds.

Joshua learned about the hazards of leadership from that spy trip: on his return, thousands of angry Israelites called for his public stoning (Numbers 14). But he stood firm, and God rewarded him. Of all the Israelites who left Egypt, only he and Caleb were allowed to enter the promised land—not even Moses had that honor. As Moses' death neared, God and Moses made Joshua their uncontested choice for a new leader for Israel. It was time for number two to become number one.

Joshua made a remarkably smooth transition into leadership. In fact, Joshua's life had many parallels to that of Moses. The miracle of crossing the Jordan River poignantly replayed Moses' crossing of the Red Sea. Moses encountered God directly at the burning bush; Joshua met God's special representative, the "commander of the army of the Lord," and likewise took off his shoes at the meeting (5:13–15).

Both Moses and Joshua wrote the law onto stones: Moses creating a permanent record for Israel, and Joshua erecting a monument for the nation to pass by on the way into the new land (8:32). Both leaders pleaded with God on behalf of their people. And both ended their terms with stirring speeches that reviewed history and challenged the people toward a critical choice.

Well-rounded Leader

Moses, who grew up in the courts of Pharaoh, obviously received a better education than Joshua. He showed a philosophical bent. Joshua, on the other hand, was action-oriented and pragmatic, a perfect military man. He had the rare combination of knowing how to follow orders as well as how to give them.

The Bible, never guilty of glossing over its heroes' flaws, reveals some of Joshua's mistakes. In one incident in the desert, he was rash (Numbers 11:26–30). During the first battle of Ai and the treaty negotiations with the Gibeonites, he acted impulsively, without first seeking God's advice. And, faced with his first major defeat at Ai, he uncharacteristically dissolved in fright, earning God's stern rebuke: "Stand up! What are you doing down on your face?" (7:6–12).

Apart from these few incidents, Joshua's life was marked by unusual faith and obedience. Joshua never let the press of military action interfere with worship and the renewal of the covenant. When he divided up the land (an immense bureaucratic burden that takes up the last half of this book), he did so with wisdom and fairness, selecting his own portion only after all others had chosen.

The Bible records this simple legacy: "Israel served the Lord throughout the lifetime of Joshua" (24:31). History would show how rarely that occurred in the life of a troublesome nation.

Life Questions: Often when a popular leader—a pastor, a politician, a teacher—retires from office, something slips. What made Joshua such an effective replacement?

yourselves that you have chosen to serve the LORD."

"Yes, we are witnesses," they replied.

23"Now then," said Joshua, "throw away the foreign gods that are among you and yield your hearts to the LORD, the God of Israel."

24And the people said to Joshua, "We will serve the LORD our God and obey him."

25On that day Joshua made a covenant for the people, and there at Shechem he drew up for them decrees and laws. 26And Joshua recorded these things in the Book of the Law of God. Then he took a large stone and set it up there under the oak near the holy place of the LORD.

27"See!" he said to all the people. "This stone

24:26 Monuments

The Israelites established at least seven memorials to remind future generations of what God had done for them. (Other stone monuments are described in chapters 4,7,8,10,22.) Even if people forgot their debt to God, the land would speak its own story.

will be a witness against us. It has heard all the words the LORD has said to us. It will be a witness against you if you are untrue to your God."

Buried in the Promised Land

28Then Joshua sent the people away, each to his own inheritance.

29After these things, Joshua son of Nun, the servant of the LORD, died at the age of a hundred and ten. 30And they buried him in the land of his inheritance, at Timnath-Serah[a] in the hill country of Ephraim, north of Mount Gaash.

31Israel served the LORD throughout the lifetime of Joshua and of the elders who outlived him and who had experienced everything the LORD had done for Israel.

32And Joseph's bones, which the Israelites had brought up from Egypt, were buried at Shechem in the tract of land that Jacob bought for a hundred pieces of silver[b] from the sons of Hamor, the father of Shechem. This became the inheritance of Joseph's descendants.

33And Eleazar son of Aaron died and was buried at Gibeah, which had been allotted to his son Phinehas in the hill country of Ephraim.

JUDGES

Freedom Fighters
These "judges" took up arms to defend their homeland

THE "JUDGES" OF THIS BOOK might be called guerrillas or freedom fighters today. These men (and one woman) were renowned not for court cases, but for their military campaigns against foreign invaders. Like all military leaders, they sometimes settled disputes; but the book of Judges, however, is preoccupied not with legal matters, but with the excitement of fighting for freedom.

Israel's judges certainly did not stick to "the rules of proper warfare." Judge Ehud tricked his opponent into a private conference; behind closed doors he pulled out a knife and plunged it into the enemy king's belly (3:12–30). Judge Gideon won a surprise victory in the middle of the night. His small band so confused the occupying army with noise and lights that the enemy soldiers stabbed each other and fled in the darkness (chapter 7). Samson never led an army; his battle tricks have been compared to the pranks of an overgrown juvenile delinquent (chapters 14–16).

Most of the time the Israelites hid in the hills while their enemies, with superior weapons, controlled the plains. (Chariots, like tanks, were devastating in level country, but almost useless in muddy or rugged terrain.) Outnumbered, the Israelites relied on ambushes and sneak attacks. They knew every gully, for they were fighting for their homeland. Strategy made up for lack of strength.

Ugliest Stories of the Bible

As a book about early Jewish military heroes, Judges inspires and fascinates. But you can't make the whole book fit that description. If you read strictly looking for heroes, you'd have to ignore half of Judges—and you would miss its most important point about God's work with Israel.

For one thing, Judges' "heroes" were badly flawed. Samson was pitifully vulnerable to his lust for women. Gideon won a battle, then led the nation into idolatry. Jephthah, a former outlaw, apparently knew very little about the God he was supposed to serve.

Add to this the "non-heroic" material: Abimelech, Gideon's son, who slaughtered 70 half brothers so he could be named king; Jephthah and Gideon, who massacred fellow Israelites who had failed to support them; and the sad characters of the last five chapters of Judges. These contain some of the ugliest stories in the Bible—tales of homosexual assault, idolatry, civil war, thievery, rape, and murder. The book of Judges runs downhill, from bad to worse. You may end up wondering what such material is doing in the Bible.

Every picture has shadows; every suspenseful novel has chapters that look truly dark. In the story of God and his people, Judges is that kind of chapter. Heroes appear sporadically, but humanity remains terribly unheroic.

Enthusiasm Fades

God wanted better things for his people than he got in Judges. He had rescued Israel from slavery in Egypt. He had given them a rich land and presented them with a grand system of worship and government centering on him. He would be no distant God in the heavens—he would live with them.

But after some initial enthusiasm, the Israelites didn't continue the way God had pointed. Instead, they learned to live with the sophisticated people they found as their neighbors—people whose faults included worshiping idols through sex orgies and child sacrifice.

The Israelites held the mountains, but the foreign-held valleys, cutting through the land, separated the tribes. Soon each group of isolated Israelites began operating independently. The next generation lost its sense of national identity. The people worshiped the idol Baal alongside the Lord. Though descended from 12 brothers, they spent more time fighting each other than the foreign oppressors.

They violated virtually every moral standard. The last verse of Judges sums it up: "Everyone did as he saw fit." What they saw fit, wasn't.

The Secret of Their Survival

The foreign invasions were no accident, Judges says: They came from God just as surely as the heroic rescuers did. A pattern developed. God allowed suffering as a consequence of the Israelites' disobedience. When things grew really terrible, their attention would turn back to God. He would respond by sending a judge to rescue them. But soon they would fail again. This pattern repeated itself time and again. The Israelites always forgot their need for God, and the dreary cycle ground on.

The secret of Israel's survival was not, then, military heroes or guerrilla tactics. It was the persistent, unwearied love of God himself. Though they forgot him, he did not forget them. He gave innumerable new beginnings. Again and again he sent "judges" to rescue them. He would not let them go. God is the real hero of Judges.

How to Read Judges

Y ou can read Judges as a collection of heroic stories, the most famous of which are Gideon's and Samson's. But together the tales tell a less heroic story.

Read Judges, therefore, on two levels at once. On one level focus on the new beginning God repeatedly offered by sending a judge to rescue Israel. These are character stories with great fascination. You can gain a great deal by studying the strengths and weaknesses of the individual judges.

On another level, read of the deterioration of a nation that quickly forgot what God had done for it. This will help you understand why, in the next stage of Israel's history, God gave the Israelites a king. For background on this change of government, read "The First King," page 308. Another interesting study is the book of Ruth, a lovely story from the time of Judges that shows a softer, more hopeful side.

PEOPLE YOU'LL MEET IN JUDGES

DEBORAH *(p. 270)*
GIDEON *(p. 272)*
SAMSON *(p. 281)*

3-TRACK READING PLAN

For an explanation and complete listing of the 3-track reading plan, turn to page 7.

TRACK 1: *Two-Week Courses on the Bible*
See page 7 for information on these courses.

TRACK 2: *An Overview of Judges in 3 Days*
□ Day 1. Read the Introduction to Judges and chapter 6, in which God calls Gideon to lead a guerrilla army.
□ Day 2. Read chapter 7, Gideon's victory in battle.
□ Day 3. Read chapter 16, the story of Samson and Delilah, and Samson's death.

Now turn to page 9 for your next Track 2 reading project.

TRACK 3: *All of Judges in 21 Days*
After you have read through Judges, turn to pages 10–14 for your next Track 3 reading project.

□1 □2 □3 □4 □5 □6 □7 □8
□9 □10 □11 □12 □13 □14 □15 □16
□17 □18 □19 □20 □21

Israel Fights the Remaining Canaanites

1 After the death of Joshua, the Israelites asked the LORD, "Who will be the first to go up and fight for us against the Canaanites?"

²The LORD answered, "Judah is to go; I have given the land into their hands."

³Then the men of Judah said to the Simeonites their brothers, "Come up with us into the territory allotted to us, to fight against the Canaanites. We in turn will go with you into yours." So the Simeonites went with them.

⁴When Judah attacked, the LORD gave the Canaanites and Perizzites into their hands, and they struck down ten thousand men at Bezek. ⁵It was there that they found Adoni-Bezek and fought against him, putting to rout the Canaanites and Perizzites. ⁶Adoni-Bezek fled, but they chased him and caught him, and cut off his thumbs and big toes.

⁷Then Adoni-Bezek said, "Seventy kings with their thumbs and big toes cut off have picked up scraps under my table. Now God has paid me back for what I did to them." They brought him to Jerusalem, and he died there.

1:7 Thumbs and Big Toes

A person lacking thumbs and big toes could not grip a weapon or run quickly. So cutting off those appendages guaranteed that a captured enemy would never fight again.

⁸The men of Judah attacked Jerusalem also and took it. They put the city to the sword and set it on fire.

⁹After that, the men of Judah went down to fight against the Canaanites living in the hill country, the Negev and the western foothills. ¹⁰They advanced against the Canaanites living in Hebron (formerly called Kiriath Arba) and defeated Sheshai, Ahiman and Talmai.

¹¹From there they advanced against the people living in Debir (formerly called Kiriath Sepher). ¹²And Caleb said, "I will give my daughter Acsah in marriage to the man who attacks and captures Kiriath Sepher." ¹³Othniel son of Kenaz, Caleb's younger brother, took it; so Caleb gave his daughter Acsah to him in marriage.

¹⁴One day when she came to Othniel, she urged him[a] to ask her father for a field. When she got off her donkey, Caleb asked her, "What can I do for you?"

¹⁵She replied, "Do me a special favor. Since you have given me land in the Negev, give me also springs of water." Then Caleb gave her the upper and lower springs.

¹⁶The descendants of Moses' father-in-law, the Kenite, went up from the City of Palms[b] with the men of Judah to live among the people of the Desert of Judah in the Negev near Arad.

¹⁷Then the men of Judah went with the Simeonites their brothers and attacked the Canaanites living in Zephath, and they totally destroyed[c] the city. Therefore it was called Hormah.[d] ¹⁸The men of Judah also took[e] Gaza, Ashkelon and Ekron—each city with its territory.

¹⁹The LORD was with the men of Judah. They took possession of the hill country, but they were

1:19 Military Setbacks

Why did the Israelites fail to take all the territory allotted them? One reason was stubborn military opposition. The Israelites had never developed the sophistication to use chariots, the equivalent of modern-day tanks. Israel controlled the hills where chariots were unwieldy, but could not win the plains. The Israelites also failed to conquer Jerusalem (verse 21); its mountainous setting made that city almost impregnable.

unable to drive the people from the plains, because they had iron chariots. ²⁰As Moses had promised, Hebron was given to Caleb, who drove from it the three sons of Anak. ²¹The Benjamites, however, failed to dislodge the Jebusites, who were living in Jerusalem; to this day the Jebusites live there with the Benjamites.

²²Now the house of Joseph attacked Bethel, and the LORD was with them. ²³When they sent men to spy out Bethel (formerly called Luz), ²⁴the spies saw a man coming out of the city and they said to him, "Show us how to get into the city and we will see that you are treated well." ²⁵So he showed them, and they put the city to the sword but spared the man and his whole family. ²⁶He then went to the land of the Hittites, where he built a city and called it Luz, which is its name to this day.

²⁷But Manasseh did not drive out the people of Beth Shan or Taanach or Dor or Ibleam or Megiddo and their surrounding settlements, for the Canaanites were determined to live in that land. ²⁸When Israel became strong, they pressed the Canaanites into forced labor but never drove them out completely. ²⁹Nor did Ephraim drive out the Canaanites living in Gezer, but the Canaanites continued to live there among them. ³⁰Neither did Zebulun drive out the Canaanites living in Kitron or Nahalol, who remained among them; but they did subject them to forced

---

a 14 Hebrew; Septuagint and Vulgate *Othniel, he urged her*   *b 16* That is, Jericho   *c 17* The Hebrew term refers to the irrevocable giving over of things or persons to the LORD, often by totally destroying them.   *d 17 Hormah* means *destruction.*   *e 18* Hebrew; Septuagint *Judah did not take*

labor. [31]Nor did Asher drive out those living in Acco or Sidon or Ahlab or Aczib or Helbah or Aphek or Rehob, [32]and because of this the people of Asher lived among the Canaanite inhabitants of the land. [33]Neither did Naphtali drive out those living in Beth Shemesh or Beth Anath; but the Naphtalites too lived among the Canaanite inhabitants of the land, and those living in Beth Shemesh and Beth Anath became forced laborers for them. [34]The Amorites confined the Danites to the hill country, not allowing them to come down into the plain. [35]And the Amorites were determined also to hold out in Mount Heres, Aijalon and Shaalbim, but when the power of the house of Joseph increased, they too were pressed into forced labor. [36]The boundary of the Amorites was from Scorpion[a] Pass to Sela and beyond.

The Angel of the LORD at Bokim

2 The angel of the LORD went up from Gilgal to Bokim and said, "I brought you up out of Egypt and led you into the land that I swore to give to your forefathers. I said, 'I will never break my covenant with you, [2]and you shall not make a covenant with the people of this land, but you shall break down their altars.' Yet you have disobeyed me. Why have you done this? [3]Now therefore I tell you that I will not drive them out before you; they will be ⌊thorns⌋ in your sides and their gods will be a snare to you."

[4]When the angel of the LORD had spoken these things to all the Israelites, the people wept aloud, [5]and they called that place Bokim.[b] There they offered sacrifices to the LORD.

Disobedience and Defeat

[6]After Joshua had dismissed the Israelites, they went to take possession of the land, each to his own inheritance. [7]The people served the LORD throughout the lifetime of Joshua and of the elders who outlived him and who had seen all the great things the LORD had done for Israel.

[8]Joshua son of Nun, the servant of the LORD, died at the age of a hundred and ten. [9]And they buried him in the land of his inheritance, at Timnath Heres[c] in the hill country of Ephraim, north of Mount Gaash.

[10]After that whole generation had been gathered to their fathers, another generation grew up, who knew neither the LORD nor what he had done for Israel. [11]Then the Israelites did evil in the eyes of the LORD and served the Baals. [12]They forsook the LORD, the God of their fathers, who had brought them out of Egypt. They followed and worshiped various gods of the peoples around them. They provoked the LORD to anger [13]because they forsook him and served Baal and the Ashtoreths. [14]In his anger against Israel the

LORD handed them over to raiders who plundered them. He sold them to their enemies all around, whom they were no longer able to resist. [15]Whenever Israel went out to fight, the hand of

2:13 Fertility Gods

Israel's neighbors worshiped Baal and Ashtoreth, male and female gods of fertility. Followers practiced ritual sex at the shrines, believing that sex with sacred prostitutes led to good crops and many children. Sometimes, too, worshipers sacrificed their children to the gods. The Israelites' attraction to these foreign religions continued for most of their history as a nation.

the LORD was against them to defeat them, just as he had sworn to them. They were in great distress.

[16]Then the LORD raised up judges,[d] who saved them out of the hands of these raiders. [17]Yet they would not listen to their judges but prostituted themselves to other gods and worshiped them. Unlike their fathers, they quickly turned from the way in which their fathers had walked, the way of obedience to the LORD's commands. [18]Whenever the LORD raised up a judge for them, he was with the judge and saved them out of the hands of their enemies as long as the judge lived; for the LORD had compassion on them as they groaned under those who oppressed and afflicted them. [19]But when the judge died, the people returned to ways even more corrupt than those of their fathers, following other gods and serving and worshiping them. They refused to give up their evil practices and stubborn ways.

[20]Therefore the LORD was very angry with Israel and said, "Because this nation has violated the covenant that I laid down for their forefathers and has not listened to me, [21]I will no longer drive out before them any of the nations Joshua left when he died. [22]I will use them to test Israel and see whether they will keep the way of the LORD and walk in it as their forefathers did." [23]The LORD had allowed those nations to remain; he did not drive them out at once by giving them into the hands of Joshua.

3 These are the nations the LORD left to test all those Israelites who had not experienced any of the wars in Canaan [2](he did this only to teach warfare to the descendants of the Israelites who had not had previous battle experience): [3]the five rulers of the Philistines, all the Canaanites, the Sidonians, and the Hivites living in the Lebanon mountains from Mount Baal Hermon to Lebo[e]

---

[a]36 Hebrew *Akrabbim*   [b]5 *Bokim* means *weepers*.   [c]9 Also known as *Timnath Serah* (see Joshua 19:50 and 24:30)   [d]16 Or *leaders*; similarly in verses 17-19   [e]3 Or *to the entrance to*

Hamath. [4]They were left to test the Israelites to see whether they would obey the LORD's commands, which he had given their forefathers through Moses.

[5]The Israelites lived among the Canaanites, Hittites, Amorites, Perizzites, Hivites and Jebusites. [6]They took their daughters in marriage and gave their own daughters to their sons, and served their gods.

3:6 Intermarriage

This passage shows why the Old Testament opposed mixed marriages, which were common in the period of the judges. Ethnic differences were not the main issue. In fact, during the period of the judges Ruth, a non-Jew, married into a Jewish family with full acceptance (see the book of Ruth). But Ruth had accepted the God of Israel. When mixed marriages meant mixed religions, they diluted faith in God.

Othniel

[7]The Israelites did evil in the eyes of the LORD; they forgot the LORD their God and served the Baals and the Asherahs. [8]The anger of the LORD burned against Israel so that he sold them into the hands of Cushan-Rishathaim king of Aram Naharaim,[a] to whom the Israelites were subject for eight years. [9]But when they cried out to the LORD, he raised up for them a deliverer, Othniel son of Kenaz, Caleb's younger brother, who saved them. [10]The Spirit of the LORD came upon him, so that he became Israel's judge[b] and went to war. The LORD gave Cushan-Rishathaim king of Aram into the hands of Othniel, who overpowered him. [11]So the land had peace for forty years, until Othniel son of Kenaz died.

Ehud

[12]Once again the Israelites did evil in the eyes of the LORD, and because they did this evil the LORD gave Eglon king of Moab power over Israel. [13]Getting the Ammonites and Amalekites to join him, Eglon came and attacked Israel, and they took possession of the City of Palms.[c] [14]The Israelites were subject to Eglon king of Moab for eighteen years.

[15]Again the Israelites cried out to the LORD, and he gave them a deliverer—Ehud, a left-handed man, the son of Gera the Benjamite. The Israelites sent him with tribute to Eglon king of Moab. [16]Now Ehud had made a double-edged sword about a foot and a half[d] long, which he strapped to his right thigh under his clothing. [17]He presented the tribute to Eglon king of Moab, who was a very fat man. [18]After Ehud had presented the tribute, he sent on their way the men who had carried it. [19]At the idols[e] near Gilgal he himself turned back and said, "I have a secret message for you, O king."

The king said, "Quiet!" And all his attendants left him.

[20]Ehud then approached him while he was sitting alone in the upper room of his summer palace[f] and said, "I have a message from God for you." As the king rose from his seat, [21]Ehud reached with his left hand, drew the sword from his right thigh and plunged it into the king's belly. [22]Even the handle sank in after the blade, which came out his back. Ehud did not pull the sword out, and the fat closed in over it. [23]Then Ehud went out to the porch;[g] he shut the doors of the upper room behind him and locked them.

[24]After he had gone, the servants came and found the doors of the upper room locked. They said, "He must be relieving himself in the inner room of the house." [25]They waited to the point of embarrassment, but when he did not open the doors of the room, they took a key and unlocked them. There they saw their lord fallen to the floor, dead.

[26]While they waited, Ehud got away. He passed by the idols and escaped to Seirah. [27]When he arrived there, he blew a trumpet in the hill country of Ephraim, and the Israelites went down with him from the hills, with him leading them.

[28]"Follow me," he ordered, "for the LORD has given Moab, your enemy, into your hands." So they followed him down and, taking possession of the fords of the Jordan that led to Moab, they allowed no one to cross over. [29]At that time they struck down about ten thousand Moabites, all vigorous and strong; not a man escaped. [30]That day Moab was made subject to Israel, and the land had peace for eighty years.

Shamgar

[31]After Ehud came Shamgar son of Anath, who struck down six hundred Philistines with an oxgoad. He too saved Israel.

Deborah

4 After Ehud died, the Israelites once again did evil in the eyes of the LORD. [2]So the LORD sold them into the hands of Jabin, a king of Canaan, who reigned in Hazor. The commander of his army was Sisera, who lived in Harosheth Haggoyim. [3]Because he had nine hundred iron chari-

---

a8 That is, Northwest Mesopotamia   *b10* Or *leader*   *c13* That is, Jericho   *d16* Hebrew *a cubit* (about 0.5 meter)   *e19* Or *the stone quarries*; also in verse 26   *f20* The meaning of the Hebrew for this phrase is uncertain. *g23* The meaning of the Hebrew for this word is uncertain.

ots and had cruelly oppressed the Israelites for twenty years, they cried to the LORD for help.

[4]Deborah, a prophetess, the wife of Lappidoth, was leading[a] Israel at that time. [5]She held court under the Palm of Deborah between Ramah and Bethel in the hill country of Ephraim, and the Israelites came to her to have their disputes decided. [6]She sent for Barak son of Abinoam from Kedesh in Naphtali and said to him, "The LORD, the God of Israel, commands you: 'Go, take with you ten thousand men of Naphtali and Zebulun and lead the way to Mount Tabor. [7]I will lure Sisera, the commander of Jabin's army, with his chariots and his troops to the Kishon River and give him into your hands.'"

[8]Barak said to her, "If you go with me, I will go; but if you don't go with me, I won't go."

[9]"Very well," Deborah said, "I will go with you. But because of the way you are going about this,[b] the honor will not be yours, for the LORD will hand Sisera over to a woman." So Deborah went with Barak to Kedesh, [10]where he summoned Zebulun and Naphtali. Ten thousand men followed him, and Deborah also went with him.

[11]Now Heber the Kenite had left the other Kenites, the descendants of Hobab, Moses' brother-in-law,[c] and pitched his tent by the great tree in Zaanannim near Kedesh.

[12]When they told Sisera that Barak son of Abinoam had gone up to Mount Tabor, [13]Sisera gathered together his nine hundred iron chariots and all the men with him, from Harosheth Haggoyim to the Kishon River.

[14]Then Deborah said to Barak, "Go! This is the day the LORD has given Sisera into your hands. Has not the LORD gone ahead of you?" So Barak went down Mount Tabor, followed by ten thousand men. [15]At Barak's advance, the LORD routed Sisera and all his chariots and army by the sword, and Sisera abandoned his chariot and fled on foot. [16]But Barak pursued the chariots and army as far as Harosheth Haggoyim. All the troops of Sisera fell by the sword; not a man was left.

[17]Sisera, however, fled on foot to the tent of Jael, the wife of Heber the Kenite, because there were friendly relations between Jabin king of Hazor and the clan of Heber the Kenite.

[18]Jael went out to meet Sisera and said to him, "Come, my lord, come right in. Don't be afraid." So he entered her tent, and she put a covering over him.

[19]"I'm thirsty," he said. "Please give me some water." She opened a skin of milk, gave him a drink, and covered him up.

[20]"Stand in the doorway of the tent," he told her. "If someone comes by and asks you, 'Is anyone here?' say 'No.'"

[21]But Jael, Heber's wife, picked up a tent peg and a hammer and went quietly to him while he lay fast asleep, exhausted. She drove the peg through his temple into the ground, and he died.

[22]Barak came by in pursuit of Sisera, and Jael went out to meet him. "Come," she said, "I will show you the man you're looking for." So he went in with her, and there lay Sisera with the tent peg through his temple—dead.

[23]On that day God subdued Jabin, the Canaanite king, before the Israelites. [24]And the hand of the Israelites grew stronger and stronger

[a]4 Traditionally *judging*   [b]9 Or *But on the expedition you are undertaking*   [c]11 Or *father-in-law*

DEBORAH *Multi-talented Woman*

WOMEN OFTEN GET OVERLOOKED IN the Old Testament, but Deborah is one spectacular exception. As a military leader, poet, prophet and judge, she used her talents to inspire Israel during a dark time.

Deborah won her fame leading a desperate nation to victory. With Israel under the thumb of a cruel foreign ruler, she gave orders for Barak to lead a revolt. He refused to go unless brave Deborah accompanied him to battle. With her giving the orders, Israel's ten thousand troops routed a better-equipped enemy. Deborah's triumph led to forty years of peace.

It is hard to think of an area in which Deborah did not excel. She was a mother and wife. Her wisdom was so renowned that people brought their disputes to her as she sat under a large palm tree, the Palm of Deborah. As a prophet, she had the ability to understand God's message and relay it to his people. When she sent Barak into battle, she stated it this way: "The LORD, the God of Israel, commands you . . ." (4:6).

Finally, Deborah was an accomplished poet, as chapter 5 demonstrates. One of the oldest and most expressive poems in the Bible, it was sung as a duet by Barak and Deborah, but the words give Deborah proper credit (5:7).

Throughout the Bible we can hardly find a more well-rounded leader, male or female, than Deborah.

Life Questions: In what areas could you strengthen your talents to become more well-rounded?

against Jabin, the Canaanite king, until they destroyed him.

The Song of Deborah

5 On that day Deborah and Barak son of Abinoam sang this song:

2"When the princes in Israel take the lead,
   when the people willingly offer
      themselves—
   praise the LORD!

3"Hear this, you kings! Listen, you rulers!
   I will sing to[a] the LORD, I will sing;
   I will make music to[b] the LORD, the God
      of Israel.

4"O LORD, when you went out from Seir,
   when you marched from the land of
      Edom,
   the earth shook, the heavens poured,
      the clouds poured down water.
5The mountains quaked before the LORD, the
      One of Sinai,
   before the LORD, the God of Israel.

6"In the days of Shamgar son of Anath,
   in the days of Jael, the roads were
      abandoned;
   travelers took to winding paths.
7Village life[c] in Israel ceased,
   ceased until I,[d] Deborah, arose,
      arose a mother in Israel.
8When they chose new gods,
   war came to the city gates,
   and not a shield or spear was seen
      among forty thousand in Israel.
9My heart is with Israel's princes,
   with the willing volunteers among the
      people.
   Praise the LORD!

10"You who ride on white donkeys,
   sitting on your saddle blankets,
   and you who walk along the road,
consider 11the voice of the singers[e] at the
      watering places.
   They recite the righteous acts of the LORD,
   the righteous acts of his warriors[f] in
      Israel.

   "Then the people of the LORD
      went down to the city gates.
12'Wake up, wake up, Deborah!
   Wake up, wake up, break out in song!
   Arise, O Barak!
      Take captive your captives, O son of
         Abinoam.'

13"Then the men who were left

came down to the nobles;
the people of the LORD
   came to me with the mighty.
14Some came from Ephraim, whose roots were
      in Amalek;
   Benjamin was with the people who
      followed you.
From Makir captains came down,
   from Zebulun those who bear a
      commander's staff.
15The princes of Issachar were with Deborah;
   yes, Issachar was with Barak,
      rushing after him into the valley.
In the districts of Reuben
   there was much searching of heart.
16Why did you stay among the campfires[g]
   to hear the whistling for the flocks?
In the districts of Reuben
   there was much searching of heart.
17Gilead stayed beyond the Jordan.
   And Dan, why did he linger by the ships?
Asher remained on the coast
   and stayed in his coves.
18The people of Zebulun risked their very
      lives;
   so did Naphtali on the heights of the field.

19"Kings came, they fought;
   the kings of Canaan fought
at Taanach by the waters of Megiddo,
   but they carried off no silver, no plunder.
20From the heavens the stars fought,
   from their courses they fought against
      Sisera.
21The river Kishon swept them away,
   the age-old river, the river Kishon.
   March on, my soul; be strong!
22Then thundered the horses' hoofs—
   galloping, galloping go his mighty steeds.
23'Curse Meroz,' said the angel of the LORD.
   'Curse its people bitterly,
because they did not come to help the LORD,
   to help the LORD against the mighty.'

24"Most blessed of women be Jael,
   the wife of Heber the Kenite,
   most blessed of tent-dwelling women.
25He asked for water, and she gave him milk;
   in a bowl fit for nobles she brought him
      curdled milk.
26Her hand reached for the tent peg,
   her right hand for the workman's
      hammer.
She struck Sisera, she crushed his head,
   she shattered and pierced his temple.
27At her feet he sank,
   he fell; there he lay.

---

*a*3 Or *of*   *b*3 Or *I with song I will praise*   *c*7 Or *Warriors*   *d*7 Or *you*   *e*11 Or *archers*; the meaning of the
Hebrew for this word is uncertain.   *f*11 Or *villagers*   *g*16 Or *saddlebags*

At her feet he sank, he fell;
  where he sank, there he fell—dead.

28"Through the window peered Sisera's
     mother;
  behind the lattice she cried out,
  'Why is his chariot so long in coming?
    Why is the clatter of his chariots delayed?'
29The wisest of her ladies answer her;
  indeed, she keeps saying to herself,
30'Are they not finding and dividing the
    spoils:
  a girl or two for each man,
  colorful garments as plunder for Sisera,
  colorful garments embroidered,
  highly embroidered garments for my
     neck—
  all this as plunder?'

31"So may all your enemies perish, O LORD!
  But may they who love you be like the
    sun
  when it rises in its strength."

Then the land had peace forty years.

Gideon

6 Again the Israelites did evil in the eyes of the LORD, and for seven years he gave them into the hands of the Midianites. ²Because the power of Midian was so oppressive, the Israelites prepared shelters for themselves in mountain clefts, caves and strongholds. ³Whenever the Israelites planted their crops, the Midianites, Amalekites and other eastern peoples invaded the country. ⁴They camped on the land and ruined the crops all the way to Gaza and did not spare a living

Unlikely Leaders
God drew out Gideon's hidden potential

GIDEON MADE AN UNLIKELY FIGHTER—HESITANT and fearful. We first meet him as he furtively threshed wheat in a winepress. To thresh wheat openly was to invite the occupying Midianite army to confiscate it. The Midianites dominated Israel so thoroughly that Israelites could rarely harvest crops; some lived in caves.

Gideon was planning no heroics until the angel of the Lord came to him with a battle commission. "Who, me?" Gideon seemed to ask, trembling.

In view of the facts, his doubts were justified. His family and village worshiped Baal, not the Lord. He himself was subject to paralyzing fears, even on the eve of battle. Gideon kept demanding miraculous proof that God really was with him—and one miracle was not enough.

At the same time, God seemed to make Gideon's job more formidable. He reduced his army from 32,000 to a pitiful 300. If an army so outnumbered were to win, that would prove beyond a doubt that God was in charge.

God knew Gideon's potential and patiently brought Gideon to the point of courage. He encouraged him, directed him, transformed him. Overnight Gideon became a strong and decisive general. He used noise and lights for scare tactics, enabling his small band to scatter the enemy. Thorough mopping-up operations followed. The little army devastated the scattered Midianites, and Gideon, triumphant, brought in an era of freedom. Perhaps no one was as surprised as he.

> The LORD said to him, "Peace! Do not be afraid. You are not going to die."
> 6:23

Cast-off Material

The selection of Gideon shows a pattern. At a time when women were regarded as second-class citizens (see 9:54; 19:24), God chose Deborah to lead. Jephthah, another judge, had been a social outcast, the leader of a gang of outlaws, before God chose him to lead.

And the pattern is found not only in Judges. Throughout the Bible, God used cast-off material. Israel was not chosen because of its great size or sophistication. (In fact, archaeologists report a drop in the culture of a city after the Israelites captured it.) God did not seek the most capable people, nor the most naturally "good." He chose a small, weak slave tribe, uncultured, with a short memory for his kindness to them. Time and again the Israelites proved themselves faulty. So did their leaders. With this unlikely material God did great things so the world could see that the glory was his and his alone.

Paul took up this theme when he wrote, over a thousand years later, "Brothers, think of what you were when you were called. Not many of you were wise by human standards; not many were influential; not many were of noble birth. But God chose the foolish things of the world to shame the wise; God chose the weak things of the world to shame the strong.... Therefore, as it is written: 'Let him who boasts boast in the Lord'" (1 Corinthians 1:26–31).

Life Questions: Do you picture yourself as a leader? Why or why not? What would God have to change to make you a leader?

thing for Israel, neither sheep nor cattle nor donkeys. [5]They came up with their livestock and their tents like swarms of locusts. It was impossible to count the men and their camels; they invaded the land to ravage it. [6]Midian so impoverished the Israelites that they cried out to the LORD for help.

6:5 Camel Power

This is the earliest mention in the Bible of camels used for military purposes. Midianite marauders let the Israelites raise their crops, then swept in and took everything when the crops were ripe. With no effective defense, the Israelites hid out in caves and other remote spots.

[7]When the Israelites cried to the LORD because of Midian, [8]he sent them a prophet, who said, "This is what the LORD, the God of Israel, says: I brought you up out of Egypt, out of the land of slavery. [9]I snatched you from the power of Egypt and from the hand of all your oppressors. I drove them from before you and gave you their land. [10]I said to you, 'I am the LORD your God; do not worship the gods of the Amorites, in whose land you live.' But you have not listened to me."

[11]The angel of the LORD came and sat down under the oak in Ophrah that belonged to Joash the Abiezrite, where his son Gideon was threshing wheat in a winepress to keep it from the Midianites. [12]When the angel of the LORD appeared to Gideon, he said, "The LORD is with you, mighty warrior."

[13]"But sir," Gideon replied, "if the LORD is with us, why has all this happened to us? Where are all his wonders that our fathers told us about when they said, 'Did not the LORD bring us up out of Egypt?' But now the LORD has abandoned us and put us into the hand of Midian."

[14]The LORD turned to him and said, "Go in the strength you have and save Israel out of Midian's hand. Am I not sending you?"

[15]"But Lord,[a]" Gideon asked, "how can I save Israel? My clan is the weakest in Manasseh, and I am the least in my family."

[16]The LORD answered, "I will be with you, and you will strike down all the Midianites together."

[17]Gideon replied, "If now I have found favor in your eyes, give me a sign that it is really you talking to me. [18]Please do not go away until I come back and bring my offering and set it before you."

And the LORD said, "I will wait until you return."

[19]Gideon went in, prepared a young goat, and from an ephah[b] of flour he made bread without yeast. Putting the meat in a basket and its broth in a pot, he brought them out and offered them to him under the oak.

[20]The angel of God said to him, "Take the meat and the unleavened bread, place them on this rock, and pour out the broth." And Gideon did so. [21]With the tip of the staff that was in his hand, the angel of the LORD touched the meat and the unleavened bread. Fire flared from the rock, consuming the meat and the bread. And the angel of the LORD disappeared. [22]When Gideon realized that it was the angel of the LORD, he exclaimed, "Ah, Sovereign LORD! I have seen the angel of the LORD face to face!"

[23]But the LORD said to him, "Peace! Do not be afraid. You are not going to die."

[24]So Gideon built an altar to the LORD there and called it The LORD is Peace. To this day it stands in Ophrah of the Abiezrites.

[25]That same night the LORD said to him, "Take the second bull from your father's herd, the one seven years old.[c] Tear down your father's altar to Baal and cut down the Asherah pole[d] beside it. [26]Then build a proper kind of[e] altar to the LORD your God on the top of this height. Using the wood of the Asherah pole that you cut down, offer the second[f] bull as a burnt offering."

[27]So Gideon took ten of his servants and did as the LORD told him. But because he was afraid of his family and the men of the town, he did it at night rather than in the daytime.

[28]In the morning when the men of the town got up, there was Baal's altar, demolished, with the Asherah pole beside it cut down and the second bull sacrificed on the newly built altar!

[29]They asked each other, "Who did this?"

When they carefully investigated, they were told, "Gideon son of Joash did it."

[30]The men of the town demanded of Joash, "Bring out your son. He must die, because he has broken down Baal's altar and cut down the Asherah pole beside it."

6:30 Topsy-turvy

Israel had turned God's commands upside down. According to Deuteronomy 13:6–10, those who worshiped idols should be stoned. But here Israelites were ready to execute Gideon for destroying their idols.

---

[a]15 Or *sir*   [b]19 That is, probably about 3/5 bushel (about 22 liters)   [c]25 Or *Take a full-grown, mature bull from your father's herd*   [d]25 That is, a symbol of the goddess Asherah; here and elsewhere in Judges   [e]26 Or *build with layers of stone an*   [f]26 Or *full-grown*; also in verse 28

³¹But Joash replied to the hostile crowd around him, "Are you going to plead Baal's cause? Are you trying to save him? Whoever fights for him shall be put to death by morning! If Baal really is a god, he can defend himself when someone breaks down his altar." ³²So that day they called Gideon "Jerub-Baal,ᵃ" saying, "Let Baal contend with him," because he broke down Baal's altar.

³³Now all the Midianites, Amalekites and other eastern peoples joined forces and crossed over the Jordan and camped in the Valley of Jezreel. ³⁴Then the Spirit of the LORD came upon Gideon, and he blew a trumpet, summoning the Abiezrites to follow him. ³⁵He sent messengers throughout Manasseh, calling them to arms, and also into Asher, Zebulun and Naphtali, so that they too went up to meet them.

³⁶Gideon said to God, "If you will save Israel by my hand as you have promised— ³⁷look, I will place a wool fleece on the threshing floor. If there is dew only on the fleece and all the ground is dry, then I will know that you will save Israel

6:37 Putting Out a Fleece

How much proof of God's will does one person need? Though the angel of the Lord had assured Gideon of success, he took fright and wanted to double-check, then triple-check, by asking for miracles. In some circles today, "putting out a fleece" has come to mean asking God to do something unusual to confirm his guidance. However, Gideon's action seems more like a lack of faith than a model of seeking God's guidance.

by my hand, as you said." ³⁸And that is what happened. Gideon rose early the next day; he squeezed the fleece and wrung out the dew—a bowlful of water.

³⁹Then Gideon said to God, "Do not be angry with me. Let me make just one more request. Allow me one more test with the fleece. This time make the fleece dry and the ground covered with dew." ⁴⁰That night God did so. Only the fleece was dry; all the ground was covered with dew.

Gideon Defeats the Midianites

7 Early in the morning, Jerub-Baal (that is, Gideon) and all his men camped at the spring of Harod. The camp of Midian was north of them in the valley near the hill of Moreh. ²The LORD said to Gideon, "You have too many men for me to deliver Midian into their hands. In order that Israel may not boast against me that her own strength has saved her, ³announce now

to the people, 'Anyone who trembles with fear may turn back and leave Mount Gilead.'" So twenty-two thousand men left, while ten thousand remained.

⁴But the LORD said to Gideon, "There are still too many men. Take them down to the water, and I will sift them for you there. If I say, 'This one shall go with you,' he shall go; but if I say, 'This one shall not go with you,' he shall not go."

⁵So Gideon took the men down to the water. There the LORD told him, "Separate those who lap the water with their tongues like a dog from those who kneel down to drink." ⁶Three hundred men lapped with their hands to their mouths. All the rest got down on their knees to drink.

⁷The LORD said to Gideon, "With the three hundred men that lapped I will save you and give the Midianites into your hands. Let all the other men go, each to his own place." ⁸So Gideon sent the rest of the Israelites to their tents but kept the three hundred, who took over the provisions and trumpets of the others.

Now the camp of Midian lay below him in the valley. ⁹During that night the LORD said to Gideon, "Get up, go down against the camp, because I am going to give it into your hands. ¹⁰If you are afraid to attack, go down to the camp with your servant Purah ¹¹and listen to what they are saying. Afterward, you will be encouraged to attack the camp." So he and Purah his servant went down to the outposts of the camp. ¹²The Midianites, the Amalekites and all the other eastern peoples had settled in the valley, thick as locusts. Their camels could no more be counted than the sand on the seashore.

¹³Gideon arrived just as a man was telling a friend his dream. "I had a dream," he was saying. "A round loaf of barley bread came tumbling into the Midianite camp. It struck the tent with such force that the tent overturned and collapsed."

¹⁴His friend responded, "This can be nothing other than the sword of Gideon son of Joash, the Israelite. God has given the Midianites and the whole camp into his hands."

¹⁵When Gideon heard the dream and its interpretation, he worshiped God. He returned to the camp of Israel and called out, "Get up! The LORD has given the Midianite camp into your hands." ¹⁶Dividing the three hundred men into three companies, he placed trumpets and empty jars in the hands of all of them, with torches inside.

¹⁷"Watch me," he told them. "Follow my lead. When I get to the edge of the camp, do exactly as I do. ¹⁸When I and all who are with me blow our trumpets, then from all around the camp blow yours and shout, 'For the LORD and for Gideon.'"

¹⁹Gideon and the hundred men with him

ᵃ *32 Jerub-Baal means let Baal contend.*

reached the edge of the camp at the beginning of the middle watch, just after they had changed the guard. They blew their trumpets and broke the jars that were in their hands. ²⁰The three companies blew the trumpets and smashed the jars. Grasping the torches in their left hands and holding in their right hands the trumpets they were to blow, they shouted, "A sword for the LORD and for Gideon!" ²¹While each man held his position around the camp, all the Midianites ran, crying out as they fled.

²²When the three hundred trumpets sounded, the LORD caused the men throughout the camp to turn on each other with their swords. The army fled to Beth Shittah toward Zererah as far as the border of Abel Meholah near Tabbath. ²³Israelites from Naphtali, Asher and all Manasseh were called out, and they pursued the Midianites. ²⁴Gideon sent messengers throughout the hill country of Ephraim, saying, "Come down against the Midianites and seize the waters of the Jordan ahead of them as far as Beth Barah."

So all the men of Ephraim were called out and they took the waters of the Jordan as far as Beth Barah. ²⁵They also captured two of the Midianite leaders, Oreb and Zeeb. They killed Oreb at the rock of Oreb, and Zeeb at the winepress of Zeeb. They pursued the Midianites and brought the heads of Oreb and Zeeb to Gideon, who was by the Jordan.

Zebah and Zalmunna

8 Now the Ephraimites asked Gideon, "Why have you treated us like this? Why didn't you call us when you went to fight Midian?" And they criticized him sharply.

²But he answered them, "What have I accomplished compared to you? Aren't the gleanings of Ephraim's grapes better than the full grape harvest of Abiezer? ³God gave Oreb and Zeeb, the Midianite leaders, into your hands. What was I able to do compared to you?" At this, their resentment against him subsided.

⁴Gideon and his three hundred men, exhausted yet keeping up the pursuit, came to the Jordan and crossed it. ⁵He said to the men of Succoth, "Give my troops some bread; they are worn out, and I am still pursuing Zebah and Zalmunna, the kings of Midian."

⁶But the officials of Succoth said, "Do you already have the hands of Zebah and Zalmunna in your possession? Why should we give bread to your troops?"

⁷Then Gideon replied, "Just for that, when the LORD has given Zebah and Zalmunna into my hand, I will tear your flesh with desert thorns and briers."

⁸From there he went up to Peniel[a] and made the same request of them, but they answered as the men of Succoth had. ⁹So he said to the men of Peniel, "When I return in triumph, I will tear down this tower."

¹⁰Now Zebah and Zalmunna were in Karkor with a force of about fifteen thousand men, all that were left of the armies of the eastern peoples; a hundred and twenty thousand swordsmen had fallen. ¹¹Gideon went up by the route of the nomads east of Nobah and Jogbehah and fell upon the unsuspecting army. ¹²Zebah and Zalmunna, the two kings of Midian, fled, but he pursued them and captured them, routing their entire army.

¹³Gideon son of Joash then returned from the battle by the Pass of Heres. ¹⁴He caught a young man of Succoth and questioned him, and the young man wrote down for him the names of the seventy-seven officials of Succoth, the elders of

> ### 8:14 Early Literacy
>
> *Some scholars argue that much of the Old Testament was handed down by word of mouth and only written at a much later time. This brief mention of a young man's ability to write suggests that literacy was widespread even at this early date—and thus that the Old Testament books could have been written soon after the events they describe.*

the town. ¹⁵Then Gideon came and said to the men of Succoth, "Here are Zebah and Zalmunna, about whom you taunted me by saying, 'Do you already have the hands of Zebah and Zalmunna in your possession? Why should we give bread to your exhausted men?'" ¹⁶He took the elders of the town and taught the men of Succoth a lesson by punishing them with desert thorns and briers. ¹⁷He also pulled down the tower of Peniel and killed the men of the town.

¹⁸Then he asked Zebah and Zalmunna, "What kind of men did you kill at Tabor?"

"Men like you," they answered, "each one with the bearing of a prince."

¹⁹Gideon replied, "Those were my brothers, the sons of my own mother. As surely as the LORD lives, if you had spared their lives, I would not kill you." ²⁰Turning to Jether, his oldest son, he said, "Kill them!" But Jether did not draw his sword, because he was only a boy and was afraid.

²¹Zebah and Zalmunna said, "Come, do it yourself. 'As is the man, so is his strength.'" So Gideon stepped forward and killed them, and took the ornaments off their camels' necks.

---

[a]8 Hebrew *Penuel*, a variant of *Peniel*; also in verses 9 and 17

Gideon's Ephod

22The Israelites said to Gideon, "Rule over us—you, your son and your grandson—because you have saved us out of the hand of Midian."

23But Gideon told them, "I will not rule over you, nor will my son rule over you. The LORD will

> ### 8:23 No King
>
> *Unlike most nations of this time, Israel had no king. Gideon, declining an opportunity to rule, explains why: God alone must rule. Generations later, when Israel insisted on royal leadership, Samuel interpreted the move as a rejection of God (1 Samuel 10:19).*
>
> *Even after Israel gained a king, the king's power had limits; rulers answered to God, the ultimate ruler. That was a novel idea in an era when people worshiped kings as gods.*

rule over you." **24**And he said, "I do have one request, that each of you give me an earring from your share of the plunder." (It was the custom of the Ishmaelites to wear gold earrings.)

25They answered, "We'll be glad to give them." So they spread out a garment, and each man threw a ring from his plunder onto it. **26**The weight of the gold rings he asked for came to seventeen hundred shekels,*a* not counting the ornaments, the pendants and the purple garments worn by the kings of Midian or the chains that were on their camels' necks. **27**Gideon made the gold into an ephod, which he placed in Ophrah, his town. All Israel prostituted themselves by worshiping it there, and it became a snare to Gideon and his family.

Gideon's Death

28Thus Midian was subdued before the Israelites and did not raise its head again. During Gideon's lifetime, the land enjoyed peace forty years.

29Jerub-Baal son of Joash went back home to live. **30**He had seventy sons of his own, for he had many wives. **31**His concubine, who lived in Shechem, also bore him a son, whom he named Abimelech. **32**Gideon son of Joash died at a good old age and was buried in the tomb of his father Joash in Ophrah of the Abiezrites.

33No sooner had Gideon died than the Israelites again prostituted themselves to the Baals. They set up Baal-Berith as their god and **34**did not remember the LORD their God, who had rescued them from the hands of all their enemies on every side. **35**They also failed to show kindness to the family of Jerub-Baal (that is, Gideon) for all the good things he had done for them.

Abimelech

9 Abimelech son of Jerub-Baal went to his mother's brothers in Shechem and said to them and to all his mother's clan, **2**"Ask all the citizens of Shechem, 'Which is better for you: to have all seventy of Jerub-Baal's sons rule over you, or just one man?' Remember, I am your flesh and blood."

3When the brothers repeated all this to the citizens of Shechem, they were inclined to follow Abimelech, for they said, "He is our brother." **4**They gave him seventy shekels*b* of silver from the temple of Baal-Berith, and Abimelech used it to hire reckless adventurers, who became his followers. **5**He went to his father's home in Ophrah and on one stone murdered his seventy brothers, the sons of Jerub-Baal. But Jotham, the youngest son of Jerub-Baal, escaped by hiding. **6**Then all the citizens of Shechem and Beth Millo gathered beside the great tree at the pillar in Shechem to crown Abimelech king.

7When Jotham was told about this, he climbed up on the top of Mount Gerizim and shouted to them, "Listen to me, citizens of Shechem, so that God may listen to you. **8**One day the trees went out to anoint a king for themselves. They said to the olive tree, 'Be our king.'

9"But the olive tree answered, 'Should I give up my oil, by which both gods and men are honored, to hold sway over the trees?'

10"Next, the trees said to the fig tree, 'Come and be our king.'

11"But the fig tree replied, 'Should I give up my fruit, so good and sweet, to hold sway over the trees?'

12"Then the trees said to the vine, 'Come and be our king.'

13"But the vine answered, 'Should I give up my wine, which cheers both gods and men, to hold sway over the trees?'

14"Finally all the trees said to the thornbush, 'Come and be our king.'

15"The thornbush said to the trees, 'If you really want to anoint me king over you, come and take refuge in my shade; but if not, then let fire come out of the thornbush and consume the cedars of Lebanon!'

16"Now if you have acted honorably and in good faith when you made Abimelech king, and if you have been fair to Jerub-Baal and his family, and if you have treated him as he deserves— **17**and to think that my father fought for you, risked his life to rescue you from the hand of Midian **18**(but today you have revolted against my father's family, murdered his seventy sons on a single stone, and made Abimelech, the son of his slave girl, king over the citizens of Shechem because he is your brother)— **19**if then you have

---

a26 That is, about 43 pounds (about 19.5 kilograms)   *b4* That is, about 1 3/4 pounds (about 0.8 kilogram)

acted honorably and in good faith toward Jerub-Baal and his family today, may Abimelech be your joy, and may you be his, too! **20**But if you have not, let fire come out from Abimelech and consume you, citizens of Shechem and Beth Millo, and let fire come out from you, citizens of Shechem and Beth Millo, and consume Abimelech!"

21Then Jotham fled, escaping to Beer, and he lived there because he was afraid of his brother Abimelech.

22After Abimelech had governed Israel three years, **23**God sent an evil spirit between Abimelech and the citizens of Shechem, who acted

> ### 9:23 Evil Spirit
>
> *The "evil spirit" God sent was not necessarily a supernatural being. "Spirit" means literally "wind" or "breath" in the Bible, and this comment might be translated, "God sent an ill wind." Perhaps an attitude of bitterness or distrust grew up between Abimelech and the people of Shechem. Characteristically, the Bible attributes this development to God, though human causes were probably involved as well.*

treacherously against Abimelech. **24**God did this in order that the crime against Jerub-Baal's seventy sons, the shedding of their blood, might be avenged on their brother Abimelech and on the citizens of Shechem, who had helped him murder his brothers. **25**In opposition to him these citizens of Shechem set men on the hilltops to ambush and rob everyone who passed by, and this was reported to Abimelech.

26Now Gaal son of Ebed moved with his brothers into Shechem, and its citizens put their confidence in him. **27**After they had gone out into the fields and gathered the grapes and trodden them, they held a festival in the temple of their god. While they were eating and drinking, they cursed Abimelech. **28**Then Gaal son of Ebed said, "Who is Abimelech, and who is Shechem, that we should be subject to him? Isn't he Jerub-Baal's son, and isn't Zebul his deputy? Serve the men of Hamor, Shechem's father! Why should we serve Abimelech? **29**If only this people were under my command! Then I would get rid of him. I would say to Abimelech, 'Call out your whole army!' "*a*

30When Zebul the governor of the city heard what Gaal son of Ebed said, he was very angry. **31**Under cover he sent messengers to Abimelech, saying, "Gaal son of Ebed and his brothers have come to Shechem and are stirring up the city

against you. **32**Now then, during the night you and your men should come and lie in wait in the fields. **33**In the morning at sunrise, advance against the city. When Gaal and his men come out against you, do whatever your hand finds to do."

34So Abimelech and all his troops set out by night and took up concealed positions near Shechem in four companies. **35**Now Gaal son of Ebed had gone out and was standing at the entrance to the city gate just as Abimelech and his soldiers came out from their hiding place.

36When Gaal saw them, he said to Zebul, "Look, people are coming down from the tops of the mountains!"

Zebul replied, "You mistake the shadows of the mountains for men."

37But Gaal spoke up again: "Look, people are coming down from the center of the land, and a company is coming from the direction of the soothsayers' tree."

38Then Zebul said to him, "Where is your big talk now, you who said, 'Who is Abimelech that we should be subject to him?' Aren't these the men you ridiculed? Go out and fight them!"

39So Gaal led out*b* the citizens of Shechem and fought Abimelech. **40**Abimelech chased him, and many fell wounded in the flight—all the way to the entrance to the gate. **41**Abimelech stayed in Arumah, and Zebul drove Gaal and his brothers out of Shechem.

42The next day the people of Shechem went out to the fields, and this was reported to Abimelech. **43**So he took his men, divided them into three companies and set an ambush in the fields. When he saw the people coming out of the city, he rose to attack them. **44**Abimelech and the companies with him rushed forward to a position at the entrance to the city gate. Then two companies rushed upon those in the fields and struck them down. **45**All that day Abimelech pressed his attack against the city until he had captured it and killed its people. Then he destroyed the city and scattered salt over it.

46On hearing this, the citizens in the tower of Shechem went into the stronghold of the temple of El-Berith. **47**When Abimelech heard that they had assembled there, **48**he and all his men went up Mount Zalmon. He took an ax and cut off some branches, which he lifted to his shoulders. He ordered the men with him, "Quick! Do what you have seen me do!" **49**So all the men cut branches and followed Abimelech. They piled them against the stronghold and set it on fire over the people inside. So all the people in the tower of Shechem, about a thousand men and women, also died.

---

a29 Septuagint; Hebrew *him."* Then he said to Abimelech, "Call out your whole army!"   *b39* Or *Gaal went out in the sight of*

⁵⁰Next Abimelech went to Thebez and besieged it and captured it. ⁵¹Inside the city, however, was a strong tower, to which all the men and women—all the people of the city—fled. They locked themselves in and climbed up on the tower roof. ⁵²Abimelech went to the tower and stormed it. But as he approached the entrance to the tower to set it on fire, ⁵³a woman dropped an upper millstone on his head and cracked his skull.

⁵⁴Hurriedly he called to his armor-bearer, "Draw your sword and kill me, so that they can't say, 'A woman killed him.'" So his servant ran

9:54 Sexist Attitudes

Abimelech preferred dying immediately to having it said that a woman killed him. Sexist attitudes clearly prevailed in the time of the judges, but nevertheless women made their marks, both good and bad. Here and in the story of Jael (4:21), women used domestic implements to kill dangerous men. (Grinding grain with millstones and setting up tents with pegs were traditionally considered "women's work.") Deborah, a judge and general, and Delilah, who seduced Samson, used their wits for good and evil, respectively.

him through, and he died. ⁵⁵When the Israelites saw that Abimelech was dead, they went home.

⁵⁶Thus God repaid the wickedness that Abimelech had done to his father by murdering his seventy brothers. ⁵⁷God also made the men of Shechem pay for all their wickedness. The curse of Jotham son of Jerub-Baal came on them.

Tola

10 After the time of Abimelech a man of Issachar, Tola son of Puah, the son of Dodo, rose to save Israel. He lived in Shamir, in the hill country of Ephraim. ²He led[a] Israel twenty-three years; then he died, and was buried in Shamir.

Jair

³He was followed by Jair of Gilead, who led Israel twenty-two years. ⁴He had thirty sons, who rode thirty donkeys. They controlled thirty towns in Gilead, which to this day are called Havvoth Jair.[b] ⁵When Jair died, he was buried in Kamon.

Jephthah

⁶Again the Israelites did evil in the eyes of the LORD. They served the Baals and the Ashtoreths, and the gods of Aram, the gods of Sidon, the gods of Moab, the gods of the Ammonites and the gods of the Philistines. And because the Israelites forsook the LORD and no longer served him, ⁷he became angry with them. He sold them into the hands of the Philistines and the Ammonites, ⁸who that year shattered and crushed them. For eighteen years they oppressed all the Israelites on the east side of the Jordan in Gilead, the land of the Amorites. ⁹The Ammonites also crossed the Jordan to fight against Judah, Benjamin and the house of Ephraim; and Israel was in great distress. ¹⁰Then the Israelites cried out to the LORD, "We have sinned against you, forsaking our God and serving the Baals."

¹¹The LORD replied, "When the Egyptians, the Amorites, the Ammonites, the Philistines, ¹²the Sidonians, the Amalekites and the Maonites[c] oppressed you and you cried to me for help, did I not save you from their hands? ¹³But you have forsaken me and served other gods, so I will no longer save you. ¹⁴Go and cry out to the gods you have chosen. Let them save you when you are in trouble!"

¹⁵But the Israelites said to the LORD, "We have sinned. Do with us whatever you think best, but please rescue us now." ¹⁶Then they got rid of the foreign gods among them and served the LORD. And he could bear Israel's misery no longer.

¹⁷When the Ammonites were called to arms and camped in Gilead, the Israelites assembled and camped at Mizpah. ¹⁸The leaders of the people of Gilead said to each other, "Whoever will launch the attack against the Ammonites will be the head of all those living in Gilead."

11 Jephthah the Gileadite was a mighty warrior. His father was Gilead; his mother was a prostitute. ²Gilead's wife also bore him sons, and when they were grown up, they drove Jephthah away. "You are not going to get any inheritance in our family," they said, "because you are the son of another woman." ³So Jephthah fled from his brothers and settled in the land of Tob, where a group of adventurers gathered around him and followed him.

⁴Some time later, when the Ammonites made war on Israel, ⁵the elders of Gilead went to get Jephthah from the land of Tob. ⁶"Come," they said, "be our commander, so we can fight the Ammonites."

⁷Jephthah said to them, "Didn't you hate me and drive me from my father's house? Why do you come to me now, when you're in trouble?"

⁸The elders of Gilead said to him, "Nevertheless, we are turning to you now; come with us to fight the Ammonites, and you will be our head over all who live in Gilead."

⁹Jephthah answered, "Suppose you take me

---

a2 Traditionally *judged*; also in verse 3   *b4* Or *called the settlements of Jair*   *c12* Hebrew; some Septuagint manuscripts *Midianites*

back to fight the Ammonites and the LORD gives them to me—will I really be your head?"

[10]The elders of Gilead replied, "The LORD is our witness; we will certainly do as you say." [11]So

11:6 A Man Like David

Jephthah, like King David to come, was an outlaw who gained leadership experience at the head of a small band of adventurers. Israel turned to him when they needed military leadership, as they later would turn to David. Yet Jephthah's reputation never equaled David's, and the reason must have had something to do with his lack of wisdom. His rash vow to God (verse 31) and his harsh answer to a complaint (12:3) each had destructive results.

Jephthah went with the elders of Gilead, and the people made him head and commander over them. And he repeated all his words before the LORD in Mizpah.

[12]Then Jephthah sent messengers to the Ammonite king with the question: "What do you have against us that you have attacked our country?"

[13]The king of the Ammonites answered Jephthah's messengers, "When Israel came up out of Egypt, they took away my land from the Arnon to the Jabbok, all the way to the Jordan. Now give it back peaceably."

[14]Jephthah sent back messengers to the Ammonite king, [15]saying:

"This is what Jephthah says: Israel did not take the land of Moab or the land of the Ammonites. [16]But when they came up out of Egypt, Israel went through the desert to the Red Sea[a] and on to Kadesh. [17]Then Israel sent messengers to the king of Edom, saying, 'Give us permission to go through your country,' but the king of Edom would not listen. They sent also to the king of Moab, and he refused. So Israel stayed at Kadesh.

[18]"Next they traveled through the desert, skirted the lands of Edom and Moab, passed along the eastern side of the country of Moab, and camped on the other side of the Arnon. They did not enter the territory of Moab, for the Arnon was its border.

[19]"Then Israel sent messengers to Sihon king of the Amorites, who ruled in Heshbon, and said to him, 'Let us pass through your country to our own place.' [20]Sihon, however, did not trust Israel[b] to pass

through his territory. He mustered all his men and encamped at Jahaz and fought with Israel.

[21]"Then the LORD, the God of Israel, gave Sihon and all his men into Israel's hands, and they defeated them. Israel took over all the land of the Amorites who lived in that country, [22]capturing all of it from the Arnon to the Jabbok and from the desert to the Jordan.

[23]"Now since the LORD, the God of Israel, has driven the Amorites out before his people Israel, what right have you to take it over? [24]Will you not take what your god Chemosh gives you? Likewise, whatever the LORD our God has given us, we will possess. [25]Are you better than Balak son of Zippor, king of Moab? Did he ever quarrel with Israel or fight with them? [26]For three hundred years Israel occupied Heshbon, Aroer, the surrounding settlements and all the towns along the Arnon. Why didn't you retake them during that time? [27]I have not wronged you, but you are doing me wrong by waging war against me. Let the LORD, the Judge,[c] decide the dispute this day between the Israelites and the Ammonites."

[28]The king of Ammon, however, paid no attention to the message Jephthah sent him.

[29]Then the Spirit of the LORD came upon Jephthah. He crossed Gilead and Manasseh, passed through Mizpah of Gilead, and from there he advanced against the Ammonites. [30]And Jephthah made a vow to the LORD: "If you give the Ammonites into my hands, [31]whatever comes out of the door of my house to meet me when I return in triumph from the Ammonites will be the LORD's, and I will sacrifice it as a burnt offering."

[32]Then Jephthah went over to fight the Ammonites, and the LORD gave them into his hands. [33]He devastated twenty towns from Aroer to the vicinity of Minnith, as far as Abel Keramim. Thus Israel subdued Ammon.

[34]When Jephthah returned to his home in Mizpah, who should come out to meet him but his daughter, dancing to the sound of tambourines! She was an only child. Except for her he had neither son nor daughter. [35]When he saw her, he tore his clothes and cried, "Oh! My daughter! You have made me miserable and wretched, because I have made a vow to the LORD that I cannot break."

[36]"My father," she replied, "you have given your word to the LORD. Do to me just as you promised, now that the LORD has avenged you of your enemies, the Ammonites. [37]But grant me

[a]16 Hebrew *Yam Suph*; that is, Sea of Reeds   [b]20 Or *however, would not make an agreement for Israel*
[c]27 Or *Ruler*

this one request," she said. "Give me two months to roam the hills and weep with my friends, because I will never marry."

38"You may go," he said. And he let her go for two months. She and the girls went into the hills and wept because she would never marry. 39After the two months, she returned to her father and he did to her as he had vowed. And she was a virgin.

From this comes the Israelite custom 40that each year the young women of Israel go out for four days to commemorate the daughter of Jephthah the Gileadite.

Jephthah and Ephraim

12 The men of Ephraim called out their forces, crossed over to Zaphon and said to Jephthah, "Why did you go to fight the Ammonites without calling us to go with you? We're going to burn down your house over your head."

12:1 A Soft Answer

"A gentle answer turns away wrath," says Proverbs 15:1. Compare Jephthah's answer to the men of Ephraim with Gideon's softer response to the same complaint in Judges 8:1–3. In Gideon's case, anger subsided. In this, civil war resulted, and 42,000 Israelites died.

2Jephthah answered, "I and my people were engaged in a great struggle with the Ammonites, and although I called, you didn't save me out of their hands. 3When I saw that you wouldn't help, I took my life in my hands and crossed over to fight the Ammonites, and the Lord gave me the victory over them. Now why have you come up today to fight me?"

4Jephthah then called together the men of Gilead and fought against Ephraim. The Gileadites struck them down because the Ephraimites had said, "You Gileadites are renegades from Ephraim and Manasseh." 5The Gileadites captured the fords of the Jordan leading to Ephraim, and whenever a survivor of Ephraim said, "Let me cross over," the men of Gilead asked him, "Are you an Ephraimite?" If he replied, "No," 6they said, "All right, say 'Shibboleth.'" If he said, "Sibboleth," because he could not pronounce the word correctly, they seized him and killed him at the fords of the Jordan. Forty-two thousand Ephraimites were killed at that time.

7Jephthah led*a* Israel six years. Then Jephthah the Gileadite died, and was buried in a town in Gilead.

Ibzan, Elon and Abdon

8After him, Ibzan of Bethlehem led Israel. 9He had thirty sons and thirty daughters. He gave his daughters away in marriage to those outside his clan, and for his sons he brought in thirty young women as wives from outside his clan. Ibzan led Israel seven years. 10Then Ibzan died, and was buried in Bethlehem.

11After him, Elon the Zebulunite led Israel ten years. 12Then Elon died, and was buried in Aijalon in the land of Zebulun.

13After him, Abdon son of Hillel, from Pirathon, led Israel. 14He had forty sons and thirty grandsons, who rode on seventy donkeys. He led Israel eight years. 15Then Abdon son of Hillel died, and was buried at Pirathon in Ephraim, in the hill country of the Amalekites.

The Birth of Samson

13 Again the Israelites did evil in the eyes of the Lord, so the Lord delivered them into the hands of the Philistines for forty years.

2A certain man of Zorah, named Manoah, from the clan of the Danites, had a wife who was sterile and remained childless. 3The angel of the Lord appeared to her and said, "You are sterile and childless, but you are going to conceive and have a son. 4Now see to it that you drink no wine or other fermented drink and that you do not eat anything unclean, 5because you will conceive and give birth to a son. No razor may be used on his head, because the boy is to be a Nazirite, set apart to God from birth, and he will begin the deliverance of Israel from the hands of the Philistines."

6Then the woman went to her husband and told him, "A man of God came to me. He looked like an angel of God, very awesome. I didn't ask him where he came from, and he didn't tell me his name. 7But he said to me, 'You will conceive and give birth to a son. Now then, drink no wine or other fermented drink and do not eat anything unclean, because the boy will be a Nazirite of God from birth until the day of his death.'"

8Then Manoah prayed to the Lord: "O Lord, I beg you, let the man of God you sent to us come again to teach us how to bring up the boy who is to be born."

9God heard Manoah, and the angel of God came again to the woman while she was out in the field; but her husband Manoah was not with her. 10The woman hurried to tell her husband, "He's here! The man who appeared to me the other day!"

11Manoah got up and followed his wife. When he came to the man, he said, "Are you the one who talked to my wife?"

"I am," he said.

a7 Traditionally judged; also in verses 8-14

¹²So Manoah asked him, "When your words are fulfilled, what is to be the rule for the boy's life and work?"

¹³The angel of the LORD answered, "Your wife must do all that I have told her. ¹⁴She must not eat anything that comes from the grapevine, nor drink any wine or other fermented drink nor eat anything unclean. She must do everything I have commanded her."

¹⁵Manoah said to the angel of the LORD, "We would like you to stay until we prepare a young goat for you."

¹⁶The angel of the LORD replied, "Even though you detain me, I will not eat any of your food. But if you prepare a burnt offering, offer it to the LORD." (Manoah did not realize that it was the angel of the LORD.)

¹⁷Then Manoah inquired of the angel of the LORD, "What is your name, so that we may honor you when your word comes true?"

¹⁸He replied, "Why do you ask my name? It is beyond understanding.ᵃ" ¹⁹Then Manoah took a young goat, together with the grain offering, and sacrificed it on a rock to the LORD. And the LORD did an amazing thing while Manoah and his wife watched: ²⁰As the flame blazed up from the altar toward heaven, the angel of the LORD ascended in the flame. Seeing this, Manoah and his wife fell with their faces to the ground. ²¹When the angel of the LORD did not show himself again to Manoah and his wife, Manoah realized that it was the angel of the LORD.

²²"We are doomed to die!" he said to his wife. "We have seen God!"

²³But his wife answered, "If the LORD had meant to kill us, he would not have accepted a

ᵃ18 Or is wonderful

Samson: A Weakness for Women
The strongest man of his generation never lived up to his promise

SAMSON, THE STRONGEST MAN OF his generation, was tragically unable to control his lust. When he saw an attractive woman, he wanted her. He first fell for a young woman he saw in a Philistine village just across the valley from his home. His parents tried to dissuade him, since her religion and culture were unacceptable, but he would not listen. Desire was his only rule. The marriage ended in a matter of days and resulted in dozens of deaths.

> "I have seen a Philistine woman . . . now get her for me as my wife."
> 14:2

The famous Delilah was at least the third woman who dallied with Samson, according to Judges. She, like his first love, was a Philistine living near his home. Where thousands of men had failed to overcome Samson, a wheedling woman succeeded. Thanks to her, he was captured, blinded, and set to work pushing a grinding machine. His final triumph was ironically fitting: Blind and bound, brought out like a freak for a hooting crowd's amusement, he destroyed himself while wreaking vengeance on the crowd. At his death, as throughout his life, it was hard to say who suffered most from Samson's hot temper: the Philistines or Samson.

Needed: A Leader

When you think of what God meant Samson to be, his life appears particularly tragic. Israel desperately needed a strong, confident leader, for the Philistines were moving in as masters, and many Israelites were willing to let them. God intended Samson for great things. Of all the judges, only Samson was announced by an angel before he was born (13:3). He was assigned to that special class of people known as Nazirites (described in Numbers 6), whose lives were specially devoted to God. Nazirites never drank wine, went near a dead body, or cut their hair.

Samson never lived up to his promise. Rule 3 was probably the only part of the Nazirite vow he kept—it required little self-discipline to let hair grow.

Despite all of Samson's weaknesses, God used him. He is mentioned in the Bible "Hall of Fame" (Hebrews 11:32) as a hero of faith along with Gideon, Barak, and Jephthah, all from Judges. Barely conscious of what it meant to live for God, and given to fits of lust and temper, Samson still had great physical strength, which came supernaturally from God. With it, he pushed back the Philistines—more by accident than by intention—and kept Israel intact.

Samson seems like a train whose engineer has fallen out of the cab, an oversized accident smashing into everything it meets. But for God, there are no accidents. He used the tragedy of Samson's life for good.

Life Questions: Which might best be said of you: "Oh, what he/she might have been!" or "He/she made the best of his/her abilities"?

burnt offering and grain offering from our hands, nor shown us all these things or now told us this."

²⁴The woman gave birth to a boy and named him Samson. He grew and the LORD blessed him, ²⁵and the Spirit of the LORD began to stir him while he was in Mahaneh Dan, between Zorah and Eshtaol.

Samson's Marriage

14 Samson went down to Timnah and saw there a young Philistine woman. ²When he

14:1 The First Sign of Trouble

Timnah was only four miles across the valley from Samson's hometown. Apparently, the Philistines and Israelites moved freely back and forth, and not all Israelites opposed the Philistines (see 15:11). Samson, making the short stroll, was attracted to a young Philistine woman. His lack of concern for differences of religion and his lack of submission to his parents were ominous signs pointing toward Samson's future troubles.

returned, he said to his father and mother, "I have seen a Philistine woman in Timnah; now get her for me as my wife."

³His father and mother replied, "Isn't there an acceptable woman among your relatives or among all our people? Must you go to the uncircumcised Philistines to get a wife?"

But Samson said to his father, "Get her for me. She's the right one for me." ⁴(His parents did not know that this was from the LORD, who was seeking an occasion to confront the Philistines; for at that time they were ruling over Israel.) ⁵Samson went down to Timnah together with his father and mother. As they approached the vineyards of Timnah, suddenly a young lion came roaring toward him. ⁶The Spirit of the LORD came upon him in power so that he tore the lion apart with his bare hands as he might have torn a young goat. But he told neither his father nor his mother what he had done. ⁷Then he went down and talked with the woman, and he liked her.

⁸Some time later, when he went back to marry her, he turned aside to look at the lion's carcass. In it was a swarm of bees and some honey, ⁹which he scooped out with his hands and ate as he went along. When he rejoined his parents, he gave them some, and they too ate it. But he did not tell them that he had taken the honey from the lion's carcass.

¹⁰Now his father went down to see the woman. And Samson made a feast there, as was custom-

ary for bridegrooms. ¹¹When he appeared, he was given thirty companions.

¹²"Let me tell you a riddle," Samson said to them. "If you can give me the answer within the seven days of the feast, I will give you thirty linen garments and thirty sets of clothes. ¹³If you can't tell me the answer, you must give me thirty linen garments and thirty sets of clothes."

"Tell us your riddle," they said. "Let's hear it."

¹⁴He replied,

"Out of the eater, something to eat;
    out of the strong, something sweet."

For three days they could not give the answer.

¹⁵On the fourth*ᵃ* day, they said to Samson's wife, "Coax your husband into explaining the riddle for us, or we will burn you and your father's household to death. Did you invite us here to rob us?"

¹⁶Then Samson's wife threw herself on him, sobbing, "You hate me! You don't really love me. You've given my people a riddle, but you haven't told me the answer."

"I haven't even explained it to my father or mother," he replied, "so why should I explain it to you?" ¹⁷She cried the whole seven days of the feast. So on the seventh day he finally told her, because she continued to press him. She in turn explained the riddle to her people.

¹⁸Before sunset on the seventh day the men of the town said to him,

"What is sweeter than honey?
    What is stronger than a lion?"

Samson said to them,

"If you had not plowed with my heifer,
    you would not have solved my riddle."

¹⁹Then the Spirit of the LORD came upon him in power. He went down to Ashkelon, struck down thirty of their men, stripped them of their belongings and gave their clothes to those who had explained the riddle. Burning with anger, he went up to his father's house. ²⁰And Samson's wife was given to the friend who had attended him at his wedding.

Samson's Vengeance on the Philistines

15 Later on, at the time of wheat harvest, Samson took a young goat and went to visit his wife. He said, "I'm going to my wife's room." But her father would not let him go in.

²"I was so sure you thoroughly hated her," he said, "that I gave her to your friend. Isn't her younger sister more attractive? Take her instead."

³Samson said to them, "This time I have a right to get even with the Philistines; I will really harm them." ⁴So he went out and caught three

---

ᵃ 15 Some Septuagint manuscripts and Syriac; Hebrew *seventh* hundred foxes and tied them tail to tail in pairs. He then fastened a torch to every pair of tails, [5]lit the torches and let the foxes loose in the standing grain of the Philistines. He burned up the shocks and standing grain, together with the vineyards and olive groves.

[6]When the Philistines asked, "Who did this?" they were told, "Samson, the Timnite's son-in-law, because his wife was given to his friend."

So the Philistines went up and burned her and her father to death. [7]Samson said to them, "Since you've acted like this, I won't stop until I get my revenge on you." [8]He attacked them viciously and slaughtered many of them. Then he went down and stayed in a cave in the rock of Etam.

[9]The Philistines went up and camped in Judah, spreading out near Lehi. [10]The men of Judah asked, "Why have you come to fight us?"

"We have come to take Samson prisoner," they answered, "to do to him as he did to us."

[11]Then three thousand men from Judah went down to the cave in the rock of Etam and said to Samson, "Don't you realize that the Philistines are rulers over us? What have you done to us?"

He answered, "I merely did to them what they did to me."

[12]They said to him, "We've come to tie you up and hand you over to the Philistines."

Samson said, "Swear to me that you won't kill me yourselves."

[13]"Agreed," they answered. "We will only tie you up and hand you over to them. We will not kill you." So they bound him with two new ropes and led him up from the rock. [14]As he approached Lehi, the Philistines came toward him shouting. The Spirit of the LORD came upon him in power. The ropes on his arms became like charred flax, and the bindings dropped from his

15:14 The Spirit and Samson

Four times (see also 13:25; 14:6,19) Judges comments that "the Spirit of the LORD" came on Samson. The same comment is made of other judges, though less frequently. But the Spirit only gave Samson great strength, as far as we can see; fruit of the Spirit like love and self-control seem lacking from his life.

hands. [15]Finding a fresh jawbone of a donkey, he grabbed it and struck down a thousand men.
[16]Then Samson said,

"With a donkey's jawbone
    I have made donkeys of them.[a]

With a donkey's jawbone
    I have killed a thousand men."

[17]When he finished speaking, he threw away the jawbone; and the place was called Ramath Lehi.[b]

[18]Because he was very thirsty, he cried out to the LORD, "You have given your servant this great victory. Must I now die of thirst and fall into the hands of the uncircumcised?" [19]Then God opened up the hollow place in Lehi, and water came out of it. When Samson drank, his strength returned and he revived. So the spring was called En Hakkore,[c] and it is still there in Lehi.

[20]Samson led[d] Israel for twenty years in the days of the Philistines.

Samson and Delilah

16 One day Samson went to Gaza, where he saw a prostitute. He went in to spend the night with her. [2]The people of Gaza were told, "Samson is here!" So they surrounded the place and lay in wait for him all night at the city gate. They made no move during the night, saying, "At dawn we'll kill him."

[3]But Samson lay there only until the middle of the night. Then he got up and took hold of the doors of the city gate, together with the two posts, and tore them loose, bar and all. He lifted them to his shoulders and carried them to the top of the hill that faces Hebron.

[4]Some time later, he fell in love with a woman in the Valley of Sorek whose name was Delilah. [5]The rulers of the Philistines went to her and said, "See if you can lure him into showing you the secret of his great strength and how we can overpower him so we may tie him up and subdue him. Each one of us will give you eleven hundred shekels[e] of silver."

[6]So Delilah said to Samson, "Tell me the secret of your great strength and how you can be tied up and subdued."

[7]Samson answered her, "If anyone ties me with seven fresh thongs[f] that have not been dried, I'll become as weak as any other man."

[8]Then the rulers of the Philistines brought her seven fresh thongs that had not been dried, and she tied him with them. [9]With men hidden in the room, she called to him, "Samson, the Philistines are upon you!" But he snapped the thongs as easily as a piece of string snaps when it comes close to a flame. So the secret of his strength was not discovered.

[10]Then Delilah said to Samson, "You have made a fool of me; you lied to me. Come now, tell me how you can be tied."

[11]He said, "If anyone ties me securely with

new ropes that have never been used, I'll become as weak as any other man."

¹²So Delilah took new ropes and tied him with them. Then, with men hidden in the room, she called to him, "Samson, the Philistines are upon you!" But he snapped the ropes off his arms as if they were threads.

¹³Delilah then said to Samson, "Until now, you have been making a fool of me and lying to me. Tell me how you can be tied."

He replied, "If you weave the seven braids of my head into the fabric ⌞on the loom⌟ and tighten it with the pin, I'll become as weak as any other man." So while he was sleeping, Delilah took the seven braids of his head, wove them into the fabric ¹⁴andᵃ tightened it with the pin.

Again she called to him, "Samson, the Philistines are upon you!" He awoke from his sleep and pulled up the pin and the loom, with the fabric.

¹⁵Then she said to him, "How can you say, 'I love you,' when you won't confide in me? This is the third time you have made a fool of me and haven't told me the secret of your great strength." ¹⁶With such nagging she prodded him day after day until he was tired to death.

¹⁷So he told her everything. "No razor has ever been used on my head," he said, "because I have been a Nazirite set apart to God since birth. If my head were shaved, my strength would leave me, and I would become as weak as any other man."

¹⁸When Delilah saw that he had told her everything, she sent word to the rulers of the Philistines, "Come back once more; he has told me everything." So the rulers of the Philistines returned with the silver in their hands. ¹⁹Having put him to sleep on her lap, she called a man to shave off the seven braids of his hair, and so began to subdue him.ᵇ And his strength left him.

²⁰Then she called, "Samson, the Philistines are upon you!"

He awoke from his sleep and thought, "I'll go out as before and shake myself free." But he did not know that the LORD had left him.

²¹Then the Philistines seized him, gouged out his eyes and took him down to Gaza. Binding him with bronze shackles, they set him to grinding in the prison. ²²But the hair on his head began to grow again after it had been shaved.

The Death of Samson

²³Now the rulers of the Philistines assembled to offer a great sacrifice to Dagon their god and to celebrate, saying, "Our god has delivered Samson, our enemy, into our hands."

²⁴When the people saw him, they praised their god, saying,

"Our god has delivered our enemy
  into our hands,
the one who laid waste our land
  and multiplied our slain."

²⁵While they were in high spirits, they shouted, "Bring out Samson to entertain us." So they called Samson out of the prison, and he performed for them.

When they stood him among the pillars, ²⁶Samson said to the servant who held his hand, "Put me where I can feel the pillars that support the temple, so that I may lean against them." ²⁷Now the temple was crowded with men and women; all the rulers of the Philistines were there, and on the roof were about three thousand men and women watching Samson perform. ²⁸Then Samson prayed to the LORD, "O Sovereign LORD, remember me. O God, please strengthen me just once more, and let me with one blow get revenge on the Philistines for my two eyes." ²⁹Then Samson reached toward the two central pillars on which the temple stood. Bracing himself against them, his right hand on the one and his left hand on the other, ³⁰Samson said, "Let me die with the Philistines!" Then he pushed with all his might, and down came the temple on the rulers and all the people in it. Thus he killed many more when he died than while he lived.

16:30 Bring the House Down

Archaeologists have excavated temples from Samson's period. Typically, wooden pillars were set close together to support a roof, which sometimes included a covered area for spectators. Quite possibly this structure was already creaking under the weight of 3,000 people, who would have crowded to one side to see Samson perform. Samson managed to push the pillars off their stone bases, and the roof collapsed.

³¹Then his brothers and his father's whole family went down to get him. They brought him back and buried him between Zorah and Eshtaol in the tomb of Manoah his father. He had ledᶜ Israel twenty years.

Micah's Idols

17 Now a man named Micah from the hill country of Ephraim ²said to his mother, "The eleven hundred shekelsᵈ of silver that were

---

ᵃ 13,14 Some Septuagint manuscripts; Hebrew "⌞I can⌟ if you weave the seven braids of my head into the fabric ⌞on the loom.⌟ ¹⁴So she   ᵇ 19 Hebrew; some Septuagint manuscripts and he began to weaken   ᶜ 31 Traditionally judged   ᵈ 2 That is, about 28 pounds (about 13 kilograms)

taken from you and about which I heard you utter a curse—I have that silver with me; I took it."

Then his mother said, "The LORD bless you, my son!"

[3]When he returned the eleven hundred shekels of silver to his mother, she said, "I solemnly consecrate my silver to the LORD for my son to make a carved image and a cast idol. I will give it back to you."

[4]So he returned the silver to his mother, and she took two hundred shekels[a] of silver and gave them to a silversmith, who made them into the image and the idol. And they were put in Micah's house.

[5]Now this man Micah had a shrine, and he made an ephod and some idols and installed one of his sons as his priest. [6]In those days Israel had no king; everyone did as he saw fit.

[7]A young Levite from Bethlehem in Judah, who had been living within the clan of Judah, [8]left that town in search of some other place to stay. On his way[b] he came to Micah's house in the hill country of Ephraim.

[9]Micah asked him, "Where are you from?"

"I'm a Levite from Bethlehem in Judah," he said, "and I'm looking for a place to stay."

[10]Then Micah said to him, "Live with me and be my father and priest, and I'll give you ten shekels[c] of silver a year, your clothes and your food." [11]So the Levite agreed to live with him, and the young man was to him like one of his

---

[a]4 That is, about 5 pounds (about 2.3 kilograms) (about 110 grams)   [b]8 Or *To carry on his profession*   [c]10 That is, about 4 ounces

---

Hanging by a Thread
Theft, rape, murder, idolatry: Israel was destroying itself

In those days Israel had no king; everyone did as he saw fit. 17:6

A TIME COMES WHEN YOU can no longer blame your problems on other people. In the comic strip character Pogo's immortal words, "We have met the enemy, and he is us."

So it is at the end of Judges. The camera zooms in for a close-up, focusing on internal violence. Foreign enemies are no longer in view: The enemy is Israel itself.

They make ugly portraits, these last five chapters. Pointless and violent, they begin with a son stealing from his mother and end with parents agreeing to let their daughters be kidnapped. In between are homosexual and heterosexual gang rape, murder, idolatry, armed robbery, mass slaughter. No enemy does all this: Israelites do it to each other. Clearly, the exalted nation of Israel, God's chosen people, has lost all sense of direction.

Who Can Rescue Them Now?

The first 16 chapters of Judges tell of repeated enemy invasions that moved Israel to call out to God. Hearing his people, God would send a freedom fighter to save them.

In the last five chapters, by contrast, God sends no freedom fighters. No military leader could rescue them from themselves. These chapters instead repeat the solemn words: "In those days Israel had no king; everyone did as he saw fit."

"Everyone did as he saw fit" may not sound very negative in our era, which places high value on individualism and personal freedom. But God prizes something more: unity. He wants his people united in love for him and each other. God's law had bound his people to a common worship in the tabernacle and to a common standard of caring for each other. For this the Israelites substituted do-as-you-please religion and a fractured society, where each family or group fought for its own rights alone. The result? These chapters tell the dismal story.

Israel's Worst Enemy

By the end of Judges, Israelites are reduced to fighting themselves. They have adopted their enemies' customs. They worship idols. They are sexually immoral. They lack respect for parents. They cannot remember the pattern of life God had set out. It is hard to say, by the end of Judges, why God should save Israel from their enemies. It is hard to say whether Israelites are the least bit different from their enemies. Israel has become, in fact, its own worst enemy.

Only one glimmer of hope appears: the Israelites' shock at the Benjamites' gang rape. They can still get together to punish such outrages, and they still consult the Lord about them. But they are a far cry from the hopeful people Joshua led into the promised land.

Life Questions: Do your troubles come more from your circumstances or from your own internal weaknesses? What kind of help do you need from God?

sons. ¹²Then Micah installed the Levite, and the young man became his priest and lived in his house. ¹³And Micah said, "Now I know that the LORD will be good to me, since this Levite has become my priest."

17:6 A State of Anarchy

Four times the final chapters of Judges mention there was "no king." Twice Judges adds that "everyone did as he saw fit." This editorial remark was probably made later, after the monarchy had begun under Saul and David; a king unified the nation. Some problems of this period are evident in verse 5: idolatry and the installation of a priest who did not come from the priestly family. The story that follows shows one group of Israelites raiding another, as though they were enemies, not relatives.

Danites Settle in Laish

18 In those days Israel had no king.

And in those days the tribe of the Danites was seeking a place of their own where they might settle, because they had not yet come into an inheritance among the tribes of Israel. ²So the Danites sent five warriors from Zorah and Eshtaol to spy out the land and explore it. These men represented all their clans. They told them, "Go, explore the land."

The men entered the hill country of Ephraim and came to the house of Micah, where they spent the night. ³When they were near Micah's house, they recognized the voice of the young Levite; so they turned in there and asked him, "Who brought you here? What are you doing in this place? Why are you here?"

⁴He told them what Micah had done for him, and said, "He has hired me and I am his priest."

⁵Then they said to him, "Please inquire of God to learn whether our journey will be successful."

⁶The priest answered them, "Go in peace. Your journey has the LORD's approval."

⁷So the five men left and came to Laish, where they saw that the people were living in safety, like the Sidonians, unsuspecting and secure. And since their land lacked nothing, they were prosperous.ᵃ Also, they lived a long way from the Sidonians and had no relationship with anyone else.ᵇ

⁸When they returned to Zorah and Eshtaol, their brothers asked them, "How did you find things?"

⁹They answered, "Come on, let's attack them! We have seen that the land is very good. Aren't you going to do something? Don't hesitate to go

there and take it over. ¹⁰When you get there, you will find an unsuspecting people and a spacious land that God has put into your hands, a land that lacks nothing whatever."

¹¹Then six hundred men from the clan of the Danites, armed for battle, set out from Zorah and Eshtaol. ¹²On their way they set up camp near Kiriath Jearim in Judah. This is why the place west of Kiriath Jearim is called Mahaneh Danᶜ to this day. ¹³From there they went on to the hill country of Ephraim and came to Micah's house.

¹⁴Then the five men who had spied out the land of Laish said to their brothers, "Do you know that one of these houses has an ephod, other household gods, a carved image and a cast idol? Now you know what to do." ¹⁵So they turned in there and went to the house of the young Levite at Micah's place and greeted him. ¹⁶The six hundred Danites, armed for battle, stood at the entrance to the gate. ¹⁷The five men who had spied out the land went inside and took the carved image, the ephod, the other household gods and the cast idol while the priest and the six hundred armed men stood at the entrance to the gate.

¹⁸When these men went into Micah's house and took the carved image, the ephod, the other household gods and the cast idol, the priest said to them, "What are you doing?"

¹⁹They answered him, "Be quiet! Don't say a word. Come with us, and be our father and priest. Isn't it better that you serve a tribe and clan in Israel as priest rather than just one man's household?" ²⁰Then the priest was glad. He took the ephod, the other household gods and the carved image and went along with the people. ²¹Putting their little children, their livestock and their possessions in front of them, they turned away and left.

²²When they had gone some distance from Micah's house, the men who lived near Micah were called together and overtook the Danites. ²³As they shouted after them, the Danites turned and said to Micah, "What's the matter with you that you called out your men to fight?"

²⁴He replied, "You took the gods I made, and my priest, and went away. What else do I have? How can you ask, 'What's the matter with you?' "

18:24 Sad Commentary

Micah's outraged cry offers a sad commentary on the state of Israel. Even though his stolen gods were obviously unable to protect themselves, let alone him, Micah knew no other refuge. Anarchy ruled, as did idolatry.

ᵃ7 The meaning of the Hebrew for this clause is uncertain. *Arameans*   ᶜ12 *Mahaneh Dan* means *Dan's camp.*

ᵇ7 Hebrew; some Septuagint manuscripts *with the*

²⁵The Danites answered, "Don't argue with us, or some hot-tempered men will attack you, and you and your family will lose your lives." ²⁶So the Danites went their way, and Micah, seeing that they were too strong for him, turned around and went back home.

²⁷Then they took what Micah had made, and his priest, and went on to Laish, against a peaceful and unsuspecting people. They attacked them with the sword and burned down their city. ²⁸There was no one to rescue them because they lived a long way from Sidon and had no relationship with anyone else. The city was in a valley near Beth Rehob.

The Danites rebuilt the city and settled there. ²⁹They named it Dan after their forefather Dan, who was born to Israel—though the city used to be called Laish. ³⁰There the Danites set up for themselves the idols, and Jonathan son of Gershom, the son of Moses,ᵃ and his sons were priests for the tribe of Dan until the time of the captivity of the land. ³¹They continued to use the idols Micah had made, all the time the house of God was in Shiloh.

A Levite and His Concubine

19 In those days Israel had no king.

Now a Levite who lived in a remote area in the hill country of Ephraim took a concubine from Bethlehem in Judah. ²But she was unfaithful to him. She left him and went back to her father's house in Bethlehem, Judah. After she had been there four months, ³her husband went to her to persuade her to return. He had with him his servant and two donkeys. She took him into her father's house, and when her father saw him, he gladly welcomed him. ⁴His father-in-law, the girl's father, prevailed upon him to stay; so he remained with him three days, eating and drinking, and sleeping there.

⁵On the fourth day they got up early and he prepared to leave, but the girl's father said to his son-in-law, "Refresh yourself with something to eat; then you can go." ⁶So the two of them sat down to eat and drink together. Afterward the girl's father said, "Please stay tonight and enjoy yourself." ⁷And when the man got up to go, his father-in-law persuaded him, so he stayed there that night. ⁸On the morning of the fifth day, when he rose to go, the girl's father said, "Refresh yourself. Wait till afternoon!" So the two of them ate together.

⁹Then when the man, with his concubine and his servant, got up to leave, his father-in-law, the girl's father, said, "Now look, it's almost evening. Spend the night here; the day is nearly over. Stay and enjoy yourself. Early tomorrow morning you can get up and be on your way home." ¹⁰But,

unwilling to stay another night, the man left and went toward Jebus (that is, Jerusalem), with his two saddled donkeys and his concubine.

¹¹When they were near Jebus and the day was almost gone, the servant said to his master, "Come, let's stop at this city of the Jebusites and spend the night."

¹²His master replied, "No. We won't go into an alien city, whose people are not Israelites. We will go on to Gibeah." ¹³He added, "Come, let's try to reach Gibeah or Ramah and spend the night in one of those places." ¹⁴So they went on, and the sun set as they neared Gibeah in Benjamin. ¹⁵There they stopped to spend the night. They went and sat in the city square, but no one took them into his home for the night.

19:15 A Breach of Hospitality

In the ancient Middle East, people took hospitality very seriously. When the Levite sat down in the city square of an Israelite city, he expected the townspeople (his relatives) to offer him a place to stay. But only an old man from his home area offered the Levite lodging—the locals were inhospitable, an ominous sign.

The old man obviously took hospitality seriously. Unfortunately, he took women much less seriously. In fact, he urged the hostile mob to rape his daughter and his guest's concubine as a substitute for the guest himself. His response was nearly identical to Lot's on the eve of Sodom's destruction (Genesis 19:6–8). The story suggests that Israel had become as bad as Sodom.

¹⁶That evening an old man from the hill country of Ephraim, who was living in Gibeah (the men of the place were Benjamites), came in from his work in the fields. ¹⁷When he looked and saw the traveler in the city square, the old man asked, "Where are you going? Where did you come from?"

¹⁸He answered, "We are on our way from Bethlehem in Judah to a remote area in the hill country of Ephraim where I live. I have been to Bethlehem in Judah and now I am going to the house of the LORD. No one has taken me into his house. ¹⁹We have both straw and fodder for our donkeys and bread and wine for ourselves your servants—me, your maidservant, and the young man with us. We don't need anything."

²⁰"You are welcome at my house," the old man said. "Let me supply whatever you need. Only don't spend the night in the square." ²¹So he took him into his house and fed his donkeys. After they had washed their feet, they had something to eat and drink.

ᵃ *30* An ancient Hebrew scribal tradition, some Septuagint manuscripts and Vulgate; Masoretic Text *Manasseh*

²²While they were enjoying themselves, some of the wicked men of the city surrounded the house. Pounding on the door, they shouted to the old man who owned the house, "Bring out the man who came to your house so we can have sex with him."

²³The owner of the house went outside and said to them, "No, my friends, don't be so vile. Since this man is my guest, don't do this disgraceful thing. ²⁴Look, here is my virgin daughter, and his concubine. I will bring them out to you now, and you can use them and do to them whatever you wish. But to this man, don't do such a disgraceful thing."

²⁵But the men would not listen to him. So the man took his concubine and sent her outside to them, and they raped her and abused her throughout the night, and at dawn they let her go. ²⁶At daybreak the woman went back to the house where her master was staying, fell down at the door and lay there until daylight.

²⁷When her master got up in the morning and opened the door of the house and stepped out to continue on his way, there lay his concubine, fallen in the doorway of the house, with her hands on the threshold. ²⁸He said to her, "Get up; let's go." But there was no answer. Then the man put her on his donkey and set out for home.

²⁹When he reached home, he took a knife and cut up his concubine, limb by limb, into twelve parts and sent them into all the areas of Israel. ³⁰Everyone who saw it said, "Such a thing has never been seen or done, not since the day the Israelites came up out of Egypt. Think about it! Consider it! Tell us what to do!"

Israelites Fight the Benjamites

20 Then all the Israelites from Dan to Beersheba and from the land of Gilead came out as one man and assembled before the LORD in Mizpah. ²The leaders of all the people of the tribes of Israel took their places in the assembly of the people of God, four hundred thousand soldiers armed with swords. ³(The Benjamites heard that the Israelites had gone up to Mizpah.) Then the Israelites said, "Tell us how this awful thing happened."

⁴So the Levite, the husband of the murdered woman, said, "I and my concubine came to Gibeah in Benjamin to spend the night. ⁵During the night the men of Gibeah came after me and surrounded the house, intending to kill me. They raped my concubine, and she died. ⁶I took my concubine, cut her into pieces and sent one piece to each region of Israel's inheritance, because they committed this lewd and disgraceful act in

Israel. ⁷Now, all you Israelites, speak up and give your verdict."

⁸All the people rose as one man, saying, "None of us will go home. No, not one of us will return to his house. ⁹But now this is what we'll do to Gibeah: We'll go up against it as the lot directs. ¹⁰We'll take ten men out of every hundred from all the tribes of Israel, and a hundred from a thousand, and a thousand from ten thousand, to get provisions for the army. Then, when the army arrives at Gibeah*ᵃ* in Benjamin, it can give them what they deserve for all this vileness done in Israel." ¹¹So all the men of Israel got together and united as one man against the city.

¹²The tribes of Israel sent men throughout the tribe of Benjamin, saying, "What about this awful crime that was committed among you? ¹³Now surrender those wicked men of Gibeah so that we may put them to death and purge the evil from Israel."

But the Benjamites would not listen to their fellow Israelites. ¹⁴From their towns they came together at Gibeah to fight against the Israelites. ¹⁵At once the Benjamites mobilized twenty-six thousand swordsmen from their towns, in addition to seven hundred chosen men from those living in Gibeah. ¹⁶Among all these soldiers there were seven hundred chosen men who were left-handed, each of whom could sling a stone at a hair and not miss.

¹⁷Israel, apart from Benjamin, mustered four hundred thousand swordsmen, all of them fighting men.

¹⁸The Israelites went up to Bethel*ᵇ* and inquired of God. They said, "Who of us shall go first to fight against the Benjamites?"

The LORD replied, "Judah shall go first."

¹⁹The next morning the Israelites got up and pitched camp near Gibeah. ²⁰The men of Israel went out to fight the Benjamites and took up battle positions against them at Gibeah. ²¹The Benjamites came out of Gibeah and cut down twenty-two thousand Israelites on the battlefield that day. ²²But the men of Israel encouraged one another and again took up their positions where they had stationed themselves the first day. ²³The Israelites went up and wept before the LORD until evening, and they inquired of the LORD. They said, "Shall we go up again to battle against the Benjamites, our brothers?"

The LORD answered, "Go up against them."

²⁴Then the Israelites drew near to Benjamin the second day. ²⁵This time, when the Benjamites came out from Gibeah to oppose them, they cut down another eighteen thousand Israelites, all of them armed with swords.

ᵃ10 One Hebrew manuscript; most Hebrew manuscripts *Geba,* a variant of *Gibeah*   *ᵇ18* Or *to the house of God*; also in verse 26

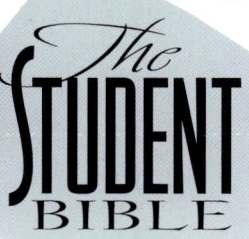

The STUDENT BIBLE

Welcome to the WoW 1997 Bible.
We're excited that you're here!

When Zondervan Publishing House and International Bible Society
approached the WoW 1997 Committee about putting together a Bible
project to accompany the WoW 1997 CD set, we were excited. When
they told us that it would be the latest edition of *The Student Bible*, one
that has sold in the millions of copies over its ten—year history, we were
even more excited!

The members of the WoW 1997 Committee, along with the people at the
International Bible Society and Zondervan Publishing House who worked
with us, sincerely hope that you enjoy this Bible. The inserts that feature
many of the artists on the WoW 1997 CD have been written personally
for you. As you read the stories and testimonies of your favorite con—
temporary Christian music artists, we hope you'll be encouraged to come
to know God in a new way. And as you read the notes and use the rich
resources included in *The Student Bible*, we hope that your spiritual life
will be enriched and renewed.

In Christ,

The WoW 1997 Committee

New International Version

Third Day

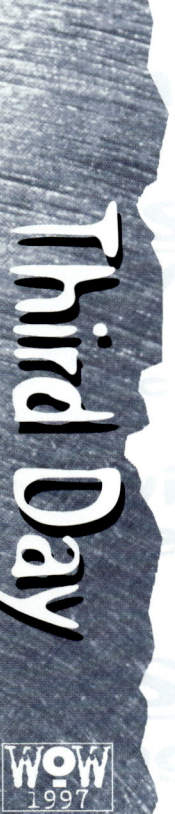

Third Day's Mac Powell talks about how Scripture influences his life and the band's work:

"One of my favorite verses from the Old Testament is Zephaniah 3:17, 'The Lord your God is with you, he is mighty to save. He will take great delight in you, he will quiet you with his love, he will rejoice over you with singing.' Being a singer, I naturally love music. I can think of so many people that I have listened to over the years who have incredible talents and beautiful voices. But none of these voices can compare to the joy of hearing our heavenly Father's voice singing to us.

"For our debut album we wrote and recorded a song entitled, 'Thief.' The idea for it came from one of my favorite stories in the Bible. Luke 23 tells the story of the conversation between Jesus and two criminals being crucified with him. We don't know what these men did, but it was probably something very serious, because crucifixion was the electric chair of the day. One of the criminals mocked Jesus along with the crowd. Looking for proof of Jesus' claims, he said, 'Aren't you the Christ? Save yourself and us!' (v. 39). To this first criminal, Jesus gave no reply.

"The second criminal, however, believed the truth. He knew that Jesus was setting up his kingdom, one that had much more significance than was involved in earthly politics and nations. He saw something eternal in Jesus that made him realize that Jesus' kingdom would be established in heaven and in the hearts of those who believe and trust in him. When the criminal said, 'Jesus, remember me when you come into your kingdom' (v. 42), Jesus responded, 'Today you will be with me in paradise' (v. 43).

"The grace and mercy offered to this hardened criminal two thousand years ago is still available for us today. Which criminal are you, the one who needs proof—flashes of lightning, puffs of smoke, and miracles—to believe? Or are you the second criminal, the one who realizes that we all would be 'punished justly' (v. 41) for our deeds were it not for the crucified King?"

²⁶Then the Israelites, all the people, went up to Bethel, and there they sat weeping before the LORD. They fasted that day until evening and presented burnt offerings and fellowship offerings^a to the LORD. ²⁷And the Israelites inquired of the LORD. (In those days the ark of the covenant of God was there, ²⁸with Phinehas son of Eleazar, the son of Aaron, ministering before it.) They asked, "Shall we go up again to battle with Benjamin our brother, or not?"

The LORD responded, "Go, for tomorrow I will give them into your hands."

²⁹Then Israel set an ambush around Gibeah. ³⁰They went up against the Benjamites on the third day and took up positions against Gibeah as they had done before. ³¹The Benjamites came out to meet them and were drawn away from the city. They began to inflict casualties on the Israelites as before, so that about thirty men fell in the open field and on the roads—the one leading to Bethel and the other to Gibeah.

³²While the Benjamites were saying, "We are defeating them as before," the Israelites were saying, "Let's retreat and draw them away from the city to the roads."

³³All the men of Israel moved from their places and took up positions at Baal Tamar, and the Israelite ambush charged out of its place on the west^b of Gibeah.^c ³⁴Then ten thousand of Israel's finest made a frontal attack on Gibeah. The fighting was so heavy that the Benjamites did not realize how near disaster was. ³⁵The LORD defeated Benjamin before Israel, and on that day the Israelites struck down 25,100 Benjamites, all armed with swords. ³⁶Then the Benjamites saw that they were beaten.

Now the men of Israel had given way before Benjamin, because they relied on the ambush they had set near Gibeah. ³⁷The men who had been in ambush made a sudden dash into Gibeah, spread out and put the whole city to the sword. ³⁸The men of Israel had arranged with the ambush that they should send up a great cloud of smoke from the city, ³⁹and then the men of Israel would turn in the battle.

The Benjamites had begun to inflict casualties on the men of Israel (about thirty), and they said, "We are defeating them as in the first battle." ⁴⁰But when the column of smoke began to rise from the city, the Benjamites turned and saw the smoke of the whole city going up into the sky. ⁴¹Then the men of Israel turned on them, and the men of Benjamin were terrified, because they realized that disaster had come upon them. ⁴²So they fled before the Israelites in the direction of the desert, but they could not escape the bat-

tle. And the men of Israel who came out of the towns cut them down there. ⁴³They surrounded the Benjamites, chased them and easily^d overran them in the vicinity of Gibeah on the east. ⁴⁴Eighteen thousand Benjamites fell, all of them valiant fighters. ⁴⁵As they turned and fled toward the desert to the rock of Rimmon, the Israelites cut down five thousand men along the roads. They kept pressing after the Benjamites as far as Gidom and struck down two thousand more.

⁴⁶On that day twenty-five thousand Benjamite swordsmen fell, all of them valiant fighters. ⁴⁷But six hundred men turned and fled into the desert to the rock of Rimmon, where they stayed four months. ⁴⁸The men of Israel went back to Benjamin and put all the towns to the sword, including the animals and everything else they found. All the towns they came across they set on fire.

Wives for the Benjamites

21 The men of Israel had taken an oath at Mizpah: "Not one of us will give his daughter in marriage to a Benjamite."

²The people went to Bethel,^e where they sat before God until evening, raising their voices and weeping bitterly. ³"O LORD, the God of Israel," they cried, "why has this happened to Israel? Why should one tribe be missing from Israel today?"

⁴Early the next day the people built an altar and presented burnt offerings and fellowship offerings.^a

⁵Then the Israelites asked, "Who from all the tribes of Israel has failed to assemble before the LORD?" For they had taken a solemn oath that anyone who failed to assemble before the LORD at Mizpah should certainly be put to death.

⁶Now the Israelites grieved for their brothers, the Benjamites. "Today one tribe is cut off from Israel," they said. ⁷"How can we provide wives for those who are left, since we have taken an oath by the LORD not to give them any of our daughters in marriage?" ⁸Then they asked, "Which one of the tribes of Israel failed to assemble before the LORD at Mizpah?" They discovered that no one from Jabesh Gilead had come to the camp for the assembly. ⁹For when they counted the people, they found that none of the people of Jabesh Gilead were there.

¹⁰So the assembly sent twelve thousand fighting men with instructions to go to Jabesh Gilead and put to the sword those living there, including the women and children. ¹¹"This is what you are to do," they said. "Kill every male and every

---

^a26,4 Traditionally *peace offerings*   ^b33 Some Septuagint manuscripts and Vulgate; the meaning of the Hebrew for this word is uncertain.   ^c33 Hebrew *Geba*, a variant of *Gibeah*   ^d43 The meaning of the Hebrew for this word is uncertain.   ^e2 Or *to the house of God*

woman who is not a virgin." 12They found among the people living in Jabesh Gilead four hundred young women who had never slept with a man, and they took them to the camp at Shiloh in Canaan.

13Then the whole assembly sent an offer of peace to the Benjamites at the rock of Rimmon. 14So the Benjamites returned at that time and were given the women of Jabesh Gilead who had been spared. But there were not enough for all of them.

15The people grieved for Benjamin, because the LORD had made a gap in the tribes of Israel. 16And the elders of the assembly said, "With the women of Benjamin destroyed, how shall we provide wives for the men who are left? 17The Benjamite survivors must have heirs," they said, "so that a tribe of Israel will not be wiped out. 18We can't give them our daughters as wives, since we Israelites have taken this oath: 'Cursed be anyone who gives a wife to a Benjamite.' 19But look, there is the annual festival of the LORD in Shiloh, to the north of Bethel, and east of the road that goes from Bethel to Shechem, and to the south of Lebonah."

20So they instructed the Benjamites, saying, "Go and hide in the vineyards 21and watch. When the girls of Shiloh come out to join in the dancing, then rush from the vineyards and each of you seize a wife from the girls of Shiloh and go to the land of Benjamin. 22When their fathers or brothers complain to us, we will say to them, 'Do us a kindness by helping them, because we did not get wives for them during the war, and you are innocent, since you did not give your daughters to them.'"

23So that is what the Benjamites did. While the girls were dancing, each man caught one and carried her off to be his wife. Then they returned to their inheritance and rebuilt the towns and settled in them.

24At that time the Israelites left that place and went home to their tribes and clans, each to his own inheritance.

25In those days Israel had no king; everyone did as he saw fit.

RUTH

A Rare Bond of Love
Ruth and Naomi lost everything, except their care for each other

RUTH AND NAOMI WERE UNLIKELY friends: a generation apart, one young and strong, the other past middle age. Stranger still, one was the other's mother-in-law and came from a completely different ethnic and religious background. Who would have put them together?

They had lost everything when their husbands died. With no man to rely on, their lives were at risk in those rough times. No one else would come to their defense: They had only each other.

The Woman's Initiative

The book of Ruth is not "two women against the world." Rather, it shows the women taking initiative to find, by God's help, a man who would care for them.

A woman's initiative rarely gets so direct as in Ruth. At her mother-in-law's direction Ruth located where Boaz, a relative, was camping out. She waited until dark, then crept to his feet and lay down. When Boaz woke and found her, he didn't have to be told what was on her mind. She wanted him for a husband. Flattered, he didn't let another sun set before making the legal arrangements for marriage.

Society the way God had designed it encouraged men like Boaz to help the needy. For instance, by Old Testament law a farmer had to leave some of his grain behind so that poor people like Ruth could harvest it. And, also by law, a helpless widow had to be taken into the home of her husband's family. This was the law by which Boaz claimed Ruth (4:1–12).

God's Invisible Presence

Behind the eloquent story of Ruth looms an invisible helper—God. He didn't intervene in the events, so far as the story tells. But nobody in Ruth doubted that life proceeded under God's direction. It was the Lord by whom Ruth swore when declaring her love to Naomi (1:17), and the Lord whom Naomi credited for bringing Ruth to Boaz's field (2:20). God's law brought Boaz and Ruth into marriage. Finally, the Lord gave them a son, in whom mother, father, and "grandmother" found deep satisfaction.

The last verses of Ruth show, furthermore, that God's plan extended beyond Ruth and Naomi's personal problems. Ruth was a member of the despised Moabites—enemies of Israel. Yet God not only accepted her into his family, but also used her to produce Israel's greatest king. Ruth's great-grandson turned out to be David. To anyone who thought that God's love was for Israelites only, Ruth's life made a striking contradiction.

> "Where you go I will go, and where you stay I will stay. Your people will be my people and your God my God. . . . May the Lord deal with me, be it ever so severely, if anything but death separates you and me." 1:16–17

How to Read Ruth

Ruth, brief enough to read in 15 minutes, is a delight. The German poet Goethe called it "the loveliest complete work on a small scale." But because Ruth's author didn't hammer his points home, it is possible to overlook his deeper meaning. As you read, concentrate on the loving bond between Ruth and Naomi. This love, which thrived in suffering, is the root of the book. It offers hope for other people in hard circumstances.

The author of Ruth assumed that readers understood the cultural and historical background of Ruth's time. You may wish to read about it for deeper understanding.

Deuteronomy 25:5–10 describes the background on marriage for a widow with a member of her husband's family, the "kinsman-redeemer." Leviticus 25:23–28 gives background on a poor person's property. The Introduction to Judges offers historical perspective, for the book of Judges is an overview of the brutal times Ruth lived in.

PEOPLE YOU'LL MEET IN RUTH

RUTH (p. 294)

3-TRACK READING PLAN

For an explanation and complete listing of the 3-track reading plan, turn to page 7.

TRACK 1: *Two-Week Courses on the Bible*

See page 7 for information on these courses.

TRACK 2: *An Overview of Ruth in 1 Day*
☐ Day 1. Read the Introduction to Ruth and chapter 1, which describes an unusual friendship developing under the unkindest of conditions.

Now turn to page 9 for your next Track 2 reading project.

TRACK 3: *All of Ruth in 4 Days*

After you have read through Ruth, turn to pages 10–14 for your next Track 3 reading project.

☐1   ☐2   ☐3   ☐4

Naomi and Ruth

1 In the days when the judges ruled,[a] there was a famine in the land, and a man from Bethlehem in Judah, together with his wife and two sons, went to live for a while in the country of Moab. ²The man's name was Elimelech, his wife's name Naomi, and the names of his two sons were Mahlon and Kilion. They were Ephrathites from Bethlehem, Judah. And they went to Moab and lived there.

³Now Elimelech, Naomi's husband, died, and she was left with her two sons. ⁴They married Moabite women, one named Orpah and the other Ruth. After they had lived there about ten years, ⁵both Mahlon and Kilion also died, and Naomi was left without her two sons and her husband.

⁶When she heard in Moab that the LORD had come to the aid of his people by providing food for them, Naomi and her daughters-in-law prepared to return home from there. ⁷With her two daughters-in-law she left the place where she had been living and set out on the road that would take them back to the land of Judah.

⁸Then Naomi said to her two daughters-in-law, "Go back, each of you, to your mother's home. May the LORD show kindness to you, as you have shown to your dead and to me. ⁹May

the LORD grant that each of you will find rest in the home of another husband."

Then she kissed them and they wept aloud ¹⁰and said to her, "We will go back with you to your people."

¹¹But Naomi said, "Return home, my daughters. Why would you come with me? Am I going to have any more sons, who could become your husbands? ¹²Return home, my daughters; I am too old to have another husband. Even if I thought there was still hope for me—even if I had a husband tonight and then gave birth to sons— ¹³would you wait until they grew up? Would you remain unmarried for them? No, my daughters. It is more bitter for me than for you, because the LORD's hand has gone out against me!"

¹⁴At this they wept again. Then Orpah kissed her mother-in-law good-by, but Ruth clung to her.

¹⁵"Look," said Naomi, "your sister-in-law is going back to her people and her gods. Go back with her."

¹⁶But Ruth replied, "Don't urge me to leave you or to turn back from you. Where you go I will go, and where you stay I will stay. Your people will be my people and your God my God. ¹⁷Where you die I will die, and there I will be

---

[a]1 Traditionally *judged*

buried. May the LORD deal with me, be it ever so severely, if anything but death separates you and me." ¹⁸When Naomi realized that Ruth was determined to go with her, she stopped urging her.

¹⁹So the two women went on until they came to Bethlehem. When they arrived in Bethlehem, the whole town was stirred because of them, and the women exclaimed, "Can this be Naomi?"

²⁰"Don't call me Naomi,ᵃ" she told them. "Call me Mara,ᵇ because the Almightyᶜ has made my life very bitter. ²¹I went away full, but the LORD has brought me back empty. Why call me Naomi? The LORD has afflictedᵈ me; the Almighty has brought misfortune upon me."

²²So Naomi returned from Moab accompanied by Ruth the Moabitess, her daughter-in-law, arriving in Bethlehem as the barley harvest was beginning.

1:22 The Worst of Times

The author stresses that Ruth was a Moabitess, a fact that would have greatly impressed the original readers. Moab and Israel were bitter enemies, and Ruth took a risk by emigrating to a land that might treat her as a despised foreigner. This story of family love and loyalty took place during the time of the judges, when murder, immorality, and general anarchy prevailed.

Ruth Meets Boaz

2 Now Naomi had a relative on her husband's side, from the clan of Elimelech, a man of standing, whose name was Boaz.

²And Ruth the Moabitess said to Naomi, "Let me go to the fields and pick up the leftover grain behind anyone in whose eyes I find favor."

Naomi said to her, "Go ahead, my daughter." ³So she went out and began to glean in the fields behind the harvesters. As it turned out, she found herself working in a field belonging to Boaz, who was from the clan of Elimelech.

⁴Just then Boaz arrived from Bethlehem and greeted the harvesters, "The LORD be with you!"

"The LORD bless you!" they called back.

⁵Boaz asked the foreman of his harvesters, "Whose young woman is that?"

⁶The foreman replied, "She is the Moabitess who came back from Moab with Naomi. ⁷She said, 'Please let me glean and gather among the sheaves behind the harvesters.' She went into the field and has worked steadily from morning till now, except for a short rest in the shelter."

⁸So Boaz said to Ruth, "My daughter, listen to me. Don't go and glean in another field and don't go away from here. Stay here with my servant girls. ⁹Watch the field where the men are harvesting, and follow along after the girls. I have told the men not to touch you. And whenever you are

2:3 Caring for the Poor

In the Old Testament God used several welfare programs to help poor people. One, reflected in this passage, was the command to leave some of the harvest in the field for the poor to gather. Poor people didn't beg for handouts, but worked for what they got. (Leviticus 19:9–10 and Deuteronomy 24:19–22 give the directions.)

Gleaning was humiliating and sometimes dangerous work. Ruth, a single woman and a foreigner, showed courage by working in the fields, and her diligence soon attracted the foreman's attention.

thirsty, go and get a drink from the water jars the men have filled."

¹⁰At this, she bowed down with her face to the ground. She exclaimed, "Why have I found such favor in your eyes that you notice me—a foreigner?"

¹¹Boaz replied, "I've been told all about what you have done for your mother-in-law since the death of your husband—how you left your father and mother and your homeland and came to live with a people you did not know before. ¹²May the LORD repay you for what you have done. May you be richly rewarded by the LORD, the God of Israel, under whose wings you have come to take refuge."

¹³"May I continue to find favor in your eyes, my lord," she said. "You have given me comfort and have spoken kindly to your servant—though I do not have the standing of one of your servant girls."

¹⁴At mealtime Boaz said to her, "Come over here. Have some bread and dip it in the wine vinegar."

When she sat down with the harvesters, he offered her some roasted grain. She ate all she wanted and had some left over. ¹⁵As she got up to glean, Boaz gave orders to his men, "Even if she gathers among the sheaves, don't embarrass her. ¹⁶Rather, pull out some stalks for her from the bundles and leave them for her to pick up, and don't rebuke her."

¹⁷So Ruth gleaned in the field until evening. Then she threshed the barley she had gathered, and it amounted to about an ephah.ᵉ ¹⁸She carried it back to town, and her mother-in-law saw how much she had gathered. Ruth also brought

---

ᵃ20 *Naomi* means *pleasant*; also in verse 21. ᵇ20 *Mara* means *bitter*. ᶜ20 Hebrew *Shaddai*; also in verse 21
ᵈ21 Or *has testified against* ᵉ17 That is, probably about 3/5 bushel (about 22 liters)

out and gave her what she had left over after she had eaten enough.

[19]Her mother-in-law asked her, "Where did you glean today? Where did you work? Blessed be the man who took notice of you!"

Then Ruth told her mother-in-law about the one at whose place she had been working. "The name of the man I worked with today is Boaz," she said.

[20]"The LORD bless him!" Naomi said to her daughter-in-law. "He has not stopped showing his kindness to the living and the dead." She added, "That man is our close relative; he is one of our kinsman-redeemers."

[21]Then Ruth the Moabitess said, "He even said to me, 'Stay with my workers until they finish harvesting all my grain.'"

[22]Naomi said to Ruth her daughter-in-law, "It will be good for you, my daughter, to go with his girls, because in someone else's field you might be harmed."

[23]So Ruth stayed close to the servant girls of Boaz to glean until the barley and wheat harvests were finished. And she lived with her mother-in-law.

Ruth and Boaz at the Threshing Floor

3 One day Naomi her mother-in-law said to her, "My daughter, should I not try to find a home[a] for you, where you will be well provided for? [2]Is not Boaz, with whose servant girls you have been, a kinsman of ours? Tonight he will be winnowing barley on the threshing floor. [3]Wash and perfume yourself, and put on your best clothes. Then go down to the threshing floor, but don't let him know you are there until he has finished eating and drinking. [4]When he lies down, note the place where he is lying. Then go and uncover his feet and lie down. He will tell you what to do."

[5]"I will do whatever you say," Ruth answered. [6]So she went down to the threshing floor and did everything her mother-in-law told her to do.

[7]When Boaz had finished eating and drinking and was in good spirits, he went over to lie down at the far end of the grain pile. Ruth approached quietly, uncovered his feet and lay down. [8]In the middle of the night something startled the man, and he turned and discovered a woman lying at his feet.

[9]"Who are you?" he asked.

"I am your servant Ruth," she said. "Spread the corner of your garment over me, since you are a kinsman-redeemer."

[10]"The LORD bless you, my daughter," he replied. "This kindness is greater than that which you showed earlier: You have not run after the younger men, whether rich or poor. [11]And now, my daughter, don't be afraid. I will do for you all you ask. All my fellow townsmen know that you are a woman of noble character. [12]Although it is true that I am near of kin, there is a kinsman-redeemer nearer than I. [13]Stay here for the night, and in the morning if he wants to redeem, good; let him redeem. But if he is not willing, as surely as the LORD lives I will do it. Lie here until morning."

[14]So she lay at his feet until morning, but got up before anyone could be recognized; and he said, "Don't let it be known that a woman came to the threshing floor."

[15]He also said, "Bring me the shawl you are

---

[a]*1 Hebrew find rest (see Ruth 1:9)

RUTH *Character Counts*

SHE ARRIVED IN ISRAEL PENNILESS, a foreigner and a widow, with her mother-in-law as her only friend. Considering that her home country Moab was often at war with Israel, and that the two nations worshiped different gods, the immigrant named Ruth hardly figured to thrive in Israel. Yet she went to work without delay.

Even though she was a foreigner, Ruth showed herself a model Israelite woman: modest, hard-working and deeply loyal to those she loved. (Her speech to Naomi is one of the world's great love poems [1:16–17]). Ruth never complained about hardship; rather, she responded with gratitude when anyone showed kindness to her. In the end she proved that character counts more than circumstances.

As this gem of a love story recounts, Ruth caught the eye of a very good man. The two married, began a new life together and had a son. Ultimately, through that son, Ruth the refugee became an ancestor of Israel's greatest king.

Ruth's life makes a lovely story in itself, but it has a larger significance. She contradicts a common assumption about the God of the Old Testament—that only members of one special tribe could be his chosen people. Ruth was fully accepted among God's people because she chose to follow the true God, despite her foreign background. Anyone could join in worshiping God, just as Ruth did.

Life Questions: Do you find it hard to accept and admire those who come from outside your group? What "qualifications" do you set up?

wearing and hold it out." When she did so, he poured into it six measures of barley and put it on her. Then he[a] went back to town.

[16]When Ruth came to her mother-in-law, Naomi asked, "How did it go, my daughter?"

Then she told her everything Boaz had done for her [17]and added, "He gave me these six measures of barley, saying, 'Don't go back to your mother-in-law empty-handed.'"

[18]Then Naomi said, "Wait, my daughter, until you find out what happens. For the man will not rest until the matter is settled today."

Boaz Marries Ruth

4 Meanwhile Boaz went up to the town gate and sat there. When the kinsman-redeemer he had mentioned came along, Boaz said, "Come over here, my friend, and sit down." So he went over and sat down.

4:1 Expensive Bride

In order to marry Ruth, Boaz had to go through a complicated legal procedure at the town gate, a public gathering place. The laws were designed to keep property in the family and to protect family members who might have suffered financial or other setbacks. As a distant relative, Boaz could purchase, or "redeem," Naomi's family property, but only after a closer relative, the "kinsman-redeemer" had declined. Along with the property, Boaz acquired marriage rights to Ruth, Naomi's relative.

[2]Boaz took ten of the elders of the town and said, "Sit here," and they did so. [3]Then he said to the kinsman-redeemer, "Naomi, who has come back from Moab, is selling the piece of land that belonged to our brother Elimelech. [4]I thought I should bring the matter to your attention and suggest that you buy it in the presence of these seated here and in the presence of the elders of my people. If you will redeem it, do so. But if you[b] will not, tell me, so I will know. For no one has the right to do it except you, and I am next in line."

"I will redeem it," he said.

[5]Then Boaz said, "On the day you buy the land from Naomi and from Ruth the Moabitess, you acquire[c] the dead man's widow, in order to maintain the name of the dead with his property."

[6]At this, the kinsman-redeemer said, "Then I cannot redeem it because I might endanger my own estate. You redeem it yourself. I cannot do it."

[7](Now in earlier times in Israel, for the redemption and transfer of property to become final, one party took off his sandal and gave it to the other. This was the method of legalizing transactions in Israel.)

[8]So the kinsman-redeemer said to Boaz, "Buy it yourself." And he removed his sandal.

[9]Then Boaz announced to the elders and all the people, "Today you are witnesses that I have bought from Naomi all the property of Elimelech, Kilion and Mahlon. [10]I have also acquired Ruth the Moabitess, Mahlon's widow, as my wife, in order to maintain the name of the dead with his property, so that his name will not disappear from among his family or from the town records. Today you are witnesses!"

[11]Then the elders and all those at the gate said, "We are witnesses. May the LORD make the woman who is coming into your home like Rachel and Leah, who together built up the house of Israel. May you have standing in Ephrathah and be famous in Bethlehem. [12]Through the offspring the LORD gives you by this young woman, may your family be like that of Perez, whom Tamar bore to Judah."

The Genealogy of David

[13]So Boaz took Ruth and she became his wife. Then he went to her, and the LORD enabled her to conceive, and she gave birth to a son. [14]The women said to Naomi: "Praise be to the LORD, who this day has not left you without a kinsman-redeemer. May he become famous throughout Israel! [15]He will renew your life and sustain you in your old age. For your daughter-in-law, who loves you and who is better to you than seven sons, has given him birth."

[16]Then Naomi took the child, laid him in her lap and cared for him. [17]The women living there said, "Naomi has a son." And they named him Obed. He was the father of Jesse, the father of David.

[18]This, then, is the family line of Perez:

Perez was the father of Hezron,
[19]Hezron the father of Ram,
Ram the father of Amminadab,
[20]Amminadab the father of Nahshon,
Nahshon the father of Salmon,[d]
[21]Salmon the father of Boaz,
Boaz the father of Obed,
[22]Obed the father of Jesse,
and Jesse the father of David.

---

[a]15 Most Hebrew manuscripts; many Hebrew manuscripts, Vulgate and Syriac *she*　　[b]4 Many Hebrew manuscripts, Septuagint, Vulgate and Syriac; most Hebrew manuscripts *he*　　[c]5 Hebrew; Vulgate and Syriac *Naomi, you acquire Ruth the Moabitess,*　　[d]20 A few Hebrew manuscripts, some Septuagint manuscripts and Vulgate (see also verse 21 and Septuagint of 1 Chron. 2:11); most Hebrew manuscripts *Salma*

1 SAMUEL

What Leadership Requires
Israel, fighting for survival, needed a leader

> "It is not by strength that one prevails; those who oppose the LORD will be shattered."
> 2:9–10

NO COUNTRY, NO ORGANIZATION, NO family is great without great leadership. But how do you get it? Israel was forced to ask that question during a critical, do-or-die period. Three men rose to the highest power: Samuel, Saul, and David. All were attractive, powerful figures who commanded admiration and respect. Two, David and Samuel, made very successful leaders. The other, Saul, had a promising beginning but ended as a failure.

Fighting for Survival

Israel was fighting for survival. The Philistines had migrated to the region about the same time Israel had escaped from Egypt. Now, from their cities near the Mediterranean coast, they were gradually pushing deeper into the mountains of Israel. They had superior weapons—chariots, in particular. Though less populous than Israel, they were apparently better organized.

Israel had neither central administration nor a regular army. A loose confederation of 12 tribes, Israelites called on each other for help only in emergencies. Occasional inspired leaders—"judges"—took charge of military defense when necessary. The nation had worked that way for well over 100 years, and the tribes seemed too independent to change. But the Philistines were pressing them. A crisis of leadership—a crisis testing the very existence of Israel—was building.

Why Begin with Hannah?

Surprisingly, 1 Samuel opens not with a battle or even with the leadership crisis, but with a very private family problem. Two bitterly jealous wives had a long-standing quarrel, one taunting the other because of her infertility. Hannah, the childless woman, turned to God in desperation, praying and promising to dedicate a son to him. The result was a little boy named Samuel.

Hannah kept her vow to God, and Samuel grew into one of the greatest leaders Israel had ever known. He had a triple role: He served as a prophet who could discern God's will, as a priest who led Israel to worship, and as a military leader. He chose, under God's direction, Israel's first two kings. Samuel's strong personality undergirds the entire book of 1 Samuel, even though he officially retired at the end of chapter 15.

Why begin 1 Samuel with Hannah? Hannah's struggles are Israel's, in miniature. Her frustration forced her to look to God, and as a result her son Samuel served in the tabernacle instead of following in his father's footsteps as a farmer. Hannah's story shows that from bitter pain may come great promise, if that pain leads you to God. The Israelites, who were going to experience a great many more troubles in their history, needed Hannah's example.

God Chooses His Own Leaders

Hannah's story also reminds us that God's leaders don't necessarily come through regulation channels. Ordinarily, Eli's corrupt sons would have carried on national leadership. But God wanted no part of them. Instead, he blessed a woman who had turned to him in her troubles, and he blessed her son as long as that son trusted in him for help. God chose a leader to suit himself, a leader who listened to him. "The LORD declares . . . Those who honor me I will honor, but those who despise me will be disdained'" (2:30).

Samuel never forgot that lesson. He anointed Saul as the first king, and then, when Saul failed to honor God, stripped him of his authority. Passing over many impressive men, Samuel chose David, a young shepherd, to replace Saul. Under David, Israel would be transformed into a wealthy, secure kingdom. Was this because David had such natural leadership qualities? First Samuel suggests a different perspective: David succeeded because God chose him for the job, and because David persistently turned to God for his direction. The best leadership, ultimately, belongs to God.

How to Read 1 Samuel

Some of the stories of 1 Samuel—David and Goliath, for instance—are justly famous as great adventures. But you should read for more than excitement. Look for insights into the character required for leadership. Samuel and David were great leaders. Saul, on the other hand, was a miserable failure.

These men led Israel during a crucial, bloody period. Israel had been dominated by a foreign power and, partly because of this, was changing its government to a monarchy. This change in governmental institutions, along with tribal tensions, form the background for the book. A good commentary can help explain this, but you can get much of it for yourself by asking, as you read, three questions: What are the most important national problems facing Israel? What kind of leadership is needed? How do these three leaders (and numerous smaller figures) respond to these needs?

PEOPLE YOU'LL MEET IN 1 SAMUEL

HANNAH (p. 299)
ELI (p. 301)

SAMUEL (p. 304)
SAUL (p. 313)

JONATHAN (p. 319)
ABIGAIL (p. 325)

3-TRACK READING PLAN

For an explanation and complete listing of the 3-track reading plan, turn to page 7.

TRACK 1: *Two-Week Courses on the Bible*
The Track 1 reading program includes one chapter from 1 Samuel. See page 8 for a complete listing of this course.

TRACK 2: *An Overview of 1 Samuel in 4 Days*
☐ Day 1. Read the Introduction to 1 Samuel and chapter 3, God's call of Samuel when he was very young.
☐ Day 2. Read chapter 16 to see how God chose David, and why.
☐ Day 3. Read chapter 17 for the exciting story of David's victory over Goliath, noting the qualities David showed.
☐ Day 4. Read chapter 20 for a glimpse of a model friendship between David and Jonathan.

Now turn to page 9 for your next Track 2 reading project.

TRACK 3: *All of 1 Samuel in 31 Days*
After you have read through 1 Samuel, turn to pages 10–14 for your next Track 3 reading project.

☐1 ☐2 ☐3 ☐4 ☐5 ☐6 ☐7 ☐8
☐9 ☐10 ☐11 ☐12 ☐13 ☐14 ☐15 ☐16
☐17 ☐18 ☐19 ☐20 ☐21 ☐22 ☐23 ☐24
☐25 ☐26 ☐27 ☐28 ☐29 ☐30 ☐31

The Birth of Samuel

1 There was a certain man from Ramathaim, a Zuphite[a] from the hill country of Ephraim, whose name was Elkanah son of Jeroham, the son of Elihu, the son of Tohu, the son of Zuph, an Ephraimite. [2]He had two wives; one was called Hannah and the other Peninnah. Peninnah had children, but Hannah had none.

[3]Year after year this man went up from his town to worship and sacrifice to the LORD Almighty at Shiloh, where Hophni and Phinehas, the two sons of Eli, were priests of the LORD. [4]Whenever the day came for Elkanah to sacrifice, he would give portions of the meat to his wife Peninnah and to all her sons and daughters. [5]But to Hannah he gave a double portion because he loved her, and the LORD had closed her womb. [6]And because the LORD had closed her womb, her rival kept provoking her in order to irritate her. [7]This went on year after year. Whenever Hannah went up to the house of the LORD, her rival provoked her till she wept and would not eat. [8]Elkanah her husband would say to her, "Hannah, why are you weeping? Why don't you eat? Why are you downhearted? Don't I mean more to you than ten sons?"

[9]Once when they had finished eating and drinking in Shiloh, Hannah stood up. Now Eli the priest was sitting on a chair by the doorpost of the LORD's temple.[b] [10]In bitterness of soul Hannah wept much and prayed to the LORD. [11]And she made a vow, saying, "O LORD Almighty, if you will only look upon your servant's misery and remember me, and not forget your servant but give her a son, then I will give him to the LORD for all the days of his life, and no razor will ever be used on his head."

[12]As she kept on praying to the LORD, Eli observed her mouth. [13]Hannah was praying in her heart, and her lips were moving but her voice was not heard. Eli thought she was drunk [14]and said

to her, "How long will you keep on getting drunk? Get rid of your wine."

[15]"Not so, my lord," Hannah replied, "I am a woman who is deeply troubled. I have not been drinking wine or beer; I was pouring out my soul to the LORD. [16]Do not take your servant for a wicked woman; I have been praying here out of my great anguish and grief."

[17]Eli answered, "Go in peace, and may the God of Israel grant you what you have asked of him."

[18]She said, "May your servant find favor in your eyes." Then she went her way and ate something, and her face was no longer downcast.

[19]Early the next morning they arose and worshiped before the LORD and then went back to their home at Ramah. Elkanah lay with Hannah his wife, and the LORD remembered her. [20]So in the course of time Hannah conceived and gave birth to a son. She named him Samuel,[c] saying, "Because I asked the LORD for him."

Hannah Dedicates Samuel

[21]When the man Elkanah went up with all his family to offer the annual sacrifice to the LORD and to fulfill his vow, [22]Hannah did not go. She said to her husband, "After the boy is weaned, I will take him and present him before the LORD, and he will live there always."

[23]"Do what seems best to you," Elkanah her husband told her. "Stay here until you have weaned him; only may the LORD make good his[d] word." So the woman stayed at home and nursed her son until she had weaned him.

[24]After he was weaned, she took the boy with her, young as he was, along with a three-year-old bull,[e] an ephah[f] of flour and a skin of wine, and brought him to the house of the LORD at Shiloh. [25]When they had slaughtered the bull, they brought the boy to Eli, [26]and she said to him, "As surely as you live, my lord, I am the woman who stood here beside you praying to the LORD. [27]I prayed for this child, and the LORD has granted me what I asked of him. [28]So now I give him to the LORD. For his whole life he will be given over to the LORD." And he worshiped the LORD there.

Hannah's Prayer

2 Then Hannah prayed and said:

"My heart rejoices in the LORD;
  in the LORD my horn[g] is lifted high.
My mouth boasts over my enemies,
  for I delight in your deliverance.

1:13 Sad, Not Drunk

Eli's mistaken assumption suggests that people sometimes came to the tabernacle drunk. Perhaps in these troubled times drunkenness was more common than heartfelt prayer. Hannah prayed with great anguish because she had no children. She is one of several barren women in the Bible whom God helped; others include Sarah (Genesis 11:30), Rebekah (Genesis 25:21), Rachel (Genesis 29:31), and Elizabeth (Luke 1:7).

---

[a]1 Or *from Ramathaim Zuphim*   [b]9 That is, tabernacle   [c]20 *Samuel* sounds like the Hebrew for *heard of God.*
[d]23 Masoretic Text; Dead Sea Scrolls, Septuagint and Syriac *your*   [e]24 Dead Sea Scrolls, Septuagint and Syriac;
Masoretic Text *with three bulls*   [f]24 That is, probably about 3/5 bushel (about 22 liters)   [g]1 *Horn* here symbolizes
strength; also in verse 10.

²"There is no one holy[a] like the LORD;
  there is no one besides you;
  there is no Rock like our God.

³"Do not keep talking so proudly
  or let your mouth speak such arrogance,
for the LORD is a God who knows,
  and by him deeds are weighed.

⁴"The bows of the warriors are broken,
  but those who stumbled are armed with
      strength.
⁵Those who were full hire themselves out for
      food,
  but those who were hungry hunger no
      more.
She who was barren has borne seven
      children,
  but she who has had many sons pines
      away.

⁶"The LORD brings death and makes alive;
  he brings down to the grave[b] and raises
      up.
⁷The LORD sends poverty and wealth;
  he humbles and he exalts.
⁸He raises the poor from the dust
  and lifts the needy from the ash heap;
he seats them with princes
  and has them inherit a throne of honor.

"For the foundations of the earth are the
      LORD's;
  upon them he has set the world.
⁹He will guard the feet of his saints,
  but the wicked will be silenced in
      darkness.

"It is not by strength that one prevails;
¹⁰   those who oppose the LORD will be
      shattered.

He will thunder against them from heaven;
  the LORD will judge the ends of the earth.

"He will give strength to his king
  and exalt the horn of his anointed."

¹¹Then Elkanah went home to Ramah, but the boy ministered before the LORD under Eli the priest.

Eli's Wicked Sons

¹²Eli's sons were wicked men; they had no regard for the LORD. ¹³Now it was the practice of the priests with the people that whenever anyone offered a sacrifice and while the meat was being boiled, the servant of the priest would come with a three-pronged fork in his hand. ¹⁴He would plunge it into the pan or kettle or caldron or pot, and the priest would take for himself whatever the fork brought up. This is how they treated all the Israelites who came to Shiloh. ¹⁵But even before the fat was burned, the servant of the priest would come and say to the man who was sacrificing, "Give the priest some meat to roast; he won't accept boiled meat from you, but only raw."

¹⁶If the man said to him, "Let the fat be burned up first, and then take whatever you want," the servant would then answer, "No, hand it over now; if you don't, I'll take it by force."

¹⁷This sin of the young men was very great in the LORD's sight, for they[c] were treating the LORD's offering with contempt.

¹⁸But Samuel was ministering before the LORD—a boy wearing a linen ephod. ¹⁹Each year his mother made him a little robe and took it to him when she went up with her husband to offer the annual sacrifice. ²⁰Eli would bless Elkanah and his wife, saying, "May the LORD give you children by this woman to take the place of the one she prayed for and gave to the LORD." Then they would go home. ²¹And the LORD was gra-

---

[a] 2 Or no Holy One   [b] 6 Hebrew Sheol   [c] 17 Or men

HANNAH *Deepest Longing*

OTHER WOMEN MIGHT ENVY HANNAH. She had, at least, a kind husband who obviously loved her. Yet for Hannah, one deep, unfulfilled longing made life miserable. Hannah wanted a child. (It hardly helped that a rival wife, Peninnah, brought the subject up at every opportunity.)

The longing for children may be the strongest in life. Today, infertile couples spend thousands of dollars in search of a medical remedy. For Hannah, who had no such recourse, her longing outweighed every blessing. Hannah wept, felt bitter and poured out her woes to God.

When God answered Hannah's prayer and gave her a son, Samuel, she poured out her joy to God as well. Remarkably, for a woman who had waited so long for a son, she took Samuel to God's tabernacle as soon as he reached an appropriate age. There she placed him in the priest's care.

Hannah certainly loved her child and never forgot him. Every year she made a garment for him—a huge expenditure in an age when cloth and even thread had to be made by hand. Yet she did not cling to her blessing any more than she had clung to her woes. She gave both to God.

Life Questions: Is some unfulfilled longing making you miserable? How can you take it to God?

cious to Hannah; she conceived and gave birth to three sons and two daughters. Meanwhile, the boy Samuel grew up in the presence of the LORD.

²²Now Eli, who was very old, heard about everything his sons were doing to all Israel and how they slept with the women who served at the entrance to the Tent of Meeting. ²³So he said to them, "Why do you do such things? I hear from all the people about these wicked deeds of yours. ²⁴No, my sons; it is not a good report that I hear spreading among the LORD's people. ²⁵If a man sins against another man, God*a* may mediate for him; but if a man sins against the LORD, who will intercede for him?" His sons, however, did not listen to their father's rebuke, for it was the LORD's will to put them to death.

2:25 God in Charge

Eli's sons disobeyed, the Bible says, because God wanted to put them to death. Does this mean that God took away their free choice? To Old Testament writers this "contradiction" seemed less troubling than to us. To them every event occurred only because, ultimately, God let it. Within his overall control people acted freely. In this case, Eli's sons were free to obey or disobey. The author wants us to know, however, that their disobedience was not beyond God's power: He planned to judge their evil activities.

²⁶And the boy Samuel continued to grow in stature and in favor with the LORD and with men.

Prophecy Against the House of Eli

²⁷Now a man of God came to Eli and said to him, "This is what the LORD says: 'Did I not clearly reveal myself to your father's house when they were in Egypt under Pharaoh? ²⁸I chose your father out of all the tribes of Israel to be my priest, to go up to my altar, to burn incense, and to wear an ephod in my presence. I also gave your father's house all the offerings made with fire by the Israelites. ²⁹Why do you*b* scorn my sacrifice and offering that I prescribed for my dwelling? Why do you honor your sons more than me by fattening yourselves on the choice parts of every offering made by my people Israel?'

³⁰"Therefore the LORD, the God of Israel, declares: 'I promised that your house and your father's house would minister before me forever.' But now the LORD declares: 'Far be it from me! Those who honor me I will honor, but those who despise me will be disdained. ³¹The time is coming when I will cut short your strength and the

strength of your father's house, so that there will not be an old man in your family line ³²and you will see distress in my dwelling. Although good will be done to Israel, in your family line there

2:30 Bad News for Eli

For Eli, this pronouncement came as bad news. He was held responsible for his sons' disgraceful behavior in the tabernacle. Eli rebuked them, but "failed to restrain them" (3:13). As the priest in charge of the tabernacle, it was his job to stop any abuse there.

will never be an old man. ³³Every one of you that I do not cut off from my altar will be spared only to blind your eyes with tears and to grieve your heart, and all your descendants will die in the prime of life.

³⁴"'And what happens to your two sons, Hophni and Phinehas, will be a sign to you—they will both die on the same day. ³⁵I will raise up for myself a faithful priest, who will do according to what is in my heart and mind. I will firmly establish his house, and he will minister before my anointed one always. ³⁶Then everyone left in your family line will come and bow down before him for a piece of silver and a crust of bread and plead, "Appoint me to some priestly office so I can have food to eat." '"

The LORD Calls Samuel

3 The boy Samuel ministered before the LORD under Eli. In those days the word of the LORD was rare; there were not many visions.

²One night Eli, whose eyes were becoming so weak that he could barely see, was lying down in his usual place. ³The lamp of God had not yet gone out, and Samuel was lying down in the temple*c* of the LORD, where the ark of God was. ⁴Then the LORD called Samuel.

Samuel answered, "Here I am." ⁵And he ran to Eli and said, "Here I am; you called me."

But Eli said, "I did not call; go back and lie down." So he went and lay down.

⁶Again the LORD called, "Samuel!" And Samuel got up and went to Eli and said, "Here I am; you called me."

"My son," Eli said, "I did not call; go back and lie down."

⁷Now Samuel did not yet know the LORD: The word of the LORD had not yet been revealed to him.

⁸The LORD called Samuel a third time, and Samuel got up and went to Eli and said, "Here I am; you called me."

Then Eli realized that the LORD was calling the

---

a25 Or the judges   *b29 The Hebrew is plural.*   *c3 That is, tabernacle* boy. ⁹So Eli told Samuel, "Go and lie down, and if he calls you, say, 'Speak, LORD, for your servant is listening.'" So Samuel went and lay down in his place.

¹⁰The LORD came and stood there, calling as at the other times, "Samuel! Samuel!"

Then Samuel said, "Speak, for your servant is listening."

¹¹And the LORD said to Samuel: "See, I am about to do something in Israel that will make the ears of everyone who hears of it tingle. ¹²At that time I will carry out against Eli everything I spoke against his family—from beginning to end. ¹³For I told him that I would judge his family forever because of the sin he knew about; his sons made themselves contemptible,ᵃ and he failed to restrain them. ¹⁴Therefore, I swore to the house of Eli, 'The guilt of Eli's house will never be atoned for by sacrifice or offering.'"

¹⁵Samuel lay down until morning and then opened the doors of the house of the LORD. He was afraid to tell Eli the vision, ¹⁶but Eli called him and said, "Samuel, my son."

Samuel answered, "Here I am."

¹⁷"What was it he said to you?" Eli asked. "Do not hide it from me. May God deal with you, be it ever so severely, if you hide from me anything he told you." ¹⁸So Samuel told him everything, hiding nothing from him. Then Eli said, "He is the LORD; let him do what is good in his eyes."

¹⁹The LORD was with Samuel as he grew up, and he let none of his words fall to the ground. ²⁰And all Israel from Dan to Beersheba recognized that Samuel was attested as a prophet of the LORD. ²¹The LORD continued to appear at Shiloh, and there he revealed himself to Samuel through his word.

4

And Samuel's word came to all Israel.

The Philistines Capture the Ark

Now the Israelites went out to fight against the Philistines. The Israelites camped at Ebenezer,

3:19 Still a Boy

While still a boy, Samuel heard God speak. He delivered God's message even though it rebuked Eli, the man who had raised him from childhood. This was one indication that Samuel was a genuine prophet, for false prophets usually delivered only good news. Samuel's message agreed with the prophecy given earlier by a man of God (2:27–36), confirming that God had indeed spoken to him.

and the Philistines at Aphek. ²The Philistines deployed their forces to meet Israel, and as the battle spread, Israel was defeated by the Philistines, who killed about four thousand of them on the battlefield. ³When the soldiers returned to camp, the elders of Israel asked, "Why did the LORD bring defeat upon us today before the Philistines? Let us bring the ark of the LORD's covenant from Shiloh, so that itᵇ may go with us and save us from the hand of our enemies."

⁴So the people sent men to Shiloh, and they brought back the ark of the covenant of the LORD Almighty, who is enthroned between the cherubim. And Eli's two sons, Hophni and Phinehas, were there with the ark of the covenant of God.

⁵When the ark of the LORD's covenant came into the camp, all Israel raised such a great shout

ᵃ13 Masoretic Text; an ancient Hebrew scribal tradition and Septuagint *sons blasphemed God*   ᵇ3 Or *he*

ELI *An End and a Beginning*

ELI'S SONS ARE THE WORST example of stereotypically rebellious "preacher's kids." They greedily grabbed from the offerings people brought to the tabernacle, and slept with the female assistants. Though they followed their father into a career as priests, they played God's tent of worship like carnival barkers, bringing contempt on the worship service.

Eli knew about his sons' antics. He talked to them and scolded them, yet he never took firm action. According to the Bible, he honored his sons more than God. As a result, God brought judgment on Eli and his family. Not only would his sons die, but his whole family line would also lose the right to serve as priests.

This tragic message came from the lips of a little boy, Samuel, who had been brought to the tabernacle for Eli to raise. While Eli's biological sons were being cursed, God blessed Eli's foster child. In the same tabernacle that Eli's sons had dishonored, a boy learned to hear God's word from the old, worn-down priest.

Samuel would go on to be the greatest leader Israel had known since Joshua. Although Eli's family legacy died out, through Samuel his best qualities lived on.

Life Questions: Often from the ruins of one era, a new one springs to life. Can you see this cycle of decay and revival in any of the families you know? In your own life?

that the ground shook. [6]Hearing the uproar, the Philistines asked, "What's all this shouting in the Hebrew camp?"

When they learned that the ark of the LORD had come into the camp, [7]the Philistines were afraid. "A god has come into the camp," they said. "We're in trouble! Nothing like this has happened before. [8]Woe to us! Who will deliver us from the hand of these mighty gods? They are the gods who struck the Egyptians with all kinds of plagues in the desert. [9]Be strong, Philistines! Be men, or you will be subject to the Hebrews, as they have been to you. Be men, and fight!"

[10]So the Philistines fought, and the Israelites were defeated and every man fled to his tent. The slaughter was very great; Israel lost thirty thousand foot soldiers. [11]The ark of God was captured, and Eli's two sons, Hophni and Phinehas, died.

Death of Eli

[12]That same day a Benjamite ran from the battle line and went to Shiloh, his clothes torn

4:12 The End of Shiloh

The Philistine victory may have led to Shiloh's capture, for the next time we encounter Eli's family, they have moved as a group to Nob. Several Bible passages mention Shiloh's destruction as a punishment for sin (Jeremiah 7:12,14; 26:6,9; Psalm 78:60). If Shiloh did fall at this time, its capture must have added greatly to Israel's general sense of despair, for the city was an important site for worship.

and dust on his head. [13]When he arrived, there was Eli sitting on his chair by the side of the road, watching, because his heart feared for the ark of God. When the man entered the town and told what had happened, the whole town sent up a cry.

[14]Eli heard the outcry and asked, "What is the meaning of this uproar?"

The man hurried over to Eli, [15]who was ninety-eight years old and whose eyes were set so that he could not see. [16]He told Eli, "I have just come from the battle line; I fled from it this very day."

Eli asked, "What happened, my son?"

[17]The man who brought the news replied, "Israel fled before the Philistines, and the army has suffered heavy losses. Also your two sons, Hophni and Phinehas, are dead, and the ark of God has been captured."

[18]When he mentioned the ark of God, Eli fell

backward off his chair by the side of the gate. His neck was broken and he died, for he was an old man and heavy. He had led[a] Israel forty years.

[19]His daughter-in-law, the wife of Phinehas, was pregnant and near the time of delivery. When she heard the news that the ark of God had been captured and that her father-in-law and her husband were dead, she went into labor and gave birth, but was overcome by her labor pains. [20]As she was dying, the women attending her said, "Don't despair; you have given birth to a son." But she did not respond or pay any attention.

[21]She named the boy Ichabod,[b] saying, "The glory has departed from Israel"—because of the capture of the ark of God and the deaths of her father-in-law and her husband. [22]She said, "The glory has departed from Israel, for the ark of God has been captured."

The Ark in Ashdod and Ekron

5 After the Philistines had captured the ark of God, they took it from Ebenezer to Ashdod. [2]Then they carried the ark into Dagon's temple and set it beside Dagon. [3]When the people of Ashdod rose early the next day, there was Dagon, fallen on his face on the ground before the ark of the LORD! They took Dagon and put him back in his place. [4]But the following morning when they rose, there was Dagon, fallen on his face on the ground before the ark of the LORD! His head and hands had been broken off and were lying on the threshold; only his body remained. [5]That is why to this day neither the priests of Dagon nor any others who enter Dagon's temple at Ashdod step on the threshold.

[6]The LORD's hand was heavy upon the people of Ashdod and its vicinity; he brought devastation upon them and afflicted them with tumors.[c] [7]When the men of Ashdod saw what was happening, they said, "The ark of the god of Israel must not stay here with us, because his hand is heavy upon us and upon Dagon our god." [8]So they called together all the rulers of the Philistines and asked them, "What shall we do with the ark of the god of Israel?"

They answered, "Have the ark of the god of Israel moved to Gath." So they moved the ark of the God of Israel.

[9]But after they had moved it, the LORD's hand was against that city, throwing it into a great panic. He afflicted the people of the city, both young and old, with an outbreak of tumors.[d] [10]So they sent the ark of God to Ekron.

As the ark of God was entering Ekron, the people of Ekron cried out, "They have brought the ark of the god of Israel around to us to kill us and our people." [11]So they called together all the

---

[a]18 Traditionally *judged*   [b]21 *Ichabod* means *no glory.*   [c]6 Hebrew; Septuagint and Vulgate *tumors. And rats appeared in their land, and death and destruction were throughout the city*   [d]9 Or *with tumors in the groin* (see Septuagint)

rulers of the Philistines and said, "Send the ark of the god of Israel away; let it go back to its own place, or it[a] will kill us and our people." For death had filled the city with panic; God's hand was very heavy upon it. [12]Those who did not die were afflicted with tumors, and the outcry of the city went up to heaven.

The Ark Returned to Israel

6 When the ark of the LORD had been in Philistine territory seven months, [2]the Philistines called for the priests and the diviners and said, "What shall we do with the ark of the LORD? Tell us how we should send it back to its place."

[3]They answered, "If you return the ark of the god of Israel, do not send it away empty, but by all means send a guilt offering to him. Then you will be healed, and you will know why his hand has not been lifted from you."

[4]The Philistines asked, "What guilt offering should we send to him?"

They replied, "Five gold tumors and five gold rats, according to the number of the Philistine rulers, because the same plague has struck both you and your rulers. [5]Make models of the tumors and of the rats that are destroying the country, and pay honor to Israel's god. Perhaps he will lift his hand from you and your gods and your land.

6:5 Magic

The Philistine strategy shows traditional magical thinking, still common in some occult or voodoo rites. By sending gold models of the tumors and rats out of the country, the Philistines hoped to send the originals out of the country too. This is similar to the voodoo practice of sticking pins into wax models of one's enemies.

The Israelites, instead of looking for a magical technique, appealed to the overwhelming power of a personal God, who could not be manipulated with magic.

[6]Why do you harden your hearts as the Egyptians and Pharaoh did? When he[b] treated them harshly, did they not send the Israelites out so they could go on their way?

[7]"Now then, get a new cart ready, with two cows that have calved and have never been yoked. Hitch the cows to the cart, but take their calves away and pen them up. [8]Take the ark of the LORD and put it on the cart, and in a chest beside it put the gold objects you are sending back to him as a guilt offering. Send it on its way, [9]but keep watching it. If it goes up to its own

territory, toward Beth Shemesh, then the LORD has brought this great disaster on us. But if it does not, then we will know that it was not his hand that struck us and that it happened to us by chance."

[10]So they did this. They took two such cows and hitched them to the cart and penned up their calves. [11]They placed the ark of the LORD on the cart and along with it the chest containing the gold rats and the models of the tumors. [12]Then the cows went straight up toward Beth Shemesh, keeping on the road and lowing all the way; they did not turn to the right or to the left. The rulers of the Philistines followed them as far as the border of Beth Shemesh.

[13]Now the people of Beth Shemesh were harvesting their wheat in the valley, and when they looked up and saw the ark, they rejoiced at the sight. [14]The cart came to the field of Joshua of Beth Shemesh, and there it stopped beside a large rock. The people chopped up the wood of the cart and sacrificed the cows as a burnt offering to the LORD. [15]The Levites took down the ark of the LORD, together with the chest containing the gold objects, and placed them on the large rock. On that day the people of Beth Shemesh offered burnt offerings and made sacrifices to the LORD. [16]The five rulers of the Philistines saw all this and then returned that same day to Ekron.

[17]These are the gold tumors the Philistines sent as a guilt offering to the LORD—one each for Ashdod, Gaza, Ashkelon, Gath and Ekron. [18]And the number of the gold rats was according to the number of Philistine towns belonging to the five rulers—the fortified towns with their country villages. The large rock, on which[c] they set the ark of the LORD, is a witness to this day in the field of Joshua of Beth Shemesh.

[19]But God struck down some of the men of Beth Shemesh, putting seventy[d] of them to death because they had looked into the ark of the LORD. The people mourned because of the heavy blow the LORD had dealt them, [20]and the men of Beth Shemesh asked, "Who can stand in the presence of the LORD, this holy God? To whom will the ark go up from here?"

[21]Then they sent messengers to the people of Kiriath Jearim, saying, "The Philistines have returned the ark of the LORD. Come down and take

7 it up to your place." [1]So the men of Kiriath Jearim came and took up the ark of the LORD. They took it to Abinadab's house on the hill and consecrated Eleazar his son to guard the ark of the LORD.

Samuel Subdues the Philistines at Mizpah

[2]It was a long time, twenty years in all, that the

---

[a]11 Or *he*   [b]6 That is, God   [c]18 A few Hebrew manuscripts (see also Septuagint); most Hebrew manuscripts *villages as far as Greater Abel, where*   [d]19 A few Hebrew manuscripts; most Hebrew manuscripts and Septuagint *50,070*

ark remained at Kiriath Jearim, and all the people of Israel mourned and sought after the LORD. ³And Samuel said to the whole house of Israel, "If you are returning to the LORD with all your hearts, then rid yourselves of the foreign gods and the Ashtoreths and commit yourselves to the LORD and serve him only, and he will deliver you out of the hand of the Philistines." ⁴So the Israelites put away their Baals and Ashtoreths, and served the LORD only.

⁵Then Samuel said, "Assemble all Israel at Mizpah and I will intercede with the LORD for you." ⁶When they had assembled at Mizpah, they drew water and poured it out before the LORD. On that day they fasted and there they confessed, "We have sinned against the LORD." And Samuel was leader*a* of Israel at Mizpah.

⁷When the Philistines heard that Israel had assembled at Mizpah, the rulers of the Philistines came up to attack them. And when the Israelites heard of it, they were afraid because of the Philistines. ⁸They said to Samuel, "Do not stop crying out to the LORD our God for us, that he may rescue us from the hand of the Philistines." ⁹Then Samuel took a suckling lamb and offered it up as a whole burnt offering to the LORD. He cried out to the LORD on Israel's behalf, and the LORD answered him.

¹⁰While Samuel was sacrificing the burnt offering, the Philistines drew near to engage Israel in battle. But that day the LORD thundered with loud thunder against the Philistines and threw them into such a panic that they were routed before the Israelites. ¹¹The men of Israel rushed out of Mizpah and pursued the Philistines, slaughtering them along the way to a point below Beth Car.

¹²Then Samuel took a stone and set it up between Mizpah and Shen. He named it Ebenezer,*b* saying, "Thus far has the LORD helped us." ¹³So the Philistines were subdued and did not invade Israelite territory again.

Throughout Samuel's lifetime, the hand of the LORD was against the Philistines. ¹⁴The towns from Ekron to Gath that the Philistines had captured from Israel were restored to her, and Israel delivered the neighboring territory from the power of the Philistines. And there was peace between Israel and the Amorites.

¹⁵Samuel continued as judge over Israel all the days of his life. ¹⁶From year to year he went on a circuit from Bethel to Gilgal to Mizpah, judging Israel in all those places. ¹⁷But he always went back to Ramah, where his home was, and there he also judged Israel. And he built an altar there to the LORD.

Israel Asks for a King

8 When Samuel grew old, he appointed his sons as judges for Israel. ²The name of his firstborn was Joel and the name of his second was Abijah, and they served at Beersheba. ³But his sons did not walk in his ways. They turned aside

---

*a*6 Traditionally *judge*   *b*12 *Ebenezer* means *stone of help.*

SAMUEL *Faithful Leadership*

TIMES OF CRISIS REQUIRE EXCEPTIONAL leadership. That's why George Washington made so great a President. In order to survive, the fledgling United States needed his flawless reputation, his decisive leadership and his wide-ranging talents.

Samuel, similarly, ruled during a difficult transition. The last judge in Israel, Eli, had failed, and Philistine armies were pressing in. With everything in flux, the Israelites needed someone worthy of their trust. Samuel was the leader for the times. He oversaw the change from a loose tribal federation to a monarchy. He anointed Israel's first two kings, wrote down the rules kings were to live by and then deposed one king, Saul, who did not measure up. Samuel ended his long career without a single black mark on his record, and the entire country mourned his death.

Samuel showed remarkable versatility. A lifelong judge, he settled disputes in a regular circuit of Israelite towns. He also gained fame as a prophet, alert to hear God's word and quick to proclaim it clearly—especially when God entrusted him with key information about the future. Finally, he functioned as a priest, presenting sacrifices and prayers on behalf of God's people. He considered prayer one of his basic duties as a leader (12:23).

Like any good leader, Samuel sometimes had to bring bad news. When he was just a boy, he heard God's message of judgment against his foster father Eli (3:11–14). Samuel also gave stern warnings about a king's potential abuses of power, abuses he later had to denounce in Saul. Yet the nation remembered him more for his positive contributions. Taking over the helm when the nation was near disaster, Samuel steered the course faithfully until he could deliver leadership to David, a young man who would become Israel's greatest king.

Life Questions: What leader do you respect most? What qualities does he or she show?

after dishonest gain and accepted bribes and perverted justice.

⁴So all the elders of Israel gathered together and came to Samuel at Ramah. ⁵They said to him, "You are old, and your sons do not walk in your ways; now appoint a king to lead*a* us, such as all the other nations have."

⁶But when they said, "Give us a king to lead us," this displeased Samuel; so he prayed to the LORD. ⁷And the LORD told him: "Listen to all that the people are saying to you; it is not you they have rejected, but they have rejected me as their king. ⁸As they have done from the day I brought them up out of Egypt until this day, forsaking me and serving other gods, so they are doing to you. ⁹Now listen to them; but warn them solemnly and let them know what the king who will reign over them will do."

¹⁰Samuel told all the words of the LORD to the people who were asking him for a king. ¹¹He said, "This is what the king who will reign over you will do: He will take your sons and make them serve with his chariots and horses, and they will run in front of his chariots. ¹²Some he will assign to be commanders of thousands and commanders of fifties, and others to plow his ground and reap his harvest, and still others to make weapons of war and equipment for his chariots. ¹³He will take your daughters to be perfumers and cooks and bakers. ¹⁴He will take the best of your fields and vineyards and olive groves and give them to his attendants. ¹⁵He will take a tenth of your grain and of your vintage and give it to his officials and attendants. ¹⁶Your menservants and maidservants and the best of your cattle*b* and donkeys he will take for his own use. ¹⁷He will take a tenth of your flocks, and you yourselves will become his slaves. ¹⁸When that day comes, you will cry out for relief from the king

you have chosen, and the LORD will not answer you in that day."

¹⁹But the people refused to listen to Samuel. "No!" they said. "We want a king over us. ²⁰Then we will be like all the other nations, with a king to lead us and to go out before us and fight our battles."

²¹When Samuel heard all that the people said, he repeated it before the LORD. ²²The LORD answered, "Listen to them and give them a king."

Then Samuel said to the men of Israel, "Everyone go back to his town."

Samuel Anoints Saul

9 There was a Benjamite, a man of standing, whose name was Kish son of Abiel, the son of Zeror, the son of Becorath, the son of Aphiah of Benjamin. ²He had a son named Saul, an impressive young man without equal among the Israelites—a head taller than any of the others.

³Now the donkeys belonging to Saul's father Kish were lost, and Kish said to his son Saul, "Take one of the servants with you and go and

look for the donkeys." ⁴So he passed through the hill country of Ephraim and through the area around Shalisha, but they did not find them. They went on into the district of Shaalim, but the donkeys were not there. Then he passed through the territory of Benjamin, but they did not find them.

⁵When they reached the district of Zuph, Saul said to the servant who was with him, "Come, let's go back, or my father will stop thinking about the donkeys and start worrying about us."

⁶But the servant replied, "Look, in this town there is a man of God; he is highly respected, and everything he says comes true. Let's go there now. Perhaps he will tell us what way to take."

⁷Saul said to his servant, "If we go, what can we give the man? The food in our sacks is gone. We have no gift to take to the man of God. What do we have?"

⁸The servant answered him again. "Look," he said, "I have a quarter of a shekel*c* of silver. I

---

a5 Traditionally *judge*; also in verses 6 and 20 (about 3 grams)   *b16* Septuagint; Hebrew *young men*   *c8* That is, about 1/10 ounce

will give it to the man of God so that he will tell us what way to take." ⁹(Formerly in Israel, if a man went to inquire of God, he would say, "Come, let us go to the seer," because the prophet of today used to be called a seer.)

¹⁰"Good," Saul said to his servant. "Come, let's go." So they set out for the town where the man of God was.

¹¹As they were going up the hill to the town, they met some girls coming out to draw water, and they asked them, "Is the seer here?"

¹²"He is," they answered. "He's ahead of you. Hurry now; he has just come to our town today, for the people have a sacrifice at the high place. ¹³As soon as you enter the town, you will find him before he goes up to the high place to eat. The people will not begin eating until he comes, because he must bless the sacrifice; afterward, those who are invited will eat. Go up now; you should find him about this time."

¹⁴They went up to the town, and as they were entering it, there was Samuel, coming toward them on his way up to the high place.

¹⁵Now the day before Saul came, the LORD had revealed this to Samuel: ¹⁶"About this time tomorrow I will send you a man from the land of Benjamin. Anoint him leader over my people Israel; he will deliver my people from the hand of the Philistines. I have looked upon my people, for their cry has reached me."

¹⁷When Samuel caught sight of Saul, the LORD said to him, "This is the man I spoke to you about; he will govern my people."

¹⁸Saul approached Samuel in the gateway and asked, "Would you please tell me where the seer's house is?"

¹⁹"I am the seer," Samuel replied. "Go up ahead of me to the high place, for today you are to eat with me, and in the morning I will let you go and will tell you all that is in your heart. ²⁰As for the donkeys you lost three days ago, do not worry about them; they have been found. And to whom is all the desire of Israel turned, if not to you and all your father's family?"

²¹Saul answered, "But am I not a Benjamite, from the smallest tribe of Israel, and is not my clan the least of all the clans of the tribe of Benjamin? Why do you say such a thing to me?"

²²Then Samuel brought Saul and his servant into the hall and seated them at the head of those who were invited—about thirty in number. ²³Samuel said to the cook, "Bring the piece of meat I gave you, the one I told you to lay aside."

²⁴So the cook took up the leg with what was on it and set it in front of Saul. Samuel said, "Here is what has been kept for you. Eat, because it was set aside for you for this occasion, from the time

I said, 'I have invited guests.'" And Saul dined with Samuel that day.

²⁵After they came down from the high place to the town, Samuel talked with Saul on the roof of his house. ²⁶They rose about daybreak and Samuel called to Saul on the roof, "Get ready, and I will send you on your way." When Saul got ready, he and Samuel went outside together. ²⁷As they were going down to the edge of the town, Samuel said to Saul, "Tell the servant to go on ahead of us"—and the servant did so—"but you stay here awhile, so that I may give you a message from God."

10 Then Samuel took a flask of oil and poured it on Saul's head and kissed him, saying, "Has not the LORD anointed you leader over his inheritance?[a] ²When you leave me today, you will meet two men near Rachel's tomb, at Zelzah on the border of Benjamin. They will say to you, 'The donkeys you set out to look for have been found. And now your father has stopped thinking about them and is worried about you. He is asking, "What shall I do about my son?"'

³"Then you will go on from there until you reach the great tree of Tabor. Three men going up to God at Bethel will meet you there. One will be carrying three young goats, another three loaves of bread, and another a skin of wine. ⁴They will greet you and offer you two loaves of bread, which you will accept from them.

⁵"After that you will go to Gibeah of God, where there is a Philistine outpost. As you approach the town, you will meet a procession of prophets coming down from the high place with lyres, tambourines, flutes and harps being played

10:5 Musical Prophets

This is one of the earliest references to prophets in the Bible. Under the kings, prophets became much more significant, possibly because they so often spoke out against the kings. The description of the prophets' musical procession is intriguing, though we can only guess what exactly they were doing. Unquestionably, the Spirit's powerful effect on Saul made a startling change in him (verse 11).

before them, and they will be prophesying. ⁶The Spirit of the LORD will come upon you in power, and you will prophesy with them; and you will be changed into a different person. ⁷Once these signs are fulfilled, do whatever your hand finds to do, for God is with you.

⁸"Go down ahead of me to Gilgal. I will surely

ᵃ1 Hebrew; Septuagint and Vulgate over his people Israel? You will reign over the LORD's people and save them from the power of their enemies round about. And this will be a sign to you that the LORD has anointed you leader over his inheritance:

come down to you to sacrifice burnt offerings and fellowship offerings,[a] but you must wait seven days until I come to you and tell you what you are to do."

Saul Made King

9As Saul turned to leave Samuel, God changed Saul's heart, and all these signs were fulfilled that day. **10**When they arrived at Gibeah, a procession of prophets met him; the Spirit of God came upon him in power, and he joined in their prophesying. **11**When all those who had formerly known him saw him prophesying with the prophets, they asked each other, "What is this that has happened to the son of Kish? Is Saul also among the prophets?"

12A man who lived there answered, "And who is their father?" So it became a saying: "Is Saul also among the prophets?" **13**After Saul stopped prophesying, he went to the high place.

14Now Saul's uncle asked him and his servant, "Where have you been?"

"Looking for the donkeys," he said. "But when we saw they were not to be found, we went to Samuel."

15Saul's uncle said, "Tell me what Samuel said to you."

16Saul replied, "He assured us that the donkeys had been found." But he did not tell his uncle what Samuel had said about the kingship.

17Samuel summoned the people of Israel to the LORD at Mizpah **18**and said to them, "This is what the LORD, the God of Israel, says: 'I brought Israel up out of Egypt, and I delivered you from the power of Egypt and all the kingdoms that oppressed you.' **19**But you have now rejected your God, who saves you out of all your calamities and distresses. And you have said, 'No, set a king over us.' So now present yourselves before the LORD by your tribes and clans."

20When Samuel brought all the tribes of Israel near, the tribe of Benjamin was chosen. **21**Then he brought forward the tribe of Benjamin, clan by clan, and Matri's clan was chosen. Finally Saul son of Kish was chosen. But when they looked for him, he was not to be found. **22**So they inquired further of the LORD, "Has the man come here yet?"

And the LORD said, "Yes, he has hidden himself among the baggage."

23They ran and brought him out, and as he stood among the people he was a head taller than any of the others. **24**Samuel said to all the people, "Do you see the man the LORD has chosen? There is no one like him among all the people."

Then the people shouted, "Long live the king!"

25Samuel explained to the people the regula-

tions of the kingship. He wrote them down on a scroll and deposited it before the LORD. Then Samuel dismissed the people, each to his own home.

10:25 Limits on the King

Though Samuel reluctantly designated Saul as the first king, he insisted on safeguards. Much as the United States government rests on a document, the Constitution, so Saul's kingship was defined and limited by certain rules, which Samuel wrote down and placed in the tabernacle as a permanent record.

26Saul also went to his home in Gibeah, accompanied by valiant men whose hearts God had touched. **27**But some troublemakers said, "How can this fellow save us?" They despised him and brought him no gifts. But Saul kept silent.

Saul Rescues the City of Jabesh

11 Nahash the Ammonite went up and besieged Jabesh Gilead. And all the men of Jabesh said to him, "Make a treaty with us, and we will be subject to you."

2But Nahash the Ammonite replied, "I will make a treaty with you only on the condition that I gouge out the right eye of every one of you and so bring disgrace on all Israel."

3The elders of Jabesh said to him, "Give us seven days so we can send messengers throughout Israel; if no one comes to rescue us, we will surrender to you."

4When the messengers came to Gibeah of Saul and reported these terms to the people, they all wept aloud. **5**Just then Saul was returning from the fields, behind his oxen, and he asked, "What is wrong with the people? Why are they weeping?" Then they repeated to him what the men of Jabesh had said.

6When Saul heard their words, the Spirit of God came upon him in power, and he burned with anger. **7**He took a pair of oxen, cut them into pieces, and sent the pieces by messengers throughout Israel, proclaiming, "This is what will be done to the oxen of anyone who does not follow Saul and Samuel." Then the terror of the LORD fell on the people, and they turned out as one man. **8**When Saul mustered them at Bezek, the men of Israel numbered three hundred thousand and the men of Judah thirty thousand.

9They told the messengers who had come, "Say to the men of Jabesh Gilead, 'By the time the sun is hot tomorrow, you will be delivered.'" When the messengers went and reported this to the men of Jabesh, they were elated. **10**They said

---

[a] *8 Traditionally peace offerings*

The First King

Every other nation had one—why not Israel?

"If both you and the king who reigns over you follow the Lᴏʀᴅ your God—good! But if you do not obey the Lᴏʀᴅ, ... his hand will be against you."
12:14–15

MAKING A SINGLE NATION OUT of a dozen tribes was not easy. Unity came hard for Israel; it also came hard for the United States. U.S. history may shed light on 1 Samuel's story.

Most people think George Washington was the first president of the United States, but that honor actually belongs to Samuel Huntington. He never achieved fame because the states he presided over weren't united. They had no Constitution, only Articles of Confederation that made them 13 independent nations loosely linked together.

Congress under Siege

Two years after Huntington took office, on June 21, 1783, 500 unpaid federal soldiers laid siege to Congress in Philadelphia, breaking windows and shouting threats because Congress, which was supposed to pay them, had no money. The jealously independent states had given them none. Driven out of town by the soldiers, Congress became nomadic, meeting in Princeton, Annapolis, Trenton, and New York City. That same June, George Washington wrote, "It is yet to be decided whether the Revolution must ultimately be considered a blessing or a curse."

Troubles continued. In Shays's Rebellion, 1,500 hostile farmers surrounded courtrooms, refusing to let courts meet. The army should have quickly dispersed them, but the national army consisted of only 700 men. Shays's Rebellion made obvious the need for a stronger central government. The next year a constitutional convention met in Philadelphia to hammer out the document that still unifies Americans. Washington was elected president.

Why Israel Needed a King

The 12 tribes of Israel, like the 13 states, were a nation in name only. They had no central government at all. Since conquering Palestine, they had worked together only during emergencies, when inspired "judges"—military heroes like Gideon, Deborah, and Samson—came forward to lead them into battle.

In Samuel's time, though, the Philistines' military threat wouldn't go away. Israel needed superior leadership, but Samuel was an old man. His sons made unappealing successors. What could be done? Looking around them, the tribes noticed that virtually every other country had a king. A king offered two advantages: first, he provided central government; second, since his sons would normally succeed a king, the nation did not have a crisis of leadership every time its leader got old. So the leaders of Israel asked Samuel to appoint a king (8:4–5).

Against God's Will

The idea seems to have been popular with everyone except Samuel and God. Samuel may have been displeased that he and his sons were being rejected. God had a deeper objection: Israel was rejecting his leadership. God told Samuel to warn the elders that a king would oppress his own citizens. Samuel warned of the military draft, of high taxation, of the king's power to make people into slaves (8:10–18).

Was God against a king? Some scholars see the monarchy as a marvelous example of God's use of a choice made against his will. God counseled Israel against the very institution that ultimately produced King David, and through him Jesus, King of kings.

Others suggest that God only opposed the motive behind the request. (Deuteronomy 17:14–20 had assumed that the Israelites would eventually want and get a king.) The key is the phrase the elders used: "Then we will be like all the other nations" (8:20). God did not want them to be like all the other nations.

The King Was a Servant

Yet God gave in to their request, bad motives and all. He not only allowed the Israelites a king, he picked out their man. He accepted the monarchy on condition that Israel still consider the Lord as its ultimate ruler (12:14).

Apparently, Israel's king didn't answer to a parliament or court system, but he did answer to God. In short order the first king, Saul, was rejected because he disobeyed God. God rebuked and punished his replacement, David. Most nations' kings held absolute power. In Israel only God was absolute, and the king was his servant.

Life Questions: Have you ever seen God take a bad request made with bad motives and use it for his own purposes?

to the Ammonites, "Tomorrow we will surrender to you, and you can do to us whatever seems good to you."

[11]The next day Saul separated his men into three divisions; during the last watch of the night they broke into the camp of the Ammonites and slaughtered them until the heat of the day. Those who survived were scattered, so that no two of them were left together.

Saul Confirmed as King

[12]The people then said to Samuel, "Who was it that asked, 'Shall Saul reign over us?' Bring these men to us and we will put them to death."

[13]But Saul said, "No one shall be put to death today, for this day the LORD has rescued Israel."

[14]Then Samuel said to the people, "Come, let us go to Gilgal and there reaffirm the kingship." [15]So all the people went to Gilgal and confirmed Saul as king in the presence of the LORD. There they sacrificed fellowship offerings[a] before the LORD, and Saul and all the Israelites held a great celebration.

Samuel's Farewell Speech

12 Samuel said to all Israel, "I have listened to everything you said to me and have set a king over you. [2]Now you have a king as your leader. As for me, I am old and gray, and my sons are here with you. I have been your leader from my youth until this day. [3]Here I stand. Testify against me in the presence of the LORD and his anointed. Whose ox have I taken? Whose donkey have I taken? Whom have I cheated? Whom have I oppressed? From whose hand have I accepted a bribe to make me shut my eyes? If I have done any of these, I will make it right."

[4]"You have not cheated or oppressed us," they replied. "You have not taken anything from anyone's hand."

[5]Samuel said to them, "The LORD is witness against you, and also his anointed is witness this day, that you have not found anything in my hand."

"He is witness," they said.

[6]Then Samuel said to the people, "It is the LORD who appointed Moses and Aaron and brought your forefathers up out of Egypt. [7]Now then, stand here, because I am going to confront you with evidence before the LORD as to all the righteous acts performed by the LORD for you and your fathers.

[8]"After Jacob entered Egypt, they cried to the LORD for help, and the LORD sent Moses and Aaron, who brought your forefathers out of Egypt and settled them in this place.

[9]"But they forgot the LORD their God; so he sold them into the hand of Sisera, the commander of the army of Hazor, and into the hands of the Philistines and the king of Moab, who fought against them. [10]They cried out to the LORD and said, 'We have sinned; we have forsaken the LORD and served the Baals and the Ashtoreths. But now deliver us from the hands of our enemies, and we will serve you.' [11]Then the LORD sent Jerub-Baal,[b] Barak,[c] Jephthah and Samuel,[d] and he delivered you from the hands of your enemies on every side, so that you lived securely.

[12]"But when you saw that Nahash king of the Ammonites was moving against you, you said to me, 'No, we want a king to rule over us'—even though the LORD your God was your king. [13]Now here is the king you have chosen, the one you asked for; see, the LORD has set a king over you. [14]If you fear the LORD and serve and obey him and do not rebel against his commands, and if both you and the king who reigns over you follow the LORD your God—good! [15]But if you do not obey the LORD, and if you rebel against his commands, his hand will be against you, as it was against your fathers.

[16]"Now then, stand still and see this great thing the LORD is about to do before your eyes! [17]Is it not wheat harvest now? I will call upon the LORD to send thunder and rain. And you will realize what an evil thing you did in the eyes of the LORD when you asked for a king."

[18]Then Samuel called upon the LORD, and that same day the LORD sent thunder and rain. So all the people stood in awe of the LORD and of Samuel.

[19]The people all said to Samuel, "Pray to the LORD your God for your servants so that we will not die, for we have added to all our other sins the evil of asking for a king."

[20]"Do not be afraid," Samuel replied. "You have done all this evil; yet do not turn away from the LORD, but serve the LORD with all your heart. [21]Do not turn away after useless idols. They can

12:4 Accuse Me!

Unlike some political and religious leaders who get caught in financial scandals, Samuel considered himself publicly accountable. He began his farewell speech by offering an opportunity for anyone to stand up and testify that he, Samuel, had been dishonest or had taken advantage of his leadership position. Before going on, he asked those present to witness aloud to his honesty.

[a]15 Traditionally *peace offerings*   [b]11 Also called *Gideon*   [c]11 Some Septuagint manuscripts and Syriac; Hebrew *Bedan*   [d]11 Hebrew; some Septuagint manuscripts and Syriac *Samson*

do you no good, nor can they rescue you, because they are useless. [22]For the sake of his great name the LORD will not reject his people, because the LORD was pleased to make you his own. [23]As for me, far be it from me that I should sin against the LORD by failing to pray for you. And I will teach you the way that is good and right. [24]But be sure to fear the LORD and serve him faithfully with all your heart; consider what great things he has done for you. [25]Yet if you persist in doing evil, both you and your king will be swept away."

Samuel Rebukes Saul

13 Saul was ⌊thirty⌋[a] years old when he became king, and he reigned over Israel ⌊forty-⌋[b] two years.

[2]Saul[c] chose three thousand men from Israel; two thousand were with him at Micmash and in the hill country of Bethel, and a thousand were with Jonathan at Gibeah in Benjamin. The rest of the men he sent back to their homes.

[3]Jonathan attacked the Philistine outpost at Geba, and the Philistines heard about it. Then Saul had the trumpet blown throughout the land and said, "Let the Hebrews hear!" [4]So all Israel heard the news: "Saul has attacked the Philistine outpost, and now Israel has become a stench to the Philistines." And the people were summoned to join Saul at Gilgal.

[5]The Philistines assembled to fight Israel, with three thousand[d] chariots, six thousand charioteers, and soldiers as numerous as the sand on the seashore. They went up and camped at Micmash, east of Beth Aven. [6]When the men of Israel saw that their situation was critical and that their army was hard pressed, they hid in caves and thickets, among the rocks, and in pits and cisterns. [7]Some Hebrews even crossed the Jordan to the land of Gad and Gilead.

Saul remained at Gilgal, and all the troops with him were quaking with fear. [8]He waited seven days, the time set by Samuel; but Samuel did not come to Gilgal, and Saul's men began to scatter. [9]So he said, "Bring me the burnt offering and the fellowship offerings.[e]" And Saul offered up the burnt offering. [10]Just as he finished making the offering, Samuel arrived, and Saul went out to greet him.

[11]"What have you done?" asked Samuel.

Saul replied, "When I saw that the men were scattering, and that you did not come at the set time, and that the Philistines were assembling at Micmash, [12]I thought, 'Now the Philistines will come down against me at Gilgal, and I have not sought the LORD's favor.' So I felt compelled to offer the burnt offering."

[13]"You acted foolishly," Samuel said. "You have not kept the command the LORD your God gave you; if you had, he would have established your kingdom over Israel for all time. [14]But now your kingdom will not endure; the LORD has sought out a man after his own heart and appointed him leader of his people, because you have not kept the LORD's command."

[15]Then Samuel left Gilgal[f] and went up to Gibeah in Benjamin, and Saul counted the men who were with him. They numbered about six hundred.

Israel Without Weapons

[16]Saul and his son Jonathan and the men with them were staying in Gibeah[g] in Benjamin, while the Philistines camped at Micmash. [17]Raiding parties went out from the Philistine camp in three detachments. One turned toward Ophrah in the vicinity of Shual, [18]another toward Beth Horon, and the third toward the borderland overlooking the Valley of Zeboim facing the desert.

[19]Not a blacksmith could be found in the whole land of Israel, because the Philistines had said, "Otherwise the Hebrews will make swords

> ### 13:19 Military Dominance
>
> *Samuel's leadership had kept the Philistines from occupying Israel (see 7:13). However, nobody could question the Philistines' military dominance. They had outposts in several central Israelite towns (10:5; 13:3) and, most important, kept a monopoly on iron weapons by outlawing local blacksmiths. Only the royal family of Israel possessed a sword or a spear (verse 22), presumably weapons that had been smuggled in and hidden.*

or spears!" [20]So all Israel went down to the Philistines to have their plowshares, mattocks, axes and sickles[h] sharpened. [21]The price was two thirds of a shekel[i] for sharpening plowshares and mattocks, and a third of a shekel[j] for sharpening forks and axes and for repointing goads.

[22]So on the day of the battle not a soldier with Saul and Jonathan had a sword or spear in his hand; only Saul and his son Jonathan had them.

---

[a]1 A few late manuscripts of the Septuagint; Hebrew does not have *thirty*.   [b]1 See the round number in Acts 13:21; Hebrew does not have *forty-*.   [c]1,2 Or *and when he had reigned over Israel two years,* [2]*he*   [d]5 Some Septuagint manuscripts and Syriac; Hebrew *thirty thousand*   [e]9 Traditionally *peace offerings*   [f]15 Hebrew; Septuagint *Gilgal and went his way; the rest of the people went after Saul to meet the army, and they went out of Gilgal*   [g]16 Two Hebrew manuscripts; most Hebrew manuscripts *Geba,* a variant of *Gibeah*   [h]20 Septuagint; Hebrew *plowshares*   [i]Hebrew *pim;* that is, about 1/4 ounce (about 8 grams)   [j]21 That is, about 1/8 ounce (about 4 grams)

Jonathan Attacks the Philistines

23Now a detachment of Philistines had gone out to the pass at Micmash. **14** **1**One day Jonathan son of Saul said to the young man bearing his armor, "Come, let's go over to the Philistine outpost on the other side." But he did not tell his father.

2Saul was staying on the outskirts of Gibeah under a pomegranate tree in Migron. With him were about six hundred men, **3**among whom was Ahijah, who was wearing an ephod. He was a son of Ichabod's brother Ahitub son of Phinehas, the son of Eli, the LORD's priest in Shiloh. No one was aware that Jonathan had left.

4On each side of the pass that Jonathan intended to cross to reach the Philistine outpost was a cliff; one was called Bozez, and the other Seneh. **5**One cliff stood to the north toward Micmash, the other to the south toward Geba.

6Jonathan said to his young armor-bearer, "Come, let's go over to the outpost of those uncircumcised fellows. Perhaps the LORD will act in our behalf. Nothing can hinder the LORD from saving, whether by many or by few."

7"Do all that you have in mind," his armor-bearer said. "Go ahead; I am with you heart and soul."

8Jonathan said, "Come, then; we will cross over toward the men and let them see us. **9**If they say to us, 'Wait there until we come to you,' we will stay where we are and not go up to them. **10**But if they say, 'Come up to us,' we will climb up, because that will be our sign that the LORD has given them into our hands."

11So both of them showed themselves to the Philistine outpost. "Look!" said the Philistines. "The Hebrews are crawling out of the holes they were hiding in." **12**The men of the outpost shouted to Jonathan and his armor-bearer, "Come up to us and we'll teach you a lesson."

So Jonathan said to his armor-bearer, "Climb up after me; the LORD has given them into the hand of Israel."

13Jonathan climbed up, using his hands and feet, with his armor-bearer right behind him. The Philistines fell before Jonathan, and his armor-bearer followed and killed behind him. **14**In that first attack Jonathan and his armor-bearer killed some twenty men in an area of about half an acre.[a]

Israel Routs the Philistines

15Then panic struck the whole army—those in the camp and field, and those in the outposts and raiding parties—and the ground shook. It was a panic sent by God.[b]

16Saul's lookouts at Gibeah in Benjamin saw the army melting away in all directions. **17**Then Saul said to the men who were with him, "Muster the forces and see who has left us." When they did, it was Jonathan and his armor-bearer who were not there.

18Saul said to Ahijah, "Bring the ark of God." (At that time it was with the Israelites.)[c] **19**While Saul was talking to the priest, the tumult in the Philistine camp increased more and more. So Saul said to the priest, "Withdraw your hand."

20Then Saul and all his men assembled and went to the battle. They found the Philistines in total confusion, striking each other with their swords. **21**Those Hebrews who had previously been with the Philistines and had gone up with them to their camp went over to the Israelites who were with Saul and Jonathan. **22**When all the Israelites who had hidden in the hill country of Ephraim heard that the Philistines were on the run, they joined the battle in hot pursuit. **23**So the LORD rescued Israel that day, and the battle moved on beyond Beth Aven.

Jonathan Eats Honey

24Now the men of Israel were in distress that day, because Saul had bound the people under an oath, saying, "Cursed be any man who eats food before evening comes, before I have avenged myself on my enemies!" So none of the troops tasted food.

14:24 Big Ego

Saul's problems surface here in two ways. First, he impulsively pronounced a curse (a very solemn vow) without thinking it through. This rash vow made his hungry army less effective, and led to trouble for his own son. Second, Saul apparently saw the battle as a personal vendetta in which he was avenging himself on his enemies. A wiser leader would have understood that God's honor and the security of his people were the issues.

25The entire army[d] entered the woods, and there was honey on the ground. **26**When they went into the woods, they saw the honey oozing out, yet no one put his hand to his mouth, because they feared the oath. **27**But Jonathan had not heard that his father had bound the people with the oath, so he reached out the end of the staff that was in his hand and dipped it into the honeycomb. He raised his hand to his mouth, and his eyes brightened.[e] **28**Then one of the soldiers told him, "Your father bound the army un-

---

[a] 14 Hebrew *half a yoke*; a "yoke" was the land plowed by a yoke of oxen in one day.   [b] 15 Or *a terrible panic*   [c] 18 Hebrew; Septuagint *"Bring the ephod." (At that time he wore the ephod before the Israelites.)*   [d] 25 Or *Now all the people of the land*   [e] 27 Or *his strength was renewed*

der a strict oath, saying, 'Cursed be any man who eats food today!' That is why the men are faint."

²⁹Jonathan said, "My father has made trouble for the country. See how my eyes brightened[a] when I tasted a little of this honey. ³⁰How much better it would have been if the men had eaten today some of the plunder they took from their enemies. Would not the slaughter of the Philistines have been even greater?"

³¹That day, after the Israelites had struck down the Philistines from Micmash to Aijalon, they were exhausted. ³²They pounced on the plunder and, taking sheep, cattle and calves, they butchered them on the ground and ate them, together with the blood. ³³Then someone said to Saul, "Look, the men are sinning against the LORD by eating meat that has blood in it."

"You have broken faith," he said. "Roll a large stone over here at once." ³⁴Then he said, "Go out among the men and tell them, 'Each of you bring me your cattle and sheep, and slaughter them here and eat them. Do not sin against the LORD by eating meat with blood still in it.'"

So everyone brought his ox that night and slaughtered it there. ³⁵Then Saul built an altar to the LORD; it was the first time he had done this.

³⁶Saul said, "Let us go down after the Philistines by night and plunder them till dawn, and let us not leave one of them alive."

"Do whatever seems best to you," they replied.

But the priest said, "Let us inquire of God here."

³⁷So Saul asked God, "Shall I go down after the Philistines? Will you give them into Israel's hand?" But God did not answer him that day.

³⁸Saul therefore said, "Come here, all you who are leaders of the army, and let us find out what sin has been committed today. ³⁹As surely as the LORD who rescues Israel lives, even if it lies with my son Jonathan, he must die." But not one of the men said a word.

⁴⁰Saul then said to all the Israelites, "You stand over there; I and Jonathan my son will stand over here."

"Do what seems best to you," the men replied.

⁴¹Then Saul prayed to the LORD, the God of Israel, "Give me the right answer."[b] And Jonathan and Saul were taken by lot, and the men were cleared. ⁴²Saul said, "Cast the lot between me and Jonathan my son." And Jonathan was taken.

⁴³Then Saul said to Jonathan, "Tell me what you have done."

So Jonathan told him, "I merely tasted a little honey with the end of my staff. And now must I die?"

⁴⁴Saul said, "May God deal with me, be it ever so severely, if you do not die, Jonathan."

⁴⁵But the men said to Saul, "Should Jonathan die—he who has brought about this great deliverance in Israel? Never! As surely as the LORD lives, not a hair of his head will fall to the ground, for he did this today with God's help." So the men rescued Jonathan, and he was not put to death.

⁴⁶Then Saul stopped pursuing the Philistines, and they withdrew to their own land.

⁴⁷After Saul had assumed rule over Israel, he fought against their enemies on every side: Moab, the Ammonites, Edom, the kings[c] of Zobah, and the Philistines. Wherever he turned, he inflicted punishment on them.[d] ⁴⁸He fought valiantly and defeated the Amalekites, delivering Israel from the hands of those who had plundered them.

Saul's Family

⁴⁹Saul's sons were Jonathan, Ishvi and Malki-Shua. The name of his older daughter was Merab, and that of the younger was Michal. ⁵⁰His wife's name was Ahinoam daughter of Ahimaaz. The name of the commander of Saul's army was Abner son of Ner, and Ner was Saul's uncle. ⁵¹Saul's father Kish and Abner's father Ner were sons of Abiel.

⁵²All the days of Saul there was bitter war with the Philistines, and whenever Saul saw a mighty or brave man, he took him into his service.

The LORD Rejects Saul as King

15 Samuel said to Saul, "I am the one the LORD sent to anoint you king over his people Israel; so listen now to the message from the LORD. ²This is what the LORD Almighty says: 'I will punish the Amalekites for what they did to Israel when they waylaid them as they came up from Egypt. ³Now go, attack the Amalekites and totally destroy[e] everything that belongs to them. Do not spare them; put to death men and women, children and infants, cattle and sheep, camels and donkeys.'"

⁴So Saul summoned the men and mustered them at Telaim—two hundred thousand foot soldiers and ten thousand men from Judah. ⁵Saul went to the city of Amalek and set an ambush in the ravine. ⁶Then he said to the Kenites, "Go away, leave the Amalekites so that I do not destroy you along with them; for you showed kindness to all the Israelites when they came up out

---

[a]29 Or *my strength was renewed*　　[b]41 Hebrew; Septuagint *"Why have you not answered your servant today? If the fault is in me or my son Jonathan, respond with Urim, but if the men of Israel are at fault, respond with Thummim."*　　[c]47 Masoretic Text; Dead Sea Scrolls and Septuagint *king*　　[d]47 Hebrew; Septuagint *he was victorious*　　[e]3 The Hebrew term refers to the irrevocable giving over of things or persons to the LORD, often by totally destroying them; also in verses 8, 9, 15, 18, 20 and 21.

Why Saul Was Rejected
A leader who failed under pressure

SAUL HAD EVERYTHING GOING FOR him. Tall and handsome, he struck people with his appearance. God chose him as the first king in the history of Israel. Soon after he was secretly anointed, God's Spirit came on him—an encounter with God that affected his entire personality.

Almost immediately Saul led a successful rescue operation, saving the people of a besieged city from mutilation. He was then publicly crowned king, even though he himself did no politicking for the office. (In fact, he hid during the selection.) He wisely refrained from allowing his opponents to be punished. Instead, he united all 12 tribes behind him, even though he himself came from a small, minority tribe.

Saul chose the best young men to serve in his army. One of them, David, was not only a skilled general, but also a loyal follower who would never oppose Saul—even when he had good reason. David married Saul's daughter, and Saul's oldest son, Jonathan, became David's best friend. This should have cemented an alliance, sealing Saul's success.

Deterioration under Pressure

Yet Saul's life went tragically wrong. The first sign of trouble, as 1 Samuel tells the story, came not long after he became king. While preparing for a campaign against the Philistines, Saul grew impatient. Samuel, scheduled to lead in the proper spiritual preparation for battle, was seven days late. Saul's men began to desert, and Saul decided he could wait no longer. He himself began to make the religious sacrifices that Samuel, as priest, was supposed to make. Just then Samuel arrived. He blasted Saul (13:13–14). Saul's hastiness, insignificant though it may seem, showed an inner weakness: his willingness to compromise God's directions under pressure.

The battle came soon afterwards, and Israel won miraculously. But in the victory Saul acted sometimes indecisively, sometimes rashly. He could not decide to attack. Then he made a boastful vow that disrupted the Israelite army, allowing the Philistines to escape.

Attempted Murder

Sometime later Saul compromised again in a high-pressure situation, not following the precise instructions God had given for a military campaign (15:3). Again, Samuel caught him in the act. This time he accused Saul of rebelling against God. Samuel's words must have rung in Saul's head the rest of his life: "Because you have rejected the word of the LORD, he has rejected you as king" (15:23).

Without God's and Samuel's support, Saul lost his sense of confidence. An evil spirit began to torment him. Instead of building an alliance with David, Saul drove David away, causing him to run for his life in the desert. Eventually fear reduced Saul to a quivering, helpless jellyfish, incapable of leadership. In that condition he and his army lost a historic battle to the Philistines, allowing them to regain control. In the battle, both Saul and Jonathan were killed.

Why Saul Failed

The book of 1 Samuel doesn't psychoanalyze Saul; it merely reports what happened. The facts do point to a moral, though. Saul had begun with all the opportunity in the world. He only lacked, it seems, a strong compulsion to obey God no matter what. Under pressure he bent the rules. He lost God's backing. He grew fearful, rash, and jealous.

Saul's poor leadership left Israel worse off than at the beginning. The kingdom David inherited from Saul was again under Philistine military domination, and it was divided between north and south. Saul shows the unique tragedy of a poor leader. He fails not just himself. Inevitably he drags others down with him.

Life Questions: When you are put in the role of leader, how do you respond to pressure? Are Saul's weaknesses your weaknesses?

of Egypt." So the Kenites moved away from the Amalekites.

7Then Saul attacked the Amalekites all the way from Havilah to Shur, to the east of Egypt. 8He

15:2 Old Enemies

The Israelites had first encountered the Amalekites, a semi-nomadic group of pitiless raiders, on their way out of Egypt. Due to the Amalekites' unprovoked attack, Moses had declared that God wanted Amalek wiped out (Exodus 17:8–16; Deuteronomy 25:17–19). The hostility continued. Typically, the Amalekites would sweep into unprotected towns and villages on the edge of the southern desert, killing and looting, leaving the survivors without food. Though Samuel's order to Saul is hard to understand, knowing the Amalekites' reputation makes it easier to sympathize with. For a more general explanation of holy war, see "Is a War Ever Holy?" page 248.

took Agag king of the Amalekites alive, and all his people he totally destroyed with the sword. 9But Saul and the army spared Agag and the best of the sheep and cattle, the fat calves*a* and lambs—everything that was good. These they were unwilling to destroy completely, but everything that was despised and weak they totally destroyed.

10Then the word of the LORD came to Samuel: 11"I am grieved that I have made Saul king, because he has turned away from me and has not carried out my instructions." Samuel was troubled, and he cried out to the LORD all that night.

12Early in the morning Samuel got up and went to meet Saul, but he was told, "Saul has gone to Carmel. There he has set up a monument in his own honor and has turned and gone on down to Gilgal."

13When Samuel reached him, Saul said, "The LORD bless you! I have carried out the LORD's instructions."

14But Samuel said, "What then is this bleating of sheep in my ears? What is this lowing of cattle that I hear?"

15Saul answered, "The soldiers brought them from the Amalekites; they spared the best of the sheep and cattle to sacrifice to the LORD your God, but we totally destroyed the rest."

16"Stop!" Samuel said to Saul. "Let me tell you what the LORD said to me last night."

"Tell me," Saul replied.

17Samuel said, "Although you were once small in your own eyes, did you not become the head of the tribes of Israel? The LORD anointed you king over Israel. 18And he sent you on a mission,

saying, 'Go and completely destroy those wicked people, the Amalekites; make war on them until you have wiped them out.' 19Why did you not obey the LORD? Why did you pounce on the plunder and do evil in the eyes of the LORD?"

20"But I did obey the LORD," Saul said. "I went on the mission the LORD assigned me. I completely destroyed the Amalekites and brought back Agag their king. 21The soldiers took sheep and cattle from the plunder, the best of what was devoted to God, in order to sacrifice them to the LORD your God at Gilgal."

22But Samuel replied:

"Does the LORD delight in burnt offerings
        and sacrifices
    as much as in obeying the voice of the
        LORD?
To obey is better than sacrifice,
    and to heed is better than the fat of rams.
23For rebellion is like the sin of divination,
    and arrogance like the evil of idolatry.
Because you have rejected the word of the
        LORD,
    he has rejected you as king."

24Then Saul said to Samuel, "I have sinned. I violated the LORD's command and your instructions. I was afraid of the people and so I gave in to them. 25Now I beg you, forgive my sin and come back with me, so that I may worship the LORD."

26But Samuel said to him, "I will not go back with you. You have rejected the word of the LORD, and the LORD has rejected you as king over Israel!"

27As Samuel turned to leave, Saul caught hold of the hem of his robe, and it tore. 28Samuel said to him, "The LORD has torn the kingdom of Israel from you today and has given it to one of your neighbors—to one better than you. 29He who is the Glory of Israel does not lie or change his mind; for he is not a man, that he should change his mind."

30Saul replied, "I have sinned. But please honor me before the elders of my people and before Israel; come back with me, so that I may worship the LORD your God." 31So Samuel went back with Saul, and Saul worshiped the LORD.

32Then Samuel said, "Bring me Agag king of the Amalekites."

Agag came to him confidently,*b* thinking, "Surely the bitterness of death is past."

33But Samuel said,

"As your sword has made women childless,
    so will your mother be childless among
        women."

---

a9 Or *the grown bulls*; the meaning of the Hebrew for this phrase is uncertain.   *b32* Or *him trembling, yet*

And Samuel put Agag to death before the LORD at Gilgal.

[34]Then Samuel left for Ramah, but Saul went up to his home in Gibeah of Saul. [35]Until the day Samuel died, he did not go to see Saul again, though Samuel mourned for him. And the LORD was grieved that he had made Saul king over Israel.

Samuel Anoints David

16 The LORD said to Samuel, "How long will you mourn for Saul, since I have rejected him as king over Israel? Fill your horn with oil and be on your way; I am sending you to Jesse of Bethlehem. I have chosen one of his sons to be king."

[2]But Samuel said, "How can I go? Saul will hear about it and kill me."

The LORD said, "Take a heifer with you and say, 'I have come to sacrifice to the LORD.' [3]Invite Jesse to the sacrifice, and I will show you what to do. You are to anoint for me the one I indicate."

[4]Samuel did what the LORD said. When he arrived at Bethlehem, the elders of the town trembled when they met him. They asked, "Do you come in peace?"

[5]Samuel replied, "Yes, in peace; I have come to sacrifice to the LORD. Consecrate yourselves and come to the sacrifice with me." Then he consecrated Jesse and his sons and invited them to the sacrifice.

[6]When they arrived, Samuel saw Eliab and thought, "Surely the LORD's anointed stands here before the LORD."

[7]But the LORD said to Samuel, "Do not consider his appearance or his height, for I have rejected him. The LORD does not look at the things man looks at. Man looks at the outward appearance, but the LORD looks at the heart."

16:7 What God Values

What qualified David to be king? Apparently he did not make an overpowering first impression, but God valued hidden qualities far more. Throughout his life David would demonstrate that he loved and trusted God with all his heart, as the law in Deuteronomy 6:4–6 demanded.

[8]Then Jesse called Abinadab and had him pass in front of Samuel. But Samuel said, "The LORD has not chosen this one either." [9]Jesse then had Shammah pass by, but Samuel said, "Nor has the LORD chosen this one." [10]Jesse had seven of his sons pass before Samuel, but Samuel said to him,

"The LORD has not chosen these." [11]So he asked Jesse, "Are these all the sons you have?"

"There is still the youngest," Jesse answered, "but he is tending the sheep."

Samuel said, "Send for him; we will not sit down[a] until he arrives."

[12]So he sent and had him brought in. He was ruddy, with a fine appearance and handsome features.

Then the LORD said, "Rise and anoint him; he is the one."

[13]So Samuel took the horn of oil and anointed him in the presence of his brothers, and from that day on the Spirit of the LORD came upon David in power. Samuel then went to Ramah.

David in Saul's Service

[14]Now the Spirit of the LORD had departed from Saul, and an evil[b] spirit from the LORD tormented him.

[15]Saul's attendants said to him, "See, an evil spirit from God is tormenting you. [16]Let our lord command his servants here to search for someone who can play the harp. He will play when the evil spirit from God comes upon you, and you will feel better."

[17]So Saul said to his attendants, "Find someone who plays well and bring him to me."

[18]One of the servants answered, "I have seen a son of Jesse of Bethlehem who knows how to play the harp. He is a brave man and a warrior. He speaks well and is a fine-looking man. And the LORD is with him."

[19]Then Saul sent messengers to Jesse and said, "Send me your son David, who is with the sheep." [20]So Jesse took a donkey loaded with bread, a skin of wine and a young goat and sent them with his son David to Saul.

[21]David came to Saul and entered his service. Saul liked him very much, and David became one of his armor-bearers. [22]Then Saul sent word to Jesse, saying, "Allow David to remain in my service, for I am pleased with him."

[23]Whenever the spirit from God came upon Saul, David would take his harp and play. Then relief would come to Saul; he would feel better, and the evil spirit would leave him.

David and Goliath

17 Now the Philistines gathered their forces for war and assembled at Socoh in Judah. They pitched camp at Ephes Dammim, between Socoh and Azekah. [2]Saul and the Israelites assembled and camped in the Valley of Elah and drew up their battle line to meet the Philistines. [3]The Philistines occupied one hill and the Israelites another, with the valley between them.

[4]A champion named Goliath, who was from

---

[a]11 Some Septuagint manuscripts; Hebrew *not gather around*   [b]14 Or *injurious*; also in verses 15, 16 and 23

Gath, came out of the Philistine camp. He was over nine feet[a] tall. [5]He had a bronze helmet on his head and wore a coat of scale armor of bronze weighing five thousand shekels[b]; [6]on his legs he

17:4 Everyone Watched Goliath

Wars in ancient times were sometimes decided by "representative combat": champions from each side would fight, and the results of their combat would decide the battle's result. People believed the outcome of the fight was controlled by the warriors' gods more than by the two sides' military strength.

Saul lacked confidence in God's support. His terror demoralized the Israelite army. David, by contrast, was as confident in his God as Goliath was scornful of God's people.

wore bronze greaves, and a bronze javelin was slung on his back. [7]His spear shaft was like a weaver's rod, and its iron point weighed six hundred shekels.[c] His shield bearer went ahead of him.

[8]Goliath stood and shouted to the ranks of Israel, "Why do you come out and line up for battle? Am I not a Philistine, and are you not the servants of Saul? Choose a man and have him come down to me. [9]If he is able to fight and kill me, we will become your subjects; but if I overcome him and kill him, you will become our subjects and serve us." [10]Then the Philistine said, "This day I defy the ranks of Israel! Give me a man and let us fight each other." [11]On hearing the Philistine's words, Saul and all the Israelites were dismayed and terrified.

[12]Now David was the son of an Ephrathite named Jesse, who was from Bethlehem in Judah. Jesse had eight sons, and in Saul's time he was old and well advanced in years. [13]Jesse's three oldest sons had followed Saul to the war: The firstborn was Eliab; the second, Abinadab; and the third, Shammah. [14]David was the youngest. The three oldest followed Saul, [15]but David went back and forth from Saul to tend his father's sheep at Bethlehem.

[16]For forty days the Philistine came forward every morning and evening and took his stand.

[17]Now Jesse said to his son David, "Take this ephah[d] of roasted grain and these ten loaves of bread for your brothers and hurry to their camp. [18]Take along these ten cheeses to the commander of their unit.[e] See how your brothers are and bring back some assurance[f] from them. [19]They are with Saul and all the men of Israel in the Valley of Elah, fighting against the Philistines."

[20]Early in the morning David left the flock with a shepherd, loaded up and set out, as Jesse had directed. He reached the camp as the army was going out to its battle positions, shouting the war cry. [21]Israel and the Philistines were drawing up their lines facing each other. [22]David left his things with the keeper of supplies, ran to the battle lines and greeted his brothers. [23]As he was talking with them, Goliath, the Philistine champion from Gath, stepped out from his lines and shouted his usual defiance, and David heard it. [24]When the Israelites saw the man, they all ran from him in great fear.

[25]Now the Israelites had been saying, "Do you see how this man keeps coming out? He comes out to defy Israel. The king will give great wealth to the man who kills him. He will also give him his daughter in marriage and will exempt his father's family from taxes in Israel."

[26]David asked the men standing near him, "What will be done for the man who kills this Philistine and removes this disgrace from Israel? Who is this uncircumcised Philistine that he should defy the armies of the living God?"

[27]They repeated to him what they had been saying and told him, "This is what will be done for the man who kills him."

[28]When Eliab, David's oldest brother, heard him speaking with the men, he burned with anger at him and asked, "Why have you come down here? And with whom did you leave those few sheep in the desert? I know how conceited you are and how wicked your heart is; you came down only to watch the battle."

[29]"Now what have I done?" said David. "Can't I even speak?" [30]He then turned away to someone else and brought up the same matter, and the men answered him as before. [31]What David said was overheard and reported to Saul, and Saul sent for him.

[32]David said to Saul, "Let no one lose heart on account of this Philistine; your servant will go and fight him."

[33]Saul replied, "You are not able to go out against this Philistine and fight him; you are only a boy, and he has been a fighting man from his youth."

[34]But David said to Saul, "Your servant has been keeping his father's sheep. When a lion or a bear came and carried off a sheep from the flock, [35]I went after it, struck it and rescued the sheep from its mouth. When it turned on me, I seized it by its hair, struck it and killed it. [36]Your servant has killed both the lion and the bear; this uncircumcised Philistine will be like one of them, because he has defied the armies of the living God. [37]The LORD who delivered me from the paw

---

[a]4 Hebrew *was six cubits and a span* (about 3 meters)   [b]5 That is, about 125 pounds (about 57 kilograms)
[c]7 That is, about 15 pounds (about 7 kilograms)   [d]17 That is, probably about 3/5 bushel (about 22 liters)
[e]18 Hebrew *thousand*   [f]18 Or *some token; or some pledge of spoils*

of the lion and the paw of the bear will deliver me from the hand of this Philistine."

Saul said to David, "Go, and the LORD be with you."

38Then Saul dressed David in his own tunic. He put a coat of armor on him and a bronze helmet on his head. 39David fastened on his sword over the tunic and tried walking around, because he was not used to them.

"I cannot go in these," he said to Saul, "because I am not used to them." So he took them off. 40Then he took his staff in his hand, chose five smooth stones from the stream, put them in the pouch of his shepherd's bag and, with his sling in his hand, approached the Philistine.

17:40 Deadly Rocks

The "five smooth stones" that David took from the stream were each probably bigger than a baseball. Someone skilled with a sling could hurl them at close to 100 miles per hour.

41Meanwhile, the Philistine, with his shield bearer in front of him, kept coming closer to David. 42He looked David over and saw that he was only a boy, ruddy and handsome, and he despised him. 43He said to David, "Am I a dog, that you come at me with sticks?" And the Philistine cursed David by his gods. 44"Come here," he said, "and I'll give your flesh to the birds of the air and the beasts of the field!"

45David said to the Philistine, "You come against me with sword and spear and javelin, but I come against you in the name of the LORD Almighty, the God of the armies of Israel, whom you have defied. 46This day the LORD will hand you over to me, and I'll strike you down and cut off your head. Today I will give the carcasses of the Philistine army to the birds of the air and the beasts of the earth, and the whole world will know that there is a God in Israel. 47All those gathered here will know that it is not by sword or spear that the LORD saves; for the battle is the LORD's, and he will give all of you into our hands."

48As the Philistine moved closer to attack him, David ran quickly toward the battle line to meet him. 49Reaching into his bag and taking out a stone, he slung it and struck the Philistine on the forehead. The stone sank into his forehead, and he fell facedown on the ground.

50So David triumphed over the Philistine with a sling and a stone; without a sword in his hand he struck down the Philistine and killed him.

51David ran and stood over him. He took hold of the Philistine's sword and drew it from the scabbard. After he killed him, he cut off his head with the sword.

When the Philistines saw that their hero was dead, they turned and ran. 52Then the men of Israel and Judah surged forward with a shout and pursued the Philistines to the entrance of Gath*a* and to the gates of Ekron. Their dead were strewn along the Shaaraim road to Gath and Ekron. 53When the Israelites returned from chasing the Philistines, they plundered their camp. 54David took the Philistine's head and brought it to Jerusalem, and he put the Philistine's weapons in his own tent.

55As Saul watched David going out to meet the Philistine, he said to Abner, commander of the army, "Abner, whose son is that young man?"

Abner replied, "As surely as you live, O king, I don't know."

56The king said, "Find out whose son this young man is."

57As soon as David returned from killing the Philistine, Abner took him and brought him before Saul, with David still holding the Philistine's head.

58"Whose son are you, young man?" Saul asked him.

David said, "I am the son of your servant Jesse of Bethlehem."

Saul's Jealousy of David

18 After David had finished talking with Saul, Jonathan became one in spirit with David, and he loved him as himself. 2From that day Saul kept David with him and did not let him return to his father's house. 3And Jonathan made a covenant with David because he loved him as himself. 4Jonathan took off the robe he was wearing and gave it to David, along with his tunic, and even his sword, his bow and his belt.

5Whatever Saul sent him to do, David did it so successfully*b* that Saul gave him a high rank in the army. This pleased all the people, and Saul's officers as well.

6When the men were returning home after David had killed the Philistine, the women came out from all the towns of Israel to meet King Saul with singing and dancing, with joyful songs and with tambourines and lutes. 7As they danced, they sang:

"Saul has slain his thousands,
    and David his tens of thousands."

8Saul was very angry; this refrain galled him. "They have credited David with tens of thousands," he thought, "but me with only thousands. What more can he get but the kingdom?" 9And from that time on Saul kept a jealous eye on David.

---

a52 Some Septuagint manuscripts; Hebrew *a valley*   *b5* Or *wisely*

10The next day an evil[a] spirit from God came forcefully upon Saul. He was prophesying in his house, while David was playing the harp, as he usually did. Saul had a spear in his hand 11and he hurled it, saying to himself, "I'll pin David to the wall." But David eluded him twice.

12Saul was afraid of David, because the LORD was with David but had left Saul. 13So he sent David away from him and gave him command over a thousand men, and David led the troops in their campaigns. 14In everything he did he had great success,[b] because the LORD was with him. 15When Saul saw how successful[c] he was, he was afraid of him. 16But all Israel and Judah loved David, because he led them in their campaigns.

17Saul said to David, "Here is my older daughter Merab. I will give her to you in marriage; only serve me bravely and fight the battles of the LORD." For Saul said to himself, "I will not raise a hand against him. Let the Philistines do that!"

18But David said to Saul, "Who am I, and what is my family or my father's clan in Israel, that I should become the king's son-in-law?" 19So[d] when the time came for Merab, Saul's daughter, to be given to David, she was given in marriage to Adriel of Meholah.

20Now Saul's daughter Michal was in love with David, and when they told Saul about it, he was pleased. 21"I will give her to him," he thought, "so that she may be a snare to him and so that the hand of the Philistines may be against him." So Saul said to David, "Now you have a second opportunity to become my son-in-law."

22Then Saul ordered his attendants: "Speak to David privately and say, 'Look, the king is pleased with you, and his attendants all like you; now become his son-in-law.'"

23They repeated these words to David. But David said, "Do you think it is a small matter to become the king's son-in-law? I'm only a poor man and little known."

24When Saul's servants told him what David had said, 25Saul replied, "Say to David, 'The king wants no other price for the bride than a hundred Philistine foreskins, to take revenge on his enemies.'" Saul's plan was to have David fall by the hands of the Philistines.

26When the attendants told David these things, he was pleased to become the king's son-in-law. So before the allotted time elapsed, 27David and his men went out and killed two hundred Philistines. He brought their foreskins and presented the full number to the king so that he might become the king's son-in-law. Then Saul gave him his daughter Michal in marriage.

28When Saul realized that the LORD was with David and that his daughter Michal loved David, 29Saul became still more afraid of him, and he remained his enemy the rest of his days.

30The Philistine commanders continued to go out to battle, and as often as they did, David met

18:27 "Scalps"

This bloody prize, something like the scalps that native Americans and white settlers collected in battles, proved that David's battle claims were not exaggerated. Foreskins would come from Philistines, since other tribes of the area, like Israel, practiced circumcision.

with more success[e] than the rest of Saul's officers, and his name became well known.

Saul Tries to Kill David

19 Saul told his son Jonathan and all the attendants to kill David. But Jonathan was very fond of David 2and warned him, "My father Saul is looking for a chance to kill you. Be on your guard tomorrow morning; go into hiding and stay there. 3I will go out and stand with my father in the field where you are. I'll speak to him about you and will tell you what I find out."

4Jonathan spoke well of David to Saul his father and said to him, "Let not the king do wrong to his servant David; he has not wronged you, and what he has done has benefited you greatly. 5He took his life in his hands when he killed the Philistine. The LORD won a great victory for all Israel, and you saw it and were glad. Why then would you do wrong to an innocent man like David by killing him for no reason?"

6Saul listened to Jonathan and took this oath: "As surely as the LORD lives, David will not be put to death."

7So Jonathan called David and told him the whole conversation. He brought him to Saul, and David was with Saul as before.

8Once more war broke out, and David went out and fought the Philistines. He struck them with such force that they fled before him.

9But an evil[a] spirit from the LORD came upon Saul as he was sitting in his house with his spear in his hand. While David was playing the harp, 10Saul tried to pin him to the wall with his spear, but David eluded him as Saul drove the spear into the wall. That night David made good his escape.

11Saul sent men to David's house to watch it and to kill him in the morning. But Michal, David's wife, warned him, "If you don't run for your

a 10,9 Or injurious more wisely   b 14 Or he was very wise   c 15 Or wise   d 19 Or However,   e 30 Or David acted life tonight, tomorrow you'll be killed." [12]So Michal let David down through a window, and he fled and escaped. [13]Then Michal took an idol[a] and laid it on the bed, covering it with a garment and putting some goats' hair at the head.

[14]When Saul sent the men to capture David, Michal said, "He is ill."

[15]Then Saul sent the men back to see David and told them, "Bring him up to me in his bed so that I may kill him." [16]But when the men entered, there was the idol in the bed, and at the head was some goats' hair.

[17]Saul said to Michal, "Why did you deceive me like this and send my enemy away so that he escaped?"

Michal told him, "He said to me, 'Let me get away. Why should I kill you?'"

[18]When David had fled and made his escape, he went to Samuel at Ramah and told him all that Saul had done to him. Then he and Samuel went to Naioth and stayed there. [19]Word came to Saul: "David is in Naioth at Ramah"; [20]so he sent men to capture him. But when they saw a group of prophets prophesying, with Samuel standing there as their leader, the Spirit of God came upon Saul's men and they also prophesied. [21]Saul was told about it, and he sent more men, and they prophesied too. Saul sent men a third time, and they also prophesied. [22]Finally, he himself left for Ramah and went to the great cistern at Secu. And he asked, "Where are Samuel and David?"

"Over in Naioth at Ramah," they said.

[23]So Saul went to Naioth at Ramah. But the Spirit of God came even upon him, and he

walked along prophesying until he came to Naioth. [24]He stripped off his robes and also prophesied in Samuel's presence. He lay that way all that day and night. This is why people say, "Is Saul also among the prophets?"

19:23 Out of Control

Prophets are usually pictured as somber figures. First Samuel reveals a different side: prophecy accompanying ecstatic worship. Saul had met a musical band of such prophets soon after he was anointed king (10:5–11). Now that he was planning evil, however, meeting the Spirit of God made him utterly lose control.

David and Jonathan

20 Then David fled from Naioth at Ramah and went to Jonathan and asked, "What have I done? What is my crime? How have I wronged your father, that he is trying to take my life?"

[2]"Never!" Jonathan replied. "You are not going to die! Look, my father doesn't do anything, great or small, without confiding in me. Why would he hide this from me? It's not so!"

[3]But David took an oath and said, "Your father knows very well that I have found favor in your eyes, and he has said to himself, 'Jonathan must not know this or he will be grieved.' Yet as surely as the LORD lives and as you live, there is only a step between me and death."

[a]13 Hebrew *teraphim*; also in verse 16

JONATHAN *Friends First*

JEALOUS FRIENDS SOMETIMES FORCE US to choose. "Who is your best friend?" they demand, when we'd prefer not to rank them. Jonathan faced that kind of loyalty dilemma with his father, who grew insanely jealous of his son's friendship with David.

Palace intrigues in those days resembled the plot of a Shakespearean play. Insecure and guilt-ridden over past misdeeds, Saul feared that young David would take away his crown. (Indeed, Samuel had secretly anointed David as Israel's future king, but David fought bravely in Saul's service and never tried to usurp the throne.)

Though Jonathan tried to stay loyal to both father and friend, his father made it impossible. Soon Jonathan realized that Saul would kill David if he caught him. Once, in a blind rage, Saul hurled a spear at his own son for standing up for David (20:32–33).

One major factor further complicated Jonathan's choice: As Saul's son, he stood next in line for the throne. By siding with David, he would ultimately harm himself. Even so, at the risk of his own neck, Jonathan chose to help David escape. He told David he would happily follow his friend as his number-two man (23:17).

Tragically, the two friends never got the chance to rule together. In a battle against the Philistines, Jonathan fought at his father's side and was killed (31:2). David, mourning his dearest friend, sang a poignant song in tribute (2 Samuel 1:17–27). Their loyalty and love make for one of the most beautiful stories of friendship ever told.

Life Questions: What friend is most loyal to you? What does that loyalty mean to you?

[4]Jonathan said to David, "Whatever you want me to do, I'll do for you."

[5]So David said, "Look, tomorrow is the New Moon festival, and I am supposed to dine with the king; but let me go and hide in the field until the evening of the day after tomorrow. [6]If your father misses me at all, tell him, 'David earnestly asked my permission to hurry to Bethlehem, his hometown, because an annual sacrifice is being made there for his whole clan.' [7]If he says, 'Very well,' then your servant is safe. But if he loses his temper, you can be sure that he is determined to harm me. [8]As for you, show kindness to your servant, for you have brought him into a covenant with you before the LORD. If I am guilty, then kill me yourself! Why hand me over to your father?"

[9]"Never!" Jonathan said. "If I had the least inkling that my father was determined to harm you, wouldn't I tell you?"

[10]David asked, "Who will tell me if your father answers you harshly?"

[11]"Come," Jonathan said, "let's go out into the field." So they went there together.

[12]Then Jonathan said to David: "By the LORD, the God of Israel, I will surely sound out my father by this time the day after tomorrow! If he is favorably disposed toward you, will I not send you word and let you know? [13]But if my father is inclined to harm you, may the LORD deal with me, be it ever so severely, if I do not let you know and send you away safely. May the LORD be with you as he has been with my father. [14]But show me unfailing kindness like that of the LORD as long as I live, so that I may not be killed, [15]and do not ever cut off your kindness from my family—not even when the LORD has cut off every one of David's enemies from the face of the earth."

[16]So Jonathan made a covenant with the house of David, saying, "May the LORD call David's enemies to account." [17]And Jonathan had David reaffirm his oath out of love for him, because he loved him as he loved himself.

[18]Then Jonathan said to David: "Tomorrow is the New Moon festival. You will be missed, because your seat will be empty. [19]The day after tomorrow, toward evening, go to the place where you hid when this trouble began, and wait by the stone Ezel. [20]I will shoot three arrows to the side of it, as though I were shooting at a target. [21]Then I will send a boy and say, 'Go, find the arrows.' If I say to him, 'Look, the arrows are on this side of you; bring them here,' then come, because, as surely as the LORD lives, you are safe; there is no danger. [22]But if I say to the boy, 'Look, the arrows are beyond you,' then you must go, because the LORD has sent you away. [23]And about the matter you and I discussed—remember, the LORD is witness between you and me forever."

[24]So David hid in the field, and when the New Moon festival came, the king sat down to eat. [25]He sat in his customary place by the wall, opposite Jonathan,[a] and Abner sat next to Saul, but David's place was empty. [26]Saul said nothing that day, for he thought, "Something must have happened to David to make him ceremonially unclean—surely he is unclean." [27]But the next day, the second day of the month, David's place was empty again. Then Saul said to his son Jonathan, "Why hasn't the son of Jesse come to the meal, either yesterday or today?"

[28]Jonathan answered, "David earnestly asked me for permission to go to Bethlehem. [29]He said, 'Let me go, because our family is observing a sacrifice in the town and my brother has ordered me to be there. If I have found favor in your eyes, let me get away to see my brothers.' That is why he has not come to the king's table."

[30]Saul's anger flared up at Jonathan and he said to him, "You son of a perverse and rebellious woman! Don't I know that you have sided with the son of Jesse to your own shame and to the shame of the mother who bore you? [31]As long as the son of Jesse lives on this earth, neither you nor your kingdom will be established. Now send and bring him to me, for he must die!"

[32]"Why should he be put to death? What has he done?" Jonathan asked his father. [33]But Saul hurled his spear at him to kill him. Then Jonathan knew that his father intended to kill David.

[34]Jonathan got up from the table in fierce anger; on that second day of the month he did not eat, because he was grieved at his father's shameful treatment of David.

[35]In the morning Jonathan went out to the field for his meeting with David. He had a small boy with him, [36]and he said to the boy, "Run and find the arrows I shoot." As the boy ran, he shot an arrow beyond him. [37]When the boy came to the place where Jonathan's arrow had fallen, Jonathan called out after him, "Isn't the arrow beyond you?" [38]Then he shouted, "Hurry! Go quickly! Don't stop!" The boy picked up the arrow and returned to his master. [39](The boy knew nothing of all this; only Jonathan and David knew.) [40]Then Jonathan gave his weapons to the boy and said, "Go, carry them back to town."

[41]After the boy had gone, David got up from the south side ⌊of the stone⌋ and bowed down before Jonathan three times, with his face to the ground. Then they kissed each other and wept together—but David wept the most.

[42]Jonathan said to David, "Go in peace, for we have sworn friendship with each other in the name of the LORD, saying, 'The LORD is witness

---

[a]25 Septuagint; Hebrew *wall.* Jonathan arose

Twila Paris

has one overarching vision when she thinks of her mission and her profession as a Christian contemporary artist. It's based on Romans 11:36: "For from him and to him and through him are all things. To him be the glory forever! Amen."

"When I picture this verse," Twila says, "I see a cycle of giving that applies to everyone in the kingdom of God. For instance, God has given me the ability to write songs and sing them. At times when I'm writing a praise song to him, I feel the words and music coming to me so clearly that I know he is giving me yet another gift—the gift of that song of praise to him. The next part of the cycle happens when I record that song or sing it to people in concert. And as people listen to the song and sing it back to God, whether in their heads as it plays on the radio or in their churches in the context of a praise service, they're using their gifts to bring my gift back to God.

"No matter what your gifts, God wants you to reflect those back to him as an act of worship. As long as God's gifts continue to flow through you (and God never stops giving gifts), that cycle continues. And each time the cycle is completed, God's kingdom is built up and his name is praised."

Twila also has an interesting story behind her WoW 1997 cut, "Love's Been Following You." As the daughter of a pastor, Twila remembers a vivid image from a sermon on Psalm 23 that she heard as a little girl. When her father would reach verse 6, "Surely goodness and love will follow me all the days of my life," he would personify both Goodness and Love as angels that followed believers wherever they went, working as God's agents to protect and to care for his children. "That image laid dormant in my mind for years, until I reread the title to this song," Twila remembers. "At one point I was struck with that image once again, of God's protecting agents following me throughout my life. I'm happy to say that this song now is a tribute to my father and that sermon. Every time I perform this song, I think of those tireless workers, Goodness and Love."

WOW
1997

PFR

Joel
Hanson,
Patrick
Andrew,
and
Mark
Nash
provide
the punch in the power
trio PFR (formerly known as
Pray for Rain). On their farewell tour at the time of this writing,
the members of PFR have found a place on the WoW 1997 CD and,
throughout their 8–year career, in the hearts of many CCM listeners. Of
their WoW 1997 offering, "Anything," lead vocalist Joel Hanson says,

"It's a simple song, really. The lyric 'It doesn't mean anything without you'
means that my life would have no meaning, no validity without my rela–
tionship with Christ. I've lived without him for a while, and it was just a
constant struggle, a search to get rid of the emptiness. There are a couple
of songs I wrote on this album that talk about just wanting to get rid of
the search, wanting to fill myself up with something other than God, and
realizing that my trusting, my obeying, my submitting to God is right."

Many of their devoted fans have questioned PFR's decision to move on and
disband. In an August., 1996 interview for CCM magazine, Joel repre–
sented the band in "A Word from PFR to Fans": "I just want to say to
anybody who's feeling bad for us not to 'cause in the midst of all this,
there's a lot of peace that's surrounded our lives. The nervousness and the
anxiety comes along with being human, but there's an underlying, maybe
even overlying peace that God provides. If we're willing to follow the foot–
steps, he'll lead us home, he'll lead us to where we're supposed to be.
Hopefully, people can rejoice that we're going to follow after what we
believe to be God's calling on our lives."

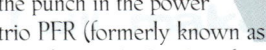

between you and me, and between your descendants and my descendants forever.'" Then David left, and Jonathan went back to the town.

David at Nob

21 David went to Nob, to Ahimelech the priest. Ahimelech trembled when he met him, and asked, "Why are you alone? Why is no one with you?"

²David answered Ahimelech the priest, "The king charged me with a certain matter and said to me, 'No one is to know anything about your mission and your instructions.' As for my men, I have told them to meet me at a certain place. ³Now then, what do you have on hand? Give me five loaves of bread, or whatever you can find."

⁴But the priest answered David, "I don't have any ordinary bread on hand; however, there is some consecrated bread here—provided the men have kept themselves from women."

21:4 Disobeying the Law

David was desperate when he reached Nob. He did not even have food. He lied about his situation. Then he ate consecrated bread that was supposed to be reserved for the priests. (A thousand years later Jesus raised the issue of the consecrated bread, suggesting that keeping the ritual laws mattered less than David's survival [Matthew 12:3–4].)

David later admitted that he had been wrong to go to Nob and endanger the priests. Saul, suspicious of their involvement, slaughtered them (22:17–18).

⁵David replied, "Indeed women have been kept from us, as usual whenever[a] I set out. The men's things[b] are holy even on missions that are not holy. How much more so today!" ⁶So the priest gave him the consecrated bread, since there was no bread there except the bread of the Presence that had been removed from before the LORD and replaced by hot bread on the day it was taken away.

⁷Now one of Saul's servants was there that day, detained before the LORD; he was Doeg the Edomite, Saul's head shepherd.

⁸David asked Ahimelech, "Don't you have a spear or a sword here? I haven't brought my sword or any other weapon, because the king's business was urgent."

⁹The priest replied, "The sword of Goliath the Philistine, whom you killed in the Valley of Elah, is here; it is wrapped in a cloth behind the ephod. If you want it, take it; there is no sword here but that one."

David said, "There is none like it; give it to me."

David at Gath

¹⁰That day David fled from Saul and went to Achish king of Gath. ¹¹But the servants of Achish said to him, "Isn't this David, the king of the land? Isn't he the one they sing about in their dances:

"'Saul has slain his thousands,
    and David his tens of thousands'?"

¹²David took these words to heart and was very much afraid of Achish king of Gath. ¹³So he pretended to be insane in their presence; and while he was in their hands he acted like a madman, making marks on the doors of the gate and letting saliva run down his beard.

¹⁴Achish said to his servants, "Look at the man! He is insane! Why bring him to me? ¹⁵Am I so short of madmen that you have to bring this fellow here to carry on like this in front of me? Must this man come into my house?"

David at Adullam and Mizpah

22 David left Gath and escaped to the cave of Adullam. When his brothers and his father's household heard about it, they went down to him there. ²All those who were in distress or in debt or discontented gathered around him, and he became their leader. About four hundred men were with him.

³From there David went to Mizpah in Moab and said to the king of Moab, "Would you let my father and mother come and stay with you until

22:3 Long-lost Relatives

Afraid that Saul would hold his family hostage, David took his parents to the neighboring kingdom of Moab for safekeeping. Why Moab? Possibly because he had distant relatives there. His great-grandmother, Ruth, had come from Moab.

I learn what God will do for me?" ⁴So he left them with the king of Moab, and they stayed with him as long as David was in the stronghold.

⁵But the prophet Gad said to David, "Do not stay in the stronghold. Go into the land of Judah." So David left and went to the forest of Hereth.

Saul Kills the Priests of Nob

⁶Now Saul heard that David and his men had been discovered. And Saul, spear in hand, was

---

[a] 5 Or *from us in the past few days since*   [b] 5 Or *bodies*

seated under the tamarisk tree on the hill at Gibeah, with all his officials standing around him. 7Saul said to them, "Listen, men of Benjamin! Will the son of Jesse give all of you fields and vineyards? Will he make all of you commanders of thousands and commanders of hundreds? 8Is that why you have all conspired against me? No one tells me when my son makes a covenant with the son of Jesse. None of you is concerned about me or tells me that my son has incited my servant to lie in wait for me, as he does today."

9But Doeg the Edomite, who was standing with Saul's officials, said, "I saw the son of Jesse come to Ahimelech son of Ahitub at Nob. 10Ahimelech inquired of the LORD for him; he also gave him provisions and the sword of Goliath the Philistine."

11Then the king sent for the priest Ahimelech son of Ahitub and his father's whole family, who were the priests at Nob, and they all came to the king. 12Saul said, "Listen now, son of Ahitub."

"Yes, my lord," he answered.

13Saul said to him, "Why have you conspired against me, you and the son of Jesse, giving him bread and a sword and inquiring of God for him, so that he has rebelled against me and lies in wait for me, as he does today?"

14Ahimelech answered the king, "Who of all your servants is as loyal as David, the king's son-in-law, captain of your bodyguard and highly respected in your household? 15Was that day the first time I inquired of God for him? Of course not! Let not the king accuse your servant or any of his father's family, for your servant knows nothing at all about this whole affair."

16But the king said, "You will surely die, Ahimelech, you and your father's whole family."

17Then the king ordered the guards at his side: "Turn and kill the priests of the LORD, because they too have sided with David. They knew he was fleeing, yet they did not tell me."

But the king's officials were not willing to raise a hand to strike the priests of the LORD.

18The king then ordered Doeg, "You turn and strike down the priests." So Doeg the Edomite turned and struck them down. That day he killed eighty-five men who wore the linen ephod. 19He also put to the sword Nob, the town of the priests, with its men and women, its children and infants, and its cattle, donkeys and sheep.

20But Abiathar, a son of Ahimelech son of Ahitub, escaped and fled to join David. 21He told David that Saul had killed the priests of the LORD. 22Then David said to Abiathar: "That day, when Doeg the Edomite was there, I knew he would be sure to tell Saul. I am responsible for the death of your father's whole family. 23Stay with me; don't be afraid; the man who is seeking your life is seeking mine also. You will be safe with me."

David Saves Keilah

23 When David was told, "Look, the Philistines are fighting against Keilah and are looting the threshing floors," 2he inquired of the LORD, saying, "Shall I go and attack these Philistines?"

The LORD answered him, "Go, attack the Philistines and save Keilah."

3But David's men said to him, "Here in Judah we are afraid. How much more, then, if we go to Keilah against the Philistine forces!"

4Once again David inquired of the LORD, and the LORD answered him, "Go down to Keilah, for I am going to give the Philistines into your hand." 5So David and his men went to Keilah, fought the Philistines and carried off their livestock. He inflicted heavy losses on the Philistines and saved the people of Keilah. 6(Now Abiathar son of Ahimelech had brought the ephod down with him when he fled to David at Keilah.)

Saul Pursues David

7Saul was told that David had gone to Keilah, and he said, "God has handed him over to me, for David has imprisoned himself by entering a town with gates and bars." 8And Saul called up all his forces for battle, to go down to Keilah to besiege David and his men.

9When David learned that Saul was plotting against him, he said to Abiathar the priest, "Bring the ephod." 10David said, "O LORD, God of Israel, your servant has heard definitely that Saul plans to come to Keilah and destroy the town on account of me. 11Will the citizens of Keilah surrender me to him? Will Saul come down, as your servant has heard? O LORD, God of Israel, tell your servant."

And the LORD said, "He will."

12Again David asked, "Will the citizens of Keilah surrender me and my men to Saul?"

And the LORD said, "They will."

13So David and his men, about six hundred in number, left Keilah and kept moving from place to place. When Saul was told that David had escaped from Keilah, he did not go there.

14David stayed in the desert strongholds and in the hills of the Desert of Ziph. Day after day Saul searched for him, but God did not give David into his hands.

15While David was at Horesh in the Desert of Ziph, he learned that Saul had come out to take his life. 16And Saul's son Jonathan went to David at Horesh and helped him find strength in God. 17"Don't be afraid," he said. "My father Saul will not lay a hand on you. You will be king over Israel, and I will be second to you. Even my father Saul knows this." 18The two of them made a covenant before the LORD. Then Jonathan went home, but David remained at Horesh.

19The Ziphites went up to Saul at Gibeah and

said, "Is not David hiding among us in the strongholds at Horesh, on the hill of Hakilah, south of Jeshimon? **20**Now, O king, come down whenever it pleases you to do so, and we will be responsible for handing him over to the king."

23:16 Final Farewell

This last, secret meeting between Jonathan and David reveals the essence of their friendship. They had grown to love each other despite Saul's (Jonathan's father's) hatred for David. Now, when David was desperate, Jonathan sought him out and "helped him find strength in God." Jonathan expected to become David's right-hand man when David became king, but Jonathan's death soon put an end to that dream (see 31:2).

21Saul replied, "The Lord bless you for your concern for me. **22**Go and make further preparation. Find out where David usually goes and who has seen him there. They tell me he is very crafty. **23**Find out about all the hiding places he uses and come back to me with definite information.*a* Then I will go with you; if he is in the area, I will track him down among all the clans of Judah."

24So they set out and went to Ziph ahead of Saul. Now David and his men were in the Desert of Maon, in the Arabah south of Jeshimon. **25**Saul and his men began the search, and when David was told about it, he went down to the rock and stayed in the Desert of Maon. When Saul heard this, he went into the Desert of Maon in pursuit of David.

26Saul was going along one side of the mountain, and David and his men were on the other side, hurrying to get away from Saul. As Saul and his forces were closing in on David and his men to capture them, **27**a messenger came to Saul, saying, "Come quickly! The Philistines are raiding the land." **28**Then Saul broke off his pursuit of David and went to meet the Philistines. That is why they call this place Sela Hammahlekoth.*b* **29**And David went up from there and lived in the strongholds of En Gedi.

David Spares Saul's Life

24 After Saul returned from pursuing the Philistines, he was told, "David is in the Desert of En Gedi." **2**So Saul took three thousand chosen men from all Israel and set out to look for David and his men near the Crags of the Wild Goats.

3He came to the sheep pens along the way; a cave was there, and Saul went in to relieve himself. David and his men were far back in the cave. **4**The men said, "This is the day the Lord spoke of when he said*c* to you, 'I will give your enemy into your hands for you to deal with as you wish.'" Then David crept up unnoticed and cut off a corner of Saul's robe.

5Afterward, David was conscience-stricken for having cut off a corner of his robe. **6**He said to his men, "The Lord forbid that I should do such a thing to my master, the Lord's anointed, or lift my hand against him; for he is the anointed of the Lord." **7**With these words David rebuked his men and did not allow them to attack Saul. And Saul left the cave and went his way.

24:5 David's Bad Conscience

David's conscience troubled him after he cut off part of Saul's robe. Why? Possibly because, to people of that day, a man looked ridiculous with his clothes cut short. See 2 Samuel 10:4–5 for a case where cutting a garment was a deliberate insult that led to war.

8Then David went out of the cave and called out to Saul, "My lord the king!" When Saul looked behind him, David bowed down and prostrated himself with his face to the ground. **9**He said to Saul, "Why do you listen when men say, 'David is bent on harming you'? **10**This day you have seen with your own eyes how the Lord delivered you into my hands in the cave. Some urged me to kill you, but I spared you; I said, 'I will not lift my hand against my master, because he is the Lord's anointed.' **11**See, my father, look at this piece of your robe in my hand! I cut off the corner of your robe but did not kill you. Now understand and recognize that I am not guilty of wrongdoing or rebellion. I have not wronged you, but you are hunting me down to take my life. **12**May the Lord judge between you and me. And may the Lord avenge the wrongs you have done to me, but my hand will not touch you. **13**As the old saying goes, 'From evildoers come evil deeds,' so my hand will not touch you.

14"Against whom has the king of Israel come out? Whom are you pursuing? A dead dog? A flea? **15**May the Lord be our judge and decide between us. May he consider my cause and uphold it; may he vindicate me by delivering me from your hand."

16When David finished saying this, Saul asked, "Is that your voice, David my son?" And he wept aloud. **17**"You are more righteous than I," he said. "You have treated me well, but I have treated you badly. **18**You have just now told me of the good you did to me; the Lord delivered me into

a23 Or me at Nacon   *b28 Sela Hammahlekoth means rock of parting.*   *c4 Or "Today the Lord is saying*

your hands, but you did not kill me. ¹⁹When a man finds his enemy, does he let him get away unharmed? May the LORD reward you well for the way you treated me today. ²⁰I know that you will surely be king and that the kingdom of Israel will be established in your hands. ²¹Now swear to me by the LORD that you will not cut off my descendants or wipe out my name from my father's family."

²²So David gave his oath to Saul. Then Saul returned home, but David and his men went up to the stronghold.

David, Nabal and Abigail

25 Now Samuel died, and all Israel assembled and mourned for him; and they buried him at his home in Ramah.

Then David moved down into the Desert of

A Sense of God's Timing
Two leaders locked in a death struggle—with one refusing to fight

> *"I have not wronged you, but you are hunting me down to take my life. May the LORD judge between you and me." 24:11–12*

IN THE WINTER OF 1777, America had two armies. One lived in comfortable homes in Philadelphia. The other camped in the snow in the hills to the northwest, at a place called Valley Forge. One showed impeccable discipline. The other tried desperately to keep its untrained recruits from deserting. One was supplied by ship with every luxury. The other fought frostbite because its soldiers had no boots.

In sum, one army had everything it could want to weather a cold winter and a war, while the other hung by a thread. Who could have thought, seeing the two, that within three years the army with nothing would defeat the army with everything?

The impoverished American army could never go head-on against the crack British forces. But it could always outwait them. George Washington's army had the support of the American people, while the British army, for all its strength, was far from home. The British had to win decisively, putting an end to the rebellion. The Americans merely had to survive and outlast them.

Washington was a military genius not at battle tactics, but at a more fundamental necessity: encouraging his men to fight on. One-quarter of them died of cold and disease that bitter winter at Valley Forge. Only his personal strength held the miserable army together. That was the key to victory.

Two Kings in Israel

David and his followers lived in a similar situation. Saul was the right and proper king, living in luxury. David had been secretly anointed as his replacement, but he lived in the desert, scrabbling to survive. Saul had a professional army, David a small band composed of family members and an assortment of outlaws.

Twice Saul accidentally fell into David's hands, but David refused to kill him. He felt that would violate God's will. He would not use his sword to become king. He fought not to win but to survive.

Survival was not easy. You can read between the lines of chapters 21–31 and see a great drama unfolding. Saul is clearly deteriorating. Can David hold on long enough to outlast him?

At first David ran from one place to another, alone and completely vulnerable. Then, when 400 outlaws gathered around him, the local people turned him in twice (23:19; 26:1). Perhaps they feared that Saul would slaughter them the way he had the Nob priests (22:6–23).

David survived and managed to keep his army intact. He even built popular support by providing military protection to his neighbors. But eventually he saw that his position was impossible. "One of these days I will be destroyed by the hand of Saul," he said (27:1). He left Israel and became, with his army, a hired soldier for one of the Philistine kings.

Sooner or later David's double-agent act would have been found out. In fact, when the Philistines planned a major military effort against Israel, David barely escaped having to fight his own people.

Time on His Side

Throughout his desert period, David's position was desperate. David had one precious asset only: God had promised he would be king. David believed this promise even when his situation looked very bad. He would wait for God's timing.

A sense of timing, people say, is essential to leadership. You must know when to act boldly and when to wait patiently; when to bend and when to stand firm. David had that critical sense of timing because he trusted God's control of events.

Life Questions: What makes you impatient? What can you learn about patience from David's life?

Maon.[a] [2]A certain man in Maon, who had property there at Carmel, was very wealthy. He had a thousand goats and three thousand sheep, which he was shearing in Carmel. [3]His name was Nabal and his wife's name was Abigail. She was an intelligent and beautiful woman, but her husband, a Calebite, was surly and mean in his dealings.

[4]While David was in the desert, he heard that Nabal was shearing sheep. [5]So he sent ten young men and said to them, "Go up to Nabal at Carmel and greet him in my name. [6]Say to him: 'Long life to you! Good health to you and your household! And good health to all that is yours!

[7]"'Now I hear that it is sheep-shearing time. When your shepherds were with us, we did not mistreat them, and the whole time they were at Carmel nothing of theirs was missing. [8]Ask your own servants and they will tell you. Therefore be favorable toward my young men, since we come at a festive time. Please give your servants and your son David whatever you can find for them.'"

[9]When David's men arrived, they gave Nabal this message in David's name. Then they waited.

[10]Nabal answered David's servants, "Who is this David? Who is this son of Jesse? Many servants are breaking away from their masters these days. [11]Why should I take my bread and water, and the meat I have slaughtered for my shearers, and give it to men coming from who knows where?"

[12]David's men turned around and went back. When they arrived, they reported every word. [13]David said to his men, "Put on your swords!" So they put on their swords, and David put on his. About four hundred men went up with David, while two hundred stayed with the supplies.

[14]One of the servants told Nabal's wife Abigail: "David sent messengers from the desert to give our master his greetings, but he hurled insults at them. [15]Yet these men were very good to us. They did not mistreat us, and the whole time we were out in the fields near them nothing was missing. [16]Night and day they were a wall around us all the time we were herding our sheep near them. [17]Now think it over and see what you can do, because disaster is hanging over our master and his whole household. He is such a wicked man that no one can talk to him."

[18]Abigail lost no time. She took two hundred loaves of bread, two skins of wine, five dressed sheep, five seahs[b] of roasted grain, a hundred cakes of raisins and two hundred cakes of pressed figs, and loaded them on donkeys. [19]Then she told her servants, "Go on ahead; I'll follow you." But she did not tell her husband Nabal.

[20]As she came riding her donkey into a mountain ravine, there were David and his men descending toward her, and she met them. [21]David had just said, "It's been useless—all my watching over this fellow's property in the desert so that nothing of his was missing. He has paid me back evil for good. [22]May God deal with David,[c] be it ever so severely, if by morning I leave alive one male of all who belong to him!"

[23]When Abigail saw David, she quickly got off her donkey and bowed down before David with her face to the ground. [24]She fell at his feet and said: "My lord, let the blame be on me alone. Please let your servant speak to you; hear what your servant has to say. [25]May my lord pay no attention to that wicked man Nabal. He is just like his name—his name is Fool, and folly goes with him. But as for me, your servant, I did not see the men my master sent.

[26]"Now since the LORD has kept you, my master, from bloodshed and from avenging yourself with your own hands, as surely as the LORD lives and as you live, may your enemies and all who intend to harm my master be like Nabal. [27]And let this gift, which your servant has brought to my master, be given to the men who follow you. [28]Please forgive your servant's offense, for the LORD will certainly make a lasting dynasty for my master, because he fights the LORD's battles. Let no wrongdoing be found in you as long as you live. [29]Even though someone is pursuing you to take your life, the life of my master will be bound securely in the bundle of the living by the LORD your God. But the lives of your enemies he will hurl away as from the pocket of a sling. [30]When the LORD has done for my master every good thing he promised concerning him and has appointed him leader over Israel, [31]my master will not have on his conscience the staggering burden of needless bloodshed or of having avenged him-

24:21 The Survival of a Family

Slaughtering the rival's entire family was normal practice when one would-be king won out over another. Such action tended to lessen the probability that the rival family would compete for the throne again. Jonathan, David's closest friend, is asking David not to follow that course when he becomes king. Because of their relationship, David let Jonathan's son Mephibosheth live (2 Samuel 9).

---

[a]1 Some Septuagint manuscripts; Hebrew *Paran*   [b]18 That is, probably about a bushel (about 37 liters)
[c]22 Some Septuagint manuscripts; Hebrew *with David's enemies*

self. And when the LORD has brought my master success, remember your servant."

³²David said to Abigail, "Praise be to the LORD, the God of Israel, who has sent you today to meet me. ³³May you be blessed for your good judgment and for keeping me from bloodshed this day and from avenging myself with my own hands. ³⁴Otherwise, as surely as the LORD, the God of Israel, lives, who has kept me from harming you, if you had not come quickly to meet me, not one male belonging to Nabal would have been left alive by daybreak."

³⁵Then David accepted from her hand what she had brought him and said, "Go home in peace. I have heard your words and granted your request."

³⁶When Abigail went to Nabal, he was in the house holding a banquet like that of a king. He was in high spirits and very drunk. So she told him nothing until daybreak. ³⁷Then in the morning, when Nabal was sober, his wife told him all these things, and his heart failed him and he became like a stone. ³⁸About ten days later, the LORD struck Nabal and he died.

³⁹When David heard that Nabal was dead, he said, "Praise be to the LORD, who has upheld my cause against Nabal for treating me with contempt. He has kept his servant from doing wrong and has brought Nabal's wrongdoing down on his own head."

Then David sent word to Abigail, asking her to become his wife. ⁴⁰His servants went to Carmel and said to Abigail, "David has sent us to you to take you to become his wife."

⁴¹She bowed down with her face to the ground and said, "Here is your maidservant, ready to serve you and wash the feet of my master's servants." ⁴²Abigail quickly got on a donkey and, attended by her five maids, went with David's messengers and became his wife. ⁴³David had also married Ahinoam of Jezreel, and they both were his wives. ⁴⁴But Saul had given his daughter Michal, David's wife, to Paltiel*a* son of Laish, who was from Gallim.

David Again Spares Saul's Life

26 The Ziphites went to Saul at Gibeah and said, "Is not David hiding on the hill of Hakilah, which faces Jeshimon?"

²So Saul went down to the Desert of Ziph, with his three thousand chosen men of Israel, to search there for David. ³Saul made his camp beside the road on the hill of Hakilah facing Jeshimon, but David stayed in the desert. When he saw that Saul had followed him there, ⁴he sent out scouts and learned that Saul had definitely arrived.*b*

⁵Then David set out and went to the place where Saul had camped. He saw where Saul and Abner son of Ner, the commander of the army, had lain down. Saul was lying inside the camp, with the army encamped around him.

⁶David then asked Ahimelech the Hittite and Abishai son of Zeruiah, Joab's brother, "Who will go down into the camp with me to Saul?"

"I'll go with you," said Abishai.

⁷So David and Abishai went to the army by night, and there was Saul, lying asleep inside the camp with his spear stuck in the ground near his head. Abner and the soldiers were lying around him.

a44 Hebrew Palti, a variant of Paltiel   *b4 Or had come to Nacon*

ABIGAIL *Beauty and Brains*

ABIGAIL WAS NOT A MAIN player in the history of Israel, but as this story shows, she had an instinctive skill for diplomacy and peace-making. A woman of beauty and brains, Abigail could defuse a dangerous situation between hot-headed men.

It is hard to imagine such a shrewd woman choosing marriage to Nabal, and indeed in those days parents, not lovers, arranged the marriages. Nabal was rich, which probably influenced Abigail's parents. She, however, knew her husband as a fool, and this incident characteristically portrays him as rude, drunk and stupid.

Though Abigail may have been trapped in a bad marriage, she was hardly helpless. When her husband mistreated David, Abigail rushed to take decisive action. She saved the day for her people as well as for David, who had lost his temper and was about to take vengeance he would doubtless regret.

A man of passion, David could lose his temper, but he also had the courage to back down when challenged with good sense. He thanked Abigail warmly and made a mental note about this remarkable woman. When her husband died a short time later, David asked the widow to be his wife. Without hesitation, without tears or mourning, Abigail agreed.

Though David was still an outlaw, Abigail sensed that a great future awaited him. As a result of her wise decisions, she became forever linked to Israel's greatest king.

Life Questions: What can you learn from Abigail's style of dealing with hot-tempered people?

⁸Abishai said to David, "Today God has delivered your enemy into your hands. Now let me pin him to the ground with one thrust of my spear; I won't strike him twice."

⁹But David said to Abishai, "Don't destroy him! Who can lay a hand on the LORD's anointed and be guiltless? ¹⁰As surely as the LORD lives," he said, "the LORD himself will strike him; either his time will come and he will die, or he will go into battle and perish. ¹¹But the LORD forbid that I should lay a hand on the LORD's anointed. Now get the spear and water jug that are near his head, and let's go."

¹²So David took the spear and water jug near Saul's head, and they left. No one saw or knew about it, nor did anyone wake up. They were all sleeping, because the LORD had put them into a deep sleep.

¹³Then David crossed over to the other side and stood on top of the hill some distance away; there was a wide space between them. ¹⁴He called out to the army and to Abner son of Ner, "Aren't you going to answer me, Abner?"

Abner replied, "Who are you who calls to the king?"

¹⁵David said, "You're a man, aren't you? And who is like you in Israel? Why didn't you guard your lord the king? Someone came to destroy your lord the king. ¹⁶What you have done is not good. As surely as the LORD lives, you and your men deserve to die, because you did not guard your master, the LORD's anointed. Look around you. Where are the king's spear and water jug that were near his head?"

¹⁷Saul recognized David's voice and said, "Is that your voice, David my son?"

David replied, "Yes it is, my lord the king." ¹⁸And he added, "Why is my lord pursuing his servant? What have I done, and what wrong am I guilty of? ¹⁹Now let my lord the king listen to his servant's words. If the LORD has incited you against me, then may he accept an offering. If, however, men have done it, may they be cursed before the LORD! They have now driven me from my share in the LORD's inheritance and have said, 'Go, serve other gods.' ²⁰Now do not let my blood fall to the ground far from the presence of the LORD. The king of Israel has come out to look for a flea—as one hunts a partridge in the mountains."

²¹Then Saul said, "I have sinned. Come back, David my son. Because you considered my life precious today, I will not try to harm you again. Surely I have acted like a fool and have erred greatly."

²²"Here is the king's spear," David answered. "Let one of your young men come over and get it. ²³The LORD rewards every man for his righteousness and faithfulness. The LORD delivered you into my hands today, but I would not lay a hand on the LORD's anointed. ²⁴As surely as I valued your life today, so may the LORD value my life and deliver me from all trouble."

²⁵Then Saul said to David, "May you be blessed, my son David; you will do great things and surely triumph."

So David went on his way, and Saul returned home.

David Among the Philistines

27 But David thought to himself, "One of these days I will be destroyed by the hand of Saul. The best thing I can do is to escape to the land of the Philistines. Then Saul will give up searching for me anywhere in Israel, and I will slip out of his hand."

²So David and the six hundred men with him left and went over to Achish son of Maoch king of Gath. ³David and his men settled in Gath with Achish. Each man had his family with him, and David had his two wives: Ahinoam of Jezreel and Abigail of Carmel, the widow of Nabal. ⁴When Saul was told that David had fled to Gath, he no longer searched for him.

⁵Then David said to Achish, "If I have found favor in your eyes, let a place be assigned to me in one of the country towns, that I may live there. Why should your servant live in the royal city with you?"

⁶So on that day Achish gave him Ziklag, and it has belonged to the kings of Judah ever since. ⁷David lived in Philistine territory a year and four months.

⁸Now David and his men went up and raided the Geshurites, the Girzites and the Amalekites. (From ancient times these peoples had lived in

27:8 David's Double Game

The Philistines accepted David because they thought he would fight against his own people. Had they known that he retained his Israelite loyalty, they would never have trusted him. So David had to pretend that he was raiding the Israelites, while actually he raided Israel's nomadic enemies. To keep his game secret, he took no prisoners, for it might be noticed that none of them were Israelites.

the land extending to Shur and Egypt.) ⁹Whenever David attacked an area, he did not leave a man or woman alive, but took sheep and cattle, donkeys and camels, and clothes. Then he returned to Achish.

¹⁰When Achish asked, "Where did you go raiding today?" David would say, "Against the Negev of Judah" or "Against the Negev of Jerahmeel" or "Against the Negev of the Kenites." ¹¹He did not leave a man or woman alive to be

brought to Gath, for he thought, "They might inform on us and say, 'This is what David did.'" And such was his practice as long as he lived in Philistine territory. ¹²Achish trusted David and said to himself, "He has become so odious to his people, the Israelites, that he will be my servant forever."

Saul and the Witch of Endor

28 In those days the Philistines gathered their forces to fight against Israel. Achish said to David, "You must understand that you and your men will accompany me in the army."

²David said, "Then you will see for yourself what your servant can do."

Achish replied, "Very well, I will make you my bodyguard for life."

³Now Samuel was dead, and all Israel had mourned for him and buried him in his own town of Ramah. Saul had expelled the mediums and spiritists from the land.

⁴The Philistines assembled and came and set up camp at Shunem, while Saul gathered all the

28:4 Battle Strategy

For their massive assault from Shunem, the Philistines tried a new tactic. They had fought previous battles in the mountains, rough terrain where their chariots were next to useless. Now they chose strategically important level ground that Israel had to defend. The Valley of Jezreel is the only part of Palestine where you can go from west to east without crossing mountains. A Philistine victory here would cut Israel in half.

Israelites and set up camp at Gilboa. ⁵When Saul saw the Philistine army, he was afraid; terror filled his heart. ⁶He inquired of the LORD, but the LORD did not answer him by dreams or Urim or prophets. ⁷Saul then said to his attendants, "Find me a woman who is a medium, so I may go and inquire of her."

"There is one in Endor," they said.

⁸So Saul disguised himself, putting on other clothes, and at night he and two men went to the woman. "Consult a spirit for me," he said, "and bring up for me the one I name."

⁹But the woman said to him, "Surely you know what Saul has done. He has cut off the mediums and spiritists from the land. Why have you set a trap for my life to bring about my death?"

¹⁰Saul swore to her by the LORD, "As surely

as the LORD lives, you will not be punished for this."

¹¹Then the woman asked, "Whom shall I bring up for you?"

"Bring up Samuel," he said.

¹²When the woman saw Samuel, she cried out at the top of her voice and said to Saul, "Why have you deceived me? You are Saul!"

28:12 The Witch of Endor

Consulting a medium or spiritist was forbidden (Leviticus 20:6,27; Deuteronomy 18:10–12), as Saul knew well. Earlier, he had banned mediums in the kingdom. But through his disobedience Saul had lost contact with God, and was desperate to know the future. Whether Samuel actually appeared or whether the woman faked it, the results were the same: Saul left more fearful than when he came.

¹³The king said to her, "Don't be afraid. What do you see?"

The woman said, "I see a spirit[a] coming up out of the ground."

¹⁴"What does he look like?" he asked.

"An old man wearing a robe is coming up," she said.

Then Saul knew it was Samuel, and he bowed down and prostrated himself with his face to the ground.

¹⁵Samuel said to Saul, "Why have you disturbed me by bringing me up?"

"I am in great distress," Saul said. "The Philistines are fighting against me, and God has turned away from me. He no longer answers me, either by prophets or by dreams. So I have called on you to tell me what to do."

¹⁶Samuel said, "Why do you consult me, now that the LORD has turned away from you and become your enemy? ¹⁷The LORD has done what he predicted through me. The LORD has torn the kingdom out of your hands and given it to one of your neighbors—to David. ¹⁸Because you did not obey the LORD or carry out his fierce wrath against the Amalekites, the LORD has done this to you today. ¹⁹The LORD will hand over both Israel and you to the Philistines, and tomorrow you and your sons will be with me. The LORD will also hand over the army of Israel to the Philistines."

²⁰Immediately Saul fell full length on the ground, filled with fear because of Samuel's words. His strength was gone, for he had eaten nothing all that day and night.

²¹When the woman came to Saul and saw that he was greatly shaken, she said, "Look, your

---

a 13 Or see spirits; or see gods

maidservant has obeyed you. I took my life in my hands and did what you told me to do. ²²Now please listen to your servant and let me give you some food so you may eat and have the strength to go on your way."

²³He refused and said, "I will not eat."

But his men joined the woman in urging him, and he listened to them. He got up from the ground and sat on the couch.

²⁴The woman had a fattened calf at the house, which she butchered at once. She took some flour, kneaded it and baked bread without yeast. ²⁵Then she set it before Saul and his men, and they ate. That same night they got up and left.

Achish Sends David Back to Ziklag

29 The Philistines gathered all their forces at Aphek, and Israel camped by the spring in Jezreel. ²As the Philistine rulers marched with their units of hundreds and thousands, David and his men were marching at the rear with Achish. ³The commanders of the Philistines asked, "What about these Hebrews?"

Achish replied, "Is this not David, who was an officer of Saul king of Israel? He has already been with me for over a year, and from the day he left Saul until now, I have found no fault in him."

⁴But the Philistine commanders were angry with him and said, "Send the man back, that he may return to the place you assigned him. He must not go with us into battle, or he will turn against us during the fighting. How better could he regain his master's favor than by taking the heads of our own men? ⁵Isn't this the David they sang about in their dances:

" 'Saul has slain his thousands,
    and David his tens of thousands'?"

⁶So Achish called David and said to him, "As surely as the LORD lives, you have been reliable, and I would be pleased to have you serve with me in the army. From the day you came to me until now, I have found no fault in you, but the rulers don't approve of you. ⁷Turn back and go in peace; do nothing to displease the Philistine rulers."

⁸"But what have I done?" asked David. "What have you found against your servant from the day I came to you until now? Why can't I go and fight against the enemies of my lord the king?"

⁹Achish answered, "I know that you have been as pleasing in my eyes as an angel of God; nevertheless, the Philistine commanders have said, 'He must not go up with us into battle.' ¹⁰Now get up early, along with your master's servants who have come with you, and leave in the morning as soon as it is light."

¹¹So David and his men got up early in the morning to go back to the land of the Philistines, and the Philistines went up to Jezreel.

David Destroys the Amalekites

30 David and his men reached Ziklag on the third day. Now the Amalekites had raided the Negev and Ziklag. They had attacked Ziklag

29:8 Faking It

For the sake of survival, David had become a mercenary in the Philistine army. But he had not yet fought against his own people, and it is doubtful that he would have done so. Now, dismissed from service because he wasn't trusted in the upcoming battle, David acted distressed. Was he genuinely upset? It's quite possible he had hoped to turn the tables against the Philistines by attacking them from behind their own lines. The Philistine commanders made a shrewd move in sending him off.

and burned it, ²and had taken captive the women and all who were in it, both young and old. They killed none of them, but carried them off as they went on their way.

³When David and his men came to Ziklag, they found it destroyed by fire and their wives and sons and daughters taken captive. ⁴So David and his men wept aloud until they had no strength left to weep. ⁵David's two wives had been captured—Ahinoam of Jezreel and Abigail, the widow of Nabal of Carmel. ⁶David was greatly distressed because the men were talking of stoning him; each one was bitter in spirit because of his sons and daughters. But David found strength in the LORD his God.

⁷Then David said to Abiathar the priest, the son of Ahimelech, "Bring me the ephod." Abiathar brought it to him, ⁸and David inquired of the LORD, "Shall I pursue this raiding party? Will I overtake them?"

"Pursue them," he answered. "You will certainly overtake them and succeed in the rescue."

⁹David and the six hundred men with him came to the Besor Ravine, where some stayed behind, ¹⁰for two hundred men were too exhausted to cross the ravine. But David and four hundred men continued the pursuit.

¹¹They found an Egyptian in a field and brought him to David. They gave him water to drink and food to eat— ¹²part of a cake of pressed figs and two cakes of raisins. He ate and was revived, for he had not eaten any food or drunk any water for three days and three nights.

¹³David asked him, "To whom do you belong, and where do you come from?"

He said, "I am an Egyptian, the slave of an Amalekite. My master abandoned me when I became ill three days ago. ¹⁴We raided the Negev of the Kerethites and the territory belonging to Judah and the Negev of Caleb. And we burned Ziklag."

¹⁵David asked him, "Can you lead me down to this raiding party?"

He answered, "Swear to me before God that you will not kill me or hand me over to my master, and I will take you down to them."

¹⁶He led David down, and there they were, scattered over the countryside, eating, drinking and reveling because of the great amount of plunder they had taken from the land of the Philistines and from Judah. ¹⁷David fought them from dusk until the evening of the next day, and none of them got away, except four hundred young men who rode off on camels and fled. ¹⁸David recovered everything the Amalekites had taken, including his two wives. ¹⁹Nothing was missing: young or old, boy or girl, plunder or anything else they had taken. David brought everything back. ²⁰He took all the flocks and herds, and his men drove them ahead of the other livestock, saying, "This is David's plunder."

²¹Then David came to the two hundred men who had been too exhausted to follow him and who were left behind at the Besor Ravine. They came out to meet David and the people with him. As David and his men approached, he greeted them. ²²But all the evil men and troublemakers among David's followers said, "Because they did not go out with us, we will not share with them the plunder we recovered. However, each man may take his wife and children and go."

²³David replied, "No, my brothers, you must not do that with what the LORD has given us. He has protected us and handed over to us the forces that came against us. ²⁴Who will listen to what you say? The share of the man who stayed with the supplies is to be the same as that of him who went down to the battle. All will share alike." ²⁵David made this a statute and ordinance for Israel from that day to this.

²⁶When David arrived in Ziklag, he sent some of the plunder to the elders of Judah, who were his friends, saying, "Here is a present for you from the plunder of the LORD's enemies."

²⁷He sent it to those who were in Bethel, Ramoth Negev and Jattir; ²⁸to those in Aroer, Siphmoth, Eshtemoa ²⁹and Racal; to those in the towns of the Jerahmeelites and the Kenites; ³⁰to those in Hormah, Bor Ashan, Athach ³¹and Hebron; and to those in all the other places where David and his men had roamed.

Saul Takes His Life

31 Now the Philistines fought against Israel; the Israelites fled before them, and many fell slain on Mount Gilboa. ²The Philistines pressed hard after Saul and his sons, and they killed his sons Jonathan, Abinadab and Malki-Shua. ³The fighting grew fierce around Saul, and when the archers overtook him, they wounded him critically.

⁴Saul said to his armor-bearer, "Draw your sword and run me through, or these uncircumcised fellows will come and run me through and abuse me."

But his armor-bearer was terrified and would not do it; so Saul took his own sword and fell on it. ⁵When the armor-bearer saw that Saul was dead, he too fell on his sword and died with him. ⁶So Saul and his three sons and his armor-bearer and all his men died together that same day.

⁷When the Israelites along the valley and those across the Jordan saw that the Israelite army had fled and that Saul and his sons had died, they abandoned their towns and fled. And the Philistines came and occupied them.

⁸The next day, when the Philistines came to strip the dead, they found Saul and his three sons fallen on Mount Gilboa. ⁹They cut off his head and stripped off his armor, and they sent messengers throughout the land of the Philistines to proclaim the news in the temple of their idols and among their people. ¹⁰They put his armor in the temple of the Ashtoreths and fastened his body to the wall of Beth Shan.

¹¹When the people of Jabesh Gilead heard of

31:11 Loyal Friends in Death

Saul's first military action as king had been the rescue of Jabesh Gilead (chapter 11). Through all these years its citizens had not forgotten. When they heard of the disgraceful display of Saul's and his sons' bodies, they undertook a dangerous night mission to steal the bodies and give them proper burial.

what the Philistines had done to Saul, ¹²all their valiant men journeyed through the night to Beth Shan. They took down the bodies of Saul and his sons from the wall of Beth Shan and went to Jabesh, where they burned them. ¹³Then they took their bones and buried them under a tamarisk tree at Jabesh, and they fasted seven days.

2 SAMUEL

The Life of King David
From herding sheep to ruling a nation

THE BIBLE IS FILLED WITH strong personalities, but none leads David in the parade. His life was a whirlwind, from which striking images flash. We see him playing his harp, writing poems, fighting battles, faking insanity, dancing jubilantly in praise of God. We watch his tear-streaked face when he learns of his closest friend's death. We see him on his rooftop, gazing down lustfully on Bathsheba's bath. We see Nathan point his finger at him, accusing him of adultery and murder. We hear David's guilty, anguished voice crying to God for the life of his infant child. We see David's bowed head as he stumbles out of Jerusalem, pursued by his murderous son.

> "'I took you from the pasture and from following the flock to be ruler over my people Israel.'"
> 7:8

David survived the crises of a dozen lives. Somehow he always bounced back. Somehow he maintained a passionate trust in God. First and Second Samuel don't paint him as a flawless character, nor as a perfect model of strength and courage. David had striking weaknesses. Yet he appeals to us as he did to the Israelites: He was completely, passionately alive. Whatever he did, right or wrong, he did with his whole heart. In his love for God, he held nothing back.

Healing the Wounds of War

While 1 Samuel tells of David's youth and his long exile, 2 Samuel focuses on David as king, leading, uniting, inspiring his people. His time in the desert was over. Different qualities of leadership were required in a king.

David inherited a country in tatters. His fellow southerners recognized him as the new king. But Saul's son, backed by a powerful general, launched a civil war for the throne. Ugly infighting followed: intrigue, murder, and treachery.

Even after David's rivals were eliminated, peace was uneasy. Unless David could heal the wounds of war, resentment might smolder in the hearts of the northerners. David's decisive action showed wisdom and firmness. He justly punished murderers who expected his gratitude. He showed respect for his enemies by mourning their deaths. From his first day in office David behaved as the king of all the people, not just his loyal followers. The northern tribes soon came over to him, submitting to his leadership (5:1–3).

David's next move was to capture Jerusalem. People said it couldn't be done; mountainous Jerusalem was impregnable. David did it, and made Jerusalem his new political and religious capital. Located on the border between north and south, Jerusalem symbolized a new national unity based on trust in God.

That was just the beginning. David led the unified tribes to do what they had barely dreamed of: They defeated the dreaded Philistines once and for all. Almost overnight the tiny, threatened nation of Israel became safe. Secure borders encouraged expanded trade, and Israel boomed. (David's son Solomon reaped most of the wealth from this.) Naturally, David's popularity increased.

A Murderer and an Adulterer

But David's reign held ironic tragedies, too. Second Samuel makes no effort to hide them. David could lead a nation but not his own children. His ineffective parenting nearly destroyed all he had done, when his heartless son Absalom led a rebellion. Second Samuel portrays David without retouching his blemishes: He was a murderer and an adulterer and a leader capable of cruelty.

Nevertheless, he was Israel's greatest king. Even at his lowest points, his great strength of character showed. He was never vengeful with his enemies. He took full responsibility for his mistakes. He managed to remember that he had started out as a mere shepherd. He held power only by the grace of God—and he believed that God had every right to take power away.

Through his love for God and his sense of astonished gratefulness for what God had done for him, David became a living embodiment of the Israel God wanted. Like all truly great leaders, he made his country thrive not just by what he did, but by who he was.

How to Read 2 Samuel

econd Samuel continues, without a break, the story begun in 1 Samuel—the two were originally one book. The difference is that David, who once sought only to survive, now seeks to unify a badly divided country. His greater responsibilities put extra stress on his leadership qualities. You can study his life with leadership in mind. You can also study chapters 11—20 to see the cancerous effects of a leader's private sins and poor family leadership.

Chapters 21—24 seem to be an appendix, bringing in other important events and facts of David's reign. Much of 2 Samuel's story is also told in 1 Chronicles 11—21, often word for word the same.

PEOPLE YOU'LL MEET IN 2 SAMUEL

DAVID (p. 331)
ABNER (p. 335)
NATHAN (p. 339)

BATHSHEBA (p. 342)
ABSALOM (p. 348)

3-TRACK READING PLAN

For an explanation and complete listing of the 3-track reading plan, turn to page 7.

TRACK 1:　**Two-Week Courses on the Bible**
The Track 1 reading program on the Old Testament includes two chapters from 2 Samuel. See page 8 for a complete listing of this course.

TRACK 2:　**An Overview of 2 Samuel in 3 Days**
☐ Day 1. Read the Introduction to 2 Samuel and chapter 6, in which the ark of the covenant was brought to Jerusalem and David danced before the Lord.
☐ Day 2. Read chapter 11, in which David's adultery with Bathsheba led to murder.
☐ Day 3. Read chapter 12 for the dramatic account of the prophet Nathan coming to confront David.

Now turn to page 9 for your next Track 2 reading project.

TRACK 3:　**All of 2 Samuel in 24 Days**
After you have read through 2 Samuel, turn to pages 10—14 for your next Track 3 reading project.

☐1	☐2	☐3	☐4	☐5	☐6	☐7	☐8
☐9	☐10	☐11	☐12	☐13	☐14	☐15	☐16
☐17	☐18	☐19	☐20	☐21	☐22	☐23	☐24

David Hears of Saul's Death

1 After the death of Saul, David returned from defeating the Amalekites and stayed in Ziklag two days. ²On the third day a man arrived from Saul's camp, with his clothes torn and with dust on his head. When he came to David, he fell to the ground to pay him honor.

³"Where have you come from?" David asked him.

He answered, "I have escaped from the Israelite camp."

⁴"What happened?" David asked. "Tell me."

He said, "The men fled from the battle. Many of them fell and died. And Saul and his son Jonathan are dead."

⁵Then David said to the young man who brought him the report, "How do you know that Saul and his son Jonathan are dead?"

⁶"I happened to be on Mount Gilboa," the young man said, "and there was Saul, leaning on his spear, with the chariots and riders almost upon him. ⁷When he turned around and saw me, he called out to me, and I said, 'What can I do?'

⁸"He asked me, 'Who are you?'

"'An Amalekite,' I answered.

⁹"Then he said to me, 'Stand over me and kill me! I am in the throes of death, but I'm still alive.'

¹⁰"So I stood over him and killed him, because I knew that after he had fallen he could not survive. And I took the crown that was on his head and the band on his arm and have brought them here to my lord."

¹¹Then David and all the men with him took hold of their clothes and tore them. ¹²They mourned and wept and fasted till evening for Saul and his son Jonathan, and for the army of the LORD and the house of Israel, because they had fallen by the sword.

¹³David said to the young man who brought him the report, "Where are you from?"

"I am the son of an alien, an Amalekite," he answered.

¹⁴David asked him, "Why were you not afraid to lift your hand to destroy the LORD's anointed?"

¹⁵Then David called one of his men and said, "Go, strike him down!" So he struck him down, and he died. ¹⁶For David had said to him, "Your blood be on your own head. Your own mouth testified against you when you said, 'I killed the LORD's anointed.'"

David's Lament for Saul and Jonathan

¹⁷David took up this lament concerning Saul and his son Jonathan, ¹⁸and ordered that the men of Judah be taught this lament of the bow (it is written in the Book of Jashar):

¹⁹"Your glory, O Israel, lies slain on your heights.
　　How the mighty have fallen!

²⁰"Tell it not in Gath,
　　proclaim it not in the streets of Ashkelon,
lest the daughters of the Philistines be glad,
　　lest the daughters of the uncircumcised rejoice.

²¹"O mountains of Gilboa,
　　may you have neither dew nor rain,
　　nor fields that yield offerings ⌊of grain⌋.
For there the shield of the mighty was defiled,
　　the shield of Saul—no longer rubbed with oil.

²²From the blood of the slain,
　　from the flesh of the mighty,
the bow of Jonathan did not turn back,
　　the sword of Saul did not return unsatisfied.

²³"Saul and Jonathan—
　　in life they were loved and gracious,
　　and in death they were not parted.
They were swifter than eagles,
　　they were stronger than lions.

²⁴"O daughters of Israel,
　　weep for Saul,
who clothed you in scarlet and finery,
　　who adorned your garments with ornaments of gold.

²⁵"How the mighty have fallen in battle!
　　Jonathan lies slain on your heights.
²⁶I grieve for you, Jonathan my brother;
　　you were very dear to me.
Your love for me was wonderful,
　　more wonderful than that of women.

²⁷"How the mighty have fallen!
　　The weapons of war have perished!"

David Anointed King Over Judah

2 In the course of time, David inquired of the LORD. "Shall I go up to one of the towns of Judah?" he asked.

The LORD said, "Go up."

David asked, "Where shall I go?"

"To Hebron," the LORD answered.

²So David went up there with his two wives, Ahinoam of Jezreel and Abigail, the widow of Nabal of Carmel. ³David also took the men who were with him, each with his family, and they settled in Hebron and its towns. ⁴Then the men of Judah came to Hebron and there they anointed David king over the house of Judah.

When David was told that it was the men of Jabesh Gilead who had buried Saul, ⁵he sent messengers to the men of Jabesh Gilead to say to them, "The LORD bless you for showing this

kindness to Saul your master by burying him.
[6]May the Lord now show you kindness and
faithfulness, and I too will show you the same
favor because you have done this. [7]Now then, be

2:5 Potential Rivals

*For their own security, dictators try to eliminate
all competitors. In the ancient world, rulers did
the same: A new king customarily killed the
former king's relatives, since they were
potential rivals. Not David! He executed the
man who claimed to have killed his old enemy
King Saul (1:14–15), he sang a painful lament
over Saul's and Jonathan's deaths, and he
blessed the people of Jabesh Gilead for their
kindness in giving Saul a decent burial. David
never abandoned his love for Saul's family.*

strong and brave, for Saul your master is dead,
and the house of Judah has anointed me king
over them."

War Between the Houses of David and Saul

[8]Meanwhile, Abner son of Ner, the commander of Saul's army, had taken Ish-Bosheth son of
Saul and brought him over to Mahanaim. [9]He
made him king over Gilead, Ashuri[a] and Jezreel,
and also over Ephraim, Benjamin and all Israel.

[10]Ish-Bosheth son of Saul was forty years old
when he became king over Israel, and he reigned
two years. The house of Judah, however, followed
David. [11]The length of time David was king in
Hebron over the house of Judah was seven years
and six months.

[12]Abner son of Ner, together with the men of
Ish-Bosheth son of Saul, left Mahanaim and went
to Gibeon. [13]Joab son of Zeruiah and David's
men went out and met them at the pool of Gibeon. One group sat down on one side of the pool
and one group on the other side.

[14]Then Abner said to Joab, "Let's have some of
the young men get up and fight hand to hand in
front of us."

"All right, let them do it," Joab said.

[15]So they stood up and were counted off—
twelve men for Benjamin and Ish-Bosheth son of
Saul, and twelve for David. [16]Then each man
grabbed his opponent by the head and thrust his
dagger into his opponent's side, and they fell
down together. So that place in Gibeon was called
Helkath Hazzurim.[b]

[17]The battle that day was very fierce, and Abner and the men of Israel were defeated by David's men.

[18]The three sons of Zeruiah were there: Joab,
Abishai and Asahel. Now Asahel was as fleet-
footed as a wild gazelle. [19]He chased Abner, turning neither to the right nor to the left as he pursued him. [20]Abner looked behind him and asked,
"Is that you, Asahel?"

"It is," he answered.

[21]Then Abner said to him, "Turn aside to the
right or to the left; take on one of the young men
and strip him of his weapons." But Asahel would
not stop chasing him.

[22]Again Abner warned Asahel, "Stop chasing
me! Why should I strike you down? How could
I look your brother Joab in the face?"

[23]But Asahel refused to give up the pursuit; so
Abner thrust the butt of his spear into Asahel's
stomach, and the spear came out through his
back. He fell there and died on the spot. And
every man stopped when he came to the place
where Asahel had fallen and died.

[24]But Joab and Abishai pursued Abner, and as
the sun was setting, they came to the hill of Ammah, near Giah on the way to the wasteland of
Gibeon. [25]Then the men of Benjamin rallied behind Abner. They formed themselves into a
group and took their stand on top of a hill.

[26]Abner called out to Joab, "Must the sword
devour forever? Don't you realize that this will
end in bitterness? How long before you order
your men to stop pursuing their brothers?"

[27]Joab answered, "As surely as God lives, if
you had not spoken, the men would have continued the pursuit of their brothers until morning.[c]"

[28]So Joab blew the trumpet, and all the men
came to a halt; they no longer pursued Israel, nor
did they fight anymore.

[29]All that night Abner and his men marched
through the Arabah. They crossed the Jordan,
continued through the whole Bithron[d] and
came to Mahanaim.

[30]Then Joab returned from pursuing Abner
and assembled all his men. Besides Asahel, nine-
teen of David's men were found missing. [31]But
David's men had killed three hundred and sixty
Benjamites who were with Abner. [32]They took
Asahel and buried him in his father's tomb at
Bethlehem. Then Joab and his men marched all
night and arrived at Hebron by daybreak.

3 The war between the house of Saul and the
house of David lasted a long time. David
grew stronger and stronger, while the house of
Saul grew weaker and weaker.

[2]Sons were born to David in Hebron:

His firstborn was Amnon the son of
Ahinoam of Jezreel;

---

[a]9 Or *Asher*   [b]16 *Helkath Hazzurim* means *field of daggers* or *field of hostilities.*   [c]27 Or *spoken this morning, the
men would not have taken up the pursuit of their brothers;* or *spoken, the men would have given up the pursuit of their
brothers by morning*   [d]29 Or *morning;* or *ravine;* the meaning of the Hebrew for this word is uncertain.

³his second, Kileab the son of Abigail the widow of Nabal of Carmel;

the third, Absalom the son of Maacah daughter of Talmai king of Geshur;

⁴the fourth, Adonijah the son of Haggith;

the fifth, Shephatiah the son of Abital;

⁵and the sixth, Ithream the son of David's wife Eglah.

These were born to David in Hebron.

Abner Goes Over to David

⁶During the war between the house of Saul and the house of David, Abner had been strengthening his own position in the house of Saul. ⁷Now Saul had had a concubine named Rizpah daughter of Aiah. And Ish-Bosheth said to Abner, "Why did you sleep with my father's concubine?"

⁸Abner was very angry because of what Ish-Bosheth said and he answered, "Am I a dog's head—on Judah's side? This very day I am loyal to the house of your father Saul and to his family and friends. I haven't handed you over to David. Yet now you accuse me of an offense involving this woman! ⁹May God deal with Abner, be it ever so severely, if I do not do for David what the LORD promised him on oath ¹⁰and transfer the kingdom from the house of Saul and establish David's throne over Israel and Judah from Dan to Beersheba." ¹¹Ish-Bosheth did not dare to say another word to Abner, because he was afraid of him.

¹²Then Abner sent messengers on his behalf to say to David, "Whose land is it? Make an agreement with me, and I will help you bring all Israel over to you."

¹³"Good," said David. "I will make an agreement with you. But I demand one thing of you: Do not come into my presence unless you bring Michal daughter of Saul when you come to see

3:7 Women in Politics

In David's time, women were political symbols. Abner's sleeping with Saul's concubine would have suggested that he had his eyes on becoming king himself. Later, when Absalom drove his father David out of Jerusalem, he slept with David's concubines in public, demonstrating to all eyes that he had taken over from his father (16:22).

David sometimes may have married for political benefit. One wife, Absalom's mother (verse 3), was a princess from a neighboring country; the marriage undoubtedly promoted good foreign relations. David's request that Michal be returned to him (though she had remarried, verses 14–16) made political sense: an alliance with Saul's daughter would tie Saul's family to the palace.

me." ¹⁴Then David sent messengers to Ish-Bosheth son of Saul, demanding, "Give me my wife Michal, whom I betrothed to myself for the price of a hundred Philistine foreskins."

¹⁵So Ish-Bosheth gave orders and had her taken away from her husband Paltiel son of Laish. ¹⁶Her husband, however, went with her, weeping behind her all the way to Bahurim. Then Abner said to him, "Go back home!" So he went back.

¹⁷Abner conferred with the elders of Israel and said, "For some time you have wanted to make

ABNER *On the Wrong Side*

WAR IS NEVER PRETTY, AND neither are most of the soldiers who fight it. Famous generals such as Rommel, Sherman, Lee or Patton do not always stand for great causes or great morals. They earn respect for their ability to lead men into battle, to kill and to triumph.

Abner was a fine general who fought most of his life for a bad king. Though he introduced David to King Saul (1 Samuel 17:55–58) and commanded David during his early campaigns, Abner ultimately followed Saul's orders and fought against David. During the years when David's band of outlaws was roaming the hills, Abner led the hunt to track them down. Along the way he and David won mutual respect as honorable enemies.

Even after Saul died, Abner remained loyal to the forces arrayed against David. He installed Saul's son as king and fought a long civil war against David's side. Abner died not from battle but from treachery. Joab, David's general, had never forgiven Abner for killing his brother. When Abner finally came to make peace with David, Joab saw his opportunity for revenge. Pretending to conference with Abner, he stuck a knife in him (3:27).

David denounced this act of treachery and gave his former enemy a state funeral. Abner, he said, was a "prince and a great man" (3:38). Israel would need more such soldiers, people who combined war-making skill with loyalty to their king.

Life Questions: Can you think of any sincere men or women today who are passionately fighting on the wrong side of an important cause?

David your king. [18]Now do it! For the LORD promised David, 'By my servant David I will rescue my people Israel from the hand of the Philistines and from the hand of all their enemies.'"

[19]Abner also spoke to the Benjamites in person. Then he went to Hebron to tell David everything that Israel and the whole house of Benjamin wanted to do. [20]When Abner, who had twenty men with him, came to David at Hebron, David prepared a feast for him and his men. [21]Then Abner said to David, "Let me go at once and assemble all Israel for my lord the king, so that they may make a compact with you, and that you may rule over all that your heart desires." So David sent Abner away, and he went in peace.

Joab Murders Abner

[22]Just then David's men and Joab returned from a raid and brought with them a great deal of plunder. But Abner was no longer with David in Hebron, because David had sent him away, and he had gone in peace. [23]When Joab and all the soldiers with him arrived, he was told that Abner son of Ner had come to the king and that the king had sent him away and that he had gone in peace.

[24]So Joab went to the king and said, "What have you done? Look, Abner came to you. Why did you let him go? Now he is gone! [25]You know Abner son of Ner; he came to deceive you and observe your movements and find out everything you are doing."

[26]Joab then left David and sent messengers after Abner, and they brought him back from the well of Sirah. But David did not know it. [27]Now when Abner returned to Hebron, Joab took him aside into the gateway, as though to speak with him privately. And there, to avenge the blood of his brother Asahel, Joab stabbed him in the stomach, and he died.

[28]Later, when David heard about this, he said, "I and my kingdom are forever innocent before the LORD concerning the blood of Abner son of Ner. [29]May his blood fall upon the head of Joab and upon all his father's house! May Joab's house never be without someone who has a running sore or leprosy[a] or who leans on a crutch or who falls by the sword or who lacks food."

[30](Joab and his brother Abishai murdered Abner because he had killed their brother Asahel in the battle at Gibeon.)

[31]Then David said to Joab and all the people with him, "Tear your clothes and put on sackcloth and walk in mourning in front of Abner." King David himself walked behind the bier. [32]They buried Abner in Hebron, and the king wept aloud at Abner's tomb. All the people wept also.

[33]The king sang this lament for Abner:

"Should Abner have died as the lawless die?
[34]   Your hands were not bound,
       your feet were not fettered.
   You fell as one falls before wicked men."

3:30 Easy on Joab

Though General Douglas MacArthur had been popular and effective during World War II, he opposed the President's Korean War policy, and finally Harry Truman fired him. David faced a similar dilemma, but made a different decision. After David had made peace with Abner, a former enemy, David's commander Joab tricked and murdered Abner. This undercut David's policy of bringing harmony to a divided land. Although David cursed Joab, he didn't punish him or strip away his power. Why not? Perhaps he needed Joab's abilities, and feared what Joab might do if alienated. Many years later, when David lay dying, he instructed Solomon to punish Joab for the crime (1 Kings 2:5–6).

And all the people wept over him again.

[35]Then they all came and urged David to eat something while it was still day; but David took an oath, saying, "May God deal with me, be it ever so severely, if I taste bread or anything else before the sun sets!"

[36]All the people took note and were pleased; indeed, everything the king did pleased them. [37]So on that day all the people and all Israel knew that the king had no part in the murder of Abner son of Ner.

[38]Then the king said to his men, "Do you not realize that a prince and a great man has fallen in Israel this day? [39]And today, though I am the anointed king, I am weak, and these sons of Zeruiah are too strong for me. May the LORD repay the evildoer according to his evil deeds!"

Ish-Bosheth Murdered

4 When Ish-Bosheth son of Saul heard that Abner had died in Hebron, he lost courage, and all Israel became alarmed. [2]Now Saul's son had two men who were leaders of raiding bands. One was named Baanah and the other Recab; they were sons of Rimmon the Beerothite from the tribe of Benjamin—Beeroth is considered part of Benjamin, [3]because the people of Beeroth fled to Gittaim and have lived there as aliens to this day.

[4](Jonathan son of Saul had a son who was lame in both feet. He was five years old when the news about Saul and Jonathan came from Jezreel.

---

[a]29 The Hebrew word was used for various diseases affecting the skin—not necessarily leprosy.

His nurse picked him up and fled, but as she hurried to leave, he fell and became crippled. His name was Mephibosheth.)

⁵Now Recab and Baanah, the sons of Rimmon the Beerothite, set out for the house of Ish-Bosheth, and they arrived there in the heat of the day while he was taking his noonday rest. ⁶They went into the inner part of the house as if to get some wheat, and they stabbed him in the stomach. Then Recab and his brother Baanah slipped away.

⁷They had gone into the house while he was lying on the bed in his bedroom. After they stabbed and killed him, they cut off his head. Taking it with them, they traveled all night by way of the Arabah. ⁸They brought the head of Ish-Bosheth to David at Hebron and said to the king, "Here is the head of Ish-Bosheth son of Saul, your enemy, who tried to take your life. This day the LORD has avenged my lord the king against Saul and his offspring."

⁹David answered Recab and his brother Baanah, the sons of Rimmon the Beerothite, "As surely as the LORD lives, who has delivered me out of all trouble, ¹⁰when a man told me, 'Saul is dead,' and thought he was bringing good news, I seized him and put him to death in Ziklag. That was the reward I gave him for his news! ¹¹How much more—when wicked men have killed an innocent man in his own house and on his own bed—should I not now demand his blood from your hand and rid the earth of you!"

¹²So David gave an order to his men, and they killed them. They cut off their hands and feet and hung the bodies by the pool in Hebron. But they took the head of Ish-Bosheth and buried it in Abner's tomb at Hebron.

David Becomes King Over Israel

5 All the tribes of Israel came to David at Hebron and said, "We are your own flesh and blood. ²In the past, while Saul was king over us, you were the one who led Israel on their military campaigns. And the LORD said to you, 'You will shepherd my people Israel, and you will become their ruler.'"

³When all the elders of Israel had come to King David at Hebron, the king made a compact with them at Hebron before the LORD, and they anointed David king over Israel.

⁴David was thirty years old when he became king, and he reigned forty years. ⁵In Hebron he reigned over Judah seven years and six months, and in Jerusalem he reigned over all Israel and Judah thirty-three years.

David Conquers Jerusalem

⁶The king and his men marched to Jerusalem to attack the Jebusites, who lived there. The Jebusites said to David, "You will not get in here; even the blind and the lame can ward you off." They thought, "David cannot get in here." ⁷Nevertheless, David captured the fortress of Zion, the City of David.

5:6 Choosing a Capital

In trying to unify the northern and southern tribes, David wanted a capital that offended neither side. He found it in Jerusalem, on the border between North and South and belonging to neither. Its choice can be compared to the U.S. capital, Washington, D.C., a compromise between North and South.

⁸On that day, David said, "Anyone who conquers the Jebusites will have to use the water shaft*ᵃ* to reach those 'lame and blind' who are David's enemies.*ᵇ*" That is why they say, "The 'blind and lame' will not enter the palace."

⁹David then took up residence in the fortress and called it the City of David. He built up the area around it, from the supporting terraces*ᶜ* inward. ¹⁰And he became more and more powerful, because the LORD God Almighty was with him.

¹¹Now Hiram king of Tyre sent messengers to David, along with cedar logs and carpenters and stonemasons, and they built a palace for David. ¹²And David knew that the LORD had established him as king over Israel and had exalted his kingdom for the sake of his people Israel.

¹³After he left Hebron, David took more concubines and wives in Jerusalem, and more sons and daughters were born to him. ¹⁴These are the names of the children born to him there: Shammua, Shobab, Nathan, Solomon, ¹⁵Ibhar, Elishua, Nepheg, Japhia, ¹⁶Elishama, Eliada and Eliphelet.

David Defeats the Philistines

¹⁷When the Philistines heard that David had been anointed king over Israel, they went up in full force to search for him, but David heard about it and went down to the stronghold. ¹⁸Now the Philistines had come and spread out in the Valley of Rephaim; ¹⁹so David inquired of the LORD, "Shall I go and attack the Philistines? Will you hand them over to me?"

The LORD answered him, "Go, for I will surely hand the Philistines over to you."

²⁰So David went to Baal Perazim, and there he defeated them. He said, "As waters break out, the LORD has broken out against my enemies before me." So that place was called Baal Perazim.*ᵈ*

ᵃ8 Or *use scaling hooks*   *ᵇ8* Or *are hated by David*   *ᶜ9* Or *the Millo*   *ᵈ20* *Baal Perazim means the lord who breaks out.*

²¹The Philistines abandoned their idols there, and David and his men carried them off.

²²Once more the Philistines came up and spread out in the Valley of Rephaim; ²³so David

inquired of the LORD, and he answered, "Do not go straight up, but circle around behind them and attack them in front of the balsam trees. ²⁴As soon as you hear the sound of marching in the tops of the balsam trees, move quickly, because that will mean the LORD has gone out in front of you to strike the Philistine army." ²⁵So David did as the LORD commanded him, and he struck down the Philistines all the way from Gibeon[a] to Gezer.

The Ark Brought to Jerusalem

6 David again brought together out of Israel chosen men, thirty thousand in all. ²He and all his men set out from Baalah of Judah[b] to bring up from there the ark of God, which is called by the Name,[c] the name of the LORD Almighty, who is enthroned between the cherubim that are on the ark. ³They set the ark of God on a new cart and brought it from the house of Abinadab, which was on the hill. Uzzah and Ahio, sons of Abinadab, were guiding the new cart ⁴with the ark of God on it,[d] and Ahio was walking in front of it. ⁵David and the whole house of Israel were celebrating with all their might before the LORD, with songs[e] and with harps, lyres, tambourines, sistrums and cymbals.

⁶When they came to the threshing floor of Nacon, Uzzah reached out and took hold of the ark of God, because the oxen stumbled. ⁷The LORD's anger burned against Uzzah because of his irreverent act; therefore God struck him down and he died there beside the ark of God.

⁸Then David was angry because the LORD's wrath had broken out against Uzzah, and to this day that place is called Perez Uzzah.[f]

⁹David was afraid of the LORD that day and said, "How can the ark of the LORD ever come to me?" ¹⁰He was not willing to take the ark of the

LORD to be with him in the City of David. Instead, he took it aside to the house of Obed-Edom the Gittite. ¹¹The ark of the LORD remained in the house of Obed-Edom the Gittite for three months, and the LORD blessed him and his entire household.

¹²Now King David was told, "The LORD has blessed the household of Obed-Edom and everything he has, because of the ark of God." So David went down and brought up the ark of God from the house of Obed-Edom to the City of David with rejoicing. ¹³When those who were carrying the ark of the LORD had taken six steps, he sacrificed a bull and a fattened calf. ¹⁴David, wearing a linen ephod, danced before the LORD with all his might, ¹⁵while he and the entire house of Israel brought up the ark of the LORD with shouts and the sound of trumpets.

¹⁶As the ark of the LORD was entering the City of David, Michal daughter of Saul watched from a window. And when she saw King David leaping and dancing before the LORD, she despised him in her heart.

¹⁷They brought the ark of the LORD and set it in its place inside the tent that David had pitched for it, and David sacrificed burnt offerings and fellowship offerings[g] before the LORD. ¹⁸After he had finished sacrificing the burnt offerings and fellowship offerings, he blessed the people in the name of the LORD Almighty. ¹⁹Then he gave a loaf of bread, a cake of dates and a cake of raisins to each person in the whole crowd of Israelites, both men and women. And all the people went to their homes.

²⁰When David returned home to bless his household, Michal daughter of Saul came out to meet him and said, "How the king of Israel has distinguished himself today, disrobing in the sight of the slave girls of his servants as any vulgar fellow would!"

²¹David said to Michal, "It was before the LORD, who chose me rather than your father or anyone from his house when he appointed me ruler over the LORD's people Israel—I will celebrate before the LORD. ²²I will become even more undignified than this, and I will be humiliated in my own eyes. But by these slave girls you spoke of, I will be held in honor."

²³And Michal daughter of Saul had no children to the day of her death.

God's Promise to David

7 After the king was settled in his palace and the LORD had given him rest from all his

---

[a]25 Septuagint (see also 1 Chron. 14:16); Hebrew *Geba*   [b]2 That is, Kiriath Jearim; Hebrew *Baale Judah*, a variant of *Baalah of Judah*   [c]2 Hebrew; Septuagint and Vulgate do not have *the Name*.   [d]3,4 Dead Sea Scrolls and some Septuagint manuscripts; Masoretic Text *cart* ⁴*and they brought it with the ark of God from the house of Abinadab, which was on the hill*   [e]5 See Dead Sea Scrolls, Septuagint and 1 Chronicles 13:8; Masoretic Text *celebrating before the LORD with all kinds of instruments made of pine.*   [f]8 *Perez Uzzah* means *outbreak against Uzzah.*   [g]17 Traditionally *peace offerings*; also in verse 18

enemies around him, ²he said to Nathan the prophet, "Here I am, living in a palace of cedar, while the ark of God remains in a tent."

³Nathan replied to the king, "Whatever you have in mind, go ahead and do it, for the LORD is with you."

⁴That night the word of the LORD came to Nathan, saying:

⁵"Go and tell my servant David, 'This is what the LORD says: Are you the one to build me a house to dwell in? ⁶I have not dwelt in a house from the day I brought the Israelites up out of Egypt to this day. I have been moving from place to place with a tent as my dwelling. ⁷Wherever I have moved with all the Israelites, did I ever say to any of their rulers whom I commanded to shepherd my people Israel, "Why have you not built me a house of cedar?" '

⁸"Now then, tell my servant David, 'This is what the LORD Almighty says: I took you from the pasture and from following the flock to be ruler over my people Israel. ⁹I have been with you wherever you have gone, and I have cut off all your enemies from before you. Now I will make your name great, like the names of the greatest men of the earth. ¹⁰And I will provide a place for my people Israel and will plant them so that they can have a home of their own and no longer be disturbed. Wicked people will not oppress them anymore, as they did at the beginning ¹¹and have done ever since the time I appointed leaders*a* over my people Israel. I will also give you rest from all your enemies.

" 'The LORD declares to you that the LORD himself will establish a house for you: ¹²When your days are over and you rest with your fathers, I will raise up your offspring to succeed you, who will come from your own body, and I will establish his kingdom. ¹³He is the one who will build a house for my Name, and I will establish the throne of his kingdom forever. ¹⁴I will be his father, and he will be my son. When he does wrong, I will punish him with the rod of men, with floggings inflicted by men. ¹⁵But my love will never be taken away from him, as I took it away from Saul, whom I removed from before you. ¹⁶Your house and your kingdom will endure forever before me*b*; your throne will be established forever.' "

¹⁷Nathan reported to David all the words of this entire revelation.

David's Prayer

¹⁸Then King David went in and sat before the LORD, and he said:

"Who am I, O Sovereign LORD, and

---

a11 Traditionally *judges*   *b16* Some Hebrew manuscripts and Septuagint; most Hebrew manuscripts *you*

NATHAN *The King's Conscience*

"LET YOUR CONSCIENCE BE YOUR guide." That's good advice only if your conscience doesn't cheat. Most people find ways to soothe their consciences by rationalizing whatever they want to do. That's why it's best to check with trustworthy people for advice.

Ancient rulers had an additional problem. Since few people had the courage to contradict an all-powerful king, such kings tended to get favorable advice even if they were doing something dead wrong. As one Roman senator said to Tiberius Caesar, "But if you speak first no one will want to refute you, and if you speak last, we will not want to have spoken against your position."

Only a few brave souls dared to be different. The prophet Nathan, for example, told the king the truth, pleasant or not. Nathan burst David's bubble by informing him that God did not want him to build the temple (7:5–16). He also spoke up to remind David of his neglected promise to crown Solomon as his successor (1 Kings 1:24–30).

Most memorably, Nathan accused David of sinning against God by committing adultery with Bathsheba and murdering her husband (2 Samuel 12). Nathan did so artfully, trapping the king with a powerful story that aroused the king's fury—until Nathan drove home the point. Nathan could have died for bringing this message, but it was a measure of David's character that he listened to Nathan even when his own conscience had gone numb. When David repented, Nathan stood beside him, assuring him of God's forgiveness.

Nathan was a true prophet. Though Biblical prophets sometimes predicted the future (as Nathan did in describing the punishments David would suffer) they were best known for telling the truth—especially the unpleasant truth that no one wanted to hear.

Life Questions: Who helps your conscience? Who can you count on to tell you the unpleasant truth about yourself?

what is my family, that you have brought me this far? ¹⁹And as if this were not enough in your sight, O Sovereign LORD, you have also spoken about the future of

your sight; for you, O Sovereign LORD, have spoken, and with your blessing the house of your servant will be blessed forever."

David's Victories

8 In the course of time, David defeated the Philistines and subdued them, and he took Metheg Ammah from the control of the Philistines.

²David also defeated the Moabites. He made them lie down on the ground and measured them off with a length of cord. Every two lengths of them were put to death, and the third length was allowed to live. So the Moabites became subject to David and brought tribute.

³Moreover, David fought Hadadezer son of Rehob, king of Zobah, when he went to restore his control along the Euphrates River. ⁴David captured a thousand of his chariots, seven thousand charioteers[b] and twenty thousand foot soldiers. He hamstrung all but a hundred of the chariot horses.

7:16 God's Great Promise

The Lord's promise to "establish David's throne forever" suggested that Israel would never lack the leadership they needed. This promise was one of a series of covenants between God and his people—with Abraham (Genesis 12), with Moses at Sinai (Exodus 20), and now with David. The New Testament sees this promise fulfilled in Jesus, a son of David, and King of kings forever (Luke 1:32–33).

---

the house of your servant. Is this your usual way of dealing with man, O Sovereign LORD?

²⁰"What more can David say to you? For you know your servant, O Sovereign LORD. ²¹For the sake of your word and according to your will, you have done this great thing and made it known to your servant.

²²"How great you are, O Sovereign LORD! There is no one like you, and there is no God but you, as we have heard with our own ears. ²³And who is like your people Israel—the one nation on earth that God went out to redeem as a people for himself, and to make a name for himself, and to perform great and awesome wonders by driving out nations and their gods from before your people, whom you redeemed from Egypt?[a] ²⁴You have established your people Israel as your very own forever, and you, O LORD, have become their God.

²⁵"And now, LORD God, keep forever the promise you have made concerning your servant and his house. Do as you promised, ²⁶so that your name will be great forever. Then men will say, 'The LORD Almighty is God over Israel!' And the house of your servant David will be established before you.

²⁷"O LORD Almighty, God of Israel, you have revealed this to your servant, saying, 'I will build a house for you.' So your servant has found courage to offer you this prayer. ²⁸O Sovereign LORD, you are God! Your words are trustworthy, and you have promised these good things to your servant. ²⁹Now be pleased to bless the house of your servant, that it may continue forever in

---

8:4 Not Ready for Chariots

Chariots were as great an innovation in weaponry as were guns centuries later. However, chariots required trained charioteers. Since David hamstrung all but 100 chariot horses, he may have lacked such trained personnel. Israel could defend the mountains, where chariots were of little use, but they were not ready to take on big armies on the surrounding plains.

---

⁵When the Arameans of Damascus came to help Hadadezer king of Zobah, David struck down twenty-two thousand of them. ⁶He put garrisons in the Aramean kingdom of Damascus, and the Arameans became subject to him and brought tribute. The LORD gave David victory wherever he went.

⁷David took the gold shields that belonged to the officers of Hadadezer and brought them to Jerusalem. ⁸From Tebah[c] and Berothai, towns that belonged to Hadadezer, King David took a great quantity of bronze.

⁹When Tou[d] king of Hamath heard that David had defeated the entire army of Hadadezer, ¹⁰he sent his son Joram[e] to King David to greet him and congratulate him on his victory in battle over Hadadezer, who had been at war with Tou. Joram brought with him articles of silver and gold and bronze.

¹¹King David dedicated these articles to the

---

a23 See Septuagint and 1 Chron. 17:21; Hebrew wonders for your land and before your people, whom you redeemed from Egypt, from the nations and their gods.   b4 Septuagint (see also Dead Sea Scrolls and 1 Chron. 18:4); Masoretic Text captured seventeen hundred of his charioteers   c8 See some Septuagint manuscripts (see also 1 Chron. 18:8); Hebrew Betah.   d9 Hebrew Toi, a variant of Tou; also in verse 10   e10 A variant of Hadoram

LORD, as he had done with the silver and gold from all the nations he had subdued: [12]Edom[a] and Moab, the Ammonites and the Philistines, and Amalek. He also dedicated the plunder taken from Hadadezer son of Rehob, king of Zobah.

[13]And David became famous after he returned from striking down eighteen thousand Edomites[b] in the Valley of Salt.

[14]He put garrisons throughout Edom, and all the Edomites became subject to David. The LORD gave David victory wherever he went.

David's Officials

[15]David reigned over all Israel, doing what was just and right for all his people. [16]Joab son of Zeruiah was over the army; Jehoshaphat son of Ahilud was recorder; [17]Zadok son of Ahitub and Ahimelech son of Abiathar were priests; Seraiah was secretary; [18]Benaiah son of Jehoiada was over the Kerethites and Pelethites; and David's sons were royal advisers.[c]

David and Mephibosheth

9 David asked, "Is there anyone still left of the house of Saul to whom I can show kindness for Jonathan's sake?"

[2]Now there was a servant of Saul's household named Ziba. They called him to appear before David, and the king said to him, "Are you Ziba?"

"Your servant," he replied.

[3]The king asked, "Is there no one still left of the house of Saul to whom I can show God's kindness?"

Ziba answered the king, "There is still a son of Jonathan; he is crippled in both feet."

[4]"Where is he?" the king asked.

Ziba answered, "He is at the house of Makir son of Ammiel in Lo Debar."

[5]So King David had him brought from Lo Debar, from the house of Makir son of Ammiel.

[6]When Mephibosheth son of Jonathan, the son of Saul, came to David, he bowed down to pay him honor.

David said, "Mephibosheth!"

"Your servant," he replied.

[7]"Don't be afraid," David said to him, "for I will surely show you kindness for the sake of your father Jonathan. I will restore to you all the land that belonged to your grandfather Saul, and you will always eat at my table."

[8]Mephibosheth bowed down and said, "What is your servant, that you should notice a dead dog like me?"

[9]Then the king summoned Ziba, Saul's servant, and said to him, "I have given your master's grandson everything that belonged to Saul and his family. [10]You and your sons and your ser-vants are to farm the land for him and bring in the crops, so that your master's grandson may be provided for. And Mephibosheth, grandson of your master, will always eat at my table." (Now Ziba had fifteen sons and twenty servants.)

> ### 9:7 Saul's Lame Grandson
>
> *Although Saul had been David's worst enemy, David consistently showed kindness and generosity to his family. In other kingdoms of that day, Mephibosheth would have been killed. David sought him out, restored his land, and welcomed him as a permanent guest at the royal table—a considerable honor. Later, when Mephibosheth suspiciously failed to join David in fleeing from Absalom's insurrection, David gave him the benefit of the doubt (19:24–30).*

[11]Then Ziba said to the king, "Your servant will do whatever my lord the king commands his servant to do." So Mephibosheth ate at David's[d] table like one of the king's sons.

[12]Mephibosheth had a young son named Mica, and all the members of Ziba's household were servants of Mephibosheth. [13]And Mephibosheth lived in Jerusalem, because he always ate at the king's table, and he was crippled in both feet.

David Defeats the Ammonites

10 In the course of time, the king of the Ammonites died, and his son Hanun succeeded him as king. [2]David thought, "I will show kindness to Hanun son of Nahash, just as his father showed kindness to me." So David sent a delegation to express his sympathy to Hanun concerning his father.

When David's men came to the land of the Ammonites, [3]the Ammonite nobles said to Hanun their lord, "Do you think David is honoring your father by sending men to you to express sympathy? Hasn't David sent them to you to explore the city and spy it out and overthrow it?" [4]So Hanun seized David's men, shaved off half of each man's beard, cut off their garments in the middle at the buttocks, and sent them away.

[5]When David was told about this, he sent messengers to meet the men, for they were greatly humiliated. The king said, "Stay at Jericho till your beards have grown, and then come back."

[6]When the Ammonites realized that they had become a stench in David's nostrils, they hired twenty thousand Aramean foot soldiers from Beth Rehob and Zobah, as well as the king of Maacah with a thousand men, and also twelve thousand men from Tob.

---

[a]12 Some Hebrew manuscripts, Septuagint and Syriac (see also 1 Chron. 18:11); most Hebrew manuscripts *Aram*   [b]13 A few Hebrew manuscripts, Septuagint and Syriac (see also 1 Chron. 18:12); most Hebrew manuscripts *Aram* (that is, Arameans)   [c]18 Or *were priests*   [d]11 Septuagint; Hebrew *my*

⁷On hearing this, David sent Joab out with the entire army of fighting men. ⁸The Ammonites came out and drew up in battle formation at the entrance to their city gate, while the Arameans of Zobah and Rehob and the men of Tob and Maacah were by themselves in the open country.

⁹Joab saw that there were battle lines in front of him and behind him; so he selected some of the best troops in Israel and deployed them against the Arameans. ¹⁰He put the rest of the men under the command of Abishai his brother and deployed them against the Ammonites. ¹¹Joab said, "If the Arameans are too strong for me, then you are to come to my rescue; but if the Ammonites are too strong for you, then I will come to rescue you. ¹²Be strong and let us fight bravely for our people and the cities of our God. The LORD will do what is good in his sight."

¹³Then Joab and the troops with him advanced to fight the Arameans, and they fled before him. ¹⁴When the Ammonites saw that the Arameans were fleeing, they fled before Abishai and went inside the city. So Joab returned from fighting the Ammonites and came to Jerusalem.

¹⁵After the Arameans saw that they had been routed by Israel, they regrouped. ¹⁶Hadadezer had Arameans brought from beyond the River*a*; they went to Helam, with Shobach the commander of Hadadezer's army leading them.

¹⁷When David was told of this, he gathered all Israel, crossed the Jordan and went to Helam. The Arameans formed their battle lines to meet David and fought against him. ¹⁸But they fled before Israel, and David killed seven hundred of their charioteers and forty thousand of their foot soldiers.*b* He also struck down Shobach the commander of their army, and he died there. ¹⁹When all the kings who were vassals of Hadadezer saw that they had been defeated by Israel, they made peace with the Israelites and became subject to them.

So the Arameans were afraid to help the Ammonites anymore.

David and Bathsheba

11 In the spring, at the time when kings go off to war, David sent Joab out with the king's men and the whole Israelite army. They destroyed the Ammonites and besieged Rabbah. But David remained in Jerusalem.

²One evening David got up from his bed and walked around on the roof of the palace. From the roof he saw a woman bathing. The woman was very beautiful, ³and David sent someone to find out about her. The man said, "Isn't this Bathsheba, the daughter of Eliam and the wife of Uriah the Hittite?" ⁴Then David sent messengers to get her. She came to him, and he slept with her. (She had purified herself from her uncleanness.) Then*c* she went back home. ⁵The woman conceived and sent word to David, saying, "I am pregnant."

⁶So David sent this word to Joab: "Send me Uriah the Hittite." And Joab sent him to David.

*a16 That is, the Euphrates   b18 Some Septuagint manuscripts (see also 1 Chron. 19:18); Hebrew *horsemen*
*c4 Or *with her. When she purified herself from her uncleanness,*

BATHSHEBA *Only Following Orders*

AFTER WORLD WAR II, NAZI soldiers made a classic defense for their war crimes: "We were only following orders." Then and ever since courts have struck down that defense. A person who knowingly does wrong is responsible, regardless of the circumstances.

Still, many people feel sympathy for the person who commits a crime under pressure or coercion. Perhaps Bathsheba fits this category. She could hardly help being beautiful, and in all probability was bathing quite innocently when she caught David's eye (houses then had no bathrooms). To complicate matters, the king—not just anybody—summoned her to sleep with him. The king's word was law, and had Bathsheba refused him she might have expected severe penalties—perhaps even death.

Certainly, Bathsheba suffered for what she did. She lost her husband and her child. Did she join with David in his repentance? The Bible does not say. After bearing another child, Solomon, she received no further mention in Scripture until the very end of David's life, when she supported Solomon's bid for the throne. The one really notable thing Bathsheba accomplished in life was the wrong thing—her affair with the king.

The way the Bible tells the story, David bore the chief responsibility for this national scandal. He initiated the adultery, followed it up with murder, and suffered the consequences throughout the rest of his life. When we consider how the repercussions of David's actions affected the entire nation, however, we can see why "I was only following orders" is no defense. Although Bathsheba was in some ways a victim, her failure to resist a sinful situation made David's sin possible.

Life Questions: Are there any situations in which you are tempted to "just go along" with sin because of pressure?

[7]When Uriah came to him, David asked him how Joab was, how the soldiers were and how the war was going. [8]Then David said to Uriah, "Go down to your house and wash your feet." So Uriah left the palace, and a gift from the king was sent after him. [9]But Uriah slept at the entrance to the palace with all his master's servants and did not go down to his house.

[10]When David was told, "Uriah did not go home," he asked him, "Haven't you just come from a distance? Why didn't you go home?"

[11]Uriah said to David, "The ark and Israel and Judah are staying in tents, and my master Joab and my lord's men are camped in the open fields. How could I go to my house to eat and drink and lie with my wife? As surely as you live, I will not do such a thing!"

11:11 A Military Hero

Israelite soldiers had no sexual relations while they were preparing for battle. (See, for instance, 1 Samuel 21:5.) Uriah refused to sleep with Bathsheba because he remembered duty before pleasure. He is mentioned (in 23:39) as one of the Thirty, a group of leading warriors under David.

[12]Then David said to him, "Stay here one more day, and tomorrow I will send you back." So Uriah remained in Jerusalem that day and the next. [13]At David's invitation, he ate and drank with him, and David made him drunk. But in the evening Uriah went out to sleep on his mat among his master's servants; he did not go home.

[14]In the morning David wrote a letter to Joab and sent it with Uriah. [15]In it he wrote, "Put Uriah in the front line where the fighting is fiercest. Then withdraw from him so he will be struck down and die."

[16]So while Joab had the city under siege, he put Uriah at a place where he knew the strongest defenders were. [17]When the men of the city came out and fought against Joab, some of the men in David's army fell; moreover, Uriah the Hittite died.

[18]Joab sent David a full account of the battle. [19]He instructed the messenger: "When you have finished giving the king this account of the battle, [20]the king's anger may flare up, and he may ask you, 'Why did you get so close to the city to fight? Didn't you know they would shoot arrows from the wall? [21]Who killed Abimelech son of Jerub-Besheth[a]? Didn't a woman throw an upper millstone on him from the wall, so that he died in Thebez? Why did you get so close to the wall?'

If he asks you this, then say to him, 'Also, your servant Uriah the Hittite is dead.'"

[22]The messenger set out, and when he arrived he told David everything Joab had sent him to say. [23]The messenger said to David, "The men overpowered us and came out against us in the open, but we drove them back to the entrance to the city gate. [24]Then the archers shot arrows at your servants from the wall, and some of the king's men died. Moreover, your servant Uriah the Hittite is dead."

[25]David told the messenger, "Say this to Joab: 'Don't let this upset you; the sword devours one as well as another. Press the attack against the city and destroy it.' Say this to encourage Joab."

[26]When Uriah's wife heard that her husband was dead, she mourned for him. [27]After the time of mourning was over, David had her brought to his house, and she became his wife and bore him a son. But the thing David had done displeased the LORD.

Nathan Rebukes David

12 The LORD sent Nathan to David. When he came to him, he said, "There were two men in a certain town, one rich and the other poor. [2]The rich man had a very large number of sheep and cattle, [3]but the poor man had nothing except one little ewe lamb he had bought. He raised it, and it grew up with him and his children. It shared his food, drank from his cup and even slept in his arms. It was like a daughter to him.

[4]"Now a traveler came to the rich man, but the rich man refrained from taking one of his own sheep or cattle to prepare a meal for the traveler who had come to him. Instead, he took the ewe lamb that belonged to the poor man and prepared it for the one who had come to him."

[5]David burned with anger against the man and said to Nathan, "As surely as the LORD lives, the man who did this deserves to die! [6]He must pay for that lamb four times over, because he did such a thing and had no pity."

[7]Then Nathan said to David, "You are the man! This is what the LORD, the God of Israel, says: 'I anointed you king over Israel, and I delivered you from the hand of Saul. [8]I gave your master's house to you, and your master's wives into your arms. I gave you the house of Israel and Judah. And if all this had been too little, I would have given you even more. [9]Why did you despise the word of the LORD by doing what is evil in his eyes? You struck down Uriah the Hittite with the sword and took his wife to be your own. You killed him with the sword of the Ammonites. [10]Now, therefore, the sword will never depart from your house, because you despised me and took the wife of Uriah the Hittite to be your own.'

[a]21 Also known as *Jerub-Baal* (that is, Gideon)

[11]"This is what the LORD says: 'Out of your own household I am going to bring calamity upon you. Before your very eyes I will take your wives and give them to one who is close to you, and he will lie with your wives in broad daylight. [12]You did it in secret, but I will do this thing in broad daylight before all Israel.'"

[13]Then David said to Nathan, "I have sinned against the LORD."

Nathan replied, "The LORD has taken away your sin. You are not going to die. [14]But because by doing this you have made the enemies of the LORD show utter contempt,[a] the son born to you will die."

[15]After Nathan had gone home, the LORD struck the child that Uriah's wife had borne to David, and he became ill. [16]David pleaded with God for the child. He fasted and went into his house and spent the nights lying on the ground. [17]The elders of his household stood beside him to get him up from the ground, but he refused, and he would not eat any food with them.

[18]On the seventh day the child died. David's servants were afraid to tell him that the child was dead, for they thought, "While the child was still living, we spoke to David but he would not listen to us. How can we tell him the child is dead? He may do something desperate."

[19]David noticed that his servants were whis-

---

[a]14 Masoretic Text; an ancient Hebrew scribal tradition *this you have shown utter contempt for the LORD*

Adultery and Murder
The king could do as he pleased—or so he thought

AN ANCIENT AND ENDURING TRADITION teaches that the people on top make the rules—they don't have to live by them. Lots of leaders in history have followed this course, taking the women they wanted, the money they wanted, the privileges they wanted.

Nobody, therefore, challenged David's right to sleep with another man's wife. David saw Bathsheba, lusted for her, and sent for her. As far as we know, neither his servants nor Bathsheba lodged a protest. Only when she got pregnant did a problem arise. Then David, who had had no thought of marrying Bathsheba, found himself in a jam. He called her husband, Uriah, home on leave from the army, hoping that Uriah would sleep with his wife and later be unable to prove the child belonged to another father.

> *David burned with anger against the man and said to Nathan, "As surely as the LORD lives, the man who did this deserves to die!" . . . Then Nathan said to David, "You are the man!" 12:5,7*

Uriah's single-minded devotion to duty spoiled David's plan. David rewarded Uriah with murder. Again, not a word of protest was filed: What the king wanted the king got, no questions asked. The murder of Uriah took other good men with him, but David showed no regrets. He was at his worst: cold as iron, arrogant in his power.

After a mourning period, Bathsheba came into his house and he married her. A good many people must have known what had happened—the servants knew, at any rate—but the Bible doesn't report that any of them were displeased. It only says, "The thing David had done displeased the LORD" (11:27).

Who Will Challenge the King?

Who would have the courage—or the authority—to challenge the king? In most nations, no one. But Israel had this distinctive: its ultimate king was not David, but God. And God had his spokesmen, the prophets. He sent Nathan to David.

Nathan cleverly captivated David with a heartrending story about a rich man who had abused his power. He offered the case to David, the highest judge in Israel. David knew exactly how to judge such a case: The man deserved death! When he said so, Nathan turned David's own judgment around: "You are the man!"

In this dramatic scene David's greatness showed itself. He could easily have had Nathan killed. Or he could have laughed and shown him out of the palace. Instead, "David said to Nathan, 'I have sinned against the LORD'" (12:13). David recognized that God was the true king of Israel.

Nathan's confrontation with David set the standard for centuries of conflict between kings and prophets. Time and again an Old Testament prophet went to the palace—sometimes risking his life—and told the king that God would punish him for what he was doing. The kings, rich and powerful by birth, did not have to listen. In fact, they rarely did. David was a great king partly because he did not act with the normal pride of a king. When confronted with the truth, he repented.

Life Questions: What determines your choices? Your own desires? Or your understanding of God's will? Think of some recent decisions you have made and apply this question to them.

pering among themselves and he realized the child was dead. "Is the child dead?" he asked.

"Yes," they replied, "he is dead."

[20]Then David got up from the ground. After

12:13 David's Finest Moment

David, who possessed absolute power, could have had Nathan killed for his daring public confrontation. Or, he could have laughed him off and thrown him out of the palace. But David knew Nathan spoke for God, and in what may have been the greatest moment of his life, he admitted, "I have sinned against the LORD." David showed what made him a man after God's own heart; though he was king, he humbled himself before the King of kings.

he had washed, put on lotions and changed his clothes, he went into the house of the LORD and worshiped. Then he went to his own house, and at his request they served him food, and he ate.

[21]His servants asked him, "Why are you acting this way? While the child was alive, you fasted and wept, but now that the child is dead, you get up and eat!"

[22]He answered, "While the child was still alive, I fasted and wept. I thought, 'Who knows? The LORD may be gracious to me and let the child live.' [23]But now that he is dead, why should I fast? Can I bring him back again? I will go to him, but he will not return to me."

[24]Then David comforted his wife Bathsheba, and he went to her and lay with her. She gave birth to a son, and they named him Solomon. The LORD loved him; [25]and because the LORD loved him, he sent word through Nathan the prophet to name him Jedidiah.[a]

[26]Meanwhile Joab fought against Rabbah of the Ammonites and captured the royal citadel. [27]Joab then sent messengers to David, saying, "I have fought against Rabbah and taken its water supply. [28]Now muster the rest of the troops and besiege the city and capture it. Otherwise I will take the city, and it will be named after me."

[29]So David mustered the entire army and went to Rabbah, and attacked and captured it. [30]He took the crown from the head of their king[b]— its weight was a talent[c] of gold, and it was set with precious stones—and it was placed on David's head. He took a great quantity of plunder from the city [31]and brought out the people who were there, consigning them to labor with saws and with iron picks and axes, and he made them work at brickmaking.[d] He did this to all the

Ammonite towns. Then David and his entire army returned to Jerusalem.

Amnon and Tamar

13 In the course of time, Amnon son of David fell in love with Tamar, the beautiful sister of Absalom son of David.

[2]Amnon became frustrated to the point of illness on account of his sister Tamar, for she was a virgin, and it seemed impossible for him to do anything to her.

[3]Now Amnon had a friend named Jonadab son of Shimeah, David's brother. Jonadab was a very shrewd man. [4]He asked Amnon, "Why do you, the king's son, look so haggard morning after morning? Won't you tell me?"

Amnon said to him, "I'm in love with Tamar, my brother Absalom's sister."

[5]"Go to bed and pretend to be ill," Jonadab said. "When your father comes to see you, say to him, 'I would like my sister Tamar to come and give me something to eat. Let her prepare the food in my sight so I may watch her and then eat it from her hand.'"

[6]So Amnon lay down and pretended to be ill. When the king came to see him, Amnon said to him, "I would like my sister Tamar to come and make some special bread in my sight, so I may eat from her hand."

[7]David sent word to Tamar at the palace: "Go to the house of your brother Amnon and prepare some food for him." [8]So Tamar went to the house of her brother Amnon, who was lying down. She took some dough, kneaded it, made the bread in his sight and baked it. [9]Then she took the pan and served him the bread, but he refused to eat.

"Send everyone out of here," Amnon said. So everyone left him. [10]Then Amnon said to Tamar, "Bring the food here into my bedroom so I may eat from your hand." And Tamar took the bread she had prepared and brought it to her brother Amnon in his bedroom. [11]But when she took it to him to eat, he grabbed her and said, "Come to bed with me, my sister."

[12]"Don't, my brother!" she said to him. "Don't force me. Such a thing should not be done in Israel! Don't do this wicked thing. [13]What about me? Where could I get rid of my disgrace? And what about you? You would be like one of the wicked fools in Israel. Please speak to the king; he will not keep me from being married to you." [14]But he refused to listen to her, and since he was stronger than she, he raped her.

[15]Then Amnon hated her with intense hatred. In fact, he hated her more than he had loved her. Amnon said to her, "Get up and get out!"

---

[a]25 *Jedidiah* means *loved by the LORD.*   [b]30 Or *of Milcom* (that is, Molech)   [c]30 That is, about 75 pounds (about 34 kilograms)   [d]31 The meaning of the Hebrew for this clause is uncertain.

16"No!" she said to him. "Sending me away would be a greater wrong than what you have already done to me."

But he refused to listen to her. 17He called his personal servant and said, "Get this woman out of here and bolt the door after her." 18So his servant put her out and bolted the door after her. She was wearing a richly ornamented*a* robe, for this was the kind of garment the virgin daughters of the king wore. 19Tamar put ashes on her head and tore the ornamented*b* robe she was wearing. She put her hand on her head and went away, weeping aloud as she went.

20Her brother Absalom said to her, "Has that Amnon, your brother, been with you? Be quiet now, my sister; he is your brother. Don't take this thing to heart." And Tamar lived in her brother Absalom's house, a desolate woman.

21When King David heard all this, he was furious. 22Absalom never said a word to Amnon, either good or bad; he hated Amnon because he had disgraced his sister Tamar.

Absalom Kills Amnon

23Two years later, when Absalom's sheepshearers were at Baal Hazor near the border of Ephraim, he invited all the king's sons to come there. 24Absalom went to the king and said, "Your servant has had shearers come. Will the king and his officials please join me?"

25"No, my son," the king replied. "All of us should not go; we would only be a burden to you." Although Absalom urged him, he still refused to go, but gave him his blessing.

26Then Absalom said, "If not, please let my brother Amnon come with us."

The king asked him, "Why should he go with you?" 27But Absalom urged him, so he sent with him Amnon and the rest of the king's sons.

28Absalom ordered his men, "Listen! When Amnon is in high spirits from drinking wine and I say to you, 'Strike Amnon down,' then kill him. Don't be afraid. Have not I given you this order? Be strong and brave." 29So Absalom's men did to Amnon what Absalom had ordered. Then all the king's sons got up, mounted their mules and fled.

30While they were on their way, the report came to David: "Absalom has struck down all the king's sons; not one of them is left." 31The king stood up, tore his clothes and lay down on the ground; and all his servants stood by with their clothes torn.

32But Jonadab son of Shimeah, David's brother, said, "My lord should not think that they killed all the princes; only Amnon is dead. This has been Absalom's expressed intention ever since the day Amnon raped his sister Tamar.

33My lord the king should not be concerned about the report that all the king's sons are dead. Only Amnon is dead."

34Meanwhile, Absalom had fled.

13:29 Vicious Children

What went wrong with David's children? Amnon raped his sister Tamar. Absalom killed Amnon in revenge. Ultimately Absalom plotted a coup against his father, driving David from Jerusalem. All through these events—rape, murder, rebellion—David failed to discipline his children. According to the law they deserved severe punishment, but David let them off with hardly a word. Perhaps his own guilt over Bathsheba had undercut his sense of moral authority.

Now the man standing watch looked up and saw many people on the road west of him, coming down the side of the hill. The watchman went and told the king, "I see men in the direction of Horonaim, on the side of the hill."*c*

35Jonadab said to the king, "See, the king's sons are here; it has happened just as your servant said."

36As he finished speaking, the king's sons came in, wailing loudly. The king, too, and all his servants wept very bitterly.

37Absalom fled and went to Talmai son of Ammihud, the king of Geshur. But King David mourned for his son every day.

38After Absalom fled and went to Geshur, he

13:38 A Refuge with His Family

Absalom ran to Geshur, a neighboring kingdom, probably because his mother was a daughter of Geshur's king. He could be assured of safety there.

stayed there three years. 39And the spirit of the king*d* longed to go to Absalom, for he was consoled concerning Amnon's death.

Absalom Returns to Jerusalem

14 Joab son of Zeruiah knew that the king's heart longed for Absalom. 2So Joab sent someone to Tekoa and had a wise woman brought from there. He said to her, "Pretend you are in mourning. Dress in mourning clothes, and don't use any cosmetic lotions. Act like a woman who has spent many days grieving for the dead.

---

a18 The meaning of the Hebrew for this phrase is uncertain. uncertain. *c34* Septuagint; Hebrew does not have this sentence. manuscripts; Masoretic Text *But ⌊the spirit of⌋ David the king*   *b19* The meaning of the Hebrew for this word is   *d39* Dead Sea Scrolls and some Septuagint

³Then go to the king and speak these words to him." And Joab put the words in her mouth.

⁴When the woman from Tekoa went[a] to the king, she fell with her face to the ground to pay him honor, and she said, "Help me, O king!"

⁵The king asked her, "What is troubling you?"

She said, "I am indeed a widow; my husband is dead. ⁶I your servant had two sons. They got into a fight with each other in the field, and no one was there to separate them. One struck the other and killed him. ⁷Now the whole clan has risen up against your servant; they say, 'Hand over the one who struck his brother down, so that we may put him to death for the life of his brother whom he killed; then we will get rid of the heir as well.' They would put out the only burning coal I have left, leaving my husband neither name nor descendant on the face of the earth."

⁸The king said to the woman, "Go home, and I will issue an order in your behalf."

⁹But the woman from Tekoa said to him, "My lord the king, let the blame rest on me and on my father's family, and let the king and his throne be without guilt."

¹⁰The king replied, "If anyone says anything to you, bring him to me, and he will not bother you again."

¹¹She said, "Then let the king invoke the LORD his God to prevent the avenger of blood from adding to the destruction, so that my son will not be destroyed."

"As surely as the LORD lives," he said, "not one hair of your son's head will fall to the ground."

¹²Then the woman said, "Let your servant speak a word to my lord the king."

"Speak," he replied.

¹³The woman said, "Why then have you devised a thing like this against the people of God? When the king says this, does he not convict himself, for the king has not brought back his banished son? ¹⁴Like water spilled on the ground, which cannot be recovered, so we must die. But God does not take away life; instead, he devises ways so that a banished person may not remain estranged from him.

¹⁵"And now I have come to say this to my lord the king because the people have made me afraid. Your servant thought, 'I will speak to the king; perhaps he will do what his servant asks. ¹⁶Perhaps the king will agree to deliver his servant from the hand of the man who is trying to cut off both me and my son from the inheritance God gave us.'

¹⁷"And now your servant says, 'May the word of my lord the king bring me rest, for my lord the king is like an angel of God in discerning good

and evil. May the LORD your God be with you.'"

¹⁸Then the king said to the woman, "Do not keep from me the answer to what I am going to ask you."

"Let my lord the king speak," the woman said.

¹⁹The king asked, "Isn't the hand of Joab with you in all this?"

The woman answered, "As surely as you live, my lord the king, no one can turn to the right or to the left from anything my lord the king says. Yes, it was your servant Joab who instructed me to do this and who put all these words into the mouth of your servant. ²⁰Your servant Joab did this to change the present situation. My lord has wisdom like that of an angel of God—he knows everything that happens in the land."

²¹The king said to Joab, "Very well, I will do it. Go, bring back the young man Absalom."

²²Joab fell with his face to the ground to pay him honor, and he blessed the king. Joab said, "Today your servant knows that he has found favor in your eyes, my lord the king, because the king has granted his servant's request."

²³Then Joab went to Geshur and brought Absalom back to Jerusalem. ²⁴But the king said, "He must go to his own house; he must not see my face." So Absalom went to his own house and did not see the face of the king.

²⁵In all Israel there was not a man so highly praised for his handsome appearance as Absalom. From the top of his head to the sole of his foot there was no blemish in him. ²⁶Whenever he cut the hair of his head—he used to cut his hair from time to time when it became too heavy for him—he would weigh it, and its weight was two hundred shekels[b] by the royal standard.

²⁷Three sons and a daughter were born to Absalom. The daughter's name was Tamar, and she became a beautiful woman.

²⁸Absalom lived two years in Jerusalem without seeing the king's face. ²⁹Then Absalom sent for Joab in order to send him to the king, but Joab refused to come to him. So he sent a second time, but he refused to come. ³⁰Then he said to his servants, "Look, Joab's field is next to mine, and he has barley there. Go and set it on fire." So Absalom's servants set the field on fire.

³¹Then Joab did go to Absalom's house and he said to him, "Why have your servants set my field on fire?"

³²Absalom said to Joab, "Look, I sent word to you and said, 'Come here so I can send you to the king to ask, "Why have I come from Geshur? It would be better for me if I were still there!"' Now then, I want to see the king's face, and if I am guilty of anything, let him put me to death."

³³So Joab went to the king and told him this.

---

^a4 Many Hebrew manuscripts, Septuagint, Vulgate and Syriac; most Hebrew manuscripts *spoke*   ^b26 That is, about 5 pounds (about 2.3 kilograms)

Then the king summoned Absalom, and he came in and bowed down with his face to the ground before the king. And the king kissed Absalom.

Absalom's Conspiracy

15 In the course of time, Absalom provided himself with a chariot and horses and with fifty men to run ahead of him. [2]He would get up early and stand by the side of the road leading to the city gate. Whenever anyone came with a complaint to be placed before the king for a decision, Absalom would call out to him, "What town are you from?" He would answer, "Your servant is from one of the tribes of Israel." [3]Then Absalom would say to him, "Look, your claims are valid and proper, but there is no representative of the king to hear you." [4]And Absalom would add, "If only I were appointed judge in the land! Then everyone who has a complaint or case could come to me and I would see that he gets justice."

[5]Also, whenever anyone approached him to bow down before him, Absalom would reach out his hand, take hold of him and kiss him. [6]Absalom behaved in this way toward all the Israelites who came to the king asking for justice, and so he stole the hearts of the men of Israel.

[7]At the end of four[a] years, Absalom said to the king, "Let me go to Hebron and fulfill a vow I made to the LORD. [8]While your servant was living at Geshur in Aram, I made this vow: 'If the LORD takes me back to Jerusalem, I will worship the LORD in Hebron.[b]'"

[9]The king said to him, "Go in peace." So he went to Hebron.

[10]Then Absalom sent secret messengers throughout the tribes of Israel to say, "As soon as you hear the sound of the trumpets, then say, 'Absalom is king in Hebron.'" [11]Two hundred men from Jerusalem had accompanied Absalom. They had been invited as guests and went quite innocently, knowing nothing about the matter. [12]While Absalom was offering sacrifices, he also sent for Ahithophel the Gilonite, David's counselor, to come from Giloh, his hometown. And so the conspiracy gained strength, and Absalom's following kept on increasing.

David Flees

[13]A messenger came and told David, "The hearts of the men of Israel are with Absalom."

[14]Then David said to all his officials who were with him in Jerusalem, "Come! We must flee, or none of us will escape from Absalom. We must leave immediately, or he will move quickly to overtake us and bring ruin upon us and put the city to the sword."

[15]The king's officials answered him, "Your servants are ready to do whatever our lord the king chooses."

[16]The king set out, with his entire household following him; but he left ten concubines to take care of the palace. [17]So the king set out, with all the people following him, and they halted at a place some distance away. [18]All his men marched past him, along with all the Kerethites and Pelethites; and all the six hundred Gittites who had

---

[a]7 Some Septuagint manuscripts, Syriac and Josephus; Hebrew *forty* not have *in Hebron.*

[b]8 Some Septuagint manuscripts; Hebrew does

ABSALOM *All That Glitters*

HE WAS THE MOST HANDSOME man of his day, a royal prince with plenty of charisma thrown in for good measure. When people had needs, Absalom seemed to care: In this way "he stole the hearts of the men of Israel" (15:6). We first meet him sheltering his sister after she had been raped (13:20). Two years later, Absalom got murderous revenge in defense of his sister's honor. Unlike his father David, he refused to let such a crime go unpunished.

Nevertheless, Absalom's glittering surface did not reveal a golden heart. As time went on it became clear that Absalom cared mainly for himself. Absalom was a tragic figure, a symbol of David's failures as a parent. For five years father and son did not speak to one another, and this simmering family feud only hardened Absalom further.

Absalom tended to act like a spoiled brat, whether getting Joab's attention by burning his barley field, or gaining the honor he thought he deserved by driving his own father out of town. Like many egotists, however, Absalom overestimated his strength and popularity.

During the bloody revolt one of David's advisers, pretending to have switched to Absalom's side, shrewdly advised a delay. David gained time to assemble his own seasoned fighters, who quickly put down Absalom's uprising. The king's son died as vainly as he had lived: While escaping on a mule, he caught his long, handsome hair in a tree and was killed by Joab and his men.

Life Questions: If someone is good-looking, gifted or naturally likable, how can such a person guard against egotism?

accompanied him from Gath marched before the king.

[19]The king said to Ittai the Gittite, "Why should you come along with us? Go back and stay with King Absalom. You are a foreigner, an exile from your homeland. [20]You came only yesterday. And today shall I make you wander about with us, when I do not know where I am going? Go back, and take your countrymen. May kindness and faithfulness be with you."

[21]But Ittai replied to the king, "As surely as the LORD lives, and as my lord the king lives, wherever my lord the king may be, whether it means life or death, there will your servant be."

[22]David said to Ittai, "Go ahead, march on." So Ittai the Gittite marched on with all his men and the families that were with him.

15:22 Mercenaries

David's army included more than just loyal Israelites; he had added mercenaries (hired soldiers). The Gittites came from the Philistine city of Gath. David had probably recruited them during his stay there (1 Samuel 27:2), and they had loyally followed him ever since.

[23]The whole countryside wept aloud as all the people passed by. The king also crossed the Kidron Valley, and all the people moved on toward the desert.

[24]Zadok was there, too, and all the Levites who were with him carrying the ark of the covenant of God. They set down the ark of God, and Abiathar offered sacrifices[a] until all the people had finished leaving the city.

[25]Then the king said to Zadok, "Take the ark of God back into the city. If I find favor in the LORD's eyes, he will bring me back and let me see it and his dwelling place again. [26]But if he says, 'I am not pleased with you,' then I am ready; let him do to me whatever seems good to him."

[27]The king also said to Zadok the priest, "Aren't you a seer? Go back to the city in peace, with your son Ahimaaz and Jonathan son of Abiathar. You and Abiathar take your two sons with you. [28]I will wait at the fords in the desert until word comes from you to inform me." [29]So Zadok and Abiathar took the ark of God back to Jerusalem and stayed there.

[30]But David continued up the Mount of Olives, weeping as he went; his head was covered and he was barefoot. All the people with him covered their heads too and were weeping as they went up. [31]Now David had been told, "Ahithophel is among the conspirators with Absalom."

So David prayed, "O LORD, turn Ahithophel's counsel into foolishness."

[32]When David arrived at the summit, where people used to worship God, Hushai the Arkite was there to meet him, his robe torn and dust on his head. [33]David said to him, "If you go with me, you will be a burden to me. [34]But if you return to the city and say to Absalom, 'I will be your servant, O king; I was your father's servant in the past, but now I will be your servant,' then you can help me by frustrating Ahithophel's advice. [35]Won't the priests Zadok and Abiathar be there with you? Tell them anything you hear in the king's palace. [36]Their two sons, Ahimaaz son of Zadok and Jonathan son of Abiathar, are there with them. Send them to me with anything you hear."

[37]So David's friend Hushai arrived at Jerusalem as Absalom was entering the city.

David and Ziba

16 When David had gone a short distance beyond the summit, there was Ziba, the steward of Mephibosheth, waiting to meet him. He had a string of donkeys saddled and loaded with two hundred loaves of bread, a hundred cakes of raisins, a hundred cakes of figs and a skin of wine.

[2]The king asked Ziba, "Why have you brought these?"

Ziba answered, "The donkeys are for the king's household to ride on, and the bread and fruit are for the men to eat, and the wine is to refresh those who become exhausted in the desert."

[3]The king then asked, "Where is your master's grandson?"

Ziba said to him, "He is staying in Jerusalem, because he thinks, 'Today the house of Israel will give me back my grandfather's kingdom.'"

[4]Then the king said to Ziba, "All that belonged to Mephibosheth is now yours."

"I humbly bow," Ziba said. "May I find favor in your eyes, my lord the king."

Shimei Curses David

[5]As King David approached Bahurim, a man from the same clan as Saul's family came out from there. His name was Shimei son of Gera, and he cursed as he came out. [6]He pelted David and all the king's officials with stones, though all the troops and the special guard were on David's right and left. [7]As he cursed, Shimei said, "Get out, get out, you man of blood, you scoundrel! [8]The LORD has repaid you for all the blood you shed in the household of Saul, in whose place you have reigned. The LORD has handed the kingdom over to your son Absalom. You have come to ruin because you are a man of blood!"

---

[a]24 Or *Abiathar went up*

⁹Then Abishai son of Zeruiah said to the king, "Why should this dead dog curse my lord the king? Let me go over and cut off his head."

¹⁰But the king said, "What do you and I have in common, you sons of Zeruiah? If he is cursing because the LORD said to him, 'Curse David,' who can ask, 'Why do you do this?'"

¹¹David then said to Abishai and all his officials, "My son, who is of my own flesh, is trying to take my life. How much more, then, this Benjamite! Leave him alone; let him curse, for the LORD has told him to. ¹²It may be that the LORD will see my distress and repay me with good for the cursing I am receiving today."

¹³So David and his men continued along the road while Shimei was going along the hillside opposite him, cursing as he went and throwing stones at him and showering him with dirt. ¹⁴The king and all the people with him arrived at their destination exhausted. And there he refreshed himself.

The Advice of Hushai and Ahithophel

¹⁵Meanwhile, Absalom and all the men of Israel came to Jerusalem, and Ahithophel was with him. ¹⁶Then Hushai the Arkite, David's friend, went to Absalom and said to him, "Long live the king! Long live the king!"

¹⁷Absalom asked Hushai, "Is this the love you show your friend? Why didn't you go with your friend?"

¹⁸Hushai said to Absalom, "No, the one chosen by the LORD, by these people, and by all the men of Israel—his I will be, and I will remain with him. ¹⁹Furthermore, whom should I serve? Should I not serve the son? Just as I served your father, so I will serve you."

²⁰Absalom said to Ahithophel, "Give us your advice. What should we do?"

²¹Ahithophel answered, "Lie with your father's concubines whom he left to take care of the palace. Then all Israel will hear that you have made yourself a stench in your father's nostrils, and the hands of everyone with you will be strengthened." ²²So they pitched a tent for Absalom on the roof, and he lay with his father's concubines in the sight of all Israel.

²³Now in those days the advice Ahithophel gave was like that of one who inquires of God. That was how both David and Absalom regarded all of Ahithophel's advice.

17 Ahithophel said to Absalom, "I would[a] choose twelve thousand men and set out tonight in pursuit of David. ²I would[b] attack him while he is weary and weak. I would[b] strike him with terror, and then all the people with him will flee. I would[b] strike down only the king ³and bring all the people back to you. The death

of the man you seek will mean the return of all; all the people will be unharmed." ⁴This plan seemed good to Absalom and to all the elders of Israel.

16:22 No Way Back

Absalom publicly slept with his father's concubines for political reasons. It made clear his claim to the throne (see 3:6 for a similar case) and was extremely offensive to David. Israelites who had held back their allegiance, thinking that father and son would reconcile their differences, knew now that the breach was permanent. They had to take sides.

⁵But Absalom said, "Summon also Hushai the Arkite, so we can hear what he has to say." ⁶When Hushai came to him, Absalom said, "Ahithophel has given this advice. Should we do what he says? If not, give us your opinion."

⁷Hushai replied to Absalom, "The advice Ahithophel has given is not good this time. ⁸You know your father and his men; they are fighters, and as fierce as a wild bear robbed of her cubs. Besides, your father is an experienced fighter; he will not spend the night with the troops. ⁹Even now, he is hidden in a cave or some other place. If he should attack your troops first,[c] whoever hears about it will say, 'There has been a slaughter among the troops who follow Absalom.' ¹⁰Then even the bravest soldier, whose heart is like the heart of a lion, will melt with fear, for all Israel knows that your father is a fighter and that those with him are brave.

¹¹"So I advise you: Let all Israel, from Dan to Beersheba—as numerous as the sand on the seashore—be gathered to you, with you yourself

17:11 Flattering Advice

Hushai, one of David's top advisers, slipped into Absalom's camp pretending to have deserted David. He deliberately gave bad advice, cleverly phrasing it to flatter Absalom. Hushai suggested that if Absalom delayed his pursuit of David, Absalom (who had never fought in battle) could gather a gigantic army to lead. Absalom fell for it, and the delay gave David enough time to consolidate his support.

leading them into battle. ¹²Then we will attack him wherever he may be found, and we will fall on him as dew settles on the ground. Neither he nor any of his men will be left alive. ¹³If he withdraws into a city, then all Israel will bring ropes

---

a1 Or *Let me*   *b2* Or *will*   *c9* Or *When some of the men fall at the first attack*

to that city, and we will drag it down to the valley until not even a piece of it can be found."

¹⁴Absalom and all the men of Israel said, "The advice of Hushai the Arkite is better than that of Ahithophel." For the LORD had determined to frustrate the good advice of Ahithophel in order to bring disaster on Absalom.

¹⁵Hushai told Zadok and Abiathar, the priests, "Ahithophel has advised Absalom and the elders of Israel to do such and such, but I have advised them to do so and so. ¹⁶Now send a message immediately and tell David, 'Do not spend the night at the fords in the desert; cross over without fail, or the king and all the people with him will be swallowed up.'"

¹⁷Jonathan and Ahimaaz were staying at En Rogel. A servant girl was to go and inform them, and they were to go and tell King David, for they could not risk being seen entering the city. ¹⁸But a young man saw them and told Absalom. So the two of them left quickly and went to the house of a man in Bahurim. He had a well in his courtyard, and they climbed down into it. ¹⁹His wife took a covering and spread it out over the opening of the well and scattered grain over it. No one knew anything about it.

²⁰When Absalom's men came to the woman at the house, they asked, "Where are Ahimaaz and Jonathan?"

The woman answered them, "They crossed over the brook."ᵃ The men searched but found no one, so they returned to Jerusalem.

²¹After the men had gone, the two climbed out of the well and went to inform King David. They said to him, "Set out and cross the river at once; Ahithophel has advised such and such against you." ²²So David and all the people with him set out and crossed the Jordan. By daybreak, no one was left who had not crossed the Jordan.

²³When Ahithophel saw that his advice had not been followed, he saddled his donkey and set out for his house in his hometown. He put his house in order and then hanged himself. So he died and was buried in his father's tomb.

²⁴David went to Mahanaim, and Absalom crossed the Jordan with all the men of Israel. ²⁵Absalom had appointed Amasa over the army in place of Joab. Amasa was the son of a man named Jether,ᵇ an Israeliteᶜ who had married Abigail,ᵈ the daughter of Nahash and sister of Zeruiah the mother of Joab. ²⁶The Israelites and Absalom camped in the land of Gilead.

²⁷When David came to Mahanaim, Shobi son of Nahash from Rabbah of the Ammonites, and Makir son of Ammiel from Lo Debar, and Barzillai the Gileadite from Rogelim ²⁸brought bedding and bowls and articles of pottery. They also brought wheat and barley, flour and roasted grain, beans and lentils,ᵉ ²⁹honey and curds, sheep, and cheese from cows' milk for David and his people to eat. For they said, "The people have become hungry and tired and thirsty in the desert."

Absalom's Death

18 David mustered the men who were with him and appointed over them commanders of thousands and commanders of hundreds. ²David sent the troops out—a third under the command of Joab, a third under Joab's brother Abishai son of Zeruiah, and a third under Ittai the Gittite. The king told the troops, "I myself will surely march out with you."

³But the men said, "You must not go out; if we are forced to flee, they won't care about us. Even if half of us die, they won't care; but you are worth ten thousand of us.ᶠ It would be better now for you to give us support from the city."

⁴The king answered, "I will do whatever seems best to you."

So the king stood beside the gate while all the men marched out in units of hundreds and of thousands. ⁵The king commanded Joab, Abishai and Ittai, "Be gentle with the young man Absalom for my sake." And all the troops heard the king giving orders concerning Absalom to each of the commanders.

⁶The army marched into the field to fight Israel, and the battle took place in the forest of Ephraim. ⁷There the army of Israel was defeated by David's men, and the casualties that day were great—twenty thousand men. ⁸The battle spread out over the whole countryside, and the forest claimed more lives that day than the sword.

⁹Now Absalom happened to meet David's men. He was riding his mule, and as the mule went under the thick branches of a large oak, Absalom's head got caught in the tree. He was left hanging in midair, while the mule he was riding kept on going.

¹⁰When one of the men saw this, he told Joab, "I just saw Absalom hanging in an oak tree."

¹¹Joab said to the man who had told him this, "What! You saw him? Why didn't you strike him to the ground right there? Then I would have had to give you ten shekelsᵍ of silver and a warrior's belt."

¹²But the man replied, "Even if a thousand

ᵃ20 Or *"They passed by the sheep pen toward the water."* ᵇ25 Hebrew *Ithra,* a variant of *Jether* ᶜ25 Hebrew *and some Septuagint manuscripts; other Septuagint manuscripts (see also 1 Chron. 2:17) Ishmaelite* or *Jezreelite* ᵈ25 Hebrew *Abigal,* a variant of *Abigail* ᵉ28 Most Septuagint manuscripts and Syriac; Hebrew *lentils, and roasted grain* ᶠ3 Two Hebrew manuscripts, some Septuagint manuscripts and Vulgate; most Hebrew manuscripts *care; for now there are ten thousand like us* ᵍ11 That is, about 4 ounces (about 115 grams)

Sin As a Cancer

First David, then his family, then a nation

SINS: MANY PEOPLE THINK OF them as parking tickets. If you get too many, the cops may track you down or give your car "the boot." However, one or two here and there won't make a big difference.

The Bible views sins more as cancer cells. One or two here and there do make a difference— often the difference between life and death. Because cancer cells grow, multiply, and take over, major surgery may be needed to save your life.

> "O my son Absalom! My son, my son Absalom! If only I had died instead of you—O Absalom, my son, my son!"
> 18:33

Second Samuel 11–20 reads like a history of a spreading cancer. In the beginning, David was on top of the world—and so was Israel. The civil war was over, the land was at peace, and Israel was entering an era of unprecedented prosperity. God had promised to ensure David's descendants a continuous reign forever. What more could David hope for? The rest of life appeared as one long celebration.

The Cancer Grows

That celebration never began. One night David caught a glimpse of Bathsheba's beautiful, naked body and impulsively sent for her. The cover-up required a murder. Nobody could deny it was an ugly business: Even David admitted it when Nathan confronted him. However, it was soon over. He repented. He married Bathsheba. He did not intend to fall to that temptation again.

But the consequences of the sin were far from over. Unknown to David, cancer was growing in his own household. David's oldest son Amnon had an eye for women too. He tricked his half sister Tamar into his bedroom, then raped her. Afterwards, filled with disgust, he threw her out.

David was furious. But, maybe because he felt his own sin had robbed him of moral authority, he did nothing to punish his son. According to the law (Leviticus 18:9,29), Amnon deserved exile, but he got off free. David apparently wanted the matter forgotten.

A Cold-blooded Character

It merely disappeared from view. Absalom waited two full years to avenge his sister's rape. Then he murdered Amnon in cold blood. Again David was long on regret, short on punishment. He wept over Amnon's death but perhaps recognized his own responsibility in it. After three years David let Absalom return to Jerusalem unpunished; two years later, when Absalom angrily demanded either a murder trial or full acceptance back into the palace (14:32), David kissed and made up completely.

Again the cancer disappeared from view. But it was not gone; it grew. Now an arrogant Absalom started a program of public relations designed to make him look better than his aging father. At the end of four years, having become quite popular, he set his coup in motion. Taken completely by surprise, David was driven out of Jerusalem, into the desert.

The shock seemed to awaken David. Though dazed and weeping as he left the city, he had enough sense to make some clever plans. When the battle came at last, David's army won, and Absalom was captured and killed.

Weeping for His Son

For David the king, Absalom's defeat was a great triumph. For David the father, it was a horrible tragedy. The worst thing that can happen to a father had happened to him. His own son had tried to kill him, and in trying, had been killed. David could not stop weeping over his son's death until Joab, his general, warned him that he was insulting the troops who had fought for him.

David pulled himself together. Piece by piece, he put his kingdom back in order. He sent conciliatory words to the rebellious leaders of his own tribe. He rewarded his supporters. He took no revenge on any rebel faction, but showed remarkable fairness. A second rebellion broke out but was soon put down. The cancer seemed finally to have run its course.

Yet it had not. David had no more trouble with rebellion in his lifetime, but after his death Solomon killed a brother who he thought was scheming for the throne (1 Kings 2:25). After Solomon's reign, the old tribal tensions rose again, and the North and the South, which David had so carefully knit together, split for good (1 Kings 12). Such may be the consequences when a leader sins. His cancer not only poisons him; it grows to affect all those he leads—and it undermines his work.

Life Questions: Many people will, at some point, see their well-run lives disintegrate. What enables someone to pick up the pieces, as David did?

shekels*a* were weighed out into my hands, I would not lift my hand against the king's son. In our hearing the king commanded you and Abishai and Ittai, 'Protect the young man Absalom for my sake.*b*' 13 And if I had put my life in jeopardy*c*—and nothing is hidden from the king—you would have kept your distance from me."

14 Joab said, "I'm not going to wait like this for you." So he took three javelins in his hand and plunged them into Absalom's heart while Absalom was still alive in the oak tree. 15 And ten of Joab's armor-bearers surrounded Absalom, struck him and killed him.

16 Then Joab sounded the trumpet, and the troops stopped pursuing Israel, for Joab halted them. 17 They took Absalom, threw him into a big pit in the forest and piled up a large heap of rocks over him. Meanwhile, all the Israelites fled to their homes.

18 During his lifetime Absalom had taken a pillar and erected it in the King's Valley as a monument to himself, for he thought, "I have no son to carry on the memory of my name." He named the pillar after himself, and it is called Absalom's Monument to this day.

David Mourns

19 Now Ahimaaz son of Zadok said, "Let me run and take the news to the king that the LORD has delivered him from the hand of his enemies."

20 "You are not the one to take the news today," Joab told him. "You may take the news another time, but you must not do so today, because the king's son is dead."

21 Then Joab said to a Cushite, "Go, tell the king what you have seen." The Cushite bowed down before Joab and ran off.

22 Ahimaaz son of Zadok again said to Joab, "Come what may, please let me run behind the Cushite."

But Joab replied, "My son, why do you want to go? You don't have any news that will bring you a reward."

23 He said, "Come what may, I want to run."

So Joab said, "Run!" Then Ahimaaz ran by way of the plain*d* and outran the Cushite.

24 While David was sitting between the inner and outer gates, the watchman went up to the roof of the gateway by the wall. As he looked out, he saw a man running alone. 25 The watchman called out to the king and reported it.

The king said, "If he is alone, he must have good news." And the man came closer and closer.

26 Then the watchman saw another man running, and he called down to the gatekeeper, "Look, another man running alone!"

The king said, "He must be bringing good news, too."

27 The watchman said, "It seems to me that the first one runs like Ahimaaz son of Zadok."

"He's a good man," the king said. "He comes with good news."

28 Then Ahimaaz called out to the king, "All is well!" He bowed down before the king with his face to the ground and said, "Praise be to the LORD your God! He has delivered up the men who lifted their hands against my lord the king."

29 The king asked, "Is the young man Absalom safe?"

Ahimaaz answered, "I saw great confusion just as Joab was about to send the king's servant and me, your servant, but I don't know what it was."

30 The king said, "Stand aside and wait here." So he stepped aside and stood there.

31 Then the Cushite arrived and said, "My lord the king, hear the good news! The LORD has delivered you today from all who rose up against you."

32 The king asked the Cushite, "Is the young man Absalom safe?"

The Cushite replied, "May the enemies of my lord the king and all who rise up to harm you be like that young man."

33 The king was shaken. He went up to the room over the gateway and wept. As he went, he said: "O my son Absalom! My son, my son Absalom! If only I had died instead of you— O Absalom, my son, my son!"

18:33 Absalom, Absalom!

David's cry is one of the most poignant in all literature. Yet here again, David's love for his children collided with his effectiveness as a leader. He wept so excessively over Absalom that it demoralized the troops who had just risked their necks for the king (19:3).

---

19 Joab was told, "The king is weeping and mourning for Absalom." 2 And for the whole army the victory that day was turned into mourning, because on that day the troops heard it said, "The king is grieving for his son." 3 The men stole into the city that day as men steal in who are ashamed when they flee from battle. 4 The king covered his face and cried aloud, "O my son Absalom! O Absalom, my son, my son!"

5 Then Joab went into the house to the king

---

*a*12 That is, about 25 pounds (about 11 kilograms)   *b*12 A few Hebrew manuscripts, Septuagint, Vulgate and Syriac; most Hebrew manuscripts may be translated *Absalom, whoever you may be,*   *c*13 Or *Otherwise, if I had acted treacherously toward him*   *d*23 That is, the plain of the Jordan

and said, "Today you have humiliated all your men, who have just saved your life and the lives of your sons and daughters and the lives of your wives and concubines. **6**You love those who hate you and hate those who love you. You have made it clear today that the commanders and their men mean nothing to you. I see that you would be pleased if Absalom were alive today and all of us were dead. **7**Now go out and encourage your men. I swear by the LORD that if you don't go out, not a man will be left with you by nightfall. This will be worse for you than all the calamities that have come upon you from your youth till now."

8So the king got up and took his seat in the gateway. When the men were told, "The king is sitting in the gateway," they all came before him.

David Returns to Jerusalem

Meanwhile, the Israelites had fled to their homes. **9**Throughout the tribes of Israel, the people were all arguing with each other, saying, "The king delivered us from the hand of our enemies; he is the one who rescued us from the hand of the Philistines. But now he has fled the country because of Absalom; **10**and Absalom, whom we anointed to rule over us, has died in battle. So why do you say nothing about bringing the king back?"

11King David sent this message to Zadok and Abiathar, the priests: "Ask the elders of Judah, 'Why should you be the last to bring the king back to his palace, since what is being said throughout Israel has reached the king at his quarters? **12**You are my brothers, my own flesh and blood. So why should you be the last to bring back the king?' **13**And say to Amasa, 'Are you not my own flesh and blood? May God deal with me, be it ever so severely, if from now on you are not the commander of my army in place of Joab.'"

14He won over the hearts of all the men of Judah as though they were one man. They sent word to the king, "Return, you and all your men." **15**Then the king returned and went as far as the Jordan.

Now the men of Judah had come to Gilgal to go out and meet the king and bring him across the Jordan. **16**Shimei son of Gera, the Benjamite from Bahurim, hurried down with the men of Judah to meet King David. **17**With him were a thousand Benjamites, along with Ziba, the steward of Saul's household, and his fifteen sons and twenty servants. They rushed to the Jordan, where the king was. **18**They crossed at the ford to take the king's household over and to do whatever he wished.

When Shimei son of Gera crossed the Jordan, he fell prostrate before the king **19**and said to him, "May my lord not hold me guilty. Do not remember how your servant did wrong on the day my lord the king left Jerusalem. May the king put

it out of his mind. **20**For I your servant know that I have sinned, but today I have come here as the first of the whole house of Joseph to come down and meet my lord the king."

21Then Abishai son of Zeruiah said, "Shouldn't Shimei be put to death for this? He cursed the LORD's anointed."

22David replied, "What do you and I have in common, you sons of Zeruiah? This day you have become my adversaries! Should anyone be put to death in Israel today? Do I not know that today I am king over Israel?" **23**So the king said to Shimei, "You shall not die." And the king promised him on oath.

24Mephibosheth, Saul's grandson, also went down to meet the king. He had not taken care of his feet or trimmed his mustache or washed his clothes from the day the king left until the day he

---

19:24 The "Traitor's" Story

Mephibosheth's servant Ziba had told David that Mephibosheth was a traitor with dreams that he, as Saul's grandson, would be made king (16:1–4). Hearing this, David had given Ziba all of Mephibosheth's property.

Now we hear Mephibosheth's side of the story. He claimed that Ziba had betrayed him, presumably by taking his donkey so he, a cripple, could not follow David. More convincing than his words was his appearance. He had not washed himself or trimmed his mustache. He looked as though he had been mourning, not grooming himself for the throne.

Did David believe him? Perhaps not completely. He ordered Ziba to give back half, but not all, of the property.

---

returned safely. **25**When he came from Jerusalem to meet the king, the king asked him, "Why didn't you go with me, Mephibosheth?"

26He said, "My lord the king, since I your servant am lame, I said, 'I will have my donkey saddled and will ride on it, so I can go with the king.' But Ziba my servant betrayed me. **27**And he has slandered your servant to my lord the king. My lord the king is like an angel of God; so do whatever pleases you. **28**All my grandfather's descendants deserved nothing but death from my lord the king, but you gave your servant a place among those who eat at your table. So what right do I have to make any more appeals to the king?"

29The king said to him, "Why say more? I order you and Ziba to divide the fields."

30Mephibosheth said to the king, "Let him take everything, now that my lord the king has arrived home safely."

31Barzillai the Gileadite also came down from

Rogelim to cross the Jordan with the king and to send him on his way from there. ³²Now Barzillai was a very old man, eighty years of age. He had provided for the king during his stay in Mahanaim, for he was a very wealthy man. ³³The king said to Barzillai, "Cross over with me and stay with me in Jerusalem, and I will provide for you."

³⁴But Barzillai answered the king, "How many more years will I live, that I should go up to Jerusalem with the king? ³⁵I am now eighty years old. Can I tell the difference between what is good and what is not? Can your servant taste what he eats and drinks? Can I still hear the voices of men and women singers? Why should your servant be an added burden to my lord the king? ³⁶Your servant will cross over the Jordan with the king for a short distance, but why should the king reward me in this way? ³⁷Let your servant return, that I may die in my own town near the tomb of my father and mother. But here is your servant Kimham. Let him cross over with my lord the king. Do for him whatever pleases you."

³⁸The king said, "Kimham shall cross over with me, and I will do for him whatever pleases you. And anything you desire from me I will do for you."

³⁹So all the people crossed the Jordan, and then the king crossed over. The king kissed Barzillai and gave him his blessing, and Barzillai returned to his home.

⁴⁰When the king crossed over to Gilgal, Kimham crossed with him. All the troops of Judah and half the troops of Israel had taken the king over.

⁴¹Soon all the men of Israel were coming to the king and saying to him, "Why did our brothers, the men of Judah, steal the king away and bring him and his household across the Jordan, together with all his men?"

⁴²All the men of Judah answered the men of Israel, "We did this because the king is closely related to us. Why are you angry about it? Have we eaten any of the king's provisions? Have we taken anything for ourselves?"

⁴³Then the men of Israel answered the men of Judah, "We have ten shares in the king; and besides, we have a greater claim on David than you have. So why do you treat us with contempt? Were we not the first to speak of bringing back our king?"

But the men of Judah responded even more harshly than the men of Israel.

Sheba Rebels Against David

20 Now a troublemaker named Sheba son of Bicri, a Benjamite, happened to be there. He sounded the trumpet and shouted,

"We have no share in David,

no part in Jesse's son!
Every man to his tent, O Israel!"

²So all the men of Israel deserted David to follow Sheba son of Bicri. But the men of Judah stayed by their king all the way from the Jordan to Jerusalem.

20:2 North Versus South

Ethnic tension crackled between North ("Israel") and South ("Judah"). Saul came from the tribe of Benjamin in the north; David was a southerner. David worked hard to heal these divisions, but this rebellion shows that many in the north remained dissatisfied. David and his son Solomon managed to keep the two regions together, but after Solomon's death they broke apart for good.

³When David returned to his palace in Jerusalem, he took the ten concubines he had left to take care of the palace and put them in a house under guard. He provided for them, but did not lie with them. They were kept in confinement till the day of their death, living as widows.

⁴Then the king said to Amasa, "Summon the men of Judah to come to me within three days, and be here yourself." ⁵But when Amasa went to summon Judah, he took longer than the time the king had set for him.

⁶David said to Abishai, "Now Sheba son of Bicri will do us more harm than Absalom did. Take your master's men and pursue him, or he will find fortified cities and escape from us." ⁷So Joab's men and the Kerethites and Pelethites and all the mighty warriors went out under the command of Abishai. They marched out from Jerusalem to pursue Sheba son of Bicri.

⁸While they were at the great rock in Gibeon, Amasa came to meet them. Joab was wearing his military tunic, and strapped over it at his waist was a belt with a dagger in its sheath. As he stepped forward, it dropped out of its sheath.

⁹Joab said to Amasa, "How are you, my brother?" Then Joab took Amasa by the beard with his right hand to kiss him. ¹⁰Amasa was not on his guard against the dagger in Joab's hand, and Joab plunged it into his belly, and his intestines spilled out on the ground. Without being stabbed again, Amasa died. Then Joab and his brother Abishai pursued Sheba son of Bicri.

¹¹One of Joab's men stood beside Amasa and said, "Whoever favors Joab, and whoever is for David, let him follow Joab!" ¹²Amasa lay wallowing in his blood in the middle of the road, and the man saw that all the troops came to a halt there. When he realized that everyone who came up to Amasa stopped, he dragged him from the road

into a field and threw a garment over him. [13]After Amasa had been removed from the road, all the men went on with Joab to pursue Sheba son of Bicri.

[14]Sheba passed through all the tribes of Israel to Abel Beth Maacah[a] and through the entire region of the Berites, who gathered together and followed him. [15]All the troops with Joab came and besieged Sheba in Abel Beth Maacah. They built a siege ramp up to the city, and it stood against the outer fortifications. While they were battering the wall to bring it down, [16]a wise woman called from the city, "Listen! Listen! Tell Joab to come here so I can speak to him." [17]He went toward her, and she asked, "Are you Joab?"

"I am," he answered.

She said, "Listen to what your servant has to say."

"I'm listening," he said.

[18]She continued, "Long ago they used to say, 'Get your answer at Abel,' and that settled it. [19]We are the peaceful and faithful in Israel. You are trying to destroy a city that is a mother in Israel. Why do you want to swallow up the LORD's inheritance?"

[20]"Far be it from me!" Joab replied, "Far be it from me to swallow up or destroy! [21]That is not the case. A man named Sheba son of Bicri, from the hill country of Ephraim, has lifted up his hand against the king, against David. Hand over this one man, and I'll withdraw from the city."

The woman said to Joab, "His head will be thrown to you from the wall."

[22]Then the woman went to all the people with her wise advice, and they cut off the head of Sheba son of Bicri and threw it to Joab. So he sounded the trumpet, and his men dispersed from the city, each returning to his home. And Joab went back to the king in Jerusalem.

[23]Joab was over Israel's entire army; Benaiah son of Jehoiada was over the Kerethites and Pelethites; [24]Adoniram[b] was in charge of forced labor; Jehoshaphat son of Ahilud was recorder; [25]Sheva was secretary; Zadok and Abiathar were priests; [26]and Ira the Jairite was David's priest.

The Gibeonites Avenged

21 During the reign of David, there was a famine for three successive years; so David sought the face of the LORD. The LORD said, "It is on account of Saul and his blood-stained house; it is because he put the Gibeonites to death."

[2]The king summoned the Gibeonites and spoke to them. (Now the Gibeonites were not a part of Israel but were survivors of the Amorites; the Israelites had sworn to ⌊spare⌋ them, but Saul in his zeal for Israel and Judah had tried to anni-

hilate them.) [3]David asked the Gibeonites, "What shall I do for you? How shall I make amends so that you will bless the LORD's inheritance?"

[4]The Gibeonites answered him, "We have no right to demand silver or gold from Saul or his family, nor do we have the right to put anyone in Israel to death."

"What do you want me to do for you?" David asked.

[5]They answered the king, "As for the man who destroyed us and plotted against us so that we have been decimated and have no place anywhere in Israel, [6]let seven of his male descendants be given to us to be killed and exposed before the LORD at Gibeah of Saul—the LORD's chosen one."

So the king said, "I will give them to you."

21:6 Needless Deaths

Is there any excuse for David's agreeing to the execution of Saul's descendants? Perhaps. One must remember that David had certain legal responsibilities as king of Israel. Having offered compensation to the Gibeonites for their mistreatment under Saul, he may have been under legal obligation to cooperate with their demand for blood. In Old Testament times, a family was considered responsible for the crimes of any individual in his family. By modern standards, however, these executions seem needless and cruel.

[7]The king spared Mephibosheth son of Jonathan, the son of Saul, because of the oath before the LORD between David and Jonathan son of Saul. [8]But the king took Armoni and Mephibosheth, the two sons of Aiah's daughter Rizpah, whom she had borne to Saul, together with the five sons of Saul's daughter Merab,[c] whom she had borne to Adriel son of Barzillai the Meholathite. [9]He handed them over to the Gibeonites, who killed and exposed them on a hill before the LORD. All seven of them fell together; they were put to death during the first days of the harvest, just as the barley harvest was beginning.

[10]Rizpah daughter of Aiah took sackcloth and spread it out for herself on a rock. From the beginning of the harvest till the rain poured down from the heavens on the bodies, she did not let the birds of the air touch them by day or the wild animals by night. [11]When David was told what Aiah's daughter Rizpah, Saul's concubine, had done, [12]he went and took the bones of Saul and his son Jonathan from the citizens of Jabesh Gilead. (They had taken them secretly

---

[a]14 Or *Abel, even Beth Maacah*; also in verse 15   [b]24 Some Septuagint manuscripts (see also 1 Kings 4:6 and 5:14); Hebrew *Adoram*   [c]8 Two Hebrew manuscripts, some Septuagint manuscripts and Syriac (see also 1 Samuel 18:19); most Hebrew and Septuagint manuscripts *Michal*

from the public square at Beth Shan, where the Philistines had hung them after they struck Saul down on Gilboa.) **13**David brought the bones of Saul and his son Jonathan from there, and the bones of those who had been killed and exposed were gathered up.

14They buried the bones of Saul and his son Jonathan in the tomb of Saul's father Kish, at Zela in Benjamin, and did everything the king commanded. After that, God answered prayer in behalf of the land.

Wars Against the Philistines

15Once again there was a battle between the Philistines and Israel. David went down with his men to fight against the Philistines, and he became exhausted. **16**And Ishbi-Benob, one of the descendants of Rapha, whose bronze spearhead weighed three hundred shekels*a* and who was armed with a new ⌊sword⌋, said he would kill David. **17**But Abishai son of Zeruiah came to David's rescue; he struck the Philistine down and killed him. Then David's men swore to him, saying, "Never again will you go out with us to battle, so that the lamp of Israel will not be extinguished."

18In the course of time, there was another battle with the Philistines, at Gob. At that time Sibbecai the Hushathite killed Saph, one of the descendants of Rapha.

19In another battle with the Philistines at Gob, Elhanan son of Jaare-Oregim*b* the Bethlehemite killed Goliath*c* the Gittite, who had a spear with a shaft like a weaver's rod.

20In still another battle, which took place at Gath, there was a huge man with six fingers on each hand and six toes on each foot—twenty-four in all. He also was descended from Rapha. **21**When he taunted Israel, Jonathan son of Shimeah, David's brother, killed him.

22These four were descendants of Rapha in Gath, and they fell at the hands of David and his men.

David's Song of Praise

22 David sang to the LORD the words of this song when the LORD delivered him from the hand of all his enemies and from the hand of Saul. **2**He said:

"The LORD is my rock, my fortress and my deliverer;
3   my God is my rock, in whom I take refuge,
    my shield and the horn*d* of my salvation.

He is my stronghold, my refuge and my savior—
    from violent men you save me.
4I call to the LORD, who is worthy of praise,
    and I am saved from my enemies.

5"The waves of death swirled about me;
    the torrents of destruction overwhelmed me.

22:1 David's Psalms

This song of praise was included in the book of Psalms as Psalm 18. Many psalms are credited to David, and some have titles suggesting the events that inspired them. You can read these as a spiritual and emotional commentary on key events in David's life:

Psalm 3. *When he fled from his son Absalom (2 Samuel 15:13)*
Psalm 18. *When the Lord delivered him from his enemies and Saul (1 Samuel 19–31)*
Psalm 51. *After Nathan confronted David over Bathsheba (2 Samuel 12)*
Psalm 52. *When Doeg turned in the high priest for helping David (1 Samuel 22:9–10)*
Psalm 54. *When the Ziphites told Saul that David was hiding in their territory (1 Samuel 23:19–20; 26:1–25)*
Psalm 56. *When the Philistines seized David in Gath (1 Samuel 21:10–15)*
Psalm 57. *When David fled from Saul into the cave (1 Samuel 22:1–2)*
Psalm 59. *When Saul sent men to watch David's house in order to kill him (1 Samuel 19:11)*
Psalm 60. *After an important battle*
Psalm 63. *When he was in the Desert of Judah*
Psalm 142. *When he was in the cave, hiding from Saul*

6The cords of the grave*e* coiled around me;
    the snares of death confronted me.
7In my distress I called to the LORD;
    I called out to my God.
From his temple he heard my voice;
    my cry came to his ears.

8"The earth trembled and quaked,
    the foundations of the heavens*f* shook;
    they trembled because he was angry.
9Smoke rose from his nostrils;
    consuming fire came from his mouth,
    burning coals blazed out of it.
10He parted the heavens and came down;
    dark clouds were under his feet.
11He mounted the cherubim and flew;

---

*a16 That is, about 7 1/2 pounds (about 3.5 kilograms)   b19 Or son of Jair the weaver   c19 Hebrew and Septuagint; 1 Chron. 20:5 son of Jair killed Lahmi the brother of Goliath   d3 Horn here symbolizes strength.
e6 Hebrew Sheol   f8 Hebrew; Vulgate and Syriac (see also Psalm 18:7) mountains*

he soared[a] on the wings of the wind.
¹²He made darkness his canopy around him—
the dark[b] rain clouds of the sky.
¹³Out of the brightness of his presence
bolts of lightning blazed forth.
¹⁴The LORD thundered from heaven;
the voice of the Most High resounded.
¹⁵He shot arrows and scattered ⌊the enemies⌋,
bolts of lightning and routed them.
¹⁶The valleys of the sea were exposed
and the foundations of the earth laid bare
at the rebuke of the LORD,
at the blast of breath from his nostrils.

¹⁷"He reached down from on high and took
hold of me;
he drew me out of deep waters.
¹⁸He rescued me from my powerful enemy,
from my foes, who were too strong for
me.
¹⁹They confronted me in the day of my
disaster,
but the LORD was my support.
²⁰He brought me out into a spacious place;
he rescued me because he delighted in
me.

²¹"The LORD has dealt with me according to
my righteousness;
according to the cleanness of my hands he
has rewarded me.
²²For I have kept the ways of the LORD;
I have not done evil by turning from my
God.
²³All his laws are before me;
I have not turned away from his decrees.
²⁴I have been blameless before him
and have kept myself from sin.
²⁵The LORD has rewarded me according to my
righteousness,
according to my cleanness[c] in his sight.

²⁶"To the faithful you show yourself faithful,
to the blameless you show yourself
blameless,
²⁷to the pure you show yourself pure,
but to the crooked you show yourself
shrewd.
²⁸You save the humble,
but your eyes are on the haughty to bring
them low.
²⁹You are my lamp, O LORD;
the LORD turns my darkness into light.
³⁰With your help I can advance against a
troop[d];
with my God I can scale a wall.

³¹"As for God, his way is perfect;
the word of the LORD is flawless.
He is a shield
for all who take refuge in him.
³²For who is God besides the LORD?
And who is the Rock except our God?
³³It is God who arms me with strength[e]
and makes my way perfect.
³⁴He makes my feet like the feet of a deer;
he enables me to stand on the heights.
³⁵He trains my hands for battle;
my arms can bend a bow of bronze.
³⁶You give me your shield of victory;
you stoop down to make me great.
³⁷You broaden the path beneath me,
so that my ankles do not turn.

³⁸"I pursued my enemies and crushed them;
I did not turn back till they were
destroyed.
³⁹I crushed them completely, and they could
not rise;
they fell beneath my feet.
⁴⁰You armed me with strength for battle;
you made my adversaries bow at my feet.
⁴¹You made my enemies turn their backs in
flight,
and I destroyed my foes.
⁴²They cried for help, but there was no one to
save them—
to the LORD, but he did not answer.
⁴³I beat them as fine as the dust of the earth;
I pounded and trampled them like mud
in the streets.

⁴⁴"You have delivered me from the attacks of
my people;
you have preserved me as the head of
nations.
People I did not know are subject to me,
⁴⁵   and foreigners come cringing to me;
as soon as they hear me, they obey me.
⁴⁶They all lose heart;
they come trembling[f] from their
strongholds.

⁴⁷"The LORD lives! Praise be to my Rock!
Exalted be God, the Rock, my Savior!
⁴⁸He is the God who avenges me,
who puts the nations under me,
⁴⁹   who sets me free from my enemies.
You exalted me above my foes;
from violent men you rescued me.
⁵⁰Therefore I will praise you, O LORD, among
the nations;
I will sing praises to your name.
⁵¹He gives his king great victories;

---

[a]11 Many Hebrew manuscripts (see also Psalm 18:10); most Hebrew manuscripts *appeared*   [b]12 Septuagint and Vulgate (see also Psalm 18:11); Hebrew *massed*   [c]25 Hebrew; Septuagint and Vulgate (see also Psalm 18:24) *to the cleanness of my hands*   [d]30 Or *can run through a barricade*   [e]33 Dead Sea Scrolls, some Septuagint manuscripts, Vulgate and Syriac (see also Psalm 18:32); Masoretic Text *who is my strong refuge*   [f]46 Some Septuagint manuscripts and Vulgate (see also Psalm 18:45); Masoretic Text *they arm themselves.*

he shows unfailing kindness to his
anointed,
to David and his descendants forever."

The Last Words of David

23 These are the last words of David:

"The oracle of David son of Jesse,
the oracle of the man exalted by the Most
High,
the man anointed by the God of Jacob,
Israel's singer of songs[a]:

23:1 Final Words

People hold on to a loved one's last words, for they sometimes sum up his or her life. This, David's final poem, shows David's deep concern to be a king who pleases God. He insists that a leader in tune with God will always be a blessing to God's people, and recalls God's promise that his descendants will always rule. A memorial to David's "mighty men" follows this psalm, honoring those who fought alongside him with unusual courage. Uriah the Hittite, whom David had murdered, makes the list. The vindictive Joab does not.

[2]"The Spirit of the LORD spoke through me;
his word was on my tongue.
[3]The God of Israel spoke,
the Rock of Israel said to me:
'When one rules over men in righteousness,
when he rules in the fear of God,
[4]he is like the light of morning at sunrise
on a cloudless morning,
like the brightness after rain
that brings the grass from the earth.'

[5]"Is not my house right with God?
Has he not made with me an everlasting
covenant,
arranged and secured in every part?
Will he not bring to fruition my salvation
and grant me my every desire?
[6]But evil men are all to be cast aside like
thorns,
which are not gathered with the hand.
[7]Whoever touches thorns
uses a tool of iron or the shaft of a spear;
they are burned up where they lie."

David's Mighty Men

[8]These are the names of David's mighty men:
Josheb-Basshebeth,[b] a Tahkemonite,[c] was
chief of the Three; he raised his spear against
eight hundred men, whom he killed[d] in one
encounter.

[9]Next to him was Eleazar son of Dodai the
Ahohite. As one of the three mighty men, he was
with David when they taunted the Philistines
gathered ⌊at Pas Dammim,⌋[e] for battle. Then the
men of Israel retreated, [10]but he stood his ground
and struck down the Philistines till his hand grew
tired and froze to the sword. The LORD brought
about a great victory that day. The troops returned to Eleazar, but only to strip the dead.

[11]Next to him was Shammah son of Agee the
Hararite. When the Philistines banded together
at a place where there was a field full of lentils,
Israel's troops fled from them. [12]But Shammah
took his stand in the middle of the field. He
defended it and struck the Philistines down, and
the LORD brought about a great victory.

[13]During harvest time, three of the thirty chief
men came down to David at the cave of Adullam,
while a band of Philistines was encamped in the
Valley of Rephaim. [14]At that time David was in
the stronghold, and the Philistine garrison was at
Bethlehem. [15]David longed for water and said,
"Oh, that someone would get me a drink of water
from the well near the gate of Bethlehem!" [16]So
the three mighty men broke through the Philistine lines, drew water from the well near the gate
of Bethlehem and carried it back to David. But he
refused to drink it; instead, he poured it out before the LORD. [17]"Far be it from me, O LORD, to
do this!" he said. "Is it not the blood of men who
went at the risk of their lives?" And David would
not drink it.

Such were the exploits of the three mighty
men.

[18]Abishai the brother of Joab son of Zeruiah
was chief of the Three.[f] He raised his spear
against three hundred men, whom he killed, and
so he became as famous as the Three. [19]Was he
not held in greater honor than the Three? He
became their commander, even though he was
not included among them.

[20]Benaiah son of Jehoiada was a valiant fighter
from Kabzeel, who performed great exploits. He
struck down two of Moab's best men. He also
went down into a pit on a snowy day and killed
a lion. [21]And he struck down a huge Egyptian.
Although the Egyptian had a spear in his hand,
Benaiah went against him with a club. He
snatched the spear from the Egyptian's hand and
killed him with his own spear. [22]Such were the
exploits of Benaiah son of Jehoiada; he too was as
famous as the three mighty men. [23]He was held

---

[a]1 Or *Israel's beloved singer*   [b]8 Hebrew; some Septuagint manuscripts suggest *Ish-Bosheth*, that is, *Esh-Baal* (see also
1 Chron. 11:11 *Jashobeam*).   [c]8 Probably a variant of *Hacmonite* (see 1 Chron. 11:11)   [d]8 Some Septuagint
manuscripts (see also 1 Chron. 11:11); Hebrew and other Septuagint manuscripts *Three; it was Adino the Eznite who killed
eight hundred men*   [e]9 See 1 Chron. 11:13; Hebrew *gathered there*.   [f]18 Most Hebrew manuscripts (see also
1 Chron. 11:20); two Hebrew manuscripts and Syriac *Thirty*

in greater honor than any of the Thirty, but he was not included among the Three. And David put him in charge of his bodyguard.

24Among the Thirty were:
  Asahel the brother of Joab,
  Elhanan son of Dodo from Bethlehem,
25Shammah the Harodite,
  Elika the Harodite,
26Helez the Paltite,
  Ira son of Ikkesh from Tekoa,
27Abiezer from Anathoth,
  Mebunnai*a* the Hushathite,
28Zalmon the Ahohite,
  Maharai the Netophathite,
29Heled*b* son of Baanah the Netophathite,
  Ithai son of Ribai from Gibeah in Benja-
    min,
30Benaiah the Pirathonite,
  Hiddai*c* from the ravines of Gaash,
31Abi-Albon the Arbathite,
  Azmaveth the Barhumite,
32Eliahba the Shaalbonite,
  the sons of Jashen,
  Jonathan 33son of*d* Shammah the Hara-
    rite,
  Ahiam son of Sharar*e* the Hararite,
34Eliphelet son of Ahasbai the Maacathite,
  Eliam son of Ahithophel the Gilonite,
35Hezro the Carmelite,
  Paarai the Arbite,
36Igal son of Nathan from Zobah,
  the son of Hagri,*f*
37Zelek the Ammonite,
  Naharai the Beerothite, the armor-
    bearer of Joab son of Zeruiah,
38Ira the Ithrite,
  Gareb the Ithrite
39and Uriah the Hittite.
  There were thirty-seven in all.

David Counts the Fighting Men

24 Again the anger of the LORD burned against Israel, and he incited David against them, saying, "Go and take a census of Israel and Judah."

2So the king said to Joab and the army commanders*g* with him, "Go throughout the tribes of Israel from Dan to Beersheba and enroll the fighting men, so that I may know how many there are."

3But Joab replied to the king, "May the LORD your God multiply the troops a hundred times over, and may the eyes of my lord the king see it.

But why does my lord the king want to do such a thing?"

4The king's word, however, overruled Joab and the army commanders; so they left the presence of the king to enroll the fighting men of Israel.

24:1 Satan or the Lord?

In a parallel account, 1 Chronicles 21:1 says that Satan incited David to take a census. Who was it—Satan or the Lord? One explanation is that both are true. The Lord, as the ultimate power, allowed the census, and as is typical in the Old Testament, he gets full credit here. The Chronicles version is more concerned about being precise: Because the census was clearly evil (David confessed it as a sin, verse 10), Satan was more directly responsible. As is so often true of evil, people (and Satan) meant it for evil, but God used it for his own purposes.

5After crossing the Jordan, they camped near Aroer, south of the town in the gorge, and then went through Gad and on to Jazer. 6They went to Gilead and the region of Tahtim Hodshi, and on to Dan Jaan and around toward Sidon. 7Then they went toward the fortress of Tyre and all the towns of the Hivites and Canaanites. Finally, they went on to Beersheba in the Negev of Judah.

8After they had gone through the entire land, they came back to Jerusalem at the end of nine months and twenty days.

9Joab reported the number of the fighting men to the king: In Israel there were eight hundred thousand able-bodied men who could handle a sword, and in Judah five hundred thousand.

10David was conscience-stricken after he had counted the fighting men, and he said to the LORD, "I have sinned greatly in what I have done. Now, O LORD, I beg you, take away the guilt of your servant. I have done a very foolish thing."

11Before David got up the next morning, the word of the LORD had come to Gad the prophet, David's seer: 12"Go and tell David, 'This is what the LORD says: I am giving you three options. Choose one of them for me to carry out against you.'"

13So Gad went to David and said to him, "Shall there come upon you three*h* years of famine in your land? Or three months of fleeing from your enemies while they pursue you? Or three days of plague in your land? Now then, think it

---

a27 Hebrew; some Septuagint manuscripts (see also 1 Chron. 11:29) *Sibbecai*   *b29* Some Hebrew manuscripts and Vulgate (see also 1 Chron. 11:30); most Hebrew manuscripts *Heleb*   *c30* Hebrew; some Septuagint manuscripts (see also 1 Chron. 11:32) *Hurai*   *d33* Some Septuagint manuscripts (see also 1 Chron. 11:34); Hebrew does not have *son of.*   *e33* Hebrew; some Septuagint manuscripts (see also 1 Chron. 11:35) *Sacar*   *f36* Some Septuagint manuscripts (see also 1 Chron. 11:38); Hebrew *Haggadi*   *g2* Septuagint (see also verse 4 and 1 Chron. 21:2); Hebrew *Joab the army commander*   *h13* Septuagint (see also 1 Chron. 21:12); Hebrew *seven*

over and decide how I should answer the one who sent me."

¹⁴David said to Gad, "I am in deep distress. Let us fall into the hands of the LORD, for his mercy is great; but do not let me fall into the hands of men."

¹⁵So the LORD sent a plague on Israel from that morning until the end of the time designated, and seventy thousand of the people from Dan to Beersheba died. ¹⁶When the angel stretched out his hand to destroy Jerusalem, the LORD was grieved because of the calamity and said to the angel who was afflicting the people, "Enough! Withdraw your hand." The angel of the LORD was then at the threshing floor of Araunah the Jebusite.

¹⁷When David saw the angel who was striking down the people, he said to the LORD, "I am the one who has sinned and done wrong. These are but sheep. What have they done? Let your hand fall upon me and my family."

David Builds an Altar

¹⁸On that day Gad went to David and said to him, "Go up and build an altar to the LORD on the threshing floor of Araunah the Jebusite." ¹⁹So David went up, as the LORD had commanded through Gad. ²⁰When Araunah looked and saw the king and his men coming toward him, he went out and bowed down before the king with his face to the ground.

²¹Araunah said, "Why has my lord the king come to his servant?"

"To buy your threshing floor," David answered, "so I can build an altar to the LORD, that the plague on the people may be stopped."

²²Araunah said to David, "Let my lord the king take whatever pleases him and offer it up.

24:24 The Cost of True Worship

David's response is timeless: He sees that worship which costs nothing is not true worship at all. It is typical of David that even after falling into sin, he was not blinded to spiritual concerns. Feeling guilty already, he might have thought "one more compromise" would make no difference. Instead he stuck to his principle.

Here are oxen for the burnt offering, and here are threshing sledges and ox yokes for the wood. ²³O king, Araunah gives all this to the king." Araunah also said to him, "May the LORD your God accept you."

²⁴But the king replied to Araunah, "No, I insist on paying you for it. I will not sacrifice to the LORD my God burnt offerings that cost me nothing."

So David bought the threshing floor and the oxen and paid fifty shekels[a] of silver for them. ²⁵David built an altar to the LORD there and sacrificed burnt offerings and fellowship offerings.[b] Then the LORD answered prayer in behalf of the land, and the plague on Israel was stopped.

---

[a]24 That is, about 1 1/4 pounds (about 0.6 kilogram)   [b]25 Traditionally *peace offerings*

1 KINGS

The Man Who Had Everything
The richest, wisest, most successful person of his time

THE FIRST HALF OF 1 KINGS describes a man who got life handed to him on a silver platter. The son of King David and Queen Bathsheba, young Solomon grew up in the royal palace. Early on, he astounded others with his talent for songwriting and natural history. He composed 1,005 songs and spun off 3,000 proverbs (a sampling of which were collected in the biblical book of Proverbs).

Solomon became king of Israel and received from God the special gift of wisdom. He was called the wisest man in the world, and kings and queens traveled hundreds of miles to meet him. They went away dazzled by the genius of Israel's king and by the prosperity of his nation.

The Best Years Ever

Israel reached its Golden Age under King Solomon, a time forever remembered with nostalgia by Jews. Almost all the promised land lay in Israel's hands, and the nation was at peace. Literature and culture flourished. Of the people, the Bible records simply that "they ate, they drank and they were happy" (4:20). "The king made silver as common in Jerusalem as stones" (10:27).

Of all Solomon's accomplishments, one stands out above the others. He built the temple of God, the finest building in the world of that day. Almost 200,000 men labored for seven years to complete it.

Despite the successes of Solomon's reign, however, later in his life the king had a dramatic downturn. His fall eventually brought the kingdom crashing down around him, and the second half of 1 Kings describes the grim process of dismemberment.

What Went Wrong?

How did it happen? How could the liveliest, wealthiest, most contented nation of its day slide so disastrously in one generation?

As 1 Kings tells it, Solomon seemed unable to control his excesses. Reared in a palace, he loved luxury. When Israel launched its first maritime expeditions, he used them to gather such exotica as gold, ivory, apes, peacocks, and silver. He plated the floor of the temple with gold, wastefully gilded over fine cedar and precious ivory, and fashioned militarily useless shields out of gold. First Kings describes the seven-year construction of the temple in elaborate detail. But then it pointedly notes that the construction of Solomon's palace—twice the temple's size—took 13 years (7:1).

Solomon showed similar extravagance in his love life. First, he married the daughter of the Egyptian pharaoh (perhaps indicating he was relying on military alliances, not on God, for the defense of his country). Then, disobeying God's specific orders, he married the princesses of Moab, Ammon, Edom, Sidon, and other nations. Seven hundred wives in all, and 300 concubines! The entire complexion of the court changed. It became un-Jewish, foreign. To please his wives, Solomon took a final, terrible step: He built altars to all their gods. The one who had built the Israelites' greatest monument to God had fallen to worshiping idols.

Rumblings of Discontent in the Land

To pay for the building projects, Solomon instituted Israel's first national taxation system. He drafted workers for employment and kept them as virtual slaves. When bills mounted, he went so far as to cede certain northern towns in the promised land to another king (9:10–14). Resentment opened up between Israel's North and South.

But the gulf separating Israel from God was even more dangerous. Previously, the people of Israel

> *"If you or your sons turn away from me and do not observe the commands and decrees I have given you and go off to serve other gods and worship them, then I will cut off Israel from the land I have given them and will reject this temple I have consecrated for my Name." 9:6–7*

had looked to God as their leader. Now, however, the focus shifted from God in heaven to the king in Jerusalem. Solomon had even made himself the unofficial religious leader of the country, and when he slid badly, the nation soon followed.

Solomon started out with every advantage of wealth, power, and wisdom. But 1 Kings gives this tragic conclusion: "So Solomon did evil in the eyes of the LORD; he did not follow the LORD completely, as David his father had done" (11:6).

Solomon seemed obsessed with a desire to outdo anyone who had ever lived. Along the way, he failed to make God the center of his life. He achieved lasting fame in history, but as a negative example. Jesus Christ himself rendered the final verdict on Solomon and his striving for glory when he pointed to a lily growing wild in the field. "Not even Solomon in all his splendor," he said, "was dressed like one of these" (Matthew 6:29).

How to Read 1 Kings

First and Second Kings were originally one book: The same Hebrew scroll contained both. Hebrew, having no vowels, is a very compact language, and when the book of Kings was translated into the wordier Greek and Latin, more space was needed. Translators arbitrarily split Kings. The two books, however, should be read as one.

First Kings divides neatly almost in half, with mostly good news in the first half. It tells of Israel's Golden Age, when King Solomon brought peace and prosperity to the nation. But he also sowed the seed for the calamities to follow. Chapter 12 marks the beginning of a civil war that ruptured Israel into two nations: Israel in the North and Judah in the South. The rest of 1, 2 Kings describes, ruler by ruler, the reigns of 19 kings in the North and 19 kings and one queen in the South.

Another book, 2 Chronicles, covers the exact same historical period as 1, 2 Kings. In some cases, 2 Chronicles adds more detail, so if a story interests you, read the parallel account there. These books of history form the background for 17 other books of the Bible: the Prophets. Famous prophets such as Isaiah, Jeremiah, Hosea, and Amos preached during the time of Kings.

Keeping 39 rulers straight can seem hopeless, especially since the books jump back and forth between two countries. Remember:

> Israel was the Northern Kingdom, with its capital in Samaria. Its kings were all unfaithful to God.
> Judah was the Southern Kingdom, with its capital in Jerusalem. Almost half of its rulers remained somewhat faithful to God; the others proved disobedient.

On pages 1361–1369, you will find a lineup of all the rulers, tracing the rise and fall of both the Northern and Southern Kingdoms. Use this handy reference as you read the history. You may find it helpful to underline the various rulers' names, using different colored marking pens (for example, red for Judah and blue for Israel). Add a star by those kings cited as doing "what was right in the eyes of the LORD." First Kings mentions two such kings: Asa and Jehoshaphat. By marking the kings and queen with some visual scheme, you can quickly refer back to them when you read references to them in the books of the prophets.

PEOPLE YOU'LL MEET IN 1 KINGS

SOLOMON (p. 362)
ABIATHAR (p. 367)
JEROBOAM (p. 379)

ELIJAH (p. 386)
AHAB (p. 393)

3-TRACK READING PLAN

For an explanation and complete listing of the 3-track reading plan, turn to page 7.

TRACK 1: **Two-Week Courses on the Bible**
The Track 1 reading program on the Old Testament includes one chapter from 1 Kings. See page 8 for a complete listing of this course.

TRACK 2: *An Overview of 1 Kings in 4 Days*
☐ Day 1. Read the Introduction to 1 Kings and then chapter 3, where Solomon asks for wisdom.
☐ Day 2. Israel reaches a high point at this ceremony: read chapter 8 through 9:9.
☐ Day 3. Elijah is one of the Bible's most dramatic and colorful characters. The third day, read about him in chapter 17.
☐ Day 4. Read chapter 18, in which Elijah takes on the prophets of Baal.

Now turn to page 9 for your next Track 2 reading project.

TRACK 3: *All of 1 Kings in 21 Days*
After you have read through 1 Kings, turn to pages 10–14 for your next Track 3 reading project.

☐1 ☐2 ☐3 ☐4–5 ☐6 ☐7 ☐8 ☐9
☐10 ☐11 ☐12 ☐13 ☐14 ☐15 ☐16 ☐17
☐18 ☐19 ☐20 ☐21 ☐22

Adonijah Sets Himself Up as King

1 When King David was old and well advanced in years, he could not keep warm even when they put covers over him. ²So his servants said to him, "Let us look for a young virgin to attend the king and take care of him. She can lie beside him so that our lord the king may keep warm."

³Then they searched throughout Israel for a beautiful girl and found Abishag, a Shunammite, and brought her to the king. ⁴The girl was very beautiful; she took care of the king and waited on him, but the king had no intimate relations with her.

⁵Now Adonijah, whose mother was Haggith, put himself forward and said, "I will be king." So he got chariots and horses[a] ready, with fifty men to run ahead of him. ⁶(His father had never interfered with him by asking, "Why do you behave as you do?" He was also very handsome and was born next after Absalom.)

⁷Adonijah conferred with Joab son of Zeruiah and with Abiathar the priest, and they gave him their support. ⁸But Zadok the priest, Benaiah son of Jehoiada, Nathan the prophet, Shimei and Rei[b] and David's special guard did not join Adonijah.

⁹Adonijah then sacrificed sheep, cattle and fattened calves at the Stone of Zoheleth near En Rogel. He invited all his brothers, the king's sons, and all the men of Judah who were royal officials, ¹⁰but he did not invite Nathan the prophet or Benaiah or the special guard or his brother Solomon.

¹¹Then Nathan asked Bathsheba, Solomon's mother, "Have you not heard that Adonijah, the son of Haggith, has become king without our lord David's knowing it? ¹²Now then, let me advise you how you can save your own life and the life of your son Solomon. ¹³Go in to King David and say to him, 'My lord the king, did you not swear to me your servant: "Surely Solomon your son shall be king after me, and he will sit on my throne"? Why then has Adonijah become king?' ¹⁴While you are still there talking to the king, I will come in and confirm what you have said."

¹⁵So Bathsheba went to see the aged king in his room, where Abishag the Shunammite was attending him. ¹⁶Bathsheba bowed low and knelt before the king.

"What is it you want?" the king asked.

¹⁷She said to him, "My lord, you yourself swore to me your servant by the LORD your God: 'Solomon your son shall be king after me, and he will sit on my throne.' ¹⁸But now Adonijah has become king, and you, my lord the king, do not know about it. ¹⁹He has sacrificed great numbers of cattle, fattened calves, and sheep, and has invited all the king's sons, Abiathar the priest and Joab the commander of the army, but he has not invited Solomon your servant. ²⁰My lord the king, the eyes of all Israel are on you, to learn from you who will sit on the throne of my lord the king after him. ²¹Otherwise, as soon as my lord the king is laid to rest with his fathers, I and my son Solomon will be treated as criminals."

²²While she was still speaking with the king, Nathan the prophet arrived. ²³And they told the king, "Nathan the prophet is here." So he went before the king and bowed with his face to the ground.

²⁴Nathan said, "Have you, my lord the king, declared that Adonijah shall be king after you, and that he will sit on your throne? ²⁵Today he has gone down and sacrificed great numbers of cattle, fattened calves, and sheep. He has invited all the king's sons, the commanders of the army and Abiathar the priest. Right now they are eating and drinking with him and saying, 'Long live

---

[a]5 Or *charioteers*   [b]8 Or *and his friends*

King Adonijah!' ²⁶But me your servant, and Zadok the priest, and Benaiah son of Jehoiada, and your servant Solomon he did not invite. ²⁷Is this something my lord the king has done without letting his servants know who should sit on the throne of my lord the king after him?"

David Makes Solomon King

²⁸Then King David said, "Call in Bathsheba." So she came into the king's presence and stood before him.

²⁹The king then took an oath: "As surely as the LORD lives, who has delivered me out of every trouble, ³⁰I will surely carry out today what I swore to you by the LORD, the God of Israel: Solomon your son shall be king after me, and he will sit on my throne in my place."

³¹Then Bathsheba bowed low with her face to the ground and, kneeling before the king, said, "May my lord King David live forever!"

³²King David said, "Call in Zadok the priest, Nathan the prophet and Benaiah son of Jehoiada." When they came before the king, ³³he said to them: "Take your lord's servants with you and set Solomon my son on my own mule and take him down to Gihon. ³⁴There have Zadok the priest and Nathan the prophet anoint him king over Israel. Blow the trumpet and shout, 'Long live King Solomon!' ³⁵Then you are to go up with him, and he is to come and sit on my throne and reign in my place. I have appointed him ruler over Israel and Judah."

³⁶Benaiah son of Jehoiada answered the king, "Amen! May the LORD, the God of my lord the king, so declare it. ³⁷As the LORD was with my lord the king, so may he be with Solomon to make his throne even greater than the throne of my lord King David!"

³⁸So Zadok the priest, Nathan the prophet, Benaiah son of Jehoiada, the Kerethites and the Pelethites went down and put Solomon on King David's mule and escorted him to Gihon. ³⁹Zadok the priest took the horn of oil from the sacred tent and anointed Solomon. Then they sounded the trumpet and all the people shouted, "Long live King Solomon!" ⁴⁰And all the people went up after him, playing flutes and rejoicing greatly, so that the ground shook with the sound.

⁴¹Adonijah and all the guests who were with him heard it as they were finishing their feast. On hearing the sound of the trumpet, Joab asked, "What's the meaning of all the noise in the city?"

⁴²Even as he was speaking, Jonathan son of Abiathar the priest arrived. Adonijah said, "Come in. A worthy man like you must be bringing good news."

⁴³"Not at all!" Jonathan answered. "Our lord King David has made Solomon king. ⁴⁴The king has sent with him Zadok the priest, Nathan the prophet, Benaiah son of Jehoiada, the Kerethites and the Pelethites, and they have put him on the king's mule, ⁴⁵and Zadok the priest and Nathan the prophet have anointed him king at Gihon. From there they have gone up cheering, and the city resounds with it. That's the noise you hear. ⁴⁶Moreover, Solomon has taken his seat on the royal throne. ⁴⁷Also, the royal officials have come to congratulate our lord King David, saying, 'May your God make Solomon's name more famous than yours and his throne greater than yours!' And the king bowed in worship on his bed ⁴⁸and said, 'Praise be to the LORD, the God of Israel, who has allowed my eyes to see a successor on my throne today.'"

⁴⁹At this, all Adonijah's guests rose in alarm and dispersed. ⁵⁰But Adonijah, in fear of Solomon, went and took hold of the horns of the altar. ⁵¹Then Solomon was told, "Adonijah is afraid of King Solomon and is clinging to the horns of the altar. He says, 'Let King Solomon swear to me today that he will not put his servant to death with the sword.'"

⁵²Solomon replied, "If he shows himself to be a worthy man, not a hair of his head will fall to the ground; but if evil is found in him, he will die." ⁵³Then King Solomon sent men, and they brought him down from the altar. And Adonijah came and bowed down to King Solomon, and Solomon said, "Go to your home."

David's Charge to Solomon

2 When the time drew near for David to die, he gave a charge to Solomon his son.

²"I am about to go the way of all the earth," he said. "So be strong, show yourself a man, ³and observe what the LORD your God requires: Walk in his ways, and keep his decrees and commands, his laws and requirements, as written in the Law of Moses, so that you may prosper in all you do and wherever you go, ⁴and that the LORD may keep his promise to me: 'If your descendants watch how they live, and if they walk faithfully before me with all their heart and soul, you will never fail to have a man on the throne of Israel.'

⁵"Now you yourself know what Joab son of Zeruiah did to me—what he did to the two commanders of Israel's armies, Abner son of Ner and Amasa son of Jether. He killed them, shedding their blood in peacetime as if in battle, and with that blood stained the belt around his waist and the sandals on his feet. ⁶Deal with him according

2:5 Paying Back Joab

For the background to David's comments about Joab, see 2 Samuel 3:17–30; 20:4–11.

to your wisdom, but do not let his gray head go down to the grave[a] in peace.

7"But show kindness to the sons of Barzillai of Gilead and let them be among those who eat at your table. They stood by me when I fled from your brother Absalom.

8"And remember, you have with you Shimei son of Gera, the Benjamite from Bahurim, who called down bitter curses on me the day I went to Mahanaim. When he came down to meet me at the Jordan, I swore to him by the LORD: 'I will not put you to death by the sword.' 9But now, do not consider him innocent. You are a man of wisdom; you will know what to do to him. Bring his gray head down to the grave in blood."

10Then David rested with his fathers and was buried in the City of David. 11He had reigned forty years over Israel—seven years in Hebron and thirty-three in Jerusalem. 12So Solomon sat on the throne of his father David, and his rule was firmly established.

Solomon's Throne Established

13Now Adonijah, the son of Haggith, went to Bathsheba, Solomon's mother. Bathsheba asked him, "Do you come peacefully?"

He answered, "Yes, peacefully." 14Then he added, "I have something to say to you."

"You may say it," she replied.

15"As you know," he said, "the kingdom was mine. All Israel looked to me as their king. But things changed, and the kingdom has gone to my brother; for it has come to him from the LORD. 16Now I have one request to make of you. Do not refuse me."

"You may make it," she said.

17So he continued, "Please ask King Solomon—he will not refuse you—to give me Abishag the Shunammite as my wife."

2:17 After More than a Wife?

Solomon had a rather harsh response (verse 23) to Adonijah's request to marry King David's companion. But asking for her may have been Adonijah's veiled attempt to regain the throne lost to Solomon. In the ancient Middle East, a person who married any of the late king's wives or concubines publicly claimed the rights of the former king (see 2 Samuel 12:8 and 16:21–22 for examples). Adonijah might have been cunningly hatching another conspiracy; Solomon, at least, seemed to think so.

18"Very well," Bathsheba replied, "I will speak to the king for you."

19When Bathsheba went to King Solomon to speak to him for Adonijah, the king stood up to meet her, bowed down to her and sat down on his throne. He had a throne brought for the king's mother, and she sat down at his right hand.

20"I have one small request to make of you," she said. "Do not refuse me."

The king replied, "Make it, my mother; I will not refuse you."

21So she said, "Let Abishag the Shunammite be given in marriage to your brother Adonijah."

22King Solomon answered his mother, "Why do you request Abishag the Shunammite for Adonijah? You might as well request the kingdom for him—after all, he is my older brother—yes, for him and for Abiathar the priest and Joab son of Zeruiah!"

23Then King Solomon swore by the LORD: "May God deal with me, be it ever so severely, if Adonijah does not pay with his life for this request! 24And now, as surely as the LORD lives—he who has established me securely on the throne of my father David and has founded a dynasty for me as he promised—Adonijah shall be put to death today!" 25So King Solomon gave orders to Benaiah son of Jehoiada, and he struck down Adonijah and he died.

26To Abiathar the priest the king said, "Go back to your fields in Anathoth. You deserve to die, but I will not put you to death now, because you carried the ark of the Sovereign LORD before my father David and shared all my father's hardships." 27So Solomon removed Abiathar from the priesthood of the LORD, fulfilling the word the LORD had spoken at Shiloh about the house of Eli.

28When the news reached Joab, who had conspired with Adonijah though not with Absalom, he fled to the tent of the LORD and took hold of the horns of the altar. 29King Solomon was told that Joab had fled to the tent of the LORD and was beside the altar. Then Solomon ordered Benaiah son of Jehoiada, "Go, strike him down!"

30So Benaiah entered the tent of the LORD and said to Joab, "The king says, 'Come out!'"

But he answered, "No, I will die here."

Benaiah reported to the king, "This is how Joab answered me."

31Then the king commanded Benaiah, "Do as he says. Strike him down and bury him, and so clear me and my father's house of the guilt of the innocent blood that Joab shed. 32The LORD will repay him for the blood he shed, because without the knowledge of my father David he attacked two men and killed them with the sword. Both of them—Abner son of Ner, commander of Israel's army, and Amasa son of Jether, commander of Judah's army—were better men and more upright than he. 33May the guilt of their blood rest on the head of Joab and his descendants forever. But on David and his descendants, his house and his throne, may there be the LORD's peace forever."

34So Benaiah son of Jehoiada went up and struck down Joab and killed him, and he was buried on his own land[a] in the desert. 35The king put Benaiah son of Jehoiada over the army in Joab's position and replaced Abiathar with Zadok the priest.

36Then the king sent for Shimei and said to him, "Build yourself a house in Jerusalem and live there, but do not go anywhere else. 37The day you leave and cross the Kidron Valley, you can be sure you will die; your blood will be on your own head."

38Shimei answered the king, "What you say is good. Your servant will do as my lord the king has said." And Shimei stayed in Jerusalem for a long time.

39But three years later, two of Shimei's slaves ran off to Achish son of Maacah, king of Gath, and Shimei was told, "Your slaves are in Gath." 40At this, he saddled his donkey and went to Achish at Gath in search of his slaves. So Shimei went away and brought the slaves back from Gath.

41When Solomon was told that Shimei had gone from Jerusalem to Gath and had returned, 42the king summoned Shimei and said to him, "Did I not make you swear by the LORD and warn you, 'On the day you leave to go anywhere else,

you can be sure you will die'? At that time you said to me, 'What you say is good. I will obey.' 43Why then did you not keep your oath to the LORD and obey the command I gave you?"

44The king also said to Shimei, "You know in your heart all the wrong you did to my father David. Now the LORD will repay you for your wrongdoing. 45But King Solomon will be blessed, and David's throne will remain secure before the LORD forever."

46Then the king gave the order to Benaiah son of Jehoiada, and he went out and struck Shimei down and killed him.

The kingdom was now firmly established in Solomon's hands.

2:46 Wise Yet Ruthless

Chapters 2 and 3 show conflicting personality traits in Solomon. In the power struggles of chapter 2 he proved more ruthless than his father David had ever been. This tendency stirred up resentment among the northern tribes of Israel and eventually led to civil war. But chapter 3 shows Solomon could also be faithful, wise, and even humble. Tragically, he gave in to his darker side more and more as his reign wore on.

Solomon Asks for Wisdom

3 Solomon made an alliance with Pharaoh king of Egypt and married his daughter. He

[a]34 Or *buried in his tomb*

ABIATHAR *Outlaw Priest*

GENERATIONS BEFORE, A PROPHET HAD predicted that Israel's chief family of priests would be destroyed (1 Samuel 2:31–36). Abiathar witnessed the horrible fulfillment of that prediction. All the men in his extended family—85 in all—were lined up and slaughtered. Abiathar's whole village—women, children, babies, even animals—perished, all because they were suspected of helping David escape from King Saul (1 Samuel 22:18).

Abiathar somehow got away and straggled into David's outlaw camp, the lone survivor bearing news of the massacre. He brought with him the ephod: the priest's garment containing the Urim and Thummim, sacred objects used to determine God's will.

From that day on David relied on Abiathar and his ephod to gain direction from God. Somewhat like Friar Tuck in Robin Hood's band, Abiathar became official priest to the outlaw band. When King Saul died and David and his guerrilla army finally came to power, David made Abiathar the nation's high priest in the new sanctuary at Jerusalem.

Abiathar's harrowing moments did not end even after he joined the power structure. When David's son Absalom led a rebellion, Abiathar remained loyal to David, returning to the conquered city as a spy (2 Samuel 15:24–29). When David grew old and feeble, Abiathar backed the wrong son to succeed the king. The aging priest might have been executed—others were—but Solomon showed mercy and banished him instead. Abiathar thus ended his career as he began: as an outcast (1 Kings 2:26).

Life Questions: Do you know anyone like Abiathar, someone who has suffered stunning losses? How can you—or someone else—be like David to him or her?

brought her to the City of David until he finished building his palace and the temple of the LORD, and the wall around Jerusalem. ²The people, however, were still sacrificing at the high places, because a temple had not yet been built for the Name of the LORD. ³Solomon showed his love for the LORD by walking according to the statutes of his father David, except that he offered sacrifices and burned incense on the high places.

⁴The king went to Gibeon to offer sacrifices, for that was the most important high place, and Solomon offered a thousand burnt offerings on that altar. ⁵At Gibeon the LORD appeared to Solomon during the night in a dream, and God said, "Ask for whatever you want me to give you."

⁶Solomon answered, "You have shown great kindness to your servant, my father David, because he was faithful to you and righteous and upright in heart. You have continued this great kindness to him and have given him a son to sit on his throne this very day.

⁷"Now, O LORD my God, you have made your servant king in place of my father David. But I am only a little child and do not know how to carry out my duties. ⁸Your servant is here among the people you have chosen, a great people, too numerous to count or number. ⁹So give your servant a discerning heart to govern your people and to distinguish between right and wrong. For who is able to govern this great people of yours?"

3:9 Solomon's Wish

By requesting the wisdom to be a good king, Solomon showed that he possessed much wisdom already. Pleased at Solomon's unselfish request, God gave Solomon even more. Unfortunately, the humility displayed in this scene did not stay with Solomon throughout his career.

¹⁰The Lord was pleased that Solomon had asked for this. ¹¹So God said to him, "Since you have asked for this and not for long life or wealth for yourself, nor have asked for the death of your enemies but for discernment in administering justice, ¹²I will do what you have asked. I will give you a wise and discerning heart, so that there will never have been anyone like you, nor will there ever be. ¹³Moreover, I will give you what you have not asked for—both riches and honor—so that in your lifetime you will have no equal among kings. ¹⁴And if you walk in my ways and obey my statutes and commands as David your father did, I will give you a long life." ¹⁵Then Solomon awoke—and he realized it had been a dream.

He returned to Jerusalem, stood before the ark of the Lord's covenant and sacrificed burnt offerings and fellowship offerings.ᵃ Then he gave a feast for all his court.

A Wise Ruling

¹⁶Now two prostitutes came to the king and stood before him. ¹⁷One of them said, "My lord, this woman and I live in the same house. I had a baby while she was there with me. ¹⁸The third day after my child was born, this woman also had a baby. We were alone; there was no one in the house but the two of us.

¹⁹"During the night this woman's son died because she lay on him. ²⁰So she got up in the middle of the night and took my son from my side while I your servant was asleep. She put him by her breast and put her dead son by my breast. ²¹The next morning, I got up to nurse my son—and he was dead! But when I looked at him closely in the morning light, I saw that it wasn't the son I had borne."

²²The other woman said, "No! The living one is my son; the dead one is yours."

But the first one insisted, "No! The dead one is yours; the living one is mine." And so they argued before the king.

²³The king said, "This one says, 'My son is alive and your son is dead,' while that one says, 'No! Your son is dead and mine is alive.'"

²⁴Then the king said, "Bring me a sword." So they brought a sword for the king. ²⁵He then gave an order: "Cut the living child in two and give half to one and half to the other."

²⁶The woman whose son was alive was filled with compassion for her son and said to the king, "Please, my lord, give her the living baby! Don't kill him!"

But the other said, "Neither I nor you shall have him. Cut him in two!"

²⁷Then the king gave his ruling: "Give the living baby to the first woman. Do not kill him; she is his mother."

²⁸When all Israel heard the verdict the king had given, they held the king in awe, because they saw that he had wisdom from God to administer justice.

Solomon's Officials and Governors

4 So King Solomon ruled over all Israel. ²And these were his chief officials:

Azariah son of Zadok—the priest;
³Elihoreph and Ahijah, sons of Shisha—secretaries;
Jehoshaphat son of Ahilud—recorder;
⁴Benaiah son of Jehoiada—commander in chief;
Zadok and Abiathar—priests;

ᵃ15 Traditionally *peace offerings*

⁵Azariah son of Nathan—in charge of the district officers;

Zabud son of Nathan—a priest and personal adviser to the king;

⁶Ahishar—in charge of the palace;

Adoniram son of Abda—in charge of forced labor.

⁷Solomon also had twelve district governors over all Israel, who supplied provisions for the king and the royal household. Each one had to provide supplies for one month in the year. ⁸These are their names:

Ben-Hur—in the hill country of Ephraim;

⁹Ben-Deker—in Makaz, Shaalbim, Beth Shemesh and Elon Bethhanan;

¹⁰Ben-Hesed—in Arubboth (Socoh and all the land of Hepher were his);

¹¹Ben-Abinadab—in Naphoth Dor*a* (he was married to Taphath daughter of Solomon);

¹²Baana son of Ahilud—in Taanach and Megiddo, and in all of Beth Shan next to Zarethan below Jezreel, from Beth Shan to Abel Meholah across to Jokmeam;

¹³Ben-Geber—in Ramoth Gilead (the settlements of Jair son of Manasseh in Gilead were his, as well as the district of Argob in Bashan and its sixty large walled cities with bronze gate bars);

¹⁴Ahinadab son of Iddo—in Mahanaim;

¹⁵Ahimaaz—in Naphtali (he had married Basemath daughter of Solomon);

¹⁶Baana son of Hushai—in Asher and in Aloth;

¹⁷Jehoshaphat son of Paruah—in Issachar;

¹⁸Shimei son of Ela—in Benjamin;

¹⁹Geber son of Uri—in Gilead (the country of Sihon king of the Amorites and the country of Og king of Bashan). He was the only governor over the district.

Solomon's Daily Provisions

²⁰The people of Judah and Israel were as numerous as the sand on the seashore; they ate, they drank and they were happy. ²¹And Solomon ruled over all the kingdoms from the River*b* to the land of the Philistines, as far as the border of Egypt. These countries brought tribute and were Solomon's subjects all his life.

²²Solomon's daily provisions were thirty cors*c* of fine flour and sixty cors*d* of meal, ²³ten head of stall-fed cattle, twenty of pasture-fed cattle and a hundred sheep and goats, as well as deer, gazelles, roebucks and choice fowl. ²⁴For he ruled over all the kingdoms west of the River,

from Tiphsah to Gaza, and had peace on all sides. ²⁵During Solomon's lifetime Judah and Israel, from Dan to Beersheba, lived in safety, each man under his own vine and fig tree.

4:21 How Large Was Israel?

Under the reigns of David and Solomon, Israel stretched from the border of Egypt to the border of Babylonia. It was approximately three times the size of the modern nation of Israel, encompassing land that now belongs to Jordan, Syria, and Lebanon.

²⁶Solomon had four*e* thousand stalls for chariot horses, and twelve thousand horses.*f*

²⁷The district officers, each in his month, supplied provisions for King Solomon and all who came to the king's table. They saw to it that nothing was lacking. ²⁸They also brought to the proper place their quotas of barley and straw for the chariot horses and the other horses.

Solomon's Wisdom

²⁹God gave Solomon wisdom and very great insight, and a breadth of understanding as measureless as the sand on the seashore. ³⁰Solomon's wisdom was greater than the wisdom of all the men of the East, and greater than all the wisdom of Egypt. ³¹He was wiser than any other man, including Ethan the Ezrahite—wiser than Heman, Calcol and Darda, the sons of Mahol. And his fame spread to all the surrounding nations. ³²He spoke three thousand proverbs and his songs numbered a thousand and five. ³³He described plant life, from the cedar of Lebanon to the hyssop that grows out of walls. He also taught about animals and birds, reptiles and fish. ³⁴Men of all nations came to listen to Solomon's wisdom, sent by all the kings of the world, who had heard of his wisdom.

Preparations for Building the Temple

5 When Hiram king of Tyre heard that Solomon had been anointed king to succeed his father David, he sent his envoys to Solomon, because he had always been on friendly terms with David. ²Solomon sent back this message to Hiram:

³"You know that because of the wars waged against my father David from all sides, he could not build a temple for the Name of the LORD his God until the LORD put his enemies under his feet. ⁴But now the LORD my God has given me rest on

---

a11 Or *in the heights of Dor*   *b21* That is, the Euphrates; also in verse 24   *c22* That is, probably about 185 bushels (about 6.6 kiloliters)   *d22* That is, probably about 375 bushels (about 13.2 kiloliters)   *e26* Some Septuagint manuscripts (see also 2 Chron. 9:25); Hebrew *forty*   *f26* Or *charioteers*

every side, and there is no adversary or disaster. ⁵I intend, therefore, to build a temple for the Name of the LORD my God, as the LORD told my father David, when he said, 'Your son whom I will put on the throne in your place will build the temple for my Name.'

⁶"So give orders that cedars of Lebanon be cut for me. My men will work with yours, and I will pay you for your men whatever wages you set. You know that we have no one so skilled in felling timber as the Sidonians."

⁷When Hiram heard Solomon's message, he was greatly pleased and said, "Praise be to the LORD today, for he has given David a wise son to rule over this great nation."

⁸So Hiram sent word to Solomon:

"I have received the message you sent me and will do all you want in providing the cedar and pine logs. ⁹My men will haul them down from Lebanon to the sea, and I will float them in rafts by sea to the place you specify. There I will separate them and you can take them away. And you are to grant my wish by providing food for my royal household."

¹⁰In this way Hiram kept Solomon supplied with all the cedar and pine logs he wanted, ¹¹and Solomon gave Hiram twenty thousand cors*a* of wheat as food for his household, in addition to twenty thousand baths*b,c* of pressed olive oil. Solomon continued to do this for Hiram year after year. ¹²The LORD gave Solomon wisdom, just as he had promised him. There were peaceful relations between Hiram and Solomon, and the two of them made a treaty.

¹³King Solomon conscripted laborers from all Israel—thirty thousand men. ¹⁴He sent them off to Lebanon in shifts of ten thousand a month, so that they spent one month in Lebanon and two months at home. Adoniram was in charge of the forced labor. ¹⁵Solomon had seventy thousand carriers and eighty thousand stonecutters in the hills, ¹⁶as well as thirty-three hundred*d* foremen who supervised the project and directed the workmen. ¹⁷At the king's command they removed from the quarry large blocks of quality stone to provide a foundation of dressed stone for the temple. ¹⁸The craftsmen of Solomon and Hiram and the men of Gebal*e* cut and prepared

the timber and stone for the building of the temple.

Solomon Builds the Temple

6 In the four hundred and eightieth*f* year after the Israelites had come out of Egypt, in the fourth year of Solomon's reign over Israel, in the month of Ziv, the second month, he began to build the temple of the LORD.

²The temple that King Solomon built for the LORD was sixty cubits long, twenty wide and thirty high.*g* ³The portico at the front of the main hall of the temple extended the width of the temple, that is twenty cubits,*h* and projected ten

6:3 History of the Temple

The Bible describes the temple architecture in some detail, though, notably, it does not record detailed instructions from God—in contrast to the very specific commands given for the tabernacle. Solomon's temple lasted about 380 years, occasionally falling into disrepair. Destroyed by Babylon's King Nebuchadnezzar, it was partially rebuilt under the leadership of Ezra and Nehemiah, and then reconstructed by King Herod in Jesus' day. Jesus walked in the temple on "Solomon's Porch." The early church met on the temple grounds, Peter preached there, and Ananias and Sapphira probably died there (Acts 5). Currently the temple site is occupied by a Muslim mosque.

cubits*i* from the front of the temple. ⁴He made narrow clerestory windows in the temple. ⁵Against the walls of the main hall and inner sanctuary he built a structure around the building, in which there were side rooms. ⁶The lowest floor was five cubits*j* wide, the middle floor six cubits*k* and the third floor seven.*l* He made offset ledges around the outside of the temple so that nothing would be inserted into the temple walls.

⁷In building the temple, only blocks dressed at the quarry were used, and no hammer, chisel or any other iron tool was heard at the temple site while it was being built.

⁸The entrance to the lowest*m* floor was on the south side of the temple; a stairway led up to the middle level and from there to the third. ⁹So he built the temple and completed it, roofing it with beams and cedar planks. ¹⁰And he built the side rooms all along the temple. The height of each

---

*a*11 That is, probably about 125,000 bushels (about 4,400 kiloliters)   *b*11 Septuagint (see also 2 Chron. 2:10); Hebrew *twenty cors*   *c*11 That is, about 115,000 gallons (about 440 kiloliters)   *d*16 Hebrew; some Septuagint manuscripts (see also 2 Chron. 2:2, 18) *thirty-six hundred*   *e*18 That is, Byblos   *f*1 Hebrew; Septuagint *four hundred and fortieth*   *g*2 That is, about 90 feet (about 27 meters) long and 30 feet (about 9 meters) wide and 45 feet (about 13.5 meters) high   *h*3 That is, about 30 feet (about 9 meters)   *i*3 That is, about 15 feet (about 4.5 meters)   *j*6 That is, about 7 1/2 feet (about 2.3 meters); also in verses 10 and 24   *k*6 That is, about 9 feet (about 2.7 meters)   *l*6 That is, about 10 1/2 feet (about 3.1 meters)   *m*8 Septuagint; Hebrew *middle*

was five cubits, and they were attached to the temple by beams of cedar.

[11]The word of the LORD came to Solomon: [12]"As for this temple you are building, if you follow my decrees, carry out my regulations and keep all my commands and obey them, I will fulfill through you the promise I gave to David your father. [13]And I will live among the Israelites and will not abandon my people Israel."

[14]So Solomon built the temple and completed it. [15]He lined its interior walls with cedar boards, paneling them from the floor of the temple to the ceiling, and covered the floor of the temple with planks of pine. [16]He partitioned off twenty cubits[a] at the rear of the temple with cedar boards from floor to ceiling to form within the temple an inner sanctuary, the Most Holy Place. [17]The main hall in front of this room was forty cubits[b] long. [18]The inside of the temple was cedar, carved with gourds and open flowers. Everything was cedar; no stone was to be seen.

[19]He prepared the inner sanctuary within the temple to set the ark of the covenant of the LORD there. [20]The inner sanctuary was twenty cubits long, twenty wide and twenty high.[c] He overlaid the inside with pure gold, and he also overlaid the altar of cedar. [21]Solomon covered the inside of the temple with pure gold, and he extended gold chains across the front of the inner sanctuary, which was overlaid with gold. [22]So he overlaid the whole interior with gold. He also overlaid with gold the altar that belonged to the inner sanctuary.

[23]In the inner sanctuary he made a pair of cherubim of olive wood, each ten cubits[d] high. [24]One wing of the first cherub was five cubits long, and the other wing five cubits—ten cubits from wing tip to wing tip. [25]The second cherub also measured ten cubits, for the two cherubim were identical in size and shape. [26]The height of each cherub was ten cubits. [27]He placed the cherubim inside the innermost room of the temple, with their wings spread out. The wing of one cherub touched one wall, while the wing of the other touched the other wall, and their wings touched each other in the middle of the room. [28]He overlaid the cherubim with gold.

[29]On the walls all around the temple, in both the inner and outer rooms, he carved cherubim, palm trees and open flowers. [30]He also covered the floors of both the inner and outer rooms of the temple with gold.

[31]For the entrance of the inner sanctuary he made doors of olive wood with five-sided jambs. [32]And on the two olive wood doors he carved cherubim, palm trees and open flowers, and overlaid the cherubim and palm trees with beaten gold. [33]In the same way he made four-sided jambs of olive wood for the entrance to the main hall. [34]He also made two pine doors, each having two leaves that turned in sockets. [35]He carved cherubim, palm trees and open flowers on them and overlaid them with gold hammered evenly over the carvings.

[36]And he built the inner courtyard of three courses of dressed stone and one course of trimmed cedar beams.

[37]The foundation of the temple of the LORD was laid in the fourth year, in the month of Ziv. [38]In the eleventh year in the month of Bul, the eighth month, the temple was finished in all its details according to its specifications. He had spent seven years building it.

Solomon Builds His Palace

7 It took Solomon thirteen years, however, to complete the construction of his palace. [2]He

7:1 Prosperity under Solomon

The magnificent temple and palace built by Solomon came to symbolize Israel's Golden Age. Solomon built many leading cities, assuming control of vital trade routes. He fortified Jerusalem, the capital, with a wall so thick that parts of it still stand. He modernized the Israelite army with 12,000 horses and the first chariot brigades, and made shrewd alliances with neighboring countries.

built the Palace of the Forest of Lebanon a hundred cubits long, fifty wide and thirty high,[e] with four rows of cedar columns supporting trimmed cedar beams. [3]It was roofed with cedar above the beams that rested on the columns—forty-five beams, fifteen to a row. [4]Its windows were placed high in sets of three, facing each other. [5]All the doorways had rectangular frames; they were in the front part in sets of three, facing each other.[f]

[6]He made a colonnade fifty cubits long and thirty wide.[g] In front of it was a portico, and in front of that were pillars and an overhanging roof.

[7]He built the throne hall, the Hall of Justice, where he was to judge, and he covered it with cedar from floor to ceiling.[h] [8]And the palace in which he was to live, set farther back, was similar in design. Solomon also made a palace like this

---

[a]16 That is, about 30 feet (about 9 meters)   [b]17 That is, about 60 feet (about 18 meters)   [c]20 That is, about 30 feet (about 9 meters) long, wide and high   [d]23 That is, about 15 feet (about 4.5 meters)   [e]2 That is, about 150 feet (about 46 meters) long, 75 feet (about 23 meters) wide and 45 feet (about 13.5 meters) high   [f]5 The meaning of the Hebrew for this verse is uncertain.   [g]6 That is, about 75 feet (about 23 meters) long and 45 feet (about 13.5 meters) wide   [h]7 Vulgate and Syriac; Hebrew *floor*

hall for Pharaoh's daughter, whom he had married.

⁹All these structures, from the outside to the great courtyard and from foundation to eaves, were made of blocks of high-grade stone cut to size and trimmed with a saw on their inner and outer faces. ¹⁰The foundations were laid with large stones of good quality, some measuring ten cubits*a* and some eight.*b* ¹¹Above were high-grade stones, cut to size, and cedar beams. ¹²The great courtyard was surrounded by a wall of three courses of dressed stone and one course of trimmed cedar beams, as was the inner courtyard of the temple of the LORD with its portico.

The Temple's Furnishings

¹³King Solomon sent to Tyre and brought Huram,*c* ¹⁴whose mother was a widow from the tribe of Naphtali and whose father was a man of Tyre and a craftsman in bronze. Huram was highly skilled and experienced in all kinds of bronze work. He came to King Solomon and did all the work assigned to him.

¹⁵He cast two bronze pillars, each eighteen cubits high and twelve cubits around,*d* by line. ¹⁶He also made two capitals of cast bronze to set on the tops of the pillars; each capital was five cubits*e* high. ¹⁷A network of interwoven chains festooned the capitals on top of the pillars, seven for each capital. ¹⁸He made pomegranates in two rows*f* encircling each network to decorate the capitals on top of the pillars.*g* He did the same for each capital. ¹⁹The capitals on top of the pillars in the portico were in the shape of lilies, four cubits*h* high. ²⁰On the capitals of both pillars, above the bowl-shaped part next to the network, were the two hundred pomegranates in rows all around. ²¹He erected the pillars at the portico of the temple. The pillar to the south he named Jakin*i* and the one to the north Boaz.*j* ²²The capitals on top were in the shape of lilies. And so the work on the pillars was completed.

²³He made the Sea of cast metal, circular in shape, measuring ten cubits*a* from rim to rim and five cubits high. It took a line of thirty cubits*k* to measure around it. ²⁴Below the rim, gourds encircled it—ten to a cubit. The gourds were cast in two rows in one piece with the Sea.

²⁵The Sea stood on twelve bulls, three facing north, three facing west, three facing south and three facing east. The Sea rested on top of them, and their hindquarters were toward the center. ²⁶It was a handbreadth*l* in thickness, and its rim was like the rim of a cup, like a lily blossom. It held two thousand baths.*m*

²⁷He also made ten movable stands of bronze; each was four cubits long, four wide and three high.*n* ²⁸This is how the stands were made: They had side panels attached to uprights. ²⁹On the panels between the uprights were lions, bulls and cherubim—and on the uprights as well. Above and below the lions and bulls were wreaths of hammered work. ³⁰Each stand had four bronze wheels with bronze axles, and each had a basin resting on four supports, cast with wreaths on each side. ³¹On the inside of the stand there was an opening that had a circular frame one cubit*o* deep. This opening was round, and with its basework it measured a cubit and a half.*p* Around its opening there was engraving. The panels of the stands were square, not round. ³²The four wheels were under the panels, and the axles of the wheels were attached to the stand. The diameter of each wheel was a cubit and a half. ³³The wheels were made like chariot wheels; the axles, rims, spokes and hubs were all of cast metal.

³⁴Each stand had four handles, one on each corner, projecting from the stand. ³⁵At the top of the stand there was a circular band half a cubit*q* deep. The supports and panels were attached to the top of the stand. ³⁶He engraved cherubim, lions and palm trees on the surfaces of the supports and on the panels, in every available space, with wreaths all around. ³⁷This is the way he made the ten stands. They were all cast in the same molds and were identical in size and shape.

³⁸He then made ten bronze basins, each holding forty baths*r* and measuring four cubits across, one basin to go on each of the ten stands. ³⁹He placed five of the stands on the south side of the temple and five on the north. He placed the Sea on the south side, at the southeast corner of the temple. ⁴⁰He also made the basins and shovels and sprinkling bowls.

So Huram finished all the work he had undertaken for King Solomon in the temple of the LORD:

⁴¹the two pillars;
  the two bowl-shaped capitals on top of the pillars;

---

a 10,23 That is, about 15 feet (about 4.5 meters)   *b 10* That is, about 12 feet (about 3.6 meters)   *c 13* Hebrew *Hiram,* a variant of *Huram;* also in verses 40 and 45   *d 15* That is, about 27 feet (about 8.1 meters) high and 18 feet (about 5.4 meters) around   *e 16* That is, about 7 1/2 feet (about 2.3 meters); also in verse 23   *f 18* Two Hebrew manuscripts and Septuagint; most Hebrew manuscripts *made the pillars, and there were two rows*   *g 18* Many Hebrew manuscripts and Syriac; most Hebrew manuscripts *pomegranates*   *h 19* That is, about 6 feet (about 1.8 meters); also in verse 38   *i 21 Jakin* probably means *he establishes.*   *j 21 Boaz* probably means *in him is strength.*   *k 23* That is, about 45 feet (about 13.5 meters)   *l 26* That is, about 3 inches (about 8 centimeters)   *m 26* That is, probably about 11,500 gallons (about 44 kiloliters); the Septuagint does not have this sentence.   *n 27* That is, about 6 feet (about 1.8 meters) long and wide and about 4 1/2 feet (about 1.3 meters) high   *o 31* That is, about 1 1/2 feet (about 0.5 meter)   *p 31* That is, about 2 1/4 feet (about 0.7 meter); also in verse 32   *q 35* That is, about 3/4 foot (about 0.2 meter)   *r 38* That is, about 230 gallons (about 880 liters)

the two sets of network decorating the two bowl-shaped capitals on top of the pillars;

⁴²the four hundred pomegranates for the two sets of network (two rows of pomegranates for each network, decorating the bowl-shaped capitals on top of the pillars);

⁴³the ten stands with their ten basins;

⁴⁴the Sea and the twelve bulls under it;

⁴⁵the pots, shovels and sprinkling bowls.

All these objects that Huram made for King Solomon for the temple of the LORD were of burnished bronze. ⁴⁶The king had them cast in clay molds in the plain of the Jordan between Succoth and Zarethan. ⁴⁷Solomon left all these things unweighed, because there were so many; the weight of the bronze was not determined.

⁴⁸Solomon also made all the furnishings that were in the LORD's temple:

the golden altar;

the golden table on which was the bread of the Presence;

⁴⁹the lampstands of pure gold (five on the right and five on the left, in front of the inner sanctuary);

the gold floral work and lamps and tongs;

⁵⁰the pure gold basins, wick trimmers, sprinkling bowls, dishes and censers;

and the gold sockets for the doors of the innermost room, the Most Holy Place, and also for the doors of the main hall of the temple.

⁵¹When all the work King Solomon had done for the temple of the LORD was finished, he brought in the things his father David had dedicated—the silver and gold and the furnishings—and he placed them in the treasuries of the LORD's temple.

The Ark Brought to the Temple

8 Then King Solomon summoned into his presence at Jerusalem the elders of Israel, all the heads of the tribes and the chiefs of the Israelite families, to bring up the ark of the LORD's covenant from Zion, the City of David. ²All the men of Israel came together to King Solomon at the time of the festival in the month of Ethanim, the seventh month.

³When all the elders of Israel had arrived, the priests took up the ark, ⁴and they brought up the ark of the LORD and the Tent of Meeting and all the sacred furnishings in it. The priests and Levites carried them up, ⁵and King Solomon and the entire assembly of Israel that had gathered about him were before the ark, sacrificing so many sheep and cattle that they could not be recorded or counted.

⁶The priests then brought the ark of the LORD's covenant to its place in the inner sanctuary of the temple, the Most Holy Place, and put it beneath the wings of the cherubim. ⁷The cherubim spread their wings over the place of the ark and overshadowed the ark and its carrying poles. ⁸These poles were so long that their ends could be seen from the Holy Place in front of the inner sanctuary, but not from outside the Holy Place; and they are still there today. ⁹There was nothing in the ark except the two stone tablets that Moses had placed in it at Horeb, where the LORD made a covenant with the Israelites after they came out of Egypt.

¹⁰When the priests withdrew from the Holy Place, the cloud filled the temple of the LORD. ¹¹And the priests could not perform their service because of the cloud, for the glory of the LORD filled his temple.

8:11 Off-limits for People

Much of the temple stayed off-limits to the general public; only priests went in. Not even priests ventured into the Most Holy Place, except on very special occasions. Solomon had not intended the building for humans—he wanted a place suitable for God to dwell. And on the memorable day described here, the awesome glory of the Lord did indeed fill the temple.

¹²Then Solomon said, "The LORD has said that he would dwell in a dark cloud; ¹³I have indeed built a magnificent temple for you, a place for you to dwell forever."

¹⁴While the whole assembly of Israel was standing there, the king turned around and blessed them. ¹⁵Then he said:

"Praise be to the LORD, the God of Israel, who with his own hand has fulfilled what he promised with his own mouth to my father David. For he said, ¹⁶'Since the day I brought my people Israel out of Egypt, I have not chosen a city in any tribe of Israel to have a temple built for my Name to be there, but I have chosen David to rule my people Israel.'

¹⁷"My father David had it in his heart to build a temple for the Name of the LORD, the God of Israel. ¹⁸But the LORD said to my father David, 'Because it was in your heart to build a temple for my Name, you did well to have this in your heart. ¹⁹Nevertheless, you are not the one to build the temple, but your son, who is your own flesh and blood—he is the one who will build the temple for my Name.'

²⁰"The LORD has kept the promise he

made: I have succeeded David my father and now I sit on the throne of Israel, just as the LORD promised, and I have built the temple for the Name of the LORD, the God of Israel. [21]I have provided a place there for the ark, in which is the covenant of the LORD that he made with our fathers when he brought them out of Egypt."

Solomon's Prayer of Dedication

[22]Then Solomon stood before the altar of the LORD in front of the whole assembly of Israel, spread out his hands toward heaven [23]and said:

"O LORD, God of Israel, there is no God like you in heaven above or on earth below—you who keep your covenant of love with your servants who continue wholeheartedly in your way. [24]You have kept your promise to your servant David my father; with your mouth you have promised and with your hand you have fulfilled it—as it is today.

[25]"Now LORD, God of Israel, keep for your servant David my father the promises you made to him when you said, 'You shall never fail to have a man to sit before me on the throne of Israel, if only your sons are careful in all they do to walk before me as you have done.' [26]And now, O God of Israel, let your word that you promised your servant David my father come true.

[27]"But will God really dwell on earth? The heavens, even the highest heaven, cannot contain you. How much less this temple I have built! [28]Yet give attention to your

8:27 Where God Dwells

King Solomon was at his most eloquent in the great speech and prayer of chapter 8. He made it clear that the Lord of the universe could not fully dwell in a building. Nevertheless, God's presence, or his "Name," would indeed live there. For that reason, Solomon began the practice of praying toward Jerusalem, a practice still followed by many Jews today (verse 29).

servant's prayer and his plea for mercy, O LORD my God. Hear the cry and the prayer that your servant is praying in your presence this day. [29]May your eyes be open toward this temple night and day, this place of which you said, 'My Name shall be there,' so that you will hear the prayer your servant prays toward this place. [30]Hear the supplication of your servant and of your people Israel when they pray toward this

place. Hear from heaven, your dwelling place, and when you hear, forgive.

[31]"When a man wrongs his neighbor and is required to take an oath and he comes and swears the oath before your altar in this temple, [32]then hear from heaven and act. Judge between your servants, condemning the guilty and bringing down on his own head what he has done. Declare the innocent not guilty, and so establish his innocence.

[33]"When your people Israel have been defeated by an enemy because they have sinned against you, and when they turn back to you and confess your name, praying and making supplication to you in this temple, [34]then hear from heaven and forgive the sin of your people Israel and bring them back to the land you gave to their fathers.

[35]"When the heavens are shut up and there is no rain because your people have sinned against you, and when they pray toward this place and confess your name and turn from their sin because you have afflicted them, [36]then hear from heaven and forgive the sin of your servants, your people Israel. Teach them the right way to live, and send rain on the land you gave your people for an inheritance.

[37]"When famine or plague comes to the land, or blight or mildew, locusts or grasshoppers, or when an enemy besieges them in any of their cities, whatever disaster or disease may come, [38]and when a prayer or plea is made by any of your people Israel—each one aware of the afflictions of his own heart, and spreading out his hands toward this temple— [39]then hear from heaven, your dwelling place. Forgive and act; deal with each man according to all he does, since you know his heart (for you alone know the hearts of all men), [40]so that they will fear you all the time they live in the land you gave our fathers.

[41]"As for the foreigner who does not belong to your people Israel but has come from a distant land because of your name— [42]for men will hear of your great name and your mighty hand and your outstretched arm—when he comes and prays toward this temple, [43]then hear from heaven, your dwelling place, and do whatever the foreigner asks of you, so that all the peoples of the earth may know your name and fear you, as do your own people Israel, and may know that this house I have built bears your Name.

[44]"When your people go to war against their enemies, wherever you send them,

and when they pray to the LORD toward the city you have chosen and the temple I have built for your Name, ⁴⁵then hear from heaven their prayer and their plea, and uphold their cause.

⁴⁶"When they sin against you—for there is no one who does not sin—and you become angry with them and give them over to the enemy, who takes them captive to his own land, far away or near; ⁴⁷and if they have a change of heart in the land where they are held captive, and repent and plead with you in the land of their conquerors and say, 'We have sinned, we have done wrong, we have acted wickedly'; ⁴⁸and if they turn back to you with all their heart and soul in the land of their enemies who took them captive, and pray to you toward the land you gave their fathers, toward the city you have chosen and the temple I have built for your Name; ⁴⁹then from heaven, your dwelling place, hear their prayer and their plea, and uphold their cause. ⁵⁰And forgive your people, who have sinned against you; forgive all the offenses they have committed against you, and cause their conquerors to show them mercy; ⁵¹for they are your people and your inheritance, whom you brought out of Egypt, out of that iron-smelting furnace.

⁵²"May your eyes be open to your servant's plea and to the plea of your people Israel, and may you listen to them whenever they cry out to you. ⁵³For you singled them out from all the nations of the world to be your own inheritance, just as you declared through your servant Moses when you, O Sovereign LORD, brought our fathers out of Egypt."

⁵⁴When Solomon had finished all these prayers and supplications to the LORD, he rose from before the altar of the LORD, where he had been kneeling with his hands spread out toward heaven. ⁵⁵He stood and blessed the whole assembly of Israel in a loud voice, saying:

⁵⁶"Praise be to the LORD, who has given rest to his people Israel just as he promised. Not one word has failed of all the good promises he gave through his servant Moses. ⁵⁷May the LORD our God be with us as he was with our fathers; may he never leave us nor forsake us. ⁵⁸May he turn our hearts to him, to walk in all his ways and to keep the commands, decrees and regulations he gave our fathers. ⁵⁹And may these words of mine, which I have prayed before the LORD, be near to the LORD our God day and night,

that he may uphold the cause of his servant and the cause of his people Israel according to each day's need, ⁶⁰so that all the peoples of the earth may know that the LORD is God and that there is no other. ⁶¹But your hearts must be fully committed to the LORD our God, to live by his decrees and obey his commands, as at this time."

The Dedication of the Temple

⁶²Then the king and all Israel with him offered sacrifices before the LORD. ⁶³Solomon offered a sacrifice of fellowship offerings^a to the LORD: twenty-two thousand cattle and a hundred and twenty thousand sheep and goats. So the king and all the Israelites dedicated the temple of the LORD.

⁶⁴On that same day the king consecrated the middle part of the courtyard in front of the temple of the LORD, and there he offered burnt offerings, grain offerings and the fat of the fellowship offerings, because the bronze altar before the LORD was too small to hold the burnt offerings, the grain offerings and the fat of the fellowship offerings.

⁶⁵So Solomon observed the festival at that time, and all Israel with him—a vast assembly, people from Lebo^b Hamath to the Wadi of Egypt. They celebrated it before the LORD our God for seven days and seven days more, fourteen days in all. ⁶⁶On the following day he sent the people away. They blessed the king and then went home, joyful and glad in heart for all the good things the LORD had done for his servant David and his people Israel.

The LORD Appears to Solomon

9 When Solomon had finished building the temple of the LORD and the royal palace, and had achieved all he had desired to do, ²the LORD appeared to him a second time, as he had appeared to him at Gibeon. ³The LORD said to him:

"I have heard the prayer and plea you have made before me; I have consecrated this temple, which you have built, by putting my Name there forever. My eyes and my heart will always be there.

⁴"As for you, if you walk before me in integrity of heart and uprightness, as David your father did, and do all I command and observe my decrees and laws, ⁵I will establish your royal throne over Israel forever, as I promised David your father when I said, 'You shall never fail to have a man on the throne of Israel.'

⁶"But if you^c or your sons turn away from me and do not observe the commands and decrees I have given you^c and

go off to serve other gods and worship them, [7]then I will cut off Israel from the land I have given them and will reject this temple I have consecrated for my Name. Israel will then become a byword and an object of ridicule among all peoples. [8]And though this temple is now imposing, all who pass by will be appalled and will scoff and say, 'Why has the LORD done such a thing to this land and to this temple?' [9]People will answer, 'Because they have forsaken the LORD their God, who brought their fathers out of Egypt, and have embraced other gods, worshiping and serving them— that is why the LORD brought all this disaster on them.'"

Solomon's Other Activities

[10]At the end of twenty years, during which Solomon built these two buildings—the temple of the LORD and the royal palace— [11]King Solomon gave twenty towns in Galilee to Hiram king of Tyre, because Hiram had supplied him with all the cedar and pine and gold he wanted. [12]But when Hiram went from Tyre to see the towns that Solomon had given him, he was not pleased with them. [13]"What kind of towns are these you have given me, my brother?" he asked. And he called them the Land of Cabul,[a] a name they

> ### 9:13 Good-for-nothing Towns
>
> *Solomon gave away part of God's promised land to a foreigner, an act that may have stirred up the resentment of northern tribes against the South. King Hiram, unimpressed with the 20 Galilean towns Solomon gave him as payment for services, called them "Cabul" (good-for-nothing). Interestingly, Jesus chose this very area as the early focal point of his ministry on earth.*

have to this day. [14]Now Hiram had sent to the king 120 talents[b] of gold.

[15]Here is the account of the forced labor King Solomon conscripted to build the LORD's temple, his own palace, the supporting terraces,[c] the wall of Jerusalem, and Hazor, Megiddo and Gezer. [16](Pharaoh king of Egypt had attacked and captured Gezer. He had set it on fire. He killed its Canaanite inhabitants and then gave it as a wedding gift to his daughter, Solomon's wife. [17]And Solomon rebuilt Gezer.) He built up Lower Beth Horon, [18]Baalath, and Tadmor[d] in the desert,

within his land, [19]as well as all his store cities and the towns for his chariots and for his horses[e]— whatever he desired to build in Jerusalem, in Lebanon and throughout all the territory he ruled.

[20]All the people left from the Amorites, Hittites, Perizzites, Hivites and Jebusites (these peoples were not Israelites), [21]that is, their descendants remaining in the land, whom the Israelites could not exterminate[f]—these Solomon conscripted for his slave labor force, as it is to this day. [22]But Solomon did not make slaves of any of the Israelites; they were his fighting men, his government officials, his officers, his captains, and the commanders of his chariots and charioteers. [23]They were also the chief officials in charge of Solomon's projects—550 officials supervising the men who did the work.

[24]After Pharaoh's daughter had come up from the City of David to the palace Solomon had built for her, he constructed the supporting terraces.

[25]Three times a year Solomon sacrificed burnt offerings and fellowship offerings[g] on the altar he had built for the LORD, burning incense before the LORD along with them, and so fulfilled the temple obligations.

[26]King Solomon also built ships at Ezion Geber, which is near Elath in Edom, on the shore of the Red Sea.[h] [27]And Hiram sent his men—sailors who knew the sea—to serve in the fleet with Solomon's men. [28]They sailed to Ophir and brought back 420 talents[i] of gold, which they delivered to King Solomon.

The Queen of Sheba Visits Solomon

10 When the queen of Sheba heard about the fame of Solomon and his relation to the name of the LORD, she came to test him with hard questions. [2]Arriving at Jerusalem with a very great caravan—with camels carrying spices, large quantities of gold, and precious stones—she came to Solomon and talked with him about all that she had on her mind. [3]Solomon answered all her questions; nothing was too hard for the king to explain to her. [4]When the queen of Sheba saw all the wisdom of Solomon and the palace he had built, [5]the food on his table, the seating of his officials, the attending servants in their robes, his cupbearers, and the burnt offerings he made at[j] the temple of the LORD, she was overwhelmed.

[6]She said to the king, "The report I heard in my own country about your achievements and your wisdom is true. [7]But I did not believe these things until I came and saw with my own eyes. Indeed, not even half was told me; in wisdom

---

[a]13 *Cabul* sounds like the Hebrew for *good-for-nothing.*   [b]14 That is, about 4 1/2 tons (about 4 metric tons)
[c]15 Or *the Millo;* also in verse 24   [d]18 The Hebrew may also be read *Tamar.*   [e]19 Or *charioteers*   [f]21 The Hebrew term refers to the irrevocable giving over of things or persons to the LORD, often by totally destroying them.
[g]25 Traditionally *peace offerings*   [h]26 Hebrew *Yam Suph;* that is, Sea of Reeds   [i]28 That is, about 16 tons (about 14.5 metric tons)   [j]5 Or *the ascent by which he went up to*

and wealth you have far exceeded the report I heard. [8]How happy your men must be! How happy your officials, who continually stand before you and hear your wisdom! [9]Praise be to the LORD your God, who has delighted in you and placed you on the throne of Israel. Because of the LORD's eternal love for Israel, he has made you king, to maintain justice and righteousness."

[10]And she gave the king 120 talents[a] of gold, large quantities of spices, and precious stones. Never again were so many spices brought in as those the queen of Sheba gave to King Solomon.

[11](Hiram's ships brought gold from Ophir; and from there they brought great cargoes of almugwood[b] and precious stones. [12]The king used the almugwood to make supports for the temple of the LORD and for the royal palace, and to make harps and lyres for the musicians. So much almugwood has never been imported or seen since that day.)

[13]King Solomon gave the queen of Sheba all she desired and asked for, besides what he had given her out of his royal bounty. Then she left and returned with her retinue to her own country.

Solomon's Splendor

[14]The weight of the gold that Solomon received yearly was 666 talents,[c] [15]not including

10:14 A King of Excess

This passage (10:14–29) graphically illustrates how far Solomon had strayed from God's ideal. The book of Deuteronomy cites Moses' forthright warnings about what kind of king should rule over Israel (Deuteronomy 17:14–20). Solomon defied those warnings by acquiring huge numbers of horses, getting involved in foreign trade, taking many wives, and accumulating silver and gold.

the revenues from merchants and traders and from all the Arabian kings and the governors of the land.

[16]King Solomon made two hundred large shields of hammered gold; six hundred bekas[d] of gold went into each shield. [17]He also made three hundred small shields of hammered gold, with three minas[e] of gold in each shield. The king put them in the Palace of the Forest of Lebanon.

[18]Then the king made a great throne inlaid with ivory and overlaid with fine gold. [19]The throne had six steps, and its back had a rounded top. On both sides of the seat were armrests, with a lion standing beside each of them. [20]Twelve lions stood on the six steps, one at either end of each step. Nothing like it had ever been made for any other kingdom. [21]All King Solomon's goblets were gold, and all the household articles in the Palace of the Forest of Lebanon were pure gold. Nothing was made of silver, because silver was considered of little value in Solomon's days. [22]The king had a fleet of trading ships[f] at sea along with the ships of Hiram. Once every three years it returned, carrying gold, silver and ivory, and apes and baboons.

[23]King Solomon was greater in riches and wisdom than all the other kings of the earth. [24]The whole world sought audience with Solomon to hear the wisdom God had put in his heart. [25]Year after year, everyone who came brought a gift — articles of silver and gold, robes, weapons and spices, and horses and mules.

[26]Solomon accumulated chariots and horses; he had fourteen hundred chariots and twelve thousand horses,[g] which he kept in the chariot cities and also with him in Jerusalem. [27]The king made silver as common in Jerusalem as stones, and cedar as plentiful as sycamore-fig trees in the foothills. [28]Solomon's horses were imported from Egypt[h] and from Kue[i] — the royal merchants purchased them from Kue. [29]They imported a chariot from Egypt for six hundred shekels[j] of silver, and a horse for a hundred and fifty.[e] They also exported them to all the kings of the Hittites and of the Arameans.

Solomon's Wives

11 King Solomon, however, loved many foreign women besides Pharaoh's daughter — Moabites, Ammonites, Edomites, Sidonians and Hittites. [2]They were from nations about which the LORD had told the Israelites, "You must not intermarry with them, because they will surely turn your hearts after their gods." Nevertheless, Solomon held fast to them in love. [3]He had seven hundred wives of royal birth and three hundred concubines, and his wives led him astray. [4]As Solomon grew old, his wives turned his heart after other gods, and his heart was not fully devoted to the LORD his God, as the heart of David his father had been. [5]He followed Ashtoreth the goddess of the Sidonians, and Molech[k] the detestable god of the Ammonites. [6]So Solomon did evil in the eyes of the LORD; he did not follow the LORD completely, as David his father had done.

[7]On a hill east of Jerusalem, Solomon built a

---

[a]10 That is, about 4 1/2 tons (about 4 metric tons)   [b]11 Probably a variant of *almugwood*; also in verse 12
[c]14 That is, about 25 tons (about 23 metric tons)   [d]16 That is, about 7 1/2 pounds (about 3.5 kilograms)
[e]17,29 That is, about 3 3/4 pounds (about 1.7 kilograms)   [f]22 Hebrew *of ships of Tarshish*   [g]26 Or *charioteers*
[h]28 Or possibly *Muzur*, a region in Cilicia; also in verse 29   [i]28 Probably *Cilicia*   [j]29 That is, about 15 pounds
(about 7 kilograms)   [k]5 Hebrew *Milcom*; also in verse 33

high place for Chemosh the detestable god of Moab, and for Molech the detestable god of the Ammonites. **8**He did the same for all his foreign wives, who burned incense and offered sacrifices to their gods.

11:3 So Many Women

Solomon's 700 wives were foreigners who worshiped other gods and had different standards of right and wrong. He probably married them as part of treaty arrangements with surrounding nations; a royal marriage was supposed to cement a bond between peoples. These marriages violated God's law (Deuteronomy 7:3–4; 17:17) and ultimately led Solomon away from God. Because of his wives' religions, he built shrines and encouraged pagan worship right in Jerusalem.

9The Lord became angry with Solomon because his heart had turned away from the Lord, the God of Israel, who had appeared to him twice. **10**Although he had forbidden Solomon to follow other gods, Solomon did not keep the Lord's command. **11**So the Lord said to Solomon, "Since this is your attitude and you have not kept my covenant and my decrees, which I commanded you, I will most certainly tear the kingdom away from you and give it to one of your subordinates. **12**Nevertheless, for the sake of David your father, I will not do it during your lifetime. I will tear it out of the hand of your son. **13**Yet I will not tear the whole kingdom from him, but will give him one tribe for the sake of David my servant and for the sake of Jerusalem, which I have chosen."

Solomon's Adversaries

14Then the Lord raised up against Solomon an adversary, Hadad the Edomite, from the royal line of Edom. **15**Earlier when David was fighting with Edom, Joab the commander of the army, who had gone up to bury the dead, had struck down all the men in Edom. **16**Joab and all the Israelites stayed there for six months, until they had destroyed all the men in Edom. **17**But Hadad, still only a boy, fled to Egypt with some Edomite officials who had served his father. **18**They set out from Midian and went to Paran. Then taking men from Paran with them, they went to Egypt, to Pharaoh king of Egypt, who gave Hadad a house and land and provided him with food.

19Pharaoh was so pleased with Hadad that he gave him a sister of his own wife, Queen Tahpenes, in marriage. **20**The sister of Tahpenes bore him a son named Genubath, whom Tahpenes

brought up in the royal palace. There Genubath lived with Pharaoh's own children.

21While he was in Egypt, Hadad heard that David rested with his fathers and that Joab the commander of the army was also dead. Then Hadad said to Pharaoh, "Let me go, that I may return to my own country."

22"What have you lacked here that you want to go back to your own country?" Pharaoh asked.

"Nothing," Hadad replied, "but do let me go!"

23And God raised up against Solomon another adversary, Rezon son of Eliada, who had fled from his master, Hadadezer king of Zobah. **24**He gathered men around him and became the leader of a band of rebels when David destroyed the forces*a* of Zobah; the rebels went to Damascus, where they settled and took control. **25**Rezon was Israel's adversary as long as Solomon lived, adding to the trouble caused by Hadad. So Rezon ruled in Aram and was hostile toward Israel.

Jeroboam Rebels Against Solomon

26Also, Jeroboam son of Nebat rebelled against the king. He was one of Solomon's officials, an Ephraimite from Zeredah, and his mother was a widow named Zeruah.

27Here is the account of how he rebelled against the king: Solomon had built the supporting terraces*b* and had filled in the gap in the wall of the city of David his father. **28**Now Jeroboam was a man of standing, and when Solomon saw how well the young man did his work, he put him in charge of the whole labor force of the house of Joseph.

29About that time Jeroboam was going out of Jerusalem, and Ahijah the prophet of Shiloh met him on the way, wearing a new cloak. The two of them were alone out in the country, **30**and Ahijah took hold of the new cloak he was wearing and tore it into twelve pieces. **31**Then he said to Jeroboam, "Take ten pieces for yourself, for this is what the Lord, the God of Israel, says: 'See, I am going to tear the kingdom out of Solomon's hand and give you ten tribes. **32**But for the sake of my servant David and the city of Jerusalem, which I have chosen out of all the tribes of Israel, he will have one tribe. **33**I will do this because they have*c* forsaken me and worshiped Ashtoreth the goddess of the Sidonians, Chemosh the god of the Moabites, and Molech the god of the Ammonites, and have not walked in my ways, nor done what is right in my eyes, nor kept my statutes and laws as David, Solomon's father, did.

34'But I will not take the whole kingdom out of Solomon's hand; I have made him ruler all the days of his life for the sake of David my servant, whom I chose and who observed my commands and statutes. **35**I will take the kingdom from his son's hands and give you ten tribes. 36I will give one tribe to his son so that David my servant may always have a lamp before me in Jerusalem, the city where I chose to put my Name. 37However, as for you, I will take you, and you will rule over all that your heart desires; you will be king over Israel. 38If you do whatever I command you and walk in my ways and do what is right in my eyes by keeping my statutes and commands, as David my servant did, I will be with you. I will build you a dynasty as enduring as the one I built for David and will give Israel to you. 39I will humble David's descendants because of this, but not forever.'"

40Solomon tried to kill Jeroboam, but Jeroboam fled to Egypt, to Shishak the king, and stayed there until Solomon's death.

Solomon's Death

41As for the other events of Solomon's reign—all he did and the wisdom he displayed—are they not written in the book of the annals of Solomon? 42Solomon reigned in Jerusalem over all Israel forty years. 43Then he rested with his fathers and was buried in the city of David his father. And Rehoboam his son succeeded him as king.

Israel Rebels Against Rehoboam

12 Rehoboam went to Shechem, for all the Israelites had gone there to make him king.

a 2 Or he remained in

2When Jeroboam son of Nebat heard this (he was still in Egypt, where he had fled from King Solomon), he returned from*a* Egypt. 3So they sent

---

11:41 Using Other Sources

The author makes liberal use of other historical records, most of which have not survived. This verse refers to "the book of the annals of Solomon." Elsewhere, 1 Kings relies on accounts of the kings of Judah (22:45) or of Israel (15:31). In all, the two books of Kings make 34 references to other sources.

---

for Jeroboam, and he and the whole assembly of Israel went to Rehoboam and said to him: 4"Your father put a heavy yoke on us, but now lighten the harsh labor and the heavy yoke he put on us, and we will serve you."

5Rehoboam answered, "Go away for three days and then come back to me." So the people went away.

6Then King Rehoboam consulted the elders who had served his father Solomon during his lifetime. "How would you advise me to answer these people?" he asked.

7They replied, "If today you will be a servant to these people and serve them and give them a

---

JEROBOAM *Blown Opportunity*

POLITICIANS WHO RUN ON A platform of reform often, when they attain power, act depressingly like the corrupt leaders they have just replaced. Such is the story of Jeroboam, a decent man who had a unique chance to stop the Israel's slide into corruption.

Jeroboam came to power by the back door. On his way out of Jerusalem, where he worked as a top official for King Solomon, Jeroboam met a prophet named Ahijah. The prophet took off the cloak he was wearing and ripped the brand-new garment into twelve pieces. Then he handed ten pieces to Jeroboam and delivered the message behind the object lesson: Because of King Solomon's failures, God would rip the kingdom of Israel apart. The bureaucrat Jeroboam would soon inherit leadership over ten of the twelve tribes.

This dramatic prophecy launched a fierce struggle for power. At first, fearing for his life, Jeroboam fled the country. Years later he came back from exile to make peace with Solomon's son, but found the son stupidly harsher than the old man. (See "Rehoboam: a Fool's Answer," p. 472.) The fed-up northern tribes rebelled, and Jeroboam became king of a new nation. God's people were irrevocably split into two camps.

Jeroboam's rule may have begun with God's approval, but the bureaucrat who would be king never lived up to God's call. Fearing that his citizens would gradually be won back to the south—they had to travel to Jerusalem to worship in the temple—Jeroboam made a clever but terrible choice. He started his own, competing religion in the north.

By outward standards the new religion succeeded, enduring as long as Israel did. God, however, who had brought Jeroboam to power, reacted with outrage. He predicted and then carried out the total destruction of Jeroboam's family (15:27–30).

Life Questions: Do you find it easier to criticize leaders than to lead? How do you usually respond when you're placed in a leadership position?

favorable answer, they will always be your servants."

⁸But Rehoboam rejected the advice the elders gave him and consulted the young men who had grown up with him and were serving him. ⁹He asked them, "What is your advice? How should we answer these people who say to me, 'Lighten the yoke your father put on us'?"

¹⁰The young men who had grown up with him replied, "Tell these people who have said to you, 'Your father put a heavy yoke on us, but make our yoke lighter'—tell them, 'My little finger is thicker than my father's waist. ¹¹My father laid on you a heavy yoke; I will make it even heavier. My father scourged you with whips; I will scourge you with scorpions.'"

¹²Three days later Jeroboam and all the people returned to Rehoboam, as the king had said, "Come back to me in three days." ¹³The king answered the people harshly. Rejecting the advice given him by the elders, ¹⁴he followed the advice of the young men and said, "My father made your yoke heavy; I will make it even heavier. My father scourged you with whips; I will scourge you with scorpions." ¹⁵So the king did not listen to the people, for this turn of events was from the LORD, to fulfill the word the LORD had spoken to Jeroboam son of Nebat through Ahijah the Shilonite.

¹⁶When all Israel saw that the king refused to listen to them, they answered the king:

"What share do we have in David,
    what part in Jesse's son?
To your tents, O Israel!
    Look after your own house, O David!"

So the Israelites went home. ¹⁷But as for the Israelites who were living in the towns of Judah, Rehoboam still ruled over them.

¹⁸King Rehoboam sent out Adoniram,[a] who was in charge of forced labor, but all Israel stoned him to death. King Rehoboam, however, managed to get into his chariot and escape to Jerusalem. ¹⁹So Israel has been in rebellion against the house of David to this day.

²⁰When all the Israelites heard that Jeroboam had returned, they sent and called him to the assembly and made him king over all Israel. Only the tribe of Judah remained loyal to the house of David.

²¹When Rehoboam arrived in Jerusalem, he mustered the whole house of Judah and the tribe of Benjamin—a hundred and eighty thousand fighting men—to make war against the house of Israel and to regain the kingdom for Rehoboam son of Solomon.

²²But this word of God came to Shemaiah the man of God: ²³"Say to Rehoboam son of Solomon king of Judah, to the whole house of Judah and Benjamin, and to the rest of the people, ²⁴'This is what the LORD says: Do not go up to fight against your brothers, the Israelites. Go home, every one of you, for this is my doing.'" So they obeyed the word of the LORD and went home again, as the LORD had ordered.

Golden Calves at Bethel and Dan

²⁵Then Jeroboam fortified Shechem in the hill country of Ephraim and lived there. From there he went out and built up Peniel.[b]

²⁶Jeroboam thought to himself, "The kingdom will now likely revert to the house of David. ²⁷If these people go up to offer sacrifices at the temple of the LORD in Jerusalem, they will again give their allegiance to their lord, Rehoboam king of Judah. They will kill me and return to King Rehoboam."

²⁸After seeking advice, the king made two golden calves. He said to the people, "It is too much for you to go up to Jerusalem. Here are your gods, O Israel, who brought you up out of Egypt." ²⁹One he set up in Bethel, and the other in Dan. ³⁰And this thing became a sin; the people went even as far as Dan to worship the one there.

³¹Jeroboam built shrines on high places and appointed priests from all sorts of people, even though they were not Levites. ³²He instituted a festival on the fifteenth day of the eighth month, like the festival held in Judah, and offered sacrifices on the altar. This he did in Bethel, sacrificing to the calves he had made. And at Bethel he also installed priests at the high places he had made. ³³On the fifteenth day of the eighth month, a month of his own choosing, he offered sacrifices on the altar he had built at Bethel. So he instituted the festival for the Israelites and went up to the altar to make offerings.

The Man of God From Judah

13 By the word of the LORD a man of God came from Judah to Bethel, as Jeroboam was standing by the altar to make an offering. ²He cried out against the altar by the word of the LORD: "O altar, altar! This is what the LORD says: 'A son named Josiah will be born to the house of David. On you he will sacrifice the priests of high places who now make offerings here, and human bones will be burned on you.'" ³That same day the man of God gave a sign: "This is the sign the LORD has declared: The altar will be split apart and the ashes on it will be poured out."

⁴When King Jeroboam heard what the man of God cried out against the altar at Bethel, he stretched out his hand from the altar and said, "Seize him!" But the hand he stretched to-

---

a 18 Some Septuagint manuscripts and Syriac (see also 1 Kings 4:6 and 5:14); Hebrew *Adoram*   *b 25* Hebrew *Penuel,* a variant of *Peniel*

ward the man shriveled up, so that he could not pull it back. ⁵Also, the altar was split apart and its ashes poured out according to the sign given by the man of God by the word of the LORD.

⁶Then the king said to the man of God, "Intercede with the LORD your God and pray for me that my hand may be restored." So the man of God interceded with the LORD, and the king's hand was restored and became as it was before.

⁷The king said to the man of God, "Come home with me and have something to eat, and I will give you a gift."

13:7–10 Standing Up to the King

Afraid that temple worship in Jerusalem would lure his northern supporters back to the South, Jeroboam lifted a page from Israel's past (Exodus 32:1–4) and put up two golden calves for worship (see 12:32). An anonymous man of God prophesied against this idol worship in the strongest terms.

Jeroboam's offer of a gift to the prophet reflects the kings' tendencies to keep "court prophets," paid to tell the kings what they wanted to hear. The anonymous man of God would have nothing to do with Jeroboam's hospitality. He had come to protest Jeroboam's new religion, and would not be bought.

⁸But the man of God answered the king, "Even if you were to give me half your possessions, I would not go with you, nor would I eat bread or drink water here. ⁹For I was commanded by the word of the LORD: 'You must not eat bread or drink water or return by the way you came.'" ¹⁰So he took another road and did not return by the way he had come to Bethel.

¹¹Now there was a certain old prophet living in Bethel, whose sons came and told him all that the man of God had done there that day. They also told their father what he had said to the king. ¹²Their father asked them, "Which way did he go?" And his sons showed him which road the man of God from Judah had taken. ¹³So he said to his sons, "Saddle the donkey for me." And when they had saddled the donkey for him, he mounted it ¹⁴and rode after the man of God. He found him sitting under an oak tree and asked, "Are you the man of God who came from Judah?"

"I am," he replied.

¹⁵So the prophet said to him, "Come home with me and eat."

¹⁶The man of God said, "I cannot turn back and go with you, nor can I eat bread or drink water with you in this place. ¹⁷I have been told by the word of the LORD: 'You must not eat bread or drink water there or return by the way you came.'"

¹⁸The old prophet answered, "I too am a prophet, as you are. And an angel said to me by the word of the LORD: 'Bring him back with you to your house so that he may eat bread and drink water.'" (But he was lying to him.) ¹⁹So the man of God returned with him and ate and drank in his house.

²⁰While they were sitting at the table, the word of the LORD came to the old prophet who had brought him back. ²¹He cried out to the man of God who had come from Judah, "This is what the LORD says: 'You have defied the word of the LORD and have not kept the command the LORD your God gave you. ²²You came back and ate bread and drank water in the place where he told you not to eat or drink. Therefore your body will not be buried in the tomb of your fathers.'"

²³When the man of God had finished eating and drinking, the prophet who had brought him back saddled his donkey for him. ²⁴As he went on his way, a lion met him on the road and killed him, and his body was thrown down on the road, with both the donkey and the lion standing beside it. ²⁵Some people who passed by saw the body thrown down there, with the lion standing beside the body, and they went and reported it in the city where the old prophet lived.

²⁶When the prophet who had brought him back from his journey heard of it, he said, "It is the man of God who defied the word of the LORD. The LORD has given him over to the lion, which has mauled him and killed him, as the word of the LORD had warned him."

²⁷The prophet said to his sons, "Saddle the donkey for me," and they did so. ²⁸Then he went out and found the body thrown down on the road, with the donkey and the lion standing beside it. The lion had neither eaten the body nor mauled the donkey. ²⁹So the prophet picked up the body of the man of God, laid it on the donkey, and brought it back to his own city to mourn for him and bury him. ³⁰Then he laid the body in his own tomb, and they mourned over him and said, "Oh, my brother!"

³¹After burying him, he said to his sons, "When I die, bury me in the grave where the man of God is buried; lay my bones beside his bones. ³²For the message he declared by the word of the LORD against the altar in Bethel and against all the shrines on the high places in the towns of Samaria will certainly come true."

³³Even after this, Jeroboam did not change his evil ways, but once more appointed priests for the high places from all sorts of people. Anyone who wanted to become a priest he consecrated for the high places. ³⁴This was the sin of the house of Jeroboam that led to its downfall and to its destruction from the face of the earth.

Ahijah's Prophecy Against Jeroboam

14 At that time Abijah son of Jeroboam became ill, ²and Jeroboam said to his wife, "Go, disguise yourself, so you won't be recognized as the wife of Jeroboam. Then go to Shiloh. Ahijah the prophet is there—the one who told me I would be king over this people. ³Take ten loaves of bread with you, some cakes and a jar of honey, and go to him. He will tell you what will happen to the boy." ⁴So Jeroboam's wife did what he said and went to Ahijah's house in Shiloh.

Now Ahijah could not see; his sight was gone because of his age. ⁵But the LORD had told Ahijah, "Jeroboam's wife is coming to ask you about her son, for he is ill, and you are to give her such and such an answer. When she arrives, she will pretend to be someone else."

⁶So when Ahijah heard the sound of her footsteps at the door, he said, "Come in, wife of Jeroboam. Why this pretense? I have been sent to you with bad news. ⁷Go, tell Jeroboam that this is what the LORD, the God of Israel, says: 'I raised you up from among the people and made you a leader over my people Israel. ⁸I tore the kingdom away from the house of David and gave it to you, but you have not been like my servant David, who kept my commands and followed me with all his heart, doing only what was right in my eyes. ⁹You have done more evil than all who lived before you. You have made for yourself other gods, idols made of metal; you have provoked me to anger and thrust me behind your back.

¹⁰"'Because of this, I am going to bring disaster on the house of Jeroboam. I will cut off from Jeroboam every last male in Israel—slave or free. I will burn up the house of Jeroboam as one burns dung, until it is all gone. ¹¹Dogs will eat those belonging to Jeroboam who die in the city, and the birds of the air will feed on those who die in the country. The LORD has spoken!'

¹²"As for you, go back home. When you set foot in your city, the boy will die. ¹³All Israel will mourn for him and bury him. He is the only one belonging to Jeroboam who will be buried, because he is the only one in the house of Jeroboam in whom the LORD, the God of Israel, has found anything good.

¹⁴"The LORD will raise up for himself a king over Israel who will cut off the family of Jeroboam. This is the day! What? Yes, even now.[a] ¹⁵And the LORD will strike Israel, so that it will be like a reed swaying in the water. He will uproot Israel from this good land that he gave to their forefathers and scatter them beyond the River,[b] because they provoked the LORD to anger by making Asherah poles.[c] ¹⁶And he will give Israel up because of the sins Jeroboam has committed and has caused Israel to commit."

¹⁷Then Jeroboam's wife got up and left and went to Tirzah. As soon as she stepped over the threshold of the house, the boy died. ¹⁸They buried him, and all Israel mourned for him, as the LORD had said through his servant the prophet Ahijah.

¹⁹The other events of Jeroboam's reign, his wars and how he ruled, are written in the book of the annals of the kings of Israel. ²⁰He reigned for twenty-two years and then rested with his fathers. And Nadab his son succeeded him as king.

Rehoboam King of Judah

²¹Rehoboam son of Solomon was king in Judah. He was forty-one years old when he became king, and he reigned seventeen years in Jerusalem, the city the LORD had chosen out of all the tribes of Israel in which to put his Name. His mother's name was Naamah; she was an Ammonite.

²²Judah did evil in the eyes of the LORD. By the sins they committed they stirred up his jealous anger more than their fathers had done. ²³They also set up for themselves high places, sacred stones and Asherah poles on every high hill and

14:23 Notorious Asherah Poles

Introduced in the reign of Rehoboam, Asherah poles became a regular feature of Judah's landscape for hundreds of years. They were dedicated to a mother-goddess and often erected alongside altars on the high places devoted to God. They came to represent Judah's slide into idolatry. When judging the failures of various kings, the authors often comment, "the high places, however, were not removed."

under every spreading tree. ²⁴There were even male shrine prostitutes in the land; the people engaged in all the detestable practices of the nations the LORD had driven out before the Israelites.

²⁵In the fifth year of King Rehoboam, Shishak king of Egypt attacked Jerusalem. ²⁶He carried off the treasures of the temple of the LORD and the treasures of the royal palace. He took everything, including all the gold shields Solomon had made. ²⁷So King Rehoboam made bronze shields to replace them and assigned these to the commanders of the guard on duty at the entrance to the royal palace. ²⁸Whenever the king went to the LORD's temple, the guards bore the shields,

---

[a]14 The meaning of the Hebrew for this sentence is uncertain. of the goddess Asherah; here and elsewhere in 1 Kings   [b]15 That is, the Euphrates   [c]15 That is, symbols

The Nation Splits Apart
A rebellion leads to civil war

There was continual warfare.
14:30

CHAPTER 12 OF 1 KINGS MARKS a decisive turning point in the nation of Israel. For 120 years Saul, David, and Solomon had consolidated power, expanded borders, and built a strong government. But immediately after Solomon's death everything began to unravel. Simmering hostility in the North boiled over at last, and the northern tribes seceded to form their own nation.

Two Nations out of One

Ten tribes joined together under Jeroboam to form a nation in the North called Israel. Only two tribes, Judah and Benjamin, remained loyal to Solomon's heir in Jerusalem. These southerners took on the name Judah and made Jerusalem, home of the temple, their capital. From that time forward, the united nation of Israel ceased to exist.

The northern rebellion brought a terrible civil war to Israel, a war that dragged on for 50 years. Despite a peace treaty, war kept breaking out.

The book of Kings records the histories of both nations. Action shifts back and forth between Israel in the North and Judah in the South. The effect resembles an account of America during Civil War years, first describing events in the North and then shifting to what was simultaneously taking place in the South.

This book does not attempt to give a full history of both nations. Rather, it focuses on their kings and queens. As guardian of the covenant with God, the king or queen came to symbolize the spiritual health of the nation. As that monarch went, so went the nation. Each ruler gets a capsule summary and usually a one-sentence rating. He or she either performed like David, who "had done what was right in the eyes of the LORD," or like the northern king Jeroboam, who "caused Israel to commit" sin.

The North: A Perpetual Slide Downward

Ironically, the northern tribes seceded as part of a reform movement, to correct some of the excesses of Solomon's reign. But starting with the first king, Jeroboam, no king of Israel did what was right in God's eyes. The books of 1, 2 Kings condemn all the northern kings.

Northern kings brought idolatry into their religion and corruption into their politics. They adopted all the oppressive ways that had sparked the original rebellion: harsh taxation, repression of prophets, abuse of power. Of 19 northern kings, eight either were murdered or committed suicide. One king, Zimri, lasted only seven days.

The worst rulers, King Ahab and Queen Jezebel, introduced the terrible practice of Baal worship (see "Why All the Fuss about Idols?" page 417). Israel hit its spiritual low point, and Ahab replaced Jeroboam as a symbol of evil. Kings to follow were called "Ahabs" much as a ruthless tyrant today is compared with Hitler. Israel's future destruction became certain; after Ahab and Jezebel, the nation was merely marking time.

The South: A Surprising Twist

While Israel—which began as a reform movement—slid toward disaster, the two tribes in the South, Judah, proved more faithful to God. They produced at least a handful of good kings. Even when other nations took advantage of Judah's weakness and plundered Jerusalem, the nation still held together.

Idolatry plagued Judah also, but not to the same extent as in the North. The temple remained a powerful symbol of worship of the true God. And every few generations a sincere, committed king arose to sweep away his predecessors' dangerous practices. The authors pointedly note that these good kings usually outlived the bad rulers.

Within 250 years the Northern Kingdom, Israel, was obliterated. Judah survived another 135 years before likewise falling to foreign invaders. In a sense, their fate was sealed from the time of the original secession. The prophet Isaiah would remember the schism as the worst disaster that had befallen his people (Isaiah 7:17).

Life Questions: Have you seen rebellion lead to "civil war" in families? Churches? Schools? When you don't like what the leaders are doing, are there alternatives to outright rebellion?

and afterward they returned them to the guard-room.

²⁹As for the other events of Rehoboam's reign, and all he did, are they not written in the book of the annals of the kings of Judah? ³⁰There was continual warfare between Rehoboam and Jeroboam. ³¹And Rehoboam rested with his fathers and was buried with them in the City of David. His mother's name was Naamah; she was an Ammonite. And Abijah[a] his son succeeded him as king.

Abijah King of Judah

15 In the eighteenth year of the reign of Jeroboam son of Nebat, Abijah[b] became king of Judah, ²and he reigned in Jerusalem three years. His mother's name was Maacah daughter of Abishalom.[c]

³He committed all the sins his father had done before him; his heart was not fully devoted to the LORD his God, as the heart of David his forefather had been. ⁴Nevertheless, for David's sake the LORD his God gave him a lamp in Jerusalem by raising up a son to succeed him and by making Jerusalem strong. ⁵For David had done what was right in the eyes of the LORD and had not failed to keep any of the LORD's commands all the days of his life—except in the case of Uriah the Hittite.

⁶There was war between Rehoboam[d] and Jeroboam throughout ⌞Abijah's⌟ lifetime. ⁷As for the other events of Abijah's reign, and all he did, are they not written in the book of the annals of the kings of Judah? There was war between Abijah and Jeroboam. ⁸And Abijah rested with his fathers and was buried in the City of David. And Asa his son succeeded him as king.

Asa King of Judah

⁹In the twentieth year of Jeroboam king of Israel, Asa became king of Judah, ¹⁰and he reigned in Jerusalem forty-one years. His grandmother's name was Maacah daughter of Abishalom.

¹¹Asa did what was right in the eyes of the LORD, as his father David had done. ¹²He expelled the male shrine prostitutes from the land and got rid of all the idols his fathers had made. ¹³He even deposed his grandmother Maacah from her position as queen mother, because she had made a repulsive Asherah pole. Asa cut the pole down and burned it in the Kidron Valley. ¹⁴Although he did not remove the high places, Asa's heart was fully committed to the LORD all his life. ¹⁵He brought into the temple of the LORD the silver and gold and the articles that he and his father had dedicated.

¹⁶There was war between Asa and Baasha king of Israel throughout their reigns. ¹⁷Baasha king of Israel went up against Judah and fortified Ramah to prevent anyone from leaving or entering the territory of Asa king of Judah.

¹⁸Asa then took all the silver and gold that was left in the treasuries of the LORD's temple and of his own palace. He entrusted it to his officials and sent them to Ben-Hadad son of Tabrimmon, the son of Hezion, the king of Aram, who was ruling in Damascus. ¹⁹"Let there be a treaty between me and you," he said, "as there was between my father and your father. See, I am sending you a gift of silver and gold. Now break your treaty with Baasha king of Israel so he will withdraw from me."

²⁰Ben-Hadad agreed with King Asa and sent the commanders of his forces against the towns of Israel. He conquered Ijon, Dan, Abel Beth Maacah and all Kinnereth in addition to Naphtali. ²¹When Baasha heard this, he stopped building Ramah and withdrew to Tirzah. ²²Then King Asa issued an order to all Judah—no one was exempt—and they carried away from Ramah the stones and timber Baasha had been using there. With them King Asa built up Geba in Benjamin, and also Mizpah.

²³As for all the other events of Asa's reign, all his achievements, all he did and the cities he built, are they not written in the book of the annals of the kings of Judah? In his old age, however, his feet became diseased. ²⁴Then Asa rested with his fathers and was buried with them in the city of his father David. And Jehoshaphat his son succeeded him as king.

Nadab King of Israel

²⁵Nadab son of Jeroboam became king of Israel in the second year of Asa king of Judah, and he reigned over Israel two years. ²⁶He did evil in the eyes of the LORD, walking in the ways of his father and in his sin, which he had caused Israel to commit.

²⁷Baasha son of Ahijah of the house of Issachar plotted against him, and he struck him down at Gibbethon, a Philistine town, while Nadab and all Israel were besieging it. ²⁸Baasha killed Nadab in the third year of Asa king of Judah and succeeded him as king.

²⁹As soon as he began to reign, he killed Jeroboam's whole family. He did not leave Jeroboam anyone that breathed, but destroyed them all,

---

*a*31 Some Hebrew manuscripts and Septuagint (see also 2 Chron. 12:16); most Hebrew manuscripts *Abijam*   *b*1 Some Hebrew manuscripts and Septuagint (see also 2 Chron. 12:16); most Hebrew manuscripts *Abijam*; also in verses 7 and 8   *c*2 A variant of *Absalom*; also in verse 10   *d*6 Most Hebrew manuscripts; some Hebrew manuscripts and Syriac *Abijam* (that is, Abijah)

according to the word of the LORD given through his servant Ahijah the Shilonite— ³⁰because of the sins Jeroboam had committed and had caused Israel to commit, and because he provoked the LORD, the God of Israel, to anger.

³¹As for the other events of Nadab's reign, and all he did, are they not written in the book of the annals of the kings of Israel? ³²There was war between Asa and Baasha king of Israel throughout their reigns.

Baasha King of Israel

³³In the third year of Asa king of Judah, Baasha son of Ahijah became king of all Israel in Tirzah, and he reigned twenty-four years. ³⁴He did evil in the eyes of the LORD, walking in the ways of Jeroboam and in his sin, which he had caused Israel to commit.

16 Then the word of the LORD came to Jehu son of Hanani against Baasha: ²"I lifted you up from the dust and made you leader of my people Israel, but you walked in the ways of Jeroboam and caused my people Israel to sin and to provoke me to anger by their sins. ³So I am about to consume Baasha and his house, and I will make your house like that of Jeroboam son of Nebat. ⁴Dogs will eat those belonging to Baasha who die in the city, and the birds of the air will feed on those who die in the country."

⁵As for the other events of Baasha's reign, what he did and his achievements, are they not written in the book of the annals of the kings of Israel? ⁶Baasha rested with his fathers and was buried in Tirzah. And Elah his son succeeded him as king.

⁷Moreover, the word of the LORD came through the prophet Jehu son of Hanani to Baasha and his house, because of all the evil he had done in the eyes of the LORD, provoking him to anger by the things he did, and becoming like the house of Jeroboam—and also because he destroyed it.

Elah King of Israel

⁸In the twenty-sixth year of Asa king of Judah, Elah son of Baasha became king of Israel, and he reigned in Tirzah two years.

⁹Zimri, one of his officials, who had command of half his chariots, plotted against him. Elah was in Tirzah at the time, getting drunk in the home of Arza, the man in charge of the palace at Tirzah. ¹⁰Zimri came in, struck him down and killed him in the twenty-seventh year of Asa king of Judah. Then he succeeded him as king.

¹¹As soon as he began to reign and was seated on the throne, he killed off Baasha's whole family. He did not spare a single male, whether relative or friend. ¹²So Zimri destroyed the whole family of Baasha, in accordance with the word

of the LORD spoken against Baasha through the prophet Jehu— ¹³because of all the sins Baasha and his son Elah had committed and had caused Israel to commit, so that they provoked the LORD, the God of Israel, to anger by their worthless idols.

¹⁴As for the other events of Elah's reign, and all he did, are they not written in the book of the annals of the kings of Israel?

Zimri King of Israel

¹⁵In the twenty-seventh year of Asa king of Judah, Zimri reigned in Tirzah seven days. The army was encamped near Gibbethon, a Philistine town. ¹⁶When the Israelites in the camp heard that Zimri had plotted against the king and murdered him, they proclaimed Omri, the commander of the army, king over Israel that very day there in the camp. ¹⁷Then Omri and all the Israelites with him withdrew from Gibbethon and laid siege to Tirzah. ¹⁸When Zimri saw that the city was taken, he went into the citadel of the royal palace and set the palace on fire around him. So he died, ¹⁹because of the sins he had committed, doing evil in the eyes of the LORD and walking in the ways of Jeroboam and in the sin he had committed and had caused Israel to commit.

²⁰As for the other events of Zimri's reign, and the rebellion he carried out, are they not written in the book of the annals of the kings of Israel?

Omri King of Israel

²¹Then the people of Israel were split into two factions; half supported Tibni son of Ginath for

16:21–28 A Strong, Weak King

King Omri gets a grand total of eight verses in 1 Kings, even though secular historians regard him as one of Israel's most powerful kings. After his firm rule, Israel was called Omriland in Assyrian records. He built the capital city of Samaria in a location that guarded all routes north and south. Yet he also started the religious heresies that led to his nation's extinction. Politically shrewd, he married off his son to a neighboring king's daughter (Jezebel). The books of 1, 2 Kings, however, are concerned with the rulers' spiritual health, and Omri scored very poorly.

king, and the other half supported Omri. ²²But Omri's followers proved stronger than those of Tibni son of Ginath. So Tibni died and Omri became king.

²³In the thirty-first year of Asa king of Judah, Omri became king of Israel, and he reigned twelve years, six of them in Tirzah. ²⁴He bought

the hill of Samaria from Shemer for two talents[a] of silver and built a city on the hill, calling it Samaria, after Shemer, the name of the former owner of the hill.

25But Omri did evil in the eyes of the LORD and sinned more than all those before him. 26He walked in all the ways of Jeroboam son of Nebat and in his sin, which he had caused Israel to commit, so that they provoked the LORD, the God of Israel, to anger by their worthless idols.

27As for the other events of Omri's reign, what he did and the things he achieved, are they not written in the book of the annals of the kings of Israel? 28Omri rested with his fathers and was buried in Samaria. And Ahab his son succeeded him as king.

Ahab Becomes King of Israel

29In the thirty-eighth year of Asa king of Judah, Ahab son of Omri became king of Israel, and he reigned in Samaria over Israel twenty-two years. 30Ahab son of Omri did more evil in the eyes of the LORD than any of those before him. 31He not only considered it trivial to commit the sins of Jeroboam son of Nebat, but he also married Jezebel daughter of Ethbaal king of the Sidonians, and began to serve Baal and worship him. 32He set up an altar for Baal in the temple of Baal that he built in Samaria. 33Ahab also made an Asherah pole and did more to provoke the LORD, the God of Israel, to anger than did all the kings of Israel before him.

34In Ahab's time, Hiel of Bethel rebuilt Jericho. He laid its foundations at the cost of his firstborn son Abiram, and he set up its gates at the cost of his youngest son Segub, in accordance with the word of the LORD spoken by Joshua son of Nun.

Elijah Fed by Ravens

17 Now Elijah the Tishbite, from Tishbe[b] in Gilead, said to Ahab, "As the LORD, the

16:34 A Curse from Joshua

Joshua 6:26 records the solemn pronouncement of what would happen to anyone who attempted to rebuild Jericho. The curse had tragic consequences for Hiel.

God of Israel, lives, whom I serve, there will be neither dew nor rain in the next few years except at my word."

2Then the word of the LORD came to Elijah: 3"Leave here, turn eastward and hide in the Kerith Ravine, east of the Jordan. 4You will drink from the brook, and I have ordered the ravens to feed you there."

5So he did what the LORD had told him. He went to the Kerith Ravine, east of the Jordan, and stayed there. 6The ravens brought him bread and meat in the morning and bread and meat in the evening, and he drank from the brook.

The Widow at Zarephath

7Some time later the brook dried up because there had been no rain in the land. 8Then the word of the LORD came to him: 9"Go at once to Zarephath of Sidon and stay there. I have commanded a widow in that place to supply you with food." 10So he went to Zarephath. When he came to the town gate, a widow was there gathering sticks. He called to her and asked, "Would you bring me a little water in a jar so I may have a

---

[a]24 That is, about 150 pounds (about 70 kilograms)   [b]1 Or *Tishbite, of the settlers*

ELIJAH *Miracle Worker*

WHEN WE SPEAK OF MIRACLES in the Bible, three names stand out: Moses, Elijah and Jesus. Those three, in fact, are the ones who met on the Mount of Transfiguration to talk about Jesus' departure from earth (Luke 9:30–31). In their lifetimes, all three saw the power—and also the limitations—of miracles.

First and Second Kings record eight amazing miracles God worked through Elijah. Some, like his contest with the prophets of Baal (1 Kings 18:16–39), were performed before a large audience. Others, like his restoration of the widow's son (17:17–24), were more private. Ironically, Elijah's experience shows the limits of miracles in encouraging faith. Right after his greatest miracle—the contest with Baal—Elijah grew depressed and afraid. It was then that God revealed his presence not through demonstrations of power, but in "a gentle whisper" (19:12).

The prophet Malachi predicted that a visit by Elijah would precede the Messiah's arrival—a prediction Jesus said that John the Baptist fulfilled (Matthew 17:9–13). All the Jews of Jesus' day—including Jesus—held Elijah in highest esteem. Even today during certain holidays Orthodox Jews leave a place at the table for Elijah, worker of wonders.

Life Questions: Have you ever witnessed a miracle? If so, how did it affect you?

drink?" ¹¹As she was going to get it, he called, "And bring me, please, a piece of bread."

¹²"As surely as the LORD your God lives," she replied, "I don't have any bread—only a handful of flour in a jar and a little oil in a jug. I am gathering a few sticks to take home and make a meal for myself and my son, that we may eat it—and die."

17:12–16 Down to the Last Meal

Elijah's unusual sources of food demanded the utmost faith in God. First, he was fed by ravens. Then, when his water supply gave out, God ordered Elijah to a very unlikely place: the home of a famished, poverty-stricken widow. The widow, not even an Israelite, lived in Jezebel's home territory, a dangerous place for a hunted prophet. Yet the widow at Zarephath showed enough faith in the prophet and his God to use up her last meager resources. The result proved her faith was well-founded. Jesus referred to this story as an example of God's reaching out to Gentiles (Luke 4:25–26).

---

¹³Elijah said to her, "Don't be afraid. Go home and do as you have said. But first make a small cake of bread for me from what you have and bring it to me, and then make something for yourself and your son. ¹⁴For this is what the LORD, the God of Israel, says: 'The jar of flour will not be used up and the jug of oil will not run dry until the day the LORD gives rain on the land.'"

¹⁵She went away and did as Elijah had told her. So there was food every day for Elijah and for the woman and her family. ¹⁶For the jar of flour was not used up and the jug of oil did not run dry, in keeping with the word of the LORD spoken by Elijah.

¹⁷Some time later the son of the woman who owned the house became ill. He grew worse and worse, and finally stopped breathing. ¹⁸She said to Elijah, "What do you have against me, man of God? Did you come to remind me of my sin and kill my son?"

¹⁹"Give me your son," Elijah replied. He took him from her arms, carried him to the upper room where he was staying, and laid him on his bed. ²⁰Then he cried out to the LORD, "O LORD my God, have you brought tragedy also upon this widow I am staying with, by causing her son to die?" ²¹Then he stretched himself out on the boy three times and cried to the LORD, "O LORD my God, let this boy's life return to him!"

²²The LORD heard Elijah's cry, and the boy's life returned to him, and he lived. ²³Elijah picked up the child and carried him down from the room into the house. He gave him to his mother and said, "Look, your son is alive!"

²⁴Then the woman said to Elijah, "Now I know that you are a man of God and that the word of the LORD from your mouth is the truth."

Elijah and Obadiah

18 After a long time, in the third year, the word of the LORD came to Elijah: "Go and present yourself to Ahab, and I will send rain on the land." ²So Elijah went to present himself to Ahab.

Now the famine was severe in Samaria, ³and Ahab had summoned Obadiah, who was in charge of his palace. (Obadiah was a devout believer in the LORD. ⁴While Jezebel was killing off the LORD's prophets, Obadiah had taken a hundred prophets and hidden them in two caves, fifty in each, and had supplied them with food and water.) ⁵Ahab had said to Obadiah, "Go through the land to all the springs and valleys. Maybe we can find some grass to keep the horses and mules alive so we will not have to kill any of our animals." ⁶So they divided the land they were to cover, Ahab going in one direction and Obadiah in another.

⁷As Obadiah was walking along, Elijah met him. Obadiah recognized him, bowed down to the ground, and said, "Is it really you, my lord Elijah?"

⁸"Yes," he replied. "Go tell your master, 'Elijah is here.'"

⁹"What have I done wrong," asked Obadiah, "that you are handing your servant over to Ahab to be put to death? ¹⁰As surely as the LORD your God lives, there is not a nation or kingdom where my master has not sent someone to look for you. And whenever a nation or kingdom claimed you were not there, he made them swear they could not find you. ¹¹But now you tell me to go to my master and say, 'Elijah is here.' ¹²I don't know where the Spirit of the LORD may carry you when I leave you. If I go and tell Ahab and he doesn't find you, he will kill me. Yet I your servant have worshiped the LORD since my youth. ¹³Haven't you heard, my lord, what I did while Jezebel was killing the prophets of the LORD? I hid a hundred of the LORD's prophets in two caves, fifty in each, and supplied them with food and water. ¹⁴And now you tell me to go to my master and say, 'Elijah is here.' He will kill me!"

¹⁵Elijah said, "As the LORD Almighty lives, whom I serve, I will surely present myself to Ahab today."

Elijah on Mount Carmel

¹⁶So Obadiah went to meet Ahab and told him, and Ahab went to meet Elijah. ¹⁷When he saw Elijah, he said to him, "Is that you, you troubler of Israel?"

¹⁸"I have not made trouble for Israel," Elijah

The Contest
One lone prophet against a thousand priests

FEW SCENES IN THE BIBLE are more dramatic than this one. The forces of evil and the forces of good collided head on. In books like J.R.R. Tolkien's *Lord of the Rings* or television shows such as the "Star Trek" series, mythmakers dream up cosmic confrontations. But the incident in 1 Kings 18 is no myth. On that day, a bedraggled desert prophet single-handedly took on a king and nearly a thousand powerful priests.

Elijah had made a grand entrance three years before. Like a wild, startling apparition, he came out of nowhere to stalk the terraced streets of affluent Samaria. Clothed in black camel's hair, he made a striking contrast to the priests of Baal in their white linen robes and high-pointed bonnets. He had a simple, unpopular message of doom: "There will be neither dew nor rain in the next few years except at my word" (17:1). It was a direct affront to followers of Baal, who believed their god could control the weather.

Having delivered his message, Elijah disappeared. For three years he was the most wanted fugitive in Israel, for he alone had the power to bring rain. And then, in the scene reported in chapter 18, the prophet Elijah returned to Samaria.

> Elijah went before the people and said, "How long will you waver between two opinions? If the LORD is God, follow him; but if Baal is God, follow him." 18:21

Elijah's Contest

Israel was at a crossroads. Other kings had introduced idolatry into Israelite religion, but King Ahab and the notorious Queen Jezebel were going much further. They wanted to wipe out all worship of the true God.

The prophet Elijah proved a worthy adversary. His very name meant "The LORD is my God." Having proposed a showdown, the ultimate contest to prove who was the true God. First Kings presents the scene in full color, complete with the priests' desperate contortions and Elijah's mocking, taunting commentary. In the final analysis, it was no contest at all. God unleashed a spectacular display of raw power.

Elijah was one of the most colorful of all Israel's prophets. He suffered from bouts of depression and self-doubt, but during times of crisis he showed amazing courage. The Mount Carmel showdown was merely one sign of the high drama going on. Elijah lived during one of the greatest outbreaks of miracles in biblical history. God was sounding a final warning to Israel.

Israel's Real Heroes

The author of the book of 1 Kings starts out by recording the history of God's anointed leaders. But as the rulers and then priests grow more and more corrupt, this book trains the spotlight on prophets like Elijah. They emerge as Israel's real heroes.

The prophets were not, to Israel, merely preachers or poets. They were channels of God's power, through word and deed. They served on the front line of the struggle between good and evil. Over time, the prophets' significance overtook and even surpassed that of kings. Kings came and went, but the message of the prophets endured.

Voices in the Desert

Whether they served in the government or wandered in occasionally from the desert, the true prophets remained accountable only to God. They decried other, "false," prophets, employed by the king, who generally told the king whatever he wished to hear.

Not all prophets left written messages (Elijah and Elisha, for example, did not). But those prophetic writings that did survive form 17 books of the Old Testament, most of them stemming from the time period described in 1 and 2 Kings.

The prophets told of a God who worked in history to accomplish his will in the world. Sometimes he seemed silent. Sometimes he worked slowly and mysteriously. But occasionally God did step in directly, spectacularly, with a display of power. And when he did, a prophet was usually right in the middle of things—like Elijah on Mount Carmel.

Life Questions: Who serves the role of "prophet" today?

replied. "But you and your father's family have. You have abandoned the LORD's commands and have followed the Baals. ¹⁹Now summon the people from all over Israel to meet me on Mount Carmel. And bring the four hundred and fifty prophets of Baal and the four hundred prophets of Asherah, who eat at Jezebel's table."

²⁰So Ahab sent word throughout all Israel and assembled the prophets on Mount Carmel. ²¹Elijah went before the people and said, "How long will you waver between two opinions? If the LORD is God, follow him; but if Baal is God, follow him."

But the people said nothing.

²²Then Elijah said to them, "I am the only one of the LORD's prophets left, but Baal has four hundred and fifty prophets. ²³Get two bulls for us. Let them choose one for themselves, and let them cut it into pieces and put it on the wood but not set fire to it. I will prepare the other bull and put it on the wood but not set fire to it. ²⁴Then you call on the name of your god, and I will call on the name of the LORD. The god who answers by fire—he is God."

Then all the people said, "What you say is good."

²⁵Elijah said to the prophets of Baal, "Choose one of the bulls and prepare it first, since there are so many of you. Call on the name of your god, but do not light the fire." ²⁶So they took the bull given them and prepared it.

Then they called on the name of Baal from morning till noon. "O Baal, answer us!" they shouted. But there was no response; no one answered. And they danced around the altar they had made.

²⁷At noon Elijah began to taunt them. "Shout louder!" he said. "Surely he is a god! Perhaps he is deep in thought, or busy, or traveling. Maybe he is sleeping and must be awakened." ²⁸So they shouted louder and slashed themselves with swords and spears, as was their custom, until their blood flowed. ²⁹Midday passed, and they continued their frantic prophesying until the time for the evening sacrifice. But there was no response, no one answered, no one paid attention.

³⁰Then Elijah said to all the people, "Come here to me." They came to him, and he repaired the altar of the LORD, which was in ruins. ³¹Elijah took twelve stones, one for each of the tribes descended from Jacob, to whom the word of the LORD had come, saying, "Your name shall be Israel." ³²With the stones he built an altar in the name of the LORD, and he dug a trench around it large enough to hold two seahs[a] of seed. ³³He arranged the wood, cut the bull into pieces and laid it on the wood. Then he said to them, "Fill four large jars with water and pour it on the offering and on the wood."

³⁴"Do it again," he said, and they did it again.

"Do it a third time," he ordered, and they did

18:33 Elijah Rubs It In

Elijah designed the contest to expose Baal, the alleged god of weather, who was often depicted carrying a thunderbolt. Elijah doused his own altar with 12 large jars of water—a precious commodity after three years of drought—before calling on God. Fire from heaven burned up the sacrifice, the wood, the stones, the soil, and even licked up the water in the trench.

it the third time. ³⁵The water ran down around the altar and even filled the trench.

³⁶At the time of sacrifice, the prophet Elijah stepped forward and prayed: "O LORD, God of Abraham, Isaac and Israel, let it be known today that you are God in Israel and that I am your servant and have done all these things at your command. ³⁷Answer me, O LORD, answer me, so these people will know that you, O LORD, are God, and that you are turning their hearts back again."

³⁸Then the fire of the LORD fell and burned up the sacrifice, the wood, the stones and the soil, and also licked up the water in the trench.

³⁹When all the people saw this, they fell prostrate and cried, "The LORD—he is God! The LORD—he is God!"

⁴⁰Then Elijah commanded them, "Seize the prophets of Baal. Don't let anyone get away!" They seized them, and Elijah had them brought down to the Kishon Valley and slaughtered there.

⁴¹And Elijah said to Ahab, "Go, eat and drink, for there is the sound of a heavy rain." ⁴²So Ahab went off to eat and drink, but Elijah climbed to the top of Carmel, bent down to the ground and put his face between his knees.

⁴³"Go and look toward the sea," he told his servant. And he went up and looked.

"There is nothing there," he said.

Seven times Elijah said, "Go back."

⁴⁴The seventh time the servant reported, "A cloud as small as a man's hand is rising from the sea."

So Elijah said, "Go and tell Ahab, 'Hitch up your chariot and go down before the rain stops you.'"

⁴⁵Meanwhile, the sky grew black with clouds, the wind rose, a heavy rain came on and Ahab rode off to Jezreel. ⁴⁶The power of the LORD came

---

a 32 That is, probably about 13 quarts (about 15 liters)

upon Elijah and, tucking his cloak into his belt, he ran ahead of Ahab all the way to Jezreel.

Elijah Flees to Horeb

19 Now Ahab told Jezebel everything Elijah had done and how he had killed all the prophets with the sword. ²So Jezebel sent a messenger to Elijah to say, "May the gods deal with me, be it ever so severely, if by this time tomorrow I do not make your life like that of one of them."

³Elijah was afraid*ᵃ* and ran for his life. When he came to Beersheba in Judah, he left his servant

---

19:3 Wicked Queen Jezebel

Queen Jezebel's reputation was such that Elijah ran from her in fear even after God had triumphantly displayed his power on Mount Carmel. The Roman historian Josephus records her family history. Her father, who had served as high priest in a pagan temple in Tyre, murdered the king and ruled there for 32 years. His reign was characterized by murderous idolatries and a reckless contempt for human rights.

Jezebel followed in her father's footsteps. Married to Ahab as part of a political alliance, she installed 950 prophets of Baal and ordered the wholesale slaughter of any prophets of God who opposed her. Ahab fell under her sway. Alone, he could be brave, chivalrous, and even conscientious. But his weakness and Jezebel's influence led him to become the most wicked king of Israel.

---

there, ⁴while he himself went a day's journey into the desert. He came to a broom tree, sat down under it and prayed that he might die. "I have had enough, LORD," he said. "Take my life; I am no better than my ancestors." ⁵Then he lay down under the tree and fell asleep.

All at once an angel touched him and said, "Get up and eat." ⁶He looked around, and there by his head was a cake of bread baked over hot coals, and a jar of water. He ate and drank and then lay down again.

⁷The angel of the LORD came back a second time and touched him and said, "Get up and eat, for the journey is too much for you." ⁸So he got up and ate and drank. Strengthened by that food, he traveled forty days and forty nights until he reached Horeb, the mountain of God. ⁹There he went into a cave and spent the night.

The LORD Appears to Elijah

And the word of the LORD came to him: "What are you doing here, Elijah?"

¹⁰He replied, "I have been very zealous for the LORD God Almighty. The Israelites have rejected your covenant, broken down your altars, and put your prophets to death with the sword. I am the only one left, and now they are trying to kill me too."

¹¹The LORD said, "Go out and stand on the mountain in the presence of the LORD, for the LORD is about to pass by."

Then a great and powerful wind tore the mountains apart and shattered the rocks before the LORD, but the LORD was not in the wind. After the wind there was an earthquake, but the LORD was not in the earthquake. ¹²After the earthquake came a fire, but the LORD was not in the fire. And after the fire came a gentle whisper. ¹³When Elijah heard it, he pulled his cloak over his face and went out and stood at the mouth of the cave.

Then a voice said to him, "What are you doing here, Elijah?"

¹⁴He replied, "I have been very zealous for the LORD God Almighty. The Israelites have rejected your covenant, broken down your altars, and put your prophets to death with the sword. I am the only one left, and now they are trying to kill me too."

¹⁵The LORD said to him, "Go back the way you came, and go to the Desert of Damascus. When you get there, anoint Hazael king over Aram. ¹⁶Also, anoint Jehu son of Nimshi king over Israel, and anoint Elisha son of Shaphat from Abel Meholah to succeed you as prophet. ¹⁷Jehu will put to death any who escape the sword of Hazael, and Elisha will put to death any who escape the sword of Jehu. ¹⁸Yet I reserve seven thousand in Israel—all whose knees have not bowed down to Baal and all whose mouths have not kissed him."

The Call of Elisha

¹⁹So Elijah went from there and found Elisha son of Shaphat. He was plowing with twelve yoke of oxen, and he himself was driving the twelfth pair. Elijah went up to him and threw his cloak around him. ²⁰Elisha then left his oxen and ran after Elijah. "Let me kiss my father and mother good-by," he said, "and then I will come with you."

"Go back," Elijah replied. "What have I done to you?"

²¹So Elisha left him and went back. He took his yoke of oxen and slaughtered them. He burned the plowing equipment to cook the meat and gave it to the people, and they ate. Then he set out to follow Elijah and became his attendant.

Ben-Hadad Attacks Samaria

20 Now Ben-Hadad king of Aram mustered his entire army. Accompanied by thirty-

---

ᵃ3 Or *Elijah saw*

two kings with their horses and chariots, he went up and besieged Samaria and attacked it. ²He sent messengers into the city to Ahab king of Israel, saying, "This is what Ben-Hadad says: ³'Your silver and gold are mine, and the best of your wives and children are mine.'"

⁴The king of Israel answered, "Just as you say, my lord the king. I and all I have are yours."

⁵The messengers came again and said, "This is what Ben-Hadad says: 'I sent to demand your silver and gold, your wives and your children. ⁶But about this time tomorrow I am going to send my officials to search your palace and the houses of your officials. They will seize everything you value and carry it away.'"

⁷The king of Israel summoned all the elders of the land and said to them, "See how this man is looking for trouble! When he sent for my wives and my children, my silver and my gold, I did not refuse him."

⁸The elders and the people all answered, "Don't listen to him or agree to his demands."

⁹So he replied to Ben-Hadad's messengers, "Tell my lord the king, 'Your servant will do all you demanded the first time, but this demand I cannot meet.'" They left and took the answer back to Ben-Hadad.

¹⁰Then Ben-Hadad sent another message to Ahab: "May the gods deal with me, be it ever so severely, if enough dust remains in Samaria to give each of my men a handful."

¹¹The king of Israel answered, "Tell him: 'One who puts on his armor should not boast like one who takes it off.'"

¹²Ben-Hadad heard this message while he and the kings were drinking in their tents,ᵃ and he ordered his men: "Prepare to attack." So they prepared to attack the city.

Ahab Defeats Ben-Hadad

¹³Meanwhile a prophet came to Ahab king of Israel and announced, "This is what the LORD says: 'Do you see this vast army? I will give it into your hand today, and then you will know that I am the LORD.'"

¹⁴"But who will do this?" asked Ahab.

The prophet replied, "This is what the LORD says: 'The young officers of the provincial commanders will do it.'"

"And who will start the battle?" he asked.

The prophet answered, "You will."

¹⁵So Ahab summoned the young officers of the provincial commanders, 232 men. Then he assembled the rest of the Israelites, 7,000 in all. ¹⁶They set out at noon while Ben-Hadad and the 32 kings allied with him were in their tents getting drunk. ¹⁷The young officers of the provincial commanders went out first.

Now Ben-Hadad had dispatched scouts, who reported, "Men are advancing from Samaria."

¹⁸He said, "If they have come out for peace, take them alive; if they have come out for war, take them alive."

¹⁹The young officers of the provincial commanders marched out of the city with the army behind them ²⁰and each one struck down his opponent. At that, the Arameans fled, with the Israelites in pursuit. But Ben-Hadad king of Aram escaped on horseback with some of his horsemen. ²¹The king of Israel advanced and overpowered the horses and chariots and inflicted heavy losses on the Arameans.

²²Afterward, the prophet came to the king of Israel and said, "Strengthen your position and see what must be done, because next spring the king of Aram will attack you again."

²³Meanwhile, the officials of the king of Aram advised him, "Their gods are gods of the hills. That is why they were too strong for us. But if we fight them on the plains, surely we will be stronger than they. ²⁴Do this: Remove all the kings from their commands and replace them with other officers. ²⁵You must also raise an army like the one you lost—horse for horse and chariot for chariot—so we can fight Israel on the plains. Then surely we will be stronger than they." He agreed with them and acted accordingly.

²⁶The next spring Ben-Hadad mustered the Arameans and went up to Aphek to fight against Israel. ²⁷When the Israelites were also mustered and given provisions, they marched out to meet them. The Israelites camped opposite them like two small flocks of goats, while the Arameans covered the countryside.

²⁸The man of God came up and told the king of Israel, "This is what the LORD says: 'Because the Arameans think the LORD is a god of the hills and not a god of the valleys, I will deliver this vast army into your hands, and you will know that I am the LORD.'"

²⁹For seven days they camped opposite each other, and on the seventh day the battle was joined. The Israelites inflicted a hundred thousand casualties on the Aramean foot soldiers in one day. ³⁰The rest of them escaped to the city of Aphek, where the wall collapsed on twenty-seven thousand of them. And Ben-Hadad fled to the city and hid in an inner room.

³¹His officials said to him, "Look, we have heard that the kings of the house of Israel are merciful. Let us go to the king of Israel with sackcloth around our waists and ropes around our heads. Perhaps he will spare your life."

³²Wearing sackcloth around their waists and ropes around their heads, they went to the king

---

ᵃ12 Or *in Succoth*; also in verse 16

of Israel and said, "Your servant Ben-Hadad says: 'Please let me live.'"

The king answered, "Is he still alive? He is my brother."

³³The men took this as a good sign and were quick to pick up his word. "Yes, your brother Ben-Hadad!" they said.

"Go and get him," the king said. When Ben-Hadad came out, Ahab had him come up into his chariot.

³⁴"I will return the cities my father took from your father," Ben-Hadad offered. "You may set up your own market areas in Damascus, as my father did in Samaria."

⌊Ahab said,⌋ "On the basis of a treaty I will set you free." So he made a treaty with him, and let him go.

A Prophet Condemns Ahab

³⁵By the word of the LORD one of the sons of the prophets said to his companion, "Strike me with your weapon," but the man refused.

³⁶So the prophet said, "Because you have not obeyed the LORD, as soon as you leave me a lion will kill you." And after the man went away, a lion found him and killed him.

³⁷The prophet found another man and said, "Strike me, please." So the man struck him and wounded him. ³⁸Then the prophet went and stood by the road waiting for the king. He disguised himself with his headband down over his eyes. ³⁹As the king passed by, the prophet called out to him, "Your servant went into the thick of the battle, and someone came to me with a captive and said, 'Guard this man. If he is missing, it will be your life for his life, or you must pay a talent[a] of silver.' ⁴⁰While your servant was busy here and there, the man disappeared."

"That is your sentence," the king of Israel said. "You have pronounced it yourself."

⁴¹Then the prophet quickly removed the headband from his eyes, and the king of Israel recognized him as one of the prophets. ⁴²He said to the king, "This is what the LORD says: 'You have set free a man I had determined should die.[b] Therefore it is your life for his life, your people for his people.'" ⁴³Sullen and angry, the king of Israel went to his palace in Samaria.

Naboth's Vineyard

21 Some time later there was an incident involving a vineyard belonging to Naboth the Jezreelite. The vineyard was in Jezreel, close to the palace of Ahab king of Samaria. ²Ahab said to Naboth, "Let me have your vineyard to use for a vegetable garden, since it is close to my palace. In exchange I will give you a better vineyard or, if you prefer, I will pay you whatever it is worth."

³But Naboth replied, "The LORD forbid that I should give you the inheritance of my fathers."

⁴So Ahab went home, sullen and angry because Naboth the Jezreelite had said, "I will not

---

21:1 A Stolen Vineyard

The incident of Naboth's vineyard shows the selective way in which Old Testament authors wove history together. In one sense, the theft was a minor incident in King Ahab's reign. Yet 1 Kings devotes more space to it than to the entire reigns of some kings. It showed the kings' abuse of power and disrespect for God's covenant. Every Israelite had the right to possess a piece of the promised land—not even a king could legally usurp that right. In fact, selling the land would break a law God gave Moses (Leviticus 25:23–31). Ahab's greed and Jezebel's intrigue led to murder and ultimately spelled doom for the kingdom.

---

give you the inheritance of my fathers." He lay on his bed sulking and refused to eat.

⁵His wife Jezebel came in and asked him, "Why are you so sullen? Why won't you eat?"

⁶He answered her, "Because I said to Naboth the Jezreelite, 'Sell me your vineyard; or if you prefer, I will give you another vineyard in its place.' But he said, 'I will not give you my vineyard.'"

⁷Jezebel his wife said, "Is this how you act as king over Israel? Get up and eat! Cheer up. I'll get you the vineyard of Naboth the Jezreelite."

⁸So she wrote letters in Ahab's name, placed his seal on them, and sent them to the elders and nobles who lived in Naboth's city with him. ⁹In those letters she wrote:

> "Proclaim a day of fasting and seat Naboth in a prominent place among the people. ¹⁰But seat two scoundrels opposite him and have them testify that he has cursed both God and the king. Then take him out and stone him to death."

¹¹So the elders and nobles who lived in Naboth's city did as Jezebel directed in the letters she had written to them. ¹²They proclaimed a fast and seated Naboth in a prominent place among the people. ¹³Then two scoundrels came and sat opposite him and brought charges against Naboth before the people, saying, "Naboth has cursed both God and the king." So they took him outside the city and stoned him to death. ¹⁴Then they sent word to Jezebel: "Naboth has been stoned and is dead."

¹⁵As soon as Jezebel heard that Naboth had

---

a39 That is, about 75 pounds (about 34 kilograms)   *b42* The Hebrew term refers to the irrevocable giving over of things or persons to the LORD, often by totally destroying them.

been stoned to death, she said to Ahab, "Get up and take possession of the vineyard of Naboth the Jezreelite that he refused to sell you. He is no longer alive, but dead." [16]When Ahab heard that Naboth was dead, he got up and went down to take possession of Naboth's vineyard.

[17]Then the word of the LORD came to Elijah the Tishbite: [18]"Go down to meet Ahab king of Israel, who rules in Samaria. He is now in Naboth's vineyard, where he has gone to take possession of it. [19]Say to him, 'This is what the LORD says: Have you not murdered a man and seized his property?' Then say to him, 'This is what the LORD says: In the place where dogs licked up Naboth's blood, dogs will lick up your blood—yes, yours!'"

[20]Ahab said to Elijah, "So you have found me, my enemy!"

"I have found you," he answered, "because you have sold yourself to do evil in the eyes of the LORD. [21]I am going to bring disaster on you. I will consume your descendants and cut off from Ahab every last male in Israel—slave or free. [22]I will make your house like that of Jeroboam son of Nebat and that of Baasha son of Ahijah, because you have provoked me to anger and have caused Israel to sin.'

[23]"And also concerning Jezebel the LORD says: 'Dogs will devour Jezebel by the wall of[a] Jezreel.'

[24]"Dogs will eat those belonging to Ahab who die in the city, and the birds of the air will feed on those who die in the country."

[25](There was never a man like Ahab, who sold himself to do evil in the eyes of the LORD, urged on by Jezebel his wife. [26]He behaved in the vilest manner by going after idols, like the Amorites the LORD drove out before Israel.)

[27]When Ahab heard these words, he tore his clothes, put on sackcloth and fasted. He lay in sackcloth and went around meekly.

[28]Then the word of the LORD came to Elijah the Tishbite: [29]"Have you noticed how Ahab has humbled himself before me? Because he has humbled himself, I will not bring this disaster in his day, but I will bring it on his house in the days of his son."

Micaiah Prophesies Against Ahab

22 For three years there was no war between Aram and Israel. [2]But in the third year Jehoshaphat king of Judah went down to see the king of Israel. [3]The king of Israel had said to his officials, "Don't you know that Ramoth Gilead belongs to us and yet we are doing nothing to retake it from the king of Aram?"

[4]So he asked Jehoshaphat, "Will you go with me to fight against Ramoth Gilead?"

Jehoshaphat replied to the king of Israel, "I am as you are, my people as your people, my horses as your horses." [5]But Jehoshaphat also said to the king of Israel, "First seek the counsel of the LORD."

[6]So the king of Israel brought together the prophets—about four hundred men—and asked them, "Shall I go to war against Ramoth Gilead, or shall I refrain?"

"Go," they answered, "for the Lord will give it into the king's hand."

[7]But Jehoshaphat asked, "Is there not a prophet of the LORD here whom we can inquire of?"

---

[a]23 Most Hebrew manuscripts; a few Hebrew manuscripts, Vulgate and Syriac (see also 2 Kings 9:26) *the plot of ground at*

AHAB *Worst King Yet*

IMAGINE THE UPROAR IF A U.S. president suddenly decided to demolish all church buildings and replace every Christian pastor with a Hindu priest. Something like that happened in King Ahab's day. True, Ahab inherited a bad situation: a divided kingdom in which religious faith was in free fall. Yet somehow he made it worse, doing "more evil in the eyes of the LORD than any of those before him" (16:30).

The Bible lays much of the blame for Ahab's performance on a bad marriage. To forge a political alliance he married Jezebel, the daughter of a neighboring king. When she brought along her idols of Baal, Ahab joined in, building a temple to Baal right in his capital. Jezebel then tried to hunt down and destroy all remnants of true Israelite faith, replacing God's prophets with her own imported substitutes.

While Ahab may seem like the passive partner in crime, he bore his share of responsibility as well. The prophet Elijah might have been his salvation; Ahab saw him instead as an enemy and a troublemaker (18:17; 21:20). Time after time Ahab rejected good and godly advice.

By secular standards of prosperity and military strength, Ahab achieved success. He built a fine palace inlaid with ivory. (Archaeologists have found ivory plaques from homes of this period.) He drove back invaders from Syria. From the Bible's point of view, however, these achievements meant nothing compared to his failures of faith and morality. As a traitor to God, Ahab was the worst king yet.

Life Questions: In today's world, how do political leaders affect a country's overall moral and spiritual climate? Should they do more?

[8]The king of Israel answered Jehoshaphat, "There is still one man through whom we can inquire of the LORD, but I hate him because he never prophesies anything good about me, but always bad. He is Micaiah son of Imlah."

22:4 Unholy Alliance

After years of warfare, peace was finally arranged between Israel and Judah. Ironically, it joined Israel's worst king, Ahab, with one of Judah's best, King Jehoshaphat. The unholy alliance with Ahab led to a fateful battle against Aram that almost cost Jehoshaphat his life (verses 29–33). Judah's king spurned later offers of cooperation (verse 49), but his son married King Ahab's daughter. This unwise marriage exposed Judah to the evil practices of the North and ultimately led to a royal bloodbath.

"The king should not say that," Jehoshaphat replied.

[9]So the king of Israel called one of his officials and said, "Bring Micaiah son of Imlah at once."

[10]Dressed in their royal robes, the king of Israel and Jehoshaphat king of Judah were sitting on their thrones at the threshing floor by the entrance of the gate of Samaria, with all the prophets prophesying before them. [11]Now Zedekiah son of Kenaanah had made iron horns and he declared, "This is what the LORD says: 'With these you will gore the Arameans until they are destroyed.'"

[12]All the other prophets were prophesying the same thing. "Attack Ramoth Gilead and be victorious," they said, "for the LORD will give it into the king's hand."

[13]The messenger who had gone to summon Micaiah said to him, "Look, as one man the other prophets are predicting success for the king. Let your word agree with theirs, and speak favorably."

[14]But Micaiah said, "As surely as the LORD lives, I can tell him only what the LORD tells me."

[15]When he arrived, the king asked him, "Micaiah, shall we go to war against Ramoth Gilead, or shall I refrain?"

"Attack and be victorious," he answered, "for the LORD will give it into the king's hand."

[16]The king said to him, "How many times must I make you swear to tell me nothing but the truth in the name of the LORD?"

[17]Then Micaiah answered, "I saw all Israel scattered on the hills like sheep without a shepherd, and the LORD said, 'These people have no master. Let each one go home in peace.'"

[18]The king of Israel said to Jehoshaphat, "Didn't I tell you that he never prophesies anything good about me, but only bad?"

[19]Micaiah continued, "Therefore hear the word of the LORD: I saw the LORD sitting on his throne with all the host of heaven standing around him on his right and on his left. [20]And the LORD said, 'Who will entice Ahab into attacking Ramoth Gilead and going to his death there?'

"One suggested this, and another that. [21]Finally, a spirit came forward, stood before the LORD and said, 'I will entice him.'

[22]"'By what means?' the LORD asked.

"'I will go out and be a lying spirit in the mouths of all his prophets,' he said.

"'You will succeed in enticing him,' said the LORD. 'Go and do it.'

[23]"So now the LORD has put a lying spirit in the mouths of all these prophets of yours. The LORD has decreed disaster for you."

[24]Then Zedekiah son of Kenaanah went up and slapped Micaiah in the face. "Which way did the spirit from[a] the LORD go when he went from me to speak to you?" he asked.

[25]Micaiah replied, "You will find out on the day you go to hide in an inner room."

[26]The king of Israel then ordered, "Take Micaiah and send him back to Amon the ruler of the city and to Joash the king's son [27]and say, 'This is what the king says: Put this fellow in prison and give him nothing but bread and water until I return safely.'"

[28]Micaiah declared, "If you ever return safely, the LORD has not spoken through me." Then he added, "Mark my words, all you people!"

Ahab Killed at Ramoth Gilead

[29]So the king of Israel and Jehoshaphat king of Judah went up to Ramoth Gilead. [30]The king of Israel said to Jehoshaphat, "I will enter the battle in disguise, but you wear your royal robes." So the king of Israel disguised himself and went into battle.

[31]Now the king of Aram had ordered his thirty-two chariot commanders, "Do not fight with anyone, small or great, except the king of Israel." [32]When the chariot commanders saw Jehoshaphat, they thought, "Surely this is the king of Israel." So they turned to attack him, but when Jehoshaphat cried out, [33]the chariot commanders saw that he was not the king of Israel and stopped pursuing him.

[34]But someone drew his bow at random and hit the king of Israel between the sections of his armor. The king told his chariot driver, "Wheel around and get me out of the fighting. I've been

wounded." [35]All day long the battle raged, and the king was propped up in his chariot facing the Arameans. The blood from his wound ran onto the floor of the chariot, and that evening he died. [36]As the sun was setting, a cry spread through the army: "Every man to his town; everyone to his land!"

[37]So the king died and was brought to Samaria, and they buried him there. [38]They washed the chariot at a pool in Samaria (where the prostitutes bathed),[a] and the dogs licked up his blood, as the word of the LORD had declared.

[39]As for the other events of Ahab's reign, including all he did, the palace he built and inlaid with ivory, and the cities he fortified, are they not written in the book of the annals of the kings of Israel? [40]Ahab rested with his fathers. And Ahaziah his son succeeded him as king.

Jehoshaphat King of Judah

[41]Jehoshaphat son of Asa became king of Judah in the fourth year of Ahab king of Israel. [42]Jehoshaphat was thirty-five years old when he became king, and he reigned in Jerusalem twenty-five years. His mother's name was Azubah daughter of Shilhi. [43]In everything he walked in the ways of his father Asa and did not stray from them; he did what was right in the eyes of the LORD. The high places, however, were not removed, and the people continued to offer sacrifices and burn incense there. [44]Jehoshaphat was also at peace with the king of Israel.

[45]As for the other events of Jehoshaphat's reign, the things he achieved and his military exploits, are they not written in the book of the annals of the kings of Judah? [46]He rid the land of the rest of the male shrine prostitutes who remained there even after the reign of his father Asa. [47]There was then no king in Edom; a deputy ruled.

[48]Now Jehoshaphat built a fleet of trading ships[b] to go to Ophir for gold, but they never set sail—they were wrecked at Ezion Geber. [49]At that time Ahaziah son of Ahab said to Jehoshaphat, "Let my men sail with your men," but Jehoshaphat refused.

[50]Then Jehoshaphat rested with his fathers and was buried with them in the city of David his father. And Jehoram his son succeeded him.

Ahaziah King of Israel

[51]Ahaziah son of Ahab became king of Israel in Samaria in the seventeenth year of Jehoshaphat king of Judah, and he reigned over Israel two years. [52]He did evil in the eyes of the LORD, because he walked in the ways of his father and mother and in the ways of Jeroboam son of Nebat, who caused Israel to sin. [53]He served and worshiped Baal and provoked the LORD, the God of Israel, to anger, just as his father had done.

---

[a]38 Or Samaria and cleaned the weapons   [b]48 Hebrew of ships of Tarshish

2 KINGS

The Great Wars of Israel
The promised land turns into a bloody battlefield

THE BOOK OF 2 KINGS TELLS of dark days in the promised land. First, the Northern Kingdom, Israel, fell to outside invaders. Then Judah, the Southern Kingdom, was conquered. To appreciate what those two events meant in Jewish history, consider our century's two great wars.

In 1918 the bloodiest war of all time came to an end. The entire planet had chosen sides. In all, nine million soldiers died. Survivors thought nothing could ever again match The Great War's ferocity and destruction. "The war to end all wars," they called it.

Yet, in a mere 20 years, a man named Adolf Hitler brought war again. In World War II, global violence stretched from London in the West to Japan in the East. The war finally closed with a blinding mushroom cloud, an ominous portent for the future.

> So the LORD said, "I will remove Judah also from my presence as I removed Israel, and I will reject Jerusalem, the city I chose, and this temple, about which I said, 'There shall my Name be.' "
> 23:27

Two Large Blots in History

No matter what else happens, the 20th century has been permanently stained by those two large blots: World War I and World War II. Everything else—art, literature, advances in science and medicine—fades into the background.

As 2 Kings tells it, something very similar occurred in the Biblical nation of Israel. Two large blots spread across the land: successive invasions by foreign giants. In the long, turbulent history of the Jews, these two invasions stand out as the Great Wars, overshadowing nearly everything else.

Israel Falls First

The kingdom had already split into two—1 Kings tells that story. Its sequel, 2 Kings, describes ever-increasing tragedy.

From the very first chapters you can sense the pending crisis in the North. Not one northern king followed the ways of God. National politics slipped into an endless cycle of intrigue and bloody revolt. Meanwhile, Elijah and Elisha intensified their attacks on the kings, and miracles broke out with unusual frequency.

Assyria's campaigns—the "World War I" in Israel's history—are reported in 2 Kings 15–18. Other records of the period tell of vicious fighting. Samaria, Israel's capital, made one final heroic stand against a two-year siege. Finally, the starving survivors surrendered, and the people of Israel were carried away into captivity.

Only two Israelite tribes remained in the promised land, holding out in the tiny Southern Kingdom of Judah. Ultimately, King Sennacherib of Assyria turned against Judah also, penetrating all the way to the gates of Jerusalem. Contemporary accounts record that he leveled 46 walled cities and carried away 200,150 people, young and old, along with all their horses, mules, cattle, and possessions. He scornfully dismissed King Hezekiah as "a bird in a cage."

A Brief Comeback

Could the tiny nation of Judah survive such an onslaught? Somehow the "caged bird" (Hezekiah) made a remarkable comeback, and Judah did survive for another 135 years. Still, Judah did not learn from the dramatic object lesson of Israel's destruction in the North. Most of the kings who followed Hezekiah failed dismally to obey God. Another foreign invader, Babylon, finally leveled Jerusalem in the "World War II" of that era.

The book of Kings ends with a bleak picture: refugees picking through the rubble of Jerusalem, and the Israelites enslaved by foreign powers. The temple itself, God's house, lay in ruins, its treasures carted off to Babylon. When the dust settled around 600 B.C., the Israelites were scattered across the earth, not to be reunited as an independent nation for 25 centuries.

All along, prophets had given eloquent warnings of what would happen to a nation that turned its back on God. But nothing makes a bigger impact than the object lesson of history itself. Ever since, Jews have looked back on their history and seen two indelible stains. Those were the dark days of Assyria and Babylon, when everything came apart.

How to Read 2 Kings

The first eight chapters of 2 Kings, full of excitement and adventure, read easily. They focus on the last days of the prophet Elijah and on the long life of his successor Elisha. But beginning with chapter 9, the book can become very confusing. It switches back and forth between two histories: that of Israel in the North and Judah in the South.

Israel was strong initially, with 10 of the 12 tribes united there. But it proved less faithful to God and was ultimately destroyed by Assyria. Chapters 18—25 cover the period after the Assyrian invasion, when only Judah existed.

Use the boldface sectional headings in this Bible for orientation: They clearly mark whether a king or queen ruled over Judah or Israel. Also, a lineup of all the rulers appears on pages 1361—1369, giving an overview of the history of each country.

One important reason for studying the books of Kings and Chronicles is that they give historical background on the prophets. Elijah and Elisha appeared at a crucial turning point in the history of the Northern Kingdom, just as Ahab was changing the official religion from worship of God to worship of Baal. Other prophets, who wrote books of the Bible, were also active during this time.

Amos and Hosea concentrated their work in the Northern Kingdom of Israel. The following prophets lived and preached in the Southern Kingdom of Judah: Obadiah, Joel, Isaiah, Micah, Nahum, Zephaniah, Jeremiah, and Habakkuk. More prophets came later, when the Israelites were still captive in Babylon or after they had returned to their homeland. The How to Read section of each book of the prophets gives a brief summary of when and where each author worked (see An Overview of the Bible, pages 17—20, for a list of the books of the prophets).

Second Kings, like its companion books, makes brief and sweeping judgments of each king or queen. As you read, look for what pleased God and what displeased him. The 39 rulers comprise a fine study of leadership of all kinds, from the inspiring to the degenerate.

PEOPLE YOU'LL MEET IN 2 KINGS

ELISHA (p. 400)
JEZEBEL (p. 409)
JOSIAH (p. 424)
ZEDEKIAH (p. 427)

3-TRACK READING PLAN

For an explanation and complete listing of the 3-track reading plan, turn to page 7.

TRACK 1: *Two-Week Courses on the Bible*
See page 7 for information on these courses.

TRACK 2: *An Overview of 2 Kings in 3 Days*
☐ Day 1. Read the Introduction to 2 Kings and then chapter 5 on Elisha's miracle of healing an enemy from Aram.
☐ Day 2. Read chapter 17, which gives a final summary of the decline and utter devastation of the Northern Kingdom of Israel.
☐ Day 3. One of the high points in 2 Kings occurred during the reign of the boy-king Josiah. Read about the beginning of his reforms in chapter 22 and the first three verses of chapter 23.

Now turn to page 9 for your next Track 2 reading project.

TRACK 3: **All of 2 Kings in 25 Days**
After you have read through 2 Kings, turn to pages 10–14 for your next Track 3 reading project.

☐1 ☐2 ☐3 ☐4 ☐5 ☐6 ☐7 ☐8
☐9 ☐10 ☐11 ☐12 ☐13 ☐14 ☐15 ☐16
☐17 ☐18 ☐19 ☐20 ☐21 ☐22 ☐23 ☐24
☐25

The LORD's Judgment on Ahaziah

1 After Ahab's death, Moab rebelled against Israel. ²Now Ahaziah had fallen through the lattice of his upper room in Samaria and injured himself. So he sent messengers, saying to them, "Go and consult Baal-Zebub, the god of Ekron, to see if I will recover from this injury."

³But the angel of the LORD said to Elijah the Tishbite, "Go up and meet the messengers of the king of Samaria and ask them, 'Is it because there is no God in Israel that you are going off to consult Baal-Zebub, the god of Ekron?' ⁴Therefore this is what the LORD says: 'You will not leave the bed you are lying on. You will certainly die!'" So Elijah went.

⁵When the messengers returned to the king, he asked them, "Why have you come back?"

⁶"A man came to meet us," they replied. "And he said to us, 'Go back to the king who sent you and tell him, "This is what the LORD says: Is it because there is no God in Israel that you are sending men to consult Baal-Zebub, the god of Ekron? Therefore you will not leave the bed you are lying on. You will certainly die!"'"

⁷The king asked them, "What kind of man was it who came to meet you and told you this?"

⁸They replied, "He was a man with a garment of hair and with a leather belt around his waist."

The king said, "That was Elijah the Tishbite."

⁹Then he sent to Elijah a captain with his company of fifty men. The captain went up to Elijah, who was sitting on the top of a hill, and said to him, "Man of God, the king says, 'Come down!'"

¹⁰Elijah answered the captain, "If I am a man of God, may fire come down from heaven and consume you and your fifty men!" Then fire fell from heaven and consumed the captain and his men.

¹¹At this the king sent to Elijah another captain with his fifty men. The captain said to him, "Man of God, this is what the king says, 'Come down at once!'"

¹²"If I am a man of God," Elijah replied, "may fire come down from heaven and consume you and your fifty men!" Then the fire of God fell from heaven and consumed him and his fifty men.

¹³So the king sent a third captain with his fifty men. This third captain went up and fell on his knees before Elijah. "Man of God," he begged, "please have respect for my life and the lives of these fifty men, your servants! ¹⁴See, fire has fallen from heaven and consumed the first two captains and all their men. But now have respect for my life!"

¹⁵The angel of the LORD said to Elijah, "Go down with him; do not be afraid of him." So Elijah got up and went down with him to the king.

¹⁶He told the king, "This is what the LORD says: Is it because there is no God in Israel for you to consult that you have sent messengers to consult Baal-Zebub, the god of Ekron? Because you have done this, you will never leave the bed you are lying on. You will certainly die!" ¹⁷So he died, according to the word of the LORD that Elijah had spoken.

Because Ahaziah had no son, Joram*ª* succeeded him as king in the second year of Jehoram son of Jehoshaphat king of Judah. ¹⁸As for all the other events of Ahaziah's reign, and what he did, are they not written in the book of the annals of the kings of Israel?

Elijah Taken Up to Heaven

2 When the LORD was about to take Elijah up to heaven in a whirlwind, Elijah and Elisha were on their way from Gilgal. ²Elijah said to Elisha, "Stay here; the LORD has sent me to Bethel."

But Elisha said, "As surely as the LORD lives and as you live, I will not leave you." So they went down to Bethel.

³The company of the prophets at Bethel came out to Elisha and asked, "Do you know that the LORD is going to take your master from you today?"

"Yes, I know," Elisha replied, "but do not speak of it."

⁴Then Elijah said to him, "Stay here, Elisha; the LORD has sent me to Jericho."

And he replied, "As surely as the LORD lives

ª 17 Hebrew *Jehoram,* a variant of *Joram*

and as you live, I will not leave you." So they went to Jericho.

[5]The company of the prophets at Jericho went up to Elisha and asked him, "Do you know that the LORD is going to take your master from you today?"

"Yes, I know," he replied, "but do not speak of it."

[6]Then Elijah said to him, "Stay here; the LORD has sent me to the Jordan."

And he replied, "As surely as the LORD lives and as you live, I will not leave you." So the two of them walked on.

[7]Fifty men of the company of the prophets went and stood at a distance, facing the place where Elijah and Elisha had stopped at the Jordan. [8]Elijah took his cloak, rolled it up and struck the water with it. The water divided to the right and to the left, and the two of them crossed over on dry ground.

[9]When they had crossed, Elijah said to Elisha, "Tell me, what can I do for you before I am taken from you?"

"Let me inherit a double portion of your spirit," Elisha replied.

[10]"You have asked a difficult thing," Elijah said, "yet if you see me when I am taken from you, it will be yours—otherwise not."

[11]As they were walking along and talking together, suddenly a chariot of fire and horses of fire appeared and separated the two of them, and Elijah went up to heaven in a whirlwind. [12]Elisha saw this and cried out, "My father! My father! The chariots and horsemen of Israel!" And Elisha saw him no more. Then he took hold of his own clothes and tore them apart.

2:12 An Obscure Compliment

Elisha's last words to Elijah were obviously a compliment, but what did they mean? Most likely they referred to Elijah's power, indicating he was worth more to the nation of Israel than a company of chariots and horsemen. Interestingly, a king of Israel said these exact words to Elisha himself as he lay dying (13:14).

[13]He picked up the cloak that had fallen from Elijah and went back and stood on the bank of the Jordan. [14]Then he took the cloak that had fallen from him and struck the water with it. "Where now is the LORD, the God of Elijah?" he asked. When he struck the water, it divided to the right and to the left, and he crossed over.

[15]The company of the prophets from Jericho, who were watching, said, "The spirit of Elijah is resting on Elisha." And they went to meet him and bowed to the ground before him. [16]"Look,"

they said, "we your servants have fifty able men. Let them go and look for your master. Perhaps the Spirit of the LORD has picked him up and set him down on some mountain or in some valley."

"No," Elisha replied, "do not send them."

[17]But they persisted until he was too ashamed to refuse. So he said, "Send them." And they sent fifty men, who searched for three days but did not find him. [18]When they returned to Elisha, who was staying in Jericho, he said to them, "Didn't I tell you not to go?"

Healing of the Water

[19]The men of the city said to Elisha, "Look, our lord, this town is well situated, as you can see, but the water is bad and the land is unproductive."

[20]"Bring me a new bowl," he said, "and put salt in it." So they brought it to him.

[21]Then he went out to the spring and threw the salt into it, saying, "This is what the LORD says: 'I have healed this water. Never again will it cause death or make the land unproductive.'" [22]And the water has remained wholesome to this day, according to the word Elisha had spoken.

Elisha Is Jeered

[23]From there Elisha went up to Bethel. As he was walking along the road, some youths came out of the town and jeered at him. "Go on up, you baldhead!" they said. "Go on up, you baldhead!" [24]He turned around, looked at them and called down a curse on them in the name of the LORD. Then two bears came out of the woods and mauled forty-two of the youths. [25]And he went on to Mount Carmel and from there returned to Samaria.

2:23 Background on the Bears

At first reading, the brief account in these three verses is very troubling. A prophet calling on bears to maul children? But, in this instance, historical background and a precise translation help cast the event in a different light. Bethel was a hotbed of Baal worship, and its residents were engaged in a life-and-death struggle with the true prophets of God. When the youths called out, "Go on up, you baldhead!" they were likely referring to what had just happened to the prophet Elijah—they were calling for Elisha to vanish into the sky, or in other words, to die. Furthermore, the word translated youths usually refers to young people in their late teens. In actuality, a large gang of teenagers was threatening a prophet's life. Elisha cursed them, but there is no indication he actually called for a bear attack.

Moab Revolts

3 Joram[a] son of Ahab became king of Israel in Samaria in the eighteenth year of Jehoshaphat king of Judah, and he reigned twelve years. ²He did evil in the eyes of the LORD, but not as his father and mother had done. He got rid of the sacred stone of Baal that his father had made. ³Nevertheless he clung to the sins of Jeroboam son of Nebat, which he had caused Israel to commit; he did not turn away from them.

⁴Now Mesha king of Moab raised sheep, and he had to supply the king of Israel with a hun-

---

a1 Hebrew *Jehoram,* a variant of *Joram;* also in verse 6

Replacing a Legend
Who could follow the great Elijah?

WHEN A PROPHET LIKE Elijah leaves the scene, who will dare to take his place? As time came to choose a successor, Elijah looked to find someone out of a different mold. He settled on his most faithful companion, a farmer named Elisha.

> When they had crossed, Elijah said to Elisha, "Tell me, what can I do for you before I am taken from you?" "Let me inherit a double portion of your spirit," Elisha replied. 2:9

Similar Names but Different Styles

The slight variance in the two men's names expresses their difference in style. Elijah, whose name meant "The LORD is my God," dueled a king and the priests of Baal in dramatic confrontations of power. He lived apart from the people and preached judgment and the need for repentance.

Elisha ("God is salvation") shifted the emphasis. He lived among people, preferring the poor and outcast, and stressed life, hope, and God's grace. All social classes had access to Elisha, from lowly widows to foreign kings. His colorful life included work as a spy, a miracle worker, an adviser to the king, a leader of a school of prophets, and an anointer of revolutionaries.

Elisha traveled widely, and his bald head and wooden walking staff became his trademarks. News of his miracles spread, making him a famous national figure for 50 years. As Elisha lay on his deathbed, the distraught king of Israel knelt beside him, asking for one last word of advice.

Serving the People and the Kingdom

Elisha's exploits fall roughly into two categories, and the Bible seems to group them that way. One set of stories concerns people with evident needs. Elisha showed a deep sensitivity for the suffering and distressed, and sometimes helped them in miraculous ways: providing food, healing diseases, even raising a young boy from the dead. He dealt far more gently with the poor and downtrodden than with kings and generals.

Another group of stories relates to the nation. Israel was reeling from the corruption brought in during King Ahab's reign (see page 1363). Politically, Israel was at the mercy of the neighboring state of Aram (the area known today as Syria), which launched periodic raids across the border.

Sometimes Elisha helped out Israel's army, using his special insight to detect bands of raiders. Twice, miracles he predicted allowed Israel's army to break out of an impossible situation and rout the enemy. Yet he refused to become a "court prophet" serving the king's whims. On at least one occasion, he blatantly insulted a king of Israel (3:13–14). Another time, he anointed a general to overthrow the king in an outright revolution.

A Dying Breed

Incidents from Elisha's life—the healing of Naaman, the chariots of fire, the widow's oil—have become among the most familiar of Old Testament stories. In a sense, Elijah and Elisha represent the last of a breed. Prophets who followed them relied less on spectacular displays and more on the power of verbal messages from God.

Elijah and Elisha used both words and dramatic events to convey their message. Everyone knew their power, especially the kings who sometimes sought them out for advice and other times tried to kill them. In a great irony, the kings and political leaders—who thought themselves the center of history at the time—all faded away. Meanwhile the stories and words of Israel's prophets live on, expressing a message as forceful today as ever.

Life Questions: Elijah and Elisha show how God uses quite different personalities to get his message across. From the description above, which of the two prophets do you more closely identify with?

dred thousand lambs and with the wool of a hundred thousand rams. ⁵But after Ahab died, the king of Moab rebelled against the king of Israel. ⁶So at that time King Joram set out from Samaria and mobilized all Israel. ⁷He also sent this message to Jehoshaphat king of Judah: "The king of Moab has rebelled against me. Will you go with me to fight against Moab?"

"I will go with you," he replied. "I am as you are, my people as your people, my horses as your horses."

⁸"By what route shall we attack?" he asked.

"Through the Desert of Edom," he answered.

⁹So the king of Israel set out with the king of Judah and the king of Edom. After a roundabout march of seven days, the army had no more water for themselves or for the animals with them.

¹⁰"What!" exclaimed the king of Israel. "Has the Lᴏʀᴅ called us three kings together only to hand us over to Moab?"

¹¹But Jehoshaphat asked, "Is there no prophet of the Lᴏʀᴅ here, that we may inquire of the Lᴏʀᴅ through him?"

An officer of the king of Israel answered, "Elisha son of Shaphat is here. He used to pour water on the hands of Elijah.ᵃ"

¹²Jehoshaphat said, "The word of the Lᴏʀᴅ is with him." So the king of Israel and Jehoshaphat and the king of Edom went down to him.

¹³Elisha said to the king of Israel, "What do we have to do with each other? Go to the prophets of your father and the prophets of your mother."

"No," the king of Israel answered, "because it was the Lᴏʀᴅ who called us three kings together to hand us over to Moab."

¹⁴Elisha said, "As surely as the Lᴏʀᴅ Almighty lives, whom I serve, if I did not have respect for the presence of Jehoshaphat king of Judah, I would not look at you or even notice you. ¹⁵But now bring me a harpist."

While the harpist was playing, the hand of the Lᴏʀᴅ came upon Elisha ¹⁶and he said, "This is what the Lᴏʀᴅ says: Make this valley full of ditches. ¹⁷For this is what the Lᴏʀᴅ says: You will see neither wind nor rain, yet this valley will be filled with water, and you, your cattle and your other animals will drink. ¹⁸This is an easy thing in the eyes of the Lᴏʀᴅ; he will also hand Moab over to you. ¹⁹You will overthrow every fortified city and every major town. You will cut down every good tree, stop up all the springs, and ruin every good field with stones."

²⁰The next morning, about the time for offering the sacrifice, there it was—water flowing from the direction of Edom! And the land was filled with water.

²¹Now all the Moabites had heard that the kings had come to fight against them; so every man, young and old, who could bear arms was called up and stationed on the border. ²²When they got up early in the morning, the sun was shining on the water. To the Moabites across the way, the water looked red—like blood. ²³"That's blood!" they said. "Those kings must have fought and slaughtered each other. Now to the plunder, Moab!"

²⁴But when the Moabites came to the camp of Israel, the Israelites rose up and fought them until they fled. And the Israelites invaded the land and slaughtered the Moabites. ²⁵They destroyed the towns, and each man threw a stone on every good field until it was covered. They stopped up all the springs and cut down every good tree. Only Kir Hareseth was left with its stones in place, but men armed with slings surrounded it and attacked it as well.

²⁶When the king of Moab saw that the battle had gone against him, he took with him seven hundred swordsmen to break through to the king of Edom, but they failed. ²⁷Then he took his firstborn son, who was to succeed him as king, and offered him as a sacrifice on the city wall. The fury against Israel was great; they withdrew and returned to their own land.

The Widow's Oil

4 The wife of a man from the company of the prophets cried out to Elisha, "Your servant my husband is dead, and you know that he revered the Lᴏʀᴅ. But now his creditor is coming to take my two boys as his slaves."

²Elisha replied to her, "How can I help you? Tell me, what do you have in your house?"

"Your servant has nothing there at all," she said, "except a little oil."

³Elisha said, "Go around and ask all your neighbors for empty jars. Don't ask for just a few. ⁴Then go inside and shut the door behind you and your sons. Pour oil into all the jars, and as each is filled, put it to one side."

⁵She left him and afterward shut the door behind her and her sons. They brought the jars to her and she kept pouring. ⁶When all the jars were full, she said to her son, "Bring me another one."

But he replied, "There is not a jar left." Then the oil stopped flowing.

⁷She went and told the man of God, and he said, "Go, sell the oil and pay your debts. You and your sons can live on what is left."

The Shunammite's Son Restored to Life

⁸One day Elisha went to Shunem. And a well-to-do woman was there, who urged him to stay for a meal. So whenever he came by, he stopped there to eat. ⁹She said to her husband, "I know that this man who often comes our way is a holy

---

ᵃ 11 That is, he was Elijah's personal servant.

man of God. ¹⁰Let's make a small room on the roof and put in it a bed and a table, a chair and a lamp for him. Then he can stay there whenever he comes to us."

¹¹One day when Elisha came, he went up to his room and lay down there. ¹²He said to his servant Gehazi, "Call the Shunammite." So he called her, and she stood before him. ¹³Elisha said to him, "Tell her, 'You have gone to all this trouble for us. Now what can be done for you? Can we speak on your behalf to the king or the commander of the army?'"

She replied, "I have a home among my own people."

¹⁴"What can be done for her?" Elisha asked.

Gehazi said, "Well, she has no son and her husband is old."

¹⁵Then Elisha said, "Call her." So he called her, and she stood in the doorway. ¹⁶"About this time next year," Elisha said, "you will hold a son in your arms."

"No, my lord," she objected. "Don't mislead your servant, O man of God!"

¹⁷But the woman became pregnant, and the next year about that same time she gave birth to a son, just as Elisha had told her.

¹⁸The child grew, and one day he went out to his father, who was with the reapers. ¹⁹"My head! My head!" he said to his father.

His father told a servant, "Carry him to his mother." ²⁰After the servant had lifted him up and carried him to his mother, the boy sat on her lap until noon, and then he died. ²¹She went up and laid him on the bed of the man of God, then shut the door and went out.

²²She called her husband and said, "Please send me one of the servants and a donkey so I can go to the man of God quickly and return."

²³"Why go to him today?" he asked. "It's not the New Moon or the Sabbath."

"It's all right," she said.

²⁴She saddled the donkey and said to her servant, "Lead on; don't slow down for me unless I tell you." ²⁵So she set out and came to the man of God at Mount Carmel.

When he saw her in the distance, the man of God said to his servant Gehazi, "Look! There's the Shunammite! ²⁶Run to meet her and ask her, 'Are you all right? Is your husband all right? Is your child all right?'"

"Everything is all right," she said.

²⁷When she reached the man of God at the mountain, she took hold of his feet. Gehazi came over to push her away, but the man of God said, "Leave her alone! She is in bitter distress, but the LORD has hidden it from me and has not told me why."

²⁸"Did I ask you for a son, my lord?" she said. "Didn't I tell you, 'Don't raise my hopes'?"

²⁹Elisha said to Gehazi, "Tuck your cloak into your belt, take my staff in your hand and run. If you meet anyone, do not greet him, and if anyone greets you, do not answer. Lay my staff on the boy's face."

³⁰But the child's mother said, "As surely as the LORD lives and as you live, I will not leave you." So he got up and followed her.

³¹Gehazi went on ahead and laid the staff on the boy's face, but there was no sound or response. So Gehazi went back to meet Elisha and told him, "The boy has not awakened."

³²When Elisha reached the house, there was the boy lying dead on his couch. ³³He went in, shut the door on the two of them and prayed to the LORD. ³⁴Then he got on the bed and lay upon the boy, mouth to mouth, eyes to eyes, hands to hands. As he stretched himself out upon him, the boy's body grew warm. ³⁵Elisha turned away and walked back and forth in the room and then got on the bed and stretched out upon him once more. The boy sneezed seven times and opened his eyes.

³⁶Elisha summoned Gehazi and said, "Call the Shunammite." And he did. When she came, he said, "Take your son." ³⁷She came in, fell at his feet and bowed to the ground. Then she took her son and went out.

Death in the Pot

³⁸Elisha returned to Gilgal and there was a famine in that region. While the company of the prophets was meeting with him, he said to his servant, "Put on the large pot and cook some stew for these men."

³⁹One of them went out into the fields to gather herbs and found a wild vine. He gathered some of its gourds and filled the fold of his cloak. When he returned, he cut them up into the pot of stew, though no one knew what they were. ⁴⁰The stew was poured out for the men, but as they began to eat it, they cried out, "O man of God, there is death in the pot!" And they could not eat it.

[41]Elisha said, "Get some flour." He put it into the pot and said, "Serve it to the people to eat." And there was nothing harmful in the pot.

Feeding of a Hundred

[42]A man came from Baal Shalishah, bringing the man of God twenty loaves of barley bread baked from the first ripe grain, along with some heads of new grain. "Give it to the people to eat," Elisha said.

[43]"How can I set this before a hundred men?" his servant asked.

But Elisha answered, "Give it to the people to eat. For this is what the LORD says: 'They will eat and have some left over.'" [44]Then he set it before them, and they ate and had some left over, according to the word of the LORD.

Naaman Healed of Leprosy

5 Now Naaman was commander of the army of the king of Aram. He was a great man in the sight of his master and highly regarded, because through him the LORD had given victory to Aram. He was a valiant soldier, but he had leprosy.[a]

[2]Now bands from Aram had gone out and had taken captive a young girl from Israel, and she served Naaman's wife. [3]She said to her mistress, "If only my master would see the prophet who is in Samaria! He would cure him of his leprosy."

5:3 A Captive's Compassion

She had been captured in a raid, taken to a foreign country, and made a slave. Yet instead of bitterness, she showed compassion toward her master. She wanted him healed, and she believed her God would do it. God used this girl's tragedy to heal and convert her enemy—a wonderful example of love reaching out.

[4]Naaman went to his master and told him what the girl from Israel had said. [5]"By all means, go," the king of Aram replied. "I will send a letter to the king of Israel." So Naaman left, taking with him ten talents[b] of silver, six thousand shekels[c] of gold and ten sets of clothing. [6]The letter that he took to the king of Israel read: "With this letter I am sending my servant Naaman to you so that you may cure him of his leprosy."

[7]As soon as the king of Israel read the letter, he tore his robes and said, "Am I God? Can I kill and bring back to life? Why does this fellow send someone to me to be cured of his leprosy? See how he is trying to pick a quarrel with me!"

[8]When Elisha the man of God heard that the king of Israel had torn his robes, he sent him this message: "Why have you torn your robes? Have the man come to me and he will know that there is a prophet in Israel." [9]So Naaman went with his horses and chariots and stopped at the door of Elisha's house. [10]Elisha sent a messenger to say to him, "Go, wash yourself seven times in the Jordan, and your flesh will be restored and you will be cleansed."

5:10–16 Harder on the Rich

Elisha's treatment of the general Naaman here, and of the king of Israel elsewhere, contrasts sharply with his mild manner around the poor and oppressed. Elisha's prescribed cure obviously offended Naaman's pride. And Elisha pointedly refused to accept payment from the wealthy general, who was used to paying his way. In this incident, and in another (8:7–15), Elisha was serving the kingdom of Aram, an enemy of Israel.

[11]But Naaman went away angry and said, "I thought that he would surely come out to me and stand and call on the name of the LORD his God, wave his hand over the spot and cure me of my leprosy. [12]Are not Abana and Pharpar, the rivers of Damascus, better than any of the waters of Israel? Couldn't I wash in them and be cleansed?" So he turned and went off in a rage.

[13]Naaman's servants went to him and said, "My father, if the prophet had told you to do some great thing, would you not have done it? How much more, then, when he tells you, 'Wash and be cleansed'!" [14]So he went down and dipped himself in the Jordan seven times, as the man of God had told him, and his flesh was restored and became clean like that of a young boy.

[15]Then Naaman and all his attendants went back to the man of God. He stood before him and said, "Now I know that there is no God in all the world except in Israel. Please accept now a gift from your servant."

[16]The prophet answered, "As surely as the LORD lives, whom I serve, I will not accept a thing." And even though Naaman urged him, he refused.

[17]"If you will not," said Naaman, "please let me, your servant, be given as much earth as a pair of mules can carry, for your servant will never again make burnt offerings and sacrifices to any other god but the LORD. [18]But may the LORD forgive your servant for this one thing: When my master enters the temple of Rimmon to bow down and he is leaning on my arm and

---

a1 The Hebrew word was used for various diseases affecting the skin—not necessarily leprosy; also in verses 3, 6, 7, 11 and 27.   *b5* That is, about 750 pounds (about 340 kilograms)   *c5* That is, about 150 pounds (about 70 kilograms)

I bow there also—when I bow down in the temple of Rimmon, may the LORD forgive your servant for this."

¹⁹"Go in peace," Elisha said.

After Naaman had traveled some distance, ²⁰Gehazi, the servant of Elisha the man of God, said to himself, "My master was too easy on Naaman, this Aramean, by not accepting from him what he brought. As surely as the LORD lives, I will run after him and get something from him."

²¹So Gehazi hurried after Naaman. When Naaman saw him running toward him, he got down from the chariot to meet him. "Is everything all right?" he asked.

²²"Everything is all right," Gehazi answered. "My master sent me to say, 'Two young men from the company of the prophets have just come to me from the hill country of Ephraim. Please give them a talent*a* of silver and two sets of clothing.'"

²³"By all means, take two talents," said Naaman. He urged Gehazi to accept them, and then tied up the two talents of silver in two bags, with two sets of clothing. He gave them to two of his servants, and they carried them ahead of Gehazi. ²⁴When Gehazi came to the hill, he took the things from the servants and put them away in the house. He sent the men away and they left. ²⁵Then he went in and stood before his master Elisha.

"Where have you been, Gehazi?" Elisha asked.

"Your servant didn't go anywhere," Gehazi answered.

²⁶But Elisha said to him, "Was not my spirit with you when the man got down from his chariot to meet you? Is this the time to take money, or to accept clothes, olive groves, vineyards, flocks, herds, or menservants and maidservants? ²⁷Naaman's leprosy will cling to you and to your descendants forever." Then Gehazi went from Elisha's presence and he was leprous, as white as snow.

An Axhead Floats

6 The company of the prophets said to Elisha, "Look, the place where we meet with you is too small for us. ²Let us go to the Jordan, where each of us can get a pole; and let us build a place there for us to live."

And he said, "Go."

³Then one of them said, "Won't you please come with your servants?"

"I will," Elisha replied. ⁴And he went with them.

They went to the Jordan and began to cut down trees. ⁵As one of them was cutting down a tree, the iron axhead fell into the water. "Oh, my lord," he cried out, "it was borrowed!"

⁶The man of God asked, "Where did it fall?" When he showed him the place, Elisha cut a stick and threw it there, and made the iron float. ⁷"Lift it out," he said. Then the man reached out his hand and took it.

Elisha Traps Blinded Arameans

⁸Now the king of Aram was at war with Israel. After conferring with his officers, he said, "I will set up my camp in such and such a place."

⁹The man of God sent word to the king of Israel: "Beware of passing that place, because the Arameans are going down there." ¹⁰So the king of Israel checked on the place indicated by the man of God. Time and again Elisha warned the king, so that he was on his guard in such places.

¹¹This enraged the king of Aram. He summoned his officers and demanded of them, "Will you not tell me which of us is on the side of the king of Israel?"

¹²"None of us, my lord the king," said one of his officers, "but Elisha, the prophet who is in Israel, tells the king of Israel the very words you speak in your bedroom."

¹³"Go, find out where he is," the king ordered, "so I can send men and capture him." The report came back: "He is in Dothan." ¹⁴Then he sent horses and chariots and a strong force there. They went by night and surrounded the city.

¹⁵When the servant of the man of God got up and went out early the next morning, an army with horses and chariots had surrounded the city. "Oh, my lord, what shall we do?" the servant asked.

¹⁶"Don't be afraid," the prophet answered. "Those who are with us are more than those who are with them."

¹⁷And Elisha prayed, "O LORD, open his eyes so he may see." Then the LORD opened the servant's eyes, and he looked and saw the hills full of horses and chariots of fire all around Elisha.

6:17 Chariots of Fire

Surrounded by an army, Elisha's servant cried, "What shall we do?" But when Elisha prayed, the servant could suddenly see that God's forces, invisible to everyone else, far outnumbered the enemy. The story offers a rare glimpse of the "invisible world" of supernatural forces. God has resources to help that we cannot see.

¹⁸As the enemy came down toward him, Elisha prayed to the LORD, "Strike these people with blindness." So he struck them with blindness, as Elisha had asked.

a22 That is, about 75 pounds (about 34 kilograms)

[19]Elisha told them, "This is not the road and this is not the city. Follow me, and I will lead you to the man you are looking for." And he led them to Samaria.

[20]After they entered the city, Elisha said, "LORD, open the eyes of these men so they can see." Then the LORD opened their eyes and they looked, and there they were, inside Samaria.

[21]When the king of Israel saw them, he asked Elisha, "Shall I kill them, my father? Shall I kill them?"

[22]"Do not kill them," he answered. "Would you kill men you have captured with your own sword or bow? Set food and water before them so that they may eat and drink and then go back to their master." [23]So he prepared a great feast for them, and after they had finished eating and drinking, he sent them away, and they returned to their master. So the bands from Aram stopped raiding Israel's territory.

Famine in Besieged Samaria

[24]Some time later, Ben-Hadad king of Aram mobilized his entire army and marched up and laid siege to Samaria. [25]There was a great famine in the city; the siege lasted so long that a donkey's head sold for eighty shekels[a] of silver, and a quarter of a cab[b] of seed pods[c] for five shekels.[d]

[26]As the king of Israel was passing by on the wall, a woman cried to him, "Help me, my lord the king!"

[27]The king replied, "If the LORD does not help you, where can I get help for you? From the threshing floor? From the winepress?" [28]Then he asked her, "What's the matter?"

She answered, "This woman said to me, 'Give up your son so we may eat him today, and tomorrow we'll eat my son.' [29]So we cooked my son and ate him. The next day I said to her, 'Give up your son so we may eat him,' but she had hidden him."

[30]When the king heard the woman's words, he tore his robes. As he went along the wall, the people looked, and there, underneath, he had sackcloth on his body. [31]He said, "May God deal with me, be it ever so severely, if the head of Elisha son of Shaphat remains on his shoulders today!"

[32]Now Elisha was sitting in his house, and the elders were sitting with him. The king sent a messenger ahead, but before he arrived, Elisha said to the elders, "Don't you see how this murderer is sending someone to cut off my head?

Look, when the messenger comes, shut the door and hold it shut against him. Is not the sound of his master's footsteps behind him?"

[33]While he was still talking to them, the messenger came down to him. And ⌊the king⌋ said, "This disaster is from the LORD. Why should I wait for the LORD any longer?"

6:31 The Prophet and Politics

Elisha's long career spanned the reigns of six kings and included some dramatic ups and downs with them. On one occasion Elisha outright insulted a king (3:14). But, as this chapter shows, he could also be an invaluable military resource, serving as a virtual spy. At Elisha's deathbed, the reigning king of Israel knelt beside him, weeping (13:14).

7 Elisha said, "Hear the word of the LORD. This is what the LORD says: About this time tomorrow, a seah[e] of flour will sell for a shekel[f] and two seahs[g] of barley for a shekel at the gate of Samaria."

[2]The officer on whose arm the king was leaning said to the man of God, "Look, even if the LORD should open the floodgates of the heavens, could this happen?"

"You will see it with your own eyes," answered Elisha, "but you will not eat any of it!"

The Siege Lifted

[3]Now there were four men with leprosy[h] at the entrance of the city gate. They said to each other, "Why stay here until we die? [4]If we say, 'We'll go into the city'—the famine is there, and we will die. And if we stay here, we will die. So let's go over to the camp of the Arameans and surrender. If they spare us, we live; if they kill us, then we die."

[5]At dusk they got up and went to the camp of the Arameans. When they reached the edge of the camp, not a man was there, [6]for the Lord had caused the Arameans to hear the sound of chariots and horses and a great army, so that they said to one another, "Look, the king of Israel has hired the Hittite and Egyptian kings to attack us!" [7]So they got up and fled in the dusk and abandoned their tents and their horses and donkeys. They left the camp as it was and ran for their lives.

[8]The men who had leprosy reached the edge

---

[a]25 That is, about 2 pounds (about 1 kilogram)   [b]25 That is, probably about 1/2 pint (about 0.3 liter)   [c]25 Or of dove's dung   [d]25 That is, about 2 ounces (about 55 grams)   [e]1 That is, probably about 7 quarts (about 7.3 liters); also in verses 16 and 18   [f]1 That is, about 2/5 ounce (about 11 grams); also in verses 16 and 18   [g]1 That is, probably about 13 quarts (about 15 liters); also in verses 16 and 18   [h]3 The Hebrew word is used for various diseases affecting the skin—not necessarily leprosy; also in verse 8.

of the camp and entered one of the tents. They ate and drank, and carried away silver, gold and clothes, and went off and hid them. They returned and entered another tent and took some things from it and hid them also.

⁹Then they said to each other, "We're not doing right. This is a day of good news and we are keeping it to ourselves. If we wait until daylight, punishment will overtake us. Let's go at once and report this to the royal palace."

¹⁰So they went and called out to the city gatekeepers and told them, "We went into the Aramean camp and not a man was there—not a sound of anyone—only tethered horses and donkeys, and the tents left just as they were." ¹¹The gatekeepers shouted the news, and it was reported within the palace.

¹²The king got up in the night and said to his officers, "I will tell you what the Arameans have done to us. They know we are starving; so they have left the camp to hide in the countryside, thinking, 'They will surely come out, and then we will take them alive and get into the city.'"

¹³One of his officers answered, "Have some men take five of the horses that are left in the city. Their plight will be like that of all the Israelites left here—yes, they will only be like all these Israelites who are doomed. So let us send them to find out what happened."

¹⁴So they selected two chariots with their horses, and the king sent them after the Aramean army. He commanded the drivers, "Go and find out what has happened." ¹⁵They followed them as far as the Jordan, and they found the whole road strewn with the clothing and equipment the Arameans had thrown away in their headlong flight. So the messengers returned and reported to the king. ¹⁶Then the people went out and plundered the camp of the Arameans. So a seah of flour sold for a shekel, and two seahs of barley sold for a shekel, as the LORD had said.

¹⁷Now the king had put the officer on whose arm he leaned in charge of the gate, and the people trampled him in the gateway, and he died, just as the man of God had foretold when the king came down to his house. ¹⁸It happened as the man of God had said to the king: "About this time tomorrow, a seah of flour will sell for a shekel and two seahs of barley for a shekel at the gate of Samaria."

¹⁹The officer had said to the man of God, "Look, even if the LORD should open the floodgates of the heavens, could this happen?" The man of God had replied, "You will see it with your own eyes, but you will not eat any of it!" ²⁰And that is exactly what happened to him, for the people trampled him in the gateway, and he died.

The Shunammite's Land Restored

8 Now Elisha had said to the woman whose son he had restored to life, "Go away with your family and stay for a while wherever you can, because the LORD has decreed a famine in the land that will last seven years." ²The woman proceeded to do as the man of God said. She and her family went away and stayed in the land of the Philistines seven years.

³At the end of the seven years she came back from the land of the Philistines and went to the king to beg for her house and land. ⁴The king was talking to Gehazi, the servant of the man of God, and had said, "Tell me about all the great things Elisha has done." ⁵Just as Gehazi was telling the king how Elisha had restored the dead to life, the woman whose son Elisha had brought back to life came to beg the king for her house and land.

Gehazi said, "This is the woman, my lord the king, and this is her son whom Elisha restored to life." ⁶The king asked the woman about it, and she told him.

Then he assigned an official to her case and said to him, "Give back everything that belonged to her, including all the income from her land from the day she left the country until now."

Hazael Murders Ben-Hadad

⁷Elisha went to Damascus, and Ben-Hadad king of Aram was ill. When the king was told, "The man of God has come all the way up here," ⁸he said to Hazael, "Take a gift with you and go to meet the man of God. Consult the LORD through him; ask him, 'Will I recover from this illness?'"

⁹Hazael went to meet Elisha, taking with him as a gift forty camel-loads of all the finest wares of Damascus. He went in and stood before him, and said, "Your son Ben-Hadad king of Aram has sent me to ask, 'Will I recover from this illness?'"

¹⁰Elisha answered, "Go and say to him, 'You will certainly recover'; but*a* the LORD has revealed to me that he will in fact die." ¹¹He stared at him with a fixed gaze until Hazael felt ashamed. Then the man of God began to weep.

¹²"Why is my lord weeping?" asked Hazael.

"Because I know the harm you will do to the Israelites," he answered. "You will set fire to their fortified places, kill their young men with the sword, dash their little children to the ground, and rip open their pregnant women."

¹³Hazael said, "How could your servant, a mere dog, accomplish such a feat?"

"The LORD has shown me that you will become king of Aram," answered Elisha.

¹⁴Then Hazael left Elisha and returned to his master. When Ben-Hadad asked, "What did Eli-

---

a 10 The Hebrew may also be read *Go and say, 'You will certainly not recover,' for.*

sha say to you?" Hazael replied, "He told me that you would certainly recover." [15]But the next day he took a thick cloth, soaked it in water and spread it over the king's face, so that he died. Then Hazael succeeded him as king.

Jehoram King of Judah

[16]In the fifth year of Joram son of Ahab king of Israel, when Jehoshaphat was king of Judah, Jehoram son of Jehoshaphat began his reign as

8:16 Two Kings, One Name

It's difficult enough to keep 39 rulers straight. When two of them from neighboring countries have the same name, the plot thickens. Joram, a son of Ahab, ruled Israel at the same time Jehoram (sometimes spelled Joram also) took over Judah's throne. Both were wicked. Jehoram's marriage to Ahab's daughter ushered in a terrible period in Judah's history. (2 Chronicles 21 gives much more detail on this king.) In addition, both Judah and Israel had a king named Ahaziah.

king of Judah. [17]He was thirty-two years old when he became king, and he reigned in Jerusalem eight years. [18]He walked in the ways of the kings of Israel, as the house of Ahab had done, for he married a daughter of Ahab. He did evil in the eyes of the LORD. [19]Nevertheless, for the sake of his servant David, the LORD was not willing to destroy Judah. He had promised to maintain a lamp for David and his descendants forever.

[20]In the time of Jehoram, Edom rebelled against Judah and set up its own king. [21]So Jehoram[a] went to Zair with all his chariots. The Edomites surrounded him and his chariot commanders, but he rose up and broke through by night; his army, however, fled back home. [22]To this day Edom has been in rebellion against Judah. Libnah revolted at the same time.

[23]As for the other events of Jehoram's reign, and all he did, are they not written in the book of the annals of the kings of Judah? [24]Jehoram rested with his fathers and was buried with them in the City of David. And Ahaziah his son succeeded him as king.

Ahaziah King of Judah

[25]In the twelfth year of Joram son of Ahab king of Israel, Ahaziah son of Jehoram king of Judah began to reign. [26]Ahaziah was twenty-two years old when he became king, and he reigned in Jerusalem one year. His mother's name was Athaliah, a granddaughter of Omri king of Israel. [27]He walked in the ways of the house of Ahab

and did evil in the eyes of the LORD, as the house of Ahab had done, for he was related by marriage to Ahab's family.

[28]Ahaziah went with Joram son of Ahab to war

8:27 Political Marriages

Ahab shrewdly arranged marriages to cement alliances with Israel's neighbors. His wife Jezebel, for example, hailed from Phoenicia, which thus became an ally of Israel. Ahab also married off his daughter to the king of Judah, bringing peace to the two warring neighbors. Later, when Jehu revolted and slaughtered all of Ahab's family members, he aroused the ire of those allies and threw Israel's foreign policy into disarray.

against Hazael king of Aram at Ramoth Gilead. The Arameans wounded Joram; [29]so King Joram returned to Jezreel to recover from the wounds the Arameans had inflicted on him at Ramoth[b] in his battle with Hazael king of Aram.

Then Ahaziah son of Jehoram king of Judah went down to Jezreel to see Joram son of Ahab, because he had been wounded.

Jehu Anointed King of Israel

9 The prophet Elisha summoned a man from the company of the prophets and said to him, "Tuck your cloak into your belt, take this flask of oil with you and go to Ramoth Gilead. [2]When you get there, look for Jehu son of Jehoshaphat, the son of Nimshi. Go to him, get him away from his companions and take him into an inner room. [3]Then take the flask and pour the oil on his head and declare, 'This is what the LORD says: I anoint you king over Israel.' Then open the door and run; don't delay!"

[4]So the young man, the prophet, went to Ramoth Gilead. [5]When he arrived, he found the army officers sitting together. "I have a message for you, commander," he said.

"For which of us?" asked Jehu.

"For you, commander," he replied.

[6]Jehu got up and went into the house. Then the prophet poured the oil on Jehu's head and declared, "This is what the LORD, the God of Israel, says: 'I anoint you king over the LORD's people Israel. [7]You are to destroy the house of Ahab your master, and I will avenge the blood of my servants the prophets and the blood of all the LORD's servants shed by Jezebel. [8]The whole house of Ahab will perish. I will cut off from Ahab every last male in Israel—slave or free. [9]I will make the house of Ahab like the house of Jeroboam son of Nebat and like the house of

[a]21 Hebrew *Joram*, a variant of *Jehoram*; also in verses 23 and 24   [b]29 Hebrew *Ramah*, a variant of *Ramoth*

Baasha son of Ahijah. ¹⁰As for Jezebel, dogs will devour her on the plot of ground at Jezreel, and no one will bury her.'" Then he opened the door and ran.

¹¹When Jehu went out to his fellow officers, one of them asked him, "Is everything all right? Why did this madman come to you?"

"You know the man and the sort of things he says," Jehu replied.

¹²"That's not true!" they said. "Tell us."

Jehu said, "Here is what he told me: 'This is what the LORD says: I anoint you king over Israel.'"

¹³They hurried and took their cloaks and spread them under him on the bare steps. Then they blew the trumpet and shouted, "Jehu is king!"

Jehu Kills Joram and Ahaziah

¹⁴So Jehu son of Jehoshaphat, the son of Nimshi, conspired against Joram. (Now Joram and all Israel had been defending Ramoth Gilead against Hazael king of Aram, ¹⁵but King Joram*a* had returned to Jezreel to recover from the wounds the Arameans had inflicted on him in the battle with Hazael king of Aram.) Jehu said, "If this is the way you feel, don't let anyone slip out of the city to go and tell the news in Jezreel." ¹⁶Then he got into his chariot and rode to Jezreel, because Joram was resting there and Ahaziah king of Judah had gone down to see him.

¹⁷When the lookout standing on the tower in Jezreel saw Jehu's troops approaching, he called out, "I see some troops coming."

"Get a horseman," Joram ordered. "Send him to meet them and ask, 'Do you come in peace?'"

¹⁸The horseman rode off to meet Jehu and said, "This is what the king says: 'Do you come in peace?'"

"What do you have to do with peace?" Jehu replied. "Fall in behind me."

The lookout reported, "The messenger has reached them, but he isn't coming back."

¹⁹So the king sent out a second horseman. When he came to them he said, "This is what the king says: 'Do you come in peace?'"

Jehu replied, "What do you have to do with peace? Fall in behind me."

²⁰The lookout reported, "He has reached them, but he isn't coming back either. The driving is like that of Jehu son of Nimshi—he drives like a madman."

²¹"Hitch up my chariot," Joram ordered. And when it was hitched up, Joram king of Israel and Ahaziah king of Judah rode out, each in his own chariot, to meet Jehu. They met him at the plot of ground that had belonged to Naboth the Jezreelite. ²²When Joram saw Jehu he asked, "Have you come in peace, Jehu?"

"How can there be peace," Jehu replied, "as long as all the idolatry and witchcraft of your mother Jezebel abound?"

²³Joram turned about and fled, calling out to Ahaziah, "Treachery, Ahaziah!"

²⁴Then Jehu drew his bow and shot Joram between the shoulders. The arrow pierced his heart and he slumped down in his chariot. ²⁵Jehu said to Bidkar, his chariot officer, "Pick him up and throw him on the field that belonged to Naboth the Jezreelite. Remember how you and I were riding together in chariots behind Ahab his father when the LORD made this prophecy about him: ²⁶'Yesterday I saw the blood of Naboth and the blood of his sons, declares the LORD, and I will surely make you pay for it on this plot of ground, declares the LORD.'*b* Now then, pick him up and throw him on that plot, in accordance with the word of the LORD."

²⁷When Ahaziah king of Judah saw what had happened, he fled up the road to Beth Haggan.*c* Jehu chased him, shouting, "Kill him too!" They wounded him in his chariot on the way up to Gur near Ibleam, but he escaped to Megiddo and died there. ²⁸His servants took him by chariot to Jerusalem and buried him with his fathers in his tomb in the City of David. ²⁹(In the eleventh year of Joram son of Ahab, Ahaziah had become king of Judah.)

Jezebel Killed

³⁰Then Jehu went to Jezreel. When Jezebel heard about it, she painted her eyes, arranged her hair and looked out of a window. ³¹As Jehu entered the gate, she asked, "Have you come in peace, Zimri, you murderer of your master?"*d*

³²He looked up at the window and called out, "Who is on my side? Who?" Two or three eunuchs looked down at him. ³³"Throw her down!" Jehu said. So they threw her down, and some of her blood spattered the wall and the horses as they trampled her underfoot.

³⁴Jehu went in and ate and drank. "Take care of that cursed woman," he said, "and bury her, for she was a king's daughter." ³⁵But when they went out to bury her, they found nothing except her skull, her feet and her hands. ³⁶They went back and told Jehu, who said, "This is the word of the LORD that he spoke through his servant Elijah the Tishbite: On the plot of ground at Jezreel dogs will devour Jezebel's flesh.*e* ³⁷Jezebel's body will be like refuse on the ground in the plot at Jezreel, so that no one will be able to say, 'This is Jezebel.'"

---

a 15 Hebrew *Jehoram,* a variant of *Joram;* also in verses 17 and 21-24   *b 26* See 1 Kings 21:19.   *c 27* Or *fled by way of the garden house*   *d 31* Or *"Did Zimri have peace, who murdered his master?"*   *e 36* See 1 Kings 21:23.

Ahab's Family Killed

10 Now there were in Samaria seventy sons of the house of Ahab. So Jehu wrote letters and sent them to Samaria: to the officials of Jezreel,[a] to the elders and to the guardians of Ahab's children. He said, 2"As soon as this letter reaches you, since your master's sons are with you and you have chariots and horses, a fortified city and weapons, 3choose the best and most worthy of your master's sons and set him on his father's throne. Then fight for your master's house."

4But they were terrified and said, "If two kings could not resist him, how can we?"

5So the palace administrator, the city governor, the elders and the guardians sent this message to Jehu: "We are your servants and we will do anything you say. We will not appoint anyone as king; you do whatever you think best."

6Then Jehu wrote them a second letter, saying, "If you are on my side and will obey me, take the heads of your master's sons and come to me in Jezreel by this time tomorrow."

Now the royal princes, seventy of them, were with the leading men of the city, who were rearing them. 7When the letter arrived, these men took the princes and slaughtered all seventy of them. They put their heads in baskets and sent them to Jehu in Jezreel. 8When the messenger arrived, he told Jehu, "They have brought the heads of the princes."

Then Jehu ordered, "Put them in two piles at the entrance of the city gate until morning."

9The next morning Jehu went out. He stood before all the people and said, "You are innocent. It was I who conspired against my master and killed him, but who killed all these? 10Know then, that not a word the LORD has spoken against the house of Ahab will fail. The LORD has done what he promised through his servant Elijah." 11So Jehu killed everyone in Jezreel who remained of the house of Ahab, as well as all his chief men, his close friends and his priests, leaving him no survivor.

12Jehu then set out and went toward Samaria. At Beth Eked of the Shepherds, 13he met some relatives of Ahaziah king of Judah and asked, "Who are you?"

They said, "We are relatives of Ahaziah, and we have come down to greet the families of the king and of the queen mother."

14"Take them alive!" he ordered. So they took them alive and slaughtered them by the well of Beth Eked—forty-two men. He left no survivor.

15After he left there, he came upon Jehonadab son of Recab, who was on his way to meet him. Jehu greeted him and said, "Are you in accord with me, as I am with you?"

"I am," Jehonadab answered.

---

a 1 Hebrew; some Septuagint manuscripts and Vulgate *of the city*

JEZEBEL *Wild and Wicked*

JEZEBEL WAS SUCH A REMARKABLE woman that her name came to define a type of person. "An impudent, shameless or abandoned woman," says the dictionary listing for jezebel. No modern jezebel ever exceeded the original, however. The proud, determined daughter of a king, Jezebel set out single-handedly to force Israel into paganism—and she nearly succeeded.

She came from Sidon on the Mediterranean coast, where her father reigned over the Phoenicians. Her royal wedding to Ahab, king of Israel, cemented an alliance between the two kingdoms. Other Israelite kings, such as Solomon, had also flouted God's law by marrying foreign wives. Typically, these women brought their religion with them (which explains why God forbade foreign marriage in the first place).

Jezebel went far beyond other foreign wives, however. Not content to worship Baal by herself, she insisted that all Israelites worship with her. She convinced Ahab to build a temple for Baal in the capital, and imported hundreds of foreign priests to work in that temple. She set out to exterminate the worship of Israel's God, killing anyone who stood in her way.

Only one man dared to oppose Jezebel publicly: the prophet Elijah. Yet even his amazing triumph on Mount Carmel (1 Kings 18) failed to faze her. God's unmistakable display of power only made her want to kill Elijah, not convert.

Jezebel died as she lived, cutting a memorable figure. When her luck ran out, she didn't beg for mercy. Like a Hollywood vamp she dressed up for the showdown and waited at the window to taunt the man who had come to deal with her. A woman who inspired no loyalty, she was tossed out the window by her own servants. As Elijah had prophesied (1 Kings 21:23), the town dogs devoured her body.

Life Questions: Some people say it doesn't matter what you believe, as long as you believe it with all your heart. What would Jezebel say to this? What would Elijah?

"If so," said Jehu, "give me your hand." So he did, and Jehu helped him up into the chariot. [16]Jehu said, "Come with me and see my zeal for the LORD." Then he had him ride along in his chariot.

10:14 Jehu's Slaughters

Jehu's bold attacks against the princes of Judah had serious consequences. To protect Israel against revenge from Judah and its friends, Jehu had to pay Assyria tribute. In fact, he is the only king of Israel whose picture has survived. A carving on an archaeological relic, the Black Obelisk, shows him paying tribute to Assyria. Although God had chosen Jehu to purge Israel, the Bible makes clear that his violence went far beyond his original assignment. God himself condemns Jehu in Hosea 1:4.

[17]When Jehu came to Samaria, he killed all who were left there of Ahab's family; he destroyed them, according to the word of the LORD spoken to Elijah.

Ministers of Baal Killed

[18]Then Jehu brought all the people together and said to them, "Ahab served Baal a little; Jehu will serve him much. [19]Now summon all the prophets of Baal, all his ministers and all his priests. See that no one is missing, because I am going to hold a great sacrifice for Baal. Anyone who fails to come will no longer live." But Jehu was acting deceptively in order to destroy the ministers of Baal.

[20]Jehu said, "Call an assembly in honor of Baal." So they proclaimed it. [21]Then he sent word throughout Israel, and all the ministers of Baal came; not one stayed away. They crowded into the temple of Baal until it was full from one end to the other. [22]And Jehu said to the keeper of the wardrobe, "Bring robes for all the ministers of Baal." So he brought out robes for them.

[23]Then Jehu and Jehonadab son of Recab went into the temple of Baal. Jehu said to the ministers of Baal, "Look around and see that no servants of the LORD are here with you—only ministers of Baal." [24]So they went in to make sacrifices and burnt offerings. Now Jehu had posted eighty men outside with this warning: "If one of you lets any of the men I am placing in your hands escape, it will be your life for his life."

[25]As soon as Jehu had finished making the burnt offering, he ordered the guards and officers: "Go in and kill them; let no one escape." So they cut them down with the sword. The guards and officers threw the bodies out and then entered the inner shrine of the temple of Baal. [26]They brought the sacred stone out of the temple of Baal and burned it. [27]They demolished the sacred stone of Baal and tore down the temple of Baal, and people have used it for a latrine to this day.

[28]So Jehu destroyed Baal worship in Israel. [29]However, he did not turn away from the sins of Jeroboam son of Nebat, which he had caused Israel to commit—the worship of the golden calves at Bethel and Dan.

[30]The LORD said to Jehu, "Because you have done well in accomplishing what is right in my eyes and have done to the house of Ahab all I had in mind to do, your descendants will sit on the throne of Israel to the fourth generation." [31]Yet Jehu was not careful to keep the law of the LORD, the God of Israel, with all his heart. He did not turn away from the sins of Jeroboam, which he had caused Israel to commit.

[32]In those days the LORD began to reduce the size of Israel. Hazael overpowered the Israelites throughout their territory [33]east of the Jordan in all the land of Gilead (the region of Gad, Reuben and Manasseh), from Aroer by the Arnon Gorge through Gilead to Bashan.

[34]As for the other events of Jehu's reign, all he did, and all his achievements, are they not written in the book of the annals of the kings of Israel?

[35]Jehu rested with his fathers and was buried in Samaria. And Jehoahaz his son succeeded him as king. [36]The time that Jehu reigned over Israel in Samaria was twenty-eight years.

Athaliah and Joash

11 When Athaliah the mother of Ahaziah saw that her son was dead, she proceeded to destroy the whole royal family. [2]But Jehosheba, the daughter of King Jehoram[a] and sister of Ahaziah, took Joash son of Ahaziah and stole him away from among the royal princes, who were about to be murdered. She put him and his nurse in a bedroom to hide him from Athaliah; so he was not killed. [3]He remained hidden with

11:2 Preserving the Royal Line

Queen Athaliah came within one baby of wiping out the royal line descending from King David. The prophets predicted that Jesus the Messiah would come from David's line, so in a sense the entire future of God's plan rested with the family's success in hiding Joash and returning him to the throne.

---

[a]2 Hebrew *Joram*, a variant of *Jehoram*

his nurse at the temple of the LORD for six years while Athaliah ruled the land.

[4]In the seventh year Jehoiada sent for the commanders of units of a hundred, the Carites and the guards and had them brought to him at the temple of the LORD. He made a covenant with them and put them under oath at the temple of the LORD. Then he showed them the king's son. [5]He commanded them, saying, "This is what you are to do: You who are in the three companies that are going on duty on the Sabbath—a third of you guarding the royal palace, [6]a third at the Sur Gate, and a third at the gate behind the guard, who take turns guarding the temple—[7]and you who are in the other two companies that normally go off Sabbath duty are all to guard the temple for the king. [8]Station yourselves around the king, each man with his weapon in his hand. Anyone who approaches your ranks[a] must be put to death. Stay close to the king wherever he goes."

[9]The commanders of units of a hundred did just as Jehoiada the priest ordered. Each one took his men—those who were going on duty on the Sabbath and those who were going off duty—and came to Jehoiada the priest. [10]Then he gave the commanders the spears and shields that had belonged to King David and that were in the temple of the LORD. [11]The guards, each with his weapon in his hand, stationed themselves around the king—near the altar and the temple, from the south side to the north side of the temple.

[12]Jehoiada brought out the king's son and put the crown on him; he presented him with a copy of the covenant and proclaimed him king. They anointed him, and the people clapped their hands and shouted, "Long live the king!"

[13]When Athaliah heard the noise made by the guards and the people, she went to the people at the temple of the LORD. [14]She looked and there was the king, standing by the pillar, as the custom was. The officers and the trumpeters were beside the king, and all the people of the land were rejoicing and blowing trumpets. Then Athaliah tore her robes and called out, "Treason! Treason!"

[15]Jehoiada the priest ordered the commanders of units of a hundred, who were in charge of the troops: "Bring her out between the ranks[b] and put to the sword anyone who follows her." For the priest had said, "She must not be put to death in the temple of the LORD." [16]So they seized her as she reached the place where the horses enter the palace grounds, and there she was put to death.

[17]Jehoiada then made a covenant between the LORD and the king and people that they would be the LORD's people. He also made a covenant between the king and the people. [18]All the people of the land went to the temple of Baal and tore it down. They smashed the altars and idols to pieces and killed Mattan the priest of Baal in front of the altars.

Then Jehoiada the priest posted guards at the temple of the LORD. [19]He took with him the commanders of hundreds, the Carites, the guards and all the people of the land, and together they brought the king down from the temple of the LORD and went into the palace, entering by way of the gate of the guards. The king then took his place on the royal throne, [20]and all the people of the land rejoiced. And the city was quiet, because Athaliah had been slain with the sword at the palace.

[21]Joash[c] was seven years old when he began to reign.

Joash Repairs the Temple

12 In the seventh year of Jehu, Joash[d] became king, and he reigned in Jerusalem forty years. His mother's name was Zibiah; she was from Beersheba. [2]Joash did what was right in the eyes of the LORD all the years Jehoiada the priest instructed him. [3]The high places, however, were not removed; the people continued to offer sacrifices and burn incense there.

[4]Joash said to the priests, "Collect all the money that is brought as sacred offerings to the temple of the LORD—the money collected in the census, the money received from personal vows and the money brought voluntarily to the temple. [5]Let every priest receive the money from one of the treasurers, and let it be used to repair whatever damage is found in the temple."

[6]But by the twenty-third year of King Joash the priests still had not repaired the temple. [7]Therefore King Joash summoned Jehoiada the priest and the other priests and asked them, "Why aren't you repairing the damage done to the temple? Take no more money from your treasurers, but hand it over for repairing the temple." [8]The priests agreed that they would not collect any more money from the people and that they would not repair the temple themselves.

[9]Jehoiada the priest took a chest and bored a hole in its lid. He placed it beside the altar, on the right side as one enters the temple of the LORD. The priests who guarded the entrance put into the chest all the money that was brought to the temple of the LORD. [10]Whenever they saw that there was a large amount of money in the chest, the royal secretary and the high priest came, counted the money that had been brought into the temple of the LORD and put it into bags.

---

[a]8 Or approaches the precincts   *[b]15 Or out from the precincts*   *[c]21 Hebrew Jehoash, a variant of Joash*
[d]1 Hebrew Jehoash, a variant of Joash; also in verses 2, 4, 6, 7 and 18

¹¹When the amount had been determined, they gave the money to the men appointed to supervise the work on the temple. With it they paid those who worked on the temple of the LORD—the carpenters and builders, ¹²the masons and stonecutters. They purchased timber and dressed stone for the repair of the temple of the LORD, and met all the other expenses of restoring the temple.

¹³The money brought into the temple was not spent for making silver basins, wick trimmers, sprinkling bowls, trumpets or any other articles of gold or silver for the temple of the LORD; ¹⁴it was paid to the workmen, who used it to repair the temple. ¹⁵They did not require an accounting from those to whom they gave the money to pay the workers, because they acted with complete honesty. ¹⁶The money from the guilt offerings and sin offerings was not brought into the temple of the LORD; it belonged to the priests.

¹⁷About this time Hazael king of Aram went up and attacked Gath and captured it. Then he turned to attack Jerusalem. ¹⁸But Joash king of Judah took all the sacred objects dedicated by his fathers—Jehoshaphat, Jehoram and Ahaziah, the kings of Judah—and the gifts he himself had dedicated and all the gold found in the treasuries of the temple of the LORD and of the royal palace, and he sent them to Hazael king of Aram, who then withdrew from Jerusalem.

¹⁹As for the other events of the reign of Joash, and all he did, are they not written in the book of the annals of the kings of Judah? ²⁰His officials conspired against him and assassinated him at Beth Millo, on the road down to Silla. ²¹The officials who murdered him were Jozabad son of Shimeath and Jehozabad son of Shomer. He died and was buried with his fathers in the City of David. And Amaziah his son succeeded him as king.

Jehoahaz King of Israel

13 In the twenty-third year of Joash son of Ahaziah king of Judah, Jehoahaz son of Jehu became king of Israel in Samaria, and he reigned seventeen years. ²He did evil in the eyes of the LORD by following the sins of Jeroboam son of Nebat, which he had caused Israel to commit, and he did not turn away from them. ³So the LORD's anger burned against Israel, and for a long time he kept them under the power of Hazael king of Aram and Ben-Hadad his son.

⁴Then Jehoahaz sought the LORD's favor, and the LORD listened to him, for he saw how severely the king of Aram was oppressing Israel. ⁵The LORD provided a deliverer for Israel, and they escaped from the power of Aram. So the Israelites lived in their own homes as they had before. ⁶But they did not turn away from the sins of the house of Jeroboam, which he had caused Israel to commit; they continued in them. Also, the Asherah pole[a] remained standing in Samaria.

13:4 Turnaround

Like so many kings of Israel, Jehoahaz started out doing "evil in the eyes of the LORD." Unlike so many kings of Israel, he repented. God, never eager to punish and always willing to relent, accepted his change of heart. Unfortunately, Jehoahaz's repentance didn't rub off. The Israelites continued their idol worship, in direct disobedience of God's command.

⁷Nothing had been left of the army of Jehoahaz except fifty horsemen, ten chariots and ten thousand foot soldiers, for the king of Aram had destroyed the rest and made them like the dust at threshing time.

⁸As for the other events of the reign of Jehoahaz, all he did and his achievements, are they not written in the book of the annals of the kings of Israel? ⁹Jehoahaz rested with his fathers and was buried in Samaria. And Jehoash[b] his son succeeded him as king.

Jehoash King of Israel

¹⁰In the thirty-seventh year of Joash king of Judah, Jehoash son of Jehoahaz became king of Israel in Samaria, and he reigned sixteen years. ¹¹He did evil in the eyes of the LORD and did not turn away from any of the sins of Jeroboam son of Nebat, which he had caused Israel to commit; he continued in them.

¹²As for the other events of the reign of Jehoash, all he did and his achievements, including his war against Amaziah king of Judah, are they not written in the book of the annals of the kings of Israel? ¹³Jehoash rested with his fathers, and Jeroboam succeeded him on the throne. Jehoash was buried in Samaria with the kings of Israel.

¹⁴Now Elisha was suffering from the illness from which he died. Jehoash king of Israel went down to see him and wept over him. "My father! My father!" he cried. "The chariots and horsemen of Israel!"

¹⁵Elisha said, "Get a bow and some arrows," and he did so. ¹⁶"Take the bow in your hands," he said to the king of Israel. When he had taken it, Elisha put his hands on the king's hands.

¹⁷"Open the east window," he said, and he opened it. "Shoot!" Elisha said, and he shot. "The

---

[a]6 That is, a symbol of the goddess Asherah; here and elsewhere in 2 Kings also in verses 12-14 and 25   [b]9 Hebrew *Joash*, a variant of *Jehoash*;

LORD's arrow of victory, the arrow of victory over Aram!" Elisha declared. "You will completely destroy the Arameans at Aphek."

¹⁸Then he said, "Take the arrows," and the king took them. Elisha told him, "Strike the ground." He struck it three times and stopped. ¹⁹The man of God was angry with him and said, "You should have struck the ground five or six times; then you would have defeated Aram and completely destroyed it. But now you will defeat it only three times."

²⁰Elisha died and was buried.

Now Moabite raiders used to enter the country every spring. ²¹Once while some Israelites

13:20 Troublesome Neighbors

Moab and Aram (Syria) often make an appearance in the books of 1, 2 Kings. They were small kingdoms much like Judah and Israel. Sometimes they fought against Israel or Judah, and sometimes they joined together in alliances to oppose a larger threat. On the world scene, constant threats came from Egypt and Assyria. Assyria cut a huge swath through history before its empire declined. Later, Babylon became the giant of the region.

were burying a man, suddenly they saw a band of raiders; so they threw the man's body into Elisha's tomb. When the body touched Elisha's bones, the man came to life and stood up on his feet.

²²Hazael king of Aram oppressed Israel throughout the reign of Jehoahaz. ²³But the LORD was gracious to them and had compassion and showed concern for them because of his covenant with Abraham, Isaac and Jacob. To this day he has been unwilling to destroy them or banish them from his presence.

²⁴Hazael king of Aram died, and Ben-Hadad his son succeeded him as king. ²⁵Then Jehoash son of Jehoahaz recaptured from Ben-Hadad son of Hazael the towns he had taken in battle from his father Jehoahaz. Three times Jehoash defeated him, and so he recovered the Israelite towns.

Amaziah King of Judah

14 In the second year of Jehoash[a] son of Jehoahaz king of Israel, Amaziah son of Joash king of Judah began to reign. ²He was twenty-five years old when he became king, and he reigned in Jerusalem twenty-nine years. His mother's name was Jehoaddin; she was from Jerusalem. ³He did what was right in the eyes of the LORD, but not as his father David had done. In

everything he followed the example of his father Joash. ⁴The high places, however, were not removed; the people continued to offer sacrifices and burn incense there.

⁵After the kingdom was firmly in his grasp, he executed the officials who had murdered his father the king. ⁶Yet he did not put the sons of the assassins to death, in accordance with what is written in the Book of the Law of Moses where the LORD commanded: "Fathers shall not be put to death for their children, nor children put to death for their fathers; each is to die for his own sins."[b]

⁷He was the one who defeated ten thousand Edomites in the Valley of Salt and captured Sela in battle, calling it Joktheel, the name it has to this day.

⁸Then Amaziah sent messengers to Jehoash son of Jehoahaz, the son of Jehu, king of Israel, with the challenge: "Come, meet me face to face."

⁹But Jehoash king of Israel replied to Amaziah king of Judah: "A thistle in Lebanon sent a message to a cedar in Lebanon, 'Give your daughter to my son in marriage.' Then a wild beast in Lebanon came along and trampled the thistle underfoot. ¹⁰You have indeed defeated Edom and now you are arrogant. Glory in your victory, but stay at home! Why ask for trouble and cause your own downfall and that of Judah also?"

¹¹Amaziah, however, would not listen, so Jehoash king of Israel attacked. He and Amaziah king of Judah faced each other at Beth Shemesh in Judah. ¹²Judah was routed by Israel, and every man fled to his home. ¹³Jehoash king of Israel captured Amaziah king of Judah, the son of Joash, the son of Ahaziah, at Beth Shemesh. Then Jehoash went to Jerusalem and broke down the wall of Jerusalem from the Ephraim Gate to the Corner Gate—a section about six hundred feet long.[c] ¹⁴He took all the gold and silver and all the articles found in the temple of the LORD and in the treasuries of the royal palace. He also took hostages and returned to Samaria.

¹⁵As for the other events of the reign of Jehoash, what he did and his achievements, including his war against Amaziah king of Judah, are they not written in the book of the annals of the kings of Israel? ¹⁶Jehoash rested with his fathers and was buried in Samaria with the kings of Israel. And Jeroboam his son succeeded him as king.

¹⁷Amaziah son of Joash king of Judah lived for fifteen years after the death of Jehoash son of Jehoahaz king of Israel. ¹⁸As for the other events of Amaziah's reign, are they not written in the book of the annals of the kings of Judah?

¹⁹They conspired against him in Jerusalem, and he fled to Lachish, but they sent men after

---

a1 Hebrew *Joash,* a variant of *Jehoash;* also in verses 13, 23 and 27   *b6* Deut. 24:16   *c13* Hebrew *four hundred cubits* (about 180 meters)

him to Lachish and killed him there. ²⁰He was brought back by horse and was buried in Jerusalem with his fathers, in the City of David.

²¹Then all the people of Judah took Azariah,ᵃ who was sixteen years old, and made him king in place of his father Amaziah. ²²He was the one who rebuilt Elath and restored it to Judah after Amaziah rested with his fathers.

Jeroboam II King of Israel

²³In the fifteenth year of Amaziah son of Joash king of Judah, Jeroboam son of Jehoash king of Israel became king in Samaria, and he reigned

14:23 Unfair Credit?

Secular historians report that Omri and Jeroboam were the strongest kings of Israel. Under them, the nation gained new heights of power and prestige. But consistently the books of 1, 2 Kings give little notice to political strength. They judge kings on the basis of spirituality, and thus both Omri and Jeroboam II are dismissed in a few paragraphs.

The wealthy-but-corrupt state of the nation during this time can be seen in the books by Amos and Hosea, both of whom prophesied in the beautiful city of Samaria. (Jonah also lived then—verse 25—but he prophesied in Nineveh, the capital city of Assyria.) Israel scoffed at these prophets' words of doom, but within 30 years all their dire predictions had come true.

forty-one years. ²⁴He did evil in the eyes of the LORD and did not turn away from any of the sins of Jeroboam son of Nebat, which he had caused Israel to commit. ²⁵He was the one who restored the boundaries of Israel from Leboᵇ Hamath to the Sea of the Arabah,ᶜ in accordance with the word of the LORD, the God of Israel, spoken through his servant Jonah son of Amittai, the prophet from Gath Hepher.

²⁶The LORD had seen how bitterly everyone in Israel, whether slave or free, was suffering; there was no one to help them. ²⁷And since the LORD had not said he would blot out the name of Israel from under heaven, he saved them by the hand of Jeroboam son of Jehoash.

²⁸As for the other events of Jeroboam's reign, all he did, and his military achievements, including how he recovered for Israel both Damascus and Hamath, which had belonged to Yaudi,ᵈ are they not written in the book of the annals of the kings of Israel? ²⁹Jeroboam rested with his fa-

thers, the kings of Israel. And Zechariah his son succeeded him as king.

Azariah King of Judah

15 In the twenty-seventh year of Jeroboam king of Israel, Azariah son of Amaziah king of Judah began to reign. ²He was sixteen years old when he became king, and he reigned in Jerusalem fifty-two years. His mother's name was Jecoliah; she was from Jerusalem. ³He did what was right in the eyes of the LORD, just as his father Amaziah had done. ⁴The high places, however, were not removed; the people continued to offer sacrifices and burn incense there.

⁵The LORD afflicted the king with leprosyᵉ until the day he died, and he lived in a separate house.ᶠ Jotham the king's son had charge of the palace and governed the people of the land.

⁶As for the other events of Azariah's reign, and all he did, are they not written in the book of the annals of the kings of Judah? ⁷Azariah rested with his fathers and was buried near them in the City of David. And Jotham his son succeeded him as king.

Zechariah King of Israel

⁸In the thirty-eighth year of Azariah king of Judah, Zechariah son of Jeroboam became king of Israel in Samaria, and he reigned six months. ⁹He did evil in the eyes of the LORD, as his fathers had done. He did not turn away from the sins of Jeroboam son of Nebat, which he had caused Israel to commit.

¹⁰Shallum son of Jabesh conspired against Zechariah. He attacked him in front of the people,ᵍ assassinated him and succeeded him as king. ¹¹The other events of Zechariah's reign are written in the book of the annals of the kings of Israel. ¹²So the word of the LORD spoken to Jehu was fulfilled: "Your descendants will sit on the throne of Israel to the fourth generation."ʰ

Shallum King of Israel

¹³Shallum son of Jabesh became king in the thirty-ninth year of Uzziah king of Judah, and he reigned in Samaria one month. ¹⁴Then Menahem son of Gadi went from Tirzah up to Samaria. He attacked Shallum son of Jabesh in Samaria, assassinated him and succeeded him as king.

¹⁵The other events of Shallum's reign, and the conspiracy he led, are written in the book of the annals of the kings of Israel.

¹⁶At that time Menahem, starting out from Tirzah, attacked Tiphsah and everyone in the city and its vicinity, because they refused to open their gates. He sacked Tiphsah and ripped open all the pregnant women.

ᵃ21 Also called *Uzziah*   ᵇ25 Or *from the entrance to*   ᶜ25 That is, the Dead Sea   ᵈ28 Or *Judah*   ᵉ5 The Hebrew word was used for various diseases affecting the skin—not necessarily leprosy.   ᶠ5 Or *in a house where he was relieved of responsibility*   ᵍ10 Hebrew; some Septuagint manuscripts *in Ibleam*   ʰ12 2 Kings 10:30

Menahem King of Israel

[17]In the thirty-ninth year of Azariah king of Judah, Menahem son of Gadi became king of Israel, and he reigned in Samaria ten years. [18]He did evil in the eyes of the LORD. During his entire reign he did not turn away from the sins of Jeroboam son of Nebat, which he had caused Israel to commit.

[19]Then Pul[a] king of Assyria invaded the land, and Menahem gave him a thousand talents[b] of silver to gain his support and strengthen his own hold on the kingdom. [20]Menahem exacted this money from Israel. Every wealthy man had to contribute fifty shekels[c] of silver to be given to the king of Assyria. So the king of Assyria withdrew and stayed in the land no longer.

[21]As for the other events of Menahem's reign, and all he did, are they not written in the book of the annals of the kings of Israel? [22]Menahem rested with his fathers. And Pekahiah his son succeeded him as king.

Pekahiah King of Israel

[23]In the fiftieth year of Azariah king of Judah, Pekahiah son of Menahem became king of Israel in Samaria, and he reigned two years. [24]Pekahiah did evil in the eyes of the LORD. He did not turn away from the sins of Jeroboam son of Nebat, which he had caused Israel to commit. [25]One of his chief officers, Pekah son of Remaliah, conspired against him. Taking fifty men of Gilead with him, he assassinated Pekahiah, along with Argob and Arieh, in the citadel of the royal palace at Samaria. So Pekah killed Pekahiah and succeeded him as king.

[26]The other events of Pekahiah's reign, and all he did, are written in the book of the annals of the kings of Israel.

Pekah King of Israel

[27]In the fifty-second year of Azariah king of Judah, Pekah son of Remaliah became king of Israel in Samaria, and he reigned twenty years. [28]He did evil in the eyes of the LORD. He did not turn away from the sins of Jeroboam son of Nebat, which he had caused Israel to commit.

[29]In the time of Pekah king of Israel, Tiglath-Pileser king of Assyria came and took Ijon, Abel Beth Maacah, Janoah, Kedesh and Hazor. He took Gilead and Galilee, including all the land of Naphtali, and deported the people to Assyria. [30]Then Hoshea son of Elah conspired against Pekah son of Remaliah. He attacked and assassinated him, and then succeeded him as king in the twentieth year of Jotham son of Uzziah.

[31]As for the other events of Pekah's reign, and all he did, are they not written in the book of the annals of the kings of Israel?

Jotham King of Judah

[32]In the second year of Pekah son of Remaliah king of Israel, Jotham son of Uzziah king of Judah began to reign. [33]He was twenty-five years old when he became king, and he reigned in Jerusalem sixteen years. His mother's name was Jerusha daughter of Zadok. [34]He did what was right in the eyes of the LORD, just as his father Uzziah had done. [35]The high places, however, were not removed; the people continued to offer sacrifices and burn incense there. Jotham rebuilt the Upper Gate of the temple of the LORD.

[36]As for the other events of Jotham's reign, and what he did, are they not written in the book of the annals of the kings of Judah? [37](In those days the LORD began to send Rezin king of Aram and Pekah son of Remaliah against Judah.) [38]Jotham rested with his fathers and was buried with them in the City of David, the city of his father. And Ahaz his son succeeded him as king.

Ahaz King of Judah

16 In the seventeenth year of Pekah son of Remaliah, Ahaz son of Jotham king of Judah began to reign. [2]Ahaz was twenty years old

16:1 Ahaz's Fateful Decisions

King Ahaz figured large in the histories of Israel and Judah. When Israel theatened his kingdom of Judah, he purchased military aid from Assyria. In response, Assyria obliterated Israel and made Judah a virtual puppet. Worse, Ahaz copied the pagan religions of his conquered territories, even to the extent of sacrificing his son in the fire.

when he became king, and he reigned in Jerusalem sixteen years. Unlike David his father, he did not do what was right in the eyes of the LORD his God. [3]He walked in the ways of the kings of Israel and even sacrificed his son in[d] the fire, following the detestable ways of the nations the LORD had driven out before the Israelites. [4]He offered sacrifices and burned incense at the high places, on the hilltops and under every spreading tree.

[5]Then Rezin king of Aram and Pekah son of Remaliah king of Israel marched up to fight against Jerusalem and besieged Ahaz, but they could not overpower him. [6]At that time, Rezin king of Aram recovered Elath for Aram by driving out the men of Judah. Edomites then moved into Elath and have lived there to this day.

---

[a]19 Also called *Tiglath-Pileser*   [b]19 That is, about 37 tons (about 34 metric tons)   [c]20 That is, about 1 1/4 pounds (about 0.6 kilogram)   [d]3 Or *even made his son pass through*

⁷Ahaz sent messengers to say to Tiglath-Pileser king of Assyria, "I am your servant and vassal. Come up and save me out of the hand of the king of Aram and of the king of Israel, who are attacking me." ⁸And Ahaz took the silver and gold found in the temple of the LORD and in the treasuries of the royal palace and sent it as a gift to the king of Assyria. ⁹The king of Assyria complied by attacking Damascus and capturing it. He deported its inhabitants to Kir and put Rezin to death.

¹⁰Then King Ahaz went to Damascus to meet Tiglath-Pileser king of Assyria. He saw an altar in Damascus and sent to Uriah the priest a sketch of the altar, with detailed plans for its construction. ¹¹So Uriah the priest built an altar in accordance with all the plans that King Ahaz had sent from Damascus and finished it before King Ahaz returned. ¹²When the king came back from Damascus and saw the altar, he approached it and presented offerings[a] on it. ¹³He offered up his burnt offering and grain offering, poured out his drink offering, and sprinkled the blood of his fellowship offerings[b] on the altar. ¹⁴The bronze altar that stood before the LORD he brought from the front of the temple—from between the new altar and the temple of the LORD—and put it on the north side of the new altar.

¹⁵King Ahaz then gave these orders to Uriah the priest: "On the large new altar, offer the morning burnt offering and the evening grain offering, the king's burnt offering and his grain offering, and the burnt offering of all the people of the land, and their grain offering and their drink offering. Sprinkle on the altar all the blood of the burnt offerings and sacrifices. But I will use the bronze altar for seeking guidance." ¹⁶And Uriah the priest did just as King Ahaz had ordered.

¹⁷King Ahaz took away the side panels and removed the basins from the movable stands. He removed the Sea from the bronze bulls that supported it and set it on a stone base. ¹⁸He took away the Sabbath canopy[c] that had been built at the temple and removed the royal entryway outside the temple of the LORD, in deference to the king of Assyria. ¹⁹As for the other events of the reign of Ahaz, and what he did, are they not written in the book of the annals of the kings of Judah? ²⁰Ahaz rested with his fathers and was buried with them in the City of David. And Hezekiah his son succeeded him as king.

Hoshea Last King of Israel

17 In the twelfth year of Ahaz king of Judah, Hoshea son of Elah became king of Israel in Samaria, and he reigned nine years. ²He did evil in the eyes of the LORD, but not like the kings of Israel who preceded him.

³Shalmaneser king of Assyria came up to attack Hoshea, who had been Shalmaneser's vassal and had paid him tribute. ⁴But the king of Assyria discovered that Hoshea was a traitor, for he had sent envoys to So[d] king of Egypt, and he no longer paid tribute to the king of Assyria, as he had done year by year. Therefore Shalmaneser seized him and put him in prison. ⁵The king of Assyria invaded the entire land, marched against Samaria and laid siege to it for three years. ⁶In the ninth year of Hoshea, the king of Assyria captured Samaria and deported the Israelites to Assyria. He settled them in Halah, in Gozan on the Habor River and in the towns of the Medes.

Israel Exiled Because of Sin

⁷All this took place because the Israelites had sinned against the LORD their God, who had brought them up out of Egypt from under the power of Pharaoh king of Egypt. They worshiped other gods ⁸and followed the practices of the nations the LORD had driven out before them, as well as the practices that the kings of Israel had introduced. ⁹The Israelites secretly did things against the LORD their God that were not right. From watchtower to fortified city they built themselves high places in all their towns. ¹⁰They set up sacred stones and Asherah poles on every high hill and under every spreading tree. ¹¹At every high place they burned incense, as the nations whom the LORD had driven out before them had done. They did wicked things that provoked the LORD to anger. ¹²They worshiped idols, though the LORD had said, "You shall not do this."[e] ¹³The LORD warned Israel and Judah through all his prophets and seers: "Turn from your evil ways. Observe my commands and decrees, in accordance with the entire Law that I commanded your fathers to obey and that I delivered to you through my servants the prophets."

¹⁴But they would not listen and were as stiff-necked as their fathers, who did not trust in the LORD their God. ¹⁵They rejected his decrees and the covenant he had made with their fathers and the warnings he had given them. They followed worthless idols and themselves became worthless. They imitated the nations around them although the LORD had ordered them, "Do not do as they do," and they did the things the LORD had forbidden them to do.

¹⁶They forsook all the commands of the LORD their God and made for themselves two idols cast in the shape of calves, and an Asherah pole. They

---

a 12 Or *and went up*   *b 13* Traditionally *peace offerings*   *c 18* Or *the dais of his throne* (see Septuagint)
d 4 Or *to Sais, to the; So* is possibly an abbreviation for *Osorkon.*   *e 12* Exodus 20:4, 5

Why All the Fuss about Idols?

The strange practice that led to a kingdom's fall

They followed worthless idols and themselves became worthless. 17:15

YOU CANNOT READ VERY FAR in the Old Testament without encountering idols, for idolatry ranks as perhaps the most common topic in the Bible. A nagging question haunts these pages: Why did the Israelites keep deserting the God who had delivered them from Egypt for the sake of carved tree trunks and bronze statues? What was the big attraction?

Idolatry seems especially strange to us in modern times. Today, idols may show up as exotic props in a movie, but does anyone truly believe in them anymore? Why do they merit so much attention in the Old Testament?

Responses to Idols Today

Actually, idols still thrive in such places as Africa and Asia, and their effect on the people there sheds light on Old Testament idolatry. In India, for example, each city and village has its own favorite god—over 1,000 different gods are worshiped. Portable idols stand on street corners of the major cities.

For devout Hindus, idolatry adds a dimension of magic to life. Hindus believe the gods control all events, including such disasters as monsoons, floods, diseases, and traffic accidents. These powerful gods must be kept happy at all costs.

But what pleases a god depends on the god's character, and gods can be fearsome and violent. Some Indians worship idols in the form of a snake; others worship the smallpox goddess. The largest city in India, Calcutta, has adopted the murderous goddess Kali, who wears a garland of gruesome heads around her waist. Devotion to such gods can easily lead to a paralyzing fear. If Kali isn't kept happy, her followers believe, she will cruelly punish them.

Other Hindus, less devout, take a different approach. They treat their gods almost as good-luck charms. A taxi driver mounts a tiny statue of a monkey god on the dashboard of his car, occasionally draping it with flowers for decoration. If you ask, he'll say he prays to the god for safety—but you know about the traffic in India, he adds with a laugh.

A Good-Luck Charm or an Evil Cult

Idolatry had similar effects on the ancient Israelites. Some Israelites took the same spirit as the Indian taxi driver: Maybe an idol will help you out, maybe not, but why not play along? They drifted carelessly from god to god, adopting the religion of whatever group seemed to be having the most success with its agriculture or armies.

No attitude could be further from that demanded by the true God. He had chosen the Israelites as a kingdom of priests, a treasured possession set apart for him. As Lord of the universe, he wanted not a casual faith, but total allegiance. He was not a good-luck charm.

Far too often, however, idols in Israel took on a more sinister form, resembling the evil goddess of Calcutta. Legends about Baal, for example, celebrated his drunkenness and debauchery. Followers worshiped him by having sex in the temple with prostitutes or even by sacrificing human babies.

Worshiping Baal meant a complete rejection of God's special relationship with the Israelites—a crime very much like adultery, as the prophets often pointed out. Baal worship could not possibly coexist with the worship of God.

What Was the Appeal?

Why did Baal and the other idols prove so appealing to the Israelites? Like peasants gawking at big-city life, the Israelites moved from 40 years of wilderness wanderings into a land of cities and more advanced technology. They had been landless nomads and shepherds. When they settled down to a new occupation of farming, they looked to a Canaanite god, Baal, as a possible means of guaranteeing good crops. In other words, they sought a shortcut through magic.

Similarly, when a mighty army threatened their borders, they smuggled in a few of that army's favorite idols, hedging their bets in case their own religion did not bring them military success. Idols became a phantom source of power, an alternative place to invest faith and hope.

Idolatry made such inroads into Israel and Judah that God had to tear apart both kingdoms in order to root it out. Second Kings clearly blames idolatry as the chief sin leading to both nations' collapse. History records that the punishment ultimately worked. After the Assyrian and Babylonian invasions, never again did the Israelites dabble in idolatry.

Life Questions: Idolatry need not involve images of wood or stone; it's possible to worship such things as money, another person, or fame. What are some "idols" you might be tempted to worship?

bowed down to all the starry hosts, and they worshiped Baal. ¹⁷They sacrificed their sons and daughters in[a] the fire. They practiced divination and sorcery and sold themselves to do evil in the eyes of the LORD, provoking him to anger.

17:17 A Higher Standard

To the casual eye, it seemed unfair. God let the Assyrians, a much crueler people, conquer Israel and take the whole nation into exile. Why? Israel was judged by a higher standard, on the basis of the great advantages God had given them. As Jesus would say hundreds of years later, "From the one who has been entrusted with much, much more will be asked" (Luke 12:48).

A hair-raising list of Israel's sins (verses 7–23) shows why they deserved judgment: they adopted their neighbors' fertility religion, even offering their own children as human sacrifices. Assyria lacked Israel's advantages, but they would be judged too—which explains why the powerful nation of Assyria no longer exists.

---

¹⁸So the LORD was very angry with Israel and removed them from his presence. Only the tribe of Judah was left, ¹⁹and even Judah did not keep the commands of the LORD their God. They followed the practices Israel had introduced. ²⁰Therefore the LORD rejected all the people of Israel; he afflicted them and gave them into the hands of plunderers, until he thrust them from his presence.

²¹When he tore Israel away from the house of David, they made Jeroboam son of Nebat their king. Jeroboam enticed Israel away from following the LORD and caused them to commit a great sin. ²²The Israelites persisted in all the sins of Jeroboam and did not turn away from them ²³until the LORD removed them from his presence, as he had warned through all his servants the prophets. So the people of Israel were taken from their homeland into exile in Assyria, and they are still there.

Samaria Resettled

²⁴The king of Assyria brought people from Babylon, Cuthah, Avva, Hamath and Sepharvaim and settled them in the towns of Samaria to replace the Israelites. They took over Samaria and lived in its towns. ²⁵When they first lived there, they did not worship the LORD; so he sent lions among them and they killed some of the people. ²⁶It was reported to the king of Assyria: "The people you deported and resettled in the towns of Samaria do not know what the god of that coun-

try requires. He has sent lions among them, which are killing them off, because the people do not know what he requires."

²⁷Then the king of Assyria gave this order: "Have one of the priests you took captive from Samaria go back to live there and teach the people what the god of the land requires." ²⁸So one of the priests who had been exiled from Samaria came to live in Bethel and taught them how to worship the LORD.

²⁹Nevertheless, each national group made its own gods in the several towns where they settled, and set them up in the shrines the people of Samaria had made at the high places. ³⁰The men from Babylon made Succoth Benoth, the men from Cuthah made Nergal, and the men from Hamath made Ashima; ³¹the Avvites made Nibhaz and Tartak, and the Sepharvites burned their children in the fire as sacrifices to Adrammelech and Anammelech, the gods of Sepharvaim. ³²They worshiped the LORD, but they also appointed all sorts of their own people to officiate for them as priests in the shrines at the high places. ³³They worshiped the LORD, but they also served their own gods in accordance with the customs of the nations from which they had been brought.

³⁴To this day they persist in their former practices. They neither worship the LORD nor adhere to the decrees and ordinances, the laws and commands that the LORD gave the descendants of Jacob, whom he named Israel. ³⁵When the LORD made a covenant with the Israelites, he commanded them: "Do not worship any other gods or bow down to them, serve them or sacrifice to them. ³⁶But the LORD, who brought you up out of Egypt with mighty power and outstretched arm, is the one you must worship. To him you shall bow down and to him offer sacrifices. ³⁷You

---

17:24 Scorched-Earth Policy

In early wars Assyrian conquerors followed a cruel policy of genocide. They exterminated their enemies and destroyed their land and property. But in later years they adopted a new technique: deporting their victims to Assyria and other countries and replacing them with foreigners from other conquered territories. In this way, they disrupted cultures and made sure the conquered peoples would never regroup and rise up as a new threat. This verse shows the origin of Samaritans, a group that still existed in New Testament times and, in fact, can still be found in modern Israel. They combined their own religions with some reverence for the true God.

---

[a] 17 Or *They made their sons and daughters pass through*

must always be careful to keep the decrees and ordinances, the laws and commands he wrote for you. Do not worship other gods. ³⁸Do not forget the covenant I have made with you, and do not worship other gods. ³⁹Rather, worship the LORD your God; it is he who will deliver you from the hand of all your enemies."

⁴⁰They would not listen, however, but persisted in their former practices. ⁴¹Even while these people were worshiping the LORD, they were serving their idols. To this day their children and grandchildren continue to do as their fathers did.

Hezekiah King of Judah

18 In the third year of Hoshea son of Elah king of Israel, Hezekiah son of Ahaz king of Judah began to reign. ²He was twenty-five years old when he became king, and he reigned in Jerusalem twenty-nine years. His mother's name was Abijah*a* daughter of Zechariah. ³He did what was right in the eyes of the LORD, just as his father David had done. ⁴He removed the high places, smashed the sacred stones and cut down the Asherah poles. He broke into pieces the bronze snake Moses had made, for up to that time the Israelites had been burning incense to it. (It was called*b* Nehushtan.*c*)

⁵Hezekiah trusted in the LORD, the God of Israel. There was no one like him among all the kings of Judah, either before him or after him. ⁶He held fast to the LORD and did not cease to follow him; he kept the commands the LORD had given Moses. ⁷And the LORD was with him; he was successful in whatever he undertook. He rebelled against the king of Assyria and did not serve him. ⁸From watchtower to fortified city, he defeated the Philistines, as far as Gaza and its territory.

⁹In King Hezekiah's fourth year, which was the seventh year of Hoshea son of Elah king of Israel, Shalmaneser king of Assyria marched against Samaria and laid siege to it. ¹⁰At the end of three years the Assyrians took it. So Samaria was captured in Hezekiah's sixth year, which was the ninth year of Hoshea king of Israel. ¹¹The king of Assyria deported Israel to Assyria and settled them in Halah, in Gozan on the Habor River and in towns of the Medes. ¹²This happened because they had not obeyed the LORD their God, but had violated his covenant—all that Moses the servant of the LORD commanded. They neither listened to the commands nor carried them out.

¹³In the fourteenth year of King Hezekiah's reign, Sennacherib king of Assyria attacked all the fortified cities of Judah and captured them. ¹⁴So Hezekiah king of Judah sent this message to the king of Assyria at Lachish: "I have done wrong. Withdraw from me, and I will pay whatever you demand of me." The king of Assyria exacted from Hezekiah king of Judah three hundred talents*d* of silver and thirty talents*e* of gold. ¹⁵So Hezekiah gave him all the silver that was found in the temple of the LORD and in the treasuries of the royal palace.

¹⁶At this time Hezekiah king of Judah stripped off the gold with which he had covered the doors and doorposts of the temple of the LORD, and gave it to the king of Assyria.

18:16 King of Contradictions

Overall, Hezekiah made a good king, trusting in God. But his life contained a mixture of wisdom and folly, vice and virtue. On the good side, Hezekiah "trusted in the LORD" (verse 5), cleansed Judah from idol worship, and won independence from the powerful nations around. When he prayed for healing, he was granted an unprecedented extension of his life (20:1–11).

On the bad side, Hezekiah foolishly tried to bribe the Assyrians with gold stripped from the temple. Later, when representatives from Babylon came (20:13), he boastfully showed them all his treasures. And when the prophet Isaiah warned that Babylon would come back to take those treasures and more, Hezekiah blithely contented himself that there would be "peace and security in my lifetime" (20:19).

Sennacherib Threatens Jerusalem

¹⁷The king of Assyria sent his supreme commander, his chief officer and his field commander with a large army, from Lachish to King Hezekiah at Jerusalem. They came up to Jerusalem and stopped at the aqueduct of the Upper Pool, on the road to the Washerman's Field. ¹⁸They called for the king; and Eliakim son of Hilkiah the palace administrator, Shebna the secretary, and Joah son of Asaph the recorder went out to them.

¹⁹The field commander said to them, "Tell Hezekiah:

" 'This is what the great king, the king of Assyria, says: On what are you basing this confidence of yours? ²⁰You say you have strategy and military strength—but you speak only empty words. On whom are you depending, that you rebel against me? ²¹Look now, you are depending on Egypt, that splintered reed of a staff, which pierces

a2 Hebrew *Abi,* a variant of *Abijah*   *b4* Or *He called it snake* and *unclean thing.*   *c4 Nehushtan* sounds like the Hebrew for *bronze* and *d14* That is, about 11 tons (about 10 metric tons)   *e14* That is, about 1 ton (about 1 metric ton)

a man's hand and wounds him if he leans on it! Such is Pharaoh king of Egypt to all who depend on him. 22And if you say to me, "We are depending on the LORD our God"—isn't he the one whose high places and altars Hezekiah removed, saying to Judah and Jerusalem, "You must worship before this altar in Jerusalem"?

23"'Come now, make a bargain with my master, the king of Assyria: I will give you two thousand horses—if you can put riders on them! 24How can you repulse one officer of the least of my master's officials, even though you are depending on Egypt for chariots and horsemen[a]? 25Furthermore, have I come to attack and destroy this place without word from the LORD? The LORD himself told me to march against this country and destroy it.'"

26Then Eliakim son of Hilkiah, and Shebna and Joah said to the field commander, "Please speak to your servants in Aramaic, since we understand it. Don't speak to us in Hebrew in the hearing of the people on the wall."

27But the commander replied, "Was it only to your master and you that my master sent me to say these things, and not to the men sitting on the wall—who, like you, will have to eat their own filth and drink their own urine?"

28Then the commander stood and called out in Hebrew: "Hear the word of the great king, the king of Assyria! 29This is what the king says: Do not let Hezekiah deceive you. He cannot deliver you from my hand. 30Do not let Hezekiah persuade you to trust in the LORD when he says, 'The LORD will surely deliver us; this city will not be given into the hand of the king of Assyria.'

31"Do not listen to Hezekiah. This is what the king of Assyria says: Make peace with me and come out to me. Then every one of you will eat from his own vine and fig tree and drink water from his own cistern, 32until I come and take you to a land like your own, a land of grain and new wine, a land of bread and vineyards, a land of olive trees and honey. Choose life and not death!

"Do not listen to Hezekiah, for he is misleading you when he says, 'The LORD will deliver us.' 33Has the god of any nation ever delivered his land from the hand of the king of Assyria? 34Where are the gods of Hamath and Arpad? Where are the gods of Sepharvaim, Hena and Ivvah? Have they rescued Samaria from my hand? 35Who of all the gods of these countries has been able to save his land from me? How then can the LORD deliver Jerusalem from my hand?"

36But the people remained silent and said nothing in reply, because the king had commanded, "Do not answer him."

37Then Eliakim son of Hilkiah the palace administrator, Shebna the secretary and Joah son of Asaph the recorder went to Hezekiah, with their clothes torn, and told him what the field commander had said.

Jerusalem's Deliverance Foretold

19 When King Hezekiah heard this, he tore his clothes and put on sackcloth and went into the temple of the LORD. 2He sent Eliakim the palace administrator, Shebna the secretary and the leading priests, all wearing sackcloth, to the prophet Isaiah son of Amoz. 3They told him, "This is what Hezekiah says: This day is a day of distress and rebuke and disgrace, as when children come to the point of birth and there is no strength to deliver them. 4It may be that the LORD your God will hear all the words of the field commander, whom his master, the king of Assyria, has sent to ridicule the living God, and that he will rebuke him for the words the LORD your God has heard. Therefore pray for the remnant that still survives."

5When King Hezekiah's officials came to Isaiah, 6Isaiah said to them, "Tell your master, 'This is what the LORD says: Do not be afraid of what you have heard—those words with which the underlings of the king of Assyria have blasphemed me. 7Listen! I am going to put such a spirit in him that when he hears a certain report, he will return to his own country, and there I will have him cut down with the sword.'"

8When the field commander heard that the king of Assyria had left Lachish, he withdrew and found the king fighting against Libnah.

9Now Sennacherib received a report that Tirhakah, the Cushite[b] king ⌊of Egypt⌋, was marching out to fight against him. So he again sent messengers to Hezekiah with this word: 10"Say to Hezekiah king of Judah: Do not let the god you depend on deceive you when he says, 'Jerusalem will not be handed over to the king of Assyria.' 11Surely you have heard what the kings of Assyria have done to all the countries, destroying them completely. And will you be delivered? 12Did the gods of the nations that were destroyed by my forefathers deliver them: the gods of Gozan, Haran, Rezeph and the people of Eden who were in Tel Assar? 13Where is the king of Hamath, the king of Arpad, the king of the city of Sepharvaim, or of Hena or Ivvah?"

Hezekiah's Prayer

14Hezekiah received the letter from the messengers and read it. Then he went up to the temple of the LORD and spread it out before the LORD.

¹⁵And Hezekiah prayed to the LORD: "O LORD, God of Israel, enthroned between the cherubim, you alone are God over all the kingdoms of the earth. You have made heaven and earth. ¹⁶Give ear, O LORD, and hear; open your eyes, O LORD, and see; listen to the words Sennacherib has sent to insult the living God.

¹⁷"It is true, O LORD, that the Assyrian kings have laid waste these nations and their lands. ¹⁸They have thrown their gods into the fire and destroyed them, for they were not gods but only wood and stone, fashioned by men's hands. ¹⁹Now, O LORD our God, deliver us from his hand, so that all kingdoms on earth may know that you alone, O LORD, are God."

Isaiah Prophesies Sennacherib's Fall

²⁰Then Isaiah son of Amoz sent a message to Hezekiah: "This is what the LORD, the God of Israel, says: I have heard your prayer concerning Sennacherib king of Assyria. ²¹This is the word that the LORD has spoken against him:

"'The Virgin Daughter of Zion
    despises you and mocks you.
The Daughter of Jerusalem
    tosses her head as you flee.
²²Who is it you have insulted and
        blasphemed?
    Against whom have you raised your voice
and lifted your eyes in pride?
    Against the Holy One of Israel!
²³By your messengers
    you have heaped insults on the Lord.
And you have said,
    "With my many chariots
I have ascended the heights of the
        mountains,
    the utmost heights of Lebanon.
I have cut down its tallest cedars,
    the choicest of its pines.
I have reached its remotest parts,
    the finest of its forests.
²⁴I have dug wells in foreign lands
    and drunk the water there.
With the soles of my feet
    I have dried up all the streams of Egypt."

²⁵"'Have you not heard?
Long ago I ordained it.
In days of old I planned it;
    now I have brought it to pass,
that you have turned fortified cities
    into piles of stone.
²⁶Their people, drained of power,
    are dismayed and put to shame.
They are like plants in the field,
    like tender green shoots,
like grass sprouting on the roof,
    scorched before it grows up.

²⁷"'But I know where you stay

and when you come and go
    and how you rage against me.
²⁸Because you rage against me
    and your insolence has reached my ears,
I will put my hook in your nose
    and my bit in your mouth,
and I will make you return
    by the way you came.'

²⁹"This will be the sign for you, O Hezekiah:

"This year you will eat what grows by itself,
    and the second year what springs from
        that.
But in the third year sow and reap,
    plant vineyards and eat their fruit.
³⁰Once more a remnant of the house of Judah
    will take root below and bear fruit above.
³¹For out of Jerusalem will come a remnant,
    and out of Mount Zion a band of
        survivors.

The zeal of the LORD Almighty will accomplish this.

19:31 Deliverance for Jerusalem

Jerusalem appeared to be a doomed city during the dark days of Assyria's siege. But two things happened to fulfill this prophecy. First, a great plague struck the Assyrians (verse 35), a plague also recorded by the historian Herodotus. Later, the murder of Assyria's leader brought internal chaos to that country, canceling out the Assyrian threat. The miraculous deliverance convinced some Israelites that Jerusalem, God's city, was indestructible—a belief that would later be proven false.

³²"Therefore this is what the LORD says concerning the king of Assyria:

"He will not enter this city
    or shoot an arrow here.
He will not come before it with shield
    or build a siege ramp against it.
³³By the way that he came he will return;
    he will not enter this city,
                            declares the LORD.
³⁴I will defend this city and save it,
    for my sake and for the sake of David my
        servant."

³⁵That night the angel of the LORD went out and put to death a hundred and eighty-five thousand men in the Assyrian camp. When the people got up the next morning—there were all the dead bodies! ³⁶So Sennacherib king of Assyria broke camp and withdrew. He returned to Nineveh and stayed there.

³⁷One day, while he was worshiping in the

temple of his god Nisroch, his sons Adrammelech and Sharezer cut him down with the sword, and they escaped to the land of Ararat. And Esarhaddon his son succeeded him as king.

Hezekiah's Illness

20 In those days Hezekiah became ill and was at the point of death. The prophet Isaiah son of Amoz went to him and said, "This is what the LORD says: Put your house in order, because you are going to die; you will not recover."

²Hezekiah turned his face to the wall and prayed to the LORD, ³"Remember, O LORD, how I have walked before you faithfully and with wholehearted devotion and have done what is good in your eyes." And Hezekiah wept bitterly.

⁴Before Isaiah had left the middle court, the word of the LORD came to him: ⁵"Go back and tell Hezekiah, the leader of my people, 'This is what the LORD, the God of your father David, says: I have heard your prayer and seen your tears; I will heal you. On the third day from now you will go up to the temple of the LORD. ⁶I will add fifteen years to your life. And I will deliver you and this city from the hand of the king of Assyria. I will defend this city for my sake and for the sake of my servant David.'"

⁷Then Isaiah said, "Prepare a poultice of figs." They did so and applied it to the boil, and he recovered.

⁸Hezekiah had asked Isaiah, "What will be the sign that the LORD will heal me and that I will go up to the temple of the LORD on the third day from now?"

⁹Isaiah answered, "This is the LORD's sign to you that the LORD will do what he has promised: Shall the shadow go forward ten steps, or shall it go back ten steps?"

¹⁰"It is a simple matter for the shadow to go forward ten steps," said Hezekiah. "Rather, have it go back ten steps."

¹¹Then the prophet Isaiah called upon the LORD, and the LORD made the shadow go back the ten steps it had gone down on the stairway of Ahaz.

Envoys From Babylon

¹²At that time Merodach-Baladan son of Baladan king of Babylon sent Hezekiah letters and a gift, because he had heard of Hezekiah's illness. ¹³Hezekiah received the messengers and showed them all that was in his storehouses—the silver, the gold, the spices and the fine oil—his armory and everything found among his treasures. There was nothing in his palace or in all his kingdom that Hezekiah did not show them.

¹⁴Then Isaiah the prophet went to King Hezekiah and asked, "What did those men say, and where did they come from?"

"From a distant land," Hezekiah replied. "They came from Babylon."

¹⁵The prophet asked, "What did they see in your palace?"

"They saw everything in my palace," Hezekiah said. "There is nothing among my treasures that I did not show them."

¹⁶Then Isaiah said to Hezekiah, "Hear the word of the LORD: ¹⁷The time will surely come when everything in your palace, and all that your fathers have stored up until this day, will be carried off to Babylon. Nothing will be left, says the LORD. ¹⁸And some of your descendants, your own flesh and blood, that will be born to you, will be taken away, and they will become eunuchs in the palace of the king of Babylon."

¹⁹"The word of the LORD you have spoken is good," Hezekiah replied. For he thought, "Will there not be peace and security in my lifetime?"

²⁰As for the other events of Hezekiah's reign, all his achievements and how he made the pool and the tunnel by which he brought water into the city, are they not written in the book of the

20:20 A Lifeline Tunnel

The tunnel, one of Hezekiah's major accomplishments, can still be seen in modern Jerusalem. In ancient days, Jerusalem had no source of water within its walls, making it vulnerable to an extended siege. Hezekiah undertook a tremendous engineering feat to bring water from a spring to a reservoir inside Jerusalem. In the late 1800s some boys swimming in the pool of Siloam happened upon a carved record, dating from Hezekiah's time, of how the tunnel had been dug. The marks of pickaxes are still clearly visible.

annals of the kings of Judah? ²¹Hezekiah rested with his fathers. And Manasseh his son succeeded him as king.

Manasseh King of Judah

21 Manasseh was twelve years old when he became king, and he reigned in Jerusalem fifty-five years. His mother's name was Hephzibah. ²He did evil in the eyes of the LORD, following the detestable practices of the nations the LORD had driven out before the Israelites. ³He rebuilt the high places his father Hezekiah had destroyed; he also erected altars to Baal and made an Asherah pole, as Ahab king of Israel had done. He bowed down to all the starry hosts and worshiped them. ⁴He built altars in the temple of the LORD, of which the LORD had said, "In Jerusalem I will put my Name." ⁵In both courts of the temple of the LORD, he built altars to all the starry hosts. [6]He sacrificed his own son in[a] the fire, practiced sorcery and divination, and consulted mediums and spiritists. He did much evil in the eyes of the LORD, provoking him to anger.

[7]He took the carved Asherah pole he had made and put it in the temple, of which the LORD had said to David and to his son Solomon, "In this temple and in Jerusalem, which I have chosen out of all the tribes of Israel, I will put my Name forever. [8]I will not again make the feet of the Israelites wander from the land I gave their forefathers, if only they will be careful to do everything I commanded them and will keep the whole Law that my servant Moses gave them." [9]But the people did not listen. Manasseh led them astray, so that they did more evil than the nations the LORD had destroyed before the Israelites.

[10]The LORD said through his servants the prophets: [11]"Manasseh king of Judah has committed these detestable sins. He has done more evil than the Amorites who preceded him and has led Judah into sin with his idols. [12]Therefore this is what the LORD, the God of Israel, says: I am going to bring such disaster on Jerusalem and Judah that the ears of everyone who hears of it will tingle. [13]I will stretch out over Jerusalem the measuring line used against Samaria and the plumb line used against the house of Ahab. I will wipe out Jerusalem as one wipes a dish, wiping it and turning it upside down. [14]I will forsake the remnant of my inheritance and hand them over to their enemies. They will be looted and plundered by all their foes, [15]because they have done evil in my eyes and have provoked me to anger from the day their forefathers came out of Egypt until this day."

[16]Moreover, Manasseh also shed so much innocent blood that he filled Jerusalem from end to end—besides the sin that he had caused Judah to commit, so that they did evil in the eyes of the LORD.

[17]As for the other events of Manasseh's reign, and all he did, including the sin he committed, are they not written in the book of the annals of the kings of Judah? [18]Manasseh rested with his fathers and was buried in his palace garden, the garden of Uzza. And Amon his son succeeded him as king.

Amon King of Judah

[19]Amon was twenty-two years old when he became king, and he reigned in Jerusalem two years. His mother's name was Meshullemeth daughter of Haruz; she was from Jotbah. [20]He did evil in the eyes of the LORD, as his father Manasseh had done. [21]He walked in all the ways of his father; he worshiped the idols his father

had worshiped, and bowed down to them. [22]He forsook the LORD, the God of his fathers, and did not walk in the way of the LORD.

[23]Amon's officials conspired against him and assassinated the king in his palace. [24]Then the people of the land killed all who had plotted against King Amon, and they made Josiah his son king in his place.

[25]As for the other events of Amon's reign, and what he did, are they not written in the book of the annals of the kings of Judah? [26]He was buried in his grave in the garden of Uzza. And Josiah his son succeeded him as king.

The Book of the Law Found

22 Josiah was eight years old when he became king, and he reigned in Jerusalem thirty-one years. His mother's name was Jedidah daughter of Adaiah; she was from Bozkath. [2]He did what was right in the eyes of the LORD and walked in all the ways of his father David, not turning aside to the right or to the left.

[3]In the eighteenth year of his reign, King Josiah sent the secretary, Shaphan son of Azaliah, the son of Meshullam, to the temple of the LORD. He said: [4]"Go up to Hilkiah the high priest and have him get ready the money that has been brought into the temple of the LORD, which the doorkeepers have collected from the people. [5]Have them entrust it to the men appointed to supervise the work on the temple. And have these men pay the workers who repair the temple of the LORD— [6]the carpenters, the builders and the masons. Also have them purchase timber and dressed stone to repair the temple. [7]But they need not account for the money entrusted to them, because they are acting faithfully."

[8]Hilkiah the high priest said to Shaphan the secretary, "I have found the Book of the Law in the temple of the LORD." He gave it to Shaphan, who read it. [9]Then Shaphan the secretary went to the king and reported to him: "Your officials have paid out the money that was in the temple of the LORD and have entrusted it to the workers and supervisors at the temple." [10]Then Shaphan the secretary informed the king, "Hilkiah the priest has given me a book." And Shaphan read from it in the presence of the king.

[11]When the king heard the words of the Book

22:11 Dramatic Discovery

Most scholars believe the Book of the Law referred to was Deuteronomy—or at least a portion of that book. The find, confirmed by a prophetess, resulted in the most thoroughgoing religious reform Judah had ever seen.

---

[a]6 Or *He made his own son pass through*

of the Law, he tore his robes. ¹²He gave these orders to Hilkiah the priest, Ahikam son of Shaphan, Acbor son of Micaiah, Shaphan the secretary and Asaiah the king's attendant: ¹³"Go and inquire of the LORD for me and for the people and for all Judah about what is written in this book that has been found. Great is the LORD's anger that burns against us because our fathers have not obeyed the words of this book; they have not acted in accordance with all that is written there concerning us."

¹⁴Hilkiah the priest, Ahikam, Acbor, Shaphan and Asaiah went to speak to the prophetess Huldah, who was the wife of Shallum son of Tikvah, the son of Harhas, keeper of the wardrobe. She lived in Jerusalem, in the Second District.

¹⁵She said to them, "This is what the LORD, the God of Israel, says: Tell the man who sent you to me, ¹⁶'This is what the LORD says: I am going to bring disaster on this place and its people, according to everything written in the book the king of Judah has read. ¹⁷Because they have forsaken me and burned incense to other gods and provoked me to anger by all the idols their hands have made,ᵃ my anger will burn against this place and will not be quenched.' ¹⁸Tell the king of Judah, who sent you to inquire of the LORD, 'This is what the LORD, the God of Israel, says concerning the words you heard: ¹⁹Because your heart was responsive and you humbled yourself before the LORD when you heard what I have spoken against this place and its people, that they would become accursed and laid waste, and because you

tore your robes and wept in my presence, I have heard you, declares the LORD. ²⁰Therefore I will gather you to your fathers, and you will be buried in peace. Your eyes will not see all the disaster I am going to bring on this place.'"

So they took her answer back to the king.

Josiah Renews the Covenant

23 Then the king called together all the elders of Judah and Jerusalem. ²He went up to the temple of the LORD with the men of Judah, the people of Jerusalem, the priests and the prophets—all the people from the least to the greatest. He read in their hearing all the words of the Book of the Covenant, which had been found in the temple of the LORD. ³The king stood by the pillar and renewed the covenant in the presence of the LORD—to follow the LORD and keep his commands, regulations and decrees with all his heart and all his soul, thus confirming the words of the covenant written in this book. Then all the people pledged themselves to the covenant.

⁴The king ordered Hilkiah the high priest, the priests next in rank and the doorkeepers to remove from the temple of the LORD all the articles made for Baal and Asherah and all the starry hosts. He burned them outside Jerusalem in the fields of the Kidron Valley and took the ashes to Bethel. ⁵He did away with the pagan priests appointed by the kings of Judah to burn incense on the high places of the towns of Judah and on those around Jerusalem—those who burned incense to Baal, to the sun and moon, to the con-

ᵃ17 Or by everything they have done

JOSIAH *Last Gasp*

JOSIAH CAME TO THE THRONE when his father, at age 24, fell to assassins. Josiah himself was a mere child of eight when he was abruptly called to fill a king's shoes. By the time he reached 16, however, the boy-king had begun to find himself.

God's holy city of Jerusalem and his chosen people, the Israelites, had sunk to historic lows. The temple featured idols, male shrine prostitutes, and carved horses dedicated to sun worshipers. In a nearby valley, people burned their children in sacrifice to the god Molech. Other pagan shrines dotted the hilltops around Jerusalem and throughout the land of Judah.

During the long slide away from God, all sacred records had disappeared. The God of Abraham, Isaac and Jacob was just a faint memory.

Perhaps Josiah had heard about his great-grandfather Hezekiah, who while king had purified the temple and restored the Passover celebration. In his youth Josiah set reforms like Hezekiah's in motion again. Then, in the process of cleaning out the temple, priests discovered an old book of Scripture. Josiah took its message to heart, spurred on by his fear of God's judgment against those who failed to obey his law.

Josiah sent to a prophetess, Huldah, for advice. (Both Jeremiah and Zephaniah were prophesying at the time, but Huldah got the call.) The nation would indeed be punished, Huldah confirmed, but because of Josiah's humility the calamity would not occur in his lifetime (22:15–20). Her words came true. After Josiah's tragic death at the age of 39, Judah went quickly downhill to total destruction. Josiah was the Israelites' last, great gasp.

Life Questions: When you see immorality all around you, what can you do to change it?

stellations and to all the starry hosts. 6He took the Asherah pole from the temple of the LORD to the Kidron Valley outside Jerusalem and burned it there. He ground it to powder and scattered the dust over the graves of the common people. 7He also tore down the quarters of the male shrine prostitutes, which were in the temple of the LORD and where women did weaving for Asherah.

8Josiah brought all the priests from the towns of Judah and desecrated the high places, from Geba to Beersheba, where the priests had burned incense. He broke down the shrines*a* at the gates—at the entrance to the Gate of Joshua, the city governor, which is on the left of the city gate. 9Although the priests of the high places did not serve at the altar of the LORD in Jerusalem, they ate unleavened bread with their fellow priests.

10He desecrated Topheth, which was in the Valley of Ben Hinnom, so no one could use it to sacrifice his son or daughter in*b* the fire to Molech. 11He removed from the entrance to the temple of the LORD the horses that the kings of Judah had dedicated to the sun. They were in the court near the room of an official named Nathan-Melech. Josiah then burned the chariots dedicated to the sun.

12He pulled down the altars the kings of Judah had erected on the roof near the upper room of Ahaz, and the altars Manasseh had built in the two courts of the temple of the LORD. He removed them from there, smashed them to pieces and threw the rubble into the Kidron Valley. 13The king also desecrated the high places that were east of Jerusalem on the south of the Hill of Corruption—the ones Solomon king of Israel had built for Ashtoreth the vile goddess of the Sidonians, for Chemosh the vile god of Moab, and for Molech*c* the detestable god of the people of Ammon. 14Josiah smashed the sacred stones and cut down the Asherah poles and covered the sites with human bones.

15Even the altar at Bethel, the high place made by Jeroboam son of Nebat, who had caused Israel to sin—even that altar and high place he demolished. He burned the high place and ground it to powder, and burned the Asherah pole also. 16Then Josiah looked around, and when he saw the tombs that were there on the hillside, he had the bones removed from them and burned on the altar to defile it, in accordance with the word of the LORD proclaimed by the man of God who foretold these things.

17The king asked, "What is that tombstone I see?"

The men of the city said, "It marks the tomb of the man of God who came from Judah and pronounced against the altar of Bethel the very things you have done to it."

18"Leave it alone," he said. "Don't let anyone disturb his bones." So they spared his bones and those of the prophet who had come from Samaria.

19Just as he had done at Bethel, Josiah removed and defiled all the shrines at the high places that the kings of Israel had built in the towns of Samaria that had provoked the LORD to anger. 20Josiah slaughtered all the priests of those high places on the altars and burned human bones on them. Then he went back to Jerusalem.

21The king gave this order to all the people: "Celebrate the Passover to the LORD your God, as it is written in this Book of the Covenant." 22Not since the days of the judges who led Israel, nor throughout the days of the kings of Israel and the kings of Judah, had any such Passover been observed. 23But in the eighteenth year of King Josiah, this Passover was celebrated to the LORD in Jerusalem.

24Furthermore, Josiah got rid of the mediums and spiritists, the household gods, the idols and all the other detestable things seen in Judah and Jerusalem. This he did to fulfill the requirements of the law written in the book that Hilkiah the priest had discovered in the temple of the LORD. 25Neither before nor after Josiah was there a king like him who turned to the LORD as he did—with all his heart and with all his soul and with all his strength, in accordance with all the Law of Moses.

26Nevertheless, the LORD did not turn away from the heat of his fierce anger, which burned against Judah because of all that Manasseh had

23:26–28 Too Little Too Late

Josiah became king when he was only eight, and at the age of 26 led a dramatic reform movement. Yet for all this wise king accomplished, the Lord still determined to punish Judah, as verse 26 tells us. Evil had become so deeply ingrained that the best efforts of one good king could not root it out. In fact, as soon as Josiah died, Judah reverted to their previous form.

done to provoke him to anger. 27So the LORD said, "I will remove Judah also from my presence as I removed Israel, and I will reject Jerusalem, the city I chose, and this temple, about which I said, 'There shall my Name be.'*d*"

28As for the other events of Josiah's reign, and all he did, are they not written in the book of the annals of the kings of Judah?

29While Josiah was king, Pharaoh Neco king of Egypt went up to the Euphrates River to help

---

a8 Or *high places*   *b10* Or *to make his son or daughter pass through*   *c13* Hebrew *Milcom*   *d27* 1 Kings 8:29

the king of Assyria. King Josiah marched out to meet him in battle, but Neco faced him and killed him at Megiddo. 30Josiah's servants brought his body in a chariot from Megiddo to Jerusalem and buried him in his own tomb. And the people of the land took Jehoahaz son of Josiah and anointed him and made him king in place of his father.

Jehoahaz King of Judah

31Jehoahaz was twenty-three years old when he became king, and he reigned in Jerusalem three months. His mother's name was Hamutal daughter of Jeremiah; she was from Libnah. 32He did evil in the eyes of the LORD, just as his fathers had done. 33Pharaoh Neco put him in chains at Riblah in the land of Hamath[a] so that he might not reign in Jerusalem, and he imposed on Judah a levy of a hundred talents[b] of silver and a talent[c] of gold. 34Pharaoh Neco made Eliakim son of Josiah king in place of his father Josiah and changed Eliakim's name to Jehoiakim. But he took Jehoahaz and carried him off to Egypt, and there he died. 35Jehoiakim paid Pharaoh Neco the silver and gold he demanded. In order to do so, he taxed the land and exacted the silver and gold from the people of the land according to their assessments.

Jehoiakim King of Judah

36Jehoiakim was twenty-five years old when he became king, and he reigned in Jerusalem eleven years. His mother's name was Zebidah daughter of Pedaiah; she was from Rumah. 37And he did evil in the eyes of the LORD, just as his fathers had done.

24 During Jehoiakim's reign, Nebuchadnezzar king of Babylon invaded the land, and Jehoiakim became his vassal for three years. But then he changed his mind and rebelled against

24:1 Jeremiah's Influence

The last two chapters, which closely parallel material in Jeremiah 52, reveal the influence of that prophet on the book of Kings. Some scholars have concluded that he wrote this historical record.

Nebuchadnezzar. 2The LORD sent Babylonian,[d] Aramean, Moabite and Ammonite raiders against him. He sent them to destroy Judah, in accordance with the word of the LORD proclaimed by his servants the prophets. 3Surely these things happened to Judah according to the LORD's command, in order to remove them from

his presence because of the sins of Manasseh and all he had done, 4including the shedding of innocent blood. For he had filled Jerusalem with innocent blood, and the LORD was not willing to forgive.

5As for the other events of Jehoiakim's reign, and all he did, are they not written in the book of the annals of the kings of Judah? 6Jehoiakim rested with his fathers. And Jehoiachin his son succeeded him as king.

7The king of Egypt did not march out from his own country again, because the king of Babylon had taken all his territory, from the Wadi of Egypt to the Euphrates River.

Jehoiachin King of Judah

8Jehoiachin was eighteen years old when he became king, and he reigned in Jerusalem three months. His mother's name was Nehushta daughter of Elnathan; she was from Jerusalem. 9He did evil in the eyes of the LORD, just as his father had done.

10At that time the officers of Nebuchadnezzar king of Babylon advanced on Jerusalem and laid siege to it, 11and Nebuchadnezzar himself came up to the city while his officers were besieging it. 12Jehoiachin king of Judah, his mother, his attendants, his nobles and his officials all surrendered to him.

In the eighth year of the reign of the king of Babylon, he took Jehoiachin prisoner. 13As the LORD had declared, Nebuchadnezzar removed all the treasures from the temple of the LORD and from the royal palace, and took away all the gold articles that Solomon king of Israel had made for the temple of the LORD. 14He carried into exile all Jerusalem: all the officers and fighting men, and all the craftsmen and artisans—a total of ten thousand. Only the poorest people of the land were left.

15Nebuchadnezzar took Jehoiachin captive to Babylon. He also took from Jerusalem to Babylon the king's mother, his wives, his officials and the leading men of the land. 16The king of Babylon also deported to Babylon the entire force of seven thousand fighting men, strong and fit for war, and a thousand craftsmen and artisans. 17He made Mattaniah, Jehoiachin's uncle, king in his place and changed his name to Zedekiah.

Zedekiah King of Judah

18Zedekiah was twenty-one years old when he became king, and he reigned in Jerusalem eleven years. His mother's name was Hamutal daughter of Jeremiah; she was from Libnah. 19He did evil in the eyes of the LORD, just as Jehoiakim had done. 20It was because of the LORD's anger that all

---

a33 Hebrew; Septuagint (see also 2 Chron. 36:3) *Neco at Riblah in Hamath removed him*   *b33* That is, about 3 3/4 tons (about 3.4 metric tons)   *c33* That is, about 75 pounds (about 34 kilograms)   *d2* Or *Chaldean*

this happened to Jerusalem and Judah, and in the end he thrust them from his presence.

The Fall of Jerusalem

Now Zedekiah rebelled against the king of Babylon.

25 So in the ninth year of Zedekiah's reign, on the tenth day of the tenth month, Nebuchadnezzar king of Babylon marched against Jerusalem with his whole army. He encamped outside the city and built siege works all around it. ²The city was kept under siege until the eleventh year of King Zedekiah. ³By the ninth day of the ⌊fourth⌋ᵃ month the famine in the city had become so severe that there was no food for the people to eat. ⁴Then the city wall was broken through, and the whole army fled at night through the gate between the two walls near the king's garden, though the Babyloniansᵇ were surrounding the city. They fled toward the Arabah,ᶜ ⁵but the Babylonianᵈ army pursued the king and overtook him in the plains of Jericho. All his soldiers were separated from him and scattered, ⁶and he was captured. He was taken to the king of Babylon at Riblah, where sentence was pronounced on him. ⁷They killed the sons of Zedekiah before his eyes. Then they put out his eyes, bound him with bronze shackles and took him to Babylon.

⁸On the seventh day of the fifth month, in the nineteenth year of Nebuchadnezzar king of Babylon, Nebuzaradan commander of the imperial guard, an official of the king of Babylon, came to Jerusalem. ⁹He set fire to the temple of the LORD, the royal palace and all the houses of Jerusalem. Every important building he burned down. ¹⁰The whole Babylonian army, under the commander of the imperial guard, broke down the walls around Jerusalem. ¹¹Nebuzaradan the commander of the guard carried into exile the people who remained in the city, along with the rest of the populace and those who had gone over to the king of Babylon. ¹²But the commander left behind some of the poorest people of the land to work the vineyards and fields.

¹³The Babylonians broke up the bronze pillars, the movable stands and the bronze Sea that were at the temple of the LORD and they carried the bronze to Babylon. ¹⁴They also took away the pots, shovels, wick trimmers, dishes and all the bronze articles used in the temple service. ¹⁵The commander of the imperial guard took away the censers and sprinkling bowls—all that were made of pure gold or silver.

¹⁶The bronze from the two pillars, the Sea and the movable stands, which Solomon had made for the temple of the LORD, was more than could be weighed. ¹⁷Each pillar was twenty-seven feetᵉ high. The bronze capital on top of one pillar was four and a half feetᶠ high and was decorated with a network and pomegranates of bronze all around. The other pillar, with its network, was similar.

¹⁸The commander of the guard took as prisoners Seraiah the chief priest, Zephaniah the priest next in rank and the three doorkeepers.

ᵃ3 See Jer. 52:6.　ᵇ4 Or *Chaldeans*; also in verses 13, 25 and 26　ᶜ4 Or *the Jordan Valley*　ᵈ5 Or *Chaldean*; also in verses 10 and 24　ᵉ17 Hebrew *eighteen cubits* (about 8.1 meters)　ᶠ17 Hebrew *three cubits* (about 1.3 meters)

ZEDEKIAH *The Bitter End*

FOR A VERY LONG TIME the kingdom of Judah had been sliding downhill. Good kings like Hezekiah and Josiah managed to stop the decline temporarily, but as soon as they passed from the scene, immorality and idolatry surged back. Prophets warned again and again of God's judgment, but few heeded them.

Fittingly, Judah endured its bitter end under the weak leadership of Zedekiah, a puppet king put on the throne by Judah's captor, the Babylonian King Nebuchadnezzar. Zedekiah personified all that was wrong with Judah. He took an oath of loyalty to Babylon, then spent his eleven-year reign cheating on it.

The great prophet Jeremiah lived during this same time, offering a strong counterpoint to Zedekiah's weakness. Zedekiah could never make up his mind whether to treat Jeremiah as a prophet of truth or as a trouble-making traitor. When Jeremiah warned against Zedekiah's policies, the king had him beaten and imprisoned. At the same time, he kept bringing Jeremiah in for secret consultations, usually ignoring his advice.

Judah paid cruelly for Zedekiah's poor leadership. Responding to his rebellion, the Babylonians put Jerusalem under a two-year siege, then utterly wrecked the city. They treated Zedekiah as a traitor, executing his sons while he watched, then putting out his eyes so that their deaths would be his last visual memory. Judah's final king was led off to Babylon, blind and in chains.

Life Questions: Under pressure, are you confident or indecisive? What do you need to gain confidence?

¹⁹Of those still in the city, he took the officer in charge of the fighting men and five royal advisers. He also took the secretary who was chief officer in charge of conscripting the people of the land and sixty of his men who were found in the city. ²⁰Nebuzaradan the commander took them all and brought them to the king of Babylon at Riblah. ²¹There at Riblah, in the land of Hamath, the king had them executed.

So Judah went into captivity, away from her land.

²²Nebuchadnezzar king of Babylon appointed Gedaliah son of Ahikam, the son of Shaphan, to be over the people he had left behind in Judah.

25:22 A Kingdom Disappears

Judah's final rebellion against mighty Babylon failed, resulting in an 18-month siege and the destruction of Jerusalem. Survivors were taken away in what became known as the "Babylonian captivity," a tragic moment in Jewish history. God spelled out the reasons for this disaster in 2 Kings 21:10–16.

²³When all the army officers and their men heard that the king of Babylon had appointed Gedaliah as governor, they came to Gedaliah at Mizpah—

Ishmael son of Nethaniah, Johanan son of Kareah, Seraiah son of Tanhumeth the Netophathite, Jaazaniah the son of the Maacathite, and their men. ²⁴Gedaliah took an oath to reassure them and their men. "Do not be afraid of the Babylonian officials," he said. "Settle down in the land and serve the king of Babylon, and it will go well with you."

²⁵In the seventh month, however, Ishmael son of Nethaniah, the son of Elishama, who was of royal blood, came with ten men and assassinated Gedaliah and also the men of Judah and the Babylonians who were with him at Mizpah. ²⁶At this, all the people from the least to the greatest, together with the army officers, fled to Egypt for fear of the Babylonians.

Jehoiachin Released

²⁷In the thirty-seventh year of the exile of Jehoiachin king of Judah, in the year Evil-Merodach[a] became king of Babylon, he released Jehoiachin from prison on the twenty-seventh day of the twelfth month. ²⁸He spoke kindly to him and gave him a seat of honor higher than those of the other kings who were with him in Babylon. ²⁹So Jehoiachin put aside his prison clothes and for the rest of his life ate regularly at the king's table. ³⁰Day by day the king gave Jehoiachin a regular allowance as long as he lived.

ª 27 Also called *Amel-Marduk*

1 CHRONICLES

A Family Record
These facts reminded Israelites of their place in God's plan

> "And who is like your people Israel—the one nation on earth whose God went out to redeem a people for himself?" 17:21

IN PIONEER DAYS, MANY AMERICAN families prized a huge black family Bible. Often the only book in the house, it served for more than reading. It was also the family memory bank. Every important event—a marriage, a birth, a death—was recorded on its flyleaves. The Bible was passed down from generation to generation, and through it, a family kept track of its past.

The book of 1 Chronicles is something like that—a record of Israel's family history, and particularly of David, Israel's greatest king. In fact, at first glance, 1 Chronicles looks like a rehash of David's life as told in 2 Samuel and 1 Kings. Some of the most dramatic episodes in David's life—his clash with Goliath, his sin with Bathsheba—don't make it into this account. But David's organization of the temple is told in great detail, and long lists and genealogies fill over half the book.

Because of that, few people read 1 Chronicles. Most of us are more interested in personalities than in institutions and genealogies.

David's Lasting Impact

First Chronicles, however, is far more interested in David's lasting accomplishments than in his ups and downs as an individual. The nation he led was more than a collection of inspired individuals. It was founded on God's unshakable promises to the children of Abraham. He had promised to be with them. He had promised to provide leadership. He had promised to make them a blessing to the world. These promises took shape in enduring institutions—the temple and the monarchy, most notably.

Why a List of Names?

The first nine chapters of 1 Chronicles trace the genealogy of Israel back to Adam. The author brings together more family records than you'll find anywhere else in the Bible. These records helped the Israelites remember their position as members in God's chosen family. God had given them unique ways to follow and worship him. First Chronicles reminded the Israelites—as it reminds us—of how different their family was meant to be.

How to Read 1 Chronicles

Few will enjoy reading 1 Chronicles's many lists and genealogies straight through. You should approach them more like a puzzle. Don't get lost in the hundreds of names. Instead, try to understand how the different parts of 1 Chronicles fit together. For each section ask, "Why was this included? What did it mean to the original audience—to the Israelites who had returned from exile in Babylon? How did it encourage them as they made a new beginning?"

First Chronicles divides cleanly into two parts. The first nine chapters are mainly lists of names. In these, the Israelites read their family tree and discovered their heritage. Chapters 10 to 29 tell David's story, focusing on the legacy he left behind for future generations—especially the temple. David, a founding father of Israel, transformed the nation in a way that lasted hundreds of years.

PEOPLE YOU'LL MEET IN 1 CHRONICLES

JOAB, ABISHAI AND ASAHEL *(p. 443)*

3-TRACK READING PLAN

For an explanation and complete listing of the 3-track reading plan, turn to page 7.

TRACK 1: *Two-Week Courses on the Bible*
See page 7 for information on these courses.

TRACK 2: *An Overview of 1 Chronicles in 1 Day*
☐ Day 1. Read the Introduction to 1 Chronicles and chapter 17, which describes God's promise to David and David's prayerful response.

Now turn to page 9 for your next Track 2 reading project.

TRACK 3: *All of 1 Chronicles in 17 Days*
You should only skim chapters 1–9 and 23–27, which contain lists and genealogies. After you have skimmed and read 1 Chronicles, turn to pages 10–14 for your next Track 3 reading project.

☐1–9 ☐10 ☐11 ☐12 ☐13 ☐14 ☐15 ☐16
☐17 ☐18 ☐19 ☐20 ☐21 ☐22 ☐23–27 ☐28
☐29

Historical Records From Adam to Abraham

To Noah's Sons

1 Adam, Seth, Enosh, ²Kenan, Mahalalel, Jared, ³Enoch, Methuselah, Lamech, Noah.

⁴The sons of Noah:ᵃ
Shem, Ham and Japheth.

The Japhethites

⁵The sonsᵇ of Japheth:
Gomer, Magog, Madai, Javan, Tubal, Meshech and Tiras.
⁶The sons of Gomer:
Ashkenaz, Riphathᶜ and Togarmah.
⁷The sons of Javan:
Elishah, Tarshish, the Kittim and the Rodanim.

The Hamites

⁸The sons of Ham:
Cush, Mizraim,ᵈ Put and Canaan.
⁹The sons of Cush:
Seba, Havilah, Sabta, Raamah and Sabteca.
The sons of Raamah:
Sheba and Dedan.

¹⁰Cush was the fatherᵉ of
Nimrod, who grew to be a mighty warrior on earth.
¹¹Mizraim was the father of
the Ludites, Anamites, Lehabites, Naphtuhites, ¹²Pathrusites, Casluhites (from whom the Philistines came) and Caphtorites.
¹³Canaan was the father of
Sidon his firstborn,ᶠ and of the Hittites, ¹⁴Jebusites, Amorites, Girgashites, ¹⁵Hivites, Arkites, Sinites, ¹⁶Arvadites, Zemarites and Hamathites.

The Semites

¹⁷The sons of Shem:
Elam, Asshur, Arphaxad, Lud and Aram.
The sons of Aramᵍ:
Uz, Hul, Gether and Meshech.
¹⁸Arphaxad was the father of Shelah, and Shelah the father of Eber.
¹⁹Two sons were born to Eber:
One was named Peleg,ʰ because in his time the earth was divided; his brother was named Joktan.
²⁰Joktan was the father of

ᵃ4 Septuagint; Hebrew does not have *The sons of Noah:*   ᵇ5 *Sons* may mean *descendants* or *successors* or *nations*; also in verses 6-10, 17 and 20.   ᶜ6 Many Hebrew manuscripts and Vulgate (see also Septuagint and Gen. 10:3); most Hebrew manuscripts *Diphath*   ᵈ8 That is, Egypt; also in verse 11   ᵉ10 *Father* may mean *ancestor* or *predecessor* or *founder*; also in verses 11, 13, 18 and 20.   ᶠ13 Or *of the Sidonians, the foremost*   ᵍ17 One Hebrew manuscript and some Septuagint manuscripts (see also Gen. 10:23); most Hebrew manuscripts do not have this line.   ʰ19 *Peleg* means *division.*

Almodad, Sheleph, Hazarmaveth, Je-rah, ²¹Hadoram, Uzal, Diklah, ²²Obal,^a Abimael, Sheba, ²³Ophir, Havilah and Jobab. All these were sons of Joktan.

²⁴Shem, Arphaxad,^b Shelah,
²⁵Eber, Peleg, Reu,
²⁶Serug, Nahor, Terah
²⁷and Abram (that is, Abraham).

The Family of Abraham

²⁸The sons of Abraham:
Isaac and Ishmael.

1:28 Compressed History

The books of 1 and 2 Chronicles, focusing on the kings of the recent past, do not pretend to give a complete history of the Israelites. But by recording individuals' names all the way back to Adam, the books underscore that God has kept his hand on this line of people from the very beginning. The Gospels complete the list begun here: Matthew traces Jesus' lineage back to Abraham, and Luke traces it back to Adam.

Descendants of Hagar

²⁹These were their descendants:
Nebaioth the firstborn of Ishmael, Ke-dar, Adbeel, Mibsam, ³⁰Mishma, Du-mah, Massa, Hadad, Tema, ³¹Jetur, Na-phish and Kedemah. These were the sons of Ishmael.

Descendants of Keturah

³²The sons born to Keturah, Abraham's concubine:
Zimran, Jokshan, Medan, Midian, Ish-bak and Shuah.
The sons of Jokshan:
Sheba and Dedan.
³³The sons of Midian:
Ephah, Epher, Hanoch, Abida and El-daah.
All these were descendants of Keturah.

Descendants of Sarah

³⁴Abraham was the father of Isaac.
The sons of Isaac:
Esau and Israel.

Esau's Sons

³⁵The sons of Esau:
Eliphaz, Reuel, Jeush, Jalam and Korah.
³⁶The sons of Eliphaz:
Teman, Omar, Zepho,^c Gatam and Kenaz;
by Timna: Amalek.^d
³⁷The sons of Reuel:
Nahath, Zerah, Shammah and Mizzah.

The People of Seir in Edom

³⁸The sons of Seir:
Lotan, Shobal, Zibeon, Anah, Dishon, Ezer and Dishan.
³⁹The sons of Lotan:
Hori and Homam. Timna was Lotan's sister.
⁴⁰The sons of Shobal:
Alvan,^e Manahath, Ebal, Shepho and Onam.
The sons of Zibeon:
Aiah and Anah.
⁴¹The son of Anah:
Dishon.
The sons of Dishon:
Hemdan,^f Eshban, Ithran and Keran.
⁴²The sons of Ezer:
Bilhan, Zaavan and Akan.^g
The sons of Dishan^h:
Uz and Aran.

The Rulers of Edom

⁴³These were the kings who reigned in Edom before any Israelite king reignedⁱ:
Bela son of Beor, whose city was named Dinhabah.
⁴⁴When Bela died, Jobab son of Zerah from Bozrah succeeded him as king.
⁴⁵When Jobab died, Husham from the land of the Temanites succeeded him as king.
⁴⁶When Husham died, Hadad son of Bedad, who defeated Midian in the country of Moab, succeeded him as king. His city was named Avith.
⁴⁷When Hadad died, Samlah from Masre-kah succeeded him as king.
⁴⁸When Samlah died, Shaul from Rehoboth on the river^j succeeded him as king.
⁴⁹When Shaul died, Baal-Hanan son of Ac-bor succeeded him as king.
⁵⁰When Baal-Hanan died, Hadad succeeded

^a22 Some Hebrew manuscripts and Syriac (see also Gen. 10:28); most Hebrew manuscripts *Ebal*   ^b24 Hebrew; some Septuagint manuscripts *Arphaxad, Cainan* (see also note at Gen. 11:10)   ^c36 Many Hebrew manuscripts, some Septuagint manuscripts and Syriac (see also Gen. 36:11); most Hebrew manuscripts *Zephi*   ^d36 Some Septuagint manuscripts (see also Gen. 36:12); Hebrew *Gatam, Kenaz, Timna and Amalek*   ^e40 Many Hebrew manuscripts and some Septuagint manuscripts (see also Gen. 36:23); most Hebrew manuscripts *Alian*   ^f41 Many Hebrew manuscripts and some Septuagint manuscripts (see also Gen. 36:26); most Hebrew manuscripts *Hamran*   ^g42 Many Hebrew and Septuagint manuscripts (see also Gen. 36:27); most Hebrew manuscripts *Zaavan, Jaakan*   ^h42 Hebrew *Dishon*, a variant of *Dishan*   ⁱ43 Or *before an Israelite king reigned over them*   ^j48 Possibly the Euphrates

him as king. His city was named Pau,[a] and his wife's name was Mehetabel daughter of Matred, the daughter of Me-Zahab. [51]Hadad also died.

The chiefs of Edom were:
Timna, Alvah, Jetheth, [52]Oholibamah, Elah, Pinon, [53]Kenaz, Teman, Mibzar, [54]Magdiel and Iram. These were the chiefs of Edom.

Israel's Sons

2 These were the sons of Israel:
Reuben, Simeon, Levi, Judah, Issachar, Zebulun, [2]Dan, Joseph, Benjamin, Naphtali, Gad and Asher.

Judah

To Hezron's Sons

[3]The sons of Judah:
Er, Onan and Shelah. These three were born to him by a Canaanite woman, the daughter of Shua. Er, Judah's firstborn, was wicked in the LORD's sight; so the LORD put him to death. [4]Tamar, Judah's daughter-in-law, bore him Perez and Zerah. Judah had five sons in all.

[5]The sons of Perez:
Hezron and Hamul.
[6]The sons of Zerah:
Zimri, Ethan, Heman, Calcol and Darda[b]—five in all.
[7]The son of Carmi:
Achar,[c] who brought trouble on Israel by violating the ban on taking devoted things.[d]
[8]The son of Ethan:
Azariah.
[9]The sons born to Hezron were:
Jerahmeel, Ram and Caleb.[e]

From Ram Son of Hezron

[10]Ram was the father of
Amminadab, and Amminadab the father of Nahshon, the leader of the people of Judah. [11]Nahshon was the father of Salmon,[f] Salmon the father of Boaz, [12]Boaz the father of Obed and Obed the father of Jesse.
[13]Jesse was the father of
Eliab his firstborn; the second son was Abinadab, the third Shimea, [14]the fourth Nethanel, the fifth Raddai, [15]the

sixth Ozem and the seventh David. [16]Their sisters were Zeruiah and Abigail. Zeruiah's three sons were Abishai, Joab and Asahel. [17]Abigail was the mother of Amasa, whose father was Jether the Ishmaelite.

Caleb Son of Hezron

[18]Caleb son of Hezron had children by his wife Azubah (and by Jerioth). These were her sons: Jesher, Shobab and Ardon. [19]When Azubah died, Caleb married Ephrath, who bore him Hur. [20]Hur was the father of Uri, and Uri the father of Bezalel.

[21]Later, Hezron lay with the daughter of Makir the father of Gilead (he had married her when he was sixty years old), and she bore him Segub. [22]Segub was the father of Jair, who controlled twenty-three towns in Gilead. [23](But Geshur and Aram captured Havvoth Jair,[g] as well as Kenath with its surrounding settlements—sixty towns.) All these were descendants of Makir the father of Gilead.

[24]After Hezron died in Caleb Ephrathah, Abijah the wife of Hezron bore him Ashhur the father[h] of Tekoa.

Jerahmeel Son of Hezron

[25]The sons of Jerahmeel the firstborn of Hezron:
Ram his firstborn, Bunah, Oren, Ozem and[i] Ahijah. [26]Jerahmeel had another wife, whose name was Atarah; she was the mother of Onam.
[27]The sons of Ram the firstborn of Jerahmeel:
Maaz, Jamin and Eker.
[28]The sons of Onam:
Shammai and Jada.
The sons of Shammai:
Nadab and Abishur.
[29]Abishur's wife was named Abihail, who bore him Ahban and Molid.
[30]The sons of Nadab:
Seled and Appaim. Seled died without children.
[31]The son of Appaim:
Ishi, who was the father of Sheshan. Sheshan was the father of Ahlai.
[32]The sons of Jada, Shammai's brother:

---

[a]50 Many Hebrew manuscripts, some Septuagint manuscripts, Vulgate and Syriac (see also Gen. 36:39); most Hebrew manuscripts *Pai*   [b]6 Many Hebrew manuscripts, some Septuagint manuscripts and Syriac (see also 1 Kings 4:31); most Hebrew manuscripts *Dara*   [c]7 *Achar* means *trouble; Achar* is called *Achan* in Joshua.   [d]7 The Hebrew term refers to the irrevocable giving over of things or persons to the LORD, often by totally destroying them.   [e]9 Hebrew *Kelubai,* a variant of *Caleb*   [f]11 Septuagint (see also Ruth 4:21); Hebrew *Salma*   [g]23 Or *captured the settlements of Jair*   [h]24 *Father* may mean *civic leader* or *military leader*; also in verses 42, 45, 49-52 and possibly elsewhere.   [i]25 Or *Oren and Ozem, by*

Jether and Jonathan. Jether died without children.

³³The sons of Jonathan:

Peleth and Zaza.

These were the descendants of Jerahmeel.

³⁴Sheshan had no sons—only daughters.

He had an Egyptian servant named Jarha. ³⁵Sheshan gave his daughter in marriage to his servant Jarha, and she bore him Attai.

³⁶Attai was the father of Nathan,

Nathan the father of Zabad,

³⁷Zabad the father of Ephlal,

Ephlal the father of Obed,

³⁸Obed the father of Jehu,

Jehu the father of Azariah,

³⁹Azariah the father of Helez,

Helez the father of Eleasah,

⁴⁰Eleasah the father of Sismai,

Sismai the father of Shallum,

⁴¹Shallum the father of Jekamiah,

and Jekamiah the father of Elishama.

The Clans of Caleb

⁴²The sons of Caleb the brother of Jerahmeel:

Mesha his firstborn, who was the father of Ziph, and his son Mareshah,[a] who was the father of Hebron.

⁴³The sons of Hebron:

Korah, Tappuah, Rekem and Shema. ⁴⁴Shema was the father of Raham, and Raham the father of Jorkeam. Rekem was the father of Shammai. ⁴⁵The son of Shammai was Maon, and Maon was the father of Beth Zur.

⁴⁶Caleb's concubine Ephah was the mother of Haran, Moza and Gazez. Haran was the father of Gazez.

⁴⁷The sons of Jahdai:

Regem, Jotham, Geshan, Pelet, Ephah and Shaaph.

⁴⁸Caleb's concubine Maacah was the mother of Sheber and Tirhanah. ⁴⁹She also gave birth to Shaaph the father of Madmannah and to Sheva the father of Macbenah and Gibea. Caleb's daughter was Acsah. ⁵⁰These were the descendants of Caleb.

The sons of Hur the firstborn of Ephrathah:

Shobal the father of Kiriath Jearim, ⁵¹Salma the father of Bethlehem, and Hareph the father of Beth Gader.

⁵²The descendants of Shobal the father of Kiriath Jearim were:

Haroeh, half the Manahathites, ⁵³and the clans of Kiriath Jearim: the Ithrites, Puthites, Shumathites and Mishraites. From these descended the Zorathites and Eshtaolites.

⁵⁴The descendants of Salma:

Bethlehem, the Netophathites, Atroth Beth Joab, half the Manahathites, the Zorites, ⁵⁵and the clans of scribes[b] who lived at Jabez: the Tirathites, Shimeathites and Sucathites. These are the Kenites who came from Hammath, the father of the house of Recab.[c]

The Sons of David

3 These were the sons of David born to him in Hebron:

The firstborn was Amnon the son of Ahinoam of Jezreel;

the second, Daniel the son of Abigail of Carmel;

²the third, Absalom the son of Maacah daughter of Talmai king of Geshur;

the fourth, Adonijah the son of Haggith;

³the fifth, Shephatiah the son of Abital; and the sixth, Ithream, by his wife Eglah.

⁴These six were born to David in Hebron, where he reigned seven years and six months.

David reigned in Jerusalem thirty-three years, ⁵and these were the children born to him there:

Shammua,[d] Shobab, Nathan and Solomon. These four were by Bathsheba[e]

3:5 Why the Cleanup?

Names like Bathsheba, Absalom, and Tamar all bring to mind unsavory scenes from David's life (see 2 Samuel 11–18). The author certainly would have known about these stories, but chose to omit them. Writing to dispirited refugees, he wanted to inspire them with a model of what the nation could become, not remind them of how it had failed in the past.

daughter of Ammiel. ⁶There were also Ibhar, Elishua,[f] Eliphelet, ⁷Nogah, Nepheg, Japhia, ⁸Elishama, Eliada and Eliphelet—nine in all. ⁹All these were the sons of David, besides his sons by

---

[a]42 The meaning of the Hebrew for this phrase is uncertain.   [b]55 Or of the Sopherites   [c]55 Or father of Beth Recab   [d]5 Hebrew Shimea, a variant of Shammua and 2 Samuel 11:3); most Hebrew manuscripts Bathshua 1 Chron. 14:5); most Hebrew manuscripts Elishama   [e]5 One Hebrew manuscript and Vulgate (see also Septuagint   [f]6 Two Hebrew manuscripts (see also 2 Samuel 5:15 and

his concubines. And Tamar was their sister.

The Kings of Judah

¹⁰Solomon's son was Rehoboam,
Abijah his son,
Asa his son,
Jehoshaphat his son,
¹¹Jehoram*ᵃ* his son,
Ahaziah his son,
Joash his son,
¹²Amaziah his son,
Azariah his son,
Jotham his son,
¹³Ahaz his son,
Hezekiah his son,
Manasseh his son,
¹⁴Amon his son,
Josiah his son.
¹⁵The sons of Josiah:
Johanan the firstborn,
Jehoiakim the second son,
Zedekiah the third,
Shallum the fourth.
¹⁶The successors of Jehoiakim:
Jehoiachin*ᵇ* his son,
and Zedekiah.

The Royal Line After the Exile

¹⁷The descendants of Jehoiachin the captive:
Shealtiel his son, ¹⁸Malkiram, Pedaiah, Shenazzar, Jekamiah, Hoshama and Nedabiah.

3:17 The Royal Line

Chronicles was written to people who no longer had a king. However, as this section reminds us, they still knew the royal line. God's promise to provide them with kingly leadership forever still held. They could expect a son of David to someday become king again. This is one reason why the New Testament takes the trouble to show that Jesus was descended from David. He was that King.

¹⁹The sons of Pedaiah:
Zerubbabel and Shimei.
The sons of Zerubbabel:
Meshullam and Hananiah.
Shelomith was their sister.
²⁰There were also five others:
Hashubah, Ohel, Berekiah, Hasadiah and Jushab-Hesed.
²¹The descendants of Hananiah:

Pelatiah and Jeshaiah, and the sons of Rephaiah, of Arnan, of Obadiah and of Shecaniah.
²²The descendants of Shecaniah:
Shemaiah and his sons:
Hattush, Igal, Bariah, Neariah and Shaphat—six in all.
²³The sons of Neariah:
Elioenai, Hizkiah and Azrikam—three in all.
²⁴The sons of Elioenai:
Hodaviah, Eliashib, Pelaiah, Akkub, Johanan, Delaiah and Anani—seven in all.

Other Clans of Judah

4 The descendants of Judah:
Perez, Hezron, Carmi, Hur and Shobal.
²Reaiah son of Shobal was the father of Jahath, and Jahath the father of Ahumai and Lahad. These were the clans of the Zorathites.
³These were the sons*ᶜ* of Etam:
Jezreel, Ishma and Idbash. Their sister was named Hazzelelponi. ⁴Penuel was the father of Gedor, and Ezer the father of Hushah.

These were the descendants of Hur, the firstborn of Ephrathah and father*ᵈ* of Bethlehem.

⁵Ashhur the father of Tekoa had two wives, Helah and Naarah.
⁶Naarah bore him Ahuzzam, Hepher, Temeni and Haahashtari. These were the descendants of Naarah.
⁷The sons of Helah:
Zereth, Zohar, Ethnan, ⁸and Koz, who was the father of Anub and Hazzobebah and of the clans of Aharhel son of Harum.

⁹Jabez was more honorable than his brothers. His mother had named him Jabez,*ᵉ* saying, "I gave birth to him in pain." ¹⁰Jabez cried out to the God of Israel, "Oh, that you would bless me and enlarge my territory! Let your hand be with me, and keep me from harm so that I will be free from pain." And God granted his request.

¹¹Kelub, Shuhah's brother, was the father of Mehir, who was the father of Eshton. ¹²Eshton was the father of Beth Rapha, Paseah and Tehinnah the father of Ir Nahash.*ᶠ* These were the men of Recah.

¹³The sons of Kenaz:

ᵃ11 Hebrew *Joram,* a variant of *Jehoram*   *ᵇ16* Hebrew *Jeconiah,* a variant of *Jehoiachin;* also in verse 17   *ᶜ3* Some Septuagint manuscripts (see also Vulgate); Hebrew *father*   *ᵈ4* *Father* may mean *civic leader* or *military leader;* also in verses 12, 14, 17, 18 and possibly elsewhere.   *ᵉ9* *Jabez* sounds like the Hebrew for *pain.*   *ᶠ12* Or *of the city of Nahash*

Othniel and Seraiah.

The sons of Othniel:

Hathath and Meonothai.[a] [14]Meonothai was the father of Ophrah.

Seraiah was the father of Joab,

the father of Ge Harashim.[b] It was called this because its people were craftsmen.

[15]The sons of Caleb son of Jephunneh:

Iru, Elah and Naam.

The son of Elah:

Kenaz.

[16]The sons of Jehallelel:

Ziph, Ziphah, Tiria and Asarel.

[17]The sons of Ezrah:

Jether, Mered, Epher and Jalon. One of Mered's wives gave birth to Miriam, Shammai and Ishbah the father of Eshtemoa. [18](His Judean wife gave birth to Jered the father of Gedor, Heber the father of Soco, and Jekuthiel the father of Zanoah.) These were the children of Pharaoh's daughter Bithiah, whom Mered had married.

[19]The sons of Hodiah's wife, the sister of Naham:

the father of Keilah the Garmite, and Eshtemoa the Maacathite.

[20]The sons of Shimon:

Amnon, Rinnah, Ben-Hanan and Tilon.

The descendants of Ishi:

Zoheth and Ben-Zoheth.

[21]The sons of Shelah son of Judah:

Er the father of Lecah, Laadah the father of Mareshah and the clans of the linen workers at Beth Ashbea, [22]Jokim, the men of Cozeba, and Joash and Saraph, who ruled in Moab and Jashubi Lehem. (These records are from ancient times.) [23]They were the potters who lived at Netaim and Gederah; they stayed there and worked for the king.

Simeon

[24]The descendants of Simeon:

Nemuel, Jamin, Jarib, Zerah and Shaul;

[25]Shallum was Shaul's son, Mibsam his son and Mishma his son.

[26]The descendants of Mishma:

Hammuel his son, Zaccur his son and Shimei his son.

[27]Shimei had sixteen sons and six daughters, but his brothers did not have many children; so their entire clan did not become as numerous as the people of Judah. [28]They lived in Beersheba,

Moladah, Hazar Shual, [29]Bilhah, Ezem, Tolad, [30]Bethuel, Hormah, Ziklag, [31]Beth Marcaboth, Hazar Susim, Beth Biri and Shaaraim. These were their towns until the reign of David. [32]Their surrounding villages were Etam, Ain, Rimmon, Token and Ashan—five towns— [33]and all the villages around these towns as far as Baalath.[c] These were their settlements. And they kept a genealogical record.

[34]Meshobab, Jamlech, Joshah son of Amaziah, [35]Joel, Jehu son of Joshibiah, the son of Seraiah, the son of Asiel, [36]also Elioenai, Jaakobah, Jeshohaiah, Asaiah, Adiel, Jesimiel, Benaiah, [37]and Ziza son of Shiphi, the son of Allon, the son of Jedaiah, the son of Shimri, the son of Shemaiah.

[38]The men listed above by name were leaders of their clans. Their families increased greatly, [39]and they went to the outskirts of Gedor to the east of the valley in search of pasture for their flocks. [40]They found rich, good pasture, and the land was spacious, peaceful and quiet. Some Hamites had lived there formerly.

[41]The men whose names were listed came in the days of Hezekiah king of Judah. They attacked the Hamites in their dwellings and also the Meunites who were there and completely destroyed[d] them, as is evident to this day. Then they settled in their place, because there was pasture for their flocks. [42]And five hundred of these Simeonites, led by Pelatiah, Neariah, Rephaiah and Uzziel, the sons of Ishi, invaded the hill country of Seir. [43]They killed the remaining Amalekites who had escaped, and they have lived there to this day.

Reuben

5 The sons of Reuben the firstborn of Israel (he was the firstborn, but when he defiled his father's marriage bed, his rights as firstborn were given to the sons of Joseph son of Israel; so he could not be listed in the genealogical record in accordance with his birthright, [2]and though Judah was the strongest of his brothers and a ruler came from him, the rights of the firstborn belonged to Joseph)— [3]the sons of Reuben the firstborn of Israel:

Hanoch, Pallu, Hezron and Carmi.

[4]The descendants of Joel:

Shemaiah his son, Gog his son,

Shimei his son, [5]Micah his son,

Reaiah his son, Baal his son,

[6]and Beerah his son, whom Tiglath-Pileser[e] king of Assyria took into exile.

Beerah was a leader of the Reubenites.

---

[a]13 Some Septuagint manuscripts and Vulgate; Hebrew does not have *and Meonothai.*   [b]14 *Ge Harashim* means *valley of craftsmen.*   [c]33 Some Septuagint manuscripts (see also Joshua 19:8); Hebrew *Baal*   [d]41 The Hebrew term refers to the irrevocable giving over of things or persons to the LORD, often by totally destroying them.   [e]6 Hebrew *Tilgath-Pilneser,* a variant of *Tiglath-Pileser;* also in verse 26

7Their relatives by clans, listed according to their genealogical records:

Jeiel the chief, Zechariah, 8and Bela son of Azaz, the son of Shema, the son of Joel. They settled in the area from Aroer to Nebo and Baal Meon. 9To the east they occupied the land up to the edge of the desert that extends to the Euphrates River, because their livestock had increased in Gilead.

10During Saul's reign they waged war against the Hagrites, who were defeated at their hands; they occupied the dwellings of the Hagrites throughout the entire region east of Gilead.

Gad

11The Gadites lived next to them in Bashan, as far as Salecah:

12Joel was the chief, Shapham the second, then Janai and Shaphat, in Bashan.

13Their relatives, by families, were:

Michael, Meshullam, Sheba, Jorai, Jacan, Zia and Eber—seven in all.

14These were the sons of Abihail son of Huri, the son of Jaroah, the son of Gilead, the son of Michael, the son of Jeshishai, the son of Jahdo, the son of Buz.

15Ahi son of Abdiel, the son of Guni, was head of their family.

16The Gadites lived in Gilead, in Bashan and its outlying villages, and on all the pasturelands of Sharon as far as they extended.

17All these were entered in the genealogical records during the reigns of Jotham king of Judah and Jeroboam king of Israel.

18The Reubenites, the Gadites and the half-tribe of Manasseh had 44,760 men ready for military service—able-bodied men who could handle shield and sword, who could use a bow, and who were trained for battle. 19They waged war against the Hagrites, Jetur, Naphish and Nodab. 20They were helped in fighting them, and God handed the Hagrites and all their allies over to them, because they cried out to him during the battle. He answered their prayers, because they trusted in him. 21They seized the livestock of the Hagrites—fifty thousand camels, two hundred fifty thousand sheep and two thousand donkeys. They also took one hundred thousand people captive, 22and many others fell slain, because the battle was God's. And they occupied the land until the exile.

The Half-Tribe of Manasseh

23The people of the half-tribe of Manasseh were numerous; they settled in the land from Bashan to Baal Hermon, that is, to Senir (Mount Hermon).

24These were the heads of their families: Epher, Ishi, Eliel, Azriel, Jeremiah, Hodaviah and Jahdiel. They were brave warriors, famous men, and heads of their families. 25But they were unfaithful to the God of their fathers and prostituted themselves to the gods of the peoples of the land, whom God had destroyed before them. 26So the God of Israel stirred up the spirit of Pul king of Assyria (that is, Tiglath-Pileser king of Assyria), who took the Reubenites, the Gadites and the half-tribe of Manasseh into exile. He took them to Halah, Habor, Hara and the river of Gozan, where they are to this day.

Levi

6 The sons of Levi:
Gershon, Kohath and Merari.

6:1 Key People

First Chronicles 1–9 form the Bible's most complete genealogical record. These chapters emphasize the two tribes most crucial to God's plans: Judahites, the tribe that David and all the later kings of Judah came from, and Levites, who had responsibility to lead Israel in worship.

It's possible that the Levite priest named Ezra wrote the two books of Chronicles, for they date from his time period. Jewish refugees had returned from exile in Babylon, and leaders like Ezra were trying to inspire the exiles to reestablish their proud nation and rebuild the temple.

2The sons of Kohath:
Amram, Izhar, Hebron and Uzziel.
3The children of Amram:
Aaron, Moses and Miriam.
The sons of Aaron:
Nadab, Abihu, Eleazar and Ithamar.
4Eleazar was the father of Phinehas,
Phinehas the father of Abishua,
5Abishua the father of Bukki,
Bukki the father of Uzzi,
6Uzzi the father of Zerahiah,
Zerahiah the father of Meraioth,
7Meraioth the father of Amariah,
Amariah the father of Ahitub,
8Ahitub the father of Zadok,
Zadok the father of Ahimaaz,
9Ahimaaz the father of Azariah,
Azariah the father of Johanan,
10Johanan the father of Azariah (it was he who served as priest in the temple Solomon built in Jerusalem),
11Azariah the father of Amariah,

Amariah the father of Ahitub,
[12]Ahitub the father of Zadok,
Zadok the father of Shallum,
[13]Shallum the father of Hilkiah,
Hilkiah the father of Azariah,
[14]Azariah the father of Seraiah,
and Seraiah the father of Jehozadak.
[15]Jehozadak was deported when the LORD sent Judah and Jerusalem into exile by the hand of Nebuchadnezzar.

[16]The sons of Levi:
Gershon,[a] Kohath and Merari.
[17]These are the names of the sons of Gershon:
Libni and Shimei.
[18]The sons of Kohath:
Amram, Izhar, Hebron and Uzziel.
[19]The sons of Merari:
Mahli and Mushi.
These are the clans of the Levites listed according to their fathers:
[20]Of Gershon:
Libni his son, Jehath his son,
Zimmah his son, [21]Joah his son,
Iddo his son, Zerah his son
and Jeatherai his son.
[22]The descendants of Kohath:
Amminadab his son, Korah his son,
Assir his son, [23]Elkanah his son,
Ebiasaph his son, Assir his son,
[24]Tahath his son, Uriel his son,
Uzziah his son and Shaul his son.
[25]The descendants of Elkanah:
Amasai, Ahimoth,
[26]Elkanah his son,[b] Zophai his son,
Nahath his son, [27]Eliab his son,
Jeroham his son, Elkanah his son
and Samuel his son.[c]
[28]The sons of Samuel:
Joel[d] the firstborn
and Abijah the second son.
[29]The descendants of Merari:
Mahli, Libni his son,
Shimei his son, Uzzah his son,
[30]Shimea his son, Haggiah his son
and Asaiah his son.

The Temple Musicians

[31]These are the men David put in charge of the music in the house of the LORD after the ark came to rest there. [32]They ministered with music before the tabernacle, the Tent of Meeting, until Solomon built the temple of the LORD in Jerusalem. They performed their duties according to the regulations laid down for them.

[33]Here are the men who served, together with their sons:
From the Kohathites:
Heman, the musician,

6:31 And Now, the Choir . . .

The author of 1 Chronicles had a special fondness for musicians. Several times he mentions David's role in establishing guilds of musicians for temple worship, and here he even records their ancestry.

the son of Joel, the son of Samuel,
[34]the son of Elkanah, the son of Jeroham,
the son of Eliel, the son of Toah,
[35]the son of Zuph, the son of Elkanah,
the son of Mahath, the son of Amasai,
[36]the son of Elkanah, the son of Joel,
the son of Azariah, the son of Zephaniah,
[37]the son of Tahath, the son of Assir,
the son of Ebiasaph, the son of Korah,
[38]the son of Izhar, the son of Kohath,
the son of Levi, the son of Israel;
[39]and Heman's associate Asaph, who served at his right hand:
Asaph son of Berekiah, the son of Shimea,
[40]the son of Michael, the son of Baaseiah,[e]
the son of Malkijah, [41]the son of Ethni,
the son of Zerah, the son of Adaiah,
[42]the son of Ethan, the son of Zimmah,
the son of Shimei, [43]the son of Jahath,
the son of Gershon, the son of Levi;
[44]and from their associates, the Merarites, at his left hand:
Ethan son of Kishi, the son of Abdi,
the son of Malluch, [45]the son of Hashabiah,
the son of Amaziah, the son of Hilkiah,
[46]the son of Amzi, the son of Bani,
the son of Shemer, [47]the son of Mahli,
the son of Mushi, the son of Merari,
the son of Levi.

[48]Their fellow Levites were assigned to all the other duties of the tabernacle, the house of God. [49]But Aaron and his descendants were the ones who presented offerings on the altar of burnt offering and on the altar of incense in connection with all that was done in the Most Holy Place, making atonement for Israel, in accordance with

---

[a]16 Hebrew *Gershom*, a variant of *Gershon*; also in verses 17, 20, 43, 62 and 71   [b]26 Some Hebrew manuscripts, Septuagint and Syriac; most Hebrew manuscripts *Ahimoth* 26*and Elkanah. The sons of Elkanah:*   [c]27 Some Septuagint manuscripts (see also 1 Samuel 1:19,20 and 1 Chron. 6:33,34); Hebrew does not have *and Samuel his son.*   [d]28 Some Septuagint manuscripts and Syriac (see also 1 Samuel 8:2 and 1 Chron. 6:33); Hebrew does not have *Joel.*   [e]40 Most Hebrew manuscripts; some Hebrew manuscripts, one Septuagint manuscript and Syriac *Maaseiah*

all that Moses the servant of God had commanded.

⁵⁰These were the descendants of Aaron:
Eleazar his son, Phinehas his son,
Abishua his son, ⁵¹Bukki his son,
Uzzi his son, Zerahiah his son,
⁵²Meraioth his son, Amariah his son,
Ahitub his son, ⁵³Zadok his son
and Ahimaaz his son.

⁵⁴These were the locations of their settlements allotted as their territory (they were assigned to the descendants of Aaron who were from the Kohathite clan, because the first lot was for them):

⁵⁵They were given Hebron in Judah with its surrounding pasturelands. ⁵⁶But the fields and villages around the city were given to Caleb son of Jephunneh.

⁵⁷So the descendants of Aaron were given Hebron (a city of refuge), and Libnah,ᵃ Jattir, Eshtemoa, ⁵⁸Hilen, Debir, ⁵⁹Ashan, Juttahᵇ and Beth Shemesh, together with their pasturelands. ⁶⁰And from the tribe of Benjamin they were given Gibeon,ᶜ Geba, Alemeth and Anathoth, together with their pasturelands.

These towns, which were distributed among the Kohathite clans, were thirteen in all.

⁶¹The rest of Kohath's descendants were allotted ten towns from the clans of half the tribe of Manasseh.

⁶²The descendants of Gershon, clan by clan, were allotted thirteen towns from the tribes of Issachar, Asher and Naphtali, and from the part of the tribe of Manasseh that is in Bashan.

⁶³The descendants of Merari, clan by clan, were allotted twelve towns from the tribes of Reuben, Gad and Zebulun.

⁶⁴So the Israelites gave the Levites these towns and their pasturelands. ⁶⁵From the tribes of Judah, Simeon and Benjamin they allotted the previously named towns.

⁶⁶Some of the Kohathite clans were given as their territory towns from the tribe of Ephraim.

⁶⁷In the hill country of Ephraim they were given Shechem (a city of refuge), and Gezer,ᵈ ⁶⁸Jokmeam, Beth Horon, ⁶⁹Aijalon and Gath Rimmon, together with their pasturelands.

⁷⁰And from half the tribe of Manasseh the Israelites gave Aner and Bileam, together with their pasturelands, to the rest of the Kohathite clans.

⁷¹The Gershonites received the following:
From the clan of the half-tribe of Manasseh
they received Golan in Bashan and also Ashtaroth, together with their pasturelands;
⁷²from the tribe of Issachar
they received Kedesh, Daberath, ⁷³Ramoth and Anem, together with their pasturelands;
⁷⁴from the tribe of Asher
they received Mashal, Abdon, ⁷⁵Hukok and Rehob, together with their pasturelands;
⁷⁶and from the tribe of Naphtali
they received Kedesh in Galilee, Hammon and Kiriathaim, together with their pasturelands.

⁷⁷The Merarites (the rest of the Levites) received the following:
From the tribe of Zebulun
they received Jokneam, Kartah,ᵉ Rimmono and Tabor, together with their pasturelands;
⁷⁸from the tribe of Reuben across the Jordan east of Jericho
they received Bezer in the desert, Jahzah, ⁷⁹Kedemoth and Mephaath, together with their pasturelands;
⁸⁰and from the tribe of Gad
they received Ramoth in Gilead, Mahanaim, ⁸¹Heshbon and Jazer, together with their pasturelands.

Issachar

7 The sons of Issachar:
Tola, Puah, Jashub and Shimron—four in all.

²The sons of Tola:
Uzzi, Rephaiah, Jeriel, Jahmai, Ibsam and Samuel—heads of their families. During the reign of David, the descendants of Tola listed as fighting men in their genealogy numbered 22,600.

³The son of Uzzi:
Izrahiah.

The sons of Izrahiah:
Michael, Obadiah, Joel and Isshiah. All five of them were chiefs. ⁴According to their family genealogy, they had 36,000 men ready for battle, for they had many wives and children.

⁵The relatives who were fighting men belonging to all the clans of Issachar, as

---

ᵃ57 See Joshua 21:13; Hebrew *given the cities of refuge: Hebron, Libnah.*   ᵇ59 Syriac (see also Septuagint and Joshua 21:16); Hebrew does not have *Juttah.*   ᶜ60 See Joshua 21:17; Hebrew does not have *Gibeon.*   ᵈ67 See Joshua 21:21; Hebrew *given the cities of refuge: Shechem, Gezer.*   ᵉ77 See Septuagint and Joshua 21:34; Hebrew does not have *Jokneam, Kartah.*

listed in their genealogy, were 87,000 in all.

Benjamin

[6]Three sons of Benjamin:

Bela, Beker and Jediael.

[7]The sons of Bela:

Ezbon, Uzzi, Uzziel, Jerimoth and Iri, heads of families—five in all. Their genealogical record listed 22,034 fighting men.

[8]The sons of Beker:

Zemirah, Joash, Eliezer, Elioenai, Omri, Jeremoth, Abijah, Anathoth and Alemeth. All these were the sons of Beker. [9]Their genealogical record listed the heads of families and 20,200 fighting men.

[10]The son of Jediael:

Bilhan.

The sons of Bilhan:

Jeush, Benjamin, Ehud, Kenaanah, Zethan, Tarshish and Ahishahar. [11]All these sons of Jediael were heads of families. There were 17,200 fighting men ready to go out to war.

[12]The Shuppites and Huppites were the descendants of Ir, and the Hushites the descendants of Aher.

Naphtali

[13]The sons of Naphtali:

Jahziel, Guni, Jezer and Shillem[a]—the descendants of Bilhah.

Manasseh

[14]The descendants of Manasseh:

Asriel was his descendant through his Aramean concubine. She gave birth to Makir the father of Gilead. [15]Makir took a

---

wife from among the Huppites and Shuppites. His sister's name was Maacah.

Another descendant was named Zelophehad, who had only daughters.

[16]Makir's wife Maacah gave birth to a son and named him Peresh. His brother was named Sheresh, and his sons were Ulam and Rakem.

[17]The son of Ulam:

Bedan.

These were the sons of Gilead son of Makir, the son of Manasseh. [18]His sister Hammoleketh gave birth to Ishhod, Abiezer and Mahlah.

[19]The sons of Shemida were:

Ahian, Shechem, Likhi and Aniam.

Ephraim

[20]The descendants of Ephraim:

Shuthelah, Bered his son,

Tahath his son, Eleadah his son,

Tahath his son, [21]Zabad his son

and Shuthelah his son.

Ezer and Elead were killed by the native-born men of Gath, when they went down to seize their livestock. [22]Their father Ephraim mourned for them many days, and his relatives came to comfort him. [23]Then he lay with his wife again, and she became pregnant and gave birth to a son. He named him Beriah,[b] because there had been misfortune in his family. [24]His daughter was Sheerah, who built Lower and Upper Beth Horon as well as Uzzen Sheerah.

[25]Rephah was his son, Resheph his son,[c]

Telah his son, Tahan his son,

[26]Ladan his son, Ammihud his son,

Elishama his son, [27]Nun his son

and Joshua his son.

[28]Their lands and settlements included Bethel and its surrounding villages, Naaran to the east, Gezer and its villages to the west, and Shechem and its villages all the way to Ayyah and its villages. [29]Along the borders of Manasseh were Beth Shan, Taanach, Megiddo and Dor, together with their villages. The descendants of Joseph son of Israel lived in these towns.

Asher

[30]The sons of Asher:

Imnah, Ishvah, Ishvi and Beriah. Their sister was Serah.

[31]The sons of Beriah:

Heber and Malkiel, who was the father of Birzaith.

[32]Heber was the father of Japhlet, Shomer and Hotham and of their sister Shua.

---

[a]13 Some Hebrew and Septuagint manuscripts (see also Gen. 46:24 and Num. 26:49); most Hebrew manuscripts *Shallum*   [b]23 *Beriah* sounds like the Hebrew for *misfortune.*   [c]25 Some Septuagint manuscripts; Hebrew does not have *his son.*

33The sons of Japhlet:
  Pasach, Bimhal and Ashvath.
  These were Japhlet's sons.
34The sons of Shomer:
  Ahi, Rohgah,ᵃ Hubbah and Aram.
35The sons of his brother Helem:
  Zophah, Imna, Shelesh and Amal.
36The sons of Zophah:
  Suah, Harnepher, Shual, Beri, Imrah,
  37Bezer, Hod, Shamma, Shilshah, Ith-
  ranᵇ and Beera.
38The sons of Jether:
  Jephunneh, Pispah and Ara.
39The sons of Ulla:
  Arah, Hanniel and Rizia.

40All these were descendants of Asher—heads of families, choice men, brave warriors and outstanding leaders. The number of men ready for battle, as listed in their genealogy, was 26,000.

The Genealogy of Saul the Benjamite

8 Benjamin was the father of Bela his firstborn, Ashbel the second son, Aharah the third,

8:1 Dynasty Rejected

Saul, Israel's first king, came from the tribe of Benjamin. Normally a royal dynasty would have followed him, descending from that same tribe. After Saul's dismal performance, however, God turned instead to the tribe of Judah and selected David, who became one of the ancestors of Jesus the Messiah.

2Nohah the fourth and Rapha the fifth.
3The sons of Bela were:
  Addar, Gera, Abihud,ᶜ 4Abishua, Naaman, Ahoah, 5Gera, Shephuphan and
  Huram.
6These were the descendants of Ehud, who were heads of families of those living in Geba and were deported to Manahath:
7Naaman, Ahijah, and Gera, who deported them and who was the father of Uzza and Ahihud.
8Sons were born to Shaharaim in Moab after he had divorced his wives Hushim and Baara. 9By his wife Hodesh he had Jobab, Zibia, Mesha, Malcam, 10Jeuz, Sakia and Mirmah. These were his sons, heads of families. 11By Hushim he had Abitub and Elpaal.
12The sons of Elpaal:
  Eber, Misham, Shemed (who built Ono

and Lod with its surrounding villages), 13and Beriah and Shema, who were heads of families of those living in Aijalon and who drove out the inhabitants of Gath.

14Ahio, Shashak, Jeremoth, 15Zebadiah, Arad, Eder, 16Michael, Ishpah and Joha were the sons of Beriah.

17Zebadiah, Meshullam, Hizki, Heber, 18Ishmerai, Izliah and Jobab were the sons of Elpaal.

19Jakim, Zicri, Zabdi, 20Elienai, Zillethai, Eliel, 21Adaiah, Beraiah and Shimrath were the sons of Shimei.

22Ishpan, Eber, Eliel, 23Abdon, Zicri, Hanan, 24Hananiah, Elam, Anthothijah, 25Iphdeiah and Penuel were the sons of Shashak.

26Shamsherai, Shehariah, Athaliah, 27Jaareshiah, Elijah and Zicri were the sons of Jeroham.

28All these were heads of families, chiefs as listed in their genealogy, and they lived in Jerusalem.

29Jeielᵈ the fatherᵉ of Gibeon lived in Gibeon.
  His wife's name was Maacah, 30and his firstborn son was Abdon, followed by Zur, Kish, Baal, Ner,ᶠ Nadab, 31Gedor, Ahio, Zeker 32and Mikloth, who was the father of Shimeah. They too lived near their relatives in Jerusalem.
33Ner was the father of Kish, Kish the father of Saul, and Saul the father of Jonathan, Malki-Shua, Abinadab and Esh-Baal.ᵍ
34The son of Jonathan:
  Merib-Baal,ʰ who was the father of Micah.
35The sons of Micah:
  Pithon, Melech, Tarea and Ahaz.
  36Ahaz was the father of Jehoaddah, Jehoaddah was the father of Alemeth, Azmaveth and Zimri, and Zimri was the father of Moza. 37Moza was the father of Binea; Raphah was his son, Eleasah his son and Azel his son.
38Azel had six sons, and these were their names:
  Azrikam, Bokeru, Ishmael, Sheariah, Obadiah and Hanan. All these were the sons of Azel.
39The sons of his brother Eshek:
  Ulam his firstborn, Jeush the second son and Eliphelet the third. 40The sons of Ulam were brave warriors who could

ᵃ34 Or of his brother Shomer: Rohgah   ᵇ37 Possibly a variant of Jether   ᶜ3 Or Gera the father of Ehud
ᵈ29 Some Septuagint manuscripts (see also 1 Chron. 9:35); Hebrew does not have Jeiel.   ᵉ29 Father may mean civic
leader or military leader.   ᶠ30 Some Septuagint manuscripts (see also 1 Chron. 9:36); Hebrew does not have Ner.
ᵍ33 Also known as Ish-Bosheth   ʰ34 Also known as Mephibosheth

handle the bow. They had many sons and grandsons—150 in all.

All these were the descendants of Benjamin.

9 All Israel was listed in the genealogies recorded in the book of the kings of Israel.

9:1 The Source of Genealogies

The author of 1 Chronicles acknowledges that he relied on older documents for his information. In 1 and 2 Chronicles (originally one book) approximately 14 sources are named. During the Israelites' exile in Babylon, historical records had been lost and family information forgotten (see Ezra 2:59). First Chronicles condenses the most important of the genealogical information. It was meant to help the Israelites reestablish their identity as God's people.

The People in Jerusalem

The people of Judah were taken captive to Babylon because of their unfaithfulness. ²Now the first to resettle on their own property in their own towns were some Israelites, priests, Levites and temple servants.

³Those from Judah, from Benjamin, and from Ephraim and Manasseh who lived in Jerusalem were:

⁴Uthai son of Ammihud, the son of Omri, the son of Imri, the son of Bani, a descendant of Perez son of Judah.

⁵Of the Shilonites:

Asaiah the firstborn and his sons.

⁶Of the Zerahites:

Jeuel.

The people from Judah numbered 690.

⁷Of the Benjamites:

Sallu son of Meshullam, the son of Hodaviah, the son of Hassenuah;

⁸Ibneiah son of Jeroham; Elah son of Uzzi, the son of Micri; and Meshullam son of Shephatiah, the son of Reuel, the son of Ibnijah.

⁹The people from Benjamin, as listed in their genealogy, numbered 956. All these men were heads of their families.

¹⁰Of the priests:

Jedaiah; Jehoiarib; Jakin;

¹¹Azariah son of Hilkiah, the son of Meshullam, the son of Zadok, the son of Meraioth, the son of Ahitub, the official in charge of the house of God;

¹²Adaiah son of Jeroham, the son of Pashhur, the son of Malkijah; and Maasai son of Adiel, the son of Jahzerah, the son of Meshullam, the son of Meshillemith, the son of Immer.

¹³The priests, who were heads of families, numbered 1,760. They were able men, responsible for ministering in the house of God.

¹⁴Of the Levites:

Shemaiah son of Hasshub, the son of Azrikam, the son of Hashabiah, a Merarite; ¹⁵Bakbakkar, Heresh, Galal and Mattaniah son of Mica, the son of Zicri, the son of Asaph; ¹⁶Obadiah son of Shemaiah, the son of Galal, the son of Jeduthun; and Berekiah son of Asa, the son of Elkanah, who lived in the villages of the Netophathites.

¹⁷The gatekeepers:

Shallum, Akkub, Talmon, Ahiman and their brothers, Shallum their chief ¹⁸being stationed at the King's Gate on the east, up to the present time. These were the gatekeepers belonging to the camp of the Levites. ¹⁹Shallum son of Kore, the son of Ebiasaph, the son of Korah, and his fellow gatekeepers from his family (the Korahites) were responsible for guarding the thresholds of the Tent[a] just as their fathers had been responsible for guarding the entrance to the dwelling of the LORD. ²⁰In earlier times Phinehas son of Eleazar was in charge of the gatekeepers, and the LORD was with him. ²¹Zechariah son of Meshelemiah was the gatekeeper at the entrance to the Tent of Meeting.

²²Altogether, those chosen to be gatekeepers at the thresholds numbered 212. They were registered by genealogy in their villages. The gatekeepers had been assigned to their positions of trust by David and Samuel the seer. ²³They and their descendants were in charge of guarding the gates of the house of the LORD—the house called the Tent. ²⁴The gatekeepers were on the four sides: east, west, north and south. ²⁵Their broth-

9:2–34 After the Exile

While most of 1 Chronicles deals with the time of David, this short section (2–34) jumps ahead 500 years to the time when a small portion of Israel had returned from exile. (See the books of Ezra, Nehemiah, Haggai, and Zechariah for more information about these returned exiles.)

---

a19 That is, the temple; also in verses 21 and 23

ers in their villages had to come from time to time and share their duties for seven-day periods. ²⁶But the four principal gatekeepers, who were Levites, were entrusted with the responsibility for the rooms and treasuries in the house of God. ²⁷They would spend the night stationed around the house of God, because they had to guard it; and they had charge of the key for opening it each morning.

²⁸Some of them were in charge of the articles used in the temple service; they counted them when they were brought in and when they were taken out. ²⁹Others were assigned to take care of the furnishings and all the other articles of the sanctuary, as well as the flour and wine, and the oil, incense and spices. ³⁰But some of the priests took care of mixing the spices. ³¹A Levite named Mattithiah, the firstborn son of Shallum the Korahite, was entrusted with the responsibility for baking the offering bread. ³²Some of their Kohathite brothers were in charge of preparing for every Sabbath the bread set out on the table.

³³Those who were musicians, heads of Levite families, stayed in the rooms of the temple and were exempt from other duties because they were responsible for the work day and night.

³⁴All these were heads of Levite families, chiefs as listed in their genealogy, and they lived in Jerusalem.

The Genealogy of Saul

³⁵Jeiel the father*ᵃ* of Gibeon lived in Gibeon.

His wife's name was Maacah, ³⁶and his firstborn son was Abdon, followed by Zur, Kish, Baal, Ner, Nadab, ³⁷Gedor, Ahio, Zechariah and Mikloth. ³⁸Mikloth was the father of Shimeam. They too lived near their relatives in Jerusalem.

³⁹Ner was the father of Kish, Kish the father of Saul, and Saul the father of Jonathan, Malki-Shua, Abinadab and Esh-Baal.*ᵇ*

⁴⁰The son of Jonathan:

Merib-Baal,*ᶜ* who was the father of Micah.

⁴¹The sons of Micah:

Pithon, Melech, Tahrea and Ahaz.*ᵈ*

⁴²Ahaz was the father of Jadah, Jadah*ᵉ* was the father of Alemeth, Azmaveth and Zimri, and Zimri was the father of Moza. ⁴³Moza was the father of Binea; Rephaiah was his son, Eleasah his son and Azel his son.

⁴⁴Azel had six sons, and these were their names:

Azrikam, Bokeru, Ishmael, Sheariah,

Obadiah and Hanan. These were the sons of Azel.

Saul Takes His Life

10 Now the Philistines fought against Israel; the Israelites fled before them, and many fell slain on Mount Gilboa. ²The Philistines pressed hard after Saul and his sons, and they killed his sons Jonathan, Abinadab and Malki-Shua. ³The fighting grew fierce around Saul, and when the archers overtook him, they wounded him.

⁴Saul said to his armor-bearer, "Draw your sword and run me through, or these uncircumcised fellows will come and abuse me."

But his armor-bearer was terrified and would not do it; so Saul took his own sword and fell on it. ⁵When the armor-bearer saw that Saul was dead, he too fell on his sword and died. ⁶So Saul and his three sons died, and all his house died together.

⁷When all the Israelites in the valley saw that the army had fled and that Saul and his sons had died, they abandoned their towns and fled. And the Philistines came and occupied them.

⁸The next day, when the Philistines came to strip the dead, they found Saul and his sons fallen on Mount Gilboa. ⁹They stripped him and took his head and his armor, and sent messengers throughout the land of the Philistines to proclaim the news among their idols and their people. ¹⁰They put his armor in the temple of their gods and hung up his head in the temple of Dagon.

¹¹When all the inhabitants of Jabesh Gilead heard of everything the Philistines had done to Saul, ¹²all their valiant men went and took the bodies of Saul and his sons and brought them to Jabesh. Then they buried their bones under the great tree in Jabesh, and they fasted seven days.

¹³Saul died because he was unfaithful to the LORD; he did not keep the word of the LORD and even consulted a medium for guidance, ¹⁴and did

10:13 Moral of the Story

First Chronicles covers much the same history as 1 Samuel, but with a distinctive approach. First Samuel gives more details about Saul's failures, while 1 Chronicles primarily concerns itself with drawing moral lessons from them. For example, 1 Samuel 28 tells the background to Saul's consulting a medium; 1 Chronicles merely alludes to it (most original readers would know the story well) and connects that act of disobedience to Saul's death.

ᵃ35 Father may mean *civic leader* or *military leader.*　*ᵇ39* Also known as *Ish-Bosheth*　*ᶜ40* Also known as *Mephibosheth*　*ᵈ41* Vulgate and Syriac (see also Septuagint and 1 Chron. 8:35); Hebrew does not have *and Ahaz.*　*ᵉ42* Some Hebrew manuscripts and Septuagint (see also 1 Chron. 8:36); most Hebrew manuscripts *Jarah, Jarah*

not inquire of the LORD. So the LORD put him to death and turned the kingdom over to David son of Jesse.

David Becomes King Over Israel

11 All Israel came together to David at Hebron and said, "We are your own flesh and blood. [2]In the past, even while Saul was king, you were the one who led Israel on their military campaigns. And the LORD your God said to you, 'You will shepherd my people Israel, and you will become their ruler.'"

[3]When all the elders of Israel had come to King David at Hebron, he made a compact with them at Hebron before the LORD, and they anointed David king over Israel, as the LORD had promised through Samuel.

David Conquers Jerusalem

[4]David and all the Israelites marched to Jerusalem (that is, Jebus). The Jebusites who lived there [5]said to David, "You will not get in here." Nevertheless, David captured the fortress of Zion, the City of David.

[6]David had said, "Whoever leads the attack on the Jebusites will become commander-in-chief." Joab son of Zeruiah went up first, and so he received the command.

[7]David then took up residence in the fortress, and so it was called the City of David. [8]He built up the city around it, from the supporting terraces[a] to the surrounding wall, while Joab restored the rest of the city. [9]And David became more and more powerful, because the LORD Almighty was with him.

David's Mighty Men

[10]These were the chiefs of David's mighty men—they, together with all Israel, gave his kingship strong support to extend it over the whole land, as the LORD had promised— [11]this is the list of David's mighty men:

Jashobeam,[b] a Hacmonite, was chief of the officers[c]; he raised his spear against three hundred men, whom he killed in one encounter.

[12]Next to him was Eleazar son of Dodai the Ahohite, one of the three mighty men. [13]He was with David at Pas Dammim when the Philistines

---

[a]8 Or the Millo also 2 Samuel 23:8) [b]11 Possibly a variant of Jashob-Baal [c]11 Or Thirty; some Septuagint manuscripts Three (see

---

JOAB, ABISHAI AND ASAHEL *Bloody Brothers*

WAR IS ALWAYS BRUTAL, AND hand-to-hand combat especially so. Allow one instant of pity as you look into your enemy's eyes, and he may stick a knife in your gut. A good warrior must be ruthless, and by that criterion Joab, Abishai and Asahel excelled. They lived violent lives, and at least two of the three died violent deaths.

Relatives of David, the brothers joined up with the future king while he was an outlaw hiding from King Saul. In a famous incident from those days, Abishai and David crept into the enemy camp at night and caught Saul fast asleep. Abishai wanted to kill Saul then and there, but David stopped him. That incident set a pattern: Several times Abishai impulsively sought to slaughter someone, only to be restrained by David.

The three brothers held to a strict code of revenge. When Asahel died in battle, the remaining brothers plotted revenge. The opportunity came some time later, when Saul's chief of the army called a truce to talk peace. Joab pretended to greet Abner and then, in an unguarded moment, stabbed him in the stomach.

David disapproved of the brothers' violent tactics, but he needed such strong and loyal soldiers. Joab proved his mettle by leading David's armies in a rout of powerful enemies. From that point on, Joab's brilliant soldiering became indispensable. David even trusted Joab with his sins: The two collaborated to murder Bathsheba's husband after David's adulterous affair. Significantly, David repented but Joab showed no interest in God or morality. He cared only about winning at war.

The bloody brothers had a fierce loyalty to David, and yet his inability to control them cost him dearly. When David's son Absalom led a rebellion, Joab and Abishai crushed the revolt. Joab caught the rebel son and dispatched him in cold blood, against David's explicit orders to let Absalom live.

Later, when David turned over the army to another general (perhaps because of the disobeyed order), Joab tricked and murdered his new rival. David never seemed capable of controlling Joab.

There is nothing pretty about these brothers and their careers in war. And as their commander-in-chief, David was inevitably drawn into their way of life. That may explain why God said to David, "You are not to build a house for my Name, because you are a warrior and have shed blood" (1 Chronicles 28:3).

Life Questions: Have you ever felt yourself being drawn in to another person's way of life, even when you disapprove? What can you do to escape?

gathered there for battle. At a place where there was a field full of barley, the troops fled from the Philistines. [14]But they took their stand in the middle of the field. They defended it and struck the Philistines down, and the LORD brought about a great victory.

[15]Three of the thirty chiefs came down to David to the rock at the cave of Adullam, while a band of Philistines was encamped in the Valley of Rephaim. [16]At that time David was in the stronghold, and the Philistine garrison was at Bethlehem. [17]David longed for water and said, "Oh, that someone would get me a drink of water from the well near the gate of Bethlehem!" [18]So the Three broke through the Philistine lines, drew water from the well near the gate of Bethlehem and carried it back to David. But he refused to drink it; instead, he poured it out before the LORD. [19]"God forbid that I should do this!" he said. "Should I drink the blood of these men who went at the risk of their lives?" Because they risked their lives to bring it back, David would not drink it.

Such were the exploits of the three mighty men.

[20]Abishai the brother of Joab was chief of the Three. He raised his spear against three hundred men, whom he killed, and so he became as famous as the Three. [21]He was doubly honored above the Three and became their commander, even though he was not included among them.

[22]Benaiah son of Jehoiada was a valiant fighter from Kabzeel, who performed great exploits. He struck down two of Moab's best men. He also went down into a pit on a snowy day and killed a lion. [23]And he struck down an Egyptian who was seven and a half feet[a] tall. Although the Egyptian had a spear like a weaver's rod in his hand, Benaiah went against him with a club. He snatched the spear from the Egyptian's hand and killed him with his own spear. [24]Such were the exploits of Benaiah son of Jehoiada; he too was as famous as the three mighty men. [25]He was held in greater honor than any of the Thirty, but he was not included among the Three. And David put him in charge of his bodyguard.

[26]The mighty men were:

Asahel the brother of Joab,
Elhanan son of Dodo from Bethlehem,
[27]Shammoth the Harorite,
Helez the Pelonite,
[28]Ira son of Ikkesh from Tekoa,
Abiezer from Anathoth,
[29]Sibbecai the Hushathite,
Ilai the Ahohite,
[30]Maharai the Netophathite,
Heled son of Baanah the Netophathite,
[31]Ithai son of Ribai from Gibeah in Benjamin,
Benaiah the Pirathonite,
[32]Hurai from the ravines of Gaash,
Abiel the Arbathite,
[33]Azmaveth the Baharumite,
Eliahba the Shaalbonite,
[34]the sons of Hashem the Gizonite,
Jonathan son of Shagee the Hararite,
[35]Ahiam son of Sacar the Hararite,
Eliphal son of Ur,
[36]Hepher the Mekerathite,
Ahijah the Pelonite,
[37]Hezro the Carmelite,
Naarai son of Ezbai,
[38]Joel the brother of Nathan,
Mibhar son of Hagri,
[39]Zelek the Ammonite,
Naharai the Berothite, the armor-bearer of Joab son of Zeruiah,
[40]Ira the Ithrite,
Gareb the Ithrite,
[41]Uriah the Hittite,
Zabad son of Ahlai,
[42]Adina son of Shiza the Reubenite, who was chief of the Reubenites, and the thirty with him,
[43]Hanan son of Maacah,
Joshaphat the Mithnite,
[44]Uzzia the Ashterathite,
Shama and Jeiel the sons of Hotham the Aroerite,
[45]Jediael son of Shimri,
his brother Joha the Tizite,
[46]Eliel the Mahavite,
Jeribai and Joshaviah the sons of Elnaam,
Ithmah the Moabite,
[47]Eliel, Obed and Jaasiel the Mezobaite.

Warriors Join David

12 These were the men who came to David at Ziklag, while he was banished from the presence of Saul son of Kish (they were among the warriors who helped him in battle; [2]they were armed with bows and were able to shoot arrows or to sling stones right-handed or left-handed; they were kinsmen of Saul from the tribe of Benjamin):

[3]Ahiezer their chief and Joash the sons of Shemaah the Gibeathite; Jeziel and Pelet the sons of Azmaveth; Beracah, Jehu the Anathothite, [4]and Ishmaiah the Gibeonite, a mighty man among the Thirty, who was a leader of the Thirty; Jeremiah, Jahaziel, Johanan, Jozabad the Gederathite, [5]Eluzai, Jerimoth, Bealiah, Shemariah and Shephatiah the Haruphite; [6]Elkanah, Isshiah, Aza-

a 23 Hebrew five cubits (about 2.3 meters)

rel, Joezer and Jashobeam the Korahites; [7]and Joelah and Zebadiah the sons of Jeroham from Gedor.

[8]Some Gadites defected to David at his stronghold in the desert. They were brave warriors, ready for battle and able to handle the shield and spear. Their faces were the faces of lions, and they were as swift as gazelles in the mountains.

[9]Ezer was the chief,
Obadiah the second in command, Eliab the third,
[10]Mishmannah the fourth, Jeremiah the fifth,
[11]Attai the sixth, Eliel the seventh,
[12]Johanan the eighth, Elzabad the ninth,
[13]Jeremiah the tenth and Macbannai the eleventh.

[14]These Gadites were army commanders; the least was a match for a hundred, and the greatest for a thousand. [15]It was they who crossed the Jordan in the first month when it was overflowing all its banks, and they put to flight everyone living in the valleys, to the east and to the west.

[16]Other Benjamites and some men from Judah also came to David in his stronghold. [17]David went out to meet them and said to them, "If you have come to me in peace, to help me, I am ready to have you unite with me. But if you have come to betray me to my enemies when my hands are free from violence, may the God of our fathers see it and judge you."

[18]Then the Spirit came upon Amasai, chief of the Thirty, and he said:

"We are yours, O David!
We are with you, O son of Jesse!
Success, success to you,
and success to those who help you,
for your God will help you."

So David received them and made them leaders of his raiding bands.

[19]Some of the men of Manasseh defected to David when he went with the Philistines to fight against Saul. (He and his men did not help the Philistines because, after consultation, their rulers sent him away. They said, "It will cost us our heads if he deserts to his master Saul.") [20]When David went to Ziklag, these were the men of Manasseh who defected to him: Adnah, Jozabad, Jediael, Michael, Jozabad, Elihu and Zillethai, leaders of units of a thousand in Manasseh. [21]They helped David against raiding bands, for all of them were brave warriors, and they were commanders in his army. [22]Day after day men came to help David, until he had a great army, like the army of God.[a]

Others Join David at Hebron

[23]These are the numbers of the men armed for battle who came to David at Hebron to turn Saul's kingdom over to him, as the LORD had said:

[24]men of Judah, carrying shield and spear— 6,800 armed for battle;
[25]men of Simeon, warriors ready for battle—7,100;
[26]men of Levi—4,600, [27]including Jehoiada, leader of the family of Aaron, with 3,700 men, [28]and Zadok, a brave young warrior, with 22 officers from his family;
[29]men of Benjamin, Saul's kinsmen—3,000, most of whom had remained loyal to Saul's house until then;
[30]men of Ephraim, brave warriors, famous in their own clans—20,800;
[31]men of half the tribe of Manasseh, designated by name to come and make David king—18,000;
[32]men of Issachar, who understood the times and knew what Israel should do—200 chiefs, with all their relatives under their command;
[33]men of Zebulun, experienced soldiers prepared for battle with every type of weapon, to help David with undivided loyalty—50,000;
[34]men of Naphtali—1,000 officers, together with 37,000 men carrying shields and spears;
[35]men of Dan, ready for battle—28,600;
[36]men of Asher, experienced soldiers prepared for battle—40,000;
[37]and from east of the Jordan, men of Reuben, Gad and the half-tribe of Manasseh, armed with every type of weapon—120,000.

[38]All these were fighting men who volunteered to serve in the ranks. They came to Hebron fully determined to make David king over all Israel. All the rest of the Israelites were also of one mind to make David king. [39]The men spent three days there with David, eating and drinking, for their families had supplied provisions for them. [40]Also,

[a]22 Or *a great and mighty army*

their neighbors from as far away as Issachar, Zebulun and Naphtali came bringing food on donkeys, camels, mules and oxen. There were plentiful supplies of flour, fig cakes, raisin cakes, wine, oil, cattle and sheep, for there was joy in Israel.

Bringing Back the Ark

13 David conferred with each of his officers, the commanders of thousands and commanders of hundreds. ²He then said to the whole assembly of Israel, "If it seems good to you and if it is the will of the LORD our God, let us send word far and wide to the rest of our brothers throughout the territories of Israel, and also to the priests and Levites who are with them in their towns and pasturelands, to come and join us. ³Let us bring the ark of our God back to us, for we did not inquire of*a* it*b* during the reign of Saul." ⁴The whole assembly agreed to do this, because it seemed right to all the people.

⁵So David assembled all the Israelites, from the Shihor River in Egypt to Lebo*c* Hamath, to bring the ark of God from Kiriath Jearim. ⁶David and all the Israelites with him went to Baalah of Judah (Kiriath Jearim) to bring up from there the ark of God the LORD, who is enthroned between the cherubim—the ark that is called by the Name.

⁷They moved the ark of God from Abinadab's house on a new cart, with Uzzah and Ahio guiding it. ⁸David and all the Israelites were celebrating with all their might before God, with songs and with harps, lyres, tambourines, cymbals and trumpets.

⁹When they came to the threshing floor of Kidon, Uzzah reached out his hand to steady the ark, because the oxen stumbled. ¹⁰The LORD's anger burned against Uzzah, and he struck him down because he had put his hand on the ark. So he died there before God.

¹¹Then David was angry because the LORD's wrath had broken out against Uzzah, and to this day that place is called Perez Uzzah.*d*

¹²David was afraid of God that day and asked, "How can I ever bring the ark of God to me?" ¹³He did not take the ark to be with him in the City of David. Instead, he took it aside to the house of Obed-Edom the Gittite. ¹⁴The ark of God remained with the family of Obed-Edom in his house for three months, and the LORD blessed his household and everything he had.

David's House and Family

14 Now Hiram king of Tyre sent messengers to David, along with cedar logs, stonemasons and carpenters to build a palace for him. ²And David knew that the LORD had established him as king over Israel and that his kingdom had

been highly exalted for the sake of his people Israel.

³In Jerusalem David took more wives and became the father of more sons and daughters.

13:9 Why Did Uzzah Die?

People who read of Uzzah's death in 2 Samuel 6:6–7 have often puzzled over why he died for trying to keep God's ark from tipping over. In 1 Chronicles the reason is clearer. David explained (15:13) that the Lord had been angry at them for moving the ark in a way disobedient to God's law.

Numbers 4:14–15 and Exodus 37:5 specify that Levites were to carry the ark with poles—and never touch it, on pain of death. Uzzah and his brother, non-Levites, were carrying it on an oxcart—the same vehicle the Philistines had used (1 Samuel 6:7). When the oxen stumbled and Uzzah stepped in to catch the ark, that was the final straw. Uzzah's death resulted from prolonged (though possibly well-intentioned) disobedience to God's direction. God had told them how to honor the ark, a sign of his presence. Their sloppiness revealed a lack of concern for God's honor.

⁴These are the names of the children born to him there: Shammua, Shobab, Nathan, Solomon, ⁵Ibhar, Elishua, Elpelet, ⁶Nogah, Nepheg, Japhia, ⁷Elishama, Beeliada*e* and Eliphelet.

David Defeats the Philistines

⁸When the Philistines heard that David had been anointed king over all Israel, they went up in full force to search for him, but David heard about it and went out to meet them. ⁹Now the Philistines had come and raided the Valley of Rephaim; ¹⁰so David inquired of God: "Shall I go and attack the Philistines? Will you hand them over to me?"

The LORD answered him, "Go, I will hand them over to you."

¹¹So David and his men went up to Baal Perazim, and there he defeated them. He said, "As waters break out, God has broken out against my enemies by my hand." So that place was called Baal Perazim.*f* ¹²The Philistines had abandoned their gods there, and David gave orders to burn them in the fire.

¹³Once more the Philistines raided the valley; ¹⁴so David inquired of God again, and God answered him, "Do not go straight up, but circle around them and attack them in front of the balsam trees. ¹⁵As soon as you hear the sound of marching in the tops of the balsam trees, move

*a*3 Or *we neglected*   *b*3 Or *him*   *c*5 Or *to the entrance to*   *d*11 *Perez Uzzah* means *outbreak against Uzzah.*
*e*7 A variant of *Eliada*   *f*11 *Baal Perazim* means *the lord who breaks out.*

out to battle, because that will mean God has gone out in front of you to strike the Philistine army." [16]So David did as God commanded him, and they struck down the Philistine army, all the way from Gibeon to Gezer.

[17]So David's fame spread throughout every land, and the LORD made all the nations fear him.

The Ark Brought to Jerusalem

15 After David had constructed buildings for himself in the City of David, he prepared a place for the ark of God and pitched a tent for it. [2]Then David said, "No one but the Levites may carry the ark of God, because the LORD chose them to carry the ark of the LORD and to minister before him forever."

[3]David assembled all Israel in Jerusalem to bring up the ark of the LORD to the place he had

15:3 Red-letter Day

Much of Chronicles summarizes and interprets history that is covered more fully in the books of Samuel. But this chapter contains mostly new material, reflecting a central concern of the author. David's bringing the ark to Jerusalem had been a landmark event, signifying the renewed presence of God in the nation (see also Psalm 132). The Chronicler yearned for a similar spirit of renewal among the people of his own time.

prepared for it. [4]He called together the descendants of Aaron and the Levites:

[5]From the descendants of Kohath,
Uriel the leader and 120 relatives;
[6]from the descendants of Merari,
Asaiah the leader and 220 relatives;
[7]from the descendants of Gershon,[a]
Joel the leader and 130 relatives;
[8]from the descendants of Elizaphan,
Shemaiah the leader and 200 relatives;
[9]from the descendants of Hebron,
Eliel the leader and 80 relatives;
[10]from the descendants of Uzziel,
Amminadab the leader and 112 relatives.

[11]Then David summoned Zadok and Abiathar the priests, and Uriel, Asaiah, Joel, Shemaiah, Eliel and Amminadab the Levites. [12]He said to them, "You are the heads of the Levitical families; you and your fellow Levites are to consecrate yourselves and bring up the ark of the LORD, the God of Israel, to the place I have prepared for it. [13]It was because you, the Levites, did not bring it up the first time that the LORD our God broke out

in anger against us. We did not inquire of him about how to do it in the prescribed way." [14]So the priests and Levites consecrated themselves in order to bring up the ark of the LORD, the God of Israel. [15]And the Levites carried the ark of God with the poles on their shoulders, as Moses had commanded in accordance with the word of the LORD.

[16]David told the leaders of the Levites to appoint their brothers as singers to sing joyful songs, accompanied by musical instruments: lyres, harps and cymbals.

[17]So the Levites appointed Heman son of Joel; from his brothers, Asaph son of Berekiah; and from their brothers the Merarites, Ethan son of Kushaiah; [18]and with them their brothers next in rank: Zechariah,[b] Jaaziel, Shemiramoth, Jehiel, Unni, Eliab, Benaiah, Maaseiah, Mattithiah, Eliphelehu, Mikneiah, Obed-Edom and Jeiel,[c] the gatekeepers.

[19]The musicians Heman, Asaph and Ethan were to sound the bronze cymbals; [20]Zechariah, Aziel, Shemiramoth, Jehiel, Unni, Eliab, Maaseiah and Benaiah were to play the lyres according to *alamoth,*[d] [21]and Mattithiah, Eliphelehu, Mikneiah, Obed-Edom, Jeiel and Azaziah were to play the harps, directing according to *sheminith.*[d] [22]Kenaniah the head Levite was in charge of the singing; that was his responsibility because he was skillful at it.

[23]Berekiah and Elkanah were to be doorkeepers for the ark. [24]Shebaniah, Joshaphat, Nethanel, Amasai, Zechariah, Benaiah and Eliezer the priests were to blow trumpets before the ark of God. Obed-Edom and Jehiah were also to be doorkeepers for the ark.

[25]So David and the elders of Israel and the commanders of units of a thousand went to bring up the ark of the covenant of the LORD from the house of Obed-Edom, with rejoicing. [26]Because God had helped the Levites who were carrying the ark of the covenant of the LORD, seven bulls and seven rams were sacrificed. [27]Now David was clothed in a robe of fine linen, as were all the Levites who were carrying the ark, and as were the singers, and Kenaniah, who was in charge of the singing of the choirs. David also wore a linen ephod. [28]So all Israel brought up the ark of the covenant of the LORD with shouts, with the sounding of rams' horns and trumpets, and of cymbals, and the playing of lyres and harps.

[29]As the ark of the covenant of the LORD was entering the City of David, Michal daughter of Saul watched from a window. And when she saw King David dancing and celebrating, she despised him in her heart.

---

[a]7 Hebrew *Gershom,* a variant of *Gershon*   [b]18 Three Hebrew manuscripts and most Septuagint manuscripts (see also verse 20 and 1 Chron. 16:5); most Hebrew manuscripts *Zechariah son and* or *Zechariah, Ben and*   [c]18 Hebrew; Septuagint (see also verse 21) *Jeiel and Azaziah*   [d]20,21 Probably a musical term

16 They brought the ark of God and set it inside the tent that David had pitched for it, and they presented burnt offerings and fellowship offerings[a] before God. [2]After David had finished sacrificing the burnt offerings and fellowship offerings, he blessed the people in the name of the LORD. [3]Then he gave a loaf of bread, a cake of dates and a cake of raisins to each Israelite man and woman.

[4]He appointed some of the Levites to minister before the ark of the LORD, to make petition, to give thanks, and to praise the LORD, the God of Israel: [5]Asaph was the chief, Zechariah second, then Jeiel, Shemiramoth, Jehiel, Mattithiah, Eliab, Benaiah, Obed-Edom and Jeiel. They were to play the lyres and harps, Asaph was to sound the cymbals, [6]and Benaiah and Jahaziel the priests were to blow the trumpets regularly before the ark of the covenant of God.

David's Psalm of Thanks

[7]That day David first committed to Asaph and his associates this psalm of thanks to the LORD:

[8]Give thanks to the LORD, call on his name;
> make known among the nations what he
> > has done.
[9]Sing to him, sing praise to him;
> tell of all his wonderful acts.
[10]Glory in his holy name;
> let the hearts of those who seek the LORD
> > rejoice.
[11]Look to the LORD and his strength;
> seek his face always.
[12]Remember the wonders he has done,
> his miracles, and the judgments he
> > pronounced,
[13]O descendants of Israel his servant,
> O sons of Jacob, his chosen ones.

[14]He is the LORD our God;
> his judgments are in all the earth.
[15]He remembers[b] his covenant forever,
> the word he commanded, for a thousand
> > generations,
[16]the covenant he made with Abraham,
> the oath he swore to Isaac.
[17]He confirmed it to Jacob as a decree,
> to Israel as an everlasting covenant:
[18]"To you I will give the land of Canaan
> as the portion you will inherit."

[19]When they were but few in number,
> few indeed, and strangers in it,
[20]they[c] wandered from nation to nation,
> from one kingdom to another.
[21]He allowed no man to oppress them;

> for their sake he rebuked kings:
[22]"Do not touch my anointed ones;
> do my prophets no harm."

[23]Sing to the LORD, all the earth;
> proclaim his salvation day after day.
[24]Declare his glory among the nations,
> his marvelous deeds among all peoples.
[25]For great is the LORD and most worthy of
> > praise;
> he is to be feared above all gods.
[26]For all the gods of the nations are idols,
> but the LORD made the heavens.
[27]Splendor and majesty are before him;
> strength and joy in his dwelling place.
[28]Ascribe to the LORD, O families of nations,
> ascribe to the LORD glory and strength,
[29] ascribe to the LORD the glory due his
> > name.
Bring an offering and come before him;
> worship the LORD in the splendor of his[d]
> > holiness.
[30]Tremble before him, all the earth!
> The world is firmly established; it cannot
> > be moved.
[31]Let the heavens rejoice, let the earth be glad;
> let them say among the nations, "The
> > LORD reigns!"
[32]Let the sea resound, and all that is in it;
> let the fields be jubilant, and everything in
> > them!
[33]Then the trees of the forest will sing,
> they will sing for joy before the LORD,
> for he comes to judge the earth.

[34]Give thanks to the LORD, for he is good;
> his love endures forever.
[35]Cry out, "Save us, O God our Savior;
> gather us and deliver us from the nations,
that we may give thanks to your holy name,
that we may glory in your praise."
[36]Praise be to the LORD, the God of Israel,
> from everlasting to everlasting.

16:39 Two Tabernacles

For a number of years, Israel had two tabernacles. David had constructed a new tent for the ark of the covenant when it came to Jerusalem. Yet the old tent, dating from Moses' time, still stood at Gibeon, five miles away. Sacrifices were offered at both locations. When the temple was built under David's son Solomon, worship was centralized at Jerusalem.

---

[a]1 Traditionally *peace offerings*; also in verse 2   [b]15 Some Septuagint manuscripts (see also Psalm 105:8); Hebrew *Remember*   [c]18-20 One Hebrew manuscript, Septuagint and Vulgate (see also Psalm 105:12); most Hebrew manuscripts *inherit, / [19]though you are but few in number, / few indeed, and strangers in it." / [20]They*   [d]29 Or LORD *with the splendor of*

Then all the people said "Amen" and "Praise the LORD."

³⁷David left Asaph and his associates before the ark of the covenant of the LORD to minister there regularly, according to each day's requirements. ³⁸He also left Obed-Edom and his sixty-eight associates to minister with them. Obed-Edom son of Jeduthun, and also Hosah, were gatekeepers.

³⁹David left Zadok the priest and his fellow priests before the tabernacle of the LORD at the high place in Gibeon ⁴⁰to present burnt offerings to the LORD on the altar of burnt offering regularly, morning and evening, in accordance with everything written in the Law of the LORD, which he had given Israel. ⁴¹With them were Heman and Jeduthun and the rest of those chosen and designated by name to give thanks to the LORD, "for his love endures forever." ⁴²Heman and Jeduthun were responsible for the sounding of the trumpets and cymbals and for the playing of the other instruments for sacred song. The sons of Jeduthun were stationed at the gate.

⁴³Then all the people left, each for his own home, and David returned home to bless his family.

God's Promise to David

17 After David was settled in his palace, he said to Nathan the prophet, "Here I am, living in a palace of cedar, while the ark of the covenant of the LORD is under a tent."

²Nathan replied to David, "Whatever you have in mind, do it, for God is with you."

³That night the word of God came to Nathan, saying:

⁴"Go and tell my servant David, 'This is what the LORD says: You are not the one to build me a house to dwell in. ⁵I have not dwelt in a house from the day I brought Israel up out of Egypt to this day. I have

Hope in a Time of Sorrow
A people starting over need to know God's promises

FIRST CHRONICLES WAS WRITTEN FOR Israelites living centuries after David. In those years Israel had gone through tremendous sorrow. None of the kings who followed David had matched him. Israel had deteriorated until God let Babylon capture and destroy Jerusalem, carrying its population into exile.

> "Who am I, O LORD God, and what is my family, that you have brought me this far?" 17:16

After half a century as captives, a small proportion of the Israelites returned to their former home. They had lost, in those beaten-down years, their own sense of identity. They were no longer self-governing. They had no king to follow in David's footsteps. Their relatives were scattered all over the Middle East. Chronicles was written to help them get in touch with what Israel had once been and could become again.

After devoting nine chapters to genealogies, 1 Chronicles tells the life of David. In keeping with its goal of encouragement, Chronicles leaves out stories of David's personal sin and failure. Nor does it tell of David's life before he became king. Instead it concentrates on the accomplishments David left behind for future generations.

The Importance of Worship

David emphasized worship as the foundation of Israel. As soon as he conquered Jerusalem, he brought the ark of the covenant there. He made preparations to build the temple and organized the priests and Levites to serve there. He established large corps of musicians to praise God. In response, God promised that a line of leaders would descend from him (17:10–14).

David's days were the high point of Israelite history: prosperous, secure, and, above all, devoted to God. How could the returned exiles recapture that grandeur? What resources could they use to begin again? First Chronicles emphasizes a legacy they still possessed. They had Jerusalem, and they had a new temple built on the site of the old one. They had the priests and Levites, so essential to proper worship. In short, they had the resources necessary to rise again, to be God's people in God's land.

Most important, they had God. They could find strength in worshiping him, as David always had. God had made them great before; he could make them great again, and provide a new leader in David's line. A sorrowful people could start over on the old foundations—foundations that depended on an unchanging God and his unchanging choice of them.

Life Questions: If you were to suffer great personal and material loss, as the Israelites did, what would you cling to?

moved from one tent site to another, from one dwelling place to another. [6]Wherever I have moved with all the Israelites, did I ever say to any of their leaders[a] whom I commanded to shepherd my people, "Why have you not built me a house of cedar?" '

[7]"Now then, tell my servant David, 'This is what the LORD Almighty says: I took you from the pasture and from following the flock, to be ruler over my people Israel. [8]I have been with you wherever you have gone, and I have cut off all your enemies from before you. Now I will make your name like the names of the greatest men of the earth. [9]And I will provide a place for my people Israel and will plant them so that they can have a home of their own and no longer be disturbed. Wicked people will not oppress them anymore, as they did at the beginning [10]and have done ever since the time I appointed leaders over my people Israel. I will also subdue all your enemies.

" 'I declare to you that the LORD will build a house for you: [11]When your days are over and you go to be with your fathers, I will raise up your offspring to succeed you, one of your own sons, and I will establish his kingdom. [12]He is the one who will build a house for me, and I will establish his throne forever. [13]I will be his father, and he will be my son. I will never take my love away from him, as I took it away from your predecessor. [14]I will set him over my house and my kingdom forever; his throne will be established forever.' "

[15]Nathan reported to David all the words of this entire revelation.

David's Prayer

[16]Then King David went in and sat before the LORD, and he said:

"Who am I, O LORD God, and what is my family, that you have brought me this far? [17]And as if this were not enough in your sight, O God, you have spoken about the future of the house of your servant. You have looked on me as though I were the most exalted of men, O LORD God.

[18]"What more can David say to you for honoring your servant? For you know your servant, [19]O LORD. For the sake of your servant and according to your will, you have done this great thing and made known all these great promises.

[20]"There is no one like you, O LORD, and there is no God but you, as we have heard with our own ears. [21]And who is like your people Israel—the one nation on earth whose God went out to redeem a people for himself, and to make a name for yourself, and to perform great and awesome wonders by driving out nations from before

17:16 Rare Trait

King David possessed in abundance that rarest of qualities in a powerful ruler: humility. Ever mindful of his modest background, he credited God's grace, not his own merit, for his success. David could have taken offense at Nathan's message; after all, God was rejecting his offer to build a temple. Instead, David accepted the news with meekness and thanksgiving.

your people, whom you redeemed from Egypt? [22]You made your people Israel your very own forever, and you, O LORD, have become their God.

[23]"And now, LORD, let the promise you have made concerning your servant and his house be established forever. Do as you promised, [24]so that it will be established and that your name will be great forever. Then men will say, 'The LORD Almighty, the God over Israel, is Israel's God!' And the house of your servant David will be established before you.

[25]"You, my God, have revealed to your servant that you will build a house for him. So your servant has found courage to pray to you. [26]O LORD, you are God! You have promised these good things to your servant. [27]Now you have been pleased to bless the house of your servant, that it may continue forever in your sight; for you, O LORD, have blessed it, and it will be blessed forever."

David's Victories

18 In the course of time, David defeated the Philistines and subdued them, and he took Gath and its surrounding villages from the control of the Philistines.

[2]David also defeated the Moabites, and they became subject to him and brought tribute.

[3]Moreover, David fought Hadadezer king of Zobah, as far as Hamath, when he went to establish his control along the Euphrates River. [4]David captured a thousand of his chariots, seven thousand charioteers and twenty thousand foot soldiers. He hamstrung all but a hundred of the chariot horses.

[5]When the Arameans of Damascus came to help Hadadezer king of Zobah, David struck

down twenty-two thousand of them. [6]He put garrisons in the Aramean kingdom of Damascus, and the Arameans became subject to him and brought tribute. The LORD gave David victory everywhere he went.

[7]David took the gold shields carried by the officers of Hadadezer and brought them to Jerusalem. [8]From Tebah[a] and Cun, towns that belonged to Hadadezer, David took a great quantity of bronze, which Solomon used to make the bronze Sea, the pillars and various bronze articles.

[9]When Tou king of Hamath heard that David had defeated the entire army of Hadadezer king of Zobah, [10]he sent his son Hadoram to King David to greet him and congratulate him on his victory in battle over Hadadezer, who had been at war with Tou. Hadoram brought all kinds of articles of gold and silver and bronze.

[11]King David dedicated these articles to the LORD, as he had done with the silver and gold he had taken from all these nations: Edom and Moab, the Ammonites and the Philistines, and Amalek.

[12]Abishai son of Zeruiah struck down eighteen thousand Edomites in the Valley of Salt. [13]He put garrisons in Edom, and all the Edomites became subject to David. The LORD gave David victory everywhere he went.

David's Officials

[14]David reigned over all Israel, doing what was just and right for all his people. [15]Joab son of Zeruiah was over the army; Jehoshaphat son of Ahilud was recorder; [16]Zadok son of Ahitub and Ahimelech[b] son of Abiathar were priests; Shavsha was secretary; [17]Benaiah son of Jehoiada was over the Kerethites and Pelethites; and David's sons were chief officials at the king's side.

The Battle Against the Ammonites

19 In the course of time, Nahash king of the Ammonites died, and his son succeeded him as king. [2]David thought, "I will show kindness to Hanun son of Nahash, because his father showed kindness to me." So David sent a delegation to express his sympathy to Hanun concerning his father.

When David's men came to Hanun in the land of the Ammonites to express sympathy to him, [3]the Ammonite nobles said to Hanun, "Do you think David is honoring your father by sending men to you to express sympathy? Haven't his men come to you to explore and spy out the country and overthrow it?" [4]So Hanun seized David's men, shaved them, cut off their garments in the middle at the buttocks, and sent them away.

[5]When someone came and told David about the men, he sent messengers to meet them, for they were greatly humiliated. The king said, "Stay at Jericho till your beards have grown, and then come back."

19:4 Comedy of Errors

Wars start for the oddest reasons. One modern war in Central America erupted after a poorly refereed soccer match. In this instance the king of Ammon misjudged the motives of a funeral delegation, and David felt obliged to respond to an insult that today seems more humorous than humiliating. The resulting war crushed one of Israel's peskiest enemies, the Ammonites, offspring of the incestuous relations between Lot and his daughter (Genesis 19).

[6]When the Ammonites realized that they had become a stench in David's nostrils, Hanun and the Ammonites sent a thousand talents[c] of silver to hire chariots and charioteers from Aram Naharaim,[d] Aram Maacah and Zobah. [7]They hired thirty-two thousand chariots and charioteers, as well as the king of Maacah with his troops, who came and camped near Medeba, while the Ammonites were mustered from their towns and moved out for battle.

[8]On hearing this, David sent Joab out with the entire army of fighting men. [9]The Ammonites came out and drew up in battle formation at the entrance to their city, while the kings who had come were by themselves in the open country.

[10]Joab saw that there were battle lines in front of him and behind him; so he selected some of the best troops in Israel and deployed them against the Arameans. [11]He put the rest of the men under the command of Abishai his brother, and they were deployed against the Ammonites. [12]Joab said, "If the Arameans are too strong for me, then you are to rescue me; but if the Ammonites are too strong for you, then I will rescue you. [13]Be strong and let us fight bravely for our people and the cities of our God. The LORD will do what is good in his sight."

[14]Then Joab and the troops with him advanced to fight the Arameans, and they fled before him. [15]When the Ammonites saw that the Arameans were fleeing, they too fled before his brother Abishai and went inside the city. So Joab went back to Jerusalem.

[16]After the Arameans saw that they had been

---

[a]8 Hebrew *Tibhath*, a variant of *Tebah*   [b]16 Some Hebrew manuscripts, Vulgate and Syriac (see also 2 Samuel 8:17); most Hebrew manuscripts *Abimelech*   [c]6 That is, about 37 tons (about 34 metric tons)   [d]6 That is, Northwest Mesopotamia

routed by Israel, they sent messengers and had Arameans brought from beyond the River,[a] with Shophach the commander of Hadadezer's army leading them.

[17]When David was told of this, he gathered all Israel and crossed the Jordan; he advanced against them and formed his battle lines opposite them. David formed his lines to meet the Arameans in battle, and they fought against him. [18]But they fled before Israel, and David killed seven thousand of their charioteers and forty thousand of their foot soldiers. He also killed Shophach the commander of their army.

[19]When the vassals of Hadadezer saw that they had been defeated by Israel, they made peace with David and became subject to him.

So the Arameans were not willing to help the Ammonites anymore.

The Capture of Rabbah

20 In the spring, at the time when kings go off to war, Joab led out the armed forces. He laid waste the land of the Ammonites and went to Rabbah and besieged it, but David remained in Jerusalem. Joab attacked Rabbah and left it in ruins. [2]David took the crown from the head of their king[b]—its weight was found to be a talent[c] of gold, and it was set with precious stones—and it was placed on David's head. He took a great quantity of plunder from the city [3]and brought out the people who were there, consigning them to labor with saws and with iron picks and axes. David did this to all the Ammonite towns. Then David and his entire army returned to Jerusalem.

War With the Philistines

[4]In the course of time, war broke out with the Philistines, at Gezer. At that time Sibbecai the Hushathite killed Sippai, one of the descendants of the Rephaites, and the Philistines were subjugated.

[5]In another battle with the Philistines, Elhanan son of Jair killed Lahmi the brother of Goliath the Gittite, who had a spear with a shaft like a weaver's rod.

[6]In still another battle, which took place at Gath, there was a huge man with six fingers on each hand and six toes on each foot—twenty-four in all. He also was descended from Rapha. [7]When he taunted Israel, Jonathan son of Shimea, David's brother, killed him.

[8]These were descendants of Rapha in Gath, and they fell at the hands of David and his men.

David Numbers the Fighting Men

21 Satan rose up against Israel and incited David to take a census of Israel. [2]So David said to Joab and the commanders of the troops, "Go and count the Israelites from Beersheba to Dan. Then report back to me so that I may know how many there are."

[3]But Joab replied, "May the LORD multiply his troops a hundred times over. My lord the king, are they not all my lord's subjects? Why does my lord want to do this? Why should he bring guilt on Israel?"

[4]The king's word, however, overruled Joab; so Joab left and went throughout Israel and then came back to Jerusalem. [5]Joab reported the number of the fighting men to David: In all Israel there were one million one hundred thousand men who could handle a sword, including four hundred and seventy thousand in Judah.

[6]But Joab did not include Levi and Benjamin in the numbering, because the king's command was repulsive to him. [7]This command was also evil in the sight of God; so he punished Israel.

21:7 Act of Pride

Taking a census was not in itself immoral— God commanded it in the book of Numbers (chapters 1,26). This census, however, came out of David's desire to survey his kingdom, now at peace, in order to glory in its size and its potential military strength. God wanted him to continue relying on divine help and guidance, not on national pride. Even Joab, a top general, sensed the grievous mistake (verse 3). For more details, see "Satan or the Lord?" page 360.

[8]Then David said to God, "I have sinned greatly by doing this. Now, I beg you, take away the guilt of your servant. I have done a very foolish thing."

[9]The LORD said to Gad, David's seer, [10]"Go and tell David, 'This is what the LORD says: I am giving you three options. Choose one of them for me to carry out against you.'"

[11]So Gad went to David and said to him, "This is what the LORD says: 'Take your choice: [12]three years of famine, three months of being swept away[d] before your enemies, with their swords overtaking you, or three days of the sword of the LORD—days of plague in the land, with the angel of the LORD ravaging every part of Israel.' Now then, decide how I should answer the one who sent me."

[13]David said to Gad, "I am in deep distress. Let me fall into the hands of the LORD, for his mercy is very great; but do not let me fall into the hands of men."

[14]So the LORD sent a plague on Israel, and

---

[a]16 That is, the Euphrates   [b]2 Or of Milcom, that is, Molech   [c]2 That is, about 75 pounds (about 34 kilograms)   [d]12 Hebrew; Septuagint and Vulgate (see also 2 Samuel 24:13) of fleeing

seventy thousand men of Israel fell dead. ¹⁵And God sent an angel to destroy Jerusalem. But as the angel was doing so, the LORD saw it and was grieved because of the calamity and said to the angel who was destroying the people, "Enough! Withdraw your hand." The angel of the LORD was then standing at the threshing floor of Araunah[a] the Jebusite.

¹⁶David looked up and saw the angel of the LORD standing between heaven and earth, with a drawn sword in his hand extended over Jerusalem. Then David and the elders, clothed in sackcloth, fell facedown.

¹⁷David said to God, "Was it not I who ordered the fighting men to be counted? I am the one who has sinned and done wrong. These are but sheep. What have they done? O LORD my God, let your hand fall upon me and my family, but do not let this plague remain on your people."

¹⁸Then the angel of the LORD ordered Gad to tell David to go up and build an altar to the LORD on the threshing floor of Araunah the Jebusite. ¹⁹So David went up in obedience to the word that Gad had spoken in the name of the LORD.

²⁰While Araunah was threshing wheat, he turned and saw the angel; his four sons who were with him hid themselves. ²¹Then David approached, and when Araunah looked and saw him, he left the threshing floor and bowed down before David with his face to the ground.

²²David said to him, "Let me have the site of your threshing floor so I can build an altar to the LORD, that the plague on the people may be stopped. Sell it to me at the full price."

²³Araunah said to David, "Take it! Let my lord the king do whatever pleases him. Look, I will give the oxen for the burnt offerings, the threshing sledges for the wood, and the wheat for the grain offering. I will give all this."

²⁴But King David replied to Araunah, "No, I insist on paying the full price. I will not take for the LORD what is yours, or sacrifice a burnt offering that costs me nothing."

²⁵So David paid Araunah six hundred shekels[b] of gold for the site. ²⁶David built an altar to the LORD there and sacrificed burnt offerings and fellowship offerings.[c] He called on the LORD, and the LORD answered him with fire from heaven on the altar of burnt offering.

²⁷Then the LORD spoke to the angel, and he put his sword back into its sheath. ²⁸At that time, when David saw that the LORD had answered him on the threshing floor of Araunah the Jebusite, he offered sacrifices there. ²⁹The tabernacle of the LORD, which Moses had made in the desert, and the altar of burnt offering were at that time on the

high place at Gibeon. ³⁰But David could not go before it to inquire of God, because he was afraid of the sword of the angel of the LORD.

22 Then David said, "The house of the LORD God is to be here, and also the altar of burnt offering for Israel."

Preparations for the Temple

²So David gave orders to assemble the aliens living in Israel, and from among them he appointed stonecutters to prepare dressed stone for building the house of God. ³He provided a large amount of iron to make nails for the doors of the gateways and for the fittings, and more bronze than could be weighed. ⁴He also provided more cedar logs than could be counted, for the Sidonians and Tyrians had brought large numbers of them to David.

⁵David said, "My son Solomon is young and inexperienced, and the house to be built for the LORD should be of great magnificence and fame and splendor in the sight of all the nations. Therefore I will make preparations for it." So David made extensive preparations before his death.

⁶Then he called for his son Solomon and charged him to build a house for the LORD, the God of Israel. ⁷David said to Solomon: "My son, I had it in my heart to build a house for the Name of the LORD my God. ⁸But this word of the LORD came to me: 'You have shed much blood and have fought many wars. You are not to build a house for my Name, because you have shed

22:8 A Man of Blood

David explained to Solomon that the Lord had not allowed him to build the temple because of his life of bloodshed. This does not suggest that David had been wrong to lead Israel in battle. God had directed him to conduct at least some of the wars. Nonetheless, war and bloodshed, even when necessary, fall short of God's ideal. He wanted the temple built by a man of peace.

much blood on the earth in my sight. ⁹But you will have a son who will be a man of peace and rest, and I will give him rest from all his enemies on every side. His name will be Solomon,[d] and I will grant Israel peace and quiet during his reign. ¹⁰He is the one who will build a house for my Name. He will be my son, and I will be his father. And I will establish the throne of his kingdom over Israel forever.'

¹¹"Now, my son, the LORD be with you, and may you have success and build the house of the

---

[a] 15 Hebrew *Ornan*, a variant of *Araunah*; also in verses 18-28   [b] 25 That is, about 15 pounds (about 7 kilograms)
[c] 26 Traditionally *peace offerings*   [d] 9 *Solomon* sounds like and may be derived from the Hebrew for *peace*.

LORD your God, as he said you would. [12]May the LORD give you discretion and understanding when he puts you in command over Israel, so that you may keep the law of the LORD your God. [13]Then you will have success if you are careful to observe the decrees and laws that the LORD gave Moses for Israel. Be strong and courageous. Do not be afraid or discouraged.

[14]"I have taken great pains to provide for the temple of the LORD a hundred thousand talents[a] of gold, a million talents[b] of silver, quantities of bronze and iron too great to be weighed, and wood and stone. And you may add to them. [15]You have many workmen: stonecutters, masons and carpenters, as well as men skilled in every kind of work [16]in gold and silver, bronze and iron—craftsmen beyond number. Now begin the work, and the LORD be with you."

[17]Then David ordered all the leaders of Israel to help his son Solomon. [18]He said to them, "Is not the LORD your God with you? And has he not granted you rest on every side? For he has handed the inhabitants of the land over to me, and the land is subject to the LORD and to his people. [19]Now devote your heart and soul to seeking the LORD your God. Begin to build the sanctuary of the LORD God, so that you may bring the ark of the covenant of the LORD and the sacred articles belonging to God into the temple that will be built for the Name of the LORD."

The Levites

23 When David was old and full of years, he made his son Solomon king over Israel.

[2]He also gathered together all the leaders of Israel, as well as the priests and Levites. [3]The Levites thirty years old or more were counted, and the total number of men was thirty-eight thousand. [4]David said, "Of these, twenty-four thousand are to supervise the work of the temple of the LORD and six thousand are to be officials and judges. [5]Four thousand are to be gatekeepers and four thousand are to praise the LORD with the musical instruments I have provided for that purpose."

[6]David divided the Levites into groups corresponding to the sons of Levi: Gershon, Kohath and Merari.

Gershonites

[7]Belonging to the Gershonites:
Ladan and Shimei.
[8]The sons of Ladan:
Jehiel the first, Zetham and Joel—three in all.
[9]The sons of Shimei:
Shelomoth, Haziel and Haran—three in all.

These were the heads of the families of Ladan.
[10]And the sons of Shimei:
Jahath, Ziza,[c] Jeush and Beriah.

23:6 Keeping the Temple

Ever since the time of Moses, the Levites had been in charge of carrying and caring for the tabernacle—the portable tent where God was worshiped. But now that the ark had been placed permanently in Jerusalem, and a temple was to be built, the Levites needed new duties and organization. Chapters 23–26 describe those duties in detail.

These were the sons of Shimei—four in all.
[11]Jahath was the first and Ziza the second, but Jeush and Beriah did not have many sons; so they were counted as one family with one assignment.

Kohathites

[12]The sons of Kohath:
Amram, Izhar, Hebron and Uzziel—four in all.
[13]The sons of Amram:
Aaron and Moses.
Aaron was set apart, he and his descendants forever, to consecrate the most holy things, to offer sacrifices before the LORD, to minister before him and to pronounce blessings in his name forever. [14]The sons of Moses the man of God were counted as part of the tribe of Levi.
[15]The sons of Moses:
Gershom and Eliezer.
[16]The descendants of Gershom:
Shubael was the first.
[17]The descendants of Eliezer:
Rehabiah was the first.
Eliezer had no other sons, but the sons of Rehabiah were very numerous.
[18]The sons of Izhar:
Shelomith was the first.
[19]The sons of Hebron:
Jeriah the first, Amariah the second, Jahaziel the third and Jekameam the fourth.
[20]The sons of Uzziel:
Micah the first and Isshiah the second.

Merarites

[21]The sons of Merari:
Mahli and Mushi.

---

[a]14 That is, about 3,750 tons (about 3,450 metric tons)   [b]14 That is, about 37,500 tons (about 34,500 metric tons)
[c]10 One Hebrew manuscript, Septuagint and Vulgate (see also verse 11); most Hebrew manuscripts *Zina*

The sons of Mahli:
Eleazar and Kish.
22Eleazar died without having sons: he had only daughters. Their cousins, the sons of Kish, married them.
23The sons of Mushi:
Mahli, Eder and Jerimoth—three in all.

24These were the descendants of Levi by their families—the heads of families as they were registered under their names and counted individually, that is, the workers twenty years old or more who served in the temple of the LORD. 25For David had said, "Since the LORD, the God of Israel, has granted rest to his people and has come to dwell in Jerusalem forever, 26the Levites no longer need to carry the tabernacle or any of the articles used in its service." 27According to the last instructions of David, the Levites were counted from those twenty years old or more.

28The duty of the Levites was to help Aaron's descendants in the service of the temple of the LORD: to be in charge of the courtyards, the side rooms, the purification of all sacred things and the performance of other duties at the house of God. 29They were in charge of the bread set out on the table, the flour for the grain offerings, the unleavened wafers, the baking and the mixing, and all measurements of quantity and size.

23:29 Little People

The best way to get volunteers is to guarantee them adequate credit, and 1 Chronicles leaves no volunteer in nation-building overlooked. After focusing on King David for several chapters, the book turns attention to those who performed menial tasks: bailiffs, bureaucrats, bread-bakers, weight-checkers, custodians, accountants, musicians, guards, a recording secretary.

30They were also to stand every morning to thank and praise the LORD. They were to do the same in the evening 31and whenever burnt offerings were presented to the LORD on Sabbaths and at New Moon festivals and at appointed feasts. They were to serve before the LORD regularly in the proper number and in the way prescribed for them.

32And so the Levites carried out their responsibilities for the Tent of Meeting, for the Holy Place and, under their brothers the descendants of Aaron, for the service of the temple of the LORD.

The Divisions of Priests

24 These were the divisions of the sons of Aaron:

The sons of Aaron were Nadab, Abihu, Eleazar and Ithamar. 2But Nadab and Abihu died before their father did, and they had no sons; so Eleazar and Ithamar served as the priests. 3With the help of Zadok a descendant of Eleazar and Ahimelech a descendant of Ithamar, David separated them into divisions for their appointed order of ministering. 4A larger number of leaders were found among Eleazar's descendants than among Ithamar's, and they were divided accordingly: sixteen heads of families from Eleazar's descendants and eight heads of families from Ithamar's descendants. 5They divided them impartially by drawing lots, for there were officials of the sanctuary and officials of God among the descendants of both Eleazar and Ithamar.

6The scribe Shemaiah son of Nethanel, a Levite, recorded their names in the presence of the king and of the officials: Zadok the priest, Ahimelech son of Abiathar and the heads of families of the priests and of the Levites—one family being taken from Eleazar and then one from Ithamar.

7The first lot fell to Jehoiarib,
the second to Jedaiah,
8the third to Harim,
the fourth to Seorim,
9the fifth to Malkijah,
the sixth to Mijamin,
10the seventh to Hakkoz,
the eighth to Abijah,
11the ninth to Jeshua,
the tenth to Shecaniah,
12the eleventh to Eliashib,
the twelfth to Jakim,
13the thirteenth to Huppah,
the fourteenth to Jeshebeab,
14the fifteenth to Bilgah,
the sixteenth to Immer,
15the seventeenth to Hezir,
the eighteenth to Happizzez,
16the nineteenth to Pethahiah,
the twentieth to Jehezkel,
17the twenty-first to Jakin,
the twenty-second to Gamul,
18the twenty-third to Delaiah
and the twenty-fourth to Maaziah.

19This was their appointed order of ministering when they entered the temple of the LORD, according to the regulations prescribed for them by their forefather Aaron, as the LORD, the God of Israel, had commanded him.

The Rest of the Levites

20As for the rest of the descendants of Levi:
from the sons of Amram: Shubael;
from the sons of Shubael: Jehdeiah.
21As for Rehabiah, from his sons:
Isshiah was the first.
22From the Izharites: Shelomoth;

from the sons of Shelomoth: Jahath.
²³The sons of Hebron: Jeriah the first,ᵃ Amariah the second, Jahaziel the third and Jekameam the fourth.
²⁴The son of Uzziel: Micah;
from the sons of Micah: Shamir.
²⁵The brother of Micah: Isshiah;
from the sons of Isshiah: Zechariah.
²⁶The sons of Merari: Mahli and Mushi. The son of Jaaziah: Beno.
²⁷The sons of Merari:
from Jaaziah: Beno, Shoham, Zaccur and Ibri.
²⁸From Mahli: Eleazar, who had no sons.
²⁹From Kish: the son of Kish: Jerahmeel.
³⁰And the sons of Mushi: Mahli, Eder and Jerimoth.

These were the Levites, according to their families. ³¹They also cast lots, just as their brothers the descendants of Aaron did, in the presence of King David and of Zadok, Ahimelech, and the heads of families of the priests and the Levites. The families of the oldest brother were treated the same as those of the youngest.

The Singers

25 David, together with the commanders of the army, set apart some of the sons of Asaph, Heman and Jeduthun for the ministry of prophesying, accompanied by harps, lyres and cymbals. Here is the list of the men who performed this service:

> **25:1 Church and State**
>
> *Israel, a theocracy ruled by God through a king, had no "separation of church and state." David even consulted with his military commanders for such decisions as appointing prophets and musicians for worship.*

²From the sons of Asaph:
Zaccur, Joseph, Nethaniah and Asarelah. The sons of Asaph were under the supervision of Asaph, who prophesied under the king's supervision.
³As for Jeduthun, from his sons:
Gedaliah, Zeri, Jeshaiah, Shimei,ᵇ Hashabiah and Mattithiah, six in all, under the supervision of their father Jeduthun, who prophesied, using the harp in thanking and praising the LORD.

⁴As for Heman, from his sons:
Bukkiah, Mattaniah, Uzziel, Shubael and Jerimoth; Hananiah, Hanani, Eliathah, Giddalti and Romamti-Ezer; Joshbekashah, Mallothi, Hothir and Mahazioth. ⁵All these were sons of Heman the king's seer. They were given him through the promises of God to exalt him.ᶜ God gave Heman fourteen sons and three daughters.

⁶All these men were under the supervision of their fathers for the music of the temple of the LORD, with cymbals, lyres and harps, for the ministry at the house of God. Asaph, Jeduthun and Heman were under the supervision of the king. ⁷Along with their relatives—all of them trained and skilled in music for the LORD—they numbered 288. ⁸Young and old alike, teacher as well as student, cast lots for their duties.

⁹The first lot, which was for Asaph, fell to Joseph,
his sons and relatives,ᵈ   12ᵉ
the second to Gedaliah,
he and his relatives and sons,   12
¹⁰the third to Zaccur,
his sons and relatives,   12
¹¹the fourth to Izri,ᶠ
his sons and relatives,   12
¹²the fifth to Nethaniah,
his sons and relatives,   12
¹³the sixth to Bukkiah,
his sons and relatives,   12
¹⁴the seventh to Jesarelah,ᵍ
his sons and relatives,   12
¹⁵the eighth to Jeshaiah,
his sons and relatives,   12
¹⁶the ninth to Mattaniah,
his sons and relatives,   12
¹⁷the tenth to Shimei,
his sons and relatives,   12
¹⁸the eleventh to Azarel,ʰ
his sons and relatives,   12
¹⁹the twelfth to Hashabiah,
his sons and relatives,   12
²⁰the thirteenth to Shubael,
his sons and relatives,   12
²¹the fourteenth to Mattithiah,
his sons and relatives,   12
²²the fifteenth to Jerimoth,
his sons and relatives,   12
²³the sixteenth to Hananiah,
his sons and relatives,   12
²⁴the seventeenth to Joshbekashah,
his sons and relatives,   12
²⁵the eighteenth to Hanani,

ᵃ23 Two Hebrew manuscripts and some Septuagint manuscripts (see also 1 Chron. 23:19); most Hebrew manuscripts *The sons of Jeriah:*   ᵇ3 One Hebrew manuscript and some Septuagint manuscripts (see also verse 17); most Hebrew manuscripts do not have *Shimei.*   ᶜ5 Hebrew *exalt the horn*   ᵈ9 See Septuagint; Hebrew does not have *his sons and relatives.*   ᵉ9 See the total in verse 7; Hebrew does not have *twelve.*   ᶠ11 A variant of *Zeri*   ᵍ14 A variant of *Asarelah*   ʰ18 A variant of *Uzziel*

his sons and relatives, 12

²⁶the nineteenth to Mallothi,
his sons and relatives, 12

²⁷the twentieth to Eliathah,
his sons and relatives, 12

²⁸the twenty-first to Hothir,
his sons and relatives, 12

²⁹the twenty-second to Giddalti,
his sons and relatives, 12

³⁰the twenty-third to Mahazioth,
his sons and relatives, 12

³¹the twenty-fourth to Romamti-Ezer,
his sons and relatives, 12

The Gatekeepers

26 The divisions of the gatekeepers:

From the Korahites: Meshelemiah son of Kore, one of the sons of Asaph.

26:1–12 Major Enterprise

To aid in worship, David appointed 4,000 gatekeepers, or temple guards, and 4,000 musicians (23:3–4). The numbers give some indication of the importance attached to worship in national life. David was preparing his nation for the day when his son Solomon would build the temple.

---

²Meshelemiah had sons:
Zechariah the firstborn,
Jediael the second,
Zebadiah the third,
Jathniel the fourth,
³Elam the fifth,
Jehohanan the sixth
and Eliehoenai the seventh.
⁴Obed-Edom also had sons:
Shemaiah the firstborn,
Jehozabad the second,
Joah the third,
Sacar the fourth,
Nethanel the fifth,
⁵Ammiel the sixth,
Issachar the seventh
and Peullethai the eighth.
(For God had blessed Obed-Edom.)

⁶His son Shemaiah also had sons, who were leaders in their father's family because they were very capable men. ⁷The sons of Shemaiah: Othni, Rephael, Obed and Elzabad; his relatives Elihu and Semakiah were also able men. ⁸All these were descendants of Obed-Edom; they and their sons and their relatives were capable men with the strength to do the work—descendants of Obed-Edom, 62 in all.

⁹Meshelemiah had sons and relatives, who were able men—18 in all.

¹⁰Hosah the Merarite had sons: Shimri the first (although he was not the firstborn, his father had appointed him the first), ¹¹Hilkiah the second, Tabaliah the third and Zechariah the fourth. The sons and relatives of Hosah were 13 in all.

¹²These divisions of the gatekeepers, through their chief men, had duties for ministering in the temple of the LORD, just as their relatives had. ¹³Lots were cast for each gate, according to their families, young and old alike.

¹⁴The lot for the East Gate fell to Shelemiah.[a] Then lots were cast for his son Zechariah, a wise counselor, and the lot for the North Gate fell to him. ¹⁵The lot for the South Gate fell to Obed-Edom, and the lot for the storehouse fell to his sons. ¹⁶The lots for the West Gate and the Shalleketh Gate on the upper road fell to Shuppim and Hosah.

Guard was alongside of guard: ¹⁷There were six Levites a day on the east, four a day on the north, four a day on the south and two at a time at the storehouse. ¹⁸As for the court to the west, there were four at the road and two at the court itself.

¹⁹These were the divisions of the gatekeepers who were descendants of Korah and Merari.

The Treasurers and Other Officials

²⁰Their fellow Levites were[b] in charge of the treasuries of the house of God and the treasuries for the dedicated things.

²¹The descendants of Ladan, who were Gershonites through Ladan and who were heads of families belonging to Ladan the Gershonite, were Jehieli, ²²the sons of Jehieli, Zetham and his brother Joel. They were in charge of the treasuries of the temple of the LORD.

²³From the Amramites, the Izharites, the Hebronites and the Uzzielites:

²⁴Shubael, a descendant of Gershom son of Moses, was the officer in charge of the treasuries. ²⁵His relatives through Eliezer: Rehabiah his son, Jeshaiah his son, Joram his son, Zicri his son and Shelomith his son. ²⁶Shelomith and his relatives were in charge of all the treasuries for the things dedicated by King David, by the heads of families who were the commanders of thousands and commanders of hundreds, and by the other army commanders. ²⁷Some of the plun-

---

[a] 14 A variant of *Meshelemiah*   [b] 20 Septuagint; Hebrew *As for the Levites, Ahijah was*

der taken in battle they dedicated for the repair of the temple of the LORD. ²⁸And everything dedicated by Samuel the seer and by Saul son of Kish, Abner son of Ner and Joab son of Zeruiah, and all the other dedicated things were in the care of Shelomith and his relatives. ²⁹From the Izharites: Kenaniah and his sons were assigned duties away from the temple, as officials and judges over Israel.

³⁰From the Hebronites: Hashabiah and his relatives—seventeen hundred able men—were responsible in Israel west of the Jordan for all the work of the LORD and for the king's service. ³¹As for the Hebronites, Jeriah was their chief according to the genealogical records of their families. In the fortieth year of David's reign a search was made in the records, and capable men among the Hebronites were found at Jazer in Gilead. ³²Jeriah had twenty-seven hundred relatives, who were able men and heads of families, and King David put them in charge of the Reubenites, the Gadites and the half-tribe of Manasseh for every matter pertaining to God and for the affairs of the king.

Army Divisions

27 This is the list of the Israelites—heads of families, commanders of thousands and commanders of hundreds, and their officers, who served the king in all that concerned the army divisions that were on duty month by month throughout the year. Each division consisted of 24,000 men.

²In charge of the first division, for the first month, was Jashobeam son of Zabdiel. There were 24,000 men in his division. ³He was a descendant of Perez and chief of all the army officers for the first month.

⁴In charge of the division for the second month was Dodai the Ahohite; Mikloth was the leader of his division. There were 24,000 men in his division.

⁵The third army commander, for the third month, was Benaiah son of Jehoiada the priest. He was chief and there were 24,000 men in his division. ⁶This was the Benaiah who was a mighty man among the Thirty and was over the Thirty. His son Ammizabad was in charge of his division.

⁷The fourth, for the fourth month, was Asahel the brother of Joab; his son Zebadiah was his successor. There were 24,000 men in his division.

⁸The fifth, for the fifth month, was the commander Shamhuth the Izrahite. There were 24,000 men in his division.

⁹The sixth, for the sixth month, was Ira the son of Ikkesh the Tekoite. There were 24,000 men in his division.

¹⁰The seventh, for the seventh month, was Helez the Pelonite, an Ephraimite. There were 24,000 men in his division.

¹¹The eighth, for the eighth month, was Sibbecai the Hushathite, a Zerahite. There were 24,000 men in his division.

¹²The ninth, for the ninth month, was Abiezer the Anathothite, a Benjamite. There were 24,000 men in his division.

¹³The tenth, for the tenth month, was Maharai the Netophathite, a Zerahite. There were 24,000 men in his division.

¹⁴The eleventh, for the eleventh month, was Benaiah the Pirathonite, an Ephraimite. There were 24,000 men in his division.

¹⁵The twelfth, for the twelfth month, was Heldai the Netophathite, from the family of Othniel. There were 24,000 men in his division.

Officers of the Tribes

¹⁶The officers over the tribes of Israel:

over the Reubenites: Eliezer son of Zicri;
over the Simeonites: Shephatiah son of Maacah;
¹⁷over Levi: Hashabiah son of Kemuel;
over Aaron: Zadok;
¹⁸over Judah: Elihu, a brother of David;
over Issachar: Omri son of Michael;
¹⁹over Zebulun: Ishmaiah son of Obadiah;
over Naphtali: Jerimoth son of Azriel;
²⁰over the Ephraimites: Hoshea son of Azaziah;
over half the tribe of Manasseh: Joel son of Pedaiah;
²¹over the half-tribe of Manasseh in Gilead: Iddo son of Zechariah;
over Benjamin: Jaasiel son of Abner;
²²over Dan: Azarel son of Jeroham.

These were the officers over the tribes of Israel.

²³David did not take the number of the men twenty years old or less, because the LORD had promised to make Israel as numerous as the stars in the sky. ²⁴Joab son of Zeruiah began to count the men but did not finish. Wrath came on Israel on account of this numbering, and the number was not entered in the book*a* of the annals of King David.

a 24 Septuagint; Hebrew *number*

The King's Overseers

25Azmaveth son of Adiel was in charge of the royal storehouses.

Jonathan son of Uzziah was in charge of the storehouses in the outlying districts, in the towns, the villages and the watchtowers.

26Ezri son of Kelub was in charge of the field workers who farmed the land.

27Shimei the Ramathite was in charge of the vineyards.

Zabdi the Shiphmite was in charge of the produce of the vineyards for the wine vats.

28Baal-Hanan the Gederite was in charge of the olive and sycamore-fig trees in the western foothills.

Joash was in charge of the supplies of olive oil.

29Shitrai the Sharonite was in charge of the herds grazing in Sharon.

Shaphat son of Adlai was in charge of the herds in the valleys.

30Obil the Ishmaelite was in charge of the camels.

Jehdeiah the Meronothite was in charge of the donkeys.

31Jaziz the Hagrite was in charge of the flocks.

All these were the officials in charge of King David's property.

32Jonathan, David's uncle, was a counselor, a man of insight and a scribe. Jehiel son of Hacmoni took care of the king's sons.

33Ahithophel was the king's counselor.

Hushai the Arkite was the king's friend. 34Ahithophel was succeeded by Jehoiada son of Benaiah and by Abiathar.

Joab was the commander of the royal army.

David's Plans for the Temple

28 David summoned all the officials of Israel to assemble at Jerusalem: the officers over the tribes, the commanders of the divisions in the service of the king, the commanders of thousands and commanders of hundreds, and the officials in charge of all the property and livestock belonging to the king and his sons, together with the palace officials, the mighty men and all the brave warriors.

2King David rose to his feet and said: "Listen to me, my brothers and my people. I had it in my heart to build a house as a place of rest for the ark of the covenant of the LORD, for the footstool of our God, and I made plans to build it. 3But God said to me, 'You are not to build a house for my Name, because you are a warrior and have shed blood.'

4"Yet the LORD, the God of Israel, chose me from my whole family to be king over Israel forever. He chose Judah as leader, and from the house of Judah he chose my family, and from my father's sons he was pleased to make me king

over all Israel. 5Of all my sons—and the LORD has given me many—he has chosen my son Solomon to sit on the throne of the kingdom of the LORD over Israel. 6He said to me: 'Solomon your son is the one who will build my house and my courts, for I have chosen him to be my son, and I will be his father. 7I will establish his kingdom forever if he is unswerving in carrying out my commands and laws, as is being done at this time.'

8"So now I charge you in the sight of all Israel and of the assembly of the LORD, and in the hearing of our God: Be careful to follow all the commands of the LORD your God, that you may possess this good land and pass it on as an inheritance to your descendants forever.

9"And you, my son Solomon, acknowledge the God of your father, and serve him with wholehearted devotion and with a willing mind, for the LORD searches every heart and understands every motive behind the thoughts. If you seek him, he will be found by you; but if you

28:9 Conditional Promise

God's promise to David of unending descendants on the throne was so important to Israel that it was reported, in different forms, several times. (See chapter 17, for instance.) Sometimes it read as though God would bless a line of successful kings regardless of their behavior. Here, though, David explained that God's favor would depend on Solomon's devotion to God.

forsake him, he will reject you forever. 10Consider now, for the LORD has chosen you to build a temple as a sanctuary. Be strong and do the work."

11Then David gave his son Solomon the plans for the portico of the temple, its buildings, its storerooms, its upper parts, its inner rooms and the place of atonement. 12He gave him the plans of all that the Spirit had put in his mind for the courts of the temple of the LORD and all the surrounding rooms, for the treasuries of the temple of God and for the treasuries for the dedicated things. 13He gave him instructions for the divisions of the priests and Levites, and for all the work of serving in the temple of the LORD, as well as for all the articles to be used in its service. 14He designated the weight of gold for all the gold articles to be used in various kinds of service, and the weight of silver for all the silver articles to be used in various kinds of service: 15the weight of gold for the gold lampstands and their lamps, with the weight for each lampstand and its lamps; and the weight of silver for each silver lampstand and its lamps, according to the use of each lampstand; **16**the weight of gold for each table for consecrated bread; the weight of silver for the silver tables; **17**the weight of pure gold for the forks, sprinkling bowls and pitchers; the weight of gold for each gold dish; the weight of silver for each silver dish; **18**and the weight of the refined gold for the altar of incense. He also gave him the plan for the chariot, that is, the cherubim of gold that spread their wings and shelter the ark of the covenant of the LORD.

19"All this," David said, "I have in writing from the hand of the LORD upon me, and he gave me understanding in all the details of the plan."

20David also said to Solomon his son, "Be strong and courageous, and do the work. Do not be afraid or discouraged, for the LORD God, my God, is with you. He will not fail you or forsake you until all the work for the service of the temple of the LORD is finished. **21**The divisions of the priests and Levites are ready for all the work on the temple of God, and every willing man skilled in any craft will help you in all the work. The officials and all the people will obey your every command."

Gifts for Building the Temple

29 Then King David said to the whole assembly: "My son Solomon, the one whom God has chosen, is young and inexperienced. The task is great, because this palatial structure is not for man but for the LORD God. **2**With all my resources I have provided for the temple of my God—gold for the gold work, silver for the silver, bronze for the bronze, iron for the iron and wood for the wood, as well as onyx for the settings, turquoise,*a* stones of various colors, and all kinds of fine stone and marble—all of these in large quantities. **3**Besides, in my devotion to the temple of my God I now give my personal treasures of gold and silver for the temple of my God, over and above everything I have provided for this holy temple: **4**three thousand talents*b* of gold (gold of Ophir) and seven thousand talents*c* of refined silver, for the overlaying of the walls of the buildings, **5**for the gold work and the silver work, and for all the work to be done by the craftsmen. Now, who is willing to consecrate himself today to the LORD?"

6Then the leaders of families, the officers of the tribes of Israel, the commanders of thousands and commanders of hundreds, and the officials in charge of the king's work gave willingly. **7**They gave toward the work on the temple of God five thousand talents*d* and ten thousand darics*e* of gold, ten thousand talents*f* of silver, eighteen thousand talents*g* of bronze and a hundred thousand talents*h* of iron. **8**Any who had precious stones gave them to the treasury of the temple of the LORD in the custody of Jehiel the Gershonite. **9**The people rejoiced at the willing response of their leaders, for they had given freely and wholeheartedly to the LORD. David the king also rejoiced greatly.

David's Prayer

10David praised the LORD in the presence of the whole assembly, saying,

"Praise be to you, O LORD,
   God of our father Israel,
   from everlasting to everlasting.

29:10 David's Great Prayer

David's prayer at the beginning of temple construction shows why he was a man after God's own heart. Despite all his achievements, he was deeply humble. He wanted glory to go to God, not himself. This passage would have reminded the original readers of Chronicles, back from exile and without a king, that David's greatest concern was for the temple, where his people could worship and serve God. They, his descendants, did not need a king to carry on David's deepest concerns.

11Yours, O LORD, is the greatness and the
      power
   and the glory and the majesty and the
      splendor,
   for everything in heaven and earth is
      yours.
Yours, O LORD, is the kingdom;
   you are exalted as head over all.
12Wealth and honor come from you;
   you are the ruler of all things.
In your hands are strength and power
   to exalt and give strength to all.
13Now, our God, we give you thanks,
   and praise your glorious name.

14"But who am I, and who are my people, that we should be able to give as generously as this? Everything comes from you, and we have given you only what comes from your hand. **15**We are aliens and strangers in your sight, as were all our forefathers. Our days on earth are like a shadow, without hope. **16**O LORD our God, as for all this abundance that we have provided for building you a temple for your Holy Name, it comes from your hand, and all of it belongs to you. **17**I know, my God, that you test the heart and are pleased

---

a2 The meaning of the Hebrew for this word is uncertain.   *b4* That is, about 110 tons (about 100 metric tons)
c4 That is, about 260 tons (about 240 metric tons)   *d7* That is, about 190 tons (about 170 metric tons)   *e7* That is, about 185 pounds (about 84 kilograms)   *f7* That is, about 375 tons (about 345 metric tons)   *g7* That is, about 675 tons (about 610 metric tons)   *h7* That is, about 3,750 tons (about 3,450 metric tons)

with integrity. All these things have I given willingly and with honest intent. And now I have seen with joy how willingly your people who are here have given to you. [18]O LORD, God of our fathers Abraham, Isaac and Israel, keep this desire in the hearts of your people forever, and keep their hearts loyal to you. [19]And give my son Solomon the wholehearted devotion to keep your commands, requirements and decrees and to do everything to build the palatial structure for which I have provided."

[20]Then David said to the whole assembly, "Praise the LORD your God." So they all praised the LORD, the God of their fathers; they bowed low and fell prostrate before the LORD and the king.

Solomon Acknowledged as King

[21]The next day they made sacrifices to the LORD and presented burnt offerings to him: a thousand bulls, a thousand rams and a thousand male lambs, together with their drink offerings, and other sacrifices in abundance for all Israel. [22]They ate and drank with great joy in the presence of the LORD that day.

Then they acknowledged Solomon son of David as king a second time, anointing him before the LORD to be ruler and Zadok to be priest. [23]So Solomon sat on the throne of the LORD as king in place of his father David. He prospered and all Israel obeyed him. [24]All the officers and mighty men, as well as all of King David's sons, pledged their submission to King Solomon.

[25]The LORD highly exalted Solomon in the sight of all Israel and bestowed on him royal splendor such as no king over Israel ever had before.

The Death of David

[26]David son of Jesse was king over all Israel.

29:24 A Second Coronation

Assuming that his readers were familiar with the family quarrels told of in 1 Kings 1, the author refers to this coronation as the "second time" (verse 22). The first coronation happened when David learned that Solomon's older brother had been conspiring to become king. David immediately called for a private coronation (1 Kings 1:32–40). Only later did this public ceremony occur, when the rebellious brother swore his loyalty. Typically, 1 Chronicles leaves out the nasty politics and emphasizes the positive result.

[27]He ruled over Israel forty years—seven in Hebron and thirty-three in Jerusalem. [28]He died at a good old age, having enjoyed long life, wealth and honor. His son Solomon succeeded him as king.

[29]As for the events of King David's reign, from beginning to end, they are written in the records of Samuel the seer, the records of Nathan the prophet and the records of Gad the seer, [30]together with the details of his reign and power, and the circumstances that surrounded him and Israel and the kingdoms of all the other lands.

2 CHRONICLES

A Time for Hope
Restoring pride to a group of refugees

I N THE EARLY 1960s, A wave of feeling known as "black pride" swept across America. It started when African-American leaders realized that far more than legal rights had been repressed for 200 years. Everything about the African-American culture, from hair texture to history, had taken a back seat to that of the white majority.

Over time, a dramatic rediscovery of the African-American heritage occurred. Textbook publishers issued new editions that for the first time included the stories of African-Americans: a soldier who rowed George Washington across the Delaware, a scientist who perfected the process of blood transfusion, an educator who founded colleges for African-Americans.

"Black pride" reminded all Americans that a minority race had made giant contributions in many fields. People encountered a heritage they had known little about. Heroes were uncovered. African-Americans everywhere began to see the past in a new light.

> *"If my people, who are called by my name, will humble themselves and pray and seek my face and turn from their wicked ways, then will I hear from heaven and will forgive their sin and will heal their land." 7:14*

Need for a Pep Talk

There was a time when the Israelites, too, desperately needed a new look at the past. Their ancestors had also been torn from home, beaten, and dragged off in chains to serve as slaves in a foreign country. In Babylon, a new generation grew up knowing little of the Israelite past: the covenant with God, the promised line of kings, the magnificent temple in Jerusalem.

When captive Israelites were finally allowed to return home, they found a pile of rubble. In Israel's Golden Age, people had traveled thousands of miles to view the majesty of Jerusalem and its temple. But to the refugees' horror, not one stone of the temple remained standing. The carved beams had all been hacked to pieces, the gold and ivory stripped away, and the furniture auctioned off or destroyed.

Outside the capital, whole villages had disappeared. Vital religious customs had gone uncelebrated for 70 years. Jewish culture was in danger of leaking away.

The book of Chronicles was written to those refugees who returned. For that dispirited group of people, the author recounted the glory days of Israel. He wanted to restore pride in the Israelite past and bring hope to their future.

History in a New Light

Chronicles (both 1 and 2) thus retells history, starting all the way at the beginning, with Adam. Most of the characters are familiar, but Chronicles tells old stories in a new light. Its author isn't just reciting facts. He is delivering a word of bright hope, a pep talk, to just-freed refugees.

Some accuse Chronicles of being a "whitewashed" history, especially in comparison to the Bible's other history books. True, the book barely mentions the Israelites' great failures—it says nothing of David's or Solomon's mistakes, for instance. Presumably, the refugees had heard plenty about the dark side of their nation's recent past: The books of Samuel and Kings, which ruthlessly exposed those failures, had been around for years.

Similarly, Chronicles ignores the chaotic Northern Kingdom of Israel, and the civil war Judah waged against it. Nothing remained of the ten scattered tribes of the North, and the book wastes little space on them. Instead, Chronicles reaches higher, seeking to restore pride in the original ideals of the nation.

A Distant Hope

The good kings of Judah, eight in all, dominate the story: Over two-thirds of 2 Chronicles is devoted to their reigns. Chronicles focuses on God's special relationship with the Israelites, recalling the covenant that had brought about their Golden Age. It reviews the religious reforms led by each king, and, above all, highlights the temple, the house where God's presence came to rest. If God had lived among them in the past, couldn't he do so again?

How to Read 2 Chronicles

You will recognize many of the stories in 2 Chronicles—about half of it closely follows other Bible passages. The author freely admits he has relied on the books of Moses, Samuel, and Kings. He also quotes from Judges, Jeremiah, Psalms, Isaiah, and Lamentations, as well as many books that have been lost to history.

But 2 Chronicles does not merely repeat. It weaves together stories and facts for a specific purpose: a Jewish philosophy of history. Chronicles sheds new light on that history by highlighting rare moments of peace and prosperity. Worship of the true God had made Israel strong. As you read, notice how 2 Chronicles underscores that fact by stressing the temple and the priests.

For comparison, you may want to read companion passages in the book of Kings (for a list, see "A Lineup of Rulers," pages 1361–1369). Read side by side, the two accounts clearly reveal the distinct purpose behind the book of Chronicles.

Look past all the names and events for the few kings who did right. (See "The Great Reformers," pages 480–481.) What made them successful? What lessons about faith can we learn from them?

PEOPLE YOU'LL MEET IN 2 CHRONICLES

REHOBOAM *(p. 472)*
ATHALIAH *(p. 482)*
HEZEKIAH *(p.488)*

3-TRACK READING PLAN

For an explanation and complete listing of the 3-track reading plan, turn to page 7.

TRACK 1: *Two-Week Courses on the Bible*
See page 7 for information on these courses.

TRACK 2: *An Overview of 2 Chronicles in 3 Days*
☐ Day 1. Read the Introduction to 2 Chronicles and then chapter 20. It tells of a high point when King Jehoshaphat brought the whole nation together in prayer.
☐ Day 2. Hezekiah had an eventful life, with soaring highs and deep lows. Read about a national high point in chapter 30.
☐ Day 3. Hezekiah lived in treacherous times. Read of his close scrape with disaster in chapter 32.

Now turn to page 9 for your next Track 2 reading project.

TRACK 3: *All of 2 Chronicles in 34 Days*
After you have read through 2 Chronicles, turn to pages 10–14 for your next Track 3 reading project.

☐1	☐2	☐3	☐4	☐5	☐6	☐7	☐8
☐9	☐10	☐11	☐12	☐13	☐14	☐15	☐16–17
☐18	☐19	☐20	☐21	☐22	☐23	☐24	☐25
☐26–27	☐28	☐29	☐30	☐31	☐32	☐33	☐34
☐35	☐36						

Solomon Asks for Wisdom

1 Solomon son of David established himself firmly over his kingdom, for the LORD his God was with him and made him exceedingly great.

²Then Solomon spoke to all Israel—to the commanders of thousands and commanders of hundreds, to the judges and to all the leaders in Israel, the heads of families— ³and Solomon and the whole assembly went to the high place at Gibeon, for God's Tent of Meeting was there, which Moses the LORD's servant had made in the desert. ⁴Now David had brought up the ark of God from Kiriath Jearim to the place he had prepared for it, because he had pitched a tent for it in Jerusalem. ⁵But the bronze altar that Bezalel son of Uri, the son of Hur, had made was in Gibeon in front of the tabernacle of the LORD; so Solomon and the assembly inquired of him there. ⁶Solomon went up to the bronze altar before the LORD in the Tent of Meeting and offered a thousand burnt offerings on it.

⁷That night God appeared to Solomon and said to him, "Ask for whatever you want me to give you."

⁸Solomon answered God, "You have shown great kindness to David my father and have made me king in his place. ⁹Now, LORD God, let your promise to my father David be confirmed, for you have made me king over a people who are as numerous as the dust of the earth. ¹⁰Give me wisdom and knowledge, that I may lead this people, for who is able to govern this great people of yours?"

¹¹God said to Solomon, "Since this is your heart's desire and you have not asked for wealth, riches or honor, nor for the death of your enemies, and since you have not asked for a long life but for wisdom and knowledge to govern my people over whom I have made you king, ¹²therefore wisdom and knowledge will be given you. And I will also give you wealth, riches and honor, such as no king who was before you ever had and none after you will have."

¹³Then Solomon went to Jerusalem from the high place at Gibeon, from before the Tent of Meeting. And he reigned over Israel.

¹⁴Solomon accumulated chariots and horses; he had fourteen hundred chariots and twelve thousand horses,ᵃ which he kept in the chariot cities and also with him in Jerusalem. ¹⁵The king made silver and gold as common in Jerusalem as stones, and cedar as plentiful as sycamore-fig trees in the foothills. ¹⁶Solomon's horses were imported from Egyptᵇ and from Kueᶜ—the royal merchants purchased them from Kue. ¹⁷They imported a chariot from Egypt for six

hundred shekelsᵈ of silver, and a horse for a hundred and fifty.ᵉ They also exported them to all the kings of the Hittites and of the Arameans.

Preparations for Building the Temple

2 Solomon gave orders to build a temple for the Name of the LORD and a royal palace for himself. ²He conscripted seventy thousand men as carriers and eighty thousand as stonecutters in the hills and thirty-six hundred as foremen over them.

2:2 Solomon's Forced Labor

King Solomon drafted laborers for his construction projects much like an army drafts soldiers. His policy of forced labor sowed dissension in the kingdom, especially among resentful northern tribes. In keeping with its morale-building purpose, 2 Chronicles has little bad to say about Solomon. The author mentions Solomon's wealth (1:14; 9:22–25) without comment, although such excess defied the rules for kings (Deuteronomy 17:15–17). Chronicles also omits reference to Solomon's palace, which Kings had pointedly described as exceeding even the temple in its splendor.

³Solomon sent this message to Hiramᶠ king of Tyre:

"Send me cedar logs as you did for my father David when you sent him cedar to build a palace to live in. ⁴Now I am about to build a temple for the Name of the LORD my God and to dedicate it to him for burning fragrant incense before him, for setting out the consecrated bread regularly, and for making burnt offerings every morning and evening and on Sabbaths and New Moons and at the appointed feasts of the LORD our God. This is a lasting ordinance for Israel.

⁵"The temple I am going to build will be great, because our God is greater than all other gods. ⁶But who is able to build a temple for him, since the heavens, even the highest heavens, cannot contain him? Who then am I to build a temple for him, except as a place to burn sacrifices before him?

⁷"Send me, therefore, a man skilled to work in gold and silver, bronze and iron, and in purple, crimson and blue yarn, and experienced in the art of engraving, to work in Judah and Jerusalem with my skilled craftsmen, whom my father David provided.

ᵃ14 Or *charioteers*   ᵇ16 Or possibly *Muzur*, a region in Cilicia; also in verse 17   ᶜ16 Probably Cilicia
ᵈ17 That is, about 15 pounds (about 7 kilograms)   ᵉ17 That is, about 3 3/4 pounds (about 1.7 kilograms)
ᶠ3 Hebrew *Huram*, a variant of *Hiram*; also in verses 11 and 12

8"Send me also cedar, pine and algum[a] logs from Lebanon, for I know that your men are skilled in cutting timber there. My men will work with yours 9to provide me with plenty of lumber, because the temple I build must be large and magnificent. 10I will give your servants, the woodsmen who cut the timber, twenty thousand cors[b] of ground wheat, twenty thousand cors of barley, twenty thousand baths[c] of wine and twenty thousand baths of olive oil."

11Hiram king of Tyre replied by letter to Solomon:

"Because the LORD loves his people, he has made you their king."

12And Hiram added:

"Praise be to the LORD, the God of Israel, who made heaven and earth! He has given King David a wise son, endowed with intelligence and discernment, who will build a temple for the LORD and a palace for himself.

13"I am sending you Huram-Abi, a man of great skill, 14whose mother was from Dan and whose father was from Tyre. He is trained to work in gold and silver, bronze and iron, stone and wood, and with purple and blue and crimson yarn and fine linen. He is experienced in all kinds of engraving and can execute any design given to him. He will work with your craftsmen and with those of my lord, David your father.

15"Now let my lord send his servants the wheat and barley and the olive oil and wine he promised, 16and we will cut all the logs from Lebanon that you need and will float them in rafts by sea down to Joppa. You can then take them up to Jerusalem."

17Solomon took a census of all the aliens who were in Israel, after the census his father David had taken; and they were found to be 153,600. 18He assigned 70,000 of them to be carriers and 80,000 to be stonecutters in the hills, with 3,600 foremen over them to keep the people working.

Solomon Builds the Temple

3 Then Solomon began to build the temple of the LORD in Jerusalem on Mount Moriah, where the LORD had appeared to his father David. It was on the threshing floor of Araunah[d] the Jebusite, the place provided by David. 2He began building on the second day of the second month in the fourth year of his reign.

3The foundation Solomon laid for building the temple of God was sixty cubits long and twenty cubits wide (using the cubit of the old standard). 4The portico at the front of the temple was twenty cubits[f] long across the width of the building and twenty cubits[g] high.

He overlaid the inside with pure gold. 5He paneled the main hall with pine and covered it with fine gold and decorated it with palm tree and chain designs. 6He adorned the temple with precious stones. And the gold he used was gold of Parvaim. 7He overlaid the ceiling beams, doorframes, walls and doors of the temple with gold, and he carved cherubim on the walls.

8He built the Most Holy Place, its length corresponding to the width of the temple—twenty cubits long and twenty cubits wide. He overlaid the inside with six hundred talents[h] of fine gold. 9The gold nails weighed fifty shekels.[i] He also overlaid the upper parts with gold.

10In the Most Holy Place he made a pair of sculptured cherubim and overlaid them with gold. 11The total wingspan of the cherubim was twenty cubits. One wing of the first cherub was five cubits[j] long and touched the temple wall, while its other wing, also five cubits long, touched the wing of the other cherub. 12Similarly one wing of the second cherub was five cubits long and touched the other temple wall, and its other wing, also five cubits long, touched the wing of the first cherub. 13The wings of these cherubim extended twenty cubits. They stood on their feet, facing the main hall.[k]

14He made the curtain of blue, purple and crimson yarn and fine linen, with cherubim worked into it.

15In the front of the temple he made two

3:14 A Temporary Separation

Just as it had in the tabernacle, a curtain in the temple separated the Holy Place and Most Holy Place. The curtain symbolized the distance between God and people. Even priests were forbidden to go beyond that curtain into the presence of God, except on the Day of Atonement. When Jesus died on the cross, this temple curtain miraculously ripped in two. That event also had symbolic meaning: Christ had opened up the way to God (Hebrews 9:7–12).

---

[a]8 Probably a variant of *almug*; possibly juniper   [b]10 That is, probably about 125,000 bushels (about 4,400 kiloliters)   [c]10 That is, probably about 115,000 gallons (about 440 kiloliters)   [d]1 Hebrew *Ornan*, a variant of *Araunah*   [e]3 That is, about 90 feet (about 27 meters) long and 30 feet (about 9 meters) wide   [f]4 That is, about 30 feet (about 9 meters); also in verses 8, 11 and 13   [g]4 Some Septuagint and Syriac manuscripts; Hebrew *and a hundred and twenty*   [h]8 That is, about 23 tons (about 21 metric tons)   [i]9 That is, about 1 1/4 pounds (about 0.6 kilogram)   [j]11 That is, about 7 1/2 feet (about 2.3 meters); also in verse 15   [k]13 Or *facing inward*

pillars, which ⌊together⌋ were thirty-five cubits[a] long, each with a capital on top measuring five cubits. [16]He made interwoven chains[b] and put them on top of the pillars. He also made a hundred pomegranates and attached them to the chains. [17]He erected the pillars in the front of the temple, one to the south and one to the north. The one to the south he named Jakin[c] and the one to the north Boaz.[d]

The Temple's Furnishings

4 He made a bronze altar twenty cubits long, twenty cubits wide and ten cubits high.[e] [2]He made the Sea of cast metal, circular in shape, measuring ten cubits from rim to rim and five cubits[f] high. It took a line of thirty cubits[g] to measure around it. [3]Below the rim, figures of bulls encircled it—ten to a cubit.[h] The bulls were cast in two rows in one piece with the Sea.

[4]The Sea stood on twelve bulls, three facing north, three facing west, three facing south and three facing east. The Sea rested on top of them, and their hindquarters were toward the center. [5]It was a handbreadth[i] in thickness, and its rim was like the rim of a cup, like a lily blossom. It held three thousand baths.[j]

[6]He then made ten basins for washing and placed five on the south side and five on the north. In them the things to be used for the burnt offerings were rinsed, but the Sea was to be used by the priests for washing.

[7]He made ten gold lampstands according to the specifications for them and placed them in the temple, five on the south side and five on the north.

[8]He made ten tables and placed them in the temple, five on the south side and five on the north. He also made a hundred gold sprinkling bowls.

[9]He made the courtyard of the priests, and the large court and the doors for the court, and overlaid the doors with bronze. [10]He placed the Sea on the south side, at the southeast corner.

[11]He also made the pots and shovels and sprinkling bowls.

So Huram finished the work he had undertaken for King Solomon in the temple of God:

[12]the two pillars;

the two bowl-shaped capitals on top of the pillars;

the two sets of network decorating the two bowl-shaped capitals on top of the pillars;

[13]the four hundred pomegranates for the two sets of network (two rows of pomegranates for each network, decorating the bowl-shaped capitals on top of the pillars);

[14]the stands with their basins;

[15]the Sea and the twelve bulls under it;

[16]the pots, shovels, meat forks and all related articles.

All the objects that Huram-Abi made for King Solomon for the temple of the LORD were of polished bronze. [17]The king had them cast in clay molds in the plain of the Jordan between Succoth and Zarethan.[k] [18]All these things that Solomon made amounted to so much that the weight of the bronze was not determined.

[19]Solomon also made all the furnishings that were in God's temple:

the golden altar;

the tables on which was the bread of the Presence;

[20]the lampstands of pure gold with their lamps, to burn in front of the inner sanctuary as prescribed;

[21]the gold floral work and lamps and tongs (they were solid gold);

[22]the pure gold wick trimmers, sprinkling bowls, dishes and censers; and the gold doors of the temple: the inner doors to the Most Holy Place and the doors of the main hall.

5 When all the work Solomon had done for the temple of the LORD was finished, he brought in the things his father David had dedicated—the silver and gold and all the furnishings—and he placed them in the treasuries of God's temple.

The Ark Brought to the Temple

[2]Then Solomon summoned to Jerusalem the elders of Israel, all the heads of the tribes and the chiefs of the Israelite families, to bring up the ark of the LORD's covenant from Zion, the City of David. [3]And all the men of Israel came together to the king at the time of the festival in the seventh month.

[4]When all the elders of Israel had arrived, the Levites took up the ark, [5]and they brought up the ark and the Tent of Meeting and all the sacred furnishings in it. The priests, who were Levites, carried them up; [6]and King Solomon and the entire assembly of Israel that had gathered about him were before the ark, sacrificing so many sheep and cattle that they could not be recorded or counted.

---

[a]15 That is, about 52 feet (about 16 meters)   [b]16 Or possibly *made chains in the inner sanctuary*; the meaning of the Hebrew for this phrase is uncertain.   [c]17 *Jakin* probably means *he establishes*.   [d]17 *Boaz* probably means *in him is strength*.   [e]1 That is, about 30 feet (about 9 meters) long and wide, and about 15 feet (about 4.5 meters) high   [f]2 That is, about 7 1/2 feet (about 2.3 meters)   [g]2 That is, about 45 feet (about 13.5 meters)   [h]3 That is, about 1 1/2 feet (about 0.5 meter)   [i]5 That is, about 3 inches (about 8 centimeters)   [j]5 That is, about 17,500 gallons (about 66 kiloliters)   [k]17 Hebrew *Zeredatha*, a variant of *Zarethan*

7The priests then brought the ark of the LORD's covenant to its place in the inner sanctuary of the temple, the Most Holy Place, and put it beneath the wings of the cherubim. 8The cherubim spread their wings over the place of the ark and covered the ark and its carrying poles. 9These poles were so long that their ends, extending from the ark, could be seen from in front of the inner sanctuary, but not from outside the Holy Place; and they are still there today. 10There was nothing in the ark except the two tablets that Moses had placed in it at Horeb, where the LORD made a covenant with the Israelites after they came out of Egypt.

5:10 Proof of the Covenant

Until the invasion by Babylon, the Israelites possessed a visible reminder of God's treaty, or "covenant," with them. It stayed in the most sacred piece of furniture in Israel, the ark. But the ark was lost during the Babylonian captivity— and has never been found.

11The priests then withdrew from the Holy Place. All the priests who were there had consecrated themselves, regardless of their divisions. 12All the Levites who were musicians—Asaph, Heman, Jeduthun and their sons and relatives— stood on the east side of the altar, dressed in fine linen and playing cymbals, harps and lyres. They were accompanied by 120 priests sounding trumpets. 13The trumpeters and singers joined in unison, as with one voice, to give praise and thanks to the LORD. Accompanied by trumpets, cymbals and other instruments, they raised their voices in praise to the LORD and sang:

"He is good;
    his love endures forever."

Then the temple of the LORD was filled with a cloud, 14and the priests could not perform their service because of the cloud, for the glory of the LORD filled the temple of God.

6 Then Solomon said, "The LORD has said that he would dwell in a dark cloud; 2I have built a magnificent temple for you, a place for you to dwell forever."

3While the whole assembly of Israel was standing there, the king turned around and blessed them. 4Then he said:

"Praise be to the LORD, the God of Israel, who with his hands has fulfilled what he promised with his mouth to my father David. For he said, 5'Since the day I brought my people out of Egypt, I have not chosen

a city in any tribe of Israel to have a temple built for my Name to be there, nor have I chosen anyone to be the leader over my people Israel. 6But now I have chosen Jerusalem for my Name to be there, and I have chosen David to rule my people Israel.'

7"My father David had it in his heart to build a temple for the Name of the LORD, the God of Israel. 8But the LORD said to my father David, 'Because it was in your heart to build a temple for my Name, you did well to have this in your heart. 9Nevertheless, you are not the one to build the temple, but your son, who is your own flesh and blood—he is the one who will build the temple for my Name.'

10"The LORD has kept the promise he made. I have succeeded David my father and now I sit on the throne of Israel, just as the LORD promised, and I have built the temple for the Name of the LORD, the God of Israel. 11There I have placed the ark, in which is the covenant of the LORD that he made with the people of Israel."

Solomon's Prayer of Dedication

12Then Solomon stood before the altar of the LORD in front of the whole assembly of Israel and spread out his hands. 13Now he had made a bronze platform, five cubits[a] long, five cubits wide and three cubits[b] high, and had placed it in the center of the outer court. He stood on the platform and then knelt down before the whole assembly of Israel and spread out his hands toward heaven. 14He said:

"O LORD, God of Israel, there is no God like you in heaven or on earth—you who keep your covenant of love with your servants who continue wholeheartedly in your

6:14 Solomon's Peak

This chapter records Solomon's high point as a leader and hints at his lost potential. Thanks to David's conquests, Israel was at peace, and prosperous. Solomon's splendid prayer reveals the depth of his wisdom and spiritual sensitivity. But from this point on, Solomon, potentially the greatest of all Israel's rulers, slid toward selfishness and overindulgence. His failings led the nation into immorality and eventual civil war.

way. 15You have kept your promise to your servant David my father; with your mouth you have promised and with your hand you have fulfilled it—as it is today.

---

a13 That is, about 7 1/2 feet (about 2.3 meters)   b13 That is, about 4 1/2 feet (about 1.3 meters)

[16]"Now LORD, God of Israel, keep for your servant David my father the promises you made to him when you said, 'You shall never fail to have a man to sit before me on the throne of Israel, if only your sons are careful in all they do to walk before me according to my law, as you have done.' [17]And now, O LORD, God of Israel, let your word that you promised your servant David come true.

[18]"But will God really dwell on earth with men? The heavens, even the highest heavens, cannot contain you. How much less this temple I have built! [19]Yet give attention to your servant's prayer and his plea for mercy, O LORD my God. Hear the cry and the prayer that your servant is praying in your presence. [20]May your eyes be open toward this temple day and night, this place of which you said you would put your Name there. May you hear the prayer your servant prays toward this place. [21]Hear the supplications of your servant and of your people Israel when they pray toward this place. Hear from heaven, your dwelling place; and when you hear, forgive.

[22]"When a man wrongs his neighbor and is required to take an oath and he comes and swears the oath before your altar in this temple, [23]then hear from heaven and act. Judge between your servants, repaying the guilty by bringing down on his own head what he has done. Declare the innocent not guilty and so establish his innocence.

[24]"When your people Israel have been defeated by an enemy because they have sinned against you and when they turn back and confess your name, praying and making supplication before you in this temple, [25]then hear from heaven and forgive the sin of your people Israel and bring them back to the land you gave to them and their fathers.

[26]"When the heavens are shut up and there is no rain because your people have sinned against you, and when they pray toward this place and confess your name and turn from their sin because you have afflicted them, [27]then hear from heaven and forgive the sin of your servants, your people Israel. Teach them the right way to live, and send rain on the land you gave your people for an inheritance.

[28]"When famine or plague comes to the land, or blight or mildew, locusts or grasshoppers, or when enemies besiege them in any of their cities, whatever disaster or disease may come, [29]and when a prayer or plea is made by any of your people Israel—each one aware of his afflictions and pains, and spreading out his hands toward this temple— [30]then hear from heaven, your dwelling place. Forgive, and deal with each man according to all he does, since you know his heart (for you alone know the hearts of men), [31]so that they will fear you and walk in your ways all the time they live in the land you gave our fathers.

[32]"As for the foreigner who does not belong to your people Israel but has come from a distant land because of your great name and your mighty hand and your outstretched arm—when he comes and prays toward this temple, [33]then hear from heaven, your dwelling place, and do whatever the foreigner asks of you, so that all the peoples of the earth may know your name and fear you, as do your own people Israel, and may know that this house I have built bears your Name.

[34]"When your people go to war against their enemies, wherever you send them, and when they pray to you toward this city you have chosen and the temple I have built for your Name, [35]then hear from heaven their prayer and their plea, and uphold their cause.

[36]"When they sin against you—for there is no one who does not sin—and you become angry with them and give them over to the enemy, who takes them captive to a land far away or near; [37]and if they have a change of heart in the land where they are held captive, and repent and plead with you in the land of their captivity and say, 'We have sinned, we have done wrong and acted wickedly'; [38]and if they turn back to you with all their heart and soul in the land of their captivity where they were taken, and pray toward the land you gave their fathers, toward the city you have chosen and toward the temple I have built for your Name; [39]then from heaven, your dwelling place, hear their prayer and their pleas, and uphold their cause. And forgive your people, who have sinned against you.

[40]"Now, my God, may your eyes be open and your ears attentive to the prayers offered in this place.

[41]"Now arise, O LORD God, and come to
　　your resting place,
　　you and the ark of your might.
May your priests, O LORD God, be
　　clothed with salvation,
　　may your saints rejoice in your
　　　goodness.
[42]O LORD God, do not reject your
　　anointed one.

Remember the great love promised to David your servant."

The Dedication of the Temple

7 When Solomon finished praying, fire came down from heaven and consumed the burnt offering and the sacrifices, and the glory of the

7:1 A High-Water Mark

Solomon's prayer in chapter 6 and God's response in chapter 7 marked a high point in Israel's existence as a nation. United, the Israelites gathered before the gleaming new temple. They saw fire come down from heaven and the glory of the Lord fill the temple. Later, when this building was destroyed, Ezra led a drive to build a new temple. But the dramatic scene of God's glory coming down was never duplicated.

Lord filled the temple. ²The priests could not enter the temple of the Lord because the glory of the Lord filled it. ³When all the Israelites saw the fire coming down and the glory of the Lord above the temple, they knelt on the pavement with their faces to the ground, and they worshiped and gave thanks to the Lord, saying,

"He is good;
his love endures forever."

⁴Then the king and all the people offered sacrifices before the Lord. ⁵And King Solomon offered a sacrifice of twenty-two thousand head of cattle and a hundred and twenty thousand sheep and goats. So the king and all the people dedicated the temple of God. ⁶The priests took their positions, as did the Levites with the Lord's musical instruments, which King David had made for praising the Lord and which were used when he gave thanks, saying, "His love endures forever." Opposite the Levites, the priests blew their trumpets, and all the Israelites were standing.

⁷Solomon consecrated the middle part of the courtyard in front of the temple of the Lord, and there he offered burnt offerings and the fat of the fellowship offerings,ᵃ because the bronze altar he had made could not hold the burnt offerings, the grain offerings and the fat portions.

⁸So Solomon observed the festival at that time for seven days, and all Israel with him—a vast assembly, people from Leboᵇ Hamath to the Wadi of Egypt. ⁹On the eighth day they held an assembly, for they had celebrated the dedication of the altar for seven days and the festival for seven days more. ¹⁰On the twenty-third day of the seventh month he sent the people to their homes, joyful and glad in heart for the good things the Lord had done for David and Solomon and for his people Israel.

The Lord Appears to Solomon

¹¹When Solomon had finished the temple of the Lord and the royal palace, and had succeeded in carrying out all he had in mind to do in the temple of the Lord and in his own palace, ¹²the Lord appeared to him at night and said:

"I have heard your prayer and have chosen this place for myself as a temple for sacrifices.

¹³"When I shut up the heavens so that there is no rain, or command locusts to devour the land or send a plague among my people, ¹⁴if my people, who are called by my name, will humble themselves and pray and seek my face and turn from their wicked ways, then will I hear from heaven and will forgive their sin and will heal their land. ¹⁵Now my eyes will be open and my ears attentive to the prayers offered in this place. ¹⁶I have chosen and consecrated this temple so that my Name may be there forever. My eyes and my heart will always be there.

¹⁷"As for you, if you walk before me as David your father did, and do all I command, and observe my decrees and laws, ¹⁸I will establish your royal throne, as I covenanted with David your father when I said, 'You shall never fail to have a man to rule over Israel.'

¹⁹"But if youᶜ turn away and forsake the decrees and commands I have given youᶜ and go off to serve other gods and worship them, ²⁰then I will uproot Israel from my land, which I have given them, and will reject this temple I have consecrated for my Name. I will make it a byword and an object of ridicule among all peoples. ²¹And though this temple is now so imposing, all who pass by will be appalled and say, 'Why has the Lord done such a thing to this land and to this temple?' ²²People will answer, 'Because they have forsaken the Lord, the God of their fathers, who brought them out of Egypt, and have embraced other gods, worshiping and serving them—that is why he brought all this disaster on them.'"

Solomon's Other Activities

8 At the end of twenty years, during which Solomon built the temple of the Lord and his own palace, ²Solomon rebuilt the villages that

---

ᵃ7 Traditionally *peace offerings* ᵇ8 Or *from the entrance to* ᶜ19 The Hebrew is plural.

Hiram[a] had given him, and settled Israelites in them. [3]Solomon then went to Hamath Zobah and captured it. [4]He also built up Tadmor in the desert and all the store cities he had built in Hamath. [5]He rebuilt Upper Beth Horon and Lower Beth Horon as fortified cities, with walls and with gates and bars, [6]as well as Baalath and all his store cities, and all the cities for his chariots and for his horses[b]—whatever he desired to build in Jerusalem, in Lebanon and throughout all the territory he ruled.

[7]All the people left from the Hittites, Amorites, Perizzites, Hivites and Jebusites (these peoples were not Israelites), [8]that is, their descendants remaining in the land, whom the Israelites had not destroyed—these Solomon conscripted for his slave labor force, as it is to this day. [9]But Solomon did not make slaves of the Israelites for his work; they were his fighting men, commanders of his captains, and commanders of his chariots and charioteers. [10]They were also King Solomon's chief officials—two hundred and fifty officials supervising the men.

[11]Solomon brought Pharaoh's daughter up from the City of David to the palace he had built for her, for he said, "My wife must not live in the palace of David king of Israel, because the places the ark of the LORD has entered are holy."

8:11 Inconsistent Ethics

Solomon scrupulously kept Pharaoh's daughter, a Gentile foreigner, apart from the Israelite sacred places. Yet as the book of Kings shows, he eventually allowed his foreign wives to bring in their own idols, which had a disastrous effect on Israel.

[12]On the altar of the LORD that he had built in front of the portico, Solomon sacrificed burnt offerings to the LORD, [13]according to the daily requirement for offerings commanded by Moses for Sabbaths, New Moons and the three annual feasts—the Feast of Unleavened Bread, the Feast of Weeks and the Feast of Tabernacles. [14]In keeping with the ordinance of his father David, he appointed the divisions of the priests for their duties, and the Levites to lead the praise and to assist the priests according to each day's requirement. He also appointed the gatekeepers by divisions for the various gates, because this was what David the man of God had ordered. [15]They did not deviate from the king's commands to the priests or to the Levites in any matter, including that of the treasuries.

[16]All Solomon's work was carried out, from the day the foundation of the temple of the LORD was laid until its completion. So the temple of the LORD was finished.

[17]Then Solomon went to Ezion Geber and Elath on the coast of Edom. [18]And Hiram sent him ships commanded by his own officers, men who knew the sea. These, with Solomon's men, sailed to Ophir and brought back four hundred and fifty talents[c] of gold, which they delivered to King Solomon.

The Queen of Sheba Visits Solomon

9 When the queen of Sheba heard of Solomon's fame, she came to Jerusalem to test him with hard questions. Arriving with a very great caravan—with camels carrying spices, large quantities of gold, and precious stones—she came to Solomon and talked with him about all she had on her mind. [2]Solomon answered all her questions; nothing was too hard for him to explain to her. [3]When the queen of Sheba saw the wisdom of Solomon, as well as the palace he had built, [4]the food on his table, the seating of his officials, the attending servants in their robes, the cupbearers in their robes and the burnt offerings he made at[d] the temple of the LORD, she was overwhelmed.

[5]She said to the king, "The report I heard in my own country about your achievements and your wisdom is true. [6]But I did not believe what they said until I came and saw with my own eyes. Indeed, not even half the greatness of your wisdom was told me; you have far exceeded the report I heard. [7]How happy your men must be! How happy your officials, who continually stand before you and hear your wisdom! [8]Praise be to the LORD your God, who has delighted in you and placed you on his throne as king to rule for the LORD your God. Because of the love of your God for Israel and his desire to uphold them forever, he has made you king over them, to maintain justice and righteousness."

[9]Then she gave the king 120 talents[e] of gold, large quantities of spices, and precious stones. There had never been such spices as those the queen of Sheba gave to King Solomon.

[10](The men of Hiram and the men of Solomon brought gold from Ophir; they also brought algumwood[f] and precious stones. [11]The king used the algumwood to make steps for the temple of the LORD and for the royal palace, and to make harps and lyres for the musicians. Nothing like them had ever been seen in Judah.)

[12]King Solomon gave the queen of Sheba all she desired and asked for; he gave her more than

she had brought to him. Then she left and returned with her retinue to her own country.

Solomon's Splendor

[13]The weight of the gold that Solomon received yearly was 666 talents,[a] [14]not including

9:12 An Unfounded Rumor

The Queen of Sheba has mistakenly gone down in legend as one of Solomon's lovers. The king had 700 wives and 300 concubines, but the Queen of Sheba was not among them.

The queen's personal visit from hundreds of miles away shows Jerusalem's reputation as the sumptuous showpiece of the Middle East. She was probably on a high-level diplomatic mission. Solomon's kingdom represented a huge threat to her land, which previously had held a trade monopoly over the land route through Israel.

Solomon financed his building projects through iron and copper-smelting industries. He traded these products to Arabia and Africa for gold, silver, ivory, and exotic animals. Evidently, he and the queen reached an agreement.

the revenues brought in by merchants and traders. Also all the kings of Arabia and the governors of the land brought gold and silver to Solomon.

[15]King Solomon made two hundred large shields of hammered gold; six hundred bekas[b] of hammered gold went into each shield. [16]He also made three hundred small shields of hammered gold, with three hundred bekas[c] of gold in each shield. The king put them in the Palace of the Forest of Lebanon.

[17]Then the king made a great throne inlaid with ivory and overlaid with pure gold. [18]The throne had six steps, and a footstool of gold was attached to it. On both sides of the seat were armrests, with a lion standing beside each of them. [19]Twelve lions stood on the six steps, one at either end of each step. Nothing like it had ever been made for any other kingdom. [20]All King Solomon's goblets were gold, and all the household articles in the Palace of the Forest of Lebanon were pure gold. Nothing was made of silver, because silver was considered of little value in Solomon's day. [21]The king had a fleet of trading ships[d] manned by Hiram's[e] men. Once every three years it returned, carrying gold, silver and ivory, and apes and baboons.

[22]King Solomon was greater in riches and wisdom than all the other kings of the earth. [23]All the kings of the earth sought audience with Solomon to hear the wisdom God had put in his heart. [24]Year after year, everyone who came brought a gift—articles of silver and gold, and robes, weapons and spices, and horses and mules.

[25]Solomon had four thousand stalls for horses and chariots, and twelve thousand horses,[f] which he kept in the chariot cities and also with him in Jerusalem. [26]He ruled over all the kings from the River[g] to the land of the Philistines, as far as the border of Egypt. [27]The king made silver as common in Jerusalem as stones, and cedar as plentiful as sycamore-fig trees in the foothills. [28]Solomon's horses were imported from Egypt[h] and from all other countries.

Solomon's Death

[29]As for the other events of Solomon's reign, from beginning to end, are they not written in the records of Nathan the prophet, in the prophecy of Ahijah the Shilonite and in the visions of Iddo the seer concerning Jeroboam son of Nebat? [30]Solomon reigned in Jerusalem over all Israel forty years. [31]Then he rested with his fathers and was buried in the city of David his father. And Rehoboam his son succeeded him as king.

Israel Rebels Against Rehoboam

10 Rehoboam went to Shechem, for all the Israelites had gone there to make him king. [2]When Jeroboam son of Nebat heard this (he was in Egypt, where he had fled from King Solomon), he returned from Egypt. [3]So they sent for Jeroboam, and he and all Israel went to Rehoboam and said to him: [4]"Your father put a heavy yoke on us, but now lighten the harsh labor and the heavy yoke he put on us, and we will serve you."

[5]Rehoboam answered, "Come back to me in three days." So the people went away.

[6]Then King Rehoboam consulted the elders who had served his father Solomon during his lifetime. "How would you advise me to answer these people?" he asked.

[7]They replied, "If you will be kind to these people and please them and give them a favorable answer, they will always be your servants."

[8]But Rehoboam rejected the advice the elders gave him and consulted the young men who had grown up with him and were serving him. [9]He asked them, "What is your advice? How should we answer these people who say to me, 'Lighten the yoke your father put on us'?"

[10]The young men who had grown up with him

---

[a]13 That is, about 25 tons (about 23 metric tons)   [b]15 That is, about 7 1/2 pounds (about 3.5 kilograms)
[c]16 That is, about 3 3/4 pounds (about 1.7 kilograms)   [d]21 Hebrew *of ships that could go to Tarshish*
[e]21 Hebrew *Huram,* a variant of *Hiram*   [f]25 Or *charioteers*   [g]26 That is, the Euphrates   [h]28 Or possibly
Muzur, a region in Cilicia

replied, "Tell the people who have said to you, 'Your father put a heavy yoke on us, but make our yoke lighter'—tell them, 'My little finger is thicker than my father's waist. [11]My father laid on you a heavy yoke; I will make it even heavier. My father scourged you with whips; I will scourge you with scorpions.'"

[12]Three days later Jeroboam and all the people returned to Rehoboam, as the king had said, "Come back to me in three days." [13]The king answered them harshly. Rejecting the advice of the elders, [14]he followed the advice of the young men and said, "My father made your yoke heavy; I will make it even heavier. My father scourged you with whips; I will scourge you with scorpions." [15]So the king did not listen to the people, for this turn of events was from God, to fulfill the word the LORD had spoken to Jeroboam son of Nebat through Ahijah the Shilonite.

[16]When all Israel saw that the king refused to listen to them, they answered the king:

"What share do we have in David,
    what part in Jesse's son?
To your tents, O Israel!
    Look after your own house, O David!"

So all the Israelites went home. [17]But as for the Israelites who were living in the towns of Judah, Rehoboam still ruled over them.

[18]King Rehoboam sent out Adoniram,[a] who was in charge of forced labor, but the Israelites stoned him to death. King Rehoboam, however, managed to get into his chariot and escape to Jerusalem. [19]So Israel has been in rebellion against the house of David to this day.

[a] 18 Hebrew *Hadoram*, a variant of *Adoniram*

11 When Rehoboam arrived in Jerusalem, he mustered the house of Judah and Benjamin—a hundred and eighty thousand fighting men—to make war against Israel and to regain the kingdom for Rehoboam.

10:19 Unified Front

Second Chronicles pays little attention to the rebellion of the ten northern tribes against the two tribes in Judah. As the book of Kings shows, the two kingdoms existed side by side, and the North, Israel, often achieved more power than the South. But Chronicles, written to survivors in the South, virtually ignores the history of the North. In fact, in several places it uses the word Israel *to refer to the South, Judah.*

[2]But this word of the LORD came to Shemaiah the man of God: [3]"Say to Rehoboam son of Solomon king of Judah and to all the Israelites in Judah and Benjamin, [4]'This is what the LORD says: Do not go up to fight against your brothers. Go home, every one of you, for this is my doing.'" So they obeyed the words of the LORD and turned back from marching against Jeroboam.

Rehoboam Fortifies Judah

[5]Rehoboam lived in Jerusalem and built up towns for defense in Judah: [6]Bethlehem, Etam, Tekoa, [7]Beth Zur, Soco, Adullam, [8]Gath, Mareshah, Ziph, [9]Adoraim, Lachish, Azekah, [10]Zorah, Aijalon and Hebron. These were fortified cities in Judah and Benjamin. [11]He strengthened their de-

REHOBOAM *A Fool's Answer*

HIS FATHER SOLOMON HAD ASKED God for wisdom as his reign began (1:10). Evidently the wisdom did not get passed down in the family DNA.

At a coronation ceremony, the northern tribes of Israel were ready to swear allegiance to Rehoboam. They asked only that the new king ease Solomon's harsh taxation and forced labor policies. Rehoboam wisely asked for three days to think about it, and wisely consulted a number of counselors. But then he foolishly followed the very worst advice of some young men he had grown up with. "My father scourged you with whips," he told the Israelites. "I will scourge you with scorpions" (10:14).

This harsh answer resulted in armed rebellion, the tragic split of Israel into two countries and a "family fight" that continued on and off as long as both nations survived. The twelve tribes of Israel, named for twelve brothers, broke into two warring factions. One man's misplaced bravado caused it all.

Rehoboam was not always so foolish. At times he listened to the right counselors. Yet in general he showed little interest in the godliness that would have strengthened his kingdom: "He did evil because he had not set his heart on seeking the LORD" (12:14). By the Bible's standard, that made him the biggest fool.

Life Questions: When pressed, do you tend to harden your position, or listen carefully to the other side? What can help you avoid a belligerent response?

fenses and put commanders in them, with supplies of food, olive oil and wine. [12]He put shields and spears in all the cities, and made them very strong. So Judah and Benjamin were his.

[13]The priests and Levites from all their districts throughout Israel sided with him. [14]The Levites even abandoned their pasturelands and property, and came to Judah and Jerusalem because Jeroboam and his sons had rejected them as priests of the LORD. [15]And he appointed his own priests for the high places and for the goat and calf idols he had made. [16]Those from every tribe of Israel who set their hearts on seeking the LORD, the God of Israel, followed the Levites to Jerusalem to offer sacrifices to the LORD, the God of their fathers. [17]They strengthened the kingdom of Judah and supported Rehoboam son of Solomon three years, walking in the ways of David and Solomon during this time.

Rehoboam's Family

[18]Rehoboam married Mahalath, who was the daughter of David's son Jerimoth and of Abihail, the daughter of Jesse's son Eliab. [19]She bore him sons: Jeush, Shemariah and Zaham. [20]Then he married Maacah daughter of Absalom, who bore him Abijah, Attai, Ziza and Shelomith. [21]Rehoboam loved Maacah daughter of Absalom more than any of his other wives and concubines. In all, he had eighteen wives and sixty concubines, twenty-eight sons and sixty daughters.

[22]Rehoboam appointed Abijah son of Maacah to be the chief prince among his brothers, in order to make him king. [23]He acted wisely, dispersing some of his sons throughout the districts of Judah and Benjamin, and to all the fortified cities. He gave them abundant provisions and took many wives for them.

Shishak Attacks Jerusalem

12 After Rehoboam's position as king was established and he had become strong, he and all Israel[a] with him abandoned the law of the LORD. [2]Because they had been unfaithful to the LORD, Shishak king of Egypt attacked Jerusalem in the fifth year of King Rehoboam. [3]With twelve hundred chariots and sixty thousand horsemen and the innumerable troops of Libyans, Sukkites and Cushites[b] that came with him from Egypt, [4]he captured the fortified cities of Judah and came as far as Jerusalem.

[5]Then the prophet Shemaiah came to Rehoboam and to the leaders of Judah who had assembled in Jerusalem for fear of Shishak, and he said to them, "This is what the LORD says, 'You have abandoned me; therefore, I now abandon you to Shishak.'"

[6]The leaders of Israel and the king humbled themselves and said, "The LORD is just."

[7]When the LORD saw that they humbled themselves, this word of the LORD came to Shemaiah: "Since they have humbled themselves, I will not destroy them but will soon give them deliverance. My wrath will not be poured out on Jerusalem through Shishak. [8]They will, however, become subject to him, so that they may learn the difference between serving me and serving the kings of other lands."

[9]When Shishak king of Egypt attacked Jerusalem, he carried off the treasures of the temple of the LORD and the treasures of the royal palace. He took everything, including the gold shields Solomon had made. [10]So King Rehoboam made bronze shields to replace them and assigned these to the commanders of the guard on duty at the entrance to the royal palace. [11]Whenever the king went to the LORD's temple, the guards went with him, bearing the shields, and afterward they returned them to the guardroom.

[12]Because Rehoboam humbled himself, the LORD's anger turned from him, and he was not totally destroyed. Indeed, there was some good in Judah.

[13]King Rehoboam established himself firmly in Jerusalem and continued as king. He was forty-one years old when he became king, and he reigned seventeen years in Jerusalem, the city the LORD had chosen out of all the tribes of Israel in which to put his Name. His mother's name was Naamah; she was an Ammonite. [14]He did evil because he had not set his heart on seeking the LORD.

[15]As for the events of Rehoboam's reign, from beginning to end, are they not written in the records of Shemaiah the prophet and of Iddo the seer that deal with genealogies? There was continual warfare between Rehoboam and Jeroboam. [16]Rehoboam rested with his fathers and was buried in the City of David. And Abijah his son succeeded him as king.

Abijah King of Judah

13 In the eighteenth year of the reign of Jeroboam, Abijah became king of Judah, [2]and he reigned in Jerusalem three years. His mother's name was Maacah,[c] a daughter[d] of Uriel of Gibeah.

There was war between Abijah and Jeroboam. [3]Abijah went into battle with a force of four hundred thousand able fighting men, and Jeroboam drew up a battle line against him with eight hundred thousand able troops.

[4]Abijah stood on Mount Zemaraim, in the hill country of Ephraim, and said, "Jeroboam and all

---

[a]1 That is, Judah, as frequently in 2 Chronicles   [b]3 That is, people from the upper Nile region   [c]2 Most Septuagint manuscripts and Syriac (see also 2 Chron. 11:20 and 1 Kings 15:2); Hebrew *Micaiah*   [d]2 Or *granddaughter*

Israel, listen to me! 5Don't you know that the Lord, the God of Israel, has given the kingship of Israel to David and his descendants forever by a covenant of salt? 6Yet Jeroboam son of Nebat, an official of Solomon son of David, rebelled against his master. 7Some worthless scoundrels gathered around him and opposed Rehoboam son of Solomon when he was young and indecisive and not strong enough to resist them.

8"And now you plan to resist the kingdom of the Lord, which is in the hands of David's descendants. You are indeed a vast army and have with you the golden calves that Jeroboam made to be your gods. 9But didn't you drive out the priests of the Lord, the sons of Aaron, and the Levites, and make priests of your own as the peoples of other lands do? Whoever comes to consecrate himself with a young bull and seven rams may become a priest of what are not gods.

10"As for us, the Lord is our God, and we have not forsaken him. The priests who serve the Lord are sons of Aaron, and the Levites assist them. 11Every morning and evening they present burnt offerings and fragrant incense to the Lord. They set out the bread on the ceremonially clean table and light the lamps on the gold lampstand every evening. We are observing the requirements of the Lord our God. But you have forsaken him. 12God is with us; he is our leader. His priests with their trumpets will sound the battle cry against you. Men of Israel, do not fight against the Lord, the God of your fathers, for you will not succeed."

13Now Jeroboam had sent troops around to the rear, so that while he was in front of Judah the ambush was behind them. 14Judah turned and saw that they were being attacked at both front and rear. Then they cried out to the Lord. The priests blew their trumpets 15and the men of Judah raised the battle cry. At the sound of their battle cry, God routed Jeroboam and all Israel before Abijah and Judah. 16The Israelites fled before Judah, and God delivered them into their hands. 17Abijah and his men inflicted heavy losses on them, so that there were five hundred thousand casualties among Israel's able men. 18The men of Israel were subdued on that occasion, and the men of Judah were victorious be-cause they relied on the Lord, the God of their fathers.

19Abijah pursued Jeroboam and took from him the towns of Bethel, Jeshanah and Ephron, with their surrounding villages. 20Jeroboam did not regain power during the time of Abijah. And the Lord struck him down and he died.

21But Abijah grew in strength. He married fourteen wives and had twenty-two sons and six-teen daughters.

22The other events of Abijah's reign, what he did and what he said, are written in the annotations of the prophet Iddo.

14 And Abijah rested with his fathers and was buried in the City of David. Asa his son succeeded him as king, and in his days the country was at peace for ten years.

Asa King of Judah

2Asa did what was good and right in the eyes of the Lord his God. 3He removed the foreign altars and the high places, smashed the sacred stones and cut down the Asherah poles.a 4He commanded Judah to seek the Lord, the God of their fathers, and to obey his laws and commands. 5He removed the high places and incense altars in every town in Judah, and the kingdom was at peace under him. 6He built up the fortified cities of Judah, since the land was at peace. No one was at war with him during those years, for the Lord gave him rest.

7"Let us build up these towns," he said to Judah, "and put walls around them, with towers, gates and bars. The land is still ours, because we have sought the Lord our God; we sought him and he has given us rest on every side." So they built and prospered.

8Asa had an army of three hundred thousand men from Judah, equipped with large shields and with spears, and two hundred and eighty thousand from Benjamin, armed with small shields and with bows. All these were brave fighting men.

9Zerah the Cushite marched out against them with a vast armyb and three hundred chariots, and came as far as Mareshah. 10Asa went out to meet him, and they took up battle positions in the Valley of Zephathah near Mareshah.

11Then Asa called to the Lord his God and said, "Lord, there is no one like you to help the powerless against the mighty. Help us, O Lord our God, for we rely on you, and in your name we have come against this vast army. O Lord, you are our God; do not let man prevail against you."

12The Lord struck down the Cushites before Asa and Judah. The Cushites fled, 13and Asa and

---

a3 That is, symbols of the goddess Asherah; here and elsewhere in 2 Chronicles b9 Hebrew *with an army of a*
thousand thousands or *with an army of thousands upon thousands*

his army pursued them as far as Gerar. Such a great number of Cushites fell that they could not recover; they were crushed before the LORD and his forces. The men of Judah carried off a large amount of plunder. ¹⁴They destroyed all the villages around Gerar, for the terror of the LORD had fallen upon them. They plundered all these villages, since there was much booty there. ¹⁵They also attacked the camps of the herdsmen and carried off droves of sheep and goats and camels. Then they returned to Jerusalem.

Asa's Reform

15 The Spirit of God came upon Azariah son of Oded. ²He went out to meet Asa and said to him, "Listen to me, Asa and all Judah and Benjamin. The LORD is with you when you are with him. If you seek him, he will be found by you, but if you forsake him, he will forsake you. ³For a long time Israel was without the true God, without a priest to teach and without the law. ⁴But in their distress they turned to the LORD, the God of Israel, and sought him, and he was found by them. ⁵In those days it was not safe to travel about, for all the inhabitants of the lands were in great turmoil. ⁶One nation was being crushed by another and one city by another, because God was troubling them with every kind of distress. ⁷But as for you, be strong and do not give up, for your work will be rewarded."

⁸When Asa heard these words and the prophecy of Azariah son of[a] Oded the prophet, he took courage. He removed the detestable idols from the whole land of Judah and Benjamin and from the towns he had captured in the hills of Ephraim. He repaired the altar of the LORD that was in front of the portico of the LORD's temple.

⁹Then he assembled all Judah and Benjamin and the people from Ephraim, Manasseh and Simeon who had settled among them, for large numbers had come over to him from Israel when they saw that the LORD his God was with him. ¹⁰They assembled at Jerusalem in the third month of the fifteenth year of Asa's reign. ¹¹At that time they sacrificed to the LORD seven hundred head of cattle and seven thousand sheep and goats from the plunder they had brought back. ¹²They entered into a covenant to seek the LORD, the God of their fathers, with all their heart and soul. ¹³All who would not seek the LORD, the God of Israel, were to be put to death, whether small or great, man or woman. ¹⁴They took an oath to the LORD with loud acclamation, with shouting and with trumpets and horns. ¹⁵All Judah rejoiced about the oath because they had sworn it wholeheartedly. They sought God eager-

ly, and he was found by them. So the LORD gave them rest on every side.

¹⁶King Asa also deposed his grandmother Maacah from her position as queen mother, because she had made a repulsive Asherah pole. Asa cut the pole down, broke it up and burned it in the

15:9–15 Northern Visitors

For the first 50 years after Jeroboam's rebellion, Israel and Judah fought a civil war. Judah was badly outnumbered, but had one great rallying point: God's temple in the city of Jerusalem. Many of the kings of Israel had built idols on "high places" as alternative worship sites to discourage their citizens from making the pilgrimage to Jerusalem. But when a southern king such as Asa launched a religious revival, members of the northern tribes would sometimes come over to Jerusalem.

Kidron Valley. ¹⁷Although he did not remove the high places from Israel, Asa's heart was fully committed ⌊to the LORD⌋ all his life. ¹⁸He brought into the temple of God the silver and gold and the articles that he and his father had dedicated.

¹⁹There was no more war until the thirty-fifth year of Asa's reign.

Asa's Last Years

16 In the thirty-sixth year of Asa's reign Baasha king of Israel went up against Judah and fortified Ramah to prevent anyone from leaving or entering the territory of Asa king of Judah.

²Asa then took the silver and gold out of the treasuries of the LORD's temple and of his own palace and sent it to Ben-Hadad king of Aram, who was ruling in Damascus. ³"Let there be a treaty between me and you," he said, "as there was between my father and your father. See, I am sending you silver and gold. Now break your treaty with Baasha king of Israel so he will withdraw from me."

⁴Ben-Hadad agreed with King Asa and sent the commanders of his forces against the towns of Israel. They conquered Ijon, Dan, Abel Maim[b] and all the store cities of Naphtali. ⁵When Baasha heard this, he stopped building Ramah and abandoned his work. ⁶Then King Asa brought all the men of Judah, and they carried away from Ramah the stones and timber Baasha had been using. With them he built up Geba and Mizpah.

⁷At that time Hanani the seer came to Asa king of Judah and said to him: "Because you

---

a8 Vulgate and Syriac (see also Septuagint and verse 1); Hebrew does not have *Azariah son of.*   *b4* Also known as *Abel Beth Maacah* relied on the king of Aram and not on the LORD your God, the army of the king of Aram has escaped from your hand. [8]Were not the Cushites[a] and Libyans a mighty army with great numbers of chariots and horsemen[b]? Yet when you relied on the LORD, he delivered them into your hand. [9]For the eyes of the LORD range throughout the earth to strengthen those whose hearts are fully committed to him. You have done a foolish thing, and from now on you will be at war."

[10]Asa was angry with the seer because of this; he was so enraged that he put him in prison. At the same time Asa brutally oppressed some of the people.

[11]The events of Asa's reign, from beginning to end, are written in the book of the kings of Judah and Israel. [12]In the thirty-ninth year of his reign Asa was afflicted with a disease in his feet. Though his disease was severe, even in his illness he did not seek help from the LORD, but only

16:12 Bad Medical Advice

King Asa suffered from a serious foot disease, which some scholars think was dropsy. The Bible criticizes his consultations with physicians because in those days "physicians" were pagan healers who used rituals that conflicted with the law of God.

from the physicians. [13]Then in the forty-first year of his reign Asa died and rested with his fathers. [14]They buried him in the tomb that he had cut out for himself in the City of David. They laid him on a bier covered with spices and various blended perfumes, and they made a huge fire in his honor.

Jehoshaphat King of Judah

17 Jehoshaphat his son succeeded him as king and strengthened himself against Israel. [2]He stationed troops in all the fortified cities of Judah and put garrisons in Judah and in the towns of Ephraim that his father Asa had captured.

[3]The LORD was with Jehoshaphat because in his early years he walked in the ways his father David had followed. He did not consult the Baals [4]but sought the God of his father and followed his commands rather than the practices of Israel. [5]The LORD established the kingdom under his control; and all Judah brought gifts to Jehoshaphat, so that he had great wealth and honor. [6]His heart was devoted to the ways of the LORD; furthermore, he removed the high places and the Asherah poles from Judah.

[7]In the third year of his reign he sent his officials Ben-Hail, Obadiah, Zechariah, Nethanel and Micaiah to teach in the towns of Judah. [8]With them were certain Levites—Shemaiah, Nethaniah, Zebadiah, Asahel, Shemiramoth, Jehonathan, Adonijah, Tobijah and Tob-Adonijah—and the priests Elishama and Jehoram. [9]They taught throughout Judah, taking with them the Book of the Law of the LORD; they went around to all the towns of Judah and taught the people.

[10]The fear of the LORD fell on all the kingdoms of the lands surrounding Judah, so that they did not make war with Jehoshaphat. [11]Some Philistines brought Jehoshaphat gifts and silver as tribute, and the Arabs brought him flocks: seven thousand seven hundred rams and seven thousand seven hundred goats.

[12]Jehoshaphat became more and more powerful; he built forts and store cities in Judah [13]and had large supplies in the towns of Judah. He also kept experienced fighting men in Jerusalem. [14]Their enrollment by families was as follows:

> From Judah, commanders of units of 1,000:
>> Adnah the commander, with 300,000 fighting men;
> [15]next, Jehohanan the commander, with 280,000;
> [16]next, Amasiah son of Zicri, who volunteered himself for the service of the LORD, with 200,000.
>
> [17]From Benjamin:
>> Eliada, a valiant soldier, with 200,000 men armed with bows and shields;
> [18]next, Jehozabad, with 180,000 men armed for battle.

[19]These were the men who served the king, besides those he stationed in the fortified cities throughout Judah.

Micaiah Prophesies Against Ahab

18 Now Jehoshaphat had great wealth and honor, and he allied himself with Ahab by marriage. [2]Some years later he went down to visit Ahab in Samaria. Ahab slaughtered many sheep and cattle for him and the people with him and urged him to attack Ramoth Gilead. [3]Ahab king of Israel asked Jehoshaphat king of Judah, "Will you go with me against Ramoth Gilead?"

Jehoshaphat replied, "I am as you are, and my people as your people; we will join you in the war." [4]But Jehoshaphat also said to the king of Israel, "First seek the counsel of the LORD."

[5]So the king of Israel brought together the prophets—four hundred men—and asked

---

[a]8 That is, people from the upper Nile region   [b]8 Or *charioteers*

them, "Shall we go to war against Ramoth Gilead, or shall I refrain?"

"Go," they answered, "for God will give it into the king's hand."

⁶But Jehoshaphat asked, "Is there not a prophet of the LORD here whom we can inquire of?"

18:6 A True or False Prophet?

Looking back from a modern perspective, it is difficult to imagine the confusion that surrounded ancient prophets. Which ones were true prophets and which were false? In this case, 400 prophets all insisted God said one thing; only one bold man contradicted them. King Jehoshaphat sensed a falseness in the 400 and insisted on listening to the true prophet. Yet, unaccountably, he failed to heed Micaiah's warning. The decision nearly cost him his life. See Deuteronomy 18:17–22 for advice on distinguishing true prophets from false.

⁷The king of Israel answered Jehoshaphat, "There is still one man through whom we can inquire of the LORD, but I hate him because he never prophesies anything good about me, but always bad. He is Micaiah son of Imlah."

"The king should not say that," Jehoshaphat replied.

⁸So the king of Israel called one of his officials and said, "Bring Micaiah son of Imlah at once."

⁹Dressed in their royal robes, the king of Israel and Jehoshaphat king of Judah were sitting on their thrones at the threshing floor by the entrance to the gate of Samaria, with all the prophets prophesying before them. ¹⁰Now Zedekiah son of Kenaanah had made iron horns, and he declared, "This is what the LORD says: 'With these you will gore the Arameans until they are destroyed.'"

¹¹All the other prophets were prophesying the same thing. "Attack Ramoth Gilead and be victorious," they said, "for the LORD will give it into the king's hand."

¹²The messenger who had gone to summon Micaiah said to him, "Look, as one man the other prophets are predicting success for the king. Let your word agree with theirs, and speak favorably."

¹³But Micaiah said, "As surely as the LORD lives, I can tell him only what my God says."

¹⁴When he arrived, the king asked him, "Micaiah, shall we go to war against Ramoth Gilead, or shall I refrain?"

"Attack and be victorious," he answered, "for they will be given into your hand."

¹⁵The king said to him, "How many times must I make you swear to tell me nothing but the truth in the name of the LORD?"

¹⁶Then Micaiah answered, "I saw all Israel scattered on the hills like sheep without a shepherd, and the LORD said, 'These people have no master. Let each one go home in peace.'"

¹⁷The king of Israel said to Jehoshaphat, "Didn't I tell you that he never prophesies anything good about me, but only bad?"

¹⁸Micaiah continued, "Therefore hear the word of the LORD: I saw the LORD sitting on his throne with all the host of heaven standing on his right and on his left. ¹⁹And the LORD said, 'Who will entice Ahab king of Israel into attacking Ramoth Gilead and going to his death there?'

"One suggested this, and another that. ²⁰Finally, a spirit came forward, stood before the LORD and said, 'I will entice him.'

"'By what means?' the LORD asked.

²¹"'I will go and be a lying spirit in the mouths of all his prophets,' he said.

"'You will succeed in enticing him,' said the LORD. 'Go and do it.'

²²"So now the LORD has put a lying spirit in the mouths of these prophets of yours. The LORD has decreed disaster for you."

²³Then Zedekiah son of Kenaanah went up and slapped Micaiah in the face. "Which way did the spirit from[a] the LORD go when he went from me to speak to you?" he asked.

²⁴Micaiah replied, "You will find out on the day you go to hide in an inner room."

²⁵The king of Israel then ordered, "Take Micaiah and send him back to Amon the ruler of the city and to Joash the king's son, ²⁶and say, 'This is what the king says: Put this fellow in prison and give him nothing but bread and water until I return safely.'"

²⁷Micaiah declared, "If you ever return safely, the LORD has not spoken through me." Then he added, "Mark my words, all you people!"

Ahab Killed at Ramoth Gilead

²⁸So the king of Israel and Jehoshaphat king of Judah went up to Ramoth Gilead. ²⁹The king of Israel said to Jehoshaphat, "I will enter the battle in disguise, but you wear your royal robes." So the king of Israel disguised himself and went into battle.

³⁰Now the king of Aram had ordered his chariot commanders, "Do not fight with anyone, small or great, except the king of Israel." ³¹When the chariot commanders saw Jehoshaphat, they thought, "This is the king of Israel." So they turned to attack him, but Jehoshaphat cried out, and the LORD helped him. God drew them away from him, ³²for when the chariot commanders

a23 Or *Spirit of*

saw that he was not the king of Israel, they stopped pursuing him. ³³But someone drew his bow at random and hit the king of Israel between the sections of his armor. The king told the chariot driver, "Wheel around and get me out of the fighting. I've been wounded." ³⁴All day long the battle raged, and the king of Israel propped himself up in his chariot facing the Arameans until evening. Then at sunset he died.

19 When Jehoshaphat king of Judah returned safely to his palace in Jerusalem, ²Jehu the seer, the son of Hanani, went out to meet him and said to the king, "Should you help the wicked and love*ᵃ* those who hate the LORD? Because of this, the wrath of the LORD is upon you. ³There is, however, some good in you, for you have rid the land of the Asherah poles and have set your heart on seeking God."

Jehoshaphat Appoints Judges

⁴Jehoshaphat lived in Jerusalem, and he went out again among the people from Beersheba to the hill country of Ephraim and turned them back to the LORD, the God of their fathers. ⁵He appointed judges in the land, in each of the fortified cities of Judah. ⁶He told them, "Consider carefully what you do, because you are not judging for man but for the LORD, who is with you whenever you give a verdict. ⁷Now let the fear of the LORD be upon you. Judge carefully, for with the LORD our God there is no injustice or partiality or bribery."

⁸In Jerusalem also, Jehoshaphat appointed some of the Levites, priests and heads of Israelite families to administer the law of the LORD and to settle disputes. And they lived in Jerusalem. ⁹He gave them these orders: "You must serve faithfully and wholeheartedly in the fear of the LORD. ¹⁰In every case that comes before you from your fellow countrymen who live in the cities — whether bloodshed or other concerns of the law, commands, decrees or ordinances — you are to warn them not to sin against the LORD; otherwise his wrath will come on you and your brothers. Do this, and you will not sin.

¹¹"Amariah the chief priest will be over you in any matter concerning the LORD, and Zebadiah son of Ishmael, the leader of the tribe of Judah, will be over you in any matter concerning the king, and the Levites will serve as officials before you. Act with courage, and may the LORD be with those who do well."

Jehoshaphat Defeats Moab and Ammon

20 After this, the Moabites and Ammonites with some of the Meunites*ᵇ* came to make war on Jehoshaphat.

²Some men came and told Jehoshaphat, "A vast army is coming against you from Edom,*ᶜ* from the other side of the Sea.*ᵈ* It is already in Hazazon Tamar" (that is, En Gedi). ³Alarmed, Jehoshaphat resolved to inquire of the LORD, and he proclaimed a fast for all Judah. ⁴The people of Judah came together to seek help from the LORD; indeed, they came from every town in Judah to seek him.

⁵Then Jehoshaphat stood up in the assembly of Judah and Jerusalem at the temple of the LORD in the front of the new courtyard ⁶and said:

"O LORD, God of our fathers, are you not the God who is in heaven? You rule over all the kingdoms of the nations. Power and might are in your hand, and no one

20:6 A Model Prayer

Second Chronicles contains two great prayers: Solomon's in chapter 6 and King Jehoshaphat's here. Commentators often point to this as a model prayer. Jehoshaphat began with adoration of God, reminded him of his promises, set forth a problem, and asked for help. Confident, Jehoshaphat thanked God for the answer even before it came.

can withstand you. ⁷O our God, did you not drive out the inhabitants of this land before your people Israel and give it forever to the descendants of Abraham your friend? ⁸They have lived in it and have built in it a sanctuary for your Name, saying, ⁹'If calamity comes upon us, whether the sword of judgment, or plague or famine, we will stand in your presence before this temple that bears your Name and will cry out to you in our distress, and you will hear us and save us.'

¹⁰"But now here are men from Ammon, Moab and Mount Seir, whose territory you would not allow Israel to invade when they came from Egypt; so they turned away from them and did not destroy them. ¹¹See how they are repaying us by coming to drive us out of the possession you gave us as an inheritance. ¹²O our God, will you not judge them? For we have no power to face this vast army that is attacking us. We do not know what to do, but our eyes are upon you."

¹³All the men of Judah, with their wives and children and little ones, stood there before the LORD.

---

*ᵃ*2 Or *and make alliances with*   *ᵇ*1 Some Septuagint manuscripts; Hebrew *Ammonites*   *ᶜ*2 One Hebrew manuscript; most Hebrew manuscripts, Septuagint and Vulgate *Aram*   *ᵈ*2 That is, the Dead Sea

¹⁴Then the Spirit of the LORD came upon Jahaziel son of Zechariah, the son of Benaiah, the son of Jeiel, the son of Mattaniah, a Levite and descendant of Asaph, as he stood in the assembly.

¹⁵He said: "Listen, King Jehoshaphat and all who live in Judah and Jerusalem! This is what the LORD says to you: 'Do not be afraid or discouraged because of this vast army. For the battle is not yours, but God's. ¹⁶Tomorrow march down against them. They will be climbing up by the Pass of Ziz, and you will find them at the end of the gorge in the Desert of Jeruel. ¹⁷You will not have to fight this battle. Take up your positions; stand firm and see the deliverance the LORD will give you, O Judah and Jerusalem. Do not be afraid; do not be discouraged. Go out to face them tomorrow, and the LORD will be with you.'"

¹⁸Jehoshaphat bowed with his face to the ground, and all the people of Judah and Jerusalem fell down in worship before the LORD. ¹⁹Then some Levites from the Kohathites and Korahites stood up and praised the LORD, the God of Israel, with very loud voice.

²⁰Early in the morning they left for the Desert of Tekoa. As they set out, Jehoshaphat stood and said, "Listen to me, Judah and people of Jerusalem! Have faith in the LORD your God and you will be upheld; have faith in his prophets and you will be successful." ²¹After consulting the people, Jehoshaphat appointed men to sing to the LORD and to praise him for the splendor of his^a holiness as they went out at the head of the army, saying:

"Give thanks to the LORD,
    for his love endures forever."

²²As they began to sing and praise, the LORD set ambushes against the men of Ammon and Moab and Mount Seir who were invading Judah, and they were defeated. ²³The men of Ammon and Moab rose up against the men from Mount Seir to destroy and annihilate them. After they finished slaughtering the men from Seir, they helped to destroy one another.

²⁴When the men of Judah came to the place that overlooks the desert and looked toward the vast army, they saw only dead bodies lying on the ground; no one had escaped. ²⁵So Jehoshaphat and his men went to carry off their plunder, and they found among them a great amount of equipment and clothing^b and also articles of value—more than they could take away. There was so much plunder that it took three days to collect it. ²⁶On the fourth day they assembled in the Valley of Beracah, where they praised the LORD. This is why it is called the Valley of Beracah^c to this day.

²⁷Then, led by Jehoshaphat, all the men of Judah and Jerusalem returned joyfully to Jerusalem, for the LORD had given them cause to rejoice over their enemies. ²⁸They entered Jerusalem and went to the temple of the LORD with harps and lutes and trumpets.

²⁹The fear of God came upon all the kingdoms of the countries when they heard how the LORD had fought against the enemies of Israel. ³⁰And the kingdom of Jehoshaphat was at peace, for his God had given him rest on every side.

The End of Jehoshaphat's Reign

³¹So Jehoshaphat reigned over Judah. He was thirty-five years old when he became king of Judah, and he reigned in Jerusalem twenty-five years. His mother's name was Azubah daughter of Shilhi. ³²He walked in the ways of his father Asa and did not stray from them; he did what was right in the eyes of the LORD. ³³The high places, however, were not removed, and the people still had not set their hearts on the God of their fathers.

³⁴The other events of Jehoshaphat's reign, from beginning to end, are written in the annals of Jehu son of Hanani, which are recorded in the book of the kings of Israel.

³⁵Later, Jehoshaphat king of Judah made an alliance with Ahaziah king of Israel, who was guilty of wickedness. ³⁶He agreed with him to construct a fleet of trading ships.^d After these were built at Ezion Geber, ³⁷Eliezer son of Dodavahu of Mareshah prophesied against Jehoshaphat, saying, "Because you have made an alliance with Ahaziah, the LORD will destroy what you have made." The ships were wrecked and were not able to set sail to trade.^e

21 Then Jehoshaphat rested with his fathers and was buried with them in the City of David. And Jehoram his son succeeded him as king. ²Jehoram's brothers, the sons of Jehoshaphat, were Azariah, Jehiel, Zechariah, Azariahu, Michael and Shephatiah. All these were sons of Jehoshaphat king of Israel.^f ³Their father had given them many gifts of silver and gold and articles of value, as well as fortified cities in Judah, but he had given the kingdom to Jehoram because he was his firstborn son.

Jehoram King of Judah

⁴When Jehoram established himself firmly over his father's kingdom, he put all his brothers to the sword along with some of the princes of Israel. ⁵Jehoram was thirty-two years old when he became king, and he reigned in Jerusalem

^a21 Or *him with the splendor of*   ^b25 Some Hebrew manuscripts and Vulgate; most Hebrew manuscripts *corpses*
^c26 *Beracah* means *praise.*   ^d36 Hebrew *of ships that could go to Tarshish*   ^e37 Hebrew *sail for Tarshish*
^f2 That is, Judah, as frequently in 2 Chronicles

eight years. 6He walked in the ways of the kings of Israel, as the house of Ahab had done, for he married a daughter of Ahab. He did evil in the eyes of the LORD. 7Nevertheless, because of the covenant the LORD had made with David, the LORD was not willing to destroy the house of David. He had promised to maintain a lamp for him and his descendants forever.

8In the time of Jehoram, Edom rebelled against Judah and set up its own king. 9So Jehoram went there with his officers and all his chariots. The Edomites surrounded him and his chariot commanders, but he rose up and broke through by night. 10To this day Edom has been in rebellion against Judah.

Libnah revolted at the same time, because Jehoram had forsaken the LORD, the God of his fathers. 11He had also built high places on the hills of Judah and had caused the people of Jerusalem to prostitute themselves and had led Judah astray.

12Jehoram received a letter from Elijah the prophet, which said:

"This is what the LORD, the God of your father David, says: 'You have not walked in the ways of your father Jehoshaphat or of Asa king of Judah. 13But you have walked in the ways of the kings of Israel, and you have led Judah and the people of Jerusalem to prostitute themselves, just as the house of Ahab did. You have also murdered your own brothers, members of your father's house, men who were better than you. 14So

The Great Reformers
Profiles in courage: the heroic kings of Judah

IN 1954 UNITED STATES SENATOR John F. Kennedy knew he would spend at least six months flat on his back. Surgeons were about to begin work on him to correct an old war injury. How could he best spend his time?

Kennedy decided to use those "idle" hours to research the most courageous individuals in American history. The idea for a book was born. *Profiles in Courage* went on to win the Pulitzer Prize and become a best seller. Kennedy's study of courageous people inspired the young senator to model his own life after them.

> "The LORD is with you when you are with him. If you seek him, he will be found by you, but if you forsake him, he will forsake you."
> 15:2

Courage in Judah

The book of 2 Chronicles can be seen as a kind of "profiles in courage" for the nation of Judah. The vast majority of kings flunked the courage test. But a few exceptions did stand out, and 2 Chronicles dwells on them.

This book records a form of courage different from what John Kennedy had in mind. Judah was drifting further and further away from the worship of the true God. It took great courage to fight against that trend and call for a return to the law of Moses. Therefore these kings excelled not so much because of military or political strength, but because of their faithfulness to God. All the great reformers described here took over in difficult times. They helped stop, at least temporarily, their nation's tragic slide away from God.

Asa: Cleaning Up the Land (chapters 14–16)

Asa inherited a country full of crime and anarchy. He led a wildfire revival, with the whole nation uniting behind him in a huge celebration in Jerusalem. Yet Asa became cocky in his later years—he jailed a prophet of God and lived out his last days plagued by war and by disease. He did much good, but fell short of the kind of courage that endures a national crisis.

Jehoshaphat: The Organizer (chapters 17–20)

Where Asa inspired the nation, Jehoshaphat organized it. He had an outstanding domestic policy: He educated his citizens in the Book of the Law and built up a national court system and large army. Curiously, Jehoshaphat's wise judgment failed to carry over into foreign policy, for he made foolish alliances with neighboring Israel's very worst king, Ahab.

Joash: Refurbishing the Temple (chapters 23–24)

Joash stepped onto the throne as a boy of seven. He reigned 40 years and accomplished much

now the LORD is about to strike your people, your sons, your wives and everything that is yours, with a heavy blow. [15]You yourself will be very ill with a lingering disease of the bowels, until the disease causes your bowels to come out.'"

21:6 Married Despots

After the benign reign of Jehoshaphat, Judah got one of its worst kings ever, Jehoram. His marriage to Athaliah, daughter of a despised pagan king, undoubtedly stirred up revolt. To eliminate rivals, Jehoram promptly killed off his brothers, along with the "princes of Israel" (possibly leaders of the revolt). Later, Athaliah would become Judah's only reigning queen—and commit even greater atrocities (22:10).

[16]The LORD aroused against Jehoram the hostility of the Philistines and of the Arabs who lived near the Cushites. [17]They attacked Judah, invaded it and carried off all the goods found in the king's palace, together with his sons and wives. Not a son was left to him except Ahaziah,[a] the youngest.

[18]After all this, the LORD afflicted Jehoram with an incurable disease of the bowels. [19]In the course of time, at the end of the second year, his bowels came out because of the disease, and he died in great pain. His people made no fire in his honor, as they had for his fathers.

[20]Jehoram was thirty-two years old when he became king, and he reigned in Jerusalem eight years. He passed away, to no one's regret, and was buried in the City of David, but not in the tombs of the kings.

Ahaziah King of Judah

22 The people of Jerusalem made Ahaziah, Jehoram's youngest son, king in his place, since the raiders, who came with the Arabs into the camp, had killed all the older sons. So Ahaziah son of Jehoram king of Judah began to reign.

[2]Ahaziah was twenty-two[b] years old when he became king, and he reigned in Jerusalem one year. His mother's name was Athaliah, a granddaughter of Omri.

[3]He too walked in the ways of the house of Ahab, for his mother encouraged him in doing wrong. [4]He did evil in the eyes of the LORD, as the house of Ahab had done, for after his father's death they became his advisers, to his undoing. [5]He also followed their counsel when he went with Joram[c] son of Ahab king of Israel to war against Hazael king of Aram at Ramoth Gilead.

---

[a]17 Hebrew *Jehoahaz*, a variant of *Ahaziah*   [b]2 Some Septuagint manuscripts and Syriac (see also 2 Kings 8:26); Hebrew *forty-two*   [c]5 Hebrew *Jehoram*, a variant of *Joram*; also in verses 6 and 7

---

good. Second Chronicles focuses mainly on his repairs of the temple, which he tried to restore to former glory.

Jehoiada: Strength behind the Throne (chapters 23–24)

King Joash hardly deserves a compliment without the mention of a priest named Jehoiada. He hid the boy Joash from a murderous queen and led the dramatic revolt against her. When Jehoiada died at a very old age, the nation gave him the extraordinary honor of a burial place alongside kings. After Jehoiada's death, everything went downhill. The boy king who had shown such promise murdered Jehoiada's son, a deed that went down as one of the great crimes of Israelite history. It became clear that the real strength of the kingdom had come from the old priest, not the young king.

Hezekiah: A Day to Remember (chapters 29–32)

Second Chronicles gives more space to the reign of Hezekiah than to that of any other reformer. He sponsored a great religious festival, an idea that first met with scorn and ridicule. But the nation did come together in a remarkable scene of happiness and unity. "There was great joy in Jerusalem," the Bible says, "for since the days of Solomon son of David king of Israel there had been nothing like this in Jerusalem" (30:26).

Josiah: The Complete Reformer (chapters 34–35)

Josiah was perhaps the most reform-conscious of all Judah's kings. When the Book of the Law (probably Deuteronomy) was discovered, Josiah realized just how far his kingdom had strayed from God's ideal. He tore his robes and wept, and led Judah back toward God. A foolish military campaign brought about Josiah's death and ruined the chances for permanent change in Judah. Known as "the good king Josiah," he was mourned by the whole nation. The prophet Jeremiah composed songs, or laments, in his memory.

Life Questions: These kings demonstrate that one person's faith can affect a great many others. Think of strong leaders you know up close. What makes them effective at inspiring and motivating others?

The Arameans wounded Joram; **6**so he returned to Jezreel to recover from the wounds they had inflicted on him at Ramoth*a* in his battle with Hazael king of Aram.

Then Ahaziah*b* son of Jehoram king of Judah went down to Jezreel to see Joram son of Ahab because he had been wounded.

7Through Ahaziah's visit to Joram, God brought about Ahaziah's downfall. When Ahaziah arrived, he went out with Joram to meet Jehu son of Nimshi, whom the LORD had anointed to destroy the house of Ahab. **8**While Jehu was executing judgment on the house of Ahab, he found the princes of Judah and the sons of Ahaziah's relatives, who had been attending Ahaziah, and he killed them. **9**He then went in search of Ahaziah, and his men captured him while he was hiding in Samaria. He was brought to Jehu and put to death. They buried him, for they said, "He was a son of Jehoshaphat, who sought the LORD with all his heart." So there was no one in the house of Ahaziah powerful enough to retain the kingdom.

Athaliah and Joash

10When Athaliah the mother of Ahaziah saw that her son was dead, she proceeded to destroy the whole royal family of the house of Judah. **11**But Jehosheba,*c* the daughter of King Jehoram, took Joash son of Ahaziah and stole him away from among the royal princes who were about to be murdered and put him and his nurse in a bedroom. Because Jehosheba,*c* the daughter of King Jehoram and wife of the priest Jehoiada, was Ahaziah's sister, she hid the child from Athaliah so she could not kill him. **12**He remained hidden with them at the temple of God for six years while Athaliah ruled the land.

23 In the seventh year Jehoiada showed his strength. He made a covenant with the commanders of units of a hundred: Azariah son of Jeroham, Ishmael son of Jehohanan, Azariah son of Obed, Maaseiah son of Adaiah, and Elishaphat son of Zicri. **2**They went throughout Judah and gathered the Levites and the heads of Israelite families from all the towns. When they came to Jerusalem, **3**the whole assembly made a covenant with the king at the temple of God.

Jehoiada said to them, "The king's son shall reign, as the LORD promised concerning the descendants of David. **4**Now this is what you are to do: A third of you priests and Levites who are going on duty on the Sabbath are to keep watch at the doors, **5**a third of you at the royal palace and a third at the Foundation Gate, and all the other men are to be in the courtyards of the temple of the LORD. **6**No one is to enter the temple of the LORD except the priests and Levites on duty; they may enter because they are consecrated, but all the other men are to guard what the LORD has assigned to them.*d* **7**The Levites are to station themselves around the king, each man with his weapons in his hand. Anyone who enters the temple must be put to death. Stay close to the king wherever he goes."

8The Levites and all the men of Judah did just as Jehoiada the priest ordered. Each one took his men—those who were going on duty on the Sabbath and those who were going off duty—for Jehoiada the priest had not released any of the divisions. **9**Then he gave the commanders of units of a hundred the spears and the large and

---

a6 Hebrew *Ramah*, a variant of *Ramoth*   *b6* Some Hebrew manuscripts, Septuagint, Vulgate and Syriac (see also 2 Kings 8:29); most Hebrew manuscripts *Azariah*   *c11* Hebrew *Jehoshabeath*, a variant of *Jehosheba*   *d6* Or *to observe the LORD's command ⸤not to enter⸥*

ATHALIAH *Live by the Sword . . .*

IN OLD TESTAMENT TIMES AMBITIOUS women usually exerted themselves through their husbands. Athaliah's wicked mother Jezebel, for example, dominated her husband Ahab, king of Israel.

Athaliah took another route, preferring to go it alone. She reigned eight years as queen to King Jehoram and a year as Queen Mother with their son Ahaziah. But when Ahaziah died a violent death, Mother decided to take charge for herself. Ruthless as Lady Macbeth, Athaliah had all potential rivals—including her own children and grandchildren—put to death. She reigned alone for six years, secure in the throne since she had eliminated all opposition.

Then appeared, in a scene as dramatic as any in the Bible, a royal heir she had overlooked. The seven-year-old boy Joash—her grandson—had been hidden in the temple all those years. This boy was now brought out and displayed on the temple steps. When Athaliah heard the tumultuous response, she went to see what the commotion was about. A revolution was underway. Rebels captured her and put her to death, and not a single person came to her defense.

Life Questions: Which type of people do you think are more likely to cause trouble: "loners," or people who have many friends and allies? Why?

small shields that had belonged to King David and that were in the temple of God. ¹⁰He stationed all the men, each with his weapon in his hand, around the king—near the altar and the

temple, from the south side to the north side of the temple.

¹¹Jehoiada and his sons brought out the king's son and put the crown on him; they presented him with a copy of the covenant and proclaimed him king. They anointed him and shouted, "Long live the king!"

¹²When Athaliah heard the noise of the people running and cheering the king, she went to them at the temple of the LORD. ¹³She looked, and there was the king, standing by his pillar at the entrance. The officers and the trumpeters were beside the king, and all the people of the land were rejoicing and blowing trumpets, and singers with musical instruments were leading the praises. Then Athaliah tore her robes and shouted, "Treason! Treason!"

¹⁴Jehoiada the priest sent out the commanders of units of a hundred, who were in charge of the troops, and said to them: "Bring her out between the ranks*ᵃ* and put to the sword anyone who follows her." For the priest had said, "Do not put her to death at the temple of the LORD." ¹⁵So they seized her as she reached the entrance of the Horse Gate on the palace grounds, and there they put her to death.

¹⁶Jehoiada then made a covenant that he and the people and the king*ᵇ* would be the LORD's people. ¹⁷All the people went to the temple of Baal and tore it down. They smashed the altars and idols and killed Mattan the priest of Baal in front of the altars.

¹⁸Then Jehoiada placed the oversight of the temple of the LORD in the hands of the priests, who were Levites, to whom David had made assignments in the temple, to present the burnt offerings of the LORD as written in the Law of Moses, with rejoicing and singing, as David had ordered. ¹⁹He also stationed doorkeepers at the gates of the LORD's temple so that no one who was in any way unclean might enter.

²⁰He took with him the commanders of hundreds, the nobles, the rulers of the people and all the people of the land and brought the king down from the temple of the LORD. They went into the palace through the Upper Gate and seated the king on the royal throne, ²¹and all the people of the land rejoiced. And the city was quiet, because Athaliah had been slain with the sword.

Joash Repairs the Temple

24 Joash was seven years old when he became king, and he reigned in Jerusalem forty years. His mother's name was Zibiah; she was from Beersheba. ²Joash did what was right in the eyes of the LORD all the years of Jehoiada the priest. ³Jehoiada chose two wives for him, and he had sons and daughters.

⁴Some time later Joash decided to restore the temple of the LORD. ⁵He called together the priests and Levites and said to them, "Go to the towns of Judah and collect the money due annually from all Israel, to repair the temple of your God. Do it now." But the Levites did not act at once.

⁶Therefore the king summoned Jehoiada the chief priest and said to him, "Why haven't you required the Levites to bring in from Judah and Jerusalem the tax imposed by Moses the servant of the LORD and by the assembly of Israel for the Tent of the Testimony?"

⁷Now the sons of that wicked woman Athaliah had broken into the temple of God and had used even its sacred objects for the Baals.

⁸At the king's command, a chest was made and placed outside, at the gate of the temple of the LORD. ⁹A proclamation was then issued in Judah and Jerusalem that they should bring to the LORD the tax that Moses the servant of God had required of Israel in the desert. ¹⁰All the officials and all the people brought their contributions gladly, dropping them into the chest until it was full. ¹¹Whenever the chest was brought in by the Levites to the king's officials and they saw that there was a large amount of money, the royal secretary and the officer of the chief priest would come and empty the chest and carry it back to its place. They did this regularly and collected a great amount of money. ¹²The king and Jehoiada gave it to the men who carried out the work required for the temple of the LORD. They hired masons and carpenters to restore the LORD's temple, and also workers in iron and bronze to repair the temple.

¹³The men in charge of the work were diligent, and the repairs progressed under them. They rebuilt the temple of God according to its original

---

ᵃ14 Or *out from the precincts*   *ᵇ16* Or *covenant between the LORD and the people and the king that they* (see 2 Kings 11:17) design and reinforced it. **14**When they had finished, they brought the rest of the money to the king and Jehoiada, and with it were made articles for the LORD's temple: articles for the service and for the burnt offerings, and also dishes and other objects of gold and silver. As long as Jehoiada lived, burnt offerings were presented continually in the temple of the LORD.

15Now Jehoiada was old and full of years, and he died at the age of a hundred and thirty. **16**He was buried with the kings in the City of David, because of the good he had done in Israel for God and his temple.

The Wickedness of Joash

17After the death of Jehoiada, the officials of Judah came and paid homage to the king, and he listened to them. **18**They abandoned the temple of the LORD, the God of their fathers, and worshiped Asherah poles and idols. Because of their guilt, God's anger came upon Judah and Jerusalem. **19**Although the LORD sent prophets to the people to bring them back to him, and though they testified against them, they would not listen.

20Then the Spirit of God came upon Zechariah son of Jehoiada the priest. He stood before the people and said, "This is what God says: 'Why do you disobey the LORD's commands? You will not prosper. Because you have forsaken the LORD, he has forsaken you.'"

21But they plotted against him, and by order of the king they stoned him to death in the courtyard of the LORD's temple. **22**King Joash did not

24:21 An Infamous Murder

Joash showed promise in his early years as king. But, like many other kings, he could not tolerate the damning words of one of God's prophets. The murder carried out on his order brought in enemy armies, inspired a conspiracy against Joash, and destroyed his reputation forever. Jesus may have been speaking of this incident when he alluded to a murder hundreds of years later (Luke 11:51; Matthew 23:35).

remember the kindness Zechariah's father Jehoiada had shown him but killed his son, who said as he lay dying, "May the LORD see this and call you to account."

23At the turn of the year,[a] the army of Aram marched against Joash; it invaded Judah and Jerusalem and killed all the leaders of the people. They sent all the plunder to their king in Damascus. **24**Although the Aramean army had come with only a few men, the LORD delivered into

their hands a much larger army. Because Judah had forsaken the LORD, the God of their fathers, judgment was executed on Joash. **25**When the Arameans withdrew, they left Joash severely wounded. His officials conspired against him for murdering the son of Jehoiada the priest, and they killed him in his bed. So he died and was buried in the City of David, but not in the tombs of the kings.

26Those who conspired against him were Zabad,[b] son of Shimeath an Ammonite woman, and Jehozabad, son of Shimrith[c] a Moabite woman. **27**The account of his sons, the many prophecies about him, and the record of the restoration of the temple of God are written in the annotations on the book of the kings. And Amaziah his son succeeded him as king.

Amaziah King of Judah

25 Amaziah was twenty-five years old when he became king, and he reigned in Jerusalem twenty-nine years. His mother's name was Jehoaddin[d]; she was from Jerusalem. **2**He did what was right in the eyes of the LORD, but not wholeheartedly. **3**After the kingdom was firmly in his control, he executed the officials who had murdered his father the king. **4**Yet he did not put their sons to death, but acted in accordance with what is written in the Law, in the Book of Moses, where the LORD commanded: "Fathers shall not be put to death for their children, nor children put to death for their fathers; each is to die for his own sins."[e]

5Amaziah called the people of Judah together and assigned them according to their families to commanders of thousands and commanders of hundreds for all Judah and Benjamin. He then mustered those twenty years old or more and found that there were three hundred thousand men ready for military service, able to handle the spear and shield. **6**He also hired a hundred thousand fighting men from Israel for a hundred talents[f] of silver.

7But a man of God came to him and said, "O king, these troops from Israel must not march with you, for the LORD is not with Israel—not with any of the people of Ephraim. **8**Even if you go and fight courageously in battle, God will overthrow you before the enemy, for God has the power to help or to overthrow."

9Amaziah asked the man of God, "But what about the hundred talents I paid for these Israelite troops?"

The man of God replied, "The LORD can give you much more than that."

10So Amaziah dismissed the troops who had come to him from Ephraim and sent them home.

a23 Probably in the spring   b26 A variant of *Jozabad*   c26 A variant of *Shomer*   d1 Hebrew *Jehoaddan*, a variant of *Jehoaddin*   e4 Deut. 24:16   f6 That is, about 3 3/4 tons (about 3.4 metric tons); also in verse 9

They were furious with Judah and left for home in a great rage.

¹¹Amaziah then marshaled his strength and led his army to the Valley of Salt, where he killed ten thousand men of Seir. ¹²The army of Judah also captured ten thousand men alive, took them to the top of a cliff and threw them down so that all were dashed to pieces.

¹³Meanwhile the troops that Amaziah had sent back and had not allowed to take part in the war raided Judean towns from Samaria to Beth Horon. They killed three thousand people and carried off great quantities of plunder.

¹⁴When Amaziah returned from slaughtering the Edomites, he brought back the gods of the people of Seir. He set them up as his own gods, bowed down to them and burned sacrifices to them. ¹⁵The anger of the LORD burned against Amaziah, and he sent a prophet to him, who said, "Why do you consult this people's gods, which could not save their own people from your hand?"

¹⁶While he was still speaking, the king said to him, "Have we appointed you an adviser to the king? Stop! Why be struck down?"

So the prophet stopped but said, "I know that God has determined to destroy you, because you have done this and have not listened to my counsel."

¹⁷After Amaziah king of Judah consulted his advisers, he sent this challenge to Jehoash[a] son of Jehoahaz, the son of Jehu, king of Israel: "Come, meet me face to face."

¹⁸But Jehoash king of Israel replied to Amaziah king of Judah: "A thistle in Lebanon sent a message to a cedar in Lebanon, 'Give your daughter to my son in marriage.' Then a wild beast in Lebanon came along and trampled the thistle underfoot. ¹⁹You say to yourself that you have defeated Edom, and now you are arrogant and proud. But stay at home! Why ask for trouble and cause your own downfall and that of Judah also?"

²⁰Amaziah, however, would not listen, for God so worked that he might hand them over to ⌊Jehoash⌋, because they sought the gods of Edom. ²¹So Jehoash king of Israel attacked. He and Amaziah king of Judah faced each other at Beth Shemesh in Judah. ²²Judah was routed by Israel, and every man fled to his home. ²³Jehoash king of Israel captured Amaziah king of Judah, the son of Joash, the son of Ahaziah,[b] at Beth Shemesh. Then Jehoash brought him to Jerusalem and broke down the wall of Jerusalem from the Ephraim Gate to the Corner Gate—a section about six hundred feet[c] long. ²⁴He took all the gold and silver and all the articles found in the temple of God that had been in the care of Obed-Edom, together with the palace treasures and the hostages, and returned to Samaria.

²⁵Amaziah son of Joash king of Judah lived for fifteen years after the death of Jehoash son of Jehoahaz king of Israel. ²⁶As for the other events of Amaziah's reign, from beginning to end, are they not written in the book of the kings of Judah and Israel? ²⁷From the time that Amaziah turned away from following the LORD, they conspired against him in Jerusalem and he fled to Lachish, but they sent men after him to Lachish and killed him there. ²⁸He was brought back by horse and was buried with his fathers in the City of Judah.

Uzziah King of Judah

26 Then all the people of Judah took Uzziah,[d] who was sixteen years old, and made him king in place of his father Amaziah. ²He was the one who rebuilt Elath and restored it to Judah after Amaziah rested with his fathers.

³Uzziah was sixteen years old when he became king, and he reigned in Jerusalem fifty-two years. His mother's name was Jecoliah; she was from Jerusalem. ⁴He did what was right in the eyes of the LORD, just as his father Amaziah had done. ⁵He sought God during the days of Zechariah, who instructed him in the fear[e] of God. As long as he sought the LORD, God gave him success.

⁶He went to war against the Philistines and broke down the walls of Gath, Jabneh and Ashdod. He then rebuilt towns near Ashdod and elsewhere among the Philistines. ⁷God helped him against the Philistines and against the Arabs who lived in Gur Baal and against the Meunites. ⁸The Ammonites brought tribute to Uzziah, and his fame spread as far as the border of Egypt, because he had become very powerful.

⁹Uzziah built towers in Jerusalem at the Corner Gate, at the Valley Gate and at the angle of the wall, and he fortified them. ¹⁰He also built towers in the desert and dug many cisterns, because he had much livestock in the foothills and in the plain. He had people working his fields and vineyards in the hills and in the fertile lands, for he loved the soil.

¹¹Uzziah had a well-trained army, ready to go out by divisions according to their numbers as mustered by Jeiel the secretary and Maaseiah the officer under the direction of Hananiah, one of the royal officials. ¹²The total number of family leaders over the fighting men was 2,600. ¹³Under their command was an army of 307,500 men trained for war, a powerful force to support the king against his enemies. ¹⁴Uzziah provided shields, spears, helmets, coats of armor, bows and slingstones for the entire army. ¹⁵In Jerusalem he

---

a17 Hebrew *Joash,* a variant of *Jehoash;* also in verses 18, 21, 23 and 25   *b23* Hebrew *Jehoahaz,* a variant of *Ahaziah*   *c23* Hebrew *four hundred cubits* (about 180 meters)   *d1* Also called *Azariah*   *e5* Many Hebrew manuscripts, Septuagint and Syriac; other Hebrew manuscripts *vision*

made machines designed by skillful men for use on the towers and on the corner defenses to shoot arrows and hurl large stones. His fame spread far and wide, for he was greatly helped until he became powerful.

¹⁶But after Uzziah became powerful, his pride led to his downfall. He was unfaithful to the LORD his God, and entered the temple of the LORD to

26:16 A King's Pride

Archaeological discoveries have verified the prosperity of Judah during Uzziah's reign. However, like many of Judah's kings, he fell victim to the sin of pride. He usurped the role of the priests and suffered ever after from a contagious skin disease.

burn incense on the altar of incense. ¹⁷Azariah the priest with eighty other courageous priests of the LORD followed him in. ¹⁸They confronted him and said, "It is not right for you, Uzziah, to burn incense to the LORD. That is for the priests, the descendants of Aaron, who have been consecrated to burn incense. Leave the sanctuary, for you have been unfaithful; and you will not be honored by the LORD God."

¹⁹Uzziah, who had a censer in his hand ready to burn incense, became angry. While he was raging at the priests in their presence before the incense altar in the LORD's temple, leprosy*ᵃ* broke out on his forehead. ²⁰When Azariah the chief priest and all the other priests looked at him, they saw that he had leprosy on his forehead, so they hurried him out. Indeed, he himself was eager to leave, because the LORD had afflicted him.

²¹King Uzziah had leprosy until the day he died. He lived in a separate house*ᵇ*—leprous, and excluded from the temple of the LORD. Jotham his son had charge of the palace and governed the people of the land.

²²The other events of Uzziah's reign, from beginning to end, are recorded by the prophet Isaiah son of Amoz. ²³Uzziah rested with his fathers and was buried near them in a field for burial that belonged to the kings, for people said, "He had leprosy." And Jotham his son succeeded him as king.

Jotham King of Judah

27 Jotham was twenty-five years old when he became king, and he reigned in Jerusalem sixteen years. His mother's name was Jerusha daughter of Zadok. ²He did what was right in the

eyes of the LORD, just as his father Uzziah had done, but unlike him he did not enter the temple of the LORD. The people, however, continued their corrupt practices. ³Jotham rebuilt the Upper Gate of the temple of the LORD and did extensive work on the wall at the hill of Ophel. ⁴He built towns in the Judean hills and forts and towers in the wooded areas.

⁵Jotham made war on the king of the Ammonites and conquered them. That year the Ammonites paid him a hundred talents*ᶜ* of silver, ten thousand cors*ᵈ* of wheat and ten thousand cors of barley. The Ammonites brought him the same amount also in the second and third years.

⁶Jotham grew powerful because he walked steadfastly before the LORD his God.

⁷The other events in Jotham's reign, including all his wars and the other things he did, are written in the book of the kings of Israel and Judah. ⁸He was twenty-five years old when he became king, and he reigned in Jerusalem sixteen years. ⁹Jotham rested with his fathers and was buried in the City of David. And Ahaz his son succeeded him as king.

Ahaz King of Judah

28 Ahaz was twenty years old when he became king, and he reigned in Jerusalem sixteen years. Unlike David his father, he did not do what was right in the eyes of the LORD. ²He walked in the ways of the kings of Israel and also made cast idols for worshiping the Baals. ³He burned sacrifices in the Valley of Ben Hinnom and sacrificed his sons in the fire, following the detestable ways of the nations the LORD had driven out before the Israelites. ⁴He offered sacrifices and burned incense at the high places, on the hilltops and under every spreading tree.

⁵Therefore the LORD his God handed him over to the king of Aram. The Arameans defeated him and took many of his people as prisoners and brought them to Damascus.

He was also given into the hands of the king of Israel, who inflicted heavy casualties on him. ⁶In one day Pekah son of Remaliah killed a hundred and twenty thousand soldiers in Judah—because Judah had forsaken the LORD, the God of their fathers. ⁷Zicri, an Ephraimite warrior, killed Maaseiah the king's son, Azrikam the officer in charge of the palace, and Elkanah, second to the king. ⁸The Israelites took captive from their kinsmen two hundred thousand wives, sons and daughters. They also took a great deal of plunder, which they carried back to Samaria.

⁹But a prophet of the LORD named Oded was there, and he went out to meet the army when it returned to Samaria. He said to them, "Because

ᵃ19 The Hebrew word was used for various diseases affecting the skin—not necessarily leprosy; also in verses 20, 21 and 23.
ᵇ21 Or *in a house where he was relieved of responsibilities*   *ᶜ5* That is, about 3 3/4 tons (about 3.4 metric tons)
ᵈ5 That is, probably about 62,000 bushels (about 2,200 kiloliters)

the Lord, the God of your fathers, was angry with Judah, he gave them into your hand. But you have slaughtered them in a rage that reaches to heaven. ¹⁰And now you intend to make the men

> ### 28:9 Limits of a Just War
>
> *Advocates of a "just war" theory sometimes cite the fascinating story in this chapter. God sanctioned Israel's attack on Judah, but the invaders from the North went too far. They slaughtered many civilians and carried away others as captives. A prophet rebuked Israel's army for their crimes committed "in a rage that reaches to heaven." The Israelites had fought a war with a just end—carrying out God's punishment—but used cruel and unjust means in waging it.*
>
> *The prophet convinced the Israelites to give up plunder and prisoners and make restitution. They fed the prisoners from Judah, gave them clothes, sandals, and medicine, and put them on donkeys to return home. This scene is one of the few in 2 Chronicles that shows the Northern Kingdom in a favorable light.*

and women of Judah and Jerusalem your slaves. But aren't you also guilty of sins against the Lord your God? ¹¹Now listen to me! Send back your fellow countrymen you have taken as prisoners, for the Lord's fierce anger rests on you."

¹²Then some of the leaders in Ephraim—Azariah son of Jehohanan, Berekiah son of Meshillemoth, Jehizkiah son of Shallum, and Amasa son of Hadlai—confronted those who were arriving from the war. ¹³"You must not bring those prisoners here," they said, "or we will be guilty before the Lord. Do you intend to add to our sin and guilt? For our guilt is already great, and his fierce anger rests on Israel."

¹⁴So the soldiers gave up the prisoners and plunder in the presence of the officials and all the assembly. ¹⁵The men designated by name took the prisoners, and from the plunder they clothed all who were naked. They provided them with clothes and sandals, food and drink, and healing balm. All those who were weak they put on donkeys. So they took them back to their fellow countrymen at Jericho, the City of Palms, and returned to Samaria.

¹⁶At that time King Ahaz sent to the king[a] of Assyria for help. ¹⁷The Edomites had again come and attacked Judah and carried away prisoners, ¹⁸while the Philistines had raided towns in the foothills and in the Negev of Judah. They captured and occupied Beth Shemesh, Aijalon and

Gederoth, as well as Soco, Timnah and Gimzo, with their surrounding villages. ¹⁹The Lord had humbled Judah because of Ahaz king of Israel,[b] for he had promoted wickedness in Judah and had been most unfaithful to the Lord. ²⁰Tiglath-Pileser[c] king of Assyria came to him, but he gave him trouble instead of help. ²¹Ahaz took some of the things from the temple of the Lord and from the royal palace and from the princes and presented them to the king of Assyria, but that did not help him.

²²In his time of trouble King Ahaz became even more unfaithful to the Lord. ²³He offered sacrifices to the gods of Damascus, who had defeated him; for he thought, "Since the gods of the kings of Aram have helped them, I will sacrifice to them so they will help me." But they were his downfall and the downfall of all Israel.

²⁴Ahaz gathered together the furnishings from the temple of God and took them away.[d] He shut the doors of the Lord's temple and set up altars at every street corner in Jerusalem. ²⁵In every town in Judah he built high places to burn sacrifices to other gods and provoked the Lord, the God of his fathers, to anger.

²⁶The other events of his reign and all his ways, from beginning to end, are written in the book of the kings of Judah and Israel. ²⁷Ahaz rested with his fathers and was buried in the city of Jerusalem, but he was not placed in the tombs of the kings of Israel. And Hezekiah his son succeeded him as king.

Hezekiah Purifies the Temple

29 Hezekiah was twenty-five years old when he became king, and he reigned in Jerusalem twenty-nine years. His mother's name was Abijah daughter of Zechariah. ²He did what was right in the eyes of the Lord, just as his father David had done.

³In the first month of the first year of his reign, he opened the doors of the temple of the Lord and repaired them. ⁴He brought in the priests and the Levites, assembled them in the square on the east side ⁵and said: "Listen to me, Levites! Consecrate yourselves now and consecrate the temple of the Lord, the God of your fathers. Remove all defilement from the sanctuary. ⁶Our fathers were unfaithful; they did evil in the eyes of the Lord our God and forsook him. They turned their faces away from the Lord's dwelling place and turned their backs on him. ⁷They also shut the doors of the portico and put out the lamps. They did not burn incense or present any burnt offerings at the sanctuary to the God of Israel. ⁸Therefore, the anger of the Lord has fall-

---

[a]16 One Hebrew manuscript, Septuagint and Vulgate (see also 2 Kings 16:7); most Hebrew manuscripts *kings*   [b]19 That is, Judah, as frequently in 2 Chronicles   [c]20 Hebrew *Tilgath-Pilneser*, a variant of *Tiglath-Pileser*   [d]24 Or *and cut them up*

en on Judah and Jerusalem; he has made them an object of dread and horror and scorn, as you can see with your own eyes. ⁹This is why our fathers have fallen by the sword and why our sons and daughters and our wives are in captivity. ¹⁰Now I intend to make a covenant with the LORD, the God of Israel, so that his fierce anger will turn away from us. ¹¹My sons, do not be negligent now, for the LORD has chosen you to stand before him and serve him, to minister before him and to burn incense."

¹²Then these Levites set to work:

from the Kohathites,

Mahath son of Amasai and Joel son of Azariah;

from the Merarites,

Kish son of Abdi and Azariah son of Jehallel;

from the Gershonites,

Joah son of Zimmah and Eden son of Joah;

¹³from the descendants of Elizaphan,

Shimri and Jeiel;

from the descendants of Asaph,

Zechariah and Mattaniah;

¹⁴from the descendants of Heman,

Jehiel and Shimei;

from the descendants of Jeduthun,

Shemaiah and Uzziel.

¹⁵When they had assembled their brothers and consecrated themselves, they went in to purify the temple of the LORD, as the king had ordered, following the word of the LORD. ¹⁶The priests went into the sanctuary of the LORD to purify it. They brought out to the courtyard of the LORD's temple everything unclean that they found in the temple of the LORD. The Levites took it and carried it out to the Kidron Valley. ¹⁷They began the consecration on the first day of the first month, and by the eighth day of the month they reached the portico of the LORD. For eight more days they consecrated the temple of the LORD itself, finishing on the sixteenth day of the first month.

¹⁸Then they went in to King Hezekiah and reported: "We have purified the entire temple of the LORD, the altar of burnt offering with all its utensils, and the table for setting out the consecrated bread, with all its articles. ¹⁹We have prepared and consecrated all the articles that King Ahaz removed in his unfaithfulness while he was king. They are now in front of the LORD's altar."

²⁰Early the next morning King Hezekiah gathered the city officials together and went up to the temple of the LORD. ²¹They brought seven bulls,

HEZEKIAH *Cleaning House*

HIS OWN FATHER HAD CLOSED the temple in Jerusalem, imported a pagan altar from Damascus and erected shrines to other gods on every street corner. Inheriting the throne as a young man, Hezekiah saw that his nation was hurtling toward disaster. He watched as the great power of Assyria invaded its sister nation Israel, demolishing its cities and sending its citizens into exile.

Unlike other kings, Hezekiah did not scurry around seeking political alliances to bolster his strength. He listened carefully to the prophet Isaiah and looked instead for God's protection. To reverse the course of his nation, he began by cleaning out God's house—the temple in Jerusalem.

When he began this task, priests and Levites who had been assigned to coordinate temple worship had dwindled away, demoralized. Hezekiah rallied them like an army and gave them marching orders: Clean up yourselves and clean up the temple. It took more than two weeks for them to dump all the idolatrous materials into a nearby ravine and to reconsecrate the temple. Worship recommenced: regular sacrifices to God, singing of the temple music written by David, even a dramatic restaging of the long-neglected Passover festival.

In these policies Hezekiah showed courage and initiative. He took risks, raising dust and probably raising hackles. Even Moses' bronze snake had to go—people were now worshiping it! (2 Kings 18:4) Hezekiah embarked on these reforms out of deep personal commitment. "In everything that he undertook in the service of God's temple and in obedience to the law and the commands, he sought his God and worked wholeheartedly. And so he prospered" (31:21).

When the powerful Assyrians camped at his gate, sneering at his God and threatening to destroy him, Hezekiah knew where to turn—to God. The prophet Isaiah prayed with Hezekiah, and Judah was miraculously saved. Later, when Hezekiah himself was close to death, God also answered his prayers for healing, extending his life by 15 years.

Hezekiah had some flaws, but overall he went down as one of the finest rulers in the Old Testament. "There was no one like him among all the kings of Judah, either before him or after him. He held fast to the LORD and did not cease to follow him; he kept the commands the LORD had given Moses" (2 Kings 18:5–6).

Life Questions: Where do you think house cleaning most needs to occur? In your life? In your church? Among your friends? In your city, state or nation?

seven rams, seven male lambs and seven male goats as a sin offering for the kingdom, for the sanctuary and for Judah. The king commanded the priests, the descendants of Aaron, to offer these on the altar of the LORD. 22So they slaughtered the bulls, and the priests took the blood and sprinkled it on the altar; next they slaughtered the rams and sprinkled their blood on the altar; then they slaughtered the lambs and sprinkled their blood on the altar. 23The goats for the sin offering were brought before the king and the assembly, and they laid their hands on them. 24The priests then slaughtered the goats and presented their blood on the altar for a sin offering to atone for all Israel, because the king had ordered the burnt offering and the sin offering for all Israel.

25He stationed the Levites in the temple of the LORD with cymbals, harps and lyres in the way prescribed by David and the king's seer and Nathan the prophet; this was commanded by the LORD through his prophets. 26So the Levites stood ready with David's instruments, and the priests with their trumpets.

27Hezekiah gave the order to sacrifice the burnt offering on the altar. As the offering began, singing to the LORD began also, accompanied by trumpets and the instruments of David king of Israel. 28The whole assembly bowed in worship, while the singers sang and the trumpeters played. All this continued until the sacrifice of the burnt offering was completed.

29When the offerings were finished, the king and everyone present with him knelt down and worshiped. 30King Hezekiah and his officials ordered the Levites to praise the LORD with the words of David and of Asaph the seer. So they sang praises with gladness and bowed their heads and worshiped.

31Then Hezekiah said, "You have now dedicated yourselves to the LORD. Come and bring sacrifices and thank offerings to the temple of the LORD." So the assembly brought sacrifices and thank offerings, and all whose hearts were willing brought burnt offerings.

32The number of burnt offerings the assembly brought was seventy bulls, a hundred rams and two hundred male lambs—all of them for burnt offerings to the LORD. 33The animals consecrated as sacrifices amounted to six hundred bulls and three thousand sheep and goats. 34The priests, however, were too few to skin all the burnt offerings; so their kinsmen the Levites helped them until the task was finished and until other priests had been consecrated, for the Levites had been more conscientious in consecrating themselves than the priests had been. 35There were burnt offerings in abundance, together with the fat of the fellowship offerings*a* and the drink offerings that accompanied the burnt offerings.

So the service of the temple of the LORD was reestablished. 36Hezekiah and all the people rejoiced at what God had brought about for his people, because it was done so quickly.

Hezekiah Celebrates the Passover

30 Hezekiah sent word to all Israel and Judah and also wrote letters to Ephraim and Manasseh, inviting them to come to the temple of the LORD in Jerusalem and celebrate the Passover

30:1 Delayed Passover

By moving the Passover date back one month, Hezekiah allowed extra time for priests to prepare and for pilgrims to make travel plans. Pointedly, Hezekiah invited tribes from the ravaged Northern Kingdom. For the first time in 200 years, the entire nation celebrated a religious festival together.

to the LORD, the God of Israel. 2The king and his officials and the whole assembly in Jerusalem decided to celebrate the Passover in the second month. 3They had not been able to celebrate it at the regular time because not enough priests had consecrated themselves and the people had not assembled in Jerusalem. 4The plan seemed right both to the king and to the whole assembly. 5They decided to send a proclamation throughout Israel, from Beersheba to Dan, calling the people to come to Jerusalem and celebrate the Passover to the LORD, the God of Israel. It had not been celebrated in large numbers according to what was written.

6At the king's command, couriers went throughout Israel and Judah with letters from the king and from his officials, which read:

"People of Israel, return to the LORD, the God of Abraham, Isaac and Israel, that he may return to you who are left, who have escaped from the hand of the kings of Assyria. 7Do not be like your fathers and brothers, who were unfaithful to the LORD, the God of their fathers, so that he made them an object of horror, as you see. 8Do not be stiff-necked, as your fathers were; submit to the LORD. Come to the sanctuary, which he has consecrated forever. Serve the LORD your God, so that his fierce anger will turn away from you. 9If you return to the LORD, then your brothers and your children will be shown compassion by their captors and will come back to this land, for the

a35 Traditionally peace offerings

LORD your God is gracious and compassionate. He will not turn his face from you if you return to him."

¹⁰The couriers went from town to town in Ephraim and Manasseh, as far as Zebulun, but the people scorned and ridiculed them. ¹¹Nevertheless, some men of Asher, Manasseh and Zebulun humbled themselves and went to Jerusalem. ¹²Also in Judah the hand of God was on the people to give them unity of mind to carry out what the king and his officials had ordered, following the word of the LORD.

¹³A very large crowd of people assembled in Jerusalem to celebrate the Feast of Unleavened Bread in the second month. ¹⁴They removed the altars in Jerusalem and cleared away the incense altars and threw them into the Kidron Valley.

¹⁵They slaughtered the Passover lamb on the fourteenth day of the second month. The priests and the Levites were ashamed and consecrated themselves and brought burnt offerings to the temple of the LORD. ¹⁶Then they took up their regular positions as prescribed in the Law of Moses the man of God. The priests sprinkled the blood handed to them by the Levites. ¹⁷Since many in the crowd had not consecrated themselves, the Levites had to kill the Passover lambs for all those who were not ceremonially clean and could not consecrate ˻their lambs˼ to the LORD. ¹⁸Although most of the many people who came from Ephraim, Manasseh, Issachar and Zebulun had not purified themselves, yet they ate the Passover, contrary to what was written. But Hezekiah prayed for them, saying, "May the LORD, who is good, pardon everyone ¹⁹who sets his heart on seeking God—the LORD, the God of his fathers—even if he is not clean according to the rules of the sanctuary." ²⁰And the LORD heard Hezekiah and healed the people.

²¹The Israelites who were present in Jerusalem celebrated the Feast of Unleavened Bread for seven days with great rejoicing, while the Levites and priests sang to the LORD every day, accompanied by the LORD's instruments of praise.ᵃ

²²Hezekiah spoke encouragingly to all the Levites, who showed good understanding of the service of the LORD. For the seven days they ate their assigned portion and offered fellowship offeringsᵇ and praised the LORD, the God of their fathers.

²³The whole assembly then agreed to celebrate the festival seven more days; so for another seven days they celebrated joyfully. ²⁴Hezekiah king of Judah provided a thousand bulls and seven thousand sheep and goats for the assembly, and the officials provided them with a thousand bulls and ten thousand sheep and goats. A great number of

priests consecrated themselves. ²⁵The entire assembly of Judah rejoiced, along with the priests and Levites and all who had assembled from Israel, including the aliens who had come from Israel and those who lived in Judah. ²⁶There was great joy in Jerusalem, for since the days of Solomon son of David king of Israel there had been nothing like this in Jerusalem. ²⁷The priests and the Levites stood to bless the people, and God heard them, for their prayer reached heaven, his holy dwelling place.

31 When all this had ended, the Israelites who were there went out to the towns of Judah, smashed the sacred stones and cut down the Asherah poles. They destroyed the high places and the altars throughout Judah and Benjamin and in Ephraim and Manasseh. After they had destroyed all of them, the Israelites returned to their own towns and to their own property.

Contributions for Worship

²Hezekiah assigned the priests and Levites to divisions—each of them according to their duties as priests or Levites—to offer burnt offerings and fellowship offerings,ᵇ to minister, to give thanks and to sing praises at the gates of LORD's dwelling. ³The king contributed from his own possessions for the morning and evening burnt offerings and for the burnt offerings on the Sabbaths, New Moons and appointed feasts as written in the Law of the LORD. ⁴He ordered the people living in Jerusalem to give the portion due the priests and Levites so they could devote themselves to the Law of the LORD. ⁵As soon as the order went out, the Israelites generously gave the firstfruits of their grain, new wine, oil and honey and all that the fields produced. They brought a great amount, a tithe of everything. ⁶The men of Israel and Judah who lived in the towns of Judah also brought a tithe of their herds and flocks and a tithe of the holy things dedicated to the LORD their God, and they piled them in heaps. ⁷They began doing this in the third month and finished in the seventh month. ⁸When Hezekiah and his officials came and saw the heaps, they praised the LORD and blessed his people Israel.

⁹Hezekiah asked the priests and Levites about the heaps; ¹⁰and Azariah the chief priest, from the family of Zadok, answered, "Since the people began to bring their contributions to the temple of the LORD, we have had enough to eat and plenty to spare, because the LORD has blessed his people, and this great amount is left over."

¹¹Hezekiah gave orders to prepare storerooms in the temple of the LORD, and this was done. ¹²Then they faithfully brought in the contribu-

---

ᵃ21 Or priests praised the LORD every day with resounding instruments belonging to the LORD   ᵇ22,2 Traditionally peace offerings

tions, tithes and dedicated gifts. Conaniah, a Levite, was in charge of these things, and his brother Shimei was next in rank. [13]Jehiel, Azaziah, Nahath, Asahel, Jerimoth, Jozabad, Eliel, Ismakiah, Mahath and Benaiah were supervisors under Conaniah and Shimei his brother, by appointment of King Hezekiah and Azariah the official in charge of the temple of God.

[14]Kore son of Imnah the Levite, keeper of the East Gate, was in charge of the freewill offerings given to God, distributing the contributions made to the LORD and also the consecrated gifts. [15]Eden, Miniamin, Jeshua, Shemaiah, Amariah and Shecaniah assisted him faithfully in the towns of the priests, distributing to their fellow priests according to their divisions, old and young alike.

[16]In addition, they distributed to the males three years old or more whose names were in the genealogical records—all who would enter the temple of the LORD to perform the daily duties of their various tasks, according to their responsibilities and their divisions. [17]And they distributed to the priests enrolled by their families in the genealogical records and likewise to the Levites twenty years old or more, according to their responsibilities and their divisions. [18]They included all the little ones, the wives, and the sons and daughters of the whole community listed in these genealogical records. For they were faithful in consecrating themselves.

[19]As for the priests, the descendants of Aaron, who lived on the farm lands around their towns or in any other towns, men were designated by name to distribute portions to every male among them and to all who were recorded in the genealogies of the Levites.

[20]This is what Hezekiah did throughout Judah, doing what was good and right and faithful before the LORD his God. [21]In everything that he undertook in the service of God's temple and in obedience to the law and the commands, he sought his God and worked wholeheartedly. And so he prospered.

Sennacherib Threatens Jerusalem

32 After all that Hezekiah had so faithfully done, Sennacherib king of Assyria came and invaded Judah. He laid siege to the fortified cities, thinking to conquer them for himself. [2]When Hezekiah saw that Sennacherib had come and that he intended to make war on Jerusalem, [3]he consulted with his officials and military staff about blocking off the water from the springs outside the city, and they helped him. [4]A large force of men assembled, and they blocked all the springs and the stream that flowed through the land. "Why should the kings[a] of Assyria come

and find plenty of water?" they said. [5]Then he worked hard repairing all the broken sections of the wall and building towers on it. He built another wall outside that one and reinforced the supporting terraces[b] of the City of David. He also made large numbers of weapons and shields.

[6]He appointed military officers over the people and assembled them before him in the square at the city gate and encouraged them with these words: [7]"Be strong and courageous. Do not be afraid or discouraged because of the king of Assyria and the vast army with him, for there is a greater power with us than with him. [8]With him is only the arm of flesh, but with us is the LORD our God to help us and to fight our battles." And the people gained confidence from what Hezekiah the king of Judah said.

[9]Later, when Sennacherib king of Assyria and all his forces were laying siege to Lachish, he sent his officers to Jerusalem with this message for Hezekiah king of Judah and for all the people of Judah who were there:

[10]"This is what Sennacherib king of Assyria says: On what are you basing your confidence, that you remain in Jerusalem under siege? [11]When Hezekiah says, 'The LORD our God will save us from the hand of the king of Assyria,' he is misleading you, to let you die of hunger and thirst. [12]Did not Hezekiah himself remove this god's high places and altars, saying to Judah and Jerusalem, 'You must worship before one altar and burn sacrifices on it'?

[13]"Do you not know what I and my fathers have done to all the peoples of the other lands? Were the gods of those nations ever able to deliver their land from my hand? [14]Who of all the gods of these nations that my fathers destroyed has been able to save his people from me? How then can your god deliver you from my hand? [15]Now do not let Hezekiah deceive you and mislead you like this. Do not believe him, for no god of any nation or kingdom has been able to deliver his people from my

32:1–21 Invasion

Sennacherib's campaign is well-documented, for he kept scrupulous records of his military ventures. Invading Palestine in 701 B.C., his armies captured 46 cities in Judah and then laid siege to Jerusalem. The Bible includes three different accounts of this major event: here, in 2 Kings 18, and in Isaiah 36.

---

[a]4 Hebrew; Septuagint and Syriac *king*   [b]5 Or *the Millo*

hand or the hand of my fathers. How much less will your god deliver you from my hand!"

[16]Sennacherib's officers spoke further against the LORD God and against his servant Hezekiah. [17]The king also wrote letters insulting the LORD, the God of Israel, and saying this against him: "Just as the gods of the peoples of the other lands did not rescue their people from my hand, so the god of Hezekiah will not rescue his people from my hand." [18]Then they called out in Hebrew to the people of Jerusalem who were on the wall, to terrify them and make them afraid in order to capture the city. [19]They spoke about the God of Jerusalem as they did about the gods of the other peoples of the world—the work of men's hands.

[20]King Hezekiah and the prophet Isaiah son of Amoz cried out in prayer to heaven about this. [21]And the LORD sent an angel, who annihilated all the fighting men and the leaders and officers in the camp of the Assyrian king. So he withdrew to his own land in disgrace. And when he went into the temple of his god, some of his sons cut him down with the sword.

Lessons from the Battlefield
What made Judah win some wars and lose others?

NO KING OF JUDAH HAD a wholly peaceful reign. As a result, much of the action in 2 Chronicles takes place on a battlefield. And, in a nutshell, here is the book's philosophy of war: "Humble yourself and rely totally on God—regardless of the odds against you. If you rely on your own military might or that of powerful neighbors, you will lose."

> *Do not be afraid or discouraged because of the king of Assyria and the vast army with him, for there is a greater power with us than with him.* 32:7

Listening to the Prophets
Chapter 12, for example, tells of a grave crisis facing Judah's very first king. Five years into Rehoboam's reign, a huge military machine from Egypt rolled in with chariots and battering rams. Surrounded, Rehoboam wanted a word of hope from a prophet. Instead, he got a rebuke: "This is what the LORD says, 'You have abandoned me; therefore, I now abandon you to Shishak' " (12:5).

God was using the armies of Egypt to punish Judah for its errors. This first invasion set a pattern: Whenever an immoral king corrupted the nation, God sent an invading army as punishment.

Often the kings of Judah ignored their prophets' hard advice. But in this first case, King Rehoboam repented and humbled himself, saving his country from even greater devastation.

A Wrong Way and a Right Way
Few kings had the faith to believe in God alone at moments of great peril. Even the best of them reached into the royal treasury and purchased help from neighboring nations. When they did, Judah usually ended up weaker than before. But 2 Chronicles concentrates on the good moments, when kings turned to God.

King Jehoshaphat was a textbook example of the proper response. He called the entire nation together in a giant prayer meeting (20:4–28). When the time came for battle, he sent a choir in front of his army to sing praises to God. Judah's enemies all turned on each other and Jehoshaphat's armies marched home victorious.

Hezekiah's Faith
Perhaps the greatest single example of a king following his prophet's advice occurred during the reign of Hezekiah. The Bible reports the incident in three places: 2 Chronicles 32, 2 Kings 18–19, and Isaiah 36–37. At the time, Judah's situation looked hopeless. Mighty Assyria had taken 27 cities and villages in Judah and was now laying siege to Jerusalem.

Hezekiah showed his true moral strength by joining together with the prophet Isaiah to humble himself in prayer. God granted a miracle that drove off the Assyrian army.

Second Chronicles stressed incidents like these as a lesson to its first readers, who had inherited a land in ruins. Looking back over their history, they could see what had gone wrong: The nation had forgotten to rely on God. To rebuild their nation they would have to relearn the simple faith that had brought them victory in the past.

Life Questions: What does it mean to trust God completely today?

²²So the LORD saved Hezekiah and the people of Jerusalem from the hand of Sennacherib king of Assyria and from the hand of all others. He took care of them[a] on every side. ²³Many brought offerings to Jerusalem for the LORD and valuable gifts for Hezekiah king of Judah. From then on he was highly regarded by all the nations.

Hezekiah's Pride, Success and Death

²⁴In those days Hezekiah became ill and was at the point of death. He prayed to the LORD, who answered him and gave him a miraculous sign. ²⁵But Hezekiah's heart was proud and he did not respond to the kindness shown him; therefore the LORD's wrath was on him and on Judah and Jerusalem. ²⁶Then Hezekiah repented of the pride of his heart, as did the people of Jerusalem; therefore the LORD's wrath did not come upon them during the days of Hezekiah.

²⁷Hezekiah had very great riches and honor, and he made treasuries for his silver and gold and for his precious stones, spices, shields and all kinds of valuables. ²⁸He also made buildings to store the harvest of grain, new wine and oil; and he made stalls for various kinds of cattle, and pens for the flocks. ²⁹He built villages and acquired great numbers of flocks and herds, for God had given him very great riches.

³⁰It was Hezekiah who blocked the upper outlet of the Gihon spring and channeled the water down to the west side of the City of David. He succeeded in everything he undertook. ³¹But when envoys were sent by the rulers of Babylon to ask him about the miraculous sign that had occurred in the land, God left him to test him and to know everything that was in his heart.

³²The other events of Hezekiah's reign and his acts of devotion are written in the vision of the prophet Isaiah son of Amoz in the book of the kings of Judah and Israel. ³³Hezekiah rested with his fathers and was buried on the hill where the tombs of David's descendants are. All Judah and the people of Jerusalem honored him when he died. And Manasseh his son succeeded him as king.

Manasseh King of Judah

33 Manasseh was twelve years old when he became king, and he reigned in Jerusalem fifty-five years. ²He did evil in the eyes of the LORD, following the detestable practices of the nations the LORD had driven out before the Israelites. ³He rebuilt the high places his father Hezekiah had demolished; he also erected altars to the Baals and made Asherah poles. He bowed down to all the starry hosts and worshiped them. ⁴He built altars in the temple of the LORD, of which the LORD had said, "My Name will remain in Jerusalem forever." ⁵In both courts of the temple

of the LORD, he built altars to all the starry hosts. ⁶He sacrificed his sons in[b] the fire in the Valley of Ben Hinnom, practiced sorcery, divination and witchcraft, and consulted mediums and spiritists. He did much evil in the eyes of the LORD, provoking him to anger.

⁷He took the carved image he had made and put it in God's temple, of which God had said to David and to his son Solomon, "In this temple and in Jerusalem, which I have chosen out of all the tribes of Israel, I will put my Name forever. ⁸I will not again make the feet of the Israelites leave the land I assigned to your forefathers, if only they will be careful to do everything I commanded them concerning all the laws, decrees and ordinances given through Moses." ⁹But Manasseh led Judah and the people of Jerusalem astray, so that they did more evil than the nations the LORD had destroyed before the Israelites.

¹⁰The LORD spoke to Manasseh and his people, but they paid no attention. ¹¹So the LORD brought against them the army commanders of the king of Assyria, who took Manasseh prisoner, put a hook in his nose, bound him with bronze shackles and took him to Babylon. ¹²In his distress he sought the favor of the LORD his God and humbled himself greatly before the God of his fathers. ¹³And when he prayed to him, the LORD was moved by his entreaty and listened to his plea; so he brought him back to Jerusalem and to his kingdom. Then Manasseh knew that the LORD is God.

33:13 A Tardy Change of Mind

Unlike the other history books, Chronicles records great moments of faith, even when they have no lasting consequences for the nation as a whole. Second Chronicles characteristically adds a new perspective on the reign of Manasseh, one of Judah's worst kings. While acknowledging his weaknesses, it adds this account of his amazing turnabout late in life. This brief episode gave an object lesson to the nation on what happens when even a wicked king repents.

¹⁴Afterward he rebuilt the outer wall of the City of David, west of the Gihon spring in the valley, as far as the entrance of the Fish Gate and encircling the hill of Ophel; he also made it much higher. He stationed military commanders in all the fortified cities in Judah.

¹⁵He got rid of the foreign gods and removed the image from the temple of the LORD, as well as all the altars he had built on the temple hill and in Jerusalem; and he threw them out of the city.

---

[a]22 Hebrew; Septuagint and Vulgate *He gave them rest*   [b]6 Or *He made his sons pass through*

16Then he restored the altar of the LORD and sacrificed fellowship offerings[a] and thank offerings on it, and told Judah to serve the LORD, the God of Israel. 17The people, however, continued to sacrifice at the high places, but only to the LORD their God.

18The other events of Manasseh's reign, including his prayer to his God and the words the seers spoke to him in the name of the LORD, the God of Israel, are written in the annals of the kings of Israel.[b] 19His prayer and how God was moved by his entreaty, as well as all his sins and unfaithfulness, and the sites where he built high places and set up Asherah poles and idols before he humbled himself—all are written in the records of the seers.[c] 20Manasseh rested with his fathers and was buried in his palace. And Amon his son succeeded him as king.

Amon King of Judah

21Amon was twenty-two years old when he became king, and he reigned in Jerusalem two years. 22He did evil in the eyes of the LORD, as his father Manasseh had done. Amon worshiped and offered sacrifices to all the idols Manasseh had made. 23But unlike his father Manasseh, he did not humble himself before the LORD; Amon increased his guilt.

24Amon's officials conspired against him and assassinated him in his palace. 25Then the people of the land killed all who had plotted against King Amon, and they made Josiah his son king in his place.

Josiah's Reforms

34 Josiah was eight years old when he became king, and he reigned in Jerusalem thirty-one years. 2He did what was right in the eyes of the LORD and walked in the ways of his father David, not turning aside to the right or to the left.

3In the eighth year of his reign, while he was still young, he began to seek the God of his father David. In his twelfth year he began to purge Judah and Jerusalem of high places, Asherah poles, carved idols and cast images. 4Under his direction the altars of the Baals were torn down; he cut to pieces the incense altars that were above them, and smashed the Asherah poles, the idols and the images. These he broke to pieces and scattered over the graves of those who had sacrificed to them. 5He burned the bones of the priests on their altars, and so he purged Judah and Jerusalem. 6In the towns of Manasseh, Ephraim and Simeon, as far as Naphtali, and in the ruins around them, 7he tore down the altars and the Asherah poles and crushed the idols to powder and cut to pieces all the incense altars throughout Israel. Then he went back to Jerusalem.

8In the eighteenth year of Josiah's reign, to purify the land and the temple, he sent Shaphan son of Azaliah and Maaseiah the ruler of the city, with Joah son of Joahaz, the recorder, to repair the temple of the LORD his God.

9They went to Hilkiah the high priest and gave him the money that had been brought into the temple of God, which the Levites who were the doorkeepers had collected from the people of Manasseh, Ephraim and the entire remnant of Israel and from all the people of Judah and Benjamin and the inhabitants of Jerusalem. 10Then they entrusted it to the men appointed to supervise the work on the LORD's temple. These men paid the workers who repaired and restored the temple. 11They also gave money to the carpenters and builders to purchase dressed stone, and timber for joists and beams for the buildings that the kings of Judah had allowed to fall into ruin.

12The men did the work faithfully. Over them to direct them were Jahath and Obadiah, Levites descended from Merari, and Zechariah and Meshullam, descended from Kohath. The Levites— all who were skilled in playing musical instruments— 13had charge of the laborers and supervised all the workers from job to job. Some of the Levites were secretaries, scribes and doorkeepers.

The Book of the Law Found

14While they were bringing out the money that had been taken into the temple of the LORD, Hilkiah the priest found the Book of the Law of the LORD that had been given through Moses. 15Hilkiah said to Shaphan the secretary, "I have found the Book of the Law in the temple of the LORD." He gave it to Shaphan.

16Then Shaphan took the book to the king and reported to him: "Your officials are doing everything that has been committed to them. 17They have paid out the money that was in the temple of the LORD and have entrusted it to the supervisors and workers." 18Then Shaphan the secretary informed the king, "Hilkiah the priest has given me a book." And Shaphan read from it in the presence of the king.

19When the king heard the words of the Law, he tore his robes. 20He gave these orders to Hilkiah, Ahikam son of Shaphan, Abdon son of Micah,[d] Shaphan the secretary and Asaiah the king's attendant: 21"Go and inquire of the LORD for me and for the remnant in Israel and Judah about what is written in this book that has been found. Great is the LORD's anger that is poured out on us because our fathers have not kept the word of the LORD; they have not acted in accordance with all that is written in this book."

a16 Traditionally peace offerings   b18 That is, Judah, as frequently in 2 Chronicles   c19 One Hebrew manuscript and Septuagint; most Hebrew manuscripts of Hozai   d20 Also called Acbor son of Micaiah

²²Hilkiah and those the king had sent with him*ᵃ* went to speak to the prophetess Huldah, who was the wife of Shallum son of Tokhath,*ᵇ* the son of Hasrah,*ᶜ* keeper of the wardrobe. She lived in Jerusalem, in the Second District.

²³She said to them, "This is what the LORD, the God of Israel, says: Tell the man who sent you to me, ²⁴This is what the LORD says: I am going to bring disaster on this place and its people—all the curses written in the book that has been read in the presence of the king of Judah. ²⁵Because they have forsaken me and burned incense to other gods and provoked me to anger by all that their hands have made,*ᵈ* my anger will be poured out on this place and will not be quenched.' ²⁶Tell the king of Judah, who sent you to inquire of the LORD, 'This is what the LORD, the God of Israel, says concerning the words you heard: ²⁷Because your heart was responsive and you humbled yourself before God when you heard what he spoke against this place and its people, and because you humbled yourself before me and tore your robes and wept in my presence, I have heard you, declares the LORD. ²⁸Now I will gather you to your fathers, and you will be buried in peace. Your eyes will not see all the disaster I am going to bring on this place and on those who live here.'"

So they took her answer back to the king.

²⁹Then the king called together all the elders of Judah and Jerusalem. ³⁰He went up to the temple of the LORD with the men of Judah, the people of Jerusalem, the priests and the Levites—all the people from the least to the greatest. He read in their hearing all the words of the Book of the Covenant, which had been found in the temple of the LORD. ³¹The king stood by his pillar and renewed the covenant in the presence of the LORD—to follow the LORD and keep his commands, regulations and decrees with all his heart and all his soul, and to obey the words of the covenant written in this book.

³²Then he had everyone in Jerusalem and Benjamin pledge themselves to it; the people of Jerusalem did this in accordance with the covenant of God, the God of their fathers.

³³Josiah removed all the detestable idols from all the territory belonging to the Israelites, and he had all who were present in Israel serve the LORD their God. As long as he lived, they did not fail to follow the LORD, the God of their fathers.

Josiah Celebrates the Passover

35 Josiah celebrated the Passover to the LORD in Jerusalem, and the Passover lamb was slaughtered on the fourteenth day of the first month. ²He appointed the priests to their duties and encouraged them in the service of the LORD's temple. ³He said to the Levites, who instructed all Israel and who had been consecrated to the LORD: "Put the sacred ark in the temple that Solomon son of David king of Israel built. It is not to be carried about on your shoulders. Now serve the LORD your God and his people Israel. ⁴Prepare yourselves by families in your divisions, according to the directions written by David king of Israel and by his son Solomon.

⁵"Stand in the holy place with a group of Levites for each subdivision of the families of your fellow countrymen, the lay people. ⁶Slaughter the Passover lambs, consecrate yourselves and prepare ⌊the lambs⌋ for your fellow countrymen, doing what the LORD commanded through Moses."

⁷Josiah provided for all the lay people who were there a total of thirty thousand sheep and goats for the Passover offerings, and also three thousand cattle—all from the king's own possessions.

⁸His officials also contributed voluntarily to the people and the priests and Levites. Hilkiah, Zechariah and Jehiel, the administrators of God's temple, gave the priests twenty-six hundred Passover offerings and three hundred cattle. ⁹Also Conaniah along with Shemaiah and Nethanel, his brothers, and Hashabiah, Jeiel and Jozabad, the leaders of the Levites, provided five thousand Passover offerings and five hundred head of cattle for the Levites.

¹⁰The service was arranged and the priests stood in their places with the Levites in their divisions as the king had ordered. ¹¹The Passover lambs were slaughtered, and the priests sprinkled the blood handed to them, while the Levites skinned the animals. ¹²They set aside the burnt offerings to give them to the subdivisions of the families of the people to offer to the LORD, as is written in the Book of Moses. They did the same with the cattle. ¹³They roasted the Passover animals over the fire as prescribed, and boiled the holy offerings in pots, caldrons and pans and served them quickly to all the people. ¹⁴After this, they made preparations for themselves and for the priests, because the priests, the descendants of Aaron, were sacrificing the burnt offerings and the fat portions until nightfall. So the Levites made preparations for themselves and for the Aaronic priests.

¹⁵The musicians, the descendants of Asaph, were in the places prescribed by David, Asaph, Heman and Jeduthun the king's seer. The gatekeepers at each gate did not need to leave their posts, because their fellow Levites made the preparations for them.

¹⁶So at that time the entire service of the LORD

---

*ᵃ*22 One Hebrew manuscript, Vulgate and Syriac; most Hebrew manuscripts do not have *had sent with him.*   *ᵇ*22 Also called *Tikvah*   *ᶜ*22 Also called *Harhas*   *ᵈ*25 Or *by everything they have done*

was carried out for the celebration of the Passover and the offering of burnt offerings on the altar of the LORD, as King Josiah had ordered. [17]The Israelites who were present celebrated the Passover at that time and observed the Feast of Unleavened Bread for seven days. [18]The Passover had not been observed like this in Israel since the days of the prophet Samuel; and none of the kings of Israel had ever celebrated such a Passover as did Josiah, with the priests, the Levites and all Judah and Israel who were there with the people of Jerusalem. [19]This Passover was celebrated in the eighteenth year of Josiah's reign.

The Death of Josiah

[20]After all this, when Josiah had set the temple in order, Neco king of Egypt went up to fight at Carchemish on the Euphrates, and Josiah marched out to meet him in battle. [21]But Neco sent messengers to him, saying, "What quarrel is there between you and me, O king of Judah? It is not you I am attacking at this time, but the house with which I am at war. God has told me to hurry; so stop opposing God, who is with me, or he will destroy you."

[22]Josiah, however, would not turn away from him, but disguised himself to engage him in battle. He would not listen to what Neco had said at God's command but went to fight him on the plain of Megiddo.

35:22 A Bloody Battlefield

Some historians estimate that the valley of Megiddo has seen more fighting and bloodshed than any other spot on earth. Sitting astride the chief north-south trade route in Canaan, it has great strategic significance. The book of Revelation records that the last battle of the age, Armageddon, will take place here (Revelation 16:16).

[23]Archers shot King Josiah, and he told his officers, "Take me away; I am badly wounded." [24]So they took him out of his chariot, put him in the other chariot he had and brought him to Jerusalem, where he died. He was buried in the tombs of his fathers, and all Judah and Jerusalem mourned for him.

[25]Jeremiah composed laments for Josiah, and to this day all the men and women singers commemorate Josiah in the laments. These became a tradition in Israel and are written in the Laments.

[26]The other events of Josiah's reign and his acts of devotion, according to what is written in the Law of the LORD— [27]all the events, from beginning to end, are written in the book of the kings of Israel and Judah.

36

[1]And the people of the land took Jehoahaz son of Josiah and made him king in Jerusalem in place of his father.

Jehoahaz King of Judah

[2]Jehoahaz[a] was twenty-three years old when he became king, and he reigned in Jerusalem three months. [3]The king of Egypt dethroned him in Jerusalem and imposed on Judah a levy of a hundred talents[b] of silver and a talent[c] of gold. [4]The king of Egypt made Eliakim, a brother of Jehoahaz, king over Judah and Jerusalem and changed Eliakim's name to Jehoiakim. But Neco took Eliakim's brother Jehoahaz and carried him off to Egypt.

Jehoiakim King of Judah

[5]Jehoiakim was twenty-five years old when he became king, and he reigned in Jerusalem eleven years. He did evil in the eyes of the LORD his God. [6]Nebuchadnezzar king of Babylon attacked him and bound him with bronze shackles to take him to Babylon. [7]Nebuchadnezzar also took to Babylon articles from the temple of the LORD and put them in his temple[d] there.

[8]The other events of Jehoiakim's reign, the detestable things he did and all that was found against him, are written in the book of the kings of Israel and Judah. And Jehoiachin his son succeeded him as king.

Jehoiachin King of Judah

[9]Jehoiachin was eighteen[e] years old when he became king, and he reigned in Jerusalem three months and ten days. He did evil in the eyes of the LORD. [10]In the spring, King Nebuchadnezzar sent for him and brought him to Babylon, together with articles of value from the temple of the LORD, and he made Jehoiachin's uncle,[f] Zedekiah, king over Judah and Jerusalem.

Zedekiah King of Judah

[11]Zedekiah was twenty-one years old when he became king, and he reigned in Jerusalem eleven years. [12]He did evil in the eyes of the LORD his God and did not humble himself before Jeremiah the prophet, who spoke the word of the LORD. [13]He also rebelled against King Nebuchadnezzar, who had made him take an oath in God's name. He became stiff-necked and hardened his heart and would not turn to the LORD, the God of Israel. [14]Furthermore, all the leaders of the priests and the people became more and more unfaith-

[a]2 Hebrew *Joahaz*, a variant of *Jehoahaz*; also in verse 4   [b]3 That is, about 3 3/4 tons (about 3.4 metric tons)
[c]3 That is, about 75 pounds (about 34 kilograms)   [d]7 Or *palace*   [e]9 One Hebrew manuscript, some Septuagint manuscripts and Syriac (see also 2 Kings 24:8); most Hebrew manuscripts *eight*   [f]10 Hebrew *brother*, that is, relative (see 2 Kings 24:17)

ful, following all the detestable practices of the nations and defiling the temple of the LORD, which he had consecrated in Jerusalem.

The Fall of Jerusalem

[15]The LORD, the God of their fathers, sent word to them through his messengers again and again, because he had pity on his people and on his dwelling place. [16]But they mocked God's messengers, despised his words and scoffed at his prophets until the wrath of the LORD was aroused against his people and there was no remedy. [17]He brought up against them the king of the Babylonians,[a] who killed their young men with the sword in the sanctuary, and spared neither young man nor young woman, old man or aged. God handed all of them over to Nebuchadnezzar. [18]He carried to Babylon all the articles from the temple of God, both large and small, and the treasures of the king and his officials. [19]They set fire to God's temple and broke down the wall of Jerusalem; they burned all the palaces and destroyed everything of value there.

[20]He carried into exile to Babylon the remnant, who escaped from the sword, and they became servants to him and his sons until the kingdom of Persia came to power. [21]The land enjoyed its sabbath rests; all the time of its desolation it rested, until the seventy years were completed in fulfillment of the word of the LORD spoken by Jeremiah.

[22]In the first year of Cyrus king of Persia, in order to fulfill the word of the LORD spoken by

36:19 Between the Temples

For about 70 years the Jews had no temple. The first local synagogues probably developed during this time, as gathering places where Jews could hear readings from the Old Testament and offer prayers. The last few verses of Chronicles hint that a more hopeful time is coming when the temple will be rebuilt. These verses are repeated at the beginning of Ezra. Most scholars believe Chronicles, Ezra, and Nehemiah were originally connected in one book.

Jeremiah, the LORD moved the heart of Cyrus king of Persia to make a proclamation throughout his realm and to put it in writing:

[23]"This is what Cyrus king of Persia says:

"'The LORD, the God of heaven, has given me all the kingdoms of the earth and he has appointed me to build a temple for him at Jerusalem in Judah. Anyone of his people among you—may the LORD his God be with him, and let him go up.'"

[a] 17 Or *Chaldeans*

EZRA

Beginning Again
For the exiles from Babylon, news almost too good to be true

EZRA BEGINS WITH EXILES RETURNING to a ruined city—a brush-covered ghost town burned and pillaged nearly 50 years before by an overpowering Babylonian army. Would Jerusalem now have a new beginning? Psalm 126 captures the returning exiles' feelings: "We were like men who dreamed. Our mouths were filled with laughter, our tongues with songs of joy." The Persian empire had conquered mighty Babylon and, under the emperor Cyrus, offered all Jews a chance to return to their land. It was too good to believe.

Many of the older priests and Levites and family heads, who had seen the former temple, wept aloud . . . while many others shouted for joy.
3:12

A New Start with God

One poet in exile had written, "If I forget you, O Jerusalem, may my right hand forget its skill" (Psalm 137:5). These returned exiles were the minority who, decades afterwards, had not forgotten. They treasured their spiritual heritage more than the houses and businesses they had built in Babylon. They wanted to live and worship in the place God had given his people. Any sacrifice was worth this opportunity. Their first impulse when they arrived was to rebuild the temple, God's home.

The tolerant Persians (whose official policy was to encourage the local religion in every area they governed) had even brought out the silver and gold temple articles, carefully preserved in a Babylonian temple as though waiting on God's timing. When the returned exiles laid the foundation to the new temple, the sound of their shouting (and noisy weeping) could be heard from far away (3:13). The temple, after all, was the place where they would meet God. It symbolized a new start with him.

The Problems of Beginning Again

God had opened the way, but the exiles needed determination to follow it. The book of Ezra divides into three parts, each one dealing with an obstacle that arose. The first part tells how, immediately after the return of the exiles, their neighbors in the surrounding countryside became hostile. After their deceptive offer of "help" was turned down, these neighbors began a campaign of opposition. They managed to stop further progress on the temple.

The temple lay in ruins for nearly 20 more years, until the prophets Haggai and Zechariah (whose messages are recorded in the books named after them) again stirred up interest in building. This "second push" is described in chapters 5 and 6. When opposition arose this time, the Jews managed to push through—again with the assistance of a Persian king.

Another problem preoccupies the final four chapters. Ezra, the man after whom this book is named, actually arrived in Jerusalem during this period, 80 years after the first party. The temple had by then been up for half a century. But the "new beginning" stood in severe jeopardy again. The Jews had begun to mingle (and compromise their faith) with the hostile people around them. Ezra's leadership, which came from deep biblical faith and genuine sorrow over sin, forced a radical, painful solution.

Ezra Leads Up to Jesus

The book of Ezra introduces an entirely new period in Israel's history—a period in which they became more like a church than a nation. Israelites before the exile had given much of their energy to fighting enemy armies. Now they focused on fighting sin and spiritual compromise.

The minority who returned could build a temple only with the permission of a foreign government in Persia. They had lost political independence, yet they clung to their religion, especially to the Old

Testament Scriptures and temple worship. They feared repeating the mistakes that had sent them into exile. True, they did flirt with spiritual compromise. Yet when God's prophets spoke, people responded.

As those who had chosen a ruined Jerusalem over a prosperous Babylon, the returned Jews looked to God instead of to government for help. Still they dreamed, more than ever, of the powerful Messiah the prophets promised. This dream, and their strong determination to obey the law of God, continued right up until the time of Jesus, about 450 years after Ezra's last words.

How to Read Ezra

The book of Ezra describes several highly emotional events. Yet it reads like a historical report, citing official documents, letters, and lists written over an 80-year span. You are often left to imagine for yourself the feelings of the returning exiles. The book can, therefore, seem confusing and dry unless you take time to imagine how the scenes must have looked and to reflect on how people must have felt.

The three distinct periods Ezra deals with all have the same theme: a new beginning for God's people. In each situation God gave opportunity and the outside world threatened it. God's people drifted back and forth in their response. Carefully take note of the "messages" from both God and the world, and how the Israelites responded. Examine Ezra's model, as an unwavering man of the law as well as of deep personal faith.

To understand how Ezra fits into Israel's long-term pattern of response to God and the world, read some historical background. Articles on "Ezra," "Haggai" or "Israel, History of" in a Bible dictionary may offer the best summary. The short book of Haggai zeroes in on the crucial months described in Ezra 5:1–2 and makes a valuable companion to any study of Ezra.

PEOPLE YOU'LL MEET IN EZRA

ARTAXERXES *(p. 505)*
EZRA *(p. 506)*

3-TRACK READING PLAN

For an explanation and complete listing of the 3-track reading plan, turn to page 7.

TRACK 1: *Two-Week Courses on the Bible*
See page 7 for information on these courses.

TRACK 2: *An Overview of Ezra in 1 Day*
☐ Day 1. Read the Introduction to Ezra and chapter 3 for the emotional story of how the returned exiles laid the foundation for the new temple.
Now turn to page 9 for your next Track 2 reading project.

TRACK 3: *All of Ezra in 9 Days*
After you have read through Ezra, turn to pages 10–14 for your next Track 3 reading project.
☐1–2   ☐3   ☐4   ☐5   ☐6   ☐7   ☐8   ☐9
☐10

Cyrus Helps the Exiles to Return

1 In the first year of Cyrus king of Persia, in order to fulfill the word of the LORD spoken by Jeremiah, the LORD moved the heart of Cyrus king of Persia to make a proclamation throughout his realm and to put it in writing:

²"This is what Cyrus king of Persia says:

"'The LORD, the God of heaven, has given me all the kingdoms of the earth and he has appointed me to build a temple for him

1:2 Prediction Fulfilled

The fulfilled prophecy was probably Jeremiah 29:10, God's promise to bring Israel back to Jerusalem after 70 years. Additionally, Isaiah 44:28 and 45:1,13 had named Cyrus of Persia as God's agent to see Jerusalem and the temple rebuilt. This is not evidence that Cyrus worshiped Israel's God. He had a policy of religious tolerance and contributed to the rebuilding of several nations' temples.

at Jerusalem in Judah. ³Anyone of his people among you—may his God be with him, and let him go up to Jerusalem in Judah and build the temple of the LORD, the God of Israel, the God who is in Jerusalem. ⁴And the people of any place where survivors may now be living are to provide him with silver and gold, with goods and livestock, and with freewill offerings for the temple of God in Jerusalem.'"

⁵Then the family heads of Judah and Benjamin, and the priests and Levites—everyone whose heart God had moved—prepared to go up and build the house of the LORD in Jerusalem. ⁶All their neighbors assisted them with articles of silver and gold, with goods and livestock, and with valuable gifts, in addition to all the freewill offerings. ⁷Moreover, King Cyrus brought out the articles belonging to the temple of the LORD, which Nebuchadnezzar had carried away from Jerusalem and had placed in the temple of his god.ᵃ ⁸Cyrus king of Persia had them brought by Mithredath the treasurer, who counted them out to Sheshbazzar the prince of Judah.

⁹This was the inventory:

gold dishes	30
silver dishes	1,000
silver pansᵇ	29
¹⁰gold bowls	30
matching silver bowls	410
other articles	1,000

¹¹In all, there were 5,400 articles of gold and of silver. Sheshbazzar brought all these along when the exiles came up from Babylon to Jerusalem.

The List of the Exiles Who Returned

2 Now these are the people of the province who came up from the captivity of the exiles,

2:1 A People Preserved

Lists of names, whether in the Bible or the telephone book, make dull reading. But the way these names are grouped reveals God's care for the people of Israel. They had not lost track of their Israelite identity during two generations in Babylon. They knew their family record, and they could place themselves according to Israelite families, Israelite towns, and Israelite religious duties in the temple. Like the temple articles, carefully stored in readiness (1:7), these were a people preserved to serve God again.

whom Nebuchadnezzar king of Babylon had taken captive to Babylon (they returned to Jerusalem and Judah, each to his own town, ²in company with Zerubbabel, Jeshua, Nehemiah, Seraiah, Reelaiah, Mordecai, Bilshan, Mispar, Bigvai, Rehum and Baanah):

The list of the men of the people of Israel:

³the descendants of Parosh	2,172
⁴of Shephatiah	372
⁵of Arah	775
⁶of Pahath-Moab (through the line of Jeshua and Joab)	2,812
⁷of Elam	1,254
⁸of Zattu	945
⁹of Zaccai	760
¹⁰of Bani	642
¹¹of Bebai	623
¹²of Azgad	1,222
¹³of Adonikam	666
¹⁴of Bigvai	2,056
¹⁵of Adin	454
¹⁶of Ater (through Hezekiah)	98
¹⁷of Bezai	323
¹⁸of Jorah	112
¹⁹of Hashum	223
²⁰of Gibbar	95
²¹the men of Bethlehem	123
²²of Netophah	56
²³of Anathoth	128
²⁴of Azmaveth	42
²⁵of Kiriath Jearim,ᶜ Kephirah and Beeroth	743

ᵃ7 Or *gods*   ᵇ9 The meaning of the Hebrew for this word is uncertain.   ᶜ25 See Septuagint (see also Neh. 7:29); Hebrew *Kiriath Arim.*

26 of Ramah and Geba	621
27 of Micmash	122
28 of Bethel and Ai	223
29 of Nebo	52
30 of Magbish	156
31 of the other Elam	1,254
32 of Harim	320
33 of Lod, Hadid and Ono	725
34 of Jericho	345
35 of Senaah	3,630

36 The priests:

the descendants of Jedaiah (through the family of Jeshua)	973
37 of Immer	1,052
38 of Pashhur	1,247
39 of Harim	1,017

40 The Levites:

the descendants of Jeshua and Kadmiel (through the line of Hodaviah)	74

41 The singers:

the descendants of Asaph	128

42 The gatekeepers of the temple:

the descendants of Shallum, Ater, Talmon, Akkub, Hatita and Shobai	139

43 The temple servants:

the descendants of
Ziha, Hasupha, Tabbaoth,
44 Keros, Siaha, Padon,
45 Lebanah, Hagabah, Akkub,
46 Hagab, Shalmai, Hanan,
47 Giddel, Gahar, Reaiah,
48 Rezin, Nekoda, Gazzam,
49 Uzza, Paseah, Besai,
50 Asnah, Meunim, Nephussim,
51 Bakbuk, Hakupha, Harhur,
52 Bazluth, Mehida, Harsha,
53 Barkos, Sisera, Temah,
54 Neziah and Hatipha

55 The descendants of the servants of Solomon:

the descendants of
Sotai, Hassophereth, Peruda,
56 Jaala, Darkon, Giddel,
57 Shephatiah, Hattil,
Pokereth-Hazzebaim and Ami

58 The temple servants and the descendants of the servants of Solomon	392

59 The following came up from the towns of Tel Melah, Tel Harsha, Kerub, Addon and Immer, but they could not show that their families were descended from Israel:

60 The descendants of Delaiah, Tobiah and Nekoda	652

61 And from among the priests:

The descendants of
Hobaiah, Hakkoz and Barzillai (a man who had married a daughter of Barzillai the Gileadite and was called by that name).

62 These searched for their family records, but they could not find them and so were excluded from the priesthood as unclean. 63 The governor ordered them not to eat any of the most sacred food until there was a priest ministering with the Urim and Thummim.

2:63 The Need for Guidance

The Urim and Thummim were probably something like dice. Priests in the Old Testament used them to determine God's will. Until the Urim and Thummim could be employed, the families whose records were lost (verse 62) had no way to establish themselves as genuine priests. For a people determined to follow God's word precisely, this mattered tremendously. God had said that only Aaron's descendants could touch the holy things in the sanctuary, on pain of death (Numbers 18:1–7).

64 The whole company numbered 42,360, 65 besides their 7,337 menservants and maidservants; and they also had 200 men and women singers. 66 They had 736 horses, 245 mules, 67 435 camels and 6,720 donkeys.

68 When they arrived at the house of the LORD in Jerusalem, some of the heads of the families gave freewill offerings toward the rebuilding of the house of God on its site. 69 According to their ability they gave to the treasury for this work 61,000 drachmas[a] of gold, 5,000 minas[b] of silver and 100 priestly garments.

70 The priests, the Levites, the singers, the gatekeepers and the temple servants settled in their own towns, along with some of the other people, and the rest of the Israelites settled in their towns.

Rebuilding the Altar

3 When the seventh month came and the Israelites had settled in their towns, the people assembled as one man in Jerusalem. 2 Then Jeshua son of Jozadak and his fellow priests and Zerubbabel son of Shealtiel and his associates began

---

[a]69 That is, about 1,100 pounds (about 500 kilograms)   [b]69 That is, about 3 tons (about 2.9 metric tons)

to build the altar of the God of Israel to sacrifice burnt offerings on it, in accordance with what is written in the Law of Moses the man of God. ³Despite their fear of the peoples around them, they built the altar on its foundation and sacrificed burnt offerings on it to the LORD, both the morning and evening sacrifices. ⁴Then in accordance with what is written, they celebrated the Feast of Tabernacles with the required number of burnt offerings prescribed for each day. ⁵After that, they presented the regular burnt offerings, the New Moon sacrifices and the sacrifices for all the appointed sacred feasts of the LORD, as well as those brought as freewill offerings to the LORD. ⁶On the first day of the seventh month they began to offer burnt offerings to the LORD, though the foundation of the LORD's temple had not yet been laid.

Rebuilding the Temple

⁷Then they gave money to the masons and carpenters, and gave food and drink and oil to the people of Sidon and Tyre, so that they would bring cedar logs by sea from Lebanon to Joppa, as authorized by Cyrus king of Persia.

⁸In the second month of the second year after their arrival at the house of God in Jerusalem, Zerubbabel son of Shealtiel, Jeshua son of Jozadak and the rest of their brothers (the priests and the Levites and all who had returned from the captivity to Jerusalem) began the work, appointing Levites twenty years of age and older to supervise the building of the house of the LORD. ⁹Jeshua and his sons and brothers and Kadmiel and his sons (descendants of Hodaviah[a]) and the sons of Henadad and their sons and brothers—all Levites—joined together in supervising those working on the house of God.

¹⁰When the builders laid the foundation of the temple of the LORD, the priests in their vestments and with trumpets, and the Levites (the sons of Asaph) with cymbals, took their places to praise the LORD, as prescribed by David king of Israel. ¹¹With praise and thanksgiving they sang to the LORD:

"He is good;
    his love to Israel endures forever."

And all the people gave a great shout of praise to the LORD, because the foundation of the house of the LORD was laid. ¹²But many of the older priests and Levites and family heads, who had seen the former temple, wept aloud when they saw the foundation of this temple being laid, while many others shouted for joy. ¹³No one could distinguish the sound of the shouts of joy from the sound of weeping, because the people made so much noise. And the sound was heard far away.

Opposition to the Rebuilding

4 When the enemies of Judah and Benjamin heard that the exiles were building a temple for the LORD, the God of Israel, ²they came to

4:1 How to Stop God's Work

Chapter 4 describes three different strategies used to hinder God's people: 1) Offer help that will lead to compromises or even a complete takeover of the project by unbelievers (verses 1–3). 2) Discourage, frighten, and frustrate God's people (verses 4–5). 3) Use official power to force them to stop (verses 23–24). Now as then, governments and opposition groups use these strategies to stop the work of believers.

Zerubbabel and to the heads of the families and said, "Let us help you build because, like you, we seek your God and have been sacrificing to him since the time of Esarhaddon king of Assyria, who brought us here."

³But Zerubbabel, Jeshua and the rest of the heads of the families of Israel answered, "You have no part with us in building a temple to our God. We alone will build it for the LORD, the God of Israel, as King Cyrus, the king of Persia, commanded us."

⁴Then the peoples around them set out to discourage the people of Judah and make them afraid to go on building.[b] ⁵They hired counselors to work against them and frustrate their plans during the entire reign of Cyrus king of Persia and down to the reign of Darius king of Persia.

Later Opposition Under Xerxes and Artaxerxes

⁶At the beginning of the reign of Xerxes,[c] they lodged an accusation against the people of Judah and Jerusalem.

4:6–23 A Flash Forward

This section is a glance forward in history. The Israelites would continue to feel opposition from their neighbors even long after the temple was successfully completed. The quarrel described here, during Xerxes' and Artaxerxes' reigns, was not over the temple but the defensive wall to be built around Jerusalem—a wall Nehemiah, with Ezra's help, completed years later.

---

[a]9 Hebrew *Yehudah*, probably a variant of *Hodaviah*   [b]4 Or *and troubled them as they built*   [c]6 Hebrew *Ahasuerus*, a variant of Xerxes' Persian name

[7]And in the days of Artaxerxes king of Persia, Bishlam, Mithredath, Tabeel and the rest of his associates wrote a letter to Artaxerxes. The letter was written in Aramaic script and in the Aramaic language.[a,b]

[8]Rehum the commanding officer and Shimshai the secretary wrote a letter against Jerusalem to Artaxerxes the king as follows:

[9]Rehum the commanding officer and Shimshai the secretary, together with the rest of their associates—the judges and officials over the men from Tripolis, Persia,[c] Erech and Babylon, the Elamites of Susa, [10]and the other people whom the great and honorable Ashurbanipal[d] deported and settled in the city of Samaria and elsewhere in Trans-Euphrates.

[11](This is a copy of the letter they sent him.)

To King Artaxerxes,

From your servants, the men of Trans-Euphrates:

[12]The king should know that the Jews who came up to us from you have gone to Jerusalem and are rebuilding that rebellious and wicked city. They are restoring the walls and repairing the foundations.

[13]Furthermore, the king should know that if this city is built and its walls are restored, no more taxes, tribute or duty will be paid, and the royal revenues will suffer. [14]Now since we are under obligation to the palace and it is not proper for us to see the king dishonored, we are sending this message to inform the king, [15]so that a search may be made in the archives of your predecessors. In these records you will find that this city is a rebellious city, troublesome to kings and provinces, a place of rebellion from ancient times. That is why this city was destroyed. [16]We inform the king that if this city is built and its walls are restored, you will be left with nothing in Trans-Euphrates.

[17]The king sent this reply:

To Rehum the commanding officer, Shimshai the secretary and the rest of their associates living in Samaria and elsewhere in Trans-Euphrates:

Greetings.

[18]The letter you sent us has been read and translated in my presence. [19]I issued an order and a search was made, and it was found that this city has a long history of revolt against kings and has been a place of rebellion and sedition. [20]Jerusalem has had powerful kings ruling over the whole of Trans-Euphrates, and taxes, tribute and duty were paid to them. [21]Now issue an order to these men to stop work, so that this city will not be rebuilt until I so order. [22]Be careful not to neglect this matter. Why let this threat grow, to the detriment of the royal interests?

[23]As soon as the copy of the letter of King Artaxerxes was read to Rehum and Shimshai the secretary and their associates, they went immediately to the Jews in Jerusalem and compelled them by force to stop.

[24]Thus the work on the house of God in Jerusalem came to a standstill until the second year of the reign of Darius king of Persia.

Tattenai's Letter to Darius

5 Now Haggai the prophet and Zechariah the prophet, a descendant of Iddo, prophesied to the Jews in Judah and Jerusalem in the name of the God of Israel, who was over them. [2]Then Zerubbabel son of Shealtiel and Jeshua son of Jozadak set to work to rebuild the house of God in Jerusalem. And the prophets of God were with them, helping them.

[3]At that time Tattenai, governor of Trans-Euphrates, and Shethar-Bozenai and their associates went to them and asked, "Who authorized you to rebuild this temple and restore this structure?" [4]They also asked, "What are the names of the men constructing this building?"[e] [5]But the eye of their God was watching over the elders of the Jews, and they were not stopped until a report could go to Darius and his written reply be received.

[6]This is a copy of the letter that Tattenai, governor of Trans-Euphrates, and Shethar-Bozenai and their associates, the officials of Trans-Euphrates, sent to King Darius. [7]The report they sent him read as follows:

To King Darius:

Cordial greetings.

[8]The king should know that we went to the district of Judah, to the temple of the great God. The people are building it with large stones and placing the timbers in the walls. The work is being carried on with diligence and is making rapid progress under their direction.

[9]We questioned the elders and asked

---

[a]7 Or *written in Aramaic and translated*   [b]7 The text of Ezra 4:8—6:18 is in Aramaic.   [c]9 Or *officials, magistrates and governors over the men from*   [d]10 Aramaic *Osnappar*, a variant of *Ashurbanipal*   [e]4 See Septuagint; Aramaic [e]4 We told them the names of the men constructing this building.

them, "Who authorized you to rebuild this temple and restore this structure?" [10]We also asked them their names, so that we could write down the names of their leaders for your information.

[11]This is the answer they gave us:

"We are the servants of the God of heaven and earth, and we are rebuilding the temple that was built many years ago, one that a great king of Israel built and finished. [12]But because our fathers angered the God of heaven, he handed them over to Nebuchadnezzar the Chaldean, king of Babylon, who destroyed this temple and deported the people to Babylon.

[13]"However, in the first year of Cyrus king of Babylon, King Cyrus issued a decree to rebuild this house of God. [14]He even removed from the temple[a] of Babylon the gold and silver articles of the house of God, which Nebuchadnezzar had taken from the temple in Jerusalem and brought to the temple[a] in Babylon.

"Then King Cyrus gave them to a man named Sheshbazzar, whom he had appointed governor, [15]and he told him, 'Take these articles and go and deposit them in the temple in Jerusalem. And rebuild the house of God on its site.' [16]So this Sheshbazzar came and laid the foundations of the house of God in Jerusalem. From that day to the present it has been under construction but is not yet finished."

[17]Now if it pleases the king, let a search be made in the royal archives of Babylon to see if King Cyrus did in fact issue a decree to rebuild this house of God in Jerusalem. Then let the king send us his decision in this matter.

The Decree of Darius

6 King Darius then issued an order, and they searched in the archives stored in the treasury at Babylon. [2]A scroll was found in the citadel of Ecbatana in the province of Media, and this was written on it:

Memorandum:

[3]In the first year of King Cyrus, the king issued a decree concerning the temple of God in Jerusalem:

Let the temple be rebuilt as a place to present sacrifices, and let its foundations be laid. It is to be ninety feet[b] high and ninety feet wide, [4]with three courses of large stones and one of timbers. The costs are to

be paid by the royal treasury. [5]Also, the gold and silver articles of the house of God, which Nebuchadnezzar took from the temple in Jerusalem and brought to Babylon,

6:2 The Ring of Truth

In a made-up legend, there is no need for insignificant, divergent details. All the loose ends tie up neatly. Real life, however, is messier. Ezra records a typical example: a document was searched for in Babylon, but it unexpectedly turned up in remote Ecbatana, where (history records) Cyrus spent the summer of his first year as king. Such details suggest that Ezra is based on accurate and detailed historical sources.

are to be returned to their places in the temple in Jerusalem; they are to be deposited in the house of God.

[6]Now then, Tattenai, governor of Trans-Euphrates, and Shethar-Bozenai and you, their fellow officials of that province, stay away from there. [7]Do not interfere with the work on this temple of God. Let the governor of the Jews and the Jewish elders rebuild this house of God on its site.

[8]Moreover, I hereby decree what you are to do for these elders of the Jews in the construction of this house of God:

The expenses of these men are to be fully paid out of the royal treasury, from the revenues of Trans-Euphrates, so that the work will not stop. [9]Whatever is needed—young bulls, rams, male lambs for burnt offerings to the God of heaven, and wheat, salt, wine and oil, as requested by the priests in Jerusalem—must be given them daily without fail, [10]so that they may offer sacrifices pleasing to the God of heaven and pray for the well-being of the king and his sons.

[11]Furthermore, I decree that if anyone changes this edict, a beam is to be pulled from his house and he is to be lifted up and impaled on it. And for this crime his house is to be made a pile of rubble. [12]May God, who has caused his Name to dwell there, overthrow any king or people who lifts a hand to change this decree or to destroy this temple in Jerusalem.

I Darius have decreed it. Let it be carried out with diligence.

Completion and Dedication of the Temple

[13]Then, because of the decree King Darius had sent, Tattenai, governor of Trans-Euphrates, and

---

a 14 Or *palace*   *b 3* Aramaic *sixty cubits* (about 27 meters)

Shethar-Bozenai and their associates carried it out with diligence. [14]So the elders of the Jews continued to build and prosper under the preaching of Haggai the prophet and Zechariah,

a descendant of Iddo. They finished building the temple according to the command of the God of Israel and the decrees of Cyrus, Darius and Artaxerxes, kings of Persia. [15]The temple was completed on the third day of the month Adar, in the sixth year of the reign of King Darius.

[16]Then the people of Israel—the priests, the Levites and the rest of the exiles—celebrated the dedication of the house of God with joy. [17]For the dedication of this house of God they offered a hundred bulls, two hundred rams, four hundred male lambs and, as a sin offering for all Israel, twelve male goats, one for each of the tribes of Israel. [18]And they installed the priests in their divisions and the Levites in their groups for the service of God at Jerusalem, according to what is written in the Book of Moses.

The Passover

[19]On the fourteenth day of the first month, the exiles celebrated the Passover. [20]The priests and Levites had purified themselves and were all ceremonially clean. The Levites slaughtered the Passover lamb for all the exiles, for their brothers the priests and for themselves. [21]So the Israelites who had returned from the exile ate it, together with all who had separated themselves from the unclean practices of their Gentile neighbors in order to seek the LORD, the God of Israel. [22]For seven days they celebrated with joy the Feast of Unleavened Bread, because the LORD had filled them with joy by changing the attitude of the king of Assyria, so that he assisted them in the work on the house of God, the God of Israel.

Ezra Comes to Jerusalem

7 After these things, during the reign of Artaxerxes king of Persia, Ezra son of Seraiah, the son of Azariah, the son of Hilkiah, [2]the son of Shallum, the son of Zadok, the son of Ahitub, [3]the son of Amariah, the son of Azariah, the son of Meraioth, [4]the son of Zerahiah, the son of Uzzi, the son of Bukki, [5]the son of Abishua, the son of Phinehas, the son of Eleazar, the son of Aaron the chief priest— [6]this Ezra came up from Babylon. He was a teacher well versed in the Law of Moses, which the LORD, the God of Israel, had given. The king had granted him everything he asked, for the hand of the LORD his God was on him. [7]Some of the Israelites, including priests, Levites, singers, gatekeepers and temple servants, also came up to Jerusalem in the seventh year of King Artaxerxes.

[8]Ezra arrived in Jerusalem in the fifth month of the seventh year of the king. [9]He had begun his journey from Babylon on the first day of the first month, and he arrived in Jerusalem on the first

day of the fifth month, for the gracious hand of his God was on him. [10]For Ezra had devoted himself to the study and observance of the Law of the LORD, and to teaching its decrees and laws in Israel.

King Artaxerxes' Letter to Ezra

[11]This is a copy of the letter King Artaxerxes had given to Ezra the priest and teacher, a man learned in matters concerning the commands and decrees of the LORD for Israel:

[a]12 The text of Ezra 7:12-26 is in Aramaic.

[12a]Artaxerxes, king of kings,

To Ezra the priest, a teacher of the Law of the God of heaven:

Greetings.

[13]Now I decree that any of the Israelites in my kingdom, including priests and Levites, who wish to go to Jerusalem with you, may go. [14]You are sent by the king and his seven advisers to inquire about Judah and

---

Ezra, a Man of the Heart
He applied God's word to himself before preaching it to others

EZRA KNEW HOW TO GET things done. He had the political savvy to win a Persian king's support for the trip back to Jerusalem, the salesmanship to convince Jewish family leaders to go along, and the organizational know-how to mount the long, complicated, and dangerous expedition. (There were no Holiday Inns.)

At the same time, Ezra was a priest who depended on God. He set aside days for fasting and prayer. He knew and lived by the Old Testament law, but used it as a path to a profound relationship with God. When he studied Scripture, he applied it to himself before applying it to others (7:10).

While Ezra was praying and confessing, weeping and throwing himself down before the house of God, a large crowd of Israelites—men, women and children—gathered around him. 10:1

A Strong Negative Reaction

Ezra's party got to Jerusalem 80 years after the first exiles had returned. Yet within four months the Jewish leaders were asking this latecomer for advice on the most sensitive matters.

They told Ezra that Israelites were marrying their idolatrous neighbors. At the news, Ezra completely lost his composure, tore his clothes, and sat down stunned (9:3). His grief-filled prayer of repentance inspired a large crowd to join him in bitter weeping. Then and there they resolved to break up the marriages. The women and children were to be sent away. Ezra, a practical man even in his emotional condition, put the machinery into operation and saw it done.

Why did Ezra react so negatively to these marriages? How could he allow children to be sent away from their fathers, families split? Some people see proof that he was racially oriented, bound to exclude non-Jews from Israel.

But racial purity was not Ezra's worry. Non-Jews like Rahab and Ruth, who converted to Judaism, had long been accepted into Israel. Ezra 6:21 suggests that outsiders who sought the Lord were still welcomed. Ezra's concern was that intermarriage represented a compromised faith that threatened the future existence of Israel.

Tossing Away One Last Chance

Marriage in those days was more than a personal matter. It created a political and religious alliance between two families. These mixed marriages were tying Israelites to other faiths—for Israel's neighbors worshiped idols, an act God hated. Ezra knew that his God must hold the only place in his people's hearts. They must be a special people with a sense of their unique destiny. The law told them not to intermarry (Exodus 34:15–16; Deuteronomy 7:3–6). (In a related situation Paul instructed Christians not to be "yoked together to unbelievers" [2 Corinthians 6:14], though he told Christians already married to non-Christians not to divorce [1 Corinthians 7:12–16].)

Ezra's prayer shows that petty technicalities of the law were far from his mind. His concerns involved the heart. He saw his people falling into the same pattern of compromise that had led God to give them up to the Babylonians years before. Had they learned nothing from their long exile? They were tossing away one last remarkable chance to start over.

Life Questions: Ezra saw intermarriage as a compromise in people's faith. Do people today make other compromises that have the same impact on their faith?

Jerusalem with regard to the Law of your God, which is in your hand. ¹⁵Moreover, you are to take with you the silver and gold that the king and his advisers have freely given to the God of Israel, whose dwelling is in Jerusalem, ¹⁶together with all the silver and gold you may obtain from the province of Babylon, as well as the freewill offerings of the people and priests for the temple of their God in Jerusalem. ¹⁷With this money be sure to buy bulls, rams and male lambs, together with their grain offerings and drink offerings, and sacrifice them on the altar of the temple of your God in Jerusalem.

¹⁸You and your brother Jews may then do whatever seems best with the rest of the silver and gold, in accordance with the will of your God. ¹⁹Deliver to the God of Jerusalem all the articles entrusted to you for worship in the temple of your God. ²⁰And anything else needed for the temple of your God that you may have occasion to supply, you may provide from the royal treasury.

²¹Now I, King Artaxerxes, order all the treasurers of Trans-Euphrates to provide with diligence whatever Ezra the priest, a teacher of the Law of the God of heaven, may ask of you— ²²up to a hundred talents*a* of silver, a hundred cors*b* of wheat, a hundred baths*c* of wine, a hundred baths*c* of olive oil, and salt without limit. ²³Whatever the God of heaven has prescribed, let it be done with diligence for the temple of the God of heaven. Why should there be wrath against the realm of the king and of his sons? ²⁴You are also to know that you have no authority to impose taxes, tribute or duty on any of the priests, Levites, singers, gatekeepers, temple servants or other workers at this house of God.

²⁵And you, Ezra, in accordance with the wisdom of your God, which you possess, appoint magistrates and judges to administer justice to all the people of Trans-Euphrates—all who know the laws of your God. And you are to teach any who do not know them. ²⁶Whoever does not obey the law of your God and the law of the king must surely be punished by death, banishment, confiscation of property, or imprisonment.

²⁷Praise be to the LORD, the God of our fathers, who has put it into the king's heart to bring honor to the house of the LORD in Jerusalem in this way ²⁸and who has extended his good favor

to me before the king and his advisers and all the king's powerful officials. Because the hand of the LORD my God was on me, I took courage and gathered leading men from Israel to go up with me.

List of the Family Heads Returning With Ezra

8 These are the family heads and those registered with them who came up with me from Babylon during the reign of King Artaxerxes:

²of the descendants of Phinehas, Gershom;
of the descendants of Ithamar, Daniel;
of the descendants of David, Hattush ³of the descendants of Shecaniah;

of the descendants of Parosh, Zechariah, and with him were registered 150 men;
⁴of the descendants of Pahath-Moab, Eliehoenai son of Zerahiah, and with him 200 men;
⁵of the descendants of Zattu,*d* Shecaniah son of Jahaziel, and with him 300 men;
⁶of the descendants of Adin, Ebed son of Jonathan, and with him 50 men;
⁷of the descendants of Elam, Jeshaiah son of Athaliah, and with him 70 men;
⁸of the descendants of Shephatiah, Zebadiah son of Michael, and with him 80 men;
⁹of the descendants of Joab, Obadiah son of Jehiel, and with him 218 men;
¹⁰of the descendants of Bani,*e* Shelomith son of Josiphiah, and with him 160 men;
¹¹of the descendants of Bebai, Zechariah son of Bebai, and with him 28 men;
¹²of the descendants of Azgad, Johanan son of Hakkatan, and with him 110 men;
¹³of the descendants of Adonikam, the last ones, whose names were Eliphelet, Jeuel and Shemaiah, and with them 60 men;
¹⁴of the descendants of Bigvai, Uthai and Zaccur, and with them 70 men.

The Return to Jerusalem

¹⁵I assembled them at the canal that flows toward Ahava, and we camped there three days. When I checked among the people and the priests, I found no Levites there. ¹⁶So I summoned Eliezer, Ariel, Shemaiah, Elnathan, Jarib, Elnathan, Nathan, Zechariah and Meshullam, who were leaders, and Joiarib and Elnathan, who were men of learning, ¹⁷and I sent them to Iddo, the leader in Casiphia. I told them what to say to

---

a22 That is, about 3 3/4 tons (about 3.4 metric tons)   *b22* That is, probably about 600 bushels (about 22 kiloliters)
c22 That is, probably about 600 gallons (about 2.2 kiloliters)   *d5* Some Septuagint manuscripts (also 1 Esdras 8:32);
Hebrew does not have *Zattu.*   *e10* Some Septuagint manuscripts (also 1 Esdras 8:36); Hebrew does not have *Bani.*

Iddo and his kinsmen, the temple servants in Casiphia, so that they might bring attendants to us for the house of our God. 18Because the gracious hand of our God was on us, they brought us Sherebiah, a capable man, from the descendants of Mahli son of Levi, the son of Israel, and Sherebiah's sons and brothers, 18 men; 19and Hashabiah, together with Jeshaiah from the descendants of Merari, and his brothers and nephews, 20 men. 20They also brought 220 of the temple servants—a body that David and the officials had established to assist the Levites. All were registered by name.

21There, by the Ahava Canal, I proclaimed a fast, so that we might humble ourselves before our God and ask him for a safe journey for us and our children, with all our possessions. 22I was ashamed to ask the king for soldiers and horsemen to protect us from enemies on the road, because we had told the king, "The gracious hand of our God is on everyone who looks to him, but his great anger is against all who forsake him."

8:22 Risk of Faith

Like gold shipments in the old Wild West, Ezra's consignment of treasure made for a dangerous journey through lawless Palestine. A military escort would surely have helped. But, having told the king that God would protect the settlers, Ezra was ashamed to ask for help that would seem to contradict his statement. His faith on the line, he determined to rely on prayer rather than soldiers.

23So we fasted and petitioned our God about this, and he answered our prayer.

24Then I set apart twelve of the leading priests, together with Sherebiah, Hashabiah and ten of their brothers, 25and I weighed out to them the offering of silver and gold and the articles that the king, his advisers, his officials and all Israel present there had donated for the house of our God. 26I weighed out to them 650 talents[a] of silver, silver articles weighing 100 talents,[b] 100 talents[b] of gold, 2720 bowls of gold valued at 1,000 darics,[c] and two fine articles of polished bronze, as precious as gold.

28I said to them, "You as well as these articles are consecrated to the LORD. The silver and gold are a freewill offering to the LORD, the God of your fathers. 29Guard them carefully until you weigh them out in the chambers of the house of the LORD in Jerusalem before the leading priests and the Levites and the family heads of Israel."

30Then the priests and Levites received the silver and gold and sacred articles that had been weighed out to be taken to the house of our God in Jerusalem.

31On the twelfth day of the first month we set out from the Ahava Canal to go to Jerusalem. The hand of our God was on us, and he protected us from enemies and bandits along the way. 32So we arrived in Jerusalem, where we rested three days.

33On the fourth day, in the house of our God, we weighed out the silver and gold and the sacred articles into the hands of Meremoth son of Uriah, the priest. Eleazar son of Phinehas was with him, and so were the Levites Jozabad son of Jeshua and Noadiah son of Binnui. 34Everything was accounted for by number and weight, and the entire weight was recorded at that time.

35Then the exiles who had returned from captivity sacrificed burnt offerings to the God of Israel: twelve bulls for all Israel, ninety-six rams, seventy-seven male lambs and, as a sin offering, twelve male goats. All this was a burnt offering to the LORD. 36They also delivered the king's orders to the royal satraps and to the governors of Trans-Euphrates, who then gave assistance to the people and to the house of God.

Ezra's Prayer About Intermarriage

9 After these things had been done, the leaders came to me and said, "The people of Israel, including the priests and the Levites, have not kept themselves separate from the neighboring peoples with their detestable practices, like those of the Canaanites, Hittites, Perizzites, Jebusites, Ammonites, Moabites, Egyptians and Amorites. 2They have taken some of their daughters as wives for themselves and their sons, and have mingled the holy race with the peoples around them. And the leaders and officials have led the way in this unfaithfulness."

3When I heard this, I tore my tunic and cloak, pulled hair from my head and beard and sat down appalled. 4Then everyone who trembled at the words of the God of Israel gathered around me because of this unfaithfulness of the exiles. And I sat there appalled until the evening sacrifice.

5Then, at the evening sacrifice, I rose from my self-abasement, with my tunic and cloak torn, and fell on my knees with my hands spread out to the LORD my God 6and prayed:

"O my God, I am too ashamed and disgraced to lift up my face to you, my God, because our sins are higher than our heads and our guilt has reached to the heavens.

---

[a]26 That is, about 25 tons (about 22 metric tons)   [b]26 That is, about 3 3/4 tons (about 3.4 metric tons)
[c]27 That is, about 19 pounds (about 8.5 kilograms)

[7]From the days of our forefathers until now, our guilt has been great. Because of our sins, we and our kings and our priests have been subjected to the sword and captivity, to pillage and humiliation at the hand of foreign kings, as it is today.

[8]"But now, for a brief moment, the LORD our God has been gracious in leaving us a remnant and giving us a firm place in his sanctuary, and so our God gives light to our eyes and a little relief in our bondage. [9]Though we are slaves, our God has not deserted us in our bondage. He has shown us kindness in the sight of the kings of Persia: He has granted us new life to rebuild the house of our God and repair its ruins, and he has given us a wall of protection in Judah and Jerusalem.

[10]"But now, O our God, what can we say after this? For we have disregarded the commands [11]you gave through your servants the prophets when you said: 'The land you are entering to possess is a land polluted by the corruption of its peoples. By their detestable practices they have filled it with their impurity from one end to the other. [12]Therefore, do not give your daughters in marriage to their sons or take their daughters for your sons. Do not seek a treaty of friendship with them at any time, that you may be strong and eat the good things of the land and leave it to your children as an everlasting inheritance.'

[13]"What has happened to us is a result of our evil deeds and our great guilt, and yet, our God, you have punished us less than our sins have deserved and have given us a remnant like this. [14]Shall we again break your commands and intermarry with the peoples who commit such detestable practices? Would you not be angry enough with us to destroy us, leaving us no remnant or survivor? [15]O LORD, God of Israel, you are righteous! We are left this day as a remnant. Here we are before you in our guilt, though because of it not one of us can stand in your presence."

The People's Confession of Sin

10 While Ezra was praying and confessing, weeping and throwing himself down before the house of God, a large crowd of Israelites—men, women and children—gathered around him. They too wept bitterly. [2]Then Shecaniah son of Jehiel, one of the descendants of Elam, said to Ezra, "We have been unfaithful to our God by marrying foreign women from the peoples around us. But in spite of this, there is still hope for Israel. [3]Now let us make a covenant before our God to send away all these women and their children, in accordance with the counsel of my lord and of those who fear the commands of our God. Let it be done according to the Law. [4]Rise up; this matter is in your hands. We will support you, so take courage and do it."

10:1 Unprecedented Response

Ezra's grief over Israel's spiritual compromise was similar to that of many prophets. But the people's response to Ezra was unprecedented. Pre-exile prophets like Amos or Jeremiah never saw such heartfelt repentance. Evidently the exile really had purified Israel.

[5]So Ezra rose up and put the leading priests and Levites and all Israel under oath to do what had been suggested. And they took the oath. [6]Then Ezra withdrew from before the house of God and went to the room of Jehohanan son of Eliashib. While he was there, he ate no food and drank no water, because he continued to mourn over the unfaithfulness of the exiles.

[7]A proclamation was then issued throughout Judah and Jerusalem for all the exiles to assemble in Jerusalem. [8]Anyone who failed to appear within three days would forfeit all his property, in accordance with the decision of the officials and elders, and would himself be expelled from the assembly of the exiles.

[9]Within the three days, all the men of Judah and Benjamin had gathered in Jerusalem. And on the twentieth day of the ninth month, all the people were sitting in the square before the house of God, greatly distressed by the occasion and because of the rain. [10]Then Ezra the priest stood up and said to them, "You have been unfaithful; you have married foreign women, adding to Israel's guilt. [11]Now make confession to the LORD, the God of your fathers, and do his will. Separate yourselves from the peoples around you and from your foreign wives."

[12]The whole assembly responded with a loud voice: "You are right! We must do as you say. [13]But there are many people here and it is the rainy season; so we cannot stand outside. Besides, this matter cannot be taken care of in a day or two, because we have sinned greatly in this thing. [14]Let our officials act for the whole assembly. Then let everyone in our towns who has married a foreign woman come at a set time, along with the elders and judges of each town, until the fierce anger of our God in this matter is turned away from us." [15]Only Jonathan son of Asahel and Jahzeiah son of Tikvah, supported by Meshullam and Shabbethai the Levite, opposed this.

[16]So the exiles did as was proposed. Ezra the

priest selected men who were family heads, one from each family division, and all of them designated by name. On the first day of the tenth month they sat down to investigate the cases, [17]and by the first day of the first month they finished dealing with all the men who had married foreign women.

10:17 Corrupt Leaders

The problem Ezra had evidently expected to solve in a day (verse 13) took, in fact, two months to sort out. Intermarriage must have been more widespread than he realized. The list of those involved shows that the priests and Levites, who were the religious leaders, had a higher proportion of intermarriage than the rest of the people.

Those Guilty of Intermarriage

[18]Among the descendants of the priests, the following had married foreign women:

From the descendants of Jeshua son of Jozadak, and his brothers: Maaseiah, Eliezer, Jarib and Gedaliah. [19](They all gave their hands in pledge to put away their wives, and for their guilt they each presented a ram from the flock as a guilt offering.)

[20]From the descendants of Immer:
Hanani and Zebadiah.

[21]From the descendants of Harim:
Maaseiah, Elijah, Shemaiah, Jehiel and Uzziah.

[22]From the descendants of Pashhur:
Elioenai, Maaseiah, Ishmael, Nethanel, Jozabad and Elasah.

[23]Among the Levites:

Jozabad, Shimei, Kelaiah (that is, Kelita), Pethahiah, Judah and Eliezer.

[24]From the singers:
Eliashib.

From the gatekeepers:
Shallum, Telem and Uri.

[25]And among the other Israelites:

From the descendants of Parosh:
Ramiah, Izziah, Malkijah, Mijamin, Eleazar, Malkijah and Benaiah.

[26]From the descendants of Elam:
Mattaniah, Zechariah, Jehiel, Abdi, Jeremoth and Elijah.

[27]From the descendants of Zattu:
Elioenai, Eliashib, Mattaniah, Jeremoth, Zabad and Aziza.

[28]From the descendants of Bebai:
Jehohanan, Hananiah, Zabbai and Athlai.

[29]From the descendants of Bani:
Meshullam, Malluch, Adaiah, Jashub, Sheal and Jeremoth.

[30]From the descendants of Pahath-Moab:
Adna, Kelal, Benaiah, Maaseiah, Mattaniah, Bezalel, Binnui and Manasseh.

[31]From the descendants of Harim:
Eliezer, Ishijah, Malkijah, Shemaiah, Shimeon, [32]Benjamin, Malluch and Shemariah.

[33]From the descendants of Hashum:
Mattenai, Mattattah, Zabad, Eliphelet, Jeremai, Manasseh and Shimei.

[34]From the descendants of Bani:
Maadai, Amram, Uel, [35]Benaiah, Bedeiah, Keluhi, [36]Vaniah, Meremoth, Eliashib, [37]Mattaniah, Mattenai and Jaasu.

[38]From the descendants of Binnui:[a]
Shimei, [39]Shelemiah, Nathan, Adaiah, [40]Macnadebai, Shashai, Sharai, [41]Azarel, Shelemiah, Shemariah, [42]Shallum, Amariah and Joseph.

[43]From the descendants of Nebo:
Jeiel, Mattithiah, Zabad, Zebina, Jaddai, Joel and Benaiah.

[44]All these had married foreign women, and some of them had children by these wives.[b]

---

[a] 37,38 See Septuagint (also 1 Esdras 9:34); Hebrew *Jaasu* [38]and Bani and Binnui, with their children   [b] 44 Or *and they sent them away with their children*

NEHEMIAH

A Man of Action
He set out to build a wall, but left an enduring legacy of leadership

> *"Don't be afraid of them. Remember the LORD, who is great and awesome, and fight." 4:14*

I N THE BOOK OF NEHEMIAH we peek inside the personal memoirs of a great leader. You can't mistake his style. He was an organizer, a pragmatic leader. That, no doubt, is why he had made his way to a top position in the Persian empire, one of the grandest in the history of the world.

Yet his heart was elsewhere—in Jerusalem, a small, troublesome place far from the center of power. When he heard of the difficulties his people were experiencing there, he took his career—and probably his life—in his hands and spoke to the king about it. Shortly thereafter he was touring, by night, the broken-down walls of a city he probably had never seen before.

Nearly 100 years had passed since his people had returned to Jerusalem from exile. Though the temple had been rebuilt, the city was barely occupied. More Jews lived in the outlying villages and towns than in the holy city. They mixed with all kinds of foreigners. They were in danger of losing their identity. Why? Partly because the city lacked a wall.

What's in a Wall?

Compared to many concerns, building a wall may not seem terribly important. But think of it this way—what if the border between Mexico and the United States was wide open, so that anyone could cross and live on either side at will? One thing is certain: The distinction between Mexico and Texas would soon dissolve.

For lack of a wall the Jews were facing assimilation into the culture of their neighbors. In those days a city without a wall was easy pickings for any robber band. Jews, concerned for security, had scattered among other nationalities in small villages outside Jerusalem. There they were intermarrying and gradually losing their own language, culture and—most important—their own religion. A wall would give them a chance to make Jerusalem a truly Jewish city, keeping it safe and controlling who came and went.

Waiting for a Leader

What had kept them from doing anything about the broken-down wall for nearly 100 years? One obstacle was local resistance: powerful politicians were determined to keep the Jews down. Perhaps another reason was the lack of a leader like Nehemiah. In his memoirs, which fill most of this book, he shows remarkable qualities of leadership: impassioned speech, prayer, organization, resolve, trust in God, quick and determined response to problems, unselfishness. Perhaps his years in the Persian court had been preparing him. Organizing a difficult building project and handling fierce opposition seemed to come easily to him.

Nehemiah was more than a good business manager. He was a man of God. He did not act without prayer, and he did not pray without acting. His prayers punctuate the book. He recognized God's role in all that happened and never forgot to give him credit. He was not looking for earthly status—if he had been, he never would have left Persia.

How to Read Nehemiah

Nehemiah's personality is the outstanding quality of the book that bears his name. No other biblical character gives such clear information about how to "practice the presence of God" while carrying a leadership role. As you read, take note of the qualities that made Nehemiah successful as a leader and man of God. You may also wish to contrast his leadership with Ezra's. They worked in tandem but had very different styles. Nehemiah was an activist, Ezra a student; Nehemiah was outspoken, Ezra more withdrawn. Yet both faced similar problems and had similar success—and the two worked smoothly together.

The books of Ezra and Nehemiah both tell how the disgraced and chastened Jews returned from exile to rebuild their country. As history, Nehemiah includes some long lists of different family groups, as well as a detailed description of who built which parts of the Jerusalem wall. Unless you are an advanced student, you should skim these lists mainly to get an understanding of why they were kept. Concentrate more on how the Israelites had been transformed and purified by exile, making them ready to meet new challenges when they returned home.

PEOPLE YOU'LL MEET IN NEHEMIAH

NEHEMIAH *(p. 511)*

3-TRACK READING PLAN

For an explanation and complete listing of the 3-track reading plan, turn to page 7.

TRACK 1: *Two-Week Courses on the Bible*
See page 7 for information on these courses.

TRACK 2: *An Overview of Nehemiah in 2 Days*
☐ Day 1. Read the Introduction to Nehemiah and chapter 2, which tells how Nehemiah began his work on the wall.
☐ Day 2. Read chapter 8, showing the power of God's Word read aloud.

Now turn to page 9 for your next Track 2 reading project.

TRACK 3: *All of Nehemiah in 12 Days*
After you have read through Nehemiah, turn to pages 10–14 for your next Track 3 reading project.

☐1 ☐2–3 ☐4 ☐5 ☐6 ☐7 ☐8 ☐9
☐10 ☐11 ☐12 ☐13

Nehemiah's Prayer

1 The words of Nehemiah son of Hacaliah:

In the month of Kislev in the twentieth year, while I was in the citadel of Susa, ²Hanani, one of my brothers, came from Judah with some other men, and I questioned them about the Jewish remnant that survived the exile, and also about Jerusalem.

³They said to me, "Those who survived the exile and are back in the province are in great trouble and disgrace. The wall of Jerusalem is broken down, and its gates have been burned with fire."

⁴When I heard these things, I sat down and wept. For some days I mourned and fasted and prayed before the God of heaven. ⁵Then I said:

"O LORD, God of heaven, the great and awesome God, who keeps his covenant of love with those who love him and obey his commands, ⁶let your ear be attentive and your eyes open to hear the prayer your servant is praying before you day and night for your servants, the people of Israel. I confess the sins we Israelites, including myself and my father's house, have committed against you. ⁷We have acted very wickedly toward you. We have not obeyed the commands, decrees and laws you gave your servant Moses.

⁸"Remember the instruction you gave your servant Moses, saying, 'If you are unfaithful, I will scatter you among the nations, ⁹but if you return to me and obey my

commands, then even if your exiled people are at the farthest horizon, I will gather them from there and bring them to the place I have chosen as a dwelling for my Name.'

[10]"They are your servants and your people, whom you redeemed by your great strength and your mighty hand. [11]O Lord, let your ear be attentive to the prayer of this your servant and to the prayer of your servants who delight in revering your name. Give your servant success today by granting him favor in the presence of this man."

I was cupbearer to the king.

Artaxerxes Sends Nehemiah to Jerusalem

2 In the month of Nisan in the twentieth year of King Artaxerxes, when wine was brought for him, I took the wine and gave it to the king. I had not been sad in his presence before; [2]so the king asked me, "Why does your face look so sad when you are not ill? This can be nothing but sadness of heart."

I was very much afraid, [3]but I said to the king, "May the king live forever! Why should my face not look sad when the city where my fathers are buried lies in ruins, and its gates have been destroyed by fire?"

[4]The king said to me, "What is it you want?"

2:4 The "Arrow Prayer"

Nehemiah characteristically prayed to God while he went about his duties. He even "shot an arrow" to God, silently asking him for help in the middle of this crucial conversation with the king. He spontaneously inserted prayers as he wrote his memoirs. Some other examples: 1:5–11; 4:4–5; 5:19; 6:9,14; 13:14,22,31.

Then I prayed to the God of heaven, [5]and I answered the king, "If it pleases the king and if your servant has found favor in his sight, let him send me to the city in Judah where my fathers are buried so that I can rebuild it."

[6]Then the king, with the queen sitting beside him, asked me, "How long will your journey take, and when will you get back?" It pleased the king to send me; so I set a time.

[7]I also said to him, "If it pleases the king, may I have letters to the governors of Trans-Euphrates, so that they will provide me safe-conduct until I arrive in Judah? [8]And may I have a letter to Asaph, keeper of the king's forest, so he will give me timber to make beams for the gates of the citadel by the temple and for the city wall and for the residence I will occupy?" And because the gracious hand of my God was upon me, the king granted my requests. [9]So I went to the governors of Trans-Euphrates and gave them the king's letters. The king had also sent army officers and cavalry with me.

[10]When Sanballat the Horonite and Tobiah the Ammonite official heard about this, they were very much disturbed that someone had come to promote the welfare of the Israelites.

2:10 Powerful Opponents

Both Sanballat and Tobiah were influential local politicians. Sanballat's family governed Samaria and had managed to marry into the high priest's family (see 13:28). Tobiah, an official in Ammon (a small country east of Judah), had family ties and influence among the top Jewish families (see 6:17–19; 13:4–5). There is some evidence both men were from Jewish backgrounds, though they preferred the political status quo in which Jewish identity was diluted.

Nehemiah Inspects Jerusalem's Walls

[11]I went to Jerusalem, and after staying there three days [12]I set out during the night with a few men. I had not told anyone what my God had put in my heart to do for Jerusalem. There were no mounts with me except the one I was riding on.

[13]By night I went out through the Valley Gate toward the Jackal[a] Well and the Dung Gate, examining the walls of Jerusalem, which had been broken down, and its gates, which had been destroyed by fire. [14]Then I moved on toward the Fountain Gate and the King's Pool, but there was not enough room for my mount to get through; [15]so I went up the valley by night, examining the wall. Finally, I turned back and reentered through the Valley Gate. [16]The officials did not know where I had gone or what I was doing, because as yet I had said nothing to the Jews or the priests or nobles or officials or any others who would be doing the work.

[17]Then I said to them, "You see the trouble we are in: Jerusalem lies in ruins, and its gates have been burned with fire. Come, let us rebuild the wall of Jerusalem, and we will no longer be in disgrace." [18]I also told them about the gracious hand of my God upon me and what the king had said to me.

They replied, "Let us start rebuilding." So they began this good work.

---

[a]13 Or *Serpent* or *Fig*

[19]But when Sanballat the Horonite, Tobiah the Ammonite official and Geshem the Arab heard about it, they mocked and ridiculed us. "What is this you are doing?" they asked. "Are you rebelling against the king?"

[20]I answered them by saying, "The God of heaven will give us success. We his servants will start rebuilding, but as for you, you have no share in Jerusalem or any claim or historic right to it."

Builders of the Wall

3 Eliashib the high priest and his fellow priests went to work and rebuilt the Sheep Gate. They dedicated it and set its doors in place, building as far as the Tower of the Hundred, which they dedicated, and as far as the Tower of

3:1–32 Lasting Credit

Archaeologists love this chapter for its valuable clues to the design of ancient Jerusalem. Other readers may find these details less inspiring, but they do give evidence of Nehemiah's organizational genius. Somehow he motivated skilled craftsmen to work alongside ordinary laborers, and he even got children to pitch in. For added motivation, he assigned families repair projects just outside their own homes. This chapter, like a brass plaque listing "Important Contributors," assured that they would receive lasting credit for their efforts.

Hananel. [2]The men of Jericho built the adjoining section, and Zaccur son of Imri built next to them.

[3]The Fish Gate was rebuilt by the sons of Hassenaah. They laid its beams and put its doors and bolts and bars in place. [4]Meremoth son of Uriah, the son of Hakkoz, repaired the next section. Next to him Meshullam son of Berekiah, the son of Meshezabel, made repairs, and next to him Zadok son of Baana also made repairs. [5]The next section was repaired by the men of Tekoa, but their nobles would not put their shoulders to the work under their supervisors.[a]

[6]The Jeshanah[b] Gate was repaired by Joiada son of Paseah and Meshullam son of Besodeiah. They laid its beams and put its doors and bolts and bars in place. [7]Next to them, repairs were made by men from Gibeon and Mizpah—Melatiah of Gibeon and Jadon of Meronoth—places under the authority of the governor of Trans-Euphrates. [8]Uzziel son of Harhaiah, one of the goldsmiths, repaired the next section; and Hananiah,

one of the perfume-makers, made repairs next to that. They restored[c] Jerusalem as far as the Broad Wall. [9]Rephaiah son of Hur, ruler of a half-district of Jerusalem, repaired the next section. [10]Adjoining this, Jedaiah son of Harumaph made repairs opposite his house, and Hattush son of Hashabneiah made repairs next to him. [11]Malkijah son of Harim and Hasshub son of Pahath-Moab repaired another section and the Tower of the Ovens. [12]Shallum son of Hallohesh, ruler of a half-district of Jerusalem, repaired the next section with the help of his daughters.

[13]The Valley Gate was repaired by Hanun and the residents of Zanoah. They rebuilt it and put its doors and bolts and bars in place. They also repaired five hundred yards[d] of the wall as far as the Dung Gate.

[14]The Dung Gate was repaired by Malkijah son of Recab, ruler of the district of Beth Hakkerem. He rebuilt it and put its doors and bolts and bars in place.

[15]The Fountain Gate was repaired by Shallun son of Col-Hozeh, ruler of the district of Mizpah. He rebuilt it, roofing it over and putting its doors and bolts and bars in place. He also repaired the wall of the Pool of Siloam,[e] by the King's Garden, as far as the steps going down from the City of David. [16]Beyond him, Nehemiah son of Azbuk, ruler of a half-district of Beth Zur, made repairs up to a point opposite the tombs[f] of David, as far as the artificial pool and the House of the Heroes.

[17]Next to him, the repairs were made by the Levites under Rehum son of Bani. Beside him, Hashabiah, ruler of half the district of Keilah, carried out repairs for his district. [18]Next to him, the repairs were made by their countrymen under Binnui[g] son of Henadad, ruler of the other half-district of Keilah. [19]Next to him, Ezer son of Jeshua, ruler of Mizpah, repaired another section, from a point facing the ascent to the armory as far as the angle. [20]Next to him, Baruch son of Zabbai zealously repaired another section, from the angle to the entrance of the house of Eliashib the high priest. [21]Next to him, Meremoth son of Uriah, the son of Hakkoz, repaired another section, from the entrance of Eliashib's house to the end of it.

[22]The repairs next to him were made by the priests from the surrounding region. [23]Beyond them, Benjamin and Hasshub made repairs in front of their house; and next to them, Azariah son of Maaseiah, the son of Ananiah, made repairs beside his house. [24]Next to him, Binnui son

---

[a]5 Or *their Lord* or *the governor*   [b]6 Or *Old*   [c]8 Or *They left out part of* (about 450 meters)   [e]15 Hebrew *Shelah,* a variant of *Shiloah,* that is, Siloam   [d]13 Hebrew *a thousand cubits*   [f]16 Hebrew; Septuagint, some Vulgate manuscripts and Syriac *tomb*   [g]18 Two Hebrew manuscripts and Syriac (see also Septuagint and verse 24); most Hebrew manuscripts *Bavvai*

of Henadad repaired another section, from Azariah's house to the angle and the corner, **25**and Palal son of Uzai worked opposite the angle and the tower projecting from the upper palace near the court of the guard. Next to him, Pedaiah son of Parosh **26**and the temple servants living on the hill of Ophel made repairs up to a point opposite the Water Gate toward the east and the projecting tower. **27**Next to them, the men of Tekoa repaired another section, from the great projecting tower to the wall of Ophel.

28Above the Horse Gate, the priests made repairs, each in front of his own house. **29**Next to them, Zadok son of Immer made repairs opposite his house. Next to him, Shemaiah son of Shecaniah, the guard at the East Gate, made repairs. **30**Next to him, Hananiah son of Shelemiah, and Hanun, the sixth son of Zalaph, repaired another section. Next to them, Meshullam son of Berekiah made repairs opposite his living quarters. **31**Next to him, Malkijah, one of the goldsmiths, made repairs as far as the house of the temple servants and the merchants, opposite the Inspection Gate, and as far as the room above the corner; **32**and between the room above the corner and the Sheep Gate the goldsmiths and merchants made repairs.

Opposition to the Rebuilding

4 When Sanballat heard that we were rebuilding the wall, he became angry and was greatly incensed. He ridiculed the Jews, **2**and in the presence of his associates and the army of Samaria, he said, "What are those feeble Jews doing? Will they restore their wall? Will they offer sacrifices? Will they finish in a day? Can they bring the stones back to life from those heaps of rubble — burned as they are?"

3Tobiah the Ammonite, who was at his side, said, "What they are building — if even a fox climbed up on it, he would break down their wall of stones!"

4Hear us, O our God, for we are despised. Turn their insults back on their own heads. Give them over as plunder in a land of captivity. **5**Do not cover up their guilt or blot out their sins from your sight, for they have thrown insults in the face of[a] the builders.

6So we rebuilt the wall till all of it reached half its height, for the people worked with all their heart.

7But when Sanballat, Tobiah, the Arabs, the Ammonites and the men of Ashdod heard that the repairs to Jerusalem's walls had gone ahead and that the gaps were being closed, they were very angry. **8**They all plotted together to come and fight against Jerusalem and stir up trouble

against it. **9**But we prayed to our God and posted a guard day and night to meet this threat.

10Meanwhile, the people in Judah said, "The strength of the laborers is giving out, and there is

4:9 Praise the Lord and Fight

Nehemiah felt no difficulty combining prayer and action, as this verse shows: "We prayed to our God and posted a guard." Verse 14 gives another unembarrassed combination of spiritual and military tactics: "Remember the Lord . . . and fight."

so much rubble that we cannot rebuild the wall."

11Also our enemies said, "Before they know it or see us, we will be right there among them and will kill them and put an end to the work."

12Then the Jews who lived near them came and told us ten times over, "Wherever you turn, they will attack us."

13Therefore I stationed some of the people behind the lowest points of the wall at the exposed places, posting them by families, with their swords, spears and bows. **14**After I looked things over, I stood up and said to the nobles, the officials and the rest of the people, "Don't be afraid of them. Remember the Lord, who is great and awesome, and fight for your brothers, your sons and your daughters, your wives and your homes."

15When our enemies heard that we were aware of their plot and that God had frustrated it, we all returned to the wall, each to his own work.

16From that day on, half of my men did the work, while the other half were equipped with spears, shields, bows and armor. The officers posted themselves behind all the people of Judah **17**who were building the wall. Those who carried materials did their work with one hand and held a weapon in the other, **18**and each of the builders wore his sword at his side as he worked. But the man who sounded the trumpet stayed with me.

19Then I said to the nobles, the officials and the rest of the people, "The work is extensive and spread out, and we are widely separated from each other along the wall. **20**Wherever you hear the sound of the trumpet, join us there. Our God will fight for us!"

21So we continued the work with half the men holding spears, from the first light of dawn till the stars came out. **22**At that time I also said to the people, "Have every man and his helper stay inside Jerusalem at night, so they can serve us as guards by night and workmen by day." **23**Neither I nor my brothers nor my men nor the guards

a 5 Or *have provoked you to anger before*

with me took off our clothes; each had his weapon, even when he went for water.[a]

Nehemiah Helps the Poor

5 Now the men and their wives raised a great outcry against their Jewish brothers. [2]Some were saying, "We and our sons and daughters are numerous; in order for us to eat and stay alive, we must get grain."

[3]Others were saying, "We are mortgaging our fields, our vineyards and our homes to get grain during the famine."

[4]Still others were saying, "We have had to borrow money to pay the king's tax on our fields and vineyards. [5]Although we are of the same flesh and blood as our countrymen and though our sons are as good as theirs, yet we have to subject our sons and daughters to slavery. Some of our daughters have already been enslaved, but we are powerless, because our fields and our vineyards belong to others."

[6]When I heard their outcry and these charges, I was very angry. [7]I pondered them in my mind and then accused the nobles and officials. I told them, "You are exacting usury from your own countrymen!" So I called together a large meeting to deal with them [8]and said: "As far as possible, we have bought back our Jewish brothers who were sold to the Gentiles. Now you are selling your brothers, only for them to be sold back to us!" They kept quiet, because they could find nothing to say.

[9]So I continued, "What you are doing is not right. Shouldn't you walk in the fear of our God to avoid the reproach of our Gentile enemies? [10]I and my brothers and my men are also lending the people money and grain. But let the exacting of usury stop! [11]Give back to them immediately their fields, vineyards, olive groves and houses, and also the usury you are charging them—the hundredth part of the money, grain, new wine and oil."

[12]"We will give it back," they said. "And we will not demand anything more from them. We will do as you say."

Then I summoned the priests and made the nobles and officials take an oath to do what they had promised. [13]I also shook out the folds of my robe and said, "In this way may God shake out of his house and possessions every man who does not keep this promise. So may such a man be shaken out and emptied!"

At this the whole assembly said, "Amen," and praised the LORD. And the people did as they had promised.

[14]Moreover, from the twentieth year of King Artaxerxes, when I was appointed to be their governor in the land of Judah, until his thirty-second year—twelve years—neither I nor my brothers ate the food allotted to the governor. [15]But the earlier governors—those preceding me—placed a heavy burden on the people and

5:14 Politician Without Greed

Nehemiah faced a daunting task similar to that confronting many leaders of developing countries today. The land was devastated, with all wealth concentrated in the hands of a few powerful families. Jews were mortgaging their property and even selling their children into slavery in order to raise money to pay taxes. Nehemiah, who apparently came from wealth, could have profited further from his political position. Instead, he set a sterling example of generosity and self-sacrifice that made a profound impression on his oppressed countrymen.

took forty shekels[b] of silver from them in addition to food and wine. Their assistants also lorded it over the people. But out of reverence for God I did not act like that. [16]Instead, I devoted myself to the work on this wall. All my men were assembled there for the work; we[c] did not acquire any land.

[17]Furthermore, a hundred and fifty Jews and officials ate at my table, as well as those who came to us from the surrounding nations. [18]Each day one ox, six choice sheep and some poultry were prepared for me, and every ten days an abundant supply of wine of all kinds. In spite of all this, I never demanded the food allotted to the governor, because the demands were heavy on these people.

[19]Remember me with favor, O my God, for all I have done for these people.

Further Opposition to the Rebuilding

6 When word came to Sanballat, Tobiah, Geshem the Arab and the rest of our enemies that I had rebuilt the wall and not a gap was left in it—though up to that time I had not set the doors in the gates— [2]Sanballat and Geshem sent me this message: "Come, let us meet together in one of the villages[d] on the plain of Ono."

But they were scheming to harm me; [3]so I sent messengers to them with this reply: "I am carrying on a great project and cannot go down. Why should the work stop while I leave it and go down to you?" [4]Four times they sent me the same message, and each time I gave them the same answer. [5]Then, the fifth time, Sanballat sent his aide to

---

[a]23 The meaning of the Hebrew for this clause is uncertain.   [b]15 That is, about 1 pound (about 0.5 kilogram)
[c]16 Most Hebrew manuscripts; some Hebrew manuscripts, Septuagint, Vulgate and Syriac I   [d]2 Or in Kephirim

me with the same message, and in his hand was an unsealed letter [6]in which was written:

"It is reported among the nations—and Geshem[a] says it is true—that you and the

6:5 Psychological Warfare

After fending off ridicule and threats of violence from his enemies (chapter 4), Nehemiah suddenly faced a new scare tactic. The author points out that this accusatory letter came "unsealed," or open to public view. Ordinarily, letters were rolled up, tied, sealed with wax, and delivered in a silk bag to guarantee privacy. Opponents were doubtless trying to intimidate Nehemiah by openly spreading rumors to arouse the suspicion of his Persian overseers. As usual, he was not easily intimidated.

Jews are plotting to revolt, and therefore you are building the wall. Moreover, according to these reports you are about to become their king [7]and have even appointed prophets to make this proclamation about you in Jerusalem: 'There is a king in Judah!' Now this report will get back to the king; so come, let us confer together."

[8]I sent him this reply: "Nothing like what you are saying is happening; you are just making it up out of your head."

[9]They were all trying to frighten us, thinking, "Their hands will get too weak for the work, and it will not be completed."

But I prayed, "Now strengthen my hands."

[10]One day I went to the house of Shemaiah son of Delaiah, the son of Mehetabel, who was shut in at his home. He said, "Let us meet in the house of God, inside the temple, and let us close the temple doors, because men are coming to kill you—by night they are coming to kill you."

[11]But I said, "Should a man like me run away? Or should one like me go into the temple to save his life? I will not go!" [12]I realized that God had not sent him, but that he had prophesied against me because Tobiah and Sanballat had hired him. [13]He had been hired to intimidate me so that I would commit a sin by doing this, and then they would give me a bad name to discredit me.

[14]Remember Tobiah and Sanballat, O my God, because of what they have done; remember also the prophetess Noadiah and the rest of the prophets who have been trying to intimidate me.

The Completion of the Wall

[15]So the wall was completed on the twenty-fifth of Elul, in fifty-two days. [16]When all our enemies heard about this, all the surrounding nations were afraid and lost their self-confidence, because they realized that this work had been done with the help of our God.

[17]Also, in those days the nobles of Judah were sending many letters to Tobiah, and replies from Tobiah kept coming to them. [18]For many in Judah were under oath to him, since he was son-in-law to Shecaniah son of Arah, and his son Jehohanan had married the daughter of Meshullam son of Berekiah. [19]Moreover, they kept reporting to me his good deeds and then telling him what I said. And Tobiah sent letters to intimidate me.

7 After the wall had been rebuilt and I had set the doors in place, the gatekeepers and the singers and the Levites were appointed. [2]I put in charge of Jerusalem my brother Hanani, along with[b] Hananiah the commander of the citadel, because he was a man of integrity and feared God more than most men do. [3]I said to them, "The gates of Jerusalem are not to be opened until the sun is hot. While the gatekeepers are still on duty, have them shut the doors and bar them. Also appoint residents of Jerusalem as guards, some at their posts and some near their own houses."

The List of the Exiles Who Returned

[4]Now the city was large and spacious, but there were few people in it, and the houses had not yet been rebuilt. [5]So my God put it into my heart to assemble the nobles, the officials and the common people for registration by families. I found the genealogical record of those who had been the first to return. This is what I found written there:

[6]These are the people of the province who came up from the captivity of the exiles whom Nebuchadnezzar king of Babylon had taken captive (they returned to Jerusalem and Judah, each to his own town,

7:6 Remembering Our Past

Because their cultural identity was threatened, the Jews in Ezra and Nehemiah kept careful track of their roots. All Jews wanted to trace their family lineage back to Abraham's grandson Israel (Jacob) in order to prove their Jewishness. In addition, descendants of Levi the priest and David the king took great pains to establish their heritage. The process had been vastly complicated by Nebuchadnezzar's burning of Jerusalem, which destroyed many records (see verses 61,64). This list (verses 8–73) almost exactly repeats the one found in Ezra 2.

---

[a]6 Hebrew *Gashmu*, a variant of *Geshem*   [b]2 Or *Hanani, that is,*

7in company with Zerubbabel, Jeshua, Nehemiah, Azariah, Raamiah, Nahamani, Mordecai, Bilshan, Mispereth, Bigvai, Nehum and Baanah):

The list of the men of Israel:

8the descendants of Parosh	2,172
9of Shephatiah	372
10of Arah	652
11of Pahath-Moab (through the line of Jeshua and Joab)	2,818
12of Elam	1,254
13of Zattu	845
14of Zaccai	760
15of Binnui	648
16of Bebai	628
17of Azgad	2,322
18of Adonikam	667
19of Bigvai	2,067
20of Adin	655
21of Ater (through Hezekiah)	98
22of Hashum	328
23of Bezai	324
24of Hariph	112
25of Gibeon	95
26the men of Bethlehem and Netophah	188
27of Anathoth	128
28of Beth Azmaveth	42
29of Kiriath Jearim, Kephirah and Beeroth	743
30of Ramah and Geba	621
31of Micmash	122
32of Bethel and Ai	123
33of the other Nebo	52
34of the other Elam	1,254
35of Harim	320
36of Jericho	345
37of Lod, Hadid and Ono	721
38of Senaah	3,930

39The priests:

the descendants of Jedaiah (through the family of Jeshua)	973
40of Immer	1,052
41of Pashhur	1,247
42of Harim	1,017

43The Levites:

the descendants of Jeshua (through Kadmiel through the line of Hodaviah)	74

44The singers:

the descendants of Asaph	148

45The gatekeepers:

the descendants of

Shallum, Ater, Talmon, Akkub, Hatita and Shobai	138

46The temple servants:

the descendants of
Ziha, Hasupha, Tabbaoth,
47Keros, Sia, Padon,
48Lebana, Hagaba, Shalmai,
49Hanan, Giddel, Gahar,
50Reaiah, Rezin, Nekoda,
51Gazzam, Uzza, Paseah,
52Besai, Meunim, Nephussim,
53Bakbuk, Hakupha, Harhur,
54Bazluth, Mehida, Harsha,
55Barkos, Sisera, Temah,
56Neziah and Hatipha

57The descendants of the servants of Solomon:

the descendants of
Sotai, Sophereth, Perida,
58Jaala, Darkon, Giddel,
59Shephatiah, Hattil,
Pokereth-Hazzebaim and Amon

60The temple servants and the descendants of the servants of Solomon	392

61The following came up from the towns of Tel Melah, Tel Harsha, Kerub, Addon and Immer, but they could not show that their families were descended from Israel:

62the descendants of Delaiah, Tobiah and Nekoda	642

63And from among the priests:

the descendants of
Hobaiah, Hakkoz and Barzillai (a man who had married a daughter of Barzillai the Gileadite and was called by that name).
64These searched for their family records, but they could not find them and so were excluded from the priesthood as unclean. 65The governor, therefore, ordered them not to eat any of the most sacred food until there should be a priest ministering with the Urim and Thummim.

66The whole company numbered 42,360, 67besides their 7,337 menservants and maidservants; and they also had 245 men and women singers. 68There were 736 horses, 245 mules,a 69435 camels and 6,720 donkeys.

70Some of the heads of the families contributed to the work. The governor gave to

---

a68 Some Hebrew manuscripts (see also Ezra 2:66); most Hebrew manuscripts do not have this verse.

the treasury 1,000 drachmas*a* of gold, 50 bowls and 530 garments for priests. [71]Some of the heads of the families gave to the treasury for the work 20,000 drachmas*b* of gold and 2,200 minas*c* of silver. [72]The total given by the rest of the people was 20,000 drachmas of gold, 2,000 minas*d* of silver and 67 garments for priests.

[73]The priests, the Levites, the gatekeepers, the singers and the temple servants, along with certain of the people and the rest of the Israelites, settled in their own towns.

Ezra Reads the Law

When the seventh month came and the Israelites had settled in their towns, [1]all the people assembled as one man in the square before the Water Gate. They told Ezra the scribe to bring out the Book of the Law of Moses, which the LORD had commanded for Israel.

[2]So on the first day of the seventh month Ezra the priest brought the Law before the assembly, which was made up of men and women and all who were able to understand. [3]He read it aloud from daybreak till noon as he faced the square before the Water Gate in the presence of the men, women and others who could understand. And all the people listened attentively to the Book of the Law.

[4]Ezra the scribe stood on a high wooden platform built for the occasion. Beside him on his right stood Mattithiah, Shema, Anaiah, Uriah, Hilkiah and Maaseiah; and on his left were Pedaiah, Mishael, Malkijah, Hashum, Hashbaddanah, Zechariah and Meshullam.

[5]Ezra opened the book. All the people could see him because he was standing above them; and as he opened it, the people all stood up. [6]Ezra praised the LORD, the great God; and all the people lifted their hands and responded, "Amen! Amen!" Then they bowed down and worshiped the LORD with their faces to the ground.

[7]The Levites—Jeshua, Bani, Sherebiah, Jamin, Akkub, Shabbethai, Hodiah, Maaseiah, Kelita, Azariah, Jozabad, Hanan and Pelaiah—instructed the people in the Law while the people were standing there. [8]They read from the Book of the Law of God, making it clear*e* and giving the meaning so that the people could understand what was being read.

[9]Then Nehemiah the governor, Ezra the priest and scribe, and the Levites who were instructing the people said to them all, "This day is sacred to the LORD your God. Do not mourn or weep." For all the people had been weeping as they listened to the words of the Law.

[10]Nehemiah said, "Go and enjoy choice food and sweet drinks, and send some to those who have nothing prepared. This day is sacred to our Lord. Do not grieve, for the joy of the LORD is your strength."

8:9 The Joy of the Lord

People sometimes think of the Old Testament as gloomy. Here, however (verses 9–12), Israel's leaders urged the people to stop weeping. Sadness, they said, did not suit a sacred day. As they discovered the next day, the law they mourned over commanded not weeping, but an eight-day celebration and campout.

[11]The Levites calmed all the people, saying, "Be still, for this is a sacred day. Do not grieve."

[12]Then all the people went away to eat and drink, to send portions of food and to celebrate with great joy, because they now understood the words that had been made known to them.

[13]On the second day of the month, the heads of all the families, along with the priests and the Levites, gathered around Ezra the scribe to give attention to the words of the Law. [14]They found written in the Law, which the LORD had commanded through Moses, that the Israelites were to live in booths during the feast of the seventh month [15]and that they should proclaim this word and spread it throughout their towns and in Jerusalem: "Go out into the hill country and bring back branches from olive and wild olive trees, and from myrtles, palms and shade trees, to make booths"—as it is written.*f*

[16]So the people went out and brought back branches and built themselves booths on their own roofs, in their courtyards, in the courts of the house of God and in the square by the Water Gate and the one by the Gate of Ephraim. [17]The whole company that had returned from exile built booths and lived in them. From the days of Joshua son of Nun until that day, the Israelites had not celebrated it like this. And their joy was very great.

[18]Day after day, from the first day to the last, Ezra read from the Book of the Law of God. They celebrated the feast for seven days, and on the eighth day, in accordance with the regulation, there was an assembly.

The Israelites Confess Their Sins

On the twenty-fourth day of the same month, the Israelites gathered together, fasting and wearing sackcloth and having dust on

---

a70 That is, about 19 pounds (about 8.5 kilograms)   *b71* That is, about 375 pounds (about 170 kilograms); also in verse 72   *c71* That is, about 1 1/3 tons (about 1.2 metric tons)   *d72* That is, about 1 1/4 tons (about 1.1 metric tons)   *e8* Or *God, translating it*   *f15* See Lev. 23:37-40.

their heads. ²Those of Israelite descent had separated themselves from all foreigners. They stood in their places and confessed their sins and the wickedness of their fathers. ³They stood where they were and read from the Book of the Law of the LORD their God for a quarter of the day, and spent another quarter in confession and in worshiping the LORD their God. ⁴Standing on the stairs were the Levites—Jeshua, Bani, Kadmiel, Shebaniah, Bunni, Sherebiah, Bani and Kenani—

who called with loud voices to the LORD their God. ⁵And the Levites—Jeshua, Kadmiel, Bani, Hashabneiah, Sherebiah, Hodiah, Shebaniah and Pethahiah—said: "Stand up and praise the LORD your God, who is from everlasting to everlasting.ᵃ"

"Blessed be your glorious name, and may it be exalted above all blessing and praise. ⁶You alone are the LORD. You made

ᵃ5 Or God for ever and ever

A People of the Book

Ezra stood on a wooden platform, reading from a simple scroll

PICTURE IT: A VAST, HUSHED crowd watching as Ezra ascends a newly built platform in the square. As he opens the book, they stand up. They praise God, hands lifted high; then they bow down, faces in the dirt. Ezra begins to read. His helpers circulate in the crowd, explaining and interpreting what God's Word says. The people listen attentively. And then a strange sound begins to rise, spreading through the multitude. It is the sound of weeping.

Ezra the priest brought the Law before the assembly. . . . He read it aloud from daybreak till noon.
8:2–3

The Law Ezra read was very ancient, but that day marked something new. The Jews were becoming, in a way they had never been before, a people of the book. They were being rebuilt, with material as strong as the stones in their newly built city wall.

Throughout their history, they had drawn strength from two sources besides the Law. One was the temple, where they worshiped God. It was a magnificently beautiful building in which they met God. The other was their leadership—first Moses, then Joshua, then the judges, and finally David and his offspring, the kings.

The Disappointing Reality

But these realities had not saved them from disgrace. The temple? For all its splendor it had become a meaningless symbol to most Jews. They had even put idols in it. God had finally allowed the Babylonians to burn the temple down.

After the exile the Jews had made rebuilding the temple their first priority (see Ezra 1—6). But it was no longer an automatic insurance policy. They could never again see the building as a substitute for real devotion to God.

Their leaders? Not one king, over hundreds of years, had come close to matching God's ideal. Most kings had been scoundrels—descendants of David in name only. After the exile, Israel had no king of its own. The Israelites were under the thumb of a Persian, who was determined to keep all power himself.

The Power of the Word

They turned to another source of power: the Word of God. The great gathering of chapter 8 stands in contrast to temples and kings. The splendor of jewels and crowns is replaced by a single man atop a wooden platform, reading from a simple scroll. Yet the words he reads, carefully explained to all, show their power in the way they affect those who hear them. The people are moved to praise God, to weep over their sins, to change their behavior, and to make renewed promises to God.

From this time on, the Jews were known as the people of the book. They lived under foreign domination, so their political leadership became secondary. Their temple, while important, was never again a guarantee of God's presence. Increasingly they studied God's law and tried to obey it. A new kind of leader emerged, following Ezra—the scribe, a student of Scripture. The nation we see at the end of Nehemiah looks very much like the nation we find, after 400 years of Scriptural silence, when Jesus appears. Israelites found their unique strength neither in government nor in worship rituals, but in reverence for God's written Word.

Life Questions: Can you point to ways in which God's Word has been powerful in your life? How has it changed you?

the heavens, even the highest heavens, and all their starry host, the earth and all that is on it, the seas and all that is in them. You give life to everything, and the multitudes of heaven worship you.

9:6 Stained-Glass Prayer

In cathedrals of medieval Europe, stained-glass windows served a dual purpose: 1) the artists designed them as aids to the worship of God; and 2) for a nonliterate society, scenes depicted in glass made it easier to learn biblical history. Old Testament Jews prohibited all images, but often their prayers served a similar purpose: they expressed worship and reminded the listeners of their providential past. This beautiful example reviews essential lessons from all of human history—an important guide for a people beginning a new life.

---

⁷"You are the LORD God, who chose Abram and brought him out of Ur of the Chaldeans and named him Abraham. ⁸You found his heart faithful to you, and you made a covenant with him to give to his descendants the land of the Canaanites, Hittites, Amorites, Perizzites, Jebusites and Girgashites. You have kept your promise because you are righteous.

⁹"You saw the suffering of our forefathers in Egypt; you heard their cry at the Red Sea.*ᵃ* ¹⁰You sent miraculous signs and wonders against Pharaoh, against all his officials and all the people of his land, for you knew how arrogantly the Egyptians treated them. You made a name for yourself, which remains to this day. ¹¹You divided the sea before them, so that they passed through it on dry ground, but you hurled their pursuers into the depths, like a stone into mighty waters. ¹²By day you led them with a pillar of cloud, and by night with a pillar of fire to give them light on the way they were to take.

¹³"You came down on Mount Sinai; you spoke to them from heaven. You gave them regulations and laws that are just and right, and decrees and commands that are good. ¹⁴You made known to them your holy Sabbath and gave them commands, decrees and laws through your servant Moses. ¹⁵In their hunger you gave them bread from heaven and in their thirst you brought them water from the rock; you told them to go in and take possession of the land you had sworn with uplifted hand to give them.

¹⁶"But they, our forefathers, became arrogant and stiff-necked, and did not obey your commands. ¹⁷They refused to listen and failed to remember the miracles you performed among them. They became stiff-necked and in their rebellion appointed a leader in order to return to their slavery. But you are a forgiving God, gracious and compassionate, slow to anger and abounding in love. Therefore you did not desert them, ¹⁸even when they cast for themselves an image of a calf and said, 'This is your god, who brought you up out of Egypt,' or when they committed awful blasphemies.

¹⁹"Because of your great compassion you did not abandon them in the desert. By day the pillar of cloud did not cease to guide them on their path, nor the pillar of fire by night to shine on the way they were to take. ²⁰You gave your good Spirit to instruct them. You did not withhold your manna from their mouths, and you gave them water for their thirst. ²¹For forty years you sustained them in the desert; they lacked nothing, their clothes did not wear out nor did their feet become swollen.

²²"You gave them kingdoms and nations, allotting to them even the remotest frontiers. They took over the country of Sihon*ᵇ* king of Heshbon and the country of Og king of Bashan. ²³You made their sons as numerous as the stars in the sky, and you brought them into the land that you told their fathers to enter and possess. ²⁴Their sons went in and took possession of the land. You subdued before them the Canaanites, who lived in the land; you handed the Canaanites over to them, along with their kings and the peoples of the land, to deal with them as they pleased. ²⁵They captured fortified cities and fertile land; they took possession of houses filled with all kinds of good things, wells already dug, vineyards, olive groves and fruit trees in abundance. They ate to the full and were well-nourished; they reveled in your great goodness.

²⁶"But they were disobedient and rebelled against you; they put your law behind their backs. They killed your prophets, who had admonished them in order to turn them back to you; they committed awful blasphemies. ²⁷So you handed them over to their enemies, who oppressed them. But when they were oppressed they cried out to you. From heaven you heard them, and in your great compassion you gave them de-

---

ᵃ9 Hebrew *Yam Suph*; that is, Sea of Reeds   *ᵇ22* One Hebrew manuscript and Septuagint; most Hebrew manuscripts *Sihon, that is, the country of the*

liverers, who rescued them from the hand of their enemies.

28"But as soon as they were at rest, they again did what was evil in your sight. Then you abandoned them to the hand of their enemies so that they ruled over them. And when they cried out to you again, you heard from heaven, and in your compassion you delivered them time after time.

29"You warned them to return to your law, but they became arrogant and disobeyed your commands. They sinned against your ordinances, by which a man will live if he obeys them. Stubbornly they turned their backs on you, became stiffnecked and refused to listen. 30For many years you were patient with them. By your Spirit you admonished them through your prophets. Yet they paid no attention, so you handed them over to the neighboring peoples. 31But in your great mercy you did not put an end to them or abandon them, for you are a gracious and merciful God.

32"Now therefore, O our God, the great, mighty and awesome God, who keeps his covenant of love, do not let all this hardship seem trifling in your eyes—the hardship that has come upon us, upon our kings and leaders, upon our priests and prophets, upon our fathers and all your people, from the days of the kings of Assyria until today. 33In all that has happened to us, you have been just; you have acted faithfully, while we did wrong. 34Our kings, our leaders, our priests and our fathers did not follow your law; they did not pay attention to your commands or the warnings you gave them. 35Even while they were in their kingdom, enjoying your great goodness to them in the spacious and fertile land you gave them, they did not serve you or turn from their evil ways.

36"But see, we are slaves today, slaves in the land you gave our forefathers so they could eat its fruit and the other good things it produces. 37Because of our sins, its abundant harvest goes to the kings you have placed over us. They rule over our bodies and our cattle as they please. We are in great distress.

The Agreement of the People

38"In view of all this, we are making a binding agreement, putting it in writing, and our leaders, our Levites and our priests are affixing their seals to it."

10 Those who sealed it were:

Nehemiah the governor, the son of Hacaliah.

Zedekiah, 2Seraiah, Azariah, Jeremiah, 3Pashhur, Amariah, Malkijah, 4Hattush, Shebaniah, Malluch, 5Harim, Meremoth, Obadiah, 6Daniel, Ginnethon, Baruch, 7Meshullam, Abijah, Mijamin, 8Maaziah, Bilgai and Shemaiah.

These were the priests.

9The Levites:

Jeshua son of Azaniah, Binnui of the sons of Henadad, Kadmiel, 10and their associates: Shebaniah, Hodiah, Kelita, Pelaiah, Hanan, 11Mica, Rehob, Hashabiah, 12Zaccur, Sherebiah, Shebaniah, 13Hodiah, Bani and Beninu.

14The leaders of the people:

Parosh, Pahath-Moab, Elam, Zattu, Bani, 15Bunni, Azgad, Bebai, 16Adonijah, Bigvai, Adin, 17Ater, Hezekiah, Azzur, 18Hodiah, Hashum, Bezai, 19Hariph, Anathoth, Nebai, 20Magpiash, Meshullam, Hezir, 21Meshezabel, Zadok, Jaddua, 22Pelatiah, Hanan, Anaiah, 23Hoshea, Hananiah, Hasshub, 24Hallohesh, Pilha, Shobek, 25Rehum, Hashabnah, Maaseiah, 26Ahiah, Hanan, Anan, 27Malluch, Harim and Baanah.

28"The rest of the people—priests, Levites, gatekeepers, singers, temple servants and all who separated themselves from the neighboring peoples for the sake of the Law of God, together with their wives and all their sons and daughters who are able to understand— 29all these now join their brothers the nobles, and bind themselves with a curse and an oath to follow the Law of God given through Moses the servant of God and to obey carefully all the com-

10:31 A Year of Freedom

According to God's law, Jews were supposed to take every seventh day—the Sabbath—off from work. Not only that, but every seventh year was a holiday from farming and a time when all debts were canceled (see Leviticus 25:1–7; Deuteronomy 15:1–11). But these rules for the seventh year were seldom if ever followed; "business as usual" generally prevailed.

mands, regulations and decrees of the LORD our Lord.

³⁰"We promise not to give our daughters in marriage to the peoples around us or take their daughters for our sons.

³¹"When the neighboring peoples bring merchandise or grain to sell on the Sabbath, we will not buy from them on the Sabbath or on any holy day. Every seventh year we will forgo working the land and will cancel all debts.

³²"We assume the responsibility for carrying out the commands to give a third of a shekel*ᵃ* each year for the service of the house of our God: ³³for the bread set out on the table; for the regular grain offerings and burnt offerings; for the offerings on the Sabbaths, New Moon festivals and appointed feasts; for the holy offerings; for sin offerings to make atonement for Israel; and for all the duties of the house of our God.

³⁴"We—the priests, the Levites and the people—have cast lots to determine when each of our families is to bring to the house of our God at set times each year a contribution of wood to burn on the altar of the LORD our God, as it is written in the Law.

³⁵"We also assume responsibility for bringing to the house of the LORD each year the firstfruits of our crops and of every fruit tree.

³⁶"As it is also written in the Law, we will bring the firstborn of our sons and of our cattle, of our herds and of our flocks to the house of our God, to the priests ministering there.

³⁷"Moreover, we will bring to the storerooms of the house of our God, to the priests, the first of our ground meal, of our ⌊grain⌋ offerings, of the fruit of all our trees and of our new wine and oil. And we will bring a tithe of our crops to the Levites, for it is the Levites who collect the tithes in all the towns where we work. ³⁸A priest descended from Aaron is to accompany the Levites when they receive the tithes, and the Levites are to bring a tenth of the tithes up to the house of our God, to the storerooms of the treasury. ³⁹The people of Israel, including the Levites, are to bring their contributions of grain, new wine and oil to the storerooms where the articles for the sanctuary are kept and where the ministering priests, the gatekeepers and the singers stay.

"We will not neglect the house of our God."

The New Residents of Jerusalem

11 Now the leaders of the people settled in Jerusalem, and the rest of the people cast lots to bring one out of every ten to live in Jerusalem, the holy city, while the remaining nine were to

11:1 City Fright

The 1990 U.S. census revealed that for the first time a majority of Americans lived in cities having more than a million in population. Worldwide, people are flocking to mega-cities such as Tokyo, London, and Mexico City. Not so in Nehemiah's day. The Israelites had learned that big cities like Jerusalem made prime targets for invading armies. In order to repopulate the city, leaders had to resort to a lottery system. (Characteristically, Nehemiah made sure the new settlers got proper credit.)

stay in their own towns. ²The people commended all the men who volunteered to live in Jerusalem.

³These are the provincial leaders who settled in Jerusalem (now some Israelites, priests, Levites, temple servants and descendants of Solomon's servants lived in the towns of Judah, each on his own property in the various towns, ⁴while other people from both Judah and Benjamin lived in Jerusalem):

From the descendants of Judah:

Athaiah son of Uzziah, the son of Zechariah, the son of Amariah, the son of Shephatiah, the son of Mahalalel, a descendant of Perez; ⁵and Maaseiah son of Baruch, the son of Col-Hozeh, the son of Hazaiah, the son of Adaiah, the son of Joiarib, the son of Zechariah, a descendant of Shelah. ⁶The descendants of Perez who lived in Jerusalem totaled 468 able men.

⁷From the descendants of Benjamin:

Sallu son of Meshullam, the son of Joed, the son of Pedaiah, the son of Kolaiah, the son of Maaseiah, the son of Ithiel, the son of Jeshaiah, ⁸and his followers, Gabbai and Sallai—928 men. ⁹Joel son of Zicri was their chief officer, and Judah son of Hassenuah was over the Second District of the city.

¹⁰From the priests:

Jedaiah; the son of Joiarib; Jakin; ¹¹Seraiah son of Hilkiah, the son of Meshullam, the son of Zadok, the son of Meraioth, the son of Ahitub, supervisor in the house of God,

ᵃ32 That is, about 1/8 ounce (about 4 grams)

12and their associates, who carried on work for the temple—822 men; Adaiah son of Jeroham, the son of Pelaliah, the son of Amzi, the son of Zechariah, the son of Pashhur, the son of Malkijah, 13and his associates, who were heads of families—242 men; Amashsai son of Azarel, the son of Ahzai, the son of Meshillemoth, the son of Immer, 14and his*a* associates, who were able men—128. Their chief officer was Zabdiel son of Haggedolim.

15From the Levites:

Shemaiah son of Hasshub, the son of Azrikam, the son of Hashabiah, the son of Bunni; 16Shabbethai and Jozabad, two of the heads of the Levites, who had charge of the outside work of the house of God; 17Mattaniah son of Mica, the son of Zabdi, the son of Asaph, the director who led in thanksgiving and prayer; Bakbukiah, second among his associates; and Abda son of Shammua, the son of Galal, the son of Jeduthun. 18The Levites in the holy city totaled 284.

19The gatekeepers:

Akkub, Talmon and their associates, who kept watch at the gates—172 men.

20The rest of the Israelites, with the priests and Levites, were in all the towns of Judah, each on his ancestral property.

21The temple servants lived on the hill of Ophel, and Ziha and Gishpa were in charge of them.

22The chief officer of the Levites in Jerusalem was Uzzi son of Bani, the son of Hashabiah, the son of Mattaniah, the son of Mica. Uzzi was one of Asaph's descendants, who were the singers responsible for the service of the house of God. 23The singers were under the king's orders, which regulated their daily activity.

24Pethahiah son of Meshezabel, one of the descendants of Zerah son of Judah, was the king's agent in all affairs relating to the people.

25As for the villages with their fields, some of the people of Judah lived in Kiriath Arba and its surrounding settlements, in Dibon and its settlements, in Jekabzeel and its villages, 26in Jeshua, in Moladah, in Beth Pelet, 27in Hazar Shual, in Beersheba and its settlements, 28in Ziklag, in Meconah and its settlements, 29in En Rimmon, in Zorah, in Jarmuth, 30Zanoah, Adullam and their villages, in Lachish and its fields, and in Azekah

and its settlements. So they were living all the way from Beersheba to the Valley of Hinnom.

31The descendants of the Benjamites from Geba lived in Micmash, Aija, Bethel and its settlements, 32in Anathoth, Nob and Ananiah, 33in Hazor, Ramah and Gittaim, 34in Hadid, Zeboim and Neballat, 35in Lod and Ono, and in the Valley of the Craftsmen.

36Some of the divisions of the Levites of Judah settled in Benjamin.

Priests and Levites

12 These were the priests and Levites who returned with Zerubbabel son of Shealtiel and with Jeshua:

Seraiah, Jeremiah, Ezra,
2Amariah, Malluch, Hattush,
3Shecaniah, Rehum, Meremoth,
4Iddo, Ginnethon,*b* Abijah,
5Mijamin,*c* Moadiah, Bilgah,
6Shemaiah, Joiarib, Jedaiah,
7Sallu, Amok, Hilkiah and Jedaiah.

These were the leaders of the priests and their associates in the days of Jeshua.

8The Levites were Jeshua, Binnui, Kadmiel, Sherebiah, Judah, and also Mattaniah, who, together with his associates, was in charge of the songs of thanksgiving. 9Bakbukiah and Unni, their associates, stood opposite them in the services.

10Jeshua was the father of Joiakim, Joiakim the father of Eliashib, Eliashib the father of Joiada, 11Joiada the father of Jonathan, and Jonathan the father of Jaddua.

12In the days of Joiakim, these were the heads of the priestly families:

of Seraiah's family, Meraiah;
of Jeremiah's, Hananiah;
13of Ezra's, Meshullam;
of Amariah's, Jehohanan;
14of Malluch's, Jonathan;
of Shecaniah's,*d* Joseph;
15of Harim's, Adna;
of Meremoth's,*e* Helkai;
16of Iddo's, Zechariah;
of Ginnethon's, Meshullam;
17of Abijah's, Zicri;
of Miniamin's and of Moadiah's, Piltai;
18of Bilgah's, Shammua;
of Shemaiah's, Jehonathan;
19of Joiarib's, Mattenai;
of Jedaiah's, Uzzi;
20of Sallu's, Kallai;
of Amok's, Eber;
21of Hilkiah's, Hashabiah;
of Jedaiah's, Nethanel.

---

a14 Most Septuagint manuscripts; Hebrew *their*   *b4* Many Hebrew manuscripts and Vulgate (see also Neh. 12:16); most Hebrew manuscripts *Ginnethoi*   *c5* A variant of *Miniamin*   *d14* Very many Hebrew manuscripts, some Septuagint manuscripts and Syriac (see also Neh. 12:3); most Hebrew manuscripts *Shebaniah's*   *e15* Some Septuagint manuscripts (see also Neh. 12:3); Hebrew *Meraioth's*

[22]The family heads of the Levites in the days of Eliashib, Joiada, Johanan and Jaddua, as well as those of the priests, were recorded in the reign of Darius the Persian. [23]The family heads among the descendants of Levi up to the time of Johanan son of Eliashib were recorded in the book of the annals. [24]And the leaders of the Levites were Hashabiah, Sherebiah, Jeshua son of Kadmiel, and their associates, who stood opposite them to give praise and thanksgiving, one section responding to the other, as prescribed by David the man of God.

[25]Mattaniah, Bakbukiah, Obadiah, Meshullam, Talmon and Akkub were gatekeepers who guarded the storerooms at the gates. [26]They served in the days of Joiakim son of Jeshua, the son of Jozadak, and in the days of Nehemiah the governor and of Ezra the priest and scribe.

Dedication of the Wall of Jerusalem

[27]At the dedication of the wall of Jerusalem, the Levites were sought out from where they lived and were brought to Jerusalem to celebrate joyfully the dedication with songs of thanksgiving and with the music of cymbals, harps and

12:27 Victory Party

Ezra, a religious leader, tried for a decade to get the wall rebuilt. Nehemiah, more pragmatic and action-oriented, managed to get the job done in 52 days (6:15). When the huge task was finished, he orchestrated a giant celebration featuring two choirs that circled the wall in opposite directions. Ezra led one of the choirs; Nehemiah, in an act of humility, brought up the rear of the other. When they met in the middle, near the temple area, they held a worship service such as Jerusalem had not seen in more than a century.

lyres. [28]The singers also were brought together from the region around Jerusalem—from the villages of the Netophathites, [29]from Beth Gilgal, and from the area of Geba and Azmaveth, for the singers had built villages for themselves around Jerusalem. [30]When the priests and Levites had purified themselves ceremonially, they purified the people, the gates and the wall.

[31]I had the leaders of Judah go up on top[a] of the wall. I also assigned two large choirs to give thanks. One was to proceed on top[b] of the wall to the right, toward the Dung Gate. [32]Hoshaiah and half the leaders of Judah followed them, [33]along with Azariah, Ezra, Meshullam, [34]Judah, Benjamin, Shemaiah, Jeremiah, [35]as well as some

priests with trumpets, and also Zechariah son of Jonathan, the son of Shemaiah, the son of Mattaniah, the son of Micaiah, the son of Zaccur, the son of Asaph, [36]and his associates—Shemaiah, Azarel, Milalai, Gilalai, Maai, Nethanel, Judah and Hanani—with musical instruments ⌊prescribed by⌋ David the man of God. Ezra the scribe led the procession. [37]At the Fountain Gate they continued directly up the steps of the City of David on the ascent to the wall and passed above the house of David to the Water Gate on the east.

[38]The second choir proceeded in the opposite direction. I followed them on top[c] of the wall, together with half the people—past the Tower of the Ovens to the Broad Wall, [39]over the Gate of Ephraim, the Jeshanah[d] Gate, the Fish Gate, the Tower of Hananel and the Tower of the Hundred, as far as the Sheep Gate. At the Gate of the Guard they stopped.

[40]The two choirs that gave thanks then took their places in the house of God; so did I, together with half the officials, [41]as well as the priests—Eliakim, Maaseiah, Miniamin, Micaiah, Elioenai, Zechariah and Hananiah with their trumpets—[42]and also Maaseiah, Shemaiah, Eleazar, Uzzi, Jehohanan, Malkijah, Elam and Ezer. The choirs sang under the direction of Jezrahiah. [43]And on that day they offered great sacrifices, rejoicing because God had given them great joy. The women and children also rejoiced. The sound of rejoicing in Jerusalem could be heard far away.

[44]At that time men were appointed to be in charge of the storerooms for the contributions, firstfruits and tithes. From the fields around the towns they were to bring into the storerooms the portions required by the Law for the priests and the Levites, for Judah was pleased with the ministering priests and Levites. [45]They performed the service of their God and the service of purification, as did also the singers and gatekeepers, according to the commands of David and his son Solomon. [46]For long ago, in the days of David and Asaph, there had been directors for the singers and for the songs of praise and thanksgiving to God. [47]So in the days of Zerubbabel and of Nehemiah, all Israel contributed the daily portions for the singers and gatekeepers. They also set aside the portion for the other Levites, and the Levites set aside the portion for the descendants of Aaron.

Nehemiah's Final Reforms

13 On that day the Book of Moses was read aloud in the hearing of the people and

---

a 31 Or *go alongside*   *b 31* Or *proceed alongside*   *c 38* Or *them alongside*   *d 39* Or *Old*

there it was found written that no Ammonite or Moabite should ever be admitted into the assembly of God, ²because they had not met the Israelites with food and water but had hired Balaam to call a curse down on them. (Our God, however, turned the curse into a blessing.) ³When the people heard this law, they excluded from Israel all who were of foreign descent.

⁴Before this, Eliashib the priest had been put in charge of the storerooms of the house of our God. He was closely associated with Tobiah, ⁵and he had provided him with a large room formerly used to store the grain offerings and incense and temple articles, and also the tithes of grain, new wine and oil prescribed for the Levites, singers and gatekeepers, as well as the contributions for the priests.

⁶But while all this was going on, I was not in Jerusalem, for in the thirty-second year of Artaxerxes king of Babylon I had returned to the king. Some time later I asked his permission ⁷and came back to Jerusalem. Here I learned about the evil thing Eliashib had done in providing Tobiah a room in the courts of the house of God. ⁸I was greatly displeased and threw all Tobiah's household goods out of the room. ⁹I gave orders to purify the rooms, and then I put back into them the equipment of the house of God, with the grain offerings and the incense.

¹⁰I also learned that the portions assigned to the Levites had not been given to them, and that all the Levites and singers responsible for the service had gone back to their own fields. ¹¹So I rebuked the officials and asked them, "Why is the house of God neglected?" Then I called them together and stationed them at their posts.

¹²All Judah brought the tithes of grain, new wine and oil into the storerooms. ¹³I put Shelemiah the priest, Zadok the scribe, and a Levite named Pedaiah in charge of the storerooms and made Hanan son of Zaccur, the son of Mattaniah, their assistant, because these men were considered trustworthy. They were made responsible for distributing the supplies to their brothers.

¹⁴Remember me for this, O my God, and do not blot out what I have so faithfully done for the house of my God and its services.

¹⁵In those days I saw men in Judah treading winepresses on the Sabbath and bringing in grain and loading it on donkeys, together with wine, grapes, figs and all other kinds of loads. And they were bringing all this into Jerusalem on the Sabbath. Therefore I warned them against selling food on that day. ¹⁶Men from Tyre who lived in Jerusalem were bringing in fish and all kinds of merchandise and selling them in Jerusalem on the Sabbath to the people of Judah. ¹⁷I rebuked the nobles of Judah and said to them, "What is this wicked thing you are doing—desecrating the Sabbath day? ¹⁸Didn't your forefathers do the same things, so that our God brought all this calamity upon us and upon this city? Now you are stirring up more wrath against Israel by desecrating the Sabbath."

¹⁹When evening shadows fell on the gates of Jerusalem before the Sabbath, I ordered the doors to be shut and not opened until the Sabbath was over. I stationed some of my own men at the gates so that no load could be brought in

13:19 Never-ending Task

Fairy tales end, "and they lived happily ever after," but real life never does. Pointedly, Nehemiah's book does not close with the triumph of chapter 12, but with a preview of the continuing hassles of leadership. Old problems recurred, new problems sprang up, and Nehemiah tackled both kinds with courage and wisdom.

on the Sabbath day. ²⁰Once or twice the merchants and sellers of all kinds of goods spent the night outside Jerusalem. ²¹But I warned them and said, "Why do you spend the night by the wall? If you do this again, I will lay hands on you." From that time on they no longer came on the Sabbath. ²²Then I commanded the Levites to purify themselves and go and guard the gates in order to keep the Sabbath day holy.

Remember me for this also, O my God, and show mercy to me according to your great love.

²³Moreover, in those days I saw men of Judah who had married women from Ashdod, Ammon and Moab. ²⁴Half of their children spoke the language of Ashdod or the language of one of the other peoples, and did not know how to speak the language of Judah. ²⁵I rebuked them and called curses down on them. I beat some of the men and pulled out their hair. I made them take an oath in God's name and said: "You are not to give your daughters in marriage to their sons, nor are you to take their daughters in marriage for your sons or for yourselves. ²⁶Was it not because of marriages like these that Solomon king of Israel sinned? Among the many nations there was no king like him. He was loved by his God, and God

made him king over all Israel, but even he was led into sin by foreign women. ²⁷Must we hear now that you too are doing all this terrible wickedness and are being unfaithful to our God by marrying foreign women?"

²⁸One of the sons of Joiada son of Eliashib the high priest was son-in-law to Sanballat the Horonite. And I drove him away from me.

²⁹Remember them, O my God, because they defiled the priestly office and the covenant of the priesthood and of the Levites.

³⁰So I purified the priests and the Levites of everything foreign, and assigned them duties, each to his own task. ³¹I also made provision for contributions of wood at designated times, and for the firstfruits.

Remember me with favor, O my God.

ESTHER

A Profile of Courage
Heroes act while others stand and watch

> "I will go to the king, even though it is against the law. And if I perish, I perish." 4:16

WHAT MAKES A HERO? ASK one, and you may find a surprising nonchalance: "I'm sure other people would have done exactly the same thing," they say. "I was just in the right place at the right time."

People become heroes because they take quick action at that "right time," while others stand watching in horror. The true hero recognizes the crisis and moves to meet it. This kind of courage made Esther great—worthy of a book in the Bible.

A Queen Risks Her Life

By the "accident" of her beauty and the "accident" of the former queen's dismissal, Esther found herself queen of one of the greatest powers of the world. Then, when all seemed smooth, her crucial moment came.

This moment has been echoed many times since. As a successful racial minority in the Persian empire, Esther's people, the Jews, had not melted into their surroundings. Others were jealous of their success and separatism. A vengeful prime minister, Haman, made up his mind to destroy them. He issued an edict of government-sponsored genocide.

Would Queen Esther intervene? Doing so would risk her life. And what difference could she make? She was a powerless sex partner to a king who strongly preferred women who never interfered with his wishes. She came only when he called, and he had not called her for a month. And yet she alone, of all the Jews, had access to the king.

Esther's cousin Mordecai reminded her of her unique place. "Who knows but that you have come to royal position for such a time as this?" Esther responded with action. Her courageous words are a classic statement of heroism: "I will go to the king, even though it is against the law. And if I perish, I perish" (4:16).

Coincidence or Plan?

The book of Esther shows, though indirectly, God's heroic concern for the Jews. The story runs on a series of extraordinary coincidences. Esther just "happened" to be chosen as the new queen. The king just "happened" to be unable to sleep, and, when he picked up some reading, just "happened" across an account of a good deed Esther's cousin Mordecai had done. The evil Haman just "happened" along at that crucial moment. These coincidences, along with Esther's courage, tilted terrible events toward the Jews' favor.

Were these really mere coincidences? Or was God behind them? The book of Esther doesn't say directly: God is not mentioned even once, and sometimes seems deliberately left out. But believing readers, whether Jews or Christians, can have no doubt. All of life is under God's command. Nothing just happens. These "coincidences" were part of God's plan to save the Jews.

God protected his people because he loved them—because he had chosen them from the beginning. Even their enemies knew the "luck" of the Jews. (See Esther 6:13, for instance.) Esther's story is another chapter in the amazing story of God's perpetual love for the Jews. Though sometimes far from his will, this tiny, often hated minority has survived and thrived down the centuries.

From Haman to Hitler, vindictive leaders have hated the Jews. Yet while no other group has been so hated, no other group has shown the Jews' ability to overcome adversity. Nor can any other ethnic group alive today point to such continuity with their ancestors. They have endured as a unique and great people. How? Esther shows that God's exquisite timing—combined with the courage of individuals who "happened" to be in the right place at the right time—made his chosen people prosper.

How to Read Esther

Esther makes such suspenseful reading that most people will find it hard to quit. As in a detective story, every detail folds into another. You don't know, from one page to the next, how the drama will turn out.

The essence of Esther lies in its characters. Study Esther, Mordecai, Haman, and King Xerxes. What kind of people were they? What were their ambitions? What were their strengths and weaknesses? What crucial moment showed the true character of each? What do you learn from them that can help you rise to the challenge when you are "the right person at the right place at the right time"?

Knowing the historical setting for Esther's story can enrich your study. A good commentary or Bible dictionary (under "Esther") will illuminate many of the details that make Esther such a convincing historical document.

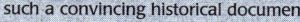

PEOPLE YOU'LL MEET IN ESTHER

ESTHER (p. 528)
MORDECAI (p. 532)

3-TRACK READING PLAN

For an explanation and complete listing of the 3-track reading plan, turn to page 7.

TRACK 1: *Two-Week Courses on the Bible*
See page 7 for information on these courses.

TRACK 2: *An Overview of Esther in 1 Day*
☐ Day 1. Read the Introduction to Esther and chapter 4, in which Esther learns that her people are in dire straits and decides to take action.
Now turn to page 9 for your next Track 2 reading project.

TRACK 3: *All of Esther in 8 Days*
After you have read through Esther, turn to pages 10–14 for your next Track 3 reading project.
☐1 ☐2 ☐3 ☐4 ☐5 ☐6–7 ☐8 ☐9–10

Queen Vashti Deposed

1 This is what happened during the time of Xerxes,[a] the Xerxes who ruled over 127 provinces stretching from India to Cush[b]: **2**At that time King Xerxes reigned from his royal throne in the citadel of Susa, **3**and in the third year of his reign he gave a banquet for all his nobles and officials. The military leaders of Persia and Media, the princes, and the nobles of the provinces were present.

4For a full 180 days he displayed the vast wealth of his kingdom and the splendor and glory of his majesty. **5**When these days were over, the king gave a banquet, lasting seven days, in the enclosed garden of the king's palace, for all the people from the least to the greatest, who were in the citadel of Susa. **6**The garden had hangings of white and blue linen, fastened with cords of white linen and purple material to silver rings on marble pillars. There were couches of gold and silver on a mosaic pavement of porphyry, marble, mother-of-pearl and other costly stones. **7**Wine was served in goblets of gold, each one different from the other, and the royal wine was abundant, in keeping with the king's liberality. **8**By the king's command each guest was allowed to drink in his own way, for the king instructed all the wine stewards to serve each man what he wished.

9Queen Vashti also gave a banquet for the women in the royal palace of King Xerxes.

10On the seventh day, when King Xerxes was in high spirits from wine, he commanded the seven eunuchs who served him—Mehuman, Biztha, Harbona, Bigtha, Abagtha, Zethar and Carcas—**11**to bring before him Queen Vashti, wearing her royal crown, in order to display her beauty to the people and nobles, for she was

a1 Hebrew *Ahasuerus*, a variant of Xerxes' Persian name; here and throughout Esther *b1* That is, the upper Nile region

lovely to look at. [12]But when the attendants delivered the king's command, Queen Vashti refused to come. Then the king became furious and burned with anger.

1:7 The Influence of Wine

Other historical sources bear out the accuracy of this verse. Greek historian Herodotus wrote that the Persians "are very fond of wine, and drink it in large quantities . . . It is also their general practice to deliberate upon affairs of weight when they are drunk . . . Sometimes, however, they are sober at their first deliberation, but in this case they always reconsider the matter under the influence of wine."

[13]Since it was customary for the king to consult experts in matters of law and justice, he spoke with the wise men who understood the times [14]and were closest to the king—Carshena, Shethar, Admatha, Tarshish, Meres, Marsena and Memucan, the seven nobles of Persia and Media who had special access to the king and were highest in the kingdom.

[15]"According to law, what must be done to Queen Vashti?" he asked. "She has not obeyed the command of King Xerxes that the eunuchs have taken to her."

[16]Then Memucan replied in the presence of the king and the nobles, "Queen Vashti has done wrong, not only against the king but also against all the nobles and the peoples of all the provinces of King Xerxes. [17]For the queen's conduct will become known to all the women, and so they will despise their husbands and say, 'King Xerxes commanded Queen Vashti to be brought before him, but she would not come.' [18]This very day the Persian and Median women of the nobility who have heard about the queen's conduct will respond to all the king's nobles in the same way. There will be no end of disrespect and discord.

[19]"Therefore, if it pleases the king, let him issue a royal decree and let it be written in the laws of Persia and Media, which cannot be repealed, that Vashti is never again to enter the presence of King Xerxes. Also let the king give her royal position to someone else who is better than she. [20]Then when the king's edict is proclaimed throughout all his vast realm, all the women will respect their husbands, from the least to the greatest."

[21]The king and his nobles were pleased with this advice, so the king did as Memucan proposed. [22]He sent dispatches to all parts of the kingdom, to each province in its own script and to each people in its own language, proclaiming in each people's tongue that every man should be ruler over his own household.

Esther Made Queen

2 Later when the anger of King Xerxes had subsided, he remembered Vashti and what she had done and what he had decreed about her. [2]Then the king's personal attendants proposed, "Let a search be made for beautiful young virgins for the king. [3]Let the king appoint commissioners in every province of his realm to bring all these beautiful girls into the harem at the citadel of Susa. Let them be placed under the care of Hegai, the king's eunuch, who is in charge of the women; and let beauty treatments be given to them. [4]Then let the girl who pleases the king be queen instead of Vashti." This advice appealed to the king, and he followed it.

[5]Now there was in the citadel of Susa a Jew of the tribe of Benjamin, named Mordecai son of Jair, the son of Shimei, the son of Kish, [6]who had been carried into exile from Jerusalem by Nebuchadnezzar king of Babylon, among those taken

2:6 Those Who Stayed Behind

Ezra and Nehemiah, the books preceding Esther, tell the inspiring story of Jews returning to Jerusalem after years of captivity. Actually, only 50,000 Jews came back to their plundered land, however. Many more—among them Mordecai's family—stayed behind, and some of these prospered. The story of Esther takes place in that foreign setting, ruled by the Persian empire. Modern-day communities of Jews in Iraq and Iran have descended from these ancient exiles.

captive with Jehoiachin[a] king of Judah. [7]Mordecai had a cousin named Hadassah, whom he had brought up because she had neither father nor mother. This girl, who was also known as Esther, was lovely in form and features, and Mordecai had taken her as his own daughter when her father and mother died.

[8]When the king's order and edict had been proclaimed, many girls were brought to the citadel of Susa and put under the care of Hegai. Esther also was taken to the king's palace and entrusted to Hegai, who had charge of the harem. [9]The girl pleased him and won his favor. Immediately he provided her with her beauty treatments and special food. He assigned to her seven maids selected from the king's palace and moved her and her maids into the best place in the harem.

---

[a]6 Hebrew *Jeconiah*, a variant of *Jehoiachin*

[10]Esther had not revealed her nationality and family background, because Mordecai had forbidden her to do so. [11]Every day he walked back and forth near the courtyard of the harem to find out how Esther was and what was happening to her.

[12]Before a girl's turn came to go in to King Xerxes, she had to complete twelve months of beauty treatments prescribed for the women, six months with oil of myrrh and six with perfumes and cosmetics. [13]And this is how she would go to the king: Anything she wanted was given her to take with her from the harem to the king's palace. [14]In the evening she would go there and in the morning return to another part of the harem to the care of Shaashgaz, the king's eunuch who was in charge of the concubines. She would not return to the king unless he was pleased with her and summoned her by name.

[15]When the turn came for Esther (the girl Mordecai had adopted, the daughter of his uncle Abihail) to go to the king, she asked for nothing other than what Hegai, the king's eunuch who was in charge of the harem, suggested. And Esther won the favor of everyone who saw her. [16]She was taken to King Xerxes in the royal residence in the tenth month, the month of Tebeth, in the seventh year of his reign.

2:16 Off at War

Between Queen Vashti's dismissal (chapter 1) and Esther's acceptance as the new queen, four years passed. Why did Xerxes wait so long? Historians say that during these four years he was off fighting, unsuccessfully trying to conquer Greece. The six-month conference described in chapter 1 was, most likely, a consultation to prepare the invasion.

[17]Now the king was attracted to Esther more than to any of the other women, and she won his favor and approval more than any of the other virgins. So he set a royal crown on her head and made her queen instead of Vashti. [18]And the king gave a great banquet, Esther's banquet, for all his nobles and officials. He proclaimed a holiday throughout the provinces and distributed gifts with royal liberality.

Mordecai Uncovers a Conspiracy

[19]When the virgins were assembled a second time, Mordecai was sitting at the king's gate. [20]But Esther had kept secret her family background and nationality just as Mordecai had told her to do, for she continued to follow Mordecai's instructions as she had done when he was bringing her up.

[21]During the time Mordecai was sitting at the king's gate, Bigthana[a] and Teresh, two of the king's officers who guarded the doorway, became angry and conspired to assassinate King Xerxes. [22]But Mordecai found out about the plot and told Queen Esther, who in turn reported it to the king, giving credit to Mordecai. [23]And when the report was investigated and found to be true, the two officials were hanged on a gallows.[b] All this was recorded in the book of the annals in the presence of the king.

Haman's Plot to Destroy the Jews

3 After these events, King Xerxes honored Haman son of Hammedatha, the Agagite, elevating him and giving him a seat of honor higher than that of all the other nobles. [2]All the royal officials at the king's gate knelt down and paid honor to Haman, for the king had commanded this concerning him. But Mordecai would not kneel down or pay him honor.

[3]Then the royal officials at the king's gate asked Mordecai, "Why do you disobey the king's command?" [4]Day after day they spoke to him but he refused to comply. Therefore they told Haman about it to see whether Mordecai's behavior would be tolerated, for he had told them he was a Jew.

[5]When Haman saw that Mordecai would not kneel down or pay him honor, he was enraged. [6]Yet having learned who Mordecai's people were, he scorned the idea of killing only Mordecai. Instead Haman looked for a way to destroy all Mordecai's people, the Jews, throughout the whole kingdom of Xerxes.

[7]In the twelfth year of King Xerxes, in the first month, the month of Nisan, they cast the *pur* (that is, the lot) in the presence of Haman to select a day and month. And the lot fell on[c] the twelfth month, the month of Adar.

[8]Then Haman said to King Xerxes, "There is a certain people dispersed and scattered among the peoples in all the provinces of your kingdom whose customs are different from those of all other people and who do not obey the king's laws; it is not in the king's best interest to tolerate them. [9]If it pleases the king, let a decree be issued to destroy them, and I will put ten thousand talents[d] of silver into the royal treasury for the men who carry out this business."

[10]So the king took his signet ring from his finger and gave it to Haman son of Hammedatha, the Agagite, the enemy of the Jews. [11]"Keep the money," the king said to Haman, "and do with the people as you please."

---

[a]21 Hebrew *Bigthan*, a variant of *Bigthana*   [b]23 Or *were hung* (or *impaled*) *on poles*; similarly elsewhere in Esther
[c]7 Septuagint; Hebrew does not have *And the lot fell on*.   [d]9 That is, about 375 tons (about 345 metric tons)

¹²Then on the thirteenth day of the first month the royal secretaries were summoned. They wrote out in the script of each province and in the language of each people all Haman's orders to the king's satraps, the governors of the various provinces and the nobles of the various peoples. These were written in the name of King Xerxes himself and sealed with his own ring. ¹³Dispatches were sent by couriers to all the king's provinces with the order to destroy, kill and annihilate all the Jews—young and old, women and little children—on a single day, the thirteenth day of the twelfth month, the month of Adar, and

3:13 Pony Express

Persia boasted one of the first efficient communication systems. The king kept men and horses stationed a day's journey apart on all major highways. Each messenger rode for a day and relayed the message on to the next station. "Nothing mortal travels so fast as these Persian messengers," wrote the historian Herodotus. Their efficiency made it essential for Mordecai and Esther to overturn the king's edict as soon as possible.

to plunder their goods. ¹⁴A copy of the text of the edict was to be issued as law in every province and made known to the people of every nationality so they would be ready for that day.

¹⁵Spurred on by the king's command, the couriers went out, and the edict was issued in the citadel of Susa. The king and Haman sat down to drink, but the city of Susa was bewildered.

Mordecai Persuades Esther to Help

4 When Mordecai learned of all that had been done, he tore his clothes, put on sackcloth and ashes, and went out into the city, wailing loudly and bitterly. ²But he went only as far as the king's gate, because no one clothed in sackcloth was allowed to enter it. ³In every province to which the edict and order of the king came, there was great mourning among the Jews, with fasting, weeping and wailing. Many lay in sackcloth and ashes.

⁴When Esther's maids and eunuchs came and told her about Mordecai, she was in great distress. She sent clothes for him to put on instead of his sackcloth, but he would not accept them. ⁵Then Esther summoned Hathach, one of the king's eunuchs assigned to attend her, and ordered him to find out what was troubling Mordecai and why.

⁶So Hathach went out to Mordecai in the open square of the city in front of the king's gate. ⁷Mordecai told him everything that had happened to him, including the exact amount of money Haman had promised to pay into the royal treasury for the destruction of the Jews. ⁸He also gave him a copy of the text of the edict for their annihilation, which had been published in Susa, to show to Esther and explain it to her, and he told him to urge her to go into the king's presence to beg for mercy and plead with him for her people.

⁹Hathach went back and reported to Esther

MORDECAI *Standing Tall*

HIS FAMILY HAD COME TO Persia as virtual slaves, captives of Jerusalem's last stand against the Babylonians. Yet even in enemy territory Mordecai succeeded in business. His relative, Esther, found more success; she was selected from all the beautiful women in the land as King Xerxes's queen.

With his connections inside the palace, Mordecai probably had high ambitions. He would have to hide his background, though, and he strongly advised Esther to keep her Jewish heritage a secret as well.

Yet when a crisis came Mordecai stood tall, showing extraordinary courage. The king had named the evil Haman his second-in-command, and everyone bowed before him—everyone except Mordecai, who stayed on his feet. His motive? Perhaps he knew of Haman's character, and of his hatred for Jews.

When Haman set out to annihilate all Jews in the empire, Mordecai urged Esther to "come out" completely, even at the risk of her life. Clearly, loyalty to their people came before success or safety.

Mordecai's stand and Esther's courage led to a dramatic turnaround for the whole community of Jewish exiles. King Xerxes rewarded Mordecai with a high position in his court. More importantly, his own community honored him, "because he worked for the good of his people and spoke up for the welfare of all the Jews" (10:3).

The feast of Purim, still celebrated by Jews today, commemorates these amazing events. Against history's dark background of anti-Semitism, Mordecai's triumph shines.

Life Questions: Whom do you speak up for? For what group would you willingly risk your life or your reputation?

what Mordecai had said. [10]Then she instructed him to say to Mordecai, [11]"All the king's officials and the people of the royal provinces know that for any man or woman who approaches the king in the inner court without being summoned the king has but one law: that he be put to death. The only exception to this is for the king to extend the gold scepter to him and spare his life. But thirty days have passed since I was called to go to the king."

[12]When Esther's words were reported to Mordecai, [13]he sent back this answer: "Do not think that because you are in the king's house you

4:13 One Safe Jew?

Esther, ensconced in the safety and luxury of the palace, was possibly the only Jew in Persia who had not heard of the extermination plans. Most likely she would have been spared, but, as Mordecai warned, the king might just as easily turn against her. Mordecai had a sophisticated view of God's providence that never lapsed into fatalism. He believed that God would somehow preserve his people; yet he also knew that God might accomplish that goal through the courageous actions of people like himself and Esther.

alone of all the Jews will escape. [14]For if you remain silent at this time, relief and deliverance for the Jews will arise from another place, but you and your father's family will perish. And who knows but that you have come to royal position for such a time as this?"

[15]Then Esther sent this reply to Mordecai: [16]"Go, gather together all the Jews who are in Susa, and fast for me. Do not eat or drink for three days, night or day. I and my maids will fast as you do. When this is done, I will go to the king, even though it is against the law. And if I perish, I perish."

[17]So Mordecai went away and carried out all of Esther's instructions.

Esther's Request to the King

5 On the third day Esther put on her royal robes and stood in the inner court of the palace, in front of the king's hall. The king was sitting on his royal throne in the hall, facing the entrance. [2]When he saw Queen Esther standing in the court, he was pleased with her and held out to her the gold scepter that was in his hand. So Esther approached and touched the tip of the scepter.

[3]Then the king asked, "What is it, Queen Es-

ther? What is your request? Even up to half the kingdom, it will be given you."

[4]"If it pleases the king," replied Esther, "let the king, together with Haman, come today to a banquet I have prepared for him."

[5]"Bring Haman at once," the king said, "so that we may do what Esther asks."

So the king and Haman went to the banquet Esther had prepared. [6]As they were drinking wine, the king again asked Esther, "Now what is your petition? It will be given you. And what is your request? Even up to half the kingdom, it will be granted."

[7]Esther replied, "My petition and my request is this: [8]If the king regards me with favor and if it pleases the king to grant my petition and fulfill my request, let the king and Haman come tomorrow to the banquet I will prepare for them. Then I will answer the king's question."

Haman's Rage Against Mordecai

[9]Haman went out that day happy and in high spirits. But when he saw Mordecai at the king's gate and observed that he neither rose nor showed fear in his presence, he was filled with rage against Mordecai. [10]Nevertheless, Haman restrained himself and went home.

Calling together his friends and Zeresh, his wife, [11]Haman boasted to them about his vast wealth, his many sons, and all the ways the king had honored him and how he had elevated him above the other nobles and officials. [12]"And that's not all," Haman added. "I'm the only person Queen Esther invited to accompany the king to the banquet she gave. And she has invited me along with the king tomorrow. [13]But all this gives me no satisfaction as long as I see that Jew Mordecai sitting at the king's gate."

[14]His wife Zeresh and all his friends said to him, "Have a gallows built, seventy-five feet[a] high, and ask the king in the morning to have Mordecai hanged on it. Then go with the king to the dinner and be happy." This suggestion delighted Haman, and he had the gallows built.

Mordecai Honored

6 That night the king could not sleep; so he ordered the book of the chronicles, the record of his reign, to be brought in and read to him. [2]It was found recorded there that Mordecai had exposed Bigthana and Teresh, two of the king's officers who guarded the doorway, who had conspired to assassinate King Xerxes.

[3]"What honor and recognition has Mordecai received for this?" the king asked.

"Nothing has been done for him," his attendants answered.

[4]The king said, "Who is in the court?" Now

---

[a]14 Hebrew *fifty cubits* (about 23 meters)

Haman had just entered the outer court of the palace to speak to the king about hanging Mordecai on the gallows he had erected for him.

[5]His attendants answered, "Haman is standing in the court."

6:1 Xerxes: A Wild Man

Other historical sources portray Xerxes as a dangerously impulsive king. When a bridge he had ordered built was destroyed in a storm, he commanded that the sea receive 300 lashes, and then had the bridge builders beheaded. When one of his loyal subjects contributed a huge sum toward a military expedition, Xerxes was so enraptured that he returned the money, along with a handsome gift of his own. But when the same man asked Xerxes to let just one of his sons go free from the draft, Xerxes, enraged, ordered the son cut into two and the army to march between the pieces.

"Bring him in," the king ordered.

[6]When Haman entered, the king asked him, "What should be done for the man the king delights to honor?"

Now Haman thought to himself, "Who is there that the king would rather honor than me?" [7]So he answered the king, "For the man the king delights to honor, [8]have them bring a royal robe the king has worn and a horse the king has ridden, one with a royal crest placed on its head. [9]Then let the robe and horse be entrusted to one of the king's most noble princes. Let them robe the man the king delights to honor, and lead him on the horse through the city streets, proclaiming before him, 'This is what is done for the man the king delights to honor!'"

[10]"Go at once," the king commanded Haman. "Get the robe and the horse and do just as you have suggested for Mordecai the Jew, who sits at the king's gate. Do not neglect anything you have recommended."

[11]So Haman got the robe and the horse. He robed Mordecai, and led him on horseback through the city streets, proclaiming before him, "This is what is done for the man the king delights to honor!"

[12]Afterward Mordecai returned to the king's gate. But Haman rushed home, with his head covered in grief, [13]and told Zeresh his wife and all his friends everything that had happened to him.

His advisers and his wife Zeresh said to him, "Since Mordecai, before whom your downfall has started, is of Jewish origin, you cannot stand against him—you will surely come to ruin!" [14]While they were still talking with him, the king's eunuchs arrived and hurried Haman away to the banquet Esther had prepared.

Haman Hanged

7 So the king and Haman went to dine with Queen Esther, [2]and as they were drinking wine on that second day, the king again asked, "Queen Esther, what is your petition? It will be given you. What is your request? Even up to half the kingdom, it will be granted."

[3]Then Queen Esther answered, "If I have found favor with you, O king, and if it pleases your majesty, grant me my life—this is my petition. And spare my people—this is my request. [4]For I and my people have been sold for destruction and slaughter and annihilation. If we had merely been sold as male and female slaves, I would have kept quiet, because no such distress would justify disturbing the king.[a]"

[5]King Xerxes asked Queen Esther, "Who is he? Where is the man who has dared to do such a thing?"

[6]Esther said, "The adversary and enemy is this vile Haman."

7:1 Subtle Approach

Esther knew well the perils of standing up to autocratic Xerxes: she had gotten her job because of the king's furious response to a queen's brashness (1:12—2:7). Esther's "banquet plot" shows that she had mastered the wiles necessary to soften the king. She grew increasingly bold and more direct, finally convincing the king to issue another decree, countering the one against the Jews—a rare turnabout for a Persian ruler (8:8).

Then Haman was terrified before the king and queen. [7]The king got up in a rage, left his wine and went out into the palace garden. But Haman, realizing that the king had already decided his fate, stayed behind to beg Queen Esther for his life.

[8]Just as the king returned from the palace garden to the banquet hall, Haman was falling on the couch where Esther was reclining.

The king exclaimed, "Will he even molest the queen while she is with me in the house?"

As soon as the word left the king's mouth, they covered Haman's face. [9]Then Harbona, one of the eunuchs attending the king, said, "A gallows seventy-five feet[b] high stands by Haman's house. He had it made for Mordecai, who spoke up to help the king."

The king said, "Hang him on it!" [10]So they

---

[a]4 Or *quiet, but the compensation our adversary offers cannot be compared with the loss the king would suffer*
[b]9 Hebrew *fifty cubits* (about 23 meters)

hanged Haman on the gallows he had prepared for Mordecai. Then the king's fury subsided.

The King's Edict in Behalf of the Jews

8 That same day King Xerxes gave Queen Esther the estate of Haman, the enemy of the Jews. And Mordecai came into the presence of the king, for Esther had told how he was related to her. [2]The king took off his signet ring, which he had reclaimed from Haman, and presented it to Mordecai. And Esther appointed him over Haman's estate.

[3]Esther again pleaded with the king, falling at his feet and weeping. She begged him to put an end to the evil plan of Haman the Agagite, which he had devised against the Jews. [4]Then the king extended the gold scepter to Esther and she arose and stood before him.

[5]"If it pleases the king," she said, "and if he regards me with favor and thinks it the right thing to do, and if he is pleased with me, let an order be written overruling the dispatches that Haman son of Hammedatha, the Agagite, devised and wrote to destroy the Jews in all the king's provinces. [6]For how can I bear to see disaster fall on my people? How can I bear to see the destruction of my family?"

[7]King Xerxes replied to Queen Esther and to Mordecai the Jew, "Because Haman attacked the Jews, I have given his estate to Esther, and they have hanged him on the gallows. [8]Now write another decree in the king's name in behalf of the Jews as seems best to you, and seal it with the king's signet ring—for no document written in the king's name and sealed with his ring can be revoked."

[9]At once the royal secretaries were summoned—on the twenty-third day of the third month, the month of Sivan. They wrote out all Mordecai's orders to the Jews, and to the satraps, governors and nobles of the 127 provinces stretching from India to Cush.[a] These orders were written in the script of each province and the language of each people and also to the Jews in their own script and language. [10]Mordecai wrote in the name of King Xerxes, sealed the dispatches with the king's signet ring, and sent them by mounted couriers, who rode fast horses especially bred for the king.

[11]The king's edict granted the Jews in every city the right to assemble and protect themselves; to destroy, kill and annihilate any armed force of any nationality or province that might attack them and their women and children; and to plunder the property of their enemies. [12]The day appointed for the Jews to do this in all the provinces of King Xerxes was the thirteenth day of the twelfth month, the month of Adar. [13]A copy of the text of the edict was to be issued as law in every province and made known to the people of every nationality so that the Jews would be ready on that day to avenge themselves on their enemies.

8:11–17 What about God?

Why is God's name not mentioned in Esther—especially in obvious places like this one? Scholars suggest several answers to this riddle. Some, reading between the lines, suggest that Esther and Mordecai were not outstanding examples of faith. They were even willing to hide Esther's Jewish background. Esther showed no reluctance to be married to a pagan king and become part of his harem. Most critically, she and Mordecai (along with all the other Jews in Esther) had chosen not to return to Jerusalem with the first wave of Jews nearly half a century before. (The story of that return is told in Ezra 1–6.) Those who stayed in Persia presumably cared more about their finances than about God's plans for the Jews to return to Jerusalem from exile. Perhaps because of this, Esther is told as a secular story, to illustrate God's care over even "secularized" Jews.

[14]The couriers, riding the royal horses, raced out, spurred on by the king's command. And the edict was also issued in the citadel of Susa.

[15]Mordecai left the king's presence wearing royal garments of blue and white, a large crown of gold and a purple robe of fine linen. And the city of Susa held a joyous celebration. [16]For the Jews it was a time of happiness and joy, gladness and honor. [17]In every province and in every city, wherever the edict of the king went, there was joy and gladness among the Jews, with feasting and celebrating. And many people of other nationalities became Jews because fear of the Jews had seized them.

Triumph of the Jews

9 On the thirteenth day of the twelfth month, the month of Adar, the edict commanded by the king was to be carried out. On this day the enemies of the Jews had hoped to overpower them, but now the tables were turned and the Jews got the upper hand over those who hated them. [2]The Jews assembled in their cities in all the provinces of King Xerxes to attack those seeking their destruction. No one could stand against them, because the people of all the other nationalities were afraid of them. [3]And all the nobles of the provinces, the satraps, the governors and the king's administrators helped the Jews, because fear of Mordecai had seized them.

[a]9 That is, the upper Nile region

[4]Mordecai was prominent in the palace; his reputation spread throughout the provinces, and he became more and more powerful.

[5]The Jews struck down all their enemies with the sword, killing and destroying them, and they did what they pleased to those who hated them. [6]In the citadel of Susa, the Jews killed and destroyed five hundred men. [7]They also killed Parshandatha, Dalphon, Aspatha, [8]Poratha, Adalia, Aridatha, [9]Parmashta, Arisai, Aridai and Vaizatha, [10]the ten sons of Haman son of Hammedatha, the enemy of the Jews. But they did not lay their hands on the plunder.

[11]The number of those slain in the citadel of Susa was reported to the king that same day. [12]The king said to Queen Esther, "The Jews have killed and destroyed five hundred men and the ten sons of Haman in the citadel of Susa. What have they done in the rest of the king's provinces? Now what is your petition? It will be given you. What is your request? It will also be granted."

[13]"If it pleases the king," Esther answered, "give the Jews in Susa permission to carry out this day's edict tomorrow also, and let Haman's ten sons be hanged on gallows."

[14]So the king commanded that this be done. An edict was issued in Susa, and they hanged the ten sons of Haman. [15]The Jews in Susa came together on the fourteenth day of the month of Adar, and they put to death in Susa three hundred men, but they did not lay their hands on the plunder.

[16]Meanwhile, the remainder of the Jews who were in the king's provinces also assembled to protect themselves and get relief from their enemies. They killed seventy-five thousand of them but did not lay their hands on the plunder. [17]This happened on the thirteenth day of the month of Adar, and on the fourteenth they rested and made it a day of feasting and joy.

Purim Celebrated

[18]The Jews in Susa, however, had assembled on the thirteenth and fourteenth, and then on the fifteenth they rested and made it a day of feasting and joy.

[19]That is why rural Jews—those living in villages—observe the fourteenth of the month of Adar as a day of joy and feasting, a day for giving presents to each other.

[20]Mordecai recorded these events, and he sent letters to all the Jews throughout the provinces of King Xerxes, near and far, [21]to have them celebrate annually the fourteenth and fifteenth days of the month of Adar [22]as the time when the Jews got relief from their enemies, and as the month when their sorrow was turned into joy and their

mourning into a day of celebration. He wrote them to observe the days as days of feasting and joy and giving presents of food to one another and gifts to the poor.

[23]So the Jews agreed to continue the celebration they had begun, doing what Mordecai had

9:19 A Day to Remember

Just as Christians retell the Christmas story each December, acting it out in church plays and manger scenes, the Jews commemorate great moments from their history. Jewish families read the book of Esther aloud on the day of Purim. The festival got its name from the casting of lots (like dice) against the Jews (3:7), a gamble that eventually backfired against Haman. The author explains the origin of celebrating Purim on two different days; even today, Jews observe Purim on the 14th everywhere except in Jerusalem, which schedules it on the 15th.

written to them. [24]For Haman son of Hammedatha, the Agagite, the enemy of all the Jews, had plotted against the Jews to destroy them and had cast the *pur* (that is, the lot) for their ruin and destruction. [25]But when the plot came to the king's attention,[a] he issued written orders that the evil scheme Haman had devised against the Jews should come back onto his own head, and that he and his sons should be hanged on the gallows. [26](Therefore these days were called Purim, from the word *pur*.) Because of everything written in this letter and because of what they had seen and what had happened to them, [27]the Jews took it upon themselves to establish the custom that they and their descendants and all who join them should without fail observe these two days every year, in the way prescribed and at the time appointed. [28]These days should be remembered and observed in every generation by every family, and in every province and in every city. And these days of Purim should never cease to be celebrated by the Jews, nor should the memory of them die out among their descendants.

[29]So Queen Esther, daughter of Abihail, along with Mordecai the Jew, wrote with full authority to confirm this second letter concerning Purim. [30]And Mordecai sent letters to all the Jews in the 127 provinces of the kingdom of Xerxes—words of goodwill and assurance— [31]to establish these days of Purim at their designated times, as Mordecai the Jew and Queen Esther had decreed for them, and as they had established for themselves and their descendants in regard to their times of fasting and lamentation. [32]Esther's decree con-

a 25 Or when Esther came before the king

firmed these regulations about Purim, and it was written down in the records.

The Greatness of Mordecai

10 King Xerxes imposed tribute throughout the empire, to its distant shores. ²And all his acts of power and might, together with a full account of the greatness of Mordecai to which the king had raised him, are they not written in the book of the annals of the kings of Media and Persia? ³Mordecai the Jew was second in rank to King Xerxes, preeminent among the Jews, and held in high esteem by his many fellow Jews, because he worked for the good of his people and spoke up for the welfare of all the Jews.

10:2 Is Esther Accurate?

Because of the many coincidences in Esther, some have considered it "just a story," having little or no historical validity. Yet as archaeologists have learned more about ancient Persian history, the details of Esther have proven remarkably reliable. Certainly the book presents itself as history: Here the author confidently asserts that readers can check the facts in the historical records. These records are lost—but evidently they were known to the early readers of Esther.

JOB

When Bad Things Happened to a Good Person
Nobody suffered more; nobody deserved it less

> "Have you considered my servant Job? There is no one on earth like him; he is blameless and upright, a man who fears God and shuns evil." 1:8

HOW COULD IT HAPPEN? ALL at once the world came crashing down on a single innocent man, a man named Job. It was the ultimate in unfairness. First, raiders stole his belongings and slaughtered his servants. Then fire from the sky burned up his sheep, and a mighty wind destroyed his house and killed his sons and daughters. Finally, Job came down with a horrible, painful disease. *What did I do to deserve such suffering?*, he wailed.

A Cosmic Contest

The book of Job reads like a detective story in which the readers know far more than the central characters. The very first chapter answers Job's main question: He had done nothing to deserve such suffering. We, the readers, know that, but nobody tells Job and his friends.

Unknown to him, Job was involved in a cosmic test, a contest proposed in heaven but staged on earth. In this extreme test of faith, the best man on earth suffered the worst calamities. Satan had claimed that people like Job love God only because of the good things he provides. Remove those good things, Satan challenged, and Job's faith would melt away along with his riches and health.

God's reputation was on the line. Would Job continue to trust him, even while his life was falling apart? This is the crucial question of the book: Would Job turn against God?

Job's wife mocked him, "Are you still holding on to your integrity? Curse God and die!" (2:9). His friends were even crueler: They argued that Job was being punished, that he fully deserved the tragedies crashing into his life. For his part, Job struggled to do what seemed impossible: to keep on believing in a loving, fair God even though all the evidence pointed against such a God.

Job on Trial

It helps to think of this book as a courtroom drama, full of long, eloquent speeches. For most of the book, Job sits in the defendant's chair listening to his friends' harangues. He knows no airtight refutations; what they say about suffering as punishment seems to make sense. Yet he also knows, deep in his soul, that they are wrong. He does not deserve the treatment he is getting. There has to be some other explanation.

Like all grieving persons, Job went through emotional cycles. He whined, exploded, cajoled, and collapsed into self-pity. He agreed with his friends, then shifted positions and contradicted himself. And occasionally he came up with a statement of brilliant hope.

Mainly, Job asked for one thing: an appearance by the one Person who could explain his miserable fate. He wanted to meet God himself, face to face. Eventually Job got his wish; God did show up in person. And when God finally spoke, no one—not Job, nor any of his friends—was prepared for what he had to say.

When We Feel Like Job

Sooner or later we all find ourselves in a position somewhat like Job's. Our world seems to crumble. Nothing makes sense any more. God seems distant and silent.

At such moments of great crisis, each one of us is put on trial. In a sense we become actors in a contest like the one Job went through. This book records every step in that process with unflinching honesty. Job's life stands as an example to every person who must go through great suffering.

How to Read Job

The book of Job is regarded as one of the world's truly great literary masterpieces. It contains some of the finest, most expressive poetry in the Bible. Yet first-time readers of Job can easily get lost because the complete "story line" is found in the first two chapters and the last one. Everything in between consists of a series of speeches.

The boldface sectional headings and the phrases that follow, such as "And Job continued his discourse" and "Then Eliphaz the Temanite replied," serve as markers or signposts throughout the book. Rather than reading large sections of the book, read one entire speech by Job, or a speech by Job and a rebuttal from one of his friends.

It may help if you try to summarize the statement behind each speech in one sentence and write that sentence in the margin (for example, "Job protests that he's innocent"). Speakers of that day impressed their audience more by eloquence than by rigorous logic, so the speeches may seem flowery. The issues Job and his friends address, however, are life-and-death ones.

As you read the speeches of Job's friends, remember that their views do not necessarily reflect God's. The book of Job merely records the friends' viewpoints; it does not endorse them.

PEOPLE YOU'LL MEET IN JOB

JOB (p. 538)

3-TRACK READING PLAN

For an explanation and complete listing of the 3-track reading plan, turn to page 7.

TRACK 1: *Two-Week Courses on the Bible*
The Track 1 reading program on the Old Testament includes one chapter from Job. See page 8 for a complete listing of this course.

TRACK 2: *An Overview of Job in 3 Days*
☐ Day 1. Read the Introduction to Job and then two short chapters, 1 and 2, which give background for the entire book.
☐ Day 2. Read chapter 38, which opens God's great speech to Job.
☐ Day 3. Read chapter 42, completing the "plot" of Job.

Now turn to page 9 for your next Track 2 reading project.

TRACK 3: *All of Job in 41 Days*
After you have read through Job, turn to pages 10–14 for your next Track 3 reading project.

☐1	☐2	☐3	☐4	☐5	☐6	☐7	☐8
☐9	☐10	☐11	☐12	☐13	☐14	☐15	☐16
☐17	☐18	☐19	☐20	☐21	☐22	☐23	☐24
☐25–26	☐27	☐28	☐29	☐30	☐31	☐32	☐33
☐34	☐35	☐36	☐37	☐38	☐39	☐40	☐41
☐42							

Prologue

1 In the land of Uz there lived a man whose name was Job. This man was blameless and upright; he feared God and shunned evil. ²He had seven sons and three daughters, ³and he owned seven thousand sheep, three thousand camels, five hundred yoke of oxen and five hundred donkeys, and had a large number of servants. He was the greatest man among all the people of the East.

⁴His sons used to take turns holding feasts in their homes, and they would invite their three sisters to eat and drink with them. ⁵When a period of feasting had run its course, Job would send and have them purified. Early in the morning he would sacrifice a burnt offering for each of them, thinking, "Perhaps my children have sinned and cursed God in their hearts." This was Job's regular custom.

Job's First Test

⁶One day the angels[a] came to present themselves before the LORD, and Satan[b] also came with them. ⁷The LORD said to Satan, "Where have you come from?"

Satan answered the LORD, "From roaming through the earth and going back and forth in it."

⁸Then the LORD said to Satan, "Have you considered my servant Job? There is no one on earth like him; he is blameless and upright, a man who fears God and shuns evil."

⁹"Does Job fear God for nothing?" Satan replied. ¹⁰"Have you not put a hedge around him and his household and everything he has? You have blessed the work of his hands, so that his flocks and herds are spread throughout the land. ¹¹But stretch out your hand and strike everything he has, and he will surely curse you to your face."

¹²The LORD said to Satan, "Very well, then, everything he has is in your hands, but on the man himself do not lay a finger."

Then Satan went out from the presence of the LORD.

¹³One day when Job's sons and daughters were feasting and drinking wine at the oldest brother's house, ¹⁴a messenger came to Job and said, "The oxen were plowing and the donkeys were grazing nearby, ¹⁵and the Sabeans attacked and carried them off. They put the servants to the sword, and I am the only one who has escaped to tell you!"

¹⁶While he was still speaking, another messenger came and said, "The fire of God fell from the sky and burned up the sheep and the servants, and I am the only one who has escaped to tell you!"

¹⁷While he was still speaking, another messenger came and said, "The Chaldeans formed three raiding parties and swept down on your camels and carried them off. They put the servants to the sword, and I am the only one who has escaped to tell you!"

1:12—2:6 The Extent of Satan's Power

Job's portrayal of Satan echoes the story in Genesis 3: Satan has supernatural power to oppress people, but is restrained by God. As John Newton said, "Satan can only go to the end of his chain." The Bible records at least one other instance where Satan specifically asked permission to attack an individual: Luke 22:31–32.

¹⁸While he was still speaking, yet another messenger came and said, "Your sons and daughters were feasting and drinking wine at the oldest brother's house, ¹⁹when suddenly a mighty wind swept in from the desert and struck the four corners of the house. It collapsed on them and they are dead, and I am the only one who has escaped to tell you!"

²⁰At this, Job got up and tore his robe and shaved his head. Then he fell to the ground in worship ²¹and said:

"Naked I came from my mother's womb,
 and naked I will depart.[c]
The LORD gave and the LORD has taken away;
 may the name of the LORD be praised."

²²In all this, Job did not sin by charging God with wrongdoing.

Job's Second Test

2 On another day the angels[a] came to present themselves before the LORD, and Satan also came with them to present himself before him. ²And the LORD said to Satan, "Where have you come from?"

Satan answered the LORD, "From roaming through the earth and going back and forth in it."

³Then the LORD said to Satan, "Have you considered my servant Job? There is no one on earth like him; he is blameless and upright, a man who fears God and shuns evil. And he still maintains his integrity, though you incited me against him to ruin him without any reason."

⁴"Skin for skin!" Satan replied. "A man will

---

[a]6,1 Hebrew *the sons of God*   [b]6 *Satan* means *accuser.*   [c]21 Or *will return there*

give all he has for his own life. ⁵But stretch out your hand and strike his flesh and bones, and he will surely curse you to your face."

⁶The LORD said to Satan, "Very well, then, he is in your hands; but you must spare his life."

⁷So Satan went out from the presence of the LORD and afflicted Job with painful sores from the soles of his feet to the top of his head. ⁸Then Job took a piece of broken pottery and scraped himself with it as he sat among the ashes.

⁹His wife said to him, "Are you still holding on to your integrity? Curse God and die!"

¹⁰He replied, "You are talking like a foolish[a] woman. Shall we accept good from God, and not trouble?"

In all this, Job did not sin in what he said.

Job's Three Friends

¹¹When Job's three friends, Eliphaz the Temanite, Bildad the Shuhite and Zophar the Naamathite, heard about all the troubles that had come upon him, they set out from their homes and met together by agreement to go and sympathize with him and comfort him. ¹²When they saw him from a distance, they could hardly recognize him; they began to weep aloud, and they tore their robes and sprinkled dust on their heads. ¹³Then they sat on the ground with him for seven days and seven nights. No one said a word to him, because they saw how great his suffering was.

2:13 Keeping Quiet

The term "Job's comforter" has come to describe how not *to act around a suffering person. These three friends proved of scant help to Job and were dismissed by God himself in the end. This verse, though, reveals the depth of their feeling for Job: They sat with him for a full week in shared, silent grief. As it turned out, compassionate silence was the most profound help they imparted to Job—a good lesson to remember for anyone who works with suffering people.*

Job Speaks

3 After this, Job opened his mouth and cursed the day of his birth. ²He said:

³"May the day of my birth perish,
 and the night it was said, 'A boy is born!'
⁴That day—may it turn to darkness;
 may God above not care about it;
 may no light shine upon it.

⁵May darkness and deep shadow[b] claim it once more;
 may a cloud settle over it;
 may blackness overwhelm its light.
⁶That night—may thick darkness seize it;
 may it not be included among the days of the year
 nor be entered in any of the months.
⁷May that night be barren;
 may no shout of joy be heard in it.
⁸May those who curse days[c] curse that day,
 those who are ready to rouse Leviathan.
⁹May its morning stars become dark;
 may it wait for daylight in vain
 and not see the first rays of dawn,
¹⁰for it did not shut the doors of the womb on me
 to hide trouble from my eyes.

¹¹"Why did I not perish at birth,
 and die as I came from the womb?
¹²Why were there knees to receive me
 and breasts that I might be nursed?
¹³For now I would be lying down in peace;
 I would be asleep and at rest
¹⁴with kings and counselors of the earth,
 who built for themselves places now lying in ruins,
¹⁵with rulers who had gold,
 who filled their houses with silver.
¹⁶Or why was I not hidden in the ground like a stillborn child,
 like an infant who never saw the light of day?
¹⁷There the wicked cease from turmoil,
 and there the weary are at rest.
¹⁸Captives also enjoy their ease;
 they no longer hear the slave driver's shout.
¹⁹The small and the great are there,
 and the slave is freed from his master.

²⁰"Why is light given to those in misery,
 and life to the bitter of soul,
²¹to those who long for death that does not come,
 who search for it more than for hidden treasure,
²²who are filled with gladness
 and rejoice when they reach the grave?
²³Why is life given to a man
 whose way is hidden,
 whom God has hedged in?
²⁴For sighing comes to me instead of food;
 my groans pour out like water.
²⁵What I feared has come upon me;
 what I dreaded has happened to me.
²⁶I have no peace, no quietness;
 I have no rest, but only turmoil."

---

[a]10 The Hebrew word rendered *foolish* denotes moral deficiency.   [b]5 Or *and the shadow of death*   [c]8 Or *the sea*

Eliphaz

4 Then Eliphaz the Temanite replied:

²"If someone ventures a word with you, will
you be impatient?
But who can keep from speaking?
³Think how you have instructed many,
how you have strengthened feeble hands.
⁴Your words have supported those who
stumbled;
you have strengthened faltering knees.
⁵But now trouble comes to you, and you are
discouraged;
it strikes you, and you are dismayed.
⁶Should not your piety be your confidence
and your blameless ways your hope?

⁷"Consider now: Who, being innocent, has
ever perished?
Where were the upright ever destroyed?
⁸As I have observed, those who plow evil
and those who sow trouble reap it.
⁹At the breath of God they are destroyed;
at the blast of his anger they perish.
¹⁰The lions may roar and growl,
yet the teeth of the great lions are broken.
¹¹The lion perishes for lack of prey,
and the cubs of the lioness are scattered.

¹²"A word was secretly brought to me,
my ears caught a whisper of it.
¹³Amid disquieting dreams in the night,
when deep sleep falls on men,

4:13 Appealing to a Vision

*The book of Job includes parallels to most
modern-day responses to people in pain. To
impress the other listeners with his religious
authority, Eliphaz appealed to a mysterious
vision in which a "spirit" restated Eliphaz's own
line of argument. In the next chapter, he hints
that Job should turn to God for a miracle
(5:8–10).*

¹⁴fear and trembling seized me
and made all my bones shake.
¹⁵A spirit glided past my face,
and the hair on my body stood on end.
¹⁶It stopped,
but I could not tell what it was.
A form stood before my eyes,
and I heard a hushed voice:
¹⁷'Can a mortal be more righteous than God?
Can a man be more pure than his Maker?
¹⁸If God places no trust in his servants,
if he charges his angels with error,

¹⁹how much more those who live in houses of
clay,
whose foundations are in the dust,
who are crushed more readily than a
moth!
²⁰Between dawn and dusk they are broken to
pieces;
unnoticed, they perish forever.
²¹Are not the cords of their tent pulled up,
so that they die without wisdom?'ᵃ

5 "Call if you will, but who will answer you?
To which of the holy ones will you turn?
²Resentment kills a fool,
and envy slays the simple.
³I myself have seen a fool taking root,
but suddenly his house was cursed.
⁴His children are far from safety,
crushed in court without a defender.
⁵The hungry consume his harvest,
taking it even from among thorns,
and the thirsty pant after his wealth.
⁶For hardship does not spring from the soil,
nor does trouble sprout from the ground.
⁷Yet man is born to trouble
as surely as sparks fly upward.

⁸"But if it were I, I would appeal to God;
I would lay my cause before him.
⁹He performs wonders that cannot be
fathomed,
miracles that cannot be counted.
¹⁰He bestows rain on the earth;
he sends water upon the countryside.
¹¹The lowly he sets on high,
and those who mourn are lifted to safety.
¹²He thwarts the plans of the crafty,
so that their hands achieve no success.
¹³He catches the wise in their craftiness,
and the schemes of the wily are swept
away.
¹⁴Darkness comes upon them in the daytime;
at noon they grope as in the night.
¹⁵He saves the needy from the sword in their
mouth;
he saves them from the clutches of the
powerful.
¹⁶So the poor have hope,
and injustice shuts its mouth.

¹⁷"Blessed is the man whom God corrects;
so do not despise the discipline of the
Almighty.ᵇ
¹⁸For he wounds, but he also binds up;
he injures, but his hands also heal.
¹⁹From six calamities he will rescue you;
in seven no harm will befall you.
²⁰In famine he will ransom you from death,
and in battle from the stroke of the
sword.

ᵃ21 Some interpreters end the quotation after verse 17.   ᵇ17 Hebrew *Shaddai*; here and throughout Job

21You will be protected from the lash of the
    tongue,
  and need not fear when destruction
    comes.

5:17 Pain as Punishment

*Job's friends sound so pious and eloquent that
it's easy to accept their words as all-
encompassing truth. Some Christians have
quoted this verse like a proverb, applying it
indiscriminately to instances of suffering. In
reality, Eliphaz was dead wrong in his theory
that God was disciplining Job. God had already
held up Job as a model of goodness (1:9).*

22You will laugh at destruction and famine,
  and need not fear the beasts of the earth.
23For you will have a covenant with the stones
    of the field,
  and the wild animals will be at peace with
    you.
24You will know that your tent is secure;
  you will take stock of your property and
    find nothing missing.
25You will know that your children will be
    many,
  and your descendants like the grass of the
    earth.
26You will come to the grave in full vigor,
  like sheaves gathered in season.

27"We have examined this, and it is true.
  So hear it and apply it to yourself."

Job

6 Then Job replied:

2"If only my anguish could be weighed
  and all my misery be placed on the scales!
3It would surely outweigh the sand of the
    seas—
  no wonder my words have been
    impetuous.
4The arrows of the Almighty are in me,
  my spirit drinks in their poison;
  God's terrors are marshaled against me.
5Does a wild donkey bray when it has grass,
  or an ox bellow when it has fodder?
6Is tasteless food eaten without salt,
  or is there flavor in the white of an egg[a]?
7I refuse to touch it;
  such food makes me ill.

8"Oh, that I might have my request,
  that God would grant what I hope for,
9that God would be willing to crush me,
  to let loose his hand and cut me off!

10Then I would still have this consolation—
  my joy in unrelenting pain—
  that I had not denied the words of the
    Holy One.

11"What strength do I have, that I should still
    hope?
  What prospects, that I should be patient?
12Do I have the strength of stone?
  Is my flesh bronze?
13Do I have any power to help myself,
  now that success has been driven from
    me?

14"A despairing man should have the devotion
    of his friends,
  even though he forsakes the fear of the
    Almighty.
15But my brothers are as undependable as
    intermittent streams,
  as the streams that overflow
16when darkened by thawing ice
  and swollen with melting snow,
17but that cease to flow in the dry season,
  and in the heat vanish from their
    channels.

6:9 Why Keep on Living?

*Job steadfastly refused to curse God, but he did
curse the day he was born. In this speech he
asked for a quick death, realizing he could not
hold out trusting in God forever. If he died
soon, at least he would die still believing. His
speeches contain some of the most profound
expressions of pain and despair in all of
literature.*

18Caravans turn aside from their routes;
  they go up into the wasteland and perish.
19The caravans of Tema look for water,
  the traveling merchants of Sheba look in
    hope.
20They are distressed, because they had been
    confident;
  they arrive there, only to be disappointed.
21Now you too have proved to be of no help;
  you see something dreadful and are afraid.
22Have I ever said, 'Give something on my
    behalf,
  pay a ransom for me from your wealth,
23deliver me from the hand of the enemy,
  ransom me from the clutches of the
    ruthless'?

24"Teach me, and I will be quiet;
  show me where I have been wrong.
25How painful are honest words!
  But what do your arguments prove?

---

[a]6 The meaning of the Hebrew for this phrase is uncertain.

²⁶Do you mean to correct what I say,
    and treat the words of a despairing man
        as wind?
²⁷You would even cast lots for the fatherless
    and barter away your friend.

²⁸"But now be so kind as to look at me.
    Would I lie to your face?
²⁹Relent, do not be unjust;
    reconsider, for my integrity is at stake. ᵃ

ᵃ29 Or *my righteousness still stands*

³⁰Is there any wickedness on my lips?
    Can my mouth not discern malice?

7 "Does not man have hard service on earth?
    Are not his days like those of a hired
        man?
²Like a slave longing for the evening shadows,
    or a hired man waiting eagerly for his
        wages,
³so I have been allotted months of futility,

What Not to Say to a Hurting Person
Job's friends only made it worse

> "Now you too have proved to be of no help." 6:21

YOU ARE SITTING IN A hospital room, where the faint smell of antiseptic lingers and the sound of lowered voices rustles all around you. The medical prognosis of your friend is bleak. You've listened to your friend's anger and despair, and a jumble of other emotions. Now it's your turn to reply. Everyone in the room waits for your response.

What do you say to a suffering person? The book of Job gives page after page of examples. Job's three friends, finding him in despair, filled the air with high-sounding advice. But unfortunately they offer models of what *not* to say. Their main argument only made Job feel worse, and at the end God dismissed them all with a scowl.

Who Were Job's Friends?

This book gives few details on time and place, but it presents Job as a very wealthy "sheik" of the Middle East. His three friends, from neighboring lands, were also prosperous and well respected. When they first saw Job, they wept aloud and sat with him on the ground, silent, for seven days and nights, overcome with grief (2:13).

After Job finally broke the silence, each friend delivered a flowery speech on Job's dilemma. There are three cycles of speeches in all, with Eliphaz, Bildad, and Zophar taking turns, allowing Job to respond to each. Eliphaz, who led off, had strong and noble ideas. Bildad was briefer and slightly less sympathetic. Zophar (who did not speak in the third cycle) showed passion and fire.

The friends seemed to crescendo in emotional intensity. In the first cycle (chapters 4—14), they showed hope of winning Job over to their point of view. In the second cycle (chapters 15—21), the speeches grew more severe and threatening. And by the time of the concluding speeches (chapters 22—25), Job's friends were making direct accusations against him.

A Flawed Theory about Suffering

Job's friends believed in a God of love and fairness; their arguments started from that fact. Surely a just God would not allow an *innocent* man to suffer so much, they reasoned. Most of their comments boil down to one simple theory: Job must have committed some great crime for which God was punishing him. All three believed that good people prosper and bad people suffer; therefore, suffering must betray some hidden sin.

"Surely God does not reject a blameless man or strengthen the hands of evildoers," they said to Job (8:20). Repent, they admonished him, and God will forgive and restore you. Their words got this response from Job: "You . . . smear me with lies; you are worthless physicians, all of you!" (13:4). Job also believed in a loving God, but he knew he was innocent.

When God finally made his appearance, he dismissed the three friends in one sentence to Eliphaz, "I am angry with you and your two friends, because you have not spoken of me what is right, as my servant Job has" (42:7).

Although the Bible elsewhere gives examples of suffering that resulted from a person's sin, Job clearly shows that such a theory cannot be applied in every case. (For a related discussion, see "Healthier, Wealthier, and Wiser," page 212.) It is not for us to try to reason out the specific cause of a person's suffering; God reserves that knowledge for himself.

Life Questions: What is the most "unfair" thing that has ever happened to you? How did it affect the way you thought about God?

and nights of misery have been assigned
 to me.
⁴When I lie down I think, 'How long before I
 get up?'
 The night drags on, and I toss till dawn.
⁵My body is clothed with worms and scabs,
 my skin is broken and festering.

⁶"My days are swifter than a weaver's shuttle,
 and they come to an end without hope.
⁷Remember, O God, that my life is but a
 breath;
 my eyes will never see happiness again.
⁸The eye that now sees me will see me no
 longer;
 you will look for me, but I will be no
 more.
⁹As a cloud vanishes and is gone,
 so he who goes down to the graveᵃ does
 not return.
¹⁰He will never come to his house again;
 his place will know him no more.

¹¹"Therefore I will not keep silent;
 I will speak out in the anguish of my
 spirit,
 I will complain in the bitterness of my
 soul.
¹²Am I the sea, or the monster of the deep,
 that you put me under guard?
¹³When I think my bed will comfort me
 and my couch will ease my complaint,
¹⁴even then you frighten me with dreams
 and terrify me with visions,
¹⁵so that I prefer strangling and death,
 rather than this body of mine.
¹⁶I despise my life; I would not live forever.
 Let me alone; my days have no meaning.

¹⁷"What is man that you make so much of
 him,
 that you give him so much attention,
¹⁸that you examine him every morning
 and test him every moment?
¹⁹Will you never look away from me,
 or let me alone even for an instant?
²⁰If I have sinned, what have I done to
 you,
 O watcher of men?
 Why have you made me your target?
 Have I become a burden to you?ᵇ
²¹Why do you not pardon my offenses
 and forgive my sins?
 For I will soon lie down in the dust;
 you will search for me, but I will be no
 more."

Bildad

8 Then Bildad the Shuhite replied:

²"How long will you say such things?
 Your words are a blustering wind.
³Does God pervert justice?
 Does the Almighty pervert what is right?
⁴When your children sinned against him,
 he gave them over to the penalty of their
 sin.

8:4 A Mixture of True and False

*Although God rejected the overall force of their
arguments, Job's three friends said some
things that were totally false and others that
were true. In this case, Bildad appealed to
common sense, ("Surely God does not reject a
blameless man," verse 20), implying that Job
sinned to deserve his suffering. But God
specifically had called Job "blameless and
upright" (2:3). Elsewhere, a statement by
Eliphaz (5:11–13) is quoted approvingly in the
New Testament (1 Corinthians 3:19).*

⁵But if you will look to God
 and plead with the Almighty,
⁶if you are pure and upright,
 even now he will rouse himself on your
 behalf
 and restore you to your rightful place.
⁷Your beginnings will seem humble,
 so prosperous will your future be.

⁸"Ask the former generations
 and find out what their fathers learned,
⁹for we were born only yesterday and know
 nothing,
 and our days on earth are but a shadow.
¹⁰Will they not instruct you and tell you?
 Will they not bring forth words from their
 understanding?
¹¹Can papyrus grow tall where there is no
 marsh?
 Can reeds thrive without water?
¹²While still growing and uncut,
 they wither more quickly than grass.
¹³Such is the destiny of all who forget God;
 so perishes the hope of the godless.
¹⁴What he trusts in is fragileᶜ;
 what he relies on is a spider's web.
¹⁵He leans on his web, but it gives way;
 he clings to it, but it does not hold.
¹⁶He is like a well-watered plant in the
 sunshine,
 spreading its shoots over the garden;

ᵃ9 Hebrew *Sheol*   ᵇ20 A few manuscripts of the Masoretic Text, an ancient Hebrew scribal tradition and Septuagint;
most manuscripts of the Masoretic Text *I have become a burden to myself.*   ᶜ14 The meaning of the Hebrew for this
word is uncertain.

¹⁷it entwines its roots around a pile of rocks
  and looks for a place among the stones.
¹⁸But when it is torn from its spot,
  that place disowns it and says, 'I never
    saw you.'
¹⁹Surely its life withers away,
  and^a from the soil other plants grow.

²⁰"Surely God does not reject a blameless man
  or strengthen the hands of evildoers.
²¹He will yet fill your mouth with laughter
  and your lips with shouts of joy.
²²Your enemies will be clothed in shame,
  and the tents of the wicked will be no
    more."

Job

9 Then Job replied:

²"Indeed, I know that this is true.
  But how can a mortal be righteous before
    God?
³Though one wished to dispute with him,
  he could not answer him one time out of
    a thousand.
⁴His wisdom is profound, his power is vast.
  Who has resisted him and come out
    unscathed?

9:4 Arms Too Short

*A gospel musical based on the book of Job took
the title "Arms Too Short to Box with God."
From the beginning Job knew he didn't stand a
chance in a dispute with God. Moreover, he
wasn't sure what to dispute—much of the time
Job demonstrated a better grasp of theology
than his friends. (For example, his words in this
chapter bear striking resemblance to what God
says at the end of the book.) But good insights
did not relieve Job's sense of being abandoned
by God. His crisis of faith was more personal
than intellectual.*

⁵He moves mountains without their knowing
    it
  and overturns them in his anger.
⁶He shakes the earth from its place
  and makes its pillars tremble.
⁷He speaks to the sun and it does not shine;
  he seals off the light of the stars.
⁸He alone stretches out the heavens
  and treads on the waves of the sea.
⁹He is the Maker of the Bear and Orion,
  the Pleiades and the constellations of the
    south.
¹⁰He performs wonders that cannot be
    fathomed,

miracles that cannot be counted.
¹¹When he passes me, I cannot see him;
  when he goes by, I cannot perceive him.
¹²If he snatches away, who can stop him?
  Who can say to him, 'What are you
    doing?'
¹³God does not restrain his anger;
  even the cohorts of Rahab cowered at his
    feet.

¹⁴"How then can I dispute with him?
  How can I find words to argue with him?
¹⁵Though I were innocent, I could not answer
    him;
  I could only plead with my Judge for
    mercy.
¹⁶Even if I summoned him and he responded,
  I do not believe he would give me a
    hearing.
¹⁷He would crush me with a storm
  and multiply my wounds for no reason.
¹⁸He would not let me regain my breath
  but would overwhelm me with misery.
¹⁹If it is a matter of strength, he is mighty!
  And if it is a matter of justice, who will
    summon him^b?
²⁰Even if I were innocent, my mouth would
    condemn me;
  if I were blameless, it would pronounce
    me guilty.

²¹"Although I am blameless,
  I have no concern for myself;
  I despise my own life.
²²It is all the same; that is why I say,
  'He destroys both the blameless and the
    wicked.'
²³When a scourge brings sudden death,
  he mocks the despair of the innocent.
²⁴When a land falls into the hands of the
    wicked,
  he blindfolds its judges.
  If it is not he, then who is it?

²⁵"My days are swifter than a runner;
  they fly away without a glimpse of joy.
²⁶They skim past like boats of papyrus,
  like eagles swooping down on their prey.
²⁷If I say, 'I will forget my complaint,
  I will change my expression, and smile,'
²⁸I still dread all my sufferings,
  for I know you will not hold me innocent.
²⁹Since I am already found guilty,
  why should I struggle in vain?
³⁰Even if I washed myself with soap^c
  and my hands with washing soda,
³¹you would plunge me into a slime pit
  so that even my clothes would detest me.

^a19 Or *Surely all the joy it has / is that*   ^b19 See Septuagint; Hebrew *me.*   ^c30 Or *snow*

³²"He is not a man like me that I might answer him,
that we might confront each other in court.
³³If only there were someone to arbitrate between us,
to lay his hand upon us both,
³⁴someone to remove God's rod from me,
so that his terror would frighten me no more.
³⁵Then I would speak up without fear of him,
but as it now stands with me, I cannot.

9:33–35 Looking for an Arbitrator

Job recognized the enormous gulf between God and people. He poignantly asked for an arbitrator "to lay his hand upon us both." A few such comments of Job, expressing great longing for an advocate, found their full realization in Jesus, who was called the "one mediator between God and men" (1 Timothy 2:5).

10 "I loathe my very life;
therefore I will give free rein to my complaint
and speak out in the bitterness of my soul.
²I will say to God: Do not condemn me,
but tell me what charges you have against me.
³Does it please you to oppress me,
to spurn the work of your hands,
while you smile on the schemes of the wicked?
⁴Do you have eyes of flesh?
Do you see as a mortal sees?
⁵Are your days like those of a mortal
or your years like those of a man,
⁶that you must search out my faults
and probe after my sin—
⁷though you know that I am not guilty
and that no one can rescue me from your hand?

⁸"Your hands shaped me and made me.
Will you now turn and destroy me?
⁹Remember that you molded me like clay.
Will you now turn me to dust again?
¹⁰Did you not pour me out like milk
and curdle me like cheese,
¹¹clothe me with skin and flesh
and knit me together with bones and sinews?
¹²You gave me life and showed me kindness,

and in your providence watched over my spirit.
¹³"But this is what you concealed in your heart,
and I know that this was in your mind:
¹⁴If I sinned, you would be watching me

10:8 Fond Memories

Author Joseph Bayly, who watched three of his sons die in their youth, said, "Don't forget in the darkness what you've learned in the light." Job lived by this same principle. Even though he could not understand God at the moment, he never belittled the blessings he had already received. In a fit of anger, a divorcée might say, "Oh, I never really loved him anyway"; Job never once turned his back on God in that way.

and would not let my offense go unpunished.
¹⁵If I am guilty—woe to me!
Even if I am innocent, I cannot lift my head,
for I am full of shame
and drowned in ᵃ my affliction.
¹⁶If I hold my head high, you stalk me like a lion
and again display your awesome power against me.
¹⁷You bring new witnesses against me
and increase your anger toward me;
your forces come against me wave upon wave.
¹⁸"Why then did you bring me out of the womb?
I wish I had died before any eye saw me.
¹⁹If only I had never come into being,
or had been carried straight from the womb to the grave!
²⁰Are not my few days almost over?
Turn away from me so I can have a moment's joy
²¹before I go to the place of no return,
to the land of gloom and deep shadow,ᵇ
²²to the land of deepest night,
of deep shadow and disorder,
where even the light is like darkness."

Zophar

11 Then Zophar the Naamathite replied:

²"Are all these words to go unanswered?
Is this talker to be vindicated?
³Will your idle talk reduce men to silence?
Will no one rebuke you when you mock?

ᵃ15 Or and aware of   ᵇ21 Or and the shadow of death; also in verse 22

⁴You say to God, 'My beliefs are flawless
and I am pure in your sight.'
⁵Oh, how I wish that God would speak,
that he would open his lips against you
⁶and disclose to you the secrets of wisdom,
for true wisdom has two sides.
Know this: God has even forgotten some
of your sin.

⁷"Can you fathom the mysteries of God?
Can you probe the limits of the Almighty?
⁸They are higher than the heavens—what can
you do?
They are deeper than the depths of the
grave*ᵃ*—what can you know?
⁹Their measure is longer than the earth
and wider than the sea.

¹⁰"If he comes along and confines you in
prison
and convenes a court, who can oppose
him?
¹¹Surely he recognizes deceitful men;
and when he sees evil, does he not take
note?
¹²But a witless man can no more become wise
than a wild donkey's colt can be born a
man.*ᵇ*

¹³"Yet if you devote your heart to him
and stretch out your hands to him,
¹⁴if you put away the sin that is in your hand
and allow no evil to dwell in your tent,

11:14 Unfair Accusation

*Zophar, the least tactful of the three friends,
made direct accusations against Job, repeating
the common refrain that Job was being
punished for some sin. In a speech recorded in
chapter 12, Job agreed in principle that God
rewards the righteous and punishes the
wicked. But in his own case he knew he was
innocent. No matter how convincing their
arguments, he had to protest against them.*

¹⁵then you will lift up your face without
shame;
you will stand firm and without fear.
¹⁶You will surely forget your trouble,
recalling it only as waters gone by.
¹⁷Life will be brighter than noonday,
and darkness will become like morning.
¹⁸You will be secure, because there is hope;
you will look about you and take your
rest in safety.
¹⁹You will lie down, with no one to make you
afraid,
and many will court your favor.

²⁰But the eyes of the wicked will fail,
and escape will elude them;
their hope will become a dying gasp."

Job

12 Then Job replied:

²"Doubtless you are the people,
and wisdom will die with you!
³But I have a mind as well as you;
I am not inferior to you.
Who does not know all these things?

⁴"I have become a laughingstock to my
friends,
though I called upon God and he
answered—
a mere laughingstock, though righteous
and blameless!
⁵Men at ease have contempt for misfortune
as the fate of those whose feet are
slipping.

12:5 Contempt, not Sympathy

*After his release from a Siberian prison,
Alexander Solzhenitsyn gained overnight fame
as a novelist. One day he was summoned to the
opulent office of an admiring Soviet official. In
those comfortable surroundings, the agony of
the Soviet prison camps seemed very far away.
"It is impossible for a man who is warm to
understand one who is cold," he concluded. Job
accused his friends—and even God—of the
same lack of sympathy. His complaint against
God would be answered finally by the
Incarnation, when God voluntarily subjected
himself to cold, hunger, and every other
human misfortune.*

⁶The tents of marauders are undisturbed,
and those who provoke God are secure—
those who carry their god in their
hands.*ᶜ*

⁷"But ask the animals, and they will teach
you,
or the birds of the air, and they will tell
you;
⁸or speak to the earth, and it will teach you,
or let the fish of the sea inform you.
⁹Which of all these does not know
that the hand of the LORD has done this?
¹⁰In his hand is the life of every creature
and the breath of all mankind.
¹¹Does not the ear test words
as the tongue tastes food?
¹²Is not wisdom found among the aged?
Does not long life bring understanding?

ᵃ8 Hebrew than Sheol   *ᵇ12 Or wild donkey can be born tame*   *ᶜ6 Or secure / in what God's hand brings them*

[13]"To God belong wisdom and power;
  counsel and understanding are his.
[14]What he tears down cannot be rebuilt;
  the man he imprisons cannot be released.
[15]If he holds back the waters, there is drought;
  if he lets them loose, they devastate the
    land.
[16]To him belong strength and victory;
  both deceived and deceiver are his.
[17]He leads counselors away stripped
  and makes fools of judges.
[18]He takes off the shackles put on by kings
  and ties a loincloth[a] around their waist.
[19]He leads priests away stripped
  and overthrows men long established.
[20]He silences the lips of trusted advisers
  and takes away the discernment of elders.
[21]He pours contempt on nobles
  and disarms the mighty.
[22]He reveals the deep things of darkness
  and brings deep shadows into the light.
[23]He makes nations great, and destroys them;
  he enlarges nations, and disperses them.
[24]He deprives the leaders of the earth of their
    reason;
  he sends them wandering through a
    trackless waste.
[25]They grope in darkness with no light;
  he makes them stagger like drunkards.

13 "My eyes have seen all this,
  my ears have heard and understood it.
[2]What you know, I also know;
  I am not inferior to you.
[3]But I desire to speak to the Almighty
  and to argue my case with God.
[4]You, however, smear me with lies;
  you are worthless physicians, all of you!
[5]If only you would be altogether silent!
  For you, that would be wisdom.
[6]Hear now my argument;
  listen to the plea of my lips.
[7]Will you speak wickedly on God's behalf?
  Will you speak deceitfully for him?
[8]Will you show him partiality?
  Will you argue the case for God?
[9]Would it turn out well if he examined you?
  Could you deceive him as you might
    deceive men?
[10]He would surely rebuke you
  if you secretly showed partiality.
[11]Would not his splendor terrify you?
  Would not the dread of him fall on you?
[12]Your maxims are proverbs of ashes;
  your defenses are defenses of clay.

[13]"Keep silent and let me speak;
  then let come to me what may.

[14]Why do I put myself in jeopardy
  and take my life in my hands?
[15]Though he slay me, yet will I hope in him;
  I will surely[b] defend my ways to his face.

13:15 A Desperate Hope

This statement more than any other shows the depth of Job's faith, and the reason he made good on God's challenge against Satan. He valued his faith in God even above his own life. He asked only for a "day in court," a chance to confront God personally and hear an explanation.

[16]Indeed, this will turn out for my deliverance,
  for no godless man would dare come
    before him!
[17]Listen carefully to my words;
  let your ears take in what I say.
[18]Now that I have prepared my case,
  I know I will be vindicated.
[19]Can anyone bring charges against me?
  If so, I will be silent and die.

[20]"Only grant me these two things, O God,
  and then I will not hide from you:
[21]Withdraw your hand far from me,
  and stop frightening me with your terrors.
[22]Then summon me and I will answer,
  or let me speak, and you reply.
[23]How many wrongs and sins have I
    committed?
  Show me my offense and my sin.
[24]Why do you hide your face
  and consider me your enemy?
[25]Will you torment a windblown leaf?
  Will you chase after dry chaff?
[26]For you write down bitter things against me
  and make me inherit the sins of my
    youth.
[27]You fasten my feet in shackles;
  you keep close watch on all my paths
  by putting marks on the soles of my feet.

[28]"So man wastes away like something rotten,
  like a garment eaten by moths.

14 "Man born of woman
  is of few days and full of trouble.
[2]He springs up like a flower and withers
    away;
  like a fleeting shadow, he does not endure.
[3]Do you fix your eye on such a one?
  Will you bring him[c] before you for
    judgment?
[4]Who can bring what is pure from the
    impure?

---

[a] 18 Or *shackles of kings / and ties a belt*   [b] 15 Or *He will surely slay me; I have no hope — / yet I will*
[c] 3 Septuagint, Vulgate and Syriac; Hebrew *me*

No one!
5Man's days are determined;
   you have decreed the number of his
      months
   and have set limits he cannot exceed.
6So look away from him and let him alone,
   till he has put in his time like a hired
      man.

7"At least there is hope for a tree:
   If it is cut down, it will sprout again,
      and its new shoots will not fail.
8Its roots may grow old in the ground
   and its stump die in the soil,
9yet at the scent of water it will bud
   and put forth shoots like a plant.
10But man dies and is laid low;
   he breathes his last and is no more.
11As water disappears from the sea
   or a riverbed becomes parched and dry,
12so man lies down and does not rise;
   till the heavens are no more, men will not
      awake
   or be roused from their sleep.

13"If only you would hide me in the grave[a]
   and conceal me till your anger has passed!
   If only you would set me a time
      and then remember me!
14If a man dies, will he live again?
   All the days of my hard service
   I will wait for my renewal[b] to come.
15You will call and I will answer you;
   you will long for the creature your hands
      have made.
16Surely then you will count my steps
   but not keep track of my sin.
17My offenses will be sealed up in a bag;
   you will cover over my sin.

18"But as a mountain erodes and crumbles
   and as a rock is moved from its place,
19as water wears away stones
   and torrents wash away the soil,
   so you destroy man's hope.
20You overpower him once for all, and he is
      gone;
   you change his countenance and send him
      away.
21If his sons are honored, he does not know it;
   if they are brought low, he does not see it.
22He feels but the pain of his own body
   and mourns only for himself."

Eliphaz

15 Then Eliphaz the Temanite replied:

2"Would a wise man answer with empty
      notions
   or fill his belly with the hot east wind?

3Would he argue with useless words,
   with speeches that have no value?
4But you even undermine piety
   and hinder devotion to God.

15:4 A Shocking Lack of Piety

*Job minced no words in his complaints against
God. As a result, his friends criticized him for
undermining piety and hindering devotion to
God. Notably, in his summing-up speech God
did not condemn Job's varying moods; he
instead dismissed the pious words of Job's
friends.*

*Counselors know that repressed feelings of
anger or disappointment don't just disappear;
they usually fester inside, and grow even more
toxic. Job expressed his feeling openly, much to
his friends' dismay.*

5Your sin prompts your mouth;
   you adopt the tongue of the crafty.
6Your own mouth condemns you, not mine;
   your own lips testify against you.

7"Are you the first man ever born?
   Were you brought forth before the hills?
8Do you listen in on God's council?
   Do you limit wisdom to yourself?
9What do you know that we do not know?
   What insights do you have that we do not
      have?
10The gray-haired and the aged are on our
      side,
   men even older than your father.
11Are God's consolations not enough for you,
   words spoken gently to you?
12Why has your heart carried you away,
   and why do your eyes flash,
13so that you vent your rage against God
   and pour out such words from your
      mouth?

14"What is man, that he could be pure,
   or one born of woman, that he could be
      righteous?
15If God places no trust in his holy ones,
   if even the heavens are not pure in his
      eyes,
16how much less man, who is vile and corrupt,
   who drinks up evil like water!

17"Listen to me and I will explain to you;
   let me tell you what I have seen,
18what wise men have declared,
   hiding nothing received from their fathers
19(to whom alone the land was given
   when no alien passed among them):
20All his days the wicked man suffers torment,

---

a 13 Hebrew *Sheol*   *b 14* Or *release*

the ruthless through all the years stored
up for him.
²¹Terrifying sounds fill his ears;
when all seems well, marauders attack
him.
²²He despairs of escaping the darkness;
he is marked for the sword.
²³He wanders about—food for vultures*ᵃ*;
he knows the day of darkness is at hand.
²⁴Distress and anguish fill him with terror;
they overwhelm him, like a king poised to
attack,
²⁵because he shakes his fist at God
and vaunts himself against the Almighty,
²⁶defiantly charging against him
with a thick, strong shield.

²⁷"Though his face is covered with fat
and his waist bulges with flesh,
²⁸he will inhabit ruined towns
and houses where no one lives,
houses crumbling to rubble.
²⁹He will no longer be rich and his wealth will
not endure,
nor will his possessions spread over the
land.
³⁰He will not escape the darkness;
a flame will wither his shoots,
and the breath of God's mouth will carry
him away.
³¹Let him not deceive himself by trusting what
is worthless,
for he will get nothing in return.
³²Before his time he will be paid in full,
and his branches will not flourish.
³³He will be like a vine stripped of its unripe
grapes,
like an olive tree shedding its blossoms.
³⁴For the company of the godless will be
barren,
and fire will consume the tents of those
who love bribes.
³⁵They conceive trouble and give birth to evil;
their womb fashions deceit."

Job

16 Then Job replied:

²"I have heard many things like these;
miserable comforters are you all!
³Will your long-winded speeches never end?
What ails you that you keep on arguing?
⁴I also could speak like you,
if you were in my place;
I could make fine speeches against you
and shake my head at you.
⁵But my mouth would encourage you;
comfort from my lips would bring you
relief.

⁶"Yet if I speak, my pain is not relieved;
and if I refrain, it does not go away.
⁷Surely, O God, you have worn me out;
you have devastated my entire household.
⁸You have bound me—and it has become a
witness;
my gauntness rises up and testifies against
me.
⁹God assails me and tears me in his anger
and gnashes his teeth at me;
my opponent fastens on me his piercing
eyes.

16:9 When God Seems Angry

*In his trauma, Job could not help feeling that he
was the object of God's anger. Many people
who undergo great pain feel the same. In Job's
case, however, we know that God was not
angry with him. God had held him up before
Satan as "a man who fears God and shuns evil"
(1:8).*

¹⁰Men open their mouths to jeer at me;
they strike my cheek in scorn
and unite together against me.
¹¹God has turned me over to evil men
and thrown me into the clutches of the
wicked.
¹²All was well with me, but he shattered me;
he seized me by the neck and crushed me.
He has made me his target;
¹³   his archers surround me.
Without pity, he pierces my kidneys
and spills my gall on the ground.
¹⁴Again and again he bursts upon me;
he rushes at me like a warrior.

¹⁵"I have sewed sackcloth over my skin
and buried my brow in the dust.
¹⁶My face is red with weeping,
deep shadows ring my eyes;
¹⁷yet my hands have been free of violence
and my prayer is pure.

¹⁸"O earth, do not cover my blood;
may my cry never be laid to rest!
¹⁹Even now my witness is in heaven;
my advocate is on high.
²⁰My intercessor is my friend*ᵇ*
as my eyes pour out tears to God;
²¹on behalf of a man he pleads with God
as a man pleads for his friend.

²²"Only a few years will pass
before I go on the journey of no return.

17 ¹My spirit is broken,
my days are cut short,

ᵃ 23 Or about, looking for food   *ᵇ 20 Or My friends treat me with scorn*

the grave awaits me.
[2]Surely mockers surround me;
my eyes must dwell on their hostility.

[3]"Give me, O God, the pledge you demand.
Who else will put up security for me?
[4]You have closed their minds to
understanding,
therefore you will not let them triumph.
[5]If a man denounces his friends for reward,
the eyes of his children will fail.

[6]"God has made me a byword to everyone,
a man in whose face people spit.
[7]My eyes have grown dim with grief;
my whole frame is but a shadow.
[8]Upright men are appalled at this;
the innocent are aroused against the
ungodly.
[9]Nevertheless, the righteous will hold to their
ways,
and those with clean hands will grow
stronger.

[10]"But come on, all of you, try again!
I will not find a wise man among you.
[11]My days have passed, my plans are shattered,
and so are the desires of my heart.
[12]These men turn night into day;
in the face of darkness they say, 'Light is
near.'
[13]If the only home I hope for is the grave,[a]
if I spread out my bed in darkness,
[14]if I say to corruption, 'You are my father,'
and to the worm, 'My mother' or 'My
sister,'
[15]where then is my hope?
Who can see any hope for me?
[16]Will it go down to the gates of death[a]?
Will we descend together into the dust?"

17:12–16 A Wrong Time for Cheer

*Falsely cheerful advice can actually make a
suffering person even more discouraged. Job's
sentiments here are echoed in a verse from
Proverbs: "Like one who takes away a garment
on a cold day, or like vinegar poured on soda,
is one who sings songs to a heavy heart"
(25:20).*

Bildad

18 Then Bildad the Shuhite replied:

[2]"When will you end these speeches?
Be sensible, and then we can talk.
[3]Why are we regarded as cattle

and considered stupid in your sight?
[4]You who tear yourself to pieces in your
anger,
is the earth to be abandoned for your
sake?
Or must the rocks be moved from their
place?

[5]"The lamp of the wicked is snuffed out;
the flame of his fire stops burning.
[6]The light in his tent becomes dark;
the lamp beside him goes out.
[7]The vigor of his step is weakened;
his own schemes throw him down.
[8]His feet thrust him into a net
and he wanders into its mesh.
[9]A trap seizes him by the heel;
a snare holds him fast.
[10]A noose is hidden for him on the ground;
a trap lies in his path.
[11]Terrors startle him on every side
and dog his every step.
[12]Calamity is hungry for him;
disaster is ready for him when he falls.
[13]It eats away parts of his skin;
death's firstborn devours his limbs.

18:13 Battle of Words

*After Job lashed out at his friends (see
17:10–12), Bildad retorted in kind, followed by
Zophar in chapter 20. These two speeches,
among the nastiest in the book, show the
danger of bitter argument about anything,
including theology. Friends who were
overwhelmed with compassion when they first
visited Job are now seen cruelly heaping more
grief upon him—just to defend their (faulty)
theological point.*

[14]He is torn from the security of his tent
and marched off to the king of terrors.
[15]Fire resides[b] in his tent;
burning sulfur is scattered over his
dwelling.
[16]His roots dry up below
and his branches wither above.
[17]The memory of him perishes from the earth;
he has no name in the land.
[18]He is driven from light into darkness
and is banished from the world.
[19]He has no offspring or descendants among
his people,
no survivor where once he lived.
[20]Men of the west are appalled at his fate;
men of the east are seized with horror.
[21]Surely such is the dwelling of an evil man;

---

[a] 13,16 Hebrew *Sheol*   [b] 15 Or *Nothing he had remains*

such is the place of one who knows not
God."

Job

19

Then Job replied:

²"How long will you torment me
and crush me with words?
³Ten times now you have reproached me;
shamelessly you attack me.
⁴If it is true that I have gone astray,
my error remains my concern alone.
⁵If indeed you would exalt yourselves above
me
and use my humiliation against me,
⁶then know that God has wronged me
and drawn his net around me.

⁷"Though I cry, 'I've been wronged!' I get no
response;
though I call for help, there is no justice.
⁸He has blocked my way so I cannot pass;
he has shrouded my paths in darkness.
⁹He has stripped me of my honor
and removed the crown from my head.
¹⁰He tears me down on every side till I am
gone;
he uproots my hope like a tree.
¹¹His anger burns against me;
he counts me among his enemies.
¹²His troops advance in force;
they build a siege ramp against me
and encamp around my tent.

¹³"He has alienated my brothers from me;
my acquaintances are completely
estranged from me.
¹⁴My kinsmen have gone away;
my friends have forgotten me.
¹⁵My guests and my maidservants count me a
stranger;
they look upon me as an alien.
¹⁶I summon my servant, but he does not
answer,
though I beg him with my own mouth.
¹⁷My breath is offensive to my wife;
I am loathsome to my own brothers.
¹⁸Even the little boys scorn me;
when I appear, they ridicule me.
¹⁹All my intimate friends detest me;
those I love have turned against me.
²⁰I am nothing but skin and bones;
I have escaped with only the skin of my
teeth.ᵃ

²¹"Have pity on me, my friends, have pity,
for the hand of God has struck me.

²²Why do you pursue me as God does?
Will you never get enough of my flesh?

²³"Oh, that my words were recorded,
that they were written on a scroll,
²⁴that they were inscribed with an iron tool
onᵇ lead,
or engraved in rock forever!
²⁵I know that my Redeemerᶜ lives,
and that in the end he will stand upon the
earth.ᵈ

19:25 An Outburst of Hope

*In the midst of his deepest agony, Job
expressed astonishing words of hope. This
prophecy expands on two other flashes of hope
(9:33; 16:19–21). Job did not try to hide his
despair and anguish, but, as this verse shows,
the trials never crushed all of his hope.*

²⁶And after my skin has been destroyed,
yetᵉ inᶠ my flesh I will see God;
²⁷I myself will see him
with my own eyes—I, and not another.
How my heart yearns within me!

²⁸"If you say, 'How we will hound him,
since the root of the trouble lies in
him,ᵍ'
²⁹you should fear the sword yourselves;
for wrath will bring punishment by the
sword,
and then you will know that there is
judgment.ʰ"

Zophar

20

Then Zophar the Naamathite replied:

²"My troubled thoughts prompt me to answer
because I am greatly disturbed.
³I hear a rebuke that dishonors me,
and my understanding inspires me to
reply.

⁴"Surely you know how it has been from of
old,
ever since manⁱ was placed on the earth,
⁵that the mirth of the wicked is brief,
the joy of the godless lasts but a moment.
⁶Though his pride reaches to the heavens
and his head touches the clouds,
⁷he will perish forever, like his own dung;
those who have seen him will say, 'Where
is he?'
⁸Like a dream he flies away, no more to be
found,

ᵃ20 Or *only my gums*   ᵇ24 Or *and*   ᶜ25 Or *defender*   ᵈ25 Or *upon my grave*   ᵉ26 Or *And after I awake, /*
though this ⌊body⌋ has been destroyed, / then   ᶠ26 Or */ apart from*   ᵍ28 Many Hebrew manuscripts, Septuagint
and Vulgate; most Hebrew manuscripts *me*   ʰ29 Or */ that you may come to know the Almighty*   ⁱ4 Or *Adam*

21"Submit to God and be at peace with him;
    in this way prosperity will come to you.
22Accept instruction from his mouth
    and lay up his words in your heart.
23If you return to the Almighty, you will be
        restored:
    If you remove wickedness far from your
        tent
24and assign your nuggets to the dust,
    your gold of Ophir to the rocks in the
        ravines,
25then the Almighty will be your gold,
    the choicest silver for you.
26Surely then you will find delight in the
        Almighty
    and will lift up your face to God.
27You will pray to him, and he will hear you,
    and you will fulfill your vows.
28What you decide on will be done,
    and light will shine on your ways.
29When men are brought low and you say,
    'Lift them up!'
    then he will save the downcast.
30He will deliver even one who is not
        innocent,
    who will be delivered through the
        cleanness of your hands."

Job

23

Then Job replied:

2"Even today my complaint is bitter;
    his hand[a] is heavy in spite of[b] my
        groaning.
3If only I knew where to find him;
    if only I could go to his dwelling!
4I would state my case before him
    and fill my mouth with arguments.
5I would find out what he would answer me,
    and consider what he would say.
6Would he oppose me with great power?
    No, he would not press charges against
        me.
7There an upright man could present his case
        before him,
    and I would be delivered forever from my
        judge.

8"But if I go to the east, he is not there;
    if I go to the west, I do not find him.
9When he is at work in the north, I do not
        see him;
    when he turns to the south, I catch no
        glimpse of him.
10But he knows the way that I take;
    when he has tested me, I will come forth
        as gold.

11My feet have closely followed his steps;
    I have kept to his way without turning
        aside.
12I have not departed from the commands of
        his lips;
    I have treasured the words of his mouth
        more than my daily bread.
13"But he stands alone, and who can oppose
        him?
    He does whatever he pleases.

23:13 Unstable Ground

*Job's friends hammered away at consistent
themes whereas Job, like most people in pain,
found himself shifting back and forth, unsure
what to believe. In the first paragraph of
chapter 23, he is ready to take God on; in the
second, he wonders if he'll ever find God to
state his case; in the third, he trembles to think
what might happen if he actually does locate
God!*

14He carries out his decree against me,
    and many such plans he still has in store.
15That is why I am terrified before him;
    when I think of all this, I fear him.
16God has made my heart faint;
    the Almighty has terrified me.
17Yet I am not silenced by the darkness,
    by the thick darkness that covers my face.

24

"Why does the Almighty not set times
    for judgment?
    Why must those who know him look in
        vain for such days?
2Men move boundary stones;
    they pasture flocks they have stolen.
3They drive away the orphan's donkey
    and take the widow's ox in pledge.
4They thrust the needy from the path
    and force all the poor of the land into
        hiding.
5Like wild donkeys in the desert,
    the poor go about their labor of foraging
        food;
    the wasteland provides food for their
        children.
6They gather fodder in the fields
    and glean in the vineyards of the wicked.
7Lacking clothes, they spend the night naked;
    they have nothing to cover themselves in
        the cold.
8They are drenched by mountain rains
    and hug the rocks for lack of shelter.

---

a2 Septuagint and Syriac; Hebrew / the hand on me   b2 Or heavy on me in

⁹The fatherless child is snatched from the
    breast;
  the infant of the poor is seized for a debt.
¹⁰Lacking clothes, they go about naked;
  they carry the sheaves, but still go hungry.
¹¹They crush olives among the terraces*ᵃ;
  they tread the winepresses, yet suffer
    thirst.
¹²The groans of the dying rise from the city,
  and the souls of the wounded cry out for
    help.
  But God charges no one with wrongdoing.

¹³"There are those who rebel against the light,
  who do not know its ways
  or stay in its paths.
¹⁴When daylight is gone, the murderer rises up
  and kills the poor and needy;
  in the night he steals forth like a thief.
¹⁵The eye of the adulterer watches for dusk;
  he thinks, 'No eye will see me,'
  and he keeps his face concealed.
¹⁶In the dark, men break into houses,
  but by day they shut themselves in;
  they want nothing to do with the light.
¹⁷For all of them, deep darkness is their
    morningᵇ;
  they make friends with the terrors of
    darkness.ᶜ

¹⁸"Yet they are foam on the surface of the
    water;
  their portion of the land is cursed,
  so that no one goes to the vineyards.
¹⁹As heat and drought snatch away the melted
    snow,
  so the graveᵈ snatches away those who
    have sinned.
²⁰The womb forgets them,
  the worm feasts on them;
  evil men are no longer remembered
  but are broken like a tree.
²¹They prey on the barren and childless
    woman,
  and to the widow show no kindness.
²²But God drags away the mighty by his
    power;
  though they become established, they have
    no assurance of life.
²³He may let them rest in a feeling of security,
  but his eyes are on their ways.
²⁴For a little while they are exalted, and then
    they are gone;
  they are brought low and gathered up like
    all others;
  they are cut off like heads of grain.

²⁵"If this is not so, who can prove me false
  and reduce my words to nothing?"

Bildad

25

Then Bildad the Shuhite replied:

²"Dominion and awe belong to God;
  he establishes order in the heights of
    heaven.

25:1–6 Where Is God?

*In the speech recorded in chapters 23–24, Job
movingly described the feeling of God's
absence at his time of greatest need. God must
also seem absent to the poor, the fatherless,
and all those suffering without relief, he said.
Bildad replied with the shortest speech in the
book (chapter 25). He questioned whether any
person ("who is but a maggot . . . a worm") had
the right to challenge God so boldly.*

³Can his forces be numbered?
  Upon whom does his light not rise?
⁴How then can a man be righteous before
    God?
  How can one born of woman be pure?
⁵If even the moon is not bright
  and the stars are not pure in his eyes,
⁶how much less man, who is but a maggot—
  a son of man, who is only a worm!"

Job

26

Then Job replied:

²"How you have helped the powerless!
  How you have saved the arm that is
    feeble!
³What advice you have offered to one without
    wisdom!
  And what great insight you have
    displayed!
⁴Who has helped you utter these words?
  And whose spirit spoke from your mouth?

⁵"The dead are in deep anguish,
  those beneath the waters and all that live
    in them.
⁶Deathᵈ is naked before God;
  Destructionᵉ lies uncovered.
⁷He spreads out the northern ⌊skies⌋ over
    empty space;
  he suspends the earth over nothing.
⁸He wraps up the waters in his clouds,
  yet the clouds do not burst under their
    weight.
⁹He covers the face of the full moon,
  spreading his clouds over it.

ᵃ11 Or *olives between the millstones*; the meaning of the Hebrew for this word is uncertain.   ᵇ17 Or *them, their
morning is like the shadow of death*   ᶜ17 Or *of the shadow of death*   ᵈ19,6 Hebrew *Sheol*   ᵉ6 Hebrew *Abaddon*

¹⁰He marks out the horizon on the face of the
waters
for a boundary between light and
darkness.

26:6–14 A Faint Whisper of God

*The book of Job contains some of the best
nature poetry ever written; it frequently cites
nature as one of the proofs of God's existence.
Job himself never denied God's power. All the
wonders of nature, he said, are "but the outer
fringe of his works," a faint whisper of God. His
complaint was not about power, but about
justice. How could a God so powerful treat him
so unfairly?*

¹¹The pillars of the heavens quake,
aghast at his rebuke.
¹²By his power he churned up the sea;
by his wisdom he cut Rahab to pieces.
¹³By his breath the skies became fair;
his hand pierced the gliding serpent.
¹⁴And these are but the outer fringe of his
works;
how faint the whisper we hear of him!
Who then can understand the thunder of
his power?"

27 And Job continued his discourse:

²"As surely as God lives, who has denied me
justice,
the Almighty, who has made me taste
bitterness of soul,
³as long as I have life within me,
the breath of God in my nostrils,
⁴my lips will not speak wickedness,
and my tongue will utter no deceit.
⁵I will never admit you are in the right;
till I die, I will not deny my integrity.
⁶I will maintain my righteousness and never
let go of it;
my conscience will not reproach me as
long as I live.

⁷"May my enemies be like the wicked,
my adversaries like the unjust!
⁸For what hope has the godless when he is
cut off,
when God takes away his life?
⁹Does God listen to his cry
when distress comes upon him?
¹⁰Will he find delight in the Almighty?
Will he call upon God at all times?

¹¹"I will teach you about the power of God;
the ways of the Almighty I will not
conceal.

¹²You have all seen this yourselves.
Why then this meaningless talk?

¹³"Here is the fate God allots to the wicked,
the heritage a ruthless man receives from
the Almighty:
¹⁴However many his children, their fate is the
sword;
his offspring will never have enough to
eat.
¹⁵The plague will bury those who survive him,
and their widows will not weep for them.
¹⁶Though he heaps up silver like dust
and clothes like piles of clay,
¹⁷what he lays up the righteous will wear,
and the innocent will divide his silver.
¹⁸The house he builds is like a moth's cocoon,
like a hut made by a watchman.
¹⁹He lies down wealthy, but will do so no
more;
when he opens his eyes, all is gone.
²⁰Terrors overtake him like a flood;
a tempest snatches him away in the night.
²¹The east wind carries him off, and he is
gone;
it sweeps him out of his place.
²²It hurls itself against him without mercy
as he flees headlong from its power.
²³It claps its hands in derision
and hisses him out of his place.

28 "There is a mine for silver
and a place where gold is refined.

28:1 A Poem on Wisdom

*In the midst of one of his most beautiful
speeches, Job included a self-contained poem
on wisdom. It uses the analogy of mining
precious metals to make the point that wisdom
cannot be found by any amount of searching
(verses 1–19). God alone knows where it
dwells. In the rest of the poem, Job admitted
some things were beyond his understanding,
then lapsed into a reminiscence of what life
was like before his time of trials.*

²Iron is taken from the earth,
and copper is smelted from ore.
³Man puts an end to the darkness;
he searches the farthest recesses
for ore in the blackest darkness.
⁴Far from where people dwell he cuts a shaft,
in places forgotten by the foot of man;
far from men he dangles and sways.
⁵The earth, from which food comes,
is transformed below as by fire;
⁶sapphires*a* come from its rocks,

a6 Or lapis lazuli; also in verse 16

and its dust contains nuggets of gold.
⁷No bird of prey knows that hidden path,
no falcon's eye has seen it.
⁸Proud beasts do not set foot on it,
and no lion prowls there.
⁹Man's hand assaults the flinty rock
and lays bare the roots of the mountains.
¹⁰He tunnels through the rock;
his eyes see all its treasures.
¹¹He searches*a* the sources of the rivers
and brings hidden things to light.

¹²"But where can wisdom be found?
Where does understanding dwell?
¹³Man does not comprehend its worth;
it cannot be found in the land of the
living.
¹⁴The deep says, 'It is not in me';
the sea says, 'It is not with me.'
¹⁵It cannot be bought with the finest gold,
nor can its price be weighed in silver.
¹⁶It cannot be bought with the gold of Ophir,
with precious onyx or sapphires.
¹⁷Neither gold nor crystal can compare with it,
nor can it be had for jewels of gold.
¹⁸Coral and jasper are not worthy of mention;
the price of wisdom is beyond rubies.
¹⁹The topaz of Cush cannot compare with it;
it cannot be bought with pure gold.

²⁰"Where then does wisdom come from?
Where does understanding dwell?
²¹It is hidden from the eyes of every living
thing,
concealed even from the birds of the air.
²²Destruction*b* and Death say,
'Only a rumor of it has reached our ears.'
²³God understands the way to it
and he alone knows where it dwells,
²⁴for he views the ends of the earth
and sees everything under the heavens.
²⁵When he established the force of the wind
and measured out the waters,
²⁶when he made a decree for the rain
and a path for the thunderstorm,
²⁷then he looked at wisdom and appraised it;
he confirmed it and tested it.
²⁸And he said to man,
'The fear of the Lord—that is wisdom,
and to shun evil is understanding.'"

29

Job continued his discourse:

²"How I long for the months gone by,
for the days when God watched over me,
³when his lamp shone upon my head
and by his light I walked through
darkness!
⁴Oh, for the days when I was in my prime,

when God's intimate friendship blessed
my house,
⁵when the Almighty was still with me
and my children were around me,
⁶when my path was drenched with cream
and the rock poured out for me streams
of olive oil.

⁷"When I went to the gate of the city
and took my seat in the public square,
⁸the young men saw me and stepped aside
and the old men rose to their feet;
⁹the chief men refrained from speaking
and covered their mouths with their
hands;
¹⁰the voices of the nobles were hushed,
and their tongues stuck to the roof of
their mouths.
¹¹Whoever heard me spoke well of me,
and those who saw me commended me,

29:11 The Good Old Days

Tenderly, Job reminisces about the "months gone by" (verse 2), before his trials began. Job could think of no reason why he might "deserve" such treatment—the point of the book of Job exactly. His recollections of life in those days refute his friends' accusations against him. He had shown concern for the poor and oppressed—a fact that must have increased his puzzlement over the unfair treatment he was receiving.

¹²because I rescued the poor who cried for
help,
and the fatherless who had none to assist
him.
¹³The man who was dying blessed me;
I made the widow's heart sing.
¹⁴I put on righteousness as my clothing;
justice was my robe and my turban.
¹⁵I was eyes to the blind
and feet to the lame.
¹⁶I was a father to the needy;
I took up the case of the stranger.
¹⁷I broke the fangs of the wicked
and snatched the victims from their teeth.

¹⁸"I thought, 'I will die in my own house,
my days as numerous as the grains of
sand.
¹⁹My roots will reach to the water,
and the dew will lie all night on my
branches.
²⁰My glory will remain fresh in me,
the bow ever new in my hand.'
²¹"Men listened to me expectantly,

a 11 Septuagint, Aquila and Vulgate; Hebrew *He dams up* *b 22* Hebrew *Abaddon*

waiting in silence for my counsel.
22After I had spoken, they spoke no more;
my words fell gently on their ears.
23They waited for me as for showers
and drank in my words as the spring rain.
24When I smiled at them, they scarcely
believed it;
the light of my face was precious to
them.*a*
25I chose the way for them and sat as their
chief;
I dwelt as a king among his troops;
I was like one who comforts mourners.

30 "But now they mock me,
men younger than I,
whose fathers I would have disdained
to put with my sheep dogs.
2Of what use was the strength of their hands
to me,
since their vigor had gone from them?
3Haggard from want and hunger,
they roamed*b* the parched land
in desolate wastelands at night.
4In the brush they gathered salt herbs,
and their food*c* was the root of the
broom tree.
5They were banished from their fellow men,
shouted at as if they were thieves.
6They were forced to live in the dry stream
beds,
among the rocks and in holes in the
ground.
7They brayed among the bushes
and huddled in the undergrowth.
8A base and nameless brood,
they were driven out of the land.

9"And now their sons mock me in song;
I have become a byword among them.
10They detest me and keep their distance;
they do not hesitate to spit in my face.
11Now that God has unstrung my bow and
afflicted me,
they throw off restraint in my presence.
12On my right the tribe*d* attacks;
they lay snares for my feet,
they build their siege ramps against me.
13They break up my road;
they succeed in destroying me—
without anyone's helping them.*e*
14They advance as through a gaping breach;
amid the ruins they come rolling in.
15Terrors overwhelm me;
my dignity is driven away as by the wind,
my safety vanishes like a cloud.

16"And now my life ebbs away;

days of suffering grip me.
17Night pierces my bones;
my gnawing pains never rest.
18In his great power ⌊God⌋ becomes like
clothing to me*f*;
he binds me like the neck of my garment.
19He throws me into the mud,
and I am reduced to dust and ashes.

20"I cry out to you, O God, but you do not
answer;
I stand up, but you merely look at me.
21You turn on me ruthlessly;
with the might of your hand you attack
me.
22You snatch me up and drive me before the
wind;
you toss me about in the storm.
23I know you will bring me down to death,
to the place appointed for all the living.

24"Surely no one lays a hand on a broken man
when he cries for help in his distress.
25Have I not wept for those in trouble?
Has not my soul grieved for the poor?
26Yet when I hoped for good, evil came;
when I looked for light, then came
darkness.
27The churning inside me never stops;
days of suffering confront me.
28I go about blackened, but not by the sun;
I stand up in the assembly and cry for
help.
29I have become a brother of jackals,
a companion of owls.
30My skin grows black and peels;
my body burns with fever.
31My harp is tuned to mourning,
and my flute to the sound of wailing.

31 "I made a covenant with my eyes
not to look lustfully at a girl.

31:1 Binding Oaths

*This chapter, Job's final line of defense, is
written in a form that had legal significance to
his hearers. Job was solemnly swearing his
innocence in response to a whole series of
accusations. He called down curses on himself
if he could be proved wrong. The oaths were
somewhat like our modern custom of swearing
on the Bible "to tell the truth, the whole truth
and nothing but the truth." Job's oaths
impressed his three friends and effectively
ended the debate. Then a new character, Elihu,
joined in.*

---

*a*24 The meaning of the Hebrew for this clause is uncertain.
the Hebrew for this word is uncertain.   *e*13 Or *me. / 'No one can help him,' ⌊they say⌋.*   *b*3 Or *gnawed*   *c*4 Or *fuel*   *d*12 The meaning of   *f*18 Hebrew; Septuagint
⌊God⌋ *grasps my clothing*

²For what is man's lot from God above,
his heritage from the Almighty on high?
³Is it not ruin for the wicked,
disaster for those who do wrong?
⁴Does he not see my ways
and count my every step?

⁵"If I have walked in falsehood
or my foot has hurried after deceit—
⁶let God weigh me in honest scales
and he will know that I am blameless—
⁷if my steps have turned from the path,
if my heart has been led by my eyes,
or if my hands have been defiled,
⁸then may others eat what I have sown,
and may my crops be uprooted.

⁹"If my heart has been enticed by a woman,
or if I have lurked at my neighbor's door,
¹⁰then may my wife grind another man's grain,
and may other men sleep with her.
¹¹For that would have been shameful,
a sin to be judged.
¹²It is a fire that burns to Destruction^a;
it would have uprooted my harvest.
¹³"If I have denied justice to my menservants
and maidservants
when they had a grievance against me,
¹⁴what will I do when God confronts me?
What will I answer when called to
account?
¹⁵Did not he who made me in the womb
make them?
Did not the same one form us both
within our mothers?

¹⁶"If I have denied the desires of the poor
or let the eyes of the widow grow weary,
¹⁷if I have kept my bread to myself,
not sharing it with the fatherless—
¹⁸but from my youth I reared him as would a
father,
and from my birth I guided the widow—
¹⁹if I have seen anyone perishing for lack of
clothing,
or a needy man without a garment,

31:16 A Habit of Trust

*This chapter gives insights into Job's life of
spiritual discipline. He had developed the habit
of obeying God. Now, with all the props
knocked out, he still turned to God for strength,
even though God seemed utterly absent. It was
as if he had a resource bank of trust in God:
The trust he had accumulated in more
comfortable times helped him survive his time
of hardship.*

²⁰and his heart did not bless me
for warming him with the fleece from my
sheep,
²¹if I have raised my hand against the
fatherless,
knowing that I had influence in court,
²²then let my arm fall from the shoulder,
let it be broken off at the joint.
²³For I dreaded destruction from God,
and for fear of his splendor I could not
do such things.

²⁴"If I have put my trust in gold
or said to pure gold, 'You are my
security,'
²⁵if I have rejoiced over my great wealth,
the fortune my hands had gained,
²⁶if I have regarded the sun in its radiance
or the moon moving in splendor,
²⁷so that my heart was secretly enticed
and my hand offered them a kiss of
homage,
²⁸then these also would be sins to be judged,
for I would have been unfaithful to God
on high.

²⁹"If I have rejoiced at my enemy's misfortune
or gloated over the trouble that came to
him—
³⁰I have not allowed my mouth to sin
by invoking a curse against his life—
³¹if the men of my household have never said,
'Who has not had his fill of Job's
meat?'—
³²but no stranger had to spend the night in
the street,
for my door was always open to the
traveler—
³³if I have concealed my sin as men do,^{b}
by hiding my guilt in my heart
³⁴because I so feared the crowd
and so dreaded the contempt of the clans
that I kept silent and would not go
outside

³⁵("Oh, that I had someone to hear me!
I sign now my defense—let the Almighty
answer me;
let my accuser put his indictment in
writing.
³⁶Surely I would wear it on my shoulder,
I would put it on like a crown.
³⁷I would give him an account of my every
step;
like a prince I would approach him.)—

³⁸"if my land cries out against me
and all its furrows are wet with tears,

---

^{a}12 Hebrew *Abaddon* ^{b}33 Or *as Adam did*

³⁹if I have devoured its yield without payment
    or broken the spirit of its tenants,
⁴⁰then let briers come up instead of wheat
    and weeds instead of barley."

The words of Job are ended.

Elihu

32 So these three men stopped answering Job,
    because he was righteous in his own eyes.
²But Elihu son of Barakel the Buzite, of the family
of Ram, became very angry with Job for justifying himself rather than God. ³He was also angry
with the three friends, because they had found no
way to refute Job, and yet had condemned him.ᵃ
⁴Now Elihu had waited before speaking to Job
because they were older than he. ⁵But when he
saw that the three men had nothing more to say,
his anger was aroused.

⁶So Elihu son of Barakel the Buzite said:

"I am young in years,
    and you are old;
that is why I was fearful,
    not daring to tell you what I know.
⁷I thought, 'Age should speak;
    advanced years should teach wisdom.'
⁸But it is the spiritᵇ in a man,
    the breath of the Almighty, that gives him
        understanding.
⁹It is not only the oldᶜ who are wise,
    not only the aged who understand what is
        right.

¹⁰"Therefore I say: Listen to me;
    I too will tell you what I know.
¹¹I waited while you spoke,
    I listened to your reasoning;
while you were searching for words,
¹²   I gave you my full attention.
But not one of you has proved Job wrong;
    none of you has answered his arguments.
¹³Do not say, 'We have found wisdom;
    let God refute him, not man.'
¹⁴But Job has not marshaled his words against
        me,
    and I will not answer him with your
        arguments.

ᵃ3 Masoretic Text; an ancient Hebrew scribal tradition *Job, and so had condemned God*   ᵇ8 Or *Spirit*; also in verse 18
ᶜ9 Or *many*; or *great*

A Silent Friend Decides to Speak Up
Elihu, out of nowhere, proposes new ideas about suffering

> "Not one of you has proved Job wrong; none of you has answered his arguments." 32:12

UP TO THIS POINT IN Job, the action has revolved around Job and his three friends. The debate among them, growing ever more heated, finally breaks off. They have reached a standoff. Job will not admit to any sin deserving of terrible punishment, and his three friends will not back down from their ideas about suffering.

Suddenly, a new voice is heard. Elihu, a young man, has been listening in silence all this time. He can restrain himself no longer. He flares up, first at Job for being so self-righteous and then at the three friends for not coming up with an answer to Job's questions. He refutes all four of them, turning their own words against them.

Is Elihu Right?

Elihu is shocked at Job's vigorous self-defense. Surely God cannot be unjust, he insists. Submit to the pain, even if you don't understand it. Don't blame God; praise him. God has shown too much of his wisdom and perfection, especially in nature, for anyone to doubt him.

Elihu offers a new explanation for Job's pain. Perhaps, he suggests, God gave suffering to Job not as punishment but as a purifying influence. God can use suffering to improve a person, if it is received in the right spirit.

Where did Elihu come from? Who is he? Are his theories right? Mystery surrounds the man. His speeches stand alone, and no one responds to them. As a result, the book of Job gives no clue on whether Elihu expressed a worthy point of view.

Some readers believe Elihu forms a bridge between the flawed theories of Job's three friends and God's own speech. Perhaps his speeches prepare the way for God's. Others see him as repeating the same fine-sounding, but not-quite-true, advice of Job's three friends.

When God does make an entrance, he dismisses Job's friends and has some mild criticism for Job. But he ignores Elihu entirely. Elihu remains a mysterious figure.

Life Questions: Do Elihu's arguments sound familiar? What do you think of friends who have similar thoughts about others who suffer?

¹⁵"They are dismayed and have no more to
say;
    words have failed them.
¹⁶Must I wait, now that they are silent,
    now that they stand there with no reply?
¹⁷I too will have my say;
    I too will tell what I know.
¹⁸For I am full of words,
    and the spirit within me compels me;
¹⁹inside I am like bottled-up wine,
    like new wineskins ready to burst.
²⁰I must speak and find relief;
    I must open my lips and reply.
²¹I will show partiality to no one,
    nor will I flatter any man;
²²for if I were skilled in flattery,
    my Maker would soon take me away.

33

    "But now, Job, listen to my words;
    pay attention to everything I say.
²I am about to open my mouth;
    my words are on the tip of my tongue.
³My words come from an upright heart;
    my lips sincerely speak what I know.
⁴The Spirit of God has made me;
    the breath of the Almighty gives me life.
⁵Answer me then, if you can;
    prepare yourself and confront me.
⁶I am just like you before God;
    I too have been taken from clay.
⁷No fear of me should alarm you,
    nor should my hand be heavy upon you.

⁸"But you have said in my hearing—
    I heard the very words—
⁹'I am pure and without sin;
    I am clean and free from guilt.
¹⁰Yet God has found fault with me;
    he considers me his enemy.
¹¹He fastens my feet in shackles;
    he keeps close watch on all my paths.'

¹²"But I tell you, in this you are not right,
    for God is greater than man.
¹³Why do you complain to him
    that he answers none of man's words[a]?
¹⁴For God does speak—now one way, now
    another—
    though man may not perceive it.
¹⁵In a dream, in a vision of the night,
    when deep sleep falls on men
    as they slumber in their beds,
¹⁶he may speak in their ears
    and terrify them with warnings,
¹⁷to turn man from wrongdoing
    and keep him from pride,
¹⁸to preserve his soul from the pit,[b]

his life from perishing by the sword.[c]
¹⁹Or a man may be chastened on a bed of
pain
    with constant distress in his bones,

33:19 Kinder, Gentler Friend

*Evidently, Elihu had sat in silence throughout
the discussions to this point (in deference to the
other speakers' age, as he explains). That fact
alone shows his calmer nature: he refused to
jump into very heated arguments. Although
Elihu introduces some new ideas, he also
follows the general line of reasoning—"You're
being punished for your sins, Job" (see verses
17–22)—that God corrects in the end.*

²⁰so that his very being finds food repulsive
    and his soul loathes the choicest meal.
²¹His flesh wastes away to nothing,
    and his bones, once hidden, now stick
    out.
²²His soul draws near to the pit,[d]
    and his life to the messengers of death.[e]

²³"Yet if there is an angel on his side
    as a mediator, one out of a thousand,
    to tell a man what is right for him,
²⁴to be gracious to him and say,
    'Spare him from going down to the pit[f];
    I have found a ransom for him'—
²⁵then his flesh is renewed like a child's;
    it is restored as in the days of his youth.
²⁶He prays to God and finds favor with him,
    he sees God's face and shouts for joy;
    he is restored by God to his righteous
    state.
²⁷Then he comes to men and says,
    'I sinned, and perverted what was right,
    but I did not get what I deserved.
²⁸He redeemed my soul from going down to
    the pit,[g]
    and I will live to enjoy the light.'

²⁹"God does all these things to a man—
    twice, even three times—
³⁰to turn back his soul from the pit,[h]
    that the light of life may shine on him.

³¹"Pay attention, Job, and listen to me;
    be silent, and I will speak.
³²If you have anything to say, answer me;
    speak up, for I want you to be cleared.
³³But if not, then listen to me;
    be silent, and I will teach you wisdom."

---

[a]13 Or *that he does not answer for any of his actions*   [b]18 Or *preserve him from the grave*   [c]18 Or *from crossing
the River*   [d]22 Or *He draws near to the grave*   [e]22 Or *to the dead*   [f]24 Or *grave*   [g]28 Or *redeemed me
from going down to the grave*   [h]30 Or *turn him back from the grave*

34

Then Elihu said:

2"Hear my words, you wise men;
 listen to me, you men of learning.
3For the ear tests words
 as the tongue tastes food.

33:30 Pain as a Warning

Elihu did not defend Job as innocent. But his arguments shifted the emphasis of suffering from punishment to warning. Perhaps, he suggested, God allows a man to suffer in order "to turn back his soul from the pit." Primarily, however, Elihu defended God's actions. "It is unthinkable that God would do wrong, that the Almighty would pervert justice" (34:12).

4Let us discern for ourselves what is right;
 let us learn together what is good.

5"Job says, 'I am innocent,
 but God denies me justice.
6Although I am right,
 I am considered a liar;
although I am guiltless,
 his arrow inflicts an incurable wound.'
7What man is like Job,
 who drinks scorn like water?
8He keeps company with evildoers;
 he associates with wicked men.
9For he says, 'It profits a man nothing
 when he tries to please God.'

10"So listen to me, you men of understanding.
 Far be it from God to do evil,
 from the Almighty to do wrong.
11He repays a man for what he has done;
 he brings upon him what his conduct
  deserves.
12It is unthinkable that God would do wrong,
 that the Almighty would pervert justice.
13Who appointed him over the earth?
 Who put him in charge of the whole
  world?
14If it were his intention
 and he withdrew his spirit*a* and breath,
15all mankind would perish together
 and man would return to the dust.

16"If you have understanding, hear this;
 listen to what I say.
17Can he who hates justice govern?
 Will you condemn the just and mighty
  One?
18Is he not the One who says to kings, 'You
  are worthless,'
 and to nobles, 'You are wicked,'

19who shows no partiality to princes
 and does not favor the rich over the poor,
 for they are all the work of his hands?
20They die in an instant, in the middle of the
  night;
 the people are shaken and they pass away;
 the mighty are removed without human
  hand.

21"His eyes are on the ways of men;
 he sees their every step.
22There is no dark place, no deep shadow,
 where evildoers can hide.
23God has no need to examine men further,
 that they should come before him for
  judgment.
24Without inquiry he shatters the mighty
 and sets up others in their place.
25Because he takes note of their deeds,
 he overthrows them in the night and they
  are crushed.
26He punishes them for their wickedness
 where everyone can see them,
27because they turned from following him
 and had no regard for any of his ways.
28They caused the cry of the poor to come
  before him,
 so that he heard the cry of the needy.
29But if he remains silent, who can condemn
  him?
 If he hides his face, who can see him?
 Yet he is over man and nation alike,
30 to keep a godless man from ruling,
 from laying snares for the people.

31"Suppose a man says to God,
 'I am guilty but will offend no more.
32Teach me what I cannot see;
 if I have done wrong, I will not do so
  again.'
33Should God then reward you on your terms,
 when you refuse to repent?
 You must decide, not I;
 so tell me what you know.

34"Men of understanding declare,
 wise men who hear me say to me,
35'Job speaks without knowledge;
 his words lack insight.'
36Oh, that Job might be tested to the utmost
 for answering like a wicked man!
37To his sin he adds rebellion;
 scornfully he claps his hands among us
 and multiplies his words against God."

35

Then Elihu said:

2"Do you think this is just?
 You say, 'I will be cleared by God.*b*'

---

a 14 Or *Spirit*   *b 2* Or *My righteousness is more than God's*

³Yet you ask him, 'What profit is it to me,ᵃ
  and what do I gain by not sinning?'

⁴"I would like to reply to you
  and to your friends with you.
⁵Look up at the heavens and see;
  gaze at the clouds so high above you.
⁶If you sin, how does that affect him?
  If your sins are many, what does that do
    to him?
⁷If you are righteous, what do you give to
    him,
  or what does he receive from your hand?
⁸Your wickedness affects only a man like
    yourself,
  and your righteousness only the sons of
    men.

⁹"Men cry out under a load of oppression;
  they plead for relief from the arm of the
    powerful.
¹⁰But no one says, 'Where is God my Maker,
  who gives songs in the night,
¹¹who teaches more to us than toᵇ the beasts
    of the earth
  and makes us wiser thanᶜ the birds of
    the air?'
¹²He does not answer when men cry out
  because of the arrogance of the wicked.
¹³Indeed, God does not listen to their empty
    plea;
  the Almighty pays no attention to it.
¹⁴How much less, then, will he listen
  when you say that you do not see him,
    that your case is before him
    and you must wait for him,

35:14 Is God Really Listening?

Readers differ on how true Elihu's words were. But in this chapter he seems to say Job had no right to argue before God or to ask for a personal appearance. Why should God be concerned about one man's wickedness or righteousness? he asks (verse 8). The opening chapters of the book, however, revealed how much hung on Job's responses. And ultimately God did step in and reveal himself. In fact, he made an entrance just as Elihu was explaining why God would not appear.

¹⁵and further, that his anger never punishes
  and he does not take the least notice of
    wickedness.ᵈ
¹⁶So Job opens his mouth with empty talk;
  without knowledge he multiplies words."

36 Elihu continued:

²"Bear with me a little longer and I will show
    you
  that there is more to be said in God's
    behalf.
³I get my knowledge from afar;
  I will ascribe justice to my Maker.
⁴Be assured that my words are not false;
  one perfect in knowledge is with you.

⁵"God is mighty, but does not despise men;
  he is mighty, and firm in his purpose.
⁶He does not keep the wicked alive
  but gives the afflicted their rights.
⁷He does not take his eyes off the righteous;
  he enthrones them with kings
  and exalts them forever.
⁸But if men are bound in chains,
  held fast by cords of affliction,
⁹he tells them what they have done—
  that they have sinned arrogantly.
¹⁰He makes them listen to correction
  and commands them to repent of their
    evil.
¹¹If they obey and serve him,
  they will spend the rest of their days in
    prosperity
  and their years in contentment.
¹²But if they do not listen,
  they will perish by the swordᵉ
  and die without knowledge.

¹³"The godless in heart harbor resentment;
  even when he fetters them, they do not
    cry for help.
¹⁴They die in their youth,
  among male prostitutes of the shrines.
¹⁵But those who suffer he delivers in their
    suffering;
  he speaks to them in their affliction.

¹⁶"He is wooing you from the jaws of distress
  to a spacious place free from restriction,
  to the comfort of your table laden with
    choice food.
¹⁷But now you are laden with the judgment
    due the wicked;
  judgment and justice have taken hold of
    you.
¹⁸Be careful that no one entices you by riches;
  do not let a large bribe turn you aside.
¹⁹Would your wealth
  or even all your mighty efforts
  sustain you so you would not be in
    distress?
²⁰Do not long for the night,
  to drag people away from their homes.ᶠ

ᵃ3 Or *you*   ᵇ11 Or *teaches us by* of the Hebrew for this word is uncertain.   ᶜ11 Or *us wise by*   ᵈ15 Symmachus, Theodotion and Vulgate; the meaning of the Hebrew for this word is uncertain. for verses 18-20 is uncertain.   ᵉ12 Or *will cross the River*   ᶠ20 The meaning of the Hebrew

²¹Beware of turning to evil,
　　which you seem to prefer to affliction.

²²"God is exalted in his power.
　　Who is a teacher like him?
²³Who has prescribed his ways for him,
　　or said to him, 'You have done wrong'?
²⁴Remember to extol his work,
　　which men have praised in song.
²⁵All mankind has seen it;
　　men gaze on it from afar.
²⁶How great is God—beyond our
　　understanding!
　　The number of his years is past finding
　　out.

²⁷"He draws up the drops of water,
　　which distill as rain to the streams*ᵃ*;
²⁸the clouds pour down their moisture
　　and abundant showers fall on mankind.
²⁹Who can understand how he spreads out
　　the clouds,
　　how he thunders from his pavilion?
³⁰See how he scatters his lightning about
　　him,
　　bathing the depths of the sea.
³¹This is the way he governs*ᵇ* the nations
　　and provides food in abundance.
³²He fills his hands with lightning
　　and commands it to strike its mark.
³³His thunder announces the coming storm;

ᵃ27 Or *distill from the mist as rain*　　*ᵇ31* Or *nourishes*

What Job Teaches about Suffering
The problem of pain and the book of Job

> "But those who suffer he delivers in their suffering; he speaks to them in their affliction."
> 36:15

　　"WHY ME?" ALMOST EVERYONE ASKS this question when terrible suffering strikes. An automobile accident, a diagnosis of cancer, a long-term disease like arthritis—each of these raises intense questions about why God allows pain.
　　Over the centuries, suffering Christians have gained help and comfort from studying the book of Job. The book gives no compact theory of why good people suffer. Nevertheless, the following insights into the problem of suffering do come out of the book of Job.

Principles from Job

　　1. *Some suffering is caused by Satan.* Chapters 1 and 2 make the important distinction that God did not cause Job's problems. He allowed them, but Satan actually caused the pain.
　　2. *God is all-powerful and good.* Nowhere does the book of Job suggest that God lacks power or goodness. Some people say that God is weak and powerless to prevent human suffering. Others, called deists, assume he runs the world at a distance, without personal involvement. But in Job, God's power is never questioned; only his fairness. And in his final summation speech, God used splendid illustrations from nature to prove his power.
　　3. *Suffering doesn't always come as a result of sin.* The Bible supports the general principle that "a man reaps what he sows," even in this life (Galatians 6:7; see Psalms 1:3; 37:25). But other people have no right to apply that *general* principle to a *particular* person. Job's friends tried with all their persuasive power. However, when God rendered the final verdict, he said simply, "You have not spoken of me what is right, as my servant Job has" (42:7). The Old Testament includes other examples of people who suffered through no fault of their own, such as Abel (Genesis 4) and Uriah (2 Samuel 11). And Jesus spoke out against the notion that suffering implies sin (see John 9:1–5 and Luke 13:1–5).
　　4. *God will reward and punish fairly in a final judgment after death.* Job's friends, along with most Old Testament folk, did not have a clearly formed belief in an afterlife. Therefore, they expected that God's fairness—his approval or disapproval of people—had to be shown in this life. Other parts of the Bible teach that God will reward and punish fairly after death.
　　5. *God does not condemn doubt and despair.* God did not condemn Job's anguished responses, only his ignorance. Job did not take his pain meekly; he cried out in anguish to God. His strong remarks scandalized his friends (see, for example, 15:1–16), but not God. Ironically, despite his bitter speeches, Job earned God's praise, while his pious friends were soundly rebuked.
　　6. *No one person has all the facts about suffering.* Neither Job nor his friends had enough facts. Job concluded God was unfair, treating him like an enemy. His friends maintained that God opposed Job because of his sin. All of them later learned they had been viewing the situation from a very limited

even the cattle make known its approach.*a*

37 "At this my heart pounds
and leaps from its place.
²Listen! Listen to the roar of his voice,
to the rumbling that comes from his mouth.
³He unleashes his lightning beneath the whole heaven
and sends it to the ends of the earth.
⁴After that comes the sound of his roar;
he thunders with his majestic voice.
When his voice resounds,
he holds nothing back.
⁵God's voice thunders in marvelous ways;
he does great things beyond our understanding.
⁶He says to the snow, 'Fall on the earth,'
and to the rain shower, 'Be a mighty downpour.'
⁷So that all men he has made may know his work,
he stops every man from his labor.*b*
⁸The animals take cover;
they remain in their dens.
⁹The tempest comes out from its chamber,

a33 Or announces his coming— / the One zealous against evil
c13 Or to favor them

the cold from the driving winds.
¹⁰The breath of God produces ice,
and the broad waters become frozen.
¹¹He loads the clouds with moisture;
he scatters his lightning through them.

37:7 The Message of a Blizzard

Anyone who has lived in a northern city can identify with Elihu's comment about a snowstorm. A blizzard "stops every man from his labor," as schools, businesses, and buses shut down. It's a reminder, says Elihu, of God's undeniable power.

¹²At his direction they swirl around
over the face of the whole earth
to do whatever he commands them.
¹³He brings the clouds to punish men,
or to water his earth*c* and show his love.

¹⁴"Listen to this, Job;
stop and consider God's wonders.
¹⁵Do you know how God controls the clouds
and makes his lightning flash?
¹⁶Do you know how the clouds hang poised,

b7 Or / he fills all men with fear by his power

perspective, blind to the real struggle being waged in heaven.

7. *God is never totally silent.* Elihu made that point convincingly, reminding Job of dreams, visions, past blessings, even the daily works of God in nature (chapter 33). God also appealed to nature as giving evidence of his wisdom and power. Although he may seem silent, some evidence of him can be found. One contemporary author expressed that truth this way, "Remember in the darkness what you have learned in the light."

8. *Well-intentioned advice can sometimes do more harm than good.* Job's friends were classic examples of people who let their pride and sense of being right interfere with their compassion. They repeated pious phrases and argued theology with Job. His response: "If only you would be altogether silent! For you, that would be wisdom" (13:5).

9. *God asks for faith.* God refocused the central issue from the *cause* of Job's suffering to his *response.* Mysteriously, God never gave an explanation for the problem of suffering. He did not even inform Job of the reason behind it: the contest recorded in chapters 1 and 2. He concentrated instead on Job's response. The real issue at stake was Job's faith—whether he would continue to trust God even when everything went wrong.

10. *Suffering can be used for a higher good.* In Job's case, God used a time of very great pain to win an important, even cosmic, victory over Satan. Looking backward, but only looking backward, we can see the "advantage" Job gained by continuing to trust God. Job is often cited as an Old Testament picture of Jesus Christ, who lived a perfectly innocent life but endured great pain and death. The terrible event of Christ's death was also transformed into a great victory.

Thousands of years later, Job's questions have not gone away. People who suffer still find themselves borrowing Job's own words as they cry out against God's seeming lack of concern. But Job affirms that God is not deaf to our cries and is in control of this world no matter how it looks. God did not answer all Job's questions, but his very appearance caused Job's doubts to melt away. Job learned that God cared about him and that God rules the world. It was enough.

Life Questions: Do these principles from Job match up with what you have heard about suffering from other Christians?

those wonders of him who is perfect in
knowledge?
17You who swelter in your clothes
when the land lies hushed under the south
wind,
18can you join him in spreading out the skies,
hard as a mirror of cast bronze?

19"Tell us what we should say to him;
we cannot draw up our case because of
our darkness.
20Should he be told that I want to speak?
Would any man ask to be swallowed up?
21Now no one can look at the sun,
bright as it is in the skies
after the wind has swept them clean.
22Out of the north he comes in golden
splendor;
God comes in awesome majesty.
23The Almighty is beyond our reach and
exalted in power;
in his justice and great righteousness, he
does not oppress.
24Therefore, men revere him,
for does he not have regard for all the
wise in heart?ᵃ"

The LORD Speaks

38 Then the LORD answered Job out of the
storm. He said:

2"Who is this that darkens my counsel
with words without knowledge?
3Brace yourself like a man;
I will question you,
and you shall answer me.

4"Where were you when I laid the earth's
foundation?
Tell me, if you understand.
5Who marked off its dimensions? Surely you
know!
Who stretched a measuring line across it?
6On what were its footings set,
or who laid its cornerstone—
7while the morning stars sang together
and all the angelsᵇ shouted for joy?

8"Who shut up the sea behind doors
when it burst forth from the womb,
9when I made the clouds its garment
and wrapped it in thick darkness,
10when I fixed limits for it
and set its doors and bars in place,
11when I said, 'This far you may come and no
farther;
here is where your proud waves halt'?

12"Have you ever given orders to the morning,
or shown the dawn its place,
13that it might take the earth by the edges
and shake the wicked out of it?
14The earth takes shape like clay under a seal;
its features stand out like those of a
garment.
15The wicked are denied their light,
and their upraised arm is broken.

16"Have you journeyed to the springs of the
sea
or walked in the recesses of the deep?
17Have the gates of death been shown to you?
Have you seen the gates of the shadow of
deathᶜ?
18Have you comprehended the vast expanses
of the earth?
Tell me, if you know all this.

19"What is the way to the abode of light?
And where does darkness reside?
20Can you take them to their places?
Do you know the paths to their dwellings?
21Surely you know, for you were already born!
You have lived so many years!

38:21 God Pulls Out the Stops

*God is not above using sarcasm, as this barb
directed at Job clearly shows. His entire speech
stresses the vast difference between a God of
all creation and one puny man like Job. "Do
you have an arm like God's?" he asks (40:9).*

22"Have you entered the storehouses of the
snow
or seen the storehouses of the hail,
23which I reserve for times of trouble,
for days of war and battle?
24What is the way to the place where the
lightning is dispersed,
or the place where the east winds are
scattered over the earth?
25Who cuts a channel for the torrents of rain,
and a path for the thunderstorm,
26to water a land where no man lives,
a desert with no one in it,
27to satisfy a desolate wasteland
and make it sprout with grass?
28Does the rain have a father?
Who fathers the drops of dew?
29From whose womb comes the ice?
Who gives birth to the frost from the
heavens
30when the waters become hard as stone,
when the surface of the deep is frozen?
31"Can you bind the beautifulᵈ Pleiades?

ᵃ24 Or for he does not have regard for any who think they are wise.
deep shadows   ᵈ31 Or the twinkling; or the chains of the
ᵇ7 Hebrew the sons of God   ᶜ17 Or gates of

Can you loose the cords of Orion?
³²Can you bring forth the constellations in
their seasons*a*
or lead out the Bear*b* with its cubs?
³³Do you know the laws of the heavens?
Can you set up ⌊God's*c*⌋ dominion over
the earth?

³⁴"Can you raise your voice to the clouds

and cover yourself with a flood of water?
³⁵Do you send the lightning bolts on their
way?
Do they report to you, 'Here we are'?
³⁶Who endowed the heart*d* with wisdom
or gave understanding to the mind*d*?
³⁷Who has the wisdom to count the
clouds?

---

a32 Or the morning star in its season   *b32* Or out Leo
for this word is uncertain.

c33 Or his; or their   *d36* The meaning of the Hebrew

God Speaks to Job
At last, Job gets what he demanded

IN THE SPAN OF A few days Job experienced more tragedy
than most people encounter in a lifetime. He scratched himself with
shards of pottery and mourned the day he was born. He could not even
suffer with dignity; he had to endure his wife's taunts and his friends' ram-
blings. Nothing anyone said helped him.

Through it all, Job steadfastly refused to turn his back on God. He had only
one request. He wanted to hear from God in person. He wanted an explanation
straight from the Source.

At last Job got his wish. God answered Job with a speech often quoted for its majesty and beauty.
In a touch of irony, God made his entrance just as Elihu was explaining why Job could not expect a
direct answer from him.

> "Will the one who
> contends with the
> Almighty correct
> him? Let him who
> accuses God answer
> him!" 40:2

Not the Expected Message

Job had saved up a long list of questions, but it was God who asked the questions, not Job. "Brace
yourself like a man," he began. "I will question you, and you shall answer me."

Author Frederick Buechner sums up what follows: "God doesn't explain. He explodes. He asks Job
who he thinks he is anyway. He says that to try to explain the kind of things Job wants explained
would be like trying to explain Einstein to a little-neck clam." God did not need Job's or anyone else's
advice on how to run the world.

God's reply resembled a nature lesson more than an explanation of the problem of suffering. He
pointed out, one by one, all the creations that gave him greatest pride. In short, God asked Job, "Do
you want to try running the universe for a while? Go ahead, try designing an ostrich, or a mountain
goat, or even a snowflake."

Astonishingly, the question of suffering itself did not even come up. Yet somehow Job seemed
satisfied—humiliated, actually. "Surely I spoke of things I did not understand," he confessed, "things too
wonderful for me to know" (42:3).

Job Passes the Test

Job had endured his terrible sufferings in the dark. When he needed God most, God had stayed
silent. And that was exactly the point of the contest begun at the beginning of the book, back in chapter 1. Satan had promised God that Job would "surely curse you to your face." He lost the challenge.
Despite everything that happened, Job did not curse God. He clung to his belief in a just God, even
when everything in his experience seemed to contradict it.

God had some words of correction for Job. No one, not Job and especially not his friends, had the
evidence needed to make judgments about how he runs the world. But mainly, God had praise for Job.
He called him "my servant," and, in an ironic twist, told the three friends to go to Job and ask for his
mercy (42:7–8). Much later, in the book of Ezekiel (14:14), God included Job in a list of the finest
human examples of righteousness.

The book of Job ends on a note of surprise. Job's friends, who had spouted all the right pieties
and clichés, ask for forgiveness. Job, who had raged and cried out, is given twice as much as he ever
had before. "And so he died, old and full of years" (42:17).

Life Questions: In Job's place, what kind of answer would you have wanted from God? Does God's
reply to Job surprise you?

Who can tip over the water jars of the
heavens
³⁸when the dust becomes hard
and the clods of earth stick together?

³⁹"Do you hunt the prey for the lioness
and satisfy the hunger of the lions
⁴⁰when they crouch in their dens
or lie in wait in a thicket?
⁴¹Who provides food for the raven
when its young cry out to God
and wander about for lack of food?

39 "Do you know when the mountain goats
give birth?
Do you watch when the doe bears her
fawn?
²Do you count the months till they bear?
Do you know the time they give birth?
³They crouch down and bring forth their
young;
their labor pains are ended.
⁴Their young thrive and grow strong in the
wilds;
they leave and do not return.

⁵"Who let the wild donkey go free?
Who untied his ropes?
⁶I gave him the wasteland as his home,
the salt flats as his habitat.
⁷He laughs at the commotion in the town;
he does not hear a driver's shout.
⁸He ranges the hills for his pasture
and searches for any green thing.

⁹"Will the wild ox consent to serve you?
Will he stay by your manger at night?

39:9 The Wildness of Animals

*God seems to take special delight in animals
with a streak of wildness: mountain goats,
lions, wild donkeys, hawks, wild oxen. They
serve as reminders that people are not as fully
in control of the world as they might think.*

¹⁰Can you hold him to the furrow with a
harness?
Will he till the valleys behind you?
¹¹Will you rely on him for his great strength?
Will you leave your heavy work to him?
¹²Can you trust him to bring in your grain
and gather it to your threshing floor?

¹³"The wings of the ostrich flap joyfully,
but they cannot compare with the pinions
and feathers of the stork.
¹⁴She lays her eggs on the ground
and lets them warm in the sand,
¹⁵unmindful that a foot may crush them,
that some wild animal may trample them.

¹⁶She treats her young harshly, as if they were
not hers;
she cares not that her labor was in vain,
¹⁷for God did not endow her with wisdom
or give her a share of good sense.
¹⁸Yet when she spreads her feathers to run,
she laughs at horse and rider.

¹⁹"Do you give the horse his strength
or clothe his neck with a flowing mane?
²⁰Do you make him leap like a locust,
striking terror with his proud snorting?
²¹He paws fiercely, rejoicing in his strength,
and charges into the fray.
²²He laughs at fear, afraid of nothing;
he does not shy away from the sword.
²³The quiver rattles against his side,
along with the flashing spear and lance.
²⁴In frenzied excitement he eats up the
ground;
he cannot stand still when the trumpet
sounds.
²⁵At the blast of the trumpet he snorts, 'Aha!'
He catches the scent of battle from afar,
the shout of commanders and the battle
cry.

²⁶"Does the hawk take flight by your wisdom
and spread his wings toward the south?
²⁷Does the eagle soar at your command
and build his nest on high?
²⁸He dwells on a cliff and stays there at night;
a rocky crag is his stronghold.
²⁹From there he seeks out his food;
his eyes detect it from afar.
³⁰His young ones feast on blood,
and where the slain are, there is he."

40 The LORD said to Job:

²"Will the one who contends with the
Almighty correct him?
Let him who accuses God answer him!"

³Then Job answered the LORD:

⁴"I am unworthy—how can I reply to you?
I put my hand over my mouth.
⁵I spoke once, but I have no answer—
twice, but I will say no more."

⁶Then the LORD spoke to Job out of the storm:

⁷"Brace yourself like a man;
I will question you,
and you shall answer me.

⁸"Would you discredit my justice?
Would you condemn me to justify
yourself?
⁹Do you have an arm like God's,
and can your voice thunder like his?
¹⁰Then adorn yourself with glory and splendor,
and clothe yourself in honor and majesty.

[11]Unleash the fury of your wrath,
    look at every proud man and bring him
        low,
[12]look at every proud man and humble him,
    crush the wicked where they stand.
[13]Bury them all in the dust together;
    shroud their faces in the grave.
[14]Then I myself will admit to you
    that your own right hand can save you.

[15]"Look at the behemoth,[a]
    which I made along with you
    and which feeds on grass like an ox.

40:15 Behemoth and Leviathan?

No one is quite sure what is meant by these two words, so the English Bible leaves them untranslated. The behemoth resembles a hippopotamus or elephant. The leviathan (41:1) has some features of a crocodile and some of a dragon. In other places, the Bible refers to the leviathan as either a whale-like creature (Psalm 104:26) or a serpent or monster of the sea (Isaiah 27:1). God used the leviathan as a symbol of something powerful and uncontrollable. Job got the message: If you can't take on one of God's fearsome creatures, don't attempt to take on God.

[16]What strength he has in his loins,
    what power in the muscles of his belly!
[17]His tail[b] sways like a cedar;
    the sinews of his thighs are close-knit.
[18]His bones are tubes of bronze,
    his limbs like rods of iron.
[19]He ranks first among the works of God,
    yet his Maker can approach him with his
        sword.
[20]The hills bring him their produce,
    and all the wild animals play nearby.
[21]Under the lotus plants he lies,
    hidden among the reeds in the marsh.
[22]The lotuses conceal him in their shadow;
    the poplars by the stream surround him.
[23]When the river rages, he is not alarmed;
    he is secure, though the Jordan should
        surge against his mouth.
[24]Can anyone capture him by the eyes,[c]
    or trap him and pierce his nose?

41 "Can you pull in the leviathan[d] with a
        fishhook
    or tie down his tongue with a rope?
[2]Can you put a cord through his nose
    or pierce his jaw with a hook?
[3]Will he keep begging you for mercy?
    Will he speak to you with gentle words?

[4]Will he make an agreement with you
    for you to take him as your slave for life?
[5]Can you make a pet of him like a bird
    or put him on a leash for your girls?
[6]Will traders barter for him?
    Will they divide him up among the
        merchants?
[7]Can you fill his hide with harpoons
    or his head with fishing spears?
[8]If you lay a hand on him,
    you will remember the struggle and never
        do it again!
[9]Any hope of subduing him is false;
    the mere sight of him is overpowering.
[10]No one is fierce enough to rouse him.
    Who then is able to stand against me?
[11]Who has a claim against me that I must pay?
    Everything under heaven belongs to me.

[12]"I will not fail to speak of his limbs,
    his strength and his graceful form.
[13]Who can strip off his outer coat?
    Who would approach him with a bridle?
[14]Who dares open the doors of his mouth,
    ringed about with his fearsome teeth?
[15]His back has[e] rows of shields
    tightly sealed together;
[16]each is so close to the next
    that no air can pass between.
[17]They are joined fast to one another;
    they cling together and cannot be parted.
[18]His snorting throws out flashes of light;
    his eyes are like the rays of dawn.
[19]Firebrands stream from his mouth;
    sparks of fire shoot out.
[20]Smoke pours from his nostrils
    as from a boiling pot over a fire of reeds.
[21]His breath sets coals ablaze,
    and flames dart from his mouth.
[22]Strength resides in his neck;
    dismay goes before him.
[23]The folds of his flesh are tightly joined;
    they are firm and immovable.
[24]His chest is hard as rock,
    hard as a lower millstone.
[25]When he rises up, the mighty are terrified;
    they retreat before his thrashing.
[26]The sword that reaches him has no effect,
    nor does the spear or the dart or the
        javelin.
[27]Iron he treats like straw
    and bronze like rotten wood.
[28]Arrows do not make him flee;
    slingstones are like chaff to him.
[29]A club seems to him but a piece of straw;
    he laughs at the rattling of the lance.
[30]His undersides are jagged potsherds,

---

[a]15 Possibly the hippopotamus or the elephant   [b]17 Possibly trunk   [c]24 Or *by a water hole*   [d]1 Possibly the
crocodile   [e]15 Or *His pride is his*

leaving a trail in the mud like a threshing
sledge.
[31]He makes the depths churn like a boiling
caldron
and stirs up the sea like a pot of
ointment.
[32]Behind him he leaves a glistening wake;
one would think the deep had white hair.
[33]Nothing on earth is his equal—
a creature without fear.
[34]He looks down on all that are haughty;
he is king over all that are proud.”

Job

42 Then Job replied to the LORD:

[2]“I know that you can do all things;
no plan of yours can be thwarted.
[3]You asked, ‘Who is this that obscures my
counsel without knowledge?’
Surely I spoke of things I did not
understand,
things too wonderful for me to know.

[4]“You said, ‘Listen now, and I will speak;
I will question you,
and you shall answer me.’
[5]My ears had heard of you
but now my eyes have seen you.
[6]Therefore I despise myself
and repent in dust and ashes.”

42:2–5 A Visit for All Time

*A personal visit from God utterly silenced all
Job's questions about unfairness. Once he saw
God, he had nothing more to say. Few people in
history have had such a direct, visible
encounter with God, but the book of Job
foreshadows a time when God paid a much
longer personal visit to earth. In Jesus, God
came not in power and majesty, but in poverty
and pain. Job stands as the clearest Old
Testament example of unfairness: an upright
man who suffered greatly. Jesus stands as the
New Testament example: a perfect man who
suffered even more. Both hint at a happy
ending after all.*

Epilogue

[7]After the LORD had said these things to Job,
he said to Eliphaz the Temanite, “I am angry with
you and your two friends, because you have not
spoken of me what is right, as my servant
Job has. [8]So now take seven bulls and seven rams
and go to my servant Job and sacrifice a burnt
offering for yourselves. My servant Job will pray
for you, and I will accept his prayer and not deal
with you according to your folly. You have not
spoken of me what is right, as my servant
Job has.” [9]So Eliphaz the Temanite, Bildad the
Shuhite and Zophar the Naamathite did what the
LORD told them; and the LORD accepted Job’s
prayer.
[10]After Job had prayed for his friends, the
LORD made him prosperous again and gave him

42:10 Seeing in the Dark

*Significantly, Job spoke his contrite words
(verse 6) before any of his losses had been
restored, while still sitting in a pile of ashes,
naked and covered with sores. Because he had
seen God, he had learned to believe God even
in the midst of suffering, with no certainty of
relief.*

twice as much as he had before. [11]All his brothers
and sisters and everyone who had known him
before came and ate with him in his house. They
comforted and consoled him over all the trouble
the LORD had brought upon him, and each one
gave him a piece of silver[a] and a gold ring.
[12]The LORD blessed the latter part of Job’s life
more than the first. He had fourteen thousand
sheep, six thousand camels, a thousand yoke of
oxen and a thousand donkeys. [13]And he also
had seven sons and three daughters. [14]The first
daughter he named Jemimah, the second Keziah
and the third Keren-Happuch. [15]Nowhere in all
the land were there found women as beautiful as
Job’s daughters, and their father granted them an
inheritance along with their brothers.
[16]After this, Job lived a hundred and forty
years; he saw his children and their children to
the fourth generation. [17]And so he died, old and
full of years.

---

[a]11 Hebrew *him a kesitah*; a kesitah was a unit of money of unknown weight and value.

PSALMS

Cries from the Heart
Songs for sorrow as well as joy

> *You are my hiding place; you will protect me from trouble and surround me with songs of deliverance. 32:7*

HERE AT THE VERY CENTER of the Bible are songs, rising up like a tune from its heart. They capture the innermost thoughts and prayers of Old Testament people—and they still speak directly to our needs.

For every emotion and mood you can find a psalm to match. The psalms wrestle with the deepest sorrow and ask God the hardest questions about suffering and injustice. Their voice is refreshingly spontaneous. They do not tip flowery compliments toward God; they cry out to him, or shout for joy before him.

After you read these poems, you can't think of the Old Testament as dry and rule-bound. Nor is the Old Testament God distant and impersonal. In almost every psalm you find the presence of God, not as a philosophical principle, but as an active, strong, and loving ruler—a God who makes a difference in life.

How Did the Psalms Come Together?

While almost half of the psalms are credited to David, at least one was written 500 years after his birth. A number of poets and writers contributed, and about a third of the psalms are completely anonymous.

How did the psalms come together? They seem to have been compiled as a hymnbook for use in temple worship. Some psalms were written from an individual's experiences, but were adapted for congregational use. Directions for musicians were added, along with a few verses to widen the psalms' meaning to everybody.

The psalms show tremendous variation, reflecting the many personalities who contributed their poems and prayers over several centuries. Yet readers have found an inner consistency in the whole book, so they can move from one psalm to the next without being particularly aware that one poem is centuries older than another. Some have called the psalms a Bible within the Bible—different books telling a single story.

Others have compared the book of Psalms to a beautiful cathedral built over centuries. Each wing and each window show the individual genius of its designers, yet all the parts are somehow harmonious. This harmony comes not merely from a common sense of style, but from unity of purpose: The whole cathedral is made for the worship of one and the same God. Just so, the psalms reflect, in a hundred moods and experiences, the never-changing reality of a strong and loving God who cares for his people.

The Presence of Real Enemies

God is not the only reality in the psalms. Equally persistent are enemies who sneer and hurt and plot violence. They, too, appear in nearly every psalm. For the psalmists, faith in God was a struggle against powerful forces that often seemed more real than God.

The psalm writers frequently asked, "Where are you, God? Why don't you help me?" Despite their love for God, they often felt abandoned, misused, betrayed. They found no guarantee of safety in their closeness to God. The joy and praise that saturate these prayers came not from an absence of problems, but from a deep conviction that a great God would overcome them.

Jesus, dying on the cross, twice expressed himself in the words of psalms (22:1 and 31:5), and his disciples, in trying to explain his life, quoted from Psalms more than any other book. They appear to have meditated on the psalms often as they considered the meaning of Jesus' life. In the psalms they could see that even the best men—even David, the great king—suffer agony and feel abandoned.

Living by faith is not easy. It was not for David; it was not for Jesus either. These powerful poems of praise and worship, some of the most beautiful ever written, offer no magical formulas to make troubles go away. Yet, while real-life questions, struggles, and discouragements have a strong voice in these poems, more powerful still is the voice of joy and security in the strength and fortress of Israel: the Lord himself.

How to Read Psalms

The best way to read the psalms is also the most common way: to make these ancient prayers your own and speak them directly to God. So many of the poems catch such deep human feelings that you can't help being moved by them.

But not all the psalms seem attractive. Some sound harsh, self-congratulatory, or boring. You will not find it easy to pray these until you understand them.

And there are so many psalms! This is the longest book in the Bible. To compensate, many people read only selected psalms, skimming over the others. But then they miss the deeper messages found there, including the messages that the New Testament writers saw when they quoted Psalms more than any other Old Testament book. The richest lessons from Psalms may come from particularly difficult poems you must read again and again until you begin to see what the author had in mind.

The original Hebrew of these poems probably used no rhyme or strict rhythm as traditional English poems do. Instead, the psalmists wrote with parallelism, following one thought by a "rhyming" thought or by its opposite. (For more on this, see "Hebrew Poetry," page 669.) Fortunately, this kind of poetry can be translated into almost any language without loss.

Readers may be confused by the psalms' frequent change of voice. In a single poem the psalmist may talk to God, then talk about him, and then return to talking to him, all in rapid succession. This would be strange English prose, but was common in Hebrew poetry.

Because so many of the psalm titles refer to David, you may find it helpful to refer to his life story. It is found in 1 Samuel 16–31, the whole book of 2 Samuel, and the first two chapters of 1 Kings. However, most of the psalms can make perfect sense without reference to any outside information. They merely ask—and reward—time and close attention. Read and reread them. They grow richer with careful study.

PEOPLE YOU'LL MEET IN PSALMS

MELCHIZEDEK *(p. 639)*

3-TRACK READING PLAN

For an explanation and complete listing of the 3-track reading plan, turn to page 7.

TRACK 1:   ***Two-Week Courses on the Bible***
The Track 1 reading program on the Old Testament includes one chapter from Psalms. See page 8 for a complete listing of this course.

TRACK 2:   ***An Overview of Psalms in 7 Days***
☐ Day 1. Read the Introduction to Psalms and Psalm 19: Perfect Harmony.
☐ Day 2. Read Psalm 23: The Shepherd Song.
☐ Day 3. Read Psalm 27: Confidence in Trouble.
☐ Day 4. Read Psalm 51: The Great Confession.
☐ Day 5. Read Psalm 84: The Delight of Worshiping God.
☐ Day 6. Read Psalm 103: God's Benefits.
☐ Day 7. Read Psalm 139: God's Care.

Now turn to page 9 for your next Track 2 reading project.

TRACK 3:   ***All of Psalms in Two Two-Month Periods (122 days)***
After you have read through Psalms, turn to pages 10–14 for your next Track 3 reading project.

Part I
☐1–2 ☐3–4 ☐5 ☐6 ☐7 ☐8 ☐9 ☐10 ☐11–12 ☐13–14
☐15–16 ☐17 ☐18 ☐19 ☐20–21 ☐22 ☐23–24 ☐25 ☐26 ☐27
☐28–29 ☐30 ☐31 ☐32 ☐33 ☐34 ☐35 ☐36 ☐37 ☐38
☐39 ☐40 ☐41 ☐42–43 ☐44 ☐45 ☐46–47 ☐48 ☐49 ☐50
☐51 ☐52 ☐53–54 ☐55 ☐56 ☐57 ☐58 ☐59 ☐60–61 ☐62
☐63–64 ☐65 ☐66 ☐67 ☐68 ☐69 ☐70 ☐71 ☐72 ☐73
☐74 ☐75

BOOK I

Psalms 1–41

Psalm 1

¹Blessed is the man
  who does not walk in the counsel of the
    wicked
or stand in the way of sinners
  or sit in the seat of mockers.
²But his delight is in the law of the LORD,
  and on his law he meditates day and
    night.
³He is like a tree planted by streams of water,
  which yields its fruit in season
and whose leaf does not wither.
  Whatever he does prospers.

⁴Not so the wicked!
  They are like chaff
  that the wind blows away.

1:4 Blowing in the Wind

*The opposite of "a tree planted by streams"
(verse 3) should be a tree withered by
drought—and so it is in Jeremiah 17:5–8, which
paints a similar contrast between good and
bad people. This image of the wicked as "chaff,"
however, is far more absolute—for chaff, utterly
worthless even for a fire, disappears in the
wind. God's judgment day is what finally
makes the wicked seem like chaff.*

⁵Therefore the wicked will not stand in the
    judgment,
  nor sinners in the assembly of the
    righteous.
⁶For the LORD watches over the way of the
    righteous,
  but the way of the wicked will perish.

Psalm 2

¹Why do the nations conspire[a]
  and the peoples plot in vain?

²The kings of the earth take their stand
  and the rulers gather together
against the LORD
  and against his Anointed One.[b]

2:2 The Messiah in the Psalms

*Israelite kings and priests were anointed with
oil when they took office. The "Anointed One"
probably originally meant "king." It came,
however, to stand for more. The Hebrew word
is* masiah, *which became* Messiah *and
translated into Greek as* Christos *or* Christ. *This
psalm was understood in the New Testament
as referring to Jesus—for no Old Testament
king ever gained the control of the nations
implied here. You can find quotations in Acts
4:25–26; 13:33; Hebrews 1:5; 5:5; and
Revelation 2:27; 12:5; and 19:15.*

³"Let us break their chains," they say,
  "and throw off their fetters."

⁴The One enthroned in heaven laughs;
  the Lord scoffs at them.
⁵Then he rebukes them in his anger
  and terrifies them in his wrath, saying,
⁶"I have installed my King[c]
  on Zion, my holy hill."

⁷I will proclaim the decree of the LORD:

He said to me, "You are my Son[d];
  today I have become your Father.[e]
⁸Ask of me,
  and I will make the nations your
    inheritance,
  the ends of the earth your possession.
⁹You will rule them with an iron scepter[f];
  you will dash them to pieces like pottery."

¹⁰Therefore, you kings, be wise;
  be warned, you rulers of the earth.
¹¹Serve the LORD with fear
  and rejoice with trembling.

---

a1 Hebrew; Septuagint *rage*   *b2* Or *anointed one*   *c6* Or *king*   *d7* Or *son*; also in verse 12   *e7* Or *have
begotten you*   *f9* Or *will break them with a rod of iron*

12Kiss the Son, lest he be angry
 and you be destroyed in your way,
for his wrath can flare up in a moment.
 Blessed are all who take refuge in him.

Psalm 3

*A psalm of David. When he fled from his son
Absalom.*

1O LORD, how many are my foes!
 How many rise up against me!
2Many are saying of me,
 "God will not deliver him."   *Selah*[a]

3But you are a shield around me, O LORD;
 you bestow glory on me and lift[b] up my
  head.
4To the LORD I cry aloud,
 and he answers me from his holy hill.
                                    Selah

5I lie down and sleep;
 I wake again, because the LORD sustains
  me.
6I will not fear the tens of thousands
 drawn up against me on every side.

7Arise, O LORD!
 Deliver me, O my God!
Strike all my enemies on the jaw;
 break the teeth of the wicked.

8From the LORD comes deliverance.
 May your blessing be on your people.
                                    Selah

Psalm 4

*For the director of music. With stringed
instruments. A psalm of David.*

1Answer me when I call to you,
 O my righteous God.
Give me relief from my distress;
 be merciful to me and hear my prayer.

2How long, O men, will you turn my glory
  into shame[c]?
 How long will you love delusions and seek
  false gods[d]?   *Selah*
3Know that the LORD has set apart the godly
  for himself;
 the LORD will hear when I call to him.

4In your anger do not sin;
 when you are on your beds,
 search your hearts and be silent.   *Selah*
5Offer right sacrifices
 and trust in the LORD.

6Many are asking, "Who can show us any
  good?"
 Let the light of your face shine upon us,
  O LORD.

4:4 Angry Inside

*Is anger sinful? No, though it can certainly lead
to sin. This prayer depicts anger springing from
anxiety, which proves especially troublesome
on sleepless nights. The psalm suggests that,
rather than venting your worry in outbursts
against others, you should examine your own
heart. Paul applied this verse to another
situation: difficult personal relationships
(Ephesians 4:26).*

7You have filled my heart with greater joy
 than when their grain and new wine
  abound.
8I will lie down and sleep in peace,
 for you alone, O LORD,
 make me dwell in safety.

Psalm 5

*For the director of music. For flutes.
A psalm of David.*

1Give ear to my words, O LORD,
 consider my sighing.
2Listen to my cry for help,
 my King and my God,
 for to you I pray.
3In the morning, O LORD, you hear my
  voice;
 in the morning I lay my requests before
  you
 and wait in expectation.

4You are not a God who takes pleasure in
  evil;
 with you the wicked cannot dwell.
5The arrogant cannot stand in your presence;
 you hate all who do wrong.
6You destroy those who tell lies;
 bloodthirsty and deceitful men
 the LORD abhors.

7But I, by your great mercy,
 will come into your house;
in reverence will I bow down
 toward your holy temple.
8Lead me, O LORD, in your righteousness
 because of my enemies—
 make straight your way before me.

---

[a]2 A word of uncertain meaning, occurring frequently in the Psalms; possibly a musical term   [b]3 Or LORD, / my
Glorious One, who lifts   [c]2 Or you dishonor my Glorious One   [d]2 Or seek lies

⁹Not a word from their mouth can be trusted;
　　their heart is filled with destruction.
Their throat is an open grave;
　　with their tongue they speak deceit.

5:9 Evil Everywhere

*Renowned for their beautiful pictures of God's
love, the psalms present equally heartfelt
portraits of evil. They often describe people
who deeply deserve God's punishment. In
Romans 3:10–18, Paul quotes from a number
of different psalms like this one, making his
case that evil infects all people, everywhere.*

---

¹⁰Declare them guilty, O God!
　　Let their intrigues be their downfall.
Banish them for their many sins,
　　for they have rebelled against you.

¹¹But let all who take refuge in you be glad;
　　let them ever sing for joy.
Spread your protection over them,
　　that those who love your name may
　　　rejoice in you.
¹²For surely, O Lord, you bless the righteous;
　　you surround them with your favor as
　　　with a shield.

Psalm 6

For the director of music. With stringed
instruments. According to *sheminith.ᵃ*
A psalm of David.

¹O Lord, do not rebuke me in your anger
　　or discipline me in your wrath.
²Be merciful to me, Lord, for I am faint;
　　O Lord, heal me, for my bones are in
　　　agony.
³My soul is in anguish.
　　How long, O Lord, how long?

⁴Turn, O Lord, and deliver me;
　　save me because of your unfailing love.
⁵No one remembers you when he is dead.
　　Who praises you from the graveᵇ?

⁶I am worn out from groaning;
　　all night long I flood my bed with
　　　weeping
　　and drench my couch with tears.
⁷My eyes grow weak with sorrow;
　　they fail because of all my foes.

⁸Away from me, all you who do evil,
　　for the Lord has heard my weeping.
⁹The Lord has heard my cry for mercy;
　　the Lord accepts my prayer.
¹⁰All my enemies will be ashamed and
　　　dismayed;
　　they will turn back in sudden disgrace.

Psalm 7

A *shiggaionᶜ* of David, which he sang to the
　　Lord concerning Cush, a Benjamite.

¹O Lord my God, I take refuge in you;
　　save and deliver me from all who pursue
　　　me,
²or they will tear me like a lion
　　and rip me to pieces with no one to
　　　rescue me.

³O Lord my God, if I have done this
　　and there is guilt on my hands—
⁴if I have done evil to him who is at peace
　　　with me
　　or without cause have robbed my foe—
⁵then let my enemy pursue and overtake me;
　　let him trample my life to the ground
　　and make me sleep in the dust.　　*Selah*

⁶Arise, O Lord, in your anger;
　　rise up against the rage of my enemies.
　　Awake, my God; decree justice.
⁷Let the assembled peoples gather around
　　　you.
　　Rule over them from on high;
⁸　let the Lord judge the peoples.
Judge me, O Lord, according to my
　　　righteousness,
　　according to my integrity, O Most High.
⁹O righteous God,
　　who searches minds and hearts,
bring to an end the violence of the wicked
　　and make the righteous secure.

¹⁰My shieldᵈ is God Most High,
　　who saves the upright in heart.
¹¹God is a righteous judge,
　　a God who expresses his wrath every day.
¹²If he does not relent,
　　heᵉ will sharpen his sword;
　　he will bend and string his bow.
¹³He has prepared his deadly weapons;
　　he makes ready his flaming arrows.

¹⁴He who is pregnant with evil
　　and conceives trouble gives birth to
　　　disillusionment.

ᵃTitle: Probably a musical term　　ᵇ5 Hebrew *Sheol*　　ᶜTitle: Probably a literary or musical term
ᵈ10 Or *sovereign*　　ᵉ12 Or *If a man does not repent, / God*

15He who digs a hole and scoops it out
   falls into the pit he has made.
16The trouble he causes recoils on himself;
   his violence comes down on his own
   head.
17I will give thanks to the LORD because of his
   righteousness
   and will sing praise to the name of the
   LORD Most High.

Psalm 8

For the director of music. According to *gittith.*a
A psalm of David.

1O LORD, our Lord,
   how majestic is your name in all the
   earth!

You have set your glory
   above the heavens.
2From the lips of children and infants
   you have ordained praiseb
because of your enemies,
   to silence the foe and the avenger.

8:2 Children's Power

*An almighty God needs no great powers to
back him. He shuts up his enemies through
little children and their spontaneous praise.
That is exactly what happened in Jesus' time
(Matthew 21:16).*

3When I consider your heavens,
   the work of your fingers,
the moon and the stars,
   which you have set in place,
4what is man that you are mindful of him,
   the son of man that you care for him?
5You made him a little lower than the
   heavenly beingsc
and crowned him with glory and honor.

6You made him ruler over the works of your
   hands;
   you put everything under his feet:
7all flocks and herds,
   and the beasts of the field,
8the birds of the air,
   and the fish of the sea,
   all that swim the paths of the seas.

9O LORD, our Lord,
   how majestic is your name in all the
   earth!

Psalm 9d

For the director of music. To the tune of "The
Death of the Son." A psalm of David.

1I will praise you, O LORD, with all my heart;
   I will tell of all your wonders.
2I will be glad and rejoice in you;
   I will sing praise to your name, O Most
   High.

3My enemies turn back;
   they stumble and perish before you.
4For you have upheld my right and my cause;
   you have sat on your throne, judging
   righteously.
5You have rebuked the nations and destroyed
   the wicked;
   you have blotted out their name for ever
   and ever.
6Endless ruin has overtaken the enemy,
   you have uprooted their cities;
   even the memory of them has perished.

7The LORD reigns forever;
   he has established his throne for
   judgment.
8He will judge the world in righteousness;
   he will govern the peoples with justice.
9The LORD is a refuge for the oppressed,
   a stronghold in times of trouble.
10Those who know your name will trust in
   you,
   for you, LORD, have never forsaken those
   who seek you.

11Sing praises to the LORD, enthroned in Zion;
   proclaim among the nations what he has
   done.
12For he who avenges blood remembers;
   he does not ignore the cry of the afflicted.

13O LORD, see how my enemies persecute me!
   Have mercy and lift me up from the gates
   of death,
14that I may declare your praises
   in the gates of the Daughter of Zion
   and there rejoice in your salvation.
15The nations have fallen into the pit they have
   dug;
   their feet are caught in the net they have
   hidden.
16The LORD is known by his justice;
   the wicked are ensnared by the work of
   their hands.   *Higgaion.e Selah*
17The wicked return to the grave,f
   all the nations that forget God.
18But the needy will not always be forgotten,
   nor the hope of the afflicted ever perish.

---

aTitle: Probably a musical term   b2 Or *strength*   c5 Or *than God*   dPsalms 9 and 10 may have been originally
a single acrostic poem, the stanzas of which begin with the successive letters of the Hebrew alphabet. In the Septuagint
they constitute one psalm.   e16 Or *Meditation*; possibly a musical notation   f17 Hebrew *Sheol*

¹⁹Arise, O LORD, let not man triumph;
　　let the nations be judged in your presence.
²⁰Strike them with terror, O LORD;
　　let the nations know they are but men.
　　　　　　　　　　　　　　　Selah

Psalm 10ᵃ

¹Why, O LORD, do you stand far off?
　　Why do you hide yourself in times of
　　　trouble?

²In his arrogance the wicked man hunts down
　　the weak,
　　who are caught in the schemes he devises.
³He boasts of the cravings of his heart;
　　he blesses the greedy and reviles the LORD.
⁴In his pride the wicked does not seek him;
　　in all his thoughts there is no room for
　　　God.
⁵His ways are always prosperous;
　　he is haughty and your laws are far from
　　　him;
　　he sneers at all his enemies.
⁶He says to himself, "Nothing will shake me;
　　I'll always be happy and never have
　　　trouble."
⁷His mouth is full of curses and lies and
　　threats;
　　trouble and evil are under his tongue.
⁸He lies in wait near the villages;
　　from ambush he murders the innocent,
　　watching in secret for his victims.
⁹He lies in wait like a lion in cover;
　　he lies in wait to catch the helpless;
　　he catches the helpless and drags them off
　　　in his net.
¹⁰His victims are crushed, they collapse;
　　they fall under his strength.
¹¹He says to himself, "God has forgotten;
　　he covers his face and never sees."

¹²Arise, LORD! Lift up your hand, O God.
　　Do not forget the helpless.
¹³Why does the wicked man revile God?
　　Why does he say to himself,
　　"He won't call me to account"?
¹⁴But you, O God, do see trouble and grief;
　　you consider it to take it in hand.
　The victim commits himself to you;
　　you are the helper of the fatherless.
¹⁵Break the arm of the wicked and evil man;
　　call him to account for his wickedness
　　that would not be found out.

¹⁶The LORD is King for ever and ever;
　　the nations will perish from his land.
¹⁷You hear, O LORD, the desire of the afflicted;

you encourage them, and you listen to
　their cry,
¹⁸defending the fatherless and the oppressed,
　　in order that man, who is of the earth,
　　may terrify no more.

Psalm 11

For the director of music. Of David.

¹In the LORD I take refuge.
　　How then can you say to me:
　　"Flee like a bird to your mountain.
²For look, the wicked bend their bows;
　　they set their arrows against the strings
to shoot from the shadows
　　at the upright in heart.
³When the foundations are being destroyed,
　　what can the righteous doᵇ?"

⁴The LORD is in his holy temple;
　　the LORD is on his heavenly throne.
　He observes the sons of men;
　　his eyes examine them.
⁵The LORD examines the righteous,
　　but the wickedᶜ and those who love
　　　violence
　　his soul hates.
⁶On the wicked he will rain
　　fiery coals and burning sulfur;
　　a scorching wind will be their lot.

⁷For the LORD is righteous,
　　he loves justice;
　　upright men will see his face.

Psalm 12

For the director of music. According to
*sheminith.*ᵈ A psalm of David.

¹Help, LORD, for the godly are no more;
　　the faithful have vanished from among
　　　men.
²Everyone lies to his neighbor;
　　their flattering lips speak with deception.

³May the LORD cut off all flattering lips

12:4 Who Owns Your Lips?

*Repeatedly the Bible stresses that talk can do
tremendous good or evil. One key distinctive is
suggested here: Wicked people use words to
build themselves up over others. They insist
that no one has the right to tell them what to
say.*

ᵃPsalms 9 and 10 may have been originally a single acrostic poem, the stanzas of which begin with the successive letters of
the Hebrew alphabet. In the Septuagint they constitute one psalm.　　ᵇ3 Or *what is the Righteous One doing*　　ᶜ5 Or
The LORD, the Righteous One, examines the wicked, /　　ᵈTitle: Probably a musical term　　ᵉ4 Or */ our lips are our
plowshares*

and every boastful tongue
[4]that says, "We will triumph with our
tongues;
we own our lips[e]—who is our master?"

[5]"Because of the oppression of the weak
and the groaning of the needy,
I will now arise," says the LORD.
"I will protect them from those who
malign them."
[6]And the words of the LORD are flawless,
like silver refined in a furnace of clay,
purified seven times.

[7]O LORD, you will keep us safe
and protect us from such people forever.
[8]The wicked freely strut about
when what is vile is honored among men.

Psalm 13

For the director of music. A psalm of David.

[1]How long, O LORD? Will you forget me
forever?
How long will you hide your face from
me?
[2]How long must I wrestle with my thoughts
and every day have sorrow in my heart?
How long will my enemy triumph over
me?
[3]Look on me and answer, O LORD my God.
Give light to my eyes, or I will sleep in
death;
[4]my enemy will say, "I have overcome him,"
and my foes will rejoice when I fall.

[5]But I trust in your unfailing love;
my heart rejoices in your salvation.
[6]I will sing to the LORD,
for he has been good to me.

Psalm 14

For the director of music. Of David.

[1]The fool[a] says in his heart,
"There is no God."
They are corrupt, their deeds are vile;
there is no one who does good.

[2]The LORD looks down from heaven
on the sons of men
to see if there are any who understand,
any who seek God.
[3]All have turned aside,
they have together become corrupt;
there is no one who does good,
not even one.

[4]Will evildoers never learn—
those who devour my people as men eat
bread
and who do not call on the LORD?

14:3 Who Seeks God?

*Though David was called a "man after God's
own heart," he is credited with this chilling
assessment of humankind—including himself.
In God's eyes, nobody—not even David—is
good. Paul quoted this in a crucial New
Testament passage, Romans 3:10–12.*

---

[5]There they are, overwhelmed with dread,
for God is present in the company of the
righteous.
[6]You evildoers frustrate the plans of the poor,
but the LORD is their refuge.

[7]Oh, that salvation for Israel would come out
of Zion!
When the LORD restores the fortunes of
his people,
let Jacob rejoice and Israel be glad!

Psalm 15

A psalm of David.

[1]LORD, who may dwell in your sanctuary?
Who may live on your holy hill?

[2]He whose walk is blameless
and who does what is righteous,
who speaks the truth from his heart
[3]   and has no slander on his tongue,
who does his neighbor no wrong
and casts no slur on his fellowman,
[4]who despises a vile man
but honors those who fear the LORD,
who keeps his oath
even when it hurts,
[5]who lends his money without usury
and does not accept a bribe against the
innocent.

He who does these things
will never be shaken.

Psalm 16

A *miktam*[b] of David.

[1]Keep me safe, O God,
for in you I take refuge.

[2]I said to the LORD, "You are my Lord;
apart from you I have no good thing."

---

[a]1 The Hebrew words rendered *fool* in Psalms denote one who is morally deficient.   [b]Title: Probably a literary or
musical term

[3]As for the saints who are in the land,
  they are the glorious ones in whom is all
    my delight.[a]
[4]The sorrows of those will increase
  who run after other gods.
 I will not pour out their libations of blood
  or take up their names on my lips.

[5]LORD, you have assigned me my portion and
    my cup;
  you have made my lot secure.
[6]The boundary lines have fallen for me in
    pleasant places;
  surely I have a delightful inheritance.

[7]I will praise the LORD, who counsels me;
  even at night my heart instructs me.
[8]I have set the LORD always before me.
  Because he is at my right hand,
  I will not be shaken.

[9]Therefore my heart is glad and my tongue
    rejoices;
  my body also will rest secure,

[10]because you will not abandon me to the
    grave,[b]
  nor will you let your Holy One[c] see
    decay.

16:9–11 Resurrection!

In this confident, happy psalm, David rejoices that the life God gives cannot be canceled by the grave. Generally, the Old Testament offers little insight into life after death, but here David's faith carries him to a deeper understanding. The apostles Peter and Paul understood this psalm as prophesying Jesus' resurrection (see Acts 2:25–28; 13:35–37). Because of Jesus' resurrection, David and all God's people would come to new life in him.

[11]You have made[d] known to me the path of
    life;
  you will fill me with joy in your presence,
  with eternal pleasures at your right hand.

[a]3 Or As for the pagan priests who are in the land / and the nobles in whom all delight, I said: [b]10 Hebrew Sheol
[c]10 Or your faithful one   [d]11 Or You will make

Life after Death
When you die, will it all be over?

> You will not abandon me to the grave, nor will you let your Holy One see decay. 16:10

WHAT HAPPENS TO YOU AFTER you die? People have always wanted an answer to that question, and the psalmists were no different. They lived in an age without effective medicine, in an age when wars were fought hand-to-hand. Dead bodies were a familiar reality. Yet death, however familiar, remained mysterious and frightening to them.

Israelites called the dark and shadowy place where dead people go "Sheol." When you got there, your life seemed thoroughly finished. The psalmists emphatically did not want to go there, and they asked God, when praying for his help, what possible good there might be in death. "Are your wonders known in the place of darkness, or your righteous deeds in the land of oblivion?" (Psalm 88:12). Sheol was the great leveler: it meant the end of plans, of worship, of a relationship with God (Psalms 30:9; 88:5; 146:4). The dead were found there, not the living.

God's Power over Death

Yet some psalms also hint at a happier view. They hold such a strong view of God's authority that they show—vaguely, but unmistakably—God's power over the grave. For instance, God is *in* Sheol (Psalm 139:8). He—and only he—can redeem a person from there (49:7–9,15). God will not let his "Holy One" see decay—a claim that both Peter and Paul saw as a clear prediction of Jesus' resurrection from the dead (Psalm 16:10, quoted in Acts 2:27; 13:35).

What did they expect life after death to be like, if God's power redeemed someone from Sheol? You won't find a clearly defined picture of heaven here—only hints. The psalmists' thoughts center on God's face and his presence. For God is the only unchangeable reality: Wherever you are, in life or in death, he will be there. He is the ultimate reward to those who love him.

The expectation of God's face shows through in Psalms 16:8–11; 17:15; 49:15; 73:23–26. But for a clearer perspective on life after death, you must read, in the Old Testament, Isaiah 26:19 and Daniel 12:1–3, and in the New Testament, 2 Corinthians 5:1–10, among many other passages.

Life Questions: Describe what you believe happens after you die. Is this a frightening or an encouraging picture to you?

Psalm 17

A prayer of David.

¹Hear, O LORD, my righteous plea;
　　listen to my cry.
　Give ear to my prayer—
　　it does not rise from deceitful lips.
²May my vindication come from you;
　　may your eyes see what is right.

³Though you probe my heart and examine
　　　me at night,
　　though you test me, you will find nothing;
　　I have resolved that my mouth will not
　　　sin.
⁴As for the deeds of men—
　　by the word of your lips
　I have kept myself
　　from the ways of the violent.
⁵My steps have held to your paths;
　　my feet have not slipped.

⁶I call on you, O God, for you will answer
　　　me;
　　give ear to me and hear my prayer.
⁷Show the wonder of your great love,
　　you who save by your right hand
　　those who take refuge in you from their
　　　foes.
⁸Keep me as the apple of your eye;
　　hide me in the shadow of your wings
⁹from the wicked who assail me,
　　from my mortal enemies who surround
　　　me.

¹⁰They close up their callous hearts,
　　and their mouths speak with arrogance.
¹¹They have tracked me down, they now
　　　surround me,
　　with eyes alert, to throw me to the
　　　ground.
¹²They are like a lion hungry for prey,
　　like a great lion crouching in cover.

¹³Rise up, O LORD, confront them, bring them
　　　down;
　　rescue me from the wicked by your
　　　sword.
¹⁴O LORD, by your hand save me from such
　　　men,
　　from men of this world whose reward is
　　　in this life.

　You still the hunger of those you cherish;
　　their sons have plenty,
　　and they store up wealth for their
　　　children.
¹⁵And I—in righteousness I will see your face;
　　when I awake, I will be satisfied with
　　　seeing your likeness.

Psalm 18

For the director of music. Of David the servant
of the LORD. He sang to the LORD the words
of this song when the LORD delivered him
from the hand of all his enemies and
from the hand of Saul. He said:

¹I love you, O LORD, my strength.

²The LORD is my rock, my fortress and my
　　deliverer;

17:15 The Face of God

*While the psalms often ask God to provide
"refuge" in a time of trouble, they also look
forward to "seeing his face"—a goal that is
valuable only to someone who deeply loves
God. To see God's face is to see and know him
personally, deeply, and without the clouds of
mystery that so often make faith difficult.*

　　my God is my rock, in whom I take
　　　refuge.
　　He is my shield and the hornᵃ of my
　　　salvation, my stronghold.
³I call to the LORD, who is worthy of praise,
　　and I am saved from my enemies.

⁴The cords of death entangled me;
　　the torrents of destruction overwhelmed
　　　me.
⁵The cords of the graveᵇ coiled around
　　　me;
　　the snares of death confronted me.
⁶In my distress I called to the LORD;
　　I cried to my God for help.
　From his temple he heard my voice;
　　my cry came before him, into his ears.

⁷The earth trembled and quaked,
　　and the foundations of the mountains
　　　shook;
　　they trembled because he was angry.
⁸Smoke rose from his nostrils;
　　consuming fire came from his mouth,
　　burning coals blazed out of it.
⁹He parted the heavens and came down;
　　dark clouds were under his feet.
¹⁰He mounted the cherubim and flew;
　　he soared on the wings of the wind.
¹¹He made darkness his covering, his canopy
　　　around him—
　　the dark rain clouds of the sky.
¹²Out of the brightness of his presence clouds
　　　advanced,

ᵃ2 *Horn* here symbolizes strength.　　ᵇ5 Hebrew *Sheol*

with hailstones and bolts of lightning.
¹³The LORD thundered from heaven;
the voice of the Most High resounded.ᵃ
¹⁴He shot his arrows and scattered ⌐the
enemies⌐,
great bolts of lightning and routed them.
¹⁵The valleys of the sea were exposed
and the foundations of the earth laid
bare
at your rebuke, O LORD,
at the blast of breath from your nostrils.

¹⁶He reached down from on high and took
hold of me;
he drew me out of deep waters.
¹⁷He rescued me from my powerful enemy,
from my foes, who were too strong for
me.
¹⁸They confronted me in the day of my
disaster,
but the LORD was my support.
¹⁹He brought me out into a spacious place;
he rescued me because he delighted in
me.

²⁰The LORD has dealt with me according to my
righteousness;
according to the cleanness of my hands he
has rewarded me.
²¹For I have kept the ways of the LORD;
I have not done evil by turning from my
God.
²²All his laws are before me;
I have not turned away from his decrees.
²³I have been blameless before him
and have kept myself from sin.
²⁴The LORD has rewarded me according to my
righteousness,
according to the cleanness of my hands in
his sight.

²⁵To the faithful you show yourself faithful,
to the blameless you show yourself
blameless,
²⁶to the pure you show yourself pure,
but to the crooked you show yourself
shrewd.
²⁷You save the humble
but bring low those whose eyes are
haughty.
²⁸You, O LORD, keep my lamp burning;
my God turns my darkness into light.
²⁹With your help I can advance against a
troopᵇ;
with my God I can scale a wall.

³⁰As for God, his way is perfect;
the word of the LORD is flawless.

He is a shield
for all who take refuge in him.
³¹For who is God besides the LORD?
And who is the Rock except our God?
³²It is God who arms me with strength
and makes my way perfect.
³³He makes my feet like the feet of a deer;
he enables me to stand on the heights.
³⁴He trains my hands for battle;
my arms can bend a bow of bronze.
³⁵You give me your shield of victory,
and your right hand sustains me;
you stoop down to make me great.
³⁶You broaden the path beneath me,
so that my ankles do not turn.

³⁷I pursued my enemies and overtook them;
I did not turn back till they were
destroyed.
³⁸I crushed them so that they could not rise;
they fell beneath my feet.
³⁹You armed me with strength for battle;
you made my adversaries bow at my
feet.
⁴⁰You made my enemies turn their backs
in flight,
and I destroyed my foes.
⁴¹They cried for help, but there was no one to
save them—
to the LORD, but he did not answer.
⁴²I beat them as fine as dust borne on the
wind;
I poured them out like mud in the streets.

⁴³You have delivered me from the attacks of
the people;
you have made me the head of nations;
people I did not know are subject to me.
⁴⁴As soon as they hear me, they obey me;
foreigners cringe before me.
⁴⁵They all lose heart;
they come trembling from their
strongholds.

18:49 Going Public

*For the psalmists, praising God was more than
a personal matter between the believer and his
God. They praised God publicly—even in front
of unbelievers—often inviting their audience to
join in. Such public praise anticipated New
Testament evangelism, the spreading of good
news to the entire world. Paul quoted this verse
in Romans 15:9 to stress that God had always
meant his love to reach out from the Jews to
the rest of humanity.*

ᵃ 13 Some Hebrew manuscripts and Septuagint (see also 2 Samuel 22:14); most Hebrew manuscripts *resounded, / amid
hailstones and bolts of lightning*   ᵇ 29 Or *can run through a barricade*

46 The LORD lives! Praise be to my Rock!
Exalted be God my Savior!
47 He is the God who avenges me,
who subdues nations under me,
48 who saves me from my enemies.
You exalted me above my foes;
from violent men you rescued me.
49 Therefore I will praise you among the
nations, O LORD;
I will sing praises to your name.
50 He gives his king great victories;
he shows unfailing kindness to his
anointed,
to David and his descendants forever.

Psalm 19

For the director of music. A psalm of David.

1 The heavens declare the glory of God;
the skies proclaim the work of his hands.
2 Day after day they pour forth speech;
night after night they display knowledge.
3 There is no speech or language
where their voice is not heard.[a]
4 Their voice[b] goes out into all the earth,
their words to the ends of the world.

In the heavens he has pitched a tent for the
sun,
5 which is like a bridegroom coming forth
from his pavilion,
like a champion rejoicing to run his
course.
6 It rises at one end of the heavens
and makes its circuit to the other;
nothing is hidden from its heat.

7 The law of the LORD is perfect,
reviving the soul.
The statutes of the LORD are trustworthy,
making wise the simple.
8 The precepts of the LORD are right,
giving joy to the heart.
The commands of the LORD are radiant,
giving light to the eyes.
9 The fear of the LORD is pure,
enduring forever.
The ordinances of the LORD are sure
and altogether righteous.
10 They are more precious than gold,
than much pure gold;
they are sweeter than honey,
than honey from the comb.
11 By them is your servant warned;
in keeping them there is great reward.

12 Who can discern his errors?
Forgive my hidden faults.

13 Keep your servant also from willful sins;
may they not rule over me.
Then will I be blameless,
innocent of great transgression.

19:7–14 The Names of God

*After describing the skies as a reflection of
God's glory in the first six verses, Psalm 19
switches gears. From the sun, moon, and stars
it turns to consider the beauty of God's law.
Reflecting that change, the poem in Hebrew
uses a different, more personal name for God.
The first six verses refer to God with a general
name that anyone, of any religion, might use—
just like our English word God. But from verse
seven on, God is called "the LORD" (a translation
of the Hebrew Yahweh)—the personal name
God revealed to Moses from the burning bush
(Exodus 3:15). The heavens declare the glory of
God, but God's law reveals even more—his
personal voice to his chosen people. He
introduces himself to them by his first name, as
it were.*

14 May the words of my mouth and the
meditation of my heart
be pleasing in your sight,
O LORD, my Rock and my Redeemer.

Psalm 20

For the director of music. A psalm of David.

1 May the LORD answer you when you are in
distress;
may the name of the God of Jacob protect
you.
2 May he send you help from the sanctuary
and grant you support from Zion.
3 May he remember all your sacrifices
and accept your burnt offerings.   *Selah*
4 May he give you the desire of your heart
and make all your plans succeed.
5 We will shout for joy when you are
victorious
and will lift up our banners in the name
of our God.
May the LORD grant all your requests.

6 Now I know that the LORD saves his
anointed;
he answers him from his holy heaven
with the saving power of his right hand.
7 Some trust in chariots and some in horses,
but we trust in the name of the LORD our
God.

a 3 Or *They have no speech, there are no words; / no sound is heard from them*   b 4 Septuagint, Jerome and Syriac;
Hebrew *line*

[8]They are brought to their knees and fall,
but we rise up and stand firm.

[9]O Lord, save the king!
Answer[a] us when we call!

Psalm 21

For the director of music. A psalm of David.

[1]O Lord, the king rejoices in your strength.
How great is his joy in the victories you give!
[2]You have granted him the desire of his heart
and have not withheld the request of his lips.   *Selah*
[3]You welcomed him with rich blessings
and placed a crown of pure gold on his head.
[4]He asked you for life, and you gave it to him—
length of days, for ever and ever.
[5]Through the victories you gave, his glory is great;
you have bestowed on him splendor and majesty.
[6]Surely you have granted him eternal blessings
and made him glad with the joy of your presence.
[7]For the king trusts in the Lord;
through the unfailing love of the Most High
he will not be shaken.

[8]Your hand will lay hold on all your enemies;
your right hand will seize your foes.
[9]At the time of your appearing
you will make them like a fiery furnace.
In his wrath the Lord will swallow them up,
and his fire will consume them.
[10]You will destroy their descendants from the earth,
their posterity from mankind.
[11]Though they plot evil against you
and devise wicked schemes, they cannot succeed;
[12]for you will make them turn their backs
when you aim at them with drawn bow.

[13]Be exalted, O Lord, in your strength;
we will sing and praise your might.

Psalm 22

For the director of music. To the tune of, "The Doe of the Morning." A psalm of David.

[1]My God, my God, why have you forsaken me?
Why are you so far from saving me,
so far from the words of my groaning?
[2]O my God, I cry out by day, but you do not answer,
by night, and am not silent.

[3]Yet you are enthroned as the Holy One;
you are the praise of Israel.[b]
[4]In you our fathers put their trust;
they trusted and you delivered them.
[5]They cried to you and were saved;
in you they trusted and were not disappointed.

[6]But I am a worm and not a man,
scorned by men and despised by the people.
[7]All who see me mock me;
they hurl insults, shaking their heads:
[8]"He trusts in the Lord;
let the Lord rescue him.
Let him deliver him,
since he delights in him."

[9]Yet you brought me out of the womb;
you made me trust in you
even at my mother's breast.
[10]From birth I was cast upon you;
from my mother's womb you have been my God.
[11]Do not be far from me,
for trouble is near
and there is no one to help.

[12]Many bulls surround me;
strong bulls of Bashan encircle me.
[13]Roaring lions tearing their prey
open their mouths wide against me.
[14]I am poured out like water,
and all my bones are out of joint.
My heart has turned to wax;
it has melted away within me.
[15]My strength is dried up like a potsherd,
and my tongue sticks to the roof of my mouth;
you lay me[c] in the dust of death.
[16]Dogs have surrounded me;
a band of evil men has encircled me,
they have pierced[d] my hands and my feet.
[17]I can count all my bones;
people stare and gloat over me.
[18]They divide my garments among them
and cast lots for my clothing.

[19]But you, O Lord, be not far off;
O my Strength, come quickly to help me.
[20]Deliver my life from the sword,
my precious life from the power of the dogs.

[a]9 Or *save! / O King, answer*   [b]3 Or *Yet you are holy, / enthroned on the praises of Israel*   [c]15 Or */ I am laid*
[d]16 Some Hebrew manuscripts, Septuagint and Syriac; most Hebrew manuscripts */ like the lion,*

21Rescue me from the mouth of the lions;
  save*a* me from the horns of the wild
    oxen.

22I will declare your name to my brothers;
  in the congregation I will praise you.
23You who fear the LORD, praise him!
  All you descendants of Jacob, honor him!
  Revere him, all you descendants of Israel!
24For he has not despised or disdained
  the suffering of the afflicted one;
  he has not hidden his face from him
    but has listened to his cry for help.

25From you comes the theme of my praise in
  the great assembly;

before those who fear you*b* will I fulfill
  my vows.
26The poor will eat and be satisfied;
  they who seek the LORD will praise
    him—
  may your hearts live forever!
27All the ends of the earth
  will remember and turn to the LORD,
and all the families of the nations
  will bow down before him,
28for dominion belongs to the LORD
  and he rules over the nations.

29All the rich of the earth will feast and
  worship;

a21 Or / you have heard   b25 Hebrew him

The Song of the Cross
Even the best people sometimes suffer

> They divide my gar-
> ments among them
> and cast lots for my
> clothing. 22:18

SUPERFICIALLY, THE OLD TESTAMENT CAN sometimes read like it's taken from old movies. The good guys are the Israelites, and they fight with the bad guys from nations around them. The Israelites have moments when they get off track, worshiping idols and acting like their "bad guy" neighbors. But when they turn back to God, they invariably win, and win big. The ending, in story after story, is happy. God *is* on their side.

Yet, in Psalm 22 and a few other places, the "good guy" story doesn't fit at all. This poem, credited to David, the great king and man "after God's own heart," tells of tremendous suffering with no relief from God. It sounds like a mob scene, a lynching. The "good guy's" enemies have him. They surround him, jeering, like a pack of dogs. He is helpless and exhausted. All he can do is cry to God.

The psalmist wavers back and forth, first crying out in misery, then taking stock of God's wonderful character, then describing his misery again. The whole poem is a prayer to God. Although this cry has gone up day and night (verse 2), God remains silent.

Whose Humiliations?

Then, at verse 22, the poem takes a dramatic turn, switching from grief to jubilation. Somehow, God has saved the sufferer, who, in great excitement, tells others about it. He sees more than his own good fortune: He foresees this deliverance spilling over into the whole world. He predicts the story of God's help told to future generations forever. God will be worshiped by the entire world.

A person might read Psalm 22 as an extravagantly poetic description of David's troubles. But Jesus and the writers of the New Testament saw something more in it. When Jesus was dying on the cross, he had this psalm on his lips (Matthew 27:46). Afterwards, when his disciples wanted to explain Jesus' life and sufferings, they turned to this psalm and others like it.

In them the disciples saw a pattern and a foreshadowing. The pattern is redemptive suffering. If good guys do not always win, if God seems actually to desert them—if David himself, the great leader and true man of God, knew these pains—then surely no one is exempt. And this suffering has a point. After it (and because of it) come victory and power, and the salvation of the world. This pattern helped Jesus' followers appreciate why Jesus, along with his followers, had to suffer.

A Fulfillment of Prophecy

Psalm 22 also helped the New Testament writers to see Jesus' life as a fulfillment of Old Testament prophecy. Jews had expected a Warrior-Messiah, a son of David who, like David, would lead his people to victory through battle. In Psalm 22 they saw that David had left another legacy: victory through suffering. The Messiah would lead his followers in suffering. Only Isaiah had put it more clearly, in his famous "servant" passages (Isaiah 42:1–9; 49:1–7; 50:4–9; 52:13–53:12). Psalm 22 stretches beyond the time of David; Jesus fits it perfectly.

Life Questions: Have you ever seen good come out of suffering for your friends or family?

all who go down to the dust will kneel
before him—
those who cannot keep themselves alive.
³⁰Posterity will serve him;
future generations will be told about the
Lord.
³¹They will proclaim his righteousness
to a people yet unborn—
for he has done it.

Psalm 23

A psalm of David.

¹The LORD is my shepherd, I shall not be in
want.
² He makes me lie down in green pastures,
he leads me beside quiet waters,
³ he restores my soul.
He guides me in paths of righteousness
for his name's sake.
⁴Even though I walk
through the valley of the shadow of
death,[a]
I will fear no evil,
for you are with me;
your rod and your staff,
they comfort me.

⁵You prepare a table before me
in the presence of my enemies.
You anoint my head with oil;
my cup overflows.
⁶Surely goodness and love will follow me
all the days of my life,
and I will dwell in the house of the LORD
forever.

Psalm 24

Of David. A psalm.

¹The earth is the LORD's, and everything in it,
the world, and all who live in it;
²for he founded it upon the seas
and established it upon the waters.

³Who may ascend the hill of the LORD?
Who may stand in his holy place?
⁴He who has clean hands and a pure heart,
who does not lift up his soul to an idol
or swear by what is false.[b]
⁵He will receive blessing from the LORD
and vindication from God his Savior.
⁶Such is the generation of those who seek
him,
who seek your face, O God of Jacob.[c]

Selah

⁷Lift up your heads, O you gates;
be lifted up, you ancient doors,
that the King of glory may come in.
⁸Who is this King of glory?
The LORD strong and mighty,
the LORD mighty in battle.
⁹Lift up your heads, O you gates;
lift them up, you ancient doors,
that the King of glory may come in.
¹⁰Who is he, this King of glory?
The LORD Almighty—
he is the King of glory.

Selah

Psalm 25[d]

Of David.

¹To you, O LORD, I lift up my soul;
² in you I trust, O my God.
Do not let me be put to shame,
nor let my enemies triumph over me.
³No one whose hope is in you
will ever be put to shame,
but they will be put to shame
who are treacherous without excuse.

⁴Show me your ways, O LORD,
teach me your paths;
⁵guide me in your truth and teach me,
for you are God my Savior,
and my hope is in you all day long.
⁶Remember, O LORD, your great mercy and
love,
for they are from of old.
⁷Remember not the sins of my youth
and my rebellious ways;
according to your love remember me,
for you are good, O LORD.

⁸Good and upright is the LORD;
therefore he instructs sinners in his ways.
⁹He guides the humble in what is right
and teaches them his way.
¹⁰All the ways of the LORD are loving and
faithful
for those who keep the demands of his
covenant.
¹¹For the sake of your name, O LORD,
forgive my iniquity, though it is great.
¹²Who, then, is the man that fears the LORD?
He will instruct him in the way chosen for
him.
¹³He will spend his days in prosperity,
and his descendants will inherit the land.
¹⁴The LORD confides in those who fear him;
he makes his covenant known to them.
¹⁵My eyes are ever on the LORD,

---

[a]4 Or *through the darkest valley* [b]4 Or *swear falsely* [c]6 Two Hebrew manuscripts and Syriac (see also
Septuagint); most Hebrew manuscripts *face, Jacob* [d]This psalm is an acrostic poem, the verses of which begin with
the successive letters of the Hebrew alphabet.

for only he will release my feet from the
snare.

16Turn to me and be gracious to me,
for I am lonely and afflicted.
17The troubles of my heart have multiplied;
free me from my anguish.
18Look upon my affliction and my distress
and take away all my sins.
19See how my enemies have increased
and how fiercely they hate me!
20Guard my life and rescue me;
let me not be put to shame,
for I take refuge in you.
21May integrity and uprightness protect me,
because my hope is in you.

22Redeem Israel, O God,
from all their troubles!

Psalm 26

Of David.

1Vindicate me, O LORD,
for I have led a blameless life;
I have trusted in the LORD
without wavering.
2Test me, O LORD, and try me,
examine my heart and my mind;
3for your love is ever before me,
and I walk continually in your truth.
4I do not sit with deceitful men,
nor do I consort with hypocrites;
5I abhor the assembly of evildoers
and refuse to sit with the wicked.
6I wash my hands in innocence,
and go about your altar, O LORD,
7proclaiming aloud your praise
and telling of all your wonderful deeds.
8I love the house where you live, O LORD,
the place where your glory dwells.

9Do not take away my soul along with
sinners,
my life with bloodthirsty men,
10in whose hands are wicked schemes,
whose right hands are full of bribes.
11But I lead a blameless life;
redeem me and be merciful to me.

12My feet stand on level ground;
in the great assembly I will praise the
LORD.

Psalm 27

Of David.

1The LORD is my light and my salvation—
whom shall I fear?

The LORD is the stronghold of my life—
of whom shall I be afraid?
2When evil men advance against me
to devour my flesh,[a]
when my enemies and my foes attack me,
they will stumble and fall.

26:11 Self-Righteous?

*This claim to be blameless or righteous—
repeated many times in other psalms—should
not be stretched too far. Whenever the
psalmists examined themselves before God,
they acknowledged their deep need for
forgiveness (see 19:12; 32:1–5; 130:3; and
143:2).*

*Here, though, the issue is God's fairness.
Knowing little about life after death, the
psalmists expected that good people would do
better in this life than bad people. They were
deeply puzzled when they did not. Didn't God
control every event? In calling for justice, they
emphasized that they had been more faithful
to God than their enemies.*

*Compared to the people plotting murder and
betrayal against him, the psalmist was
blameless. In a wholehearted, sincere way he
had followed God. He was no hypocrite. He
responds like a person swearing in court about
his traffic accident: "My driving is blameless."
He doesn't mean he never makes a mistake. He
means only that he doesn't deserve
punishment.*

3Though an army besiege me,
my heart will not fear;
though war break out against me,
even then will I be confident.

4One thing I ask of the LORD,
this is what I seek:
that I may dwell in the house of the LORD
all the days of my life,
to gaze upon the beauty of the LORD
and to seek him in his temple.
5For in the day of trouble
he will keep me safe in his dwelling;
he will hide me in the shelter of his
tabernacle
and set me high upon a rock.
6Then my head will be exalted
above the enemies who surround me;
at his tabernacle will I sacrifice with shouts
of joy;
I will sing and make music to the LORD.

7Hear my voice when I call, O LORD;
be merciful to me and answer me.
8My heart says of you, "Seek his[b] face!"

a2 Or to slander me   b8 Or To you, O my heart, he has said, "Seek my

Your face, LORD, I will seek.
⁹Do not hide your face from me,
 do not turn your servant away in anger;
 you have been my helper.
Do not reject me or forsake me,
 O God my Savior.
¹⁰Though my father and mother forsake me,
 the LORD will receive me.
¹¹Teach me your way, O LORD;
 lead me in a straight path
 because of my oppressors.
¹²Do not turn me over to the desire of my
 foes,
 for false witnesses rise up against me,
 breathing out violence.

¹³I am still confident of this:
 I will see the goodness of the LORD
 in the land of the living.
¹⁴Wait for the LORD;
 be strong and take heart
 and wait for the LORD.

Psalm 28

Of David.

¹To you I call, O LORD my Rock;
 do not turn a deaf ear to me.
For if you remain silent,
 I will be like those who have gone down
 to the pit.
²Hear my cry for mercy
 as I call to you for help,
as I lift up my hands
 toward your Most Holy Place.

³Do not drag me away with the wicked,
 with those who do evil,
who speak cordially with their neighbors
 but harbor malice in their hearts.
⁴Repay them for their deeds
 and for their evil work;
repay them for what their hands have done
 and bring back upon them what they
 deserve.
⁵Since they show no regard for the works of
 the LORD
 and what his hands have done,
he will tear them down
 and never build them up again.

⁶Praise be to the LORD,
 for he has heard my cry for mercy.
⁷The LORD is my strength and my shield;
 my heart trusts in him, and I am helped.
My heart leaps for joy
 and I will give thanks to him in song.

⁸The LORD is the strength of his people,

a fortress of salvation for his anointed
 one.
⁹Save your people and bless your inheritance;
 be their shepherd and carry them forever.

Psalm 29

A psalm of David.

¹Ascribe to the LORD, O mighty ones,
 ascribe to the LORD glory and strength.
²Ascribe to the LORD the glory due his name;
 worship the LORD in the splendor of his[a]
 holiness.

³The voice of the LORD is over the waters;
 the God of glory thunders,
 the LORD thunders over the mighty waters.
⁴The voice of the LORD is powerful;
 the voice of the LORD is majestic.
⁵The voice of the LORD breaks the cedars;
 the LORD breaks in pieces the cedars of
 Lebanon.
⁶He makes Lebanon skip like a calf,
 Sirion[b] like a young wild ox.
⁷The voice of the LORD strikes
 with flashes of lightning.
⁸The voice of the LORD shakes the desert;
 the LORD shakes the Desert of Kadesh.
⁹The voice of the LORD twists the oaks[c]
 and strips the forests bare.
And in his temple all cry, "Glory!"

¹⁰The LORD sits[d] enthroned over the flood;
 the LORD is enthroned as King forever.
¹¹The LORD gives strength to his people;
 the LORD blesses his people with peace.

Psalm 30

A psalm. A song. For the dedication of the
temple.[e] Of David.

¹I will exalt you, O LORD,
 for you lifted me out of the depths
 and did not let my enemies gloat over me.
²O LORD my God, I called to you for help
 and you healed me.
³O LORD, you brought me up from the
 grave[f];
 you spared me from going down into the
 pit.

⁴Sing to the LORD, you saints of his;
 praise his holy name.
⁵For his anger lasts only a moment,
 but his favor lasts a lifetime;
weeping may remain for a night,
 but rejoicing comes in the morning.

ᵃ2 Or LORD *with the splendor of*   ᵇ6 That is, Mount Hermon
ᵈ10 Or *sat*   ᵉTitle: Or *palace*   ᶠ3 Hebrew *Sheol*   ᶜ9 Or LORD *makes the deer give birth*

⁶When I felt secure, I said,
  "I will never be shaken."
⁷O LORD, when you favored me,
  you made my mountain[a] stand firm;
but when you hid your face,
  I was dismayed.

30:5 One-night Guest

The Bible never ignores the emotions of the moment. Here, the psalmist acknowledges the tough times that come with living as God's child. But the Bible also insists on a long-range perspective. Difficulties don't last; God's care does. This psalm pictures "weeping" as a guest who comes to stay for just a single night.

⁸To you, O LORD, I called;
  to the Lord I cried for mercy:
⁹"What gain is there in my destruction,[b]
  in my going down into the pit?
Will the dust praise you?
  Will it proclaim your faithfulness?
¹⁰Hear, O LORD, and be merciful to me;
  O LORD, be my help."

¹¹You turned my wailing into dancing;
  you removed my sackcloth and clothed
    me with joy,
¹²that my heart may sing to you and not be
    silent.
  O LORD my God, I will give you thanks
    forever.

Psalm 31

For the director of music. A psalm of David.

¹In you, O LORD, I have taken refuge;
  let me never be put to shame;
  deliver me in your righteousness.
²Turn your ear to me,
  come quickly to my rescue;
be my rock of refuge,
  a strong fortress to save me.
³Since you are my rock and my fortress,
  for the sake of your name lead and guide
    me.
⁴Free me from the trap that is set for me,
  for you are my refuge.
⁵Into your hands I commit my spirit;
  redeem me, O LORD, the God of truth.

⁶I hate those who cling to worthless idols;
  I trust in the LORD.
⁷I will be glad and rejoice in your love,
  for you saw my affliction
  and knew the anguish of my soul.

⁸You have not handed me over to the enemy
  but have set my feet in a spacious place.

⁹Be merciful to me, O LORD, for I am in
    distress;
  my eyes grow weak with sorrow,
  my soul and my body with grief.
¹⁰My life is consumed by anguish
  and my years by groaning;
my strength fails because of my affliction,[c]
  and my bones grow weak.
¹¹Because of all my enemies,
  I am the utter contempt of my neighbors;
I am a dread to my friends—
  those who see me on the street flee from
    me.
¹²I am forgotten by them as though I were
    dead;
  I have become like broken pottery.
¹³For I hear the slander of many;
  there is terror on every side;
they conspire against me
  and plot to take my life.

¹⁴But I trust in you, O LORD;
  I say, "You are my God."
¹⁵My times are in your hands;
  deliver me from my enemies
  and from those who pursue me.
¹⁶Let your face shine on your servant;
  save me in your unfailing love.
¹⁷Let me not be put to shame, O LORD,
  for I have cried out to you;
but let the wicked be put to shame
  and lie silent in the grave.[d]
¹⁸Let their lying lips be silenced,
  for with pride and contempt
  they speak arrogantly against the
    righteous.

¹⁹How great is your goodness,
  which you have stored up for those who
    fear you,
  which you bestow in the sight of men
  on those who take refuge in you.
²⁰In the shelter of your presence you hide
    them
  from the intrigues of men;
in your dwelling you keep them safe
  from accusing tongues.

²¹Praise be to the LORD,
  for he showed his wonderful love to me
  when I was in a besieged city.
²²In my alarm I said,
  "I am cut off from your sight!"
Yet you heard my cry for mercy
  when I called to you for help.

²³Love the LORD, all his saints!
  The LORD preserves the faithful,

---

[a]7 Or *hill country*   [b]9 Or *there if I am silenced*   [c]10 Or *guilt*   [d]17 Hebrew *Sheol*

but the proud he pays back in full.

²⁴Be strong and take heart,
  all you who hope in the LORD.

Psalm 32

Of David. A *maskil.*ᵃ

¹Blessed is he
  whose transgressions are forgiven,
  whose sins are covered.
²Blessed is the man
  whose sin the LORD does not count
    against him
  and in whose spirit is no deceit.

32:2 The Benefits of Faith

Paul quoted this verse in Romans 4:6–8, while making his case that we do not earn status in God's eyes: God must credit righteousness on the basis of faith.

³When I kept silent,
  my bones wasted away
  through my groaning all day long.
⁴For day and night
  your hand was heavy upon me;
my strength was sapped
  as in the heat of summer.   *Selah*
⁵Then I acknowledged my sin to you
  and did not cover up my iniquity.
I said, "I will confess
  my transgressions to the LORD"—
and you forgave
  the guilt of my sin.   *Selah*

⁶Therefore let everyone who is godly pray to
    you
  while you may be found;
surely when the mighty waters rise,
  they will not reach him.
⁷You are my hiding place;
  you will protect me from trouble
  and surround me with songs of
    deliverance.   *Selah*

⁸I will instruct you and teach you in the way
  you should go;
  I will counsel you and watch over you.
⁹Do not be like the horse or the mule,
  which have no understanding
but must be controlled by bit and bridle
  or they will not come to you.
¹⁰Many are the woes of the wicked,
  but the LORD's unfailing love
  surrounds the man who trusts in him.

¹¹Rejoice in the LORD and be glad, you
  righteous;
  sing, all you who are upright in heart!

Psalm 33

¹Sing joyfully to the LORD, you righteous;
  it is fitting for the upright to praise him.
²Praise the LORD with the harp;
  make music to him on the ten-stringed
    lyre.
³Sing to him a new song;
  play skillfully, and shout for joy.

⁴For the word of the LORD is right and true;
  he is faithful in all he does.
⁵The LORD loves righteousness and justice;
  the earth is full of his unfailing love.

⁶By the word of the LORD were the heavens
  made,
  their starry host by the breath of his
    mouth.
⁷He gathers the waters of the sea into jarsᵇ;
  he puts the deep into storehouses.
⁸Let all the earth fear the LORD;
  let all the people of the world revere him.
⁹For he spoke, and it came to be;
  he commanded, and it stood firm.
¹⁰The LORD foils the plans of the nations;
  he thwarts the purposes of the peoples.
¹¹But the plans of the LORD stand firm forever,
  the purposes of his heart through all
    generations.

¹²Blessed is the nation whose God is the LORD,
  the people he chose for his inheritance.
¹³From heaven the LORD looks down
  and sees all mankind;
¹⁴from his dwelling place he watches
  all who live on earth—
¹⁵he who forms the hearts of all,
  who considers everything they do.

¹⁶No king is saved by the size of his army;
  no warrior escapes by his great strength.
¹⁷A horse is a vain hope for deliverance;
  despite all its great strength it cannot save.
¹⁸But the eyes of the LORD are on those who
  fear him,
  on those whose hope is in his unfailing
    love,
¹⁹to deliver them from death
  and keep them alive in famine.

²⁰We wait in hope for the LORD;
  he is our help and our shield.
²¹In him our hearts rejoice,
  for we trust in his holy name.
²²May your unfailing love rest upon us,
  O LORD,
  even as we put our hope in you.

ᵃTitle: Probably a literary or musical term   ᵇ7 Or *sea as into a heap*

Psalm 34[a]

Of David. When he pretended to be insane
before Abimelech, who drove him away,
and he left.

[1]I will extol the LORD at all times;
his praise will always be on my lips.
[2]My soul will boast in the LORD;
let the afflicted hear and rejoice.
[3]Glorify the LORD with me;
let us exalt his name together.

[4]I sought the LORD, and he answered me;
he delivered me from all my fears.
[5]Those who look to him are radiant;
their faces are never covered with shame.

[6]This poor man called, and the LORD heard
him;
he saved him out of all his troubles.
[7]The angel of the LORD encamps around those
who fear him,
and he delivers them.

[8]Taste and see that the LORD is good;
blessed is the man who takes refuge in
him.
[9]Fear the LORD, you his saints,
for those who fear him lack nothing.
[10]The lions may grow weak and hungry,
but those who seek the LORD lack no good
thing.

[11]Come, my children, listen to me;

[a]This psalm is an acrostic poem, the verses of which begin with the successive letters of the Hebrew alphabet.

Lyrics for the Living God
The psalms were meant to be sung—and shouted

> Sing to him a new song; play skillfully, and shout for joy.
> 33:3

WILLIAM BOOTH, BELIEVING THE 19TH-CENTURY English church had become too refined to reach the cities' poor, took the gospel into the streets. He organized his workers into a "salvation army," complete with uniforms and military rank.

With hecklers and drunks abounding, the "army" didn't always find preaching easy or safe. A local builder, Charles William Fry, offered himself and his three sons as bodyguards. As it happened all four played brass instruments, which they carried along to accompany singing.

Booth's rowdier supporters were soon dragging along concertinas, bells, hunting horns, banjos, tambourines, and drums to praise the Lord. Said one leader, "It sounds as if a brass band's gone out of its mind."

Salvation Army recruits did not stick to traditional hymns but invented their own words for rousing popular tunes. "Here's to Good Old Whiskey" became "Storm the Forts of Darkness." Booth had his doubts about this trend until one night, hearing a beautiful rendition of "Bless His Name, He Sets Me Free," he asked about the tune. "Why, Mr. Booth, that's 'Champagne Charlie Is My Name,'" the embarrassed singer replied.

"That settles it," Booth said. "Why *should* the devil have all the best tunes?" Soon 400 bands were crashing about England, playing hit tunes with Christian words.

The Best Music Available

David and his people would have liked that spirit. Many of the psalms were meant to be sung, and sung joyfully. Modern church formality seems far removed from their frequent command: "Sing for joy! Shout aloud!" Their instruments included cymbals, tambourines, trumpets, ram's horns, harps, and lyres. Sometimes dancing erupted. The world, in the psalmist's imagination, can't contain the delight God inspires. A *new* song must be sung. "Shout for joy to the LORD, all the earth, burst into jubilant song" (98:4).

First Chronicles 15:16 and 23:5 report that David appointed 4,000 professional musicians to provide their services to the temple. They offered the best music available, and the congregation joined in. Nobody knows exactly what it sounded like, but scholars doubt it was all soft and soothing. Musicians improvised. Most of the instruments used suggest rousing, rhythmic sound.

Every generation of Christians renews the discovery of this "new song," sometimes through the music of their forebears, sometimes in a form that shocks their solemn elders. The Salvation Army did, as did the Jesus Movement in the 60s and Christian rock music in the 80s and 90s. David would not have been surprised. He jolted his own wife with spontaneous dancing (see 1 Chronicles 15:29). When people know God, they come to life with a jubilant song on their lips.

Life Questions: When you sing to God, what kind of emotions do you hope to feel? What kind of music contributes to that?

I will teach you the fear of the LORD.
¹²Whoever of you loves life
and desires to see many good days,
¹³keep your tongue from evil

and your lips from speaking lies.
¹⁴Turn from evil and do good;
seek peace and pursue it.

¹⁵The eyes of the LORD are on the righteous
and his ears are attentive to their cry;
¹⁶the face of the LORD is against those who do evil,
to cut off the memory of them from the earth.

¹⁷The righteous cry out, and the LORD hears them;
he delivers them from all their troubles.
¹⁸The LORD is close to the brokenhearted
and saves those who are crushed in spirit.

¹⁹A righteous man may have many troubles,
but the LORD delivers him from them all;
²⁰he protects all his bones,
not one of them will be broken.

²¹Evil will slay the wicked;
the foes of the righteous will be condemned.
²²The LORD redeems his servants;
no one will be condemned who takes refuge in him.

Psalm 35

Of David.

¹Contend, O LORD, with those who contend with me;
fight against those who fight against me.
²Take up shield and buckler;
arise and come to my aid.
³Brandish spear and javelin*a*
against those who pursue me.
Say to my soul,
"I am your salvation."

⁴May those who seek my life
be disgraced and put to shame;
may those who plot my ruin
be turned back in dismay.
⁵May they be like chaff before the wind,
with the angel of the LORD driving them away;
⁶may their path be dark and slippery,
with the angel of the LORD pursuing them.
⁷Since they hid their net for me without cause
and without cause dug a pit for me,
⁸may ruin overtake them by surprise—
may the net they hid entangle them,
may they fall into the pit, to their ruin.
⁹Then my soul will rejoice in the LORD
and delight in his salvation.
¹⁰My whole being will exclaim,
"Who is like you, O LORD?
You rescue the poor from those too strong for them,
the poor and needy from those who rob them."

¹¹Ruthless witnesses come forward;
they question me on things I know nothing about.
¹²They repay me evil for good
and leave my soul forlorn.
¹³Yet when they were ill, I put on sackcloth
and humbled myself with fasting.
When my prayers returned to me unanswered,
¹⁴ I went about mourning
as though for my friend or brother.
I bowed my head in grief
as though weeping for my mother.
¹⁵But when I stumbled, they gathered in glee;
attackers gathered against me when I was unaware.
They slandered me without ceasing.
¹⁶Like the ungodly they maliciously mocked*b*;
they gnashed their teeth at me.
¹⁷O Lord, how long will you look on?
Rescue my life from their ravages,
my precious life from these lions.
¹⁸I will give you thanks in the great assembly;
among throngs of people I will praise you.

¹⁹Let not those gloat over me
who are my enemies without cause;
let not those who hate me without reason
maliciously wink the eye.
²⁰They do not speak peaceably,
but devise false accusations
against those who live quietly in the land.
²¹They gape at me and say, "Aha! Aha!
With our own eyes we have seen it."
²²O LORD, you have seen this; be not silent.
Do not be far from me, O Lord.

a 3 Or *and block the way*   *b 16* Septuagint; Hebrew may mean *ungodly circle of mockers.*

²³Awake, and rise to my defense!
Contend for me, my God and Lord.
²⁴Vindicate me in your righteousness, O LORD
my God;
do not let them gloat over me.
²⁵Do not let them think, "Aha, just what we
wanted!"
or say, "We have swallowed him up."

²⁶May all who gloat over my distress
be put to shame and confusion;
may all who exalt themselves over me
be clothed with shame and disgrace.
²⁷May those who delight in my vindication
shout for joy and gladness;
may they always say, "The LORD be exalted,
who delights in the well-being of his
servant."
²⁸My tongue will speak of your righteousness
and of your praises all day long.

Psalm 36

For the director of music. Of David the servant
of the LORD.

¹An oracle is within my heart
concerning the sinfulness of the wicked:^a
There is no fear of God
before his eyes.
²For in his own eyes he flatters himself
too much to detect or hate his sin.
³The words of his mouth are wicked and
deceitful;
he has ceased to be wise and to do good.
⁴Even on his bed he plots evil;
he commits himself to a sinful course
and does not reject what is wrong.

⁵Your love, O LORD, reaches to the heavens,
your faithfulness to the skies.
⁶Your righteousness is like the mighty
mountains,
your justice like the great deep.
O LORD, you preserve both man and beast.
⁷ How priceless is your unfailing love!
Both high and low among men
find^b refuge in the shadow of your wings.
⁸They feast on the abundance of your house;
you give them drink from your river of
delights.
⁹For with you is the fountain of life;
in your light we see light.

¹⁰Continue your love to those who know you,
your righteousness to the upright in heart.
¹¹May the foot of the proud not come against
me,

nor the hand of the wicked drive me
away.
¹²See how the evildoers lie fallen—
thrown down, not able to rise!

36:9 Light Makes Light

*By itself, light is invisible; and yet everything is
invisible until light strikes it. So it is with God:
we can't see him, but "in his light" (under his
loving influence) we see and understand his
love in all that surrounds us. God's
overwhelming generosity stands in complete
contrast to the self-important plotting of
wicked human beings (verses 1–4).*

Psalm 37^c

Of David.

¹Do not fret because of evil men
or be envious of those who do wrong;
²for like the grass they will soon wither,
like green plants they will soon die away.

³Trust in the LORD and do good;
dwell in the land and enjoy safe pasture.
⁴Delight yourself in the LORD
and he will give you the desires of your
heart.

⁵Commit your way to the LORD;
trust in him and he will do this:
⁶He will make your righteousness shine like
the dawn,
the justice of your cause like the noonday
sun.

⁷Be still before the LORD and wait patiently
for him;
do not fret when men succeed in their
ways,
when they carry out their wicked schemes.

⁸Refrain from anger and turn from wrath;
do not fret—it leads only to evil.
⁹For evil men will be cut off,
but those who hope in the LORD will
inherit the land.

¹⁰A little while, and the wicked will be no
more;
though you look for them, they will not
be found.
¹¹But the meek will inherit the land
and enjoy great peace.

¹²The wicked plot against the righteous
and gnash their teeth at them;

13but the Lord laughs at the wicked,
for he knows their day is coming.

14The wicked draw the sword
and bend the bow
to bring down the poor and needy,
to slay those whose ways are upright.
15But their swords will pierce their own hearts,
and their bows will be broken.

16Better the little that the righteous have
than the wealth of many wicked;
17for the power of the wicked will be broken,
but the LORD upholds the righteous.

18The days of the blameless are known to the
LORD,
and their inheritance will endure forever.
19In times of disaster they will not wither;
in days of famine they will enjoy plenty.

20But the wicked will perish:
The LORD's enemies will be like the beauty
of the fields,
they will vanish—vanish like smoke.

21The wicked borrow and do not repay,
but the righteous give generously;
22those the LORD blesses will inherit the land,
but those he curses will be cut off.

23If the LORD delights in a man's way,
he makes his steps firm;
24though he stumble, he will not fall,
for the LORD upholds him with his hand.

25I was young and now I am old,
yet I have never seen the righteous
forsaken
or their children begging bread.

37:25 Never Abandoned

*Is life unfair? Psalm 37 ponders that
perplexing question. Its basic conclusion: The
success of wicked people won't last, while in the
long run people who do right will flourish. The
psalmist adds this observation, based on
experience: Through a lifetime of troubles and
anxieties, he has yet to see the righteous
abandoned by God and unable to provide the
basics of life for their children. Their generosity
doesn't bankrupt them.*

26They are always generous and lend freely;
their children will be blessed.

27Turn from evil and do good;
then you will dwell in the land forever.
28For the LORD loves the just
and will not forsake his faithful ones.

They will be protected forever,
but the offspring of the wicked will be cut
off;
29the righteous will inherit the land
and dwell in it forever.

30The mouth of the righteous man utters
wisdom,
and his tongue speaks what is just.
31The law of his God is in his heart;
his feet do not slip.

32The wicked lie in wait for the righteous,
seeking their very lives;
33but the LORD will not leave them in their
power
or let them be condemned when brought
to trial.

34Wait for the LORD
and keep his way.
He will exalt you to inherit the land;
when the wicked are cut off, you will see
it.

35I have seen a wicked and ruthless man
flourishing like a green tree in its native
soil,
36but he soon passed away and was no more;
though I looked for him, he could not be
found.

37Consider the blameless, observe the upright;
there is a future[a] for the man of peace.
38But all sinners will be destroyed;
the future[b] of the wicked will be cut off.

39The salvation of the righteous comes from
the LORD;
he is their stronghold in time of trouble.
40The LORD helps them and delivers them;
he delivers them from the wicked and
saves them,
because they take refuge in him.

Psalm 38

A psalm of David. A petition.

1O LORD, do not rebuke me in your anger
or discipline me in your wrath.
2For your arrows have pierced me,
and your hand has come down upon me.
3Because of your wrath there is no health in
my body;
my bones have no soundness because of
my sin.
4My guilt has overwhelmed me
like a burden too heavy to bear.
5My wounds fester and are loathsome
because of my sinful folly.

---

a37 Or *there will be posterity*   *b38* Or *posterity*

⁶I am bowed down and brought very low;
    all day long I go about mourning.
⁷My back is filled with searing pain;
    there is no health in my body.
⁸I am feeble and utterly crushed;
    I groan in anguish of heart.

⁹All my longings lie open before you, O Lord;
    my sighing is not hidden from you.
¹⁰My heart pounds, my strength fails me;
    even the light has gone from my eyes.
¹¹My friends and companions avoid me
    because of my wounds;
    my neighbors stay far away.
¹²Those who seek my life set their traps,
    those who would harm me talk of my
      ruin;
    all day long they plot deception.

¹³I am like a deaf man, who cannot hear,
    like a mute, who cannot open his mouth;
¹⁴I have become like a man who does not
      hear,
    whose mouth can offer no reply.
¹⁵I wait for you, O LORD;
    you will answer, O Lord my God.
¹⁶For I said, "Do not let them gloat
    or exalt themselves over me when my foot
      slips."

¹⁷For I am about to fall,
    and my pain is ever with me.
¹⁸I confess my iniquity;
    I am troubled by my sin.
¹⁹Many are those who are my vigorous
      enemies;
    those who hate me without reason are
      numerous.
²⁰Those who repay my good with evil
    slander me when I pursue what is good.

²¹O LORD, do not forsake me;
    be not far from me, O my God.
²²Come quickly to help me,
    O Lord my Savior.

Psalm 39

For the director of music. For Jeduthun.
A psalm of David.

¹I said, "I will watch my ways
    and keep my tongue from sin;
 I will put a muzzle on my mouth
    as long as the wicked are in my presence."
²But when I was silent and still,
    not even saying anything good,
    my anguish increased.
³My heart grew hot within me,
    and as I meditated, the fire burned;
    then I spoke with my tongue:

⁴"Show me, O LORD, my life's end

and the number of my days;
    let me know how fleeting is my life.
⁵You have made my days a mere
      handbreadth;
    the span of my years is as nothing before
      you.
    Each man's life is but a breath.   *Selah*
⁶Man is a mere phantom as he goes to and
      fro:
    He bustles about, but only in vain;
    he heaps up wealth, not knowing who will
      get it.

⁷"But now, Lord, what do I look for?
    My hope is in you.
⁸Save me from all my transgressions;
    do not make me the scorn of fools.
⁹I was silent; I would not open my mouth,
    for you are the one who has done this.
¹⁰Remove your scourge from me;
    I am overcome by the blow of your hand.

39:10 Wrestling with God

Not all the psalms are happy. Some, such as this one and Psalms 44 and 88, are intensely sad. They try to make sense out of suffering, and fail. They ask God for help and receive none. The Bible's inclusion of such hopeless cries eloquently testifies to God's acceptance of human struggles. These psalms are not the final word on suffering. They show, however, that wrestling with God has value even when we fail to find answers.

¹¹You rebuke and discipline men for their sin;
    you consume their wealth like a moth—
    each man is but a breath.   *Selah*

¹²"Hear my prayer, O LORD,
    listen to my cry for help;
    be not deaf to my weeping.
For I dwell with you as an alien,
    a stranger, as all my fathers were.
¹³Look away from me, that I may rejoice again
    before I depart and am no more."

Psalm 40

For the director of music. Of David. A psalm.

¹I waited patiently for the LORD;
    he turned to me and heard my cry.
²He lifted me out of the slimy pit,
    out of the mud and mire;
he set my feet on a rock
    and gave me a firm place to stand.
³He put a new song in my mouth,
    a hymn of praise to our God.

Many will see and fear
  and put their trust in the LORD.

[4]Blessed is the man
  who makes the LORD his trust,
who does not look to the proud,
  to those who turn aside to false gods.[a]
[5]Many, O LORD my God,
  are the wonders you have done.
The things you planned for us
  no one can recount to you;
were I to speak and tell of them,
  they would be too many to declare.

[6]Sacrifice and offering you did not desire,
  but my ears you have pierced[b,c];
burnt offerings and sin offerings
  you did not require.

40:6 A Better Sacrifice

While the Old Testament law prescribed animal and grain sacrifices to deal with the problem of sin, Old Testament writers made clear that God really wanted obedient lives, not ritual performances. Hebrews 10:5–9 quotes these verses (6–8) in explaining that Jesus' sacrifice made all the animal sacrifices obsolete. Only Jesus' sacrifice has the power to actually forgive sins and change lives.

[7]Then I said, "Here I am, I have come—
  it is written about me in the scroll.[d]
[8]I desire to do your will, O my God;
  your law is within my heart."

[9]I proclaim righteousness in the great
      assembly;
  I do not seal my lips,
  as you know, O LORD.
[10]I do not hide your righteousness in my
      heart;
  I speak of your faithfulness and salvation.
I do not conceal your love and your truth
  from the great assembly.

[11]Do not withhold your mercy from me,
      O LORD;
  may your love and your truth always
      protect me.
[12]For troubles without number surround me;
  my sins have overtaken me, and I cannot
      see.
They are more than the hairs of my head,
  and my heart fails within me.

[13]Be pleased, O LORD, to save me;
  O LORD, come quickly to help me.
[14]May all who seek to take my life

be put to shame and confusion;
may all who desire my ruin
  be turned back in disgrace.
[15]May those who say to me, "Aha! Aha!"
  be appalled at their own shame.
[16]But may all who seek you
  rejoice and be glad in you;
may those who love your salvation always
      say,
  "The LORD be exalted!"

[17]Yet I am poor and needy;
  may the Lord think of me.
You are my help and my deliverer;
  O my God, do not delay.

Psalm 41

For the director of music. A psalm of David.

[1]Blessed is he who has regard for the weak;
  the LORD delivers him in times of trouble.

41:1 A Key Characteristic

The psalmist was severely ill. Enemies and rivals—and even a close friend, verse 9—whispered that he was dying. What made him so confident that God would heal him? He knew that God helps those who show "regard for the weak." Because he had shown integrity in this, he confidently expected God to show mercy to him. Jesus reflected this value when he said, "Blessed are the merciful, for they will be shown mercy" (Matthew 5:7).

[2]The LORD will protect him and preserve his
      life;
  he will bless him in the land
  and not surrender him to the desire of his
      foes.
[3]The LORD will sustain him on his sickbed
  and restore him from his bed of illness.

[4]I said, "O LORD, have mercy on me;
  heal me, for I have sinned against you."
[5]My enemies say of me in malice,
  "When will he die and his name perish?"
[6]Whenever one comes to see me,
  he speaks falsely, while his heart gathers
      slander;
  then he goes out and spreads it abroad.

[7]All my enemies whisper together against me;
  they imagine the worst for me, saying,
[8]"A vile disease has beset him;
  he will never get up from the place where
      he lies."

---

[a]4 Or *to falsehood*   [b]6 Hebrew; Septuagint *but a body you have prepared for me* (see also Symmachus and Theodotion)   [c]6 Or *opened*   [d]7 Or *come / with the scroll written for me*

⁹Even my close friend, whom I trusted,
  he who shared my bread,
  has lifted up his heel against me.

¹⁰But you, O LORD, have mercy on me;
  raise me up, that I may repay them.
¹¹I know that you are pleased with me,
  for my enemy does not triumph over me.
¹²In my integrity you uphold me
  and set me in your presence forever.

¹³Praise be to the LORD, the God of Israel,
  from everlasting to everlasting.
        Amen and Amen.

BOOK II

Psalms 42–72

Psalm 42ᵃ

For the director of music. A *maskil*ᵇ of the
Sons of Korah.

¹As the deer pants for streams of water,
  so my soul pants for you, O God.
²My soul thirsts for God, for the living God.
  When can I go and meet with God?
³My tears have been my food
  day and night,
while men say to me all day long,
  "Where is your God?"
⁴These things I remember
  as I pour out my soul:
how I used to go with the multitude,
  leading the procession to the house of
    God,
with shouts of joy and thanksgiving
  among the festive throng.

⁵Why are you downcast, O my soul?
  Why so disturbed within me?
Put your hope in God,
  for I will yet praise him,
  my Savior and ⁶my God.

Myᶜ soul is downcast within me;
  therefore I will remember you
from the land of the Jordan,
  the heights of Hermon—from Mount
    Mizar.
⁷Deep calls to deep
  in the roar of your waterfalls;
all your waves and breakers
  have swept over me.

⁸By day the LORD directs his love,
  at night his song is with me—
  a prayer to the God of my life.

⁹I say to God my Rock,
  "Why have you forgotten me?
Why must I go about mourning,
  oppressed by the enemy?"
¹⁰My bones suffer mortal agony
  as my foes taunt me,
saying to me all day long,
  "Where is your God?"

¹¹Why are you downcast, O my soul?
  Why so disturbed within me?
Put your hope in God,
  for I will yet praise him,
  my Savior and my God.

Psalm 43ᵃ

¹Vindicate me, O God,
  and plead my cause against an ungodly
    nation;
  rescue me from deceitful and wicked men.
²You are God my stronghold.
  Why have you rejected me?
Why must I go about mourning,
  oppressed by the enemy?
³Send forth your light and your truth,
  let them guide me;
let them bring me to your holy mountain,
  to the place where you dwell.
⁴Then will I go to the altar of God,
  to God, my joy and my delight.
I will praise you with the harp,
  O God, my God.

⁵Why are you downcast, O my soul?
  Why so disturbed within me?
Put your hope in God,
  for I will yet praise him,
  my Savior and my God.

Psalm 44

For the director of music. Of the Sons of Korah.
A *maskil.*ᵇ

¹We have heard with our ears, O God;
  our fathers have told us
what you did in their days,
  in days long ago.
²With your hand you drove out the nations
  and planted our fathers;
you crushed the peoples
  and made our fathers flourish.
³It was not by their sword that they won the
    land,
  nor did their arm bring them victory;
it was your right hand, your arm,
  and the light of your face, for you loved
    them.

ᵃIn many Hebrew manuscripts Psalms 42 and 43 constitute one psalm. ᵇTitle: Probably a literary or musical term
ᶜ5,6 A few Hebrew manuscripts, Septuagint and Syriac; most Hebrew manuscripts *praise him for his saving help.* / ⁶O my
God, my

[4]You are my King and my God,
who decrees[a] victories for Jacob.
[5]Through you we push back our enemies;
through your name we trample our foes.
[6]I do not trust in my bow,
my sword does not bring me victory;
[7]but you give us victory over our enemies,
you put our adversaries to shame.
[8]In God we make our boast all day long,
and we will praise your name forever.

Selah

[9]But now you have rejected and humbled us;
you no longer go out with our armies.
[10]You made us retreat before the enemy,
and our adversaries have plundered us.
[11]You gave us up to be devoured like sheep
and have scattered us among the nations.
[12]You sold your people for a pittance,
gaining nothing from their sale.

[13]You have made us a reproach to our
neighbors,
the scorn and derision of those around us.
[14]You have made us a byword among the
nations;
the peoples shake their heads at us.
[15]My disgrace is before me all day long,
and my face is covered with shame
[16]at the taunts of those who reproach and
revile me,
because of the enemy, who is bent on
revenge.

[17]All this happened to us,
though we had not forgotten you
or been false to your covenant.
[18]Our hearts had not turned back;
our feet had not strayed from your path.
[19]But you crushed us and made us a haunt for
jackals
and covered us over with deep darkness.

[20]If we had forgotten the name of our God
or spread out our hands to a foreign god,
[21]would not God have discovered it,
since he knows the secrets of the heart?
[22]Yet for your sake we face death all day long;
we are considered as sheep to be
slaughtered.

[23]Awake, O Lord! Why do you sleep?
Rouse yourself! Do not reject us forever.
[24]Why do you hide your face
and forget our misery and oppression?

[25]We are brought down to the dust;
our bodies cling to the ground.
[26]Rise up and help us;
redeem us because of your unfailing love.

Psalm 45

For the director of music. To ⌊the tune of⌋
"Lilies." Of the Sons of Korah. A *maskil*.[b]
A wedding song.

[1]My heart is stirred by a noble theme
as I recite my verses for the king;
my tongue is the pen of a skillful writer.

44:22 No Happy Ending

Not all the psalms have happy endings. This one, while beginning with distant memories of what God did in the past, ends with a poignant plea for help. Prayers and faith in God have not produced any results. Is God asleep?

Yet God works in bigger patterns than we can see. The apostle Paul, considering the place of suffering in a Christian's life, quoted this verse to remind his readers that suffering was nothing new for believers (Romans 8:36). He asked, "Who shall separate us from the love of Christ?" His response: "No one! Nothing!" He would have loved to go back in time and tell the suffering psalmist about all the good things in store for God's people.

[2]You are the most excellent of men
and your lips have been anointed with
grace,
since God has blessed you forever.
[3]Gird your sword upon your side, O mighty
one;
clothe yourself with splendor and majesty.
[4]In your majesty ride forth victoriously
in behalf of truth, humility and
righteousness;
let your right hand display awesome
deeds.
[5]Let your sharp arrows pierce the hearts of
the king's enemies;
let the nations fall beneath your feet.
[6]Your throne, O God, will last for ever and
ever;
a scepter of justice will be the scepter of
your kingdom.
[7]You love righteousness and hate wickedness;
therefore God, your God, has set you
above your companions
by anointing you with the oil of joy.
[8]All your robes are fragrant with myrrh and
aloes and cassia;
from palaces adorned with ivory
the music of the strings makes you glad.
[9]Daughters of kings are among your honored
women;

---

[a]4 Septuagint, Aquila and Syriac; Hebrew *King, O God; / command*   [b]Title: Probably a literary or musical term

at your right hand is the royal bride in
gold of Ophir.

¹⁰Listen, O daughter, consider and give ear:
Forget your people and your father's
house.
¹¹The king is enthralled by your beauty;
honor him, for he is your lord.
¹²The Daughter of Tyre will come with a
gift,^a
men of wealth will seek your favor.

¹³All glorious is the princess within ˌher
chamberˌ;
her gown is interwoven with gold.
¹⁴In embroidered garments she is led to the
king;
her virgin companions follow her
and are brought to you.

¹⁵They are led in with joy and gladness;
they enter the palace of the king.

¹⁶Your sons will take the place of your fathers;
you will make them princes throughout
the land.
¹⁷I will perpetuate your memory through all
generations;
therefore the nations will praise you for
ever and ever.

Psalm 46

For the director of music. Of the Sons of Korah.
According to *alamoth.*^b A song.

¹God is our refuge and strength,
an ever-present help in trouble.
²Therefore we will not fear, though the earth
give way

---

^a12 Or *A Tyrian robe is among the gifts*   ^bTitle: Probably a musical term

---

A Wedding Fit for a King
Why should this poem be found in a book of prayers?

IN THE MIDDLE OF A book of heartfelt prayers, a wedding
poem suddenly appears. Does Psalm 45 belong here? Its "noble theme"
(verse 1) is not God's kindness, but the excellence of his majesty the king
as he prepares to take a bride. While most of the psalms express an intimacy with God that could
have been written yesterday, thrones, scepters, and royal robes make us think of an old Hollywood
epic.

> Your throne, O God,
> will last for ever
> and ever. 45:6

To understand why this psalm was included we need to know, first, that the king in biblical times
was more than just a symbol. He was the president and the commanding general and the chief justice
of the Supreme Court, all rolled into one. An unjust or cowardly king could cost his people their lives. A
clever, successful king, on the other hand, could assure them of prosperity.

When the Israelites wished the king well, therefore, they wished themselves well. Seeing their king
decked out in finery was like looking at a picture of their own success. And when their king made a
happy and fruitful marriage, it assured them of stable leadership for years to come. The king's welfare
represented the welfare of God's people.

The Promise to David

David was the first good king Israel had known. God had told David that his "house" would
endure forever (2 Samuel 7:16). This meant that Israel would endure, too. When David's people combined this promise with the other benefits God had promised to Abraham and Moses, they could foresee a great future for their small, poor, war-weary nation.

Yet David's descendants disappointed these hopes. Israel remained a small, hemmed-in nation.
Gradually, Israelites began to expect another king who would live up to the Bible's praises and
promises. They called him "the Anointed" (for kings and priests took office through an official anointing
with oil, like our swearing in). When they read psalms that mentioned the king, they thought of this
coming ruler.

As the years went by and Israel's kings failed miserably, Israel's longing grew stronger and
stronger. People looked for "the consolation of Israel" (Luke 2:25). The word for "the Anointed" became
Messiah, or (in Greek) *Christ.*

Only when "the Anointed" came—in Jesus—did the extravagant language of Psalm 45:6–7 (along
with unusual descriptions in Psalms 2 and 110) make sense. These verses were quoted in Hebrews
1:8–9 to show that the king the Jews had long expected could be no ordinary man. The king turned
out to *be* God—as verse 6 had suggested. The poem that seemed to be only about a king's marriage
turned out, in the end, to be about God's marriage to humanity.

and the mountains fall into the heart of
    the sea,
3though its waters roar and foam
    and the mountains quake with their
        surging.   *Selah*

4There is a river whose streams make glad the
        city of God,
    the holy place where the Most High
        dwells.
5God is within her, she will not fall;
    God will help her at break of day.
6Nations are in uproar, kingdoms fall;
    he lifts his voice, the earth melts.

7The LORD Almighty is with us;
    the God of Jacob is our fortress.   *Selah*

8Come and see the works of the LORD,
    the desolations he has brought on the
        earth.
9He makes wars cease to the ends of the
        earth;
    he breaks the bow and shatters the spear,
    he burns the shields[a] with fire.
10"Be still, and know that I am God;
    I will be exalted among the nations,
    I will be exalted in the earth."

11The LORD Almighty is with us;
    the God of Jacob is our fortress.   *Selah*

Psalm 47

For the director of music. Of the Sons of Korah.
A psalm.

1Clap your hands, all you nations;
    shout to God with cries of joy.
2How awesome is the LORD Most High,
    the great King over all the earth!
3He subdued nations under us,
    peoples under our feet.
4He chose our inheritance for us,
    the pride of Jacob, whom he loved.   *Selah*

5God has ascended amid shouts of joy,
    the LORD amid the sounding of trumpets.
6Sing praises to God, sing praises;
    sing praises to our King, sing praises.

7For God is the King of all the earth;
    sing to him a psalm[b] of praise.
8God reigns over the nations;
    God is seated on his holy throne.
9The nobles of the nations assemble
    as the people of the God of Abraham,
for the kings[c] of the earth belong to God;
    he is greatly exalted.

Psalm 48

A song. A psalm of the Sons of Korah.

1Great is the LORD, and most worthy of
    praise,

> ### 47:7–9 Who Are God's People?
>
> *While the Israelites often thought of themselves as exclusively God's people, Psalms contains frequent references to a day when "the nations" —that is, all ethnic groups—will exultantly praise God. In this psalm they not only join in, they do so as "the people of the God of Abraham"—that is, as insiders included in God's covenant with the Israelites.*

in the city of our God, his holy mountain.
2It is beautiful in its loftiness,
    the joy of the whole earth.
Like the utmost heights of Zaphon[d] is
        Mount Zion,
    the[e] city of the Great King.
3God is in her citadels;
    he has shown himself to be her fortress.

4When the kings joined forces,
    when they advanced together,
5they saw ⌊her⌋ and were astounded;
    they fled in terror.
6Trembling seized them there,
    pain like that of a woman in labor.
7You destroyed them like ships of Tarshish
    shattered by an east wind.

8As we have heard,
    so have we seen
in the city of the LORD Almighty,
    in the city of our God:
    God makes her secure forever.   *Selah*

9Within your temple, O God,
    we meditate on your unfailing love.
10Like your name, O God,
    your praise reaches to the ends of the
        earth;
    your right hand is filled with
        righteousness.
11Mount Zion rejoices,
    the villages of Judah are glad
    because of your judgments.

12Walk about Zion, go around her,
    count her towers,
13consider well her ramparts,
    view her citadels,
    that you may tell of them to the next
        generation.

---

a9 Or *chariots*   b7 Or *a maskil* (probably a literary or musical term)   c9 Or *shields*   d2 *Zaphon* can refer to a sacred mountain or the direction north.   e2 Or *earth*, / *Mount Zion, on the northern side* / *of the*

¹⁴For this God is our God for ever and ever;
he will be our guide even to the end.

Psalm 49

For the director of music. Of the Sons of Korah.
A psalm.

¹Hear this, all you peoples;
listen, all who live in this world,
²both low and high,
rich and poor alike:
³My mouth will speak words of wisdom;
the utterance from my heart will give
understanding.
⁴I will turn my ear to a proverb;
with the harp I will expound my riddle:

⁵Why should I fear when evil days come,
when wicked deceivers surround me—

49:5–20 Money Can't Buy Life

*How do you make sense of a world in which
bad people get rich and actually oppress good
people? This psalm ponders this riddle and
finds the answer on the other side of death.
Money can do many things, but it simply
cannot buy an escape from the grave. "No man
can redeem the life of another . . . no payment
is ever enough—that he should live on forever"
(verses 7–9). But "God will redeem my life from
the grave," says verse 15; "he will surely take
me to himself."*

⁶those who trust in their wealth
and boast of their great riches?
⁷No man can redeem the life of another
or give to God a ransom for him—
⁸the ransom for a life is costly,
no payment is ever enough—
⁹that he should live on forever
and not see decay.

¹⁰For all can see that wise men die;
the foolish and the senseless alike perish
and leave their wealth to others.
¹¹Their tombs will remain their houses*a*
forever,
their dwellings for endless generations,
though they had*b* named lands after
themselves.

¹²But man, despite his riches, does not endure;
he is*c* like the beasts that perish.

¹³This is the fate of those who trust in
themselves,
and of their followers, who approve their
sayings.   *Selah*
¹⁴Like sheep they are destined for the grave,*d*
and death will feed on them.
The upright will rule over them in the
morning;
their forms will decay in the grave,*d*
far from their princely mansions.
¹⁵But God will redeem my life*e* from the
grave;
he will surely take me to himself.   *Selah*

¹⁶Do not be overawed when a man grows rich,
when the splendor of his house increases;
¹⁷for he will take nothing with him when he
dies,
his splendor will not descend with him.
¹⁸Though while he lived he counted himself
blessed—
and men praise you when you prosper—
¹⁹he will join the generation of his fathers,
who will never see the light ⌊of life⌋.

²⁰A man who has riches without
understanding
is like the beasts that perish.

Psalm 50

A psalm of Asaph.

¹The Mighty One, God, the LORD,
speaks and summons the earth
from the rising of the sun to the place
where it sets.
²From Zion, perfect in beauty,
God shines forth.
³Our God comes and will not be silent;
a fire devours before him,
and around him a tempest rages.
⁴He summons the heavens above,
and the earth, that he may judge his
people:
⁵"Gather to me my consecrated ones,
who made a covenant with me by
sacrifice."
⁶And the heavens proclaim his righteousness,
for God himself is judge.   *Selah*

⁷"Hear, O my people, and I will speak,
O Israel, and I will testify against you:
I am God, your God.
⁸I do not rebuke you for your sacrifices
or your burnt offerings, which are ever
before me.

*a11 Septuagint and Syriac; Hebrew In their thoughts their houses will remain   b11 Or / for they have   c12 Hebrew;
Septuagint and Syriac read verse 12 the same as verse 20.   d14 Hebrew Sheol; also in verse 15   e15 Or soul*

⁹I have no need of a bull from your stall
    or of goats from your pens,
¹⁰for every animal of the forest is mine,
    and the cattle on a thousand hills.
¹¹I know every bird in the mountains,
    and the creatures of the field are mine.
¹²If I were hungry I would not tell you,
    for the world is mine, and all that is in it.

50:9–12 Does God Need Our Gifts?

People often try to bargain with God, thinking that by their good deeds they can get God to do what they want. Old Testament people sometimes viewed their animal sacrifices this way: not as an act of commitment and fellowship with God, but as a way to manipulate God into putting his stamp of approval on their plans. These majestic words from God scorn such a view. He is rich beyond their dreams; he has no need of their offerings. What matters to him is the attitude they take toward him.

¹³Do I eat the flesh of bulls
    or drink the blood of goats?
¹⁴Sacrifice thank offerings to God,
    fulfill your vows to the Most High,
¹⁵and call upon me in the day of trouble;
    I will deliver you, and you will honor
        me.”

¹⁶But to the wicked, God says:

“What right have you to recite my laws
    or take my covenant on your lips?
¹⁷You hate my instruction
    and cast my words behind you.
¹⁸When you see a thief, you join with him;
    you throw in your lot with adulterers.
¹⁹You use your mouth for evil
    and harness your tongue to deceit.
²⁰You speak continually against your brother
    and slander your own mother’s son.
²¹These things you have done and I kept
        silent;
    you thought I was altogether[a] like you.
But I will rebuke you
    and accuse you to your face.

²²“Consider this, you who forget God,
    or I will tear you to pieces, with none to
        rescue:
²³He who sacrifices thank offerings honors me,
    and he prepares the way
so that I may show him[b] the salvation of
        God.”

Psalm 51

For the director of music. A psalm of David.
When the prophet Nathan came to him after
David had committed adultery with Bathsheba.

¹Have mercy on me, O God,
    according to your unfailing love;
according to your great compassion
    blot out my transgressions.
²Wash away all my iniquity
    and cleanse me from my sin.

³For I know my transgressions,
    and my sin is always before me.
⁴Against you, you only, have I sinned
    and done what is evil in your sight,
so that you are proved right when you speak
    and justified when you judge.
⁵Surely I was sinful at birth,
    sinful from the time my mother conceived
        me.
⁶Surely you desire truth in the inner parts[c];
    you teach[d] me wisdom in the inmost
        place.

⁷Cleanse me with hyssop, and I will be clean;
    wash me, and I will be whiter than snow.
⁸Let me hear joy and gladness;
    let the bones you have crushed rejoice.
⁹Hide your face from my sins
    and blot out all my iniquity.

¹⁰Create in me a pure heart, O God,
    and renew a steadfast spirit within me.
¹¹Do not cast me from your presence
    or take your Holy Spirit from me.
¹²Restore to me the joy of your salvation
    and grant me a willing spirit, to sustain
        me.

¹³Then I will teach transgressors your ways,
    and sinners will turn back to you.
¹⁴Save me from bloodguilt, O God,
    the God who saves me,
    and my tongue will sing of your
        righteousness.
¹⁵O Lord, open my lips,
    and my mouth will declare your praise.
¹⁶You do not delight in sacrifice, or I would
        bring it;
    you do not take pleasure in burnt
        offerings.
¹⁷The sacrifices of God are[e] a broken spirit;
    a broken and contrite heart,
    O God, you will not despise.

¹⁸In your good pleasure make Zion prosper;
    build up the walls of Jerusalem.

---

a 21 Or thought the ‘I AM’ was   *b 23 Or and to him who considers his way / I will show*   *c 6 The meaning of the Hebrew for this phrase is uncertain.*   *d 6 Or you desired . . . ; / you taught*   *e 17 Or My sacrifice, O God, is*

19Then there will be righteous sacrifices,
    whole burnt offerings to delight you;
    then bulls will be offered on your altar.

Psalm 52

For the director of music. A *maskil*[a] of David.
When Doeg the Edomite had gone to Saul and
told him: "David has gone to the house of
Ahimelech."

1Why do you boast of evil, you mighty man?
    Why do you boast all day long,
    you who are a disgrace in the eyes of
        God?
2Your tongue plots destruction;
    it is like a sharpened razor,
    you who practice deceit.
3You love evil rather than good,
    falsehood rather than speaking the truth.
                                    Selah
4You love every harmful word,
    O you deceitful tongue!

[a]Title: Probably a literary or musical term

5Surely God will bring you down to
        everlasting ruin:
    He will snatch you up and tear you from
        your tent;
    he will uproot you from the land of the
        living.   *Selah*
6The righteous will see and fear;
    they will laugh at him, saying,
7"Here now is the man
    who did not make God his stronghold
    but trusted in his great wealth
    and grew strong by destroying others!"

8But I am like an olive tree
    flourishing in the house of God;
    I trust in God's unfailing love
    for ever and ever.
9I will praise you forever for what you have
        done;
    in your name I will hope, for your name
        is good.
    I will praise you in the presence of your
        saints.

David Caught in the Act
Israel had a strange way to remember its heroes

> Against you, you only, have I sinned and done what is evil in your sight.
> 51:4

DAVID FOUND A PLACE IN the hearts of Israelites something like the one Abraham Lincoln found in the hearts of Americans. Both men led their nations through dark hours with courage, wisdom, and deep faith.

But there are essential differences in the way they are remembered. Suppose, for example, that Abraham Lincoln had been caught in the act of adultery. Would his private outpouring of grief before God have been included in America's July 4th celebration? Hardly: America tends to cover up the faults of its heroes, and even invent stories about their spotless honesty.

Yet, for David, no cover-up was attempted. Just the opposite: Psalm 51 publishes David's anguished reaction when he was caught in sin. The story behind the psalm is told in 2 Samuel 11 and 12—a sordid tale of adultery, intrigue, and murder. David, the greatest king in Israel's history, acted like the worst.

David apparently thought nothing of his crime until the prophet Nathan accused him to his face. Then, in tears, David confessed—and this poem was one result. It was recorded (along with the story of David's deeds) in the holy Scriptures. It may well have been used in worship services, as a guide for others' confession.

David's Greatest Legacy

All nations have heroes. Israel may have been alone in making heroic literature about its heroes' failings. In confessing his failures openly, David was certainly unique among all leaders of his day. He knew his place before God, and this humility made him an example for his people.

Ultimately Israel remembered David more for his devotion to God than for his military achievements. In centuries to come, Israel looked for a "son of David" to come and save them. They wanted a truly strong leader—one humble enough to know that God must lead the leaders.

Life Questions: When you fail, what is your response—to cover up your failure, or to publicize your confession?

Psalm 53

For the director of music. According to
mahalath.[a] A *maskil*[b] of David.

[1]The fool says in his heart,
  "There is no God."
They are corrupt, and their ways are vile;
  there is no one who does good.

[2]God looks down from heaven
  on the sons of men
to see if there are any who understand,
  any who seek God.
[3]Everyone has turned away,
  they have together become corrupt;
there is no one who does good,
  not even one.

53:3 Sound Familiar?

Psalm 53 is nearly identical to Psalm 14.
Scholars think the book of Psalms bundled
together several different collections of hymns;
this duplication is one reason they believe so.

[4]Will the evildoers never learn—
  those who devour my people as men eat
  bread
and who do not call on God?
[5]There they were, overwhelmed with dread,
  where there was nothing to dread.
God scattered the bones of those who
  attacked you;
  you put them to shame, for God despised
  them.

[6]Oh, that salvation for Israel would come out
  of Zion!
  When God restores the fortunes of his
  people,
  let Jacob rejoice and Israel be glad!

Psalm 54

For the director of music. With stringed
instruments. A *maskil*[b] of David. When the
Ziphites had gone to Saul and said, "Is not
David hiding among us?"

[1]Save me, O God, by your name;
  vindicate me by your might.
[2]Hear my prayer, O God;
  listen to the words of my mouth.

[3]Strangers are attacking me;
  ruthless men seek my life—
  men without regard for God.   *Selah*

[4]Surely God is my help;
  the Lord is the one who sustains me.

[5]Let evil recoil on those who slander me;
  in your faithfulness destroy them.

[6]I will sacrifice a freewill offering to you;
  I will praise your name, O LORD,
  for it is good.
[7]For he has delivered me from all my
  troubles,
  and my eyes have looked in triumph on
  my foes.

Psalm 55

For the director of music. With stringed
instruments. A *maskil*[b] of David.

[1]Listen to my prayer, O God,
  do not ignore my plea;
[2] hear me and answer me.
My thoughts trouble me and I am distraught
[3] at the voice of the enemy,
  at the stares of the wicked;
for they bring down suffering upon me
  and revile me in their anger.

[4]My heart is in anguish within me;
  the terrors of death assail me.
[5]Fear and trembling have beset me;
  horror has overwhelmed me.
[6]I said, "Oh, that I had the wings of a dove!
  I would fly away and be at rest—
[7]I would flee far away
  and stay in the desert;   *Selah*
[8]I would hurry to my place of shelter,
  far from the tempest and storm."

[9]Confuse the wicked, O Lord, confound their
  speech,
  for I see violence and strife in the city.
[10]Day and night they prowl about on its walls;
  malice and abuse are within it.
[11]Destructive forces are at work in the city;
  threats and lies never leave its streets.

[12]If an enemy were insulting me,
  I could endure it;
if a foe were raising himself against me,
  I could hide from him.
[13]But it is you, a man like myself,
  my companion, my close friend,
[14]with whom I once enjoyed sweet fellowship
  as we walked with the throng at the house
  of God.

[15]Let death take my enemies by surprise;
  let them go down alive to the grave,[c]
  for evil finds lodging among them.

[16]But I call to God,

---

[a]Title: Probably a musical term   [b]Title: Probably a literary or musical term   [c]15 Hebrew *Sheol*

and the LORD saves me.
[17]Evening, morning and noon
I cry out in distress,
and he hears my voice.

55:14 Betrayed by a Friend

It is hard enough to deal with enemies, but far harder to face the fact of betrayal by a close friend. Feeling that he can no longer trust anyone, the psalmist turns to God for help. God, he knows, will never betray him.

[18]He ransoms me unharmed
from the battle waged against me,
even though many oppose me.
[19]God, who is enthroned forever,
will hear them and afflict them—   *Selah*
men who never change their ways
and have no fear of God.

[20]My companion attacks his friends;
he violates his covenant.
[21]His speech is smooth as butter,
yet war is in his heart;
his words are more soothing than oil,
yet they are drawn swords.

[22]Cast your cares on the LORD
and he will sustain you;
he will never let the righteous fall.
[23]But you, O God, will bring down the wicked
into the pit of corruption;
bloodthirsty and deceitful men
will not live out half their days.

But as for me, I trust in you.

Psalm 56

For the director of music. To ⌊the tune of⌋ "A Dove on Distant Oaks." Of David. A *miktam*.[a] When the Philistines had seized him in Gath.

[1]Be merciful to me, O God, for men hotly pursue me;
all day long they press their attack.
[2]My slanderers pursue me all day long;
many are attacking me in their pride.

[3]When I am afraid,
I will trust in you.
[4]In God, whose word I praise,
in God I trust; I will not be afraid.
What can mortal man do to me?

[5]All day long they twist my words;
they are always plotting to harm me.
[6]They conspire, they lurk,

they watch my steps,
eager to take my life.
[7]On no account let them escape;
in your anger, O God, bring down the nations.
[8]Record my lament;
list my tears on your scroll[b]—
are they not in your record?

[9]Then my enemies will turn back
when I call for help.
By this I will know that God is for me.
[10]In God, whose word I praise,
in the LORD, whose word I praise—
[11]in God I trust; I will not be afraid.
What can man do to me?

[12]I am under vows to you, O God;
I will present my thank offerings to you.
[13]For you have delivered me[c] from death
and my feet from stumbling,
that I may walk before God
in the light of life.[d]

Psalm 57

For the director of music. ⌊To the tune of⌋ "Do Not Destroy." Of David. A *miktam*.[a] When he had fled from Saul into the cave.

[1]Have mercy on me, O God, have mercy on me,
for in you my soul takes refuge.
I will take refuge in the shadow of your wings
until the disaster has passed.

[2]I cry out to God Most High,
to God, who fulfills ⌊his purpose⌋ for me.
[3]He sends from heaven and saves me,
rebuking those who hotly pursue me;
                                        Selah
God sends his love and his faithfulness.

[4]I am in the midst of lions;
I lie among ravenous beasts—
men whose teeth are spears and arrows,
whose tongues are sharp swords.

[5]Be exalted, O God, above the heavens;
let your glory be over all the earth.

[6]They spread a net for my feet—
I was bowed down in distress.
They dug a pit in my path—
but they have fallen into it themselves.
                                        Selah

[7]My heart is steadfast, O God,
my heart is steadfast;
I will sing and make music.

---

[a]Title: Probably a literary or musical term   [b]8 Or *I put my tears in your wineskin*   [c]13 Or *my soul*
[d]13 Or *the land of the living*

⁸Awake, my soul!
    Awake, harp and lyre!
    I will awaken the dawn.

⁹I will praise you, O Lord, among the nations;
    I will sing of you among the peoples.
¹⁰For great is your love, reaching to the
        heavens;
    your faithfulness reaches to the skies.

¹¹Be exalted, O God, above the heavens;
    let your glory be over all the earth.

Psalm 58

For the director of music. ⌞To the tune of⌟ "Do
Not Destroy." Of David. A *miktam*.ᵃ

¹Do you rulers indeed speak justly?
    Do you judge uprightly among men?
²No, in your heart you devise injustice,
    and your hands mete out violence on the
        earth.
³Even from birth the wicked go astray;
    from the womb they are wayward and
        speak lies.
⁴Their venom is like the venom of a snake,
    like that of a cobra that has stopped its
        ears,
⁵that will not heed the tune of the charmer,
    however skillful the enchanter may be.

⁶Break the teeth in their mouths, O God;
    tear out, O Lord, the fangs of the lions!
⁷Let them vanish like water that flows away;
    when they draw the bow, let their arrows
        be blunted.
⁸Like a slug melting away as it moves along,
    like a stillborn child, may they not see the
        sun.

58:8 Rough Words

*The psalmist's white-hot anger is never more
obvious than in these ardent words asking God
to punish wicked people. His demand for
retribution is a far cry from Jesus' command to
love your enemies; no Christian should make
this a model of prayer. We ought to remember,
though, that the psalmist is asking God for
justice—not planning how he will bring it about
himself. For more on this subject, see "What
About Curses?" page 654.*

⁹Before your pots can feel ⌞the heat of⌟ the
        thorns—
    whether they are green or dry—the wicked
        will be swept away.ᵇ

¹⁰The righteous will be glad when they are
        avenged,
    when they bathe their feet in the blood of
        the wicked.
¹¹Then men will say,
    "Surely the righteous still are rewarded;
    surely there is a God who judges the
        earth."

Psalm 59

For the director of music. ⌞To the tune of⌟ "Do
Not Destroy." Of David. A *miktam*.ᵃ When
Saul had sent men to watch David's house in
order to kill him.

¹Deliver me from my enemies, O God;
    protect me from those who rise up against
        me.
²Deliver me from evildoers
    and save me from bloodthirsty men.

³See how they lie in wait for me!
    Fierce men conspire against me
    for no offense or sin of mine, O Lord.
⁴I have done no wrong, yet they are ready to
        attack me.
    Arise to help me; look on my plight!
⁵O Lord God Almighty, the God of Israel,
    rouse yourself to punish all the nations;
    show no mercy to wicked traitors.   *Selah*

⁶They return at evening,
    snarling like dogs,
    and prowl about the city.
⁷See what they spew from their mouths—
    they spew out swords from their lips,
    and they say, "Who can hear us?"
⁸But you, O Lord, laugh at them;
    you scoff at all those nations.

⁹O my Strength, I watch for you;
    you, O God, are my fortress, ¹⁰my loving
        God.

God will go before me
    and will let me gloat over those who
        slander me.
¹¹But do not kill them, O Lord our shield,ᶜ
    or my people will forget.
In your might make them wander about,
    and bring them down.
¹²For the sins of their mouths,
    for the words of their lips,
    let them be caught in their pride.
For the curses and lies they utter,
¹³   consume them in wrath,
    consume them till they are no more.

ᵃTitle: Probably a literary or musical term   ᵇ9 The meaning of the Hebrew for this verse is uncertain.
ᶜ11 Or *sovereign*

Then it will be known to the ends of the
  earth
  that God rules over Jacob. *Selah*

¹⁴They return at evening,
  snarling like dogs,
  and prowl about the city.
¹⁵They wander about for food
  and howl if not satisfied.
¹⁶But I will sing of your strength,
  in the morning I will sing of your love;
for you are my fortress,
  my refuge in times of trouble.

¹⁷O my Strength, I sing praise to you;
  you, O God, are my fortress, my loving
    God.

Psalm 60

For the director of music. To the tune of, "The
Lily of the Covenant." A *miktam*^a of David.
For teaching. When he fought Aram
Naharaim^b and Aram Zobah,^c and when Joab
returned and struck down twelve thousand
Edomites in the Valley of Salt.

¹You have rejected us, O God, and burst
    forth upon us;
  you have been angry—now restore us!
²You have shaken the land and torn it open;
  mend its fractures, for it is quaking.
³You have shown your people desperate
    times;
  you have given us wine that makes us
    stagger.

⁴But for those who fear you, you have raised
    a banner
  to be unfurled against the bow. *Selah*

⁵Save us and help us with your right hand,
  that those you love may be delivered.
⁶God has spoken from his sanctuary:
  "In triumph I will parcel out Shechem
  and measure off the Valley of Succoth.
⁷Gilead is mine, and Manasseh is mine;
  Ephraim is my helmet,
  Judah my scepter.
⁸Moab is my washbasin,
  upon Edom I toss my sandal;
  over Philistia I shout in triumph."

⁹Who will bring me to the fortified city?
  Who will lead me to Edom?
¹⁰Is it not you, O God, you who have rejected
    us
  and no longer go out with our armies?
¹¹Give us aid against the enemy,
  for the help of man is worthless.

¹²With God we will gain the victory,
  and he will trample down our enemies.

Psalm 61

For the director of music. With stringed
instruments. Of David.

¹Hear my cry, O God;
  listen to my prayer.

²From the ends of the earth I call to you,
  I call as my heart grows faint;
  lead me to the rock that is higher than I.
³For you have been my refuge,
  a strong tower against the foe.

⁴I long to dwell in your tent forever
  and take refuge in the shelter of your
    wings. *Selah*
⁵For you have heard my vows, O God;
  you have given me the heritage of those
    who fear your name.

⁶Increase the days of the king's life,
  his years for many generations.
⁷May he be enthroned in God's presence
    forever;
  appoint your love and faithfulness to
    protect him.

⁸Then will I ever sing praise to your name
  and fulfill my vows day after day.

Psalm 62

For the director of music. For Jeduthun.
A psalm of David.

¹My soul finds rest in God alone;
  my salvation comes from him.
²He alone is my rock and my salvation;
  he is my fortress, I will never be shaken.

³How long will you assault a man?
  Would all of you throw him down—
  this leaning wall, this tottering fence?
⁴They fully intend to topple him
  from his lofty place;
  they take delight in lies.
  With their mouths they bless,
  but in their hearts they curse. *Selah*

⁵Find rest, O my soul, in God alone;
  my hope comes from him.
⁶He alone is my rock and my salvation;
  he is my fortress, I will not be shaken.
⁷My salvation and my honor depend on
    God^d;
  he is my mighty rock, my refuge.
⁸Trust in him at all times, O people;

---

^aTitle: Probably a literary or musical term   ^bTitle: That is, Arameans of Northwest Mesopotamia   ^cTitle: That is,
Arameans of central Syria   ^d7 Or *God Most High is my salvation and my honor*

pour out your hearts to him,
for God is our refuge. *Selah*

⁹Lowborn men are but a breath,
the highborn are but a lie;

62:7 The Hideout

In the years when David was an outlaw from King Saul, his hideouts included a "rock" in the desert (1 Samuel 23:25–28), as well as a "stronghold" (1 Samuel 22:4). As an experienced fighter, David knew the value of such defenses. He recognized, however, that he owed his safety to God, his true rock and fortress.

if weighed on a balance, they are nothing;
together they are only a breath.
¹⁰Do not trust in extortion
or take pride in stolen goods;
though your riches increase,
do not set your heart on them.

¹¹One thing God has spoken,
two things have I heard:
that you, O God, are strong,
¹²   and that you, O Lord, are loving.
Surely you will reward each person
according to what he has done.

Psalm 63

A psalm of David. When he was in the Desert of Judah.

¹O God, you are my God,
earnestly I seek you;
my soul thirsts for you,
my body longs for you,
in a dry and weary land
where there is no water.

²I have seen you in the sanctuary
and beheld your power and your glory.
³Because your love is better than life,
my lips will glorify you.
⁴I will praise you as long as I live,
and in your name I will lift up my hands.
⁵My soul will be satisfied as with the richest
of foods;
with singing lips my mouth will praise
you.

⁶On my bed I remember you;
I think of you through the watches of the
night.
⁷Because you are my help,
I sing in the shadow of your wings.

⁸My soul clings to you;
your right hand upholds me.

⁹They who seek my life will be destroyed;
they will go down to the depths of the
earth.
¹⁰They will be given over to the sword
and become food for jackals.

¹¹But the king will rejoice in God;
all who swear by God's name will praise
him,
while the mouths of liars will be silenced.

Psalm 64

For the director of music. A psalm of David.

¹Hear me, O God, as I voice my complaint;
protect my life from the threat of the
enemy.
²Hide me from the conspiracy of the wicked,
from that noisy crowd of evildoers.

³They sharpen their tongues like swords
and aim their words like deadly arrows.
⁴They shoot from ambush at the innocent
man;
they shoot at him suddenly, without fear.

⁵They encourage each other in evil plans,
they talk about hiding their snares;
they say, "Who will see them*a*?"
⁶They plot injustice and say,
"We have devised a perfect plan!"
Surely the mind and heart of man are
cunning.

⁷But God will shoot them with arrows;
suddenly they will be struck down.
⁸He will turn their own tongues against them
and bring them to ruin;
all who see them will shake their heads in
scorn.

⁹All mankind will fear;
they will proclaim the works of God
and ponder what he has done.
¹⁰Let the righteous rejoice in the LORD
and take refuge in him;
let all the upright in heart praise him!

Psalm 65

For the director of music. A psalm of David.
A song.

¹Praise awaits*b* you, O God, in Zion;
to you our vows will be fulfilled.
²O you who hear prayer,
to you all men will come.
³When we were overwhelmed by sins,

---

*a*5 Or *us*   *b*1 Or *befits*; the meaning of the Hebrew for this word is uncertain.

you forgave[a] our transgressions.
⁴Blessed are those you choose
and bring near to live in your courts!
We are filled with the good things of your
house,
of your holy temple.

⁵You answer us with awesome deeds of
righteousness,
O God our Savior,
the hope of all the ends of the earth
and of the farthest seas,
⁶who formed the mountains by your power,
having armed yourself with strength,
⁷who stilled the roaring of the seas,
the roaring of their waves,
and the turmoil of the nations.
⁸Those living far away fear your wonders;
where morning dawns and evening fades
you call forth songs of joy.

65:8 God Reaches Out

*God's Old Testament people primarily came
from a specially chosen ethnic group. Some
outsiders joined them in their faith (Ruth, for
instance), but the Israelites didn't issue blanket
invitations. Nevertheless, they recognized that
God's love extended to people over the horizon.
His care for the earth, so beautifully described
here, called for a response everywhere, not just
in Israel.*

⁹You care for the land and water it;
you enrich it abundantly.
The streams of God are filled with water
to provide the people with grain,
for so you have ordained it.[b]
¹⁰You drench its furrows
and level its ridges;
you soften it with showers
and bless its crops.
¹¹You crown the year with your bounty,
and your carts overflow with abundance.
¹²The grasslands of the desert overflow;
the hills are clothed with gladness.
¹³The meadows are covered with flocks
and the valleys are mantled with grain;
they shout for joy and sing.

Psalm 66

For the director of music. A song. A psalm.

¹Shout with joy to God, all the earth!
²   Sing the glory of his name;
make his praise glorious!
³Say to God, "How awesome are your deeds!

So great is your power
that your enemies cringe before you.
⁴All the earth bows down to you;
they sing praise to you,
they sing praise to your name."   *Selah*

⁵Come and see what God has done,
how awesome his works in man's behalf!
⁶He turned the sea into dry land,
they passed through the waters on foot—
come, let us rejoice in him.
⁷He rules forever by his power,
his eyes watch the nations—
let not the rebellious rise up against him.
Selah

⁸Praise our God, O peoples,
let the sound of his praise be heard;
⁹he has preserved our lives
and kept our feet from slipping.
¹⁰For you, O God, tested us;
you refined us like silver.
¹¹You brought us into prison
and laid burdens on our backs.
¹²You let men ride over our heads;
we went through fire and water,
but you brought us to a place of
abundance.

¹³I will come to your temple with burnt
offerings
and fulfill my vows to you—
¹⁴vows my lips promised and my mouth spoke
when I was in trouble.
¹⁵I will sacrifice fat animals to you
and an offering of rams;
I will offer bulls and goats.   *Selah*

¹⁶Come and listen, all you who fear God;
let me tell you what he has done for me.
¹⁷I cried out to him with my mouth;
his praise was on my tongue.
¹⁸If I had cherished sin in my heart,
the Lord would not have listened;
¹⁹but God has surely listened
and heard my voice in prayer.
²⁰Praise be to God,
who has not rejected my prayer
or withheld his love from me!

Psalm 67

For the director of music. With stringed
instruments. A psalm. A song.

¹May God be gracious to us and bless us
and make his face shine upon us,   *Selah*
²that your ways may be known on earth,
your salvation among all nations.

³May the peoples praise you, O God;

ᵃ3 Or *made atonement for*   ᵇ9 Or *for that is how you prepare the land*

may all the peoples praise you.
⁴May the nations be glad and sing for joy,
for you rule the peoples justly
and guide the nations of the earth.   *Selah*
⁵May the peoples praise you, O God;
may all the peoples praise you.

⁶Then the land will yield its harvest,
and God, our God, will bless us.
⁷God will bless us,
and all the ends of the earth will fear him.

Psalm 68

For the director of music. Of David. A psalm.
A song.

¹May God arise, may his enemies be
scattered;
may his foes flee before him.
²As smoke is blown away by the wind,
may you blow them away;
as wax melts before the fire,
may the wicked perish before God.
³But may the righteous be glad
and rejoice before God;
may they be happy and joyful.

⁴Sing to God, sing praise to his name,
extol him who rides on the clouds*ᵃ*—
his name is the LORD—
and rejoice before him.
⁵A father to the fatherless, a defender of
widows,
is God in his holy dwelling.
⁶God sets the lonely in families,*ᵇ*
he leads forth the prisoners with singing;
but the rebellious live in a sun-scorched
land.

⁷When you went out before your people,
O God,
when you marched through the wasteland,
Selah
⁸the earth shook,
the heavens poured down rain,
before God, the One of Sinai,
before God, the God of Israel.
⁹You gave abundant showers, O God;
you refreshed your weary inheritance.
¹⁰Your people settled in it,
and from your bounty, O God, you
provided for the poor.

¹¹The Lord announced the word,
and great was the company of those who
proclaimed it:
¹²"Kings and armies flee in haste;
in the camps men divide the plunder.
¹³Even while you sleep among the campfires,*ᶜ*

the wings of ⌐my⌐ dove are sheathed with
silver,
its feathers with shining gold."
¹⁴When the Almighty*ᵈ* scattered the kings in
the land,
it was like snow fallen on Zalmon.

¹⁵The mountains of Bashan are majestic
mountains;
rugged are the mountains of Bashan.
¹⁶Why gaze in envy, O rugged mountains,
at the mountain where God chooses to
reign,
where the LORD himself will dwell forever?
¹⁷The chariots of God are tens of thousands
and thousands of thousands;
the Lord ⌐has come⌐ from Sinai into his
sanctuary.
¹⁸When you ascended on high,
you led captives in your train;
you received gifts from men,
even from*ᵉ* the rebellious—
that you,*ᶠ* O LORD God, might dwell
there.

¹⁹Praise be to the Lord, to God our Savior,
who daily bears our burdens.   *Selah*
²⁰Our God is a God who saves;
from the Sovereign LORD comes escape
from death.

²¹Surely God will crush the heads of his
enemies,
the hairy crowns of those who go on in
their sins.
²²The Lord says, "I will bring them from
Bashan;
I will bring them from the depths of the
sea,
²³that you may plunge your feet in the blood
of your foes,
while the tongues of your dogs have their
share."

²⁴Your procession has come into view, O God,
the procession of my God and King into
the sanctuary.
²⁵In front are the singers, after them the
musicians;
with them are the maidens playing
tambourines.
²⁶Praise God in the great congregation;
praise the LORD in the assembly of Israel.
²⁷There is the little tribe of Benjamin, leading
them,
there the great throng of Judah's princes,
and there the princes of Zebulun and of
Naphtali.

ᵃ4 Or / *prepare the way for him who rides through the deserts*   *ᵇ6* Or *The desolate in a homeland*
ᶜ13 Or *saddlebags*   *ᵈ14* Hebrew *Shaddai*   *ᵉ18* Or *gifts for men, / even*   *ᶠ18* Or *they*

28Summon your power, O God[a];
  show us your strength, O God, as you
    have done before.
29Because of your temple at Jerusalem

68:24 The Way They Worshiped

Many of the psalms were sung in the temple, to worship God. Exactly how people worshiped, however, is difficult to know. This verse offers unmistakable clues to how this psalm was used—in a procession leading to the temple. It may have first been sung when David brought the ark—the sign of God's actual presence—into Jerusalem (2 Samuel 6; 1 Chronicles 15–16). Or it may have been used in one of the annual festivals that drew Israelites from all over to the capital.

  kings will bring you gifts.
30Rebuke the beast among the reeds,
  the herd of bulls among the calves of the
    nations.
  Humbled, may it bring bars of silver.
  Scatter the nations who delight in war.
31Envoys will come from Egypt;
  Cush[b] will submit herself to God.

32Sing to God, O kingdoms of the earth,
  sing praise to the Lord,   *Selah*
33to him who rides the ancient skies above,
  who thunders with mighty voice.
34Proclaim the power of God,
  whose majesty is over Israel,
  whose power is in the skies.
35You are awesome, O God, in your sanctuary;
  the God of Israel gives power and strength
    to his people.

  Praise be to God!

Psalm 69

For the director of music. To ⌞the tune of⌟
"Lilies." Of David.

1Save me, O God,
  for the waters have come up to my neck.
2I sink in the miry depths,
  where there is no foothold.
  I have come into the deep waters;
    the floods engulf me.
3I am worn out calling for help;
  my throat is parched.
  My eyes fail,
    looking for my God.
4Those who hate me without reason
  outnumber the hairs of my head;

many are my enemies without cause,
  those who seek to destroy me.
I am forced to restore
  what I did not steal.

5You know my folly, O God;
  my guilt is not hidden from you.

6May those who hope in you
  not be disgraced because of me,
    O Lord, the LORD Almighty;
  may those who seek you
    not be put to shame because of me,
      O God of Israel.
7For I endure scorn for your sake,
  and shame covers my face.
8I am a stranger to my brothers,
  an alien to my own mother's sons;
9for zeal for your house consumes me,
  and the insults of those who insult you
    fall on me.

69:9 Foreshadowing Jesus

Psalm 69 was quoted repeatedly by New Testament writers, who identify Jesus as the righteous sufferer. "Zeal for your house consumes me" was quoted in John 2:17, for instance, when Jesus drove out the money changers. And Romans 15:3 quoted the second half of that verse, referring to Jesus' self-sacrificial attitude.

Why did the New Testament writers see Jesus in this psalm? The psalm was attributed to David, the great king. Yet it is not David's greatness and majesty that are described here. Instead, the psalm is a cry of suffering from a righteous man, alienated even from his family because of his zeal for God. It is strange: Israel's greatest hero is portrayed as a helpless victim because of his faith in God. Yet Jesus filled this pattern completely. He did not, however, follow every part of the psalm: Instead of the curses this psalm directs toward enemies, Jesus prayed that God would forgive the men murdering him.

10When I weep and fast,
  I must endure scorn;
11when I put on sackcloth,
  people make sport of me.
12Those who sit at the gate mock me,
  and I am the song of the drunkards.

13But I pray to you, O LORD,
  in the time of your favor;
in your great love, O God,
  answer me with your sure salvation.
14Rescue me from the mire,

---

[a]28 Many Hebrew manuscripts, Septuagint and Syriac; most Hebrew manuscripts *Your God has summoned power for you*
[b]31 That is, the upper Nile region

do not let me sink;
deliver me from those who hate me,
from the deep waters.
¹⁵Do not let the floodwaters engulf me
or the depths swallow me up
or the pit close its mouth over me.
¹⁶Answer me, O LORD, out of the goodness of
your love;
in your great mercy turn to me.
¹⁷Do not hide your face from your servant;
answer me quickly, for I am in trouble.
¹⁸Come near and rescue me;
redeem me because of my foes.

¹⁹You know how I am scorned, disgraced and
shamed;
all my enemies are before you.
²⁰Scorn has broken my heart
and has left me helpless;
I looked for sympathy, but there was none,
for comforters, but I found none.
²¹They put gall in my food
and gave me vinegar for my thirst.

²²May the table set before them become a
snare;
may it become retribution and[a] a trap.
²³May their eyes be darkened so they cannot
see,
and their backs be bent forever.
²⁴Pour out your wrath on them;
let your fierce anger overtake them.
²⁵May their place be deserted;
let there be no one to dwell in their tents.
²⁶For they persecute those you wound
and talk about the pain of those you hurt.
²⁷Charge them with crime upon crime;
do not let them share in your salvation.
²⁸May they be blotted out of the book of life
and not be listed with the righteous.

²⁹I am in pain and distress;
may your salvation, O God, protect me.

³⁰I will praise God's name in song
and glorify him with thanksgiving.
³¹This will please the LORD more than an ox,
more than a bull with its horns and hoofs.
³²The poor will see and be glad—
you who seek God, may your hearts live!
³³The LORD hears the needy
and does not despise his captive people.

³⁴Let heaven and earth praise him,
the seas and all that move in them,
³⁵for God will save Zion
and rebuild the cities of Judah.
Then people will settle there and possess it;
³⁶   the children of his servants will inherit it,
and those who love his name will dwell
there.

Psalm 70

For the director of music. Of David. A petition.

¹Hasten, O God, to save me;
O LORD, come quickly to help me.
²May those who seek my life
be put to shame and confusion;
may all who desire my ruin
be turned back in disgrace.
³May those who say to me, "Aha! Aha!"
turn back because of their shame.
⁴But may all who seek you
rejoice and be glad in you;
may those who love your salvation always
say,
"Let God be exalted!"

⁵Yet I am poor and needy;
come quickly to me, O God.
You are my help and my deliverer;
O LORD, do not delay.

Psalm 71

¹In you, O LORD, I have taken refuge;
let me never be put to shame.
²Rescue me and deliver me in your
righteousness;
turn your ear to me and save me.
³Be my rock of refuge,
to which I can always go;
give the command to save me,
for you are my rock and my fortress.
⁴Deliver me, O my God, from the hand of the
wicked,
from the grasp of evil and cruel men.

⁵For you have been my hope, O Sovereign
LORD,
my confidence since my youth.
⁶From birth I have relied on you;
you brought me forth from my mother's
womb.
I will ever praise you.
⁷I have become like a portent to many,
but you are my strong refuge.
⁸My mouth is filled with your praise,
declaring your splendor all day long.

⁹Do not cast me away when I am old;
do not forsake me when my strength is
gone.
¹⁰For my enemies speak against me;
those who wait to kill me conspire
together.
¹¹They say, "God has forsaken him;
pursue him and seize him,
for no one will rescue him."
¹²Be not far from me, O my God;
come quickly, O my God, to help me.

¹³May my accusers perish in shame;
  may those who want to harm me
    be covered with scorn and disgrace.

¹⁴But as for me, I will always have hope;
  I will praise you more and more.
¹⁵My mouth will tell of your righteousness,
  of your salvation all day long,
    though I know not its measure.
¹⁶I will come and proclaim your mighty acts,
    O Sovereign LORD;
  I will proclaim your righteousness, yours
    alone.
¹⁷Since my youth, O God, you have taught
    me,
  and to this day I declare your marvelous
    deeds.
¹⁸Even when I am old and gray,
  do not forsake me, O God,
till I declare your power to the next
    generation,
  your might to all who are to come.

71:18 A View from Old Age

Older people have a peculiar privilege: the chance to see God's faithfulness over a lifetime. Their troubles do not grow smaller as the years go by (see verses 9–11), but their experiences can strengthen confidence that God will deliver as he always has (verses 20–21).

¹⁹Your righteousness reaches to the skies,
    O God,
  you who have done great things.
  Who, O God, is like you?
²⁰Though you have made me see troubles,
    many and bitter,
  you will restore my life again;
from the depths of the earth
  you will again bring me up.
²¹You will increase my honor
  and comfort me once again.

²²I will praise you with the harp
  for your faithfulness, O my God;
  I will sing praise to you with the lyre,
    O Holy One of Israel.
²³My lips will shout for joy
  when I sing praise to you—
  I, whom you have redeemed.
²⁴My tongue will tell of your righteous acts
  all day long,
for those who wanted to harm me
  have been put to shame and confusion.

Psalm 72

Of Solomon.

¹Endow the king with your justice, O God,
  the royal son with your righteousness.
²He will^a judge your people in righteousness,
  your afflicted ones with justice.
³The mountains will bring prosperity to the
    people,
  the hills the fruit of righteousness.
⁴He will defend the afflicted among the
    people
  and save the children of the needy;
  he will crush the oppressor.

⁵He will endure^b as long as the sun,
  as long as the moon, through all
    generations.
⁶He will be like rain falling on a mown field,
  like showers watering the earth.
⁷In his days the righteous will flourish;
  prosperity will abound till the moon is no
    more.

⁸He will rule from sea to sea
  and from the River^c to the ends of the
    earth.^d
⁹The desert tribes will bow before him
  and his enemies will lick the dust.
¹⁰The kings of Tarshish and of distant shores
  will bring tribute to him;
  the kings of Sheba and Seba
  will present him gifts.
¹¹All kings will bow down to him
  and all nations will serve him.

¹²For he will deliver the needy who cry out,
  the afflicted who have no one to help.
¹³He will take pity on the weak and the needy
  and save the needy from death.
¹⁴He will rescue them from oppression and
    violence,
  for precious is their blood in his sight.

¹⁵Long may he live!
  May gold from Sheba be given him.
  May people ever pray for him
  and bless him all day long.
¹⁶Let grain abound throughout the land;
  on the tops of the hills may it sway.
  Let its fruit flourish like Lebanon;
  let it thrive like the grass of the field.
¹⁷May his name endure forever;
  may it continue as long as the sun.

All nations will be blessed through him,
  and they will call him blessed.

¹⁸Praise be to the LORD God, the God of Israel,

^a2 Or *May he*; similarly in verses 3–11 and 17   ^b5 Septuagint; Hebrew *You will be feared*   ^c8 That is, the
Euphrates   ^d8 Or *the end of the land*

who alone does marvelous deeds.
[19] Praise be to his glorious name forever;
  may the whole earth be filled with his
    glory.
        Amen and Amen.

[20] This concludes the prayers of David son of
  Jesse.

BOOK III

Psalms 73–89

Psalm 73

A psalm of Asaph.

[1] Surely God is good to Israel,
  to those who are pure in heart.
[2] But as for me, my feet had almost slipped;
  I had nearly lost my foothold.
[3] For I envied the arrogant
  when I saw the prosperity of the wicked.
[4] They have no struggles;
  their bodies are healthy and strong.[a]
[5] They are free from the burdens common to
    man;
  they are not plagued by human ills.
[6] Therefore pride is their necklace;
  they clothe themselves with violence.
[7] From their callous hearts comes iniquity[b];
  the evil conceits of their minds know no
    limits.
[8] They scoff, and speak with malice;
  in their arrogance they threaten
    oppression.

[9] Their mouths lay claim to heaven,
  and their tongues take possession of the
    earth.
[10] Therefore their people turn to them
  and drink up waters in abundance.[c]
[11] They say, "How can God know?
  Does the Most High have knowledge?"

[12] This is what the wicked are like—
  always carefree, they increase in wealth.

[13] Surely in vain have I kept my heart pure;
  in vain have I washed my hands in
    innocence.
[14] All day long I have been plagued;
  I have been punished every morning.

[15] If I had said, "I will speak thus,"
  I would have betrayed your children.
[16] When I tried to understand all this,
  it was oppressive to me
[17] till I entered the sanctuary of God;
  then I understood their final destiny.

[18] Surely you place them on slippery ground;
  you cast them down to ruin.
[19] How suddenly are they destroyed,
  completely swept away by terrors!
[20] As a dream when one awakes,
  so when you arise, O Lord,
  you will despise them as fantasies.

[21] When my heart was grieved
  and my spirit embittered,
[22] I was senseless and ignorant;
  I was a brute beast before you.

[23] Yet I am always with you;
  you hold me by my right hand.
[24] You guide me with your counsel,
  and afterward you will take me into glory.
[25] Whom have I in heaven but you?
  And earth has nothing I desire besides
    you.
[26] My flesh and my heart may fail,
  but God is the strength of my heart
  and my portion forever.

[a]4 With a different word division of the Hebrew; Masoretic Text *struggles at their death; / their bodies are healthy*
[b]7 Syriac (see also Septuagint); Hebrew *Their eyes bulge with fat*   [c]10 The meaning of the Hebrew for this verse is
uncertain.

27Those who are far from you will perish;
  you destroy all who are unfaithful to you.
28But as for me, it is good to be near God.
  I have made the Sovereign LORD my
    refuge;
  I will tell of all your deeds.

Psalm 74

A maskil[a] of Asaph.

1Why have you rejected us forever, O God?
  Why does your anger smolder against the
    sheep of your pasture?
2Remember the people you purchased of old,
  the tribe of your inheritance, whom you
    redeemed—
  Mount Zion, where you dwelt.
3Turn your steps toward these everlasting
    ruins,
  all this destruction the enemy has brought
    on the sanctuary.

4Your foes roared in the place where you met
    with us;
  they set up their standards as signs.
5They behaved like men wielding axes
  to cut through a thicket of trees.
6They smashed all the carved paneling
  with their axes and hatchets.
7They burned your sanctuary to the ground;
  they defiled the dwelling place of your
    Name.
8They said in their hearts, "We will crush
    them completely!"
  They burned every place where God was
    worshiped in the land.
9We are given no miraculous signs;
  no prophets are left,
  and none of us knows how long this will
    be.

10How long will the enemy mock you, O God?
  Will the foe revile your name forever?
11Why do you hold back your hand, your
    right hand?
  Take it from the folds of your garment
    and destroy them!

12But you, O God, are my king from of old;
  you bring salvation upon the earth.
13It was you who split open the sea by your
    power;
  you broke the heads of the monster in the
    waters.
14It was you who crushed the heads of
    Leviathan
  and gave him as food to the creatures of
    the desert.

15It was you who opened up springs and
    streams;
  you dried up the ever flowing rivers.
16The day is yours, and yours also the night;
  you established the sun and moon.
17It was you who set all the boundaries of the
    earth;
  you made both summer and winter.

18Remember how the enemy has mocked you,
    O LORD,
  how foolish people have reviled your
    name.
19Do not hand over the life of your dove to
    wild beasts;
  do not forget the lives of your afflicted
    people forever.
20Have regard for your covenant,
  because haunts of violence fill the dark
    places of the land.
21Do not let the oppressed retreat in disgrace;
  may the poor and needy praise your
    name.

22Rise up, O God, and defend your cause;
  remember how fools mock you all day
    long.
23Do not ignore the clamor of your
    adversaries,
  the uproar of your enemies, which rises
    continually.

Psalm 75

*For the director of music. ₍To the tune of₎ "Do
Not Destroy." A psalm of Asaph. A song.*

1We give thanks to you, O God,
  we give thanks, for your Name is near;
  men tell of your wonderful deeds.

2You say, "I choose the appointed time;
  it is I who judge uprightly.
3When the earth and all its people quake,
  it is I who hold its pillars firm.   *Selah*
4To the arrogant I say, 'Boast no more,'
  and to the wicked, 'Do not lift up your
    horns.
5Do not lift your horns against heaven;
  do not speak with outstretched neck.'"

6No one from the east or the west
  or from the desert can exalt a man.
7But it is God who judges:
  He brings one down, he exalts another.
8In the hand of the LORD is a cup
  full of foaming wine mixed with spices;
 he pours it out, and all the wicked of the
    earth
  drink it down to its very dregs.

---

a Title: Probably a literary or musical term

9As for me, I will declare this forever;
  I will sing praise to the God of Jacob.
10I will cut off the horns of all the wicked,
  but the horns of the righteous will be
    lifted up.

Psalm 76

For the director of music. With stringed
instruments. A psalm of Asaph. A song.

1In Judah God is known;
  his name is great in Israel.
2His tent is in Salem,
  his dwelling place in Zion.
3There he broke the flashing arrows,
  the shields and the swords, the weapons
    of war.   *Selah*

4You are resplendent with light,
  more majestic than mountains rich with
    game.
5Valiant men lie plundered,
  they sleep their last sleep;
not one of the warriors
  can lift his hands.
6At your rebuke, O God of Jacob,
  both horse and chariot lie still.
7You alone are to be feared.
  Who can stand before you when you are
    angry?
8From heaven you pronounced judgment,
  and the land feared and was quiet—
9when you, O God, rose up to judge,
  to save all the afflicted of the land.   *Selah*
10Surely your wrath against men brings you
    praise,
  and the survivors of your wrath are
    restrained.*a*
11Make vows to the LORD your God and fulfill
    them;
  let all the neighboring lands
  bring gifts to the One to be feared.
12He breaks the spirit of rulers;
  he is feared by the kings of the earth.

Psalm 77

For the director of music. For Jeduthun.
Of Asaph. A psalm.

1I cried out to God for help;
  I cried out to God to hear me.
2When I was in distress, I sought the Lord;
  at night I stretched out untiring hands
  and my soul refused to be comforted.

3I remembered you, O God, and I groaned;
  I mused, and my spirit grew faint.   *Selah*
4You kept my eyes from closing;

I was too troubled to speak.
5I thought about the former days,
  the years of long ago;
6I remembered my songs in the night.
  My heart mused and my spirit inquired:

77:3–12 Sleepless Nights

*Sleeplessness afflicts millions, and this psalm
shows it is nothing new. Anxiety tormented the
psalmist while he lay awake at night. What to
do? He deliberately turned his thoughts to the
past, remembering what God had done for him
and for his people.*

7"Will the Lord reject forever?
  Will he never show his favor again?
8Has his unfailing love vanished forever?
  Has his promise failed for all time?
9Has God forgotten to be merciful?
  Has he in anger withheld his
    compassion?"   *Selah*

10Then I thought, "To this I will appeal:
  the years of the right hand of the Most
    High."
11I will remember the deeds of the LORD;
  yes, I will remember your miracles of long
    ago.
12I will meditate on all your works
  and consider all your mighty deeds.

13Your ways, O God, are holy.
  What god is so great as our God?
14You are the God who performs miracles;
  you display your power among the
    peoples.
15With your mighty arm you redeemed your
    people,
  the descendants of Jacob and Joseph.   *Selah*

16The waters saw you, O God,
  the waters saw you and writhed;
  the very depths were convulsed.
17The clouds poured down water,
  the skies resounded with thunder;
  your arrows flashed back and forth.
18Your thunder was heard in the whirlwind,
  your lightning lit up the world;
  the earth trembled and quaked.
19Your path led through the sea,
  your way through the mighty waters,
  though your footprints were not seen.

20You led your people like a flock
  by the hand of Moses and Aaron.

---

a10 Or Surely the wrath of men brings you praise, / and with the remainder of wrath you arm yourself

Psalm 78

A *maskil*[a] of Asaph.

[1]O my people, hear my teaching;
  listen to the words of my mouth.
[2]I will open my mouth in parables,
  I will utter hidden things, things from of
    old—
[3]what we have heard and known,
  what our fathers have told us.
[4]We will not hide them from their children;
  we will tell the next generation
the praiseworthy deeds of the LORD,
  his power, and the wonders he has done.
[5]He decreed statutes for Jacob
  and established the law in Israel,

which he commanded our forefathers
  to teach their children,
[6]so the next generation would know them,
  even the children yet to be born,
  and they in turn would tell their children.
[7]Then they would put their trust in God
  and would not forget his deeds
  but would keep his commands.
[8]They would not be like their forefathers—
  a stubborn and rebellious generation,
whose hearts were not loyal to God,
  whose spirits were not faithful to him.

[9]The men of Ephraim, though armed with
    bows,
  turned back on the day of battle;
[10]they did not keep God's covenant

[a]Title: Probably a literary or musical term

Remembering Back

The past can give you hope for the future

> I will remember the
> deeds of the LORD.
> 77:11

MARRIED PEOPLE MAKE IT THEIR business to remember how love began. Anniversaries recall their wedding day, year after year. Wedding rings remind them of their commitment. Wedding photos capture the moment when "two become one." In remembering the beginning of their love, couples often find new hope for the future.

Forgetting, on the other hand, amounts to treason. If one person forgets the all-important anniversary, tears and anger may follow.

An Anniversary Day

The book of Psalms remembers too. When things get bad, these poems often refer to the past—particularly to the great events when, under Moses, the Israelite nation began. God freed the Israelites from Egyptian slavery, carried them through the Red Sea, gave them directions for living, and ushered them into the promised land. This miraculous beginning was as significant to Jews as the cross is to Christians.

The Israelites even had an "anniversary day"—known as Passover—to remember it. Every spring Passover reminded them of their escape from Egypt. It's no accident that Easter often falls on the same week. Both days celebrate liberation from slavery.

The memories weren't all positive. The Israelites could, in fact, be brutally frank about their early failings. Even as they remembered how persistently wonderful God had been, they also remembered how rebellious, complaining, and forgetful they had been. Yet they had one great, happy reason to celebrate: God had kept his promise to love them.

Hope in a Time of Despair

Psalm 77 is a "remembering" poem. It starts with deep despair. "Will the Lord reject forever? Will he never show his favor again? Has God forgotten to be merciful? Has he in anger withheld his compassion?" (77:7,9). Imagine a wife asking such questions about her husband.

Then thoughts turn, deliberately, to the past. Remember the turmoil at the banks of the Red Sea? Could anything be worse? But in that turbulent water they had seen the Lord's power: God had led them through to safety. He would do the same again.

The historical psalms (77, 78, 105, 106) invite us, along with the Israelites, to relive history. Like married couples remembering back, we can recall God's work—his powerful victories recorded all through Scripture, his promises and proofs of love toward his people. And we can refer to God's history with us as individuals, too. Who cannot count some blessings, some undeserved favors? Through such remembering we are strengthened to face the future, and to recommit ourselves to trusting God's care.

Life Questions: If you were to refer to a single past event for encouragement, what would it be?

and refused to live by his law.
11They forgot what he had done,
   the wonders he had shown them.
12He did miracles in the sight of their fathers
   in the land of Egypt, in the region of
      Zoan.

78:2 Speaking in Parables

Matthew saw this verse as foreshadowing Jesus' teaching style (Matthew 13:35). A "parable" or "proverb" (the Hebrew word is the same) simply compares one thing with another. This psalm compares the present to the past. By going over the great things God has done—and the great indifference God's people have often shown—the psalmist warns against making the same mistakes again.

13He divided the sea and led them through;
   he made the water stand firm like a wall.
14He guided them with the cloud by day
   and with light from the fire all night.
15He split the rocks in the desert
   and gave them water as abundant as the
      seas;
16he brought streams out of a rocky crag
   and made water flow down like rivers.

17But they continued to sin against him,
   rebelling in the desert against the Most
      High.
18They willfully put God to the test
   by demanding the food they craved.
19They spoke against God, saying,
   "Can God spread a table in the desert?
20When he struck the rock, water gushed out,
   and streams flowed abundantly.
But can he also give us food?
   Can he supply meat for his people?"
21When the LORD heard them, he was very
      angry;
   his fire broke out against Jacob,
   and his wrath rose against Israel,
22for they did not believe in God
   or trust in his deliverance.
23Yet he gave a command to the skies above
   and opened the doors of the heavens;
24he rained down manna for the people to eat,
   he gave them the grain of heaven.
25Men ate the bread of angels;
   he sent them all the food they could eat.
26He let loose the east wind from the heavens
   and led forth the south wind by his
      power.
27He rained meat down on them like dust,
   flying birds like sand on the seashore.
28He made them come down inside their
      camp,

all around their tents.
29They ate till they had more than enough,
   for he had given them what they craved.
30But before they turned from the food they
      craved,
   even while it was still in their mouths,
31God's anger rose against them;
   he put to death the sturdiest among them,
   cutting down the young men of Israel.

32In spite of all this, they kept on sinning;
   in spite of his wonders, they did not
      believe.
33So he ended their days in futility
   and their years in terror.
34Whenever God slew them, they would seek
      him;
   they eagerly turned to him again.
35They remembered that God was their Rock,
   that God Most High was their Redeemer.
36But then they would flatter him with their
      mouths,
   lying to him with their tongues;
37their hearts were not loyal to him,
   they were not faithful to his covenant.
38Yet he was merciful;
   he forgave their iniquities
   and did not destroy them.
Time after time he restrained his anger
   and did not stir up his full wrath.
39He remembered that they were but flesh,
   a passing breeze that does not return.

40How often they rebelled against him in the
      desert
   and grieved him in the wasteland!
41Again and again they put God to the test;
   they vexed the Holy One of Israel.
42They did not remember his power—
   the day he redeemed them from the
      oppressor,
43the day he displayed his miraculous signs in
      Egypt,
   his wonders in the region of Zoan.
44He turned their rivers to blood;
   they could not drink from their streams.
45He sent swarms of flies that devoured them,
   and frogs that devastated them.
46He gave their crops to the grasshopper,
   their produce to the locust.
47He destroyed their vines with hail
   and their sycamore-figs with sleet.
48He gave over their cattle to the hail,
   their livestock to bolts of lightning.
49He unleashed against them his hot anger,
   his wrath, indignation and hostility—
   a band of destroying angels.
50He prepared a path for his anger;
   he did not spare them from death
   but gave them over to the plague.
51He struck down all the firstborn of Egypt,

the firstfruits of manhood in the tents of
Ham.
⁵²But he brought his people out like a flock;
he led them like sheep through the desert.
⁵³He guided them safely, so they were
unafraid;
but the sea engulfed their enemies.
⁵⁴Thus he brought them to the border of his
holy land,
to the hill country his right hand had
taken.
⁵⁵He drove out nations before them
and allotted their lands to them as an
inheritance;
he settled the tribes of Israel in their
homes.

⁵⁶But they put God to the test
and rebelled against the Most High;
they did not keep his statutes.
⁵⁷Like their fathers they were disloyal and
faithless,
as unreliable as a faulty bow.
⁵⁸They angered him with their high places;
they aroused his jealousy with their idols.
⁵⁹When God heard them, he was very angry;
he rejected Israel completely.
⁶⁰He abandoned the tabernacle of Shiloh,
the tent he had set up among men.
⁶¹He sent ˌthe ark of⸴ his might into captivity,
his splendor into the hands of the enemy.
⁶²He gave his people over to the sword;
he was very angry with his inheritance.
⁶³Fire consumed their young men,
and their maidens had no wedding songs;
⁶⁴their priests were put to the sword,
and their widows could not weep.

78:64 The Bad Old Days

*From the time they entered the promised land
to the time when Saul was named their first
king, Israelites had no central government.
Instead they were governed by "judges,"
colorful volunteer leaders like Deborah, Gideon,
and Samson. Israel had few nostalgic
memories of those days. Psalm 78 portrays
them as a time when Israel abandoned God—
and God rejected Israel. These verses (59–64)
draw from the events described in 1 Samuel 4.*

⁶⁵Then the Lord awoke as from sleep,
as a man wakes from the stupor of wine.
⁶⁶He beat back his enemies;
he put them to everlasting shame.
⁶⁷Then he rejected the tents of Joseph,
he did not choose the tribe of Ephraim;
⁶⁸but he chose the tribe of Judah,
Mount Zion, which he loved.
⁶⁹He built his sanctuary like the heights,

like the earth that he established forever.
⁷⁰He chose David his servant
and took him from the sheep pens;
⁷¹from tending the sheep he brought him
to be the shepherd of his people Jacob,
of Israel his inheritance.
⁷²And David shepherded them with integrity
of heart;
with skillful hands he led them.

Psalm 79

A psalm of Asaph.

¹O God, the nations have invaded your
inheritance;
they have defiled your holy temple,
they have reduced Jerusalem to rubble.
²They have given the dead bodies of your
servants
as food to the birds of the air,
the flesh of your saints to the beasts of the
earth.
³They have poured out blood like water
all around Jerusalem,
and there is no one to bury the dead.
⁴We are objects of reproach to our neighbors,
of scorn and derision to those around us.

⁵How long, O LORD? Will you be angry
forever?
How long will your jealousy burn like fire?
⁶Pour out your wrath on the nations
that do not acknowledge you,
on the kingdoms
that do not call on your name;
⁷for they have devoured Jacob
and destroyed his homeland.
⁸Do not hold against us the sins of the
fathers;
may your mercy come quickly to meet us,
for we are in desperate need.

⁹Help us, O God our Savior,
for the glory of your name;
deliver us and forgive our sins
for your name's sake.
¹⁰Why should the nations say,
"Where is their God?"
Before our eyes, make known among the
nations
that you avenge the outpoured blood of
your servants.
¹¹May the groans of the prisoners come before
you;
by the strength of your arm
preserve those condemned to die.

¹²Pay back into the laps of our neighbors
seven times
the reproach they have hurled at you,
O Lord.

¹³Then we your people, the sheep of your
    pasture,
  will praise you forever;
from generation to generation
  we will recount your praise.

Psalm 80

For the director of music. To the tune of, "The
Lilies of the Covenant." Of Asaph. A psalm.

¹Hear us, O Shepherd of Israel,
  you who lead Joseph like a flock;
you who sit enthroned between the
    cherubim, shine forth
² before Ephraim, Benjamin and Manasseh.
Awaken your might;
  come and save us.

³Restore us, O God;
  make your face shine upon us,
  that we may be saved.

⁴O LORD God Almighty,
  how long will your anger smolder
  against the prayers of your people?
⁵You have fed them with the bread of tears;
  you have made them drink tears by the
    bowlful.
⁶You have made us a source of contention to
    our neighbors,
  and our enemies mock us.

⁷Restore us, O God Almighty;
  make your face shine upon us,
  that we may be saved.

⁸You brought a vine out of Egypt;
  you drove out the nations and planted it.
⁹You cleared the ground for it,
  and it took root and filled the land.
¹⁰The mountains were covered with its shade,
  the mighty cedars with its branches.
¹¹It sent out its boughs to the Sea,ᵃ
  its shoots as far as the River.ᵇ

¹²Why have you broken down its walls
  so that all who pass by pick its grapes?
¹³Boars from the forest ravage it
  and the creatures of the field feed on it.
¹⁴Return to us, O God Almighty!
  Look down from heaven and see!
  Watch over this vine,
¹⁵ the root your right hand has planted,
  the sonᶜ you raised up for yourself.

¹⁶Your vine is cut down, it is burned with fire;
  at your rebuke your people perish.
¹⁷Let your hand rest on the man at your right
    hand,

the son of man you have raised up for
    yourself.
¹⁸Then we will not turn away from you;
  revive us, and we will call on your name.

¹⁹Restore us, O LORD God Almighty;
  make your face shine upon us,
  that we may be saved.

80:14 Grapevines

*The Old Testament often portrays God's people
as a vineyard. Jesus, too, used the image (see
Mark 12:1–9; John 15:1–5). Raising grapes
was as familiar to Israelites as playing baseball
is to Americans. Many sermon illustrations
have been made from both.*

Psalm 81

For the director of music. According to *gittith.*ᵈ
Of Asaph.

¹Sing for joy to God our strength;
  shout aloud to the God of Jacob!
²Begin the music, strike the tambourine,
  play the melodious harp and lyre.

³Sound the ram's horn at the New Moon,
  and when the moon is full, on the day of
    our Feast;
⁴this is a decree for Israel,
  an ordinance of the God of Jacob.
⁵He established it as a statute for Joseph
  when he went out against Egypt,
  where we heard a language we did not
    understand.ᵉ

⁶He says, "I removed the burden from their
    shoulders;
  their hands were set free from the basket.
⁷In your distress you called and I rescued
    you,
  I answered you out of a thundercloud;
  I tested you at the waters of Meribah.
                                    Selah

⁸"Hear, O my people, and I will warn you—
  if you would but listen to me, O Israel!
⁹You shall have no foreign god among you;
  you shall not bow down to an alien god.
¹⁰I am the LORD your God,
  who brought you up out of Egypt.
  Open wide your mouth and I will fill it.

¹¹"But my people would not listen to me;
  Israel would not submit to me.
¹²So I gave them over to their stubborn hearts
  to follow their own devices.

ᵃ11 Probably the Mediterranean   ᵇ11 That is, the Euphrates   ᶜ15 Or *branch*   ᵈTitle: Probably a musical term
ᵉ5 Or *I and we heard a voice we had not known*

13"If my people would but listen to me,
    if Israel would follow my ways,
14how quickly would I subdue their enemies
    and turn my hand against their foes!
15Those who hate the LORD would cringe
    before him,
    and their punishment would last forever.
16But you would be fed with the finest of
    wheat;
    with honey from the rock I would satisfy
    you."

Psalm 82

A psalm of Asaph.

1God presides in the great assembly;
    he gives judgment among the "gods":

82:1 Among "the Gods"

Human beings like to think of themselves as godlike—able to do whatever they like. Many commentators believe this psalm's snort of disdain is aimed at human judges and "powers that be" who set themselves up as little gods. What will become of their arrogance if they defy God? They will "die like mere men" (verse 7). The grave is a perfect answer to their pretensions.

When Jesus was accused of blasphemy for claiming to be God's Son, he referred his critics to this psalm (John 10:35). If Scripture could apply such lofty terminology to sinful human beings, was it not possible that a perfect man could be God's own Son?

2"How long will you[a] defend the unjust
    and show partiality to the wicked?   *Selah*
3Defend the cause of the weak and fatherless;
    maintain the rights of the poor and
    oppressed.
4Rescue the weak and needy;
    deliver them from the hand of the wicked.

5"They know nothing, they understand
    nothing.
    They walk about in darkness;
    all the foundations of the earth are
    shaken.

6"I said, 'You are "gods";
    you are all sons of the Most High.'
7But you will die like mere men;
    you will fall like every other ruler."

8Rise up, O God, judge the earth,
    for all the nations are your inheritance.

Psalm 83

A song. A psalm of Asaph.

1O God, do not keep silent;
    be not quiet, O God, be not still.
2See how your enemies are astir,
    how your foes rear their heads.
3With cunning they conspire against your
    people;
    they plot against those you cherish.
4"Come," they say, "let us destroy them as a
    nation,
    that the name of Israel be remembered no
    more."

5With one mind they plot together;
    they form an alliance against you—
6the tents of Edom and the Ishmaelites,
    of Moab and the Hagrites,
7Gebal,[b] Ammon and Amalek,
    Philistia, with the people of Tyre.
8Even Assyria has joined them
    to lend strength to the descendants of Lot.
        Selah

9Do to them as you did to Midian,
    as you did to Sisera and Jabin at the river
    Kishon,
10who perished at Endor
    and became like refuse on the ground.
11Make their nobles like Oreb and Zeeb,
    all their princes like Zebah and Zalmunna,
12who said, "Let us take possession
    of the pasturelands of God."

13Make them like tumbleweed, O my God,
    like chaff before the wind.
14As fire consumes the forest
    or a flame sets the mountains ablaze,
15so pursue them with your tempest
    and terrify them with your storm.
16Cover their faces with shame
    so that men will seek your name, O LORD.

17May they ever be ashamed and dismayed;
    may they perish in disgrace.
18Let them know that you, whose name is the
    LORD—
    that you alone are the Most High over all
    the earth.

Psalm 84

For the director of music. According to *gittith*.[c]
Of the Sons of Korah. A psalm.

1How lovely is your dwelling place,
    O LORD Almighty!
2My soul yearns, even faints,
    for the courts of the LORD;

---

[a]2 The Hebrew is plural.   [b]7 That is, Byblos   [c]Title: Probably a musical term

my heart and my flesh cry out
  for the living God.

³Even the sparrow has found a home,
  and the swallow a nest for herself,
  where she may have her young—
a place near your altar,
  O Lord Almighty, my King and my God.
⁴Blessed are those who dwell in your house;
  they are ever praising you.   *Selah*

⁵Blessed are those whose strength is in you,
  who have set their hearts on pilgrimage.
⁶As they pass through the Valley of Baca,
  they make it a place of springs;
  the autumn rains also cover it with
    pools.ᵃ
⁷They go from strength to strength,
  till each appears before God in Zion.

⁸Hear my prayer, O Lord God Almighty;
  listen to me, O God of Jacob.   *Selah*
⁹Look upon our shield,ᵇ O God;
  look with favor on your anointed one.

¹⁰Better is one day in your courts
  than a thousand elsewhere;
I would rather be a doorkeeper in the house
    of my God
  than dwell in the tents of the wicked.

84:10 Homecoming

*"Home Sweet Home" probably adorns more
plaques than any other motto. Home is a place
where you can lay down your tired body and
bruised ego in safety. Psalm 84 contains the
same idea, but with a dramatic difference.
Home is in God's house, a place that brings
comfort right down into your bones. You'd
rather spend one day near God, praising him,
than a thousand days anywhere else.*

¹¹For the Lord God is a sun and shield;
  the Lord bestows favor and honor;
no good thing does he withhold
  from those whose walk is blameless.

¹²O Lord Almighty,
  blessed is the man who trusts in you.

Psalm 85

For the director of music. Of the Sons of Korah.
A psalm.

¹You showed favor to your land, O Lord;
  you restored the fortunes of Jacob.
²You forgave the iniquity of your people
  and covered all their sins.   *Selah*

³You set aside all your wrath
  and turned from your fierce anger.

⁴Restore us again, O God our Savior,
  and put away your displeasure toward us.
⁵Will you be angry with us forever?
  Will you prolong your anger through all
    generations?
⁶Will you not revive us again,
  that your people may rejoice in you?
⁷Show us your unfailing love, O Lord,
  and grant us your salvation.

⁸I will listen to what God the Lord will say;
  he promises peace to his people, his
    saints—
  but let them not return to folly.
⁹Surely his salvation is near those who fear
    him,
  that his glory may dwell in our land.

¹⁰Love and faithfulness meet together;
  righteousness and peace kiss each other.
¹¹Faithfulness springs forth from the earth,
  and righteousness looks down from
    heaven.
¹²The Lord will indeed give what is good,
  and our land will yield its harvest.
¹³Righteousness goes before him
  and prepares the way for his steps.

Psalm 86

A prayer of David.

¹Hear, O Lord, and answer me,
  for I am poor and needy.
²Guard my life, for I am devoted to you.
  You are my God; save your servant
  who trusts in you.
³Have mercy on me, O Lord,
  for I call to you all day long.
⁴Bring joy to your servant,
  for to you, O Lord,
  I lift up my soul.

⁵You are forgiving and good, O Lord,
  abounding in love to all who call to you.
⁶Hear my prayer, O Lord;
  listen to my cry for mercy.
⁷In the day of my trouble I will call to you,
  for you will answer me.

⁸Among the gods there is none like you,
    O Lord;
  no deeds can compare with yours.
⁹All the nations you have made
  will come and worship before you,
    O Lord;
  they will bring glory to your name.

ᵃ6 Or *blessings*   ᵇ9 Or *sovereign*

10For you are great and do marvelous deeds;
    you alone are God.

11Teach me your way, O LORD,
    and I will walk in your truth;
give me an undivided heart,
    that I may fear your name.

86:11 Heart Surgery

David prays for an undivided heart, in order to give all of it to God in his praise. "Heart" in the Bible doesn't refer merely to emotions, but to the whole person. David's prayer means, "Help me aim myself in a single direction!"

12I will praise you, O Lord my God, with all
        my heart;
    I will glorify your name forever.
13For great is your love toward me;
        you have delivered me from the depths of
        the grave.[a]

14The arrogant are attacking me, O God;
        a band of ruthless men seeks my life—
    men without regard for you.
15But you, O Lord, are a compassionate and
        gracious God,
    slow to anger, abounding in love and
        faithfulness.
16Turn to me and have mercy on me;
    grant your strength to your servant
    and save the son of your maidservant.[b]
17Give me a sign of your goodness,
    that my enemies may see it and be put to
        shame,
    for you, O LORD, have helped me and
        comforted me.

Psalm 87

Of the Sons of Korah. A psalm. A song.

1He has set his foundation on the holy
        mountain;
2   the LORD loves the gates of Zion
    more than all the dwellings of Jacob.
3Glorious things are said of you,
    O city of God: *Selah*
4"I will record Rahab[c] and Babylon
    among those who acknowledge me—
Philistia too, and Tyre, along with Cush[d]—
    and will say, 'This[e] one was born in
        Zion.'"

5Indeed, of Zion it will be said,
    "This one and that one were born in her,

and the Most High himself will establish
        her."
6The LORD will write in the register of the
        peoples:
    "This one was born in Zion."   *Selah*
7As they make music they will sing,
    "All my fountains are in you."

Psalm 88

A song. A psalm of the Sons of Korah. For the
    director of music. According to *mahalath
    leannoth.[f]* A *maskil[g]* of Heman the Ezrahite.

1O LORD, the God who saves me,
    day and night I cry out before you.

88:1 Bad Father, Good Kids

Psalm 88 is the last of 12 psalms ascribed to "the Sons of Korah." Korah, a rebel against Moses' leadership, died in his rebellion (Numbers 16). His children were spared, and many years later David chose their clan to found a temple choir (1 Chronicles 6:31–37). Apparently these psalms were part of a musical collection they used.

2May my prayer come before you;
    turn your ear to my cry.

3For my soul is full of trouble
    and my life draws near the grave.[a]
4I am counted among those who go down to
        the pit;
    I am like a man without strength.
5I am set apart with the dead,
    like the slain who lie in the grave,
whom you remember no more,
    who are cut off from your care.

6You have put me in the lowest pit,
    in the darkest depths.
7Your wrath lies heavily upon me;
    you have overwhelmed me with all your
        waves.   *Selah*
8You have taken from me my closest friends
    and have made me repulsive to them.
I am confined and cannot escape;
9   my eyes are dim with grief.

I call to you, O LORD, every day;
    I spread out my hands to you.
10Do you show your wonders to the dead?
    Do those who are dead rise up and praise
        you?   *Selah*
11Is your love declared in the grave,

---

[a]13,3 Hebrew *Sheol*   [b]16 Or *save your faithful son*   [c]4 A poetic name for Egypt   [d]4 That is, the upper Nile region   [e]4 Or *"O Rahab and Babylon, / Philistia, Tyre and Cush, / I will record concerning those who acknowledge me:* / *'This*   [f]Title: Possibly a tune, "The Suffering of Affliction"   [g]Title: Probably a literary or musical term

your faithfulness in Destruction[a]?
¹²Are your wonders known in the place of
darkness,
or your righteous deeds in the land of
oblivion?

¹³But I cry to you for help, O LORD;
in the morning my prayer comes before
you.
¹⁴Why, O LORD, do you reject me
and hide your face from me?

¹⁵From my youth I have been afflicted and
close to death;
I have suffered your terrors and am in
despair.
¹⁶Your wrath has swept over me;
your terrors have destroyed me.
¹⁷All day long they surround me like a flood;
they have completely engulfed me.
¹⁸You have taken my companions and loved
ones from me;
the darkness is my closest friend.

Psalm 89

A *maskil*[b] of Ethan the Ezrahite.

¹I will sing of the LORD's great love forever;
with my mouth I will make your
faithfulness known through all
generations.
²I will declare that your love stands firm
forever,
that you established your faithfulness in
heaven itself.

³You said, "I have made a covenant with my
chosen one,
I have sworn to David my servant,
⁴'I will establish your line forever
and make your throne firm through all
generations.'"   *Selah*

⁵The heavens praise your wonders, O LORD,
your faithfulness too, in the assembly of
the holy ones.
⁶For who in the skies above can compare
with the LORD?
Who is like the LORD among the heavenly
beings?
⁷In the council of the holy ones God is
greatly feared;
he is more awesome than all who
surround him.
⁸O LORD God Almighty, who is like you?
You are mighty, O LORD, and your
faithfulness surrounds you.

⁹You rule over the surging sea;

when its waves mount up, you still them.
¹⁰You crushed Rahab like one of the slain;
with your strong arm you scattered your
enemies.
¹¹The heavens are yours, and yours also the
earth;
you founded the world and all that is in
it.
¹²You created the north and the south;
Tabor and Hermon sing for joy at your
name.
¹³Your arm is endued with power;
your hand is strong, your right hand
exalted.

¹⁴Righteousness and justice are the foundation
of your throne;
love and faithfulness go before you.
¹⁵Blessed are those who have learned to
acclaim you,
who walk in the light of your presence,
O LORD.
¹⁶They rejoice in your name all day long;
they exult in your righteousness.
¹⁷For you are their glory and strength,
and by your favor you exalt our horn.[c]
¹⁸Indeed, our shield[d] belongs to the LORD,
our king to the Holy One of Israel.

¹⁹Once you spoke in a vision,
to your faithful people you said:
"I have bestowed strength on a warrior;
I have exalted a young man from among
the people.
²⁰I have found David my servant;
with my sacred oil I have anointed him.
²¹My hand will sustain him;
surely my arm will strengthen him.
²²No enemy will subject him to tribute;
no wicked man will oppress him.
²³I will crush his foes before him
and strike down his adversaries.
²⁴My faithful love will be with him,
and through my name his horn[e] will be
exalted.
²⁵I will set his hand over the sea,
his right hand over the rivers.
²⁶He will call out to me, 'You are my Father,
my God, the Rock my Savior.'
²⁷I will also appoint him my firstborn,
the most exalted of the kings of the earth.
²⁸I will maintain my love to him forever,
and my covenant with him will never fail.
²⁹I will establish his line forever,
his throne as long as the heavens endure.

³⁰"If his sons forsake my law
and do not follow my statutes,
³¹if they violate my decrees

---

[a]11 Hebrew *Abaddon*   [b]Title: Probably a literary or musical term   [c]17 *Horn* here symbolizes strong one.
[d]18 Or *sovereign*   [e]24 *Horn* here symbolizes strength.

and fail to keep my commands,
[32]I will punish their sin with the rod,
their iniquity with flogging;
[33]but I will not take my love from him,

89:30–49 Shame Forever?

God, as this psalm notes, had made tremendous promises to David and to his descendants (see 2 Samuel 7:4–17). But what do you do when God's promises don't match your experience? This psalm was probably written after the Babylonians had deported the young king Jehoiachin (see here and 2 Kings 24:8,15) and torn down Jerusalem (see verse 40 and 2 Kings 25:10). It gives no explanation of how God's promises fit with this humiliation and suffering. But it offers a model of how to respond, taking the problem straight to God in the frankest terms. Only when Jesus came centuries later did Israel see God fulfill these promises to honor and love a "son of David" as his own Son (verses 26–29).

nor will I ever betray my faithfulness.
[34]I will not violate my covenant
or alter what my lips have uttered.
[35]Once for all, I have sworn by my holiness—
and I will not lie to David—
[36]that his line will continue forever
and his throne endure before me like the
sun;
[37]it will be established forever like the moon,
the faithful witness in the sky." *Selah*

[38]But you have rejected, you have spurned,
you have been very angry with your
anointed one.
[39]You have renounced the covenant with your
servant
and have defiled his crown in the dust.
[40]You have broken through all his walls
and reduced his strongholds to ruins.
[41]All who pass by have plundered him;
he has become the scorn of his neighbors.
[42]You have exalted the right hand of his foes;
you have made all his enemies rejoice.
[43]You have turned back the edge of his sword
and have not supported him in battle.
[44]You have put an end to his splendor
and cast his throne to the ground.
[45]You have cut short the days of his youth;
you have covered him with a mantle of
shame. *Selah*

[46]How long, O LORD? Will you hide yourself
forever?
How long will your wrath burn like fire?
[47]Remember how fleeting is my life.

For what futility you have created all men!
[48]What man can live and not see death,
or save himself from the power of the
grave[a]? *Selah*

[49]O Lord, where is your former great love,
which in your faithfulness you swore to
David?
[50]Remember, Lord, how your servant has[b]
been mocked,
how I bear in my heart the taunts of all
the nations,
[51]the taunts with which your enemies have
mocked, O LORD,
with which they have mocked every step
of your anointed one.

[52]Praise be to the LORD forever!
Amen and Amen.

BOOK IV

Psalms 90–106

Psalm 90

A prayer of Moses the man of God.

[1]Lord, you have been our dwelling place
throughout all generations.
[2]Before the mountains were born
or you brought forth the earth and the
world,
from everlasting to everlasting you are
God.

[3]You turn men back to dust,
saying, "Return to dust, O sons of men."
[4]For a thousand years in your sight
are like a day that has just gone by,
or like a watch in the night.
[5]You sweep men away in the sleep of death;
they are like the new grass of the
morning—
[6]though in the morning it springs up new,
by evening it is dry and withered.

[7]We are consumed by your anger
and terrified by your indignation.
[8]You have set our iniquities before you,
our secret sins in the light of your
presence.
[9]All our days pass away under your wrath;
we finish our years with a moan.
[10]The length of our days is seventy years—
or eighty, if we have the strength;
yet their span[c] is but trouble and sorrow,
for they quickly pass, and we fly away.
[11]Who knows the power of your anger?
For your wrath is as great as the fear that
is due you.

---

[a]48 Hebrew *Sheol*   [b]50 Or *your servants have*   [c]10 Or *yet the best of them*

¹²Teach us to number our days aright,
  that we may gain a heart of wisdom.

¹³Relent, O LORD! How long will it be?
  Have compassion on your servants.
¹⁴Satisfy us in the morning with your unfailing
    love,
  that we may sing for joy and be glad all
    our days.
¹⁵Make us glad for as many days as you have
    afflicted us,
  for as many years as we have seen trouble.
¹⁶May your deeds be shown to your servants,
  your splendor to their children.

¹⁷May the favor*ᵃ* of the Lord our God rest
    upon us;
  establish the work of our hands for us—
  yes, establish the work of our hands.

Psalm 91

¹He who dwells in the shelter of the Most
    High
  will rest in the shadow of the Almighty.*ᵇ*
²I will say*ᶜ* of the LORD, "He is my refuge
    and my fortress,
  my God, in whom I trust."

³Surely he will save you from the fowler's
    snare
  and from the deadly pestilence.
⁴He will cover you with his feathers,
  and under his wings you will find refuge;
  his faithfulness will be your shield and
    rampart.
⁵You will not fear the terror of night,
  nor the arrow that flies by day,
⁶nor the pestilence that stalks in the darkness,
  nor the plague that destroys at midday.
⁷A thousand may fall at your side,
  ten thousand at your right hand,
  but it will not come near you.
⁸You will only observe with your eyes
  and see the punishment of the wicked.

⁹If you make the Most High your dwelling—
  even the LORD, who is my refuge—
¹⁰then no harm will befall you,
  no disaster will come near your tent.
¹¹For he will command his angels concerning
    you
  to guard you in all your ways;
¹²they will lift you up in their hands,
  so that you will not strike your foot
    against a stone.
¹³You will tread upon the lion and the cobra;
  you will trample the great lion and the
    serpent.

¹⁴"Because he loves me," says the LORD, "I will
    rescue him;
  I will protect him, for he acknowledges
    my name.

91:12 Satan and the Bible

*Satan knows Scripture. He quoted this promise
to Jesus when tempting him to spiritual
arrogance (see Matthew 4:6). Jesus recognized
that Satan had twisted its meaning. The
magnificent assurances in this psalm
encourage us to rest in God, not test him.*

¹⁵He will call upon me, and I will answer him;
  I will be with him in trouble,
  I will deliver him and honor him.
¹⁶With long life will I satisfy him
  and show him my salvation."

Psalm 92

A psalm. A song. For the Sabbath day.

¹It is good to praise the LORD
  and make music to your name, O Most
    High,
²to proclaim your love in the morning
  and your faithfulness at night,
³to the music of the ten-stringed lyre
  and the melody of the harp.

⁴For you make me glad by your deeds,
    O LORD;
  I sing for joy at the works of your hands.
⁵How great are your works, O LORD,
  how profound your thoughts!
⁶The senseless man does not know,
  fools do not understand,
⁷that though the wicked spring up like grass
  and all evildoers flourish,
  they will be forever destroyed.

⁸But you, O LORD, are exalted forever.

⁹For surely your enemies, O LORD,
  surely your enemies will perish;
  all evildoers will be scattered.
¹⁰You have exalted my horn*ᵈ* like that of a
    wild ox;
  fine oils have been poured upon me.
¹¹My eyes have seen the defeat of my
    adversaries;
  my ears have heard the rout of my wicked
    foes.

¹²The righteous will flourish like a palm tree,
  they will grow like a cedar of Lebanon;
¹³planted in the house of the LORD,

ᵃ17 Or *beauty*   *ᵇ1* Hebrew *Shaddai*   *ᶜ2* Or *He says*   *ᵈ10 Horn* here symbolizes strength.

they will flourish in the courts of our
    God.
14They will still bear fruit in old age,
    they will stay fresh and green,
15proclaiming, "The LORD is upright;
    he is my Rock, and there is no wickedness
      in him."

Psalm 93

1The LORD reigns, he is robed in majesty;
    the LORD is robed in majesty
    and is armed with strength.
The world is firmly established;
    it cannot be moved.
2Your throne was established long ago;
    you are from all eternity.

3The seas have lifted up, O LORD,
    the seas have lifted up their voice;
    the seas have lifted up their pounding
      waves.
4Mightier than the thunder of the great
    waters,
    mightier than the breakers of the sea—
    the LORD on high is mighty.

5Your statutes stand firm;
    holiness adorns your house
    for endless days, O LORD.

Psalm 94

1O LORD, the God who avenges,
    O God who avenges, shine forth.
2Rise up, O Judge of the earth;
    pay back to the proud what they deserve.
3How long will the wicked, O LORD,
    how long will the wicked be jubilant?

4They pour out arrogant words;
    all the evildoers are full of boasting.
5They crush your people, O LORD;
    they oppress your inheritance.
6They slay the widow and the alien;
    they murder the fatherless.
7They say, "The LORD does not see;
    the God of Jacob pays no heed."

8Take heed, you senseless ones among the
    people;
    you fools, when will you become wise?
9Does he who implanted the ear not hear?
    Does he who formed the eye not see?
10Does he who disciplines nations not punish?
    Does he who teaches man lack
      knowledge?
11The LORD knows the thoughts of man;
    he knows that they are futile.

12Blessed is the man you discipline, O LORD,
    the man you teach from your law;

13you grant him relief from days of trouble,
    till a pit is dug for the wicked.
14For the LORD will not reject his people;
    he will never forsake his inheritance.
15Judgment will again be founded on
    righteousness,
    and all the upright in heart will follow it.

16Who will rise up for me against the wicked?
    Who will take a stand for me against
      evildoers?
17Unless the LORD had given me help,
    I would soon have dwelt in the silence of
      death.
18When I said, "My foot is slipping,"
    your love, O LORD, supported me.
19When anxiety was great within me,
    your consolation brought joy to my soul.

20Can a corrupt throne be allied with you—
    one that brings on misery by its decrees?
21They band together against the righteous
    and condemn the innocent to death.
22But the LORD has become my fortress,
    and my God the rock in whom I take
      refuge.
23He will repay them for their sins
    and destroy them for their wickedness;
    the LORD our God will destroy them.

Psalm 95

1Come, let us sing for joy to the LORD;
    let us shout aloud to the Rock of our
      salvation.
2Let us come before him with thanksgiving
    and extol him with music and song.

3For the LORD is the great God,
    the great King above all gods.
4In his hand are the depths of the earth,
    and the mountain peaks belong to him.
5The sea is his, for he made it,
    and his hands formed the dry land.

6Come, let us bow down in worship,
    let us kneel before the LORD our Maker;
7for he is our God
    and we are the people of his pasture,
    the flock under his care.

Today, if you hear his voice,
8   do not harden your hearts as you did at
      Meribah,a
    as you did that day at Massahb in the
      desert,
9where your fathers tested and tried me,
    though they had seen what I did.
10For forty years I was angry with that
    generation;

---

a8 Meribah means quarreling.   b8 Massah means testing.

I said, "They are a people whose hearts go
astray,
and they have not known my ways."
¹¹So I declared on oath in my anger,
"They shall never enter my rest."

95:8 Rebellion

*One of Israel's worst memories involved a place
known as Massah and Meribah. There, on their
way to the promised land, the Israelites ran out
of water (Exodus 17:1–7) and rebelled against
Moses and God. Because of their lack of faith,
God made them wander the wilderness for 40
years.*

*Now, hundreds of years later, Psalm 95
warns another generation of Israelites not to
repeat the mistake that had made their
forebears miss "God's rest." In the New
Testament, Hebrews 4:1–13 argues that "God's
rest" means not merely the promised land of
Israel, but a state of peaceful unity with God.
The warning still applies.*

Psalm 96

¹Sing to the LORD a new song;
sing to the LORD, all the earth.
²Sing to the LORD, praise his name;
proclaim his salvation day after day.
³Declare his glory among the nations,
his marvelous deeds among all peoples.

⁴For great is the LORD and most worthy of
praise;
he is to be feared above all gods.
⁵For all the gods of the nations are idols,
but the LORD made the heavens.
⁶Splendor and majesty are before him;
strength and glory are in his sanctuary.

⁷Ascribe to the LORD, O families of nations,
ascribe to the LORD glory and strength.
⁸Ascribe to the LORD the glory due his name;
bring an offering and come into his
courts.
⁹Worship the LORD in the splendor of his*a*
holiness;
tremble before him, all the earth.

¹⁰Say among the nations, "The LORD reigns."
The world is firmly established, it cannot
be moved;
he will judge the peoples with equity.
¹¹Let the heavens rejoice, let the earth be glad;
let the sea resound, and all that is in it;
¹² let the fields be jubilant, and everything in
them.

Then all the trees of the forest will sing for
joy;
¹³ they will sing before the LORD, for he
comes,
he comes to judge the earth.
He will judge the world in righteousness
and the peoples in his truth.

Psalm 97

¹The LORD reigns, let the earth be glad;
let the distant shores rejoice.

²Clouds and thick darkness surround him;
righteousness and justice are the
foundation of his throne.
³Fire goes before him
and consumes his foes on every side.
⁴His lightning lights up the world;
the earth sees and trembles.
⁵The mountains melt like wax before the
LORD,
before the Lord of all the earth.
⁶The heavens proclaim his righteousness,
and all the peoples see his glory.

⁷All who worship images are put to shame,
those who boast in idols—
worship him, all you gods!

⁸Zion hears and rejoices
and the villages of Judah are glad
because of your judgments, O LORD.
⁹For you, O LORD, are the Most High over all
the earth;
you are exalted far above all gods.

¹⁰Let those who love the LORD hate evil,
for he guards the lives of his faithful ones
and delivers them from the hand of the
wicked.
¹¹Light is shed upon the righteous
and joy on the upright in heart.
¹²Rejoice in the LORD, you who are righteous,
and praise his holy name.

Psalm 98

A psalm.

¹Sing to the LORD a new song,
for he has done marvelous things;
his right hand and his holy arm
have worked salvation for him.
²The LORD has made his salvation known
and revealed his righteousness to the
nations.
³He has remembered his love
and his faithfulness to the house of Israel;
all the ends of the earth have seen
the salvation of our God.

a9 Or LORD with the splendor of

⁴Shout for joy to the LORD, all the earth,
   burst into jubilant song with music;
⁵make music to the LORD with the harp,
   with the harp and the sound of singing,
⁶with trumpets and the blast of the ram's
      horn—
   shout for joy before the LORD, the King.

⁷Let the sea resound, and everything in it,
   the world, and all who live in it.
⁸Let the rivers clap their hands,
   let the mountains sing together for joy;

98:8 Ecological Choir

Seas, rivers, and mountains crown this psalm with their praise. God's salvation doesn't just affect human beings. When rebellion against God finally ends, nature itself will celebrate. Romans 8:18–22 takes up this theme as part of the wonderful salvation God offers to all people.

⁹let them sing before the LORD,
   for he comes to judge the earth.
He will judge the world in righteousness
   and the peoples with equity.

Psalm 99

¹The LORD reigns,
   let the nations tremble;
he sits enthroned between the cherubim,
   let the earth shake.
²Great is the LORD in Zion;
   he is exalted over all the nations.
³Let them praise your great and awesome
      name—
   he is holy.

⁴The King is mighty, he loves justice—
   you have established equity;
in Jacob you have done
   what is just and right.
⁵Exalt the LORD our God
   and worship at his footstool;
   he is holy.

⁶Moses and Aaron were among his priests,
   Samuel was among those who called on
      his name;
they called on the LORD
   and he answered them.
⁷He spoke to them from the pillar of cloud;
   they kept his statutes and the decrees he
      gave them.

⁸O LORD our God,
   you answered them;
you were to Israel*ᵃ* a forgiving God,
   though you punished their misdeeds.*ᵇ*
⁹Exalt the LORD our God
   and worship at his holy mountain,
   for the LORD our God is holy.

Psalm 100

A psalm. For giving thanks.

¹Shout for joy to the LORD, all the earth.
²   Worship the LORD with gladness;
   come before him with joyful songs.
³Know that the LORD is God.
   It is he who made us, and we are his*ᶜ*;
   we are his people, the sheep of his
      pasture.

⁴Enter his gates with thanksgiving
   and his courts with praise;
   give thanks to him and praise his name.
⁵For the LORD is good and his love endures
      forever;
   his faithfulness continues through all
      generations.

Psalm 101

Of David. A psalm.

¹I will sing of your love and justice;
   to you, O LORD, I will sing praise.
²I will be careful to lead a blameless life—
   when will you come to me?

I will walk in my house
   with blameless heart.
³I will set before my eyes
   no vile thing.

The deeds of faithless men I hate;
   they will not cling to me.
⁴Men of perverse heart shall be far from me;
   I will have nothing to do with evil.

⁵Whoever slanders his neighbor in secret,
   him will I put to silence;
whoever has haughty eyes and a proud heart,
   him will I not endure.

⁶My eyes will be on the faithful in the land,
   that they may dwell with me;
he whose walk is blameless
   will minister to me.

⁷No one who practices deceit
   will dwell in my house;

ᵃ8 Hebrew them   *ᵇ8 Or / an avenger of the wrongs done to them*   *ᶜ3 Or and not we ourselves*

no one who speaks falsely
    will stand in my presence.

8Every morning I will put to silence
    all the wicked in the land;
I will cut off every evildoer
    from the city of the LORD.

Psalm 102

A prayer of an afflicted man. When he is faint
and pours out his lament before the LORD.

1Hear my prayer, O LORD;
    let my cry for help come to you.

101:7 The Company You Keep

*Some friends build you up, others tear you
down. That's true for people in influential
positions as well. "Politics makes strange
bedfellows," they say, because a politician must
work with people from various political
factions, whether he or she admires them or
not. But here David, the head of state, pledges
to steer clear of all shady alliances. He wants a
clean administration, from the top down.*

2Do not hide your face from me
    when I am in distress.
Turn your ear to me;
    when I call, answer me quickly.

3For my days vanish like smoke;
    my bones burn like glowing embers.
4My heart is blighted and withered like grass;
    I forget to eat my food.
5Because of my loud groaning
    I am reduced to skin and bones.
6I am like a desert owl,
    like an owl among the ruins.
7I lie awake; I have become
    like a bird alone on a roof.
8All day long my enemies taunt me;
    those who rail against me use my name as
        a curse.
9For I eat ashes as my food
    and mingle my drink with tears
10because of your great wrath,
    for you have taken me up and thrown me
        aside.
11My days are like the evening shadow;
    I wither away like grass.

12But you, O LORD, sit enthroned forever;
    your renown endures through all
        generations.
13You will arise and have compassion on Zion,

for it is time to show favor to her;
    the appointed time has come.
14For her stones are dear to your servants;
    her very dust moves them to pity.
15The nations will fear the name of the LORD,
    all the kings of the earth will revere your
        glory.
16For the LORD will rebuild Zion
    and appear in his glory.
17He will respond to the prayer of the
        destitute;
    he will not despise their plea.

18Let this be written for a future generation,
    that a people not yet created may praise
        the LORD:
19"The LORD looked down from his sanctuary
        on high,
    from heaven he viewed the earth,
20to hear the groans of the prisoners
    and release those condemned to death."
21So the name of the LORD will be declared in
        Zion
    and his praise in Jerusalem
22when the peoples and the kingdoms
    assemble to worship the LORD.

23In the course of my life*a* he broke my
        strength;
    he cut short my days.
24So I said:
"Do not take me away, O my God, in the
        midst of my days;
    your years go on through all generations.
25In the beginning you laid the foundations of
        the earth,
    and the heavens are the work of your
        hands.
26They will perish, but you remain;
    they will all wear out like a garment.
Like clothing you will change them
    and they will be discarded.

102:26 Outlasting the Universe

*Is a diamond forever? Not according to the
psalmist, who predicts that the universe, which
God made, will wear out like old clothes. But
God remains the same forever—and he will
preserve his people, whom he is committed to
far more than to his universe.*

27But you remain the same,
    and your years will never end.
28The children of your servants will live in
        your presence;
    their descendants will be established
        before you."

a23 Or By his power

Psalm 103

Of David.

[1] Praise the LORD, O my soul;
  all my inmost being, praise his holy name.
[2] Praise the LORD, O my soul,
  and forget not all his benefits—
[3] who forgives all your sins
  and heals all your diseases,
[4] who redeems your life from the pit
  and crowns you with love and
    compassion,
[5] who satisfies your desires with good things
  so that your youth is renewed like the
    eagle's.

[6] The LORD works righteousness
  and justice for all the oppressed.

[7] He made known his ways to Moses,
  his deeds to the people of Israel:
[8] The LORD is compassionate and gracious,
  slow to anger, abounding in love.
[9] He will not always accuse,
  nor will he harbor his anger forever;
[10] he does not treat us as our sins deserve
  or repay us according to our iniquities.
[11] For as high as the heavens are above the
    earth,
  so great is his love for those who fear
    him;
[12] as far as the east is from the west,
  so far has he removed our transgressions
    from us.
[13] As a father has compassion on his children,
  so the LORD has compassion on those who
    fear him;
[14] for he knows how we are formed,
  he remembers that we are dust.
[15] As for man, his days are like grass,
  he flourishes like a flower of the field;
[16] the wind blows over it and it is gone,
  and its place remembers it no more.
[17] But from everlasting to everlasting
  the LORD's love is with those who fear
    him,
  and his righteousness with their children's
    children—
[18] with those who keep his covenant
  and remember to obey his precepts.

[19] The LORD has established his throne in
    heaven,
  and his kingdom rules over all.

[20] Praise the LORD, you his angels,
  you mighty ones who do his bidding,
  who obey his word.
[21] Praise the LORD, all his heavenly hosts,
  you servants who do his will.

[22] Praise the LORD, all his works
  everywhere in his dominion.

Praise the LORD, O my soul.

Psalm 104

[1] Praise the LORD, O my soul.

O LORD my God, you are very great;
  you are clothed with splendor and
    majesty.
[2] He wraps himself in light as with a garment;
  he stretches out the heavens like a tent
[3]   and lays the beams of his upper chambers
    on their waters.
He makes the clouds his chariot
  and rides on the wings of the wind.
[4] He makes winds his messengers,[a]
  flames of fire his servants.

[5] He set the earth on its foundations;
  it can never be moved.
[6] You covered it with the deep as with a
    garment;
  the waters stood above the mountains.
[7] But at your rebuke the waters fled,
  at the sound of your thunder they took to
    flight;
[8] they flowed over the mountains,
  they went down into the valleys,
  to the place you assigned for them.
[9] You set a boundary they cannot cross;
  never again will they cover the earth.

[10] He makes springs pour water into the
    ravines;
  it flows between the mountains.
[11] They give water to all the beasts of the field;
  the wild donkeys quench their thirst.
[12] The birds of the air nest by the waters;
  they sing among the branches.
[13] He waters the mountains from his upper
    chambers;
  the earth is satisfied by the fruit of his
    work.
[14] He makes grass grow for the cattle,
  and plants for man to cultivate—
  bringing forth food from the earth:
[15] wine that gladdens the heart of man,
  oil to make his face shine,
  and bread that sustains his heart.
[16] The trees of the LORD are well watered,
  the cedars of Lebanon that he planted.
[17] There the birds make their nests;
  the stork has its home in the pine trees.
[18] The high mountains belong to the wild
    goats;
  the crags are a refuge for the coneys.[b]

[19] The moon marks off the seasons,

---

[a]4 Or *angels*   [b]18 That is, the hyrax or rock badger

and the sun knows when to go down.
²⁰You bring darkness, it becomes night,
    and all the beasts of the forest prowl.
²¹The lions roar for their prey
    and seek their food from God.
²²The sun rises, and they steal away;
    they return and lie down in their dens.
²³Then man goes out to his work,
    to his labor until evening.

²⁴How many are your works, O Lᴏʀᴅ!
    In wisdom you made them all;
    the earth is full of your creatures.
²⁵There is the sea, vast and spacious,
    teeming with creatures beyond number—
    living things both large and small.
²⁶There the ships go to and fro,
    and the leviathan, which you formed to
        frolic there.

²⁷These all look to you
    to give them their food at the proper
        time.
²⁸When you give it to them,
    they gather it up;

104:26 Just for Fun

What good is a leviathan (possibly a whale, but to the landlocked Israelites a frightening sea monster)? Why would God make such a creature? Simply "to frolic." God makes and delights in each creature for its own sake.

when you open your hand,
    they are satisfied with good things.
²⁹When you hide your face,

Ecology Plus
Creation sings God's praise

How many are your works, O Lᴏʀᴅ! In wisdom you made them all. 104:24

IN 1962 BIOLOGIST RACHEL CARSON published *Silent Spring*, a book tracing the effects of pesticides—DDT in particular. Until then, DDT had been treated like a wonder chemical, sprayed almost at random to kill pests. Carson showed how it worked its way up the food chain, killing larger animals—like songbirds. If no birds were left to sing, we would have an ominously "silent spring."

Until then, *ecology* had been a word known only to specialists. But with Carson's book, ordinary people began to take an interest in what only biologists had known: the delicate balance of nature, in which each creature is intertwined with every other. The ecology movement had begun.

The Value in "Useless" Creatures

Ecology was new, but its ideas were old. You could have learned its basic principles from Psalm 104. It shows appreciation for every aspect of nature, even creatures like wild goats, lions, and the "leviathan," the crocodile or sea monster. The Israelites, as herders and farmers, had no romantic idealization of the outdoors. Nobody who herds sheep thinks of them as soft and fluffy pets. But to the poet who wrote Psalm 104, creatures that are of no "use" to anyone still have intrinsic worth—especially to God.

The author saw how the world fits together, everything in its proper sphere. At night wild animals hunt; at daybreak humans go out to work. The rain falls, nourishing crops for people and grass for cattle, but also watering the forest to provide a place for birds to nest.

Ecology Is God's Work

The intertwining of nature is not, for the psalmist, like a complex machine, dangerously sensitive. Things fit together because of an intimate, personal God watches over his creation. Animals eat on schedule not just because their habitat contains adequate food, but because God gives them their food "at the proper time." Every breath of life depends on his will. So do the weather, the winds and clouds, the water supply, the very stability of the earth. The psalmist doesn't just marvel over the complexity and beauty of nature; in it he sees the work of God.

When modern people think of ecology, they are preoccupied with the fear of overcrowding and of poisoning the planet with landfills, oil spills, and toxic chemicals. The psalms show no such fear, for overcrowding and pollution were not major problems in that preindustrial civilization. Yet interestingly enough, this psalm ends with a wish that God would clean up the earth—cleanse it of sinners, who mar its perfection by their rejection of God's will. The beauty of the earth, made by God, calls out for purity—purity of the heart.

Life Questions: How does nature affect you? How do you affect it?

they are terrified;
when you take away their breath,
  they die and return to the dust.
30When you send your Spirit,
  they are created,
  and you renew the face of the earth.

31May the glory of the LORD endure forever;
  may the LORD rejoice in his works—
32he who looks at the earth, and it trembles,
  who touches the mountains, and they
    smoke.

33I will sing to the LORD all my life;
  I will sing praise to my God as long as I
    live.
34May my meditation be pleasing to him,
  as I rejoice in the LORD.
35But may sinners vanish from the earth
  and the wicked be no more.

Praise the LORD, O my soul.

Praise the LORD.*a*

Psalm 105

1Give thanks to the LORD, call on his name;
  make known among the nations what he
    has done.
2Sing to him, sing praise to him;
  tell of all his wonderful acts.
3Glory in his holy name;
  let the hearts of those who seek the LORD
    rejoice.
4Look to the LORD and his strength;
  seek his face always.

5Remember the wonders he has done,
  his miracles, and the judgments he
    pronounced,
6O descendants of Abraham his servant,
  O sons of Jacob, his chosen ones.
7He is the LORD our God;
  his judgments are in all the earth.

8He remembers his covenant forever,
  the word he commanded, for a thousand
    generations,
9the covenant he made with Abraham,
  the oath he swore to Isaac.
10He confirmed it to Jacob as a decree,
  to Israel as an everlasting covenant:
11"To you I will give the land of Canaan
  as the portion you will inherit."

12When they were but few in number,
  few indeed, and strangers in it,
13they wandered from nation to nation,
  from one kingdom to another.
14He allowed no one to oppress them;
  for their sake he rebuked kings:

15"Do not touch my anointed ones;
  do my prophets no harm."

16He called down famine on the land
  and destroyed all their supplies of food;
17and he sent a man before them—
  Joseph, sold as a slave.
18They bruised his feet with shackles,
  his neck was put in irons,
19till what he foretold came to pass,
  till the word of the LORD proved him true.
20The king sent and released him,
  the ruler of peoples set him free.
21He made him master of his household,
  ruler over all he possessed,
22to instruct his princes as he pleased
  and teach his elders wisdom.

23Then Israel entered Egypt;
  Jacob lived as an alien in the land of
    Ham.
24The LORD made his people very fruitful;
  he made them too numerous for their
    foes,
25whose hearts he turned to hate his people,
  to conspire against his servants.
26He sent Moses his servant,
  and Aaron, whom he had chosen.
27They performed his miraculous signs among
    them,
  his wonders in the land of Ham.
28He sent darkness and made the land dark—
  for had they not rebelled against his
    words?
29He turned their waters into blood,
  causing their fish to die.
30Their land teemed with frogs,
  which went up into the bedrooms of their
    rulers.
31He spoke, and there came swarms of flies,
  and gnats throughout their country.
32He turned their rain into hail,
  with lightning throughout their land;
33he struck down their vines and fig trees
  and shattered the trees of their country.
34He spoke, and the locusts came,
  grasshoppers without number;
35they ate up every green thing in their land,
  ate up the produce of their soil.
36Then he struck down all the firstborn in
    their land,
  the firstfruits of all their manhood.

37He brought out Israel, laden with silver and
    gold,
  and from among their tribes no one
    faltered.
38Egypt was glad when they left,
  because dread of Israel had fallen on
    them.

a 35 Hebrew *Hallelu Yah*; in the Septuagint this line stands at the beginning of Psalm 105.

[39]He spread out a cloud as a covering,
and a fire to give light at night.
[40]They asked, and he brought them quail
and satisfied them with the bread of
heaven.
[41]He opened the rock, and water gushed out;
like a river it flowed in the desert.

[42]For he remembered his holy promise
given to his servant Abraham.
[43]He brought out his people with rejoicing,
his chosen ones with shouts of joy;
[44]he gave them the lands of the nations,
and they fell heir to what others had
toiled for—
[45]that they might keep his precepts
and observe his laws.

Praise the LORD.[a]

Psalm 106

[1]Praise the LORD.[b]

Give thanks to the LORD, for he is good;
his love endures forever.
[2]Who can proclaim the mighty acts of the
LORD
or fully declare his praise?
[3]Blessed are they who maintain justice,
who constantly do what is right.
[4]Remember me, O LORD, when you show
favor to your people,
come to my aid when you save them,
[5]that I may enjoy the prosperity of your
chosen ones,
that I may share in the joy of your nation
and join your inheritance in giving praise.

[6]We have sinned, even as our fathers did;
we have done wrong and acted wickedly.
[7]When our fathers were in Egypt,
they gave no thought to your miracles;
they did not remember your many
kindnesses,
and they rebelled by the sea, the Red
Sea.[c]
[8]Yet he saved them for his name's sake,
to make his mighty power known.
[9]He rebuked the Red Sea, and it dried up;
he led them through the depths as
through a desert.
[10]He saved them from the hand of the foe;
from the hand of the enemy he redeemed
them.
[11]The waters covered their adversaries;
not one of them survived.

[12]Then they believed his promises
and sang his praise.

[13]But they soon forgot what he had done
and did not wait for his counsel.
[14]In the desert they gave in to their craving;
in the wasteland they put God to the test.

106:12 The Turning Point

When the Israelites praised God, their thoughts turned naturally back to the time when God (through Moses) freed them from slavery and gave them a country all their own. In it they saw God's pure graciousness. They had done nothing to win their freedom; God had done it all. Similarly, Christians look back to Jesus' death and resurrection, which freed them from sin's slavery.

[15]So he gave them what they asked for,
but sent a wasting disease upon them.

[16]In the camp they grew envious of Moses
and of Aaron, who was consecrated to the
LORD.
[17]The earth opened up and swallowed Dathan;
it buried the company of Abiram.
[18]Fire blazed among their followers;
a flame consumed the wicked.

[19]At Horeb they made a calf
and worshiped an idol cast from metal.
[20]They exchanged their Glory
for an image of a bull, which eats grass.
[21]They forgot the God who saved them,
who had done great things in Egypt,
[22]miracles in the land of Ham
and awesome deeds by the Red Sea.
[23]So he said he would destroy them—
had not Moses, his chosen one,
stood in the breach before him
to keep his wrath from destroying them.

[24]Then they despised the pleasant land;
they did not believe his promise.
[25]They grumbled in their tents
and did not obey the LORD.
[26]So he swore to them with uplifted hand
that he would make them fall in the
desert,
[27]make their descendants fall among the
nations
and scatter them throughout the lands.

[28]They yoked themselves to the Baal of Peor

---

[a]45 Hebrew *Hallelu Yah*; also in verses 9 and 22   [b]1 Hebrew *Hallelu Yah*; also in verse 48   [c]7 Hebrew *Yam Suph*; that is, Sea of Reeds;

and ate sacrifices offered to lifeless gods;
29they provoked the LORD to anger by their
wicked deeds,
and a plague broke out among them.
30But Phinehas stood up and intervened,
and the plague was checked.
31This was credited to him as righteousness
for endless generations to come.

32By the waters of Meribah they angered the
LORD,
and trouble came to Moses because of
them;
33for they rebelled against the Spirit of God,
and rash words came from Moses' lips. ᵃ

34They did not destroy the peoples
as the LORD had commanded them,
35but they mingled with the nations
and adopted their customs.
36They worshiped their idols,
which became a snare to them.
37They sacrificed their sons
and their daughters to demons.
38They shed innocent blood,
the blood of their sons and daughters,
whom they sacrificed to the idols of Canaan,
and the land was desecrated by their
blood.
39They defiled themselves by what they did;
by their deeds they prostituted themselves.

40Therefore the LORD was angry with his
people
and abhorred his inheritance.
41He handed them over to the nations,
and their foes ruled over them.
42Their enemies oppressed them
and subjected them to their power.
43Many times he delivered them,
but they were bent on rebellion
and they wasted away in their sin.

44But he took note of their distress
when he heard their cry;
45for their sake he remembered his covenant
and out of his great love he relented.
46He caused them to be pitied
by all who held them captive.

47Save us, O LORD our God,
and gather us from the nations,
that we may give thanks to your holy name
and glory in your praise.

48Praise be to the LORD, the God of Israel,
from everlasting to everlasting.
Let all the people say, "Amen!"

Praise the LORD.

BOOK V

Psalms 107–150

Psalm 107

1Give thanks to the LORD, for he is good;
his love endures forever.
2Let the redeemed of the LORD say this—
those he redeemed from the hand of the
foe,
3those he gathered from the lands,
from east and west, from north and
south.ᵇ

4Some wandered in desert wastelands,
finding no way to a city where they could
settle.
5They were hungry and thirsty,
and their lives ebbed away.
6Then they cried out to the LORD in their
trouble,
and he delivered them from their distress.
7He led them by a straight way
to a city where they could settle.
8Let them give thanks to the LORD for his
unfailing love
and his wonderful deeds for men,
9for he satisfies the thirsty
and fills the hungry with good things.

10Some sat in darkness and the deepest gloom,
prisoners suffering in iron chains,
11for they had rebelled against the words of
God
and despised the counsel of the Most
High.
12So he subjected them to bitter labor;
they stumbled, and there was no one to
help.
13Then they cried to the LORD in their trouble,
and he saved them from their distress.
14He brought them out of darkness and the
deepest gloom
and broke away their chains.
15Let them give thanks to the LORD for his
unfailing love
and his wonderful deeds for men,
16for he breaks down gates of bronze
and cuts through bars of iron.

17Some became fools through their rebellious
ways
and suffered affliction because of their
iniquities.
18They loathed all food
and drew near the gates of death.
19Then they cried to the LORD in their trouble,
and he saved them from their distress.

ᵃ33 Or *against his spirit, / and rash words came from his lips*   ᵇ3 Hebrew *north and the sea*

²⁰He sent forth his word and healed them;
  he rescued them from the grave.
²¹Let them give thanks to the LORD for his
    unfailing love
  and his wonderful deeds for men.
²²Let them sacrifice thank offerings
  and tell of his works with songs of joy.

²³Others went out on the sea in ships;
  they were merchants on the mighty
    waters.
²⁴They saw the works of the LORD,
  his wonderful deeds in the deep.
²⁵For he spoke and stirred up a tempest
  that lifted high the waves.
²⁶They mounted up to the heavens and went
    down to the depths;
  in their peril their courage melted away.
²⁷They reeled and staggered like drunken men;
  they were at their wits' end.

107:27 Worst Case

*No problem is too great for God. This psalm
imagines the worst calamities a Jew could
think of: homelessness and starvation (verses
4–5), imprisonment (10–12), self-inflicted
disease (17–18), and—the ultimate—imminent
shipwreck (23–27). (Since Israel was
landlocked, Jews had little experience with
turbulent seas—and they dreaded them.) In all
these cases, God was able to rescue those who
called for his help.*

²⁸Then they cried out to the LORD in their
    trouble,
  and he brought them out of their distress.
²⁹He stilled the storm to a whisper;
  the waves of the sea were hushed.
³⁰They were glad when it grew calm,
  and he guided them to their desired
    haven.
³¹Let them give thanks to the LORD for his
    unfailing love
  and his wonderful deeds for men.
³²Let them exalt him in the assembly of the
    people
  and praise him in the council of the
    elders.

³³He turned rivers into a desert,
  flowing springs into thirsty ground,
³⁴and fruitful land into a salt waste,
  because of the wickedness of those who
    lived there.
³⁵He turned the desert into pools of water
  and the parched ground into flowing
    springs;

³⁶there he brought the hungry to live,
  and they founded a city where they could
    settle.
³⁷They sowed fields and planted vineyards
  that yielded a fruitful harvest;
³⁸he blessed them, and their numbers greatly
    increased,
  and he did not let their herds diminish.

³⁹Then their numbers decreased, and they
    were humbled
  by oppression, calamity and sorrow;
⁴⁰he who pours contempt on nobles
  made them wander in a trackless waste.
⁴¹But he lifted the needy out of their affliction
  and increased their families like flocks.
⁴²The upright see and rejoice,
  but all the wicked shut their mouths.

⁴³Whoever is wise, let him heed these things
  and consider the great love of the LORD.

Psalm 108

A song. A psalm of David.

¹My heart is steadfast, O God;
  I will sing and make music with all my
    soul.
²Awake, harp and lyre!
  I will awaken the dawn.
³I will praise you, O LORD, among the
    nations;
  I will sing of you among the peoples.
⁴For great is your love, higher than the
    heavens;
  your faithfulness reaches to the skies.
⁵Be exalted, O God, above the heavens,
  and let your glory be over all the earth.

⁶Save us and help us with your right hand,
  that those you love may be delivered.
⁷God has spoken from his sanctuary:
  "In triumph I will parcel out Shechem
  and measure off the Valley of Succoth.
⁸Gilead is mine, Manasseh is mine;
  Ephraim is my helmet,
  Judah my scepter.
⁹Moab is my washbasin,
  upon Edom I toss my sandal;
  over Philistia I shout in triumph."

¹⁰Who will bring me to the fortified city?
  Who will lead me to Edom?
¹¹Is it not you, O God, you who have rejected
    us
  and no longer go out with our armies?
¹²Give us aid against the enemy,
  for the help of man is worthless.
¹³With God we will gain the victory,
  and he will trample down our enemies.

Psalm 109

For the director of music. Of David. A psalm.

[1]O God, whom I praise,
     do not remain silent,
[2]for wicked and deceitful men
     have opened their mouths against me;
     they have spoken against me with lying
        tongues.
[3]With words of hatred they surround me;
     they attack me without cause.
[4]In return for my friendship they accuse me,
     but I am a man of prayer.
[5]They repay me evil for good,
     and hatred for my friendship.

[6]Appoint[a] an evil man[b] to oppose him;
     let an accuser[c] stand at his right hand.
[7]When he is tried, let him be found guilty,
     and may his prayers condemn him.
[8]May his days be few;
     may another take his place of leadership.

109:8 The Judas Principle

*Peter applied this verse to Judas (Acts 1:20).
The New Testament writers saw David's life as
the pattern and foreshadowing of the Messiah,
David's son. The savage betrayal recorded in
this poem shows, as do many psalms, that
unexplained suffering comes to the most
devoted of God's people: first David, then Jesus.*

[9]May his children be fatherless
     and his wife a widow.
[10]May his children be wandering beggars;
     may they be driven[d] from their ruined
        homes.
[11]May a creditor seize all he has;
     may strangers plunder the fruits of his
        labor.
[12]May no one extend kindness to him
     or take pity on his fatherless children.
[13]May his descendants be cut off,
     their names blotted out from the next
        generation.
[14]May the iniquity of his fathers be
     remembered before the LORD;
     may the sin of his mother never be
        blotted out.
[15]May their sins always remain before the
     LORD,
     that he may cut off the memory of them
        from the earth.

[16]For he never thought of doing a kindness,
     but hounded to death the poor
     and the needy and the brokenhearted.
[17]He loved to pronounce a curse—
     may it[e] come on him;
  he found no pleasure in blessing—
     may it be[f] far from him.
[18]He wore cursing as his garment;
     it entered into his body like water,
     into his bones like oil.
[19]May it be like a cloak wrapped about him,
     like a belt tied forever around him.
[20]May this be the LORD's payment to my
        accusers,
     to those who speak evil of me.

[21]But you, O Sovereign LORD,
     deal well with me for your name's sake;
     out of the goodness of your love, deliver
        me.
[22]For I am poor and needy,
     and my heart is wounded within me.
[23]I fade away like an evening shadow;
     I am shaken off like a locust.
[24]My knees give way from fasting;
     my body is thin and gaunt.
[25]I am an object of scorn to my accusers;
     when they see me, they shake their heads.

[26]Help me, O LORD my God;
     save me in accordance with your love.
[27]Let them know that it is your hand,
     that you, O LORD, have done it.
[28]They may curse, but you will bless;
     when they attack they will be put to
        shame,
     but your servant will rejoice.
[29]My accusers will be clothed with disgrace
     and wrapped in shame as in a cloak.

[30]With my mouth I will greatly extol the LORD;
     in the great throng I will praise him.
[31]For he stands at the right hand of the needy
        one,
     to save his life from those who condemn
        him.

Psalm 110

Of David. A psalm.

[1]The LORD says to my Lord:
     "Sit at my right hand
  until I make your enemies
     a footstool for your feet."

[2]The LORD will extend your mighty scepter
        from Zion;
     you will rule in the midst of your
        enemies.

---

[a]6 Or ⌊They say:⌋ "Appoint (with quotation marks at the end of verse 19)   [b]6 Or the Evil One   [c]6 Or let Satan
[d]10 Septuagint; Hebrew sought   [e]17 Or curse, / and it has   [f]17 Or blessing, / and it is

³Your troops will be willing
    on your day of battle.
Arrayed in holy majesty,
    from the womb of the dawn
    you will receive the dew of your youth.*ᵃ*

⁴The LORD has sworn
    and will not change his mind:

ᵃ3 Or / your young men will come to you like the dew

"You are a priest forever,
    in the order of Melchizedek."

⁵The Lord is at your right hand;
    he will crush kings on the day of his
        wrath.
⁶He will judge the nations, heaping up the
        dead

The Twelfth Man
He came "out of nowhere" to win great respect

> "You are a priest forever, in the order of Melchizedek."
> 110:4

IN DALLAS, TEXAS, ON JANUARY 1, 1922, Texas A&M fought it out in the first bowl game ever played in the Southwest. Coach Dana Bible watched helplessly as, one by one, his running backs limped off the field with injuries. As the game neared halftime, he had only one reserve left.

What to do? He remembered a small, wiry back who had not made the traveling team. He had told Coach Bible, "I'll be in the stands if you need me." Bible sent a messenger to search for the young player, King Gill, and get him to suit up for the second half. The Texas A&M tradition of "the twelfth man" began.

Since then, a series of "twelfth men" have come from the student body to help Texas A&M teams. At some schools football players are a breed apart. But Texas A&M, with its "twelfth man" tradition, remembers that a football player may come "out of nowhere." Help doesn't always arrive in the proper uniform.

Mystery Man

The Bible has a kind of twelfth man, a shadowy figure who is mentioned only three times, yet has great importance. Melchizedek came "out of nowhere" in Genesis 14:18–20 as a priest whom Abraham honored. Melchizedek never reappeared. But Psalm 110 mentions him in referring to the Messiah, the conquering king whom Israelites expected. And in the New Testament, the book of Hebrews devotes more than a chapter to Melchizedek's significance. Why so? The answer has to do with Israel's longing for great leadership.

Much as the United States government recognizes three branches of government, Israel had three important kinds of leaders: prophets, priests, and kings. Prophets told the truth, revealing God's righteousness. Kings were to put righteousness into effect, as head of the government. Priests were to see that God met his people in worship: they represented God to the people, and the people to God. According to the God-given Israelite constitution, kings and priests always came from different tribes: a priest from the family of Levi and a king from the family of Judah. Ordinarily, a king could not be a priest.

Total Leadership

The Messiah, however, must be a total leader: a perfect king governing justly, a perfect prophet revealing God's truth, a perfect priest bringing God and people together. But how could he be all three, when priests and kings were supposed to come from different families? Wouldn't that violate God's law?

Psalm 110 suggests (and Hebrews 7 amplifies) the answer. Just as a football player need not necessarily come from the athletic dorm, so Melchizedek's example proves that a priest need not necessarily come from the proper family. Melchizedek was not even an Israelite, let alone from the Levite family. He knew nothing about the temple or the Old Testament law, for these came after his time. Yet his spiritual power impressed Abraham. Melchizedek showed the kind of leadership Christ was to bring. He was both a priest and a king.

Psalm 110's brief praise provides a thread between the Old and New Testaments. It hints that the Messiah would be greater than David, while David's descendant. And by tracing the Messiah's roots to Melchizedek, it established his credibility as both priest and king.

Life Questions: What are the "proper channels" you expect to see spiritual leadership come from? Has God ever led you through someone outside those channels?

and crushing the rulers of the whole earth.
[7]He will drink from a brook beside the
way[a];
therefore he will lift up his head.

110:1 The Son of God

Jesus quoted this verse in Mark 12:35–37 to show that the Messiah would not be merely a human military leader, as many Jews expected. Here David refers to the coming King (David's descendant) as "my Lord." If the Messiah were strictly his human descendant, David would not address him so respectfully.

Psalm 111[b]

[1]Praise the LORD.[c]

I will extol the LORD with all my heart
in the council of the upright and in the
assembly.
[2]Great are the works of the LORD;
they are pondered by all who delight in
them.
[3]Glorious and majestic are his deeds,
and his righteousness endures forever.
[4]He has caused his wonders to be
remembered;
the LORD is gracious and compassionate.
[5]He provides food for those who fear him;
he remembers his covenant forever.
[6]He has shown his people the power of his
works,
giving them the lands of other nations.
[7]The works of his hands are faithful and just;
all his precepts are trustworthy.
[8]They are steadfast for ever and ever,
done in faithfulness and uprightness.
[9]He provided redemption for his people;
he ordained his covenant forever—
holy and awesome is his name.

[10]The fear of the LORD is the beginning of
wisdom;
all who follow his precepts have good
understanding.
To him belongs eternal praise.

Psalm 112[b]

[1]Praise the LORD.[c]

Blessed is the man who fears the LORD,
who finds great delight in his commands.

[2]His children will be mighty in the land;

the generation of the upright will be
blessed.
[3]Wealth and riches are in his house,
and his righteousness endures forever.
[4]Even in darkness light dawns for the upright,
for the gracious and compassionate and
righteous man.[d]
[5]Good will come to him who is generous and
lends freely,
who conducts his affairs with justice.
[6]Surely he will never be shaken;
a righteous man will be remembered
forever.
[7]He will have no fear of bad news;
his heart is steadfast, trusting in the LORD.
[8]His heart is secure, he will have no fear;
in the end he will look in triumph on his
foes.
[9]He has scattered abroad his gifts to the poor,
his righteousness endures forever;
his horn[e] will be lifted high in honor.

[10]The wicked man will see and be vexed,
he will gnash his teeth and waste away;
the longings of the wicked will come to
nothing.

Psalm 113

[1]Praise the LORD.[f]

Praise, O servants of the LORD,
praise the name of the LORD.

113:1 Psalms of the Last Supper

Psalms 113 to 118 were traditionally sung at the Passover meal—the first two before the meal, the last four after. These were probably the last songs Jesus sang with his disciples before his death (Mark 14:26).

[2]Let the name of the LORD be praised,
both now and forevermore.
[3]From the rising of the sun to the place
where it sets,
the name of the LORD is to be praised.

[4]The LORD is exalted over all the nations,
his glory above the heavens.
[5]Who is like the LORD our God,
the One who sits enthroned on high,
[6]who stoops down to look
on the heavens and the earth?

[7]He raises the poor from the dust
and lifts the needy from the ash heap;

---

[a]7 Or / *The One who grants succession will set him in authority*   [b]This psalm is an acrostic poem, the lines of which begin with the successive letters of the Hebrew alphabet.   [c]1 Hebrew *Hallelu Yah*   [d]4 Or / *for* ⌊*the LORD*⌋ *is gracious and compassionate and righteous*   [e]9 *Horn* here symbolizes dignity.   [f]1 Hebrew *Hallelu Yah*; also in verse 9

Margaret Becker

Margaret Becker, represented on WoW 1997 by her song "True Devotion," speaks out about what inspired her most recent release, *Grace.*

"This album is all about... living life passionately.

"The lyrical content of the project is taken from some recent developments in my spiritual life. Most of it has to do with living boldly in the grace that God has granted us. I think once we understand, wholly and completely, the love that God has for us, it should energize us, push us to new heights in all areas of our lives. To reiterate a well-known Scripture, 'If God is for us, who can be against us?' (Romans 8:31).

"While we breathe, we have hope because God is with us. Even if you're at a particularly bad chapter in your life, that's all it is—a chapter. One chapter blends into the next, and so it goes. The true concern is the entire story. What will we get from our difficulties? An ulcer? A bitter streak? Maybe for a while, but I pray that we can attempt to inwardly turn the corner of difficulty with confidence, taking chances in all areas of our lives...

"After losing my aunt, I find that I am more aware of how little time we have in this world. I want to spend it learning how to use all that God has given me to his glory. I want to move in all that he has granted me, with passion! If I am crying, I want to cry from my toes up. I want to allow myself to feel sad. If I'm laughing, I want to laugh long and hard. I want every fiber of my being to feel the joy in that instant. Doesn't God grant it all, all these moments? Shouldn't we, or rather I, live like I mean it, not like this is a dress rehearsal and time is of no consequence?

"My prayer is that we will enjoy all that God has given, and learn true devotion to him along the way."

Margaret Becker's comments are taken from her newsletter, "The Wire."

Margaret Becker

WOW
1997

Kirk Franklin

Kirk Franklin was born and raised in Fort Worth, Texas. Abandoned by his teenage mother and father at the age of three, the orphaned Franklin was adopted by a distant 64-year old aunt, Gertrude. Franklin began playing piano at the age of four. On Saturday mornings, his aunt would collect cans to return so that she could pay for his music lessons. On Sunday mornings that same woman, the only mother Franklin ever knew, made sure he was in church.

In three short years Kirk Franklin has become a musical superstar. He has broken barriers, crossed musical boundary lines, and achieved levels of success previously unknown to any other gospel artist. His first album, *Kirk Franklin and the Family*, was certified platinum. It was the first time in the history of Gospel music that a debut album sold over a million copies. Franklin has established himself as one of the leaders of the new gospel music renaissance.

Kirk states, "I wanted to do church music, but I had no idea I was going to be put in front of these audiences. Slowly but surely I realized that [God] was putting me in front of non-Christian people." Because of this startling series of events, Franklin began to ask God to reveal his divine purpose. "This is not the direction that I wanted to go," Franklin confess-es. He wondered what God was doing. "Because of that, I began fasting and praying, laying before God and asking him to show me his purpose for my life." God revealed that plan. Franklin is now determined to spread the gospel wherever he can, especially outside of the church walls and to young people.

Asked what makes his brand of gospel music unique, Franklin quips, "This isn't gospel music. It's Christian Love music." Taking a serious tone, he adds, "the form sculpts each delivery with the intention of touching hearts. Sometimes music needs to let you know you are not on your own, and that you're not alone."

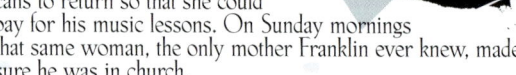

WOW
1997

⁸he seats them with princes,
    with the princes of their people.
⁹He settles the barren woman in her home
    as a happy mother of children.

Praise the LORD.

Psalm 114

¹When Israel came out of Egypt,
    the house of Jacob from a people of
        foreign tongue,
²Judah became God's sanctuary,
    Israel his dominion.

³The sea looked and fled,
    the Jordan turned back;
⁴the mountains skipped like rams,
    the hills like lambs.

⁵Why was it, O sea, that you fled,
    O Jordan, that you turned back,
⁶you mountains, that you skipped like rams,
    you hills, like lambs?

⁷Tremble, O earth, at the presence of the
        Lord,
    at the presence of the God of Jacob,
⁸who turned the rock into a pool,
    the hard rock into springs of water.

Psalm 115

¹Not to us, O LORD, not to us
    but to your name be the glory,
    because of your love and faithfulness.

²Why do the nations say,
    "Where is their God?"
³Our God is in heaven;
    he does whatever pleases him.
⁴But their idols are silver and gold,
    made by the hands of men.
⁵They have mouths, but cannot speak,
    eyes, but they cannot see;
⁶they have ears, but cannot hear,
    noses, but they cannot smell;
⁷they have hands, but cannot feel,
    feet, but they cannot walk;
    nor can they utter a sound with their
        throats.
⁸Those who make them will be like them,
    and so will all who trust in them.

⁹O house of Israel, trust in the LORD—
    he is their help and shield.
¹⁰O house of Aaron, trust in the LORD—
    he is their help and shield.
¹¹You who fear him, trust in the LORD—
    he is their help and shield.

¹²The LORD remembers us and will bless us:
    He will bless the house of Israel,

    he will bless the house of Aaron,
¹³he will bless those who fear the LORD—
    small and great alike.

¹⁴May the LORD make you increase,
    both you and your children.
¹⁵May you be blessed by the LORD,
    the Maker of heaven and earth.

¹⁶The highest heavens belong to the LORD,
    but the earth he has given to man.
¹⁷It is not the dead who praise the LORD,
    those who go down to silence;
¹⁸it is we who extol the LORD,
    both now and forevermore.

Praise the LORD.ᵃ

Psalm 116

¹I love the LORD, for he heard my voice;
    he heard my cry for mercy.
²Because he turned his ear to me,
    I will call on him as long as I live.

³The cords of death entangled me,
    the anguish of the graveᵇ came upon me;
    I was overcome by trouble and sorrow.
⁴Then I called on the name of the LORD:
    "O LORD, save me!"

⁵The LORD is gracious and righteous;
    our God is full of compassion.
⁶The LORD protects the simplehearted;
    when I was in great need, he saved me.

⁷Be at rest once more, O my soul,
    for the LORD has been good to you.

⁸For you, O LORD, have delivered my soul
        from death,
    my eyes from tears,
    my feet from stumbling,
⁹that I may walk before the LORD
    in the land of the living.
¹⁰I believed; thereforeᶜ I said,
    "I am greatly afflicted."
¹¹And in my dismay I said,
    "All men are liars."

¹²How can I repay the LORD
    for all his goodness to me?
¹³I will lift up the cup of salvation
    and call on the name of the LORD.
¹⁴I will fulfill my vows to the LORD
    in the presence of all his people.

¹⁵Precious in the sight of the LORD
    is the death of his saints.
¹⁶O LORD, truly I am your servant;
    I am your servant, the son of your
        maidservantᵈ;
    you have freed me from my chains.

ᵃ 18 Hebrew Hallelu Yah   ᵇ 3 Hebrew Sheol   ᶜ 10 Or believed even when   ᵈ 16 Or servant, your faithful son

17I will sacrifice a thank offering to you
and call on the name of the LORD.
18I will fulfill my vows to the LORD
in the presence of all his people,
19in the courts of the house of the LORD—
in your midst, O Jerusalem.

Praise the LORD.[a]

116:15 Precious Death

This verse, often read at funerals, in no way implies that God enjoys the death of his people. Instead, it means that he carefully watches over their death, and that it matters deeply to him. The whole psalm praises God for saving from death. Psalm 72:14 uses a similar phrase in a similar way: "precious is their blood in his sight."

Psalm 117

1Praise the LORD, all you nations;
extol him, all you peoples.
2For great is his love toward us,
and the faithfulness of the LORD endures forever.

Praise the LORD.[a]

Psalm 118

1Give thanks to the LORD, for he is good;
his love endures forever.

2Let Israel say:
"His love endures forever."
3Let the house of Aaron say:
"His love endures forever."
4Let those who fear the LORD say:
"His love endures forever."

5In my anguish I cried to the LORD,
and he answered by setting me free.
6The LORD is with me; I will not be afraid.
What can man do to me?
7The LORD is with me; he is my helper.
I will look in triumph on my enemies.

8It is better to take refuge in the LORD
than to trust in man.
9It is better to take refuge in the LORD
than to trust in princes.

10All the nations surrounded me,
but in the name of the LORD I cut them off.
11They surrounded me on every side,
but in the name of the LORD I cut them off.

12They swarmed around me like bees,
but they died out as quickly as burning thorns;
in the name of the LORD I cut them off.

13I was pushed back and about to fall,
but the LORD helped me.
14The LORD is my strength and my song;
he has become my salvation.

15Shouts of joy and victory
resound in the tents of the righteous:
"The LORD's right hand has done mighty things!
16   The LORD's right hand is lifted high;
the LORD's right hand has done mighty things!"

17I will not die but live,
and will proclaim what the LORD has done.
18The LORD has chastened me severely,
but he has not given me over to death.

19Open for me the gates of righteousness;
I will enter and give thanks to the LORD.
20This is the gate of the LORD
through which the righteous may enter.
21I will give you thanks, for you answered me;
you have become my salvation.

22The stone the builders rejected
has become the capstone;

118:22 Last-place Winner

God has a habit of reversing people's status. The poor and needy end up satisfied, while the rich and arrogant lose their position. As Jesus said, "many who are first will be last, and many who are last will be first" (Matthew 19:30). This psalm expresses the concept with an image: A stone builders considered unusable ends up holding the whole building together. Jesus applied it to himself, and it was quoted by Peter as a prophecy fulfilled by Jesus' death and resurrection (see Matthew 21:42; 1 Peter 2:7; and Acts 4:11).

23the LORD has done this,
and it is marvelous in our eyes.
24This is the day the LORD has made;
let us rejoice and be glad in it.

25O LORD, save us;
O LORD, grant us success.
26Blessed is he who comes in the name of the LORD.
From the house of the LORD we bless you.[b]

[a]19,2 Hebrew *Hallelu Yah*   [b]26 The Hebrew is plural.

27The LORD is God,
and he has made his light shine upon us.
With boughs in hand, join in the festal
procession
up[a] to the horns of the altar.

28You are my God, and I will give you thanks;
you are my God, and I will exalt you.

29Give thanks to the LORD, for he is good;
his love endures forever.

Psalm 119[b]

א Aleph

1Blessed are they whose ways are blameless,
who walk according to the law of the
LORD.
2Blessed are they who keep his statutes
and seek him with all their heart.
3They do nothing wrong;
they walk in his ways.
4You have laid down precepts
that are to be fully obeyed.
5Oh, that my ways were steadfast
in obeying your decrees!
6Then I would not be put to shame
when I consider all your commands.
7I will praise you with an upright heart
as I learn your righteous laws.
8I will obey your decrees;
do not utterly forsake me.

ב Beth

9How can a young man keep his way pure?
By living according to your word.
10I seek you with all my heart;
do not let me stray from your commands.
11I have hidden your word in my heart
that I might not sin against you.
12Praise be to you, O LORD;
teach me your decrees.
13With my lips I recount
all the laws that come from your mouth.
14I rejoice in following your statutes
as one rejoices in great riches.
15I meditate on your precepts
and consider your ways.
16I delight in your decrees;
I will not neglect your word.

ג Gimel

17Do good to your servant, and I will live;
I will obey your word.
18Open my eyes that I may see
wonderful things in your law.
19I am a stranger on earth;
do not hide your commands from me.

20My soul is consumed with longing
for your laws at all times.
21You rebuke the arrogant, who are cursed
and who stray from your commands.
22Remove from me scorn and contempt,
for I keep your statutes.
23Though rulers sit together and slander me,
your servant will meditate on your
decrees.
24Your statutes are my delight;
they are my counselors.

ד Daleth

25I am laid low in the dust;
preserve my life according to your word.
26I recounted my ways and you answered me;
teach me your decrees.
27Let me understand the teaching of your
precepts;
then I will meditate on your wonders.
28My soul is weary with sorrow;
strengthen me according to your word.
29Keep me from deceitful ways;
be gracious to me through your law.
30I have chosen the way of truth;
I have set my heart on your laws.
31I hold fast to your statutes, O LORD;
do not let me be put to shame.
32I run in the path of your commands,
for you have set my heart free.

ה He

33Teach me, O LORD, to follow your decrees;
then I will keep them to the end.
34Give me understanding, and I will keep your
law
and obey it with all my heart.
35Direct me in the path of your commands,
for there I find delight.
36Turn my heart toward your statutes
and not toward selfish gain.
37Turn my eyes away from worthless things;
preserve my life according to your
word.[c]
38Fulfill your promise to your servant,
so that you may be feared.
39Take away the disgrace I dread,
for your laws are good.
40How I long for your precepts!
Preserve my life in your righteousness.

ו Waw

41May your unfailing love come to me,
O LORD,
your salvation according to your promise;
42then I will answer the one who taunts me,
for I trust in your word.

---

[a]27 Or *Bind the festal sacrifice with ropes / and take it
begin with the same letter of the Hebrew alphabet.*   [c]37 Two manuscripts of the Masoretic Text and Dead Sea Scrolls;
most manuscripts of the Masoretic Text *life in your way*   [b]This psalm is an acrostic poem; the verses of each stanza

⁴³Do not snatch the word of truth from my
      mouth,
   for I have put my hope in your laws.
⁴⁴I will always obey your law,
   for ever and ever.
⁴⁵I will walk about in freedom,
   for I have sought out your precepts.

ᵃ48 Or for

⁴⁶I will speak of your statutes before kings
      and will not be put to shame,
⁴⁷for I delight in your commands
      because I love them.
⁴⁸I lift up my hands toᵃ your commands,
      which I love,
   and I meditate on your decrees.

A Love Poem to God's Law

How could Scripture inspire such poetry?

> *I lift up my hands to your commands, which I love.*
> 119:48

FOR ALL THE HUNDREDS OF books written about William
Shakespeare, he remains a mysterious figure. His "dark lady" prompts
endless guesses. He wrote 26 passionate poems to her, yet we do not
even know her name. Numerous books try to guess it, "proving" that one
lady or another must have been the one.

One thing we do know: She had captivated Shakespeare. Seldom has love produced such
writhing emotion as his sonnets express. Helplessly ravished by her unfashionable "black (brunette)
beauty," Shakespeare longed to forget her, to escape her evil character. Yet he was uncontrollably
drawn.

> *My thoughts and my discourse as madman's are . . .*
> *For I have sworn thee fair, and thought thee bright,*
> *Who art as black as hell, as dark as night.*

But what an oddity to express such fevered emotion in sonnets! The sonnets require discipline:
precisely 14 lines, an exact rhyming scheme, and iambic pentameter rhythm. How can a raging storm
be reflected in such a small, still pond? Yet the evidence of the poems is unmistakable. The discipline
gave wild emotion a backbone.

A Love Poem to the Law

Psalm 119 contains even greater oddities. As emotional as Shakespeare's sonnets, this poem also
takes a very systematic form: the acrostic, where each line of each stanza begins with a letter from the
Hebrew alphabet, *A* in the first stanza, *B* in the second, and so on, through all 22 letters of the Hebrew
alphabet.

But the subject is the biggest surprise. Psalm 119 is a long, passionate love poem about God's law.

How do you fall in love with law? Most people admit that rules are necessary, and appreciate
them grudgingly. But no one writes love poems to the federal drug abuse statutes.

The word translated "law" doesn't merely mean rules. It expresses the totality of God's written
instructions. The poet sees life full of uncertainties, of enemies, of pain. But God has given a reliable
guide for living—like pavement underfoot after you have been stuck in mud. Obeying God's law, to the
psalmist, is no slavery—rather it is freedom. "I run in the path of your commands, for you have set my
heart free" (verse 32).

On the Edge of Death

Psalm 119 is not written from an ivory tower. The poet has apparently been near death (verse 87),
and even as he writes, "the wicked are waiting to destroy" him (verse 95). But in this dangerous situation he has learned to hang on to God's wisdom. The lesson is so valuable he has become grateful for
his sufferings: "It was good for me to be afflicted so that I might learn your decrees" (verse 71).

The psalmist simply does not see God's law as a dusty, rigid rulebook. He hears God's loving
voice in it. "The earth is filled with your love, O LORD; teach me your decrees" (verse 64). "Your statutes
. . . are the joy of my heart" (verse 111).

God's laws channel God's love into the poet's life. They protect him from doing wrong and give
him wisdom to understand his situation. They make new life flow into him. No wonder he writes with
such thankfulness. In God's word he finds more than direction. He finds God himself.

Life Questions: Do you ever feel with the psalmist that life has become frighteningly out of control?
How can God's law help you regain confidence?

ז   Zayin

⁴⁹Remember your word to your servant,
      for you have given me hope.
⁵⁰My comfort in my suffering is this:
      Your promise preserves my life.
⁵¹The arrogant mock me without restraint,
      but I do not turn from your law.
⁵²I remember your ancient laws, O Lord,
      and I find comfort in them.
⁵³Indignation grips me because of the wicked,
      who have forsaken your law.
⁵⁴Your decrees are the theme of my song
      wherever I lodge.
⁵⁵In the night I remember your name,
      O Lord,
      and I will keep your law.

119:55 Lying in Bed

*The psalms consider every aspect of life—even
the thoughts that come while lying in bed at
night. You can easily become obsessed with
other people's wrongs against you. But you
can also turn your thoughts to God and quiet
your anxieties while strengthening your
commitment. Other psalms that refer to such
nighttime thoughts, good and bad, are these:
4:4; 6:6; 16:7; 17:3; 63:6; 77:2; 102:7; and
119:62,148.*

⁵⁶This has been my practice:
      I obey your precepts.

ח   Heth

⁵⁷You are my portion, O Lord;
      I have promised to obey your words.
⁵⁸I have sought your face with all my heart;
      be gracious to me according to your
         promise.
⁵⁹I have considered my ways
      and have turned my steps to your statutes.
⁶⁰I will hasten and not delay
      to obey your commands.
⁶¹Though the wicked bind me with ropes,
      I will not forget your law.
⁶²At midnight I rise to give you thanks
      for your righteous laws.
⁶³I am a friend to all who fear you,
      to all who follow your precepts.
⁶⁴The earth is filled with your love, O Lord;
      teach me your decrees.

ט   Teth

⁶⁵Do good to your servant
      according to your word, O Lord.
⁶⁶Teach me knowledge and good judgment,
      for I believe in your commands.
⁶⁷Before I was afflicted I went astray,
      but now I obey your word.

⁶⁸You are good, and what you do is good;
      teach me your decrees.
⁶⁹Though the arrogant have smeared me with
         lies,
      I keep your precepts with all my heart.
⁷⁰Their hearts are callous and unfeeling,
      but I delight in your law.
⁷¹It was good for me to be afflicted
      so that I might learn your decrees.
⁷²The law from your mouth is more precious
         to me
      than thousands of pieces of silver and
         gold.

י   Yodh

⁷³Your hands made me and formed me;
      give me understanding to learn your
         commands.
⁷⁴May those who fear you rejoice when they
         see me,
      for I have put my hope in your word.
⁷⁵I know, O Lord, that your laws are
         righteous,
      and in faithfulness you have afflicted me.
⁷⁶May your unfailing love be my comfort,
      according to your promise to your
         servant.
⁷⁷Let your compassion come to me that I may
         live,
      for your law is my delight.
⁷⁸May the arrogant be put to shame for
         wronging me without cause;
      but I will meditate on your precepts.
⁷⁹May those who fear you turn to me,
      those who understand your statutes.
⁸⁰May my heart be blameless toward your
         decrees,
      that I may not be put to shame.

כ   Kaph

⁸¹My soul faints with longing for your
         salvation,
      but I have put my hope in your word.
⁸²My eyes fail, looking for your promise;
      I say, "When will you comfort me?"
⁸³Though I am like a wineskin in the smoke,
      I do not forget your decrees.
⁸⁴How long must your servant wait?
      When will you punish my persecutors?
⁸⁵The arrogant dig pitfalls for me,
      contrary to your law.
⁸⁶All your commands are trustworthy;
      help me, for men persecute me without
         cause.
⁸⁷They almost wiped me from the earth,
      but I have not forsaken your precepts.
⁸⁸Preserve my life according to your love,
      and I will obey the statutes of your
         mouth.

ל Lamedh

89Your word, O LORD, is eternal;
  it stands firm in the heavens.
90Your faithfulness continues through all
    generations;
  you established the earth, and it endures.
91Your laws endure to this day,
  for all things serve you.
92If your law had not been my delight,
  I would have perished in my affliction.
93I will never forget your precepts,
  for by them you have preserved my life.
94Save me, for I am yours;
  I have sought out your precepts.
95The wicked are waiting to destroy me,
  but I will ponder your statutes.
96To all perfection I see a limit;
  but your commands are boundless.

119:96 Free At Last

*People often wonder if following God's law will
restrict them, but actual experience shows that
God's law liberates—by freeing us from the
destructive impact of sinful behavior, and by
introducing us to the mind-expanding realm of
God's wisdom. Like the author of Ecclesiastes,
the psalmist had looked around and seen limits
to everything. Only in following God's
commands, he sees, can a person escape this
frustrating sense of boundaries.*

מ Mem

97Oh, how I love your law!
  I meditate on it all day long.
98Your commands make me wiser than my
    enemies,
  for they are ever with me.
99I have more insight than all my teachers,
  for I meditate on your statutes.
100I have more understanding than the elders,
  for I obey your precepts.
101I have kept my feet from every evil path
  so that I might obey your word.
102I have not departed from your laws,
  for you yourself have taught me.
103How sweet are your words to my taste,
  sweeter than honey to my mouth!
104I gain understanding from your precepts;
  therefore I hate every wrong path.

נ Nun

105Your word is a lamp to my feet
  and a light for my path.
106I have taken an oath and confirmed it,
  that I will follow your righteous laws.
107I have suffered much;

preserve my life, O LORD, according to
    your word.
108Accept, O LORD, the willing praise of my
    mouth,
  and teach me your laws.
109Though I constantly take my life in my
    hands,
  I will not forget your law.
110The wicked have set a snare for me,
  but I have not strayed from your precepts.
111Your statutes are my heritage forever;
  they are the joy of my heart.
112My heart is set on keeping your decrees
  to the very end.

ס Samekh

113I hate double-minded men,
  but I love your law.
114You are my refuge and my shield;
  I have put my hope in your word.
115Away from me, you evildoers,
  that I may keep the commands of my
    God!
116Sustain me according to your promise, and
    I will live;
  do not let my hopes be dashed.
117Uphold me, and I will be delivered;
  I will always have regard for your decrees.
118You reject all who stray from your decrees,
  for their deceitfulness is in vain.
119All the wicked of the earth you discard like
    dross;
  therefore I love your statutes.
120My flesh trembles in fear of you;
  I stand in awe of your laws.

ע Ayin

121I have done what is righteous and just;
  do not leave me to my oppressors.
122Ensure your servant's well-being;
  let not the arrogant oppress me.
123My eyes fail, looking for your salvation,
  looking for your righteous promise.
124Deal with your servant according to your
    love
  and teach me your decrees.
125I am your servant; give me discernment
  that I may understand your statutes.
126It is time for you to act, O LORD;
  your law is being broken.
127Because I love your commands
  more than gold, more than pure gold,
128and because I consider all your precepts
    right,
  I hate every wrong path.

פ Pe

129Your statutes are wonderful;
  therefore I obey them.
130The unfolding of your words gives light;

it gives understanding to the simple.
¹³¹I open my mouth and pant,
longing for your commands.
¹³²Turn to me and have mercy on me,
as you always do to those who love your
name.
¹³³Direct my footsteps according to your word;
let no sin rule over me.
¹³⁴Redeem me from the oppression of men,
that I may obey your precepts.
¹³⁵Make your face shine upon your servant
and teach me your decrees.
¹³⁶Streams of tears flow from my eyes,
for your law is not obeyed.

צ   Tsadhe

¹³⁷Righteous are you, O LORD,
and your laws are right.
¹³⁸The statutes you have laid down are
righteous;
they are fully trustworthy.
¹³⁹My zeal wears me out,
for my enemies ignore your words.
¹⁴⁰Your promises have been thoroughly tested,
and your servant loves them.
¹⁴¹Though I am lowly and despised,
I do not forget your precepts.
¹⁴²Your righteousness is everlasting
and your law is true.
¹⁴³Trouble and distress have come upon me,
but your commands are my delight.
¹⁴⁴Your statutes are forever right;
give me understanding that I may live.

ק   Qoph

¹⁴⁵I call with all my heart; answer me, O LORD,
and I will obey your decrees.
¹⁴⁶I call out to you; save me
and I will keep your statutes.
¹⁴⁷I rise before dawn and cry for help;
I have put my hope in your word.
¹⁴⁸My eyes stay open through the watches of
the night,
that I may meditate on your promises.
¹⁴⁹Hear my voice in accordance with your
love;
preserve my life, O LORD, according to
your laws.
¹⁵⁰Those who devise wicked schemes are near,
but they are far from your law.
¹⁵¹Yet you are near, O LORD,
and all your commands are true.
¹⁵²Long ago I learned from your statutes
that you established them to last forever.

ר   Resh

¹⁵³Look upon my suffering and deliver me,
for I have not forgotten your law.
¹⁵⁴Defend my cause and redeem me;

preserve my life according to your
promise.
¹⁵⁵Salvation is far from the wicked,
for they do not seek out your decrees.

119:151 Near and Nearer

The psalmist doesn't claim that God makes problem people disappear. He merely points out that while they are near, so is God. Big problems gain a different perspective when we remember the nearness of a bigger God.

¹⁵⁶Your compassion is great, O LORD;
preserve my life according to your laws.
¹⁵⁷Many are the foes who persecute me,
but I have not turned from your statutes.
¹⁵⁸I look on the faithless with loathing,
for they do not obey your word.
¹⁵⁹See how I love your precepts;
preserve my life, O LORD, according to
your love.
¹⁶⁰All your words are true;
all your righteous laws are eternal.

ש   Sin and Shin

¹⁶¹Rulers persecute me without cause,
but my heart trembles at your word.
¹⁶²I rejoice in your promise
like one who finds great spoil.
¹⁶³I hate and abhor falsehood
but I love your law.
¹⁶⁴Seven times a day I praise you
for your righteous laws.
¹⁶⁵Great peace have they who love your law,
and nothing can make them stumble.
¹⁶⁶I wait for your salvation, O LORD,
and I follow your commands.
¹⁶⁷I obey your statutes,
for I love them greatly.
¹⁶⁸I obey your precepts and your statutes,
for all my ways are known to you.

ת   Taw

¹⁶⁹May my cry come before you, O LORD;
give me understanding according to your
word.
¹⁷⁰May my supplication come before you;
deliver me according to your promise.
¹⁷¹May my lips overflow with praise,
for you teach me your decrees.
¹⁷²May my tongue sing of your word,
for all your commands are righteous.
¹⁷³May your hand be ready to help me,
for I have chosen your precepts.
¹⁷⁴I long for your salvation, O LORD,
and your law is my delight.
¹⁷⁵Let me live that I may praise you,
and may your laws sustain me.

¹⁷⁶I have strayed like a lost sheep.
  Seek your servant,
    for I have not forgotten your commands.

Psalm 120

A song of ascents.

¹I call on the LORD in my distress,
  and he answers me.
²Save me, O LORD, from lying lips
  and from deceitful tongues.

³What will he do to you,
  and what more besides, O deceitful
    tongue?
⁴He will punish you with a warrior's sharp
    arrows,
  with burning coals of the broom tree.

⁵Woe to me that I dwell in Meshech,
  that I live among the tents of Kedar!
⁶Too long have I lived
  among those who hate peace.
⁷I am a man of peace;
  but when I speak, they are for war.

Psalm 121

A song of ascents.

¹I lift up my eyes to the hills—
  where does my help come from?
²My help comes from the LORD,
  the Maker of heaven and earth.

³He will not let your foot slip—
  he who watches over you will not
    slumber;
⁴indeed, he who watches over Israel
  will neither slumber nor sleep.

⁵The LORD watches over you—
  the LORD is your shade at your right hand;
⁶the sun will not harm you by day,
  nor the moon by night.

⁷The LORD will keep you from all harm—
  he will watch over your life;
⁸the LORD will watch over your coming and
    going
  both now and forevermore.

Psalm 122

A song of ascents. Of David.

¹I rejoiced with those who said to me,
  "Let us go to the house of the LORD."
²Our feet are standing
  in your gates, O Jerusalem.

³Jerusalem is built like a city
  that is closely compacted together.

⁴That is where the tribes go up,
  the tribes of the LORD,
 to praise the name of the LORD
  according to the statute given to Israel.
⁵There the thrones for judgment stand,
  the thrones of the house of David.

⁶Pray for the peace of Jerusalem:
  "May those who love you be secure.
⁷May there be peace within your walls
  and security within your citadels."
⁸For the sake of my brothers and friends,
  I will say, "Peace be within you."
⁹For the sake of the house of the LORD our
    God,
  I will seek your prosperity.

Psalm 123

A song of ascents.

¹I lift up my eyes to you,
  to you whose throne is in heaven.
²As the eyes of slaves look to the hand of
    their master,
  as the eyes of a maid look to the hand of
    her mistress,
 so our eyes look to the LORD our God,
  till he shows us his mercy.

³Have mercy on us, O LORD, have mercy on
    us,
  for we have endured much contempt.
⁴We have endured much ridicule from the
    proud,
  much contempt from the arrogant.

Psalm 124

A song of ascents. Of David.

¹If the LORD had not been on our side—
  let Israel say—
²if the LORD had not been on our side
  when men attacked us,
³when their anger flared against us,
  they would have swallowed us alive;
⁴the flood would have engulfed us,
  the torrent would have swept over us,
⁵the raging waters
  would have swept us away.

⁶Praise be to the LORD,
  who has not let us be torn by their teeth.
⁷We have escaped like a bird
  out of the fowler's snare;
 the snare has been broken,
  and we have escaped.
⁸Our help is in the name of the LORD,
  the Maker of heaven and earth.

Psalm 125

A song of ascents.

¹Those who trust in the LORD are like Mount
Zion,
which cannot be shaken but endures
forever.
²As the mountains surround Jerusalem,
so the LORD surrounds his people
both now and forevermore.

124:7 Deeper and Deeper

*Some trouble is quick—bang and it's over. If you
get caught speeding, for instance, you pay your
fine and that ends the whole affair. But with
other trouble, trying to escape only gets you
more deeply entangled. Spreading gossip, for
instance, may lead you into all kinds of
unexpected consequences as the gossip
spreads. If you try to undo the damage, you
only make it worse.*

*That's exactly the picture of "the fowler's
snare." The bird that caught its neck in the
noose only tightened the snare's choke-hold by
struggling. The bird could not get out by its
own effort. But this time, says David, the snare
has miraculously broken, and the bird has
flown to safety. When you escape that way,
there's only one person to thank: the Lord.*

³The scepter of the wicked will not remain
over the land allotted to the righteous,
for then the righteous might use
their hands to do evil.

⁴Do good, O LORD, to those who are good,
to those who are upright in heart.
⁵But those who turn to crooked ways
the LORD will banish with the evildoers.

Peace be upon Israel.

Psalm 126

A song of ascents.

¹When the LORD brought back the captives
to*a* Zion,
we were like men who dreamed.*b*
²Our mouths were filled with laughter,
our tongues with songs of joy.
Then it was said among the nations,
"The LORD has done great things for
them."
³The LORD has done great things for us,

and we are filled with joy.

⁴Restore our fortunes,*c* O LORD,
like streams in the Negev.
⁵Those who sow in tears
will reap with songs of joy.
⁶He who goes out weeping,
carrying seed to sow,
will return with songs of joy,
carrying sheaves with him.

Psalm 127

A song of ascents. Of Solomon.

¹Unless the LORD builds the house,
its builders labor in vain.
Unless the LORD watches over the city,
the watchmen stand guard in vain.
²In vain you rise early
and stay up late,
toiling for food to eat—
for he grants sleep to*d* those he loves.

³Sons are a heritage from the LORD,
children a reward from him.
⁴Like arrows in the hands of a warrior
are sons born in one's youth.
⁵Blessed is the man
whose quiver is full of them.
They will not be put to shame
when they contend with their enemies in
the gate.

Psalm 128

A song of ascents.

¹Blessed are all who fear the LORD,
who walk in his ways.
²You will eat the fruit of your labor;
blessings and prosperity will be yours.
³Your wife will be like a fruitful vine
within your house;
your sons will be like olive shoots
around your table.
⁴Thus is the man blessed
who fears the LORD.

⁵May the LORD bless you from Zion
all the days of your life;
may you see the prosperity of Jerusalem,
⁶   and may you live to see your children's
children.

Peace be upon Israel.

a1 Or LORD *restored the fortunes of*   *b1* Or *men restored to health*   *c4* Or *Bring back our captives*
d2 Or *eat— / for while they sleep he provides for*

Psalm 129

A song of ascents.

¹They have greatly oppressed me from my
    youth—
        let Israel say—
²they have greatly oppressed me from my
    youth,
        but they have not gained the victory over
        me.
³Plowmen have plowed my back
    and made their furrows long.

129:3 The Right Words

*You can't improve on the vivid images used in
great poetry. If someone asks you, "What's it
about?" you can only quote the poem. The
psalms are full of such unforgettable language.
"Plowmen have plowed my back and made
their furrows long" makes you grit your teeth
with the sense of oppression. "May they be like
grass on the roof, which withers before it can
grow" (verse 6) says it better than any
alternate phrase like, "Let their successes
amount to nothing."*

⁴But the LORD is righteous;
    he has cut me free from the cords of the
    wicked.

⁵May all who hate Zion
    be turned back in shame.
⁶May they be like grass on the roof,
    which withers before it can grow;
⁷with it the reaper cannot fill his hands,
    nor the one who gathers fill his arms.
⁸May those who pass by not say,
    "The blessing of the LORD be upon you;
    we bless you in the name of the LORD."

Psalm 130

A song of ascents.

¹Out of the depths I cry to you, O LORD;
²   O Lord, hear my voice.
 Let your ears be attentive
    to my cry for mercy.

³If you, O LORD, kept a record of sins,
    O Lord, who could stand?
⁴But with you there is forgiveness;
    therefore you are feared.

⁵I wait for the LORD, my soul waits,
    and in his word I put my hope.
⁶My soul waits for the Lord
    more than watchmen wait for the
    morning,
more than watchmen wait for the
    morning.

⁷O Israel, put your hope in the LORD,
    for with the LORD is unfailing love
    and with him is full redemption.
⁸He himself will redeem Israel
    from all their sins.

Psalm 131

A song of ascents. Of David.

¹My heart is not proud, O LORD,
    my eyes are not haughty;
 I do not concern myself with great matters
    or things too wonderful for me.
²But I have stilled and quieted my soul;
    like a weaned child with its mother,
    like a weaned child is my soul within me.

131:2 A Child with Its Mother

*How trusting is a baby? Not very, some would
say, for babies cry violently as soon as they
feel the slightest hunger. It is the weaned child,
a little older, who has learned to trust its
mother, to fret less and simply ask for food
instead of wailing. The profound simplicity of
this patience is David's model for how he, and
all Israel, should wait on the Lord. The apostle
Paul comments similarly, "I have learned the
secret of being content in any and every
situation . . . I can do everything through him
who gives me strength" (Philippians 4:12–13).*

³O Israel, put your hope in the LORD
    both now and forevermore.

Psalm 132

A song of ascents.

¹O LORD, remember David
    and all the hardships he endured.

²He swore an oath to the LORD
    and made a vow to the Mighty One of
    Jacob:
³"I will not enter my house
    or go to my bed—
⁴I will allow no sleep to my eyes,
    no slumber to my eyelids,
⁵till I find a place for the LORD,
    a dwelling for the Mighty One of Jacob."

⁶We heard it in Ephrathah,

we came upon it in the fields of Jaar:*a;b*
7"Let us go to his dwelling place;
let us worship at his footstool—
8arise, O LORD, and come to your resting
place,
you and the ark of your might.
9May your priests be clothed with
righteousness;
may your saints sing for joy."

10For the sake of David your servant,
do not reject your anointed one.

11The LORD swore an oath to David,
a sure oath that he will not revoke:
"One of your own descendants
I will place on your throne—

132:11–18 Promise to David

*God's covenant with David promised that he
and his descendants would always reign over
Israel. For Israel, this promise meant that God
would never let the nation disintegrate, that he
would always provide a leader. Over the
centuries, when Israel chafed under the
domination of other nations, Jews remembered
this promise and looked for a "Messiah" or
"anointed one" (a king) who would provide this
leadership. That is why the New Testament
often refers to Jesus as a "son of David."*

12if your sons keep my covenant
and the statutes I teach them,
then their sons will sit
on your throne for ever and ever."

13For the LORD has chosen Zion,
he has desired it for his dwelling:
14"This is my resting place for ever and ever;
here I will sit enthroned, for I have
desired it—
15I will bless her with abundant provisions;
her poor will I satisfy with food.
16I will clothe her priests with salvation,
and her saints will ever sing for joy.

17"Here I will make a horn*c* grow for David
and set up a lamp for my anointed one.
18I will clothe his enemies with shame,
but the crown on his head will be
resplendent."

Psalm 133

A song of ascents. Of David.

1How good and pleasant it is
when brothers live together in unity!

2It is like precious oil poured on the head,
running down on the beard,
running down on Aaron's beard,
down upon the collar of his robes.
3It is as if the dew of Hermon
were falling on Mount Zion.
For there the LORD bestows his blessing,
even life forevermore.

Psalm 134

A song of ascents.

1Praise the LORD, all you servants of the LORD
who minister by night in the house of the
LORD.
2Lift up your hands in the sanctuary
and praise the LORD.

3May the LORD, the Maker of heaven and
earth,
bless you from Zion.

Psalm 135

1Praise the LORD.*d*

Praise the name of the LORD;
praise him, you servants of the LORD,
2you who minister in the house of the LORD,
in the courts of the house of our God.

3Praise the LORD, for the LORD is good;
sing praise to his name, for that is
pleasant.
4For the LORD has chosen Jacob to be his
own,
Israel to be his treasured possession.

5I know that the LORD is great,
that our Lord is greater than all gods.
6The LORD does whatever pleases him,
in the heavens and on the earth,
in the seas and all their depths.
7He makes clouds rise from the ends of the
earth;
he sends lightning with the rain
and brings out the wind from his
storehouses.

8He struck down the firstborn of Egypt,
the firstborn of men and animals.
9He sent his signs and wonders into your
midst, O Egypt,
against Pharaoh and all his servants.
10He struck down many nations
and killed mighty kings—
11Sihon king of the Amorites,
Og king of Bashan
and all the kings of Canaan—

---

a6 That is, Kiriath Jearim   *b6* Or *heard of it in Ephrathah, / we found it in the fields of Jaar.* (And no quotes around
verses 7-9)   *c17 Horn* here symbolizes strong one, that is, king.   *d1* Hebrew *Hallelu Yah*; also in verses 3 and 21

¹²and he gave their land as an inheritance,
  an inheritance to his people Israel.

¹³Your name, O LORD, endures forever,
  your renown, O LORD, through all
    generations.
¹⁴For the LORD will vindicate his people
  and have compassion on his servants.

¹⁵The idols of the nations are silver and gold,
  made by the hands of men.
¹⁶They have mouths, but cannot speak,
  eyes, but they cannot see;
¹⁷they have ears, but cannot hear,
  nor is there breath in their mouths.
¹⁸Those who make them will be like them,
  and so will all who trust in them.

¹⁹O house of Israel, praise the LORD;
  O house of Aaron, praise the LORD;
²⁰O house of Levi, praise the LORD;
  you who fear him, praise the LORD.
²¹Praise be to the LORD from Zion,
  to him who dwells in Jerusalem.

  Praise the LORD.

Psalm 136

¹Give thanks to the LORD, for he is good.
          His love endures forever.

136:1 Call and Response

Scholars think most of the psalms were used in temple worship, but they are unsure how they were sung. This psalm seems like an example of what is known in African-American music as "call and response." A leader sings out a story, and the congregation shouts back a rhythmic refrain.

²Give thanks to the God of gods.
          His love endures forever.
³Give thanks to the Lord of lords:
          His love endures forever.

⁴to him who alone does great wonders,
          His love endures forever.
⁵who by his understanding made the heavens,
          His love endures forever.
⁶who spread out the earth upon the waters,
          His love endures forever.
⁷who made the great lights—
          His love endures forever.
⁸the sun to govern the day,
          His love endures forever.
⁹the moon and stars to govern the night;
          His love endures forever.

¹⁰to him who struck down the firstborn of
    Egypt
          His love endures forever.
¹¹and brought Israel out from among them
          His love endures forever.
¹²with a mighty hand and outstretched arm;
          His love endures forever.

¹³to him who divided the Red Sea*ᵃ* asunder
          His love endures forever.
¹⁴and brought Israel through the midst of it,
          His love endures forever.
¹⁵but swept Pharaoh and his army into the
    Red Sea;
          His love endures forever.

¹⁶to him who led his people through the
    desert,
          His love endures forever.
¹⁷who struck down great kings,
          His love endures forever.
¹⁸and killed mighty kings—
          His love endures forever.
¹⁹Sihon king of the Amorites
          His love endures forever.
²⁰and Og king of Bashan—
          His love endures forever.
²¹and gave their land as an inheritance,
          His love endures forever.
²²an inheritance to his servant Israel;
          His love endures forever.

²³to the One who remembered us in our low
    estate
          His love endures forever.
²⁴and freed us from our enemies,
          His love endures forever.
²⁵and who gives food to every creature.
          His love endures forever.

²⁶Give thanks to the God of heaven.
          His love endures forever.

Psalm 137

¹By the rivers of Babylon we sat and wept
  when we remembered Zion.
²There on the poplars
  we hung our harps,
³for there our captors asked us for songs,
  our tormentors demanded songs of joy;
  they said, "Sing us one of the songs of
    Zion!"

⁴How can we sing the songs of the LORD
  while in a foreign land?
⁵If I forget you, O Jerusalem,
  may my right hand forget ⸤its skill⸥.
⁶May my tongue cling to the roof of my
    mouth
  if I do not remember you,

ᵃ13 Hebrew Yam Suph; that is, Sea of Reeds; also in verse 15

if I do not consider Jerusalem
my highest joy.

⁷Remember, O LORD, what the Edomites
did
on the day Jerusalem fell.
"Tear it down," they cried,
"tear it down to its foundations!"

⁸O Daughter of Babylon, doomed to
destruction,
happy is he who repays you
for what you have done to us—
⁹he who seizes your infants
and dashes them against the rocks.

Psalm 138

Of David.

¹I will praise you, O LORD, with all my heart;
before the "gods" I will sing your praise.
²I will bow down toward your holy temple
and will praise your name
for your love and your faithfulness,
for you have exalted above all things
your name and your word.
³When I called, you answered me;
you made me bold and stouthearted.

⁴May all the kings of the earth praise you,
O LORD,
when they hear the words of your mouth.
⁵May they sing of the ways of the LORD,
for the glory of the LORD is great.

⁶Though the LORD is on high, he looks upon
the lowly,
but the proud he knows from afar.
⁷Though I walk in the midst of trouble,
you preserve my life;
you stretch out your hand against the anger
of my foes,
with your right hand you save me.
⁸The LORD will fulfill ⌊his purpose⌋ for me;
your love, O LORD, endures forever—
do not abandon the works of your hands.

Psalm 139

For the director of music. Of David. A psalm.

¹O LORD, you have searched me
and you know me.
²You know when I sit and when I rise;
you perceive my thoughts from afar.
³You discern my going out and my lying
down;
you are familiar with all my ways.

⁴Before a word is on my tongue
you know it completely, O LORD.
⁵You hem me in—behind and before;
you have laid your hand upon me.
⁶Such knowledge is too wonderful for me,
too lofty for me to attain.

⁷Where can I go from your Spirit?
Where can I flee from your presence?
⁸If I go up to the heavens, you are there;
if I make my bed in the depths,ᵃ you are
there.
⁹If I rise on the wings of the dawn,
if I settle on the far side of the sea,
¹⁰even there your hand will guide me,
your right hand will hold me fast.
¹¹If I say, "Surely the darkness will hide me
and the light become night around me,"
¹²even the darkness will not be dark to you;
the night will shine like the day,
for darkness is as light to you.

¹³For you created my inmost being;
you knit me together in my mother's
womb.

139:13–16 Love Before Birth

**Does life begin at conception, or at birth? This
psalm doesn't directly answer that question,
but it does make clear that God's loving
involvement with our lives starts long before
birth. Nothing can escape God's concern,
according to this psalm—no person, no
thought, no place, no time.**

¹⁴I praise you because I am fearfully and
wonderfully made;
your works are wonderful,
I know that full well.
¹⁵My frame was not hidden from you
when I was made in the secret place.
When I was woven together in the depths of
the earth,
¹⁶   your eyes saw my unformed body.
All the days ordained for me
were written in your book
before one of them came to be.

¹⁷How precious toᵇ me are your thoughts,
O God!
How vast is the sum of them!
¹⁸Were I to count them,
they would outnumber the grains of sand.
When I awake,
I am still with you.

ᵃ8 Hebrew *Sheol*   ᵇ17 Or *concerning*

19If only you would slay the wicked, O God!
  Away from me, you bloodthirsty men!
20They speak of you with evil intent;
  your adversaries misuse your name.
21Do I not hate those who hate you, O LORD,
  and abhor those who rise up against you?
22I have nothing but hatred for them;
  I count them my enemies.

23Search me, O God, and know my heart;
  test me and know my anxious thoughts.
24See if there is any offensive way in me,
  and lead me in the way everlasting.

Psalm 140

For the director of music. A psalm of David.

1Rescue me, O LORD, from evil men;
  protect me from men of violence,
2who devise evil plans in their hearts
  and stir up war every day.

3They make their tongues as sharp as a
    serpent's;
  the poison of vipers is on their lips.   Selah

4Keep me, O LORD, from the hands of the
    wicked;
  protect me from men of violence
  who plan to trip my feet.
5Proud men have hidden a snare for me;
  they have spread out the cords of their
    net
  and have set traps for me along my path.
                                          Selah

6O LORD, I say to you, "You are my God."
  Hear, O LORD, my cry for mercy.
7O Sovereign LORD, my strong deliverer,
  who shields my head in the day of
    battle—
8do not grant the wicked their desires,
  O LORD;

What about Curses?
Bitter emotions expressed in sorrow

THE SO-CALLED "CURSING PSALMS" COME as a shock. Psalm 137 is the most famous example. In a gorgeous lament from exile, the poet crescendoes to wish that God would bless anyone who knocks a Babylonian baby's brains out.

> Happy is he . . . who seizes your infants and dashes them against the rocks. 137:8–9

To many people, this wish seems too bitter to belong in the Bible. Aren't Christians supposed to love their enemies and pray for those who persecute them (Matthew 5:44)? Even in the Old Testament, enemies were not to be treated unkindly (Exodus 23:4). How does this outburst fit into God's Word?

A Cry for Justice

To answer we must go to the courtroom, where more and more judges are allowing the victims of a crime to testify during sentencing. A mother who has lost her child to a murderer may spout wild and even vindictive emotions as she stands to demand the death sentence. Still the court needs to hear her. She alone knows fully what was lost. She alone feels the full outrage of the crime.

The cursing psalms voice such "victim testimony" to God, the judge. They always assume that the punishment they ask for is deserved. For example, Psalm 109 calls down curses on a man who "hounded to death the poor and the needy and the brokenhearted. He loved to pronounce a curse— may it come on him" (109:16–17).

Psalm 137 was written out of similar anguish. As a nation, Babylon had callously murdered, earning punishment. The Bible says that God hears the cries of the innocent. He promises to punish those who have hurt them.

With all his teaching on forgiving enemies, Jesus did not change this idea of justice. He taught that justice will be done by God after death. (See, for instance, Matthew 25:31–46.) But Old Testament Israelites had only vague ideas about life after death. For them, justice had to be done in this life, before their eyes. They asked for it in the cursing psalms.

Mercy for Your Enemies

What about mercy? Isn't our duty to forgive our enemies, and love them? How do the cursing psalms fit with that?

Three things must be said. First, while no mercy shows through in the cursing psalms, that doesn't mean the people who wrote them were wholly unmerciful. David, credited with some of the strongest cursing psalms, showed extraordinary mercy toward Saul, his vengeful enemy. The cursing psalms are

do not let their plans succeed,
or they will become proud.   *Selah*

[9] Let the heads of those who surround me
be covered with the trouble their lips have
caused.
[10] Let burning coals fall upon them;
may they be thrown into the fire,
into miry pits, never to rise.
[11] Let slanderers not be established in the
land;
may disaster hunt down men of violence.

[12] I know that the LORD secures justice for the
poor
and upholds the cause of the needy.

140:12 Justice for the Poor

*In ancient societies (and in most of the world
today) poor people lose all status. Nobody of
influence will listen to them or take up their
cause. In the Bible, though, God emphasizes his
concern for the poor. He will see that they get
just treatment. Naturally he expects his
followers to do the same.*

[13] Surely the righteous will praise your name
and the upright will live before you.

a5 Or Let the Righteous One

Psalm 141

A psalm of David.

[1] O LORD, I call to you; come quickly to me.
Hear my voice when I call to you.
[2] May my prayer be set before you like
incense;
may the lifting up of my hands be like the
evening sacrifice.

[3] Set a guard over my mouth, O LORD;
keep watch over the door of my lips.
[4] Let not my heart be drawn to what is evil,
to take part in wicked deeds
with men who are evildoers;
let me not eat of their delicacies.

[5] Let a righteous man*a* strike me—it is a
kindness;
let him rebuke me—it is oil on my head.
My head will not refuse it.

Yet my prayer is ever against the deeds of
evildoers;
[6] their rulers will be thrown down from the
cliffs,
and the wicked will learn that my words
were well spoken.
[7] ⌊They will say,⌋ "As one plows and breaks up
the earth,

---

unbridled cries of agony. They honestly reflect the way people felt. Their authors' lives sometimes balanced this cry with compassion.

Second, the psalmists wrote before Jesus offered forgiveness to all by dying, as God's Son, in people's place. Even today many people find it difficult to accept Jesus' teaching on forgiving enemies, for it means forgiving rapists, child molesters, mass murderers. We can only forgive them because Jesus paid the price for their crimes. The psalmists lived before that payment.

Third, the cursing psalms prepared the way for forgiveness. You can only be genuinely merciful if you start with a full appreciation of guilt. The judge who carelessly lets a criminal off on a technicality is not showing mercy. Maybe he or she just lacks sympathy for the crime's victim. True mercy comes when victims themselves turn and forgive the people who hurt them, releasing them to liberty.

Jesus the Victim

The cursing psalms express the hideousness of violence and injustice. Unless you feel the depth of this, you cannot understand the depth of God's forgiveness, offered freely to anyone who pleads for mercy. God is not merely letting people off on a legal technicality. He hears the cry of their victims, and more: He shares it. In Jesus, God was the victim, beaten, cursed, killed.

The New Testament actually quoted two of the cursing psalms, referring to Judas's betrayal of Jesus. These psalms speak of bitter injustice, and Jesus suffered the ultimate injustice. But the final word comes from Jesus himself: "Father, forgive them, for they do not know what they are doing."

If we follow Jesus' example, we dare not mouth the cursing psalms when we think of our enemies. These psalms are not for us to borrow from, as are other psalms. Yet these cursing psalms remind us of the bitter suffering many experience, and reading them can impel us to fight for justice. More, they remind us to forgive. For God, hearing such cries from the victim, having suffered as they suffer, forgives. So can we.

Life Questions: What is the worst injustice you have ever experienced? Did you feel some of the anger expressed in the cursing psalms? Were you able to forgive?

so our bones have been scattered at the
mouth of the grave.[a]"

8But my eyes are fixed on you, O Sovereign
LORD;
in you I take refuge—do not give me
over to death.
9Keep me from the snares they have laid for
me,
from the traps set by evildoers.
10Let the wicked fall into their own nets,
while I pass by in safety.

Psalm 142

A *maskil*[b] of David. When he was in the cave.
A prayer.

1I cry aloud to the LORD;
I lift up my voice to the LORD for mercy.
2I pour out my complaint before him;
before him I tell my trouble.

3When my spirit grows faint within me,
it is you who know my way.
In the path where I walk
men have hidden a snare for me.
4Look to my right and see;
no one is concerned for me.
I have no refuge;
no one cares for my life.

5I cry to you, O LORD;
I say, "You are my refuge,
my portion in the land of the living."
6Listen to my cry,
for I am in desperate need;
rescue me from those who pursue me,
for they are too strong for me.
7Set me free from my prison,
that I may praise your name.

Then the righteous will gather about me
because of your goodness to me.

Psalm 143

A psalm of David.

1O LORD, hear my prayer,
listen to my cry for mercy;
in your faithfulness and righteousness
come to my relief.
2Do not bring your servant into judgment,
for no one living is righteous before you.

3The enemy pursues me,
he crushes me to the ground;
he makes me dwell in darkness
like those long dead.

4So my spirit grows faint within me;
my heart within me is dismayed.

5I remember the days of long ago;
I meditate on all your works
and consider what your hands have done.
6I spread out my hands to you;
my soul thirsts for you like a parched
land.   *Selah*

7Answer me quickly, O LORD;
my spirit fails.
Do not hide your face from me
or I will be like those who go down to the
pit.
8Let the morning bring me word of your
unfailing love,
for I have put my trust in you.
Show me the way I should go,
for to you I lift up my soul.
9Rescue me from my enemies, O LORD,
for I hide myself in you.
10Teach me to do your will,
for you are my God;
may your good Spirit
lead me on level ground.

11For your name's sake, O LORD, preserve my
life;
in your righteousness, bring me out of
trouble.
12In your unfailing love, silence my enemies;
destroy all my foes,
for I am your servant.

Psalm 144

Of David.

1Praise be to the LORD my Rock,
who trains my hands for war,
my fingers for battle.
2He is my loving God and my fortress,
my stronghold and my deliverer,
my shield, in whom I take refuge,
who subdues peoples[c] under me.

3O LORD, what is man that you care for him,
the son of man that you think of him?
4Man is like a breath;
his days are like a fleeting shadow.

5Part your heavens, O LORD, and come down;
touch the mountains, so that they smoke.
6Send forth lightning and scatter ⌊the
enemies⌋;
shoot your arrows and rout them.
7Reach down your hand from on high;
deliver me and rescue me
from the mighty waters,

---

a7 Hebrew *Sheol*   *b*Title: Probably a literary or musical term   *c2* Many manuscripts of the Masoretic Text, Dead
Sea Scrolls, Aquila, Jerome and Syriac; most manuscripts of the Masoretic Text *subdues my people*

from the hands of foreigners
[8]whose mouths are full of lies,
whose right hands are deceitful.

[9]I will sing a new song to you, O God;
on the ten-stringed lyre I will make music
to you,
[10]to the One who gives victory to kings,
who delivers his servant David from the
deadly sword.

[11]Deliver me and rescue me
from the hands of foreigners
whose mouths are full of lies,
whose right hands are deceitful.

[12]Then our sons in their youth
will be like well-nurtured plants,
and our daughters will be like pillars
carved to adorn a palace.
[13]Our barns will be filled
with every kind of provision.
Our sheep will increase by thousands,
by tens of thousands in our fields;
[14]   our oxen will draw heavy loads.[a]
There will be no breaching of walls,
no going into captivity,
no cry of distress in our streets.

[15]Blessed are the people of whom this is true;
blessed are the people whose God is the
LORD.

Psalm 145[b]

A psalm of praise. Of David.

[1]I will exalt you, my God the King;
I will praise your name for ever and ever.
[2]Every day I will praise you
and extol your name for ever and ever.

[3]Great is the LORD and most worthy of praise;
his greatness no one can fathom.
[4]One generation will commend your works to
another;
they will tell of your mighty acts.
[5]They will speak of the glorious splendor of
your majesty,
and I will meditate on your wonderful
works.[c]
[6]They will tell of the power of your awesome
works,
and I will proclaim your great deeds.
[7]They will celebrate your abundant goodness
and joyfully sing of your righteousness.

[8]The LORD is gracious and compassionate,

slow to anger and rich in love.
[9]The LORD is good to all;
he has compassion on all he has made.
[10]All you have made will praise you, O LORD;
your saints will extol you.
[11]They will tell of the glory of your kingdom
and speak of your might,
[12]so that all men may know of your mighty
acts
and the glorious splendor of your
kingdom.
[13]Your kingdom is an everlasting kingdom,
and your dominion endures through all
generations.

The LORD is faithful to all his promises
and loving toward all he has made.[d]
[14]The LORD upholds all those who fall
and lifts up all who are bowed down.
[15]The eyes of all look to you,
and you give them their food at the
proper time.
[16]You open your hand
and satisfy the desires of every living
thing.

[17]The LORD is righteous in all his ways
and loving toward all he has made.
[18]The LORD is near to all who call on him,
to all who call on him in truth.
[19]He fulfills the desires of those who fear him;
he hears their cry and saves them.
[20]The LORD watches over all who love him,
but all the wicked he will destroy.

[21]My mouth will speak in praise of the LORD.
Let every creature praise his holy name
for ever and ever.

Psalm 146

[1]Praise the LORD.[e]

Praise the LORD, O my soul.
[2]   I will praise the LORD all my life;
I will sing praise to my God as long as I
live.

[3]Do not put your trust in princes,
in mortal men, who cannot save.
[4]When their spirit departs, they return to the
ground;
on that very day their plans come to
nothing.

[5]Blessed is he whose help is the God of Jacob,
whose hope is in the LORD his God,
[6]the Maker of heaven and earth,

---

[a]14 Or *our chieftains will be firmly established*   [b]This psalm is an acrostic poem, the verses of which (including verse 13b) begin with the successive letters of the Hebrew alphabet.   [c]5 Dead Sea Scrolls and Syriac (see also Septuagint); Masoretic Text *On the glorious splendor of your majesty / and on your wonderful works I will meditate*   [d]13 One manuscript of the Masoretic Text, Dead Sea Scrolls and Syriac (see also Septuagint); most manuscripts of the Masoretic Text do not have the last two lines of verse 13.   [e]1 Hebrew *Hallelu Yah*; also in verse 10

the sea, and everything in them—
the LORD, who remains faithful forever.
⁷He upholds the cause of the oppressed
and gives food to the hungry.
The LORD sets prisoners free,
⁸ the LORD gives sight to the blind,
the LORD lifts up those who are bowed down,
the LORD loves the righteous.
⁹The LORD watches over the alien
and sustains the fatherless and the widow,
but he frustrates the ways of the wicked.

¹⁰The LORD reigns forever,
your God, O Zion, for all generations.

Praise the LORD.

Psalm 147

¹Praise the LORD.ᵃ

How good it is to sing praises to our God,
how pleasant and fitting to praise him!

²The LORD builds up Jerusalem;
he gathers the exiles of Israel.
³He heals the brokenhearted
and binds up their wounds.

⁴He determines the number of the stars
and calls them each by name.
⁵Great is our Lord and mighty in power;
his understanding has no limit.
⁶The LORD sustains the humble
but casts the wicked to the ground.

⁷Sing to the LORD with thanksgiving;
make music to our God on the harp.
⁸He covers the sky with clouds;
he supplies the earth with rain
and makes grass grow on the hills.
⁹He provides food for the cattle
and for the young ravens when they call.

¹⁰His pleasure is not in the strength of the
horse,
nor his delight in the legs of a man;
¹¹the LORD delights in those who fear him,
who put their hope in his unfailing love.

¹²Extol the LORD, O Jerusalem;
praise your God, O Zion,

147:11 God's Great Concern

*The Lord is a God of strength, as this song
amply demonstrates. But power doesn't delight
him (verse 10). More than anything he loves to
be in a close relationship to people who
respond to his love.*

¹³for he strengthens the bars of your gates
and blesses your people within you.
¹⁴He grants peace to your borders
and satisfies you with the finest of wheat.

¹⁵He sends his command to the earth;
his word runs swiftly.
¹⁶He spreads the snow like wool
and scatters the frost like ashes.
¹⁷He hurls down his hail like pebbles.
Who can withstand his icy blast?
¹⁸He sends his word and melts them;
he stirs up his breezes, and the waters
flow.

¹⁹He has revealed his word to Jacob,
his laws and decrees to Israel.
²⁰He has done this for no other nation;
they do not know his laws.

Praise the LORD.

Psalm 148

¹Praise the LORD.ᵇ

Praise the LORD from the heavens,
praise him in the heights above.
²Praise him, all his angels,
praise him, all his heavenly hosts.
³Praise him, sun and moon,
praise him, all you shining stars.
⁴Praise him, you highest heavens
and you waters above the skies.
⁵Let them praise the name of the LORD,
for he commanded and they were created.
⁶He set them in place for ever and ever;
he gave a decree that will never pass away.

⁷Praise the LORD from the earth,
you great sea creatures and all ocean
depths,
⁸lightning and hail, snow and clouds,
stormy winds that do his bidding,
⁹you mountains and all hills,
fruit trees and all cedars,
¹⁰wild animals and all cattle,
small creatures and flying birds,
¹¹kings of the earth and all nations,
you princes and all rulers on earth,
¹²young men and maidens,
old men and children.

¹³Let them praise the name of the LORD,
for his name alone is exalted;
his splendor is above the earth and the
heavens.
¹⁴He has raised up for his people a horn,ᶜ

ᵃ1 Hebrew *Hallelu Yah;* also in verse 20   ᵇ1 Hebrew *Hallelu Yah;* also in verse 14   ᶜ14 *Horn* here symbolizes
strong one, that is, king.

the praise of all his saints,
of Israel, the people close to his heart.

Praise the LORD.

Psalm 149

[1]Praise the LORD.[a]

Sing to the LORD a new song,
his praise in the assembly of the saints.

[2]Let Israel rejoice in their Maker;
let the people of Zion be glad in their
King.
[3]Let them praise his name with dancing
and make music to him with tambourine
and harp.
[4]For the LORD takes delight in his people;
he crowns the humble with salvation.
[5]Let the saints rejoice in this honor
and sing for joy on their beds.

[6]May the praise of God be in their mouths
and a double-edged sword in their hands,
[7]to inflict vengeance on the nations
and punishment on the peoples,
[8]to bind their kings with fetters,
their nobles with shackles of iron,
[9]to carry out the sentence written against
them.
This is the glory of all his saints.

Praise the LORD.

Psalm 150

[1]Praise the LORD.[b]

Praise God in his sanctuary;
praise him in his mighty heavens.
[2]Praise him for his acts of power;
praise him for his surpassing greatness.
[3]Praise him with the sounding of the trumpet,
praise him with the harp and lyre,
[4]praise him with tambourine and dancing,
praise him with the strings and flute,
[5]praise him with the clash of cymbals,
praise him with resounding cymbals.

[6]Let everything that has breath praise the
LORD.

Praise the LORD.

---

[a]1 Hebrew *Hallelu Yah*; also in verse 9   [b]1 Hebrew *Hallelu Yah*; also in verse 6

PROVERBS

Uncommon Sense
A most down-to-earth book

"SESAME STREET," THE EDUCATIONAL TV show, has changed a lot of people's ideas about education. It offers a kaleidoscopic mix of gentle fun that seems to have nothing to do with education at all. One episode may start with a band of puppet rock stars—the Beetles—singing an ode entitled "Letter B" (to a tune that sounds surprisingly like the Beatles' "Let It Be"). Then the picture cuts to Big Bird asking Oscar the Grouch to help him write a letter to his uncle—Uncle Bird, whose name just happens to start with the letter *B*. Five minutes later, a cartoon letter *B* is jumping in front of various letter combinations while a voice intones the words spelled out: "B-b-boy." "B-b-bathtub." "B-b-bicycle."

"Sesame Street" showed that teaching kids doesn't always mean forcing them to sit down and memorize lists. By watching Big Bird, Cookie Monster, and Oscar the Grouch, children painlessly learn the letter *B* as well as colors, shapes, and a lot more.

> If you call out for insight and cry aloud for understanding, and if you look for it as for silver and search for it as for hidden treasure, then you will understand the fear of the LORD and find the knowledge of God. 2:3–5

The book of Proverbs does for wisdom what "Sesame Street" does for the ABCs. Much of Proverbs reads like a collection of one-liners, moving quickly (and apparently illogically) from one subject to another. A proverb pleases the ear much as "Sesame Street" pleases the eye, using "shortness, sense and salt" to compress life into a handful of memorable words. But just as with the TV program, Proverbs has an overall objective behind its disorder. If you spend enough time in Proverbs, you will gain a subtle and practical understanding of life.

A Father's Guidance

Proverbs is probably the most down-to-earth book in the Bible. Its education prepares you for the street and the marketplace, not the schoolroom. (Proverbs 1:20–21 expresses this poetically.) The book offers the warm advice you get by growing up in a good family: practical guidance for successfully making your way in the world. It covers small questions as well as large: talking too much, visiting neighbors too often, being unbearably cheerful too early in the morning.

The first nine chapters, which explain the purpose of Proverbs's wisdom, are spoken from father to son. Fifteen times the fatherly voice says, "My son." Some of the advice seems particularly well suited to young people: warnings against joining gangs, for instance, or urgent cautions against sex outside marriage. But the central message of Proverbs applies to anyone, old or young: "Get wisdom at all costs." It is a plea to strain your mind and your ears searching for the wise way to live.

Virtue Is Not Its Only Reward

Anybody with a brain can find exceptions to Proverbs's generalities. For instance, Proverbs 28:19 proclaims that "he who works his land will have abundant food, but the one who chases fantasies will have his fill of poverty." Yet farmers who work hard go hungry in a drought, and dreamers win $10 million in a lottery.

Proverbs simply tells how life works most of the time. You can worry about the exceptions after you have learned the rule. Try to live by the exceptions, and you court disaster.

The rule is that the godly, moral, hardworking, and wise will reap many rewards. Those who learn the practical and godly wisdom of Proverbs not only sleep better, they succeed and become able to help their family and friends. Fools and scoffers, though they appear successful, will eventually pay the cost of their lifestyle.

Much of Proverbs's practical advice makes no mention of God, and its concern for success may therefore seem quite secular. But if you take the book as a whole, it becomes obvious that the lifestyle Proverbs teaches depends on a healthy respect for God (1:7) affecting every aspect of life (3:5–7).

Proverbs frankly concedes that the wise path will not be chosen by many; it is easier to live carelessly and godlessly. But those who choose to live by Proverbs will get success and safety, and more: They will get to know God himself. "Then you will understand the fear of the LORD and find the knowledge of God" (2:5).

How to Read Proverbs

People love to quote proverbs. Often they express truth about life in an elegant, witty kernel. You'll find more humor in Proverbs than anywhere else in the Bible.

Yet Proverbs may well be the most abused book in the Bible. People often quote the proverbs as though they were absolute promises from God or rigid rules for living. In fact, few of the proverbs should be read that way. And some proverbs, read alone, would give you a distorted point of view.

To understand Proverbs, you should not hunt through it for proverbs you like. You should study the whole book to get its overall point of view. This takes time, for Proverbs covers dozens of subjects in subtle detail.

Each of the more than 500 proverbs is a tough nut you have to crack before you get the inner meat. Read Proverbs slowly, but not for too long at one sitting.

Some people like to read a small number of proverbs each day in addition to their regular Bible readings. Others concentrate on memorizing proverbs, so they can run them through their heads as they go on about the day. Whatever technique you use, keep two things in mind: Think carefully about each proverb, and try to put each into the bigger context of the teachings of all of Proverbs. To help you see the total picture of Proverbs's teaching on some key subjects, ten Insights scattered throughout Proverbs briefly introduce ten subjects and list relevant proverbs.

The book of Proverbs is divided into two main parts: an introduction in the first nine chapters and the proverbs themselves in the remaining 22 chapters. If you skip the introduction, you won't understand the point of Proverbs as a book. It introduces "Lady Wisdom," and explains what she can do for you.

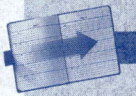

3-TRACK READING PLAN

For an explanation and complete listing of the 3-track reading plan, turn to page 7.

TRACK 1: *Two-Week Courses on the Bible*
See page 7 for information on these courses.

TRACK 2: *An Overview of Proverbs in 3 Days*
☐ Day 1. Read the Introduction to Proverbs and chapter 4, which gives an introduction to the importance of wisdom and the style of life you need to pursue it.
☐ Day 2. Read chapter 10, which covers a fairly typical range of subject matter.
☐ Day 3. Read all the proverbs listed in "Verbal Dynamite," on page 676.

Now turn to page 9 for your next Track 2 reading project.

TRACK 3: *All of Proverbs in 31 Days*
After you have read through Proverbs, turn to pages 10–14 for your next Track 3 reading project.

☐1 ☐2 ☐3 ☐4 ☐5 ☐6 ☐7 ☐8
☐9 ☐10 ☐11 ☐12 ☐13 ☐14 ☐15 ☐16
☐17 ☐18 ☐19 ☐20 ☐21 ☐22 ☐23 ☐24
☐25 ☐26 ☐27 ☐28 ☐29 ☐30 ☐31

Prologue: Purpose and Theme

1 The proverbs of Solomon son of David, king of Israel:

[2] for attaining wisdom and discipline;
  for understanding words of insight;
[3] for acquiring a disciplined and prudent life,
  doing what is right and just and fair;
[4] for giving prudence to the simple,
  knowledge and discretion to the young—
[5] let the wise listen and add to their learning,
  and let the discerning get guidance—
[6] for understanding proverbs and parables,
  the sayings and riddles of the wise.

[7] The fear of the LORD is the beginning of knowledge,
  but fools[a] despise wisdom and discipline.

Exhortations to Embrace Wisdom

Warning Against Enticement

[8] Listen, my son, to your father's instruction
  and do not forsake your mother's teaching.
[9] They will be a garland to grace your head
  and a chain to adorn your neck.

[10] My son, if sinners entice you,
  do not give in to them.
[11] If they say, "Come along with us;
  let's lie in wait for someone's blood,
  let's waylay some harmless soul;
[12] let's swallow them alive, like the grave,[b]
  and whole, like those who go down to the pit;
[13] we will get all sorts of valuable things
  and fill our houses with plunder;
[14] throw in your lot with us,
  and we will share a common purse"—
[15] my son, do not go along with them,
  do not set foot on their paths;
[16] for their feet rush into sin,
  they are swift to shed blood.
[17] How useless to spread a net
  in full view of all the birds!
[18] These men lie in wait for their own blood;
  they waylay only themselves!
[19] Such is the end of all who go after ill-gotten gain;
  it takes away the lives of those who get it.

Warning Against Rejecting Wisdom

[20] Wisdom calls aloud in the street,
  she raises her voice in the public squares;
[21] at the head of the noisy streets[c] she cries out,
  in the gateways of the city she makes her speech:

[22] "How long will you simple ones[d] love your simple ways?
  How long will mockers delight in mockery
  and fools hate knowledge?

1:22 Three Problem People

Mockers, fools, the simple: *Proverbs keeps using these words to define the "bad characters" we should stay away from. What kind of people are they? The "simple" are the least harmful group: they live without thinking and are too lazy to change. But they, like the others, will end up sorry. "Fools" have more smarts but have made a conscious decision to live by their own wits, independent of God and independent of advice. "Mockers," worst of all, are rebels against God who make their prideful position known to everyone. They mock God, but God will mock them in the end (verse 26).*

[23] If you had responded to my rebuke,
  I would have poured out my heart to you
  and made my thoughts known to you.
[24] But since you rejected me when I called
  and no one gave heed when I stretched out my hand,
[25] since you ignored all my advice
  and would not accept my rebuke,
[26] I in turn will laugh at your disaster;
  I will mock when calamity overtakes you—
[27] when calamity overtakes you like a storm,
  when disaster sweeps over you like a whirlwind,
  when distress and trouble overwhelm you.

[28] "Then they will call to me but I will not answer;
  they will look for me but will not find me.
[29] Since they hated knowledge
  and did not choose to fear the LORD,
[30] since they would not accept my advice
  and spurned my rebuke,
[31] they will eat the fruit of their ways
  and be filled with the fruit of their schemes.
[32] For the waywardness of the simple will kill them,
  and the complacency of fools will destroy them;
[33] but whoever listens to me will live in safety
  and be at ease, without fear of harm."

---

a7 The Hebrew words rendered *fool* in Proverbs, and often elsewhere in the Old Testament, denote one who is morally deficient. *b12* Hebrew *Sheol* *c21* Hebrew; Septuagint / *on the tops of the walls* *d22* The Hebrew word rendered *simple* in Proverbs generally denotes one without moral direction and inclined to evil.

Moral Benefits of Wisdom

2 My son, if you accept my words
  and store up my commands within you,
[2]turning your ear to wisdom
  and applying your heart to understanding,
[3]and if you call out for insight
  and cry aloud for understanding,
[4]and if you look for it as for silver
  and search for it as for hidden treasure,
[5]then you will understand the fear of the
  LORD
  and find the knowledge of God.
[6]For the LORD gives wisdom,
  and from his mouth come knowledge and
  understanding.
[7]He holds victory in store for the upright,
  he is a shield to those whose walk is
  blameless,
[8]for he guards the course of the just
  and protects the way of his faithful ones.

[9]Then you will understand what is right and
  just
  and fair—every good path.
[10]For wisdom will enter your heart,
  and knowledge will be pleasant to your
  soul.
[11]Discretion will protect you,
  and understanding will guard you.

[12]Wisdom will save you from the ways of
  wicked men,
  from men whose words are perverse,
[13]who leave the straight paths
  to walk in dark ways,
[14]who delight in doing wrong
  and rejoice in the perverseness of evil,
[15]whose paths are crooked
  and who are devious in their ways.

[16]It will save you also from the adulteress,
  from the wayward wife with her seductive
  words,
[17]who has left the partner of her youth
  and ignored the covenant she made before
  God.[a]
[18]For her house leads down to death
  and her paths to the spirits of the dead.
[19]None who go to her return
  or attain the paths of life.

[20]Thus you will walk in the ways of good
  men
  and keep to the paths of the righteous.
[21]For the upright will live in the land,
  and the blameless will remain in it;
[22]but the wicked will be cut off from the land,
  and the unfaithful will be torn from it.

Further Benefits of Wisdom

3 My son, do not forget my teaching,
  but keep my commands in your heart,
[2]for they will prolong your life many years
  and bring you prosperity.

[3]Let love and faithfulness never leave you;
  bind them around your neck,
  write them on the tablet of your heart.
[4]Then you will win favor and a good name
  in the sight of God and man.

[5]Trust in the LORD with all your heart
  and lean not on your own understanding;
[6]in all your ways acknowledge him,
  and he will make your paths straight.[b]

3:6 Walking with God

*In the original Hebrew, "in all your ways
acknowledge him" is more literally "in all your
ways know him." This fundamental statement
of how to relate to God implies more than mere
reverence. Nodding in God's direction is not
enough: You must know him by living closely
with him, relating to him personally in every
aspect of your life.*

[7]Do not be wise in your own eyes;
  fear the LORD and shun evil.
[8]This will bring health to your body
  and nourishment to your bones.

[9]Honor the LORD with your wealth,
  with the firstfruits of all your crops;
[10]then your barns will be filled to overflowing,
  and your vats will brim over with new
  wine.

[11]My son, do not despise the LORD's discipline
  and do not resent his rebuke,
[12]because the LORD disciplines those he loves,
  as a father[c] the son he delights in.

[13]Blessed is the man who finds wisdom,
  the man who gains understanding,
[14]for she is more profitable than silver
  and yields better returns than gold.
[15]She is more precious than rubies;
  nothing you desire can compare with her.
[16]Long life is in her right hand;
  in her left hand are riches and honor.
[17]Her ways are pleasant ways,
  and all her paths are peace.
[18]She is a tree of life to those who embrace
  her;
  those who lay hold of her will be blessed.

[19]By wisdom the LORD laid the earth's
  foundations,

---

[a]17 Or *covenant of her God*   [b]6 Or *will direct your paths*   [c]12 Hebrew; Septuagint / *and he punishes*

by understanding he set the heavens in
place;
[20] by his knowledge the deeps were divided,
and the clouds let drop the dew.

[21] My son, preserve sound judgment and
discernment,
do not let them out of your sight;
[22] they will be life for you,
an ornament to grace your neck.
[23] Then you will go on your way in safety,
and your foot will not stumble;
[24] when you lie down, you will not be afraid;
when you lie down, your sleep will be
sweet.
[25] Have no fear of sudden disaster
or of the ruin that overtakes the wicked,
[26] for the LORD will be your confidence
and will keep your foot from being
snared.

[27] Do not withhold good from those who
deserve it,
when it is in your power to act.
[28] Do not say to your neighbor,
"Come back later; I'll give it tomorrow"—
when you now have it with you.

[29] Do not plot harm against your neighbor,
who lives trustfully near you.
[30] Do not accuse a man for no reason—
when he has done you no harm.

[31] Do not envy a violent man
or choose any of his ways,
[32] for the LORD detests a perverse man
but takes the upright into his confidence.

[33] The LORD's curse is on the house of the
wicked,
but he blesses the home of the righteous.
[34] He mocks proud mockers
but gives grace to the humble.
[35] The wise inherit honor,
but fools he holds up to shame.

Wisdom Is Supreme

4 Listen, my sons, to a father's instruction;
pay attention and gain understanding.
[2] I give you sound learning,
so do not forsake my teaching.
[3] When I was a boy in my father's house,
still tender, and an only child of my
mother,
[4] he taught me and said,
"Lay hold of my words with all your
heart;
keep my commands and you will live.
[5] Get wisdom, get understanding;
do not forget my words or swerve from
them.

[6] Do not forsake wisdom, and she will protect
you;
love her, and she will watch over you.
[7] Wisdom is supreme; therefore get wisdom.
Though it cost all you have,[a] get
understanding.

4:7 A Lifelong Quest

*A father's advice can easily degenerate into,
"Don't do this, don't do that." But the fatherly
advice of Proverbs isn't preoccupied with rules.
Instead, this father tries to help his son develop
a love for the best things in life—just as his
father did for him. This love for the best—and
most of all for wisdom—begins with listening to
your father's advice, but it goes beyond taking
instructions. The love of wisdom becomes a
lifelong quest that may make you wiser than
your father.*

[8] Esteem her, and she will exalt you;
embrace her, and she will honor you.
[9] She will set a garland of grace on your head
and present you with a crown of
splendor."

[10] Listen, my son, accept what I say,
and the years of your life will be many.
[11] I guide you in the way of wisdom
and lead you along straight paths.
[12] When you walk, your steps will not be
hampered;
when you run, you will not stumble.
[13] Hold on to instruction, do not let it go;
guard it well, for it is your life.
[14] Do not set foot on the path of the wicked
or walk in the way of evil men.
[15] Avoid it, do not travel on it;
turn from it and go on your way.
[16] For they cannot sleep till they do evil;
they are robbed of slumber till they make
someone fall.
[17] They eat the bread of wickedness
and drink the wine of violence.

[18] The path of the righteous is like the first
gleam of dawn,
shining ever brighter till the full light of
day.
[19] But the way of the wicked is like deep
darkness;
they do not know what makes them
stumble.

[20] My son, pay attention to what I say;
listen closely to my words.
[21] Do not let them out of your sight,
keep them within your heart;

a 7 Or Whatever else you get

22for they are life to those who find them
  and health to a man's whole body.
23Above all else, guard your heart,
  for it is the wellspring of life.
24Put away perversity from your mouth;
  keep corrupt talk far from your lips.
25Let your eyes look straight ahead,
  fix your gaze directly before you.
26Make level[a] paths for your feet
  and take only ways that are firm.
27Do not swerve to the right or the left;
  keep your foot from evil.

Warning Against Adultery

5 My son, pay attention to my wisdom,
  listen well to my words of insight,
2that you may maintain discretion
  and your lips may preserve knowledge.
3For the lips of an adulteress drip honey,
  and her speech is smoother than oil;
4but in the end she is bitter as gall,
  sharp as a double-edged sword.
5Her feet go down to death;
  her steps lead straight to the grave.[b]
6She gives no thought to the way of life;
  her paths are crooked, but she knows it
    not.

7Now then, my sons, listen to me;
  do not turn aside from what I say.
8Keep to a path far from her,
  do not go near the door of her house,
9lest you give your best strength to others
  and your years to one who is cruel,
10lest strangers feast on your wealth
  and your toil enrich another man's house.
11At the end of your life you will groan,
  when your flesh and body are spent.
12You will say, "How I hated discipline!
  How my heart spurned correction!
13I would not obey my teachers
  or listen to my instructors.
14I have come to the brink of utter ruin
  in the midst of the whole assembly."

15Drink water from your own cistern,
  running water from your own well.
16Should your springs overflow in the streets,
  your streams of water in the public
    squares?
17Let them be yours alone,
  never to be shared with strangers.
18May your fountain be blessed,
  and may you rejoice in the wife of your
    youth.
19A loving doe, a graceful deer—
  may her breasts satisfy you always,
  may you ever be captivated by her love.

20Why be captivated, my son, by an
    adulteress?
  Why embrace the bosom of another
    man's wife?
21For a man's ways are in full view of the
    LORD,
  and he examines all his paths.
22The evil deeds of a wicked man ensnare him;
  the cords of his sin hold him fast.
23He will die for lack of discipline,
  led astray by his own great folly.

Warnings Against Folly

6 My son, if you have put up security for
    your neighbor,
  if you have struck hands in pledge for
    another,

6:1–3 Danger in Debt

*Proverbs warns against "putting up security"
for a neighbor—something like co-signing a
loan for a friend who doesn't otherwise qualify.
Proverbs supports generosity, but not open-
ended charity in which the amount you must
give and the timing are determined by
circumstances beyond your control. Too often it
leads to disaster. (See also 11:15; 17:18;
22:26–27.)*

2if you have been trapped by what you said,
  ensnared by the words of your mouth,
3then do this, my son, to free yourself,
  since you have fallen into your neighbor's
    hands:
  Go and humble yourself;
    press your plea with your neighbor!
4Allow no sleep to your eyes,
  no slumber to your eyelids.
5Free yourself, like a gazelle from the hand of
    the hunter,
  like a bird from the snare of the fowler.

6Go to the ant, you sluggard;
  consider its ways and be wise!
7It has no commander,
  no overseer or ruler,
8yet it stores its provisions in summer
  and gathers its food at harvest.
9How long will you lie there, you sluggard?
  When will you get up from your sleep?
10A little sleep, a little slumber,
  a little folding of the hands to rest—
11and poverty will come on you like a bandit
  and scarcity like an armed man.[c]

12A scoundrel and villain,

---

a26 Or *Consider the*   b5 Hebrew *Sheol*   c11 Or *like a vagrant / and scarcity like a beggar*

who goes about with a corrupt mouth,
¹³ who winks with his eye,
signals with his feet
and motions with his fingers,
¹⁴ who plots evil with deceit in his heart—
he always stirs up dissension.
¹⁵Therefore disaster will overtake him in an
instant;
he will suddenly be destroyed—without
remedy.

¹⁶There are six things the LORD hates,
seven that are detestable to him:
¹⁷ haughty eyes,
a lying tongue,
hands that shed innocent blood,
¹⁸ a heart that devises wicked schemes,
feet that are quick to rush into evil,
¹⁹ a false witness who pours out lies
and a man who stirs up dissension
among brothers.

Warning Against Adultery

²⁰My son, keep your father's commands
and do not forsake your mother's
teaching.
²¹Bind them upon your heart forever;
fasten them around your neck.
²²When you walk, they will guide you;
when you sleep, they will watch over you;
when you awake, they will speak to you.
²³For these commands are a lamp,
this teaching is a light,
and the corrections of discipline
are the way to life,
²⁴keeping you from the immoral woman,
from the smooth tongue of the wayward
wife.
²⁵Do not lust in your heart after her beauty
or let her captivate you with her eyes,
²⁶for the prostitute reduces you to a loaf of
bread,
and the adulteress preys upon your very
life.
²⁷Can a man scoop fire into his lap
without his clothes being burned?
²⁸Can a man walk on hot coals
without his feet being scorched?
²⁹So is he who sleeps with another man's wife;
no one who touches her will go
unpunished.

³⁰Men do not despise a thief if he steals
to satisfy his hunger when he is starving.
³¹Yet if he is caught, he must pay sevenfold,
though it costs him all the wealth of his
house.
³²But a man who commits adultery lacks
judgment;
whoever does so destroys himself.

³³Blows and disgrace are his lot,
and his shame will never be wiped away;
³⁴for jealousy arouses a husband's fury,
and he will show no mercy when he takes
revenge.
³⁵He will not accept any compensation;
he will refuse the bribe, however great
it is.

Warning Against the Adulteress

7 My son, keep my words
and store up my commands within you.
²Keep my commands and you will live;
guard my teachings as the apple of your
eye.

7:2 The Apple of Your Eye

The "apple of your eye" is an Old English expression for the eye's center, or pupil. The whole body is tuned to protect that pupil from harm: eyelids reflexively snap shut at the slightest hint of danger; tear ducts bathe your eye with a cleansing liquid if any irritant enters; nerve endings scream "danger" at the slightest pain or pressure. Proverbs urges you to take as much care of its teachings as you do of your eye.

³Bind them on your fingers;
write them on the tablet of your heart.
⁴Say to wisdom, "You are my sister,"
and call understanding your kinsman;
⁵they will keep you from the adulteress,
from the wayward wife with her seductive
words.

⁶At the window of my house
I looked out through the lattice.
⁷I saw among the simple,
I noticed among the young men,
a youth who lacked judgment.
⁸He was going down the street near her
corner,
walking along in the direction of her
house
⁹at twilight, as the day was fading,
as the dark of night set in.

¹⁰Then out came a woman to meet him,
dressed like a prostitute and with crafty
intent.
¹¹(She is loud and defiant,
her feet never stay at home;
¹²now in the street, now in the squares,
at every corner she lurks.)
¹³She took hold of him and kissed him
and with a brazen face she said:

¹⁴"I have fellowship offerings[a] at home;
today I fulfilled my vows.
¹⁵So I came out to meet you;
I looked for you and have found you!
¹⁶I have covered my bed
with colored linens from Egypt.
¹⁷I have perfumed my bed
with myrrh, aloes and cinnamon.
¹⁸Come, let's drink deep of love till morning;
let's enjoy ourselves with love!
¹⁹My husband is not at home;
he has gone on a long journey.
²⁰He took his purse filled with money
and will not be home till full moon."

²¹With persuasive words she led him
astray;
she seduced him with her smooth
talk.
²²All at once he followed her
like an ox going to the slaughter,
like a deer[b] stepping into a noose[c]
²³   till an arrow pierces his liver,
like a bird darting into a snare,
little knowing it will cost him his life.

²⁴Now then, my sons, listen to me;
pay attention to what I say.
²⁵Do not let your heart turn to her ways
or stray into her paths.
²⁶Many are the victims she has brought down;
her slain are a mighty throng.

²⁷Her house is a highway to the grave,[d]
leading down to the chambers of death.

Wisdom's Call

8 Does not wisdom call out?
Does not understanding raise her voice?
²On the heights along the way,
where the paths meet, she takes her stand;
³beside the gates leading into the city,
at the entrances, she cries aloud:
⁴"To you, O men, I call out;
I raise my voice to all mankind.
⁵You who are simple, gain prudence;
you who are foolish, gain understanding.
⁶Listen, for I have worthy things to say;
I open my lips to speak what is right.
⁷My mouth speaks what is true,
for my lips detest wickedness.
⁸All the words of my mouth are just;
none of them is crooked or perverse.
⁹To the discerning all of them are right;
they are faultless to those who have
knowledge.
¹⁰Choose my instruction instead of silver,
knowledge rather than choice gold,
¹¹for wisdom is more precious than rubies,
and nothing you desire can compare with
her.

¹²"I, wisdom, dwell together with prudence;

---

[a] 14 Traditionally *peace offerings*   [b] 22 Syriac (see also Septuagint); Hebrew *fool*   [c] 22 The meaning of the Hebrew for this line is uncertain.   [d] 27 Hebrew *Sheol*

God and "How-to-Succeed"
Does Proverbs care more for success than for God?

> *"The fear of the LORD is the beginning of wisdom." 9:10*

BOOKSTORES ARE FULL OF "HOW-TO" books, each promising to teach you how to make a success of yourself by just following a few simple rules. Is Proverbs an ancient "how-to" book? It seems, at first look, more interested in success and prosperity than in God. Many of the proverbs can be adopted by those who have no love for God.

But if you look at Proverbs as a book, rather than a collection of unrelated fragments, you will find that its "how-tos" of wise living can't be separated from God. While some proverbs observe the hard facts of life—that bribes are effective, for instance, or that money does buy friends of a kind—the book never for a moment endorses success techniques that involve immorality. More important, a deep sense of people's sin and their utter dependence on God pervades Proverbs. Wisdom, that fundamental tool for living, starts with the fear of God and leads to a knowledge of him.

The words *Lord* or *God* are actually mentioned nearly 100 times, so a complete study of God's place in Proverbs takes you through virtually the entire book.
Proverbs on God's relationship to wisdom: 1:7; 2:5–9; 8:22–31; 9:10; 22:17–19.
Proverbs on sin: 15:8; 16:6; 20:9; 24:11–12; 28:9,13.
Proverbs on trust in God: 3:5–12; 14:26–27; 16:20; 18:10; 19:21; 21:31; 29:25–26; 30:5–9.
Proverbs on God's blessing: 10:22,27,29; 15:16.
Other proverbs of particular interest: 11:1; 17:3; 19:3; 20:12; 21:3; 28:5.

Life Questions: What are your plans for success? Is God's will the basis of your plans, or is it an afterthought?

I possess knowledge and discretion.
¹³To fear the LORD is to hate evil;
I hate pride and arrogance,
evil behavior and perverse speech.

8:13 The Fear of the Lord

The phrase "fear of the LORD" doesn't mean fright or terror. It means "a good relationship with God," based on reverence and respect for him and his commands. Here, for instance, the fear of the Lord means righteous living.

¹⁴Counsel and sound judgment are mine;
I have understanding and power.
¹⁵By me kings reign
and rulers make laws that are just;
¹⁶by me princes govern,
and all nobles who rule on earth.ᵃ
¹⁷I love those who love me,
and those who seek me find me.
¹⁸With me are riches and honor,
enduring wealth and prosperity.
¹⁹My fruit is better than fine gold;
what I yield surpasses choice silver.
²⁰I walk in the way of righteousness,
along the paths of justice,
²¹bestowing wealth on those who love me
and making their treasuries full.

²²"The LORD brought me forth as the first of his works,ᵇ, ᶜ
before his deeds of old;
²³I was appointedᵈ from eternity,
from the beginning, before the world began.
²⁴When there were no oceans, I was given birth,
when there were no springs abounding with water;
²⁵before the mountains were settled in place,
before the hills, I was given birth,
²⁶before he made the earth or its fields
or any of the dust of the world.
²⁷I was there when he set the heavens in place,
when he marked out the horizon on the face of the deep,
²⁸when he established the clouds above
and fixed securely the fountains of the deep,
²⁹when he gave the sea its boundary
so the waters would not overstep his command,
and when he marked out the foundations of the earth.
³⁰   Then I was the craftsman at his side.
I was filled with delight day after day,

rejoicing always in his presence,
³¹rejoicing in his whole world
and delighting in mankind.

³²"Now then, my sons, listen to me;
blessed are those who keep my ways.
³³Listen to my instruction and be wise;
do not ignore it.
³⁴Blessed is the man who listens to me,
watching daily at my doors,
waiting at my doorway.
³⁵For whoever finds me finds life
and receives favor from the LORD.
³⁶But whoever fails to find me harms himself;
all who hate me love death."

Invitations of Wisdom and of Folly

9 Wisdom has built her house;
she has hewn out its seven pillars.
²She has prepared her meat and mixed her wine;
she has also set her table.
³She has sent out her maids, and she calls
from the highest point of the city.
⁴"Let all who are simple come in here!"
she says to those who lack judgment.
⁵"Come, eat my food
and drink the wine I have mixed.
⁶Leave your simple ways and you will live;
walk in the way of understanding.

⁷"Whoever corrects a mocker invites insult;
whoever rebukes a wicked man incurs abuse.
⁸Do not rebuke a mocker or he will hate you;
rebuke a wise man and he will love you.
⁹Instruct a wise man and he will be wiser still;
teach a righteous man and he will add to his learning.

¹⁰"The fear of the LORD is the beginning of wisdom,
and knowledge of the Holy One is understanding.
¹¹For through me your days will be many,
and years will be added to your life.
¹²If you are wise, your wisdom will reward you;
if you are a mocker, you alone will suffer."

¹³The woman Folly is loud;
she is undisciplined and without knowledge.
¹⁴She sits at the door of her house,
on a seat at the highest point of the city,
¹⁵calling out to those who pass by,
who go straight on their way.
¹⁶"Let all who are simple come in here!"
she says to those who lack judgment.
¹⁷"Stolen water is sweet;

ᵃ16 Many Hebrew manuscripts and Septuagint; most Hebrew manuscripts *and nobles—all righteous rulers*   ᵇ22 Or *way*; or *dominion*   ᶜ22 Or *The LORD possessed me at the beginning of his work*; or *The LORD brought me forth at the beginning of his work*   ᵈ23 Or *fashioned*

food eaten in secret is delicious!"
¹⁸But little do they know that the dead are there,

that her guests are in the depths of the grave.ᵃ

Proverbs of Solomon

10 The proverbs of Solomon:

A wise son brings joy to his father,
but a foolish son grief to his mother.

²Ill-gotten treasures are of no value,
but righteousness delivers from death.

³The LORD does not let the righteous go hungry
but he thwarts the craving of the wicked.

⁴Lazy hands make a man poor,
but diligent hands bring wealth.

⁵He who gathers crops in summer is a wise son,
but he who sleeps during harvest is a disgraceful son.

⁶Blessings crown the head of the righteous,
but violence overwhelms the mouth of the wicked.ᵇ

⁷The memory of the righteous will be a blessing,
but the name of the wicked will rot.

⁸The wise in heart accept commands,
but a chattering fool comes to ruin.

⁹The man of integrity walks securely,
but he who takes crooked paths will be found out.

¹⁰He who winks maliciously causes grief,
and a chattering fool comes to ruin.

10:1 Hebrew Poetry

"Parallelism" is a technical term for the form of Hebrew poetry that repeats a thought in slightly different ways. "Synonymous parallelism" is found in Proverbs 15:30, "A cheerful look brings joy to the heart, and good news gives health to the bones." "Antithetical parallelism," in which a thought is followed by its opposite, is found in 14:30, "A heart at peace gives life to the body, but envy rots the bones."

In studying parallelism the trick is to compare each part with its pair in the other half of the proverb. For instance, in 14:30 "a heart at peace" pairs with its opposite, "envy," and "rots the bones" is the opposite of "gives life to the body." Sometimes these comparisons bare subtle shades of meaning.

¹¹The mouth of the righteous is a fountain of life,
but violence overwhelms the mouth of the wicked.

¹²Hatred stirs up dissension,
but love covers over all wrongs.

ᵃ18 Hebrew *Sheol* ᵇ6 Or *but the mouth of the wicked conceals violence*; also in verse 11

What Makes People Poor?
A clear-eyed view of wealth and poverty

The wealth of the rich is their fortified city, but poverty is the ruin of the poor.
10:15

POOR PEOPLE ARE LAZY," SAYS one person. Someone else claims the opposite: "They are poor because the rich control the system." People tend to oversimplify when they discuss wealth and poverty. Curiously, both sides may quote Proverbs to prove their point.

You have to read all of Proverbs to get its subtle view. It says people are poor for various reasons: because of laziness and drunkenness, but also because the rich oppress them. People get rich for various reasons too: because of hard work, because of the Lord's blessing, because they cheated.

Proverbs gives an evenhanded view of what money does for people. Wealth brings benefits, including eager friends, Proverbs says; but it also brings worries and troubles. Proverbs strongly urges the rich and powerful to be generous and fair to poor people. It remains remarkably clear-eyed about the tangled causes of poverty and about the dangers and benefits of wealth.

Proverbs on money: 10:4,15,22; 11:4,16,28; 13:8,18,22–23; 14:20,23,31; 15:16; 18:23; 19:1,4,17; 20:13; 21:5,17; 22:1–2,4,7,9,16,22–23; 23:5; 28:3,6,8,11,19,20,22,27; 29:7,14; 30:7–9.

Life Questions: Think of the richest and the poorest people you know. Have stereotypes about wealth and poverty affected your attitude toward them?

[13]Wisdom is found on the lips of the
discerning,
but a rod is for the back of him who lacks
judgment.

10:12 Love Is the Greatest

*If you think of love as restricted to the New
Testament, Proverbs will surprise you. Here
love is the all-purpose cure, covering all
wrongs. It is worth searching for. It should be
expressed openly.*

*Some of the proverbs on love are found in
the following passages: 3:3–4; 9:8; 10:12;
14:22; 15:17; 16:6; 17:9; 19:22; 20:6,28; 21:21;
27:5.*

[14]Wise men store up knowledge,
but the mouth of a fool invites ruin.

[15]The wealth of the rich is their fortified city,
but poverty is the ruin of the poor.

[16]The wages of the righteous bring them life,
but the income of the wicked brings them
punishment.

[17]He who heeds discipline shows the way to
life,
but whoever ignores correction leads
others astray.

[18]He who conceals his hatred has lying lips,
and whoever spreads slander is a fool.

[19]When words are many, sin is not absent,
but he who holds his tongue is wise.

[20]The tongue of the righteous is choice silver,
but the heart of the wicked is of little
value.

[21]The lips of the righteous nourish many,
but fools die for lack of judgment.

[22]The blessing of the LORD brings wealth,
and he adds no trouble to it.

[23]A fool finds pleasure in evil conduct,
but a man of understanding delights in
wisdom.

[24]What the wicked dreads will overtake him;
what the righteous desire will be granted.

[25]When the storm has swept by, the wicked
are gone,
but the righteous stand firm forever.

[26]As vinegar to the teeth and smoke to the
eyes,
so is a sluggard to those who send him.

[27]The fear of the LORD adds length to life,
but the years of the wicked are cut short.

[28]The prospect of the righteous is joy,
but the hopes of the wicked come to
nothing.

[29]The way of the LORD is a refuge for the
righteous,
but it is the ruin of those who do evil.

[30]The righteous will never be uprooted,
but the wicked will not remain in the
land.

[31]The mouth of the righteous brings forth
wisdom,
but a perverse tongue will be cut out.

[32]The lips of the righteous know what is
fitting,
but the mouth of the wicked only what is
perverse.

11 The LORD abhors dishonest scales,
but accurate weights are his delight.

[2]When pride comes, then comes disgrace,
but with humility comes wisdom.

[3]The integrity of the upright guides them,
but the unfaithful are destroyed by their
duplicity.

[4]Wealth is worthless in the day of wrath,
but righteousness delivers from death.

[5]The righteousness of the blameless makes a
straight way for them,
but the wicked are brought down by their
own wickedness.

[6]The righteousness of the upright delivers
them,
but the unfaithful are trapped by evil
desires.

[7]When a wicked man dies, his hope perishes;
all he expected from his power comes to
nothing.

[8]The righteous man is rescued from trouble,
and it comes on the wicked instead.

[9]With his mouth the godless destroys his
neighbor,
but through knowledge the righteous
escape.

[10]When the righteous prosper, the city rejoices;
when the wicked perish, there are shouts
of joy.

[11]Through the blessing of the upright a city is
exalted,
but by the mouth of the wicked it is
destroyed.

[12]A man who lacks judgment derides his
neighbor,

but a man of understanding holds his
tongue.

¹³A gossip betrays a confidence,
but a trustworthy man keeps a secret.

¹⁴For lack of guidance a nation falls,
but many advisers make victory sure.

¹⁵He who puts up security for another will
surely suffer,
but whoever refuses to strike hands in
pledge is safe.

¹⁶A kindhearted woman gains respect,
but ruthless men gain only wealth.

¹⁷A kind man benefits himself,
but a cruel man brings trouble on himself.

¹⁸The wicked man earns deceptive wages,
but he who sows righteousness reaps a
sure reward.

¹⁹The truly righteous man attains life,
but he who pursues evil goes to his death.

²⁰The LORD detests men of perverse heart
but he delights in those whose ways are
blameless.

²¹Be sure of this: The wicked will not go
unpunished,
but those who are righteous will go free.

²²Like a gold ring in a pig's snout
is a beautiful woman who shows no
discretion.

²³The desire of the righteous ends only in
good,
but the hope of the wicked only in wrath.

²⁴One man gives freely, yet gains even more;
another withholds unduly, but comes to
poverty.

²⁵A generous man will prosper;
he who refreshes others will himself be
refreshed.

²⁶People curse the man who hoards grain,
but blessing crowns him who is willing to
sell.

²⁷He who seeks good finds goodwill,
but evil comes to him who searches for it.

11:22 Skin-deep Beauty

*Throughout Proverbs, character is what counts.
When not matched by inward beauty, good
looks seem ridiculous, as this saying
humorously suggests.*

²⁸Whoever trusts in his riches will fall,
but the righteous will thrive like a green
leaf.

²⁹He who brings trouble on his family will
inherit only wind,
and the fool will be servant to the wise.

³⁰The fruit of the righteous is a tree of life,
and he who wins souls is wise.

³¹If the righteous receive their due on earth,
how much more the ungodly and the
sinner!

The Supreme Gift of Wisdom
First, learn to listen

> *He who walks with
> the wise grows wise,
> but a companion of
> fools suffers harm.
> 13:20*

PROVERBS JUDGES EVERY THOUGHT OR action by one stan-
dard: "Is this wise?" The word *wisdom* brings up pictures of gray-haired
old men muttering obscure philosophic maxims. But that is almost the
opposite of what Proverbs means by the word. Wisdom is above all practical
and down to earth. Young people as well as old can and should have it. Wisdom teaches you how to live. It combines understanding with discipline—the
kind of discipline an athlete needs in training. It also adds a healthy dose of good common sense—
except that common sense isn't, and never has been, common.

How do you become a wise person? You must first begin to listen. Wisdom is freely available to
those who will stop talking and start paying attention—to God and his Word, to parents, to wise counselors. Anybody can become wise, Proverbs says. Wisdom is not reserved for a brainy elite. But becoming wise requires self-discipline to study and humbly seek wisdom at every opportunity.

Proverbs on becoming a wise person: 2:1–6; 9:1–10; 10:1,5,8,14,19,23; 11:2; 12:18; 13:10,20; 14:8;
15:7,31; 16:23; 17:24; 18:15; 19:11,20; 20:1; 21:11,20,30; 23:4; 29:3,8,11,15; 30:5–6.

Life Questions: Think over the last two years of your life. To whom do you listen? Who has the greatest
influence on you?

12 Whoever loves discipline loves
knowledge,
but he who hates correction is stupid.

²A good man obtains favor from the LORD,
but the LORD condemns a crafty man.

³A man cannot be established through
wickedness,
but the righteous cannot be uprooted.

⁴A wife of noble character is her husband's
crown,
but a disgraceful wife is like decay in his
bones.

⁵The plans of the righteous are just,
but the advice of the wicked is deceitful.

⁶The words of the wicked lie in wait for
blood,
but the speech of the upright rescues
them.

⁷Wicked men are overthrown and are no
more,
but the house of the righteous stands firm.

⁸A man is praised according to his wisdom,
but men with warped minds are despised.

⁹Better to be a nobody and yet have a servant
than pretend to be somebody and have no
food.

¹⁰A righteous man cares for the needs of his
animal,
but the kindest acts of the wicked are
cruel.

¹¹He who works his land will have abundant
food,
but he who chases fantasies lacks
judgment.

¹²The wicked desire the plunder of evil men,
but the root of the righteous flourishes.

¹³An evil man is trapped by his sinful talk,
but a righteous man escapes trouble.

¹⁴From the fruit of his lips a man is filled with
good things
as surely as the work of his hands rewards
him.

¹⁵The way of a fool seems right to him,
but a wise man listens to advice.

¹⁶A fool shows his annoyance at once,
but a prudent man overlooks an insult.

¹⁷A truthful witness gives honest testimony,
but a false witness tells lies.

¹⁸Reckless words pierce like a sword,
but the tongue of the wise brings healing.

¹⁹Truthful lips endure forever,
but a lying tongue lasts only a moment.

²⁰There is deceit in the hearts of those who
plot evil,
but joy for those who promote peace.

²¹No harm befalls the righteous,
but the wicked have their fill of trouble.

²²The LORD detests lying lips,
but he delights in men who are truthful.

12:17 Deeper Meanings

*Some proverbs, disarmingly obvious at first
glance, offer deep truth when chewed on. For
instance, verse 17 seems to merely repeat the
obvious. But its underlying meaning is that a
person's character determines his or her
actions. You can reflect at length on what this
implies about why you do what you do.*

²³A prudent man keeps his knowledge to
himself,
but the heart of fools blurts out folly.

²⁴Diligent hands will rule,
but laziness ends in slave labor.

²⁵An anxious heart weighs a man down,
but a kind word cheers him up.

²⁶A righteous man is cautious in friendship,ᵃ
but the way of the wicked leads them
astray.

²⁷The lazy man does not roastᵇ his game,
but the diligent man prizes his
possessions.

²⁸In the way of righteousness there is life;
along that path is immortality.

13 A wise son heeds his father's instruction,
but a mocker does not listen to rebuke.

²From the fruit of his lips a man enjoys good
things,
but the unfaithful have a craving for
violence.

³He who guards his lips guards his life,
but he who speaks rashly will come to
ruin.

⁴The sluggard craves and gets nothing,
but the desires of the diligent are fully
satisfied.

⁵The righteous hate what is false,
but the wicked bring shame and disgrace.

ᵃ26 Or *man is a guide to his neighbor*   ᵇ27 The meaning of the Hebrew for this word is uncertain.

Clay Crosse

WoW 1997 participant Clay Crosse speaks candidly about how God's Word has pulled him through some tough times:

"On November 1st of 1993, my daughter Shelby was born prematurely. My wife Renna had developed a condition known as toxemia, and was forced to deliver eight weeks early. Shelby weighed in at a meager three pounds and two ounces.

"During the days surrounding the birth, Renna and I agonized over the possibility that Shelby might not pull through. After she was born, the nursing staff placed her in a special intensive care nursery for premature babies. We could visit our daughter in this nursery, but we weren't allowed to take her home with us until she reached a target weight of four pounds and eight ounces. Finally, on December 4th, 1993, we brought Shelby home. Renna and I looked on this occasion as the greatest Christmas gift we could ever receive.

"Throughout this trying time, I held Philippians 4:13 close to my heart. It says, 'I can do everything through him who gives me strength.' Notice that it doesn't say that I can do 'this thing' or maybe 'that thing.' It promises that we can do everything in Christ's power. I know that he was with Renna, Shelby and me through this experience, and that I can rely on him to strengthen me during all the difficult times of my life.

"Looking at Shelby now, three years later, I realize that God had his hand on her the whole time. She has grown into a beautiful little girl who continues to grow and learn and melt my heart daily."

Clay Crosse

Sierra

Ecclesiastes 4:12 says that "a cord of three strands is not quickly broken." Sierra, a trio of Texas natives, provide living proof of the truth of that verse. Their friendship is evident to their concertgoers, interviewers, and, in fact, anyone who comes into contact with them.

So is their commitment to producing the best Christian contemporary music that they possibly can. Their mission statement, the first thing to catch the eye when one opens their latest release, *Devotion*, is as follows:

"It is our desire to influence the believer and non-believer alike, with songs that we feel reflect a real walk with Jesus Christ. We do not want to candy-coat life, or the problems that we go through, but we want to let people know that God is the author of our lives and that he has a perfect plan for us and because of him, we can live a life filled with peace and joy.

"Day by day, we want to be vessels that he can mold and use in any way he sees fit. We are striving to be spiritually devoted, not only to you, the listener, but to each other, and, most importantly, to Jesus Christ our Savior."

Sierra

⁶Righteousness guards the man of integrity,
  but wickedness overthrows the sinner.

⁷One man pretends to be rich, yet has
    nothing;
  another pretends to be poor, yet has great
    wealth.

⁸A man's riches may ransom his life,
  but a poor man hears no threat.

⁹The light of the righteous shines brightly,
  but the lamp of the wicked is snuffed out.

¹⁰Pride only breeds quarrels,
  but wisdom is found in those who take
    advice.

¹¹Dishonest money dwindles away,
  but he who gathers money little by little
    makes it grow.

¹²Hope deferred makes the heart sick,
  but a longing fulfilled is a tree of life.

¹³He who scorns instruction will pay for it,
  but he who respects a command is
    rewarded.

¹⁴The teaching of the wise is a fountain of life,
  turning a man from the snares of death.

¹⁵Good understanding wins favor,
  but the way of the unfaithful is hard.ᵃ

¹⁶Every prudent man acts out of knowledge,
  but a fool exposes his folly.

¹⁷A wicked messenger falls into trouble,
  but a trustworthy envoy brings healing.

¹⁸He who ignores discipline comes to poverty
    and shame,
  but whoever heeds correction is honored.

¹⁹A longing fulfilled is sweet to the soul,
  but fools detest turning from evil.

²⁰He who walks with the wise grows wise,
  but a companion of fools suffers harm.

²¹Misfortune pursues the sinner,
  but prosperity is the reward of the
    righteous.

²²A good man leaves an inheritance for his
    children's children,
  but a sinner's wealth is stored up for the
    righteous.

²³A poor man's field may produce abundant
    food,
  but injustice sweeps it away.

²⁴He who spares the rod hates his son,
  but he who loves him is careful to
    discipline him.

²⁵The righteous eat to their hearts' content,
  but the stomach of the wicked goes
    hungry.

14 The wise woman builds her house,
  but with her own hands the foolish one
    tears hers down.

²He whose walk is upright fears the LORD,
  but he whose ways are devious despises
    him.

³A fool's talk brings a rod to his back,
  but the lips of the wise protect them.

ᵃ15 Or *unfaithful does not endure*

A Matter of Life and Death
More than mere survival

PROVERBS FREQUENTLY TALKS ABOUT LIFE and death. Wise living, it says, tends to make you live longer, while foolish living will push you into an early grave.

> There is a way that seems right to a man, but in the end it leads to death.
> 14:12

If you take this observation at face value, you'll have a problem: Plenty of people who live foolishly survive into old age. But the concept of life and death in Proverbs includes much more than physical survival. By life, Proverbs means "real living" full of peace and joy and wisdom. By death, it means spiritual as well as physical decay. A person who misses the way of wisdom may be as good as dead, even though he or she is still walking around.

Proverbs on "real living": 3:18,21–22; 4:23; 8:34–36; 10:11,16; 12:28; 13:12; 14:27,30; 15:4,27; 18:21; 19:23; 21:21; 28:16.

Proverbs on "real dying": 2:16–18; 5:3–6,22–23; 10:21; 14:12,32; 15:10; 19:16; 21:25; 27:20.

Life Questions: Can you remember a specific experience that represents, for you, "real living"? How about "real dying"?

⁴Where there are no oxen, the manger is
empty,
but from the strength of an ox comes an
abundant harvest.

⁵A truthful witness does not deceive,
but a false witness pours out lies.

⁶The mocker seeks wisdom and finds none,
but knowledge comes easily to the
discerning.

⁷Stay away from a foolish man,
for you will not find knowledge on his
lips.

⁸The wisdom of the prudent is to give
thought to their ways,
but the folly of fools is deception.

⁹Fools mock at making amends for sin,
but goodwill is found among the upright.

¹⁰Each heart knows its own bitterness,
and no one else can share its joy.

¹¹The house of the wicked will be destroyed,
but the tent of the upright will flourish.

¹²There is a way that seems right to a man,
but in the end it leads to death.

14:12 Be Careful

*Proverbs offers common sense, but doesn't
encourage simply trusting your own sense.
Choices that seem perfectly right may end up
destroying you. That is precisely why people
need to cultivate wisdom: What looks good
often isn't.*

¹³Even in laughter the heart may ache,
and joy may end in grief.

¹⁴The faithless will be fully repaid for their
ways,
and the good man rewarded for his.

¹⁵A simple man believes anything,
but a prudent man gives thought to his
steps.

¹⁶A wise man fears the Lord and shuns evil,
but a fool is hotheaded and reckless.

¹⁷A quick-tempered man does foolish things,
and a crafty man is hated.

¹⁸The simple inherit folly,
but the prudent are crowned with
knowledge.

¹⁹Evil men will bow down in the presence of
the good,
and the wicked at the gates of the
righteous.

²⁰The poor are shunned even by their
neighbors,
but the rich have many friends.

²¹He who despises his neighbor sins,

14:20 Lucky Rich

*Rich people have many friends, whereas the
poor often get ignored. That's the way life is.
But, according to the next proverb (verse 21),
life isn't meant to be "the way it is." Verse 31
goes on to show God himself closely involved
in the way we treat poor people.*

but blessed is he who is kind to the
needy.

²²Do not those who plot evil go astray?
But those who plan what is good find*ᵃ*
love and faithfulness.

²³All hard work brings a profit,
but mere talk leads only to poverty.

²⁴The wealth of the wise is their crown,
but the folly of fools yields folly.

²⁵A truthful witness saves lives,
but a false witness is deceitful.

²⁶He who fears the Lord has a secure fortress,
and for his children it will be a refuge.

²⁷The fear of the Lord is a fountain of life,
turning a man from the snares of death.

²⁸A large population is a king's glory,
but without subjects a prince is ruined.

²⁹A patient man has great understanding,
but a quick-tempered man displays folly.

³⁰A heart at peace gives life to the body,
but envy rots the bones.

³¹He who oppresses the poor shows contempt
for their Maker,
but whoever is kind to the needy honors
God.

³²When calamity comes, the wicked are
brought down,
but even in death the righteous have a
refuge.

³³Wisdom reposes in the heart of the
discerning
and even among fools she lets herself be
known.*ᵇ*

ᵃ22 Or show   ᵇ33 Hebrew; Septuagint and Syriac / but in the heart of fools she is not known

³⁴Righteousness exalts a nation,
  but sin is a disgrace to any people.

³⁵A king delights in a wise servant,
  but a shameful servant incurs his wrath.

15

A gentle answer turns away wrath,
  but a harsh word stirs up anger.

²The tongue of the wise commends
    knowledge,
  but the mouth of the fool gushes folly.

³The eyes of the LORD are everywhere,
  keeping watch on the wicked and the
    good.

⁴The tongue that brings healing is a tree of
    life,
  but a deceitful tongue crushes the spirit.

⁵A fool spurns his father's discipline,
  but whoever heeds correction shows
    prudence.

⁶The house of the righteous contains great
    treasure,
  but the income of the wicked brings them
    trouble.

⁷The lips of the wise spread knowledge;
  not so the hearts of fools.

⁸The LORD detests the sacrifice of the wicked,
  but the prayer of the upright pleases him.

⁹The LORD detests the way of the wicked
  but he loves those who pursue
    righteousness.

¹⁰Stern discipline awaits him who leaves the
    path;
  he who hates correction will die.

¹¹Death and Destruction[a] lie open before the
    LORD—
  how much more the hearts of men!

¹²A mocker resents correction;
  he will not consult the wise.

¹³A happy heart makes the face cheerful,
  but heartache crushes the spirit.

¹⁴The discerning heart seeks knowledge,
  but the mouth of a fool feeds on folly.

¹⁵All the days of the oppressed are wretched,
  but the cheerful heart has a continual
    feast.

¹⁶Better a little with the fear of the LORD
  than great wealth with turmoil.

¹⁷Better a meal of vegetables where there is
    love
  than a fattened calf with hatred.

¹⁸A hot-tempered man stirs up dissension,
  but a patient man calms a quarrel.

¹⁹The way of the sluggard is blocked with
    thorns,
  but the path of the upright is a highway.

²⁰A wise son brings joy to his father,
  but a foolish man despises his mother.

²¹Folly delights a man who lacks judgment,
  but a man of understanding keeps a
    straight course.

²²Plans fail for lack of counsel,
  but with many advisers they succeed.

²³A man finds joy in giving an apt reply—
  and how good is a timely word!

²⁴The path of life leads upward for the wise
  to keep him from going down to the
    grave.[b]

²⁵The LORD tears down the proud man's house
  but he keeps the widow's boundaries
    intact.

15:25 Poor and Helpless

In Old Testament society the most helpless person was the widow. With no one to protect her, she could only watch as her late husband's land was grabbed by bullying neighbors. But a widow was never completely helpless. The Lord was on her side. In the final analysis her condition was more secure than that of her proud, rich neighbor.

²⁶The LORD detests the thoughts of the wicked,
  but those of the pure are pleasing to him.

²⁷A greedy man brings trouble to his family,
  but he who hates bribes will live.

²⁸The heart of the righteous weighs its
    answers,
  but the mouth of the wicked gushes evil.

²⁹The LORD is far from the wicked
  but he hears the prayer of the righteous.

³⁰A cheerful look brings joy to the heart,
  and good news gives health to the bones.

³¹He who listens to a life-giving rebuke
  will be at home among the wise.

³²He who ignores discipline despises himself,
  but whoever heeds correction gains
    understanding.

³³The fear of the LORD teaches a man wisdom,[c]
  and humility comes before honor.

---

[a]11 Hebrew *Sheol and Abaddon*   [b]24 Hebrew *Sheol*   [c]33 Or *Wisdom teaches the fear of the LORD*

16 To man belong the plans of the heart,
but from the LORD comes the reply of
the tongue.

[2]All a man's ways seem innocent to him,
but motives are weighed by the LORD.

[3]Commit to the LORD whatever you do,
and your plans will succeed.

[4]The LORD works out everything for his own
ends—
even the wicked for a day of disaster.

[5]The LORD detests all the proud of heart.
Be sure of this: They will not go
unpunished.

[6]Through love and faithfulness sin is atoned
for;
through the fear of the LORD a man avoids
evil.

[7]When a man's ways are pleasing to the
LORD,
he makes even his enemies live at peace
with him.

[8]Better a little with righteousness
than much gain with injustice.

[9]In his heart a man plans his course,
but the LORD determines his steps.

[10]The lips of a king speak as an oracle,
and his mouth should not betray justice.

[a]21 Or words make a man persuasive

[11]Honest scales and balances are from the
LORD;
all the weights in the bag are of his
making.

[12]Kings detest wrongdoing,
for a throne is established through
righteousness.

[13]Kings take pleasure in honest lips;
they value a man who speaks the truth.

[14]A king's wrath is a messenger of death,
but a wise man will appease it.

[15]When a king's face brightens, it means life;
his favor is like a rain cloud in spring.

[16]How much better to get wisdom than gold,
to choose understanding rather than
silver!

[17]The highway of the upright avoids evil;
he who guards his way guards his life.

[18]Pride goes before destruction,
a haughty spirit before a fall.

[19]Better to be lowly in spirit and among the
oppressed
than to share plunder with the proud.

[20]Whoever gives heed to instruction prospers,
and blessed is he who trusts in the LORD.

[21]The wise in heart are called discerning,
and pleasant words promote instruction.[a]

Verbal Dynamite
Even truthful words can damage other people

> A perverse man stirs
> up dissension, and a
> gossip separates
> close friends. 16:28

WHAT COULD BE WRONG WITH just talking, as long as you
don't actually lie? Proverbs sees plenty of danger. Words are dynamite;
they can destroy people. They should be carefully weighed before they are
spoken. Even truthful words can damage. Yet they can also save a friend
from going wrong. Proverbs speaks strongly about both the danger of gossip and the good done
when someone justly rebukes his or her friend.

"The tongue has the power of life and death," Proverbs 18:21 says, "and those who love it will eat
its fruit." Proverbs teaches the skill of speaking so as to give life.

Proverbs on the importance of words: 10:11,20; 12:14; 15:4; 17:10; 18:21; 25:11.

Proverbs on the wrong way to speak: 6:16–19; 11:9,12–13; 12:18; 13:3; 16:27–28; 18:8,13; 26:23–28;
29:5.

Proverbs on the right way to speak: 10:14,21,32; 12:25; 15:1,23,28; 16:13,23–24; 17:27–28; 25:12,15;
27:5–6; 28:23.

Proverbs on the dangers of words: 10:19; 14:23.

Life Questions: Have you said anything recently that you wish you could take back? What are the most
life-giving words you've spoken lately?

²²Understanding is a fountain of life to those
who have it,
but folly brings punishment to fools.

²³A wise man's heart guides his mouth,
and his lips promote instruction.ᵃ

²⁴Pleasant words are a honeycomb,
sweet to the soul and healing to the
bones.

²⁵There is a way that seems right to a man,
but in the end it leads to death.

²⁶The laborer's appetite works for him;
his hunger drives him on.

²⁷A scoundrel plots evil,
and his speech is like a scorching fire.

²⁸A perverse man stirs up dissension,
and a gossip separates close friends.

²⁹A violent man entices his neighbor
and leads him down a path that is not
good.

³⁰He who winks with his eye is plotting
perversity;
he who purses his lips is bent on evil.

³¹Gray hair is a crown of splendor;
it is attained by a righteous life.

³²Better a patient man than a warrior,
a man who controls his temper than one
who takes a city.

³³The lot is cast into the lap,
but its every decision is from the LORD.

17 Better a dry crust with peace and quiet
than a house full of feasting,ᵇ with
strife.

²A wise servant will rule over a disgraceful
son,
and will share the inheritance as one of
the brothers.

³The crucible for silver and the furnace for
gold,
but the LORD tests the heart.

⁴A wicked man listens to evil lips;
a liar pays attention to a malicious tongue.

⁵He who mocks the poor shows contempt for
their Maker;
whoever gloats over disaster will not go
unpunished.

⁶Children's children are a crown to the aged,
and parents are the pride of their
children.

⁷Arrogantᶜ lips are unsuited to a fool—
how much worse lying lips to a ruler!

⁸A bribe is a charm to the one who gives it;
wherever he turns, he succeeds.

17:8 Bribery Works Wonders!

*Proverbs is utterly realistic about the hard facts
of life. One is that bribery works. A complete
education ought to include that fact! But does
that make bribery right? No—just a few verses
later (verse 23), Proverbs condemns bribery.*

⁹He who covers over an offense promotes
love,
but whoever repeats the matter separates
close friends.

¹⁰A rebuke impresses a man of discernment
more than a hundred lashes a fool.

¹¹An evil man is bent only on rebellion;
a merciless official will be sent against
him.

¹²Better to meet a bear robbed of her cubs
than a fool in his folly.

¹³If a man pays back evil for good,
evil will never leave his house.

¹⁴Starting a quarrel is like breaching a dam;
so drop the matter before a dispute breaks
out.

¹⁵Acquitting the guilty and condemning the
innocent—
the LORD detests them both.

¹⁶Of what use is money in the hand of a fool,
since he has no desire to get wisdom?

¹⁷A friend loves at all times,
and a brother is born for adversity.

¹⁸A man lacking in judgment strikes hands in
pledge
and puts up security for his neighbor.

¹⁹He who loves a quarrel loves sin;
he who builds a high gate invites
destruction.

²⁰A man of perverse heart does not prosper;
he whose tongue is deceitful falls into
trouble.

²¹To have a fool for a son brings grief;
there is no joy for the father of a fool.

²²A cheerful heart is good medicine,
but a crushed spirit dries up the bones.

ᵃ23 Or *mouth / and makes his lips persuasive*   ᵇ1 Hebrew *sacrifices*   ᶜ7 Or *Eloquent*

²³A wicked man accepts a bribe in secret
   to pervert the course of justice.

²⁴A discerning man keeps wisdom in view,
   but a fool's eyes wander to the ends of the
   earth.

17:17 How to Be a Good Friend

*The Old Testament puts great emphasis on
close family relationships. Surprisingly,
Proverbs rates a good friend even higher, for
he or she "sticks closer than a brother" (18:24).
Fair-weather friends are common (14:20), and
the wrong kind of companions will bring you
trouble. But a true friend loves you at all times,
even when things are bad.*

*Some key proverbs on being a good friend
and neighbor can be found in the following
passages: 3:27–28; 11:12; 12:26; 17:9,17;
18:24; 22:24–25; 25:20; 26:18–19;
27:6,9–10,14,17; 28:23; 29:5.*

---

²⁵A foolish son brings grief to his father
   and bitterness to the one who bore him.

²⁶It is not good to punish an innocent man,
   or to flog officials for their integrity.

²⁷A man of knowledge uses words with
      restraint,
   and a man of understanding is
      even-tempered.

²⁸Even a fool is thought wise if he keeps silent,
   and discerning if he holds his tongue.

18 An unfriendly man pursues selfish ends;
   he defies all sound judgment.

²A fool finds no pleasure in understanding
   but delights in airing his own opinions.

³When wickedness comes, so does contempt,
   and with shame comes disgrace.

⁴The words of a man's mouth are deep
      waters,
   but the fountain of wisdom is a bubbling
      brook.

⁵It is not good to be partial to the wicked
   or to deprive the innocent of justice.

⁶A fool's lips bring him strife,
   and his mouth invites a beating.

⁷A fool's mouth is his undoing,
   and his lips are a snare to his soul.

⁸The words of a gossip are like choice
      morsels;
   they go down to a man's inmost parts.

⁹One who is slack in his work
   is brother to one who destroys.

¹⁰The name of the LORD is a strong tower;
   the righteous run to it and are safe.

¹¹The wealth of the rich is their fortified city;
   they imagine it an unscalable wall.

¹²Before his downfall a man's heart is proud,
   but humility comes before honor.

¹³He who answers before listening—
   that is his folly and his shame.

¹⁴A man's spirit sustains him in sickness,
   but a crushed spirit who can bear?

¹⁵The heart of the discerning acquires
      knowledge;
   the ears of the wise seek it out.

¹⁶A gift opens the way for the giver
   and ushers him into the presence of the
      great.

¹⁷The first to present his case seems right,
   till another comes forward and questions
      him.

¹⁸Casting the lot settles disputes
   and keeps strong opponents apart.

¹⁹An offended brother is more unyielding than
      a fortified city,
   and disputes are like the barred gates of a
      citadel.

²⁰From the fruit of his mouth a man's
      stomach is filled;
   with the harvest from his lips he is
      satisfied.

²¹The tongue has the power of life and death,
   and those who love it will eat its fruit.

²²He who finds a wife finds what is good
   and receives favor from the LORD.

²³A poor man pleads for mercy,
   but a rich man answers harshly.

²⁴A man of many companions may come to
      ruin,
   but there is a friend who sticks closer than
      a brother.

19 Better a poor man whose walk is
      blameless
   than a fool whose lips are perverse.

²It is not good to have zeal without
      knowledge,
   nor to be hasty and miss the way.

³A man's own folly ruins his life,
   yet his heart rages against the LORD.

⁴Wealth brings many friends,
   but a poor man's friend deserts him.

⁵A false witness will not go unpunished,
   and he who pours out lies will not go free.

⁶Many curry favor with a ruler,
and everyone is the friend of a man who
gives gifts.

⁷A poor man is shunned by all his relatives—
how much more do his friends avoid him!
Though he pursues them with pleading,
they are nowhere to be found.ᵃ

⁸He who gets wisdom loves his own soul;
he who cherishes understanding prospers.

⁹A false witness will not go unpunished,
and he who pours out lies will perish.

¹⁰It is not fitting for a fool to live in luxury—
how much worse for a slave to rule over
princes!

¹¹A man's wisdom gives him patience;
it is to his glory to overlook an offense.

¹²A king's rage is like the roar of a lion,
but his favor is like dew on the grass.

¹³A foolish son is his father's ruin,
and a quarrelsome wife is like a constant
dripping.

¹⁴Houses and wealth are inherited from
parents,
but a prudent wife is from the LORD.

¹⁵Laziness brings on deep sleep,
and the shiftless man goes hungry.

¹⁶He who obeys instructions guards his life,
but he who is contemptuous of his ways
will die.

¹⁷He who is kind to the poor lends to the
LORD,
and he will reward him for what he has
done.

¹⁸Discipline your son, for in that there is hope;
do not be a willing party to his death.

¹⁹A hot-tempered man must pay the penalty;
if you rescue him, you will have to do it
again.

²⁰Listen to advice and accept instruction,
and in the end you will be wise.

²¹Many are the plans in a man's heart,
but it is the LORD's purpose that prevails.

²²What a man desires is unfailing loveᵇ;
better to be poor than a liar.

²³The fear of the LORD leads to life:
Then one rests content, untouched by
trouble.

²⁴The sluggard buries his hand in the dish;

he will not even bring it back to his
mouth!

²⁵Flog a mocker, and the simple will learn
prudence;
rebuke a discerning man, and he will gain
knowledge.

²⁶He who robs his father and drives out his
mother
is a son who brings shame and disgrace.

²⁷Stop listening to instruction, my son,
and you will stray from the words of
knowledge.

²⁸A corrupt witness mocks at justice,
and the mouth of the wicked gulps down
evil.

²⁹Penalties are prepared for mockers,
and beatings for the backs of fools.

20 Wine is a mocker and beer a brawler;
whoever is led astray by them is not
wise.

²A king's wrath is like the roar of a lion;
he who angers him forfeits his life.

³It is to a man's honor to avoid strife,
but every fool is quick to quarrel.

⁴A sluggard does not plow in season;
so at harvest time he looks but finds
nothing.

⁵The purposes of a man's heart are deep
waters,
but a man of understanding draws them
out.

⁶Many a man claims to have unfailing love,
but a faithful man who can find?

⁷The righteous man leads a blameless life;
blessed are his children after him.

⁸When a king sits on his throne to judge,
he winnows out all evil with his eyes.

⁹Who can say, "I have kept my heart pure;
I am clean and without sin"?

¹⁰Differing weights and differing measures—
the LORD detests them both.

¹¹Even a child is known by his actions,
by whether his conduct is pure and right.

¹²Ears that hear and eyes that see—
the LORD has made them both.

¹³Do not love sleep or you will grow poor;
stay awake and you will have food to
spare.

¹⁴"It's no good, it's no good!" says the buyer;

ᵃ7 The meaning of the Hebrew for this sentence is uncertain.   ᵇ22 Or A man's greed is his shame

then off he goes and boasts about his
purchase.

¹⁵Gold there is, and rubies in abundance,
but lips that speak knowledge are a rare
jewel.

¹⁶Take the garment of one who puts up
security for a stranger;
hold it in pledge if he does it for a
wayward woman.

¹⁷Food gained by fraud tastes sweet to a man,
but he ends up with a mouth full of
gravel.

¹⁸Make plans by seeking advice;
if you wage war, obtain guidance.

¹⁹A gossip betrays a confidence;
so avoid a man who talks too much.

²⁰If a man curses his father or mother,
his lamp will be snuffed out in pitch
darkness.

²¹An inheritance quickly gained at the
beginning
will not be blessed at the end.

²²Do not say, "I'll pay you back for this
wrong!"
Wait for the LORD, and he will deliver
you.

²³The LORD detests differing weights,
and dishonest scales do not please him.

²⁴A man's steps are directed by the LORD.

a27 Or *The spirit of man is the LORD's lamp*

How then can anyone understand his own
way?

²⁵It is a trap for a man to dedicate something
rashly
and only later to consider his vows.

²⁶A wise king winnows out the wicked;
he drives the threshing wheel over them.

²⁷The lamp of the LORD searches the spirit of a
man*a*;
it searches out his inmost being.

²⁸Love and faithfulness keep a king safe;
through love his throne is made secure.

²⁹The glory of young men is their strength,
gray hair the splendor of the old.

³⁰Blows and wounds cleanse away evil,
and beatings purge the inmost being.

21 The king's heart is in the hand of the
LORD;
he directs it like a watercourse wherever
he pleases.

²All a man's ways seem right to him,
but the LORD weighs the heart.

³To do what is right and just
is more acceptable to the LORD than
sacrifice.

⁴Haughty eyes and a proud heart,
the lamp of the wicked, are sin!

Whom Should You Marry?
A good partner can make or break your life

IN ANCIENT TIMES WOMEN WERE often viewed as men's
property, good for bearing children and not much more. Proverbs,
addressed to young men approaching the age of marriage, takes a different view. It holds up marriage as a crucial choice, to be made with great
care.

> Better to live on a
> corner of the roof
> than share a house
> with a quarrelsome
> wife. 21:9

A good wife (or husband, we can assume) will make or break her partner's
life. Her duties lay the foundation for her family's welfare (14:1; 31:10–31). She shares with her husband the most significant task of teaching their children the way of wisdom (1:8–9; 6:20). Therefore,
her character matters far more than her physical beauty.

Not that Proverbs ignores the physical side of love. It urges marriage partners to rejoice in their
love, to be captivated by it (5:18–19). It warns young people against sexual sin precisely because this
wastes sexuality on unsatisfying, unloving relationships. Sex ought to be saved for the long-lasting,
productive joy of marriage.

Proverbs on sexual sin: 2:16–19; 5:1–23; 6:20–35; 7:6–27; 23:26–28.
Proverbs on marriage: 5:15–19; 12:4; 14:1; 18:22; 19:13–14; 21:9,19; 27:15–16; 31:10–31.

Life Questions: What do you look for in a mate? How does your list compare with Proverbs's rating of
attributes such as physical attractiveness?

⁵The plans of the diligent lead to profit
   as surely as haste leads to poverty.

⁶A fortune made by a lying tongue
   is a fleeting vapor and a deadly snare.ᵃ

⁷The violence of the wicked will drag them
      away,
   for they refuse to do what is right.

⁸The way of the guilty is devious,
   but the conduct of the innocent is upright.

⁹Better to live on a corner of the roof
   than share a house with a quarrelsome
      wife.

¹⁰The wicked man craves evil;
   his neighbor gets no mercy from him.

¹¹When a mocker is punished, the simple gain
      wisdom;
   when a wise man is instructed, he gets
      knowledge.

21:11 Learning the Easy Way

*"The simple"—those who live without thinking—
are rarely persuaded to change, because they
don't listen. One lesson may get through to
them, though: seeing a troublemaker—the
"mocker"—get punished. Wise people learn in a
much less painful way. When told something,
they pay attention.*

¹²The Righteous Oneᵇ takes note of the house
      of the wicked
   and brings the wicked to ruin.

¹³If a man shuts his ears to the cry of the
      poor,
   he too will cry out and not be answered.

¹⁴A gift given in secret soothes anger,
   and a bribe concealed in the cloak pacifies
      great wrath.

¹⁵When justice is done, it brings joy to the
      righteous
   but terror to evildoers.

¹⁶A man who strays from the path of
      understanding
   comes to rest in the company of the dead.

¹⁷He who loves pleasure will become poor;
   whoever loves wine and oil will never be
      rich.

¹⁸The wicked become a ransom for the
      righteous,
   and the unfaithful for the upright.

¹⁹Better to live in a desert
   than with a quarrelsome and ill-tempered
      wife.

²⁰In the house of the wise are stores of choice
      food and oil,
   but a foolish man devours all he has.

²¹He who pursues righteousness and love
   finds life, prosperityᶜ and honor.

²²A wise man attacks the city of the mighty
   and pulls down the stronghold in which
      they trust.

²³He who guards his mouth and his tongue
   keeps himself from calamity.

²⁴The proud and arrogant man—"Mocker" is
      his name;
   he behaves with overweening pride.

²⁵The sluggard's craving will be the death of
      him,
   because his hands refuse to work.

²⁶All day long he craves for more,
   but the righteous give without sparing.

²⁷The sacrifice of the wicked is detestable—
   how much more so when brought with
      evil intent!

²⁸A false witness will perish,
   and whoever listens to him will be
      destroyed forever.ᵈ

²⁹A wicked man puts up a bold front,
   but an upright man gives thought to his
      ways.

³⁰There is no wisdom, no insight, no plan
   that can succeed against the LORD.

³¹The horse is made ready for the day of
      battle,
   but victory rests with the LORD.

22 A good name is more desirable than
   great riches;
   to be esteemed is better than silver or
      gold.

²Rich and poor have this in common:
   The LORD is the Maker of them all.

³A prudent man sees danger and takes refuge,
   but the simple keep going and suffer for
      it.

⁴Humility and the fear of the LORD
   bring wealth and honor and life.

⁵In the paths of the wicked lie thorns and
      snares,

ᵃ6 Some Hebrew manuscripts, Septuagint and Vulgate; most Hebrew manuscripts *vapor for those who seek death*
ᵇ12 Or *The righteous man*   ᶜ21 Or *righteousness*   ᵈ28 Or / *but the words of an obedient man will live on*

but he who guards his soul stays far from
them.

⁶Train*a* a child in the way he should go,
and when he is old he will not turn
from it.

22:6 Good Parenting

*An individual proverb shouldn't be read as
either an invariable rule or a binding promise
from God. Proverbs 10:4 generalizes truthfully,
"diligent hands bring wealth," but you would
not have to look too far to find an exception to
the rule. Verse 6, a famous proverb, reinforces
the importance of early training in forming a
person's lifelong character. But you can find
individuals who, though well brought up,
choose to reject their training. Proverbs studies
life the way it normally works. The general rule
is this: Good parents raise good children.*

---

⁷The rich rule over the poor,
and the borrower is servant to the lender.

⁸He who sows wickedness reaps trouble,
and the rod of his fury will be destroyed.

⁹A generous man will himself be blessed,
for he shares his food with the poor.

¹⁰Drive out the mocker, and out goes strife;
quarrels and insults are ended.

¹¹He who loves a pure heart and whose speech
is gracious
will have the king for his friend.

¹²The eyes of the LORD keep watch over
knowledge,
but he frustrates the words of the
unfaithful.

¹³The sluggard says, "There is a lion outside!"
or, "I will be murdered in the streets!"

¹⁴The mouth of an adulteress is a deep pit;
he who is under the LORD's wrath will fall
into it.

¹⁵Folly is bound up in the heart of a child,
but the rod of discipline will drive it far
from him.

¹⁶He who oppresses the poor to increase his
wealth
and he who gives gifts to the rich—both
come to poverty.

Sayings of the Wise

¹⁷Pay attention and listen to the sayings of the
wise;
apply your heart to what I teach,
¹⁸for it is pleasing when you keep them in
your heart
and have all of them ready on your lips.
¹⁹So that your trust may be in the LORD,
I teach you today, even you.
²⁰Have I not written thirty*b* sayings for you,
sayings of counsel and knowledge,
²¹teaching you true and reliable words,
so that you can give sound answers
to him who sent you?

a6 Or Start   b20 Or not formerly written; or not written excellent

---

How to Raise Children
Family members should be allies, not adversaries

"SPARE THE ROD AND SPOIL the child" may be the most
famous of the Bible's proverbs. Proverbs calls punishment a form of love
and says that parents who won't discipline their children are in danger of
ruining them (29:15). But that much-quoted maxim is only a small part of
what Proverbs has to offer on the subject of bringing up children.

The overwhelming emphasis of Proverbs is on verbal encouragement and
teaching. The whole book is framed as a father's words to his son, teaching him those "facts of life"
that have nothing to do with biology. Again and again he pleads, "Listen, my son." Mother has equally
important words (1:8; 6:20). The parent-child conversation is a warm one, and Proverbs 17:6 bears out
what the whole book implies: Parents and children are not meant to be adversaries, but allies in life
who are proud of each other.

Proverbs on parent-child relationships: 3:11–12; 10:1,5; 13:1,24; 14:26; 15:20; 17:6,21; 19:18,26–27;
20:20; 22:6,15; 23:13–16,22–25; 27:11; 29:15,17; 31:28.

> *Train a child in the
> way he should go,
> and when he is old
> he will not turn
> from it. 22:6*

Life Questions: In your upbringing, which had the most effect: punishment and discipline, or verbal
instruction and encouragement?

²²Do not exploit the poor because they are
poor
and do not crush the needy in court,
²³for the LORD will take up their case
and will plunder those who plunder them.

²⁴Do not make friends with a hot-tempered
man,
do not associate with one easily angered,
²⁵or you may learn his ways
and get yourself ensnared.

²⁶Do not be a man who strikes hands in
pledge
or puts up security for debts;
²⁷if you lack the means to pay,
your very bed will be snatched from
under you.

²⁸Do not move an ancient boundary stone
set up by your forefathers.

²⁹Do you see a man skilled in his work?
He will serve before kings;
he will not serve before obscure men.

23 When you sit to dine with a ruler,
note well what*a* is before you,
²and put a knife to your throat
if you are given to gluttony.
³Do not crave his delicacies,
for that food is deceptive.

⁴Do not wear yourself out to get rich;
have the wisdom to show restraint.
⁵Cast but a glance at riches, and they are
gone,
for they will surely sprout wings
and fly off to the sky like an eagle.

⁶Do not eat the food of a stingy man,
do not crave his delicacies;
⁷for he is the kind of man
who is always thinking about the cost.*b*
"Eat and drink," he says to you,
but his heart is not with you.
⁸You will vomit up the little you have eaten
and will have wasted your compliments.

⁹Do not speak to a fool,
for he will scorn the wisdom of your
words.

¹⁰Do not move an ancient boundary stone
or encroach on the fields of the fatherless,
¹¹for their Defender is strong;
he will take up their case against you.

¹²Apply your heart to instruction
and your ears to words of knowledge.

¹³Do not withhold discipline from a child;

if you punish him with the rod, he will
not die.
¹⁴Punish him with the rod
and save his soul from death.*c*

¹⁵My son, if your heart is wise,
then my heart will be glad;
¹⁶my inmost being will rejoice
when your lips speak what is right.

¹⁷Do not let your heart envy sinners,
but always be zealous for the fear of the
LORD.
¹⁸There is surely a future hope for you,
and your hope will not be cut off.

¹⁹Listen, my son, and be wise,
and keep your heart on the right path.
²⁰Do not join those who drink too much wine
or gorge themselves on meat,
²¹for drunkards and gluttons become poor,
and drowsiness clothes them in rags.

²²Listen to your father, who gave you life,
and do not despise your mother when she
is old.
²³Buy the truth and do not sell it;
get wisdom, discipline and understanding.
²⁴The father of a righteous man has great joy;
he who has a wise son delights in him.
²⁵May your father and mother be glad;
may she who gave you birth rejoice!

²⁶My son, give me your heart
and let your eyes keep to my ways,
²⁷for a prostitute is a deep pit
and a wayward wife is a narrow well.
²⁸Like a bandit she lies in wait,
and multiplies the unfaithful among men.

²⁹Who has woe? Who has sorrow?
Who has strife? Who has complaints?
Who has needless bruises? Who has
bloodshot eyes?
³⁰Those who linger over wine,
who go to sample bowls of mixed wine.
³¹Do not gaze at wine when it is red,
when it sparkles in the cup,
when it goes down smoothly!
³²In the end it bites like a snake
and poisons like a viper.
³³Your eyes will see strange sights
and your mind imagine confusing things.
³⁴You will be like one sleeping on the high
seas,
lying on top of the rigging.
³⁵"They hit me," you will say, "but I'm not
hurt!
They beat me, but I don't feel it!
When will I wake up
so I can find another drink?"

a1 Or *who*   *b7* Or *for as he thinks within himself, / so he is; or for as he puts on a feast, / so he is*
c14 Hebrew *Sheol*

24

Do not envy wicked men,
do not desire their company;
²for their hearts plot violence,
and their lips talk about making trouble.

23:35 The Dangers of Wine

Wine was common in biblical times, but its dangers were recognized. Proverbs contains some of the Bible's strongest warnings against overindulgence: 20:1; 21:17; 23:20–21, 30–35; 31:4–7.

---

³By wisdom a house is built,
and through understanding it is
established;
⁴through knowledge its rooms are filled
with rare and beautiful treasures.

⁵A wise man has great power,
and a man of knowledge increases
strength;
⁶for waging war you need guidance,
and for victory many advisers.

⁷Wisdom is too high for a fool;
in the assembly at the gate he has nothing
to say.

⁸He who plots evil
will be known as a schemer.
⁹The schemes of folly are sin,
and men detest a mocker.

¹⁰If you falter in times of trouble,
how small is your strength!

¹¹Rescue those being led away to death;
hold back those staggering toward
slaughter.
¹²If you say, "But we knew nothing about
this,"
does not he who weighs the heart perceive
it?
Does not he who guards your life know it?
Will he not repay each person according
to what he has done?

¹³Eat honey, my son, for it is good;
honey from the comb is sweet to your
taste.
¹⁴Know also that wisdom is sweet to your soul;
if you find it, there is a future hope for
you,
and your hope will not be cut off.

¹⁵Do not lie in wait like an outlaw against a
righteous man's house,
do not raid his dwelling place;
¹⁶for though a righteous man falls seven times,
he rises again,
but the wicked are brought down by
calamity.

¹⁷Do not gloat when your enemy falls;
when he stumbles, do not let your heart
rejoice,
¹⁸or the LORD will see and disapprove
and turn his wrath away from him.

¹⁹Do not fret because of evil men
or be envious of the wicked,
²⁰for the evil man has no future hope,
and the lamp of the wicked will be
snuffed out.

²¹Fear the LORD and the king, my son,

The Problem with Laziness
Becoming a sluggard requires little effort

A little sleep, a little slumber, a little folding of the hands to rest—and poverty will come on you like a bandit. 24:33

THE "SLUGGARD" IS LAZIER THAN a pig on vacation. His only exercise is turning on his bed; Proverbs says he is *hinged* to it. Any far-fetched excuse—"there is a lion in the road!"—will keep him from going to work. Proverbs laughs at the sluggard a little, but uses him to teach serious lessons. You can be like him very easily, for it doesn't require much: "A little sleep, a little slumber, a little folding of the hands to rest." Putting things off, making excuses, sleeping in—who doesn't sometimes fall victim to these tendencies?

The result of such a life? Poverty, frustration, broken relationships. The sluggard still wants the luxuries hard work earns, but he never gets them. "The sluggard's craving will be the death of him" (21:25).

Proverbs on laziness: 6:6–11; 10:4,26; 12:24,27; 13:4; 15:19; 19:15,24; 20:4; 21:25; 22:13; 24:30–34; 26:13–16.

Life Questions: What attributes of a sluggard do you recognize in yourself? Do you think of these as serious?

and do not join with the rebellious,
²²for those two will send sudden destruction
    upon them,
and who knows what calamities they can
    bring?

Further Sayings of the Wise

²³These also are sayings of the wise:

To show partiality in judging is not good:
²⁴Whoever says to the guilty, "You are
    innocent"—
peoples will curse him and nations
    denounce him.
²⁵But it will go well with those who convict the
    guilty,
and rich blessing will come upon them.

²⁶An honest answer
    is like a kiss on the lips.

²⁷Finish your outdoor work
    and get your fields ready;
    after that, build your house.

²⁸Do not testify against your neighbor without
    cause,
    or use your lips to deceive.
²⁹Do not say, "I'll do to him as he has done to
    me;
    I'll pay that man back for what he did."

³⁰I went past the field of the sluggard,
    past the vineyard of the man who lacks
        judgment;
³¹thorns had come up everywhere,
    the ground was covered with weeds,
    and the stone wall was in ruins.
³²I applied my heart to what I observed
    and learned a lesson from what I saw:
³³A little sleep, a little slumber,
    a little folding of the hands to rest—
³⁴and poverty will come on you like a bandit
    and scarcity like an armed man. [a]

More Proverbs of Solomon

25 These are more proverbs of Solomon,
    copied by the men of Hezekiah king of
Judah:

²It is the glory of God to conceal a matter;
    to search out a matter is the glory of
        kings.

³As the heavens are high and the earth is
        deep,
    so the hearts of kings are unsearchable.

⁴Remove the dross from the silver,
    and out comes material for [b] the
        silversmith;

⁵remove the wicked from the king's presence,
    and his throne will be established through
        righteousness.

⁶Do not exalt yourself in the king's presence,

25:1 Good Government

*Proverbs lists three kings in its credits:
Solomon (1:1; 10:1), Hezekiah (25:1), and
Lemuel (31:1). So, naturally, it shows concern
for what makes good government. The
qualities needed in a king still apply to
governmental heads today. Proverbs doesn't
mention political philosophy or administrative
efficiency. Justice and fairness matter most.*
*Proverbs on good government include the
following: 14:35; 16:10,12–13; 20:26; 22:11;
25:4–5; 29:4,14; 31:3–5.*

and do not claim a place among great
    men;
⁷it is better for him to say to you, "Come up
    here,"
than for him to humiliate you before a
    nobleman.

What you have seen with your eyes
⁸   do not bring [c] hastily to court,
for what will you do in the end
    if your neighbor puts you to shame?

⁹If you argue your case with a neighbor,
    do not betray another man's confidence,
¹⁰or he who hears it may shame you
    and you will never lose your bad
        reputation.

¹¹A word aptly spoken
    is like apples of gold in settings of silver.

¹²Like an earring of gold or an ornament of
        fine gold
    is a wise man's rebuke to a listening ear.

¹³Like the coolness of snow at harvest time
    is a trustworthy messenger to those who
        send him;
he refreshes the spirit of his masters.

¹⁴Like clouds and wind without rain
    is a man who boasts of gifts he does not
        give.

¹⁵Through patience a ruler can be persuaded,
    and a gentle tongue can break a bone.

¹⁶If you find honey, eat just enough—
    too much of it, and you will vomit.
¹⁷Seldom set foot in your neighbor's house—
    too much of you, and he will hate you.

---

[a] 34 Or *like a vagrant / and scarcity like a beggar
had set your eyes. /* [b] Do not go   [b] 4 Or *comes a vessel from*   [c] 7,8 Or *nobleman / on whom you*

¹⁸Like a club or a sword or a sharp arrow
  is the man who gives false testimony
    against his neighbor.

¹⁹Like a bad tooth or a lame foot
  is reliance on the unfaithful in times of
    trouble.

²⁰Like one who takes away a garment on a
    cold day,
  or like vinegar poured on soda,
  is one who sings songs to a heavy heart.

²¹If your enemy is hungry, give him food to
    eat;
  if he is thirsty, give him water to drink.
²²In doing this, you will heap burning coals on
    his head,
  and the LORD will reward you.

²³As a north wind brings rain,
  so a sly tongue brings angry looks.

²⁴Better to live on a corner of the roof
  than share a house with a quarrelsome
    wife.

²⁵Like cold water to a weary soul
  is good news from a distant land.

²⁶Like a muddied spring or a polluted well
  is a righteous man who gives way to the
    wicked.

²⁷It is not good to eat too much honey,
  nor is it honorable to seek one's own
    honor.

²⁸Like a city whose walls are broken down
  is a man who lacks self-control.

26 Like snow in summer or rain in harvest,
  honor is not fitting for a fool.

²Like a fluttering sparrow or a darting
    swallow,
  an undeserved curse does not come to
    rest.

³A whip for the horse, a halter for the
    donkey,
  and a rod for the backs of fools!

⁴Do not answer a fool according to his folly,
  or you will be like him yourself.

⁵Answer a fool according to his folly,
  or he will be wise in his own eyes.

⁶Like cutting off one's feet or drinking
    violence
  is the sending of a message by the hand
    of a fool.

⁷Like a lame man's legs that hang limp
  is a proverb in the mouth of a fool.

⁸Like tying a stone in a sling
  is the giving of honor to a fool.

⁹Like a thornbush in a drunkard's hand
  is a proverb in the mouth of a fool.

¹⁰Like an archer who wounds at random
  is he who hires a fool or any passer-by.

¹¹As a dog returns to its vomit,
  so a fool repeats his folly.

¹²Do you see a man wise in his own eyes?
  There is more hope for a fool than for
    him.

¹³The sluggard says, "There is a lion in the
    road,
  a fierce lion roaming the streets!"

The Making of a Fool
Even a genius can be one

FOOLS, IN MODERN ENGLISH, ARE people who lack brains. But the word has a different meaning in the Bible. Fools may have high IQs. People may admire their reputation for success. Yet a wise person views them as a disaster.

> As a dog returns to its vomit, so a fool repeats his folly.
> 26:11

One of the Bible's worst insults is "You fool!" People become fools by ignoring the wisdom God offers them, preferring to follow the crowd or their own conceited opinions. They may think themselves very clever, but their cleverness will land them in trouble.

Proverbs aims its sharpest warnings, not against acting immorally, but against becoming a fool. If you develop such a character, no set of rules can keep you out of trouble. A wise person ought to learn to recognize a fool from far away, and stay out of his or her path.

Poignant proverbs on foolishness: 1:7; 10:8; 12:15–16,23; 14:8–9,16,24; 15:14; 17:10,12,16; 18:2,6; 20:3; 26:3,11; 27:22; 28:26; 29:11.

Life Questions: Do you know anyone whom Proverbs would call a fool? If so, how should you relate to him or her?

¹⁴As a door turns on its hinges,
so a sluggard turns on his bed.

¹⁵The sluggard buries his hand in the dish;
he is too lazy to bring it back to his
mouth.

26:13 The Excuses of a Lazy Man

*At first glance some proverbs, like this one,
appear incomplete and pointless. But this
proverb cleverly pinpoints a lazy man's habit of
seeing dangerous obstacles to every plan and
making incredible excuses. He will not go
anywhere (on a road) or even get out of his
house (into the streets) because his imagination
conjures up all the things that could go wrong.*

¹⁶The sluggard is wiser in his own eyes
than seven men who answer discreetly.

¹⁷Like one who seizes a dog by the ears
is a passer-by who meddles in a quarrel
not his own.

¹⁸Like a madman shooting
firebrands or deadly arrows
¹⁹is a man who deceives his neighbor
and says, "I was only joking!"

²⁰Without wood a fire goes out;
without gossip a quarrel dies down.

²¹As charcoal to embers and as wood to fire,
so is a quarrelsome man for kindling
strife.

²²The words of a gossip are like choice
morsels;
they go down to a man's inmost parts.

²³Like a coating of glaze*ᵃ* over earthenware
are fervent lips with an evil heart.

²⁴A malicious man disguises himself with his
lips,
but in his heart he harbors deceit.
²⁵Though his speech is charming, do not
believe him,
for seven abominations fill his heart.
²⁶His malice may be concealed by deception,
but his wickedness will be exposed in the
assembly.

²⁷If a man digs a pit, he will fall into it;
if a man rolls a stone, it will roll back on
him.

²⁸A lying tongue hates those it hurts,
and a flattering mouth works ruin.

27 Do not boast about tomorrow,
for you do not know what a day may
bring forth.

²Let another praise you, and not your own
mouth;
someone else, and not your own lips.

³Stone is heavy and sand a burden,
but provocation by a fool is heavier than
both.

⁴Anger is cruel and fury overwhelming,
but who can stand before jealousy?

⁵Better is open rebuke
than hidden love.

⁶Wounds from a friend can be trusted,
but an enemy multiplies kisses.

⁷He who is full loathes honey,
but to the hungry even what is bitter
tastes sweet.

⁸Like a bird that strays from its nest
is a man who strays from his home.

⁹Perfume and incense bring joy to the heart,
and the pleasantness of one's friend
springs from his earnest counsel.

¹⁰Do not forsake your friend and the friend of
your father,
and do not go to your brother's house
when disaster strikes you—
better a neighbor nearby than a brother
far away.

¹¹Be wise, my son, and bring joy to my heart;
then I can answer anyone who treats me
with contempt.

¹²The prudent see danger and take refuge,
but the simple keep going and suffer for
it.

¹³Take the garment of one who puts up
security for a stranger;
hold it in pledge if he does it for a
wayward woman.

¹⁴If a man loudly blesses his neighbor early in
the morning,
it will be taken as a curse.

¹⁵A quarrelsome wife is like
a constant dripping on a rainy day;
¹⁶restraining her is like restraining the wind
or grasping oil with the hand.

¹⁷As iron sharpens iron,
so one man sharpens another.

¹⁸He who tends a fig tree will eat its fruit,

ᵃ23 With a different word division of the Hebrew; Masoretic Text *of silver dross*

and he who looks after his master will be
   honored.

¹⁹As water reflects a face,
   so a man's heart reflects the man.

²⁰Death and Destruction[a] are never satisfied,
   and neither are the eyes of man.

²¹The crucible for silver and the furnace for
      gold,
   but man is tested by the praise he
      receives.

²²Though you grind a fool in a mortar,
   grinding him like grain with a pestle,
   you will not remove his folly from him.

²³Be sure you know the condition of your
      flocks,
   give careful attention to your herds;
²⁴for riches do not endure forever,
   and a crown is not secure for all
      generations.
²⁵When the hay is removed and new growth
      appears
   and the grass from the hills is gathered in,
²⁶the lambs will provide you with clothing,
   and the goats with the price of a field.
²⁷You will have plenty of goats' milk
   to feed you and your family
   and to nourish your servant girls.

28 The wicked man flees though no one
      pursues,
   but the righteous are as bold as a lion.

²When a country is rebellious, it has many
      rulers,
   but a man of understanding and
      knowledge maintains order.

³A ruler[b] who oppresses the poor
   is like a driving rain that leaves no crops.

⁴Those who forsake the law praise the wicked,
   but those who keep the law resist them.

⁵Evil men do not understand justice,
   but those who seek the LORD understand
      it fully.

⁶Better a poor man whose walk is blameless
   than a rich man whose ways are perverse.

⁷He who keeps the law is a discerning son,
   but a companion of gluttons disgraces his
      father.

⁸He who increases his wealth by exorbitant
      interest
   amasses it for another, who will be kind
      to the poor.

⁹If anyone turns a deaf ear to the law,
   even his prayers are detestable.

¹⁰He who leads the upright along an evil path
   will fall into his own trap,
   but the blameless will receive a good
      inheritance.

¹¹A rich man may be wise in his own eyes,
   but a poor man who has discernment sees
      through him.

¹²When the righteous triumph, there is great
      elation;
   but when the wicked rise to power, men
      go into hiding.

¹³He who conceals his sins does not prosper,
   but whoever confesses and renounces
      them finds mercy.

¹⁴Blessed is the man who always fears the
      LORD,
   but he who hardens his heart falls into
      trouble.

¹⁵Like a roaring lion or a charging bear
   is a wicked man ruling over a helpless
      people.

¹⁶A tyrannical ruler lacks judgment,
   but he who hates ill-gotten gain will enjoy
      a long life.

¹⁷A man tormented by the guilt of murder
   will be a fugitive till death;
   let no one support him.

¹⁸He whose walk is blameless is kept safe,
   but he whose ways are perverse will
      suddenly fall.

¹⁹He who works his land will have abundant
      food,
   but the one who chases fantasies will have
      his fill of poverty.

²⁰A faithful man will be richly blessed,
   but one eager to get rich will not go
      unpunished.

²¹To show partiality is not good—
   yet a man will do wrong for a piece of
      bread.

²²A stingy man is eager to get rich
   and is unaware that poverty awaits him.

²³He who rebukes a man will in the end gain
      more favor
   than he who has a flattering tongue.

²⁴He who robs his father or mother
   and says, "It's not wrong"—
   he is partner to him who destroys.

[a]20 Hebrew Sheol and Abaddon   [b]3 Or A poor man

²⁵A greedy man stirs up dissension,
but he who trusts in the LORD will
prosper.

²⁶He who trusts in himself is a fool,
but he who walks in wisdom is kept safe.

²⁷He who gives to the poor will lack nothing,
but he who closes his eyes to them
receives many curses.

²⁸When the wicked rise to power, people go
into hiding;
but when the wicked perish, the righteous
thrive.

29 A man who remains stiff-necked after
many rebukes
will suddenly be destroyed—without
remedy.

²When the righteous thrive, the people
rejoice;
when the wicked rule, the people groan.

³A man who loves wisdom brings joy to his
father,
but a companion of prostitutes squanders
his wealth.

⁴By justice a king gives a country stability,
but one who is greedy for bribes tears it
down.

⁵Whoever flatters his neighbor
is spreading a net for his feet.

⁶An evil man is snared by his own sin,
but a righteous one can sing and be glad.

⁷The righteous care about justice for the poor,
but the wicked have no such concern.

⁸Mockers stir up a city,
but wise men turn away anger.

⁹If a wise man goes to court with a fool,
the fool rages and scoffs, and there is no
peace.

¹⁰Bloodthirsty men hate a man of integrity
and seek to kill the upright.

29:5 Dangerous Flattery

"Flattery can get you anywhere," some say. But flattery—the art of making someone feel good by stretching the truth—can be downright harmful. It can leave a trusting friend unprepared for troubles ahead. Instead of flattering, we should warn a friend where he or she is headed (see 28:23).

¹¹A fool gives full vent to his anger,
but a wise man keeps himself under
control.

¹²If a ruler listens to lies,
all his officials become wicked.

¹³The poor man and the oppressor have this
in common:
The LORD gives sight to the eyes of both.

¹⁴If a king judges the poor with fairness,
his throne will always be secure.

¹⁵The rod of correction imparts wisdom,
but a child left to himself disgraces his
mother.

¹⁶When the wicked thrive, so does sin,
but the righteous will see their downfall.

¹⁷Discipline your son, and he will give you
peace;
he will bring delight to your soul.

¹⁸Where there is no revelation, the people cast
off restraint;
but blessed is he who keeps the law.

Five Dangerous Responses
Inner attitudes can destroy you

A wise man keeps himself under control. 29:11

ANGER WILL DESTROY YOU BEFORE it destroys anyone else. Control your temper! Read Proverbs 14:17; 14:29; 15:18; 19:19; 22:24–25; 29:11; 29:22.

Pride will lead to your downfall. Humility is far more rewarding. See Proverbs 3:34; 11:2; 13:10; 16:5,18–19; 18:12; 21:4.

Jealousy grows like a cancer. Read Proverbs 14:30; 23:17; 24:1; 27:4.

Fear of people is unnecessary if you trust God. See Proverbs 3:25–26; 29:25.

Conceit is ugly. A conceited person forgets God's place in his or her life. Read Proverbs 16:2; 25:27; 26:12; 27:2; 28:11,13.

Life Questions: Which of these responses tempts you most? Why?

¹⁹A servant cannot be corrected by mere
words;
though he understands, he will not
respond.

²⁰Do you see a man who speaks in haste?
There is more hope for a fool than for
him.

²¹If a man pampers his servant from youth,
he will bring grief^a in the end.

²²An angry man stirs up dissension,
and a hot-tempered one commits many
sins.

²³A man's pride brings him low,
but a man of lowly spirit gains honor.

²⁴The accomplice of a thief is his own enemy;
he is put under oath and dare not testify.

²⁵Fear of man will prove to be a snare,
but whoever trusts in the LORD is kept
safe.

²⁶Many seek an audience with a ruler,
but it is from the LORD that man gets
justice.

²⁷The righteous detest the dishonest;
the wicked detest the upright.

Sayings of Agur

30 The sayings of Agur son of Jakeh—an oracle^b:

This man declared to Ithiel,
to Ithiel and to Ucal:^c

²"I am the most ignorant of men;
I do not have a man's understanding.
³I have not learned wisdom,
nor have I knowledge of the Holy One.
⁴Who has gone up to heaven and come
down?
Who has gathered up the wind in the
hollow of his hands?
Who has wrapped up the waters in his
cloak?
Who has established all the ends of the
earth?
What is his name, and the name of his son?
Tell me if you know!

⁵"Every word of God is flawless;
he is a shield to those who take refuge in
him.
⁶Do not add to his words,
or he will rebuke you and prove you a
liar.

⁷"Two things I ask of you, O LORD;
do not refuse me before I die:
⁸Keep falsehood and lies far from me;
give me neither poverty nor riches,
but give me only my daily bread.
⁹Otherwise, I may have too much and disown
you
and say, 'Who is the LORD?'
Or I may become poor and steal,
and so dishonor the name of my God.

¹⁰"Do not slander a servant to his master,
or he will curse you, and you will pay
for it.

¹¹"There are those who curse their fathers
and do not bless their mothers;
¹²those who are pure in their own eyes
and yet are not cleansed of their filth;
¹³those whose eyes are ever so haughty,
whose glances are so disdainful;
¹⁴those whose teeth are swords
and whose jaws are set with knives
to devour the poor from the earth,
the needy from among mankind.

¹⁵"The leech has two daughters.
'Give! Give!' they cry.

"There are three things that are never
satisfied,
four that never say, 'Enough!':
¹⁶the grave,^d the barren womb,
land, which is never satisfied with water,
and fire, which never says, 'Enough!'

¹⁷"The eye that mocks a father,
that scorns obedience to a mother,
will be pecked out by the ravens of the
valley,
will be eaten by the vultures.

¹⁸"There are three things that are too amazing
for me,
four that I do not understand:
¹⁹the way of an eagle in the sky,
the way of a snake on a rock,
the way of a ship on the high seas,
and the way of a man with a maiden.

²⁰"This is the way of an adulteress:
She eats and wipes her mouth
and says, 'I've done nothing wrong.'

²¹"Under three things the earth trembles,
under four it cannot bear up:
²²a servant who becomes king,
a fool who is full of food,
²³an unloved woman who is married,

---

^a21 The meaning of the Hebrew for this word is uncertain.   ^b1 Or *Jakeh of Massa*   ^c1 Masoretic Text; with a
different word division of the Hebrew *declared, "I am weary, O God; / I am weary, O God, and faint.*   ^d16 Hebrew
Sheol

and a maidservant who displaces her
mistress.

²⁴"Four things on earth are small,
yet they are extremely wise:
²⁵Ants are creatures of little strength,
yet they store up their food in the
summer;
²⁶coneys[a] are creatures of little power,
yet they make their home in the crags;
²⁷locusts have no king,
yet they advance together in ranks;
²⁸a lizard can be caught with the hand,
yet it is found in kings' palaces.

²⁹"There are three things that are stately in
their stride,
four that move with stately bearing:
³⁰a lion, mighty among beasts,
who retreats before nothing;
³¹a strutting rooster, a he-goat,
and a king with his army around him.[b]

³²"If you have played the fool and exalted
yourself,
or if you have planned evil,
clap your hand over your mouth!
³³For as churning the milk produces butter,
and as twisting the nose produces blood,
so stirring up anger produces strife."

Sayings of King Lemuel

31 The sayings of King Lemuel—an oracle[c]
his mother taught him:

²"O my son, O son of my womb,
O son of my vows,[d]
³do not spend your strength on women,
your vigor on those who ruin kings.

⁴"It is not for kings, O Lemuel—
not for kings to drink wine,
not for rulers to crave beer,
⁵lest they drink and forget what the law
decrees,
and deprive all the oppressed of their
rights.
⁶Give beer to those who are perishing,
wine to those who are in anguish;
⁷let them drink and forget their poverty
and remember their misery no more.

⁸"Speak up for those who cannot speak for
themselves,
for the rights of all who are destitute.
⁹Speak up and judge fairly;
defend the rights of the poor and needy."

Epilogue: The Wife of Noble Character

¹⁰[e]A wife of noble character who can find?
She is worth far more than rubies.
¹¹Her husband has full confidence in her
and lacks nothing of value.
¹²She brings him good, not harm,
all the days of her life.

31:8 For the Voiceless

*The German pastor Dietrich Bonhoeffer
frequently quoted this verse in the years before
World War II. He was urging his fellow
Christians to speak up for Hitler's victims,
particularly Jews who had been stripped of
their civil rights.*

¹³She selects wool and flax
and works with eager hands.
¹⁴She is like the merchant ships,
bringing her food from afar.
¹⁵She gets up while it is still dark;
she provides food for her family
and portions for her servant girls.
¹⁶She considers a field and buys it;
out of her earnings she plants a vineyard.
¹⁷She sets about her work vigorously;
her arms are strong for her tasks.
¹⁸She sees that her trading is profitable,
and her lamp does not go out at night.
¹⁹In her hand she holds the distaff
and grasps the spindle with her fingers.
²⁰She opens her arms to the poor
and extends her hands to the needy.
²¹When it snows, she has no fear for her
household;
for all of them are clothed in scarlet.
²²She makes coverings for her bed;
she is clothed in fine linen and purple.
²³Her husband is respected at the city gate,
where he takes his seat among the elders
of the land.
²⁴She makes linen garments and sells them,
and supplies the merchants with sashes.
²⁵She is clothed with strength and dignity;
she can laugh at the days to come.
²⁶She speaks with wisdom,
and faithful instruction is on her tongue.
²⁷She watches over the affairs of her household
and does not eat the bread of idleness.

---

a 26 That is, the hyrax or rock badger   *b 31* Or *king secure against revolt*   *c 1* Or *of Lemuel king of Massa, which*
d 2 Or */ the answer to my prayers*   *e 10* Verses 10-31 are an acrostic, each verse beginning with a successive letter of the
Hebrew alphabet.

²⁸Her children arise and call her blessed;
  her husband also, and he praises her:
²⁹"Many women do noble things,
  but you surpass them all."
³⁰Charm is deceptive, and beauty is fleeting;

but a woman who fears the LORD is to be
  praised.
³¹Give her the reward she has earned,
  and let her works bring her praise at the
  city gate.

ECCLESIASTES

When Life Seems Senseless
A book for our time

I
N THIS WORLD THERE ARE only two tragedies," said Irish writer Oscar Wilde. "One is not getting what one wants, and the other is getting it." This paradoxical proverb has often proved true. Consider a larger-than-life character from the 20th century, a man named Howard Hughes.

> *"Meaningless! Meaningless!" says the Teacher. "Utterly meaningless! Everything is meaningless." 1:2*

World's Richest Man

At age 45 Hughes was one of the most glamorous men in America. He courted actresses, piloted exotic test aircraft, and worked on top-secret CIA contracts. He owned a string of hotels around the world, and even an airline—TWA—to carry him on global jaunts.

Twenty years later, at 65, Howard Hughes still had plenty of money—$2.3 billion, to be exact. But the world's richest man had become one of its most pathetic. He lived in small, dark rooms atop his hotels, without sun and without joy. He was unkempt: A scraggly beard had grown waist-length, his hair fell well down his back, and his fingernails were two inches long. His once-powerful 6'4" frame had shrunk to about 100 pounds.

This famous man spent most of his time watching movies over and over, with the same movie showing as many as 150 times. He lay naked in bed, deathly afraid of germs. Life held no meaning for him. Finally, emaciated and hooked on drugs, he died at age 67, for lack of a medical device his own company had helped to develop.

A King's Charmed Life

Howard Hughes is an extreme example of a syndrome that can afflict the rich and famous. His attitude toward life closely followed the thoughts of another successful man, a great king who ruled Israel long ago. This book, Ecclesiastes, records what happened to that man who had everything.

The author of Ecclesiastes had tasted just about everything life has to offer. Wealth? No one could exceed him in luxurious lifestyle (2:4–9). Wisdom? His was world-renowned (1:13–18). Fame? He was king, the most famous man of his time (1:12). Systematically, he sampled all of life's powers and pleasures, yet all ultimately disappointed him. All proved meaningless.

What is the point of life? he asked. You work hard, and someone else gets all the credit. You struggle to be good, and evil people take advantage of you. You accumulate money, and it just goes to spoiled heirs. You seek pleasure, and it turns sour on you. And everyone—rich or poor, good or evil—meets the same end. We all die. There is only one word to describe this life: meaningless!

Life Under the Sun

Ecclesiastes strikes a responsive chord in our age. Its words show up in folk songs and at presidential inaugurations. No century has seen such progress, and yet such despair. What is the purpose of life anyway? Is there any ultimate meaning? "Is that all there is?" asked one songwriter after listing life's pleasures.

A key phrase in this book, "under the sun," describes the world lived on one level, apart from God and without any belief in the afterlife. If you live on that level, you may well conclude that life is meaningless.

Ecclesiastes gives some words of hope, including the final summary: "Fear God and keep his commandments, for this is the whole ⸤duty⸥ of man" (12:13). That's the positive message, the "lesson" of

Ecclesiastes. But such positive words are almost overwhelmed by the author's powerful negative example. You could summarize his whole life in Jesus' one statement, "What good will it be for a man if he gains the whole world, yet forfeits his soul?" (Matthew 16:26).

How to Read Ecclesiastes

Ecclesiastes attracts extreme reactions. For several hundred years, Jewish scholars fiercely debated whether the book should even be included in the Old Testament. Yet American novelist Thomas Wolfe said of it, "Ecclesiastes is the greatest single piece of writing I have ever known, and the wisdom expressed in it the most lasting and profound."

Because of the book's unique nature, it is important to keep certain principles in mind while reading it. Consider Ecclesiastes as a whole. The Teacher was exploring various philosophies of life. During his search, he tried different approaches, including hedonism, the unrestrained pursuit of pleasure. The book honestly records the author's search without endorsing it.

At times the author concludes with despairing statements that directly contradict other parts of the Bible (for example, the recurring phrase, "Everything is meaningless!"). Read such individual statements in their context. Just as the book of Job contains arguments that God directly refuted later, so Ecclesiastes contains many isolated statements that contradict its final conclusion.

Ecclesiastes performs two very valuable functions. First, it should stimulate compassion for those who are trapped in despair and live in a meaningless world, alone, without God. The author brilliantly captures the futility and meaninglessness of that world, expressing a philosophy of life widespread in the 20th century.

But the book includes more than despair. It also blends in proverbs about how life should be lived, pungent observations that can be easily overlooked. Look for these nuggets of wisdom, especially toward the end of the book. (You may also find it helpful to balance out Ecclesiastes with the more confident advice of Proverbs.)

By asking questions, the author of Ecclesiastes helped prepare for the answers God ultimately provided. The Teacher concluded, "Everything is meaningless!" under the sun, but when Jesus Christ came, he promised life "to the full" (John 10:10).

3-TRACK READING PLAN

For an explanation and complete listing of the 3-track reading plan, turn to page 7.

TRACK 1: **_Two-Week Courses on the Bible_**
See page 7 for information on these courses.

TRACK 2: **_An Overview of Ecclesiastes in 1 Day_**
☐ Day 1. Read the Introduction to Ecclesiastes and then chapter 3, perhaps the most enduring portion of the book's poetry. Folksinger Pete Seeger used the first part verbatim in a famous song, and former United States president John F. Kennedy had these words read at his inauguration.

Now turn to page 9 for your next Track 2 reading project.

TRACK 3: **_All of Ecclesiastes in 12 Days_**
After you have read through Ecclesiastes, turn to pages 10–14 for your next Track 3 reading project.
☐1 ☐2 ☐3 ☐4 ☐5 ☐6 ☐7 ☐8
☐9 ☐10 ☐11 ☐12

Everything Is Meaningless

1 The words of the Teacher,[a] son of David, king in Jerusalem:

[2] "Meaningless! Meaningless!"
  says the Teacher.
"Utterly meaningless!
  Everything is meaningless."

[3] What does man gain from all his labor
  at which he toils under the sun?
[4] Generations come and generations go,
  but the earth remains forever.
[5] The sun rises and the sun sets,
  and hurries back to where it rises.
[6] The wind blows to the south
  and turns to the north;
round and round it goes,
  ever returning on its course.
[7] All streams flow into the sea,
  yet the sea is never full.
To the place the streams come from,
  there they return again.
[8] All things are wearisome,
  more than one can say.
The eye never has enough of seeing,
  nor the ear its fill of hearing.
[9] What has been will be again,
  what has been done will be done again;
  there is nothing new under the sun.
[10] Is there anything of which one can say,
  "Look! This is something new"?
It was here already, long ago;
  it was here before our time.
[11] There is no remembrance of men of old,
  and even those who are yet to come
  will not be remembered
    by those who follow.

Wisdom Is Meaningless

[12] I, the Teacher, was king over Israel in Jerusalem. [13] I devoted myself to study and to explore by wisdom all that is done under heaven. What a heavy burden God has laid on men! [14] I have seen all the things that are done under the sun; all of them are meaningless, a chasing after the wind.

[15] What is twisted cannot be straightened;
  what is lacking cannot be counted.

[16] I thought to myself, "Look, I have grown and increased in wisdom more than anyone who has ruled over Jerusalem before me; I have experienced much of wisdom and knowledge." [17] Then I applied myself to the understanding of wisdom, and also of madness and folly, but I learned that this, too, is a chasing after the wind.

[18] For with much wisdom comes much sorrow;
  the more knowledge, the more grief.

Pleasures Are Meaningless

2 I thought in my heart, "Come now, I will test you with pleasure to find out what is good."

2:1 Outside the Palace

The first two chapters of Ecclesiastes tell of "the Teacher's" own experience of despair and meaninglessness. The life described in this autobiographical section resembles that of King Solomon. In the rest of the book, the Teacher examines the world around him to see if others have found answers to life "under the sun." To his disappointment, he finds the same pattern repeated over and over.

But that also proved to be meaningless. [2] "Laughter," I said, "is foolish. And what does pleasure accomplish?" [3] I tried cheering myself with wine, and embracing folly—my mind still guiding me with wisdom. I wanted to see what was worthwhile for men to do under heaven during the few days of their lives.

[4] I undertook great projects: I built houses for myself and planted vineyards. [5] I made gardens and parks and planted all kinds of fruit trees in them. [6] I made reservoirs to water groves of flourishing trees. [7] I bought male and female slaves and had other slaves who were born in my house. I also owned more herds and flocks than anyone in Jerusalem before me. [8] I amassed silver and gold for myself, and the treasure of kings and provinces. I acquired men and women singers, and a harem[b] as well—the delights of the heart of man. [9] I became greater by far than anyone in Jerusalem before me. In all this my wisdom stayed with me.

[10] I denied myself nothing my eyes desired;
  I refused my heart no pleasure.
My heart took delight in all my work,
  and this was the reward for all my labor.
[11] Yet when I surveyed all that my hands had
    done
  and what I had toiled to achieve,
everything was meaningless, a chasing after
    the wind;
  nothing was gained under the sun.

Wisdom and Folly Are Meaningless

[12] Then I turned my thoughts to consider
    wisdom,
  and also madness and folly.
What more can the king's successor do
  than what has already been done?

---

[a]1 Or *leader of the assembly*; also in verses 2 and 12   [b]8 The meaning of the Hebrew for this phrase is uncertain.

[13]I saw that wisdom is better than folly,
  just as light is better than darkness.
[14]The wise man has eyes in his head,
  while the fool walks in the darkness;
but I came to realize
  that the same fate overtakes them both.

[15]Then I thought in my heart,

"The fate of the fool will overtake me also.
  What then do I gain by being wise?"
I said in my heart,
  "This too is meaningless."
[16]For the wise man, like the fool, will not be
  long remembered;
  in days to come both will be forgotten.
Like the fool, the wise man too must die!

Toil Is Meaningless

[17]So I hated life, because the work that is done
under the sun was grievous to me. All of it is
meaningless, a chasing after the wind. [18]I hated
all the things I had toiled for under the sun,
because I must leave them to the one who comes
after me. [19]And who knows whether he will be a
wise man or a fool? Yet he will have control over
all the work into which I have poured my effort
and skill under the sun. This too is meaningless.
[20]So my heart began to despair over all my toilsome labor under the sun. [21]For a man may do
his work with wisdom, knowledge and skill, and
then he must leave all he owns to someone who
has not worked for it. This too is meaningless
and a great misfortune. [22]What does a man get
for all the toil and anxious striving with which he
labors under the sun? [23]All his days his work is
pain and grief; even at night his mind does not
rest. This too is meaningless.

[24]A man can do nothing better than to eat and
drink and find satisfaction in his work. This too,
I see, is from the hand of God, [25]for without him,
who can eat or find enjoyment? [26]To the man
who pleases him, God gives wisdom, knowledge
and happiness, but to the sinner he gives the task
of gathering and storing up wealth to hand it
over to the one who pleases God. This too is
meaningless, a chasing after the wind.

A Time for Everything

3 There is a time for everything,
  and a season for every activity under
    heaven:

[2] a time to be born and a time to die,
  a time to plant and a time to uproot,
[3] a time to kill and a time to heal,
  a time to tear down and a time to build,
[4] a time to weep and a time to laugh,
  a time to mourn and a time to dance,

[5] a time to scatter stones and a time to
    gather them,
  a time to embrace and a time to refrain,
[6] a time to search and a time to give up,
  a time to keep and a time to throw away,
[7] a time to tear and a time to mend,
  a time to be silent and a time to speak,
[8] a time to love and a time to hate,
  a time for war and a time for peace.

3:4 Change or No Change?

*At first the Teacher complained that nothing
ever changes (1:10–14). Now in this passage—
made famous by a popular song in the 1960s—
he indicates that life is full of changes. The
French proverb, "The more things change, the
more they stay the same," expresses this same
paradox. For someone in despair who can see
no meaning in life, everything that happens
seems like an endless, repetitive cycle of futility.*

[9]What does the worker gain from his toil? [10]I
have seen the burden God has laid on men. [11]He
has made everything beautiful in its time. He has
also set eternity in the hearts of men; yet they
cannot fathom what God has done from beginning to end. [12]I know that there is nothing better
for men than to be happy and do good while they
live. [13]That everyone may eat and drink, and find
satisfaction in all his toil—this is the gift of God.
[14]I know that everything God does will endure
forever; nothing can be added to it and nothing
taken from it. God does it so that men will revere
him.

[15]Whatever is has already been,
  and what will be has been before;
  and God will call the past to account.[a]

[16]And I saw something else under the sun:

In the place of judgment—wickedness was
    there,
  in the place of justice—wickedness was
    there.

[17]I thought in my heart,

"God will bring to judgment
  both the righteous and the wicked,
for there will be a time for every activity,
  a time for every deed."

[18]I also thought, "As for men, God tests them
so that they may see that they are like the animals. [19]Man's fate is like that of the animals; the
same fate awaits them both: As one dies, so dies
the other. All have the same breath[b]; man has

---

[a]15 Or *God calls back the past*   [b]19 Or *spirit*

no advantage over the animal. Everything is meaningless. ²⁰All go to the same place; all come from dust, and to dust all return. ²¹Who knows if the spirit of man rises upward and if the spirit of the animal*a* goes down into the earth?"

3:20 Is There an Afterlife?

Old Testament writers said very little about the afterlife. Not until Jesus' coming did God reveal details about heaven and hell. In this passage, the author wonders aloud whether death will be the end of everything. Yet he also adds some intriguing hints about the future. God "has also set eternity in the hearts of men," he declares (verse 11). He also refers to a time of future judgment (verse 17).

---

²²So I saw that there is nothing better for a man than to enjoy his work, because that is his lot. For who can bring him to see what will happen after him?

Oppression, Toil, Friendlessness

4 Again I looked and saw all the oppression that was taking place under the sun:

I saw the tears of the oppressed—
and they have no comforter;
power was on the side of their oppressors—
and they have no comforter.
²And I declared that the dead,
who had already died,
are happier than the living,
who are still alive.
³But better than both
is he who has not yet been,
who has not seen the evil
that is done under the sun.

⁴And I saw that all labor and all achievement spring from man's envy of his neighbor. This too is meaningless, a chasing after the wind.

⁵The fool folds his hands
and ruins himself.
⁶Better one handful with tranquillity
than two handfuls with toil
and chasing after the wind.

⁷Again I saw something meaningless under the sun:

⁸There was a man all alone;
he had neither son nor brother.
There was no end to his toil,
yet his eyes were not content with his
wealth.
"For whom am I toiling," he asked,

"and why am I depriving myself of
enjoyment?"
This too is meaningless—
a miserable business!

⁹Two are better than one,
because they have a good return for their
work:
¹⁰If one falls down,
his friend can help him up.
But pity the man who falls
and has no one to help him up!
¹¹Also, if two lie down together, they will keep
warm.
But how can one keep warm alone?
¹²Though one may be overpowered,
two can defend themselves.
A cord of three strands is not quickly
broken.

Advancement Is Meaningless

¹³Better a poor but wise youth than an old but foolish king who no longer knows how to take warning. ¹⁴The youth may have come from prison to the kingship, or he may have been born in poverty within his kingdom. ¹⁵I saw that all who lived and walked under the sun followed the youth, the king's successor. ¹⁶There was no end to all the people who were before them. But those who came later were not pleased with the successor. This too is meaningless, a chasing after the wind.

Stand in Awe of God

5 Guard your steps when you go to the house of God. Go near to listen rather than to offer the sacrifice of fools, who do not know that they do wrong.

²Do not be quick with your mouth,
do not be hasty in your heart
to utter anything before God.
God is in heaven
and you are on earth,
so let your words be few.
³As a dream comes when there are many
cares,
so the speech of a fool when there are
many words.

⁴When you make a vow to God, do not delay in fulfilling it. He has no pleasure in fools; fulfill your vow. ⁵It is better not to vow than to make a vow and not fulfill it. ⁶Do not let your mouth lead you into sin. And do not protest to the ˏtempleˏ messenger, "My vow was a mistake." Why should God be angry at what you say and destroy

---

a21 Or Who knows the spirit of man, which rises upward, or the spirit of the animal, which

the work of your hands? ⁷Much dreaming and many words are meaningless. Therefore stand in awe of God.

Riches Are Meaningless

⁸If you see the poor oppressed in a district, and justice and rights denied, do not be surprised at such things; for one official is eyed by a higher one, and over them both are others higher still. ⁹The increase from the land is taken by all; the king himself profits from the fields.

¹⁰Whoever loves money never has money
 enough;
 whoever loves wealth is never satisfied
  with his income.
 This too is meaningless.

5:10 Never Enough

Someone asked John D. Rockefeller, the richest man of his time, how much money is enough. He replied with a perfect definition of greed: "Just a little bit more." A real estate tycoon said something similar: "I don't want all the land in the world, just whatever touches mine."

¹¹As goods increase,
 so do those who consume them.
 And what benefit are they to the owner
  except to feast his eyes on them?

¹²The sleep of a laborer is sweet,
 whether he eats little or much,
 but the abundance of a rich man
  permits him no sleep.

¹³I have seen a grievous evil under the sun:

 wealth hoarded to the harm of its owner,
¹⁴ or wealth lost through some misfortune,
 so that when he has a son
  there is nothing left for him.
¹⁵Naked a man comes from his mother's
  womb,
 and as he comes, so he departs.
 He takes nothing from his labor
  that he can carry in his hand.

¹⁶This too is a grievous evil:

 As a man comes, so he departs,
 and what does he gain,
  since he toils for the wind?
¹⁷All his days he eats in darkness,
 with great frustration, affliction and anger.

¹⁸Then I realized that it is good and proper for a man to eat and drink, and to find satisfaction in his toilsome labor under the sun during the few days of life God has given him—for this is

his lot. ¹⁹Moreover, when God gives any man wealth and possessions, and enables him to enjoy them, to accept his lot and be happy in his work—this is a gift of God. ²⁰He seldom reflects on the days of his life, because God keeps him occupied with gladness of heart.

5:18 Good for Something

As he tasted various attractions in life—work, food, drink, success—the Teacher decided that all are "meaningless." None gave ultimate satisfaction. But in passages like this one, he admits that such good things are gifts from God and have a temporary value. Some possessions are better than none, wisdom is better than ignorance, life is better than death.

6 I have seen another evil under the sun, and it weighs heavily on men: ²God gives a man wealth, possessions and honor, so that he lacks nothing his heart desires, but God does not enable him to enjoy them, and a stranger enjoys them instead. This is meaningless, a grievous evil.

³A man may have a hundred children and live many years; yet no matter how long he lives, if he cannot enjoy his prosperity and does not receive proper burial, I say that a stillborn child is better off than he. ⁴It comes without meaning, it departs in darkness, and in darkness its name is shrouded. ⁵Though it never saw the sun or knew anything, it has more rest than does that man— ⁶even if he lives a thousand years twice over but fails to enjoy his prosperity. Do not all go to the same place?

⁷All man's efforts are for his mouth,
 yet his appetite is never satisfied.
⁸What advantage has a wise man
 over a fool?
What does a poor man gain
 by knowing how to conduct himself
  before others?
⁹Better what the eye sees
 than the roving of the appetite.
This too is meaningless,
 a chasing after the wind.

¹⁰Whatever exists has already been named,
 and what man is has been known;
no man can contend
 with one who is stronger than he.
¹¹The more the words,
 the less the meaning,
 and how does that profit anyone?

¹²For who knows what is good for a man in life, during the few and meaningless days he passes through like a shadow? Who can tell him what will happen under the sun after he is gone?

Wisdom

7 A good name is better than fine perfume,
    and the day of death better than the day
        of birth.
[2] It is better to go to a house of mourning
    than to go to a house of feasting,
for death is the destiny of every man;
    the living should take this to heart.
[3] Sorrow is better than laughter,
    because a sad face is good for the heart.
[4] The heart of the wise is in the house of
        mourning,
    but the heart of fools is in the house of
        pleasure.
[5] It is better to heed a wise man's rebuke
    than to listen to the song of fools.
[6] Like the crackling of thorns under the pot,
    so is the laughter of fools.
    This too is meaningless.

[7] Extortion turns a wise man into a fool,
    and a bribe corrupts the heart.

[8] The end of a matter is better than its
        beginning,
    and patience is better than pride.
[9] Do not be quickly provoked in your spirit,
    for anger resides in the lap of fools.

[10] Do not say, "Why were the old days better
        than these?"
    For it is not wise to ask such questions.

[11] Wisdom, like an inheritance, is a good thing
    and benefits those who see the sun.
[12] Wisdom is a shelter
    as money is a shelter,
but the advantage of knowledge is this:
    that wisdom preserves the life of its
        possessor.

[13] Consider what God has done:

Who can straighten
    what he has made crooked?
[14] When times are good, be happy;
    but when times are bad, consider:
God has made the one
    as well as the other.
Therefore, a man cannot discover
    anything about his future.

[15] In this meaningless life of mine I have seen
both of these:

a righteous man perishing in his
        righteousness,
    and a wicked man living long in his
        wickedness.
[16] Do not be overrighteous,
    neither be overwise—
    why destroy yourself?

[17] Do not be overwicked,
    and do not be a fool—
    why die before your time?
[18] It is good to grasp the one
    and not let go of the other.
    The man who fears God will avoid all
    ⌊extremes⌋.[a]

7:15 Companion Book

*Passages in Ecclesiastes sound eerily like the
book of Job. Both books are "philosophical,"
asking the hardest questions about life. Both
authors battled despair, but for opposite
reasons: Job was overwhelmed by tragedy and
pain while the Teacher was jaded by luxury
and success. No matter what their status in life,
everyone has to face the same basic issues: Is
there a God? Is life unfair? Does it have
meaning?*

[19] Wisdom makes one wise man more powerful
    than ten rulers in a city.

[20] There is not a righteous man on earth
    who does what is right and never sins.

[21] Do not pay attention to every word people
        say,
    or you may hear your servant cursing
        you—
[22] for you know in your heart
    that many times you yourself have cursed
        others.

[23] All this I tested by wisdom and I said,

"I am determined to be wise"—
    but this was beyond me.
[24] Whatever wisdom may be,
    it is far off and most profound—
    who can discover it?
[25] So I turned my mind to understand,
    to investigate and to search out wisdom
        and the scheme of things
and to understand the stupidity of
        wickedness
    and the madness of folly.

[26] I find more bitter than death
    the woman who is a snare,
whose heart is a trap
    and whose hands are chains.
The man who pleases God will escape her,
    but the sinner she will ensnare.

[27] "Look," says the Teacher,[b] "this is what I
have discovered:

"Adding one thing to another to discover the
        scheme of things—

---

[a] 18 Or *will follow them both*   [b] 27 Or *leader of the assembly*

28 while I was still searching
    but not finding—
I found one ⌊upright⌋ man among a
        thousand,
    but not one ⌊upright⌋ woman among them
        all.
29 This only have I found:
    God made mankind upright,
    but men have gone in search of many
        schemes."

8 Who is like the wise man?
    Who knows the explanation of things?
Wisdom brightens a man's face
    and changes its hard appearance.

Obey the King

2 Obey the king's command, I say, because you took an oath before God. 3 Do not be in a hurry to leave the king's presence. Do not stand up for a bad cause, for he will do whatever he pleases. 4 Since a king's word is supreme, who can say to him, "What are you doing?"

5 Whoever obeys his command will come to
        no harm,
    and the wise heart will know the proper
        time and procedure.
6 For there is a proper time and procedure for
        every matter,
    though a man's misery weighs heavily
        upon him.

7 Since no man knows the future,
    who can tell him what is to come?
8 No man has power over the wind to contain
        it[a];
    so no one has power over the day of his
        death.
As no one is discharged in time of war,
    so wickedness will not release those who
        practice it.

9 All this I saw, as I applied my mind to everything done under the sun. There is a time when a man lords it over others to his own[b] hurt. 10 Then too, I saw the wicked buried—those who used to come and go from the holy place and receive praise[c] in the city where they did this. This too is meaningless.

11 When the sentence for a crime is not quickly carried out, the hearts of the people are filled with schemes to do wrong. 12 Although a wicked man commits a hundred crimes and still lives a long time, I know that it will go better with God-fearing men, who are reverent before God. 13 Yet because the wicked do not fear God, it will not go well with them, and their days will not lengthen like a shadow.

14 There is something else meaningless that occurs on earth: righteous men who get what the wicked deserve, and wicked men who get what the righteous deserve. This too, I say, is meaningless. 15 So I commend the enjoyment of life, because nothing is better for a man under the sun than to eat and drink and be glad. Then joy will accompany him in his work all the days of the life God has given him under the sun.

16 When I applied my mind to know wisdom and to observe man's labor on earth—his eyes not seeing sleep day or night— 17 then I saw all that God has done. No one can comprehend what goes on under the sun. Despite all his efforts to search it out, man cannot discover its meaning. Even if a wise man claims he knows, he cannot really comprehend it.

8:17 God's Fault?

Despite their similarities, Job and Ecclesiastes reveal important differences. As this verse shows, the Teacher never really expected to solve life's riddles; his attitude of resignation contrasts with Job's combativeness. Also, in his anguish, Job sometimes questioned the character of God himself, demanding a personal explanation. At no time did the Teacher blame God for the unfairness and meaninglessness he saw around him. "God made mankind upright," he concludes, "but men have gone in search of many schemes" (7:29).

A Common Destiny for All

9 So I reflected on all this and concluded that the righteous and the wise and what they do are in God's hands, but no man knows whether love or hate awaits him. 2 All share a common destiny—the righteous and the wicked, the good and the bad,[d] the clean and the unclean, those who offer sacrifices and those who do not.

As it is with the good man,
    so with the sinner;
as it is with those who take oaths,
    so with those who are afraid to take them.

3 This is the evil in everything that happens under the sun: The same destiny overtakes all. The hearts of men, moreover, are full of evil and there is madness in their hearts while they live, and afterward they join the dead. 4 Anyone who is among the living has hope[e]—even a live dog is better off than a dead lion!

5 For the living know that they will die,

---

[a]8 Or over his spirit to retain it   [b]9 Or to their   [c]10 Some Hebrew manuscripts and Septuagint (Aquila); most Hebrew manuscripts and are forgotten   [d]2 Septuagint (Aquila), Vulgate and Syriac; Hebrew does not have and the bad.   [e]4 Or What then is to be chosen? With all who live, there is hope

but the dead know nothing;
they have no further reward,
    and even the memory of them is
        forgotten.
⁶Their love, their hate
    and their jealousy have long since
        vanished;
never again will they have a part
    in anything that happens under the sun.

⁷Go, eat your food with gladness, and drink
your wine with a joyful heart, for it is now that
God favors what you do. ⁸Always be clothed in
white, and always anoint your head with oil. ⁹En-
joy life with your wife, whom you love, all the
days of this meaningless life that God has given
you under the sun— all your meaningless days.
For this is your lot in life and in your toilsome
labor under the sun. ¹⁰Whatever your hand finds
to do, do it with all your might, for in the
grave,ᵃ where you are going, there is neither
working nor planning nor knowledge nor wisdom.

¹¹I have seen something else under the sun:

The race is not to the swift
    or the battle to the strong,
nor does food come to the wise
    or wealth to the brilliant
    or favor to the learned;
but time and chance happen to them all.

9:11 Life Is Unfair

*Chapters 8 and 9 eloquently voice the
unfairness of life. People don't get what they
deserve, claims the Teacher. Good people suffer
while wicked people prosper. Everything seems
determined only by time and chance. The
Teacher's doubts about the afterlife (see 3:20)
affected all his thinking, because he saw the
utter unfairness of life around him. In contrast,
New Testament authors, with a solid belief in
the afterlife, showed confidence that God would
ultimately judge all people with fairness.*

¹²Moreover, no man knows when his hour will
come:

As fish are caught in a cruel net,
    or birds are taken in a snare,
so men are trapped by evil times
    that fall unexpectedly upon them.

Wisdom Better Than Folly

¹³I also saw under the sun this example of
wisdom that greatly impressed me: ¹⁴There was
once a small city with only a few people in it. And

a powerful king came against it, surrounded it
and built huge siegeworks against it. ¹⁵Now there
lived in that city a man poor but wise, and he
saved the city by his wisdom. But nobody remembered that poor man. ¹⁶So I said, "Wisdom
is better than strength." But the poor man's wisdom is despised, and his words are no longer
heeded.

¹⁷The quiet words of the wise are more to be
        heeded
    than the shouts of a ruler of fools.
¹⁸Wisdom is better than weapons of war,
    but one sinner destroys much good.

10 As dead flies give perfume a bad smell,
    so a little folly outweighs wisdom and
        honor.
²The heart of the wise inclines to the right,
    but the heart of the fool to the left.
³Even as he walks along the road,
    the fool lacks sense
    and shows everyone how stupid he is.
⁴If a ruler's anger rises against you,
    do not leave your post;
    calmness can lay great errors to rest.

⁵There is an evil I have seen under the sun,
    the sort of error that arises from a ruler:
⁶Fools are put in many high positions,
    while the rich occupy the low ones.
⁷I have seen slaves on horseback,
    while princes go on foot like slaves.

⁸Whoever digs a pit may fall into it;
    whoever breaks through a wall may be
        bitten by a snake.
⁹Whoever quarries stones may be injured by
        them;
    whoever splits logs may be endangered by
        them.

¹⁰If the ax is dull
    and its edge unsharpened,
    more strength is needed
    but skill will bring success.

¹¹If a snake bites before it is charmed,
    there is no profit for the charmer.

¹²Words from a wise man's mouth are
        gracious,
    but a fool is consumed by his own lips.
¹³At the beginning his words are folly;
    at the end they are wicked madness—
¹⁴   and the fool multiplies words.

No one knows what is coming—
    who can tell him what will happen after
        him?

¹⁵A fool's work wearies him;
    he does not know the way to town.

ᵃ10 Hebrew *Sheol*

¹⁶Woe to you, O land whose king was a
  servant[a]
  and whose princes feast in the morning.
¹⁷Blessed are you, O land whose king is of
  noble birth
  and whose princes eat at a proper time—
  for strength and not for drunkenness.

¹⁸If a man is lazy, the rafters sag;
  if his hands are idle, the house leaks.

¹⁹A feast is made for laughter,
  and wine makes life merry,
  but money is the answer for everything.

²⁰Do not revile the king even in your
  thoughts,
  or curse the rich in your bedroom,
  because a bird of the air may carry your
  words,
  and a bird on the wing may report what
  you say.

Bread Upon the Waters

11 Cast your bread upon the waters,
  for after many days you will find it again.
²Give portions to seven, yes to eight,
  for you do not know what disaster may
  come upon the land.

³If clouds are full of water,
  they pour rain upon the earth.
Whether a tree falls to the south or to the
  north,
  in the place where it falls, there will it lie.
⁴Whoever watches the wind will not plant;
  whoever looks at the clouds will not reap.

⁵As you do not know the path of the wind,
  or how the body is formed[b] in a
  mother's womb,
  so you cannot understand the work of God,
  the Maker of all things.

⁶Sow your seed in the morning,
  and at evening let not your hands be idle,
  for you do not know which will succeed,
  whether this or that,
  or whether both will do equally well.

Remember Your Creator While Young

⁷Light is sweet,
  and it pleases the eyes to see the sun.
⁸However many years a man may live,
  let him enjoy them all.
But let him remember the days of darkness,
  for they will be many.
  Everything to come is meaningless.

⁹Be happy, young man, while you are young,

and let your heart give you joy in the days
  of your youth.
Follow the ways of your heart
  and whatever your eyes see,
but know that for all these things
  God will bring you to judgment.

11:5 Beyond Understanding

*Even the Teacher, a man who possessed
brilliant powers of wisdom and observation,
had to conclude some things are beyond
understanding. Failing in his attempt to "figure
out" life, he fell back on simple advice: Fear God
and obey him, no matter how things seem to
you. In essence, he concluded in favor of a life
of faith. For him, an old man, much of life had
already passed; in eloquent poetry he
describes the decay that was already at work
in his body (12:1–7). Thus he stressed,
"Remember your Creator in the days of your
youth" (12:1).*

¹⁰So then, banish anxiety from your heart
  and cast off the troubles of your body,
  for youth and vigor are meaningless.

12 Remember your Creator
  in the days of your youth,
before the days of trouble come
  and the years approach when you will say,
  "I find no pleasure in them"—
²before the sun and the light
  and the moon and the stars grow dark,
  and the clouds return after the rain;
³when the keepers of the house tremble,
  and the strong men stoop,
when the grinders cease because they are
  few,
  and those looking through the windows
  grow dim;
⁴when the doors to the street are closed
  and the sound of grinding fades;
when men rise up at the sound of birds,
  but all their songs grow faint;
⁵when men are afraid of heights
  and of dangers in the streets;
when the almond tree blossoms
  and the grasshopper drags himself along
  and desire no longer is stirred.
Then man goes to his eternal home
  and mourners go about the streets.

⁶Remember him—before the silver cord is
  severed,
  or the golden bowl is broken;
before the pitcher is shattered at the spring,
  or the wheel broken at the well,

---

a16 Or *king is a child*   *b5* Or *know how life* (or *the spirit*) / *enters the body being formed*

⁷and the dust returns to the ground it came
from,
and the spirit returns to God who gave it.

⁸"Meaningless! Meaningless!" says the
Teacher.ᵃ

12:13 The Gamble

*Having tried everything life has to offer, the
Teacher circles back to this uncomplicated
formula for making sense of our time on earth.
Although Ecclesiastes displays little of the
confidence of the book of Proverbs preceding it,
both arrive at exactly the same conclusion (see
Proverbs 1:7).*

*The 17th-century mathematician and
philosopher Blaise Pascal, who similarly
struggled with issues of meaninglessness,
concluded that faith sometimes resembles a
wager. He told his friends, "If I believe in God
and life after death and you do not, and if there
is no God, we both lose when we die. However,
if there is a God, you still lose and I gain
everything."*

"Everything is meaningless!"

The Conclusion of the Matter

⁹Not only was the Teacher wise, but also he
imparted knowledge to the people. He pondered
and searched out and set in order many proverbs. ¹⁰The Teacher searched to find just the
right words, and what he wrote was upright and
true.

¹¹The words of the wise are like goads, their
collected sayings like firmly embedded nails—
given by one Shepherd. ¹²Be warned, my son, of
anything in addition to them.

Of making many books there is no end, and
much study wearies the body.

¹³Now all has been heard;
here is the conclusion of the
matter:
Fear God and keep his commandments,
for this is the whole ⌊duty⌋ of man.

¹⁴For God will bring every deed into
judgment,
including every hidden thing,
whether it is good or evil.

ᵃ8 Or *the leader of the assembly*; also in verses 9 and 10

SONG OF SONGS

An Intoxicating Love
A poem about love the way it's meant to be

> *Many waters cannot quench love; rivers cannot wash it away. 8:7*

SNAP THE RADIO ON, ZIP to any station, and what are you likely to hear? Love songs. Songs of new love, songs of disappointed love, songs of grateful love, songs of crazy love. Times change, but through history the flow of love songs is a constant.

Plenty of people are shocked to find an explicit love song in the Bible—complete with erotic lyrics. But Song of Songs is exactly that. It shows no embarrassment about lovers enjoying each other's bodies, and talking about it. Consequently, intermittent attempts have been made to rule Song of Songs out of the Bible or to make it for "Adults Only." In 16th-century Spain, for instance, professor Fray Luis de Leon was dragged out of his classroom and imprisoned for four years. His crime? He translated Song of Songs into Spanish.

Allegorical Interpretation

More often, Song of Songs has been read as though it had nothing to do with lovers at all. Many have interpreted it as an allegory of love between God and his people. Some of these interpretations identify every poetic detail with some corresponding facet of our relationship to God. For instance, the bride's hair may be interpreted as non-Jewish nations who come to Christ. The famous 12th-century monk Saint Bernard of Clairvaux, using this allegorical approach, wrote 86 sermons on the first two chapters of Song of Songs.

Nowadays, few follow that kind of interpretation. Most scholars believe that the poem was intended to celebrate love between a newly married couple. God values love between a man and a woman. That's why he placed this song in his holy Bible. It may have been sung first at a wedding.

Naked and Unashamed

These lovers love to look at each other. They love to tell each other what they feel. They revel in the sensuous: the beauty of nature, the scent of perfumes and spices. They are openly erotic.

Their intoxication with love sounds quite up-to-date, not so different from what you hear on the radio. Yet Song of Songs conveys a very different atmosphere from most modern love songs. The explicit lyrics never become even slightly dirty. This love comes from the Garden of Eden, when both man and woman were naked and unashamed. It is tender, filled with delight, natural. You sense no shame or guilt; you feel that God is with the two as they love.

The lovers act as equals. Both woman and man take the initiative in praising each other. They don't flirt or play games: they say what they mean.

Yet they show caution and dignity in their love. While at the peak of joy, the lovers repeatedly warn others not to stir up love prematurely (2:7; 3:5; 8:4). They recognize the dangerously explosive side of love. "For love is as strong as death, its jealousy unyielding as the grave. It burns like blazing fire, like a mighty flame" (8:6).

How to Read Song of Songs

Since love songs are always popular, many people approach Song of Songs with great expectations. However, readers often find the book different from what they had expected.

Two main problems may hinder today's reader. One is the poetic imagery. No modern lover would say, "Your hair is like a flock of goats" (4:1), or, "Your nose is like the tower of Lebanon" (7:4). While some images in Song of Songs appeal—"His banner over me is love" (2:4) or "Love is as strong as death" (8:6)—the majority of the book's metaphors sound strange to our ears.

Most of the comparisons aren't visual, but emotional. For instance, when the lover tells his beloved that "your two breasts are like two fawns" (4:5), he isn't saying that her breasts look like deer. He is saying that they bring out the same tender feelings baby deer do. When you read strange-sounding metaphors in Song of Songs, don't ask, "What did these things (pomegranates, myrrh, a flock of sheep) look like?" but ask, "What did the lovers *feel* when they thought of them?"

A second problem: Song of Songs is hard to follow. One part doesn't seem connected to the next. Think of it as a series of snapshots of a couple in love—snapshots not necessarily in order. Put together in one photo album, they show the profound feelings of newly married lovers.

Though Song of Songs is primarily about love on the human level, many Christians and Jews have read it as a book about God's love. This was probably not the author's original intent, but it is a legitimate and inspiring way to look at the book. After all, God made human love, and other parts of the Bible suggest its similarity to God's love. (See Hosea 1—3 and Ephesians 5:22–33.) Song of Songs never makes this connection, but it does present a love so rich, so full, so unashamed that it's natural to think of God and his love for us.

3-TRACK READING PLAN

For an explanation and complete listing of the 3-track reading plan, turn to page 7

TRACK 1: *Two-Week Courses on the Bible*
See page 7 for information on these courses.

TRACK 2: *An Overview of Song of Songs in 1 Day*
☐ Day 1. Read the Introduction to Song of Songs and chapter 2, a beautiful love poem.

Now turn to page 9 for your next Track 2 reading project.

TRACK 3: *All of Song of Songs in 8 Days*
After you have read through Song of Songs, turn to pages 10–14 for your next Track 3 reading project.
☐1 ☐2 ☐3 ☐4 ☐5 ☐6 ☐7 ☐8

1

Solomon's Song of Songs.

Beloved[a]

²Let him kiss me with the kisses of his
      mouth—
   for your love is more delightful than wine.
³Pleasing is the fragrance of your perfumes;
   your name is like perfume poured out.
   No wonder the maidens love you!
⁴Take me away with you—let us hurry!
   Let the king bring me into his chambers.

Friends

We rejoice and delight in you[b];
   we will praise your love more than wine.

Beloved

How right they are to adore you!

⁵Dark am I, yet lovely,
   O daughters of Jerusalem,
   dark like the tents of Kedar,
   like the tent curtains of Solomon.[c]
⁶Do not stare at me because I am dark,
   because I am darkened by the sun.
   My mother's sons were angry with me
   and made me take care of the vineyards;
   my own vineyard I have neglected.
⁷Tell me, you whom I love, where you graze
      your flock
   and where you rest your sheep at
      midday.

[a]Primarily on the basis of the gender of the Hebrew pronouns used, male and female speakers are indicated in the margins by the captions *Lover* and *Beloved* respectively. The words of others are marked *Friends*. In some instances the divisions and their captions are debatable.   [b]4 The Hebrew is masculine singular.   [c]5 Or *Salma*

Why should I be like a veiled woman
  beside the flocks of your friends?

Friends

[8] If you do not know, most beautiful of
    women,
  follow the tracks of the sheep
and graze your young goats
  by the tents of the shepherds.

1:6 Tan Lines

Modern Americans, who lavish millions of dollars on tanning lotions and tanning salons, consider a suntan desirable, despite its health risks. Not so in Victorian times—or in Solomon's time. Soft white skin marked a more refined person who had not been required to work outdoors.

Lover

[9] I liken you, my darling, to a mare
  harnessed to one of the chariots of
    Pharaoh.
[10] Your cheeks are beautiful with earrings,
  your neck with strings of jewels.
[11] We will make you earrings of gold,
  studded with silver.

Beloved

[12] While the king was at his table,
  my perfume spread its fragrance.
[13] My lover is to me a sachet of myrrh
  resting between my breasts.
[14] My lover is to me a cluster of henna
    blossoms
  from the vineyards of En Gedi.

Lover

[15] How beautiful you are, my darling!
  Oh, how beautiful!
  Your eyes are doves.

Beloved

[16] How handsome you are, my lover!
  Oh, how charming!
  And our bed is verdant.

Lover

[17] The beams of our house are cedars;
  our rafters are firs.

Beloved[a]

2 I am a rose[b] of Sharon,
  a lily of the valleys.

Lover

[2] Like a lily among thorns
  is my darling among the maidens.

Beloved

[3] Like an apple tree among the trees of the
    forest
  is my lover among the young men.
I delight to sit in his shade,
  and his fruit is sweet to my taste.
[4] He has taken me to the banquet hall,
  and his banner over me is love.

2:4 His Banner over Me

A "banner" was a large military flag that held a fighting unit together in battle. In the noise and dust of the fight, soldiers needed a visible sign to keep them oriented. For these lovers, a public and visible declaration of love forms a "banner," keeping them together.

[5] Strengthen me with raisins,
  refresh me with apples,
  for I am faint with love.
[6] His left arm is under my head,
  and his right arm embraces me.
[7] Daughters of Jerusalem, I charge you
  by the gazelles and by the does of the
    field:
Do not arouse or awaken love
  until it so desires.

[8] Listen! My lover!
  Look! Here he comes,
leaping across the mountains,
  bounding over the hills.
[9] My lover is like a gazelle or a young stag.
  Look! There he stands behind our wall,
gazing through the windows,
  peering through the lattice.
[10] My lover spoke and said to me,
  "Arise, my darling,
  my beautiful one, and come with me.
[11] See! The winter is past;
  the rains are over and gone.
[12] Flowers appear on the earth;
  the season of singing has come,
the cooing of doves
  is heard in our land.
[13] The fig tree forms its early fruit;
  the blossoming vines spread their
    fragrance.
Arise, come, my darling;
  my beautiful one, come with me."

---

[a] 1 Or *Lover*   [b] 1 Possibly a member of the crocus family

Lover

[14]My dove in the clefts of the rock,
in the hiding places on the mountainside,
show me your face,
let me hear your voice;
for your voice is sweet,
and your face is lovely.
[15]Catch for us the foxes,
the little foxes
that ruin the vineyards,
our vineyards that are in bloom.

Beloved

[16]My lover is mine and I am his;
he browses among the lilies.
[17]Until the day breaks
and the shadows flee,
turn, my lover,
and be like a gazelle
or like a young stag
on the rugged hills.[a]

3 All night long on my bed
I looked for the one my heart loves;
I looked for him but did not find him.
[2]I will get up now and go about the city,
through its streets and squares;
I will search for the one my heart loves.
So I looked for him but did not find him.
[3]The watchmen found me
as they made their rounds in the city.
"Have you seen the one my heart loves?"
[4]Scarcely had I passed them
when I found the one my heart loves.
I held him and would not let him go
till I had brought him to my mother's
house,
to the room of the one who conceived
me.
[5]Daughters of Jerusalem, I charge you
by the gazelles and by the does of the
field:
Do not arouse or awaken love
until it so desires.

[6]Who is this coming up from the desert
like a column of smoke,

3:5 Let Love Sleep

*If love is so wonderful, as this poem beautifully
sings, shouldn't people pursue it recklessly? Yet
the beloved warns them not to. Three times she
urges others not to force love, but to let it
develop at its own rate. Love should wait for its
proper time.*

perfumed with myrrh and incense
made from all the spices of the merchant?
[7]Look! It is Solomon's carriage,
escorted by sixty warriors,
the noblest of Israel,
[8]all of them wearing the sword,
all experienced in battle,
each with his sword at his side,
prepared for the terrors of the night.
[9]King Solomon made for himself the carriage;
he made it of wood from Lebanon.
[10]Its posts he made of silver,
its base of gold.
Its seat was upholstered with purple,
its interior lovingly inlaid
by[b] the daughters of Jerusalem.
[11]Come out, you daughters of Zion,
and look at King Solomon wearing the
crown,
the crown with which his mother crowned
him
on the day of his wedding,
the day his heart rejoiced.

Lover

4 How beautiful you are, my darling!
Oh, how beautiful!
Your eyes behind your veil are doves.
Your hair is like a flock of goats
descending from Mount Gilead.
[2]Your teeth are like a flock of sheep just
shorn,
coming up from the washing.
Each has its twin;
not one of them is alone.
[3]Your lips are like a scarlet ribbon;
your mouth is lovely.
Your temples behind your veil
are like the halves of a pomegranate.
[4]Your neck is like the tower of David,
built with elegance[c];
on it hang a thousand shields,
all of them shields of warriors.
[5]Your two breasts are like two fawns,
like twin fawns of a gazelle
that browse among the lilies.
[6]Until the day breaks
and the shadows flee,
I will go to the mountain of myrrh
and to the hill of incense.
[7]All beautiful you are, my darling;
there is no flaw in you.

[8]Come with me from Lebanon, my bride,
come with me from Lebanon.
Descend from the crest of Amana,
from the top of Senir, the summit of
Hermon,

---

[a]17 Or *the hills of Bether*   [b]10 Or *its inlaid interior a gift of love / from*   [c]4 The meaning of the Hebrew for this
word is uncertain.

from the lions' dens
    and the mountain haunts of the leopards.
[9]You have stolen my heart, my sister, my
    bride;
  you have stolen my heart
with one glance of your eyes,
  with one jewel of your necklace.
[10]How delightful is your love, my sister, my
    bride!
  How much more pleasing is your love
    than wine,
  and the fragrance of your perfume than
    any spice!
[11]Your lips drop sweetness as the honeycomb,
    my bride;
  milk and honey are under your tongue.
  The fragrance of your garments is like
    that of Lebanon.
[12]You are a garden locked up, my sister, my
    bride;
  you are a spring enclosed, a sealed
    fountain.
[13]Your plants are an orchard of pomegranates
    with choice fruits,
  with henna and nard,
[14]   nard and saffron,
    calamus and cinnamon,
  with every kind of incense tree,
  with myrrh and aloes
    and all the finest spices.
[15]You are[a] a garden fountain,
  a well of flowing water
    streaming down from Lebanon.

Beloved

[16]Awake, north wind,
    and come, south wind!
Blow on my garden,
  that its fragrance may spread abroad.
Let my lover come into his garden
  and taste its choice fruits.

Lover

5 I have come into my garden, my sister, my
    bride;
  I have gathered my myrrh with my spice.
I have eaten my honeycomb and my honey;
  I have drunk my wine and my milk.

Friends

Eat, O friends, and drink;
  drink your fill, O lovers.

Beloved

[2]I slept but my heart was awake.
  Listen! My lover is knocking:
"Open to me, my sister, my darling,
  my dove, my flawless one.

My head is drenched with dew,
  my hair with the dampness of the night."
[3]I have taken off my robe—
  must I put it on again?

5:2–8 A Nightmare

This short passage and the first five verses of chapter 3 are strange and troubling interludes. Many scholars think they are dream sequences, nightmares showing that the beauty of love also brings an increased vulnerability to pain and fear. Here, the beloved is slow to get out of bed to welcome her lover. As a result, he is gone when she reaches the door.

I have washed my feet—
  must I soil them again?
[4]My lover thrust his hand through the
    latch-opening;
  my heart began to pound for him.
[5]I arose to open for my lover,
  and my hands dripped with myrrh,
my fingers with flowing myrrh,
  on the handles of the lock.
[6]I opened for my lover,
  but my lover had left; he was gone.
  My heart sank at his departure.[b]
I looked for him but did not find him.
  I called him but he did not answer.
[7]The watchmen found me
  as they made their rounds in the city.
They beat me, they bruised me;
  they took away my cloak,
  those watchmen of the walls!
[8]O daughters of Jerusalem, I charge you—
  if you find my lover,
what will you tell him?
  Tell him I am faint with love.

Friends

[9]How is your beloved better than others,
  most beautiful of women?
How is your beloved better than others,
  that you charge us so?

Beloved

[10]My lover is radiant and ruddy,
  outstanding among ten thousand.
[11]His head is purest gold;
  his hair is wavy
    and black as a raven.
[12]His eyes are like doves
  by the water streams,
washed in milk,
  mounted like jewels.

---

a 15 Or I am (spoken by the Beloved)   *b 6 Or heart had gone out to him when he spoke*

¹³His cheeks are like beds of spice
  yielding perfume.
His lips are like lilies
  dripping with myrrh.
¹⁴His arms are rods of gold
  set with chrysolite.
His body is like polished ivory
  decorated with sapphires.ᵃ
¹⁵His legs are pillars of marble
  set on bases of pure gold.
His appearance is like Lebanon,
  choice as its cedars.
¹⁶His mouth is sweetness itself;
  he is altogether lovely.
This is my lover, this my friend,
  O daughters of Jerusalem.

Friends

6 Where has your lover gone,
  most beautiful of women?
Which way did your lover turn,
  that we may look for him with you?

Beloved

²My lover has gone down to his garden,
  to the beds of spices,
to browse in the gardens
  and to gather lilies.
³I am my lover's and my lover is mine;
  he browses among the lilies.

Lover

⁴You are beautiful, my darling, as Tirzah,
  lovely as Jerusalem,
  majestic as troops with banners.
⁵Turn your eyes from me;
  they overwhelm me.
Your hair is like a flock of goats
  descending from Gilead.
⁶Your teeth are like a flock of sheep
  coming up from the washing.
Each has its twin,
  not one of them is alone.
⁷Your temples behind your veil
  are like the halves of a pomegranate.
⁸Sixty queens there may be,
  and eighty concubines,
  and virgins beyond number;
⁹but my dove, my perfect one, is unique,
  the only daughter of her mother,
  the favorite of the one who bore her.
The maidens saw her and called her blessed;
  the queens and concubines praised her.

Friends

¹⁰Who is this that appears like the dawn,
  fair as the moon, bright as the sun,
  majestic as the stars in procession?

Lover

¹¹I went down to the grove of nut trees
  to look at the new growth in the valley,
to see if the vines had budded
  or the pomegranates were in bloom.
¹²Before I realized it,
  my desire set me among the royal chariots
   of my people.ᵇ

Friends

¹³Come back, come back, O Shulammite;
  come back, come back, that we may gaze
   on you!

Lover

Why would you gaze on the Shulammite
  as on the dance of Mahanaim?

7 How beautiful your sandaled feet,
  O prince's daughter!
Your graceful legs are like jewels,
  the work of a craftsman's hands.
²Your navel is a rounded goblet
  that never lacks blended wine.
Your waist is a mound of wheat
  encircled by lilies.
³Your breasts are like two fawns,
  twins of a gazelle.
⁴Your neck is like an ivory tower.
Your eyes are the pools of Heshbon
  by the gate of Bath Rabbim.
Your nose is like the tower of Lebanon
  looking toward Damascus.
⁵Your head crowns you like Mount Carmel.
Your hair is like royal tapestry;
  the king is held captive by its tresses.
⁶How beautiful you are and how pleasing,
  O love, with your delights!
⁷Your stature is like that of the palm,
  and your breasts like clusters of fruit.
⁸I said, "I will climb the palm tree;
  I will take hold of its fruit."
May your breasts be like the clusters of the
  vine,
  the fragrance of your breath like apples,
⁹ and your mouth like the best wine.

Beloved

May the wine go straight to my lover,
  flowing gently over lips and teeth.ᶜ
¹⁰I belong to my lover,
  and his desire is for me.
¹¹Come, my lover, let us go to the countryside,
  let us spend the night in the villages.ᵈ
¹²Let us go early to the vineyards
  to see if the vines have budded,
if their blossoms have opened,
  and if the pomegranates are in bloom—

ᵃ14 Or *lapis lazuli* ᵇ12 Or *among the chariots of Amminadab;* or *among the chariots of the people of the prince*
ᶜ9 Septuagint, Aquila, Vulgate and Syriac; Hebrew *lips of sleepers* ᵈ11 Or *henna bushes*

there I will give you my love.
¹³The mandrakes send out their fragrance,
    and at our door is every delicacy,
both new and old,
    that I have stored up for you, my lover.

8 If only you were to me like a brother,
    who was nursed at my mother's breasts!
Then, if I found you outside,
    I would kiss you,
    and no one would despise me.

8:1 A Brotherly Kiss

In oriental culture, even a married couple could not express their love publicly. Only a brother and sister could openly kiss. The beloved is wishing she had the right to show their love to the world.

²I would lead you
    and bring you to my mother's house—
    she who has taught me.
I would give you spiced wine to drink,
    the nectar of my pomegranates.
³His left arm is under my head
    and his right arm embraces me.
⁴Daughters of Jerusalem, I charge you:
    Do not arouse or awaken love
    until it so desires.

Friends

⁵Who is this coming up from the desert
    leaning on her lover?

Beloved

Under the apple tree I roused you;
    there your mother conceived you,
    there she who was in labor gave you birth.
⁶Place me like a seal over your heart,
    like a seal on your arm;
for love is as strong as death,
    its jealousy*ᵃ* unyielding as the grave.*ᵇ*
It burns like blazing fire,
    like a mighty flame.*ᶜ*
⁷Many waters cannot quench love;
    rivers cannot wash it away.
If one were to give

all the wealth of his house for love,
    it*ᵈ* would be utterly scorned.

Friends

⁸We have a young sister,
    and her breasts are not yet grown.
What shall we do for our sister
    for the day she is spoken for?
⁹If she is a wall,
    we will build towers of silver on her.
If she is a door,
    we will enclose her with panels of cedar.

Beloved

¹⁰I am a wall,
    and my breasts are like towers.
Thus I have become in his eyes
    like one bringing contentment.
¹¹Solomon had a vineyard in Baal Hamon;
    he let out his vineyard to tenants.
Each was to bring for its fruit
    a thousand shekels*ᵉ* of silver.
¹²But my own vineyard is mine to give;
    the thousand shekels are for you,
        O Solomon,
    and two hundred*ᶠ* are for those who
        tend its fruit.

8:6 Love and Death

Death sweeps everything away. It yields to no one, and once you are in its power you cannot escape. So with love: It takes control of your life, and like a gigantic fire, it cannot be doused. Love must be treated with the greatest caution and respect.

Lover

¹³You who dwell in the gardens
    with friends in attendance,
    let me hear your voice!

Beloved

¹⁴Come away, my lover,
    and be like a gazelle
or like a young stag
    on the spice-laden mountains.

ᵃ6 Or *ardor*   *ᵇ6* Hebrew *Sheol*   *ᶜ6* Or / *like the very flame of the* LORD   *ᵈ7* Or *he*   *ᵉ11* That is, about 25
pounds (about 11.5 kilograms); also in verse 12   *ᶠ12* That is, about 5 pounds (about 2.3 kilograms)

ISAIAH

Prophet, Poet, and Politician
His nation at a crossroads, Isaiah rose to meet the challenge

T HE PROPHET ISAIAH WAS A giant of Jewish history. He was the Shakespeare of Hebrew literature, and the New Testament quotes him more than
all the other prophets combined. No other biblical author can match his
rich vocabulary and use of imagery.

And yet Isaiah spent his days not in an ivory tower, but in the corridors of
power. He served as adviser to the kings of Judah and helped set the course of
his nation.

> *And he looked for justice, but saw bloodshed; for righteousness, but heard cries of distress. 5:7*

Days of Crisis

Isaiah lived at a crucial time, midway between the founding of the kingdom under Saul and
David and its eventual destruction. A civil war had split the Israelites into North (Israel) and
South (Judah), and Isaiah lived in the more pious Southern Kingdom.

When Isaiah began his work, the nation seemed strong and wealthy. But Isaiah saw signs of
grave danger. People were using their power to harass the poor. Men went around drunk; women
cared more about their clothes than about their neighbors' hunger. People gave lip service to God and
kept up the outward appearance of religion but did little more.

Outside dangers loomed even larger. The armies of neighboring Israel were rattling swords and
spears at the border. On all sides, monster empires were growing, especially Egypt and Assyria. Judah
was caught in a pincers. Should the nation choose one of the empires as an ally?

Harsh Words from an Uncompromising Prophet

The nation of Judah, said Isaiah, stood at a crossroads: It could either regain its footing or begin a
dangerous slide downward. The prophet did not temper his message for the sake of popular opinion.
He had harsh and unyielding words about what changes must take place.

Although he moved in royal circles, Isaiah was hardly a yes-man in politics. Sometimes he stood
alone against a tide of optimism. His very name meant "The LORD saves," and he warned kings that
relying on military power or wealth or any force other than God would lead to disaster.

Isaiah outlasted four kings, but he finally offended one beyond repair. King Manasseh (notorious for
practicing infant sacrifice) found Isaiah's strong words too much to bear. Tradition records that he had
Isaiah killed by fastening him between two planks of wood and sawing his body in half.

Manasseh has long since disappeared into obscurity. But Isaiah, through this book, endures as one
of the great authors of all time. Sometimes the pen *is* mightier than the sword.

How to Read Isaiah

I n the eighth century B.C., about the time Homer was writing *The Iliad* and *The Odyssey*,
Isaiah wrote the book that bears his name. It is arguably the most eloquent book in the
Old Testament, and you will likely recognize many verses and phrases.

Isaiah is full of profound insights into the nature of God and his plan for the earth. Due to
its length and its peculiar organization, however, the book may seem hard to grasp.

Remember that Isaiah consists of a collection of many messages on various topics, pulled together into groupings. To understand Isaiah, it helps to think of "road markers" that set off the major groupings. Here is a summary of them:

Isaiah 1–12: Isaiah's call and messages of warning to Judah during the prosperous days of the kingdom. (These came mostly in the reigns of Jotham and Ahaz: see "A Lineup of Rulers," pages 1361–1369.)

Isaiah 13–23: Isaiah's messages to all the nations around Judah—including enemies and close allies.

Isaiah 24–35: A view of the earth's future (24–27) and specific messages to the people of Judah as they faced Assyria's imminent invasion.

Isaiah 36–39: An interlude telling of great crises faced by King Hezekiah. The focus of the book moves from Assyria to Babylon.

Isaiah 40–48: Prophecies addressed to a very different situation, 200 years into the future. Now Babylon, not Assyria, is the great enemy.

Isaiah 49–55: A word of hope about final deliverance through the "suffering servant."

Isaiah 56–66: General warnings to Judah, and a view of the future.

PEOPLE YOU'LL MEET IN ISAIAH

ISAIAH (p. 711)
CYRUS (p. 755)

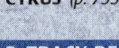

3-TRACK READING PLAN

For an explanation and complete listing of the 3-track reading plan, turn to page 7.

TRACK 1: **Two-Week Courses on the Bible**
The Track 1 reading program on the Old Testament includes one chapter from Isaiah. See page 8 for a complete listing of this course.

TRACK 2: **An Overview of Isaiah in 6 Days**
☐ Day 1. Read the Introduction to Isaiah and also chapter 6. This chapter describes Isaiah's dramatic call.
☐ Day 2. Read chapter 25, a song of praise.
☐ Day 3. Read chapter 40, a great description of God and his power over the whole earth.
☐ Day 4. Read chapter 52, which gives detailed descriptions of God's ultimate plan.
☐ Day 5. Read chapter 53, a remarkable prophecy quoted at least ten times in the New Testament.
☐ Day 6. Read chapter 55, a word of great comfort from God.

Now turn to page 9 for your next Track 2 reading project.

TRACK 3: **All of Isaiah in 63 Days**
After you have read through Isaiah, turn to pages 10–14 for your next Track 3 reading project.

☐1	☐2	☐3	☐4–5	☐6	☐7	☐8	☐9
☐10	☐11	☐12	☐13	☐14	☐15	☐16	☐17
☐18	☐19–20	☐21	☐22	☐23	☐24	☐25	☐26
☐27	☐28	☐29	☐30	☐31	☐32	☐33	☐34
☐35	☐36	☐37	☐38–39	☐40	☐41	☐42	☐43
☐44	☐45	☐46	☐47	☐48	☐49	☐50	☐51
☐52	☐53	☐54	☐55	☐56	☐57	☐58	☐59
☐60	☐61	☐62	☐63	☐64	☐65	☐66	

1

The vision concerning Judah and Jerusalem that Isaiah son of Amoz saw during the reigns of Uzziah, Jotham, Ahaz and Hezekiah, kings of Judah.

A Rebellious Nation

²Hear, O heavens! Listen, O earth!
  For the LORD has spoken:
"I reared children and brought them up,
  but they have rebelled against me.
³The ox knows his master,
  the donkey his owner's manger,
but Israel does not know,
  my people do not understand."

⁴Ah, sinful nation,
  a people loaded with guilt,
a brood of evildoers,
  children given to corruption!
They have forsaken the LORD;
  they have spurned the Holy One of Israel
  and turned their backs on him.

⁵Why should you be beaten anymore?
  Why do you persist in rebellion?
Your whole head is injured,
  your whole heart afflicted.
⁶From the sole of your foot to the top of
    your head
  there is no soundness—
only wounds and welts
  and open sores,
not cleansed or bandaged
  or soothed with oil.

⁷Your country is desolate,
  your cities burned with fire;
your fields are being stripped by foreigners
  right before you,
  laid waste as when overthrown by
    strangers.
⁸The Daughter of Zion is left
  like a shelter in a vineyard,
like a hut in a field of melons,
  like a city under siege.
⁹Unless the LORD Almighty
  had left us some survivors,
we would have become like Sodom,
  we would have been like Gomorrah.

¹⁰Hear the word of the LORD,
  you rulers of Sodom;
listen to the law of our God,
  you people of Gomorrah!
¹¹"The multitude of your sacrifices—
  what are they to me?" says the LORD.
"I have more than enough of burnt offerings,
  of rams and the fat of fattened animals;
I have no pleasure
  in the blood of bulls and lambs and goats.

¹²When you come to appear before me,
  who has asked this of you,
  this trampling of my courts?
¹³Stop bringing meaningless offerings!
  Your incense is detestable to me.
New Moons, Sabbaths and convocations—
  I cannot bear your evil assemblies.
¹⁴Your New Moon festivals and your
    appointed feasts
  my soul hates.
They have become a burden to me;
  I am weary of bearing them.

1:14 The New Sodom

Is God finished with Israel? He denounces them as "Sodom and Gomorrah" (verse 10), judging their worship worthless, and their prayers an insult. But just when his tirade reaches its peak, God invites the Israelites to "come . . . reason" with him. Sins "like scarlet" shall be "as white as snow" (verse 18). God judges his people not to destroy them, but to bring them to repentance, forgiveness, and redemption.

¹⁵When you spread out your hands in prayer,
  I will hide my eyes from you;
even if you offer many prayers,
  I will not listen.
Your hands are full of blood;
¹⁶ wash and make yourselves clean.
Take your evil deeds
  out of my sight!
Stop doing wrong,
¹⁷ learn to do right!
Seek justice,
  encourage the oppressed.ᵃ
Defend the cause of the fatherless,
  plead the case of the widow.

¹⁸"Come now, let us reason together,"
  says the LORD.
"Though your sins are like scarlet,
  they shall be as white as snow;
though they are red as crimson,
  they shall be like wool.
¹⁹If you are willing and obedient,
  you will eat the best from the land;
²⁰but if you resist and rebel,
  you will be devoured by the sword."
            For the mouth of the LORD
              has spoken.

²¹See how the faithful city
  has become a harlot!
She once was full of justice;
  righteousness used to dwell in her—
  but now murderers!

ᵃ17 Or / rebuke the oppressor

²²Your silver has become dross,
    your choice wine is diluted with water.
²³Your rulers are rebels,
    companions of thieves;
they all love bribes
    and chase after gifts.
They do not defend the cause of the
      fatherless;
    the widow's case does not come before
      them.

1:23 Justice, Not Religion

*Isaiah 1 paints a striking picture of conditions
in Judah. Descriptions of luxury indicate the
nation was prospering economically. There
was no shortage of offerings, prayers, and
religious celebrations (verses 11–17). But Isaiah
condemned Judah for not putting religion into
practice by defending weak people, such as
widows and the fatherless. The country's
prosperity had come at the poor's expense.*

²⁴Therefore the Lord, the LORD Almighty,
    the Mighty One of Israel, declares:
"Ah, I will get relief from my foes
    and avenge myself on my enemies.
²⁵I will turn my hand against you;
    I will thoroughly purge away your dross
    and remove all your impurities.
²⁶I will restore your judges as in days of old,
    your counselors as at the beginning.
Afterward you will be called
    the City of Righteousness,
    the Faithful City."

²⁷Zion will be redeemed with justice,
    her penitent ones with righteousness.
²⁸But rebels and sinners will both be broken,
    and those who forsake the LORD will
      perish.

²⁹"You will be ashamed because of the sacred
      oaks
    in which you have delighted;
you will be disgraced because of the gardens
    that you have chosen.
³⁰You will be like an oak with fading leaves,
    like a garden without water.
³¹The mighty man will become tinder
    and his work a spark;
both will burn together,
    with no one to quench the fire."

The Mountain of the LORD

2 This is what Isaiah son of Amoz saw concerning Judah and Jerusalem:

²In the last days

the mountain of the LORD's temple will be
      established
    as chief among the mountains;
it will be raised above the hills,
    and all nations will stream to it.

³Many peoples will come and say,

"Come, let us go up to the mountain of the
      LORD,
    to the house of the God of Jacob.
He will teach us his ways,
    so that we may walk in his paths."
The law will go out from Zion,
    the word of the LORD from Jerusalem.
⁴He will judge between the nations
    and will settle disputes for many peoples.
They will beat their swords into plowshares
    and their spears into pruning hooks.
Nation will not take up sword against nation,
    nor will they train for war anymore.

⁵Come, O house of Jacob,
    let us walk in the light of the LORD.

The Day of the LORD

⁶You have abandoned your people,
    the house of Jacob.
They are full of superstitions from the East;
    they practice divination like the Philistines
    and clasp hands with pagans.
⁷Their land is full of silver and gold;
    there is no end to their treasures.
Their land is full of horses;
    there is no end to their chariots.
⁸Their land is full of idols;
    they bow down to the work of their
      hands,
    to what their fingers have made.
⁹So man will be brought low
    and mankind humbled—
    do not forgive them.ᵃ

¹⁰Go into the rocks,
    hide in the ground
from dread of the LORD
    and the splendor of his majesty!
¹¹The eyes of the arrogant man will be
      humbled
    and the pride of men brought low;
the LORD alone will be exalted in that day.

¹²The LORD Almighty has a day in store
    for all the proud and lofty,
    for all that is exalted
    (and they will be humbled),
¹³for all the cedars of Lebanon, tall and lofty,
    and all the oaks of Bashan,
¹⁴for all the towering mountains
    and all the high hills,
¹⁵for every lofty tower

ᵃ9 Or *not raise them up*

and every fortified wall,
[16]for every trading ship[a]
and every stately vessel.
[17]The arrogance of man will be brought low
and the pride of men humbled;
the LORD alone will be exalted in that day,
[18] and the idols will totally disappear.

[19]Men will flee to caves in the rocks
and to holes in the ground
from dread of the LORD
and the splendor of his majesty,
when he rises to shake the earth.
[20]In that day men will throw away
to the rodents and bats
their idols of silver and idols of gold,
which they made to worship.
[21]They will flee to caverns in the rocks
and to the overhanging crags
from dread of the LORD
and the splendor of his majesty,
when he rises to shake the earth.

[22]Stop trusting in man,
who has but a breath in his nostrils.
Of what account is he?

Judgment on Jerusalem and Judah

3 See now, the Lord,
the LORD Almighty,
is about to take from Jerusalem and Judah
both supply and support:
all supplies of food and all supplies of water,
[2] the hero and warrior,
the judge and prophet,
the soothsayer and elder,
[3]the captain of fifty and man of rank,
the counselor, skilled craftsman and clever
enchanter.

[4]I will make boys their officials;
mere children will govern them.
[5]People will oppress each other—
man against man, neighbor against
neighbor.
The young will rise up against the old,
the base against the honorable.

[6]A man will seize one of his brothers
at his father's home, and say,
"You have a cloak, you be our leader;
take charge of this heap of ruins!"
[7]But in that day he will cry out,
"I have no remedy.
I have no food or clothing in my house;
do not make me the leader of the people."

[8]Jerusalem staggers,
Judah is falling;
their words and deeds are against the LORD,
defying his glorious presence.

[9]The look on their faces testifies against them;
they parade their sin like Sodom;
they do not hide it.
Woe to them!
They have brought disaster upon
themselves.

3:6 Total Anarchy

*Isaiah foresees a time of judgment on Judah,
when total anarchy will prevail. Leaders will be
chosen at random, and the nation's supply of
young men will be decimated by war (verse
25). The vivid passage on the haughty women
of Zion (3:16—4:1) shows why this book is
admired for its writing style.*

[10]Tell the righteous it will be well with them,
for they will enjoy the fruit of their deeds.
[11]Woe to the wicked! Disaster is upon them!
They will be paid back for what their hands
have done.

[12]Youths oppress my people,
women rule over them.
O my people, your guides lead you astray;
they turn you from the path.

[13]The LORD takes his place in court;
he rises to judge the people.
[14]The LORD enters into judgment
against the elders and leaders of his
people:
"It is you who have ruined my vineyard;
the plunder from the poor is in your
houses.
[15]What do you mean by crushing my people
and grinding the faces of the poor?"
declares the Lord,
the LORD Almighty.

[16]The LORD says,
"The women of Zion are haughty,
walking along with outstretched necks,
flirting with their eyes,
tripping along with mincing steps,
with ornaments jingling on their ankles.
[17]Therefore the Lord will bring sores on the
heads of the women of Zion;
the LORD will make their scalps bald."

[18]In that day the Lord will snatch away their
finery: the bangles and headbands and crescent
necklaces, [19]the earrings and bracelets and veils,
[20]the headdresses and ankle chains and sashes,
the perfume bottles and charms, [21]the signet
rings and nose rings, [22]the fine robes and the

---

[a] 16 Hebrew *every ship of Tarshish*

capes and cloaks, the purses ²³and mirrors, and the linen garments and tiaras and shawls.

²⁴Instead of fragrance there will be a stench;
    instead of a sash, a rope;
instead of well-dressed hair, baldness,
    instead of fine clothing, sackcloth;
    instead of beauty, branding.
²⁵Your men will fall by the sword,
    your warriors in battle.
²⁶The gates of Zion will lament and mourn;
    destitute, she will sit on the ground.

4 In that day seven women
    will take hold of one man
and say, "We will eat our own food
    and provide our own clothes;
only let us be called by your name.
    Take away our disgrace!"

The Branch of the LORD

²In that day the Branch of the LORD will be beautiful and glorious, and the fruit of the land will be the pride and glory of the survivors in Israel. ³Those who are left in Zion, who remain in Jerusalem, will be called holy, all who are recorded among the living in Jerusalem. ⁴The Lord will wash away the filth of the women of Zion; he will cleanse the bloodstains from Jerusalem by a spirit*a* of judgment and a spirit*a* of fire. ⁵Then the LORD will create over all of Mount Zion and over those who assemble there a cloud of smoke by day and a glow of flaming fire by night; over all the glory will be a canopy. ⁶It will be a shelter and shade from the heat of the day, and a refuge and hiding place from the storm and rain.

The Song of the Vineyard

5 I will sing for the one I love
    a song about his vineyard:
My loved one had a vineyard
    on a fertile hillside.
²He dug it up and cleared it of stones
    and planted it with the choicest vines.
He built a watchtower in it
    and cut out a winepress as well.
Then he looked for a crop of good grapes,
    but it yielded only bad fruit.

³"Now you dwellers in Jerusalem and men of
        Judah,
    judge between me and my vineyard.
⁴What more could have been done for my
        vineyard
    than I have done for it?
When I looked for good grapes,
    why did it yield only bad?
⁵Now I will tell you
    what I am going to do to my vineyard:

I will take away its hedge,
    and it will be destroyed;
I will break down its wall,
    and it will be trampled.
⁶I will make it a wasteland,

5:4 What Can God Do?

The "Song of the Vineyard" beautifully summarizes God's message to Judah. Although he had done everything possible to care for the nation, his "vineyard"—the house of Israel—had produced only wild grapes. What else could he do but allow it to grow wild and uncultivated? Jesus used a related analogy in some of his parables (Matthew 20:1–16; 21:33–46; Mark 12:1–12; Luke 13:6–9; 20:9–19).

    neither pruned nor cultivated,
    and briers and thorns will grow there.
I will command the clouds
    not to rain on it."

⁷The vineyard of the LORD Almighty
    is the house of Israel,
and the men of Judah
    are the garden of his delight.
And he looked for justice, but saw
        bloodshed;
    for righteousness, but heard cries of
        distress.

Woes and Judgments

⁸Woe to you who add house to house
    and join field to field
till no space is left
    and you live alone in the land.

⁹The LORD Almighty has declared in my hearing:

"Surely the great houses will become
        desolate,
    the fine mansions left without occupants.
¹⁰A ten-acre*b* vineyard will produce only a
        bath*c* of wine,
    a homer*d* of seed only an ephah*e* of
        grain."

¹¹Woe to those who rise early in the morning
    to run after their drinks,
who stay up late at night
    till they are inflamed with wine.
¹²They have harps and lyres at their banquets,
    tambourines and flutes and wine,
but they have no regard for the deeds of the
        LORD,

---

*a*4 Or *the Spirit*   *b*10 Hebrew *ten-yoke,* that is, the land plowed by 10 yoke of oxen in one day   *c*10 That is,
probably about 6 gallons (about 22 liters)   *d*10 That is, probably about 6 bushels (about 220 liters)   *e*10 That is,
probably about 3/5 bushel (about 22 liters)

no respect for the work of his hands.
¹³Therefore my people will go into exile
for lack of understanding;
their men of rank will die of hunger
and their masses will be parched with
thirst.
¹⁴Therefore the grave*a* enlarges its appetite
and opens its mouth without limit;
into it will descend their nobles and masses
with all their brawlers and revelers.
¹⁵So man will be brought low
and mankind humbled,
the eyes of the arrogant humbled.
¹⁶But the LORD Almighty will be exalted by his
justice,
and the holy God will show himself holy
by his righteousness.
¹⁷Then sheep will graze as in their own
pasture;
lambs will feed*b* among the ruins of the
rich.

¹⁸Woe to those who draw sin along with cords
of deceit,
and wickedness as with cart ropes,
¹⁹to those who say, "Let God hurry,
let him hasten his work
so we may see it.
Let it approach,
let the plan of the Holy One of Israel
come,
so we may know it."

²⁰Woe to those who call evil good
and good evil,
who put darkness for light
and light for darkness,
who put bitter for sweet
and sweet for bitter.

²¹Woe to those who are wise in their own eyes
and clever in their own sight.

²²Woe to those who are heroes at drinking
wine
and champions at mixing drinks,
²³who acquit the guilty for a bribe,
but deny justice to the innocent.

²⁴Therefore, as tongues of fire lick up straw
and as dry grass sinks down in the flames,
so their roots will decay
and their flowers blow away like dust;
for they have rejected the law of the LORD
Almighty
and spurned the word of the Holy One of
Israel.
²⁵Therefore the LORD's anger burns against his
people;
his hand is raised and he strikes them
down.

The mountains shake,
and the dead bodies are like refuse in the
streets.

Yet for all this, his anger is not turned away,
his hand is still upraised.

²⁶He lifts up a banner for the distant nations,
he whistles for those at the ends of the
earth.
Here they come,
swiftly and speedily!
²⁷Not one of them grows tired or stumbles,
not one slumbers or sleeps;
not a belt is loosened at the waist,
not a sandal thong is broken.
²⁸Their arrows are sharp,
all their bows are strung;
their horses' hoofs seem like flint,
their chariot wheels like a whirlwind.
²⁹Their roar is like that of the lion,
they roar like young lions;
they growl as they seize their prey
and carry it off with no one to rescue.
³⁰In that day they will roar over it
like the roaring of the sea.
And if one looks at the land,
he will see darkness and distress;
even the light will be darkened by the
clouds.

Isaiah's Commission

6 In the year that King Uzziah died, I saw the
Lord seated on a throne, high and exalted,
and the train of his robe filled the temple. ²Above
him were seraphs, each with six wings: With two
wings they covered their faces, with two they covered their feet, and with two they were flying.
³And they were calling to one another:

6:2 A Message from God

*Isaiah experienced a dramatic call from God to
become a prophet. The message was
personally delivered by seraphs, a term that
appears only here and means "something
burning and dazzling." Evidently, seraphs were
angels who acted as spokesmen for God.*

"Holy, holy, holy is the LORD Almighty;
the whole earth is full of his glory."

⁴At the sound of their voices the doorposts and
thresholds shook and the temple was filled with
smoke.
⁵"Woe to me!" I cried. "I am ruined! For I am
a man of unclean lips, and I live among a people

---

a 14 Hebrew *Sheol*   *b* 17 Septuagint; Hebrew / *strangers will eat*

of unclean lips, and my eyes have seen the King, the LORD Almighty."

⁶Then one of the seraphs flew to me with a live coal in his hand, which he had taken with tongs from the altar. ⁷With it he touched my mouth and said, "See, this has touched your lips; your guilt is taken away and your sin atoned for."

⁸Then I heard the voice of the Lord saying, "Whom shall I send? And who will go for us?"

And I said, "Here am I. Send me!"

⁹He said, "Go and tell this people:

" 'Be ever hearing, but never understanding;
    be ever seeing, but never perceiving.'
¹⁰Make the heart of this people calloused;
    make their ears dull
    and close their eyes.ᵃ
Otherwise they might see with their eyes,
    hear with their ears,
    understand with their hearts,
and turn and be healed."

¹¹Then I said, "For how long, O Lord?"

And he answered:

"Until the cities lie ruined
    and without inhabitant,
until the houses are left deserted
    and the fields ruined and ravaged,
¹²until the LORD has sent everyone far away
    and the land is utterly forsaken.
¹³And though a tenth remains in the land,
    it will again be laid waste.
But as the terebinth and oak
    leave stumps when they are cut down,
    so the holy seed will be the stump in the
        land."

The Sign of Immanuel

7 When Ahaz son of Jotham, the son of Uzziah, was king of Judah, King Rezin of Aram and Pekah son of Remaliah king of Israel marched up to fight against Jerusalem, but they could not overpower it.

²Now the house of David was told, "Aram has allied itself withᵇ Ephraim"; so the hearts of Ahaz and his people were shaken, as the trees of the forest are shaken by the wind.

³Then the LORD said to Isaiah, "Go out, you and your son Shear-Jashub,ᶜ to meet Ahaz at the end of the aqueduct of the Upper Pool, on the road to the Washerman's Field. ⁴Say to him, 'Be careful, keep calm and don't be afraid. Do not lose heart because of these two smoldering stubs of firewood—because of the fierce anger of Rezin and Aram and of the son of Remaliah. ⁵Aram, Ephraim and Remaliah's son have plotted your

ruin, saying, ⁶"Let us invade Judah; let us tear it apart and divide it among ourselves, and make the son of Tabeel king over it." ⁷Yet this is what the Sovereign LORD says:

" 'It will not take place,
    it will not happen,
⁸for the head of Aram is Damascus,
    and the head of Damascus is only Rezin.
Within sixty-five years
    Ephraim will be too shattered to be a
        people.
⁹The head of Ephraim is Samaria,
    and the head of Samaria is only
        Remaliah's son.
If you do not stand firm in your faith,
    you will not stand at all.' "

¹⁰Again the LORD spoke to Ahaz, ¹¹"Ask the LORD your God for a sign, whether in the deepest depths or in the highest heights."

¹²But Ahaz said, "I will not ask; I will not put the LORD to the test."

¹³Then Isaiah said, "Hear now, you house of David! Is it not enough to try the patience of men? Will you try the patience of my God also? ¹⁴Therefore the Lord himself will give youᵈ a sign: The virgin will be with child and will give birth to a son, andᵉ will call him Immanuel.ᶠ

7:14 A Famous Sign

Like so many prophecies, this one probably had two meanings: one for Isaiah's time and another much later. Isaiah urged King Ahaz to seek a sign from God about Judah's safety from its neighbors. Ahaz, notoriously stubborn and ungodly, refused.

Isaiah told of the sign anyway: A young boy would be born, and before he grew out of childhood Judah's feared enemies would be destroyed. Only 12 years after this prediction, the Northern Kingdom of Israel fell. The New Testament sees a further meaning in this prophecy, applying it to the birth of Jesus Christ (Matthew 1:23).

¹⁵He will eat curds and honey when he knows enough to reject the wrong and choose the right. ¹⁶But before the boy knows enough to reject the wrong and choose the right, the land of the two kings you dread will be laid waste. ¹⁷The LORD will bring on you and on your people and on the house of your father a time unlike any since Ephraim broke away from Judah—he will bring the king of Assyria."

ᵃ9,10 Hebrew; Septuagint 'You will be ever hearing, but never understanding; / you will be ever seeing, but never perceiving.' / ¹⁰This people's heart has become calloused; / they hardly hear with their ears, / and they have closed their eyes   ᵇ2 Or has set up camp in   ᶜ3 Shear-Jashub means a remnant will return.   ᵈ14 The Hebrew is plural.   ᵉ14 Masoretic Text; Dead Sea Scrolls and he or and they   ᶠ14 Immanuel means God with us.

[18]In that day the LORD will whistle for flies from the distant streams of Egypt and for bees from the land of Assyria. [19]They will all come and settle in the steep ravines and in the crevices in the rocks, on all the thornbushes and at all the water holes. [20]In that day the Lord will use a razor hired from beyond the River[a]—the king of Assyria—to shave your head and the hair of your legs, and to take off your beards also. [21]In that day, a man will keep alive a young cow and two goats. [22]And because of the abundance of the milk they give, he will have curds to eat. All who remain in the land will eat curds and honey. [23]In that day, in every place where there were a thousand vines worth a thousand silver shekels,[b] there will be only briers and thorns. [24]Men will go there with bow and arrow, for the land will be covered with briers and thorns. [25]As for all the hills once cultivated by the hoe, you will no longer go there for fear of the briers and thorns; they will become places where cattle are turned loose and where sheep run.

Assyria, the LORD's Instrument

8 The LORD said to me, "Take a large scroll and write on it with an ordinary pen: Maher-Shalal-Hash-Baz.[c] [2]And I will call in Uriah the priest and Zechariah son of Jeberekiah as reliable witnesses for me."

[3]Then I went to the prophetess, and she conceived and gave birth to a son. And the LORD said to me, "Name him Maher-Shalal-Hash-Baz. [4]Before the boy knows how to say 'My father' or 'My mother,' the wealth of Damascus and the plunder of Samaria will be carried off by the king of Assyria."

[5]The LORD spoke to me again:

[6]"Because this people has rejected
    the gently flowing waters of Shiloah
and rejoices over Rezin
    and the son of Remaliah,
[7]therefore the Lord is about to bring against
        them
    the mighty floodwaters of the River[a]—
    the king of Assyria with all his pomp.
It will overflow all its channels,
    run over all its banks
[8]and sweep on into Judah, swirling over it,
    passing through it and reaching up to the
        neck.
Its outspread wings will cover the breadth of
        your land,
    O Immanuel[d]!"

[9]Raise the war cry,[e] you nations, and be
        shattered!
    Listen, all you distant lands.

Prepare for battle, and be shattered!
Prepare for battle, and be shattered!
[10]Devise your strategy, but it will be thwarted;
    propose your plan, but it will not stand,
for God is with us.[f]

Fear God

[11]The LORD spoke to me with his strong hand upon me, warning me not to follow the way of this people. He said:

[12]"Do not call conspiracy
        everything that these people call
        conspiracy[g];
    do not fear what they fear,
        and do not dread it.
[13]The LORD Almighty is the one you are to
        regard as holy,
    he is the one you are to fear,
    he is the one you are to dread,
[14]and he will be a sanctuary;
    but for both houses of Israel he will be
a stone that causes men to stumble
    and a rock that makes them fall.
And for the people of Jerusalem he will be
    a trap and a snare.
[15]Many of them will stumble;
    they will fall and be broken,
    they will be snared and captured."

[16]Bind up the testimony
    and seal up the law among my disciples.
[17]I will wait for the LORD,
    who is hiding his face from the house of
        Jacob.
I will put my trust in him.

[18]Here am I, and the children the LORD has given me. We are signs and symbols in Israel from the LORD Almighty, who dwells on Mount Zion.

[19]When men tell you to consult mediums and spiritists, who whisper and mutter, should not a people inquire of their God? Why consult the dead on behalf of the living? [20]To the law and to the testimony! If they do not speak according to

8:20 Whom to Believe?

King Ahaz and his people sought guidance from every source but the right one. They consulted mediums, spiritists, even the dead. Isaiah suggests ironically that they try God. "To the law and to the testimony!" he says—that is, to the Scriptures, which give God's commandments and the testimony of what great things he has done.

---

[a]20,7 That is, the Euphrates   [b]23 That is, about 25 pounds (about 11.5 kilograms)   [c]1 Maher-Shalal-Hash-Baz means quick to the plunder, swift to the spoil; also in verse 3.   [d]8 Immanuel means God with us.   [e]9 Or Do your worst   [f]10 Hebrew Immanuel   [g]12 Or Do not call for a treaty / every time these people call for a treaty

this word, they have no light of dawn. [21]Distressed and hungry, they will roam through the land; when they are famished, they will become enraged and, looking upward, will curse their king and their God. [22]Then they will look toward the earth and see only distress and darkness and fearful gloom, and they will be thrust into utter darkness.

To Us a Child Is Born

9 Nevertheless, there will be no more gloom for those who were in distress. In the past he humbled the land of Zebulun and the land of Naphtali, but in the future he will honor Galilee of the Gentiles, by the way of the sea, along the Jordan—

[2]The people walking in darkness
    have seen a great light;
on those living in the land of the shadow of death[a]
    a light has dawned.
[3]You have enlarged the nation
    and increased their joy;
they rejoice before you
    as people rejoice at the harvest,
as men rejoice
    when dividing the plunder.
[4]For as in the day of Midian's defeat,
    you have shattered
the yoke that burdens them,
    the bar across their shoulders,
    the rod of their oppressor.
[5]Every warrior's boot used in battle
    and every garment rolled in blood
will be destined for burning,
    will be fuel for the fire.
[6]For to us a child is born,
    to us a son is given,
    and the government will be on his
        shoulders.
And he will be called
    Wonderful Counselor,[b] Mighty God,
    Everlasting Father, Prince of Peace.
[7]Of the increase of his government and peace
    there will be no end.
He will reign on David's throne
    and over his kingdom,
establishing and upholding it
    with justice and righteousness
    from that time on and forever.
The zeal of the LORD Almighty
    will accomplish this.

The LORD's Anger Against Israel

[8]The Lord has sent a message against Jacob;
    it will fall on Israel.
[9]All the people will know it—
    Ephraim and the inhabitants of Samaria—

who say with pride
    and arrogance of heart,
[10]"The bricks have fallen down,
    but we will rebuild with dressed stone;

9:6 A Child Is Born

Isaiah includes many direct predictions of the coming Messiah, including this passage, which established that the Messiah will come from Galilee (verse 1). The lands Isaiah mentions as "humbled" in verse 1 are the very regions devastated by Assyria's armies (2 Kings 15:29). Thus Isaiah offers a word of distant hope for those parts of his nation most affected by war.

---

the fig trees have been felled,
    but we will replace them with cedars."
[11]But the LORD has strengthened Rezin's foes
        against them
    and has spurred their enemies on.
[12]Arameans from the east and Philistines from
        the west
    have devoured Israel with open mouth.

Yet for all this, his anger is not turned away,
    his hand is still upraised.

[13]But the people have not returned to him
        who struck them,
    nor have they sought the LORD Almighty.
[14]So the LORD will cut off from Israel both
        head and tail,
    both palm branch and reed in a single
        day;
[15]the elders and prominent men are the head,
    the prophets who teach lies are the tail.
[16]Those who guide this people mislead them,
    and those who are guided are led astray.
[17]Therefore the Lord will take no pleasure in
        the young men,
    nor will he pity the fatherless and widows,
for everyone is ungodly and wicked,
    every mouth speaks vileness.

Yet for all this, his anger is not turned away,
    his hand is still upraised.

[18]Surely wickedness burns like a fire;
    it consumes briers and thorns,
it sets the forest thickets ablaze,
    so that it rolls upward in a column of
        smoke.
[19]By the wrath of the LORD Almighty
    the land will be scorched
and the people will be fuel for the fire;
    no one will spare his brother.
[20]On the right they will devour,
    but still be hungry;

---

[a]2 Or *land of darkness*   [b]6 Or *Wonderful, Counselor*

on the left they will eat,
but not be satisfied.
Each will feed on the flesh of his own
offspring*:
21 Manasseh will feed on Ephraim, and
Ephraim on Manasseh;
together they will turn against Judah.

Yet for all this, his anger is not turned away,
his hand is still upraised.

10 Woe to those who make unjust laws,
to those who issue oppressive decrees,
[2]to deprive the poor of their rights
and withhold justice from the oppressed
of my people,
making widows their prey
and robbing the fatherless.
[3]What will you do on the day of reckoning,
when disaster comes from afar?
To whom will you run for help?
Where will you leave your riches?
[4]Nothing will remain but to cringe among the
captives
or fall among the slain.

Yet for all this, his anger is not turned away,
his hand is still upraised.

God's Judgment on Assyria

[5]"Woe to the Assyrian, the rod of my anger,
in whose hand is the club of my wrath!
[6]I send him against a godless nation,
I dispatch him against a people who anger
me,
to seize loot and snatch plunder,
and to trample them down like mud in
the streets.
[7]But this is not what he intends,
this is not what he has in mind;
his purpose is to destroy,
to put an end to many nations.

10:7 God's Hand in History

*In this comment, God reveals how he works
through history in hidden, indirect ways. The
pagan empire Assyria had no idea it was being
used by the true God—it dealt with Jerusalem
just as it dealt with any nation and its idols
(verse 11). Nevertheless, Assyria would serve
God's purpose, and would one day be punished
for its own pride and greed (verse 12).*

[8]'Are not my commanders all kings?' he says.
[9] 'Has not Calno fared like Carchemish?
Is not Hamath like Arpad,
and Samaria like Damascus?

[10]As my hand seized the kingdoms of the
idols,
kingdoms whose images excelled those of
Jerusalem and Samaria—
[11]shall I not deal with Jerusalem and her
images
as I dealt with Samaria and her idols?'"

[12]When the Lord has finished all his work
against Mount Zion and Jerusalem, he will say, "I
will punish the king of Assyria for the willful
pride of his heart and the haughty look in his
eyes. [13]For he says:

"'By the strength of my hand I have done
this,
and by my wisdom, because I have
understanding.
I removed the boundaries of nations,
I plundered their treasures;
like a mighty one I subdued[b] their kings.
[14]As one reaches into a nest,
so my hand reached for the wealth of the
nations;
as men gather abandoned eggs,
so I gathered all the countries;
not one flapped a wing,
or opened its mouth to chirp.'"

[15]Does the ax raise itself above him who
swings it,
or the saw boast against him who uses it?
As if a rod were to wield him who lifts it up,
or a club brandish him who is not wood!
[16]Therefore, the Lord, the LORD Almighty,
will send a wasting disease upon his
sturdy warriors;
under his pomp a fire will be kindled
like a blazing flame.
[17]The Light of Israel will become a fire,
their Holy One a flame;
in a single day it will burn and consume
his thorns and his briers.
[18]The splendor of his forests and fertile fields
it will completely destroy,
as when a sick man wastes away.
[19]And the remaining trees of his forests will be
so few
that a child could write them down.

The Remnant of Israel

[20]In that day the remnant of Israel,
the survivors of the house of Jacob,
will no longer rely on him
who struck them down
but will truly rely on the LORD,
the Holy One of Israel.
[21]A remnant will return,[c] a remnant of Jacob
will return to the Mighty God.

[a]20 Or arm [b]13 Or / I subdued the mighty, [c]21 Hebrew shear-jashub; also in verse 22

22Though your people, O Israel, be like the
  sand by the sea,
  only a remnant will return.
Destruction has been decreed,
  overwhelming and righteous.
23The Lord, the LORD Almighty, will carry out
  the destruction decreed upon the whole
  land.

24Therefore, this is what the Lord, the LORD
Almighty, says:

"O my people who live in Zion,
  do not be afraid of the Assyrians,
who beat you with a rod
  and lift up a club against you, as Egypt
  did.
25Very soon my anger against you will end
  and my wrath will be directed to their
  destruction."

26The LORD Almighty will lash them with a
  whip,
  as when he struck down Midian at the
  rock of Oreb;
and he will raise his staff over the waters,
  as he did in Egypt.
27In that day their burden will be lifted from
  your shoulders,
  their yoke from your neck;
the yoke will be broken
  because you have grown so fat.*a*

28They enter Aiath;
  they pass through Migron;
  they store supplies at Micmash.
29They go over the pass, and say,
  "We will camp overnight at Geba."
Ramah trembles;
  Gibeah of Saul flees.
30Cry out, O Daughter of Gallim!
  Listen, O Laishah!
  Poor Anathoth!
31Madmenah is in flight;
  the people of Gebim take cover.
32This day they will halt at Nob;
  they will shake their fist
at the mount of the Daughter of Zion,
  at the hill of Jerusalem.

33See, the Lord, the LORD Almighty,
  will lop off the boughs with great power.
The lofty trees will be felled,
  the tall ones will be brought low.
34He will cut down the forest thickets with an
  ax;
  Lebanon will fall before the Mighty One.

The Branch From Jesse

11 A shoot will come up from the stump of
    Jesse;

from his roots a Branch will bear fruit.
2The Spirit of the LORD will rest on him—
  the Spirit of wisdom and of
  understanding,

> ### 11:1–16 The Good Old Days
>
> *To express his message of hope to the Israelite
> people, Isaiah appealed to their fondest
> memories. This chapter borrows images from
> three of the greatest events from the past: the
> prosperous dynasty of David when Israel was
> united (verse 1); the Garden of Eden (verses
> 6–9); and the miracles of the exodus from
> Egypt (verse 15). Whatever the state of "the
> good old days," the future time of peace will
> exceed it.*

the Spirit of counsel and of power,
  the Spirit of knowledge and of the fear of
  the LORD—
3and he will delight in the fear of the LORD.

He will not judge by what he sees with his
  eyes,
  or decide by what he hears with his ears;
4but with righteousness he will judge the
  needy,
  with justice he will give decisions for the
  poor of the earth.
He will strike the earth with the rod of his
  mouth;
  with the breath of his lips he will slay the
  wicked.
5Righteousness will be his belt
  and faithfulness the sash around his waist.

6The wolf will live with the lamb,
  the leopard will lie down with the goat,
the calf and the lion and the yearling*b*
  together;
  and a little child will lead them.
7The cow will feed with the bear,
  their young will lie down together,
  and the lion will eat straw like the ox.
8The infant will play near the hole of the
  cobra,
  and the young child put his hand into the
  viper's nest.
9They will neither harm nor destroy
  on all my holy mountain,
for the earth will be full of the knowledge of
  the LORD
  as the waters cover the sea.

10In that day the Root of Jesse will stand as a
banner for the peoples; the nations will rally to
him, and his place of rest will be glorious. 11In
that day the Lord will reach out his hand a sec-

---

a27 Hebrew; Septuagint *broken / from your shoulders*   *b6* Hebrew; Septuagint *lion will feed* ond time to reclaim the remnant that is left of his people from Assyria, from Lower Egypt, from Upper Egypt,[a] from Cush,[b] from Elam, from Babylonia,[c] from Hamath and from the islands of the sea.

[12]He will raise a banner for the nations
and gather the exiles of Israel;
he will assemble the scattered people of Judah
from the four quarters of the earth.
[13]Ephraim's jealousy will vanish,
and Judah's enemies[d] will be cut off;
Ephraim will not be jealous of Judah,
nor Judah hostile toward Ephraim.
[14]They will swoop down on the slopes of Philistia to the west;
together they will plunder the people to the east.
They will lay hands on Edom and Moab,
and the Ammonites will be subject to them.
[15]The LORD will dry up
the gulf of the Egyptian sea;
with a scorching wind he will sweep his hand over the Euphrates River.[e]
He will break it up into seven streams
so that men can cross over in sandals.
[16]There will be a highway for the remnant of his people
that is left from Assyria,
as there was for Israel
when they came up from Egypt.

Songs of Praise

12 In that day you will say:

"I will praise you, O LORD.
Although you were angry with me,
your anger has turned away
and you have comforted me.
[2]Surely God is my salvation;
I will trust and not be afraid.
The LORD, the LORD, is my strength and my song;
he has become my salvation."
[3]With joy you will draw water
from the wells of salvation.

[4]In that day you will say:

"Give thanks to the LORD, call on his name;
make known among the nations what he has done,
and proclaim that his name is exalted.
[5]Sing to the LORD, for he has done glorious things;
let this be known to all the world.
[6]Shout aloud and sing for joy, people of Zion,

for great is the Holy One of Israel among you."

A Prophecy Against Babylon

13 An oracle concerning Babylon that Isaiah son of Amoz saw:

12:6 A Key Phrase

The first 12 chapters contain specific messages to Judah. But now Isaiah shifts his focus to surrounding nations. He ends the first section with a reference to the "Holy One of Israel," a key phrase that hints at the special relationship between God and his covenant nation. The phrase appears only five times in the rest of the Old Testament, but 26 times in Isaiah.

[2]Raise a banner on a bare hilltop,
shout to them;
beckon to them
to enter the gates of the nobles.
[3]I have commanded my holy ones;
I have summoned my warriors to carry out my wrath—
those who rejoice in my triumph.

[4]Listen, a noise on the mountains,
like that of a great multitude!
Listen, an uproar among the kingdoms,
like nations massing together!
The LORD Almighty is mustering
an army for war.
[5]They come from faraway lands,
from the ends of the heavens—
the LORD and the weapons of his wrath—
to destroy the whole country.

[6]Wail, for the day of the LORD is near;
it will come like destruction from the Almighty.[f]
[7]Because of this, all hands will go limp,
every man's heart will melt.
[8]Terror will seize them,
pain and anguish will grip them;
they will writhe like a woman in labor.
They will look aghast at each other,
their faces aflame.

[9]See, the day of the LORD is coming
—a cruel day, with wrath and fierce anger—
to make the land desolate
and destroy the sinners within it.
[10]The stars of heaven and their constellations
will not show their light.
The rising sun will be darkened
and the moon will not give its light.

---

[a] 11 Hebrew *from Pathros*   [b] 11 That is, the upper Nile region   [c] 11 Hebrew *Shinar*   [d] 13 Or *hostility*
[e] 15 Hebrew *the River*   [f] 6 Hebrew *Shaddai*

¹¹I will punish the world for its evil,
  the wicked for their sins.
I will put an end to the arrogance of the
    haughty
  and will humble the pride of the ruthless.
¹²I will make man scarcer than pure gold,
  more rare than the gold of Ophir.
¹³Therefore I will make the heavens tremble;
  and the earth will shake from its place
at the wrath of the LORD Almighty,
  in the day of his burning anger.

¹⁴Like a hunted gazelle,
  like sheep without a shepherd,
each will return to his own people,
  each will flee to his native land.
¹⁵Whoever is captured will be thrust through;
  all who are caught will fall by the sword.
¹⁶Their infants will be dashed to pieces before
    their eyes;
  their houses will be looted and their wives
    ravished.

¹⁷See, I will stir up against them the Medes,
  who do not care for silver
  and have no delight in gold.
¹⁸Their bows will strike down the young men;
  they will have no mercy on infants
  nor will they look with compassion on
    children.
¹⁹Babylon, the jewel of kingdoms,
  the glory of the Babylonians'ᵃ pride,
will be overthrown by God
  like Sodom and Gomorrah.
²⁰She will never be inhabited
  or lived in through all generations;
no Arab will pitch his tent there,
  no shepherd will rest his flocks there.
²¹But desert creatures will lie there,
  jackals will fill her houses;
there the owls will dwell,
  and there the wild goats will leap about.
²²Hyenas will howl in her strongholds,
  jackals in her luxurious palaces.
Her time is at hand,
  and her days will not be prolonged.

14 The LORD will have compassion on Jacob;
  once again he will choose Israel
and will settle them in their own land.
Aliens will join them
  and unite with the house of Jacob.
²Nations will take them
  and bring them to their own place.
And the house of Israel will possess the
    nations
  as menservants and maidservants in the
    LORD's land.

They will make captives of their captors
  and rule over their oppressors.

³On the day the LORD gives you relief from
suffering and turmoil and cruel bondage, ⁴you
will take up this taunt against the king of Babylon:

How the oppressor has come to an end!
  How his furyᵇ has ended!
⁵The LORD has broken the rod of the wicked,
  the scepter of the rulers,
⁶which in anger struck down peoples
  with unceasing blows,
and in fury subdued nations
  with relentless aggression.
⁷All the lands are at rest and at peace;
  they break into singing.
⁸Even the pine trees and the cedars of
    Lebanon
  exult over you and say,
"Now that you have been laid low,
  no woodsman comes to cut us down."

⁹The graveᶜ below is all astir
  to meet you at your coming;
it rouses the spirits of the departed to greet
    you—
  all those who were leaders in the world;
it makes them rise from their thrones—
  all those who were kings over the nations.
¹⁰They will all respond,
  they will say to you,
"You also have become weak, as we are;
  you have become like us."
¹¹All your pomp has been brought down to
    the grave,
  along with the noise of your harps;
maggots are spread out beneath you
  and worms cover you.

¹²How you have fallen from heaven,
  O morning star, son of the dawn!
You have been cast down to the earth,
  you who once laid low the nations!
¹³You said in your heart,
  "I will ascend to heaven;
I will raise my throne
  above the stars of God;
I will sit enthroned on the mount of
    assembly,
  on the utmost heights of the sacred
    mountain.ᵈ
¹⁴I will ascend above the tops of the clouds;
  I will make myself like the Most High."
¹⁵But you are brought down to the grave,
  to the depths of the pit.

¹⁶Those who see you stare at you,
  they ponder your fate:

ᵃ19 Or *Chaldeans'*   ᵇ4 Dead Sea Scrolls, Septuagint and Syriac; the meaning of the word in the Masoretic Text is
uncertain.   ᶜ9 Hebrew *Sheol*; also in verses 11 and 15   ᵈ13 Or *the north*; Hebrew *Zaphon*

"Is this the man who shook the earth
and made kingdoms tremble,
[17]the man who made the world a desert,
who overthrew its cities
and would not let his captives go home?"

[18]All the kings of the nations lie in state,
each in his own tomb.
[19]But you are cast out of your tomb
like a rejected branch;
you are covered with the slain,
with those pierced by the sword,
those who descend to the stones of the
pit.
Like a corpse trampled underfoot,
[20] you will not join them in burial,
for you have destroyed your land
and killed your people.

The offspring of the wicked
will never be mentioned again.
[21]Prepare a place to slaughter his sons
for the sins of their forefathers;
they are not to rise to inherit the land
and cover the earth with their cities.

14:12 Fall of the Morning Star

A name used of Satan—"Lucifer," or "morning star,"—comes from this verse. The word Lucifer *refers to Venus, one of the brightest objects in the sky. Yet, when the sun rises, the light of even the brightest morning star is totally eclipsed.*

In context, Isaiah was describing the cruelly oppressive king of Babylon, who swelled with pride but would be brought down to defeat. However, Isaiah may be hinting at a force behind the human king: Satan himself. Isaiah's metaphor of the faded morning star aptly describes the eclipse of the haughty king of Babylon—and of Satan.

[22]"I will rise up against them,"
declares the LORD Almighty.
"I will cut off from Babylon her name and
survivors,
her offspring and descendants,"
declares the LORD.
[23]"I will turn her into a place for owls
and into swampland;
I will sweep her with the broom of
destruction,"
declares the LORD Almighty.

A Prophecy Against Assyria

[24]The LORD Almighty has sworn,

"Surely, as I have planned, so it will be,
and as I have purposed, so it will stand.

[25]I will crush the Assyrian in my land;
on my mountains I will trample him down.
His yoke will be taken from my people,
and his burden removed from their
shoulders."

[26]This is the plan determined for the whole
world;
this is the hand stretched out over all
nations.
[27]For the LORD Almighty has purposed, and
who can thwart him?
His hand is stretched out, and who can
turn it back?

A Prophecy Against the Philistines

[28]This oracle came in the year King Ahaz died:

[29]Do not rejoice, all you Philistines,
that the rod that struck you is broken;
from the root of that snake will spring up a
viper,
its fruit will be a darting, venomous
serpent.
[30]The poorest of the poor will find pasture,
and the needy will lie down in safety.
But your root I will destroy by famine;
it will slay your survivors.

[31]Wail, O gate! Howl, O city!
Melt away, all you Philistines!
A cloud of smoke comes from the north,
and there is not a straggler in its ranks.
[32]What answer shall be given
to the envoys of that nation?
"The LORD has established Zion,
and in her his afflicted people will find
refuge."

A Prophecy Against Moab

15 An oracle concerning Moab:

Ar in Moab is ruined,
destroyed in a night!
Kir in Moab is ruined,
destroyed in a night!
[2]Dibon goes up to its temple,
to its high places to weep;
Moab wails over Nebo and Medeba.
Every head is shaved
and every beard cut off.
[3]In the streets they wear sackcloth;
on the roofs and in the public squares
they all wail,
prostrate with weeping.
[4]Heshbon and Elealeh cry out,
their voices are heard all the way to Jahaz.
Therefore the armed men of Moab cry out,
and their hearts are faint.
[5]My heart cries out over Moab;

her fugitives flee as far as Zoar,
as far as Eglath Shelishiyah.
They go up the way to Luhith,
weeping as they go;
on the road to Horonaim
they lament their destruction.
⁶The waters of Nimrim are dried up
and the grass is withered;
the vegetation is gone

and nothing green is left.
⁷So the wealth they have acquired and stored
up
they carry away over the Ravine of the
Poplars.
⁸Their outcry echoes along the border of
Moab;
their wailing reaches as far as Eglaim,
their lamentation as far as Beer Elim.

Faith in God or the Military?

Where does a weak nation turn for help?

IN 1944, WILD CHEERING GREETED the Russian tanks that
rolled into Poland. The Russians were freeing Poland from the Nazis, and
grateful Poles showered the liberating soldiers with fresh flowers.

But 45 years later, Russian troops had worn out their welcome, and the
Polish government asked them to leave. The Polish experience offers living
proof of a painful lesson of history: Military help from great powers usually
comes with strings attached.

> *This is the plan determined for the whole world; this is the hand stretched out over all nations.*
> *14:26*

A Small Nation Seeks Help

What can a small nation do when facing a military giant? Judah found itself in that predicament
early in Isaiah's career. When two neighboring nations invaded, the tiny kingdom suffered heavy
losses. King Ahaz and the people of Judah were shaken, "as the trees of the forest are shaken by the
wind" (7:2). Panicked, Ahaz sought Isaiah's advice.

Isaiah had received a "call" to ministry as dramatic as any recorded in the Bible (chapter 6). King
Ahaz knew that Isaiah would deliver a message straight from God, no matter how unpopular. Still,
Ahaz was hardly prepared for what Isaiah said: Stay calm, don't worry, simply trust God.

The attacking kings were mere "smoldering stubs of firewood," Isaiah declared (7:4). Whatever
happens, don't seek help from an empire like Assyria; if you do, you will invite in the very army that
will one day destroy you.

The Long Slide Begins

But Ahaz, reeling from the invasion, wanted quick relief. Ignoring Isaiah's warnings, he negotiated
a treaty with mighty Assyria, using as a bribe the treasury of the temple in Jerusalem.

In the short term, Ahaz's decision brought results. No army of that day could match the Assyrian
war machine, and all Judah's enemies fell to the onslaught. Israel, to the north, was wiped off the map.
At last Judah had peace. But at what cost?

Perhaps as part of the treaty with Assyria, Ahaz began corrupting Judah's religion. He first closed
the doors of the temple to worship, and later replaced the sacred altar to God with a foreign one. He
officially adopted Assyria's state religion, going so far as to make a human sacrifice of his sons in a
fire. In every way King Ahaz became a puppet king, under the thumb of Assyria. Foreign armies stayed
in Judah. Indeed, Assyria's help had come with strings attached.

Messages for Then and Now

The prophet Isaiah was furious. He had grown up in a boom time in Judah, under a good king.
Suddenly he saw his country become a mere pawn of Assyria, trading away even its great religious
heritage.

Chapters 7–19 record his passionate words, not only against Judah, but against her neighbors
also. He told of a reckoning day, when each nation would be punished for its sin and rebellion. The
immediate future looked very bleak, and Isaiah minced no words in describing it.

But Isaiah did not stop there. He went on to project far into the future, in familiar words that still
stir up hope and longing. This section begins with a question from a king about where to turn for help.
It ends with a grand sweep of all of history.

Life Questions: What do you think Isaiah would say if he were writing today about such superpower
countries as the United States and Russia?

⁹Dimon's^a waters are full of blood,
  but I will bring still more upon
    Dimon^a—
a lion upon the fugitives of Moab
  and upon those who remain in the land.

16 Send lambs as tribute
  to the ruler of the land,
from Sela, across the desert,
  to the mount of the Daughter of Zion.
²Like fluttering birds
  pushed from the nest,
so are the women of Moab
  at the fords of the Arnon.

³"Give us counsel,
  render a decision.
Make your shadow like night—
  at high noon.
Hide the fugitives,
  do not betray the refugees.
⁴Let the Moabite fugitives stay with you;
  be their shelter from the destroyer."

The oppressor will come to an end,
  and destruction will cease;
  the aggressor will vanish from the land.
⁵In love a throne will be established;
  in faithfulness a man will sit on it—
    one from the house^b of David—
one who in judging seeks justice
  and speeds the cause of righteousness.

⁶We have heard of Moab's pride—
  her overweening pride and conceit,
  her pride and her insolence—
    but her boasts are empty.
⁷Therefore the Moabites wail,
  they wail together for Moab.
Lament and grieve
  for the men^c of Kir Hareseth.
⁸The fields of Heshbon wither,
  the vines of Sibmah also.
The rulers of the nations
  have trampled down the choicest vines,
which once reached Jazer
  and spread toward the desert.
Their shoots spread out
  and went as far as the sea.
⁹So I weep, as Jazer weeps,
  for the vines of Sibmah.
O Heshbon, O Elealeh,
  I drench you with tears!
The shouts of joy over your ripened fruit
  and over your harvests have been stilled.
¹⁰Joy and gladness are taken away from the
    orchards;
  no one sings or shouts in the vineyards;
no one treads out wine at the presses,

for I have put an end to the shouting.
¹¹My heart laments for Moab like a harp,
  my inmost being for Kir Hareseth.
¹²When Moab appears at her high place,

16:9 A Prophet's Pain

Although Isaiah often delivered bad news to the nations around him, he never took pleasure in it. Remarkably, he often deeply identified with the pain of other, non-Israelite nations such as Moab (see 15:5). Chapters 15–16 were likely used as sources for Jeremiah 48. (Jeremiah was another prophet who suffered greatly.)

she only wears herself out;
when she goes to her shrine to pray,
  it is to no avail.

¹³This is the word the LORD has already spoken concerning Moab. ¹⁴But now the LORD says: "Within three years, as a servant bound by contract would count them, Moab's splendor and all her many people will be despised, and her survivors will be very few and feeble."

An Oracle Against Damascus

17 An oracle concerning Damascus:

"See, Damascus will no longer be a city
  but will become a heap of ruins.
²The cities of Aroer will be deserted
  and left to flocks, which will lie down,
  with no one to make them afraid.
³The fortified city will disappear from
    Ephraim,
  and royal power from Damascus;
the remnant of Aram will be
  like the glory of the Israelites,"
                declares the LORD Almighty.

⁴"In that day the glory of Jacob will fade;
  the fat of his body will waste away.
⁵It will be as when a reaper gathers the
    standing grain
  and harvests the grain with his arm—
as when a man gleans heads of grain
  in the Valley of Rephaim.
⁶Yet some gleanings will remain,
  as when an olive tree is beaten,
leaving two or three olives on the topmost
    branches,
  four or five on the fruitful boughs,"
                declares the LORD, the God of Israel.

⁷In that day men will look to their Maker

---

^a9 Masoretic Text; Dead Sea Scrolls, some Septuagint manuscripts and Vulgate *Dibon*   ^b5 Hebrew *tent*
^c7 Or "*raisin cakes*," a wordplay

and turn their eyes to the Holy One of
    Israel.
[8]They will not look to the altars,
    the work of their hands,
and they will have no regard for the Asherah
    poles[a]
    and the incense altars their fingers have
        made.

[9]In that day their strong cities, which they left
because of the Israelites, will be like places abandoned to thickets and undergrowth. And all will
be desolation.

[10]You have forgotten God your Savior;
    you have not remembered the Rock, your
        fortress.
Therefore, though you set out the finest
        plants
    and plant imported vines,
[11]though on the day you set them out, you
        make them grow,
    and on the morning when you plant
        them, you bring them to bud,
yet the harvest will be as nothing
    in the day of disease and incurable pain.

[12]Oh, the raging of many nations—
    they rage like the raging sea!
Oh, the uproar of the peoples—
    they roar like the roaring of great waters!
[13]Although the peoples roar like the roar of
        surging waters,
    when he rebukes them they flee far away,
driven before the wind like chaff on the hills,
    like tumbleweed before a gale.
[14]In the evening, sudden terror!
    Before the morning, they are gone!
This is the portion of those who loot us,
    the lot of those who plunder us.

A Prophecy Against Cush

18 Woe to the land of whirring wings[b]
    along the rivers of Cush,[c]
[2]which sends envoys by sea
    in papyrus boats over the water.

Go, swift messengers,
to a people tall and smooth-skinned,
    to a people feared far and wide,
an aggressive nation of strange speech,
    whose land is divided by rivers.

[3]All you people of the world,
    you who live on the earth,
when a banner is raised on the mountains,
    you will see it,
and when a trumpet sounds,
    you will hear it.
[4]This is what the Lord says to me:

"I will remain quiet and will look on from
    my dwelling place,
like shimmering heat in the sunshine,
    like a cloud of dew in the heat of
        harvest."

18:2 Foreign Policy

*Isaiah never balked at direct political
involvement. He consistently lobbied against
alliances with any foreign powers. Here, he
warned against the "envoys by sea" coming
from Cush, a region near Ethiopia or Sudan.
Judah's king was often tempted to make
alliances with Ethiopia or Egypt, but according
to Isaiah, both nations would meet disaster.*

[5]For, before the harvest, when the blossom is
        gone
    and the flower becomes a ripening grape,
he will cut off the shoots with pruning
        knives,
    and cut down and take away the
        spreading branches.
[6]They will all be left to the mountain birds of
        prey
    and to the wild animals;
the birds will feed on them all summer,
    the wild animals all winter.

[7]At that time gifts will be brought to the Lord
Almighty

from a people tall and smooth-skinned,
    from a people feared far and wide,
an aggressive nation of strange speech,
    whose land is divided by rivers—

the gifts will be brought to Mount Zion, the place
of the Name of the Lord Almighty.

A Prophecy About Egypt

19 An oracle concerning Egypt:

See, the Lord rides on a swift cloud
    and is coming to Egypt.
The idols of Egypt tremble before him,
    and the hearts of the Egyptians melt
        within them.

[2]"I will stir up Egyptian against Egyptian—
    brother will fight against brother,
    neighbor against neighbor,
    city against city,
    kingdom against kingdom.
[3]The Egyptians will lose heart,
    and I will bring their plans to nothing;
they will consult the idols and the spirits of
        the dead,

---

[a]8 That is, symbols of the goddess Asherah   [b]1 Or *of locusts*   [c]1 That is, the upper Nile region

the mediums and the spiritists.
[4]I will hand the Egyptians over
  to the power of a cruel master,
and a fierce king will rule over them,"
  declares the Lord, the LORD Almighty.

[5]The waters of the river will dry up,
  and the riverbed will be parched and dry.
[6]The canals will stink;
  the streams of Egypt will dwindle and dry
    up.
The reeds and rushes will wither,
[7] also the plants along the Nile,
  at the mouth of the river.
Every sown field along the Nile
  will become parched, will blow away and
    be no more.
[8]The fishermen will groan and lament,
  all who cast hooks into the Nile;
those who throw nets on the water
  will pine away.
[9]Those who work with combed flax will
    despair,
  the weavers of fine linen will lose hope.
[10]The workers in cloth will be dejected,
  and all the wage earners will be sick at
    heart.

[11]The officials of Zoan are nothing but fools;
  the wise counselors of Pharaoh give
    senseless advice.
How can you say to Pharaoh,
  "I am one of the wise men,
  a disciple of the ancient kings"?

[12]Where are your wise men now?
  Let them show you and make known
what the LORD Almighty
  has planned against Egypt.
[13]The officials of Zoan have become fools,
  the leaders of Memphis[a] are deceived;
the cornerstones of her peoples
  have led Egypt astray.
[14]The LORD has poured into them
  a spirit of dizziness;
they make Egypt stagger in all that she does,
  as a drunkard staggers around in his
    vomit.
[15]There is nothing Egypt can do—
  head or tail, palm branch or reed.

[16]In that day the Egyptians will be like women. They will shudder with fear at the uplifted hand that the LORD Almighty raises against them. [17]And the land of Judah will bring terror to the Egyptians; everyone to whom Judah is mentioned will be terrified, because of what the LORD Almighty is planning against them.

[18]In that day five cities in Egypt will speak the language of Canaan and swear allegiance to the LORD Almighty. One of them will be called the City of Destruction.[b]

[19]In that day there will be an altar to the LORD in the heart of Egypt, and a monument to the LORD at its border. [20]It will be a sign and witness to the LORD Almighty in the land of Egypt. When they cry out to the LORD because of their oppressors, he will send them a savior and defender, and he will rescue them. [21]So the LORD will make himself known to the Egyptians, and in that day they will acknowledge the LORD. They will worship with sacrifices and grain offerings; they will make vows to the LORD and keep them. [22]The LORD will strike Egypt with a plague; he will strike them and heal them. They will turn to the LORD, and he will respond to their pleas and heal them.

[23]In that day there will be a highway from Egypt to Assyria. The Assyrians will go to Egypt and the Egyptians to Assyria. The Egyptians and Assyrians will worship together. [24]In that day Israel will be the third, along with Egypt and Assyria, a blessing on the earth. [25]The LORD Almighty will bless them, saying, "Blessed be Egypt my people, Assyria my handiwork, and Israel my inheritance."

A Prophecy Against Egypt and Cush

20 In the year that the supreme commander, sent by Sargon king of Assyria, came to Ashdod and attacked and captured it— [2]at that time the LORD spoke through Isaiah son of Amoz. He said to him, "Take off the sackcloth from your body and the sandals from your feet." And he did so, going around stripped and barefoot.

20:2 A Dramatic Object Lesson

Isaiah was an educated and urbane prophet, at home in the corridors of power. His reputation must have made this object lesson very shocking: For three years he walked around stripped and barefoot, in the guise of a slave, to protest a planned alliance with Egypt and Cush. He had originally opposed an alliance with Assyria. Now he opposed a treaty with other nations as well.

[3]Then the LORD said, "Just as my servant Isaiah has gone stripped and barefoot for three years, as a sign and portent against Egypt and Cush,[c] [4]so the king of Assyria will lead away stripped and barefoot the Egyptian captives and Cushite exiles, young and old, with buttocks bared—to Egypt's shame. [5]Those who trusted in

---

[a]13 Hebrew *Noph*   [b]18 Most manuscripts of the Masoretic Text; some manuscripts of the Masoretic Text, Dead Sea Scrolls and Vulgate *City of the Sun* (that is, Heliopolis)   [c]3 That is, the upper Nile region; also in verse 5

Cush and boasted in Egypt will be afraid and put to shame. ⁶In that day the people who live on this coast will say, 'See what has happened to those we relied on, those we fled to for help and deliverance from the king of Assyria! How then can we escape?'"

A Prophecy Against Babylon

21 An oracle concerning the Desert by the Sea:

Like whirlwinds sweeping through the
   southland,
an invader comes from the desert,
   from a land of terror.

²A dire vision has been shown to me:
   The traitor betrays, the looter takes loot.
Elam, attack! Media, lay siege!
   I will bring to an end all the groaning she
      caused.

³At this my body is racked with pain,
   pangs seize me, like those of a woman in
      labor;
I am staggered by what I hear,
   I am bewildered by what I see.
⁴My heart falters,
   fear makes me tremble;
the twilight I longed for
   has become a horror to me.

⁵They set the tables,
   they spread the rugs,
   they eat, they drink!
Get up, you officers,
   oil the shields!

⁶This is what the Lord says to me:

"Go, post a lookout
   and have him report what he sees.
⁷When he sees chariots
   with teams of horses,
riders on donkeys

Catastrophes Through God's Eyes
An endless cycle of war and death—what did it mean?

> At this my body is racked with pain, pangs seize me, like those of a woman in labor; I am staggered by what I hear, I am bewildered by what I see.
> *21:3*

THERE IS ONE EASY WAY to picture the Middle East of Isaiah's day: Simply follow today's newspaper headlines and project backward in time. Then, as now, one nation would invade its neighbor, leveling cities and devastating the land and its people. The prophet Isaiah longed for an end to the cycle, much as modern-day residents of Lebanon or Israel do today.

Isaiah looked at the world with a kind of split vision. Around him he saw spiritual decay and the dreary cycle of war and death. Yet God had given him a clear vision of what his nation could one day become: a pure people, faithful to God, living in peace with "war no more."

A Kingdom for a Purpose

With God's view of the future shining brightly before him, Isaiah went about reinterpreting history. Others in Judah looked upon military invasions as terrible catastrophes. In contrast, Isaiah—though he felt anguish over the events—saw glimpses of a higher purpose.

Isaiah said that Judah had to endure pain and suffering in order to be purified. He counseled against making political alliances to forestall the punishment. God's people had to go through the fire, and from the trials a remnant—a small remaining number of persons—would emerge that God could then use to accomplish his work. Isaiah went so far as to name his own son "a remnant will return" as a walking object lesson of his message to Judah (see Isaiah 7:3 and footnote).

Why had the Jews been called by God in the first place? They were to be a "light for the Gentiles," Isaiah said, a nation used by God to bring his truth to other nations. And out of the land of Judah God would raise up a great Prince who would rule over all the earth.

Who Is in Charge?

In short, God had not discarded his people, no matter how bleak things looked. The Israelites would ultimately become a missionary nation, pointing others to God.

Above all messages, Isaiah stressed this one: God is in charge of history. To Judah—surrounded by enemies, staggering from invasion, weary of bloodshed—God seemed far away and distant. Isaiah assured them that the great powers of earth were mere tools in God's hands; he would use them and fling them aside.

Life Questions: Isaiah described people who felt afraid and abandoned by God. Have you ever felt like that? How does Isaiah's message offer hope for us today?

or riders on camels,
let him be alert,
 fully alert."

[8]And the lookout[a] shouted,

"Day after day, my lord, I stand on the
  watchtower;
 every night I stay at my post.
[9]Look, here comes a man in a chariot
  with a team of horses.
And he gives back the answer:
 'Babylon has fallen, has fallen!
All the images of its gods
 lie shattered on the ground!'"

[10]O my people, crushed on the threshing floor,
  I tell you what I have heard
from the LORD Almighty,
 from the God of Israel.

A Prophecy Against Edom

[11]An oracle concerning Dumah[b]:

Someone calls to me from Seir,
 "Watchman, what is left of the night?
 Watchman, what is left of the night?"
[12]The watchman replies,
 "Morning is coming, but also the night.
If you would ask, then ask;
 and come back yet again."

A Prophecy Against Arabia

[13]An oracle concerning Arabia:

You caravans of Dedanites,
 who camp in the thickets of Arabia,
[14] bring water for the thirsty;
you who live in Tema,
 bring food for the fugitives.
[15]They flee from the sword,
 from the drawn sword,
from the bent bow
 and from the heat of battle.

[16]This is what the Lord says to me: "Within
one year, as a servant bound by contract would
count it, all the pomp of Kedar will come to an
end. [17]The survivors of the bowmen, the warriors
of Kedar, will be few." The LORD, the God of
Israel, has spoken.

A Prophecy About Jerusalem

22 An oracle concerning the Valley of Vision:

What troubles you now,
 that you have all gone up on the roofs,
[2]O town full of commotion,
 O city of tumult and revelry?
Your slain were not killed by the sword,
 nor did they die in battle.
[3]All your leaders have fled together;

they have been captured without using the
  bow.
All you who were caught were taken prisoner
  together,
 having fled while the enemy was still far
  away.
[4]Therefore I said, "Turn away from me;
 let me weep bitterly.
Do not try to console me
 over the destruction of my people."

[5]The Lord, the LORD Almighty, has a day
 of tumult and trampling and terror
  in the Valley of Vision,
a day of battering down walls
 and of crying out to the mountains.
[6]Elam takes up the quiver,
 with her charioteers and horses;
 Kir uncovers the shield.
[7]Your choicest valleys are full of chariots,
 and horsemen are posted at the city gates;
[8] the defenses of Judah are stripped away.

And you looked in that day
 to the weapons in the Palace of the Forest;
[9]you saw that the City of David
 had many breaches in its defenses;
you stored up water
 in the Lower Pool.
[10]You counted the buildings in Jerusalem
 and tore down houses to strengthen the
  wall.
[11]You built a reservoir between the two walls
 for the water of the Old Pool,
but you did not look to the One who made
  it,
 or have regard for the One who planned
  it long ago.

[12]The Lord, the LORD Almighty,
 called you on that day
to weep and to wail,
 to tear out your hair and put on
  sackcloth.

22:12 Smiles Instead of Tears

*This chapter may refer to Jerusalem's
deliverance recorded in Isaiah 36–37. Isaiah
was distressed because, although great
devastation was prophesied, Jerusalem was
celebrating, not mourning. People had
reinforced walls and built water reservoirs to
prepare for war, but had not turned to God for
help (verse 11). Israelites at that time had a
certain cockiness about the city of Jerusalem,
believing that God would never allow it to fall
into enemy hands.*

---

[a]8 Dead Sea Scrolls and Syriac; Masoretic Text *A lion*   [b]11 *Dumah* means *silence* or *stillness*, a wordplay on *Edom*.

13But see, there is joy and revelry,
  slaughtering of cattle and killing of sheep,
  eating of meat and drinking of wine!
"Let us eat and drink," you say,
  "for tomorrow we die!"

14The LORD Almighty has revealed this in my
hearing: "Till your dying day this sin will not be
atoned for," says the Lord, the LORD Almighty.

15This is what the Lord, the LORD Almighty,
says:

"Go, say to this steward,
  to Shebna, who is in charge of the palace:
16What are you doing here and who gave you
    permission
  to cut out a grave for yourself here,
hewing your grave on the height
  and chiseling your resting place in the
    rock?

17"Beware, the LORD is about to take firm hold
    of you
  and hurl you away, O you mighty man.
18He will roll you up tightly like a ball
  and throw you into a large country.
There you will die
  and there your splendid chariots will
    remain—
  you disgrace to your master's house!
19I will depose you from your office,
  and you will be ousted from your
    position.

20"In that day I will summon my servant, Eliakim son of Hilkiah. 21I will clothe him with your
robe and fasten your sash around him and hand
your authority over to him. He will be a father to
those who live in Jerusalem and to the house of
Judah. 22I will place on his shoulder the key to the
house of David; what he opens no one can shut,
and what he shuts no one can open. 23I will drive
him like a peg into a firm place; he will be a seat[a]
of honor for the house of his father. 24All the
glory of his family will hang on him: its offspring
and offshoots—all its lesser vessels, from the
bowls to all the jars.

25"In that day," declares the LORD Almighty,
"the peg driven into the firm place will give way;
it will be sheared off and will fall, and the load
hanging on it will be cut down." The LORD has
spoken.

A Prophecy About Tyre

23 An oracle concerning Tyre:

Wail, O ships of Tarshish!
  For Tyre is destroyed

and left without house or harbor.
From the land of Cyprus[b]
  word has come to them.

2Be silent, you people of the island
  and you merchants of Sidon,

23:1 The Decline of Tyre

*In Isaiah's day the city of Tyre was a major
power, dominating the sea trade in the eastern
Mediterranean. Her many colonies included the
island of Cyprus, and her merchants traveled
as far as the Indian Ocean and the English
Channel. But not long after this prophecy
Assyria conquered the city, and Tyre's king fled
to Cyprus.*

whom the seafarers have enriched.
3On the great waters
  came the grain of the Shihor;
the harvest of the Nile[c] was the revenue of
    Tyre,
  and she became the marketplace of the
    nations.

4Be ashamed, O Sidon, and you, O fortress of
    the sea,
  for the sea has spoken:
"I have neither been in labor nor given birth;
  I have neither reared sons nor brought up
    daughters."
5When word comes to Egypt,
  they will be in anguish at the report from
    Tyre.

6Cross over to Tarshish;
  wail, you people of the island.
7Is this your city of revelry,
  the old, old city,
whose feet have taken her
  to settle in far-off lands?
8Who planned this against Tyre,
  the bestower of crowns,
whose merchants are princes,
  whose traders are renowned in the earth?
9The LORD Almighty planned it,
  to bring low the pride of all glory
  and to humble all who are renowned on
    the earth.

10Till[d] your land as along the Nile,
  O Daughter of Tarshish,
  for you no longer have a harbor.
11The LORD has stretched out his hand over
    the sea
  and made its kingdoms tremble.

---

a23 Or *throne*   b1 Hebrew *Kittim*   c2,3 Masoretic Text; one Dead Sea Scroll *Sidon, / who cross over the sea; / your
envoys* 3*are on the great waters. / The grain of the Shihor, / the harvest of the Nile,*   d10 Dead Sea Scrolls and some
Septuagint manuscripts; Masoretic Text *Go through*

He has given an order concerning
    Phoenicia[a]
  that her fortresses be destroyed.
[12]He said, "No more of your reveling,
    O Virgin Daughter of Sidon, now crushed!

"Up, cross over to Cyprus[b];
  even there you will find no rest."
[13]Look at the land of the Babylonians,[c]
  this people that is now of no account!
The Assyrians have made it
  a place for desert creatures;
they raised up their siege towers,
  they stripped its fortresses bare
  and turned it into a ruin.

[14]Wail, you ships of Tarshish;
  your fortress is destroyed!

[15]At that time Tyre will be forgotten for seventy years, the span of a king's life. But at the end of these seventy years, it will happen to Tyre as in the song of the prostitute:

[16]"Take up a harp, walk through the city,
    O prostitute forgotten;
play the harp well, sing many a song,
  so that you will be remembered."

[17]At the end of seventy years, the LORD will deal with Tyre. She will return to her hire as a prostitute and will ply her trade with all the kingdoms on the face of the earth. [18]Yet her profit and her earnings will be set apart for the LORD; they will not be stored up or hoarded. Her profits will go to those who live before the LORD, for abundant food and fine clothes.

The LORD's Devastation of the Earth

24 See, the LORD is going to lay waste the
    earth
  and devastate it;
he will ruin its face
  and scatter its inhabitants—
[2]it will be the same
  for priest as for people,
  for master as for servant,
  for mistress as for maid,
  for seller as for buyer,
  for borrower as for lender,
  for debtor as for creditor.
[3]The earth will be completely laid waste
  and totally plundered.
      The LORD has spoken this word.

[4]The earth dries up and withers,
  the world languishes and withers,
  the exalted of the earth languish.
[5]The earth is defiled by its people;
  they have disobeyed the laws,
  violated the statutes

and broken the everlasting covenant.
[6]Therefore a curse consumes the earth;
  its people must bear their guilt.
Therefore earth's inhabitants are burned up,
  and very few are left.
[7]The new wine dries up and the vine withers;
  all the merrymakers groan.
[8]The gaiety of the tambourines is stilled,
  the noise of the revelers has stopped,
  the joyful harp is silent.
[9]No longer do they drink wine with a song;
  the beer is bitter to its drinkers.
[10]The ruined city lies desolate;
  the entrance to every house is barred.
[11]In the streets they cry out for wine;
  all joy turns to gloom,
  all gaiety is banished from the earth.
[12]The city is left in ruins,
  its gate is battered to pieces.
[13]So will it be on the earth
  and among the nations,
as when an olive tree is beaten,
  or as when gleanings are left after the
    grape harvest.

[14]They raise their voices, they shout for joy;
  from the west they acclaim the LORD's
    majesty.
[15]Therefore in the east give glory to the LORD;
  exalt the name of the LORD, the God of
    Israel,
  in the islands of the sea.
[16]From the ends of the earth we hear singing:
  "Glory to the Righteous One."

But I said, "I waste away, I waste away!
  Woe to me!
The treacherous betray!
  With treachery the treacherous betray!"
[17]Terror and pit and snare await you,
  O people of the earth.
[18]Whoever flees at the sound of terror
  will fall into a pit;
whoever climbs out of the pit
  will be caught in a snare.

The floodgates of the heavens are opened,
  the foundations of the earth shake.
[19]The earth is broken up,
  the earth is split asunder,
  the earth is thoroughly shaken.
[20]The earth reels like a drunkard,
  it sways like a hut in the wind;
so heavy upon it is the guilt of its rebellion
  that it falls—never to rise again.

[21]In that day the LORD will punish
  the powers in the heavens above
  and the kings on the earth below.
[22]They will be herded together

---

[a]11 Hebrew *Canaan*   [b]12 Hebrew *Kittim*   [c]13 Or *Chaldeans*

like prisoners bound in a dungeon;
they will be shut up in prison
and be punished[a] after many days.
²³The moon will be abashed, the sun ashamed;
for the LORD Almighty will reign
on Mount Zion and in Jerusalem,
and before its elders, gloriously.

Praise to the LORD

25 O LORD, you are my God;
I will exalt you and praise your name,
for in perfect faithfulness
you have done marvelous things,
things planned long ago.
²You have made the city a heap of rubble,
the fortified town a ruin,
the foreigners' stronghold a city no more;
it will never be rebuilt.
³Therefore strong peoples will honor you;
cities of ruthless nations will revere you.
⁴You have been a refuge for the poor,
a refuge for the needy in his distress,
a shelter from the storm
and a shade from the heat.
For the breath of the ruthless
is like a storm driving against a wall
⁵ and like the heat of the desert.
You silence the uproar of foreigners;
as heat is reduced by the shadow of a
cloud,
so the song of the ruthless is stilled.

⁶On this mountain the LORD Almighty will
prepare
a feast of rich food for all peoples,
a banquet of aged wine—
the best of meats and the finest of wines.

25:6 A Promise of Eternal Life

*The Old Testament includes only a few hints
about resurrection and the afterlife, and this is
one of the strongest. Isaiah follows a
devastating chapter on God's judgment of the
whole earth (chapter 24) with a bright promise
of a future life. Then, death and pain will be
abolished (see verses 7–8 and 26:19), and God
will reign with perfect justice.*

⁷On this mountain he will destroy
the shroud that enfolds all peoples,
the sheet that covers all nations;
⁸ he will swallow up death forever.
The Sovereign LORD will wipe away the tears
from all faces;
he will remove the disgrace of his people
from all the earth.
The LORD has spoken.

⁹In that day they will say,

"Surely this is our God;
we trusted in him, and he saved us.
This is the LORD, we trusted in him;
let us rejoice and be glad in his salvation."

¹⁰The hand of the LORD will rest on this
mountain;
but Moab will be trampled under him
as straw is trampled down in the manure.
¹¹They will spread out their hands in it,
as a swimmer spreads out his hands to
swim.
God will bring down their pride
despite the cleverness[b] of their hands.
¹²He will bring down your high fortified walls
and lay them low;
he will bring them down to the ground,
to the very dust.

A Song of Praise

26 In that day this song will be sung in the
land of Judah:

We have a strong city;
God makes salvation
its walls and ramparts.
²Open the gates
that the righteous nation may enter,
the nation that keeps faith.
³You will keep in perfect peace
him whose mind is steadfast,
because he trusts in you.

26:3 Perfect Peace

*Isaiah, who lived in a time of tremendous
turmoil, predicted more of the same. Godly
people would suffer along with everybody else,
he said. How should believers cope? Isaiah
urged them to focus on a reality greater than
their current troubles: to keep their minds
steady on God, who never loses control over
events.*

⁴Trust in the LORD forever,
for the LORD, the LORD, is the Rock
eternal.
⁵He humbles those who dwell on high,
he lays the lofty city low;
he levels it to the ground
and casts it down to the dust.
⁶Feet trample it down—
the feet of the oppressed,
the footsteps of the poor.

⁷The path of the righteous is level;

ᵃ22 Or *released*   ᵇ11 The meaning of the Hebrew for this word is uncertain.

O upright One, you make the way of the
righteous smooth.
[8]Yes, LORD, walking in the way of your
laws,[a]
we wait for you;
your name and renown
are the desire of our hearts.
[9]My soul yearns for you in the night;
in the morning my spirit longs for you.
When your judgments come upon the earth,
the people of the world learn
righteousness.
[10]Though grace is shown to the wicked,
they do not learn righteousness;
even in a land of uprightness they go on
doing evil
and regard not the majesty of the LORD.
[11]O LORD, your hand is lifted high,
but they do not see it.
Let them see your zeal for your people and
be put to shame;
let the fire reserved for your enemies
consume them.

[12]LORD, you establish peace for us;
all that we have accomplished you have
done for us.
[13]O LORD, our God, other lords besides you
have ruled over us,
but your name alone do we honor.
[14]They are now dead, they live no more;
those departed spirits do not rise.
You punished them and brought them to
ruin;
you wiped out all memory of them.
[15]You have enlarged the nation, O LORD;
you have enlarged the nation.
You have gained glory for yourself;
you have extended all the borders of the
land.

[16]LORD, they came to you in their distress;
when you disciplined them,
they could barely whisper a prayer.[b]
[17]As a woman with child and about to give
birth
writhes and cries out in her pain,
so were we in your presence, O LORD.
[18]We were with child, we writhed in pain,
but we gave birth to wind.
We have not brought salvation to the earth;
we have not given birth to people of the
world.

[19]But your dead will live;
their bodies will rise.
You who dwell in the dust,
wake up and shout for joy.

Your dew is like the dew of the morning;
the earth will give birth to her dead.

[20]Go, my people, enter your rooms
and shut the doors behind you;
hide yourselves for a little while
until his wrath has passed by.
[21]See, the LORD is coming out of his dwelling
to punish the people of the earth for their
sins.
The earth will disclose the blood shed upon
her;
she will conceal her slain no longer.

Deliverance of Israel

27 In that day,

the LORD will punish with his sword,
his fierce, great and powerful sword,
Leviathan the gliding serpent,
Leviathan the coiling serpent;
he will slay the monster of the sea.

27:1 A Prophecy for the World

*Most of Isaiah 1–39 concerns specific nations
in the prophet's own time. But chapters 24 to
27 form a unit that seems to sum up all world
history. Those chapters contain some of
Isaiah's strongest imagery.*

[2]In that day—

"Sing about a fruitful vineyard:
[3]   I, the LORD, watch over it;
I water it continually.
I guard it day and night
so that no one may harm it.
[4]   I am not angry.
If only there were briers and thorns
confronting me!
I would march against them in battle;
I would set them all on fire.
[5]Or else let them come to me for refuge;
let them make peace with me,
yes, let them make peace with me."

[6]In days to come Jacob will take root,
Israel will bud and blossom
and fill all the world with fruit.

[7]Has ⌊the LORD⌋ struck her
as he struck down those who struck her?
Has she been killed
as those were killed who killed her?
[8]By warfare[c] and exile you contend with
her—
with his fierce blast he drives her out,

---

[a]8 Or *judgments*   [b]16 The meaning of the Hebrew for this clause is uncertain.   [c]8 See Septuagint; the meaning of
the Hebrew for this word is uncertain.

as on a day the east wind blows.
⁹By this, then, will Jacob's guilt be atoned for,
and this will be the full fruitage of the
removal of his sin:
When he makes all the altar stones
to be like chalk stones crushed to pieces,
no Asherah poles*a* or incense altars
will be left standing.
¹⁰The fortified city stands desolate,
an abandoned settlement, forsaken like the
desert;
there the calves graze,
there they lie down;
they strip its branches bare.
¹¹When its twigs are dry, they are broken off
and women come and make fires with
them.
For this is a people without understanding;
so their Maker has no compassion on
them,
and their Creator shows them no favor.

¹²In that day the LORD will thresh from the
flowing Euphrates*b* to the Wadi of Egypt, and
you, O Israelites, will be gathered up one by one.
¹³And in that day a great trumpet will sound.
Those who were perishing in Assyria and those
who were exiled in Egypt will come and worship
the LORD on the holy mountain in Jerusalem.

Woe to Ephraim

28 Woe to that wreath, the pride of
Ephraim's drunkards,
to the fading flower, his glorious beauty,
set on the head of a fertile valley—
to that city, the pride of those laid low by
wine!
²See, the Lord has one who is powerful and
strong.
Like a hailstorm and a destructive wind,
like a driving rain and a flooding downpour,
he will throw it forcefully to the ground.
³That wreath, the pride of Ephraim's
drunkards,
will be trampled underfoot.
⁴That fading flower, his glorious beauty,
set on the head of a fertile valley,
will be like a fig ripe before harvest—
as soon as someone sees it and takes it in
his hand,
he swallows it.

⁵In that day the LORD Almighty
will be a glorious crown,
a beautiful wreath
for the remnant of his people.
⁶He will be a spirit of justice
to him who sits in judgment,

a source of strength
to those who turn back the battle at the
gate.

⁷And these also stagger from wine
and reel from beer:
Priests and prophets stagger from beer
and are befuddled with wine;
they reel from beer,
they stagger when seeing visions,
they stumble when rendering decisions.
⁸All the tables are covered with vomit
and there is not a spot without filth.

⁹"Who is it he is trying to teach?
To whom is he explaining his message?
To children weaned from their milk,
to those just taken from the breast?
¹⁰For it is:
Do and do, do and do,
rule on rule, rule on rule*c*;
a little here, a little there."

¹¹Very well then, with foreign lips and strange
tongues
God will speak to this people,
¹²to whom he said,
"This is the resting place, let the weary
rest";
and, "This is the place of repose"—
but they would not listen.
¹³So then, the word of the LORD to them will
become:
Do and do, do and do,
rule on rule, rule on rule;
a little here, a little there—
so that they will go and fall backward,
be injured and snared and captured.

¹⁴Therefore hear the word of the LORD, you
scoffers
who rule this people in Jerusalem.
¹⁵You boast, "We have entered into a
covenant with death,
with the grave*d* we have made an
agreement.
When an overwhelming scourge sweeps by,
it cannot touch us,
for we have made a lie our refuge
and falsehood*e* our hiding place."

¹⁶So this is what the Sovereign LORD says:

"See, I lay a stone in Zion,
a tested stone,
a precious cornerstone for a sure foundation;
the one who trusts will never be
dismayed.
¹⁷I will make justice the measuring line
and righteousness the plumb line;

---

a 9 That is, symbols of the goddess Asherah   *b 12* Hebrew *River*   *c 10* Hebrew / *sav lasav sav lasav / kav lakav kav lakav* (possibly meaningless sounds; perhaps a mimicking of the prophet's words); also in verse 13   *d 15* Hebrew *Sheol*; also in verse 18   *e 15* Or *false gods*

hail will sweep away your refuge, the lie,
and water will overflow your hiding place.
[18]Your covenant with death will be annulled;
your agreement with the grave will not
stand.

When the overwhelming scourge sweeps by,
you will be beaten down by it.
[19]As often as it comes it will carry you away;
morning after morning, by day and by
night,
it will sweep through."

The understanding of this message
will bring sheer terror.
[20]The bed is too short to stretch out on,
the blanket too narrow to wrap around
you.
[21]The LORD will rise up as he did at Mount
Perazim,
he will rouse himself as in the Valley of
Gibeon—
to do his work, his strange work,
and perform his task, his alien task.
[22]Now stop your mocking,
or your chains will become heavier;
the Lord, the LORD Almighty, has told me
of the destruction decreed against the
whole land.

[23]Listen and hear my voice;
pay attention and hear what I say.
[24]When a farmer plows for planting, does he
plow continually?
Does he keep on breaking up and
harrowing the soil?

28:24 Like a Wise Farmer

*Drawing an analogy from farming, Isaiah
shows that God varies his treatment of nations,
depending on conditions. Just as different
crops—grain, barley, caraway, cummin—
require different farming techniques, so each
nation requires individual treatment. Those
who readily repent need only light punishment,
while stubborn nations need further discipline.*

[25]When he has leveled the surface,
does he not sow caraway and scatter
cummin?
Does he not plant wheat in its place,[a]
barley in its plot,[a]
and spelt in its field?
[26]His God instructs him
and teaches him the right way.

[27]Caraway is not threshed with a sledge,
nor is a cartwheel rolled over cummin;

caraway is beaten out with a rod,
and cummin with a stick.
[28]Grain must be ground to make bread;
so one does not go on threshing it
forever.
Though he drives the wheels of his threshing
cart over it,
his horses do not grind it.
[29]All this also comes from the LORD Almighty,
wonderful in counsel and magnificent in
wisdom.

Woe to David's City

29 Woe to you, Ariel, Ariel,
the city where David settled!
Add year to year
and let your cycle of festivals go on.
[2]Yet I will besiege Ariel;
she will mourn and lament,
she will be to me like an altar hearth.[b]
[3]I will encamp against you all around;
I will encircle you with towers
and set up my siege works against you.
[4]Brought low, you will speak from the
ground;
your speech will mumble out of the dust.
Your voice will come ghostlike from the
earth;
out of the dust your speech will whisper.

[5]But your many enemies will become like fine
dust,
the ruthless hordes like blown chaff.
Suddenly, in an instant,
[6]   the LORD Almighty will come
with thunder and earthquake and great
noise,
with windstorm and tempest and flames
of a devouring fire.
[7]Then the hordes of all the nations that fight
against Ariel,
that attack her and her fortress and
besiege her,
will be as it is with a dream,
with a vision in the night—
[8]as when a hungry man dreams that he is
eating,
but he awakens, and his hunger remains;
as when a thirsty man dreams that he is
drinking,
but he awakens faint, with his thirst
unquenched.
So will it be with the hordes of all the
nations
that fight against Mount Zion.

[9]Be stunned and amazed,
blind yourselves and be sightless;

---

[a]25 The meaning of the Hebrew for this word is uncertain.
for *Ariel.*

[b]2 The Hebrew for *altar hearth* sounds like the Hebrew

be drunk, but not from wine,
    stagger, but not from beer.
¹⁰The LORD has brought over you a deep sleep:
    He has sealed your eyes (the prophets);
he has covered your heads (the seers).

¹¹For you this whole vision is nothing but words sealed in a scroll. And if you give the scroll to someone who can read, and say to him, "Read this, please," he will answer, "I can't; it is sealed." ¹²Or if you give the scroll to someone who cannot read, and say, "Read this, please," he will answer, "I don't know how to read."

¹³The Lord says:

"These people come near to me with their
    mouth
    and honor me with their lips,
but their hearts are far from me.
Their worship of me
    is made up only of rules taught by men.ᵃ

29:13 Hypocrites

Again and again, Isaiah blasts the Israelites for a superficial faith—all words and no heart. Hundreds of years later, Jesus quoted this verse, saying that it applied precisely to people of his day (Mark 7:6–7).

---

¹⁴Therefore once more I will astound these
    people
    with wonder upon wonder;
the wisdom of the wise will perish,
    the intelligence of the intelligent will
    vanish."
¹⁵Woe to those who go to great depths
    to hide their plans from the LORD,
who do their work in darkness and think,
    "Who sees us? Who will know?"
¹⁶You turn things upside down,
    as if the potter were thought to be like the
    clay!
Shall what is formed say to him who formed
    it,
    "He did not make me"?
Can the pot say of the potter,
    "He knows nothing"?

¹⁷In a very short time, will not Lebanon be
    turned into a fertile field
    and the fertile field seem like a forest?
¹⁸In that day the deaf will hear the words of
    the scroll,
    and out of gloom and darkness
    the eyes of the blind will see.
¹⁹Once more the humble will rejoice in the
    LORD;

the needy will rejoice in the Holy One of
    Israel.
²⁰The ruthless will vanish,
    the mockers will disappear,
and all who have an eye for evil will be
    cut down—
²¹those who with a word make a man out to
    be guilty,
who ensnare the defender in court
    and with false testimony deprive the
    innocent of justice.

²²Therefore this is what the LORD, who redeemed Abraham, says to the house of Jacob:

"No longer will Jacob be ashamed;
    no longer will their faces grow pale.
²³When they see among them their children,
    the work of my hands,
they will keep my name holy;
    they will acknowledge the holiness of the
    Holy One of Jacob,
and will stand in awe of the God of Israel.
²⁴Those who are wayward in spirit will gain
    understanding;
    those who complain will accept
    instruction."

Woe to the Obstinate Nation

30 "Woe to the obstinate children,"
    declares the LORD,
"to those who carry out plans that are not
    mine,
    forming an alliance, but not by my Spirit,
    heaping sin upon sin;

30:1 Isaiah in His Prime

Isaiah delivered the messages of chapters 28–35 at the peak of his ministry, under Hezekiah. He unleashed six great "woes," or warnings: (1) to drunken, scoffing politicians, 28:1; (2) to those who carry on the form of religion, without true faith, 29:1; (3) to those who hide their plans from God (possibly referring to secret political intrigues), 29:15; (4) to the pro-Egyptian party lobbying for a political alliance, 30:1; (5) to those who trust in military power (horses and chariots) instead of God, 31:1; and (6) to the Assyrian destroyer, 33:1. Seemingly invincible at the time, the Assyrian empire would face a judgment day.

---

²who go down to Egypt
    without consulting me;
who look for help to Pharaoh's protection,
    to Egypt's shade for refuge.
³But Pharaoh's protection will be to your
    shame,

ᵃ13 Hebrew; Septuagint *They worship me in vain, / their teachings are but rules taught by men*

Egypt's shade will bring you disgrace.
[4] Though they have officials in Zoan
and their envoys have arrived in Hanes,
[5] everyone will be put to shame
because of a people useless to them,
who bring neither help nor advantage,
but only shame and disgrace."

[6] An oracle concerning the animals of the Negev:

Through a land of hardship and distress,
of lions and lionesses,
of adders and darting snakes,
the envoys carry their riches on donkeys'
backs,
their treasures on the humps of camels,
to that unprofitable nation,
[7] to Egypt, whose help is utterly useless.
Therefore I call her
Rahab the Do-Nothing.

[8] Go now, write it on a tablet for them,
inscribe it on a scroll,
that for the days to come
it may be an everlasting witness.
[9] These are rebellious people, deceitful
children,
children unwilling to listen to the LORD's
instruction.
[10] They say to the seers,
"See no more visions!"
and to the prophets,
"Give us no more visions of what is right!
Tell us pleasant things,
prophesy illusions.
[11] Leave this way,
get off this path,
and stop confronting us
with the Holy One of Israel!"

[12] Therefore, this is what the Holy One of Israel says:

"Because you have rejected this message,
relied on oppression
and depended on deceit,
[13] this sin will become for you
like a high wall, cracked and bulging,
that collapses suddenly, in an instant.
[14] It will break in pieces like pottery,
shattered so mercilessly
that among its pieces not a fragment will be
found
for taking coals from a hearth
or scooping water out of a cistern."

[15] This is what the Sovereign LORD, the Holy One of Israel, says:

"In repentance and rest is your salvation,
in quietness and trust is your strength,
but you would have none of it.
[16] You said, 'No, we will flee on horses.'
Therefore you will flee!
You said, 'We will ride off on swift horses.'
Therefore your pursuers will be swift!
[17] A thousand will flee
at the threat of one;
at the threat of five
you will all flee away,
till you are left
like a flagstaff on a mountaintop,
like a banner on a hill."

[18] Yet the LORD longs to be gracious to you;
he rises to show you compassion.
For the LORD is a God of justice.
Blessed are all who wait for him!

[19] O people of Zion, who live in Jerusalem, you will weep no more. How gracious he will be when you cry for help! As soon as he hears, he will answer you. [20] Although the Lord gives you the bread of adversity and the water of affliction, your teachers will be hidden no more; with your own eyes you will see them. [21] Whether you turn to the right or to the left, your ears will hear a voice behind you, saying, "This is the way; walk in it." [22] Then you will defile your idols overlaid with silver and your images covered with gold; you will throw them away like a menstrual cloth and say to them, "Away with you!"

[23] He will also send you rain for the seed you sow in the ground, and the food that comes from the land will be rich and plentiful. In that day your cattle will graze in broad meadows. [24] The oxen and donkeys that work the soil will eat fodder and mash, spread out with fork and shovel. [25] In the day of great slaughter, when the towers fall, streams of water will flow on every high mountain and every lofty hill. [26] The moon will shine like the sun, and the sunlight will be seven times brighter, like the light of seven full days, when the LORD binds up the bruises of his people and heals the wounds he inflicted.

[27] See, the Name of the LORD comes from afar,
with burning anger and dense clouds of
smoke;
his lips are full of wrath,
and his tongue is a consuming fire.

30:27 An End to Punishment

Isaiah minces no words in his fierce descriptions of the punishment awaiting Judah. But as this chapter shows, the punishment will reach an end, and then God will turn on the surrounding evil nations. The fire of judgment will culminate in Topheth (verse 33), a valley near Jerusalem where human sacrifices were offered to the god Molech.

²⁸His breath is like a rushing torrent,
　　rising up to the neck.
He shakes the nations in the sieve of
　　　destruction;
　　he places in the jaws of the peoples
　　a bit that leads them astray.
²⁹And you will sing
　　as on the night you celebrate a holy
　　　festival;
your hearts will rejoice
　　as when people go up with flutes
to the mountain of the LORD,
　　to the Rock of Israel.
³⁰The LORD will cause men to hear his majestic
　　　voice
　　and will make them see his arm coming
　　　down
with raging anger and consuming fire,
　　with cloudburst, thunderstorm and hail.
³¹The voice of the LORD will shatter Assyria;
　　with his scepter he will strike them down.
³²Every stroke the LORD lays on them
　　with his punishing rod
will be to the music of tambourines and
　　　harps,
　　as he fights them in battle with the blows
　　　of his arm.
³³Topheth has long been prepared;
　　it has been made ready for the king.
Its fire pit has been made deep and wide,
　　with an abundance of fire and wood;
the breath of the LORD,
　　like a stream of burning sulfur,
　　sets it ablaze.

Woe to Those Who Rely on Egypt

31 Woe to those who go down to Egypt for
　　help,
who rely on horses,
who trust in the multitude of their chariots
　　and in the great strength of their
　　　horsemen,
but do not look to the Holy One of Israel,
　　or seek help from the LORD.
²Yet he too is wise and can bring disaster;
　　he does not take back his words.
He will rise up against the house of the
　　wicked,
　　against those who help evildoers.
³But the Egyptians are men and not God;
　　their horses are flesh and not spirit.
When the LORD stretches out his hand,
　　he who helps will stumble,
　　he who is helped will fall;
　　both will perish together.

⁴This is what the LORD says to me:

"As a lion growls,
　　a great lion over his prey—
and though a whole band of shepherds

is called together against him,
he is not frightened by their shouts
　　or disturbed by their clamor—
so the LORD Almighty will come down
　　to do battle on Mount Zion and on its
　　　heights.
⁵Like birds hovering overhead,
　　the LORD Almighty will shield Jerusalem;
he will shield it and deliver it,
　　he will 'pass over' it and will rescue it."

⁶Return to him you have so greatly revolted
against, O Israelites. ⁷For in that day every one of
you will reject the idols of silver and gold your
sinful hands have made.

⁸"Assyria will fall by a sword that is not of
　　man;
　　a sword, not of mortals, will devour them.
They will flee before the sword
　　and their young men will be put to forced
　　　labor.
⁹Their stronghold will fall because of terror;
　　at sight of the battle standard their
　　　commanders will panic,"
declares the LORD,
　　whose fire is in Zion,
　　whose furnace is in Jerusalem.

The Kingdom of Righteousness

32 See, a king will reign in righteousness
　　and rulers will rule with justice.

32:1–20 Shifting Stance in Time

*Isaiah's writings often shift confusingly,
describing the present surroundings and then
moving on to predict the future. At times Isaiah
even projects himself into the future, writing in
the past tense about events that have not yet
happened. Note the shifting time sequence in
this chapter.*

²Each man will be like a shelter from the
　　wind
　　and a refuge from the storm,
like streams of water in the desert
　　and the shadow of a great rock in a
　　　thirsty land.

³Then the eyes of those who see will no
　　longer be closed,
　　and the ears of those who hear will listen.
⁴The mind of the rash will know and
　　understand,
　　and the stammering tongue will be fluent
　　　and clear.
⁵No longer will the fool be called noble
　　nor the scoundrel be highly respected.
⁶For the fool speaks folly,

his mind is busy with evil:
He practices ungodliness
and spreads error concerning the LORD;
the hungry he leaves empty
and from the thirsty he withholds water.
[7]The scoundrel's methods are wicked,
he makes up evil schemes
to destroy the poor with lies,
even when the plea of the needy is just.
[8]But the noble man makes noble plans,
and by noble deeds he stands.

The Women of Jerusalem

[9]You women who are so complacent,
rise up and listen to me;
you daughters who feel secure,
hear what I have to say!
[10]In little more than a year
you who feel secure will tremble;
the grape harvest will fail,
and the harvest of fruit will not come.
[11]Tremble, you complacent women;
shudder, you daughters who feel secure!
Strip off your clothes,
put sackcloth around your waists.
[12]Beat your breasts for the pleasant fields,
for the fruitful vines
[13]and for the land of my people,

A Time of Crisis
Defeat seemed certain to everyone but Isaiah

"Assyria will fall by a sword that is not of man." 31:8

AFTER TWO DISMAL DECADES UNDER King Ahaz, Judah finally saw a ray of hope when Hezekiah ascended the throne. Second Kings summarizes his reign this way: "There was no one like him among all the kings of Judah, either before him or after him" (2 Kings 18:5).

Isaiah reached the peak of his ministry under King Hezekiah, who often sought his advice. The king needed Isaiah's help; he had inherited a kingdom in mortal danger from Assyria.

Protesting a Foolish Rebellion

How could Judah break free from Assyrian domination? Like other kings before him, Hezekiah thought of joining with other countries. Both Egypt and a rising Babylon seemed eager to court Judah as an ally.

Isaiah, however, said no. He urged Hezekiah to trust only in God. To dramatize his point, the court prophet did a shocking thing: he stalked around stripped and barefoot for three years as a protest against the pro-Egypt lobby (20:1–6). This protest forms the background for some of the strongest speeches in Isaiah's book (chapters 18–20; 30–31).

Isaiah's protest failed, however. Not even Hezekiah could resist the temptation to oppose Assyria. First, he shored up the defenses of Jerusalem and built up the city's water supplies. Then he formed an alliance of small kingdoms and led an outright rebellion against Assyria.

Revenge of an Empire

Assyria lowered the boom. Its armies smashed into Judah, leveling 46 walled cities and carrying away 200,150 captives. The Assyrian king demanded huge sums of money from Hezekiah, whom he mockingly described as "a bird in a cage."

Hezekiah, cowering under siege in Jerusalem, once more turned to Isaiah for advice. Should he surrender? Assyrian soldiers were already pressing in around the walls, hurling insults at the demoralized citizens inside.

Isaiah avoided an "I told you so" attitude. Against all odds, he again recommended prayer and reliance on the power of God. Have faith, he said; don't surrender, don't fear. Assyria will return home, wounded (37:5–7).

Isaiah's deep courage and optimism raised the morale of all Jerusalem. And in a spectacular way (37:36; also 2 Kings 19), God took care of the Assyrian army.

An Authentic Hero

Chapters 18–35 contain Isaiah's messages from this period, including many of the very words that stirred a desperate nation to faith. Without his inspiring example, Jerusalem might have surrendered.

Many of the prophets of Israel and Judah were loners, voices "crying in the desert." Isaiah was an exception. He had the king's ear at a critical moment in Judah's history. Because of his effectiveness, Isaiah went down in history as a great statesman and hero.

Life Questions: In your life, what experience has called for the most courage and faith? How did you respond at the time?

a land overgrown with thorns and
briers—
yes, mourn for all houses of merriment
and for this city of revelry.
¹⁴The fortress will be abandoned,
the noisy city deserted;
citadel and watchtower will become a
wasteland forever,
the delight of donkeys, a pasture for
flocks,
¹⁵till the Spirit is poured upon us from on
high,
and the desert becomes a fertile field,
and the fertile field seems like a forest.
¹⁶Justice will dwell in the desert
and righteousness live in the fertile field.
¹⁷The fruit of righteousness will be peace;
the effect of righteousness will be
quietness and confidence forever.
¹⁸My people will live in peaceful dwelling
places,
in secure homes,
in undisturbed places of rest.
¹⁹Though hail flattens the forest
and the city is leveled completely,
²⁰how blessed you will be,
sowing your seed by every stream,
and letting your cattle and donkeys range
free.

Distress and Help

33 Woe to you, O destroyer,
you who have not been destroyed!
Woe to you, O traitor,
you who have not been betrayed!
When you stop destroying,
you will be destroyed;
when you stop betraying,
you will be betrayed.

²O LORD, be gracious to us;
we long for you.
Be our strength every morning,
our salvation in time of distress.
³At the thunder of your voice, the peoples
flee;
when you rise up, the nations scatter.
⁴Your plunder, O nations, is harvested as by
young locusts;
like a swarm of locusts men pounce on it.

⁵The LORD is exalted, for he dwells on high;
he will fill Zion with justice and
righteousness.
⁶He will be the sure foundation for your
times,
a rich store of salvation and wisdom and
knowledge;

the fear of the LORD is the key to this
treasure.ᵃ

⁷Look, their brave men cry aloud in the
streets;
the envoys of peace weep bitterly.
⁸The highways are deserted,
no travelers are on the roads.
The treaty is broken,
its witnessesᵇ are despised,
no one is respected.
⁹The land mournsᶜ and wastes away,
Lebanon is ashamed and withers;
Sharon is like the Arabah,
and Bashan and Carmel drop their leaves.

¹⁰"Now will I arise," says the LORD.
"Now will I be exalted;
now will I be lifted up.
¹¹You conceive chaff,
you give birth to straw;
your breath is a fire that consumes you.
¹²The peoples will be burned as if to lime;
like cut thornbushes they will be set
ablaze."

¹³You who are far away, hear what I have
done;
you who are near, acknowledge my
power!
¹⁴The sinners in Zion are terrified;
trembling grips the godless:
"Who of us can dwell with the consuming
fire?
Who of us can dwell with everlasting
burning?"
¹⁵He who walks righteously
and speaks what is right,
who rejects gain from extortion
and keeps his hand from accepting bribes,
who stops his ears against plots of murder
and shuts his eyes against contemplating
evil—
¹⁶this is the man who will dwell on the
heights,
whose refuge will be the mountain
fortress.
His bread will be supplied,
and water will not fail him.

¹⁷Your eyes will see the king in his beauty
and view a land that stretches afar.
¹⁸In your thoughts you will ponder the former
terror:
"Where is that chief officer?
Where is the one who took the revenue?
Where is the officer in charge of the
towers?"
¹⁹You will see those arrogant people no more,
those people of an obscure speech,

ᵃ6 Or is a treasure from him   ᵇ8 Dead Sea Scrolls; Masoretic Text / the cities   ᶜ9 Or dries up

with their strange, incomprehensible
    tongue.

²⁰Look upon Zion, the city of our festivals;
    your eyes will see Jerusalem,
    a peaceful abode, a tent that will not be
        moved;
    its stakes will never be pulled up,
    nor any of its ropes broken.
²¹There the LORD will be our Mighty One.
    It will be like a place of broad rivers and
        streams.
    No galley with oars will ride them,
    no mighty ship will sail them.
²²For the LORD is our judge,
    the LORD is our lawgiver,
    the LORD is our king;
    it is he who will save us.

²³Your rigging hangs loose:
    The mast is not held secure,
    the sail is not spread.
    Then an abundance of spoils will be divided
    and even the lame will carry off plunder.
²⁴No one living in Zion will say, "I am ill";
    and the sins of those who dwell there will
        be forgiven.

Judgment Against the Nations

34 Come near, you nations, and listen;
    pay attention, you peoples!
Let the earth hear, and all that is in it,
    the world, and all that comes out of it!

34:1 Isaiah the Historian

*Isaiah's book includes many references to
nations and leaders of his day. Perhaps more
than any other prophet, Isaiah had a deep
sense of history. In fact, he wrote an account of
the life of King Uzziah and a record of the
rulers of Israel and Judah (see 2 Chronicles
26:22; 32:32). Although neither of these books
has survived, the one that bears his name
gives a blow-by-blow analysis of all the
nations of his time.*

²The LORD is angry with all nations;
    his wrath is upon all their armies.
    He will totally destroy[a] them,
    he will give them over to slaughter.
³Their slain will be thrown out,
    their dead bodies will send up a stench;
    the mountains will be soaked with their
        blood.
⁴All the stars of the heavens will be dissolved
    and the sky rolled up like a scroll;

all the starry host will fall
    like withered leaves from the vine,
    like shriveled figs from the fig tree.

⁵My sword has drunk its fill in the heavens;
    see, it descends in judgment on Edom,
    the people I have totally destroyed.
⁶The sword of the LORD is bathed in blood,
    it is covered with fat—
    the blood of lambs and goats,
    fat from the kidneys of rams.
For the LORD has a sacrifice in Bozrah
    and a great slaughter in Edom.
⁷And the wild oxen will fall with them,
    the bull calves and the great bulls.
    Their land will be drenched with blood,
    and the dust will be soaked with fat.

⁸For the LORD has a day of vengeance,
    a year of retribution, to uphold Zion's
        cause.
⁹Edom's streams will be turned into pitch,
    her dust into burning sulfur;
    her land will become blazing pitch!
¹⁰It will not be quenched night and day;
    its smoke will rise forever.
    From generation to generation it will lie
        desolate;
    no one will ever pass through it again.
¹¹The desert owl[b] and screech owl[b] will
        possess it;
    the great owl[b] and the raven will nest
        there.
God will stretch out over Edom
    the measuring line of chaos
    and the plumb line of desolation.
¹²Her nobles will have nothing there to be
        called a kingdom,
    all her princes will vanish away.
¹³Thorns will overrun her citadels,
    nettles and brambles her strongholds.
    She will become a haunt for jackals,
    a home for owls.
¹⁴Desert creatures will meet with hyenas,
    and wild goats will bleat to each other;
    there the night creatures will also repose
    and find for themselves places of rest.
¹⁵The owl will nest there and lay eggs,
    she will hatch them, and care for her
        young under the shadow of her
        wings;
    there also the falcons will gather,
    each with its mate.

¹⁶Look in the scroll of the LORD and read:

None of these will be missing,
    not one will lack her mate.
    For it is his mouth that has given the order,

---

[a]2 The Hebrew term refers to the irrevocable giving over of things or persons to the LORD, often by totally destroying them; also in verse 5.   [b]11 The precise identification of these birds is uncertain.

and his Spirit will gather them together.
[17]He allots their portions;
  his hand distributes them by measure.
They will possess it forever
  and dwell there from generation to
    generation.

Joy of the Redeemed

35 The desert and the parched land will be
  glad;
  the wilderness will rejoice and blossom.
Like the crocus, [2]it will burst into bloom;
  it will rejoice greatly and shout for joy.
The glory of Lebanon will be given to it,
  the splendor of Carmel and Sharon;
they will see the glory of the LORD,
  the splendor of our God.

[3]Strengthen the feeble hands,
  steady the knees that give way;
[4]say to those with fearful hearts,
  "Be strong, do not fear;
your God will come,
  he will come with vengeance;
with divine retribution
  he will come to save you."

[5]Then will the eyes of the blind be opened
  and the ears of the deaf unstopped,
[6]Then will the lame leap like a deer,
  and the mute tongue shout for joy.
Water will gush forth in the wilderness
  and streams in the desert.
[7]The burning sand will become a pool,
  the thirsty ground bubbling springs.
In the haunts where jackals once lay,
  grass and reeds and papyrus will grow.

[8]And a highway will be there;
  it will be called the Way of Holiness.
The unclean will not journey on it;
  it will be for those who walk in that Way;
  wicked fools will not go about on it.[a]
[9]No lion will be there,
  nor will any ferocious beast get up on it;
  they will not be found there.
But only the redeemed will walk there,
[10] and the ransomed of the LORD will return.
They will enter Zion with singing;
  everlasting joy will crown their heads.
Gladness and joy will overtake them,
  and sorrow and sighing will flee away.

Sennacherib Threatens Jerusalem

36 In the fourteenth year of King Hezekiah's
  reign, Sennacherib king of Assyria attacked all the fortified cities of Judah and captured them. [2]Then the king of Assyria sent his
field commander with a large army from Lachish
to King Hezekiah at Jerusalem. When the commander stopped at the aqueduct of the Upper
Pool, on the road to the Washerman's Field, [3]Eli-
akim son of Hilkiah the palace administrator,
Shebna the secretary, and Joah son of Asaph the
recorder went out to him.

36:1 Bridge Chapters

After a beautiful poem describing the renewed world God will make, Isaiah plunges into a historical account of Judah's troubles with the superpower Assyria. These next four historical chapters (which closely follow 2 Kings 18:13–20:19) form a bridge between problems with Assyria (chapters 1–35) and those with Babylon (chapters 40–66). They record some of the greatest crises in Isaiah's and King Hezekiah's lives, beginning with Assyria's final assault on Jerusalem and ending with Hezekiah's biggest blunder. That blunder led to Isaiah's prediction that Babylon would someday destroy Judah.

[4]The field commander said to them, "Tell Hezekiah,

"'This is what the great king, the king of Assyria, says: On what are you basing this confidence of yours? [5]You say you have strategy and military strength—but you speak only empty words. On whom are you depending, that you rebel against me? [6]Look now, you are depending on Egypt, that splintered reed of a staff, which pierces a man's hand and wounds him if he leans on it! Such is Pharaoh king of Egypt to all who depend on him. [7]And if you say to me, "We are depending on the LORD our God"—isn't he the one whose high places and altars Hezekiah removed, saying to Judah and Jerusalem, "You must worship before this altar"?

[8]"'Come now, make a bargain with my master, the king of Assyria: I will give you two thousand horses—if you can put riders on them! [9]How then can you repulse one officer of the least of my master's officials, even though you are depending on Egypt for chariots and horsemen? [10]Furthermore, have I come to attack and destroy this land without the LORD? The LORD himself told me to march against this country and destroy it.'"

[11]Then Eliakim, Shebna and Joah said to the field commander, "Please speak to your servants in Aramaic, since we understand it. Don't speak to us in Hebrew in the hearing of the people on the wall."

---

[a]8 Or / the simple will not stray from it

¹²But the commander replied, "Was it only to your master and you that my master sent me to say these things, and not to the men sitting on the wall—who, like you, will have to eat their own filth and drink their own urine?"

36:11 Fear in the City

The Assyrian commander showed great skill in demoralizing the besieged residents of Jerusalem. King Hezekiah's own officials were terrified (36:22–37:4). Only Isaiah stood firm in believing that God could save the city. Earlier (see 22:15–25), God had expressed through Isaiah utter contempt for these very officials of Hezekiah.

¹³Then the commander stood and called out in Hebrew, "Hear the words of the great king, the king of Assyria! ¹⁴This is what the king says: Do not let Hezekiah deceive you. He cannot deliver you! ¹⁵Do not let Hezekiah persuade you to trust in the LORD when he says, 'The LORD will surely deliver us; this city will not be given into the hand of the king of Assyria.'

¹⁶"Do not listen to Hezekiah. This is what the king of Assyria says: Make peace with me and come out to me. Then every one of you will eat from his own vine and fig tree and drink water from his own cistern, ¹⁷until I come and take you to a land like your own—a land of grain and new wine, a land of bread and vineyards.

¹⁸"Do not let Hezekiah mislead you when he says, 'The LORD will deliver us.' Has the god of any nation ever delivered his land from the hand of the king of Assyria? ¹⁹Where are the gods of Hamath and Arpad? Where are the gods of Sepharvaim? Have they rescued Samaria from my hand? ²⁰Who of all the gods of these countries has been able to save his land from me? How then can the LORD deliver Jerusalem from my hand?"

²¹But the people remained silent and said nothing in reply, because the king had commanded, "Do not answer him."

²²Then Eliakim son of Hilkiah the palace administrator, Shebna the secretary, and Joah son of Asaph the recorder went to Hezekiah, with their clothes torn, and told him what the field commander had said.

Jerusalem's Deliverance Foretold

37 When King Hezekiah heard this, he tore his clothes and put on sackcloth and went into the temple of the LORD. ²He sent Eliakim the palace administrator, Shebna the secretary, and the leading priests, all wearing sackcloth, to the

prophet Isaiah son of Amoz. ³They told him, "This is what Hezekiah says: This day is a day of distress and rebuke and disgrace, as when children come to the point of birth and there is no strength to deliver them. ⁴It may be that the LORD your God will hear the words of the field commander, whom his master, the king of Assyria, has sent to ridicule the living God, and that he will rebuke him for the words the LORD your God has heard. Therefore pray for the remnant that still survives."

⁵When King Hezekiah's officials came to Isaiah, ⁶Isaiah said to them, "Tell your master, 'This is what the LORD says: Do not be afraid of what you have heard—those words with which the underlings of the king of Assyria have blasphemed me. ⁷Listen! I am going to put a spirit in him so that when he hears a certain report, he will return to his own country, and there I will have him cut down with the sword.'"

⁸When the field commander heard that the king of Assyria had left Lachish, he withdrew and found the king fighting against Libnah.

⁹Now Sennacherib received a report that Tirhakah, the Cushite[a] king of Egypt, was marching out to fight against him. When he heard it, he sent messengers to Hezekiah with this word: ¹⁰"Say to Hezekiah king of Judah: Do not let the god you depend on deceive you when he says, 'Jerusalem will not be handed over to the king of Assyria.' ¹¹Surely you have heard what the kings of Assyria have done to all the countries, destroying them completely. And will you be delivered? ¹²Did the gods of the nations that were destroyed by my forefathers deliver them—the gods of Gozan, Haran, Rezeph and the people of Eden who were in Tel Assar? ¹³Where is the king of Hamath, the king of Arpad, the king of the city of Sepharvaim, or of Hena or Ivvah?"

Hezekiah's Prayer

¹⁴Hezekiah received the letter from the messengers and read it. Then he went up to the temple of the LORD and spread it out before the LORD. ¹⁵And Hezekiah prayed to the LORD: ¹⁶"O LORD Almighty, God of Israel, enthroned between the cherubim, you alone are God over all the kingdoms of the earth. You have made heaven and earth. ¹⁷Give ear, O LORD, and hear; open your eyes, O LORD, and see; listen to all the words Sennacherib has sent to insult the living God.

¹⁸"It is true, O LORD, that the Assyrian kings have laid waste all these peoples and their lands. ¹⁹They have thrown their gods into the fire and destroyed them, for they were not gods but only wood and stone, fashioned by human hands. ²⁰Now, O LORD our God, deliver us from his

a9 That is, from the upper Nile region

hand, so that all kingdoms on earth may know that you alone, O LORD, are God.[a]"

Sennacherib's Fall

[21]Then Isaiah son of Amoz sent a message to Hezekiah: "This is what the LORD, the God of Israel, says: Because you have prayed to me concerning Sennacherib king of Assyria, [22]this is the word the LORD has spoken against him:

"The Virgin Daughter of Zion
    despises and mocks you.
The Daughter of Jerusalem
    tosses her head as you flee.
[23]Who is it you have insulted and
    blasphemed?
    Against whom have you raised your voice
and lifted your eyes in pride?
    Against the Holy One of Israel!
[24]By your messengers
    you have heaped insults on the Lord.
And you have said,
    'With my many chariots
I have ascended the heights of the
    mountains,
    the utmost heights of Lebanon.
I have cut down its tallest cedars,
    the choicest of its pines.
I have reached its remotest heights,
    the finest of its forests.
[25]I have dug wells in foreign lands[b]
    and drunk the water there.
With the soles of my feet
    I have dried up all the streams of Egypt.'

[26]"Have you not heard?
    Long ago I ordained it.
In days of old I planned it;
    now I have brought it to pass,
that you have turned fortified cities
    into piles of stone.
[27]Their people, drained of power,
    are dismayed and put to shame.
They are like plants in the field,
    like tender green shoots,
like grass sprouting on the roof,
    scorched[c] before it grows up.

[28]"But I know where you stay
    and when you come and go
    and how you rage against me.
[29]Because you rage against me
    and because your insolence has reached
        my ears,
I will put my hook in your nose
    and my bit in your mouth,

and I will make you return
    by the way you came.

[30]"This will be the sign for you, O Hezekiah:

"This year you will eat what grows by itself,
    and the second year what springs from
        that.
But in the third year sow and reap,
    plant vineyards and eat their fruit.
[31]Once more a remnant of the house of Judah
    will take root below and bear fruit above.
[32]For out of Jerusalem will come a remnant,
    and out of Mount Zion a band of
        survivors.
The zeal of the LORD Almighty
    will accomplish this.

[33]"Therefore this is what the LORD says concerning the king of Assyria:

"He will not enter this city
    or shoot an arrow here.
He will not come before it with shield
    or build a siege ramp against it.
[34]By the way that he came he will return;
    he will not enter this city,"
                            declares the LORD.
[35]"I will defend this city and save it,
    for my sake and for the sake of David my
        servant!"

[36]Then the angel of the LORD went out and put to death a hundred and eighty-five thousand men in the Assyrian camp. When the people got up the next morning—there were all the dead bodies! [37]So Sennacherib king of Assyria broke camp and withdrew. He returned to Nineveh and stayed there.

[38]One day, while he was worshiping in the temple of his god Nisroch, his sons Adrammelech and Sharezer cut him down with the sword, and they escaped to the land of Ararat. And Esarhaddon his son succeeded him as king.

Hezekiah's Illness

38 In those days Hezekiah became ill and was at the point of death. The prophet Isaiah son of Amoz went to him and said, "This is what the LORD says: Put your house in order, because you are going to die; you will not recover."

[2]Hezekiah turned his face to the wall and prayed to the LORD, [3]"Remember, O LORD, how I have walked before you faithfully and with wholehearted devotion and have done what is good in your eyes." And Hezekiah wept bitterly.

[4]Then the word of the LORD came to Isaiah: [5]"Go and tell Hezekiah, 'This is what the LORD,

---

[a]20 Dead Sea Scrolls (see also 2 Kings 19:19); Masoretic Text *alone are the LORD*   [b]25 Dead Sea Scrolls (see also 2 Kings 19:24); Masoretic Text does not have *in foreign lands*.   [c]27 Some manuscripts of the Masoretic Text, Dead Sea Scrolls and some Septuagint manuscripts (see also 2 Kings 19:26); most manuscripts of the Masoretic Text *roof / and terraced fields*

the God of your father David, says: I have heard your prayer and seen your tears; I will add fifteen years to your life. [6]And I will deliver you and this city from the hand of the king of Assyria. I will defend this city.

38:1 Fifteen More Years

When the doctor solemnly pronounces a disease terminal, who doesn't crave a second chance? After Isaiah announced to Hezekiah that his disease would be fatal, Hezekiah did not give up. He went bitterly and asked God to remember his devotion. In response, God sent Isaiah back with an amazing message: He had granted Hezekiah fifteen additional years. Here, as so often in the Bible, God changes events because of prayer.

[7]"This is the LORD's sign to you that the LORD will do what he has promised: [8]I will make the shadow cast by the sun go back the ten steps it has gone down on the stairway of Ahaz.'" So the sunlight went back the ten steps it had gone down.

[9]A writing of Hezekiah king of Judah after his illness and recovery:

[10]I said, "In the prime of my life
    must I go through the gates of death[a]
    and be robbed of the rest of my years?"
[11]I said, "I will not again see the LORD,
    the LORD, in the land of the living;
no longer will I look on mankind,
    or be with those who now dwell in this
        world.[b]
[12]Like a shepherd's tent my house
    has been pulled down and taken from me.
Like a weaver I have rolled up my life,
    and he has cut me off from the loom;
    day and night you made an end of me.
[13]I waited patiently till dawn,
    but like a lion he broke all my bones;
    day and night you made an end of me.
[14]I cried like a swift or thrush,
    I moaned like a mourning dove.
My eyes grew weak as I looked to the
        heavens.
    I am troubled; O Lord, come to my aid!"

[15]But what can I say?
    He has spoken to me, and he himself has
        done this.
I will walk humbly all my years
    because of this anguish of my soul.
[16]Lord, by such things men live;
    and my spirit finds life in them too.
You restored me to health

and let me live.
[17]Surely it was for my benefit
    that I suffered such anguish.
In your love you kept me
    from the pit of destruction;
you have put all my sins
    behind your back.
[18]For the grave[a] cannot praise you,
    death cannot sing your praise;
those who go down to the pit
    cannot hope for your faithfulness.
[19]The living, the living—they praise you,
    as I am doing today;
fathers tell their children
    about your faithfulness.

[20]The LORD will save me,
    and we will sing with stringed instruments
all the days of our lives
    in the temple of the LORD.

[21]Isaiah had said, "Prepare a poultice of figs and apply it to the boil, and he will recover."
[22]Hezekiah had asked, "What will be the sign that I will go up to the temple of the LORD?"

Envoys From Babylon

39 At that time Merodach-Baladan son of Baladan king of Babylon sent Hezekiah letters and a gift, because he had heard of his illness and recovery. [2]Hezekiah received the envoys gladly and showed them what was in his storehouses—the silver, the gold, the spices, the fine oil, his entire armory and everything found among his treasures. There was nothing in his palace or in all his kingdom that Hezekiah did not show them.

[3]Then Isaiah the prophet went to King Hezekiah and asked, "What did those men say, and where did they come from?"

"From a distant land," Hezekiah replied. "They came to me from Babylon."

[4]The prophet asked, "What did they see in your palace?"

"They saw everything in my palace," Hezekiah said. "There is nothing among my treasures that I did not show them."

[5]Then Isaiah said to Hezekiah, "Hear the word of the LORD Almighty: [6]The time will surely come when everything in your palace, and all that your fathers have stored up until this day, will be carried off to Babylon. Nothing will be left, says the LORD. [7]And some of your descendants, your own flesh and blood who will be born to you, will be taken away, and they will become eunuchs in the palace of the king of Babylon."

[8]"The word of the LORD you have spoken is good," Hezekiah replied. For he thought, "There will be peace and security in my lifetime."

---

[a] 10,18 Hebrew *Sheol*   [b] 11 A few Hebrew manuscripts; most Hebrew manuscripts *in the place of cessation*

Comfort for God's People

40 Comfort, comfort my people,
  says your God.
²Speak tenderly to Jerusalem,
  and proclaim to her
that her hard service has been completed,
  that her sin has been paid for,
that she has received from the LORD's hand
  double for all her sins.

³A voice of one calling:
"In the desert prepare
  the way for the LORD*ᵃ*;
make straight in the wilderness
  a highway for our God.*ᵇ*

40:3 Voice in the Wilderness

Beginning here, Isaiah's emphasis shifts away from judgment and toward comfort. The comfort will ultimately come through God's glorious arrival, which God's people should prepare for by building a "highway" for God to travel on. In the New Testament, John the Baptist identified himself as the "voice" calling for this preparation (John 1:23). The "earthmoving" he demanded was repentance from sin, a preparation for Jesus' arrival.

⁴Every valley shall be raised up,
  every mountain and hill made low;
the rough ground shall become level,
  the rugged places a plain.
⁵And the glory of the LORD will be revealed,
  and all mankind together will see it.
                For the mouth of the
                  LORD has spoken."

⁶A voice says, "Cry out."
  And I said, "What shall I cry?"

"All men are like grass,
  and all their glory is like the flowers of the
    field.
⁷The grass withers and the flowers fall,
  because the breath of the LORD blows on
    them.
  Surely the people are grass.
⁸The grass withers and the flowers fall,
  but the word of our God stands forever."

⁹You who bring good tidings to Zion,
  go up on a high mountain.
You who bring good tidings to Jerusalem,*ᶜ*
  lift up your voice with a shout,
lift it up, do not be afraid;
  say to the towns of Judah,

"Here is your God!"
¹⁰See, the Sovereign LORD comes with power,
  and his arm rules for him.
See, his reward is with him,
  and his recompense accompanies him.
¹¹He tends his flock like a shepherd:
  He gathers the lambs in his arms
and carries them close to his heart;
  he gently leads those that have young.

¹²Who has measured the waters in the hollow
      of his hand,
  or with the breadth of his hand marked
      off the heavens?
Who has held the dust of the earth in a
      basket,
  or weighed the mountains on the scales
    and the hills in a balance?
¹³Who has understood the mind*ᵈ* of the
      LORD,
  or instructed him as his counselor?
¹⁴Whom did the LORD consult to enlighten
      him,
  and who taught him the right way?
Who was it that taught him knowledge
  or showed him the path of understanding?

¹⁵Surely the nations are like a drop in a
      bucket;
  they are regarded as dust on the scales;
he weighs the islands as though they were
    fine dust.
¹⁶Lebanon is not sufficient for altar fires,
  nor its animals enough for burnt offerings.
¹⁷Before him all the nations are as nothing;
  they are regarded by him as worthless
    and less than nothing.

¹⁸To whom, then, will you compare God?
  What image will you compare him to?
¹⁹As for an idol, a craftsman casts it,
  and a goldsmith overlays it with gold
    and fashions silver chains for it.
²⁰A man too poor to present such an offering
  selects wood that will not rot.
He looks for a skilled craftsman
  to set up an idol that will not topple.

²¹Do you not know?
  Have you not heard?
Has it not been told you from the
      beginning?
  Have you not understood since the earth
      was founded?
²²He sits enthroned above the circle of the
      earth,
  and its people are like grasshoppers.
He stretches out the heavens like a canopy,

ᵃ3 Or A voice of one calling in the desert: / "Prepare the way for the LORD   *ᵇ3 Hebrew; Septuagint make straight the paths of our God*   *ᶜ9 Or O Zion, bringer of good tidings, / go up on a high mountain. / O Jerusalem, bringer of good tidings*   *ᵈ13 Or Spirit; or spirit*

A New Song

A dramatic change in tone: comfort and hope for the worst of times

YOU CAN SENSE THE CHANGE in the very first words of chapter 40. "Comfort, comfort my people, says your God. Speak tenderly to Jerusalem, and proclaim to her that her hard service has been completed." Soft, reassuring words replace the harsh warnings of Isaiah's earlier chapters.

During much of Isaiah's life, Judah was confident and strong. But the prophecies beginning in chapter 40 project forward to a radically different scene. The land of Judah has been devastated, and the Jews have been taken captive. Jerusalem lies in ruins. Some 200 years separate what is described in the first part of Isaiah from the latter part. (Many scholars believe these later prophecies were given by another prophet.)

> Those who hope in the LORD will renew their strength. They will soar on wings like eagles; they will run and not grow weary, they will walk and not be faint. 40:31

What Happened in the Meantime

To understand the rest of the book of Isaiah, you need to understand what happened in those 200 years. The confident nation Isaiah once knew slid further and further downward. At the same time a new empire, Babylon, gained strength. This new enemy invaded Judah.

The armies of Babylon did something no army had accomplished since King David's time: they conquered Jerusalem itself. Siege engines breached the walls. Judah's king was led out of Jerusalem, blinded. Their homes destroyed, most of the city's inhabitants followed their king in chains. The dark period of Babylonian captivity began.

Prophets of this period, and those who prophesied in advance about the coming catastrophes, faced huge questions. Was God abandoning his "eternal" throne of David? How could he watch in silence as his own nation—his own temple—was ripped to shreds by pagan armies?

Three Great Hopes

Reflecting the change in circumstances, Isaiah 40–66 shifts into a new key. Gone are the bleak predictions of judgment on the Jews. Instead, a majestic message of hope and joy and light breaks in, beginning with the opening words of comfort. The prophet sets out to reestablish faith in God.

What happened to Judah, Isaiah teaches, was not God's defeat. God had in mind a new thing, a plan far more grand than anything seen before.

The author of Isaiah expresses the plan as a series of wonderful reasons for hope. First, he says, will come deliverance from the Babylonian captivity. A new star, a ruler named Cyrus, will arise in the east and set the Jews free. He will allow them to return to Jerusalem to begin the long task of rebuilding a city and a nation. Chapters 40–48 detail God's confident predictions about Cyrus and the relief he would give captive Jews.

Indeed, just such a ruler did ascend to the throne in ancient Persia (present-day Iran). Cyrus smashed Babylon's armies in one decisive battle. As recorded in Ezra 1:1–4, he granted the Jews permission to return to their city and rebuild.

In words that have become very familiar, the book of Isaiah tells of two further hopes for the future. A mysterious figure called "the servant" appears in chapter 49. That servant, through his suffering, would provide a way to rescue the entire world. Finally, in conclusion, the prophet turns to a faraway time, when God will usher in peace for all in a new heaven and new earth. "The Holy One of Israel" (one of Isaiah's favorite names for God) will rule as the God of the whole earth.

Surviving Tough Times

Isaiah 40–66 had immense practical value for the people who first heard it. The Jews, facing a series of great crises, needed the prophet's message of hope: Forgiveness was on the way; the Jews, though scattered, would one day be gathered "one by one."

Further, Isaiah teaches that no matter how difficult the circumstances, God can use them for our benefit. Again and again in the Israelites' history, good times led to decadence. In contrast, times of suffering tested and refined the true people of God. Ultimately, suffering would lead to the salvation of all the world.

Life Questions: Try to put yourself in the circumstances of the Jews back then. Would you have found the prophet's words comforting?

and spreads them out like a tent to live
in.
²³He brings princes to naught
and reduces the rulers of this world to
nothing.
²⁴No sooner are they planted,
no sooner are they sown,
no sooner do they take root in the
ground,
than he blows on them and they wither,
and a whirlwind sweeps them away like
chaff.

²⁵"To whom will you compare me?
Or who is my equal?" says the Holy One.
²⁶Lift your eyes and look to the heavens:
Who created all these?
He who brings out the starry host one by
one,
and calls them each by name.
Because of his great power and mighty
strength,
not one of them is missing.

²⁷Why do you say, O Jacob,
and complain, O Israel,
"My way is hidden from the LORD;
my cause is disregarded by my God"?
²⁸Do you not know?
Have you not heard?
The LORD is the everlasting God,
the Creator of the ends of the earth.
He will not grow tired or weary,
and his understanding no one can fathom.
²⁹He gives strength to the weary
and increases the power of the weak.
³⁰Even youths grow tired and weary,
and young men stumble and fall;
³¹but those who hope in the LORD
will renew their strength.
They will soar on wings like eagles;
they will run and not grow weary,
they will walk and not be faint.

The Helper of Israel

41 "Be silent before me, you islands!
Let the nations renew their strength!
Let them come forward and speak;
let us meet together at the place of
judgment.

²"Who has stirred up one from the east,
calling him in righteousness to his
serviceᵃ?
He hands nations over to him
and subdues kings before him.
He turns them to dust with his sword,
to windblown chaff with his bow.
³He pursues them and moves on unscathed,

by a path his feet have not traveled
before.
⁴Who has done this and carried it through,
calling forth the generations from the
beginning?
I, the LORD—with the first of them
and with the last—I am he."

41:4 How to Understand God

*Chapters 40–46 echo the majestic chapters at
the end of Job. God shows himself as master of
the universe. Before him, nations are like a
drop in a bucket (40:15) and people are like
grasshoppers (40:22). He taunts all other so-
called "gods": such idols are carved of the same
tree used to cook supper! (44:12–20). The true
God, the God of the Israelites, is the One who
created the universe (45:12,18), who called
Abraham (41:8), who rescued the Israelites
from slavery in Egypt. For the dispirited Jewish
survivors of Babylon's invasion, this exalted
view of God was a reminder that God had
neither vanished nor rejected them.*

⁵The islands have seen it and fear;
the ends of the earth tremble.
They approach and come forward;
⁶ each helps the other
and says to his brother, "Be strong!"
⁷The craftsman encourages the goldsmith,
and he who smooths with the hammer
spurs on him who strikes the anvil.
He says of the welding, "It is good."
He nails down the idol so it will not
topple.

⁸"But you, O Israel, my servant,
Jacob, whom I have chosen,
you descendants of Abraham my friend,
⁹I took you from the ends of the earth,
from its farthest corners I called you.
I said, 'You are my servant';
I have chosen you and have not rejected
you.
¹⁰So do not fear, for I am with you;
do not be dismayed, for I am your God.
I will strengthen you and help you;
I will uphold you with my righteous right
hand.

¹¹"All who rage against you
will surely be ashamed and disgraced;
those who oppose you
will be as nothing and perish.
¹²Though you search for your enemies,
you will not find them.
Those who wage war against you
will be as nothing at all.

ᵃ2 Or / whom victory meets at every step

¹³For I am the LORD, your God,
who takes hold of your right hand
and says to you, Do not fear;
I will help you.
¹⁴Do not be afraid, O worm Jacob,
O little Israel,
for I myself will help you," declares the
LORD,
your Redeemer, the Holy One of Israel.
¹⁵"See, I will make you into a threshing sledge,
new and sharp, with many teeth.
You will thresh the mountains and crush
them,
and reduce the hills to chaff.
¹⁶You will winnow them, the wind will pick
them up,
and a gale will blow them away.
But you will rejoice in the LORD
and glory in the Holy One of Israel.

¹⁷"The poor and needy search for water,
but there is none;
their tongues are parched with thirst.
But I the LORD will answer them;
I, the God of Israel, will not forsake them.
¹⁸I will make rivers flow on barren heights,
and springs within the valleys.
I will turn the desert into pools of water,
and the parched ground into springs.
¹⁹I will put in the desert
the cedar and the acacia, the myrtle and
the olive.
I will set pines in the wasteland,
the fir and the cypress together,
²⁰so that people may see and know,
may consider and understand,
that the hand of the LORD has done this,
that the Holy One of Israel has created it.

²¹"Present your case," says the LORD.
"Set forth your arguments," says Jacob's
King.
²²"Bring in ⌊ your idols ⌋ to tell us
what is going to happen.
Tell us what the former things were,
so that we may consider them
and know their final outcome.
Or declare to us the things to come,
²³   tell us what the future holds,
so we may know that you are gods.
Do something, whether good or bad,
so that we will be dismayed and filled
with fear.
²⁴But you are less than nothing
and your works are utterly worthless;
he who chooses you is detestable.

²⁵"I have stirred up one from the north, and
he comes—
one from the rising sun who calls on my
name.
He treads on rulers as if they were mortar,

as if he were a potter treading the clay.
²⁶Who told of this from the beginning, so we
could know,
or beforehand, so we could say, 'He was
right'?
No one told of this,
no one foretold it,
no one heard any words from you.
²⁷I was the first to tell Zion, 'Look, here they
are!'
I gave to Jerusalem a messenger of good
tidings.
²⁸I look but there is no one—
no one among them to give counsel,
no one to give answer when I ask them.
²⁹See, they are all false!
Their deeds amount to nothing;
their images are but wind and confusion.

The Servant of the LORD

42 "Here is my servant, whom I uphold,
my chosen one in whom I delight;
I will put my Spirit on him
and he will bring justice to the nations.

42:1 The Solution

Having described shocking injustice, Isaiah now gives the solution: God's servant, who in a quiet, gentle, steady way will bring justice not only to Israel but to "the nations"—that is, the entire earth. Matthew 12:18–21, quoting this passage, identifies the servant as Jesus.

²He will not shout or cry out,
or raise his voice in the streets.
³A bruised reed he will not break,
and a smoldering wick he will not snuff
out.
In faithfulness he will bring forth justice;
⁴   he will not falter or be discouraged
till he establishes justice on earth.
In his law the islands will put their hope."

⁵This is what God the LORD says—
he who created the heavens and stretched
them out,
who spread out the earth and all that
comes out of it,
who gives breath to its people,
and life to those who walk on it:
⁶"I, the LORD, have called you in
righteousness;
I will take hold of your hand.
I will keep you and will make you
to be a covenant for the people
and a light for the Gentiles,
⁷to open eyes that are blind,
to free captives from prison

and to release from the dungeon those
who sit in darkness.

[8]"I am the LORD; that is my name!
I will not give my glory to another
or my praise to idols.
[9]See, the former things have taken place,
and new things I declare;
before they spring into being
I announce them to you."

Song of Praise to the LORD

[10]Sing to the LORD a new song,
his praise from the ends of the earth,
you who go down to the sea, and all that is
in it,
you islands, and all who live in them.
[11]Let the desert and its towns raise their
voices;
let the settlements where Kedar lives
rejoice.
Let the people of Sela sing for joy;
let them shout from the mountaintops.
[12]Let them give glory to the LORD
and proclaim his praise in the islands.
[13]The LORD will march out like a mighty man,
like a warrior he will stir up his zeal;
with a shout he will raise the battle cry
and will triumph over his enemies.

[14]"For a long time I have kept silent,
I have been quiet and held myself back.
But now, like a woman in childbirth,
I cry out, I gasp and pant.

42:14 Does God Care?

*After telling of his power, God goes on to
describe the depth of his feelings for his people.
He uses tender and sometimes shocking
language, especially in this comparison of his
pain to that of childbirth.*

[15]I will lay waste the mountains and hills
and dry up all their vegetation;
I will turn rivers into islands
and dry up the pools.
[16]I will lead the blind by ways they have not
known,
along unfamiliar paths I will guide them;
I will turn the darkness into light before
them
and make the rough places smooth.
These are the things I will do;
I will not forsake them.
[17]But those who trust in idols,
who say to images, 'You are our gods,'
will be turned back in utter shame.

Israel Blind and Deaf

[18]"Hear, you deaf;
look, you blind, and see!
[19]Who is blind but my servant,
and deaf like the messenger I send?
Who is blind like the one committed to me,
blind like the servant of the LORD?
[20]You have seen many things, but have paid
no attention;
your ears are open, but you hear
nothing."
[21]It pleased the LORD
for the sake of his righteousness
to make his law great and glorious.
[22]But this is a people plundered and looted,
all of them trapped in pits
or hidden away in prisons.
They have become plunder,
with no one to rescue them;
they have been made loot,
with no one to say, "Send them back."

[23]Which of you will listen to this
or pay close attention in time to come?
[24]Who handed Jacob over to become loot,
and Israel to the plunderers?
Was it not the LORD,
against whom we have sinned?
For they would not follow his ways;
they did not obey his law.
[25]So he poured out on them his burning
anger,
the violence of war.
It enveloped them in flames, yet they did not
understand;
it consumed them, but they did not take
it to heart.

Israel's Only Savior

43 But now, this is what the LORD says—
he who created you, O Jacob,
he who formed you, O Israel:
"Fear not, for I have redeemed you;
I have summoned you by name; you are
mine.
[2]When you pass through the waters,
I will be with you;
and when you pass through the rivers,
they will not sweep over you.
When you walk through the fire,
you will not be burned;
the flames will not set you ablaze.
[3]For I am the LORD, your God,
the Holy One of Israel, your Savior;
I give Egypt for your ransom,
Cush[a] and Seba in your stead.
[4]Since you are precious and honored in my
sight,

---

[a] 3 That is, the upper Nile region

and because I love you,
I will give men in exchange for you,
and people in exchange for your life.
⁵Do not be afraid, for I am with you;

I will bring your children from the east
and gather you from the west.
⁶I will say to the north, 'Give them up!'
and to the south, 'Do not hold them
back.'
Bring my sons from afar
and my daughters from the ends of the
earth—
⁷everyone who is called by my name,
whom I created for my glory,
whom I formed and made."

⁸Lead out those who have eyes but are blind,
who have ears but are deaf.
⁹All the nations gather together
and the peoples assemble.
Which of them foretold this
and proclaimed to us the former things?
Let them bring in their witnesses to prove
they were right,
so that others may hear and say, "It is
true."

¹⁰"You are my witnesses," declares the LORD,
"and my servant whom I have chosen,
so that you may know and believe me
and understand that I am he.
Before me no god was formed,
nor will there be one after me.

¹¹I, even I, am the LORD,
and apart from me there is no savior.
¹²I have revealed and saved and proclaimed—
I, and not some foreign god among you.
You are my witnesses," declares the LORD,
"that I am God.
¹³ Yes, and from ancient days I am he.
No one can deliver out of my hand.
When I act, who can reverse it?"

God's Mercy and Israel's Unfaithfulness

¹⁴This is what the LORD says—
your Redeemer, the Holy One of Israel:
"For your sake I will send to Babylon
and bring down as fugitives all the
Babylonians,ᵃ
in the ships in which they took pride.
¹⁵I am the LORD, your Holy One,
Israel's Creator, your King."

¹⁶This is what the LORD says—
he who made a way through the sea,
a path through the mighty waters,
¹⁷who drew out the chariots and horses,
the army and reinforcements together,
and they lay there, never to rise again,
extinguished, snuffed out like a wick:
¹⁸"Forget the former things;
do not dwell on the past.
¹⁹See, I am doing a new thing!
Now it springs up; do you not perceive it?
I am making a way in the desert
and streams in the wasteland.
²⁰The wild animals honor me,
the jackals and the owls,
because I provide water in the desert
and streams in the wasteland,
to give drink to my people, my chosen,
²¹ the people I formed for myself
that they may proclaim my praise.

²²"Yet you have not called upon me, O Jacob,
you have not wearied yourselves for me,
O Israel.
²³You have not brought me sheep for burnt
offerings,
nor honored me with your sacrifices.
I have not burdened you with grain offerings
nor wearied you with demands for
incense.
²⁴You have not bought any fragrant calamus
for me,
or lavished on me the fat of your
sacrifices.
But you have burdened me with your sins
and wearied me with your offenses.

²⁵"I, even I, am he who blots out
your transgressions, for my own sake,
and remembers your sins no more.

ᵃ*14 Or Chaldeans*

²⁶Review the past for me,
  let us argue the matter together;
  state the case for your innocence.
²⁷Your first father sinned;
  your spokesmen rebelled against me.
²⁸So I will disgrace the dignitaries of your
    temple,
  and I will consign Jacob to destruction*ᵃ*
  and Israel to scorn.

Israel the Chosen

44 "But now listen, O Jacob, my servant,
  Israel, whom I have chosen.
²This is what the LORD says—
  he who made you, who formed you in the
    womb,
  and who will help you:
  Do not be afraid, O Jacob, my servant,
  Jeshurun, whom I have chosen.
³For I will pour water on the thirsty land,
  and streams on the dry ground;
  I will pour out my Spirit on your offspring,
  and my blessing on your descendants.
⁴They will spring up like grass in a meadow,
  like poplar trees by flowing streams.
⁵One will say, 'I belong to the LORD';
  another will call himself by the name of
    Jacob;
  still another will write on his hand, 'The
    LORD's,'
  and will take the name Israel.

The LORD, Not Idols

⁶"This is what the LORD says—
  Israel's King and Redeemer, the LORD
    Almighty:
  I am the first and I am the last;
  apart from me there is no God.
⁷Who then is like me? Let him proclaim it.
  Let him declare and lay out before me
  what has happened since I established my
    ancient people,
  and what is yet to come—
  yes, let him foretell what will come.
⁸Do not tremble, do not be afraid.
  Did I not proclaim this and foretell it long
    ago?
  You are my witnesses. Is there any God
    besides me?
  No, there is no other Rock; I know not
    one."

⁹All who make idols are nothing,
  and the things they treasure are worthless.
  Those who would speak up for them are
    blind;
  they are ignorant, to their own shame.
¹⁰Who shapes a god and casts an idol,

which can profit him nothing?
¹¹He and his kind will be put to shame;
  craftsmen are nothing but men.
  Let them all come together and take their
    stand;
  they will be brought down to terror and
    infamy.

¹²The blacksmith takes a tool
  and works with it in the coals;
  he shapes an idol with hammers,
  he forges it with the might of his arm.
  He gets hungry and loses his strength;
  he drinks no water and grows faint.
¹³The carpenter measures with a line
  and makes an outline with a marker;
  he roughs it out with chisels
  and marks it with compasses.
  He shapes it in the form of man,
  of man in all his glory,
  that it may dwell in a shrine.
¹⁴He cut down cedars,
  or perhaps took a cypress or oak.
  He let it grow among the trees of the forest,
  or planted a pine, and the rain made it
    grow.
¹⁵It is man's fuel for burning;
  some of it he takes and warms himself,
  he kindles a fire and bakes bread.
  But he also fashions a god and worships it;
  he makes an idol and bows down to it.
¹⁶Half of the wood he burns in the fire;
  over it he prepares his meal,
  he roasts his meat and eats his fill.
  He also warms himself and says,
  "Ah! I am warm; I see the fire."
¹⁷From the rest he makes a god, his idol;
  he bows down to it and worships.
  He prays to it and says,
  "Save me; you are my god."
¹⁸They know nothing, they understand
    nothing;
  their eyes are plastered over so they
    cannot see,
  and their minds closed so they cannot
    understand.
¹⁹No one stops to think,
  no one has the knowledge or
    understanding to say,
  "Half of it I used for fuel;
  I even baked bread over its coals,
  I roasted meat and I ate.
  Shall I make a detestable thing from what is
    left?
  Shall I bow down to a block of wood?"
²⁰He feeds on ashes, a deluded heart misleads
    him;

ᵃ 28 The Hebrew term refers to the irrevocable giving over of things or persons to the LORD, often by totally destroying them.

he cannot save himself, or say,
"Is not this thing in my right hand a lie?"

²¹"Remember these things, O Jacob,
for you are my servant, O Israel.
I have made you, you are my servant;
O Israel, I will not forget you.
²²I have swept away your offenses like a cloud,
your sins like the morning mist.
Return to me,
for I have redeemed you."

²³Sing for joy, O heavens, for the LORD has
done this;
shout aloud, O earth beneath.
Burst into song, you mountains,
you forests and all your trees,
for the LORD has redeemed Jacob,
he displays his glory in Israel.

Jerusalem to Be Inhabited

²⁴"This is what the LORD says—
your Redeemer, who formed you in the
womb:

I am the LORD,
who has made all things,
who alone stretched out the heavens,
who spread out the earth by myself,

²⁵who foils the signs of false prophets
and makes fools of diviners,
who overthrows the learning of the wise
and turns it into nonsense,
²⁶who carries out the words of his servants
and fulfills the predictions of his
messengers,

who says of Jerusalem, 'It shall be inhabited,'
of the towns of Judah, 'They shall be
built,'
and of their ruins, 'I will restore them,'
²⁷who says to the watery deep, 'Be dry,
and I will dry up your streams,'
²⁸who says of Cyrus, 'He is my shepherd
and will accomplish all that I please;
he will say of Jerusalem, "Let it be
rebuilt,"
and of the temple, "Let its foundations be
laid." '

45 "This is what the LORD says to his
anointed,
to Cyrus, whose right hand I take hold of
to subdue nations before him
and to strip kings of their armor,
to open doors before him
so that gates will not be shut:
²I will go before you
and will level the mountains*ᵃ*;
I will break down gates of bronze
and cut through bars of iron.
³I will give you the treasures of darkness,
riches stored in secret places,
so that you may know that I am the LORD,
the God of Israel, who summons you by
name.
⁴For the sake of Jacob my servant,
of Israel my chosen,
I summon you by name
and bestow on you a title of honor,
though you do not acknowledge me.
⁵I am the LORD, and there is no other;

ᵃ2 Dead Sea Scrolls and Septuagint; the meaning of the word in the Masoretic Text is uncertain.

CYRUS *Good Shepherd?*

GOD REFERRED TO HIM AS "my shepherd," delegated to him the rebuilding of Jerusalem
and the temple (44:28), summoned him by name and bestowed on him "a title of honor"
(45:4). Who was this ruler so favored by God? Surprisingly, Cyrus was not one of God's faithful followers at all. He was a foreigner, the emperor and founder of the great Persian Empire. A political and military genius, Cyrus had melded the Medes and the Persians into a unified nation and used his power to
overthrow the cruel Babylonians.

Cyrus introduced a genuinely fresh idea onto the world stage: tolerance. Rather than smashing
small countries, killing or deporting their people and destroying their religion and identity, Cyrus began
a policy of encouraging ethnic minorities. He let them return to their homelands and helped them
reestablish their places of worship.

The Jews benefited greatly from this policy (as the book of Ezra recounts in detail). Cyrus allowed
the captive Jews to return to Jerusalem and rebuild their temple. Some 42,360 made the long trek
home. Amazingly, Cyrus restored to the Jews the temple vessels stolen by the Babylonians and even
contributed financially to the Jewish cause.

From the story of Cyrus, Isaiah draws the strong lesson that God has complete control over
human history. He can use anybody to accomplish his work, even a great emperor who does not
acknowledge him. All people of the earth belong to God, whether they know it or not.

Life Questions: Do you think God is using powerful leaders today to accomplish his will? How?

apart from me there is no God.
I will strengthen you,
　　though you have not acknowledged me,
⁶so that from the rising of the sun
　　to the place of its setting
men may know there is none besides me.
　　I am the LORD, and there is no other.
⁷I form the light and create darkness,
　　I bring prosperity and create disaster;
　　I, the LORD, do all these things.

⁸"You heavens above, rain down
　　　　righteousness;
　　let the clouds shower it down.
Let the earth open wide,
　　let salvation spring up,
let righteousness grow with it;
　　I, the LORD, have created it.

⁹"Woe to him who quarrels with his Maker,
　　to him who is but a potsherd among the
　　　　potsherds on the ground.
Does the clay say to the potter,
　　'What are you making?'
Does your work say,
　　'He has no hands'?

45:9 Quarrels with God

*Quarreling with your Maker goes far beyond
the spirited dialogue that Moses, Job, and
Jeremiah engaged in. Isaiah is describing an
insolent assault on God's competence. Not only
is it wrong, it is ridiculous—as ridiculous as a
pot complaining about the shape the potter
gives it. In Romans 9:20, Paul applies this
analogy to complaints that God had treated the
Jews unfairly.*

¹⁰Woe to him who says to his father,
　　'What have you begotten?'
or to his mother,
　　'What have you brought to birth?'

¹¹"This is what the LORD says—
　　the Holy One of Israel, and its Maker:
Concerning things to come,
　　do you question me about my children,
　　or give me orders about the work of my
　　　　hands?
¹²It is I who made the earth
　　and created mankind upon it.
My own hands stretched out the heavens;
　　I marshaled their starry hosts.
¹³I will raise up Cyrus[a] in my righteousness:
　　I will make all his ways straight.
He will rebuild my city
　　and set my exiles free,

but not for a price or reward,
　　says the LORD Almighty."

¹⁴This is what the LORD says:

"The products of Egypt and the merchandise
　　　　of Cush,[b]
　　and those tall Sabeans—
they will come over to you
　　and will be yours;
they will trudge behind you,
　　coming over to you in chains.
They will bow down before you
　　and plead with you, saying,
'Surely God is with you, and there is no
　　　　other;
　　there is no other god.'"

¹⁵Truly you are a God who hides himself,
　　O God and Savior of Israel.
¹⁶All the makers of idols will be put to shame
　　　　and disgraced;
　　they will go off into disgrace together.
¹⁷But Israel will be saved by the LORD
　　with an everlasting salvation;
you will never be put to shame or disgraced,
　　to ages everlasting.

¹⁸For this is what the LORD says—
　　he who created the heavens,
　　　　he is God;
he who fashioned and made the earth,
　　he founded it;
he did not create it to be empty,
　　but formed it to be inhabited—
he says:
"I am the LORD,
　　and there is no other.
¹⁹I have not spoken in secret,
　　from somewhere in a land of darkness;
I have not said to Jacob's descendants,
　　'Seek me in vain.'
I, the LORD, speak the truth;
　　I declare what is right.

²⁰"Gather together and come;
　　assemble, you fugitives from the nations.
Ignorant are those who carry about idols of
　　　　wood,
　　who pray to gods that cannot save.
²¹Declare what is to be, present it—
　　let them take counsel together.
Who foretold this long ago,
　　who declared it from the distant past?
Was it not I, the LORD?
　　And there is no God apart from me,
a righteous God and a Savior;
　　there is none but me.
²²"Turn to me and be saved,
　　all you ends of the earth;

---

a 13 Hebrew *him*　　*b 14* That is, the upper Nile region

for I am God, and there is no other.
²³By myself I have sworn,
my mouth has uttered in all integrity
a word that will not be revoked:
Before me every knee will bow;
by me every tongue will swear.

45:21 Foretelling the Future

Isaiah contains many predictions of future events. These chapters tell of Cyrus's rise from the east. Elsewhere, the prophet gives specific predictions about the coming Messiah and about events near the end of time. God uses these predictions as proof of his power and knowledge, challenging the pagan gods to foretell anything (41:23).

²⁴They will say of me, 'In the LORD alone
are righteousness and strength.'"
All who have raged against him
will come to him and be put to shame.
²⁵But in the LORD all the descendants of Israel
will be found righteous and will exult.

Gods of Babylon

46 Bel bows down, Nebo stoops low;
their idols are borne by beasts of
burden.ᵃ
The images that are carried about are
burdensome,
a burden for the weary.
²They stoop and bow down together;
unable to rescue the burden,
they themselves go off into captivity.

³"Listen to me, O house of Jacob,
all you who remain of the house of Israel,
you whom I have upheld since you were
conceived,
and have carried since your birth.
⁴Even to your old age and gray hairs
I am he, I am he who will sustain you.
I have made you and I will carry you;
I will sustain you and I will rescue you.

46:4 I Carried You

Is religion a burden? For idol worshipers, certainly, in the most literal sense: Their helpless gods had to be carried around on carts (verse 1). In contrast, God carries his people, and has done so from the time of their conception and birth. He won't stop; he will sustain and rescue them in their old age.

⁵"To whom will you compare me or count
me equal?
To whom will you liken me that we may
be compared?
⁶Some pour out gold from their bags
and weigh out silver on the scales;
they hire a goldsmith to make it into a god,
and they bow down and worship it.
⁷They lift it to their shoulders and carry it;
they set it up in its place, and there it
stands.
From that spot it cannot move.
Though one cries out to it, it does not
answer;
it cannot save him from his troubles.

⁸"Remember this, fix it in mind,
take it to heart, you rebels.
⁹Remember the former things, those of long
ago;
I am God, and there is no other;
I am God, and there is none like me.
¹⁰I make known the end from the beginning,
from ancient times, what is still to come.
I say: My purpose will stand,
and I will do all that I please.
¹¹From the east I summon a bird of prey;
from a far-off land, a man to fulfill my
purpose.
What I have said, that will I bring about;
what I have planned, that will I do.
¹²Listen to me, you stubborn-hearted,
you who are far from righteousness.
¹³I am bringing my righteousness near,
it is not far away;
and my salvation will not be delayed.
I will grant salvation to Zion,
my splendor to Israel.

The Fall of Babylon

47 "Go down, sit in the dust,
Virgin Daughter of Babylon;
sit on the ground without a throne,
Daughter of the Babylonians.ᵇ
No more will you be called
tender or delicate.
²Take millstones and grind flour;
take off your veil.
Lift up your skirts, bare your legs,
and wade through the streams.
³Your nakedness will be exposed
and your shame uncovered.
I will take vengeance;
I will spare no one."

⁴Our Redeemer—the LORD Almighty is his
name—
is the Holy One of Israel.

ᵃ1 Or *are but beasts and cattle*   ᵇ1 Or *Chaldeans*; also in verse 5

⁵"Sit in silence, go into darkness,
    Daughter of the Babylonians;
no more will you be called
    queen of kingdoms.
⁶I was angry with my people
    and desecrated my inheritance;
I gave them into your hand,
    and you showed them no mercy.
Even on the aged
    you laid a very heavy yoke.
⁷You said, 'I will continue forever—
    the eternal queen!'
But you did not consider these things
    or reflect on what might happen.

47:7 An Evil Queen

*Over the centuries, Babylon became a byword
for evil among the Jews, for she was the nation
that had destroyed Jerusalem and its temple.
Psalm 137, composed by captive Jews in
Babylon, expresses their anguish. But in this
chapter God predicts that the great queen will
become a prostitute, surprised by a sudden
catastrophe. The same theme is echoed in the
book of Revelation, which applies the
symbolism of "Babylon the Great" to another
evil empire (Revelation 18).*

⁸"Now then, listen, you wanton creature,
    lounging in your security
and saying to yourself,
    'I am, and there is none besides me.
I will never be a widow
    or suffer the loss of children.'
⁹Both of these will overtake you
    in a moment, on a single day:
loss of children and widowhood.
They will come upon you in full measure,
    in spite of your many sorceries
    and all your potent spells.
¹⁰You have trusted in your wickedness
    and have said, 'No one sees me.'
Your wisdom and knowledge mislead you
    when you say to yourself,
    'I am, and there is none besides me.'
¹¹Disaster will come upon you,
    and you will not know how to conjure it
        away.
A calamity will fall upon you
    that you cannot ward off with a ransom;
a catastrophe you cannot foresee
    will suddenly come upon you.

¹²"Keep on, then, with your magic spells
    and with your many sorceries,
    which you have labored at since
        childhood.
Perhaps you will succeed,
    perhaps you will cause terror.

¹³All the counsel you have received has only
        worn you out!
Let your astrologers come forward,
    those stargazers who make predictions
        month by month,
    let them save you from what is coming
        upon you.
¹⁴Surely they are like stubble;
    the fire will burn them up.
They cannot even save themselves
    from the power of the flame.
Here are no coals to warm anyone;
    here is no fire to sit by.
¹⁵That is all they can do for you—
    these you have labored with
    and trafficked with since childhood.
Each of them goes on in his error;
    there is not one that can save you.

Stubborn Israel

48 "Listen to this, O house of Jacob,
    you who are called by the name of Israel
    and come from the line of Judah,
you who take oaths in the name of the LORD
    and invoke the God of Israel—
    but not in truth or righteousness—
²you who call yourselves citizens of the holy
        city
    and rely on the God of Israel—
    the LORD Almighty is his name:
³I foretold the former things long ago,
    my mouth announced them and I made
        them known;
    then suddenly I acted, and they came to
        pass.
⁴For I knew how stubborn you were;
    the sinews of your neck were iron,
    your forehead was bronze.
⁵Therefore I told you these things long ago;
    before they happened I announced them
        to you
so that you could not say,
    'My idols did them;
    my wooden image and metal god
        ordained them.'
⁶You have heard these things; look at them
        all.
    Will you not admit them?

"From now on I will tell you of new things,
    of hidden things unknown to you.
⁷They are created now, and not long ago;
    you have not heard of them before today.
So you cannot say,
    'Yes, I knew of them.'
⁸You have neither heard nor understood;
    from of old your ear has not been open.
Well do I know how treacherous you are;
    you were called a rebel from birth.
⁹For my own name's sake I delay my wrath;

for the sake of my praise I hold it back
from you,
so as not to cut you off.
¹⁰See, I have refined you, though not as silver;
I have tested you in the furnace of
affliction.
¹¹For my own sake, for my own sake, I do
this.
How can I let myself be defamed?
I will not yield my glory to another.

Israel Freed

¹²"Listen to me, O Jacob,
Israel, whom I have called:
I am he;
I am the first and I am the last.
¹³My own hand laid the foundations of the
earth,
and my right hand spread out the
heavens;
when I summon them,
they all stand up together.

¹⁴"Come together, all of you, and listen:
Which of ⌊the idols⌋ has foretold these
things?
The LORD's chosen ally
will carry out his purpose against Babylon;
his arm will be against the Babylonians.ᵃ
¹⁵I, even I, have spoken;
yes, I have called him.
I will bring him,
and he will succeed in his mission.

¹⁶"Come near me and listen to this:

"From the first announcement I have not
spoken in secret;
at the time it happens, I am there."

And now the Sovereign LORD has sent me,
with his Spirit.

¹⁷This is what the LORD says—
your Redeemer, the Holy One of Israel:
"I am the LORD your God,
who teaches you what is best for you,
who directs you in the way you should go.
¹⁸If only you had paid attention to my
commands,
your peace would have been like a river,
your righteousness like the waves of the
sea.
¹⁹Your descendants would have been like the
sand,
your children like its numberless grains;
their name would never be cut off
nor destroyed from before me."

²⁰Leave Babylon,
flee from the Babylonians!
Announce this with shouts of joy
and proclaim it.
Send it out to the ends of the earth;
say, "The LORD has redeemed his servant
Jacob."
²¹They did not thirst when he led them
through the deserts;
he made water flow for them from the
rock;
he split the rock
and water gushed out.

²²"There is no peace," says the LORD, "for the
wicked."

The Servant of the LORD

49 Listen to me, you islands;
hear this, you distant nations:
Before I was born the LORD called me;
from my birth he has made mention of
my name.
²He made my mouth like a sharpened sword,
in the shadow of his hand he hid me;
he made me into a polished arrow
and concealed me in his quiver.
³He said to me, "You are my servant,
Israel, in whom I will display my
splendor."
⁴But I said, "I have labored to no purpose;
I have spent my strength in vain and for
nothing.
Yet what is due me is in the LORD's hand,
and my reward is with my God."

⁵And now the LORD says—
he who formed me in the womb to be his
servant
to bring Jacob back to him
and gather Israel to himself,
for I am honored in the eyes of the LORD
and my God has been my strength—
⁶he says:
"It is too small a thing for you to be my
servant
to restore the tribes of Jacob
and bring back those of Israel I have kept.
I will also make you a light for the Gentiles,
that you may bring my salvation to the
ends of the earth."

⁷This is what the LORD says—
the Redeemer and Holy One of Israel—
to him who was despised and abhorred by
the nation,
to the servant of rulers:
"Kings will see you and rise up,
princes will see and bow down,
because of the LORD, who is faithful,
the Holy One of Israel, who has chosen
you."

ᵃ14 Or Chaldeans; also in verse 20

Restoration of Israel

[8]This is what the LORD says:

"In the time of my favor I will answer you,
  and in the day of salvation I will help you;

49:6 Israel's Final Destiny

*The book of Isaiah spells out Israel's ultimate
destiny: to be a light for the Gentiles and to
bring salvation to the ends of the earth. Isaiah
is not introducing a brand-new thought—God
had made clear his intentions in the original
covenant (Genesis 22:18). But, along the way,
Israel and Judah's desire for political greatness
had obscured their original calling.*

I will keep you and will make you
  to be a covenant for the people,
to restore the land
  and to reassign its desolate inheritances,
[9]to say to the captives, 'Come out,'
  and to those in darkness, 'Be free!'

"They will feed beside the roads
  and find pasture on every barren hill.
[10]They will neither hunger nor thirst,
  nor will the desert heat or the sun beat
    upon them.
He who has compassion on them will guide
    them
  and lead them beside springs of water.
[11]I will turn all my mountains into roads,
  and my highways will be raised up.
[12]See, they will come from afar—
  some from the north, some from the west,
  some from the region of Aswan.[a]"

[13]Shout for joy, O heavens;
  rejoice, O earth;
  burst into song, O mountains!
For the LORD comforts his people
  and will have compassion on his afflicted
    ones.

[14]But Zion said, "The LORD has forsaken me,
  the Lord has forgotten me."

[15]"Can a mother forget the baby at her breast
  and have no compassion on the child she
    has borne?
Though she may forget,
  I will not forget you!
[16]See, I have engraved you on the palms of my
    hands;
  your walls are ever before me.
[17]Your sons hasten back,

and those who laid you waste depart from
    you.
[18]Lift up your eyes and look around;
  all your sons gather and come to you.
As surely as I live," declares the LORD,
  "you will wear them all as ornaments;
  you will put them on, like a bride.

[19]"Though you were ruined and made desolate
  and your land laid waste,
now you will be too small for your people,
  and those who devoured you will be far
    away.
[20]The children born during your bereavement
  will yet say in your hearing,
'This place is too small for us;
  give us more space to live in.'
[21]Then you will say in your heart,
  'Who bore me these?
I was bereaved and barren;
  I was exiled and rejected.
  Who brought these up?
I was left all alone,
  but these—where have they come from?'"

[22]This is what the Sovereign LORD says:

"See, I will beckon to the Gentiles,
  I will lift up my banner to the peoples;
they will bring your sons in their arms
  and carry your daughters on their
    shoulders.
[23]Kings will be your foster fathers,
  and their queens your nursing mothers.
They will bow down before you with their
    faces to the ground;
  they will lick the dust at your feet.
Then you will know that I am the LORD;
  those who hope in me will not be
    disappointed."

[24]Can plunder be taken from warriors,
  or captives rescued from the fierce[b]?

[25]But this is what the LORD says:

"Yes, captives will be taken from warriors,
  and plunder retrieved from the fierce;
I will contend with those who contend with
    you,
  and your children I will save.
[26]I will make your oppressors eat their own
    flesh;
  they will be drunk on their own blood, as
    with wine.
Then all mankind will know
  that I, the LORD, am your Savior,
  your Redeemer, the Mighty One of
    Jacob."

---

[a]12 Dead Sea Scrolls; Masoretic Text *Sinim*   [b]24 Dead Sea Scrolls, Vulgate and Syriac (see also Septuagint and
verse 25); Masoretic Text *righteous*

Israel's Sin and the Servant's Obedience

50 This is what the LORD says:

"Where is your mother's certificate of
      divorce
    with which I sent her away?
Or to which of my creditors
    did I sell you?
Because of your sins you were sold;
    because of your transgressions your
      mother was sent away.
²When I came, why was there no one?
    When I called, why was there no one to
      answer?
Was my arm too short to ransom you?
    Do I lack the strength to rescue you?
By a mere rebuke I dry up the sea,
    I turn rivers into a desert;
their fish rot for lack of water
    and die of thirst.
³I clothe the sky with darkness
    and make sackcloth its covering."

⁴The Sovereign LORD has given me an
      instructed tongue,
    to know the word that sustains the weary.
He wakens me morning by morning,
    wakens my ear to listen like one being
      taught.
⁵The Sovereign LORD has opened my ears,
    and I have not been rebellious;
    I have not drawn back.
⁶I offered my back to those who beat me,
    my cheeks to those who pulled out my
      beard;
I did not hide my face
    from mocking and spitting.
⁷Because the Sovereign LORD helps me,
    I will not be disgraced.
Therefore have I set my face like flint,
    and I know I will not be put to shame.
⁸He who vindicates me is near.
    Who then will bring charges against me?
    Let us face each other!
Who is my accuser?
    Let him confront me!
⁹It is the Sovereign LORD who helps me.
    Who is he that will condemn me?
They will all wear out like a garment;
    the moths will eat them up.

¹⁰Who among you fears the LORD
    and obeys the word of his servant?
Let him who walks in the dark,
    who has no light,
trust in the name of the LORD
    and rely on his God.
¹¹But now, all you who light fires
    and provide yourselves with flaming
      torches,
go, walk in the light of your fires

and of the torches you have set ablaze.
This is what you shall receive from my hand:
    You will lie down in torment.

Everlasting Salvation for Zion

51 "Listen to me, you who pursue
      righteousness
    and who seek the LORD:
Look to the rock from which you were cut
    and to the quarry from which you were
      hewn;
²look to Abraham, your father,
    and to Sarah, who gave you birth.
When I called him he was but one,
    and I blessed him and made him many.
³The LORD will surely comfort Zion
    and will look with compassion on all her
      ruins;
he will make her deserts like Eden,
    her wastelands like the garden of the
      LORD.
Joy and gladness will be found in her,
    thanksgiving and the sound of singing.

⁴"Listen to me, my people;
    hear me, my nation:
The law will go out from me;
    my justice will become a light to the
      nations.
⁵My righteousness draws near speedily,
    my salvation is on the way,
    and my arm will bring justice to the
      nations.
The islands will look to me
    and wait in hope for my arm.
⁶Lift up your eyes to the heavens,
    look at the earth beneath;
the heavens will vanish like smoke,
    the earth will wear out like a garment
    and its inhabitants die like flies.
But my salvation will last forever,
    my righteousness will never fail.

⁷"Hear me, you who know what is right,
    you people who have my law in your
      hearts:
Do not fear the reproach of men
    or be terrified by their insults.
⁸For the moth will eat them up like a
      garment;
    the worm will devour them like wool.
But my righteousness will last forever,
    my salvation through all generations."

⁹Awake, awake! Clothe yourself with strength,
    O arm of the LORD;
awake, as in days gone by,
    as in generations of old.
Was it not you who cut Rahab to pieces,
    who pierced that monster through?
¹⁰Was it not you who dried up the sea,
    the waters of the great deep,

who made a road in the depths of the sea
  so that the redeemed might cross over?
[11]The ransomed of the LORD will return.
  They will enter Zion with singing;

everlasting joy will crown their heads.
Gladness and joy will overtake them,
  and sorrow and sighing will flee away.

[12]"I, even I, am he who comforts you.
  Who are you that you fear mortal men,
    the sons of men, who are but grass,
[13]that you forget the LORD your Maker,
  who stretched out the heavens
    and laid the foundations of the earth,
that you live in constant terror every day
  because of the wrath of the oppressor,
    who is bent on destruction?
For where is the wrath of the oppressor?
[14] The cowering prisoners will soon be set
      free;
  they will not die in their dungeon,
    nor will they lack bread.
[15]For I am the LORD your God,
  who churns up the sea so that its waves
    roar—
    the LORD Almighty is his name.
[16]I have put my words in your mouth
  and covered you with the shadow of my
    hand—
I who set the heavens in place,
  who laid the foundations of the earth,
  and who say to Zion, 'You are my
    people.'"

The Cup of the LORD's Wrath

[17]Awake, awake!
  Rise up, O Jerusalem,
you who have drunk from the hand of the
    LORD
  the cup of his wrath,
you who have drained to its dregs
  the goblet that makes men stagger.
[18]Of all the sons she bore
  there was none to guide her;
of all the sons she reared

  there was none to take her by the hand.
[19]These double calamities have come upon
    you—
  who can comfort you?—
ruin and destruction, famine and sword—
  who can[a] console you?
[20]Your sons have fainted;
  they lie at the head of every street,
    like antelope caught in a net.
They are filled with the wrath of the LORD
  and the rebuke of your God.

[21]Therefore hear this, you afflicted one,
  made drunk, but not with wine.
[22]This is what your Sovereign LORD says,
  your God, who defends his people:
"See, I have taken out of your hand
  the cup that made you stagger;
from that cup, the goblet of my wrath,
  you will never drink again.
[23]I will put it into the hands of your
    tormentors,
  who said to you,
    'Fall prostrate that we may walk over you.'
And you made your back like the ground,
  like a street to be walked over."

52

Awake, awake, O Zion,
  clothe yourself with strength.
Put on your garments of splendor,
  O Jerusalem, the holy city.
The uncircumcised and defiled
  will not enter you again.
[2]Shake off your dust;
  rise up, sit enthroned, O Jerusalem.
Free yourself from the chains on your neck,
  O captive Daughter of Zion.

[3]For this is what the LORD says:

"You were sold for nothing,
  and without money you will be
    redeemed."

[4]For this is what the Sovereign LORD says:

"At first my people went down to Egypt to
    live;
  lately, Assyria has oppressed them.

[5]"And now what do I have here?" declares the
    LORD.

"For my people have been taken away for
    nothing,
  and those who rule them mock,[b]"
                              declares the LORD.
"And all day long
  my name is constantly blasphemed.
[6]Therefore my people will know my name;
  therefore in that day they will know

---

[a]19 Dead Sea Scrolls, Septuagint, Vulgate and Syriac; Masoretic Text / *how can I*   [b]5 Dead Sea Scrolls and Vulgate;
Masoretic Text *wail*

that it is I who foretold it.
Yes, it is I."

[7]How beautiful on the mountains
are the feet of those who bring good
news,
who proclaim peace,
who bring good tidings,
who proclaim salvation,
who say to Zion,
"Your God reigns!"

52:7 Beautiful Feet

Isaiah portrays the joy of carrying good news to those desperately hoping for it—perhaps a city waiting for news of a battle in which all their young men were at risk. But Isaiah's news is not of war; it is of God's people returning from exile, with the Lord himself leading the way. In Romans 10:15, Paul applied this joyful cheer to the messengers who, like himself, bore the good news of Jesus Christ.

[8]Listen! Your watchmen lift up their voices;
together they shout for joy.
When the LORD returns to Zion,
they will see it with their own eyes.
[9]Burst into songs of joy together,
you ruins of Jerusalem,
for the LORD has comforted his people,
he has redeemed Jerusalem.
[10]The LORD will lay bare his holy arm
in the sight of all the nations,
and all the ends of the earth will see
the salvation of our God.

[11]Depart, depart, go out from there!
Touch no unclean thing!
Come out from it and be pure,
you who carry the vessels of the LORD.
[12]But you will not leave in haste
or go in flight;
for the LORD will go before you,
the God of Israel will be your rear guard.

The Suffering and Glory of the Servant

[13]See, my servant will act wisely[a];
he will be raised and lifted up and highly
exalted.
[14]Just as there were many who were appalled
at him[b]—
his appearance was so disfigured beyond
that of any man
and his form marred beyond human
likeness—

[15]so will he sprinkle many nations,[c]
and kings will shut their mouths because
of him.
For what they were not told, they will see,
and what they have not heard, they will
understand.

53 Who has believed our message
and to whom has the arm of the LORD
been revealed?
[2]He grew up before him like a tender shoot,
and like a root out of dry ground.
He had no beauty or majesty to attract us to
him,
nothing in his appearance that we should
desire him.
[3]He was despised and rejected by men,
a man of sorrows, and familiar with
suffering.
Like one from whom men hide their faces
he was despised, and we esteemed him
not.

[4]Surely he took up our infirmities
and carried our sorrows,
yet we considered him stricken by God,
smitten by him, and afflicted.
[5]But he was pierced for our transgressions,
he was crushed for our iniquities;
the punishment that brought us peace was
upon him,
and by his wounds we are healed.

53:5 Healing Wounds

Throughout the New Testament, the Suffering Servant described here is understood to be Jesus. This astounding verse claims that his wounds heal us. Peter explained it this way: when Jesus died on the cross, his suffering and death "healed" us of our sins, enabling us to live for righteousness (1 Peter 2:24).

[6]We all, like sheep, have gone astray,
each of us has turned to his own way;
and the LORD has laid on him
the iniquity of us all.

[7]He was oppressed and afflicted,
yet he did not open his mouth;
he was led like a lamb to the slaughter,
and as a sheep before her shearers is
silent,
so he did not open his mouth.
[8]By oppression[d] and judgment he was taken
away.

---

[a]13 Or *will prosper*   [b]14 Hebrew *you*   [c]15 Hebrew; Septuagint *so will many nations marvel at him*
[d]8 Or *From arrest*

And who can speak of his descendants?
For he was cut off from the land of the
    living;
    for the transgression of my people he was
        stricken.[a]

⁹He was assigned a grave with the wicked,
    and with the rich in his death,
    though he had done no violence,
        nor was any deceit in his mouth.

¹⁰Yet it was the LORD's will to crush him and
    cause him to suffer,
    and though the LORD makes[b] his life a
        guilt offering,
he will see his offspring and prolong his
    days,
    and the will of the LORD will prosper in
        his hand.

¹¹After the suffering of his soul,

---

[a]8 Or away. / Yet who of his generation considered / that he was cut off from the land of the living / for the transgression of
my people, / to whom the blow was due?   [b]10 Hebrew though you make

The Suffering Servant
A great victory looked at first like defeat

CHAPTERS 49–55 OF ISAIAH TELL of a "suffering servant" who
will come from Israel to bring light to all nations. Who is this suffering
servant?

Jewish scholars puzzled over these passages for centuries. Many considered them the most significant part of the entire Old Testament, and yet they could not agree on exactly what the prophet meant. (Four passages especially are called the "servant songs": 42:1–9; 49:1–13; 50:4–9; 52:13–53:12.)

> He was despised
> and rejected by
> men, a man of sor-
> rows, and familiar
> with suffering.
> 53:3

A Nation or a Person?

Sometimes the verses speak about the nation of Israel as a whole: "You are my servant, Israel, in whom I will display my splendor" (49:3). But in other places the servant seems to refer to a specific individual, a great leader who suffers terribly.

Isaiah presents the servant as the deliverer of all humankind. And yet it portrays him more as a tragic figure than as a hero: "He had no beauty or majesty to attract us to him. . . . He was oppressed and afflicted, yet he did not open his mouth; he was led like a lamb to the slaughter" (53:2,7).

Some Jewish scholars guessed the prophet was describing himself or another prophet, such as Jeremiah. Still others focused their hopes on a Messiah to come. They expected a king from very humble origins, whose power would depend not on swords, but on the spirits of people committed to him.

An Answer from the New Testament

The idea of the suffering servant did not really catch on among the Jewish nation. They longed for a victorious Messiah, not a suffering one. The image of the suffering servant went underground, as it were, lying dormant for centuries.

Then, in a very dramatic scene early in his ministry, Jesus quoted from one of the servant passages in Isaiah (Luke 4:18–19). "Then he rolled up the scroll, gave it back to the attendant and sat down. The eyes of everyone in the synagogue were fastened on him, and he began by saying to them, 'Today this scripture is fulfilled in your hearing' " (Luke 4:20–21).

Following his example, the New Testament writers named Jesus as the servant, at least ten times. In one instance, Philip corrected an Ethiopian official who had wondered if the suffering servant referred to an ancient prophet (Acts 8:26–35).

The Final Sacrifice

Isaiah 49–55 includes vivid scenes of the servant's sufferings, predictions that found their fulfillment in Jesus' death on the cross. Written like an eyewitness account, they were actually composed centuries before Christ's death.

According to Isaiah, the servant died for a very specific purpose: "He was pierced for our transgressions" (53:5). Through his wounds, the suffering servant won a great victory. His death made possible a future when all that is wrong on earth will be set right. Significantly, the book of Isaiah does not end with the suffering servant image. It goes on to describe a wonderful life in a new heaven and new earth made possible by the servant's death.

Life Questions: If you had been a Jew in Jesus' day, would you have been disappointed in the Messiah? Why did Jesus choose to come as a suffering servant rather than, say, a triumphant army general?

he will see the light ⌊of life⌋[a] and be
  satisfied[b];
by his knowledge[c] my righteous servant will
    justify many,
  and he will bear their iniquities.
[12]Therefore I will give him a portion among
    the great,[d]
  and he will divide the spoils with the
    strong,[e]
because he poured out his life unto death,
  and was numbered with the transgressors.
For he bore the sin of many,
  and made intercession for the
    transgressors.

The Future Glory of Zion

54 "Sing, O barren woman,
  you who never bore a child;
burst into song, shout for joy,
  you who were never in labor;
because more are the children of the desolate
    woman
  than of her who has a husband,"
                        says the LORD.
[2]"Enlarge the place of your tent,
  stretch your tent curtains wide,
    do not hold back;
lengthen your cords,
  strengthen your stakes.
[3]For you will spread out to the right and to
    the left;
  your descendants will dispossess nations
  and settle in their desolate cities.

[4]"Do not be afraid; you will not suffer shame.
  Do not fear disgrace; you will not be
    humiliated.
You will forget the shame of your youth
  and remember no more the reproach of
    your widowhood.
[5]For your Maker is your husband—
  the LORD Almighty is his name—
the Holy One of Israel is your Redeemer;
  he is called the God of all the earth.
[6]The LORD will call you back
  as if you were a wife deserted and
    distressed in spirit—
a wife who married young,
  only to be rejected," says your God.
[7]"For a brief moment I abandoned you,
  but with deep compassion I will bring you
    back.
[8]In a surge of anger
  I hid my face from you for a moment,
but with everlasting kindness
  I will have compassion on you,"
  says the LORD your Redeemer.

[9]"To me this is like the days of Noah,
  when I swore that the waters of Noah
    would never again cover the earth.
So now I have sworn not to be angry with
  you,

54:6 Jerusalem's Future

*The book of Isaiah insists that God will not
permanently divorce the nation of Israel. It
foretells a time when the ruined capital city will
be rebuilt and achieve a greatness it has never
known. Yet the description in these chapters
goes far beyond what has ever been realized in
Jerusalem. It merges into a vision of the future,
when sin and sorrow will be no more and
people will live in final peace with God.*

  never to rebuke you again.
[10]Though the mountains be shaken
  and the hills be removed,
yet my unfailing love for you will not be
  shaken
  nor my covenant of peace be removed,"
  says the LORD, who has compassion on
    you.

[11]"O afflicted city, lashed by storms and not
    comforted,
  I will build you with stones of
    turquoise,[f]
  your foundations with sapphires.[g]
[12]I will make your battlements of rubies,
  your gates of sparkling jewels,
  and all your walls of precious stones.
[13]All your sons will be taught by the LORD,
  and great will be your children's peace.
[14]In righteousness you will be established:
  Tyranny will be far from you;
    you will have nothing to fear.
Terror will be far removed;
  it will not come near you.
[15]If anyone does attack you, it will not be my
    doing;
  whoever attacks you will surrender to you.

[16]"See, it is I who created the blacksmith
  who fans the coals into flame
  and forges a weapon fit for its work.
And it is I who have created the destroyer to
    work havoc;
[17] no weapon forged against you will prevail,
  and you will refute every tongue that
    accuses you.
This is the heritage of the servants of the
    LORD,

---

[a]11 Dead Sea Scrolls (see also Septuagint); Masoretic Text does not have *the light ⌊of life⌋*   [b]11 Or (with Masoretic
Text) [11]*He will see the result of the suffering of his soul / and be satisfied*   [c]11 Or *by knowledge of him*   [d]12 Or
many   [e]12 Or *numerous*   [f]11 The meaning of the Hebrew for this word is uncertain.   [g]11 Or *lapis lazuli*

and this is their vindication from me,"
                    declares the LORD.

Invitation to the Thirsty

55 "Come, all you who are thirsty,
    come to the waters;
and you who have no money,
    come, buy and eat!
Come, buy wine and milk
    without money and without cost.

²Why spend money on what is not bread,
    and your labor on what does not satisfy?
Listen, listen to me, and eat what is good,
    and your soul will delight in the richest of
        fare.
³Give ear and come to me;
    hear me, that your soul may live.
I will make an everlasting covenant with you,
    my faithful love promised to David.
⁴See, I have made him a witness to the
        peoples,
    a leader and commander of the peoples.
⁵Surely you will summon nations you know
        not,
    and nations that do not know you will
        hasten to you,
because of the LORD your God,
    the Holy One of Israel,
    for he has endowed you with splendor."

⁶Seek the LORD while he may be found;
    call on him while he is near.
⁷Let the wicked forsake his way
    and the evil man his thoughts.
Let him turn to the LORD, and he will have
        mercy on him,
    and to our God, for he will freely pardon.

⁸"For my thoughts are not your thoughts,
    neither are your ways my ways,"
                    declares the LORD.
⁹"As the heavens are higher than the earth,
    so are my ways higher than your ways
    and my thoughts than your thoughts.
¹⁰As the rain and the snow
    come down from heaven,
and do not return to it
    without watering the earth
and making it bud and flourish,

so that it yields seed for the sower and
        bread for the eater,
¹¹so is my word that goes out from my
        mouth:
It will not return to me empty,
    but will accomplish what I desire
    and achieve the purpose for which I sent
        it.
¹²You will go out in joy
    and be led forth in peace;
the mountains and hills
    will burst into song before you,
and all the trees of the field
    will clap their hands.
¹³Instead of the thornbush will grow the pine
        tree,
    and instead of briers the myrtle will grow.
This will be for the LORD's renown,
    for an everlasting sign,
    which will not be destroyed."

Salvation for Others

56 This is what the LORD says:

"Maintain justice
    and do what is right,
for my salvation is close at hand
    and my righteousness will soon be
        revealed.
²Blessed is the man who does this,
    the man who holds it fast,
who keeps the Sabbath without desecrating
        it,
    and keeps his hand from doing any evil."

³Let no foreigner who has bound himself to
        the LORD say,
    "The LORD will surely exclude me from
        his people."
And let not any eunuch complain,
    "I am only a dry tree."

⁴For this is what the LORD says:

"To the eunuchs who keep my Sabbaths,
    who choose what pleases me
    and hold fast to my covenant—
⁵to them I will give within my temple and its
        walls
    a memorial and a name
    better than sons and daughters;
I will give them an everlasting name
    that will not be cut off.
⁶And foreigners who bind themselves to the
        LORD
    to serve him,
to love the name of the LORD,
    and to worship him,
all who keep the Sabbath without desecrating
        it
    and who hold fast to my covenant—
⁷these I will bring to my holy mountain

and give them joy in my house of prayer.
Their burnt offerings and sacrifices
    will be accepted on my altar;
for my house will be called
    a house of prayer for all nations."

56:7 House of Prayer

Traditionally, foreigners and eunuchs were excluded from worshiping God (see Exodus 12:43; Deuteronomy 23:1,3,7–8). But now God promises to welcome all those once excluded. The New Testament church welcomed foreigners and eunuchs into God's family; in contrast, the temple in Jerusalem never made non-Jews welcome. Jesus complained that rather than creating a "house of prayer for all nations," merchants had turned it into a "den of robbers" (Mark 11:17).

⁸The Sovereign LORD declares—
    he who gathers the exiles of Israel:
"I will gather still others to them
    besides those already gathered."

God's Accusation Against the Wicked

⁹Come, all you beasts of the field,
    come and devour, all you beasts of the
    forest!
¹⁰Israel's watchmen are blind,
    they all lack knowledge;
they are all mute dogs,
    they cannot bark;
they lie around and dream,
    they love to sleep.

56:10–11 Doglike Prophets

This passage gives one of the most scathing denunciations of Israel's corrupt spiritual leaders in the entire Bible.

¹¹They are dogs with mighty appetites;
    they never have enough.
They are shepherds who lack understanding;
    they all turn to their own way,
    each seeks his own gain.
¹²"Come," each one cries, "let me get wine!
    Let us drink our fill of beer!
And tomorrow will be like today,
    or even far better."

57 The righteous perish,
    and no one ponders it in his heart;
devout men are taken away,
    and no one understands

that the righteous are taken away
    to be spared from evil.
²Those who walk uprightly
    enter into peace;
    they find rest as they lie in death.

³"But you—come here, you sons of a
    sorceress,
    you offspring of adulterers and prostitutes!
⁴Whom are you mocking?
    At whom do you sneer
    and stick out your tongue?
Are you not a brood of rebels,
    the offspring of liars?
⁵You burn with lust among the oaks
    and under every spreading tree;
you sacrifice your children in the ravines
    and under the overhanging crags.
⁶ʟThe idolsˌ among the smooth stones of the
    ravines are your portion;
    they, they are your lot.
Yes, to them you have poured out drink
    offerings
    and offered grain offerings.
In the light of these things, should I
    relent?
⁷You have made your bed on a high and lofty
    hill;
    there you went up to offer your sacrifices.
⁸Behind your doors and your doorposts
    you have put your pagan symbols.
Forsaking me, you uncovered your bed,
    you climbed into it and opened it wide;
you made a pact with those whose beds you
    love,
    and you looked on their nakedness.
⁹You went to Molech*ᵃ* with olive oil
    and increased your perfumes.
You sent your ambassadors*ᵇ* far away;
    you descended to the grave*ᶜ* itself!
¹⁰You were wearied by all your ways,
    but you would not say, 'It is hopeless.'
You found renewal of your strength,
    and so you did not faint.

¹¹"Whom have you so dreaded and feared
    that you have been false to me,
and have neither remembered me
    nor pondered this in your hearts?
Is it not because I have long been silent
    that you do not fear me?
¹²I will expose your righteousness and your
    works,
    and they will not benefit you.
¹³When you cry out for help,
    let your collection ʟof idolsˌ save you!
The wind will carry all of them off,
    a mere breath will blow them away.
But the man who makes me his refuge

ᵃ9 Or *to the king*   *ᵇ9* Or *idols*   *ᶜ9* Hebrew *Sheol*

will inherit the land
and possess my holy mountain."

Comfort for the Contrite

¹⁴And it will be said:

"Build up, build up, prepare the road!
    Remove the obstacles out of the way of
        my people."
¹⁵For this is what the high and lofty One
    says—
    he who lives forever, whose name is holy:
"I live in a high and holy place,
    but also with him who is contrite and
        lowly in spirit,
to revive the spirit of the lowly
    and to revive the heart of the contrite.
¹⁶I will not accuse forever,
    nor will I always be angry,
for then the spirit of man would grow faint
        before me—
    the breath of man that I have created.
¹⁷I was enraged by his sinful greed;
    I punished him, and hid my face in anger,
    yet he kept on in his willful ways.
¹⁸I have seen his ways, but I will heal him;
    I will guide him and restore comfort to
        him,
¹⁹   creating praise on the lips of the mourners
        in Israel.
Peace, peace, to those far and near,"
    says the LORD. "And I will heal them."
²⁰But the wicked are like the tossing sea,
    which cannot rest,
    whose waves cast up mire and mud.
²¹"There is no peace," says my God, "for the
    wicked."

True Fasting

58 "Shout it aloud, do not hold back.
    Raise your voice like a trumpet.
Declare to my people their rebellion
    and to the house of Jacob their sins.
²For day after day they seek me out;
    they seem eager to know my ways,
as if they were a nation that does what is
        right
    and has not forsaken the commands of its
        God.
They ask me for just decisions
    and seem eager for God to come near
        them.
³'Why have we fasted,' they say,
    'and you have not seen it?
Why have we humbled ourselves,
    and you have not noticed?'

"Yet on the day of your fasting, you do as
    you please

and exploit all your workers.
⁴Your fasting ends in quarreling and strife,
    and in striking each other with wicked
        fists.
You cannot fast as you do today
    and expect your voice to be heard on
        high.
⁵Is this the kind of fast I have chosen,
    only a day for a man to humble himself?
Is it only for bowing one's head like a reed
    and for lying on sackcloth and ashes?
Is that what you call a fast,
    a day acceptable to the LORD?

⁶"Is not this the kind of fasting I have chosen:
to loose the chains of injustice
    and untie the cords of the yoke,
to set the oppressed free
    and break every yoke?

58:6 Religion at Its Best

*The book of Isaiah begins in chapter 1 by
exposing false religion that had the right form
and ritual, but no true sincerity. This chapter
gives the other side: the spiritual work God
prefers. The book of James includes a similar
perspective (1:27).*

⁷Is it not to share your food with the hungry
    and to provide the poor wanderer with
        shelter—
when you see the naked, to clothe him,
    and not to turn away from your own flesh
        and blood?
⁸Then your light will break forth like the
        dawn,
    and your healing will quickly appear;
then your righteousness[a] will go before you,
    and the glory of the LORD will be your
        rear guard.
⁹Then you will call, and the LORD will answer;
    you will cry for help, and he will say:
        Here am I.

"If you do away with the yoke of oppression,
    with the pointing finger and malicious
        talk,
¹⁰and if you spend yourselves in behalf of the
        hungry
    and satisfy the needs of the oppressed,
then your light will rise in the darkness,
    and your night will become like the
        noonday.
¹¹The LORD will guide you always;
    he will satisfy your needs in a
        sun-scorched land
    and will strengthen your frame.

---

a8 Or your righteous One

You will be like a well-watered garden,
   like a spring whose waters never fail.
[12]Your people will rebuild the ancient ruins
   and will raise up the age-old foundations;
you will be called Repairer of Broken Walls,
   Restorer of Streets with Dwellings.

[13]"If you keep your feet from breaking the
      Sabbath
   and from doing as you please on my holy
      day,
if you call the Sabbath a delight
   and the LORD's holy day honorable,
and if you honor it by not going your own
      way
   and not doing as you please or speaking
      idle words,
[14]then you will find your joy in the LORD,
   and I will cause you to ride on the heights
      of the land
   and to feast on the inheritance of your
      father Jacob."
            The mouth of the LORD has spoken.

Sin, Confession and Redemption

59 Surely the arm of the LORD is not too
      short to save,
   nor his ear too dull to hear.
[2]But your iniquities have separated
   you from your God;
your sins have hidden his face from you,
   so that he will not hear.
[3]For your hands are stained with blood,
   your fingers with guilt.
Your lips have spoken lies,
   and your tongue mutters wicked things.
[4]No one calls for justice;
   no one pleads his case with integrity.
They rely on empty arguments and speak
      lies;
   they conceive trouble and give birth to
      evil.
[5]They hatch the eggs of vipers
   and spin a spider's web.
Whoever eats their eggs will die,
   and when one is broken, an adder is
      hatched.
[6]Their cobwebs are useless for clothing;
   they cannot cover themselves with what
      they make.
Their deeds are evil deeds,
   and acts of violence are in their hands.
[7]Their feet rush into sin;
   they are swift to shed innocent blood.
Their thoughts are evil thoughts;
   ruin and destruction mark their ways.
[8]The way of peace they do not know;
   there is no justice in their paths.
They have turned them into crooked roads;

no one who walks in them will know
      peace.

[9]So justice is far from us,
   and righteousness does not reach us.
We look for light, but all is darkness;
   for brightness, but we walk in deep
      shadows.
[10]Like the blind we grope along the wall,
   feeling our way like men without eyes.
At midday we stumble as if it were twilight;
   among the strong, we are like the dead.
[11]We all growl like bears;
   we moan mournfully like doves.
We look for justice, but find none;
   for deliverance, but it is far away.

[12]For our offenses are many in your sight,
   and our sins testify against us.
Our offenses are ever with us,
   and we acknowledge our iniquities:
[13]rebellion and treachery against the LORD,
   turning our backs on our God,
fomenting oppression and revolt,
   uttering lies our hearts have conceived.
[14]So justice is driven back,
   and righteousness stands at a distance;
truth has stumbled in the streets,
   honesty cannot enter.
[15]Truth is nowhere to be found,
   and whoever shuns evil becomes a prey.

The LORD looked and was displeased
   that there was no justice.
[16]He saw that there was no one,
   he was appalled that there was no one to
      intervene;
so his own arm worked salvation for him,
   and his own righteousness sustained him.
[17]He put on righteousness as his breastplate,
   and the helmet of salvation on his head;
he put on the garments of vengeance
   and wrapped himself in zeal as in a cloak.
[18]According to what they have done,
   so will he repay
wrath to his enemies
   and retribution to his foes;
   he will repay the islands their due.
[19]From the west, men will fear the name of the
      LORD,
   and from the rising of the sun, they will
      revere his glory.
For he will come like a pent-up flood
   that the breath of the LORD drives along.[a]

[20]"The Redeemer will come to Zion,
   to those in Jacob who repent of their
      sins,"
            declares the LORD.

[21]"As for me, this is my covenant with them,"

---

[a]19 Or *When the enemy comes in like a flood, / the Spirit of the LORD will put him to flight*

says the LORD. "My Spirit, who is on you, and my words that I have put in your mouth will not depart from your mouth, or from the mouths of your children, or from the mouths of their descendants from this time on and forever," says the LORD.

The Glory of Zion

60 "Arise, shine, for your light has come,
and the glory of the LORD rises upon you.
²See, darkness covers the earth
and thick darkness is over the peoples,
but the LORD rises upon you
and his glory appears over you.
³Nations will come to your light,
and kings to the brightness of your dawn.

⁴"Lift up your eyes and look about you:
All assemble and come to you;
your sons come from afar,
and your daughters are carried on the arm.
⁵Then you will look and be radiant,
your heart will throb and swell with joy;
the wealth on the seas will be brought to you,
to you the riches of the nations will come.
⁶Herds of camels will cover your land,
young camels of Midian and Ephah.
And all from Sheba will come,
bearing gold and incense
and proclaiming the praise of the LORD.
⁷All Kedar's flocks will be gathered to you,
the rams of Nebaioth will serve you;
they will be accepted as offerings on my altar,
and I will adorn my glorious temple.

⁸"Who are these that fly along like clouds,
like doves to their nests?
⁹Surely the islands look to me;
in the lead are the ships of Tarshish,[a]
bringing your sons from afar,
with their silver and gold,
to the honor of the LORD your God,
the Holy One of Israel,
for he has endowed you with splendor.

¹⁰"Foreigners will rebuild your walls,
and their kings will serve you.
Though in anger I struck you,
in favor I will show you compassion.
¹¹Your gates will always stand open,
they will never be shut, day or night,
so that men may bring you the wealth of the nations—
their kings led in triumphal procession.

¹²For the nation or kingdom that will not serve you will perish;
it will be utterly ruined.

¹³"The glory of Lebanon will come to you,
the pine, the fir and the cypress together,
to adorn the place of my sanctuary;
and I will glorify the place of my feet.
¹⁴The sons of your oppressors will come bowing before you;
all who despise you will bow down at your feet
and will call you the City of the LORD,
Zion of the Holy One of Israel.

¹⁵"Although you have been forsaken and hated,
with no one traveling through,
I will make you the everlasting pride
and the joy of all generations.
¹⁶You will drink the milk of nations
and be nursed at royal breasts.
Then you will know that I, the LORD, am your Savior,
your Redeemer, the Mighty One of Jacob.
¹⁷Instead of bronze I will bring you gold,
and silver in place of iron.
Instead of wood I will bring you bronze,
and iron in place of stones.
I will make peace your governor
and righteousness your ruler.
¹⁸No longer will violence be heard in your land,
nor ruin or destruction within your borders,
but you will call your walls Salvation
and your gates Praise.
¹⁹The sun will no more be your light by day,
nor will the brightness of the moon shine on you,
for the LORD will be your everlasting light,
and your God will be your glory.
²⁰Your sun will never set again,
and your moon will wane no more;
the LORD will be your everlasting light,
and your days of sorrow will end.
²¹Then will all your people be righteous
and they will possess the land forever.
They are the shoot I have planted,
the work of my hands,
for the display of my splendor.
²²The least of you will become a thousand,
the smallest a mighty nation.
I am the LORD;
in its time I will do this swiftly."

The Year of the LORD's Favor

61 The Spirit of the Sovereign LORD is on me,

---

a 9 Or the trading ships

because the LORD has anointed me
to preach good news to the poor.
He has sent me to bind up the
brokenhearted,
to proclaim freedom for the captives
and release from darkness for the
prisoners,[a]

61:1 Jesus Began Here

*When Jesus was ready to announce himself
and his mission, he began with a dramatic
quotation of this passage (Luke 4:18–19).
Notably, he stopped in mid-sentence, before he
reached the phrase "the day of vengeance of
our God." Jesus taught that this day of
vengeance would indeed take place, but at the
time of his second coming, not his first.*

---

²to proclaim the year of the LORD's favor
and the day of vengeance of our God,
to comfort all who mourn,
³ and provide for those who grieve in
Zion—
to bestow on them a crown of beauty
instead of ashes,
the oil of gladness
instead of mourning,
and a garment of praise
instead of a spirit of despair.
They will be called oaks of righteousness,
a planting of the LORD
for the display of his splendor.

⁴They will rebuild the ancient ruins
and restore the places long devastated;
they will renew the ruined cities
that have been devastated for generations.
⁵Aliens will shepherd your flocks;
foreigners will work your fields and
vineyards.
⁶And you will be called priests of the LORD,
you will be named ministers of our God.
You will feed on the wealth of nations,
and in their riches you will boast.

⁷Instead of their shame
my people will receive a double portion,
and instead of disgrace
they will rejoice in their inheritance;
and so they will inherit a double portion in
their land,
and everlasting joy will be theirs.

⁸"For I, the LORD, love justice;
I hate robbery and iniquity.
In my faithfulness I will reward them

and make an everlasting covenant with
them.
⁹Their descendants will be known among the
nations
and their offspring among the peoples.
All who see them will acknowledge
that they are a people the LORD has
blessed."

¹⁰I delight greatly in the LORD;
my soul rejoices in my God.
For he has clothed me with garments of
salvation
and arrayed me in a robe of
righteousness,
as a bridegroom adorns his head like a
priest,
and as a bride adorns herself with her
jewels.
¹¹For as the soil makes the sprout come up
and a garden causes seeds to grow,
so the Sovereign LORD will make
righteousness and praise
spring up before all nations.

Zion's New Name

62 For Zion's sake I will not keep silent,
for Jerusalem's sake I will not remain
quiet,
till her righteousness shines out like the
dawn,
her salvation like a blazing torch.
²The nations will see your righteousness,
and all kings your glory;
you will be called by a new name
that the mouth of the LORD will bestow.
³You will be a crown of splendor in the
LORD's hand,
a royal diadem in the hand of your God.
⁴No longer will they call you Deserted,
or name your land Desolate.
But you will be called Hephzibah,[b]
and your land Beulah[c];
for the LORD will take delight in you,
and your land will be married.
⁵As a young man marries a maiden,
so will your sons[d] marry you;
as a bridegroom rejoices over his bride,
so will your God rejoice over you.

⁶I have posted watchmen on your walls,
O Jerusalem;
they will never be silent day or night.
You who call on the LORD,
give yourselves no rest,
⁷and give him no rest till he establishes
Jerusalem
and makes her the praise of the earth.

---

a 1 Hebrew; Septuagint the blind   *b 4 Hephzibah means my delight is in her.*   *c 4 Beulah means married.*
d 5 Or Builder

8The LORD has sworn by his right hand
    and by his mighty arm:
"Never again will I give your grain
    as food for your enemies,
and never again will foreigners drink the new
        wine
    for which you have toiled;
9but those who harvest it will eat it
    and praise the LORD,
and those who gather the grapes will drink it
    in the courts of my sanctuary."

10Pass through, pass through the gates!
    Prepare the way for the people.
Build up, build up the highway!
    Remove the stones.
Raise a banner for the nations.

11The LORD has made proclamation
    to the ends of the earth:
"Say to the Daughter of Zion,
    'See, your Savior comes!
See, his reward is with him,

and his recompense accompanies him.'"
12They will be called the Holy People,
    the Redeemed of the LORD;
and you will be called Sought After,
    the City No Longer Deserted.

God's Day of Vengeance and Redemption

63 Who is this coming from Edom,
    from Bozrah, with his garments stained
        crimson?
Who is this, robed in splendor,
    striding forward in the greatness of his
        strength?

"It is I, speaking in righteousness,
    mighty to save."

2Why are your garments red,
    like those of one treading the winepress?

3"I have trodden the winepress alone;
    from the nations no one was with me.
I trampled them in my anger
    and trod them down in my wrath;

A Glimpse of Things to Come
When all our best dreams will come true

EVERYBODY WANTS A GLIMPSE INTO the future, and the last part of Isaiah gives just that. It tells what will happen at the end of our age on earth. The account is not easy to decipher, however, because the prophet shifts back and forth between his own time and the final events on earth.

> "Behold, I will create new heavens and a new earth. The former things will not be remembered, nor will they come to mind."
> 65:17

A Missionary Book

To the original audience of Israelites, Isaiah makes one thing clear: God would not permanently divorce Israel. "For a brief moment I abandoned you," says God, "but with deep compassion I will bring you back" (54:7). There is a future for his chosen people.

Isaiah declares that Israel's future involves other nations. Foreigners will flock to Jerusalem: "My house will be called a house of prayer for all nations" (56:7). Word about God will go out to nations nearby and far away, and to distant islands that have never heard of him (66:18–21).

Thus the last part of Isaiah, addressed to a people facing deep despair, opens the door for the Jews to become a gift to all people. This prophecy saw fulfillment in Jesus, who recruited disciples to take his message to everyone. Through his life and death, the suffering servant indeed introduced the gospel to the entire world.

What Isaiah Says to Us

The book of Isaiah goes on to describe a new beginning, a time of final triumph and peace. In that day, there will be no need for tears. Wild animals will tamely lie down together. The sun and moon will fade, overwhelmed by the brightness of God's glory.

In chapters 60 and 65, the prophet describes the future with such eloquence that New Testament books like Revelation could not improve on the language; they merely quoted Isaiah. Even today some of these phrases—"beat their swords into plowshares," for example—surface in popular language, expressing our deepest longings for peace.

We dream of a time of peace, without pain or fear or disease or death. Isaiah assures us that one day those dreams will come true.

Life Questions: What would you most like to see changed about your world? Does Isaiah speak to that change?

their blood spattered my garments,
and I stained all my clothing.
[4]For the day of vengeance was in my heart,
and the year of my redemption has come.
[5]I looked, but there was no one to help,
I was appalled that no one gave support;
so my own arm worked salvation for me,
and my own wrath sustained me.
[6]I trampled the nations in my anger;
in my wrath I made them drunk
and poured their blood on the ground."

Praise and Prayer

[7]I will tell of the kindnesses of the LORD,
the deeds for which he is to be praised,
according to all the LORD has done for
us—
yes, the many good things he has done
for the house of Israel,
according to his compassion and many
kindnesses.
[8]He said, "Surely they are my people,
sons who will not be false to me";
and so he became their Savior.
[9]In all their distress he too was distressed,
and the angel of his presence saved them.
In his love and mercy he redeemed them;
he lifted them up and carried them
all the days of old.

63:9–17 A Lesson from History

The Babylonian captivity brought a grave crisis to the Israelites. To them, God's own integrity was at stake. They had a treaty, or covenant, with him. Had he abandoned them? In this chapter, the prophet reviews all the good things God has done for the Israelites and says that, even in the worst times, "in all their distress he too was distressed." If God had been with them in the past, then he would be with them in the future. Then he turns to God directly and makes an impassioned appeal for help: "Oh, that you would rend the heavens and come down" (64:1).

[10]Yet they rebelled
and grieved his Holy Spirit.
So he turned and became their enemy
and he himself fought against them.

[11]Then his people recalled[a] the days of old,
the days of Moses and his people—
where is he who brought them through the
sea,
with the shepherd of his flock?
Where is he who set
his Holy Spirit among them,

[12]who sent his glorious arm of power
to be at Moses' right hand,
who divided the waters before them,
to gain for himself everlasting renown,
[13]who led them through the depths?
Like a horse in open country,
they did not stumble;
[14]like cattle that go down to the plain,
they were given rest by the Spirit of the
LORD.
This is how you guided your people
to make for yourself a glorious name.

[15]Look down from heaven and see
from your lofty throne, holy and glorious.
Where are your zeal and your might?
Your tenderness and compassion are
withheld from us.
[16]But you are our Father,
though Abraham does not know us
or Israel acknowledge us;
you, O LORD, are our Father,
our Redeemer from of old is your name.
[17]Why, O LORD, do you make us wander from
your ways
and harden our hearts so we do not
revere you?
Return for the sake of your servants,
the tribes that are your inheritance.
[18]For a little while your people possessed your
holy place,
but now our enemies have trampled down
your sanctuary.
[19]We are yours from of old;
but you have not ruled over them,
they have not been called by your name.[b]

64 Oh, that you would rend the heavens
and come down,
that the mountains would tremble before
you!
[2]As when fire sets twigs ablaze
and causes water to boil,
come down to make your name known to
your enemies
and cause the nations to quake before
you!
[3]For when you did awesome things that we
did not expect,
you came down, and the mountains
trembled before you.
[4]Since ancient times no one has heard,
no ear has perceived,
no eye has seen any God besides you,
who acts on behalf of those who wait for
him.
[5]You come to the help of those who gladly do
right,
who remember your ways.

[a]11 Or *But may he recall*   [b]19 Or *We are like those you have never ruled, / like those never called by your name*

But when we continued to sin against them,
  you were angry.
How then can we be saved?
⁶All of us have become like one who is
    unclean,
  and all our righteous acts are like filthy
    rags;
we all shrivel up like a leaf,
  and like the wind our sins sweep us away.
⁷No one calls on your name
  or strives to lay hold of you;
for you have hidden your face from us
  and made us waste away because of our
    sins.

⁸Yet, O LORD, you are our Father.
  We are the clay, you are the potter;
  we are all the work of your hand.
⁹Do not be angry beyond measure, O LORD;
  do not remember our sins forever.
Oh, look upon us, we pray,
  for we are all your people.
¹⁰Your sacred cities have become a desert;
  even Zion is a desert, Jerusalem a
    desolation.
¹¹Our holy and glorious temple, where our
    fathers praised you,
  has been burned with fire,
  and all that we treasured lies in ruins.
¹²After all this, O LORD, will you hold yourself
    back?
  Will you keep silent and punish us
    beyond measure?

Judgment and Salvation

65 "I revealed myself to those who did not
    ask for me;
  I was found by those who did not seek
    me.
To a nation that did not call on my name,
  I said, 'Here am I, here am I.'
²All day long I have held out my hands
  to an obstinate people,
who walk in ways not good,
  pursuing their own imaginations—
³a people who continually provoke me
  to my very face,
offering sacrifices in gardens
  and burning incense on altars of brick;
⁴who sit among the graves
  and spend their nights keeping secret vigil;
who eat the flesh of pigs,
  and whose pots hold broth of unclean
    meat;
⁵who say, 'Keep away; don't come near me,
  for I am too sacred for you!'
Such people are smoke in my nostrils,
  a fire that keeps burning all day.

⁶"See, it stands written before me:

I will not keep silent but will pay back in
    full;
I will pay it back into their laps—
⁷both your sins and the sins of your fathers,"
  says the LORD.
"Because they burned sacrifices on the
    mountains
  and defied me on the hills,
I will measure into their laps
  the full payment for their former deeds."

65:3 Provoking God

*In this speech, God is directly attacking the
most repulsive practices of Judah, notably its
idolatry. "Gardens" refers to the gardens that
usually surrounded pagan shrines. Verse 4
mentions the superstitious practice of sitting in
cemeteries to seek help from the dead. And the
"flesh of pigs" was eaten in a sacrificial meal
for a pagan god—faithful Jews did not eat pork.*

⁸This is what the LORD says:

"As when juice is still found in a cluster of
    grapes
  and men say, 'Don't destroy it,
    there is yet some good in it,'
so will I do in behalf of my servants;
  I will not destroy them all.
⁹I will bring forth descendants from Jacob,
  and from Judah those who will possess
    my mountains;
my chosen people will inherit them,
  and there will my servants live.
¹⁰Sharon will become a pasture for flocks,
  and the Valley of Achor a resting place
    for herds,
  for my people who seek me.

¹¹"But as for you who forsake the LORD
  and forget my holy mountain,
who spread a table for Fortune
  and fill bowls of mixed wine for Destiny,
¹²I will destine you for the sword,
  and you will all bend down for the
    slaughter;
for I called but you did not answer,
  I spoke but you did not listen.
You did evil in my sight
  and chose what displeases me."

¹³Therefore this is what the Sovereign LORD
says:

"My servants will eat,
  but you will go hungry;
my servants will drink,
  but you will go thirsty;
my servants will rejoice,

but you will be put to shame.
¹⁴My servants will sing
out of the joy of their hearts,
but you will cry out
from anguish of heart
and wail in brokenness of spirit.
¹⁵You will leave your name
to my chosen ones as a curse;
the Sovereign LORD will put you to death,
but to his servants he will give another
name.
¹⁶Whoever invokes a blessing in the land
will do so by the God of truth;
he who takes an oath in the land
will swear by the God of truth.
For the past troubles will be forgotten
and hidden from my eyes.

New Heavens and a New Earth

¹⁷"Behold, I will create
new heavens and a new earth.
The former things will not be remembered,
nor will they come to mind.

65:17 New Earth

Human beings have always longed for a utopia. Isaiah repeatedly promises just that, here and in chapters 11 and 35. He has in mind a whole new earth, in which people will build and farm, work and raise children—but without frustration. The violence and sadness that mark our earth will vanish. The key to that new era will be an intimate relationship with God. "Before they call I will answer; while they are still speaking I will hear" (verse 24).

¹⁸But be glad and rejoice forever
in what I will create,
for I will create Jerusalem to be a delight
and its people a joy.
¹⁹I will rejoice over Jerusalem
and take delight in my people;
the sound of weeping and of crying
will be heard in it no more.

²⁰"Never again will there be in it
an infant who lives but a few days,
or an old man who does not live out his
years;
he who dies at a hundred
will be thought a mere youth;
he who fails to reachᵃ a hundred
will be considered accursed.
²¹They will build houses and dwell in them;
they will plant vineyards and eat their
fruit.

²²No longer will they build houses and others
live in them,
or plant and others eat.
For as the days of a tree,
so will be the days of my people;
my chosen ones will long enjoy
the works of their hands.
²³They will not toil in vain
or bear children doomed to misfortune;
for they will be a people blessed by the
LORD,
they and their descendants with them.
²⁴Before they call I will answer;
while they are still speaking I will hear.
²⁵The wolf and the lamb will feed together,
and the lion will eat straw like the ox,
but dust will be the serpent's food.
They will neither harm nor destroy
on all my holy mountain,"
says the LORD.

Judgment and Hope

66 This is what the LORD says:

"Heaven is my throne,
and the earth is my footstool.
Where is the house you will build for me?
Where will my resting place be?
²Has not my hand made all these things,
and so they came into being?"
declares the LORD.

"This is the one I esteem:
he who is humble and contrite in spirit,
and trembles at my word.
³But whoever sacrifices a bull
is like one who kills a man,
and whoever offers a lamb,
like one who breaks a dog's neck;
whoever makes a grain offering
is like one who presents pig's blood,
and whoever burns memorial incense,
like one who worships an idol.
They have chosen their own ways,
and their souls delight in their
abominations;
⁴so I also will choose harsh treatment for
them
and will bring upon them what they
dread.
For when I called, no one answered,
when I spoke, no one listened.
They did evil in my sight
and chose what displeases me."

⁵Hear the word of the LORD,
you who tremble at his word:
"Your brothers who hate you,

ᵃ20 Or / the sinner who reaches

and exclude you because of my name,
have said,
'Let the LORD be glorified,
that we may see your joy!'
Yet they will be put to shame.
[6]Hear that uproar from the city,
hear that noise from the temple!
It is the sound of the LORD
repaying his enemies all they deserve.

[7]"Before she goes into labor,
she gives birth;
before the pains come upon her,
she delivers a son.
[8]Who has ever heard of such a thing?
Who has ever seen such things?
Can a country be born in a day
or a nation be brought forth in a
moment?
Yet no sooner is Zion in labor
than she gives birth to her children.
[9]Do I bring to the moment of birth
and not give delivery?" says the LORD.
"Do I close up the womb
when I bring to delivery?" says your God.

66:9 Pain with a Purpose

Nowhere does the book of Isaiah minimize the pain Israel went through; the prophet shared the nation's agony. But God makes clear that the pain was not arbitrary and purposeless. Like childbirth, this pain will lead to something happy and good. "As a mother comforts her child, so will I comfort you" (verse 13). In one last word of triumph, God reaffirms that the suffering of the Israelites will one day lead to a great missionary outreach among all humanity (verses 19,23).

[10]"Rejoice with Jerusalem and be glad for her,
all you who love her;
rejoice greatly with her,
all you who mourn over her.
[11]For you will nurse and be satisfied
at her comforting breasts;
you will drink deeply
and delight in her overflowing
abundance."

[12]For this is what the LORD says:

"I will extend peace to her like a river,
and the wealth of nations like a flooding
stream;
you will nurse and be carried on her arm

and dandled on her knees.
[13]As a mother comforts her child,
so will I comfort you;
and you will be comforted over
Jerusalem."

[14]When you see this, your heart will rejoice
and you will flourish like grass;
the hand of the LORD will be made known to
his servants,
but his fury will be shown to his foes.
[15]See, the LORD is coming with fire,
and his chariots are like a whirlwind;
he will bring down his anger with fury,
and his rebuke with flames of fire.
[16]For with fire and with his sword
the LORD will execute judgment upon all
men,
and many will be those slain by the LORD.

[17]"Those who consecrate and purify themselves to go into the gardens, following the one in the midst of[a] those who eat the flesh of pigs and rats and other abominable things—they will meet their end together," declares the LORD.

[18]"And I, because of their actions and their imaginations, am about to come[b] and gather all nations and tongues, and they will come and see my glory.

[19]"I will set a sign among them, and I will send some of those who survive to the nations—to Tarshish, to the Libyans[c] and Lydians (famous as archers), to Tubal and Greece, and to the distant islands that have not heard of my fame or seen my glory. They will proclaim my glory among the nations. [20]And they will bring all your brothers, from all the nations, to my holy mountain in Jerusalem as an offering to the LORD—on horses, in chariots and wagons, and on mules and camels," says the LORD. "They will bring them, as the Israelites bring their grain offerings, to the temple of the LORD in ceremonially clean vessels. [21]And I will select some of them also to be priests and Levites," says the LORD.

[22]"As the new heavens and the new earth that I make will endure before me," declares the LORD, "so will your name and descendants endure. [23]From one New Moon to another and from one Sabbath to another, all mankind will come and bow down before me," says the LORD. [24]"And they will go out and look upon the dead bodies of those who rebelled against me; their worm will not die, nor will their fire be quenched, and they will be loathsome to all mankind."

[a]17 Or *gardens behind one of your temples, and*   [b]18 The meaning of the Hebrew for this clause is uncertain.
[c]19 Some Septuagint manuscripts *Put* (Libyans); Hebrew *Pul*

JEREMIAH

God's Reluctant Messenger
Jeremiah felt frightened and insecure—but he burned with a message

> *"Do not be afraid of them, for I am with you and will rescue you," declares the LORD. 1:8*

JEREMIAH LIVED ONE OF THE most dramatic lives in the Bible, and that is saying something. But he never learned to like his role. Through all the excitement he remained reluctant, insecure, and often unhappy.

God chose him to be "over nations and kingdoms to uproot and tear down, to destroy and overthrow, to build and to plant" (1:10). To accomplish that, Jeremiah had only one resource—his mouth. How did he respond to such an awesome challenge? "Ah, Sovereign LORD," he said, "I do not know how to speak; I am only a child" (1:6). He didn't stride forward; he barely hung on. He wanted out of the job.

His only encouragement was God's promise: "Today I have made you a fortified city, an iron pillar and a bronze wall to stand against the whole land" (1:18). For 40 years Jeremiah gave top officials a warning they hated to hear and refused to heed. Several times they arrested and imprisoned him; they nearly killed him.

His message? With God's approval, the savage Babylonians would sweep down into Judah. Clever alliances with other powers like Egypt would not help, said Jeremiah. Neither would Judah's half-hearted religion. Judah's only hope lay in renewing an alliance with the living God.

A Disturbing Glimpse of Jeremiah's Mind

The book of Jeremiah stands out not for beautiful poetry or great ideas. Its power comes from its disturbing glimpse of Jeremiah's mind. Jeremiah talked like a man who has awakened from a nightmare, convinced that the nightmare is coming true. His words were sledgehammer blows designed to crack the hardest, most indifferent skull. Though he wished to keep quiet, he found that God's "word is in my heart like a fire, a fire shut up in my bones" (20:9).

No prophet exposed his feelings more than Jeremiah. His relationship with God was streaked with quarrels, reproaches, and outbursts. He told God he wished he were dead (20:14–18). He accused God of being unreliable (15:18). But God offered no sympathy. Rather, he promised more of the same, reminding Jeremiah of his promise to stand by him (12:5–6; 15:19–20). Their relationship, doubts and all, forms one of the best examples in the Bible of what it means to follow God in spite of everything.

Reason to Fear

Jeremiah frankly feared death. He wearied of ridicule. He hated standing alone against the crowd. He told God how he felt. Yet he obeyed God, and in the end his message proved true. He stands as a far greater man than the kings in their luxurious palaces who imprisoned him and burned his writings.

He spoke a gloomy message in a gloomy time, and as a result his words are not always pleasant to read. He reminds us, in an era of artificial cheer and television smiles, that God's message is not always comforting and encouraging. People who disregard God will have reason to fear. For a world that defies him, he plans judgment. And no one, not even his chosen messengers, will escape suffering. God's presence will make them strong enough to face it.

How to Read Jeremiah

Suppose you find, in an old trunk, a thick packet of letters written by your great uncle. You soon realize they are all out of order. One he wrote from the trenches of France during World War I. The next also refers to a war, but from the references to British prime minister Winston Churchill you soon recognize it as World War II, over 20 years later.

Those letters might contain the whole of your uncle's life, but to get his story straight, you'd have to read the whole packet. A reader of Jeremiah finds a very similar situation. The book is an anthology of prophecies given at different times. They jump forward and backward in history, and if you imagine that the book is in chronological order, you will become very confused. Fortunately, it is not hard to reconstruct the order of the main events of Jeremiah's life.

Jeremiah spoke to a nation about to be destroyed by war. Three hundred years before him, the Israelites had split into two countries, Israel in the North and Judah in the South. About 100 years before Jeremiah, Assyria had conquered the Northern Kingdom. This disaster was "World War I" in Old Testament history.

Now, during Jeremiah's life, World War II threatened. Another fierce kingdom, Babylon, assembled troops against the remaining Southern Kingdom. Would God save his chosen people? Jeremiah loudly insisted for more than 20 years that God would punish Judah just as he had Israel, by letting Babylon take them into captivity. He lived to see his predictions come true.

Many passages in Jeremiah refer to the five kings he knew. When you see their names, use them as a reference point in figuring out the order of events:

Josiah (17 years)
Jehoahaz (3 months)
Jehoiakim (12 years)
Jehoiachin (3 months)
Zedekiah (11 years)

Second Kings 23—25 or 2 Chronicles 34—36 gives an overall historical summary of their reigns. You can read a brief synopsis in "A Lineup of Rulers," pages 1361–1369. The better you grasp the historical situation Jeremiah lived in, the more insight you will have into his words.

To capture the full emotion of Jeremiah, you may want to read the first few chapters out loud.

PEOPLE YOU'LL MEET IN JEREMIAH

JEREMIAH *(p. 777)*

3-TRACK READING PLAN

For an explanation and complete listing of the 3-track reading plan, turn to page 7.

TRACK 1: **Two-Week Courses on the Bible**
See page 7 for information on these courses.

TRACK 2: **An Overview of Jeremiah in 4 Days**
☐ Day 1. Read the Introduction to Jeremiah and chapter 2, for God's passionate indictment of his people.
☐ Day 2. Read chapter 15, part of an emotional dialogue between Jeremiah and God.
☐ Day 3. Read chapter 31, God's promise of restoration and a new covenant.
☐ Day 4. Read chapter 38, for Jeremiah's dramatic skirmishes with death in the last days of Jerusalem.

Now turn to page 9 for your next Track 2 reading project.

TRACK 3: **All of Jeremiah in 51 Days**
After you have read through Jeremiah, turn to pages 10–14 for your next Track 3 reading project.

☐1	☐2	☐3	☐4	☐5	☐6	☐7	☐8
☐9	☐10	☐11	☐12	☐13	☐14	☐15	☐16
☐17	☐18	☐19	☐20	☐21	☐22	☐23	☐24
☐25	☐26	☐27	☐28	☐29	☐30	☐31	☐32
☐33	☐34	☐35	☐36	☐37	☐38	☐39	☐40
☐41	☐42	☐43	☐44–45	☐46	☐47	☐48	☐49
☐50	☐51	☐52					

1 The words of Jeremiah son of Hilkiah, one of the priests at Anathoth in the territory of Benjamin. ²The word of the LORD came to him in the thirteenth year of the reign of Josiah son of Amon king of Judah, ³and through the reign of Jehoiakim son of Josiah king of Judah, down to the fifth month of the eleventh year of Zedekiah son of Josiah king of Judah, when the people of Jerusalem went into exile.

The Call of Jeremiah

⁴The word of the LORD came to me, saying,

⁵"Before I formed you in the womb I knew*a* you,
>   before you were born I set you apart;
>   I appointed you as a prophet to the
>   nations."

⁶"Ah, Sovereign LORD," I said, "I do not know how to speak; I am only a child."

⁷But the LORD said to me, "Do not say, 'I am only a child.' You must go to everyone I send you to and say whatever I command you. ⁸Do not be afraid of them, for I am with you and will rescue you," declares the LORD.

⁹Then the LORD reached out his hand and touched my mouth and said to me, "Now, I have put my words in your mouth. ¹⁰See, today I appoint you over nations and kingdoms to uproot and tear down, to destroy and overthrow, to build and to plant."

¹¹The word of the LORD came to me: "What do you see, Jeremiah?"

"I see the branch of an almond tree," I replied.

¹²The LORD said to me, "You have seen correctly, for I am watching*b* to see that my word is fulfilled."

¹³The word of the LORD came to me again: "What do you see?"

"I see a boiling pot, tilting away from the north," I answered.

¹⁴The LORD said to me, "From the north disaster will be poured out on all who live in the land. ¹⁵I am about to summon all the peoples of the northern kingdoms," declares the LORD.

"Their kings will come and set up their
>   thrones
>   in the entrance of the gates of Jerusalem;
> they will come against all her surrounding
>   walls
>   and against all the towns of Judah.
¹⁶I will pronounce my judgments on my
>   people
> because of their wickedness in forsaking
>   me,
>   in burning incense to other gods

and in worshiping what their hands have
    made.

¹⁷"Get yourself ready! Stand up and say to them whatever I command you. Do not be terrified by them, or I will terrify you before them. ¹⁸Today I have made you a fortified city, an iron pillar and a bronze wall to stand against the whole land—against the kings of Judah, its officials, its priests and the people of the land. ¹⁹They

1:18 Too Young?

Like Moses before him, Jeremiah responded reluctantly to God's call. "I am only a child," he protested, feeling too inexperienced to carry such responsibility (verse 6). But God contradicted him. Age and experience did not matter; God's presence did (verse 8). In the face of powerful opposition, God would make Jeremiah as strong as iron.

will fight against you but will not overcome you, for I am with you and will rescue you," declares the LORD.

Israel Forsakes God

2 The word of the LORD came to me: ²"Go and proclaim in the hearing of Jerusalem:

"'I remember the devotion of your youth,
>   how as a bride you loved me
> and followed me through the desert,
>   through a land not sown.
³Israel was holy to the LORD,
>   the firstfruits of his harvest;
> all who devoured her were held guilty,
>   and disaster overtook them,'"
>   declares the LORD.

⁴Hear the word of the LORD, O house of
>   Jacob,
>   all you clans of the house of Israel.

⁵This is what the LORD says:

"What fault did your fathers find in me,
>   that they strayed so far from me?
> They followed worthless idols
>   and became worthless themselves.
⁶They did not ask, 'Where is the LORD,
>   who brought us up out of Egypt
> and led us through the barren wilderness,
>   through a land of deserts and rifts,
> a land of drought and darkness,*c*
>   a land where no one travels and no one
>   lives?'
⁷I brought you into a fertile land
>   to eat its fruit and rich produce.

---

a5 Or *chose*   *b12* The Hebrew for *watching* sounds like the Hebrew for *almond tree.*   *c6* Or *and the shadow of death*

But you came and defiled my land
and made my inheritance detestable.
⁸The priests did not ask,
'Where is the LORD?'
Those who deal with the law did not know
me;
the leaders rebelled against me.
The prophets prophesied by Baal,
following worthless idols.

⁹"Therefore I bring charges against you
again,"
declares the LORD.
"And I will bring charges against your
children's children.
¹⁰Cross over to the coasts of Kittim*a* and
look,
send to Kedar*b* and observe closely;
see if there has ever been anything like
this:
¹¹Has a nation ever changed its gods?
(Yet they are not gods at all.)
But my people have exchanged their*c* Glory
for worthless idols.
¹²Be appalled at this, O heavens,
and shudder with great horror,"
declares the LORD.
¹³"My people have committed two sins:
They have forsaken me,
the spring of living water,
and have dug their own cisterns,
broken cisterns that cannot hold water.

2:13 An Astounding Trade

*Jeremiah piles image on top of image,
searching for a way to express the astounding
fact that Israelites had traded the living God for
the idols of their neighbors. Here he compares
the deed to exchanging a spring of living water
for a leaky cistern. In verse 20 he graphically
compares idolatry to sexual promiscuity. In an
interesting twist, Jesus offered "living water" to
a sexually promiscuous Samaritan woman in
John 4:10.*

¹⁴Is Israel a servant, a slave by birth?
Why then has he become plunder?
¹⁵Lions have roared;
they have growled at him.
They have laid waste his land;
his towns are burned and deserted.
¹⁶Also, the men of Memphis*d* and Tahpanhes
have shaved the crown of your head.*e*
¹⁷Have you not brought this on yourselves
by forsaking the LORD your God

when he led you in the way?
¹⁸Now why go to Egypt
to drink water from the Shihor*f*?
And why go to Assyria
to drink water from the River*g*?
¹⁹Your wickedness will punish you;
your backsliding will rebuke you.
Consider then and realize
how evil and bitter it is for you
when you forsake the LORD your God
and have no awe of me,"
declares the Lord,
the LORD Almighty.

²⁰"Long ago you broke off your yoke
and tore off your bonds;
you said, 'I will not serve you!'
Indeed, on every high hill
and under every spreading tree
you lay down as a prostitute.
²¹I had planted you like a choice vine
of sound and reliable stock.
How then did you turn against me
into a corrupt, wild vine?
²²Although you wash yourself with soda
and use an abundance of soap,
the stain of your guilt is still before me,"
declares the Sovereign LORD.
²³"How can you say, 'I am not defiled;
I have not run after the Baals'?
See how you behaved in the valley;
consider what you have done.
You are a swift she-camel
running here and there,
²⁴a wild donkey accustomed to the desert,
sniffing the wind in her craving—
in her heat who can restrain her?
Any males that pursue her need not tire
themselves;
at mating time they will find her.
²⁵Do not run until your feet are bare
and your throat is dry.
But you said, 'It's no use!
I love foreign gods,
and I must go after them.'

²⁶"As a thief is disgraced when he is caught,
so the house of Israel is disgraced—
they, their kings and their officials,
their priests and their prophets.
²⁷They say to wood, 'You are my father,'
and to stone, 'You gave me birth.'
They have turned their backs to me
and not their faces;
yet when they are in trouble, they say,
'Come and save us!'
²⁸Where then are the gods you made for
yourselves?

---

a10 That is, Cyprus and western coastlands   *b10* The home of Bedouin tribes in the Syro-Arabian desert
c11 Masoretic Text; an ancient Hebrew scribal tradition *my*   *d16* Hebrew *Noph*   *e16* Or *have cracked your skull*
f18 That is, a branch of the Nile   *g18* That is, the Euphrates

Let them come if they can save you
when you are in trouble!
For you have as many gods
as you have towns, O Judah.

29"Why do you bring charges against me?
You have all rebelled against me,"
declares the LORD.
30"In vain I punished your people;
they did not respond to correction.
Your sword has devoured your prophets
like a ravening lion.

31"You of this generation, consider the word
of the LORD:

"Have I been a desert to Israel
or a land of great darkness?
Why do my people say, 'We are free to
roam;
we will come to you no more'?
32Does a maiden forget her jewelry,
a bride her wedding ornaments?
Yet my people have forgotten me,
days without number.
33How skilled you are at pursuing love!
Even the worst of women can learn from
your ways.
34On your clothes men find
the lifeblood of the innocent poor,
though you did not catch them breaking
in.
Yet in spite of all this
35   you say, 'I am innocent;
he is not angry with me.'
But I will pass judgment on you
because you say, 'I have not sinned.'
36Why do you go about so much,
changing your ways?
You will be disappointed by Egypt
as you were by Assyria.
37You will also leave that place
with your hands on your head,
for the LORD has rejected those you trust;
you will not be helped by them.

3 "If a man divorces his wife
and she leaves him and marries another
man,
should he return to her again?
Would not the land be completely defiled?
But you have lived as a prostitute with many
lovers—
would you now return to me?"
declares the LORD.
2"Look up to the barren heights and see.
Is there any place where you have not
been ravished?
By the roadside you sat waiting for lovers,
sat like a nomad[a] in the desert.

You have defiled the land
with your prostitution and wickedness.
3Therefore the showers have been withheld,
and no spring rains have fallen.

3:2 Ritual Sex

*Today, the news that a minister or priest has
committed adultery sends shock waves
through the community. But Israel's neighbors
in ancient times actually incorporated adultery
into their religious rites. Pagans worshiped
their gods through cultic prostitution, believing
sex would put them in tune with divine power.
This ritual sex went on at religious shrines
located on the "high places" (hilltops). When
Israel joined in their neighbors' worship, God
properly called it adultery—both physical and
spiritual. Israel was going out with every god
in town.*

Yet you have the brazen look of a prostitute;
you refuse to blush with shame.
4Have you not just called to me:
'My Father, my friend from my youth,
5will you always be angry?
Will your wrath continue forever?'
This is how you talk,
but you do all the evil you can."

Unfaithful Israel

6During the reign of King Josiah, the LORD
said to me, "Have you seen what faithless Israel
has done? She has gone up on every high hill and
under every spreading tree and has committed
adultery there. 7I thought that after she had done
all this she would return to me but she did not,
and her unfaithful sister Judah saw it. 8I gave
faithless Israel her certificate of divorce and sent
her away because of all her adulteries. Yet I saw
that her unfaithful sister Judah had no fear; she
also went out and committed adultery. 9Because
Israel's immorality mattered so little to her, she
defiled the land and committed adultery with
stone and wood. 10In spite of all this, her unfaithful sister Judah did not return to me with all her

3:10 A Superficial Change

*King Josiah, one of the few good kings in
Judah's history, led a massive religious reform
(see 2 Kings 22 and 23). While Josiah was
unquestionably sincere, Jeremiah saw that the
nation's return to God wasn't. Jeremiah's
accusation was borne out after King Josiah's
death: Judah returned quickly to her former
ways.*

a2 Or an Arab

heart, but only in pretense," declares the LORD. [11]The LORD said to me, "Faithless Israel is more righteous than unfaithful Judah. [12]Go, proclaim this message toward the north:

"'Return, faithless Israel,' declares the LORD,
  'I will frown on you no longer,
for I am merciful,' declares the LORD,
  'I will not be angry forever.
[13]Only acknowledge your guilt—
  you have rebelled against the LORD your
    God,
you have scattered your favors to foreign gods
  under every spreading tree,
  and have not obeyed me,'"

                    declares the LORD.

[14]"Return, faithless people," declares the LORD, "for I am your husband. I will choose you—one from a town and two from a clan—and bring you to Zion. [15]Then I will give you shepherds after my own heart, who will lead you with knowledge and understanding. [16]In those days, when your numbers have increased greatly in the land," declares the LORD, "men will no longer say, 'The ark of the covenant of the LORD.' It will never enter their minds or be remembered; it will not be missed, nor will another one be made. [17]At that time they will call Jerusalem The Throne of the LORD, and all nations will gather in Jerusalem to honor the name of the LORD. No longer will they follow the stubbornness of their evil

A Lover's Quarrel
The violent emotions of a scorned lover

THE CALL COMES LATE, AFTER midnight, to a police officer who grimaces and shakes his head. Then, siren screaming, he races toward the house. Neighbors heard a woman's cries. Someone saw a man threatening her with a knife. As the police officer pulls up to the house, he hears her high-pitched shrieks. She is begging for mercy—from her husband.

"You have lived as a prostitute with many lovers—would you now return to me?" declares the LORD. 3:1

Such cases are called "domestic disturbances." They happen nearly every night, and particularly on weekends. The police usually dislike getting called in. Both husband and wife can turn on the person who is "interfering."

Lovers' quarrels may seem silly to outsiders, but they are deadly serious to those involved. Some turn violent, even murderous. The most precious, desired gift anyone can offer has been abused. Love has been betrayed. Lovers react to that with violent emotions.

Words that Tear His Heart

It is a lovers' quarrel that Jeremiah exposes in chapters 2 and 3, and the emotions are violent and helpless. Again and again God makes his charge against Judah. Of all the nations, he had picked her; he had tenderly offered his protection and care. But she keeps sleeping with other men. He warns her again and again, but she ignores him. She saw how he divorced her sister Israel. Doesn't she know he will do the same to her?

God's words bleed pain. He accuses as though he cannot help himself, although his words tear his own heart. First, he is tender, full of memories: "I remember . . . how as a bride you loved me and followed me through the desert" (2:2). But then you "tore off your bonds; you said, 'I will not serve you!' Indeed, on every high hill and under every spreading tree you lay down as a prostitute" (2:20). In disgust God compares Judah to a donkey in heat, "sniffing the wind in her craving. . . . Any males that pursue her need not tire themselves" (2:24). But the comparison hurts him more than her. His love, not hers, is scorned.

Married to a Whore

The prophet Hosea was the first to draw the picture of God married to a prostitute. Jeremiah amplifies it. The comparison cries out both the passionate love God feels for his people and the terrible, wounded pain he feels at their betrayal. Jeremiah's imagery is violent and dark, but underneath it, something wonderful shines out: the tender and personal love of God for his people.

The "adultery" Jeremiah wrote about focuses on the worship of idols. Most modern people find it hard to understand why Israelites felt any impulse to kneel before wooden or metal statues, or why their doing so made God furious. But when Jeremiah refers to it as adultery, God's hatred of idolatry becomes understandable. God meant his people to have only one true love in their lives—God himself. God the lover will not take second place; he refuses to share his bride.

Life Questions: Have you ever fought with God? What issues were you fighting about?

hearts. [18]In those days the house of Judah will join the house of Israel, and together they will come from a northern land to the land I gave your forefathers as an inheritance.

[19]"I myself said,

"'How gladly would I treat you like sons
    and give you a desirable land,
    the most beautiful inheritance of any
        nation.'
I thought you would call me 'Father'
    and not turn away from following me.
[20]But like a woman unfaithful to her husband,
    so you have been unfaithful to me,
        O house of Israel,"
                declares the LORD.

[21]A cry is heard on the barren heights,
    the weeping and pleading of the people of
        Israel,
because they have perverted their ways
    and have forgotten the LORD their God.

[22]"Return, faithless people;
    I will cure you of backsliding."

"Yes, we will come to you,
    for you are the LORD our God.
[23]Surely the ⌊idolatrous⌋ commotion on the
        hills
    and mountains is a deception;
surely in the LORD our God
    is the salvation of Israel.
[24]From our youth shameful gods have
        consumed
    the fruits of our fathers' labor—
their flocks and herds,
    their sons and daughters.
[25]Let us lie down in our shame,
    and let our disgrace cover us.
We have sinned against the LORD our God,
    both we and our fathers;
from our youth till this day
    we have not obeyed the LORD our God."

4 "If you will return, O Israel,
    return to me,"
                declares the LORD.
"If you put your detestable idols out of my
        sight
    and no longer go astray,
[2]and if in a truthful, just and righteous way
    you swear, 'As surely as the LORD lives,'
then the nations will be blessed by him
    and in him they will glory."

[3]This is what the LORD says to the men of
Judah and to Jerusalem:

"Break up your unplowed ground
    and do not sow among thorns.
[4]Circumcise yourselves to the LORD,
    circumcise your hearts,
    you men of Judah and people of
        Jerusalem,
or my wrath will break out and burn like fire
    because of the evil you have done—
    burn with no one to quench it.

4:4 Circumcised Hearts

All male Jewish babies underwent circumcision, a sign of their "set-apartness" as God's chosen people. Often, though, circumcision became just a ritual, not reflecting any real difference in the way people lived. Jeremiah used a startling metaphor—"circumcise your hearts"—to remind the Israelites that membership in God's family should make a difference inside, not just on the surface. The apostle Paul wrote that Christ brings about this inner circumcision (Colossians 2:11).

Disaster From the North

[5]"Announce in Judah and proclaim in
        Jerusalem and say:
    'Sound the trumpet throughout the
        land!'
Cry aloud and say:
    'Gather together!
    Let us flee to the fortified cities!'
[6]Raise the signal to go to Zion!
    Flee for safety without delay!
For I am bringing disaster from the north,
    even terrible destruction.

[7]A lion has come out of his lair;
    a destroyer of nations has set out.
He has left his place
    to lay waste your land.
Your towns will lie in ruins
    without inhabitant.
[8]So put on sackcloth,
    lament and wail,
for the fierce anger of the LORD
    has not turned away from us.

[9]"In that day," declares the LORD,
    "the king and the officials will lose heart,
the priests will be horrified,
    and the prophets will be appalled."

[10]Then I said, "Ah, Sovereign LORD, how completely you have deceived this people and Jerusalem by saying, 'You will have peace,' when the sword is at our throats."

[11]At that time this people and Jerusalem will be told, "A scorching wind from the barren heights in the desert blows toward my people, but not to winnow or cleanse; [12]a wind too strong

for that comes from me.ᵃ Now I pronounce my
judgments against them."

¹³Look! He advances like the clouds,
    his chariots come like a whirlwind,
his horses are swifter than eagles.
    Woe to us! We are ruined!
¹⁴O Jerusalem, wash the evil from your heart
        and be saved.
    How long will you harbor wicked
        thoughts?
¹⁵A voice is announcing from Dan,
    proclaiming disaster from the hills of
        Ephraim.
¹⁶"Tell this to the nations,
    proclaim it to Jerusalem:
'A besieging army is coming from a distant
    land,
    raising a war cry against the cities of
        Judah.
¹⁷They surround her like men guarding a field,
    because she has rebelled against me,'"
                            declares the LORD.
¹⁸"Your own conduct and actions
    have brought this upon you.
This is your punishment.
    How bitter it is!
    How it pierces to the heart!"

¹⁹Oh, my anguish, my anguish!
    I writhe in pain.
Oh, the agony of my heart!
    My heart pounds within me,
    I cannot keep silent.
For I have heard the sound of the trumpet;
    I have heard the battle cry.
²⁰Disaster follows disaster;
    the whole land lies in ruins.
In an instant my tents are destroyed,
    my shelter in a moment.
²¹How long must I see the battle standard
    and hear the sound of the trumpet?

²²"My people are fools;
    they do not know me.
They are senseless children;
    they have no understanding.
They are skilled in doing evil;
    they know not how to do good."

²³I looked at the earth,
    and it was formless and empty;
and at the heavens,
    and their light was gone.
²⁴I looked at the mountains,
    and they were quaking;
    all the hills were swaying.
²⁵I looked, and there were no people;
    every bird in the sky had flown away.
²⁶I looked, and the fruitful land was a desert;

all its towns lay in ruins
    before the LORD, before his fierce anger.

²⁷This is what the LORD says:

"The whole land will be ruined,
    though I will not destroy it completely.
²⁸Therefore the earth will mourn
    and the heavens above grow dark,
because I have spoken and will not relent,
    I have decided and will not turn back."

4:23 Return to the Void

*Jeremiah used words from Genesis 1:2 to
describe the effect of the Israelites' sin. It was as
though the Israelites were carrying the earth
back to the chaos before creation, destroying
all the beauty and order God had made.*

²⁹At the sound of horsemen and archers
    every town takes to flight.
Some go into the thickets;
    some climb up among the rocks.
All the towns are deserted;
    no one lives in them.

³⁰What are you doing, O devastated one?
    Why dress yourself in scarlet
    and put on jewels of gold?
Why shade your eyes with paint?
    You adorn yourself in vain.
Your lovers despise you;
    they seek your life.

³¹I hear a cry as of a woman in labor,
    a groan as of one bearing her first child—
the cry of the Daughter of Zion gasping for
    breath,
    stretching out her hands and saying,
"Alas! I am fainting;
    my life is given over to murderers."

Not One Is Upright

5 "Go up and down the streets of Jerusalem,
        look around and consider,

5:1 Search for an Honest Person

*In Genesis 18:22–33, Abraham tried to
convince God not to destroy Sodom and
Gomorrah if as many as ten righteous people
could be found. God agreed, but evidently the
ten did not exist. Here, God offers to forgive
Jerusalem if a single honest person can be
found. God's people had sunk to Sodom's level
(23:14).*

ᵃ 12 Or *comes at my command*

search through her squares.
If you can find but one person
  who deals honestly and seeks the truth,
  I will forgive this city.
[2]Although they say, 'As surely as the LORD
    lives,'
  still they are swearing falsely."

[3]O LORD, do not your eyes look for truth?
  You struck them, but they felt no pain;
  you crushed them, but they refused
    correction.
They made their faces harder than stone
  and refused to repent.
[4]I thought, "These are only the poor;
  they are foolish,
for they do not know the way of the LORD,
  the requirements of their God.
[5]So I will go to the leaders
  and speak to them;
surely they know the way of the LORD,
  the requirements of their God."
But with one accord they too had broken off
    the yoke
  and torn off the bonds.
[6]Therefore a lion from the forest will attack
    them,
  a wolf from the desert will ravage them,
a leopard will lie in wait near their towns
  to tear to pieces any who venture out,
for their rebellion is great
  and their backslidings many.

[7]"Why should I forgive you?
  Your children have forsaken me
  and sworn by gods that are not gods.
I supplied all their needs,
  yet they committed adultery
  and thronged to the houses of prostitutes.
[8]They are well-fed, lusty stallions,
  each neighing for another man's wife.
[9]Should I not punish them for this?"
    declares the LORD.
  "Should I not avenge myself
    on such a nation as this?

[10]"Go through her vineyards and ravage them,
  but do not destroy them completely.
Strip off her branches,
  for these people do not belong to the
    LORD.
[11]The house of Israel and the house of Judah
  have been utterly unfaithful to me,"
    declares the LORD.

[12]They have lied about the LORD;
  they said, "He will do nothing!
No harm will come to us;
  we will never see sword or famine.
[13]The prophets are but wind

and the word is not in them;
  so let what they say be done to them."

[14]Therefore this is what the LORD God Almighty says:

"Because the people have spoken these
    words,
  I will make my words in your mouth a
    fire
  and these people the wood it consumes.
[15]O house of Israel," declares the LORD,
  "I am bringing a distant nation against
    you—
an ancient and enduring nation,
  a people whose language you do not
    know,
  whose speech you do not understand.
[16]Their quivers are like an open grave;
  all of them are mighty warriors.
[17]They will devour your harvests and food,
  devour your sons and daughters;
they will devour your flocks and herds,
  devour your vines and fig trees.
With the sword they will destroy
  the fortified cities in which you trust.

[18]"Yet even in those days," declares the LORD,
"I will not destroy you completely. [19]And when
the people ask, 'Why has the LORD our God done
all this to us?' you will tell them, 'As you have
forsaken me and served foreign gods in your own
land, so now you will serve foreigners in a land
not your own.'

[20]"Announce this to the house of Jacob
  and proclaim it in Judah:
[21]Hear this, you foolish and senseless people,
  who have eyes but do not see,
  who have ears but do not hear:
[22]Should you not fear me?" declares the LORD.
  "Should you not tremble in my presence?
I made the sand a boundary for the sea,
  an everlasting barrier it cannot cross.
The waves may roll, but they cannot prevail;
  they may roar, but they cannot cross it.
[23]But these people have stubborn and
    rebellious hearts;
  they have turned aside and gone away.
[24]They do not say to themselves,

'Let us fear the LORD our God,
who gives autumn and spring rains in
season,
who assures us of the regular weeks of
harvest.'
²⁵Your wrongdoings have kept these away;
your sins have deprived you of good.

²⁶"Among my people are wicked men
who lie in wait like men who snare birds
and like those who set traps to catch men.
²⁷Like cages full of birds,
their houses are full of deceit;
they have become rich and powerful
²⁸ and have grown fat and sleek.
Their evil deeds have no limit;
they do not plead the case of the
fatherless to win it,
they do not defend the rights of the poor.
²⁹Should I not punish them for this?"
declares the LORD.
"Should I not avenge myself
on such a nation as this?

³⁰"A horrible and shocking thing
has happened in the land:
³¹The prophets prophesy lies,
the priests rule by their own authority,
and my people love it this way.
But what will you do in the end?

Jerusalem Under Siege

6 "Flee for safety, people of Benjamin!
Flee from Jerusalem!
Sound the trumpet in Tekoa!
Raise the signal over Beth Hakkerem!
For disaster looms out of the north,
even terrible destruction.
²I will destroy the Daughter of Zion,
so beautiful and delicate.
³Shepherds with their flocks will come against
her;
they will pitch their tents around her,
each tending his own portion."

⁴"Prepare for battle against her!
Arise, let us attack at noon!
But, alas, the daylight is fading,
and the shadows of evening grow long.
⁵So arise, let us attack at night
and destroy her fortresses!"

⁶This is what the LORD Almighty says:

"Cut down the trees
and build siege ramps against Jerusalem.
This city must be punished;
it is filled with oppression.
⁷As a well pours out its water,
so she pours out her wickedness.
Violence and destruction resound in her;

her sickness and wounds are ever before
me.
⁸Take warning, O Jerusalem,
or I will turn away from you
and make your land desolate
so no one can live in it."

⁹This is what the LORD Almighty says:

"Let them glean the remnant of Israel
as thoroughly as a vine;
pass your hand over the branches again,
like one gathering grapes."

¹⁰To whom can I speak and give warning?
Who will listen to me?
Their ears are closed^a
so they cannot hear.
The word of the LORD is offensive to them;
they find no pleasure in it.
¹¹But I am full of the wrath of the LORD,
and I cannot hold it in.

"Pour it out on the children in the street
and on the young men gathered together;
both husband and wife will be caught in it,
and the old, those weighed down with
years.
¹²Their houses will be turned over to others,
together with their fields and their wives,
when I stretch out my hand
against those who live in the land,"
declares the LORD.
¹³"From the least to the greatest,
all are greedy for gain;
prophets and priests alike,
all practice deceit.
¹⁴They dress the wound of my people
as though it were not serious.
'Peace, peace,' they say,
when there is no peace.

6:14 Greedy Doctors

*A good doctor sometimes has to convey bad
tidings, delivering a diagnosis of cancer, for
example. But in Judah the spiritual "doctors"
(prophets and priests) only gave out good
news. They covered up serious wounds with a
Band-Aid.*

¹⁵Are they ashamed of their loathsome
conduct?
No, they have no shame at all;
they do not even know how to blush.
So they will fall among the fallen;
they will be brought down when I punish
them,"
says the LORD.

^a10 Hebrew *uncircumcised*

[16]This is what the LORD says:

"Stand at the crossroads and look;
  ask for the ancient paths,
ask where the good way is, and walk in it,
  and you will find rest for your souls.
  But you said, 'We will not walk in it.'
[17]I appointed watchmen over you and said,
  'Listen to the sound of the trumpet!'
  But you said, 'We will not listen.'
[18]Therefore hear, O nations;
  observe, O witnesses,
  what will happen to them.
[19]Hear, O earth:
I am bringing disaster on this people,
  the fruit of their schemes,
because they have not listened to my words
  and have rejected my law.
[20]What do I care about incense from Sheba
  or sweet calamus from a distant land?
Your burnt offerings are not acceptable;
  your sacrifices do not please me."

[21]Therefore this is what the LORD says:

"I will put obstacles before this people.
  Fathers and sons alike will stumble over
    them;
  neighbors and friends will perish."

[22]This is what the LORD says:

"Look, an army is coming
  from the land of the north;
a great nation is being stirred up
  from the ends of the earth.
[23]They are armed with bow and spear;
  they are cruel and show no mercy.
They sound like the roaring sea
  as they ride on their horses;
they come like men in battle formation
  to attack you, O Daughter of Zion."

[24]We have heard reports about them,
  and our hands hang limp.
Anguish has gripped us,
  pain like that of a woman in labor.
[25]Do not go out to the fields
  or walk on the roads,
for the enemy has a sword,
  and there is terror on every side.
[26]O my people, put on sackcloth
  and roll in ashes;
mourn with bitter wailing
  as for an only son,
for suddenly the destroyer
  will come upon us.

[27]"I have made you a tester of metals
  and my people the ore,
that you may observe
  and test their ways.

[28]They are all hardened rebels,
  going about to slander.
They are bronze and iron;
  they all act corruptly.
[29]The bellows blow fiercely
  to burn away the lead with fire,
but the refining goes on in vain;
  the wicked are not purged out.
[30]They are called rejected silver,
  because the LORD has rejected them."

False Religion Worthless

7 This is the word that came to Jeremiah from the LORD: [2]"Stand at the gate of the LORD's house and there proclaim this message:

" 'Hear the word of the LORD, all you people of Judah who come through these gates to worship the LORD. [3]This is what the LORD Almighty, the God of Israel, says: Reform your ways and your actions, and I will let you live in this place. [4]Do not trust in deceptive words and say, "This is the temple of the LORD, the temple of the LORD, the temple of the LORD!" [5]If you really change your ways and your actions and deal with each other justly, [6]if you do not oppress the alien, the fatherless or the widow and do not shed innocent blood in this place, and if you do not follow other gods to your own harm, [7]then I will let you live in this place, in the land I gave your forefathers for ever and ever. [8]But look, you are trusting in deceptive words that are worthless.

[9]" 'Will you steal and murder, commit adultery and perjury,[a] burn incense to Baal and follow other gods you have not known, [10]and then come and stand before me in this house, which bears my Name, and say, "We are safe"—safe to do all these detestable things? [11]Has this house, which bears my Name, become a den of robbers to you? But I have been watching! declares the LORD.

[12]" 'Go now to the place in Shiloh where I first made a dwelling for my Name, and see what I did

7:11 A Den of Robbers

Israelites of Jeremiah's time felt they were safe from invasion as long as they had the temple. After all, they thought, God would not let his home be destroyed (verse 4). But the Lord, through Jeremiah, said that the temple had become "a den of robbers" and would be demolished. In Jeremiah's lifetime this prediction came true. Jesus quoted the reference to a den of robbers when driving out money changers from the rebuilt temple (Mark 11:17).

[a]9 Or and swear by false gods

to it because of the wickedness of my people Israel. [13]While you were doing all these things, declares the LORD, I spoke to you again and again, but you did not listen; I called you, but you did not answer. [14]Therefore, what I did to Shiloh I will now do to the house that bears my Name, the temple you trust in, the place I gave to you and your fathers. [15]I will thrust you from my presence, just as I did all your brothers, the people of Ephraim.'

[16]"So do not pray for this people nor offer any plea or petition for them; do not plead with me, for I will not listen to you. [17]Do you not see what they are doing in the towns of Judah and in the streets of Jerusalem? [18]The children gather wood, the fathers light the fire, and the women knead the dough and make cakes of bread for the Queen of Heaven. They pour out drink offerings to other gods to provoke me to anger. [19]But am I the one they are provoking? declares the LORD. Are they not rather harming themselves, to their own shame?

[20]"Therefore this is what the Sovereign LORD says: My anger and my wrath will be poured out on this place, on man and beast, on the trees of the field and on the fruit of the ground, and it will burn and not be quenched.

[21]"This is what the LORD Almighty, the God of Israel, says: Go ahead, add your burnt offerings to your other sacrifices and eat the meat yourselves! [22]For when I brought your forefathers out of Egypt and spoke to them, I did not just give them commands about burnt offerings and sacrifices, [23]but I gave them this command: Obey me, and I will be your God and you will be my people. Walk in all the ways I command you, that it may go well with you. [24]But they did not listen or pay attention; instead, they followed the stubborn inclinations of their evil hearts. They went backward and not forward. [25]From the time your forefathers left Egypt until now, day after day, again and again I sent you my servants the prophets. [26]But they did not listen to me or pay attention. They were stiff-necked and did more evil than their forefathers.'

[27]"When you tell them all this, they will not listen to you; when you call to them, they will not answer. [28]Therefore say to them, 'This is the nation that has not obeyed the LORD its God or responded to correction. Truth has perished; it has vanished from their lips. [29]Cut off your hair and throw it away; take up a lament on the barren heights, for the LORD has rejected and abandoned this generation that is under his wrath.

The Valley of Slaughter

[30]"The people of Judah have done evil in my eyes, declares the LORD. They have set up their detestable idols in the house that bears my Name and have defiled it. [31]They have built the high places of Topheth in the Valley of Ben Hinnom to burn their sons and daughters in the fire—something I did not command, nor did it enter my mind. [32]So beware, the days are coming, declares the LORD, when people will no longer call it Topheth or the Valley of Ben Hinnom, but the Valley of Slaughter, for they will bury the dead in Topheth until there is no more room. [33]Then the carcasses of this people will become food for the birds of the air and the beasts of the earth, and there will be no one to frighten them away. [34]I will bring an end to the sounds of joy and gladness and to the voices of bride and bridegroom in the towns of Judah and the streets of Jerusalem, for the land will become desolate.

8 "'At that time, declares the LORD, the bones of the kings and officials of Judah, the bones of the priests and prophets, and the bones of the people of Jerusalem will be removed from their graves. [2]They will be exposed to the sun and the moon and all the stars of the heavens, which they have loved and served and which they have followed and consulted and worshiped. They will not be gathered up or buried, but will be like refuse lying on the ground. [3]Wherever I banish them, all the survivors of this evil nation will prefer death to life, declares the LORD Almighty.'

Sin and Punishment

[4]"Say to them, 'This is what the LORD says:

"'When men fall down, do they not get up?
   When a man turns away, does he not
      return?
[5]Why then have these people turned away?
   Why does Jerusalem always turn away?
They cling to deceit;
   they refuse to return.
[6]I have listened attentively,
   but they do not say what is right.
No one repents of his wickedness,
   saying, "What have I done?"
Each pursues his own course
   like a horse charging into battle.
[7]Even the stork in the sky
   knows her appointed seasons,
and the dove, the swift and the thrush
   observe the time of their migration.
But my people do not know
   the requirements of the LORD.

[8]"'How can you say, "We are wise,
   for we have the law of the LORD,"
when actually the lying pen of the scribes
   has handled it falsely?
[9]The wise will be put to shame;
   they will be dismayed and trapped.
Since they have rejected the word of the
      LORD,
   what kind of wisdom do they have?

[10]Therefore I will give their wives to other
men
and their fields to new owners.
From the least to the greatest,
all are greedy for gain;
prophets and priests alike,
all practice deceit.
[11]They dress the wound of my people
as though it were not serious.
"Peace, peace," they say,
when there is no peace.
[12]Are they ashamed of their loathsome
conduct?
No, they have no shame at all;
they do not even know how to blush.
So they will fall among the fallen;
they will be brought down when they are
punished,
says the LORD.

[13]" 'I will take away their harvest,
declares the LORD.
There will be no grapes on the vine.
There will be no figs on the tree,
and their leaves will wither.
What I have given them
will be taken from them.[a]' "

[14]"Why are we sitting here?
Gather together!
Let us flee to the fortified cities
and perish there!
For the LORD our God has doomed us to
perish
and given us poisoned water to drink,
because we have sinned against him.
[15]We hoped for peace
but no good has come,
for a time of healing
but there was only terror.
[16]The snorting of the enemy's horses
is heard from Dan;
at the neighing of their stallions
the whole land trembles.
They have come to devour
the land and everything in it,
the city and all who live there."

[17]"See, I will send venomous snakes among
you,
vipers that cannot be charmed,
and they will bite you,"
declares the LORD.

[18]O my Comforter[b] in sorrow,
my heart is faint within me.
[19]Listen to the cry of my people
from a land far away:

"Is the LORD not in Zion?
Is her King no longer there?"

"Why have they provoked me to anger with
their images,
with their worthless foreign idols?"

[20]"The harvest is past,
the summer has ended,
and we are not saved."

[21]Since my people are crushed, I am crushed;
I mourn, and horror grips me.
[22]Is there no balm in Gilead?
Is there no physician there?
Why then is there no healing
for the wound of my people?

9 [1]Oh, that my head were a spring of water
and my eyes a fountain of tears!
I would weep day and night
for the slain of my people.

9:1 A Fountain of Tears

*Jeremiah never stood aside like a stern
moralist, enjoying others' well-deserved
sufferings. He felt the bitterness of the
judgment he announced. "Since my people are
crushed, I am crushed; I mourn, and horror
grips me" (8:21). In the end, Jeremiah
swallowed the bitter medicine of exile like the
others.*

*Jeremiah reminds us of another "man of
sorrows." Like Jesus, Jeremiah wept over
Jerusalem. Like Jesus, he was rejected by his
own hometown (11:18–23). Jeremiah even
compared himself to a lamb led to the
slaughter (11:19), language that would later be
applied to Jesus' sacrifice for our sins.*

[2]Oh, that I had in the desert
a lodging place for travelers,
so that I might leave my people
and go away from them;
for they are all adulterers,
a crowd of unfaithful people.

[3]"They make ready their tongue
like a bow, to shoot lies;
it is not by truth
that they triumph[c] in the land.
They go from one sin to another;
they do not acknowledge me,"
declares the LORD.

[4]"Beware of your friends;
do not trust your brothers.
For every brother is a deceiver,[d]
and every friend a slanderer.
[5]Friend deceives friend,

---

[a]13 The meaning of the Hebrew for this sentence is uncertain.   [c]3 Or lies; / they are not valiant for truth   [b]18 The meaning of the Hebrew for this word is uncertain.   [d]4 Or a deceiving Jacob

and no one speaks the truth.
They have taught their tongues to lie;
they weary themselves with sinning.
[6] You[a] live in the midst of deception;
in their deceit they refuse to acknowledge
me,"

declares the LORD.

[7] Therefore this is what the LORD Almighty
says:

"See, I will refine and test them,
for what else can I do
because of the sin of my people?
[8] Their tongue is a deadly arrow;
it speaks with deceit.
With his mouth each speaks cordially to his
neighbor,
but in his heart he sets a trap for him.
[9] Should I not punish them for this?"
declares the LORD.
"Should I not avenge myself
on such a nation as this?"

[10] I will weep and wail for the mountains
and take up a lament concerning the
desert pastures.
They are desolate and untraveled,
and the lowing of cattle is not heard.
The birds of the air have fled
and the animals are gone.

[11] "I will make Jerusalem a heap of ruins,
a haunt of jackals;
and I will lay waste the towns of Judah
so no one can live there."

[12] What man is wise enough to understand
this? Who has been instructed by the LORD and
can explain it? Why has the land been ruined and
laid waste like a desert that no one can cross?

[13] The LORD said, "It is because they have forsaken my law, which I set before them; they have
not obeyed me or followed my law. [14] Instead,
they have followed the stubbornness of their
hearts; they have followed the Baals, as their fathers taught them." [15] Therefore, this is what the
LORD Almighty, the God of Israel, says: "See, I
will make this people eat bitter food and drink
poisoned water. [16] I will scatter them among nations that neither they nor their fathers have
known, and I will pursue them with the sword
until I have destroyed them."

[17] This is what the LORD Almighty says:

"Consider now! Call for the wailing women
to come;
send for the most skillful of them.
[18] Let them come quickly
and wail over us
till our eyes overflow with tears

and water streams from our eyelids.
[19] The sound of wailing is heard from Zion:
'How ruined we are!
How great is our shame!
We must leave our land
because our houses are in ruins.'"

[20] Now, O women, hear the word of the LORD;
open your ears to the words of his mouth.
Teach your daughters how to wail;
teach one another a lament.
[21] Death has climbed in through our windows
and has entered our fortresses;
it has cut off the children from the streets
and the young men from the public
squares.

[22] Say, "This is what the LORD declares:

"'The dead bodies of men will lie
like refuse on the open field,
like cut grain behind the reaper,
with no one to gather them.'"

[23] This is what the LORD says:

"Let not the wise man boast of his wisdom
or the strong man boast of his strength
or the rich man boast of his riches,
[24] but let him who boasts boast about this:
that he understands and knows me,
that I am the LORD, who exercises kindness,
justice and righteousness on earth,
for in these I delight,"

declares the LORD.

9:24 Bragging on God

*In dire circumstances like those Jeremiah
predicts, what has value? Wisdom? Strength?
Money? In the midst of a devastating invasion,
these will get you nothing. Only one thing will
count: a living, confident relationship with God.
If you have that, it's worth boasting about. Paul
quoted this verse in writing to the Corinthians
(1 Corinthians 1:31); he said God seems to
prefer to work through weak and poor people,
those who have little else to brag about.*

[25] "The days are coming," declares the LORD,
"when I will punish all who are circumcised only
in the flesh— [26] Egypt, Judah, Edom, Ammon,
Moab and all who live in the desert in distant
places.[b] For all these nations are really uncircumcised, and even the whole house of Israel is
uncircumcised in heart."

God and Idols

10 Hear what the LORD says to you, O house
of Israel. [2] This is what the LORD says:

a 6 That is, Jeremiah (the Hebrew is singular)   b 26 Or desert and who clip the hair by their foreheads

"Do not learn the ways of the nations
 or be terrified by signs in the sky,
 though the nations are terrified by them.
[3]For the customs of the peoples are worthless;
 they cut a tree out of the forest,
 and a craftsman shapes it with his chisel.
[4]They adorn it with silver and gold;
 they fasten it with hammer and nails
 so it will not totter.
[5]Like a scarecrow in a melon patch,
 their idols cannot speak;
they must be carried
 because they cannot walk.
Do not fear them;
 they can do no harm
 nor can they do any good."

[6]No one is like you, O LORD;
 you are great,
 and your name is mighty in power.
[7]Who should not revere you,
 O King of the nations?
 This is your due.
Among all the wise men of the nations
 and in all their kingdoms,
 there is no one like you.
[8]They are all senseless and foolish;
 they are taught by worthless wooden idols.
[9]Hammered silver is brought from Tarshish
 and gold from Uphaz.
What the craftsman and goldsmith have
 made
 is then dressed in blue and purple—
 all made by skilled workers.
[10]But the LORD is the true God;
 he is the living God, the eternal King.
When he is angry, the earth trembles;
 the nations cannot endure his wrath.

[11]"Tell them this: 'These gods, who did not
make the heavens and the earth, will perish from
the earth and from under the heavens.'"[a]

[12]But God made the earth by his power;
 he founded the world by his wisdom
 and stretched out the heavens by his
 understanding.
[13]When he thunders, the waters in the heavens
 roar;
 he makes clouds rise from the ends of the
 earth.
He sends lightning with the rain
 and brings out the wind from his
 storehouses.

[14]Everyone is senseless and without knowledge;
 every goldsmith is shamed by his idols.
His images are a fraud;
 they have no breath in them.
[15]They are worthless, the objects of mockery;

when their judgment comes, they will
 perish.
[16]He who is the Portion of Jacob is not like
 these,
 for he is the Maker of all things,
including Israel, the tribe of his
 inheritance—
 the LORD Almighty is his name.

Coming Destruction

[17]Gather up your belongings to leave the land,
 you who live under siege.
[18]For this is what the LORD says:
 "At this time I will hurl out
 those who live in this land;
 I will bring distress on them
 so that they may be captured."

[19]Woe to me because of my injury!
 My wound is incurable!
Yet I said to myself,
 "This is my sickness, and I must endure
 it."
[20]My tent is destroyed;
 all its ropes are snapped.
My sons are gone from me and are no more;
 no one is left now to pitch my tent
 or to set up my shelter.
[21]The shepherds are senseless
 and do not inquire of the LORD;
 so they do not prosper
 and all their flock is scattered.
[22]Listen! The report is coming—
 a great commotion from the land of the
 north!
It will make the towns of Judah desolate,
 a haunt of jackals.

Jeremiah's Prayer

[23]I know, O LORD, that a man's life is not his
 own;
 it is not for man to direct his steps.
[24]Correct me, LORD, but only with justice—
 not in your anger,
 lest you reduce me to nothing.
[25]Pour out your wrath on the nations
 that do not acknowledge you,
 on the peoples who do not call on your
 name.
For they have devoured Jacob;
 they have devoured him completely
 and destroyed his homeland.

The Covenant Is Broken

11 This is the word that came to Jeremiah from
the LORD: [2]"Listen to the terms of this covenant and tell them to the people of Judah and to
those who live in Jerusalem. [3]Tell them that this
is what the LORD, the God of Israel, says: 'Cursed

---

[a]11 The text of this verse is in Aramaic.

is the man who does not obey the terms of this covenant— [4]the terms I commanded your forefathers when I brought them out of Egypt, out of the iron-smelting furnace.' I said, 'Obey me and do everything I command you, and you will be my people, and I will be your God. [5]Then I will fulfill the oath I swore to your forefathers, to give them a land flowing with milk and honey'—the land you possess today."

I answered, "Amen, LORD."

[6]The LORD said to me, "Proclaim all these words in the towns of Judah and in the streets of Jerusalem: 'Listen to the terms of this covenant and follow them. [7]From the time I brought your forefathers up from Egypt until today, I warned them again and again, saying, "Obey me." [8]But they did not listen or pay attention; instead, they followed the stubbornness of their evil hearts. So I brought on them all the curses of the covenant I had commanded them to follow but that they did not keep.'"

11:8 Day of Reckoning

If you sign a note to buy a house, you have to follow through. Miss too many payments, and the bank will evict you. So it was with Israel. Hundreds of years before Jeremiah's time, God had made a "covenant" with them—a treaty binding him to be their God, in exchange for their obedience (see "The Covenant," page 104). This was formally ratified, along with a series of "blessings" and "curses"—good consequences for obedience, bad consequences for disobedience—as recorded in Deuteronomy 28. Now, God announces, because the covenant has been broken, severe punishment must follow.

[9]Then the LORD said to me, "There is a conspiracy among the people of Judah and those who live in Jerusalem. [10]They have returned to the sins of their forefathers, who refused to listen to my words. They have followed other gods to serve them. Both the house of Israel and the house of Judah have broken the covenant I made with their forefathers. [11]Therefore this is what the LORD says: 'I will bring on them a disaster they cannot escape. Although they cry out to me, I will not listen to them. [12]The towns of Judah and the people of Jerusalem will go and cry out to the gods to whom they burn incense, but they will not help them at all when disaster strikes. [13]You have as many gods as you have towns, O Judah; and the altars you have set up to burn incense to that shameful god Baal are as many as the streets of Jerusalem.'

[14]"Do not pray for this people nor offer any

plea or petition for them, because I will not listen when they call to me in the time of their distress.

[15]"What is my beloved doing in my temple
 as she works out her evil schemes with
  many?
Can consecrated meat avert ₍ your
  punishment₎?
When you engage in your wickedness,
 then you rejoice.[a]"

[16]The LORD called you a thriving olive tree
 with fruit beautiful in form.
But with the roar of a mighty storm
 he will set it on fire,
 and its branches will be broken.

[17]The LORD Almighty, who planted you, has decreed disaster for you, because the house of Israel and the house of Judah have done evil and provoked me to anger by burning incense to Baal.

Plot Against Jeremiah

[18]Because the LORD revealed their plot to me, I knew it, for at that time he showed me what they were doing. [19]I had been like a gentle lamb led to the slaughter; I did not realize that they had plotted against me, saying,

"Let us destroy the tree and its fruit;
 let us cut him off from the land of the
  living,
that his name be remembered no more."

[20]But, O LORD Almighty, you who judge
 righteously
 and test the heart and mind,
let me see your vengeance upon them,
 for to you I have committed my cause.

[21]"Therefore this is what the LORD says about the men of Anathoth who are seeking your life and saying, 'Do not prophesy in the name of the LORD or you will die by our hands'— [22]therefore this is what the LORD Almighty says: 'I will punish them. Their young men will die by the sword, their sons and daughters by famine. [23]Not even a remnant will be left to them, because I will bring disaster on the men of Anathoth in the year of their punishment.'"

11:23 Hometown Enemies

Jeremiah's life was endangered several times because of his message. On this occasion, men from his hometown were plotting against him. Though Jeremiah was completely unprepared for their attack, God protected him. Other prophets, however, had been killed (2:30).

---

[a]15 Or *Could consecrated meat avert your punishment? / Then you would rejoice*

Jeremiah's Complaint

12 You are always righteous, O Lord,
when I bring a case before you.
Yet I would speak with you about your
justice:
Why does the way of the wicked prosper?
Why do all the faithless live at ease?
[2]You have planted them, and they have taken
root;
they grow and bear fruit.
You are always on their lips
but far from their hearts.
[3]Yet you know me, O Lord;
you see me and test my thoughts about
you.
Drag them off like sheep to be butchered!
Set them apart for the day of slaughter!
[4]How long will the land lie parched[a]
and the grass in every field be withered?
Because those who live in it are wicked,
the animals and birds have perished.
Moreover, the people are saying,
"He will not see what happens to us."

God's Answer

[5]"If you have raced with men on foot
and they have worn you out,
how can you compete with horses?
If you stumble in safe country,[b]
how will you manage in the thickets by[c]
the Jordan?
[6]Your brothers, your own family—
even they have betrayed you;
they have raised a loud cry against you.
Do not trust them,
though they speak well of you.

[7]"I will forsake my house,
abandon my inheritance;
I will give the one I love
into the hands of her enemies.
[8]My inheritance has become to me
like a lion in the forest.
She roars at me;
therefore I hate her.
[9]Has not my inheritance become to me
like a speckled bird of prey
that other birds of prey surround and
attack?
Go and gather all the wild beasts;
bring them to devour.
[10]Many shepherds will ruin my vineyard
and trample down my field;
they will turn my pleasant field
into a desolate wasteland.
[11]It will be made a wasteland,
parched and desolate before me;
the whole land will be laid waste

because there is no one who cares.
[12]Over all the barren heights in the desert
destroyers will swarm,
for the sword of the Lord will devour
from one end of the land to the other;
no one will be safe.
[13]They will sow wheat but reap thorns;
they will wear themselves out but gain
nothing.
So bear the shame of your harvest
because of the Lord's fierce anger."

[14]This is what the Lord says: "As for all my
wicked neighbors who seize the inheritance I
gave my people Israel, I will uproot them from
their lands and I will uproot the house of Judah
from among them. [15]But after I uproot them, I
will again have compassion and will bring each of
them back to his own inheritance and his own
country. [16]And if they learn well the ways of my
people and swear by my name, saying, 'As surely
as the Lord lives'—even as they once taught my

12:16 Hope for the Gentiles

*Through most of the Old Testament, Israel's
Gentile neighbors seem to have no part in
God's plan. Here, though, God clearly promises
them his salvation.*

people to swear by Baal—then they will be established among my people. [17]But if any nation does
not listen, I will completely uproot and destroy
it," declares the Lord.

A Linen Belt

13 This is what the Lord said to me: "Go and
buy a linen belt and put it around your
waist, but do not let it touch water." [2]So I bought
a belt, as the Lord directed, and put it around my
waist.

[3]Then the word of the Lord came to me a
second time: [4]"Take the belt you bought and are
wearing around your waist, and go now to Perath[d] and hide it there in a crevice in the rocks."
[5]So I went and hid it at Perath, as the Lord
told me.

[6]Many days later the Lord said to me, "Go
now to Perath and get the belt I told you to hide
there." [7]So I went to Perath and dug up the belt
and took it from the place where I had hidden it,
but now it was ruined and completely useless.

[8]Then the word of the Lord came to me:
[9]"This is what the Lord says: 'In the same way I
will ruin the pride of Judah and the great pride of
Jerusalem. [10]These wicked people, who refuse to

---

[a]4 Or *land mourn*   [b]5 Or *If you put your trust in a land of safety*   [c]5 Or *the flooding of*   [d]4 Or possibly *the
Euphrates*; also in verses 5-7

listen to my words, who follow the stubbornness of their hearts and go after other gods to serve and worship them, will be like this belt—completely useless! [11]For as a belt is bound around a man's waist, so I bound the whole house of Israel and the whole house of Judah to me,' declares the LORD, 'to be my people for my renown and praise and honor. But they have not listened.'

Wineskins

[12]"Say to them: 'This is what the LORD, the God of Israel, says: Every wineskin should be filled with wine.' And if they say to you, 'Don't we know that every wineskin should be filled with wine?' [13]then tell them, 'This is what the LORD says: I am going to fill with drunkenness all who live in this land, including the kings who sit on David's throne, the priests, the prophets and all those living in Jerusalem. [14]I will smash them one against the other, fathers and sons alike, declares the LORD. I will allow no pity or mercy or compassion to keep me from destroying them.' "

Threat of Captivity

[15]Hear and pay attention,
  do not be arrogant,
    for the LORD has spoken.
[16]Give glory to the LORD your God
  before he brings the darkness,
before your feet stumble
  on the darkening hills.
You hope for light,
  but he will turn it to thick darkness
  and change it to deep gloom.
[17]But if you do not listen,
  I will weep in secret
  because of your pride;
my eyes will weep bitterly,
  overflowing with tears,
  because the LORD's flock will be taken
    captive.

[18]Say to the king and to the queen mother,
  "Come down from your thrones,
for your glorious crowns
  will fall from your heads."
[19]The cities in the Negev will be shut up,
  and there will be no one to open them.
All Judah will be carried into exile,
  carried completely away.

[20]Lift up your eyes and see
  those who are coming from the north.
Where is the flock that was entrusted to you,
  the sheep of which you boasted?
[21]What will you say when ⌊the LORD⌋ sets over
    you
  those you cultivated as your special allies?
Will not pain grip you

like that of a woman in labor?
[22]And if you ask yourself,
  "Why has this happened to me?"—
it is because of your many sins
  that your skirts have been torn off
  and your body mistreated.
[23]Can the Ethiopian[a] change his skin
  or the leopard its spots?
Neither can you do good
  who are accustomed to doing evil.

[24]"I will scatter you like chaff
  driven by the desert wind.
[25]This is your lot,
  the portion I have decreed for you,"
              declares the LORD,
"because you have forgotten me
  and trusted in false gods.
[26]I will pull up your skirts over your face
  that your shame may be seen—
[27]your adulteries and lustful neighings,
  your shameless prostitution!
I have seen your detestable acts
  on the hills and in the fields.
Woe to you, O Jerusalem!
  How long will you be unclean?"

Drought, Famine, Sword

14 This is the word of the LORD to Jeremiah concerning the drought:

[2]"Judah mourns,
  her cities languish;
they wail for the land,
  and a cry goes up from Jerusalem.
[3]The nobles send their servants for water;
  they go to the cisterns
  but find no water.
They return with their jars unfilled;
  dismayed and despairing,
  they cover their heads.
[4]The ground is cracked
  because there is no rain in the land;
the farmers are dismayed
  and cover their heads.
[5]Even the doe in the field
  deserts her newborn fawn
  because there is no grass.
[6]Wild donkeys stand on the barren heights
  and pant like jackals;
their eyesight fails
  for lack of pasture."

[7]Although our sins testify against us,
  O LORD, do something for the sake of
    your name.
For our backsliding is great;
  we have sinned against you.
[8]O Hope of Israel,
  its Savior in times of distress,

---

[a] 23 Hebrew *Cushite* (probably a person from the upper Nile region)

why are you like a stranger in the land,
like a traveler who stays only a night?
[9]Why are you like a man taken by surprise,
like a warrior powerless to save?
You are among us, O LORD,
and we bear your name;
do not forsake us!

[10]This is what the LORD says about this people:

"They greatly love to wander;
they do not restrain their feet.
So the LORD does not accept them;
he will now remember their wickedness
and punish them for their sins."

[11]Then the LORD said to me, "Do not pray for the well-being of this people. [12]Although they

14:11 God's Patience Exhausted

God gave Jeremiah these dreaded instructions, repeated nowhere else in the Bible: "Do not pray for this people . . . because I will not listen" (11:14). He repeated that message twice (7:16; 14:11). He told Jeremiah, "Even if Moses and Samuel were to stand before me, my heart would not go out to this people. Send them away from my presence!" (15:1).

fast, I will not listen to their cry; though they offer burnt offerings and grain offerings, I will not accept them. Instead, I will destroy them with the sword, famine and plague."

[13]But I said, "Ah, Sovereign LORD, the prophets keep telling them, 'You will not see the sword or suffer famine. Indeed, I will give you lasting peace in this place.'"

[14]Then the LORD said to me, "The prophets are prophesying lies in my name. I have not sent them or appointed them or spoken to them. They are prophesying to you false visions, divinations, idolatries[a] and the delusions of their own minds. [15]Therefore, this is what the LORD says about the prophets who are prophesying in my name: I did not send them, yet they are saying, 'No sword or famine will touch this land.' Those same prophets will perish by sword and famine. [16]And the people they are prophesying to will be thrown out into the streets of Jerusalem because of the famine and sword. There will be no one to bury them or their wives, their sons or their daughters. I will pour out on them the calamity they deserve.

[17]"Speak this word to them:

"'Let my eyes overflow with tears
night and day without ceasing;
for my virgin daughter—my people—

has suffered a grievous wound,
a crushing blow.
[18]If I go into the country,
I see those slain by the sword;
if I go into the city,
I see the ravages of famine.
Both prophet and priest
have gone to a land they know not.'"

[19]Have you rejected Judah completely?
Do you despise Zion?
Why have you afflicted us
so that we cannot be healed?
We hoped for peace
but no good has come,
for a time of healing
but there is only terror.
[20]O LORD, we acknowledge our wickedness
and the guilt of our fathers;
we have indeed sinned against you.
[21]For the sake of your name do not despise us;
do not dishonor your glorious throne.
Remember your covenant with us
and do not break it.
[22]Do any of the worthless idols of the nations
bring rain?
Do the skies themselves send down
showers?
No, it is you, O LORD our God.
Therefore our hope is in you,
for you are the one who does all this.

15 Then the LORD said to me: "Even if Moses and Samuel were to stand before me, my heart would not go out to this people. Send them away from my presence! Let them go! [2]And if they ask you, 'Where shall we go?' tell them, 'This is what the LORD says:

"'Those destined for death, to death;
those for the sword, to the sword;
those for starvation, to starvation;
those for captivity, to captivity.'

[3]"I will send four kinds of destroyers against them," declares the LORD, "the sword to kill and the dogs to drag away and the birds of the air and the beasts of the earth to devour and destroy. [4]I will make them abhorrent to all the kingdoms of the earth because of what Manasseh son of Hezekiah king of Judah did in Jerusalem.

[5]"Who will have pity on you, O Jerusalem?
Who will mourn for you?
Who will stop to ask how you are?
[6]You have rejected me," declares the LORD.
"You keep on backsliding.
So I will lay hands on you and destroy you;
I can no longer show compassion.
[7]I will winnow them with a winnowing fork
at the city gates of the land.

---

[a] 14 Or *visions, worthless divinations*

I will bring bereavement and destruction on
　　my people,
　　for they have not changed their ways.
⁸I will make their widows more numerous
　　than the sand of the sea.
At midday I will bring a destroyer
　　against the mothers of their young men;
suddenly I will bring down on them
　　anguish and terror.
⁹The mother of seven will grow faint
　　and breathe her last.
Her sun will set while it is still day;
　　she will be disgraced and humiliated.
I will put the survivors to the sword
　　before their enemies,"
　　　　　　　　　　　　　declares the LORD.

¹⁰Alas, my mother, that you gave me birth,
　　a man with whom the whole land strives
　　　　and contends!
I have neither lent nor borrowed,
　　yet everyone curses me.

¹¹The LORD said,

"Surely I will deliver you for a good purpose;
　surely I will make your enemies plead
　　　with you
in times of disaster and times of distress.

¹²"Can a man break iron—
　　iron from the north—or bronze?
¹³Your wealth and your treasures
　　I will give as plunder, without charge,
because of all your sins
　　throughout your country.
¹⁴I will enslave you to your enemies
　　inᵃ a land you do not know,
for my anger will kindle a fire
　　that will burn against you."

¹⁵You understand, O LORD;
　　remember me and care for me.
　　Avenge me on my persecutors.
You are long-suffering—do not take me
　　away;
　　think of how I suffer reproach for your
　　　sake.
¹⁶When your words came, I ate them;
　　they were my joy and my heart's delight,
for I bear your name,
　　O LORD God Almighty.
¹⁷I never sat in the company of revelers,
　　never made merry with them;
I sat alone because your hand was on me
　　and you had filled me with indignation.
¹⁸Why is my pain unending
　　and my wound grievous and incurable?
Will you be to me like a deceptive brook,
　　like a spring that fails?

¹⁹Therefore this is what the LORD says:

"If you repent, I will restore you
　　that you may serve me;
if you utter worthy, not worthless, words,
　　you will be my spokesman.
Let this people turn to you,
　　but you must not turn to them.
²⁰I will make you a wall to this people,
　　a fortified wall of bronze;
they will fight against you
　　but will not overcome you,
for I am with you
　　to rescue and save you,"
　　　　　　　　　　　　　declares the LORD.
²¹"I will save you from the hands of the
　　wicked
　　and redeem you from the grasp of the
　　　cruel."

Day of Disaster

16 Then the word of the LORD came to me:
²"You must not marry and have sons or
daughters in this place." ³For this is what the
LORD says about the sons and daughters born in
this land and about the women who are their
mothers and the men who are their fathers:
⁴"They will die of deadly diseases. They will not
be mourned or buried but will be like refuse lying
on the ground. They will perish by sword and
famine, and their dead bodies will become food
for the birds of the air and the beasts of the
earth."

⁵For this is what the LORD says: "Do not enter
a house where there is a funeral meal; do not go
to mourn or show sympathy, because I have
withdrawn my blessing, my love and my pity
from this people," declares the LORD. ⁶"Both high
and low will die in this land. They will not be
buried or mourned, and no one will cut himself
or shave his head for them. ⁷No one will offer
food to comfort those who mourn for the dead—
not even for a father or a mother—nor will anyone give them a drink to console them.

⁸"And do not enter a house where there is
feasting and sit down to eat and drink. ⁹For this
is what the LORD Almighty, the God of Israel,
says: Before your eyes and in your days I will
bring an end to the sounds of joy and gladness
and to the voices of bride and bridegroom in this
place.

¹⁰"When you tell these people all this and they
ask you, 'Why has the LORD decreed such a great
disaster against us? What wrong have we done?
What sin have we committed against the LORD
our God?' ¹¹then say to them, 'It is because your
fathers forsook me,' declares the LORD, 'and followed other gods and served and worshiped

---

ᵃ 14 Some Hebrew manuscripts, Septuagint and Syriac (see also Jer. 17:4); most Hebrew manuscripts *I will cause your
enemies to bring you / into*

them. They forsook me and did not keep my law. [12]But you have behaved more wickedly than your fathers. See how each of you is following the stubbornness of his evil heart instead of obeying

16:8 No Social Life

Jeremiah was a man swallowed up in his work. He had no family and little social life, because God told him never to marry and not to attend weddings, funerals, or any other ceremonial feasts (verses 1–9). God's message through him was so negative that a tale of woe or complaint came to be known as a "jeremiad." Other prophets kept predicting peace (14:13), but Jeremiah couldn't say what people wanted to hear. He told the truth, and the truth was bleak. Nevertheless, Jeremiah experienced the joy and delight of receiving God's word, and bearing God's name (15:16).

me. [13]So I will throw you out of this land into a land neither you nor your fathers have known, and there you will serve other gods day and night, for I will show you no favor.'

[14]"However, the days are coming," declares the LORD, "when men will no longer say, 'As surely as the LORD lives, who brought the Israelites up out of Egypt,' [15]but they will say, 'As surely as the LORD lives, who brought the Israelites up out of the land of the north and out of all the countries where he had banished them.' For I will restore them to the land I gave their forefathers.

[16]"But now I will send for many fishermen," declares the LORD, "and they will catch them. After that I will send for many hunters, and they will hunt them down on every mountain and hill and from the crevices of the rocks. [17]My eyes are on all their ways; they are not hidden from me, nor is their sin concealed from my eyes. [18]I will repay them double for their wickedness and their sin, because they have defiled my land with the lifeless forms of their vile images and have filled my inheritance with their detestable idols."

[19]O LORD, my strength and my fortress,
 my refuge in time of distress,
to you the nations will come
 from the ends of the earth and say,
"Our fathers possessed nothing but false
 gods,
 worthless idols that did them no good.
[20]Do men make their own gods?
 Yes, but they are not gods!"

[21]"Therefore I will teach them—
 this time I will teach them

my power and might.
Then they will know
 that my name is the LORD.

17 "Judah's sin is engraved with an iron
 tool,
 inscribed with a flint point,
on the tablets of their hearts
 and on the horns of their altars.
[2]Even their children remember
 their altars and Asherah poles[a]
beside the spreading trees
 and on the high hills.
[3]My mountain in the land
 and your[b] wealth and all your treasures
I will give away as plunder,
 together with your high places,
 because of sin throughout your country.
[4]Through your own fault you will lose
 the inheritance I gave you.
I will enslave you to your enemies
 in a land you do not know,
for you have kindled my anger,
 and it will burn forever."

[5]This is what the LORD says:

"Cursed is the one who trusts in man,
 who depends on flesh for his strength
 and whose heart turns away from the
 LORD.
[6]He will be like a bush in the wastelands;
 he will not see prosperity when it comes.
He will dwell in the parched places of the
 desert,
 in a salt land where no one lives.

17:6 Whom to Trust?

Buy two identical plants in a nursery. Plant one in a desert, and one by a river. For a few days they'll look alike, but what happens after a few weeks? That's the image Jeremiah uses. The person who trusts in human beings will end up like a shriveled bush (verse 6), while the person who trusts God will be like a tree that has its roots sunk deep beside a stream (verse 8).

[7]"But blessed is the man who trusts in the
 LORD,
 whose confidence is in him.
[8]He will be like a tree planted by the water
 that sends out its roots by the stream.
It does not fear when heat comes;
 its leaves are always green.
It has no worries in a year of drought
 and never fails to bear fruit."

[9]The heart is deceitful above all things

---

[a]2 That is, symbols of the goddess Asherah   [b]2,3 Or hills / [3]and the mountains of the land. / Your

and beyond cure.
Who can understand it?

¹⁰"I the LORD search the heart
and examine the mind,
to reward a man according to his conduct,
according to what his deeds deserve."

¹¹Like a partridge that hatches eggs it did not
lay
is the man who gains riches by unjust
means.
When his life is half gone, they will desert
him,
and in the end he will prove to be a fool.

¹²A glorious throne, exalted from the
beginning,
is the place of our sanctuary.
¹³O LORD, the hope of Israel,
all who forsake you will be put to shame.
Those who turn away from you will be
written in the dust
because they have forsaken the LORD,
the spring of living water.

¹⁴Heal me, O LORD, and I will be healed;
save me and I will be saved,
for you are the one I praise.
¹⁵They keep saying to me,
"Where is the word of the LORD?
Let it now be fulfilled!"
¹⁶I have not run away from being your
shepherd;
you know I have not desired the day of
despair.
What passes my lips is open before you.
¹⁷Do not be a terror to me;
you are my refuge in the day of disaster.
¹⁸Let my persecutors be put to shame,
but keep me from shame;
let them be terrified,
but keep me from terror.
Bring on them the day of disaster;
destroy them with double destruction.

Keeping the Sabbath Holy

¹⁹This is what the LORD said to me: "Go and
stand at the gate of the people, through which the
kings of Judah go in and out; stand also at all the
other gates of Jerusalem. ²⁰Say to them, 'Hear
the word of the LORD, O kings of Judah and all
people of Judah and everyone living in Jerusalem
who come through these gates. ²¹This is what the
LORD says: Be careful not to carry a load on the
Sabbath day or bring it through the gates of Jerusalem. ²²Do not bring a load out of your houses
or do any work on the Sabbath, but keep the
Sabbath day holy, as I commanded your forefathers. ²³Yet they did not listen or pay attention;
they were stiff-necked and would not listen or
respond to discipline. ²⁴But if you are careful to

obey me, declares the LORD, and bring no load
through the gates of this city on the Sabbath, but
keep the Sabbath day holy by not doing any work
on it, ²⁵then kings who sit on David's throne will
come through the gates of this city with their
officials. They and their officials will come riding
in chariots and on horses, accompanied by the
men of Judah and those living in Jerusalem, and
this city will be inhabited forever. ²⁶People will
come from the towns of Judah and the villages
around Jerusalem, from the territory of Benjamin
and the western foothills, from the hill country
and the Negev, bringing burnt offerings and sacrifices, grain offerings, incense and thank offerings to the house of the LORD. ²⁷But if you do not
obey me to keep the Sabbath day holy by not
carrying any load as you come through the gates
of Jerusalem on the Sabbath day, then I will kindle an unquenchable fire in the gates of Jerusalem
that will consume her fortresses.' "

At the Potter's House

18 This is the word that came to Jeremiah
from the LORD: ²"Go down to the potter's
house, and there I will give you my message." ³So
I went down to the potter's house, and I saw him
working at the wheel. ⁴But the pot he was shaping
from the clay was marred in his hands; so the
potter formed it into another pot, shaping it as
seemed best to him.

⁵Then the word of the LORD came to me:
⁶"O house of Israel, can I not do with you as
this potter does?" declares the LORD. "Like clay in
the hand of the potter, so are you in my hand,

18:6 The Potter and the Clay

*God is in control—a message vividly portrayed
to Jeremiah as he watched a potter start over
on a pot that did not take the shape he wanted
it to take. Israelites had gradually come to
think that God, because he had chosen them as
his people, was obliged to protect them. But
their unnatural behavior toward him had
brought God to the point of "starting over." In
Romans 9:21, Paul returned to this metaphor to
answer people who were claiming God was
unjust.*

O house of Israel. ⁷If at any time I announce
that a nation or kingdom is to be uprooted, torn
down and destroyed, ⁸and if that nation I warned
repents of its evil, then I will relent and not inflict on it the disaster I had planned. ⁹And if at another time I announce that a nation or kingdom is to be built up and planted, ¹⁰and if it does
evil in my sight and does not obey me, then I will
reconsider the good I had intended to do for it.

¹¹"Now therefore say to the people of Judah

and those living in Jerusalem, 'This is what the LORD says: Look! I am preparing a disaster for you and devising a plan against you. So turn from your evil ways, each one of you, and reform your ways and your actions.' 12But they will reply, 'It's no use. We will continue with our own plans; each of us will follow the stubbornness of his evil heart.'"

13Therefore this is what the LORD says:

"Inquire among the nations:
    Who has ever heard anything like this?
A most horrible thing has been done
    by Virgin Israel.
14Does the snow of Lebanon
    ever vanish from its rocky slopes?
Do its cool waters from distant sources
    ever cease to flow?[a]
15Yet my people have forgotten me;
    they burn incense to worthless idols,
which made them stumble in their ways
    and in the ancient paths.
They made them walk in bypaths
    and on roads not built up.
16Their land will be laid waste,
    an object of lasting scorn;
all who pass by will be appalled
    and will shake their heads.
17Like a wind from the east,
    I will scatter them before their enemies;
I will show them my back and not my face
    in the day of their disaster."

18They said, "Come, let's make plans against Jeremiah; for the teaching of the law by the priest will not be lost, nor will counsel from the wise, nor the word from the prophets. So come, let's attack him with our tongues and pay no attention to anything he says."

19Listen to me, O LORD;
    hear what my accusers are saying!
20Should good be repaid with evil?
    Yet they have dug a pit for me.
Remember that I stood before you
    and spoke in their behalf
    to turn your wrath away from them.
21So give their children over to famine;
    hand them over to the power of the
        sword.
Let their wives be made childless and
        widows;
    let their men be put to death,
    their young men slain by the sword in
        battle.
22Let a cry be heard from their houses
    when you suddenly bring invaders against
        them,

for they have dug a pit to capture me
    and have hidden snares for my feet.
23But you know, O LORD,
    all their plots to kill me.
Do not forgive their crimes
    or blot out their sins from your sight.
Let them be overthrown before you;
    deal with them in the time of your anger.

19 This is what the LORD says: "Go and buy a clay jar from a potter. Take along some of the elders of the people and of the priests 2and go out to the Valley of Ben Hinnom, near the entrance of the Potsherd Gate. There proclaim the words I tell you, 3and say, 'Hear the word of the LORD, O kings of Judah and people of Jerusalem. This is what the LORD Almighty, the God of Israel, says: Listen! I am going to bring a disaster on this place that will make the ears of everyone who hears of it tingle. 4For they have forsaken me and made this a place of foreign gods; they have burned sacrifices in it to gods that neither they nor their fathers nor the kings of Judah ever knew, and they have filled this place with the blood of the innocent. 5They have built the high places of Baal to burn their sons in the fire as offerings to Baal—something I did not command or mention, nor did it enter my mind. 6So beware, the days are coming, declares the LORD, when people will no longer call this place Topheth or the Valley of Ben Hinnom, but the Valley of Slaughter.

7"'In this place I will ruin[b] the plans of Judah and Jerusalem. I will make them fall by the sword before their enemies, at the hands of those who seek their lives, and I will give their carcasses as food to the birds of the air and the beasts of the earth. 8I will devastate this city and make it an object of scorn; all who pass by will be appalled and will scoff because of all its wounds. 9I will make them eat the flesh of their sons and daughters, and they will eat one another's flesh during the stress of the siege imposed on them by the enemies who seek their lives.'

10"Then break the jar while those who go with you are watching, 11and say to them, 'This is what the LORD Almighty says: I will smash this nation and this city just as this potter's jar is smashed and cannot be repaired. They will bury the dead in Topheth until there is no more room. 12This is what I will do to this place and to those who live here, declares the LORD. I will make this city like Topheth. 13The houses in Jerusalem and those of the kings of Judah will be defiled like this place, Topheth—all the houses where they burned incense on the roofs to all the starry hosts and poured out drink offerings to other gods.'"

---

[a]14 The meaning of the Hebrew for this sentence is uncertain. *jar* (see verses 1 and 10).

[b]7 The Hebrew for *ruin* sounds like the Hebrew for

¹⁴Jeremiah then returned from Topheth, where the LORD had sent him to prophesy, and stood in the court of the LORD's temple and said to all the people, ¹⁵"This is what the LORD Almighty, the God of Israel, says: 'Listen! I am going to bring on this city and the villages around it every disaster I pronounced against them, be-

cause they were stiff-necked and would not listen to my words.'"

Jeremiah and Pashhur

20 When the priest Pashhur son of Immer, the chief officer in the temple of the LORD, heard Jeremiah prophesying these things, ²he

---

Idolatry
It still flourishes, even without statues

> "They have forsaken me and made this a place of foreign gods." 19:4

SUPPOSE YOU FOUND A FRIEND carving a small statue out of a piece of wood. "What are you going to do with that?" you ask. "I'm going to worship it," he says. "I've got a nice spot in my bedroom where I can kneel down and ask it for things."

Or imagine people on a suburban street pooling their wedding rings and other jewelry to make a statue they can put in the park. They plan to kill animals and leave the meat out in front of the statue.

To moderns, idolatry is as weird as cannibalism; we're not tempted to try it. But since a great part of the Old Testament is concerned with idolatry, we need to get some idea of what people saw in it—and why God condemned it.

Mixing Religions

In Jeremiah's day, practically everybody practiced idolatry. Israelites had a hard time seeing that a few statues interfered with their relationship with the one true God. They worshiped the God of Abraham, but mixed in the gods of countries surrounding them. They had idols right in the Jerusalem temple (7:30). They could go to worship God right after burning incense to Baal (7:9–10).

They had built shrines on top of many hills—the "high places"—and under the tallest trees so that worship could be carried out conveniently, without a trip to Jerusalem. They ignored the prophets' warnings that God hated this "mixed" religion.

Judah's neighbors believed in many gods, each having its sphere of influence. The Jews themselves had begun to wonder: Why should their God be so different? Why should he want to knock out all competition? If idols were a fraud, mere carvings (10:4), why should God worry about them?

The Evils Idols Stood For

Idols were far from innocent, however. They stood for vile, angry gods who could hurt you unless you bartered for peace. The highest sacrifice? Slaughter your own son. The Israelites had adopted this practice (19:5).

According to these idol-worshiping religions, success came through the fertile power of nature and the gods. You could tune in to such power by having sex with temple prostitutes, either male or female. The Israelites also borrowed this (2 Kings 23:7). These ideas disgusted the God of Israel. By mixing such practices with their devotion to him, God's people were becoming confused about his true character. (For more on idolatry, see "Why All the Fuss about Idols?" page 417.)

Idolatry Today

The New Testament broadens the definition of idolatry so that it applies to us, even though we worship no statues. Paul said that greed is idolatry (Ephesians 5:5; Colossians 3:5). The things people get greedy for—money, sex, power, even food—can function as little gods. When we feel depressed, we turn to them for comfort. When we're happy, we give them the credit. We gradually become their slaves. But this is exactly the place for God in our lives, and God alone. If something else takes his place, we are as guilty of idolatry as the people Jeremiah spoke to. God cannot share us. He is either the only God, or he is not God at all.

Jealousy is an ugly emotion, but in some situations it is the only appropriate response. A father is jealous of his children; he will fight never to give them up to another family. A husband is jealous of his wife; he will not share her most intimate love with anyone else. So God feels about his people. They belong to him, and to him alone.

Life Questions: Where do you turn when you're troubled? Do money, success, popularity, or other factors serve as substitutes for God?

had Jeremiah the prophet beaten and put in the stocks at the Upper Gate of Benjamin at the LORD's temple. ³The next day, when Pashhur released him from the stocks, Jeremiah said to him, "The LORD's name for you is not Pashhur, but Magor-Missabib.ᵃ ⁴For this is what the LORD says: 'I will make you a terror to yourself and to all your friends; with your own eyes you will see them fall by the sword of their enemies. I will hand all Judah over to the king of Babylon, who will carry them away to Babylon or put them to the sword. ⁵I will hand over to their enemies all the wealth of this city—all its products, all its valuables and all the treasures of the kings of Judah. They will take it away as plunder and carry it off to Babylon. ⁶And you, Pashhur, and all who live in your house will go into exile to Babylon. There you will die and be buried, you and all your friends to whom you have prophesied lies.'"

Jeremiah's Complaint

⁷O LORD, you deceivedᵇ me, and I was
        deceivedᵇ;
    you overpowered me and prevailed.
I am ridiculed all day long;
        everyone mocks me.
⁸Whenever I speak, I cry out
        proclaiming violence and destruction.
So the word of the LORD has brought me
        insult and reproach all day long.
⁹But if I say, "I will not mention him
        or speak any more in his name,"
his word is in my heart like a fire,
        a fire shut up in my bones.
I am weary of holding it in;
        indeed, I cannot.

20:9 Fire in His Bones

When Jeremiah spoke to God, he often complained angrily about the role God had given him. Here he claimed that God "overpowered" him into carrying a message that people ridiculed (verse 7). Jeremiah cursed his own birth, wishing he had been stillborn (verses 14–18). Just how did God "overpower" Jeremiah? God's message was like fire in his bones, so powerful that he could not resist telling it. The "force" God used on Jeremiah was the power of truth.

¹⁰I hear many whispering,
        "Terror on every side!
        Report him! Let's report him!"
All my friends

are waiting for me to slip, saying,
"Perhaps he will be deceived;
        then we will prevail over him
        and take our revenge on him."

¹¹But the LORD is with me like a mighty
        warrior;
    so my persecutors will stumble and not
        prevail.
They will fail and be thoroughly disgraced;
    their dishonor will never be forgotten.
¹²O LORD Almighty, you who examine the
        righteous
    and probe the heart and mind,
let me see your vengeance upon them,
    for to you I have committed my cause.

¹³Sing to the LORD!
    Give praise to the LORD!
He rescues the life of the needy
    from the hands of the wicked.

¹⁴Cursed be the day I was born!
    May the day my mother bore me not be
        blessed!
¹⁵Cursed be the man who brought my father
        the news,
    who made him very glad, saying,
    "A child is born to you—a son!"
¹⁶May that man be like the towns
        the LORD overthrew without pity.
    May he hear wailing in the morning,
        a battle cry at noon.
¹⁷For he did not kill me in the womb,
    with my mother as my grave,
    her womb enlarged forever.
¹⁸Why did I ever come out of the womb
    to see trouble and sorrow
    and to end my days in shame?

God Rejects Zedekiah's Request

21 The word came to Jeremiah from the LORD when King Zedekiah sent to him Pashhur son of Malkijah and the priest Zephaniah son of Maaseiah. They said: ²"Inquire now of the LORD for us because Nebuchadnezzarᶜ king of Babylon is attacking us. Perhaps the LORD will perform wonders for us as in times past so that he will withdraw from us."

³But Jeremiah answered them, "Tell Zedekiah, ⁴'This is what the LORD, the God of Israel, says: I am about to turn against you the weapons of war that are in your hands, which you are using to fight the king of Babylon and the Babyloniansᵈ who are outside the wall besieging you. And I will gather them inside this city. ⁵I myself will fight against you with an outstretched hand and a mighty arm in anger and fury and great wrath. ⁶I will strike down those who live in this city—both

---

ᵃ3 *Magor-Missabib* means *terror on every side.*   ᵇ7 Or *persuaded*
Nebuchadnezzar is a variant; here and often in Jeremiah and Ezekiel   ᶜ2 Hebrew *Nebuchadrezzar*, of which
ᵈ4 Or *Chaldeans*; also in verse 9

men and animals—and they will die of a terrible plague. [7]After that, declares the LORD, I will hand over Zedekiah king of Judah, his officials and the people in this city who survive the plague, sword and famine, to Nebuchadnezzar king of Babylon and to their enemies who seek their lives. He will put them to the sword; he will show them no mercy or pity or compassion.'

21:7 God's Answer: No

Prayer changes things, but the results depend on who's asking and what their motives are. Faced with a crisis, King Zedekiah asked Jeremiah to pray to God on his behalf. He hoped for a miracle, but the answer Jeremiah received was anything but good news. Not only would God not help, he would fight against Zedekiah and his people. Why was God's response so negative? Because nobody had paid attention to his warnings. Judah wanted to be rescued—not to alter its behavior.

[8]"Furthermore, tell the people, 'This is what the LORD says: See, I am setting before you the way of life and the way of death. [9]Whoever stays in this city will die by the sword, famine or plague. But whoever goes out and surrenders to the Babylonians who are besieging you will live; he will escape with his life. [10]I have determined to do this city harm and not good, declares the LORD. It will be given into the hands of the king of Babylon, and he will destroy it with fire.'

[11]"Moreover, say to the royal house of Judah, 'Hear the word of the LORD; [12]O house of David, this is what the LORD says:

" 'Administer justice every morning;
    rescue from the hand of his oppressor
    the one who has been robbed,
or my wrath will break out and burn like fire
    because of the evil you have done—
    burn with no one to quench it.
[13]I am against you, ⌊Jerusalem,⌋
    you who live above this valley
    on the rocky plateau,
                         declares the LORD—
you who say, "Who can come against us?
    Who can enter our refuge?"
[14]I will punish you as your deeds deserve,
                         declares the LORD.
I will kindle a fire in your forests
    that will consume everything around
        you.' "

Judgment Against Evil Kings

22 This is what the LORD says: "Go down to the palace of the king of Judah and pro-

claim this message there: [2]'Hear the word of the LORD, O king of Judah, you who sit on David's throne—you, your officials and your people who come through these gates. [3]This is what the LORD says: Do what is just and right. Rescue from the hand of his oppressor the one who has been robbed. Do no wrong or violence to the alien, the fatherless or the widow, and do not shed innocent blood in this place. [4]For if you are careful to carry out these commands, then kings who sit on David's throne will come through the gates of this palace, riding in chariots and on horses, accompanied by their officials and their people. [5]But if you do not obey these commands, declares the LORD, I swear by myself that this palace will become a ruin.' "

[6]For this is what the LORD says about the palace of the king of Judah:

"Though you are like Gilead to me,
    like the summit of Lebanon,
I will surely make you like a desert,
    like towns not inhabited.
[7]I will send destroyers against you,
    each man with his weapons,
and they will cut up your fine cedar beams
    and throw them into the fire.

[8]"People from many nations will pass by this city and will ask one another, 'Why has the LORD done such a thing to this great city?' [9]And the answer will be: 'Because they have forsaken the covenant of the LORD their God and have worshiped and served other gods.' "

[10]Do not weep for the dead ⌊king⌋ or mourn
        his loss;
    rather, weep bitterly for him who is exiled,
because he will never return
    nor see his native land again.

[11]For this is what the LORD says about Shallum[a] son of Josiah, who succeeded his father as king of Judah but has gone from this place: "He will never return. [12]He will die in the place where they have led him captive; he will not see this land again."

[13]"Woe to him who builds his palace by
        unrighteousness,
    his upper rooms by injustice,
making his countrymen work for nothing,
    not paying them for their labor.
[14]He says, 'I will build myself a great palace
    with spacious upper rooms.'
So he makes large windows in it,
    panels it with cedar
    and decorates it in red.

[15]"Does it make you a king
    to have more and more cedar?

---

a 11 Also called *Jehoahaz*

Did not your father have food and drink?
He did what was right and just,
so all went well with him.
16He defended the cause of the poor and
needy,
and so all went well.
Is that not what it means to know me?"
declares the LORD.
17"But your eyes and your heart
are set only on dishonest gain,
on shedding innocent blood
and on oppression and extortion."

18Therefore this is what the LORD says about Jehoiakim son of Josiah king of Judah:

"They will not mourn for him:
'Alas, my brother! Alas, my sister!'
They will not mourn for him:
'Alas, my master! Alas, his splendor!'
19He will have the burial of a donkey—
dragged away and thrown
outside the gates of Jerusalem."

20"Go up to Lebanon and cry out,
let your voice be heard in Bashan,
cry out from Abarim,
for all your allies are crushed.
21I warned you when you felt secure,
but you said, 'I will not listen!'
This has been your way from your youth;
you have not obeyed me.
22The wind will drive all your shepherds away,
and your allies will go into exile.
Then you will be ashamed and disgraced
because of all your wickedness.
23You who live in 'Lebanon,'a'
who are nestled in cedar buildings,
how you will groan when pangs come upon
you,
pain like that of a woman in labor!

24"As surely as I live," declares the LORD, "even
if you, Jehoiachinb son of Jehoiakim king of
Judah, were a signet ring on my right hand, I
would still pull you off. 25I will hand you over
to those who seek your life, those you fear—to
Nebuchadnezzar king of Babylon and to the Bab-
yloniansc 26I will hurl you and the mother who
gave you birth into another country, where neither of you was born, and there you both will die.
27You will never come back to the land you long
to return to."

28Is this man Jehoiachin a despised, broken
pot,
an object no one wants?
Why will he and his children be hurled out,
cast into a land they do not know?
29O land, land, land,

hear the word of the LORD!
30This is what the LORD says:
"Record this man as if childless,
a man who will not prosper in his
lifetime,
for none of his offspring will prosper,
none will sit on the throne of David
or rule anymore in Judah."

The Righteous Branch

23 "Woe to the shepherds who are destroying
and scattering the sheep of my pasture!"
declares the LORD. 2Therefore this is what the
LORD, the God of Israel, says to the shepherds
who tend my people: "Because you have scattered my flock and driven them away and have
not bestowed care on them, I will bestow punishment on you for the evil you have done," declares
the LORD. 3"I myself will gather the remnant of
my flock out of all the countries where I have
driven them and will bring them back to their
pasture, where they will be fruitful and increase
in number. 4I will place shepherds over them
who will tend them, and they will no longer be
afraid or terrified, nor will any be missing," declares the LORD.

5"The days are coming," declares the LORD,
"when I will raise up to Davidd a
righteous Branch,
a King who will reign wisely
and do what is just and right in the land.
6In his days Judah will be saved
and Israel will live in safety.
This is the name by which he will be called:
The LORD Our Righteousness.

23:6 The Messianic Promise

*Long before, God had promised David that his
descendants would always rule Israel. But the
kings who followed David had been more like
wolves than shepherds of God's people.
Jeremiah predicted that the kings of his day
would either be killed or carried into captivity—
which in fact occurred. He also predicted that a
good king would replace them—the Messiah.*

7"So then, the days are coming," declares the
LORD, "when people will no longer say, 'As surely
as the LORD lives, who brought the Israelites up
out of Egypt,' 8but they will say, 'As surely as the
LORD lives, who brought the descendants of Israel
up out of the land of the north and out of all the
countries where he had banished them.' Then
they will live in their own land."

---

a23 That is, the palace in Jerusalem (see 1 Kings 7:2)   b24 Hebrew Coniah, a variant of Jehoiachin; also in verse 28
c25 Or Chaldeans   d5 Or up from David's line

Lying Prophets

[9]Concerning the prophets:

My heart is broken within me;
  all my bones tremble.
I am like a drunken man,
  like a man overcome by wine,
because of the LORD
  and his holy words.
[10]The land is full of adulterers;
  because of the curse[a] the land lies
    parched[b]
  and the pastures in the desert are
    withered.
The ʟprophets₌ follow an evil course
  and use their power unjustly.

[11]"Both prophet and priest are godless;
  even in my temple I find their
    wickedness,"
                    declares the LORD.
[12]"Therefore their path will become slippery;
  they will be banished to darkness
  and there they will fall.
I will bring disaster on them
  in the year they are punished,"
                    declares the LORD.

[13]"Among the prophets of Samaria
  I saw this repulsive thing:
They prophesied by Baal
  and led my people Israel astray.
[14]And among the prophets of Jerusalem
  I have seen something horrible:
They commit adultery and live a lie.
They strengthen the hands of evildoers,
  so that no one turns from his wickedness.
They are all like Sodom to me;
  the people of Jerusalem are like
    Gomorrah."

[15]Therefore, this is what the LORD Almighty
says concerning the prophets:

"I will make them eat bitter food
  and drink poisoned water,
because from the prophets of Jerusalem
  ungodliness has spread throughout the
    land."

[16]This is what the LORD Almighty says:

"Do not listen to what the prophets are
    prophesying to you;
  they fill you with false hopes.
They speak visions from their own minds,
  not from the mouth of the LORD.
[17]They keep saying to those who despise me,
  'The LORD says: You will have peace.'
And to all who follow the stubbornness of
    their hearts

they say, 'No harm will come to you.'
[18]But which of them has stood in the council
    of the LORD
  to see or to hear his word?
  Who has listened and heard his word?
[19]See, the storm of the LORD
  will burst out in wrath,
a whirlwind swirling down
  on the heads of the wicked.
[20]The anger of the LORD will not turn back
  until he fully accomplishes
  the purposes of his heart.
In days to come
  you will understand it clearly.
[21]I did not send these prophets,
  yet they have run with their message;
I did not speak to them,
  yet they have prophesied.
[22]But if they had stood in my council,
  they would have proclaimed my words to
    my people
and would have turned them from their evil
    ways
  and from their evil deeds.

[23]"Am I only a God nearby,"
                    declares the LORD,
  "and not a God far away?
[24]Can anyone hide in secret places
  so that I cannot see him?"
                    declares the LORD.
  "Do not I fill heaven and earth?"
                    declares the LORD.

[25]"I have heard what the prophets say who
prophesy lies in my name. They say, 'I had a

23:25 Questionable Dreams

*For the casual observer, it must have been
difficult to tell real prophets from false prophets
in Jeremiah's day. Jeremiah was outnumbered
by optimists who claimed God gave them
dreams and messages. In reality, their dreams
had nothing to do with God's word, and
anyone who compared their message with
Scripture could have seen the difference. They
predicted peace when God had promised severe
punishment for his people's sins.*

dream! I had a dream!' [26]How long will this continue in the hearts of these lying prophets, who
prophesy the delusions of their own minds?
[27]They think the dreams they tell one another will
make my people forget my name, just as their
fathers forgot my name through Baal worship.
[28]Let the prophet who has a dream tell his dream,
but let the one who has my word speak it faithful-

---

[a]10 Or *because of these things*   [b]10 Or *land mourns*

ly. For what has straw to do with grain?" declares the LORD. [29]"Is not my word like fire," declares the LORD, "and like a hammer that breaks a rock in pieces?

[30]"Therefore," declares the LORD, "I am against the prophets who steal from one another words supposedly from me. [31]Yes," declares the LORD, "I am against the prophets who wag their own tongues and yet declare, 'The LORD declares.' [32]Indeed, I am against those who prophesy false dreams," declares the LORD. "They tell them and lead my people astray with their reckless lies, yet I did not send or appoint them. They do not benefit these people in the least," declares the LORD.

False Oracles and False Prophets

[33]"When these people, or a prophet or a priest, ask you, 'What is the oracle[a] of the LORD?' say to them, 'What oracle?[b] I will forsake you, declares the LORD.' [34]If a prophet or a priest or anyone else claims, 'This is the oracle of the LORD,' I will punish that man and his household. [35]This is what each of you keeps on saying to his friend or relative: 'What is the LORD's answer?' or 'What has the LORD spoken?' [36]But you must not mention 'the oracle of the LORD' again, because every man's own word becomes his oracle and so you distort the words of the living God, the LORD Almighty, our God. [37]This is what you keep saying to a prophet: 'What is the LORD's answer to you?' or 'What has the LORD spoken?' [38]Although you claim, 'This is the oracle of the LORD,' this is what the LORD says: You used the words, 'This is the oracle of the LORD,' even though I told you that you must not claim, 'This is the oracle of the LORD.' [39]Therefore, I will surely forget you and cast you out of my presence along with the city I gave to you and your fathers. [40]I will bring upon you everlasting disgrace—everlasting shame that will not be forgotten."

Two Baskets of Figs

24 After Jehoiachin[c] son of Jehoiakim king of Judah and the officials, the craftsmen and the artisans of Judah were carried into exile from Jerusalem to Babylon by Nebuchadnezzar king of Babylon, the LORD showed me two baskets of figs placed in front of the temple of the LORD. [2]One basket had very good figs, like those that ripen early; the other basket had very poor figs, so bad they could not be eaten. [3]Then the LORD asked me, "What do you see, Jeremiah?"

"Figs," I answered. "The good ones are very good, but the poor ones are so bad they cannot be eaten."

[4]Then the word of the LORD came to me: [5]"This is what the LORD, the God of Israel, says: 'Like these good figs, I regard as good the exiles from Judah, whom I sent away from this place to the land of the Babylonians.[d] [6]My eyes will watch over them for their good, and I will bring them back to this land. I will build them up and not tear them down; I will plant them and not uproot them. [7]I will give them a heart to know me, that I am the LORD. They will be my people, and I will be their God, for they will return to me with all their heart.

[8]"'But like the poor figs, which are so bad they cannot be eaten,' says the LORD, 'so will I deal with Zedekiah king of Judah, his officials and the survivors from Jerusalem, whether they remain in this land or live in Egypt. [9]I will make them abhorrent and an offense to all the kingdoms of the earth, a reproach and a byword, an object of ridicule and cursing, wherever I banish them. [10]I will send the sword, famine and plague against them until they are destroyed from the land I gave to them and their fathers.'"

Seventy Years of Captivity

25 The word came to Jeremiah concerning all the people of Judah in the fourth year of Jehoiakim son of Josiah king of Judah, which was the first year of Nebuchadnezzar king of Babylon. [2]So Jeremiah the prophet said to all the people of Judah and to all those living in Jerusalem: [3]For twenty-three years—from the thirteenth year of Josiah son of Amon king of Judah until this very day—the word of the LORD has come to me and I have spoken to you again and again, but you have not listened.

[4]And though the LORD has sent all his servants the prophets to you again and again, you have not listened or paid any attention. [5]They said, "Turn now, each of you, from your evil ways and your evil practices, and you can stay in the land the LORD gave to you and your fathers for ever and ever. [6]Do not follow other gods to serve and worship them; do not provoke me to anger with what your hands have made. Then I will not harm you."

[7]"But you did not listen to me," declares the LORD, "and you have provoked me with what your hands have made, and you have brought harm to yourselves."

[8]Therefore the LORD Almighty says this: "Because you have not listened to my words, [9]I will summon all the peoples of the north and my servant Nebuchadnezzar king of Babylon," declares the LORD, "and I will bring them against this land and its inhabitants and against all the surrounding nations. I will completely destroy[e]

---

[a]33 Or burden (see Septuagint and Vulgate)   [b]33 Hebrew; Septuagint and Vulgate 'You are the burden. (The Hebrew for oracle and burden is the same.)   [c]1 Hebrew Jeconiah, a variant of Jehoiachin   [d]5 Or Chaldeans   [e]9 The Hebrew term refers to the irrevocable giving over of things or persons to the LORD, often by totally destroying them.

them and make them an object of horror and scorn, and an everlasting ruin. ¹⁰I will banish from them the sounds of joy and gladness, the voices of bride and bridegroom, the sound of millstones and the light of the lamp. ¹¹This whole country will become a desolate wasteland, and these nations will serve the king of Babylon seventy years.

25:11–12 Gone, But Not Forever

Seventy years of captivity, God predicted. This probably represents a rounded-off number; the precise length of the captivity can be calculated in different ways, since several waves of captives were taken away and several waves of exiles returned. The number 70 has a deeper significance, though: It says that the punishment, though long and severe (at least two generations would die far from home), will not last forever. Unlike other nations taken into captivity, Israel will return. God's judgment is limited, but his mercy is forever.

¹²"But when the seventy years are fulfilled, I will punish the king of Babylon and his nation, the land of the Babylonians,ᵃ for their guilt," declares the LORD, "and will make it desolate forever. ¹³I will bring upon that land all the things I have spoken against it, all that are written in this book and prophesied by Jeremiah against all the nations. ¹⁴They themselves will be enslaved by many nations and great kings; I will repay them according to their deeds and the work of their hands."

The Cup of God's Wrath

¹⁵This is what the LORD, the God of Israel, said to me: "Take from my hand this cup filled with the wine of my wrath and make all the nations to whom I send you drink it. ¹⁶When they drink it, they will stagger and go mad because of the sword I will send among them."

¹⁷So I took the cup from the LORD's hand and made all the nations to whom he sent me drink it: ¹⁸Jerusalem and the towns of Judah, its kings and officials, to make them a ruin and an object of horror and scorn and cursing, as they are today; ¹⁹Pharaoh king of Egypt, his attendants, his officials and all his people, ²⁰and all the foreign people there; all the kings of Uz; all the kings of the Philistines (those of Ashkelon, Gaza, Ekron, and the people left at Ashdod); ²¹Edom, Moab and Ammon; ²²all the kings of Tyre and Sidon; the kings of the coastlands across the sea; ²³Dedan, Tema, Buz and all who are in distant placesᵇ; ²⁴all the kings of Arabia and all the

kings of the foreign people who live in the desert; ²⁵all the kings of Zimri, Elam and Media; ²⁶and all the kings of the north, near and far, one after the other—all the kingdoms on the face of the earth. And after all of them, the king of Sheshachᶜ will drink it too.

²⁷"Then tell them, 'This is what the LORD Almighty, the God of Israel, says: Drink, get drunk and vomit, and fall to rise no more because of the sword I will send among you.' ²⁸But if they refuse to take the cup from your hand and drink, tell them, 'This is what the LORD Almighty says: You must drink it! ²⁹See, I am beginning to bring disaster on the city that bears my Name, and will you indeed go unpunished? You will not go unpunished, for I am calling down a sword upon all who live on the earth, declares the LORD Almighty.'

³⁰"Now prophesy all these words against them and say to them:

"'The LORD will roar from on high;
    he will thunder from his holy dwelling
    and roar mightily against his land.
He will shout like those who tread the grapes,
    shout against all who live on the earth.
³¹The tumult will resound to the ends of the earth,
    for the LORD will bring charges against the nations;
he will bring judgment on all mankind
    and put the wicked to the sword,'"
                        declares the LORD.

³²This is what the LORD Almighty says:

"Look! Disaster is spreading
    from nation to nation;
a mighty storm is rising
    from the ends of the earth."

³³At that time those slain by the LORD will be everywhere—from one end of the earth to the other. They will not be mourned or gathered up or buried, but will be like refuse lying on the ground.

³⁴Weep and wail, you shepherds;
    roll in the dust, you leaders of the flock.
For your time to be slaughtered has come;
    you will fall and be shattered like fine pottery.
³⁵The shepherds will have nowhere to flee,
    the leaders of the flock no place to escape.
³⁶Hear the cry of the shepherds,
    the wailing of the leaders of the flock,
    for the LORD is destroying their pasture.
³⁷The peaceful meadows will be laid waste
    because of the fierce anger of the LORD.
³⁸Like a lion he will leave his lair,

ᵃ12 Or *Chaldeans*   ᵇ23 Or *who clip the hair by their foreheads*   ᶜ26 *Sheshach* is a cryptogram for Babylon.

and their land will become desolate
because of the sword[a] of the oppressor
and because of the LORD's fierce anger.

Jeremiah Threatened With Death

26 Early in the reign of Jehoiakim son of Josiah king of Judah, this word came from the LORD: 2"This is what the LORD says: Stand in the courtyard of the LORD's house and speak to all the people of the towns of Judah who come to worship in the house of the LORD. Tell them everything I command you; do not omit a word. 3Perhaps they will listen and each will turn from his evil way. Then I will relent and not bring on them the disaster I was planning because of the evil they have done. 4Say to them, 'This is what the LORD says: If you do not listen to me and follow my law, which I have set before you, 5and if you do not listen to the words of my servants the prophets, whom I have sent to you again and again (though you have not listened), 6then I will make this house like Shiloh and this city an object of cursing among all the nations of the earth.'"

7The priests, the prophets and all the people heard Jeremiah speak these words in the house of the LORD. 8But as soon as Jeremiah finished telling all the people everything the LORD had commanded him to say, the priests, the prophets and all the people seized him and said, "You must die! 9Why do you prophesy in the LORD's name that this house will be like Shiloh and this city will be desolate and deserted?" And all the people crowded around Jeremiah in the house of the LORD.

10When the officials of Judah heard about these things, they went up from the royal palace to the house of the LORD and took their places at the entrance of the New Gate of the LORD's house. 11Then the priests and the prophets said to the officials and all the people, "This man should be sentenced to death because he has prophesied against this city. You have heard it with your own ears!"

12Then Jeremiah said to all the officials and all the people: "The LORD sent me to prophesy against this house and this city all the things you have heard. 13Now reform your ways and your actions and obey the LORD your God. Then the LORD will relent and not bring the disaster he has pronounced against you. 14As for me, I am in your hands; do with me whatever you think is good and right. 15Be assured, however, that if you put me to death, you will bring the guilt of innocent blood on yourselves and on this city and on those who live in it, for in truth the LORD has sent

me to you to speak all these words in your hearing."

16Then the officials and all the people said to the priests and the prophets, "This man should not be sentenced to death! He has spoken to us in the name of the LORD our God."

17Some of the elders of the land stepped forward and said to the entire assembly of people, 18"Micah of Moresheth prophesied in the days of Hezekiah king of Judah. He told all the people of Judah, 'This is what the LORD Almighty says:

" 'Zion will be plowed like a field,
Jerusalem will become a heap of rubble,
the temple hill a mound overgrown with
thickets.'[b]

19"Did Hezekiah king of Judah or anyone else in Judah put him to death? Did not Hezekiah fear the LORD and seek his favor? And did not the LORD relent, so that he did not bring the disaster he pronounced against them? We are about to bring a terrible disaster on ourselves!"

26:19 Scripture Saves a Life

Jeremiah's scorn for the temple was considered sacrilege and might have cost him his life. (Another prophet, Uriah, was assassinated for the same message—see verses 20–23.) But some of the elders remembered the treatment given Micah years before. Hezekiah—a good king—had listened to Micah. Based on this precedent, Jeremiah was allowed to live.

20(Now Uriah son of Shemaiah from Kiriath Jearim was another man who prophesied in the name of the LORD; he prophesied the same things against this city and this land as Jeremiah did. 21When King Jehoiakim and all his officers and officials heard his words, the king sought to put him to death. But Uriah heard of it and fled in fear to Egypt. 22King Jehoiakim, however, sent Elnathan son of Acbor to Egypt, along with some other men. 23They brought Uriah out of Egypt and took him to King Jehoiakim, who had him struck down with a sword and his body thrown into the burial place of the common people.)

24Furthermore, Ahikam son of Shaphan supported Jeremiah, and so he was not handed over to the people to be put to death.

Judah to Serve Nebuchadnezzar

27 Early in the reign of Zedekiah[c] son of Josiah king of Judah, this word came to Jeremiah from the LORD: 2This is what the LORD

---

[a]38 Some Hebrew manuscripts and Septuagint (see also Jer. 46:16 and 50:16); most Hebrew manuscripts *anger*   [b]18 Micah 3:12   [c]1 A few Hebrew manuscripts and Syriac (see also Jer. 27:3, 12 and 28:1); most Hebrew manuscripts *Jehoiakim* (Most Septuagint manuscripts do not have this verse.)

said to me: "Make a yoke out of straps and crossbars and put it on your neck. [3]Then send word to the kings of Edom, Moab, Ammon, Tyre and Sidon through the envoys who have come to Jerusalem to Zedekiah king of Judah. [4]Give them a message for their masters and say, 'This is what the LORD Almighty, the God of Israel, says: "Tell this to your masters: [5]With my great power and outstretched arm I made the earth and its people and the animals that are on it, and I give it to anyone I please. [6]Now I will hand all your countries over to my servant Nebuchadnezzar king of Babylon; I will make even the wild animals subject to him. [7]All nations will serve him and his son and his grandson until the time for his land comes; then many nations and great kings will subjugate him.

[8]" 'If, however, any nation or kingdom will not serve Nebuchadnezzar king of Babylon or bow its neck under his yoke, I will punish that nation with the sword, famine and plague, declares the LORD, until I destroy it by his hand. [9]So do not listen to your prophets, your diviners, your interpreters of dreams, your mediums or your sorcerers who tell you, 'You will not serve the king of Babylon.' [10]They prophesy lies to you that will only serve to remove you far from your lands; I will banish you and you will perish. [11]But if any nation will bow its neck under the yoke of the king of Babylon and serve him, I will let that nation remain in its own land to till it and to live there, declares the LORD.' "'

[12]I gave the same message to Zedekiah king of Judah. I said, "Bow your neck under the yoke of the king of Babylon; serve him and his people,

---

27:12 Counseling Surrender

By the time Zedekiah took office, Israel had twice surrendered to Babylon. Two groups of Israelites had already been exiled, including in their number King Jehoiachin. The desire for independence did not die easily, however. Zedekiah, who had been put into office as a puppet king, soon began scheming for revolution. Jeremiah persistently counseled submission to Babylon—unpopular advice that nearly cost him his life when he was accused of treason.

---

and you will live. [13]Why will you and your people die by the sword, famine and plague with which the LORD has threatened any nation that will not serve the king of Babylon? [14]Do not listen to the words of the prophets who say to you, 'You will not serve the king of Babylon,' for they are prophesying lies to you. [15]'I have not sent them,'

declares the LORD. 'They are prophesying lies in my name. Therefore, I will banish you and you will perish, both you and the prophets who prophesy to you.' "

[16]Then I said to the priests and all these people, "This is what the LORD says: Do not listen to the prophets who say, 'Very soon now the articles from the LORD's house will be brought back from Babylon.' They are prophesying lies to you. [17]Do not listen to them. Serve the king of Babylon, and you will live. Why should this city become a ruin? [18]If they are prophets and have the word of the LORD, let them plead with the LORD Almighty that the furnishings remaining in the house of the LORD and in the palace of the king of Judah and in Jerusalem not be taken to Babylon. [19]For this is what the LORD Almighty says about the pillars, the Sea, the movable stands and the other furnishings that are left in this city, [20]which Nebuchadnezzar king of Babylon did not take away when he carried Jehoiachin[a] son of Jehoiakim king of Judah into exile from Jerusalem to Babylon, along with all the nobles of Judah and Jerusalem— [21]yes, this is what the LORD Almighty, the God of Israel, says about the things that are left in the house of the LORD and in the palace of the king of Judah and in Jerusalem: [22]They will be taken to Babylon and there they will remain until the day I come for them,' declares the LORD. 'Then I will bring them back and restore them to this place.' "

The False Prophet Hananiah

28 In the fifth month of that same year, the fourth year, early in the reign of Zedekiah king of Judah, the prophet Hananiah son of Azzur, who was from Gibeon, said to me in the house of the LORD in the presence of the priests and all the people: [2]"This is what the LORD Almighty, the God of Israel, says: 'I will break the yoke of the king of Babylon. [3]Within two years I will bring back to this place all the articles of the LORD's house that Nebuchadnezzar king of Babylon removed from here and took to Babylon. [4]I will also bring back to this place Jehoiachin[a] son of Jehoiakim king of Judah and all the other exiles from Judah who went to Babylon,' declares the LORD, 'for I will break the yoke of the king of Babylon.' "

[5]Then the prophet Jeremiah replied to the prophet Hananiah before the priests and all the people who were standing in the house of the LORD. [6]He said, "Amen! May the LORD do so! May the LORD fulfill the words you have prophesied by bringing the articles of the LORD's house and all the exiles back to this place from Babylon. [7]Nevertheless, listen to what I have to say in your hearing and in the hearing of all the people:

---

[a]20,4 Hebrew *Jeconiah*, a variant of *Jehoiachin*

[8]From early times the prophets who preceded you and me have prophesied war, disaster and plague against many countries and great kingdoms. [9]But the prophet who prophesies peace will be recognized as one truly sent by the LORD only if his prediction comes true."

[10]Then the prophet Hananiah took the yoke off the neck of the prophet Jeremiah and broke it, [11]and he said before all the people, "This is what the LORD says: 'In the same way will I break the yoke of Nebuchadnezzar king of Babylon off the neck of all the nations within two years.'" At this, the prophet Jeremiah went on his way.

[12]Shortly after the prophet Hananiah had broken the yoke off the neck of the prophet Jeremiah, the word of the LORD came to Jeremiah: [13]"Go and tell Hananiah, 'This is what the LORD says: You have broken a wooden yoke, but in its place you will get a yoke of iron. [14]This is what the LORD Almighty, the God of Israel, says: I will put an iron yoke on the necks of all these nations to make them serve Nebuchadnezzar king of Babylon, and they will serve him. I will even give him control over the wild animals.'"

[15]Then the prophet Jeremiah said to Hananiah the prophet, "Listen, Hananiah! The LORD has not sent you, yet you have persuaded this nation to trust in lies. [16]Therefore, this is what the LORD says: 'I am about to remove you from the face of the earth. This very year you are going to die, because you have preached rebellion against the LORD.'"

[17]In the seventh month of that same year, Hananiah the prophet died.

A Letter to the Exiles

29 This is the text of the letter that the prophet Jeremiah sent from Jerusalem to the surviving elders among the exiles and to the priests, the prophets and all the other people Nebuchadnezzar had carried into exile from Jerusalem to Babylon. [2](This was after King Jehoiachin[a] and the queen mother, the court officials and the leaders of Judah and Jerusalem, the craftsmen and the artisans had gone into exile from Jerusalem.) [3]He entrusted the letter to Elasah son of Shaphan and to Gemariah son of Hilkiah, whom Zedekiah king of Judah sent to King Nebuchadnezzar in Babylon. It said:

[4]This is what the LORD Almighty, the God of Israel, says to all those I carried into exile from Jerusalem to Babylon: [5]"Build houses and settle down; plant gardens and eat what they produce. [6]Marry and have sons and daughters; find wives for your sons and give your daughters in marriage, so that they too may have sons and daughters. Increase in number there; do not decrease. [7]Also, seek the peace and prosperity of the city to which I have carried you into exile. Pray to the LORD for it, because if it prospers, you too will prosper." [8]Yes, this is

29:5 Writing to Ezekiel

During the last years of Jeremiah's work, a sizable community of exiles were already living in Babylon. Among them were Daniel, a young man who would rise to tremendous power in court, and the prophet Ezekiel. Ezekiel was preaching at the same time as Jeremiah, and their messages are similar in many ways. Since neither one mentions the other, however, we can't be sure whether they were acquainted.

what the LORD Almighty, the God of Israel, says: "Do not let the prophets and diviners among you deceive you. Do not listen to the dreams you encourage them to have. [9]They are prophesying lies to you in my name. I have not sent them," declares the LORD.

[10]This is what the LORD says: "When seventy years are completed for Babylon, I will come to you and fulfill my gracious promise to bring you back to this place. [11]For I know the plans I have for you," declares the LORD, "plans to prosper you and not to harm you, plans to give you hope and a future. [12]Then you will call upon me and come and pray to me, and I will listen to you. [13]You will seek me and find me when you seek me with all your heart. [14]I will be found by you," declares the LORD, "and will bring you back from captivity.[b] I will gather you from all the nations and places where I have banished you," declares the LORD, "and will bring you back to the place from which I carried you into exile."

[15]You may say, "The LORD has raised up prophets for us in Babylon," [16]but this is what the LORD says about the king who sits on David's throne and all the people who remain in this city, your countrymen who did not go with you into exile— [17]yes, this is what the LORD Almighty says: "I will send the sword, famine and plague against them and I will make them like poor figs that are so bad they cannot be eaten. [18]I will pursue them with the sword, famine and plague and will make them abhorrent to all the kingdoms of the earth and an object of cursing and horror, of scorn and reproach, among all the nations where I drive them. [19]For they have not listened to my words,"

---

a 2 Hebrew Jeconiah, a variant of Jehoiachin   *b 14 Or will restore your fortunes*

JEREMIAH 29:20

declares the LORD, "words that I sent to them again and again by my servants the prophets. And you exiles have not listened either," declares the LORD.

²⁰Therefore, hear the word of the LORD, all you exiles whom I have sent away from Jerusalem to Babylon. ²¹This is what the LORD Almighty, the God of Israel, says about Ahab son of Kolaiah and Zedekiah son of Maaseiah, who are prophesying lies to you in my name: "I will hand them over to Nebuchadnezzar king of Babylon, and he will put them to death before your very eyes. ²²Because of them, all the exiles from Judah who are in Babylon will use this curse: 'The LORD treat you like Zedekiah and Ahab, whom the king of Babylon burned in the fire.' ²³For they have done outrageous things in Israel; they have committed adultery with their neighbors' wives and in my name have spoken lies, which I did not tell them to do. I know it and am a witness to it," declares the LORD.

Message to Shemaiah

²⁴Tell Shemaiah the Nehelamite, ²⁵"This is what the LORD Almighty, the God of Israel, says: You sent letters in your own name to all the people in Jerusalem, to Zephaniah son of Maaseiah the priest, and to all the other priests. You said to Zephaniah, ²⁶'The LORD has appointed you priest in place of Jehoiada to be in charge of the house of the LORD; you should put any madman who acts like a prophet into the stocks and neck-irons. ²⁷So why have you not reprimanded Jeremiah from Anathoth, who poses as a prophet among you? ²⁸He has sent this message to us in Babylon: It will be a long time. Therefore build houses and settle down; plant gardens and eat what they produce.'"

²⁹Zephaniah the priest, however, read the letter to Jeremiah the prophet. ³⁰Then the word of the LORD came to Jeremiah: ³¹"Send this message to all the exiles: 'This is what the LORD says about Shemaiah the Nehelamite: Because Shemaiah has prophesied to you, even though I did not send him, and has led you to believe a lie, ³²this is what the LORD says: I will surely punish Shemaiah the Nehelamite and his descendants. He will have no one left among this people, nor will he see the good things I will do for my people, declares the LORD, because he has preached rebellion against me.'"

Restoration of Israel

30 This is the word that came to Jeremiah from the LORD: ²"This is what the LORD, the God of Israel, says: 'Write in a book all the words I have spoken to you. ³The days are coming,' declares the LORD, 'when I will bring my people Israel and Judah back from captivity^a and restore them to the land I gave their forefathers to possess,' says the LORD."

⁴These are the words the LORD spoke concerning Israel and Judah: ⁵"This is what the LORD says:

"'Cries of fear are heard—
    terror, not peace.
⁶Ask and see:
    Can a man bear children?
Then why do I see every strong man
    with his hands on his stomach like a
        woman in labor,
    every face turned deathly pale?
⁷How awful that day will be!
    None will be like it.
It will be a time of trouble for Jacob,
    but he will be saved out of it.

⁸"'In that day,' declares the LORD Almighty,
    'I will break the yoke off their necks
and will tear off their bonds;
    no longer will foreigners enslave them.
⁹Instead, they will serve the LORD their God
    and David their king,
    whom I will raise up for them.

¹⁰"'So do not fear, O Jacob my servant;
    do not be dismayed, O Israel,'
                        declares the LORD.
'I will surely save you out of a distant place,
    your descendants from the land of their
        exile.
Jacob will again have peace and security,
    and no one will make him afraid.
¹¹I am with you and will save you,'
    declares the LORD.
'Though I completely destroy all the nations
    among which I scatter you,
    I will not completely destroy you.
I will discipline you but only with justice;
    I will not let you go entirely unpunished.'

¹²"This is what the LORD says:

30:11 Free Again

Though Jeremiah mainly spoke of God's judgment, he also offered hope beyond judgment. Someday, Israel would be free again. The prophecy of this verse has been fulfilled: not one of the powerful cultures surrounding Israel has endured, but the Jews have survived with their language, customs, and religion intact.

^a3 Or will restore the fortunes of my people Israel and Judah

The People Who Refuse to Die

Their powerful neighbors have disappeared—but the Jews live on

IF YOU GET LOST IN Brooklyn, New York, and wander into the section called Williamsburg, prepare to do a double take. Boys playing baseball look odd: long, uncut curls of hair trail from above their ears down to their chests. Men in black, with long, untrimmed beards, coach from the sidelines. All the women you see wear wigs because they've shaved their heads completely. Is this a new cult from California? The latest punk fashion from London?

You've stumbled into a community of Hasidic Jews. They live, not by the latest fad, but by ancient rules based on Old Testament laws. They follow complicated dietary regulations. They keep one set of bowls for meat, and another for dairy products. Young men devote long hours of study to the Hebrew Old Testament. Though they are Americans living in New York, their cultural compass points to Mount Sinai, where God gave Moses the Law.

> "'I will surely save you out of a distant place, your descendants from the land of their exile. Jacob will again have peace and security, and no one will make him afraid.'"
> 30:10

Jews Outlived Their Enemies

The Jewish people have survived, astonishingly. Who in Jeremiah's time could have predicted their persistence, when they were hemmed in and threatened with total destruction? The Babylonians conquered and carried them into exile. But where are the Babylonians today? They have vanished. Desert sand covers their capital.

The story of the Jews is a long chronicle of discrimination, exile, punishment, and slaughter. Against no other people have such destructive measures been taken. Yet they have survived, and thrived. Their language endures. Their book, the Old Testament, is part of the great best seller of all time. They have rebuilt their nation.

Even more remarkably, this durability was predicted in writing 2,500 years ago. God promised in the clearest terms that he would never reject his people.

The New Covenant

Jeremiah, known for his stinging denunciations and repeated predictions of savage destruction, also brought word of God's eternal faithfulness and of a new covenant replacing the old, broken one. The new covenant would improve generously on the old one, Jeremiah said. God would no longer simply list rules for his people to obey. He would plant those rules in their hearts, so they would want to obey (31:33). Each individual would know the Lord personally. God would offer forgiveness for sins.

Jeremiah promised more than that. He said a new king from David's line would come to rule. He would be called "The LORD Our Righteousness" (23:5–8). Israel would return from exile to their land. They would farm there again. They would rebuild Jerusalem and again worship God there. Jeremiah wrote these rosy words in the face of Israel's worst catastrophe.

Jeremiah didn't just deliver these messages. He acted them out. He made what was either one of the stupidest financial investments of all time, or a remarkable act of faith. He bought property from a relative at the height of the Babylonian siege (chapter 32). God had promised Jeremiah that someday the property would be worth money again to his family. He believed and invested in that distant prospect. He bet on the survival of Israel.

The Fulfillment of Prophecy

Christians agree that the new king Jeremiah predicted was Jesus. They agree that Jesus brought the new covenant, which puts the law into people's hearts and enables them to know God. But on the restoration of Israel Christians hold different opinions. Some feel that the modern nation of Israel is, at least partly, the reincarnated nation Jeremiah wrote about. Others feel that the New Testament teaches that Christians of all races form Jeremiah's "new nation" of God's people, and that the promises apply allegorically to them.

All agree, though, that what Jesus set out to do is not yet finished. Someday he will destroy the forces of evil and fully establish his new kingdom.

Life Questions: Jeremiah bought a field as a sign of his faith in the future of Israel. By what "investments" can you demonstrate practical faith in God's kingdom?

" 'Your wound is incurable,
    your injury beyond healing.
[13]There is no one to plead your cause,
    no remedy for your sore,
    no healing for you.
[14]All your allies have forgotten you;
    they care nothing for you.
I have struck you as an enemy would
    and punished you as would the cruel,
because your guilt is so great
    and your sins so many.
[15]Why do you cry out over your wound,
    your pain that has no cure?
Because of your great guilt and many sins
    I have done these things to you.

[16]" 'But all who devour you will be devoured;
    all your enemies will go into exile.
Those who plunder you will be plundered;
    all who make spoil of you I will despoil.
[17]But I will restore you to health
    and heal your wounds,'
                declares the LORD,
'because you are called an outcast,
    Zion for whom no one cares.'

[18]"This is what the LORD says:

" 'I will restore the fortunes of Jacob's tents
    and have compassion on his dwellings;
the city will be rebuilt on her ruins,
    and the palace will stand in its proper
        place.
[19]From them will come songs of thanksgiving
    and the sound of rejoicing.
I will add to their numbers,
    and they will not be decreased;
I will bring them honor,
    and they will not be disdained.
[20]Their children will be as in days of old,
    and their community will be established
        before me;
I will punish all who oppress them.
[21]Their leader will be one of their own;
    their ruler will arise from among them.
I will bring him near and he will come close
        to me,
for who is he who will devote himself
    to be close to me?'
                declares the LORD.
[22]" 'So you will be my people,
    and I will be your God.' "

[23]See, the storm of the LORD
    will burst out in wrath,
a driving wind swirling down
    on the heads of the wicked.
[24]The fierce anger of the LORD will not turn
        back
until he fully accomplishes

the purposes of his heart.
In days to come
    you will understand this.

31 "At that time," declares the LORD, "I will be the God of all the clans of Israel, and they will be my people."
[2]This is what the LORD says:

"The people who survive the sword
    will find favor in the desert;
    I will come to give rest to Israel."

[3]The LORD appeared to us in the past,[a] saying:

"I have loved you with an everlasting love;
    I have drawn you with loving-kindness.
[4]I will build you up again
    and you will be rebuilt, O Virgin Israel.
Again you will take up your tambourines
    and go out to dance with the joyful.
[5]Again you will plant vineyards
    on the hills of Samaria;
the farmers will plant them
    and enjoy their fruit.
[6]There will be a day when watchmen cry out
    on the hills of Ephraim,
'Come, let us go up to Zion,
    to the LORD our God.' "

[7]This is what the LORD says:

"Sing with joy for Jacob;
    shout for the foremost of the nations.
Make your praises heard, and say,
    'O LORD, save your people,
    the remnant of Israel.'
[8]See, I will bring them from the land of the
        north
    and gather them from the ends of the
        earth.
Among them will be the blind and the lame,
    expectant mothers and women in labor;
    a great throng will return.
[9]They will come with weeping;
    they will pray as I bring them back.
I will lead them beside streams of water
    on a level path where they will not
        stumble,
because I am Israel's father,
    and Ephraim is my firstborn son.

[10]"Hear the word of the LORD, O nations;
    proclaim it in distant coastlands:
'He who scattered Israel will gather them
    and will watch over his flock like a
        shepherd.'
[11]For the LORD will ransom Jacob
    and redeem them from the hand of those
        stronger than they.

---

[a]3 Or LORD *has appeared to us from afar*

¹²They will come and shout for joy on the
heights of Zion;
they will rejoice in the bounty of the
LORD—
the grain, the new wine and the oil,
the young of the flocks and herds.
They will be like a well-watered garden,
and they will sorrow no more.
¹³Then maidens will dance and be glad,
young men and old as well.
I will turn their mourning into gladness;
I will give them comfort and joy instead
of sorrow.
¹⁴I will satisfy the priests with abundance,
and my people will be filled with my
bounty,"
declares the LORD.

¹⁵This is what the LORD says:

"A voice is heard in Ramah,
mourning and great weeping,
Rachel weeping for her children
and refusing to be comforted,
because her children are no more."

31:15 Pain in Redemption

*The Babylonians used Ramah, a town north of
Jerusalem, as a collection point for the captives
they were about to exile. Rachel, the "mother of
Israel," was buried near there, and she is
portrayed as weeping over the exiles. But the
Lord's voice answers hers, offering hope for
their return. Matthew related this verse to King
Herod's slaughter of all baby boys in the
vicinity of Bethlehem (Matthew 2:18). In
deepest grief, God is not absent: He is planning
redemption.*

¹⁶This is what the LORD says:

"Restrain your voice from weeping
and your eyes from tears,
for your work will be rewarded,"
declares the LORD.
"They will return from the land of the
enemy.
¹⁷So there is hope for your future,"
declares the LORD.
"Your children will return to their own
land.

¹⁸"I have surely heard Ephraim's moaning:
'You disciplined me like an unruly calf,
and I have been disciplined.
Restore me, and I will return,
because you are the LORD my God.
¹⁹After I strayed,

I repented;
after I came to understand,
I beat my breast.
I was ashamed and humiliated
because I bore the disgrace of my youth.'
²⁰Is not Ephraim my dear son,
the child in whom I delight?
Though I often speak against him,
I still remember him.
Therefore my heart yearns for him;
I have great compassion for him,"
declares the LORD.

²¹"Set up road signs;
put up guideposts.
Take note of the highway,
the road that you take.
Return, O Virgin Israel,
return to your towns.
²²How long will you wander,
O unfaithful daughter?
The LORD will create a new thing on earth—
a woman will surround*a* a man."

²³This is what the LORD Almighty, the God of
Israel, says: "When I bring them back from captivity,*b* the people in the land of Judah and in its
towns will once again use these words: 'The LORD
bless you, O righteous dwelling, O sacred mountain.' ²⁴People will live together in Judah and all
its towns—farmers and those who move about
with their flocks. ²⁵I will refresh the weary and
satisfy the faint."

²⁶At this I awoke and looked around. My sleep
had been pleasant to me.

²⁷"The days are coming," declares the LORD,
"when I will plant the house of Israel and the
house of Judah with the offspring of men and of
animals. ²⁸Just as I watched over them to uproot
and tear down, and to overthrow, destroy and
bring disaster, so I will watch over them to build
and to plant," declares the LORD. ²⁹"In those days
people will no longer say,

'The fathers have eaten sour grapes,
and the children's teeth are set on edge.'

³⁰Instead, everyone will die for his own sin; whoever eats sour grapes—his own teeth will be set
on edge.

³¹"The time is coming," declares the LORD,
"when I will make a new covenant
with the house of Israel
and with the house of Judah.
³²It will not be like the covenant
I made with their forefathers
when I took them by the hand
to lead them out of Egypt,
because they broke my covenant,

---

a 22 Or *will go about ₍seeking₎;* or *will protect*   *b 23* Or *I restore their fortunes*

though I was a husband to[a] them,[b]".
>
> declares the LORD.

33"This is the covenant I will make with the
house of Israel
after that time," declares the LORD.
"I will put my law in their minds
and write it on their hearts.
I will be their God,
and they will be my people.

31:33-34 Law in Their Hearts

The book of Hebrews quotes this passage (Hebrews 8:8–12) in explaining why Christians no longer live by Old Testament regulations. The written law was useful, and God-given. But as the history of Israel proved, it didn't have the power to transform people's inner attitudes. Something more was needed. God would have to change his people from the inside out, putting his law into their hearts through his Holy Spirit.

34No longer will a man teach his neighbor,
or a man his brother, saying, 'Know the
LORD,'
because they will all know me,
from the least of them to the greatest,"
declares the LORD.
"For I will forgive their wickedness
and will remember their sins no more."

35This is what the LORD says,

he who appoints the sun
to shine by day,
who decrees the moon and stars
to shine by night,
who stirs up the sea
so that its waves roar—
the LORD Almighty is his name:
36"Only if these decrees vanish from my sight,"
declares the LORD,
"will the descendants of Israel ever cease
to be a nation before me."

37This is what the LORD says:

"Only if the heavens above can be measured
and the foundations of the earth below be
searched out
will I reject all the descendants of Israel
because of all they have done,"
declares the LORD.

38"The days are coming," declares the LORD,
"when this city will be rebuilt for me from the
Tower of Hananel to the Corner Gate. 39The
measuring line will stretch from there straight to

the hill of Gareb and then turn to Goah. 40The
whole valley where dead bodies and ashes are
thrown, and all the terraces out to the Kidron
Valley on the east as far as the corner of the
Horse Gate, will be holy to the LORD. The city will
never again be uprooted or demolished."

Jeremiah Buys a Field

32 This is the word that came to Jeremiah
from the LORD in the tenth year of Zedekiah king of Judah, which was the eighteenth year
of Nebuchadnezzar. 2The army of the king of
Babylon was then besieging Jerusalem, and Jeremiah the prophet was confined in the courtyard
of the guard in the royal palace of Judah.

3Now Zedekiah king of Judah had imprisoned
him there, saying, "Why do you prophesy as you
do? You say, 'This is what the LORD says: I am
about to hand this city over to the king of Babylon, and he will capture it. 4Zedekiah king of
Judah will not escape out of the hands of the
Babylonians[c] but will certainly be handed over
to the king of Babylon, and will speak with him
face to face and see him with his own eyes. 5He
will take Zedekiah to Babylon, where he will remain until I deal with him, declares the LORD. If
you fight against the Babylonians, you will not
succeed.'"

6Jeremiah said, "The word of the LORD came
to me: 7Hanamel son of Shallum your uncle is
going to come to you and say, 'Buy my field at
Anathoth, because as nearest relative it is your
right and duty to buy it.'

32:7 Bargain Hunting

Jerusalem, under siege from the most powerful army in the world, hardly looked like a prime market for real estate. Nevertheless, God told Jeremiah to buy up family property that was presently occupied by Babylonians. Though worthless in the short run, it would grow valuable when Jeremiah's heirs returned from exile. Through his outrageous investment, Jeremiah put his money where his mouth was. He showed practical faith that God would bring his people back.

8"Then, just as the LORD had said, my cousin
Hanamel came to me in the courtyard of the
guard and said, 'Buy my field at Anathoth in the
territory of Benjamin. Since it is your right to
redeem it and possess it, buy it for yourself.'

"I knew that this was the word of the LORD; 9so
I bought the field at Anathoth from my cousin
Hanamel and weighed out for him seventeen

---

[a]32 Hebrew; Septuagint and Syriac / *and I turned away from*
verses 5, 24, 25, 28, 29 and 43   [b]32 Or *was their master*   [c]4 Or *Chaldeans*; also in

shekels[a] of silver. [10]I signed and sealed the deed, had it witnessed, and weighed out the silver on the scales. [11]I took the deed of purchase—the sealed copy containing the terms and conditions, as well as the unsealed copy— [12]and I gave this deed to Baruch son of Neriah, the son of Mahseiah, in the presence of my cousin Hanamel and of the witnesses who had signed the deed and of all the Jews sitting in the courtyard of the guard.

[13]"In their presence I gave Baruch these instructions: [14]'This is what the LORD Almighty, the God of Israel, says: Take these documents, both the sealed and unsealed copies of the deed of purchase, and put them in a clay jar so they will last a long time. [15]For this is what the LORD Almighty, the God of Israel, says: Houses, fields and vineyards will again be bought in this land.'

[16]"After I had given the deed of purchase to Baruch son of Neriah, I prayed to the LORD:

[17]"Ah, Sovereign LORD, you have made the heavens and the earth by your great power and outstretched arm. Nothing is too hard for you. [18]You show love to thousands but bring the punishment for the fathers' sins into the laps of their children after them. O great and powerful God, whose name is the LORD Almighty, [19]great are your purposes and mighty are your deeds. Your eyes are open to all the ways of men; you reward everyone according to his conduct and as his deeds deserve. [20]You performed miraculous signs and wonders in Egypt and have continued them to this day, both in Israel and among all mankind, and have gained the renown that is still yours. [21]You brought your people Israel out of Egypt with signs and wonders, by a mighty hand and an outstretched arm and with great terror. [22]You gave them this land you had sworn to give their forefathers, a land flowing with milk and honey. [23]They came in and took possession of it, but they did not obey you or follow your law; they did not do what you commanded them to do. So you brought all this disaster upon them.

[24]"See how the siege ramps are built up to take the city. Because of the sword, famine and plague, the city will be handed over to the Babylonians who are attacking it. What you said has happened, as you now see. [25]And though the city will be handed over to the Babylonians, you, O Sovereign LORD, say to me, 'Buy the field with silver and have the transaction witnessed.'"

[26]Then the word of the LORD came to Jeremiah: [27]"I am the LORD, the God of all mankind. Is anything too hard for me? [28]Therefore, this is what the LORD says: I am about to hand this city over to the Babylonians and to Nebuchadnezzar king of Babylon, who will capture it. [29]The Babylonians who are attacking this city will come in and set it on fire; they will burn it down, along with the houses where the people provoked me to anger by burning incense on the roofs to Baal and by pouring out drink offerings to other gods.

[30]"The people of Israel and Judah have done nothing but evil in my sight from their youth; indeed, the people of Israel have done nothing but provoke me with what their hands have made, declares the LORD. [31]From the day it was built until now, this city has so aroused my anger and wrath that I must remove it from my sight. [32]The people of Israel and Judah have provoked me by all the evil they have done—they, their kings and officials, their priests and prophets, the men of Judah and the people of Jerusalem. [33]They turned their backs to me and not their faces; though I taught them again and again, they would not listen or respond to discipline. [34]They set up their abominable idols in the house that bears my Name and defiled it. [35]They built high places for Baal in the Valley of Ben Hinnom to sacrifice their sons and daughters[b] to Molech, though I never commanded, nor did it enter my mind, that they should do such a detestable thing and so make Judah sin.

[36]"You are saying about this city, 'By the sword, famine and plague it will be handed over to the king of Babylon'; but this is what the LORD, the God of Israel, says: [37]I will surely gather them from all the lands where I banish them in my furious anger and great wrath; I will bring them back to this place and let them live in safety. [38]They will be my people, and I will be their God. [39]I will give them singleness of heart and action, so that they will always fear me for their own good and the good of their children after them. [40]I will make an everlasting covenant with them: I will never stop doing good to them, and I will inspire them to fear me, so that they will never turn away from me. [41]I will rejoice in doing them

32:40 A New Covenant

The foundation of Israel was its covenant with God. It bound both sides together on the basis of clear-cut expectations (see "The Covenant," page 104). Israel had never really lived up to the covenant, however. Here (and in 31:31–34) God promised a new covenant, far better than the old one. It would change the people's thinking. Paul amplified the contrast in 2 Corinthians 2:12–3:18. The new covenant came in Christ.

[a]9 That is, about 7 ounces (about 200 grams)   [b]35 Or to make their sons and daughters pass through ⌐the fire⌐

good and will assuredly plant them in this land with all my heart and soul.

⁴²"This is what the LORD says: As I have brought all this great calamity on this people, so I will give them all the prosperity I have promised them. ⁴³Once more fields will be bought in this land of which you say, 'It is a desolate waste, without men or animals, for it has been handed over to the Babylonians.' ⁴⁴Fields will be bought for silver, and deeds will be signed, sealed and witnessed in the territory of Benjamin, in the villages around Jerusalem, in the towns of Judah and in the towns of the hill country, of the western foothills and of the Negev, because I will restore their fortunes,[a] declares the LORD."

Promise of Restoration

33 While Jeremiah was still confined in the courtyard of the guard, the word of the LORD came to him a second time: ²"This is what the LORD says, he who made the earth, the LORD who formed it and established it—the LORD is his name: ³'Call to me and I will answer you and tell you great and unsearchable things you do not know.' ⁴For this is what the LORD, the God of Israel, says about the houses in this city and the royal palaces of Judah that have been torn down to be used against the siege ramps and the sword ⁵in the fight with the Babylonians[b]: 'They will be filled with the dead bodies of the men I will slay in my anger and wrath. I will hide my face from this city because of all its wickedness.

⁶" 'Nevertheless, I will bring health and healing to it; I will heal my people and will let them enjoy abundant peace and security. ⁷I will bring Judah and Israel back from captivity[c] and will rebuild them as they were before. ⁸I will cleanse them from all the sin they have committed against me and will forgive all their sins of rebellion against me. ⁹Then this city will bring me renown, joy, praise and honor before all nations on earth that hear of all the good things I do for it; and they will be in awe and will tremble at the abundant prosperity and peace I provide for it.'

¹⁰"This is what the LORD says: 'You say about this place, "It is a desolate waste, without men or animals." Yet in the towns of Judah and the streets of Jerusalem that are deserted, inhabited by neither men nor animals, there will be heard once more ¹¹the sounds of joy and gladness, the voices of bride and bridegroom, and the voices of those who bring thank offerings to the house of the LORD, saying,

"Give thanks to the LORD Almighty,
    for the LORD is good;
    his love endures forever."

For I will restore the fortunes of the land as they were before,' says the LORD.

¹²"This is what the LORD Almighty says: 'In this place, desolate and without men or animals—in all its towns there will again be pastures for shepherds to rest their flocks. ¹³In the towns of the hill country, of the western foothills and of the Negev, in the territory of Benjamin, in the villages around Jerusalem and in the towns of Judah, flocks will again pass under the hand of the one who counts them,' says the LORD.

¹⁴" 'The days are coming,' declares the LORD, 'when I will fulfill the gracious promise I made to the house of Israel and to the house of Judah.

¹⁵" 'In those days and at that time
    I will make a righteous Branch sprout
        from David's line;
    he will do what is just and right in the
        land.
¹⁶In those days Judah will be saved
    and Jerusalem will live in safety.
This is the name by which it[d] will be called:
    The LORD Our Righteousness.'

¹⁷For this is what the LORD says: 'David will never fail to have a man to sit on the throne of the house of Israel, ¹⁸nor will the priests, who are Levites, ever fail to have a man to stand before me continually to offer burnt offerings, to burn grain offerings and to present sacrifices.' "

33:18 Unchanged Promises

Jerusalem lay in rubble, and survivors must surely have wondered whether God's covenants had been irrevocably broken. In this message through Jeremiah, God says that his promises still stand. Israel will always have an heir of David to provide leadership, and priests to lead in worship. The New Testament, and particularly the book of Hebrews, teaches that these promises are fulfilled forever in Jesus, who is both priest and king.

¹⁹The word of the LORD came to Jeremiah: ²⁰"This is what the LORD says: 'If you can break my covenant with the day and my covenant with the night, so that day and night no longer come at their appointed time, ²¹then my covenant with David my servant—and my covenant with the Levites who are priests ministering before me—can be broken and David will no longer have a descendant to reign on his throne. ²²I will make the descendants of David my servant and the Levites who minister before me as countless as

---

[a]44 Or *will bring them back from captivity*   [b]5 Or *Chaldeans*   [c]7 Or *will restore the fortunes of Judah and Israel*
[d]16 Or *he*

the stars of the sky and as measureless as the sand on the seashore.'"

²³The word of the LORD came to Jeremiah: ²⁴"Have you not noticed that these people are saying, 'The LORD has rejected the two kingdoms[a] he chose'? So they despise my people and no longer regard them as a nation. ²⁵This is what the LORD says: 'If I have not established my covenant with day and night and the fixed laws of heaven and earth, ²⁶then I will reject the descendants of Jacob and David my servant and will not choose any one of his sons to rule over the descendants of Abraham, Isaac and Jacob. For I will restore their fortunes[b] and have compassion on them.'"

Warning to Zedekiah

34 While Nebuchadnezzar king of Babylon and all his army and all the kingdoms and peoples in the empire he ruled were fighting against Jerusalem and all its surrounding towns, this word came to Jeremiah from the LORD: ²"This is what the LORD, the God of Israel, says: Go to Zedekiah king of Judah and tell him, 'This is what the LORD says: I am about to hand this city over to the king of Babylon, and he will burn it down. ³You will not escape from his grasp but will surely be captured and handed over to him. You will see the king of Babylon with your own eyes, and he will speak with you face to face. And you will go to Babylon.

⁴"'Yet hear the promise of the LORD, O Zedekiah king of Judah. This is what the LORD says concerning you: You will not die by the sword; ⁵you will die peacefully. As people made a funeral fire in honor of your fathers, the former kings who preceded you, so they will make a fire in your honor and lament, "Alas, O master!" I myself make this promise, declares the LORD.'"

⁶Then Jeremiah the prophet told all this to Zedekiah king of Judah, in Jerusalem, ⁷while the army of the king of Babylon was fighting against Jerusalem and the other cities of Judah that were still holding out—Lachish and Azekah. These were the only fortified cities left in Judah.

Freedom for Slaves

⁸The word came to Jeremiah from the LORD after King Zedekiah had made a covenant with all the people in Jerusalem to proclaim freedom for the slaves. ⁹Everyone was to free his Hebrew slaves, both male and female; no one was to hold a fellow Jew in bondage. ¹⁰So all the officials and people who entered into this covenant agreed that they would free their male and female slaves and no longer hold them in bondage. They agreed, and set them free. ¹¹But afterward they changed their minds and took back the slaves they had freed and enslaved them again.

¹²Then the word of the LORD came to Jeremiah: ¹³"This is what the LORD, the God of Israel, says: I made a covenant with your forefathers when I brought them out of Egypt, out of the land of slavery. I said, ¹⁴'Every seventh year each of you must free any fellow Hebrew who has sold himself to you. After he has served you six years, you must let him go free.'[c] Your fathers, however, did not listen to me or pay attention to me. ¹⁵Recently you repented and did what is right in my sight: Each of you proclaimed freedom to his countrymen. You even made a covenant before me in the house that bears my Name. ¹⁶But now you have turned around and profaned my name; each of you has taken back the male and female slaves you had set free to go where they wished. You have forced them to become your slaves again.

¹⁷"Therefore, this is what the LORD says: You have not obeyed me; you have not proclaimed freedom for your fellow countrymen. So I now proclaim 'freedom' for you, declares the LORD—'freedom' to fall by the sword, plague and famine. I will make you abhorrent to all the kingdoms of the earth. ¹⁸The men who have violated my covenant and have not fulfilled the terms of the covenant they made before me, I will treat like the calf they cut in two and then walked between its pieces. ¹⁹The leaders of Judah and Jerusalem, the court officials, the priests and all the people of the land who walked between the pieces of the calf, ²⁰I will hand over to their enemies who seek their lives. Their dead bodies will become food for the birds of the air and the beasts of the earth.

²¹"I will hand Zedekiah king of Judah and his officials over to their enemies who seek their lives, to the army of the king of Babylon, which has withdrawn from you. ²²I am going to give the order, declares the LORD, and I will bring them back to this city. They will fight against it, take it and burn it down. And I will lay waste the towns of Judah so no one can live there."

The Recabites

35 This is the word that came to Jeremiah from the LORD during the reign of Jehoiakim son of Josiah king of Judah: ²"Go to the Recabite family and invite them to come to one of the side rooms of the house of the LORD and give them wine to drink."

³So I went to get Jaazaniah son of Jeremiah, the son of Habazziniah, and his brothers and all his sons—the whole family of the Recabites. ⁴I brought them into the house of the LORD, into the room of the sons of Hanan son of Igdaliah the man of God. It was next to the room of the

---

a24 Or *families*   *b26* Or *will bring them back from captivity*   *c14* Deut. 15:12

officials, which was over that of Maaseiah son of Shallum the doorkeeper. [5]Then I set bowls full of wine and some cups before the men of the Recabite family and said to them, "Drink some wine."

[6]But they replied, "We do not drink wine, because our forefather Jonadab son of Recab gave us this command: 'Neither you nor your descendants must ever drink wine. [7]Also you must never build houses, sow seed or plant vineyards; you must never have any of these things, but must always live in tents. Then you will live a long time in the land where you are nomads.' [8]We have obeyed everything our forefather Jonadab son of Recab commanded us. Neither we nor our wives nor our sons and daughters have ever drunk wine [9]or built houses to live in or had vineyards, fields or crops. [10]We have lived in tents and have fully obeyed everything our forefather Jonadab commanded us. [11]But when Nebuchadnezzar king of Babylon invaded this land, we said,

'Come, we must go to Jerusalem to escape the Babylonian[a] and Aramean armies.' So we have remained in Jerusalem."

[12]Then the word of the LORD came to Jeremiah, saying: [13]"This is what the LORD Almighty, the God of Israel, says: Go and tell the men of Judah and the people of Jerusalem, 'Will you not learn a lesson and obey my words?' declares the LORD. [14]Jonadab son of Recab ordered his sons not to drink wine and this command has been kept. To this day they do not drink wine, because they obey their forefather's command. But I have spoken to you again and again, yet you have not obeyed me. [15]Again and again I sent all my servants the prophets to you. They said, "Each of you must turn from your wicked ways and reform your actions; do not follow other gods to serve them. Then you will live in the land I have given to you and your fathers." But you have not paid attention or listened to me. [16]The descendants of Jonadab son of Recab have carried out

[a]11 Or *Chaldean*

Living Parables
Jeremiah's bizarre protests

OCCASIONALLY THE EVENING NEWS BRINGS us word of someone's bizarre protest. Anti-military demonstrators pour pigs' blood on a sidewalk. Monks set themselves on fire. Environmental activists chain themselves to trees to protest logging. Marchers block the entrance to a nuclear power station. Such protests leave many people feeling uneasy. We can't easily imagine a serious political figure, or a respectable pastor, acting that way.

> *"'You have not paid attention or listened to me.'"*
> 35:15

But Jeremiah's life was full of such protests, at the express command of God. He made an ox yoke and wore it everywhere until the false prophet Hananiah took it off and broke it in the temple one day. (Jeremiah prophesied Hananiah's death, and within two months he was gone.) Jeremiah's point? He wanted to emphasize the yoke of captivity the king of Babylon would put on Judah's shoulders. The story is in chapters 27–28.

On another occasion (chapter 35) Jeremiah invited a group of well-known nondrinkers into a room in the temple and offered them wine. They refused, and that made another sermon. If they could remember their vows not to drink, then why couldn't the people of Judah and Jerusalem remember the words of the living God?

Nothing Was Too Undignified

Jeremiah bought a beautiful linen sash and buried it in a hole until it was ruined (chapter 13). He invited the rulers of Jerusalem on a trip outside the city, and in the midst of a sermon about God's anger smashed a pot to smithereens (chapter 19). And in his most famous "enacted parable," Jeremiah bought a farm while the Babylonian army was knocking at Jerusalem's door (chapter 32). He might as well have been a Jew buying property within a German concentration camp during World War II, for all the hope he had of using it. But his action demonstrated bold hope. Someday his family would farm there again.

Why such weird activity? It says less about Jeremiah than it does about the God who gave the orders. God would not let go of his people until he had done all in his power to turn them around. Nothing was too undignified; no carnival ploy was too corny. So long as he had the slightest hope of breaking through to them, he would keep shouting.

Life Questions: How does God get through to you? Does he use dramatic means like Jeremiah's or quieter methods?

the command their forefather gave them, but these people have not obeyed me.'

¹⁷"Therefore, this is what the LORD God Almighty, the God of Israel, says: 'Listen! I am going to bring on Judah and on everyone living in Jerusalem every disaster I pronounced against them. I spoke to them, but they did not listen; I called to them, but they did not answer.'"

¹⁸Then Jeremiah said to the family of the Recabites, "This is what the LORD Almighty, the God of Israel, says: 'You have obeyed the command of your forefather Jonadab and have followed all his instructions and have done everything he ordered.' ¹⁹Therefore, this is what the LORD Almighty, the God of Israel, says: 'Jonadab son of Recab will never fail to have a man to serve me.'"

Jehoiakim Burns Jeremiah's Scroll

36 In the fourth year of Jehoiakim son of Josiah king of Judah, this word came to Jeremiah from the LORD: ²"Take a scroll and write on it all the words I have spoken to you concerning Israel, Judah and all the other nations from the time I began speaking to you in the reign of Josiah till now. ³Perhaps when the people of Judah hear about every disaster I plan to inflict on them, each of them will turn from his wicked way; then I will forgive their wickedness and their sin."

⁴So Jeremiah called Baruch son of Neriah, and while Jeremiah dictated all the words the LORD had spoken to him, Baruch wrote them on the scroll. ⁵Then Jeremiah told Baruch, "I am restricted; I cannot go to the LORD's temple. ⁶So you go to the house of the LORD on a day of fasting and read to the people from the scroll the words of the LORD that you wrote as I dictated. Read them to all the people of Judah who come in from their towns. ⁷Perhaps they will bring their petition before the LORD, and each will turn from his wicked ways, for the anger and wrath pronounced against this people by the LORD are great."

⁸Baruch son of Neriah did everything Jeremiah the prophet told him to do; at the LORD's temple he read the words of the LORD from the scroll. ⁹In the ninth month of the fifth year of Jehoiakim son of Josiah king of Judah, a time of fasting before the LORD was proclaimed for all the

people in Jerusalem and those who had come from the towns of Judah. ¹⁰From the room of Gemariah son of Shaphan the secretary, which was in the upper courtyard at the entrance of the New Gate of the temple, Baruch read to all the people at the LORD's temple the words of Jeremiah from the scroll.

¹¹When Micaiah son of Gemariah, the son of Shaphan, heard all the words of the LORD from the scroll, ¹²he went down to the secretary's room in the royal palace, where all the officials were sitting: Elishama the secretary, Delaiah son of Shemaiah, Elnathan son of Acbor, Gemariah son of Shaphan, Zedekiah son of Hananiah, and all the other officials. ¹³After Micaiah told them everything he had heard Baruch read to the people from the scroll, ¹⁴all the officials sent Jehudi son of Nethaniah, the son of Shelemiah, the son of Cushi, to say to Baruch, "Bring the scroll from which you have read to the people and come." So Baruch son of Neriah went to them with the scroll in his hand. ¹⁵They said to him, "Sit down, please, and read it to us."

So Baruch read it to them. ¹⁶When they heard all these words, they looked at each other in fear and said to Baruch, "We must report all these words to the king." ¹⁷Then they asked Baruch, "Tell us, how did you come to write all this? Did Jeremiah dictate it?"

¹⁸"Yes," Baruch replied, "he dictated all these words to me, and I wrote them in ink on the scroll."

¹⁹Then the officials said to Baruch, "You and Jeremiah, go and hide. Don't let anyone know where you are."

²⁰After they put the scroll in the room of Elishama the secretary, they went to the king in the courtyard and reported everything to him. ²¹The king sent Jehudi to get the scroll, and Jehudi brought it from the room of Elishama the secretary and read it to the king and all the officials standing beside him. ²²It was the ninth month and the king was sitting in the winter apartment, with a fire burning in the firepot in front of him. ²³Whenever Jehudi had read three or four columns of the scroll, the king cut them off with a scribe's knife and threw them into the firepot, until the entire scroll was burned in the fire. ²⁴The king and all his attendants who heard all these words showed no fear, nor did they tear their clothes. ²⁵Even though Elnathan, Delaiah and Gemariah urged the king not to burn the scroll, he would not listen to them. ²⁶Instead, the king commanded Jerahmeel, a son of the king, Seraiah son of Azriel and Shelemiah son of Abdeel to arrest Baruch the scribe and Jeremiah the prophet. But the LORD had hidden them.

²⁷After the king burned the scroll containing the words that Baruch had written at Jeremiah's dictation, the word of the LORD came to Jeremi-

---

35:14 Teetotalers

The Recabites had a family tradition of not drinking, and nothing Jeremiah said or did could budge them from it. He made their tenacity the basis of a sermon. If family traditions are carried on for generations, why not God's traditions?

ah: **28**"Take another scroll and write on it all the words that were on the first scroll, which Jehoiakim king of Judah burned up. **29**Also tell Jehoiakim king of Judah, 'This is what the LORD says: You burned that scroll and said, "Why did you write on it that the king of Babylon would certainly come and destroy this land and cut off both men and animals from it?" **30**Therefore, this is what the LORD says about Jehoiakim king of Judah: He will have no one to sit on the throne of David; his body will be thrown out and exposed to the heat by day and the frost by night. **31**I will punish him and his children and his attendants for their wickedness; I will bring on them and those living in Jerusalem and the people of Judah every disaster I pronounced against them, because they have not listened.'"

32So Jeremiah took another scroll and gave it to the scribe Baruch son of Neriah, and as Jeremiah dictated, Baruch wrote on it all the words of the scroll that Jehoiakim king of Judah had burned in the fire. And many similar words were added to them.

Jeremiah in Prison

37 Zedekiah son of Josiah was made king of Judah by Nebuchadnezzar king of Babylon; he reigned in place of Jehoiachin[a] son of Jehoiakim. **2**Neither he nor his attendants nor the people of the land paid any attention to the words the LORD had spoken through Jeremiah the prophet.

3King Zedekiah, however, sent Jehucal son of Shelemiah with the priest Zephaniah son of Maaseiah to Jeremiah the prophet with this message: "Please pray to the LORD our God for us."

4Now Jeremiah was free to come and go among the people, for he had not yet been put in prison. **5**Pharaoh's army had marched out of Egypt, and when the Babylonians[b] who were besieging Jerusalem heard the report about them, they withdrew from Jerusalem.

6Then the word of the LORD came to Jeremiah the prophet: **7**"This is what the LORD, the God of Israel, says: Tell the king of Judah, who sent you to inquire of me, 'Pharaoh's army, which has marched out to support you, will go back to its own land, to Egypt. **8**Then the Babylonians will return and attack this city; they will capture it and burn it down.'

9"This is what the LORD says: Do not deceive yourselves, thinking, 'The Babylonians will surely leave us.' They will not! **10**Even if you were to defeat the entire Babylonian[c] army that is attacking you and only wounded men were left in their tents, they would come out and burn this city down."

11After the Babylonian army had withdrawn from Jerusalem because of Pharaoh's army, **12**Jeremiah started to leave the city to go to the territory of Benjamin to get his share of the property

37:5 The Siege Lifted

Israel was a small nation, hemmed in by bigger powers such as Egypt and Babylon. Israelite kings often attempted to keep their independence by playing off the big powers against each other. King Zedekiah tried to get Egypt to intervene against Babylon, and during this brief period it seemed he had succeeded. Because the Egyptian army marched out, Nebuchadnezzar lifted his siege of Jerusalem. Jeremiah, who had warned that this foreign policy must ultimately fail, was arrested for treason.

among the people there. **13**But when he reached the Benjamin Gate, the captain of the guard, whose name was Irijah son of Shelemiah, the son of Hananiah, arrested him and said, "You are deserting to the Babylonians!"

14"That's not true!" Jeremiah said. "I am not deserting to the Babylonians." But Irijah would not listen to him; instead, he arrested Jeremiah and brought him to the officials. **15**They were angry with Jeremiah and had him beaten and imprisoned in the house of Jonathan the secretary, which they had made into a prison.

16Jeremiah was put into a vaulted cell in a dungeon, where he remained a long time. **17**Then King Zedekiah sent for him and had him brought to the palace, where he asked him privately, "Is there any word from the LORD?"

"Yes," Jeremiah replied, "you will be handed over to the king of Babylon."

18Then Jeremiah said to King Zedekiah, "What crime have I committed against you or your officials or this people, that you have put me in prison? **19**Where are your prophets who prophesied to you, 'The king of Babylon will not attack you or this land'? **20**But now, my lord the king, please listen. Let me bring my petition before you: Do not send me back to the house of Jonathan the secretary, or I will die there."

21King Zedekiah then gave orders for Jeremiah to be placed in the courtyard of the guard and given bread from the street of the bakers each day until all the bread in the city was gone. So Jeremiah remained in the courtyard of the guard.

Jeremiah Thrown Into a Cistern

38 Shephatiah son of Mattan, Gedaliah son of Pashhur, Jehucal[d] son of Shelemiah, and

---

[a]1 Hebrew *Coniah,* a variant of *Jehoiachin*   [b]5 Or *Chaldeans;* also in verses 8, 9, 13 and 14   [c]10 Or *Chaldean;* also in verse 11   [d]1 Hebrew *Jucal,* a variant of *Jehucal*

Pashhur son of Malkijah heard what Jeremiah was telling all the people when he said, ²"This is what the LORD says: 'Whoever stays in this city will die by the sword, famine or plague, but whoever goes over to the Babylonians[a] will live. He will escape with his life; he will live.' ³And this is what the LORD says: 'This city will certainly be handed over to the army of the king of Babylon, who will capture it.'"

⁴Then the officials said to the king, "This man should be put to death. He is discouraging the soldiers who are left in this city, as well as all the people, by the things he is saying to them. This man is not seeking the good of these people but their ruin."

⁵"He is in your hands," King Zedekiah answered. "The king can do nothing to oppose you."

⁶So they took Jeremiah and put him into the cistern of Malkijah, the king's son, which was in the courtyard of the guard. They lowered Jeremiah by ropes into the cistern; it had no water in it, only mud, and Jeremiah sank down into the mud.

⁷But Ebed-Melech, a Cushite,[b] an official[c] in the royal palace, heard that they had put Jeremiah into the cistern. While the king was sitting in the Benjamin Gate, ⁸Ebed-Melech went out of the palace and said to him, ⁹"My lord the king, these men have acted wickedly in all they have done to Jeremiah the prophet. They have thrown him into a cistern, where he will starve to death when there is no longer any bread in the city."

38:9 Close to Death

Jeremiah was arrested during the long, final siege of Jerusalem—a time when food became so short some Israelites resorted to cannibalism. Imprisoned at the bottom of an empty cistern, the prophet could easily have starved to death. Interestingly, only a foreigner cared enough to go to the king and convince him to let Jeremiah out. For this, Ebed-Melech received a special message from God (39:15–18).

¹⁰Then the king commanded Ebed-Melech the Cushite, "Take thirty men from here with you and lift Jeremiah the prophet out of the cistern before he dies." ¹¹So Ebed-Melech took the men with him and went to a room under the treasury in the palace. He took some old rags and worn-out clothes from there and let them down with ropes to Jeremiah in the cistern. ¹²Ebed-Melech the Cushite

said to Jeremiah, "Put these old rags and worn-out clothes under your arms to pad the ropes." Jeremiah did so, ¹³and they pulled him up with the ropes and lifted him out of the cistern. And Jeremiah remained in the courtyard of the guard.

Zedekiah Questions Jeremiah Again

¹⁴Then King Zedekiah sent for Jeremiah the prophet and had him brought to the third entrance to the temple of the LORD. "I am going to ask you something," the king said to Jeremiah. "Do not hide anything from me."

¹⁵Jeremiah said to Zedekiah, "If I give you an answer, will you not kill me? Even if I did give you counsel, you would not listen to me."

¹⁶But King Zedekiah swore this oath secretly to Jeremiah: "As surely as the LORD lives, who has given us breath, I will neither kill you nor hand you over to those who are seeking your life."

¹⁷Then Jeremiah said to Zedekiah, "This is what the LORD God Almighty, the God of Israel, says: 'If you surrender to the officers of the king of Babylon, your life will be spared and this city will not be burned down; you and your family will live. ¹⁸But if you will not surrender to the officers of the king of Babylon, this city will be handed over to the Babylonians and they will burn it down; you yourself will not escape from their hands.'"

¹⁹King Zedekiah said to Jeremiah, "I am afraid of the Jews who have gone over to the Babylonians, for the Babylonians may hand me over to them and they will mistreat me."

²⁰"They will not hand you over," Jeremiah replied. "Obey the LORD by doing what I tell you. Then it will go well with you, and your life will be spared. ²¹But if you refuse to surrender, this is what the LORD has revealed to me: ²²All the women left in the palace of the king of Judah will be brought out to the officials of the king of Babylon. Those women will say to you:

"'They misled you and overcame you—
    those trusted friends of yours.
Your feet are sunk in the mud;
    your friends have deserted you.'

²³"All your wives and children will be brought out to the Babylonians. You yourself will not escape from their hands but will be captured by the king of Babylon; and this city will[d] be burned down."

²⁴Then Zedekiah said to Jeremiah, "Do not let anyone know about this conversation, or you may die. ²⁵If the officials hear that I talked with you, and they come to you and say, 'Tell us what you said to the king and what the king said to you; do not hide it from us or we will kill you,'

---

*a 2 Or *Chaldeans*; also in verses 18, 19 and 23   *b 7 Probably from the upper Nile region   *c 7 Or *a eunuch*
*d 23 Or *and you will cause this city to*

[26]then tell them, 'I was pleading with the king not to send me back to Jonathan's house to die there.'"

[27]All the officials did come to Jeremiah and question him, and he told them everything the king had ordered him to say. So they said no more to him, for no one had heard his conversation with the king.

[28]And Jeremiah remained in the courtyard of the guard until the day Jerusalem was captured.

The Fall of Jerusalem

39 This is how Jerusalem was taken: [1]In the ninth year of Zedekiah king of Judah, in the tenth month, Nebuchadnezzar king of Babylon marched against Jerusalem with his whole army and laid siege to it. [2]And on the ninth day of the fourth month of Zedekiah's eleventh year, the city wall was broken through. [3]Then all the officials of the king of Babylon came and took seats in the Middle Gate: Nergal-Sharezer of Samgar, Nebo-Sarsekim[a] a chief officer, Nergal-Sharezer a high official and all the other officials of the king of Babylon. [4]When Zedekiah king of Judah and all the soldiers saw them, they fled; they left the city at night by way of the king's garden, through the gate between the two walls, and headed toward the Arabah.[b]

[5]But the Babylonian[c] army pursued them and overtook Zedekiah in the plains of Jericho. They captured him and took him to Nebuchadnezzar king of Babylon at Riblah in the land of Hamath, where he pronounced sentence on him. [6]There at Riblah the king of Babylon slaughtered the sons of Zedekiah before his eyes and also killed all the nobles of Judah. [7]Then he put out Zedekiah's eyes and bound him with bronze shackles to take him to Babylon.

[8]The Babylonians[d] set fire to the royal palace and the houses of the people and broke down the walls of Jerusalem. [9]Nebuzaradan commander of the imperial guard carried into exile to Babylon the people who remained in the city, along with those who had gone over to him, and the rest of the people. [10]But Nebuzaradan the commander of the guard left behind in the land of Judah some of the poor people, who owned nothing; and at that time he gave them vineyards and fields.

[11]Now Nebuchadnezzar king of Babylon had given these orders about Jeremiah through Nebuzaradan commander of the imperial guard: [12]"Take him and look after him; don't harm him but do for him whatever he asks." [13]So Nebuzaradan the commander of the guard, Nebushazban a chief officer, Nergal-Sharezer a high official and all the other officers of the king of Babylon [14]sent and had Jeremiah taken out of the courtyard of the guard. They turned him over to Gedaliah son of Ahikam, the son of Shaphan, to take him back to his home. So he remained among his own people.

39:12 Influential Prisoner

Jeremiah's message of doom made him unpopular in Jerusalem but evidently impressed the conquering Babylonians. The highest officials knew about the prophet and gave explicit instructions to see that he was not hurt. Later they offered him his freedom (40:4).

[15]While Jeremiah had been confined in the courtyard of the guard, the word of the LORD came to him: [16]"Go and tell Ebed-Melech the Cushite, 'This is what the LORD Almighty, the God of Israel, says: I am about to fulfill my words against this city through disaster, not prosperity. At that time they will be fulfilled before your eyes. [17]But I will rescue you on that day, declares the LORD; you will not be handed over to those you fear. [18]I will save you; you will not fall by the sword but will escape with your life, because you trust in me, declares the LORD.'"

Jeremiah Freed

40 The word came to Jeremiah from the LORD after Nebuzaradan commander of the imperial guard had released him at Ramah. He had found Jeremiah bound in chains among all the captives from Jerusalem and Judah who were being carried into exile to Babylon. [2]When the commander of the guard found Jeremiah, he said to him, "The LORD your God decreed this disaster for this place. [3]And now the LORD has brought it about; he has done just as he said he would. All this happened because you people sinned against the LORD and did not obey him. [4]But today I am freeing you from the chains on your wrists. Come with me to Babylon, if you like, and I will look after you; but if you do not want to, then don't come. Look, the whole country lies before you; go wherever you please." [5]However, before Jeremiah turned to go,[e] Nebuzaradan added, "Go back to Gedaliah son of Ahikam, the son of Shaphan, whom the king of Babylon has appointed over the towns of Judah, and live with him among the people, or go anywhere else you please."

Then the commander gave him provisions and a present and let him go. [6]So Jeremiah went to Gedaliah son of Ahikam at Mizpah and stayed

---

[a]3 Or *Nergal-Sharezer, Samgar-Nebo, Sarsekim*   [b]4 Or *the Jordan Valley*   [c]5 Or *Chaldean*   [d]8 Or *Chaldeans*
[e]5 Or *Jeremiah answered*

with him among the people who were left behind in the land.

Gedaliah Assassinated

⁷When all the army officers and their men who were still in the open country heard that the king of Babylon had appointed Gedaliah son of Ahikam as governor over the land and had put him in charge of the men, women and children who were the poorest in the land and who had not been carried into exile to Babylon, ⁸they came to Gedaliah at Mizpah—Ishmael son of Nethaniah, Johanan and Jonathan the sons of Kareah, Seraiah son of Tanhumeth, the sons of Ephai the Netophathite, and Jaazaniah[a] the son of the Maacathite, and their men. ⁹Gedaliah son of Ahikam, the son of Shaphan, took an oath to reassure them and their men. "Do not be afraid to serve the Babylonians,[b]" he said. "Settle down in the land and serve the king of Babylon, and it will go well with you. ¹⁰I myself will stay at Mizpah to represent you before the Babylonians who come to us, but you are to harvest the wine, summer fruit and oil, and put them in your storage jars, and live in the towns you have taken over."

¹¹When all the Jews in Moab, Ammon, Edom and all the other countries heard that the king of Babylon had left a remnant in Judah and had appointed Gedaliah son of Ahikam, the son of Shaphan, as governor over them, ¹²they all came back to the land of Judah, to Gedaliah at Mizpah, from all the countries where they had been scattered. And they harvested an abundance of wine and summer fruit.

40:12 False Hopes

The Babylonians, once they had captured rebel Jerusalem, left some of the common people behind under a governor. When other Jews scattered in the region heard news of this, they came home and gathered an excellent harvest—undoubtedly from fields the exiles had left behind. But even this small nucleus of Jews was to be scattered—this time due to local political infighting.

¹³Johanan son of Kareah and all the army officers still in the open country came to Gedaliah at Mizpah ¹⁴and said to him, "Don't you know that Baalis king of the Ammonites has sent Ishmael son of Nethaniah to take your life?" But Gedaliah son of Ahikam did not believe them.

¹⁵Then Johanan son of Kareah said privately to Gedaliah in Mizpah, "Let me go and kill Ish-

mael son of Nethaniah, and no one will know it. Why should he take your life and cause all the Jews who are gathered around you to be scattered and the remnant of Judah to perish?"

¹⁶But Gedaliah son of Ahikam said to Johanan son of Kareah, "Don't do such a thing! What you are saying about Ishmael is not true."

41 In the seventh month Ishmael son of Nethaniah, the son of Elishama, who was of royal blood and had been one of the king's officers, came with ten men to Gedaliah son of Ahikam at Mizpah. While they were eating together there, ²Ishmael son of Nethaniah and the ten men who were with him got up and struck down Gedaliah son of Ahikam, the son of Shaphan, with the sword, killing the one whom the king of Babylon had appointed as governor over the land. ³Ishmael also killed all the Jews who were with Gedaliah at Mizpah, as well as the Babylonian[c] soldiers who were there.

⁴The day after Gedaliah's assassination, before anyone knew about it, ⁵eighty men who had shaved off their beards, torn their clothes and cut themselves came from Shechem, Shiloh and Samaria, bringing grain offerings and incense with them to the house of the LORD. ⁶Ishmael son of Nethaniah went out from Mizpah to meet them, weeping as he went. When he met them, he said, "Come to Gedaliah son of Ahikam." ⁷When they went into the city, Ishmael son of Nethaniah and the men who were with him slaughtered them and threw them into a cistern. ⁸But ten of them said to Ishmael, "Don't kill us! We have wheat and barley, oil and honey, hidden in a field." So he let them alone and did not kill them with the others. ⁹Now the cistern where he threw all the bodies of the men he had killed along with Gedaliah was the one King Asa had made as part of his defense against Baasha king of Israel. Ishmael son of Nethaniah filled it with the dead.

¹⁰Ishmael made captives of all the rest of the people who were in Mizpah—the king's daughters along with all the others who were left there, over whom Nebuzaradan commander of the imperial guard had appointed Gedaliah son of Ahikam. Ishmael son of Nethaniah took them captive and set out to cross over to the Ammonites.

¹¹When Johanan son of Kareah and all the army officers who were with him heard about all the crimes Ishmael son of Nethaniah had committed, ¹²they took all their men and went to fight Ishmael son of Nethaniah. They caught up with him near the great pool in Gibeon. ¹³When all the people Ishmael had with him saw Johanan son of Kareah and the army officers who were with him, they were glad. ¹⁴All the people Ishmael had taken captive at Mizpah turned and went over to Johanan son of Kareah. ¹⁵But Ishmael son

---

[a] 8 Hebrew *Jezaniah*, a variant of *Jaazaniah*   [b] 9 Or *Chaldeans*; also in verse 10   [c] 3 Or *Chaldean*

of Nethaniah and eight of his men escaped from Johanan and fled to the Ammonites.

Flight to Egypt

[16]Then Johanan son of Kareah and all the army officers who were with him led away all the survivors from Mizpah whom he had recovered from Ishmael son of Nethaniah after he had assassinated Gedaliah son of Ahikam: the soldiers, women, children and court officials he had brought from Gibeon. [17]And they went on, stopping at Geruth Kimham near Bethlehem on their way to Egypt [18]to escape the Babylonians.[a] They were afraid of them because Ishmael son of Nethaniah had killed Gedaliah son of Ahikam, whom the king of Babylon had appointed as governor over the land.

42 Then all the army officers, including Johanan son of Kareah and Jezaniah[b] son of Hoshaiah, and all the people from the least to the greatest approached [2]Jeremiah the prophet and said to him, "Please hear our petition and pray to the LORD your God for this entire remnant. For as you now see, though we were once many, now only a few are left. [3]Pray that the LORD your God will tell us where we should go and what we should do."

[4]"I have heard you," replied Jeremiah the prophet. "I will certainly pray to the LORD your God as you have requested; I will tell you everything the LORD says and will keep nothing back from you."

[5]Then they said to Jeremiah, "May the LORD be a true and faithful witness against us if we do not act in accordance with everything the LORD your God sends you to tell us. [6]Whether it is favorable or unfavorable, we will obey the LORD our God, to whom we are sending you, so that it will go well with us, for we will obey the LORD our God."

[7]Ten days later the word of the LORD came to Jeremiah. [8]So he called together Johanan son of Kareah and all the army officers who were with him and all the people from the least to the greatest. [9]He said to them, "This is what the LORD, the God of Israel, to whom you sent me to present your petition, says: [10]'If you stay in this land, I will build you up and not tear you down; I will plant you and not uproot you, for I am grieved over the disaster I have inflicted on you. [11]Do not be afraid of the king of Babylon, whom you now fear. Do not be afraid of him, declares the LORD, for I am with you and will save you and deliver you from his hands. [12]I will show you compassion so that he will have compassion on you and restore you to your land.'

[13]"However, if you say, 'We will not stay in this land,' and so disobey the LORD your God, [14]and if you say, 'No, we will go and live in Egypt, where we will not see war or hear the trumpet or be hungry for bread,' [15]then hear the word of the LORD, O remnant of Judah. This is what the LORD Almighty, the God of Israel, says: 'If you are determined to go to Egypt and you do go to settle there, [16]then the sword you fear will overtake you there, and the famine you dread will follow you into Egypt, and there you will die. [17]Indeed, all who are determined to go to Egypt to settle there will die by the sword, famine and plague; not one of them will survive or escape the disaster I will bring on them.' [18]This is what the LORD Almighty, the God of Israel, says: 'As my anger and wrath have been poured out on those who lived in Jerusalem, so will my wrath be poured out on you when you go to Egypt. You will be an object of cursing and horror, of condemnation and reproach; you will never see this place again.'

[19]"O remnant of Judah, the LORD has told you, 'Do not go to Egypt.' Be sure of this: I warn you today [20]that you made a fatal mistake[c] when you sent me to the LORD your God and said, 'Pray to the LORD our God for us; tell us everything he says and we will do it.' [21]I have told you today, but you still have not obeyed the LORD your God in all he sent me to tell you. [22]So now, be sure of this: You will die by the sword, famine and plague in the place where you want to go to settle."

43 When Jeremiah finished telling the people all the words of the LORD their God—everything the LORD had sent him to tell them— [2]Azariah son of Hoshaiah and Johanan son of Kareah and all the arrogant men said to Jeremiah, "You are lying! The LORD our God has not sent you to say, 'You must not go to Egypt to settle there.' [3]But Baruch son of Neriah is inciting you against us to hand us over to the Babylonians,[a] so they may kill us or carry us into exile to Babylon."

[4]So Johanan son of Kareah and all the army

43:3 Closed Minds

Jeremiah was kidnapped by the few Israelites remaining in Jerusalem. Fearful that the Babylonians would blame them for the governor's murder, they took Jeremiah with them as they headed for Egypt. They stopped near Bethlehem to ask Jeremiah if they were doing the right thing. When he told them God wanted them to go back, they called him a liar. Jeremiah was disbelieved from the beginning to the end of his ministry, even by those who had seen some of his predictions come true.

officers and all the people disobeyed the LORD's command to stay in the land of Judah. [5]Instead, Johanan son of Kareah and all the army officers led away all the remnant of Judah who had come back to live in the land of Judah from all the nations where they had been scattered. [6]They also led away all the men, women and children and the king's daughters whom Nebuzaradan commander of the imperial guard had left with Gedaliah son of Ahikam, the son of Shaphan, and Jeremiah the prophet and Baruch son of Neriah. [7]So they entered Egypt in disobedience to the LORD and went as far as Tahpanhes.

[8]In Tahpanhes the word of the LORD came to Jeremiah: [9]"While the Jews are watching, take some large stones with you and bury them in clay in the brick pavement at the entrance to Pharaoh's palace in Tahpanhes. [10]Then say to them, 'This is what the LORD Almighty, the God of Israel, says: I will send for my servant Nebuchadnezzar king of Babylon, and I will set his throne over these stones I have buried here; he will spread his royal canopy above them. [11]He will come and attack Egypt, bringing death to those destined for death, captivity to those destined for captivity, and the sword to those destined for the sword. [12]He[a] will set fire to the temples of the gods of Egypt; he will burn their temples and take their gods captive. As a shepherd wraps his garment around him, so will he wrap Egypt around himself and depart from there unscathed. [13]There in the temple of the sun[b] in Egypt he will demolish the sacred pillars and will burn down the temples of the gods of Egypt.'"

Disaster Because of Idolatry

44 This word came to Jeremiah concerning all the Jews living in Lower Egypt—in Migdol, Tahpanhes and Memphis[c]—and in Upper Egypt[d]: [2]"This is what the LORD Almighty, the God of Israel, says: You saw the great disaster I brought on Jerusalem and on all the towns of Judah. Today they lie deserted and in ruins [3]because of the evil they have done. They provoked me to anger by burning incense and by worshiping other gods that neither they nor you nor your fathers ever knew. [4]Again and again I sent my servants the prophets, who said, 'Do not do this detestable thing that I hate!' [5]But they did not listen or pay attention; they did not turn from their wickedness or stop burning incense to other gods. [6]Therefore, my fierce anger was poured out; it raged against the towns of Judah and the streets of Jerusalem and made them the desolate ruins they are today.

[7]"Now this is what the LORD God Almighty, the God of Israel, says: Why bring such great disaster on yourselves by cutting off from Judah the men and women, the children and infants, and so leave yourselves without a remnant? [8]Why provoke me to anger with what your hands have made, burning incense to other gods in Egypt, where you have come to live? You will destroy yourselves and make yourselves an object of cursing and reproach among all the nations on earth. [9]Have you forgotten the wickedness committed by your fathers and by the kings and queens of Judah and the wickedness committed by you and your wives in the land of Judah and the streets of Jerusalem? [10]To this day they have not humbled themselves or shown reverence, nor have they followed my law and the decrees I set before you and your fathers.

[11]"Therefore, this is what the LORD Almighty, the God of Israel, says: I am determined to bring disaster on you and to destroy all Judah. [12]I will take away the remnant of Judah who were determined to go to Egypt to settle there. They will all perish in Egypt; they will fall by the sword or die from famine. From the least to the greatest, they will die by sword or famine. They will become an object of cursing and horror, of condemnation and reproach. [13]I will punish those who live in Egypt with the sword, famine and plague, as I punished Jerusalem. [14]None of the remnant of Judah who have gone to live in Egypt will escape or survive to return to the land of Judah, to which they long to return and live; none will return except a few fugitives."

[15]Then all the men who knew that their wives were burning incense to other gods, along with all the women who were present—a large assembly—and all the people living in Lower and Upper Egypt,[e] said to Jeremiah, [16]"We will not listen to the message you have spoken to us in the name of the LORD! [17]We will certainly do everything we said we would: We will burn incense to the Queen of Heaven and will pour out drink offerings to her just as we and our fathers, our kings and our officials did in the towns of Judah and in the streets of Jerusalem. At that time we had plenty of food and were well off and suffered no harm. [18]But ever since we stopped burning incense to the Queen of Heaven and pouring out drink offerings to her, we have had nothing and have been perishing by sword and famine."

[19]The women added, "When we burned incense to the Queen of Heaven and poured out drink offerings to her, did not our husbands know that we were making cakes like her image and pouring out drink offerings to her?"

[20]Then Jeremiah said to all the people, both

men and women, who were answering him, [21]"Did not the LORD remember and think about the incense burned in the towns of Judah and the streets of Jerusalem by you and your fathers, your kings and your officials and the people of the land? [22]When the LORD could no longer endure your wicked actions and the detestable

44:18 Queen of Heaven

"Queen of Heaven" was a title for Ishtar, a Babylonian goddess of fertility. Israelites— women especially—had worshiped her for a very long time, until the revival sparked by King Josiah put a stop to the practice (2 Kings 22). Now, about 35 years after Josiah's campaign, Israelites blamed their downfall on his reform. Jeremiah tried to set the record straight: It was persistence in pagan worship that had led to their destruction.

things you did, your land became an object of cursing and a desolate waste without inhabitants, as it is today. [23]Because you have burned incense and have sinned against the LORD and have not obeyed him or followed his law or his decrees or his stipulations, this disaster has come upon you, as you now see."

[24]Then Jeremiah said to all the people, including the women, "Hear the word of the LORD, all you people of Judah in Egypt. [25]This is what the LORD Almighty, the God of Israel, says: You and your wives have shown by your actions what you promised when you said, 'We will certainly carry out the vows we made to burn incense and pour out drink offerings to the Queen of Heaven.'

"Go ahead then, do what you promised! Keep your vows! [26]But hear the word of the LORD, all Jews living in Egypt: 'I swear by my great name,' says the LORD, 'that no one from Judah living anywhere in Egypt will ever again invoke my name or swear, "As surely as the Sovereign LORD lives." [27]For I am watching over them for harm, not for good; the Jews in Egypt will perish by sword and famine until they are all destroyed. [28]Those who escape the sword and return to the land of Judah from Egypt will be very few. Then the whole remnant of Judah who came to live in Egypt will know whose word will stand—mine or theirs.

[29]"'This will be the sign to you that I will punish you in this place,' declares the LORD, 'so that you will know that my threats of harm against you will surely stand.' [30]This is what the LORD says: 'I am going to hand Pharaoh Hophra king of Egypt over to his enemies who seek his life, just as I handed Zedekiah king of Judah over to Nebuchadnezzar king of Babylon, the enemy who was seeking his life.'"

A Message to Baruch

45 This is what Jeremiah the prophet told Baruch son of Neriah in the fourth year of Jehoiakim son of Josiah king of Judah, after Baruch had written on a scroll the words Jeremiah was then dictating: [2]"This is what the LORD, the God of Israel, says to you, Baruch: [3]You said, 'Woe to me! The LORD has added sorrow to my pain; I am worn out with groaning and find no rest.'"

[4]The LORD said, "Say this to him: 'This is what the LORD says: I will overthrow what I have built and uproot what I have planted, throughout the land. [5]Should you then seek great things for yourself? Seek them not. For I will bring disaster on all people, declares the LORD, but wherever you go I will let you escape with your life.'"

A Message About Egypt

46 This is the word of the LORD that came to Jeremiah the prophet concerning the nations:

[2]Concerning Egypt:

This is the message against the army of Pharaoh Neco king of Egypt, which was defeated at Carchemish on the Euphrates River by Nebuchadnezzar king of Babylon in the fourth year of Jehoiakim son of Josiah king of Judah:

[3]"Prepare your shields, both large and small,
    and march out for battle!
[4]Harness the horses,
    mount the steeds!
Take your positions
    with helmets on!
Polish your spears,
    put on your armor!
[5]What do I see?
    They are terrified,
they are retreating,
    their warriors are defeated.
They flee in haste
    without looking back,
    and there is terror on every side,"
                        declares the LORD.
[6]"The swift cannot flee
    nor the strong escape.
In the north by the River Euphrates
    they stumble and fall.

[7]"Who is this that rises like the Nile,
    like rivers of surging waters?
[8]Egypt rises like the Nile,
    like rivers of surging waters.
She says, 'I will rise and cover the earth;
    I will destroy cities and their people.'
[9]Charge, O horses!
    Drive furiously, O charioteers!

March on, O warriors—
men of Cush[a] and Put who carry shields,
men of Lydia who draw the bow.
¹⁰But that day belongs to the Lord, the LORD
Almighty—
a day of vengeance, for vengeance on his
foes.
The sword will devour till it is satisfied,
till it has quenched its thirst with blood.
For the Lord, the LORD Almighty, will offer
sacrifice
in the land of the north by the River
Euphrates.

¹¹"Go up to Gilead and get balm,
O Virgin Daughter of Egypt.
But you multiply remedies in vain;
there is no healing for you.
¹²The nations will hear of your shame;
your cries will fill the earth.
One warrior will stumble over another;
both will fall down together."

¹³This is the message the LORD spoke to Jeremiah the prophet about the coming of Nebuchadnezzar king of Babylon to attack Egypt:

¹⁴"Announce this in Egypt, and proclaim it in
Migdol;
proclaim it also in Memphis[b] and
Tahpanhes:
'Take your positions and get ready,
for the sword devours those around you.'
¹⁵Why will your warriors be laid low?
They cannot stand, for the LORD will push
them down.
¹⁶They will stumble repeatedly;
they will fall over each other.
They will say, 'Get up, let us go back
to our own people and our native lands,
away from the sword of the oppressor.'
¹⁷There they will exclaim,
'Pharaoh king of Egypt is only a loud
noise;
he has missed his opportunity.'

¹⁸"As surely as I live," declares the King,
whose name is the LORD Almighty,
"one will come who is like Tabor among the
mountains,
like Carmel by the sea.
¹⁹Pack your belongings for exile,
you who live in Egypt,

---

[a]9 That is, the upper Nile region   [b]14 Hebrew Noph; also in verse 19

World at War
While nations battle, God is in control

> "The sword will devour till it is satisfied, till it has quenched its thirst with blood." 46:10

FLIP ON THE TV NEWS. Scenes from around the world flash across the screen. In the Middle East, a bomb explodes and a building collapses. Bodies lie in the gutter. Women howl with anguish over their dead.

Seconds later you are in Africa. Revolutionaries, rifles brandished over their heads, march through captured streets. The camera zeroes in on the crumpled body of their former president.

The scene shifts to a Central American capital. Sirens scream around a burning restaurant while stretcher-bearers carry out the moaning victims of a drug-lord attack. Next, in Africa again, starving children grimace at you, too far gone to beg for food. Then you see snatches of violence in United States ghettoes, scenes of ethnic unrest in Europe, and political protests in Tibet and India. The world is whirling out of control. Your mind cannot take it in; one disaster muddles with another.

God Is in Control
In chapters 46 to 50, Jeremiah gives a similar portrait of the world. We flash by imagination from one country to the next. We smell the rotting bodies; we hear the exultant cries of conquerors. Jeremiah shows, in vivid color, a world as frightening as ours.

But there is a difference. TV news leaves viewers with a dizzy feeling that chaos reigns. But Jeremiah's vision shows, paradoxically, that God is in control. Through these disasters God punishes those who have opposed his will. As Israel's neighbors are destroyed, exiled Jews are freed to return to their land. History is not just "one thing after another." God gives it a sense of direction.

Jeremiah delivered his longest and most biting message to Babylon, Judah's conqueror. Their sheer arrogance, their assumption that they could do whatever they liked, drew God's fury. To a lesser degree, other countries followed the same pattern. God did not judge them by his law, because they never knew it. He judged them for their pride. They ought to have shown humility before God.

Life Questions: Can you discern any pattern or purpose to the violence in the world today?

for Memphis will be laid waste
    and lie in ruins without inhabitant.

20"Egypt is a beautiful heifer,
    but a gadfly is coming
    against her from the north.
21The mercenaries in her ranks
    are like fattened calves.
They too will turn and flee together,
    they will not stand their ground,
for the day of disaster is coming upon them,
    the time for them to be punished.
22Egypt will hiss like a fleeing serpent
    as the enemy advances in force;
they will come against her with axes,
    like men who cut down trees.
23They will chop down her forest,"
                            declares the LORD,
    "dense though it be.
They are more numerous than locusts,
    they cannot be counted.
24The Daughter of Egypt will be put to shame,
    handed over to the people of the north."

25The LORD Almighty, the God of Israel, says:
"I am about to bring punishment on Amon god
of Thebes,a on Pharaoh, on Egypt and her gods
and her kings, and on those who rely on Pharaoh. 26I will hand them over to those who seek
their lives, to Nebuchadnezzar king of Babylon
and his officers. Later, however, Egypt will be
inhabited as in times past," declares the LORD.

27"Do not fear, O Jacob my servant;
    do not be dismayed, O Israel.
I will surely save you out of a distant place,
    your descendants from the land of their
        exile.
Jacob will again have peace and security,
    and no one will make him afraid.
28Do not fear, O Jacob my servant,
    for I am with you," declares the LORD.
"Though I completely destroy all the nations
    among which I scatter you,
I will not completely destroy you.
I will discipline you but only with justice;
    I will not let you go entirely unpunished."

A Message About the Philistines

47 This is the word of the LORD that came to
Jeremiah the prophet concerning the Philistines before Pharaoh attacked Gaza:

2This is what the LORD says:

"See how the waters are rising in the north;
    they will become an overflowing torrent.
They will overflow the land and everything
        in it,

the towns and those who live in them.
The people will cry out;
    all who dwell in the land will wail
3at the sound of the hoofs of galloping steeds,
    at the noise of enemy chariots
    and the rumble of their wheels.
Fathers will not turn to help their children;
    their hands will hang limp.
4For the day has come
    to destroy all the Philistines
and to cut off all survivors
    who could help Tyre and Sidon.
The LORD is about to destroy the Philistines,
    the remnant from the coasts of Caphtor.b
5Gaza will shave her head in mourning;
    Ashkelon will be silenced.
O remnant on the plain,
    how long will you cut yourselves?

6"'Ah, sword of the LORD,' ⌐you cry,⌐
    'how long till you rest?
Return to your scabbard;
    cease and be still.'
7But how can it rest
    when the LORD has commanded it,
when he has ordered it
    to attack Ashkelon and the coast?"

A Message About Moab

48 Concerning Moab:

This is what the LORD Almighty, the God of
Israel, says:

"Woe to Nebo, for it will be ruined.
    Kiriathaim will be disgraced and captured;
    the strongholdc will be disgraced and
        shattered.
2Moab will be praised no more;
    in Heshbond men will plot her downfall:
    'Come, let us put an end to that nation.'
You too, O Madmen,e will be silenced;
    the sword will pursue you.
3Listen to the cries from Horonaim,
    cries of great havoc and destruction.
4Moab will be broken;
    her little ones will cry out.f
5They go up the way to Luhith,
    weeping bitterly as they go;
on the road down to Horonaim
    anguished cries over the destruction are
        heard.
6Flee! Run for your lives;
    become like a bushg in the desert.
7Since you trust in your deeds and riches,
    you too will be taken captive,
and Chemosh will go into exile,
    together with his priests and officials.

a25 Hebrew No   b4 That is, Crete   c1 Or / Misgab
plot.   e2 The name of the Moabite town Madmen sounds like the Hebrew for be silenced.   f4 Hebrew; Septuagint
/ proclaim it to Zoar   g6 Or like Aroer   d2 The Hebrew for Heshbon sounds like the Hebrew for

⁸The destroyer will come against every town,
　　and not a town will escape.
The valley will be ruined
　　and the plateau destroyed,
　　because the LORD has spoken.

48:7 An Exiled God

The gods of the Middle East tended to occupy a certain territory—thus each city had its own god. Chemosh, the chief god of Moab, was worshiped through child sacrifice (2 Kings 3:27). Here Jeremiah predicts that not only would the Moabites go into exile—their god would too. These gods were powerless before the God of Israel.

⁹Put salt on Moab,
　　for she will be laid waste[a];
her towns will become desolate,
　　with no one to live in them.

¹⁰"A curse on him who is lax in doing the
　　　LORD's work!
　　A curse on him who keeps his sword
　　　from bloodshed!

¹¹"Moab has been at rest from youth,
　　like wine left on its dregs,
not poured from one jar to another—
　　she has not gone into exile.
So she tastes as she did,
　　and her aroma is unchanged.
¹²But days are coming,"
　　declares the LORD,
　　"when I will send men who pour from jars,
　　and they will pour her out;
they will empty her jars
　　and smash her jugs.
¹³Then Moab will be ashamed of Chemosh,
　　as the house of Israel was ashamed
　　when they trusted in Bethel.

¹⁴"How can you say, 'We are warriors,
　　men valiant in battle'?
¹⁵Moab will be destroyed and her towns
　　　invaded;
　　her finest young men will go down in the
　　　slaughter,"
　　declares the King, whose name is the
　　　LORD Almighty.
¹⁶"The fall of Moab is at hand;
　　her calamity will come quickly.
¹⁷Mourn for her, all who live around her,
　　all who know her fame;
say, 'How broken is the mighty scepter,
　　how broken the glorious staff!'

¹⁸"Come down from your glory
　　and sit on the parched ground,
　　O inhabitants of the Daughter of Dibon,
for he who destroys Moab
　　will come up against you
　　and ruin your fortified cities.
¹⁹Stand by the road and watch,
　　you who live in Aroer.
Ask the man fleeing and the woman
　　　escaping,
　　ask them, 'What has happened?'
²⁰Moab is disgraced, for she is shattered.
　　Wail and cry out!
Announce by the Arnon
　　that Moab is destroyed.
²¹Judgment has come to the plateau—
　　to Holon, Jahzah and Mephaath,
²² 　to Dibon, Nebo and Beth Diblathaim,
²³ 　to Kiriathaim, Beth Gamul and Beth
　　　Meon,
²⁴ 　to Kerioth and Bozrah—
　　to all the towns of Moab, far and near.
²⁵Moab's horn[b] is cut off;
　　her arm is broken,"
　　　　　　　　　　　　declares the LORD.

²⁶"Make her drunk,
　　for she has defied the LORD.
Let Moab wallow in her vomit;
　　let her be an object of ridicule.
²⁷Was not Israel the object of your ridicule?
　　Was she caught among thieves,
that you shake your head in scorn
　　whenever you speak of her?
²⁸Abandon your towns and dwell among the
　　　rocks,
　　you who live in Moab.
Be like a dove that makes its nest
　　at the mouth of a cave.

²⁹"We have heard of Moab's pride—
　　her overweening pride and conceit,
her pride and arrogance
　　and the haughtiness of her heart.
³⁰I know her insolence but it is futile,"
　　　　　　　　　　　　declares the LORD,
　　"and her boasts accomplish nothing.
³¹Therefore I wail over Moab,
　　for all Moab I cry out,
　　I moan for the men of Kir Hareseth.
³²I weep for you, as Jazer weeps,
　　O vines of Sibmah.
Your branches spread as far as the sea;
　　they reached as far as the sea of Jazer.
The destroyer has fallen
　　on your ripened fruit and grapes.
³³Joy and gladness are gone
　　from the orchards and fields of Moab.
I have stopped the flow of wine from the
　　　presses;

---

a 9 Or Give wings to Moab, / for she will fly away　　*b 25 Horn here symbolizes strength.*

no one treads them with shouts of joy.
Although there are shouts,
  they are not shouts of joy.

³⁴"The sound of their cry rises
  from Heshbon to Elealeh and Jahaz,
from Zoar as far as Horonaim and Eglath
    Shelishiyah,
  for even the waters of Nimrim are dried
    up.
³⁵In Moab I will put an end
  to those who make offerings on the high
    places
  and burn incense to their gods,"
                    declares the LORD.
³⁶"So my heart laments for Moab like a flute;
  it laments like a flute for the men of Kir
    Hareseth.
The wealth they acquired is gone.
³⁷Every head is shaved
  and every beard cut off;
every hand is slashed
  and every waist is covered with sackcloth.
³⁸On all the roofs in Moab
  and in the public squares
there is nothing but mourning,
  for I have broken Moab
  like a jar that no one wants,"
                    declares the LORD.
³⁹"How shattered she is! How they wail!
  How Moab turns her back in shame!
Moab has become an object of ridicule,
  an object of horror to all those around
    her."

⁴⁰This is what the LORD says:

"Look! An eagle is swooping down,
  spreading its wings over Moab.
⁴¹Kerioth*ᵃ* will be captured
  and the strongholds taken.
In that day the hearts of Moab's warriors
  will be like the heart of a woman in labor.
⁴²Moab will be destroyed as a nation
  because she defied the LORD.
⁴³Terror and pit and snare await you,
  O people of Moab,"
                    declares the LORD.
⁴⁴"Whoever flees from the terror
  will fall into a pit,
whoever climbs out of the pit
  will be caught in a snare;
for I will bring upon Moab
  the year of her punishment,"
                    declares the LORD.

⁴⁵"In the shadow of Heshbon
  the fugitives stand helpless,
for a fire has gone out from Heshbon,
  a blaze from the midst of Sihon;

it burns the foreheads of Moab,
  the skulls of the noisy boasters.
⁴⁶Woe to you, O Moab!
  The people of Chemosh are destroyed;

48:43 Well-turned Phrase

Some of Jeremiah's language eludes translation, especially when, as here, he chooses Hebrew words for the sake of sound. "Terror, pit, snare" are translations of "pahad, pahat, pah." Isaiah (or some poet before him) had already minted the phrase, generations before Jeremiah (see Isaiah 24:17).

your sons are taken into exile
  and your daughters into captivity.

⁴⁷"Yet I will restore the fortunes of Moab
  in days to come,"
                    declares the LORD.

Here ends the judgment on Moab.

A Message About Ammon

49
Concerning the Ammonites:

This is what the LORD says:

"Has Israel no sons?
  Has she no heirs?
Why then has Molech*ᵇ* taken possession of
    Gad?
  Why do his people live in its towns?
²But the days are coming,"
    declares the LORD,
"when I will sound the battle cry
  against Rabbah of the Ammonites;
it will become a mound of ruins,
  and its surrounding villages will be set on
    fire.
Then Israel will drive out
  those who drove her out,"
                    says the LORD.
³"Wail, O Heshbon, for Ai is destroyed!
  Cry out, O inhabitants of Rabbah!
Put on sackcloth and mourn;
  rush here and there inside the walls,
for Molech will go into exile,
  together with his priests and officials.
⁴Why do you boast of your valleys,
  boast of your valleys so fruitful?
O unfaithful daughter,
  you trust in your riches and say,
  'Who will attack me?'
⁵I will bring terror on you

ᵃ41 Or *The cities*   ᵇ1 Or *their king*; Hebrew *malcam*; also in verse 3

from all those around you,"

> declares the Lord,
> the LORD Almighty.

"Every one of you will be driven away,
  and no one will gather the fugitives.

⁶"Yet afterward, I will restore the fortunes of
  the Ammonites,"

> declares the LORD.

A Message About Edom

⁷Concerning Edom:

This is what the LORD Almighty says:

"Is there no longer wisdom in Teman?
  Has counsel perished from the prudent?
  Has their wisdom decayed?
⁸Turn and flee, hide in deep caves,
  you who live in Dedan,
for I will bring disaster on Esau
  at the time I punish him.
⁹If grape pickers came to you,
  would they not leave a few grapes?
If thieves came during the night,
  would they not steal only as much as they
    wanted?
¹⁰But I will strip Esau bare;
  I will uncover his hiding places,
  so that he cannot conceal himself.
His children, relatives and neighbors will
    perish,
  and he will be no more.
¹¹Leave your orphans; I will protect their lives.
  Your widows too can trust in me."

¹²This is what the LORD says: "If those who do
not deserve to drink the cup must drink it, why
should you go unpunished? You will not go unpunished, but must drink it. ¹³I swear by myself,"
declares the LORD, "that Bozrah will become a
ruin and an object of horror, of reproach and of
cursing; and all its towns will be in ruins forever."

¹⁴I have heard a message from the LORD:
  An envoy was sent to the nations to say,
"Assemble yourselves to attack it!
  Rise up for battle!"

¹⁵"Now I will make you small among the
    nations,
  despised among men.
¹⁶The terror you inspire
  and the pride of your heart have deceived
    you,
you who live in the clefts of the rocks,
  who occupy the heights of the hill.
Though you build your nest as high as the
    eagle's,
  from there I will bring you down,"

> declares the LORD.

¹⁷"Edom will become an object of horror;
  all who pass by will be appalled and will
    scoff
because of all its wounds.
¹⁸As Sodom and Gomorrah were overthrown,
  along with their neighboring towns,"

> says the LORD,

"so no one will live there;
  no man will dwell in it.

¹⁹"Like a lion coming up from Jordan's
    thickets
  to a rich pastureland,
I will chase Edom from its land in an
    instant.
  Who is the chosen one I will appoint for
    this?
Who is like me and who can challenge me?
  And what shepherd can stand against
    me?"
²⁰Therefore, hear what the LORD has planned
    against Edom,
  what he has purposed against those who
    live in Teman:
The young of the flock will be dragged away;
  he will completely destroy their pasture
    because of them.
²¹At the sound of their fall the earth will
    tremble;
  their cry will resound to the Red Sea.ᵃ
²²Look! An eagle will soar and swoop down,
  spreading its wings over Bozrah.
In that day the hearts of Edom's warriors
  will be like the heart of a woman in labor.

A Message About Damascus

²³Concerning Damascus:

"Hamath and Arpad are dismayed,
  for they have heard bad news.
They are disheartened,
  troubled likeᵇ the restless sea.
²⁴Damascus has become feeble,
  she has turned to flee
  and panic has gripped her;
anguish and pain have seized her,
  pain like that of a woman in labor.
²⁵Why has the city of renown not been
    abandoned,
  the town in which I delight?
²⁶Surely, her young men will fall in the streets;
  all her soldiers will be silenced in that
    day,"

> declares the LORD Almighty.

²⁷"I will set fire to the walls of Damascus;
  it will consume the fortresses of
    Ben-Hadad."

ᵃ21 Hebrew *Yam Suph*; that is, Sea of Reeds   ᵇ23 Hebrew *on* or *by*

A Message About Kedar and Hazor

28Concerning Kedar and the kingdoms of Hazor, which Nebuchadnezzar king of Babylon attacked:

This is what the LORD says:

"Arise, and attack Kedar
  and destroy the people of the East.
29Their tents and their flocks will be taken;
  their shelters will be carried off
  with all their goods and camels.
Men will shout to them,
  'Terror on every side!'

30"Flee quickly away!
  Stay in deep caves, you who live in
    Hazor,"
                    declares the LORD.
"Nebuchadnezzar king of Babylon has
    plotted against you;
  he has devised a plan against you.

31"Arise and attack a nation at ease,
  which lives in confidence,"
                    declares the LORD,
"a nation that has neither gates nor bars;
  its people live alone.
32Their camels will become plunder,
  and their large herds will be booty.
I will scatter to the winds those who are in
    distant places[a]
  and will bring disaster on them from
    every side,"
                    declares the LORD.
33"Hazor will become a haunt of jackals,
  a desolate place forever.
No one will live there;
  no man will dwell in it."

A Message About Elam

34This is the word of the LORD that came to Jeremiah the prophet concerning Elam, early in the reign of Zedekiah king of Judah:

35This is what the LORD Almighty says:

"See, I will break the bow of Elam,
  the mainstay of their might.
36I will bring against Elam the four winds
  from the four quarters of the heavens;
I will scatter them to the four winds,
  and there will not be a nation
  where Elam's exiles do not go.
37I will shatter Elam before their foes,
  before those who seek their lives;
I will bring disaster upon them,
  even my fierce anger,"
                    declares the LORD.
"I will pursue them with the sword
  until I have made an end of them.

38I will set my throne in Elam
  and destroy her king and officials,"
                    declares the LORD.

39"Yet I will restore the fortunes of Elam
  in days to come,"
                    declares the LORD.

A Message About Babylon

50 This is the word the LORD spoke through Jeremiah the prophet concerning Babylon and the land of the Babylonians[b]:

2"Announce and proclaim among the nations,
  lift up a banner and proclaim it;
  keep nothing back, but say,
'Babylon will be captured;
  Bel will be put to shame,
  Marduk filled with terror.
Her images will be put to shame
  and her idols filled with terror.'
3A nation from the north will attack her
  and lay waste her land.
No one will live in it;
  both men and animals will flee away.

50:1–3 None Escape

Chapters 46–50 record a virtual catalog of Israel's enemies. Jeremiah begins with Egypt, goes on to Israel's immediate (small) neighbors, and ends with archenemy Babylon. No nation is exempt from God's justice.

4"In those days, at that time,"
  declares the LORD,
"the people of Israel and the people of Judah
    together
  will go in tears to seek the LORD their
    God.
5They will ask the way to Zion
  and turn their faces toward it.
They will come and bind themselves to the
    LORD
  in an everlasting covenant
  that will not be forgotten.

6"My people have been lost sheep;
  their shepherds have led them astray
  and caused them to roam on the
    mountains.
They wandered over mountain and hill
  and forgot their own resting place.
7Whoever found them devoured them;
  their enemies said, 'We are not guilty,
for they sinned against the LORD, their true
    pasture,
  the LORD, the hope of their fathers.'

---

a32 Or *who clip the hair by their foreheads*   b1 Or *Chaldeans*; also in verses 8, 25, 35 and 45

8"Flee out of Babylon;
     leave the land of the Babylonians,
     and be like the goats that lead the flock.
9For I will stir up and bring against Babylon
     an alliance of great nations from the land
          of the north.
They will take up their positions against her,
     and from the north she will be captured.
Their arrows will be like skilled warriors
     who do not return empty-handed.
10So Babylonia[a] will be plundered;
     all who plunder her will have their fill,"
                              declares the LORD.

11"Because you rejoice and are glad,
     you who pillage my inheritance,
because you frolic like a heifer threshing
          grain
     and neigh like stallions,
12your mother will be greatly ashamed;
     she who gave you birth will be disgraced.
She will be the least of the nations—
     a wilderness, a dry land, a desert.
13Because of the LORD's anger she will not be
          inhabited
     but will be completely desolate.
All who pass Babylon will be horrified and
          scoff
     because of all her wounds.

14"Take up your positions around Babylon,
     all you who draw the bow.
Shoot at her! Spare no arrows,
     for she has sinned against the LORD.
15Shout against her on every side!
     She surrenders, her towers fall,
     her walls are torn down.
Since this is the vengeance of the LORD,
     take vengeance on her;
     do to her as she has done to others.
16Cut off from Babylon the sower,
     and the reaper with his sickle at harvest.
Because of the sword of the oppressor
     let everyone return to his own people,
     let everyone flee to his own land.

17"Israel is a scattered flock
     that lions have chased away.
The first to devour him
     was the king of Assyria;
the last to crush his bones
     was Nebuchadnezzar king of Babylon."

18Therefore this is what the LORD Almighty,
the God of Israel, says:

     "I will punish the king of Babylon and his
          land
     as I punished the king of Assyria.

19But I will bring Israel back to his own
          pasture
     and he will graze on Carmel and Bashan;
his appetite will be satisfied
     on the hills of Ephraim and Gilead.
20In those days, at that time,"
                    declares the LORD,
"search will be made for Israel's guilt,
     but there will be none,
and for the sins of Judah,
     but none will be found,
     for I will forgive the remnant I spare.

50:20 An End to Guilt

For 50 chapters the book of Jeremiah hammers away at Israel's guilt. Because of it, punishment was bound to come. Yet the forgiveness to come from God will be as absolute as the guilt: A search for Israel's sins will not uncover a single one.

21"Attack the land of Merathaim
     and those who live in Pekod.
Pursue, kill and completely destroy[b] them,"
                              declares the LORD.
     "Do everything I have commanded you.
22The noise of battle is in the land,
     the noise of great destruction!
23How broken and shattered
     is the hammer of the whole earth!
How desolate is Babylon
     among the nations!
24I set a trap for you, O Babylon,
     and you were caught before you knew it;
you were found and captured
     because you opposed the LORD.
25The LORD has opened his arsenal
     and brought out the weapons of his
          wrath,
for the Sovereign LORD Almighty has work to
          do
     in the land of the Babylonians.
26Come against her from afar.
     Break open her granaries;
     pile her up like heaps of grain.
Completely destroy her
     and leave her no remnant.
27Kill all her young bulls;
     let them go down to the slaughter!
Woe to them! For their day has come,
     the time for them to be punished.
28Listen to the fugitives and refugees from
          Babylon
     declaring in Zion

---

[a]10 Or *Chaldea*   [b]21 The Hebrew term refers to the irrevocable giving over of things or persons to the LORD, often by totally destroying them; also in verse 26.

how the LORD our God has taken vengeance,
    vengeance for his temple.

²⁹"Summon archers against Babylon,
    all those who draw the bow.
Encamp all around her;
    let no one escape.
Repay her for her deeds;
    do to her as she has done.
For she has defied the LORD,
    the Holy One of Israel.
³⁰Therefore, her young men will fall in the
    streets;
    all her soldiers will be silenced in that
      day,"
                      declares the LORD.
³¹"See, I am against you, O arrogant one,"
    declares the Lord, the LORD Almighty,
"for your day has come,
    the time for you to be punished.
³²The arrogant one will stumble and fall
    and no one will help her up;
I will kindle a fire in her towns
    that will consume all who are around
      her."

³³This is what the LORD Almighty says:

"The people of Israel are oppressed,
    and the people of Judah as well.
All their captors hold them fast,
    refusing to let them go.
³⁴Yet their Redeemer is strong;
    the LORD Almighty is his name.
He will vigorously defend their cause
    so that he may bring rest to their land,
    but unrest to those who live in Babylon.

³⁵"A sword against the Babylonians!"
    declares the LORD—
"against those who live in Babylon
    and against her officials and wise men!
³⁶A sword against her false prophets!
    They will become fools.
A sword against her warriors!
    They will be filled with terror.
³⁷A sword against her horses and chariots
    and all the foreigners in her ranks!
    They will become women.
A sword against her treasures!
    They will be plundered.
³⁸A drought on^a her waters!
    They will dry up.
For it is a land of idols,
    idols that will go mad with terror.

³⁹"So desert creatures and hyenas will live
    there,
    and there the owl will dwell.

It will never again be inhabited
    or lived in from generation to generation.
⁴⁰As God overthrew Sodom and Gomorrah
    along with their neighboring towns,"
                declares the LORD,
"so no one will live there;
    no man will dwell in it.

⁴¹"Look! An army is coming from the north;
    a great nation and many kings
    are being stirred up from the ends of the
      earth.
⁴²They are armed with bows and spears;
    they are cruel and without mercy.
They sound like the roaring sea
    as they ride on their horses;
they come like men in battle formation
    to attack you, O Daughter of Babylon.
⁴³The king of Babylon has heard reports about
    them,
    and his hands hang limp.
Anguish has gripped him,
    pain like that of a woman in labor.
⁴⁴Like a lion coming up from Jordan's thickets
    to a rich pastureland,
I will chase Babylon from its land in an
    instant.
    Who is the chosen one I will appoint for
      this?
Who is like me and who can challenge me?
    And what shepherd can stand against
      me?"
⁴⁵Therefore, hear what the LORD has planned
    against Babylon,
    what he has purposed against the land of
      the Babylonians:
The young of the flock will be dragged away;
    he will completely destroy their pasture
      because of them.
⁴⁶At the sound of Babylon's capture the earth
    will tremble;
    its cry will resound among the nations.

51 This is what the LORD says:

"See, I will stir up the spirit of a destroyer
    against Babylon and the people of Leb
      Kamai.^b
²I will send foreigners to Babylon
    to winnow her and to devastate her land;
they will oppose her on every side
    in the day of her disaster.
³Let not the archer string his bow,
    nor let him put on his armor.
Do not spare her young men;
    completely destroy^c her army.
⁴They will fall down slain in Babylon,^d

---

^a38 Or *A sword against*   ^b1 *Leb Kamai* is a cryptogram for Chaldea, that is, Babylonia.   ^c3 The Hebrew term refers to the irrevocable giving over of things or persons to the LORD, often by totally destroying them.   ^d4 Or *Chaldea*

fatally wounded in her streets.
[5]For Israel and Judah have not been forsaken
by their God, the LORD Almighty,
though their land[a] is full of guilt
before the Holy One of Israel.

[6]"Flee from Babylon!
Run for your lives!
Do not be destroyed because of her sins.
It is time for the LORD's vengeance;
he will pay her what she deserves.
[7]Babylon was a gold cup in the LORD's hand;
she made the whole earth drunk.
The nations drank her wine;
therefore they have now gone mad.
[8]Babylon will suddenly fall and be broken.
Wail over her!
Get balm for her pain;
perhaps she can be healed.

[9]"'We would have healed Babylon,
but she cannot be healed;
let us leave her and each go to his own land,
for her judgment reaches to the skies,
it rises as high as the clouds.'

[10]"'The LORD has vindicated us;
come, let us tell in Zion
what the LORD our God has done.'

[11]"Sharpen the arrows,
take up the shields!
The LORD has stirred up the kings of the
Medes,
because his purpose is to destroy Babylon.
The LORD will take vengeance,
vengeance for his temple.
[12]Lift up a banner against the walls of
Babylon!
Reinforce the guard,
station the watchmen,
prepare an ambush!
The LORD will carry out his purpose,
his decree against the people of Babylon.
[13]You who live by many waters
and are rich in treasures,
your end has come,
the time for you to be cut off.
[14]The LORD Almighty has sworn by himself:
I will surely fill you with men, as with a
swarm of locusts,
and they will shout in triumph over you.

[15]"He made the earth by his power;
he founded the world by his wisdom
and stretched out the heavens by his
understanding.
[16]When he thunders, the waters in the heavens
roar;
he makes clouds rise from the ends of the
earth.

He sends lightning with the rain
and brings out the wind from his
storehouses.

[17]"Every man is senseless and without
knowledge;
every goldsmith is shamed by his idols.

51:13 Waters of Babylon

Water has always been precious in the Middle East, and Babylon's mighty Euphrates River, complemented by a magnificent system of irrigation canals, was a major source of wealth and security in times of drought. The modern-day nations of Iraq, Iran, and Turkey still argue—and sometimes fight—over this resource.

His images are a fraud;
they have no breath in them.
[18]They are worthless, the objects of mockery;
when their judgment comes, they will
perish.
[19]He who is the Portion of Jacob is not like
these,
for he is the Maker of all things,
including the tribe of his inheritance—
the LORD Almighty is his name.

[20]"You are my war club,
my weapon for battle—
with you I shatter nations,
with you I destroy kingdoms,
[21]with you I shatter horse and rider,
with you I shatter chariot and driver,
[22]with you I shatter man and woman,
with you I shatter old man and youth,
with you I shatter young man and
maiden,
[23]with you I shatter shepherd and flock,
with you I shatter farmer and oxen,
with you I shatter governors and officials.

[24]"Before your eyes I will repay Babylon and
all who live in Babylonia[b] for all the wrong they
have done in Zion," declares the LORD.

[25]"I am against you, O destroying mountain,
you who destroy the whole earth,"
declares the LORD.
"I will stretch out my hand against you,
roll you off the cliffs,
and make you a burned-out mountain.
[26]No rock will be taken from you for a
cornerstone,
nor any stone for a foundation,
for you will be desolate forever,"
declares the LORD.

[a]5 Or *I and the land ⌊of the Babylonians⌋*   [b]24 Or *Chaldea*; also in verse 35

27"Lift up a banner in the land!
  Blow the trumpet among the nations!
Prepare the nations for battle against her;
  summon against her these kingdoms:
  Ararat, Minni and Ashkenaz.
Appoint a commander against her;
  send up horses like a swarm of locusts.
28Prepare the nations for battle against her—
  the kings of the Medes,
their governors and all their officials,
  and all the countries they rule.
29The land trembles and writhes,
  for the LORD's purposes against Babylon
    stand—
to lay waste the land of Babylon
  so that no one will live there.
30Babylon's warriors have stopped fighting;
  they remain in their strongholds.
Their strength is exhausted;
  they have become like women.
Her dwellings are set on fire;
  the bars of her gates are broken.
31One courier follows another
  and messenger follows messenger
to announce to the king of Babylon
  that his entire city is captured,
32the river crossings seized,
  the marshes set on fire,
  and the soldiers terrified."

33This is what the LORD Almighty, the God of
Israel, says:

  "The Daughter of Babylon is like a threshing
    floor
    at the time it is trampled;
  the time to harvest her will soon come."

34"Nebuchadnezzar king of Babylon has
    devoured us,
  he has thrown us into confusion,
  he has made us an empty jar.
Like a serpent he has swallowed us
  and filled his stomach with our delicacies,
  and then has spewed us out.
35May the violence done to our flesh*a* be
    upon Babylon,"
  say the inhabitants of Zion.
"May our blood be on those who live in
    Babylonia,"
  says Jerusalem.

36Therefore, this is what the LORD says:

"See, I will defend your cause
  and avenge you;
I will dry up her sea
  and make her springs dry.
37Babylon will be a heap of ruins,
  a haunt of jackals,
  an object of horror and scorn,

  a place where no one lives.
38Her people all roar like young lions,
  they growl like lion cubs.
39But while they are aroused,
  I will set out a feast for them
  and make them drunk,
so that they shout with laughter—
  then sleep forever and not awake,"
                    declares the LORD.
40"I will bring them down
  like lambs to the slaughter,
  like rams and goats.

41"How Sheshach*b* will be captured,
  the boast of the whole earth seized!
What a horror Babylon will be
  among the nations!
42The sea will rise over Babylon;
  its roaring waves will cover her.
43Her towns will be desolate,
  a dry and desert land,
a land where no one lives,
  through which no man travels.
44I will punish Bel in Babylon
  and make him spew out what he has
    swallowed.
The nations will no longer stream to him.
  And the wall of Babylon will fall.

45"Come out of her, my people!
  Run for your lives!
  Run from the fierce anger of the LORD.
46Do not lose heart or be afraid
  when rumors are heard in the land;
one rumor comes this year, another the next,
  rumors of violence in the land
  and of ruler against ruler.
47For the time will surely come
  when I will punish the idols of Babylon;
  her whole land will be disgraced
  and her slain will all lie fallen within her.
48Then heaven and earth and all that is in
    them
  will shout for joy over Babylon,
for out of the north
  destroyers will attack her,"
                    declares the LORD.

49"Babylon must fall because of Israel's slain,
  just as the slain in all the earth
  have fallen because of Babylon.
50You who have escaped the sword,
  leave and do not linger!
Remember the LORD in a distant land,
  and think on Jerusalem."

51"We are disgraced,
  for we have been insulted
  and shame covers our faces,

a35 Or *done to us and to our children*   *b41 Sheshach* is a cryptogram for Babylon.

because foreigners have entered
   the holy places of the LORD's house."

⁵²"But days are coming," declares the LORD,
   "when I will punish her idols,
and throughout her land
   the wounded will groan.
⁵³Even if Babylon reaches the sky
   and fortifies her lofty stronghold,
I will send destroyers against her,"
                         declares the LORD.

51:53 Apocalyptic Arrogance

*The arrogance of Babylon—her sense of
absolute, untouchable power—became an
emblem of the forces God will ultimately
destroy. Jeremiah probably was thinking only
of Babylon's towering ziggurat (or temple) and
double wall defenses. But Babylon's "reaching
for the sky" suggested an image of a nation
trying to compete with God. Revelation 18—
written long after Jeremiah's Babylon had been
destroyed—described the fall of another proud
and wealthy "Babylon" at the end of the age.*

⁵⁴"The sound of a cry comes from Babylon,
   the sound of great destruction
   from the land of the Babylonians.ᵃ
⁵⁵The LORD will destroy Babylon;
   he will silence her noisy din.
Waves ⌊of enemies⌋ will rage like great
     waters;
   the roar of their voices will resound.
⁵⁶A destroyer will come against Babylon;
   her warriors will be captured,
   and their bows will be broken.
For the LORD is a God of retribution;
   he will repay in full.
⁵⁷I will make her officials and wise men drunk,
   her governors, officers and warriors as
     well;
they will sleep forever and not awake,"
   declares the King, whose name is the
     LORD Almighty.

⁵⁸This is what the LORD Almighty says:

"Babylon's thick wall will be leveled
   and her high gates set on fire;
the peoples exhaust themselves for nothing,
   the nations' labor is only fuel for the
     flames."

⁵⁹This is the message Jeremiah gave to the staff
officer Seraiah son of Neriah, the son of Mahseiah, when he went to Babylon with Zedekiah king
of Judah in the fourth year of his reign. ⁶⁰Jeremi-

ah had written on a scroll about all the disasters
that would come upon Babylon—all that had
been recorded concerning Babylon. ⁶¹He said to
Seraiah, "When you get to Babylon, see that you
read all these words aloud. ⁶²Then say, 'O LORD,
you have said you will destroy this place, so that
neither man nor animal will live in it; it will be
desolate forever.' ⁶³When you finish reading this
scroll, tie a stone to it and throw it into the Euphrates. ⁶⁴Then say, 'So will Babylon sink to rise
no more because of the disaster I will bring upon
her. And her people will fall.' "

The words of Jeremiah end here.

The Fall of Jerusalem

52 Zedekiah was twenty-one years old when
he became king, and he reigned in Jerusalem eleven years. His mother's name was Hamutal daughter of Jeremiah; she was from Libnah.
²He did evil in the eyes of the LORD, just as Jehoiakim had done. ³It was because of the LORD's
anger that all this happened to Jerusalem and
Judah, and in the end he thrust them from his
presence.

Now Zedekiah rebelled against the king of
Babylon.

⁴So in the ninth year of Zedekiah's reign, on
the tenth day of the tenth month, Nebuchadnezzar king of Babylon marched against Jerusalem
with his whole army. They camped outside the
city and built siege works all around it. ⁵The city
was kept under siege until the eleventh year of
King Zedekiah.

⁶By the ninth day of the fourth month the
famine in the city had become so severe that
there was no food for the people to eat. ⁷Then the
city wall was broken through, and the whole
army fled. They left the city at night through the
gate between the two walls near the king's garden, though the Babyloniansᵇ were surrounding
the city. They fled toward the Arabah,ᶜ ⁸but the
Babylonianᵈ army pursued King Zedekiah and
overtook him in the plains of Jericho. All his
soldiers were separated from him and scattered,
⁹and he was captured.

He was taken to the king of Babylon at Riblah
in the land of Hamath, where he pronounced
sentence on him. ¹⁰There at Riblah the king of
Babylon slaughtered the sons of Zedekiah before
his eyes; he also killed all the officials of Judah.
¹¹Then he put out Zedekiah's eyes, bound him
with bronze shackles and took him to Babylon,
where he put him in prison till the day of his
death.

¹²On the tenth day of the fifth month, in the
nineteenth year of Nebuchadnezzar king of Babylon, Nebuzaradan commander of the imperial

---

ᵃ54 Or *Chaldeans*; also   ᵇ7 Or *Chaldeans*; also in verse 17   ᶜ7 Or *the Jordan Valley*   ᵈ8 Or *Chaldean*; also
in verse 14

guard, who served the king of Babylon, came to Jerusalem. [13]He set fire to the temple of the LORD, the royal palace and all the houses of Jerusalem. Every important building he burned down. [14]The

whole Babylonian army under the commander of the imperial guard broke down all the walls around Jerusalem. [15]Nebuzaradan the commander of the guard carried into exile some of the poorest people and those who remained in the city, along with the rest of the craftsmen[a] and those who had gone over to the king of Babylon. [16]But Nebuzaradan left behind the rest of the poorest people of the land to work the vineyards and fields.

[17]The Babylonians broke up the bronze pillars, the movable stands and the bronze Sea that were at the temple of the LORD and they carried all the bronze to Babylon. [18]They also took away the pots, shovels, wick trimmers, sprinkling bowls, dishes and all the bronze articles used in the temple service. [19]The commander of the imperial guard took away the basins, censers, sprinkling bowls, pots, lampstands, dishes and bowls used for drink offerings—all that were made of pure gold or silver.

[20]The bronze from the two pillars, the Sea and the twelve bronze bulls under it, and the movable stands, which King Solomon had made for the temple of the LORD, was more than could be weighed. [21]Each of the pillars was eighteen cubits high and twelve cubits in circumference[b]; each was four fingers thick, and hollow. [22]The bronze capital on top of the one pillar was five cubits[c] high and was decorated with a network and pomegranates of bronze all around. The other pillar, with its pomegranates, was similar. [23]There were ninety-six pomegranates on the sides; the total number of pomegranates above the surrounding network was a hundred.

[24]The commander of the guard took as prisoners Seraiah the chief priest, Zephaniah the priest next in rank and the three doorkeepers. [25]Of those still in the city, he took the officer in charge of the fighting men, and seven royal advisers. He also took the secretary who was chief officer in charge of conscripting the people of the land and sixty of his men who were found in the city. [26]Nebuzaradan the commander took them all and brought them to the king of Babylon at Riblah. [27]There at Riblah, in the land of Hamath, the king had them executed.

So Judah went into captivity, away from her land. [28]This is the number of the people Nebuchadnezzar carried into exile:

in the seventh year, 3,023 Jews;
[29]in Nebuchadnezzar's eighteenth year,
   832 people from Jerusalem;
[30]in his twenty-third year,
   745 Jews taken into exile by Nebuzaradan the commander of the imperial guard.
There were 4,600 people in all.

Jehoiachin Released

[31]In the thirty-seventh year of the exile of Jehoiachin king of Judah, in the year Evil-Merodach[d] became king of Babylon, he released Jehoiachin king of Judah and freed him from prison on the twenty-fifth day of the twelfth month. [32]He spoke kindly to him and gave him a seat of honor higher than those of the other kings who were with him in Babylon. [33]So Jehoiachin put aside his prison clothes and for the rest of his life ate regularly at the king's table. [34]Day by day the king of Babylon gave Jehoiachin a regular allowance as long as he lived, till the day of his death.

---

[a]15 Or *populace*   [b]21 That is, about 27 feet (about 8.1 meters) high and 18 feet (about 5.4 meters) in circumference   [c]22 That is, about 7 1/2 feet (about 2.3 meters)   [d]31 Also called *Amel-Marduk*

LAMENTATIONS

A City in Ruins
There was nothing left to do but weep

"Is it nothing to you, all you who pass by?" 1:12

EVERY YEAR THE WORLD PAUSES to remember one awful day in Hiroshima, Japan, when the power of the atom came out of the sky. Opinions vary over whether an atom bomb was necessary to end World War II. Necessary or not, however, Hiroshima was a horrible tragedy. Though the survivors have gone on with their lives, they cannot forget. Nor can the rest of the world. Hiroshima's shadow stretches through to our time.

Five Poems of Grief

Lamentations offers five poems written from a state of dazed grief worthy of Hiroshima. A whole city has been destroyed. Brothers, sisters, children, friends are all gone. Men the town admired wander the body-littered streets, their skins shriveled and their faces barely recognizable. Starvation has even compelled women to cook their own children (4:10).

And so the author mourns. He carefully reviews everything he has seen and felt, his pain darkening every line. He writes the first four poems in an acrostic style, following the Hebrew alphabet, one letter for each stanza. Perhaps this system helps him to pursue the subject thoroughly and not to break down in spasms of emotion. When he thinks of the starving children, he nearly does (2:11).

God Caused the Carnage

The author of Lamentations—tradition ascribes it to Jeremiah—evidently had seen the siege and destruction of Jerusalem in 586 B.C., when the Babylonian army burned and destroyed all the principal buildings and carried most of the surviving inhabitants into exile. Lamentations conducts a kind of postmortem on the death of Jerusalem, examining the body in clinical detail.

Like a doctor, Lamentations's author seeks to know the cause of death. He has no final doubt: Though the Babylonians did the work, ultimately God was responsible. But could God willingly create such misery? The author seems stunned that God has actually destroyed his own people, though he admits they richly deserved the punishment. "The Lord is like an enemy," he cries in astonishment (2:5). "Even when I call out or cry for help, he shuts out my prayer" (3:8). "He dragged me from the path and mangled me and left me without help" (3:11). "He has broken my teeth with gravel" (3:16).

But, though astonished and grief-stricken, the author never doubts God's justice. Jerusalem's destruction came as a result of sin (1:5). This fact prompts quiet hope, based on the character of God. "Though he brings grief, he will show compassion, so great is his unfailing love. For he does not willingly bring affliction or grief to the children of men" (3:32–33). When sin is eliminated, the Lord acts quickly to forgive and heal.

Looking for Recovery

Though the grief of Lamentations is as deep and heavy as any ever written, hope lies at the bottom. The author does not say "Cheer up!" to himself or anyone else. He mourns passionately and fully. But in mourning he looks to recovery. Lamentations ends with a prayer to God, asking him to restore his people, "unless you have utterly rejected us and are angry with us beyond measure" (5:22). Behind that "unless" lies confidence. God can never be angry without limits.

The author of Lamentations doesn't soften his words to God for fear of offending him. He expresses the full and dreadful horror of what he has seen, and he gives God full responsibility. But, remembering that the Lord is a loving God, he counts on God to heal Israel's wounds. This time of mourning will be followed by another time, a time to dance.

How to Read Lamentations

Lamentations is poetry, one poem per chapter. Its main purpose is not to describe events, nor to teach lessons, though it does both. Its intent is to express grief, to pour out before God the horror and bitterness of what has happened to Jerusalem. These five poems can help you to understand what it meant for Jews to see Jerusalem destroyed. They can also help you learn to deal appropriately with grief, your own or others'. Read them expressively, preferably out loud, so that you catch the deep emotion. Note that the author does not rush to express his hope in God, but fully grieves for the tragedy he was involved in.

Lamentations is not difficult to understand, though some of the poetical allusions may become clearer if you use a Bible dictionary or a commentary. For a summary of the destruction that inspired Lamentations, read 2 Kings 25.

3-TRACK READING PLAN

For an explanation and complete listing of the 3-track reading plan, turn to page 7.

TRACK 1: **_Two-Week Courses on the Bible_**
See page 7 for information on these courses.

TRACK 2: **_An Overview of Lamentations in 1 Day_**
☐ Day 1. Read the Introduction to Lamentations and chapter 3, which contains both bitter grief and quiet hope.
Now turn to page 9 for your next Track 2 reading project.

TRACK 3: **_All of Lamentations in 5 Days_**
After you have read through Lamentations, turn to pages 10–14 for your next Track 3 reading project.
☐1   ☐2   ☐3   ☐4   ☐5

---

1 [a]How deserted lies the city,
    once so full of people!
How like a widow is she,
    who once was great among the nations!
She who was queen among the provinces
    has now become a slave.

[2]Bitterly she weeps at night,
    tears are upon her cheeks.
Among all her lovers
    there is none to comfort her.
All her friends have betrayed her;
    they have become her enemies.

[3]After affliction and harsh labor,
    Judah has gone into exile.
She dwells among the nations;
    she finds no resting place.
All who pursue her have overtaken her
    in the midst of her distress.

[4]The roads to Zion mourn,
    for no one comes to her appointed feasts.
All her gateways are desolate,
    her priests groan,
her maidens grieve,
    and she is in bitter anguish.

[5]Her foes have become her masters;
    her enemies are at ease.
The LORD has brought her grief
    because of her many sins.
Her children have gone into exile,
    captive before the foe.

1:4–5 Structured Passion

Middle Easterners often commemorated catastrophes in poetry and song, as a kind of dirge in memory of the event. (See Psalm 137 for another example.) Lamentations, a response to the destruction of Jerusalem, contains as much passion as any book in the Bible. Yet, remarkably, the author has poured his passion into a highly structured form of poetry. Note that each chapter contains exactly 22 verses, or "stanzas," except for chapter 3, which has 66 verses (3 times 22). There were 22 letters in the Hebrew alphabet, and all but one of these poems follow an acrostic form, with each stanza beginning with a different letter of the alphabet.

---

[a]This chapter is an acrostic poem, the verses of which begin with the successive letters of the Hebrew alphabet.

⁶All the splendor has departed
from the Daughter of Zion.
Her princes are like deer
that find no pasture;
in weakness they have fled
before the pursuer.

⁷In the days of her affliction and wandering
Jerusalem remembers all the treasures
that were hers in days of old.
When her people fell into enemy hands,
there was no one to help her.
Her enemies looked at her
and laughed at her destruction.

⁸Jerusalem has sinned greatly
and so has become unclean.
All who honored her despise her,
for they have seen her nakedness;
she herself groans
and turns away.

⁹Her filthiness clung to her skirts;
she did not consider her future.
Her fall was astounding;
there was none to comfort her.
"Look, O Lord, on my affliction,
for the enemy has triumphed."

¹⁰The enemy laid hands
on all her treasures;
she saw pagan nations
enter her sanctuary—
those you had forbidden
to enter your assembly.

1:10 The Temple Destroyed

Non-Jews were barred from the holy places of the temple. But when the Babylonians conquered Jerusalem, they not only entered the temple; they looted and burned it. This shook devout Jews deeply; more than anything else it showed that God had given them up. Even today Orthodox Jews observe the anniversary of the temple's destruction by reading the book of Lamentations aloud, and pilgrims daily recite its prayers at the Wailing Wall in Jerusalem.

¹¹All her people groan
as they search for bread;
they barter their treasures for food
to keep themselves alive.
"Look, O Lord, and consider,
for I am despised."

¹²"Is it nothing to you, all you who pass by?
Look around and see.
Is any suffering like my suffering
that was inflicted on me,
that the Lord brought on me
in the day of his fierce anger?

¹³"From on high he sent fire,
sent it down into my bones.
He spread a net for my feet
and turned me back.
He made me desolate,
faint all the day long.

¹⁴"My sins have been bound into a yoke*a*;
by his hands they were woven together.
They have come upon my neck
and the Lord has sapped my strength.
He has handed me over
to those I cannot withstand.

¹⁵"The Lord has rejected
all the warriors in my midst;
he has summoned an army against me
to*b* crush my young men.
In his winepress the Lord has trampled
the Virgin Daughter of Judah.

¹⁶"This is why I weep
and my eyes overflow with tears.
No one is near to comfort me,
no one to restore my spirit.
My children are destitute
because the enemy has prevailed."

¹⁷Zion stretches out her hands,
but there is no one to comfort her.
The Lord has decreed for Jacob
that his neighbors become his foes;
Jerusalem has become
an unclean thing among them.

¹⁸"The Lord is righteous,
yet I rebelled against his command.
Listen, all you peoples;
look upon my suffering.
My young men and maidens
have gone into exile.

¹⁹"I called to my allies
but they betrayed me.
My priests and my elders
perished in the city
while they searched for food
to keep themselves alive.

²⁰"See, O Lord, how distressed I am!
I am in torment within,
and in my heart I am disturbed,
for I have been most rebellious.
Outside, the sword bereaves;
inside, there is only death.

a 14 Most Hebrew manuscripts; Septuagint *He kept watch over my sins*   *b 15* Or *has set a time for me / when he will*

²¹"People have heard my groaning,
   but there is no one to comfort me.
All my enemies have heard of my distress;
   they rejoice at what you have done.
May you bring the day you have announced
   so they may become like me.

²²"Let all their wickedness come before you;
   deal with them
as you have dealt with me
   because of all my sins.
My groans are many
   and my heart is faint."

2 ^aHow the Lord has covered the Daughter
      of Zion
   with the cloud of his anger^b!
He has hurled down the splendor of Israel
   from heaven to earth;
he has not remembered his footstool
   in the day of his anger.

²Without pity the Lord has swallowed up
   all the dwellings of Jacob;
in his wrath he has torn down
   the strongholds of the Daughter of Judah.
He has brought her kingdom and its princes
   down to the ground in dishonor.

³In fierce anger he has cut off
   every horn^c of Israel.
He has withdrawn his right hand
   at the approach of the enemy.
He has burned in Jacob like a flaming fire
   that consumes everything around it.

⁴Like an enemy he has strung his bow;
   his right hand is ready.
Like a foe he has slain
   all who were pleasing to the eye;
he has poured out his wrath like fire
   on the tent of the Daughter of Zion.

⁵The Lord is like an enemy;
   he has swallowed up Israel.
He has swallowed up all her palaces
   and destroyed her strongholds.
He has multiplied mourning and lamentation
   for the Daughter of Judah.

⁶He has laid waste his dwelling like a garden;
   he has destroyed his place of meeting.
The LORD has made Zion forget
   her appointed feasts and her Sabbaths;
in his fierce anger he has spurned
   both king and priest.

⁷The Lord has rejected his altar
   and abandoned his sanctuary.
He has handed over to the enemy
   the walls of her palaces;
they have raised a shout in the house of the
      LORD
   as on the day of an appointed feast.

⁸The LORD determined to tear down
   the wall around the Daughter of Zion.
He stretched out a measuring line
   and did not withhold his hand from
      destroying.
He made ramparts and walls lament;
   together they wasted away.

⁹Her gates have sunk into the ground;
   their bars he has broken and destroyed.
Her king and her princes are exiled among
      the nations,
   the law is no more,
and her prophets no longer find
   visions from the LORD.

¹⁰The elders of the Daughter of Zion
   sit on the ground in silence;
they have sprinkled dust on their heads
   and put on sackcloth.
The young women of Jerusalem
   have bowed their heads to the ground.

¹¹My eyes fail from weeping,
   I am in torment within,
my heart is poured out on the ground
   because my people are destroyed,
because children and infants faint
   in the streets of the city.

¹²They say to their mothers,
   "Where is bread and wine?"
as they faint like wounded men
   in the streets of the city,
as their lives ebb away
   in their mothers' arms.

2:12 Pity the Children

Everyone suffered in the destruction of Jerusalem, rich and poor, young and old, male and female. Lamentations grieves for them all, but especially for the children, who were dying of hunger. During the long siege, hunger grew so fierce that mothers ate their own children (2:20; 4:10). Compassion for children had disappeared (4:3–4).

¹³What can I say for you?
   With what can I compare you,
   O Daughter of Jerusalem?
To what can I liken you,
   that I may comfort you,

---

^aThis chapter is an acrostic poem, the verses of which begin with the successive letters of the Hebrew alphabet.
^b1 Or *How the Lord in his anger / has treated the Daughter of Zion with contempt*   ^c3 Or / *all the strength*; or
every king; horn here symbolizes strength.

O Virgin Daughter of Zion?
Your wound is as deep as the sea.
Who can heal you?

¹⁴The visions of your prophets
were false and worthless;
they did not expose your sin
to ward off your captivity.
The oracles they gave you
were false and misleading.

¹⁵All who pass your way
clap their hands at you;
they scoff and shake their heads
at the Daughter of Jerusalem:
"Is this the city that was called
the perfection of beauty,
the joy of the whole earth?"

¹⁶All your enemies open their mouths
wide against you;
they scoff and gnash their teeth
and say, "We have swallowed her up.
This is the day we have waited for;
we have lived to see it."

¹⁷The LORD has done what he planned;
he has fulfilled his word,
which he decreed long ago.
He has overthrown you without pity,
he has let the enemy gloat over you,
he has exalted the horn*a* of your foes.

¹⁸The hearts of the people
cry out to the Lord.
O wall of the Daughter of Zion,
let your tears flow like a river
day and night;
give yourself no relief,
your eyes no rest.

¹⁹Arise, cry out in the night,
as the watches of the night begin;
pour out your heart like water
in the presence of the Lord.
Lift up your hands to him
for the lives of your children,
who faint from hunger
at the head of every street.

²⁰"Look, O LORD, and consider:
Whom have you ever treated like this?
Should women eat their offspring,
the children they have cared for?
Should priest and prophet be killed
in the sanctuary of the Lord?

²¹"Young and old lie together
in the dust of the streets;
my young men and maidens
have fallen by the sword.

You have slain them in the day of your
anger;
you have slaughtered them without pity.

²²"As you summon to a feast day,
so you summoned against me terrors on
every side.
In the day of the LORD's anger
no one escaped or survived;
those I cared for and reared,
my enemy has destroyed."

3 *b*I am the man who has seen affliction
by the rod of his wrath.

3:1 Autobiography of Pain

*Ancient traditions say that Jeremiah wrote the
book of Lamentations, and if so, this chapter
records that doleful prophet's autobiography of
pain. He was persecuted by enemies, thrown in
a well, dragged captive, and jailed. Jeremiah
knew, of course, that the people who did those
things were God's enemies too, and he had
delivered strong pronouncements against
them. Yet to a person in pain—like Job, like
Jeremiah—it often feels as if God himself has
turned his back.*

²He has driven me away and made me walk
in darkness rather than light;
³indeed, he has turned his hand against me
again and again, all day long.

⁴He has made my skin and my flesh grow old
and has broken my bones.
⁵He has besieged me and surrounded me
with bitterness and hardship.
⁶He has made me dwell in darkness
like those long dead.

⁷He has walled me in so I cannot escape;
he has weighed me down with chains.
⁸Even when I call out or cry for help,
he shuts out my prayer.
⁹He has barred my way with blocks of stone;
he has made my paths crooked.

¹⁰Like a bear lying in wait,
like a lion in hiding,
¹¹he dragged me from the path and mangled
me
and left me without help.
¹²He drew his bow
and made me the target for his arrows.

¹³He pierced my heart
with arrows from his quiver.
¹⁴I became the laughingstock of all my people;

---

a 17 *Horn* here symbolizes strength.   *b*This chapter is an acrostic poem; the verses of each stanza begin with the
successive letters of the Hebrew alphabet, and the verses within each stanza begin with the same letter.

they mock me in song all day long.
15He has filled me with bitter herbs
  and sated me with gall.

16He has broken my teeth with gravel;
  he has trampled me in the dust.
17I have been deprived of peace;
  I have forgotten what prosperity is.
18So I say, "My splendor is gone
  and all that I had hoped from the LORD."

19I remember my affliction and my wandering,
  the bitterness and the gall.
20I well remember them,
  and my soul is downcast within me.
21Yet this I call to mind
  and therefore I have hope:

22Because of the LORD's great love we are not
    consumed,
  for his compassions never fail.
23They are new every morning;
  great is your faithfulness.
24I say to myself, "The LORD is my portion;
  therefore I will wait for him."

25The LORD is good to those whose hope is in
    him,
  to the one who seeks him;
26it is good to wait quietly
  for the salvation of the LORD.
27It is good for a man to bear the yoke
  while he is young.

28Let him sit alone in silence,
  for the LORD has laid it on him.
29Let him bury his face in the dust—
  there may yet be hope.
30Let him offer his cheek to one who would
    strike him,
  and let him be filled with disgrace.

31For men are not cast off
  by the Lord forever.
32Though he brings grief, he will show
    compassion,
  so great is his unfailing love.
33For he does not willingly bring affliction
  or grief to the children of men.

34To crush underfoot
  all prisoners in the land,
35to deny a man his rights
  before the Most High,
36to deprive a man of justice—
  would not the Lord see such things?

37Who can speak and have it happen
  if the Lord has not decreed it?
38Is it not from the mouth of the Most High
  that both calamities and good things
    come?
39Why should any living man complain
  when punished for his sins?

40Let us examine our ways and test them,
  and let us return to the LORD.
41Let us lift up our hearts and our hands
  to God in heaven, and say:

3:33 Hope for the Grieving

Lamentations bares the full horror of suffering, yet offers hope based on the character of God. He has let some survive (verse 22), and he is not a God to be angry with them forever. Their duty is to accept fully their grief, and quietly meditate on its meaning while waiting for the Lord.

42"We have sinned and rebelled
  and you have not forgiven.

43"You have covered yourself with anger and
    pursued us;
  you have slain without pity.
44You have covered yourself with a cloud
  so that no prayer can get through.
45You have made us scum and refuse
  among the nations.

46"All our enemies have opened their mouths
  wide against us.
47We have suffered terror and pitfalls,
  ruin and destruction."
48Streams of tears flow from my eyes
  because my people are destroyed.

49My eyes will flow unceasingly,
  without relief,
50until the LORD looks down
  from heaven and sees.
51What I see brings grief to my soul
  because of all the women of my city.

52Those who were my enemies without cause
  hunted me like a bird.
53They tried to end my life in a pit
  and threw stones at me;
54the waters closed over my head,
  and I thought I was about to be cut off.

55I called on your name, O LORD,
  from the depths of the pit.
56You heard my plea: "Do not close your ears
  to my cry for relief."
57You came near when I called you,
  and you said, "Do not fear."

58O Lord, you took up my case;
  you redeemed my life.
59You have seen, O LORD, the wrong done to
    me.
  Uphold my cause!
60You have seen the depth of their vengeance,
  all their plots against me.

⁶¹O LORD, you have heard their insults,
    all their plots against me—
⁶²what my enemies whisper and mutter
    against me all day long.
⁶³Look at them! Sitting or standing,
    they mock me in their songs.

⁶⁴Pay them back what they deserve, O LORD,
    for what their hands have done.
⁶⁵Put a veil over their hearts,
    and may your curse be on them!
⁶⁶Pursue them in anger and destroy them
    from under the heavens of the LORD.

4 ᵃ"How the gold has lost its luster,
    the fine gold become dull!
The sacred gems are scattered
    at the head of every street.

²How the precious sons of Zion,
    once worth their weight in gold,
are now considered as pots of clay,
    the work of a potter's hands!

³Even jackals offer their breasts
    to nurse their young,
but my people have become heartless
    like ostriches in the desert.

⁴Because of thirst the infant's tongue
    sticks to the roof of its mouth;
the children beg for bread,
    but no one gives it to them.

4:4 Starving to Death

Horrible scenes of starvation, like those shown in documentaries of African famines in recent times, were seen in the streets of Jerusalem during the Babylonian invasion. Foreign armies encircled the city for two years, cutting off all sources of food. The residents of this once-proud city resorted to eating their own children (verse 10) just to stay alive.

⁵Those who once ate delicacies
    are destitute in the streets.
Those nurtured in purple
    now lie on ash heaps.

⁶The punishment of my people
    is greater than that of Sodom,
which was overthrown in a moment
    without a hand turned to help her.

⁷Their princes were brighter than snow
    and whiter than milk,
their bodies more ruddy than rubies,
    their appearance like sapphires.ᵇ

⁸But now they are blacker than soot;
    they are not recognized in the streets.
Their skin has shriveled on their bones;
    it has become as dry as a stick.

⁹Those killed by the sword are better off
    than those who die of famine;
racked with hunger, they waste away
    for lack of food from the field.

¹⁰With their own hands compassionate women
    have cooked their own children,
who became their food
    when my people were destroyed.

¹¹The LORD has given full vent to his wrath;
    he has poured out his fierce anger.
He kindled a fire in Zion
    that consumed her foundations.

¹²The kings of the earth did not believe,
    nor did any of the world's people,
that enemies and foes could enter
    the gates of Jerusalem.

¹³But it happened because of the sins of her
        prophets
    and the iniquities of her priests,
who shed within her
    the blood of the righteous.

¹⁴Now they grope through the streets
    like men who are blind.
They are so defiled with blood
    that no one dares to touch their garments.

¹⁵"Go away! You are unclean!" men cry to
    them.
    "Away! Away! Don't touch us!"
When they flee and wander about,
    people among the nations say,
    "They can stay here no longer."

¹⁶The LORD himself has scattered them;
    he no longer watches over them.
The priests are shown no honor,
    the elders no favor.

¹⁷Moreover, our eyes failed,
    looking in vain for help;
from our towers we watched
    for a nation that could not save us.

¹⁸Men stalked us at every step,
    so we could not walk in our streets.
Our end was near, our days were numbered,
    for our end had come.

¹⁹Our pursuers were swifter
    than eagles in the sky;
they chased us over the mountains
    and lay in wait for us in the desert.

ᵃThis chapter is an acrostic poem, the verses of which begin with the successive letters of the Hebrew alphabet.
ᵇ7 Or *lapis lazuli*

20The LORD's anointed, our very life breath,
    was caught in their traps.
We thought that under his shadow
    we would live among the nations.

21Rejoice and be glad, O Daughter of Edom,
    you who live in the land of Uz.
But to you also the cup will be passed;
    you will be drunk and stripped naked.

22O Daughter of Zion, your punishment will
        end;
    he will not prolong your exile.
But, O Daughter of Edom, he will punish
        your sin
    and expose your wickedness.

5 Remember, O LORD, what has happened to
        us;
    look, and see our disgrace.
2Our inheritance has been turned over to
        aliens,
    our homes to foreigners.
3We have become orphans and fatherless,
    our mothers like widows.
4We must buy the water we drink;
    our wood can be had only at a price.
5Those who pursue us are at our heels;

we are weary and find no rest.
6We submitted to Egypt and Assyria
    to get enough bread.
7Our fathers sinned and are no more,
    and we bear their punishment.
8Slaves rule over us,
    and there is none to free us from their
        hands.
9We get our bread at the risk of our lives
    because of the sword in the desert.
10Our skin is hot as an oven,
    feverish from hunger.
11Women have been ravished in Zion,
    and virgins in the towns of Judah.
12Princes have been hung up by their hands;
    elders are shown no respect.
13Young men toil at the millstones;
    boys stagger under loads of wood.
14The elders are gone from the city gate;
    the young men have stopped their music.
15Joy is gone from our hearts;
    our dancing has turned to mourning.
16The crown has fallen from our head.
    Woe to us, for we have sinned!
17Because of this our hearts are faint,
    because of these things our eyes grow dim
18for Mount Zion, which lies desolate,
    with jackals prowling over it.

19You, O LORD, reign forever;
    your throne endures from generation to
        generation.
20Why do you always forget us?
    Why do you forsake us so long?
21Restore us to yourself, O LORD, that we may
        return;
    renew our days as of old
22unless you have utterly rejected us
    and are angry with us beyond measure.

EZEKIEL

Seeing the Unseen God
God showed himself to Ezekiel in unearthly radiance

EZEKIEL BEGINS WITH A DESCRIPTION so unearthly that some have suggested the prophet saw a UFO. Indeed, there are similarities: glowing lights, quick movements, inhuman figures shrouded with fire. But at least one critical difference sets Ezekiel's story apart. UFOs typically appear in remote places and then mysteriously zoom off, never to be heard from again. The majestic being Ezekiel described was not rushing off to disappear. He wanted to be known—by everyone.

For Ezekiel was quite sure that he had seen and heard the God of the Bible. While few have been privileged to see him as Ezekiel did, this God had been speaking plainly for generations. His words were on record.

> *Like the appearance of a rainbow in the clouds on a rainy day, so was the radiance around him. . . . When I saw it, I fell facedown.*
> 1:28

Before such splendor Ezekiel felt utterly weak and inadequate, just as Isaiah had during a similar vision (Isaiah 6). He fell on his face, repeatedly. But God raised Ezekiel to his feet and gave him a message to deliver.

A Stunning Portrait of God

In describing his call by God, Ezekiel groped for words. He portrayed a God of stunning grandeur, above and beyond our world. Yet this supernatural God was inescapably near and real. He demanded complete obedience. Surprisingly, he appeared to Ezekiel in Babylon—the last place an Israelite expected to see him. This God could not be locked in by national or geographical boxes. He ruled the earth.

Ezekiel repeated this classic message over 60 times: "Then they will know that I am the LORD." God said it when promising the destruction of Jerusalem in the first 24 chapters. He said it when predicting the downfall of Israel's neighbors in chapters 25 through 32. And, after Jerusalem had fallen, God said it when promising a great future in the last 16 chapters. God did not want to remain vague or far off. He wanted his people to know him. More, Ezekiel's God wanted to live with his people. He wanted to make his home in the center of their city.

A Strange Book

Ezekiel has a reputation for strangeness, partly because of the unearthly visions with which his book begins and ends, and partly because Ezekiel acted out God's messages through some bizarre behavior. (For instance, for months at a time he lay in public on his side, bound by ropes, facing a clay model of Jerusalem.) Strange? When a car is speeding down a road unaware of a bridge washout, you may take strange measures to get the driver's attention. You may scream and gesture so wildly people think you are insane. So it was with Ezekiel. His message came in the most vivid form possible, meant to force people to pay attention.

Ezekiel lived in perhaps the most tragic period of his people's existence. They had been tempting fate for generations, ignoring God's messengers (prophets like Micah, Amos, Isaiah) who warned that if they didn't listen to God, they would be destroyed. Finally, Babylonian armies swept through Judah, deporting large groups of citizens.

Ezekiel had gone into exile in one of the first groups, as had Daniel. Ezekiel became God's messenger as a captive in Babylon. His voice blended in stereo with Jeremiah's, still in Jerusalem. Both prophets warned their people (who kept plotting ways to break free of Babylon) that the captives were going to be in Babylon for a long time. They predicted that Babylon's oppression would grow heavier: Jerusalem and the temple would be destroyed. Since Judah had ignored God's repeated warnings, God would use another means to get their attention: suffering.

A New Jerusalem

Yet even while punishing them, God's aim remained the same: to make himself known. God had warned Ezekiel that the Israelites were unlikely to listen (3:7), even from captivity. They preferred idols to the living God. Yet Ezekiel's messages and dramas and visions continued to come, year after year. It's as though God were saying through him, "Some way, some day, I will get through to them. If the message doesn't reach their hearts one way, I'll try another."

Ezekiel ends with hope. The final chapters show a new Jerusalem rising from the ruins of the old. The renewed city would never die, for it would be built on an unshifting reality: "They will know that I am the LORD." The burning vision of God that Ezekiel had seen would become accessible to all. God would make himself at home there forever. Ezekiel's last verse says it all: "And the name of the city from that time on will be: THE LORD IS THERE."

How to Read Ezekiel

The special difficulty in reading Ezekiel is the dizzying variety of forms he used to get his message across. The book is like a multimedia package—a mix of visions, messages, dramas, poems. But three remarkable visions of God bracket the package, beginning, middle, and end (1:1–3:15; 8:1–6 and 11:16–25; 40:1–4 and 43:1–9). And throughout, one line is repeated: "Then they will know that I am the LORD." All God's messages are meant to shock his people into restoring a living relationship with him.

As you read Ezekiel, note down when each prophecy was made and its dominant image—Jerusalem as a prostitute, as a spreading grapevine, as a shaved head, etc. (For insight into why Ezekiel sometimes acted out his message in bizarre fashion, read "Living Parables," page 818.) Don't skip ahead too fast as you read—take time to think about the message in each section. Remember that the book of Ezekiel compresses messages God gave over 22 years. Try to imagine the impact of each message on the people who first heard or saw it.

Most of what Ezekiel said in Babylonia concerned a dramatic military situation hundreds of miles away in Jerusalem. His message changed from doom to hope in chapter 33; the turning point came with news of Jerusalem's fall. You can get to know the historical situation by reading 2 Kings 23:36–25:12. "A Lineup of Rulers," page 1361–1369, can help you place Ezekiel in Israel's history.

A fascinating though difficult study is the design of the renewed temple, which Ezekiel described in chapters 40–43. A commentary on Ezekiel or a Bible dictionary (under "Ezekiel" or "temple") can help immensely in understanding these visions.

PEOPLE YOU'LL MEET IN EZEKIEL

EZEKIEL *(p. 851)*

3-TRACK READING PLAN

For an explanation and complete listing of the 3-track reading plan, turn to page 7.

TRACK 1: ***Two-Week Courses on the Bible***
See page 7 for information on these courses.

TRACK 2: ***An Overview of Ezekiel in 4 Days***
☐ Day 1. Read the Introduction to Ezekiel and chapter 1, the majestic vision of a living God who appeared to Ezekiel.
☐ Day 2. Read chapters 2–3, which tell how God called Ezekiel to deliver a difficult message.
☐ Day 3. Read chapter 4, one of the most dramatic of the "enacted parables" Ezekiel performed.
☐ Day 4. Read chapter 37, a message of hope and resurrection for a defeated people.

Now turn to page 9 for your next Track 2 reading project.

TRACK 3: **All of Ezekiel in 47 Days**
After you have read through Ezekiel, turn to pages 10–14 for your next Track 3 reading project.

□1	□2–3	□4	□5	□6	□7	□8	□9
□10	□11	□12	□13	□14	□15	□16	□17
□18	□19	□20	□21	□22	□23	□24	□25
□26	□27	□28	□29	□30	□31	□32	□33
□34	□35	□36	□37	□38	□39	□40	□41
□42	□43	□44	□45	□46	□47	□48	

The Living Creatures and the Glory of the LORD

1 In the[a] thirtieth year, in the fourth month on the fifth day, while I was among the exiles by the Kebar River, the heavens were opened and I saw visions of God.

²On the fifth of the month—it was the fifth year of the exile of King Jehoiachin— ³the word of the LORD came to Ezekiel the priest, the son of Buzi,[b] by the Kebar River in the land of the Babylonians.[c] There the hand of the LORD was upon him.

1:3 Foreign Appearance

Most ancient religions worshiped tribal gods, whose rule extended only within the tribal territory. As an exile, Ezekiel may have wondered whether the God of Israel would still speak so far from home. But it was in Babylon that God appeared. The terrifying vision in a windstorm revealed a God who ruled over the entire world, awesome, magnificent, exalted, far more powerful than the Babylonian armies.

⁴I looked, and I saw a windstorm coming out of the north—an immense cloud with flashing lightning and surrounded by brilliant light. The center of the fire looked like glowing metal, ⁵and in the fire was what looked like four living creatures. In appearance their form was that of a man, ⁶but each of them had four faces and four wings. ⁷Their legs were straight; their feet were like those of a calf and gleamed like burnished bronze. ⁸Under their wings on their four sides they had the hands of a man. All four of them had faces and wings, ⁹and their wings touched one another. Each one went straight ahead; they did not turn as they moved.

¹⁰Their faces looked like this: Each of the four had the face of a man, and on the right side each had the face of a lion, and on the left the face of an ox; each also had the face of an eagle. ¹¹Such were their faces. Their wings were spread out upward; each had two wings, one touching the wing of another creature on either side, and two wings covering its body. ¹²Each one went straight ahead. Wherever the spirit would go, they would go, without turning as they went. ¹³The appearance of the living creatures was like burning coals of fire or like torches. Fire moved back and forth among the creatures; it was bright, and lightning flashed out of it. ¹⁴The creatures sped back and forth like flashes of lightning.

¹⁵As I looked at the living creatures, I saw a wheel on the ground beside each creature with its four faces. ¹⁶This was the appearance and structure of the wheels: They sparkled like chrysolite, and all four looked alike. Each appeared to be made like a wheel intersecting a wheel. ¹⁷As they moved, they would go in any one of the four directions the creatures faced; the wheels did not turn about[d] as the creatures went. ¹⁸Their rims were high and awesome, and all four rims were full of eyes all around.

¹⁹When the living creatures moved, the wheels beside them moved; and when the living creatures rose from the ground, the wheels also rose. ²⁰Wherever the spirit would go, they would go, and the wheels would rise along with them, because the spirit of the living creatures was in the wheels. ²¹When the creatures moved, they also moved; when the creatures stood still, they also stood still; and when the creatures rose from the ground, the wheels rose along with them, because the spirit of the living creatures was in the wheels.

²²Spread out above the heads of the living creatures was what looked like an expanse, sparkling like ice, and awesome. ²³Under the expanse their wings were stretched out one toward the other, and each had two wings covering its body. ²⁴When the creatures moved, I heard the sound of their wings, like the roar of rushing waters, like the voice of the Almighty,[e] like the tumult of an army. When they stood still, they lowered their wings.

²⁵Then there came a voice from above the expanse over their heads as they stood with lowered wings. ²⁶Above the expanse over their heads was

---

[a]1 Or ⌞my⌟   [b]3 Or Ezekiel son of Buzi the priest   [c]3 Or Chaldeans   [d]17 Or aside   [e]24 Hebrew Shaddai

what looked like a throne of sapphire,[a] and high above on the throne was a figure like that of a man. [27]I saw that from what appeared to be his waist up he looked like glowing metal, as if full of fire, and that from there down he looked like fire; and brilliant light surrounded him. [28]Like the appearance of a rainbow in the clouds on a rainy day, so was the radiance around him.

This was the appearance of the likeness of the glory of the LORD. When I saw it, I fell facedown, and I heard the voice of one speaking.

Ezekiel's Call

2 He said to me, "Son of man, stand up on your feet and I will speak to you." [2]As he spoke, the Spirit came into me and raised me to my feet, and I heard him speaking to me.

[3]He said: "Son of man, I am sending you to the Israelites, to a rebellious nation that has rebelled against me; they and their fathers have been in revolt against me to this very day. [4]The people to whom I am sending you are obstinate and stubborn. Say to them, 'This is what the Sovereign LORD says.' [5]And whether they listen or fail to listen—for they are a rebellious house—they will know that a prophet has been among them. [6]And you, son of man, do not be afraid of them or their words. Do not be afraid, though briers and thorns are all around you and you live among scorpions. Do not be afraid of what they say or terrified by them, though they are a rebellious house. [7]You must speak my words to them, whether they listen or fail to listen, for they are rebellious. [8]But you, son of man, listen to what I say to you. Do not rebel like that rebellious house; open your mouth and eat what I give you."

[9]Then I looked, and I saw a hand stretched out to me. In it was a scroll, [10]which he unrolled before me. On both sides of it were written words of lament and mourning and woe.

3 And he said to me, "Son of man, eat what is before you, eat this scroll; then go and speak to the house of Israel." [2]So I opened my mouth, and he gave me the scroll to eat.

[3]Then he said to me, "Son of man, eat this scroll I am giving you and fill your stomach with it." So I ate it, and it tasted as sweet as honey in my mouth.

[4]He then said to me: "Son of man, go now to the house of Israel and speak my words to them. [5]You are not being sent to a people of obscure speech and difficult language, but to the house of Israel— [6]not to many peoples of obscure speech and difficult language, whose words you cannot understand. Surely if I had sent you to them, they would have listened to you. [7]But the house of Israel is not willing to listen to you because they

are not willing to listen to me, for the whole house of Israel is hardened and obstinate. [8]But I will make you as unyielding and hardened as they are. [9]I will make your forehead like the

3:3 Eat the Scroll

The scroll with words of woe looked inedible, but tasted sweet as honey to Ezekiel. Most of God's prophets gave bitter messages of warning, but God's word sustained and strengthened them as they served him. (See also Jeremiah's experience, in Jeremiah 15:16.) Similarly, the book of Revelation tells of a scroll being eaten (Revelation 10:9–11). Many of Ezekiel's images are paralleled in that book.

hardest stone, harder than flint. Do not be afraid of them or terrified by them, though they are a rebellious house."

[10]And he said to me, "Son of man, listen carefully and take to heart all the words I speak to you. [11]Go now to your countrymen in exile and speak to them. Say to them, 'This is what the Sovereign LORD says,' whether they listen or fail to listen."

[12]Then the Spirit lifted me up, and I heard behind me a loud rumbling sound—May the glory of the LORD be praised in his dwelling place!— [13]the sound of the wings of the living creatures brushing against each other and the sound of the wheels beside them, a loud rumbling sound. [14]The Spirit then lifted me up and took me away, and I went in bitterness and in the anger of my spirit, with the strong hand of the LORD upon me. [15]I came to the exiles who lived at Tel Abib near the Kebar River. And there, where they were living, I sat among them for seven days—overwhelmed.

Warning to Israel

[16]At the end of seven days the word of the LORD came to me: [17]"Son of man, I have made you a watchman for the house of Israel; so hear the word I speak and give them warning from me. [18]When I say to a wicked man, 'You will surely die,' and you do not warn him or speak out to dissuade him from his evil ways in order to save his life, that wicked man will die for[b] his sin, and I will hold you accountable for his blood. [19]But if you do warn the wicked man and he does not turn from his wickedness or from his evil ways, he will die for his sin; but you will have saved yourself.

[20]"Again, when a righteous man turns from his righteousness and does evil, and I put a stumbling block before him, he will die. Since you did

---

[a]26 Or *lapis lazuli*   [b]18 Or *in*; also in verses 19 and 20

not warn him, he will die for his sin. The righteous things he did will not be remembered, and I will hold you accountable for his blood. ²¹But if you do warn the righteous man not to sin and he does not sin, he will surely live because he took warning, and you will have saved yourself."

²²The hand of the LORD was upon me there, and he said to me, "Get up and go out to the plain, and there I will speak to you." ²³So I got up and went out to the plain. And the glory of the LORD was standing there, like the glory I had seen by the Kebar River, and I fell facedown.

²⁴Then the Spirit came into me and raised me to my feet. He spoke to me and said: "Go, shut yourself inside your house. ²⁵And you, son of man, they will tie with ropes; you will be bound so that you cannot go out among the people. ²⁶I will make your tongue stick to the roof of your mouth so that you will be silent and unable to rebuke them, though they are a rebellious house. ²⁷But when I speak to you, I will open your mouth and you shall say to them, 'This is what the Sovereign LORD says.' Whoever will listen let him listen, and whoever will refuse let him refuse; for they are a rebellious house.

Siege of Jerusalem Symbolized

4 "Now, son of man, take a clay tablet, put it in front of you and draw the city of Jerusalem on it. ²Then lay siege to it: Erect siege works

against it, build a ramp up to it, set up camps against it and put battering rams around it. ³Then take an iron pan, place it as an iron wall between you and the city and turn your face toward it. It will be under siege, and you shall besiege it. This will be a sign to the house of Israel.

⁴"Then lie on your left side and put the sin of the house of Israel upon yourself.ᵃ You are to bear their sin for the number of days you lie on your side. ⁵I have assigned you the same number of days as the years of their sin. So for 390 days you will bear the sin of the house of Israel.

⁶"After you have finished this, lie down again, this time on your right side, and bear the sin of the house of Judah. I have assigned you 40 days, a day for each year. ⁷Turn your face toward the siege of Jerusalem and with bared arm prophesy against her. ⁸I will tie you up with ropes so that you cannot turn from one side to the other until you have finished the days of your siege.

⁹"Take wheat and barley, beans and lentils, millet and spelt; put them in a storage jar and use them to make bread for yourself. You are to eat it during the 390 days you lie on your side. ¹⁰Weigh out twenty shekelsᵇ of food to eat each day and eat it at set times. ¹¹Also measure out a sixth of a hinᶜ of water and drink it at set times. ¹²Eat the food as you would a barley cake; bake it in the sight of the people, using human excrement for fuel." ¹³The LORD said, "In this way the

---

ᵃ4 Or *your side*   ᵇ10 That is, about 8 ounces (about 0.2 kilogram)   ᶜ11 That is, about 2/3 quart (about 0.6 liter)

EZEKIEL *Radical Priest*

SOME GREAT HISTORICAL FIGURES ARE known only by their accomplishments. The artists who created the great European cathedrals, for example—in most cases we do not even know their names. They fashioned beautiful monuments to God, not to themselves.

In some ways Ezekiel fits this pattern. He created a major book of the Bible and acted as God's messenger in some hinge moments of history. We know what he did, yet we know next to nothing about *him:* his personality, his background, his family life. Ezekiel recounted his calling as a prophet in detail and mentioned his work as a priest, but otherwise his book includes only a few shreds of personal information (such as the fact that he was married). His work swallowed up his life.

Ezekiel's story begins with King Nebuchadnezzar taking him captive from Jerusalem to Babylon—the site of present-day Iraq. No doubt the foreign setting made him feel lonely and homesick. He was a priest far from God's temple, as fruitless a combination as a basketball coach without a gym. What could Ezekiel do?

Complicating Ezekiel's life, God told him to deliver a very unpopular message—that God would continue to punish his people because they had not repented from their sin. Moreover, God instructed Ezekiel to dramatize that message in bizarre ways. At various times he ate a book, shaved his head, cooked with cow manure, and lay outdoors beside a model of Jerusalem. Looking back, some of Ezekiel's "object lessons" seem downright weird.

For one short period, when his predictions came true, Ezekiel enjoyed popularity and acceptance (33:30–32). More often, though, he needed God's prodding and encouragement: "Do not be afraid, though briers and thorns are all around you and you live among scorpions' (2:6). God had vital work for him to do. For Ezekiel, that made for a worthy life, regardless of the cost.

Life Questions: If you were to die today, what "monument" would you leave behind?

people of Israel will eat defiled food among the nations where I will drive them."

[14]Then I said, "Not so, Sovereign LORD! I have never defiled myself. From my youth until now I have never eaten anything found dead or torn by wild animals. No unclean meat has ever entered my mouth."

[15]"Very well," he said, "I will let you bake your bread over cow manure instead of human excrement."

[16]He then said to me: "Son of man, I will cut off the supply of food in Jerusalem. The people will eat rationed food in anxiety and drink rationed water in despair, [17]for food and water will be scarce. They will be appalled at the sight of each other and will waste away because of[a] their sin.

5 "Now, son of man, take a sharp sword and use it as a barber's razor to shave your head and your beard. Then take a set of scales and divide up the hair. [2]When the days of your siege come to an end, burn a third of the hair with fire inside the city. Take a third and strike it with the sword all around the city. And scatter a third to the wind. For I will pursue them with drawn sword. [3]But take a few strands of hair and tuck them away in the folds of your garment. [4]Again, take a few of these and throw them into the fire and burn them up. A fire will spread from there to the whole house of Israel.

[5]"This is what the Sovereign LORD says: This is Jerusalem, which I have set in the center of the

5:5 Navel of the Universe

Maps dating from the Middle Ages often showed Jerusalem and Israel as the center of a flat world. The practice probably stemmed from several verses like this one, referring to Jerusalem as "the center of the nations." Geography was not what God had in mind, however. Jerusalem was at the center of his love. A lover might say something similar: "You're the center of my universe."

nations, with countries all around her. [6]Yet in her wickedness she has rebelled against my laws and decrees more than the nations and countries around her. She has rejected my laws and has not followed my decrees.

[7]"Therefore this is what the Sovereign LORD says: You have been more unruly than the nations around you and have not followed my decrees or kept my laws. You have not even[b] conformed to the standards of the nations around you.

[8]"Therefore this is what the Sovereign LORD

says: I myself am against you, Jerusalem, and I will inflict punishment on you in the sight of the nations. [9]Because of all your detestable idols, I will do to you what I have never done before and will never do again. [10]Therefore in your midst fathers will eat their children, and children will eat their fathers. I will inflict punishment on you and will scatter all your survivors to the winds. [11]Therefore as surely as I live, declares the Sovereign LORD, because you have defiled my sanctuary with all your vile images and detestable practices, I myself will withdraw my favor; I will not look on you with pity or spare you. [12]A third of your people will die of the plague or perish by famine inside you; a third will fall by the sword outside your walls; and a third I will scatter to the winds and pursue with drawn sword.

[13]"Then my anger will cease and my wrath against them will subside, and I will be avenged. And when I have spent my wrath upon them, they will know that I the LORD have spoken in my zeal.

[14]"I will make you a ruin and a reproach among the nations around you, in the sight of all who pass by. [15]You will be a reproach and a taunt, a warning and an object of horror to the nations around you when I inflict punishment on you in anger and in wrath and with stinging rebuke. I the LORD have spoken. [16]When I shoot at you with my deadly and destructive arrows of famine, I will shoot to destroy you. I will bring more and more famine upon you and cut off your supply of food. [17]I will send famine and wild beasts against you, and they will leave you childless. Plague and bloodshed will sweep through you, and I will bring the sword against you. I the LORD have spoken."

A Prophecy Against the Mountains of Israel

6 The word of the LORD came to me: [2]"Son of man, set your face against the mountains of Israel; prophesy against them [3]and say: 'O mountains of Israel, hear the word of the Sovereign LORD. This is what the Sovereign LORD says to the mountains and hills, to the ravines and valleys: I am about to bring a sword against you, and I will destroy your high places. [4]Your altars will be demolished and your incense altars will be smashed; and I will slay your people in front of your idols. [5]I will lay the dead bodies of the Israelites in front of their idols, and I will scatter your bones around your altars. [6]Wherever you live, the towns will be laid waste and the high places demolished, so that your altars will be laid waste and devastated, your idols smashed and ruined, your incense altars broken down, and what you have made wiped out. [7]Your people

---

[a]17 Or *away in*   [b]7 Most Hebrew manuscripts; some Hebrew manuscripts and Syriac *You have*

will fall slain among you, and you will know that I am the LORD.

⁸"'But I will spare some, for some of you will escape the sword when you are scattered among the lands and nations. ⁹Then in the nations where they have been carried captive, those who escape will remember me—how I have been grieved by their adulterous hearts, which have turned away from me, and by their eyes, which have lusted after their idols. They will loathe themselves for the evil they have done and for all their detestable

practices. ¹⁰And they will know that I am the LORD; I did not threaten in vain to bring this calamity on them.

¹¹"'This is what the Sovereign LORD says: Strike your hands together and stamp your feet and cry out "Alas!" because of all the wicked and detestable practices of the house of Israel, for they will fall by the sword, famine and plague. ¹²He that is far away will die of the plague, and he that is near will fall by the sword, and he that survives and is spared will die of famine. So will I spend my wrath upon them. ¹³And they will know that I am the LORD, when their people lie slain among their idols around their altars, on every high hill and on all the mountaintops, under every spreading tree and every leafy oak—places where they offered fragrant incense to all their idols. ¹⁴And I will stretch out my hand against them and make the land a desolate waste from the desert to Diblah[a]—wherever they live. Then they will know that I am the LORD.'"

The End Has Come

7 The word of the LORD came to me: ²"Son of man, this is what the Sovereign LORD says to the land of Israel: The end! The end has come upon the four corners of the land. ³The end is now upon you and I will unleash my anger against you. I will judge you according to your conduct and repay you for all your detestable practices. ⁴I will not look on you with pity or spare you; I will surely repay you for your con-

duct and the detestable practices among you. Then you will know that I am the LORD.

⁵"This is what the Sovereign LORD says: Disaster! An unheard-of[b] disaster is coming. ⁶The end has come! The end has come! It has roused itself against you. It has come! ⁷Doom has come upon you—you who dwell in the land. The time has come, the day is near; there is panic, not joy, upon the mountains. ⁸I am about to pour out my wrath on you and spend my anger against you; I will judge you according to your conduct and repay you for all your detestable practices. ⁹I will not look on you with pity or spare you; I will repay you in accordance with your conduct and the detestable practices among you. Then you will know that it is I the LORD who strikes the blow.

¹⁰"The day is here! It has come! Doom has burst forth, the rod has budded, arrogance has blossomed! ¹¹Violence has grown into[c] a rod to punish wickedness; none of the people will be left, none of that crowd—no wealth, nothing of value. ¹²The time has come, the day has arrived. Let not the buyer rejoice nor the seller grieve, for wrath is upon the whole crowd. ¹³The seller will not recover the land he has sold as long as both of them live, for the vision concerning the whole crowd will not be reversed. Because of their sins, not one of them will preserve his life. ¹⁴Though they blow the trumpet and get everything ready, no one will go into battle, for my wrath is upon the whole crowd.

¹⁵"Outside is the sword, inside are plague and famine; those in the country will die by the sword, and those in the city will be devoured by famine and plague. ¹⁶All who survive and escape will be in the mountains, moaning like doves of the valleys, each because of his sins. ¹⁷Every hand will go limp, and every knee will become as weak as water. ¹⁸They will put on sackcloth and be clothed with terror. Their faces will be covered with shame and their heads will be shaved. ¹⁹They will throw their silver into the streets, and their gold will be an unclean thing. Their silver and gold will not be able to save them in the day of the LORD's wrath. They will not satisfy their hunger or fill their stomachs with it, for it has made them stumble into sin. ²⁰They were proud of their beautiful jewelry and used it to make their detestable idols and vile images. Therefore I will turn these into an unclean thing for them. ²¹I will hand it all over as plunder to foreigners and as loot to the wicked of the earth, and they will defile it. ²²I will turn my face away from them, and they will desecrate my treasured place; robbers will enter it and desecrate it.

²³"Prepare chains, because the land is full of

bloodshed and the city is full of violence. ²⁴I will bring the most wicked of the nations to take possession of their houses; I will put an end to the pride of the mighty, and their sanctuaries will be desecrated. ²⁵When terror comes, they will seek peace, but there will be none. ²⁶Calamity upon calamity will come, and rumor upon rumor. They will try to get a vision from the prophet; the teaching of the law by the priest will be lost, as will the counsel of the elders. ²⁷The king will mourn, the prince will be clothed with despair, and the hands of the people of the land will tremble. I will deal with them according to their conduct, and by their own standards I will judge them. Then they will know that I am the LORD."

Idolatry in the Temple

8 In the sixth year, in the sixth month on the fifth day, while I was sitting in my house and the elders of Judah were sitting before me, the hand of the Sovereign LORD came upon me there. ²I looked, and I saw a figure like that of a man.ᵃ From what appeared to be his waist down he was like fire, and from there up his appearance was as bright as glowing metal. ³He stretched out what looked like a hand and took me by the hair of my head. The Spirit lifted me up between earth and heaven and in visions of God he took me to Jerusalem, to the entrance to the north gate of the inner court, where the idol that provokes to jealousy stood. ⁴And there before me was the glory of the God of Israel, as in the vision I had seen in the plain.

⁵Then he said to me, "Son of man, look toward the north." So I looked, and in the entrance north of the gate of the altar I saw this idol of jealousy.

⁶And he said to me, "Son of man, do you see what they are doing—the utterly detestable things the house of Israel is doing here, things that will drive me far from my sanctuary? But you will see things that are even more detestable."

⁷Then he brought me to the entrance to the court. I looked, and I saw a hole in the wall. ⁸He said to me, "Son of man, now dig into the wall." So I dug into the wall and saw a doorway there.

⁹And he said to me, "Go in and see the wicked and detestable things they are doing here." ¹⁰So I went in and looked, and I saw portrayed all over the walls all kinds of crawling things and detestable animals and all the idols of the house of Israel. ¹¹In front of them stood seventy elders of the house of Israel, and Jaazaniah son of Shaphan was standing among them. Each had a censer in his hand, and a fragrant cloud of incense was rising.

¹²He said to me, "Son of man, have you seen what the elders of the house of Israel are doing in the darkness, each at the shrine of his own idol? They say, 'The LORD does not see us; the LORD has forsaken the land.'" ¹³Again, he said, "You will see them doing things that are even more detestable."

¹⁴Then he brought me to the entrance to the north gate of the house of the LORD, and I saw women sitting there, mourning for Tammuz. ¹⁵He said to me, "Do you see this, son of man? You will see things that are even more detestable than this."

¹⁶He then brought me into the inner court of the house of the LORD, and there at the entrance to the temple, between the portico and the altar, were about twenty-five men. With their backs toward the temple of the LORD and their faces toward the east, they were bowing down to the sun in the east.

¹⁷He said to me, "Have you seen this, son of man? Is it a trivial matter for the house of Judah to do the detestable things they are doing here? Must they also fill the land with violence and continually provoke me to anger? Look at them putting the branch to their nose! ¹⁸Therefore I will deal with them in anger; I will not look on them with pity or spare them. Although they shout in my ears, I will not listen to them."

Idolaters Killed

9 Then I heard him call out in a loud voice, "Bring the guards of the city here, each with a weapon in his hand." ²And I saw six men coming from the direction of the upper gate, which faces north, each with a deadly weapon in his hand. With them was a man clothed in linen who had a writing kit at his side. They came in and stood beside the bronze altar.

³Now the glory of the God of Israel went up from above the cherubim, where it had been, and moved to the threshold of the temple. Then the LORD called to the man clothed in linen who had the writing kit at his side ⁴and said to him, "Go throughout the city of Jerusalem and put a mark

---

8:6 Detestable Things

Ezekiel, a priest, had a special concern about the abuses going on in the temple. Here, in a vision, he sees painful details of these practices, notably idol worship (verses 5,10) and sun worship (verse 16). The leaders of Israel had lost faith in their God, and were desperately trying alternatives. Here and elsewhere Ezekiel accuses leaders by name; his original audience would have known them well.

ᵃ2 Or *saw a fiery figure*

on the foreheads of those who grieve and lament over all the detestable things that are done in it."

⁵As I listened, he said to the others, "Follow him through the city and kill, without showing

pity or compassion. ⁶Slaughter old men, young men and maidens, women and children, but do not touch anyone who has the mark. Begin at my sanctuary." So they began with the elders who were in front of the temple.

⁷Then he said to them, "Defile the temple and fill the courts with the slain. Go!" So they went out and began killing throughout the city. ⁸While they were killing and I was left alone, I fell facedown, crying out, "Ah, Sovereign LORD! Are you going to destroy the entire remnant of Israel in this outpouring of your wrath on Jerusalem?"

⁹He answered me, "The sin of the house of Israel and Judah is exceedingly great; the land is full of bloodshed and the city is full of injustice. They say, 'The LORD has forsaken the land; the LORD does not see.' ¹⁰So I will not look on them with pity or spare them, but I will bring down on their own heads what they have done."

¹¹Then the man in linen with the writing kit at his side brought back word, saying, "I have done as you commanded."

The Glory Departs From the Temple

10 I looked, and I saw the likeness of a throne of sapphire[a] above the expanse that was over the heads of the cherubim. ²The LORD said to the man clothed in linen, "Go in among the wheels beneath the cherubim. Fill your hands with burning coals from among the cherubim and scatter them over the city." And as I watched, he went in.

³Now the cherubim were standing on the south side of the temple when the man went in, and a cloud filled the inner court. ⁴Then the glory of the LORD rose from above the cherubim and moved to the threshold of the temple. The cloud filled the temple, and the court was full of the radiance of the glory of the LORD. ⁵The sound of the wings of the cherubim could be heard as far away as the outer court, like the voice of God Almighty[b] when he speaks.

⁶When the LORD commanded the man in linen, "Take fire from among the wheels, from among the cherubim," the man went in and stood beside a wheel. ⁷Then one of the cherubim reached out his hand to the fire that was among them. He took up some of it and put it into the hands of the man in linen, who took it and went out. ⁸(Under the wings of the cherubim could be seen what looked like the hands of a man.)

⁹I looked, and I saw beside the cherubim four wheels, one beside each of the cherubim; the wheels sparkled like chrysolite. ¹⁰As for their appearance, the four of them looked alike; each was like a wheel intersecting a wheel. ¹¹As they moved, they would go in any one of the four directions the cherubim faced; the wheels did not turn about[c] as the cherubim went. The cherubim went in whatever direction the head faced, without turning as they went. ¹²Their entire bodies, including their backs, their hands and their wings, were completely full of eyes, as were their four wheels. ¹³I heard the wheels being called "the whirling wheels." ¹⁴Each of the cherubim had four faces: One face was that of a cherub, the second the face of a man, the third the face of a lion, and the fourth the face of an eagle.

¹⁵Then the cherubim rose upward. These were the living creatures I had seen by the Kebar River. ¹⁶When the cherubim moved, the wheels beside them moved; and when the cherubim spread their wings to rise from the ground, the wheels did not leave their side. ¹⁷When the cherubim stood still, they also stood still; and when the cherubim rose, they rose with them, because the spirit of the living creatures was in them.

¹⁸Then the glory of the LORD departed from over the threshold of the temple and stopped above the cherubim.

above the cherubim. ¹⁹While I watched, the cherubim spread their wings and rose from the ground, and as they went, the wheels went with them. They stopped at the entrance to the east gate of the LORD's house, and the glory of the God of Israel was above them.

²⁰These were the living creatures I had seen beneath the God of Israel by the Kebar River, and I realized that they were cherubim. ²¹Each had

---

a1 Or *lapis lazuli*   *b5* Hebrew *El-Shaddai*   *c11* Or *aside* four faces and four wings, and under their wings was what looked like the hands of a man. [22]Their faces had the same appearance as those I had seen by the Kebar River. Each one went straight ahead.

Judgment on Israel's Leaders

11 Then the Spirit lifted me up and brought me to the gate of the house of the LORD that faces east. There at the entrance to the gate were twenty-five men, and I saw among them Jaazaniah son of Azzur and Pelatiah son of Benaiah, leaders of the people. [2]The LORD said to me, "Son of man, these are the men who are plotting evil and giving wicked advice in this city. [3]They say, 'Will it not soon be time to build houses?[a] This city is a cooking pot, and we are the meat.' [4]Therefore prophesy against them; prophesy, son of man."

[5]Then the Spirit of the LORD came upon me, and he told me to say: "This is what the LORD says: That is what you are saying, O house of Israel, but I know what is going through your mind. [6]You have killed many people in this city and filled its streets with the dead.

[7]"Therefore this is what the Sovereign LORD says: The bodies you have thrown there are the meat and this city is the pot, but I will drive you out of it. [8]You fear the sword, and the sword is what I will bring against you, declares the Sovereign LORD. [9]I will drive you out of the city and hand you over to foreigners and inflict punishment on you. [10]You will fall by the sword, and I will execute judgment on you at the borders of Israel. Then you will know that I am the LORD. [11]This city will not be a pot for you, nor will you be the meat in it; I will execute judgment on you at the borders of Israel. [12]And you will know that I am the LORD, for you have not followed my decrees or kept my laws but have conformed to the standards of the nations around you."

[13]Now as I was prophesying, Pelatiah son of Benaiah died. Then I fell facedown and cried out in a loud voice, "Ah, Sovereign LORD! Will you completely destroy the remnant of Israel?"

[14]The word of the LORD came to me: [15]"Son of man, your brothers—your brothers who are your blood relatives[b] and the whole house of Israel—are those of whom the people of Jerusalem have said, 'They are[c] far away from the LORD; this land was given to us as our possession.'

Promised Return of Israel

[16]"Therefore say: 'This is what the Sovereign LORD says: Although I sent them far away among the nations and scattered them among the countries, yet for a little while I have been a sanctuary for them in the countries where they have gone.'

[17]"Therefore say: 'This is what the Sovereign LORD says: I will gather you from the nations and bring you back from the countries where you have been scattered, and I will give you back the land of Israel again.'

[18]"They will return to it and remove all its vile images and detestable idols. [19]I will give them an undivided heart and put a new spirit in them; I will remove from them their heart of stone and give them a heart of flesh. [20]Then they will follow my decrees and be careful to keep my laws. They will be my people, and I will be their God. [21]But as for those whose hearts are devoted to their vile images and detestable idols, I will bring down on their own heads what they have done, declares the Sovereign LORD."

[22]Then the cherubim, with the wheels beside them, spread their wings, and the glory of the God of Israel was above them. [23]The glory of the LORD went up from within the city and stopped above the mountain east of it. [24]The Spirit lifted me up and brought me to the exiles in Babylonia[d] in the vision given by the Spirit of God.

Then the vision I had seen went up from me, [25]and I told the exiles everything the LORD had shown me.

The Exile Symbolized

12 The word of the LORD came to me: [2]"Son of man, you are living among a rebellious people. They have eyes to see but do not see and ears to hear but do not hear, for they are a rebellious people.

[3]"Therefore, son of man, pack your belongings for exile and in the daytime, as they watch, set out and go from where you are to another place. Perhaps they will understand, though they are a rebellious house. [4]During the daytime, while they watch, bring out your belongings packed for exile. Then in the evening, while they are watching, go out like those who go into exile. [5]While they watch, dig through the wall and take your belongings out through it. [6]Put them on your shoulder as they are watching and carry them out at dusk. Cover your face so that you cannot see the land, for I have made you a sign to the house of Israel."

[7]So I did as I was commanded. During the day I brought out my things packed for exile. Then in the evening I dug through the wall with my hands. I took my belongings out at dusk, carrying them on my shoulders while they watched.

[8]In the morning the word of the LORD came to me: [9]"Son of man, did not that rebellious house of Israel ask you, 'What are you doing?'

[10]"Say to them, 'This is what the Sovereign

---

[a]3 Or *This is not the time to build houses.* [b]15 Or *are in exile with you* (see Septuagint and Syriac) [c]15 Or *those to whom the people of Jerusalem have said, 'Stay* [d]24 Or *Chaldea*

LORD says: This oracle concerns the prince in Jerusalem and the whole house of Israel who are there.' ¹¹Say to them, 'I am a sign to you.'

"As I have done, so it will be done to them. They will go into exile as captives.

¹²"The prince among them will put his things on his shoulder at dusk and leave, and a hole will be dug in the wall for him to go through. He will

12:12 Out Through the Hole

Ezekiel's prediction of Jerusalem's leader leaving through a hole in the wall was literally fulfilled. You can read about it in 2 Kings 25:4–7 or Jeremiah 39:4–7.

cover his face so that he cannot see the land. ¹³I will spread my net for him, and he will be caught in my snare; I will bring him to Babylonia, the land of the Chaldeans, but he will not see it, and there he will die. ¹⁴I will scatter to the winds all those around him—his staff and all his troops—and I will pursue them with drawn sword.

¹⁵"They will know that I am the LORD, when I disperse them among the nations and scatter them through the countries. ¹⁶But I will spare a few of them from the sword, famine and plague, so that in the nations where they go they may acknowledge all their detestable practices. Then they will know that I am the LORD."

¹⁷The word of the LORD came to me: ¹⁸"Son of man, tremble as you eat your food, and shudder in fear as you drink your water. ¹⁹Say to the people of the land: 'This is what the Sovereign LORD says about those living in Jerusalem and in the land of Israel: They will eat their food in anxiety and drink their water in despair, for their land will be stripped of everything in it because of the violence of all who live there. ²⁰The inhabited towns will be laid waste and the land will be desolate. Then you will know that I am the LORD.'"

²¹The word of the LORD came to me: ²²"Son of man, what is this proverb you have in the land of Israel: 'The days go by and every vision comes to nothing'? ²³Say to them, 'This is what the Sovereign LORD says: I am going to put an end to this proverb, and they will no longer quote it in Israel.' Say to them, 'The days are near when every vision will be fulfilled. ²⁴For there will be no more false visions or flattering divinations among the people of Israel. ²⁵But I the LORD will speak what I will, and it shall be fulfilled without delay. For in your days, you rebellious house, I will fulfill whatever I say, declares the Sovereign LORD.'"

²⁶The word of the LORD came to me: ²⁷"Son of man, the house of Israel is saying, 'The vision he

sees is for many years from now, and he prophesies about the distant future.'

²⁸"Therefore say to them, 'This is what the Sovereign LORD says: None of my words will be delayed any longer; whatever I say will be fulfilled, declares the Sovereign LORD.'"

False Prophets Condemned

13 The word of the LORD came to me: ²"Son of man, prophesy against the prophets of Israel who are now prophesying. Say to those who prophesy out of their own imagination: 'Hear the word of the LORD! ³This is what the Sovereign LORD says: Woe to the foolish[a] prophets who follow their own spirit and have seen nothing! ⁴Your prophets, O Israel, are like jackals among ruins. ⁵You have not gone up to the breaks in the wall to repair it for the house of Israel so that it will stand firm in the battle on the day of the LORD. ⁶Their visions are false and their divinations a lie. They say, "The LORD declares," when the LORD has not sent them; yet they expect their words to be fulfilled. ⁷Have you not seen false visions and uttered lying divinations when you say, "The LORD declares," though I have not spoken?

⁸"'Therefore this is what the Sovereign LORD says: Because of your false words and lying visions, I am against you, declares the Sovereign LORD. ⁹My hand will be against the prophets who see false visions and utter lying divinations. They will not belong to the council of my people or be listed in the records of the house of Israel, nor will they enter the land of Israel. Then you will know that I am the Sovereign LORD.

¹⁰"'Because they lead my people astray, saying, "Peace," when there is no peace, and because, when a flimsy wall is built, they cover it with whitewash, ¹¹therefore tell those who cover it with whitewash that it is going to fall. Rain will come in torrents, and I will send hailstones hurtling down, and violent winds will burst forth. ¹²When the wall collapses, will people not ask you, "Where is the whitewash you covered it with?"

¹³"'Therefore this is what the Sovereign LORD says: In my wrath I will unleash a violent wind, and in my anger hailstones and torrents of rain will fall with destructive fury. ¹⁴I will tear down the wall you have covered with whitewash and will level it to the ground so that its foundation will be laid bare. When it[b] falls, you will be destroyed in it; and you will know that I am the LORD. ¹⁵So I will spend my wrath against the wall and against those who covered it with whitewash. I will say to you, "The wall is gone and so are those who whitewashed it, ¹⁶those prophets of Israel who prophesied to Jerusalem and saw vi-

---

a 3 Or *wicked*   *b* 14 Or *the city*

sions of peace for her when there was no peace, declares the Sovereign LORD." '

¹⁷"Now, son of man, set your face against the daughters of your people who prophesy out of

---

13:10–16 Whitewash

The Hebrew word translated "whitewash" means "to plaster over." The picture is of a poorly constructed wall that is carefully plastered so it looks well built. False prophets, wanting everyone to be happy, spoke cheerfully about the future. But they were only covering up the surface of fundamental problems. A storm, God warns, will strip off their coat of whitewash, and the flawed wall will collapse. In contrast, real prophets were unafraid of exposing the truth, however bad, for only then could problems be remedied.

Ezekiel 13:6–9 asserts that the false prophets thought up messages, then attributed them to God. Ezekiel, on the other hand, was repeatedly seized by a supernatural power. See, for examples, Ezekiel 8:1–5; 10:1–2; 24:1–2; and 33:21–22.

---

their own imagination. Prophesy against them ¹⁸and say, 'This is what the Sovereign LORD says: Woe to the women who sew magic charms on all their wrists and make veils of various lengths for their heads in order to ensnare people. Will you ensnare the lives of my people but preserve your own? ¹⁹You have profaned me among my people for a few handfuls of barley and scraps of bread. By lying to my people, who listen to lies, you have killed those who should not have died and have spared those who should not live.

²⁰" 'Therefore this is what the Sovereign LORD says: I am against your magic charms with which you ensnare people like birds and I will tear them from your arms; I will set free the people that you ensnare like birds. ²¹I will tear off your veils and save my people from your hands, and they will no longer fall prey to your power. Then you will know that I am the LORD. ²²Because you disheartened the righteous with your lies, when I had brought them no grief, and because you encouraged the wicked not to turn from their evil ways and so save their lives, ²³therefore you will no longer see false visions or practice divination. I will save my people from your hands. And then you will know that I am the LORD.' "

Idolaters Condemned

14 Some of the elders of Israel came to me and sat down in front of me. ²Then the word of the LORD came to me: ³"Son of man, these men have set up idols in their hearts and put wicked

stumbling blocks before their faces. Should I let them inquire of me at all? ⁴Therefore speak to them and tell them, 'This is what the Sovereign LORD says: When any Israelite sets up idols in his heart and puts a wicked stumbling block before his face and then goes to a prophet, I the LORD will answer him myself in keeping with his great idolatry. ⁵I will do this to recapture the hearts of the people of Israel, who have all deserted me for their idols.'

⁶"Therefore say to the house of Israel, 'This is what the Sovereign LORD says: Repent! Turn from your idols and renounce all your detestable practices!

⁷" 'When any Israelite or any alien living in Israel separates himself from me and sets up idols in his heart and puts a wicked stumbling block before his face and then goes to a prophet to inquire of me, I the LORD will answer him myself. ⁸I will set my face against that man and make him an example and a byword. I will cut him off from my people. Then you will know that I am the LORD.

⁹" 'And if the prophet is enticed to utter a prophecy, I the LORD have enticed that prophet, and I will stretch out my hand against him and destroy him from among my people Israel. ¹⁰They will bear their guilt—the prophet will be as guilty as the one who consults him. ¹¹Then the people of Israel will no longer stray from me, nor will they defile themselves anymore with all their sins. They will be my people, and I will be their God, declares the Sovereign LORD.' "

Judgment Inescapable

¹²The word of the LORD came to me: ¹³"Son of man, if a country sins against me by being unfaithful and I stretch out my hand against it to cut off its food supply and send famine upon it and kill its men and their animals, ¹⁴even if these three men—Noah, Daniel*a* and Job—were in it, they could save only themselves by their righteousness, declares the Sovereign LORD.

¹⁵"Or if I send wild beasts through that country and they leave it childless and it becomes desolate so that no one can pass through it because of the beasts, ¹⁶as surely as I live, declares the Sovereign LORD, even if these three men were in it, they could not save their own sons or daughters. They alone would be saved, but the land would be desolate.

¹⁷"Or if I bring a sword against that country and say, 'Let the sword pass throughout the land,' and I kill its men and their animals, ¹⁸as surely as I live, declares the Sovereign LORD, even if these three men were in it, they could not save their own sons or daughters. They alone would be saved.

---

a14 Or *Danel*; the Hebrew spelling may suggest a person other than the prophet Daniel; also in verse 20.

[19]"Or if I send a plague into that land and pour out my wrath upon it through bloodshed, killing its men and their animals, [20]as surely as I live, declares the Sovereign LORD, even if Noah, Daniel and Job were in it, they could save neither son nor daughter. They would save only themselves by their righteousness.

[21]"For this is what the Sovereign LORD says: How much worse will it be when I send against Jerusalem my four dreadful judgments—sword and famine and wild beasts and plague—to kill its men and their animals! [22]Yet there will be some survivors—sons and daughters who will be brought out of it. They will come to you, and when you see their conduct and their actions, you will be consoled regarding the disaster I have brought upon Jerusalem—every disaster I have brought upon it. [23]You will be consoled when you see their conduct and their actions, for you will know that I have done nothing in it without cause, declares the Sovereign LORD."

Jerusalem, A Useless Vine

15 The word of the LORD came to me: [2]"Son of man, how is the wood of a vine better than that of a branch on any of the trees in the forest? [3]Is wood ever taken from it to make anything useful? Do they make pegs from it to hang things on? [4]And after it is thrown on the fire as fuel and the fire burns both ends and chars the middle, is it then useful for anything? [5]If it was not useful for anything when it was whole, how much less can it be made into something useful when the fire has burned it and it is charred?

[6]"Therefore this is what the Sovereign LORD says: As I have given the wood of the vine among the trees of the forest as fuel for the fire, so will I treat the people living in Jerusalem. [7]I will set my face against them. Although they have come out of the fire, the fire will yet consume them. And when I set my face against them, you will know that I am the LORD. [8]I will make the land desolate because they have been unfaithful, declares the Sovereign LORD."

An Allegory of Unfaithful Jerusalem

16 The word of the LORD came to me: [2]"Son of man, confront Jerusalem with her detestable practices [3]and say, 'This is what the Sovereign LORD says to Jerusalem: Your ancestry and birth were in the land of the Canaanites; your father was an Amorite and your mother a Hittite. [4]On the day you were born your cord was not cut, nor were you washed with water to make you clean, nor were you rubbed with salt or wrapped in cloths. [5]No one looked on you with pity or had

compassion enough to do any of these things for you. Rather, you were thrown out into the open field, for on the day you were born you were despised.

[6]"'Then I passed by and saw you kicking about in your blood, and as you lay there in your blood I said to you, "Live!"[a] [7]I made you grow like a plant of the field. You grew up and developed and became the most beautiful of jewels.[b] Your breasts were formed and your hair grew, you who were naked and bare.

[8]"'Later I passed by, and when I looked at you and saw that you were old enough for love, I spread the corner of my garment over you and covered your nakedness. I gave you my solemn oath and entered into a covenant with you, declares the Sovereign LORD, and you became mine.

[9]"'I bathed[c] you with water and washed the blood from you and put ointments on you. [10]I clothed you with an embroidered dress and put leather sandals on you. I dressed you in fine linen and covered you with costly garments. [11]I adorned you with jewelry: I put bracelets on your arms and a necklace around your neck, [12]and I put a ring on your nose, earrings on your ears and a beautiful crown on your head. [13]So you were adorned with gold and silver; your clothes were of fine linen and costly fabric and embroidered cloth. Your food was fine flour, honey and olive oil. You became very beautiful and rose to be a queen. [14]And your fame spread among the nations on account of your beauty, because the splendor I had given you made your beauty perfect, declares the Sovereign LORD.

[15]"'But you trusted in your beauty and used your fame to become a prostitute. You lavished your favors on anyone who passed by and your beauty became his.[d] [16]You took some of your garments to make gaudy high places, where you carried on your prostitution. Such things should not happen, nor should they ever occur. [17]You also took the fine jewelry I gave you, the jewelry made of my gold and silver, and you made for yourself male idols and engaged in prostitution with them. [18]And you took your embroidered clothes to put on them, and you offered my oil and incense before them. [19]Also the food I provided for you—the fine flour, olive oil and honey I gave you to eat—you offered as fragrant incense before them. That is what happened, declares the Sovereign LORD.

[20]"'And you took your sons and daughters whom you bore to me and sacrificed them as food to the idols. Was your prostitution not enough? [21]You slaughtered my children and sacrificed them[e] to the idols. [22]In all your detest-

---

[a]6 A few Hebrew manuscripts, Septuagint and Syriac; most Hebrew manuscripts *"Live!" And as you lay there in your blood I said to you, "Live!"* [b]7 Or *became mature* [c]9 Or *I had bathed* [d]15 Most Hebrew manuscripts; one Hebrew manuscript (see some Septuagint manuscripts) *by. Such a thing should not happen* [e]21 Or *and made them pass through ⌊the fire⌋*

able practices and your prostitution you did not remember the days of your youth, when you were naked and bare, kicking about in your blood.

23 "Woe! Woe to you, declares the Sovereign LORD. In addition to all your other wickedness, 24 you built a mound for yourself and made a lofty shrine in every public square. 25 At the head of every street you built your lofty shrines and degraded your beauty, offering your body with increasing promiscuity to anyone who passed by. 26 You engaged in prostitution with the Egyptians, your lustful neighbors, and provoked me to anger with your increasing promiscuity. 27 So I

16:26 Worse than a Whore

In this graphic allegory, Ezekiel compares Jerusalem to an abandoned baby whom God rescues and raises with great tenderness. (Female children, often unwanted, were sometimes left to die.) Yet she rebels, preferring life on the wild side. She becomes a prostitute, then sinks even lower. Rather than being paid for her services, she actually pays for sex (verse 34). Ezekiel is depicting Israel's eagerness to adopt the religious practices of her neighbors.

stretched out my hand against you and reduced your territory; I gave you over to the greed of your enemies, the daughters of the Philistines, who were shocked by your lewd conduct. 28 You engaged in prostitution with the Assyrians too, because you were insatiable; and even after that, you still were not satisfied. 29 Then you increased your promiscuity to include Babylonia,[a] a land of merchants, but even with this you were not satisfied.

30 "How weak-willed you are, declares the Sovereign LORD, when you do all these things, acting like a brazen prostitute! 31 When you built your mounds at the head of every street and made your lofty shrines in every public square, you were unlike a prostitute, because you scorned payment.

32 "You adulterous wife! You prefer strangers to your own husband! 33 Every prostitute receives a fee, but you give gifts to all your lovers, bribing them to come to you from everywhere for your illicit favors. 34 So in your prostitution you are the opposite of others; no one runs after you for your favors. You are the very opposite, for you give payment and none is given to you.

35 "Therefore, you prostitute, hear the word of the LORD! 36 This is what the Sovereign LORD says: Because you poured out your wealth[b] and ex-

posed your nakedness in your promiscuity with your lovers, and because of all your detestable idols, and because you gave them your children's blood, 37 therefore I am going to gather all your lovers, with whom you found pleasure, those you loved as well as those you hated. I will gather them against you from all around and will strip you in front of them, and they will see all your nakedness. 38 I will sentence you to the punishment of women who commit adultery and who shed blood; I will bring upon you the blood vengeance of my wrath and jealous anger. 39 Then I will hand you over to your lovers, and they will tear down your mounds and destroy your lofty shrines. They will strip you of your clothes and take your fine jewelry and leave you naked and bare. 40 They will bring a mob against you, who will stone you and hack you to pieces with their swords. 41 They will burn down your houses and inflict punishment on you in the sight of many women. I will put a stop to your prostitution, and you will no longer pay your lovers. 42 Then my wrath against you will subside and my jealous anger will turn away from you; I will be calm and no longer angry.

43 "Because you did not remember the days of your youth but enraged me with all these things, I will surely bring down on your head what you have done, declares the Sovereign LORD. Did you not add lewdness to all your other detestable practices?

44 "Everyone who quotes proverbs will quote this proverb about you: "Like mother, like daughter." 45 You are a true daughter of your mother, who despised her husband and her children; and you are a true sister of your sisters, who despised their husbands and their children. Your mother was a Hittite and your father an Amorite. 46 Your older sister was Samaria, who lived to the north of you with her daughters; and your younger sister, who lived to the south of you with her daughters, was Sodom. 47 You not only walked in their ways and copied their detestable practices, but in all your ways you soon became more depraved than they. 48 As surely as I live, declares the Sovereign LORD, your sister Sodom and her daughters never did what you and your daughters have done.

49 "Now this was the sin of your sister Sodom: She and her daughters were arrogant, overfed and unconcerned; they did not help the poor and needy. 50 They were haughty and did detestable things before me. Therefore I did away with them as you have seen. 51 Samaria did not commit half the sins you did. You have done more detestable things than they, and have made your sisters seem righteous by all these things you have done. 52 Bear your disgrace, for you have furnished

---

a29 Or Chaldea   *b36 Or lust*

some justification for your sisters. Because your sins were more vile than theirs, they appear more righteous than you. So then, be ashamed and bear your disgrace, for you have made your sisters appear righteous.

53 " 'However, I will restore the fortunes of Sodom and her daughters and of Samaria and her daughters, and your fortunes along with them, 54 so that you may bear your disgrace and be ashamed of all you have done in giving them comfort. 55 And your sisters, Sodom with her daughters and Samaria with her daughters, will return to what they were before; and you and your daughters will return to what you were before. 56 You would not even mention your sister Sodom in the day of your pride, 57 before your wickedness was uncovered. Even so, you are now scorned by the daughters of Edom[a] and all her neighbors and the daughters of the Philistines—all those around you who despise you. 58 You will bear the consequences of your lewdness and your detestable practices, declares the LORD.

59 " 'This is what the Sovereign LORD says: I will deal with you as you deserve, because you have despised my oath by breaking the covenant. 60 Yet I will remember the covenant I made with you in the days of your youth, and I will establish an everlasting covenant with you. 61 Then you will remember your ways and be ashamed when you receive your sisters, both those who are older than you and those who are younger. I will give them to you as daughters, but not on the basis of my covenant with you. 62 So I will establish my covenant with you, and you will know that I am the LORD. 63 Then, when I make atonement for you for all you have done, you will remember and be ashamed and never again open your mouth because of your humiliation, declares the Sovereign LORD.' "

Two Eagles and a Vine

17 The word of the LORD came to me: 2 "Son of man, set forth an allegory and tell the house of Israel a parable. 3 Say to them, 'This is what the Sovereign LORD says: A great eagle with powerful wings, long feathers and full plumage of varied colors came to Lebanon. Taking hold of the top of a cedar, 4 he broke off its topmost shoot and carried it away to a land of merchants, where he planted it in a city of traders.

5 " 'He took some of the seed of your land and put it in fertile soil. He planted it like a willow by abundant water, 6 and it sprouted and became a low, spreading vine. Its branches turned toward him, but its roots remained under it. So it became a vine and produced branches and put out leafy boughs.

7 " 'But there was another great eagle with powerful wings and full plumage. The vine now sent out its roots toward him from the plot where it was planted and stretched out its branches to him for water. 8 It had been planted in good soil by abundant water so that it would produce branches, bear fruit and become a splendid vine.'

9 "Say to them, 'This is what the Sovereign LORD says: Will it thrive? Will it not be uprooted and stripped of its fruit so that it withers? All its new growth will wither. It will not take a strong arm or many people to pull it up by the roots. 10 Even if it is transplanted, will it thrive? Will it not wither completely when the east wind strikes it—wither away in the plot where it grew?' "

11 Then the word of the LORD came to me: 12 "Say to this rebellious house, 'Do you not know what these things mean?' Say to them: 'The king of Babylon went to Jerusalem and carried off her king and her nobles, bringing them back with him to Babylon. 13 Then he took a member of the royal family and made a treaty with him, putting him under oath. He also carried away the leading men of the land, 14 so that the kingdom would be brought low, unable to rise again, surviving only by keeping his treaty. 15 But the king rebelled against him by sending his envoys to Egypt to get horses and a large army. Will he succeed? Will he who does such things escape? Will he break the treaty and yet escape?

16 " 'As surely as I live, declares the Sovereign LORD, he shall die in Babylon, in the land of the king who put him on the throne, whose oath he despised and whose treaty he broke. 17 Pharaoh with his mighty army and great horde will be of no help to him in war, when ramps are built and siege works erected to destroy many lives. 18 He despised the oath by breaking the covenant. Because he had given his hand in pledge and yet did all these things, he shall not escape.

19 " 'Therefore this is what the Sovereign LORD says: As surely as I live, I will bring down on his head my oath that he despised and my covenant that he broke. 20 I will spread my net for him, and he will be caught in my snare. I will bring him to Babylon and execute judgment upon him there because he was unfaithful to me. 21 All his fleeing

---

[a] 57 Many Hebrew manuscripts and Syriac; most Hebrew manuscripts, Septuagint and Vulgate *Aram*

troops will fall by the sword, and the survivors will be scattered to the winds. Then you will know that I the LORD have spoken.

22"'This is what the Sovereign LORD says: I myself will take a shoot from the very top of a cedar and plant it; I will break off a tender sprig from its topmost shoots and plant it on a high and lofty mountain. 23On the mountain heights of Israel I will plant it; it will produce branches and bear fruit and become a splendid cedar. Birds of every kind will nest in it; they will find shelter in the shade of its branches. 24All the trees of the field will know that I the LORD bring down the tall tree and make the low tree grow tall. I dry up the green tree and make the dry tree flourish.

"'I the LORD have spoken, and I will do it.'"

The Soul Who Sins Will Die

18 The word of the LORD came to me: 2"What do you people mean by quoting this proverb about the land of Israel:

"'The fathers eat sour grapes,
    and the children's teeth are set on edge'?

18:2 Jeremiah and Ezekiel

This proverb, which suggests the way children pay for their parents' sins, was also quoted by Jeremiah (Jeremiah 31:29). While Ezekiel did his work in Babylon, Jeremiah carried out a parallel work in Jerusalem. Neither mentions the other, but their messages carry many similarities. Note particularly Jeremiah 1:14–19; 3:6–13; 6:27–30; 8:10–11; 15:1–2; 16:5–8; 23:16–40; 24; 29; 31:27–34; 39—all passages that have close parallels in Ezekiel.

3"As surely as I live, declares the Sovereign LORD, you will no longer quote this proverb in Israel. 4For every living soul belongs to me, the father as well as the son—both alike belong to me. The soul who sins is the one who will die.

5"Suppose there is a righteous man
    who does what is just and right.
6He does not eat at the mountain shrines
    or look to the idols of the house of Israel.
He does not defile his neighbor's wife
    or lie with a woman during her period.
7He does not oppress anyone,
    but returns what he took in pledge for a loan.
He does not commit robbery
    but gives his food to the hungry
    and provides clothing for the naked.
8He does not lend at usury

or take excessive interest.[a]
He withholds his hand from doing wrong
    and judges fairly between man and man.
9He follows my decrees
    and faithfully keeps my laws.
That man is righteous;
    he will surely live,
                    declares the Sovereign LORD.

10"Suppose he has a violent son, who sheds blood or does any of these other things[b] 11(though the father has done none of them):

"He eats at the mountain shrines.
He defiles his neighbor's wife.
12He oppresses the poor and needy.
He commits robbery.
He does not return what he took in pledge.
He looks to the idols.
He does detestable things.
13He lends at usury and takes excessive
    interest.

Will such a man live? He will not! Because he has done all these detestable things, he will surely be put to death and his blood will be on his own head.

14"But suppose this son has a son who sees all the sins his father commits, and though he sees them, he does not do such things:

15"He does not eat at the mountain shrines
    or look to the idols of the house of Israel.
He does not defile his neighbor's wife.
16He does not oppress anyone
    or require a pledge for a loan.
He does not commit robbery
    but gives his food to the hungry
    and provides clothing for the naked.
17He withholds his hand from sin[c]
    and takes no usury or excessive interest.
He keeps my laws and follows my decrees.

He will not die for his father's sin; he will surely live. 18But his father will die for his own sin, because he practiced extortion, robbed his brother and did what was wrong among his people.

19"Yet you ask, 'Why does the son not share the guilt of his father?' Since the son has done what is just and right and has been careful to keep all my decrees, he will surely live. 20The soul who sins is the one who will die. The son will not share the guilt of the father, nor will the father share the guilt of the son. The righteousness of the righteous man will be credited to him, and the wickedness of the wicked will be charged against him.

21"But if a wicked man turns away from all the sins he has committed and keeps all my decrees and does what is just and right, he will surely live;

---

a8 Or take interest; similarly in verses 13 and 17   b10 Or things to a brother   c17 Septuagint (see also verse 8);
Hebrew from the poor

he will not die. [22]None of the offenses he has committed will be remembered against him. Because of the righteous things he has done, he will live. [23]Do I take any pleasure in the death of the wicked? declares the Sovereign LORD. Rather, am I not pleased when they turn from their ways and live?

[24]"But if a righteous man turns from his righteousness and commits sin and does the same detestable things the wicked man does, will he live? None of the righteous things he has done will be remembered. Because of the unfaithfulness he is guilty of and because of the sins he has committed, he will die.

[25]"Yet you say, 'The way of the Lord is not just.' Hear, O house of Israel: Is my way unjust?

18:25 God Is Unfair?

"The way of the Lord is not just" probably was less a complaint than a fatalistic sigh, much like our saying, "Life isn't fair." People had lost any sense that they were suffering because of their sins. They were saying that it made no difference how they acted. Determined to break down this attitude, God guaranteed forgiveness for those who turn away from their sins.

Is it not your ways that are unjust? [26]If a righteous man turns from his righteousness and commits sin, he will die for it; because of the sin he has committed he will die. [27]But if a wicked man turns away from the wickedness he has committed and does what is just and right, he will save his life. [28]Because he considers all the offenses he has committed and turns away from them, he will surely live; he will not die. [29]Yet the house of Israel says, 'The way of the Lord is not just.' Are my ways unjust, O house of Israel? Is it not your ways that are unjust?

[30]"Therefore, O house of Israel, I will judge you, each one according to his ways, declares the Sovereign LORD. Repent! Turn away from all your offenses; then sin will not be your downfall. [31]Rid yourselves of all the offenses you have committed, and get a new heart and a new spirit. Why will you die, O house of Israel? [32]For I take no pleasure in the death of anyone, declares the Sovereign LORD. Repent and live!

A Lament for Israel's Princes

19 "Take up a lament concerning the princes of Israel [2]and say:

"'What a lioness was your mother
  among the lions!

She lay down among the young lions
  and reared her cubs.
[3]She brought up one of her cubs,
  and he became a strong lion.
He learned to tear the prey
  and he devoured men.
[4]The nations heard about him,
  and he was trapped in their pit.
They led him with hooks
  to the land of Egypt.

[5]"'When she saw her hope unfulfilled,
  her expectation gone,
she took another of her cubs
  and made him a strong lion.
[6]He prowled among the lions,
  for he was now a strong lion.
He learned to tear the prey
  and he devoured men.
[7]He broke down[a] their strongholds
  and devastated their towns.
The land and all who were in it
  were terrified by his roaring.
[8]Then the nations came against him,
  those from regions round about.
They spread their net for him,
  and he was trapped in their pit.
[9]With hooks they pulled him into a cage
  and brought him to the king of Babylon.
They put him in prison,
  so his roar was heard no longer
  on the mountains of Israel.

[10]"'Your mother was like a vine in your
      vineyard[b]
  planted by the water;
it was fruitful and full of branches
  because of abundant water.
[11]Its branches were strong,
  fit for a ruler's scepter.
It towered high
  above the thick foliage,
conspicuous for its height
  and for its many branches.
[12]But it was uprooted in fury
  and thrown to the ground.
The east wind made it shrivel,
  it was stripped of its fruit;
its strong branches withered
  and fire consumed them.
[13]Now it is planted in the desert,
  in a dry and thirsty land.
[14]Fire spread from one of its main[c] branches
  and consumed its fruit.
No strong branch is left on it
  fit for a ruler's scepter.'

This is a lament and is to be used as a lament."

---

[a]7 Targum (see Septuagint); Hebrew *He knew*   [b]10 Two Hebrew manuscripts; most Hebrew manuscripts *your blood*
[c]14 Or *from under its*

Rebellious Israel

20 In the seventh year, in the fifth month on the tenth day, some of the elders of Israel came to inquire of the LORD, and they sat down in front of me.

²Then the word of the LORD came to me: ³"Son of man, speak to the elders of Israel and say to them, 'This is what the Sovereign LORD says: Have you come to inquire of me? As surely as I live, I will not let you inquire of me, declares the Sovereign LORD.'

20:3 Don't Ask God

Does God always want people to pray? According to this passage, time sometimes runs out on prayer. When elders came to Ezekiel to ask God for direction, God said: Don't bother. What is the use, when he has told them over and over what the problem is? He has nothing more to say.

⁴"Will you judge them? Will you judge them, son of man? Then confront them with the detestable practices of their fathers ⁵and say to them: 'This is what the Sovereign LORD says: On the day I chose Israel, I swore with uplifted hand to the descendants of the house of Jacob and revealed myself to them in Egypt. With uplifted hand I said to them, "I am the LORD your God." ⁶On that day I swore to them that I would bring them out of Egypt into a land I had searched out for them, a land flowing with milk and honey, the most beautiful of all lands. ⁷And I said to them, "Each of you, get rid of the vile images you have set your eyes on, and do not defile yourselves with the idols of Egypt. I am the LORD your God."

⁸"'But they rebelled against me and would not listen to me; they did not get rid of the vile images they had set their eyes on, nor did they forsake the idols of Egypt. So I said I would pour out my wrath on them and spend my anger against them in Egypt. ⁹But for the sake of my name I did what would keep it from being profaned in the eyes of the nations they lived among and in whose sight I had revealed myself to the Israelites by bringing them out of Egypt. ¹⁰Therefore I led them out of Egypt and brought them into the desert. ¹¹I gave them my decrees and made known to them my laws, for the man who obeys them will live by them. ¹²Also I gave them my Sabbaths as a sign between us, so they would know that I the LORD made them holy.

¹³"'Yet the people of Israel rebelled against me in the desert. They did not follow my decrees but rejected my laws—although the man who obeys them will live by them—and they utterly dese-

crated my Sabbaths. So I said I would pour out my wrath on them and destroy them in the desert. ¹⁴But for the sake of my name I did what would keep it from being profaned in the eyes of the nations in whose sight I had brought them out. ¹⁵Also with uplifted hand I swore to them in the desert that I would not bring them into the land I had given them—a land flowing with milk and honey, most beautiful of all lands— ¹⁶because they rejected my laws and did not follow my decrees and desecrated my Sabbaths. For their hearts were devoted to their idols. ¹⁷Yet I looked on them with pity and did not destroy them or put an end to them in the desert. ¹⁸I said to their children in the desert, "Do not follow the statutes of your fathers or keep their laws or defile yourselves with their idols. ¹⁹I am the LORD your God; follow my decrees and be careful to keep my laws. ²⁰Keep my Sabbaths holy, that they may be a sign between us. Then you will know that I am the LORD your God."

²¹"'But the children rebelled against me: They did not follow my decrees, they were not careful to keep my laws—although the man who obeys them will live by them—and they desecrated my Sabbaths. So I said I would pour out my wrath on them and spend my anger against them in the desert. ²²But I withheld my hand, and for the sake of my name I did what would keep it from being profaned in the eyes of the nations in whose sight I had brought them out. ²³Also with uplifted hand I swore to them in the desert that I would disperse them among the nations and scatter them through the countries, ²⁴because they had not obeyed my laws but had rejected my decrees and desecrated my Sabbaths, and their eyes ⌊lusted⌋ after their fathers' idols. ²⁵I also gave them over to statutes that were not good and laws they could not live by; ²⁶I let them become defiled through their gifts—the sacrifice of every firstborn[a]—that I might fill them with horror so they would know that I am the LORD.'

²⁷"Therefore, son of man, speak to the people of Israel and say to them, 'This is what the Sovereign LORD says: In this also your fathers blasphemed me by forsaking me: ²⁸When I brought them into the land I had sworn to give them and they saw any high hill or any leafy tree, there they offered their sacrifices, made offerings that provoked me to anger, presented their fragrant incense and poured out their drink offerings. ²⁹Then I said to them: What is this high place you go to?'" (It is called Bamah[b] to this day.)

Judgment and Restoration

³⁰"Therefore say to the house of Israel: 'This is what the Sovereign LORD says: Will you defile yourselves the way your fathers did and lust after

---

[a]26 Or —*making every firstborn pass through* ⌊*the fire*⌋   [b]29 *Bamah* means *high place.*

their vile images? [31]When you offer your gifts—the sacrifice of your sons in[a] the fire—you continue to defile yourselves with all your idols to this day. Am I to let you inquire of me, O house of Israel? As surely as I live, declares the Sovereign LORD, I will not let you inquire of me.

[32]"You say, "We want to be like the nations, like the peoples of the world, who serve wood and stone." But what you have in mind will never

20:32 Like Everybody Else

"Everybody does it!" children sometimes whine to their parents. Good parents aren't swayed, however. They want their children to live up to their own potential, not mimic everybody else.
Like those children, Israelites grew tired of their calling. They wanted to relax and live like other nations. But God swears he will never let it happen. He will remain strict, even putting them through another desert experience to purify them, but he absolutely refuses to let them conform.

happen. [33]As surely as I live, declares the Sovereign LORD, I will rule over you with a mighty hand and an outstretched arm and with outpoured wrath. [34]I will bring you from the nations and gather you from the countries where you have been scattered—with a mighty hand and an outstretched arm and with outpoured wrath. [35]I will bring you into the desert of the nations and there, face to face, I will execute judgment upon you. [36]As I judged your fathers in the desert of the land of Egypt, so I will judge you, declares the Sovereign LORD. [37]I will take note of you as you pass under my rod, and I will bring you into the bond of the covenant. [38]I will purge you of those who revolt and rebel against me. Although I will bring them out of the land where they are living, yet they will not enter the land of Israel. Then you will know that I am the LORD.

[39]"As for you, O house of Israel, this is what the Sovereign LORD says: Go and serve your idols, every one of you! But afterward you will surely listen to me and no longer profane my holy name with your gifts and idols. [40]For on my holy mountain, the high mountain of Israel, declares the Sovereign LORD, there in the land the entire house of Israel will serve me, and there I will accept them. There I will require your offerings and your choice gifts,[b] along with all your holy sacrifices. [41]I will accept you as fragrant incense when I bring you out from the nations and gather you from the countries where you have been scattered, and I will show myself holy among you in the sight of the nations. [42]Then you will know

that I am the LORD, when I bring you into the land of Israel, the land I had sworn with uplifted hand to give to your fathers. [43]There you will remember your conduct and all the actions by which you have defiled yourselves, and you will loathe yourselves for all the evil you have done. [44]You will know that I am the LORD, when I deal with you for my name's sake and not according to your evil ways and your corrupt practices, O house of Israel, declares the Sovereign LORD.'"

Prophecy Against the South

[45]The word of the LORD came to me: [46]"Son of man, set your face toward the south; preach against the south and prophesy against the forest of the southland. [47]Say to the southern forest: 'Hear the word of the LORD. This is what the Sovereign LORD says: I am about to set fire to you, and it will consume all your trees, both green and dry. The blazing flame will not be quenched, and every face from south to north will be scorched by it. [48]Everyone will see that I the LORD have kindled it; it will not be quenched.'"

[49]Then I said, "Ah, Sovereign LORD! They are saying of me, 'Isn't he just telling parables?'"

Babylon, God's Sword of Judgment

21 The word of the LORD came to me: [2]"Son of man, set your face against Jerusalem and preach against the sanctuary. Prophesy against the land of Israel [3]and say to her: 'This is what the LORD says: I am against you. I will draw my sword from its scabbard and cut off from you both the righteous and the wicked. [4]Because I am going to cut off the righteous and the wicked, my sword will be unsheathed against everyone from south to north. [5]Then all people will know that I the LORD have drawn my sword from its scabbard; it will not return again.'

[6]"Therefore groan, son of man! Groan before them with broken heart and bitter grief. [7]And when they ask you, 'Why are you groaning?' you shall say, 'Because of the news that is coming. Every heart will melt and every hand go limp; every spirit will become faint and every knee become as weak as water.' It is coming! It will surely take place, declares the Sovereign LORD."

[8]The word of the LORD came to me: [9]"Son of man, prophesy and say, 'This is what the Lord says:

"'A sword, a sword,
    sharpened and polished—
[10]sharpened for the slaughter,
    polished to flash like lightning!

"'Shall we rejoice in the scepter of my son Judah? The sword despises every such stick.

11 "'The sword is appointed to be polished,
    to be grasped with the hand;
  it is sharpened and polished,
    made ready for the hand of the slayer.
12 Cry out and wail, son of man,
    for it is against my people;
  it is against all the princes of Israel.
They are thrown to the sword
    along with my people.
Therefore beat your breast.

13 "'Testing will surely come. And what if the
scepter ⌊of Judah⌋, which the sword despises,
does not continue? declares the Sovereign LORD.'

14 "So then, son of man, prophesy
    and strike your hands together.
Let the sword strike twice,
    even three times.
It is a sword for slaughter—
    a sword for great slaughter,
    closing in on them from every side.
15 So that hearts may melt
    and the fallen be many,
I have stationed the sword for slaughter[a]
    at all their gates.
Oh! It is made to flash like lightning,
    it is grasped for slaughter.
16 O sword, slash to the right,
    then to the left,
    wherever your blade is turned.
17 I too will strike my hands together,
    and my wrath will subside.
I the LORD have spoken."

18 The word of the LORD came to me: 19 "Son of
man, mark out two roads for the sword of the
king of Babylon to take, both starting from the
same country. Make a signpost where the road
branches off to the city. 20 Mark out one road for
the sword to come against Rabbah of the Ammonites and another against Judah and fortified
Jerusalem. 21 For the king of Babylon will stop at
the fork in the road, at the junction of the two
roads, to seek an omen: He will cast lots with
arrows, he will consult his idols, he will examine
the liver. 22 Into his right hand will come the lot
for Jerusalem, where he is to set up battering
rams, to give the command to slaughter, to
sound the battle cry, to set battering rams against
the gates, to build a ramp and to erect siege
works. 23 It will seem like a false omen to those
who have sworn allegiance to him, but he will
remind them of their guilt and take them captive.

24 "Therefore this is what the Sovereign LORD
says: 'Because you people have brought to mind
your guilt by your open rebellion, revealing your
sins in all that you do—because you have done
this, you will be taken captive.

25 "'O profane and wicked prince of Israel,
whose day has come, whose time of punishment
has reached its climax, 26 this is what the Sovereign LORD says: Take off the turban, remove the
crown. It will not be as it was: The lowly will be

21:21 Liver-Gazing

*This verse shows how an ancient Babylonian
king might seek direction from his gods.
Casting lots with arrows apparently meant
marking arrows with various alternatives,
putting them in a quiver, and drawing one out.
Consulting idols would mean praying to them,
perhaps hoping for a dream or an omen. The
livers of animals, like tea leaves today, were
often studied in ancient times; their shape or
color was supposed to tell the future.*

exalted and the exalted will be brought low. 27 A
ruin! A ruin! I will make it a ruin! It will not be
restored until he comes to whom it rightfully
belongs; to him I will give it.'

28 "And you, son of man, prophesy and say,
'This is what the Sovereign LORD says about the
Ammonites and their insults:

"'A sword, a sword,
    drawn for the slaughter,
polished to consume
    and to flash like lightning!
29 Despite false visions concerning you
    and lying divinations about you,
it will be laid on the necks
    of the wicked who are to be slain,
whose day has come,
    whose time of punishment has reached its
      climax.
30 Return the sword to its scabbard.
    In the place where you were created,
in the land of your ancestry,
    I will judge you.
31 I will pour out my wrath upon you
    and breathe out my fiery anger against
      you;
I will hand you over to brutal men,
    men skilled in destruction.
32 You will be fuel for the fire,
    your blood will be shed in your land,
you will be remembered no more;
    for I the LORD have spoken.'"

Jerusalem's Sins

22 The word of the LORD came to me: 2 "Son
of man, will you judge her? Will you judge
this city of bloodshed? Then confront her with all
her detestable practices 3 and say: 'This is what
the Sovereign LORD says: O city that brings on
herself doom by shedding blood in her midst and

---

[a] 15 Septuagint; the meaning of the Hebrew for this word is uncertain.

defiles herself by making idols, **4**you have become guilty because of the blood you have shed and have become defiled by the idols you have made. You have brought your days to a close, and the end of your years has come. Therefore I will make you an object of scorn to the nations and a laughingstock to all the countries. **5**Those who are near and those who are far away will mock you, O infamous city, full of turmoil.

6"'See how each of the princes of Israel who are in you uses his power to shed blood. **7**In you they have treated father and mother with contempt; in you they have oppressed the alien and mistreated the fatherless and the widow. **8**You have despised my holy things and desecrated my Sabbaths. **9**In you are slanderous men bent on shedding blood; in you are those who eat at the mountain shrines and commit lewd acts. **10**In you are those who dishonor their fathers' bed; in you are those who violate women during their period, when they are ceremonially unclean. **11**In you one man commits a detestable offense with his neighbor's wife, another shamefully defiles his daughter-in-law, and another violates his sister, his own father's daughter. **12**In you men accept bribes to shed blood; you take usury and excessive interest*a* and make unjust gain from your neighbors by extortion. And you have forgotten me, declares the Sovereign LORD.

13"'I will surely strike my hands together at the unjust gain you have made and at the blood you have shed in your midst. **14**Will your courage endure or your hands be strong in the day I deal with you? I the LORD have spoken, and I will do it. **15**I will disperse you among the nations and scatter you through the countries; and I will put an end to your uncleanness. **16**When you have been defiled*b* in the eyes of the nations, you will know that I am the LORD.'"

17Then the word of the LORD came to me: **18**"Son of man, the house of Israel has become dross to me; all of them are the copper, tin, iron and lead left inside a furnace. They are but the dross of silver. **19**Therefore this is what the Sovereign LORD says: 'Because you have all become dross, I will gather you into Jerusalem. **20**As men gather silver, copper, iron, lead and tin into a furnace to melt it with a fiery blast, so will I gather you in my anger and my wrath and put you inside the city and melt you. **21**I will gather you and I will blow on you with my fiery wrath, and you will be melted inside her. **22**As silver is melted in a furnace, so you will be melted inside her, and you will know that I the LORD have poured out my wrath upon you.'"

23Again the word of the LORD came to me: **24**"Son of man, say to the land, 'You are a land that has had no rain or showers*c* in the day of wrath.' **25**There is a conspiracy of her princes*d* within her like a roaring lion tearing its prey; they devour people, take treasures and precious things and make many widows within her. **26**Her priests do violence to my law and profane my holy things; they do not distinguish between the holy and the common; they teach that there is no difference between the unclean and the clean; and they shut their eyes to the keeping of my Sabbaths, so that I am profaned among them. **27**Her officials within her are like wolves tearing their prey; they shed blood and kill people to make unjust gain. **28**Her prophets whitewash these deeds for them by false visions and lying divinations. They say, 'This is what the Sovereign LORD says'—when the LORD has not spoken. **29**The people of the land practice extortion and commit robbery; they oppress the poor and needy and mistreat the alien, denying them justice.

30"I looked for a man among them who would build up the wall and stand before me in the gap on behalf of the land so I would not have to destroy it, but I found none. **31**So I will pour out my wrath on them and consume them with my fiery anger, bringing down on their own heads all they have done, declares the Sovereign LORD."

Two Adulterous Sisters

23 The word of the LORD came to me: **2**"Son of man, there were two women, daughters of the same mother. **3**They became prostitutes in Egypt, engaging in prostitution from their youth. In that land their breasts were fondled and their virgin bosoms caressed. **4**The older was named Oholah, and her sister was Oholibah. They were mine and gave birth to sons and daughters. Oholah is Samaria, and Oholibah is Jerusalem.

5"Oholah engaged in prostitution while she was still mine; and she lusted after her lovers, the Assyrians—warriors **6**clothed in blue, governors and commanders, all of them handsome young men, and mounted horsemen. **7**She gave herself as a prostitute to all the elite of the Assyrians and defiled herself with all the idols of everyone she lusted after. **8**She did not give up the prostitution she began in Egypt, when during her youth men slept with her, caressed her virgin bosom and poured out their lust upon her.

9"Therefore I handed her over to her lovers, the Assyrians, for whom she lusted. **10**They stripped her naked, took away her sons and daughters and killed her with the sword. She became a byword among women, and punishment was inflicted on her.

11"Her sister Oholibah saw this, yet in her lust

---

a12 Or *usury and interest* *b16* Or *When I have allotted you your inheritance* *c24* Septuagint; Hebrew *has not*
been cleansed or rained on *d25* Septuagint; Hebrew *prophets*

and prostitution she was more depraved than her sister. ¹²She too lusted after the Assyrians—governors and commanders, warriors in full dress, mounted horsemen, all handsome young men. ¹³I saw that she too defiled herself; both of them went the same way.

¹⁴"But she carried her prostitution still further. She saw men portrayed on a wall, figures of Chaldeans[a] portrayed in red, ¹⁵with belts around their waists and flowing turbans on their heads; all of them looked like Babylonian chariot officers, natives of Chaldea.[b] ¹⁶As soon as she saw them, she lusted after them and sent messengers to them in Chaldea. ¹⁷Then the Babylonians came to her, to the bed of love, and in their lust they defiled her. After she had been defiled by them, she turned away from them in disgust. ¹⁸When she carried on her prostitution openly and exposed her nakedness, I turned away from her in disgust, just as I had turned away from her

sister. ¹⁹Yet she became more and more promiscuous as she recalled the days of her youth, when she was a prostitute in Egypt. ²⁰There she lusted after her lovers, whose genitals were like those of donkeys and whose emission was like that of horses. ²¹So you longed for the lewdness of your youth, when in Egypt your bosom was caressed and your young breasts fondled.[c]

²²"Therefore, Oholibah, this is what the Sovereign Lord says: I will stir up your lovers against you, those you turned away from in disgust, and I will bring them against you from every side— ²³the Babylonians and all the Chaldeans, the men of Pekod and Shoa and Koa, and all the Assyrians with them, handsome young men, all of them governors and commanders, chariot officers and men of high rank, all mounted on horses. ²⁴They will come against you with weapons,[d] chariots and wagons and with a throng of people; they will take up positions against you on every side

---

[a] 14 Or *Babylonians*   [b] 15 Or *Babylonia*; also in verse 16   [c] 21 Syriac (see also verse 3); Hebrew *caressed because of your young breasts*   [d] 24 The meaning of the Hebrew for this word is uncertain.

The Runaways
A story meant to make you sick

> *"'Now let them use her as a prostitute, for that is all she is.'" 23:43*

THIS STORY, WHICH USES SEXUALLY explicit language, turns you off, not on. It tells of two sisters who choose promiscuous sex. Once they are involved, nothing satisfies them. They go from one man to the next. God calls them prostitutes, but they don't do it for the money. They do it because they like to live perversely.

Finally, in grief and frustration, God turns them over to their chosen lovers, who treat them like trash. God seems to take angry satisfaction in this. Love makes him angry—angry enough to weep.

An Allegory of Love

Ezekiel doesn't pretend that these two sisters are real people. From the beginning he identifies them with the capitals of the two halves of Israel—Samaria in the North, which the Assyrians had wiped out over 100 years before, and Jerusalem in the South. Samaria was properly rewarded for her prostitution, Ezekiel says, and Jerusalem will be too. The story of the two sisters is, in a sense, one more graphic way of saying that God has been patient with Jerusalem long enough. (A similar story is told in Ezekiel 16.)

A Drastic Dose of Reality

God had promised the Israelites everything their hearts desired if they would stick by him. But they were always cozying up to other nations whose prosperity and power they envied. In those days, a little nation like Israel couldn't just sign a friendship pact with a big power. Political alliances meant accepting the big power's religion and worshiping its gods alongside your own. God warned Israel against this repeatedly, but they ignored the warning. Therefore, Ezekiel says, they will get their wish. They will experience firsthand the care and concern of their Babylonian "lovers."

God responds like a father who has finally given up trying to regulate his daughter's bad habits. He tells her, "Get out! Find out for yourself what life is like on the street!" God says, "You will drink your sister's cup, a cup large and deep; it will bring scorn and derision, for it holds so much. . . . You will drink it and drain it dry; you will dash it to pieces and tear your breasts" (23:32–34). He says it in anger, but also in hope that such bitter grief will awaken Israel to the disastrous choices she made in rejecting God's care.

Life Questions: Have you ever loved someone who didn't love you back? What emotions did you feel?

with large and small shields and with helmets. I will turn you over to them for punishment, and they will punish you according to their standards. 25I will direct my jealous anger against you, and they will deal with you in fury. They will cut off your noses and your ears, and those of you who are left will fall by the sword. They will take away your sons and daughters, and those of you who are left will be consumed by fire. 26They will also strip you of your clothes and take your fine jewelry. 27So I will put a stop to the lewdness and prostitution you began in Egypt. You will not look on these things with longing or remember Egypt anymore.

28"For this is what the Sovereign LORD says: I am about to hand you over to those you hate, to those you turned away from in disgust. 29They will deal with you in hatred and take away everything you have worked for. They will leave you naked and bare, and the shame of your prostitution will be exposed. Your lewdness and promiscuity 30have brought this upon you, because you lusted after the nations and defiled yourself with their idols. 31You have gone the way of your sister; so I will put her cup into your hand.

32This is what the Sovereign LORD says:

"You will drink your sister's cup,
    a cup large and deep;
it will bring scorn and derision,
    for it holds so much.
33You will be filled with drunkenness and
        sorrow,
    the cup of ruin and desolation,
    the cup of your sister Samaria.
34You will drink it and drain it dry;
    you will dash it to pieces
    and tear your breasts.

I have spoken, declares the Sovereign LORD.

35"Therefore this is what the Sovereign LORD says: Since you have forgotten me and thrust me behind your back, you must bear the consequences of your lewdness and prostitution."

36The LORD said to me: "Son of man, will you judge Oholah and Oholibah? Then confront them with their detestable practices, 37for they have committed adultery and blood is on their hands. They committed adultery with their idols; they even sacrificed their children, whom they bore to me,a as food for them. 38They have also done this to me: At that same time they defiled my sanctuary and desecrated my Sabbaths. 39On the very day they sacrificed their children to their idols, they entered my sanctuary and desecrated it. That is what they did in my house.

40"They even sent messengers for men who came from far away, and when they arrived you bathed yourself for them, painted your eyes and put on your jewelry. 41You sat on an elegant couch, with a table spread before it on which you had placed the incense and oil that belonged to me.

42"The noise of a carefree crowd was around her; Sabeansb were brought from the desert along with men from the rabble, and they put bracelets on the arms of the woman and her sister and beautiful crowns on their heads. 43Then I said about the one worn out by adultery, 'Now let them use her as a prostitute, for that is all she is.' 44And they slept with her. As men sleep with a prostitute, so they slept with those lewd women, Oholah and Oholibah. 45But righteous men will sentence them to the punishment of women who commit adultery and shed blood, because they are adulterous and blood is on their hands.

46"This is what the Sovereign LORD says: Bring a mob against them and give them over to terror and plunder. 47The mob will stone them and cut them down with their swords; they will kill their sons and daughters and burn down their houses.

48"So I will put an end to lewdness in the land, that all women may take warning and not imitate you. 49You will suffer the penalty for your lewdness and bear the consequences of your sins of idolatry. Then you will know that I am the Sovereign LORD."

The Cooking Pot

24 In the ninth year, in the tenth month on the tenth day, the word of the LORD came to me: 2"Son of man, record this date, this very date, because the king of Babylon has laid siege

24:2 Prophet's Proof

With Ezekiel living in Babylon, news from Israel took months to reach him. By recording the date when God told him the final siege of Jerusalem had begun, Ezekiel would have evidence that he was genuinely a prophet of God.

to Jerusalem this very day. 3Tell this rebellious house a parable and say to them: 'This is what the Sovereign LORD says:

" 'Put on the cooking pot; put it on
    and pour water into it.
4Put into it the pieces of meat,
    all the choice pieces—the leg and the
        shoulder.
Fill it with the best of these bones;
5   take the pick of the flock.
Pile wood beneath it for the bones;

---

a37 Or *even made the children they bore to me pass through ⌊the fire⌋*   b42 Or *drunkards*

bring it to a boil
and cook the bones in it.

6 "'For this is what the Sovereign LORD says:

"'Woe to the city of bloodshed,
to the pot now encrusted,
whose deposit will not go away!
Empty it piece by piece
without casting lots for them.

7 "'For the blood she shed is in her midst:
She poured it on the bare rock;
she did not pour it on the ground,
where the dust would cover it.
8 To stir up wrath and take revenge
I put her blood on the bare rock,
so that it would not be covered.

9 "'Therefore this is what the Sovereign LORD says:

"'Woe to the city of bloodshed!
I, too, will pile the wood high.
10 So heap on the wood
and kindle the fire.
Cook the meat well,
mixing in the spices;
and let the bones be charred.
11 Then set the empty pot on the coals
till it becomes hot and its copper glows
so its impurities may be melted
and its deposit burned away.
12 It has frustrated all efforts;
its heavy deposit has not been removed,
not even by fire.

13 "'Now your impurity is lewdness. Because I tried to cleanse you but you would not be cleansed from your impurity, you will not be clean again until my wrath against you has subsided.

14 "'I the LORD have spoken. The time has come for me to act. I will not hold back; I will not have pity, nor will I relent. You will be judged according to your conduct and your actions, declares the Sovereign LORD.'"

Ezekiel's Wife Dies

15 The word of the LORD came to me: 16 "Son of man, with one blow I am about to take away from you the delight of your eyes. Yet do not lament or weep or shed any tears. 17 Groan quietly; do not mourn for the dead. Keep your turban fastened and your sandals on your feet; do not cover the lower part of your face or eat the customary food ⌊of mourners⌋."

18 So I spoke to the people in the morning, and in the evening my wife died. The next morning I did as I had been commanded.

19 Then the people asked me, "Won't you tell us what these things have to do with us?"

20 So I said to them, "The word of the LORD came to me: 21 Say to the house of Israel, 'This is what the Sovereign LORD says: I am about to desecrate my sanctuary—the stronghold in which you take pride, the delight of your eyes, the object of your affection. The sons and daughters you left behind will fall by the sword. 22 And you will do as I have done. You will not cover the lower part of your face or eat the customary food ⌊of mourners⌋. 23 You will keep your turbans on your heads and your sandals on your feet. You will not mourn or weep but will waste away because of[a] your sins and groan among yourselves. 24 Ezekiel will be a sign to you; you will do just as he has done. When this happens, you will know that I am the Sovereign LORD.'

25 "And you, son of man, on the day I take away their stronghold, their joy and glory, the delight of their eyes, their heart's desire, and their sons and daughters as well— 26 on that day a fugitive will come to tell you the news. 27 At that time your mouth will be opened; you will speak with him and will no longer be silent. So you will be a sign to them, and they will know that I am the LORD."

A Prophecy Against Ammon

25 The word of the LORD came to me: 2 "Son of man, set your face against the Ammonites and prophesy against them. 3 Say to them, 'Hear the word of the Sovereign LORD. This is what the Sovereign LORD says: Because you said "Aha!" over my sanctuary when it was desecrated and over the land of Israel when it was laid waste and over the people of Judah when they went into exile, 4 therefore I am going to give you to the people of the East as a possession. They will set up their camps and pitch their tents among you; they will eat your fruit and drink your milk. 5 I will turn Rabbah into a pasture for camels and Ammon into a resting place for sheep. Then you will know that I am the LORD. 6 For this is what the Sovereign LORD says: Because you have clapped your hands and stamped your feet, rejoicing with all the malice of your heart against the land of Israel, 7 therefore I will stretch out my hand against you and give you as plunder to the nations. I will cut you off from the nations and exterminate you from the countries. I will destroy you, and you will know that I am the LORD.'"

A Prophecy Against Moab

8 "This is what the Sovereign LORD says: 'Because Moab and Seir said, "Look, the house of Judah has become like all the other nations,"

⁹therefore I will expose the flank of Moab, beginning at its frontier towns—Beth Jeshimoth, Baal Meon and Kiriathaim—the glory of that land. ¹⁰I will give Moab along with the Ammonites to the people of the East as a possession, so that the Ammonites will not be remembered among the nations; ¹¹and I will inflict punishment on Moab. Then they will know that I am the LORD.'"

A Prophecy Against Edom

¹²"This is what the Sovereign LORD says: 'Because Edom took revenge on the house of Judah and became very guilty by doing so, ¹³therefore this is what the Sovereign LORD says: I will stretch out my hand against Edom and kill its men and their animals. I will lay it waste, and from Teman to Dedan they will fall by the sword. ¹⁴I will take vengeance on Edom by the hand of my people Israel, and they will deal with Edom in accordance with my anger and my wrath; they will know my vengeance, declares the Sovereign LORD.'"

Just What They Deserved
God will judge every nation in the world

WORLD WAR II ENDED IN Europe with the surrender of the German army. People danced in the streets.

But the victorious allies could not simply pack and go home. They had captured thousands of Nazis. Among them were some of the most brutal murderers the world has ever known– monsters, really, who had enriched themselves with the gold and jewelry of the millions of Jews they had exterminated.

> "'I will carry out great vengeance on them and punish them in my wrath. Then they will know that I am the LORD.'" 25:17

A question came up: Under what law could the Nazis be tried? American, British, or French law didn't apply in Germany. Faced with this dilemma, the Allies invented something new: the Nuremberg trials for war crimes. Judgments were based on a belief in a higher law–an international code of right and wrong that applies to every person, regardless of country. Under this unwritten law many Nazi leaders were condemned to death.

Nations on Trial

Ezekiel introduces a similar concept of justice, beginning in chapter 25. In the first 24 chapters he had spoken harsh words to the Israelites, who had repeatedly broken the law God had given them. But now Ezekiel's vision expands to nations who never had that law. Ezekiel marches through Ammon, Moab, Edom, Philistia–four nations that, on the small scale of Palestinian geography, could be seen with the naked eye from Jerusalem.

Each nation has its moment in court, and each is condemned for its inhumane malice against Israel. (The sentences Ezekiel gave were soon carried out historically. The nations listed vanished from the face of the earth, victims of the same violence they had used against Israel.)

Ezekiel goes on to Tyre, 100 miles up the coast. Tyre's soul was profit; its merchants controlled trade for the whole Mediterranean. Because of their wealth and success, they considered themselves virtual gods (28:2,6). They had callously rejoiced in Jerusalem's downfall, seeing it as a chance for increased trade (26:2). For such unfeeling arrogance, God would sentence them. Nebuchadnezzar began this punishment in Ezekiel's era, and centuries later Alexander the Great finished it off by razing the city. Tyre became, as Ezekiel had predicted, "a bare rock, and . . . a place to spread fishnets" (26:14).

A Comic Condemnation

Pausing briefly to give a judgment against Sidon, Ezekiel travels on to Egypt. His words might have seemed comic. Who does he think he is, passing judgment on one of the great powers of his day? Ezekiel, a captive from a two-bit country about to be overrun, sounds rather like a refugee from Haiti shaking his fist at the United States. Yet Ezekiel confidently asserts that Egypt can start mourning now. As it happened, Egypt, a great power for many centuries, lost its dominance and has never regained it (29:15).

Perhaps, in taking up these nations' fates, Ezekiel intended to build suspense for the climactic tragedy of Jerusalem's fall. But certainly this trial of the nations demonstrated that Jerusalem had not been singled out for justice. Every nation would be judged by the standard of right and wrong that they knew. If God was harder on Judah, it was only because Judah knew so much more about God and his expectations.

Life Questions: Do you believe in universal standards of right and wrong? What "code of conduct" applies to everybody, regardless of their upbringing?

A Prophecy Against Philistia

15"This is what the Sovereign LORD says: 'Because the Philistines acted in vengeance and took revenge with malice in their hearts, and with ancient hostility sought to destroy Judah, 16therefore this is what the Sovereign LORD says: I am about to stretch out my hand against the Philistines, and I will cut off the Kerethites and destroy those remaining along the coast. 17I will carry out great vengeance on them and punish them in my wrath. Then they will know that I am the LORD, when I take vengeance on them.'"

A Prophecy Against Tyre

26 In the eleventh year, on the first day of the month, the word of the LORD came to me: 2"Son of man, because Tyre has said of Jerusalem, 'Aha! The gate to the nations is broken, and its doors have swung open to me; now that she lies in ruins I will prosper,' 3therefore this is what the Sovereign LORD says: I am against you, O Tyre, and I will bring many nations against you, like the sea casting up its waves. 4They will destroy the walls of Tyre and pull down her towers; I will scrape away her rubble and make her a bare rock. 5Out in the sea she will become a place to spread fishnets, for I have spoken, declares the Sovereign LORD. She will become plunder for the nations, 6and her settlements on the mainland will be ravaged by the sword. Then they will know that I am the LORD.

7"For this is what the Sovereign LORD says: From the north I am going to bring against Tyre Nebuchadnezzar[a] king of Babylon, king of kings, with horses and chariots, with horsemen and a great army. 8He will ravage your settlements on the mainland with the sword; he will set up siege works against you, build a ramp up to your walls and raise his shields against you. 9He will direct the blows of his battering rams against your walls and demolish your towers with his weapons. 10His horses will be so many that they will cover you with dust. Your walls will tremble at the noise of the war horses, wagons and chariots when he enters your gates as men enter a city whose walls have been broken through. 11The hoofs of his horses will trample all your streets; he will kill your people with the sword, and your strong pillars will fall to the ground. 12They will plunder your wealth and loot your merchandise; they will break down your walls and demolish your fine houses and throw your stones, timber and rubble into the sea. 13I will put an end to your noisy songs, and the music of your harps will be heard no more. 14I will make you a bare rock, and you will become a place to spread fish-

nets. You will never be rebuilt, for I the LORD have spoken, declares the Sovereign LORD.

15"This is what the Sovereign LORD says to Tyre: Will not the coastlands tremble at the sound of your fall, when the wounded groan and the slaughter takes place in you? 16Then all the

26:14 Alexander the Great

Tyre, a city on the Mediterranean coast, included two rocky offshore islands. Nebuchadnezzar captured the mainland city in 572 B.C., just 12 years after the fall of Jerusalem. But the islands were not taken until Alexander the Great destroyed them two centuries later. True to this prophecy, the city has never been rebuilt.

princes of the coast will step down from their thrones and lay aside their robes and take off their embroidered garments. Clothed with terror, they will sit on the ground, trembling every moment, appalled at you. 17Then they will take up a lament concerning you and say to you:

"'How you are destroyed, O city of renown,
    peopled by men of the sea!
You were a power on the seas,
    you and your citizens;
you put your terror
    on all who lived there.
18Now the coastlands tremble
    on the day of your fall;
the islands in the sea
    are terrified at your collapse.'

19"This is what the Sovereign LORD says: When I make you a desolate city, like cities no longer inhabited, and when I bring the ocean depths over you and its vast waters cover you, 20then I will bring you down with those who go down to the pit, to the people of long ago. I will make you dwell in the earth below, as in ancient ruins, with those who go down to the pit, and you will not return or take your place[b] in the land of the living. 21I will bring you to a horrible end and you will be no more. You will be sought, but you will never again be found, declares the Sovereign LORD."

A Lament for Tyre

27 The word of the LORD came to me: 2"Son of man, take up a lament concerning Tyre. 3Say to Tyre, situated at the gateway to the sea, merchant of peoples on many coasts, 'This is what the Sovereign LORD says:

"'You say, O Tyre,

---

a 7 Hebrew *Nebuchadrezzar,* of which *Nebuchadnezzar* is a variant; here and often in Ezekiel and Jeremiah
b 20 Septuagint; Hebrew *return, and I will give glory*

"I am perfect in beauty."
[4]Your domain was on the high seas;
  your builders brought your beauty to
      perfection.
[5]They made all your timbers
      of pine trees from Senir[a];
  they took a cedar from Lebanon
      to make a mast for you.
[6]Of oaks from Bashan
      they made your oars;
  of cypress wood[b] from the coasts of
      Cyprus[c]
  they made your deck, inlaid with ivory.
[7]Fine embroidered linen from Egypt was your
      sail
      and served as your banner;
  your awnings were of blue and purple
      from the coasts of Elishah.
[8]Men of Sidon and Arvad were your
      oarsmen;
  your skilled men, O Tyre, were aboard as
      your seamen.
[9]Veteran craftsmen of Gebal[d] were on board
      as shipwrights to caulk your seams.
  All the ships of the sea and their sailors
      came alongside to trade for your wares.

[10]"Men of Persia, Lydia and Put
      served as soldiers in your army.
  They hung their shields and helmets on your
      walls,
      bringing you splendor.
[11]Men of Arvad and Helech
      manned your walls on every side;
  men of Gammad
      were in your towers.
  They hung their shields around your walls;
      they brought your beauty to perfection.

[12]"Tarshish did business with you because of
your great wealth of goods; they exchanged silver, iron, tin and lead for your merchandise.

[13]"Greece, Tubal and Meshech traded with
you; they exchanged slaves and articles of bronze
for your wares.

[14]"Men of Beth Togarmah exchanged work
horses, war horses and mules for your merchandise.

[15]"The men of Rhodes[e] traded with you,
and many coastlands were your customers; they
paid you with ivory tusks and ebony.

[16]"Aram[f] did business with you because of
your many products; they exchanged turquoise,
purple fabric, embroidered work, fine linen, coral
and rubies for your merchandise.

[17]"Judah and Israel traded with you; they exchanged wheat from Minnith and confections,[g]
honey, oil and balm for your wares.

[18]"Damascus, because of your many products
and great wealth of goods, did business with you
in wine from Helbon and wool from Zahar.

[19]"Danites and Greeks from Uzal bought
your merchandise; they exchanged wrought iron,
cassia and calamus for your wares.

[20]"Dedan traded in saddle blankets with you.

[21]"Arabia and all the princes of Kedar were
your customers; they did business with you in
lambs, rams and goats.

[22]"The merchants of Sheba and Raamah traded with you; for your merchandise they exchanged the finest of all kinds of spices and precious stones, and gold.

[23]"Haran, Canneh and Eden and merchants
of Sheba, Asshur and Kilmad traded with you.
[24]In your marketplace they traded with you
beautiful garments, blue fabric, embroidered
work and multicolored rugs with cords twisted
and tightly knotted.

[25]"The ships of Tarshish serve
      as carriers for your wares.
  You are filled with heavy cargo
      in the heart of the sea.
[26]Your oarsmen take you
      out to the high seas.
  But the east wind will break you to pieces
      in the heart of the sea.
[27]Your wealth, merchandise and wares,
      your mariners, seamen and shipwrights,
  your merchants and all your soldiers,
      and everyone else on board
  will sink into the heart of the sea
      on the day of your shipwreck.
[28]The shorelands will quake
      when your seamen cry out.
[29]All who handle the oars
      will abandon their ships;
  the mariners and all the seamen
      will stand on the shore.
[30]They will raise their voice
      and cry bitterly over you;
  they will sprinkle dust on their heads
      and roll in ashes.
[31]They will shave their heads because of you
      and will put on sackcloth.
  They will weep over you with anguish of
      soul
      and with bitter mourning.
[32]As they wail and mourn over you,
      they will take up a lament concerning you:
  "Who was ever silenced like Tyre,
      surrounded by the sea?"
[33]When your merchandise went out on the
      seas,
      you satisfied many nations;

[a]5 That is, Hermon   [b]6 Targum; the Masoretic Text has a different division of the consonants.   [c]6 Hebrew
Kittim   [d]9 That is, Byblos   [e]15 Septuagint; Hebrew Dedan   [f]16 Most Hebrew manuscripts; some Hebrew
manuscripts and Syriac Edom   [g]17 The meaning of the Hebrew for this word is uncertain.

with your great wealth and your wares
    you enriched the kings of the earth.
³⁴Now you are shattered by the sea
    in the depths of the waters;
your wares and all your company
    have gone down with you.
³⁵All who live in the coastlands
    are appalled at you;
their kings shudder with horror
    and their faces are distorted with fear.
³⁶The merchants among the nations hiss at
    you;
    you have come to a horrible end
    and will be no more.'"

A Prophecy Against the King of Tyre

28 The word of the LORD came to me: ²"Son of man, say to the ruler of Tyre, 'This is what the Sovereign LORD says:

"'In the pride of your heart
    you say, "I am a god;
I sit on the throne of a god
    in the heart of the seas."
But you are a man and not a god,
    though you think you are as wise as a
    god.
³Are you wiser than Daniel*ᵃ*?
    Is no secret hidden from you?

28:3 Different Daniel

This Daniel, also mentioned in 14:14, is probably not the prophet Daniel, but an earlier patriarch revered for his wisdom. The prophet Daniel, Ezekiel's fellow exile in Babylon, would not likely have gained such renown so soon. Also, his name is spelled slightly differently in Hebrew.

⁴By your wisdom and understanding
    you have gained wealth for yourself
and amassed gold and silver
    in your treasuries.
⁵By your great skill in trading
    you have increased your wealth,
and because of your wealth
    your heart has grown proud.

⁶"'Therefore this is what the Sovereign LORD says:

"'Because you think you are wise,
    as wise as a god,
⁷I am going to bring foreigners against you,
    the most ruthless of nations;

they will draw their swords against your
    beauty and wisdom
    and pierce your shining splendor.
⁸They will bring you down to the pit,
    and you will die a violent death
    in the heart of the seas.
⁹Will you then say, "I am a god,"
    in the presence of those who kill you?
You will be but a man, not a god,
    in the hands of those who slay you.
¹⁰You will die the death of the uncircumcised
    at the hands of foreigners.

I have spoken, declares the Sovereign LORD.'"

¹¹The word of the LORD came to me: ¹²"Son of man, take up a lament concerning the king of Tyre and say to him: 'This is what the Sovereign LORD says:

"'You were the model of perfection,
    full of wisdom and perfect in beauty.
¹³You were in Eden,
    the garden of God;
every precious stone adorned you:
    ruby, topaz and emerald,
    chrysolite, onyx and jasper,
    sapphire,ᵇ turquoise and beryl.ᶜ
Your settings and mountingsᵈ were made of
    gold;
    on the day you were created they were
    prepared.
¹⁴You were anointed as a guardian cherub,
    for so I ordained you.
You were on the holy mount of God;
    you walked among the fiery stones.
¹⁵You were blameless in your ways
    from the day you were created
    till wickedness was found in you.
¹⁶Through your widespread trade
    you were filled with violence,
    and you sinned.
So I drove you in disgrace from the mount
    of God,
    and I expelled you, O guardian cherub,
    from among the fiery stones.
¹⁷Your heart became proud
    on account of your beauty,
and you corrupted your wisdom
    because of your splendor.
So I threw you to the earth;
    I made a spectacle of you before kings.
¹⁸By your many sins and dishonest trade
    you have desecrated your sanctuaries.
So I made a fire come out from you,
    and it consumed you,
and I reduced you to ashes on the ground
    in the sight of all who were watching.

ᵃ3 Or *Danel*; the Hebrew spelling may suggest a person other than the prophet Daniel.   ᵇ13 Or *lapis lazuli*
ᶜ13 The precise identification of some of these precious stones is uncertain.   ᵈ13 The meaning of the Hebrew for this phrase is uncertain.

19All the nations who knew you
  are appalled at you;
you have come to a horrible end
  and will be no more.' "

A Prophecy Against Sidon

20The word of the LORD came to me: 21"Son
of man, set your face against Sidon; prophesy
against her 22and say: 'This is what the Sovereign
LORD says:

" 'I am against you, O Sidon,
  and I will gain glory within you.
They will know that I am the LORD,
  when I inflict punishment on her
  and show myself holy within her.
23I will send a plague upon her
  and make blood flow in her streets.
The slain will fall within her,
  with the sword against her on every side.
Then they will know that I am the LORD.

24" 'No longer will the people of Israel have
malicious neighbors who are painful briers and
sharp thorns. Then they will know that I am the
Sovereign LORD.

25" 'This is what the Sovereign LORD says:
When I gather the people of Israel from the nations where they have been scattered, I will show
myself holy among them in the sight of the nations. Then they will live in their own land, which
I gave to my servant Jacob. 26They will live there
in safety and will build houses and plant vineyards; they will live in safety when I inflict punishment on all their neighbors who maligned
them. Then they will know that I am the LORD
their God.' "

A Prophecy Against Egypt

29 In the tenth year, in the tenth month on
the twelfth day, the word of the LORD came
to me: 2"Son of man, set your face against Pharaoh king of Egypt and prophesy against him and
against all Egypt. 3Speak to him and say: 'This is
what the Sovereign LORD says:

" 'I am against you, Pharaoh king of Egypt,
  you great monster lying among your
    streams.
You say, "The Nile is mine;
  I made it for myself."
4But I will put hooks in your jaws
  and make the fish of your streams stick to
    your scales.
I will pull you out from among your
    streams,
  with all the fish sticking to your scales.
5I will leave you in the desert,
  you and all the fish of your streams.

You will fall on the open field
  and not be gathered or picked up.
I will give you as food
  to the beasts of the earth and the birds of
    the air.

6Then all who live in Egypt will know that I am
the LORD.

" 'You have been a staff of reed for the house
of Israel. 7When they grasped you with their
hands, you splintered and you tore open their
shoulders; when they leaned on you, you broke
and their backs were wrenched. [a]

29:7 Unreliable Egypt

*When threatened by another superpower
(Babylon or Assyria), Israel often turned to
Egypt for help. Each time that nation let Israel
down. Right up until the final destruction of
Jerusalem, the Israelites expected Egypt to
come to their rescue, but its mighty armies
never appeared.*

8" 'Therefore this is what the Sovereign LORD
says: I will bring a sword against you and kill
your men and their animals. 9Egypt will become
a desolate wasteland. Then they will know that I
am the LORD.

" 'Because you said, "The Nile is mine; I made
it," 10therefore I am against you and against your
streams, and I will make the land of Egypt a ruin
and a desolate waste from Migdol to Aswan, as
far as the border of Cush. [b] 11No foot of man or
animal will pass through it; no one will live there
for forty years. 12I will make the land of Egypt
desolate among devastated lands, and her cities
will lie desolate forty years among ruined cities.
And I will disperse the Egyptians among the nations and scatter them through the countries.

13" 'Yet this is what the Sovereign LORD says:
At the end of forty years I will gather the Egyptians from the nations where they were scattered.
14I will bring them back from captivity and return them to Upper Egypt, [c] the land of their
ancestry. There they will be a lowly kingdom. 15It
will be the lowliest of kingdoms and will never
again exalt itself above the other nations. I will
make it so weak that it will never again rule over
the nations. 16Egypt will no longer be a source of
confidence for the people of Israel but will be a
reminder of their sin in turning to her for help.
Then they will know that I am the Sovereign
LORD.' "

17In the twenty-seventh year, in the first
month on the first day, the word of the LORD

---

[a]7 Syriac (see also Septuagint and Vulgate); Hebrew *and you caused their backs to stand*   [b]10 That is, the upper Nile
region   [c]14 Hebrew *to Pathros*

came to me: [18]"Son of man, Nebuchadnezzar king of Babylon drove his army in a hard campaign against Tyre; every head was rubbed bare and every shoulder made raw. Yet he and his army got no reward from the campaign he led against Tyre. [19]Therefore this is what the Sovereign LORD says: I am going to give Egypt to Nebuchadnezzar king of Babylon, and he will carry off its wealth. He will loot and plunder the land as pay for his army. [20]I have given him Egypt as a reward for his efforts because he and his army did it for me, declares the Sovereign LORD. [21]"On that day I will make a horn[a] grow for the house of Israel, and I will open your mouth among them. Then they will know that I am the LORD."

A Lament for Egypt

30 The word of the LORD came to me: [2]"Son of man, prophesy and say: 'This is what the Sovereign LORD says:

"'Wail and say,
      "Alas for that day!"
[3]For the day is near,
      the day of the LORD is near—
a day of clouds,
      a time of doom for the nations.
[4]A sword will come against Egypt,
      and anguish will come upon Cush.[b]
When the slain fall in Egypt,
      her wealth will be carried away
      and her foundations torn down.

[5]Cush and Put, Lydia and all Arabia, Libya[c] and the people of the covenant land will fall by the sword along with Egypt.

[6]"'This is what the LORD says:

"'The allies of Egypt will fall
      and her proud strength will fail.
From Migdol to Aswan
      they will fall by the sword within her,
                  declares the Sovereign LORD.
[7]"'They will be desolate
      among desolate lands,
and their cities will lie
      among ruined cities.
[8]Then they will know that I am the LORD,
      when I set fire to Egypt
      and all her helpers are crushed.

[9]"'On that day messengers will go out from me in ships to frighten Cush out of her complacency. Anguish will take hold of them on the day of Egypt's doom, for it is sure to come.

[10]"'This is what the Sovereign LORD says:

"'I will put an end to the hordes of Egypt

by the hand of Nebuchadnezzar king of Babylon.
[11]He and his army—the most ruthless of nations—
      will be brought in to destroy the land.
They will draw their swords against Egypt
      and fill the land with the slain.

30:11 Most Ruthless

Babylonians had a well-deserved reputation for cruelty. When they finally took Jerusalem at the end of a two-and-a-half-year siege, they executed all of King Zedekiah's sons while he watched. Then they put out his eyes and carted him off to Babylon (see 2 Kings 25:7).

[12]I will dry up the streams of the Nile
      and sell the land to evil men;
by the hand of foreigners
      I will lay waste the land and everything in it.

I the LORD have spoken.

[13]"'This is what the Sovereign LORD says:

"'I will destroy the idols
      and put an end to the images in
            Memphis.[d]
No longer will there be a prince in Egypt,
      and I will spread fear throughout the land.
[14]I will lay waste Upper Egypt,[e]
      set fire to Zoan
      and inflict punishment on Thebes.[f]
[15]I will pour out my wrath on Pelusium,[g]
      the stronghold of Egypt,
      and cut off the hordes of Thebes.
[16]I will set fire to Egypt;
      Pelusium will writhe in agony.
Thebes will be taken by storm;
      Memphis will be in constant distress.
[17]The young men of Heliopolis[h] and
            Bubastis[i]
      will fall by the sword,
      and the cities themselves will go into
            captivity.
[18]Dark will be the day at Tahpanhes
      when I break the yoke of Egypt;
      there her proud strength will come to an
            end.
She will be covered with clouds,
      and her villages will go into captivity.
[19]So I will inflict punishment on Egypt,
      and they will know that I am the LORD.'"

[20]In the eleventh year, in the first month on

---

[a]21 *Horn* here symbolizes strength.   [b]4 That is, the upper Nile region; also in verses 5 and 9   [c]5 Hebrew *Cub*
[d]13 Hebrew *Noph*; also in verse 16   [e]14 Hebrew *waste Pathros*   [f]14 Hebrew *No*; also in verses 15 and 16
[g]15 Hebrew *Sin*; also in verse 16   [h]17 Hebrew *Awen* (or *On*)   [i]17 Hebrew *Pi Beseth*

the seventh day, the word of the LORD came to me: ²¹"Son of man, I have broken the arm of Pharaoh king of Egypt. It has not been bound up for healing or put in a splint so as to become strong enough to hold a sword. ²²Therefore this is what the Sovereign LORD says: I am against Pharaoh king of Egypt. I will break both his arms, the good arm as well as the broken one, and make the sword fall from his hand. ²³I will disperse the Egyptians among the nations and scatter them through the countries. ²⁴I will strengthen the arms of the king of Babylon and put my sword in his hand, but I will break the arms of Pharaoh, and he will groan before him like a mortally wounded man. ²⁵I will strengthen the arms of the king of Babylon, but the arms of Pharaoh will fall limp. Then they will know that I am the LORD, when I put my sword into the hand of the king of Babylon and he brandishes it against Egypt. ²⁶I will disperse the Egyptians among the nations and scatter them through the countries. Then they will know that I am the LORD."

A Cedar in Lebanon

31 In the eleventh year, in the third month on the first day, the word of the LORD came to me: ²"Son of man, say to Pharaoh king of Egypt and to his hordes:

"'Who can be compared with you in
      majesty?
³Consider Assyria, once a cedar in Lebanon,
   with beautiful branches overshadowing the
      forest;
 it towered on high,
   its top above the thick foliage.
⁴The waters nourished it,
   deep springs made it grow tall;
 their streams flowed
   all around its base
 and sent their channels
   to all the trees of the field.
⁵So it towered higher
   than all the trees of the field;
 its boughs increased
   and its branches grew long,
   spreading because of abundant waters.
⁶All the birds of the air
   nested in its boughs,
 all the beasts of the field
   gave birth under its branches;
 all the great nations
   lived in its shade.
⁷It was majestic in beauty,
   with its spreading boughs,
 for its roots went down
   to abundant waters.
⁸The cedars in the garden of God

could not rival it,
 nor could the pine trees
   equal its boughs,
 nor could the plane trees
   compare with its branches—
 no tree in the garden of God
   could match its beauty.
⁹I made it beautiful
   with abundant branches,
 the envy of all the trees of Eden
   in the garden of God.

¹⁰"'Therefore this is what the Sovereign LORD says: Because it towered on high, lifting its top above the thick foliage, and because it was proud of its height, ¹¹I handed it over to the ruler of the nations, for him to deal with according to its wickedness. I cast it aside, ¹²and the most ruthless of foreign nations cut it down and left it. Its boughs fell on the mountains and in all the valleys; its branches lay broken in all the ravines of the land. All the nations of the earth came out from under its shade and left it. ¹³All the birds of the air settled on the fallen tree, and all the beasts of the field were among its branches. ¹⁴Therefore no other trees by the waters are ever to tower proudly on high, lifting their tops above the thick foliage. No other trees so well-watered are ever to reach such a height; they are all destined for death, for the earth below, among mortal men, with those who go down to the pit.

¹⁵"'This is what the Sovereign LORD says: On the day it was brought down to the grave[a] I covered the deep springs with mourning for it; I held back its streams, and its abundant waters were restrained. Because of it I clothed Lebanon with gloom, and all the trees of the field withered away. ¹⁶I made the nations tremble at the sound of its fall when I brought it down to the grave with those who go down to the pit. Then all the trees of Eden, the choicest and best of Lebanon, all the trees that were well-watered, were consoled in the earth below. ¹⁷Those who lived in its shade, its allies among the nations, had also gone down to the grave with it, joining those killed by the sword.

¹⁸"'Which of the trees of Eden can be compared with you in splendor and majesty? Yet you, too, will be brought down with the trees of Eden to the earth below; you will lie among the uncircumcised, with those killed by the sword.

"'This is Pharaoh and all his hordes, declares the Sovereign LORD.'"

A Lament for Pharaoh

32 In the twelfth year, in the twelfth month on the first day, the word of the LORD came to me: ²"Son of man, take up a lament

---

a 15 Hebrew *Sheol*; also in verses 16 and 17

concerning Pharaoh king of Egypt and say to him:

"'You are like a lion among the nations;
  you are like a monster in the seas
thrashing about in your streams,
  churning the water with your feet
  and muddying the streams.

³"'This is what the Sovereign LORD says:

"'With a great throng of people
  I will cast my net over you,
  and they will haul you up in my net.
⁴I will throw you on the land
  and hurl you on the open field.
I will let all the birds of the air settle on you
  and all the beasts of the earth gorge
    themselves on you.
⁵I will spread your flesh on the mountains
  and fill the valleys with your remains.
⁶I will drench the land with your flowing
    blood
  all the way to the mountains,
  and the ravines will be filled with your
    flesh.
⁷When I snuff you out, I will cover the
    heavens
  and darken their stars;
I will cover the sun with a cloud,
  and the moon will not give its light.
⁸All the shining lights in the heavens
  I will darken over you;
  I will bring darkness over your land,
    declares the Sovereign LORD.
⁹I will trouble the hearts of many peoples
  when I bring about your destruction
    among the nations,
  among[a] lands you have not known.
¹⁰I will cause many peoples to be appalled at
    you,
  and their kings will shudder with horror
    because of you
  when I brandish my sword before them.
On the day of your downfall
  each of them will tremble
  every moment for his life.

¹¹"'For this is what the Sovereign LORD says:

"'The sword of the king of Babylon
  will come against you.
¹²I will cause your hordes to fall
  by the swords of mighty men—
  the most ruthless of all nations.
They will shatter the pride of Egypt,
  and all her hordes will be overthrown.
¹³I will destroy all her cattle
  from beside abundant waters
no longer to be stirred by the foot of man
  or muddied by the hoofs of cattle.

¹⁴Then I will let her waters settle
  and make her streams flow like oil,
    declares the Sovereign LORD.
¹⁵When I make Egypt desolate
  and strip the land of everything in it,
when I strike down all who live there,
  then they will know that I am the LORD.'

¹⁶"'This is the lament they will chant for her. The daughters of the nations will chant it; for Egypt and all her hordes they will chant it, declares the Sovereign LORD.'"

¹⁷In the twelfth year, on the fifteenth day of the month, the word of the LORD came to me: ¹⁸"Son of man, wail for the hordes of Egypt and consign to the earth below both her and the daughters of mighty nations, with those who go down to the pit. ¹⁹Say to them, 'Are you more favored than others? Go down and be laid among the uncircumcised.' ²⁰They will fall among those killed by the sword. The sword is drawn; let her be dragged off with all her hordes. ²¹From within the grave[b] the mighty leaders will say of Egypt and her allies, 'They have come down and they lie with the uncircumcised, with those killed by the sword.'

32:21 The Afterlife

Though eternal life shines through a few Old Testament passages (see "Life after Death," page 581), life after death was extremely vague in most of the Old Testament. The grave was represented by a place called "Sheol." The fate of the nations described here as "within the grave" gives a vivid, eerie sense of death.

²²"Assyria is there with her whole army; she is surrounded by the graves of all her slain, all who have fallen by the sword. ²³Their graves are in the depths of the pit and her army lies around her grave. All who had spread terror in the land of the living are slain, fallen by the sword.

²⁴"Elam is there, with all her hordes around her grave. All of them are slain, fallen by the sword. All who had spread terror in the land of the living went down uncircumcised to the earth below. They bear their shame with those who go down to the pit. ²⁵A bed is made for her among the slain, with all her hordes around her grave. All of them are uncircumcised, killed by the sword. Because their terror had spread in the land of the living, they bear their shame with those who go down to the pit; they are laid among the slain.

²⁶"Meshech and Tubal are there, with all their hordes around their graves. All of them are un-

---

[a]9 Hebrew; Septuagint *bring you into captivity among the nations, / to*   [b]21 Hebrew *Sheol*; also in verse 27

circumcised, killed by the sword because they spread their terror in the land of the living. ²⁷Do they not lie with the other uncircumcised warriors who have fallen, who went down to the grave with their weapons of war, whose swords were placed under their heads? The punishment for their sins rested on their bones, though the terror of these warriors had stalked through the land of the living.

²⁸"You too, O Pharaoh, will be broken and will lie among the uncircumcised, with those killed by the sword.

²⁹"Edom is there, her kings and all her princes; despite their power, they are laid with those killed by the sword. They lie with the uncircumcised, with those who go down to the pit.

³⁰"All the princes of the north and all the Sidonians are there; they went down with the slain in disgrace despite the terror caused by their power. They lie uncircumcised with those killed by the sword and bear their shame with those who go down to the pit.

³¹"Pharaoh—he and all his army—will see them and he will be consoled for all his hordes that were killed by the sword, declares the Sovereign LORD. ³²Although I had him spread terror in the land of the living, Pharaoh and all his hordes will be laid among the uncircumcised, with those

The Turning Point
From here forward, Ezekiel offers good news

TO THEIR CHILDREN PARENTS CAN seem frighteningly inconsistent. One minute a father is gripping his son's wrist, shouting about something. The next moment, punishment over, he is talking about going camping together next summer. How can he change so drastically? Why so angry one minute and so loving the next?

The sudden change makes sense only if you grasp that most parents hate the role of disciplinarian. They punish in order to correct something they see as harmful. Afterwards, they put punishment behind them as quickly as possible, because they dream of better times in the future.

> *In the twelfth year of our exile . . . a man who had escaped from Jerusalem came to me and said, "The city has fallen!"*
> 33:21

A Happier Life for Ezekiel

Ezekiel portrays just such a drastic change between God and Israel. Until chapter 33 he had offered mostly anger and threats. Suddenly, in verse 21, the news of Jerusalem's fall reached Ezekiel. The punishment, long threatened, had come. From this point on, Ezekiel's message from God became dominated by dreams of the future—happy dreams. Ezekiel's life became happier too. After seven years of virtual silence (3:26–27—he spoke only what God told him to), he opened his mouth freely again.

God, speaking through Ezekiel, began to paint the future with the same vivid colors he had used to promise punishment. He spoke of Israel as a flock of sheep and himself as their loving shepherd (chapter 34). He previewed the mountains of Israel as they will look under his full blessing (chapter 36)—very different from the prediction given those same mountains in chapter 6.

God showed Ezekiel a valley of dry bones rising up and taking life (chapter 37), a vision that has inspired musicians and preachers ever since. He forecast a fantastic battle with evil forces from the north, Gog and Magog, in which God's people would triumph magnificently (chapters 38–39). Then, in his final vision, God showed Ezekiel the nation of Israel restored, with its boundaries extended far into hostile territory, its temple rebuilt in new splendor (chapters 40–48). The Lord would come back to his home, to live with his people.

The Temple's Significance

The temple, to Israel, was a sign of God's love. By taking up a home there, he committed himself to be with them permanently—not to come and go but to be available at any and all times to his people. When he left the temple (10:18) and let it be razed by the Babylonians (2 Kings 25:9), he communicated clearly that Israel had forfeited any right to his care.

So Ezekiel's vision of a rebuilt temple, with God's glory filling it, was a promise of new hope. The temple has never been rebuilt according to the precise description Ezekiel gave (chapters 40–43), and many scholars understand his portrayal as symbolic. But the central beauty of the temple is this: "THE LORD IS THERE." The glorious, astonishing God whom Ezekiel first saw in the Babylonian desert will make his home in the center of the land. He will not always be angry. He has great plans for the happiness of his people.

Life Questions: In your relationship with God, are you more concerned with past failures? Or with hopes for the future?

killed by the sword, declares the Sovereign LORD."

Ezekiel a Watchman

33 The word of the LORD came to me: [2]"Son of man, speak to your countrymen and say to them: 'When I bring the sword against a land, and the people of the land choose one of their men and make him their watchman, [3]and he sees the sword coming against the land and blows the trumpet to warn the people, [4]then if anyone hears the trumpet but does not take warning and the sword comes and takes his life, his blood will be on his own head. [5]Since he heard the sound of the trumpet but did not take warning, his blood will be on his own head. If he had taken warning, he would have saved himself. [6]But if the watchman sees the sword coming and does not blow the trumpet to warn the people and the sword comes and takes the life of one of them, that man will be taken away because of his sin, but I will hold the watchman accountable for his blood.'

[7]"Son of man, I have made you a watchman for the house of Israel; so hear the word I speak

33:7 Watch Out

You don't hire a watchman to fight off robbers single-handed; he is responsible for sounding the alarm. God assigns Ezekiel the watchman's role, here and earlier (3:18). It's tragic when someone dies for his or her sins, but when he or she dies without being warned, that is inexcusable—for the watchman was assigned to offer a chance to repent.

and give them warning from me. [8]When I say to the wicked, 'O wicked man, you will surely die,' and you do not speak out to dissuade him from his ways, that wicked man will die for[a] his sin, and I will hold you accountable for his blood. [9]But if you do warn the wicked man to turn from his ways and he does not do so, he will die for his sin, but you will have saved yourself.

[10]"Son of man, say to the house of Israel, 'This is what you are saying: "Our offenses and sins weigh us down, and we are wasting away because of[b] them. How then can we live?"' [11]Say to them, 'As surely as I live, declares the Sovereign LORD, I take no pleasure in the death of the wicked, but rather that they turn from their ways and live. Turn! Turn from your evil ways! Why will you die, O house of Israel?'

[12]"Therefore, son of man, say to your countrymen, 'The righteousness of the righteous man will not save him when he disobeys, and the

wickedness of the wicked man will not cause him to fall when he turns from it. The righteous man, if he sins, will not be allowed to live because of his former righteousness.' [13]If I tell the righteous man that he will surely live, but then he trusts in his righteousness and does evil, none of the righteous things he has done will be remembered; he will die for the evil he has done. [14]And if I say to the wicked man, 'You will surely die,' but he then turns away from his sin and does what is just and right— [15]if he gives back what he took in pledge for a loan, returns what he has stolen, follows the decrees that give life, and does no evil, he will surely live; he will not die. [16]None of the sins he has committed will be remembered against him. He has done what is just and right; he will surely live.

[17]"Yet your countrymen say, 'The way of the Lord is not just.' But it is their way that is not just. [18]If a righteous man turns from his righteousness and does evil, he will die for it. [19]And if a wicked man turns away from his wickedness and does what is just and right, he will live by doing so. [20]Yet, O house of Israel, you say, 'The way of the Lord is not just.' But I will judge each of you according to his own ways."

Jerusalem's Fall Explained

[21]In the twelfth year of our exile, in the tenth month on the fifth day, a man who had escaped from Jerusalem came to me and said, "The city has fallen!" [22]Now the evening before the man arrived, the hand of the LORD was upon me, and he opened my mouth before the man came to me in the morning. So my mouth was opened and I was no longer silent.

33:22 End of the Silence

For nearly eight years, since the beginning of his ministry, Ezekiel had been silent except when giving God's words. Now, an exile arrived in Babylon with bad news from Jerusalem: The temple had been burned, the city destroyed. Ezekiel's long silence ended, by God's permission. His message of doom ended too, for his prediction of punishment had come true. From this point on, Ezekiel's prophecies take up a more hopeful theme, of rebuilding a broken people.

[23]Then the word of the LORD came to me: [24]"Son of man, the people living in those ruins in the land of Israel are saying, 'Abraham was only one man, yet he possessed the land. But we are many; surely the land has been given to us as our possession.' [25]Therefore say to them, 'This is

---

[a]8 Or *in;* also in verse 9   [b]10 Or *away in*

what the Sovereign LORD says: Since you eat meat with the blood still in it and look to your idols and shed blood, should you then possess the land? 26You rely on your sword, you do detestable things, and each of you defiles his neighbor's wife. Should you then possess the land?'

27"Say this to them: 'This is what the Sovereign LORD says: As surely as I live, those who are left in the ruins will fall by the sword, those out in the country I will give to the wild animals to be devoured, and those in strongholds and caves will die of a plague. 28I will make the land a desolate waste, and her proud strength will come to an end, and the mountains of Israel will become desolate so that no one will cross them. 29Then they will know that I am the LORD, when I have made the land a desolate waste because of all the detestable things they have done.'

30"As for you, son of man, your countrymen are talking together about you by the walls and at the doors of the houses, saying to each other, 'Come and hear the message that has come from the LORD.' 31My people come to you, as they usually do, and sit before you to listen to your words, but they do not put them into practice. With their mouths they express devotion, but their hearts are greedy for unjust gain. 32Indeed, to them you are nothing more than one who sings love songs with a beautiful voice and plays an instrument well, for they hear your words but do not put them into practice.

33:32 Prophetic Entertainment

Ezekiel's popularity soared after Jerusalem's fall, for his warnings had all come true. Even so, his audience listened just for entertainment, as they would to music. God reminds Ezekiel that the true purpose of prophecy is to change people's lives, not to draw a crowd.

33"When all this comes true—and it surely will—then they will know that a prophet has been among them."

Shepherds and Sheep

34 The word of the LORD came to me: 2"Son of man, prophesy against the shepherds of Israel; prophesy and say to them: 'This is what the Sovereign LORD says: Woe to the shepherds of Israel who only take care of themselves! Should not shepherds take care of the flock? 3You eat the curds, clothe yourselves with the wool and slaughter the choice animals, but you do not take care of the flock. 4You have not strengthened the weak or healed the sick or bound up the injured. You have not brought back the strays or searched for the lost. You have ruled them harshly and brutally. 5So they were scattered because there

was no shepherd, and when they were scattered they became food for all the wild animals. 6My sheep wandered over all the mountains and on every high hill. They were scattered over the whole earth, and no one searched or looked for them.

7" 'Therefore, you shepherds, hear the word of the LORD: 8As surely as I live, declares the Sovereign LORD, because my flock lacks a shepherd and so has been plundered and has become food for all the wild animals, and because my shepherds did not search for my flock but cared for themselves rather than for my flock, 9therefore, O shepherds, hear the word of the LORD: 10This is what the Sovereign LORD says: I am against the shepherds and will hold them accountable for my flock. I will remove them from tending the flock so that the shepherds can no longer feed themselves. I will rescue my flock from their mouths, and it will no longer be food for them.

11" 'For this is what the Sovereign LORD says: I myself will search for my sheep and look after them. 12As a shepherd looks after his scattered flock when he is with them, so will I look after my sheep. I will rescue them from all the places where they were scattered on a day of clouds and darkness. 13I will bring them out from the nations and gather them from the countries, and I will bring them into their own land. I will pasture them on the mountains of Israel, in the ravines and in all the settlements in the land. 14I will tend them in a good pasture, and the mountain heights of Israel will be their grazing land. There they will lie down in good grazing land, and there they will feed in a rich pasture on the mountains of Israel. 15I myself will tend my sheep and have them lie down, declares the Sovereign LORD. 16I will search for the lost and bring back the strays. I will bind up the injured and strengthen the

34:11-16 The Good Shepherd

Ezekiel, who used strong imagery throughout his writing, developed the image of God as a shepherd with more detail than any other author in the Bible. To people who herded sheep for a living, the simile had tremendous impact.

The same comparison is used repeatedly throughout the Bible. One much-loved passage is Psalm 23, which begins, "The LORD is my shepherd." Jesus called himself "the good shepherd" (John 10:11–16) and had compassion on crowds because they were like "sheep without a shepherd" (Mark 6:34). The image of God as a shepherd begins with Jacob (Genesis 48:15) and ends with Revelation 7:17.

weak, but the sleek and the strong I will destroy. I will shepherd the flock with justice.

17 " 'As for you, my flock, this is what the Sovereign LORD says: I will judge between one sheep and another, and between rams and goats. 18 Is it not enough for you to feed on the good pasture? Must you also trample the rest of your pasture with your feet? Is it not enough for you to drink clear water? Must you also muddy the rest with your feet? 19 Must my flock feed on what you have trampled and drink what you have muddied with your feet?

20 " 'Therefore this is what the Sovereign LORD says to them: See, I myself will judge between the fat sheep and the lean sheep. 21 Because you shove with flank and shoulder, butting all the weak sheep with your horns until you have driven them away, 22 I will save my flock, and they will no longer be plundered. I will judge between one sheep and another. 23 I will place over them one shepherd, my servant David, and he will tend them; he will tend them and be their shepherd. 24 I the LORD will be their God, and my servant David will be prince among them. I the LORD have spoken.

25 " 'I will make a covenant of peace with them and rid the land of wild beasts so that they may live in the desert and sleep in the forests in safety. 26 I will bless them and the places surrounding my hill.ᵃ I will send down showers in season; there will be showers of blessing. 27 The trees of the field will yield their fruit and the ground will yield its

ᵃ26 Or I will make them and the places surrounding my hill a blessing

---

The Sad Truth
Ezekiel became popular overnight—but the praise was empty

> "My people come to you . . . and sit before you to listen to your words, but they do not put them into practice."
> 33:31

GOD WARNED EZEKIEL IT WOULD be a terrible job. Nobody would listen to his message. He would find his own people "hardened and obstinate" (3:7). And how would God help him? "I will make you as unyielding and hardened as they are" (3:8).

As a result Ezekiel lived a lonely life. Those few who believed his prophecies expected nothing to happen in their lifetime (12:27). People thought of Ezekiel as someone just telling stories (20:49). They couldn't believe that God would let Jerusalem fall, as Ezekiel was stubbornly predicting.

Then, after years of prophecy, news came that Babylon had conquered Jerusalem (33:21). Suddenly Ezekiel was popular. People talked about him, flocked to hear his words, expressed devotion. But they listened to Ezekiel without changing their hearts. He was just someone "who sings love songs with a beautiful voice" (33:32). The people heard his words but did not put them into practice.

A Dreadful Message

In some ways Ezekiel could sympathize with the people's negative attitude. He did not like his message either; sometimes it horrified him. Twice, seeing God's judgment, he fell facedown in horror, crying out (9:8; 11:13). When God told him to cook food over human excrement, a symbol of defilement, he was too shocked to agree (4:14). When his wife, "the delight of his eyes," died, he was not even allowed to weep (24:15–24).

Ezekiel had to subordinate ordinary human emotions to the unpleasant task God had given him: to tell the truth, the whole truth, and nothing but the truth, and to tell it in a way that the Israelites could not ignore. "As surely as I live, declares the Sovereign LORD, I take no pleasure in the death of the wicked, but rather that they turn from their ways and live. Turn! Turn from your evil ways! Why will you die, O house of Israel?" (33:11).

Phony Optimism

The false prophets, by contrast, tended to be optimists. They overlooked their nation's corruption and predicted that everything would work out. Chapter 13 records Ezekiel's words against them. "Woe to the foolish prophets who follow their own spirit and have seen nothing!" he said (13:3). They would "whitewash" a bad situation with claims that God could never let Jerusalem be destroyed (13:10–16).

In the end Ezekiel got to deliver genuine good news: the promise of restored life. He saw a vision that still lives in song: scattered, bleached bones coming to life (37:1–14). In another vision, he saw God return to live in Jerusalem (43:1–5). Ezekiel didn't live to see these hopeful predictions fulfilled. But you can be sure he enjoyed making them far more than he enjoyed his predictions of disaster.

Life Questions: Is there any place today for "bad news" of the kind Ezekiel proclaimed?

crops; the people will be secure in their land. They will know that I am the LORD, when I break the bars of their yoke and rescue them from the hands of those who enslaved them. ²⁸They will no longer be plundered by the nations, nor will wild animals devour them. They will live in safety, and no one will make them afraid. ²⁹I will provide for them a land renowned for its crops, and they will no longer be victims of famine in the land or bear the scorn of the nations. ³⁰Then they will know that I, the LORD their God, am with them and that they, the house of Israel, are my people, declares the Sovereign LORD. ³¹You my sheep, the sheep of my pasture, are people, and I am your God, declares the Sovereign LORD.'"

A Prophecy Against Edom

35 The word of the LORD came to me: ²"Son of man, set your face against Mount Seir; prophesy against it ³and say: 'This is what the Sovereign LORD says: I am against you, Mount Seir, and I will stretch out my hand against you and make you a desolate waste. ⁴I will turn your towns into ruins and you will be desolate. Then you will know that I am the LORD.

⁵"'Because you harbored an ancient hostility and delivered the Israelites over to the sword at the time of their calamity, the time their punishment reached its climax, ⁶therefore as surely as I

35:5 Bad Blood

Ill will between two clans dated from the beginning, when Jacob cheated his brother Esau out of the family inheritance. Over the centuries Esau's descendants became the nation of Edom, and Jacob's became Israel. Bad feelings persisted. To Israelites, however, this incident was the ultimate offense: When Babylon burned down Jerusalem, the Edomites looted the city and egged on the Babylonians.

live, declares the Sovereign LORD, I will give you over to bloodshed and it will pursue you. Since you did not hate bloodshed, bloodshed will pursue you. ⁷I will make Mount Seir a desolate waste and cut off from it all who come and go. ⁸I will fill your mountains with the slain; those killed by the sword will fall on your hills and in your valleys and in all your ravines. ⁹I will make you desolate forever; your towns will not be inhabited. Then you will know that I am the LORD.

¹⁰"'Because you have said, "These two nations and countries will be ours and we will take possession of them," even though I the LORD was there, ¹¹therefore as surely as I live, declares the Sovereign LORD, I will treat you in accordance with the anger and jealousy you showed in your hatred of them and I will make myself known among them when I judge you. ¹²Then you will know that I the LORD have heard all the contemptible things you have said against the mountains of Israel. You said, "They have been laid waste and have been given over to us to devour." ¹³You boasted against me and spoke against me without restraint, and I heard it. ¹⁴This is what the Sovereign LORD says: While the whole earth rejoices, I will make you desolate. ¹⁵Because you rejoiced when the inheritance of the house of Israel became desolate, that is how I will treat you. You will be desolate, O Mount Seir, you and all of Edom. Then they will know that I am the LORD.'"

A Prophecy to the Mountains of Israel

36 "Son of man, prophesy to the mountains of Israel and say, 'O mountains of Israel, hear the word of the LORD. ²This is what the Sovereign LORD says: The enemy said of you, "Aha! The ancient heights have become our possession."' ³Therefore prophesy and say, 'This is what the Sovereign LORD says: Because they ravaged and hounded you from every side so that you became the possession of the rest of the nations and the object of people's malicious talk and slander, ⁴therefore, O mountains of Israel, hear the word of the Sovereign LORD: This is what the Sovereign LORD says to the mountains and hills, to the ravines and valleys, to the desolate ruins and the deserted towns that have been plundered and ridiculed by the rest of the nations around you— ⁵this is what the Sovereign LORD says: In my burning zeal I have spoken against the rest of the nations, and against all Edom, for with glee and with malice in their hearts they made my land their own possession so that they might plunder its pastureland.' ⁶Therefore prophesy concerning the land of Israel and say to the mountains and hills, to the ravines and valleys: 'This is what the Sovereign LORD says: I speak in my jealous wrath because you have suffered the scorn of the nations. ⁷Therefore this is what the Sovereign LORD says: I swear with uplifted hand that the nations around you will also suffer scorn.

⁸"'But you, O mountains of Israel, will produce branches and fruit for my people Israel, for they will soon come home. ⁹I am concerned for you and will look on you with favor; you will be plowed and sown, ¹⁰and I will multiply the number of people upon you, even the whole house of Israel. The towns will be inhabited and the ruins rebuilt. ¹¹I will increase the number of men and animals upon you, and they will be fruitful and become numerous. I will settle people on you as in the past and will make you prosper more than before. Then you will know that I am the LORD. ¹²I will cause people, my people Israel, to walk upon you. They will possess you, and you will be

their inheritance; you will never again deprive them of their children.

[13] "This is what the Sovereign LORD says: Because people say to you, "You devour men and deprive your nation of its children," [14]therefore you will no longer devour men or make your nation childless, declares the Sovereign LORD. [15]No longer will I make you hear the taunts of the nations, and no longer will you suffer the scorn of the peoples or cause your nation to fall, declares the Sovereign LORD.'"

[16]Again the word of the LORD came to me: [17]"Son of man, when the people of Israel were living in their own land, they defiled it by their conduct and their actions. Their conduct was like a woman's monthly uncleanness in my sight. [18]So I poured out my wrath on them because they had shed blood in the land and because they had defiled it with their idols. [19]I dispersed them among the nations, and they were scattered through the countries; I judged them according to their conduct and their actions. [20]And wherever they went among the nations they profaned my holy name, for it was said of them, 'These are the LORD's people, and yet they had to leave his land.' [21]I had concern for my holy name, which the house of Israel profaned among the nations where they had gone.

[22]"Therefore say to the house of Israel, 'This is what the Sovereign LORD says: It is not for your sake, O house of Israel, that I am going to do these things, but for the sake of my holy name, which you have profaned among the nations where you have gone. [23]I will show the holiness of my great name, which has been profaned among the nations, the name you have profaned among them. Then the nations will know that I am the LORD, declares the Sovereign LORD, when I show myself holy through you before their eyes.

[24]"'For I will take you out of the nations; I will gather you from all the countries and bring you back into your own land. [25]I will sprinkle clean water on you, and you will be clean; I will cleanse you from all your impurities and from all your idols. [26]I will give you a new heart and put a new spirit in you; I will remove from you your heart of stone and give you a heart of flesh. [27]And I will put my Spirit in you and move you to follow my decrees and be careful to keep my laws. [28]You will live in the land I gave your forefathers; you will be my people, and I will be your God. [29]I will save you from all your uncleanness. I will call for the grain and make it plentiful and will not bring famine upon you. [30]I will increase the fruit of the trees and the crops of the field, so that you will no longer suffer disgrace among the nations because of famine. [31]Then you will remember your evil ways and wicked deeds, and you will loathe

yourselves for your sins and detestable practices. [32]I want you to know that I am not doing this for your sake, declares the Sovereign LORD. Be ashamed and disgraced for your conduct, O house of Israel!

[33]"'This is what the Sovereign LORD says: On

36:27 A New Spirit

Like Jeremiah, Ezekiel realized that Israel needed more than a fresh start. To avoid making the same mistakes all over again, they needed new motivation and orientation. God must work radical surgery on them, to implant a new heart and a new spirit. Jesus' followers believed that this began when the Holy Spirit came at Pentecost (Acts 2:17–21).

the day I cleanse you from all your sins, I will resettle your towns, and the ruins will be rebuilt. [34]The desolate land will be cultivated instead of lying desolate in the sight of all who pass through it. [35]They will say, "This land that was laid waste has become like the garden of Eden; the cities that were lying in ruins, desolate and destroyed, are now fortified and inhabited." [36]Then the nations around you that remain will know that I the LORD have rebuilt what was destroyed and have replanted what was desolate. I the LORD have spoken, and I will do it.'

[37]"This is what the Sovereign LORD says: Once again I will yield to the plea of the house of Israel and do this for them: I will make their people as numerous as sheep, [38]as numerous as the flocks for offerings at Jerusalem during her appointed feasts. So will the ruined cities be filled with flocks of people. Then they will know that I am the LORD."

The Valley of Dry Bones

37 The hand of the LORD was upon me, and he brought me out by the Spirit of the LORD and set me in the middle of a valley; it was full of bones. [2]He led me back and forth among them, and I saw a great many bones on the floor of the valley, bones that were very dry. [3]He asked me, "Son of man, can these bones live?"

I said, "O Sovereign LORD, you alone know."

[4]Then he said to me, "Prophesy to these bones and say to them, 'Dry bones, hear the word of the LORD! [5]This is what the Sovereign LORD says to these bones: I will make breath[a] enter you, and you will come to life. [6]I will attach tendons to you and make flesh come upon you and cover you with skin; I will put breath in you, and you will come to life. Then you will know that I am the LORD.'"

---

[a]5 The Hebrew for this word can also mean *wind* or *spirit* (see verses 6–14).

[7]So I prophesied as I was commanded. And as I was prophesying, there was a noise, a rattling sound, and the bones came together, bone to bone. [8]I looked, and tendons and flesh appeared on them and skin covered them, but there was no breath in them.

[9]Then he said to me, "Prophesy to the breath; prophesy, son of man, and say to it, 'This is what the Sovereign LORD says: Come from the four winds, O breath, and breathe into these slain,

37:9 Dry Bones

This marvelous vision, celebrated in a famous song, begins with a collection of bones littering a valley floor. Before Ezekiel's eyes, the bones come together, assembling from skeletons and growing flesh and skin. The bodies stay dead, however, until in a dramatic moment God puts breath into them. The Hebrew for "breath" also means Spirit, and the vision would have reminded any Jew of Genesis 2:7, where God breathed life into the first man.

God is reminding Ezekiel that it would take a miracle to bring the remnants of Israel back together from the many locations where they were scattered. But to be truly alive, Israel will need a greater miracle: a new Spirit, breathed by God. Only a new creation can resurrect Israel or anyone else.

that they may live.'" [10]So I prophesied as he commanded me, and breath entered them; they came to life and stood up on their feet—a vast army.

[11]Then he said to me: "Son of man, these bones are the whole house of Israel. They say, 'Our bones are dried up and our hope is gone; we are cut off.' [12]Therefore prophesy and say to them: 'This is what the Sovereign LORD says: O my people, I am going to open your graves and bring you up from them; I will bring you back to the land of Israel. [13]Then you, my people, will know that I am the LORD, when I open your graves and bring you up from them. [14]I will put my Spirit in you and you will live, and I will settle you in your own land. Then you will know that I the LORD have spoken, and I have done it, declares the LORD.'"

One Nation Under One King

[15]The word of the LORD came to me: [16]"Son of man, take a stick of wood and write on it, 'Belonging to Judah and the Israelites associated with him.' Then take another stick of wood, and write on it, 'Ephraim's stick, belonging to Joseph and all the house of Israel associated with him.'

[17]Join them together into one stick so that they will become one in your hand.

[18]"When your countrymen ask you, 'Won't you tell us what you mean by this?' [19]say to them, 'This is what the Sovereign LORD says: I am going to take the stick of Joseph—which is in Ephraim's hand—and of the Israelite tribes associated with him, and join it to Judah's stick, making them a single stick of wood, and they will become one in my hand.' [20]Hold before their eyes the sticks you have written on [21]and say to them, 'This is what the Sovereign LORD says: I will take the Israelites out of the nations where they have gone. I will gather them from all around and bring them back into their own land. [22]I will make them one nation in the land, on the mountains of Israel. There will be one king over all of them and they will never again be two nations or

37:22 North and South Reunited

Israel longed to be reunited. The Jews had been split into two nations (sometimes at war) since the days of Solomon, over 300 years before. Yet, like East and West Germany, now united again, and North and South Korea today, they had not forgotten their common origin. God promised to reunite the two—even though one had been in exile, scattered among other nations, for over 100 years.

be divided into two kingdoms. [23]They will no longer defile themselves with their idols and vile images or with any of their offenses, for I will save them from all their sinful backsliding,[a] and I will cleanse them. They will be my people, and I will be their God.

[24]"'My servant David will be king over them, and they will all have one shepherd. They will follow my laws and be careful to keep my decrees. [25]They will live in the land I gave to my servant Jacob, the land where your fathers lived. They and their children and their children's children will live there forever, and David my servant will be their prince forever. [26]I will make a covenant of peace with them; it will be an everlasting covenant. I will establish them and increase their numbers, and I will put my sanctuary among them forever. [27]My dwelling place will be with them; I will be their God, and they will be my people. [28]Then the nations will know that I the LORD make Israel holy, when my sanctuary is among them forever.'"

A Prophecy Against Gog

38 The word of the LORD came to me: [2]"Son of man, set your face against Gog, of the

---

[a]23 Many Hebrew manuscripts (see also Septuagint); most Hebrew manuscripts *all their dwelling places where they sinned*

land of Magog, the chief prince of[a] Meshech and Tubal; prophesy against him ³and say: 'This is what the Sovereign LORD says: I am against you, O Gog, chief prince of[b] Meshech and Tubal. ⁴I will turn you around, put hooks in your jaws and bring you out with your whole army—your horses, your horsemen fully armed, and a great horde with large and small shields, all of them brandishing their swords. ⁵Persia, Cush[c] and Put will be with them, all with shields and helmets, ⁶also Gomer with all its troops, and Beth Togarmah from the far north with all its troops—the many nations with you.

⁷"'Get ready; be prepared, you and all the hordes gathered about you, and take command of them. ⁸After many days you will be called to arms. In future years you will invade a land that has recovered from war, whose people were gathered from many nations to the mountains of Israel, which had long been desolate. They had been brought out from the nations, and now all of them live in safety. ⁹You and all your troops and the many nations with you will go up, advancing like a storm; you will be like a cloud covering the land.

¹⁰"'This is what the Sovereign LORD says: On that day thoughts will come into your mind and you will devise an evil scheme. ¹¹You will say, "I will invade a land of unwalled villages; I will attack a peaceful and unsuspecting people—all of them living without walls and without gates and bars. ¹²I will plunder and loot and turn my hand against the resettled ruins and the people gathered from the nations, rich in livestock and goods, living at the center of the land." ¹³Sheba and Dedan and the merchants of Tarshish and all her villages[d] will say to you, "Have you come to plunder? Have you gathered your hordes to loot, to carry off silver and gold, to take away livestock and goods and to seize much plunder?"'

¹⁴"Therefore, son of man, prophesy and say to Gog: 'This is what the Sovereign LORD says: In that day, when my people Israel are living in safety, will you not take notice of it? ¹⁵You will come from your place in the far north, you and many nations with you, all of them riding on horses, a great horde, a mighty army. ¹⁶You will advance against my people Israel like a cloud that covers the land. In days to come, O Gog, I will bring you against my land, so that the nations may know me when I show myself holy through you before their eyes.

¹⁷"'This is what the Sovereign LORD says: Are you not the one I spoke of in former days by my servants the prophets of Israel? At that time they prophesied for years that I would bring you against them. ¹⁸This is what will happen in that day: When Gog attacks the land of Israel, my hot anger will be aroused, declares the Sovereign LORD. ¹⁹In my zeal and fiery wrath I declare that at that time there shall be a great earthquake in the land of Israel. ²⁰The fish of the sea, the birds of the air, the beasts of the field, every creature that moves along the ground, and all the people on the face of the earth will tremble at my presence. The mountains will be overturned, the cliffs will crumble and every wall will fall to the ground. ²¹I will summon a sword against Gog on all my mountains, declares the Sovereign LORD. Every man's sword will be against his brother. ²²I will execute judgment upon him with plague and bloodshed; I will pour down torrents of rain, hailstones and burning sulfur on him and on his troops and on the many nations with him. ²³And so I will show my greatness and my holiness, and I will make myself known in the sight of many nations. Then they will know that I am the LORD.'

39 "Son of man, prophesy against Gog and say: 'This is what the Sovereign LORD says: I am against you, O Gog, chief prince of[b] Me-

39:1 Gog and Magog

Who are Gog and Magog? Bible interpreters disagree. At the very least, they represent an evil empire that attacks Israel from the north. More than ordinary enemies, they are a personification of evil—the evil that has fought God's people from the very beginning. These chapters show God delivering his people by destroying Gog. The two names, Gog and Magog, reappear in Revelation 20:8, participating in the final battle with evil.

shech and Tubal. ²I will turn you around and drag you along. I will bring you from the far north and send you against the mountains of Israel. ³Then I will strike your bow from your left hand and make your arrows drop from your right hand. ⁴On the mountains of Israel you will fall, you and all your troops and the nations with you. I will give you as food to all kinds of carrion birds and to the wild animals. ⁵You will fall in the open field, for I have spoken, declares the Sovereign LORD. ⁶I will send fire on Magog and on those who live in safety in the coastlands, and they will know that I am the LORD.

⁷"'I will make known my holy name among my people Israel. I will no longer let my holy name be profaned, and the nations will know that I the LORD am the Holy One in Israel. ⁸It is coming! It will surely take place, declares the Sovereign LORD. This is the day I have spoken of.

---

[a]2 Or *the prince of Rosh,* [b]3,1 Or *Gog, prince of Rosh,* [c]5 That is, the upper Nile region [d]13 Or *her*
strong lions

⁹"Then those who live in the towns of Israel will go out and use the weapons for fuel and burn them up—the small and large shields, the bows and arrows, the war clubs and spears. For seven years they will use them for fuel. ¹⁰They will not need to gather wood from the fields or cut it from the forests, because they will use the weapons for fuel. And they will plunder those who plundered them and loot those who looted them, declares the Sovereign LORD.

¹¹"On that day I will give Gog a burial place in Israel, in the valley of those who travel east toward*ᵃ* the Sea.*ᵇ* It will block the way of travelers, because Gog and all his hordes will be buried there. So it will be called the Valley of Hamon Gog.*ᶜ*

¹²"For seven months the house of Israel will be burying them in order to cleanse the land. ¹³All the people of the land will bury them, and the day I am glorified will be a memorable day for them, declares the Sovereign LORD.

¹⁴"'Men will be regularly employed to cleanse the land. Some will go throughout the land and, in addition to them, others will bury those that remain on the ground. At the end of the seven months they will begin their search. ¹⁵As they go through the land and one of them sees a human bone, he will set up a marker beside it until the gravediggers have buried it in the Valley of Hamon Gog. ¹⁶(Also a town called Hamonah*ᵈ* will be there.) And so they will cleanse the land.'

¹⁷"Son of man, this is what the Sovereign LORD says: Call out to every kind of bird and all the wild animals: 'Assemble and come together from all around to the sacrifice I am preparing for you, the great sacrifice on the mountains of Israel. There you will eat flesh and drink blood. ¹⁸You will eat the flesh of mighty men and drink the blood of the princes of the earth as if they were rams and lambs, goats and bulls—all of them fattened animals from Bashan. ¹⁹At the sacrifice I am preparing for you, you will eat fat till you are glutted and drink blood till you are drunk. ²⁰At my table you will eat your fill of horses and riders, mighty men and soldiers of every kind,' declares the Sovereign LORD.

²¹"I will display my glory among the nations, and all the nations will see the punishment I inflict and the hand I lay upon them. ²²From that day forward the house of Israel will know that I am the LORD their God. ²³And the nations will know that the people of Israel went into exile for their sin, because they were unfaithful to me. So I hid my face from them and handed them over to their enemies, and they all fell by the sword. ²⁴I

dealt with them according to their uncleanness and their offenses, and I hid my face from them.

²⁵"Therefore this is what the Sovereign LORD says: I will now bring Jacob back from captivity*ᵉ* and will have compassion on all the people of Israel, and I will be zealous for my holy name. ²⁶They will forget their shame and all the unfaithfulness they showed toward me when they lived in safety in their land with no one to make them afraid. ²⁷When I have brought them back from the nations and have gathered them from the countries of their enemies, I will show myself holy through them in the sight of many nations. ²⁸Then they will know that I am the LORD their God, for though I sent them into exile among the nations, I will gather them to their own land, not leaving any behind. ²⁹I will no longer hide my face from them, for I will pour out my Spirit on the house of Israel, declares the Sovereign LORD."

The New Temple Area

40 In the twenty-fifth year of our exile, at the beginning of the year, on the tenth of the month, in the fourteenth year after the fall of the city—on that very day the hand of the LORD was upon me and he took me there. ²In visions of God he took me to the land of Israel and set me on a very high mountain, on whose south side were some buildings that looked like a city. ³He took me there, and I saw a man whose appearance was like bronze; he was standing in the gateway with a linen cord and a measuring rod in his hand. ⁴The man said to me, "Son of man, look with your eyes and hear with your ears and pay attention to everything I am going to show you, for that is why you have been brought here. Tell the house of Israel everything you see."

The East Gate to the Outer Court

⁵I saw a wall completely surrounding the temple area. The length of the measuring rod in the man's hand was six long cubits, each of which was a cubit*ᶠ* and a handbreadth.*ᵍ* He measured the wall; it was one measuring rod thick and one rod high.

⁶Then he went to the gate facing east. He climbed its steps and measured the threshold of the gate; it was one rod deep.*ʰ* ⁷The alcoves for the guards were one rod long and one rod wide, and the projecting walls between the alcoves were five cubits thick. And the threshold of the gate next to the portico facing the temple was one rod deep.

⁸Then he measured the portico of the gateway; ⁹it*ⁱ* was eight cubits deep and its jambs were two

---

*ᵃ*11 Or *of*   *ᵇ*11 That is, the Dead Sea   *ᶜ*11 *Hamon Gog* means *hordes of Gog.*   *ᵈ*16 *Hamonah* means *horde.*
*ᵉ*25 Or *now restore the fortunes of Jacob*   *ᶠ*5 The common cubit was about 1 1/2 feet (about 0.5 meter).   *ᵍ*5 That
is, about 3 inches (about 8 centimeters)   *ʰ*6 Septuagint; Hebrew *deep, the first threshold, one rod deep*   *ⁱ*8,9 Many
Hebrew manuscripts, Septuagint, Vulgate and Syriac; most Hebrew manuscripts *gateway facing the temple; it was one rod
deep.* ⁹*Then he measured the portico of the gateway; it*

cubits thick. The portico of the gateway faced the temple.

[10]Inside the east gate were three alcoves on each side; the three had the same measurements,

---

40:5 Taking Measurements

When Moses and Solomon supervised the building of God's dwelling place, they placed great emphasis on exact specifications for its construction. Ezekiel does the same, even though the temple he measured with such care was never constructed. Some scholars see the details as symbolic, emphasizing how important renewed worship in the temple would be. The symmetry and beauty of the new temple witness to the perfection of God's plan for his people.

---

and the faces of the projecting walls on each side had the same measurements. [11]Then he measured the width of the entrance to the gateway; it was ten cubits and its length was thirteen cubits. [12]In front of each alcove was a wall one cubit high, and the alcoves were six cubits square. [13]Then he measured the gateway from the top of the rear wall of one alcove to the top of the opposite one; the distance was twenty-five cubits from one parapet opening to the opposite one. [14]He measured along the faces of the projecting walls all around the inside of the gateway—sixty cubits. The measurement was up to the portico[a] facing the courtyard.[b] [15]The distance from the entrance of the gateway to the far end of its portico was fifty cubits. [16]The alcoves and the projecting walls inside the gateway were surmounted by narrow parapet openings all around, as was the portico; the openings all around faced inward. The faces of the projecting walls were decorated with palm trees.

The Outer Court

[17]Then he brought me into the outer court. There I saw some rooms and a pavement that had been constructed all around the court; there were thirty rooms along the pavement. [18]It abutted the sides of the gateways and was as wide as they were long; this was the lower pavement. [19]He measured the distance from the inside of the lower gateway to the outside of the inner court; it was a hundred cubits on the east side as well as on the north.

The North Gate

[20]Then he measured the length and width of the gate facing north, leading into the outer

court. [21]Its alcoves—three on each side—its projecting walls and its portico had the same measurements as those of the first gateway. It was fifty cubits long and twenty-five cubits wide. [22]Its openings, its portico and its palm tree decorations had the same measurements as those of the gate facing east. Seven steps led up to it, with its portico opposite them. [23]There was a gate to the inner court facing the north gate, just as there was on the east. He measured from one gate to the opposite one; it was a hundred cubits.

The South Gate

[24]Then he led me to the south side and I saw a gate facing south. He measured its jambs and its portico, and they had the same measurements as the others. [25]The gateway and its portico had narrow openings all around, like the openings of the others. It was fifty cubits long and twenty-five cubits wide. [26]Seven steps led up to it, with its portico opposite them; it had palm tree decorations on the faces of the projecting walls on each side. [27]The inner court also had a gate facing south, and he measured from this gate to the outer gate on the south side; it was a hundred cubits.

Gates to the Inner Court

[28]Then he brought me into the inner court through the south gate, and he measured the south gate; it had the same measurements as the others. [29]Its alcoves, its projecting walls and its portico had the same measurements as the others. The gateway and its portico had openings all around. It was fifty cubits long and twenty-five cubits wide. [30](The porticoes of the gateways around the inner court were twenty-five cubits wide and five cubits deep.) [31]Its portico faced the outer court; palm trees decorated its jambs, and eight steps led up to it.

[32]Then he brought me to the inner court on the east side, and he measured the gateway; it had the same measurements as the others. [33]Its alcoves, its projecting walls and its portico had the same measurements as the others. The gateway and its portico had openings all around. It was fifty cubits long and twenty-five cubits wide. [34]Its portico faced the outer court; palm trees decorated the jambs on either side, and eight steps led up to it.

[35]Then he brought me to the north gate and measured it. It had the same measurements as the others, [36]as did its alcoves, its projecting walls and its portico, and it had openings all around. It was fifty cubits long and twenty-five cubits wide. [37]Its portico[c] faced the outer court; palm trees decorated the jambs on either side, and eight steps led up to it.

---

[a]14 Septuagint; Hebrew *projecting wall*   [b]14 The meaning of the Hebrew for this verse is uncertain.
[c]37 Septuagint (see also verses 31 and 34); Hebrew *jambs*

The Rooms for Preparing Sacrifices

[38]A room with a doorway was by the portico in each of the inner gateways, where the burnt offerings were washed. [39]In the portico of the gateway were two tables on each side, on which the burnt offerings, sin offerings and guilt offerings were slaughtered. [40]By the outside wall of the portico of the gateway, near the steps at the entrance to the north gateway were two tables, on the other side of the steps were two tables. [41]So there were four tables on one side of the gateway and four on the other—eight tables in all—on which the sacrifices were slaughtered. [42]There were also four tables of dressed stone for the burnt offerings, each a cubit and a half long, a cubit and a half wide and a cubit high. On them were placed the utensils for slaughtering the burnt offerings and the other sacrifices. [43]And double-pronged hooks, each a handbreadth long, were attached to the wall all around. The tables were for the flesh of the offerings.

Rooms for the Priests

[44]Outside the inner gate, within the inner court, were two rooms, one[a] at the side of the north gate and facing south, and another at the side of the south[b] gate and facing north. [45]He said to me, "The room facing south is for the priests who have charge of the temple, [46]and the room facing north is for the priests who have charge of the altar. These are the sons of Zadok, who are the only Levites who may draw near to the LORD to minister before him."

[47]Then he measured the court: It was square—a hundred cubits long and a hundred cubits wide. And the altar was in front of the temple.

The Temple

[48]He brought me to the portico of the temple and measured the jambs of the portico; they were five cubits wide on either side. The width of the entrance was fourteen cubits and its projecting walls were[c] three cubits wide on either side. [49]The portico was twenty cubits wide, and twelve[d] cubits from front to back. It was reached by a flight of stairs,[e] and there were pillars on each side of the jambs.

41 Then the man brought me to the outer sanctuary and measured the jambs; the width of the jambs was six cubits[f] on each side.[g] [2]The entrance was ten cubits wide, and the projecting walls on each side of it were five cubits wide. He also measured the outer sanctu-

ary; it was forty cubits long and twenty cubits wide.

[3]Then he went into the inner sanctuary and measured the jambs of the entrance; each was

41:2 Seeing the New Temple

You'll find it easier to visualize Ezekiel's temple if you look at a sketch from a Bible dictionary. (Look under "Temple" or "Ezekiel.") Ezekiel's description reveals fascinating insights. For instance, the number of steps up toward the Holy Place grows greater at each stage, so that a worshiper mounts increasingly higher. But the doorways grow narrower (40:48; 41:2–3)—suggesting that the nearer to God's presence one climbs, the narrower the path he or she must follow.

two cubits wide. The entrance was six cubits wide, and the projecting walls on each side of it were seven cubits wide. [4]And he measured the length of the inner sanctuary; it was twenty cubits, and its width was twenty cubits across the end of the outer sanctuary. He said to me, "This is the Most Holy Place."

[5]Then he measured the wall of the temple; it was six cubits thick, and each side room around the temple was four cubits wide. [6]The side rooms were on three levels, one above another, thirty on each level. There were ledges all around the wall of the temple to serve as supports for the side rooms, so that the supports were not inserted into the wall of the temple. [7]The side rooms all around the temple were wider at each successive level. The structure surrounding the temple was built in ascending stages, so that the rooms widened as one went upward. A stairway went up from the lowest floor to the top floor through the middle floor.

[8]I saw that the temple had a raised base all around it, forming the foundation of the side rooms. It was the length of the rod, six long cubits. [9]The outer wall of the side rooms was five cubits thick. The open area between the side rooms of the temple [10]and the ⌞priests'⌟ rooms was twenty cubits wide all around the temple. [11]There were entrances to the side rooms from the open area, one on the north and another on the south; and the base adjoining the open area was five cubits wide all around.

[12]The building facing the temple courtyard on the west side was seventy cubits wide. The wall of the building was five cubits thick all around, and its length was ninety cubits.

---

[a]44 Septuagint; Hebrew *were rooms for singers, which were entrance was*   [d]49 Septuagint; Hebrew *eleven*   cubit was about 1 1/2 feet (about 0.5 meter).   [g]1 One Hebrew manuscript and Septuagint; most Hebrew manuscripts *side, the width of the tent*

[b]44 Septuagint; Hebrew *east*   [c]48 Septuagint; Hebrew   [e]49 Hebrew; Septuagint *Ten steps led up to it*   [f]1 The common

¹³Then he measured the temple; it was a hundred cubits long, and the temple courtyard and the building with its walls were also a hundred cubits long. ¹⁴The width of the temple courtyard on the east, including the front of the temple, was a hundred cubits.

¹⁵Then he measured the length of the building facing the courtyard at the rear of the temple, including its galleries on each side; it was a hundred cubits.

The outer sanctuary, the inner sanctuary and the portico facing the court, ¹⁶as well as the thresholds and the narrow windows and galleries around the three of them—everything beyond and including the threshold was covered with wood. The floor, the wall up to the windows, and the windows were covered. ¹⁷In the space above the outside of the entrance to the inner sanctuary and on the walls at regular intervals all around the inner and outer sanctuary ¹⁸were carved cherubim and palm trees. Palm trees alternated with cherubim. Each cherub had two faces: ¹⁹the face of a man toward the palm tree on one side and the face of a lion toward the palm tree on the other. They were carved all around the whole temple. ²⁰From the floor to the area above the entrance, cherubim and palm trees were carved on the wall of the outer sanctuary.

²¹The outer sanctuary had a rectangular doorframe, and the one at the front of the Most Holy Place was similar. ²²There was a wooden altar three cubits high and two cubits square*a*; its corners, its base*b* and its sides were of wood. The man said to me, "This is the table that is before the LORD." ²³Both the outer sanctuary and the Most Holy Place had double doors. ²⁴Each door had two leaves—two hinged leaves for each door. ²⁵And on the doors of the outer sanctuary were carved cherubim and palm trees like those carved on the walls, and there was a wooden overhang on the front of the portico. ²⁶On the sidewalls of the portico were narrow windows with palm trees carved on each side. The side rooms of the temple also had overhangs.

Rooms for the Priests

42 Then the man led me northward into the outer court and brought me to the rooms opposite the temple courtyard and opposite the outer wall on the north side. ²The building whose door faced north was a hundred cubits*c* long and fifty cubits wide. ³Both in the section twenty cubits from the inner court and in the section opposite the pavement of the outer court, gallery faced gallery at the three levels. ⁴In front of the rooms was an inner passageway ten cubits wide and a hundred cubits*d* long. Their doors were

on the north. ⁵Now the upper rooms were narrower, for the galleries took more space from them than from the rooms on the lower and middle floors of the building. ⁶The rooms on the third floor had no pillars, as the courts had; so they were smaller in floor space than those on the lower and middle floors. ⁷There was an outer wall parallel to the rooms and the outer court; it extended in front of the rooms for fifty cubits. ⁸While the row of rooms on the side next to the outer court was fifty cubits long, the row on the side nearest the sanctuary was a hundred cubits long. ⁹The lower rooms had an entrance on the east side as one enters them from the outer court.

¹⁰On the south side*e* along the length of the wall of the outer court, adjoining the temple courtyard and opposite the outer wall, were rooms ¹¹with a passageway in front of them. These were like the rooms on the north; they had the same length and width, with similar exits and dimensions. Similar to the doorways on the north ¹²were the doorways of the rooms on the south. There was a doorway at the beginning of the passageway that was parallel to the corresponding wall extending eastward, by which one enters the rooms.

¹³Then he said to me, "The north and south rooms facing the temple courtyard are the priests' rooms, where the priests who approach the LORD will eat the most holy offerings. There they will put the most holy offerings—the grain offerings, the sin offerings and the guilt offerings—for the place is holy. ¹⁴Once the priests enter the holy precincts, they are not to go into the outer court until they leave behind the garments in which they minister, for these are holy. They are to put on other clothes before they go near the places that are for the people."

¹⁵When he had finished measuring what was inside the temple area, he led me out by the east gate and measured the area all around: ¹⁶He measured the east side with the measuring rod; it was five hundred cubits.*f* ¹⁷He measured the north side; it was five hundred cubits*g* by the measuring rod. ¹⁸He measured the south side; it was five hundred cubits by the measuring rod. ¹⁹Then he turned to the west side and measured; it was five hundred cubits by the measuring rod. ²⁰So he measured the area on all four sides. It had a wall around it, five hundred cubits long and five hundred cubits wide, to separate the holy from the common.

The Glory Returns to the Temple

43 Then the man brought me to the gate facing east, ²and I saw the glory of the God of Israel coming from the east. His voice was like

---

*a*22 Septuagint; Hebrew *long*   *b*22 Septuagint; Hebrew *length* 0.5 meter).   *d*4 Septuagint and Syriac; Hebrew *and one cubit* Septuagint of verse 17; Hebrew *rods*; also in verses 18 and 19.

*c*2 The common cubit was about 1 1/2 feet (about *e*10 Septuagint; Hebrew *Eastward*   *f*16 See *g*17 Septuagint; Hebrew *rods*

the roar of rushing waters, and the land was radiant with his glory. ³The vision I saw was like the vision I had seen when he[a] came to destroy the city and like the visions I had seen by the Kebar River, and I fell facedown. ⁴The glory of the LORD entered the temple through the gate facing east.

43:4–9 The Glory Returns

Nineteen years had passed since Ezekiel saw the glory of the Lord leave the temple (11:22–23). That temple was now dust and ashes and broken stones: The conquering Babylonians had burnt and destroyed it. The new temple Ezekiel saw in this vision symbolized that God would again live with his renewed people.

⁵Then the Spirit lifted me up and brought me into the inner court, and the glory of the LORD filled the temple.

⁶While the man was standing beside me, I heard someone speaking to me from inside the temple. ⁷He said: "Son of man, this is the place of my throne and the place for the soles of my feet. This is where I will live among the Israelites forever. The house of Israel will never again defile my holy name—neither they nor their kings—by their prostitution[b] and the lifeless idols[c] of their kings at their high places. ⁸When they placed their threshold next to my threshold and their doorposts beside my doorposts, with only a wall between me and them, they defiled my holy name by their detestable practices. So I destroyed them in my anger. ⁹Now let them put away from me their prostitution and the lifeless idols of their kings, and I will live among them forever.

¹⁰"Son of man, describe the temple to the people of Israel, that they may be ashamed of their sins. Let them consider the plan, ¹¹and if they are ashamed of all they have done, make known to them the design of the temple—its arrangement, its exits and entrances—its whole design and all its regulations[d] and laws. Write these down before them so that they may be faithful to its design and follow all its regulations.

¹²"This is the law of the temple: All the surrounding area on top of the mountain will be most holy. Such is the law of the temple.

The Altar

¹³"These are the measurements of the altar in long cubits, that cubit being a cubit[e] and a handbreadth[f]: Its gutter is a cubit deep and a

cubit wide, with a rim of one span[g] around the edge. And this is the height of the altar: ¹⁴From the gutter on the ground up to the lower ledge it is two cubits high and a cubit wide, and from the smaller ledge up to the larger ledge it is four cubits high and a cubit wide. ¹⁵The altar hearth is four cubits high, and four horns project upward from the hearth. ¹⁶The altar hearth is square, twelve cubits long and twelve cubits wide. ¹⁷The upper ledge also is square, fourteen cubits long and fourteen cubits wide, with a rim of half a cubit and a gutter of a cubit all around. The steps of the altar face east."

¹⁸Then he said to me, "Son of man, this is what the Sovereign LORD says: These will be the regulations for sacrificing burnt offerings and sprinkling blood upon the altar when it is built: ¹⁹You are to give a young bull as a sin offering to the priests, who are Levites, of the family of Zadok, who come near to minister before me, declares the Sovereign LORD. ²⁰You are to take some of its blood and put it on the four horns of the altar and on the four corners of the upper ledge and all around the rim, and so purify the altar and make atonement for it. ²¹You are to take the bull for the sin offering and burn it in the designated part of the temple area outside the sanctuary.

²²"On the second day you are to offer a male goat without defect for a sin offering, and the altar is to be purified as it was purified with the bull. ²³When you have finished purifying it, you are to offer a young bull and a ram from the flock, both without defect. ²⁴You are to offer them before the LORD, and the priests are to sprinkle salt on them and sacrifice them as a burnt offering to the LORD.

²⁵"For seven days you are to provide a male goat daily for a sin offering; you are also to provide a young bull and a ram from the flock, both without defect. ²⁶For seven days they are to make atonement for the altar and cleanse it; thus they will dedicate it. ²⁷At the end of these days, from the eighth day on, the priests are to present your burnt offerings and fellowship offerings[h] on the altar. Then I will accept you, declares the Sovereign LORD."

The Prince, the Levites, the Priests

44 Then the man brought me back to the outer gate of the sanctuary, the one facing east, and it was shut. ²The LORD said to me, "This gate is to remain shut. It must not be opened; no one may enter through it. It is to remain shut because the LORD, the God of Israel, has entered

---

[a]3 Some Hebrew manuscripts and Vulgate; most Hebrew manuscripts *I*   [b]7 Or *their spiritual adultery;* also in verse 9
[c]7 Or *the corpses;* also in verse 9   [d]11 Some Hebrew manuscripts and Septuagint; most Hebrew manuscripts *regulations and its whole design*   [e]13 The common cubit was about 1 1/2 feet (about 0.5 meter).   [f]13 That is, about 3 inches (about 8 centimeters)   [g]13 That is, about 9 inches (about 22 centimeters)   [h]27 Traditionally *peace offerings*

through it. [3]The prince himself is the only one who may sit inside the gateway to eat in the presence of the LORD. He is to enter by way of the portico of the gateway and go out the same way."

[4]Then the man brought me by way of the north gate to the front of the temple. I looked and saw the glory of the LORD filling the temple of the LORD, and I fell facedown.

[5]The LORD said to me, "Son of man, look carefully, listen closely and give attention to everything I tell you concerning all the regulations regarding the temple of the LORD. Give attention to the entrance of the temple and all the exits of the sanctuary. [6]Say to the rebellious house of Israel, 'This is what the Sovereign LORD says: Enough of your detestable practices, O house of Israel! [7]In addition to all your other detestable practices, you brought foreigners uncircumcised in heart and flesh into my sanctuary, desecrating my temple while you offered me food, fat and blood, and you broke my covenant. [8]Instead of carrying out your duty in regard to my holy things, you put others in charge of my sanctuary. [9]This is what the Sovereign LORD says: No foreigner uncircumcised in heart and flesh is to enter my sanctuary, not even the foreigners who live among the Israelites.

[10]"'The Levites who went far from me when Israel went astray and who wandered from me after their idols must bear the consequences of their sin. [11]They may serve in my sanctuary, having charge of the gates of the temple and serving in it; they may slaughter the burnt offerings and sacrifices for the people and stand before them and serve them. [12]But because they served them in the presence of their idols and made the house of Israel fall into sin, therefore I have sworn with uplifted hand that they must bear the consequences of their sin, declares the Sovereign LORD. [13]They are not to come near to serve me as priests or come near any of my holy things or my most holy offerings; they must bear the shame of their detestable practices. [14]Yet I will put them in charge of the duties of the temple and all the work that is to be done in it.

[15]"'But the priests, who are Levites and descendants of Zadok and who faithfully carried out the duties of my sanctuary when the Israelites went astray from me, are to come near to minister before me; they are to stand before me to offer sacrifices of fat and blood, declares the Sovereign LORD. [16]They alone are to enter my sanctuary; they alone are to come near my table to minister before me and perform my service.

[17]"'When they enter the gates of the inner court, they are to wear linen clothes; they must not wear any woolen garment while ministering at the gates of the inner court or inside the temple. [18]They are to wear linen turbans on their heads and linen undergarments around their waists. They must not wear anything that makes them perspire. [19]When they go out into the outer court where the people are, they are to take off the clothes they have been ministering in and are to leave them in the sacred rooms, and put on other clothes, so that they do not consecrate the people by means of their garments.

[20]"'They must not shave their heads or let their hair grow long, but they are to keep the hair of their heads trimmed. [21]No priest is to drink wine when he enters the inner court. [22]They must not marry widows or divorced women; they may marry only virgins of Israelite descent or widows of priests. [23]They are to teach my people the difference between the holy and the common and show them how to distinguish between the unclean and the clean.

[24]"'In any dispute, the priests are to serve as judges and decide it according to my ordinances. They are to keep my laws and my decrees for all my appointed feasts, and they are to keep my Sabbaths holy.

[25]"'A priest must not defile himself by going near a dead person; however, if the dead person was his father or mother, son or daughter, brother or unmarried sister, then he may defile himself. [26]After he is cleansed, he must wait seven days. [27]On the day he goes into the inner court of the sanctuary to minister in the sanctuary, he is to offer a sin offering for himself, declares the Sovereign LORD.

[28]"'I am to be the only inheritance the priests have. You are to give them no possession in Israel; I will be their possession. [29]They will eat the grain offerings, the sin offerings and the guilt offerings; and everything in Israel devoted[a] to the LORD will belong to them. [30]The best of all the firstfruits and of all your special gifts will belong to the priests. You are to give them the first portion of your ground meal so that a blessing may rest on your household. [31]The priests must not eat anything, bird or animal, found dead or torn by wild animals.

Division of the Land

45 "'When you allot the land as an inheritance, you are to present to the LORD a portion of the land as a sacred district, 25,000 cubits long and 20,000[b] cubits wide; the entire area will be holy. [2]Of this, a section 500 cubits square is to be for the sanctuary, with 50 cubits around it for open land. [3]In the sacred district, measure off a section 25,000 cubits[c] long and 10,000 cubits[d] wide. In it will be the sanctuary,

---

[a]29 The Hebrew term refers to the irrevocable giving over of things or persons to the LORD. verses 3 and 5 and 48:9); Hebrew *10,000*   [c]3 That is, about 7 miles (about 12 kilometers)   miles (about 5 kilometers)   [b]1 Septuagint (see also   [d]3 That is, about 3

the Most Holy Place. [4]It will be the sacred portion of the land for the priests, who minister in the sanctuary and who draw near to minister before the LORD. It will be a place for their houses as well as a holy place for the sanctuary. [5]An area 25,000 cubits long and 10,000 cubits wide will belong to the Levites, who serve in the temple, as their possession for towns to live in.[a]

[6]"'You are to give the city as its property an area 5,000 cubits wide and 25,000 cubits long, adjoining the sacred portion; it will belong to the whole house of Israel.

[7]"'The prince will have the land bordering each side of the area formed by the sacred district and the property of the city. It will extend westward from the west side and eastward from the east side, running lengthwise from the western to the eastern border parallel to one of the tribal portions. [8]This land will be his possession in Israel. And my princes will no longer oppress my people but will allow the house of Israel to possess the land according to their tribes.

[9]"'This is what the Sovereign LORD says: You have gone far enough, O princes of Israel! Give up your violence and oppression and do what is just and right. Stop dispossessing my people, declares the Sovereign LORD. [10]You are to use accurate scales, an accurate ephah[b] and an accurate

45:10 Honest Weight

The Bible, always practical, doesn't bother to define honesty in philosophic terms. It merely says, "Don't cheat on your measures." Such cheating was a common problem in Judah (see, for instance, Micah 6:10–12). Archaeologists have found many weights once used in Hebrew marketplaces, but very few have weighed exactly the weight inscribed on them.

bath.[c] [11]The ephah and the bath are to be the same size, the bath containing a tenth of a homer[d] and the ephah a tenth of a homer; the homer is to be the standard measure for both. [12]The shekel[e] is to consist of twenty gerahs. Twenty shekels plus twenty-five shekels plus fifteen shekels equal one mina.[f]

Offerings and Holy Days

[13]"'This is the special gift you are to offer: a sixth of an ephah from each homer of wheat and a sixth of an ephah from each homer of barley. [14]The prescribed portion of oil, measured by the bath, is a tenth of a bath from each cor (which

consists of ten baths or one homer, for ten baths are equivalent to a homer). [15]Also one sheep is to be taken from every flock of two hundred from the well-watered pastures of Israel. These will be used for the grain offerings, burnt offerings and fellowship offerings[g] to make atonement for the people, declares the Sovereign LORD. [16]All the people of the land will participate in this special gift for the use of the prince in Israel. [17]It will be the duty of the prince to provide the burnt offerings, grain offerings and drink offerings at the festivals, the New Moons and the Sabbaths—at all the appointed feasts of the house of Israel. He will provide the sin offerings, grain offerings, burnt offerings and fellowship offerings to make atonement for the house of Israel.

[18]"'This is what the Sovereign LORD says: In the first month on the first day you are to take a young bull without defect and purify the sanctuary. [19]The priest is to take some of the blood of the sin offering and put it on the doorposts of the temple, on the four corners of the upper ledge of the altar and on the gateposts of the inner court. [20]You are to do the same on the seventh day of the month for anyone who sins unintentionally or through ignorance; so you are to make atonement for the temple.

[21]"'In the first month on the fourteenth day you are to observe the Passover, a feast lasting seven days, during which you shall eat bread made without yeast. [22]On that day the prince is to provide a bull as a sin offering for himself and for all the people of the land. [23]Every day during the seven days of the Feast he is to provide seven bulls and seven rams without defect as a burnt offering to the LORD, and a male goat for a sin offering. [24]He is to provide as a grain offering an ephah for each bull and an ephah for each ram, along with a hin[h] of oil for each ephah.

[25]"'During the seven days of the Feast, which begins in the seventh month on the fifteenth day, he is to make the same provision for sin offerings, burnt offerings, grain offerings and oil.

46 "'This is what the Sovereign LORD says: The gate of the inner court facing east is to be shut on the six working days, but on the Sabbath day and on the day of the New Moon it is to be opened. [2]The prince is to enter from the outside through the portico of the gateway and stand by the gatepost. The priests are to sacrifice his burnt offering and his fellowship offerings.[i] He is to worship at the threshold of the gateway and then go out, but the gate will not be shut until evening. [3]On the Sabbaths and New Moons the people of the land are to worship in the pres-

---

[a]5 Septuagint; Hebrew *temple; they will have as their possession 20 rooms*   [b]10 An ephah was a dry measure.
[c]10 A bath was a liquid measure.   [d]11 A homer was a dry measure.   [e]12 A shekel weighed about 2/5 ounce
(about 11.5 grams).   [f]12 That is, 60 shekels; the common mina was 50 shekels.   [g]15 Traditionally *peace offerings*;
also in verse 17   [h]24 That is, probably about 4 quarts (about 4 liters)   [i]2 Traditionally *peace offerings*; also in
verse 12

ence of the LORD at the entrance to that gateway. ⁴The burnt offering the prince brings to the LORD on the Sabbath day is to be six male lambs and a ram, all without defect. ⁵The grain offering given with the ram is to be an ephah,ᵃ and the grain offering with the lambs is to be as much as he pleases, along with a hinᵇ of oil for each ephah. ⁶On the day of the New Moon he is to offer a young bull, six lambs and a ram, all without defect. ⁷He is to provide as a grain offering one ephah with the bull, one ephah with the ram, and with the lambs as much as he wants to give, along with a hin of oil with each ephah. ⁸When the prince enters, he is to go in through the portico of the gateway, and he is to come out the same way.

⁹"'When the people of the land come before the LORD at the appointed feasts, whoever enters by the north gate to worship is to go out the south gate; and whoever enters by the south gate is to go out the north gate. No one is to return through the gate by which he entered, but each is to go out the opposite gate. ¹⁰The prince is to be among them, going in when they go in and going out when they go out.

¹¹"'At the festivals and the appointed feasts, the grain offering is to be an ephah with a bull, an ephah with a ram, and with the lambs as much as one pleases, along with a hin of oil for each ephah. ¹²When the prince provides a freewill offering to the LORD—whether a burnt offering or fellowship offerings—the gate facing east is to be opened for him. He shall offer his burnt offering or his fellowship offerings as he does on the Sabbath day. Then he shall go out, and after he has gone out, the gate shall be shut.

¹³"'Every day you are to provide a year-old lamb without defect for a burnt offering to the LORD; morning by morning you shall provide it. ¹⁴You are also to provide with it morning by morning a grain offering, consisting of a sixth of an ephah with a third of a hin of oil to moisten the flour. The presenting of this grain offering to the LORD is a lasting ordinance. ¹⁵So the lamb and the grain offering and the oil shall be provided morning by morning for a regular burnt offering.

¹⁶"'This is what the Sovereign LORD says: If the prince makes a gift from his inheritance to one of his sons, it will also belong to his descendants; it is to be their property by inheritance. ¹⁷If, however, he makes a gift from his inheritance to one of his servants, the servant may keep it until the year of freedom; then it will revert to the prince. His inheritance belongs to his sons only; it is theirs. ¹⁸The prince must not take any of the inheritance of the people, driving them off their property. He is to give his sons their inheritance out of his own property, so that none of my people will be separated from his property.'"

¹⁹Then the man brought me through the entrance at the side of the gate to the sacred rooms facing north, which belonged to the priests, and showed me a place at the western end. ²⁰He said to me, "This is the place where the priests will cook the guilt offering and the sin offering and bake the grain offering, to avoid bringing them into the outer court and consecrating the people."

²¹He then brought me to the outer court and led me around to its four corners, and I saw in each corner another court. ²²In the four corners of the outer court were enclosedᶜ courts, forty cubits long and thirty cubits wide; each of the courts in the four corners was the same size. ²³Around the inside of each of the four courts was a ledge of stone, with places for fire built all around under the ledge. ²⁴He said to me, "These are the kitchens where those who minister at the temple will cook the sacrifices of the people."

The River From the Temple

47 The man brought me back to the entrance of the temple, and I saw water coming out from under the threshold of the temple toward the east (for the temple faced east). The water was coming down from under the south side of the temple, south of the altar. ²He then brought me out through the north gate and led me around the outside to the outer gate facing east, and the water was flowing from the south side.

³As the man went eastward with a measuring line in his hand, he measured off a thousand cubitsᵈ and then led me through water that was ankle-deep. ⁴He measured off another thousand cubits and led me through water that was knee-deep. He measured off another thousand and led me through water that was up to the waist. ⁵He measured off another thousand, but now it was a river that I could not cross, because the water had risen and was deep enough to swim in—a river that no one could cross. ⁶He asked me, "Son of man, do you see this?"

Then he led me back to the bank of the river. ⁷When I arrived there, I saw a great number of trees on each side of the river. ⁸He said to me, "This water flows toward the eastern region and goes down into the Arabah,ᵉ where it enters the Sea.ᶠ When it empties into the Sea,ᶠ the water there becomes fresh. ⁹Swarms of living creatures will live wherever the river flows. There will be large numbers of fish, because this water flows there and makes the salt water fresh; so where the river flows everything will live. ¹⁰Fishermen will stand along the shore; from En Gedi to En

---

ᵃ5 That is, probably about 3/5 bushel (about 22 liters)   ᵇ5 That is, probably about 4 quarts (about 4 liters)
ᶜ22 The meaning of the Hebrew for this word is uncertain.   ᵈ3 That is, about 1,500 feet (about 450 meters)
ᵉ8 Or *the Jordan Valley*   ᶠ8 That is, the Dead Sea

Eglaim there will be places for spreading nets. The fish will be of many kinds—like the fish of the Great Sea.[a] [11]But the swamps and marshes will not become fresh; they will be left for salt. [12]Fruit trees of all kinds will grow on both banks of the river. Their leaves will not wither, nor will their fruit fail. Every month they will bear, because the water from the sanctuary flows to them. Their fruit will serve for food and their leaves for healing."

47:12 River from the Temple

This river, flowing from the temple, had miraculous properties: it reversed the deadly saltiness of the Dead Sea and produced healing fruit on its banks. The early Christians used similar symbolism; in John's vision of a new Jerusalem (Revelation 22), he saw a river of life flowing from the throne of God.

The Boundaries of the Land

[13]This is what the Sovereign LORD says: "These are the boundaries by which you are to divide the land for an inheritance among the twelve tribes of Israel, with two portions for Joseph. [14]You are to divide it equally among them. Because I swore with uplifted hand to give it to your forefathers, this land will become your inheritance.

[15]"This is to be the boundary of the land:

"On the north side it will run from the Great Sea by the Hethlon road past Lebo[b] Hamath to Zedad, [16]Berothah[c] and Sibraim (which lies on the border between Damascus and Hamath), as far as Hazer Hatticon, which is on the border of Hauran. [17]The boundary will extend from the sea to Hazar Enan,[d] along the northern border of Damascus, with the border of Hamath to the north. This will be the north boundary.

[18]"On the east side the boundary will run between Hauran and Damascus, along the Jordan between Gilead and the land of Israel, to the eastern sea and as far as Tamar.[e] This will be the east boundary.

[19]"On the south side it will run from Tamar as far as the waters of Meribah Kadesh, then along the Wadi ˻of Egypt˼ to the Great Sea. This will be the south boundary.

[20]"On the west side, the Great Sea will be the boundary to a point opposite Lebo[f] Hamath. This will be the west boundary.

[21]"You are to distribute this land among yourselves according to the tribes of Israel. [22]You are to allot it as an inheritance for yourselves and for the aliens who have settled among you and who have children. You are to consider them as native-born Israelites; along with you they are to be allotted an inheritance among the tribes of Israel. [23]In whatever tribe the alien settles, there you are to give him his inheritance," declares the Sovereign LORD.

The Division of the Land

48 "These are the tribes, listed by name: At the northern frontier, Dan will have one portion; it will follow the Hethlon road to Lebo[g] Hamath; Hazar Enan and the northern border of Damascus next to Hamath will be part of its border from the east side to the west side.

[2]"Asher will have one portion; it will border the territory of Dan from east to west.

[3]"Naphtali will have one portion; it will border the territory of Asher from east to west.

[4]"Manasseh will have one portion; it will border the territory of Naphtali from east to west.

[5]"Ephraim will have one portion; it will border the territory of Manasseh from east to west.

[6]"Reuben will have one portion; it will border the territory of Ephraim from east to west.

[7]"Judah will have one portion; it will border the territory of Reuben from east to west.

[8]"Bordering the territory of Judah from east to west will be the portion you are to present as a special gift. It will be 25,000 cubits[h] wide, and its length from east to west will equal one of the tribal portions; the sanctuary will be in the center of it.

[9]"The special portion you are to offer to the LORD will be 25,000 cubits long and 10,000 cubits[i] wide. [10]This will be the sacred portion for the priests. It will be 25,000 cubits long on the north side, 10,000 cubits wide on the west side, 10,000 cubits wide on the east side and 25,000 cubits long on the south side. In the center of it will be the sanctuary of the LORD. [11]This will be for the consecrated priests, the Zadokites, who were faithful in serving me and did not go astray as the Levites did when the Israelites went astray. [12]It will be a special gift to them from the sacred portion of the land, a most holy portion, bordering the territory of the Levites.

[13]"Alongside the territory of the priests, the Levites will have an allotment 25,000 cubits long and 10,000 cubits wide. Its total length will be 25,000 cubits and its width 10,000 cubits. [14]They must not sell or exchange any of it. This is the

---

[a]10 That is, the Mediterranean; also in verses 15, 19 and 20 and Ezekiel 48:1; Hebrew *road to go into Zedad,* [16]*Hamath, Berothah* [b]15 Or *past the entrance to* [c]15,16 See Septuagint [d]17 Hebrew *Enon,* a variant of *Enan* [e]18 Septuagint and Syriac; Hebrew *Israel. You will measure to the eastern sea* [f]20 Or *opposite the entrance to* [g]1 Or *to the entrance to* [h]8 That is, about 7 miles (about 12 kilometers) [i]9 That is, about 3 miles (about 5 kilometers)

best of the land and must not pass into other hands, because it is holy to the LORD.

15"The remaining area, 5,000 cubits wide and 25,000 cubits long, will be for the common use of the city, for houses and for pastureland. The city will be in the center of it 16and will have these measurements: the north side 4,500 cubits, the south side 4,500 cubits, the east side 4,500 cubits, and the west side 4,500 cubits. 17The pastureland for the city will be 250 cubits on the north, 250 cubits on the south, 250 cubits on the east, and 250 cubits on the west. 18What remains of the area, bordering on the sacred portion and running the length of it, will be 10,000 cubits on the east side and 10,000 cubits on the west side. Its produce will supply food for the workers of the city. 19The workers from the city who farm it will come from all the tribes of Israel. 20The entire portion will be a square, 25,000 cubits on each side. As a special gift you will set aside the sacred portion, along with the property of the city.

21"What remains on both sides of the area formed by the sacred portion and the city property will belong to the prince. It will extend eastward from the 25,000 cubits of the sacred portion to the eastern border, and westward from the 25,000 cubits to the western border. Both these areas running the length of the tribal portions will belong to the prince, and the sacred portion with the temple sanctuary will be in the center of them. 22So the property of the Levites and the property of the city will lie in the center of the area that belongs to the prince. The area belonging to the prince will lie between the border of Judah and the border of Benjamin.

23"As for the rest of the tribes: Benjamin will have one portion; it will extend from the east side to the west side.

24"Simeon will have one portion; it will border the territory of Benjamin from east to west.

25"Issachar will have one portion; it will border the territory of Simeon from east to west.

26"Zebulun will have one portion; it will border the territory of Issachar from east to west.

27"Gad will have one portion; it will border the territory of Zebulun from east to west.

28"The southern boundary of Gad will run south from Tamar to the waters of Meribah Kadesh, then along the Wadi ⌐of Egypt⌐ to the Great Sea.[a]

29"This is the land you are to allot as an inheritance to the tribes of Israel, and these will be their portions," declares the Sovereign LORD.

The Gates of the City

30"These will be the exits of the city: Beginning on the north side, which is 4,500 cubits long, 31the gates of the city will be named after the tribes of Israel. The three gates on the north side will be the gate of Reuben, the gate of Judah and the gate of Levi.

32"On the east side, which is 4,500 cubits long,

48:30 Gates to the City

These twelve gates, named after the twelve tribes of Israel, are also described in the new Jerusalem (Revelation 21:12). Other details of Ezekiel's vision are echoed in Revelation 21–22: for example, the view from a high mountain (Ezekiel 40:2), the angel guide (40:3), and the healing river (47:12). The most important similarity is reflected in the name of Ezekiel's city: "THE LORD IS THERE" (48:35). As Revelation expresses it, "Now the dwelling of God is with men, and he will live with them" (Revelation 21:3).

will be three gates: the gate of Joseph, the gate of Benjamin and the gate of Dan.

33"On the south side, which measures 4,500 cubits, will be three gates: the gate of Simeon, the gate of Issachar and the gate of Zebulun.

34"On the west side, which is 4,500 cubits long, will be three gates: the gate of Gad, the gate of Asher and the gate of Naphtali.

35"The distance all around will be 18,000 cubits.

"And the name of the city from that time on will be:

THE LORD IS THERE."

DANIEL

"Kidnapped"
Even as prime minister, Daniel remained a lonely outsider

A S A YOUNG MAN, DANIEL could have anticipated an outstanding future in Jerusalem. He came from a prominent family, and he had a first-rate mind (1:4). But, when the Babylonian army dragged him captive to a faraway country, they didn't ask about his plans and dreams.

True, the Babylonians recognized Daniel's potential and put him into a top civil service training program. But even the study material was distasteful to a Jew: It covered sorcery, magic, and a pagan, multigod religion. After graduation Daniel was put to work for the Babylonian king, who continued to war against Daniel's people for nearly 20 more years.

Anyone far from home feels lonely. But Daniel was one of those whose lives got lost in the shuffle of history—refugees, captives. He was destined to spend his life as an alien in Babylon. We have no record that he ever married or had family members nearby.

> Daniel resolved not to defile himself with the royal food and wine, and he asked the chief official for permission not to defile himself this way. 1:8

Great Personal Courage

Through his ability and God's blessing he rose to the post of prime minister of Babylon. Yet he remained an outsider. The higher he rose, the more prominent a target he became. Babylonians resented his foreign background and his political success. Their plots put him under pressure to compromise his faith, to fit in, to bend his principles. His life was often at risk.

Daniel's career near the top lasted at least 66 years, so that by the time he was thrown into the lions' den (chapter 6), he must have been in his 80s. Throughout these years he labored with great effectiveness for Babylon. He was respectful and diligent, even though working for pagan kings. Yet he never compromised his faith. He would not bend, even when threatened with death. The Bible gives no better model of how to live with and serve those who don't share or respect your beliefs.

The Shape of the Future

Near the end of Daniel's life God gave him a series of visions, described in chapters 7—12. In graphic images God showed Daniel the pattern of future history. Daniel's people would duplicate his own experience, but on a world stage.

The Jews, Daniel's visions showed, would be caught in a political storm, battered about by a series of world empires. Daniel foresaw nations raging in battle against each other. He foresaw God's people thrown in between these nations, suffering through no fault of their own. They would be helpless until God himself rescued them from their troubles. Daniel foresaw, in the end, all people falling down to worship "one like a son of man" (7:13). This was the title Jesus applied to himself when he came, nearly six centuries after Daniel, to bring the good news of salvation for all people.

Spreading the Word

Daniel's people had thought of God in terms of their own small community, their own capital city and the temple there. Not only were the Jews God's chosen people, but (they tended to think) they held exclusive rights to him.

But God had never intended his blessings to stop with the Jews. He had the world in mind. At the time he called Abraham, he had promised that through Abraham's offspring he would bless the whole earth (Genesis 12:3).

The Jews had found it difficult enough to keep their own faith, let alone spread it to others. Only while captives in Babylon, unwillingly dragged far from home, did they begin to convince others that their God deserved honor. The proclamations Nebuchadnezzar and Darius made because of Daniel (4:2–3; 6:26–27) honored God more than anything a king of Judah had done in years.

How to Read Daniel

Daniel breaks into two parts, each quite different from the other. The first six chapters tell the "famous" Daniel stories—including the stories of three men thrown into a fiery furnace and Daniel in the lions' den. Any of these chapters would make a script for a thriller. As you read them, reflect on the principles Daniel lived by, far from home and in dangerous circumstances. Ask yourself what Daniel can teach you about faithfulness to God in similarly "alien" circumstances.

Most people find chapters 7–12 far more difficult: They record Daniel's visions about the future of world history. Such symbolism was a familiar mode of expression in the ancient world, but it reads very strangely now—almost like science fiction. Look for broad impressions of how God's people can live, caught in the jaws of brutal world politics. Let the visual symbols engage your emotions and imagination.

If you seek a more detailed understanding of these visions, a commentary on Daniel will be a great help. In some passages, background information on ancient world history is essential. A good commentary can offer this, along with an interpretation of difficult symbols.

You can place Daniel's message in the context of Israelite history by looking at "A Lineup of Rulers," pages 1361–1369.

PEOPLE YOU'LL MEET IN DANIEL

DANIEL (p. 897)
NEBUCHADNEZZAR (p. 902)

3-TRACK READING PLAN

For an explanation and complete listing of the 3-track reading plan, turn to page 7.

TRACK 1: ***Two-Week Courses on the Bible***
The Track 1 reading program on the Old Testament includes one chapter from Daniel. See page 8 for a complete listing of this course.

TRACK 2: ***An Overview of Daniel in 4 Days***
☐ Day 1. Read the Introduction to Daniel and chapter 1, which describes Daniel's courage in rejecting compromise. He set a lifelong pattern.
☐ Day 2. Read chapter 3, the famous story of three men thrown into a fiery furnace.
☐ Day 3. Read chapter 5, the "handwriting on the wall" that announced the destruction of a great empire.
☐ Day 4. Read chapter 6, Daniel in the lions' den.
Now turn to page 9 for your next Track 2 reading project.

TRACK 3: ***All of Daniel in 12 Days***
After you have read through Daniel, turn to pages 10–14 for your next Track 3 reading project.

☐1 ☐2 ☐3 ☐4 ☐5 ☐6 ☐7 ☐8
☐9 ☐10 ☐11 ☐12

Daniel's Training in Babylon

1 In the third year of the reign of Jehoiakim king of Judah, Nebuchadnezzar king of Babylon came to Jerusalem and besieged it. ²And the Lord delivered Jehoiakim king of Judah into his hand, along with some of the articles from the temple of God. These he carried off to the temple of his god in Babylonia*ᵃ* and put in the treasure house of his god.

³Then the king ordered Ashpenaz, chief of his court officials, to bring in some of the Israelites from the royal family and the nobility— ⁴young men without any physical defect, handsome, showing aptitude for every kind of learning, well informed, quick to understand, and qualified to serve in the king's palace. He was to teach them the language and literature of the Babylonians.*ᵇ* ⁵The king assigned them a daily amount of food and wine from the king's table. They were to be trained for three years, and after that they were to enter the king's service.

⁶Among these were some from Judah: Daniel, Hananiah, Mishael and Azariah. ⁷The chief official gave them new names: to Daniel, the name Belteshazzar; to Hananiah, Shadrach; to Mishael, Meshach; and to Azariah, Abednego.

⁸But Daniel resolved not to defile himself with the royal food and wine, and he asked the chief official for permission not to defile himself this way. ⁹Now God had caused the official to show favor and sympathy to Daniel, ¹⁰but the official told Daniel, "I am afraid of my lord the king, who has assigned your*ᶜ* food and drink. Why should he see you looking worse than the other young men your age? The king would then have my head because of you."

¹¹Daniel then said to the guard whom the chief official had appointed over Daniel, Hananiah, Mishael and Azariah, ¹²"Please test your servants for ten days: Give us nothing but vegetables to eat and water to drink. ¹³Then compare our appearance with that of the young men who eat the royal food, and treat your servants in accordance with what you see." ¹⁴So he agreed to this and tested them for ten days.

¹⁵At the end of the ten days they looked healthier and better nourished than any of the young men who ate the royal food. ¹⁶So the guard took away their choice food and the wine they were to drink and gave them vegetables instead.

¹⁷To these four young men God gave knowledge and understanding of all kinds of literature and learning. And Daniel could understand visions and dreams of all kinds.

¹⁸At the end of the time set by the king to bring them in, the chief official presented them to Nebuchadnezzar. ¹⁹The king talked with them, and he found none equal to Daniel, Hananiah, Mishael and Azariah; so they entered the king's service. ²⁰In every matter of wisdom and understanding about which the king questioned them, he found them ten times better than all the magicians and enchanters in his whole kingdom.

²¹And Daniel remained there until the first year of King Cyrus.

Nebuchadnezzar's Dream

2 In the second year of his reign, Nebuchadnezzar had dreams; his mind was troubled and he could not sleep. ²So the king summoned the magicians, enchanters, sorcerers and astrologers*ᵈ* to tell him what he had dreamed. When they came in and stood before the king, ³he said to them, "I have had a dream that troubles me and I want to know what it means.*ᵉ*"

⁴Then the astrologers answered the king in Aramaic,*ᶠ* "O king, live forever! Tell your servants the dream, and we will interpret it."

2:4 A Change in Language

The astrologers spoke in Aramaic, the most common language of the Middle East during this period. From this point through chapter 7, Daniel was written in Aramaic, instead of Hebrew. Only the book of Ezra is similarly split into two languages. Some theorize that these chapters would have been of general interest throughout the Middle East and so were put in a language everyone could understand.

⁵The king replied to the astrologers, "This is what I have firmly decided: If you do not tell me what my dream was and interpret it, I will have you cut into pieces and your houses turned into piles of rubble. ⁶But if you tell me the dream and explain it, you will receive from me gifts and rewards and great honor. So tell me the dream and interpret it for me."

⁷Once more they replied, "Let the king tell his servants the dream, and we will interpret it."

⁸Then the king answered, "I am certain that you are trying to gain time, because you realize that this is what I have firmly decided: ⁹If you do not tell me the dream, there is just one penalty for you. You have conspired to tell me misleading and wicked things, hoping the situation will change. So then, tell me the dream, and I will know that you can interpret it for me."

¹⁰The astrologers answered the king, "There is not a man on earth who can do what the king asks! No king, however great and mighty, has

---

*ᵃ*2 Hebrew *Shinar*   *ᵇ*4 Or *Chaldeans*   *ᶜ*10 The Hebrew for *your* and *you* in this verse is plural.   *ᵈ*2 Or *Chaldeans*; also in verses 4, 5 and 10   *ᵉ*3 Or *was*   *ᶠ*4 The text from here through chapter 7 is in Aramaic.

ever asked such a thing of any magician or enchanter or astrologer. [11]What the king asks is too difficult. No one can reveal it to the king except the gods, and they do not live among men."

[12]This made the king so angry and furious that he ordered the execution of all the wise men of Babylon. [13]So the decree was issued to put the wise men to death, and men were sent to look for Daniel and his friends to put them to death.

[14]When Arioch, the commander of the king's guard, had gone out to put to death the wise men of Babylon, Daniel spoke to him with wisdom and tact. [15]He asked the king's officer, "Why did the king issue such a harsh decree?" Arioch then explained the matter to Daniel. [16]At this, Daniel went in to the king and asked for time, so that he might interpret the dream for him.

[17]Then Daniel returned to his house and explained the matter to his friends Hananiah, Mishael and Azariah. [18]He urged them to plead for mercy from the God of heaven concerning this mystery, so that he and his friends might not be executed with the rest of the wise men of Babylon. [19]During the night the mystery was revealed to Daniel in a vision. Then Daniel praised the God of heaven [20]and said:

"Praise be to the name of God for ever and
        ever;
    wisdom and power are his.

2:20 Revealing Prayer

This brief "psalm" gives insight into Daniel's spiritual life. It begins by expressing absolute confidence in God's control over the world: Daniel clung to such faith even while living in an enemy nation that had just destroyed God's temple in Jerusalem. Also, the prayer shows Daniel's spirit of humility and praise in the midst of crisis: He paused to give God credit before rushing to the king to interpret his dream.

[21]He changes times and seasons;
    he sets up kings and deposes them.
He gives wisdom to the wise
    and knowledge to the discerning.
[22]He reveals deep and hidden things;
    he knows what lies in darkness,
    and light dwells with him.
[23]I thank and praise you, O God of my
        fathers:
    You have given me wisdom and power,
you have made known to me what we asked
        of you,
    you have made known to us the dream of
        the king."

Daniel Interprets the Dream

[24]Then Daniel went to Arioch, whom the king had appointed to execute the wise men of Babylon, and said to him, "Do not execute the wise men of Babylon. Take me to the king, and I will interpret his dream for him."

[25]Arioch took Daniel to the king at once and said, "I have found a man among the exiles from Judah who can tell the king what his dream means."

[26]The king asked Daniel (also called Belteshazzar), "Are you able to tell me what I saw in my dream and interpret it?"

[27]Daniel replied, "No wise man, enchanter, magician or diviner can explain to the king the mystery he has asked about, [28]but there is a God in heaven who reveals mysteries. He has shown King Nebuchadnezzar what will happen in days to come. Your dream and the visions that passed through your mind as you lay on your bed are these:

[29]"As you were lying there, O king, your mind turned to things to come, and the revealer of mysteries showed you what is going to happen. [30]As for me, this mystery has been revealed to me, not because I have greater wisdom than other living men, but so that you, O king, may know the interpretation and that you may understand what went through your mind.

[31]"You looked, O king, and there before you stood a large statue—an enormous, dazzling statue, awesome in appearance. [32]The head of the statue was made of pure gold, its chest and arms of silver, its belly and thighs of bronze, [33]its legs of iron, its feet partly of iron and partly of baked clay. [34]While you were watching, a rock was cut out, but not by human hands. It struck the statue on its feet of iron and clay and smashed them. [35]Then the iron, the clay, the bronze, the silver and the gold were broken to pieces at the same time and became like chaff on a threshing floor in the summer. The wind swept them away without leaving a trace. But the rock that struck the statue became a huge mountain and filled the whole earth.

[36]"This was the dream, and now we will interpret it to the king. [37]You, O king, are the king of kings. The God of heaven has given you dominion and power and might and glory; [38]in your hands he has placed mankind and the beasts of the field and the birds of the air. Wherever they live, he has made you ruler over them all. You are that head of gold.

[39]"After you, another kingdom will rise, inferior to yours. Next, a third kingdom, one of bronze, will rule over the whole earth. [40]Finally, there will be a fourth kingdom, strong as iron—for iron breaks and smashes everything—and as iron breaks things to pieces, so it will crush and break all the others. [41]Just as you saw that the feet

and toes were partly of baked clay and partly of iron, so this will be a divided kingdom; yet it will have some of the strength of iron in it, even as you saw iron mixed with clay. [42]As the toes were partly iron and partly clay, so this kingdom will be partly strong and partly brittle. [43]And just as you saw the iron mixed with baked clay, so the people will be a mixture and will not remain united, any more than iron mixes with clay.

[44]"In the time of those kings, the God of heaven will set up a kingdom that will never be destroyed, nor will it be left to another people. It will crush all those kingdoms and bring them to an end, but it will itself endure forever. [45]This is the meaning of the vision of the rock cut out of a mountain, but not by human hands—a rock that broke the iron, the bronze, the clay, the silver and the gold to pieces.

"The great God has shown the king what will take place in the future. The dream is true and the interpretation is trustworthy."

[46]Then King Nebuchadnezzar fell prostrate before Daniel and paid him honor and ordered that an offering and incense be presented to him. [47]The king said to Daniel, "Surely your God is the God of gods and the Lord of kings and a revealer of mysteries, for you were able to reveal this mystery."

[48]Then the king placed Daniel in a high position and lavished many gifts on him. He made him ruler over the entire province of Babylon and placed him in charge of all its wise men.

2:48 A Nation of Dreamers

The Babylonians highly valued dream interpretation, for they believed the gods spoke to them through dreams. "If a man cannot remember the dream he saw, his personal god is angry with him," says one Babylonian proverb. That proverb helps explain Nebuchadnezzar's panic over forgetting his dream—and his lavish reward to Daniel for recalling and interpreting it.

[49]Moreover, at Daniel's request the king appointed Shadrach, Meshach and Abednego administrators over the province of Babylon, while Daniel himself remained at the royal court.

The Image of Gold and the Fiery Furnace

3 King Nebuchadnezzar made an image of gold, ninety feet high and nine feet[a] wide, and set it up on the plain of Dura in the province of Babylon. [2]He then summoned the satraps, prefects, governors, advisers, treasurers, judges, magistrates and all the other provincial officials to come to the dedication of the image he had set up. [3]So the satraps, prefects, governors, advisers, treasurers, judges, magistrates and all the other provincial officials assembled for the dedication of the image that King Nebuchadnezzar had set up, and they stood before it.

[4]Then the herald loudly proclaimed, "This is what you are commanded to do, O peoples, nations and men of every language: [5]As soon as you hear the sound of the horn, flute, zither, lyre, harp, pipes and all kinds of music, you must fall down and worship the image of gold that King Nebuchadnezzar has set up. [6]Whoever does not fall down and worship will immediately be thrown into a blazing furnace."

[7]Therefore, as soon as they heard the sound of the horn, flute, zither, lyre, harp and all kinds of music, all the peoples, nations and men of every language fell down and worshiped the image of gold that King Nebuchadnezzar had set up.

[8]At this time some astrologers[b] came forward and denounced the Jews. [9]They said to King Nebuchadnezzar, "O king, live forever! [10]You have issued a decree, O king, that everyone who hears the sound of the horn, flute, zither, lyre, harp, pipes and all kinds of music must fall down and worship the image of gold, [11]and that whoever does not fall down and worship will be thrown into a blazing furnace. [12]But there are some Jews whom you have set over the affairs of the province of Babylon—Shadrach, Meshach and Abednego—who pay no attention to you, O king. They neither serve your gods nor worship the image of gold you have set up."

[13]Furious with rage, Nebuchadnezzar summoned Shadrach, Meshach and Abednego. So these men were brought before the king, [14]and Nebuchadnezzar said to them, "Is it true, Shadrach, Meshach and Abednego, that you do not serve my gods or worship the image of gold I have set up? [15]Now when you hear the sound of the horn, flute, zither, lyre, harp, pipes and all kinds of music, if you are ready to fall down and worship the image I made, very good. But if you do not worship it, you will be thrown immediately into a blazing furnace. Then what god will be able to rescue you from my hand?"

[16]Shadrach, Meshach and Abednego replied to the king, "O Nebuchadnezzar, we do not need to defend ourselves before you in this matter. [17]If we are thrown into the blazing furnace, the God we serve is able to save us from it, and he will rescue us from your hand, O king. [18]But even if he does not, we want you to know, O king, that we will not serve your gods or worship the image of gold you have set up."

[19]Then Nebuchadnezzar was furious with Shadrach, Meshach and Abednego, and his attitude

---

[a]1 Aramaic *sixty cubits high and six cubits wide* (about 27 meters high and 2.7 meters wide) [b]8 Or *Chaldeans*

toward them changed. He ordered the furnace heated seven times hotter than usual [20]and commanded some of the strongest soldiers in his army to tie up Shadrach, Meshach and Abednego

and throw them into the blazing furnace. [21]So these men, wearing their robes, trousers, turbans and other clothes, were bound and thrown into the blazing furnace. [22]The king's command was so urgent and the furnace so hot that the flames of the fire killed the soldiers who took up Shadrach, Meshach and Abednego, [23]and these three men, firmly tied, fell into the blazing furnace.

[24]Then King Nebuchadnezzar leaped to his feet in amazement and asked his advisers, "Weren't there three men that we tied up and threw into the fire?"

They replied, "Certainly, O king."

[25]He said, "Look! I see four men walking around in the fire, unbound and unharmed, and the fourth looks like a son of the gods."

[26]Nebuchadnezzar then approached the opening of the blazing furnace and shouted, "Shadrach, Meshach and Abednego, servants of the Most High God, come out! Come here!"

So Shadrach, Meshach and Abednego came out of the fire, [27]and the satraps, prefects, governors and royal advisers crowded around them. They saw that the fire had not harmed their bodies, nor was a hair of their heads singed; their robes were not scorched, and there was no smell of fire on them.

[28]Then Nebuchadnezzar said, "Praise be to the God of Shadrach, Meshach and Abednego, who has sent his angel and rescued his servants! They trusted in him and defied the king's command and were willing to give up their lives rather than serve or worship any god except their own God. [29]Therefore I decree that the people of any nation or language who say anything against the God of Shadrach, Meshach and Abednego be cut into pieces and their houses be turned into piles of rubble, for no other god can save in this way."

[30]Then the king promoted Shadrach, Meshach and Abednego in the province of Babylon.

Nebuchadnezzar's Dream of a Tree

4 King Nebuchadnezzar,

To the peoples, nations and men of every language, who live in all the world:

May you prosper greatly!

[2]It is my pleasure to tell you about the

NEBUCHADNEZZAR *Power and Pride*

NEBUCHADNEZZAR, THE WORLD'S MOST POWERFUL man, had reason to be proud. He captained the mighty Babylonian army (based in what is now Iraq) on its march through the Middle East, annihilating all opposition and demanding tribute. No one could withstand him.

The kingdom of Judah, vastly reduced by previous wars, was just one small country among many that sent money and captives to try to appease this tyrant. Ultimately Nebuchadnezzar destroyed Jerusalem and its temple and dragged its remaining citizens into exile. Jews still look back on that time as one of the darkest periods of Jewish history.

On the home front, Nebuchadnezzar went on a lavish building campaign. He decorated the sacred Procession Way with 120 lions flanking its length of nearly a mile. He adorned the Ishtar Gate with enameled brickwork depicting 575 dragons and bulls. He built spectacular palaces and temples and also the "Hanging Gardens of Babylon," one of the Seven Wonders of the Ancient World.

The book of Daniel, however, shows Nebuchadnezzar in a different light: as a vulnerable man who needed to recognize the King of kings. Some of the hapless Jews whom Nebuchadnezzar carried into exile became his trusted officials. Through them, and through a humiliating (but God-given) bout of insanity, Nebuchadnezzar came to terms with his pride. He learned his lesson while living out in the fields like a wild animal, eating grass.

In the end, the mighty Nebuchadnezzar himself wrote of Daniel's God: "Those who walk in pride he is able to humble" (4:37).

Life Questions: Do the most powerful people you know recognize God's "higher power?" What could you do to help them see it?

miraculous signs and wonders that the Most High God has performed for me.

³How great are his signs,
how mighty his wonders!
His kingdom is an eternal kingdom;
his dominion endures from
generation to generation.

⁴I, Nebuchadnezzar, was at home in my palace, contented and prosperous. ⁵I had a dream that made me afraid. As I was lying in my bed, the images and visions that passed through my mind terrified me. ⁶So I commanded that all the wise men of Babylon be brought before me to interpret the dream for me. ⁷When the magicians, enchanters, astrologers*a* and diviners came, I told them the dream, but they could not interpret it for me. ⁸Finally, Daniel came into my presence and I told him the dream. (He is called Belteshazzar, after the name of my god, and the spirit of the holy gods is in him.)

4:8 The Name of a God

Names were extremely important in Biblical times, for they conveyed something of a person's identity. Thus God sometimes gave a person a new name to indicate a changed life. However, the name the Babylonians presented to Daniel, Belteshazzar, was no gift from God. It was taken from "Bel," a title for the Babylonian god Marduk. Daniel was surrounded by an alien culture and could not avoid every aspect of it.

⁹I said, "Belteshazzar, chief of the magicians, I know that the spirit of the holy gods is in you, and no mystery is too difficult for you. Here is my dream; interpret it for me. ¹⁰These are the visions I saw while lying in my bed: I looked, and there before me stood a tree in the middle of the land. Its height was enormous. ¹¹The tree grew large and strong and its top touched the sky; it was visible to the ends of the earth. ¹²Its leaves were beautiful, its fruit abundant, and on it was food for all. Under it the beasts of the field found shelter, and the birds of the air lived in its branches; from it every creature was fed.

¹³"In the visions I saw while lying in my bed, I looked, and there before me was a messenger,*b* a holy one, coming down from heaven. ¹⁴He called in a loud voice: 'Cut down the tree and trim off its branches; strip off its leaves and scatter its fruit. Let the animals flee from under it and the birds from its branches. ¹⁵But let the stump and its roots, bound with iron and bronze, remain in the ground, in the grass of the field.

"'Let him be drenched with the dew of heaven, and let him live with the animals among the plants of the earth. ¹⁶Let his mind be changed from that of a man and let him be given the mind of an animal, till seven times*c* pass by for him.

¹⁷"'The decision is announced by messengers, the holy ones declare the verdict, so that the living may know that the Most High is sovereign over the kingdoms of men and gives them to anyone he wishes and sets over them the lowliest of men.'

¹⁸"This is the dream that I, King Nebuchadnezzar, had. Now, Belteshazzar, tell me what it means, for none of the wise men in my kingdom can interpret it for me. But you can, because the spirit of the holy gods is in you."

Daniel Interprets the Dream

¹⁹Then Daniel (also called Belteshazzar) was greatly perplexed for a time, and his thoughts terrified him. So the king said, "Belteshazzar, do not let the dream or its meaning alarm you."

Belteshazzar answered, "My lord, if only the dream applied to your enemies and its meaning to your adversaries! ²⁰The tree you saw, which grew large and strong, with its top touching the sky, visible to the whole earth, ²¹with beautiful leaves and abundant fruit, providing food for all, giving shelter to the beasts of the field, and having nesting places in its branches for the birds of the air— ²²you, O king, are that tree! You have become great and strong; your greatness has grown until it reaches the sky, and your dominion extends to distant parts of the earth.

²³"You, O king, saw a messenger, a holy one, coming down from heaven and saying, 'Cut down the tree and destroy it, but leave the stump, bound with iron and bronze, in the grass of the field, while its roots remain in the ground. Let him be drenched with the dew of heaven; let him live like the wild animals, until seven times pass by for him.'

²⁴"This is the interpretation, O king, and this is the decree the Most High has issued against my lord the king: ²⁵You will be driven away from people and will live with the wild animals; you will eat grass like cattle

---

a7 Or *Chaldeans*   *b13* Or *watchman*; also in verses 17 and 23   *c16* Or *years*; also in verses 23, 25 and 32

and be drenched with the dew of heaven. Seven times will pass by for you until you acknowledge that the Most High is sovereign over the kingdoms of men and gives them to anyone he wishes. ²⁶The command to leave the stump of the tree with its roots means that your kingdom will be restored to you when you acknowledge that Heaven rules. ²⁷Therefore, O king, be pleased to accept my advice: Renounce your sins by doing what is right, and your wickedness by being kind to the oppressed. It may be that then your prosperity will continue."

The Dream Is Fulfilled

²⁸All this happened to King Nebuchadnezzar. ²⁹Twelve months later, as the king was walking on the roof of the royal palace of Babylon, ³⁰he said, "Is not this the great Babylon I have built as the royal residence, by my mighty power and for the glory of my majesty?"

³¹The words were still on his lips when a voice came from heaven, "This is what is decreed for you, King Nebuchadnezzar: Your royal authority has been taken from you. ³²You will be driven away from people and will live with the wild animals; you will eat grass like cattle. Seven times will pass by for you until you acknowledge that the Most High is sovereign over the kingdoms of men and gives them to anyone he wishes."

³³Immediately what had been said about Nebuchadnezzar was fulfilled. He was driven away from people and ate grass like cattle. His body was drenched with the dew of heaven until his hair grew like the feathers of an eagle and his nails like the claws of a bird.

³⁴At the end of that time, I, Nebuchadnezzar, raised my eyes toward heaven, and my sanity was restored. Then I praised the Most High; I honored and glorified him who lives forever.

His dominion is an eternal dominion;
    his kingdom endures from generation to
        generation.
³⁵All the peoples of the earth
    are regarded as nothing.
He does as he pleases
    with the powers of heaven
    and the peoples of the earth.
No one can hold back his hand
    or say to him: "What have you done?"

³⁶At the same time that my sanity was restored, my honor and splendor were returned to me for the glory of my kingdom. My advisers and nobles sought me out, and I was restored to my throne and became even greater than before. ³⁷Now I, Nebuchadnezzar, praise and exalt and glorify the King of heaven, because everything he does is right and all his ways are just. And those who walk in pride he is able to humble.

The Writing on the Wall

5 King Belshazzar gave a great banquet for a thousand of his nobles and drank wine with

> #### 5:1 The Throne Room
>
> *Modern archaeological excavation has found, in the Babylonian palace, a large room (about 150 feet by 50 feet—one quarter the size of a football field) that has become known as the Throne Room. One wall had a design of blue enameled bricks, but the other three were covered in white plaster (see verse 5).*

them. ²While Belshazzar was drinking his wine, he gave orders to bring in the gold and silver goblets that Nebuchadnezzar his father[a] had taken from the temple in Jerusalem, so that the king and his nobles, his wives and his concubines might drink from them. ³So they brought in the gold goblets that had been taken from the temple of God in Jerusalem, and the king and his nobles, his wives and his concubines drank from them. ⁴As they drank the wine, they praised the gods of gold and silver, of bronze, iron, wood and stone.

⁵Suddenly the fingers of a human hand appeared and wrote on the plaster of the wall, near the lampstand in the royal palace. The king watched the hand as it wrote. ⁶His face turned pale and he was so frightened that his knees knocked together and his legs gave way.

⁷The king called out for the enchanters, astrologers[b] and diviners to be brought and said to these wise men of Babylon, "Whoever reads this writing and tells me what it means will be clothed in purple and have a gold chain placed around his neck, and he will be made the third highest ruler in the kingdom."

⁸Then all the king's wise men came in, but they could not read the writing or tell the king what it meant. ⁹So King Belshazzar became even more terrified and his face grew more pale. His nobles were baffled.

¹⁰The queen,[c] hearing the voices of the king and his nobles, came into the banquet hall. "O king, live forever!" she said. "Don't be

---

a2 Or *ancestor;* or *predecessor;* also in verses 11, 13 and 18 *mother*   *b7* Or *Chaldeans;* also in verse 11   *c10* Or *queen*

alarmed! Don't look so pale! **11**There is a man in your kingdom who has the spirit of the holy gods in him. In the time of your father he was found to have insight and intelligence and wisdom like that of the gods. King Nebuchadnezzar your father—your father the king, I say—appointed him chief of the magicians, enchanters, astrologers and diviners. **12**This man Daniel, whom the king called Belteshazzar, was found to have a keen mind and knowledge and understanding, and also the ability to interpret dreams, explain riddles and solve difficult problems. Call for Daniel, and he will tell you what the writing means."

13So Daniel was brought before the king, and the king said to him, "Are you Daniel, one of the exiles my father the king brought from Judah? **14**I have heard that the spirit of the gods is in you and that you have insight, intelligence and outstanding wisdom. **15**The wise men and enchanters were brought before me to read this writing and tell me what it means, but they could not explain it. **16**Now I have heard that you are able to give interpretations and to solve difficult problems. If you can read this writing and tell me what it means, you will be clothed in purple and have a gold chain placed around your neck, and you will be made the third highest ruler in the kingdom."

17Then Daniel answered the king, "You may keep your gifts for yourself and give your rewards to someone else. Nevertheless, I will read the writing for the king and tell him what it means.

18"O king, the Most High God gave your father Nebuchadnezzar sovereignty and greatness and glory and splendor. **19**Because of the high position he gave him, all the peoples and nations and men of every language dreaded and feared him. Those the king wanted to put to death, he put to death; those he wanted to spare, he spared; those he wanted to promote, he promoted; and those he wanted to humble, he humbled. **20**But when his heart became arrogant and hardened with pride, he was deposed from his royal throne and stripped of his glory. **21**He was driven away from people and given the mind of an animal; he lived with the wild donkeys and ate grass like cattle; and his body was drenched with the dew of heaven, until he acknowledged that the Most High God is sovereign over the kingdoms of men and sets over them anyone he wishes.

22"But you his son,*a* O Belshazzar, have not humbled yourself, though you knew all this. **23**Instead, you have set yourself up against the Lord of heaven. You had the goblets from his temple brought to you, and you and your nobles, your wives and your concubines drank wine from

them. You praised the gods of silver and gold, of bronze, iron, wood and stone, which cannot see or hear or understand. But you did not honor the God who holds in his hand your life and all your ways. **24**Therefore he sent the hand that wrote the inscription.

25"This is the inscription that was written:

MENE, MENE, TEKEL, PARSIN*b*

26"This is what these words mean:

*Mene*c: God has numbered the days of your reign and brought it to an end.
27*Tekel*d: You have been weighed on the scales and found wanting.
28*Peres*e: Your kingdom is divided and given to the Medes and Persians."

29Then at Belshazzar's command, Daniel was clothed in purple, a gold chain was placed around his neck, and he was proclaimed the third highest ruler in the kingdom.

30That very night Belshazzar, king of the Babylonians,*f* was slain, **31**and Darius the Mede took over the kingdom, at the age of sixty-two.

5:30 Sneak Attack

Two empires, the Medes and the Persians, joined forces to overthrow Babylon, the dominant power of the day. Invading armies diverted the river Euphrates to another channel, then marched along the dry riverbed underneath the city walls. The site of ancient Babylon lies about fifty miles from modern-day Baghdad, Iraq.

Daniel in the Den of Lions

6 It pleased Darius to appoint 120 satraps to rule throughout the kingdom, **2**with three administrators over them, one of whom was Daniel. The satraps were made accountable to them so that the king might not suffer loss. **3**Now Daniel so distinguished himself among the administrators and the satraps by his exceptional qualities that the king planned to set him over the whole kingdom. **4**At this, the administrators and the satraps tried to find grounds for charges against Daniel in his conduct of government affairs, but they were unable to do so. They could find no corruption in him, because he was trustworthy and neither corrupt nor negligent. **5**Finally these men said, "We will never find any basis for

---

a22 Or *descendant*; or *successor*   *b25* Aramaic UPARSIN (that is, AND PARSIN)   *c26* Mene can mean *numbered* or *mina* (a unit of money).   *d27* Tekel can mean *weighed* or *shekel*.   *e28* Peres (the singular of *Parsin*) can mean *divided* or *Persia* or *a half mina* or *a half shekel*.   *f30* Or *Chaldeans*

charges against this man Daniel unless it has something to do with the law of his God."

6So the administrators and the satraps went as a group to the king and said: "O King Darius, live forever! 7The royal administrators, prefects, satraps, advisers and governors have all agreed that the king should issue an edict and enforce the decree that anyone who prays to any god or man during the next thirty days, except to you, O king, shall be thrown into the lions' den. 8Now, O king, issue the decree and put it in writing so that it cannot be altered—in accordance with the laws of the Medes and Persians, which cannot be repealed." 9So King Darius put the decree in writing.

10Now when Daniel learned that the decree had been published, he went home to his upstairs room where the windows opened toward Jerusalem. Three times a day he got down on his knees and prayed, giving thanks to his God, just as he

6:10–11 A Jewish Orientation

Daniel had lost much of his Jewish heritage— even his name had been changed to a Babylonian one (1:7). Certainly he could not worship God in the way God's law commanded, through sacrifices at the temple in Jerusalem. He did, however, point himself toward the promised land three times a day in prayer. Not even the threat of death could make him vary this practice. By this time Daniel had been in Babylon over 60 years; he was probably in his 80s.

had done before. 11Then these men went as a group and found Daniel praying and asking God for help. 12So they went to the king and spoke to him about his royal decree: "Did you not publish a decree that during the next thirty days anyone who prays to any god or man except to you, O king, would be thrown into the lions' den?"

The king answered, "The decree stands—in accordance with the laws of the Medes and Persians, which cannot be repealed."

13Then they said to the king, "Daniel, who is one of the exiles from Judah, pays no attention to you, O king, or to the decree you put in writing. He still prays three times a day." 14When the king heard this, he was greatly distressed; he was determined to rescue Daniel and made every effort until sundown to save him.

15Then the men went as a group to the king and said to him, "Remember, O king, that according to the law of the Medes and Persians no decree or edict that the king issues can be changed."

16So the king gave the order, and they brought Daniel and threw him into the lions' den. The king said to Daniel, "May your God, whom you serve continually, rescue you!"

17A stone was brought and placed over the mouth of the den, and the king sealed it with his own signet ring and with the rings of his nobles, so that Daniel's situation might not be changed. 18Then the king returned to his palace and spent the night without eating and without any entertainment being brought to him. And he could not sleep.

19At the first light of dawn, the king got up and hurried to the lions' den. 20When he came near the den, he called to Daniel in an anguished voice, "Daniel, servant of the living God, has your God, whom you serve continually, been able to rescue you from the lions?"

21Daniel answered, "O king, live forever! 22My God sent his angel, and he shut the mouths of the lions. They have not hurt me, because I was found innocent in his sight. Nor have I ever done any wrong before you, O king."

23The king was overjoyed and gave orders to lift Daniel out of the den. And when Daniel was lifted from the den, no wound was found on him, because he had trusted in his God.

24At the king's command, the men who had falsely accused Daniel were brought in and thrown into the lions' den, along with their wives and children. And before they reached the floor of the den, the lions overpowered them and crushed all their bones.

25Then King Darius wrote to all the peoples, nations and men of every language throughout the land:

"May you prosper greatly!

26"I issue a decree that in every part of my kingdom people must fear and reverence the God of Daniel.

"For he is the living God
   and he endures forever;
his kingdom will not be destroyed,
   his dominion will never end.
27He rescues and he saves;
   he performs signs and wonders
   in the heavens and on the earth.
He has rescued Daniel
   from the power of the lions."

28So Daniel prospered during the reign of Darius and the reign of Cyrus*a* the Persian.

Daniel's Dream of Four Beasts

7 In the first year of Belshazzar king of Babylon, Daniel had a dream, and visions

a28 Or Darius, that is, the reign of Cyrus

passed through his mind as he was lying on his bed. He wrote down the substance of his dream.

²Daniel said: "In my vision at night I looked, and there before me were the four winds of heaven churning up the great sea. ³Four great beasts, each different from the others, came up out of the sea.

⁴"The first was like a lion, and it had the wings of an eagle. I watched until its wings were torn off and it was lifted from the ground so that it stood on two feet like a man, and the heart of a man was given to it.

⁵"And there before me was a second beast, which looked like a bear. It was raised up on one of its sides, and it had three ribs in its mouth between its teeth. It was told, 'Get up and eat your fill of flesh!'

⁶"After that, I looked, and there before me was another beast, one that looked like a leopard. And on its back it had four wings like those of a bird. This beast had four heads, and it was given authority to rule.

⁷"After that, in my vision at night I looked, and there before me was a fourth beast—terrifying and frightening and very powerful. It had large iron teeth; it crushed and devoured its victims and trampled underfoot whatever was left. It

was different from all the former beasts, and it had ten horns.

⁸"While I was thinking about the horns, there before me was another horn, a little one, which came up among them; and three of the first horns were uprooted before it. This horn had eyes like the eyes of a man and a mouth that spoke boastfully.

⁹"As I looked,

"thrones were set in place,
    and the Ancient of Days took his seat.
His clothing was as white as snow;
    the hair of his head was white like wool.
His throne was flaming with fire,
    and its wheels were all ablaze.
¹⁰A river of fire was flowing,
    coming out from before him.
Thousands upon thousands attended him;
    ten thousand times ten thousand stood
        before him.
The court was seated,
    and the books were opened.

¹¹"Then I continued to watch because of the boastful words the horn was speaking. I kept looking until the beast was slain and its body destroyed and thrown into the blazing fire. ¹²(The other beasts had been stripped of their

Symbols of Power
The bigger the tyrant, the more statues litter the landscape

IT'S NO SURPRISE THAT NEBUCHADNEZZAR erected a gold image for people to worship (chapter 3). Kings and rulers love to display statues or gigantic photos as symbols of their power. The bigger the tyrants, the more of their statues litter the landscape.

It seems reasonable, then, that Daniel's visions depict political realms through statues and symbolic animals. But since each of the visions uses a different set of symbols, you can easily lose track of what the symbols stand for. This chart may help you coordinate Daniel's view of four great empires—and the almighty God who overwhelms their power in the end:

"In my vision at night I looked, and there before me was a fourth beast—terrifying and frightening and very powerful. It had large iron teeth; it crushed and devoured its victims." 7:7

	Babylon	Medo-Persia	Greece	Rome	Kingdom of God
Chapter 2	gold	silver	bronze	iron	supernatural rock
Chapter 7	lion	bear	leopard	beast with horns	Ancient of Days, Son of Man
Chapter 8	–	ram	goat	–	–
Chapter 11	–	–	king of North	–	–

Life Questions: What images 'litter the landscape' in our time? Are they symbols of power? If so, how does that power affect you?

authority, but were allowed to live for a period of time."

[13]"In my vision at night I looked, and there before me was one like a son of man, coming with the clouds of heaven. He approached the Ancient of Days and was led into his presence.

7:13–14 A Son of Man

God's power is given to one "like a son of man" rather than to those like beasts. The contrast suggests God's kingdom has power that is humane, not savage or bestial. Jesus adopted this term for himself.

[14]He was given authority, glory and sovereign power; all peoples, nations and men of every language worshiped him. His dominion is an everlasting dominion that will not pass away, and his kingdom is one that will never be destroyed.

The Interpretation of the Dream

[15]"I, Daniel, was troubled in spirit, and the visions that passed through my mind disturbed me. [16]I approached one of those standing there and asked him the true meaning of all this.

"So he told me and gave me the interpretation of these things: [17]'The four great beasts are four kingdoms that will rise from the earth. [18]But the saints of the Most High will receive the kingdom and will possess it forever—yes, for ever and ever.'

[19]"Then I wanted to know the true meaning of the fourth beast, which was different from all the others and most terrifying, with its iron teeth and bronze claws—the beast that crushed and devoured its victims and trampled underfoot whatever was left. [20]I also wanted to know about the ten horns on its head and about the other horn that came up, before which three of them fell— the horn that looked more imposing than the others and that had eyes and a mouth that spoke boastfully. [21]As I watched, this horn was waging war against the saints and defeating them, [22]until the Ancient of Days came and pronounced judgment in favor of the saints of the Most High, and the time came when they possessed the kingdom.

[23]"He gave me this explanation: 'The fourth beast is a fourth kingdom that will appear on earth. It will be different from all the other kingdoms and will devour the whole earth, trampling it down and crushing it. [24]The ten horns are ten kings who will come from this kingdom. After them another king will arise, different from the earlier ones; he will subdue three kings. [25]He will speak against the Most High and oppress his saints and try to change the set times and the

laws. The saints will be handed over to him for a time, times and half a time.[a]

[26]"'But the court will sit, and his power will be taken away and completely destroyed forever. [27]Then the sovereignty, power and greatness of the kingdoms under the whole heaven will be handed over to the saints, the people of the Most High. His kingdom will be an everlasting kingdom, and all rulers will worship and obey him.'

[28]"This is the end of the matter. I, Daniel, was deeply troubled by my thoughts, and my face turned pale, but I kept the matter to myself."

Daniel's Vision of a Ram and a Goat

8 In the third year of King Belshazzar's reign, I, Daniel, had a vision, after the one that had already appeared to me. [2]In my vision I saw myself in the citadel of Susa in the province of Elam; in the vision I was beside the Ulai Canal. [3]I looked up, and there before me was a ram with two horns, standing beside the canal, and the horns were long. One of the horns was longer than the other but grew up later. [4]I watched the ram as he charged toward the west and the north and the south. No animal could stand against him, and none could rescue from his power. He did as he pleased and became great.

[5]As I was thinking about this, suddenly a goat with a prominent horn between his eyes came from the west, crossing the whole earth without touching the ground. [6]He came toward the two-horned ram I had seen standing beside the canal and charged at him in great rage. [7]I saw him attack the ram furiously, striking the ram and shattering his two horns. The ram was powerless to stand against him; the goat knocked him to the ground and trampled on him, and none could rescue the ram from his power. [8]The goat became very great, but at the height of his power his large horn was broken off, and in its place four prominent horns grew up toward the four winds of heaven.

[9]Out of one of them came another horn, which started small but grew in power to the south and to the east and toward the Beautiful Land. [10]It grew until it reached the host of the heavens, and it threw some of the starry host down to the earth and trampled on them. [11]It set itself up to be as great as the Prince of the host; it took away the daily sacrifice from him, and the place of his sanctuary was brought low. [12]Because of rebellion, the host ⌊of the saints⌋[b] and the daily sacrifice were given over to it. It prospered in everything it did, and truth was thrown to the ground.

[13]Then I heard a holy one speaking, and another holy one said to him, "How long will it take

---

[a]25 Or *for a year, two years and half a year*   [b]12 Or *rebellion, the armies*

for the vision to be fulfilled—the vision concerning the daily sacrifice, the rebellion that causes desolation, and the surrender of the sanctuary and of the host that will be trampled underfoot?"

¹⁴He said to me, "It will take 2,300 evenings and mornings; then the sanctuary will be reconsecrated."

The Interpretation of the Vision

¹⁵While I, Daniel, was watching the vision and trying to understand it, there before me stood one who looked like a man. ¹⁶And I heard a man's voice from the Ulai calling, "Gabriel, tell this man the meaning of the vision."

¹⁷As he came near the place where I was standing, I was terrified and fell prostrate. "Son of man," he said to me, "understand that the vision concerns the time of the end."

¹⁸While he was speaking to me, I was in a deep sleep, with my face to the ground. Then he touched me and raised me to my feet.

¹⁹He said: "I am going to tell you what will happen later in the time of wrath, because the vision concerns the appointed time of the end.ᵃ ²⁰The two-horned ram that you saw represents the kings of Media and Persia. ²¹The shaggy goat is the king of Greece, and the large horn between his eyes is the first king. ²²The four horns that replaced the one that was broken off represent four kingdoms that will emerge from his nation but will not have the same power.

²³"In the latter part of their reign, when rebels have become completely wicked, a stern-faced king, a master of intrigue, will arise. ²⁴He will become very strong, but not by his own power. He will cause astounding devastation and will succeed in whatever he does. He will destroy the mighty men and the holy people. ²⁵He will cause deceit to prosper, and he will consider himself superior. When they feel secure, he will destroy many and take his stand against the Prince of princes. Yet he will be destroyed, but not by human power.

²⁶"The vision of the evenings and mornings

8:26 Long Delay

Twice (here and 12:4) the angel tells Daniel to seal up the vision because it concerns the distant future. Pointedly, in Revelation, the last book of the Bible, an angel tells John, "Do not seal up the words of the prophecy of this book, because the time is near" (Revelation 22:10). Daniel and Revelation, written hundreds of years apart, arrive at the same conclusion: No matter how bad things look, God is in control of history and will one day reclaim the earth.

that has been given you is true, but seal up the vision, for it concerns the distant future."

²⁷I, Daniel, was exhausted and lay ill for several days. Then I got up and went about the king's business. I was appalled by the vision; it was beyond understanding.

Daniel's Prayer

9 In the first year of Darius son of Xerxesᵇ (a Mede by descent), who was made ruler over the Babylonianᶜ kingdom— ²in the first year of his reign, I, Daniel, understood from the Scriptures, according to the word of the LORD given to Jeremiah the prophet, that the desolation of Jerusalem would last seventy years. ³So I turned to

9:2 Favored by God and Kings

This chapter gives a rare glimpse of one prophet, Daniel, being comforted by the words of another, Jeremiah. Daniel's response shows that, despite his government service to two enemy empires (Babylon and Persia), loyalty to his homeland never faltered. The remarkable prayer that follows expresses well his intimate relationship with God.

the Lord God and pleaded with him in prayer and petition, in fasting, and in sackcloth and ashes.

⁴I prayed to the LORD my God and confessed:

"O Lord, the great and awesome God, who keeps his covenant of love with all who love him and obey his commands, ⁵we have sinned and done wrong. We have been wicked and have rebelled; we have turned away from your commands and laws. ⁶We have not listened to your servants the prophets, who spoke in your name to our kings, our princes and our fathers, and to all the people of the land.

⁷"Lord, you are righteous, but this day we are covered with shame—the men of Judah and people of Jerusalem and all Israel, both near and far, in all the countries where you have scattered us because of our unfaithfulness to you. ⁸O LORD, we and our kings, our princes and our fathers are covered with shame because we have sinned against you. ⁹The Lord our God is merciful and forgiving, even though we have rebelled against him; ¹⁰we have not obeyed the LORD our God or kept the laws he gave us through his servants the prophets. ¹¹All Israel has transgressed your law and turned away, refusing to obey you.

"Therefore the curses and sworn judg-

ᵃ19 Or *because the end will be at the appointed time*   ᵇ1 Hebrew *Ahasuerus*   ᶜ1 Or *Chaldean*

ments written in the Law of Moses, the servant of God, have been poured out on us, because we have sinned against you. ¹²You have fulfilled the words spoken against us and against our rulers by bringing upon us great disaster. Under the whole heaven nothing has ever been done like what has been done to Jerusalem. ¹³Just as it is written in the Law of Moses, all this disaster has come upon us, yet we have not sought the favor of the LORD our God by turning from our sins and giving attention to your truth. ¹⁴The LORD did not hesitate to bring the disaster upon us, for the LORD our God is righteous in everything he does; yet we have not obeyed him.

¹⁵"Now, O Lord our God, who brought your people out of Egypt with a mighty hand and who made for yourself a name that endures to this day, we have sinned, we have done wrong. ¹⁶O Lord, in keeping with all your righteous acts, turn away your anger and your wrath from Jerusalem, your city, your holy hill. Our sins and the iniquities of our fathers have made Jerusalem and your people an object of scorn to all those around us.

¹⁷"Now, our God, hear the prayers and petitions of your servant. For your sake, O Lord, look with favor on your desolate sanctuary. ¹⁸Give ear, O God, and hear; open your eyes and see the desolation of the city that bears your Name. We do not make requests of you because we are righteous, but because of your great mercy. ¹⁹O Lord, listen! O Lord, forgive! O Lord, hear and act! For your sake, O my God, do not delay, because your city and your people bear your Name."

The Seventy "Sevens"

²⁰While I was speaking and praying, confessing my sin and the sin of my people Israel and making my request to the LORD my God for his holy hill— ²¹while I was still in prayer, Gabriel, the man I had seen in the earlier vision, came to me in swift flight about the time of the evening sacrifice. ²²He instructed me and said to me, "Daniel, I have now come to give you insight and understanding. ²³As soon as you began to pray, an answer was given, which I have come to tell you, for you are highly esteemed. Therefore, consider the message and understand the vision:

²⁴"Seventy 'sevens'ᵃ are decreed for your people and your holy city to finishᵇ transgression, to put an end to sin, to atone for wicked-

ness, to bring in everlasting righteousness, to seal up vision and prophecy and to anoint the most holy.ᶜ

²⁵"Know and understand this: From the issuing of the decreeᵈ to restore and rebuild Jerusalem until the Anointed One,ᵉ the ruler, comes, there will be seven 'sevens,' and sixty-two 'sevens.' It will be rebuilt with streets and a trench, but in times of trouble. ²⁶After the sixty-two 'sevens,' the Anointed One will be cut off and will have nothing.ᶠ The people of the ruler who will come will destroy the city and the sanctuary. The end will come like a flood: War will continue until the end, and desolations have been decreed. ²⁷He will confirm a covenant with many for one 'seven.'ᵍ In the middle of the 'seven'ᵍ he will put an end to sacrifice and offering. And on a wing ⌞of the temple⌟ he will set up an abomination that causes desolation, until the end that is decreed is poured out on him.ʰ"ⁱ

Daniel's Vision of a Man

10 In the third year of Cyrus king of Persia, a revelation was given to Daniel (who was called Belteshazzar). Its message was true and it concerned a great war.ʲ The understanding of the message came to him in a vision.

²At that time I, Daniel, mourned for three weeks. ³I ate no choice food; no meat or wine touched my lips; and I used no lotions at all until the three weeks were over.

⁴On the twenty-fourth day of the first month, as I was standing on the bank of the great river, the Tigris, ⁵I looked up and there before me was a man dressed in linen, with a belt of the finest gold around his waist. ⁶His body was like chrysolite, his face like lightning, his eyes like flaming torches, his arms and legs like the gleam of burnished bronze, and his voice like the sound of a multitude.

⁷I, Daniel, was the only one who saw the vision; the men with me did not see it, but such terror overwhelmed them that they fled and hid themselves. ⁸So I was left alone, gazing at this great vision; I had no strength left, my face turned deathly pale and I was helpless. ⁹Then I heard him speaking, and as I listened to him, I fell into a deep sleep, my face to the ground.

¹⁰A hand touched me and set me trembling on my hands and knees. ¹¹He said, "Daniel, you who are highly esteemed, consider carefully the words I am about to speak to you, and stand up, for I have now been sent to you." And when he said this to me, I stood up trembling.

¹²Then he continued, "Do not be afraid, Daniel. Since the first day that you set your mind to

---

ᵃ24 Or 'weeks'; also in verses 25 and 26   ᵇ24 Or restrain
ᵈ25 Or word   ᵉ25 Or an anointed one; also in verse 26   ᶜ24 Or Most Holy Place; or most holy One
ᵍ27 Or 'week'   ʰ27 Or it   ⁱ27 Or And one who causes desolation will come upon the pinnacle of the abominable
⌞temple⌟, until the end that is decreed is poured out on the desolated ⌞city⌟   ᶠ26 Or off and will have no one; or off, but not for himself
ʲ1 Or true and burdensome

[fragment of overlapping torn page, partially legible]
...will rise to power;
...feel secure, he will
...eve what neither his
...'s did. He will distri...
...among his...

16 "Then one who looked like a man touched my lips, and I opened my mouth and began to speak. I said to the one standing before me, "I am overcome with anguish because of the vision, my lord, and I am helpless. 17 How can I, your servant, talk with you, my lord? My strength is gone and I can hardly breathe."

18 Again the one who looked like a man touched me and gave me strength. 19 "Do not be afraid, O man highly esteemed," he said. "Peace! Be strong now; be strong."

When he spoke to me, I was strengthened and said, "Speak, my lord, since you have given me strength."

20 So he said, "Do you know why I have come to you? Soon I will return to fight against the prince of Persia, and when I go, the prince of

10:20 Slow to Answer Prayer

These comments come from what seems to be an angelic messenger. They hint at heavenly warfare human beings know little about. When prayers go unanswered for long periods, more may be involved than we ever dream.

Greece will come; 21 but first I will tell you what is written in the Book of Truth. (No one supports me against them except Michael, your prince.

11 1 And in the first year of Darius the Mede, I took my stand to support and protect him.)

The Kings of the South and the North

2 "Now then, I tell you the truth: Three more kings will appear in Persia, and then a fourth, who will be far richer than all the others. When he has gained power by his wealth, he will stir up everyone against the kingdom of Greece. 3 Then a mighty king will appear, who will rule with great power and do as he pleases. 4 After he has appeared, his empire will be broken up and parceled out toward the four winds of heaven. It will not go to his descendants, nor will it have the power he exercised, because his empire will be uprooted and given to others.

5 "The king of the South will become strong, but one of his commanders will become even ...ger than he and will rule his own kingdom ...power. 6 After some years, they will ...her. ...The daughter of the king of the ...king of the North to make an ...tain her power, and he ...her power... In those days she ...her royal es-...

7 "One from her family line will arise to take her place. He will attack the forces of the king of the North and enter his fortress; he will fight against them and be victorious. 8 He will also seize their gods, their metal images and their valuable articles of silver and gold and carry them off to Egypt. For some years he will leave the king of the North alone. 9 Then the king of the North will invade the realm of the king of the South but will retreat to his own country. 10 His sons will prepare for war and assemble a great army, which will sweep on like an irresistible flood and carry the battle as far as his fortress.

11 "Then the king of the South will march out in a rage and fight against the king of the North, who will raise a large army, but it will be defeated. 12 When the army is carried off, the king of the South will be filled with pride and will slaughter many thousands, yet he will not remain triumphant. 13 For the king of the North will muster another army, larger than the first; and after several years, he will advance with a huge army fully equipped.

14 "In those times many will rise against the king of the South. The violent men among your own people will rebel in fulfillment of the vision, but without success. 15 Then the king of the North will come and build up siege ramps and will capture a fortified city. The forces of the South will be powerless to resist; even their best troops will not have the strength to stand. 16 The invader will do as he pleases; no one will be able to stand against him. He will establish himself in the Beautiful Land and will have the power to destroy it. 17 He will determine to come with the might of his entire kingdom and will make an alliance with the king of the South. And he will give him a daughter in marriage in order to overthrow the kingdom, but his plans will not succeed or help him. 18 Then he will turn his attention to the coastlands and will take many of them, but a commander will put an end to his insolence and will turn his insolence back upon him. 19 After this, he will turn back toward the

---

a 16 Most manuscripts of the Masoretic Text; one manuscript of the Masoretic Text, Dead Sea Scrolls and Septuagint *Then something that looked like a man's hand*   b 6 Or *offspring*   c 6 Or *child* (see Vulgate and Syriac)   d 17 Or *but she*

fortresses of his own country but will s... and fall, to be seen no more. 20"His successor will send out a ... ... maintain the royal splendor. In a ...tough ever, he will be destroyed, ... battle.

21"He will be su...ceding army will be person who has royalty. He ...ve him; both it and a prince of people feel ...ve him; both it and a prince of intrigue.sweet will be destroyed. 23After coming to an agreement with him, he will act deceitfully,

...ollowers. He ...or fortresses—but only

...with a large army he will stir up his strength and courage against the king of the South. The king of the South will wage war with a large and very powerful army, but he will not be able to stand because of the plots devised against him. 26Those who eat from the king's provisions will try to destroy him; his army will be swept

In the Hands of Tyrants
Daniel's visions portray history as one bestial empire after another

JOSEF STALIN, HEAD OF THE Soviet Union from 1924 to 1953, murdered millions. His supporters knew that the slightest slip would lead them to the executioner. Of 1,966 delegates to one Party Congress, Stalin had 1,108—all Stalin supporters—arrested and killed. Of the 139 Central Committee members, 98 were shot.

In spite of this, the nation virtually worshiped Stalin. He had made himself a god. Every public park displayed his statue. Every newspaper published lavish tributes daily. For one of his birthdays, an entire museum in Moscow was stripped so it could be filled with his birthday presents. He was called Father of the Peoples, the Greatest Genius in History, the Shining Sun of Humanity, the Life-giving Force of Socialism.

> "The king will do as he pleases. He will exalt and magnify himself above every god and will say unheard-of things against the God of gods." 11:36

He was not the first, nor the last, of his kind. Increasingly, it seems, totalitarian leaders promise everything—and demand everything. They brutally dispose of anyone who opposes them. Hitler, Stalin, Idi Amin, Chairman Mao, the Ayatollah Khomeini, Saddam Hussein . . . the list grows longer.

A Single, Cruel King

Daniel's visions predicted such tyrants. History, in these visions, is one terrible empire after another. Each is stronger but more bestial than the last.

The focus narrows (in 8:23–25 and 11:21–45) to a single, cruel king. Most scholars agree the description matches Antiochus IV of Syria. An obscure tyrant who ruled a century and a half before Jesus, he was the Jews' worst enemy in history, until Hitler.

Antiochus, never totally victorious against archenemy Egypt, took out his frustrations on little Jerusalem. He determined to make that city Greek rather than Jewish by rooting out its religion. He sold the high priest's position to an opportunist and transformed the temple into an altar for the Greek god Zeus. This desecration sparked one of history's earliest guerrilla wars, the Maccabean revolt that began in 168 B.C. Antiochus conquered Jerusalem twice, slaughtering thousands. He outlawed Judaism and proclaimed himself to be God incarnate.

The End of the Tyrant

And yet, for all his power and terror, Antiochus died raving from insanity, and his mark on history has virtually disappeared. Ironically, the religion he sought to destroy has endured and touched the whole world. This is just what you could expect from reading Daniel. Terrible rulers rise up one after another, but they disappear just as quickly. We can expect political terror. But we can count on God.

The New Testament suggests that Antiochus's brutal pattern will culminate someday in the antichrist, an arrogant leader who will dominate the world and persecute God's people as never before. Many scholars believe that the last part of Daniel's final vision refers to this character. Yet despite the antichrist's power, he too will fall in the end. God's justice will rule the earth. Those who believe in such an outcome have reason to be as brave as Daniel.

Life Questions: How does Daniel's view of history affect your perspective on world politics? How should a Christian regard the human "powers-that-be"?

away, and many will fall in battle. ²⁷The two kings, with their hearts bent on evil, will sit at the same table and lie to each other, but to no avail, because an end will still come at the appointed time. ²⁸The king of the North will return to his own country with great wealth, but his heart will be set against the holy covenant. He will take action against it and then return to his own country.

²⁹At the appointed time he will invade the South again, but this time the outcome will be different from what it was before. ³⁰Ships of the western coastlands*a* will oppose him, and he will lose heart. Then he will turn back and vent his fury against the holy covenant. He will return and show favor to those who forsake the holy covenant.

³¹"His armed forces will rise up to desecrate the temple fortress and will abolish the daily sacrifice. Then they will set up the abomination that causes desolation. ³²With flattery he will corrupt those who have violated the covenant, but the people who know their God will firmly resist him.

³³"Those who are wise will instruct many, though for a time they will fall by the sword or be burned or captured or plundered. ³⁴When they fall, they will receive a little help, and many who are not sincere will join them. ³⁵Some of the wise will stumble, so that they may be refined, purified and made spotless until the time of the end, for it will still come at the appointed time.

The King Who Exalts Himself

³⁶"The king will do as he pleases. He will exalt and magnify himself above every god and will say unheard-of things against the God of gods. He will be successful until the time of wrath is completed, for what has been determined must take place. ³⁷He will show no regard for the gods of his fathers or for the one desired by women, nor will he regard any god, but will exalt himself above them all. ³⁸Instead of them, he will honor a god of fortresses; a god unknown to his fathers he will honor with gold and silver, with precious stones and costly gifts. ³⁹He will attack the mightiest fortresses with the help of a foreign god and will greatly honor those who acknowledge him. He will make them rulers over many people and will distribute the land at a price.*b*

⁴⁰"At the time of the end the king of the South will engage him in battle, and the king of the North will storm out against him with chariots and cavalry and a great fleet of ships. He will invade many countries and sweep through them like a flood. ⁴¹He will also invade the Beautiful Land. Many countries will fall, but Edom, Moab and the leaders of Ammon will be delivered from his hand. ⁴²He will extend his power over many countries; Egypt will not escape. ⁴³He will gain control of the treasures of gold and silver and all the riches of Egypt, with the Libyans and Nubians in submission. ⁴⁴But reports from the east and the north will alarm him, and he will set out in a great rage to destroy and annihilate many.

11:37 Exalted above the Gods

The tyrant Antiochus IV, whom most commentators believe is described here, minted many coins showing his portrait. The early coins were merely stamped, "King Antiochus." But, as he grew more obsessed with his own importance, he added features to his portrait that made him look like the Greek gods Apollo or Zeus, and to his given name he appended the title "Epiphanes"—"God Manifest." Such behavior earned him the nickname "Antiochus Epimanes"—"crazy Antiochus."

⁴⁵He will pitch his royal tents between the seas at*c* the beautiful holy mountain. Yet he will come to his end, and no one will help him.

The End Times

12 "At that time Michael, the great prince who protects your people, will arise. There will be a time of distress such as has not happened from the beginning of nations until then. But at that time your people—everyone whose name is found written in the book—will be delivered. ²Multitudes who sleep in the dust of the earth will awake: some to everlasting life, others to shame

12:2 Resurrection

While eternal life is usually portrayed cloudily in the Old Testament, this verse clearly predicts that we will live forever.

and everlasting contempt. ³Those who are wise*d* will shine like the brightness of the heavens, and those who lead many to righteousness, like the stars for ever and ever. ⁴But you, Daniel, close up and seal the words of the scroll until the time of the end. Many will go here and there to increase knowledge."

⁵Then I, Daniel, looked, and there before me stood two others, one on this bank of the river and one on the opposite bank. ⁶One of them said

---

a 30 Hebrew of Kittim   *b* 39 Or land for a reward   *c* 45 Or the sea and   *d* 3 Or who impart wisdom to the man clothed in linen, who was above the waters of the river, "How long will it be before these astonishing things are fulfilled?"

7The man clothed in linen, who was above the waters of the river, lifted his right hand and his left hand toward heaven, and I heard him swear by him who lives forever, saying, "It will be for a time, times and half a time.[a] When the power of the holy people has been finally broken, all these things will be completed."

8I heard, but I did not understand. So I asked, "My lord, what will the outcome of all this be?"

9He replied, "Go your way, Daniel, because the words are closed up and sealed until the time of the end. 10Many will be purified, made spotless and refined, but the wicked will continue to be wicked. None of the wicked will understand, but those who are wise will understand.

11"From the time that the daily sacrifice is abolished and the abomination that causes desolation is set up, there will be 1,290 days. 12Blessed is the one who waits for and reaches the end of the 1,335 days.

13"As for you, go your way till the end. You will rest, and then at the end of the days you will rise to receive your allotted inheritance."

HOSEA

Tearing God's Heart
Why would he love such a woman?

HOSEA BEGINS WITH A LOVE story—a painful, personal love story, the prophet's very own. Hosea had married a woman who acted like a prostitute. Yet the more she went out on him, the more Hosea loved her. He gave her everything a good wife deserved: his love, his home, his name, his reputation. She responded by sleeping around with other men. He warned her, he pleaded with her, he punished her. She humiliated him until he wanted to cry, yet still he clung to her.

> *"She decked herself with rings and jewelry, and went after her lovers, but me she forgot," declares the* LORD. *2:13*

Why did Hosea begin with his personal life? Because God had expressly told him to relate it to another, more tragic love story: the painful love of God for his people. God could have simply declared, "Israel is like a wife to me—an adulterous wife." Instead, he used Hosea to act out the treachery in real life—and to show in living color God's fury, his jealousy, and above all else, his love for his people.

Winding Down to a Bitter End

Virtually every chapter of Hosea talks about the "prostitution" or "adultery" of God's people (1:2; 2:2,4; 3:1; 4:2,10–15,18; 5:3–4; 6:10; 7:4; 8:9; 9:1). Underlying some hard words is a remarkably tender revelation: God doesn't want to be only "master" to his people. He wants to be a husband, giving all of himself in intimate love.

Hosea spoke and acted these messages to the northern part of God's divided country—Israel or "Ephraim," as Hosea sometimes called it. King Jeroboam II's reign was a time of prosperity; the prophet Amos blasted the rich for their greedy injustices toward the poor. But soon after Jeroboam's death the national fabric began to unravel. In just over 20 years six kings took the throne—four of them by murdering the previous king. Hosea probably lived to see the massive Assyrian armies storm the capital and deport all the Israelite citizens to other lands. God's "wife" was carried off, just as he had warned.

God Is a Lover

When most people must have been preoccupied with politics and military matters, Hosea kept his message aimed at idol worship, which he referred to as adultery. He saw that as the root of Israel's problems.

Israel tended to mix religions freely—to think that everybody's religion had a little truth in it, and the more religion you got, the better off you would be. Many prophets attacked Israel's idol worship. Hosea shows that God's concern about idolatry is no fussy, religious matter. It is terribly personal. God, the lover, will not share his bride with anyone else.

God's anger and jealousy, expressed so often throughout the Old Testament, reflect his powerful love. Sin does not merely break God's law, it breaks his heart. He punishes to get his lover's attention. Yet even when she turns her back on him, he sticks with her. He is willing to suffer, in the hope that someday she will change. Hosea shows that God longs not to punish, but to love.

How to Read Hosea

Hosea is one of the most emotional books in the Bible, an outpouring of suffering love from God's heart. This shows in the writing, which jumps impulsively from one thought to the next. Read a chapter dramatically aloud, and you will get this sense. It is almost like listening in on a husband-and-wife fight.

The book divides into two parts. In the first three chapters, the prophet Hosea briefly describes his marriage to an adulterous woman and makes the connection to Israel's unfaithfulness to God. From chapter 4 onward this dramatic, personal beginning is not mentioned again. But it has set the stage. God's deep love, his disappointment and anger, and his determination to persevere with his unfaithful wife pour out in a series of vivid speeches.

For a historical perspective on Hosea's times, read from 2 Kings 14:23 to 17:41, noting that some sections describe Judah, the southern nation, while the rest relate to the deteriorating Israel Hosea knew. This history is summarized in "A Lineup of Rulers," pages 1361–1369. The prophet Amos spoke to the North at about the same time as Hosea, but from a noticeably different point of view. Amos concentrated on law and justice, with special concern for the poor, while Hosea concentrated on the broken relationship with God that led to this injustice. Together, these two prophets provide a three-dimensional view of Israel's problems.

Because Hosea is so emotional, he doesn't stop to explain a large number of images or biblical references. A Bible dictionary will help you understand the names and places you aren't familiar with.

3-TRACK READING PLAN

For an explanation and complete listing of the 3-track reading plan, turn to page 7.

TRACK 1: *Two-Week Courses on the Bible*
See page 7 for information on these courses.

TRACK 2: *An Overview of Hosea in 2 Days*
☐ Day 1. Read the Introduction to Hosea and chapters 2 and 3, which compare Hosea's marriage to Israel's relationship with God.
☐ Day 2. Read chapter 11, which shows God's powerful, competing emotions as he thinks of Israel.

Now turn to page 9 for your next Track 2 reading project.

TRACK 3: *All of Hosea in 10 Days*
After you have read through Hosea, turn to pages 10–14 for your next Track 3 reading project.
☐1 ☐2–3 ☐4 ☐5 ☐6–7 ☐8 ☐9 ☐10
☐11–12 ☐13–14

1 The word of the LORD that came to Hosea son of Beeri during the reigns of Uzziah, Jotham, Ahaz and Hezekiah, kings of Judah, and during the reign of Jeroboam son of Jehoash[a] king of Israel:

Hosea's Wife and Children

²When the LORD began to speak through Hosea, the LORD said to him, "Go, take to yourself an adulterous wife and children of unfaithfulness, because the land is guilty of the vilest adultery in departing from the LORD." ³So he married Gomer daughter of Diblaim, and she conceived and bore him a son.

⁴Then the LORD said to Hosea, "Call him Jezreel, because I will soon punish the house of Jehu for the massacre at Jezreel, and I will put an end to the kingdom of Israel. ⁵In that day I will break Israel's bow in the Valley of Jezreel."

⁶Gomer conceived again and gave birth to a daughter. Then the LORD said to Hosea, "Call her Lo-Ruhamah,[b] for I will no longer show love to the house of Israel, that I should at all forgive them. ⁷Yet I will show love to the house of Judah; and I will save them—not by bow, sword or battle, or by horses and horsemen, but by the LORD their God."

⁸After she had weaned Lo-Ruhamah, Gomer had another son. ⁹Then the LORD said, "Call him Lo-Ammi,[c] for you are not my people, and I am not your God.

¹⁰"Yet the Israelites will be like the sand on the seashore, which cannot be measured or counted. In the place where it was said to them, 'You are not my people,' they will be called 'sons of the living God.' ¹¹The people of Judah and the people of Israel will be reunited, and they will appoint one leader and will come up out of the land, for great will be the day of Jezreel.

---

[a]1 Hebrew *Joash*, a variant of *Jehoash* [b]6 *Lo-Ruhamah* means *not loved*. [c]9 *Lo-Ammi* means *not my people*.

2 "Say of your brothers, 'My people,' and of your sisters, 'My loved one.'

Israel Punished and Restored

²"Rebuke your mother, rebuke her,
    for she is not my wife,
    and I am not her husband.

Let her remove the adulterous look from her face
    and the unfaithfulness from between her breasts.
³Otherwise I will strip her naked
    and make her as bare as on the day she was born;
I will make her like a desert,
    turn her into a parched land,
    and slay her with thirst.
⁴I will not show my love to her children,
    because they are the children of adultery.
⁵Their mother has been unfaithful
    and has conceived them in disgrace.
She said, 'I will go after my lovers,
    who give me my food and my water,
    my wool and my linen, my oil and my drink.'
⁶Therefore I will block her path with thornbushes;
    I will wall her in so that she cannot find her way.
⁷She will chase after her lovers but not catch them;
    she will look for them but not find them.
Then she will say,

'I will go back to my husband as at first,
    for then I was better off than now.'
⁸She has not acknowledged that I was the one
    who gave her the grain, the new wine and oil,
who lavished on her the silver and gold—
    which they used for Baal.

⁹"Therefore I will take away my grain when it ripens,
    and my new wine when it is ready.
I will take back my wool and my linen,
    intended to cover her nakedness.
¹⁰So now I will expose her lewdness
    before the eyes of her lovers;
    no one will take her out of my hands.
¹¹I will stop all her celebrations:
    her yearly festivals, her New Moons,
    her Sabbath days—all her appointed feasts.
¹²I will ruin her vines and her fig trees,
    which she said were her pay from her lovers;
I will make them a thicket,
    and wild animals will devour them.
¹³I will punish her for the days
    she burned incense to the Baals;
she decked herself with rings and jewelry,
    and went after her lovers,
    but me she forgot,"

declares the LORD.

¹⁴"Therefore I am now going to allure her;
    I will lead her into the desert
    and speak tenderly to her.
¹⁵There I will give her back her vineyards,
    and will make the Valley of Achor^a a door of hope.
There she will sing^b as in the days of her youth,
    as in the day she came up out of Egypt.

¹⁶"In that day," declares the LORD,
    "you will call me 'my husband';
    you will no longer call me 'my master.'^c
¹⁷I will remove the names of the Baals from her lips;
    no longer will their names be invoked.
¹⁸In that day I will make a covenant for them
    with the beasts of the field and the birds of the air
    and the creatures that move along the ground.
Bow and sword and battle
    I will abolish from the land,
    so that all may lie down in safety.
¹⁹I will betroth you to me forever;
    I will betroth you in^d righteousness and justice,
    in^e love and compassion.

20I will betroth you in faithfulness,
and you will acknowledge the LORD.

21"In that day I will respond,"
declares the LORD—
"I will respond to the skies,
and they will respond to the earth;
22and the earth will respond to the grain,
the new wine and oil,
and they will respond to Jezreel.ᵃ
23I will plant her for myself in the land;
I will show my love to the one I called
'Not my loved one.'ᵇ'
I will say to those called 'Not my people,'ᶜ'
'You are my people';
and they will say, 'You are my God.'"

3:1 Parable of Love

No other prophet lived out an object lesson with quite the same emotional force as Hosea did. Gomer had sunk so low as to sell herself into slavery, but Hosea purchased her back and reclaimed her as his wife. That remarkable deed, certainly the subject of his countrymen's gossip, symbolized God's undying love for his people. Though they had dragged his name in the mud, still he welcomed them back.

Hosea's Reconciliation With His Wife

3 The LORD said to me, "Go, show your love to your wife again, though she is loved by another and is an adulteress. Love her as the LORD loves the Israelites, though they turn to other gods and love the sacred raisin cakes."

2So I bought her for fifteen shekelsᵈ of silver and about a homer and a lethekᵉ of barley. 3Then I told her, "You are to live withᶠ me many days; you must not be a prostitute or be intimate with any man, and I will live withᶠ you."

4For the Israelites will live many days without king or prince, without sacrifice or sacred stones, without ephod or idol. 5Afterward the Israelites will return and seek the LORD their God and David their king. They will come trembling to the LORD and to his blessings in the last days.

The Charge Against Israel

4 Hear the word of the LORD, you Israelites, because the LORD has a charge to bring against you who live in the land:
"There is no faithfulness, no love,
no acknowledgment of God in the land.

2There is only cursing,ᵍ lying and murder,
stealing and adultery;
they break all bounds,
and bloodshed follows bloodshed.
3Because of this the land mourns,ʰ
and all who live in it waste away;
the beasts of the field and the birds of the air
and the fish of the sea are dying.

4"But let no man bring a charge,
let no man accuse another,
for your people are like those
who bring charges against a priest.
5You stumble day and night,
and the prophets stumble with you.
So I will destroy your mother—
6   my people are destroyed from lack of
knowledge.

"Because you have rejected knowledge,
I also reject you as my priests;
because you have ignored the law of your
God,
I also will ignore your children.
7The more the priests increased,
the more they sinned against me;
they exchangedⁱ theirʲ Glory for
something disgraceful.

4:7 Poor Trade

Early in its history, the Northern Kingdom of Israel began appointing its own priests from ineligible tribes (1 Kings 12:31). These priests led the people in the worship of golden calves— idols—instead of in the worship of the God of Abraham and Moses. This verse has an echo in Romans 1:23, where Paul blasts pagans who exchange the glory of immortal God for mere statues of birds, animals, and reptiles.

8They feed on the sins of my people
and relish their wickedness.
9And it will be: Like people, like priests.
I will punish both of them for their ways
and repay them for their deeds.

10"They will eat but not have enough;
they will engage in prostitution but not
increase,
because they have deserted the LORD
to give themselves 11to prostitution,
to old wine and new,
which take away the understanding 12of
my people.
They consult a wooden idol

ᵃ22 *Jezreel* means *God plants.*   ᵇ23 Hebrew *Lo-Ruhamah* (about 170 grams)   ᵉ2 That is, probably about 10 bushels (about 330 liters)   ᶜ23 Hebrew *Lo-Ammi*   ᵈ2 That is, about 6 ounces   ᶠ3 Or *wait for*   ᵍ2 That is, to pronounce a curse upon   ʰ3 Or *dries up*   ⁱ7 Syriac and an ancient Hebrew scribal tradition; Masoretic Text *I will exchange*   ʲ7 Masoretic Text; an ancient Hebrew scribal tradition *my*

and are answered by a stick of wood.
A spirit of prostitution leads them astray;
   they are unfaithful to their God.
¹³They sacrifice on the mountaintops
   and burn offerings on the hills,
under oak, poplar and terebinth,
   where the shade is pleasant.
Therefore your daughters turn to prostitution
   and your daughters-in-law to adultery.

4:13 Real Prostitution

In each of the first nine chapters of his book, Hosea describes Israel's sin as prostitution or adultery. This is primarily symbolism meant to emphasize God's deep, personal love for Israel and his pain when the Israelites desert him to go after other gods.

But prostitution has a literal meaning also. The religions Israel pursued taught that human sexuality was tied to agricultural fertility. To encourage good crops, believers in these religions practiced their human fertility. This meant organized prostitution, done as part of their worship experience.

¹⁴"I will not punish your daughters
   when they turn to prostitution,
nor your daughters-in-law
   when they commit adultery,
because the men themselves consort with
      harlots
   and sacrifice with shrine prostitutes—
a people without understanding will come
      to ruin!

¹⁵"Though you commit adultery, O Israel,
   let not Judah become guilty.

"Do not go to Gilgal;
   do not go up to Beth Aven.ᵃ
And do not swear, 'As surely as the LORD
      lives!'
¹⁶The Israelites are stubborn,
   like a stubborn heifer.
How then can the LORD pasture them
   like lambs in a meadow?
¹⁷Ephraim is joined to idols;
   leave him alone!
¹⁸Even when their drinks are gone,
   they continue their prostitution;
   their rulers dearly love shameful ways.
¹⁹A whirlwind will sweep them away,
   and their sacrifices will bring them shame.

Judgment Against Israel

5 "Hear this, you priests!
   Pay attention, you Israelites!

Listen, O royal house!
   This judgment is against you:
You have been a snare at Mizpah,
   a net spread out on Tabor.
²The rebels are deep in slaughter.
   I will discipline all of them.
³I know all about Ephraim;
   Israel is not hidden from me.
Ephraim, you have now turned to
      prostitution;
   Israel is corrupt.

⁴"Their deeds do not permit them
   to return to their God.
A spirit of prostitution is in their heart;
   they do not acknowledge the LORD.
⁵Israel's arrogance testifies against them;
   the Israelites, even Ephraim, stumble in
      their sin;
   Judah also stumbles with them.
⁶When they go with their flocks and herds
   to seek the LORD,
they will not find him;
   he has withdrawn himself from them.
⁷They are unfaithful to the LORD;
   they give birth to illegitimate children.
Now their New Moon festivals
   will devour them and their fields.

⁸"Sound the trumpet in Gibeah,
   the horn in Ramah.
Raise the battle cry in Beth Avenᵃ;
   lead on, O Benjamin.
⁹Ephraim will be laid waste
   on the day of reckoning.
Among the tribes of Israel
   I proclaim what is certain.
¹⁰Judah's leaders are like those
   who move boundary stones.
I will pour out my wrath on them
   like a flood of water.
¹¹Ephraim is oppressed,
   trampled in judgment,
   intent on pursuing idols.ᵇ
¹²I am like a moth to Ephraim,
   like rot to the people of Judah.

¹³"When Ephraim saw his sickness,
   and Judah his sores,
then Ephraim turned to Assyria,
   and sent to the great king for help.
But he is not able to cure you,
   not able to heal your sores.
¹⁴For I will be like a lion to Ephraim,
   like a great lion to Judah.
I will tear them to pieces and go away;
   I will carry them off, with no one to
      rescue them.
¹⁵Then I will go back to my place

ᵃ 15,8 *Beth Aven* means *house of wickedness* (a name for Bethel, which means *house of God*).   ᵇ 11 The meaning of the Hebrew for this word is uncertain.

until they admit their guilt.
And they will seek my face;
　in their misery they will earnestly seek
　　me."

Israel Unrepentant

6 "Come, let us return to the LORD.
He has torn us to pieces
　but he will heal us;
he has injured us
　but he will bind up our wounds.
²After two days he will revive us;
　on the third day he will restore us,
　that we may live in his presence.
³Let us acknowledge the LORD;
　let us press on to acknowledge him.
As surely as the sun rises,
　he will appear;
he will come to us like the winter rains,
　like the spring rains that water the earth."

⁴"What can I do with you, Ephraim?
　What can I do with you, Judah?
Your love is like the morning mist,
　like the early dew that disappears.
⁵Therefore I cut you in pieces with my
　　prophets,
　I killed you with the words of my mouth;
　my judgments flashed like lightning upon
　　you.
⁶For I desire mercy, not sacrifice,
　and acknowledgment of God rather than
　　burnt offerings.
⁷Like Adam,ᵃ they have broken the
　　covenant—
　they were unfaithful to me there.
⁸Gilead is a city of wicked men,
　stained with footprints of blood.
⁹As marauders lie in ambush for a man,
　so do bands of priests;
they murder on the road to Shechem,
　committing shameful crimes.
¹⁰I have seen a horrible thing
　in the house of Israel.
There Ephraim is given to prostitution
　and Israel is defiled.

¹¹"Also for you, Judah,
　a harvest is appointed.

"Whenever I would restore the fortunes of
　my people,

7 ¹whenever I would heal Israel,
the sins of Ephraim are exposed
　and the crimes of Samaria revealed.
They practice deceit,
　thieves break into houses,
　bandits rob in the streets;
²but they do not realize
　that I remember all their evil deeds.

Their sins engulf them;
　they are always before me.

³"They delight the king with their wickedness,
　the princes with their lies.
⁴They are all adulterers,
　burning like an oven
whose fire the baker need not stir
　from the kneading of the dough till it
　　rises.

7:4 Smoldering Passion

*In parts of the Middle East, ovens are made of
clay and shaped like a large cone or beehive.
The baker builds a fire inside and tends it until
the clay gets very hot. Then, fire and wood ash
can be pulled out and the fresh dough placed
inside. It rises due to the heat contained inside
the oven, which stays hot long after the fire has
been removed. Such was Israel's lust for other
gods: It kept on smoldering, like a self-fueling
oven (verse 6).*

⁵On the day of the festival of our king
　the princes become inflamed with wine,
　and he joins hands with the mockers.
⁶Their hearts are like an oven;
　they approach him with intrigue.
Their passion smolders all night;
　in the morning it blazes like a flaming
　　fire.
⁷All of them are hot as an oven;
　they devour their rulers.
All their kings fall,
　and none of them calls on me.

⁸"Ephraim mixes with the nations;
　Ephraim is a flat cake not turned over.
⁹Foreigners sap his strength,
　but he does not realize it.
His hair is sprinkled with gray,
　but he does not notice.
¹⁰Israel's arrogance testifies against him,
　but despite all this
he does not return to the LORD his God
　or search for him.

¹¹"Ephraim is like a dove,
　easily deceived and senseless—
now calling to Egypt,
　now turning to Assyria.
¹²When they go, I will throw my net over
　　them;
　I will pull them down like birds of the air.
When I hear them flocking together,
　I will catch them.
¹³Woe to them,
　because they have strayed from me!

ᵃ7 Or *As at Adam*; or *Like men*

Destruction to them,
because they have rebelled against me!
I long to redeem them
but they speak lies against me.
¹⁴They do not cry out to me from their hearts
but wail upon their beds.
They gather together[a] for grain and new
wine
but turn away from me.
¹⁵I trained them and strengthened them,
but they plot evil against me.
¹⁶They do not turn to the Most High;
they are like a faulty bow.
Their leaders will fall by the sword
because of their insolent words.
For this they will be ridiculed
in the land of Egypt.

Israel to Reap the Whirlwind

8 "Put the trumpet to your lips!
An eagle is over the house of the LORD
because the people have broken my covenant
and rebelled against my law.
²Israel cries out to me,
'O our God, we acknowledge you!'
³But Israel has rejected what is good;
an enemy will pursue him.
⁴They set up kings without my consent;
they choose princes without my approval.
With their silver and gold
they make idols for themselves
to their own destruction.
⁵Throw out your calf-idol, O Samaria!
My anger burns against them.
How long will they be incapable of purity?
⁶ They are from Israel!
This calf—a craftsman has made it;
it is not God.
It will be broken in pieces,
that calf of Samaria.

⁷"They sow the wind
and reap the whirlwind.
The stalk has no head;
it will produce no flour.
Were it to yield grain,
foreigners would swallow it up.
⁸Israel is swallowed up;
now she is among the nations
like a worthless thing.
⁹For they have gone up to Assyria
like a wild donkey wandering alone.
Ephraim has sold herself to lovers.
¹⁰Although they have sold themselves among
the nations,
I will now gather them together.
They will begin to waste away
under the oppression of the mighty king.

¹¹"Though Ephraim built many altars for sin
offerings,
these have become altars for sinning.
¹²I wrote for them the many things of my law,
but they regarded them as something
alien.

8:11 How to Be Religious Without Pleasing God
The Israelites didn't think they were rejecting God. In fact, they became increasingly pious. (See 6:1–3; 8:2,11,13; and 10:1 for their expressions of faith.) But they wanted to worship on their terms, not God's. While their sacrifices to God increased, they kept on worshiping idols as well.

¹³They offer sacrifices given to me
and they eat the meat,
but the LORD is not pleased with them.
Now he will remember their wickedness
and punish their sins:
They will return to Egypt.
¹⁴Israel has forgotten his Maker
and built palaces;
Judah has fortified many towns.
But I will send fire upon their cities
that will consume their fortresses."

Punishment for Israel

9 Do not rejoice, O Israel;
do not be jubilant like the other nations.
For you have been unfaithful to your God;
you love the wages of a prostitute
at every threshing floor.
²Threshing floors and winepresses will not
feed the people;
the new wine will fail them.
³They will not remain in the LORD's land;
Ephraim will return to Egypt
and eat unclean[b] food in Assyria.
⁴They will not pour out wine offerings to the
LORD,
nor will their sacrifices please him.
Such sacrifices will be to them like the bread
of mourners;
all who eat them will be unclean.
This food will be for themselves;
it will not come into the temple of the
LORD.

⁵What will you do on the day of your
appointed feasts,
on the festival days of the LORD?
⁶Even if they escape from destruction,
Egypt will gather them,

a14 Most Hebrew manuscripts; some Hebrew manuscripts and Septuagint *They slash themselves*   b3 That is, ceremonially unclean

and Memphis will bury them.
Their treasures of silver will be taken over by
briers,
and thorns will overrun their tents.
⁷The days of punishment are coming,
the days of reckoning are at hand.
Let Israel know this.
Because your sins are so many
and your hostility so great,
the prophet is considered a fool,
the inspired man a maniac.
⁸The prophet, along with my God,
is the watchman over Ephraim,ᵃ
yet snares await him on all his paths,
and hostility in the house of his God.
⁹They have sunk deep into corruption,
as in the days of Gibeah.
God will remember their wickedness
and punish them for their sins.

9:9 Two Instances of Evil

The "days of Gibeah" evidently refers to the vicious murder of a woman, told in Judges 19–21. This horrifying incident was a version of Sodom and Gomorrah right in Israel. Another incident (verse 10), equally bad in its own way, occurred at Baal Peor (see Numbers 25:1–3). Israelite men en route to the promised land slept with Moabite women and worshiped their gods. From both these incidents, Hosea proves that sin is nothing new to Israel.

¹⁰"When I found Israel,
it was like finding grapes in the desert;
when I saw your fathers,
it was like seeing the early fruit on the fig
tree.
But when they came to Baal Peor,
they consecrated themselves to that
shameful idol
and became as vile as the thing they
loved.
¹¹Ephraim's glory will fly away like a bird—
no birth, no pregnancy, no conception.
¹²Even if they rear children,
I will bereave them of every one.
Woe to them
when I turn away from them!
¹³I have seen Ephraim, like Tyre,
planted in a pleasant place.
But Ephraim will bring out
their children to the slayer."

¹⁴Give them, O LORD—
what will you give them?

Give them wombs that miscarry
and breasts that are dry.

¹⁵"Because of all their wickedness in Gilgal,
I hated them there.
Because of their sinful deeds,
I will drive them out of my house.
I will no longer love them;
all their leaders are rebellious.
¹⁶Ephraim is blighted,
their root is withered,
they yield no fruit.
Even if they bear children,
I will slay their cherished offspring."

¹⁷My God will reject them
because they have not obeyed him;
they will be wanderers among the nations.

10 Israel was a spreading vine;
he brought forth fruit for himself.
As his fruit increased,
he built more altars;
as his land prospered,
he adorned his sacred stones.
²Their heart is deceitful,
and now they must bear their guilt.
The LORD will demolish their altars
and destroy their sacred stones.

³Then they will say, "We have no king
because we did not revere the LORD.
But even if we had a king,
what could he do for us?"
⁴They make many promises,
take false oaths
and make agreements;
therefore lawsuits spring up
like poisonous weeds in a plowed field.
⁵The people who live in Samaria fear
for the calf-idol of Beth Aven.ᵇ

10:5 The New Golden Calf

Beth Aven ("house of wickedness") is a sarcastic reference to Bethel ("house of God"), which is mentioned more times in the Bible than any other city except Jerusalem. When Israel split into North and South, the northern king, Jeroboam I, made Bethel the chief religious sanctuary, to replace Jerusalem. There he put up a golden calf for people to worship (1 Kings 12:26–30). Mixing worship of the one true God with the idol worship of Baal was, according to Hosea, the root of Israel's trouble.

ᵃ8 Or *The prophet is the watchman over Ephraim, / the people of my God* (a name for Bethel, which means *house of God*).   ᵇ5 *Beth Aven* means *house of wickedness*

Its people will mourn over it,
and so will its idolatrous priests,
those who had rejoiced over its splendor,
because it is taken from them into exile.
⁶It will be carried to Assyria
as tribute for the great king.
Ephraim will be disgraced;
Israel will be ashamed of its wooden
idols.ᵃ
⁷Samaria and its king will float away
like a twig on the surface of the waters.
⁸The high places of wickednessᵇ will be
destroyed—
it is the sin of Israel.
Thorns and thistles will grow up
and cover their altars.
Then they will say to the mountains, "Cover
us!"
and to the hills, "Fall on us!"

⁹"Since the days of Gibeah, you have sinned,
O Israel,
and there you have remained.ᶜ
Did not war overtake
the evildoers in Gibeah?
¹⁰When I please, I will punish them;
nations will be gathered against them
to put them in bonds for their double sin.
¹¹Ephraim is a trained heifer
that loves to thresh;
so I will put a yoke
on her fair neck.
I will drive Ephraim,
Judah must plow,
and Jacob must break up the ground.
¹²Sow for yourselves righteousness,
reap the fruit of unfailing love,
and break up your unplowed ground;
for it is time to seek the LORD,
until he comes
and showers righteousness on you.
¹³But you have planted wickedness,
you have reaped evil,
you have eaten the fruit of deception.
Because you have depended on your own
strength
and on your many warriors,
¹⁴the roar of battle will rise against your people,
so that all your fortresses will be
devastated—
as Shalman devastated Beth Arbel on the day
of battle,
when mothers were dashed to the ground
with their children.
¹⁵Thus will it happen to you, O Bethel,
because your wickedness is great.
When that day dawns,

the king of Israel will be completely
destroyed.

God's Love for Israel

11 "When Israel was a child, I loved him,
and out of Egypt I called my son.

> **11:1 Rebel Son**
>
> *God has already illustrated his unquenchable
> love for Israel through the real-life parable of
> Hosea and his unfaithful wife. Now he
> introduces yet another picture: a rebellious son.
> According to the laws of Deuteronomy, a rebel
> son could be sentenced to death by stoning
> (Deuteronomy 21:18–21). But God cannot
> make himself carry out that sentence (verses
> 8–9). He gives his people one more chance.*

²But the more Iᵈ called Israel,
the further they went from me.ᵉ
They sacrificed to the Baals
and they burned incense to images.
³It was I who taught Ephraim to walk,
taking them by the arms;
but they did not realize
it was I who healed them.
⁴I led them with cords of human kindness,
with ties of love;
I lifted the yoke from their neck
and bent down to feed them.

⁵"Will they not return to Egypt
and will not Assyria rule over them
because they refuse to repent?
⁶Swords will flash in their cities,
will destroy the bars of their gates
and put an end to their plans.
⁷My people are determined to turn from me.
Even if they call to the Most High,
he will by no means exalt them.

⁸"How can I give you up, Ephraim?
How can I hand you over, Israel?
How can I treat you like Admah?
How can I make you like Zeboiim?
My heart is changed within me;
all my compassion is aroused.
⁹I will not carry out my fierce anger,
nor will I turn and devastate Ephraim.
For I am God, and not man—
the Holy One among you.
I will not come in wrath.ᶠ
¹⁰They will follow the LORD;
he will roar like a lion.
When he roars,

ᵃ6 Or *its counsel*   ᵇ8 Hebrew *aven*, a reference to Beth Aven (a derogatory name for Bethel)   ᶜ9 Or *there a stand
was taken*   ᵈ2 Some Septuagint manuscripts; Hebrew *they*   ᵉ2 Septuagint; Hebrew *them*
ᶠ9 Or *come against any city*

his children will come trembling from the
west.

¹¹They will come trembling
like birds from Egypt,
like doves from Assyria.
I will settle them in their homes,"
declares the LORD.

Israel's Sin

¹²Ephraim has surrounded me with lies,
the house of Israel with deceit.
And Judah is unruly against God,
even against the faithful Holy One.

12 ¹Ephraim feeds on the wind;
he pursues the east wind all day
and multiplies lies and violence.
He makes a treaty with Assyria
and sends olive oil to Egypt.
²The LORD has a charge to bring against
Judah;
he will punish Jacob[a] according to his
ways
and repay him according to his deeds.

12:2–5 Jacob, a Man and a Country

*"Israel" was a nation named after a man—a
man also known as Jacob, whose story is told
principally in Genesis 25–35. He was greedy
and grasping, and he went into exile for it. Yet
he had another side: an eagerness to meet God
and be blessed by him, culminating in his
nighttime "wrestling with God" (Genesis 32).
Though Jacob went into exile, as would Israel,
he came back with God's blessing on his future.
So, Hosea suggests, could the nation that
carried his name.*

³In the womb he grasped his brother's heel;
as a man he struggled with God.
⁴He struggled with the angel and overcame
him;
he wept and begged for his favor.
He found him at Bethel
and talked with him there—
⁵the LORD God Almighty,
the LORD is his name of renown!
⁶But you must return to your God;
maintain love and justice,
and wait for your God always.

⁷The merchant uses dishonest scales;
he loves to defraud.
⁸Ephraim boasts,
"I am very rich; I have become wealthy.
With all my wealth they will not find in me
any iniquity or sin."

⁹"I am the LORD your God,
⌞who brought you⌟ out of[b] Egypt;
I will make you live in tents again,
as in the days of your appointed feasts.
¹⁰I spoke to the prophets,
gave them many visions
and told parables through them."

¹¹Is Gilead wicked?
Its people are worthless!
Do they sacrifice bulls in Gilgal?
Their altars will be like piles of stones
on a plowed field.
¹²Jacob fled to the country of Aram[c];
Israel served to get a wife,
and to pay for her he tended sheep.
¹³The LORD used a prophet to bring Israel up
from Egypt,
by a prophet he cared for him.
¹⁴But Ephraim has bitterly provoked him to
anger;
his Lord will leave upon him the guilt of
his bloodshed
and will repay him for his contempt.

The LORD's Anger Against Israel

13 When Ephraim spoke, men trembled;
he was exalted in Israel.
But he became guilty of Baal worship and
died.
²Now they sin more and more;
they make idols for themselves from their
silver,
cleverly fashioned images,
all of them the work of craftsmen.
It is said of these people,
"They offer human sacrifice
and kiss[d] the calf-idols."
³Therefore they will be like the morning mist,
like the early dew that disappears,
like chaff swirling from a threshing floor,
like smoke escaping through a window.

13:3 As Reliable as the Wind

*The fruitlessness of Israel's deeds is beautifully
expressed in the metaphor of wind: They feed
on it, they pursue it all day (12:1), they sow it,
and they reap the whirlwind (8:7). Their love is
like the morning mist, or dew (6:4), and their
lives will be as lasting as the early dew or as
chaff or as smoke escaping out a window
(13:3).*

⁴"But I am the LORD your God,
⌞who brought you⌟ out of[b] Egypt.
You shall acknowledge no God but me,

---

[a]2 *Jacob* means *he grasps the heel* (figuratively, *he deceives*).
Northwest Mesopotamia   [d]2 Or *"Men who sacrifice / kiss*   [b]9,4 Or *God / ever since you were in*   [c]12 That is,

no Savior except me.
⁵I cared for you in the desert,
in the land of burning heat.
⁶When I fed them, they were satisfied;
when they were satisfied, they became
proud;
then they forgot me.
⁷So I will come upon them like a lion,
like a leopard I will lurk by the path.
⁸Like a bear robbed of her cubs,
I will attack them and rip them open.
Like a lion I will devour them;
a wild animal will tear them apart.

⁹"You are destroyed, O Israel,
because you are against me, against your
helper.
¹⁰Where is your king, that he may save you?
Where are your rulers in all your towns,
of whom you said,
'Give me a king and princes'?
¹¹So in my anger I gave you a king,
and in my wrath I took him away.
¹²The guilt of Ephraim is stored up,
his sins are kept on record.
¹³Pains as of a woman in childbirth come to
him,
but he is a child without wisdom;
when the time arrives,
he does not come to the opening of the
womb.
¹⁴"I will ransom them from the power of the
grave[a];
I will redeem them from death.
Where, O death, are your plagues?
Where, O grave,[a] is your destruction?

"I will have no compassion,
15   even though he thrives among his
brothers.
An east wind from the LORD will come,
blowing in from the desert;
his spring will fail
and his well dry up.
His storehouse will be plundered
of all its treasures.
¹⁶The people of Samaria must bear their guilt,
because they have rebelled against their
God.
They will fall by the sword;
their little ones will be dashed to the
ground,
their pregnant women ripped open."

Repentance to Bring Blessing

14 Return, O Israel, to the LORD your God.
Your sins have been your downfall!

²Take words with you
and return to the LORD.
Say to him:
"Forgive all our sins
and receive us graciously,
that we may offer the fruit of our lips.[b]
³Assyria cannot save us;
we will not mount war-horses.
We will never again say 'Our gods'
to what our own hands have made,
for in you the fatherless find compassion."

⁴"I will heal their waywardness
and love them freely,
for my anger has turned away from
them.
⁵I will be like the dew to Israel;
he will blossom like a lily.
Like a cedar of Lebanon
he will send down his roots;

14:5 New Hope

*In its conclusion the book of Hosea, so full of
torment, dissolves into a series of serene
images of what Israel can become. God
compares the nation to a lily (beauty), a cedar
(strength), an olive tree (value), a fragrant tree
(delight), grain (abundance), a grapevine
(fruitfulness). Thus a book dominated by
images of unfaithfulness—an adulterous wife, a
rebellious son—ends with the firm promise of
restoration.*

⁶   his young shoots will grow.
His splendor will be like an olive tree,
his fragrance like a cedar of Lebanon.
⁷Men will dwell again in his shade.
He will flourish like the grain.
He will blossom like a vine,
and his fame will be like the wine from
Lebanon.
⁸O Ephraim, what more have I[c] to do with
idols?
I will answer him and care for him.
I am like a green pine tree;
your fruitfulness comes from me."

⁹Who is wise? He will realize these things.
Who is discerning? He will understand
them.
The ways of the LORD are right;
the righteous walk in them,
but the rebellious stumble in them.

---

a14 Hebrew *Sheol*   *b2* Or *offer our lips as sacrifices of bulls*   *c8* Or *What more has Ephraim*

JOEL

The Meaning of a Natural Disaster
What's behind a devastating locust plague?

THEIR NUMBER WAS ASTOUNDING; THE whole face of the mountain was black with them. On they came like a living deluge. We dug trenches, and kindled fires, and beat and burned to death 'heaps upon heaps'; but the effort was utterly useless. Wave after wave rolled up the mountainside and poured over rocks, walls, ditches and hedges—those behind covering up and bridging over the masses already killed. It was perfectly appalling to watch this animated river as it flowed up the road and ascended the hill above my house. For four days they continued to pass on toward the east . . . ."

> *Before them the earth shakes, the sky trembles, the sun and moon are darkened, and the stars no longer shine.*
> *2:10*

Eyewitness W. M. Thomson is describing a locust plague. Descriptions of the aftermath sound just as awful. When locusts have passed, the terrain looks as though it has been swept by a scorching fire.

Why Have I Lived?

Many awestruck observers have written accounts of locust swarms, but none more graphically than the prophet Joel. In striking, polished imagery he described the devastation. His people faced starvation. Joel drew a verbal portrait of grief and fear.

Natural disasters provoke questions. Why did God allow this disaster to happen? Why have I lived and others died? Is there a lesson here? For Joel, a plague of locusts led to deep insights into God's universal plan.

Joel had no doubt that God was behind the plague. In fact, he pictured God leading the locusts like an army into battle (2:11). They represented "the day of the Lord," a judgment on Israel. Unlike many of the other prophets, Joel did not devote time to an analysis of Israel's failings. He concentrated, instead, on a cure.

Joel urged the priests to call a nationwide day of prayer and fasting to lead the people back to God. Then God would roll back the damage done by the locusts, and more: "You will have plenty to eat, until you are full, and you will praise the name of the Lord your God, who has worked wonders for you" (2:26). They would emerge from the experience with new, durable confidence in God's love. So it has often proved for God's people: A disaster has pressed them to a deeper relationship with him.

God's Bigger Plans

Though the locust plague was by far the worst Joel had ever heard of (1:2–3), no historical record of this particular invasion has endured, other than the one Joel left us. The truth is, even the worst natural disasters fade from memory. Joel wanted the disaster to turn people's attention toward something more lasting—toward an eternal God.

Joel wanted God's people to believe that God controlled the locusts, and, even more important, that God shaped the entire course of history to his plan. As terribly as the locusts had destroyed, and as wonderfully as God had rolled back their destruction, these events only foreshadowed far more terrible and wonderful things. Joel saw that God's Spirit would transform his people into those who love him constantly, not just when a disaster catches their attention. After a time of terrible judgment, God would create a renewed, secure city for his people, in which he himself would live.

How to Read Joel

Joel breaks naturally into two parts. Up to 2:28, it talks about a locust invasion and the response of God's people to such a natural disaster. From that verse on, however, Joel's view rises above the local situation and deals with the far-off future.

Joel rarely refers to unfamiliar people, places, or events, so you can read it fairly easily without using any outside reference like a Bible dictionary. The challenge is to connect his understanding of a natural disaster—a locust plague—with his vision of the future.

The Bible often refers to "the day of the LORD" as the time when God will completely take charge of our world. But Joel seems to see "the day of the LORD" partly revealed in the disasters of his day. As you read, try to see the similarities Joel draws between the locust invasion and the final consummation of history. Ask yourself: How do I respond to disaster? How would Joel want me to respond?

3-TRACK READING PLAN

For an explanation and complete listing of the 3-track reading plan, turn to page 7.

TRACK 1: **Two-Week Courses on the Bible**
See page 7 for information on these courses.

TRACK 2: **An Overview of Joel in 1 Day**
☐ Day 1. Read the Introduction to Joel and chapter 2, which describes the locust plague and its effect on the people's relationship with God.
Now turn to page 9 for your next Track 2 reading project.

TRACK 3: **All of Joel in 3 Days**
After you have read through Joel, turn to pages 10–14 for your next Track 3 reading project.
☐1   ☐2   ☐3

---

1 The word of the LORD that came to Joel son of Pethuel.

An Invasion of Locusts

²Hear this, you elders;
    listen, all who live in the land.
Has anything like this ever happened in your
        days
    or in the days of your forefathers?
³Tell it to your children,
    and let your children tell it to their
        children,
    and their children to the next generation.
⁴What the locust swarm has left
    the great locusts have eaten;
what the great locusts have left
    the young locusts have eaten;
what the young locusts have left
    other locusts^a have eaten.

⁵Wake up, you drunkards, and weep!
    Wail, all you drinkers of wine;
wail because of the new wine,
    for it has been snatched from your lips.
⁶A nation has invaded my land,

powerful and without number;
    it has the teeth of a lion,
        the fangs of a lioness.

1:4 Doomsday

Nowadays we tend to think of doomsday in terms of nuclear holocaust. But until recent times the most powerful weapons in the world belonged to nature. Earthquakes, floods, and plagues of illness caused far more destruction than arrows, spears, and swords. Natural disasters were frightening and unpredictable: A plague of locusts, for example, could wipe out an entire food supply overnight.

⁷It has laid waste my vines
    and ruined my fig trees.
It has stripped off their bark
    and thrown it away,
        leaving their branches white.

⁸Mourn like a virgin^b in sackcloth
    grieving for the husband^c of her youth.
⁹Grain offerings and drink offerings

---

^a 4 The precise meaning of the four Hebrew words used here for locusts is uncertain.   ^b 8 Or *young woman*
^c 8 Or *betrothed*

are cut off from the house of the LORD.
The priests are in mourning,
  those who minister before the LORD.
[10]The fields are ruined,
  the ground is dried up[a];
the grain is destroyed,
  the new wine is dried up,
  the oil fails.
[11]Despair, you farmers,
  wail, you vine growers;
grieve for the wheat and the barley,
  because the harvest of the field is
    destroyed.
[12]The vine is dried up
  and the fig tree is withered;
the pomegranate, the palm and the apple
    tree—
  all the trees of the field—are dried up.
Surely the joy of mankind
  is withered away.

A Call to Repentance

[13]Put on sackcloth, O priests, and mourn;
  wail, you who minister before the altar.
Come, spend the night in sackcloth,
  you who minister before my God;
for the grain offerings and drink offerings
  are withheld from the house of your
    God.
[14]Declare a holy fast;
  call a sacred assembly.
Summon the elders
  and all who live in the land
to the house of the LORD your God,
  and cry out to the LORD.

[15]Alas for that day!
  For the day of the LORD is near;
  it will come like destruction from the
    Almighty.[b]

[16]Has not the food been cut off
  before our very eyes—
joy and gladness
  from the house of our God?
[17]The seeds are shriveled
  beneath the clods.[c]
The storehouses are in ruins,
  the granaries have been broken down,
  for the grain has dried up.
[18]How the cattle moan!
  The herds mill about
because they have no pasture;
  even the flocks of sheep are suffering.

[19]To you, O LORD, I call,
  for fire has devoured the open pastures

and flames have burned up all the trees of
  the field.
[20]Even the wild animals pant for you;
  the streams of water have dried up
  and fire has devoured the open pastures.

1:18 Total Devastation

No wine for the drunkards, no husbands for young brides, no crops for the farmers, no offerings for the priests—the disaster was affecting every part of society. Cattle moaned, sheep wandered in starvation. People had nowhere to turn but God, concluded Joel. So why didn't they?

An Army of Locusts

2 Blow the trumpet in Zion;
  sound the alarm on my holy hill.
Let all who live in the land tremble,
  for the day of the LORD is coming.
It is close at hand—
[2] a day of darkness and gloom,
  a day of clouds and blackness.
Like dawn spreading across the mountains
  a large and mighty army comes,
such as never was of old
  nor ever will be in ages to come.

[3]Before them fire devours,
  behind them a flame blazes.
Before them the land is like the garden of
    Eden,
  behind them, a desert waste—
  nothing escapes them.
[4]They have the appearance of horses;
  they gallop along like cavalry.
[5]With a noise like that of chariots
  they leap over the mountaintops,
like a crackling fire consuming stubble,
  like a mighty army drawn up for battle.

[6]At the sight of them, nations are in anguish;
  every face turns pale.
[7]They charge like warriors;
  they scale walls like soldiers.
They all march in line,
  not swerving from their course.
[8]They do not jostle each other;
  each marches straight ahead.
They plunge through defenses
  without breaking ranks.
[9]They rush upon the city;
  they run along the wall.
They climb into the houses;
  like thieves they enter through the
    windows.

---

[a]10 Or *ground mourns*   [b]15 Hebrew *Shaddai*   [c]17 The meaning of the Hebrew for this word is uncertain.

¹⁰Before them the earth shakes,
　the sky trembles,
the sun and moon are darkened,
　and the stars no longer shine.
¹¹The LORD thunders
　at the head of his army;
his forces are beyond number,
　and mighty are those who obey his
　　command.
The day of the LORD is great;
　it is dreadful.
　Who can endure it?

Rend Your Heart

¹²"Even now," declares the LORD,
　"return to me with all your heart,
　with fasting and weeping and mourning."

¹³Rend your heart
　and not your garments.
Return to the LORD your God,
　for he is gracious and compassionate,
slow to anger and abounding in love,
　and he relents from sending calamity.

2:13 Torn Hearts

*In the Old Testament, men and women tore
their robes as a sign of sorrow and mourning.
(Some Middle Easterners do so still.) Jacob,
Moses, Joshua, Elijah, David, and Job all tore
their clothes as an expression of grief or
anguish. In Joel's day, however, God looked for
change on the inside, not just another outward
show of remorse. He sought broken hearts, not
torn garments.*

¹⁴Who knows? He may turn and have pity
　and leave behind a blessing—
grain offerings and drink offerings
　for the LORD your God.

¹⁵Blow the trumpet in Zion,
　declare a holy fast,
　call a sacred assembly.
¹⁶Gather the people,
　consecrate the assembly;
bring together the elders,
　gather the children,
　those nursing at the breast.
Let the bridegroom leave his room
　and the bride her chamber.
¹⁷Let the priests, who minister before the
　　LORD,
　weep between the temple porch and the
　　altar.

Let them say, "Spare your people, O LORD.
Do not make your inheritance an object
　of scorn,
　a byword among the nations.
Why should they say among the peoples,
　'Where is their God?'"

The LORD's Answer

¹⁸Then the LORD will be jealous for his land
　and take pity on his people.

¹⁹The LORD will reply^a to them:

"I am sending you grain, new wine and oil,
　enough to satisfy you fully;
never again will I make you
　an object of scorn to the nations.

²⁰"I will drive the northern army far from you,
　pushing it into a parched and barren land,
with its front columns going into the eastern
　　sea^b
　and those in the rear into the western
　　sea.^{c}
And its stench will go up;
　its smell will rise."

Surely he has done great things.^{d}
²¹　Be not afraid, O land;
　be glad and rejoice.
Surely the LORD has done great things.
²²　Be not afraid, O wild animals,
　for the open pastures are becoming green.
The trees are bearing their fruit;
　the fig tree and the vine yield their riches.
²³Be glad, O people of Zion,
　rejoice in the LORD your God,
for he has given you
　the autumn rains in righteousness.^{e}
He sends you abundant showers,
　both autumn and spring rains, as before.
²⁴The threshing floors will be filled with grain;
　the vats will overflow with new wine and
　　oil.

²⁵"I will repay you for the years the locusts
　　have eaten—
　the great locust and the young locust,
　the other locusts and the locust
　　swarm^f—
my great army that I sent among you.
²⁶You will have plenty to eat, until you are
　　full,
　and you will praise the name of the LORD
　　your God,
　who has worked wonders for you;
never again will my people be shamed.
²⁷Then you will know that I am in Israel,
　that I am the LORD your God,

---

^{a}18,19 Or LORD was jealous . . . / and took pity . . . / ¹⁹The LORD replied　　^{b}20 That is, the Dead Sea　^{c}20 That is,
the Mediterranean　　^{d}20 Or rise. / Surely it has done great things."　^{e}23 Or / the teacher for righteousness:
^{f}25 The precise meaning of the four Hebrew words used here for locusts is uncertain.

and that there is no other;
never again will my people be shamed.

The Day of the LORD

28"And afterward,
I will pour out my Spirit on all people.
Your sons and daughters will prophesy,
your old men will dream dreams,
your young men will see visions.
29Even on my servants, both men and women,
I will pour out my Spirit in those days.

2:29 The Spirit Poured Out

This prophecy was quoted by Peter on the day of Pentecost (Acts 2:17–21). He said it had been fulfilled when the Holy Spirit came on Jesus' disciples. Paul also quoted verse 32 in Romans 10:12–13, making the point that God would respond to Jews and non-Jews without distinction.

30I will show wonders in the heavens
and on the earth,
blood and fire and billows of smoke.
31The sun will be turned to darkness
and the moon to blood
before the coming of the great and
dreadful day of the LORD.
32And everyone who calls
on the name of the LORD will be saved;
for on Mount Zion and in Jerusalem
there will be deliverance,
as the LORD has said,
among the survivors
whom the LORD calls.

The Nations Judged

3 "In those days and at that time,
when I restore the fortunes of Judah and
Jerusalem,
2I will gather all nations
and bring them down to the Valley of
Jehoshaphat.[a]
There I will enter into judgment against
them
concerning my inheritance, my people
Israel,
for they scattered my people among the
nations
and divided up my land.
3They cast lots for my people
and traded boys for prostitutes;
they sold girls for wine
that they might drink.

4"Now what have you against me, O Tyre and

Sidon and all you regions of Philistia? Are you repaying me for something I have done? If you are paying me back, I will swiftly and speedily return on your own heads what you have done.

3:3 Gambling Prizes

The Babylonians who invaded Judah fulfilled this prophecy literally: They seized captives as part of the spoils of war, divided them up by casting lots, then traded them for prostitutes and wine. In this section, God promises vengeance on such war crimes.

5For you took my silver and my gold and carried off my finest treasures to your temples. 6You sold the people of Judah and Jerusalem to the Greeks, that you might send them far from their homeland.
7"See, I am going to rouse them out of the places to which you sold them, and I will return on your own heads what you have done. 8I will sell your sons and daughters to the people of Judah, and they will sell them to the Sabeans, a nation far away." The LORD has spoken.

9Proclaim this among the nations:
Prepare for war!
Rouse the warriors!
Let all the fighting men draw near and
attack.
10Beat your plowshares into swords
and your pruning hooks into spears.
Let the weakling say,
"I am strong!"
11Come quickly, all you nations from every
side,
and assemble there.

Bring down your warriors, O LORD!

12"Let the nations be roused;
let them advance into the Valley of
Jehoshaphat,
for there I will sit
to judge all the nations on every side.
13Swing the sickle,
for the harvest is ripe.
Come, trample the grapes,
for the winepress is full
and the vats overflow—
so great is their wickedness!"

14Multitudes, multitudes
in the valley of decision!
For the day of the LORD is near
in the valley of decision.
15The sun and moon will be darkened,
and the stars no longer shine.

a 2 Jehoshaphat means the LORD judges; also in verse 12.

¹⁶The LORD will roar from Zion
and thunder from Jerusalem;
the earth and the sky will tremble.
But the LORD will be a refuge for his
people,
a stronghold for the people of Israel.

Blessings for God's People

¹⁷"Then you will know that I, the LORD your
God,
dwell in Zion, my holy hill.
Jerusalem will be holy;
never again will foreigners invade her.

¹⁸"In that day the mountains will drip new
wine,
and the hills will flow with milk;
all the ravines of Judah will run with
water.
A fountain will flow out of the LORD's house
and will water the valley of acacias. [a]
¹⁹But Egypt will be desolate,
Edom a desert waste,
because of violence done to the people of
Judah,
in whose land they shed innocent blood.
²⁰Judah will be inhabited forever
and Jerusalem through all generations.
²¹Their bloodguilt, which I have not pardoned,
I will pardon."

The LORD dwells in Zion!

---

[a] 18 Or *Valley of Shittim*

AMOS

Justice!
A simple farmer takes on a materialistic nation

> "Let justice roll on like a river, righteousness like a never-failing stream!" 5:24

BUSINESS HAD NEVER BEEN BETTER. For the first time in generations, Israel faced no military threat. Since they controlled the crucial trade routes, merchants piled up big profits. Luxuries became readily available—new stone houses, ivory-inlaid furniture, top-grade meat and fine wine, the best body lotions.

Amid such peace and prosperity, one lone voice scraped like fingernails on a blackboard. Amos spoke bluntly with a farmer's vocabulary, calling the city socialites "cows" (4:1). A mere shepherd—among the poorest of all professions—he treated luxury with scorn. Worst of all, Amos was a foreigner from the South—from Tekoa, a small town in Judah. Since Israel had split from the South about 170 years before, Israelite leaders did not take kindly to criticism from a southerner.

But to Amos, social acceptance didn't matter. He was no professional prophet, making his living talking smoothly about God (7:14). God had called him to leave his job and carry a message. God had said go, and Amos had obeyed.

God's View of "Religion"

The people Amos addressed had plenty of "religion." They went regularly to shrines for worship. They looked forward to "the day of the Lord," when God would fulfill all their expectations for their country. But Amos brought unexpected bad news from God: "I hate, I despise your religious feasts" (5:21). God didn't want sacrifice or singing. He demanded justice.

Amos listed all Israel's neighbors, announcing God's judgment for their crimes against humanity. Israelites liked this kind of talk; they felt superior to all these nations. But having caught the Israelites' attention, Amos circled dramatically home. God would judge Israel too. The people, their beautiful homes, their sacred altars—all would be destroyed.

The Character of God

More than any other book in the Bible, Amos concentrates on injustice. Israel had plenty of other faults he might have blasted. Their religious system, for instance, centered on two calf-idols. But Amos wasted little breath on that. He focused on the facts that met his eyes and ears in every marketplace: oppression of the poor, dishonest business, bribery in court, privilege bought with money.

The wealthy Israelites were getting their luxuries at the expense of the poor. They congratulated themselves on their devotion to God with no sense that they had cut the heart out of their relationship to him. They wanted God to fit conveniently into life as an additive. God showed himself through Amos as lordly, absolute, inescapable. He must be master over all of life, including business affairs.

How to Read Amos

Perhaps because he was a farmer, Amos used a plain writing style, filled with strong country language. The organization of his book is clear too: chapters 1–2 line up the Middle Eastern nations for trial, chapters 3–6 give a series of messages from God (usually beginning with "Hear this word"), and the last three chapters convey God's judgment through five graphic visions.

Throughout, Amos sticks close to his main concern: cruelty and inhumanity between people. The injustices Amos condemns often sound familiar today. As you read, ask yourself, "What would Amos say about me and about my people?"

It is a good idea to read Amos and Hosea together, for they give two views of the same situation. A visitor from the South, Amos was shocked by the injustices he saw in every marketplace. Hosea emphasized the inner dimension, an abused relationship to a loving God.

Amos predicted that Israel would be punished, and his prediction proved right. After King Jeroboam, the government deteriorated. Five kings took the throne in the next 13 years; four were assassinated. In 30 years Israel was permanently dismantled by Assyrian armies. For historical background, read 2 Kings 14:23—17:41, noting that the kings of both Israel and Judah are interspersed. For a briefer account, read the summaries of their reigns in "A Lineup of Rulers," pages 1361–1369.

3-TRACK READING PLAN

For an explanation and complete listing of the 3-track reading plan, turn to page 7.

TRACK 1: **Two-Week Courses on the Bible**
The Track 1 reading program on the Old Testament includes one chapter from Amos. See page 8 for a complete listing of this course.

TRACK 2: **An Overview of Amos in 1 Day**
☐ Day 1. Read the Introduction to Amos and chapter 4, which sums up God's majestic anger against his people.

Now turn to page 9 for your next Track 2 reading project.

TRACK 3: **All of Amos in 9 Days**
After you have read through Amos, turn to pages 10–14 for your next Track 3 reading project.

☐1 ☐2 ☐3 ☐4 ☐5 ☐6 ☐7 ☐8
☐9

---

1 The words of Amos, one of the shepherds of Tekoa—what he saw concerning Israel two years before the earthquake, when Uzziah was king of Judah and Jeroboam son of Jehoash[a] was king of Israel.

²He said:

"The LORD roars from Zion
and thunders from Jerusalem;
the pastures of the shepherds dry up,[b]
and the top of Carmel withers."

Judgment on Israel's Neighbors

³This is what the LORD says:

"For three sins of Damascus,
even for four, I will not turn back ⌊my wrath⌋.
Because she threshed Gilead
with sledges having iron teeth,
⁴I will send fire upon the house of Hazael
that will consume the fortresses of Ben-Hadad.
⁵I will break down the gate of Damascus;

I will destroy the king who is in[c] the Valley of Aven[d]
and the one who holds the scepter in Beth Eden.
The people of Aram will go into exile to Kir,"

says the LORD.

⁶This is what the LORD says:

"For three sins of Gaza,
even for four, I will not turn back ⌊my wrath⌋.
Because she took captive whole communities
and sold them to Edom,
⁷I will send fire upon the walls of Gaza
that will consume her fortresses.
⁸I will destroy the king[e] of Ashdod
and the one who holds the scepter in Ashkelon.
I will turn my hand against Ekron,
till the last of the Philistines is dead,"

says the Sovereign LORD.

⁹This is what the LORD says:

---

a 1 Hebrew Joash, a variant of Jehoash   *b 2 Or shepherds mourn*   *c 5 Or the inhabitants of*   *d 5 Aven means wickedness.*   *e 8 Or inhabitants*

"For three sins of Tyre,
   even for four, I will not turn back ⌐my
      wrath⌐.
Because she sold whole communities of
      captives to Edom,
   disregarding a treaty of brotherhood,

1:9 Atrocities

*Amos began with thundering pronouncements
against the enemies of Israel and Judah. His
local audience must have cheered as he called
down judgment on the blatant misdeeds of
their neighbors: selling slaves, breaking
treaties, ripping open pregnant women,
desecrating the dead. But then Amos turned his
attention to his own countrymen (2:4–16). God
held his people to a far higher standard of
morality. Israelites failed by breaking God's
law; their neighbors were judged guilty of
"crimes against humanity," for breaking laws
of common decency.*

¹⁰I will send fire upon the walls of Tyre
   that will consume her fortresses."

¹¹This is what the LORD says:

"For three sins of Edom,
   even for four, I will not turn back ⌐my
      wrath⌐.
Because he pursued his brother with a
      sword,
   stifling all compassion,ᵃ
because his anger raged continually
   and his fury flamed unchecked,
¹²I will send fire upon Teman
   that will consume the fortresses of
      Bozrah."

¹³This is what the LORD says:

"For three sins of Ammon,
   even for four, I will not turn back ⌐my
      wrath⌐.
Because he ripped open the pregnant women
      of Gilead
   in order to extend his borders,
¹⁴I will set fire to the walls of Rabbah
   that will consume her fortresses
amid war cries on the day of battle,
   amid violent winds on a stormy day.
¹⁵Her kingᵇ will go into exile,
   he and his officials together,"
                          says the LORD.

2 This is what the LORD says:

"For three sins of Moab,

even for four, I will not turn back ⌐my
      wrath⌐.
Because he burned, as if to lime,
   the bones of Edom's king,
²I will send fire upon Moab
   that will consume the fortresses of
      Kerioth.ᶜ
Moab will go down in great tumult
   amid war cries and the blast of the
      trumpet.
³I will destroy her ruler
   and kill all her officials with him,"
                          says the LORD.

⁴This is what the LORD says:

"For three sins of Judah,
   even for four, I will not turn back ⌐my
      wrath⌐.
Because they have rejected the law of the
      LORD
   and have not kept his decrees,
because they have been led astray by false
      gods,ᵈ
   the godsᵉ their ancestors followed,
⁵I will send fire upon Judah
   that will consume the fortresses of
      Jerusalem."

Judgment on Israel

⁶This is what the LORD says:

"For three sins of Israel,
   even for four, I will not turn back ⌐my
      wrath⌐.
They sell the righteous for silver,
   and the needy for a pair of sandals.
⁷They trample on the heads of the poor
   as upon the dust of the ground
   and deny justice to the oppressed.
Father and son use the same girl
   and so profane my holy name.
⁸They lie down beside every altar
   on garments taken in pledge.
In the house of their god
   they drink wine taken as fines.

2:8 Ruthless Bill Collectors

*Bankers making loans usually want collateral
to back up the promise to repay. In Amos's day
poor people resorted to pledging the very
clothes on their backs as collateral. Bill
collectors who took a debtor's garments
flagrantly violated God's law (Exodus
22:25–27). Worse, they were using the clothes
as bedding when they went to their shrines to
worship God.*

ᵃ11 Or *sword / and destroyed his allies*   ᵇ15 Or *l Molech*; Hebrew *malcam*   ᶜ2 Or *of her cities*   ᵈ4 Or *by lies*
ᵉ4 Or *lies*

⁹"I destroyed the Amorite before them,
  though he was tall as the cedars
  and strong as the oaks.
I destroyed his fruit above
  and his roots below.

¹⁰"I brought you up out of Egypt,
  and I led you forty years in the desert
  to give you the land of the Amorites.
¹¹I also raised up prophets from among your
    sons
  and Nazirites from among your young
    men.
Is this not true, people of Israel?"
                        declares the LORD.
¹²"But you made the Nazirites drink wine
  and commanded the prophets not to
    prophesy.

¹³"Now then, I will crush you
  as a cart crushes when loaded with grain.
¹⁴The swift will not escape,
  the strong will not muster their strength,
  and the warrior will not save his life.
¹⁵The archer will not stand his ground,
  the fleet-footed soldier will not get away,
  and the horseman will not save his life.
¹⁶Even the bravest warriors
  will flee naked on that day,"
                        declares the LORD.

Witnesses Summoned Against Israel

3 Hear this word the LORD has spoken against
you, O people of Israel—against the whole
family I brought up out of Egypt:

²"You only have I chosen
  of all the families of the earth;
therefore I will punish you
  for all your sins."

³Do two walk together
  unless they have agreed to do so?
⁴Does a lion roar in the thicket
  when he has no prey?
Does he growl in his den
  when he has caught nothing?
⁵Does a bird fall into a trap on the ground
  where no snare has been set?
Does a trap spring up from the earth
  when there is nothing to catch?
⁶When a trumpet sounds in a city,
  do not the people tremble?
When disaster comes to a city,
  has not the LORD caused it?

⁷Surely the Sovereign LORD does nothing
  without revealing his plan
  to his servants the prophets.

⁸The lion has roared—

who will not fear?
The Sovereign LORD has spoken—
  who can but prophesy?

⁹Proclaim to the fortresses of Ashdod
  and to the fortresses of Egypt:
"Assemble yourselves on the mountains of
    Samaria;
  see the great unrest within her
  and the oppression among her people."

¹⁰"They do not know how to do right,"
                  declares the LORD,
  "who hoard plunder and loot in their
    fortresses."

¹¹Therefore this is what the Sovereign LORD
says:

  "An enemy will overrun the land;
    he will pull down your strongholds
    and plunder your fortresses."

¹²This is what the LORD says:

  "As a shepherd saves from the lion's mouth
    only two leg bones or a piece of an ear,
    so will the Israelites be saved,
  those who sit in Samaria
    on the edge of their beds
    and in Damascus on their couches.ᵃ"

¹³"Hear this and testify against the house of
Jacob," declares the Lord, the LORD God Almighty.

¹⁴"On the day I punish Israel for her sins,
  I will destroy the altars of Bethel;
  the horns of the altar will be cut off
  and fall to the ground.
¹⁵I will tear down the winter house
  along with the summer house;
  the houses adorned with ivory will be
    destroyed
  and the mansions will be demolished,"
                        declares the LORD.

Israel Has Not Returned to God

4 Hear this word, you cows of Bashan on
    Mount Samaria,
  you women who oppress the poor and
    crush the needy
  and say to your husbands, "Bring us some
    drinks!"
²The Sovereign LORD has sworn by his
    holiness:
  "The time will surely come
  when you will be taken away with hooks,
    the last of you with fishhooks.
³You will each go straight out
  through breaks in the wall,

ᵃ12 The meaning of the Hebrew for this line is uncertain.

and you will be cast out toward
Harmon,ᵃ"
                                    declares the LORD.

⁴"Go to Bethel and sin;
    go to Gilgal and sin yet more.
Bring your sacrifices every morning,
    your tithes every three years.ᵇ

4:1 Prize Cows

With searing scornfulness, Amos paints a picture of women living in sheer luxury. These "cows" thought only of their pleasure, not of the oppressed poor who made their life of luxury possible. Amos paints their punishment just as vividly. The brutal Assyrian armies, who later captured Israel and took its people into exile, left monuments portraying their captives being dragged off with hooks in their mouths.

⁵Burn leavened bread as a thank offering
    and brag about your freewill offerings—
boast about them, you Israelites,
    for this is what you love to do,"
                        declares the Sovereign LORD.

⁶"I gave you empty stomachsᶜ in every city
    and lack of bread in every town,
yet you have not returned to me,"
                                    declares the LORD.

⁷"I also withheld rain from you
    when the harvest was still three months
        away.
I sent rain on one town,
    but withheld it from another.
One field had rain;
    another had none and dried up.
⁸People staggered from town to town for
        water
    but did not get enough to drink,
yet you have not returned to me,"
                                    declares the LORD.

⁹"Many times I struck your gardens and
        vineyards,
    I struck them with blight and mildew.
Locusts devoured your fig and olive trees,
    yet you have not returned to me,"
                                    declares the LORD.

¹⁰"I sent plagues among you
    as I did to Egypt.
I killed your young men with the sword,
    along with your captured horses.
I filled your nostrils with the stench of your
        camps,

yet you have not returned to me,"
                                    declares the LORD.

¹¹"I overthrew some of you
    as Iᵈ overthrew Sodom and Gomorrah.
You were like a burning stick snatched from
        the fire,
    yet you have not returned to me,"
                                    declares the LORD.

¹²"Therefore this is what I will do to you,
        Israel,
    and because I will do this to you,
    prepare to meet your God, O Israel."

4:12 Before It's Too Late

This is the most famous verse in Amos, thanks to graffiti artists who write "Prepare to meet thy God!" in unlikely places. Amos has just reviewed a series of natural disasters—famine, drought, blight, plagues, war—any of which should have been enough to turn the nation to God. But Israel did not respond, and now Amos is holding out one last chance for repentance.

¹³He who forms the mountains,
        creates the wind,
    and reveals his thoughts to man,
he who turns dawn to darkness,
    and treads the high places of the earth—
    the LORD God Almighty is his name.

A Lament and Call to Repentance

5 Hear this word, O house of Israel, this lament
    I take up concerning you:

²"Fallen is Virgin Israel,
        never to rise again,
deserted in her own land,
    with no one to lift her up."

³This is what the Sovereign LORD says:

"The city that marches out a thousand
        strong for Israel
    will have only a hundred left;
the town that marches out a hundred strong
    will have only ten left."

⁴This is what the LORD says to the house of
    Israel:

"Seek me and live;
⁵   do not seek Bethel,
    do not go to Gilgal,
    do not journey to Beersheba.
For Gilgal will surely go into exile,
    and Bethel will be reduced to nothing.ᵉ"

ᵃ3 Masoretic Text; with a different word division of the Hebrew (see Septuagint) *out, O mountain of oppression*
ᵇ4 Or *tithes on the third day*   ᶜ6 Hebrew *you cleanness of teeth*   ᵈ11 Hebrew *God*   ᵉ5 Or *grief*; or *wickedness*;
Hebrew *aven*, a reference to Beth Aven (a derogatory name for Bethel)

[6]Seek the LORD and live,
or he will sweep through the house of
Joseph like a fire;
it will devour,
and Bethel will have no one to quench it.

[7]You who turn justice into bitterness
and cast righteousness to the ground
[8](he who made the Pleiades and Orion,
who turns blackness into dawn
and darkens day into night,
who calls for the waters of the sea
and pours them out over the face of the
land—
the LORD is his name—
[9]he flashes destruction on the stronghold
and brings the fortified city to ruin),
[10]you hate the one who reproves in court
and despise him who tells the truth.

[11]You trample on the poor
and force him to give you grain.
Therefore, though you have built stone
mansions,
you will not live in them;
though you have planted lush vineyards,
you will not drink their wine.
[12]For I know how many are your offenses
and how great your sins.

You oppress the righteous and take bribes
and you deprive the poor of justice in the
courts.
[13]Therefore the prudent man keeps quiet in
such times,
for the times are evil.

[14]Seek good, not evil,
that you may live.
Then the LORD God Almighty will be with
you,
just as you say he is.
[15]Hate evil, love good;
maintain justice in the courts.
Perhaps the LORD God Almighty will have
mercy
on the remnant of Joseph.

[16]Therefore this is what the Lord, the LORD
God Almighty, says:

"There will be wailing in all the streets
and cries of anguish in every public
square.
The farmers will be summoned to weep
and the mourners to wail.
[17]There will be wailing in all the vineyards,
for I will pass through your midst,"
says the LORD.

The Day of the LORD

[18]Woe to you who long
for the day of the LORD!
Why do you long for the day of the LORD?
That day will be darkness, not light.
[19]It will be as though a man fled from a lion
only to meet a bear,
as though he entered his house
and rested his hand on the wall
only to have a snake bite him.
[20]Will not the day of the LORD be darkness,
not light—
pitch-dark, without a ray of brightness?

5:20 The Day of the Lord

*In Amos's day as today, some religious people
looked forward to "the day of the LORD," when
God will intervene personally in history and
save his people. Israelites, assuming that "God
is on our side," thought it would be a great day
for them. But Amos contradicted their
expectations. In a few words he depicted "the
day of the LORD" as a nightmare.*

[21]"I hate, I despise your religious feasts;
I cannot stand your assemblies.
[22]Even though you bring me burnt offerings
and grain offerings,
I will not accept them.
Though you bring choice fellowship
offerings,[a]
I will have no regard for them.
[23]Away with the noise of your songs!
I will not listen to the music of your
harps.
[24]But let justice roll on like a river,
righteousness like a never-failing stream!

[25]"Did you bring me sacrifices and offerings
forty years in the desert, O house of
Israel?
[26]You have lifted up the shrine of your king,
the pedestal of your idols,
the star of your god[b]—
which you made for yourselves.
[27]Therefore I will send you into exile beyond
Damascus,"
says the LORD, whose name is God
Almighty.

Woe to the Complacent

6 Woe to you who are complacent in Zion,
and to you who feel secure on Mount
Samaria,
you notable men of the foremost nation,

[a]22 Traditionally *peace offerings*   [b]26 Or *lifted up Sakkuth your king / and Kaiwan your idols, / your star-gods*;
Septuagint *lifted up the shrine of Molech / and the star of your god Rephan, / their idols*

to whom the people of Israel come!
²Go to Calneh and look at it;
go from there to great Hamath,
and then go down to Gath in Philistia.

6:1 Soft and Fat

Amos is at his sarcastic best in this message to "the notable men of the foremost nation." Consistently, Israel proved much better at handling hardship than success. In prosperous times like Amos's they grew addicted to luxury and power, forgetting all about God. Hundreds of years before, Moses had warned against this very syndrome (Deuteronomy 8:10–20).

Are they better off than your two kingdoms?
Is their land larger than yours?
³You put off the evil day
and bring near a reign of terror.
⁴You lie on beds inlaid with ivory
and lounge on your couches.
You dine on choice lambs
and fattened calves.
⁵You strum away on your harps like David
and improvise on musical instruments.
⁶You drink wine by the bowlful
and use the finest lotions,
but you do not grieve over the ruin of
Joseph.
⁷Therefore you will be among the first to go
into exile;
your feasting and lounging will end.

The LORD Abhors the Pride of Israel

⁸The Sovereign LORD has sworn by himself—
the LORD God Almighty declares:

"I abhor the pride of Jacob
and detest his fortresses;
I will deliver up the city
and everything in it."

⁹If ten men are left in one house, they too will die. ¹⁰And if a relative who is to burn the bodies comes to carry them out of the house and asks anyone still hiding there, "Is anyone with you?" and he says, "No," then he will say, "Hush! We must not mention the name of the LORD."

¹¹For the LORD has given the command,
and he will smash the great house into
pieces
and the small house into bits.

¹²Do horses run on the rocky crags?
Does one plow there with oxen?
But you have turned justice into poison

and the fruit of righteousness into
bitterness—
¹³you who rejoice in the conquest of Lo
Debar[a]
and say, "Did we not take Karnaim[b] by
our own strength?"

¹⁴For the LORD God Almighty declares,
"I will stir up a nation against you,
O house of Israel,
that will oppress you all the way
from Lebo[c] Hamath to the valley of the
Arabah."

Locusts, Fire and a Plumb Line

7 This is what the Sovereign LORD showed me: He was preparing swarms of locusts after the king's share had been harvested and just as the second crop was coming up. ²When they had stripped the land clean, I cried out, "Sovereign LORD, forgive! How can Jacob survive? He is so small!"

³So the LORD relented.

"This will not happen," the LORD said.

⁴This is what the Sovereign LORD showed me: The Sovereign LORD was calling for judgment by fire; it dried up the great deep and devoured the land. ⁵Then I cried out, "Sovereign LORD, I beg you, stop! How can Jacob survive? He is so small!"

⁶So the LORD relented.

"This will not happen either," the Sovereign LORD said.

⁷This is what he showed me: The Lord was standing by a wall that had been built true to plumb, with a plumb line in his hand. ⁸And the LORD asked me, "What do you see, Amos?"

"A plumb line," I replied.

Then the Lord said, "Look, I am setting a plumb line among my people Israel; I will spare them no longer.

7:8 A Plumb Line

A plumb line is a weight on the end of a string; builders use it to make certain that their walls stand straight. A wall may look right, but if it doesn't match a plumb line, it is out of kilter. Similarly God will use a plumb line to judge whether Israel is "straight" by his standards.

⁹"The high places of Isaac will be destroyed
and the sanctuaries of Israel will be
ruined;
with my sword I will rise against the
house of Jeroboam."

---

a13 Lo Debar means *nothing.*   *b13 Karnaim* means *horns; horn* here symbolizes strength.   *c14 Or from the entrance to*

Amos and Amaziah

¹⁰Then Amaziah the priest of Bethel sent a message to Jeroboam king of Israel: "Amos is raising a conspiracy against you in the very heart of Israel. The land cannot bear all his words. ¹¹For this is what Amos is saying:

"'Jeroboam will die by the sword,
  and Israel will surely go into exile,
  away from their native land.'"

¹²Then Amaziah said to Amos, "Get out, you seer! Go back to the land of Judah. Earn your bread there and do your prophesying there. ¹³Don't prophesy anymore at Bethel, because this is the king's sanctuary and the temple of the kingdom."

¹⁴Amos answered Amaziah, "I was neither a prophet nor a prophet's son, but I was a shepherd, and I also took care of sycamore-fig trees. ¹⁵But the LORD took me from tending the flock and said to me, 'Go, prophesy to my people Israel.' ¹⁶Now then, hear the word of the LORD. You say,

"'Do not prophesy against Israel,
  and stop preaching against the house of
    Isaac.'

¹⁷"Therefore this is what the LORD says:

"'Your wife will become a prostitute in the
    city,
  and your sons and daughters will fall by
    the sword.
Your land will be measured and divided up,
  and you yourself will die in a pagan*ᵃ*
    country.
And Israel will certainly go into exile,
  away from their native land.'"

A Basket of Ripe Fruit

8 This is what the Sovereign LORD showed me: a basket of ripe fruit. ²"What do you see, Amos?" he asked.

"A basket of ripe fruit," I answered.

Then the LORD said to me, "The time is ripe for my people Israel; I will spare them no longer.

³"In that day," declares the Sovereign LORD, "the songs in the temple will turn to wailing.*ᵇ* Many, many bodies—flung everywhere! Silence!"

⁴Hear this, you who trample the needy
  and do away with the poor of the land,

⁵saying,

"When will the New Moon be over
  that we may sell grain,

and the Sabbath be ended
  that we may market wheat?"—
skimping the measure,
  boosting the price
  and cheating with dishonest scales,
⁶buying the poor with silver
  and the needy for a pair of sandals,
  selling even the sweepings with the wheat.

⁷The LORD has sworn by the Pride of Jacob: "I will never forget anything they have done.

⁸"Will not the land tremble for this,
  and all who live in it mourn?
The whole land will rise like the Nile;
  it will be stirred up and then sink
  like the river of Egypt.

⁹"In that day," declares the Sovereign LORD,

"I will make the sun go down at noon
  and darken the earth in broad daylight.
¹⁰I will turn your religious feasts into
    mourning
  and all your singing into weeping.
I will make all of you wear sackcloth
  and shave your heads.
I will make that time like mourning for an
    only son
  and the end of it like a bitter day.

¹¹"The days are coming," declares the
    Sovereign LORD,
  "when I will send a famine through the
    land—
not a famine of food or a thirst for water,
  but a famine of hearing the words of the
    LORD.

8:11 Worst of All Famines

In this chapter, God describes devastations that will fall upon Israel if they do not repent. One judgment, however stands out above all others: The nation will experience the silence of God, a famine of the words of the Lord. A few more prophets succeeded Amos, but after Malachi no prophet appeared in Israel for four centuries, until John the Baptist came to announce Jesus.

¹²Men will stagger from sea to sea
  and wander from north to east,
searching for the word of the LORD,
  but they will not find it.

ᵃ 17 Hebrew an unclean   *ᵇ 3 Or "the temple singers will wail*

13"In that day

"the lovely young women and strong young
    men
    will faint because of thirst.
14They who swear by the shame[a] of Samaria,
    or say, 'As surely as your god lives,
        O Dan,'
    or, 'As surely as the god[b] of Beersheba
        lives' —
they will fall,
    never to rise again."

Israel to Be Destroyed

9 I saw the Lord standing by the altar, and he
    said:

"Strike the tops of the pillars
    so that the thresholds shake.
Bring them down on the heads of all the
    people;
    those who are left I will kill with the
        sword.
Not one will get away,
    none will escape.
2Though they dig down to the depths of the
    grave,[c]
    from there my hand will take them.
Though they climb up to the heavens,
    from there I will bring them down.
3Though they hide themselves on the top of
    Carmel,
    there I will hunt them down and seize
        them.
Though they hide from me at the bottom of
    the sea,
    there I will command the serpent to bite
        them.
4Though they are driven into exile by their
    enemies,
    there I will command the sword to slay
        them.
I will fix my eyes upon them
    for evil and not for good."

9:4 An Inescapable God

*The beautiful verses of Psalm 139:7–12
describe God's inescapable presence as a
comfort. Here, in similar poetry, Amos gives the
opposite side of that truth. Those whom God
opposes can find no refuge. They may hide on
top of Mount Carmel, or even at the very
bottom of the sea, but God's eye will follow
them.*

5The Lord, the LORD Almighty,
    he who touches the earth and it melts,
    and all who live in it mourn—
the whole land rises like the Nile,
    then sinks like the river of Egypt—
6he who builds his lofty palace[d] in the
    heavens
    and sets its foundation[e] on the earth,
who calls for the waters of the sea
    and pours them out over the face of the
        land—
    the LORD is his name.

7"Are not you Israelites
    the same to me as the Cushites[f]?"
                        declares the LORD.
"Did I not bring Israel up from Egypt,
    the Philistines from Caphtor[g]
    and the Arameans from Kir?

8"Surely the eyes of the Sovereign LORD
    are on the sinful kingdom.
I will destroy it
    from the face of the earth—
yet I will not totally destroy
    the house of Jacob,"
                        declares the LORD.
9"For I will give the command,
    and I will shake the house of Israel
        among all the nations
as grain is shaken in a sieve,
    and not a pebble will reach the ground.
10All the sinners among my people
    will die by the sword,
all those who say,
    'Disaster will not overtake or meet us.'

Israel's Restoration

11"In that day I will restore
    David's fallen tent.
I will repair its broken places,
    restore its ruins,
    and build it as it used to be,
12so that they may possess the remnant of
        Edom
    and all the nations that bear my name,[h]"
                        declares the LORD,
                        who will do these things.

13"The days are coming," declares the LORD,

"when the reaper will be overtaken by the
    plowman
    and the planter by the one treading
        grapes.
New wine will drip from the mountains

---

[a] 14 Or by Ashima; or by the idol   [b] 14 Or power   [c] 2 Hebrew to Sheol   [d] 6 The meaning of the Hebrew for this
phrase is uncertain.   [e] 6 The meaning of the Hebrew for this word is uncertain.   [f] 7 That is, people from
the upper Nile region   [g] 7 That is, Crete   [h] 12 Hebrew; Septuagint so that the remnant of men / and all the
nations that bear my name may seek ⌊the Lord⌋

and flow from all the hills.
14I will bring back my exiled*a* people Israel;
 they will rebuild the ruined cities and live
  in them.
They will plant vineyards and drink their
 wine;

they will make gardens and eat their fruit.
15I will plant Israel in their own land,
 never again to be uprooted
 from the land I have given them,"

says the LORD your God.

---

a 14 Or *will restore the fortunes of my*

OBADIAH

Poetic Justice
Obadiah gave the final word on a blood feud

> *"As you have done, it will be done to you." 15*

THE FEUD BEGAN WITH TWIN brothers, Jacob and Esau. Esau, the older by minutes, would have inherited family leadership, but in a moment of hunger he traded it for a meal (Genesis 25:19–34). Jacob went on to become the founding father of the nation of Israel. Esau, a born hunter, moved southeast to desolate mountain country. He founded the nation of Edom.

Their descendants continued the quarrel. Over hundreds of years the two nations battled repeatedly but inconclusively. The Edomites' capital, Sela, sat on a high plateau above a sheer cliff; the only access was by a deep ravine. From that well-protected enclave, the Edomites raided Israel.

Though the Israelites had been commanded, "Do not abhor an Edomite, for he is your brother" (Deuteronomy 23:7), they grew to regard the Edomites as cruel and heartless. Repeatedly the prophets predicted Edom's punishment by God. The final straw came when Babylon dismembered Jerusalem and took its citizens into exile. The Edomites egged on the conquering army, preyed on fleeing Israelites, and helped plunder Jerusalem. Psalm 137, one of the saddest passages in the Bible, records the Israelite bitterness over this. As Esau had cared more for a meal than for the family name, so his descendants cared more for the profit they could get from plunder than for the compassion they owed a brother.

Fair Return for Cruelty

Obadiah predicts poetic justice for proud Edom: their treachery toward Judah (verses 11–12) repaid with treachery from their own allies (7), their robbery (13) repaid with robbery (5–6), their violence (10) with violence (9), their love of destruction (12–14) repaid with utter destruction (10,18). Obadiah predicts that downtrodden Israel will rise again, while Edom will disappear from the face of the earth.

This prediction came precisely true. Edom was destroyed, not by Israel but by a series of foreign invaders. The last remnant of Edomites were destroyed in the Roman siege of Jerusalem in A.D. 70. Ironically, the nation that had tormented Jews in Jerusalem later died defending that city.

Why does this blood feud earn a place in Scripture? It demonstrates God's ongoing protection of his people from their enemies. It also shows that God's standards extend beyond his chosen people. Every nation will be judged, like Edom, by their own standard: "As you have done, it will be done to you" (15).

How to Read Obadiah

The shortest book in the Old Testament, Obadiah can easily be read and understood in one sitting. Many readers, however, have a hard time seeing the importance of this ongoing border feud between blood relatives.

A Bible dictionary can summarize the centuries of violence. Look under "Edom." Perhaps, though, you can only fully appreciate Israel's feelings by reflecting on your own when a close relative treats you cruelly. A family betrayal is uniquely offensive to God and humanity. Obadiah reminds us that justice will be done.

3-TRACK READING PLAN

For an explanation and complete listing of the 3-track reading plan, turn to page 7.

TRACK 1: ***Two-Week Courses on the Bible***
See page 7 for information on these courses.

TRACK 2: ***An Overview of Obadiah in 1 Day***
☐ Day 1. Read the Introduction to Obadiah and all of Obadiah.
Now turn to page 9 for your next Track 2 reading project.

TRACK 3: ***All of Obadiah in 1 Day***
After you have read through Obadiah, turn to pages 10–14 for your next Track 3 reading project.
☐ Obadiah

¹The vision of Obadiah.

This is what the Sovereign LORD says about Edom—

We have heard a message from the LORD:
　An envoy was sent to the nations to say,
　"Rise, and let us go against her for battle"—

²"See, I will make you small among the nations;
　you will be utterly despised.
³The pride of your heart has deceived you,
　you who live in the clefts of the rocks*a*
　and make your home on the heights,
you who say to yourself,
　'Who can bring me down to the ground?'
⁴Though you soar like the eagle
　and make your nest among the stars,
　from there I will bring you down,"
　　　　　　　　　　　declares the LORD.
⁵"If thieves came to you,
　if robbers in the night—
Oh, what a disaster awaits you—
　would they not steal only as much as they wanted?
If grape pickers came to you,
　would they not leave a few grapes?
⁶But how Esau will be ransacked,
　his hidden treasures pillaged!
⁷All your allies will force you to the border;
　your friends will deceive and overpower you;
those who eat your bread will set a trap for you,*b*
　but you will not detect it.

⁸"In that day," declares the LORD,
　"will I not destroy the wise men of Edom,
　men of understanding in the mountains of Esau?

⁹Your warriors, O Teman, will be terrified,
　and everyone in Esau's mountains
　will be cut down in the slaughter.
¹⁰Because of the violence against your brother Jacob,
　you will be covered with shame;
　you will be destroyed forever.
¹¹On the day you stood aloof
　while strangers carried off his wealth
and foreigners entered his gates
　and cast lots for Jerusalem,
　you were like one of them.
¹²You should not look down on your brother
　in the day of his misfortune,
nor rejoice over the people of Judah
　in the day of their destruction,
nor boast so much
　in the day of their trouble.
¹³You should not march through the gates of my people
　in the day of their disaster,
nor look down on them in their calamity
　in the day of their disaster,
nor seize their wealth
　in the day of their disaster.
¹⁴You should not wait at the crossroads
　to cut down their fugitives,
nor hand over their survivors
　in the day of their trouble.

¹⁵"The day of the LORD is near
　for all nations.
As you have done, it will be done to you;
　your deeds will return upon your own head.
¹⁶Just as you drank on my holy hill,
　so all the nations will drink continually;
they will drink and drink
　and be as if they had never been.

---

*a*3 Or *of Sela*　　*b*7 The meaning of the Hebrew for this clause is uncertain.

¹⁷But on Mount Zion will be deliverance;
   it will be holy,
and the house of Jacob
   will possess its inheritance.
¹⁸The house of Jacob will be a fire
   and the house of Joseph a flame;
the house of Esau will be stubble,
   and they will set it on fire and consume it.
There will be no survivors
   from the house of Esau."
                The Lord has spoken.

¹⁹People from the Negev will occupy
   the mountains of Esau,
and people from the foothills will possess
   the land of the Philistines.
They will occupy the fields of Ephraim and
   Samaria,
and Benjamin will possess Gilead.
²⁰This company of Israelite exiles who are in
   Canaan
will possess ⌊the land⌋ as far as Zarephath;
the exiles from Jerusalem who are in
   Sepharad
will possess the towns of the Negev.
²¹Deliverers will go up on[a] Mount Zion
   to govern the mountains of Esau.
And the kingdom will be the Lord's.

---

a 21 Or *from*

JONAH

Good News for the Enemy?
Jonah balked at loving the cruel Assyrians

JESUS TOLD HIS FOLLOWERS, "LOVE your enemies and pray for those who persecute you" (Matthew 5:44). While everyone talks admiringly about that command, loving your enemies is no easy thing. Many people doubt whether it is even right. Should we forgive the Nazis? Should we make a point to be kind to the Ku Klux Klan? Should we have compassion on dictators like Saddam Hussein?

> "Nineveh has more than a hundred and twenty thousand people. . . . Should I not be concerned about that great city?" 4:11

The book of Jonah tells the story of a man whom God instructed to love his enemies in Nineveh. True to life, the prophet Jonah did just the opposite of what God commanded. He refused to go to the people he hated. Instead, he tried to run away from the Lord.

Nineveh was a large, important city in Assyria, situated on the river Tigris. It posed a grave military threat to tiny Israel. God sent Jonah there, and he responded without hesitation: In Joppa he caught a boat going in the opposite direction. Obviously, Jonah didn't want to warn Nineveh's citizens they were about to be destroyed. He suspected they would repent and God would forgive them.

Why Jonah Didn't Want to Go

We can't be sure why Jonah hated Assyria, but another short Old Testament book, Nahum, gives a clue. This book, also completely dedicated to Nineveh, describes a ruthless, bloodthirsty people. The Assyrians themselves left monuments to their cruelty—long, boastful inscriptions describing their torture and slaughter of people who opposed them.

Israelites had reasons to hate and fear Nineveh. But God *loved* Nineveh. He wanted to save the city, not destroy it. He knew Nineveh was ripe for change. When Jonah finally preached there, the entire city believed his message and repented. Though cruel and hardened, Nineveh was ready to believe God. Israel had never responded to a prophet like these Assyrians did.

An Attitude Like God's

Since God repeatedly warned the Israelites not to intermarry with people of other religions, and even ordered them to drive other nations out of the promised land, some readers conclude that the Old Testament is racially narrow-minded. They say the New Testament gives the first indication that God cares for non-Jewish people.

The book of Jonah contradicts that view. It shows, instead, that God wanted to use Israelites like Jonah as agents of his concern. They would preach doom but always with the hope that the warning would lead to repentance.

Jonah needed to develop an attitude like God's toward his enemies. Insistently, God led Jonah to this understanding of his own mind and heart. The book of Jonah is a story of a miraculous change in Nineveh, but even more a story of miraculous change in Jonah.

How to Read Jonah

Like Esther and Ruth, Jonah is a delightful short narrative by a master writer. Its spiritual implications are powerful and obvious. You can easily read it at one sitting.

As you read Jonah, notice the changes that the city of Nineveh goes through. Try also to trace the changes that occur in Jonah, and observe how God pushes him to make these changes. Then ask yourself: What did this book say to its original Jewish readers? What does it say to me?

You may also be interested in following Nineveh's entire history. Though the Ninevites repented in Jonah's time, they later returned to old patterns. Later prophets (Nahum and Zephaniah) predicted Nineveh's downfall for "endless cruelty" (Nahum 3:19), and in 612 B.C. that city was destroyed, never to be inhabited again. A Bible dictionary can summarize Nineveh's long history as a world power; look under "Assyria." To place Jonah in Israelite history, see "A Lineup of Rulers," pages 1361–1369.

Is Jonah a "fish story"? Interpreters differ over whether it should be read as a parable (not necessarily factual) or as historical fact. At least one reliable account exists of a man swallowed by a sperm whale and later found, alive, in the whale's stomach. Jonah's historical basis cannot be dismissed simply because of the "great fish."

More to the point, Jesus compared himself to Jonah, and the people of his time to the Ninevites (Matthew 12:39–41; Luke 11:29–32). He predicted that "the men of Nineveh will stand up at the judgment with this generation and condemn it; for they repented at the preaching of Jonah, and now one greater than Jonah is here." It is hard to see how fictional characters could stand up at an event Jesus evidently believed would be historical.

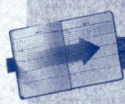

3-TRACK READING PLAN

For an explanation and complete listing of the 3-track reading plan, turn to page 7.

TRACK 1: **Two-Week Courses on the Bible**
See page 7 for information on these courses.

TRACK 2: **An Overview of Jonah in 1 Day**
☐ Day 1. Read the Introduction to Jonah and chapters 3 and 4. These two short chapters tell the less familiar part of the story: How Jonah got to Nineveh and became more bitter than before.

Now turn to page 9 for your next Track 2 reading project.

TRACK 3: **All of Jonah in 2 Days**
After you have read through Jonah, turn to pages 10–14 for your next Track 3 reading project.
☐1–2   ☐3–4

Jonah Flees From the LORD

1 The word of the LORD came to Jonah son of Amittai: ²"Go to the great city of Nineveh and preach against it, because its wickedness has come up before me."

³But Jonah ran away from the LORD and headed for Tarshish. He went down to Joppa, where he found a ship bound for that port. After paying the fare, he went aboard and sailed for Tarshish to flee from the LORD.

⁴Then the LORD sent a great wind on the sea, and such a violent storm arose that the ship threatened to break up. ⁵All the sailors were afraid and each cried out to his own god. And they threw the cargo into the sea to lighten the ship.

But Jonah had gone below deck, where he lay down and fell into a deep sleep. ⁶The captain went to him and said, "How can you sleep? Get up and call on your god! Maybe he will take notice of us, and we will not perish."

⁷Then the sailors said to each other, "Come, let us cast lots to find out who is responsible for this calamity." They cast lots and the lot fell on Jonah.

⁸So they asked him, "Tell us, who is responsible for making all this trouble for us? What do you do? Where do you come from? What is your country? From what people are you?"

⁹He answered, "I am a Hebrew and I worship the LORD, the God of heaven, who made the sea and the land."

¹⁰This terrified them and they asked, "What have you done?" (They knew he was running away from the LORD, because he had already told them so.)

¹¹The sea was getting rougher and rougher. So they asked him, "What should we do to you to make the sea calm down for us?"

¹²"Pick me up and throw me into the sea," he replied, "and it will become calm. I know that it is my fault that this great storm has come upon you."

¹³Instead, the men did their best to row back

to land. But they could not, for the sea grew even wilder than before. [14]Then they cried to the LORD, "O LORD, please do not let us die for taking this man's life. Do not hold us accountable for killing an innocent man, for you, O LORD, have done as you pleased." [15]Then they took Jonah and threw him overboard, and the raging sea grew calm. [16]At this the men greatly feared the LORD, and they offered a sacrifice to the LORD and made vows to him.

[17]But the LORD provided a great fish to swallow Jonah, and Jonah was inside the fish three days and three nights.

Jonah's Prayer

2 From inside the fish Jonah prayed to the LORD his God. [2]He said:

"In my distress I called to the LORD,
    and he answered me.
From the depths of the grave[a] I called for
        help,
    and you listened to my cry.
[3]You hurled me into the deep,
    into the very heart of the seas,
    and the currents swirled about me;
all your waves and breakers
        swept over me.
[4]I said, 'I have been banished
        from your sight;
    yet I will look again
        toward your holy temple.'
[5]The engulfing waters threatened me,[b]
    the deep surrounded me;
    seaweed was wrapped around my head.
[6]To the roots of the mountains I sank down;
    the earth beneath barred me in forever.
But you brought my life up from the pit,
    O LORD my God.

[7]"When my life was ebbing away,
    I remembered you, LORD,
and my prayer rose to you,
    to your holy temple.

[8]"Those who cling to worthless idols
    forfeit the grace that could be theirs.
[9]But I, with a song of thanksgiving,
    will sacrifice to you.
What I have vowed I will make good.
    Salvation comes from the LORD."

[10]And the LORD commanded the fish, and it vomited Jonah onto dry land.

Jonah Goes to Nineveh

3 Then the word of the LORD came to Jonah a second time: [2]"Go to the great city of Nineveh and proclaim to it the message I give you."

[3]Jonah obeyed the word of the LORD and went to Nineveh. Now Nineveh was a very important city—a visit required three days. [4]On the first day, Jonah started into the city. He proclaimed:

3:3 How Big a City?

Archaeologists who have dug up Nineveh report that at its peak its walls were 7¾ miles in circumference. Since it would not take three days to go around a city of that size, most probably the "three days" refers to the administrative district of which Nineveh was the capital. This comprised four cities with a circumference of about 60 miles. Another possibility: Perhaps it took Jonah three days to go to every neighborhood, marketplace, and city gate with his message.

"Forty more days and Nineveh will be overturned." [5]The Ninevites believed God. They declared a fast, and all of them, from the greatest to the least, put on sackcloth.

[6]When the news reached the king of Nineveh, he rose from his throne, took off his royal robes, covered himself with sackcloth and sat down in the dust. [7]Then he issued a proclamation in Nineveh:

"By the decree of the king and his nobles:

    Do not let any man or beast, herd or flock, taste anything; do not let them eat or drink. [8]But let man and beast be covered with sackcloth. Let everyone call urgently on God. Let them give up their evil ways and their violence. [9]Who knows? God may yet relent and with compassion turn from his fierce anger so that we will not perish."

[10]When God saw what they did and how they turned from their evil ways, he had compassion and did not bring upon them the destruction he had threatened.

Jonah's Anger at the LORD's Compassion

4 But Jonah was greatly displeased and became angry. [2]He prayed to the LORD, "O LORD, is this not what I said when I was still at home? That is why I was so quick to flee to Tarshish. I knew that you are a gracious and compassionate God, slow to anger and abounding in love, a God who relents from sending calamity. [3]Now, O LORD, take away my life, for it is better for me to die than to live."

[4]But the LORD replied, "Have you any right to be angry?"

[5]Jonah went out and sat down at a place east of the city. There he made himself a shelter, sat

---

[a]2 Hebrew *Sheol*   [b]5 Or *waters were at my throat*

in its shade and waited to see what would happen to the city. [6]Then the LORD God provided a vine and made it grow up over Jonah to give shade for his head to ease his discomfort, and Jonah was

very happy about the vine. [7]But at dawn the next day God provided a worm, which chewed the vine so that it withered. [8]When the sun rose, God provided a scorching east wind, and the sun blazed on Jonah's head so that he grew faint. He wanted to die, and said, "It would be better for me to die than to live."

[9]But God said to Jonah, "Do you have a right to be angry about the vine?"

"I do," he said. "I am angry enough to die."

[10]But the LORD said, "You have been concerned about this vine, though you did not tend it or make it grow. It sprang up overnight and died overnight. [11]But Nineveh has more than a hundred and twenty thousand people who cannot tell their right hand from their left, and many cattle as well. Should I not be concerned about that great city?"

4:2 Too Merciful a God?

The poet Robert Frost said, "After Jonah, you could never trust God not to be merciful again." The balky prophet discloses why he ran away from God in the first place: He was afraid God would forgive his archenemies. In fact, God did just that, after Nineveh repented with an eagerness that the Jews themselves often lacked (see Matthew 12:41). Pointedly, the book of Jonah ends with a question. Can anyone put limits on God's mercy and forgiveness?

MICAH

Light in a Dark Time
Evil and violence were creeping south toward Jerusalem

COUNTRY BOYS OFTEN LOSE PERSPECTIVE in the big city. They gawk at the tall buildings, the fancy clothes, and the showy symbols of power. Micah was a country boy from Moresheth, a small village in the no-man's-land southwest of Jerusalem. While his contemporary, Isaiah, moved in and out of the king's palace, Micah shows no sign of traveling in such circles.

And what does the LORD require of you? To act justly and to love mercy and to walk humbly with your God. 6:8

Yet this country boy kept his sense of perspective. The blood and violence of his day did not overwhelm him, nor was he intimidated by powerful and wealthy people. He spoke like a person who had seen the world through God's eyes.

Micah lived in one of the darkest times in Israel's history, a time of brutal warfare. The country had long been split into North and South. Micah saw war break out between these sides, with 120,000 deaths on the southern side alone (2 Chronicles 28:6). Then Assyria, the brutal chief power of the day, smashed the Northern Kingdom after a three-year siege of its capital, Samaria. Only a miracle kept those same Assyrian armies out of Jerusalem (2 Chronicles 32). But for how long would the South remain free?

The Sin of the South

Micah had no doubt how to interpret these chaotic events. God had punished the northern nation of Israel for sins summarized in 2 Kings 17:16–17: idolatry, Baal worship, child sacrifice, magic and sorcery. Now these same activities were creeping south into Judah—so much so that Micah referred in disgust to Jerusalem as a "high place," the traditional setting for pagan idol worship (1:5). The same judgment the North had suffered would come to Judah if people continued to disobey God.

Other historical accounts give more details of the South's sins. They describe how King Ahaz set up a foreign altar in God's temple, altering the temple construction "in deference to the king of Assyria" (2 Kings 16:18). He gave his own children in human sacrifice and shut the Lord's temple, substituting altars on every street corner (2 Chronicles 28:3,24–25). Along with this religious corruption came every other kind of sin: dishonesty (Micah 6:10–11), bribery (3:11), injustice (2:2), and distrust that destroyed families (7:5–6).

Beyond the Darkness

Yet Micah saw light ahead. He perceived a majestic God over all events, who punished his people only to purify and restore them. Along with making some of the Bible's frankest predictions of destruction, Micah gave some of the clearest predictions of the Messiah, the leader who would come to save Israel. Micah's perspective encompassed not only the events of his time but events far into the future, when the nations "will beat their swords into plowshares" (4:3).

Micah looked straight at the darkness of his time and at the darkness yet to come. But his perspective—God's perspective—enabled him to see beyond darkness. "Do not gloat over me, my enemy! Though I have fallen, I will rise. Though I sit in darkness, the LORD will be my light" (7:8).

How to Read Micah

Micah had the big view of history, and thus he covered a lot of ground. His book, only seven chapters, is loaded with pronouncements on the events of several thousand years. Because so much is jammed into so short a space, reading Micah can be confusing. A fragment may deal with the Messiah, for instance, and without warning the next few verses shift to the battle against Assyria.

To grasp Micah's message, think of his book as a collection of short speeches. One speech doesn't necessarily lead into the next. Instead of reading quickly from start to finish, pause after each short section to see whether you understand what it says. Try to understand who is speaking. Sometimes God speaks, sometimes Micah, sometimes the rebellious people.

In general, Micah follows this outline: chapters 1—3 indict both Northern and Southern Kingdoms, with their leaders; chapters 4 and 5 turn to the wonderful future God is planning; the last two chapters give the trial, punishment, and hope of the guilty nations.

It's very helpful to understand Micah's historical situation. Micah 1:1 names the kings of Judah he worked under. You can read about these kings, and their northern counterparts, in 2 Kings 15:27—20:21 and 2 Chronicles 27—32. For a brief summary, see "A Lineup of Rulers," pages 1361—1369.

3-TRACK READING PLAN

For an explanation and complete listing of the 3-track reading plan, turn to page 7.

TRACK 1: **Two-Week Courses on the Bible**
See page 7 for information on these courses.

TRACK 2: **An Overview of Micah in 1 Day**
☐ Day 1. Read the Introduction to Micah and chapter 6, which includes one of the most succinct statements in the Old Testament of what God wants our lives to be.

Now turn to page 9 for your next Track 2 reading project.

TRACK 3: **All of Micah in 7 Days**
After you have read through Micah, turn to pages 10—14 for your next Track 3 reading project.

☐1   ☐2   ☐3   ☐4   ☐5   ☐6   ☐7

---

1 The word of the LORD that came to Micah of Moresheth during the reigns of Jotham, Ahaz and Hezekiah, kings of Judah—the vision he saw concerning Samaria and Jerusalem.

²Hear, O peoples, all of you,
  listen, O earth and all who are in it,
that the Sovereign LORD may witness against you,
  the Lord from his holy temple.

Judgment Against Samaria and Jerusalem

³Look! The LORD is coming from his dwelling place;
  he comes down and treads the high places of the earth.
⁴The mountains melt beneath him
  and the valleys split apart,
like wax before the fire,
  like water rushing down a slope.
⁵All this is because of Jacob's transgression,
  because of the sins of the house of Israel.
What is Jacob's transgression?
  Is it not Samaria?

What is Judah's high place?
  Is it not Jerusalem?

⁶"Therefore I will make Samaria a heap of rubble,
  a place for planting vineyards.
I will pour her stones into the valley
  and lay bare her foundations.
⁷All her idols will be broken to pieces;
  all her temple gifts will be burned with fire;
  I will destroy all her images.
Since she gathered her gifts from the wages of prostitutes,
  as the wages of prostitutes they will again be used."

Weeping and Mourning

⁸Because of this I will weep and wail;
  I will go about barefoot and naked.
I will howl like a jackal
  and moan like an owl.
⁹For her wound is incurable;
  it has come to Judah.

It[a] has reached the very gate of my people,
    even to Jerusalem itself.
[10]Tell it not in Gath[b];
    weep not at all.[c]
In Beth Ophrah[d]
    roll in the dust.

1:10 A Passion for Punning

Puns stump even the best translators. In verses 10–15 Micah plays on the names of a series of Israelite towns—probably marking the path Assyrian invaders followed. The puns were not meant to be funny. They extracted grief from the place-names of the invasion. NIV footnotes explain Micah's Hebrew puns, which are virtually untranslatable.

[11]Pass on in nakedness and shame,
    you who live in Shaphir.[e]
Those who live in Zaanan[f]
    will not come out.
Beth Ezel is in mourning;
    its protection is taken from you.
[12]Those who live in Maroth[g] writhe in pain,
    waiting for relief,
because disaster has come from the LORD,
    even to the gate of Jerusalem.
[13]You who live in Lachish,[h]
    harness the team to the chariot.
You were the beginning of sin
    to the Daughter of Zion,
for the transgressions of Israel
    were found in you.
[14]Therefore you will give parting gifts
    to Moresheth Gath.
The town of Aczib[i] will prove deceptive
    to the kings of Israel.
[15]I will bring a conqueror against you
    who live in Mareshah.[j]
He who is the glory of Israel
    will come to Adullam.
[16]Shave your heads in mourning
    for the children in whom you delight;
make yourselves as bald as the vulture,
    for they will go from you into exile.

Man's Plans and God's

2 Woe to those who plan iniquity,
    to those who plot evil on their beds!
At morning's light they carry it out
    because it is in their power to do it.
[2]They covet fields and seize them,
    and houses, and take them.

They defraud a man of his home,
    a fellowman of his inheritance.

[3]Therefore, the LORD says:

"I am planning disaster against this people,
    from which you cannot save yourselves.
You will no longer walk proudly,
    for it will be a time of calamity.
[4]In that day men will ridicule you;
    they will taunt you with this mournful
        song:
'We are utterly ruined;
    my people's possession is divided up.
He takes it from me!
    He assigns our fields to traitors.'"

[5]Therefore you will have no one in the
        assembly of the LORD
    to divide the land by lot.

False Prophets

[6]"Do not prophesy," their prophets say.
    "Do not prophesy about these things;
    disgrace will not overtake us."
[7]Should it be said, O house of Jacob:
    "Is the Spirit of the LORD angry?
    Does he do such things?"

"Do not my words do good
    to him whose ways are upright?
[8]Lately my people have risen up
    like an enemy.
You strip off the rich robe
    from those who pass by without a care,
    like men returning from battle.
[9]You drive the women of my people
    from their pleasant homes.
You take away my blessing
    from their children forever.
[10]Get up, go away!
    For this is not your resting place,
because it is defiled,
    it is ruined, beyond all remedy.
[11]If a liar and deceiver comes and says,
    'I will prophesy for you plenty of wine
        and beer,'
he would be just the prophet for this
        people!

Deliverance Promised

[12]"I will surely gather all of you, O Jacob;
    I will surely bring together the remnant of
        Israel.
I will bring them together like sheep in a
        pen,
    like a flock in its pasture;

---

[a]9 Or He   *[b]10 Gath sounds like the Hebrew for tell. Hebrew for in Acco sounds like the Hebrew for weep.*   *[c]10 Hebrew; Septuagint may suggest not in Acco. The*   *[d]10 Beth Ophrah means house of dust.*   *[e]11 Shaphir means pleasant.*   *[f]11 Zaanan sounds like the Hebrew for come out.*   *[g]12 Maroth sounds like the Hebrew for bitter.*   *[h]13 Lachish sounds like the Hebrew for team.*   *[i]14 Aczib means deception.*   *[j]15 Mareshah sounds like the Hebrew for conqueror.*

the place will throng with people.
[13]One who breaks open the way will go up
before them;
they will break through the gate and go
out.
Their king will pass through before them,
the LORD at their head."

2:11 Plenty of Beer

Modern politicians avoid the phrase like poison: "tax hike." They love to proclaim "a new day in America," and hate to bring bad news. Prophets in Micah's time were just the same. They insisted that Micah stop predicting bad news (2:6; 3:5) and join their peace bandwagon. In fact, says Micah sarcastically, the ideal prophet for feel-good Israel would predict plenty of wine and beer.

Leaders and Prophets Rebuked

3 Then I said,

"Listen, you leaders of Jacob,
you rulers of the house of Israel.
Should you not know justice,
[2]   you who hate good and love evil;
who tear the skin from my people
and the flesh from their bones;
[3]who eat my people's flesh,
strip off their skin
and break their bones in pieces;
who chop them up like meat for the pan,
like flesh for the pot?"

[4]Then they will cry out to the LORD,
but he will not answer them.
At that time he will hide his face from them
because of the evil they have done.

[5]This is what the LORD says:

"As for the prophets
who lead my people astray,
if one feeds them,
they proclaim 'peace';
if he does not,
they prepare to wage war against him.
[6]Therefore night will come over you, without
visions,
and darkness, without divination.
The sun will set for the prophets,
and the day will go dark for them.
[7]The seers will be ashamed
and the diviners disgraced.
They will all cover their faces
because there is no answer from God."

[8]But as for me, I am filled with power,
with the Spirit of the LORD,

and with justice and might,
to declare to Jacob his transgression,
to Israel his sin.
[9]Hear this, you leaders of the house of Jacob,
you rulers of the house of Israel,
who despise justice
and distort all that is right;
[10]who build Zion with bloodshed,
and Jerusalem with wickedness.
[11]Her leaders judge for a bribe,
her priests teach for a price,
and her prophets tell fortunes for money.
Yet they lean upon the LORD and say,
"Is not the LORD among us?
No disaster will come upon us."
[12]Therefore because of you,
Zion will be plowed like a field,
Jerusalem will become a heap of rubble,
the temple hill a mound overgrown with
thickets.

3:12 Life-saving Prophecy

One hundred years after this clear prophecy of its destruction, Jerusalem still stood. By that time Jeremiah was making similar predictions, which led to his arrest for treason. Some of the city leaders, however, quoted Micah's "ancient" prophecy, pointing out that since Micah had not been put to death, neither should Jeremiah be (Jeremiah 26:18–19). Their memory probably saved Jeremiah's life.
Within another 20 years, both Micah's and Jeremiah's predictions came true and Jerusalem was reduced to rubble.

The Mountain of the LORD

4 In the last days

the mountain of the LORD's temple will be
established
as chief among the mountains;
it will be raised above the hills,
and peoples will stream to it.

[2]Many nations will come and say,

"Come, let us go up to the mountain of the
LORD,
to the house of the God of Jacob.
He will teach us his ways,
so that we may walk in his paths."
The law will go out from Zion,
the word of the LORD from Jerusalem.
[3]He will judge between many peoples
and will settle disputes for strong nations
far and wide.
They will beat their swords into plowshares
and their spears into pruning hooks.
Nation will not take up sword against nation,

nor will they train for war anymore.
⁴Every man will sit under his own vine
 and under his own fig tree,
and no one will make them afraid,
 for the LORD Almighty has spoken.
⁵All the nations may walk
 in the name of their gods;
we will walk in the name of the LORD
 our God for ever and ever.

4:3 Parallel with Isaiah

Micah 4:1–3, which describes the wonderful future in store for the world, has an almost exact parallel in Isaiah 2:2–4. Isaiah must have quoted Micah, or vice versa, or perhaps both quoted a third unknown prophet. Both prophets spoke in Jerusalem at about the same time.

The LORD's Plan

⁶"In that day," declares the LORD,

"I will gather the lame;
 I will assemble the exiles
 and those I have brought to grief.
⁷I will make the lame a remnant,
 those driven away a strong nation.
The LORD will rule over them in Mount Zion
 from that day and forever.
⁸As for you, O watchtower of the flock,
 O stronghold*ᵃ* of the Daughter of Zion,
the former dominion will be restored to you;
 kingship will come to the Daughter of
 Jerusalem."

⁹Why do you now cry aloud—
 have you no king?
Has your counselor perished,
 that pain seizes you like that of a woman
 in labor?
¹⁰Writhe in agony, O Daughter of Zion,
 like a woman in labor,
for now you must leave the city
 to camp in the open field.
You will go to Babylon;
 there you will be rescued.
There the LORD will redeem you
 out of the hand of your enemies.

¹¹But now many nations
 are gathered against you.
They say, "Let her be defiled,
 let our eyes gloat over Zion!"
¹²But they do not know
 the thoughts of the LORD;
they do not understand his plan,

he who gathers them like sheaves to the
 threshing floor.

¹³"Rise and thresh, O Daughter of Zion,
 for I will give you horns of iron;
I will give you hoofs of bronze
 and you will break to pieces many
 nations."

You will devote their ill-gotten gains to the
 LORD,
 their wealth to the Lord of all the earth.

A Promised Ruler From Bethlehem

5 Marshal your troops, O city of troops,*ᵇ*
 for a siege is laid against us.
They will strike Israel's ruler
 on the cheek with a rod.

²"But you, Bethlehem Ephrathah,
 though you are small among the clans*ᶜ*
 of Judah,
out of you will come for me
 one who will be ruler over Israel,
whose origins*ᵈ* are from of old,
 from ancient times.*ᵉ*"

5:2 Messiah's Birthplace

When the Magi came looking for a newborn "king of the Jews," King Herod asked the biblical scholars where to search. They referred him to this passage (see Matthew 2:6), which predicted that the Messiah would come from the small town of Bethlehem. Micah also describes Christ as a shepherd who will not merely bring peace, but be Israel's peace.

³Therefore Israel will be abandoned
 until the time when she who is in labor
 gives birth
and the rest of his brothers return
 to join the Israelites.

⁴He will stand and shepherd his flock
 in the strength of the LORD,
 in the majesty of the name of the LORD
 his God.
And they will live securely, for then his
 greatness
 will reach to the ends of the earth.
⁵ And he will be their peace.

Deliverance and Destruction

When the Assyrian invades our land
 and marches through our fortresses,
we will raise against him seven shepherds,
 even eight leaders of men.

ᵃ8 Or hill   ᵇ1 Or Strengthen your walls, O walled city   ᶜ2 Or rulers   ᵈ2 Hebrew goings out   ᵉ2 Or from days of eternity

⁶They will rule[a] the land of Assyria with the
        sword,
    the land of Nimrod with drawn sword.[b]
He will deliver us from the Assyrian
    when he invades our land
    and marches into our borders.

⁷The remnant of Jacob will be
    in the midst of many peoples
like dew from the LORD,
    like showers on the grass,
which do not wait for man
    or linger for mankind.
⁸The remnant of Jacob will be among the
        nations,
    in the midst of many peoples,
like a lion among the beasts of the forest,
    like a young lion among flocks of sheep,
which mauls and mangles as it goes,
    and no one can rescue.
⁹Your hand will be lifted up in triumph over
        your enemies,
    and all your foes will be destroyed.

¹⁰"In that day," declares the LORD,

"I will destroy your horses from among you
    and demolish your chariots.
¹¹I will destroy the cities of your land
    and tear down all your strongholds.
¹²I will destroy your witchcraft
    and you will no longer cast spells.
¹³I will destroy your carved images
    and your sacred stones from among you;

you will no longer bow down
    to the work of your hands.
¹⁴I will uproot from among you your Asherah
        poles[c]
    and demolish your cities.
¹⁵I will take vengeance in anger and wrath
    upon the nations that have not obeyed
        me."

The LORD's Case Against Israel

6 Listen to what the LORD says:

"Stand up, plead your case before the
        mountains;
    let the hills hear what you have to say.
²Hear, O mountains, the LORD's accusation;
    listen, you everlasting foundations of the
        earth.
For the LORD has a case against his people;
    he is lodging a charge against Israel.

³"My people, what have I done to you?
    How have I burdened you? Answer me.
⁴I brought you up out of Egypt
    and redeemed you from the land of
        slavery.
I sent Moses to lead you,
    also Aaron and Miriam.
⁵My people, remember
    what Balak king of Moab counseled
    and what Balaam son of Beor answered.
Remember ⌊your journey⌋ from Shittim to
        Gilgal,

---

[a]6 Or *crush*   [b]6 Or *Nimrod in its gates*   [c]14 That is, symbols of the goddess Asherah

Seeing in Two Dimensions
Little distinction between next week and the next thousand years

> They will beat their swords into plowshares and their spears into pruning hooks. 4:3

WHEN YOU SEE A MOUNTAIN range from a distance, it's very difficult to tell which peak is highest. A smaller mountain may loom largest simply because it is closer to you than a higher peak.

Micah, and many of the other Old Testament prophets, saw the future like that. They made little distinction between events coming next week and events that would come a thousand years later. They seemed to see the future with limited "depth perception."

In the space of one verse, for instance, Micah shifts from a prediction (3:12) that Jerusalem will become a mound of rubble—a prophecy fulfilled about 100 years later—to a prophecy (4:1) that the same mountain will be lifted up as "chief among the mountains"—something that has yet to be fulfilled today. In 5:2 comes a prediction that Matthew 2:6 records as fulfilled by Jesus' birth in Bethlehem 700 years later.

In Micah, the thousands of years between these fulfillments are unclear. They all seem to be about the same distance into the future. Almost certainly, Micah himself saw them unclearly. First Peter 1:10–11 comments that "the prophets . . . searched intently and with the greatest care, trying to find out the time and circumstances to which the Spirit of Christ in them was pointing when he predicted the sufferings of Christ and the glories that would follow."

Life Questions: What emotions do you feel knowing that some prophecies have not yet been fulfilled?

that you may know the righteous acts of
the LORD."

⁶With what shall I come before the LORD
and bow down before the exalted God?

6:5 Names with Meaning

*Speaking to people who knew their own
history well, Micah needed only to mention
names like Balaam and Balak to recall God's
goodness and humankind's disobedience.
Numbers 22–24 tells the story of Balaam, in
which Balak tried to get Balaam to curse Israel.
Balaam gave this famous reply: "How can I
curse those whom God has not cursed?"
(Numbers 23:8). The trip from Shittim to Gilgal
apparently refers to Israel's miraculous
crossing of the Jordan River (Joshua 3:1;
4:19–20), the final stage in their journey from
slavery in Egypt to freedom in the promised
land. These events, which had occurred about
500 years before, were as real to the Israelites
as yesterday.*

*Verse 16 offers a different kind of memory:
"The statutes of Omri and all the practices of
Ahab's house." Omri and his son Ahab were
two of the most notoriously wicked kings in
Israelite history (1 Kings 16:21–33). Ahab went
so far as to marry Jezebel, a Phoenician
princess, and set up a temple for her god, Baal,
in the new capital of Samaria. He sponsored
her massacre of genuine prophets.*

Shall I come before him with burnt offerings,
with calves a year old?
⁷Will the LORD be pleased with thousands of
rams,
with ten thousand rivers of oil?
Shall I offer my firstborn for my
transgression,
the fruit of my body for the sin of my
soul?
⁸He has showed you, O man, what is good.
And what does the LORD require of you?
To act justly and to love mercy
and to walk humbly with your God.

Israel's Guilt and Punishment

⁹Listen! The LORD is calling to the city—
and to fear your name is wisdom—
"Heed the rod and the One who
appointed it.*a*
¹⁰Am I still to forget, O wicked house,
your ill-gotten treasures
and the short ephah,*b* which is accursed?
¹¹Shall I acquit a man with dishonest scales,
with a bag of false weights?

¹²Her rich men are violent;
her people are liars
and their tongues speak deceitfully.
¹³Therefore, I have begun to destroy you,
to ruin you because of your sins.
¹⁴You will eat but not be satisfied;
your stomach will still be empty.*c*
You will store up but save nothing,
because what you save I will give to the
sword.
¹⁵You will plant but not harvest;
you will press olives but not use the oil on
yourselves,
you will crush grapes but not drink the
wine.
¹⁶You have observed the statutes of Omri
and all the practices of Ahab's house,
and you have followed their traditions.
Therefore I will give you over to ruin
and your people to derision;
you will bear the scorn of the nations.*d*"

Israel's Misery

7 What misery is mine!
I am like one who gathers summer fruit
at the gleaning of the vineyard;
there is no cluster of grapes to eat,
none of the early figs that I crave.
²The godly have been swept from the land;
not one upright man remains.
All men lie in wait to shed blood;
each hunts his brother with a net.

6:8 What God Wants

*Micah's most famous pronouncement
summarizes the qualities that matter to God.
Jesus spoke in similar terms to the Pharisees
about their religious hypocrisy: They gave a
tenth of even their spices to God, yet they
neglected justice, mercy, and faithfulness
(Matthew 23:23).*

³Both hands are skilled in doing evil;
the ruler demands gifts,
the judge accepts bribes,
the powerful dictate what they desire—
they all conspire together.
⁴The best of them is like a brier,
the most upright worse than a thorn
hedge.
The day of your watchmen has come,
the day God visits you.
Now is the time of their confusion.
⁵Do not trust a neighbor;
put no confidence in a friend.

---

a9 The meaning of the Hebrew for this line is uncertain.
the Hebrew for this word is uncertain.   *d16* Septuagint; Hebrew *scorn due my people*   *b10* An ephah was a dry measure.   *c14* The meaning of

Even with her who lies in your embrace
    be careful of your words.
[6]For a son dishonors his father,
    a daughter rises up against her mother,
a daughter-in-law against her
        mother-in-law—
a man's enemies are the members of his
    own household.

[7]But as for me, I watch in hope for the LORD,
    I wait for God my Savior;
    my God will hear me.

Israel Will Rise

[8]Do not gloat over me, my enemy!
    Though I have fallen, I will rise.
Though I sit in darkness,
    the LORD will be my light.
[9]Because I have sinned against him,
    I will bear the LORD's wrath,
until he pleads my case
    and establishes my right.
He will bring me out into the light;
    I will see his righteousness.
[10]Then my enemy will see it
    and will be covered with shame,
she who said to me,
    "Where is the LORD your God?"
My eyes will see her downfall;
    even now she will be trampled underfoot
    like mire in the streets.

[11]The day for building your walls will come,
    the day for extending your boundaries.
[12]In that day people will come to you
    from Assyria and the cities of Egypt,
even from Egypt to the Euphrates
    and from sea to sea
    and from mountain to mountain.
[13]The earth will become desolate because of its
        inhabitants,
    as the result of their deeds.

Prayer and Praise

[14]Shepherd your people with your staff,
the flock of your inheritance,
which lives by itself in a forest,
    in fertile pasturelands.[a]
Let them feed in Bashan and Gilead
    as in days long ago.

[15]"As in the days when you came out of
        Egypt,
    I will show them my wonders."

[16]Nations will see and be ashamed,
    deprived of all their power.
They will lay their hands on their mouths
    and their ears will become deaf.
[17]They will lick dust like a snake,
    like creatures that crawl on the ground.
They will come trembling out of their dens;
    they will turn in fear to the LORD our God
    and will be afraid of you.
[18]Who is a God like you,
    who pardons sin and forgives the
        transgression
    of the remnant of his inheritance?
You do not stay angry forever
    but delight to show mercy.

7:18 Nobody Like God

Theologians use big words to describe God's unique qualities: transcendence, omnipotence, omnipresence. Micah marveled even more over this: God's forgiveness. Unlike the angry gods of other nations, Israel's God delighted to show mercy.

[19]You will again have compassion on us;
    you will tread our sins underfoot
    and hurl all our iniquities into the depths
        of the sea.
[20]You will be true to Jacob,
    and show mercy to Abraham,
as you pledged on oath to our fathers
    in days long ago.

---

[a]14 Or *in the middle of Carmel*

NAHUM

God's Answer to Injustice
A power above the powers

> *Who can withstand his indignation? Who can endure his fierce anger? 1:6*

IS LIFE FAIR? IT RARELY seems so, especially in international politics. The most vicious dictators thrive, and raw power is the key ingredient in a successful foreign policy. Weak people get trampled.

As a citizen of Judah, the prophet Nahum felt the force of such injustice. His message from God concerned the greatest city of the time, Nineveh. This city, the capital of Assyria, represented raw, brutal power—"endless cruelty," as Nahum put it (3:19). Though Nineveh was hundreds of miles northeast of Judah, Assyrian power dominated the Middle East. In contrast, Judah was a small, fragile state barely clinging to independence.

Nahum's Nerve

Judah's sister nation to the north, Israel, had already been defeated by Assyria and carried into exile. Only God's miraculous intervention had saved Judah on that occasion. And now, in Nahum's time, the Assyrians had returned. They dragged off Manasseh, the king, with a hook in his nose (2 Chronicles 33:11). Judah was forced to pay tribute as a vassal state.

Few people can stare into the face of such raw power and come away unimpressed. Nahum did so only because he had seen a far greater power—the power of a God whose wrath could shatter rocks. If God was angry, how could Nineveh stand? Nahum's absolute confidence in God is underlined throughout this book.

It took nerve to stand up and predict the downfall of the most powerful nation in the world. Yet, in this book, Nahum sounds unintimidated, almost lordly. He spoke with confidence because he knew God's character: "The LORD will not leave the guilty unpunished" (1:3).

Decline and Fall of Nineveh

Within a few years, Nahum's predictions came true. Nineveh did fall, never to rise again. The greatest city in the world became a pile of rubble overgrown with grass. Both Alexander the Great and Napoleon camped near it but had no idea a city had ever been there. The site became known as "the mound of many sheep."

The name *Nahum* means "comfort." Though Nahum describes God's anger, his message offers comfort to those who live with injustice and evil. "The LORD is good," said Nahum, "a refuge in times of trouble. He cares for those who trust in him, but with an overwhelming flood . . . he will pursue his foes into darkness" (1:7–8). Nineveh is gone, but Nahum's testimony lives on, reminding us that though God's justice may seem slow, nothing can ultimately escape it.

How to Read Nahum

Nahum stands out from the other short prophetic books in two ways. He addressed a foreign city—Nineveh—instead of his own home nation, and he used unusually vivid language.

You can read more background on Judah and its relationship to Nineveh in the following historical accounts: 2 Kings 17–19 and 2 Chronicles 32—33:13. The background will help you understand why God was so angry at Nineveh.

As you read Nahum, pay special attention to the vivid imagery. Some of the best examples are the following:

Descriptions of warfare: 2:3–7; 3:1–3
Nineveh like a pool with its water draining out: 2:8
Nineveh like a lions' den, full of bones: 2:11–12
Nineveh like a prostitute shamed in the streets: 3:5–6
Nineveh's fortresses like fig trees, with fruit shaken into the mouth of their attacker: 3:12
Nineveh's numerous citizens like grasshoppers: prolific, voracious, and quickly disappearing: 3:15–17

3-TRACK READING PLAN

For an explanation and complete listing of the 3-track reading plan, turn to page 7.

TRACK 1: *Two-Week Courses on the Bible*
See page 7 for information on these courses.

TRACK 2: *An Overview of Nahum in 1 Day*
☐ Day 1. Read the Introduction to Nahum and chapter 1, which portrays God's anger against Nineveh's injustice.
Now turn to page 9 for your next Track 2 reading project.

TRACK 3: *All of Nahum in 3 Days*
After you have read through Nahum, turn to pages 10–14 for your next Track 3 reading project.
☐1 ☐2 ☐3

1 An oracle concerning Nineveh. The book of the vision of Nahum the Elkoshite.

The Lord's Anger Against Nineveh

²The Lord is a jealous and avenging God;
  the Lord takes vengeance and is filled
    with wrath.
The Lord takes vengeance on his foes
  and maintains his wrath against his
    enemies.
³The Lord is slow to anger and great in
    power;
  the Lord will not leave the guilty
    unpunished.
His way is in the whirlwind and the
    storm,
  and clouds are the dust of his feet.
⁴He rebukes the sea and dries it up;
  he makes all the rivers run dry.
Bashan and Carmel wither
  and the blossoms of Lebanon fade.
⁵The mountains quake before him
  and the hills melt away.
The earth trembles at his presence,
  the world and all who live in it.
⁶Who can withstand his indignation?
  Who can endure his fierce anger?
His wrath is poured out like fire;
  the rocks are shattered before him.

⁷The Lord is good,
  a refuge in times of trouble.
He cares for those who trust in him,
⁸ but with an overwhelming flood
he will make an end of ⌊Nineveh⌋;
  he will pursue his foes into darkness.

⁹Whatever they plot against the Lord
  he[a] will bring to an end;

1:3 God Is Slow to Anger

God's anger against Nineveh had not appeared overnight. Assyria had been the dominant world power for at least 300 years. Once before, Jonah had carried a message of condemnation to its chief city, Nineveh. As was always true with God's prophets, Jonah's condemnation sounded absolute. Actually, it included an escape clause. In Jeremiah 18:7–10, God spelled it out: "If at any time I announce that a nation or kingdom is to be uprooted, torn down and destroyed, and if that nation I warned repents of its evil, then I will relent." Hearing Jonah, the Ninevites had repented, and God had spared their city.

The repentance had not lasted, however. By Nahum's time, Nineveh had returned to her evil ways. God's anger, while slow to develop, was sure.

---

a 9 Or *What do you foes plot against the Lord? / He*

trouble will not come a second time.
[10]They will be entangled among thorns
    and drunk from their wine;
    they will be consumed like dry stubble.[a]
[11]From you, ⌞O Nineveh,⌟ has one come forth
    who plots evil against the LORD
    and counsels wickedness.

[12]This is what the LORD says:

"Although they have allies and are
        numerous,
    they will be cut off and pass away.
Although I have afflicted you, ⌞O Judah,⌟
    I will afflict you no more.
[13]Now I will break their yoke from your neck
    and tear your shackles away."

[14]The LORD has given a command concerning
        you, ⌞Nineveh⌟:
    "You will have no descendants to bear
        your name.
I will destroy the carved images and cast
        idols
    that are in the temple of your gods.
I will prepare your grave,
    for you are vile."

[15]Look, there on the mountains,
    the feet of one who brings good news,
    who proclaims peace!
Celebrate your festivals, O Judah,
    and fulfill your vows.
No more will the wicked invade you;
    they will be completely destroyed.

Nineveh to Fall

2 An attacker advances against you,
        ⌞Nineveh⌟.
    Guard the fortress,
    watch the road,
    brace yourselves,
    marshal all your strength!

[2]The LORD will restore the splendor of Jacob
    like the splendor of Israel,
though destroyers have laid them waste
    and have ruined their vines.

[3]The shields of his soldiers are red;
    the warriors are clad in scarlet.
The metal on the chariots flashes
    on the day they are made ready;
    the spears of pine are brandished.[b]
[4]The chariots storm through the streets,
    rushing back and forth through the
        squares.
They look like flaming torches;
    they dart about like lightning.

[5]He summons his picked troops,

yet they stumble on their way.
They dash to the city wall;
    the protective shield is put in place.
[6]The river gates are thrown open
    and the palace collapses.

[7]It is decreed[c] that ⌞the city⌟
    be exiled and carried away.
Its slave girls moan like doves
    and beat upon their breasts.
[8]Nineveh is like a pool,
    and its water is draining away.
"Stop! Stop!" they cry,
    but no one turns back.
[9]Plunder the silver!
    Plunder the gold!
The supply is endless,
    the wealth from all its treasures!
[10]She is pillaged, plundered, stripped!
    Hearts melt, knees give way,
    bodies tremble, every face grows pale.

[11]Where now is the lions' den,
    the place where they fed their young,
where the lion and lioness went,
    and the cubs, with nothing to fear?
[12]The lion killed enough for his cubs
    and strangled the prey for his mate,
filling his lairs with the kill
    and his dens with the prey.

[13]"I am against you,"
    declares the LORD Almighty.
"I will burn up your chariots in smoke,
    and the sword will devour your young
        lions.
    I will leave you no prey on the earth.
The voices of your messengers
    will no longer be heard."

Woe to Nineveh

3 Woe to the city of blood,
        full of lies,
    full of plunder,

---

[a]10 The meaning of the Hebrew for this verse is uncertain.   [b]3 Hebrew; Septuagint and Syriac / *the horsemen rush to*
and fro   [c]7 The meaning of the Hebrew for this word is uncertain.

never without victims!
²The crack of whips,
    the clatter of wheels,
galloping horses
    and jolting chariots!
³Charging cavalry,
    flashing swords
    and glittering spears!
Many casualties,
    piles of dead,
bodies without number,
    people stumbling over the corpses—
⁴all because of the wanton lust of a harlot,
    alluring, the mistress of sorceries,
who enslaved nations by her prostitution
    and peoples by her witchcraft.

⁵"I am against you," declares the LORD
        Almighty.
    "I will lift your skirts over your face.
I will show the nations your nakedness
    and the kingdoms your shame.
⁶I will pelt you with filth,
    I will treat you with contempt
    and make you a spectacle.
⁷All who see you will flee from you and say,
    'Nineveh is in ruins—who will mourn for
        her?'
    Where can I find anyone to comfort
        you?"

⁸Are you better than Thebes,ᵃ
    situated on the Nile,
    with water around her?
The river was her defense,
    the waters her wall.

3:8 Another Powerful City

In approximately 663 B.C. Assyria overwhelmed Thebes, the ancient, wealthy capital of Upper Egypt. This victory seemed to symbolize Assyria's absolute power. To Nahum, however, the battle told a different tale. If Thebes was vulnerable, so was proud Nineveh. About 50 years after capturing Thebes, Nineveh fell to the Babylonians. The mention of Thebes's downfall enables us to date Nahum's message within that 50-year period.

⁹Cushᵇ and Egypt were her boundless
        strength;
    Put and Libya were among her allies.

¹⁰Yet she was taken captive
    and went into exile.
Her infants were dashed to pieces
    at the head of every street.
Lots were cast for her nobles,
    and all her great men were put in chains.
¹¹You too will become drunk;
    you will go into hiding
    and seek refuge from the enemy.

¹²All your fortresses are like fig trees
    with their first ripe fruit;
when they are shaken,
    the figs fall into the mouth of the eater.
¹³Look at your troops—
    they are all women!
The gates of your land
    are wide open to your enemies;
    fire has consumed their bars.

¹⁴Draw water for the siege,
    strengthen your defenses!
Work the clay,
    tread the mortar,
    repair the brickwork!
¹⁵There the fire will devour you;
    the sword will cut you down
    and, like grasshoppers, consume you.
Multiply like grasshoppers,
    multiply like locusts!
¹⁶You have increased the number of your
        merchants
    till they are more than the stars of the
        sky,
but like locusts they strip the land
    and then fly away.
¹⁷Your guards are like locusts,
    your officials like swarms of locusts
    that settle in the walls on a cold day—
but when the sun appears they fly away,
    and no one knows where.

¹⁸O king of Assyria, your shepherdsᶜ
        slumber;
    your nobles lie down to rest.
Your people are scattered on the mountains
    with no one to gather them.
¹⁹Nothing can heal your wound;
    your injury is fatal.
Everyone who hears the news about you
    claps his hands at your fall,
for who has not felt
    your endless cruelty?

ᵃ8 Hebrew *No Amon*   ᵇ9 That is, the upper Nile region   ᶜ18 Or *rulers*

HABAKKUK

The Problem of Evil

Habakkuk's question: "Why is God silent while the wicked succeed?"

> "The righteous will
> live by his faith."
> 2:4

THE BOOK OF HABAKKUK BEGINS with a complaint. The prophet saw injustice, violence, and evil in his own country, yet God remained silent and invisible. Why didn't God intervene? Why did he give no answer when Habakkuk called out for help? Habakkuk took these questions directly to God, in prayer.

God answered him, but hardly in the way Habakkuk had anticipated. God said he was sending the Babylonians to punish Judah. God's words described a ruthless, savage army that would tear Israel apart.

So Habakkuk complained again. Could this be justice—punishing Judah through an even more evil nation? Deeply perplexed, Habakkuk waited to see what answer God would give to his second complaint.

How long he had to wait, we do not know. But God did reply, and his answer is perhaps the best explanation we have of God's attitude toward evil. It satisfied Habakkuk, so that his book, which begins with a complaint, ends with one of the most beautiful songs in the Bible.

Two Certainties to Live By

God pointed out two certainties to Habakkuk. First, the violent, proud Babylonians would be paid back with the very weapons they had used on others. Just as they destroyed nations, they would be destroyed. "Has not the LORD Almighty determined ... that the nations exhaust themselves for nothing?" (2:13). Evil may dominate the earth, but it always wears itself out.

The second certainty was God's character. He may be silent for a time, but not forever. "The earth will be filled with the knowledge of the glory of the LORD, as the waters cover the sea" (2:14). In chapter 3, Habakkuk "saw" this powerful glory, and his heart pounded. It changed his attitude from complaining to joy.

Because the future belongs to God, a believer can cling to the truth embodied in 2:4: "The righteous shall live by his faith." Habakkuk beautifully expressed this attitude of faith in the last three verses of his book: No matter how hard life might become, he would rejoice and find strength in the Lord.

Living by Faith

Did Habakkuk explain why God allows evil? Not precisely. He did affirm that God has not lost control. Evil is moving toward its own logical end of self-destruction, and God's glory will someday fill the earth. Habakkuk offers no proof of this, merely the record of God's communication to him. A believer can find hope and joy through faith in God, regardless of circumstances. Habakkuk's capsule of faith was quoted at three crucial points in the New Testament: Romans 1:17; Galatians 3:11; and Hebrews 10:38.

Though Habakkuk probably did not live to see it, the Babylonians were destroyed. Today they are merely a memory. Yet we, like Habakkuk, must still wait in faith to see the earth "filled with the knowledge of the glory of the LORD."

How to Read Habakkuk

Other prophets carried messages from God to humankind; Habakkuk addressed God alone. He pondered deep riddles of life while wrestling with two terrible realities: the degeneration of his own nation and the certainty that it was about to be overrun by another, worse nation. How can a just God allow, even use, such evil? To fully delve into

Habakkuk's questions, you may want to read the book of Job and Psalm 73, which explore related issues.

The first two chapters of Habakkuk tell of two "complaints" and two answers. As you read, try to imagine the emotional changes Habakkuk experienced as he talked with God. Then read the joyful psalm of chapter 3 (set to music, either by Habakkuk or someone else) and ask yourself: Where did this joyful confidence come from?

3-TRACK READING PLAN

For an explanation and complete listing of the 3-track reading plan, turn to page 7.

TRACK 1:   ***Two-Week Courses on the Bible***
See page 7 for information on these courses.

TRACK 2:   ***An Overview of Habakkuk in 1 Day***
☐ Day 1. Read the Introduction to Habakkuk and chapter 1, which gives you a flavor of the dialogue between God and the prophet.

Now turn to page 9 for your next Track 2 reading project.

TRACK 3:   ***All of Habakkuk in 3 Days***
After you have read through Habakkuk, turn to pages 10–14 for your next Track 3 reading project.
☐1   ☐2   ☐3

1 The oracle that Habakkuk the prophet received.

Habakkuk's Complaint

²How long, O Lord, must I call for help,
  but you do not listen?
Or cry out to you, "Violence!"
  but you do not save?
³Why do you make me look at injustice?
  Why do you tolerate wrong?
Destruction and violence are before me;
  there is strife, and conflict abounds.
⁴Therefore the law is paralyzed,
  and justice never prevails.
The wicked hem in the righteous,
  so that justice is perverted.

The Lord's Answer

⁵"Look at the nations and watch—
  and be utterly amazed.
For I am going to do something in your days
  that you would not believe,
  even if you were told.
⁶I am raising up the Babylonians,ᵃ
  that ruthless and impetuous people,
who sweep across the whole earth
  to seize dwelling places not their own.
⁷They are a feared and dreaded people;
  they are a law to themselves
  and promote their own honor.
⁸Their horses are swifter than leopards,

fiercer than wolves at dusk.
Their cavalry gallops headlong;
  their horsemen come from afar.
They fly like a vulture swooping to devour;

1:5 Unbelievable!

To Habakkuk and his fellow Israelites, it seemed unbelievable. How could God hand his own people over to the cruel and arrogant Babylonians? But incredible reversals can happen to people who think they have an automatic entitlement with God. Hundreds of years later the apostle Paul quoted this verse to a synagogue congregation (Acts 13:41), urging them not to let complacency keep them from accepting Jesus.

⁹   they all come bent on violence.
Their hordesᵇ advance like a desert wind
  and gather prisoners like sand.
¹⁰They deride kings
  and scoff at rulers.
They laugh at all fortified cities;
  they build earthen ramps and capture them.
¹¹Then they sweep past like the wind and go on—
  guilty men, whose own strength is their god."

ᵃ6 Or *Chaldeans*   ᵇ9 The meaning of the Hebrew for this word is uncertain.

Habakkuk's Second Complaint

[12]O LORD, are you not from everlasting?
My God, my Holy One, we will not die.
O LORD, you have appointed them to execute
judgment;

1:11 Worshiping the Military

The Babylonians had their own gods, but Habakkuk claimed that they really worshiped their "net," that is, their military might (verse 16). God described them as "guilty men, whose own strength is their god" (verse 11).

O Rock, you have ordained them to
punish.
[13]Your eyes are too pure to look on evil;
you cannot tolerate wrong.
Why then do you tolerate the treacherous?
Why are you silent while the wicked
swallow up those more righteous than
themselves?
[14]You have made men like fish in the sea,
like sea creatures that have no ruler.
[15]The wicked foe pulls all of them up with
hooks,
he catches them in his net,
he gathers them up in his dragnet;
and so he rejoices and is glad.
[16]Therefore he sacrifices to his net
and burns incense to his dragnet,
for by his net he lives in luxury
and enjoys the choicest food.
[17]Is he to keep on emptying his net,
destroying nations without mercy?

2 I will stand at my watch
and station myself on the ramparts;
I will look to see what he will say to me,
and what answer I am to give to this
complaint.[a]

The LORD's Answer

[2]Then the LORD replied:

"Write down the revelation
and make it plain on tablets
so that a herald[b] may run with it.
[3]For the revelation awaits an appointed time;
it speaks of the end
and will not prove false.
Though it linger, wait for it;
it[c] will certainly come and will not delay.

[4]"See, he is puffed up;
his desires are not upright—
but the righteous will live by his faith[d]—

[5]indeed, wine betrays him;
he is arrogant and never at rest.
Because he is as greedy as the grave[e]
and like death is never satisfied,
he gathers to himself all the nations
and takes captive all the peoples.

[6]"Will not all of them taunt him with ridicule
and scorn, saying,

"'Woe to him who piles up stolen goods
and makes himself wealthy by extortion!
How long must this go on?'
[7]Will not your debtors[f] suddenly arise?
Will they not wake up and make you
tremble?
Then you will become their victim.
[8]Because you have plundered many nations,
the peoples who are left will plunder you.
For you have shed man's blood;
you have destroyed lands and cities and
everyone in them.

2:4 Righteous by Faith

Has any brief slogan made a bigger impact than this one? For Habakkuk, "the righteous will live by his faith" meant that righteous people must patiently trust God in a difficult time. The New Testament quoted Habakkuk in a wider context (Romans 1:17; Galatians 3:11; Hebrews 10:38–39), saying not only that believers must live by faith, but that they are saved by grace through faith. When Martin Luther read that quote in Romans, it changed his life, and "righteousness by faith" became a rallying cry of the Protestant Reformation.

[9]"Woe to him who builds his realm by unjust
gain
to set his nest on high,
to escape the clutches of ruin!
[10]You have plotted the ruin of many peoples,
shaming your own house and forfeiting
your life.
[11]The stones of the wall will cry out,
and the beams of the woodwork will echo
it.

[12]"Woe to him who builds a city with
bloodshed
and establishes a town by crime!
[13]Has not the LORD Almighty determined
that the people's labor is only fuel for the
fire,
that the nations exhaust themselves for
nothing?

---

[a]1 Or *and what to answer when I am rebuked*   [b]2 Or *so that whoever reads it*   [c]3 Or *Though he linger, wait for him; / he*   [d]4 Or *faithfulness*   [e]5 Hebrew *Sheol*   [f]7 Or *creditors*

¹⁴For the earth will be filled with the
        knowledge of the glory of the LORD,
    as the waters cover the sea.

¹⁵"Woe to him who gives drink to his
        neighbors,
    pouring it from the wineskin till they are
        drunk,
    so that he can gaze on their naked bodies.
¹⁶You will be filled with shame instead of
        glory.
    Now it is your turn! Drink and be
        exposed*a*!
The cup from the LORD's right hand is
        coming around to you,
    and disgrace will cover your glory.
¹⁷The violence you have done to Lebanon will
        overwhelm you,
    and your destruction of animals will
        terrify you.
For you have shed man's blood;
    you have destroyed lands and cities and
        everyone in them.

¹⁸"Of what value is an idol, since a man has
        carved it?
    Or an image that teaches lies?
For he who makes it trusts in his own
        creation;
    he makes idols that cannot speak.
¹⁹Woe to him who says to wood, 'Come to
        life!'
    Or to lifeless stone, 'Wake up!'
Can it give guidance?
    It is covered with gold and silver;
        there is no breath in it.
²⁰But the LORD is in his holy temple;
    let all the earth be silent before him."

Habakkuk's Prayer

3 A prayer of Habakkuk the prophet. On *shigi-
    onoth.*b

²LORD, I have heard of your fame;
    I stand in awe of your deeds, O LORD.
Renew them in our day,
    in our time make them known;
    in wrath remember mercy.

³God came from Teman,
    the Holy One from Mount Paran.   *Selah*c
His glory covered the heavens
    and his praise filled the earth.
⁴His splendor was like the sunrise;
    rays flashed from his hand,
    where his power was hidden.
⁵Plague went before him;
    pestilence followed his steps.

⁶He stood, and shook the earth;
    he looked, and made the nations tremble.
The ancient mountains crumbled
    and the age-old hills collapsed.
    His ways are eternal.
⁷I saw the tents of Cushan in distress,
    the dwellings of Midian in anguish.

⁸Were you angry with the rivers, O LORD?
    Was your wrath against the streams?
Did you rage against the sea
    when you rode with your horses
    and your victorious chariots?
⁹You uncovered your bow,
    you called for many arrows.   *Selah*
You split the earth with rivers;
¹⁰   the mountains saw you and writhed.
Torrents of water swept by;
    the deep roared
    and lifted its waves on high.

¹¹Sun and moon stood still in the heavens
    at the glint of your flying arrows,
    at the lightning of your flashing spear.
¹²In wrath you strode through the earth
    and in anger you threshed the nations.
¹³You came out to deliver your people,
    to save your anointed one.
You crushed the leader of the land of
        wickedness,
    you stripped him from head to foot.   *Selah*
¹⁴With his own spear you pierced his head
    when his warriors stormed out to scatter
        us,
gloating as though about to devour
    the wretched who were in hiding.

3:14 God at Work

*"With his own spear you pierced his head" is
how Habakkuk sees God overcoming the
leader of evil. Earlier (2:6–7), Habakkuk had
demonstrated how this would work out: The
Babylonians' own enemies would treat them
just as they had treated others. Violence turns
back on the violent. On the surface, God's
power is not always visible, but the person of
faith knows God is behind it all.*

¹⁵You trampled the sea with your horses,
    churning the great waters.

¹⁶I heard and my heart pounded,
    my lips quivered at the sound;
decay crept into my bones,
    and my legs trembled.
Yet I will wait patiently for the day of
        calamity

---

a 16 Masoretic Text; Dead Sea Scrolls, Aquila, Vulgate and Syriac (see also Septuagint) *and stagger*   *b 1* Probably a
literary or musical term   *c 3* A word of uncertain meaning; possibly a musical term; also in verses 9 and 13

to come on the nation invading
us.
17Though the fig tree does not bud
and there are no grapes on the vines,
though the olive crop fails
and the fields produce no food,
though there are no sheep in the pen
and no cattle in the stalls,

18yet I will rejoice in the LORD,
I will be joyful in God my Savior.

19The Sovereign LORD is my strength;
he makes my feet like the feet of a deer,
he enables me to go on the heights.

For the director of music. On my stringed
instruments.

ZEPHANIAH

Beyond Darkness
A worldwide catastrophe and a shining light

> "The LORD . . . will quiet you with his love, he will rejoice over you with singing." 3:17

EPHANIAH WROTE NOT LONG AFTER Manasseh had ended his 50-year reign in Judah. One of the worst kings on record, Manasseh had made idol worship and child sacrifice common practice. He had built altars for star worshipers in God's temple and had encouraged male prostitution as part of the religious ritual. He had also "shed so much innocent blood that he filled Jerusalem from end to end" (2 Kings 21:16). His son Amon carried on in the same way during his short reign.

Then came King Josiah, who took the throne at the age of eight, after his father's assassination. The Bible says there was never a king like Josiah (2 Kings 23:25). He led a reform, destroying all the pagan idols and restoring the temple. He organized the first Passover celebration in generations.

Zephaniah, who was probably related to the king through his great-great-grandfather King Hezekiah, apparently spoke just before the big changes. The nation's future hung in the balance, and Zephaniah's words may well have helped tip it toward renewal of faith in God.

From Gloom to Exultation

Zephaniah's book begins in deep gloom. Like other prophets, he condemned the sins of his nation and predicted judgment from God. But he went one big step further. He talked repeatedly about "the day of the LORD" and saw that it would be a supernatural event sweeping clean the whole planet. Zephaniah offered no hope that it could be avoided. The Lord had warned and pleaded, but to no avail (3:6–7). Zephaniah saw hope for a minority only. A faithful, humble remnant could be sheltered from disaster if they would seek God.

Beyond the judgment fires Zephaniah saw something remarkably bright. He predicted that a purified remnant of God's people, truthful and humble, would trust in God. He foresaw a remade world learning to worship God.

Therefore this short book, which starts with such gloom, ends with an ecstatic song of joy: an anticipation of the kingdom to come after the judgment. God's blessing will flow freely as every nation worships him. Zephaniah's words may have been influential in encouraging Josiah's reforms, but his vision extended far beyond. The New Testament speaks often, like Zephaniah, of the worldwide judgment and a renewed world to come.

How to Read Zephaniah

ephaniah will seem more interesting if you grasp the historical situation in which he wrote. For the decadence that led to King Josiah's reforms, read 2 Kings 21. Josiah's history is told in chapters 22 and 23. Second Chronicles 33—35 tells the same story with slightly different details. You can find a brief summary of these reigns in "A Lineup of Rulers," pages 1361–1369.

Zephaniah is easily understood. It has a clear and symmetrical structure, opening (after a brief introduction) with a warning of judgment for Judah and its capital of Jerusalem, then extending the judgment to Judah's neighbors, and closing in chapter 3 with good news about Jerusalem.

3-TRACK READING PLAN

For an explanation and complete listing of the 3-track reading plan, turn to page 7.

TRACK 1: *Two-Week Courses on the Bible*
See page 7 for information on these courses.

TRACK 2: *An Overview of Zephaniah in 1 Day*
☐ Day 1: Read the Introduction to Zephaniah and chapter 3, with its hopeful portrait of Jerusalem after the judgment.

Now turn to page 9 for your next Track 2 reading project.

TRACK 3: *All of Zephaniah in 3 Days*
After you have read through Zephaniah, turn to pages 10–14 for your next Track 3 reading project.
☐1   ☐2   ☐3

1 The word of the LORD that came to Zephaniah son of Cushi, the son of Gedaliah, the son of Amariah, the son of Hezekiah, during the reign of Josiah son of Amon king of Judah:

> ### 1:1 Royal Blood
>
> *Prophets had to be hand-picked by God. Education or family background didn't qualify them for the job. Zephaniah, however, came from an impressive family. His great-great-grandfather was King Hezekiah. Despite his royal blood, Zephaniah was blunt and uncompromising; he took no white-glove approach to prophecy.*

Warning of Coming Destruction

²"I will sweep away everything
  from the face of the earth,"
                              declares the LORD.
³"I will sweep away both men and animals;
  I will sweep away the birds of the air
  and the fish of the sea.
The wicked will have only heaps of rubble^a
  when I cut off man from the face of the earth,"
                              declares the LORD.

Against Judah

⁴"I will stretch out my hand against Judah
  and against all who live in Jerusalem.
I will cut off from this place every remnant of Baal,
  the names of the pagan and the idolatrous priests—
⁵those who bow down on the roofs
  to worship the starry host,
those who bow down and swear by the LORD
  and who also swear by Molech,^b
⁶those who turn back from following the LORD
  and neither seek the LORD nor inquire of him.

⁷Be silent before the Sovereign LORD,
  for the day of the LORD is near.
The LORD has prepared a sacrifice;
  he has consecrated those he has invited.
⁸On the day of the LORD's sacrifice
  I will punish the princes
  and the king's sons
and all those clad
  in foreign clothes.
⁹On that day I will punish
  all who avoid stepping on the threshold,^c
who fill the temple of their gods
  with violence and deceit.

¹⁰"On that day," declares the LORD,
  "a cry will go up from the Fish Gate,
  wailing from the New Quarter,
  and a loud crash from the hills.
¹¹Wail, you who live in the market district^d;
  all your merchants will be wiped out,
  all who trade with^e silver will be ruined.
¹²At that time I will search Jerusalem with lamps
  and punish those who are complacent,
  who are like wine left on its dregs,
who think, 'The LORD will do nothing,
  either good or bad.'
¹³Their wealth will be plundered,
  their houses demolished.
They will build houses
  but not live in them;

---

^a3 The meaning of the Hebrew for this line is uncertain.   ^b5 Hebrew *Malcam*, that is, Milcom
^c9 See 1 Samuel 5:5.   ^d11 Or *the Mortar*   ^e11 Or *in*

they will plant vineyards
but not drink the wine.

The Great Day of the LORD

14"The great day of the LORD is near—
near and coming quickly.

1:12 Practical Atheism

The people of Judah did terrible things, such as worshiping Molech (verse 5), the Ammonite god who sometimes required child sacrifice. Zephaniah singled out another sin, however, that was just as damaging: complacency. They weren't formal atheists, but they acted like it.

Listen! The cry on the day of the LORD will
be bitter,
the shouting of the warrior there.
15That day will be a day of wrath,
a day of distress and anguish,
a day of trouble and ruin,
a day of darkness and gloom,
a day of clouds and blackness,
16a day of trumpet and battle cry
against the fortified cities
and against the corner towers.
17I will bring distress on the people
and they will walk like blind men,
because they have sinned against the
LORD.
Their blood will be poured out like dust
and their entrails like filth.
18Neither their silver nor their gold
will be able to save them
on the day of the LORD's wrath.
In the fire of his jealousy
the whole world will be consumed,
for he will make a sudden end
of all who live in the earth."

2 Gather together, gather together,
O shameful nation,
2before the appointed time arrives
and that day sweeps on like chaff,
before the fierce anger of the LORD comes
upon you,
before the day of the LORD's wrath comes
upon you.
3Seek the LORD, all you humble of the land,
you who do what he commands.
Seek righteousness, seek humility;
perhaps you will be sheltered
on the day of the LORD's anger.

Against Philistia

4Gaza will be abandoned

and Ashkelon left in ruins.
At midday Ashdod will be emptied
and Ekron uprooted.
5Woe to you who live by the sea,
O Kerethite people;
the word of the LORD is against you,
O Canaan, land of the Philistines.

"I will destroy you,
and none will be left."

6The land by the sea, where the Kerethites[a]
dwell,
will be a place for shepherds and sheep
pens.
7It will belong to the remnant of the house of
Judah;
there they will find pasture.
In the evening they will lie down
in the houses of Ashkelon.
The LORD their God will care for them;
he will restore their fortunes.[b]

Against Moab and Ammon

8"I have heard the insults of Moab
and the taunts of the Ammonites,
who insulted my people
and made threats against their land.
9Therefore, as surely as I live,"
declares the LORD Almighty, the God of
Israel,
"surely Moab will become like Sodom,
the Ammonites like Gomorrah—
a place of weeds and salt pits,
a wasteland forever.
The remnant of my people will plunder
them;
the survivors of my nation will inherit
their land."

10This is what they will get in return for their
pride,
for insulting and mocking the people of
the LORD Almighty.
11The LORD will be awesome to them
when he destroys all the gods of the land.
The nations on every shore will worship him,
every one in its own land.

Against Cush

12"You too, O Cushites,[c]
will be slain by my sword."

Against Assyria

13He will stretch out his hand against the
north
and destroy Assyria,
leaving Nineveh utterly desolate
and dry as the desert.

---

[a]6 The meaning of the Hebrew for this word is uncertain.
people from the upper Nile region
[b]7 Or *will bring back their captives*   [c]12 That is,

¹⁴Flocks and herds will lie down there,
   creatures of every kind.
The desert owl and the screech owl
   will roost on her columns.
Their calls will echo through the windows,
   rubble will be in the doorways,
   the beams of cedar will be exposed.
¹⁵This is the carefree city
   that lived in safety.
She said to herself,
   "I am, and there is none besides me."
What a ruin she has become,
   a lair for wild beasts!
All who pass by her scoff
   and shake their fists.

The Future of Jerusalem

3 Woe to the city of oppressors,
   rebellious and defiled!
²She obeys no one,
   she accepts no correction.
She does not trust in the LORD,
   she does not draw near to her God.
³Her officials are roaring lions,
   her rulers are evening wolves,
   who leave nothing for the morning.
⁴Her prophets are arrogant;
   they are treacherous men.
Her priests profane the sanctuary
   and do violence to the law.
⁵The LORD within her is righteous;
   he does no wrong.
Morning by morning he dispenses his justice,
   and every new day he does not fail,
   yet the unrighteous know no shame.

⁶"I have cut off nations;
   their strongholds are demolished.
I have left their streets deserted,
   with no one passing through.
Their cities are destroyed;
   no one will be left—no one at all.
⁷I said to the city,
   'Surely you will fear me
   and accept correction!'
Then her dwelling would not be cut off,
   nor all my punishments come upon her.
But they were still eager
   to act corruptly in all they did.
⁸Therefore wait for me," declares the LORD,
   "for the day I will stand up to testify.[a]
I have decided to assemble the nations,
   to gather the kingdoms
and to pour out my wrath on them—
   all my fierce anger.
The whole world will be consumed
   by the fire of my jealous anger.

⁹"Then will I purify the lips of the peoples,
   that all of them may call on the name of
      the LORD
   and serve him shoulder to shoulder.
¹⁰From beyond the rivers of Cush[b]
   my worshipers, my scattered people,
   will bring me offerings.
¹¹On that day you will not be put to shame
   for all the wrongs you have done to me,
because I will remove from this city
   those who rejoice in their pride.
Never again will you be haughty
   on my holy hill.
¹²But I will leave within you
   the meek and humble,
   who trust in the name of the LORD.

3:12 Meek Will Inherit

As on Wall Street, as in the streets of many cities, "survival of the fittest" might have been Jerusalem's motto. Its officials were like wolves, devouring everything in sight (verse 3). Could only the ruthless survive? Zephaniah said no. In fact, he claimed, only the meek and the humble, those who trust God and simply tell the truth, would live in security. Jesus said something similar: "Blessed are the meek, for they will inherit the earth" (Matthew 5:5).

¹³The remnant of Israel will do no wrong;
   they will speak no lies,
   nor will deceit be found in their mouths.
They will eat and lie down
   and no one will make them afraid."

¹⁴Sing, O Daughter of Zion;
   shout aloud, O Israel!
Be glad and rejoice with all your heart,
   O Daughter of Jerusalem!
¹⁵The LORD has taken away your punishment,
   he has turned back your enemy.
The LORD, the King of Israel, is with you;
   never again will you fear any harm.
¹⁶On that day they will say to Jerusalem,
   "Do not fear, O Zion;
   do not let your hands hang limp.
¹⁷The LORD your God is with you,
   he is mighty to save.
He will take great delight in you,
   he will quiet you with his love,
   he will rejoice over you with singing."

¹⁸"The sorrows for the appointed feasts
   I will remove from you;
   they are a burden and a reproach to
      you.[c]

---

[a] 8 Septuagint and Syriac; Hebrew *will rise up to plunder you who mourn for the appointed feasts; / your reproach is a burden to you*   [b] 10 That is, the upper Nile region   [c] 18 Or *"I will gather*

19At that time I will deal
    with all who oppressed you;
I will rescue the lame
    and gather those who have been scattered.
I will give them praise and honor
    in every land where they were put to
    shame.

20At that time I will gather you;
    at that time I will bring you home.
I will give you honor and praise
    among all the peoples of the earth
when I restore your fortunes*a*
    before your very eyes,"

              says the LORD.

a20 Or I bring back your captives

HAGGAI

The Prophet Who Got Results
For once, God's people listened

SOMETIMES, AT CRUCIAL MOMENTS, A single voice can stir a directionless mass of people to action. Prime minister Winston Churchill's inspiring oratory may have saved Britain in World War II. American clergyman and civil rights leader Martin Luther King's sermons and speeches captured America's conscience in the 1950s and 60s.

Haggai's words, similarly, rang clear in a time of confusion. The Jews had come back from their exile in Babylon nearly 20 years before. But they seemed to have forgotten the point of returning. After one false start on the temple, the returned exiles had devoted their energy to building their own houses. The ruins of Solomon's temple stood as a nagging reminder that they had neglected God.

> *The whole remnant of the people obeyed the voice of the LORD their God and the message of the prophet Haggai, because the LORD their God had sent him. 1:12*

Now Haggai urged these pioneers to "give careful thought" to their situation. He did not rage like Jeremiah or build eloquent poems like Isaiah. He put it simply and logically. They had worked hard, but what had it earned them? Their crops were unsuccessful. Their money disappeared as soon as they earned it. Why? Haggai asked. Because they had mistaken their priorities. They needed to put God first. They needed to rebuild his temple.

A Response from the Heart

People responded to Haggai immediately. Prophets before him, such as Amos, Isaiah, and Jeremiah, had spoken for decades without seeing such a heartfelt reaction. Haggai's messages span a mere four months, but he accomplished everything he set out to do. In four years the temple was complete.

What made the temple so important? After all, the proper sacrifices and rituals could be carried out on a makeshift altar. But God's reputation was at stake. He could not be properly honored so long as the house he called home lay in ruins. The temple symbolized God's presence, and Israel's priorities.

Would rebuilding the temple change Israel's financial situation? Haggai's first words promised nothing. He simply said, "Give careful thought to your ways," and pointed out that Israel's lack of prosperity was God's doing. They had worked hard, but God had withheld the rain their crops needed. A month later (2:1–9) Haggai said that God had glorious plans for Israel, plans that would shake the whole earth. But he referred to God's presence with them, not to good crops.

Only on the last day accounted for in this brief book did Haggai get back to the subject of harvests. He said that God wanted his people to "give careful thought" again—this time to the dramatic difference they would see in their harvests now that they had put God first. "From this day on I will bless you," God said through Haggai (2:18–19).

How to Read Haggai

One of the shortest books in the Bible, Haggai can easily be read at one sitting. Haggai's words came at a critical time in the life of the nation of Israel. They mark one of the few times in all history when God spoke and his people quickly and unquestioningly obeyed. For the historical background, read Ezra 1–6. Haggai's crucial message is mentioned in Ezra 5:1–2. "A Lineup of Rulers," pages 1361–1369, can help you place Haggai in Israelite history.

There is a progression to God's warnings and his promises through Haggai. Study each of Haggai's messages, and note what *encouragement*, what *warning*, and what *hope* God offered Israel. How did God motivate them to obey him?

3-TRACK READING PLAN

For an explanation and complete listing of the 3-track reading plan, turn to page 7.

TRACK 1: *Two-Week Courses on the Bible*
See page 7 for information on these courses.

TRACK 2: *An Overview of Haggai in 1 Day*
☐ Day 1. Read the Introduction to Haggai and chapter 1, which tells how Haggai's message changed Israel's direction.

Now turn to page 9 for your next Track 2 reading project.

TRACK 3: *All of Haggai in 2 Days*
After you have read through Haggai, turn to pages 10–14 for your next Track 3 reading project.
☐ 1   ☐ 2

A Call to Build the House of the LORD

1 In the second year of King Darius, on the first day of the sixth month, the word of the LORD came through the prophet Haggai to Zerubbabel son of Shealtiel, governor of Judah, and to Joshua*ᵃ* son of Jehozadak, the high priest:

²This is what the LORD Almighty says: "These people say, 'The time has not yet come for the LORD's house to be built.'"

1:2–13 Change of Tone

For two decades the Israelites had ignored God's strong desire for them to rebuild the temple. When they finally responded and got to work, however, God's sternness melted immediately. "I am with you," he told them. And though the new temple going up seemed a sad imitation of Solomon's masterpiece, God still spoke with gentleness and kindness (2:2–5). Haggai, one of the last prophets, indicates God's eagerness to respond with mercy.

³Then the word of the LORD came through the prophet Haggai: ⁴"Is it a time for you yourselves to be living in your paneled houses, while this house remains a ruin?"

⁵Now this is what the LORD Almighty says: "Give careful thought to your ways. ⁶You have planted much, but have harvested little. You eat, but never have enough. You drink, but never have your fill. You put on clothes, but are not warm. You earn wages, only to put them in a purse with holes in it."

⁷This is what the LORD Almighty says: "Give careful thought to your ways. ⁸Go up into the mountains and bring down timber and build the house, so that I may take pleasure in it and be honored," says the LORD. ⁹"You expected much, but see, it turned out to be little. What you brought home, I blew away. Why?" declares the LORD Almighty. "Because of my house, which remains a ruin, while each of you is busy with his own house. ¹⁰Therefore, because of you the heavens have withheld their dew and the earth its crops. ¹¹I called for a drought on the fields and the mountains, on the grain, the new wine, the oil and whatever the ground produces, on men and cattle, and on the labor of your hands."

¹²Then Zerubbabel son of Shealtiel, Joshua son of Jehozadak, the high priest, and the whole remnant of the people obeyed the voice of the LORD their God and the message of the prophet Haggai, because the LORD their God had sent him. And the people feared the LORD.

¹³Then Haggai, the LORD's messenger, gave this message of the LORD to the people: "I am with you," declares the LORD. ¹⁴So the LORD stirred up the spirit of Zerubbabel son of Shealtiel, governor of Judah, and the spirit of Joshua son of Jehozadak, the high priest, and the spirit of the whole remnant of the people. They came and began to work on the house of the LORD Almighty, their God, ¹⁵on the twenty-fourth day of the sixth month in the second year of King Darius.

The Promised Glory of the New House

2 On the twenty-first day of the seventh month, the word of the LORD came through the prophet Haggai: ²"Speak to Zerubbabel son of Shealtiel, governor of Judah, to Joshua son of Jehozadak, the high priest, and to the remnant of the people. Ask them, ³'Who of you is left who saw this house in its former glory? How does it

ᵃ1 A variant of Jeshua; here and elsewhere in Haggai

look to you now? Does it not seem to you like nothing? [4]But now be strong, O Zerubbabel,' declares the LORD. 'Be strong, O Joshua son of Jehozadak, the high priest. Be strong, all you people of the land,' declares the LORD, 'and work. For I am with you,' declares the LORD Almighty. [5]This is what I covenanted with you when you came out of Egypt. And my Spirit remains among you. Do not fear.'

[6]"This is what the LORD Almighty says: 'In a little while I will once more shake the heavens and the earth, the sea and the dry land. [7]I will shake all nations, and the desired of all nations will come, and I will fill this house with glory,' says the LORD Almighty. [8]'The silver is mine and the gold is mine,' declares the LORD Almighty. [9]'The glory of this present house will be greater than the glory of the former house,' says the LORD Almighty. 'And in this place I will grant peace,' declares the LORD Almighty."

Blessings for a Defiled People

[10]On the twenty-fourth day of the ninth month, in the second year of Darius, the word of the LORD came to the prophet Haggai: [11]"This is what the LORD Almighty says: 'Ask the priests what the law says: [12]If a person carries consecrated meat in the fold of his garment, and that fold touches some bread or stew, some wine, oil or other food, does it become consecrated?' "

The priests answered, "No."

2:12 One-way Contamination

"One bad apple spoils the barrel," the saying goes; but one good apple doesn't clean up the rotten ones. In a similar vein, Haggai asked, "Which is contagious, good or evil?" In the Old Testament law, he found that consecrated meat—set aside to be used in sacrificial worship—did not "spread" its holiness. But a person who became "unclean" did spread his or her defilement. Under the Old Testament law, evil spread, but goodness did not. The Israelites' failure to rebuild the temple had defiled everything they touched—even their good deeds.

[13]Then Haggai said, "If a person defiled by contact with a dead body touches one of these things, does it become defiled?"

"Yes," the priests replied, "it becomes defiled."
[14]Then Haggai said, " 'So it is with this people

and this nation in my sight,' declares the LORD. 'Whatever they do and whatever they offer there is defiled.

[15]" 'Now give careful thought to this from this day on[a]—consider how things were before one stone was laid on another in the LORD's temple. [16]When anyone came to a heap of twenty measures, there were only ten. When anyone went to a wine vat to draw fifty measures, there were only twenty. [17]I struck all the work of your hands with blight, mildew and hail, yet you did not turn to me,' declares the LORD. [18]'From this day on, from this twenty-fourth day of the ninth month, give careful thought to the day when the foundation of the LORD's temple was laid. Give careful thought: [19]Is there yet any seed left in the barn? Until now, the vine and the fig tree, the pomegranate and the olive tree have not borne fruit.

" 'From this day on I will bless you.' "

2:23 The Imprint of the Master

Some 78 years before, King Jehoiachin had been captured and taken to Babylon. God had rejected him: "Even if you, Jehoiachin . . . , were a signet ring on my right hand, I would still pull you off" (Jeremiah 22:24).

But now his grandson Zerubbabel had come back to Jerusalem, chosen again as the Lord's "signet ring." Such a ring was used in place of a signature, to impress the king's seal on important documents. God had accepted men from the royal line of David as his chosen leaders again. The complete fulfillment of this prophecy would have to wait for Zerubbabel's descendant Jesus, a son of David who fully printed God's image on humanity.

Zerubbabel the LORD's Signet Ring

[20]The word of the LORD came to Haggai a second time on the twenty-fourth day of the month: [21]"Tell Zerubbabel governor of Judah that I will shake the heavens and the earth. [22]I will overturn royal thrones and shatter the power of the foreign kingdoms. I will overthrow chariots and their drivers; horses and their riders will fall, each by the sword of his brother.

[23]" 'On that day,' declares the LORD Almighty, 'I will take you, my servant Zerubbabel son of Shealtiel,' declares the LORD, 'and I will make you like my signet ring, for I have chosen you,' declares the LORD Almighty."

ZECHARIAH

Starting Over
How could they rebuild with broken pieces?

WHEN THE JEWS REVIEWED THEIR history, it looked like a long slide downhill. Consistently, they had responded to God's love by grumbling against him, by disobeying his law, by worshiping idols. Finally, after centuries of warning, punishment had come. Jerusalem was flattened. The survivors marched off in chains toward the other end of the world.

> "The LORD says,
> 'I will return to
> Jerusalem with
> mercy, and there my
> house will be
> rebuilt.'" 1:16

They had not merely lost a battle. They had lost, seemingly, their place in God's heart and their future as his special people.

But hope for a new start came in exile. When Persian emperor Cyrus took power, he offered Jews a chance to return to their land and rebuild their temple. Some jumped at the chance. They took the long journey to a homeland most of them had never seen (you can read about the trip in the first chapters of Ezra). They wanted not merely to rebuild; they hoped somehow to escape the downward, anti-God trend that had plagued their nation from its beginnings.

Hope Begins to Fade

They found a disheartening scene. Their once-beautiful city was a ghost town. Everything of value had been destroyed. Fertile fields were overgrown. The region was almost empty of people.

The small band of returned exiles built an altar on the grounds of the ruined temple. But soon they grew discouraged about actual rebuilding. They had enough trouble finding shelter and scratching out a living from the land. When their non-Jewish neighbors fought against rebuilding the temple, the former exiles gave up. Their hopes of a glorious "new beginning" began to fade.

The temple stayed in a state of disrepair for nearly 20 years, until the prophets Haggai and Zechariah stirred up renewed interest. These prophets saw that as long as the temple lay in ruins, Israel's distinctive character as a people of God was ruined, too. At their urging, the Jews organized to build again.

The book of Zechariah is a record from that critical period of rebuilding. Its first recorded message dates from approximately two months after the temple foundation was laid. The temple was completed four years later, at least partly due to Zechariah's encouraging words.

Needed: A Change of Heart

Zechariah wasn't mainly interested in a building, however. More important was the relationship with God that the temple symbolized. In his first recorded words Zechariah warned his people not to be like their ancestors. What good had a temple done them? A really new beginning required a change of heart. "'Return to me,' declares the LORD Almighty, 'and I will return to you'" (1:3).

The last half of Zechariah widens its view to the whole world. The small refugee community of Jews, Zechariah says, holds the world's future. Their new beginning would become the hope of the world.

How to Read Zechariah

Most people find Zechariah difficult to understand. Throughout the book you will find references to people and events that are hard to interpret. A commentary can be a great help, clarifying the meaning of these details. For historical background on Zechariah's times, read Ezra 1–6. Zechariah is mentioned by name in Ezra 5:1.

The book of Zechariah breaks into three parts. The first six chapters offer eight symbolic visions, which were meant to encourage the builders of the temple. They are not too difficult to understand if you take them one at a time and don't rush through them. Their main emphasis: God is at work again. He plans to live with his people in Jerusalem. He will protect them from their enemies, cleanse them from their sins, banish evil. He is making a new beginning for them.

Chapters 7–8 address the quality of life God wants his renewed people to enjoy. These words contain many encouraging promises to Israel.

The last six chapters are packed with puzzling references to the struggles Israel must endure in becoming what God wants. You will find predictions of terrible suffering and absolute victory. These chapters, as complex as they are, helped the Gospel writers understand Jesus' suffering, death, and resurrection. The writers quoted these chapters as they wrote of Jesus' final days. The book of Revelation, telling of the final goal of history, also drew on Zechariah's predictions.

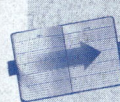

3-TRACK READING PLAN

For an explanation and complete listing of the 3-track reading plan, turn to page 7.

TRACK 1: *Two-Week Courses on the Bible*
See page 7 for information on these courses.

TRACK 2: *An Overview of Zechariah in 1 Day*
☐ Day 1. Read the Introduction to Zechariah and chapter 8, which describes the future God has in mind for his people.

Now turn to page 9 for your next Track 2 reading project.

TRACK 3: *All of Zechariah in 11 Days*
After you have read through Zechariah, turn to pages 10–14 for your next Track 3 reading project.

☐1   ☐2–3   ☐4–5   ☐6   ☐7   ☐8   ☐9   ☐10
☐11   ☐12–13 ☐14

A Call to Return to the LORD

1 In the eighth month of the second year of Darius, the word of the LORD came to the prophet Zechariah son of Berekiah, the son of Iddo:

²"The LORD was very angry with your forefathers. ³Therefore tell the people: This is what the LORD Almighty says: 'Return to me,' declares the LORD Almighty, 'and I will return to you,' says the LORD Almighty. ⁴Do not be like your forefathers, to whom the earlier prophets proclaimed: This is what the LORD Almighty says: 'Turn from your evil ways and your evil practices.' But they would not listen or pay attention to me, declares the LORD. ⁵Where are your forefathers now? And the prophets, do they live forever? ⁶But did not my words and my decrees, which I commanded my servants the prophets, overtake your forefathers?

"Then they repented and said, 'The LORD Almighty has done to us what our ways and practices deserve, just as he determined to do.'"

The Man Among the Myrtle Trees

⁷On the twenty-fourth day of the eleventh month, the month of Shebat, in the second year of Darius, the word of the LORD came to the prophet Zechariah son of Berekiah, the son of Iddo.

⁸During the night I had a vision—and there before me was a man riding a red horse! He was standing among the myrtle trees in a ravine. Behind him were red, brown and white horses.

⁹I asked, "What are these, my lord?"

The angel who was talking with me answered, "I will show you what they are."

¹⁰Then the man standing among the myrtle trees explained, "They are the ones the LORD has sent to go throughout the earth."

¹¹And they reported to the angel of the LORD, who was standing among the myrtle trees, "We have gone throughout the earth and found the whole world at rest and in peace."

¹²Then the angel of the LORD said, "LORD Almighty, how long will you withhold mercy from Jerusalem and from the towns of Judah, which you have been angry with these seventy years?" ¹³So the LORD spoke kind and comforting words to the angel who talked with me.

¹⁴Then the angel who was speaking to me said,

"Proclaim this word: This is what the LORD Almighty says: 'I am very jealous for Jerusalem and Zion, ¹⁵but I am very angry with the nations that feel secure. I was only a little angry, but they added to the calamity.'

¹⁶"Therefore, this is what the LORD says: 'I will return to Jerusalem with mercy, and there my house will be rebuilt. And the measuring line will be stretched out over Jerusalem,' declares the LORD Almighty.

¹⁷"Proclaim further: This is what the LORD Almighty says: 'My towns will again overflow with prosperity, and the LORD will again comfort Zion and choose Jerusalem.' "

Four Horns and Four Craftsmen

¹⁸Then I looked up—and there before me were four horns! ¹⁹I asked the angel who was speaking to me, "What are these?"

1:18 Brute Power

In an agricultural society that does its plowing with oxen, nothing is stronger than a bull. Probably because of this, horns are frequently used as symbols of power in the Old Testament. In our day we might say "bulldozer."

He answered me, "These are the horns that scattered Judah, Israel and Jerusalem."

²⁰Then the LORD showed me four craftsmen. ²¹I asked, "What are these coming to do?"

He answered, "These are the horns that scattered Judah so that no one could raise his head, but the craftsmen have come to terrify them and throw down these horns of the nations who lifted up their horns against the land of Judah to scatter its people."

A Man With a Measuring Line

2 Then I looked up—and there before me was a man with a measuring line in his hand! ²I asked, "Where are you going?"

He answered me, "To measure Jerusalem, to find out how wide and how long it is."

³Then the angel who was speaking to me left, and another angel came to meet him ⁴and said to him: "Run, tell that young man, 'Jerusalem will be a city without walls because of the great number of men and livestock in it. ⁵And I myself will be a wall of fire around it,' declares the LORD, 'and I will be its glory within.'

⁶"Come! Come! Flee from the land of the north," declares the LORD, "for I have scattered you to the four winds of heaven," declares the LORD.

⁷"Come, O Zion! Escape, you who live in the Daughter of Babylon!" ⁸For this is what the LORD Almighty says: "After he has honored me and has sent me against the nations that have plundered you—for whoever touches you touches the apple of his eye— ⁹I will surely raise my hand against them so that their slaves will plunder them.ᵃ Then you will know that the LORD Almighty has sent me.

¹⁰"Shout and be glad, O Daughter of Zion. For I am coming, and I will live among you," declares the LORD. ¹¹"Many nations will be joined with the LORD in that day and will become my people. I will live among you and you will know that the LORD Almighty has sent me to you. ¹²The LORD will inherit Judah as his portion in the holy land and will again choose Jerusalem. ¹³Be still before the LORD, all mankind, because he has roused himself from his holy dwelling."

Clean Garments for the High Priest

3 Then he showed me Joshuaᵇ the high priest standing before the angel of the LORD, and Satanᶜ standing at his right side to accuse him. ²The LORD said to Satan, "The LORD rebuke you, Satan! The LORD, who has chosen Jerusalem, rebuke you! Is not this man a burning stick snatched from the fire?"

³Now Joshua was dressed in filthy clothes as he stood before the angel. ⁴The angel said to those who were standing before him, "Take off his filthy clothes."

Then he said to Joshua, "See, I have taken away your sin, and I will put rich garments on you."

3:1–4 Bad News, Good News

References to the high priest Joshua also appear throughout Haggai. Whereas Zechariah uses him as a symbol of the rebellious nation, Haggai tells of Joshua's later transformation and obedience to God. Although Haggai and Zechariah cover the same time period, they show radically different styles. Haggai emphasizes the positive and gives a very straightforward message; Zechariah warns of danger and conveys his message in visions and symbols.

⁵Then I said, "Put a clean turban on his head." So they put a clean turban on his head and clothed him, while the angel of the LORD stood by.

⁶The angel of the LORD gave this charge to Joshua: ⁷"This is what the LORD Almighty says: 'If

---

ᵃ8,9 Or says after . . . eye: ⁹"I . . . plunder them."   ᵇ1 A variant of Jeshua; here and elsewhere in Zechariah
ᶜ1 Satan means accuser.

you will walk in my ways and keep my requirements, then you will govern my house and have charge of my courts, and I will give you a place among these standing here.

8"'Listen, O high priest Joshua and your associates seated before you, who are men symbolic of things to come: I am going to bring my servant, the Branch. 9See, the stone I have set in front of Joshua! There are seven eyes[a] on that one stone, and I will engrave an inscription on it,' says the LORD Almighty, 'and I will remove the sin of this land in a single day.

10"'In that day each of you will invite his neighbor to sit under his vine and fig tree,' declares the LORD Almighty."

The Gold Lampstand and the Two Olive Trees

4 Then the angel who talked with me returned and wakened me, as a man is wakened from his sleep. 2He asked me, "What do you see?"

I answered, "I see a solid gold lampstand with a bowl at the top and seven lights on it, with seven channels to the lights. 3Also there are two olive trees by it, one on the right of the bowl and the other on its left."

4I asked the angel who talked with me, "What are these, my lord?"

5He answered, "Do you not know what these are?"

"No, my lord," I replied.

6So he said to me, "This is the word of the LORD to Zerubbabel: 'Not by might nor by power, but by my Spirit,' says the LORD Almighty.

7"What[b] are you, O mighty mountain? Before Zerubbabel you will become level ground. Then he will bring out the capstone to shouts of 'God bless it! God bless it!'"

8Then the word of the LORD came to me: 9"The hands of Zerubbabel have laid the foundation of this temple; his hands will also complete it. Then you will know that the LORD Almighty has sent me to you.

10"Who despises the day of small things? Men will rejoice when they see the plumb line in the hand of Zerubbabel.

"(These seven are the eyes of the LORD, which range throughout the earth.)"

11Then I asked the angel, "What are these two olive trees on the right and the left of the lampstand?"

12Again I asked him, "What are these two olive branches beside the two gold pipes that pour out golden oil?"

13He replied, "Do you not know what these are?"

"No, my lord," I said.

14So he said, "These are the two who are anointed to[c] serve the Lord of all the earth."

The Flying Scroll

5 I looked again—and there before me was a flying scroll!

2He asked me, "What do you see?"

I answered, "I see a flying scroll, thirty feet long and fifteen feet wide.[d]"

3And he said to me, "This is the curse that is going out over the whole land; for according to what it says on one side, every thief will be banished, and according to what it says on the other, everyone who swears falsely will be banished. 4The LORD Almighty declares, 'I will send it out, and it will enter the house of the thief and the house of him who swears falsely by my name. It will remain in his house and destroy it, both its timbers and its stones.'"

The Woman in a Basket

5Then the angel who was speaking to me came forward and said to me, "Look up and see what this is that is appearing."

6I asked, "What is it?"

He replied, "It is a measuring basket.[e]" And he added, "This is the iniquity[f] of the people throughout the land."

7Then the cover of lead was raised, and there in the basket sat a woman! 8He said, "This is wickedness," and he pushed her back into the basket and pushed the lead cover down over its mouth.

9Then I looked up—and there before me were two women, with the wind in their wings! They had wings like those of a stork, and they lifted up the basket between heaven and earth.

10"Where are they taking the basket?" I asked the angel who was speaking to me.

11He replied, "To the country of Babylonia[g] to build a house for it. When it is ready, the basket will be set there in its place."

Four Chariots

6 I looked up again—and there before me were four chariots coming out from between two mountains—mountains of bronze! 2The first

---

a9 Or facets   *b7 Or Who*   *c14 Or two who bring oil and* (about 9 meters long and 4.5 meters wide)   *e6 Hebrew an ephah; also in verses 7–11*   *d2 Hebrew twenty cubits long and ten cubits wide*   *f6 Or appearance*   *g11 Hebrew Shinar*

chariot had red horses, the second black, ³the third white, and the fourth dappled—all of them powerful. ⁴I asked the angel who was speaking to me, "What are these, my lord?"

⁵The angel answered me, "These are the four spirits*a* of heaven, going out from standing in the presence of the Lord of the whole world. ⁶The one with the black horses is going toward the north country, the one with the white horses toward the west,*b* and the one with the dappled horses toward the south."

⁷When the powerful horses went out, they were straining to go throughout the earth. And he said, "Go throughout the earth!" So they went throughout the earth.

⁸Then he called to me, "Look, those going toward the north country have given my Spirit*c* rest in the land of the north."

A Crown for Joshua

⁹The word of the LORD came to me: ¹⁰"Take ⌊silver and gold⌋ from the exiles Heldai, Tobijah and Jedaiah, who have arrived from Babylon. Go the same day to the house of Josiah son of Zephaniah. ¹¹Take the silver and gold and make a crown, and set it on the head of the high priest, Joshua son of Jehozadak. ¹²Tell him this is what the LORD Almighty says: 'Here is the man whose name is the Branch, and he will branch out from his place and build the temple of the LORD. ¹³It is he who will build the temple of the LORD, and he will be clothed with majesty and will sit and rule on his throne. And he will be a priest on his throne. And there will be harmony between the two.' ¹⁴The crown will be given to Heldai,*d* Tobijah, Jedaiah and Hen*e* son of Zephaniah as a memorial in the temple of the LORD. ¹⁵Those who are far away will come and help to build the temple of the LORD, and you will know that the LORD Almighty has sent me to you. This will happen if you diligently obey the LORD your God."

Justice and Mercy, Not Fasting

7 In the fourth year of King Darius, the word of the LORD came to Zechariah on the fourth day of the ninth month, the month of Kislev. ²The people of Bethel had sent Sharezer and Regem-Melech, together with their men, to entreat the LORD ³by asking the priests of the house of the LORD Almighty and the prophets, "Should I mourn and fast in the fifth month, as I have done for so many years?"

⁴Then the word of the LORD Almighty came to me: ⁵"Ask all the people of the land and the priests, 'When you fasted and mourned in the fifth and seventh months for the past seventy years, was it really for me that you fasted? ⁶And

when you were eating and drinking, were you not just feasting for yourselves? ⁷Are these not the words the LORD proclaimed through the earlier prophets when Jerusalem and its surrounding

7:3 Repent for How Long?

While in exile, Jews had fasted and mourned on certain days in memory of the siege and overthrow of Jerusalem. Now that they had returned to Jerusalem they wanted to know: Should we keep fasting? Zechariah's answer came in 8:19: Fasting should now be replaced with feasting. But Zechariah warned that all religious ceremonies, however proper, were meaningless unless people's lives were controlled by God.

towns were at rest and prosperous, and the Negev and the western foothills were settled?'"

⁸And the word of the LORD came again to Zechariah: ⁹"This is what the LORD Almighty says: 'Administer true justice; show mercy and compassion to one another. ¹⁰Do not oppress the widow or the fatherless, the alien or the poor. In your hearts do not think evil of each other.'

¹¹"But they refused to pay attention; stubbornly they turned their backs and stopped up their ears. ¹²They made their hearts as hard as flint and would not listen to the law or to the words that the LORD Almighty had sent by his Spirit through the earlier prophets. So the LORD Almighty was very angry.

¹³"When I called, they did not listen; so when they called, I would not listen,' says the LORD Almighty. ¹⁴'I scattered them with a whirlwind among all the nations, where they were strangers. The land was left so desolate behind them that no one could come or go. This is how they made the pleasant land desolate.'"

The LORD Promises to Bless Jerusalem

8 Again the word of the LORD Almighty came to me. ²This is what the LORD Almighty says: "I am very jealous for Zion; I am burning with jealousy for her."

³This is what the LORD says: "I will return to Zion and dwell in Jerusalem. Then Jerusalem will be called the City of Truth, and the mountain of the LORD Almighty will be called the Holy Mountain."

⁴This is what the LORD Almighty says: "Once again men and women of ripe old age will sit in the streets of Jerusalem, each with cane in hand because of his age. ⁵The city streets will be filled with boys and girls playing there."

---

*a*5 Or *winds*   *b*6 Or *horses after them*   *c*8 Or *spirit*   *d*14 Syriac; Hebrew *Helem*   *e*14 Or *and the gracious one, the*

⁶This is what the LORD Almighty says: "It may seem marvelous to the remnant of this people at that time, but will it seem marvelous to me?" declares the LORD Almighty.

⁷This is what the LORD Almighty says: "I will save my people from the countries of the east and the west. ⁸I will bring them back to live in Jerusalem; they will be my people, and I will be faithful and righteous to them as their God."

⁹This is what the LORD Almighty says: "You who now hear these words spoken by the prophets who were there when the foundation was laid for the house of the LORD Almighty, let your hands be strong so that the temple may be built. ¹⁰Before that time there were no wages for man or beast. No one could go about his business safely because of his enemy, for I had turned every man against his neighbor. ¹¹But now I will not deal with the remnant of this people as I did in the past," declares the LORD Almighty.

¹²"The seed will grow well, the vine will yield its fruit, the ground will produce its crops, and the heavens will drop their dew. I will give all these things as an inheritance to the remnant of this people. ¹³As you have been an object of cursing among the nations, O Judah and Israel, so will I save you, and you will be a blessing. Do not be afraid, but let your hands be strong."

¹⁴This is what the LORD Almighty says: "Just as I had determined to bring disaster upon you and showed no pity when your fathers angered me," says the LORD Almighty, ¹⁵"so now I have determined to do good again to Jerusalem and Judah. Do not be afraid. ¹⁶These are the things you are to do: Speak the truth to each other, and render true and sound judgment in your courts; ¹⁷do not plot evil against your neighbor, and do not love to swear falsely. I hate all this," declares the LORD.

¹⁸Again the word of the LORD Almighty came to me. ¹⁹This is what the LORD Almighty says: "The fasts of the fourth, fifth, seventh and tenth months will become joyful and glad occasions and happy festivals for Judah. Therefore love truth and peace."

²⁰This is what the LORD Almighty says: "Many peoples and the inhabitants of many cities will yet come, ²¹and the inhabitants of one city will go to another and say, 'Let us go at once to entreat the LORD and seek the LORD Almighty. I myself am going.' ²²And many peoples and powerful nations will come to Jerusalem to seek the LORD Almighty and to entreat him."

²³This is what the LORD Almighty says: "In those days ten men from all languages and nations will take firm hold of one Jew by the hem of his robe and say, 'Let us go with you, because we have heard that God is with you.'"

Judgment on Israel's Enemies

An Oracle

9 The word of the LORD is against the land of Hadrach
  and will rest upon Damascus—
for the eyes of men and all the tribes of Israel
  are on the LORD—ᵃ
²and upon Hamath too, which borders on it,
  and upon Tyre and Sidon, though they are very skillful.
³Tyre has built herself a stronghold;
  she has heaped up silver like dust,
  and gold like the dirt of the streets.
⁴But the Lord will take away her possessions
  and destroy her power on the sea,
  and she will be consumed by fire.
⁵Ashkelon will see it and fear;
  Gaza will writhe in agony,
  and Ekron too, for her hope will wither.
Gaza will lose her king
  and Ashkelon will be deserted.
⁶Foreigners will occupy Ashdod,
  and I will cut off the pride of the Philistines.
⁷I will take the blood from their mouths,
  the forbidden food from between their teeth.
Those who are left will belong to our God
  and become leaders in Judah,
  and Ekron will be like the Jebusites.
⁸But I will defend my house
  against marauding forces.
Never again will an oppressor overrun my people,
  for now I am keeping watch.

The Coming of Zion's King

⁹Rejoice greatly, O Daughter of Zion!
  Shout, Daughter of Jerusalem!
See, your kingᵇ comes to you,
  righteous and having salvation,
  gentle and riding on a donkey,
  on a colt, the foal of a donkey.
¹⁰I will take away the chariots from Ephraim

ᵃ1 Or *Damascus. / For the eye of the LORD is on all mankind, / as well as on the tribes of Israel,*   ᵇ9 Or *King*

and the war-horses from Jerusalem,
and the battle bow will be broken.
He will proclaim peace to the nations.
His rule will extend from sea to sea

and from the River*a* to the ends of the earth.*b*
¹¹As for you, because of the blood of my covenant with you,
    I will free your prisoners from the waterless pit.

---

a 10 That is, the Euphrates   *b 10* Or *the end of the land*

¹²Return to your fortress, O prisoners of hope;
    even now I announce that I will restore twice as much to you.
¹³I will bend Judah as I bend my bow
    and fill it with Ephraim.
I will rouse your sons, O Zion,
    against your sons, O Greece,
    and make you like a warrior's sword.

The LORD Will Appear

¹⁴Then the LORD will appear over them;
    his arrow will flash like lightning.
The Sovereign LORD will sound the trumpet;
    he will march in the storms of the south,
¹⁵   and the LORD Almighty will shield them.
They will destroy
    and overcome with slingstones.
They will drink and roar as with wine;
    they will be full like a bowl
    used for sprinkling*c* the corners of the altar.
¹⁶The LORD their God will save them on that day
    as the flock of his people.
They will sparkle in his land

---

c 15 Or *bowl, / like*

New King, New Kingdom
The paradox of leadership that triumphs through suffering

THE BOOK OF ZECHARIAH TAKES a radical turn at chapter 9. A series of messages from God, expressed in fragmented images, tells the future of the world—and the role of God's people in it.

These chapters are difficult to understand, even in our day. The ultimate future is clearly good, however: Instead of remaining a small, subject nation, God's people will shake the world. The nations will worship at Jerusalem. 'The LORD will be king over the whole earth' (14:9).

> *Your king comes to you, righteous and having salvation, gentle and riding on a donkey. 9:9*

How could it be? Even for the Israelites this dream sounded farfetched. In Zechariah's day they needed clearance from the far-off Persian government just to rebuild their temple. Persia was the center of their world. Jerusalem hardly mattered. How could Israel become a great nation?

A Rejected Leader

These chapters of Zechariah show Israel's greatness emerging through struggle and suffering. No one who reads these words could have a glib idea that God makes things easy. Evil and misery virtually triumph before God's final intervention.

The key to Israel's future is a coming leader—a very unusual leader. People naturally expected the Messiah to be a triumphant warrior, especially since many Old Testament prophecies spoke of him that way. But this king would come on a donkey instead of a war-horse (9:9). Zechariah speaks of a shepherd—a term for 'leader'—who would be rejected by the nation (11:4–17). It describes a nation in mourning for 'the one they have pierced' (12:10).

All these predictions of a coming leader were quoted in the New Testament as applying to Jesus: a king without an army, whose crown was made of thorns. In all the Old Testament, only Isaiah (especially in chapter 53) captures so fully the paradox of Jesus' life: gentle leadership that triumphs through suffering.

Life Questions: Who is the 'greatest' person you've known up close? Did some kind of suffering contribute to his or her greatness?

like jewels in a crown.
[17]How attractive and beautiful they will be!
 Grain will make the young men thrive,
 and new wine the young women.

The LORD Will Care for Judah

10 Ask the LORD for rain in the springtime;
 it is the LORD who makes the storm
 clouds.
He gives showers of rain to men,
 and plants of the field to everyone.
[2]The idols speak deceit,
 diviners see visions that lie;
they tell dreams that are false,
 they give comfort in vain.
Therefore the people wander like sheep
 oppressed for lack of a shepherd.

[3]"My anger burns against the shepherds,
 and I will punish the leaders;
for the LORD Almighty will care
 for his flock, the house of Judah,
 and make them like a proud horse in
 battle.
[4]From Judah will come the cornerstone,
 from him the tent peg,
 from him the battle bow,
 from him every ruler.
[5]Together they[a] will be like mighty men
 trampling the muddy streets in battle.
Because the LORD is with them,
 they will fight and overthrow the
 horsemen.

[6]"I will strengthen the house of Judah
 and save the house of Joseph.
I will restore them
 because I have compassion on them.
They will be as though
 I had not rejected them,
for I am the LORD their God
 and I will answer them.
[7]The Ephraimites will become like mighty
 men,
 and their hearts will be glad as with wine.
Their children will see it and be joyful;
 their hearts will rejoice in the LORD.
[8]I will signal for them
 and gather them in.
Surely I will redeem them;
 they will be as numerous as before.
[9]Though I scatter them among the peoples,
 yet in distant lands they will remember
 me.
They and their children will survive,
 and they will return.
[10]I will bring them back from Egypt
 and gather them from Assyria.
I will bring them to Gilead and Lebanon,

and there will not be room enough for
 them.
[11]They will pass through the sea of trouble;
 the surging sea will be subdued
 and all the depths of the Nile will dry up.
Assyria's pride will be brought down
 and Egypt's scepter will pass away.
[12]I will strengthen them in the LORD
 and in his name they will walk,"
                                declares the LORD.

11 Open your doors, O Lebanon,
 so that fire may devour your cedars!
[2]Wail, O pine tree, for the cedar has fallen;
 the stately trees are ruined!
Wail, oaks of Bashan;
 the dense forest has been cut down!
[3]Listen to the wail of the shepherds;
 their rich pastures are destroyed!
Listen to the roar of the lions;
 the lush thicket of the Jordan is ruined!

Two Shepherds

[4]This is what the LORD my God says: "Pasture the flock marked for slaughter. [5]Their buyers slaughter them and go unpunished. Those who sell them say, 'Praise the LORD, I am rich!' Their own shepherds do not spare them. [6]For I will no longer have pity on the people of the land," declares the LORD. "I will hand everyone over to his neighbor and his king. They will oppress the land, and I will not rescue them from their hands."

[7]So I pastured the flock marked for slaughter, particularly the oppressed of the flock. Then I took two staffs and called one Favor and the

11:7 Who Are the Shepherds?

The prophets' messages often had a double meaning: one for the people who first heard them, and another, deeper meaning for future times. In this passage, Zechariah plays the role of the good shepherd who is rejected, an image that Jesus later applied to himself. Similarly, the Jews in Zechariah's day had many "foolish shepherd" leaders, but this description (verses 15–17) may also foreshadow the New Testament's "antichrist."

other Union, and I pastured the flock. [8]In one month I got rid of the three shepherds.

The flock detested me, and I grew weary of them [9]and said, "I will not be your shepherd. Let the dying die, and the perishing perish. Let those who are left eat one another's flesh."

[10]Then I took my staff called Favor and broke it, revoking the covenant I had made with all the

[a]4,5 Or *ruler, all of them together.* / [5]*They*

nations. [11]It was revoked on that day, and so the afflicted of the flock who were watching me knew it was the word of the LORD.

[12]I told them, "If you think it best, give me my pay; but if not, keep it." So they paid me thirty pieces of silver.

[13]And the LORD said to me, "Throw it to the potter"—the handsome price at which they priced me! So I took the thirty pieces of silver and threw them into the house of the LORD to the potter.

[14]Then I broke my second staff called Union, breaking the brotherhood between Judah and Israel.

[15]Then the LORD said to me, "Take again the equipment of a foolish shepherd. [16]For I am going to raise up a shepherd over the land who will not care for the lost, or seek the young, or heal the injured, or feed the healthy, but will eat the meat of the choice sheep, tearing off their hoofs.

[17]"Woe to the worthless shepherd,
    who deserts the flock!
May the sword strike his arm and his right
        eye!
    May his arm be completely withered,
        his right eye totally blinded!"

Jerusalem's Enemies to Be Destroyed

An Oracle

12 This is the word of the LORD concerning Israel. The LORD, who stretches out the heavens, who lays the foundation of the earth, and who forms the spirit of man within him, declares: [2]"I am going to make Jerusalem a cup that sends all the surrounding peoples reeling. Judah will be besieged as well as Jerusalem. [3]On that day, when all the nations of the earth are gathered against her, I will make Jerusalem an immovable rock for all the nations. All who try to move it will injure themselves. [4]On that day I will strike every horse with panic and its rider with madness," declares the LORD. "I will keep a watchful eye over the house of Judah, but I will blind all the horses of the nations. [5]Then the leaders of Judah will say in their hearts, 'The people of Jerusalem are strong, because the LORD Almighty is their God.'

[6]"On that day I will make the leaders of Judah like a firepot in a woodpile, like a flaming torch among sheaves. They will consume right and left all the surrounding peoples, but Jerusalem will remain intact in her place.

[7]"The LORD will save the dwellings of Judah first, so that the honor of the house of David and of Jerusalem's inhabitants may not be greater than that of Judah. [8]On that day the LORD will shield those who live in Jerusalem, so that the feeblest among them will be like David, and the house of David will be like God, like the Angel of the LORD going before them. [9]On that day I will set out to destroy all the nations that attack Jerusalem.

Mourning for the One They Pierced

[10]"And I will pour out on the house of David and the inhabitants of Jerusalem a spirit[a] of grace and supplication. They will look on[b] me, the one they have pierced, and they will mourn for him as one mourns for an only child, and grieve bitterly for him as one grieves for a firstborn son. [11]On that day the weeping in Jerusalem will be great, like the weeping of Hadad Rimmon in the plain of Megiddo. [12]The land will mourn, each clan by itself, with their wives by themselves: the clan of the house of David and their wives, the clan of the house of Nathan and their wives, [13]the clan of the house of Levi and their wives, the clan of Shimei and their wives, [14]and all the rest of the clans and their wives.

Cleansing From Sin

13 "On that day a fountain will be opened to the house of David and the inhabitants of Jerusalem, to cleanse them from sin and impurity.

[2]"On that day, I will banish the names of the idols from the land, and they will be remembered no more," declares the LORD Almighty. "I will remove both the prophets and the spirit of impurity from the land. [3]And if anyone still prophesies, his father and mother, to whom he was born, will say to him, 'You must die, because you have told lies in the LORD's name.' When he prophesies, his own parents will stab him.

[4]"On that day every prophet will be ashamed of his prophetic vision. He will not put on a prophet's garment of hair in order to deceive. [5]He will say, 'I am not a prophet. I am a farmer; the land has been my livelihood since my youth.[c]' [6]If someone asks him, 'What are these wounds on your body[d]?' he will answer, 'The wounds I was given at the house of my friends.'

13:7 A Prophecy of Jesus

Jesus applied this verse to himself just before he died (Matthew 26:31). Some commentators believe that his words about the shepherd who "lays down his life for the sheep" (John 10:11) also drew on this passage. Zechariah's prophecies were on the minds of the Gospel writers: 9:9 is quoted in Matthew 21:5; 12:10 in John 19:37; and 11:12–13 in Matthew 27:9.

---

[a]10 Or *the Spirit*   [b]10 Or *to*   [c]5 Or *farmer; a man sold me in my youth*   [d]6 Or *wounds between your hands*

The Shepherd Struck, the Sheep Scattered

⁷"Awake, O sword, against my shepherd,
　against the man who is close to me!"
　　declares the LORD Almighty.
"Strike the shepherd,
　and the sheep will be scattered,
　and I will turn my hand against the little
　　ones.
⁸In the whole land," declares the LORD,
　"two-thirds will be struck down and
　　perish;
　yet one-third will be left in it.
⁹This third I will bring into the fire;
　I will refine them like silver
　and test them like gold.
They will call on my name
　and I will answer them;
I will say, 'They are my people,'
　and they will say, 'The LORD is our God.'"

The LORD Comes and Reigns

14 A day of the LORD is coming when your
plunder will be divided among you.
²I will gather all the nations to Jerusalem to
fight against it; the city will be captured, the
houses ransacked, and the women raped. Half of
the city will go into exile, but the rest of the
people will not be taken from the city. ³Then the LORD will go out and fight against
those nations, as he fights in the day of battle.
⁴On that day his feet will stand on the Mount of
Olives, east of Jerusalem, and the Mount of Olives will be split in two from east to west, forming
a great valley, with half of the mountain moving
north and half moving south. ⁵You will flee by
my mountain valley, for it will extend to Azel.
You will flee as you fled from the earthquake*a* in
the days of Uzziah king of Judah. Then the LORD
my God will come, and all the holy ones with
him.

⁶On that day there will be no light, no cold or
frost. ⁷It will be a unique day, without daytime or
nighttime—a day known to the LORD. When
evening comes, there will be light.

⁸On that day living water will flow out from
Jerusalem, half to the eastern sea*b* and half to
the western sea,*c* in summer and in winter.

⁹The LORD will be king over the whole earth.
On that day there will be one LORD, and his name
the only name.

¹⁰The whole land, from Geba to Rimmon,
south of Jerusalem, will become like the Arabah.
But Jerusalem will be raised up and remain in its
place, from the Benjamin Gate to the site of the
First Gate, to the Corner Gate, and from the
Tower of Hananel to the royal winepresses. ¹¹It

will be inhabited; never again will it be destroyed.
Jerusalem will be secure.

¹²This is the plague with which the LORD will
strike all the nations that fought against Jerusa-

14:9 Catastrophes to Come?

*Biblical scholars disagree on how to
understand the images in this chapter. To
some, the catastrophes portrayed—a mountain
splitting in two, a day without light or cold,
people rotting on their feet (verses 4,6,12)—take
on added significance in an era of nuclear
weapons and a possible greenhouse effect.
Others interpret these images in more symbolic
ways. Regardless, Zechariah makes clear that
the end result of the earth's turmoil will be
good news for all followers of God.*

lem: Their flesh will rot while they are still standing on their feet, their eyes will rot in their sockets, and their tongues will rot in their mouths.
¹³On that day men will be stricken by the LORD
with great panic. Each man will seize the hand of
another, and they will attack each other. ¹⁴Judah
too will fight at Jerusalem. The wealth of all the
surrounding nations will be collected—great
quantities of gold and silver and clothing. ¹⁵A
similar plague will strike the horses and mules,
the camels and donkeys, and all the animals in
those camps.

14:21 No More Separation

*The priests and the temple had always been
separate and more holy than the rest of Israel.
HOLY TO THE LORD had been inscribed on the
priests' turbans (Exodus 28:36) as a symbol of
this. But, Zechariah predicted, in the future such
words would decorate even horses. Ordinary
kitchen pots would become as sacred as the
holy sacramental vessels. There would no
longer be a distinction between the sacred and
secular, for everything would be sacred.*

¹⁶Then the survivors from all the nations that
have attacked Jerusalem will go up year after year
to worship the King, the LORD Almighty, and to
celebrate the Feast of Tabernacles. ¹⁷If any of the
peoples of the earth do not go up to Jerusalem to
worship the King, the LORD Almighty, they will
have no rain. ¹⁸If the Egyptian people do not go
up and take part, they will have no rain. The
LORD*d* will bring on them the plague he inflicts

---

*a5 Or ⁵My mountain valley will be blocked and will extend to Azel. It will be blocked as it was blocked because of the
earthquake* ᵇ8 That is, the Dead Sea ᶜ8 That is, the Mediterranean ᵈ18 Or part, then the LORD

on the nations that do not go up to celebrate the Feast of Tabernacles. [19]This will be the punishment of Egypt and the punishment of all the nations that do not go up to celebrate the Feast of Tabernacles.

[20]On that day HOLY TO THE LORD will be inscribed on the bells of the horses, and the cooking pots in the LORD's house will be like the sacred bowls in front of the altar. [21]Every pot in Jerusalem and Judah will be holy to the LORD Almighty, and all who come to sacrifice will take some of the pots and cook in them. And on that day there will no longer be a Canaanite[a] in the house of the LORD Almighty.

MALACHI

When Faith Grows Weary

Malachi spoke to people "going through the motions"

> *"A son honors his father, and a servant his master. If I am a father, where is the honor due me?" 1:6*

SUCCESS HAS DANGERS OF ITS own. When you reach the top, you may tend to slack off. Spiritual life can gradually deteriorate too.

Malachi, in this short book, tried to awaken Israel from slackness in relating to God. Years before, they had optimistically returned to Jerusalem after a long exile. Their faith had grown deeper through difficulties. Despite fierce opposition they had rebuilt the temple, the symbol of their hope in God. They had expected God to supernaturally fill it with his glory and make their nation the center of the world.

By Malachi's time Israel's hope had faded. In fact, life seemed to have passed the Israelites by. They could not see that God loved them (1:2), and they felt that serving God brought no reward (2:17; 3:14).

No Big Sinners

The people of Jerusalem had become lukewarm. Their complaints showed it, and so did their actions. They were not "big" sinners like the people before the exile, who had practiced child sacrifice and brought idols into the temple. Malachi's people had kept their religion, but they had lost contact with the God whom the religion was all about.

While Malachi mentioned the same injustices and evils earlier prophets had blasted (3:5), he concentrated most of his energy on problems that may seem petty in comparison: mixed marriages, divorce, and apathetic worship (shown in their second-rate offerings). Through Malachi's eyes, we see the Israelites going through the motions of their faith, doing the bare minimum.

How do you heat up a lukewarm faith? Malachi used several tactics. He began with God's love. To his audience, it was not apparent. But if they would compare their situation with neighboring Edom's, they would see that God had been caring for them all along.

Curing a Careless Attitude

Malachi then challenged the Jews to take obedience seriously. They were bringing injured or sick animals to God for offerings. "Try offering them to your governor!" Malachi said. "Would he be pleased with you?" (1:8). Malachi urged them to bring the perfect animals God's law demands and his honor requires. Malachi further demanded that they stop marrying women of other religions, a practice that inevitably introduced religious compromise. They must also put an end to divorce. And finally, they must bring a full tenth—the "tithe"—of their income to God at the temple. Their skimping amounted to robbery—robbery from God.

Malachi didn't demand these changes just because they were in the rulebook. They were actions meant to symbolize an inner attitude. The people must practice their faith seriously. " 'Test me in this,' says the Lord Almighty, 'and see if I will not throw open the floodgates of heaven and pour out so much blessing that you will not have room enough for it' " (3:10).

The Last Voice

Malachi's was the last Old Testament voice. It reverberated through 400 or more years of biblical silence. During those years at least some of Malachi's message took hold. Led by the Pharisees, Jews became increasingly devoted to keeping the Old Testament law. Unfortunately, many of them lost Malachi's main point. They forgot that the law was not an end in itself. It was a means by which to give God the honor he deserves.

How to Read Malachi

God's voice dominates Malachi, the voice of a loving father pleading with his children. The people's response is given in the form of seven questions or complaints. The result is a kind of dialogue—almost an argument—which lets you see into the personal attitudes of God and the people he is speaking to.

As in most arguments, a variety of issues are raised, but they are all rooted in a few basic attitudes. As you read through Malachi, try to see what attitudes lay behind the questions, complaints, and problems of God's people. Also note what attitudes lay behind God's words and promises to them.

You can place Malachi's message in the context of Israelite history by looking up "A Lineup of Rulers," pages 1361–1369.

3-TRACK READING PLAN

For an explanation and complete listing of the 3-track reading plan, turn to page 7.

TRACK 1: *Two-Week Courses on the Bible*
See page 7 for information on these courses.

TRACK 2: *An Overview of Malachi in 1 Day*
☐ Day 1. Read the Introduction to Malachi and chapter 3, which lays out some of God's promises and expectations for his people.

Now turn to page 9 for your next Track 2 reading project.

TRACK 3: *All of Malachi in 3 Days*
After you have read through Malachi, turn to pages 10–14 for your next Track 3 reading project.
☐1   ☐2   ☐3–4

---

1 An oracle: The word of the LORD to Israel through Malachi.[a]

Jacob Loved, Esau Hated

²"I have loved you," says the LORD.

"But you ask, 'How have you loved us?'

"Was not Esau Jacob's brother?" the LORD says. "Yet I have loved Jacob, ³but Esau I have hated, and I have turned his mountains into a wasteland and left his inheritance to the desert jackals."

⁴Edom may say, "Though we have been crushed, we will rebuild the ruins."

But this is what the LORD Almighty says: "They may build, but I will demolish. They will be called the Wicked Land, a people always under the wrath of the LORD. ⁵You will see it with your own eyes and say, 'Great is the LORD—even beyond the borders of Israel!'

Blemished Sacrifices

⁶"A son honors his father, and a servant his master. If I am a father, where is the honor due me? If I am a master, where is the respect due me?" says the LORD Almighty. "It is you, O priests, who show contempt for my name.

"But you ask, 'How have we shown contempt for your name?'

⁷"You place defiled food on my altar.

"But you ask, 'How have we defiled you?'

"By saying that the LORD's table is contemptible. ⁸When you bring blind animals for sacrifice, is that not wrong? When you sacrifice crippled or diseased animals, is that not wrong? Try offering

1:2 Spurned

Lovers remember when they first fell for someone. They also remember how that person responded, especially if their love met rejection.

In Malachi, God starts the conversation: "I have loved you." Then he traces all of Israel's sins back to their underlying contempt for that love. They have not honored him as a father (verse 6) or worshiped him as the great King he is (verse 11). Instead, they have shown contempt, bringing second-rate offerings (verse 8), saying, "What a burden!" and sniffing contemptuously at his table (verse 13).

---

[a]1 *Malachi* means *my messenger.*

them to your governor! Would he be pleased with you? Would he accept you?" says the LORD Almighty.

⁹"Now implore God to be gracious to us. With such offerings from your hands, will he accept you?"—says the LORD Almighty.

¹⁰"Oh, that one of you would shut the temple doors, so that you would not light useless fires on my altar! I am not pleased with you," says the LORD Almighty, "and I will accept no offering from your hands. ¹¹My name will be great among the nations, from the rising to the setting of the sun. In every place incense and pure offerings will be brought to my name, because my name will be great among the nations," says the LORD Almighty.

¹²"But you profane it by saying of the Lord's table, 'It is defiled,' and of its food, 'It is contemptible.' ¹³And you say, 'What a burden!' and you sniff at it contemptuously," says the LORD Almighty.

"When you bring injured, crippled or diseased animals and offer them as sacrifices, should I accept them from your hands?" says the LORD. ¹⁴"Cursed is the cheat who has an acceptable male in his flock and vows to give it, but then sacrifices a blemished animal to the Lord. For I am a great king," says the LORD Almighty, "and my name is to be feared among the nations.

Admonition for the Priests

2 "And now this admonition is for you, O priests. ²If you do not listen, and if you do not set your heart to honor my name," says the LORD Almighty, "I will send a curse upon you, and I will curse your blessings. Yes, I have already cursed them, because you have not set your heart to honor me.

³"Because of you I will rebuke[a] your descendants[b]; I will spread on your faces the offal from your festival sacrifices, and you will be carried off with it. ⁴And you will know that I have sent you this admonition so that my covenant with Levi may continue," says the LORD Almighty. ⁵"My covenant was with him, a covenant of life and peace, and I gave them to him; this called for reverence and he revered me and stood in awe of my name. ⁶True instruction was in his mouth and nothing false was found on his lips. He walked with me in peace and uprightness, and turned many from sin.

⁷"For the lips of a priest ought to preserve knowledge, and from his mouth men should seek instruction—because he is the messenger of the

LORD Almighty. ⁸But you have turned from the way and by your teaching have caused many to stumble; you have violated the covenant with Levi," says the LORD Almighty. ⁹"So I have caused you to be despised and humiliated before all the people, because you have not followed my ways but have shown partiality in matters of the law."

Judah Unfaithful

¹⁰Have we not all one Father[c]? Did not one God create us? Why do we profane the covenant of our fathers by breaking faith with one another?

¹¹Judah has broken faith. A detestable thing has been committed in Israel and in Jerusalem: Judah has desecrated the sanctuary the LORD loves, by marrying the daughter of a foreign god. ¹²As for the man who does this, whoever he may be, may the LORD cut him off from the tents of Jacob[d]—even though he brings offerings to the LORD Almighty.

¹³Another thing you do: You flood the LORD's altar with tears. You weep and wail because he no longer pays attention to your offerings or accepts them with pleasure from your hands. ¹⁴You ask, "Why?" It is because the LORD is acting as the witness between you and the wife of your youth, because you have broken faith with her, though she is your partner, the wife of your marriage covenant.

¹⁵Has not ⌊the LORD⌋ made them one? In flesh and spirit they are his. And why one? Because he was seeking godly offspring.[e] So guard yourself in your spirit, and do not break faith with the wife of your youth.

¹⁶"I hate divorce," says the LORD God of Israel, "and I hate a man's covering himself[f] with violence as well as with his garment," says the LORD Almighty.

So guard yourself in your spirit, and do not break faith.

> ### 2:16 I Hate Divorce
> *Divorce was legal in Israel (see Deuteronomy 24:1–4), so perhaps people made no connection between their troubles and the divorce statistics. Malachi straightens them out. God hates divorce, legal or not. The marriage covenant between a man and woman should be kept faithfully. Jesus said much the same thing in Matthew 19:1–9.*

---

[a]3 Or cut off (see Septuagint)   [b]3 Or will blight your grain   [c]10 Or father   [d]12 Or ¹²May the LORD cut off from the tents of Jacob anyone who gives testimony in behalf of the man who does this   [e]15 Or ¹⁵But the one ⌊who is our father⌋ did not do this, not as long as life remained in him. And what was he seeking? An offspring from God   [f]16 Or his wife

The Day of Judgment

[17]You have wearied the LORD with your words.
"How have we wearied him?" you ask.

By saying, "All who do evil are good in the
eyes of the LORD, and he is pleased with them" or
"Where is the God of justice?"

3 "See, I will send my messenger, who will prepare the way before me. Then suddenly the
Lord you are seeking will come to his temple; the
messenger of the covenant, whom you desire,
will come," says the LORD Almighty.

2:17 Why Serve God?

*Here and in 3:14 people harshly complained
they could see no point in serving God, when
you got no special reward. In responding, God
did not try to convince them that the righteous
were, in fact, better off. He told them that he
keeps a "scroll of remembrance" (3:16), on
which he records those who fear him, and that
sometime in the future he will come as judge,
destroying the wicked and preserving those
who fear him. The value of serving him will be
obvious someday, even if it is not today.*

[2]But who can endure the day of his coming?
Who can stand when he appears? For he will be
like a refiner's fire or a launderer's soap. [3]He will
sit as a refiner and purifier of silver; he will purify
the Levites and refine them like gold and silver.
Then the LORD will have men who will bring
offerings in righteousness, [4]and the offerings of
Judah and Jerusalem will be acceptable to the
LORD, as in days gone by, as in former years.

[5]"So I will come near to you for judgment. I
will be quick to testify against sorcerers, adulterers and perjurers, against those who defraud laborers of their wages, who oppress the widows
and the fatherless, and deprive aliens of justice,
but do not fear me," says the LORD Almighty.

Robbing God

[6]"I the LORD do not change. So you,
O descendants of Jacob, are not destroyed. [7]Ever
since the time of your forefathers you have
turned away from my decrees and have not kept
them. Return to me, and I will return to you,"
says the LORD Almighty.

"But you ask, 'How are we to return?'

[8]"Will a man rob God? Yet you rob me.

"But you ask, 'How do we rob you?'

"In tithes and offerings. [9]You are under a
curse—the whole nation of you—because you
are robbing me. [10]Bring the whole tithe into the
storehouse, that there may be food in my house.

Test me in this," says the LORD Almighty, "and
see if I will not throw open the floodgates of
heaven and pour out so much blessing that you
will not have room enough for it. [11]I will prevent
pests from devouring your crops, and the vines
in your fields will not cast their fruit," says the
LORD Almighty. [12]"Then all the nations will call

3:10 Testing the Tithe

*Like a salesman offering a free sample, God
urges the Israelites to test him out. If they bring
their tithes to the temple, they will see how God
blesses them, opening the "floodgates of
heaven" to pour out an abundance. The "tithe"
was at least a tenth of their income, used to
feed the priests, pay temple expenses, and help
the poor.*

you blessed, for yours will be a delightful land,"
says the LORD Almighty.

[13]"You have said harsh things against me,"
says the LORD.

"Yet you ask, 'What have we said against you?'

[14]"You have said, 'It is futile to serve God.
What did we gain by carrying out his requirements and going about like mourners before the
LORD Almighty? [15]But now we call the arrogant
blessed. Certainly the evildoers prosper, and even
those who challenge God escape.'"

[16]Then those who feared the LORD talked with
each other, and the LORD listened and heard. A
scroll of remembrance was written in his presence concerning those who feared the LORD and
honored his name.

[17]"They will be mine," says the LORD Almighty, "in the day when I make up my treasured possession.[a] I will spare them, just as in
compassion a man spares his son who serves
him. [18]And you will again see the distinction between the righteous and the wicked, between
those who serve God and those who do not.

The Day of the LORD

4 "Surely the day is coming; it will burn like a
furnace. All the arrogant and every evildoer
will be stubble, and that day that is coming will
set them on fire," says the LORD Almighty. "Not
a root or a branch will be left to them. [2]But for
you who revere my name, the sun of righteousness will rise with healing in its wings. And you
will go out and leap like calves released from the
stall. [3]Then you will trample down the wicked;
they will be ashes under the soles of your feet on
the day when I do these things," says the LORD
Almighty.

---

[a]17 Or *Almighty, "my treasured possession, in the day when I act*

⁴"Remember the law of my servant Moses, the decrees and laws I gave him at Horeb for all Israel.

⁵"See, I will send you the prophet Elijah before that great and dreadful day of the LORD comes. ⁶He will turn the hearts of the fathers to their children, and the hearts of the children to their fathers; or else I will come and strike the land with a curse."

4:5 The Second Elijah

The prophet Elijah, Malachi predicted, would precede the Lord. This prophecy was carefully noted in the New Testament. Jesus identified John the Baptist as the one predicted (Matthew 11:14; 17:9–13).

Outline of Old Testament History

This outline emphasizes broad historical periods rather than specific events. Dates, which often depend on scholarly interpretation, are approximate.

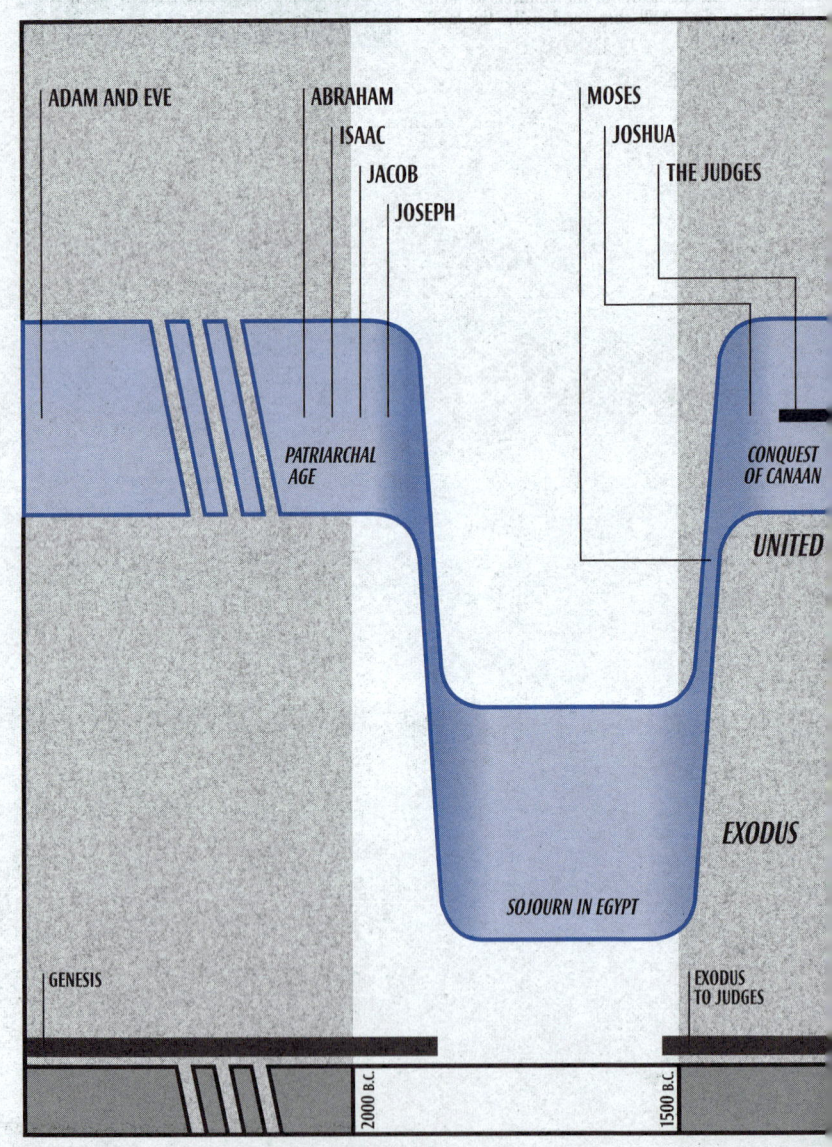

ADAM AND EVE

ABRAHAM

ISAAC

JACOB

JOSEPH

MOSES

JOSHUA

THE JUDGES

PATRIARCHAL AGE

CONQUEST OF CANAAN

UNITED

EXODUS

SOJOURN IN EGYPT

GENESIS

EXODUS TO JUDGES

2000 B.C.

1500 B.C.

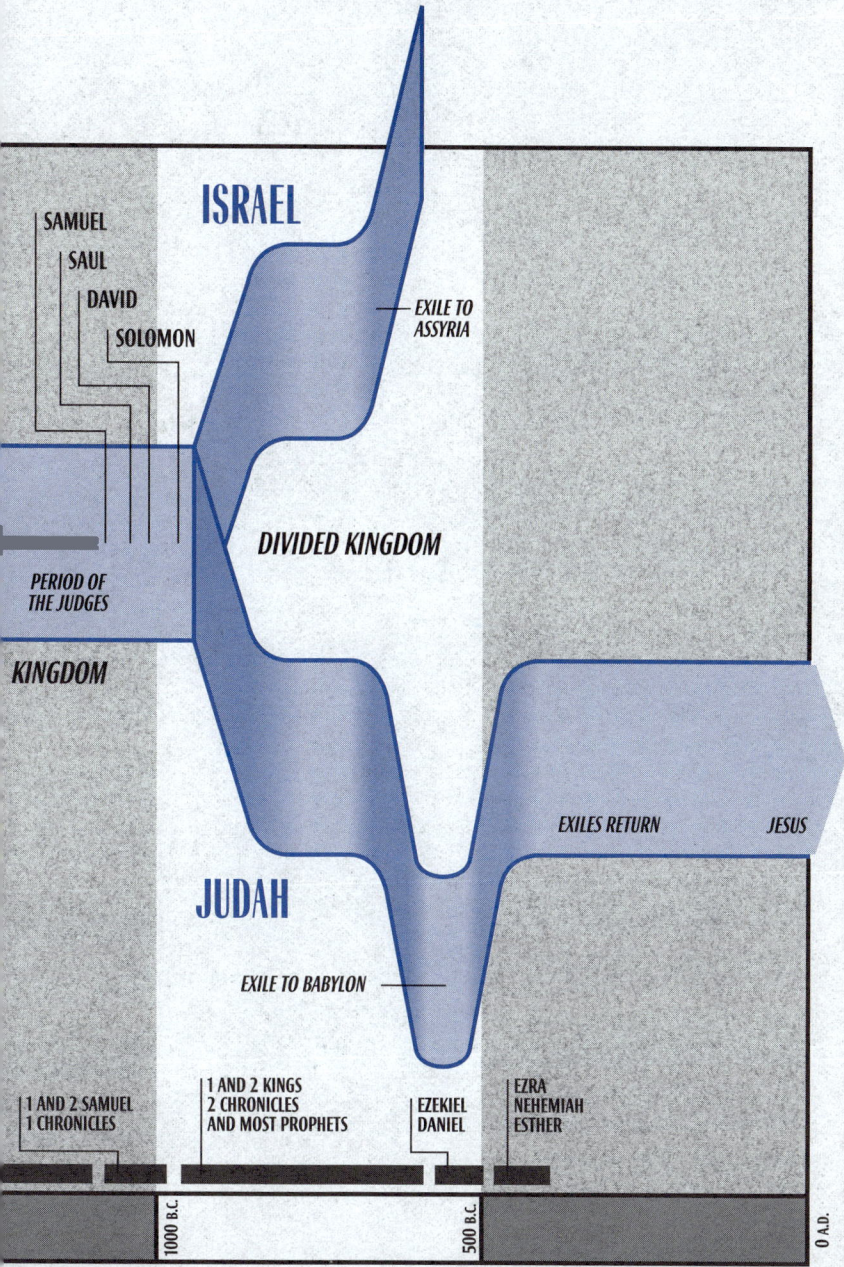

ISRAEL

SAMUEL
SAUL
DAVID
SOLOMON

EXILE TO
ASSYRIA

DIVIDED KINGDOM

PERIOD OF
THE JUDGES

KINGDOM

EXILES RETURN   JESUS

JUDAH

EXILE TO BABYLON

1 AND 2 SAMUEL
1 CHRONICLES

1 AND 2 KINGS
2 CHRONICLES
AND MOST PROPHETS

EZEKIEL
DANIEL

EZRA
NEHEMIAH
ESTHER

1000 B.C.

500 B.C.

0 A.D.

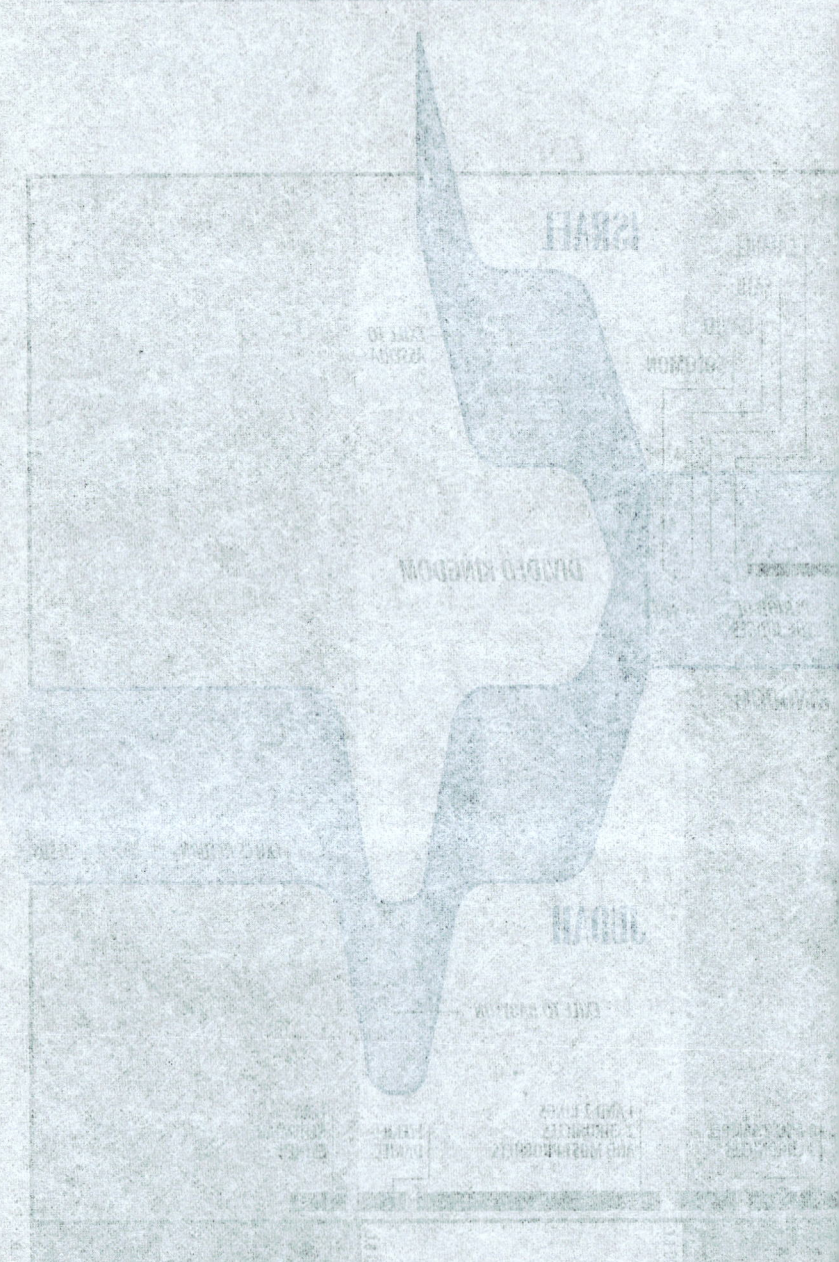

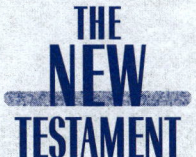

THE
NEW
TESTAMENT

MATTHEW

A Bridge from Old to New
Why start with a list of names?

> "She will give birth to a son, and you are to give him the name Jesus, because he will save his people from their sins."
> 1:21

FOR FOUR HUNDRED YEARS, NOTHING new was added to the Bible. The prophets fell silent. During this time, Middle Eastern empires rose and fell, and the tiny nation of Israel suffered under the domination of greater powers like Greece and Rome.

And then something momentous happened. A baby was born—a baby unlike any who had ever come before. By introducing this baby who grew into the man Jesus, the book of Matthew opens a whole new section of the Bible—the New Testament.

Matthew makes his intentions clear from the very first sentence: He connects Jesus' arrival with the Old Testament story line. Jesus was a Jew, he says, the son of Abraham. And also a king, the son of David. Matthew then sets out to prove an audacious claim: This Jesus, from the humble town of Nazareth, is the very "Messiah," the deliverer promised back in the Old Testament. (*Christ* is a Greek translation of the word *Messiah*.)

Jesus' Family Tree

People all over the world, especially Jews, had been eagerly awaiting the Messiah. His coming would change the entire history of the world, they believed. Could this carpenter's son be the long-expected king? To answer that question, Matthew starts with a genealogy.

Genealogies—long lists of names—rarely prove interesting to anyone but the people directly involved. To those people, however, the lists are anything but boring.

Listen to one modern author describe what it was like to hear an ancient genealogy: "There is an expression, 'the peak experience,' a moment which emotionally can never again be equaled in your life. I had mine, that first day in the village of Juffure, in black west Africa . . . Goose bumps came out on me the size of marbles." With those words, Alex Haley, author of *Roots*, recalls the day he first heard, from the lips of an aged storyteller, the account of young Kunta Kinte being taken captive by slave traders in 1752.

The Importance of Roots

Haley's ancestors in Tennessee and Virginia had descended directly from a native African captured in a tiny village in Gambia. The day he listened to the gentle African elder recite, "And so-and-so took as a wife so-and-so, and begat so-and-so," the final link in Haley's family chain snapped into place. *Roots* tells the story of this connection.

In a similar way, the book of Matthew doesn't begin with Jesus' birth, but reaches back further to establish his roots. If indeed Jesus is the Messiah, his ancestors must match up to that claim. As any student of history knows, kings don't merely declare themselves; they must belong to a royal line. Matthew traces Jesus' lineage to the father of the Jewish race, Abraham—who first received the promise of the Messiah—then to the great Jewish king David.

Links to the Old Testament

After recording Jesus' bloodline, Matthew narrates the story of Jesus' life on earth. He relies heavily on the Old Testament, quoting it more frequently than does any other New Testament author. (Note such phrases as "So was fulfilled what was said through the prophets.")

The first book in the New Testament, then, stands as the Gospel that pulls things together, the link between the old and the new. Matthew starts with Jesus' roots, but he also contrasts Jesus with the traditional Jewish picture of the Messiah. Jesus, a king, ended thousands of years of eager waiting.

But he came to establish a wholly new kind of kingdom—a kingdom different from what anyone expected.

How to Read Matthew

Anybody who has looked over an Internal Revenue Service (IRS) form knows what tax collectors like: neat, orderly rows of figures, with all expenses and income classified by type and source. Fittingly, the Gospel attributed to former tax collector Matthew reflects systematic, ledger-sheet thinking. He doesn't tell Jesus' story chronologically; he groups facts topically.

Matthew collects Jesus' sayings in five main places. First comes the famous Sermon on the Mount in chapters 5–7. Chapter 10 records Jesus' instructions to his disciples about their mission; chapter 13, a series of parables on the kingdom; chapter 18, Christ's words on the church as a community; and chapters 23–25, Jesus' thoughts on religious hypocrisy and his predictions of the future. Sandwiched in among these five great discourses you'll find connected scenes of Jesus in action.

The skillful blending of Jesus' action and teaching has helped earn this Gospel an esteemed place in literature. Artists are often drawn to it as a capsule summary of Jesus' ministry: witness J.S. Bach's greatest choral work, *Saint Matthew's Passion*, the joyous play *Godspell*, and Italian film maker Pasolini's film *The Gospel according to Saint Matthew*. The French skeptic Renan praised Matthew as "the most important book of Christendom—the most important book that has ever been written."

Two approaches will help in a detailed study of Matthew. First, consider how it differs from the other three Gospels; this will give you some idea of Matthew's distinctive purpose. Then, you will find it enlightening to look up many of Matthew's references to the Old Testament. Most are cited in the NIV footnotes.

PEOPLE YOU'LL MEET IN MATTHEW

JOSEPH *(p. 999)*
JOHN THE BAPTIST *(p. 1008)*
THE HERODS *(p. 1014)*

3-TRACK READING PLAN

For an explanation and complete listing of the 3-track reading plan, turn to page 7.

TRACK 1: *Two-Week Courses on the Bible*
The Track 1 reading program on the Life and Teachings of Jesus includes four chapters from Matthew. See page 7 for a complete listing of this course.

TRACK 2: *An Overview of Matthew in 7 Days*
☐ Day 1. Read the Introduction to Matthew. Then turn to Matthew 5 and begin the Sermon on the Mount.
☐ Day 2. Read chapter 6, a continuation of Jesus' longest single speech, perhaps the most familiar passage in the entire Bible.
☐ Day 3. Matthew 13 records some of Jesus' parables—concise stories with a powerful meaning behind them. Read these parables about the "kingdom of heaven," referring to "What Should a Leader Look Like?" page 1011, for help in understanding.
☐ Day 4. As a former tax collector, Matthew was especially sensitive to what Jesus had to say about money. Read his comments on this and other topics in chapter 19.
☐ Day 5. The last three chapters of Matthew give a complete, factual account of Jesus' death. Read chapter 26, the story of the arrest and trial.
☐ Day 6. Continue the crucifixion story with chapter 27.
☐ Day 7. Read chapter 28, which tells of Jesus' resurrection.

Now turn to page 9 for your next Track 2 reading project.

TRACK 3: **All of Matthew in 28 Days**
After you have read through Matthew a chapter a day, turn to pages 10–14 for your next Track 3 reading project.

☐1 ☐2 ☐3 ☐4 ☐5 ☐6 ☐7 ☐8
☐9 ☐10 ☐11 ☐12 ☐13 ☐14 ☐15 ☐16
☐17 ☐18 ☐19 ☐20 ☐21 ☐22 ☐23 ☐24
☐25 ☐26 ☐27 ☐28

The Genealogy of Jesus

▶ See Ruth 4:18–22; 1 Chronicles 3:10–17; Luke 3:23–38

1 A record of the genealogy of Jesus Christ the son of David, the son of Abraham:

²Abraham was the father of Isaac,
Isaac the father of Jacob,
Jacob the father of Judah and his brothers,
³Judah the father of Perez and Zerah,
whose mother was Tamar,
Perez the father of Hezron,
Hezron the father of Ram,
⁴Ram the father of Amminadab,
Amminadab the father of Nahshon,
Nahshon the father of Salmon,
⁵Salmon the father of Boaz, whose mother was Rahab,
Boaz the father of Obed, whose mother was Ruth,
Obed the father of Jesse,
⁶and Jesse the father of King David.

David was the father of Solomon, whose mother had been Uriah's wife,

1:6 Shady Ancestors

Matthew's list differs from many Jewish genealogies by including women, and a surprising selection of women at that. Tamar, a Gentile, tricked and seduced her father-in-law, then bore illegitimate twins (Genesis 38); Rahab, another Gentile, once worked as a prostitute (Joshua 2; 6); Ruth also grew up as a pagan Gentile (Ruth 1–4); and Uriah's wife Bathsheba committed adultery with King David (2 Samuel 11–12). Many of the men listed had unsavory pasts as well; taken together, these ancestors of Jesus vividly demonstrate God's ability to work with all sorts of people.

⁷Solomon the father of Rehoboam,
Rehoboam the father of Abijah,
Abijah the father of Asa,

⁸Asa the father of Jehoshaphat,
Jehoshaphat the father of Jehoram,
Jehoram the father of Uzziah,
⁹Uzziah the father of Jotham,
Jotham the father of Ahaz,
Ahaz the father of Hezekiah,
¹⁰Hezekiah the father of Manasseh,
Manasseh the father of Amon,
Amon the father of Josiah,
¹¹and Josiah the father of Jeconiah[a] and his brothers at the time of the exile to Babylon.

¹²After the exile to Babylon:
Jeconiah was the father of Shealtiel,
Shealtiel the father of Zerubbabel,
¹³Zerubbabel the father of Abiud,
Abiud the father of Eliakim,
Eliakim the father of Azor,
¹⁴Azor the father of Zadok,
Zadok the father of Akim,
Akim the father of Eliud,
¹⁵Eliud the father of Eleazar,
Eleazar the father of Matthan,
Matthan the father of Jacob,
¹⁶and Jacob the father of Joseph, the husband of Mary, of whom was born Jesus, who is called Christ.

¹⁷Thus there were fourteen generations in all from Abraham to David, fourteen from David to the exile to Babylon, and fourteen from the exile to the Christ.[b]

The Birth of Jesus Christ

¹⁸This is how the birth of Jesus Christ came about: His mother Mary was pledged to be married to Joseph, but before they came together, she was found to be with child through the Holy Spirit. ¹⁹Because Joseph her husband was a righteous man and did not want to expose her to public disgrace, he had in mind to divorce her quietly.

²⁰But after he had considered this, an angel of the Lord appeared to him in a dream and said, "Joseph son of David, do not be afraid to take Mary home as your wife, because what is conceived in her is from the Holy Spirit. ²¹She will

---

[a]11 That is, Jehoiachin; also in verse 12   [b]17 Or *Messiah.* "The Christ" (Greek) and "the Messiah" (Hebrew) both mean "the Anointed One."

give birth to a son, and you are to give him the name Jesus,[a] because he will save his people from their sins."

[22]All this took place to fulfill what the Lord

had said through the prophet: [23]"The virgin will be with child and will give birth to a son, and they will call him Immanuel"[b]—which means, "God with us."

[24]When Joseph woke up, he did what the angel of the Lord had commanded him and took Mary home as his wife. [25]But he had no union with her until she gave birth to a son. And he gave him the name Jesus.

The Visit of the Magi

2 After Jesus was born in Bethlehem in Judea, during the time of King Herod, Magi[c] from the east came to Jerusalem [2]and asked, "Where is the one who has been born king of the Jews? We saw his star in the east[d] and have come to worship him."

[3]When King Herod heard this he was disturbed, and all Jerusalem with him. [4]When he had called together all the people's chief priests and teachers of the law, he asked them where the Christ[e] was to be born. [5]"In Bethlehem in Judea," they replied, "for this is what the prophet has written:

[6]" 'But you, Bethlehem, in the land of Judah,
    are by no means least among the rulers of
        Judah;
for out of you will come a ruler
    who will be the shepherd of my people
        Israel.'[f]"

[7]Then Herod called the Magi secretly and found out from them the exact time the star had appeared. [8]He sent them to Bethlehem and said, "Go and make a careful search for the child. As soon as you find him, report to me, so that I too may go and worship him."

[9]After they had heard the king, they went on their way, and the star they had seen in the east[g] went ahead of them until it stopped over the place where the child was. [10]When they saw the star, they were overjoyed. [11]On coming to the house, they saw the child with his mother Mary, and they bowed down and worshiped him. Then they opened their treasures and presented him with gifts of gold and of incense and of

myrrh. [12]And having been warned in a dream not to go back to Herod, they returned to their country by another route.

The Escape to Egypt

[13]When they had gone, an angel of the Lord appeared to Joseph in a dream. "Get up," he said, "take the child and his mother and escape to Egypt. Stay there until I tell you, for Herod is going to search for the child to kill him."

[14]So he got up, took the child and his mother during the night and left for Egypt, [15]where he stayed until the death of Herod. And so was fulfilled what the Lord had said through the prophet: "Out of Egypt I called my son."[h]

[16]When Herod realized that he had been outwitted by the Magi, he was furious, and he gave orders to kill all the boys in Bethlehem and its vicinity who were two years old and under, in accordance with the time he had learned from the Magi. [17]Then what was said through the prophet Jeremiah was fulfilled:

[18]"A voice is heard in Ramah,
    weeping and great mourning,
Rachel weeping for her children
    and refusing to be comforted,
because they are no more."[i]

The Return to Nazareth

[19]After Herod died, an angel of the Lord appeared in a dream to Joseph in Egypt [20]and said, "Get up, take the child and his mother and go to the land of Israel, for those who were trying to take the child's life are dead."

[21]So he got up, took the child and his mother and went to the land of Israel. [22]But when he

---

[a]21 *Jesus* is the Greek form of *Joshua,* which means *the LORD saves.*   [b]23 Isaiah 7:14   [c]1 Traditionally *Wise Men*   [d]2 Or *star when it rose*   [e]4 Or *Messiah*   [f]6 Micah 5:2   [g]9 Or *seen when it rose*   [h]15 Hosea 11:1   [i]18 Jer. 31:15

heard that Archelaus was reigning in Judea in place of his father Herod, he was afraid to go there. Having been warned in a dream, he withdrew to the district of Galilee, [23]and he went and lived in a town called Nazareth. So was fulfilled what was said through the prophets: "He will be called a Nazarene."

John the Baptist Prepares the Way

▶ See Mark 1:3–8; Luke 3:2–17

3 In those days John the Baptist came, preaching in the Desert of Judea [2]and saying, "Repent, for the kingdom of heaven is near." [3]This is he who was spoken of through the prophet Isaiah:

"A voice of one calling in the desert,
'Prepare the way for the Lord,
    make straight paths for him.'"[a]

[4]John's clothes were made of camel's hair, and he had a leather belt around his waist. His food was locusts and wild honey. [5]People went out to him from Jerusalem and all Judea and the whole region of the Jordan. [6]Confessing their sins, they were baptized by him in the Jordan River.

[7]But when he saw many of the Pharisees and Sadducees coming to where he was baptizing, he said to them: "You brood of vipers! Who warned you to flee from the coming wrath? [8]Produce fruit in keeping with repentance. [9]And do not think you can say to yourselves, 'We have Abraham as our father.' I tell you that out of these stones God can raise up children for Abraham. [10]The ax is already at the root of the trees, and

every tree that does not produce good fruit will be cut down and thrown into the fire.

[11]"I baptize you with[b] water for repentance. But after me will come one who is more powerful than I, whose sandals I am not fit to carry. He will baptize you with the Holy Spirit and with fire. [12]His winnowing fork is in his hand, and he will clear his threshing floor, gathering his wheat into the barn and burning up the chaff with unquenchable fire."

The Baptism of Jesus

▶ See Mark 1:9–11; Luke 3:21–22; John 1:31–34

[13]Then Jesus came from Galilee to the Jordan to be baptized by John. [14]But John tried to deter him, saying, "I need to be baptized by you, and do you come to me?"

[15]Jesus replied, "Let it be so now; it is proper for us to do this to fulfill all righteousness." Then John consented.

[16]As soon as Jesus was baptized, he went up out of the water. At that moment heaven was opened, and he saw the Spirit of God descending like a dove and lighting on him. [17]And a voice from heaven said, "This is my Son, whom I love; with him I am well pleased."

The Temptation of Jesus

▶ See Mark 1:12–13; Luke 4:1–13

4 Then Jesus was led by the Spirit into the desert to be tempted by the devil. [2]After fasting forty days and forty nights, he was hungry. [3]The tempter came to him and said, "If you are

[a]3 Isaiah 40:3   [b]11 Or in

JOSEPH Stepfather

STEPPARENTS TAKE ON ONE OF the hardest tasks in life—raising a child who isn't biologically theirs. When Joseph first learned that his fiancée Mary was bearing someone else's child, he must have felt deep heartache. By law, he had the right to accuse Mary of adultery and have her executed. Then an angel brought instructions in a dream: Joseph was to stay with Mary, for her child was from God.

Three times Joseph received angelic messages in dreams, and each time they called for moves he had not planned and could hardly wish. First he was called to care for a wife he had never slept with and a child who was not his. Then he was ordered to flee as a refugee to far-off Egypt. Finally an angel told him to return home, where skeptical neighbors probably remembered that Mary had been pregnant before her marriage.

We know one thing about Joseph: He obeyed, following the angel's orders in each difficult case. A dutiful stepfather, he treated his son as his own, raising him according to the Jewish law. As a carpenter, he taught Jesus to hammer and saw. As a righteous man, he modeled for him an obedient life.

We last hear of Joseph when Jesus was 12. After that, the Bible only mentions Jesus' mother, Mary, and Jesus' brothers. (Joseph probably died before Jesus began his ministry. From the cross, Jesus committed the care of his mother to one of his disciples [John 19:25–27].) Through his faithfulness as a stepfather, however, Joseph made a lasting contribution to the world.

Life Questions: Has God asked you to do any thankless tasks? What were they, and how did they turn out?

the Son of God, tell these stones to become bread."

⁴Jesus answered, "It is written: 'Man does not live on bread alone, but on every word that comes from the mouth of God.'ᵃ"

⁵Then the devil took him to the holy city and had him stand on the highest point of the temple. ⁶"If you are the Son of God," he said, "throw yourself down. For it is written:

"'He will command his angels concerning you,
    and they will lift you up in their hands,
so that you will not strike your foot against a stone.'ᵇ"

⁷Jesus answered him, "It is also written: 'Do not put the Lord your God to the test.'ᶜ"

⁸Again, the devil took him to a very high mountain and showed him all the kingdoms of the world and their splendor. ⁹"All this I will give you," he said, "if you will bow down and worship me."

¹⁰Jesus said to him, "Away from me, Satan! For it is written: 'Worship the Lord your God, and serve him only.'ᵈ"

¹¹Then the devil left him, and angels came and attended him.

Jesus Begins to Preach

¹²When Jesus heard that John had been put in prison, he returned to Galilee. ¹³Leaving Nazareth, he went and lived in Capernaum, which was by the lake in the area of Zebulun and Naphtali— ¹⁴to fulfill what was said through the prophet Isaiah:

¹⁵"Land of Zebulun and land of Naphtali,
    the way to the sea, along the Jordan,
    Galilee of the Gentiles—
¹⁶the people living in darkness
    have seen a great light;
on those living in the land of the shadow of death
    a light has dawned."ᵉ

¹⁷From that time on Jesus began to preach, "Repent, for the kingdom of heaven is near."

The Calling of the First Disciples

▶ *See Mark 1:16–20; Luke 5:2–11; John 1:35–42*

¹⁸As Jesus was walking beside the Sea of Galilee, he saw two brothers, Simon called Peter and his brother Andrew. They were casting a net into the lake, for they were fishermen. ¹⁹"Come, follow me," Jesus said, "and I will make you fishers of men." ²⁰At once they left their nets and followed him.

²¹Going on from there, he saw two other brothers, James son of Zebedee and his brother John. They were in a boat with their father Zebedee, preparing their nets. Jesus called them, ²²and immediately they left the boat and their father and followed him.

4:17 Words for Jewish Readers

Matthew wrote for a primarily Jewish audience. Starting with his opening chapter, he affirms that Jesus is the Messiah, backing up that claim by constant reference to the Old Testament. Often Matthew leaves Jewish phrases and customs unexplained, assuming that his readers are familiar with them. And, where other Gospel writers say, "kingdom of God," he uses the phrase "kingdom of heaven," out of respect for Jews, who never wrote out the word God.

Jesus Heals the Sick

²³Jesus went throughout Galilee, teaching in their synagogues, preaching the good news of the kingdom, and healing every disease and sickness among the people. ²⁴News about him spread all over Syria, and people brought to him all who were ill with various diseases, those suffering severe pain, the demon-possessed, those having seizures, and the paralyzed, and he healed them. ²⁵Large crowds from Galilee, the Decapolis,ᶠ Jerusalem, Judea and the region across the Jordan followed him.

The Beatitudes

▶ *See Luke 6:20–23*

5 Now when he saw the crowds, he went up on a mountainside and sat down. His disciples came to him, ²and he began to teach them, saying:

³"Blessed are the poor in spirit,
    for theirs is the kingdom of heaven.
⁴Blessed are those who mourn,
    for they will be comforted.
⁵Blessed are the meek,
    for they will inherit the earth.
⁶Blessed are those who hunger and thirst for righteousness,
    for they will be filled.
⁷Blessed are the merciful,
    for they will be shown mercy.
⁸Blessed are the pure in heart,
    for they will see God.
⁹Blessed are the peacemakers,
    for they will be called sons of God.

ᵃ4 Deut. 8:3   ᵇ6 Psalm 91:11,12   ᶜ7 Deut. 6:16   ᵈ10 Deut. 6:13   ᵉ16 Isaiah 9:1,2   ᶠ25 That is, the Ten Cities

[10]Blessed are those who are persecuted because
of righteousness,
for theirs is the kingdom of heaven.

[11]"Blessed are you when people insult you,
persecute you and falsely say all kinds of evil
against you because of me. [12]Rejoice and be glad,
because great is your reward in heaven, for in the
same way they persecuted the prophets who were
before you.

Salt and Light

[13]"You are the salt of the earth. But if the salt
loses its saltiness, how can it be made salty again?
It is no longer good for anything, except to be
thrown out and trampled by men.

[14]"You are the light of the world. A city on a
hill cannot be hidden. [15]Neither do people light a
lamp and put it under a bowl. Instead they put it
on its stand, and it gives light to everyone in the
house. [16]In the same way, let your light shine
before men, that they may see your good deeds
and praise your Father in heaven.

The Fulfillment of the Law

[17]"Do not think that I have come to abolish
the Law or the Prophets; I have not come to

5:17 Jesus and Moses' Law

*In this statement, Jesus clarifies his
relationship to the Law of Moses. The next
verses get more specific, contrasting Jesus'
teaching with many common interpretations of
that Law. "You have heard that it was
said . . . ," he begins, and then concludes, "But I
tell you . . ." Jesus revealed the true intent of the
Old Testament law, rather than its legalistic
interpretations.*

abolish them but to fulfill them. [18]I tell you the
truth, until heaven and earth disappear, not the
smallest letter, not the least stroke of a pen, will
by any means disappear from the Law until everything is accomplished. [19]Anyone who breaks
one of the least of these commandments and
teaches others to do the same will be called least
in the kingdom of heaven, but whoever practices
and teaches these commands will be called great
in the kingdom of heaven. [20]For I tell you that
unless your righteousness surpasses that of the
Pharisees and the teachers of the law, you will
certainly not enter the kingdom of heaven.

Murder

[21]"You have heard that it was said to the people long ago, 'Do not murder,[a] and anyone who

murders will be subject to judgment.' [22]But I tell
you that anyone who is angry with his brother[b]
will be subject to judgment. Again, anyone who
says to his brother, 'Raca,[c]' is answerable to the
Sanhedrin. But anyone who says, 'You fool!' will
be in danger of the fire of hell.

[23]"Therefore, if you are offering your gift at
the altar and there remember that your brother
has something against you, [24]leave your gift there
in front of the altar. First go and be reconciled to
your brother; then come and offer your gift.

[25]"Settle matters quickly with your adversary
who is taking you to court. Do it while you are
still with him on the way, or he may hand you
over to the judge, and the judge may hand you
over to the officer, and you may be thrown into
prison. [26]I tell you the truth, you will not get out
until you have paid the last penny.[d]

Adultery

[27]"You have heard that it was said, 'Do not
commit adultery.'[e] [28]But I tell you that anyone
who looks at a woman lustfully has already committed adultery with her in his heart. [29]If your
right eye causes you to sin, gouge it out and
throw it away. It is better for you to lose one part
of your body than for your whole body to be
thrown into hell. [30]And if your right hand causes
you to sin, cut it off and throw it away. It is better
for you to lose one part of your body than for
your whole body to go into hell.

Divorce

[31]"It has been said, 'Anyone who divorces his
wife must give her a certificate of divorce.'[f]
[32]But I tell you that anyone who divorces his wife,
except for marital unfaithfulness, causes her to
become an adulteress, and anyone who marries
the divorced woman commits adultery.

Oaths

[33]"Again, you have heard that it was said to
the people long ago, 'Do not break your oath, but
keep the oaths you have made to the Lord.' [34]But
I tell you, Do not swear at all: either by heaven,
for it is God's throne; [35]or by the earth, for it is
his footstool; or by Jerusalem, for it is the city of
the Great King. [36]And do not swear by your head,
for you cannot make even one hair white or
black. [37]Simply let your 'Yes' be 'Yes,' and your
'No,' 'No'; anything beyond this comes from the
evil one.

An Eye for an Eye

[38]"You have heard that it was said, 'Eye for
eye, and tooth for tooth.'[g] [39]But I tell you, Do
not resist an evil person. If someone strikes you
on the right cheek, turn to him the other also.

[a]21 Exodus 20:13   [b]22 Some manuscripts *brother without cause*   [c]22 An Aramaic term of contempt
[d]26 Greek *kodrantes*   [e]27 Exodus 20:14   [f]31 Deut. 24:1   [g]38 Exodus 21:24; Lev. 24:20; Deut. 19:21

40And if someone wants to sue you and take your tunic, let him have your cloak as well. 41If someone forces you to go one mile, go with him two miles. 42Give to the one who asks you, and do not turn away from the one who wants to borrow from you.

Love for Enemies

43"You have heard that it was said, 'Love your neighbor*a* and hate your enemy.' 44But I tell you: Love your enemies*b* and pray for those who persecute you, 45that you may be sons of your Father in heaven. He causes his sun to rise on the evil and the good, and sends rain on the righteous and the unrighteous. 46If you love those who love you, what reward will you get? Are not even the tax collectors doing that? 47And if you greet only your brothers, what are you doing more than others? Do not even pagans do that? 48Be perfect, therefore, as your heavenly Father is perfect.

Giving to the Needy

6 "Be careful not to do your 'acts of righteousness' before men, to be seen by them. If you do, you will have no reward from your Father in heaven.

2"So when you give to the needy, do not announce it with trumpets, as the hypocrites do in the synagogues and on the streets, to be honored by men. I tell you the truth, they have received their reward in full. 3But when you give to the needy, do not let your left hand know what your right hand is doing, 4so that your giving may be in secret. Then your Father, who sees what is done in secret, will reward you.

a43 Lev. 19:18   *b44* Some late manuscripts *enemies, bless those who curse you, do good to those who hate you*

Letting the Inside Match the Outside
Is everyone a hypocrite?

ALMOST ALL OF US LIVE two lives: what people see outside and what is really going on inside. In school we learn what outward signs of attention will please the teacher. At a job we learn to "put up a good front" whenever the boss happens to stroll by. As if putting on masks, we style our hair, choose our clothes, and use body language to impress those around us. Over time, we learn to excel at hiding truly serious problems.

"Your Father, who sees what is done in secret, will reward you." 6:4

People tend to judge by outward appearances and so can easily be fooled. Acquaintances are often shocked when a mass-murderer is arrested. "He seemed like such a nice man!" they insist. The outside appearance did not match the inside reality.

A Blast at Hypocrites

Chapters 5–7 announce that the time has come for us to change not just the outside, but also the inside. In Jesus' day, religious people tried to impress each other with showy outward behavior. They wore gaunt and hungry looks during a brief fast, prayed grandiosely if people were watching, and went so far as to wear Bible verses strapped to their foreheads and left arms.

In his famous Sermon on the Mount, Jesus blasts the hypocrisy behind such seemingly harmless practices. God is not fooled by appearances. We cannot fake behavior to impress him. He knows that inside the best of us lurk dark thoughts of hatred, pride, and lust—internal problems only he can deal with. Jesus goes on to present a truly radical way of life, free of pretense.

Familiar Yet Startling Words

These three chapters, among the most analyzed in the entire Bible, present a fresh view of the world. You will likely recognize many familiar sections, including the Golden Rule and the Lord's Prayer.

In one sense, Jesus says, the truths presented here are not new: they fulfill, rather than abolish the Old Testament law. In another sense the way of life described is more radical than anything before or since. Jesus' words turn many normal assumptions upside down. With statements like, "Blessed are the poor in spirit . . . those who mourn . . . the meek . . . the peacemakers . . . those who are persecuted," Jesus attacks those who strive to build a good image by appearing powerful, successful, and assertive.

Perhaps most radical of all, The Sermon on the Mount introduces the possibility of living solely for God and not for appearances. At last we can bring our inner and outer lives together.

Life Questions: Do other people see what you're really like inside? How do your friends try to impress each other?

Prayer

▶ See Luke 11:2–4

⁵"And when you pray, do not be like the hypocrites, for they love to pray standing in the synagogues and on the street corners to be seen by men. I tell you the truth, they have received their

reward in full. ⁶But when you pray, go into your room, close the door and pray to your Father, who is unseen. Then your Father, who sees what is done in secret, will reward you. ⁷And when you pray, do not keep on babbling like pagans, for they think they will be heard because of their many words. ⁸Do not be like them, for your Father knows what you need before you ask him.

⁹"This, then, is how you should pray:

"'Our Father in heaven,
hallowed be your name,
¹⁰your kingdom come,
your will be done
on earth as it is in heaven.
¹¹Give us today our daily bread.
¹²Forgive us our debts,
as we also have forgiven our debtors.
¹³And lead us not into temptation,
but deliver us from the evil one.ᵃ'

¹⁴For if you forgive men when they sin against you, your heavenly Father will also forgive you. ¹⁵But if you do not forgive men their sins, your Father will not forgive your sins.

Fasting

¹⁶"When you fast, do not look somber as the hypocrites do, for they disfigure their faces to show men they are fasting. I tell you the truth, they have received their reward in full. ¹⁷But when you fast, put oil on your head and wash your face, ¹⁸so that it will not be obvious to men that you are fasting, but only to your Father, who is unseen; and your Father, who sees what is done in secret, will reward you.

Treasures in Heaven

¹⁹"Do not store up for yourselves treasures on earth, where moth and rust destroy, and where

thieves break in and steal. ²⁰But store up for yourselves treasures in heaven, where moth and rust do not destroy, and where thieves do not break in and steal. ²¹For where your treasure is, there your heart will be also.

²²"The eye is the lamp of the body. If your eyes are good, your whole body will be full of light. ²³But if your eyes are bad, your whole body will be full of darkness. If then the light within you is darkness, how great is that darkness!

²⁴"No one can serve two masters. Either he will hate the one and love the other, or he will be devoted to the one and despise the other. You cannot serve both God and Money.

Do Not Worry

▶ See Luke 12:22–31

²⁵"Therefore I tell you, do not worry about your life, what you will eat or drink; or about your body, what you will wear. Is not life more important than food, and the body more important than clothes? ²⁶Look at the birds of the air; they do not sow or reap or store away in barns, and yet your heavenly Father feeds them. Are you not much more valuable than they? ²⁷Who of you by worrying can add a single hour to his lifeᵇ?

²⁸"And why do you worry about clothes? See how the lilies of the field grow. They do not labor or spin. ²⁹Yet I tell you that not even Solomon in all his splendor was dressed like one of these. ³⁰If that is how God clothes the grass of the field, which is here today and tomorrow is thrown into the fire, will he not much more clothe you, O you of little faith? ³¹So do not worry, saying, 'What shall we eat?' or 'What shall we drink?' or 'What shall we wear?' ³²For the pagans run after all these things, and your heavenly Father knows that you need them. ³³But seek first his kingdom and his righteousness, and all these things will be given to you as well. ³⁴Therefore do not worry about tomorrow, for tomorrow will worry about itself. Each day has enough trouble of its own.

Judging Others

▶ See Luke 6:41–42

7 "Do not judge, or you too will be judged. ²For in the same way you judge others, you will be judged, and with the measure you use, it will be measured to you.

³"Why do you look at the speck of sawdust in your brother's eye and pay no attention to the plank in your own eye? ⁴How can you say to your brother, 'Let me take the speck out of your eye,' when all the time there is a plank in your own eye? ⁵You hypocrite, first take the plank out of

ᵃ13 Or *from evil*; some late manuscripts *one, / for yours is the kingdom and the power and the glory forever. Amen.*
ᵇ27 Or *single cubit to his height*

your own eye, and then you will see clearly to remove the speck from your brother's eye.

6"Do not give dogs what is sacred; do not throw your pearls to pigs. If you do, they may trample them under their feet, and then turn and tear you to pieces.

Ask, Seek, Knock

▶ See Luke 11:9–13

7"Ask and it will be given to you; seek and you will find; knock and the door will be opened to you. 8For everyone who asks receives; he who seeks finds; and to him who knocks, the door will be opened.

9"Which of you, if his son asks for bread, will give him a stone? 10Or if he asks for a fish, will give him a snake? 11If you, then, though you are evil, know how to give good gifts to your children, how much more will your Father in heaven give good gifts to those who ask him! 12So in everything, do to others what you would have them do to you, for this sums up the Law and the Prophets.

7:12 Golden Rule

Other religions (Judaism, Hinduism, Buddhism, Confucianism) had some form of this saying, but most were stated negatively: "Don't do to others what you wouldn't want them to do to you." Jesus' version is far more open-ended and challenging.

The Narrow and Wide Gates

13"Enter through the narrow gate. For wide is the gate and broad is the road that leads to destruction, and many enter through it. 14But small is the gate and narrow the road that leads to life, and only a few find it.

A Tree and Its Fruit

15"Watch out for false prophets. They come to you in sheep's clothing, but inwardly they are ferocious wolves. 16By their fruit you will recognize them. Do people pick grapes from thornbushes, or figs from thistles? 17Likewise every good tree bears good fruit, but a bad tree bears bad fruit. 18A good tree cannot bear bad fruit, and a bad tree cannot bear good fruit. 19Every tree that does not bear good fruit is cut down and thrown into the fire. 20Thus, by their fruit you will recognize them.

21"Not everyone who says to me, 'Lord, Lord,' will enter the kingdom of heaven, but only he who does the will of my Father who is in heaven.

22Many will say to me on that day, 'Lord, Lord, did we not prophesy in your name, and in your name drive out demons and perform many miracles?' 23Then I will tell them plainly, 'I never knew you. Away from me, you evildoers!'

The Wise and Foolish Builders

▶ See Luke 6:47–49

24"Therefore everyone who hears these words of mine and puts them into practice is like a wise man who built his house on the rock. 25The rain came down, the streams rose, and the winds blew and beat against that house; yet it did not fall, because it had its foundation on the rock. 26But everyone who hears these words of mine and does not put them into practice is like a foolish man who built his house on sand. 27The rain came down, the streams rose, and the winds blew and beat against that house, and it fell with a great crash."

28When Jesus had finished saying these things, the crowds were amazed at his teaching, 29because he taught as one who had authority, and not as their teachers of the law.

The Man With Leprosy

▶ See Mark 1:40–44; Luke 5:12–14

8 When he came down from the mountainside, large crowds followed him. 2A man with leprosy[a] came and knelt before him and said, "Lord, if you are willing, you can make me clean."

3Jesus reached out his hand and touched the man. "I am willing," he said. "Be clean!" Immediately he was cured[b] of his leprosy. 4Then Jesus said to him, "See that you don't tell anyone. But go, show yourself to the priest and offer the gift Moses commanded, as a testimony to them."

The Faith of the Centurion

▶ See Luke 7:1–10

5When Jesus had entered Capernaum, a centurion came to him, asking for help. 6"Lord," he said, "my servant lies at home paralyzed and in terrible suffering."

7Jesus said to him, "I will go and heal him."

8The centurion replied, "Lord, I do not deserve to have you come under my roof. But just say the word, and my servant will be healed. 9For I myself am a man under authority, with soldiers under me. I tell this one, 'Go,' and he goes; and that one, 'Come,' and he comes. I say to my servant, 'Do this,' and he does it."

10When Jesus heard this, he was astonished and said to those following him, "I tell you the

a2 The Greek word was used for various diseases affecting the skin—not necessarily leprosy.   b3 Greek made clean

truth, I have not found anyone in Israel with such great faith. 11I say to you that many will come from the east and the west, and will take their places at the feast with Abraham, Isaac and Jacob in the kingdom of heaven. 12But the subjects of the kingdom will be thrown outside, into the darkness, where there will be weeping and gnashing of teeth."

13Then Jesus said to the centurion, "Go! It will be done just as you believed it would." And his servant was healed at that very hour.

Jesus Heals Many

▶ See Mark 1:29–34; Luke 4:38–41

14When Jesus came into Peter's house, he saw Peter's mother-in-law lying in bed with a fever.

8:14 Actions Follow Words

Typically, Matthew blends together Jesus' words and actions. Chapters 5–7 contain Jesus' longest recorded speech, the Sermon on the Mount—a speech that greatly impressed the audience. The next few chapters mention ten miracles performed by Jesus, which further established his authority. Those who benefited—a despised leprosy victim, a Roman officer, a housewife, two violent demoniacs, a quadriplegic, a synagogue ruler—demonstrate the "wideness in God's mercy" Jesus had just described.

15He touched her hand and the fever left her, and she got up and began to wait on him.

16When evening came, many who were demon-possessed were brought to him, and he drove out the spirits with a word and healed all the sick. 17This was to fulfill what was spoken through the prophet Isaiah:

"He took up our infirmities
    and carried our diseases."[a]

The Cost of Following Jesus

▶ See Luke 9:57–60

18When Jesus saw the crowd around him, he gave orders to cross to the other side of the lake. 19Then a teacher of the law came to him and said, "Teacher, I will follow you wherever you go."

20Jesus replied, "Foxes have holes and birds of the air have nests, but the Son of Man has no place to lay his head."

21Another disciple said to him, "Lord, first let me go and bury my father."

22But Jesus told him, "Follow me, and let the dead bury their own dead."

Jesus Calms the Storm

▶ See Mark 4:36–41; Luke 8:22–25

23Then he got into the boat and his disciples followed him. 24Without warning, a furious storm came up on the lake, so that the waves swept over the boat. But Jesus was sleeping. 25The disciples went and woke him, saying, "Lord, save us! We're going to drown!"

26He replied, "You of little faith, why are you so afraid?" Then he got up and rebuked the winds and the waves, and it was completely calm.

27The men were amazed and asked, "What kind of man is this? Even the winds and the waves obey him!"

The Healing of Two Demon-possessed Men

▶ See Mark 5:1–17; Luke 8:26–37

28When he arrived at the other side in the region of the Gadarenes,[b] two demon-possessed men coming from the tombs met him. They were so violent that no one could pass that way. 29"What do you want with us, Son of God?" they shouted. "Have you come here to torture us before the appointed time?"

30Some distance from them a large herd of pigs was feeding. 31The demons begged Jesus, "If you drive us out, send us into the herd of pigs."

32He said to them, "Go!" So they came out and went into the pigs, and the whole herd rushed down the steep bank into the lake and died in the water. 33Those tending the pigs ran off, went into the town and reported all this, including what had happened to the demon-possessed men. 34Then the whole town went out to meet Jesus. And when they saw him, they pleaded with him to leave their region.

Jesus Heals a Paralytic

▶ See Mark 2:3–12; Luke 5:18–26

9 Jesus stepped into a boat, crossed over and came to his own town. 2Some men brought to him a paralytic, lying on a mat. When Jesus saw their faith, he said to the paralytic, "Take heart, son; your sins are forgiven."

3At this, some of the teachers of the law said to themselves, "This fellow is blaspheming!"

4Knowing their thoughts, Jesus said, "Why do you entertain evil thoughts in your hearts? 5Which is easier: to say, 'Your sins are forgiven,' or to say, 'Get up and walk'? 6But so that you may know that the Son of Man has authority on earth to forgive sins . . ." Then he said to the paralytic, "Get up, take your mat and go home." 7And the man got up and went home. 8When the crowd saw this, they were filled with awe; and they

---

a 17 Isaiah 53:4   *b 28* Some manuscripts *Gergesenes*; others *Gerasenes*

praised God, who had given such authority to men.

The Calling of Matthew

▶ *See Mark 2:14–17; Luke 5:27–32*

⁹As Jesus went on from there, he saw a man named Matthew sitting at the tax collector's booth. "Follow me," he told him, and Matthew got up and followed him.

9:9 Unpopular Profession

Tax collectors like Matthew were even less popular in Jesus' day than now. Many Jews viewed them as traitors serving the hated Roman empire. To make things worse, they worked on a commission basis, allowing them to set their own rates, which often led to extortion.

In this poignant scene, the Gospel tells how Jesus first called Matthew and then came to his house to mingle freely with "tax collectors and 'sinners'." By following Jesus, Matthew turned his back on a lucrative government job. He was gradually transformed into a loyal disciple who applied his orderly mind to organize this account of Jesus' life.

¹⁰While Jesus was having dinner at Matthew's house, many tax collectors and "sinners" came and ate with him and his disciples. ¹¹When the Pharisees saw this, they asked his disciples, "Why does your teacher eat with tax collectors and 'sinners'?"

¹²On hearing this, Jesus said, "It is not the healthy who need a doctor, but the sick. ¹³But go and learn what this means: 'I desire mercy, not sacrifice.'[a] For I have not come to call the righteous, but sinners."

Jesus Questioned About Fasting

▶ *See Mark 2:18–22; Luke 5:33–39*

¹⁴Then John's disciples came and asked him, "How is it that we and the Pharisees fast, but your disciples do not fast?"

¹⁵Jesus answered, "How can the guests of the bridegroom mourn while he is with them? The time will come when the bridegroom will be taken from them; then they will fast.

¹⁶"No one sews a patch of unshrunk cloth on an old garment, for the patch will pull away from the garment, making the tear worse. ¹⁷Neither do men pour new wine into old wineskins. If they do, the skins will burst, the wine will run out and the wineskins will be ruined. No, they pour new wine into new wineskins, and both are preserved."

A Dead Girl and a Sick Woman

▶ *See Mark 5:22–43; Luke 8:41–56*

¹⁸While he was saying this, a ruler came and knelt before him and said, "My daughter has just died. But come and put your hand on her, and she will live." ¹⁹Jesus got up and went with him, and so did his disciples.

²⁰Just then a woman who had been subject to bleeding for twelve years came up behind him and touched the edge of his cloak. ²¹She said to herself, "If I only touch his cloak, I will be healed."

²²Jesus turned and saw her. "Take heart, daughter," he said, "your faith has healed you." And the woman was healed from that moment.

²³When Jesus entered the ruler's house and saw the flute players and the noisy crowd, ²⁴he said, "Go away. The girl is not dead but asleep." But they laughed at him. ²⁵After the crowd had been put outside, he went in and took the girl by the hand, and she got up. ²⁶News of this spread through all that region.

Jesus Heals the Blind and Mute

²⁷As Jesus went on from there, two blind men followed him, calling out, "Have mercy on us, Son of David!"

²⁸When he had gone indoors, the blind men came to him, and he asked them, "Do you believe that I am able to do this?"

"Yes, Lord," they replied.

²⁹Then he touched their eyes and said, "According to your faith will it be done to you"; ³⁰and their sight was restored. Jesus warned them sternly, "See that no one knows about this." ³¹But they went out and spread the news about him all over that region.

³²While they were going out, a man who was demon-possessed and could not talk was brought to Jesus. ³³And when the demon was driven out, the man who had been mute spoke. The crowd was amazed and said, "Nothing like this has ever been seen in Israel."

³⁴But the Pharisees said, "It is by the prince of demons that he drives out demons."

The Workers Are Few

³⁵Jesus went through all the towns and villages, teaching in their synagogues, preaching the good news of the kingdom and healing every disease and sickness. ³⁶When he saw the crowds, he had compassion on them, because they were harassed and helpless, like sheep without a shepherd. ³⁷Then he said to his disciples, "The harvest is plentiful but the workers are few. ³⁸Ask the Lord of the harvest, therefore, to send out workers into his harvest field."

---

a 13 Hosea 6:6

Jesus Sends Out the Twelve

▶ *See Mark 6:8–11; Luke 9:3–5; 10:4–12*

10 He called his twelve disciples to him and gave them authority to drive out evil[a] spirits and to heal every disease and sickness.

[2]These are the names of the twelve apostles: first, Simon (who is called Peter) and his brother Andrew; James son of Zebedee, and his brother John; [3]Philip and Bartholomew; Thomas and Matthew the tax collector; James son of Alphaeus, and Thaddaeus; [4]Simon the Zealot and Judas Iscariot, who betrayed him.

[5]These twelve Jesus sent out with the following instructions: "Do not go among the Gentiles or enter any town of the Samaritans. [6]Go rather to the lost sheep of Israel. [7]As you go, preach this message: 'The kingdom of heaven is near.' [8]Heal the sick, raise the dead, cleanse those who have leprosy,[b] drive out demons. Freely you have received, freely give. [9]Do not take along any gold or silver or copper in your belts; [10]take no bag for the journey, or extra tunic, or sandals or a staff; for the worker is worth his keep.

[11]"Whatever town or village you enter, search for some worthy person there and stay at his house until you leave. [12]As you enter the home, give it your greeting. [13]If the home is deserving, let your peace rest on it; if it is not, let your peace return to you. [14]If anyone will not welcome you or listen to your words, shake the dust off your feet when you leave that home or town. [15]I tell you the truth, it will be more bearable for Sodom and Gomorrah on the day of judgment than for that town. [16]I am sending you out like sheep among wolves. Therefore be as shrewd as snakes and as innocent as doves.

[17]"Be on your guard against men; they will hand you over to the local councils and flog you in their synagogues. [18]On my account you will be brought before governors and kings as witnesses to them and to the Gentiles. [19]But when they arrest you, do not worry about what to say or how to say it. At that time you will be given what to say, [20]for it will not be you speaking, but the Spirit of your Father speaking through you.

[21]"Brother will betray brother to death, and a father his child; children will rebel against their parents and have them put to death. [22]All men will hate you because of me, but he who stands firm to the end will be saved. [23]When you are persecuted in one place, flee to another. I tell you the truth, you will not finish going through the cities of Israel before the Son of Man comes.

[24]"A student is not above his teacher, nor a servant above his master. [25]It is enough for the student to be like his teacher, and the servant like his master. If the head of the house has been called Beelzebub,[c] how much more the members of his household!

[26]"So do not be afraid of them. There is nothing concealed that will not be disclosed, or hidden that will not be made known. [27]What I tell you in the dark, speak in the daylight; what is whispered in your ear, proclaim from the roofs. [28]Do not be afraid of those who kill the body but cannot kill the soul. Rather, be afraid of the One who can destroy both soul and body in hell. [29]Are not two sparrows sold for a penny[d]? Yet not one of them will fall to the ground apart from the will of your Father. [30]And even the very hairs of your head are all numbered. [31]So don't be afraid; you are worth more than many sparrows.

[32]"Whoever acknowledges me before men, I will also acknowledge him before my Father in heaven. [33]But whoever disowns me before men, I will disown him before my Father in heaven.

[34]"Do not suppose that I have come to bring peace to the earth. I did not come to bring peace, but a sword. [35]For I have come to turn

> "'a man against his father,
>   a daughter against her mother,
> a daughter-in-law against her
>   mother-in-law—
> [36]   a man's enemies will be the members of
>   his own household.'[e]

[37]"Anyone who loves his father or mother more than me is not worthy of me; anyone who loves his son or daughter more than me is not worthy of me; [38]and anyone who does not take his cross and follow me is not worthy of me. [39]Whoever finds his life will lose it, and whoever loses his life for my sake will find it.

[40]"He who receives you receives me, and he who receives me receives the one who sent me. [41]Anyone who receives a prophet because he is a prophet will receive a prophet's reward, and anyone who receives a righteous man because he is a righteous man will receive a righteous man's reward. [42]And if anyone gives even a cup of cold water to one of these little ones because he is my disciple, I tell you the truth, he will certainly not lose his reward."

Jesus and John the Baptist

▶ *See Luke 7:18–35*

11 After Jesus had finished instructing his twelve disciples, he went on from there to teach and preach in the towns of Galilee.[f]

[2]When John heard in prison what Christ was doing, he sent his disciples [3]to ask him, "Are you the one who was to come, or should we expect someone else?"

[4]Jesus replied, "Go back and report to John

---

[a]1 Greek *unclean*   [b]8 The Greek word was used for various diseases affecting the skin—not necessarily leprosy.   [c]25 Greek *Beezeboul* or *Beelzeboul*   [d]29 Greek *an assarion*   [e]36 Micah 7:6   [f]1 Greek *in their towns*

what you hear and see: [5]The blind receive sight, the lame walk, those who have leprosy[a] are cured, the deaf hear, the dead are raised, and the good news is preached to the poor. [6]Blessed is the man who does not fall away on account of me."

11:2 The One to Come?

John's question here may reflect confusion over the Messiah's role. If, like many Jews, John was expecting a political Messiah who would overthrow the Romans, his imprisonment may have caused him to wonder why Jesus wasn't taking action. Jesus responded by clarifying the kind of kingdom he came to establish: a kingdom that brought healing, liberation, and good news—but not necessarily political power.

[7]As John's disciples were leaving, Jesus began to speak to the crowd about John: "What did you go out into the desert to see? A reed swayed by the wind? [8]If not, what did you go out to see? A man dressed in fine clothes? No, those who wear fine clothes are in kings' palaces. [9]Then what did you go out to see? A prophet? Yes, I tell you, and more than a prophet. [10]This is the one about whom it is written:

"'I will send my messenger ahead of you,
    who will prepare your way before you.'[b]

[11]I tell you the truth: Among those born of women there has not risen anyone greater than John the Baptist; yet he who is least in the kingdom of heaven is greater than he. [12]From the days of John the Baptist until now, the kingdom of heaven has been forcefully advancing, and forceful men lay hold of it. [13]For all the Prophets and the Law prophesied until John. [14]And if you are willing to accept it, he is the Elijah who was to come. [15]He who has ears, let him hear.

[16]"To what can I compare this generation? They are like children sitting in the marketplaces and calling out to others:

[17]"'We played the flute for you,
    and you did not dance;
  we sang a dirge,
    and you did not mourn.'

[18]For John came neither eating nor drinking, and they say, 'He has a demon.' [19]The Son of Man came eating and drinking, and they say, 'Here is a glutton and a drunkard, a friend of tax collectors and "sinners." ' But wisdom is proved right by her actions."

---

[a]5 The Greek word was used for various diseases affecting the skin—not necessarily leprosy.   [b]10 Mal. 3:1

JOHN THE BAPTIST *Something New*

FASHION STARTS WITH A SINGLE purpose: to turn people's heads. At first the new look is a shock. Many say, "Wow"; some say, "Ugh!" Whether it's short skirts or long, nose rings or earrings, paisleys or pastels, the new must stand out to gain attention.

John the Baptist was something new, and he certainly stood out from his surroundings. Though he could have been a priest like his father, he exchanged those linen robes for a garment of coarse camel's hair. He took to the wilderness, scavenging grasshoppers and wild honey rather than settling in Jerusalem where he could have savored a portion of the offerings people presented to God.

John's unusual style helped direct attention to his burning message: The Messiah was about to arrive, and people must change their ways. Crowds flocked to hear John, and he baptized them in the Jordan River as a sign of their repentance, thus earning himself the nickname "the Baptist."

No less an authority than Jesus said that John was as great as any man who had ever lived (11:11). In the same breath Jesus added that the lowest-ranking person in the kingdom of God, now drawing near, was even greater than John. Although John represented the best of the old order, the new order of God's kingdom would outshine his greatness by far.

John had no difficulty accepting this comparison. When he saw Jesus he recognized "the Lamb of God, who takes away the sin of the world" (John 1:29). He considered himself unworthy even to untie Jesus' sandals. John the Baptist did not intend to attract attention to himself; rather, he pointed to Jesus.

When Herod Antipas arrested and executed John (14:1–12), most of John's disciples followed Jesus. It took a long time, however, for some who lived in far-off parts of the world to get the full message about Jesus (see Acts 18:24–26, 19:1–7). They, too, quickly adopted the Christian way. Despite John's great influence, it was a mark of his success that he left no distinctive "church" of his own. His followers were ready for Jesus.

Life Questions: How can your lifestyle help prepare people for Jesus?

Woe on Unrepentant Cities

▶ See Luke 10:13–15

²⁰Then Jesus began to denounce the cities in which most of his miracles had been performed,

---

11:20 Miracles Aren't Enough

Surprisingly, seeing supernatural miracles didn't lead people to repent and follow Jesus' teaching. Throughout his ministry, Jesus showed annoyance with crowds who flocked to see a popular leader do something supernatural. He wanted from them not applause, but commitment. Gradually, he relied more and more on parables, which, in private, he would explain to his disciples (see 13:11–17).

---

because they did not repent. ²¹"Woe to you, Korazin! Woe to you, Bethsaida! If the miracles that were performed in you had been performed in Tyre and Sidon, they would have repented long ago in sackcloth and ashes. ²²But I tell you, it will be more bearable for Tyre and Sidon on the day of judgment than for you. ²³And you, Capernaum, will you be lifted up to the skies? No, you will go down to the depths.ᵃ If the miracles that were performed in you had been performed in Sodom, it would have remained to this day. ²⁴But I tell you that it will be more bearable for Sodom on the day of judgment than for you."

Rest for the Weary

▶ See Luke 10:21–22

²⁵At that time Jesus said, "I praise you, Father, Lord of heaven and earth, because you have hidden these things from the wise and learned, and revealed them to little children. ²⁶Yes, Father, for this was your good pleasure.

²⁷"All things have been committed to me by my Father. No one knows the Son except the Father, and no one knows the Father except the Son and those to whom the Son chooses to reveal him.

²⁸"Come to me, all you who are weary and burdened, and I will give you rest. ²⁹Take my yoke upon you and learn from me, for I am gentle and humble in heart, and you will find rest for your souls. ³⁰For my yoke is easy and my burden is light."

Lord of the Sabbath

▶ See Mark 2:23 — 3:6; Luke 6:1–11

12 At that time Jesus went through the grainfields on the Sabbath. His disciples were hungry and began to pick some heads of grain and eat them. ²When the Pharisees saw this, they said to him, "Look! Your disciples are doing what is unlawful on the Sabbath."

³He answered, "Haven't you read what David did when he and his companions were hungry? ⁴He entered the house of God, and he and his companions ate the consecrated bread—which was not lawful for them to do, but only for the priests. ⁵Or haven't you read in the Law that on the Sabbath the priests in the temple desecrate the day and yet are innocent? ⁶I tell you that oneᵇ greater than the temple is here. ⁷If you had known what these words mean, 'I desire mercy, not sacrifice,'ᶜ you would not have condemned the innocent. ⁸For the Son of Man is Lord of the Sabbath."

⁹Going on from that place, he went into their synagogue, ¹⁰and a man with a shriveled hand was there. Looking for a reason to accuse Jesus, they asked him, "Is it lawful to heal on the Sabbath?"

¹¹He said to them, "If any of you has a sheep and it falls into a pit on the Sabbath, will you not take hold of it and lift it out? ¹²How much more valuable is a man than a sheep! Therefore it is lawful to do good on the Sabbath."

12:12 Pharisees Take Offense

Chapter 12 gives insight into why the Pharisees were offended by Jesus. First, his disciples picked grain on the Sabbath (verses 1–7), something forbidden by the Pharisees. A provocative healing on the Sabbath followed. Jesus accused the Pharisees of caring more for the letter of the law than the spirit, so much so that they showed more concern for animal life than human.

---

¹³Then he said to the man, "Stretch out your hand." So he stretched it out and it was completely restored, just as sound as the other. ¹⁴But the Pharisees went out and plotted how they might kill Jesus.

God's Chosen Servant

¹⁵Aware of this, Jesus withdrew from that place. Many followed him, and he healed all their sick, ¹⁶warning them not to tell who he was. ¹⁷This was to fulfill what was spoken through the prophet Isaiah:

¹⁸"Here is my servant whom I have chosen,
    the one I love, in whom I delight;
I will put my Spirit on him,
    and he will proclaim justice to the nations.
¹⁹He will not quarrel or cry out;
    no one will hear his voice in the streets.
²⁰A bruised reed he will not break,

ᵃ23 Greek Hades   ᵇ6 Or *something*; also in verses 41 and 42   ᶜ7 Hosea 6:6

and a smoldering wick he will not snuff
out,
till he leads justice to victory.
21 In his name the nations will put their
hope."[a]

Jesus and Beelzebub

▶ See Mark 3:23–27; Luke 11:17–22

22Then they brought him a demon-possessed
man who was blind and mute, and Jesus healed
him, so that he could both talk and see. 23All the
people were astonished and said, "Could this be
the Son of David?"

24But when the Pharisees heard this, they said,
"It is only by Beelzebub,[b] the prince of demons,
that this fellow drives out demons."

25Jesus knew their thoughts and said to them,
"Every kingdom divided against itself will be ruined, and every city or household divided against
itself will not stand. 26If Satan drives out Satan,
he is divided against himself. How then can his
kingdom stand? 27And if I drive out demons by
Beelzebub, by whom do your people drive them
out? So then, they will be your judges. 28But if I
drive out demons by the Spirit of God, then the
kingdom of God has come upon you.

29"Or again, how can anyone enter a strong
man's house and carry off his possessions unless
he first ties up the strong man? Then he can rob
his house.

30"He who is not with me is against me, and he
who does not gather with me scatters. 31And so
I tell you, every sin and blasphemy will be forgiv-
en men, but the blasphemy against the Spirit will
not be forgiven. 32Anyone who speaks a word
against the Son of Man will be forgiven, but anyone who speaks against the Holy Spirit will not
be forgiven, either in this age or in the age to
come.

33"Make a tree good and its fruit will be good,
or make a tree bad and its fruit will be bad, for
a tree is recognized by its fruit. 34You brood of
vipers, how can you who are evil say anything
good? For out of the overflow of the heart the
mouth speaks. 35The good man brings good
things out of the good stored up in him, and the
evil man brings evil things out of the evil stored
up in him. 36But I tell you that men will have to
give account on the day of judgment for every
careless word they have spoken. 37For by your
words you will be acquitted, and by your words
you will be condemned."

The Sign of Jonah

▶ See Luke 11:29–32

38Then some of the Pharisees and teachers of
the law said to him, "Teacher, we want to see a
miraculous sign from you."

39He answered, "A wicked and adulterous
generation asks for a miraculous sign! But none
will be given it except the sign of the prophet
Jonah. 40For as Jonah was three days and three
nights in the belly of a huge fish, so the Son of
Man will be three days and three nights in the
heart of the earth. 41The men of Nineveh will
stand up at the judgment with this generation
and condemn it; for they repented at the preaching of Jonah, and now one[c] greater than Jonah
is here. 42The Queen of the South will rise at the
judgment with this generation and condemn it;
for she came from the ends of the earth to listen
to Solomon's wisdom, and now one greater than
Solomon is here.

43"When an evil[d] spirit comes out of a man,
it goes through arid places seeking rest and does
not find it. 44Then it says, 'I will return to the
house I left.' When it arrives, it finds the house
unoccupied, swept clean and put in order.
45Then it goes and takes with it seven other spirits more wicked than itself, and they go in and
live there. And the final condition of that man is
worse than the first. That is how it will be with
this wicked generation."

Jesus' Mother and Brothers

▶ See Mark 3:31–35; Luke 8:19–21

46While Jesus was still talking to the crowd, his
mother and brothers stood outside, wanting to
speak to him. 47Someone told him, "Your mother
and brothers are standing outside, wanting to
speak to you."[e]

48He replied to him, "Who is my mother, and
who are my brothers?" 49Pointing to his disciples,
he said, "Here are my mother and my brothers.
50For whoever does the will of my Father in heav-
en is my brother and sister and mother."

The Parable of the Sower

▶ See Mark 4:1–20; Luke 8:4–15

13 That same day Jesus went out of the house
and sat by the lake. 2Such large crowds
gathered around him that he got into a boat and
sat in it, while all the people stood on the shore.
3Then he told them many things in parables, saying: "A farmer went out to sow his seed. 4As he
was scattering the seed, some fell along the path,
and the birds came and ate it up. 5Some fell on
rocky places, where it did not have much soil. It
sprang up quickly, because the soil was shallow.
6But when the sun came up, the plants were
scorched, and they withered because they had no
root. 7Other seed fell among thorns, which grew

---

a21 Isaiah 42:1-4   b24 Greek Beezeboul or Beelzeboul; also in verse 27   c41 Or something; also in verse 42
d43 Greek unclean   e47 Some manuscripts do not have verse 47.

up and choked the plants. [8]Still other seed fell on good soil, where it produced a crop—a hundred, sixty or thirty times what was sown. [9]He who has ears, let him hear."

[10]The disciples came to him and asked, "Why do you speak to the people in parables?"

[11]He replied, "The knowledge of the secrets of the kingdom of heaven has been given to you, but not to them. [12]Whoever has will be given more, and he will have an abundance. Whoever does not have, even what he has will be taken from him. [13]This is why I speak to them in parables:

"Though seeing, they do not see;
    though hearing, they do not hear or
        understand.

[14]In them is fulfilled the prophecy of Isaiah:

What Should a Leader Look Like?

Not everyone wanted Jesus' kind of kingdom

IMPORTANT LEADERS, SUCH AS PRESIDENTS and prime ministers, work hard to convey an impression of confidence and power. A leader, they assume, should look like a leader, and many of them hire an "image specialist" to learn how. Wherever they go, press agents, bodyguards, loyal assistants, and throngs of eager admirers follow in their wake.

Matthew depicts Jesus as a true leader—a king, in fact—but one who broke stereotypes. Jesus had undeniable power. He could quiet an angry storm and even walk on the surface of a lake. Yet he used that power compassionately, for the sake of others: to feed the hungry and heal the sick. He wasn't concerned about a powerful image.

> "Where did this man get this wisdom and these miraculous powers?" they asked. "Isn't this the carpenter's son?"
> 13:54–55

A New Kind of Kingdom

First-century Jews, who hated the Roman empire, would have rallied eagerly around a militant Jewish king. They rebelled often until a vengeful Roman general flattened Jerusalem in A.D. 70. The kingdom Jesus presented, however, didn't meet their expectations.

At the beginning of his ministry, Jesus turned down a tempting offer of glory and territory (4:8–11), and he consistently bucked the pressures of the crowd. Although he was the most powerful leader ever, he spent his time telling stories, not raising an army. As a true Messiah, he sought not to satisfy people's false image of him, but to please God.

In chapter 13, Matthew collects several of the stories Jesus told to describe his "kingdom of heaven"—a phrase used 32 times in Matthew. Although Jesus never concisely defined the phrase, he gave many clues about the nature of his kingdom. The kingdom is so important, he said, that belonging to it is worth selling everything a person owns.

Jesus said his kingdom doesn't have geographical boundaries. Unlike, say, Greece or China or Spain, it can't be charted on a map. Its followers live right among their enemies, not separated from them by a moat or a wall. Yet Jesus predicted that his kingdom would show remarkable growth even in an evil environment bent on its destruction.

The Disciples Fail to Understand

The "kingdom of heaven" consists of the rule of God in the world. It's made up of people of all races and from all nations who loyally follow God's will on earth. Jesus stressed that this new kingdom was a major advance in God's plan: its least member, he said, is even greater than John the Baptist (11:11).

The disciples, accustomed to more traditional images of power and leadership, couldn't quite grasp Jesus' concept of the kingdom. They kept asking him to explain his parables even as they jockeyed vainly for status.

As the days passed, the disciples became convinced that Jesus was "the Christ, the Son of the living God!" — Peter won warm praise for that assertion (16:17). But he received Jesus' strongest rebuke in the next scene when he recoiled from the idea that his leader might soon suffer and die.

The paradoxes of Jesus' style of leadership deepened as he neared Jerusalem, the capital city. He allowed one moment of public triumph, on the day we call Palm Sunday. Yet, even then he rode not a chariot or a stallion, but a donkey colt. And a few days later he left his followers an enduring emblem: not a royal banner or a scepter, but an executioner's cross.

Life Questions: Could Jesus run for political office in the United States? What kind of leader do people want today?

" 'You will be ever hearing but never
        understanding;
    you will be ever seeing but never
        perceiving.

> ### 13:10 Stories to Remember
>
> *An illiterate society (like much of Palestine in
> Jesus' day) passes down wisdom in the form of
> proverbs and stories. Everybody likes a story,
> and stories are easier to remember than
> concepts or logical outlines. Jesus spoke in
> terms that would hold the interest of a society
> of farmers and fishermen, and about 30 of his
> masterful parables—stories with a point—have
> survived in the Gospels.*

¹⁵For this people's heart has become calloused;
    they hardly hear with their ears,
    and they have closed their eyes.
Otherwise they might see with their eyes,
    hear with their ears,
    understand with their hearts
and turn, and I would heal them.' ᵃ

¹⁶But blessed are your eyes because they see, and
your ears because they hear. ¹⁷For I tell you the
truth, many prophets and righteous men longed
to see what you see but did not see it, and to hear
what you hear but did not hear it.

¹⁸"Listen then to what the parable of the sower
means: ¹⁹When anyone hears the message about
the kingdom and does not understand it, the evil
one comes and snatches away what was sown in
his heart. This is the seed sown along the path.
²⁰The one who received the seed that fell on
rocky places is the man who hears the word and
at once receives it with joy. ²¹But since he has no
root, he lasts only a short time. When trouble
or persecution comes because of the word, he
quickly falls away. ²²The one who received the
seed that fell among the thorns is the man who
hears the word, but the worries of this life and the
deceitfulness of wealth choke it, making it unfruitful. ²³But the one who received the seed that
fell on good soil is the man who hears the word
and understands it. He produces a crop, yielding
a hundred, sixty or thirty times what was sown."

The Parable of the Weeds

²⁴Jesus told them another parable: "The kingdom of heaven is like a man who sowed good
seed in his field. ²⁵But while everyone was sleeping, his enemy came and sowed weeds among the
wheat, and went away. ²⁶When the wheat sprouted and formed heads, then the weeds also appeared.

²⁷"The owner's servants came to him and said,

'Sir, didn't you sow good seed in your field?
Where then did the weeds come from?'

²⁸"'An enemy did this,' he replied.

"The servants asked him, 'Do you want us to
go and pull them up?'

²⁹"'No,' he answered, 'because while you are
pulling the weeds, you may root up the wheat
with them. ³⁰Let both grow together until the
harvest. At that time I will tell the harvesters: First
collect the weeds and tie them in bundles to be
burned; then gather the wheat and bring it into
my barn.' "

The Parables of the Mustard Seed and the Yeast

▶ *See Mark 4:30–32; Luke 13:18–21*

³¹He told them another parable: "The kingdom of heaven is like a mustard seed, which a
man took and planted in his field. ³²Though it is
the smallest of all your seeds, yet when it grows,
it is the largest of garden plants and becomes a
tree, so that the birds of the air come and perch
in its branches."

³³He told them still another parable: "The
kingdom of heaven is like yeast that a woman
took and mixed into a large amountᵇ of flour
until it worked all through the dough."

³⁴Jesus spoke all these things to the crowd in
parables; he did not say anything to them without using a parable. ³⁵So was fulfilled what was
spoken through the prophet:

"I will open my mouth in parables,
    I will utter things hidden since the
        creation of the world."ᶜ

The Parable of the Weeds Explained

³⁶Then he left the crowd and went into the
house. His disciples came to him and said, "Explain to us the parable of the weeds in the field."

³⁷He answered, "The one who sowed the good
seed is the Son of Man. ³⁸The field is the world,
and the good seed stands for the sons of the
kingdom. The weeds are the sons of the evil one,
³⁹and the enemy who sows them is the devil. The
harvest is the end of the age, and the harvesters
are angels.

⁴⁰"As the weeds are pulled up and burned in
the fire, so it will be at the end of the age. ⁴¹The
Son of Man will send out his angels, and they will
weed out of his kingdom everything that causes
sin and all who do evil. ⁴²They will throw them
into the fiery furnace, where there will be weeping and gnashing of teeth. ⁴³Then the righteous
will shine like the sun in the kingdom of their
Father. He who has ears, let him hear.

ᵃ15 Isaiah 6:9,10   ᵇ33 Greek *three satas* (probably about 1/2 bushel or 22 liters)   ᶜ35 Psalm 78:2

The Parables of the Hidden Treasure and the Pearl

44"The kingdom of heaven is like treasure hidden in a field. When a man found it, he hid it again, and then in his joy went and sold all he had and bought that field.

45"Again, the kingdom of heaven is like a merchant looking for fine pearls. 46When he found one of great value, he went away and sold everything he had and bought it.

The Parable of the Net

47"Once again, the kingdom of heaven is like a net that was let down into the lake and caught all kinds of fish. 48When it was full, the fishermen pulled it up on the shore. Then they sat down and collected the good fish in baskets, but threw the bad away. 49This is how it will be at the end of the age. The angels will come and separate the wicked from the righteous 50and throw them into the fiery furnace, where there will be weeping and gnashing of teeth.

51"Have you understood all these things?" Jesus asked.

"Yes," they replied.

52He said to them, "Therefore every teacher of the law who has been instructed about the kingdom of heaven is like the owner of a house who brings out of his storeroom new treasures as well as old."

A Prophet Without Honor

▶ See Mark 6:1–6

53When Jesus had finished these parables, he moved on from there. 54Coming to his hometown, he began teaching the people in their synagogue, and they were amazed. "Where did this man get this wisdom and these miraculous powers?" they asked. 55"Isn't this the carpenter's son? Isn't his mother's name Mary, and aren't his brothers James, Joseph, Simon and Judas? 56Aren't all his sisters with us? Where then did this man get all these things?" 57And they took offense at him.

But Jesus said to them, "Only in his hometown and in his own house is a prophet without honor."

58And he did not do many miracles there because of their lack of faith.

John the Baptist Beheaded

▶ See Mark 6:14–29

14 At that time Herod the tetrarch heard the reports about Jesus, 2and he said to his attendants, "This is John the Baptist; he has risen from the dead! That is why miraculous powers are at work in him."

3Now Herod had arrested John and bound him and put him in prison because of Herodias, his brother Philip's wife, 4for John had been saying to him: "It is not lawful for you to have her." 5Herod wanted to kill John, but he was afraid of the people, because they considered him a prophet.

14:5 A Wife's Revenge

John the Baptist offended King Herod with his blunt accusations, but Mark 6 points out that most of the venom came from Herod's wife (whom the king had stolen from his brother Philip). Herod had mixed feelings about John. He liked to listen to the prophet and had a respectful fear of him and his stern message. After falling into a trap set by his wife and stepdaughter, however, he succumbed to peer pressure and ordered John's execution.

6On Herod's birthday the daughter of Herodias danced for them and pleased Herod so much 7that he promised with an oath to give her whatever she asked. 8Prompted by her mother, she said, "Give me here on a platter the head of John the Baptist." 9The king was distressed, but because of his oaths and his dinner guests, he ordered that her request be granted 10and had John beheaded in the prison. 11His head was brought in on a platter and given to the girl, who carried it to her mother. 12John's disciples came and took his body and buried it. Then they went and told Jesus.

Jesus Feeds the Five Thousand

▶ See Mark 6:32–44; Luke 9:10–17; John 6:1–13

13When Jesus heard what had happened, he withdrew by boat privately to a solitary place. Hearing of this, the crowds followed him on foot from the towns. 14When Jesus landed and saw a large crowd, he had compassion on them and healed their sick.

15As evening approached, the disciples came to him and said, "This is a remote place, and it's already getting late. Send the crowds away, so

13:57 No Respect at Home

Jesus had opened his ministry at home in a synagogue, an occasion marked by a near-riot. When he returned later, he aroused great curiosity but little belief. The townsfolk couldn't fathom that one who'd been raised in their midst by a carpenter was now teaching like a rabbi and performing miracles. Jesus declined to display his supernatural power for them, and quietly withdrew.

they can go to the villages and buy themselves some food."

[16]Jesus replied, "They do not need to go away. You give them something to eat."

[17]"We have here only five loaves of bread and two fish," they answered.

[18]"Bring them here to me," he said. [19]And he directed the people to sit down on the grass. Taking the five loaves and the two fish and looking up to heaven, he gave thanks and broke the loaves. Then he gave them to the disciples, and the disciples gave them to the people. [20]They all ate and were satisfied, and the disciples picked up twelve basketfuls of broken pieces that were left over. [21]The number of those who ate was about five thousand men, besides women and children.

Jesus Walks on the Water

▶ See Mark 6:45–51; John 6:15–21

[22]Immediately Jesus made the disciples get into the boat and go on ahead of him to the other side, while he dismissed the crowd. [23]After he had dismissed them, he went up on a mountainside by himself to pray. When evening came, he was there alone, [24]but the boat was already a considerable distance[a] from land, buffeted by the waves because the wind was against it.

[25]During the fourth watch of the night Jesus went out to them, walking on the lake. [26]When the disciples saw him walking on the lake, they were terrified. "It's a ghost," they said, and cried out in fear.

[27]But Jesus immediately said to them: "Take courage! It is I. Don't be afraid."

[28]"Lord, if it's you," Peter replied, "tell me to come to you on the water."

[29]"Come," he said.

Then Peter got down out of the boat, walked on the water and came toward Jesus. [30]But when he saw the wind, he was afraid and, beginning to sink, cried out, "Lord, save me!"

[31]Immediately Jesus reached out his hand and caught him. "You of little faith," he said, "why did you doubt?"

[32]And when they climbed into the boat, the wind died down. [33]Then those who were in the boat worshiped him, saying, "Truly you are the Son of God."

[34]When they had crossed over, they landed at Gennesaret. [35]And when the men of that place

[a]24 Greek *many stadia*

THE HERODS *Lower Authority*

THE HEROD FAMILY WEAVES ITS way through the background of the New Testament, like minor supporting characters in a play. Oddly enough, in their own minds—and in the minds of most people then—they were major players.

Like the Kennedys in modern America, or the many royal families in European history, the Herods were a family dynasty. They ruled on behalf of the Romans with nearly absolute power. Such power did not impress the early Christians, however. They worshiped a higher authority, one whom the Herods were too spiritually dense to recognize.

Three different rulers go by the name of Herod in the New Testament. (A fourth, Agrippa, descended from the same family [see Agrippa, page 1169].) All three clashed with Jesus or his followers.

Herod the Great reigned as king when Jesus was born. He met the Magi, pointed them toward Bethlehem and then, when they disappeared without identifying the baby king, had all the infants in the area slaughtered (Matthew 2). Other historical sources suggest that such behavior was all too typical of this Herod—he even had his own sons murdered when he thought they threatened his power.

Herod the tetrarch, also known as Herod Antipas, was among Herod the Great's sons who survived the violence. At his father's death, he took command over Jesus' home area of Galilee. When John the Baptist offended Herod and his mistress by criticizing their morals, Herod imprisoned John and later had him beheaded. Jesus himself fell into this Herod's hands during his trial. Herod had heard of Jesus and hoped to see him do a miracle; when Jesus wouldn't cooperate, Herod ridiculed him and sent him back to Pilate (Luke 23:6–12).

Herod Agrippa I, grandson of Herod the Great, continued the pattern into the next generation. He ruled Jerusalem when the church first began growing there. He clamped down on the early Christians, executing James and arresting a number of others, including Peter. When Peter "escaped" with God's help, Herod had the guards executed (Acts 12). Acts tells us that Herod Agrippa died a sudden death, because he "did not give praise to God" when a crowd of admirers hailed him as divine (Acts 12:23).

As modern people we tend to focus on the Herods' brutal behavior, but most rulers behaved brutally in those days. Even more importantly, in the Bible's eyes, the Herods failed to recognize the real power on earth—that belonging to God.

Life Questions: What dangers do Christians in the modern world face from the "lower authority" of politicians and rulers?

recognized Jesus, they sent word to all the surrounding country. People brought all their sick to him [36] and begged him to let the sick just touch the edge of his cloak, and all who touched him were healed.

Clean and Unclean

▶ See Mark 7:1–23

15 Then some Pharisees and teachers of the law came to Jesus from Jerusalem and

---

15:1 Attacking Legalism

The Pharisees and teachers of the law considered their own strict traditions as binding as Old Testament law. In this passage, Jesus points out glaring inconsistencies in those traditions.

---

asked, [2]"Why do your disciples break the tradition of the elders? They don't wash their hands before they eat!"

[3]Jesus replied, "And why do you break the command of God for the sake of your tradition? [4]For God said, 'Honor your father and mother'[a] and 'Anyone who curses his father or mother must be put to death.'[b] [5]But you say that if a man says to his father or mother, 'Whatever help you might otherwise have received from me is a gift devoted to God,' [6]he is not to 'honor his father[c]' with it. Thus you nullify the word of God for the sake of your tradition. [7]You hypocrites! Isaiah was right when he prophesied about you:

[8]" 'These people honor me with their lips,
    but their hearts are far from me.
[9]They worship me in vain;
    their teachings are but rules taught by
        men.'[d]

[10]Jesus called the crowd to him and said, "Listen and understand. [11]What goes into a man's mouth does not make him 'unclean,' but what comes out of his mouth, that is what makes him 'unclean.'"

[12]Then the disciples came to him and asked, "Do you know that the Pharisees were offended when they heard this?"

[13]He replied, "Every plant that my heavenly Father has not planted will be pulled up by the roots. [14]Leave them; they are blind guides.[e] If a blind man leads a blind man, both will fall into a pit."

[15]Peter said, "Explain the parable to us."

[16]"Are you still so dull?" Jesus asked them. [17]"Don't you see that whatever enters the mouth goes into the stomach and then out of the body? [18]But the things that come out of the mouth come from the heart, and these make a man 'unclean.' [19]For out of the heart come evil thoughts, murder, adultery, sexual immorality, theft, false testimony, slander. [20]These are what make a man 'unclean'; but eating with unwashed hands does not make him 'unclean.' "

The Faith of the Canaanite Woman

▶ See Mark 7:24–30

[21]Leaving that place, Jesus withdrew to the region of Tyre and Sidon. [22]A Canaanite woman from that vicinity came to him, crying out, "Lord, Son of David, have mercy on me! My daughter is suffering terribly from demon-possession."

[23]Jesus did not answer a word. So his disciples came to him and urged him, "Send her away, for she keeps crying out after us."

[24]He answered, "I was sent only to the lost sheep of Israel."

[25]The woman came and knelt before him. "Lord, help me!" she said.

[26]He replied, "It is not right to take the children's bread and toss it to their dogs."

[27]"Yes, Lord," she said, "but even the dogs eat the crumbs that fall from their masters' table."

[28]Then Jesus answered, "Woman, you have great faith! Your request is granted." And her daughter was healed from that very hour.

Jesus Feeds the Four Thousand

▶ See Mark 8:1–10

[29]Jesus left there and went along the Sea of Galilee. Then he went up on a mountainside and

---

15:29–39 Two Feedings

In back-to-back chapters, Matthew reports on two incidents that can be easily confused. The feeding of the 5,000 (chapter 14) came at the height of Jesus' popularity and made a huge impression: all four Gospels report on it. Only Matthew and Mark, however, record this separate miracle performed for a slightly smaller crowd. In Mark's account (Mark 8:1–10), Jesus seems amazed that his disciples, having seen the first miracle, doubt his ability to supply a crowd's needs this second time.

---

sat down. [30]Great crowds came to him, bringing the lame, the blind, the crippled, the mute and many others, and laid them at his feet; and he healed them. [31]The people were amazed when they saw the mute speaking, the crippled made

---

[a]4 Exodus 20:12; Deut. 5:16   [b]4 Exodus 21:17; Lev. 20:9   [c]6 Some manuscripts *father or his mother*
[d]9 Isaiah 29:13   [e]14 Some manuscripts *guides of the blind*

well, the lame walking and the blind seeing. And they praised the God of Israel.

32Jesus called his disciples to him and said, "I have compassion for these people; they have already been with me three days and have nothing to eat. I do not want to send them away hungry, or they may collapse on the way."

33His disciples answered, "Where could we get enough bread in this remote place to feed such a crowd?"

34"How many loaves do you have?" Jesus asked.

"Seven," they replied, "and a few small fish."

35He told the crowd to sit down on the ground. 36Then he took the seven loaves and the fish, and when he had given thanks, he broke them and gave them to the disciples, and they in turn to the people. 37They all ate and were satisfied. Afterward the disciples picked up seven basketfuls of broken pieces that were left over. 38The number of those who ate was four thousand, besides women and children. 39After Jesus had sent the crowd away, he got into the boat and went to the vicinity of Magadan.

The Demand for a Sign

▶ See Mark 8:11-21

16 The Pharisees and Sadducees came to Jesus and tested him by asking him to show them a sign from heaven.

2He replied,[a] "When evening comes, you say, 'It will be fair weather, for the sky is red,' 3and in the morning, 'Today it will be stormy, for the sky is red and overcast.' You know how to interpret the appearance of the sky, but you cannot interpret the signs of the times. 4A wicked and adulterous generation looks for a miraculous sign, but none will be given it except the sign of Jonah." Jesus then left them and went away.

The Yeast of the Pharisees and Sadducees

5When they went across the lake, the disciples forgot to take bread. 6"Be careful," Jesus said to them. "Be on your guard against the yeast of the Pharisees and Sadducees."

7They discussed this among themselves and said, "It is because we didn't bring any bread."

8Aware of their discussion, Jesus asked, "You of little faith, why are you talking among yourselves about having no bread? 9Do you still not understand? Don't you remember the five loaves for the five thousand, and how many basketfuls you gathered? 10Or the seven loaves for the four thousand, and how many basketfuls you gathered? 11How is it you don't understand that I was not talking to you about bread? But be on your guard against the yeast of the Pharisees and Sad-

ducees." 12Then they understood that he was not telling them to guard against the yeast used in bread, but against the teaching of the Pharisees and Sadducees.

Peter's Confession of Christ

▶ See Mark 8:27-29; Luke 9:18-20

13When Jesus came to the region of Caesarea Philippi, he asked his disciples, "Who do people say the Son of Man is?"

16:13 Peter's Highs and Lows

The disciple Peter earned a reputation for impulsiveness, and this chapter shows him at his very best and very worst. He won highest praise for discerning Jesus' true identity, but in the very next paragraph he made one of his biggest blunders. He wanted Jesus to avoid pain, not understanding that the pain of the cross would bring salvation to the whole world.

14They replied, "Some say John the Baptist; others say Elijah; and still others, Jeremiah or one of the prophets."

15"But what about you?" he asked. "Who do you say I am?"

16Simon Peter answered, "You are the Christ,[b] the Son of the living God."

17Jesus replied, "Blessed are you, Simon son of Jonah, for this was not revealed to you by man, but by my Father in heaven. 18And I tell you that you are Peter,[c] and on this rock I will build my church, and the gates of Hades[d] will not overcome it.[e] 19I will give you the keys of the kingdom of heaven; whatever you bind on earth will be[f] bound in heaven, and whatever you loose on earth will be[f] loosed in heaven." 20Then he warned his disciples not to tell anyone that he was the Christ.

Jesus Predicts His Death

▶ See Mark 8:31— 9:1; Luke 9:22-27

21From that time on Jesus began to explain to his disciples that he must go to Jerusalem and suffer many things at the hands of the elders, chief priests and teachers of the law, and that he must be killed and on the third day be raised to life.

22Peter took him aside and began to rebuke him. "Never, Lord!" he said. "This shall never happen to you!"

23Jesus turned and said to Peter, "Get behind me, Satan! You are a stumbling block to me; you do not have in mind the things of God, but the things of men."

---

[a]2 Some early manuscripts do not have the rest of verse 2 and all of verse 3.   [b]16 Or Messiah; also in verse 20
[c]18 Peter means rock.   [d]18 Or hell   [e]18 Or not prove stronger than it   [f]19 Or have been

[24]Then Jesus said to his disciples, "If anyone would come after me, he must deny himself and take up his cross and follow me. [25]For whoever wants to save his life[a] will lose it, but whoever loses his life for me will find it. [26]What good will it be for a man if he gains the whole world, yet forfeits his soul? Or what can a man give in exchange for his soul? [27]For the Son of Man is going to come in his Father's glory with his angels, and then he will reward each person according to what he has done. [28]I tell you the truth, some who are standing here will not taste death before they see the Son of Man coming in his kingdom."

The Transfiguration

▶ See Mark 9:2–13; Luke 9:28–36

17 After six days Jesus took with him Peter, James and John the brother of James, and led them up a high mountain by themselves. [2]There he was transfigured before them. His face shone like the sun, and his clothes became as white as the light. [3]Just then there appeared before them Moses and Elijah, talking with Jesus.

[4]Peter said to Jesus, "Lord, it is good for us to be here. If you wish, I will put up three shelters—one for you, one for Moses and one for Elijah."

[5]While he was still speaking, a bright cloud enveloped them, and a voice from the cloud said, "This is my Son, whom I love; with him I am well pleased. Listen to him!"

17:5 Unforgettable Moment

Three of Jesus' disciples had the opportunity to observe this dramatic scene of God's approving of his Son Jesus. Moses, the first great lawgiver, and Elijah, the first great prophet, appeared with Jesus, and God spoke from heaven. The apostle Peter described the impact of this experience in 2 Peter 1:16–18.

[6]When the disciples heard this, they fell facedown to the ground, terrified. [7]But Jesus came and touched them. "Get up," he said. "Don't be afraid." [8]When they looked up, they saw no one except Jesus.

[9]As they were coming down the mountain, Jesus instructed them, "Don't tell anyone what you have seen, until the Son of Man has been raised from the dead."

[10]The disciples asked him, "Why then do the teachers of the law say that Elijah must come first?"

[11]Jesus replied, "To be sure, Elijah comes and will restore all things. [12]But I tell you, Elijah has already come, and they did not recognize him, but have done to him everything they wished. In the same way the Son of Man is going to suffer at their hands." [13]Then the disciples understood that he was talking to them about John the Baptist.

The Healing of a Boy With a Demon

▶ See Mark 9:14–28; Luke 9:37–42

[14]When they came to the crowd, a man approached Jesus and knelt before him. [15]"Lord, have mercy on my son," he said. "He has seizures and is suffering greatly. He often falls into the fire or into the water. [16]I brought him to your disciples, but they could not heal him."

[17]"O unbelieving and perverse generation," Jesus replied, "how long shall I stay with you? How long shall I put up with you? Bring the boy here to me." [18]Jesus rebuked the demon, and it came out of the boy, and he was healed from that moment.

[19]Then the disciples came to Jesus in private and asked, "Why couldn't we drive it out?"

[20]He replied, "Because you have so little faith. I tell you the truth, if you have faith as small as a mustard seed, you can say to this mountain, 'Move from here to there' and it will move. Nothing will be impossible for you.[b]"

[22]When they came together in Galilee, he said to them, "The Son of Man is going to be betrayed into the hands of men. [23]They will kill him, and on the third day he will be raised to life." And the disciples were filled with grief.

The Temple Tax

[24]After Jesus and his disciples arrived in Capernaum, the collectors of the two-drachma tax came to Peter and asked, "Doesn't your teacher pay the temple tax[c]?"

[25]"Yes, he does," he replied.

When Peter came into the house, Jesus was the first to speak. "What do you think, Simon?" he asked. "From whom do the kings of the earth collect duty and taxes—from their own sons or from others?"

[26]"From others," Peter answered.

"Then the sons are exempt," Jesus said to him. [27]"But so that we may not offend them, go to the lake and throw out your line. Take the first fish you catch; open its mouth and you will find a four-drachma coin. Take it and give it to them for my tax and yours."

The Greatest in the Kingdom of Heaven

▶ See Mark 9:33–37; Luke 9:46–48

18 At that time the disciples came to Jesus and asked, "Who is the greatest in the kingdom of heaven?"

---

[a]25 The Greek word means either *life* or *soul*; also in verse 26.   [c]24 Greek *the two drachmas*   [b]20 Some manuscripts *you.* [21]*But this kind does not go out except by prayer and fasting.*

²He called a little child and had him stand among them. ³And he said: "I tell you the truth, unless you change and become like little children, you will never enter the kingdom of heaven. ⁴Therefore, whoever humbles himself like this child is the greatest in the kingdom of heaven.

⁵"And whoever welcomes a little child like this in my name welcomes me. ⁶But if anyone causes one of these little ones who believe in me to sin, it would be better for him to have a large millstone hung around his neck and to be drowned in the depths of the sea.

⁷"Woe to the world because of the things that cause people to sin! Such things must come, but woe to the man through whom they come! ⁸If your hand or your foot causes you to sin, cut it off and throw it away. It is better for you to enter life maimed or crippled than to have two hands or two feet and be thrown into eternal fire. ⁹And if your eye causes you to sin, gouge it out and throw it away. It is better for you to enter life with one eye than to have two eyes and be thrown into the fire of hell.

The Parable of the Lost Sheep

▶ See Luke 15:4–7

¹⁰"See that you do not look down on one of these little ones. For I tell you that their angels in heaven always see the face of my Father in heaven.ᵃ ¹²"What do you think? If a man owns a hundred sheep, and one of them wanders away, will he not leave the ninety-nine on the hills and go to look for the one that wandered off? ¹³And if he finds it, I tell you the truth, he is happier about that one sheep than about the ninety-nine that did not wander off. ¹⁴In the same way your Father in heaven is not willing that any of these little ones should be lost.

A Brother Who Sins Against You

¹⁵"If your brother sins against you,ᵇ go and show him his fault, just between the two of you. If he listens to you, you have won your brother over. ¹⁶But if he will not listen, take one or two others along, so that 'every matter may be established by the testimony of two or three witnesses.'ᶜ ¹⁷If he refuses to listen to them, tell it to the church; and if he refuses to listen even to the church, treat him as you would a pagan or a tax collector.

¹⁸"I tell you the truth, whatever you bind on earth will beᵈ bound in heaven, and whatever you loose on earth will beᵈ loosed in heaven.

¹⁹"Again, I tell you that if two of you on earth agree about anything you ask for, it will be done for you by my Father in heaven. ²⁰For where two or three come together in my name, there am I with them."

The Parable of the Unmerciful Servant

²¹Then Peter came to Jesus and asked, "Lord, how many times shall I forgive my brother when he sins against me? Up to seven times?"

²²Jesus answered, "I tell you, not seven times, but seventy-seven times.ᵉ

²³"Therefore, the kingdom of heaven is like a king who wanted to settle accounts with his servants. ²⁴As he began the settlement, a man who

> ### 18:23 Matthew and Money
>
> *Just as Luke, a doctor, gives more descriptive accounts of physical healings, Matthew, a former tax collector, highlights stories about money. This story in chapter 18, as well as others in chapters 20 and 25, appears only in Matthew's Gospel. Significantly, the former tax collector records Jesus' strongest words on treatment of the poor and needy.*

owed him ten thousand talentsᶠ was brought to him. ²⁵Since he was not able to pay, the master ordered that he and his wife and his children and all that he had be sold to repay the debt.

²⁶"The servant fell on his knees before him. 'Be patient with me,' he begged, 'and I will pay back everything.' ²⁷The servant's master took pity on him, canceled the debt and let him go.

²⁸"But when that servant went out, he found one of his fellow servants who owed him a hundred denarii.ᵍ He grabbed him and began to choke him. 'Pay back what you owe me!' he demanded.

²⁹"His fellow servant fell to his knees and begged him, 'Be patient with me, and I will pay you back.'

³⁰"But he refused. Instead, he went off and had the man thrown into prison until he could pay the debt. ³¹When the other servants saw what had happened, they were greatly distressed and went and told their master everything that had happened.

³²"Then the master called the servant in. 'You wicked servant,' he said, 'I canceled all that debt of yours because you begged me to. ³³Shouldn't you have had mercy on your fellow servant just as I had on you?' ³⁴In anger his master turned him over to the jailers to be tortured, until he should pay back all he owed.

³⁵"This is how my heavenly Father will treat

ᵃ10 Some manuscripts *heaven.* ¹¹*The Son of Man came to save what was lost.*   ᵇ15 Some manuscripts do not have *against you.*   ᶜ16 Deut. 19:15   ᵈ18 Or *have been*   ᵉ22 Or *seventy times seven*   ᶠ24 That is, millions of dollars   ᵍ28 That is, a few dollars

each of you unless you forgive your brother from your heart."

Divorce

▶ See Mark 10:1–12

19 When Jesus had finished saying these things, he left Galilee and went into the region of Judea to the other side of the Jordan. ²Large crowds followed him, and he healed them there.

³Some Pharisees came to him to test him. They asked, "Is it lawful for a man to divorce his wife for any and every reason?"

⁴"Haven't you read," he replied, "that at the beginning the Creator 'made them male and female,'ᵃ ⁵and said, 'For this reason a man will leave his father and mother and be united to his wife, and the two will become one flesh'ᵇ? ⁶So they are no longer two, but one. Therefore what God has joined together, let man not separate."

⁷"Why then," they asked, "did Moses command that a man give his wife a certificate of divorce and send her away?"

⁸Jesus replied, "Moses permitted you to divorce your wives because your hearts were hard. But it was not this way from the beginning. ⁹I tell you that anyone who divorces his wife, except for marital unfaithfulness, and marries another woman commits adultery."

19:9 No-Fault Divorce?

In Jesus' day Pharisees debated how to interpret Old Testament rules concerning divorce. As usual, they tried to pull Jesus into the dispute. A famous rabbi named Hillel taught that a man could divorce his wife if she did anything at all to displease him, such as burning his food. A stricter school headed by Shammai limited grounds for divorce to marital infidelity. Jesus clearly sided with Shammai but pointed much deeper, beyond the technicalities of divorce to God's original design for marriage.

¹⁰The disciples said to him, "If this is the situation between a husband and wife, it is better not to marry."

¹¹Jesus replied, "Not everyone can accept this word, but only those to whom it has been given. ¹²For some are eunuchs because they were born that way; others were made that way by men; and others have renounced marriageᶜ because of the kingdom of heaven. The one who can accept this should accept it."

The Little Children and Jesus

▶ See Mark 10:13–16; Luke 18:15–17

¹³Then little children were brought to Jesus for him to place his hands on them and pray for them. But the disciples rebuked those who brought them.

¹⁴Jesus said, "Let the little children come to me, and do not hinder them, for the kingdom of heaven belongs to such as these." ¹⁵When he had placed his hands on them, he went on from there.

The Rich Young Man

▶ See Mark 10:17–30; Luke 18:18–30

¹⁶Now a man came up to Jesus and asked, "Teacher, what good thing must I do to get eternal life?"

¹⁷"Why do you ask me about what is good?" Jesus replied. "There is only One who is good. If you want to enter life, obey the commandments."

¹⁸"Which ones?" the man inquired.

Jesus replied, "'Do not murder, do not commit adultery, do not steal, do not give false testimony, ¹⁹honor your father and mother,'ᵈ and 'love your neighbor as yourself.'ᵉ"

²⁰"All these I have kept," the young man said. "What do I still lack?"

²¹Jesus answered, "If you want to be perfect, go, sell your possessions and give to the poor, and you will have treasure in heaven. Then come, follow me."

²²When the young man heard this, he went away sad, because he had great wealth.

²³Then Jesus said to his disciples, "I tell you the truth, it is hard for a rich man to enter the kingdom of heaven. ²⁴Again I tell you, it is easier for a camel to go through the eye of a needle than for a rich man to enter the kingdom of God."

²⁵When the disciples heard this, they were greatly astonished and asked, "Who then can be saved?"

²⁶Jesus looked at them and said, "With man this is impossible, but with God all things are possible."

²⁷Peter answered him, "We have left everything to follow you! What then will there be for us?"

²⁸Jesus said to them, "I tell you the truth, at the renewal of all things, when the Son of Man sits on his glorious throne, you who have followed me will also sit on twelve thrones, judging the twelve tribes of Israel. ²⁹And everyone who has left houses or brothers or sisters or father or motherᶠ or children or fields for my sake will receive a hundred times as much and will inherit eternal life. ³⁰But many who are first will be last, and many who are last will be first.

ᵃ4 Gen. 1:27   ᵇ5 Gen. 2:24   ᶜ12 Or *have made themselves eunuchs*   ᵈ19 Exodus 20:12-16; Deut. 5:16-20
ᵉ19 Lev. 19:18   ᶠ29 Some manuscripts *mother or wife*

The Parable of the Workers in the Vineyard

20 "For the kingdom of heaven is like a landowner who went out early in the morning

> ### 20:1 Unfair Pay
>
> *Jesus' story makes little economic sense, which was his point exactly. He is giving a parable about grace, and you can't calculate the grace of God like you can a day's wages. We receive it as a gift from God, not as something we work hard to earn. The person who comes to God at the end of life—like the robber on the cross— enjoys the same ultimate benefits as someone who follows God from early childhood. Jealousy of another's "unfair" rewards can take the joy from your own.*

to hire men to work in his vineyard. ²He agreed to pay them a denarius for the day and sent them into his vineyard.

³"About the third hour he went out and saw others standing in the marketplace doing nothing. ⁴He told them, 'You also go and work in my vineyard, and I will pay you whatever is right.' ⁵So they went.

"He went out again about the sixth hour and the ninth hour and did the same thing. ⁶About the eleventh hour he went out and found still others standing around. He asked them, 'Why have you been standing here all day long doing nothing?'

⁷"'Because no one has hired us,' they answered.

"He said to them, 'You also go and work in my vineyard.'

⁸"When evening came, the owner of the vineyard said to his foreman, 'Call the workers and pay them their wages, beginning with the last ones hired and going on to the first.'

⁹"The workers who were hired about the eleventh hour came and each received a denarius. ¹⁰So when those came who were hired first, they expected to receive more. But each one of them also received a denarius. ¹¹When they received it, they began to grumble against the landowner. ¹²These men who were hired last worked only one hour,' they said, 'and you have made them equal to us who have borne the burden of the work and the heat of the day.'

¹³"But he answered one of them, 'Friend, I am not being unfair to you. Didn't you agree to work for a denarius? ¹⁴Take your pay and go. I want to give the man who was hired last the same as I gave you. ¹⁵Don't I have the right to do what I want with my own money? Or are you envious because I am generous?'

¹⁶"So the last will be first, and the first will be last."

Jesus Again Predicts His Death

▶ *See Mark 10:32–34; Luke 18:31–33*

¹⁷Now as Jesus was going up to Jerusalem, he took the twelve disciples aside and said to them, ¹⁸"We are going up to Jerusalem, and the Son of Man will be betrayed to the chief priests and the teachers of the law. They will condemn him to death ¹⁹and will turn him over to the Gentiles to be mocked and flogged and crucified. On the third day he will be raised to life!"

A Mother's Request

▶ *See Mark 10:35–45*

²⁰Then the mother of Zebedee's sons came to Jesus with her sons and, kneeling down, asked a favor of him.

²¹"What is it you want?" he asked.

She said, "Grant that one of these two sons of mine may sit at your right and the other at your left in your kingdom."

²²"You don't know what you are asking," Jesus said to them. "Can you drink the cup I am going to drink?"

"We can," they answered.

²³Jesus said to them, "You will indeed drink from my cup, but to sit at my right or left is not for me to grant. These places belong to those for whom they have been prepared by my Father."

²⁴When the ten heard about this, they were indignant with the two brothers. ²⁵Jesus called them together and said, "You know that the rulers of the Gentiles lord it over them, and their high officials exercise authority over them. ²⁶Not so with you. Instead, whoever wants to become great among you must be your servant, ²⁷and whoever wants to be first must be your slave— ²⁸just as the Son of Man did not come to be served, but to serve, and to give his life as a ransom for many."

Two Blind Men Receive Sight

▶ *See Mark 10:46–52; Luke 18:35–43*

²⁹As Jesus and his disciples were leaving Jericho, a large crowd followed him. ³⁰Two blind men were sitting by the roadside, and when they heard that Jesus was going by, they shouted, "Lord, Son of David, have mercy on us!"

³¹The crowd rebuked them and told them to be quiet, but they shouted all the louder, "Lord, Son of David, have mercy on us!"

³²Jesus stopped and called them. "What do you want me to do for you?" he asked.

³³"Lord," they answered, "we want our sight."

³⁴Jesus had compassion on them and touched their eyes. Immediately they received their sight and followed him.

The Triumphal Entry

▶ *See Mark 11:1–10; Luke 19:29–38; John 12:12–15*

21 As they approached Jerusalem and came to Bethphage on the Mount of Olives, Jesus sent two disciples, ²saying to them, "Go to the village ahead of you, and at once you will find a donkey tied there, with her colt by her. Untie them and bring them to me. ³If anyone says any-

*a*5 Zech. 9:9

thing to you, tell him that the Lord needs them, and he will send them right away."

⁴This took place to fulfill what was spoken through the prophet:

⁵"Say to the Daughter of Zion,
  'See, your king comes to you,
gentle and riding on a donkey,
  on a colt, the foal of a donkey.' "*a*

Out to Get Jesus
Jesus confronts his enemies

THE MERE BIRTH OF JESUS had threatened King Herod so much that he had ordered a bloody slaughter of boy babies. The pattern of opposition continued. Early on, Jesus openly predicted his own death.

Beginning in chapter 19, Matthew explains some of the escalating tensions between Jesus and the groups who resisted him. Enemies followed him from town to town, setting traps. Even so, Jesus neither tempered his words nor tried to hide. Instead, he used the occasions of conflict to warn his disciples and the watching crowds against those enemies, whose fury only increased.

Chapter 22 shows Jesus confronting three different groups of enemies on the same day: two religious sects, the Pharisees and the Sadducees, as well as the political Herodians. Jesus easily avoided their carefully devised verbal traps. In fact, he succeeded so brilliantly that Matthew concludes, "From that day on no one dared to ask him any more questions" (22:46).

> *When the chief priests and the Pharisees heard Jesus' parables, they knew he was talking about them. They looked for a way to arrest him, but they were afraid of the crowd. 21:45–46*

What Did Jesus Have Against the Pharisees?

Students of history have often puzzled over why Jesus lashed out so strongly at one Jewish sect, the Pharisees—a group the New Testament mentions 100 times. At first glance, they seem like people Jesus should have liked. They were the most religious people of the day. More than any other group, they strove to follow the letter of the Old Testament law. Their very name, meaning "separatists," hinted at their desire to rise above normal behavior.

Pharisees were legalists. Besides unduly focusing on minute details of the law, they embellished it with their own strict traditions. For example, a person could ride a donkey without breaking the Sabbath rules, but if he carried a switch to speed up the animal, he would be guilty of laying a burden on it.

A Pharisee could give to a beggar on the Sabbath only if the beggar stuck his hand inside the home of the Pharisee so that the Pharisee needn't reach outside. A woman couldn't look in the mirror on the Sabbath—she might see a gray hair and be tempted to pull it out.

Matthew 23 records Jesus' eloquent verdict on the Pharisees. He chastised them for being proud and cliquish and petty, and for refusing to admit their wrongs. External, showy forms of legalism, he said, tend to divert attention away from a person's inner attitude toward God and other people.

Are There Pharisees Now?

As he entered into the last weeks of his life on earth, Jesus polarized people. He boldly contrasted his own teaching with that of his opponents. In addition, he warned his followers about what to expect after his death. Opposition from enemies like the Pharisees wouldn't fade away when he departed. Rather, it would crescendo until the day of final judgment.

Jesus singled out the Pharisees as an example of legalism carried to an extreme. But he wasn't talking merely against an ancient Jewish sect. His words describe persistent tendencies of human beings, then and now. The errors he mentioned have characterized the church throughout its history. Christians still battle against pride and intolerance and a religion based on deeds.

Life Questions: Jesus describes characteristics of Pharisees in the first century. But what about our own time? What Pharisee-like qualities exist in your church? In you?

⁶The disciples went and did as Jesus had instructed them. ⁷They brought the donkey and the colt, placed their cloaks on them, and Jesus sat on them. ⁸A very large crowd spread their cloaks on the road, while others cut branches from the trees and spread them on the road. ⁹The crowds that went ahead of him and those that followed shouted,

"Hosanna*a* to the Son of David!"

"Blessed is he who comes in the name of the Lord!"*b*

"Hosanna*a* in the highest!"

¹⁰When Jesus entered Jerusalem, the whole city was stirred and asked, "Who is this?"

¹¹The crowds answered, "This is Jesus, the prophet from Nazareth in Galilee."

Jesus at the Temple

▶ See Mark 11:15–18; Luke 19:45–47

¹²Jesus entered the temple area and drove out all who were buying and selling there. He overturned the tables of the money changers and the

21:12 Drastic Action

In Jesus' day, activities at the temple, supposedly the center for worship of God, had taken on a commercial cast. Merchants sold sacrificial animals to pilgrims and foreigners at inflated prices. The system was designed more for profit than for true worship. Jesus responded first by aggressively turning out these "robbers," and then by turning his attention to the people with real needs, the blind and the lame.

benches of those selling doves. ¹³"It is written," he said to them, "'My house will be called a house of prayer,'*c* but you are making it a 'den of robbers.'*d*"

¹⁴The blind and the lame came to him at the temple, and he healed them. ¹⁵But when the chief priests and the teachers of the law saw the wonderful things he did and the children shouting in the temple area, "Hosanna to the Son of David," they were indignant.

¹⁶"Do you hear what these children are saying?" they asked him.

"Yes," replied Jesus, "have you never read,

"'From the lips of children and infants
   you have ordained praise'*e*?"

¹⁷And he left them and went out of the city to Bethany, where he spent the night.

The Fig Tree Withers

▶ See Mark 11:12–14,20–24

¹⁸Early in the morning, as he was on his way back to the city, he was hungry. ¹⁹Seeing a fig tree by the road, he went up to it but found nothing on it except leaves. Then he said to it, "May you never bear fruit again!" Immediately the tree withered.

²⁰When the disciples saw this, they were amazed. "How did the fig tree wither so quickly?" they asked.

²¹Jesus replied, "I tell you the truth, if you have faith and do not doubt, not only can you do what was done to the fig tree, but also you can say to this mountain, 'Go, throw yourself into the sea,' and it will be done. ²²If you believe, you will receive whatever you ask for in prayer."

The Authority of Jesus Questioned

▶ See Mark 11:27–33; Luke 20:1–8

²³Jesus entered the temple courts, and, while he was teaching, the chief priests and the elders of the people came to him. "By what authority are you doing these things?" they asked. "And who gave you this authority?"

²⁴Jesus replied, "I will also ask you one question. If you answer me, I will tell you by what authority I am doing these things. ²⁵John's baptism—where did it come from? Was it from heaven, or from men?"

They discussed it among themselves and said, "If we say, 'From heaven,' he will ask, 'Then why didn't you believe him?' ²⁶But if we say, 'From men'—we are afraid of the people, for they all hold that John was a prophet."

²⁷So they answered Jesus, "We don't know."

Then he said, "Neither will I tell you by what authority I am doing these things.

The Parable of the Two Sons

²⁸"What do you think? There was a man who had two sons. He went to the first and said, 'Son, go and work today in the vineyard.'

²⁹"'I will not,' he answered, but later he changed his mind and went.

³⁰"Then the father went to the other son and said the same thing. He answered, 'I will, sir,' but he did not go.

³¹"Which of the two did what his father wanted?"

"The first," they answered.

Jesus said to them, "I tell you the truth, the tax collectors and the prostitutes are entering the kingdom of God ahead of you. ³²For John came to you to show you the way of righteousness, and you did not believe him, but the tax collectors

---

*a*9 A Hebrew expression meaning "Save!" which became an exclamation of praise; also in verse 15   *b*9 Psalm 118:26
*c*13 Isaiah 56:7   *d*13 Jer. 7:11   *e*16 Psalm 8:2

and the prostitutes did. And even after you saw this, you did not repent and believe him.

The Parable of the Tenants

▶ See Mark 12:1–12; Luke 20:9–19

33"Listen to another parable: There was a landowner who planted a vineyard. He put a wall around it, dug a winepress in it and built a watchtower. Then he rented the vineyard to some farmers and went away on a journey. 34When the harvest time approached, he sent his servants to the tenants to collect his fruit.

35"The tenants seized his servants; they beat one, killed another, and stoned a third. 36Then he sent other servants to them, more than the first time, and the tenants treated them the same way. 37Last of all, he sent his son to them. 'They will respect my son,' he said.

38"But when the tenants saw the son, they said to each other, 'This is the heir. Come, let's kill him and take his inheritance.' 39So they took him and threw him out of the vineyard and killed him.

40"Therefore, when the owner of the vineyard comes, what will he do to those tenants?"

41"He will bring those wretches to a wretched end," they replied, "and he will rent the vineyard to other tenants, who will give him his share of the crop at harvest time."

42Jesus said to them, "Have you never read in the Scriptures:

"'The stone the builders rejected
    has become the capstone[a];
the Lord has done this,
    and it is marvelous in our eyes'[b]?

43"Therefore I tell you that the kingdom of God will be taken away from you and given to a people who will produce its fruit. 44He who falls on this stone will be broken to pieces, but he on whom it falls will be crushed."[c]

45When the chief priests and the Pharisees heard Jesus' parables, they knew he was talking about them. 46They looked for a way to arrest him, but they were afraid of the crowd because the people held that he was a prophet.

The Parable of the Wedding Banquet

22 Jesus spoke to them again in parables, saying: 2"The kingdom of heaven is like a king who prepared a wedding banquet for his son. 3He sent his servants to those who had been invited to the banquet to tell them to come, but they refused to come.

4"Then he sent some more servants and said, 'Tell those who have been invited that I have prepared my dinner: My oxen and fattened cattle have been butchered, and everything is ready. Come to the wedding banquet.'

5"But they paid no attention and went off—one to his field, another to his business. 6The rest seized his servants, mistreated them and killed them. 7The king was enraged. He sent his army and destroyed those murderers and burned their city.

8"Then he said to his servants, 'The wedding banquet is ready, but those I invited did not deserve to come. 9Go to the street corners and invite to the banquet anyone you find.' 10So the servants went out into the streets and gathered all the people they could find, both good and bad, and the wedding hall was filled with guests.

11"But when the king came in to see the guests, he noticed a man there who was not wearing wedding clothes. 12'Friend,' he asked, 'how did you get in here without wedding clothes?' The man was speechless.

13"Then the king told the attendants, 'Tie him hand and foot, and throw him outside, into the darkness, where there will be weeping and gnashing of teeth.'

14"For many are invited, but few are chosen."

Paying Taxes to Caesar

▶ See Mark 12:13–17; Luke 20:20–26

15Then the Pharisees went out and laid plans to trap him in his words. 16They sent their disciples to him along with the Herodians. "Teacher," they said, "we know you are a man of integrity and that you teach the way of God in accordance with the truth. You aren't swayed by men, because you pay no attention to who they are. 17Tell us then, what is your opinion? Is it right to pay taxes to Caesar or not?"

22:17 A Double Bind

The Pharisees, allied with a party following King Herod, posed a question designed to trap Jesus regardless of his answer. If Jesus said, Pay the taxes, he would lose the support of the independence-minded Jews; if he said, Don't pay, he could be turned in to Rome for breaking the law.

18But Jesus, knowing their evil intent, said, "You hypocrites, why are you trying to trap me? 19Show me the coin used for paying the tax." They brought him a denarius, 20and he asked them, "Whose portrait is this? And whose inscription?"

21"Caesar's," they replied.

Then he said to them, "Give to Caesar what is Caesar's, and to God what is God's."

---

[a]42 Or cornerstone   [b]42 Psalm 118:22,23   [c]44 Some manuscripts do not have verse 44.

[22]When they heard this, they were amazed. So they left him and went away.

Marriage at the Resurrection

▶ *See Mark 12:18–27; Luke 20:27–40*

[23]That same day the Sadducees, who say there is no resurrection, came to him with a question. [24]"Teacher," they said, "Moses told us that if a man dies without having children, his brother must marry the widow and have children for him. [25]Now there were seven brothers among us. The first one married and died, and since he had no children, he left his wife to his brother. [26]The same thing happened to the second and third brother, right on down to the seventh. [27]Finally, the woman died. [28]Now then, at the resurrection, whose wife will she be of the seven, since all of them were married to her?"

[29]Jesus replied, "You are in error because you do not know the Scriptures or the power of God. [30]At the resurrection people will neither marry nor be given in marriage; they will be like the angels in heaven. [31]But about the resurrection of the dead—have you not read what God said to you, [32]'I am the God of Abraham, the God of Isaac, and the God of Jacob'[a]? He is not the God of the dead but of the living."

[33]When the crowds heard this, they were astonished at his teaching.

The Greatest Commandment

▶ *See Mark 12:28–31*

[34]Hearing that Jesus had silenced the Sadducees, the Pharisees got together. [35]One of them, an expert in the law, tested him with this question: [36]"Teacher, which is the greatest commandment in the Law?"

[37]Jesus replied: " 'Love the Lord your God with all your heart and with all your soul and with all your mind.'[b] [38]This is the first and greatest commandment. [39]And the second is like it: 'Love your neighbor as yourself.'[c] [40]All the Law and the Prophets hang on these two commandments."

Whose Son Is the Christ?

▶ *See Mark 12:35–37; Luke 20:41–44*

[41]While the Pharisees were gathered together, Jesus asked them, [42]"What do you think about the Christ[d]? Whose son is he?"

"The son of David," they replied.

[43]He said to them, "How is it then that David, speaking by the Spirit, calls him 'Lord'? For he says,

[44]" 'The Lord said to my Lord:

"Sit at my right hand
until I put your enemies
under your feet." '[e]

[45]If then David calls him 'Lord,' how can he be his son?" [46]No one could say a word in reply, and from that day on no one dared to ask him any more questions.

Seven Woes

▶ *See Mark 12:38–39; Luke 20:45–46*

23 Then Jesus said to the crowds and to his disciples: [2]"The teachers of the law and the Pharisees sit in Moses' seat. [3]So you must obey them and do everything they tell you. But do not do what they do, for they do not practice what they preach. [4]They tie up heavy loads and put them on men's shoulders, but they themselves are not willing to lift a finger to move them.

[5]"Everything they do is done for men to see: They make their phylacteries[f] wide and the tassels on their garments long; [6]they love the place of honor at banquets and the most important seats in the synagogues; [7]they love to be greeted in the marketplaces and to have men call them 'Rabbi.'

[8]"But you are not to be called 'Rabbi,' for you have only one Master and you are all brothers. [9]And do not call anyone on earth 'father,' for you have one Father, and he is in heaven. [10]Nor are you to be called 'teacher,' for you have one Teacher, the Christ.[d] [11]The greatest among you will be your servant. [12]For whoever exalts himself will be humbled, and whoever humbles himself will be exalted.

[13]"Woe to you, teachers of the law and Pharisees, you hypocrites! You shut the kingdom of heaven in men's faces. You yourselves do not enter, nor will you let those enter who are trying to.[g]

[15]"Woe to you, teachers of the law and Pharisees, you hypocrites! You travel over land and sea to win a single convert, and when he becomes one, you make him twice as much a son of hell as you are.

[16]"Woe to you, blind guides! You say, 'If anyone swears by the temple, it means nothing; but if anyone swears by the gold of the temple, he is bound by his oath.' [17]You blind fools! Which is greater: the gold, or the temple that makes the gold sacred? [18]You also say, 'If anyone swears by the altar, it means nothing; but if anyone swears by the gift on it, he is bound by his oath.' [19]You blind men! Which is greater: the gift, or the altar that makes the gift sacred? [20]Therefore, he who swears by the altar swears by it and by everything

---

[a]32 Exodus 3:6   [b]37 Deut. 6:5   [c]39 Lev. 19:18   [d]42,10 Or *Messiah*   [e]44 Psalm 110:1   [f]5 That is, boxes containing Scripture verses, worn on forehead and arm   [g]13 Some manuscripts *to. 14Woe to you, teachers of the law and Pharisees, you hypocrites! You devour widows' houses and for a show make lengthy prayers. Therefore you will be punished more severely.*

on it. ²¹And he who swears by the temple swears by it and by the one who dwells in it. ²²And he who swears by heaven swears by God's throne and by the one who sits on it.

²³"Woe to you, teachers of the law and Pharisees, you hypocrites! You give a tenth of your spices—mint, dill and cummin. But you have neglected the more important matters of the law—justice, mercy and faithfulness. You should have practiced the latter, without neglecting the former. ²⁴You blind guides! You strain out a gnat but swallow a camel.

23:24–28 Straining at Gnats

The Pharisees, who literally strained water through a cloth to filter out unclean gnats, could hardly miss the point of Jesus' biting humor. Jesus was not attacking them for being strict per se, but rather for fixating on trivial matters while ignoring more important issues: justice, mercy, faithfulness. He blasted their smug, hypocritical sense of superiority.

²⁵"Woe to you, teachers of the law and Pharisees, you hypocrites! You clean the outside of the cup and dish, but inside they are full of greed and self-indulgence. ²⁶Blind Pharisee! First clean the inside of the cup and dish, and then the outside also will be clean.

²⁷"Woe to you, teachers of the law and Pharisees, you hypocrites! You are like whitewashed tombs, which look beautiful on the outside but on the inside are full of dead men's bones and everything unclean. ²⁸In the same way, on the outside you appear to people as righteous but on the inside you are full of hypocrisy and wickedness.

²⁹"Woe to you, teachers of the law and Pharisees, you hypocrites! You build tombs for the prophets and decorate the graves of the righteous. ³⁰And you say, 'If we had lived in the days of our forefathers, we would not have taken part with them in shedding the blood of the prophets.' ³¹So you testify against yourselves that you are the descendants of those who murdered the prophets. ³²Fill up, then, the measure of the sin of your forefathers!

³³"You snakes! You brood of vipers! How will you escape being condemned to hell? ³⁴Therefore I am sending you prophets and wise men and teachers. Some of them you will kill and crucify; others you will flog in your synagogues and pursue from town to town. ³⁵And so upon you will come all the righteous blood that has been shed on earth, from the blood of righteous Abel to the

blood of Zechariah son of Berekiah, whom you murdered between the temple and the altar. ³⁶I tell you the truth, all this will come upon this generation.

³⁷"O Jerusalem, Jerusalem, you who kill the prophets and stone those sent to you, how often I have longed to gather your children together, as a hen gathers her chicks under her wings, but you were not willing. ³⁸Look, your house is left to you desolate. ³⁹For I tell you, you will not see me again until you say, 'Blessed is he who comes in the name of the Lord.'ᵃ"

Signs of the End of the Age

▶ *See Mark 13:1–37; Luke 21:5–36*

24 Jesus left the temple and was walking away when his disciples came up to him to call his attention to its buildings. ²"Do you see all these things?" he asked. "I tell you the truth, not one stone here will be left on another; every one will be thrown down."

24:2 Stones Overturned

Jesus' prediction came true four decades after his death, in A.D. 70, when the Roman army crushed a Jewish rebellion in Jerusalem. Soldiers knocked down the massive stones of the temple in search of the melted gold that had run down between the stones as the temple burned. The largest stones weighed over 400 tons, but General Titus's soldiers leveled them all.

³As Jesus was sitting on the Mount of Olives, the disciples came to him privately. "Tell us," they said, "when will this happen, and what will be the sign of your coming and of the end of the age?"

⁴Jesus answered: "Watch out that no one deceives you. ⁵For many will come in my name, claiming, 'I am the Christ,ᵇ' and will deceive many. ⁶You will hear of wars and rumors of wars, but see to it that you are not alarmed. Such things must happen, but the end is still to come. ⁷Nation will rise against nation, and kingdom against kingdom. There will be famines and earthquakes in various places. ⁸All these are the beginning of birth pains.

⁹"Then you will be handed over to be persecuted and put to death, and you will be hated by all nations because of me. ¹⁰At that time many will turn away from the faith and will betray and hate each other, ¹¹and many false prophets will appear and deceive many people. ¹²Because of the increase of wickedness, the love of most

---

ᵃ39 Psalm 118:26   ᵇ5 Or *Messiah*; also in verse 23

will grow cold, ¹³but he who stands firm to the end will be saved. ¹⁴And this gospel of the kingdom will be preached in the whole world as a testimony to all nations, and then the end will come.

¹⁵"So when you see standing in the holy place 'the abomination that causes desolation,'ᵃ spoken of through the prophet Daniel—let the reader understand— ¹⁶then let those who are in Judea flee to the mountains. ¹⁷Let no one on the roof of his house go down to take anything out of the house. ¹⁸Let no one in the field go back to get his cloak. ¹⁹How dreadful it will be in those days for pregnant women and nursing mothers! ²⁰Pray that your flight will not take place in winter or on the Sabbath. ²¹For then there will be great distress, unequaled from the beginning of the world until now—and never to be equaled again. ²²If those days had not been cut short, no one would survive, but for the sake of the elect those days will be shortened. ²³At that time if anyone says to you, 'Look, here is the Christ!' or, 'There he is!' do not believe it. ²⁴For false Christs and false prophets will appear and perform great signs and miracles to deceive even the elect—if that were possible. ²⁵See, I have told you ahead of time.

²⁶"So if anyone tells you, 'There he is, out in the desert,' do not go out; or, 'Here he is, in the inner rooms,' do not believe it. ²⁷For as lightning that comes from the east is visible even in the west, so will be the coming of the Son of Man. ²⁸Wherever there is a carcass, there the vultures will gather.

²⁹"Immediately after the distress of those days

" 'the sun will be darkened,
    and the moon will not give its light;
the stars will fall from the sky,
    and the heavenly bodies will be shaken.'ᵇ

³⁰"At that time the sign of the Son of Man will appear in the sky, and all the nations of the earth will mourn. They will see the Son of Man coming on the clouds of the sky, with power and great glory. ³¹And he will send his angels with a loud trumpet call, and they will gather his elect from the four winds, from one end of the heavens to the other.

³²"Now learn this lesson from the fig tree: As soon as its twigs get tender and its leaves come out, you know that summer is near. ³³Even so, when you see all these things, you know that itᶜ is near, right at the door. ³⁴I tell you the truth, this generationᵈ will certainly not pass away until all these things have happened. ³⁵Heaven and earth will pass away, but my words will never pass away.

The Day and Hour Unknown

▶ See Luke 12:42–46; 17:26–27

³⁶"No one knows about that day or hour, not even the angels in heaven, nor the Son,ᵉ but

24:36 When Will Jesus Return?

Matthew 24 records one of Jesus' longest statements about the future. Jesus gives direct clues to events that will precede his second coming. But, notably, almost half the chapter consists of warnings that no one can predict the precise time of his coming.

only the Father. ³⁷As it was in the days of Noah, so it will be at the coming of the Son of Man. ³⁸For in the days before the flood, people were eating and drinking, marrying and giving in marriage, up to the day Noah entered the ark; ³⁹and they knew nothing about what would happen until the flood came and took them all away. That is how it will be at the coming of the Son of Man. ⁴⁰Two men will be in the field; one will be taken and the other left. ⁴¹Two women will be grinding with a hand mill; one will be taken and the other left.

⁴²"Therefore keep watch, because you do not know on what day your Lord will come. ⁴³But understand this: If the owner of the house had known at what time of night the thief was coming, he would have kept watch and would not have let his house be broken into. ⁴⁴So you also must be ready, because the Son of Man will come at an hour when you do not expect him.

⁴⁵"Who then is the faithful and wise servant, whom the master has put in charge of the servants in his household to give them their food at the proper time? ⁴⁶It will be good for that servant whose master finds him doing so when he returns. ⁴⁷I tell you the truth, he will put him in charge of all his possessions. ⁴⁸But suppose that servant is wicked and says to himself, 'My master is staying away a long time,' ⁴⁹and he then begins to beat his fellow servants and to eat and drink with drunkards. ⁵⁰The master of that servant will come on a day when he does not expect him and at an hour he is not aware of. ⁵¹He will cut him to pieces and assign him a place with the hypocrites, where there will be weeping and gnashing of teeth.

The Parable of the Ten Virgins

25 "At that time the kingdom of heaven will be like ten virgins who took their lamps and went out to meet the bridegroom. ²Five of

ᵃ15 Daniel 9:27; 11:31; 12:11   ᵇ29 Isaiah 13:10; 34:4   ᶜ33 Or he   ᵈ34 Or race   ᵉ36 Some manuscripts do not have *nor the Son.*

them were foolish and five were wise. ³The foolish ones took their lamps but did not take any oil with them. ⁴The wise, however, took oil in jars along with their lamps. ⁵The bridegroom was a long time in coming, and they all became drowsy and fell asleep.

⁶"At midnight the cry rang out: 'Here's the bridegroom! Come out to meet him!'

⁷"Then all the virgins woke up and trimmed their lamps. ⁸The foolish ones said to the wise, 'Give us some of your oil; our lamps are going out.'

⁹"'No,' they replied, 'there may not be enough for both us and you. Instead, go to those who sell oil and buy some for yourselves.'

¹⁰"But while they were on their way to buy the oil, the bridegroom arrived. The virgins who were ready went in with him to the wedding banquet. And the door was shut.

¹¹"Later the others also came. 'Sir! Sir!' they said. 'Open the door for us!'

¹²"But he replied, 'I tell you the truth, I don't know you.'

¹³"Therefore keep watch, because you do not know the day or the hour.

The Parable of the Talents

¹⁴"Again, it will be like a man going on a journey, who called his servants and entrusted his property to them. ¹⁵To one he gave five talents*a* of money, to another two talents, and to another one talent, each according to his ability. Then he

went on his journey. ¹⁶The man who had received the five talents went at once and put his money to work and gained five more. ¹⁷So also, the one with the two talents gained two more. ¹⁸But the man who had received the one talent went off, dug a hole in the ground and hid his master's money.

¹⁹"After a long time the master of those servants returned and settled accounts with them. ²⁰The man who had received the five talents brought the other five. 'Master,' he said, 'you

entrusted me with five talents. See, I have gained five more.'

²¹"His master replied, 'Well done, good and faithful servant! You have been faithful with a few things; I will put you in charge of many things. Come and share your master's happiness!'

²²"The man with the two talents also came. 'Master,' he said, 'you entrusted me with two talents; see, I have gained two more.'

²³"His master replied, 'Well done, good and faithful servant! You have been faithful with a few things; I will put you in charge of many things. Come and share your master's happiness!'

²⁴"Then the man who had received the one talent came. 'Master,' he said, 'I knew that you are a hard man, harvesting where you have not sown and gathering where you have not scattered seed. ²⁵So I was afraid and went out and hid your talent in the ground. See, here is what belongs to you.'

²⁶"His master replied, 'You wicked, lazy servant! So you knew that I harvest where I have not sown and gather where I have not scattered seed? ²⁷Well then, you should have put my money on deposit with the bankers, so that when I returned I would have received it back with interest.

²⁸"'Take the talent from him and give it to the one who has the ten talents. ²⁹For everyone who has will be given more, and he will have an abundance. Whoever does not have, even what he has will be taken from him. ³⁰And throw that worthless servant outside, into the darkness, where there will be weeping and gnashing of teeth.'

The Sheep and the Goats

³¹"When the Son of Man comes in his glory, and all the angels with him, he will sit on his throne in heavenly glory. ³²All the nations will be gathered before him, and he will separate the people one from another as a shepherd separates the sheep from the goats. ³³He will put the sheep on his right and the goats on his left.

³⁴"Then the King will say to those on his right, 'Come, you who are blessed by my Father; take your inheritance, the kingdom prepared for you since the creation of the world. ³⁵For I was hungry and you gave me something to eat, I was thirsty and you gave me something to drink, I was a stranger and you invited me in, ³⁶I needed clothes and you clothed me, I was sick and you looked after me, I was in prison and you came to visit me.'

³⁷"Then the righteous will answer him, 'Lord, when did we see you hungry and feed you, or thirsty and give you something to drink? ³⁸When did we see you a stranger and invite you in, or needing clothes and clothe you? ³⁹When did we see you sick or in prison and go to visit you?'

---

a 15 A talent was worth more than a thousand dollars.

40"The King will reply, 'I tell you the truth, whatever you did for one of the least of these brothers of mine, you did for me.'

41"Then he will say to those on his left, 'Depart from me, you who are cursed, into the eternal fire prepared for the devil and his angels. 42For I was hungry and you gave me nothing to eat, I was thirsty and you gave me nothing to drink, 43I was a stranger and you did not invite me in, I needed clothes and you did not clothe me, I was sick and in prison and you did not look after me.'

44"They also will answer, 'Lord, when did we see you hungry or thirsty or a stranger or needing clothes or sick or in prison, and did not help you?'

45"He will reply, 'I tell you the truth, whatever you did not do for one of the least of these, you did not do for me.'

46"Then they will go away to eternal punishment, but the righteous to eternal life."

The Plot Against Jesus

▶ See Mark 14:1–2; Luke 22:1–2

26 When Jesus had finished saying all these things, he said to his disciples, 2"As you know, the Passover is two days away—and the Son of Man will be handed over to be crucified."

3Then the chief priests and the elders of the people assembled in the palace of the high priest, whose name was Caiaphas, 4and they plotted to

26:4 "Some Sly Way"

The religious leaders failed in their plan to dispose of Jesus quietly. He was killed during a national holiday while Jerusalem swarmed with pilgrims. Yet his death sparked no riots, and in the end even his devoted followers abandoned him. The chief priests and elders might have congratulated themselves on a successful mission—except for what happened on Easter Sunday.

arrest Jesus in some sly way and kill him. 5"But not during the Feast," they said, "or there may be a riot among the people."

Jesus Anointed at Bethany

▶ See Mark 14:3–9

6While Jesus was in Bethany in the home of a man known as Simon the Leper, 7a woman came to him with an alabaster jar of very expensive perfume, which she poured on his head as he was reclining at the table.

8When the disciples saw this, they were indignant. "Why this waste?" they asked. 9"This per-

fume could have been sold at a high price and the money given to the poor."

10Aware of this, Jesus said to them, "Why are you bothering this woman? She has done a beautiful thing to me. 11The poor you will always have with you, but you will not always have me. 12When she poured this perfume on my body, she did it to prepare me for burial. 13I tell you the truth, wherever this gospel is preached throughout the world, what she has done will also be told, in memory of her."

Judas Agrees to Betray Jesus

▶ See Mark 14:10–11; Luke 22:3–6

14Then one of the Twelve—the one called Judas Iscariot—went to the chief priests 15and asked, "What are you willing to give me if I hand him over to you?" So they counted out for him thirty silver coins. 16From then on Judas watched for an opportunity to hand him over.

The Lord's Supper

▶ See Mark 14:12–25; Luke 22:7–13

17On the first day of the Feast of Unleavened Bread, the disciples came to Jesus and asked, "Where do you want us to make preparations for you to eat the Passover?"

18He replied, "Go into the city to a certain man and tell him, 'The Teacher says: My appointed time is near. I am going to celebrate the Passover with my disciples at your house.'" 19So the disciples did as Jesus had directed them and prepared the Passover.

20When evening came, Jesus was reclining at the table with the Twelve. 21And while they were eating, he said, "I tell you the truth, one of you will betray me."

22They were very sad and began to say to him one after the other, "Surely not I, Lord?"

23Jesus replied, "The one who has dipped his hand into the bowl with me will betray me. 24The Son of Man will go just as it is written about him. But woe to that man who betrays the Son of Man! It would be better for him if he had not been born."

25Then Judas, the one who would betray him, said, "Surely not I, Rabbi?"

Jesus answered, "Yes, it is you."[a]

26While they were eating, Jesus took bread, gave thanks and broke it, and gave it to his disciples, saying, "Take and eat; this is my body."

27Then he took the cup, gave thanks and offered it to them, saying, "Drink from it, all of you. 28This is my blood of the[b] covenant, which is poured out for many for the forgiveness of sins. 29I tell you, I will not drink of this fruit of the vine from now on until that day when I drink it anew with you in my Father's kingdom."

---

[a]25 Or "You yourself have said it"   [b]28 Some manuscripts the new

[30]When they had sung a hymn, they went out to the Mount of Olives.

Jesus Predicts Peter's Denial

▶ *See Mark 14:27–31; Luke 22:31–34*

[31]Then Jesus told them, "This very night you will all fall away on account of me, for it is written:

"'I will strike the shepherd,
  and the sheep of the flock will be
    scattered.'[a]

[32]But after I have risen, I will go ahead of you into Galilee."

[33]Peter replied, "Even if all fall away on account of you, I never will."

[34]"I tell you the truth," Jesus answered, "this very night, before the rooster crows, you will disown me three times."

[35]But Peter declared, "Even if I have to die with you, I will never disown you." And all the other disciples said the same.

Gethsemane

▶ *See Mark 14:32–42; Luke 22:40–46*

[36]Then Jesus went with his disciples to a place called Gethsemane, and he said to them, "Sit here while I go over there and pray." [37]He took Peter and the two sons of Zebedee along with him, and he began to be sorrowful and troubled. [38]Then he said to them, "My soul is overwhelmed with sorrow to the point of death. Stay here and keep watch with me."

[39]Going a little farther, he fell with his face to the ground and prayed, "My Father, if it is possible, may this cup be taken from me. Yet not as I will, but as you will."

[40]Then he returned to his disciples and found them sleeping. "Could you men not keep watch with me for one hour?" he asked Peter. [41]"Watch and pray so that you will not fall into temptation. The spirit is willing, but the body is weak."

[42]He went away a second time and prayed, "My Father, if it is not possible for this cup to be taken away unless I drink it, may your will be done."

[43]When he came back, he again found them sleeping, because their eyes were heavy. [44]So he left them and went away once more and prayed the third time, saying the same thing.

[45]Then he returned to the disciples and said to them, "Are you still sleeping and resting? Look, the hour is near, and the Son of Man is betrayed into the hands of sinners. [46]Rise, let us go! Here comes my betrayer!"

Jesus Arrested

▶ *See Mark 14:43–50; Luke 22:47–53*

[47]While he was still speaking, Judas, one of the Twelve, arrived. With him was a large crowd armed with swords and clubs, sent from the chief

26:47 A Name Disgraced

Judas (like Jesus) was a common name for Jewish men in those days; it is the Greek form of Judah. He came from a region called Judea, whereas all the other disciples came from Galilee. Yet he gained enough trust to be named the disciples' treasurer. The Bible gives few details on Judas's motive for betraying Jesus. He may have become disillusioned when Jesus didn't fulfill his expectations of a powerful king and Messiah.

priests and the elders of the people. [48]Now the betrayer had arranged a signal with them: "The one I kiss is the man; arrest him." [49]Going at once to Jesus, Judas said, "Greetings, Rabbi!" and kissed him.

[50]Jesus replied, "Friend, do what you came for."[b]

Then the men stepped forward, seized Jesus and arrested him. [51]With that, one of Jesus' companions reached for his sword, drew it out and struck the servant of the high priest, cutting off his ear.

[52]"Put your sword back in its place," Jesus said to him, "for all who draw the sword will die by the sword. [53]Do you think I cannot call on my Father, and he will at once put at my disposal more than twelve legions of angels? [54]But how then would the Scriptures be fulfilled that say it must happen in this way?"

[55]At that time Jesus said to the crowd, "Am I leading a rebellion, that you have come out with swords and clubs to capture me? Every day I sat in the temple courts teaching, and you did not arrest me. [56]But this has all taken place that the writings of the prophets might be fulfilled." Then all the disciples deserted him and fled.

Before the Sanhedrin

▶ *See Mark 14:53–65; John 18:12–13,19–24*

[57]Those who had arrested Jesus took him to Caiaphas, the high priest, where the teachers of the law and the elders had assembled. [58]But Peter followed him at a distance, right up to the courtyard of the high priest. He entered and sat down with the guards to see the outcome.

[59]The chief priests and the whole Sanhedrin were looking for false evidence against Jesus so

---

[a]31 Zech. 13:7   [b]50 Or *"Friend, why have you come?"*

that they could put him to death. ⁶⁰But they did not find any, though many false witnesses came forward.

Finally two came forward ⁶¹and declared, "This fellow said, 'I am able to destroy the temple of God and rebuild it in three days.'"

⁶²Then the high priest stood up and said to Jesus, "Are you not going to answer? What is this testimony that these men are bringing against you?" ⁶³But Jesus remained silent.

The high priest said to him, "I charge you under oath by the living God: Tell us if you are the Christ,*a* the Son of God."

⁶⁴"Yes, it is as you say," Jesus replied. "But I say to all of you: In the future you will see the Son of Man sitting at the right hand of the Mighty One and coming on the clouds of heaven."

⁶⁵Then the high priest tore his clothes and said, "He has spoken blasphemy! Why do we need any more witnesses? Look, now you have heard the blasphemy. ⁶⁶What do you think?"

"He is worthy of death," they answered.

⁶⁷Then they spit in his face and struck him with their fists. Others slapped him ⁶⁸and said, "Prophesy to us, Christ. Who hit you?"

Peter Disowns Jesus

▶ *See Mark 14:66–72; Luke 22:52–62; John 18:16–18,25–27*

⁶⁹Now Peter was sitting out in the courtyard, and a servant girl came to him. "You also were with Jesus of Galilee," she said.

⁷⁰But he denied it before them all. "I don't know what you're talking about," he said.

⁷¹Then he went out to the gateway, where another girl saw him and said to the people there, "This fellow was with Jesus of Nazareth."

⁷²He denied it again, with an oath: "I don't know the man!"

⁷³After a little while, those standing there went up to Peter and said, "Surely you are one of them, for your accent gives you away."

26:73 Telltale Accent

Revolutionaries and troublemakers in Palestine usually operated in the rugged countryside. In Jerusalem, a city abuzz with rumors, Peter's Galilean accent made him suspect, for it marked him as a non-local. Jesus, also from Galilee, had already been arrested.

⁷⁴Then he began to call down curses on himself and he swore to them, "I don't know the man!"

Immediately a rooster crowed. ⁷⁵Then Peter remembered the word Jesus had spoken: "Before the rooster crows, you will disown me three times." And he went outside and wept bitterly.

Judas Hangs Himself

27 Early in the morning, all the chief priests and the elders of the people came to the decision to put Jesus to death. ²They bound him, led him away and handed him over to Pilate, the governor.

³When Judas, who had betrayed him, saw that Jesus was condemned, he was seized with remorse and returned the thirty silver coins to the chief priests and the elders. ⁴"I have sinned," he said, "for I have betrayed innocent blood."

"What is that to us?" they replied. "That's your responsibility."

⁵So Judas threw the money into the temple and left. Then he went away and hanged himself.

⁶The chief priests picked up the coins and said, "It is against the law to put this into the treasury, since it is blood money." ⁷So they decided to use the money to buy the potter's field as a burial place for foreigners. ⁸That is why it has been called the Field of Blood to this day. ⁹Then what was spoken by Jeremiah the prophet was fulfilled: "They took the thirty silver coins, the price set on him by the people of Israel, ¹⁰and they used them to buy the potter's field, as the Lord commanded me."*b*

Jesus Before Pilate

▶ *See Mark 15:2–15; Luke 23:2–3,18–25; John 18:29—19:16*

¹¹Meanwhile Jesus stood before the governor, and the governor asked him, "Are you the king of the Jews?"

"Yes, it is as you say," Jesus replied.

¹²When he was accused by the chief priests and the elders, he gave no answer. ¹³Then Pilate asked him, "Don't you hear the testimony they are bringing against you?" ¹⁴But Jesus made no reply, not even to a single charge—to the great amazement of the governor.

¹⁵Now it was the governor's custom at the Feast to release a prisoner chosen by the crowd. ¹⁶At that time they had a notorious prisoner, called Barabbas. ¹⁷So when the crowd had gathered, Pilate asked them, "Which one do you want me to release to you: Barabbas, or Jesus who is called Christ?" ¹⁸For he knew it was out of envy that they had handed Jesus over to him.

¹⁹While Pilate was sitting on the judge's seat, his wife sent him this message: "Don't have anything to do with that innocent man, for I have suffered a great deal today in a dream because of him."

²⁰But the chief priests and the elders persuad-

---

a63 Or Messiah; also in verse 68   b10 See Zech. 11:12,13; Jer. 19:1-13; 32:6-9.

ed the crowd to ask for Barabbas and to have Jesus executed.

21"Which of the two do you want me to release to you?" asked the governor.

"Barabbas," they answered.

22"What shall I do, then, with Jesus who is called Christ?" Pilate asked.

They all answered, "Crucify him!"

23"Why? What crime has he committed?" asked Pilate.

But they shouted all the louder, "Crucify him!"

24When Pilate saw that he was getting nowhere, but that instead an uproar was starting, he took water and washed his hands in front of the crowd. "I am innocent of this man's blood," he said. "It is your responsibility!"

25All the people answered, "Let his blood be on us and on our children!"

26Then he released Barabbas to them. But he had Jesus flogged, and handed him over to be crucified.

The Soldiers Mock Jesus

▶ See Mark 15:16–20

27Then the governor's soldiers took Jesus into the Praetorium and gathered the whole company of soldiers around him. 28They stripped him and put a scarlet robe on him, 29and then twisted together a crown of thorns and set it on his head. They put a staff in his right hand and knelt in front of him and mocked him. "Hail, king of the Jews!" they said. 30They spit on him, and took the staff and struck him on the head again and again. 31After they had mocked him, they took off the robe and put his own clothes on him. Then they led him away to crucify him.

The Crucifixion

▶ See Mark 15:22–32; Luke 23:33–43; John 19:17–24

32As they were going out, they met a man from Cyrene, named Simon, and they forced him to carry the cross. 33They came to a place called Golgotha (which means The Place of the Skull). 34There they offered Jesus wine to drink, mixed with gall; but after tasting it, he refused to drink it. 35When they had crucified him, they divided up his clothes by casting lots.*a* 36And sitting down, they kept watch over him there. 37Above his head they placed the written charge against him: THIS IS JESUS, THE KING OF THE JEWS. 38Two robbers were crucified with him, one on his right

a35 A few late manuscripts lots that the word spoken by the prophet might be fulfilled: "They divided my garments among themselves and cast lots for my clothing" (Psalm 22:18)

The Killing of a King
Arrest, trial, and execution

IN SPARE, UNADORNED LANGUAGE THE last three chapters of Matthew draw together the deep ironies of Jesus' life. From the first sentence, Matthew has stressed that Jesus is the Messiah, a true king. This Gospel is sometimes called the "royal" Gospel because it refers so many times to kingship.

But at the end of his life, the man whom wise men had crossed a continent to worship was sold, like a slave, for thirty pieces of silver. Jesus got a royal robe and crown at last—but as a cruel, mocking joke. Blood from the wounds on his back clotted on the robe, and the crown of thorns streaked his face with more blood.

A short time before, he had blistered the religious leaders with accusations. But when they put him on the stand and accused him, his strong voice stayed mostly silent.

> "What shall I do, then, with Jesus who is called Christ?" Pilate asked. They all answered, "Crucify him!" 27:22

Jesus' Self-Defense

Jesus' enemies asked him two chief questions: "Are you the king of the Jews?" and "Are you the Messiah?" He answered with a simple "Yes, it is as you say" (27:11), confirming the major themes woven throughout Matthew's book. Finally he was executed, with his "crime"—being a king—posted above his sagging body.

Jesus was indeed a king, but not the kind of king people expected. Even his disciples, who had known Jesus intimately for three years, slipped away in doubt.

The story, however, doesn't end with the death scene in chapter 27. Good Friday would never have been called "good" without the miracle described next. The king came back! And the writer who opened his book by tracing Jesus' Jewish roots ends it with Jesus' stirring call to take the good news to all nations.

Life Questions: The people who crucified Jesus—what did they hate in him? Is it the same today?

and one on his left. [39]Those who passed by hurled insults at him, shaking their heads [40]and saying, "You who are going to destroy the temple and build it in three days, save yourself! Come down from the cross, if you are the Son of God!"

[41]In the same way the chief priests, the teachers of the law and the elders mocked him. [42]"He saved others," they said, "but he can't save himself! He's the King of Israel! Let him come down now from the cross, and we will believe in him. [43]He trusts in God. Let God rescue him now if he wants him, for he said, 'I am the Son of God.'" [44]In the same way the robbers who were crucified with him also heaped insults on him.

The Death of Jesus

▶ See Mark 15:33–41; Luke 23:44–49

[45]From the sixth hour until the ninth hour darkness came over all the land. [46]About the ninth hour Jesus cried out in a loud voice, "Eloi, Eloi,[a] lama sabachthani?"—which means, "My God, my God, why have you forsaken me?"[b]

[47]When some of those standing there heard this, they said, "He's calling Elijah."

[48]Immediately one of them ran and got a sponge. He filled it with wine vinegar, put it on a stick, and offered it to Jesus to drink. [49]The rest said, "Now leave him alone. Let's see if Elijah comes to save him."

[50]And when Jesus had cried out again in a loud voice, he gave up his spirit.

[51]At that moment the curtain of the temple was torn in two from top to bottom. The earth

27:51 A Curtain Is Torn

At Jesus' death, the massive, thick curtain in the temple in Jerusalem ripped in two. This curtain sealed off the Most Holy Place. No one except the high priest was allowed into the presence of God in that Most Holy Place. And the high priest was permitted in only once a year, on a special day. The author of Hebrews looked on the miraculously torn curtain as symbolic: it signified the immediate access to God made possible by Jesus' death (Hebrews 10:19–20).

shook and the rocks split. [52]The tombs broke open and the bodies of many holy people who had died were raised to life. [53]They came out of the tombs, and after Jesus' resurrection they went into the holy city and appeared to many people.

[54]When the centurion and those with him who were guarding Jesus saw the earthquake and all that had happened, they were terrified, and exclaimed, "Surely he was the Son[c] of God!"

[55]Many women were there, watching from a distance. They had followed Jesus from Galilee to care for his needs. [56]Among them were Mary Magdalene, Mary the mother of James and Joses, and the mother of Zebedee's sons.

The Burial of Jesus

▶ See Mark 15:42–47; Luke 23:50–56; John 19:38–42

[57]As evening approached, there came a rich man from Arimathea, named Joseph, who had himself become a disciple of Jesus. [58]Going to Pilate, he asked for Jesus' body, and Pilate ordered that it be given to him. [59]Joseph took the body, wrapped it in a clean linen cloth, [60]and placed it in his own new tomb that he had cut out of the rock. He rolled a big stone in front of the entrance to the tomb and went away. [61]Mary Magdalene and the other Mary were sitting there opposite the tomb.

The Guard at the Tomb

[62]The next day, the one after Preparation Day, the chief priests and the Pharisees went to Pilate. [63]"Sir," they said, "we remember that while he was still alive that deceiver said, 'After three days I will rise again.' [64]So give the order for the tomb to be made secure until the third day. Otherwise, his disciples may come and steal the body and tell the people that he has been raised from the dead. This last deception will be worse than the first." [65]"Take a guard," Pilate answered. "Go, make the tomb as secure as you know how." [66]So they went and made the tomb secure by putting a seal on the stone and posting the guard.

The Resurrection

▶ See Mark 16:1–8; Luke 24:1–10

28 After the Sabbath, at dawn on the first day of the week, Mary Magdalene and the other Mary went to look at the tomb.

[2]There was a violent earthquake, for an angel of the Lord came down from heaven and, going to the tomb, rolled back the stone and sat on it. [3]His appearance was like lightning, and his clothes were white as snow. [4]The guards were so afraid of him that they shook and became like dead men.

[5]The angel said to the women, "Do not be afraid, for I know that you are looking for Jesus, who was crucified. [6]He is not here; he has risen, just as he said. Come and see the place where he lay. [7]Then go quickly and tell his disciples: 'He has risen from the dead and is going ahead of you into Galilee. There you will see him.' Now I have told you."

[8]So the women hurried away from the tomb, afraid yet filled with joy, and ran to tell his disciples. [9]Suddenly Jesus met them. "Greetings," he said. They came to him, clasped his feet and wor-

[a]46 Some manuscripts *Eli, Eli*   [b]46 Psalm 22:1   [c]54 Or *a son*

shiped him. ¹⁰Then Jesus said to them, "Do not be afraid. Go and tell my brothers to go to Galilee; there they will see me."

The Guards' Report

¹¹While the women were on their way, some

28:4 Coverup

Throughout Jesus' extraordinary life, people found all sorts of reasons to doubt him, even in the face of unexplainable events. These guards, for instance, were virtual eyewitnesses of the greatest miracle of all time, Jesus' resurrection. Yet a few hours later they made a deal with the chief priests to cover up the story (verses 11–15). Then, as now, people who choose not to believe can always find a rationale.

of the guards went into the city and reported to the chief priests everything that had happened. ¹²When the chief priests had met with the elders

and devised a plan, they gave the soldiers a large sum of money, ¹³telling them, "You are to say, 'His disciples came during the night and stole him away while we were asleep.' ¹⁴If this report gets to the governor, we will satisfy him and keep you out of trouble." ¹⁵So the soldiers took the money and did as they were instructed. And this story has been widely circulated among the Jews to this very day.

The Great Commission

¹⁶Then the eleven disciples went to Galilee, to the mountain where Jesus had told them to go. ¹⁷When they saw him, they worshiped him; but some doubted. ¹⁸Then Jesus came to them and said, "All authority in heaven and on earth has been given to me. ¹⁹Therefore go and make disciples of all nations, baptizing them in[a] the name of the Father and of the Son and of the Holy Spirit, ²⁰and teaching them to obey everything I have commanded you. And surely I am with you always, to the very end of the age."

---

[a]19 Or *into*; see Acts 8:16; 19:5; Romans 6:3; 1 Cor. 1:13; 10:2 and Gal. 3:27.

MARK

The Fast-paced Gospel
Mark reads like the script for an action movie

News about him spread quickly over the whole region of Galilee. 1:28

BRIEF INTRODUCTORY CREDITS FLASH ON the screen. Then the camera pans across an expanse of bleached sand, inhabited mostly by scorpions, lizards, and tarantulas. At last, through the shimmering heat, a lone figure appears: an eccentric wearing camel's hair and crying something in the thin desert air. So begins Mark.

It helps to imagine the book of Mark as a concisely edited documentary film. Unlike the other Gospels, this one has little tolerance for dialogue and personal reflection. The author is writing to a restless, impatient audience—people more like moviegoers than readers.

Mark deftly controls camera angles, alternately panning across large crowds and zooming in on individual people. He leaves no doubt about the main character. After the opening shot of John the Baptist, he moves Jesus to center stage and the camera follows him everywhere.

An Emphasis on Action

Those who look for an outline in Mark come away baffled: all the spliced-together scenes defy structure. One author observed that Mark shows Jesus "scattering miracles like rice at a wedding." Matthew and Luke each give four chapters of historical warm-up before recording a miracle by Jesus; Mark covers three miracles and a group event in the first chapter alone.

In contrast to all its action scenes, the book includes only a sampling of Jesus' parables. It focuses on events, not speeches or editorial comments. Mark shows gymnasium-size crowds pressing around Jesus so tightly that he launches a boat to escape them. Wherever he goes, the crowds follow, buzzing about his remarkable life. "Is he the Holy One of God?" "Is he mad?" "Isn't this the carpenter's boy?"

A Breathless Pace

By dispensing with all but bare-bones action, Mark manages to achieve more drama than perhaps any other biblical writer. Action guarantees an attentive audience, and Mark jams sequences together breathlessly. *At once* the Spirit sends Jesus into the desert; *at once* the disciples respond to Jesus' call to follow him; Jesus' touch *immediately* heals a man with leprosy—42 times this book uses the Greek hurry-up adverb translated several different ways into English.

Characters rush from place to place, jostle among crowds, are astonished at mighty works. Mark is a Gospel of exclamation points, full of words like *amazed, overwhelmed, terrified.* A phenomenon is loose on the earth, and the author is determined to capture its impact for future generations.

How to Read Mark

About 90 percent of Mark's content appears in the other three Gospels, but the book makes an ideal starting place for someone who knows little about Jesus. Its style—simple sentences, without complicated transitions or long speeches—makes understanding easier. In fact, Mark was probably written as a missionary book to people who knew next to nothing about the new Christian faith.

Except where he cites Jesus' own quotations, Mark quotes the Old Testament directly in only one place (1:2–3). In addition, Mark doesn't refer to the Old Testament Law, a striking difference from the other Gospels. Such facts indicate his book was written to a non-Jewish audience, probably the Romans.

You'll need no special instructions on reading Mark. This book's breezy style makes it as understandable as a newspaper. Because it loosely follows the chronology of Jesus' life, Mark offers an excellent introduction to the life of Jesus. As you read, stop and ponder the events Mark records. Why did the author select these facts? What meaning did they have for the people in Jesus' day? What about for you?

PEOPLE YOU'LL MEET IN MARK

JAMES *(p. 1050)*

3-TRACK READING PLAN

For an explanation and complete listing of the 3-track reading plan, turn to page 7.

TRACK 1: ***Two-Week Courses on the Bible***
The Track 1 reading program on the Life and Teachings of Jesus includes two chapters from Mark. See page 7 for a complete listing of this course.

TRACK 2: ***An Overview of Mark in 15 Days***
Reading Mark will give you a quick summary of Jesus' acts on this earth. For this reason, plan to spend two weeks reading all 16 chapters of Mark.

☐ Day 1. Read the Introduction to Mark, then chapter 1.
☐ Day 2. Read chapter 2's record of scenes from Jesus' life during a period of popular acclaim.
☐ Day 3. Read chapter 3, which shows Jesus calling his 12 disciples.
☐ Day 4. Read the brief parables and the account of the calming of a storm in chapter 4.
☐ Day 5. Mark 5 tells of three miracles of healing; note the different crowd reaction to each one.
☐ Day 6. Read chapter 6, which includes several famous miracles and also the story of John the Baptist's beheading.
☐ Day 7. Read chapter 7, which shows the Pharisees' opposition to Jesus beginning to mount.
☐ Day 8. As you read chapter 8, notice, on the one hand, Jesus' increasing popularity and, on the other, the growing tension that will eventually culminate in his death.
☐ Day 9. Read the account of Jesus' transfiguration and the other events recorded in chapter 9.
☐ Day 10. Mark 10 records Jesus' teaching on divorce, humility, and wealth.
☐ Day 11. Read chapter 11's account of Jesus' entry into Jerusalem for the last week of his life.
☐ Day 12. Read chapter 12, which includes Jesus' teaching on a variety of topics.
☐ Day 13. Read chapter 13 for Jesus' predictions of the end of the world.
☐ Day 14. Mark 14 records the events leading up to Jesus' arrest, as well as his trial before a Jewish court.
☐ Day 15. Read chapters 15 and 16, which report the last events in Jesus' life on earth.

Now turn to page 9 for your next Track 2 reading project.

TRACK 3: ***All of Mark in 15 Days***
After you have read through Mark, turn to pages 10–14 for your next Track 3 reading project.

☐1 ☐2 ☐3 ☐4 ☐5 ☐6 ☐7 ☐8
☐9 ☐10 ☐11 ☐12 ☐13 ☐14 ☐15–16

John the Baptist Prepares the Way

▶ *See Matthew 3:1–11; Luke 3:2–16*

1 The beginning of the gospel about Jesus Christ, the Son of God.[a]

²It is written in Isaiah the prophet:

"I will send my messenger ahead of you,
    who will prepare your way"[b]—
³"a voice of one calling in the desert,
'Prepare the way for the Lord,
    make straight paths for him.'"[c]

⁴And so John came, baptizing in the desert region and preaching a baptism of repentance for the forgiveness of sins. ⁵The whole Judean countryside and all the people of Jerusalem went out to him. Confessing their sins, they were baptized by him in the Jordan River. ⁶John wore clothing made of camel's hair, with a leather belt around his waist, and he ate locusts and wild honey. ⁷And this was his message: "After me will come one more powerful than I, the thongs of whose sandals I am not worthy to stoop down and untie. ⁸I baptize you with[d] water, but he will baptize you with the Holy Spirit."

The Baptism and Temptation of Jesus

▶ *See Matthew 3:13–17; 4:1–11; Luke 3:21–22; 4:1–13*

⁹At that time Jesus came from Nazareth in Galilee and was baptized by John in the Jordan. ¹⁰As Jesus was coming up out of the water, he saw heaven being torn open and the Spirit descending on him like a dove. ¹¹And a voice came from heaven: "You are my Son, whom I love; with you I am well pleased."

¹²At once the Spirit sent him out into the desert, ¹³and he was in the desert forty days, being tempted by Satan. He was with the wild animals, and angels attended him.

The Calling of the First Disciples

▶ *See Matthew 4:18–22; Luke 5:2–11; John 1:35–42*

¹⁴After John was put in prison, Jesus went into Galilee, proclaiming the good news of God. ¹⁵"The time has come," he said. "The kingdom of God is near. Repent and believe the good news!"

¹⁶As Jesus walked beside the Sea of Galilee, he saw Simon and his brother Andrew casting a net into the lake, for they were fishermen. ¹⁷"Come, follow me," Jesus said, "and I will make you fishers of men." ¹⁸At once they left their nets and followed him.

¹⁹When he had gone a little farther, he saw James son of Zebedee and his brother John in a boat, preparing their nets. ²⁰Without delay he called them, and they left their father Zebedee in the boat with the hired men and followed him.

Jesus Drives Out an Evil Spirit

▶ *See Luke 4:31–37*

²¹They went to Capernaum, and when the

1:14 Into the Countryside

Possibly, Jesus withdrew to Galilee in order to escape the political turmoil spawned by John's arrest. He went on to spend almost two-thirds of his working life in this rather remote northern region, the lushest and most picturesque portion of Palestine. Except for festival times when he traveled to Jerusalem, Jesus showed a marked preference for rural and small-town areas.

Sabbath came, Jesus went into the synagogue and began to teach. ²²The people were amazed at his teaching, because he taught them as one who had authority, not as the teachers of the law. ²³Just then a man in their synagogue who was possessed by an evil[e] spirit cried out, ²⁴"What do you want with us, Jesus of Nazareth? Have you come to destroy us? I know who you are—the Holy One of God!"

²⁵"Be quiet!" said Jesus sternly. "Come out of him!" ²⁶The evil spirit shook the man violently and came out of him with a shriek.

²⁷The people were all so amazed that they asked each other, "What is this? A new teaching—and with authority! He even gives orders to evil spirits and they obey him." ²⁸News about him spread quickly over the whole region of Galilee.

Jesus Heals Many

▶ *See Matthew 8:14–17; Luke 4:38–41*

²⁹As soon as they left the synagogue, they went with James and John to the home of Simon and Andrew. ³⁰Simon's mother-in-law was in bed with a fever, and they told Jesus about her. ³¹So he went to her, took her hand and helped her up. The fever left her and she began to wait on them.

³²That evening after sunset the people brought to Jesus all the sick and demon-possessed. ³³The whole town gathered at the door, ³⁴and Jesus healed many who had various diseases. He also drove out many demons, but he would not let the demons speak because they knew who he was.

Jesus Prays in a Solitary Place

▶ *See Luke 4:42–43*

³⁵Very early in the morning, while it was still

---

a 1 Some manuscripts do not have *the Son of God.* *b 2* Mal. 3:1 *c 3* Isaiah 40:3 *d 8* Or *in* *e 23* Greek *unclean;* also in verses 26 and 27

dark, Jesus got up, left the house and went off to a solitary place, where he prayed. ³⁶Simon and his companions went to look for him, ³⁷and when they found him, they exclaimed: "Everyone is looking for you!"

³⁸Jesus replied, "Let us go somewhere else—to the nearby villages—so I can preach there also. That is why I have come." ³⁹So he traveled throughout Galilee, preaching in their synagogues and driving out demons.

A Man With Leprosy

▶ See Matthew 8:2–4; Luke 5:12–14

⁴⁰A man with leprosy[a] came to him and begged him on his knees, "If you are willing, you can make me clean."

⁴¹Filled with compassion, Jesus reached out his hand and touched the man. "I am willing," he said. "Be clean!" ⁴²Immediately the leprosy left him and he was cured.

⁴³Jesus sent him away at once with a strong warning: ⁴⁴"See that you don't tell this to anyone. But go, show yourself to the priest and offer the sacrifices that Moses commanded for your cleansing, as a testimony to them." ⁴⁵Instead he went out and began to talk freely, spreading the news. As a result, Jesus could no longer enter a town openly but stayed outside in lonely places. Yet the people still came to him from everywhere.

Jesus Heals a Paralytic

▶ See Matthew 9:2–8; Luke 5:18–26

2 A few days later, when Jesus again entered Capernaum, the people heard that he had come home. ²So many gathered that there was no room left, not even outside the door, and he preached the word to them. ³Some men came, bringing to him a paralytic, carried by four of them. ⁴Since they could not get him to Jesus because of the crowd, they made an opening in the roof above Jesus and, after digging through it,

2:4 Barriers to the Disabled

One disabled person has pointed out this story's relevance to the modern controversy over accessibility. "Any disabled person can supply lots of stories like this one—entering a church through the sacristy (or, worse, having to be carried up the front steps like a child), coming into a lecture hall by means of a freight elevator and then through the kitchen or utility room before being able to join the 'normal' people who come in the front door." The paralytic's friends found a rather drastic solution to the problem, and Jesus, impressed, honored their (plural) faith.

lowered the mat the paralyzed man was lying on. ⁵When Jesus saw their faith, he said to the paralytic, "Son, your sins are forgiven."

⁶Now some teachers of the law were sitting there, thinking to themselves, ⁷"Why does this fellow talk like that? He's blaspheming! Who can forgive sins but God alone?"

⁸Immediately Jesus knew in his spirit that this was what they were thinking in their hearts, and he said to them, "Why are you thinking these things? ⁹Which is easier: to say to the paralytic, 'Your sins are forgiven,' or to say, 'Get up, take your mat and walk'? ¹⁰But that you may know that the Son of Man has authority on earth to forgive sins . . ." He said to the paralytic, ¹¹"I tell you, get up, take your mat and go home." ¹²He got up, took his mat and walked out in full view of them all. This amazed everyone and they praised God, saying, "We have never seen anything like this!"

The Calling of Levi

▶ See Matthew 9:9–13; Luke 5:27–32

¹³Once again Jesus went out beside the lake. A large crowd came to him, and he began to teach them. ¹⁴As he walked along, he saw Levi son of Alphaeus sitting at the tax collector's booth. "Follow me," Jesus told him, and Levi got up and followed him.

¹⁵While Jesus was having dinner at Levi's house, many tax collectors and "sinners" were eating with him and his disciples, for there were many who followed him. ¹⁶When the teachers of the law who were Pharisees saw him eating with the "sinners" and tax collectors, they asked his disciples: "Why does he eat with tax collectors and 'sinners'?"

¹⁷On hearing this, Jesus said to them, "It is not the healthy who need a doctor, but the sick. I have not come to call the righteous, but sinners."

Jesus Questioned About Fasting

▶ See Matthew 9:14–17; Luke 5:33–38

¹⁸Now John's disciples and the Pharisees were fasting. Some people came and asked Jesus, "How is it that John's disciples and the disciples of the Pharisees are fasting, but yours are not?"

¹⁹Jesus answered, "How can the guests of the bridegroom fast while he is with them? They cannot, so long as they have him with them. ²⁰But the time will come when the bridegroom will be taken from them, and on that day they will fast.

²¹"No one sews a patch of unshrunk cloth on an old garment. If he does, the new piece will pull away from the old, making the tear worse. ²²And no one pours new wine into old wineskins. If he does, the wine will burst the skins, and both the

---

[a]40 The Greek word was used for various diseases affecting the skin—not necessarily leprosy.

wine and the wineskins will be ruined. No, he pours new wine into new wineskins."

Lord of the Sabbath

▶ *See Matthew 12:1–14; Luke 6:1–11*

23One Sabbath Jesus was going through the grainfields, and as his disciples walked along, they began to pick some heads of grain. 24The Pharisees said to him, "Look, why are they doing what is unlawful on the Sabbath?"

25He answered, "Have you never read what David did when he and his companions were hungry and in need? 26In the days of Abiathar the high priest, he entered the house of God and ate the consecrated bread, which is lawful only for priests to eat. And he also gave some to his companions."

27Then he said to them, "The Sabbath was made for man, not man for the Sabbath. 28So the Son of Man is Lord even of the Sabbath."

3 Another time he went into the synagogue, and a man with a shriveled hand was there. 2Some of them were looking for a reason to accuse Jesus, so they watched him closely to see if he would heal him on the Sabbath. 3Jesus said to the man with the shriveled hand, "Stand up in front of everyone."

4Then Jesus asked them, "Which is lawful on the Sabbath: to do good or to do evil, to save life or to kill?" But they remained silent.

5He looked around at them in anger and, deeply distressed at their stubborn hearts, said to the man, "Stretch out your hand." He stretched it out, and his hand was completely restored. 6Then the Pharisees went out and began to plot with the Herodians how they might kill Jesus.

Crowds Follow Jesus

▶ *See Matthew 12:15–16; Luke 6:17–19*

7Jesus withdrew with his disciples to the lake, and a large crowd from Galilee followed. 8When they heard all he was doing, many people came to him from Judea, Jerusalem, Idumea, and the regions across the Jordan and around Tyre and Sidon. 9Because of the crowd he told his disciples to have a small boat ready for him, to keep the people from crowding him. 10For he had healed many, so that those with diseases were pushing forward to touch him. 11Whenever the evil[a] spirits saw him, they fell down before him and cried out, "You are the Son of God." 12But he gave them strict orders not to tell who he was.

The Appointing of the Twelve Apostles

13Jesus went up on a mountainside and called to him those he wanted, and they came to him. 14He appointed twelve—designating them apostles[b]—that they might be with him and that he might send them out to preach 15and to have authority to drive out demons. 16These are the twelve he appointed: Simon (to whom he gave the name Peter); 17James son of Zebedee and his brother John (to them he gave the name Boanerges, which means Sons of Thunder); 18Andrew, Philip, Bartholomew, Matthew, Thomas, James son of Alphaeus, Thaddaeus, Simon the Zealot 19and Judas Iscariot, who betrayed him.

Jesus and Beelzebub

▶ *See Matthew 12:25–29; Luke 11:17–22*

20Then Jesus entered a house, and again a crowd gathered, so that he and his disciples were not even able to eat. 21When his family heard about this, they went to take charge of him, for they said, "He is out of his mind."

22And the teachers of the law who came down from Jerusalem said, "He is possessed by Beelzebub[c]! By the prince of demons he is driving out demons."

23So Jesus called them and spoke to them in parables: "How can Satan drive out Satan? 24If a kingdom is divided against itself, that kingdom cannot stand. 25If a house is divided against itself, that house cannot stand. 26And if Satan opposes himself and is divided, he cannot stand; his end has come. 27In fact, no one can enter a strong man's house and carry off his possessions unless he first ties up the strong man. Then he can rob his house. 28I tell you the truth, all the sins and blasphemies of men will be forgiven them. 29But whoever blasphemes against the Holy Spirit will never be forgiven; he is guilty of an eternal sin."

30He said this because they were saying, "He has an evil spirit."

3:30 Out of His Mind?

Jesus provoked a strong reaction in just about everyone. In this instance, Jesus' own family members questioned his sanity, and teachers of the law wondered about demon-possession. He aroused the fiercest opposition among his own neighbors and among the religious "professionals" of his day. But, as Mark shows, throngs of other people were amazed by his authoritative teaching and his miraculous powers. Personal contact with Jesus left virtually no one unmoved.

Jesus' Mother and Brothers

▶ *See Matthew 12:46–50; Luke 8:19–21*

31Then Jesus' mother and brothers arrived. Standing outside, they sent someone in to call

---

[a]11 Greek *unclean*; also in verse 30   [b]14 Some manuscripts do not have *designating them apostles*.   [c]22 Greek *Beezeboul* or *Beelzeboul*

him. ³²A crowd was sitting around him, and they told him, "Your mother and brothers are outside looking for you."

³³"Who are my mother and my brothers?" he asked.

³⁴Then he looked at those seated in a circle around him and said, "Here are my mother and my brothers! ³⁵Whoever does God's will is my brother and sister and mother."

The Parable of the Sower

▶ See Matthew 13:1–15,18–23; Luke 8:4–15

4 Again Jesus began to teach by the lake. The crowd that gathered around him was so large

Why Come to Earth?
The only way God could get through

AMERICAN RADIO BROADCASTER PAUL HARVEY once told a modern parable about a religious skeptic who worked as a farmer. One raw winter night the man heard an irregular thumping sound against the kitchen storm door. He went to a window and watched as tiny, shivering sparrows, attracted to the evident warmth inside, beat in vain against the glass.

> *They were terrified and asked each other, "Who is this? Even the wind and the waves obey him!" 4:41*

Touched, the farmer bundled up and trudged through fresh snow to open the barn door for the struggling birds. He turned on the lights and tossed some hay in a corner. But the sparrows, which had scattered in all directions when he emerged from the house, hid in the darkness, afraid.

The man tried various tactics to get them into the barn. He laid down a trail of Saltine cracker crumbs to direct them. He tried circling behind the birds to drive them toward the barn. Nothing worked. He, a huge, alien creature, had terrified them; the birds couldn't comprehend that he actually desired to help.

The farmer withdrew to his house and watched the doomed sparrows through a window. As he stared, a thought hit him like lightning from a clear blue sky: *If only I could become a bird—one of them— just for a moment. Then I wouldn't frighten them so. I could show them the way to warmth and safety.*

At the same moment, another thought dawned on him. He had grasped the reason Jesus was born.

When God Came to Earth

A man becoming a bird is nothing compared to God becoming a man. The concept of a sovereign eternal being who created the universe, confining himself to a human body was—and is—too much for some people to believe. But how else could God truly communicate with us?

We don't know what God looked like as a man; no Gospel writer described the physical appearance of Jesus. But, in other ways, Mark painted a full picture of his humanity. Jesus, who claimed to be God, didn't have a supernatural "glow" about him. His own neighbors and family marveled that he seemed so, well, normal.

Mark does not diminish Jesus. He shows the power of a man who healed the blind with a simple touch (8:25), and the authority of a teacher so captivating that people sat three days straight, with empty stomachs, just to hear him (8:2). Even after Jesus hushed them, people wouldn't stop talking about his miracles.

But Mark also reveals the full range of Jesus' emotions: a surge of compassion for a person with leprosy (1:41), a deep sigh in response to nagging Pharisees (8:12), a look of anger and distress at cold-hearted legalists (3:5), and then an awful cry on the cross, "My God, my God, why have you forsaken me?" (15:34). Jesus was sometimes witty, and he sometimes cried. He got tired: Five times, Mark records, he sought a quiet place for rest away from the crowds.

Like No One Else

Jesus was like no other person who ever lived. Twelve men left their jobs and families at a single command to follow him. Yet Jesus was also fully "one of us." He needed food and friends. He got lonely and tired. He showed anger and disappointment. Because Jesus experienced all we experience as human beings, he can understand us completely, and share in our joys and sorrows.

Mark portrays both sides of Jesus—the divine and the human. The disciples needed to see both dimensions to give their lives to him.

Life Questions: Suppose that Jesus had never come, that God had merely sent an elaborate love note. What difference would that make?

that he got into a boat and sat in it out on the lake, while all the people were along the shore at the water's edge. ²He taught them many things by parables, and in his teaching said: ³"Listen! A farmer went out to sow his seed. ⁴As he was scattering the seed, some fell along the path, and the birds came and ate it up. ⁵Some fell on rocky places, where it did not have much soil. It sprang up quickly, because the soil was shallow. ⁶But when the sun came up, the plants were scorched, and they withered because they had no root. ⁷Other seed fell among thorns, which grew up and choked the plants, so that they did not bear grain. ⁸Still other seed fell on good soil. It came up, grew and produced a crop, multiplying thirty, sixty, or even a hundred times."

⁹Then Jesus said, "He who has ears to hear, let him hear."

¹⁰When he was alone, the Twelve and the others around him asked him about the parables. ¹¹He told them, "The secret of the kingdom of God has been given to you. But to those on the outside everything is said in parables ¹²so that,

"'they may be ever seeing but never
        perceiving,
    and ever hearing but never understanding;
    otherwise they might turn and be
        forgiven!'ᵃ"

¹³Then Jesus said to them, "Don't you understand this parable? How then will you understand any parable? ¹⁴The farmer sows the word. ¹⁵Some people are like seed along the path, where the word is sown. As soon as they hear it, Satan comes and takes away the word that was sown in them. ¹⁶Others, like seed sown on rocky places, hear the word and at once receive it with joy. ¹⁷But since they have no root, they last only a short time. When trouble or persecution comes because of the word, they quickly fall away. ¹⁸Still others, like seed sown among thorns, hear the word; ¹⁹but the worries of this life, the deceitfulness of wealth and the desires for other things come in and choke the word, making it unfruitful. ²⁰Others, like seed sown on good soil, hear the word, accept it, and produce a crop—thirty, sixty or even a hundred times what was sown."

A Lamp on a Stand

²¹He said to them, "Do you bring in a lamp to put it under a bowl or a bed? Instead, don't you put it on its stand? ²²For whatever is hidden is meant to be disclosed, and whatever is concealed is meant to be brought out into the open. ²³If anyone has ears to hear, let him hear."

²⁴"Consider carefully what you hear," he continued. "With the measure you use, it will be measured to you—and even more. ²⁵Whoever has will be given more; whoever does not have, even what he has will be taken from him."

The Parable of the Growing Seed

²⁶He also said, "This is what the kingdom of God is like. A man scatters seed on the ground. ²⁷Night and day, whether he sleeps or gets up, the seed sprouts and grows, though he does not know how. ²⁸All by itself the soil produces grain—first the stalk, then the head, then the full kernel in the head. ²⁹As soon as the grain is ripe, he puts the sickle to it, because the harvest has come."

The Parable of the Mustard Seed

▶ See Matthew 13:31–32; Luke 13:18–19

³⁰Again he said, "What shall we say the kingdom of God is like, or what parable shall we use

> **4:30 Scarce Parables**
>
> *Unlike Matthew and Luke, Mark devotes little space to parables, the unique form of teaching Jesus often relied on. Yet Mark includes as many miracles as does any Gospel. Clearly, this book emphasizes action over words.*

to describe it? ³¹It is like a mustard seed, which is the smallest seed you plant in the ground. ³²Yet when planted, it grows and becomes the largest of all garden plants, with such big branches that the birds of the air can perch in its shade."

³³With many similar parables Jesus spoke the word to them, as much as they could understand. ³⁴He did not say anything to them without using a parable. But when he was alone with his own disciples, he explained everything.

Jesus Calms the Storm

▶ See Matthew 8:18,23–27; Luke 8:22–25

³⁵That day when evening came, he said to his disciples, "Let us go over to the other side." ³⁶Leaving the crowd behind, they took him along, just as he was, in the boat. There were also other boats with him. ³⁷A furious squall came up, and the waves broke over the boat, so that it was nearly swamped. ³⁸Jesus was in the stern, sleeping on a cushion. The disciples woke him and said to him, "Teacher, don't you care if we drown?"

³⁹He got up, rebuked the wind and said to the waves, "Quiet! Be still!" Then the wind died down and it was completely calm.

ᵃ12 Isaiah 6:9,10

⁴⁰He said to his disciples, "Why are you so afraid? Do you still have no faith?"

⁴¹They were terrified and asked each other, "Who is this? Even the wind and the waves obey him!"

The Healing of a Demon-possessed Man

▶ *See Matthew 8:28–34; Luke 8:26–39*

5 They went across the lake to the region of the Gerasenes.ᵃ ²When Jesus got out of the boat, a man with an evilᵇ spirit came from the tombs to meet him. ³This man lived in the tombs, and no one could bind him any more, not even with a chain. ⁴For he had often been chained hand and foot, but he tore the chains apart and broke the irons on his feet. No one was strong enough to subdue him. ⁵Night and day among the tombs and in the hills he would cry out and cut himself with stones.

⁶When he saw Jesus from a distance, he ran and fell on his knees in front of him. ⁷He shouted at the top of his voice, "What do you want with me, Jesus, Son of the Most High God? Swear to God that you won't torture me!" ⁸For Jesus had said to him, "Come out of this man, you evil spirit!"

⁹Then Jesus asked him, "What is your name?"

"My name is Legion," he replied, "for we are many." ¹⁰And he begged Jesus again and again not to send them out of the area.

¹¹A large herd of pigs was feeding on the nearby hillside. ¹²The demons begged Jesus, "Send us among the pigs; allow us to go into them." ¹³He gave them permission, and the evil spirits came out and went into the pigs. The herd, about two thousand in number, rushed down the steep bank into the lake and were drowned.

¹⁴Those tending the pigs ran off and reported this in the town and countryside, and the people went out to see what had happened. ¹⁵When they came to Jesus, they saw the man who had been possessed by the legion of demons, sitting there, dressed and in his right mind; and they were afraid. ¹⁶Those who had seen it told the people what had happened to the demon-possessed man—and told about the pigs as well. ¹⁷Then the people began to plead with Jesus to leave their region.

¹⁸As Jesus was getting into the boat, the man who had been demon-possessed begged to go with him. ¹⁹Jesus did not let him, but said, "Go home to your family and tell them how much the Lord has done for you, and how he has had mercy on you." ²⁰So the man went away and began to tell in the Decapolisᶜ how much Jesus had done for him. And all the people were amazed.

A Dead Girl and a Sick Woman

▶ *See Matthew 9:18–26; Luke 8:41–56*

²¹When Jesus had again crossed over by boat to the other side of the lake, a large crowd gathered around him while he was by the lake. ²²Then one of the synagogue rulers, named Jairus, came there. Seeing Jesus, he fell at his feet ²³and pleaded earnestly with him, "My little daughter is dying. Please come and put your hands on her so that she will be healed and live." ²⁴So Jesus went with him.

A large crowd followed and pressed around him. ²⁵And a woman was there who had been subject to bleeding for twelve years. ²⁶She had suffered a great deal under the care of many doctors and had spent all she had, yet instead of getting better she grew worse. ²⁷When she heard about Jesus, she came up behind him in the crowd and touched his cloak, ²⁸because she thought, "If I just touch his clothes, I will be healed." ²⁹Immediately her bleeding stopped and she felt in her body that she was freed from her suffering.

³⁰At once Jesus realized that power had gone out from him. He turned around in the crowd and asked, "Who touched my clothes?"

³¹"You see the people crowding against you," his disciples answered, "and yet you can ask, 'Who touched me?'"

³²But Jesus kept looking around to see who had done it. ³³Then the woman, knowing what had happened to her, came and fell at his feet and, trembling with fear, told him the whole truth. ³⁴He said to her, "Daughter, your faith has healed you. Go in peace and be freed from your suffering."

³⁵While Jesus was still speaking, some men came from the house of Jairus, the synagogue ruler. "Your daughter is dead," they said. "Why bother the teacher any more?"

³⁶Ignoring what they said, Jesus told the synagogue ruler, "Don't be afraid; just believe."

³⁷He did not let anyone follow him except Peter, James and John the brother of James. ³⁸When they came to the home of the synagogue ruler, Jesus saw a commotion, with people crying and wailing loudly. ³⁹He went in and said to them, "Why all this commotion and wailing? The child is not dead but asleep." ⁴⁰But they laughed at him.

After he put them all out, he took the child's father and mother and the disciples who were with him, and went in where the child was. ⁴¹He took her by the hand and said to her, *"Talitha koum!"* (which means, "Little girl, I say to you, get up!"). ⁴²Immediately the girl stood up and

---

ᵃ1 Some manuscripts *Gadarenes*; other manuscripts *Gergesenes*   ᵇ2 Greek *unclean*; also in verses 8 and 13
ᶜ20 That is, the Ten Cities

walked around (she was twelve years old). At this they were completely astonished. **⁴³**He gave strict orders not to let anyone know about this, and told them to give her something to eat.

5:43 Don't Tell

Seven times in Mark, Jesus asked people who had seen a miracle not to tell anyone. He was protecting himself from the crush of crowds that flocked to him when word of his miracles spread—as it usually did, despite his orders— and from the opposition forces who were already tailing him. Jesus recognized early on that the kind of excitement generated by miracles did not automatically convert into the life-changing faith he sought to arouse.

ª3 Greek *Joses,* a variant of *Joseph*

A Prophet Without Honor

▶ *See Matthew 13:54–58*

6 Jesus left there and went to his hometown, accompanied by his disciples. **²**When the Sabbath came, he began to teach in the synagogue, and many who heard him were amazed. "Where did this man get these things?" they asked. "What's this wisdom that has been given him, that he even does miracles! **³**Isn't this the carpenter? Isn't this Mary's son and the brother of James, Joseph,*ª* Judas and Simon? Aren't his sisters here with us?" And they took offense at him.

⁴Jesus said to them, "Only in his hometown, among his relatives and in his own house is a prophet without honor." **⁵**He could not do any miracles there, except lay his hands on a few sick people and heal them. **⁶**And he was amazed at their lack of faith.

Eyewitness Reports
Where did Mark get his facts?

WHEN PEOPLE TRANSLATE THE BIBLE into a new language, they have a lot of explaining to do. How do you convey Christianity to someone who has never heard of Abraham or Moses or the apostles Peter and Paul? Where do you start?

More often than not, translators begin with the book of Mark. Its simple sentences and brief, action-filled scenes allow for easier translation. It reads like a newspaper. And the book seems written for a foreign culture (perhaps the Romans) in the first place: Common Jewish customs are explained in parentheses.

> *He did not let any-one follow him except Peter, James and John the brother of James. 5:37*

The Peter Connection

Perhaps the most compelling feature of Mark to an unfamiliar reader, though, is its vividness. It has the feel of an eyewitness account. Those who study such things have concluded that Mark probably got his facts from Peter, one of Jesus' intimate disciples. Peter, or someone like him, provided believable, close-up details.

Jesus spent his time in the desert "with the wild animals" (1:13). When he went to pray, he got up "very early in the morning, while it was still dark" (1:35)—a memorable detail to Jesus' disciples, sometimes known for their untimely sleeping habits. In the midst of a furious squall Jesus lay in a boat "sleeping on a cushion" (4:38).

Whoever told Mark about the scene on the Mount of Transfiguration described Jesus' clothes as "dazzling white, whiter than anyone in the world could bleach them" (9:3). And only Mark tells us that Peter sat with the guards during Jesus' trial, warming himself by the fire.

Why Details Matter

You can say these details don't matter, and it's true that Matthew and Luke recounted the same events without them. But as any good writer knows, details like these make a story come alive. Vivid images that stuck in the eyewitness's memory will likely stick with the reader as well.

For example, Mark could have matter-of-factly told of people being healed, but it just didn't happen that way. A blind man, "throwing his cloak aside ... jumped to his feet and came to Jesus" (10:50). And after the paralytic stood up, "This amazed everyone and they praised God, saying, 'We have never seen anything like this!'" (2:12).

Life Questions: As you read Mark, what "eyewitness details" stand out to you?

Jesus Sends Out the Twelve

▶ *See Matthew 10:1,9–14; Luke 9:1,3–5*

Then Jesus went around teaching from village to village. [7]Calling the Twelve to him, he sent them out two by two and gave them authority over evil[a] spirits.

[8]These were his instructions: "Take nothing for the journey except a staff—no bread, no bag, no money in your belts. [9]Wear sandals but not an extra tunic. [10]Whenever you enter a house, stay there until you leave that town. [11]And if any place will not welcome you or listen to you, shake the dust off your feet when you leave, as a testimony against them."

[12]They went out and preached that people should repent. [13]They drove out many demons and anointed many sick people with oil and healed them.

John the Baptist Beheaded

▶ *See Matthew 14:1–12*

[14]King Herod heard about this, for Jesus' name had become well known. Some were saying,[b] "John the Baptist has been raised from the dead, and that is why miraculous powers are at work in him."

[15]Others said, "He is Elijah."

And still others claimed, "He is a prophet, like one of the prophets of long ago."

[16]But when Herod heard this, he said, "John, the man I beheaded, has been raised from the dead!"

[17]For Herod himself had given orders to have John arrested, and he had him bound and put in prison. He did this because of Herodias, his brother Philip's wife, whom he had married. [18]For John had been saying to Herod, "It is not lawful for you to have your brother's wife." [19]So Herodias nursed a grudge against John and wanted to kill him. But she was not able to, [20]because Herod feared John and protected him, knowing him to be a righteous and holy man. When Herod heard John, he was greatly puzzled[c]; yet he liked to listen to him.

[21]Finally the opportune time came. On his birthday Herod gave a banquet for his high officials and military commanders and the leading men of Galilee. [22]When the daughter of Herodias came in and danced, she pleased Herod and his dinner guests.

The king said to the girl, "Ask me for anything you want, and I'll give it to you." [23]And he promised her with an oath, "Whatever you ask I will give you, up to half my kingdom."

[24]She went out and said to her mother, "What shall I ask for?"

"The head of John the Baptist," she answered.

[25]At once the girl hurried in to the king with the request: "I want you to give me right now the head of John the Baptist on a platter."

[26]The king was greatly distressed, but because of his oaths and his dinner guests, he did not want to refuse her. [27]So he immediately sent an executioner with orders to bring John's head. The man went, beheaded John in the prison, [28]and brought back his head on a platter. He presented it to the girl, and she gave it to her mother. [29]On hearing of this, John's disciples came and took his body and laid it in a tomb.

6:29 New Recruits

Jesus got some of his original disciples from John the Baptist (see John 1:35,40), and after John's execution even more of them joined up with Jesus. But as Acts 19:1–5 makes clear, some of John's disciples never got the word about Jesus. Two decades after John's death, Paul stumbled across a group of loyal followers in Ephesus, hundreds of miles away.

Jesus Feeds the Five Thousand

▶ *See Matthew 14:13–21; Luke 9:10–17; John 6:5–13*

[30]The apostles gathered around Jesus and reported to him all they had done and taught. [31]Then, because so many people were coming and going that they did not even have a chance to eat, he said to them, "Come with me by yourselves to a quiet place and get some rest."

6:31 The Need to Get Away

Mark graphically shows the press of the crowds around Jesus. Wherever he went, people followed, bringing him the sick to heal and challenging him with questions. In five separate places (3:7–9; 6:31; 6:45; 7:24; 9:30) Mark records that Jesus took his disciples aside to some quiet place to escape the crush of the crowd.

[32]So they went away by themselves in a boat to a solitary place. [33]But many who saw them leaving recognized them and ran on foot from all the towns and got there ahead of them. [34]When Jesus landed and saw a large crowd, he had compassion on them, because they were like sheep without a shepherd. So he began teaching them many things.

[35]By this time it was late in the day, so his disciples came to him. "This is a remote place," they said, "and it's already very late. [36]Send the

---

[a]7 Greek *unclean*   [b]14 Some early manuscripts *He was saying*   [c]20 Some early manuscripts *he did many things*

people away so they can go to the surrounding countryside and villages and buy themselves something to eat."

³⁷But he answered, "You give them something to eat."

They said to him, "That would take eight months of a man's wages*ᵃ*! Are we to go and spend that much on bread and give it to them to eat?"

³⁸"How many loaves do you have?" he asked. "Go and see."

When they found out, they said, "Five—and two fish."

³⁹Then Jesus directed them to have all the people sit down in groups on the green grass. ⁴⁰So they sat down in groups of hundreds and fifties. ⁴¹Taking the five loaves and the two fish and looking up to heaven, he gave thanks and broke the loaves. Then he gave them to his disciples to set before the people. He also divided the two fish among them all. ⁴²They all ate and were satisfied, ⁴³and the disciples picked up twelve basketfuls of broken pieces of bread and fish. ⁴⁴The number of the men who had eaten was five thousand.

Jesus Walks on the Water

▶ *See Matthew 14:22–32; John 6:15–21*

⁴⁵Immediately Jesus made his disciples get into the boat and go on ahead of him to Bethsaida, while he dismissed the crowd. ⁴⁶After leaving them, he went up on a mountainside to pray.

⁴⁷When evening came, the boat was in the middle of the lake, and he was alone on land. ⁴⁸He saw the disciples straining at the oars, because the wind was against them. About the fourth watch of the night he went out to them, walking on the lake. He was about to pass by them, ⁴⁹but when they saw him walking on the lake, they thought he was a ghost. They cried out, ⁵⁰because they all saw him and were terrified.

Immediately he spoke to them and said, "Take courage! It is I. Don't be afraid." ⁵¹Then he climbed into the boat with them, and the wind died down. They were completely amazed, ⁵²for they had not understood about the loaves; their hearts were hardened.

⁵³When they had crossed over, they landed at Gennesaret and anchored there. ⁵⁴As soon as they got out of the boat, people recognized Jesus. ⁵⁵They ran throughout that whole region and carried the sick on mats to wherever they heard he was. ⁵⁶And wherever he went—into villages, towns or countryside—they placed the sick in the marketplaces. They begged him to let them touch even the edge of his cloak, and all who touched him were healed.

Clean and Unclean

▶ *See Matthew 15:1–20*

7 The Pharisees and some of the teachers of the law who had come from Jerusalem gathered around Jesus and ²saw some of his disciples eating food with hands that were "unclean," that is, unwashed. ³(The Pharisees and all the Jews do not eat unless they give their hands a ceremonial washing, holding to the tradition of the elders.

7:3 Explaining Jewish Customs

The parenthetical remark in verses 3–4 explains a common Jewish custom of ceremonial hand-washing. Such remarks as these indicate Mark was writing to a non-Jewish audience who needed background explanations.

⁴When they come from the marketplace they do not eat unless they wash. And they observe many other traditions, such as the washing of cups, pitchers and kettles.*ᵇ*)

⁵So the Pharisees and teachers of the law asked Jesus, "Why don't your disciples live according to the tradition of the elders instead of eating their food with 'unclean' hands?"

⁶He replied, "Isaiah was right when he prophesied about you hypocrites; as it is written:

" 'These people honor me with their lips,
    but their hearts are far from me.
⁷They worship me in vain;
    their teachings are but rules taught by
        men.'*ᶜ*

⁸You have let go of the commands of God and are holding on to the traditions of men."

⁹And he said to them: "You have a fine way of setting aside the commands of God in order to observe*ᵈ* your own traditions! ¹⁰For Moses said, 'Honor your father and your mother,'*ᵉ* and, 'Anyone who curses his father or mother must be put to death.'*ᶠ* ¹¹But you say that if a man says to his father or mother: 'Whatever help you might otherwise have received from me is Corban' (that is, a gift devoted to God), ¹²then you no longer let him do anything for his father or mother. ¹³Thus you nullify the word of God by your tradition that you have handed down. And you do many things like that."

¹⁴Again Jesus called the crowd to him and said, "Listen to me, everyone, and understand this. ¹⁵Nothing outside a man can make him 'unclean' by going into him. Rather, it is what comes out of a man that makes him 'unclean.'*ᵍ* "

ᵃ37 Greek *take two hundred denarii*   *ᵇ4* Some early manuscripts *pitchers, kettles and dining couches*   *ᶜ6,7* Isaiah 29:13   *ᵈ9* Some manuscripts *set up*   *ᵉ10* Exodus 20:12; Deut. 5:16   *ᶠ10* Exodus 21:17; Lev. 20:9   *ᵍ15* Some early manuscripts *'unclean.'* *¹⁶If anyone has ears to hear, let him hear.*

17After he had left the crowd and entered the house, his disciples asked him about this parable. 18"Are you so dull?" he asked. "Don't you see that nothing that enters a man from the outside can make him 'unclean'? 19For it doesn't go into his heart but into his stomach, and then out of his body." (In saying this, Jesus declared all foods "clean.")

20He went on: "What comes out of a man is what makes him 'unclean.' 21For from within, out of men's hearts, come evil thoughts, sexual immorality, theft, murder, adultery, 22greed, malice, deceit, lewdness, envy, slander, arrogance and folly. 23All these evils come from inside and make a man 'unclean.'"

The Faith of a Syrophoenician Woman

▶ *See Matthew 15:21–28*

24Jesus left that place and went to the vicinity of Tyre.*a* He entered a house and did not want anyone to know it; yet he could not keep his presence secret. 25In fact, as soon as she heard about him, a woman whose little daughter was possessed by an evil*b* spirit came and fell at his feet. 26The woman was a Greek, born in Syrian Phoenicia. She begged Jesus to drive the demon out of her daughter.

27"First let the children eat all they want," he told her, "for it is not right to take the children's bread and toss it to their dogs."

28"Yes, Lord," she replied, "but even the dogs under the table eat the children's crumbs."

29Then he told her, "For such a reply, you may go; the demon has left your daughter."

30She went home and found her child lying on the bed, and the demon gone.

The Healing of a Deaf and Mute Man

▶ *See Matthew 15:29–31*

31Then Jesus left the vicinity of Tyre and went through Sidon, down to the Sea of Galilee and into the region of the Decapolis.*c* 32There some people brought to him a man who was deaf and could hardly talk, and they begged him to place his hand on the man.

33After he took him aside, away from the crowd, Jesus put his fingers into the man's ears. Then he spit and touched the man's tongue. 34He looked up to heaven and with a deep sigh said to him, *"Ephphatha!"* (which means, "Be opened!"). 35At this, the man's ears were opened, his tongue was loosened and he began to speak plainly.

36Jesus commanded them not to tell anyone. But the more he did so, the more they kept talking about it. 37People were overwhelmed with amazement. "He has done everything well," they said. "He even makes the deaf hear and the mute speak."

Jesus Feeds the Four Thousand

▶ *See Matthew 15:32–39*

8 During those days another large crowd gathered. Since they had nothing to eat, Jesus called his disciples to him and said, 2"I have compassion for these people; they have already been with me three days and have nothing to eat. 3If I send them home hungry, they will collapse on the way, because some of them have come a long distance."

4His disciples answered, "But where in this remote place can anyone get enough bread to feed them?"

5"How many loaves do you have?" Jesus asked.

"Seven," they replied.

6He told the crowd to sit down on the ground. When he had taken the seven loaves and given thanks, he broke them and gave them to his disciples to set before the people, and they did so. 7They had a few small fish as well; he gave thanks for them also and told the disciples to distribute them. 8The people ate and were satisfied. Afterward the disciples picked up seven basketfuls of

---

8:8 Lost in Translation

Often details get lost when a book is translated from one language to another. For example, the Greek word for the "baskets" used in the feeding of the 5,000 (6:43) is used for small, lunchbox-size baskets. In the feeding of the 4,000, leftovers filled seven large baskets; the same word describes the basket the apostle Paul would hide in to escape from Damascus (Acts 9:25).

---

broken pieces that were left over. 9About four thousand men were present. And having sent them away, 10he got into the boat with his disciples and went to the region of Dalmanutha.

11The Pharisees came and began to question Jesus. To test him, they asked him for a sign from heaven. 12He sighed deeply and said, "Why does this generation ask for a miraculous sign? I tell you the truth, no sign will be given to it." 13Then he left them, got back into the boat and crossed to the other side.

The Yeast of the Pharisees and Herod

14The disciples had forgotten to bring bread, except for one loaf they had with them in the boat. 15"Be careful," Jesus warned them. "Watch out for the yeast of the Pharisees and that of Herod."

16They discussed this with one another and said, "It is because we have no bread."

---

a24 Many early manuscripts *Tyre and Sidon*   *b25* Greek *unclean*   *c31* That is, the Ten Cities

[17] Aware of their discussion, Jesus asked them: "Why are you talking about having no bread? Do you still not see or understand? Are your hearts hardened? [18] Do you have eyes but fail to see, and ears but fail to hear? And don't you remember? [19] When I broke the five loaves for the five thousand, how many basketfuls of pieces did you pick up?"

"Twelve," they replied.

[20] "And when I broke the seven loaves for the four thousand, how many basketfuls of pieces did you pick up?"

They answered, "Seven."

[21] He said to them, "Do you still not understand?"

The Healing of a Blind Man at Bethsaida

[22] They came to Bethsaida, and some people brought a blind man and begged Jesus to touch him. [23] He took the blind man by the hand and led him outside the village. When he had spit on the man's eyes and put his hands on him, Jesus asked, "Do you see anything?"

[24] He looked up and said, "I see people; they look like trees walking around."

[25] Once more Jesus put his hands on the man's eyes. Then his eyes were opened, his sight was restored, and he saw everything clearly. [26] Jesus sent him home, saying, "Don't go into the village.[a]"

Peter's Confession of Christ

▶ See Matthew 16:13–16; Luke 9:18–20

[27] Jesus and his disciples went on to the villages around Caesarea Philippi. On the way he asked them, "Who do people say I am?"

[28] They replied, "Some say John the Baptist; others say Elijah; and still others, one of the prophets."

[29] "But what about you?" he asked. "Who do you say I am?"

Peter answered, "You are the Christ.[b]"

[30] Jesus warned them not to tell anyone about him.

Jesus Predicts His Death

▶ See Matthew 16:21–28; Luke 9:22–27

[31] He then began to teach them that the Son of Man must suffer many things and be rejected by the elders, chief priests and teachers of the law, and that he must be killed and after three days rise again. [32] He spoke plainly about this, and Peter took him aside and began to rebuke him.

[33] But when Jesus turned and looked at his disciples, he rebuked Peter. "Get behind me, Satan!" he said. "You do not have in mind the things of God, but the things of men."

[34] Then he called the crowd to him along with his disciples and said: "If anyone would come after me, he must deny himself and take up his cross and follow me. [35] For whoever wants to save

8:29 Peter Learns Humility

Most scholars believe that Mark got his eyewitness details from the disciple Peter. If so, the book reveals something about how Peter changed. Mark tells of three separate instances when Jesus rebuked Peter (see, for example, verse 33), but omits several compliments paid him. For example, compare this passage to a parallel account in Matthew 16:13–20, where Jesus commended Peter highly. Evidently, brash Peter learned a few lessons about humility along the way.

his life[c] will lose it, but whoever loses his life for me and for the gospel will save it. [36] What good is it for a man to gain the whole world, yet forfeit his soul? [37] Or what can a man give in exchange for his soul? [38] If anyone is ashamed of me and my words in this adulterous and sinful generation, the Son of Man will be ashamed of him when he comes in his Father's glory with the holy angels."

9 And he said to them, "I tell you the truth, some who are standing here will not taste death before they see the kingdom of God come with power."

The Transfiguration

▶ See Matthew 17:1–13; Luke 9:28–36

[2] After six days Jesus took Peter, James and John with him and led them up a high mountain, where they were all alone. There he was transfigured before them. [3] His clothes became dazzling white, whiter than anyone in the world could bleach them. [4] And there appeared before them Elijah and Moses, who were talking with Jesus.

[5] Peter said to Jesus, "Rabbi, it is good for us to be here. Let us put up three shelters—one for you, one for Moses and one for Elijah." [6] (He did not know what to say, they were so frightened.)

[7] Then a cloud appeared and enveloped them, and a voice came from the cloud: "This is my Son, whom I love. Listen to him!"

[8] Suddenly, when they looked around, they no longer saw anyone with them except Jesus.

[9] As they were coming down the mountain, Jesus gave them orders not to tell anyone what they had seen until the Son of Man had risen from the dead. [10] They kept the matter to them-

---

[a]26 Some manuscripts *Don't go and tell anyone in the village*   [b]29 Or *Messiah*. "The Christ" (Greek) and "the Messiah" (Hebrew) both mean "the Anointed One."   [c]35 The Greek word means either *life* or *soul*; also in verse 36.

selves, discussing what "rising from the dead" meant.

¹¹And they asked him, "Why do the teachers of the law say that Elijah must come first?"

¹²Jesus replied, "To be sure, Elijah does come first, and restores all things. Why then is it written that the Son of Man must suffer much and be rejected? ¹³But I tell you, Elijah has come, and they have done to him everything they wished, just as it is written about him."

The Healing of a Boy With an Evil Spirit

▶ *See Matthew 17:14–19,22–23; Luke 9:37–45*

¹⁴When they came to the other disciples, they saw a large crowd around them and the teachers of the law arguing with them. ¹⁵As soon as all the people saw Jesus, they were overwhelmed with wonder and ran to greet him.

¹⁶"What are you arguing with them about?" he asked.

¹⁷A man in the crowd answered, "Teacher, I brought you my son, who is possessed by a spirit that has robbed him of speech. ¹⁸Whenever it seizes him, it throws him to the ground. He foams at the mouth, gnashes his teeth and becomes rigid. I asked your disciples to drive out the spirit, but they could not."

¹⁹"O unbelieving generation," Jesus replied, "how long shall I stay with you? How long shall I put up with you? Bring the boy to me."

²⁰So they brought him. When the spirit saw Jesus, it immediately threw the boy into a convulsion. He fell to the ground and rolled around, foaming at the mouth.

²¹Jesus asked the boy's father, "How long has he been like this?"

"From childhood," he answered. ²²"It has often thrown him into fire or water to kill him. But if you can do anything, take pity on us and help us."

Training the 12 Disciples
A most unpromising group of recruits

> "Do you have eyes but fail to see, and ears but fail to hear?" 8:18

A SKILLED DRAMATIST, MARK DESCRIBES THE crowd reactions to Jesus all through his account. He shows people astonished, confused, and upset by Jesus' actions. Always, twelve people, the disciples, linger in the background, working out the logistics of Jesus' ministry.

At first, the disciples did not distinguish themselves—to put it mildly. Their most obvious trait was denseness: "Are you so dull?" Jesus asked (7:18), and again, "How long shall I put up with you?" (9:19).

Dense Disciples

About halfway through the book of Mark (chapter 8), the focus shifts away from the crowds and onto the disciples. In spite of their erratic performance, Jesus devoted much of his time to them. Outsiders still gathered to watch and listen, but Jesus concentrated on training the Twelve, preparing them to carry on his work after his departure.

How did the disciples handle the increased attention? If anything, they proved even more inept. When Jesus referred to his coming death, they either missed the point or foolishly protested his plans. Sometimes they squabbled about who deserved the most favored position. They obviously didn't understand the dazzling events going on around them. In short, the disciples amply demonstrated the mixture of good and bad present in all of us.

Near the end of Mark, as events conspired toward Jesus' death, the disciples grew more anxious and assertive. Jesus singled out two followers in particular, John and Peter, for his strongest reprimands. Ultimately, despite vigorous pronouncements of loyalty, each one of the Twelve sneaked quietly and ashamedly away from Jesus in his moment of deepest need.

A Decisive Change

One event, however, dramatically altered them. Something passed through their lives like a flame: Jesus' resurrection from death. After that, Jesus' patient hours of training seemed to bear fruit at last.

The disciples' change in behavior is astonishing. Of the proofs for the resurrection of Jesus, one of the most compelling is simply to compare these cowering disciples as portrayed in a Gospel like Mark with the bold, confident figures in the book of Acts. There, in a remarkable irony, we see the incredible advance of the early church being led by the two disciples with the thickest heads of all: Peter and John.

Life Questions: Sometimes we think of the disciples as saints or heroes, but Mark shows their weak spots. What weak spots keep you from following Jesus as you might?

23"'If you can'?" said Jesus. "Everything is possible for him who believes."

24Immediately the boy's father exclaimed, "I do believe; help me overcome my unbelief!"

25When Jesus saw that a crowd was running to the scene, he rebuked the evil[a] spirit. "You deaf and mute spirit," he said, "I command you, come out of him and never enter him again."

26The spirit shrieked, convulsed him violently and came out. The boy looked so much like a corpse that many said, "He's dead." 27But Jesus took him by the hand and lifted him to his feet, and he stood up.

28After Jesus had gone indoors, his disciples asked him privately, "Why couldn't we drive it out?"

29He replied, "This kind can come out only by prayer.[b]"

30They left that place and passed through Galilee. Jesus did not want anyone to know where they were, 31because he was teaching his disciples. He said to them, "The Son of Man is going to be betrayed into the hands of men. They will

> ## 9:31 Baffling Thoughts
>
> *At the height of his popularity, as throngs of people were following him, Jesus began to talk about his suffering and death. Such talk baffled his disciples, whose image of a Messiah included no such dark notions. (When reality finally hit, they would all desert him and flee 14:50.) Although Jesus made a point of mentioning his resurrection whenever he talked about his death, the disciples grasped neither concept—until he had died and then come back.*

kill him, and after three days he will rise." 32But they did not understand what he meant and were afraid to ask him about it.

Who Is the Greatest?

▶ *See Matthew 18:1–5; Luke 9:46–48*

33They came to Capernaum. When he was in the house, he asked them, "What were you arguing about on the road?" 34But they kept quiet because on the way they had argued about who was the greatest.

35Sitting down, Jesus called the Twelve and said, "If anyone wants to be first, he must be the very last, and the servant of all."

36He took a little child and had him stand among them. Taking him in his arms, he said to them, 37"Whoever welcomes one of these little

children in my name welcomes me; and whoever welcomes me does not welcome me but the one who sent me."

Whoever Is Not Against Us Is for Us

▶ *See Luke 9:49–50*

38"Teacher," said John, "we saw a man driving out demons in your name and we told him to stop, because he was not one of us."

39"Do not stop him," Jesus said. "No one who does a miracle in my name can in the next moment say anything bad about me, 40for whoever is not against us is for us. 41I tell you the truth, anyone who gives you a cup of water in my name because you belong to Christ will certainly not lose his reward.

Causing to Sin

42"And if anyone causes one of these little ones who believe in me to sin, it would be better for him to be thrown into the sea with a large millstone tied around his neck. 43If your hand causes you to sin, cut it off. It is better for you to enter life maimed than with two hands to go into hell, where the fire never goes out.[c] 45And if your foot causes you to sin, cut it off. It is better for you to enter life crippled than to have two feet and be thrown into hell.[d] 47And if your eye causes you to sin, pluck it out. It is better for you to enter the kingdom of God with one eye than to have two eyes and be thrown into hell, 48where

> "'their worm does not die,
>   and the fire is not quenched.'[e]

49Everyone will be salted with fire.

50"Salt is good, but if it loses its saltiness, how can you make it salty again? Have salt in yourselves, and be at peace with each other."

Divorce

▶ *See Matthew 19:1–9*

10 Jesus then left that place and went into the region of Judea and across the Jordan. Again crowds of people came to him, and as was his custom, he taught them.

2Some Pharisees came and tested him by asking, "Is it lawful for a man to divorce his wife?"

3"What did Moses command you?" he replied.

4They said, "Moses permitted a man to write a certificate of divorce and send her away."

5"It was because your hearts were hard that Moses wrote you this law," Jesus replied. 6"But at the beginning of creation God 'made them male and female.'[f] 7For this reason a man will leave his father and mother and be united to his wife,[g]

---

[a]25 Greek *unclean*   [b]29 Some manuscripts *prayer and fasting*   [c]43 Some manuscripts *out,* 44*where* / "'*their worm does not die, / and the fire is not quenched.'*   [d]45 Some manuscripts *hell,* 46*where* / "'*their worm does not die, / and the fire is not quenched.'*   [e]48 Isaiah 66:24   [f]6 Gen. 1:27   [g]7 Some early manuscripts do not have *and be united to his wife.*

[8]and the two will become one flesh.'[a] So they are no longer two, but one. [9]Therefore what God has joined together, let man not separate."

[10]When they were in the house again, the disciples asked Jesus about this. [11]He answered,

---

10:2–12 Teaching on Divorce

The Pharisees tested Jesus with questions about common practices of divorce and remarriage. Jesus responded by pointing back to the origin of marriage at creation. His disciples were surprised by his strict views on divorce, and questioned him further in private. For other passages on this topic, see Matthew 19:1–12 and 1 Corinthians 7:1–16.

"Anyone who divorces his wife and marries another woman commits adultery against her. [12]And if she divorces her husband and marries another man, she commits adultery."

The Little Children and Jesus

▶ *See Matthew 19:13–15; Luke 18:15–17*

[13]People were bringing little children to Jesus to have him touch them, but the disciples rebuked them. [14]When Jesus saw this, he was indignant. He said to them, "Let the little children come to me, and do not hinder them, for the kingdom of God belongs to such as these. [15]I tell you the truth, anyone who will not receive the kingdom of God like a little child will never enter it." [16]And he took the children in his arms, put his hands on them and blessed them.

The Rich Young Man

▶ *See Matthew 19:16–30; Luke 18:18–30*

[17]As Jesus started on his way, a man ran up to him and fell on his knees before him. "Good teacher," he asked, "what must I do to inherit eternal life?"

[18]"Why do you call me good?" Jesus answered. "No one is good—except God alone. [19]You know the commandments: 'Do not murder, do not commit adultery, do not steal, do not give false testimony, do not defraud, honor your father and mother.'[b]"

[20]"Teacher," he declared, "all these I have kept since I was a boy."

[21]Jesus looked at him and loved him. "One thing you lack," he said. "Go, sell everything you have and give to the poor, and you will have treasure in heaven. Then come, follow me."

[22]At this the man's face fell. He went away sad, because he had great wealth.

[23]Jesus looked around and said to his disci-

ples, "How hard it is for the rich to enter the kingdom of God!"

[24]The disciples were amazed at his words. But Jesus said again, "Children, how hard it is[c] to enter the kingdom of God! [25]It is easier for a camel to go through the eye of a needle than for a rich man to enter the kingdom of God."

[26]The disciples were even more amazed, and said to each other, "Who then can be saved?"

10:26 The Wealth Barrier

Religious teachers of that time saw wealth as a positive sign of God's approval, which explains the disciples' bewilderment. Jesus contradicted such ideas by teaching that wealth can actually be a barrier keeping people out of the kingdom of God.

---

[27]Jesus looked at them and said, "With man this is impossible, but not with God; all things are possible with God."

[28]Peter said to him, "We have left everything to follow you!"

[29]"I tell you the truth," Jesus replied, "no one who has left home or brothers or sisters or mother or father or children or fields for me and the gospel [30]will fail to receive a hundred times as much in this present age (homes, brothers, sisters, mothers, children and fields—and with them, persecutions) and in the age to come, eternal life. [31]But many who are first will be last, and the last first."

Jesus Again Predicts His Death

▶ *See Matthew 20:17–19; Luke 18:31–33*

[32]They were on their way up to Jerusalem, with Jesus leading the way, and the disciples were astonished, while those who followed were afraid. Again he took the Twelve aside and told them what was going to happen to him. [33]"We are going up to Jerusalem," he said, "and the Son of Man will be betrayed to the chief priests and teachers of the law. They will condemn him to death and will hand him over to the Gentiles, [34]who will mock him and spit on him, flog him and kill him. Three days later he will rise."

The Request of James and John

▶ *See Matthew 20:20–28*

[35]Then James and John, the sons of Zebedee, came to him. "Teacher," they said, "we want you to do for us whatever we ask."

[36]"What do you want me to do for you?" he asked.

---

a8 Gen. 2:24   *b19 Exodus 20:12-16; Deut. 5:16-20*   *c24 Some manuscripts is for those who trust in riches*

[37]They replied, "Let one of us sit at your right and the other at your left in your glory."

[38]"You don't know what you are asking," Jesus said. "Can you drink the cup I drink or be baptized with the baptism I am baptized with?"

[39]"We can," they answered.

Jesus said to them, "You will drink the cup I drink and be baptized with the baptism I am baptized with, [40]but to sit at my right or left is not for me to grant. These places belong to those for whom they have been prepared."

[41]When the ten heard about this, they became indignant with James and John. [42]Jesus called them together and said, "You know that those who are regarded as rulers of the Gentiles lord it over them, and their high officials exercise authority over them. [43]Not so with you. Instead, whoever wants to become great among you must be your servant, [44]and whoever wants to be first must be slave of all. [45]For even the Son of Man did not come to be served, but to serve, and to give his life as a ransom for many."

Blind Bartimaeus Receives His Sight

▶ See Matthew 20:29–34; Luke 18:35–43

[46]Then they came to Jericho. As Jesus and his disciples, together with a large crowd, were leaving the city, a blind man, Bartimaeus (that is, the Son of Timaeus), was sitting by the roadside begging. [47]When he heard that it was Jesus of Nazareth, he began to shout, "Jesus, Son of David, have mercy on me!"

[48]Many rebuked him and told him to be quiet, but he shouted all the more, "Son of David, have mercy on me!"

[49]Jesus stopped and said, "Call him."

So they called to the blind man, "Cheer up! On your feet! He's calling you." [50]Throwing his cloak aside, he jumped to his feet and came to Jesus.

[51]"What do you want me to do for you?" Jesus asked him.

The blind man said, "Rabbi, I want to see."

[52]"Go," said Jesus, "your faith has healed you." Immediately he received his sight and followed Jesus along the road.

The Triumphal Entry

▶ See Matthew 21:1–9; Luke 19:29–38; John 12:12–15

11 As they approached Jerusalem and came to Bethphage and Bethany at the Mount of Olives, Jesus sent two of his disciples, [2]saying to them, "Go to the village ahead of you, and just as you enter it, you will find a colt tied there, which no one has ever ridden. Untie it and bring it here. [3]If anyone asks you, 'Why are you doing this?' tell him, 'The Lord needs it and will send it back here shortly.'"

[4]They went and found a colt outside in the street, tied at a doorway. As they untied it, [5]some people standing there asked, "What are you doing, untying that colt?" [6]They answered as Jesus had told them to, and the people let them go.

JAMES *Inner Circle*

THINK OF YOUR FRIENDS AS a series of concentric circles. The outer circle holds casual acquaintances: the drug store clerk, the neighbor who waves when she drives past. Closer in are real friends, people you trust and care about–perhaps classmates or friends from work. The innermost circle–the bullseye–includes only a handful: those people whose company you seek for the most important events of your life.

Jesus had a wide outer circle. He ministered to thousands of people who crowded around him wherever he went. Closer in were his disciples, the group of people who seriously followed him. The twelve apostles formed a smaller, more committed group. And near the center was an inner core: Peter, James and John.

James and his brother John worked alongside their father and another pair of brothers, Peter and Andrew, in a modest fishing fleet on the Sea of Galilee. These were the first disciples whom Jesus called, and from them Jesus chose his inner circle. During the critical times of his life, Jesus sought the company of his inner circle. At Jairus's house, only James, Peter and John accompanied him to see the dead child (5:37). At the transfiguration, the same three were chosen to climb the mountain (Matthew 17:1). In Gethsemane, Jesus sought their company and their prayers during his time of agony (14:33).

Belonging to Jesus' inner circle brought privileges but also temptations. Jesus' closest companions were susceptible to pride, a trap that caught James and his brother John at least twice. Once, when people failed to give Jesus the reception they thought appropriate, James and John were ready to call down fire from heaven (Luke 9:51–56).

In another incident reported in this chapter, the two brothers asked for special treatment when Jesus came to power. Gently, Jesus told them they did not know what they were asking. To be in the inner circle, Jesus said, meant living as a servant, not as a king.

Life Questions: Who is in your inner circle? How does your inner circle treat those who are outside?

[7]When they brought the colt to Jesus and threw their cloaks over it, he sat on it. [8]Many people spread their cloaks on the road, while others spread branches they had cut in the fields. [9]Those who went ahead and those who followed shouted,

"Hosanna![a]"

"Blessed is he who comes in the name of the Lord!"[b]

11:9 Short-lived Acceptance

During much of his ministry, Jesus hushed up news about his miraculous power and his identity as the true Messiah. But in this rare scene, large crowds clearly recognized him as the Messiah and honored him as such. The next few chapters, however, demonstrate how tragically short-lived public acceptance proved to be.

[10]"Blessed is the coming kingdom of our father David!"

"Hosanna in the highest!"

[11]Jesus entered Jerusalem and went to the temple. He looked around at everything, but since it was already late, he went out to Bethany with the Twelve.

Jesus Clears the Temple

▶ *See Matthew 21:12–16; Luke 19:45–47; John 2:13–16*

[12]The next day as they were leaving Bethany, Jesus was hungry. [13]Seeing in the distance a fig tree in leaf, he went to find out if it had any fruit. When he reached it, he found nothing but leaves, because it was not the season for figs. [14]Then he said to the tree, "May no one ever eat fruit from you again." And his disciples heard him say it.

[15]On reaching Jerusalem, Jesus entered the temple area and began driving out those who were buying and selling there. He overturned the tables of the money changers and the benches of those selling doves, [16]and would not allow anyone to carry merchandise through the temple courts. [17]And as he taught them, he said, "Is it not written:

" 'My house will be called
a house of prayer for all nations'[c]?

But you have made it 'a den of robbers.'[d]"

[18]The chief priests and the teachers of the law

heard this and began looking for a way to kill him, for they feared him, because the whole crowd was amazed at his teaching.

[19]When evening came, they[e] went out of the city.

11:16 Big Business

The outer court of the temple, accessible to non-Jews, encompassed a huge area the size of ten football fields. Some business there was legitimate: Out-of-town pilgrims needed a way to obtain sacrificial animals and to change money into local currency. Apparently, though, the business had fallen into the hands of people more interested in profit than in worship.

The Withered Fig Tree

▶ *See Matthew 21:19–22*

[20]In the morning, as they went along, they saw the fig tree withered from the roots. [21]Peter remembered and said to Jesus, "Rabbi, look! The fig tree you cursed has withered!"

[22]"Have[f] faith in God," Jesus answered. [23]"I tell you the truth, if anyone says to this mountain, 'Go, throw yourself into the sea,' and does not doubt in his heart but believes that what he says will happen, it will be done for him. [24]Therefore I tell you, whatever you ask for in prayer, believe that you have received it, and it will be yours. [25]And when you stand praying, if you hold anything against anyone, forgive him, so that your Father in heaven may forgive you your sins.[g]"

The Authority of Jesus Questioned

▶ *See Matthew 21:23–27; Luke 20:1–8*

[27]They arrived again in Jerusalem, and while Jesus was walking in the temple courts, the chief priests, the teachers of the law and the elders came to him. [28]"By what authority are you doing these things?" they asked. "And who gave you authority to do this?"

[29]Jesus replied, "I will ask you one question. Answer me, and I will tell you by what authority I am doing these things. [30]John's baptism—was it from heaven, or from men? Tell me!"

[31]They discussed it among themselves and said, "If we say, 'From heaven,' he will ask, 'Then why didn't you believe him?' [32]But if we say, 'From men'...." (They feared the people, for everyone held that John really was a prophet.)

[33]So they answered Jesus, "We don't know."

---

[a]9 A Hebrew expression meaning "Save!" which became an exclamation of praise; also in verse 10
[b]9 Psalm 118:25,26   [c]17 Isaiah 56:7   [d]17 Jer. 7:11   [e]19 Some early manuscripts *he*
[f]22 Some early manuscripts *If you have*   [g]25 Some manuscripts *sins.* [26]*But if you do not forgive, neither will your Father who is in heaven forgive your sins.*

Jesus said, "Neither will I tell you by what authority I am doing these things."

The Parable of the Tenants

▶ *See Matthew 21:33–46; Luke 20:9–19*

12 He then began to speak to them in parables: "A man planted a vineyard. He put a wall around it, dug a pit for the winepress and built a watchtower. Then he rented the vineyard to some farmers and went away on a journey. [2]At harvest time he sent a servant to the tenants to collect from them some of the fruit of the vineyard. [3]But they seized him, beat him and sent him away empty-handed. [4]Then he sent another servant to them; they struck this man on the head and treated him shamefully. [5]He sent still another, and that one they killed. He sent many others; some of them they beat, others they killed.

[6]"He had one left to send, a son, whom he loved. He sent him last of all, saying, 'They will respect my son.'

[7]"But the tenants said to one another, 'This is the heir. Come, let's kill him, and the inheritance will be ours.' [8]So they took him and killed him, and threw him out of the vineyard.

[9]"What then will the owner of the vineyard do? He will come and kill those tenants and give the vineyard to others. [10]Haven't you read this scripture:

" 'The stone the builders rejected
    has become the capstone[a];
[11]the Lord has done this,
    and it is marvelous in our eyes'[b]?"

[12]Then they looked for a way to arrest him because they knew he had spoken the parable against them. But they were afraid of the crowd; so they left him and went away.

Paying Taxes to Caesar

▶ *See Matthew 22:15–22; Luke 20:20–26*

[13]Later they sent some of the Pharisees and Herodians to Jesus to catch him in his words. [14]They came to him and said, "Teacher, we know you are a man of integrity. You aren't swayed by men, because you pay no attention to who they are; but you teach the way of God in accordance with the truth. Is it right to pay taxes to Caesar or not? [15]Should we pay or shouldn't we?"

But Jesus knew their hypocrisy. "Why are you trying to trap me?" he asked. "Bring me a denarius and let me look at it." [16]They brought the coin, and he asked them, "Whose portrait is this? And whose inscription?"

"Caesar's," they replied.

[17]Then Jesus said to them, "Give to Caesar what is Caesar's and to God what is God's."

And they were amazed at him.

Marriage at the Resurrection

▶ *See Matthew 22:23–33; Luke 20:27–38*

[18]Then the Sadducees, who say there is no resurrection, came to him with a question. [19]"Teacher," they said, "Moses wrote for us that if a man's brother dies and leaves a wife but no children, the man must marry the widow and have children for his brother. [20]Now there were seven brothers. The first one married and died without leaving any children. [21]The second one married the widow, but he also died, leaving no child. It was the same with the third. [22]In fact, none of the seven left any children. Last of all, the woman died too. [23]At the resurrection[c] whose wife will she be, since the seven were married to her?"

[24]Jesus replied, "Are you not in error because you do not know the Scriptures or the power of God? [25]When the dead rise, they will neither marry nor be given in marriage; they will be like the angels in heaven. [26]Now about the dead rising—have you not read in the book of Moses, in the account of the bush, how God said to him, 'I am the God of Abraham, the God of Isaac, and the God of Jacob'[d]? [27]He is not the God of the dead, but of the living. You are badly mistaken!"

The Greatest Commandment

▶ *See Matthew 22:34–40*

[28]One of the teachers of the law came and heard them debating. Noticing that Jesus had given them a good answer, he asked him, "Of all the commandments, which is the most important?"

[29]"The most important one," answered Jesus, "is this: 'Hear, O Israel, the Lord our God, the Lord is one.[e] [30]Love the Lord your God with all your heart and with all your soul and with all your mind and with all your strength.'[f] [31]The second is this: 'Love your neighbor as yourself.'[g] There is no commandment greater than these."

[32]"Well said, teacher," the man replied. "You are right in saying that God is one and there is no

12:13 Opposition Heats Up

While in Jerusalem, Jesus was surrounded by hostile groups. Mark 12 records a series of attempts to bait him: by the Pharisees and Sadducees, by the political Herodians, and by the teachers of the law. Each group challenged Jesus with a situation designed to trap him and anger the crowd.

---

[a]10 Or *cornerstone*   [b]11 Psalm 118:22,23   [c]23 Some manuscripts *resurrection, when men rise from the dead,*   [d]26 Exodus 3:6   [e]29 Or *the Lord our God is one Lord*   [f]30 Deut. 6:4,5   [g]31 Lev. 19:18

other but him. ³³To love him with all your heart, with all your understanding and with all your strength, and to love your neighbor as yourself is more important than all burnt offerings and sacrifices."

³⁴When Jesus saw that he had answered wisely, he said to him, "You are not far from the kingdom of God." And from then on no one dared ask him any more questions.

Whose Son Is the Christ?

▶ See Matthew 22:41–46; Luke 20:41–47

³⁵While Jesus was teaching in the temple courts, he asked, "How is it that the teachers of the law say that the Christ*ᵃ* is the son of David? ³⁶David himself, speaking by the Holy Spirit, declared:

" 'The Lord said to my Lord:
   "Sit at my right hand
until I put your enemies
   under your feet." ' *ᵇ*

³⁷David himself calls him 'Lord.' How then can he be his son?"

The large crowd listened to him with delight.

³⁸As he taught, Jesus said, "Watch out for the teachers of the law. They like to walk around in flowing robes and be greeted in the marketplaces, ³⁹and have the most important seats in the synagogues and the places of honor at banquets. ⁴⁰They devour widows' houses and for a show make lengthy prayers. Such men will be punished most severely."

The Widow's Offering

▶ See Luke 21:1–4

⁴¹Jesus sat down opposite the place where the offerings were put and watched the crowd putting their money into the temple treasury. Many rich people threw in large amounts. ⁴²But a poor widow came and put in two very small copper coins,*ᶜ* worth only a fraction of a penny.*ᵈ*

12:42 Exploiting Widows

The simple act of faithfulness by an impoverished widow made a stark contrast to others' pompous public displays. Some teachers "devour widows' houses," Jesus had said (verse 40). Teachers of the law lived off the gifts of supporters, and, then as now, the gullible poor made a tempting target.

⁴³Calling his disciples to him, Jesus said, "I tell you the truth, this poor widow has put more into the treasury than all the others. ⁴⁴They all gave

out of their wealth; but she, out of her poverty, put in everything—all she had to live on."

Signs of the End of the Age

▶ See Matthew 24:1–51; Luke 21:5–36

13 As he was leaving the temple, one of his disciples said to him, "Look, Teacher! What massive stones! What magnificent buildings!"

²"Do you see all these great buildings?" replied Jesus. "Not one stone here will be left on another; every one will be thrown down."

³As Jesus was sitting on the Mount of Olives opposite the temple, Peter, James, John and Andrew asked him privately, ⁴"Tell us, when will these things happen? And what will be the sign that they are all about to be fulfilled?"

⁵Jesus said to them: "Watch out that no one deceives you. ⁶Many will come in my name, claiming, 'I am he,' and will deceive many. ⁷When you hear of wars and rumors of wars, do not be alarmed. Such things must happen, but the end is still to come. ⁸Nation will rise against nation, and kingdom against kingdom. There will be earthquakes in various places, and famines. These are the beginning of birth pains.

⁹"You must be on your guard. You will be handed over to the local councils and flogged in the synagogues. On account of me you will stand before governors and kings as witnesses to them. ¹⁰And the gospel must first be preached to all

13:10 To All Nations

Preaching the gospel to all nations was probably a new thought to the disciples, who still thought in terms of a Messiah for the Jews. But some of them would spend the remainder of their lives making this prophecy come true.

nations. ¹¹Whenever you are arrested and brought to trial, do not worry beforehand about what to say. Just say whatever is given you at the time, for it is not you speaking, but the Holy Spirit.

¹²"Brother will betray brother to death, and a father his child. Children will rebel against their parents and have them put to death. ¹³All men will hate you because of me, but he who stands firm to the end will be saved.

¹⁴"When you see 'the abomination that causes desolation'*ᵉ* standing where it*ᶠ* does not belong—let the reader understand—then let those who are in Judea flee to the mountains. ¹⁵Let no one on the roof of his house go down or enter the house to take anything out. ¹⁶Let no one in the

field go back to get his cloak. ¹⁷How dreadful it will be in those days for pregnant women and nursing mothers! ¹⁸Pray that this will not take place in winter, ¹⁹because those will be days of distress unequaled from the beginning, when God created the world, until now—and never to be equaled again. ²⁰If the Lord had not cut short those days, no one would survive. But for the sake of the elect, whom he has chosen, he has shortened them. ²¹At that time if anyone says to you, 'Look, here is the Christ[a]!' or, 'Look, there he is!' do not believe it. ²²For false Christs and false prophets will appear and perform signs and miracles to deceive the elect—if that were possible. ²³So be on your guard; I have told you everything ahead of time.

²⁴"But in those days, following that distress,

"'the sun will be darkened,
  and the moon will not give its light;
²⁵the stars will fall from the sky,
  and the heavenly bodies will be shaken.'[b]

²⁶"At that time men will see the Son of Man coming in clouds with great power and glory. ²⁷And he will send his angels and gather his elect from the four winds, from the ends of the earth to the ends of the heavens.

²⁸"Now learn this lesson from the fig tree: As soon as its twigs get tender and its leaves come out, you know that summer is near. ²⁹Even so, when you see these things happening, you know that it is near, right at the door. ³⁰I tell you the truth, this generation[c] will certainly not pass away until all these things have happened. ³¹Heaven and earth will pass away, but my words will never pass away.

The Day and Hour Unknown

³²"No one knows about that day or hour, not even the angels in heaven, nor the Son, but only the Father. ³³Be on guard! Be alert[d]! You do not know when that time will come. ³⁴It's like a man going away: He leaves his house and puts his servants in charge, each with his assigned task, and tells the one at the door to keep watch.

³⁵"Therefore keep watch because you do not know when the owner of the house will come back—whether in the evening, or at midnight, or when the rooster crows, or at dawn. ³⁶If he comes suddenly, do not let him find you sleeping. ³⁷What I say to you, I say to everyone: 'Watch!'"

Jesus Anointed at Bethany

▶ See Matthew 26:2–16; Luke 22:1–6

14 Now the Passover and the Feast of Unleavened Bread were only two days away, and the chief priests and the teachers of the law were looking for some sly way to arrest Jesus and kill him. ²"But not during the Feast," they said, "or the people may riot."

³While he was in Bethany, reclining at the table in the home of a man known as Simon the

14:1 Festival Time in Jerusalem

The Passover, celebrating the Jews' deliverance from Egypt, was one of the high points of the Jewish calendar. All males older than age 12 went to Jerusalem for the holiday. Thus the city was filled with hundreds of thousands of pilgrims at the time of Jesus' death.

Leper, a woman came with an alabaster jar of very expensive perfume, made of pure nard. She broke the jar and poured the perfume on his head.

⁴Some of those present were saying indignantly to one another, "Why this waste of perfume? ⁵It could have been sold for more than a year's wages[e] and the money given to the poor." And they rebuked her harshly.

⁶"Leave her alone," said Jesus. "Why are you bothering her? She has done a beautiful thing to me. ⁷The poor you will always have with you, and you can help them any time you want. But you will not always have me. ⁸She did what she could. She poured perfume on my body beforehand to prepare for my burial. ⁹I tell you the truth, wherever the gospel is preached throughout the world, what she has done will also be told, in memory of her."

¹⁰Then Judas Iscariot, one of the Twelve, went to the chief priests to betray Jesus to them. ¹¹They were delighted to hear this and promised to give him money. So he watched for an opportunity to hand him over.

The Lord's Supper

▶ See Matthew 26:17–30; Luke 22:7–23

¹²On the first day of the Feast of Unleavened Bread, when it was customary to sacrifice the Passover lamb, Jesus' disciples asked him, "Where do you want us to go and make preparations for you to eat the Passover?"

¹³So he sent two of his disciples, telling them, "Go into the city, and a man carrying a jar of water will meet you. Follow him. ¹⁴Say to the owner of the house he enters, 'The Teacher asks: Where is my guest room, where I may eat the Passover with my disciples?' ¹⁵He will show you a large upper room, furnished and ready. Make preparations for us there."

¹⁶The disciples left, went into the city and

---

[a]21 Or *Messiah* [b]25 Isaiah 13:10; 34:4 [c]30 Or *race than three hundred denarii* [d]33 Some manuscripts *alert and pray* [e]5 Greek

found things just as Jesus had told them. So they prepared the Passover.

[17]When evening came, Jesus arrived with the Twelve. [18]While they were reclining at the table eating, he said, "I tell you the truth, one of you will betray me—one who is eating with me."

[19]They were saddened, and one by one they said to him, "Surely not I?"

[20]"It is one of the Twelve," he replied, "one who dips bread into the bowl with me. [21]The Son of Man will go just as it is written about him. But woe to that man who betrays the Son of Man! It would be better for him if he had not been born."

[22]While they were eating, Jesus took bread, gave thanks and broke it, and gave it to his disciples, saying, "Take it; this is my body."

14:22–26 Original Lord's Supper

Virtually all Christian churches celebrate the practice of Communion (Mass, Eucharist, or Lord's Supper) in some form. Matthew, Mark, and Luke each record the original Passover meal when Jesus instituted the practice.

[23]Then he took the cup, gave thanks and offered it to them, and they all drank from it.

[24]"This is my blood of the[a] covenant, which is poured out for many," he said to them. [25]"I tell you the truth, I will not drink again of the fruit of the vine until that day when I drink it anew in the kingdom of God."

[26]When they had sung a hymn, they went out to the Mount of Olives.

Jesus Predicts Peter's Denial

▶ *See Matthew 26:31–35*

[27]"You will all fall away," Jesus told them, "for it is written:

" 'I will strike the shepherd,
    and the sheep will be scattered.'[b]

[28]But after I have risen, I will go ahead of you into Galilee."

[29]Peter declared, "Even if all fall away, I will not."

[30]"I tell you the truth," Jesus answered, "today—yes, tonight—before the rooster crows twice[c] you yourself will disown me three times."

[31]But Peter insisted emphatically, "Even if I have to die with you, I will never disown you." And all the others said the same.

Gethsemane

▶ *See Matthew 26:36–46; Luke 22:40–46*

[32]They went to a place called Gethsemane, and

Jesus said to his disciples, "Sit here while I pray." [33]He took Peter, James and John along with him, and he began to be deeply distressed and troubled. [34]"My soul is overwhelmed with sorrow to

14:32 Seeking Privacy

Where to pray? The temple was crowded, and synagogues were reserved for public meetings. In order to find some privacy, Jesus would often rise early in the morning or spend all night in prayer. Luke reports that this garden was one of Jesus' favorite places (Luke 22:39).

the point of death," he said to them. "Stay here and keep watch."

[35]Going a little farther, he fell to the ground and prayed that if possible the hour might pass from him. [36]"Abba,[d] Father," he said, "everything is possible for you. Take this cup from me. Yet not what I will, but what you will."

[37]Then he returned to his disciples and found them sleeping. "Simon," he said to Peter, "are you asleep? Could you not keep watch for one hour? [38]Watch and pray so that you will not fall into temptation. The spirit is willing, but the body is weak."

[39]Once more he went away and prayed the same thing. [40]When he came back, he again found them sleeping, because their eyes were heavy. They did not know what to say to him.

[41]Returning the third time, he said to them, "Are you still sleeping and resting? Enough! The hour has come. Look, the Son of Man is betrayed into the hands of sinners. [42]Rise! Let us go! Here comes my betrayer!"

Jesus Arrested

▶ *See Matthew 26:47–56; Luke 22:47–50; John 18:3–11*

[43]Just as he was speaking, Judas, one of the Twelve, appeared. With him was a crowd armed with swords and clubs, sent from the chief priests, the teachers of the law, and the elders.

[44]Now the betrayer had arranged a signal with them: "The one I kiss is the man; arrest him and lead him away under guard." [45]Going at once to Jesus, Judas said, "Rabbi!" and kissed him. [46]The men seized Jesus and arrested him. [47]Then one of those standing near drew his sword and struck the servant of the high priest, cutting off his ear.

[48]"Am I leading a rebellion," said Jesus, "that you have come out with swords and clubs to capture me? [49]Every day I was with you, teaching in the temple courts, and you did not arrest me.

---

[a]24 Some manuscripts *the new*   [b]27 Zech. 13:7   [c]30 Some early manuscripts do not have *twice.*   [d]36 Aramaic for *Father*

But the Scriptures must be fulfilled." ⁵⁰Then everyone deserted him and fled.

⁵¹A young man, wearing nothing but a linen garment, was following Jesus. When they seized him, ⁵²he fled naked, leaving his garment behind.

14:51 The Anonymous Author?

Many scholars believe the young man in this verse was none other than Mark himself, author of this Gospel. Often, in ancient days, an author wouldn't use his name, but would plant a clue such as this (see John 21:24).

Before the Sanhedrin

▶ *See Matthew 26:57–68; John 18:12–13,19–24*

⁵³They took Jesus to the high priest, and all the chief priests, elders and teachers of the law came together. ⁵⁴Peter followed him at a distance, right into the courtyard of the high priest. There he sat with the guards and warmed himself at the fire.

⁵⁵The chief priests and the whole Sanhedrin were looking for evidence against Jesus so that they could put him to death, but they did not find any. ⁵⁶Many testified falsely against him, but their statements did not agree.

⁵⁷Then some stood up and gave this false testimony against him: ⁵⁸"We heard him say, 'I will destroy this man-made temple and in three days will build another, not made by man.'" ⁵⁹Yet even then their testimony did not agree.

⁶⁰Then the high priest stood up before them and asked Jesus, "Are you not going to answer? What is this testimony that these men are bringing against you?" ⁶¹But Jesus remained silent and gave no answer.

Again the high priest asked him, "Are you the Christ,ᵃ the Son of the Blessed One?"

⁶²"I am," said Jesus. "And you will see the Son of Man sitting at the right hand of the Mighty One and coming on the clouds of heaven."

⁶³The high priest tore his clothes. "Why do we need any more witnesses?" he asked. ⁶⁴"You have heard the blasphemy. What do you think?"

They all condemned him as worthy of death. ⁶⁵Then some began to spit at him; they blindfolded him, struck him with their fists, and said, "Prophesy!" And the guards took him and beat him.

Peter Disowns Jesus

▶ *See Matthew 26:69–75; Luke 22:56–62; John 18:16–18,25–27*

⁶⁶While Peter was below in the courtyard, one of the servant girls of the high priest came by.

⁶⁷When she saw Peter warming himself, she looked closely at him.

"You also were with that Nazarene, Jesus," she said.

⁶⁸But he denied it. "I don't know or understand what you're talking about," he said, and went out into the entryway.ᵇ

⁶⁹When the servant girl saw him there, she said again to those standing around, "This fellow is one of them." ⁷⁰Again he denied it.

After a little while, those standing near said to Peter, "Surely you are one of them, for you are a Galilean."

⁷¹He began to call down curses on himself, and he swore to them, "I don't know this man you're talking about."

⁷²Immediately the rooster crowed the second time.ᶜ Then Peter remembered the word Jesus had spoken to him: "Before the rooster crows twiceᵈ you will disown me three times." And he broke down and wept.

Jesus Before Pilate

▶ *See Matthew 27:11–26; Luke 23:2–3,18–25; John 18:29—19:16*

15 Very early in the morning, the chief priests, with the elders, the teachers of the law and the whole Sanhedrin, reached a decision. They bound Jesus, led him away and handed him over to Pilate.

15:1 Appeal for a Death Penalty

Roman law granted the Jews many freedoms, including the right to their Jewish court system, a council called the Sanhedrin. However, the Sanhedrin had no authority to order the death penalty. Seeking that sentence, Jesus' opponents sent him to Pilate, the Roman governor.

²"Are you the king of the Jews?" asked Pilate.

"Yes, it is as you say," Jesus replied.

³The chief priests accused him of many things. ⁴So again Pilate asked him, "Aren't you going to answer? See how many things they are accusing you of."

⁵But Jesus still made no reply, and Pilate was amazed.

⁶Now it was the custom at the Feast to release a prisoner whom the people requested. ⁷A man called Barabbas was in prison with the insurrectionists who had committed murder in the uprising. ⁸The crowd came up and asked Pilate to do for them what he usually did.

⁹"Do you want me to release to you the king

ᵃ61 Or *Messiah*   ᵇ68 Some early manuscripts *entryway and the rooster crowed*   ᶜ72 Some early manuscripts do not have *the second time.*   ᵈ72 Some early manuscripts do not have *twice.*

of the Jews?" asked Pilate, [10]knowing it was out of envy that the chief priests had handed Jesus over to him. [11]But the chief priests stirred up the crowd to have Pilate release Barabbas instead.

[12]"What shall I do, then, with the one you call the king of the Jews?" Pilate asked them.

[13]"Crucify him!" they shouted.

[14]"Why? What crime has he committed?" asked Pilate.

But they shouted all the louder, "Crucify him!"

[15]Wanting to satisfy the crowd, Pilate released Barabbas to them. He had Jesus flogged, and handed him over to be crucified.

The Soldiers Mock Jesus

▶ See Matthew 27:27–31

[16]The soldiers led Jesus away into the palace (that is, the Praetorium) and called together the whole company of soldiers. [17]They put a purple robe on him, then twisted together a crown of thorns and set it on him. [18]And they began to call out to him, "Hail, king of the Jews!" [19]Again and again they struck him on the head with a staff

---

The Day of Execution
The disciples were totally unprepared

EVENTS IN JESUS' LIFE—THE BIRTH in a manger, the death on a cross—can become so familiar that we miss the point. They're too close to us. In thinking about them, it sometimes helps to let the mind wander and search out whole new images.

A Bible study group was asked to suggest word images that might apply to Jesus. Common ones surfaced first: a shepherd, a lamb, a door. Then out of nowhere came a wildly different metaphor: "fireworks in reverse." Everyone turned, puzzled, to the middle-aged woman who had spoken.

"Think about it," she said. "Fireworks explode with brilliant, dazzling colors and loud noises . . . yet they start out in an ordinary-looking paper package. When God became a man, the opposite happened. The Creator of everything in the universe confined himself to an unimpressive human package."

> And when the centurion, who stood there in front of Jesus, heard his cry and saw how he died, he said, "Surely this man was the Son of God!" 15:39

When the Impossible Happened

No event in the life of Jesus fits the woman's metaphor better than his execution in Jerusalem. The idea was inconceivable, even to Jesus' closest followers. The Son of God die? How could this be?

Could the Creator of all things succumb to his creation? Disciples who had slogged through every other confrontation by his side now forsook him. It made no sense for Jesus, the Messiah, to die.

Not until later would other thoughts click into place: memories of Old Testament customs that hauntingly pointed to a cross, prophecies of a Messiah who was King but also a Suffering Servant (see Isaiah 53). To die was, after all, the central reason Jesus came to earth; he had insisted on that from the beginning.

The Most Important Week

Jesus' last week so impressed the disciples that the four chroniclers of his life, including Mark, devoted one-third of their space to that final week in Jerusalem. By the time they wrote it down, of course, they could see his death in a new light: as a mournful prelude to the greatest miracle of all, his resurrection.

Even so, nothing could erase the impact of those fear-filled, final days. When the eerie darkness had lifted and Jesus had breathed his last, the disciples had learned something profound about God, and about love.

Dorothy Sayers put it this way: "Whatever game He is playing with His creation, He has kept His own rules and played fair. He can exact nothing from man that He has not exacted from Himself. He has Himself gone through the whole of human experience, from the trivial irritations of family life and the cramping restriction of hard work and lack of money to the worst horrors of pain and humiliation, defeat, despair, and death. When He was a man, He played the man. He was born in poverty and died in disgrace and thought it well worthwhile" (from Christian Letters to a Post-Christian World).

At no other point in history did the fireworks appear so powerless as the day Jesus died. They had not yet been lit.

Life Questions: Put yourself in the disciples' place. How would you have responded to news of Jesus' death? Would you have believed in him still?

and spit on him. Falling on their knees, they paid homage to him. 20And when they had mocked him, they took off the purple robe and put his own clothes on him. Then they led him out to crucify him.

The Crucifixion

▶ *See Matthew 27:33–44; Luke 23:33–43; John 19:17–24*

21A certain man from Cyrene, Simon, the father of Alexander and Rufus, was passing by on his way in from the country, and they forced him to carry the cross. 22They brought Jesus to the place called Golgotha (which means The Place of the Skull). 23Then they offered him wine mixed with myrrh, but he did not take it. 24And they crucified him. Dividing up his clothes, they cast lots to see what each would get.

25It was the third hour when they crucified

15:25 Death Without Dignity

Romans reserved their cruelest form of execution—crucifixion—for slaves and the worst criminals. Skeletons of crucifixion victims show that thick nails were pounded through the wrist and heel bones. Death (from asphyxiation) usually took many hours or even several days.

him. 26The written notice of the charge against him read: THE KING OF THE JEWS. 27They crucified two robbers with him, one on his right and one on his left.a 29Those who passed by hurled insults at him, shaking their heads and saying, "So! You who are going to destroy the temple and build it in three days, 30come down from the cross and save yourself!"

31In the same way the chief priests and the teachers of the law mocked him among themselves. "He saved others," they said, "but he can't save himself! 32Let this Christ,b this King of Israel, come down now from the cross, that we may see and believe." Those crucified with him also heaped insults on him.

The Death of Jesus

▶ *See Matthew 27:45–56; Luke 23:44–49*

33At the sixth hour darkness came over the whole land until the ninth hour. 34And at the ninth hour Jesus cried out in a loud voice, *"Eloi, Eloi, lama sabachthani?"*—which means, "My God, my God, why have you forsaken me?"c

35When some of those standing near heard this, they said, "Listen, he's calling Elijah."

36One man ran, filled a sponge with wine vinegar, put it on a stick, and offered it to Jesus to drink. "Now leave him alone. Let's see if Elijah comes to take him down," he said.

37With a loud cry, Jesus breathed his last.

38The curtain of the temple was torn in two from top to bottom. 39And when the centurion, who stood there in front of Jesus, heard his cry andd saw how he died, he said, "Surely this man was the Sone of God!"

40Some women were watching from a distance. Among them were Mary Magdalene, Mary the mother of James the younger and of Joses, and Salome. 41In Galilee these women had followed him and cared for his needs. Many other women who had come up with him to Jerusalem were also there.

The Burial of Jesus

▶ *See Matthew 27:57–61; Luke 23:50–56; John 19:38–42*

42It was Preparation Day (that is, the day before the Sabbath). So as evening approached, 43Joseph of Arimathea, a prominent member of the Council, who was himself waiting for the kingdom of God, went boldly to Pilate and asked for Jesus' body. 44Pilate was surprised to hear that he was already dead. Summoning the centurion, he asked him if Jesus had already died. 45When he learned from the centurion that it was so, he gave the body to Joseph. 46So Joseph bought some linen cloth, took down the body, wrapped it in the linen, and placed it in a tomb cut out of rock. Then he rolled a stone against the entrance of the tomb. 47Mary Magdalene and Mary the mother of Joses saw where he was laid.

The Resurrection

▶ *See Matthew 28:1–8; Luke 24:1–10*

16 When the Sabbath was over, Mary Magdalene, Mary the mother of James, and

16:1 A Late Anointing

Jewish rules forbade handling dead bodies during the Sabbath. Because Jesus died during the Sabbath celebration, his friends and relatives couldn't properly embalm and prepare his body. They returned to the tomb later for this purpose, only to find the greatest surprise of their lives.

---

a27 Some manuscripts *left, 28and the scripture was fulfilled which says, "He was counted with the lawless ones"* (Isaiah 53:12)   b32 Or *Messiah*   c34 Psalm 22:1   d39 Some manuscripts do not have *heard his cry and*   e39 Or *a son*

Salome bought spices so that they might go to anoint Jesus' body. [2]Very early on the first day of the week, just after sunrise, they were on their way to the tomb [3]and they asked each other, "Who will roll the stone away from the entrance of the tomb?"

[4]But when they looked up, they saw that the stone, which was very large, had been rolled away. [5]As they entered the tomb, they saw a young man dressed in a white robe sitting on the right side, and they were alarmed.

[6]"Don't be alarmed," he said. "You are looking for Jesus the Nazarene, who was crucified. He has risen! He is not here. See the place where they laid him. [7]But go, tell his disciples and Peter, 'He is going ahead of you into Galilee. There you will see him, just as he told you.'"

16:7 . . . and Peter

The messenger who informed the women about Jesus' resurrection pointedly asked them to tell "his disciples and Peter," singling out the disciple who had vehemently denied Jesus. John 21 records a further, moving scene in which Jesus specifically reinstated Peter.

[8]Trembling and bewildered, the women went out and fled from the tomb. They said nothing to anyone, because they were afraid.

[The earliest manuscripts and some other ancient witnesses do not have Mark 16:9–20.]

[9]When Jesus rose early on the first day of the week, he appeared first to Mary Magdalene, out of whom he had driven seven demons. [10]She went and told those who had been with him and who were mourning and weeping. [11]When they heard that Jesus was alive and that she had seen him, they did not believe it.

[12]Afterward Jesus appeared in a different form to two of them while they were walking in the country. [13]These returned and reported it to the rest; but they did not believe them either.

[14]Later Jesus appeared to the Eleven as they were eating; he rebuked them for their lack of faith and their stubborn refusal to believe those who had seen him after he had risen.

[15]He said to them, "Go into all the world and preach the good news to all creation. [16]Whoever believes and is baptized will be saved, but whoever does not believe will be condemned. [17]And these signs will accompany those who believe: In my name they will drive out demons; they will speak in new tongues; [18]they will pick up snakes with their hands; and when they drink deadly poison, it will not hurt them at all; they will place their hands on sick people, and they will get well."

[19]After the Lord Jesus had spoken to them, he was taken up into heaven and he sat at the right hand of God. [20]Then the disciples went out and preached everywhere, and the Lord worked with them and confirmed his word by the signs that accompanied it.

Like a Joy-filled Musical
Something was brewing on planet Earth

ALTHOUGH LUKE COVERS THE SAME basic territory as Matthew and Mark, he gives away his own slant in the very first chapters. Matthew begins with a formal family genealogy; Mark opens with a bleached desert scene. In contrast, Luke describes a hearty celebration.

The way Luke tells it, events surrounding Jesus' birth resembled a joy-filled musical. Characters crowded into the scene: a white-haired great-uncle, an astonished virgin, a tottery old prophetess. They all smiled broadly and, as likely as not, burst into song.

Once Mary had recovered from the shock of seeing an angel, she let loose with a beautiful hymn. The old priest Zechariah broke nine months of muteness with a rousing poem, and even the unborn John the Baptist kicked for joy inside his mother's womb (1:44). When Jesus finally made an entrance, in an inconspicuous stable, the sky filled with singing angels. Clearly, something was brewing on planet Earth.

> *But the angel said to them, "Do not be afraid. I bring you good news of great joy that will be for all the people."*
> *2:10*

History Split in Two

You get the feeling when you read his account that Luke wanted to capture in words the spirit of "great joy" that the angel predicted (2:10). Among dreary, defeated villagers in a remote corner of the Roman empire, something climactically good was bursting out.

The author tells us (1:1–4) that he researched many accounts of Jesus' life. Intimate details in these first two chapters show he relied heavily on eyewitnesses, for no other Gospel writer picked up so many facts. Careful attention to detail and an undergirding tone of joy characterize Luke's book.

Jesus' birth literally split history into two parts; we memorialize the event whenever we write a date. The book of Luke takes us back to the world before there was an A.D. or B.C., when Jesus' life was just beginning.

Even now, almost 2,000 years later, the commemoration of Jesus' birth still gives cause for joy. We eat better during the Christmas season, buy gifts for others, donate to charity, and sing more often. Our feelings of celebration are gentle aftershocks, reminders of the remarkable moment when God became a man and lived on earth.

How to Read Luke

Luke probably did not know Jesus personally. But as a dedicated convert in the early church, he accompanied the apostle Paul on missionary trips. In three of his letters, Paul refers to Luke with great affection.

As he mentions in his introduction, Luke eventually saw the need to draw up a carefully researched account of the life of Christ. Many accounts of varying quality existed then, but Luke set out to interview eyewitnesses and compose a thoughtful summary. His book shows thoroughness and detail. It starts before Jesus' birth, and ends with his ascension into heaven.

You should find Luke a very appealing book to read. Luke was a gifted writer, and the stories he recorded have won their place among the classics of literature: the Good Samaritan, the Lost Son, the Rich Man and Lazarus. If Mark is a Gospel of action, Luke is a Gospel of relationships. It contains very good character descriptions.

Look for the many different ethnic, religious, economic, and social groups in Luke. Think of the diverse groups in a country like the United States today. How do you think each of them would respond to Jesus in the flesh?

Note especially two large sections of Luke that present material found nowhere else: chapters 1–2 and chapters 10–19.

PEOPLE YOU'LL MEET IN LUKE

ELIZABETH AND ZECHARIAH (p. 1062)
MARY, MOTHER OF JESUS (p. 1064)
MARTHA AND MARY OF BETHANY (p. 1079)

3-TRACK READING PLAN

For an explanation and complete listing of the 3-track reading plan, turn to page 7.

TRACK 1: *Two-Week Courses on the Bible*
The Track 1 reading program on the Life and Teachings of Jesus includes four chapters from Luke. See page 7 for a complete listing of this course.

TRACK 2: *An Overview of Luke in 8 Days*
Over the next eight days, read from the material that's found in no other Gospel but Luke's.

☐ Day 1. Read the Introduction to Luke and then Luke's account in chapter 1 of the events preceding Jesus' birth.
☐ Day 2. Read the familiar Christmas passage, chapter 2.
☐ Day 3. Read chapter 10, which includes the parable of the Good Samaritan.
☐ Day 4. Read chapter 12, in which Jesus draws a strong contrast between those who trust him, no matter how poor, and haughty rich people.
☐ Day 5. Read the famous parables, or short stories, that Jesus tells in chapter 15.
☐ Day 6. Read chapter 16's two familiar stories: the shrewd manager and the rich man and Lazarus.
☐ Day 7. Read chapter 18.
☐ Day 8. How did Jesus' disciples react to his resurrection? Read a good description in chapter 24.

Now turn to page 9 for your next Track 2 reading project.

TRACK 3: *All of Luke in 24 Days*
After you have read through Luke, turn to pages 10–14 for your next Track 3 reading project.

☐1   ☐2   ☐3   ☐4   ☐5   ☐6   ☐7   ☐8
☐9   ☐10   ☐11   ☐12   ☐13   ☐14   ☐15   ☐16
☐17   ☐18   ☐19   ☐20   ☐21   ☐22   ☐23   ☐24

Introduction

1 Many have undertaken to draw up an account of the things that have been fulfilled[a] among us, ²just as they were handed down to us by those who from the first were eyewitnesses and servants of the word. ³Therefore, since I myself have carefully investigated everything from the beginning, it seemed good also to me to write an orderly account for you, most excellent Theophilus, ⁴so that you may know the certainty of the things you have been taught.

The Birth of John the Baptist Foretold

⁵In the time of Herod king of Judea there was a priest named Zechariah, who belonged to the priestly division of Abijah; his wife Elizabeth was also a descendant of Aaron. ⁶Both of them were upright in the sight of God, observing all the

a 1 Or been surely believed

Lord's commandments and regulations blamelessly. 7But they had no children, because Elizabeth was barren; and they were both well along in years.

8Once when Zechariah's division was on duty and he was serving as priest before God, 9he was chosen by lot, according to the custom of the priesthood, to go into the temple of the Lord and burn incense. 10And when the time for the burning of incense came, all the assembled worshipers were praying outside.

> ## 1:3 Luke the Historian
>
> *A historian looks for original sources of information—people who were personally involved in the events being described. Luke doesn't claim to be an eyewitness himself, but he had carefully interviewed many who were. As the apostle Paul's traveling companion, Luke must have met many such sources. The Gospel of Luke is the first of a two-part work; the book of Acts continues the story.*

11Then an angel of the Lord appeared to him, standing at the right side of the altar of incense. 12When Zechariah saw him, he was startled and was gripped with fear. 13But the angel said to him: "Do not be afraid, Zechariah; your prayer has been heard. Your wife Elizabeth will bear you a son, and you are to give him the name John. 14He will be a joy and delight to you, and many will rejoice because of his birth, 15for he will be great in the sight of the Lord. He is never to take wine or other fermented drink, and he will be filled with the Holy Spirit even from birth.*a* 16Many of the people of Israel will he bring back to the Lord their God. 17And he will go on before the Lord, in the spirit and power of Elijah, to turn the hearts of the fathers to their children and the disobedient to the wisdom of the righteous—to make ready a people prepared for the Lord."

18Zechariah asked the angel, "How can I be sure of this? I am an old man and my wife is well along in years."

19The angel answered, "I am Gabriel. I stand in the presence of God, and I have been sent to speak to you and to tell you this good news. 20And now you will be silent and not able to speak until the day this happens, because you did not believe my words, which will come true at their proper time."

21Meanwhile, the people were waiting for Zechariah and wondering why he stayed so long in the temple. 22When he came out, he could not speak to them. They realized he had seen a vision in the temple, for he kept making signs to them but remained unable to speak.

23When his time of service was completed, he returned home. 24After this his wife Elizabeth became pregnant and for five months remained in seclusion. 25"The Lord has done this for me," she said. "In these days he has shown his favor and taken away my disgrace among the people."

a 15 Or from his mother's womb

ELIZABETH AND ZECHARIAH *End of an Era*

"THE END OF AN ERA," people say when a retiring coach hands over his clipboard to a young assistant. Similarly, when a new president, a new pastor or a new principal moves in, one era ends and another begins. As fresh faces take over, new ways surely follow.

Elizabeth and Zechariah were among the very first to sense the change that came with Jesus. Devout believers from priestly families, they represented the best of the old order. They had devoted many years to serving God under the Old Testament law. Yet a cloud of sadness hung over their lives, for they were growing old and the greatest blessing they could imagine had been denied them. Childless, they knew their line would die out when they passed away.

Then the new era abruptly broke in. One day as Zechariah was performing his duties in the temple, an angel brought some astounding news: He would have a son! Zechariah, long past the age of parenthood, asked for proof and got perhaps more than he bargained for (1:20).

A short while later a relative of Elizabeth's named Mary brought even greater news. The Messiah, the Savior the Jews had been longing for, was on the way! Not only had God answered Elizabeth's and Zechariah's personal prayers, their nation's long waiting would soon come to an end as well.

Soon the old priest Zechariah and his elderly wife Elizabeth were bringing up the young and vigorous John the Baptist, a true original who would prepare the way for Jesus. With unusual foresight, the old couple greeted the new era with joy. In it they saw not the loss of their old order, but the fulfillment of their dreams.

Life Questions: Think of a time in your life when an 'old era' ended and something quite new began: a move, a marriage, a new job or perhaps an experience with God. What made the change difficult? What made it joyful? How was God involved?

The Birth of Jesus Foretold

²⁶In the sixth month, God sent the angel Gabriel to Nazareth, a town in Galilee, ²⁷to a virgin pledged to be married to a man named Joseph, a descendant of David. The virgin's name was Mary. ²⁸The angel went to her and said, "Greetings, you who are highly favored! The Lord is with you."

²⁹Mary was greatly troubled at his words and wondered what kind of greeting this might be. ³⁰But the angel said to her, "Do not be afraid, Mary, you have found favor with God. ³¹You will be with child and give birth to a son, and you are to give him the name Jesus. ³²He will be great and will be called the Son of the Most High. The Lord God will give him the throne of his father David, ³³and he will reign over the house of Jacob forever; his kingdom will never end."

³⁴"How will this be," Mary asked the angel, "since I am a virgin?"

³⁵The angel answered, "The Holy Spirit will come upon you, and the power of the Most High will overshadow you. So the holy one to be born will be called^a the Son of God. ³⁶Even Elizabeth your relative is going to have a child in her old age, and she who was said to be barren is in her sixth month. ³⁷For nothing is impossible with God."

³⁸"I am the Lord's servant," Mary answered. "May it be to me as you have said." Then the angel left her.

Mary Visits Elizabeth

³⁹At that time Mary got ready and hurried to a town in the hill country of Judea, ⁴⁰where she entered Zechariah's home and greeted Elizabeth. ⁴¹When Elizabeth heard Mary's greeting, the baby leaped in her womb, and Elizabeth was filled with the Holy Spirit. ⁴²In a loud voice she exclaimed: "Blessed are you among women, and blessed is the child you will bear! ⁴³But why am I so favored, that the mother of my Lord should come to me? ⁴⁴As soon as the sound of your greeting reached my ears, the baby in my womb leaped for joy. ⁴⁵Blessed is she who has believed that what the Lord has said to her will be accomplished!"

Mary's Song

▶ See 1 Samuel 2:1–10

⁴⁶And Mary said:

"My soul glorifies the Lord
⁴⁷   and my spirit rejoices in God my Savior,
⁴⁸for he has been mindful
    of the humble state of his servant.
From now on all generations will call me
    blessed,

⁴⁹   for the Mighty One has done great things
        for me—
    holy is his name.
⁵⁰His mercy extends to those who fear him,
    from generation to generation.
⁵¹He has performed mighty deeds with his
        arm;
    he has scattered those who are proud in
        their inmost thoughts.
⁵²He has brought down rulers from their
        thrones
    but has lifted up the humble.
⁵³He has filled the hungry with good things
    but has sent the rich away empty.
⁵⁴He has helped his servant Israel,
    remembering to be merciful
⁵⁵to Abraham and his descendants forever,
    even as he said to our fathers."

⁵⁶Mary stayed with Elizabeth for about three months and then returned home.

The Birth of John the Baptist

⁵⁷When it was time for Elizabeth to have her baby, she gave birth to a son. ⁵⁸Her neighbors and relatives heard that the Lord had shown her great mercy, and they shared her joy.

⁵⁹On the eighth day they came to circumcise the child, and they were going to name him after his father Zechariah, ⁶⁰but his mother spoke up and said, "No! He is to be called John."

⁶¹They said to her, "There is no one among your relatives who has that name."

⁶²Then they made signs to his father, to find out what he would like to name the child. ⁶³He asked for a writing tablet, and to everyone's astonishment he wrote, "His name is John." ⁶⁴Immediately his mouth was opened and his tongue was loosed, and he began to speak, praising God. ⁶⁵The neighbors were all filled with awe, and throughout the hill country of Judea people were talking about all these things. ⁶⁶Everyone who heard this wondered about it, asking, "What then is this child going to be?" For the Lord's hand was with him.

Zechariah's Song

⁶⁷His father Zechariah was filled with the Holy Spirit and prophesied:

⁶⁸"Praise be to the Lord, the God of Israel,
    because he has come and has redeemed
        his people.
⁶⁹He has raised up a horn^b of salvation for us
    in the house of his servant David
⁷⁰(as he said through his holy prophets of long
        ago),
⁷¹salvation from our enemies
    and from the hand of all who hate us—

---

^a35 Or *So the child to be born will be called holy,*   ^b69 *Horn* here symbolizes strength.

72to show mercy to our fathers
  and to remember his holy covenant,
73 the oath he swore to our father Abraham:
74to rescue us from the hand of our enemies,
  and to enable us to serve him without fear
75 in holiness and righteousness before him
  all our days.

76And you, my child, will be called a prophet
    of the Most High;
  for you will go on before the Lord to
    prepare the way for him,
77to give his people the knowledge of salvation
    through the forgiveness of their sins,
78because of the tender mercy of our God,
  by which the rising sun will come to us
    from heaven
79to shine on those living in darkness
  and in the shadow of death,
  to guide our feet into the path of peace."

80And the child grew and became strong in spirit; and he lived in the desert until he appeared publicly to Israel.

The Birth of Jesus

In those days Caesar Augustus issued a decree that a census should be taken of the entire Roman world. 2(This was the first census that took place while Quirinius was governor of Syria.) 3And everyone went to his own town to register.

4So Joseph also went up from the town of Nazareth in Galilee to Judea, to Bethlehem the town of David, because he belonged to the house and line of David. 5He went there to register with Mary, who was pledged to be married to him and was expecting a child. 6While they were there, the time came for the baby to be born, 7and she gave birth to her firstborn, a son. She wrapped him in cloths and placed him in a manger, because there was no room for them in the inn.

The Shepherds and the Angels

8And there were shepherds living out in the

2:1 Dating by Emperors

Among biblical writers, only Luke dated the events he wrote about by referring to Roman emperors. He had determined (1:1–4) to write a thorough, factual account of Jesus' life, which included setting the events in historical context. Because of the Roman census mentioned here, Mary had to travel from her hometown in a very advanced state of pregnancy. As a result, the Messiah was born in Bethlehem, fulfilling an ancient prophecy.

fields nearby, keeping watch over their flocks at night. 9An angel of the Lord appeared to them, and the glory of the Lord shone around them, and they were terrified. 10But the angel said to them, "Do not be afraid. I bring you good news of great joy that will be for all the people. 11Today in the town of David a Savior has been born to you; he is Christ*a* the Lord. 12This will be a sign to you: You will find a baby wrapped in cloths and lying in a manger."

13Suddenly a great company of the heavenly host appeared with the angel, praising God and saying,

14"Glory to God in the highest,
    and on earth peace to men on whom his
      favor rests."

a 11 Or Messiah. "The Christ" (Greek) and "the Messiah" (Hebrew) both mean "the Anointed One"; also in verse 26.

MARY, MOTHER OF JESUS *Saying Yes to God*

MARY RECEIVED THE GREATEST HONOR God can pay: He chose her to mother his son. Probably a teenager at the time, Mary had done nothing to deserve such favor. Yet her simple response spoke deeply of her humble faith. "I am the Lord's servant . . . May it be to me as you have said" (Luke 1:38). Without hesitation, Mary said yes to God's plan to take over her life.

Saying yes to God usually involves sacrifice. It did for Mary, who endured the doubts of her fiancé and the scorn of neighbors who saw her pregnant before marriage. Saying yes meant bearing the pain of childbirth. It meant fleeing to far-off Egypt to protect her baby from Herod's soldiers. It meant raising a child she did not completely understand. (Once during his ministry she came to take charge of Jesus, thinking him out of his mind [Mark 3:21].) Most of all, it meant watching her son die on the cross.

Our last glimpse of Mary, though, shows her among the disciples after the resurrection, praying for the Holy Spirit Jesus had promised (Acts 1:14). Mary had begun her relationship with Jesus by holding his tiny form in her arms. In the end she realized she must let Jesus hold her. He was not only her child, he was her Lord. To that, too, Mary said yes.

Life Questions: To what is God asking you to say yes? What sacrifice may be involved?

¹⁵When the angels had left them and gone into heaven, the shepherds said to one another, "Let's go to Bethlehem and see this thing that has happened, which the Lord has told us about."

¹⁶So they hurried off and found Mary and Joseph, and the baby, who was lying in the manger. ¹⁷When they had seen him, they spread the

2:16 Cast of Characters

If a public relations firm planned the introduction of God's Son on earth, whom would they invite? Certainly not the group Luke introduces. No Roman emperor or Greek philosopher attended. Instead, Luke tells of an obscure priest and his wife, a carpenter and his young fiancée, a group of shepherds, and two elderly people. Jesus never had much to do with the high and mighty, except during his trial and execution. He would change the world through the lives of ordinary people.

word concerning what had been told them about this child, ¹⁸ and all who heard it were amazed at what the shepherds said to them. ¹⁹ But Mary treasured up all these things and pondered them in her heart. ²⁰ The shepherds returned, glorifying and praising God for all the things they had heard and seen, which were just as they had been told.

Jesus Presented in the Temple

²¹On the eighth day, when it was time to circumcise him, he was named Jesus, the name the angel had given him before he had been conceived.

²²When the time of their purification according to the Law of Moses had been completed, Joseph and Mary took him to Jerusalem to present him to the Lord ²³(as it is written in the Law of the Lord, "Every firstborn male is to be consecrated to the Lord"ᵃ), ²⁴and to offer a sacrifice in keeping with what is said in the Law of the Lord: "a pair of doves or two young pigeons."ᵇ

²⁵Now there was a man in Jerusalem called Simeon, who was righteous and devout. He was waiting for the consolation of Israel, and the Holy Spirit was upon him. ²⁶It had been revealed to him by the Holy Spirit that he would not die before he had seen the Lord's Christ. ²⁷Moved by the Spirit, he went into the temple courts. When the parents brought in the child Jesus to do for him what the custom of the Law required, ²⁸Simeon took him in his arms and praised God, saying:

²⁹"Sovereign Lord, as you have promised,
    you now dismissᶜ your servant in peace.

³⁰For my eyes have seen your salvation,
³¹   which you have prepared in the sight of
        all people,
³²a light for revelation to the Gentiles
    and for glory to your people Israel."

³³The child's father and mother marveled at what was said about him. ³⁴Then Simeon blessed them and said to Mary, his mother: "This child is destined to cause the falling and rising of many in Israel, and to be a sign that will be spoken against, ³⁵so that the thoughts of many hearts will be revealed. And a sword will pierce your own soul too."

³⁶There was also a prophetess, Anna, the daughter of Phanuel, of the tribe of Asher. She was very old; she had lived with her husband seven years after her marriage, ³⁷and then was a widow until she was eighty-four.ᵈ She never left the temple but worshiped night and day, fasting and praying. ³⁸Coming up to them at that very moment, she gave thanks to God and spoke about the child to all who were looking forward to the redemption of Jerusalem.

³⁹When Joseph and Mary had done everything required by the Law of the Lord, they returned to Galilee to their own town of Nazareth. ⁴⁰And the child grew and became strong; he was filled with wisdom, and the grace of God was upon him.

The Boy Jesus at the Temple

⁴¹Every year his parents went to Jerusalem for

2:41 Jesus' Childhood

Most Christmas pageants rely heavily on Luke because of his thoroughness in reporting the facts of Jesus' birth. And only Luke recorded the brief glimpses of Jesus' early years given in this chapter. For this reason, many scholars believe Luke must have interviewed Mary, mother of Jesus, during his investigations into Jesus' life.

the Feast of the Passover. ⁴²When he was twelve years old, they went up to the Feast, according to the custom. ⁴³After the Feast was over, while his parents were returning home, the boy Jesus stayed behind in Jerusalem, but they were unaware of it. ⁴⁴Thinking he was in their company, they traveled on for a day. Then they began looking for him among their relatives and friends. ⁴⁵When they did not find him, they went back to Jerusalem to look for him. ⁴⁶After three days they found him in the temple courts, sitting among the teachers, listening to them and asking them questions. ⁴⁷Everyone who heard him was amazed at his understanding and his answers. ⁴⁸When his parents saw him, they were aston-

---

ᵃ23 Exodus 13:2,12   ᵇ24 Lev. 12:8   ᶜ29 Or *promised, / now dismiss*   ᵈ37 Or *widow for eighty-four years*

ished. His mother said to him, "Son, why have you treated us like this? Your father and I have been anxiously searching for you."

49"Why were you searching for me?" he asked. "Didn't you know I had to be in my Father's house?" 50But they did not understand what he was saying to them.

51Then he went down to Nazareth with them and was obedient to them. But his mother treasured all these things in her heart. 52And Jesus grew in wisdom and stature, and in favor with God and men.

John the Baptist Prepares the Way

▶ *See Matthew 3:1–10; Mark 1:3–5*

3 In the fifteenth year of the reign of Tiberius Caesar—when Pontius Pilate was governor of Judea, Herod tetrarch of Galilee, his brother Philip tetrarch of Iturea and Traconitis, and Lysanias tetrarch of Abilene— 2during the high priesthood of Annas and Caiaphas, the word of God came to John son of Zechariah in the desert. 3He went into all the country around the Jordan, preaching a baptism of repentance for the forgiveness of sins. 4As is written in the book of the words of Isaiah the prophet:

"A voice of one calling in the desert,
'Prepare the way for the Lord,
  make straight paths for him.
5Every valley shall be filled in,
  every mountain and hill made low.
The crooked roads shall become straight,
  the rough ways smooth.
6And all mankind will see God's salvation.'"*a*

7John said to the crowds coming out to be baptized by him, "You brood of vipers! Who warned you to flee from the coming wrath? 8Produce fruit in keeping with repentance. And do not begin to say to yourselves, 'We have Abraham as our father.' For I tell you that out of these stones God can raise up children for Abraham. 9The ax is already at the root of the trees, and every tree that does not produce good fruit will be cut down and thrown into the fire."

10"What should we do then?" the crowd asked.

11John answered, "The man with two tunics should share with him who has none, and the one who has food should do the same."

12Tax collectors also came to be baptized. "Teacher," they asked, "what should we do?"

13"Don't collect any more than you are required to," he told them.

14Then some soldiers asked him, "And what should we do?"

He replied, "Don't extort money and don't accuse people falsely—be content with your pay."

15The people were waiting expectantly and were all wondering in their hearts if John might possibly be the Christ.*b* 16John answered them all, "I baptize you with*c* water. But one more powerful than I will come, the thongs of whose sandals I am not worthy to untie. He will baptize you with the Holy Spirit and with fire. 17His winnowing fork is in his hand to clear his threshing floor and to gather the wheat into his barn, but he will burn up the chaff with unquenchable fire." 18And with many other words John exhorted the people and preached the good news to them.

19But when John rebuked Herod the tetrarch because of Herodias, his brother's wife, and all the other evil things he had done, 20Herod added this to them all: He locked John up in prison.

The Baptism and Genealogy of Jesus

▶ *See Matthew 1:1–17; 3:13–17; Mark 1:9–11*

21When all the people were being baptized, Jesus was baptized too. And as he was praying, heaven was opened 22and the Holy Spirit descended on him in bodily form like a dove. And a voice came from heaven: "You are my Son, whom I love; with you I am well pleased."

23Now Jesus himself was about thirty years old when he began his ministry. He was the son, so it was thought, of Joseph,

the son of Heli, 24the son of Matthat,
the son of Levi, the son of Melki,
the son of Jannai, the son of Joseph,
25the son of Mattathias, the son of Amos,
the son of Nahum, the son of Esli,
the son of Naggai, 26the son of Maath,
the son of Mattathias, the son of Semein,
the son of Josech, the son of Joda,
27the son of Joanan, the son of Rhesa,
the son of Zerubbabel, the son of Shealtiel,
the son of Neri, 28the son of Melki,
the son of Addi, the son of Cosam,
the son of Elmadam, the son of Er,
29the son of Joshua, the son of Eliezer,
the son of Jorim, the son of Matthat,
the son of Levi, 30the son of Simeon,
the son of Judah, the son of Joseph,
the son of Jonam, the son of Eliakim,
31the son of Melea, the son of Menna,
the son of Mattatha, the son of Nathan,
the son of David, 32the son of Jesse,
the son of Obed, the son of Boaz,
the son of Salmon,*d* the son of Nahshon,
33the son of Amminadab, the son of Ram,*e*
the son of Hezron, the son of Perez,
the son of Judah, 34the son of Jacob,

a6 Isaiah 40:3-5   *b15* Or *Messiah*   *c16* Or *in*   *d32* Some early manuscripts *Sala*   *e33* Some manuscripts *Amminadab, the son of Admin, the son of Arni*; other manuscripts vary widely.

the son of Isaac, the son of Abraham,
the son of Terah, the son of Nahor,
35the son of Serug, the son of Reu,
the son of Peleg, the son of Eber,
the son of Shelah, 36the son of Cainan,
the son of Arphaxad, the son of Shem,
the son of Noah, the son of Lamech,
37the son of Methuselah, the son of Enoch,
the son of Jared, the son of Mahalalel,
the son of Kenan, 38the son of Enosh,
the son of Seth, the son of Adam,
the son of God.

3:38 A Gospel for the Gentiles

Matthew's Gospel traced Jesus' roots back to Abraham, father of the Jewish race. But Luke, probably the only Gentile writer of the New Testament, emphasized that Jesus' good news was for all people, not just the Jews. In keeping with that purpose, he carried Jesus' lineage all the way back to the first man, Adam.

The Temptation of Jesus

▶ *See Matthew 4:1–11; Mark 1:12–13*

4 Jesus, full of the Holy Spirit, returned from the Jordan and was led by the Spirit in the desert, 2where for forty days he was tempted by the devil. He ate nothing during those days, and at the end of them he was hungry.

3The devil said to him, "If you are the Son of God, tell this stone to become bread."

4Jesus answered, "It is written: 'Man does not live on bread alone.'[a]"

5The devil led him up to a high place and showed him in an instant all the kingdoms of the world. 6And he said to him, "I will give you all their authority and splendor, for it has been given to me, and I can give it to anyone I want to. 7So if you worship me, it will all be yours."

8Jesus answered, "It is written: 'Worship the Lord your God and serve him only.'[b]"

9The devil led him to Jerusalem and had him stand on the highest point of the temple. "If you are the Son of God," he said, "throw yourself down from here. 10For it is written:

" 'He will command his angels concerning you
to guard you carefully;
11they will lift you up in their hands,
so that you will not strike your foot against a stone.'[c]"

12Jesus answered, "It says: 'Do not put the Lord your God to the test.'[d]"

13When the devil had finished all this tempting, he left him until an opportune time.

Jesus Rejected at Nazareth

14Jesus returned to Galilee in the power of the Spirit, and news about him spread through the whole countryside. 15He taught in their synagogues, and everyone praised him.

16He went to Nazareth, where he had been brought up, and on the Sabbath day he went into the synagogue, as was his custom. And he stood up to read. 17The scroll of the prophet Isaiah was handed to him. Unrolling it, he found the place where it is written:

18"The Spirit of the Lord is on me,
because he has anointed me
to preach good news to the poor.
He has sent me to proclaim freedom for the prisoners
and recovery of sight for the blind,
to release the oppressed,
19 to proclaim the year of the Lord's favor."[e]

20Then he rolled up the scroll, gave it back to the attendant and sat down. The eyes of everyone in the synagogue were fastened on him, 21and he began by saying to them, "Today this scripture is fulfilled in your hearing."

22All spoke well of him and were amazed at the gracious words that came from his lips. "Isn't this Joseph's son?" they asked.

23Jesus said to them, "Surely you will quote this proverb to me: 'Physician, heal yourself! Do here in your hometown what we have heard that you did in Capernaum.'"

24"I tell you the truth," he continued, "no prophet is accepted in his hometown. 25I assure you that there were many widows in Israel in Elijah's time, when the sky was shut for three and a half years and there was a severe famine

4:26 Hard Words for the Jews

Luke's book stresses the universal appeal of the gospel. In both of these Old Testament stories (the Zarephath widow and Naaman), God sent a prophet to perform a miracle for foreigners (non-Jews). Such an emphasis scandalized the Jews, who saw themselves as God's uniquely chosen people. Jesus' words proved so inflammatory that a mob attempted to kill him. As far as is known, Jesus never returned to his home territory of Nazareth.

a4 Deut. 8:3   b8 Deut. 6:13   c11 Psalm 91:11,12   d12 Deut. 6:16   e19 Isaiah 61:1,2

throughout the land. [26]Yet Elijah was not sent to any of them, but to a widow in Zarephath in the region of Sidon. [27]And there were many in Israel with leprosy[a] in the time of Elisha the prophet, yet not one of them was cleansed—only Naaman the Syrian."

[28]All the people in the synagogue were furious when they heard this. [29]They got up, drove him out of the town, and took him to the brow of the hill on which the town was built, in order to throw him down the cliff. [30]But he walked right through the crowd and went on his way.

Jesus Drives Out an Evil Spirit

[31]Then he went down to Capernaum, a town in Galilee, and on the Sabbath began to teach the people. [32]They were amazed at his teaching, because his message had authority.

[33]In the synagogue there was a man possessed by a demon, an evil[b] spirit. He cried out at the top of his voice, [34]"Ha! What do you want with us, Jesus of Nazareth? Have you come to destroy us? I know who you are—the Holy One of God!"

[35]"Be quiet!" Jesus said sternly. "Come out of him!" Then the demon threw the man down before them all and came out without injuring him.

[36]All the people were amazed and said to each other, "What is this teaching? With authority and power he gives orders to evil spirits and they come out!" [37]And the news about him spread throughout the surrounding area.

Jesus Heals Many

▶ See Matthew 8:14–17; Mark 1:29–38

[38]Jesus left the synagogue and went to the home of Simon. Now Simon's mother-in-law was suffering from a high fever, and they asked Jesus to help her. [39]So he bent over her and rebuked the fever, and it left her. She got up at once and began to wait on them.

[40]When the sun was setting, the people brought to Jesus all who had various kinds of sickness, and laying his hands on each one, he healed them. [41]Moreover, demons came out of many people, shouting, "You are the Son of God!" But he rebuked them and would not allow them to speak, because they knew he was the Christ.[c]

[42]At daybreak Jesus went out to a solitary place. The people were looking for him and when they came to where he was, they tried to keep him from leaving them. [43]But he said, "I must preach the good news of the kingdom of God to the other towns also, because that is why I was sent." [44]And he kept on preaching in the synagogues of Judea.[d]

The Calling of the First Disciples

▶ See Matthew 4:18–22; Mark 1:16–20; John 1:40–42

5 One day as Jesus was standing by the Lake of Gennesaret,[e] with the people crowding around him and listening to the word of God, [2]he saw at the water's edge two boats, left there by the fishermen, who were washing their nets. [3]He got into one of the boats, the one belonging to Simon, and asked him to put out a little from shore. Then he sat down and taught the people from the boat.

[4]When he had finished speaking, he said to Simon, "Put out into deep water, and let down[f] the nets for a catch."

[5]Simon answered, "Master, we've worked hard all night and haven't caught anything. But because you say so, I will let down the nets."

[6]When they had done so, they caught such a large number of fish that their nets began to break. [7]So they signaled their partners in the other boat to come and help them, and they came and filled both boats so full that they began to sink.

[8]When Simon Peter saw this, he fell at Jesus' knees and said, "Go away from me, Lord; I am a sinful man!" [9]For he and all his companions were astonished at the catch of fish they had taken, [10]and so were James and John, the sons of Zebedee, Simon's partners.

Then Jesus said to Simon, "Don't be afraid; from now on you will catch men." [11]So they pulled their boats up on shore, left everything and followed him.

The Man With Leprosy

▶ See Matthew 8:2–4; Mark 1:40–44

[12]While Jesus was in one of the towns, a man came along who was covered with leprosy.[a]

5:20 Group Faith

The paralytic's friends showed remarkable determination to get him to Jesus. Luke writes that their faith—the man's and his friends'— moved Jesus to forgive and to heal. Jesus recognized that a helpless man needed help to come to him. Often an individual comes to Christ only with the persistent encouragement of friends and family.

---

[a]27,12 The Greek word was used for various diseases affecting the skin—not necessarily leprosy; also in verse 36   [c]41 Or *Messiah*   [d]44 Or *the land of the Jews*; some manuscripts *Galilee*   [b]33 Greek *unclean*;   [e]1 That is, Sea of Galilee   [f]4 The Greek verb is plural.

When he saw Jesus, he fell with his face to the ground and begged him, "Lord, if you are willing, you can make me clean."

[13]Jesus reached out his hand and touched the man. "I am willing," he said. "Be clean!" And immediately the leprosy left him.

[14]Then Jesus ordered him, "Don't tell anyone, but go, show yourself to the priest and offer the sacrifices that Moses commanded for your cleansing, as a testimony to them."

[15]Yet the news about him spread all the more, so that crowds of people came to hear him and to be healed of their sicknesses. [16]But Jesus often withdrew to lonely places and prayed.

Jesus Heals a Paralytic

▶ See Matthew 9:2–8; Mark 2:3–12

[17]One day as he was teaching, Pharisees and teachers of the law, who had come from every village of Galilee and from Judea and Jerusalem, were sitting there. And the power of the Lord was present for him to heal the sick. [18]Some men came carrying a paralytic on a mat and tried to take him into the house to lay him before Jesus. [19]When they could not find a way to do this because of the crowd, they went up on the roof and lowered him on his mat through the tiles into the middle of the crowd, right in front of Jesus.

[20]When Jesus saw their faith, he said, "Friend, your sins are forgiven."

[21]The Pharisees and the teachers of the law began thinking to themselves, "Who is this fellow who speaks blasphemy? Who can forgive sins but God alone?"

[22]Jesus knew what they were thinking and

A Physician Looks at the Poor
The surprising emphasis of an upper-class writer

A GREAT DOCTOR ONCE COMPARED HIS professional duties to working at the complaint desk of a large department store. "All through medical school I studied the body's wonderful engineering. A healthy body is perfect—absolutely beautiful to observe. But in practice I spend my time treating people whose bodies don't work right. I hear only complaints. After a while, it's easy to lose perspective."

"It is not the healthy who need a doctor, but the sick." 5:31

Luke, a physician, knew firsthand about sick and suffering people; he, too, heard their daily complaints. Yet somehow he never became callous. In fact, his Gospel focuses on Jesus' ministry to society's "complaint desk": the poor, the sick, and the neglected.

Jesus Announces His Mission

In Luke, even Mary's opening song strikes a chord for the poor and hungry (1:46–55). Using his favorite title for Jesus ("Son of Man") 25 times, Luke reveals him as a true servant of all humanity.

Luke 4 shows Jesus boldly declaring why he came to earth. He had just resisted temptations of wealth and power, and returned from the desert to his hometown. There Jesus, a local village boy, announced his unique mission from God: to preach good news to the poor, to free prisoners, heal the blind, and release the oppressed (4:18–19).

With little editorial comment, Luke follows Jesus from town to town. Jesus avoided such fashionable places as the resort town of Tiberias. He stayed near the farming communities and fishing villages clustered around the Sea of Galilee, serving the needs of humble people.

Reaction to Jesus varied. Naturally, the sick clamored for his attention, begging for healing. Even a few powerful people believed in him, including a respected Roman centurion and a synagogue ruler. But the religious leaders constantly challenged his actions, and his own neighbors angrily chased him out of town.

An Unlikely Friend of the Poor

Luke skillfully brings his characters to life in vignettes. Learned and sophisticated, he uses the finest Greek of any Gospel writer; but, ironically, he focuses mainly on the poor and the outcast. Women, largely ignored by ancient historians, play a large role: Luke introduces 13 women mentioned in no other Gospel. He also shows a delight and appreciation for children.

It may seem strange that Luke, by education and profession a member of the upper class, emerged as a champion of the poor and the oppressed. Evidently Jesus' message had affected him deeply. As Jesus said, "It is not the healthy who need a doctor, but the sick. I have not come to call the righteous, but sinners to repentance" (5:31–32).

Life Questions: As Luke tells it, Jesus threatened the rich and powerful, but appealed to the poor and outcast. If Jesus came today, how would those two groups in our society respond to him?

asked, "Why are you thinking these things in your hearts? 23Which is easier: to say, 'Your sins are forgiven,' or to say, 'Get up and walk'? 24But that you may know that the Son of Man has authority on earth to forgive sins . . ." He said to the paralyzed man, "I tell you, get up, take your mat and go home." 25Immediately he stood up in front of them, took what he had been lying on and went home praising God. 26Everyone was amazed and gave praise to God. They were filled with awe and said, "We have seen remarkable things today."

The Calling of Levi

▶ See Matthew 9:9–13; Mark 2:14–17

27After this, Jesus went out and saw a tax collector by the name of Levi sitting at his tax booth. "Follow me," Jesus said to him, 28and Levi got up, left everything and followed him.

29Then Levi held a great banquet for Jesus at his house, and a large crowd of tax collectors and others were eating with them. 30But the Pharisees and the teachers of the law who belonged to their sect complained to his disciples, "Why do you eat and drink with tax collectors and 'sinners'?"

31Jesus answered them, "It is not the healthy who need a doctor, but the sick. 32I have not come to call the righteous, but sinners to repentance."

Jesus Questioned About Fasting

▶ See Matthew 9:14–17; Mark 2:18–22

33They said to him, "John's disciples often fast and pray, and so do the disciples of the Pharisees, but yours go on eating and drinking."

34Jesus answered, "Can you make the guests of the bridegroom fast while he is with them? 35But the time will come when the bridegroom will be taken from them; in those days they will fast."

36He told them this parable: "No one tears a patch from a new garment and sews it on an old one. If he does, he will have torn the new garment, and the patch from the new will not match the old. 37And no one pours new wine into old wineskins. If he does, the new wine will burst the skins, the wine will run out and the wineskins will be ruined. 38No, new wine must be poured into new wineskins. 39And no one after drinking old wine wants the new, for he says, 'The old is better.'"

Lord of the Sabbath

▶ See Matthew 12:1–14; Mark 2:23—3:6

6 One Sabbath Jesus was going through the grainfields, and his disciples began to pick some heads of grain, rub them in their hands and eat the kernels. 2Some of the Pharisees asked, "Why are you doing what is unlawful on the Sabbath?"

3Jesus answered them, "Have you never read what David did when he and his companions were hungry? 4He entered the house of God, and taking the consecrated bread, he ate what is lawful only for priests to eat. And he also gave some to his companions." 5Then Jesus said to them, "The Son of Man is Lord of the Sabbath."

6On another Sabbath he went into the synagogue and was teaching, and a man was there whose right hand was shriveled. 7The Pharisees and the teachers of the law were looking for a reason to accuse Jesus, so they watched him closely to see if he would heal on the Sabbath. 8But Jesus knew what they were thinking and said to the man with the shriveled hand, "Get up and stand in front of everyone." So he got up and stood there.

9Then Jesus said to them, "I ask you, which is lawful on the Sabbath: to do good or to do evil, to save life or to destroy it?"

6:9 Rules Without Love

Luke's vignettes on Jesus and the Sabbath (see also 13:10–17) demonstrate the legalism Jesus opposed. Jews of his day observed very strict rules governing what could be done on the Sabbath. Religious leaders became furious at Jesus for "breaking" the traditions. His crime? Healing people on the Sabbath. Jesus refused to let traditions interfere with compassion for needy people.

10He looked around at them all, and then said to the man, "Stretch out your hand." He did so, and his hand was completely restored. 11But they were furious and began to discuss with one another what they might do to Jesus.

The Twelve Apostles

▶ See Matthew 10:2–4; Mark 3:16–19; Acts 1:13

12One of those days Jesus went out to a mountainside to pray, and spent the night praying to God. 13When morning came, he called his disciples to him and chose twelve of them, whom he also designated apostles: 14Simon (whom he named Peter), his brother Andrew, James, John, Philip, Bartholomew, 15Matthew, Thomas, James son of Alphaeus, Simon who was called the Zealot, 16Judas son of James, and Judas Iscariot, who became a traitor.

Blessings and Woes

▶ See Matthew 5:3–12

17He went down with them and stood on a level place. A large crowd of his disciples was there and a great number of people from all over Judea, from Jerusalem, and from the coast of Tyre and Sidon, 18who had come to hear him and to be healed of their diseases. Those troubled by evil*a* spirits were cured, ¹⁹and the people all tried to touch him, because power was coming from him and healing them all.

²⁰Looking at his disciples, he said:

"Blessed are you who are poor,
　for yours is the kingdom of God.
²¹Blessed are you who hunger now,
　for you will be satisfied.
Blessed are you who weep now,
　for you will laugh.
²²Blessed are you when men hate you,
　when they exclude you and insult you
　and reject your name as evil,
　　because of the Son of Man.

²³"Rejoice in that day and leap for joy, because great is your reward in heaven. For that is how their fathers treated the prophets.

²⁴"But woe to you who are rich,
　for you have already received your
　　comfort.
²⁵Woe to you who are well fed now,
　for you will go hungry.
Woe to you who laugh now,
　for you will mourn and weep.
²⁶Woe to you when all men speak well of you,
　for that is how their fathers treated the
　　false prophets.

Love for Enemies

²⁷"But I tell you who hear me: Love your enemies, do good to those who hate you, ²⁸bless those who curse you, pray for those who mistreat you. ²⁹If someone strikes you on one cheek, turn to him the other also. If someone takes your cloak, do not stop him from taking your tunic. ³⁰Give to everyone who asks you, and if anyone takes what belongs to you, do not demand it back. ³¹Do to others as you would have them do to you.

³²"If you love those who love you, what credit is that to you? Even 'sinners' love those who love them. ³³And if you do good to those who are good to you, what credit is that to you? Even 'sinners' do that. ³⁴And if you lend to those from whom you expect repayment, what credit is that to you? Even 'sinners' lend to 'sinners,' expecting to be repaid in full. ³⁵But love your enemies, do good to them, and lend to them without expecting to get anything back. Then your reward will be great, and you will be sons of the Most High, because he is kind to the ungrateful and wicked. ³⁶Be merciful, just as your Father is merciful.

Judging Others

▶ *See Matthew 7:1–5*

³⁷"Do not judge, and you will not be judged. Do not condemn, and you will not be con-

demned. Forgive, and you will be forgiven. ³⁸Give, and it will be given to you. A good measure, pressed down, shaken together and running over, will be poured into your lap. For with the measure you use, it will be measured to you."

³⁹He also told them this parable: "Can a blind man lead a blind man? Will they not both fall into a pit? ⁴⁰A student is not above his teacher, but everyone who is fully trained will be like his teacher.

⁴¹"Why do you look at the speck of sawdust in your brother's eye and pay no attention to the plank in your own eye? ⁴²How can you say to your brother, 'Brother, let me take the speck out of your eye,' when you yourself fail to see the plank in your own eye? You hypocrite, first take the plank out of your eye, and then you will see clearly to remove the speck from your brother's eye.

A Tree and Its Fruit

▶ *See Matthew 7:16,18,20*

⁴³"No good tree bears bad fruit, nor does a bad tree bear good fruit. ⁴⁴Each tree is recognized by its own fruit. People do not pick figs from thornbushes, or grapes from briers. ⁴⁵The good man brings good things out of the good stored up in his heart, and the evil man brings evil things out of the evil stored up in his heart. For out of the overflow of his heart his mouth speaks.

The Wise and Foolish Builders

▶ *See Matthew 7:24–27*

⁴⁶"Why do you call me, 'Lord, Lord,' and do not do what I say? ⁴⁷I will show you what he is like who comes to me and hears my words and puts them into practice. ⁴⁸He is like a man building a house, who dug down deep and laid the foundation on rock. When a flood came, the torrent struck that house but could not shake it, because it was well built. ⁴⁹But the one who hears my words and does not put them into practice is like a man who built a house on the ground without a foundation. The moment the torrent struck that house, it collapsed and its destruction was complete."

The Faith of the Centurion

▶ *See Matthew 8:5–13*

7 When Jesus had finished saying all this in the hearing of the people, he entered Capernaum. ²There a centurion's servant, whom his master valued highly, was sick and about to die. ³The centurion heard of Jesus and sent some elders of the Jews to him, asking him to come and heal his servant. ⁴When they came to Jesus, they pleaded earnestly with him, "This man deserves to have you do this, ⁵because he loves our nation and has

built our synagogue." [6]So Jesus went with them.

He was not far from the house when the centurion sent friends to say to him: "Lord, don't trouble yourself, for I do not deserve to have you come under my roof. [7]That is why I did not even consider myself worthy to come to you. But say the word, and my servant will be healed. [8]For I myself am a man under authority, with soldiers under me. I tell this one, 'Go,' and he goes; and that one, 'Come,' and he comes. I say to my servant, 'Do this,' and he does it."

[9]When Jesus heard this, he was amazed at him, and turning to the crowd following him, he said, "I tell you, I have not found such great faith even in Israel." [10]Then the men who had been sent returned to the house and found the servant well.

Jesus Raises a Widow's Son

[11]Soon afterward, Jesus went to a town called Nain, and his disciples and a large crowd went along with him. [12]As he approached the town gate, a dead person was being carried out—the only son of his mother, and she was a widow. And a large crowd from the town was with her. [13]When the Lord saw her, his heart went out to her and he said, "Don't cry."

[14]Then he went up and touched the coffin, and those carrying it stood still. He said, "Young man, I say to you, get up!" [15]The dead man sat up and began to talk, and Jesus gave him back to his mother.

[16]They were all filled with awe and praised God. "A great prophet has appeared among us," they said. "God has come to help his people." [17]This news about Jesus spread throughout Judea[a] and the surrounding country.

Jesus and John the Baptist

▶ See Matthew 11:2–19

[18]John's disciples told him about all these things. Calling two of them, [19]he sent them to the Lord to ask, "Are you the one who was to come, or should we expect someone else?"

[20]When the men came to Jesus, they said, "John the Baptist sent us to you to ask, 'Are you the one who was to come, or should we expect someone else?'"

[21]At that very time Jesus cured many who had diseases, sicknesses and evil spirits, and gave sight to many who were blind. [22]So he replied to the messengers, "Go back and report to John what you have seen and heard: The blind receive sight, the lame walk, those who have leprosy[b] are cured, the deaf hear, the dead are raised, and the good news is preached to the poor. [23]Blessed is the man who does not fall away on account of me."

[24]After John's messengers left, Jesus began to speak to the crowd about John: "What did you

7:19 Even John Questioned

The crowds Jesus attracted wavered between enthusiastic support and outright rejection of him. Evidently, some of the controversy even affected John the Baptist, who had baptized Jesus and pronounced him the Son of God (see John 1:34). John, then in prison, sent his disciples to confirm whether Jesus was the true Messiah. Jesus reassured him with a direct reference to the prophecies of Isaiah 61 (see also Luke 4:18–21).

go out into the desert to see? A reed swayed by the wind? [25]If not, what did you go out to see? A man dressed in fine clothes? No, those who wear expensive clothes and indulge in luxury are in palaces. [26]But what did you go out to see? A prophet? Yes, I tell you, and more than a prophet. [27]This is the one about whom it is written:

"'I will send my messenger ahead of you,
who will prepare your way before you.'[c]

[28]I tell you, among those born of women there is no one greater than John; yet the one who is least in the kingdom of God is greater than he."

[29](All the people, even the tax collectors, when they heard Jesus' words, acknowledged that God's way was right, because they had been baptized by John. [30]But the Pharisees and experts in the law rejected God's purpose for themselves, because they had not been baptized by John.)

[31]"To what, then, can I compare the people of this generation? What are they like? [32]They are like children sitting in the marketplace and calling out to each other:

"'We played the flute for you,
    and you did not dance;
we sang a dirge,
    and you did not cry.'

[33]For John the Baptist came neither eating bread nor drinking wine, and you say, 'He has a demon.' [34]The Son of Man came eating and drinking, and you say, 'Here is a glutton and a drunkard, a friend of tax collectors and "sinners."' [35]But wisdom is proved right by all her children."

Jesus Anointed by a Sinful Woman

[36]Now one of the Pharisees invited Jesus to have dinner with him, so he went to the Phari-

---

[a]17 Or *the land of the Jews*   [b]22 The Greek word was used for various diseases affecting the skin—not necessarily leprosy.   [c]27 Mal. 3:1

see's house and reclined at the table. ³⁷When a woman who had lived a sinful life in that town learned that Jesus was eating at the Pharisee's house, she brought an alabaster jar of perfume, ³⁸and as she stood behind him at his feet weeping, she began to wet his feet with her tears. Then she wiped them with her hair, kissed them and poured perfume on them.

³⁹When the Pharisee who had invited him saw this, he said to himself, "If this man were a prophet, he would know who is touching him and what kind of woman she is—that she is a sinner."

⁴⁰Jesus answered him, "Simon, I have something to tell you."

"Tell me, teacher," he said.

⁴¹"Two men owed money to a certain moneylender. One owed him five hundred denarii,[a] and the other fifty. ⁴²Neither of them had the money to pay him back, so he canceled the debts of both. Now which of them will love him more?"

⁴³Simon replied, "I suppose the one who had the bigger debt canceled."

"You have judged correctly," Jesus said.

⁴⁴Then he turned toward the woman and said to Simon, "Do you see this woman? I came into your house. You did not give me any water for my feet, but she wet my feet with her tears and wiped them with her hair. ⁴⁵You did not give me a kiss, but this woman, from the time I entered, has not stopped kissing my feet. ⁴⁶You did not put oil on my head, but she has poured perfume on my feet. ⁴⁷Therefore, I tell you, her many sins have been forgiven—for she loved much. But he who has been forgiven little loves little."

⁴⁸Then Jesus said to her, "Your sins are forgiven."

⁴⁹The other guests began to say among themselves, "Who is this who even forgives sins?"

⁵⁰Jesus said to the woman, "Your faith has saved you; go in peace."

The Parable of the Sower

▶ See Matthew 13:2–23; Mark 4:1–20

8 After this, Jesus traveled about from one town and village to another, proclaiming the good news of the kingdom of God. The Twelve were with him, ²and also some women who had been cured of evil spirits and diseases: Mary (called Magdalene) from whom seven demons had come out; ³Joanna the wife of Cuza, the manager of Herod's household; Susanna; and many others. These women were helping to support them out of their own means.

⁴While a large crowd was gathering and people were coming to Jesus from town after town, he told this parable: ⁵"A farmer went out to sow his seed. As he was scattering the seed, some fell along the path; it was trampled on, and the birds of the air ate it up. ⁶Some fell on rock, and when it came up, the plants withered because they had no moisture. ⁷Other seed fell among thorns,

8:3 Jesus' Support

In the Middle East of that day, teachers traveled from town to town, accepting the gifts of appreciative listeners. Luke points out that certain women who had been healed by Jesus helped provide for him. In all, Luke introduces 13 women who do not appear in the other Gospels.

which grew up with it and choked the plants. ⁸Still other seed fell on good soil. It came up and yielded a crop, a hundred times more than was sown."

When he said this, he called out, "He who has ears to hear, let him hear."

⁹His disciples asked him what this parable meant. ¹⁰He said, "The knowledge of the secrets of the kingdom of God has been given to you, but to others I speak in parables, so that,

> "'though seeing, they may not see;
> though hearing, they may not
> understand.'[b]

¹¹"This is the meaning of the parable: The seed is the word of God. ¹²Those along the path are the ones who hear, and then the devil comes and takes away the word from their hearts, so that they may not believe and be saved. ¹³Those on the rock are the ones who receive the word with joy when they hear it, but they have no root. They believe for a while, but in the time of testing they fall away. ¹⁴The seed that fell among thorns stands for those who hear, but as they go on their way they are choked by life's worries, riches and pleasures, and they do not mature. ¹⁵But the seed on good soil stands for those with a noble and good heart, who hear the word, retain it, and by persevering produce a crop.

A Lamp on a Stand

¹⁶"No one lights a lamp and hides it in a jar or puts it under a bed. Instead, he puts it on a stand, so that those who come in can see the light. ¹⁷For there is nothing hidden that will not be disclosed, and nothing concealed that will not be known or brought out into the open. ¹⁸Therefore consider carefully how you listen. Whoever has will be given more; whoever does not have, even what he thinks he has will be taken from him."

---

[a]41 A denarius was a coin worth about a day's wages.   [b]10 Isaiah 6:9

Jesus' Mother and Brothers

▶ *See Matthew 12:46–50; Mark 3:31–35*

[19] Now Jesus' mother and brothers came to see him, but they were not able to get near him because of the crowd. [20] Someone told him, "Your mother and brothers are standing outside, wanting to see you."

[21] He replied, "My mother and brothers are those who hear God's word and put it into practice."

Jesus Calms the Storm

▶ *See Matthew 8:23–27; Mark 4:36–41*

[22] One day Jesus said to his disciples, "Let's go over to the other side of the lake." So they got into a boat and set out. [23] As they sailed, he fell asleep. A squall came down on the lake, so that the boat was being swamped, and they were in great danger.

[24] The disciples went and woke him, saying, "Master, Master, we're going to drown!"

He got up and rebuked the wind and the raging waters; the storm subsided, and all was calm. [25] "Where is your faith?" he asked his disciples.

In fear and amazement they asked one another, "Who is this? He commands even the winds and the water, and they obey him."

The Healing of a Demon-possessed Man

▶ *See Matthew 8:28–34; Mark 5:1–20*

[26] They sailed to the region of the Gerasenes,[a] which is across the lake from Galilee. [27] When Jesus stepped ashore, he was met by a demon-possessed man from the town. For a long time this man had not worn clothes or lived in a

8:27 Homeless

Much as some mentally troubled people live under bridges today, this disturbed man had fled society to live in the tombs. Cemeteries in the ancient world were located far from town, because people feared the spirits of the dead. The man was violent and uncontrollable, and he greeted Jesus with bizarre behavior. Jesus, rather than avoiding him, went straight to the heart of his problem.

house, but had lived in the tombs. [28] When he saw Jesus, he cried out and fell at his feet, shouting at the top of his voice, "What do you want with me, Jesus, Son of the Most High God? I beg you, don't torture me!" [29] For Jesus had commanded the evil[b] spirit to come out of the man. Many times it had seized him, and though he was

chained hand and foot and kept under guard, he had broken his chains and had been driven by the demon into solitary places.

[30] Jesus asked him, "What is your name?"

"Legion," he replied, because many demons had gone into him. [31] And they begged him repeatedly not to order them to go into the Abyss.

[32] A large herd of pigs was feeding there on the hillside. The demons begged Jesus to let them go into them, and he gave them permission. [33] When the demons came out of the man, they went into the pigs, and the herd rushed down the steep bank into the lake and was drowned.

[34] When those tending the pigs saw what had happened, they ran off and reported this in the town and countryside, [35] and the people went out to see what had happened. When they came to Jesus, they found the man from whom the demons had gone out, sitting at Jesus' feet, dressed and in his right mind; and they were afraid. [36] Those who had seen it told the people how the demon-possessed man had been cured. [37] Then all the people of the region of the Gerasenes asked Jesus to leave them, because they were overcome with fear. So he got into the boat and left.

[38] The man from whom the demons had gone out begged to go with him, but Jesus sent him away, saying, [39] "Return home and tell how much God has done for you." So the man went away and told all over town how much Jesus had done for him.

A Dead Girl and a Sick Woman

▶ *See Matthew 9:18–26; Mark 5:22–43*

[40] Now when Jesus returned, a crowd welcomed him, for they were all expecting him. [41] Then a man named Jairus, a ruler of the synagogue, came and fell at Jesus' feet, pleading with him to come to his house [42] because his only daughter, a girl of about twelve, was dying.

As Jesus was on his way, the crowds almost crushed him. [43] And a woman was there who had been subject to bleeding for twelve years,[c] but no one could heal her. [44] She came up behind him and touched the edge of his cloak, and immediately her bleeding stopped.

[45] "Who touched me?" Jesus asked.

When they all denied it, Peter said, "Master, the people are crowding and pressing against you."

[46] But Jesus said, "Someone touched me; I know that power has gone out from me."

[47] Then the woman, seeing that she could not go unnoticed, came trembling and fell at his feet. In the presence of all the people, she told why she had touched him and how she had been instantly

[a] 26 Some manuscripts *Gadarenes*; other manuscripts *Gergesenes*; also in verse 37   [b] 29 Greek *unclean*   [c] 43 Many manuscripts *years, and she had spent all she had on doctors*

healed. 48Then he said to her, "Daughter, your faith has healed you. Go in peace."

49While Jesus was still speaking, someone came from the house of Jairus, the synagogue ruler. "Your daughter is dead," he said. "Don't bother the teacher any more."

50Hearing this, Jesus said to Jairus, "Don't be afraid; just believe, and she will be healed."

51When he arrived at the house of Jairus, he did not let anyone go in with him except Peter, John and James, and the child's father and mother. 52Meanwhile, all the people were wailing and mourning for her. "Stop wailing," Jesus said. "She is not dead but asleep."

53They laughed at him, knowing that she was dead. 54But he took her by the hand and said, "My child, get up!" 55Her spirit returned, and at once she stood up. Then Jesus told them to give her something to eat. 56Her parents were astonished, but he ordered them not to tell anyone what had happened.

Jesus Sends Out the Twelve

▶ See Matthew 10:9–15; Mark 6:8–11

9 When Jesus had called the Twelve together, he gave them power and authority to drive out all demons and to cure diseases, 2and he sent them out to preach the kingdom of God and to heal the sick. 3He told them: "Take nothing for the journey—no staff, no bag, no bread, no money, no extra tunic. 4Whatever house you enter, stay there until you leave that town. 5If people do not welcome you, shake the dust off your feet when you leave their town, as a testimony against them." 6So they set out and went from village to village, preaching the gospel and healing people everywhere.

7Now Herod the tetrarch heard about all that was going on. And he was perplexed, because some were saying that John had been raised from the dead, 8others that Elijah had appeared, and still others that one of the prophets of long ago had come back to life. 9But Herod said, "I beheaded John. Who, then, is this I hear such things about?" And he tried to see him.

Jesus Feeds the Five Thousand

▶ See Matthew 14:13–21; Mark 6:32–44; John 6:5–13

10When the apostles returned, they reported to Jesus what they had done. Then he took them with him and they withdrew by themselves to a town called Bethsaida, 11but the crowds learned about it and followed him. He welcomed them and spoke to them about the kingdom of God, and healed those who needed healing.

12Late in the afternoon the Twelve came to him and said, "Send the crowd away so they can go to the surrounding villages and countryside and find food and lodging, because we are in a remote place here."

13He replied, "You give them something to eat."

They answered, "We have only five loaves of bread and two fish—unless we go and buy food for all this crowd." 14(About five thousand men were there.)

But he said to his disciples, "Have them sit down in groups of about fifty each." 15The disciples did so, and everybody sat down. 16Taking the five loaves and the two fish and looking up to heaven, he gave thanks and broke them. Then he gave them to the disciples to set before the people. 17They all ate and were satisfied, and the disciples picked up twelve basketfuls of broken pieces that were left over.

Peter's Confession of Christ

▶ See Matthew 16:13–16; Mark 8:27–29

18Once when Jesus was praying in private and his disciples were with him, he asked them, "Who do the crowds say I am?"

19They replied, "Some say John the Baptist; others say Elijah; and still others, that one of the prophets of long ago has come back to life."

20"But what about you?" he asked. "Who do you say I am?"

Peter answered, "The Christ[a] of God."

21Jesus strictly warned them not to tell this to anyone. 22And he said, "The Son of Man must suffer many things and be rejected by the elders, chief priests and teachers of the law, and he must be killed and on the third day be raised to life."

23Then he said to them all: "If anyone would come after me, he must deny himself and take up his cross daily and follow me. 24For whoever wants to save his life will lose it, but whoever loses his life for me will save it. 25What good is it for a man to gain the whole world, and yet lose or forfeit his very self? 26If anyone is ashamed of me and my words, the Son of Man will be ashamed of him when he comes in his glory and in the glory of the Father and of the holy angels. 27I tell you the truth, some who are standing here will not taste death before they see the kingdom of God."

The Transfiguration

▶ See Matthew 17:1–8; Mark 9:2–8

28About eight days after Jesus said this, he took Peter, John and James with him and went up onto a mountain to pray. 29As he was praying, the appearance of his face changed, and his clothes became as bright as a flash of lightning. 30Two men, Moses and Elijah, 31appeared in glorious splendor, talking with Jesus. They spoke about his departure, which he was about to bring to fulfillment at Jerusalem. ³²Peter and his companions were very sleepy, but when they became fully awake, they saw his glory and the two men

9:28–33 Seeing the Kingdom

Jesus predicted that some of his disciples would "see the kingdom of God" (verse 27) before tasting death. Eight days later, three of them witnessed Jesus gleaming like a flash of lightning and talking with the long-dead Moses and Elijah (verses 29–30). Many scholars think the Transfiguration fulfilled Jesus' "seeing the kingdom" prediction. Apart from this moment, Jesus looked like any other man during his years on earth. He had none of the brilliant glory associated with God in the Old Testament (see Exodus 40:34).

standing with him. ³³As the men were leaving Jesus, Peter said to him, "Master, it is good for us to be here. Let us put up three shelters—one for you, one for Moses and one for Elijah." (He did not know what he was saying.)

³⁴While he was speaking, a cloud appeared and enveloped them, and they were afraid as they entered the cloud. ³⁵A voice came from the cloud, saying, "This is my Son, whom I have chosen; listen to him." ³⁶When the voice had spoken, they found that Jesus was alone. The disciples kept this to themselves, and told no one at that time what they had seen.

The Healing of a Boy With an Evil Spirit

▶ *See Matthew 17:14–18,22–23; Mark 9:14–27,30–32*

³⁷The next day, when they came down from the mountain, a large crowd met him. ³⁸A man in the crowd called out, "Teacher, I beg you to look at my son, for he is my only child. ³⁹A spirit seizes him and he suddenly screams; it throws him into convulsions so that he foams at the mouth. It scarcely ever leaves him and is destroying him. ⁴⁰I begged your disciples to drive it out, but they could not."

⁴¹"O unbelieving and perverse generation," Jesus replied, "how long shall I stay with you and put up with you? Bring your son here."

⁴²Even while the boy was coming, the demon threw him to the ground in a convulsion. But Jesus rebuked the evil*ᵃ* spirit, healed the boy and gave him back to his father. ⁴³And they were all amazed at the greatness of God.

While everyone was marveling at all that Jesus

did, he said to his disciples, ⁴⁴"Listen carefully to what I am about to tell you: The Son of Man is going to be betrayed into the hands of men." ⁴⁵But they did not understand what this meant. It was hidden from them, so that they did not grasp it, and they were afraid to ask him about it.

Who Will Be the Greatest?

▶ *See Matthew 18:1–5; Mark 9:33–40*

⁴⁶An argument started among the disciples as to which of them would be the greatest. ⁴⁷Jesus, knowing their thoughts, took a little child and had him stand beside him. ⁴⁸Then he said to them, "Whoever welcomes this little child in my name welcomes me; and whoever welcomes me welcomes the one who sent me. For he who is least among you all—he is the greatest."

⁴⁹"Master," said John, "we saw a man driving out demons in your name and we tried to stop him, because he is not one of us."

⁵⁰"Do not stop him," Jesus said, "for whoever is not against you is for you."

Samaritan Opposition

⁵¹As the time approached for him to be taken up to heaven, Jesus resolutely set out for Jerusalem. ⁵²And he sent messengers on ahead, who went into a Samaritan village to get things ready for him; ⁵³but the people there did not welcome him, because he was heading for Jerusalem. ⁵⁴When the disciples James and John saw this, they asked, "Lord, do you want us to call fire down from heaven to destroy them*ᵇ*?" ⁵⁵But Jesus turned and rebuked them, ⁵⁶and*ᶜ* they went to another village.

The Cost of Following Jesus

▶ *See Matthew 8:19–22*

⁵⁷As they were walking along the road, a man said to him, "I will follow you wherever you go."

⁵⁸Jesus replied, "Foxes have holes and birds of the air have nests, but the Son of Man has no place to lay his head."

⁵⁹He said to another man, "Follow me."

9:59 Burying His Father

The man's request to "let me go and bury my father" didn't necessarily mean that the man's father had just died. Possibly the expression was a figure of speech, a way of saying, "Let me wait until my father has died." Jesus instead stressed the urgency of his mission.

ᵃ42 Greek *unclean* *ᵇ54* Some manuscripts *them, even as Elijah did* *ᶜ55,56* Some manuscripts *them. And he said, "You do not know what kind of spirit you are of, for the Son of Man did not come to destroy men's lives, but to save them."* ⁵⁶*And*

But the man replied, "Lord, first let me go and bury my father."

⁶⁰Jesus said to him, "Let the dead bury their own dead, but you go and proclaim the kingdom of God."

⁶¹Still another said, "I will follow you, Lord; but first let me go back and say good-by to my family."

⁶²Jesus replied, "No one who puts his hand to the plow and looks back is fit for service in the kingdom of God."

a 1 Some manuscripts seventy; also in verse 17

Jesus Sends Out the Seventy-two

▶ See Luke 9:3-5

10 After this the Lord appointed seventy-two[a] others and sent them two by two ahead of him to every town and place where he was about to go. ²He told them, "The harvest is plentiful, but the workers are few. Ask the Lord of the harvest, therefore, to send out workers into his harvest field. ³Go! I am sending you out like lambs among wolves. ⁴Do not take a purse or bag

The Power of a Name
Jesus' time on earth was running out

CHRISTIANS SPEAK "IN THE NAME of Jesus." But that familiar phrase may have lost meaning for some of us. Consider:

College sophomore Tom Bowers took a summer job as an intern on the governor of Michigan's staff. He spent the first few weeks cranking out memos, returning mundane phone calls, and straightening files. But one day a harried manager asked Tom to write a public statement on the state's new law enforcement program. Tom composed a brief announcement and took it to the governor.

The next day, as he rounded the corner of a newsstand, his eyes snapped wide open. Headlined across the front page of the *Detroit News* was the announcement he had composed. It dawned on him that, all over the city, people would be reading his very own words as the governor's.

Throughout that summer, Tom discovered the power of the governor's name. If he sent a letter to a mayor under his own signature, it would likely be filed under "Ignore." Who was Tom Bowers, sophomore summer intern? If, however, the governor put his name at the bottom, the letter got instant attention anywhere in the state. That summer Tom worked "in the name of the governor"—he represented the governor.

> "He who listens to you listens to me; he who rejects you rejects me." 10:16

Jesus' Crash Training Course

It is one thing to represent the governor of Michigan; it is quite another to represent God and use his name. Yet Jesus had exactly that plan in mind for his followers. He hand-selected simple folk like James and Andrew to bear his name and represent him to the world. In the same way that a governor or president delegates authority to people acting on his behalf, Jesus gave his followers his own authority and power.

Jesus' time on earth was running out. Luke 9:51 records that he "resolutely set out for Jerusalem," on his way to die. Only a few weeks remained for him to train those people who would be left behind to carry his name: "Christ-ians." Jesus used the time as a crash training course for his followers.

Chapters 9–19 contain many of Jesus' events and sayings found nowhere else in the Bible. First he sent out the Twelve, then 72 others, to announce his message to all who would listen. These chapters convey Jesus' last detailed instructions to his loyal followers.

Final Instructions

Everything about Jesus' life increased in intensity along the treacherous road to Jerusalem. As he taught his small group of disciples, gawking crowds shoved in from all sides, sometimes even trampling each other. From those crowds, Pharisees tossed out loaded questions, seeking to trap Jesus.

Jesus did not soften his words in the face of danger. Instead, he emphasized the severe cost of following him. Frequently he talked about prayer, the church's life-giving connection to the Father.

Later, the apostle Paul would say that we, the church, actually form Christ's body in the world. By coming to earth and then leaving, Jesus ushered in a completely new chapter in history. And, as he prepared for departure, he called on his people—the disciples and us—to represent him. In every sense, we bear his name.

Life Questions: What does it mean to pray "in Jesus' name"? How can your life have the power and authority of Jesus behind it?

or sandals; and do not greet anyone on the road.
⁵"When you enter a house, first say, 'Peace to this house.' ⁶If a man of peace is there, your peace will rest on him; if not, it will return to you. ⁷Stay in that house, eating and drinking whatever they give you, for the worker deserves his wages. Do not move around from house to house.

⁸"When you enter a town and are welcomed, eat what is set before you. ⁹Heal the sick who are there and tell them, 'The kingdom of God is near you.' ¹⁰But when you enter a town and are not welcomed, go into its streets and say, ¹¹'Even the dust of your town that sticks to our feet we wipe off against you. Yet be sure of this: The kingdom of God is near.' ¹²I tell you, it will be more bearable on that day for Sodom than for that town.

¹³"Woe to you, Korazin! Woe to you, Bethsaida! For if the miracles that were performed in you had been performed in Tyre and Sidon, they would have repented long ago, sitting in sackcloth and ashes. ¹⁴But it will be more bearable for Tyre and Sidon at the judgment than for you. ¹⁵And you, Capernaum, will you be lifted up to the skies? No, you will go down to the depths.[a]

¹⁶"He who listens to you listens to me; he who rejects you rejects me; but he who rejects me rejects him who sent me."

¹⁷The seventy-two returned with joy and said, "Lord, even the demons submit to us in your name."

¹⁸He replied, "I saw Satan fall like lightning from heaven. ¹⁹I have given you authority to trample on snakes and scorpions and to overcome all the power of the enemy; nothing will harm you. ²⁰However, do not rejoice that the spirits submit to you, but rejoice that your names are written in heaven."

10:20 Taste of Power

Power can go to your head, especially if you've never had any. The disciples—mainly farmers and fishermen—were overwhelmed to discover their spiritual authority. Jesus urged them to keep it in perspective. Their salvation, he said— their names written in heaven—mattered more than their power. The Bible often speaks of God's people having their names recorded in a heavenly book (Daniel 12:1; Revelation 3:5).

²¹At that time Jesus, full of joy through the Holy Spirit, said, "I praise you, Father, Lord of heaven and earth, because you have hidden these things from the wise and learned, and revealed them to little children. Yes, Father, for this was your good pleasure.

²²"All things have been committed to me by my Father. No one knows who the Son is except the Father, and no one knows who the Father is except the Son and those to whom the Son chooses to reveal him."

²³Then he turned to his disciples and said privately, "Blessed are the eyes that see what you see. ²⁴For I tell you that many prophets and kings wanted to see what you see but did not see it, and to hear what you hear but did not hear it."

The Parable of the Good Samaritan

▶ *See Matthew 22:34–40; Mark 12:28–31*

²⁵On one occasion an expert in the law stood up to test Jesus. "Teacher," he asked, "what must I do to inherit eternal life?"

²⁶"What is written in the Law?" he replied. "How do you read it?"

²⁷He answered: "'Love the Lord your God with all your heart and with all your soul and with all your strength and with all your mind'[b]; and, 'Love your neighbor as yourself.'[c]"

²⁸"You have answered correctly," Jesus replied. "Do this and you will live."

²⁹But he wanted to justify himself, so he asked Jesus, "And who is my neighbor?"

³⁰In reply Jesus said: "A man was going down from Jerusalem to Jericho, when he fell into the hands of robbers. They stripped him of his clothes, beat him and went away, leaving him half dead. ³¹A priest happened to be going down the same road, and when he saw the man, he passed

10:31 Which One Showed Love?

The priest saw the robbery victim in a half-dead state. According to Old Testament law, a priest who touched a dead body made himself ceremonially impure (Leviticus 21:1–4). The priest and religious Levite decided not to get involved. Jesus' audience might have been expecting the third character to be a Jewish layperson. But Jesus added a twist by making the one who showed love a Samaritan—a racial minority despised in Israel. In this way, Jesus contrasted mere religious beliefs with true love.

by on the other side. ³²So too, a Levite, when he came to the place and saw him, passed by on the other side. ³³But a Samaritan, as he traveled, came where the man was; and when he saw him, he took pity on him. ³⁴He went to him and bandaged his wounds, pouring on oil and wine. Then he put the man on his own donkey, took him to an inn and took care of him. ³⁵The next day he took out two silver coins[d] and gave them to the innkeeper. 'Look after him,' he said, 'and

---

[a] 15 Greek *Hades*   [b] 27 Deut. 6:5   [c] 27 Lev. 19:18   [d] 35 Greek *two denarii*

when I return, I will reimburse you for any extra expense you may have.'

36"Which of these three do you think was a neighbor to the man who fell into the hands of robbers?"

37The expert in the law replied, "The one who had mercy on him."

Jesus told him, "Go and do likewise."

At the Home of Martha and Mary

38As Jesus and his disciples were on their way, he came to a village where a woman named Martha opened her home to him. 39She had a sister called Mary, who sat at the Lord's feet listening to what he said. 40But Martha was distracted by all the preparations that had to be made. She came to him and asked, "Lord, don't you care that my sister has left me to do the work by myself? Tell her to help me!"

41"Martha, Martha," the Lord answered, "you are worried and upset about many things, 42but only one thing is needed.*a* Mary has chosen what is better, and it will not be taken away from her."

Jesus' Teaching on Prayer

▶ *See Matthew 6:9–13; 7:7–11*

11 One day Jesus was praying in a certain place. When he finished, one of his disciples said to him, "Lord, teach us to pray, just as John taught his disciples."

2He said to them, "When you pray, say:

" 'Father,*b*
hallowed be your name,
your kingdom come.*c*

3Give us each day our daily bread.
4Forgive us our sins,
    for we also forgive everyone who sins
        against us.*d*
And lead us not into temptation.*e* ' "

5Then he said to them, "Suppose one of you has a friend, and he goes to him at midnight and says, 'Friend, lend me three loaves of bread, 6because a friend of mine on a journey has come to me, and I have nothing to set before him.'

7"Then the one inside answers, 'Don't bother me. The door is already locked, and my children are with me in bed. I can't get up and give you anything.' 8I tell you, though he will not get up and give him the bread because he is his friend, yet because of the man's boldness*f* he will get up and give him as much as he needs.

9"So I say to you: Ask and it will be given to you; seek and you will find; knock and the door will be opened to you. 10For everyone who asks receives; he who seeks finds; and to him who knocks, the door will be opened.

11"Which of you fathers, if your son asks for*g* a fish, will give him a snake instead? 12Or if he asks for an egg, will give him a scorpion? 13If you then, though you are evil, know how to give good gifts to your children, how much more will your Father in heaven give the Holy Spirit to those who ask him!"

Jesus and Beelzebub

▶ *See Matthew 12:22,24–29,43–45; Mark 3:23–27*

14Jesus was driving out a demon that was mute. When the demon left, the man who had been mute spoke, and the crowd was amazed.

---

a42 Some manuscripts *but few things are needed—or only one*   *b2* Some manuscripts *Our Father in heaven*
c2 Some manuscripts *come. May your will be done on earth as it is in heaven.*   *d4* Greek *everyone who is indebted to us*
e4 Some manuscripts *temptation but deliver us from the evil one*   *f8* Or *persistence*   *g11* Some manuscripts
for bread, will give him a stone; or if he asks for

MARTHA AND MARY OF BETHANY   *Doer and Seeker*

MARY AND MARTHA BOTH HAD a close relationship with Jesus, who loved them deeply. He visited the sisters' home three times that we know of, and probably many more. They lived with their brother Lazarus in Bethany, a village just outside Jerusalem. Like many sisters, Mary and Martha had quite different personalities, and we can see the difference clearly in how they related to Jesus.

Mary could drop everything and listen to Jesus. When he called, she answered instantly. She showed her love for him in extravagant ways, once lavishing a huge amount of expensive perfume on his feet (John 12:3). For Mary, everything stopped when Jesus was present.

Mary's ways sometimes annoyed her sister Martha, who showed more obsessive concern about getting things done. "Duty first" was Martha's motto. She served Jesus by preparing meals and doing the work of hosting.

Which way was better? Martha preferred her own hard-working style, and she asked Jesus to set Mary straight. Jesus gently disagreed. Mary, who simply sat at his feet and listened, did the one really necessary thing in life, he said, and he would not reprove her (10:41).

Life Questions: Are you more like Mary or like Martha? Why do you think Jesus preferred Mary's way?

[15]But some of them said, "By Beelzebub,[a] the prince of demons, he is driving out demons." [16]Others tested him by asking for a sign from heaven.

11:17 Jesus or Lincoln?

Abraham Lincoln is often credited with saying, "A house divided against itself cannot stand." Actually, Lincoln quoted Jesus, who was refuting a frivolous accusation that his power came from Satan (Beelzebub). Jesus suggested that if Satan used his power against his own cause, Satan's kingdom would soon fall. Lincoln applied this principle to the not-so-United States just before the Civil War: A nation divided over such a fundamental issue as slavery could not endure.

[17]Jesus knew their thoughts and said to them: "Any kingdom divided against itself will be ruined, and a house divided against itself will fall. [18]If Satan is divided against himself, how can his kingdom stand? I say this because you claim that I drive out demons by Beelzebub. [19]Now if I drive out demons by Beelzebub, by whom do your followers drive them out? So then, they will be your judges. [20]But if I drive out demons by the finger of God, then the kingdom of God has come to you.

[21]"When a strong man, fully armed, guards his own house, his possessions are safe. [22]But when someone stronger attacks and overpowers him, he takes away the armor in which the man trusted and divides up the spoils.

[23]"He who is not with me is against me, and he who does not gather with me, scatters.

[24]"When an evil[b] spirit comes out of a man, it goes through arid places seeking rest and does not find it. Then it says, 'I will return to the house I left.' [25]When it arrives, it finds the house swept clean and put in order. [26]Then it goes and takes seven other spirits more wicked than itself, and they go in and live there. And the final condition of that man is worse than the first."

[27]As Jesus was saying these things, a woman in the crowd called out, "Blessed is the mother who gave you birth and nursed you."

[28]He replied, "Blessed rather are those who hear the word of God and obey it."

The Sign of Jonah

▶ *See Matthew 12:39–42*

[29]As the crowds increased, Jesus said, "This is a wicked generation. It asks for a miraculous sign, but none will be given it except the sign of Jonah. [30]For as Jonah was a sign to the Ninevites, so also will the Son of Man be to this generation. [31]The Queen of the South will rise at the judgment with the men of this generation and condemn them; for she came from the ends of the earth to listen to Solomon's wisdom, and now one[c] greater than Solomon is here. [32]The men of Nineveh will stand up at the judgment with this generation and condemn it; for they repented at the preaching of Jonah, and now one greater than Jonah is here.

11:29 Sensation-Seekers

Jesus had no tolerance for people who begged for miraculous signs. Here and elsewhere he declared that no amount of proof would convince those who stubbornly refused to believe in him. In contrast, certain Old Testament Gentiles believed even though they had far less evidence.

The Lamp of the Body

▶ *See Matthew 6:22–23*

[33]"No one lights a lamp and puts it in a place where it will be hidden, or under a bowl. Instead he puts it on its stand, so that those who come in may see the light. [34]Your eye is the lamp of your body. When your eyes are good, your whole body also is full of light. But when they are bad, your body also is full of darkness. [35]See to it, then, that the light within you is not darkness. [36]Therefore, if your whole body is full of light, and no part of it dark, it will be completely lighted, as when the light of a lamp shines on you."

Six Woes

[37]When Jesus had finished speaking, a Pharisee invited him to eat with him; so he went in and reclined at the table. [38]But the Pharisee, noticing that Jesus did not first wash before the meal, was surprised.

[39]Then the Lord said to him, "Now then, you Pharisees clean the outside of the cup and dish, but inside you are full of greed and wickedness. [40]You foolish people! Did not the one who made the outside make the inside also? [41]But give what is inside ˎthe dishˏ[d] to the poor, and everything will be clean for you.

[42]"Woe to you Pharisees, because you give God a tenth of your mint, rue and all other kinds of garden herbs, but you neglect justice and the love of God. You should have practiced the latter without leaving the former undone.

[43]"Woe to you Pharisees, because you love the

---

[a] 15 Greek *Beezeboul* or *Beelzeboul*; also in verses 18 and 19   [b] 24 Greek *unclean*   [c] 31 Or *something*; also in verse 32
[d] 41 Or *what you have*

most important seats in the synagogues and greetings in the marketplaces.

44"Woe to you, because you are like unmarked graves, which men walk over without knowing it."

45One of the experts in the law answered him, "Teacher, when you say these things, you insult us also."

46Jesus replied, "And you experts in the law, woe to you, because you load people down with burdens they can hardly carry, and you yourselves will not lift one finger to help them.

47"Woe to you, because you build tombs for the prophets, and it was your forefathers who killed them. 48So you testify that you approve of what your forefathers did; they killed the prophets, and you build their tombs. 49Because of this, God in his wisdom said, 'I will send them prophets and apostles, some of whom they will kill and others they will persecute.' 50Therefore this generation will be held responsible for the blood of all the prophets that has been shed since the beginning of the world, 51from the blood of Abel to the blood of Zechariah, who was killed between the altar and the sanctuary. Yes, I tell you, this generation will be held responsible for it all.

52"Woe to you experts in the law, because you have taken away the key to knowledge. You yourselves have not entered, and you have hindered those who were entering."

53When Jesus left there, the Pharisees and the teachers of the law began to oppose him fiercely and to besiege him with questions, 54waiting to catch him in something he might say.

Warnings and Encouragements

▶ See Matthew 10:26–33

12 Meanwhile, when a crowd of many thousands had gathered, so that they were trampling on one another, Jesus began to speak first to his disciples, saying: "Be on your guard against the yeast of the Pharisees, which is hypocrisy. 2There is nothing concealed that will not be disclosed, or hidden that will not be made known. 3What you have said in the dark will be heard in the daylight, and what you have whispered in the ear in the inner rooms will be proclaimed from the roofs.

4"I tell you, my friends, do not be afraid of those who kill the body and after that can do no more. 5But I will show you whom you should fear: Fear him who, after the killing of the body, has power to throw you into hell. Yes, I tell you, fear him. 6Are not five sparrows sold for two pennies[a]? Yet not one of them is forgotten by God. 7Indeed, the very hairs of your head are all numbered. Don't be afraid; you are worth more than many sparrows.

8"I tell you, whoever acknowledges me before men, the Son of Man will also acknowledge him before the angels of God. 9But he who disowns me before men will be disowned before the angels of God. 10And everyone who speaks a word against the Son of Man will be forgiven, but anyone who blasphemes against the Holy Spirit will not be forgiven.

11"When you are brought before synagogues, rulers and authorities, do not worry about how you will defend yourselves or what you will say, 12for the Holy Spirit will teach you at that time what you should say."

The Parable of the Rich Fool

13Someone in the crowd said to him, "Teacher, tell my brother to divide the inheritance with me."

14Jesus replied, "Man, who appointed me a judge or an arbiter between you?" 15Then he said to them, "Watch out! Be on your guard against all kinds of greed; a man's life does not consist in the abundance of his possessions."

12:15 When Money Is Useless

Jesus refused to get involved in a family dispute about money. In this statement, he neatly summarized his usual approach to money. He did not condemn the possession of it. But he did warn against putting faith in money to secure the future. The rich man's money did him absolutely no good the night of his death. To emphasize this point, Jesus referred back to King Solomon, the richest man in the Old Testament (verse 27). The lesson: Trust in God and his kingdom, and free yourself of worry about money and possessions.

16And he told them this parable: "The ground of a certain rich man produced a good crop. 17He thought to himself, 'What shall I do? I have no place to store my crops.'

18"Then he said, 'This is what I'll do. I will tear down my barns and build bigger ones, and there I will store all my grain and my goods. 19And I'll say to myself, "You have plenty of good things laid up for many years. Take life easy; eat, drink and be merry."'

20"But God said to him, 'You fool! This very night your life will be demanded from you. Then who will get what you have prepared for yourself?'

21"This is how it will be with anyone who stores up things for himself but is not rich toward God."

a6 Greek *two assaria*

Do Not Worry

▶ *See Matthew 6:25–33*

22Then Jesus said to his disciples: "Therefore I tell you, do not worry about your life, what you will eat; or about your body, what you will wear. 23Life is more than food, and the body more than clothes. 24Consider the ravens: They do not sow or reap, they have no storeroom or barn; yet God feeds them. And how much more valuable you are than birds! 25Who of you by worrying can add a single hour to his life*a*? 26Since you cannot do this very little thing, why do you worry about the rest?

27"Consider how the lilies grow. They do not labor or spin. Yet I tell you, not even Solomon in all his splendor was dressed like one of these. 28If that is how God clothes the grass of the field, which is here today, and tomorrow is thrown into the fire, how much more will he clothe you, O you of little faith! 29And do not set your heart on what you will eat or drink; do not worry about it. 30For the pagan world runs after all such things, and your Father knows that you need them. 31But seek his kingdom, and these things will be given to you as well.

32"Do not be afraid, little flock, for your Father has been pleased to give you the kingdom. 33Sell your possessions and give to the poor. Provide purses for yourselves that will not wear out, a treasure in heaven that will not be exhausted, where no thief comes near and no moth destroys. 34For where your treasure is, there your heart will be also.

Watchfulness

▶ *See Matthew 24:43–51; Mark 13:33–37*

35"Be dressed ready for service and keep your lamps burning, 36like men waiting for their master to return from a wedding banquet, so that when he comes and knocks they can immediately open the door for him. 37It will be good for those servants whose master finds them watching when he comes. I tell you the truth, he will dress himself to serve, will have them recline at the table and will come and wait on them. 38It will be good for those servants whose master finds them ready, even if he comes in the second or third watch of the night. 39But understand this: If the owner of the house had known at what hour the thief was coming, he would not have let his house be broken into. 40You also must be ready, because the Son of Man will come at an hour when you do not expect him."

41Peter asked, "Lord, are you telling this parable to us, or to everyone?"

42The Lord answered, "Who then is the faithful and wise manager, whom the master puts in charge of his servants to give them their food allowance at the proper time? 43It will be good for that servant whom the master finds doing so when he returns. 44I tell you the truth, he will put him in charge of all his possessions. 45But suppose the servant says to himself, 'My master is taking a long time in coming,' and he then begins to beat the menservants and maidservants and to eat and drink and get drunk. 46The master of that servant will come on a day when he does not expect him and at an hour he is not aware of. He will cut him to pieces and assign him a place with the unbelievers.

47"That servant who knows his master's will and does not get ready or does not do what his master wants will be beaten with many blows. 48But the one who does not know and does things deserving punishment will be beaten with few blows. From everyone who has been given much, much will be demanded; and from the one who has been entrusted with much, much more will be asked.

Not Peace but Division

▶ *See Matthew 10:34–36*

49"I have come to bring fire on the earth, and how I wish it were already kindled! 50But I have a baptism to undergo, and how distressed I am until it is completed! 51Do you think I came to bring peace on earth? No, I tell you, but division. 52From now on there will be five in one family divided against each other, three against two and two against three. 53They will be divided, father against son and son against father, mother against daughter and daughter against mother, mother-in-law against daughter-in-law and daughter-in-law against mother-in-law."

Interpreting the Times

54He said to the crowd: "When you see a cloud rising in the west, immediately you say, 'It's going to rain,' and it does. 55And when the south wind blows, you say, 'It's going to be hot,' and it is. 56Hypocrites! You know how to interpret the appearance of the earth and the sky. How is it that you don't know how to interpret this present time?

57"Why don't you judge for yourselves what is right? 58As you are going with your adversary to the magistrate, try hard to be reconciled to him on the way, or he may drag you off to the judge, and the judge turn you over to the officer, and the officer throw you into prison. 59I tell you, you will not get out until you have paid the last penny.*b*"

Repent or Perish

13 Now there were some present at that time who told Jesus about the Galileans whose

*a*25 Or *single cubit to his height*   *b*59 Greek *lepton* blood Pilate had mixed with their sacrifices. [2]Jesus answered, "Do you think that these Galileans were worse sinners than all the other Galileans because they suffered this way? [3]I tell you, no! But unless you repent, you too will all perish. [4]Or those eighteen who died when the tower in Siloam fell on them—do you think they were more guilty than all the others living in Jerusalem? [5]I tell you, no! But unless you repent, you too will all perish."

[6]Then he told this parable: "A man had a fig tree, planted in his vineyard, and he went to look for fruit on it, but did not find any. [7]So he said to the man who took care of the vineyard, 'For three years now I've been coming to look for fruit on this fig tree and haven't found any. Cut it down! Why should it use up the soil?'

[8]"'Sir,' the man replied, 'leave it alone for one more year, and I'll dig around it and fertilize it. [9]If it bears fruit next year, fine! If not, then cut it down.'"

A Crippled Woman Healed on the Sabbath

[10]On a Sabbath Jesus was teaching in one of the synagogues, [11]and a woman was there who had been crippled by a spirit for eighteen years. She was bent over and could not straighten up at all. [12]When Jesus saw her, he called her forward and said to her, "Woman, you are set free from your infirmity." [13]Then he put his hands on her, and immediately she straightened up and praised God.

[14]Indignant because Jesus had healed on the Sabbath, the synagogue ruler said to the people, "There are six days for work. So come and be healed on those days, not on the Sabbath."

[15]The Lord answered him, "You hypocrites! Doesn't each of you on the Sabbath untie his ox or donkey from the stall and lead it out to give it water? [16]Then should not this woman, a daughter of Abraham, whom Satan has kept bound for eighteen long years, be set free on the Sabbath day from what bound her?"

[17]When he said this, all his opponents were humiliated, but the people were delighted with all the wonderful things he was doing.

The Parables of the Mustard Seed and the Yeast

▶ See Matthew 13:31–33; Mark 4:30–32

[18]Then Jesus asked, "What is the kingdom of God like? What shall I compare it to? [19]It is like a mustard seed, which a man took and planted in his garden. It grew and became a tree, and the birds of the air perched in its branches."

[20]Again he said, "What shall I compare the kingdom of God to? [21]It is like yeast that a wom-

an took and mixed into a large amount[a] of flour until it worked all through the dough."

The Narrow Door

[22]Then Jesus went through the towns and villages, teaching as he made his way to Jerusalem. [23]Someone asked him, "Lord, are only a few people going to be saved?"

He said to them, [24]"Make every effort to enter through the narrow door, because many, I tell you, will try to enter and will not be able to. [25]Once the owner of the house gets up and closes the door, you will stand outside knocking and pleading, 'Sir, open the door for us.'

"But he will answer, 'I don't know you or where you come from.'

[26]"Then you will say, 'We ate and drank with you, and you taught in our streets.'

[27]"But he will reply, 'I don't know you or where you come from. Away from me, all you evildoers!'

[28]"There will be weeping there, and gnashing of teeth, when you see Abraham, Isaac and Jacob and all the prophets in the kingdom of God, but you yourselves thrown out. [29]People will come from east and west and north and south, and will take their places at the feast in the kingdom of God. [30]Indeed there are those who are last who will be first, and first who will be last."

Jesus' Sorrow for Jerusalem

▶ See Matthew 23:37–39

[31]At that time some Pharisees came to Jesus and said to him, "Leave this place and go somewhere else. Herod wants to kill you."

[32]He replied, "Go tell that fox, 'I will drive out demons and heal people today and tomorrow,

13:32 Who Had Real Power?

Jesus was executed by powerful political authorities, among them the Roman official Herod. But this statement, spoken before his arrest, reveals who had the real power. Jesus dismissed Herod as "that fox," a Jewish expression for a worthless or insignificant person. Jesus' death on a cross came as no surprise to him; in fact, here Jesus calls it his "goal."

and on the third day I will reach my goal.' [33]In any case, I must keep going today and tomorrow and the next day—for surely no prophet can die outside Jerusalem!

[34]"O Jerusalem, Jerusalem, you who kill the prophets and stone those sent to you, how often I have longed to gather your children together, as

---

[a]21 Greek *three satas* (probably about 1/2 bushel or 22 liters)

a hen gathers her chicks under her wings, but you were not willing! [35]Look, your house is left to you desolate. I tell you, you will not see me again until you say, 'Blessed is he who comes in the name of the Lord.'[a]"

Jesus at a Pharisee's House

14 One Sabbath, when Jesus went to eat in the house of a prominent Pharisee, he was being carefully watched. [2]There in front of him was a man suffering from dropsy. [3]Jesus asked the Pharisees and experts in the law, "Is it lawful to heal on the Sabbath or not?" [4]But they remained silent. So taking hold of the man, he healed him and sent him away.

[5]Then he asked them, "If one of you has a son[b] or an ox that falls into a well on the Sabbath day, will you not immediately pull him out?" [6]And they had nothing to say.

[7]When he noticed how the guests picked the places of honor at the table, he told them this parable: [8]"When someone invites you to a wedding feast, do not take the place of honor, for a person more distinguished than you may have been invited. [9]If so, the host who invited both of you will come and say to you, 'Give this man your seat.' Then, humiliated, you will have to take the least important place. [10]But when you are invited, take the lowest place, so that when your host comes, he will say to you, 'Friend, move up to a better place.' Then you will be honored in the presence of all your fellow guests. [11]For everyone who exalts himself will be humbled, and he who humbles himself will be exalted."

[12]Then Jesus said to his host, "When you give a luncheon or dinner, do not invite your friends, your brothers or relatives, or your rich neighbors; if you do, they may invite you back and so you will be repaid. [13]But when you give a banquet, invite the poor, the crippled, the lame, the blind, [14]and you will be blessed. Although they cannot repay you, you will be repaid at the resurrection of the righteous."

The Parable of the Great Banquet

[15]When one of those at the table with him heard this, he said to Jesus, "Blessed is the man who will eat at the feast in the kingdom of God."

[16]Jesus replied: "A certain man was preparing a great banquet and invited many guests. [17]At the time of the banquet he sent his servant to tell those who had been invited, 'Come, for everything is now ready.'

[18]"But they all alike began to make excuses. The first said, 'I have just bought a field, and I must go and see it. Please excuse me.'

[19]"Another said, 'I have just bought five yoke of oxen, and I'm on my way to try them out. Please excuse me.'

[20]"Still another said, 'I just got married, so I can't come.'

[21]"The servant came back and reported this to his master. Then the owner of the house became angry and ordered his servant, 'Go out quickly into the streets and alleys of the town and bring in the poor, the crippled, the blind and the lame.'

[22]"'Sir,' the servant said, 'what you ordered has been done, but there is still room.'

[23]"Then the master told his servant, 'Go out to the roads and country lanes and make them come in, so that my house will be full. [24]I tell you, not one of those men who were invited will get a taste of my banquet.'"

The Cost of Being a Disciple

[25]Large crowds were traveling with Jesus, and turning to them he said: [26]"If anyone comes to me and does not hate his father and mother, his wife and children, his brothers and sisters—yes, even his own life—he cannot be my disciple. [27]And anyone who does not carry his cross and follow me cannot be my disciple.

[28]"Suppose one of you wants to build a tower. Will he not first sit down and estimate the cost to see if he has enough money to complete it? [29]For if he lays the foundation and is not able to finish it, everyone who sees it will ridicule him, [30]saying, 'This fellow began to build and was not able to finish.'

[31]"Or suppose a king is about to go to war against another king. Will he not first sit down and consider whether he is able with ten thousand men to oppose the one coming against him with twenty thousand? [32]If he is not able, he will send a delegation while the other is still a long way off and will ask for terms of peace. [33]In the same way, any of you who does not give up everything he has cannot be my disciple.

[34]"Salt is good, but if it loses its saltiness, how can it be made salty again? [35]It is fit neither for the soil nor for the manure pile; it is thrown out.

"He who has ears to hear, let him hear."

The Parable of the Lost Sheep

▶ *See Matthew 18:12–14*

15 Now the tax collectors and "sinners" were all gathering around to hear him. [2]But the Pharisees and the teachers of the law muttered, "This man welcomes sinners and eats with them."

[3]Then Jesus told them this parable: [4]"Suppose one of you has a hundred sheep and loses one of them. Does he not leave the ninety-nine in the open country and go after the lost sheep until he finds it? [5]And when he finds it, he joyfully puts it

---

[a]35 Psalm 118:26   [b]5 Some manuscripts *donkey*

on his shoulders ⁶and goes home. Then he calls his friends and neighbors together and says, 'Rejoice with me; I have found my lost sheep.' ⁷I tell you that in the same way there will be more

15:3 Severe and Gentle Stories

The collection of stories in chapters 14 and 15, found only in Luke's Gospel, shows the two-edged thrust of Jesus' message. The stern warnings in chapter 14 are directed to the proud, who either see no need for God or refuse to pay the cost of following him. The three stories in the next chapter progressively show the limitless love of God for those in real need. He stands ready to forgive all who turn to him.

rejoicing in heaven over one sinner who repents than over ninety-nine righteous persons who do not need to repent.

The Parable of the Lost Coin

⁸"Or suppose a woman has ten silver coins*a* and loses one. Does she not light a lamp, sweep the house and search carefully until she finds it? ⁹And when she finds it, she calls her friends and neighbors together and says, 'Rejoice with me; I have found my lost coin.' ¹⁰In the same way, I tell you, there is rejoicing in the presence of the angels of God over one sinner who repents."

The Parable of the Lost Son

¹¹Jesus continued: "There was a man who had two sons. ¹²The younger one said to his father, 'Father, give me my share of the estate.' So he divided his property between them.

¹³"Not long after that, the younger son got together all he had, set off for a distant country and there squandered his wealth in wild living. ¹⁴After he had spent everything, there was a severe famine in that whole country, and he began to be in need. ¹⁵So he went and hired himself out to a citizen of that country, who sent him to his fields to feed pigs. ¹⁶He longed to fill his stomach with the pods that the pigs were eating, but no one gave him anything.

¹⁷"When he came to his senses, he said, 'How many of my father's hired men have food to spare, and here I am starving to death! ¹⁸I will set out and go back to my father and say to him: Father, I have sinned against heaven and against you. ¹⁹I am no longer worthy to be called your son; make me like one of your hired men.' ²⁰So he got up and went to his father.

"But while he was still a long way off, his father saw him and was filled with compassion for him;

he ran to his son, threw his arms around him and kissed him.

²¹"The son said to him, 'Father, I have sinned against heaven and against you. I am no longer worthy to be called your son.*b*' ²²But the father said to his servants, 'Quick! Bring the best robe and put it on him. Put a ring on his finger and sandals on his feet. ²³Bring the fattened calf and kill it. Let's have a feast and celebrate. ²⁴For this son of mine was dead and is alive again; he was lost and is found.' So they began to celebrate.

²⁵"Meanwhile, the older son was in the field. When he came near the house, he heard music and dancing. ²⁶So he called one of the servants and asked him what was going on. ²⁷'Your brother has come,' he replied, 'and your father has killed the fattened calf because he has him back safe and sound.'

²⁸"The older brother became angry and refused to go in. So his father went out and pleaded

15:28 Two Lost Brothers?

The parable of the Lost Son actually tells of two sons, one irresponsible, the other hardworking. One wastes his life and comes home humbled; the other proudly refuses to celebrate his brother's homecoming. The story ends with one son in a joyful family celebration, and his brother outside, bitterly unwilling to forgive. Which son is really lost?

with him. ²⁹But he answered his father, 'Look! All these years I've been slaving for you and never disobeyed your orders. Yet you never gave me even a young goat so I could celebrate with my friends. ³⁰But when this son of yours who has squandered your property with prostitutes comes home, you kill the fattened calf for him!'

³¹"'My son,' the father said, 'you are always with me, and everything I have is yours. ³²But we had to celebrate and be glad, because this brother of yours was dead and is alive again; he was lost and is found.'"

The Parable of the Shrewd Manager

16 Jesus told his disciples: "There was a rich man whose manager was accused of wasting his possessions. ²So he called him in and asked him, 'What is this I hear about you? Give an account of your management, because you cannot be manager any longer.'

³"The manager said to himself, 'What shall I do now? My master is taking away my job. I'm not strong enough to dig, and I'm ashamed to

a8 Greek *ten drachmas,* each worth about a day's wages *b21* Some early manuscripts *son. Make me like one of your*
hired men.

beg— [4]I know what I'll do so that, when I lose my job here, people will welcome me into their houses.'

[5]"So he called in each one of his master's debtors. He asked the first, 'How much do you owe my master?'

[6]" 'Eight hundred gallons[a] of olive oil,' he replied.

"The manager told him, 'Take your bill, sit down quickly, and make it four hundred.'

[7]"Then he asked the second, 'And how much do you owe?'

" 'A thousand bushels[b] of wheat,' he replied.

"He told him, 'Take your bill and make it eight hundred.'

[8]"The master commended the dishonest manager because he had acted shrewdly. For the people of this world are more shrewd in dealing with their own kind than are the people of the light. [9]I tell you, use worldly wealth to gain friends for yourselves, so that when it is gone, you will be welcomed into eternal dwellings.

[10]"Whoever can be trusted with very little can also be trusted with much, and whoever is dishonest with very little will also be dishonest with much. [11]So if you have not been trustworthy in handling worldly wealth, who will trust you with true riches? [12]And if you have not been trustworthy with someone else's property, who will give you property of your own?

[13]"No servant can serve two masters. Either he will hate the one and love the other, or he will be devoted to the one and despise the other. You cannot serve both God and Money."

[14]The Pharisees, who loved money, heard all this and were sneering at Jesus. [15]He said to them, "You are the ones who justify yourselves in the eyes of men, but God knows your hearts. What is highly valued among men is detestable in God's sight.

Additional Teachings

[16]"The Law and the Prophets were proclaimed until John. Since that time, the good news of the kingdom of God is being preached, and everyone is forcing his way into it. [17]It is easier for heaven and earth to disappear than for the least stroke of a pen to drop out of the Law.

[18]"Anyone who divorces his wife and marries another woman commits adultery, and the man who marries a divorced woman commits adultery.

The Rich Man and Lazarus

[19]"There was a rich man who was dressed in purple and fine linen and lived in luxury every day. [20]At his gate was laid a beggar named Lazarus, covered with sores [21]and longing to eat what fell from the rich man's table. Even the dogs came and licked his sores.

[22]"The time came when the beggar died and the angels carried him to Abraham's side. The rich man also died and was buried. [23]In hell,[c] where he was in torment, he looked up and saw Abraham far away, with Lazarus by his side. [24]So he called to him, 'Father Abraham, have pity on me and send Lazarus to dip the tip of his finger in water and cool my tongue, because I am in agony in this fire.'

[25]"But Abraham replied, 'Son, remember that in your lifetime you received your good things, while Lazarus received bad things, but now he is comforted here and you are in agony. [26]And besides all this, between us and you a great chasm has been fixed, so that those who want to go from here to you cannot, nor can anyone cross over from there to us.'

[27]"He answered, 'Then I beg you, father, send Lazarus to my father's house, [28]for I have five brothers. Let him warn them, so that they will not also come to this place of torment.'

[29]"Abraham replied, 'They have Moses and the Prophets; let them listen to them.'

[30]" 'No, father Abraham,' he said, 'but if someone from the dead goes to them, they will repent.'

[31]"He said to him, 'If they do not listen to Moses and the Prophets, they will not be convinced even if someone rises from the dead.' "

16:31 Stubbornly Unconvinced

With the concluding statement in this famous story of Lazarus, Jesus made a poignant prophecy, although his listeners at the time probably missed the point. Many of them, especially the Pharisees, refused to believe him even after he rose from the dead.

Sin, Faith, Duty

17 Jesus said to his disciples: "Things that cause people to sin are bound to come, but woe to that person through whom they come. [2]It would be better for him to be thrown into the sea with a millstone tied around his neck than for him to cause one of these little ones to sin. [3]So watch yourselves.

"If your brother sins, rebuke him, and if he repents, forgive him. [4]If he sins against you seven times in a day, and seven times comes back to you and says, 'I repent,' forgive him."

[5]The apostles said to the Lord, "Increase our faith!"

[6]He replied, "If you have faith as small as a mustard seed, you can say to this mulberry tree,

---

[a]6 Greek *one hundred batous* (probably about 3 kiloliters)
kiloliters)   [c]23 Greek *Hades*

[b]7 Greek *one hundred korous* (probably about 35

'Be uprooted and planted in the sea,' and it will obey you.

⁷"Suppose one of you had a servant plowing or looking after the sheep. Would he say to the servant when he comes in from the field, 'Come along now and sit down to eat'? ⁸Would he not rather say, 'Prepare my supper, get yourself ready and wait on me while I eat and drink; after that you may eat and drink'? ⁹Would he thank the servant because he did what he was told to do? ¹⁰So you also, when you have done everything you were told to do, should say, 'We are unworthy servants; we have only done our duty.'"

Ten Healed of Leprosy

¹¹Now on his way to Jerusalem, Jesus traveled along the border between Samaria and Galilee. ¹²As he was going into a village, ten men who had leprosy*a* met him. They stood at a distance ¹³and called out in a loud voice, "Jesus, Master, have pity on us!"

¹⁴When he saw them, he said, "Go, show yourselves to the priests." And as they went, they were cleansed.

¹⁵One of them, when he saw he was healed, came back, praising God in a loud voice. ¹⁶He threw himself at Jesus' feet and thanked him— and he was a Samaritan.

¹⁷Jesus asked, "Were not all ten cleansed? Where are the other nine? ¹⁸Was no one found to return and give praise to God except this foreigner?" ¹⁹Then he said to him, "Rise and go; your faith has made you well."

The Coming of the Kingdom of God

²⁰Once, having been asked by the Pharisees when the kingdom of God would come, Jesus replied, "The kingdom of God does not come with your careful observation, ²¹nor will people say, 'Here it is,' or 'There it is,' because the kingdom of God is within*b* you."

²²Then he said to his disciples, "The time is coming when you will long to see one of the days of the Son of Man, but you will not see it. ²³Men will tell you, 'There he is!' or 'Here he is!' Do not go running off after them. ²⁴For the Son of Man in his day*c* will be like the lightning, which flashes and lights up the sky from one end to the other. ²⁵But first he must suffer many things and be rejected by this generation.

²⁶"Just as it was in the days of Noah, so also will it be in the days of the Son of Man. ²⁷People were eating, drinking, marrying and being given in marriage up to the day Noah entered the ark. Then the flood came and destroyed them all.

²⁸"It was the same in the days of Lot. People were eating and drinking, buying and selling, planting and building. ²⁹But the day Lot left Sodom, fire and sulfur rained down from heaven and destroyed them all.

³⁰"It will be just like this on the day the Son of Man is revealed. ³¹On that day no one who is on the roof of his house, with his goods inside, should go down to get them. Likewise, no one in the field should go back for anything. ³²Remember Lot's wife! ³³Whoever tries to keep his life will lose it, and whoever loses his life will preserve it. ³⁴I tell you, on that night two people will be in one bed; one will be taken and the other left. ³⁵Two women will be grinding grain together; one will be taken and the other left.*d*"

³⁷"Where, Lord?" they asked.

He replied, "Where there is a dead body, there the vultures will gather."

The Parable of the Persistent Widow

18 Then Jesus told his disciples a parable to show them that they should always pray and not give up. ²He said: "In a certain town there was a judge who neither feared God nor cared about men. ³And there was a widow in that town who kept coming to him with the plea, 'Grant me justice against my adversary.'

⁴"For some time he refused. But finally he said to himself, 'Even though I don't fear God or care about men, ⁵yet because this widow keeps bothering me, I will see that she gets justice, so that she won't eventually wear me out with her coming!'"

⁶And the Lord said, "Listen to what the unjust judge says. ⁷And will not God bring about justice for his chosen ones, who cry out to him day and night? Will he keep putting them off? ⁸I tell you, he will see that they get justice, and quickly. However, when the Son of Man comes, will he find faith on the earth?"

The Parable of the Pharisee and the Tax Collector

⁹To some who were confident of their own righteousness and looked down on everybody

---

18:9 Luke and the Underdog

Luke's concern for the humble comes through clearly in the stories he selected, especially in chapters 18 and 19. The parable of the Pharisee and the tax collector, for example, draws a sharp contrast between the proud and the humble. Stories that follow also feature the humble: little children, a blind beggar, another tax collector.

---

*a*12 The Greek word was used for various diseases affecting the skin—not necessarily leprosy.   *b*21 Or *among*
*c*24 Some manuscripts do not have *in his day.*   *d*35 Some manuscripts *left. 36Two men will be in the field; one will be taken and the other left.*

else, Jesus told this parable: [10]"Two men went up to the temple to pray, one a Pharisee and the other a tax collector. [11]The Pharisee stood up and prayed about[a] himself: 'God, I thank you that I am not like other men—robbers, evildoers, adulterers—or even like this tax collector. [12]I fast twice a week and give a tenth of all I get.'

[13]"But the tax collector stood at a distance. He would not even look up to heaven, but beat his breast and said, 'God, have mercy on me, a sinner.'

[14]"I tell you that this man, rather than the other, went home justified before God. For everyone who exalts himself will be humbled, and he who humbles himself will be exalted."

The Little Children and Jesus

▶ See Matthew 19:13–15; Mark 10:13–16

[15]People were also bringing babies to Jesus to have him touch them. When the disciples saw this, they rebuked them. [16]But Jesus called the children to him and said, "Let the little children come to me, and do not hinder them, for the kingdom of God belongs to such as these. [17]I tell you the truth, anyone who will not receive the kingdom of God like a little child will never enter it."

The Rich Ruler

▶ See Matthew 19:16–29; Mark 10:17–30

[18]A certain ruler asked him, "Good teacher, what must I do to inherit eternal life?"

[19]"Why do you call me good?" Jesus answered. "No one is good—except God alone. [20]You know the commandments: 'Do not commit adultery, do not murder, do not steal, do not give false testimony, honor your father and mother.'[b]"

[21]"All these I have kept since I was a boy," he said.

[22]When Jesus heard this, he said to him, "You still lack one thing. Sell everything you have and give to the poor, and you will have treasure in heaven. Then come, follow me."

[23]When he heard this, he became very sad, because he was a man of great wealth. [24]Jesus looked at him and said, "How hard it is for the rich to enter the kingdom of God! [25]Indeed, it is easier for a camel to go through the eye of a needle than for a rich man to enter the kingdom of God."

[26]Those who heard this asked, "Who then can be saved?"

[27]Jesus replied, "What is impossible with men is possible with God."

[28]Peter said to him, "We have left all we had to follow you!"

[29]"I tell you the truth," Jesus said to them, "no one who has left home or wife or brothers or parents or children for the sake of the kingdom of God [30]will fail to receive many times as much in this age and, in the age to come, eternal life."

Jesus Again Predicts His Death

▶ See Matthew 20:17–19; Mark 10:32–34

[31]Jesus took the Twelve aside and told them, "We are going up to Jerusalem, and everything that is written by the prophets about the Son of Man will be fulfilled. [32]He will be handed over to the Gentiles. They will mock him, insult him, spit on him, flog him and kill him. [33]On the third day he will rise again."

[34]The disciples did not understand any of this. Its meaning was hidden from them, and they did not know what he was talking about.

A Blind Beggar Receives His Sight

▶ See Matthew 20:29–34; Mark 10:46–52

[35]As Jesus approached Jericho, a blind man was sitting by the roadside begging. [36]When he heard the crowd going by, he asked what was happening. [37]They told him, "Jesus of Nazareth is passing by."

[38]He called out, "Jesus, Son of David, have mercy on me!"

[39]Those who led the way rebuked him and told him to be quiet, but he shouted all the more, "Son of David, have mercy on me!"

[40]Jesus stopped and ordered the man to be brought to him. When he came near, Jesus asked him, [41]"What do you want me to do for you?"

"Lord, I want to see," he replied.

[42]Jesus said to him, "Receive your sight; your faith has healed you." [43]Immediately he received his sight and followed Jesus, praising God. When all the people saw it, they also praised God.

Zacchaeus the Tax Collector

19 Jesus entered Jericho and was passing through. [2]A man was there by the name of Zacchaeus; he was a chief tax collector and was wealthy. [3]He wanted to see who Jesus was, but being a short man he could not, because of the crowd. [4]So he ran ahead and climbed a sycamore-fig tree to see him, since Jesus was coming that way.

[5]When Jesus reached the spot, he looked up and said to him, "Zacchaeus, come down immediately. I must stay at your house today." [6]So he came down at once and welcomed him gladly.

[7]All the people saw this and began to mutter, "He has gone to be the guest of a 'sinner.'"

[8]But Zacchaeus stood up and said to the Lord, "Look, Lord! Here and now I give half of my possessions to the poor, and if I have cheated

a 11 Or to   b 20 Exodus 20:12-16; Deut. 5:16-20

anybody out of anything, I will pay back four times the amount."

⁹Jesus said to him, "Today salvation has come to this house, because this man, too, is a son of Abraham. ¹⁰For the Son of Man came to seek and to save what was lost."

The Parable of the Ten Minas

¹¹While they were listening to this, he went on to tell them a parable, because he was near Jeru-

salem and the people thought that the kingdom of God was going to appear at once. ¹²He said: "A man of noble birth went to a distant country to have himself appointed king and then to return. ¹³So he called ten of his servants and gave them ten minas.*a* 'Put this money to work,' he said, 'until I come back.'

¹⁴"But his subjects hated him and sent a delegation after him to say, 'We don't want this man to be our king.'

a 13 A mina was about three months' wages.

Handling Tough Questions
Why so many stories?

SUFFERING STRIKES LIKE AN EARTHQUAKE, without warning, causing sudden devastation. Twenty-nine teenagers die when a school bus plunges off a bridge. A hurricane smashes into Mexico. An epidemic of cholera breaks out in South America.

Psychological tremors follow, often in the form of questions. "Why did God let this happen? Did we do something wrong? Why does God permit such suffering?"

In Jesus' day, rumors buzzed about two catastrophes: Pontius Pilate's slaughter of Galileans and the collapse of a tower (13:1–4). Naturally, people around Jesus questioned him about these events, but his answers puzzled them. He refused to be drawn into a discussion of the age-old problem of pain. He merely dismissed the common opinion that tragedies happen to people who deserve them and deflected the issue back to the questioners as a general warning (13:4–5; see also "What Job Teaches about Suffering," page 566).

> The chief priests, the teachers of the law and the leaders among the people were trying to kill him. Yet they could not find any way to do it, because all the people hung on his words.
> 19:47–48

The Heart of the Question

Jesus' response to the questions on suffering illustrate how he dealt with difficult issues. Religious leaders and philosophical types were constantly trying to stop him with an arsenal of tough questions. Usually their tactics backfired as Jesus expertly turned their questions back on them.

Conscious of the listening crowds, Jesus avoided long arguments, instead emphasizing the need for people to change behavior. His answers cut to the heart of the question, and to the hearts of his listeners.

When teaching, Jesus often relied on a parable—a compact short story with a moral. Speaking in parables allowed him to continue training his disciples "privately," despite the throngs of onlookers (8:10). He could explain the meaning to the disciples later on when they were alone together. Parables also helped preserve his message: Years later, as people reflected on what Jesus taught, his parables came to mind in vivid detail.

Simple Stories with a Profound Point

Luke, a master storyteller, collected 18 parables that appear nowhere else, and he also retold some of the most familiar. While Matthew emphasizes parables of the kingdom, Luke adds those that focus on people: the good Samaritan, a persistent widow, the lost son. His parables speak to heavy subjects, but in an unexpectedly disarming way.

Jesus' style of handling tough questions contrasts sharply with Paul's. The apostle Paul wrapped concepts in theological words and gave formal explanations. In careful prose he patiently probed such complex words as *forgiveness* and *justification.*

Jesus, speaking to a restless crowd of thousands, communicated the same message in three progressive stories—the Lost Sheep, the Lost Coin, and the Lost Son (15:1–32). Scottish Christians like to call that last story "The Wonderful Father." It expresses the heart of Jesus' message about as well as any ten-volume theological work.

Life Questions: What one question would you most like to ask Jesus in person? Given how he handled tough questions in Luke, can you imagine how he might respond to yours?

¹⁵"He was made king, however, and returned home. Then he sent for the servants to whom he had given the money, in order to find out what they had gained with it.

19:10 Seek and Save

A Jew who had sided with the hated Roman oppressors, Zacchaeus still had enough religious sensitivity to be curious about Jesus. Seeing his interest, Jesus took the initiative. He stopped the procession and called out to Zacchaeus, inviting himself to a meal at Zacchaeus's home. Though befriending this tax collector upset the crowd, Jesus proclaimed it as typical of his ministry: to seek and to save the lost.

¹⁶"The first one came and said, 'Sir, your mina has earned ten more.'

¹⁷"'Well done, my good servant!' his master replied. 'Because you have been trustworthy in a very small matter, take charge of ten cities.'

¹⁸"The second one came and said, 'Sir, your mina has earned five more.'

¹⁹"His master answered, 'You take charge of five cities.'

²⁰"Then another servant came and said, 'Sir, here is your mina; I have kept it laid away in a piece of cloth. ²¹I was afraid of you, because you are a hard man. You take out what you did not put in and reap what you did not sow.'

²²"His master replied, 'I will judge you by your own words, you wicked servant! You knew, did you, that I am a hard man, taking out what I did not put in, and reaping what I did not sow? ²³Why then didn't you put my money on deposit, so that when I came back, I could have collected it with interest?'

²⁴"Then he said to those standing by, 'Take his mina away from him and give it to the one who has ten minas.'

²⁵"'Sir,' they said, 'he already has ten!'

²⁶"He replied, 'I tell you that to everyone who has, more will be given, but as for the one who has nothing, even what he has will be taken away. ²⁷But those enemies of mine who did not want me to be king over them—bring them here and kill them in front of me.'"

The Triumphal Entry

▶ *See Matthew 21:1–9; Mark 11:1–10; John 12:12–15*

²⁸After Jesus had said this, he went on ahead, going up to Jerusalem. ²⁹As he approached Bethphage and Bethany at the hill called the Mount of Olives, he sent two of his disciples, saying to

them, ³⁰"Go to the village ahead of you, and as you enter it, you will find a colt tied there, which no one has ever ridden. Untie it and bring it here. ³¹If anyone asks you, 'Why are you untying it?' tell him, 'The Lord needs it.'"

³²Those who were sent ahead went and found it just as he had told them. ³³As they were untying the colt, its owners asked them, "Why are you untying the colt?"

³⁴They replied, "The Lord needs it."

³⁵They brought it to Jesus, threw their cloaks on the colt and put Jesus on it. ³⁶As he went along, people spread their cloaks on the road.

³⁷When he came near the place where the road goes down the Mount of Olives, the whole crowd of disciples began joyfully to praise God in loud voices for all the miracles they had seen:

³⁸"Blessed is the king who comes in the name
of the Lord!"ᵃ

"Peace in heaven and glory in the highest!"

³⁹Some of the Pharisees in the crowd said to Jesus, "Teacher, rebuke your disciples!"

⁴⁰"I tell you," he replied, "if they keep quiet, the stones will cry out."

⁴¹As he approached Jerusalem and saw the city, he wept over it ⁴²and said, "If you, even you, had only known on this day what would bring you peace—but now it is hidden from your eyes. ⁴³The days will come upon you when your enemies will build an embankment against you and encircle you and hem you in on every side. ⁴⁴They will dash you to the ground, you and the children within your walls. They will not leave one stone on another, because you did not recognize the time of God's coming to you."

19:44 Wailing Wall

Jesus' tearful prediction of total destruction was fulfilled in A.D. 70, when the Romans crushed a Jewish revolt by razing the city. In modern Jerusalem, the Wailing Wall is one of the few places where some of the original stonework of Jerusalem can still be seen.

Jesus at the Temple

▶ *See Matthew 21:12–16; Mark 11:15–18; John 2:13–16*

⁴⁵Then he entered the temple area and began driving out those who were selling. ⁴⁶"It is written," he said to them, "'My house will be a house of prayer'ᵇ; but you have made it 'a den of robbers.'ᶜ"

⁴⁷Every day he was teaching at the temple. But the chief priests, the teachers of the law and the

---

ᵃ38 Psalm 118:26   ᵇ46 Isaiah 56:7   ᶜ46 Jer. 7:11

leaders among the people were trying to kill him. ⁴⁸Yet they could not find any way to do it, because all the people hung on his words.

The Authority of Jesus Questioned

▶ See Matthew 21:23–27; Mark 11:27–33

20 One day as he was teaching the people in the temple courts and preaching the gospel, the chief priests and the teachers of the law, together with the elders, came up to him. ²"Tell us by what authority you are doing these things," they said. "Who gave you this authority?"

³He replied, "I will also ask you a question. Tell me, ⁴John's baptism—was it from heaven, or from men?"

⁵They discussed it among themselves and said, "If we say, 'From heaven,' he will ask, 'Why didn't you believe him?' ⁶But if we say, 'From men,' all the people will stone us, because they are persuaded that John was a prophet."

⁷So they answered, "We don't know where it was from."

⁸Jesus said, "Neither will I tell you by what authority I am doing these things."

The Parable of the Tenants

▶ See Matthew 21:33–46; Mark 12:1–12

⁹He went on to tell the people this parable: "A man planted a vineyard, rented it to some farmers and went away for a long time. ¹⁰At harvest time he sent a servant to the tenants so they would give him some of the fruit of the vineyard. But the tenants beat him and sent him away empty-handed. ¹¹He sent another servant, but that one also they beat and treated shamefully and sent away empty-handed. ¹²He sent still a third, and they wounded him and threw him out.

¹³"Then the owner of the vineyard said, 'What shall I do? I will send my son, whom I love; perhaps they will respect him.'

¹⁴"But when the tenants saw him, they talked the matter over. 'This is the heir,' they said. 'Let's kill him, and the inheritance will be ours.' ¹⁵So they threw him out of the vineyard and killed him.

"What then will the owner of the vineyard do to them? ¹⁶He will come and kill those tenants and give the vineyard to others."

When the people heard this, they said, "May this never be!"

¹⁷Jesus looked directly at them and asked, "Then what is the meaning of that which is written:

"'The stone the builders rejected
    has become the capstone*ᵃ*ᵇ?

¹⁸Everyone who falls on that stone will be broken

to pieces, but he on whom it falls will be crushed."

¹⁹The teachers of the law and the chief priests looked for a way to arrest him immediately, because they knew he had spoken this parable against them. But they were afraid of the people.

Paying Taxes to Caesar

▶ See Matthew 22:15–22; Mark 12:13–17

²⁰Keeping a close watch on him, they sent spies, who pretended to be honest. They hoped to catch Jesus in something he said so that they might hand him over to the power and authority of the governor. ²¹So the spies questioned him: "Teacher, we know that you speak and teach what is right, and that you do not show partiality but teach the way of God in accordance with the truth. ²²Is it right for us to pay taxes to Caesar or not?"

²³He saw through their duplicity and said to them, ²⁴"Show me a denarius. Whose portrait and inscription are on it?"

²⁵"Caesar's," they replied.

He said to them, "Then give to Caesar what is Caesar's, and to God what is God's."

²⁶They were unable to trap him in what he had said there in public. And astonished by his answer, they became silent.

The Resurrection and Marriage

▶ See Matthew 22:23–33; Mark 12:18–27

²⁷Some of the Sadducees, who say there is no resurrection, came to Jesus with a question. ²⁸"Teacher," they said, "Moses wrote for us that if a man's brother dies and leaves a wife but no children, the man must marry the widow and have children for his brother. ²⁹Now there were seven brothers. The first one married a woman and died childless. ³⁰The second ³¹and then the third married her, and in the same way the seven died, leaving no children. ³²Finally, the woman died too. ³³Now then, at the resurrection whose wife will she be, since the seven were married to her?"

³⁴Jesus replied, "The people of this age marry and are given in marriage. ³⁵But those who are considered worthy of taking part in that age and in the resurrection from the dead will neither marry nor be given in marriage, ³⁶and they can no longer die; for they are like the angels. They are God's children, since they are children of the resurrection. ³⁷But in the account of the bush, even Moses showed that the dead rise, for he calls the Lord 'the God of Abraham, and the God of Isaac, and the God of Jacob.'ᶜ ³⁸He is not the God of the dead, but of the living, for to him all are alive."

³⁹Some of the teachers of the law responded,

ᵃ17 Or *cornerstone*   *ᵇ17* Psalm 118:22   *ᶜ37* Exodus 3:6

"Well said, teacher!" [40]And no one dared to ask him any more questions.

Whose Son Is the Christ?

▶ *See Matthew 22:41—23:7; Mark 12:35–40*

[41]Then Jesus said to them, "How is it that they

20:41–44 Jesus Asks a Question

In the midst of many questions thrown at him, Jesus offers one back. The passage, quoting Psalm 110:1, is difficult to understand, but Jesus may have been trying to clear up a misunderstanding about the Messiah. Nationalistic Jews of that day were expecting a Messiah, or a "Son of David," out of the same mold as the great Jewish king who defeated Israel's enemies. But Jesus shows that David himself acknowledged the Messiah to come as "Lord," or One far greater than a mere earthly king.

say the Christ[a] is the Son of David? [42]David himself declares in the Book of Psalms:

"'The Lord said to my Lord:
    "Sit at my right hand
[43]until I make your enemies
    a footstool for your feet." '[b]

[44]David calls him 'Lord.' How then can he be his son?"

[45]While all the people were listening, Jesus said to his disciples, [46]"Beware of the teachers of the law. They like to walk around in flowing robes and love to be greeted in the marketplaces and have the most important seats in the synagogues and the places of honor at banquets. [47]They devour widows' houses and for a show make lengthy prayers. Such men will be punished most severely."

The Widow's Offering

▶ *See Mark 12:41–44*

21 As he looked up, Jesus saw the rich putting their gifts into the temple treasury. [2]He also saw a poor widow put in two very small copper coins.[c] [3]"I tell you the truth," he said, "this poor widow has put in more than all the others. [4]All these people gave their gifts out of their wealth; but she out of her poverty put in all she had to live on."

Signs of the End of the Age

▶ *See Matthew 24; Mark 13*

[5]Some of his disciples were remarking about how the temple was adorned with beautiful stones and with gifts dedicated to God. But Jesus said, [6]"As for what you see here, the time will come when not one stone will be left on another; every one of them will be thrown down."

[7]"Teacher," they asked, "when will these things happen? And what will be the sign that they are about to take place?"

[8]He replied: "Watch out that you are not deceived. For many will come in my name, claiming, 'I am he,' and, 'The time is near.' Do not follow them. [9]When you hear of wars and revolutions, do not be frightened. These things must happen first, but the end will not come right away."

[10]Then he said to them: "Nation will rise against nation, and kingdom against kingdom. [11]There will be great earthquakes, famines and pestilences in various places, and fearful events and great signs from heaven.

[12]"But before all this, they will lay hands on you and persecute you. They will deliver you to synagogues and prisons, and you will be brought before kings and governors, and all on account of my name. [13]This will result in your being witnesses to them. [14]But make up your mind not to worry beforehand how you will defend yourselves. [15]For I will give you words and wisdom that none of your adversaries will be able to resist or contradict. [16]You will be betrayed even by parents, brothers, relatives and friends, and they will put some of you to death. [17]All men will hate you because of me. [18]But not a hair of your head will perish. [19]By standing firm you will gain life.

[20]"When you see Jerusalem being surrounded by armies, you will know that its desolation is near. [21]Then let those who are in Judea flee to the mountains, let those in the city get out, and let those in the country not enter the city. [22]For this is the time of punishment in fulfillment of all that has been written. [23]How dreadful it will be in those days for pregnant women and nursing mothers! There will be great distress in the land and wrath against this people. [24]They will fall by the sword and will be taken as prisoners to all the nations. Jerusalem will be trampled on by the Gentiles until the times of the Gentiles are fulfilled.

[25]"There will be signs in the sun, moon and stars. On the earth, nations will be in anguish and perplexity at the roaring and tossing of the sea. [26]Men will faint from terror, apprehensive of what is coming on the world, for the heavenly bodies will be shaken. [27]At that time they will see the Son of Man coming in a cloud with power and great glory. [28]When these things begin to take place, stand up and lift up your heads, because your redemption is drawing near."

[29]He told them this parable: "Look at the fig tree and all the trees. [30]When they sprout leaves,

[a]41 Or *Messiah*   [b]43 Psalm 110:1   [c]2 Greek *two lepta*

you can see for yourselves and know that summer is near. ³¹Even so, when you see these things happening, you know that the kingdom of God is near.

³²"I tell you the truth, this generation[a] will certainly not pass away until all these things have happened. ³³Heaven and earth will pass away, but my words will never pass away.

³⁴"Be careful, or your hearts will be weighed down with dissipation, drunkenness and the anxieties of life, and that day will close on you unexpectedly like a trap. ³⁵For it will come upon all those who live on the face of the whole earth. ³⁶Be always on the watch, and pray that you may be able to escape all that is about to happen, and that you may be able to stand before the Son of Man."

³⁷Each day Jesus was teaching at the temple, and each evening he went out to spend the night on the hill called the Mount of Olives, ³⁸and all the people came early in the morning to hear him at the temple.

Judas Agrees to Betray Jesus

▶ See Matthew 26:2–5; Mark 14:1–2,10–11

22 Now the Feast of Unleavened Bread, called the Passover, was approaching, ²and the chief priests and the teachers of the law were looking for some way to get rid of Jesus, for they were afraid of the people. ³Then Satan entered Judas, called Iscariot, one of the Twelve. ⁴And Judas went to the chief priests and the officers of the temple guard and discussed with them how he might betray Jesus. ⁵They were delighted and agreed to give him money. ⁶He consented, and watched for an opportunity to hand Jesus over to them when no crowd was present.

The Last Supper

▶ See Matthew 26:17–19,26–29;
Mark 14:12–16,22–25

⁷Then came the day of Unleavened Bread on which the Passover lamb had to be sacrificed. ⁸Jesus sent Peter and John, saying, "Go and make preparations for us to eat the Passover."

⁹"Where do you want us to prepare for it?" they asked.

¹⁰He replied, "As you enter the city, a man carrying a jar of water will meet you. Follow him to the house that he enters, ¹¹and say to the owner of the house, 'The Teacher asks: Where is the guest room, where I may eat the Passover with my disciples?' ¹²He will show you a large upper room, all furnished. Make preparations there."

¹³They left and found things just as Jesus had told them. So they prepared the Passover.

¹⁴When the hour came, Jesus and his apostles reclined at the table. ¹⁵And he said to them, "I have eagerly desired to eat this Passover with you before I suffer. ¹⁶For I tell you, I will not eat it again until it finds fulfillment in the kingdom of God."

¹⁷After taking the cup, he gave thanks and said, "Take this and divide it among you. ¹⁸For I tell you I will not drink again of the fruit of the vine until the kingdom of God comes."

¹⁹And he took bread, gave thanks and broke it, and gave it to them, saying, "This is my body given for you; do this in remembrance of me."

²⁰In the same way, after the supper he took the cup, saying, "This cup is the new covenant in my blood, which is poured out for you. ²¹But the hand of him who is going to betray me is with mine on the table. ²²The Son of Man will go as it has been decreed, but woe to that man who betrays him." ²³They began to question among themselves which of them it might be who would do this.

²⁴Also a dispute arose among them as to which of them was considered to be greatest.

22:24 Status-conscious Disciples

Even at the emotional Last Supper scene described here, the disciples fell into their habit of worrying about rank and status. Not until after Jesus had died and returned did they understand the true nature of the kingdom he was setting into motion. It is a kingdom primarily of spiritual, not political, power. And in it, the greatest is the one who serves others.

²⁵Jesus said to them, "The kings of the Gentiles lord it over them; and those who exercise authority over them call themselves Benefactors. ²⁶But you are not to be like that. Instead, the greatest among you should be like the youngest, and the one who rules like the one who serves. ²⁷For who is greater, the one who is at the table or the one who serves? Is it not the one who is at the table? But I am among you as one who serves. ²⁸You are those who have stood by me in my trials. ²⁹And I confer on you a kingdom, just as my Father conferred one on me, ³⁰so that you may eat and drink at my table in my kingdom and sit on thrones, judging the twelve tribes of Israel.

³¹"Simon, Simon, Satan has asked to sift you[b] as wheat. ³²But I have prayed for you, Simon, that your faith may not fail. And when you have turned back, strengthen your brothers."

³³But he replied, "Lord, I am ready to go with you to prison and to death."

³⁴Jesus answered, "I tell you, Peter, before the

ᵃ32 Or race   ᵇ31 The Greek is plural.

rooster crows today, you will deny three times that you know me."

³⁵Then Jesus asked them, "When I sent you without purse, bag or sandals, did you lack anything?"

"Nothing," they answered.

³⁶He said to them, "But now if you have a purse, take it, and also a bag; and if you don't have a sword, sell your cloak and buy one. ³⁷It is written: 'And he was numbered with the transgressors'ᵃ; and I tell you that this must be fulfilled in me. Yes, what is written about me is reaching its fulfillment."

³⁸The disciples said, "See, Lord, here are two swords."

"That is enough," he replied.

Jesus Prays on the Mount of Olives

▶ See Matthew 26:36–46; Mark 14:32–42

³⁹Jesus went out as usual to the Mount of Olives, and his disciples followed him. ⁴⁰On reaching the place, he said to them, "Pray that you will not fall into temptation." ⁴¹He withdrew about a stone's throw beyond them, knelt down and prayed, ⁴²"Father, if you are willing, take this cup from me; yet not my will, but yours be done." ⁴³An angel from heaven appeared to him and strengthened him. ⁴⁴And being in anguish, he prayed more earnestly, and his sweat was like drops of blood falling to the ground.ᵇ

⁴⁵When he rose from prayer and went back to the disciples, he found them asleep, exhausted from sorrow. ⁴⁶"Why are you sleeping?" he asked them. "Get up and pray so that you will not fall into temptation."

Jesus Arrested

▶ See Matthew 26:47–56; Mark 14:43–50; John 18:3–11

⁴⁷While he was still speaking a crowd came up, and the man who was called Judas, one of the Twelve, was leading them. He approached Jesus to kiss him, ⁴⁸but Jesus asked him, "Judas, are you betraying the Son of Man with a kiss?"

⁴⁹When Jesus' followers saw what was going to happen, they said, "Lord, should we strike with our swords?" ⁵⁰And one of them struck the servant of the high priest, cutting off his right ear.

⁵¹But Jesus answered, "No more of this!" And he touched the man's ear and healed him.

⁵²Then Jesus said to the chief priests, the officers of the temple guard, and the elders, who had come for him, "Am I leading a rebellion, that you have come with swords and clubs? ⁵³Every day I was with you in the temple courts, and you did not lay a hand on me. But this is your hour—when darkness reigns."

Peter Disowns Jesus

▶ See Matthew 26:69–75; Mark 14:66–72; John 18:16–18,25–27

⁵⁴Then seizing him, they led him away and took him into the house of the high priest. Peter followed at a distance. ⁵⁵But when they had kindled a fire in the middle of the courtyard and had sat down together, Peter sat down with them. ⁵⁶A servant girl saw him seated there in the firelight. She looked closely at him and said, "This man was with him."

⁵⁷But he denied it. "Woman, I don't know him," he said.

⁵⁸A little later someone else saw him and said, "You also are one of them."

"Man, I am not!" Peter replied.

22:58 Deserted by His Friends

Peter showed courage by following Jesus, rather than going into hiding. Perhaps trying to gain information, he even went into the high priest's courtyard. But there he was recognized, partly because of his Galilean accent (see Matthew 26:73). After denying that he knew Jesus, Peter remembered with pain his boast that he would be willing to die with Jesus (verse 33). Jesus had accurately predicted even Peter would desert him.

⁵⁹About an hour later another asserted, "Certainly this fellow was with him, for he is a Galilean."

⁶⁰Peter replied, "Man, I don't know what you're talking about!" Just as he was speaking, the rooster crowed. ⁶¹The Lord turned and looked straight at Peter. Then Peter remembered the word the Lord had spoken to him: "Before the rooster crows today, you will disown me three times." ⁶²And he went outside and wept bitterly.

The Guards Mock Jesus

▶ See Matthew 26:67–68; Mark 14:65; John 18:22–23

⁶³The men who were guarding Jesus began mocking and beating him. ⁶⁴They blindfolded him and demanded, "Prophesy! Who hit you?" ⁶⁵And they said many other insulting things to him.

Jesus Before Pilate and Herod

▶ See Matthew 26:63–66; Mark 14:61–63; John 18:19–21

⁶⁶At daybreak the council of the elders of the people, both the chief priests and teachers of the

---

ᵃ37 Isaiah 53:12   ᵇ44 Some early manuscripts do not have verses 43 and 44.

law, met together, and Jesus was led before them. [67]"If you are the Christ,[a]" they said, "tell us."

Jesus answered, "If I tell you, you will not believe me, [68]and if I asked you, you would not answer. [69]But from now on, the Son of Man will be seated at the right hand of the mighty God."

[70]They all asked, "Are you then the Son of God?"

He replied, "You are right in saying I am."

[71]Then they said, "Why do we need any more testimony? We have heard it from his own lips."

[a]67 Or *Messiah*   [b]2 Or *Messiah*; also in verses 35 and 39

23 Then the whole assembly rose and led him off to Pilate. [2]And they began to accuse him, saying, "We have found this man subverting our nation. He opposes payment of taxes to Caesar and claims to be Christ,[b] a king."

[3]So Pilate asked Jesus, "Are you the king of the Jews?"

"Yes, it is as you say," Jesus replied.

[4]Then Pilate announced to the chief priests and the crowd, "I find no basis for a charge against this man."

Final Glimpses of Jesus
The most important week in history

EVERYTHING ABOUT JESUS SEEMED TO come together during his last few days on earth, and surely those days offer a key to understanding him. As if on a roller coaster, people's reactions to him plunged from heady exhilaration to murderous rejection overnight.

> But with loud shouts they insistently demanded that he be crucified, and their shouts prevailed. 23:23

Those last days included one scene of triumph, a grand entry into Jerusalem. Pilgrims were filling the streets in holiday celebration. In a gallant gesture for Jesus, they laid their coats before him, and they roared their approval as he approached. But against that tumultuous background, Jesus sat weeping, painfully aware that their praise was hollow.

Even as Jesus' popularity with the masses was soaring, spies joined the ranks of onlookers, assailing him with questions and verbal traps. Jesus knew he wasn't safe anywhere, even in an intimate gathering with his disciples. During his and his disciples' last meal together, one of the Twelve rose and left the room to bargain for Jesus' life.

The Darkest Day and the Brightest

At Jesus' arrest, the religious and political power brokers had a look at him at last. They had heard many intriguing rumors, and hoped he would perform for them like a magician (23:8). Jesus declined. He had never sought their kind of power, and would not then, even with his life at stake.

Outside, the crowd that previously had shouted, "Blessed is the king!" took up a very different chant: "Crucify him!" Jesus' life was doomed. The one who had come to save the world was about to be destroyed by it.

In two back-to-back closing chapters Luke records the darkest day in history ... and the brightest. No one was more surprised than Jesus' disciples to hear reports that the man they had seen die on Friday was walking around on Sunday. It seemed like hysterical nonsense at first—until he did appear, and they could deny it no longer.

Ordinary People, an Extraordinary Discovery

Luke adds one scene that captures the terrible confusion of those final days. Two of Jesus' disciples were walking away from Jerusalem, downhearted. Their dream was over; all the mounting hopes of the last few years had died with Jesus on the cross.

A strange man appeared beside the two forlorn disciples. Bizarrely, he seemed the only man alive who hadn't heard about the incredible week in Jerusalem. He talked with them, tracing the whole story of the gospel, beginning with Moses and the prophets.

The stranger intrigued them, and they asked him to stay longer. At mealtime the last link snapped into place. It was Jesus! No one else. Without a doubt, he was alive.

Ordinary people, with more than a touch of cowardice, had followed Jesus, listened to him, and watched him die (from a distance, to keep themselves safe). But seeing Jesus alive changed all that. Luke's story began with joy, and it ends that way: "Then they worshiped him and returned to Jerusalem with great joy" (24:52). Before long they were out telling the world about it.

Life Questions: Suppose you had been in the room to hear the first news of Jesus' resurrection. Would you have believed it? What makes you believe it now?

[5]But they insisted, "He stirs up the people all over Judea[a] by his teaching. He started in Galilee and has come all the way here."

[6]On hearing this, Pilate asked if the man was a Galilean. [7]When he learned that Jesus was under Herod's jurisdiction, he sent him to Herod, who was also in Jerusalem at that time.

[8]When Herod saw Jesus, he was greatly pleased, because for a long time he had been wanting to see him. From what he had heard about him, he hoped to see him perform some miracle. [9]He plied him with many questions, but Jesus gave him no answer. [10]The chief priests and the teachers of the law were standing there, vehemently accusing him. [11]Then Herod and his soldiers ridiculed and mocked him. Dressing him in an elegant robe, they sent him back to Pilate. [12]That day Herod and Pilate became friends—before this they had been enemies.

[13]Pilate called together the chief priests, the rulers and the people, [14]and said to them, "You brought me this man as one who was inciting the people to rebellion. I have examined him in your presence and have found no basis for your charges against him. [15]Neither has Herod, for he sent him back to us; as you can see, he has done nothing to deserve death. [16]Therefore, I will punish him and then release him.[b]"

[18]With one voice they cried out, "Away with this man! Release Barabbas to us!" [19](Barabbas had been thrown into prison for an insurrection in the city, and for murder.)

[20]Wanting to release Jesus, Pilate appealed to them again. [21]But they kept shouting, "Crucify him! Crucify him!"

[22]For the third time he spoke to them: "Why? What crime has this man committed? I have found in him no grounds for the death penalty. Therefore I will have him punished and then release him."

[23]But with loud shouts they insistently demanded that he be crucified, and their shouts prevailed. [24]So Pilate decided to grant their demand. [25]He released the man who had been thrown into prison for insurrection and murder, the one they asked for, and surrendered Jesus to their will.

The Crucifixion

▶ *See Matthew 27:33–44; Mark 15:22–32; John 19:17–24*

[26]As they led him away, they seized Simon from Cyrene, who was on his way in from the country, and put the cross on him and made him carry it behind Jesus. [27]A large number of people followed him, including women who mourned and wailed for him. [28]Jesus turned and said to them, "Daughters of Jerusalem, do not weep for me; weep for yourselves and for your children. [29]For the time will come when you will say, 'Blessed are the barren women, the wombs that never bore and the breasts that never nursed!' [30]Then

> "'they will say to the mountains, "Fall on us!"
> and to the hills, "Cover us!"'[c]

[31]For if men do these things when the tree is green, what will happen when it is dry?"

[32]Two other men, both criminals, were also led out with him to be executed. [33]When they came to the place called the Skull, there they crucified him, along with the criminals—one on his right, the other on his left. [34]Jesus said, "Father, forgive them, for they do not know what they are doing."[d] And they divided up his clothes by casting lots.

[35]The people stood watching, and the rulers even sneered at him. They said, "He saved others; let him save himself if he is the Christ of God, the Chosen One."

[36]The soldiers also came up and mocked him. They offered him wine vinegar [37]and said, "If you are the king of the Jews, save yourself."

[38]There was a written notice above him, which read: THIS IS THE KING OF THE JEWS.

[39]One of the criminals who hung there hurled insults at him: "Aren't you the Christ? Save yourself and us!"

[40]But the other criminal rebuked him. "Don't you fear God," he said, "since you are under the same sentence? [41]We are punished justly, for we

---

[a]5 Or *over the land of the Jews*   [b]16 Some manuscripts *him.* [17]*Now he was obliged to release one man to them at the Feast.*   [c]30 Hosea 10:8   [d]34 Some early manuscripts do not have this sentence.

are getting what our deeds deserve. But this man has done nothing wrong."

⁴²Then he said, "Jesus, remember me when you come into your kingdom.ᵃ"

⁴³Jesus answered him, "I tell you the truth, today you will be with me in paradise."

Jesus' Death

▶ *See Matthew 27:45–56; Mark 15:33–41*

⁴⁴It was now about the sixth hour, and darkness came over the whole land until the ninth hour, ⁴⁵for the sun stopped shining. And the curtain of the temple was torn in two. ⁴⁶Jesus called out with a loud voice, "Father, into your hands I commit my spirit." When he had said this, he breathed his last.

⁴⁷The centurion, seeing what had happened, praised God and said, "Surely this was a righteous man." ⁴⁸When all the people who had gathered to witness this sight saw what took place, they beat their breasts and went away. ⁴⁹But all those who knew him, including the women who had followed him from Galilee, stood at a distance, watching these things.

Jesus' Burial

▶ *See Matthew 27:57–61; Mark 15:42–47; John 19:38–42*

⁵⁰Now there was a man named Joseph, a member of the Council, a good and upright man, ⁵¹who had not consented to their decision and action. He came from the Judean town of Arimathea and he was waiting for the kingdom of God. ⁵²Going to Pilate, he asked for Jesus' body. ⁵³Then he took it down, wrapped it in linen cloth and placed it in a tomb cut in the rock, one in which no one had yet been laid. ⁵⁴It was Preparation Day, and the Sabbath was about to begin.

⁵⁵The women who had come with Jesus from Galilee followed Joseph and saw the tomb and how his body was laid in it. ⁵⁶Then they went home and prepared spices and perfumes. But they rested on the Sabbath in obedience to the commandment.

The Resurrection

▶ *See Matthew 28:1–8; Mark 16:1–8; John 20:1–8*

24 On the first day of the week, very early in the morning, the women took the spices they had prepared and went to the tomb. ²They found the stone rolled away from the tomb, ³but when they entered, they did not find the body of the Lord Jesus. ⁴While they were wondering about this, suddenly two men in clothes that gleamed like lightning stood beside them. ⁵In their fright the women bowed down with their faces to the ground, but the men said to them,

"Why do you look for the living among the dead? ⁶He is not here; he has risen! Remember how he told you, while he was still with you in Galilee: ⁷'The Son of Man must be delivered into the hands of sinful men, be crucified and on the third day be raised again.' " ⁸Then they remembered his words.

⁹When they came back from the tomb, they told all these things to the Eleven and to all the others. ¹⁰It was Mary Magdalene, Joanna, Mary the mother of James, and the others with them who told this to the apostles. ¹¹But they did not believe the women, because their words seemed to them like nonsense. ¹²Peter, however, got up and ran to the tomb. Bending over, he saw the strips of linen lying by themselves, and he went away, wondering to himself what had happened.

On the Road to Emmaus

¹³Now that same day two of them were going to a village called Emmaus, about seven milesᵇ from Jerusalem. ¹⁴They were talking with each other about everything that had happened. ¹⁵As they talked and discussed these things with each other, Jesus himself came up and walked along with them; ¹⁶but they were kept from recognizing him.

¹⁷He asked them, "What are you discussing together as you walk along?"

They stood still, their faces downcast. ¹⁸One of them, named Cleopas, asked him, "Are you only a visitor to Jerusalem and do not know the things that have happened there in these days?"

¹⁹"What things?" he asked.

"About Jesus of Nazareth," they replied. "He was a prophet, powerful in word and deed before God and all the people. ²⁰The chief priests and our rulers handed him over to be sentenced to death, and they crucified him; ²¹but we had hoped that he was the one who was going to redeem Israel. And what is more, it is the third day since all this took place. ²²In addition, some of our women amazed us. They went to the tomb early this morning ²³but didn't find his body. They came and told us that they had seen a vision of angels, who said he was alive. ²⁴Then some of our companions went to the tomb and found it just as the women had said, but him they did not see."

²⁵He said to them, "How foolish you are, and how slow of heart to believe all that the prophets have spoken! ²⁶Did not the Christᶜ have to suffer these things and then enter his glory?" ²⁷And beginning with Moses and all the Prophets, he explained to them what was said in all the Scriptures concerning himself.

²⁸As they approached the village to which they

ᵃ42 Some manuscripts *come with your kingly power*   ᵇ13 Greek *sixty stadia* (about 11 kilometers)
ᶜ26 Or *Messiah*; also in verse 46

were going, Jesus acted as if he were going farther. ²⁹But they urged him strongly, "Stay with us, for it is nearly evening; the day is almost over." So he went in to stay with them.

24:27 Old Testament 101

When the disciples first began to tell about Jesus' resurrection, they quoted Old Testament scriptures and explained how Jesus fulfilled their predictions. (See, for example, Peter's sermons in Acts 2 and 3.) They were probably following what Jesus had taught on the road to Emmaus. Jesus went through the entire Old Testament, explaining how his life crowned centuries of God's work.

³⁰When he was at the table with them, he took bread, gave thanks, broke it and began to give it to them. ³¹Then their eyes were opened and they recognized him, and he disappeared from their sight. ³²They asked each other, "Were not our hearts burning within us while he talked with us on the road and opened the Scriptures to us?"

³³They got up and returned at once to Jerusalem. There they found the Eleven and those with them, assembled together ³⁴and saying, "It is true! The Lord has risen and has appeared to Simon." ³⁵Then the two told what had happened on the way, and how Jesus was recognized by them when he broke the bread.

Jesus Appears to the Disciples

³⁶While they were still talking about this, Jesus himself stood among them and said to them, "Peace be with you."

³⁷They were startled and frightened, thinking they saw a ghost. ³⁸He said to them, "Why are you troubled, and why do doubts rise in your minds? ³⁹Look at my hands and my feet. It is I myself! Touch me and see; a ghost does not have flesh and bones, as you see I have."

⁴⁰When he had said this, he showed them his hands and feet. ⁴¹And while they still did not believe it because of joy and amazement, he asked them, "Do you have anything here to eat?" ⁴²They gave him a piece of broiled fish, ⁴³and he took it and ate it in their presence.

⁴⁴He said to them, "This is what I told you while I was still with you: Everything must be fulfilled that is written about me in the Law of Moses, the Prophets and the Psalms."

⁴⁵Then he opened their minds so they could understand the Scriptures. ⁴⁶He told them, "This is what is written: The Christ will suffer and rise from the dead on the third day, ⁴⁷and repentance and forgiveness of sins will be preached in his name to all nations, beginning at Jerusalem. ⁴⁸You are witnesses of these things. ⁴⁹I am going to send you what my Father has promised; but stay in the city until you have been clothed with power from on high."

The Ascension

⁵⁰When he had led them out to the vicinity of Bethany, he lifted up his hands and blessed them. ⁵¹While he was blessing them, he left them and was taken up into heaven. ⁵²Then they worshiped him and returned to Jerusalem with great joy. ⁵³And they stayed continually at the temple, praising God.

JOHN

God Breaks the Silence
He spoke in the only way we could truly understand

U NLESS A PERSON COMMUNICATES TO you, in speech or gestures or even facial expressions, you can't get to know him or her. What goes on behind the mask of skin will always remain a mystery.

> *The Word became flesh and made his dwelling among us.*
> *1:14*

God, too, was a mystery until he broke his silence. He spoke once, and all creation sprang to life—quasars, oceans, whales, giraffes, orchids, and beetles. He spoke again, says John, and this time the Word took the form of a man, Jesus Christ. John's book tells the story of that Word who became flesh.

Different from Other Gospels

It's clear from the first few paragraphs that John broke sharply from the style of Matthew, Mark, and Luke. The other Gospel writers focused on events, following Jesus through the bustling marketplaces and villages.

Unlike them, John assumed readers knew the basic facts about Jesus. Instead of focusing on facts, he mulled over the profound meaning of what Jesus had said and done. The book of John reads as if it were written under a great, shady tree by an author who had lots of time for reflection.

In his first sentence, John highlights Christ's nature. There are no Christmas scenes here: no stables, shepherds, or wise men. John tells nothing of Jesus' birth and youth. He introduces him as the adult Son of God. After an eloquent prologue, the book shows John the Baptist humbly pointing to Jesus, "the thongs of whose sandals I am not worthy to untie" (1:27).

Jesus Sent with a Mission

John selected vignettes from no more than 20 days in Jesus' life, and arranged them so that they present a Messiah who knows "where I came from and where I am going" (8:14). Jesus was not simply a "man who fell to earth," but God's Son, sent to do the work of the Father. His repeated references to the One "who sent me" give a cadence to the book.

According to John, Christ participated in the original creation act. But later he was sent to earth as the Word, the sum of all that God wanted to say. God spoke in the only way we could truly understand: by becoming one of us.

How to Read John

N ew Christians often turn to the book of John because it spells out so clearly the basics of the faith. Jesus proves who he is, diagnoses humanity's problems, and bluntly describes what is necessary for conversion. You will likely recognize familiar verses and phrases in this remarkable book (such as Jesus' "I am" sayings).

John selected seven "signs" or miracles (five of which aren't reported elsewhere) and built a story around them. As you read John, note how the author weaves together his story and its meaning.

It's best to read John in units. Don't just read a paragraph or a chapter. Follow the bold-face sectional headings and read a complete section, both the action and the commentary on it. John does not primarily relate events; he interprets those events.

Look carefully for the audiences Jesus addresses. Is he talking to his disciples? To his opponents? To the large crowds? He treats each audience differently.

PEOPLE YOU'LL MEET IN JOHN

NICODEMAS *(p. 1103)*   **THOMAS** *(p. 1121)*
ANDREW *(p. 1107)*   **PONTIUS PILATE** *(p. 1126)*
JUDAS *(p. 1110)*   **MARY MAGDALENE** *(p. 1128)*
ANNAS AND CAIAPHAS *(p. 1117)* **JOHN** *(p. 1129)*

3-TRACK READING PLAN

For an explanation and complete listing of the 3-track reading plan, turn to page 7.

TRACK 1:   ***Two-Week Courses on the Bible***
The Track 1 reading program on the Life and Teachings of Jesus includes four chapters from John. See page 7 for a complete listing of this course.

TRACK 2:   ***An Overview of John in 8 Days***
☐ Day 1. Read the Introduction to John and then turn to John 3, which contains perhaps the best-known verse in the entire Bible (verse 16). Read Jesus' conversation with Nicodemus.
☐ Day 2. John 5 and 6 contain Jesus' blunt teaching about who he was and why he came to earth. Read chapter 6, noting how John weaves together a miracle, the crowd's reaction to it, then Jesus' comments on it.
☐ Day 3. Read chapter 10, another familiar passage.
☐ Day 4. The next four readings are taken from John's report of the Last Supper. Begin with chapter 14.
☐ Day 5. Read chapter 15, where Jesus explains the image of a vine and its branches.
☐ Day 6. Read chapter 16, noting especially what Jesus says about the Holy Spirit. John contains more teaching about the Holy Spirit than any other Gospel.
☐ Day 7. Read chapter 17, a farewell prayer Jesus prayed for his disciples.
☐ Day 8. Read John's account of Jesus' resurrection, chapter 20.

Now turn to page 9 for your next Track 2 reading project.

TRACK 3:   ***All of John in 21 Days***
After you have read through John, turn to pages 10–14 for your next Track 3 reading project.

☐1	☐2	☐3	☐4	☐5	☐6	☐7	☐8
☐9	☐10	☐11	☐12	☐13	☐14	☐15	☐16
☐17	☐18	☐19	☐20	☐21			

The Word Became Flesh

1 In the beginning was the Word, and the Word was with God, and the Word was God. ²He was with God in the beginning.

³Through him all things were made; without him nothing was made that has been made. ⁴In him was life, and that life was the light of men. ⁵The light shines in the darkness, but the darkness has not understood*a* it.

⁶There came a man who was sent from God; his name was John. ⁷He came as a witness to testify concerning that light, so that through him all men might believe. ⁸He himself was not the light; he came only as a witness to the light. ⁹The true light that gives light to every man was coming into the world.*b*

¹⁰He was in the world, and though the world was made through him, the world did not recognize him. ¹¹He came to that which was his own, but his own did not receive him. ¹²Yet to all who received him, to those who believed in his name, he gave the right to become children of God— ¹³children born not of natural descent,*c* nor of human decision or a husband's will, but born of God.

¹⁴The Word became flesh and made his dwell-

a5 Or *darkness, and the darkness has not overcome comes into the world*   *b9* Or *This was the true light that gives light to every man who*   *c13* Greek *of bloods*

ing among us. We have seen his glory, the glory of the One and Only,[a] who came from the Father, full of grace and truth.

[15]John testifies concerning him. He cries out, saying, "This was he of whom I said, 'He who comes after me has surpassed me because he was before me.'" [16]From the fullness of his grace we have all received one blessing after another. [17]For the law was given through Moses; grace and truth came through Jesus Christ. [18]No one has ever seen God, but God the One and Only,[a,b] who is at the Father's side, has made him known.

1:14 Jesus the Word

John used language with special meaning for both Greek and Jewish readers. In Greek philosophy, "word" (logos) was a key term, often referring to the power of reason undergirding all creation. For Jews, too, "word" had great significance, for God spoke his word to create the world and to transform his people. Yet John's meaning passed beyond the Greek and Jewish ideas. An eight-year-old girl expressed it well. When asked why Jesus was called the Word, she said, "Because Jesus is all God wanted to say to us."

John the Baptist Denies Being the Christ

[19]Now this was John's testimony when the Jews of Jerusalem sent priests and Levites to ask him who he was. [20]He did not fail to confess, but confessed freely, "I am not the Christ.[c]"

[21]They asked him, "Then who are you? Are you Elijah?"

He said, "I am not."

"Are you the Prophet?"

He answered, "No."

[22]Finally they said, "Who are you? Give us an answer to take back to those who sent us. What do you say about yourself?"

[23]John replied in the words of Isaiah the prophet, "I am the voice of one calling in the desert, 'Make straight the way for the Lord.'"[d]

[24]Now some Pharisees who had been sent [25]questioned him, "Why then do you baptize if you are not the Christ, nor Elijah, nor the Prophet?"

[26]"I baptize with[e] water," John replied, "but among you stands one you do not know. [27]He is the one who comes after me, the thongs of whose sandals I am not worthy to untie."

[28]This all happened at Bethany on the other side of the Jordan, where John was baptizing.

Jesus the Lamb of God

[29]The next day John saw Jesus coming toward him and said, "Look, the Lamb of God, who takes away the sin of the world! [30]This is the one I meant when I said, 'A man who comes after me has surpassed me because he was before me.' [31]I myself did not know him, but the reason I came baptizing with water was that he might be revealed to Israel."

[32]Then John gave this testimony: "I saw the Spirit come down from heaven as a dove and remain on him. [33]I would not have known him, except that the one who sent me to baptize with water told me, 'The man on whom you see the Spirit come down and remain is he who will baptize with the Holy Spirit.' [34]I have seen and I testify that this is the Son of God."

Jesus' First Disciples

[35]The next day John was there again with two of his disciples. [36]When he saw Jesus passing by, he said, "Look, the Lamb of God!"

[37]When the two disciples heard him say this, they followed Jesus. [38]Turning around, Jesus saw them following and asked, "What do you want?"

They said, "Rabbi" (which means Teacher), "where are you staying?"

[39]"Come," he replied, "and you will see."

So they went and saw where he was staying, and spent that day with him. It was about the tenth hour.

1:39 Gradual Disciples

Other Gospels show the disciples dropping their nets and following Jesus instantly. John describes a more gradual process. When two of John the Baptist's disciples grew curious, Jesus invited them to come and spend a day with him. Soon, they were ready to tell others what they had seen and heard.

[40]Andrew, Simon Peter's brother, was one of the two who heard what John had said and who had followed Jesus. [41]The first thing Andrew did was to find his brother Simon and tell him, "We have found the Messiah" (that is, the Christ). [42]And he brought him to Jesus.

Jesus looked at him and said, "You are Simon son of John. You will be called Cephas" (which, when translated, is Peter[f]).

Jesus Calls Philip and Nathanael

[43]The next day Jesus decided to leave for Galilee. Finding Philip, he said to him, "Follow me."

---

[a]14,18 Or *the Only Begotten*   [b]18 Some manuscripts *but the only* (or *only begotten*) *Son*   [c]20 Or *Messiah*. "The Christ" (Greek) and "the Messiah" (Hebrew) both mean "the Anointed One"; also in verse 25.   [d]23 Isaiah 40:3   [e]26 Or *in*; also in verses 31 and 33   [f]42 Both *Cephas* (Aramaic) and *Peter* (Greek) mean *rock*.

[44]Philip, like Andrew and Peter, was from the town of Bethsaida. [45]Philip found Nathanael and told him, "We have found the one Moses wrote about in the Law, and about whom the prophets also wrote—Jesus of Nazareth, the son of Joseph."

[46]"Nazareth! Can anything good come from there?" Nathanael asked.

"Come and see," said Philip.

[47]When Jesus saw Nathanael approaching, he said of him, "Here is a true Israelite, in whom there is nothing false."

[48]"How do you know me?" Nathanael asked.

Jesus answered, "I saw you while you were still under the fig tree before Philip called you."

[49]Then Nathanael declared, "Rabbi, you are the Son of God; you are the King of Israel."

[50]Jesus said, "You believe[a] because I told you I saw you under the fig tree. You shall see greater things than that." [51]He then added, "I tell you[b] the truth, you[b] shall see heaven open, and the angels of God ascending and descending on the Son of Man."

Jesus Changes Water to Wine

2 On the third day a wedding took place at Cana in Galilee. Jesus' mother was there, [2]and Jesus and his disciples had also been invited to the wedding. [3]When the wine was gone, Jesus' mother said to him, "They have no more wine."

[4]"Dear woman, why do you involve me?" Jesus replied. "My time has not yet come."

[5]His mother said to the servants, "Do whatever he tells you."

[6]Nearby stood six stone water jars, the kind used by the Jews for ceremonial washing, each holding from twenty to thirty gallons.[c]

2:6 Eyewitness Details

Numerous specific details show that an eyewitness wrote the book of John. Here, the author describes stone water jars; elsewhere, he records the exact number of fish caught (21:11).

[7]Jesus said to the servants, "Fill the jars with water"; so they filled them to the brim.

[8]Then he told them, "Now draw some out and take it to the master of the banquet."

They did so, [9]and the master of the banquet tasted the water that had been turned into wine. He did not realize where it had come from, though the servants who had drawn the water knew. Then he called the bridegroom aside [10]and said, "Everyone brings out the choice wine first

and then the cheaper wine after the guests have had too much to drink; but you have saved the best till now."

[11]This, the first of his miraculous signs, Jesus performed at Cana in Galilee. He thus revealed his glory, and his disciples put their faith in him.

Jesus Clears the Temple

▶ *See Matthew 21:12–13; Mark 11:15–17; Luke 19:45–46*

[12]After this he went down to Capernaum with his mother and brothers and his disciples. There they stayed for a few days.

[13]When it was almost time for the Jewish Passover, Jesus went up to Jerusalem. [14]In the temple courts he found men selling cattle, sheep and doves, and others sitting at tables exchanging money. [15]So he made a whip out of cords, and drove all from the temple area, both sheep and cattle; he scattered the coins of the money changers and overturned their tables. [16]To those who sold doves he said, "Get these out of here! How dare you turn my Father's house into a market!"

[17]His disciples remembered that it is written: "Zeal for your house will consume me."[d]

[18]Then the Jews demanded of him, "What miraculous sign can you show us to prove your authority to do all this?"

[19]Jesus answered them, "Destroy this temple, and I will raise it again in three days."

[20]The Jews replied, "It has taken forty-six years to build this temple, and you are going to raise it in three days?" [21]But the temple he had spoken of was his body. [22]After he was raised from the dead, his disciples recalled what he had said. Then they believed the Scripture and the words that Jesus had spoken.

[23]Now while he was in Jerusalem at the Passover Feast, many people saw the miraculous signs he was doing and believed in his name.[e] [24]But Jesus would not entrust himself to them, for he knew all men. [25]He did not need man's testimony about man, for he knew what was in a man.

Jesus Teaches Nicodemus

3 Now there was a man of the Pharisees named Nicodemus, a member of the Jewish ruling council. [2]He came to Jesus at night and said, "Rabbi, we know you are a teacher who has come from God. For no one could perform the miraculous signs you are doing if God were not with him."

[3]In reply Jesus declared, "I tell you the truth, no one can see the kingdom of God unless he is born again.[f]"

[4]"How can a man be born when he is old?"

---

[a]50 Or *Do you believe . . . ?*   [b]51 The Greek is plural.   [c]6 Greek *two to three metretes* (probably about 75 to 115 liters)   [d]17 Psalm 69:9   [e]23 Or *and believed in him*   [f]3 Or *born from above*; also in verse 7

Nicodemus asked. "Surely he cannot enter a second time into his mother's womb to be born!"

[5]Jesus answered, "I tell you the truth, no one can enter the kingdom of God unless he is born of water and the Spirit. [6]Flesh gives birth to flesh, but the Spirit[a] gives birth to spirit. [7]You should not be surprised at my saying, 'You[b] must be born again.' [8]The wind blows wherever it pleases. You hear its sound, but you cannot tell where it comes from or where it is going. So it is with everyone born of the Spirit."

[9]"How can this be?" Nicodemus asked.

[10]"You are Israel's teacher," said Jesus, "and do you not understand these things? [11]I tell you the truth, we speak of what we know, and we testify to what we have seen, but still you people do not accept our testimony. [12]I have spoken to you of earthly things and you do not believe; how then will you believe if I speak of heavenly things? [13]No one has ever gone into heaven except the one who came from heaven—the Son of Man.[c] [14]Just as Moses lifted up the snake in the desert, so the Son of Man must be lifted up, [15]that everyone who believes in him may have eternal life.[d]

[16]"For God so loved the world that he gave his one and only Son,[e] that whoever believes in him shall not perish but have eternal life. [17]For God did not send his Son into the world to condemn the world, but to save the world through him. [18]Whoever believes in him is not condemned, but whoever does not believe stands condemned already because he has not believed in the name of God's one and only Son.[f] [19]This is the verdict: Light has come into the world, but men loved darkness instead of light because their deeds were evil. [20]Everyone who does evil hates the light, and will not come into the light for fear that his deeds will be exposed. [21]But whoever

---

3:16 The Gospel in a Nutshell

This verse has probably been memorized more than any other in the Bible. In a few words it tells the story of salvation: God's love for the world, God's gift of his Son, and the opportunity for anyone who believes to be saved.

---

lives by the truth comes into the light, so that it may be seen plainly that what he has done has been done through God."[g]

John the Baptist's Testimony About Jesus

[22]After this, Jesus and his disciples went out into the Judean countryside, where he spent some time with them, and baptized. [23]Now John also was baptizing at Aenon near Salim, because there was plenty of water, and people were constantly coming to be baptized. [24](This was before John was put in prison.) [25]An argument developed between some of John's disciples and a certain Jew[h] over the matter of ceremonial washing. [26]They came to John and said to him, "Rabbi, that man who was with you on the other side of the Jordan—the one you testified

---

a6 Or *but spirit*　　*b7* The Greek is plural.　　*c13* Some manuscripts *Man, who is in heaven*　　*d15* Or *believes may have eternal life in him*　　*e16* Or *his only begotten Son*　　*f18* Or *God's only begotten Son*　　*g21* Some interpreters end the quotation after verse 15.　　*h25* Some manuscripts *and certain Jews*

NICODEMUS　*A Reputation at Stake*

MOST OF JESUS' DISCIPLES WERE ordinary people with no status to worry about losing. A fisherman or tax collector would not forfeit much standing if he followed an unorthodox teacher. In contrast, Nicodemus had quite a reputation at stake. As a member of the Jewish Sanhedrin, he held an important ruling post. As a Pharisee, he was committed to a certain set of beliefs. And as a prominent religious teacher, he was a respected interpreter of God's law.

No doubt that is why Nicodemus first asked Jesus to meet him at night. As time went on, however, Nicodemus grew more bold. When the Sanhedrin discussed Jesus, he spoke out against their willingness to condemn the man without talking to him. For that, Nicodemus received scalding criticism (7:50–52).

After Jesus' death, Nicodemus let his sentiments become more public. Along with Joseph of Arimathea, he took Jesus' body from Calvary and prepared it for burial.

The Bible tells us no more about Nicodemus, so we can't be sure whether he ever openly confessed faith in Jesus. It seems likely, however, that John mentions these incidents because Nicodemus was willing to talk about what he had seen and heard and believed. How else would John have learned the intimate details of Nicodemus's actions? This Gospel gives reason to hope that Nicodemus sacrificed his reputation—and gained a new birth—in the end.

Life Questions: Are there questions about God you feel you cannot ask in public? What are they, and who could you ask in private?

about—well, he is baptizing, and everyone is going to him."

[27]To this John replied, "A man can receive only what is given him from heaven. [28]You yourselves can testify that I said, 'I am not the Christ[a] but am sent ahead of him.' [29]The bride belongs to the bridegroom. The friend who attends the bridegroom waits and listens for him, and is full of joy when he hears the bridegroom's voice. That joy is mine, and it is now complete. [30]He must become greater; I must become less.

[31]"The one who comes from above is above all; the one who is from the earth belongs to the earth, and speaks as one from the earth. The one who comes from heaven is above all. [32]He testifies to what he has seen and heard, but no one accepts his testimony. [33]The man who has accepted it has certified that God is truthful. [34]For the one whom God has sent speaks the words of God, for God[b] gives the Spirit without limit. [35]The Father loves the Son and has placed everything in his hands. [36]Whoever believes in the Son has eternal life, but whoever rejects the Son will not see life, for God's wrath remains on him."[c]

Jesus Talks With a Samaritan Woman

4 The Pharisees heard that Jesus was gaining and baptizing more disciples than John, [2]although in fact it was not Jesus who baptized, but his disciples. [3]When the Lord learned of this, he left Judea and went back once more to Galilee. [4]Now he had to go through Samaria. [5]So he

---

[a]28 Or Messiah   [b]34 Greek he   [c]36 Some interpreters end the quotation after verse 30.

Conversations with Jesus
How did Jesus talk to ordinary people?

WATER. WHERE IT'S PLENTIFUL, WE tend to take it for granted, like air. We linger in the shower, hose down a dusty driveway, let a sprinkler spurt for hours to keep the lawn green.

Not so in the desert, where even plants hoard water with bristly defenses. There, water takes on a mythical aura. Taunting visions of pools and streams dance in the heat waves. A craving for water crowds out all other thoughts, and one spoonful, on a parched tongue, is worth gold.

To a woman in a dry land who spent part of each day hauling clay jugs to and from a well, water was the most powerful symbol imaginable. Little wonder that when Jesus offered "living water" that would never run dry (4:10,14), the Samaritan woman paid attention.

> The woman said, "I know that Messiah" (called Christ) "is coming. When he comes, he will explain everything to us." Then Jesus declared, "I who speak to you am he." 4:25–26

Profoundly Simple Words

A simple word or phrase with a profound meaning: that is the style of Jesus' teaching as presented in John. No biblical author used simpler, more commonplace words: *water, world, light, life, birth, love, truth*. Yet John used them with such depth that hundreds of authors since have tried to plumb their meaning.

Reading John is like sitting in a canoe in the middle of a deep, pristine lake. The clarity of the water reveals everything under the surface—you think. Yet, as you gaze deeper, you can never see the bottom. Something always remains hidden.

Those who look for a neat scheme of organization in John usually fail. John's Gospel omits many of the events recorded in Mark, most of the long public speeches of Matthew, and all of the parables of Luke. Its teaching emerges mainly through Jesus' intimate encounters with diverse people.

Listening in on Private Conversations

Jesus uttered some of his most memorable sayings in the midst of very ordinary conversations. The book of John rarely shows him speaking to large crowds. Instead, we see Jesus meeting secretly with a nervous religious leader (3:1–21), or talking with a promiscuous woman (4:5–26) beside a well. Both visitors carried away simple-yet-profound images (a second birth, living water), and today we recall those words as among the most familiar in all the Bible.

John paints close-ups of individuals who responded to Jesus on earth. Some followed him courageously, others remained skeptical, and still others reacted with hostility. Often, John reports, people simply "did not understand," despite Jesus' use of visual images. In short, response to the Son of God on earth nearly 2,000 years ago bears a striking resemblance to the world's response to him now.

Life Questions: Imagine yourself in a private conversation with Jesus, much like the Samaritan woman's. What would you want to talk about?

came to a town in Samaria called Sychar, near the plot of ground Jacob had given to his son Joseph. [6]Jacob's well was there, and Jesus, tired as he was from the journey, sat down by the well. It was about the sixth hour.

[7]When a Samaritan woman came to draw water, Jesus said to her, "Will you give me a drink?" [8](His disciples had gone into the town to buy food.)

[9]The Samaritan woman said to him, "You are a Jew and I am a Samaritan woman. How can you ask me for a drink?" (For Jews do not associate with Samaritans.[a])

4:9 Bridging Differences

When one church brands another a cult, it usually creates long-standing bitterness. The Samaritans and the Jews felt that way about each other. Samaritan religion closely resembled Judaism, but on key issues its followers had gone their own way. They accepted only the first five books of the Old Testament, and insisted that Mount Gerizim, not Jerusalem, was the proper place to worship God. Though Jews and Samaritans usually avoided each other, Jesus reached across these barriers.

[10]Jesus answered her, "If you knew the gift of God and who it is that asks you for a drink, you would have asked him and he would have given you living water."

[11]"Sir," the woman said, "you have nothing to draw with and the well is deep. Where can you get this living water? [12]Are you greater than our father Jacob, who gave us the well and drank from it himself, as did also his sons and his flocks and herds?"

[13]Jesus answered, "Everyone who drinks this water will be thirsty again, [14]but whoever drinks the water I give him will never thirst. Indeed, the water I give him will become in him a spring of water welling up to eternal life."

[15]The woman said to him, "Sir, give me this water so that I won't get thirsty and have to keep coming here to draw water."

[16]He told her, "Go, call your husband and come back."

[17]"I have no husband," she replied.

Jesus said to her, "You are right when you say you have no husband. [18]The fact is, you have had five husbands, and the man you now have is not your husband. What you have just said is quite true."

[19]"Sir," the woman said, "I can see that you are a prophet. [20]Our fathers worshiped on this mountain, but you Jews claim that the place where we must worship is in Jerusalem."

[21]Jesus declared, "Believe me, woman, a time is coming when you will worship the Father neither on this mountain nor in Jerusalem. [22]You Samaritans worship what you do not know; we worship what we do know, for salvation is from the Jews. [23]Yet a time is coming and has now come when the true worshipers will worship the Father in spirit and truth, for they are the kind of worshipers the Father seeks. [24]God is spirit, and his worshipers must worship in spirit and in truth."

[25]The woman said, "I know that Messiah" (called Christ) "is coming. When he comes, he will explain everything to us."

[26]Then Jesus declared, "I who speak to you am he."

The Disciples Rejoin Jesus

[27]Just then his disciples returned and were surprised to find him talking with a woman. But no one asked, "What do you want?" or "Why are you talking with her?"

[28]Then, leaving her water jar, the woman went back to the town and said to the people, [29]"Come, see a man who told me everything I ever did. Could this be the Christ[b]?" [30]They came out of the town and made their way toward him.

[31]Meanwhile his disciples urged him, "Rabbi, eat something."

[32]But he said to them, "I have food to eat that you know nothing about."

[33]Then his disciples said to each other, "Could someone have brought him food?"

[34]"My food," said Jesus, "is to do the will of him who sent me and to finish his work. [35]Do you not say, 'Four months more and then the harvest'? I tell you, open your eyes and look at the fields! They are ripe for harvest. [36]Even now the reaper draws his wages, even now he harvests the crop for eternal life, so that the sower and the reaper may be glad together. [37]Thus the saying 'One sows and another reaps' is true. [38]I sent you to reap what you have not worked for. Others have done the hard work, and you have reaped the benefits of their labor."

Many Samaritans Believe

[39]Many of the Samaritans from that town believed in him because of the woman's testimony, "He told me everything I ever did." [40]So when the Samaritans came to him, they urged him to stay with them, and he stayed two days. [41]And because of his words many more became believers.

[42]They said to the woman, "We no longer be-

---

[a]9 Or *do not use dishes Samaritans have used*   [b]29 Or *Messiah*

lieve just because of what you said; now we have heard for ourselves, and we know that this man really is the Savior of the world."

Jesus Heals the Official's Son

[43]After the two days he left for Galilee. [44](Now Jesus himself had pointed out that a prophet has no honor in his own country.) [45]When he arrived in Galilee, the Galileans welcomed him. They had seen all that he had done in Jerusalem at the Passover Feast, for they also had been there.

[46]Once more he visited Cana in Galilee, where he had turned the water into wine. And there was a certain royal official whose son lay sick at Capernaum. [47]When this man heard that Jesus had arrived in Galilee from Judea, he went to him and begged him to come and heal his son, who was close to death.

[48]"Unless you people see miraculous signs and wonders," Jesus told him, "you will never believe."

[49]The royal official said, "Sir, come down before my child dies."

[50]Jesus replied, "You may go. Your son will live."

The man took Jesus at his word and departed.

4:50 A Long-distance Miracle

This miracle has certain similarities to another performed at the request of a Roman centurion (Luke 7:2–10; Matthew 8:5–13). Of Jesus' two dozen recorded miracles of healing, only these occurred over a distance.

[51]While he was still on the way, his servants met him with the news that his boy was living. [52]When he inquired as to the time when his son got better, they said to him, "The fever left him yesterday at the seventh hour."

[53]Then the father realized that this was the exact time at which Jesus had said to him, "Your son will live." So he and all his household believed.

[54]This was the second miraculous sign that Jesus performed, having come from Judea to Galilee.

The Healing at the Pool

5 Some time later, Jesus went up to Jerusalem for a feast of the Jews. [2]Now there is in Jerusalem near the Sheep Gate a pool, which in Aramaic is called Bethesda[a] and which is surrounded by five covered colonnades. [3]Here a great number of disabled people used to lie—the

blind, the lame, the paralyzed.[b] [5]One who was there had been an invalid for thirty-eight years. [6]When Jesus saw him lying there and learned that he had been in this condition for a long time, he asked him, "Do you want to get well?"

[7]"Sir," the invalid replied, "I have no one to help me into the pool when the water is stirred. While I am trying to get in, someone else goes down ahead of me."

[8]Then Jesus said to him, "Get up! Pick up your mat and walk." [9]At once the man was cured; he picked up his mat and walked.

The day on which this took place was a Sabbath, [10]and so the Jews said to the man who had been healed, "It is the Sabbath; the law forbids you to carry your mat."

[11]But he replied, "The man who made me well said to me, 'Pick up your mat and walk.' "

[12]So they asked him, "Who is this fellow who told you to pick it up and walk?"

[13]The man who was healed had no idea who it was, for Jesus had slipped away into the crowd that was there.

[14]Later Jesus found him at the temple and said to him, "See, you are well again. Stop sinning or something worse may happen to you." [15]The man went away and told the Jews that it was Jesus who had made him well.

Life Through the Son

[16]So, because Jesus was doing these things on the Sabbath, the Jews persecuted him. [17]Jesus said to them, "My Father is always at his work to this very day, and I, too, am working." [18]For this reason the Jews tried all the harder to kill him; not only was he breaking the Sabbath, but he was even calling God his own Father, making himself equal with God.

[19]Jesus gave them this answer: "I tell you the truth, the Son can do nothing by himself; he can do only what he sees his Father doing, because whatever the Father does the Son also does. [20]For the Father loves the Son and shows him all he does. Yes, to your amazement he will show him even greater things than these. [21]For just as the Father raises the dead and gives them life, even so the Son gives life to whom he is pleased to give it. [22]Moreover, the Father judges no one, but has entrusted all judgment to the Son, [23]that all may honor the Son just as they honor the Father. He who does not honor the Son does not honor the Father, who sent him.

[24]"I tell you the truth, whoever hears my word and believes him who sent me has eternal life and will not be condemned; he has crossed over from death to life. [25]I tell you the truth, a time is coming and has now come when the dead will hear

---

[a]2 Some manuscripts *Bethzatha*; other manuscripts *Bethsaida*   [b]3 Some less important manuscripts *paralyzed—and they waited for the moving of the waters.* [4]*From time to time an angel of the Lord would come down and stir up the waters. The first one into the pool after each such disturbance would be cured of whatever disease he had.*

the voice of the Son of God and those who hear will live. ²⁶For as the Father has life in himself, so he has granted the Son to have life in himself. ²⁷And he has given him authority to judge because he is the Son of Man.

²⁸"Do not be amazed at this, for a time is coming when all who are in their graves will hear his voice ²⁹and come out—those who have done good will rise to live, and those who have done evil will rise to be condemned. ³⁰By myself I can do nothing; I judge only as I hear, and my judgment is just, for I seek not to please myself but him who sent me.

Testimonies About Jesus

³¹"If I testify about myself, my testimony is not valid. ³²There is another who testifies in my favor, and I know that his testimony about me is valid.

³³"You have sent to John and he has testified to the truth. ³⁴Not that I accept human testimony; but I mention it that you may be saved. ³⁵John was a lamp that burned and gave light, and you chose for a time to enjoy his light.

³⁶"I have testimony weightier than that of John. For the very work that the Father has given me to finish, and which I am doing, testifies that the Father has sent me. ³⁷And the Father who sent me has himself testified concerning me. You have never heard his voice nor seen his form, ³⁸nor does his word dwell in you, for you do not believe the one he sent. ³⁹You diligently study*a* the Scriptures because you think that by them you possess eternal life. These are the Scriptures that testify about me, ⁴⁰yet you refuse to come to me to have life.

⁴¹"I do not accept praise from men, ⁴²but I know you. I know that you do not have the love of God in your hearts. ⁴³I have come in my Father's name, and you do not accept me; but if someone else comes in his own name, you will

accept him. ⁴⁴How can you believe if you accept praise from one another, yet make no effort to obtain the praise that comes from the only God*b*?

⁴⁵"But do not think I will accuse you before the Father. Your accuser is Moses, on whom your hopes are set. ⁴⁶If you believed Moses, you would believe me, for he wrote about me. ⁴⁷But since you do not believe what he wrote, how are you going to believe what I say?"

Jesus Feeds the Five Thousand

▶ *See Matthew 14:13–21; Mark 6:32–44; Luke 9:10–17*

6 Some time after this, Jesus crossed to the far shore of the Sea of Galilee (that is, the Sea of Tiberias), ²and a great crowd of people followed him because they saw the miraculous signs he had performed on the sick. ³Then Jesus went up on a mountainside and sat down with his disciples. ⁴The Jewish Passover Feast was near.

⁵When Jesus looked up and saw a great crowd coming toward him, he said to Philip, "Where shall we buy bread for these people to eat?" ⁶He asked this only to test him, for he already had in mind what he was going to do.

⁷Philip answered him, "Eight months' wages*c* would not buy enough bread for each one to have a bite!"

⁸Another of his disciples, Andrew, Simon Peter's brother, spoke up, ⁹"Here is a boy with five small barley loaves and two small fish, but how far will they go among so many?"

¹⁰Jesus said, "Have the people sit down." There was plenty of grass in that place, and the men sat down, about five thousand of them. ¹¹Jesus then took the loaves, gave thanks, and distributed to those who were seated as much as they wanted. He did the same with the fish.

¹²When they had all had enough to eat, he said to his disciples, "Gather the pieces that are left

a39 Or Study diligently (the imperative)   *b44 Some early manuscripts the Only One*   *c7 Greek two hundred denarii*

ANDREW *Out of the Spotlight*

ANDREW OPERATED MOSTLY BEHIND THE scenes. As Simon Peter's brother and one of Jesus' first followers, he got involved in many important happenings. Yet all of Andrew's appearances in the Gospels show him directing attention to someone else, not himself.

His greatest recorded achievement was making an introduction. When Andrew heard John the Baptist commend Jesus as "the Lamb of God," he dropped everything to follow Jesus. (He was one of the first to recognize Jesus as the "Messiah.") Then, after spending the day with Jesus, he went to fetch Peter, his brother and fishing partner. Andrew introduced the two, and the rest is history (see 1:35–42).

The Gospels show two other occasions on which Andrew served as a facilitator: He drew Jesus' attention to a boy carrying a lunch (6:8–9) and helped introduce Jesus to some Greek visitors (12:20). Both incidents led to impressive miracles.

Life Questions: How can a behind-the-scenes person today have a role in introducing others to Jesus?

over. Let nothing be wasted." [13]So they gathered them and filled twelve baskets with the pieces of the five barley loaves left over by those who had eaten.

6:9 Better Bread

The feeding of the five thousand is the only miracle (except Jesus' resurrection) that all four Gospels record. It shows Jesus meeting the most basic human need, using barley loaves, the least expensive kind of bread. Many Jews believed that the Messiah would renew the miraculous manna that their ancestors had eaten under Moses. Jesus pointed to a better, life-changing meal—himself. As the bread of life (verse 35), he would nourish his people far better than any miraculous meal.

[14]After the people saw the miraculous sign that Jesus did, they began to say, "Surely this is the Prophet who is to come into the world." [15]Jesus, knowing that they intended to come and make him king by force, withdrew again to a mountain by himself.

Jesus Walks on the Water

▶ See Matthew 14:22–33; Mark 6:47–51

[16]When evening came, his disciples went down to the lake, [17]where they got into a boat and set off across the lake for Capernaum. By now it was dark, and Jesus had not yet joined them. [18]A strong wind was blowing and the waters grew rough. [19]When they had rowed three or three and a half miles,[a] they saw Jesus approaching the boat, walking on the water; and they were terrified. [20]But he said to them, "It is I; don't be afraid." [21]Then they were willing to take him into the boat, and immediately the boat reached the shore where they were heading.

[22]The next day the crowd that had stayed on the opposite shore of the lake realized that only one boat had been there, and that Jesus had not entered it with his disciples, but that they had gone away alone. [23]Then some boats from Tiberias landed near the place where the people had eaten the bread after the Lord had given thanks. [24]Once the crowd realized that neither Jesus nor his disciples were there, they got into the boats and went to Capernaum in search of Jesus.

Jesus the Bread of Life

[25]When they found him on the other side of the lake, they asked him, "Rabbi, when did you get here?"

[26]Jesus answered, "I tell you the truth, you are looking for me, not because you saw miraculous signs but because you ate the loaves and had your fill. [27]Do not work for food that spoils, but for food that endures to eternal life, which the Son of Man will give you. On him God the Father has placed his seal of approval."

[28]Then they asked him, "What must we do to do the works God requires?"

[29]Jesus answered, "The work of God is this: to believe in the one he has sent."

[30]So they asked him, "What miraculous sign then will you give that we may see it and believe you? What will you do? [31]Our forefathers ate the manna in the desert; as it is written: 'He gave them bread from heaven to eat.'[b]"

[32]Jesus said to them, "I tell you the truth, it is not Moses who has given you the bread from heaven, but it is my Father who gives you the true bread from heaven. [33]For the bread of God is he who comes down from heaven and gives life to the world."

[34]"Sir," they said, "from now on give us this bread."

[35]Then Jesus declared, "I am the bread of life. He who comes to me will never go hungry, and he who believes in me will never be thirsty. [36]But as I told you, you have seen me and still you do not believe. [37]All that the Father gives me will come to me, and whoever comes to me I will never drive away. [38]For I have come down from heaven not to do my will but to do the will of him who sent me. [39]And this is the will of him who sent me, that I shall lose none of all that he has given me, but raise them up at the last day. [40]For my Father's will is that everyone who looks to the Son and believes in him shall have eternal life, and I will raise him up at the last day."

[41]At this the Jews began to grumble about him because he said, "I am the bread that came down from heaven." [42]They said, "Is this not Jesus, the son of Joseph, whose father and mother we know? How can he now say, 'I came down from heaven'?"

[43]"Stop grumbling among yourselves," Jesus answered. [44]"No one can come to me unless the Father who sent me draws him, and I will raise him up at the last day. [45]It is written in the Prophets: 'They will all be taught by God.'[c] Everyone who listens to the Father and learns from him comes to me. [46]No one has seen the Father except the one who is from God; only he has seen the Father. [47]I tell you the truth, he who believes has everlasting life. [48]I am the bread of life. [49]Your forefathers ate the manna in the desert, yet they died. [50]But here is the bread that comes down from heaven, which a man may eat and not die. [51]I am the living bread that came down from

---

[a]19 Greek *rowed twenty-five or thirty stadia* (about 5 or 6 kilometers) [b]31 Exodus 16:4; Neh. 9:15; Psalm 78:24,25
[c]45 Isaiah 54:13

heaven. If anyone eats of this bread, he will live forever. This bread is my flesh, which I will give for the life of the world."

⁵²Then the Jews began to argue sharply among themselves, "How can this man give us his flesh to eat?"

⁵³Jesus said to them, "I tell you the truth, unless you eat the flesh of the Son of Man and drink his blood, you have no life in you. ⁵⁴Whoever eats my flesh and drinks my blood has eternal life, and I will raise him up at the last day. ⁵⁵For my flesh is real food and my blood is real drink. ⁵⁶Whoever eats my flesh and drinks my blood remains in me, and I in him. ⁵⁷Just as the living Father sent me and I live because of the Father, so the one who feeds on me will live because of me. ⁵⁸This is the bread that came down from heaven. Your forefathers ate manna and died, but he who feeds on this bread will live forever." ⁵⁹He said this while teaching in the synagogue in Capernaum.

Many Disciples Desert Jesus

⁶⁰On hearing it, many of his disciples said, "This is a hard teaching. Who can accept it?"

6:60 Too Hard to Swallow

Chapter 6 shows the full cycle of people's response to Jesus. At first, excited by his miracle of feeding the 5,000, people tried to make him king. But Jesus escaped. The next day he rebuked them for having an interest only in physical concerns, not in spiritual truth (verse 26). He used the miracle of the feeding to give an important lesson on the bread of life, using words that were later applied to the Lord's Supper, or the Eucharist. These words, however, so disappointed the sensation-seeking crowd that many turned away from him.

⁶¹Aware that his disciples were grumbling about this, Jesus said to them, "Does this offend you? ⁶²What if you see the Son of Man ascend to where he was before! ⁶³The Spirit gives life; the flesh counts for nothing. The words I have spoken to you are spirit*ᵃ* and they are life. ⁶⁴Yet there are some of you who do not believe." For Jesus had known from the beginning which of them did not believe and who would betray him. ⁶⁵He went on to say, "This is why I told you that no one can come to me unless the Father has enabled him."

⁶⁶From this time many of his disciples turned back and no longer followed him.

⁶⁷"You do not want to leave too, do you?" Jesus asked the Twelve.

⁶⁸Simon Peter answered him, "Lord, to whom shall we go? You have the words of eternal life. ⁶⁹We believe and know that you are the Holy One of God."

⁷⁰Then Jesus replied, "Have I not chosen you, the Twelve? Yet one of you is a devil!" ⁷¹(He meant Judas, the son of Simon Iscariot, who, though one of the Twelve, was later to betray him.)

Jesus Goes to the Feast of Tabernacles

7 After this, Jesus went around in Galilee, purposely staying away from Judea because the Jews there were waiting to take his life. ²But when the Jewish Feast of Tabernacles was near, ³Jesus' brothers said to him, "You ought to leave here and go to Judea, so that your disciples may see the miracles you do. ⁴No one who wants to become a public figure acts in secret. Since you are doing these things, show yourself to the world." ⁵For even his own brothers did not believe in him.

⁶Therefore Jesus told them, "The right time for me has not yet come; for you any time is right. ⁷The world cannot hate you, but it hates me because I testify that what it does is evil. ⁸You go to the Feast. I am not yet*ᵇ* going up to this Feast, because for me the right time has not yet come." ⁹Having said this, he stayed in Galilee.

¹⁰However, after his brothers had left for the Feast, he went also, not publicly, but in secret. ¹¹Now at the Feast the Jews were watching for him and asking, "Where is that man?"

¹²Among the crowds there was widespread whispering about him. Some said, "He is a good man."

Others replied, "No, he deceives the people."

7:12 Public Opinion

At one time a musician who wanted a national reputation had to play at New York's Carnegie Hall, the nation's cultural center. Similarly, Jesus' brothers wanted him to appear in Jerusalem, Israel's political and religious center. But Jesus had less faith than they in public opinion, and John shows why. The crowds that came to Jerusalem were curious but skeptical. Some thought Jesus a good man, some considered him a con artist. They were amazed at his knowledge of Scripture, but attributed his ideas to demon-possession (verse 20). They couldn't agree whether he was the Messiah (verse 43).

ᵃ63 Or *Spirit* *ᵇ8* Some early manuscripts do not have *yet.*

13But no one would say anything publicly about him for fear of the Jews.

Jesus Teaches at the Feast

14Not until halfway through the Feast did Jesus go up to the temple courts and begin to teach. 15The Jews were amazed and asked, "How did this man get such learning without having studied?"

16Jesus answered, "My teaching is not my own. It comes from him who sent me. 17If anyone chooses to do God's will, he will find out whether my teaching comes from God or whether I speak on my own. 18He who speaks on his own does so to gain honor for himself, but he who works for the honor of the one who sent him is a man of truth; there is nothing false about him. 19Has not Moses given you the law? Yet not one of you keeps the law. Why are you trying to kill me?"

20"You are demon-possessed," the crowd answered. "Who is trying to kill you?"

21Jesus said to them, "I did one miracle, and you are all astonished. 22Yet, because Moses gave you circumcision (though actually it did not come from Moses, but from the patriarchs), you circumcise a child on the Sabbath. 23Now if a child can be circumcised on the Sabbath so that the law of Moses may not be broken, why are you angry with me for healing the whole man on the Sabbath? 24Stop judging by mere appearances, and make a right judgment."

Is Jesus the Christ?

25At that point some of the people of Jerusalem began to ask, "Isn't this the man they are trying to kill? 26Here he is, speaking publicly, and they are not saying a word to him. Have the authorities really concluded that he is the Christ[a]? 27But we know where this man is from; when the Christ comes, no one will know where he is from."

28Then Jesus, still teaching in the temple courts, cried out, "Yes, you know me, and you know where I am from. I am not here on my own, but he who sent me is true. You do not know him, 29but I know him because I am from him and he sent me."

30At this they tried to seize him, but no one laid a hand on him, because his time had not yet come. 31Still, many in the crowd put their faith in him. They said, "When the Christ comes, will he do more miraculous signs than this man?"

32The Pharisees heard the crowd whispering such things about him. Then the chief priests and the Pharisees sent temple guards to arrest him.

33Jesus said, "I am with you for only a short time, and then I go to the one who sent me. 34You will look for me, but you will not find me; and where I am, you cannot come."

a26 Or Messiah; also in verses 27, 31, 41 and 42

JUDAS Devil Man

HUMAN BEINGS ARE BOTH "THE scum and glory of the universe," said Blaise Pascal. The Bible, too, paints a realistic picture of people as definite mixtures of good and bad. Apart from Jesus, no one is as good as to be flawless, and rarely is anyone portrayed as all bad.

Judas Iscariot is a major exception. No doubt he had some good qualities, or else why would Jesus have picked him as a disciple? Yet these good qualities were swallowed up by characteristics the Bible clearly labels satanic. In fact, Jesus himself described Judas as a devil (6:70).

How does a human being fall so low? From the evidence of the New Testament, it seems that Judas let greed get the better of him. While handling the cash as the disciples' treasurer, he began to take money for himself (12:6).

Possibly, too, Judas became frustrated over Jesus' unwillingness to be crowned king and lead a revolt against the Romans. Although other disciples struggled with that same issue, only Judas left himself so open to evil that Satan took control. Both John and Luke say that Satan entered into Judas (Luke 22:3; John 13:27). In a final, terrible act, he betrayed his Master, identifying him with a kiss in a crowd on a dark night.

Afterward, Judas felt shame and remorse. But so did the other disciples, who had also abandoned and denied Jesus. Judas should have gone to Jesus for forgiveness—after all, Jesus mercifully forgave Peter's brazen denial. Instead Judas went to the wrong people, attempting to undo his betrayal by meeting with the very ones who had financed it.

Rebuffed by his co-conspirators, Judas killed himself (Matthew 27:5). He went down in history as perhaps the most famous of all of Jesus' disciples—famous as an object lesson of what can happen, even among Jesus' followers, if they let evil have its way.

Life Questions: In Judas's life, one sin led to other, bigger ones. Have you ever seen this process in action? Where and how? What steps can you take to counteract this process?

³⁵The Jews said to one another, "Where does this man intend to go that we cannot find him? Will he go where our people live scattered among the Greeks, and teach the Greeks? ³⁶What did he mean when he said, 'You will look for me, but you will not find me,' and 'Where I am, you cannot come'?"

³⁷On the last and greatest day of the Feast, Jesus stood and said in a loud voice, "If anyone is thirsty, let him come to me and drink. ³⁸Whoever believes in me, as*ᵃ* the Scripture has said, streams of living water will flow from within him." ³⁹By this he meant the Spirit, whom those who believed in him were later to receive. Up to that time the Spirit had not been given, since Jesus had not yet been glorified.

⁴⁰On hearing his words, some of the people said, "Surely this man is the Prophet."

⁴¹Others said, "He is the Christ."

Still others asked, "How can the Christ come from Galilee? ⁴²Does not the Scripture say that the Christ will come from David's family*ᵇ* and from Bethlehem, the town where David lived?" ⁴³Thus the people were divided because of Jesus. ⁴⁴Some wanted to seize him, but no one laid a hand on him.

Unbelief of the Jewish Leaders

⁴⁵Finally the temple guards went back to the chief priests and Pharisees, who asked them, "Why didn't you bring him in?"

⁴⁶"No one ever spoke the way this man does," the guards declared.

⁴⁷"You mean he has deceived you also?" the Pharisees retorted. ⁴⁸"Has any of the rulers or of the Pharisees believed in him? ⁴⁹No! But this mob that knows nothing of the law—there is a curse on them."

⁵⁰Nicodemus, who had gone to Jesus earlier and who was one of their own number, asked, ⁵¹"Does our law condemn anyone without first hearing him to find out what he is doing?"

⁵²They replied, "Are you from Galilee, too? Look into it, and you will find that a prophet*ᶜ* does not come out of Galilee."

[The earliest manuscripts and many other ancient witnesses do not have John 7:53–8:11.]

⁵³Then each went to his own home.

8 But Jesus went to the Mount of Olives. ²At dawn he appeared again in the temple courts, where all the people gathered around him, and he sat down to teach them. ³The teachers of the law and the Pharisees brought in a woman caught in adultery. They made her stand before the group ⁴and said to Jesus, "Teacher, this woman was caught in the act of adultery. ⁵In the Law Moses commanded us to stone such women. Now what do you say?" ⁶They were using this question as a trap, in order to have a basis for accusing him.

But Jesus bent down and started to write on

8:6 Belong in the Bible?

Because most ancient manuscripts don't include this story about the woman caught in adultery, many scholars question whether it was added later or perhaps originally fell at a different place in the Gospel. According to the story, the Pharisees weren't following Moses' law, which required the woman's partner in crime to appear also. Interestingly, verse 6 records the only scene of Jesus writing.

the ground with his finger. ⁷When they kept on questioning him, he straightened up and said to them, "If any one of you is without sin, let him be the first to throw a stone at her." ⁸Again he stooped down and wrote on the ground.

⁹At this, those who heard began to go away one at a time, the older ones first, until only Jesus was left, with the woman still standing there. ¹⁰Jesus straightened up and asked her, "Woman, where are they? Has no one condemned you?"

¹¹"No one, sir," she said.

"Then neither do I condemn you," Jesus declared. "Go now and leave your life of sin."

The Validity of Jesus' Testimony

¹²When Jesus spoke again to the people, he said, "I am the light of the world. Whoever follows me will never walk in darkness, but will have the light of life."

¹³The Pharisees challenged him, "Here you are, appearing as your own witness; your testimony is not valid."

¹⁴Jesus answered, "Even if I testify on my own behalf, my testimony is valid, for I know where I came from and where I am going. But you have no idea where I come from or where I am going. ¹⁵You judge by human standards; I pass judgment on no one. ¹⁶But if I do judge, my decisions are right, because I am not alone. I stand with the Father, who sent me. ¹⁷In your own Law it is written that the testimony of two men is valid. ¹⁸I am one who testifies for myself; my other witness is the Father, who sent me."

ᵃ37,38 Or *If anyone is thirsty, let him come to me. / And let him drink,* *³⁸who believes in me. / As*   *ᵇ42* Greek *seed*
ᶜ52 Two early manuscripts *the Prophet*

[19]Then they asked him, "Where is your father?"

"You do not know me or my Father," Jesus replied. "If you knew me, you would know my Father also." [20]He spoke these words while teaching in the temple area near the place where the offerings were put. Yet no one seized him, because his time had not yet come.

[21]Once more Jesus said to them, "I am going away, and you will look for me, and you will die in your sin. Where I go, you cannot come."

[22]This made the Jews ask, "Will he kill himself? Is that why he says, 'Where I go, you cannot come'?"

[23]But he continued, "You are from below; I am from above. You are of this world; I am not of this world. [24]I told you that you would die in your sins; if you do not believe that I am [the one I claim to be],[a] you will indeed die in your sins."

[25]"Who are you?" they asked.

"Just what I have been claiming all along," Jesus replied. [26]"I have much to say in judgment of you. But he who sent me is reliable, and what I have heard from him I tell the world."

[27]They did not understand that he was telling them about his Father. [28]So Jesus said, "When you have lifted up the Son of Man, then you will know that I am [the one I claim to be] and that I do nothing on my own but speak just what the Father has taught me. [29]The one who sent me is with me; he has not left me alone, for I always do what pleases him." [30]Even as he spoke, many put their faith in him.

The Children of Abraham

[31]To the Jews who had believed him, Jesus said, "If you hold to my teaching, you are really my disciples. [32]Then you will know the truth, and the truth will set you free."

[33]They answered him, "We are Abraham's descendants[b] and have never been slaves of anyone. How can you say that we shall be set free?"

[34]Jesus replied, "I tell you the truth, everyone who sins is a slave to sin. [35]Now a slave has no permanent place in the family, but a son belongs to it forever. [36]So if the Son sets you free, you will be free indeed. [37]I know you are Abraham's descendants. Yet you are ready to kill me, because you have no room for my word. [38]I am telling you what I have seen in the Father's presence, and you do what you have heard from your father.[c]"

[39]"Abraham is our father," they answered.

"If you were Abraham's children," said Jesus, "then you would[d] do the things Abraham did. [40]As it is, you are determined to kill me, a man who has told you the truth that I heard from God. Abraham did not do such things. [41]You are doing the things your own father does."

"We are not illegitimate children," they protested. "The only Father we have is God himself."

The Children of the Devil

[42]Jesus said to them, "If God were your Father, you would love me, for I came from God and now am here. I have not come on my own; but he sent me. [43]Why is my language not clear to you? Because you are unable to hear what I say. [44]You belong to your father, the devil, and you want to carry out your father's desire. He was a murderer from the beginning, not holding to the truth, for there is no truth in him. When he lies, he speaks his native language, for he is a liar and the father of lies. [45]Yet because I tell the truth, you do not believe me! [46]Can any of you prove me guilty of sin? If I am telling the truth, why don't you believe me? [47]He who belongs to God hears what God says. The reason you do not hear is that you do not belong to God."

The Claims of Jesus About Himself

[48]The Jews answered him, "Aren't we right in saying that you are a Samaritan and demon-possessed?"

[49]"I am not possessed by a demon," said Jesus, "but I honor my Father and you dishonor me. [50]I am not seeking glory for myself; but there is one who seeks it, and he is the judge. [51]I tell you the truth, if anyone keeps my word, he will never see death."

[52]At this the Jews exclaimed, "Now we know that you are demon-possessed! Abraham died and so did the prophets, yet you say that if anyone keeps your word, he will never taste death. [53]Are you greater than our father Abraham? He died, and so did the prophets. Who do you think you are?"

[54]Jesus replied, "If I glorify myself, my glory means nothing. My Father, whom you claim as your God, is the one who glorifies me. [55]Though you do not know him, I know him. If I said I did not, I would be a liar like you, but I do know him and keep his word. [56]Your father Abraham rejoiced at the thought of seeing my day; he saw it and was glad."

[57]"You are not yet fifty years old," the Jews said to him, "and you have seen Abraham!"

[58]"I tell you the truth," Jesus answered, "before Abraham was born, I am!" [59]At this, they picked up stones to stone him, but Jesus hid himself, slipping away from the temple grounds.

Jesus Heals a Man Born Blind

9 As he went along, he saw a man blind from birth. [2]His disciples asked him, "Rabbi, who

---

[a]24 Or I am he; also in verse 28   [b]33 Greek seed; also in verse 37   [c]38 Or presence. Therefore do what you have heard from the Father.   [d]39 Some early manuscripts "If you are Abraham's children," said Jesus, "then

sinned, this man or his parents, that he was born blind?"

3"Neither this man nor his parents sinned," said Jesus, "but this happened so that the work of

9:2 Suffering and Sin

In this story, Jesus corrects a commonly held notion that suffering comes because of sin. The healed man became a loyal spokesman for Jesus. His testimony, however, failed to convince the Pharisees, who also rejected Jesus' teaching about why the man had been born blind (verse 34). In typical style, John wove together the incident with Jesus' comments on a different kind of blindness.

God might be displayed in his life. 4As long as it is day, we must do the work of him who sent me. Night is coming, when no one can work. 5While I am in the world, I am the light of the world."

6Having said this, he spit on the ground, made some mud with the saliva, and put it on the man's eyes. 7"Go," he told him, "wash in the Pool of Siloam" (this word means Sent). So the man went and washed, and came home seeing.

8His neighbors and those who had formerly seen him begging asked, "Isn't this the same man who used to sit and beg?" 9Some claimed that he was.

Others said, "No, he only looks like him."

But he himself insisted, "I am the man."

10"How then were your eyes opened?" they demanded.

11He replied, "The man they call Jesus made some mud and put it on my eyes. He told me to go to Siloam and wash. So I went and washed, and then I could see."

12"Where is this man?" they asked him.

"I don't know," he said.

The Pharisees Investigate the Healing

13They brought to the Pharisees the man who had been blind. 14Now the day on which Jesus had made the mud and opened the man's eyes was a Sabbath. 15Therefore the Pharisees also asked him how he had received his sight. "He put mud on my eyes," the man replied, "and I washed, and now I see."

16Some of the Pharisees said, "This man is not from God, for he does not keep the Sabbath."

But others asked, "How can a sinner do such miraculous signs?" So they were divided.

17Finally they turned again to the blind man, "What have you to say about him? It was your eyes he opened."

The man replied, "He is a prophet."

18The Jews still did not believe that he had been blind and had received his sight until they sent for the man's parents. 19"Is this your son?" they asked. "Is this the one you say was born blind? How is it that now he can see?"

20"We know he is our son," the parents answered, "and we know he was born blind. 21But how he can see now, or who opened his eyes, we don't know. Ask him. He is of age; he will speak for himself." 22His parents said this because they were afraid of the Jews, for already the Jews had decided that anyone who acknowledged that Jesus was the Christ[a] would be put out of the synagogue. 23That was why his parents said, "He is of age; ask him."

24A second time they summoned the man who had been blind. "Give glory to God,[b]" they said. "We know this man is a sinner."

25He replied, "Whether he is a sinner or not, I don't know. One thing I do know. I was blind but now I see!"

26Then they asked him, "What did he do to you? How did he open your eyes?"

27He answered, "I have told you already and you did not listen. Why do you want to hear it again? Do you want to become his disciples, too?"

28Then they hurled insults at him and said, "You are this fellow's disciple! We are disciples of Moses! 29We know that God spoke to Moses, but as for this fellow, we don't even know where he comes from."

30The man answered, "Now that is remarkable! You don't know where he comes from, yet he opened my eyes. 31We know that God does not listen to sinners. He listens to the godly man who does his will. 32Nobody has ever heard of opening the eyes of a man born blind. 33If this man were not from God, he could do nothing."

34To this they replied, "You were steeped in sin at birth; how dare you lecture us!" And they threw him out.

Spiritual Blindness

35Jesus heard that they had thrown him out, and when he found him, he said, "Do you believe in the Son of Man?"

36"Who is he, sir?" the man asked. "Tell me so that I may believe in him."

37Jesus said, "You have now seen him; in fact, he is the one speaking with you."

38Then the man said, "Lord, I believe," and he worshiped him.

39Jesus said, "For judgment I have come into this world, so that the blind will see and those who see will become blind."

40Some Pharisees who were with him heard

---

a22 Or Messiah   b24 A solemn charge to tell the truth (see Joshua 7:19) him say this and asked, "What? Are we blind too?"

⁴¹Jesus said, "If you were blind, you would not be guilty of sin; but now that you claim you can see, your guilt remains.

The Shepherd and His Flock

10 "I tell you the truth, the man who does not enter the sheep pen by the gate, but climbs in by some other way, is a thief and a robber. ²The man who enters by the gate is the shepherd of his sheep. ³The watchman opens the gate for him, and the sheep listen to his voice. He calls his own sheep by name and leads them out. ⁴When he has brought out all his own, he goes on ahead of them, and his sheep follow him because they know his voice. ⁵But they will never follow a stranger; in fact, they will run away from him because they do not recognize a stranger's voice."

A Modern Shepherd
What a "good shepherd" would look like today

> "I have come that they may have life, and have it to the full." 10:10

SOME OF THE BIBLE'S RURAL illustrations simply do not transfer easily into modern life. What is a "good shepherd" like? What did Jesus mean by the term?

A small drama that took place on the slopes of Washington's Mount Rainier may shed light on the meaning of the "good shepherd." One Memorial Day weekend a Christian dentist named James Reddick was teaching his 12-year-old daughter and 11-year-old son the joy of mountain hiking. A sudden storm came up, battering them with hurricane-force winds and thick, wet sheets of snow. A blinding "whiteout" made it impossible to see or move on the steep slopes.

Willing to Die

Reddick laboriously dug an oblong trench with an aluminum mess kit, then tucked his children into sleeping bags away from the entrance. He covered the opening with a tarp, but it kept blowing away, exposing the trench to the swirling snow outside. Reddick found he had to lie directly across the opening, using his own weight to hold down the edges of the tarp. His body protected his son and daughter from the howling wind.

Two days passed before searchers finally noticed the corner of a backpack protruding from deep snow. They rushed to the site, hoping the snow-covered mound would contain the three missing hikers. Inside, they found Sharon and David Reddick, very much alive. But the stiff body of their father lay against one wall of the snow cave. He had "taken the cold spot," in one searcher's words, by using his own back as the outer wall.

An image something like that must have filled the minds of Jesus' listeners as he described a good shepherd who "lays down his life" for his sheep (10:11). Nothing—not ravaging cold, thieves, or wolves—would come between the good shepherd and his sheep. He would die for their protection.

Popularity, for a While

As Jesus headed toward final tragedy in Jerusalem, the theme of death, *his* death, kept surfacing in his parables and direct statements. Ironically, his followers were growing in numbers. His popularity had reached a peak with the feeding of 5,000 people on a handful of morsels, a miracle mentioned by all four Gospel writers.

The ground swell of support to make Jesus king deeply impressed his followers; Jesus, however, escaped into the hills (6:15). He would not be a king on the crowd's terms. He continued on his lonely mission, stirring up controversy and hatred by healing people on the Sabbath and by proclaiming himself equal with God.

Ignoring an Impressive Miracle

Many Jews came over to Jesus after one of his most impressive signs: bringing Lazarus back to life. But, simultaneously, religious leaders concluded callously that it was best for one man (Jesus) to die rather than upset the whole world (11:50). Four separate times they tried to seize him.

Jesus came to offer "life"—one of those one-syllable words, swollen with meaning, that John threaded through his narrative. Lazarus received that life in an astonishingly literal way, providing yet another sign of Jesus' ultimate power. Jesus, though, made preparations to give up his own life, making the ultimate sacrifice of the good shepherd.

Life Questions: What have you sacrificed for the sake of another person?

⁶Jesus used this figure of speech, but they did not understand what he was telling them.

⁷Therefore Jesus said again, "I tell you the truth, I am the gate for the sheep. ⁸All who ever

10:4 Good Shepherd

Unlike modern-day shepherds, who use dogs to drive their flocks, Palestinian shepherds walked ahead, calling the sheep to follow. Only a familiar voice would make them come. In the Old Testament, God was called the "Shepherd of Israel" (Psalm 80:1), and God's appointed leaders were often referred to as shepherds. In claiming to be the good shepherd, Jesus was asserting his leadership over a flock he was willing to die for.

came before me were thieves and robbers, but the sheep did not listen to them. ⁹I am the gate; whoever enters through me will be saved.ᵃ He will come in and go out, and find pasture. ¹⁰The thief comes only to steal and kill and destroy; I have come that they may have life, and have it to the full.

¹¹"I am the good shepherd. The good shepherd lays down his life for the sheep. ¹²The hired hand is not the shepherd who owns the sheep. So when he sees the wolf coming, he abandons the sheep and runs away. Then the wolf attacks the flock and scatters it. ¹³The man runs away because he is a hired hand and cares nothing for the sheep.

¹⁴"I am the good shepherd; I know my sheep and my sheep know me— ¹⁵just as the Father knows me and I know the Father—and I lay down my life for the sheep. ¹⁶I have other sheep that are not of this sheep pen. I must bring them also. They too will listen to my voice, and there shall be one flock and one shepherd. ¹⁷The reason my Father loves me is that I lay down my life—only to take it up again. ¹⁸No one takes it from me, but I lay it down of my own accord. I have authority to lay it down and authority to take it up again. This command I received from my Father."

¹⁹At these words the Jews were again divided. ²⁰Many of them said, "He is demon-possessed and raving mad. Why listen to him?"

²¹But others said, "These are not the sayings of a man possessed by a demon. Can a demon open the eyes of the blind?"

The Unbelief of the Jews

²²Then came the Feast of Dedicationᵇ at Jerusalem. It was winter, ²³and Jesus was in the tem-

ple area walking in Solomon's Colonnade. ²⁴The Jews gathered around him, saying, "How long will you keep us in suspense? If you are the Christ,ᶜ tell us plainly."

²⁵Jesus answered, "I did tell you, but you do not believe. The miracles I do in my Father's name speak for me, ²⁶but you do not believe because you are not my sheep. ²⁷My sheep listen to my voice; I know them, and they follow me. ²⁸I give them eternal life, and they shall never perish; no one can snatch them out of my hand. ²⁹My Father, who has given them to me, is greater than all ᵈ; no one can snatch them out of my Father's hand. ³⁰I and the Father are one."

³¹Again the Jews picked up stones to stone him, ³²but Jesus said to them, "I have shown you many great miracles from the Father. For which of these do you stone me?"

³³"We are not stoning you for any of these," replied the Jews, "but for blasphemy, because you, a mere man, claim to be God."

³⁴Jesus answered them, "Is it not written in your Law, 'I have said you are gods'ᵉ? ³⁵If he called them 'gods,' to whom the word of God came—and the Scripture cannot be broken— ³⁶what about the one whom the Father set apart as his very own and sent into the world? Why then do you accuse me of blasphemy because I said, 'I am God's Son'? ³⁷Do not believe me unless I do what my Father does. ³⁸But if I do it, even though you do not believe me, believe the miracles, that you may know and understand that the Father is in me, and I in the Father." ³⁹Again they tried to seize him, but he escaped their grasp.

⁴⁰Then Jesus went back across the Jordan to the place where John had been baptizing in the early days. Here he stayed ⁴¹and many people came to him. They said, "Though John never performed a miraculous sign, all that John said about this man was true." ⁴²And in that place many believed in Jesus.

The Death of Lazarus

11 Now a man named Lazarus was sick. He was from Bethany, the village of Mary and her sister Martha. ²This Mary, whose brother Lazarus now lay sick, was the same one who poured perfume on the Lord and wiped his feet with her hair. ³So the sisters sent word to Jesus, "Lord, the one you love is sick."

⁴When he heard this, Jesus said, "This sickness will not end in death. No, it is for God's glory so that God's Son may be glorified through it." ⁵Jesus loved Martha and her sister and Lazarus. ⁶Yet when he heard that Lazarus was sick, he stayed where he was two more days.

ᵃ9 Or *kept safe*   ᵇ22 That is, Hanukkah   ᶜ24 Or *Messiah*   ᵈ29 Many early manuscripts *What my Father has given me is greater than all*   ᵉ34 Psalm 82:6

[7]Then he said to his disciples, "Let us go back to Judea."

[8]"But Rabbi," they said, "a short while ago the Jews tried to stone you, and yet you are going back there?"

[9]Jesus answered, "Are there not twelve hours of daylight? A man who walks by day will not stumble, for he sees by this world's light. [10]It is when he walks by night that he stumbles, for he has no light."

[11]After he had said this, he went on to tell them, "Our friend Lazarus has fallen asleep; but I am going there to wake him up."

[12]His disciples replied, "Lord, if he sleeps, he will get better." [13]Jesus had been speaking of his death, but his disciples thought he meant natural sleep.

[14]So then he told them plainly, "Lazarus is dead, [15]and for your sake I am glad I was not there, so that you may believe. But let us go to him."

[16]Then Thomas (called Didymus) said to the rest of the disciples, "Let us also go, that we may die with him."

Jesus Comforts the Sisters

[17]On his arrival, Jesus found that Lazarus had already been in the tomb for four days. [18]Bethany was less than two miles[a] from Jerusalem, [19]and many Jews had come to Martha and Mary to comfort them in the loss of their brother. [20]When Martha heard that Jesus was coming, she went out to meet him, but Mary stayed at home.

[21]"Lord," Martha said to Jesus, "if you had

11:21 If Only . . .

Mary and Martha had very different personalities, but the same response to pain. Both sisters, meeting Jesus, said the same thing: "If you had been here, my brother would not have died" (verses 21,32). They had asked Jesus to come, and for reasons they could not understand, he had delayed. The healing they longed for had not occurred. Jesus gave the sisters no explanation of his timing, but showed he had a reason: to demonstrate his power over death.

been here, my brother would not have died. [22]But I know that even now God will give you whatever you ask."

[23]Jesus said to her, "Your brother will rise again."

[24]Martha answered, "I know he will rise again in the resurrection at the last day."

[25]Jesus said to her, "I am the resurrection and the life. He who believes in me will live, even though he dies; [26]and whoever lives and believes in me will never die. Do you believe this?"

[27]"Yes, Lord," she told him, "I believe that you are the Christ,[b] the Son of God, who was to come into the world."

[28]And after she had said this, she went back and called her sister Mary aside. "The Teacher is here," she said, "and is asking for you." [29]When Mary heard this, she got up quickly and went to him. [30]Now Jesus had not yet entered the village, but was still at the place where Martha had met him. [31]When the Jews who had been with Mary in the house, comforting her, noticed how quickly she got up and went out, they followed her, supposing she was going to the tomb to mourn there.

[32]When Mary reached the place where Jesus was and saw him, she fell at his feet and said, "Lord, if you had been here, my brother would not have died."

[33]When Jesus saw her weeping, and the Jews who had come along with her also weeping, he was deeply moved in spirit and troubled. [34]"Where have you laid him?" he asked.

"Come and see, Lord," they replied.

[35]Jesus wept.

[36]Then the Jews said, "See how he loved him!"

[37]But some of them said, "Could not he who opened the eyes of the blind man have kept this man from dying?"

Jesus Raises Lazarus From the Dead

[38]Jesus, once more deeply moved, came to the tomb. It was a cave with a stone laid across the entrance. [39]"Take away the stone," he said.

"But, Lord," said Martha, the sister of the dead man, "by this time there is a bad odor, for he has been there four days."

[40]Then Jesus said, "Did I not tell you that if you believed, you would see the glory of God?"

[41]So they took away the stone. Then Jesus looked up and said, "Father, I thank you that you have heard me. [42]I knew that you always hear me, but I said this for the benefit of the people standing here, that they may believe that you sent me."

[43]When he had said this, Jesus called in a loud voice, "Lazarus, come out!" [44]The dead man came out, his hands and feet wrapped with strips of linen, and a cloth around his face.

Jesus said to them, "Take off the grave clothes and let him go."

The Plot to Kill Jesus

[45]Therefore many of the Jews who had come to visit Mary, and had seen what Jesus did, put their faith in him. [46]But some of them went to the Pharisees and told them what Jesus had done.

---

[a]18 Greek *fifteen stadia* (about 3 kilometers)   [b]27 Or *Messiah*

47Then the chief priests and the Pharisees called a meeting of the Sanhedrin.

"What are we accomplishing?" they asked. "Here is this man performing many miraculous signs. 48If we let him go on like this, everyone will believe in him, and then the Romans will come and take away both our place[a] and our nation."

49Then one of them, named Caiaphas, who was high priest that year, spoke up, "You know nothing at all! 50You do not realize that it is better for you that one man die for the people than that the whole nation perish."

51He did not say this on his own, but as high priest that year he prophesied that Jesus would die for the Jewish nation, 52and not only for that nation but also for the scattered children of God, to bring them together and make them one. 53So from that day on they plotted to take his life.

54Therefore Jesus no longer moved about publicly among the Jews. Instead he withdrew to a region near the desert, to a village called Ephraim, where he stayed with his disciples.

55When it was almost time for the Jewish Passover, many went up from the country to Jerusalem for their ceremonial cleansing before the Passover. 56They kept looking for Jesus, and as they stood in the temple area they asked one another, "What do you think? Isn't he coming to the Feast at all?" 57But the chief priests and Pharisees had given orders that if anyone found out where Jesus was, he should report it so that they might arrest him.

Jesus Anointed at Bethany

12 Six days before the Passover, Jesus arrived at Bethany, where Lazarus lived, whom Jesus had raised from the dead. 2Here a dinner

11:53 Climax of the Drama

John wrote his book with a great sense of drama. The first six chapters reveal the identity of Jesus. The next six chapters (7–12) show the increasingly divided opinions about Jesus. On the one hand, his disciples were won over, and Jesus gained a loyal following among the people. On the other hand, his enemies rejected all the evidence about him. Their opposition culminated in this plot, which finally brought about Jesus' death.

was given in Jesus' honor. Martha served, while Lazarus was among those reclining at the table with him. 3Then Mary took about a pint[b] of pure nard, an expensive perfume; she poured it on Jesus' feet and wiped his feet with her hair. And the house was filled with the fragrance of the perfume.

4But one of his disciples, Judas Iscariot, who was later to betray him, objected, 5"Why wasn't this perfume sold and the money given to the poor? It was worth a year's wages.[c]" 6He did not say this because he cared about the poor but because he was a thief; as keeper of the money

---

[a]48 Or *temple*   [b]3 Greek *a litra* (probably about 0.5 liter)   [c]5 Greek *three hundred denarii*

ANNAS AND CAIAPHAS *Collaborators*

THE ANCIENT ROMANS KNEW HOW the Jews valued their faith, which is why they insisted on appointing Israel's high priest. Much like the Soviet Communists and German Nazis in our own century, first-century Romans sought to keep the religious dimension of life under their control.

Annas and Caiaphas fit the Romans' plans perfectly. Caiaphas held office during Jesus' ministry, but Annas, his father-in-law and a former high priest, retained so much influence that he was sometimes called by the title. Both were Sadducees, an aristocratic group who had a very this-worldly understanding of Judaism. Sadducees bent over backward to cooperate with whatever group held political power, and as a result they prospered.

When Jesus started making waves in Israel, Annas and Caiaphas viewed him as a political threat. As John explains it, they feared Jesus would attract so many followers that the Romans would grow alarmed and step in. In classic "Don't rock the boat" thinking, Caiaphas concluded it was better to do away with Jesus than jeopardize the future of Israel. Jesus' miracles, his teachings and his character made no difference to Caiaphas. Political survival mattered above all (11:45–53).

With that in mind, religious leaders secretly kidnapped Jesus, put him on trial, and brought him to the Romans for execution. They later persecuted the church that sprang up after Jesus' resurrection.

The nation of Israel did survive, though not for long. In AD 70 the Romans wiped Israel out of existence, in the process destroying the temple where the high priest officiated. Not until 1948 would the Jews again control Jerusalem.

Life Questions: Is it possible to be so concerned with keeping the peace that you end up opposing what God is doing? What examples can you think of today?

bag, he used to help himself to what was put into it.

[7]"Leave her alone," Jesus replied. "⌊It was intended⌋ that she should save this perfume for the day of my burial. [8]You will always have the poor among you, but you will not always have me."

[9]Meanwhile a large crowd of Jews found out that Jesus was there and came, not only because of him but also to see Lazarus, whom he had raised from the dead. [10]So the chief priests made plans to kill Lazarus as well, [11]for on account of him many of the Jews were going over to Jesus and putting their faith in him.

The Triumphal Entry

▶ See Matthew 21:4–9; Mark 11:7–10; Luke 19:35–38

[12]The next day the great crowd that had come for the Feast heard that Jesus was on his way to Jerusalem. [13]They took palm branches and went out to meet him, shouting,

"Hosanna![a]"

"Blessed is he who comes in the name of the Lord!"[b]

"Blessed is the King of Israel!"

[14]Jesus found a young donkey and sat upon it, as it is written,

[15]"Do not be afraid, O Daughter of Zion;
    see, your king is coming,
    seated on a donkey's colt."[c]

[16]At first his disciples did not understand all this. Only after Jesus was glorified did they realize that these things had been written about him and that they had done these things to him.

[17]Now the crowd that was with him when he called Lazarus from the tomb and raised him from the dead continued to spread the word. [18]Many people, because they had heard that he had given this miraculous sign, went out to meet him. [19]So the Pharisees said to one another, "See, this is getting us nowhere. Look how the whole world has gone after him!"

Jesus Predicts His Death

[20]Now there were some Greeks among those who went up to worship at the Feast. [21]They came to Philip, who was from Bethsaida in Galilee, with a request. "Sir," they said, "we would like to see Jesus." [22]Philip went to tell Andrew; Andrew and Philip in turn told Jesus.

[23]Jesus replied, "The hour has come for the Son of Man to be glorified. [24]I tell you the truth, unless a kernel of wheat falls to the ground and dies, it remains only a single seed. But if it dies,

it produces many seeds. [25]The man who loves his life will lose it, while the man who hates his life in this world will keep it for eternal life. [26]Whoever serves me must follow me; and where I am, my servant also will be. My Father will honor the one who serves me.

[27]"Now my heart is troubled, and what shall I say? 'Father, save me from this hour'? No, it was for this very reason I came to this hour. [28]Father, glorify your name!"

Then a voice came from heaven, "I have glorified it, and will glorify it again." [29]The crowd that was there and heard it said it had thundered; others said an angel had spoken to him.

[30]Jesus said, "This voice was for your benefit, not mine. [31]Now is the time for judgment on this world; now the prince of this world will be driven out. [32]But I, when I am lifted up from the earth, will draw all men to myself." [33]He said this to show the kind of death he was going to die.

[34]The crowd spoke up, "We have heard from the Law that the Christ[d] will remain forever, so how can you say, 'The Son of Man must be lifted up'? Who is this 'Son of Man'?"

[35]Then Jesus told them, "You are going to have the light just a little while longer. Walk while you have the light, before darkness overtakes you. The man who walks in the dark does not know where he is going. [36]Put your trust in the light while you have it, so that you may become sons of light." When he had finished speaking, Jesus left and hid himself from them.

The Jews Continue in Their Unbelief

[37]Even after Jesus had done all these miraculous signs in their presence, they still would not believe in him. [38]This was to fulfill the word of Isaiah the prophet:

"Lord, who has believed our message
    and to whom has the arm of the Lord
        been revealed?"[e]

[39]For this reason they could not believe, because, as Isaiah says elsewhere:

[40]"He has blinded their eyes
    and deadened their hearts,
so they can neither see with their eyes,
    nor understand with their hearts,
    nor turn—and I would heal them."[f]

[41]Isaiah said this because he saw Jesus' glory and spoke about him.

[42]Yet at the same time many even among the leaders believed in him. But because of the Pharisees they would not confess their faith for fear they would be put out of the synagogue; [43]for

---

[a]13 A Hebrew expression meaning "Save!" which became an exclamation of praise   [b]13 Psalm 118:25, 26
[c]15 Zech. 9:9   [d]34 Or Messiah   [e]38 Isaiah 53:1   [f]40 Isaiah 6:10

they loved praise from men more than praise from God.

44Then Jesus cried out, "When a man believes in me, he does not believe in me only, but in the one who sent me. 45When he looks at me, he sees the one who sent me. 46I have come into the world as a light, so that no one who believes in me should stay in darkness.

47"As for the person who hears my words but does not keep them, I do not judge him. For I did not come to judge the world, but to save it. 48There is a judge for the one who rejects me and does not accept my words; that very word which I spoke will condemn him at the last day. 49For I did not speak of my own accord, but the Father who sent me commanded me what to say and how to say it. 50I know that his command leads to eternal life. So whatever I say is just what the Father has told me to say."

Jesus Washes His Disciples' Feet

13 It was just before the Passover Feast. Jesus knew that the time had come for him to

John's Reason for Writing
Handpicked incidents that prove a point

> "Believe me when I say that I am in the Father and the Father is in me; or at least believe on the evidence of the miracles themselves." 14:11

PRESIDENT ABRAHAM LINCOLN ATTRACTS BIOGRAPHERS like candy attracts ants; books about his life would easily fill a large room. Some explore his religious beliefs, some his military strategy, some his eloquence, and others his character. Imagine, though, a biography written about only one aspect of the man: Lincoln the lawyer.

Stories from the childhood of Abe—his reading by light filtered through chinks in the wall or his traipsing across town to return a customer's change—would likely never make it into such a book. Yet the precise wording of the Emancipation Proclamation might merit an entire chapter. Long chapters would dwell on an obscure period in Springfield, Illinois, when Lincoln practiced law. But his political campaigns would get scarce mention.

Such an incomplete biography would serve one purpose: to establish Lincoln's ability in law. All other details would fade into the background.

Everything for a Purpose

Like such a biographer, John wrote his book about Jesus for a similarly limited purpose, which he states very clearly: "These are written that you may believe that Jesus is the Christ, the Son of God, and that by believing you may have life in his name" (20:31). The book is not so much a biography as an argument. Its author has handpicked incidents to demonstrate that Jesus is unlike any man who has ever lived; he is the Son of God.

This purpose shows up, for example, in how John treats Jesus' miracles. Although Matthew, Mark, and Luke all record miracles, John goes one step further and calls them "signs." A sign points to something. In John, supernatural acts are one more proof of Jesus' unique nature. Jesus refused to perform miracles as magic to dazzle the crowds but used them instead as object lessons to teach about himself.

After feeding 5,000 people from one sack lunch, Jesus described himself as the bread of life (6:1–59). Just before restoring sight to a blind man, he called himself the light of the world (9:1–7). Nothing "just happens" in John; everything underscores the author's overall theme.

Merely a Great Man?

Because Jesus is so clear in describing his own nature, a statement like "I'm ready to accept Jesus as a great moral teacher, but I don't accept his claim to be God" doesn't hold up. As C.S. Lewis has said, "That is the one thing we must not say. A man who was merely a man and said the sort of things Jesus said would not be a great moral teacher. He would either be a lunatic—on a level with the man who says he is a poached egg—or else he would be the Devil of Hell. You must make your choice. Either this man was, and is, the Son of God: or else a madman or something worse."

According to John, not everyone believed Jesus was divine: "Who do you think you are?" some indignantly demanded (8:53). Doubters had him killed for making such an audacious claim. But it is hardly possible to read John without being convinced that Jesus himself claimed to be God.

Life Questions: Despite what C.S. Lewis says, many people do think of Jesus as "merely a great man." How do they rationalize it?

leave this world and go to the Father. Having loved his own who were in the world, he now showed them the full extent of his love.ᵃ

²The evening meal was being served, and the devil had already prompted Judas Iscariot, son of Simon, to betray Jesus. ³Jesus knew that the Father had put all things under his power, and that he had come from God and was returning to God; ⁴so he got up from the meal, took off his outer clothing, and wrapped a towel around his

13:4 The Role of a Servant

Before beginning an intimate meal with his disciples, Jesus gave them a lesson about humility. Normally, slaves performed the act of washing the feet of dinner guests. Here Jesus, the guest of honor, dressed himself like a slave, with a towel around his waist, and insisted on washing the feet of his disciples. Paul comments on Jesus' servanthood in Philippians 2:5–11.

waist. ⁵After that, he poured water into a basin and began to wash his disciples' feet, drying them with the towel that was wrapped around him.

⁶He came to Simon Peter, who said to him, "Lord, are you going to wash my feet?"

⁷Jesus replied, "You do not realize now what I am doing, but later you will understand."

⁸"No," said Peter, "you shall never wash my feet."

Jesus answered, "Unless I wash you, you have no part with me."

⁹"Then, Lord," Simon Peter replied, "not just my feet but my hands and my head as well!"

¹⁰Jesus answered, "A person who has had a bath needs only to wash his feet; his whole body is clean. And you are clean, though not every one of you." ¹¹For he knew who was going to betray him, and that was why he said not every one was clean.

¹²When he had finished washing their feet, he put on his clothes and returned to his place. "Do you understand what I have done for you?" he asked them. ¹³"You call me 'Teacher' and 'Lord,' and rightly so, for that is what I am. ¹⁴Now that I, your Lord and Teacher, have washed your feet, you also should wash one another's feet. ¹⁵I have set you an example that you should do as I have done for you. ¹⁶I tell you the truth, no servant is greater than his master, nor is a messenger greater than the one who sent him. ¹⁷Now that you know these things, you will be blessed if you do them.

Jesus Predicts His Betrayal

¹⁸"I am not referring to all of you; I know those I have chosen. But this is to fulfill the scripture: 'He who shares my bread has lifted up his heel against me.'ᵇ

¹⁹"I am telling you now before it happens, so that when it does happen you will believe that I am He. ²⁰I tell you the truth, whoever accepts anyone I send accepts me; and whoever accepts me accepts the one who sent me."

²¹After he had said this, Jesus was troubled in spirit and testified, "I tell you the truth, one of you is going to betray me."

²²His disciples stared at one another, at a loss to know which of them he meant. ²³One of them, the disciple whom Jesus loved, was reclining next to him. ²⁴Simon Peter motioned to this disciple and said, "Ask him which one he means."

²⁵Leaning back against Jesus, he asked him, "Lord, who is it?"

²⁶Jesus answered, "It is the one to whom I will give this piece of bread when I have dipped it in the dish." Then, dipping the piece of bread, he gave it to Judas Iscariot, son of Simon. ²⁷As soon as Judas took the bread, Satan entered into him.

"What you are about to do, do quickly," Jesus told him, ²⁸but no one at the meal understood why Jesus said this to him. ²⁹Since Judas had charge of the money, some thought Jesus was telling him to buy what was needed for the Feast, or to give something to the poor. ³⁰As soon as Judas had taken the bread, he went out. And it was night.

Jesus Predicts Peter's Denial

▶ *See Matthew 26:33–35; Mark 14:29–31; Luke 22:33–34*

³¹When he was gone, Jesus said, "Now is the Son of Man glorified and God is glorified in him. ³²If God is glorified in him,ᶜ God will glorify the Son in himself, and will glorify him at once.

³³"My children, I will be with you only a little longer. You will look for me, and just as I told the Jews, so I tell you now: Where I am going, you cannot come.

³⁴"A new command I give you: Love one another. As I have loved you, so you must love one another. ³⁵By this all men will know that you are my disciples, if you love one another."

³⁶Simon Peter asked him, "Lord, where are you going?"

Jesus replied, "Where I am going, you cannot follow now, but you will follow later."

³⁷Peter asked, "Lord, why can't I follow you now? I will lay down my life for you."

³⁸Then Jesus answered, "Will you really lay

ᵃ1 Or *he loved them to the last*   ᵇ18 Psalm 41:9   ᶜ32 Many early manuscripts do not have *If God is glorified in him.*

SC Chapman

When asked to select a verse to meditate on for the WoW 1997 Bible, Steven Curtis Chapman selected 2 Corinthians 5:7: "We live by faith, not by sight."

Reflecting on his song "Sometimes He Comes in the Clouds" from the *My Utmost for His Highest* CD compilation, Steven comments on this verse:

"The shadows of life...we've all been there. The bright sky suddenly begins to turn black and the sun's warmth is consumed by a chilling breeze. Just as we're beginning to really enjoy the sunshine, the clouds come rolling in.

"There was a point in my life when I had developed an understanding of God that can be basically summed up like this: 'If times are good, God is near. If times are bad, God is far away.' The obvious remedy for this problem was to pray hard, make the right 'positive confessions' and God would come and clear the skies ASAP. If I looked up and saw a sky full of dark and intimidating clouds, I immediately began praying for God to come and break through the darkness in my life.

"But I've learned that sometimes God comes in the clouds. Sometimes he uses the seasons of shadowy darkness to teach his people the reality of walking by faith and not by sight. Although I would ask to have my head examined if I ever prayed that God would come in the clouds, I have come to treasure those times when he has allowed me to wrestle with doubt, to search his Word for answers. In so doing, God takes me deeper into faith and trust in him."

Steven Curtis Chapman

Cindy Morgan

Though Cindy Morgan's earlier albums met success featuring a youthful dance–pop sound, it was her last project, *Under The Waterfall*, that hinted at a new direction for this sensitive, passionate songwriter.

"When I first came to Nashville from east Tennessee, I didn't know exactly who I was as an artist. I was more than willing to listen to suggestions and take direction, and the dance–pop direction we took was an honest attempt to reach kids. It wasn't anything anyone forced me to do... it was a process of peeling back the layers, of personal growth as an artist and as a believer."

The process of change wasn't difficult, but a natural evolution. "I've always been writing on the piano, and for the last year or so, I've been traveling with a combination of piano, acoustic guitar and percussion, for the more intimate sound that I love." That's the sound that is most evident on Cindy's latest release, *Listen*.

Cindy's own father will hear something familiar in the title track. Years ago, as an aspiring young songwriter, he wrote a gentle ballad called "Listen." Secretly, Cindy resurrected the song from memory, giving it a completely different art–rock feel while preserving the lyrics virtually intact, and recorded it as the centerpiece of her signature artistic statement. "I kept it a surprise from Dad until the release of the album. He made the ultimate sacrifice of his own artistic desires, turning down opportunities to try song writing for the good of his family. This song is a way to say, 'Thanks, Dad—now we've done this together...God's made your dream come true.'"

Excerpts taken from "CINDY MORGAN....LISTEN" by Bernie Sheahan

WOW
1997

down your life for me? I tell you the truth, before the rooster crows, you will disown me three times!

Jesus Comforts His Disciples

14 "Do not let your hearts be troubled. Trust in God[a]; trust also in me. [2]In my Father's house are many rooms; if it were not so, I would have told you. I am going there to prepare a place for you. [3]And if I go and prepare a place for you, I will come back and take you to be with me that you also may be where I am. [4]You know the way to the place where I am going."

Jesus the Way to the Father

[5]Thomas said to him, "Lord, we don't know where you are going, so how can we know the way?"

[6]Jesus answered, "I am the way and the truth and the life. No one comes to the Father except through me. [7]If you really knew me, you would know[b] my Father as well. From now on, you do know him and have seen him."

[8]Philip said, "Lord, show us the Father and that will be enough for us."

[9]Jesus answered: "Don't you know me, Philip, even after I have been among you such a long time? Anyone who has seen me has seen the Father. How can you say, 'Show us the Father'? [10]Don't you believe that I am in the Father, and that the Father is in me? The words I say to you are not just my own. Rather, it is the Father, living in me, who is doing his work. [11]Believe me when I say that I am in the Father and the Father is in me; or at least believe on the evidence of the miracles themselves. [12]I tell you the truth, anyone who has faith in me will do what I have been doing. He will do even greater things than these, because I am going to the Father. [13]And I will do whatever you ask in my name, so that the Son may bring glory to the Father. [14]You may ask me for anything in my name, and I will do it.

Jesus Promises the Holy Spirit

[15]"If you love me, you will obey what I command. [16]And I will ask the Father, and he will give you another Counselor to be with you forever— [17]the Spirit of truth. The world cannot accept him, because it neither sees him nor knows him. But you know him, for he lives with you and will be[c] in you. [18]I will not leave you as orphans; I will come to you. [19]Before long, the world will not see me anymore, but you will see me. Because I live, you also will live. [20]On that day you will realize that I am in my Father, and you are in me, and I am in you. [21]Whoever has my commands and obeys them, he is the one who loves me. He who loves me will be loved by my Father, and I too will love him and show myself to him."

[22]Then Judas (not Judas Iscariot) said, "But, Lord, why do you intend to show yourself to us and not to the world?"

[23]Jesus replied, "If anyone loves me, he will obey my teaching. My Father will love him, and we will come to him and make our home with him. [24]He who does not love me will not obey my teaching. These words you hear are not my own; they belong to the Father who sent me.

[25]"All this I have spoken while still with you. [26]But the Counselor, the Holy Spirit, whom the Father will send in my name, will teach you all

---

[a]1 Or You trust in God   [b]7 Some early manuscripts If you really have known me, you will know   [c]17 Some early manuscripts and is

---

THOMAS *Honest Questions*

BETWEEN STUBBORN SKEPTICISM AND HONEST questioning there is a huge gap, and the disciple named Thomas illustrates the difference. Popularly known as "Doubting Thomas," this disciple stands out for his practical honesty, not for his unbelief.

When Jesus' friend Lazarus died, Thomas frankly showed his despondency along with his intense loyalty to Jesus: "Let us also go [to Lazarus' grave], that we may die with him" (11:16). At Jesus' last meal with his disciples, he expressed the confusion that was surely on all the disciples' minds (14:5). Thomas never pretended. If he didn't understand something, he said so; if he felt discouraged, he acted like it.

Thomas got his reputation as a doubter primarily because of his reaction when told of Jesus' resurrection. He simply insisted, "I need to see it for myself." The implications of a risen Jesus were too great, he believed, to take someone else's word for it. Jesus honored this honest doubt, and when he visited Thomas in person to offer proof, Thomas responded with the ultimate statement of faith: "My Lord and my God" (20:28). He was, in fact, the only disciple who specifically addressed Jesus as God.

Thomas's questions led to faith because he expressed them sincerely and looked for answers. The last mention of him in the Bible shows Thomas not questioning but praying, waiting with the other disciples for the Holy Spirit to come (Acts 1:12–14).

Life Questions: What honest questions do you need to bring before God?

things and will remind you of everything I have said to you. 27Peace I leave with you; my peace I give you. I do not give to you as the world gives. Do not let your hearts be troubled and do not be afraid.

28"You heard me say, 'I am going away and I am coming back to you.' If you loved me, you would be glad that I am going to the Father, for the Father is greater than I. 29I have told you now before it happens, so that when it does happen you will believe. 30I will not speak with you much longer, for the prince of this world is coming. He has no hold on me, 31but the world must learn that I love the Father and that I do exactly what my Father has commanded me.

"Come now; let us leave.

The Vine and the Branches

15 "I am the true vine, and my Father is the gardener. 2He cuts off every branch in me

15:1 Jesus as the Vine

Old Testament prophets referred to the Israelites as God's "vine," or "vineyard." But as Jesus often pointed out, the Jews had failed to bear fruit. Here he claims the image for himself, "I am the vine."

John frequently records Jesus' use of the words I am: "I am the bread of life," "I am the way and the truth and the life." The phrase stood out sharply to Jewish leaders, because God had been known as the great I AM to the Jews (Exodus 3:14). Jewish unbelievers, recognizing that Jesus was claiming to be God, reacted with shock and outrage.

that bears no fruit, while every branch that does bear fruit he prunes[a] so that it will be even more fruitful. 3You are already clean because of the word I have spoken to you. 4Remain in me, and I will remain in you. No branch can bear fruit by itself; it must remain in the vine. Neither can you bear fruit unless you remain in me.

5"I am the vine; you are the branches. If a man remains in me and I in him, he will bear much fruit; apart from me you can do nothing. 6If anyone does not remain in me, he is like a branch that is thrown away and withers; such branches are picked up, thrown into the fire and burned. 7If you remain in me and my words remain in you, ask whatever you wish, and it will be given you. 8This is to my Father's glory, that you bear much fruit, showing yourselves to be my disciples.

9"As the Father has loved me, so have I loved you. Now remain in my love. 10If you obey my commands, you will remain in my love, just as I have obeyed my Father's commands and remain in his love. 11I have told you this so that my joy may be in you and that your joy may be complete. 12My command is this: Love each other as I have loved you. 13Greater love has no one than this, that he lay down his life for his friends. 14You are my friends if you do what I command. 15I no longer call you servants, because a servant does not know his master's business. Instead, I have called you friends, for everything that I learned from my Father I have made known to you. 16You did not choose me, but I chose you and appointed you to go and bear fruit—fruit that will last. Then the Father will give you whatever you ask in my name. 17This is my command: Love each other.

The World Hates the Disciples

18"If the world hates you, keep in mind that it hated me first. 19If you belonged to the world, it would love you as its own. As it is, you do not belong to the world, but I have chosen you out of the world. That is why the world hates you. 20Remember the words I spoke to you: 'No servant is greater than his master.'[b] If they persecuted me, they will persecute you also. If they obeyed my teaching, they will obey yours also. 21They will treat you this way because of my name, for they do not know the One who sent me. 22If I had not come and spoken to them, they would not be guilty of sin. Now, however, they have no excuse for their sin. 23He who hates me hates my Father as well. 24If I had not done among them what no one else did, they would not be guilty of sin. But now they have seen these miracles, and yet they have hated both me and my Father. 25But this is to fulfill what is written in their Law: 'They hated me without reason.'[c]

26"When the Counselor comes, whom I will send to you from the Father, the Spirit of truth who goes out from the Father, he will testify about me. 27And you also must testify, for you have been with me from the beginning.

16 "All this I have told you so that you will not go astray. 2They will put you out of the synagogue; in fact, a time is coming when anyone who kills you will think he is offering a service to God. 3They will do such things because they have not known the Father or me. 4I have told you this, so that when the time comes you will remember that I warned you. I did not tell you this at first because I was with you.

The Work of the Holy Spirit

5"Now I am going to him who sent me, yet none of you asks me, 'Where are you going?' 6Because I have said these things, you are filled

---

[a]2 The Greek for *prunes* also means *cleans.* [b]20 John 13:16 [c]25 Psalms 35:19; 69:4

with grief. 7But I tell you the truth: It is for your good that I am going away. Unless I go away, the Counselor will not come to you; but if I go, I will send him to you. 8When he comes, he will convict the world of guilt*a* in regard to sin and righteousness and judgment: 9in regard to sin, because men do not believe in me; 10in regard to righteousness, because I am going to the Father, where you can see me no longer; 11and in regard to judgment, because the prince of this world now stands condemned.

12"I have much more to say to you, more than you can now bear. 13But when he, the Spirit of truth, comes, he will guide you into all truth. He will not speak on his own; he will speak only what he hears, and he will tell you what is yet to come.

14He will bring glory to me by taking from what is mine and making it known to you. 15All that belongs to the Father is mine. That is why I said the Spirit will take from what is mine and make it known to you.

16"In a little while you will see me no more, and then after a little while you will see me."

The Disciples' Grief Will Turn to Joy

17Some of his disciples said to one another, "What does he mean by saying, 'In a little while you will see me no more, and then after a little while you will see me,' and 'Because I am going to the Father'?" 18They kept asking, "What does he mean by 'a little while'? We don't understand what he is saying."

a8 Or will expose the guilt of the world

The Last Meal Together
The longest, most emotional night of Jesus' life

> "You will grieve, but your grief will turn to joy." 16:20

JOHN DEVOTED ONE-THIRD OF HIS book to the last 24-hour period Jesus spent on earth. Five chapters (13—17) describe one of the scenes from that period, and nothing like these chapters exists elsewhere in the Bible. In their slow-motion, realistic detail, they provide an intimate memoir of Jesus' most anguished evening.

Leonardo da Vinci immortalized the setting in his famous painting *The Last Supper*, with the participants arranged on one side of the table as if posing for the artist. But John gives few physical details; instead, he focuses on a whirlpool of emotional currents.

John holds a light to the disciples' faces, and you can almost see the awareness flickering in their eyes. All that Jesus had told them was slowly settling in. As for Jesus, "having loved his own who were in the world, he now showed them the full extent of his love" (13:1).

Jesus Prepares to Leave

Never before had Jesus been so direct with them. Around the table he avoided parables and painstakingly answered the disciples' redundant questions. Never was he more "theological." He alone fully recognized the significance of this last evening before his death. The world was about to undergo a convulsive trauma, and the 11 fearful men with him were his hope for that world.

"It is for your good that I am going away," Jesus said (16:7), but the disciples were too busy discussing the meaning of "going away" to comprehend the good that would follow.

Nevertheless, Jesus kept explaining until at last the disciples showed signs of understanding. God's Son had entered the world to reside in one body. He was leaving earth to return to the Father. But the Spirit would come and reside in many bodies. Jesus seemed aware that much of what they nodded their heads at now would not sink in until later.

Pain before Joy

Jesus concluded his words with a ringing declaration, "Take heart! I have overcome the world" (16:33). How hollow this statement would seem the next evening, when his pale, abused body hung on an executioner's cross. The disciples' emotions—and faith—would rise and plummet in one unforgettable day. Jesus predicted this, too, likening the pain to the spasms of childbirth before great joy breaks through (16:21—22).

In his longest recorded prayer, Jesus summed up his feelings and his plans for the tight circle of friends gathered around him. He prayed, too, for the others who would follow them, stretching in an unbroken chain throughout history. And then he led the little band to his appointment with death.

Life Questions: Have you ever been around someone facing death? How did he or she act? What does Jesus' response to impending death reveal about why he came to earth?

[19]Jesus saw that they wanted to ask him about this, so he said to them, "Are you asking one another what I meant when I said, 'In a little while you will see me no more, and then after a little while you will see me'? [20]I tell you the truth, you will weep and mourn while the world rejoices. You will grieve, but your grief will turn to

16:20 Filled with Grief

Good-byes are always sad, and for the disciples this farewell speech was especially so. They had staked their lives on Jesus, and without him they could see no future. Jesus, however, promised that he was leaving for their own good. He would send the Holy Spirit to guide them into "all truth" (verse 13). In fact, as Acts shows, only after Jesus' departure did these confused disciples fully grasp the meaning of his death and resurrection and begin to proclaim it joyfully to everyone around them.

joy. [21]A woman giving birth to a child has pain because her time has come; but when her baby is born she forgets the anguish because of her joy that a child is born into the world. [22]So with you: Now is your time of grief, but I will see you again and you will rejoice, and no one will take away your joy. [23]In that day you will no longer ask me anything. I tell you the truth, my Father will give you whatever you ask in my name. [24]Until now you have not asked for anything in my name. Ask and you will receive, and your joy will be complete.

[25]"Though I have been speaking figuratively, a time is coming when I will no longer use this kind of language but will tell you plainly about my Father. [26]In that day you will ask in my name. I am not saying that I will ask the Father on your behalf. [27]No, the Father himself loves you because you have loved me and have believed that I came from God. [28]I came from the Father and entered the world; now I am leaving the world and going back to the Father."

[29]Then Jesus' disciples said, "Now you are speaking clearly and without figures of speech. [30]Now we can see that you know all things and that you do not even need to have anyone ask you questions. This makes us believe that you came from God."

[31]"You believe at last!"[a] Jesus answered. [32]"But a time is coming, and has come, when you will be scattered, each to his own home. You will leave me all alone. Yet I am not alone, for my Father is with me.

[33]"I have told you these things, so that in me you may have peace. In this world you will have trouble. But take heart! I have overcome the world."

Jesus Prays for Himself

17 After Jesus said this, he looked toward heaven and prayed:

"Father, the time has come. Glorify your Son, that your Son may glorify you. [2]For you granted him authority over all people that he might give eternal life to all those you have given him. [3]Now this is eternal life: that they may know you, the only true God, and Jesus Christ, whom you have sent. [4]I have brought you glory on earth by completing the work you gave me to do. [5]And now, Father, glorify me in your presence with the glory I had with you before the world began.

Jesus Prays for His Disciples

[6]"I have revealed you[b] to those whom you gave me out of the world. They were yours; you gave them to me and they have obeyed your word. [7]Now they know that everything you have given me comes from you. [8]For I gave them the words you gave me and they accepted them. They knew with certainty that I came from you, and they believed that you sent me. [9]I pray for them. I am not praying for the world, but for those you have given me, for they are yours. [10]All I have is yours, and all you have is mine. And glory has come to me through them. [11]I will remain in the world no longer, but they are still in the world, and I am coming to you. Holy Father, protect them by the power of your name—the name you gave me—so that they may be one as we are one. [12]While I was with them, I protected them and kept them safe by that name you gave me. None has been lost except the one doomed to destruction so that Scripture would be fulfilled.

[13]"I am coming to you now, but I say these things while I am still in the world, so that they may have the full measure of my joy within them. [14]I have given them your word and the world has hated them, for they are not of the world any more than I am of the world. [15]My prayer is not that you take them out of the world but that you protect them from the evil one. [16]They are not of the world, even as I am not of it. [17]Sanctify[c] them by the truth; your word is truth. [18]As you sent me into the world, I

[a]31 Or *"Do you now believe?"*   [b]6 Greek *your name*; also in verse 26   [c]17 Greek *hagiazo* (set apart for sacred use or make holy); also in verse 19

have sent them into the world. [19]For them I sanctify myself, that they too may be truly sanctified.

Jesus Prays for All Believers

[20]"My prayer is not for them alone. I pray also for those who will believe in me through their message, [21]that all of them may be one, Father, just as you are in me and I am in you. May they also be in us so that the world may believe that you have

17:21 Jesus' Longest Prayer

The famous prayer recorded here concludes a kind of commissioning or graduation. In it, Jesus turns over his mission to the disciples and, by extension, to all believers who would follow.

sent me. [22]I have given them the glory that you gave me, that they may be one as we are one: [23]I in them and you in me. May they be brought to complete unity to let the world know that you sent me and have loved them even as you have loved me.

[24]"Father, I want those you have given me to be with me where I am, and to see my glory, the glory you have given me because you loved me before the creation of the world. [25]"Righteous Father, though the world does not know you, I know you, and they know that you have sent me. [26]I have made you known to them, and will continue to make you known in order that the love you have for me may be in them and that I myself may be in them."

Jesus Arrested

▶ *See Matthew 26:47–56; Mark 14:43–50; Luke 22:47–53*

18 When he had finished praying, Jesus left with his disciples and crossed the Kidron Valley. On the other side there was an olive grove, and he and his disciples went into it.

[2]Now Judas, who betrayed him, knew the place, because Jesus had often met there with his disciples. [3]So Judas came to the grove, guiding a detachment of soldiers and some officials from the chief priests and Pharisees. They were carrying torches, lanterns and weapons.

[4]Jesus, knowing all that was going to happen to him, went out and asked them, "Who is it you want?"

[5]"Jesus of Nazareth," they replied.

"I am he," Jesus said. (And Judas the traitor

was standing there with them.) [6]When Jesus said, "I am he," they drew back and fell to the ground.

[7]Again he asked them, "Who is it you want?"

And they said, "Jesus of Nazareth."

[8]"I told you that I am he," Jesus answered. "If you are looking for me, then let these men go." [9]This happened so that the words he had spoken would be fulfilled: "I have not lost one of those you gave me."[a]

[10]Then Simon Peter, who had a sword, drew it and struck the high priest's servant, cutting off his right ear. (The servant's name was Malchus.)

[11]Jesus commanded Peter, "Put your sword away! Shall I not drink the cup the Father has given me?"

Jesus Taken to Annas

▶ *See Matthew 26:57*

[12]Then the detachment of soldiers with its commander and the Jewish officials arrested Jesus. They bound him [13]and brought him first to Annas, who was the father-in-law of Caiaphas, the high priest that year. [14]Caiaphas was the one who had advised the Jews that it would be good if one man died for the people.

Peter's First Denial

▶ *See Matthew 26:69–70; Mark 14:66–68; Luke 22:55–57*

[15]Simon Peter and another disciple were following Jesus. Because this disciple was known to the high priest, he went with Jesus into the high priest's courtyard, [16]but Peter had to wait outside at the door. The other disciple, who was known to the high priest, came back, spoke to the girl on duty there and brought Peter in.

[17]"You are not one of his disciples, are you?" the girl at the door asked Peter.

He replied, "I am not."

[18]It was cold, and the servants and officials stood around a fire they had made to keep warm. Peter also was standing with them, warming himself.

The High Priest Questions Jesus

▶ *See Matthew 26:59–68; Mark 14:55–65; Luke 22:63–71*

[19]Meanwhile, the high priest questioned Jesus about his disciples and his teaching.

[20]"I have spoken openly to the world," Jesus replied. "I always taught in synagogues or at the temple, where all the Jews come together. I said nothing in secret. [21]Why question me? Ask those who heard me. Surely they know what I said."

[22]When Jesus said this, one of the officials nearby struck him in the face. "Is this the way you answer the high priest?" he demanded.

[23]"If I said something wrong," Jesus replied,

[a]9 John 6:39

"testify as to what is wrong. But if I spoke the truth, why did you strike me?" 24Then Annas sent him, still bound, to Caiaphas the high priest.*a*

Peter's Second and Third Denials

▶ *See Matthew 26:71–75; Mark 14:69–72; Luke 22:58–62*

25As Simon Peter stood warming himself, he was asked, "You are not one of his disciples, are you?"

He denied it, saying, "I am not."

26One of the high priest's servants, a relative of the man whose ear Peter had cut off, challenged him, "Didn't I see you with him in the olive grove?" 27Again Peter denied it, and at that moment a rooster began to crow.

Jesus Before Pilate

▶ *See Matthew 27:11–18,20–23; Mark 15:2–15; Luke 23:2–3,18–25*

28Then the Jews led Jesus from Caiaphas to the palace of the Roman governor. By now it was early morning, and to avoid ceremonial uncleanness the Jews did not enter the palace; they wanted to be able to eat the Passover. 29So Pilate came out to them and asked, "What charges are you bringing against this man?"

30"If he were not a criminal," they replied, "we would not have handed him over to you."

31Pilate said, "Take him yourselves and judge him by your own law."

"But we have no right to execute anyone," the Jews objected. 32This happened so that the words Jesus had spoken indicating the kind of death he was going to die would be fulfilled.

33Pilate then went back inside the palace, summoned Jesus and asked him, "Are you the king of the Jews?"

34"Is that your own idea," Jesus asked, "or did others talk to you about me?"

35"Am I a Jew?" Pilate replied. "It was your people and your chief priests who handed you over to me. What is it you have done?"

36Jesus said, "My kingdom is not of this world. If it were, my servants would fight to prevent my arrest by the Jews. But now my kingdom is from another place."

37"You are a king, then!" said Pilate.

Jesus answered, "You are right in saying I am a king. In fact, for this reason I was born, and for this I came into the world, to testify to the truth. Everyone on the side of truth listens to me."

38"What is truth?" Pilate asked. With this he went out again to the Jews and said, "I find no basis for a charge against him. 39But it is your custom for me to release to you one prisoner at the time of the Passover. Do you want me to release 'the king of the Jews'?"

40They shouted back, "No, not him! Give us Barabbas!" Now Barabbas had taken part in a rebellion.

a 24 Or *(Now Annas had sent him, still bound, to Caiaphas the high priest.)*

PONTIUS PILATE *Governor Cynic*

WHENEVER LOCAL RULERS FAILED TO keep the colonies in line, Rome appointed its own strongmen, called "procurators" or "governors." Pilate served as Roman procurator of Judea, a regional ruler for the most powerful empire in the history of the planet up to that time. Yet, as Pilate discovered, having absolute power does not guarantee peace. The Jews hated Roman rule, and religious and nationalist emotions constantly flared up in Judea.

According to the first-century historian Josephus, Pilate marched Roman soldiers into Jerusalem, learning too late that Jews would die to keep Rome's military emblems out. (They considered images of the emperor blasphemous.) When Pilate set out to build an aqueduct for Jerusalem, he caused a bloody riot by appropriating temple offerings to pay the bill. Pilate's soldiers brutally put down many such disturbances.

When Pilate met Jesus, he mainly saw one more source of trouble. Pilate tried to pass the buck (to Herod). He even offered to set the prisoner free. But in the end Pilate was willing to sacrifice Jesus if that would buy order. Pilate's most famous words were a cynical question, "What is truth?" (18:38). The answer was standing right in front of him, but Pilate didn't really want to know.

Pilate must have considered Jesus' execution a success (it didn't start any riots), but his balancing act was upturned just a few years later. Some Samaritans—the mixed-race group whom Jews despised—heard a crazy report that Moses had buried treasures on Mt. Gerizim. A crowd gathered to climb the mountain. Pilate, thinking these pilgrims might be dangerous, sent in troops. Soon he had a massacre on his hands. For his overreaction he was relieved from command and sent back to Rome to stand trial.

Life Questions: Are there situations in your life where you would buy peace at any cost? What happens to the truth when you do so?

Jesus Sentenced to be Crucified

▶ See Matthew 27:27–31; Mark 15:16–20

19 Then Pilate took Jesus and had him flogged. ²The soldiers twisted together a crown of thorns and put it on his head. They clothed him in a purple robe ³and went up to him again and again, saying, "Hail, king of the Jews!" And they struck him in the face.

⁴Once more Pilate came out and said to the Jews, "Look, I am bringing him out to you to let you know that I find no basis for a charge against him." ⁵When Jesus came out wearing the crown of thorns and the purple robe, Pilate said to them, "Here is the man!"

⁶As soon as the chief priests and their officials saw him, they shouted, "Crucify! Crucify!"

But Pilate answered, "You take him and crucify him. As for me, I find no basis for a charge against him."

⁷The Jews insisted, "We have a law, and according to that law he must die, because he claimed to be the Son of God."

⁸When Pilate heard this, he was even more afraid, ⁹and he went back inside the palace. "Where do you come from?" he asked Jesus, but Jesus gave him no answer. ¹⁰"Do you refuse to speak to me?" Pilate said. "Don't you realize I have power either to free you or to crucify you?"

¹¹Jesus answered, "You would have no power over me if it were not given to you from above. Therefore the one who handed me over to you is guilty of a greater sin."

¹²From then on, Pilate tried to set Jesus free, but the Jews kept shouting, "If you let this man go, you are no friend of Caesar. Anyone who claims to be a king opposes Caesar."

¹³When Pilate heard this, he brought Jesus out and sat down on the judge's seat at a place known as the Stone Pavement (which in Aramaic is Gabbatha). ¹⁴It was the day of Preparation of Passover Week, about the sixth hour.

"Here is your king," Pilate said to the Jews.

¹⁵But they shouted, "Take him away! Take him away! Crucify him!"

"Shall I crucify your king?" Pilate asked.

"We have no king but Caesar," the chief priests answered.

¹⁶Finally Pilate handed him over to them to be crucified.

The Crucifixion

▶ See Matthew 27:33–44; Mark 15:22–32; Luke 23:33–43

So the soldiers took charge of Jesus. ¹⁷Carrying his own cross, he went out to the place of the Skull (which in Aramaic is called Golgotha). ¹⁸Here they crucified him, and with him two others— one on each side and Jesus in the middle.

¹⁹Pilate had a notice prepared and fastened to the cross. It read: JESUS OF NAZARETH, THE KING OF THE JEWS. ²⁰Many of the Jews read this sign, for the place where Jesus was crucified was near the city, and the sign was written in Aramaic, Latin and Greek. ²¹The chief priests of the Jews protested to Pilate, "Do not write 'The King of the Jews,' but that this man claimed to be king of the Jews."

²²Pilate answered, "What I have written, I have written."

²³When the soldiers crucified Jesus, they took his clothes, dividing them into four shares, one for each of them, with the undergarment remaining. This garment was seamless, woven in one piece from top to bottom.

²⁴"Let's not tear it," they said to one another. "Let's decide by lot who will get it."

This happened that the scripture might be fulfilled which said,

"They divided my garments among them
and cast lots for my clothing."ᵃ

So this is what the soldiers did.

²⁵Near the cross of Jesus stood his mother, his mother's sister, Mary the wife of Clopas, and Mary Magdalene. ²⁶When Jesus saw his mother there, and the disciple whom he loved standing nearby, he said to his mother, "Dear woman, here is your son," ²⁷and to the disciple, "Here is your mother." From that time on, this disciple took her into his home.

The Death of Jesus

▶ See Matthew 27:48,50; Mark 15:36–37; Luke 23:36

²⁸Later, knowing that all was now completed, and so that the Scripture would be fulfilled, Jesus said, "I am thirsty." ²⁹A jar of wine vinegar was there, so they soaked a sponge in it, put the sponge on a stalk of the hyssop plant, and lifted it to Jesus' lips. ³⁰When he had received the drink, Jesus said, "It is finished." With that, he bowed his head and gave up his spirit.

³¹Now it was the day of Preparation, and the next day was to be a special Sabbath. Because the Jews did not want the bodies left on the crosses during the Sabbath, they asked Pilate to have the

19:31 Speeding up Death

Soldiers broke the bones of crucified men to speed up their dying, here so the bodies could be removed before the holy day that followed. Jesus had already died, so his bones were left intact. This fulfilled Old Testament promises that the Messiah's bones would not be broken and that his side would be pierced with a spear (Exodus 12:46; Zechariah 12:10).

ᵃ24 Psalm 22:18

legs broken and the bodies taken down. ³²The soldiers therefore came and broke the legs of the first man who had been crucified with Jesus, and then those of the other. ³³But when they came to Jesus and found that he was already dead, they did not break his legs. ³⁴Instead, one of the soldiers pierced Jesus' side with a spear, bringing a sudden flow of blood and water. ³⁵The man who saw it has given testimony, and his testimony is true. He knows that he tells the truth, and he testifies so that you also may believe. ³⁶These things happened so that the scripture would be fulfilled: "Not one of his bones will be broken,"[a] ³⁷and, as another scripture says, "They will look on the one they have pierced."[b]

The Burial of Jesus

▶ See Matthew 27:57–61; Mark 15:42–47; Luke 23:50–56

³⁸Later, Joseph of Arimathea asked Pilate for the body of Jesus. Now Joseph was a disciple of Jesus, but secretly because he feared the Jews. With Pilate's permission, he came and took the body away. ³⁹He was accompanied by Nicodemus, the man who earlier had visited Jesus at night. Nicodemus brought a mixture of myrrh and aloes, about seventy-five pounds.[c] ⁴⁰Taking Jesus' body, the two of them wrapped it, with the spices, in strips of linen. This was in accordance with Jewish burial customs. ⁴¹At the place where Jesus was crucified, there was a garden, and in the garden a new tomb, in which no one had ever been laid. ⁴²Because it was the Jewish day of Preparation and since the tomb was nearby, they laid Jesus there.

The Empty Tomb

▶ See Matthew 28:1–8; Mark 16:1–8; Luke 24:1–10

20 Early on the first day of the week, while it was still dark, Mary Magdalene went to the tomb and saw that the stone had been removed from the entrance. ²So she came running to Simon Peter and the other disciple, the one Jesus loved, and said, "They have taken the Lord out of the tomb, and we don't know where they have put him!"

³So Peter and the other disciple started for the tomb. ⁴Both were running, but the other disciple outran Peter and reached the tomb first. ⁵He bent over and looked in at the strips of linen lying there but did not go in. ⁶Then Simon Peter, who was behind him, arrived and went into the tomb. He saw the strips of linen lying there, ⁷as well as the burial cloth that had been around Jesus' head. The cloth was folded up by itself, separate from the linen. ⁸Finally the other disciple, who had reached the tomb first, also went inside. He saw and believed. ⁹(They still did not understand from Scripture that Jesus had to rise from the dead.)

Jesus Appears to Mary Magdalene

¹⁰Then the disciples went back to their homes, ¹¹but Mary stood outside the tomb crying. As she wept, she bent over to look into the tomb ¹²and saw two angels in white, seated where Jesus' body had been, one at the head and the other at the foot.

¹³They asked her, "Woman, why are you crying?"

"They have taken my Lord away," she said, "and I don't know where they have put him."

a36 Exodus 12:46; Num. 9:12; Psalm 34:20   *b37* Zech. 12:10   *c39* Greek *a hundred litrai* (about 34 kilograms)

MARY MAGDALENE *First to See*

MARY MAGDALENE HAS BECOME FAMOUS. *Jesus Christ Superstar* and other plays and movies have portrayed her as a sensuous woman, sometimes as a reformed prostitute. In reality, the Bible gives no indication of anything tawdry about her. All we know is that she came from Magdala, a city on the Sea of Galilee, and that Jesus drove seven demons from her. Having been healed by him, she dedicated her life to Jesus.

The Gospels, which focus on Jesus' twelve disciples, also mention that a good-sized crowd of women left their homes and families to follow Jesus (Matthew 27:55–56). Mary Magdalene heads the list of the women who helped finance his ministry.

When Jesus was crucified in Jerusalem, far from his home in Galilee, Mary Magdalene stayed near him. She carefully observed where he was buried and faithfully went there at the earliest opportunity to care for his body. As a result, she was the very first person to see Jesus risen from the dead and the first to spread the word (20:18).

Women in that time were usually given second place, if any place at all. Jewish courts did not even accept their testimony. At the great miracle of Jesus' resurrection, however, Mary Magdalene had the honor of being the first witness on the scene.

Life Questions: Have you been able to witness God's work? Where and how?

14At this, she turned around and saw Jesus standing there, but she did not realize that it was Jesus.

15"Woman," he said, "why are you crying? Who is it you are looking for?"

Thinking he was the gardener, she said, "Sir, if you have carried him away, tell me where you have put him, and I will get him."

16Jesus said to her, "Mary."

She turned toward him and cried out in Aramaic, "Rabboni!" (which means Teacher).

17Jesus said, "Do not hold on to me, for I have not yet returned to the Father. Go instead to my brothers and tell them, 'I am returning to my Father and your Father, to my God and your God.'"

18Mary Magdalene went to the disciples with the news: "I have seen the Lord!" And she told them that he had said these things to her.

Jesus Appears to His Disciples

19On the evening of that first day of the week, when the disciples were together, with the doors locked for fear of the Jews, Jesus came and stood among them and said, "Peace be with you!" 20After he said this, he showed them his hands and side. The disciples were overjoyed when they saw the Lord.

21Again Jesus said, "Peace be with you! As the Father has sent me, I am sending you." 22And with that he breathed on them and said, "Receive the Holy Spirit. 23If you forgive anyone his sins, they are forgiven; if you do not forgive them, they are not forgiven."

Jesus Appears to Thomas

24Now Thomas (called Didymus), one of the Twelve, was not with the disciples when Jesus came. 25So the other disciples told him, "We have seen the Lord!"

But he said to them, "Unless I see the nail marks in his hands and put my finger where the

nails were, and put my hand into his side, I will not believe it."

26A week later his disciples were in the house again, and Thomas was with them. Though the doors were locked, Jesus came and stood among them and said, "Peace be with you!" 27Then he said to Thomas, "Put your finger here; see my hands. Reach out your hand and put it into my side. Stop doubting and believe."

28Thomas said to him, "My Lord and my God!"

29Then Jesus told him, "Because you have seen me, you have believed; blessed are those who have not seen and yet have believed."

30Jesus did many other miraculous signs in the presence of his disciples, which are not recorded in this book. 31But these are written that you may*a* believe that Jesus is the Christ, the Son of God, and that by believing you may have life in his name.

Jesus and the Miraculous Catch of Fish

21 Afterward Jesus appeared again to his disciples, by the Sea of Tiberias.*b* It happened this way: 2Simon Peter, Thomas (called Didymus), Nathanael from Cana in Galilee, the sons of Zebedee, and two other disciples were together. 3"I'm going out to fish," Simon Peter told them, and they said, "We'll go with you." So they went out and got into the boat, but that night they caught nothing.

4Early in the morning, Jesus stood on the shore, but the disciples did not realize that it was Jesus.

5He called out to them, "Friends, haven't you any fish?"

"No," they answered.

6He said, "Throw your net on the right side of the boat and you will find some." When they did, they were unable to haul the net in because of the large number of fish.

7Then the disciple whom Jesus loved said to Peter, "It is the Lord!" As soon as Simon Peter heard him say, "It is the Lord," he wrapped his outer garment around him (for he had taken it off) and jumped into the water. 8The other disciples followed in the boat, towing the net full of fish, for they were not far from shore, about a hundred yards.*c* 9When they landed, they saw a fire of burning coals there with fish on it, and some bread.

10Jesus said to them, "Bring some of the fish you have just caught."

11Simon Peter climbed aboard and dragged the net ashore. It was full of large fish, 153, but even with so many the net was not torn. 12Jesus

20:25 Doubting Thomas

The skeptical Thomas is sometimes singled out, as though he had unusual doubts. In reality, none of the disciples believed in Jesus' resurrection until they saw him for themselves. Thomas had been absent, though, when Jesus first appeared to the others. He stayed skeptical until Jesus appeared again, and summoned Thomas to touch him. Seeing was believing for all the disciples, but Jesus specially commended those who believed without such firsthand evidence.

*a*31 Some manuscripts *may continue to*   *b*1 That is, Sea of Galilee   *c*8 Greek *about two hundred cubits* (about 90 meters)

said to them, "Come and have breakfast." None of the disciples dared ask him, "Who are you?" They knew it was the Lord. [13]Jesus came, took the bread and gave it to them, and did the same with the fish. [14]This was now the third time Jesus appeared to his disciples after he was raised from the dead.

Jesus Reinstates Peter

[15]When they had finished eating, Jesus said to Simon Peter, "Simon son of John, do you truly love me more than these?"

"Yes, Lord," he said, "you know that I love you."

Jesus said, "Feed my lambs."

[16]Again Jesus said, "Simon son of John, do you truly love me?"

He answered, "Yes, Lord, you know that I love you."

Jesus said, "Take care of my sheep."

[17]The third time he said to him, "Simon son of John, do you love me?"

Peter was hurt because Jesus asked him the third time, "Do you love me?" He said, "Lord, you know all things; you know that I love you."

Jesus said, "Feed my sheep. [18]I tell you the truth, when you were younger you dressed yourself and went where you wanted; but when you are old you will stretch out your hands, and someone else will dress you and lead you where you do not want to go." [19]Jesus said this to indicate the kind of death by which Peter would glorify God. Then he said to him, "Follow me!"

[20]Peter turned and saw that the disciple whom Jesus loved was following them. (This was the one who had leaned back against Jesus at the supper and had said, "Lord, who is going to betray you?") [21]When Peter saw him, he asked, "Lord, what about him?"

[22]Jesus answered, "If I want him to remain alive until I return, what is that to you? You must

21:15 Do You Love Me?

John ends his book with a moving scene in which Jesus spoke to Peter and "the disciple whom Jesus loved," presumably John himself. Jesus asked Peter the same question three times, a painful reminder of Peter's three denials of him. But this reinstatement helped embolden Peter to become one of the early church's most fearless spokesmen.

A Change of Heart and Mind
Whatever happened to the "Son of Thunder"?

THE DISCIPLE JOHN HAD BEEN favored to share private moments with Jesus. As part of an inner circle of three, he saw Jesus transfigured, watched him bring Jairus's daughter back to life, and waited for him in the Garden of Gethsemane.

After Jesus was arrested, John witnessed the sequence of his trials. He was the only disciple mentioned as being near the cross at Jesus' death and one of the very first to learn of Christ's resurrection. Somehow, this process changed John.

This is the disciple who testifies to these things and who wrote them down. We know that his testimony is true. 21:24

From Thunder to Love

John wore an amusing nickname, "Son of Thunder" (Mark 3:17), and several incidents in the Gospels hint that this name reflected his stormy personality. John jealously resented competition from rival miracle workers (Mark 9:38), and he insisted on the best seat in the kingdom of heaven for himself. Once, he wanted to call fire down from heaven to destroy a hostile town (Luke 9:54).

Somewhere in his life, the thunderclouds broke apart. Eventually he got a new nickname: "the apostle of love." John's books—this Gospel and the letters John wrote later—are marked by a recurring emphasis on love.

Naturally, John's spiritual pilgrimage influenced his written record of Jesus' life. His changed personality may provide a clue to his unique style of telling Jesus' story through a handful of poignant episodes. Perhaps these few scenes are the memories of Jesus that finally convinced John himself that Jesus was, indeed, the Son of God.

Life Questions: Getting to know Jesus changes a person. How have you been changed?

follow me." [23]Because of this, the rumor spread among the brothers that this disciple would not die. But Jesus did not say that he would not die; he only said, "If I want him to remain alive until I return, what is that to you?"

[24]This is the disciple who testifies to these things and who wrote them down. We know that his testimony is true.

[25]Jesus did many other things as well. If every one of them were written down, I suppose that even the whole world would not have room for the books that would be written.

ACTS

The Linking Book
Imagine a Bible without the book of Acts

> "You will receive power when the Holy Spirit comes on you; and you will be my witnesses." 1:8

THE NEW TESTAMENT DIVIDES NEATLY into two nearly equal sections. The first consists of four Gospels that tell about Jesus' life on earth. The second section, beginning with Romans, concerns churches that sprang up after Jesus left. In between stands the book of Acts.

The best way to appreciate Acts is to imagine a Bible without it. You have just read the life of Jesus, underscored by four different authors, and you turn to Romans: "Paul, a servant of Christ Jesus ... to all in Rome who are loved by God and called to be saints." Rome? How did the story get there from Jerusalem?

Next you'd find two books, also from Paul (who's he?), addressed to "the church of God in Corinth." Another book follows, written to the church in Galatia, then one to Ephesus, and so on with more letters to other exotic locales. Obviously, something is missing. Without Acts, the New Testament leaps from an orderly history of one man, Jesus, to a collection of unexplained personal correspondence.

A Plan Revealed by Jesus

With Acts, everything fits into place. This book gives a transition from the life of Christ to the new church. It introduces Paul and explains how a minority religion crossed the sea to Rome, the capital of the empire. A reader of Acts visits key cities sprinkled around the Mediterranean, meets the principal leaders of the new movement, and gets a strong scent of the problems that will occupy Paul's letters.

Luke, a physician, had written the third Gospel as an account of "all that Jesus began to do and to teach" (Acts 1:1). The book of Acts resumes the story, hinting that this history, too, will show Jesus at work, but in a quite different form. "I will build my church," Jesus had promised (Matthew 16:18), and Acts graphically shows how that process began.

Jesus himself had laid out the plot in his last recorded words on earth: "You will be my witnesses in Jerusalem, and in all Judea and Samaria, and to the ends of the earth" (1:8). Acts faithfully follows that outline: The first seven chapters show the church in Jerusalem, the next five focus on Judea and Samaria, and the rest of the book follows the spread of the gospel to the outposts of Roman civilization.

Boisterous Beginnings

The book opens in Jerusalem, during the Pentecost holiday. Over a million pilgrims were milling about the city when suddenly a group of 120 believers came alive. Jesus' followers hit the streets with a bold new style, and 3,000 joined up on the first day alone. Starting with that boisterous scene, Luke spins a historical adventure tale.

Due to Luke's writing skill, Acts reads like a novel, skipping from one exhilarating scene to the next. Wherever the apostles went, action swirled, riots erupted, and a small church took root. In an era when new religions were a dime a dozen, the Christian faith became a worldwide phenomenon. Acts tells how.

How to Read Acts

Acts reads like well-written history. It follows a logical plan, includes fascinating details, and focuses on the most dramatic events. In that sense, it is self-explanatory.

The first twelve chapters concentrate mainly on the apostle Peter. The rest of Acts features Paul (also called Saul), and the book explains how he became accepted as the first and foremost Christian missionary. Paul made three extensive trips in Acts, then a final voyage in chains to Rome (see map, "Paul's Missionary Journeys," at the back of this Bible).

Acts records the early history of relations between the church and the Roman empire. It also gives important background information on such cities as Corinth, Ephesus, and Philippi—cities Paul later wrote letters to. The material in Acts will help you understand what Paul is writing about in 1 and 2 Corinthians, Ephesians, Philippians, and the other letters.

Acts also summarizes 18 different speeches by Paul, Peter, and a few others. These speeches make a fascinating study in themselves: The apostles were beginning to interpret the facts of Jesus' life in light of their spiritual significance. As you read them, note how the speakers chose their words and content with the audience in mind, and then note audience reaction.

PEOPLE YOU'LL MEET IN ACTS

STEPHEN (p. 1141)
PHILIP (p. 1145)
CORNELIUS (p. 1148)
BARNABAS (p. 1152)

MARK (JOHN MARK) (p. 1155)
SILAS (p. 1157)
PRISCILLA AND AQUILA (p. 1160)
AGRIPPA (p. 1169)

3-TRACK READING PLAN

For an explanation and complete listing of the 3-track reading plan, turn to page 7.

TRACK 1: **Two-Week Courses on the Bible**
The Track 1 reading program on the Life and Teachings of Paul includes six chapters from Acts. See page 7 for a complete listing of this course.

TRACK 2: **An Overview of Acts in 9 Days**
☐ Day 1. Read the Introduction to Acts and then Acts 1, which describes Jesus' last appearance to the disciples.
☐ Day 2. Read about the remarkable events of Pentecost in chapter 2.
☐ Day 3. Chapter 5 gives a glimpse of life in the early Christian church—some good parts and also a tragic scene of failure.
☐ Day 4. Read Acts 9 to learn the details of Saul's conversion.
☐ Day 5. Chapter 16 tells of Paul's dramatic experiences in Philippi, a city that produced one of Paul's favorite churches.
☐ Day 6. Chapter 17 shows Paul on some of the most difficult assignments of his missionary journeys.
☐ Day 7. Read chapter 26, Paul's recounting of his personal story to a king.
☐ Day 8. Read chapter 27, which tells of Paul's shipwreck on the way to Rome.
☐ Day 9. Read chapter 28, which describes Paul's last setting, under house arrest in Rome, where he probably wrote some of his New Testament letters.

Now turn to page 9 for your next Track 2 reading project.

TRACK 3: **All of Acts in 28 Days**
After you have read through Acts, turn to pages 10–14 for your next Track 3 reading project.

☐1	☐2	☐3	☐4	☐5	☐6	☐7	☐8
☐9	☐10	☐11	☐12	☐13	☐14	☐15	☐16
☐17	☐18	☐19	☐20	☐21	☐22	☐23	☐24
☐25	☐26	☐27	☐28				

Jesus Taken Up Into Heaven

1 In my former book, Theophilus, I wrote about all that Jesus began to do and to teach [2]until the day he was taken up to heaven, after giving instructions through the Holy Spirit to the apostles he had chosen. [3]After his suffering, he showed himself to these men and gave many convincing proofs that he was alive. He appeared to them over a period of forty days and spoke about the kingdom of God. [4]On one occasion, while he was eating with them, he gave them this command: "Do not leave Jerusalem, but wait for the gift my Father promised, which you have heard me speak about. [5]For John baptized with[a] water, but in a few days you will be baptized with the Holy Spirit."

[6]So when they met together, they asked him, "Lord, are you at this time going to restore the kingdom to Israel?"

[7]He said to them: "It is not for you to know the times or dates the Father has set by his own authority. [8]But you will receive power when the Holy Spirit comes on you; and you will be my witnesses in Jerusalem, and in all Judea and Samaria, and to the ends of the earth."

[9]After he said this, he was taken up before their very eyes, and a cloud hid him from their sight.

[10]They were looking intently up into the sky as he was going, when suddenly two men dressed in white stood beside them. [11]"Men of Galilee," they said, "why do you stand here looking into the sky? This same Jesus, who has been taken from you into heaven, will come back in the same way you have seen him go into heaven."

Matthias Chosen to Replace Judas

[12]Then they returned to Jerusalem from the hill called the Mount of Olives, a Sabbath day's walk[b] from the city. [13]When they arrived, they went upstairs to the room where they were staying. Those present were Peter, John, James and Andrew; Philip and Thomas, Bartholomew and Matthew; James son of Alphaeus and Simon the Zealot, and Judas son of James. [14]They all joined together constantly in prayer, along with the women and Mary the mother of Jesus, and with his brothers.

[15]In those days Peter stood up among the believers[c] (a group numbering about a hundred and twenty) [16]and said, "Brothers, the Scripture had to be fulfilled which the Holy Spirit spoke long ago through the mouth of David concerning Judas, who served as guide for those who arrested Jesus— [17]he was one of our number and shared in this ministry."

[18](With the reward he got for his wickedness, Judas bought a field; there he fell headlong, his body burst open and all his intestines spilled out. [19]Everyone in Jerusalem heard about this, so they called that field in their language Akeldama, that is, Field of Blood.)

[20]"For," said Peter, "it is written in the book of Psalms,

> "'May his place be deserted;
> let there be no one to dwell in it,'[d]

and,

> "'May another take his place of
> leadership.'[e]

[21]Therefore it is necessary to choose one of the men who have been with us the whole time the

1:21 Inner Circle

The group of Jesus' closest disciples known as the Twelve became "the Eleven" after Judas's death. In choosing a replacement for the betrayer, the disciples favored an old-timer who had been with Jesus from the very beginning. Evidently several people qualified, and the group cast lots between two to make the final choice. This is the Bible's last mention of casting lots, a method used in the Old Testament to discern God's will; after Pentecost the disciples relied directly on the Holy Spirit for guidance.

Lord Jesus went in and out among us, [22]beginning from John's baptism to the time when Jesus was taken up from us. For one of these must become a witness with us of his resurrection."

[23]So they proposed two men: Joseph called Barsabbas (also known as Justus) and Matthias. [24]Then they prayed, "Lord, you know everyone's heart. Show us which of these two you have chosen [25]to take over this apostolic ministry, which Judas left to go where he belongs." [26]Then they cast lots, and the lot fell to Matthias; so he was added to the eleven apostles.

The Holy Spirit Comes at Pentecost

2 When the day of Pentecost came, they were all together in one place. [2]Suddenly a sound like the blowing of a violent wind came from heaven and filled the whole house where they were sitting. [3]They saw what seemed to be tongues of fire that separated and came to rest on each of them. [4]All of them were filled with the Holy Spirit and began to speak in other tongues[f] as the Spirit enabled them.

[5]Now there were staying in Jerusalem God-

---

[a]5 Or *in*   [b]12 That is, about 3/4 mile (about 1,100 meters)
[e]20 Psalm 109:8   [f]4 Or *languages*; also in verse 11   [c]15 Greek *brothers*   [d]20 Psalm 69:25

fearing Jews from every nation under heaven. [6]When they heard this sound, a crowd came together in bewilderment, because each one heard them speaking in his own language. [7]Utterly amazed, they asked: "Are not all these men who are speaking Galileans? [8]Then how is it that each of us hears them in his own native language? [9]Parthians, Medes and Elamites; residents of Mesopotamia, Judea and Cappadocia, Pontus and Asia, [10]Phrygia and Pamphylia, Egypt and the parts of Libya near Cyrene; visitors from Rome [11](both Jews and converts to Judaism); Cretans and Arabs—we hear them declaring the wonders of God in our own tongues!" [12]Amazed and perplexed, they asked one another, "What does this mean?"

[13]Some, however, made fun of them and said, "They have had too much wine.[a]"

Peter Addresses the Crowd

[14]Then Peter stood up with the Eleven, raised his voice and addressed the crowd: "Fellow Jews and all of you who live in Jerusalem, let me explain this to you; listen carefully to what I say. [15]These men are not drunk, as you suppose. It's only nine in the morning! [16]No, this is what was spoken by the prophet Joel:

[17]" 'In the last days, God says,
  I will pour out my Spirit on all people.
Your sons and daughters will prophesy,
  your young men will see visions,
  your old men will dream dreams.
[18]Even on my servants, both men and women,
  I will pour out my Spirit in those days,
  and they will prophesy.
[19]I will show wonders in the heaven above
  and signs on the earth below,
  blood and fire and billows of smoke.
[20]The sun will be turned to darkness
  and the moon to blood
  before the coming of the great and
    glorious day of the Lord.
[21]And everyone who calls
  on the name of the Lord will be saved.'[b]

[22]"Men of Israel, listen to this: Jesus of Nazareth was a man accredited by God to you by miracles, wonders and signs, which God did among you through him, as you yourselves know. [23]This man was handed over to you by God's set purpose and foreknowledge; and you, with the help of wicked men,[c] put him to death by nailing him to the cross. [24]But God raised him from the dead, freeing him from the agony of death, because it was impossible for death to keep its hold on him. [25]David said about him:

" 'I saw the Lord always before me.
  Because he is at my right hand,
  I will not be shaken.
[26]Therefore my heart is glad and my tongue
    rejoices;
  my body also will live in hope,
[27]because you will not abandon me to the
    grave,
  nor will you let your Holy One see decay.
[28]You have made known to me the paths of
    life;
  you will fill me with joy in your
    presence.'[d]

[29]"Brothers, I can tell you confidently that the patriarch David died and was buried, and his tomb is here to this day. [30]But he was a prophet and knew that God had promised him on oath that he would place one of his descendants on his throne. [31]Seeing what was ahead, he spoke of the resurrection of the Christ,[e] that he was not abandoned to the grave, nor did his body see decay. [32]God has raised this Jesus to life, and we are all witnesses of the fact. [33]Exalted to the right hand of God, he has received from the Father the promised Holy Spirit and has poured out what you now see and hear. [34]For David did not ascend to heaven, and yet he said,

" 'The Lord said to my Lord:
  "Sit at my right hand
[35]until I make your enemies
    a footstool for your feet." '[f]

[36]"Therefore let all Israel be assured of this: God has made this Jesus, whom you crucified, both Lord and Christ."

[37]When the people heard this, they were cut to the heart and said to Peter and the other apostles, "Brothers, what shall we do?"

[38]Peter replied, "Repent and be baptized, every one of you, in the name of Jesus Christ for the forgiveness of your sins. And you will receive the gift of the Holy Spirit. [39]The promise is for you

2:42 Infant Church

Acts records a series of stages through which the Christian church became a separate movement. At this point, the followers of Jesus were still keeping the pattern of traditional Jewish worship: prayers in the temple at 9 A.M., 3 P.M., and sunset (3:1). Yet this paragraph shows them also developing a new form of "house churches" based on communal sharing and fellowship.

[a]13 Or *sweet wine*   [b]21 Joel 2:28-32   [c]23 Or *of those not having the law* (that is, Gentiles)   [d]28 Psalm 16:8-11   [e]31 Or *Messiah*. "The Christ" (Greek) and "the Messiah" (Hebrew) both mean "the Anointed One"; also in verse 36.   [f]35 Psalm 110:1

and your children and for all who are far off—for all whom the Lord our God will call."

⁴⁰With many other words he warned them; and he pleaded with them, "Save yourselves from this corrupt generation." ⁴¹Those who accepted his message were baptized, and about three thousand were added to their number that day.

The Fellowship of the Believers

⁴²They devoted themselves to the apostles' teaching and to the fellowship, to the breaking of bread and to prayer. ⁴³Everyone was filled with awe, and many wonders and miraculous signs were done by the apostles. ⁴⁴All the believers were together and had everything in common.

⁴⁵Selling their possessions and goods, they gave to anyone as he had need. ⁴⁶Every day they continued to meet together in the temple courts. They broke bread in their homes and ate together with glad and sincere hearts, ⁴⁷praising God and enjoying the favor of all the people. And the Lord added to their number daily those who were being saved.

Peter Heals the Crippled Beggar

3 One day Peter and John were going up to the temple at the time of prayer—at three in the afternoon. ²Now a man crippled from birth was being carried to the temple gate called Beautiful, where he was put every day to beg from those

More than a Ghost
The best proof that Jesus is alive

"HE LOOKS AS IF HE'S seen a ghost!" What image comes to mind when you hear that? A face drained of blood, a trembling jaw, pasty skin and thin lips, a look of terror.

Seeing a ghost doesn't make a person stronger and more confident. The witness is usually reluctant to talk about the experience. Self-doubt attacks in waves: *Was it real? Maybe I was hallucinating . . . it was so dark and eerie.*

"You killed the author of life, but God raised him from the dead. We are witnesses of this." 3:15

A Convincing Change

When Jesus showed up after his death, his disciples went through a did-we-see-a-ghost? phase, complete with terror, disbelief, and wild rumors. But it didn't last long. In 40 days Jesus made enough undeniable appearances to convince each of his disciples—even skeptical Thomas—that he had indeed overthrown death.

As Acts shows, the disciples began acting the opposite of people who think they've seen a ghost. Rather, they acted like people who had just witnessed the most astounding event in all history. They couldn't wait to tell the world about it.

Exuberance, not fear, lit up the disciples' faces. In the streets of Jerusalem and in the temple, to anyone who would listen, they cried out the news that couldn't be true, but was. "Jesus is alive! The man who died has come back—he's the Messiah we've been waiting for!"

If you're ever tempted to doubt Jesus' resurrection, take a sober look at his changed followers in Acts. Consider Peter, for instance. He had cowered in the shadows at the trial scene, trying to look inconspicuous. Out of fear of arrest, he had even cursed and denied knowing Jesus. Could this be the same man, standing before the most distinguished religious leaders in the land, blasting them as murderers (chapter 3)? Something ignited Peter that would not easily be snuffed out.

Response to a New Message

When Jesus was on earth he mostly preached "the kingdom," sometimes even warning his followers not to mention he was the Messiah. In Acts, the word is out. Jesus is the theme of every speech, whether delivered in the temple square or in the luxurious setting of a royal palace, to working-class pagans or cultured Greek philosophers. Reports of his resurrection resound throughout Acts.

To those who heard, the message sounded like the first note of music to people born deaf. Five thousand men believed (4:4), as did many priests (6:7) and many thousands of Jews (21:20). The scanty band of followers Jesus had left behind was soon organizing and electing officers to handle the needs of a growing church.

Acts follows the core of leaders from place to place, as a remarkable drama unfolds. A few men, mostly unlearned, were setting into motion a worldwide outreach that would ultimately reshape civilization. A revolution was underway, but not one with weapons. This one was powered by the work of God in simple men who had seen a miracle. As Peter said, "We cannot help speaking about what we have seen and heard" (4:20).

Life Questions: The disciples led mass conversions to Christ. What made them such effective spokesmen?

going into the temple courts. ³When he saw Peter and John about to enter, he asked them for money. ⁴Peter looked straight at him, as did John. Then Peter said, "Look at us!" ⁵So the man gave them his attention, expecting to get something from them.

⁶Then Peter said, "Silver or gold I do not have, but what I have I give you. In the name of Jesus Christ of Nazareth, walk." ⁷Taking him by the right hand, he helped him up, and instantly the man's feet and ankles became strong. ⁸He jumped to his feet and began to walk. Then he went with them into the temple courts, walking and jumping, and praising God. ⁹When all the people saw him walking and praising God, ¹⁰they recognized him as the same man who used to sit begging at the temple gate called Beautiful, and they were filled with wonder and amazement at what had happened to him.

Peter Speaks to the Onlookers

¹¹While the beggar held on to Peter and John, all the people were astonished and came running to them in the place called Solomon's Colonnade. ¹²When Peter saw this, he said to them: "Men of Israel, why does this surprise you? Why do you stare at us as if by our own power or godliness we

3:12 Knowing the Audience

Peter's speeches in chapters 2 and 3 offer excellent examples of adapting the gospel message to a particular audience. Preaching to Jews gathered in Jerusalem to celebrate Pentecost, he relied heavily on quotations from the Old Testament. Although his main intent was to tell them about Jesus, he referred to Joel, David, Abraham, Isaac, Jacob, Moses, and Samuel. His words proved so effective that 3,000 people were converted the first day. Jewish leaders soon arrested Peter and John.

had made this man walk? ¹³The God of Abraham, Isaac and Jacob, the God of our fathers, has glorified his servant Jesus. You handed him over to be killed, and you disowned him before Pilate, though he had decided to let him go. ¹⁴You disowned the Holy and Righteous One and asked that a murderer be released to you. ¹⁵You killed the author of life, but God raised him from the dead. We are witnesses of this. ¹⁶By faith in the name of Jesus, this man whom you see and know was made strong. It is Jesus' name and the faith that comes through him that has given this complete healing to him, as you can all see.

¹⁷"Now, brothers, I know that you acted in ignorance, as did your leaders. ¹⁸But this is how God fulfilled what he had foretold through all the prophets, saying that his Christ*ᵃ* would suffer. ¹⁹Repent, then, and turn to God, so that your sins may be wiped out, that times of refreshing may come from the Lord, ²⁰and that he may send the Christ, who has been appointed for you—even Jesus. ²¹He must remain in heaven until the time comes for God to restore everything, as he promised long ago through his holy prophets. ²²For Moses said, 'The Lord your God will raise up for you a prophet like me from among your own people; you must listen to everything he tells you. ²³Anyone who does not listen to him will be completely cut off from among his people.'*ᵇ*

²⁴"Indeed, all the prophets from Samuel on, as many as have spoken, have foretold these days. ²⁵And you are heirs of the prophets and of the covenant God made with your fathers. He said to Abraham, 'Through your offspring all peoples on earth will be blessed.'*ᶜ* ²⁶When God raised up his servant, he sent him first to you to bless you by turning each of you from your wicked ways."

Peter and John Before the Sanhedrin

4 The priests and the captain of the temple guard and the Sadducees came up to Peter and John while they were speaking to the people. ²They were greatly disturbed because the apostles were teaching the people and proclaiming in Jesus the resurrection of the dead. ³They seized Peter and John, and because it was evening, they put them in jail until the next day. ⁴But many who heard the message believed, and the number of men grew to about five thousand.

⁵The next day the rulers, elders and teachers of the law met in Jerusalem. ⁶Annas the high priest was there, and so were Caiaphas, John, Alexander and the other men of the high priest's family. ⁷They had Peter and John brought before them and began to question them: "By what power or what name did you do this?"

4:1 Alarmed Sadducees

The coalition arrayed against the disciples resembled the group that had arrested Jesus in Gethsemane. The priests were working hand in hand with Roman rulers, who allowed them to maintain a police force (or "temple guard") to keep order in the temple. Reports of Jesus' resurrection from the dead especially alarmed the Sadducees, a party of priests who denied there would ever be a resurrection from the dead (see also 5:17 and 23:6–8).

ᵃ18 Or *Messiah*; also in verse 20   *ᵇ23* Deut. 18:15,18,19   *ᶜ25* Gen. 22:18; 26:4

[8]Then Peter, filled with the Holy Spirit, said to them: "Rulers and elders of the people! [9]If we are being called to account today for an act of kindness shown to a cripple and are asked how he was healed, [10]then know this, you and all the people of Israel: It is by the name of Jesus Christ of Nazareth, whom you crucified but whom God raised from the dead, that this man stands before you healed. [11]He is

" 'the stone you builders rejected,
which has become the capstone.[a'b]

[12]Salvation is found in no one else, for there is no other name under heaven given to men by which we must be saved."

[13]When they saw the courage of Peter and John and realized that they were unschooled, ordinary men, they were astonished and they took note that these men had been with Jesus. [14]But since they could see the man who had been healed standing there with them, there was nothing they could say. [15]So they ordered them to withdraw from the Sanhedrin and then conferred together. [16]"What are we going to do with these men?" they asked. "Everybody living in Jerusalem knows they have done an outstanding miracle, and we cannot deny it. [17]But to stop this thing from spreading any further among the people, we must warn these men to speak no longer to anyone in this name."

[18]Then they called them in again and commanded them not to speak or teach at all in the name of Jesus. [19]But Peter and John replied, "Judge for yourselves whether it is right in God's sight to obey you rather than God. [20]For we cannot help speaking about what we have seen and heard."

[21]After further threats they let them go. They could not decide how to punish them, because all the people were praising God for what had happened. [22]For the man who was miraculously healed was over forty years old.

The Believers' Prayer

[23]On their release, Peter and John went back to their own people and reported all that the chief priests and elders had said to them. [24]When they heard this, they raised their voices together in prayer to God. "Sovereign Lord," they said, "you made the heaven and the earth and the sea, and everything in them. [25]You spoke by the Holy Spirit through the mouth of your servant, our father David:

" 'Why do the nations rage
and the peoples plot in vain?
[26]The kings of the earth take their stand
and the rulers gather together

against the Lord
and against his Anointed One.[c'd]

[27]Indeed Herod and Pontius Pilate met together with the Gentiles and the people[e] of Israel in this city to conspire against your holy servant Jesus, whom you anointed. [28]They did what your power and will had decided beforehand should happen. [29]Now, Lord, consider their threats and enable your servants to speak your word with great boldness. [30]Stretch out your hand to heal and perform miraculous signs and wonders through the name of your holy servant Jesus."

[31]After they prayed, the place where they were meeting was shaken. And they were all filled with the Holy Spirit and spoke the word of God boldly.

The Believers Share Their Possessions

[32]All the believers were one in heart and mind. No one claimed that any of his possessions was his own, but they shared everything they had. [33]With great power the apostles continued to testify to the resurrection of the Lord Jesus, and much grace was upon them all. [34]There were no needy persons among them. For from time to time those who owned lands or houses sold them, brought the money from the sales [35]and put it at the apostles' feet, and it was distributed to anyone as he had need.

[36]Joseph, a Levite from Cyprus, whom the apostles called Barnabas (which means Son of Encouragement), [37]sold a field he owned and brought the money and put it at the apostles' feet.

Ananias and Sapphira

5 Now a man named Ananias, together with his wife Sapphira, also sold a piece of property. [2]With his wife's full knowledge he kept back part of the money for himself, but brought the rest and put it at the apostles' feet.

[3]Then Peter said, "Ananias, how is it that Satan has so filled your heart that you have lied to the Holy Spirit and have kept for yourself some of the money you received for the land? [4]Didn't

5:4 Deadly Deceit

As Peter makes clear, Ananias and Sapphira were punished not for holding back money but for lying about it. They were misrepresenting themselves spiritually, trying to appear especially pious and generous. At the very beginning of the church (the word first appears in Acts in verse 11), God set a stern standard of absolute honesty and integrity.

---

[a]11 Or *cornerstone*   [b]11 Psalm 118:22   [c]26 That is, Christ or Messiah   [d]26 Psalm 2:1,2   [e]27 The Greek is plural.

it belong to you before it was sold? And after it was sold, wasn't the money at your disposal? What made you think of doing such a thing? You have not lied to men but to God."

⁵When Ananias heard this, he fell down and died. And great fear seized all who heard what had happened. ⁶Then the young men came forward, wrapped up his body, and carried him out and buried him.

⁷About three hours later his wife came in, not knowing what had happened. ⁸Peter asked her, "Tell me, is this the price you and Ananias got for the land?"

"Yes," she said, "that is the price."

⁹Peter said to her, "How could you agree to test the Spirit of the Lord? Look! The feet of the men who buried your husband are at the door, and they will carry you out also."

¹⁰At that moment she fell down at his feet and died. Then the young men came in and, finding her dead, carried her out and buried her beside her husband. ¹¹Great fear seized the whole church and all who heard about these events.

The Apostles Heal Many

¹²The apostles performed many miraculous signs and wonders among the people. And all the believers used to meet together in Solomon's Colonnade. ¹³No one else dared join them, even though they were highly regarded by the people. ¹⁴Nevertheless, more and more men and women believed in the Lord and were added to their number. ¹⁵As a result, people brought the sick into the streets and laid them on beds and mats so that at least Peter's shadow might fall on some of them as he passed by. ¹⁶Crowds gathered also from the towns around Jerusalem, bringing their sick and those tormented by evil*a* spirits, and all of them were healed.

The Apostles Persecuted

¹⁷Then the high priest and all his associates,

a 16 Greek unclean

The Secret to the Early Church
The real power at work in Acts

AUTHOR J.B. PHILLIPS, AFTER SPENDING 14 years translating the New Testament, sat back and reflected on his most lasting impressions. He kept returning to the book of Acts and its portrait of an infant church. "The sick are not merely prayed about," said Phillips, "they are healed, often suddenly and dramatically.... Human nature is changed. The fresh air of Heaven blows gustily through these pages.

"The early church lived dangerously, but never before has such a handful of people exerted such widespread influence.... To put it shortly, the lasting excitement which follows the reading of the book is this: *the thing works!*"

> "Leave these men alone! Let them go! For if their purpose or activity is of human origin, it will fail. But if it is from God, you will not be able to stop these men; you will only find yourselves fighting against God." 5:38–39

Who Was behind the Success?

Why did it work? Acts points decisively to the power of God, through his Holy Spirit. Luke carefully notes that every major decision of the young church was made under the Spirit's guidance. Indeed, some have suggested Acts should really be titled *Acts of the Holy Spirit* because of his dominant role. Luke mentions the Holy Spirit 57 times in Acts.

The disciples waited on the Spirit in Jerusalem before beginning to preach (2:4). According to Luke, the Holy Spirit fell on each new group of believers: on Jews (4:31), then on Samaritans (8:17), then on Gentiles (10:44), and finally on John the Baptist's disciples (19:6).

For Their Good

As the church grew, the disciples gradually began to understand what Jesus had meant when he said, "It is for your good that I am going away. Unless I go away, the Counselor will not come to you; but if I go, I will send him to you" (John 16:7). Although Jesus himself departed, God became present in each one of them, making his activity in the world more widespread than ever before.

The Spirit personally directed each major advance of the church. He sent Philip into the desert to meet an Ethiopian (8:29), set apart missionaries in Antioch (13:2), guided the first big church council (15:1–28), and helped plan Paul's itinerary (13:4; 16:6). As presented in Acts, the Spirit was no vague mist but a living person who spoke, guided in decisions, and fueled the church with the energy of faith.

Life Questions: How is the Holy Spirit active in your life?

who were members of the party of the Sadducees, were filled with jealousy. [18]They arrested the apostles and put them in the public jail. [19]But during the night an angel of the Lord opened the doors of the jail and brought them out. [20]"Go, stand in the temple courts," he said, "and tell the people the full message of this new life."

[21]At daybreak they entered the temple courts, as they had been told, and began to teach the people.

When the high priest and his associates arrived, they called together the Sanhedrin—the full assembly of the elders of Israel—and sent to the jail for the apostles. [22]But on arriving at the jail, the officers did not find them there. So they went back and reported, [23]"We found the jail securely locked, with the guards standing at the doors; but when we opened them, we found no one inside." [24]On hearing this report, the captain of the temple guard and the chief priests were puzzled, wondering what would come of this.

[25]Then someone came and said, "Look! The men you put in jail are standing in the temple courts teaching the people." [26]At that, the captain went with his officers and brought the apostles. They did not use force, because they feared that the people would stone them.

[27]Having brought the apostles, they made them appear before the Sanhedrin to be questioned by the high priest. [28]"We gave you strict orders not to teach in this name," he said. "Yet you have filled Jerusalem with your teaching and are determined to make us guilty of this man's blood."

[29]Peter and the other apostles replied: "We must obey God rather than men! [30]The God of our fathers raised Jesus from the dead—whom you had killed by hanging him on a tree. [31]God exalted him to his own right hand as Prince and Savior that he might give repentance and forgiveness of sins to Israel. [32]We are witnesses of these things, and so is the Holy Spirit, whom God has given to those who obey him."

[33]When they heard this, they were furious and wanted to put them to death. [34]But a Pharisee named Gamaliel, a teacher of the law, who was honored by all the people, stood up in the Sanhedrin and ordered that the men be put outside for a little while. [35]Then he addressed them: "Men of Israel, consider carefully what you intend to do to these men. [36]Some time ago Theudas appeared, claiming to be somebody, and about four hundred men rallied to him. He was killed, all his followers were dispersed, and it all came to nothing. [37]After him, Judas the Galilean appeared in the days of the census and led a band of people in revolt. He too was killed, and all his followers were scattered. [38]Therefore, in the present case I

advise you: Leave these men alone! Let them go! For if their purpose or activity is of human origin, it will fail. [39]But if it is from God, you will not be able to stop these men; you will only find yourselves fighting against God."

[40]His speech persuaded them. They called the

5:34 Ancient Terrorism

Terrorist acts have had a long history in the Middle East, as Gamaliel's speech shows. During the years surrounding Jesus' life, several revolutionaries had led armed uprisings, two of whom Gamaliel refers to here. Several decades later, the apostle Paul was mistaken for an Egyptian who had staged a terrorist revolt in the desert (21:38).

Gamaliel, who urged a cautious approach on the issue, was a revered and wise rabbi in his day. He followed the progressive branch of Judaism that originated with the rabbi Hillel, and Saul (who became the apostle Paul) was one of his pupils (22:3).

apostles in and had them flogged. Then they ordered them not to speak in the name of Jesus, and let them go.

[41]The apostles left the Sanhedrin, rejoicing because they had been counted worthy of suffering disgrace for the Name. [42]Day after day, in the temple courts and from house to house, they never stopped teaching and proclaiming the good news that Jesus is the Christ.[a]

The Choosing of the Seven

6 In those days when the number of disciples was increasing, the Grecian Jews among them complained against the Hebraic Jews because their widows were being overlooked in the daily distribution of food. [2]So the Twelve gathered all the disciples together and said, "It would not be right for us to neglect the ministry of the word of God in order to wait on tables. [3]Brothers, choose seven men from among you who are known to be full of the Spirit and wisdom. We will turn this responsibility over to them [4]and will give our attention to prayer and the ministry of the word."

[5]This proposal pleased the whole group. They chose Stephen, a man full of faith and of the Holy Spirit; also Philip, Procorus, Nicanor, Timon, Parmenas, and Nicolas from Antioch, a convert to Judaism. [6]They presented these men to the apostles, who prayed and laid their hands on them.

[7]So the word of God spread. The number of disciples in Jerusalem increased rapidly, and a

large number of priests became obedient to the faith.

Stephen Seized

[8]Now Stephen, a man full of God's grace and

power, did great wonders and miraculous signs among the people. [9]Opposition arose, however, from members of the Synagogue of the Freedmen (as it was called)—Jews of Cyrene and Alexandria as well as the provinces of Cilicia and Asia. These men began to argue with Stephen, [10]but they could not stand up against his wisdom or the Spirit by whom he spoke.

[a]3 Gen. 12:1

[11]Then they secretly persuaded some men to say, "We have heard Stephen speak words of blasphemy against Moses and against God."

[12]So they stirred up the people and the elders and the teachers of the law. They seized Stephen and brought him before the Sanhedrin. [13]They produced false witnesses, who testified, "This fellow never stops speaking against this holy place and against the law. [14]For we have heard him say that this Jesus of Nazareth will destroy this place and change the customs Moses handed down to us."

[15]All who were sitting in the Sanhedrin looked intently at Stephen, and they saw that his face was like the face of an angel.

Stephen's Speech to the Sanhedrin

7 Then the high priest asked him, "Are these charges true?"

[2]To this he replied: "Brothers and fathers, listen to me! The God of glory appeared to our father Abraham while he was still in Mesopotamia, before he lived in Haran. [3]'Leave your country and your people,' God said, 'and go to the land I will show you.'[a]

[4]"So he left the land of the Chaldeans and settled in Haran. After the death of his father, God sent him to this land where you are now living. [5]He gave him no inheritance here, not even a foot of ground. But God promised him

---

STEPHEN *Dying to Live*

THOUSANDS OF CHRISTIANS HAVE DIED for their faith over the centuries. Even today Christians are persecuted in countries like Algeria, Iran, Sudan and China. Stephen was the first martyr, setting the standard for all Christians who have come under fire for their faith.

While on trial, Stephen spoke so courageously and clearly that members of the sophisticated Sanhedrin lost all control. They gnashed their teeth, covered their ears and, yelling at the top of their voices, rushed at Stephen in their fury. Then, in a mob action, they stoned him to death.

Stephen had begun his public service for Christ when the apostles chose him, with six others, to make sure that Greek-speaking widows got their fair share of food. As it turned out, he did far more than administrate charity. God gave him the power to do miracles and to speak convincingly to other Greek-speaking Jews.

Stephen angered the religious establishment for some of the same reasons Jesus did. The Jews claimed that he had dishonored their revered temple and the Old Testament Law. There was a shred of truth in the charges. For Stephen, God's grace was greater than any building or any rule book.

At his trial, Stephen presented his case loud and clear. He recast the history of Israel as the story of God saving his people *in spite of* their stubborn resistance. Had anything changed? The very people who most honored the temple and the Law—weren't these the same ones who "betrayed and murdered" Jesus?

Like Jesus, Stephen was tried and executed because he upset the establishment. Like Jesus, he died breathing forgiveness, not condemnation. Even while dying, he prayed for those who stoned him. Stephen's final prayer was answered spectacularly, for a man named Saul stood among the persecutors. As Augustine said, "If Stephen had not prayed, the church would not have had Paul."

Life Questions: How would you react if you were put on trial and asked to justify your faith in Christ? What would you say?

that he and his descendants after him would possess the land, even though at that time Abraham had no child. [6]God spoke to him in this way: 'Your descendants will be strangers in a country not their own, and they will be enslaved and mistreated four hundred years. [7]But I will punish the nation they serve as slaves,' God said, 'and afterward they will come out of that country and worship me in this place.'[a] [8]Then he gave Abraham the covenant of circumcision. And Abraham became the father of Isaac and circumcised him eight days after his birth. Later Isaac became the father of Jacob, and Jacob became the father of the twelve patriarchs.

[9]"Because the patriarchs were jealous of Joseph, they sold him as a slave into Egypt. But God was with him [10]and rescued him from all his troubles. He gave Joseph wisdom and enabled him to gain the goodwill of Pharaoh king of Egypt; so he made him ruler over Egypt and all his palace.

[11]"Then a famine struck all Egypt and Canaan, bringing great suffering, and our fathers could not find food. [12]When Jacob heard that there was grain in Egypt, he sent our fathers on their first visit. [13]On their second visit, Joseph told his brothers who he was, and Pharaoh learned about Joseph's family. [14]After this, Joseph sent for his father Jacob and his whole family, seventy-five in all. [15]Then Jacob went down to Egypt, where he and our fathers died. [16]Their bodies were brought back to Shechem and placed in the tomb that Abraham had bought from the sons of Hamor at Shechem for a certain sum of money.

[17]"As the time drew near for God to fulfill his promise to Abraham, the number of our people in Egypt greatly increased. [18]Then another king, who knew nothing about Joseph, became ruler of Egypt. [19]He dealt treacherously with our people and oppressed our forefathers by forcing them to throw out their newborn babies so that they would die.

[20]"At that time Moses was born, and he was no ordinary child.[b] For three months he was cared for in his father's house. [21]When he was placed outside, Pharaoh's daughter took him and brought him up as her own son. [22]Moses was educated in all the wisdom of the Egyptians and was powerful in speech and action.

[23]"When Moses was forty years old, he decided to visit his fellow Israelites. [24]He saw one of them being mistreated by an Egyptian, so he went to his defense and avenged him by killing the Egyptian. [25]Moses thought that his own people would realize that God was using him to rescue them, but they did not. [26]The next day Moses came upon two Israelites who were fighting. He

tried to reconcile them by saying, 'Men, you are brothers; why do you want to hurt each other?'

[27]"But the man who was mistreating the other pushed Moses aside and said, 'Who made you ruler and judge over us? [28]Do you want to kill me as you killed the Egyptian yesterday?'[c] [29]When Moses heard this, he fled to Midian, where he settled as a foreigner and had two sons.

[30]"After forty years had passed, an angel appeared to Moses in the flames of a burning bush in the desert near Mount Sinai. [31]When he saw this, he was amazed at the sight. As he went over to look more closely, he heard the Lord's voice: [32]'I am the God of your fathers, the God of Abraham, Isaac and Jacob.'[d] Moses trembled with fear and did not dare to look.

[33]"Then the Lord said to him, 'Take off your sandals; the place where you are standing is holy ground. [34]I have indeed seen the oppression of my people in Egypt. I have heard their groaning and have come down to set them free. Now come, I will send you back to Egypt.'[e]

[35]"This is the same Moses whom they had rejected with the words, 'Who made you ruler and judge?' He was sent to be their ruler and deliverer by God himself, through the angel who

7:35 Provocative Words

The early part of Stephen's speech must have pleased his Jewish audience. He was, in effect, giving a capsule view of history from the Jewish point of view, featuring such famous ancestors as Abraham, Joseph, Moses, and David. But then Stephen turned the tables, directly attacking the Jewish establishment.

He compared their treatment of Jesus with earlier Jewish rejection of God's messengers. He also called into question Jewish temple worship, claiming that "the Most High does not live in houses made by men" (verse 48). He ended the speech by calling them traitors and murderers. Stephen's death and the resulting persecution in Jerusalem scattered the disciples, helping to fulfill what Jesus had predicted just before leaving the earth (1:8).

appeared to him in the bush. [36]He led them out of Egypt and did wonders and miraculous signs in Egypt, at the Red Sea[f] and for forty years in the desert.

[37]"This is that Moses who told the Israelites, 'God will send you a prophet like me from your own people.'[g] [38]He was in the assembly in the desert, with the angel who spoke to him on Mount Sinai, and with our fathers; and he received living words to pass on to us.

---

[a]7 Gen. 15:13,14   [b]20 Or *was fair in the sight of God*
[c]34 Exodus 3:5,7,8,10   [f]36 That is, Sea of Reeds   [c]28 Exodus 2:14   [d]32 Exodus 3:6
[g]37 Deut. 18:15

³⁹"But our fathers refused to obey him. Instead, they rejected him and in their hearts turned back to Egypt. ⁴⁰They told Aaron, 'Make us gods who will go before us. As for this fellow Moses who led us out of Egypt—we don't know what has happened to him!'ᵃ ⁴¹That was the time they made an idol in the form of a calf. They brought sacrifices to it and held a celebration in honor of what their hands had made. ⁴²But God turned away and gave them over to the worship of the heavenly bodies. This agrees with what is written in the book of the prophets:

> " 'Did you bring me sacrifices and offerings
>   forty years in the desert, O house of Israel?
> ⁴³You have lifted up the shrine of Molech
>   and the star of your god Rephan,
>   the idols you made to worship.
> Therefore I will send you into exile'ᵇ
>   beyond Babylon.

⁴⁴"Our forefathers had the tabernacle of the Testimony with them in the desert. It had been made as God directed Moses, according to the pattern he had seen. ⁴⁵Having received the tabernacle, our fathers under Joshua brought it with them when they took the land from the nations God drove out before them. It remained in the land until the time of David, ⁴⁶who enjoyed God's favor and asked that he might provide a dwelling place for the God of Jacob.ᶜ ⁴⁷But it was Solomon who built the house for him.

ᵃ40 Exodus 32:1   ᵇ43 Amos 5:25-27   ᶜ46 Some early manuscripts *the house of Jacob*

The Danger in Being a Christian
It began as a Jewish sect; fierce persecution only helped it spread

> On that day a great persecution broke out against the church at Jerusalem, and all except the apostles were scattered throughout Judea and Samaria.   8:1

IN SOME COUNTRIES, A PERSON who becomes a Christian forfeits a good education and job. And in a few countries, a person who converts risks his or her life. One church historian estimates more Christians have been martyred in this century than in all preceding centuries put together.

Yet, strangely, more often than not, intense persecution of Christians leads to a spurt of growth in the church. An ancient saying expresses this phenomenon, 'The blood of martyrs is the seed of the church.'

The First Big Advance

For a while, the new faith enjoyed popular favor. But very soon it involved grave risk. In the book of Acts, the persecution that produced the first Christian martyr, Stephen, ironically brought about the advance of Christianity outside its Jewish base. Forced out of stormy Jerusalem, the scattering Jewish Christians turned to other races and ethnic groups. Philip preached first to the despised Samaritans, and then crossed racial barriers by helping to convert an official from Ethiopia.

Acts documents a dramatic change in the faith. What had been viewed as an offshoot of the Jewish religion, a "sect of the Nazarenes," began to encompass people from other religions, races, and cultures. Before long, the center of church activity moved from Jerusalem to the city of Antioch. There, people coined the word *Christian*, indicating how separate the new faith had become. Never again would it be considered "just a Jewish thing."

Breaking the Jewish Mold

As Luke tells it, the transition to other ethnic groups required some adjustments. Jewish disciples balked at letting go of their centuries-old traditions and allowing the church to be flooded with non-Jews.

Peter, one of the most loyal Jews, explained his dilemma this way, "Who was I to think that I could oppose God?" (11:17). A direct, unmistakable vision from God (10:9–23) overcame Peter's resistance to accepting non-Jews, and later a decisive church council settled on a policy toward them (15:1–21).

As the pages of Acts turn, whole provinces and cultures open up to the gospel. The faith that had been guarded by a small knot of intimates, all Jews who knew Jesus personally, broke out into a rough world of soldiers, sorcerers, merchants, and antagonists from other religions. This process was not without its bloody and frightening moments.

Life Questions: If severe persecution came to the church in your region today, what would happen to your faith?

48"However, the Most High does not live in houses made by men. As the prophet says:

49" 'Heaven is my throne,
    and the earth is my footstool.
What kind of house will you build for me?
                          says the Lord.
    Or where will my resting place be?
50Has not my hand made all these things?'a

51"You stiff-necked people, with uncircumcised hearts and ears! You are just like your fathers: You always resist the Holy Spirit! 52Was there ever a prophet your fathers did not persecute? They even killed those who predicted the coming of the Righteous One. And now you have betrayed and murdered him— 53you who have received the law that was put into effect through angels but have not obeyed it."

The Stoning of Stephen

54When they heard this, they were furious and gnashed their teeth at him. 55But Stephen, full of the Holy Spirit, looked up to heaven and saw the glory of God, and Jesus standing at the right hand of God. 56"Look," he said, "I see heaven open and the Son of Man standing at the right hand of God."

57At this they covered their ears and, yelling at the top of their voices, they all rushed at him, 58dragged him out of the city and began to stone him. Meanwhile, the witnesses laid their clothes at the feet of a young man named Saul.

59While they were stoning him, Stephen prayed, "Lord Jesus, receive my spirit." 60Then he fell on his knees and cried out, "Lord, do not hold this sin against them." When he had said this, he fell asleep.

8 And Saul was there, giving approval to his death.

The Church Persecuted and Scattered

On that day a great persecution broke out against the church at Jerusalem, and all except the apostles were scattered throughout Judea and Samaria. 2Godly men buried Stephen and mourned deeply for him. 3But Saul began to destroy the church. Going from house to house, he dragged off men and women and put them in prison.

Philip in Samaria

4Those who had been scattered preached the word wherever they went. 5Philip went down to a city in Samaria and proclaimed the Christb there. 6When the crowds heard Philip and saw the miraculous signs he did, they all paid close attention to what he said. 7With shrieks, evilc spirits came out of many, and many paralytics and cripples were healed. 8So there was great joy in that city.

> ### 8:5 Crossing Racial Barriers
>
> *Philip's visit to Samaria was quite remarkable in its day. Jewish people had little to do with the Samaritans, whom they looked down on for racial and religious reasons. Later, Philip met with an Ethiopian official on a mission that crossed racial barriers. The modern Christian church in Ethiopia claims an uninterrupted descent from the conversion described in chapter 8.*

Simon the Sorcerer

9Now for some time a man named Simon had practiced sorcery in the city and amazed all the people of Samaria. He boasted that he was someone great, 10and all the people, both high and low, gave him their attention and exclaimed, "This man is the divine power known as the Great Power." 11They followed him because he had amazed them for a long time with his magic. 12But when they believed Philip as he preached the good news of the kingdom of God and the name of Jesus Christ, they were baptized, both men and women. 13Simon himself believed and was baptized. And he followed Philip everywhere, astonished by the great signs and miracles he saw.

14When the apostles in Jerusalem heard that Samaria had accepted the word of God, they sent Peter and John to them. 15When they arrived, they prayed for them that they might receive the Holy Spirit, 16because the Holy Spirit had not yet come upon any of them; they had simply been baptized intod the name of the Lord Jesus. 17Then Peter and John placed their hands on them, and they received the Holy Spirit.

18When Simon saw that the Spirit was given at the laying on of the apostles' hands, he offered them money 19and said, "Give me also this ability so that everyone on whom I lay my hands may receive the Holy Spirit."

20Peter answered: "May your money perish with you, because you thought you could buy the gift of God with money! 21You have no part or share in this ministry, because your heart is not right before God. 22Repent of this wickedness and pray to the Lord. Perhaps he will forgive you for having such a thought in your heart. 23For I see that you are full of bitterness and captive to sin."

a50 Isaiah 66:1,2   b5 Or Messiah   c7 Greek unclean   d16 Or in

²⁴Then Simon answered, "Pray to the Lord for me so that nothing you have said may happen to me."

²⁵When they had testified and proclaimed the

8:20 Gospel Greed

The tendency to exploit spiritual power for material profit did not originate with the television age. Simon, a local magician, saw the gospel as a way to increase his own fame. The disciples had no more tolerance for his attitude than they had for the lies of Ananias and Sapphira (Acts 5).

---

word of the Lord, Peter and John returned to Jerusalem, preaching the gospel in many Samaritan villages.

Philip and the Ethiopian

²⁶Now an angel of the Lord said to Philip, "Go south to the road—the desert road—that goes down from Jerusalem to Gaza." ²⁷So he started out, and on his way he met an Ethiopianª eunuch, an important official in charge of all the treasury of Candace, queen of the Ethiopians.

This man had gone to Jerusalem to worship, ²⁸and on his way home was sitting in his chariot reading the book of Isaiah the prophet. ²⁹The Spirit told Philip, "Go to that chariot and stay near it."

³⁰Then Philip ran up to the chariot and heard the man reading Isaiah the prophet. "Do you understand what you are reading?" Philip asked.

³¹"How can I," he said, "unless someone explains it to me?" So he invited Philip to come up and sit with him.

³²The eunuch was reading this passage of Scripture:

"He was led like a sheep to the slaughter,
   and as a lamb before the shearer is silent,
   so he did not open his mouth.
³³In his humiliation he was deprived of justice.
   Who can speak of his descendants?
   For his life was taken from the earth."ᵇ

³⁴The eunuch asked Philip, "Tell me, please, who is the prophet talking about, himself or someone else?" ³⁵Then Philip began with that very passage of Scripture and told him the good news about Jesus.

³⁶As they traveled along the road, they came to some water and the eunuch said, "Look, here is water. Why shouldn't I be baptized?"ᶜ ³⁸And he

---

ª27 That is, from the upper Nile region   ᵇ33 Isaiah 53:7,8   ᶜ36 Some late manuscripts *baptized?"* ³⁷*Philip said, "If you believe with all your heart, you may." The eunuch answered, "I believe that Jesus Christ is the Son of God."*

PHILIP *Breakthrough Man*

RELIGION EASILY GETS ASSOCIATED WITH ethnic groups. Arabs are stereotypically Muslim, Indians are Hindu, Japanese are Shinto or Buddhist. Initially, that same pattern held true for early Christians as well. All the original disciples were Jews, and although Jesus had told them to spread the good news to all ethnic groups they found such a prospect hard to imagine.

Philip (not to be confused with the apostle Philip, one of Jesus' original Twelve) was one of the very first to put the Great Commission into practice. He was a pioneer in carrying Jesus' love across racial lines.

Philip originally came to prominence as one of seven men named by the early church to care for poor widows (6:1–7). Greek-speaking Jews had complained about being overlooked, and the apostles wanted someone to take on the problems of providing food and care for these and other individuals. By appointing Philip and six of his colleagues (all Greek-speaking themselves, to judge from their Greek names), the apostles showed their concern for Christians who were not traditional Hebrews.

Still, no one thought of inviting Samaritans-people who had some Jewish blood but were disdained by Jews as heretics and half-breeds-into the fellowship. Then Philip, pushed out of Jerusalem by persecution, began preaching to Samaritans, with amazing results. For the first time, non-Jews joined in following Jesus.

And Philip was just beginning. Next he brought the word about Jesus to a traveling Ethiopian official. Thus Philip was responsible for the first African Christian (8:26–40), and legend has it that the strong North African church of the first few centuries could be traced back to this convert.

Years later the apostle Paul visited Philip, staying with him on his way to Jerusalem (21:7–16). Acts mentions that Philip "the evangelist" had four daughters who prophesied. Since women rarely had a public role in those days, this may indicate that Philip was involved in one more breakthrough–this time involving his own family.

Life Questions: Think of some barriers that you would like to see the gospel "break through." What kind of men or women of God will be needed for that to happen? Are you one of those individuals?

gave orders to stop the chariot. Then both Philip and the eunuch went down into the water and Philip baptized him. [39]When they came up out of the water, the Spirit of the Lord suddenly took Philip away, and the eunuch did not see him again, but went on his way rejoicing. [40]Philip, however, appeared at Azotus and traveled about, preaching the gospel in all the towns until he reached Caesarea.

Saul's Conversion

9 Meanwhile, Saul was still breathing out murderous threats against the Lord's disciples. He went to the high priest [2]and asked him for letters to the synagogues in Damascus, so that if he found any there who belonged to the Way, whether men or women, he might take them as

---

9:2 Naming the New Religion

In the early days of the church, its believers were given a variety of labels. Here, they are called members of "the Way"; elsewhere, "the brothers" (9:30), "all the believers" (2:44), and "the Nazarene sect" (24:5). Luke reports (11:26) that in the city of Antioch they were first called "Christians," a name that stuck. Roman writers often used the word Christian *in a derisive sense, reflecting the hostility that greeted the first believers.*

---

prisoners to Jerusalem. [3]As he neared Damascus on his journey, suddenly a light from heaven flashed around him. [4]He fell to the ground and heard a voice say to him, "Saul, Saul, why do you persecute me?"

[5]"Who are you, Lord?" Saul asked.

"I am Jesus, whom you are persecuting," he replied. [6]"Now get up and go into the city, and you will be told what you must do."

[7]The men traveling with Saul stood there speechless; they heard the sound but did not see anyone. [8]Saul got up from the ground, but when he opened his eyes he could see nothing. So they led him by the hand into Damascus. [9]For three days he was blind, and did not eat or drink anything.

[10]In Damascus there was a disciple named Ananias. The Lord called to him in a vision, "Ananias!"

"Yes, Lord," he answered.

[11]The Lord told him, "Go to the house of Judas on Straight Street and ask for a man from Tarsus named Saul, for he is praying. [12]In a vision he has seen a man named Ananias come and place his hands on him to restore his sight."

[13]"Lord," Ananias answered, "I have heard many reports about this man and all the harm he has done to your saints in Jerusalem. [14]And he has come here with authority from the chief priests to arrest all who call on your name."

[15]But the Lord said to Ananias, "Go! This man is my chosen instrument to carry my name before the Gentiles and their kings and before the people of Israel. [16]I will show him how much he must suffer for my name."

[17]Then Ananias went to the house and entered it. Placing his hands on Saul, he said, "Brother Saul, the Lord—Jesus, who appeared to you on the road as you were coming here—has sent me so that you may see again and be filled with the Holy Spirit." [18]Immediately, something like scales fell from Saul's eyes, and he could see again. He got up and was baptized, [19]and after taking some food, he regained his strength.

Saul in Damascus and Jerusalem

Saul spent several days with the disciples in Damascus. [20]At once he began to preach in the synagogues that Jesus is the Son of God. [21]All those who heard him were astonished and asked, "Isn't he the man who raised havoc in Jerusalem among those who call on this name? And hasn't he come here to take them as prisoners to the

---

9:21 Altered Mission

Damascus, said to be the oldest continually occupied city in the world, is now capital of present-day Syria. Saul undertook the 150-mile journey from Jerusalem in order to persecute Christians there, but on the "Damascus Road" he had an encounter that changed his life forever. In the end, Paul had to flee the Jewish zealots he had originally come to aid.

Although Luke does not mention it, sometime during this period Paul withdrew to Arabia, where he had an extended time to think through his new faith and mission (Galatians 1:17).

---

chief priests?" [22]Yet Saul grew more and more powerful and baffled the Jews living in Damascus by proving that Jesus is the Christ.[a]

[23]After many days had gone by, the Jews conspired to kill him, [24]but Saul learned of their plan. Day and night they kept close watch on the city gates in order to kill him. [25]But his followers took him by night and lowered him in a basket through an opening in the wall.

[26]When he came to Jerusalem, he tried to join the disciples, but they were all afraid of him, not believing that he really was a disciple. [27]But Barnabas took him and brought him to the apostles.

[a]22 Or *Messiah*

He told them how Saul on his journey had seen the Lord and that the Lord had spoken to him, and how in Damascus he had preached fearlessly in the name of Jesus. ²⁸So Saul stayed with them and moved about freely in Jerusalem, speaking boldly in the name of the Lord. ²⁹He talked and debated with the Grecian Jews, but they tried to kill him. ³⁰When the brothers learned of this, they took him down to Caesarea and sent him off to Tarsus.

³¹Then the church throughout Judea, Galilee and Samaria enjoyed a time of peace. It was strengthened; and encouraged by the Holy Spirit, it grew in numbers, living in the fear of the Lord.

Aeneas and Dorcas

³²As Peter traveled about the country, he went to visit the saints in Lydda. ³³There he found a man named Aeneas, a paralytic who had been bedridden for eight years. ³⁴"Aeneas," Peter said to him, "Jesus Christ heals you. Get up and take care of your mat." Immediately Aeneas got up. ³⁵All those who lived in Lydda and Sharon saw him and turned to the Lord.

³⁶In Joppa there was a disciple named Tabitha (which, when translated, is Dorcas[a]), who was always doing good and helping the poor. ³⁷About that time she became sick and died, and her body was washed and placed in an upstairs room. ³⁸Lydda was near Joppa; so when the disciples heard that Peter was in Lydda, they sent two men to him and urged him, "Please come at once!"

³⁹Peter went with them, and when he arrived he was taken upstairs to the room. All the widows stood around him, crying and showing him the robes and other clothing that Dorcas had made while she was still with them.

⁴⁰Peter sent them all out of the room; then he got down on his knees and prayed. Turning toward the dead woman, he said, "Tabitha, get up." She opened her eyes, and seeing Peter she sat up. ⁴¹He took her by the hand and helped her to her feet. Then he called the believers and the widows and presented her to them alive. ⁴²This became known all over Joppa, and many people believed in the Lord. ⁴³Peter stayed in Joppa for some time with a tanner named Simon.

Cornelius Calls for Peter

10 At Caesarea there was a man named Cornelius, a centurion in what was known as the Italian Regiment. ²He and all his family were devout and God-fearing; he gave generously to those in need and prayed to God regularly. ³One day at about three in the afternoon he had a vision. He distinctly saw an angel of God, who came to him and said, "Cornelius!"

⁴Cornelius stared at him in fear. "What is it, Lord?" he asked.

The angel answered, "Your prayers and gifts to the poor have come up as a memorial offering before God. ⁵Now send men to Joppa to bring back a man named Simon who is called Peter. ⁶He is staying with Simon the tanner, whose house is by the sea."

⁷When the angel who spoke to him had gone, Cornelius called two of his servants and a devout soldier who was one of his attendants. ⁸He told them everything that had happened and sent them to Joppa.

Peter's Vision

⁹About noon the following day as they were on their journey and approaching the city, Peter

10:9 A Shift from Peter to Paul

The first part of Acts, especially chapters 9–12, concentrates on the life of Peter. He represented the conservative Jewish contingent, and Acts reports that God gave him direct revelation to understand his plan of outreach to the Gentiles. But a man named Saul had been converted, and beginning with chapter 13, Acts follows his story almost exclusively.

went up on the roof to pray. ¹⁰He became hungry and wanted something to eat, and while the meal was being prepared, he fell into a trance. ¹¹He saw heaven opened and something like a large sheet being let down to earth by its four corners. ¹²It contained all kinds of four-footed animals, as well as reptiles of the earth and birds of the air. ¹³Then a voice told him, "Get up, Peter. Kill and eat."

¹⁴"Surely not, Lord!" Peter replied. "I have never eaten anything impure or unclean."

¹⁵The voice spoke to him a second time, "Do not call anything impure that God has made clean."

¹⁶This happened three times, and immediately the sheet was taken back to heaven.

¹⁷While Peter was wondering about the meaning of the vision, the men sent by Cornelius found out where Simon's house was and stopped at the gate. ¹⁸They called out, asking if Simon who was known as Peter was staying there.

¹⁹While Peter was still thinking about the vision, the Spirit said to him, "Simon, three[b] men are looking for you. ²⁰So get up and go downstairs. Do not hesitate to go with them, for I have sent them."

²¹Peter went down and said to the men, "I'm

---

[a]36 Both *Tabitha* (Aramaic) and *Dorcas* (Greek) mean *gazelle*, not have the number.

[b]19 One early manuscript *two*; other manuscripts do

the one you're looking for. Why have you come?"

²²The men replied, "We have come from Cornelius the centurion. He is a righteous and God-fearing man, who is respected by all the Jewish people. A holy angel told him to have you come to his house so that he could hear what you have to say." ²³Then Peter invited the men into the house to be his guests.

Peter at Cornelius' House

The next day Peter started out with them, and some of the brothers from Joppa went along. ²⁴The following day he arrived in Caesarea. Cornelius was expecting them and had called together his relatives and close friends. ²⁵As Peter entered the house, Cornelius met him and fell at his feet in reverence. ²⁶But Peter made him get up. "Stand up," he said, "I am only a man myself."

²⁷Talking with him, Peter went inside and found a large gathering of people. ²⁸He said to them: "You are well aware that it is against our law for a Jew to associate with a Gentile or visit him. But God has shown me that I should not call any man impure or unclean. ²⁹So when I was sent for, I came without raising any objection. May I ask why you sent for me?"

³⁰Cornelius answered: "Four days ago I was in my house praying at this hour, at three in the afternoon. Suddenly a man in shining clothes stood before me ³¹and said, 'Cornelius, God has heard your prayer and remembered your gifts to the poor. ³²Send to Joppa for Simon who is called Peter. He is a guest in the home of Simon the

tanner, who lives by the sea.' ³³So I sent for you immediately, and it was good of you to come. Now we are all here in the presence of God to listen to everything the Lord has commanded you to tell us."

³⁴Then Peter began to speak: "I now realize how true it is that God does not show favoritism ³⁵but accepts men from every nation who fear him and do what is right. ³⁶You know the message God sent to the people of Israel, telling the good news of peace through Jesus Christ, who is Lord of all. ³⁷You know what has happened throughout Judea, beginning in Galilee after the baptism that John preached— ³⁸how God anointed Jesus of Nazareth with the Holy Spirit and power, and how he went around doing good and healing all who were under the power of the devil, because God was with him.

³⁹"We are witnesses of everything he did in the country of the Jews and in Jerusalem. They killed him by hanging him on a tree, ⁴⁰but God raised him from the dead on the third day and caused him to be seen. ⁴¹He was not seen by all the people, but by witnesses whom God had already chosen—by us who ate and drank with him after he rose from the dead. ⁴²He commanded us to preach to the people and to testify that he is the one whom God appointed as judge of the living and the dead. ⁴³All the prophets testify about him that everyone who believes in him receives forgiveness of sins through his name."

⁴⁴While Peter was still speaking these words, the Holy Spirit came on all who heard the message. ⁴⁵The circumcised believers who had come

CORNELIUS *Least Likely Convert*

WHO WOULD YOU NOMINATE AS 'least likely to become a Christian?' A fundamentalist Muslim from Iran? A drug dealer? A hardened, hate-filled criminal? Most of us have a stereotype of who is—and is not—a candidate for Christianity.

To Jesus' first disciples, Cornelius certainly fit the "least likely" description. He was a Roman, which meant that he represented the absolute opposite of Jewish culture and religion. A good Jew could never even enter the home of a Roman, let alone share a meal with him.

Furthermore, Cornelius held the position of centurion, an officer in the brutal occupying army that all good Jews resented and despised. A Jewish fisherman like Simon Peter would never have expected such a man to become a Christian. And Cornelius never would have, had not God used supernatural means to bring Cornelius and Peter together. (The vision Peter received helps explain why Christians today eat such foods as pork and shrimp rather than following Jewish dietary laws.)

While Cornelius the Roman soldier made an unlikely candidate for conversion, Cornelius the *man* was far more ready than most. Acts tells us he gave generously to the poor, prayed often and actively sought God. In short, he had a sterling character. When an angel told him where to seek help, Cornelius responded immediately. Not only did he send for Peter, but he had enough faith to assemble friends and relatives in his home in expectation of Peter's arrival.

Peter, who probably had never stepped inside a non-Jewish house before, was stunned when he heard Cornelius's story. He quickly grasped the point: "I now realize how true it is that God does not show favoritism but accepts men from every nation who fear him and do what is right" (10:34,35).

Life Questions: Who in your circle do you feel is "least likely" to become a Christian? Do you really know what goes on underneath the surface, or are you making assumptions?

with Peter were astonished that the gift of the Holy Spirit had been poured out even on the Gentiles. ⁴⁶For they heard them speaking in tongues*ᵃ* and praising God.

Then Peter said, ⁴⁷"Can anyone keep these people from being baptized with water? They have received the Holy Spirit just as we have." ⁴⁸So he ordered that they be baptized in the name of Jesus Christ. Then they asked Peter to stay with them for a few days.

Peter Explains His Actions

11 The apostles and the brothers throughout Judea heard that the Gentiles also had received the word of God. ²So when Peter went up

11:1 Earthshaking Change

Nearly 2,000 years later, the decision to accept Gentiles into the church on equal footing with Jews may seem minor, but at the time it was a hotly debated issue of enormous consequence. Antioch, the first church with a large number of Gentile members, sparked a major controversy with the Jewish-dominated church in Jerusalem (see Acts 15). The third largest city in the Roman empire, Antioch was a crossroads between the Mediterranean and the eastern world, and from here the first missionaries went out to other nations and cultures.

to Jerusalem, the circumcised believers criticized him ³and said, "You went into the house of uncircumcised men and ate with them."

⁴Peter began and explained everything to them precisely as it had happened: ⁵"I was in the city of Joppa praying, and in a trance I saw a vision. I saw something like a large sheet being let down from heaven by its four corners, and it came down to where I was. ⁶I looked into it and saw four-footed animals of the earth, wild beasts, reptiles, and birds of the air. ⁷Then I heard a voice telling me, 'Get up, Peter. Kill and eat.'

⁸"I replied, 'Surely not, Lord! Nothing impure or unclean has ever entered my mouth.'

⁹"The voice spoke from heaven a second time, 'Do not call anything impure that God has made clean.' ¹⁰This happened three times, and then it was all pulled up to heaven again.

¹¹"Right then three men who had been sent to me from Caesarea stopped at the house where I was staying. ¹²The Spirit told me to have no hesitation about going with them. These six brothers also went with me, and we entered the man's house. ¹³He told us how he had seen an angel appear in his house and say, 'Send to Joppa for Simon who is called Peter. ¹⁴He will bring you a

message through which you and all your household will be saved.'

¹⁵"As I began to speak, the Holy Spirit came on them as he had come on us at the beginning. ¹⁶Then I remembered what the Lord had said: 'John baptized with*ᵇ* water, but you will be baptized with the Holy Spirit.' ¹⁷So if God gave them the same gift as he gave us, who believed in the Lord Jesus Christ, who was I to think that I could oppose God?"

¹⁸When they heard this, they had no further objections and praised God, saying, "So then, God has granted even the Gentiles repentance unto life."

The Church in Antioch

¹⁹Now those who had been scattered by the persecution in connection with Stephen traveled as far as Phoenicia, Cyprus and Antioch, telling the message only to Jews. ²⁰Some of them, however, men from Cyprus and Cyrene, went to Antioch and began to speak to Greeks also, telling them the good news about the Lord Jesus. ²¹The Lord's hand was with them, and a great number of people believed and turned to the Lord.

²²News of this reached the ears of the church at Jerusalem, and they sent Barnabas to Antioch. ²³When he arrived and saw the evidence of the grace of God, he was glad and encouraged them all to remain true to the Lord with all their hearts. ²⁴He was a good man, full of the Holy Spirit and faith, and a great number of people were brought to the Lord.

²⁵Then Barnabas went to Tarsus to look for Saul, ²⁶and when he found him, he brought him to Antioch. So for a whole year Barnabas and Saul met with the church and taught great numbers of people. The disciples were called Christians first at Antioch.

²⁷During this time some prophets came down from Jerusalem to Antioch. ²⁸One of them, named Agabus, stood up and through the Spirit predicted that a severe famine would spread over the entire Roman world. (This happened during

11:28 During the Reign of . . .

The historian Luke is the only New Testament author who dates his books by referring to Roman emperors. He refers to Claudius three times in Acts; the events in Luke's Gospel occur during the reigns of Tiberius and Augustus.

the reign of Claudius.) ²⁹The disciples, each according to his ability, decided to provide help for the brothers living in Judea. ³⁰This they did,

ᵃ46 Or other languages   ᵇ16 Or in

sending their gift to the elders by Barnabas and Saul.

Peter's Miraculous Escape From Prison

12 It was about this time that King Herod arrested some who belonged to the church, intending to persecute them. ²He had James, the brother of John, put to death with the sword. ³When he saw that this pleased the Jews, he proceeded to seize Peter also. This happened during the Feast of Unleavened Bread. ⁴After arresting him, he put him in prison, handing him over to be guarded by four squads of four soldiers each. Herod intended to bring him out for public trial after the Passover.

⁵So Peter was kept in prison, but the church was earnestly praying to God for him.

⁶The night before Herod was to bring him to trial, Peter was sleeping between two soldiers, bound with two chains, and sentries stood guard at the entrance. ⁷Suddenly an angel of the Lord appeared and a light shone in the cell. He struck Peter on the side and woke him up. "Quick, get up!" he said, and the chains fell off Peter's wrists.

⁸Then the angel said to him, "Put on your clothes and sandals." And Peter did so. "Wrap your cloak around you and follow me," the angel told him. ⁹Peter followed him out of the prison, but he had no idea that what the angel was doing was really happening; he thought he was seeing a vision. ¹⁰They passed the first and second guards and came to the iron gate leading to the city. It opened for them by itself, and they went through it. When they had walked the length of one street, suddenly the angel left him.

¹¹Then Peter came to himself and said, "Now I know without a doubt that the Lord sent his angel and rescued me from Herod's clutches and from everything the Jewish people were anticipating."

¹²When this had dawned on him, he went to the house of Mary the mother of John, also called Mark, where many people had gathered and were praying. ¹³Peter knocked at the outer entrance, and a servant girl named Rhoda came to answer the door. ¹⁴When she recognized Peter's voice, she was so overjoyed she ran back without opening it and exclaimed, "Peter is at the door!"

¹⁵"You're out of your mind," they told her. When she kept insisting that it was so, they said, "It must be his angel."

¹⁶But Peter kept on knocking, and when they opened the door and saw him, they were astonished. ¹⁷Peter motioned with his hand for them to be quiet and described how the Lord had brought him out of prison. "Tell James and the brothers about this," he said, and then he left for another place.

¹⁸In the morning, there was no small commotion among the soldiers as to what had become of Peter. ¹⁹After Herod had a thorough search made for him and did not find him, he cross-examined the guards and ordered that they be executed.

12:19 Guards Without Allies

The soldiers who had unsuccessfully guarded Jesus' tomb were protected by a conspiracy hatched by the Jewish establishment (Matthew 28:12–15). This passage sheds light on their eagerness to agree to a cover-up plan: Rome dealt harshly with guards who did not perform their duty. In contrast, the guards who had been on duty when Peter "escaped" (he was set free by an angel) had no one to plead for them. Herod ordered their execution.

Herod's Death

Then Herod went from Judea to Caesarea and stayed there a while. ²⁰He had been quarreling with the people of Tyre and Sidon; they now joined together and sought an audience with him. Having secured the support of Blastus, a trusted personal servant of the king, they asked for peace, because they depended on the king's country for their food supply.

²¹On the appointed day Herod, wearing his royal robes, sat on his throne and delivered a public address to the people. ²²They shouted, "This is the voice of a god, not of a man." ²³Immediately, because Herod did not give praise to God, an angel of the Lord struck him down, and he was eaten by worms and died.

²⁴But the word of God continued to increase and spread.

²⁵When Barnabas and Saul had finished their mission, they returned from*ᵃ* Jerusalem, taking with them John, also called Mark.

Barnabas and Saul Sent Off

13 In the church at Antioch there were prophets and teachers: Barnabas, Simeon called Niger, Lucius of Cyrene, Manaen (who had been brought up with Herod the tetrarch) and Saul. ²While they were worshiping the Lord and fasting, the Holy Spirit said, "Set apart for me Barnabas and Saul for the work to which I have called them." ³So after they had fasted and prayed, they placed their hands on them and sent them off.

On Cyprus

⁴The two of them, sent on their way by the Holy Spirit, went down to Seleucia and sailed from there to Cyprus. ⁵When they arrived at Sal-

---

ᵃ25 Some manuscripts to

Recruiting from the Opposition
A former bounty hunter breaks through to the Gentiles

WITH A TOUCH OF THEATRICS, the Indianapolis judge shook his head very slowly back and forth as his clerk read off John Erwin's offenses from a red record book. He had skipped school too many times to count. He had stolen petty items, like flashlight batteries, only to discard them. He had stolen bicycles, ridden them to the junkyard, and destroyed them.

Most recently, twelve-year-old John had joined a gang of young toughs and threatened his foster parents with a .22 rifle. The judge leaned forward and announced, "Young man, I don't know how any one boy can be as mean as they say you are. But I'm convinced you'll never change. I'm going to send you to a Manual Labor Institute for correction, and I predict you'll spend most of your life in institutions."

> *All those who heard him [Saul] were astonished and asked, "Isn't he the man who raised havoc in Jerusalem among those who call on this name?"*
> *9:21*

Voluntary Life Imprisonment

Three decades later the judge's prophecy has been partially fulfilled: In all, John Erwin has spent over 25 years in a large, notorious institution—Chicago's Cook County jail. But not as an inmate. The judge was mostly wrong: John did change. Remarkably.

During a stint in the army, Erwin met a family who adopted him, determined to show him the same love they had shown their own children. The defenses he had built up in a childhood of violence and sexual abuse slowly melted. He experienced God's love and forgiveness, and he became a new person.

As a free man determined to help set others free, he founded and led the PACE Institute, one of America's most successful prison rehabilitation programs. Then he went on to join the staff of Charles Colson's Prison Fellowship.

When asked why he has been so effective in the failure-littered field of prison work, Erwin replies, "Maybe it's because I've been behind bars, like these prisoners. Most of them came from miserable homes also, and were abused by their parents. I understand what makes life so hard for them—and my story gives them hope. I don't give up on people. If God can change me, he can change them too."

A Complete Turnaround

Converts like John Erwin often make the best crusaders. Former alcoholics can convince others of drinking's dangers. Exiles from Communist countries, such as Alexander Solzhenitsyn, often become the most vehement anti-Communists. And when the book of Acts introduces the most effective Christian missionary of all time, he turns out to be a former bounty hunter of Christians.

How did a Jewish sect become the largest Gentile religion? How did an Asian faith become associated with European civilization? The answers trace back to the remarkable career of Paul, apostle to the Gentiles.

Paul (formerly called Saul) made his first appearance in Acts (8:1), assisting at the brutal stoning of Stephen. Later, he led a gang of persecutors on a violent campaign against Christian believers. But then came a miraculous turnabout on the road to Damascus (9:1–19).

A Courageous Career

Acts is constructed like a drama that delays introducing the hero until the stage is finally set. Beginning in chapter 13, the spotlight in Acts moves from Peter to Paul and follows him throughout the rest of the book. Other Christians, knowing Paul's old reputation, were initially skeptical about his conversion. But he soon proved to be as fiery and intense in preaching Christ as he had been in working against him.

Paul spearheaded the campaign to grant Gentiles full acceptance without subjecting them to Jewish law. He had himself been liberated from bondage to confining laws, and he insisted on a life based on God's free forgiveness, not legalism.

During his journeys, Paul wrote half the New Testament books, and in them he laid the groundwork for much of Christian theology. All the while he carried on a courageous career despite jailings, beatings and riots. He was perhaps the most thoroughly converted man who ever lived.

Life Questions: Has your life changed quickly and dramatically, as Paul's did, or slowly and gradually?

amis, they proclaimed the word of God in the Jewish synagogues. John was with them as their helper.

⁶They traveled through the whole island until they came to Paphos. There they met a Jewish sorcerer and false prophet named Bar-Jesus, ⁷who was an attendant of the proconsul, Sergius Paulus. The proconsul, an intelligent man, sent for Barnabas and Saul because he wanted to hear the word of God. ⁸But Elymas the sorcerer (for that is what his name means) opposed them and tried to turn the proconsul from the faith. ⁹Then Saul, who was also called Paul, filled with the Holy Spirit, looked straight at Elymas and said, ¹⁰"You are a child of the devil and an enemy of everything that is right! You are full of all kinds of deceit and trickery. Will you never stop perverting the right ways of the Lord? ¹¹Now the hand of the Lord is against you. You are going to be blind, and for a time you will be unable to see the light of the sun."

Immediately mist and darkness came over him, and he groped about, seeking someone to lead him by the hand. ¹²When the proconsul saw what had happened, he believed, for he was amazed at the teaching about the Lord.

In Pisidian Antioch

¹³From Paphos, Paul and his companions sailed to Perga in Pamphylia, where John left them to return to Jerusalem. ¹⁴From Perga they went on to Pisidian Antioch. On the Sabbath they entered the synagogue and sat down. ¹⁵After the reading from the Law and the Prophets, the synagogue rulers sent word to them, saying, "Broth-

---

a18 Some manuscripts and cared for them

---

ers, if you have a message of encouragement for the people, please speak."

¹⁶Standing up, Paul motioned with his hand and said: "Men of Israel and you Gentiles who worship God, listen to me! ¹⁷The God of the people of Israel chose our fathers; he made the

---

13:15 Visiting Speaker

Synagogue rulers customarily invited a visiting rabbi to address the congregation, and in this case the apostle Paul responded by delivering his longest-recorded sermon. The rulers got more than they bargained for: The next week virtually the whole city turned out to hear him, resulting in a near-riot (verses 44–45).

---

people prosper during their stay in Egypt, with mighty power he led them out of that country, ¹⁸he endured their conduct*a* for about forty years in the desert, ¹⁹he overthrew seven nations in Canaan and gave their land to his people as their inheritance. ²⁰All this took about 450 years.

"After this, God gave them judges until the time of Samuel the prophet. ²¹Then the people asked for a king, and he gave them Saul son of Kish, of the tribe of Benjamin, who ruled forty years. ²²After removing Saul, he made David their king. He testified concerning him: 'I have found David son of Jesse a man after my own heart; he will do everything I want him to do.'

²³"From this man's descendants God has brought to Israel the Savior Jesus, as he promised. ²⁴Before the coming of Jesus, John preached

---

BARNABAS *The Encourager*

THOUGH HIS REAL NAME WAS Joseph, he became known as "Barnabas," an apt nickname meaning "Son of Encouragement." Barnabas had a knack for recognizing and encouraging others' potential. His most notable beneficiary? None other than the apostle Paul.

Even after his dramatic conversion, Paul frightened Jewish Christians—so much so that when he reached Jerusalem they all kept their distance. Wasn't this the fire-breather who had hurt so many believers? But Barnabas took his life in his hands and went to see Paul. Convinced that his conversion was genuine, Barnabas led Paul to the apostles and introduced them (9:26–27).

Later, when the first Gentile church sprang to life in Antioch, Barnabas encouraged these new Christians and then thought of a role for Paul (11:25–26). Barnabas helped Paul find his real calling: to nurture churches that crossed Jewish-Gentile lines. (Paul would eventually become known as the "Apostle to the Gentiles.") Soon God would hand-pick the two of them to leave Antioch on the first missionary journey (13:1–3).

Ironically, Barnabas's encouraging outlook put him at odds with Paul. On that first trip they took along Barnabas's young cousin John Mark, who quit in mid-journey. When they were planning a second trip, Barnabas wanted to give Mark another chance, but Paul refused. Consequently they split and went their separate ways (15:36–40). Barnabas proved right on this point, for Mark proved trustworthy and Paul ultimately came to depend on him (2 Timothy 4:11).

Life Questions: Whom do you encourage, and how do you do it? Who encourages you?

Carman

Throughout his career as a Christian recording and performance artist, Carman's ministry has extended to many different parts of the world. His no-excuses, in-your-face recordings, videos, kids' shows, and concerts leave no question as to what he feels is his purpose—to turn the hearts of unbelievers to Christ.

One of Carman's favorite Scripture verses is 1 Corinthians 2:9-10: "'No eye has seen, no ear has heard, no mind has conceived what God has prepared for those who love him'—but God has revealed it to us by his Spirit." This verse, which Carman calls "one of the greatest promises in all of God's Word," inspires him as he proclaims the Gospel message around the world.

Carman's genius comes in spanning the range of musical genres to get the message out. "Once you've found the right message, then you look long and hard for the best way to house it. If the message isn't there," Carman says, "it's not going to get into the spirit. It'll get into the head, it'll get into the body, but it won't get into the spirit."

Carman's mission comes through clearly when he reflects on his long career as an artist and entertainer for God. "I have to follow, ultimately, what I feel is my number one call, and that is to minister through music. And the purpose of music, at least according to the Scriptures, primarily is to bring people to an attitude of praise and worship. Ultimately, that's the number one purpose of me walking up on that platform. I'm only doing what I've been trained to do for the last 20 years, and that's to bring people to praise and worship and then lead them to Christ."

Carman

Bryan Duncan

Those who are familiar with Bryan Duncan's insightful song writing are well aware of his commitment to spiritual growth. His albums reflect the fact that he's constantly moving forward in his relationship with God, and he takes those who listen to his music along on that journey. Bryan notes that the Scriptures help him out in his daily walk, giving him encouragement for each day.

"The Bible reminds me over and over that there is hope for me, that I don't have to have my Christian walk figured out all the time. The hardest thing for me to believe is that God even knows that I'm here, let alone knowing that he really loves me. That's why I continue to read 'the old, old story of Jesus and his love.'

"The song I've included in the WoW 1997 compilation, 'After This Day Is Gone,' is my most recent favorite from the songs I have written for my new album *Blue Skies*. It has been so reassuring for me to sing, 'I believe...there's still a place in your heart for me.' Understanding that God can see me as I really am—separate from my circumstances—strengthens my faith, even though I don't know what the future holds. My days sometimes seem long and full of mistakes, yet my only plan is to follow Jesus throughout each day.

"Some days I wonder if I'll be able to recover from the mistakes I've made in that day. Still, I am grateful for each new morning. Each one is an opportunity for me to consider yesterday as past history and to start fresh; a new chance to live right now and appreciate each moment God has given me."

repentance and baptism to all the people of Israel. 25As John was completing his work, he said: 'Who do you think I am? I am not that one. No, but he is coming after me, whose sandals I am not worthy to untie.'

26"Brothers, children of Abraham, and you God-fearing Gentiles, it is to us that this message of salvation has been sent. 27The people of Jerusalem and their rulers did not recognize Jesus, yet in condemning him they fulfilled the words of the prophets that are read every Sabbath. 28Though they found no proper ground for a death sentence, they asked Pilate to have him executed. 29When they had carried out all that was written about him, they took him down from the tree and laid him in a tomb. 30But God raised him from the dead, 31and for many days he was seen by those who had traveled with him from Galilee to Jerusalem. They are now his witnesses to our people.

32"We tell you the good news: What God promised our fathers 33he has fulfilled for us, their children, by raising up Jesus. As it is written in the second Psalm:

"'You are my Son;
today I have become your Father.'*a*'*b*

34The fact that God raised him from the dead, never to decay, is stated in these words:

"'I will give you the holy and sure blessings promised to David.'*c*

35So it is stated elsewhere:

"'You will not let your Holy One see decay.'*d*

36"For when David had served God's purpose in his own generation, he fell asleep; he was buried with his fathers and his body decayed. 37But the one whom God raised from the dead did not see decay.

38"Therefore, my brothers, I want you to know that through Jesus the forgiveness of sins is proclaimed to you. 39Through him everyone who believes is justified from everything you could not be justified from by the law of Moses. 40Take care that what the prophets have said does not happen to you:

41"'Look, you scoffers,
wonder and perish,
for I am going to do something in your days
that you would never believe,
even if someone told you.'*e*"

42As Paul and Barnabas were leaving the synagogue, the people invited them to speak further about these things on the next Sabbath. 43When the congregation was dismissed, many of the Jews and devout converts to Judaism followed Paul and Barnabas, who talked with them and urged them to continue in the grace of God.

44On the next Sabbath almost the whole city gathered to hear the word of the Lord. 45When the Jews saw the crowds, they were filled with jealousy and talked abusively against what Paul was saying.

46Then Paul and Barnabas answered them boldly: "We had to speak the word of God to you first. Since you reject it and do not consider yourselves worthy of eternal life, we now turn to

13:46 Apostle to the Gentiles

This incident is the first of several occasions in Acts showing Paul turning away from the Jews (see 18:6; 19:9). When the Jews rejected his message, he went to the Gentiles. Eventually he became known as the "apostle to the Gentiles," even though he maintained a deep love for his own people (see Romans 9:1–5).

the Gentiles. 47For this is what the Lord has commanded us:

"'I have made you*f* a light for the Gentiles,
that you*f* may bring salvation to the
ends of the earth.'*g*"

48When the Gentiles heard this, they were glad and honored the word of the Lord; and all who were appointed for eternal life believed.

49The word of the Lord spread through the whole region. 50But the Jews incited the God-fearing women of high standing and the leading men of the city. They stirred up persecution against Paul and Barnabas, and expelled them from their region. 51So they shook the dust from their feet in protest against them and went to Iconium. 52And the disciples were filled with joy and with the Holy Spirit.

In Iconium

14 At Iconium Paul and Barnabas went as usual into the Jewish synagogue. There they spoke so effectively that a great number of Jews and Gentiles believed. 2But the Jews who refused to believe stirred up the Gentiles and poisoned their minds against the brothers. 3So Paul and Barnabas spent considerable time there, speaking boldly for the Lord, who confirmed the message of his grace by enabling them to do miraculous signs and wonders. 4The people of the city were divided; some sided with the Jews, others with the apostles. 5There was a plot afoot

---

*a*33 Or *have begotten you*   *b*33 Psalm 2:7   *c*34 Isaiah 55:3   *d*35 Psalm 16:10   *e*41 Hab. 1:5
*f*47 The Greek is singular.   *g*47 Isaiah 49:6

among the Gentiles and Jews, together with their leaders, to mistreat them and stone them. **6**But they found out about it and fled to the Lycaonian cities of Lystra and Derbe and to the surrounding country, **7**where they continued to preach the good news.

In Lystra and Derbe

8In Lystra there sat a man crippled in his feet, who was lame from birth and had never walked. **9**He listened to Paul as he was speaking. Paul looked directly at him, saw that he had faith to be healed **10**and called out, "Stand up on your feet!" At that, the man jumped up and began to walk.

11When the crowd saw what Paul had done, they shouted in the Lycaonian language, "The gods have come down to us in human form!" **12**Barnabas they called Zeus, and Paul they called Hermes because he was the chief speaker. **13**The priest of Zeus, whose temple was just outside the city, brought bulls and wreaths to the city gates because he and the crowd wanted to offer sacrifices to them.

14But when the apostles Barnabas and Paul heard of this, they tore their clothes and rushed out into the crowd, shouting: **15**"Men, why are you doing this? We too are only men, human like you. We are bringing you good news, telling you to turn from these worthless things to the living God, who made heaven and earth and sea and everything in them. **16**In the past, he let all nations go their own way. **17**Yet he has not left himself without testimony: He has shown kindness by giving you rain from heaven and crops in their seasons; he provides you with plenty of food and fills your hearts with joy." **18**Even with these words, they had difficulty keeping the crowd from sacrificing to them.

19Then some Jews came from Antioch and Iconium and won the crowd over. They stoned Paul and dragged him outside the city, thinking he was dead. **20**But after the disciples had gathered around him, he got up and went back into the city. The next day he and Barnabas left for Derbe.

The Return to Antioch in Syria

21They preached the good news in that city and won a large number of disciples. Then they returned to Lystra, Iconium and Antioch, **22**strengthening the disciples and encouraging them to remain true to the faith. "We must go through many hardships to enter the kingdom of God," they said. **23**Paul and Barnabas appointed elders*a* for them in each church and, with prayer and fasting, committed them to the Lord, in whom they had put their trust. **24**After going through Pisidia, they came into Pamphylia, **25**and

when they had preached the word in Perga, they went down to Attalia.

26From Attalia they sailed back to Antioch, where they had been committed to the grace of God for the work they had now completed. **27**On arriving there, they gathered the church together and reported all that God had done through them and how he had opened the door of faith to the Gentiles. **28**And they stayed there a long time with the disciples.

The Council at Jerusalem

15 Some men came down from Judea to Antioch and were teaching the brothers: "Unless you are circumcised, according to the custom taught by Moses, you cannot be saved." **2**This brought Paul and Barnabas into sharp dispute and debate with them. So Paul and Barnabas were appointed, along with some other believers, to go up to Jerusalem to see the apostles and elders about this question. **3**The church sent them on their way, and as they traveled through Phoenicia and Samaria, they told how the Gentiles had been converted. This news made all the brothers very glad. **4**When they came to Jerusalem, they were welcomed by the church and the apostles and elders, to whom they reported everything God had done through them.

5Then some of the believers who belonged to the party of the Pharisees stood up and said, "The Gentiles must be circumcised and required to obey the law of Moses."

6The apostles and elders met to consider this question. **7**After much discussion, Peter got up and addressed them: "Brothers, you know that some time ago God made a choice among you that the Gentiles might hear from my lips the

---

15:7 The First Church Council

Chapter 15 gives a fascinating glimpse into Jewish/Gentile politics in the early church, recounting a debate between such leaders as Peter, Paul, and James. "Some time ago," Peter began his speech—about ten years had passed since his startling experience with Gentiles recorded in Acts 10. By now Gentiles probably outnumbered Jewish believers worldwide.

The leaders agreed on a compromise position that removed some of the barriers between the two groups. They issued a formal position paper, reproduced here, in which Jewish Christians asked the Gentiles to honor four of their practices, two moral issues and two cultural. The two on food relate to a "kosher" method of food preparation designed to keep people from ingesting any animal blood.

---

*a*23 Or *Barnabas ordained elders*; or *Barnabas had elders elected*

message of the gospel and believe. ⁸God, who knows the heart, showed that he accepted them by giving the Holy Spirit to them, just as he did to us. ⁹He made no distinction between us and them, for he purified their hearts by faith. ¹⁰Now then, why do you try to test God by putting on the necks of the disciples a yoke that neither we nor our fathers have been able to bear? ¹¹No! We believe it is through the grace of our Lord Jesus that we are saved, just as they are."

¹²The whole assembly became silent as they listened to Barnabas and Paul telling about the miraculous signs and wonders God had done among the Gentiles through them. ¹³When they finished, James spoke up: "Brothers, listen to me. ¹⁴Simon*ᵃ* has described to us how God at first showed his concern by taking from the Gentiles a people for himself. ¹⁵The words of the prophets are in agreement with this, as it is written:

¹⁶" 'After this I will return
    and rebuild David's fallen tent.
  Its ruins I will rebuild,
    and I will restore it,
¹⁷that the remnant of men may seek the Lord,
    and all the Gentiles who bear my name,
  says the Lord, who does these things'ᵇ
¹⁸   that have been known for ages.ᶜ

¹⁹"It is my judgment, therefore, that we should not make it difficult for the Gentiles who are turning to God. ²⁰Instead we should write to them, telling them to abstain from food polluted by idols, from sexual immorality, from the meat of strangled animals and from blood. ²¹For Moses has been preached in every city from the earliest times and is read in the synagogues on every Sabbath."

The Council's Letter to Gentile Believers

²²Then the apostles and elders, with the whole church, decided to choose some of their own men and send them to Antioch with Paul and Barnabas. They chose Judas (called Barsabbas) and Silas, two men who were leaders among the brothers. ²³With them they sent the following letter:

The apostles and elders, your brothers,

To the Gentile believers in Antioch, Syria and Cilicia:

Greetings.

²⁴We have heard that some went out from us without our authorization and disturbed you, troubling your minds by what they said. ²⁵So we all agreed to choose some men and send them to you with our dear friends Barnabas and Paul— ²⁶men who have risked their lives for the name of our Lord Jesus Christ. ²⁷Therefore we are sending Judas and Silas to confirm by word of mouth what we are writing. ²⁸It seemed good to the Holy Spirit and to us not to burden you with anything beyond the following requirements: ²⁹You are to abstain from food sacrificed to idols, from

---

ᵃ14 Greek *Simeon*, a variant of *Simon*; that is, Peter   ᵇ17 Amos 9:11,12   ᶜ17,18 Some manuscripts *things'*—
/ ¹⁸known to the Lord for ages is his work

MARK (JOHN MARK) *Slow Starter*

FOR MORE THAN 75 YEARS, England has chosen an All-England soccer team for players under the age of 15. Selections each year represent the very best young players, England's future. Yet a long-term study of these players unearthed a disturbing fact. Of more than 1,200 young players, only 29 went on to play for the All-England adult team. In other words, only two percent of the best remained the best as adults.

It's risky to size someone up too early. Why? Because people change. That was the case with John Mark. As a young man living in Jerusalem, he had a ringside seat for the coming of Christ and the early days of the church. His mother Mary, apparently a widow, opened her home to the early Christians. His cousin Barnabas served as one of the early deacons. Surely Mark would become an outstanding Christian leader!

Paul and Barnabas certainly must have thought so when they took Mark along on their first missionary journey. But the young man failed, deserting them in the middle of the trip. Terribly disappointed, Paul refused to allow Mark on the next journey. This refusal led to a rift with Barnabas (15:39).

Although Paul may have sized up the young man as hopeless, he later changed his opinion. Mark eventually became a valued assistant to Paul, and three of the apostle's letters mention him with gratitude.

Another apostle, Peter, refers warmly to Mark as "my son" (1 Peter 5:13). Tradition has it that Mark accompanied Peter to Rome, where Peter helped him write the Gospel account that bears Mark's name.

Life Questions: If someone were to evaluate you now, as against five years ago, would you show improvement?

blood, from the meat of strangled animals and from sexual immorality. You will do well to avoid these things.

Farewell.

30The men were sent off and went down to Antioch, where they gathered the church together and delivered the letter. 31The people read it and were glad for its encouraging message. 32Judas and Silas, who themselves were prophets, said much to encourage and strengthen the brothers. 33After spending some time there, they were sent off by the brothers with the blessing of peace to return to those who had sent them.*a 35But Paul and Barnabas remained in Antioch, where they and many others taught and preached the word of the Lord.

Disagreement Between Paul and Barnabas

36Some time later Paul said to Barnabas, "Let us go back and visit the brothers in all the towns where we preached the word of the Lord and see how they are doing." 37Barnabas wanted to take John, also called Mark, with them, 38but Paul did not think it wise to take him, because he had deserted them in Pamphylia and had not continued with them in the work. 39They had such a sharp disagreement that they parted company. Barnabas took Mark and sailed for Cyprus, 40but Paul chose Silas and left, commended by the brothers to the grace of the Lord. 41He went through Syria and Cilicia, strengthening the churches.

Timothy Joins Paul and Silas

16 He came to Derbe and then to Lystra, where a disciple named Timothy lived, whose mother was a Jewess and a believer, but whose father was a Greek. 2The brothers at Lystra and Iconium spoke well of him. 3Paul wanted to take him along on the journey, so he circumcised him because of the Jews who lived in that area, for they all knew that his father was a Greek. 4As they traveled from town to town, they delivered the decisions reached by the apostles and elders in Jerusalem for the people to obey. 5So the churches were strengthened in the faith and grew daily in numbers.

Paul's Vision of the Man of Macedonia

6Paul and his companions traveled throughout the region of Phrygia and Galatia, having been kept by the Holy Spirit from preaching the word in the province of Asia. 7When they came to the border of Mysia, they tried to enter Bithynia, but the Spirit of Jesus would not allow them to. 8So they passed by Mysia and went down to Troas. 9During the night Paul had a vision of a man of Macedonia standing and begging him, "Come over to Macedonia and help us." 10After Paul had seen the vision, we got ready at once to leave for Macedonia, concluding that God had called us to preach the gospel to them.

16:10 Firsthand Report

In Acts 16, 21, and 28, Luke uses "we" in writing, for he accompanied the apostle Paul on some of his trips. His close association with Paul meant he had immediate access to the central character in Acts 13–28.

Lydia's Conversion in Philippi

11From Troas we put out to sea and sailed straight for Samothrace, and the next day on to Neapolis. 12From there we traveled to Philippi, a Roman colony and the leading city of that district of Macedonia. And we stayed there several days.

13On the Sabbath we went outside the city gate to the river, where we expected to find a place of prayer. We sat down and began to speak to the women who had gathered there. 14One of those listening was a woman named Lydia, a dealer in purple cloth from the city of Thyatira, who was a worshiper of God. The Lord opened her heart to respond to Paul's message. 15When she and the members of her household were baptized, she invited us to her home. "If you consider me a believer in the Lord," she said, "come and stay at my house." And she persuaded us.

Paul and Silas in Prison

16Once when we were going to the place of prayer, we were met by a slave girl who had a spirit by which she predicted the future. She earned a great deal of money for her owners by fortune-telling. 17This girl followed Paul and the rest of us, shouting, "These men are servants of the Most High God, who are telling you the way to be saved." 18She kept this up for many days. Finally Paul became so troubled that he turned around and said to the spirit, "In the name of Jesus Christ I command you to come out of her!" At that moment the spirit left her.

19When the owners of the slave girl realized that their hope of making money was gone, they seized Paul and Silas and dragged them into the marketplace to face the authorities. 20They brought them before the magistrates and said, "These men are Jews, and are throwing our city into an uproar 21by advocating customs unlawful for us Romans to accept or practice."

22The crowd joined in the attack against Paul and Silas, and the magistrates ordered them to be stripped and beaten. 23After they had been se-

---

a 33 Some manuscripts them, 34but Silas decided to remain there verely flogged, they were thrown into prison, and the jailer was commanded to guard them carefully. [24]Upon receiving such orders, he put them in the inner cell and fastened their feet in the stocks.

[25]About midnight Paul and Silas were praying and singing hymns to God, and the other prisoners were listening to them. [26]Suddenly there was such a violent earthquake that the foundations of the prison were shaken. At once all the prison doors flew open, and everybody's chains came loose. [27]The jailer woke up, and when he saw the prison doors open, he drew his sword and was about to kill himself because he thought the prisoners had escaped. [28]But Paul shouted, "Don't harm yourself! We are all here!"

[29]The jailer called for lights, rushed in and fell trembling before Paul and Silas. [30]He then brought them out and asked, "Sirs, what must I do to be saved?"

[31]They replied, "Believe in the Lord Jesus, and you will be saved—you and your household." [32]Then they spoke the word of the Lord to him and to all the others in his house. [33]At that hour of the night the jailer took them and washed their wounds; then immediately he and all his family were baptized. [34]The jailer brought them into his house and set a meal before them; he was filled with joy because he had come to believe in God—he and his whole family.

[35]When it was daylight, the magistrates sent their officers to the jailer with the order: "Release those men." [36]The jailer told Paul, "The magistrates have ordered that you and Silas be released. Now you can leave. Go in peace."

[37]But Paul said to the officers: "They beat us publicly without a trial, even though we are Roman citizens, and threw us into prison. And now do they want to get rid of us quietly? No! Let them come themselves and escort us out."

[38]The officers reported this to the magistrates, and when they heard that Paul and Silas were Roman citizens, they were alarmed. [39]They came to appease them and escorted them from the prison, requesting them to leave the city. [40]After Paul and Silas came out of the prison, they went to Lydia's house, where they met with the brothers and encouraged them. Then they left.

In Thessalonica

17 When they had passed through Amphipolis and Apollonia, they came to Thessalonica, where there was a Jewish synagogue. [2]As his custom was, Paul went into the synagogue, and on three Sabbath days he reasoned with them from the Scriptures, [3]explaining and proving that the Christ[a] had to suffer and rise from the dead. "This Jesus I am proclaiming to you is the Christ,[a]" he said. [4]Some of the Jews were persuaded and joined Paul and Silas, as did a large number of God-fearing Greeks and not a few prominent women.

[5]But the Jews were jealous; so they rounded up some bad characters from the marketplace, formed a mob and started a riot in the city. They rushed to Jason's house in search of Paul and Silas in order to bring them out to the crowd.[b] [6]But when they did not find them, they dragged Jason and some other brothers before the city officials, shouting: "These men who have caused trouble all over the world have now come here,

a3 Or Messiah   b5 Or the assembly of the people

SILAS *Singing in Prison*

THE NEW CHURCH EXPLODED OUTWARD, persecution pounded inward and change hung everywhere in the air. Boredom never troubled the early Christians—especially the small band who, with the apostle Paul, boldly carried the good news into uncharted territory.

Silas was one of that elite, brave group. A leader in the Jerusalem church, he journeyed to Antioch with an official church message. Something about that city's multicultural church apparently got under his skin, because he volunteered to accompany the apostle Paul on a lengthy missionary trip. Any trip with the fearless Paul guaranteed excitement.

Even today, in some parts of the world, missionary work can be risky business. In those early days of the church, Paul and Silas found trouble ready at hand. In Philippi, the authorities beat up the two missionaries and threw them in jail. While they were singing hymns at midnight behind bars, an earthquake freed them, yet the two stayed around to lead the jailer to faith in Christ. At the next stop, Thessalonica, the pair inadvertently started a riot. Narrowly escaping injury, they went on to Berea, where more trouble ensued.

Such excitement came with the job. The message about Jesus proved challenging and sometimes offensive to those who heard. Silas dedicated his life to spreading the word. Besides preaching the good news, he evidently helped in the writing of 1 and 2 Thessalonians and 1 Peter (1 Thessalonians 1:1; 2 Thessalonians 1:1; 1 Peter 5:12).

Life Questions: Can you imagine serving God as exciting? What would make it so for you?

⁷and Jason has welcomed them into his house. They are all defying Caesar's decrees, saying that there is another king, one called Jesus." ⁸When they heard this, the crowd and the city officials were thrown into turmoil. ⁹Then they made Jason and the others post bond and let them go.

In Berea

¹⁰As soon as it was night, the brothers sent Paul and Silas away to Berea. On arriving there, they went to the Jewish synagogue. ¹¹Now the Bereans were of more noble character than the Thessalonians, for they received the message with great eagerness and examined the Scriptures every day to see if what Paul said was true. ¹²Many of the Jews believed, as did also a number of prominent Greek women and many Greek men.

¹³When the Jews in Thessalonica learned that Paul was preaching the word of God at Berea, they went there too, agitating the crowds and stirring them up. ¹⁴The brothers immediately sent Paul to the coast, but Silas and Timothy stayed at Berea. ¹⁵The men who escorted Paul brought him to Athens and then left with instructions for Silas and Timothy to join him as soon as possible.

In Athens

¹⁶While Paul was waiting for them in Athens, he was greatly distressed to see that the city was

17:16 Flexible Approach

In places like Thessalonica and Berea, Paul went first to the synagogues, where he tried to convince fellow Jews that Jesus Christ was the Messiah promised in the Old Testament. In Athens he initially took that same approach, but few Athenians had the Old Testament background to understand his argument. Paul soon began comparing his God to the many gods they worshiped. The ancients used to say, "It is easier to find a god than a man in Athens."

full of idols. ¹⁷So he reasoned in the synagogue with the Jews and the God-fearing Greeks, as well as in the marketplace day by day with those who happened to be there. ¹⁸A group of Epicurean and Stoic philosophers began to dispute with him. Some of them asked, "What is this babbler trying to say?" Others remarked, "He seems to be advocating foreign gods." They said this because Paul was preaching the good news about Jesus and the resurrection. ¹⁹Then they took him and brought him to a meeting of the Areopagus, where they said to him, "May we know what this new teaching is that you are presenting? ²⁰You

are bringing some strange ideas to our ears, and we want to know what they mean." ²¹(All the Athenians and the foreigners who lived there spent their time doing nothing but talking about and listening to the latest ideas.)

²²Paul then stood up in the meeting of the Areopagus and said: "Men of Athens! I see that in every way you are very religious. ²³For as I walked around and looked carefully at your objects of worship, I even found an altar with this inscription: TO AN UNKNOWN GOD. Now what you worship as something unknown I am going to proclaim to you.

²⁴"The God who made the world and everything in it is the Lord of heaven and earth and does not live in temples built by hands. ²⁵And he is not served by human hands, as if he needed anything, because he himself gives all men life and breath and everything else. ²⁶From one man he made every nation of men, that they should inhabit the whole earth; and he determined the times set for them and the exact places where they should live. ²⁷God did this so that men would seek him and perhaps reach out for him and find him, though he is not far from each one of us. ²⁸'For in him we live and move and have our being.' As some of your own poets have said, 'We are his offspring.'

²⁹"Therefore since we are God's offspring, we should not think that the divine being is like gold or silver or stone—an image made by man's design and skill. ³⁰In the past God overlooked such ignorance, but now he commands all people everywhere to repent. ³¹For he has set a day when he will judge the world with justice by the man he has appointed. He has given proof of this to all men by raising him from the dead."

³²When they heard about the resurrection of the dead, some of them sneered, but others said,

17:32 A Tough Audience

Paul gave a remarkable speech to a gathering of philosophers and thinkers in the sophisticated university city of Athens. It appears he met with little success, and the results may have troubled him greatly. Acts 18:5 hints at a shift in his approach. Some scholars believe that the first four chapters of 1 Corinthians, reflecting on this period of time, may describe the strong impact of his experience in Athens.

"We want to hear you again on this subject." ³³At that, Paul left the Council. ³⁴A few men became followers of Paul and believed. Among them was Dionysius, a member of the Areopagus, also a woman named Damaris, and a number of others.

In Corinth

18 After this, Paul left Athens and went to Corinth. [2]There he met a Jew named Aquila, a native of Pontus, who had recently come from Italy with his wife Priscilla, because Claudius had ordered all the Jews to leave Rome. Paul went to see them, [3]and because he was a tentmaker as they were, he stayed and worked with them. [4]Every Sabbath he reasoned in the synagogue, trying to persuade Jews and Greeks.

[5]When Silas and Timothy came from Macedonia, Paul devoted himself exclusively to preaching, testifying to the Jews that Jesus was the Christ.[a] [6]But when the Jews opposed Paul and became abusive, he shook out his clothes in protest and said to them, "Your blood be on your own heads! I am clear of my responsibility. From now on I will go to the Gentiles."

[7]Then Paul left the synagogue and went next door to the house of Titius Justus, a worshiper of God. [8]Crispus, the synagogue ruler, and his entire household believed in the Lord; and many of the Corinthians who heard him believed and were baptized.

[9]One night the Lord spoke to Paul in a vision: "Do not be afraid; keep on speaking, do not be silent. [10]For I am with you, and no one is going to attack and harm you, because I have many

a5 Or Messiah; also in verse 28

On the Road with the Apostle Paul
Paul, both Jewish and Roman, took the gospel into the melting pot

THE BOOK OF ACTS FOLLOWS Paul on three distinct missionary journeys along the northeastern shores of the Mediterranean Sea. Normally in the ancient world, travel posed great hazards, with pirates, barbarian armies, and hostile border guards clogging up the roads. But by Paul's lifetime, Rome had established absolute mastery over a vast territory. Empire-wide peace, the famous *Pax Romana*—a condition that existed only twice in 700 years—prevailed.

Roman engineers had crisscrossed the empire with a network of roads (built so well that many still survive), and as a Roman citizen Paul had a passport to any destination. Language, too, was unified. The Greek tongue, as well as the Greek style of thinking, crossed ethnic barriers.

> But when the Jews opposed Paul and became abusive, he shook out his clothes in protest and said to them, "Your blood be on your own heads! I am clear of my responsibility. From now on I will go to the Gentiles." **18:6**

Paul's Strategy

In his missionary ventures, Paul focused primarily on chief trade towns, capital cities, and Roman colonies. Like modern cities today, these comprised a melting pot of diverse cultures. From these places, the gospel message would be carried across the globe.

Usually, Paul began with a visit to a local synagogue, establishing contact with fellow Jews. If they rejected his message, as often happened, he quickly turned to a non-Jewish audience.

When a promising church was established, Paul stayed on—sometimes as long as three years—to teach and to direct its spiritual growth. His letters glow with affection for the friends he developed in this way. (Acts 20 gives a glimpse of the intimacy he shared with one such group.) On his second and third journeys Paul revisited many of the churches he had founded.

Unusual Qualifications, Impressive Results

Paul's background uniquely qualified him for his adventures. A Pharisee who had studied with the famous teacher Gamaliel, he fully understood the Jewish mind. Roman citizenship gave him the status and respect he needed to gain official recognition and to survive threatening legal scrapes.

Paul's mastery of languages helped him also. He used Aramaic to relate to the early church leaders in Jerusalem, and fluency in Greek made possible a speech before philosophers in Athens.

Sometimes Paul was used by God to work miracles. In one tragicomic episode, a sleepy listener succumbed to Paul's all-night sermon and fell out of a third-story window (20:7–12); Paul raised him from the dead.

By the end of his eventful life, Paul had left a ring of burgeoning churches around the eastern Mediterranean. To make sure his work would go on, he trained such leaders as Silas, Titus, Timothy, and the man who recorded much of what we know about Paul's life—Luke himself.

Life Questions: Why did God choose Paul to lead the early church? What special qualifications do you have that God could use?

people in this city." [11]So Paul stayed for a year and a half, teaching them the word of God.

[12]While Gallio was proconsul of Achaia, the Jews made a united attack on Paul and brought him into court. [13]"This man," they charged, "is persuading the people to worship God in ways contrary to the law."

18:15 A Secular View

Like many Roman officials, Gallio showed little interest in religious matters. However, his decision not to hear charges against Paul had far-reaching consequences. Gallio was an important ruler—brother of the philosopher Seneca and in line for a high office in Rome. By treating Christianity as a part of Judaism he was granting it a form of official protection, for Judaism had already been formally recognized as a religion.

Ironically, when Gallio eventually returned to Rome, he was killed on the orders of Nero—one of the first emperors to begin persecuting Christians.

[14]Just as Paul was about to speak, Gallio said to the Jews, "If you Jews were making a complaint about some misdemeanor or serious crime, it would be reasonable for me to listen to you. [15]But since it involves questions about words and names and your own law—settle the matter yourselves. I will not be a judge of such things." [16]So he had them ejected from the court.

[a]25 Or *with fervor in the Spirit*

[17]Then they all turned on Sosthenes the synagogue ruler and beat him in front of the court. But Gallio showed no concern whatever.

Priscilla, Aquila and Apollos

[18]Paul stayed on in Corinth for some time. Then he left the brothers and sailed for Syria, accompanied by Priscilla and Aquila. Before he sailed, he had his hair cut off at Cenchrea because of a vow he had taken. [19]They arrived at Ephesus, where Paul left Priscilla and Aquila. He himself went into the synagogue and reasoned with the Jews. [20]When they asked him to spend more time with them, he declined. [21]But as he left, he promised, "I will come back if it is God's will." Then he set sail from Ephesus. [22]When he landed at Caesarea, he went up and greeted the church and then went down to Antioch.

[23]After spending some time in Antioch, Paul set out from there and traveled from place to place throughout the region of Galatia and Phrygia, strengthening all the disciples.

[24]Meanwhile a Jew named Apollos, a native of Alexandria, came to Ephesus. He was a learned man, with a thorough knowledge of the Scriptures. [25]He had been instructed in the way of the Lord, and he spoke with great fervor[a] and taught about Jesus accurately, though he knew only the baptism of John. [26]He began to speak boldly in the synagogue. When Priscilla and Aquila heard him, they invited him to their home and explained to him the way of God more adequately.

PRISCILLA AND AQUILA *Power Couple*

MOST LEADERS IN THE NEW Testament were married, but Priscilla and Aquila stand out for making their impact together as a married couple. The Bible never mentions one without the other. Together they worked as tentmakers (18:3), as a couple they sponsored churches in their home (1 Corinthians 16:19; Romans 16:3–5), and in tandem they quietly straightened out a powerful evangelist's doctrine (18:26). More often than not, Priscilla's name comes first—which certainly leaves an impression that in the eyes of their friends she was at least her husband's equal.

Priscilla and Aquila rank among the apostle Paul's closest friends. They first met when Paul arrived alone and weary in the sophisticated, immoral city of Corinth. Priscilla and Aquila were recent arrivals as well—refugees, in fact. Along with all Jews, they had been evicted from Rome by the emperor Claudius. Paul stayed with them and—since he, too, had been trained as a tentmaker—worked alongside them. No doubt the three talked long and thoughtfully as they worked together making tents.

Later Priscilla and Aquila accompanied Paul to the port city of Ephesus, where they became leaders in that new and dynamic church. Churches often met in homes then, just as they do today in places such as Communist China. Under such circumstances the hospitality of hosts like Priscilla and Aquila was crucial to the believers' fellowship.

Since Paul was constantly on the go, he had to rely on letters and occasional visits to sustain his friendship with Priscilla and Aquila. At some point they risked their lives for him (Romans 16:4). When he sent greetings in public letters, this couple headed the list (Romans 16:3; 2 Timothy 4:19).

Life Questions: Think of a married couple you know who have a ministry together. What attitudes toward each other do they show?

²⁷When Apollos wanted to go to Achaia, the brothers encouraged him and wrote to the disciples there to welcome him. On arriving, he was a great help to those who by grace had believed. ²⁸For he vigorously refuted the Jews in public debate, proving from the Scriptures that Jesus was the Christ.

Paul in Ephesus

19 While Apollos was at Corinth, Paul took the road through the interior and arrived at Ephesus. There he found some disciples ²and asked them, "Did you receive the Holy Spirit when*a* you believed?"

They answered, "No, we have not even heard that there is a Holy Spirit."

³So Paul asked, "Then what baptism did you receive?"

"John's baptism," they replied.

⁴Paul said, "John's baptism was a baptism of repentance. He told the people to believe in the one coming after him, that is, in Jesus." ⁵On hearing this, they were baptized into*b* the name of the Lord Jesus. ⁶When Paul placed his hands on them, the Holy Spirit came on them, and they spoke in tongues*c* and prophesied. ⁷There were about twelve men in all.

⁸Paul entered the synagogue and spoke boldly there for three months, arguing persuasively about the kingdom of God. ⁹But some of them became obstinate; they refused to believe and publicly maligned the Way. So Paul left them. He took the disciples with him and had discussions daily in the lecture hall of Tyrannus. ¹⁰This went on for two years, so that all the Jews and Greeks who lived in the province of Asia heard the word of the Lord.

¹¹God did extraordinary miracles through Paul, ¹²so that even handkerchiefs and aprons that had touched him were taken to the sick, and their illnesses were cured and the evil spirits left them.

¹³Some Jews who went around driving out evil

19:9 Sports and Education

Greek lecture halls or gymnasiums, such as this one at Tyrannus, often were built as training rooms for Olympic athletes and later converted to educational purposes. (The word "gymnasium" comes from a Greek word that means, literally, "to train in the nude.") Modern Americans use this ancient word for athletic facilities; Europeans, especially Germans, use it in referring to college-prep schools.

spirits tried to invoke the name of the Lord Jesus over those who were demon-possessed. They would say, "In the name of Jesus, whom Paul preaches, I command you to come out." ¹⁴Seven sons of Sceva, a Jewish chief priest, were doing this. ¹⁵One day, the evil spirit answered them, "Jesus I know, and I know about Paul, but who are you?" ¹⁶Then the man who had the evil spirit jumped on them and overpowered them all. He gave them such a beating that they ran out of the house naked and bleeding.

¹⁷When this became known to the Jews and Greeks living in Ephesus, they were all seized with fear, and the name of the Lord Jesus was held in high honor. ¹⁸Many of those who believed now came and openly confessed their evil deeds. ¹⁹A number who had practiced sorcery brought their scrolls together and burned them publicly. When they calculated the value of the scrolls, the total came to fifty thousand drachmas.*d* ²⁰In this way the word of the Lord spread widely and grew in power.

²¹After all this had happened, Paul decided to go to Jerusalem, passing through Macedonia and Achaia. "After I have been there," he said, "I must visit Rome also." ²²He sent two of his helpers, Timothy and Erastus, to Macedonia, while he stayed in the province of Asia a little longer.

The Riot in Ephesus

²³About that time there arose a great disturbance about the Way. ²⁴A silversmith named Demetrius, who made silver shrines of Artemis, brought in no little business for the craftsmen.

19:24 Commercialized Religion

Ephesus was devoted to idolatry and to profit, and Paul's message threatened both. The citizens took great pride in their temple, one of the seven wonders of the ancient world, and were outraged at anyone who might interfere with their profitable businesses dependent on religious pilgrims. The story presents a clear case of mob psychology. Paul started a riot, but he also founded one of his strongest churches, a community that later inspired the book of Ephesians.

²⁵He called them together, along with the workmen in related trades, and said: "Men, you know we receive a good income from this business. ²⁶And you see and hear how this fellow Paul has convinced and led astray large numbers of people here in Ephesus and in practically the whole province of Asia. He says that man-made gods

---

a2 Or after   b5 Or in   c6 Or other languages   d19 A drachma was a silver coin worth about a day's wages.

are no gods at all. [27]There is danger not only that our trade will lose its good name, but also that the temple of the great goddess Artemis will be discredited, and the goddess herself, who is worshiped throughout the province of Asia and the world, will be robbed of her divine majesty."

[28]When they heard this, they were furious and began shouting: "Great is Artemis of the Ephesians!" [29]Soon the whole city was in an uproar. The people seized Gaius and Aristarchus, Paul's traveling companions from Macedonia, and rushed as one man into the theater. [30]Paul wanted to appear before the crowd, but the disciples would not let him. [31]Even some of the officials of the province, friends of Paul, sent him a message begging him not to venture into the theater.

[32]The assembly was in confusion: Some were shouting one thing, some another. Most of the people did not even know why they were there. [33]The Jews pushed Alexander to the front, and some of the crowd shouted instructions to him. He motioned for silence in order to make a defense before the people. [34]But when they realized he was a Jew, they all shouted in unison for about two hours: "Great is Artemis of the Ephesians!"

[35]The city clerk quieted the crowd and said: "Men of Ephesus, doesn't all the world know that the city of Ephesus is the guardian of the temple of the great Artemis and of her image, which fell from heaven? [36]Therefore, since these facts are undeniable, you ought to be quiet and not do anything rash. [37]You have brought these men here, though they have neither robbed temples nor blasphemed our goddess. [38]If, then, Demetrius and his fellow craftsmen have a grievance against anybody, the courts are open and there are proconsuls. They can press charges. [39]If there is anything further you want to bring up, it must be settled in a legal assembly. [40]As it is, we are in danger of being charged with rioting because of today's events. In that case we would not be able to account for this commotion, since there is no reason for it." [41]After he had said this, he dismissed the assembly.

Through Macedonia and Greece

20 When the uproar had ended, Paul sent for the disciples and, after encouraging them, said good-by and set out for Macedonia. [2]He traveled through that area, speaking many words of encouragement to the people, and finally arrived in Greece, [3]where he stayed three months. Because the Jews made a plot against him just as he was about to sail for Syria, he decided to go back through Macedonia. [4]He was accompanied by Sopater son of Pyrrhus from Berea, Aristarchus and Secundus from Thessalonica, Gaius from Derbe, Timothy also, and Tychicus and Trophimus from the province of Asia. [5]These men went on ahead and waited for us at Troas.

[6]But we sailed from Philippi after the Feast of Unleavened Bread, and five days later joined the others at Troas, where we stayed seven days.

Eutychus Raised From the Dead at Troas

[7]On the first day of the week we came together to break bread. Paul spoke to the people and, because he intended to leave the next day, kept on talking until midnight. [8]There were many lamps in the upstairs room where we were meeting. [9]Seated in a window was a young man named Eutychus, who was sinking into a deep sleep as Paul talked on and on. When he was sound asleep, he fell to the ground from the third

20:4 No Cheating

In the days before electronic banking, money had to be carried in person. Thus Paul's plan to transfer the famine relief funds collected in Greece and Asia to the churches in Judea (see 24:17) posed some problems. Eager to avoid suspicion, Paul invited representatives from the donating churches to accompany him. That way he could assure everyone the money was used as promised, and not for personal gain. Second Corinthians 8 gives more details about this offering.

story and was picked up dead. [10]Paul went down, threw himself on the young man and put his arms around him. "Don't be alarmed," he said. "He's alive!" [11]Then he went upstairs again and broke bread and ate. After talking until daylight, he left. [12]The people took the young man home alive and were greatly comforted.

Paul's Farewell to the Ephesian Elders

[13]We went on ahead to the ship and sailed for Assos, where we were going to take Paul aboard. He had made this arrangement because he was going there on foot. [14]When he met us at Assos, we took him aboard and went on to Mitylene. [15]The next day we set sail from there and arrived off Kios. The day after that we crossed over to Samos, and on the following day arrived at Miletus. [16]Paul had decided to sail past Ephesus to avoid spending time in the province of Asia, for he was in a hurry to reach Jerusalem, if possible, by the day of Pentecost.

[17]From Miletus, Paul sent to Ephesus for the elders of the church. [18]When they arrived, he said to them: "You know how I lived the whole time I was with you, from the first day I came into the province of Asia. [19]I served the Lord with great humility and with tears, although I was severely tested by the plots of the Jews. [20]You know that I have not hesitated to preach anything that would be helpful to you but have taught you

publicly and from house to house. ²¹I have declared to both Jews and Greeks that they must turn to God in repentance and have faith in our Lord Jesus.

²²"And now, compelled by the Spirit, I am going to Jerusalem, not knowing what will happen to me there. ²³I only know that in every city the Holy Spirit warns me that prison and hardships are facing me. ²⁴However, I consider my life worth nothing to me, if only I may finish the race and complete the task the Lord Jesus has given me—the task of testifying to the gospel of God's grace.

²⁵"Now I know that none of you among whom I have gone about preaching the kingdom will ever see me again. ²⁶Therefore, I declare to you

today that I am innocent of the blood of all men. ²⁷For I have not hesitated to proclaim to you the whole will of God. ²⁸Keep watch over yourselves and all the flock of which the Holy Spirit has made you overseers.ᵃ Be shepherds of the church of God,ᵇ which he bought with his own blood. ²⁹I know that after I leave, savage wolves will come in among you and will not spare the flock. ³⁰Even from your own number men will arise and distort the truth in order to draw away disciples after them. ³¹So be on your guard! Remember that for three years I never stopped warning each of you night and day with tears.

³²"Now I commit you to God and to the word of his grace, which can build you up and give you an inheritance among all those who are sancti-

ᵃ28 Traditionally *bishops*   ᵇ28 Many manuscripts *of the Lord*

Paul's Legal Battles
470 Roman soldiers protected him from a lynch mob

THE DRUMBEAT STARTS WITH THE last verse in chapter 20: "What grieved them most was his statement that they would never see his face again." After this, wherever he went, Paul's friends begged him not to go to Jerusalem. One of them bound his own hands and feet with Paul's belt, publicly role-playing what was in store for Paul (21:10–11).

But Paul had survived shipwrecks, a stoning, beatings, and long nights in jail, and fear had never stopped him. Besides, he knew that God wanted him to take his word to Rome, and no disaster in Jerusalem could prevent that.

> "And now, compelled by the Spirit, I am going to Jerusalem, not knowing what will happen to me there. I only know that in every city the Holy Spirit warns me that prison and hardships are facing me." 20:22–23

A Dangerous Revolutionary?

Thus, against all advice Paul went to Jerusalem. His reputation as a Christian missionary had spread, to such an extent that it took a brigade of 470 Roman soldiers to protect him from a Jewish lynch mob.

Luke details the process of Roman justice so thoroughly that some have speculated he wrote Acts as a legal brief for Paul's defense. Was Paul a violent terrorist intent on inciting revolt? Luke meticulously records that, no, Paul had no political ambitions and consistently worked within Roman law.

Most of the time, Roman law found Paul innocent. An official in Corinth dismissed charges against him (18:15), as did the town clerk at Ephesus (19:35–41). In Judea Governor Festus and King Agrippa both concluded Paul might have been freed outright had he not appealed to Caesar (26:32).

The Beginning of the End

Paul's last days of freedom summarize his turbulent life. His friends' fears regarding Jerusalem proved well-founded. A murderous mob there assailed him with trumped-up charges, and he had to be rescued bodily by soldiers.

In typical brazen style, Paul asked to address the unruly crowd, using the chance to confront them with his life's testimony. The crowd listened until he got to the part about a mission to the Gentiles; then it erupted.

In his speech (22:3–21), Paul referred back to the day he stood on the sidelines cheering as Stephen, the first Christian martyr, was killed. That violent scene was forever etched in Paul's mind as a reminder of his former life. But another memory was even more powerful: the blinding light on the road to Damascus. Ever after that event in Damascus, Paul seemed determined to stun the human race as he had been stunned on that desert road. No matter how many nights in jail it cost him.

Life Questions: Acts 20 shows Paul's closeness to other Christians. What produced such intense feelings? What could increase your closeness with others?

fied. ³³I have not coveted anyone's silver or gold or clothing. ³⁴You yourselves know that these hands of mine have supplied my own needs and the needs of my companions. ³⁵In everything I did, I showed you that by this kind of hard work we must help the weak, remembering the words the Lord Jesus himself said: 'It is more blessed to give than to receive.'"

20:35 Emotional Farewell

Paul had worked in Ephesus longer than any other city. Before leaving on his fateful trip to Jerusalem, he called the elders to Miletus for a final farewell (verse 17). In his speech, he quotes a saying from Jesus—the only New Testament quotation from Jesus not found in the Gospels.

³⁶When he had said this, he knelt down with all of them and prayed. ³⁷They all wept as they embraced him and kissed him. ³⁸What grieved them most was his statement that they would never see his face again. Then they accompanied him to the ship.

On to Jerusalem

21 After we had torn ourselves away from them, we put out to sea and sailed straight to Cos. The next day we went to Rhodes and from there to Patara. ²We found a ship crossing over to Phoenicia, went on board and set sail. ³After sighting Cyprus and passing to the south of it, we sailed on to Syria. We landed at Tyre, where our ship was to unload its cargo. ⁴Finding the disciples there, we stayed with them seven days. Through the Spirit they urged Paul not to go on to Jerusalem. ⁵But when our time was up, we left and continued on our way. All the disciples and their wives and children accompanied us out of the city, and there on the beach we knelt to pray. ⁶After saying good-by to each other, we went aboard the ship, and they returned home.

⁷We continued our voyage from Tyre and landed at Ptolemais, where we greeted the brothers and stayed with them for a day. ⁸Leaving the next day, we reached Caesarea and stayed at the house of Philip the evangelist, one of the Seven. ⁹He had four unmarried daughters who prophesied.

¹⁰After we had been there a number of days, a prophet named Agabus came down from Judea. ¹¹Coming over to us, he took Paul's belt, tied his own hands and feet with it and said, "The Holy Spirit says, 'In this way the Jews of Jerusalem will bind the owner of this belt and will hand him over to the Gentiles.'"

¹²When we heard this, we and the people there pleaded with Paul not to go up to Jerusalem.

¹³Then Paul answered, "Why are you weeping and breaking my heart? I am ready not only to be bound, but also to die in Jerusalem for the name of the Lord Jesus." ¹⁴When he would not be dissuaded, we gave up and said, "The Lord's will be done."

¹⁵After this, we got ready and went up to Jerusalem. ¹⁶Some of the disciples from Caesarea accompanied us and brought us to the home of Mnason, where we were to stay. He was a man from Cyprus and one of the early disciples.

Paul's Arrival at Jerusalem

¹⁷When we arrived at Jerusalem, the brothers received us warmly. ¹⁸The next day Paul and the rest of us went to see James, and all the elders were present. ¹⁹Paul greeted them and reported in detail what God had done among the Gentiles through his ministry.

²⁰When they heard this, they praised God. Then they said to Paul: "You see, brother, how many thousands of Jews have believed, and all of them are zealous for the law. ²¹They have been informed that you teach all the Jews who live among the Gentiles to turn away from Moses, telling them not to circumcise their children or live according to our customs. ²²What shall we do? They will certainly hear that you have come, ²³so do what we tell you. There are four men with us who have made a vow. ²⁴Take these men, join in their purification rites and pay their expenses, so that they can have their heads shaved. Then everybody will know there is no truth in these reports about you, but that you yourself are living in obedience to the law. ²⁵As for the Gentile believers, we have written to them our decision that they should abstain from food sacrificed to idols, from blood, from the meat of strangled animals and from sexual immorality."

²⁶The next day Paul took the men and purified himself along with them. Then he went to the temple to give notice of the date when the days of purification would end and the offering would be made for each of them.

Paul Arrested

²⁷When the seven days were nearly over, some Jews from the province of Asia saw Paul at the temple. They stirred up the whole crowd and seized him, ²⁸shouting, "Men of Israel, help us! This is the man who teaches all men everywhere against our people and our law and this place. And besides, he has brought Greeks into the temple area and defiled this holy place." ²⁹(They had previously seen Trophimus the Ephesian in the city with Paul and assumed that Paul had brought him into the temple area.)

³⁰The whole city was aroused, and the people came running from all directions. Seizing Paul, they dragged him from the temple, and immedi-

ately the gates were shut. ³¹While they were trying to kill him, news reached the commander of the Roman troops that the whole city of Jerusalem was in an uproar. ³²He at once took some

---

21:28 A Trumped-up Charge

Ironically, the arrest that led to Paul's final imprisonment came because of a misunderstanding. He was actually trying to reassure the Jerusalem church of his loyalty by agreeing to take Jewish vows. But a rumor spread that Paul had illegally taken an "unclean" Gentile into a forbidden part of the temple, and a mob scene ensued. The remainder of Acts reports on various stages of Paul's legal appeals.

---

officers and soldiers and ran down to the crowd. When the rioters saw the commander and his soldiers, they stopped beating Paul.

³³The commander came up and arrested him and ordered him to be bound with two chains. Then he asked who he was and what he had done. ³⁴Some in the crowd shouted one thing and some another, and since the commander could not get at the truth because of the uproar, he ordered that Paul be taken into the barracks. ³⁵When Paul reached the steps, the violence of the mob was so great he had to be carried by the soldiers. ³⁶The crowd that followed kept shouting, "Away with him!"

Paul Speaks to the Crowd

³⁷As the soldiers were about to take Paul into the barracks, he asked the commander, "May I say something to you?"

"Do you speak Greek?" he replied. ³⁸"Aren't you the Egyptian who started a revolt and led four thousand terrorists out into the desert some time ago?"

³⁹Paul answered, "I am a Jew, from Tarsus in Cilicia, a citizen of no ordinary city. Please let me speak to the people."

⁴⁰Having received the commander's permission, Paul stood on the steps and motioned to the crowd. When they were all silent, he said to them **22** in Aramaic[a]: ¹"Brothers and fathers, listen now to my defense."

²When they heard him speak to them in Aramaic, they became very quiet.

Then Paul said: ³"I am a Jew, born in Tarsus of Cilicia, but brought up in this city. Under Gamaliel I was thoroughly trained in the law of our fathers and was just as zealous for God as any of you are today. ⁴I persecuted the followers of this Way to their death, arresting both men and

women and throwing them into prison, ⁵as also the high priest and all the Council can testify. I even obtained letters from them to their brothers in Damascus, and went there to bring these people as prisoners to Jerusalem to be punished.

⁶"About noon as I came near Damascus, suddenly a bright light from heaven flashed around me. ⁷I fell to the ground and heard a voice say to me, 'Saul! Saul! Why do you persecute me?'

⁸"'Who are you, Lord?' I asked.

"'I am Jesus of Nazareth, whom you are persecuting,' he replied. ⁹My companions saw the light, but they did not understand the voice of him who was speaking to me.

¹⁰"'What shall I do, Lord?' I asked.

"'Get up,' the Lord said, 'and go into Damascus. There you will be told all that you have been assigned to do.' ¹¹My companions led me by the hand into Damascus, because the brilliance of the light had blinded me.

22:6 Three Versions

Paul's change from persecutor to Christian missionary makes for one of the most dramatic conversion stories in the New Testament. Acts gives three versions: Luke's historical report in chapter 9; Paul's self-defense here before a Jewish mob; and his formal testimony before Agrippa (chapter 26), a descendant of the ruler who tried to kill the infant Jesus in Bethlehem. Each version adds new details custom-tailored to the specific audience.

---

¹²"A man named Ananias came to see me. He was a devout observer of the law and highly respected by all the Jews living there. ¹³He stood beside me and said, 'Brother Saul, receive your sight!' And at that very moment I was able to see him.

¹⁴"Then he said: 'The God of our fathers has chosen you to know his will and to see the Righteous One and to hear words from his mouth. ¹⁵You will be his witness to all men of what you have seen and heard. ¹⁶And now what are you waiting for? Get up, be baptized and wash your sins away, calling on his name.'

¹⁷"When I returned to Jerusalem and was praying at the temple, I fell into a trance ¹⁸and saw the Lord speaking. 'Quick!' he said to me. 'Leave Jerusalem immediately, because they will not accept your testimony about me.'

¹⁹"'Lord,' I replied, 'these men know that I went from one synagogue to another to imprison and beat those who believe[b] in you. ²⁰And when the blood of your martyr[b] Stephen was shed, I

ᵃ40 Or possibly Hebrew; also in 22:2   *ᵇ20 Or witness*

stood there giving my approval and guarding the clothes of those who were killing him.'

²¹"Then the Lord said to me, 'Go; I will send you far away to the Gentiles.' "

Paul the Roman Citizen

²²The crowd listened to Paul until he said this. Then they raised their voices and shouted, "Rid the earth of him! He's not fit to live!"

²³As they were shouting and throwing off their cloaks and flinging dust into the air, ²⁴the commander ordered Paul to be taken into the barracks. He directed that he be flogged and questioned in order to find out why the people were shouting at him like this. ²⁵As they stretched him out to flog him, Paul said to the centurion standing there, "Is it legal for you to flog a Roman citizen who hasn't even been found guilty?"

²⁶When the centurion heard this, he went to the commander and reported it. "What are you going to do?" he asked. "This man is a Roman citizen."

²⁷The commander went to Paul and asked, "Tell me, are you a Roman citizen?"

"Yes, I am," he answered.

²⁸Then the commander said, "I had to pay a big price for my citizenship."

"But I was born a citizen," Paul replied.

²⁹Those who were about to question him withdrew immediately. The commander himself was alarmed when he realized that he had put Paul, a Roman citizen, in chains.

Before the Sanhedrin

³⁰The next day, since the commander wanted to find out exactly why Paul was being accused by the Jews, he released him and ordered the chief priests and all the Sanhedrin to assemble. Then he brought Paul and had him stand before them.

23 Paul looked straight at the Sanhedrin and said, "My brothers, I have fulfilled my duty to God in all good conscience to this day." ²At this the high priest Ananias ordered those standing near Paul to strike him on the mouth. ³Then Paul said to him, "God will strike you, you whitewashed wall! You sit there to judge me according to the law, yet you yourself violate the law by commanding that I be struck!"

⁴Those who were standing near Paul said, "You dare to insult God's high priest?"

⁵Paul replied, "Brothers, I did not realize that he was the high priest; for it is written: 'Do not speak evil about the ruler of your people.'ᵃ"

⁶Then Paul, knowing that some of them were Sadducees and the others Pharisees, called out in the Sanhedrin, "My brothers, I am a Pharisee, the son of a Pharisee. I stand on trial because of my hope in the resurrection of the dead." ⁷When he said this, a dispute broke out between the Pharisees and the Sadducees, and the assembly was divided. ⁸(The Sadducees say that there is no

23:6 Paul under Attack

Under pressure, Paul proved to be a formidable opponent. In this scene, he spoke back to a priest who struck him on the mouth. Using great skill, Paul divided his accusers by exploiting the differences between two Jewish sects, the Pharisees and Sadducees (see note on 4:1). Paul managed to arouse such intense opposition that a group of 40 conspirators vowed not to eat or drink until they had killed him.

resurrection, and that there are neither angels nor spirits, but the Pharisees acknowledge them all.)

⁹There was a great uproar, and some of the teachers of the law who were Pharisees stood up and argued vigorously. "We find nothing wrong with this man," they said. "What if a spirit or an angel has spoken to him?" ¹⁰The dispute became so violent that the commander was afraid Paul would be torn to pieces by them. He ordered the troops to go down and take him away from them by force and bring him into the barracks.

¹¹The following night the Lord stood near Paul and said, "Take courage! As you have testified about me in Jerusalem, so you must also testify in Rome."

The Plot to Kill Paul

¹²The next morning the Jews formed a conspiracy and bound themselves with an oath not to eat or drink until they had killed Paul. ¹³More than forty men were involved in this plot. ¹⁴They went to the chief priests and elders and said, "We have taken a solemn oath not to eat anything until we have killed Paul. ¹⁵Now then, you and the Sanhedrin petition the commander to bring him before you on the pretext of wanting more accurate information about his case. We are ready to kill him before he gets here."

¹⁶But when the son of Paul's sister heard of this plot, he went into the barracks and told Paul.

¹⁷Then Paul called one of the centurions and said, "Take this young man to the commander; he has something to tell him." ¹⁸So he took him to the commander.

The centurion said, "Paul, the prisoner, sent for me and asked me to bring this young man to you because he has something to tell you."

¹⁹The commander took the young man by the

ᵃ5 Exodus 22:28

hand, drew him aside and asked, "What is it you want to tell me?"

[20]He said: "The Jews have agreed to ask you to bring Paul before the Sanhedrin tomorrow on

23:16 Paul's Family

This mention of Paul's nephew is the only reference to Paul's family. Born a Roman citizen in Tarsus (22:28), Paul likely came from a rather prominent family. Only a minority of people in the Roman empire held citizenship, especially in occupied lands. Citizenship could be purchased at a great price or awarded by Roman authorities, but Paul specifies his came through inheritance.

the pretext of wanting more accurate information about him. [21]Don't give in to them, because more than forty of them are waiting in ambush for him. They have taken an oath not to eat or drink until they have killed him. They are ready now, waiting for your consent to their request."

[22]The commander dismissed the young man and cautioned him, "Don't tell anyone that you have reported this to me."

Paul Transferred to Caesarea

[23]Then he called two of his centurions and ordered them, "Get ready a detachment of two hundred soldiers, seventy horsemen and two hundred spearmen[a] to go to Caesarea at nine tonight. [24]Provide mounts for Paul so that he may be taken safely to Governor Felix."

[25]He wrote a letter as follows:

[26]Claudius Lysias,

To His Excellency, Governor Felix:

Greetings.

[27]This man was seized by the Jews and they were about to kill him, but I came with my troops and rescued him, for I had learned that he is a Roman citizen. [28]I wanted to know why they were accusing him, so I brought him to their Sanhedrin. [29]I found that the accusation had to do with questions about their law, but there was no charge against him that deserved death or imprisonment. [30]When I was informed of a plot to be carried out against the man, I sent him to you at once. I also ordered his accusers to present to you their case against him.

[31]So the soldiers, carrying out their orders, took Paul with them during the night and brought him as far as Antipatris. [32]The next day they let the cavalry go on with him, while they returned to the barracks. [33]When the cavalry arrived in Caesarea, they delivered the letter to the governor and handed Paul over to him. [34]The governor read the letter and asked what province he was from. Learning that he was from Cilicia, [35]he said, "I will hear your case when your accusers get here." Then he ordered that Paul be kept under guard in Herod's palace.

The Trial Before Felix

24 Five days later the high priest Ananias went down to Caesarea with some of the elders and a lawyer named Tertullus, and they brought their charges against Paul before the governor. [2]When Paul was called in, Tertullus presented his case before Felix: "We have enjoyed a long period of peace under you, and your foresight has brought about reforms in this nation. [3]Everywhere and in every way, most excellent Felix, we acknowledge this with profound gratitude. [4]But in order not to weary you further, I would request that you be kind enough to hear us briefly.

[5]"We have found this man to be a troublemaker, stirring up riots among the Jews all over the world. He is a ringleader of the Nazarene sect [6]and even tried to desecrate the temple; so we seized him. [8]By[b] examining him yourself you will be able to learn the truth about all these charges we are bringing against him."

[9]The Jews joined in the accusation, asserting that these things were true.

[10]When the governor motioned for him to speak, Paul replied: "I know that for a number of years you have been a judge over this nation; so I gladly make my defense. [11]You can easily verify that no more than twelve days ago I went up to Jerusalem to worship. [12]My accusers did not find me arguing with anyone at the temple, or stirring up a crowd in the synagogues or anywhere else in the city. [13]And they cannot prove to you the charges they are now making against me. [14]However, I admit that I worship the God of our fathers as a follower of the Way, which they call a sect. I believe everything that agrees with the Law and that is written in the Prophets, [15]and I have the same hope in God as these men, that there will be a resurrection of both the righteous and the wicked. [16]So I strive always to keep my conscience clear before God and man.

[17]"After an absence of several years, I came to Jerusalem to bring my people gifts for the poor and to present offerings. [18]I was ceremonially

---

[a]23 The meaning of the Greek for this word is uncertain.   [b]6-8 Some manuscripts *him and wanted to judge him according to our law.* [7]*But the commander, Lysias, came and with the use of much force snatched him from our hands* [8]*and ordered his accusers to come before you. By*

clean when they found me in the temple courts doing this. There was no crowd with me, nor was I involved in any disturbance. [19]But there are some Jews from the province of Asia, who ought to be here before you and bring charges if they have anything against me. [20]Or these who are here should state what crime they found in me when I stood before the Sanhedrin— [21]unless it was this one thing I shouted as I stood in their presence: 'It is concerning the resurrection of the dead that I am on trial before you today.'"

[22]Then Felix, who was well acquainted with the Way, adjourned the proceedings. "When Lysias the commander comes," he said, "I will decide your case." [23]He ordered the centurion to keep Paul under guard but to give him some freedom and permit his friends to take care of his needs.

[24]Several days later Felix came with his wife Drusilla, who was a Jewess. He sent for Paul and listened to him as he spoke about faith in Christ Jesus. [25]As Paul discoursed on righteousness, self-control and the judgment to come, Felix was afraid and said, "That's enough for now! You may leave. When I find it convenient, I will send for you." [26]At the same time he was hoping that Paul would offer him a bribe, so he sent for him frequently and talked with him.

[27]When two years had passed, Felix was succeeded by Porcius Festus, but because Felix wanted to grant a favor to the Jews, he left Paul in prison.

24:27 Left in Chains

Felix was unpopular with the Jews of Palestine. The brief report in Acts shows him to be shrewd and even corrupt (verse 26). Recalled by Rome because of his troubles with the Jews, Felix left Paul in chains for a period of two years. When the new Roman ruler arrived, the controversy over Paul hadn't died down. Jewish leaders immediately confronted Festus with their charges against Paul.

The Trial Before Festus

25 Three days after arriving in the province, Festus went up from Caesarea to Jerusalem, [2]where the chief priests and Jewish leaders appeared before him and presented the charges against Paul. [3]They urgently requested Festus, as a favor to them, to have Paul transferred to Jerusalem, for they were preparing an ambush to kill him along the way. [4]Festus answered, "Paul is being held at Caesarea, and I myself am going there soon. [5]Let some of your leaders come with me and press charges against the man there, if he has done anything wrong."

[6]After spending eight or ten days with them, he went down to Caesarea, and the next day he convened the court and ordered that Paul be brought before him. [7]When Paul appeared, the Jews who had come down from Jerusalem stood around him, bringing many serious charges against him, which they could not prove.

[8]Then Paul made his defense: "I have done nothing wrong against the law of the Jews or against the temple or against Caesar."

[9]Festus, wishing to do the Jews a favor, said to Paul, "Are you willing to go up to Jerusalem and stand trial before me there on these charges?"

[10]Paul answered: "I am now standing before Caesar's court, where I ought to be tried. I have not done any wrong to the Jews, as you yourself know very well. [11]If, however, I am guilty of doing anything deserving death, I do not refuse to die. But if the charges brought against me by these Jews are not true, no one has the right to hand me over to them. I appeal to Caesar!"

[12]After Festus had conferred with his council, he declared: "You have appealed to Caesar. To Caesar you will go!"

Festus Consults King Agrippa

[13]A few days later King Agrippa and Bernice arrived at Caesarea to pay their respects to Festus. [14]Since they were spending many days there,

25:13 Two Rulers

In Jesus' day Rome ruled Palestine through local rulers (the Herods) and their overseer Pilate, a governor who reported directly to Rome. Now, around A.D. 59 or 60, their counterparts were the Roman governor Festus and the last of the Herods, Agrippa II. Festus, a responsible leader, dealt with Paul's case promptly, whereas his predecessor Felix had stalled for two years, leaving Paul in prison. Festus used the visit of Herod Agrippa to schedule this special inquiry into Paul's case.

Festus discussed Paul's case with the king. He said: "There is a man here whom Felix left as a prisoner. [15]When I went to Jerusalem, the chief priests and elders of the Jews brought charges against him and asked that he be condemned.

[16]"I told them that it is not the Roman custom to hand over any man before he has faced his accusers and has had an opportunity to defend himself against their charges. [17]When they came here with me, I did not delay the case, but convened the court the next day and ordered the man to be brought in. [18]When his accusers got up to speak, they did not charge him with any of the crimes I had expected. [19]Instead, they had some points of dispute with him about their own religion and about a dead man named Jesus who

Paul claimed was alive. ²⁰I was at a loss how to investigate such matters; so I asked if he would be willing to go to Jerusalem and stand trial there on these charges. ²¹When Paul made his appeal to be held over for the Emperor's decision, I ordered him held until I could send him to Caesar."

²²Then Agrippa said to Festus, "I would like to hear this man myself."

He replied, "Tomorrow you will hear him."

Paul Before Agrippa

²³The next day Agrippa and Bernice came with great pomp and entered the audience room with the high ranking officers and the leading men of the city. At the command of Festus, Paul was brought in. ²⁴Festus said: "King Agrippa, and all who are present with us, you see this man! The whole Jewish community has petitioned me about him in Jerusalem and here in Caesarea, shouting that he ought not to live any longer. ²⁵I found he had done nothing deserving of death, but because he made his appeal to the Emperor I decided to send him to Rome. ²⁶But I have nothing definite to write to His Majesty about him. Therefore I have brought him before all of you, and especially before you, King Agrippa, so that as a result of this investigation I may have something to write. ²⁷For I think it is unreasonable to send on a prisoner without specifying the charges against him."

26 Then Agrippa said to Paul, "You have permission to speak for yourself."

So Paul motioned with his hand and began his defense: ²"King Agrippa, I consider myself fortunate to stand before you today as I make my defense against all the accusations of the Jews, ³and especially so because you are well acquainted with all the Jewish customs and controversies. Therefore, I beg you to listen to me patiently.

⁴"The Jews all know the way I have lived ever since I was a child, from the beginning of my life in my own country, and also in Jerusalem. ⁵They have known me for a long time and can testify, if they are willing, that according to the strictest sect of our religion, I lived as a Pharisee. ⁶And now it is because of my hope in what God has promised our fathers that I am on trial today. ⁷This is the promise our twelve tribes are hoping to see fulfilled as they earnestly serve God day and night. O king, it is because of this hope that the Jews are accusing me. ⁸Why should any of you consider it incredible that God raises the dead?

⁹"I too was convinced that I ought to do all that was possible to oppose the name of Jesus of Nazareth. ¹⁰And that is just what I did in Jerusalem. On the authority of the chief priests I put many of the saints in prison, and when they were put to death, I cast my vote against them. ¹¹Many a time I went from one synagogue to another to have them punished, and I tried to force them to blaspheme. In my obsession against them, I even went to foreign cities to persecute them.

¹²"On one of these journeys I was going to Damascus with the authority and commission of the chief priests. ¹³About noon, O king, as I was on the road, I saw a light from heaven, brighter than the sun, blazing around me and my companions. ¹⁴We all fell to the ground, and I heard

AGRIPPA *Roman Heart*

MEMBERS OF THE HEROD FAMILY were native to Palestine, but their loyalties lay elsewhere—in Rome, where their bread was buttered. The Herods play a leading role in New Testament history, but mostly a negative one.

Agrippa, known to historians as Herod Agrippa II, was the last of a series of Herods who ruled Palestine on Rome's behalf. His great uncle had beheaded John the Baptist and presided over one of Jesus' trials; that man's father had ordered the massacre of babies after Jesus' birth. Now, Agrippa had to pass judgment on the apostle Paul, fiery missionary of the new cause.

Educated in Rome, Agrippa came to power at the age of 17 when his father died. Apparently Agrippa picked up some loose morals in Rome as well; his sister Bernice, who accompanied him to hear Paul's trial, was also his mistress. She tried marriage a number of times, and was mistress to other powerful men, but always she returned to her brother. Their incest fueled Roman gossip.

Nonetheless Paul assumed that Agrippa had some background knowledge of the gospel. As overseer of the Jewish temple, he knew about the increasing number of Jesus-followers and their claims that the prophets' predictions of a Messiah had been fulfilled. Agrippa, however, brushed off Paul's appeal. He was not about to get into a Biblical discussion in front of a Roman governor.

As far as we know, Agrippa stayed loyal to Rome until the end. When Jerusalem revolted against Nero in the year 66, Agrippa backed Rome completely. He was involved in Rome's complete destruction of Jerusalem and its temple in AD 70. His death marked the end of the Herods.

Life Questions: Agrippa put his loyalty to Rome above God's claims. Do you feel any conflict between competing loyalties? Where and why?

a voice saying to me in Aramaic,[a] 'Saul, Saul, why do you persecute me? It is hard for you to kick against the goads.'

15"Then I asked, 'Who are you, Lord?'

26:14 Kicking the Oxgoads

The proverb comes from a sharp "goad" farmers used to control their oxen hitched to a plow. It means something like, "You are only hurting yourself."

" 'I am Jesus, whom you are persecuting,' the Lord replied. 16'Now get up and stand on your feet. I have appeared to you to appoint you as a servant and as a witness of what you have seen of me and what I will show you. 17I will rescue you from your own people and from the Gentiles. I am sending you to them 18to open their eyes and turn them from darkness to light, and from the power of Satan to God, so that they may receive forgiveness of sins and a place among those who are sanctified by faith in me.'

19"So then, King Agrippa, I was not disobedient to the vision from heaven. 20First to those in Damascus, then to those in Jerusalem and in all Judea, and to the Gentiles also, I preached that they should repent and turn to God and prove their repentance by their deeds. 21That is why the Jews seized me in the temple courts and tried to kill me. 22But I have had God's help to this very day, and so I stand here and testify to small and great alike. I am saying nothing beyond what the prophets and Moses said would happen— 23that the Christ[b] would suffer and, as the first to rise from the dead, would proclaim light to his own people and to the Gentiles."

24At this point Festus interrupted Paul's defense. "You are out of your mind, Paul!" he shouted. "Your great learning is driving you insane."

25"I am not insane, most excellent Festus," Paul replied. "What I am saying is true and reasonable. 26The king is familiar with these things, and I can speak freely to him. I am convinced that none of this has escaped his notice, because it was not done in a corner. 27King Agrippa, do you believe the prophets? I know you do."

28Then Agrippa said to Paul, "Do you think that in such a short time you can persuade me to be a Christian?"

29Paul replied, "Short time or long—I pray God that not only you but all who are listening to me today may become what I am, except for these chains."

30The king rose, and with him the governor and Bernice and those sitting with them. 31They left the room, and while talking with one another, they said, "This man is not doing anything that deserves death or imprisonment."

32Agrippa said to Festus, "This man could have been set free if he had not appealed to Caesar."

Paul Sails for Rome

27 When it was decided that we would sail for Italy, Paul and some other prisoners were handed over to a centurion named Julius, who belonged to the Imperial Regiment. 2We boarded a ship from Adramyttium about to sail for ports along the coast of the province of Asia, and we put out to sea. Aristarchus, a Macedonian from Thessalonica, was with us.

3The next day we landed at Sidon; and Julius, in kindness to Paul, allowed him to go to his friends so they might provide for his needs. 4From there we put out to sea again and passed to the lee of Cyprus because the winds were against us. 5When we had sailed across the open sea off the coast of Cilicia and Pamphylia, we landed at Myra in Lycia. 6There the centurion found an Alexandrian ship sailing for Italy and put us on board. 7We made slow headway for many days and had difficulty arriving off Cnidus. When the wind did not allow us to hold our course, we sailed to the lee of Crete, opposite Salmone. 8We moved along the coast with difficulty and came to a place called Fair Havens, near the town of Lasea.

9Much time had been lost, and sailing had already become dangerous because by now it was after the Fast.[c] So Paul warned them, 10"Men, I can see that our voyage is going to be disastrous and bring great loss to ship and cargo, and to our own lives also." 11But the centurion, instead of listening to what Paul said, followed the advice of the pilot and of the owner of the ship. 12Since the harbor was unsuitable to winter in, the majority decided that we should sail on, hoping to reach Phoenix and winter there. This was a harbor in Crete, facing both southwest and northwest.

The Storm

13When a gentle south wind began to blow, they thought they had obtained what they wanted; so they weighed anchor and sailed along the shore of Crete. 14Before very long, a wind of hurricane force, called the "northeaster," swept down from the island. 15The ship was caught by the storm and could not head into the wind; so we gave way to it and were driven along. 16As we passed to the lee of a small island called Cauda, we were hardly able to make the lifeboat secure. 17When the men had hoisted it aboard, they passed ropes under the ship itself to hold it to-

---

[a]14 Or *Hebrew*   [b]23 Or *Messiah*   [c]9 That is, the Day of Atonement (Yom Kippur)

gether. Fearing that they would run aground on the sandbars of Syrtis, they lowered the sea anchor and let the ship be driven along. [18]We took such a violent battering from the storm that the

next day they began to throw the cargo overboard. [19]On the third day, they threw the ship's tackle overboard with their own hands. [20]When neither sun nor stars appeared for many days and the storm continued raging, we finally gave up all hope of being saved.

[21]After the men had gone a long time without food, Paul stood up before them and said: "Men, you should have taken my advice not to sail from Crete; then you would have spared yourselves this damage and loss. [22]But now I urge you to keep up your courage, because not one of you will be lost; only the ship will be destroyed. [23]Last night an angel of the God whose I am and whom I serve stood beside me [24]and said, 'Do not be afraid, Paul. You must stand trial before Caesar; and God has graciously given you the lives of all who sail with you.' [25]So keep up your courage, men, for I have faith in God that it will happen just as he told me. [26]Nevertheless, we must run aground on some island."

The Shipwreck

[27]On the fourteenth night we were still being driven across the Adriatic[a] Sea, when about midnight the sailors sensed they were approaching land. [28]They took soundings and found that the water was a hundred and twenty feet[b] deep. A short time later they took soundings again and found it was ninety feet[c] deep. [29]Fearing that we would be dashed against the rocks, they dropped four anchors from the stern and prayed for daylight. [30]In an attempt to escape from the ship, the

[a]27 In ancient times the name referred to an area extending well south of Italy.   [b]28 Greek *twenty orguias* (about 37 meters)   [c]28 Greek *fifteen orguias* (about 27 meters)

Rome at Last
Paul finally made it to the capital—in chains

ACTS RECORDS 18 SPEECHES IN all, the last three of which were delivered before a very select audience. Roman officials, intrigued by the most talked-about prisoner in their corner of the empire, brought Paul out and asked him to perform, like a trained bear. As a result of their inquisition, he got his long-awaited trip to Rome.

It is hard for us today to realize how completely the city of Rome then dominated the world. "All roads lead to Rome" was more than a figure of speech. Like a center of gravity, the city attracted all the roads and commerce, all the leaders and thinkers and fortune-seekers of the empire. Political and military power fanned out from Rome. It was the indisputable capital of the world. If Christianity was to gain a foothold anywhere, it had to be in Rome.

> *From morning till evening he explained and declared to them the kingdom of God and tried to convince them about Jesus from the Law of Moses and from the Prophets.*
> **28:23**

A Missionary in Chains

Ironically, Paul, the greatest spokesman for the Christian faith, arrived in Rome as a prisoner. He was exhausted, having just survived a harrowing shipwreck. In Rome, Paul got hours of quiet solitude to work on fond letters to the churches he had left behind.

In one sense, Acts ends anticlimactically, for Luke leaves Paul's life dangling. Most scholars believe Paul was released from this imprisonment and expanded his ministry into new frontiers. Luke records nothing of this period, and nothing about the trial of Paul or his eventual fate. He ends with a single memory, frozen in time: Paul, confined to his house, welcoming and preaching to all who come.

Paul could no longer choose his audience; they had to seek him. But boldly, in the heart of mighty Rome, he talked of a new kingdom and a new king. Christianity had made the journey, and the transition, from Jerusalem to Rome.

Life Questions: Is it better for Christianity to be popular or unpopular?

sailors let the lifeboat down into the sea, pretending they were going to lower some anchors from the bow. ³¹Then Paul said to the centurion and the soldiers, "Unless these men stay with the ship, you cannot be saved." ³²So the soldiers cut the ropes that held the lifeboat and let it fall away.

³³Just before dawn Paul urged them all to eat. "For the last fourteen days," he said, "you have been in constant suspense and have gone without food—you haven't eaten anything. ³⁴Now I urge you to take some food. You need it to survive. Not one of you will lose a single hair from his head." ³⁵After he said this, he took some bread and gave thanks to God in front of them all. Then he broke it and began to eat. ³⁶They were all encouraged and ate some food themselves. ³⁷Altogether there were 276 of us on board. ³⁸When they had eaten as much as they wanted, they lightened the ship by throwing the grain into the sea.

³⁹When daylight came, they did not recognize the land, but they saw a bay with a sandy beach, where they decided to run the ship aground if they could. ⁴⁰Cutting loose the anchors, they left them in the sea and at the same time untied the ropes that held the rudders. Then they hoisted the foresail to the wind and made for the beach. ⁴¹But the ship struck a sandbar and ran aground. The bow stuck fast and would not move, and the stern was broken to pieces by the pounding of the surf.

⁴²The soldiers planned to kill the prisoners to prevent any of them from swimming away and escaping. ⁴³But the centurion wanted to spare Paul's life and kept them from carrying out their plan. He ordered those who could swim to jump overboard first and get to land. ⁴⁴The rest were to get there on planks or on pieces of the ship. In this way everyone reached land in safety.

Ashore on Malta

28 Once safely on shore, we found out that the island was called Malta. ²The islanders showed us unusual kindness. They built a fire and welcomed us all because it was raining and cold. ³Paul gathered a pile of brushwood and, as he put it on the fire, a viper, driven out by the heat, fastened itself on his hand. ⁴When the islanders saw the snake hanging from his hand, they said to each other, "This man must be a murderer; for though he escaped from the sea, Justice has not allowed him to live." ⁵But Paul shook the snake off into the fire and suffered no ill effects. ⁶The people expected him to swell up or suddenly fall dead, but after waiting a long time and seeing nothing unusual happen to him, they changed their minds and said he was a god.

⁷There was an estate nearby that belonged to Publius, the chief official of the island. He welcomed us to his home and for three days entertained us hospitably. ⁸His father was sick in bed, suffering from fever and dysentery. Paul went in to see him and, after prayer, placed his hands on him and healed him. ⁹When this had happened, the rest of the sick on the island came and were cured. ¹⁰They honored us in many ways and when we were ready to sail, they furnished us with the supplies we needed.

Arrival at Rome

¹¹After three months we put out to sea in a ship that had wintered in the island. It was an Alexandrian ship with the figurehead of the twin gods Castor and Pollux. ¹²We put in at Syracuse and stayed there three days. ¹³From there we set sail and arrived at Rhegium. The next day the south wind came up, and on the following day we reached Puteoli. ¹⁴There we found some brothers who invited us to spend a week with them. And so we came to Rome. ¹⁵The brothers there had heard that we were coming, and they traveled as far as the Forum of Appius and the Three Taverns to meet us. At the sight of these men Paul thanked God and was encouraged. ¹⁶When we got to Rome, Paul was allowed to live by himself, with a soldier to guard him.

28:16 Time on His Hands

Luke reports that controversy about the Christian "sect" had preceded Paul to Rome (verse 22). The apostle put his time of house arrest to good use, evangelizing all who came to see him and writing to the churches he had founded along the way. Such New Testament books as Philippians, Colossians, Ephesians, and Philemon came out of this period of protective custody, which may have lasted four years.

Paul Preaches at Rome Under Guard

¹⁷Three days later he called together the leaders of the Jews. When they had assembled, Paul said to them: "My brothers, although I have done nothing against our people or against the customs of our ancestors, I was arrested in Jerusalem and handed over to the Romans. ¹⁸They examined me and wanted to release me, because I was not guilty of any crime deserving death. ¹⁹But when the Jews objected, I was compelled to appeal to Caesar—not that I had any charge to bring against my own people. ²⁰For this reason I have asked to see you and talk with you. It is because of the hope of Israel that I am bound with this chain."

²¹They replied, "We have not received any letters from Judea concerning you, and none of the brothers who have come from there has reported or said anything bad about you. ²²But we want to

hear what your views are, for we know that people everywhere are talking against this sect."

[23]They arranged to meet Paul on a certain day, and came in even larger numbers to the place where he was staying. From morning till evening he explained and declared to them the kingdom of God and tried to convince them about Jesus from the Law of Moses and from the Prophets. [24]Some were convinced by what he said, but others would not believe. [25]They disagreed among themselves and began to leave after Paul had made this final statement: "The Holy Spirit spoke the truth to your forefathers when he said through Isaiah the prophet:

[26]" 'Go to this people and say,
  "You will be ever hearing but never
      understanding;
    you will be ever seeing but never
      perceiving."
[27]For this people's heart has become calloused;
    they hardly hear with their ears,
    and they have closed their eyes.
  Otherwise they might see with their eyes,
    hear with their ears,
    understand with their hearts
  and turn, and I would heal them.' [a]

[28]"Therefore I want you to know that God's salvation has been sent to the Gentiles, and they will listen!" [b]

[30]For two whole years Paul stayed there in his own rented house and welcomed all who came to see him. [31]Boldly and without hindrance he preached the kingdom of God and taught about the Lord Jesus Christ.

---

[a]27 Isaiah 6:9,10   [b]28 Some manuscripts listen!" [29]After he said this, the Jews left, arguing vigorously among themselves.

ROMANS

A Most Demanding Audience
If you were stranded on a deserted island, what book would you want along?

I MAGINE YOURSELF IN A COLLEGE speech course. Your assignment: a brief speech on "the meaning of life." Over late-night cups of coffee, you outline the Christian faith and what it means to you. You devote a lot of time to this assignment—after all, this speech may be the only clear expression of faith your classmates will ever hear.

But what if you were asked to write up the speech for your local paper? Instead of a few dozen listeners, you would have thousands of readers. Undoubtedly, you would devote even more time and care to preparation.

> I thank my God through Jesus Christ for all of you, because your faith is being reported all over the world. 1:8

Letter to the Center of the World

Let your imagination run even further. How would you react if you were asked to adapt this same speech for a front-page story in the *New York Times*? This newspaper has sophisticated, demanding readers. In writing for them, you would meticulously pore over every word, polishing phrases and making sure your thoughts were complete and well-expressed.

You can see a similar process at work in the apostle Paul's various letters. Some of his letters were, like a college speech, addressed to a small cluster of people he knew by name. Often they consisted of warm, personal words of advice or even fatherly scolding.

But, *Romans* . . . the very title of this book conjures up images of the powerful empire that ruled the western world. To people of Paul's day, Rome was the center of the world in every way: law, culture, power, and learning. A letter to this sophisticated audience had to be impressive indeed.

In Romans, Paul brilliantly set down the whole scope of Christian doctrine, which, at that time, was still being passed along orally from town to town. Paul wanted to convince those demanding readers that Christ held the answers to all of life's important questions.

One-Volume Summary

Literary types are often asked questions like this: "What one book would you most want along if you were stranded on a deserted island?" (Victorian author G.K. Chesterton gave a classic reply: *"Thomas's Guide to Practical Shipbuilding"*!) If asked the same question about a single book of the Bible, many Christians would choose Romans. Compact enough to fit on one spread of a modern newspaper, Romans yet manages to encompass all essentials of the Christian faith.

Despite its thoroughness, however, Romans does not read like a dry book of theology. Great revivals in church history have been spawned by a study of this book. Augustine, Martin Luther, and John Wesley all trace their spiritual renewals to a reading of Romans. It gives the apostle Paul's final answer to questions about the "meaning of life."

How to Read Romans

Romans is a book to savor, slowly and carefully. Paul is developing an argument, and his logic unfolds thought by thought from the very first chapter. You may recognize many well-known verses in Romans; note these in their context as a part of Paul's overall presentation.

Romans divides into a clear outline. Chapters 1—3 introduce the book and give the need for the good news of the gospel. The end of chapter 3, called the "central theological passage in the Bible," compresses the core message in a brief paragraph. Chapters 4 and 5 expand on that message.

Romans 6—8 discuss the working out of the gospel in a Christian's life. Paul then pauses for three chapters (9—11) to link his argument to the Old Testament history of the Jews. From there, he proceeds to give practical advice on specific problems (12—16).

It will require time and concentration to grasp fully the teachings of Romans; few people would claim to have "mastered" this book. But it has no equal as a concise, reasonable statement of the Christian faith.

PEOPLE YOU'LL MEET IN ROMANS

PAUL *(p. 1177)*

3-TRACK READING PLAN

For an explanation and complete listing of the 3-track reading plan, turn to page 7.

TRACK 1: *Two-Week Courses on the Bible*
The Track 1 reading program on the Life and Teachings of Paul includes three chapters from Romans. See page 7 for a complete listing of this course.

TRACK 2: *An Overview of Romans in 4 Days*
☐ Day 1. Read the Introduction to Romans and then read chapter 3 as a summary of the whole book. Take your time as you read the end, verses 21—31.
☐ Day 2. Read of Paul's struggles against sin in chapter 7.
☐ Day 3. Paul concludes this great section on the Christian life with the triumphant message of chapter 8.
☐ Day 4. Paul gets practical toward the end of the book. Read his direct instructions on how to live in chapter 12.

Now turn to page 9 for your next Track 2 reading project.

TRACK 3: *All of Romans in 14 Days*
After you have read through Romans, turn to pages 10—14 for your next Track 3 reading project.

☐1 ☐2 ☐3 ☐4 ☐5 ☐6 ☐7 ☐8
☐9 ☐10 ☐11 ☐12–13 ☐14 ☐15–16

1 Paul, a servant of Christ Jesus, called to be an apostle and set apart for the gospel of God— [2]the gospel he promised beforehand through his prophets in the Holy Scriptures [3]regarding his Son, who as to his human nature was a descendant of David, [4]and who through the Spirit[a] of holiness was declared with power to be the Son of God[b] by his resurrection from the dead: Jesus Christ our Lord. [5]Through him and for his name's sake, we received grace and apostleship to call people from among all the Gentiles to the obedience that comes from faith. [6]And you also are among those who are called to belong to Jesus Christ.

[7]To all in Rome who are loved by God and called to be saints:

Grace and peace to you from God our Father and from the Lord Jesus Christ.

Paul's Longing to Visit Rome

[8]First, I thank my God through Jesus Christ for all of you, because your faith is being reported all over the world. [9]God, whom I serve with my whole heart in preaching the gospel of his Son, is my witness how constantly I remember you [10]in my prayers at all times; and I pray that now at last by God's will the way may be opened for me to come to you.

[11]I long to see you so that I may impart to you some spiritual gift to make you strong— [12]that is, that you and I may be mutually encouraged by each other's faith. [13]I do not want you to be unaware, brothers, that I planned many times to

---

a4 Or who as to his spirit   *b4 Or was appointed to be the Son of God with power*

come to you (but have been prevented from doing so until now) in order that I might have a harvest among you, just as I have had among the other Gentiles. ¹⁴I am obligated both to Greeks and non-Greeks, both to the wise and the foolish. ¹⁵That is why I am so eager to preach the gospel also to you who are at Rome.

¹⁶I am not ashamed of the gospel, because it is the power of God for the salvation of everyone who believes: first for the Jew, then for the Gentile. ¹⁷For in the gospel a righteousness from God is revealed, a righteousness that is by faith from first to last,ᵃ just as it is written: "The righteous will live by faith."ᵇ

1:17 Luther's Gateway

Verses 16–17, a capsule summary of Paul's message to the Romans, changed Martin Luther forever. After he finally understood the phrase "righteousness from God," Luther said, "I felt myself to be reborn and to have gone through open doors into paradise. The whole of Scripture took on a new meaning . . . . This passage of Paul became to me a gateway to heaven."

God's Wrath Against Mankind

¹⁸The wrath of God is being revealed from heaven against all the godlessness and wickedness of men who suppress the truth by their wickedness, ¹⁹since what may be known about God is plain to them, because God has made it plain to them. ²⁰For since the creation of the world God's invisible qualities—his eternal power and divine nature—have been clearly seen, being understood from what has been made, so that men are without excuse.

1:20 No Excuses

From Adam and Eve onward, people have tended to blame others, not themselves, for what goes wrong. Romans 1–3 sets forth an important principle that has been widely recognized by recovery groups such as Alcoholics Anonymous: Unless you first accept responsibility for wrong behavior and stop blaming others, you'll never get well.

²¹For although they knew God, they neither glorified him as God nor gave thanks to him, but their thinking became futile and their foolish hearts were darkened. ²²Although they claimed to be wise, they became fools ²³and exchanged the glory of the immortal God for images made to look like mortal man and birds and animals and reptiles.

²⁴Therefore God gave them over in the sinful desires of their hearts to sexual impurity for the degrading of their bodies with one another. ²⁵They exchanged the truth of God for a lie, and worshiped and served created things rather than the Creator—who is forever praised. Amen.

²⁶Because of this, God gave them over to shameful lusts. Even their women exchanged natural relations for unnatural ones. ²⁷In the same way the men also abandoned natural relations with women and were inflamed with lust for one another. Men committed indecent acts with other men, and received in themselves the due penalty for their perversion.

²⁸Furthermore, since they did not think it worthwhile to retain the knowledge of God, he gave them over to a depraved mind, to do what ought not to be done. ²⁹They have become filled with every kind of wickedness, evil, greed and depravity. They are full of envy, murder, strife, deceit and malice. They are gossips, ³⁰slanderers, God-haters, insolent, arrogant and boastful; they invent ways of doing evil; they disobey their parents; ³¹they are senseless, faithless, heartless, ruthless. ³²Although they know God's righteous decree that those who do such things deserve death, they not only continue to do these very things but also approve of those who practice them.

God's Righteous Judgment

2 You, therefore, have no excuse, you who pass judgment on someone else, for at whatever point you judge the other, you are condemning yourself, because you who pass judgment do the

2:1 Unsettling Proverbs

"It takes one to know one." "The pot calls the kettle black." Or, as the Spanish say, "The donkey calls the pig 'long ears.' " All these proverbs echo Paul's point: We often criticize in others the very thing we ourselves say or do.

same things. ²Now we know that God's judgment against those who do such things is based on truth. ³So when you, a mere man, pass judgment on them and yet do the same things, do you think you will escape God's judgment? ⁴Or do you show contempt for the riches of his kindness, tolerance and patience, not realizing that God's kindness leads you toward repentance?

⁵But because of your stubbornness and your

ᵃ17 Or *is from faith to faith*   ᵇ17 Hab. 2:4

unrepentant heart, you are storing up wrath against yourself for the day of God's wrath, when his righteous judgment will be revealed. ⁶God "will give to each person according to what he has done."ᵃ ⁷To those who by persistence in doing good seek glory, honor and immortality, he will give eternal life. ⁸But for those who are self-seeking and who reject the truth and follow evil, there will be wrath and anger. ⁹There will be trouble and distress for every human being who does evil: first for the Jew, then for the Gentile; ¹⁰but glory, honor and peace for everyone who does good: first for the Jew, then for the Gentile. ¹¹For God does not show favoritism.

¹²All who sin apart from the law will also perish apart from the law, and all who sin under the law will be judged by the law. ¹³For it is not those who hear the law who are righteous in God's sight, but it is those who obey the law who will be declared righteous. ¹⁴(Indeed, when Gentiles, who do not have the law, do by nature things required by the law, they are a law for themselves, even though they do not have the law, ¹⁵since

they show that the requirements of the law are written on their hearts, their consciences also bearing witness, and their thoughts now accusing, now even defending them.) ¹⁶This will take place on the day when God will judge men's secrets through Jesus Christ, as my gospel declares.

The Jews and the Law

¹⁷Now you, if you call yourself a Jew; if you rely on the law and brag about your relationship to God; ¹⁸if you know his will and approve of what is superior because you are instructed by the law; ¹⁹if you are convinced that you are a guide for the blind, a light for those who are in the dark, ²⁰an instructor of the foolish, a teacher of infants, because you have in the law the embodiment of knowledge and truth— ²¹you, then, who teach others, do you not teach yourself? You who preach against stealing, do you steal? ²²You who say that people should not commit adultery, do you commit adultery? You who abhor idols, do you rob temples? ²³You who brag

ᵃ6 Psalm 62:12; Prov. 24:12

PAUL *Turnaround*

THOUGH PAUL BEGAN HIS CAREER as a fanatical enemy of Christianity, he became its greatest leader. After Jesus, he is unquestionably the most important person in the New Testament. Paul was not just an activist committed to the cause, and not just a theologian thinking deep thoughts about God. He was *both*—and his passionate, committed life still serves as a model.

Unlike the twelve apostles, Paul started out with status and education. He was born a Roman citizen, a rare and precious privilege for any Jew. Paul's fluent Greek writings show him to be a man of the world, well versed in secular literature.

Fundamentally, though, Paul saw himself as a devout Jew. He had studied theology in Jerusalem under the famous rabbi Gamaliel. He joined the campaign to arrest, imprison and even execute Christians because he believed they were blaspheming God by worshiping a man, and he was determined to stamp out such heresy.

Jesus' searing appearance on the road to Damascus turned Paul's life upside down (Acts 9:1–19). In one of the most dramatic conversions ever, Paul became the very thing he had so hated—a Christian. Paul later wrote to the Philippian believers, "For to me, to live is Christ" (Philippians 1:21). Nobody could doubt it. A passionate focus on Jesus shines through every line he wrote and was the reason for every mile he traveled. He remains what every Christian means by "Christ-centered."

Some years passed, though, before Paul found his role. He discovered it in Antioch, an important Roman city in modern-day Turkey, where the first sizable congregation of non-Jewish Christians sprang up. From then on Paul was every inch a missionary, taking the Good News about Jesus to the whole world. He traveled almost incessantly, moving from city to city around the Mediterranean Sea, preaching to both Jews and Gentiles.

Paul's life was marked with excitement: a shipwreck, a snakebite, beatings, narrow escapes. He started many churches, and thirteen letters of the New Testament have his name on them—all of them addressing problems in those first churches.

Though Paul never stopped thinking of himself as a devout Jew, he spent much of his life explaining that Jews and Gentiles were equally loved by God. Many people talk about racial reconciliation. Paul was one of the first to fight for it. He struggled hard against those who wanted Gentiles to submit to the whole Jewish law. Non-Jewish Christians, he was determined, should be considered first-class citizens of the kingdom of God. Faith in Jesus was all that God required.

Life Questions: To what role does God call you? How does your pursuit of that compare with the apostle Paul's?

about the law, do you dishonor God by breaking the law? [24]As it is written: "God's name is blasphemed among the Gentiles because of you."[a]

[25]Circumcision has value if you observe the law, but if you break the law, you have become as though you had not been circumcised. [26]If those who are not circumcised keep the law's requirements, will they not be regarded as though they were circumcised? [27]The one who is not circumcised physically and yet obeys the law will condemn you who, even though you have the[b] written code and circumcision, are a lawbreaker.

[28]A man is not a Jew if he is only one outwardly, nor is circumcision merely outward and physical. [29]No, a man is a Jew if he is one inwardly; and circumcision is circumcision of the heart, by the Spirit, not by the written code. Such a man's praise is not from men, but from God.

God's Faithfulness

3 What advantage, then, is there in being a Jew, or what value is there in circumcision? [2]Much in every way! First of all, they have been entrusted with the very words of God.

[3]What if some did not have faith? Will their lack of faith nullify God's faithfulness? [4]Not at all! Let God be true, and every man a liar. As it is written:

"So that you may be proved right when you speak
and prevail when you judge."[c]

[5]But if our unrighteousness brings out God's righteousness more clearly, what shall we say? That God is unjust in bringing his wrath on us? (I am using a human argument.) [6]Certainly not! If that were so, how could God judge the world? [7]Someone might argue, "If my falsehood enhances God's truthfulness and so increases his glory, why am I still condemned as a sinner?" [8]Why not say—as we are being slanderously reported as saying and as some claim that we say— "Let us do evil that good may result"? Their condemnation is deserved.

No One Is Righteous

[9]What shall we conclude then? Are we any better[d]? Not at all! We have already made the charge that Jews and Gentiles alike are all under sin. [10]As it is written:

"There is no one righteous, not even one;
[11] there is no one who understands,
  no one who seeks God.
[12]All have turned away,
  they have together become worthless;
  there is no one who does good,

not even one."[e]
[13]"Their throats are open graves;
  their tongues practice deceit."[f]
"The poison of vipers is on their lips."[g]
[14] "Their mouths are full of cursing and
  bitterness."[h]

3:10–18 Need for a Cure

If a doctor suddenly appeared on a television news program announcing, in an excited voice, a cure for the Paraguayan flu, who would notice? For his discovery to impress us so deeply that we would seek vaccination, he would first need to prove the terrible danger of the unknown virus.

Paul's message in Romans is the great news about God's amazing grace: A complete cure is available to all. But people won't seek a cure until they know they are ill. Thus, Romans begins with one of the darkest descriptions in the Bible. Paul concludes, "There is no one righteous, not even one." The entire world is doomed to spiritual death unless a cure can be found.

[15]"Their feet are swift to shed blood;
[16] ruin and misery mark their ways,
[17]and the way of peace they do not know."[i]
[18] "There is no fear of God before their
  eyes."[j]

[19]Now we know that whatever the law says, it says to those who are under the law, so that every mouth may be silenced and the whole world held accountable to God. [20]Therefore no one will be declared righteous in his sight by observing the law; rather, through the law we become conscious of sin.

Righteousness Through Faith

[21]But now a righteousness from God, apart from law, has been made known, to which the Law and the Prophets testify. [22]This righteousness from God comes through faith in Jesus Christ to all who believe. There is no difference, [23]for all have sinned and fall short of the glory of God, [24]and are justified freely by his grace through the redemption that came by Christ Jesus. [25]God presented him as a sacrifice of atonement,[k] through faith in his blood. He did this to demonstrate his justice, because in his forbearance he had left the sins committed beforehand unpunished— [26]he did it to demonstrate his justice at the present time, so as to be

[a]24 Isaiah 52:5; Ezek. 36:22   [b]27 Or who, by means of a   [c]4 Psalm 51:4   [d]9 Or worse   [e]12 Psalms 14:1-3;
53:1-3; Eccles. 7:20   [f]13 Psalm 5:9   [g]13 Psalm 140:3   [h]14 Psalm 10:7   [i]17 Isaiah 59:7,8
[j]18 Psalm 36:1   [k]25 Or as the one who would turn aside his wrath, taking away sin

just and the one who justifies those who have faith in Jesus.

[27]Where, then, is boasting? It is excluded. On what principle? On that of observing the law? No, but on that of faith. [28]For we maintain that a man is justified by faith apart from observing the law. [29]Is God the God of Jews only? Is he not the God of Gentiles too? Yes, of Gentiles too, [30]since there is only one God, who will justify the circumcised by faith and the uncircumcised through that same faith. [31]Do we, then, nullify the law by this faith? Not at all! Rather, we uphold the law.

Abraham Justified by Faith

4 What then shall we say that Abraham, our forefather, discovered in this matter? [2]If, in fact, Abraham was justified by works, he had something to boast about—but not before God. [3]What does the Scripture say? "Abraham believed God, and it was credited to him as righteousness."[a]

[4]Now when a man works, his wages are not credited to him as a gift, but as an obligation. [5]However, to the man who does not work but trusts God who justifies the wicked, his faith is credited as righteousness. [6]David says the same thing when he speaks of the blessedness of the man to whom God credits righteousness apart from works:

[7]"Blessed are they
    whose transgressions are forgiven,
    whose sins are covered.
[8]Blessed is the man
    whose sin the Lord will never count
        against him."[b]

[9]Is this blessedness only for the circumcised, or also for the uncircumcised? We have been saying that Abraham's faith was credited to him as righteousness. [10]Under what circumstances was it credited? Was it after he was circumcised, or before? It was not after, but before! [11]And he received the sign of circumcision, a seal of the righteousness that he had by faith while he was still uncircumcised. So then, he is the father of all who believe but have not been circumcised, in order that righteousness might be credited to them. [12]And he is also the father of the circumcised who not only are circumcised but who also walk in the footsteps of the faith that our father Abraham had before he was circumcised.

[13]It was not through law that Abraham and his offspring received the promise that he would be heir of the world, but through the righteousness that comes by faith. [14]For if those who live by law are heirs, faith has no value and the promise is worthless, [15]because law brings wrath. And where there is no law there is no transgression.

[16]Therefore, the promise comes by faith, so that it may be by grace and may be guaranteed to all Abraham's offspring—not only to those who are of the law but also to those who are of the

4:13 How to Please God

Paul goes to great lengths in chapter 4 to make a theological point. He traces the Jewish heritage back to Abraham, who lived hundreds of years before Moses and the Old Testament law. Abraham, says Paul, pleased God exactly as we do: through faith. The Old Testament law was never meant to bridge the gap between God and people. Only Jesus Christ could do that. Paul stresses that the law was given not to bring about redemption, but to point up the need for it (5:20).

faith of Abraham. He is the father of us all. [17]As it is written: "I have made you a father of many nations."[c] He is our father in the sight of God, in whom he believed—the God who gives life to the dead and calls things that are not as though they were.

[18]Against all hope, Abraham in hope believed and so became the father of many nations, just as it had been said to him, "So shall your offspring be."[d] [19]Without weakening in his faith, he faced the fact that his body was as good as dead—since he was about a hundred years old—and that Sarah's womb was also dead. [20]Yet he did not waver through unbelief regarding the promise of God, but was strengthened in his faith and gave glory to God, [21]being fully persuaded that God had power to do what he had promised. [22]This is why "it was credited to him as righteousness." [23]The words "it was credited to him" were written not for him alone, [24]but also for us, to whom God will credit righteousness—for us who believe in him who raised Jesus our Lord from the dead. [25]He was delivered over to death for our sins and was raised to life for our justification.

Peace and Joy

5 Therefore, since we have been justified through faith, we[e] have peace with God through our Lord Jesus Christ, [2]through whom we have gained access by faith into this grace in which we now stand. And we[e] rejoice in the hope of the glory of God. [3]Not only so, but we[e] also rejoice in our sufferings, because we know that suffering produces perseverance; [4]perseverance, character; and character, hope. [5]And hope does not disappoint us, because God has poured out his love into our hearts by the Holy Spirit, whom he has given us.

[a]3 Gen. 15:6; also in verse 22   [b]8 Psalm 32:1,2   [c]17 Gen. 17:5   [d]18 Gen. 15:5   [e]1,2,3 Or *let us*

A Modern Peace Child

God spans the gulf

DON RICHARDSON SPENT SEVERAL FRUSTRATING years among the Sawi tribe in New Guinea. He had come from America as an anthropologist/missionary, hoping to bring the Christian message to a nearly stone-age tribe. But his message kept colliding with the tribe's unusual beliefs.

Christian values of love and forgiveness had no appeal to the Sawi, for they held up deceit as the highest virtue. They saw no reason to change their patterns of cruelty and cannibalism. In fact, when Richardson told them the story of Jesus, only one incident sparked their interest: the story of Judas's betrayal! To the Sawi, Judas was a genuine hero; he had shrewdly penetrated the trusted inner circle of disciples before turning against Jesus.

> *Very rarely will anyone die for a righteous man, though for a good man someone might possibly dare to die. But God demonstrates his own love for us in this: While we were still sinners, Christ died for us.*
> *5:7–8*

A Mysterious Ceremony

Every time Richardson tried to share Christ with the Sawi, the attempt miscarried. Finally, after watching the fourteenth bloody battle fought outside his home, Richardson reached the end of his patience. How could he ever break through to such violent people? He decided to leave New Guinea, despite the Sawi's pleas that he stay.

Just before Richardson left, the Sawi and their deadly enemies, the Haenam tribe, staged an elaborate ceremony in front of his home. It was their final effort to convince the missionary to stay.

The entire village gathered to watch the event. All were silent except the Sawi chief's wife. She screamed loudly as the chief seized their six-month-old baby from her arms and held him high in the air. The chief then carried his son to the enemy chief and gave him to his enemies. A member of the tribe explained to Richardson that the Haenam tribe would rename the baby and rear him as one of its own.

Breakthrough

Richardson knew that no Sawi could be fully trusted, since any action might be part of an elaborate deception. But that memorable day he learned of the one great exception: the peace child. A chief's giving his own son to his enemies—that profound, painful act would overcome all suspicion. By mutual agreement, as long as the peace child lived, no wars could be fought between the two tribes.

Something clicked in Don Richardson's mind as he watched the spectacle. At last he had found an analogy—a parallel story—built into the Sawi's culture that could convey the message of a forgiving God. He gathered members of the tribe around him and, with a pounding heart and dry throat, told them of God's peace child. God had sent his own Son, Jesus, to live among enemies, to make peace with humankind.

A Key Passage

Perhaps Paul felt that same pounding heart and dry throat as he presented in 11 concise verses, Romans 3:21–31, the meaning of God's offering of his peace child Jesus. The first part of Romans spelled out the vast gulf between God and people. Now Paul describes how God spanned this gulf. Some have called this section "the central theological passage in the Bible."

After stating the facts, Paul backs them up with historical proofs in chapters 4 and 5. American politicians often defend their positions by appealing to founding fathers, men like George Washington and Abraham Lincoln. Similarly, Paul keeps his Jewish audience in mind. He supports his concepts by citing Abraham, Moses, and even Adam.

Christ's death, says Paul, was not a new idea, an addition to the Old Testament law. Rather, it was the completion of the law, what the Old Testament implied and foreshadowed. Like the Sawi, the Jewish culture had its own "redemptive analogies"; and they all found true fulfillment in Jesus Christ.

Life Questions: Have you ever felt far from God? Does Romans 3–5 say anything that might help during those times?

[6]You see, at just the right time, when we were still powerless, Christ died for the ungodly. [7]Very rarely will anyone die for a righteous man, though for a good man someone might possibly

5:1 What It's There For

In Romans, Paul constructs a step-by-step argument much like a legal brief, as shown by his frequent use of the legalese word "therefore" (20 times in all). Step one: No one is righteous and we all need help (3:20); Step two: God has provided that help in the form of his Son, making peace with us (5:11); Step three: Therefore God no longer condemns those who are in Christ (8:1).

dare to die. [8]But God demonstrates his own love for us in this: While we were still sinners, Christ died for us.

[9]Since we have now been justified by his blood, how much more shall we be saved from God's wrath through him! [10]For if, when we were God's enemies, we were reconciled to him through the death of his Son, how much more, having been reconciled, shall we be saved through his life! [11]Not only is this so, but we also rejoice in God through our Lord Jesus Christ, through whom we have now received reconciliation.

Death Through Adam, Life Through Christ

[12]Therefore, just as sin entered the world through one man, and death through sin, and in this way death came to all men, because all sinned— [13]for before the law was given, sin was in the world. But sin is not taken into account when there is no law. [14]Nevertheless, death reigned from the time of Adam to the time of Moses, even over those who did not sin by breaking a command, as did Adam, who was a pattern of the one to come.

[15]But the gift is not like the trespass. For if the many died by the trespass of the one man, how much more did God's grace and the gift that came by the grace of the one man, Jesus Christ, overflow to the many! [16]Again, the gift of God is not like the result of the one man's sin: The judgment followed one sin and brought condemnation, but the gift followed many trespasses and brought justification. [17]For if, by the trespass of the one man, death reigned through that one man, how much more will those who receive God's abundant provision of grace and of the gift of righteousness reign in life through the one man, Jesus Christ.

[18]Consequently, just as the result of one trespass was condemnation for all men, so also the result of one act of righteousness was justification that brings life for all men. [19]For just as through the disobedience of the one man the many were made sinners, so also through the obedience of the one man the many will be made righteous.

[20]The law was added so that the trespass might increase. But where sin increased, grace increased all the more, [21]so that, just as sin reigned in death, so also grace might reign through righteousness to bring eternal life through Jesus Christ our Lord.

Dead to Sin, Alive in Christ

6 What shall we say, then? Shall we go on sinning so that grace may increase? [2]By no means! We died to sin; how can we live in it any longer? [3]Or don't you know that all of us who were baptized into Christ Jesus were baptized into his death? [4]We were therefore buried with him through baptism into death in order that, just as Christ was raised from the dead through the glory of the Father, we too may live a new life.

6:1 More Sin, More Forgiveness?

Paul often uses this writing technique: He pauses in the middle of an argument to answer objections or questions that may be occurring to the reader. Some people have actually reached the conclusion that horrifies Paul in this passage. The Russian monk Rasputin, for example, concluded, "I'll sin more to earn more forgiveness." He lived a bizarre life of immorality.

[5]If we have been united with him like this in his death, we will certainly also be united with him in his resurrection. [6]For we know that our old self was crucified with him so that the body of sin might be done away with,[a] that we should no longer be slaves to sin— [7]because anyone who has died has been freed from sin.

[8]Now if we died with Christ, we believe that we will also live with him. [9]For we know that since Christ was raised from the dead, he cannot die again; death no longer has mastery over him. [10]The death he died, he died to sin once for all; but the life he lives, he lives to God.

[11]In the same way, count yourselves dead to sin but alive to God in Christ Jesus. [12]Therefore do not let sin reign in your mortal body so that you obey its evil desires. [13]Do not offer the parts of your body to sin, as instruments of wickedness, but rather offer yourselves to God, as those who have been brought from death to life; and

---

[a]6 Or *be rendered powerless*

offer the parts of your body to him as instruments of righteousness. ¹⁴For sin shall not be your master, because you are not under law, but under grace.

Slaves to Righteousness

¹⁵What then? Shall we sin because we are not under law but under grace? By no means! ¹⁶Don't you know that when you offer yourselves to someone to obey him as slaves, you are slaves to the one whom you obey—whether you are slaves to sin, which leads to death, or to obedience, which leads to righteousness? ¹⁷But thanks be to God that, though you used to be slaves to sin, you wholeheartedly obeyed the form of teaching to which you were entrusted. ¹⁸You have been set free from sin and have become slaves to righteousness.

¹⁹I put this in human terms because you are weak in your natural selves. Just as you used to offer the parts of your body in slavery to impurity and to ever-increasing wickedness, so now offer them in slavery to righteousness leading to holiness. ²⁰When you were slaves to sin, you were free from the control of righteousness. ²¹What benefit did you reap at that time from the things you are now ashamed of? Those things result in death! ²²But now that you have been set free from sin and have become slaves to God, the benefit you reap leads to holiness, and the result is eternal life. ²³For the wages of sin is death, but the gift of God is eternal life in*ᵃ* Christ Jesus our Lord.

An Illustration From Marriage

7 Do you not know, brothers—for I am speaking to men who know the law—that the law has authority over a man only as long as he lives? ²For example, by law a married woman is bound

ᵃ23 Or through

Inner Struggles
A battle, and a victory

> So I find this law at work: When I want to do good, evil is right there with me.
> 7:21

THE FIRST PART OF ROMANS paints a grand picture of God's grace and forgiveness, so grand that Paul opens himself up to some tricky questions. "I think I like what I'm hearing," a devious person may exclaim as he or she finishes the first part of Romans. "The more I sin, the more opportunity God has to forgive me, right? Then I can live any way I want!"

In chapter 6, Paul reacts to the "Now I have an excuse to sin" line of thinking with shock and outrage. And then he turns to practical issues in the Christian life. Why is it that sin is so hard to overcome? Does God forgive every sin, no matter how bad? What really happens when we become Christians? Do we change or don't we?

Illustrations from Life

When Paul was trying to be a good person (by keeping all the law) in his own strength, he was ultimately defeated by his own problem. Although his intentions were good, he was attempting to win the battle over sin by his own plan and ability. There is only one solution to that kind of struggle. Paul concludes at the end, "What a wretched man I am! Who will rescue me from this body of death? Thanks be to God—through Jesus Christ our Lord!" (7:24–25a).

The very best proof of the Christian faith is a believer with a changed life. Paul calls Christians to "count yourselves dead to sin but alive to God in Christ Jesus" (6:11), and he wrote as if this were really possible!

A Final Answer

Then, like a gust of fresh air, chapter 8 follows with one of the most hopeful passages in the Bible. The Holy Spirit is its theme, and Paul defines the Spirit's role in our lives. The Spirit works alongside us as we relate to God, even praying for us when we don't know what to ask (8:26). Mainly, the Spirit teaches us the benefits of being a child of God.

Conflict won't disappear completely yet, says Paul, for we are part of a "groaning," imperfect creation (8:18–25). But with God working for us, we can be *more than* conquerors, and one day God will make all of creation perfect again. That promise should assure us that nothing can separate us from God's love (8:38–39).

Life Questions: Which person do you identify with—the one who is struggling to please God on personal strength alone, or the one who is trusting in Christ for victory over sin?

to her husband as long as he is alive, but if her husband dies, she is released from the law of marriage. [3]So then, if she marries another man while her husband is still alive, she is called an adulteress. But if her husband dies, she is released from that law and is not an adulteress, even though she marries another man.

[4]So, my brothers, you also died to the law through the body of Christ, that you might belong to another, to him who was raised from the dead, in order that we might bear fruit to God. [5]For when we were controlled by the sinful nature,[a] the sinful passions aroused by the law were at work in our bodies, so that we bore fruit for death. [6]But now, by dying to what once bound us, we have been released from the law so that we serve in the new way of the Spirit, and not in the old way of the written code.

Struggling With Sin

[7]What shall we say, then? Is the law sin? Certainly not! Indeed I would not have known what sin was except through the law. For I would not have known what coveting really was if the law

7:7 Hidden Dangers

A strict disciplinarian like Paul had little trouble keeping most of the Ten Commandments. Outward actions such as swearing, murder, adultery, stealing, and lying could be measured and controlled. But the internal, invisible sin of coveting proved far more bedeviling. As Jesus made clear in the Sermon on the Mount, invisible sins like coveting, lust, and anger can have the same toxic effects as the more outward manifestations of stealing, adultery, and murder.

had not said, "Do not covet."[b] [8]But sin, seizing the opportunity afforded by the commandment, produced in me every kind of covetous desire. For apart from law, sin is dead. [9]Once I was alive apart from law; but when the commandment came, sin sprang to life and I died. [10]I found that the very commandment that was intended to bring life actually brought death. [11]For sin, seizing the opportunity afforded by the commandment, deceived me, and through the commandment put me to death. [12]So then, the law is holy, and the commandment is holy, righteous and good.

[13]Did that which is good, then, become death to me? By no means! But in order that sin might be recognized as sin, it produced death in me

through what was good, so that through the commandment sin might become utterly sinful.

[14]We know that the law is spiritual; but I am unspiritual, sold as a slave to sin. [15]I do not understand what I do. For what I want to do I do not do, but what I hate I do. [16]And if I do what I do not want to do, I agree that the law is good. [17]As it is, it is no longer I myself who do it, but it is sin living in me. [18]I know that nothing good lives in me, that is, in my sinful nature.[c] For I have the desire to do what is good, but I cannot carry it out. [19]For what I do is not the good I want to do; no, the evil I do not want to do—this I keep on doing. [20]Now if I do what I do not want to do, it is no longer I who do it, but it is sin living in me that does it.

[21]So I find this law at work: When I want to do good, evil is right there with me. [22]For in my inner being I delight in God's law; [23]but I see another law at work in the members of my body, waging war against the law of my mind and making me a prisoner of the law of sin at work within my members. [24]What a wretched man I am! Who will rescue me from this body of death? [25]Thanks be to God—through Jesus Christ our Lord!

So then, I myself in my mind am a slave to God's law, but in the sinful nature a slave to the law of sin.

Life Through the Spirit

8 Therefore, there is now no condemnation for those who are in Christ Jesus,[d] [2]because through Christ Jesus the law of the Spirit of life set me free from the law of sin and death. [3]For what the law was powerless to do in that it was weakened by the sinful nature,[e] God did by sending his own Son in the likeness of sinful man to be a sin offering.[f] And so he condemned sin in sinful man,[g] [4]in order that the righteous requirements of the law might be fully met in us, who do not live according to the sinful nature but according to the Spirit.

[5]Those who live according to the sinful nature have their minds set on what that nature desires; but those who live in accordance with the Spirit have their minds set on what the Spirit desires. [6]The mind of sinful man[h] is death, but the mind controlled by the Spirit is life and peace; [7]the sinful mind[i] is hostile to God. It does not submit to God's law, nor can it do so. [8]Those controlled by the sinful nature cannot please God.

[9]You, however, are controlled not by the sinful nature but by the Spirit, if the Spirit of God lives in you. And if anyone does not have the Spirit of Christ, he does not belong to Christ. [10]But if Christ is in you, your body is dead because of sin,

a5 Or the flesh; also in verse 25   b7 Exodus 20:17; Deut. 5:21   c18 Or my flesh   d1 Some later manuscripts Jesus, who do not live according to the sinful nature but according to the Spirit,   e3 Or the flesh; also in verses 4, 5, 8, 9, 12 and 13   f3 Or man, for sin   g3 Or in the flesh   h6 Or mind set on the flesh   i7 Or the mind set on the flesh

yet your spirit is alive because of righteousness. [11]And if the Spirit of him who raised Jesus from the dead is living in you, he who raised Christ from the dead will also give life to your mortal bodies through his Spirit, who lives in you.

[12]Therefore, brothers, we have an obligation—but it is not to the sinful nature, to live according to it. [13]For if you live according to the sinful nature, you will die; but if by the Spirit you put to death the misdeeds of the body, you will live, [14]because those who are led by the Spirit of God are sons of God. [15]For you did not receive a spirit that makes you a slave again to fear, but you received the Spirit of sonship.[a] And by him we cry, "Abba,[b] Father." [16]The Spirit himself testifies with our spirit that we are God's children. [17]Now if we are children, then we are heirs—heirs of God and co-heirs with Christ, if indeed we share in his sufferings in order that we may also share in his glory.

Future Glory

[18]I consider that our present sufferings are not worth comparing with the glory that will be revealed in us. [19]The creation waits in eager expectation for the sons of God to be revealed. [20]For the creation was subjected to frustration, not by its own choice, but by the will of the one who subjected it, in hope [21]that[c] the creation itself will be liberated from its bondage to decay and brought into the glorious freedom of the children of God.

8:18 Worth the Struggle

Paul never minimizes suffering; after all, his own life included beatings, imprisonment, shipwrecks, assassination attempts, and chronic illness. But he insists with absolute conviction that future rewards will outweigh all present sufferings.

Olympic athletes endure years of eight-hour practice sessions and much discipline and pain for the goal of winning a gold medal. Similarly, the Christian's life on earth may involve many difficulties (verses 22–23), but the end result will make them seem worthwhile.

[22]We know that the whole creation has been groaning as in the pains of childbirth right up to the present time. [23]Not only so, but we ourselves, who have the firstfruits of the Spirit, groan inwardly as we wait eagerly for our adoption as sons, the redemption of our bodies. [24]For in this hope we were saved. But hope that is seen is no hope at all. Who hopes for what he already has? [25]But if we hope for what we do not yet have, we wait for it patiently.

[26]In the same way, the Spirit helps us in our weakness. We do not know what we ought to pray for, but the Spirit himself intercedes for us with groans that words cannot express. [27]And he who searches our hearts knows the mind of the Spirit, because the Spirit intercedes for the saints in accordance with God's will.

More Than Conquerors

[28]And we know that in all things God works for the good of those who love him,[d] who[e] have

8:28 Only Good Things?

This famous verse is often misquoted or stretched to mean more than it says. It should be read along with the next two paragraphs. Paul doesn't promise that only good, or pleasurable, things will come to the Christian. What he does say is that even the difficult experiences described in verses 35–39 can be used in God's overall plan for good. And nothing can separate us from the love of God.

been called according to his purpose. [29]For those God foreknew he also predestined to be conformed to the likeness of his Son, that he might be the firstborn among many brothers. [30]And those he predestined, he also called; those he called, he also justified; those he justified, he also glorified.

[31]What, then, shall we say in response to this? If God is for us, who can be against us? [32]He who did not spare his own Son, but gave him up for us all—how will he not also, along with him, graciously give us all things? [33]Who will bring any charge against those whom God has chosen? It is God who justifies. [34]Who is he that condemns? Christ Jesus, who died—more than that, who was raised to life—is at the right hand of God and is also interceding for us. [35]Who shall separate us from the love of Christ? Shall trouble or hardship or persecution or famine or nakedness or danger or sword? [36]As it is written:

"For your sake we face death all day long;
    we are considered as sheep to be
        slaughtered."[f]

[37]No, in all these things we are more than conquerors through him who loved us. [38]For I am convinced that neither death nor life, neither angels nor demons,[g] neither the present nor the future, nor any powers, [39]neither height nor

depth, nor anything else in all creation, will be able to separate us from the love of God that is in Christ Jesus our Lord.

God's Sovereign Choice

9 I speak the truth in Christ—I am not lying, my conscience confirms it in the Holy Spirit— ²I have great sorrow and unceasing anguish in my heart. ³For I could wish that I myself were cursed and cut off from Christ for the sake of my brothers, those of my own race, ⁴the people of Israel. Theirs is the adoption as sons; theirs the divine glory, the covenants, the receiving of the law, the temple worship and the promises. ⁵Theirs are the patriarchs, and from them is traced the human ancestry of Christ, who is God over all, forever praised!ᵃ Amen.

⁶It is not as though God's word had failed. For not all who are descended from Israel are Israel. ⁷Nor because they are his descendants are they all Abraham's children. On the contrary, "It is through Isaac that your offspring will be reckoned."ᵇ ⁸In other words, it is not the natural children who are God's children, but it is the children of the promise who are regarded as Abraham's offspring. ⁹For this was how the promise was stated: "At the appointed time I will return, and Sarah will have a son."ᶜ

¹⁰Not only that, but Rebekah's children had one and the same father, our father Isaac. ¹¹Yet, before the twins were born or had done anything good or bad—in order that God's purpose in election might stand: ¹²not by works but by him who calls—she was told, "The older will serve the younger."ᵈ ¹³Just as it is written: "Jacob I loved, but Esau I hated."ᵉ

¹⁴What then shall we say? Is God unjust? Not at all! ¹⁵For he says to Moses,

"I will have mercy on whom I have mercy,
and I will have compassion on whom I
have compassion."ᶠ

¹⁶It does not, therefore, depend on man's desire or effort, but on God's mercy. ¹⁷For the Scripture says to Pharaoh: "I raised you up for this very purpose, that I might display my power in you and that my name might be proclaimed in all the earth."ᵍ ¹⁸Therefore God has mercy on whom he wants to have mercy, and he hardens whom he wants to harden.

¹⁹One of you will say to me: "Then why does God still blame us? For who resists his will?" ²⁰But who are you, O man, to talk back to God?

ᵃ5 Or *Christ, who is over all. God be forever praised!* Or *Christ. God who is over all be forever praised!*   ᵇ7 Gen. 21:12
ᶜ9 Gen. 18:10,14   ᵈ12 Gen. 25:23   ᵉ13 Mal. 1:2,3   ᶠ15 Exodus 33:19   ᵍ17 Exodus 9:16

A Crushing Blow to Paul
Does God break his promises?

> *I have great sorrow and unceasing anguish in my heart. 9:2*

DOES ANYTHING BRING MORE PAIN to a new Christian than family rejection? A teenager converts to Christianity. Her parents overreact, assuming their daughter has fallen for some weird cult. They slap away all her attempts to present the appealing facts of the gospel. What is good news for her is seen as bad news by the family.

Some new Christians can melt down the walls of suspicion and hostility. But others are treated like diseased persons by other family members and forced to live in a state of emotional quarantine.

Anyone who has lived through such an experience can understand the agonizing dilemma Paul faced. Members of his own race, the Jews, were rejecting the gospel he had committed his life to.

Can God Be Trusted?

Rejection by the Jews was a crushing blow to Paul, and he interrupted his letter to the Romans to consider the dilemma. These three chapters (9—11) contain some of his strongest words ever, including an offer to forfeit his own relationship with Christ for the sake of his race (9:3).

The issues discussed here apply to non-Jews as well, for they raise basic questions about God. Had he given up on the Jewish people, ignoring the promises he made to them in Old Testament times? If so, couldn't he also break promises made to us today?

For Paul, a Jew who called himself an apostle to the Gentiles, no other issue was so important to resolve. He couldn't rest until he linked the brilliant theology set forth in Romans to God's past, present, and future activity among the Jews.

Life Questions: Romans 9—11 explains how God worked with people disappointed in him: the Jews. Have you ever been deeply disappointed in God? What does Paul say that might help answer your questions?

"Shall what is formed say to him who formed it, 'Why did you make me like this?'"[a] 21Does not the potter have the right to make out of the same lump of clay some pottery for noble purposes and some for common use?

9:19 Questions, Anyone?

Frequently Paul interrupts his writing with a question or series of questions. In doing so, he is imitating the style he learned from rabbis in his earlier training. The story is told of one student who asked, "Why do you rabbis so often put your teaching in the form of a question?" The reply: "So what's wrong with a question?"

22What if God, choosing to show his wrath and make his power known, bore with great patience the objects of his wrath—prepared for destruction? 23What if he did this to make the riches of his glory known to the objects of his mercy, whom he prepared in advance for glory— 24even us, whom he also called, not only from the Jews but also from the Gentiles? 25As he says in Hosea:

"I will call them 'my people' who are not my people;
    and I will call her 'my loved one' who is not my loved one,"[b]

26and,

"It will happen that in the very place where it was said to them,
    'You are not my people,'
they will be called 'sons of the living God.'"[c]

27Isaiah cries out concerning Israel:

"Though the number of the Israelites be like the sand by the sea,
    only the remnant will be saved.
28For the Lord will carry out
    his sentence on earth with speed and finality."[d]

29It is just as Isaiah said previously:

"Unless the Lord Almighty
    had left us descendants,
we would have become like Sodom,
    we would have been like Gomorrah."[e]

Israel's Unbelief

30What then shall we say? That the Gentiles, who did not pursue righteousness, have obtained it, a righteousness that is by faith; 31but Israel,

who pursued a law of righteousness, has not attained it. 32Why not? Because they pursued it not by faith but as if it were by works. They stumbled over the "stumbling stone." 33As it is written:

"See, I lay in Zion a stone that causes men to stumble
    and a rock that makes them fall,
and the one who trusts in him will never be put to shame."[f]

10 Brothers, my heart's desire and prayer to God for the Israelites is that they may be saved. 2For I can testify about them that they are zealous for God, but their zeal is not based on knowledge. 3Since they did not know the righteousness that comes from God and sought to establish their own, they did not submit to God's righteousness. 4Christ is the end of the law so that there may be righteousness for everyone who believes.

5Moses describes in this way the righteousness that is by the law: "The man who does these things will live by them."[g] 6But the righteousness that is by faith says: "Do not say in your heart, 'Who will ascend into heaven?'[h]" (that is, to bring Christ down) 7"or 'Who will descend into the deep?'[i]" (that is, to bring Christ up from the dead). 8But what does it say? "The word is near you; it is in your mouth and in your heart,"[j] that is, the word of faith we are proclaiming: 9That if you confess with your mouth, "Jesus is Lord," and believe in your heart that God raised him from the dead, you will be saved. 10For it is with your heart that you believe and are justified, and it is with your mouth that you confess and are saved. 11As the Scripture says, "Anyone who trusts in him will never be put to shame."[k] 12For there is no difference between Jew and Gentile—the same Lord is Lord of all and richly blesses all who call on him, 13for, "Everyone who calls on the name of the Lord will be saved."[l]

14How, then, can they call on the one they have not believed in? And how can they believe in the one of whom they have not heard? And how can they hear without someone preaching to them? 15And how can they preach unless they are sent? As it is written, "How beautiful are the feet of those who bring good news!"[m]

16But not all the Israelites accepted the good news. For Isaiah says, "Lord, who has believed our message?"[n] 17Consequently, faith comes from hearing the message, and the message is heard through the word of Christ. 18But I ask: Did they not hear? Of course they did:

---

[a]20 Isaiah 29:16; 45:9   [b]25 Hosea 2:23   [c]26 Hosea 1:10
[f]33 Isaiah 8:14; 28:16   [g]5 Lev. 18:5   [h]6 Deut. 30:12
[l]13 Joel 2:32   [m]15 Isaiah 52:7   [n]16 Isaiah 53:1
[d]28 Isaiah 10:22,23   [e]29 Isaiah 1:9
[i]7 Deut. 30:13   [j]8 Deut. 30:14   [k]11 Isaiah 28:16

"Their voice has gone out into all the earth,
their words to the ends of the world."[a]

[19]Again I ask: Did Israel not understand? First, Moses says,

"I will make you envious by those who are
not a nation;
I will make you angry by a nation that
has no understanding."[b]

[20]And Isaiah boldly says,

"I was found by those who did not seek me;
I revealed myself to those who did not ask
for me."[c]

[21]But concerning Israel he says,

"All day long I have held out my hands
to a disobedient and obstinate people."[d]

The Remnant of Israel

11 I ask then: Did God reject his people? By no means! I am an Israelite myself, a descendant of Abraham, from the tribe of Benjamin. [2]God did not reject his people, whom he foreknew. Don't you know what the Scripture says in the passage about Elijah—how he appealed to God against Israel: [3]"Lord, they have killed your prophets and torn down your altars; I am the only one left, and they are trying to kill me"[e]? [4]And what was God's answer to him? "I have reserved for myself seven thousand who have not bowed the knee to Baal."[f] [5]So too, at the present time there is a remnant chosen by grace. [6]And if by grace, then it is no longer by works; if it were, grace would no longer be grace.[g]

[7]What then? What Israel sought so earnestly it did not obtain, but the elect did. The others were hardened, [8]as it is written:

"God gave them a spirit of stupor,
eyes so that they could not see
and ears so that they could not hear,
to this very day."[h]

[9]And David says:

"May their table become a snare and a trap,
a stumbling block and a retribution for
them.
[10]May their eyes be darkened so they cannot
see,
and their backs be bent forever."[i]

Ingrafted Branches

[11]Again I ask: Did they stumble so as to fall beyond recovery? Not at all! Rather, because of their transgression, salvation has come to the Gentiles to make Israel envious. [12]But if their transgression means riches for the world, and their loss means riches for the Gentiles, how much greater riches will their fullness bring!

[13]I am talking to you Gentiles. Inasmuch as I

11:11 The Future of the Jews

In chapters 9 and 10, Paul painfully admits that, on the whole, the Jews did not believe in Christ. Despite all the advantages of Old Testament history, they "stumbled over the 'stumbling stone' " (9:32). In chapter 11, Paul goes back over that history and asks whether it was futile. Will the Jews come to believe in Christ some day? Did their tragic experience produce any advantage for the rest of the world? This chapter clearly shows God's eternal love for his chosen people. Paul concludes with a poetic outburst, celebrating God's mysterious ways of working on earth.

am the apostle to the Gentiles, I make much of my ministry [14]in the hope that I may somehow arouse my own people to envy and save some of them. [15]For if their rejection is the reconciliation of the world, what will their acceptance be but life from the dead? [16]If the part of the dough offered as firstfruits is holy, then the whole batch is holy; if the root is holy, so are the branches.

[17]If some of the branches have been broken off, and you, though a wild olive shoot, have been grafted in among the others and now share in the nourishing sap from the olive root, [18]do not boast over those branches. If you do, consider this: You do not support the root, but the root supports you. [19]You will say then, "Branches were broken off so that I could be grafted in." [20]Granted. But they were broken off because of unbelief, and you stand by faith. Do not be arrogant, but be afraid. [21]For if God did not spare the natural branches, he will not spare you either.

[22]Consider therefore the kindness and sternness of God: sternness to those who fell, but

11:17 Unnatural Botany

Botanists and orchard growers commonly use grafting to improve their stock of flowers and fruit. Usually they graft a weaker, cultivated branch onto a wild but sturdy root stock. Paul admits that "contrary to nature" God has grafted the wild branches (Gentiles) onto the cultivated roots (Jews)—a reverse technique sometimes used to reinvigorate an olive tree.

---

[a]18 Psalm 19:4 [b]19 Deut. 32:21 [c]20 Isaiah 65:1 [d]21 Isaiah 65:2 [e]3 1 Kings 19:10,14
[f]4 1 Kings 19:18 [g]6 Some manuscripts *by grace. But if by works, then it is no longer grace; if it were, work would no longer be work.* [h]8 Deut. 29:4; Isaiah 29:10 [i]10 Psalm 69:22,23

kindness to you, provided that you continue in his kindness. Otherwise, you also will be cut off. [23]And if they do not persist in unbelief, they will be grafted in, for God is able to graft them in again. [24]After all, if you were cut out of an olive tree that is wild by nature, and contrary to nature were grafted into a cultivated olive tree, how much more readily will these, the natural branches, be grafted into their own olive tree!

All Israel Will Be Saved

[25]I do not want you to be ignorant of this mystery, brothers, so that you may not be conceited: Israel has experienced a hardening in part until the full number of the Gentiles has come in. [26]And so all Israel will be saved, as it is written:

"The deliverer will come from Zion;
    he will turn godlessness away from Jacob.
[27]And this is[a] my covenant with them
    when I take away their sins."[b]

[28]As far as the gospel is concerned, they are enemies on your account; but as far as election is concerned, they are loved on account of the patriarchs, [29]for God's gifts and his call are irrevocable. [30]Just as you who were at one time disobedient to God have now received mercy as a result of their disobedience, [31]so they too have now become disobedient in order that they too may now[c] receive mercy as a result of God's mercy to you. [32]For God has bound all men over to disobedience so that he may have mercy on them all.

Doxology

[33]Oh, the depth of the riches of the wisdom
        and[d] knowledge of God!
    How unsearchable his judgments,
        and his paths beyond tracing out!
[34]"Who has known the mind of the Lord?
        Or who has been his counselor?"[e]
[35]"Who has ever given to God,
        that God should repay him?"[f]
[36]For from him and through him and to him
        are all things.
    To him be the glory forever! Amen.

Living Sacrifices

12 Therefore, I urge you, brothers, in view of God's mercy, to offer your bodies as living sacrifices, holy and pleasing to God—this is your spiritual[g] act of worship. [2]Do not conform any longer to the pattern of this world, but be transformed by the renewing of your mind. Then you will be able to test and approve what God's will is—his good, pleasing and perfect will.

[3]For by the grace given me I say to every one of you: Do not think of yourself more highly than

---

[a]27 Or will be   [b]27 Isaiah 59:20,21; 27:9; Jer. 31:33,34
[d]33 Or riches and the wisdom and the   [e]34 Isaiah 40:13
[c]31 Some manuscripts do not have now.
[f]35 Job 41:11   [g]1 Or reasonable

Down-To-Earth Problems
When Christians disagree about what's right and wrong

TOO OFTEN THEOLOGY IS VIEWED as stuff for hermits and marooned shipwreck victims. When there's nothing else to do, *then* is the time to ask abstract questions about God.

> Hate what is evil; cling to what is good. 12:9

Such a notion would surely have exasperated the apostle Paul. To him, theology *was* worthless unless it made a difference in how people lived. Therefore, he concluded the most concise theological book in the Bible with a down-to-earth discussion of contemporary problems.

Revolutionaries and Weaker Brothers

The issue of politics surfaces in Romans (13:1–7). How should a Christian relate to government? In Paul's day, when Christians were living under Nero's tyrannical regime, that question was hotly debated, as it still is in our revolution-oriented era.

Christians in Rome were also disagreeing on what was proper behavior for a Christian (14:1–15:4). One person was sure another was sinning; but that "offender" was convinced his accuser was hopelessly narrow-minded. Who was right? The specific issues change with each culture, but Paul's guidelines on the proper attitudes apply to all.

Paul did not live as an intellectual recluse. He applied his theology to life, practicing what he preached. In fact, the lofty book of Romans was written while he was out raising money for famine victims in Jerusalem (15:25–27).

Life Questions: Christians in Paul's day hotly debated such issues as eating meat, celebrating holidays, and drinking wine. What issues do Christians debate today? What attitude should we have toward Christians we differ with?

you ought, but rather think of yourself with sober judgment, in accordance with the measure of faith God has given you. ⁴Just as each of us has one body with many members, and these members do not all have the same function, ⁵so in Christ we who are many form one body, and each member belongs to all the others. ⁶We have different gifts, according to the grace given us. If a man's gift is prophesying, let him use it in proportion to his* faith. ⁷If it is serving, let him serve; if it is teaching, let him teach; ⁸if it is encouraging, let him encourage; if it is contributing to the needs of others, let him give generously; if it is leadership, let him govern diligently; if it is showing mercy, let him do it cheerfully.

Love

⁹Love must be sincere. Hate what is evil; cling to what is good. ¹⁰Be devoted to one another in brotherly love. Honor one another above yourselves. ¹¹Never be lacking in zeal, but keep your spiritual fervor, serving the Lord. ¹²Be joyful in hope, patient in affliction, faithful in prayer. ¹³Share with God's people who are in need. Practice hospitality.

¹⁴Bless those who persecute you; bless and do not curse. ¹⁵Rejoice with those who rejoice; mourn with those who mourn. ¹⁶Live in harmony with one another. Do not be proud, but be willing to associate with people of low position.*ᵇ Do not be conceited.

¹⁷Do not repay anyone evil for evil. Be careful to do what is right in the eyes of everybody. ¹⁸If it is possible, as far as it depends on you, live at peace with everyone. ¹⁹Do not take revenge, my friends, but leave room for God's wrath, for it is written: "It is mine to avenge; I will repay,"ᶜ says the Lord. ²⁰On the contrary:

"If your enemy is hungry, feed him;
    if he is thirsty, give him something to drink.
In doing this, you will heap burning coals on his head."ᵈ

²¹Do not be overcome by evil, but overcome evil with good.

Submission to the Authorities

13 Everyone must submit himself to the governing authorities, for there is no authority except that which God has established. The authorities that exist have been established by God. ²Consequently, he who rebels against the authority is rebelling against what God has instituted, and those who do so will bring judgment on themselves. ³For rulers hold no terror for those who do right, but for those who do wrong. Do you want to be free from fear of the one in au-

thority? Then do what is right and he will commend you. ⁴For he is God's servant to do you good. But if you do wrong, be afraid, for he does not bear the sword for nothing. He is God's servant, an agent of wrath to bring punishment on

13:1 Christians and the Empire

For most of his ministry, Paul benefited from the legal protection of the Roman empire. The first generation of Christians received the same freedom of worship and legal protection as did the Jews. But soon emperors such as Nero vengefully turned on Christians, torturing and murdering thousands of them, probably including Paul himself. History shows that most of them followed Paul's difficult advice in this passage, refusing to revolt against the government no matter how hostile it became.

the wrongdoer. ⁵Therefore, it is necessary to submit to the authorities, not only because of possible punishment but also because of conscience.

⁶This is also why you pay taxes, for the authorities are God's servants, who give their full time to governing. ⁷Give everyone what you owe him: If you owe taxes, pay taxes; if revenue, then revenue; if respect, then respect; if honor, then honor.

Love, for the Day Is Near

⁸Let no debt remain outstanding, except the continuing debt to love one another, for he who loves his fellowman has fulfilled the law. ⁹The commandments, "Do not commit adultery," "Do not murder," "Do not steal," "Do not covet,"ᵉ and whatever other commandment there may be, are summed up in this one rule: "Love your neighbor as yourself."ᶠ ¹⁰Love does no harm to its neighbor. Therefore love is the fulfillment of the law.

¹¹And do this, understanding the present time. The hour has come for you to wake up from your slumber, because our salvation is nearer now than when we first believed. ¹²The night is nearly over; the day is almost here. So let us put aside the deeds of darkness and put on the armor of light. ¹³Let us behave decently, as in the daytime, not in orgies and drunkenness, not in sexual immorality and debauchery, not in dissension and jealousy. ¹⁴Rather, clothe yourselves with the Lord Jesus Christ, and do not think about how to gratify the desires of the sinful nature.ᵍ

The Weak and the Strong

14 Accept him whose faith is weak, without passing judgment on disputable matters.

ᵃ6 Or in agreement with the   *ᵇ16 Or willing to do menial work*   *ᶜ19 Deut. 32:35*   *ᵈ20 Prov. 25:21,22*   *ᵉ9 Exodus 20:13-15,17; Deut. 5:17-19,21*   *ᶠ9 Lev. 19:18*   *ᵍ14 Or the flesh*

²One man's faith allows him to eat everything, but another man, whose faith is weak, eats only vegetables. ³The man who eats everything must not look down on him who does not, and the

man who does not eat everything must not condemn the man who does, for God has accepted him. ⁴Who are you to judge someone else's servant? To his own master he stands or falls. And he will stand, for the Lord is able to make him stand.

⁵One man considers one day more sacred than another; another man considers every day alike. Each one should be fully convinced in his own mind. ⁶He who regards one day as special, does so to the Lord. He who eats meat, eats to the Lord, for he gives thanks to God; and he who abstains, does so to the Lord and gives thanks to God. ⁷For none of us lives to himself alone and none of us dies to himself alone. ⁸If we live, we live to the Lord; and if we die, we die to the Lord. So, whether we live or die, we belong to the Lord.

⁹For this very reason, Christ died and returned to life so that he might be the Lord of both the dead and the living. ¹⁰You, then, why do you judge your brother? Or why do you look down on your brother? For we will all stand before God's judgment seat. ¹¹It is written:

"'As surely as I live,' says the Lord,
'every knee will bow before me;
    every tongue will confess to God.'"ᵃ

¹²So then, each of us will give an account of himself to God.

¹³Therefore let us stop passing judgment on one another. Instead, make up your mind not to put any stumbling block or obstacle in your brother's way. ¹⁴As one who is in the Lord Jesus, I am fully convinced that no foodᵇ is unclean in itself. But if anyone regards something as unclean, then for him it is unclean. ¹⁵If your brother is distressed because of what you eat, you are no longer acting in love. Do not by your eating destroy your brother for whom Christ died. ¹⁶Do not allow what you consider good to be spoken of as evil. ¹⁷For the kingdom of God is not a matter of eating and drinking, but of righteousness, peace and joy in the Holy Spirit, ¹⁸because anyone who serves Christ in this way is pleasing to God and approved by men.

¹⁹Let us therefore make every effort to do what leads to peace and to mutual edification. ²⁰Do not destroy the work of God for the sake of food. All food is clean, but it is wrong for a man to eat anything that causes someone else to stumble. ²¹It is better not to eat meat or drink wine or to do anything else that will cause your brother to fall.

²²So whatever you believe about these things keep between yourself and God. Blessed is the man who does not condemn himself by what he approves. ²³But the man who has doubts is condemned if he eats, because his eating is not from faith; and everything that does not come from faith is sin.

15 We who are strong ought to bear with the failings of the weak and not to please ourselves. ²Each of us should please his neighbor for his good, to build him up. ³For even Christ did not please himself but, as it is written: "The insults of those who insult you have fallen on me."ᶜ ⁴For everything that was written in the past was written to teach us, so that through endurance and the encouragement of the Scriptures we might have hope.

⁵May the God who gives endurance and encouragement give you a spirit of unity among yourselves as you follow Christ Jesus, ⁶so that with one heart and mouth you may glorify the God and Father of our Lord Jesus Christ.

⁷Accept one another, then, just as Christ accepted you, in order to bring praise to God. ⁸For I tell you that Christ has become a servant of the Jewsᵈ on behalf of God's truth, to confirm the promises made to the patriarchs ⁹so that the Gentiles may glorify God for his mercy, as it is written:

"Therefore I will praise you among the
    Gentiles;
    I will sing hymns to your name."ᵉ

¹⁰Again, it says,

"Rejoice, O Gentiles, with his people."ᶠ

¹¹And again,

"Praise the Lord, all you Gentiles,
    and sing praises to him, all you
        peoples."ᵍ

ᵃ11 Isaiah 45:23   ᵇ14 Or *that nothing*   ᶜ3 Psalm 69:9
Psalm 18:49   ᶠ10 Deut. 32:43   ᵍ11 Psalm 117:1   ᵈ8 Greek *circumcision*   ᵉ9 2 Samuel 22:50;

12And again, Isaiah says,

"The Root of Jesse will spring up,
　　one who will arise to rule over the
　　　　nations;
the Gentiles will hope in him."*a*

13May the God of hope fill you with all joy and peace as you trust in him, so that you may overflow with hope by the power of the Holy Spirit.

Paul the Minister to the Gentiles

14I myself am convinced, my brothers, that you yourselves are full of goodness, complete in knowledge and competent to instruct one another. 15I have written you quite boldly on some points, as if to remind you of them again, because of the grace God gave me 16to be a minister of Christ Jesus to the Gentiles with the priestly duty of proclaiming the gospel of God, so that the Gentiles might become an offering acceptable to God, sanctified by the Holy Spirit.

17Therefore I glory in Christ Jesus in my service to God. 18I will not venture to speak of anything except what Christ has accomplished through me in leading the Gentiles to obey God by what I have said and done— 19by the power of signs and miracles, through the power of the Spirit. So from Jerusalem all the way around to Illyricum, I have fully proclaimed the gospel of Christ. 20It has always been my ambition to preach the gospel where Christ was not known, so that I would not be building on someone else's foundation. 21Rather, as it is written:

"Those who were not told about him will
　　see,
and those who have not heard will
　　understand."*b*

22This is why I have often been hindered from coming to you.

Paul's Plan to Visit Rome

23But now that there is no more place for me to work in these regions, and since I have been longing for many years to see you, 24I plan to do so when I go to Spain. I hope to visit you while passing through and to have you assist me on my journey there, after I have enjoyed your company for a while. 25Now, however, I am on my way to Jerusalem in the service of the saints there. 26For Macedonia and Achaia were pleased to make a contribution for the poor among the saints in Jerusalem. 27They were pleased to do it, and indeed they owe it to them. For if the Gentiles have shared in the Jews' spiritual blessings, they owe it to the Jews to share with them their material blessings. 28So after I have completed this task and have made sure that they have received this fruit, I will go to Spain and visit you on the way. 29I know that when I come to you, I will come in the full measure of the blessing of Christ.

30I urge you, brothers, by our Lord Jesus

15:26 Paul the Fund-raiser

Paul wrote Romans while traveling to raise funds for famine relief. Another letter (2 Corinthians 8) gives more details on this mercy mission on behalf of the Jews in Jerusalem. Paul's actions set an example of unity for a church composed of both Jews and Gentiles—unity sorely needed by groups racked by the divisions described in chapter 14.

Christ and by the love of the Spirit, to join me in my struggle by praying to God for me. 31Pray that I may be rescued from the unbelievers in Judea and that my service in Jerusalem may be acceptable to the saints there, 32so that by God's will I may come to you with joy and together with you be refreshed. 33The God of peace be with you all. Amen.

Personal Greetings

16 I commend to you our sister Phoebe, a servant*c* of the church in Cenchrea. 2I ask you to receive her in the Lord in a way worthy of the saints and to give her any help she may need from you, for she has been a great help to many people, including me.

3Greet Priscilla*d* and Aquila, my fellow workers in Christ Jesus. 4They risked their lives for me. Not only I but all the churches of the Gentiles are grateful to them.

5Greet also the church that meets at their house.
Greet my dear friend Epenetus, who was the first convert to Christ in the province of Asia.

6Greet Mary, who worked very hard for you.

7Greet Andronicus and Junias, my relatives who have been in prison with me. They are outstanding among the apostles, and they were in Christ before I was.

8Greet Ampliatus, whom I love in the Lord.

9Greet Urbanus, our fellow worker in Christ, and my dear friend Stachys.

10Greet Apelles, tested and approved in Christ.
Greet those who belong to the household of Aristobulus.

11Greet Herodion, my relative.
Greet those in the household of Narcissus who are in the Lord.

12Greet Tryphena and Tryphosa, those women who work hard in the Lord.
Greet my dear friend Persis, another woman who has worked very hard in the Lord.

---

a12 Isaiah 11:10　　*b21* Isaiah 52:15　　*c1 Or deaconess*　　*d3* Greek *Prisca*, a variant of *Priscilla*

[13]Greet Rufus, chosen in the Lord, and his mother, who has been a mother to me, too. [14]Greet Asyncritus, Phlegon, Hermes, Patrobas, Hermas and the brothers with them. [15]Greet Philologus, Julia, Nereus and his sister, and Olympas and all the saints with them. [16]Greet one another with a holy kiss.

All the churches of Christ send greetings.

[17]I urge you, brothers, to watch out for those who cause divisions and put obstacles in your way that are contrary to the teaching you have learned. Keep away from them. [18]For such people are not serving our Lord Christ, but their own appetites. By smooth talk and flattery they deceive the minds of naive people. [19]Everyone has heard about your obedience, so I am full of joy over you; but I want you to be wise about what is good, and innocent about what is evil.

[20]The God of peace will soon crush Satan under your feet.

The grace of our Lord Jesus be with you.

[21]Timothy, my fellow worker, sends his greetings to you, as do Lucius, Jason and Sosipater, my relatives.

[22]I, Tertius, who wrote down this letter, greet you in the Lord.

[23]Gaius, whose hospitality I and the whole church here enjoy, sends you his greetings.

Erastus, who is the city's director of public works, and our brother Quartus send you their greetings.[a]

[25]Now to him who is able to establish you by my gospel and the proclamation of Jesus Christ, according to the revelation of the mystery hidden for long ages past, [26]but now revealed and made known through the prophetic writings by the command of the eternal God, so that all nations might believe and obey him— [27]to the only wise God be glory forever through Jesus Christ! Amen.

16:23 Paul's Friends

This chapter contains a fascinating list of Paul's friends and co-workers, many of whom would be unknown apart from their mention here. Although Paul himself had not yet visited Rome, a Christian community had taken root in the imperial capital. The list includes prominent women in the church (Phoebe, Priscilla, Junias, Tryphena, Tryphosa, Persis), common slave names (Ampliatus, Urbanus, Stachys, Apelles), and possible royalty (the household of Aristobulus—probably the grandson of Herod the Great).

Paul was writing from Corinth, where his friends included the city's director of public works. At Corinth archaeologists have dug up a block of stone that may refer to this man: It bears the Latin inscription "Erastus, commissioner of public works, bore the expense of this pavement."

---

[a]23 Some manuscripts *their greetings. [24]May the grace of our Lord Jesus Christ be with all of you. Amen.*

1 CORINTHIANS

The Last Place to Start a Church
No one expected much from crazy Corinth

EVERY LARGE CITY HAS ONE pocket where prostitutes, strippers, gamblers, and drug dealers hang out. Tourists stroll by to gawk at the sights. In New York, it's Times Square; in San Francisco, the North Beach district; in New Orleans, Bourbon Street; and in Las Vegas, it's virtually anywhere.

In the ancient world, the whole city of Corinth was known for that kind of lifestyle. Romans made the Corinthians the butt of dirty jokes, and playwrights consistently portrayed them as drunken brawlers. The Greek verb "to Corinthianize" meant to live shamelessly and immorally.

A Wide-Open City

Everyone knew what the Corinthians worshiped: money and the kinky things it could buy. Money flowed freely, for Corinth straddled one of the Roman empire's most vital trade routes. When a ship wrecked nearby, salvage companies housed the hapless sailors at inflated prices while they scrambled to auction off the ship's cargo. The city was a sprawling open-air market, filled with slaves, Orientals, Jews, Greeks, Egyptians, sailors, athletes, gamblers, and charioteers.

Brothers, think of what you were when you were called. Not many of you were wise by human standards; not many were influential; not many were of noble birth. But God chose the foolish things of the world to shame the wise; God chose the weak things of the world to shame the strong. 1:26–27

Yet Corinth was no blue-collar town. It had a population of 700,000, second only to Rome's, and as the capital of a large province, the city hosted a parade of Roman diplomats and dignitaries. Its clever citizens showcased new "Corinthian" architecture and prided themselves on having a cosmopolitan outlook.

For their religious ideal, the fun-loving Corinthians adopted Venus, the goddess of love. A temple built in her honor employed more than 1,000 prostitutes.

Paul Takes on the Corinthians

Due to all these influences, Corinth loomed as the one city "least likely to convert" to the Christian faith. What crazy cults and new religions did spring up there quickly gave in to the prevailing good-time atmosphere.

The mighty Paul, reeling from one of his most difficult missionary assignments in Athens, came to Corinth "in weakness and fear, and with much trembling" (2:3). He knew its strategic importance: If the gospel could take root there, it could transplant anywhere—and probably would, considering Corinth's crossroads location.

Paul worked in Corinth for 18 months. To everyone's surprise , the church he founded became one of the largest in the first century. But several years later he heard reports that the church, true to its city's heritage, had broken out in a series of spiritual ills. The distressing news prompted the letter known as 1 Corinthians.

The tone of this letter differs drastically from the one that precedes it. If Romans was stylistically carved in stone, 1 Corinthians was dashed off in tears and anger. One of Paul's longest letters, it covers the greatest variety of topics, partly because the Corinthians added bizarre new twists to ethical issues. In it, Paul gives practical advice on a series of church problems as well as a fascinating glimpse into the personal lives of early Christians.

How to Read 1 Corinthians

To fully appreciate Paul's letters, keep in mind that they are personal correspondence. We are actually reading someone else's mail.

In 1 Corinthians a riled-up apostle gives direct, forthright advice to a troubled local church. Paul saw alarming trends at work, and he used his full literary powers to set its members on the right course. He tried sarcasm, emotional pleas, autobiography, poetry, and lengthy arguments.

First, you will encounter the problems that had been reported to Paul: divisions in the church, a case of incest, court cases, the abuse of Christian freedom, chaos in the worship services. Paul lunges into these problems early in the book. Then, beginning with chapter 7, he takes up some other problems the Corinthians had written him about: marriage and the single life, pagan festivals, behavior of women, spiritual gifts, and the resurrection of the dead.

This first letter to the Corinthians presents a foundation for practical Christian ethics. Use the boldface sectional headings throughout the book to locate those issues that especially trouble you. Not all the problems discussed will apply directly to modern situations. But the general principles underlying Paul's advice do apply. As you read, look for those principles behind Paul's arguments.

PEOPLE YOU'LL MEET IN 1 CORINTHIANS

APOLLOS *(p. 1198)*

3-TRACK READING PLAN

For an explanation and complete listing of the 3-track reading plan, turn to page 7.

TRACK 1: *Two-Week Courses on the Bible*
The Track 1 reading program on the Life and Teachings of Paul includes two chapters from 1 Corinthians. See page 7 for a complete listing of this course.

TRACK 2: *An Overview of 1 Corinthians in 2 Days*
The emotional tone of 1 Corinthians makes for exciting reading throughout, but two chapters especially can't be missed.
☐ Day 1. Read the Introduction to 1 Corinthians, then chapter 13. Paul is at the top of his literary form as he defines love in one of the most famous passages in all of literature.
☐ Day 2. Read chapter 15, a crucial passage on life after death and resurrection from the dead.

Now turn to page 9 for your next Track 2 reading project.

TRACK 3: *All of 1 Corinthians in 14 Days*
After you have read through 1 Corinthians, turn to pages 10–14 for your next Track 3 reading project.

☐1 ☐2 ☐3 ☐4–5 ☐6 ☐7 ☐8–9 ☐10
☐11 ☐12 ☐13 ☐14 ☐15 ☐16

1 Paul, called to be an apostle of Christ Jesus by the will of God, and our brother Sosthenes,

[2] To the church of God in Corinth, to those sanctified in Christ Jesus and called to be holy, together with all those everywhere who call on the name of our Lord Jesus Christ—their Lord and ours:

[3] Grace and peace to you from God our Father and the Lord Jesus Christ.

Thanksgiving

[4] I always thank God for you because of his grace given you in Christ Jesus. [5] For in him you have been enriched in every way—in all your speaking and in all your knowledge— [6] because our testimony about Christ was confirmed in you. [7] Therefore you do not lack any spiritual gift as you eagerly wait for our Lord Jesus Christ to be revealed. [8] He will keep you strong to the end, so that you will be blameless on the day of our Lord Jesus Christ. [9] God, who has called you into fellowship with his Son Jesus Christ our Lord, is faithful.

Divisions in the Church

[10] I appeal to you, brothers, in the name of our Lord Jesus Christ, that all of you agree with one another so that there may be no divisions among you and that you may be perfectly united in mind and thought. [11] My brothers, some from Chloe's household have informed me that there are quarrels among you. [12] What I mean is this: One of you says, "I follow Paul"; another, "I follow Apollos[a]"; another, "I follow Cephas[a]"; still another, "I follow Christ."

[13] Is Christ divided? Was Paul crucified for you? Were you baptized into[b] the name of Paul? [14] I am thankful that I did not baptize any of you except Crispus and Gaius, [15] so no one can say that you were baptized into my name. [16] (Yes, I also baptized the household of Stephanas; beyond that, I don't remember if I baptized anyone else.) [17] For Christ did not send me to baptize, but to preach the gospel—not with words of human wisdom, lest the cross of Christ be emptied of its power.

Christ the Wisdom and Power of God

[18] For the message of the cross is foolishness to those who are perishing, but to us who are being saved it is the power of God. [19] For it is written:

"I will destroy the wisdom of the wise;
    the intelligence of the intelligent I will
        frustrate."[c]

[20] Where is the wise man? Where is the scholar? Where is the philosopher of this age? Has not God made foolish the wisdom of the world? [21] For since in the wisdom of God the world through its wisdom did not know him, God was pleased through the foolishness of what was preached to save those who believe. [22] Jews demand miraculous signs and Greeks look for wisdom, [23] but we preach Christ crucified: a stumbling block to Jews and foolishness to Gentiles, [24] but to those whom God has called, both Jews and Greeks, Christ the power of God and the wisdom of God. [25] For the foolishness of God is wiser than man's wisdom, and the weakness of God is stronger than man's strength.

[26] Brothers, think of what you were when you were called. Not many of you were wise by human standards; not many were influential; not many were of noble birth. [27] But God chose the foolish things of the world to shame the wise; God chose the weak things of the world to shame the strong. [28] He chose the lowly things of this world and the despised things—and the things that are not—to nullify the things that are, [29] so that no one may boast before him. [30] It is because of him that you are in Christ Jesus, who has become for us wisdom from God—that is, our righteousness, holiness and redemption. [31] Therefore, as it is written: "Let him who boasts boast in the Lord."[d]

2 When I came to you, brothers, I did not come with eloquence or superior wisdom as I proclaimed to you the testimony about God.[e] [2] For I resolved to know nothing while I was with you except Jesus Christ and him crucified. [3] I came to you in weakness and fear, and with

2:3 Paul at a Crossroads

This brief paragraph hints at a grave personal crisis in the apostle Paul's ministry, and Acts 16–18 gives important background. In three cities Paul saw a promising beginning crushed by fanatical Jews. Then in Athens he met little success in communicating to the intelligentsia. Many scholars believe that he reached Corinth shaken and discouraged and that he resolved to make Christ the sole subject of his teaching and preaching while there.

much trembling. [4] My message and my preaching were not with wise and persuasive words, but with a demonstration of the Spirit's power, [5] so that your faith might not rest on men's wisdom, but on God's power.

Wisdom From the Spirit

[6] We do, however, speak a message of wisdom

---

[a]12 That is, Peter   [b]13 Or in; also in verse 15   [c]19 Isaiah 29:14   [d]31 Jer. 9:24   [e]1 Some manuscripts as I proclaimed to you God's mystery

among the mature, but not the wisdom of this age or of the rulers of this age, who are coming to nothing. [7]No, we speak of God's secret wisdom, a wisdom that has been hidden and that God destined for our glory before time began. [8]None of the rulers of this age understood it, for if they had, they would not have crucified the Lord of glory. [9]However, as it is written:

"No eye has seen,
   no ear has heard,
no mind has conceived
   what God has prepared for those who love him"[a]—

[10]but God has revealed it to us by his Spirit.

The Spirit searches all things, even the deep things of God. [11]For who among men knows the thoughts of a man except the man's spirit within him? In the same way no one knows the thoughts of God except the Spirit of God. [12]We have not received the spirit of the world but the Spirit who is from God, that we may understand what God has freely given us. [13]This is what we speak, not in words taught us by human wisdom but in words taught by the Spirit, expressing spiritual truths in spiritual words.[b] [14]The man without the Spirit does not accept the things that come from the Spirit of God, for they are foolishness to him, and he cannot understand them, because they are spiritually discerned. [15]The spiritual man makes judgments about all things, but he himself is not subject to any man's judgment:

[16]"For who has known the mind of the Lord
   that he may instruct him?"[c]

But we have the mind of Christ.

On Divisions in the Church

3 Brothers, I could not address you as spiritual but as worldly—mere infants in Christ. [2]I gave you milk, not solid food, for you were not yet ready for it. Indeed, you are still not ready. [3]You are still worldly. For since there is jealousy and quarreling among you, are you not worldly? Are you not acting like mere men? [4]For when one says, "I follow Paul," and another, "I follow Apollos," are you not mere men?

[5]What, after all, is Apollos? And what is Paul?

---

[a]9 Isaiah 64:4   [b]13 Or *Spirit, interpreting spiritual truths to spiritual men*   [c]16 Isaiah 40:13

Like an Angry Letter from Home
A well-deserved scolding from a grieving "parent"

IMAGINE A COLLEGE FRESHMAN, STANDING in a corridor amid a swirl of chattering students. In two minutes the next class will begin. But, for her, time has stopped. She has just opened a tearstained, 12-page letter from her parents.

The tone of the letter takes her by surprise. Her parents are normally reserved, not given to emotional outbursts. Their letters are warm and friendly. Not this time. Somehow they have heard about her recent behavior on campus, and they are very hurt. In a torrent of words, they pour out their feelings for her and their equally deep disappointment.

First Corinthians reflects the same tone: it is an intimate, well-deserved scolding from a grieved parent. "I am not writing this to shame you," says Paul, "but to warn you, as my dear children" (4:14).

> I am not writing this to shame you, but to warn you, as my dear children. 4:14

Paul's Shifting Moods

No other letter in the New Testament reveals such a wide range of Paul's emotions. At his own financial expense, he had invested 18 risk-filled months in Corinth. But afterwards his rebellious "children" had launched personal attacks against him. Paul reacted like any parent first informed of his child's shocking behavior. His moods in 1 Corinthians bounce from anger to shame, from sorrow to indignation.

Chapter 3, for example, begins with a stern lecture to "mere infants in Christ." This leads to biting sarcasm (4:8), which melts into the tender pleas of a spiritual father. Six times in chapter 6 Paul asks, "Do you not know . . . ?" Finally, in chapter 7, he gets to the practical questions that had prompted his letter in the first place.

The apostle Paul was a superbly educated logician who could skillfully weave together history and philosophy. But he also brooded over his missionary churches like a parent. He asked the Corinthians pointedly, "Shall I come to you with a whip, or in love and with a gentle spirit?" (4:21). In this letter, we see a little of both.

Life Questions: How do you react when someone—a parent, teacher, boss, pastor—tries to straighten you out?

Only servants, through whom you came to believe—as the Lord has assigned to each his task. [6]I planted the seed, Apollos watered it, but God made it grow. [7]So neither he who plants nor

Apostles of Christ

4 So then, men ought to regard us as servants of Christ and as those entrusted with the secret things of God. [2]Now it is required that those who have been given a trust must prove faithful. [3]I care very little if I am judged by you or by any human court; indeed, I do not even judge myself. [4]My conscience is clear, but that does not make me innocent. It is the Lord who judges me. [5]Therefore judge nothing before the appointed time; wait till the Lord comes. He will bring to light what is hidden in darkness and will expose the motives of men's hearts. At that time each will receive his praise from God.

[6]Now, brothers, I have applied these things to myself and Apollos for your benefit, so that you may learn from us the meaning of the saying, "Do not go beyond what is written." Then you will not take pride in one man over against another. [7]For who makes you different from anyone else? What do you have that you did not receive? And if you did receive it, why do you boast as though you did not?

[8]Already you have all you want! Already you have become rich! You have become kings—and that without us! How I wish that you really had become kings so that we might be kings with

3:5–9 Personality Cults

In this chapter, Paul expands on a theme first introduced in 1:12. Converts were lining up behind various church leaders: Peter, who had walked and talked with Christ on earth; Apollos, with his sophisticated, cultivated style; Paul, the famous missionary; and Christ himself. Paul had no tolerance for that kind of hero worship. He stressed vigorously that the Corinthians belonged only to God, not to any human worker.

he who waters is anything, but only God, who makes things grow. [8]The man who plants and the man who waters have one purpose, and each will be rewarded according to his own labor. [9]For we are God's fellow workers; you are God's field, God's building.

[10]By the grace God has given me, I laid a foundation as an expert builder, and someone else is building on it. But each one should be careful how he builds. [11]For no one can lay any foundation other than the one already laid, which is Jesus Christ. [12]If any man builds on this foundation using gold, silver, costly stones, wood, hay or straw, [13]his work will be shown for what it is, because the Day will bring it to light. It will be revealed with fire, and the fire will test the quality of each man's work. [14]If what he has built survives, he will receive his reward. [15]If it is burned up, he will suffer loss; he himself will be saved, but only as one escaping through the flames.

[16]Don't you know that you yourselves are God's temple and that God's Spirit lives in you? [17]If anyone destroys God's temple, God will destroy him; for God's temple is sacred, and you are that temple.

[18]Do not deceive yourselves. If any one of you thinks he is wise by the standards of this age, he should become a "fool" so that he may become wise. [19]For the wisdom of this world is foolishness in God's sight. As it is written: "He catches the wise in their craftiness"[a]; [20]and again, "The Lord knows that the thoughts of the wise are futile."[b] [21]So then, no more boasting about men! All things are yours, [22]whether Paul or Apollos or Cephas[c] or the world or life or death or the present or the future—all are yours, [23]and you are of Christ, and Christ is of God.

4:8–13 A Hint of Trials to Come

Paul's intense feelings come to the surface in this paragraph, as sharply worded as any in the New Testament. He alludes (verse 9) to the Roman practice of parading the gladiators condemned to death—a poignant reference in light of the martyr's fate that awaited him and other apostles.

you! [9]For it seems to me that God has put us apostles on display at the end of the procession, like men condemned to die in the arena. We have been made a spectacle to the whole universe, to angels as well as to men. [10]We are fools for Christ, but you are so wise in Christ! We are weak, but you are strong! You are honored, we are dishonored! [11]To this very hour we go hungry and thirsty, we are in rags, we are brutally treated, we are homeless. [12]We work hard with our own hands. When we are cursed, we bless; when we are persecuted, we endure it; [13]when we are slandered, we answer kindly. Up to this moment we have become the scum of the earth, the refuse of the world.

[14]I am not writing this to shame you, but to warn you, as my dear children. [15]Even though you have ten thousand guardians in Christ, you

[a]19 Job 5:13   [b]20 Psalm 94:11   [c]22 That is, Peter

do not have many fathers, for in Christ Jesus I became your father through the gospel. [16]Therefore I urge you to imitate me. [17]For this reason I am sending to you Timothy, my son whom I love, who is faithful in the Lord. He will remind you of my way of life in Christ Jesus, which agrees with what I teach everywhere in every church.

[18]Some of you have become arrogant, as if I were not coming to you. [19]But I will come to you very soon, if the Lord is willing, and then I will find out not only how these arrogant people are talking, but what power they have. [20]For the kingdom of God is not a matter of talk but of power. [21]What do you prefer? Shall I come to you with a whip, or in love and with a gentle spirit?

Expel the Immoral Brother!

5 It is actually reported that there is sexual immorality among you, and of a kind that does not occur even among pagans: A man has his father's wife. [2]And you are proud! Shouldn't you rather have been filled with grief and have put out of your fellowship the man who did this? [3]Even though I am not physically present, I am with you in spirit. And I have already passed judgment on the one who did this, just as if I were present. [4]When you are assembled in the name of our Lord Jesus and I am with you in spirit, and the power of our Lord Jesus is present, [5]hand this man over to Satan, so that the sinful nature[a] may be destroyed and his spirit saved on the day of the Lord.

[6]Your boasting is not good. Don't you know that a little yeast works through the whole batch of dough? [7]Get rid of the old yeast that you may be a new batch without yeast—as you really are.

For Christ, our Passover lamb, has been sacrificed. [8]Therefore let us keep the Festival, not with the old yeast, the yeast of malice and wickedness, but with bread without yeast, the bread of sincerity and truth.

[9]I have written you in my letter not to associate with sexually immoral people— [10]not at all meaning the people of this world who are immoral, or the greedy and swindlers, or idolaters. In that case you would have to leave this world. [11]But now I am writing you that you must not associate with anyone who calls himself a brother but is sexually immoral or greedy, an idolater or a slanderer, a drunkard or a swindler. With such a man do not even eat.

[12]What business is it of mine to judge those outside the church? Are you not to judge those inside? [13]God will judge those outside. "Expel the wicked man from among you."[b]

5:5 Handed Over to Satan

The strong phrase used in this verse has a Biblical parallel in 1 Timothy 1:20. To Paul, expelling someone from the church and Christian privileges meant pushing them out into the world ruled by Satan. In both references, however, Paul stresses that the action was designed to teach the offender a lesson.

Lawsuits Among Believers

6 If any of you has a dispute with another, dare he take it before the ungodly for judgment instead of before the saints? [2]Do you not know that the saints will judge the world? And if you

---

[a]5 Or *that his body*; or *that the flesh*   [b]13 Deut. 17:7; 19:19; 21:21; 22:21,24; 24:7

APOLLOS *Brimming with Confidence*

APOLLOS CAME ON THE SCENE at Ephesus like a whirlwind (Acts 18:24–26). He knew the Scriptures inside out and went immediately to the Jewish synagogue to present Jesus as their long-awaited Messiah. Apollos had a few things to learn (Priscilla and Aquila found it necessary to update his information privately), but he was fearless in telling what he knew.

Brimming with confidence, Apollos hailed from one of the largest, most cultured cities in the world. Alexandria in Egypt boasted a centuries-old university and library, and had a thriving, scholarly Jewish sector. It was in Alexandria that the Old Testament had been translated into Greek.

Apollos later traveled to Corinth, where he became an extremely effective leader in the church. Indeed, he made such an impact that a "pro-Apollos" faction gathered around him, threatening to split the church in two. The apostle Paul had to warn the Corinthians to stay together, rather than taking sides.

When Paul wrote this letter, Apollos apparently was with him (16:12). Paul urged Apollos to return to Corinth, but he declined. Divisions in the church were no doubt as troubling to Apollos as they were to Paul.

Life Questions: How can charismatic leaders avoid attracting attention to themselves rather than their message?

are to judge the world, are you not competent to judge trivial cases? [3]Do you not know that we will judge angels? How much more the things of this life! [4]Therefore, if you have disputes about such matters, appoint as judges even men of little account in the church![a] [5]I say this to shame you. Is it possible that there is nobody among you wise enough to judge a dispute between believers? [6]But instead, one brother goes to law against another—and this in front of unbelievers!

[7]The very fact that you have lawsuits among you means you have been completely defeated already. Why not rather be wronged? Why not rather be cheated? [8]Instead, you yourselves cheat and do wrong, and you do this to your brothers.

[9]Do you not know that the wicked will not inherit the kingdom of God? Do not be deceived: Neither the sexually immoral nor idolaters nor adulterers nor male prostitutes nor homosexual offenders [10]nor thieves nor the greedy nor drunkards nor slanderers nor swindlers will inherit the kingdom of God. [11]And that is what some of you were. But you were washed, you were sanctified, you were justified in the name of the Lord Jesus Christ and by the Spirit of our God.

Sexual Immorality

[12]"Everything is permissible for me"—but not everything is beneficial. "Everything is permissible for me"—but I will not be mastered by anything. [13]"Food for the stomach and the stomach

6:12 Corinthian Slogans

The phrases given here in quotes ("Everything is permissible for me"; "Food for the stomach and the stomach for food") appear to be slogans the Corinthians had used in justifying their loose behavior. Paul doesn't refute their ideas outright, but rather points to the ultimate effect of their excesses.

for food"—but God will destroy them both. The body is not meant for sexual immorality, but for the Lord, and the Lord for the body. [14]By his power God raised the Lord from the dead, and he will raise us also. [15]Do you not know that your bodies are members of Christ himself? Shall I then take the members of Christ and unite them with a prostitute? Never! [16]Do you not know that he who unites himself with a prostitute is one with her in body? For it is said, "The two will become one flesh."[b] [17]But he who unites himself with the Lord is one with him in spirit.

[18]Flee from sexual immorality. All other sins a

man commits are outside his body, but he who sins sexually sins against his own body. [19]Do you not know that your body is a temple of the Holy Spirit, who is in you, whom you have received from God? You are not your own; [20]you were bought at a price. Therefore honor God with your body.

Marriage

7 Now for the matters you wrote about: It is good for a man not to marry.[c] [2]But since there is so much immorality, each man should have his own wife, and each woman her own husband. [3]The husband should fulfill his marital duty to his wife, and likewise the wife to her husband. [4]The wife's body does not belong to her alone but also to her husband. In the same way, the husband's body does not belong to him alone but also to his wife. [5]Do not deprive each other except by mutual consent and for a time, so that you may devote yourselves to prayer. Then come together again so that Satan will not tempt you because of your lack of self-control. [6]I say this as a concession, not as a command. [7]I wish that all men were as I am. But each man has his own gift from God; one has this gift, another has that.

[8]Now to the unmarried and the widows I say: It is good for them to stay unmarried, as I am. [9]But if they cannot control themselves, they should marry, for it is better to marry than to burn with passion.

[10]To the married I give this command (not I, but the Lord): A wife must not separate from her husband. [11]But if she does, she must remain unmarried or else be reconciled to her husband. And a husband must not divorce his wife.

[12]To the rest I say this (I, not the Lord): If any brother has a wife who is not a believer and she is willing to live with him, he must not divorce her. [13]And if a woman has a husband who is not a believer and he is willing to live with her, she must not divorce him. [14]For the unbelieving husband has been sanctified through his wife, and the unbelieving wife has been sanctified through her believing husband. Otherwise your children would be unclean, but as it is, they are holy.

[15]But if the unbeliever leaves, let him do so. A believing man or woman is not bound in such circumstances; God has called us to live in peace. [16]How do you know, wife, whether you will save your husband? Or, how do you know, husband, whether you will save your wife?

[17]Nevertheless, each one should retain the place in life that the Lord assigned to him and to which God has called him. This is the rule I lay down in all the churches. [18]Was a man already circumcised when he was called? He should not

---

[a]4 Or *matters, do you appoint as judges men of little account in the church?*   [b]16 Gen. 2:24   [c]1 Or "*It is good for a man not to have sexual relations with a woman.*"

become uncircumcised. Was a man uncircumcised when he was called? He should not be circumcised. [19]Circumcision is nothing and uncircumcision is nothing. Keeping God's commands is what counts. [20]Each one should remain in the situation which he was in when God called him. [21]Were you a slave when you were called? Don't let it trouble you—although if you can gain your freedom, do so. [22]For he who was a slave when he was called by the Lord is the Lord's freedman; similarly, he who was a free man when he was called is Christ's slave. [23]You were bought at a price; do not become slaves of men. [24]Brothers, each man, as responsible to God, should remain in the situation God called him to.

[25]Now about virgins: I have no command from the Lord, but I give a judgment as one who

7:25 Paul's Personal Opinions

In discussing the thorny issue of singleness and marriage, Paul carefully distinguishes what is his personal opinion and what is a clear revelation from God. He explains in verse 29 why he reached these conclusions.

by the Lord's mercy is trustworthy. [26]Because of the present crisis, I think that it is good for you to remain as you are. [27]Are you married? Do not seek a divorce. Are you unmarried? Do not look for a wife. [28]But if you do marry, you have not sinned; and if a virgin marries, she has not sinned. But those who marry will face many troubles in this life, and I want to spare you this.

[29]What I mean, brothers, is that the time is short. From now on those who have wives should live as if they had none; [30]those who mourn, as if they did not; those who are happy, as if they were not; those who buy something, as if it were not theirs to keep; [31]those who use the things of the world, as if not engrossed in them. For this world in its present form is passing away.

[32]I would like you to be free from concern. An unmarried man is concerned about the Lord's affairs—how he can please the Lord. [33]But a married man is concerned about the affairs of this world—how he can please his wife— [34]and his interests are divided. An unmarried woman or virgin is concerned about the Lord's affairs: Her aim is to be devoted to the Lord in both body and spirit. But a married woman is concerned about the affairs of this world—how she can please her husband. [35]I am saying this for your own good, not to restrict you, but that you

may live in a right way in undivided devotion to the Lord.

[36]If anyone thinks he is acting improperly toward the virgin he is engaged to, and if she is getting along in years and he feels he ought to marry, he should do as he wants. He is not sinning. They should get married. [37]But the man who has settled the matter in his own mind, who is under no compulsion but has control over his own will, and who has made up his mind not to marry the virgin—this man also does the right thing. [38]So then, he who marries the virgin does right, but he who does not marry her does even better.[a]

[39]A woman is bound to her husband as long as he lives. But if her husband dies, she is free to marry anyone she wishes, but he must belong to the Lord. [40]In my judgment, she is happier if she stays as she is—and I think that I too have the Spirit of God.

Food Sacrificed to Idols

8 Now about food sacrificed to idols: We know that we all possess knowledge.[b] Knowledge puffs up, but love builds up. [2]The man who thinks he knows something does not yet know as he ought to know. [3]But the man who loves God is known by God.

[4]So then, about eating food sacrificed to idols: We know that an idol is nothing at all in the world and that there is no God but one. [5]For even if there are so-called gods, whether in heaven or on earth (as indeed there are many "gods" and many "lords"), [6]yet for us there is but one God, the Father, from whom all things came and for whom we live; and there is but one Lord, Jesus Christ, through whom all things came and through whom we live.

[7]But not everyone knows this. Some people are still so accustomed to idols that when they eat such food they think of it as having been sacrificed to an idol, and since their conscience is weak, it is defiled. [8]But food does not bring us near to God; we are no worse if we do not eat, and no better if we do.

[9]Be careful, however, that the exercise of your freedom does not become a stumbling block to the weak. [10]For if anyone with a weak conscience sees you who have this knowledge eating in an idol's temple, won't he be emboldened to eat what has been sacrificed to idols? [11]So this weak brother, for whom Christ died, is destroyed by your knowledge. [12]When you sin against your brothers in this way and wound their weak conscience, you sin against Christ. [13]Therefore, if

---

[a] 36-38 Or [36]*If anyone thinks he is not treating his daughter properly, and if she is getting along in years, and he feels she ought to marry, he should do as he wants. He is not sinning. He should let her get married.* [37]*But the man who has settled the matter in his own mind, who is under no compulsion but has control over his own will, and who has made up his mind to keep the virgin unmarried—this man also does the right thing.* [38]*So then, he who gives his virgin in marriage does right, but he who does not give her in marriage does even better.*   [b] 1 Or *"We all possess knowledge,"* as you say

what I eat causes my brother to fall into sin, I will never eat meat again, so that I will not cause him to fall.

The Rights of an Apostle

9 Am I not free? Am I not an apostle? Have I not seen Jesus our Lord? Are you not the result of my work in the Lord? [2]Even though I may not be an apostle to others, surely I am to you! For you are the seal of my apostleship in the Lord.

[3]This is my defense to those who sit in judgment on me. [4]Don't we have the right to food and drink? [5]Don't we have the right to take a believing wife along with us, as do the other apostles and the Lord's brothers and Cephas[a]? [6]Or is it only I and Barnabas who must work for a living?

[7]Who serves as a soldier at his own expense? Who plants a vineyard and does not eat of its grapes? Who tends a flock and does not drink of the milk? [8]Do I say this merely from a human point of view? Doesn't the Law say the same thing? [9]For it is written in the Law of Moses: "Do not muzzle an ox while it is treading out the grain."[b] Is it about oxen that God is concerned? [10]Surely he says this for us, doesn't he? Yes, this was written for us, because when the plowman plows and the thresher threshes, they ought to do

so in the hope of sharing in the harvest. [11]If we have sown spiritual seed among you, is it too much if we reap a material harvest from you? [12]If others have this right of support from you, shouldn't we have it all the more?

But we did not use this right. On the contrary, we put up with anything rather than hinder the gospel of Christ. [13]Don't you know that those who work in the temple get their food from the temple, and those who serve at the altar share in what is offered on the altar? [14]In the same way, the Lord has commanded that those who preach the gospel should receive their living from the gospel.

[15]But I have not used any of these rights. And I am not writing this in the hope that you will do such things for me. I would rather die than have anyone deprive me of this boast. [16]Yet when I preach the gospel, I cannot boast, for I am compelled to preach. Woe to me if I do not preach the gospel! [17]If I preach voluntarily, I have a reward; if not voluntarily, I am simply discharging the trust committed to me. [18]What then is my reward? Just this: that in preaching the gospel I may offer it free of charge, and so not make use of my rights in preaching it.

[19]Though I am free and belong to no man, I make myself a slave to everyone, to win as many as possible. [20]To the Jews I became like a Jew, to

[a]5 That is, Peter   [b]9 Deut. 25:4

When Everything Goes Wrong
A church of former idolaters, adulterers, thieves, and drunkards

Now for the matters you wrote about . . .
7:1

"IF ANYTHING CAN GO WRONG, it will." This tongue-in-cheek principle, known as Murphy's Law, is cited by economists, sports team owners, and big-city mayors. Human nature somehow guarantees that nothing turns out quite the way it's supposed to. And the church at Corinth provides a darkly shining example of Murphy's Law.

To be sure, Corinthian Christians started out with the odds stacked against them. Imagine a church composed of converted idolaters, adulterers, male prostitutes, thieves, drunkards, and swindlers (6:9–11). The church made up of people from such backgrounds soon encountered a thicket of problems. Paul faced a huge challenge: For one thing, he had to convince these people of the immorality of sexual activities that had been a part of everyday worship under their old religion.

Local and Universal Issues

First Corinthians is Paul's careful response to that thicket of problems, some of which had been posed to him as questions in a letter (7:1). Many of his answers relate directly to Corinth's local situation. In that culture, as in Muslim countries today, whether or not to wear a veil was a major issue for women (11:3–10). Eating meat sacrificed to pagan idols also disturbed some new Christians (10:18–33).

But other problems discussed here turn up in every culture: divisions in the church, lawsuits, immorality, the single life, the extent of Christian freedoms, differing views of worship and the place of tongue-speaking and other spiritual gifts. Not every breakdown in Corinth will recur in churches today, but Paul's principles apply to our own unpredictable experiences with Murphy's Law.

Life Questions: Think of the most "Corinthian" television show you know. Then imagine: If the lead characters became Christians, what problems would they encounter?

win the Jews. To those under the law I became like one under the law (though I myself am not under the law), so as to win those under the law. [21]To those not having the law I became like one not having the law (though I am not free from God's law but am under Christ's law), so as to win those not having the law. [22]To the weak I became weak, to win the weak. I have become all things to all men so that by all possible means I

might save some. [23]I do all this for the sake of the gospel, that I may share in its blessings.

[24]Do you not know that in a race all the runners run, but only one gets the prize? Run in such a way as to get the prize. [25]Everyone who competes in the games goes into strict training. They do it to get a crown that will not last; but we do it to get a crown that will last forever. [26]Therefore I do not run like a man running aimlessly; I do not fight like a man beating the air. [27]No, I beat my body and make it my slave so that after I have preached to others, I myself will not be disqualified for the prize.

Warnings From Israel's History

10 For I do not want you to be ignorant of the fact, brothers, that our forefathers were all under the cloud and that they all passed through the sea. [2]They were all baptized into Moses in the cloud and in the sea. [3]They all ate the same spiritual food [4]and drank the same spiritual drink; for they drank from the spiritual rock that accompanied them, and that rock was Christ. [5]Nevertheless, God was not pleased with most of them; their bodies were scattered over the desert.

[6]Now these things occurred as examples[a] to keep us from setting our hearts on evil things as they did. [7]Do not be idolaters, as some of them were; as it is written: "The people sat down to eat and drink and got up to indulge in pagan revelry."[b] [8]We should not commit sexual immorality, as some of them did—and in one day twenty-

three thousand of them died. [9]We should not test the Lord, as some of them did—and were killed by snakes. [10]And do not grumble, as some of them did—and were killed by the destroying angel.

[11]These things happened to them as examples and were written down as warnings for us, on whom the fulfillment of the ages has come. [12]So, if you think you are standing firm, be careful that you don't fall! [13]No temptation has seized you except what is common to man. And God is faithful; he will not let you be tempted beyond what you can bear. But when you are tempted, he will also provide a way out so that you can stand up under it.

Idol Feasts and the Lord's Supper

[14]Therefore, my dear friends, flee from idolatry. [15]I speak to sensible people; judge for yourselves what I say. [16]Is not the cup of thanksgiving for which we give thanks a participation in the blood of Christ? And is not the bread that we break a participation in the body of Christ? [17]Because there is one loaf, we, who are many, are one body, for we all partake of the one loaf.

[18]Consider the people of Israel: Do not those who eat the sacrifices participate in the altar? [19]Do I mean then that a sacrifice offered to an idol is anything, or that an idol is anything? [20]No, but the sacrifices of pagans are offered to demons, not to God, and I do not want you to be participants with demons. [21]You cannot drink the cup of the Lord and the cup of demons too; you cannot have a part in both the Lord's table and the table of demons. [22]Are we trying to arouse the Lord's jealousy? Are we stronger than he?

The Believer's Freedom

[23]"Everything is permissible"—but not everything is beneficial. "Everything is permissible"—but not everything is constructive. [24]Nobody should seek his own good, but the good of others.

[25]Eat anything sold in the meat market without raising questions of conscience, [26]for, "The earth is the Lord's, and everything in it."[c]

[27]If some unbeliever invites you to a meal and you want to go, eat whatever is put before you without raising questions of conscience. [28]But if anyone says to you, "This has been offered in sacrifice," then do not eat it, both for the sake of the man who told you and for conscience' sake[d]— [29]the other man's conscience, I mean, not yours. For why should my freedom be judged by another's conscience? [30]If I take part in the meal with thankfulness, why am I denounced because of something I thank God for?

[31]So whether you eat or drink or whatever you

---

[a]6 Or *types*; also in verse 11   [b]7 Exodus 32:6   [c]26 Psalm 24:1   [d]28 Some manuscripts *conscience' sake, for "the earth is the Lord's and everything in it"*

do, do it all for the glory of God. [32]Do not cause anyone to stumble, whether Jews, Greeks or the church of God— [33]even as I try to please everybody in every way. For I am not seeking my own good but the good of many, so that they may be saved. **11** [1]Follow my example, as I follow the example of Christ.

Propriety in Worship

[2]I praise you for remembering me in everything and for holding to the teachings,[a] just as I passed them on to you.

[3]Now I want you to realize that the head of every man is Christ, and the head of the woman is man, and the head of Christ is God. [4]Every man who prays or prophesies with his head covered dishonors his head. [5]And every woman who prays or prophesies with her head uncovered dishonors her head—it is just as though her head

11:5 Women in Corinth

In the Middle East, a woman who appeared in public barefaced, without a veil, showed loose morals. Some Muslim countries today still retain that custom. Paul's advice applied directly to the cultural situation in Corinth, where unruly women were disrupting the worship services.

were shaved. [6]If a woman does not cover her head, she should have her hair cut off; and if it is a disgrace for a woman to have her hair cut or shaved off, she should cover her head. [7]A man ought not to cover his head,[b] since he is the image and glory of God; but the woman is the glory of man. [8]For man did not come from woman, but woman from man; [9]neither was man created for woman, but woman for man. [10]For this reason, and because of the angels, the woman ought to have a sign of authority on her head. [11]In the Lord, however, woman is not independent of man, nor is man independent of woman. [12]For as woman came from man, so also man is born of woman. But everything comes from God. [13]Judge for yourselves: Is it proper for a woman to pray to God with her head uncovered? [14]Does not the very nature of things teach you that if a man has long hair, it is a disgrace to him, [15]but that if a woman has long hair, it is her glory? For long hair is given to her as a covering. [16]If anyone wants to be contentious about this, we have no other practice—nor do the churches of God.

The Lord's Supper

[17]In the following directives I have no praise for you, for your meetings do more harm than good. [18]In the first place, I hear that when you come together as a church, there are divisions among you, and to some extent I believe it. [19]No doubt there have to be differences among you to show which of you have God's approval. [20]When you come together, it is not the Lord's Supper you eat, [21]for as you eat, each of you goes ahead without waiting for anybody else. One remains hungry, another gets drunk. [22]Don't you have homes to eat and drink in? Or do you despise the church of God and humiliate those who have nothing? What shall I say to you? Shall I praise you for this? Certainly not!

[23]For I received from the Lord what I also passed on to you: The Lord Jesus, on the night he was betrayed, took bread, [24]and when he had given thanks, he broke it and said, "This is my body, which is for you; do this in remembrance of me." [25]In the same way, after supper he took the cup, saying, "This cup is the new covenant in my blood; do this, whenever you drink it, in remembrance of me." [26]For whenever you eat this bread and drink this cup, you proclaim the Lord's death until he comes.

[27]Therefore, whoever eats the bread or drinks the cup of the Lord in an unworthy manner will be guilty of sinning against the body and blood of the Lord. [28]A man ought to examine himself before he eats of the bread and drinks of the cup. [29]For anyone who eats and drinks without recognizing the body of the Lord eats and drinks judgment on himself. [30]That is why many among you are weak and sick, and a number of you have fallen asleep. [31]But if we judged ourselves, we would not come under judgment. [32]When we are judged by the Lord, we are being disciplined so that we will not be condemned with the world.

[33]So then, my brothers, when you come together to eat, wait for each other. [34]If anyone is hungry, he should eat at home, so that when you meet together it may not result in judgment.

And when I come I will give further directions.

Spiritual Gifts

12 Now about spiritual gifts, brothers, I do not want you to be ignorant. [2]You know that when you were pagans, somehow or other you were influenced and led astray to mute idols. [3]Therefore I tell you that no one who is speaking by the Spirit of God says, "Jesus be cursed," and no one can say, "Jesus is Lord," except by the Holy Spirit.

---

[a]2 Or *traditions* [b]4-7 Or *4Every man who prays or prophesies with long hair dishonors his head. 5And every woman who prays or prophesies with no covering [of hair] on her head dishonors her head—she is just like one of the "shorn women." 6If a woman has no covering, let her be for now with short hair, but since it is a disgrace for a woman to have her hair shorn or shaved, she should grow it again. 7A man ought not to have long hair*

⁴There are different kinds of gifts, but the same Spirit. ⁵There are different kinds of service, but the same Lord. ⁶There are different kinds of working, but the same God works all of them in all men.

⁷Now to each one the manifestation of the Spirit is given for the common good. ⁸To one there is given through the Spirit the message of wisdom, to another the message of knowledge by means of the same Spirit, ⁹to another faith by the same Spirit, to another gifts of healing by that one Spirit, ¹⁰to another miraculous powers, to another prophecy, to another distinguishing between spirits, to another speaking in different kinds of tongues,*a* and to still another the interpretation of tongues.*a* ¹¹All these are the work of one and the same Spirit, and he gives them to each one, just as he determines.

One Body, Many Parts

¹²The body is a unit, though it is made up of many parts; and though all its parts are many, they form one body. So it is with Christ. ¹³For we were all baptized by*b* one Spirit into one body—whether Jews or Greeks, slave or free—and we were all given the one Spirit to drink.

¹⁴Now the body is not made up of one part but of many. ¹⁵If the foot should say, "Because I am not a hand, I do not belong to the body," it would not for that reason cease to be part of the body. ¹⁶And if the ear should say, "Because I am not an eye, I do not belong to the body," it would not for that reason cease to be part of the body. ¹⁷If the whole body were an eye, where would the sense of hearing be? If the whole body were an ear, where would the sense of smell be? ¹⁸But in fact God has arranged the parts in the body,

---

a 10 Or *languages*; also in verse 28   *b 13* Or *with*; or *in*

Lessons from the Human Body
The body needs an eye, and the eye needs a body

CAN YOU GET ALONG IN life without eyes? Of course, but you must make adjustments. You must rely more on other senses and depend on friends, or perhaps a seeing-eye dog, for extra help. Regardless of what adjustments you make, however, your body will remain incomplete without eyes. You will miss out on color and design and all the visual delights this world offers.

An eyeless body can cope, but a bodyless eye is unimaginable. The most beautiful eyes in the world, when detached from a body, are lifeless and worthless. Eyes need a body that will bring them blood and receive their nerve impulses.

> The body is a unit, though it is made up of many parts; and though all its parts are many, they form one body. So it is with Christ. 12:12

Many Parts, All Working Together

In chapter 12 Paul gives a clever anatomy lesson, with a purpose. By comparing members of the church of Christ to parts of a human body, he neatly explains two complementary truths the Corinthians had failed to comprehend. Any part of a body, he says—such as an eye or a foot—makes a valuable contribution to the whole body. Whenever a single member is missing, the entire body suffers.

And, he continues, no member can survive if isolated from the rest. Alone, an eye is useless. All parts must cooperate to form a single, unified body.

Paul relied on body images to explain both the diversity and unity of God's followers. The body analogy fit so well that he referred to it two dozen times in his various letters. It became his favorite way of portraying the church.

An Emphasis on Unity

A church as diverse as Corinth knew about the differences among various members, so Paul's letter to them stressed the unity part of the analogy. How can diverse people work together in a spiritual body? He answered that question with the famous lyrical description of love in chapter 13. After that eloquent statement, he went on to discuss the Corinthians' various spiritual gifts.

Chapters 12–14 address issues that troubled the patchwork Corinthian church and that still disturb the church today. The solution, in our time as well as Paul's, is for each person to respect other members of the body and to take direction from Jesus Christ, the head.

Life Questions: Of Paul's list of spiritual gifts, which are prominent in your church? Are any overlooked? How do you fit in?

every one of them, just as he wanted them to be. ¹⁹If they were all one part, where would the body be? ²⁰As it is, there are many parts, but one body.

²¹The eye cannot say to the hand, "I don't need you!" And the head cannot say to the feet, "I don't need you!" ²²On the contrary, those parts of the body that seem to be weaker are indispensable, ²³and the parts that we think are less honorable we treat with special honor. And the parts that are unpresentable are treated with special modesty, ²⁴while our presentable parts need no special treatment. But God has combined the members of the body and has given greater honor to the parts that lacked it, ²⁵so that there should be no division in the body, but that its parts should have equal concern for each other. ²⁶If one part suffers, every part suffers with it; if one part is honored, every part rejoices with it.

²⁷Now you are the body of Christ, and each one of you is a part of it. ²⁸And in the church God has appointed first of all apostles, second prophets, third teachers, then workers of miracles, also those having gifts of healing, those able to help others, those with gifts of administration, and those speaking in different kinds of tongues. ²⁹Are all apostles? Are all prophets? Are all teachers? Do all work miracles? ³⁰Do all have gifts of healing? Do all speak in tongues*ᵃ*? Do all interpret? ³¹But eagerly desire*ᵇ* the greater gifts.

Love

And now I will show you the most excellent way.

13 If I speak in the tongues*ᶜ* of men and of angels, but have not love, I am only a resounding gong or a clanging cymbal. ²If I have the gift of prophecy and can fathom all mysteries and all knowledge, and if I have a faith that can move mountains, but have not love, I am nothing. ³If I give all I possess to the poor and surrender my body to the flames,*ᵈ* but have not love, I gain nothing.

⁴Love is patient, love is kind. It does not envy, it does not boast, it is not proud. ⁵It is not rude, it is not self-seeking, it is not easily angered, it keeps no record of wrongs. ⁶Love does not delight in evil but rejoices with the truth. ⁷It always protects, always trusts, always hopes, always perseveres.

⁸Love never fails. But where there are prophecies, they will cease; where there are tongues, they will be stilled; where there is knowledge, it will pass away. ⁹For we know in part and we prophesy in part, ¹⁰but when perfection comes, the imperfect disappears. ¹¹When I was a child, I talked like a child, I thought like a child, I reasoned like a child. When I became a man, I put childish

ways behind me. ¹²Now we see but a poor reflection as in a mirror; then we shall see face to face. Now I know in part; then I shall know fully, even as I am fully known.

¹³And now these three remain: faith, hope and love. But the greatest of these is love.

Gifts of Prophecy and Tongues

14 Follow the way of love and eagerly desire spiritual gifts, especially the gift of prophecy. ²For anyone who speaks in a tongue*ᵉ* does not speak to men but to God. Indeed, no one understands him; he utters mysteries with his

---

14:2 Speaking in Tongues

1 Corinthians 12–14 gives the New Testament's most complete teaching on supernatural gifts such as healing and speaking in tongues. Paul stresses two concerns: (1) "Sensational" gifts must not be given higher rank than they deserve (chapter 13 stresses the superiority of simple love). (2) These gifts should contribute to orderly and proper worship, not confusion. The Corinthians seemed to take everything to excess—whether practicing immorality, celebrating the Lord's Supper, or exercising spiritual gifts.

---

spirit.*ᶠ* ³But everyone who prophesies speaks to men for their strengthening, encouragement and comfort. ⁴He who speaks in a tongue edifies himself, but he who prophesies edifies the church. ⁵I would like every one of you to speak in tongues,*ᵍ* but I would rather have you prophesy. He who prophesies is greater than one who speaks in tongues,*ᵍ* unless he interprets, so that the church may be edified.

⁶Now, brothers, if I come to you and speak in tongues, what good will I be to you, unless I bring you some revelation or knowledge or prophecy or word of instruction? ⁷Even in the case of lifeless things that make sounds, such as the flute or harp, how will anyone know what tune is being played unless there is a distinction in the notes? ⁸Again, if the trumpet does not sound a clear call, who will get ready for battle? ⁹So it is with you. Unless you speak intelligible words with your tongue, how will anyone know what you are saying? You will just be speaking into the air. ¹⁰Undoubtedly there are all sorts of languages in the world, yet none of them is without meaning. ¹¹If then I do not grasp the meaning of what someone is saying, I am a foreigner to the speaker, and he is a foreigner to me. ¹²So it is with you. Since you are eager to have spiritu-

---

ᵃ30 Or *other languages*   *ᵇ31* Or *But you are eagerly desiring the body that I may boast*   *ᶜ1* Or *languages*   *ᵈ3* Some early manuscripts *body that I may boast*   *ᵉ2* Or *another language*; also in verses 4, 13, 14, 19, 26 and 27   *ᶠ2* Or *by the Spirit*   *ᵍ5* Or *other languages*; also in verses 6, 18, 22, 23 and 39

al gifts, try to excel in gifts that build up the church.

¹³For this reason anyone who speaks in a tongue should pray that he may interpret what he says. ¹⁴For if I pray in a tongue, my spirit prays, but my mind is unfruitful. ¹⁵So what shall I do? I will pray with my spirit, but I will also pray with my mind; I will sing with my spirit, but I will also sing with my mind. ¹⁶If you are praising God with your spirit, how can one who finds himself among those who do not understand*ᵃ* say "Amen" to your thanksgiving, since he does not know what you are saying? ¹⁷You may be giving thanks well enough, but the other man is not edified.

¹⁸I thank God that I speak in tongues more than all of you. ¹⁹But in the church I would rather speak five intelligible words to instruct others than ten thousand words in a tongue.

²⁰Brothers, stop thinking like children. In regard to evil be infants, but in your thinking be adults. ²¹In the Law it is written:

"Through men of strange tongues
    and through the lips of foreigners
I will speak to this people,
    but even then they will not listen to
        me,"ᵇ

says the Lord.

²²Tongues, then, are a sign, not for believers but for unbelievers; prophecy, however, is for believers, not for unbelievers. ²³So if the whole church comes together and everyone speaks in tongues, and some who do not understandᶜ or some unbelievers come in, will they not say that you are out of your mind? ²⁴But if an unbeliever or someone who does not understandᵈ comes in while everybody is prophesying, he will be convinced by all that he is a sinner and will be judged by all, ²⁵and the secrets of his heart will be laid bare. So he will fall down and worship God, exclaiming, "God is really among you!"

Orderly Worship

²⁶What then shall we say, brothers? When you come together, everyone has a hymn, or a word of instruction, a revelation, a tongue or an interpretation. All of these must be done for the strengthening of the church. ²⁷If anyone speaks in a tongue, two—or at the most three—should speak, one at a time, and someone must interpret. ²⁸If there is no interpreter, the speaker should keep quiet in the church and speak to himself and God.

²⁹Two or three prophets should speak, and the others should weigh carefully what is said. ³⁰And if a revelation comes to someone who is sitting down, the first speaker should stop. ³¹For you can all prophesy in turn so that everyone may be instructed and encouraged. ³²The spirits of prophets are subject to the control of prophets. ³³For God is not a God of disorder but of peace.

As in all the congregations of the saints, ³⁴women should remain silent in the churches. They are not allowed to speak, but must be in submission, as the Law says. ³⁵If they want to inquire about something, they should ask their own husbands at home; for it is disgraceful for a woman to speak in the church.

³⁶Did the word of God originate with you? Or are you the only people it has reached? ³⁷If anybody thinks he is a prophet or spiritually gifted, let him acknowledge that what I am writing to you is the Lord's command. ³⁸If he ignores this, he himself will be ignored.ᵉ

³⁹Therefore, my brothers, be eager to prophesy, and do not forbid speaking in tongues. ⁴⁰But everything should be done in a fitting and orderly way.

The Resurrection of Christ

15 Now, brothers, I want to remind you of the gospel I preached to you, which you received and on which you have taken your stand. ²By this gospel you are saved, if you hold firmly to the word I preached to you. Otherwise, you have believed in vain.

³For what I received I passed on to you as of first importanceᶠ: that Christ died for our sins according to the Scriptures, ⁴that he was buried, that he was raised on the third day according to the Scriptures, ⁵and that he appeared to Peter,ᵍ and then to the Twelve. ⁶After that, he appeared to more than five hundred of the brothers at the same time, most of whom are still living, though some have fallen asleep. ⁷Then he appeared to James, then to all the apostles, ⁸and last of all he appeared to me also, as to one abnormally born.

15:8 Basic Christianity

Paul stresses the basics every Christian must believe: that Christ died for our sins, that he was buried (really dead), and that he rose again. Listing some of the many people who saw Jesus after his resurrection, Paul includes himself last of all. He is referring to his encounter with Christ on the road to Damascus (see Acts 9).

⁹For I am the least of the apostles and do not even deserve to be called an apostle, because I persecuted the church of God. ¹⁰But by the grace

---

ᵃ16 Or *among the inquirers*   ᵇ21 Isaiah 28:11,12   ᶜ23 Or *some inquirers*   ᵈ24 Or *or some inquirer*
ᵉ38 Some manuscripts *If he is ignorant of this, let him be ignorant*   ᶠ3 Or *you at the first*   ᵍ5 Greek *Cephas*

of God I am what I am, and his grace to me was not without effect. No, I worked harder than all of them—yet not I, but the grace of God that was with me. ¹¹Whether, then, it was I or they, this is what we preach, and this is what you believed.

The Resurrection of the Dead

¹²But if it is preached that Christ has been raised from the dead, how can some of you say that there is no resurrection of the dead? ¹³If there is no resurrection of the dead, then not even Christ has been raised. ¹⁴And if Christ has not been raised, our preaching is useless and so is your faith. ¹⁵More than that, we are then found to be false witnesses about God, for we have testified about God that he raised Christ from the dead. But he did not raise him if in fact the dead are not raised. ¹⁶For if the dead are not raised, then Christ has not been raised either. ¹⁷And if Christ has not been raised, your faith is futile; you are still in your sins. ¹⁸Then those also who have fallen asleep in Christ are lost. ¹⁹If only for this life we have hope in Christ, we are to be pitied more than all men.

²⁰But Christ has indeed been raised from the dead, the firstfruits of those who have fallen asleep. ²¹For since death came through a man, the resurrection of the dead comes also through a man. ²²For as in Adam all die, so in Christ all will be made alive. ²³But each in his own turn: Christ, the firstfruits; then, when he comes, those

who belong to him. ²⁴Then the end will come, when he hands over the kingdom to God the Father after he has destroyed all dominion, authority and power. ²⁵For he must reign until he has put all his enemies under his feet. ²⁶The last enemy to be destroyed is death. ²⁷For he "has put everything under his feet."[a] Now when it says that "everything" has been put under him, it is clear that this does not include God himself, who put everything under Christ. ²⁸When he has done this, then the Son himself will be made subject to him who put everything under him, so that God may be all in all.

²⁹Now if there is no resurrection, what will those do who are baptized for the dead? If the dead are not raised at all, why are people baptized for them? ³⁰And as for us, why do we endanger ourselves every hour? ³¹I die every day— I mean that, brothers—just as surely as I glory over you in Christ Jesus our Lord. ³²If I fought wild beasts in Ephesus for merely human reasons, what have I gained? If the dead are not raised,

"Let us eat and drink,
    for tomorrow we die."[b]

³³Do not be misled: "Bad company corrupts good character." ³⁴Come back to your senses as you ought, and stop sinning; for there are some who are ignorant of God—I say this to your shame.

---

[a]27 Psalm 8:6   [b]32 Isaiah 22:13

The Worst Danger of All
Why believe in life after death?

> If there is no resurrection of the dead, then not even Christ has been raised. And if Christ has not been raised, our preaching is useless and so is your faith. 15:13–14

MOST OF THE PROBLEMS RAISED by the church at Corinth concerned personal behavior. After tackling each of those problems, Paul turned to one last question, a matter of doctrine. Some people in the church were challenging the Christian belief in an afterlife. Death, they said, is the end.

Many people have questioned the afterlife. In Jesus' day, a Jewish sect called Sadducees denied the resurrection from the dead. Doubters persist today (among them: many Black Muslims, Buddhists, and Marxists and most atheists). But Paul saw the matter of life after death as the most explosive issue in the Corinthian church.

Pitiable Christians

If there's no future life, he thundered, the entire Christian message would be a lie. He, Paul, would have no reason to continue as a minister; Christ's death would have merely wasted blood; and Christians would be the most pitiable of all people.

Chapter 15 weaves together the threads of Christian belief about death. It shows how death is finally conquered and becomes, not an end, but a beginning. Cheered by such a triumphant note, the apostle Paul sums up his counsel to the Corinthians with a ringing challenge to "stand firm."

Life Questions: Which of Paul's arguments in chapter 15 do you find most convincing? How does belief in an afterlife affect you?

The Resurrection Body

35But someone may ask, "How are the dead raised? With what kind of body will they come?" 36How foolish! What you sow does not come to life unless it dies. 37When you sow, you do not plant the body that will be, but just a seed, perhaps of wheat or of something else. 38But God gives it a body as he has determined, and to each kind of seed he gives its own body. 39All flesh is not the same: Men have one kind of flesh, animals have another, birds another and fish another. 40There are also heavenly bodies and there are earthly bodies; but the splendor of the heavenly bodies is one kind, and the splendor of the earthly bodies is another. 41The sun has one kind of splendor, the moon another and the stars another; and star differs from star in splendor.

42So will it be with the resurrection of the dead. The body that is sown is perishable, it is raised imperishable; 43it is sown in dishonor, it is raised in glory; it is sown in weakness, it is raised in power; 44it is sown a natural body, it is raised a spiritual body.

If there is a natural body, there is also a spiritual body. 45So it is written: "The first man Adam became a living being"[a]; the last Adam, a lifegiving spirit. 46The spiritual did not come first, but the natural, and after that the spiritual. 47The first man was of the dust of the earth, the second man from heaven. 48As was the earthly man, so are those who are of the earth; and as is the man from heaven, so also are those who are of heaven. 49And just as we have borne the likeness of the earthly man, so shall we[b] bear the likeness of the man from heaven.

50I declare to you, brothers, that flesh and blood cannot inherit the kingdom of God, nor does the perishable inherit the imperishable. 51Listen, I tell you a mystery: We will not all sleep, but we will all be changed— 52in a flash, in the twinkling of an eye, at the last trumpet. For the trumpet will sound, the dead will be raised imperishable, and we will be changed. 53For the perishable must clothe itself with the imperishable, and the mortal with immortality. 54When the perishable has been clothed with the imperishable, and the mortal with immortality, then the saying that is written will come true: "Death has been swallowed up in victory."[c]

55"Where, O death, is your victory?
  Where, O death, is your sting?"[d]

56The sting of death is sin, and the power of sin is the law. 57But thanks be to God! He gives us the victory through our Lord Jesus Christ.

58Therefore, my dear brothers, stand firm. Let nothing move you. Always give yourselves fully to the work of the Lord, because you know that your labor in the Lord is not in vain.

The Collection for God's People

16 Now about the collection for God's people: Do what I told the Galatian churches to do.

16:1 Remembering the Poor

Paul's deep concern for the poor in Jerusalem comes up often in the New Testament. He mentions taking a collection here, as well as in Romans and 2 Corinthians. He knew that widespread concern for the mother church in Jerusalem would do much to further unity between Jewish and Gentile Christians.

2On the first day of every week, each one of you should set aside a sum of money in keeping with his income, saving it up, so that when I come no collections will have to be made. 3Then, when I arrive, I will give letters of introduction to the men you approve and send them with your gift to Jerusalem. 4If it seems advisable for me to go also, they will accompany me.

Personal Requests

5After I go through Macedonia, I will come to you—for I will be going through Macedonia. 6Perhaps I will stay with you awhile, or even spend the winter, so that you can help me on my journey, wherever I go. 7I do not want to see you now and make only a passing visit; I hope to spend some time with you, if the Lord permits. 8But I will stay on at Ephesus until Pentecost, 9because a great door for effective work has opened to me, and there are many who oppose me.

10If Timothy comes, see to it that he has nothing to fear while he is with you, for he is carrying on the work of the Lord, just as I am. 11No one, then, should refuse to accept him. Send him on his way in peace so that he may return to me. I am expecting him along with the brothers.

12Now about our brother Apollos: I strongly urged him to go to you with the brothers. He was quite unwilling to go now, but he will go when he has the opportunity.

13Be on your guard; stand firm in the faith; be men of courage; be strong. 14Do everything in love.

15You know that the household of Stephanas were the first converts in Achaia, and they have devoted themselves to the service of the saints. I urge you, brothers, 16to submit to such as these and to everyone who joins in the work, and labors at it. 17I was glad when Stephanas, Fortuna-

---

a45 Gen. 2:7   *b49* Some early manuscripts *so let us*   *c54* Isaiah 25:8   *d55* Hosea 13:14

tus and Achaicus arrived, because they have supplied what was lacking from you. **18**For they refreshed my spirit and yours also. Such men deserve recognition.

Final Greetings

19The churches in the province of Asia send you greetings. Aquila and Priscilla*a* greet you warmly in the Lord, and so does the church that meets at their house. **20**All the brothers here send you greetings. Greet one another with a holy kiss.

21I, Paul, write this greeting in my own hand. **22**If anyone does not love the Lord—a curse be on him. Come, O Lord*b*!

23The grace of the Lord Jesus be with you.

24My love to all of you in Christ Jesus. Amen.*c*

---

a19 Greek *Prisca*, a variant of *Priscilla* manuscripts do not have *Amen*. *b22* In Aramaic the expression *Come, O Lord* is *Marana tha*. *c24* Some

2 CORINTHIANS

A Book of Joy and Sadness
Why isn't Paul celebrating his victory?

> Indeed, in our hearts we felt the sentence of death. But this happened that we might not rely on ourselves but on God, who raises the dead. 1:9

ATHLETES SOMETIMES HAVE A STRANGE reaction to a great victory. Some call it "morning-after sickness." An Olympic gymnast who has trained for 15 years wakes up the day after her gold medal performance feeling oddly depressed. Paradoxically, the sweet taste of victory can take on a bitter edge.

An even more pungent feeling may hit those who prevail in personal disputes. The man who wins a crucial court case is stabbed by sympathy for those he defeated. The politician who waves jubilantly to a cheering crowd on primary night winces inwardly at the bruises she suffered—and inflicted—during the campaign. The husband who insisted on a divorce leaves the final settlement feeling sad and burdened.

Lingering Pain

Something like that bittersweet state must have plagued the apostle Paul when he wrote 2 Corinthians. He had just won a great victory in convincing the Corinthians to come over to his side. His spirit had surged upon hearing Titus's news of their wave of support for him (7:6–16). His previous letter, a personal risk, had paid off. Reflecting Paul's triumph, this letter spontaneously breaks out in jubilant praise and thanksgiving.

And yet, in no other letter does Paul so openly admit his frustrations. Immediately after a spare greeting he mentions hardships so severe that "we despaired even of life" (1:8). Numerous references crop up regarding the tense relations he and the Corinthians have had. Paul wonders aloud if he has been too hard on them; he acknowledges his own lingering pain.

A Diary for Two Audiences

Second Corinthians, full of allusions and personal references, reads more like a diary than a public document. If 1 Corinthians analyzes the problems of the Corinthian church, this sequel reveals the problems Paul himself experienced.

He doesn't gloat over his victory in getting the Corinthians' support. Rather, he makes himself vulnerable and opens a window into his inner self. He summarizes his state as "hard pressed on every side, but not crushed; perplexed, but not in despair; persecuted, but not abandoned; struck down, but not destroyed" (4:8–9).

Although random selections from 2 Corinthians demonstrate the author's seesawing moods, the book as a whole reveals a tenacious man on the rebound. Paul expresses relief that the Corinthians' problems are being resolved, even as he points out new danger signs in the church. Always he keeps in mind a dual readership: the majority who support him, for whom he has warm, loving words, and the minority of dissenters who pose a grave threat to church unity.

How to Read 2 Corinthians

Of all Paul's letters, 2 Corinthians reads most like a personal letter and least like a public document. He wrote it when an intense struggle with the Corinthian church was coming to a head. As a result, it reveals much about Paul's troubled state. He half-apologized for speaking so freely, for appearing to be boasting, and for spending time on "foolishness."

Read 2 Corinthians like you would read any personal letter. Try to visualize the mood of the apostle Paul as he was writing, and look between the lines for clues that would help explain his relationship with the church at Corinth. What were his enemies accusing him of? Watch especially for Paul's spirited reply to criticism, especially in the last four chapters. He tells about certain events in his life that are recorded nowhere else.

You will likely notice that Paul is tying up loose ends in this letter: for example, he is preparing for a third visit to Corinth and asking them to get a collection ready. Yet amid these practical matters he pauses to write profound words on such topics as suffering, giving, and personal ministry.

3-TRACK READING PLAN

For an explanation and complete listing of the 3-track reading plan, turn to page 7.

TRACK 1: *Two-Week Courses on the Bible*
See page 7 for information on these courses.

TRACK 2: *An Overview of 2 Corinthians in 2 Days*
☐ Day 1. Read the Introduction to 2 Corinthians, then chapter 4. It helps explain how Paul kept going despite all his hardships.
☐ Day 2. Read chapter 12, which includes a brief description of Paul's "out-of-the-body" experience and his mysterious "thorn in the flesh."

Now turn to page 9 for your next Track 2 reading project.

TRACK 3: *All of 2 Corinthians in 10 Days*
After you have read through 2 Corinthians, turn to pages 10–14 for your next Track 3 reading project.

☐1   ☐2–3   ☐4   ☐5   ☐6   ☐7   ☐8–9   ☐10
☐11   ☐12–13

1 Paul, an apostle of Christ Jesus by the will of God, and Timothy our brother,

To the church of God in Corinth, together with all the saints throughout Achaia:

²Grace and peace to you from God our Father and the Lord Jesus Christ.

The God of All Comfort

³Praise be to the God and Father of our Lord Jesus Christ, the Father of compassion and the God of all comfort, ⁴who comforts us in all our troubles, so that we can comfort those in any trouble with the comfort we ourselves have received from God. ⁵For just as the sufferings of Christ flow over into our lives, so also through Christ our comfort overflows. ⁶If we are distressed, it is for your comfort and salvation; if we are comforted, it is for your comfort, which produces in you patient endurance of the same sufferings we suffer. ⁷And our hope for you is firm, because we know that just as you share in our sufferings, so also you share in our comfort.

⁸We do not want you to be uninformed, brothers, about the hardships we suffered in the province of Asia. We were under great pressure,

far beyond our ability to endure, so that we despaired even of life. ⁹Indeed, in our hearts we felt the sentence of death. But this happened that we might not rely on ourselves but on God, who raises the dead. ¹⁰He has delivered us from such a deadly peril, and he will deliver us. On him we have set our hope that he will continue to deliver

1:8 On the Rebound

Paul does not tell what specific hardships he had faced in Asia; they were probably known to the original audience. But four separate places in this letter (chapters 4, 6, 11, 12) he spells out an accumulation of hardships that plagued his ministry. Such life-threatening trials had recently driven him into a deep state of despair. He survived, though, and was now using his newfound vitality to comfort and reassure concerned friends in Corinth.

us, ¹¹as you help us by your prayers. Then many will give thanks on our*ᵃ* behalf for the gracious favor granted us in answer to the prayers of many.

ᵃ 11 Many manuscripts your

Paul's Change of Plans

[12]Now this is our boast: Our conscience testifies that we have conducted ourselves in the world, and especially in our relations with you, in the holiness and sincerity that are from God. We have done so not according to worldly wisdom but according to God's grace. [13]For we do not write you anything you cannot read or understand. And I hope that, [14]as you have understood us in part, you will come to understand fully that you can boast of us just as we will boast of you in the day of the Lord Jesus.

[15]Because I was confident of this, I planned to visit you first so that you might benefit twice. [16]I planned to visit you on my way to Macedonia and to come back to you from Macedonia, and then to have you send me on my way to Judea. [17]When I planned this, did I do it lightly? Or do I make my plans in a worldly manner so that in the same breath I say, "Yes, yes" and "No, no"?

[18]But as surely as God is faithful, our message to you is not "Yes" and "No." [19]For the Son of God, Jesus Christ, who was preached among you by me and Silas[a] and Timothy, was not "Yes" and "No," but in him it has always been "Yes." [20]For no matter how many promises God has made, they are "Yes" in Christ. And so through him the "Amen" is spoken by us to the glory of God. [21]Now it is God who makes both us and you stand firm in Christ. He anointed us, [22]set his seal of ownership on us, and put his Spirit in our hearts as a deposit, guaranteeing what is to come.

[23]I call God as my witness that it was in order to spare you that I did not return to Corinth. [24]Not that we lord it over your faith, but we work with you for your joy, because it is by faith you stand firm.

2 [1]So I made up my mind that I would not make another painful visit to you. [2]For if I grieve you, who is left to make me glad but you whom I have grieved? [3]I wrote as I did so that when I came I should not be distressed by those who ought to make me rejoice. I had confidence in all of you, that you would all share my joy. [4]For I wrote you out of great distress and anguish of heart and with many tears, not to grieve you but to let you know the depth of my love for you.

Forgiveness for the Sinner

[5]If anyone has caused grief, he has not so much grieved me as he has grieved all of you, to some extent—not to put it too severely. [6]The punishment inflicted on him by the majority is sufficient for him. [7]Now instead, you ought to forgive and comfort him, so that he will not be overwhelmed by excessive sorrow. [8]I urge you, therefore, to reaffirm your love for him. [9]The reason I wrote you was to see if you would stand

the test and be obedient in everything. [10]If you forgive anyone, I also forgive him. And what I have forgiven—if there was anything to forgive—I have forgiven in the sight of Christ for your sake, [11]in order that Satan might not outwit us. For we are not unaware of his schemes.

Ministers of the New Covenant

[12]Now when I went to Troas to preach the gospel of Christ and found that the Lord had opened a door for me, [13]I still had no peace of mind, because I did not find my brother Titus there. So I said good-by to them and went on to Macedonia.

[14]But thanks be to God, who always leads us in triumphal procession in Christ and through us spreads everywhere the fragrance of the knowl-

2:14 Victory Party

On their return from battle, Roman generals were honored with a triumphal procession, much like the ticker-tape parades given modern heroes. As the victorious army paraded their loot and conquered captives, the streets would be filled with fragrance from burning incense and the smells of the victory feast being prepared.

edge of him. [15]For we are to God the aroma of Christ among those who are being saved and those who are perishing. [16]To the one we are the smell of death; to the other, the fragrance of life. And who is equal to such a task? [17]Unlike so many, we do not peddle the word of God for profit. On the contrary, in Christ we speak before God with sincerity, like men sent from God.

3 [1]Are we beginning to commend ourselves again? Or do we need, like some people, letters of recommendation to you or from you? [2]You yourselves are our letter, written on our

3:2 A Human Letter

Chapters 3–5 form one of the Bible's great passages on professional ministry: what is involved in representing Christ on earth. Responding to attacks, Paul defends his "style" of ministry. He discusses the ultimate goal of ministry and the grace of God in using mere "jars of clay" (4:7) to accomplish his work. But the final proof of effectiveness, he says, is people's lives. In this way, the Corinthians themselves are his best letter of recommendation, for he brought them the gospel in the first place.

---

[a] 19 Greek *Silvanus*, a variant of *Silas*

hearts, known and read by everybody. ³You show that you are a letter from Christ, the result of our ministry, written not with ink but with the Spirit of the living God, not on tablets of stone but on tablets of human hearts.

⁴Such confidence as this is ours through Christ before God. ⁵Not that we are competent in ourselves to claim anything for ourselves, but our competence comes from God. ⁶He has made us competent as ministers of a new covenant—not of the letter but of the Spirit; for the letter kills, but the Spirit gives life.

The Glory of the New Covenant

⁷Now if the ministry that brought death, which was engraved in letters on stone, came with glory, so that the Israelites could not look steadily at the face of Moses because of its glory, fading though it was, ⁸will not the ministry of the Spirit be even more glorious? ⁹If the ministry that condemns men is glorious, how much more glorious is the ministry that brings righteousness! ¹⁰For what was glorious has no glory now in comparison with the surpassing glory. ¹¹And if what was fading away came with glory, how much greater is the glory of that which lasts!

¹²Therefore, since we have such a hope, we are very bold. ¹³We are not like Moses, who would put a veil over his face to keep the Israelites from gazing at it while the radiance was fading away. ¹⁴But their minds were made dull, for to this day the same veil remains when the old covenant is read. It has not been removed, because only in Christ is it taken away. ¹⁵Even to this day when Moses is read, a veil covers their hearts. ¹⁶But whenever anyone turns to the Lord, the veil is taken away. ¹⁷Now the Lord is the Spirit, and where the Spirit of the Lord is, there is freedom.

A Mysterious Visit
Paul's break with the Corinthians

THOSE WHO TRY TO PIECE together Paul's life story from fragments in the two Corinthian letters and the book of Acts usually come away puzzled. Paul, addressing friends who knew that history intimately, saw no need to review every stage of their relationship. Yet for us, reading centuries later, some chronology would help explain his allusions and his emotional state.

> So I made up my mind that I would not make another painful visit to you.
> 2:1

Many scholars believe two events occurred to which Paul refers only in passing: the "painful visit" and the letter written "out of great distress."

A Change in Plans

In the first two chapters Paul explains a change of plans whereby he decided not to visit Corinth because he didn't want to make "another painful visit" (2:1). What visit was he referring to?

During his first visit to Corinth, spanning 18 months, the church took shape (Acts 18:11). Paul probably would not have described that time as a "painful visit," for his relationship with them at that time was basically positive. Evidently he made a second visit to Corinth, not recorded in Acts, that included a painful confrontation.

Paul planned a third visit to Corinth, but postponed it because he didn't want to stir up the conflict. Later, he wondered about rescheduling that third visit (12:14; 13:1).

The Longed-for Reconciliation

Second Corinthians also mentions a letter written out of great distress and with many tears (2:4; 7:8). This letter, coming after Paul's unsettling second visit, contained such strong wording that he feared the Corinthians' response. He fleetingly regretted having written the letter. Had it ruptured their relationship? While he preached in the seaport town of Troas, Paul anxiously awaited some report of their reaction, through Titus.

One can imagine Paul rushing to the dock as ships from Macedonia came to unload, fervently scanning the vessels for some sign of Titus. Finally, unable to find peace of mind, he left his ministry in Troas to seek out Titus in Macedonia.

News from Titus at last calmed Paul. The Corinthians had indeed repented (7:7–9) and now wanted to restore ties with him. Feeling encouraged, Paul contemplated a third visit as he wrote 2 Corinthians. He used the letter to rebuild his relationship with them and to spell out his reasons for coming.

Life Questions: Have you ever experienced a tear in a relationship like the one described here? How have you found healing?

18And we, who with unveiled faces all reflect[a] the Lord's glory, are being transformed into his likeness with ever-increasing glory, which comes from the Lord, who is the Spirit.

Treasures in Jars of Clay

4 Therefore, since through God's mercy we have this ministry, we do not lose heart. 2Rather, we have renounced secret and shameful ways; we do not use deception, nor do we distort the word of God. On the contrary, by setting forth the truth plainly we commend ourselves to every man's conscience in the sight of God. 3And even if our gospel is veiled, it is veiled to those who are perishing. 4The god of this age has blinded the minds of unbelievers, so that they cannot see the light of the gospel of the glory of Christ, who is the image of God. 5For we do not preach ourselves, but Jesus Christ as Lord, and ourselves as your servants for Jesus' sake. 6For God, who said, "Let light shine out of darkness,"[b] made his light shine in our hearts to give us the light of the knowledge of the glory of God in the face of Christ.

7But we have this treasure in jars of clay to show that this all-surpassing power is from God

4:7 A Picture of Weakness

Where would you keep expensive jewelry? You would want a safe, secure place. You wouldn't stash valuables in, say, a tattered cardboard box. Yet this image comes close to the one Paul used to describe his ministry: "jars of clay." In his day jars were about as common—and as safe—as cardboard boxes are today.

The treasure Paul refers to is the incredible message of the gospel: God's good news of forgiveness and the promise of life forever. Yet, amazingly, God chose to enclose that treasure in people who are like "jars of clay." Clay jars are ordinary and highly breakable, and Paul tells us he is both. An immortal God chooses mere humans as his personal representatives. "And who is equal to such a task?" Paul asks (2:16). He determines to draw attention to the treasure inside him, not to himself.

and not from us. 8We are hard pressed on every side, but not crushed; perplexed, but not in despair; 9persecuted, but not abandoned; struck down, but not destroyed. 10We always carry around in our body the death of Jesus, so that the life of Jesus may also be revealed in our body. 11For we who are alive are always being given over to death for Jesus' sake, so that his life may be revealed in our mortal body. 12So then, death is at work in us, but life is at work in you.

13It is written: "I believed; therefore I have spoken."[c] With that same spirit of faith we also believe and therefore speak, 14because we know that the one who raised the Lord Jesus from the dead will also raise us with Jesus and present us with you in his presence. 15All this is for your benefit, so that the grace that is reaching more and more people may cause thanksgiving to overflow to the glory of God.

16Therefore we do not lose heart. Though outwardly we are wasting away, yet inwardly we are being renewed day by day. 17For our light and momentary troubles are achieving for us an eternal glory that far outweighs them all. 18So we fix our eyes not on what is seen, but on what is unseen. For what is seen is temporary, but what is unseen is eternal.

Our Heavenly Dwelling

5 Now we know that if the earthly tent we live in is destroyed, we have a building from God, an eternal house in heaven, not built by human

5:1 The Body as a Tent

Paul often refers to his frail and abused body in this letter. But in this passage he looks past life on earth to a future life when, he says, we will have new bodies "not built by human hands." The contrast between tent and house shows the temporary nature of a body in this life compared to what is to come.

hands. 2Meanwhile we groan, longing to be clothed with our heavenly dwelling, 3because when we are clothed, we will not be found naked. 4For while we are in this tent, we groan and are burdened, because we do not wish to be unclothed but to be clothed with our heavenly dwelling, so that what is mortal may be swallowed up by life. 5Now it is God who has made us for this very purpose and has given us the Spirit as a deposit, guaranteeing what is to come.

6Therefore we are always confident and know that as long as we are at home in the body we are away from the Lord. 7We live by faith, not by sight. 8We are confident, I say, and would prefer to be away from the body and at home with the Lord. 9So we make it our goal to please him, whether we are at home in the body or away from it. 10For we must all appear before the judgment seat of Christ, that each one may receive what is due him for the things done while in the body, whether good or bad.

The Ministry of Reconciliation

11Since, then, we know what it is to fear the

a18 Or *contemplate*   b6 Gen. 1:3   c13 Psalm 116:10

Lord, we try to persuade men. What we are is plain to God, and I hope it is also plain to your conscience. [12]We are not trying to commend ourselves to you again, but are giving you an opportunity to take pride in us, so that you can answer those who take pride in what is seen rather than in what is in the heart. [13]If we are out of our mind, it is for the sake of God; if we are in our right mind, it is for you. [14]For Christ's love compels us, because we are convinced that one died for all, and therefore all died. [15]And he died for all, that those who live should no longer live for themselves but for him who died for them and was raised again.

[16]So from now on we regard no one from a worldly point of view. Though we once regarded Christ in this way, we do so no longer. [17]Therefore, if anyone is in Christ, he is a new creation; the old has gone, the new has come! [18]All this is from God, who reconciled us to himself through Christ and gave us the ministry of reconciliation: [19]that God was reconciling the world to himself in Christ, not counting men's sins against them. And he has committed to us the message of reconciliation. [20]We are therefore Christ's ambassadors, as though God were making his appeal through us. We implore you on Christ's behalf: Be reconciled to God. [21]God made him who had no sin to be sin[a] for us, so that in him we might become the righteousness of God.

6 As God's fellow workers we urge you not to receive God's grace in vain. [2]For he says,

"In the time of my favor I heard you,
and in the day of salvation I helped
you."[b]

I tell you, now is the time of God's favor, now is the day of salvation.

Paul's Hardships

[3]We put no stumbling block in anyone's path, so that our ministry will not be discredited. [4]Rather, as servants of God we commend ourselves in every way: in great endurance; in troubles, hardships and distresses; [5]in beatings, imprisonments and riots; in hard work, sleepless nights and hunger; [6]in purity, understanding, patience and kindness; in the Holy Spirit and in sincere love; [7]in truthful speech and in the power of God; with weapons of righteousness in the right hand and in the left; [8]through glory and dishonor, bad report and good report; genuine, yet regarded as impostors; [9]known, yet regarded as unknown; dying, and yet we live on; beaten, and yet not killed; [10]sorrowful, yet always rejoicing; poor, yet making many rich; having nothing, and yet possessing everything.

[11]We have spoken freely to you, Corinthians, and opened wide our hearts to you. [12]We are not withholding our affection from you, but you are withholding yours from us. [13]As a fair exchange—I speak as to my children—open wide your hearts also.

Do Not Be Yoked With Unbelievers

[14]Do not be yoked together with unbelievers. For what do righteousness and wickedness have in common? Or what fellowship can light have

6:14 Unequal Yokes

A yoke is a curved wooden bar that fits across the necks of two animals used to pull a plow or wagon. Yoke together a short, speedy calf with a tall, sluggish ox, and you're asking for trouble. Paul probably had in mind the false teachers who so often bedeviled the Corinthians, but his wise principle applies to many other alliances between believers and unbelievers.

with darkness? [15]What harmony is there between Christ and Belial[c]? What does a believer have in common with an unbeliever? [16]What agreement is there between the temple of God and idols? For we are the temple of the living God. As God has said: "I will live with them and walk among them, and I will be their God, and they will be my people."[d]

[17]"Therefore come out from them
and be separate,
says the Lord.
Touch no unclean thing,
and I will receive you."[e]
[18]"I will be a Father to you,
and you will be my sons and daughters,
says the Lord Almighty."[f]

7 Since we have these promises, dear friends, let us purify ourselves from everything that contaminates body and spirit, perfecting holiness out of reverence for God.

Paul's Joy

[2]Make room for us in your hearts. We have wronged no one, we have corrupted no one, we have exploited no one. [3]I do not say this to condemn you; I have said before that you have such a place in our hearts that we would live or die with you. [4]I have great confidence in you; I take great pride in you. I am greatly encouraged; in all our troubles my joy knows no bounds.

[5]For when we came into Macedonia, this body

[a]21 Or *be a sin offering*   [b]2 Isaiah 49:8   [c]15 Greek *Beliar*, a variant of *Belial*   [d]16 Lev. 26:12; Jer. 32:38; Ezek. 37:27   [e]17 Isaiah 52:11; Ezek. 20:34,41   [f]18 2 Samuel 7:14; 7:8

of ours had no rest, but we were harassed at every turn—conflicts on the outside, fears within. ⁶But God, who comforts the downcast, comforted us by the coming of Titus, ⁷and not only by his coming but also by the comfort you had given him. He told us about your longing for me, your deep sorrow, your ardent concern for me, so that my joy was greater than ever.

⁸Even if I caused you sorrow by my letter, I do not regret it. Though I did regret it—I see that my letter hurt you, but only for a little while— ⁹yet now I am happy, not because you were made sorry, but because your sorrow led you to repentance. For you became sorrowful as God intended and so were not harmed in any way by us. ¹⁰Godly sorrow brings repentance that leads to salvation and leaves no regret, but worldly sorrow brings death. ¹¹See what this godly sorrow has produced in you: what earnestness, what eagerness to clear yourselves, what indignation, what alarm, what longing, what concern, what readiness to see justice done. At every point you have proved yourselves to be innocent in this matter. ¹²So even though I wrote to you, it was not on account of the one who did the wrong or of the injured party, but rather that before God you could see for yourselves how devoted to us you are. ¹³By all this we are encouraged.

In addition to our own encouragement, we were especially delighted to see how happy Titus

was, because his spirit has been refreshed by all of you. ¹⁴I had boasted to him about you, and you have not embarrassed me. But just as everything we said to you was true, so our boasting

---

7:11 What Suffering Produces

When he wrote about suffering, Paul concentrated not merely on the pain itself, but on what qualities it produced in those who had faith. In this case, he cites the emotional suffering the Corinthians had experienced because of his letter. Although the suffering was unpleasant, it produced something of great value: an abrupt change in their attitudes.

---

about you to Titus has proved to be true as well. ¹⁵And his affection for you is all the greater when he remembers that you were all obedient, receiving him with fear and trembling. ¹⁶I am glad I can have complete confidence in you.

Generosity Encouraged

8 And now, brothers, we want you to know about the grace that God has given the Macedonian churches. ²Out of the most severe trial, their overflowing joy and their extreme poverty welled up in rich generosity. ³For I testify that

---

Don't Forget the Poor
A fund-raising letter from Paul himself

EVERY DAY IN MILLIONS OF mailboxes across the United States, letters with special "non-profit" postage stamps appear, stuffed among catalogs, magazines, and flyers from retail stores. Fund-raising through the mail is big business for Jews, Catholics, Protestants and a passel of charitable organizations.

The apostle Paul assuredly never engineered a million-piece charity appeal—the empire's postal service and the cost of papyrus made such an idea unthinkable. But 2 Corinthians does present a direct appeal for funds (chapters 8–9). Jewish Christians near Jerusalem were reportedly on the edge of starvation. Paul seized on the crisis as a perfect chance for Gentile Christians to reach out in compassion and demonstrate their spiritual unity with Jewish Christians.

> *Each man should give what he has decided in his heart to give, not reluctantly or under compulsion, for God loves a cheerful giver. 9:7*

Practicing What He Preached

In these two chapters, Paul outlines a philosophy of Christian giving, holding up Jesus Christ as a model. He explains the goal of such giving and the proper attitude of the givers. He even applies a little pressure by citing examples of Christians less well-heeled than the Corinthians (8:1–6; 9:1–5).

This brief passage on giving shows Paul's holistic concerns. While still recuperating from personal trauma, he had agreed to head up a major fund-raising drive on behalf of the needy in Jerusalem. Later, working on that very project, he paused to write the profoundly theological book of Romans (Romans 15:25–26). His scholarship didn't dampen a zeal for practical Christian love; his concern for souls didn't crowd out concern for their hungry bodies.

Life Questions: Compare Paul's appeal for funds with those you see in the mail and in the media. Is there a different emphasis?

Anointed

For the members of Anointed, music is more than a job, more than an adventure, more than a passion – it's a calling. It's not always easy. The path is not always clear and there are sacrifices to be made, but there's nothing they'd rather do than follow the will of the Lord.

"We've been called to do what we do," Anointed's Steve Crawford says. "It's more than just doing music and singing and recording albums. It all started with a word from God—a vision from him, and we've been walking in that vision ever since. Then it just started to expand nationally and internationally. Our vision is to reach a lot of people—young and old—with our music, music of encouragement, music of inspiration."

Steve's sister Da'dra agrees. "I think all of us, from a very young age, had sense that God had something very special for our lives," she relates. "I think in the process of seeking God as teenagers, we were in a position to be able to sense when God was moving us toward this ministry. The most miraculous thing is that all four of us were just immediately on one accord about the whole thing. We just knew it was right."

Denise ("Nee-C") Walls rounded out the group's membership, and before long the group's powerful vocals and passionate performances had made them one of the most popular ensembles in their hometown of Columbus, Ohio. They admit at first they had no intentions of ever signing a record deal or performing beyond their hometown, but God had bigger plans.

Nee-C reflects on Anointed's latest release, *Under the Influence*: "I want people to feel a lot of love," she says, "and a lot of hope from this album that they can go on in their ministry whatever it may be...I want them to feel God's love and their hearts to be encouraged. I want to see people touched and lives changed."

Touching people and changing lives – that's what Anointed is all about.

WOW
1997

Ray Boltz

"One Drop of Blood" is the inspiring song from CCM artist Ray Boltz that appears on the WoW 1997 CD. Ray writes,

"I have written many songs about people who have made sacrifices—Sunday school teachers, pastors, missionaries, and even Christians who have been martyred for their faith. But without question, I consider the sacrifice of Jesus Christ, God's own Son, the greatest sacrifice of all!

"I have stood in Calcutta, India, and watched as animals have been sacrificed at one of the temples. I remember thinking of Hebrews 9:12 in that situation: 'He did not enter by means of the blood of goats and calves; but he entered the Most Holy Place once for all by his own blood, having obtained eternal redemption.'

"Hebrews 10:5-7 says, 'Therefore, when Christ came into the world, he said: "Sacrifice and offering you did not desire, but a body you prepared for me; with burnt offerings and sin offerings you were not pleased." Then I said, "Here I am—it is written about me in the scroll—I have come to do your will, O God."'

"I am so thankful that Jesus did the will of the Father and offered himself to us. I am so glad that the only sacrifice we need to make is to trust in him and in his perfect sacrifice for us."

"By one sacrifice he has made perfect forever those who are being made holy" (Hebrews 10:14).

they gave as much as they were able, and even beyond their ability. Entirely on their own, [4]they urgently pleaded with us for the privilege of sharing in this service to the saints. [5]And they did not do as we expected, but they gave themselves first to the Lord and then to us in keeping with God's will. [6]So we urged Titus, since he had earlier made a beginning, to bring also to completion this act of grace on your part. [7]But just as you excel in everything—in faith, in speech, in knowledge, in complete earnestness and in your love for us[a]—see that you also excel in this grace of giving.

[8]I am not commanding you, but I want to test the sincerity of your love by comparing it with the earnestness of others. [9]For you know the grace of our Lord Jesus Christ, that though he was rich, yet for your sakes he became poor, so that you through his poverty might become rich.

[10]And here is my advice about what is best for you in this matter: Last year you were the first not only to give but also to have the desire to do so. [11]Now finish the work, so that your eager willingness to do it may be matched by your completion of it, according to your means. [12]For if the willingness is there, the gift is acceptable according to what one has, not according to what he does not have.

[13]Our desire is not that others might be relieved while you are hard pressed, but that there might be equality. [14]At the present time your plenty will supply what they need, so that in turn their plenty will supply what you need. Then there will be equality, [15]as it is written: "He who gathered much did not have too much, and he who gathered little did not have too little."[b]

Titus Sent to Corinth

[16]I thank God, who put into the heart of Titus the same concern I have for you. [17]For Titus not only welcomed our appeal, but he is coming to you with much enthusiasm and on his own initiative. [18]And we are sending along with him the brother who is praised by all the churches for his service to the gospel. [19]What is more, he was chosen by the churches to accompany us as we carry the offering, which we administer in order to honor the Lord himself and to show our eagerness to help. [20]We want to avoid any criticism of the way we administer this liberal gift. [21]For we are taking pains to do what is right, not only in the eyes of the Lord but also in the eyes of men.

[22]In addition, we are sending with them our brother who has often proved to us in many ways that he is zealous, and now even more so because of his great confidence in you. [23]As for Titus, he is my partner and fellow worker among you; as for our brothers, they are representatives of the churches and an honor to Christ. [24]Therefore show these men the proof of your love and the reason for our pride in you, so that the churches can see it.

9 There is no need for me to write to you about this service to the saints. [2]For I know your eagerness to help, and I have been boasting about it to the Macedonians, telling them that since last year you in Achaia were ready to give; and your enthusiasm has stirred most of them to action. [3]But I am sending the brothers in order that our boasting about you in this matter should not prove hollow, but that you may be ready, as I said you would be. [4]For if any Macedonians come with me and find you unprepared, we—not to say anything about you—would be ashamed of having been so confident. [5]So I thought it necessary to urge the brothers to visit you in advance and finish the arrangements for the generous gift you had promised. Then it will be ready as a generous gift, not as one grudgingly given.

Sowing Generously

[6]Remember this: Whoever sows sparingly will also reap sparingly, and whoever sows generously

9:6 Bonuses of Giving

In taking his collection for poor people, Paul mainly appealed to the Christian responsibility to help those in need. But in this passage he details generosity's side effects. Giving actually enriches and benefits the giver, he says. Also, a gift can serve as an act of worship to God and can inspire other people's faith and thanksgiving.

will also reap generously. [7]Each man should give what he has decided in his heart to give, not reluctantly or under compulsion, for God loves a cheerful giver. [8]And God is able to make all grace abound to you, so that in all things at all times, having all that you need, you will abound in every good work. [9]As it is written:

"He has scattered abroad his gifts to the poor;
    his righteousness endures forever."[c]

[10]Now he who supplies seed to the sower and bread for food will also supply and increase your store of seed and will enlarge the harvest of your righteousness. [11]You will be made rich in every way so that you can be generous on every occasion, and through us your generosity will result in thanksgiving to God.

[12]This service that you perform is not only supplying the needs of God's people but is also

---

[a]7 Some manuscripts *in our love for you*   [b]15 Exodus 16:18   [c]9 Psalm 112:9

overflowing in many expressions of thanks to God. [13]Because of the service by which you have proved yourselves, men will praise God for the obedience that accompanies your confession of the gospel of Christ, and for your generosity in sharing with them and with everyone else. [14]And in their prayers for you their hearts will go out to you, because of the surpassing grace God has given you. [15]Thanks be to God for his indescribable gift!

Paul's Defense of His Ministry

10 By the meekness and gentleness of Christ, I appeal to you—I, Paul, who am "timid" when face to face with you, but "bold" when away! [2]I beg you that when I come I may not have to be as bold as I expect to be toward some people who think that we live by the standards of this world. [3]For though we live in the world, we do not wage war as the world does. [4]The weapons we fight with are not the weapons of the world. On the contrary, they have divine power to demolish strongholds. [5]We demolish arguments and every pretension that sets itself up against the knowledge of God, and we take captive every thought to make it obedient to Christ. [6]And we will be ready to punish every act of disobedience, once your obedience is complete.

[7]You are looking only on the surface of things.[a] If anyone is confident that he belongs to Christ, he should consider again that we belong to Christ just as much as he. [8]For even if I boast somewhat freely about the authority the Lord gave us for building you up rather than pulling you down, I will not be ashamed of it. [9]I do not want to seem to be trying to frighten you with my letters. [10]For some say, "His letters are weighty and forceful, but in person he is unimpressive and his speaking amounts to nothing." [11]Such people should realize that what we are in our letters when we are absent, we will be in our actions when we are present.

[12]We do not dare to classify or compare ourselves with some who commend themselves. When they measure themselves by themselves and compare themselves with themselves, they

[a]7 Or Look at the obvious facts

Paul Has Had Enough
Answering his critics

> I repeat: Let no one take me for a fool.
> 11:16

VERSE 1 OF CHAPTER 10 introduces a dramatic shift in tone. The first nine chapters mainly show Paul's relief at seeing encouraging signs in Corinth. But these last four chapters make clear that hostility was still raging. In fact, some have guessed this section was taken from the painful letter Paul referred to earlier (2:4). Here at the end of 2 Corinthians, Paul boldly confronts his critics.

Who were his antagonists? A picture of them emerges if you compile all the accusations Paul answers throughout the letter. Basically, they were carping troublemakers. In their eyes, Paul could do nothing right.

Paul's enemies in Corinth had blasted him for not visiting them as promised; yet when he did visit they gossiped, "In person he is unimpressive and his speaking amounts to nothing" (10:10). They had criticized him for not taking a salary and then hinted he was misusing funds (8:20; 11:7–9). To these "super-apostles" (11:5), Paul somehow appeared simultaneously unimpressive and yet crafty; overly strict and yet worldly. Some even hinted he was out of his mind (5:13).

A Ringing Self-Defense

You can almost sense Paul declaring "I've had it!" and then rolling up his sleeves to refute the charges. He insists that the future of the Corinthian church, not just his own reputation, is at stake. What does he feel? Something like the burning jealousy of a father who watches his virgin daughter being seduced away from her true lover (11:2–3).

These four remarkable chapters show Paul's passionate nature. Frustrated by having to defend himself, he almost stammers in print. He is determined to convince the Corinthians that he is motivated by a desire to serve God, not by any schemes of profit or power. Along the way, he lists an amazing catalog of his physical sufferings and reveals intimate details of his spiritual life, including one incident still shrouded in mystery (12:1–6).

Judge for yourself, Paul seems to say, to the Corinthians and to all of us. Look at my life and decide, Whose fool am I?

Life Questions: Have you ever been wrongly accused of something? How did you react to your accusers?

are not wise. [13]We, however, will not boast beyond proper limits, but will confine our boasting to the field God has assigned to us, a field that reaches even to you. [14]We are not going too far

10:7–18 Style or Substance?

Paul had an image problem, and his enemies were taking advantage of it by ridiculing his unimpressive personal style. Though a powerful, direct, and engaging speaker, Paul was spurned by those who preferred a more golden-tongued style, with lots of rhetorical flourish (verse 10). Such orators may have attracted applause and money, but Paul was looking for results in the form of changed lives, not profit or fame.

In the next two chapters, Paul reviews his qualifications, but he also ironically "boasts" of his weaknesses. Judge a messenger by the substance of the gospel he or she preaches, Paul seems to say—not by fancy words or a flashy style.

in our boasting, as would be the case if we had not come to you, for we did get as far as you with the gospel of Christ. [15]Neither do we go beyond our limits by boasting of work done by others.[a] Our hope is that, as your faith continues to grow, our area of activity among you will greatly expand, [16]so that we can preach the gospel in the regions beyond you. For we do not want to boast about work already done in another man's territory. [17]But, "Let him who boasts boast in the Lord."[b] [18]For it is not the one who commends himself who is approved, but the one whom the Lord commends.

Paul and the False Apostles

11 I hope you will put up with a little of my foolishness; but you are already doing that. [2]I am jealous for you with a godly jealousy. I promised you to one husband, to Christ, so that I might present you as a pure virgin to him. [3]But I am afraid that just as Eve was deceived by the serpent's cunning, your minds may somehow be led astray from your sincere and pure devotion to Christ. [4]For if someone comes to you and preaches a Jesus other than the Jesus we preached, or if you receive a different spirit from the one you received, or a different gospel from the one you accepted, you put up with it easily enough. [5]But I do not think I am in the least inferior to those "super-apostles." [6]I may not be a trained speaker, but I do have knowledge. We

have made this perfectly clear to you in every way.

[7]Was it a sin for me to lower myself in order to elevate you by preaching the gospel of God to you free of charge? [8]I robbed other churches by receiving support from them so as to serve you. [9]And when I was with you and needed something, I was not a burden to anyone, for the brothers who came from Macedonia supplied what I needed. I have kept myself from being a burden to you in any way, and will continue to do so. [10]As surely as the truth of Christ is in me, nobody in the regions of Achaia will stop this boasting of mine. [11]Why? Because I do not love you? God knows I do! [12]And I will keep on doing what I am doing in order to cut the ground from under those who want an opportunity to be considered equal with us in the things they boast about.

[13]For such men are false apostles, deceitful workmen, masquerading as apostles of Christ. [14]And no wonder, for Satan himself masquerades as an angel of light. [15]It is not surprising, then, if his servants masquerade as servants of righteousness. Their end will be what their actions deserve.

Paul Boasts About His Sufferings

[16]I repeat: Let no one take me for a fool. But if you do, then receive me just as you would a fool, so that I may do a little boasting. [17]In this self-confident boasting I am not talking as the Lord would, but as a fool. [18]Since many are boasting in the way the world does, I too will boast. [19]You gladly put up with fools since you are so wise! [20]In fact, you even put up with anyone who enslaves you or exploits you or takes advantage of you or pushes himself forward or slaps you in the face. [21]To my shame I admit that we were too weak for that!

What anyone else dares to boast about—I am speaking as a fool—I also dare to boast about. [22]Are they Hebrews? So am I. Are they Israelites? So am I. Are they Abraham's descendants? So am I. [23]Are they servants of Christ? (I am out of my mind to talk like this.) I am more. I have worked much harder, been in prison more frequently, been flogged more severely, and been exposed to death again and again. [24]Five times I received from the Jews the forty lashes minus one. [25]Three times I was beaten with rods, once I was stoned, three times I was shipwrecked, I spent a night and a day in the open sea, [26]I have been constantly on the move. I have been in danger from rivers, in danger from bandits, in danger from my own countrymen, in danger from Gentiles; in danger in the city, in danger in the country, in danger at sea; and in danger from false brothers.

[a]13-15 Or [13]We, however, will not boast about things that cannot be measured, but we will boast according to the standard of measurement that the God of measure has assigned us—a measurement that relates even to you. [14] . . . . [15]Neither do we boast about things that cannot be measured in regard to the work done by others.   [b]17 Jer. 9:24

[27]I have labored and toiled and have often gone without sleep; I have known hunger and thirst and have often gone without food; I have been cold and naked. [28]Besides everything else, I face

11:24 Paul's Many Trials

Acts records many of the apostle Paul's adventures and trials, but this passage shows that other disasters occurred as well. "Forty lashes minus one" was the maximum punishment allowed under Jewish law—five times Paul had been judged and sentenced by the Jews for his activities as a Christian. In addition, he was often imprisoned under Roman law and sometimes beaten with rods (an illegal punishment for a Roman citizen such as Paul).

daily the pressure of my concern for all the churches. [29]Who is weak, and I do not feel weak? Who is led into sin, and I do not inwardly burn?

[30]If I must boast, I will boast of the things that show my weakness. [31]The God and Father of the Lord Jesus, who is to be praised forever, knows that I am not lying. [32]In Damascus the governor under King Aretas had the city of the Damascenes guarded in order to arrest me. [33]But I was lowered in a basket from a window in the wall and slipped through his hands.

Paul's Vision and His Thorn

12 I must go on boasting. Although there is nothing to be gained, I will go on to visions and revelations from the Lord. [2]I know a man in Christ who fourteen years ago was caught up to the third heaven. Whether it was in the body or out of the body I do not know—God knows. [3]And I know that this man—whether in the body or apart from the body I do not know, but God knows— [4]was caught up to paradise. He heard inexpressible things, things that man is not permitted to tell. [5]I will boast about a man like that, but I will not boast about myself, except about my weaknesses. [6]Even if I should choose to boast, I would not be a fool, because I would be speaking the truth. But I refrain, so no one will think more of me than is warranted by what I do or say.

[7]To keep me from becoming conceited because of these surpassingly great revelations, there was given me a thorn in my flesh, a messenger of Satan, to torment me. [8]Three times I pleaded with the Lord to take it away from me. [9]But he said to me, "My grace is sufficient for you, for my power is made perfect in weakness." Therefore I will boast all the more gladly about my weaknesses, so that Christ's power may rest on me. [10]That is why, for Christ's sake, I delight

in weaknesses, in insults, in hardships, in persecutions, in difficulties. For when I am weak, then I am strong.

Paul's Concern for the Corinthians

[11]I have made a fool of myself, but you drove me to it. I ought to have been commended by you, for I am not in the least inferior to the "super-apostles," even though I am nothing. [12]The things that mark an apostle—signs, wonders and miracles—were done among you with great perseverance. [13]How were you inferior to the other churches, except that I was never a burden to you? Forgive me this wrong!

12:7 The Thorn in Paul's Flesh

Bible scholars don't agree on the precise nature of Paul's "thorn." Some suggest a physical ailment, such as an eye disease, malaria, or epilepsy. Others interpret it as a spiritual temptation, or a sequence of failures in his ministry. The Bible gives no clear evidence on the precise nature of this affliction. Regardless, Paul stresses that God permitted the thorn to continue, despite his prayers for relief, to teach him an important lesson about grace and dependence. This conclusion echoes Paul's thoughts on the Corinthians' suffering in chapter 7.

[14]Now I am ready to visit you for the third time, and I will not be a burden to you, because what I want is not your possessions but you. After all, children should not have to save up for their parents, but parents for their children. [15]So I will very gladly spend for you everything I have and expend myself as well. If I love you more, will you love me less? [16]Be that as it may, I have not been a burden to you. Yet, crafty fellow that I am, I caught you by trickery! [17]Did I exploit you through any of the men I sent you? [18]I urged Titus to go to you and I sent our brother with him. Titus did not exploit you, did he? Did we not act in the same spirit and follow the same course?

[19]Have you been thinking all along that we have been defending ourselves to you? We have been speaking in the sight of God as those in Christ; and everything we do, dear friends, is for your strengthening. [20]For I am afraid that when I come I may not find you as I want you to be, and you may not find me as you want me to be. I fear that there may be quarreling, jealousy, outbursts of anger, factions, slander, gossip, arrogance and disorder. [21]I am afraid that when I come again my God will humble me before you, and I will be grieved over many who have sinned earlier and have not repented of the impurity,

sexual sin and debauchery in which they have indulged.

Final Warnings

13 This will be my third visit to you. "Every matter must be established by the testimony of two or three witnesses."[a] [2]I already gave you a warning when I was with you the second time. I now repeat it while absent: On my return I will not spare those who sinned earlier or any of the others, [3]since you are demanding proof that Christ is speaking through me. He is not weak in dealing with you, but is powerful among you. [4]For to be sure, he was crucified in weakness, yet he lives by God's power. Likewise, we are weak in him, yet by God's power we will live with him to serve you.

[5]Examine yourselves to see whether you are in the faith; test yourselves. Do you not realize that Christ Jesus is in you—unless, of course, you fail the test? [6]And I trust that you will discover that we have not failed the test. [7]Now we pray to God that you will not do anything wrong. Not that people will see that we have stood the test but that you will do what is right even though we may seem to have failed. [8]For we cannot do anything against the truth, but only for the truth. [9]We are glad whenever we are weak but you are strong; and our prayer is for your perfection. [10]This is why I write these things when I am absent, that when I come I may not have to be harsh in my use of authority—the authority the Lord gave me for building you up, not for tearing you down.

Final Greetings

[11]Finally, brothers, good-by. Aim for perfection, listen to my appeal, be of one mind, live in peace. And the God of love and peace will be with you.

[12]Greet one another with a holy kiss. [13]All the saints send their greetings.

[14]May the grace of the Lord Jesus Christ, and the love of God, and the fellowship of the Holy Spirit be with you all.

a 1 Deut. 19:15

GALATIANS

No Second-Class Christians
A protest against treason

> But even if we or an angel from heaven should preach a gospel other than the one we preached to you, let him be eternally condemned! 1:8

PAUL IS ANGRY. YOU CAN almost see his face: flushed red, with lines of tension working in his jaw. Typically, he greets his readers briefly and then launches into warm praise of them. But in this letter shock and dismay replace the usual warmth. A crisis threatens the Galatians, and Paul opens with a withering blast against the people responsible.

What's the Problem?

Yet, when you read a few chapters, you may wonder why the apostle is so upset. Galatia seems innocent of the kinkiness of Corinth; Paul describes no incest or idolatry here. Instead, he brings up common, everyday Jewish affairs such as the observance of festival days and the practice of ancient traditions, especially circumcision. Where is the big crisis?

Paul could foresee the outcome of the Galatians' thinking: By unduly stressing their Jewish heritage, the Galatians would soon devalue what Christ had done. They would start trusting in their own human effort (their keeping of "the law") to gain acceptance by God (3:1–5).

If the Galatians continued their policies, the bedrock of the gospel would crumble. Faith in Christ would become just one of many steps in salvation, not the only one. The gospel itself would be perverted (1:6–9).

A Dangerous Class Structure

Paul saw other ominous dangers ahead for the fledgling Christian church. As a Jewish Roman citizen who spoke Greek, he knew well the innate human tendency to look down on people. Roman citizens snubbed non-Romans; Greeks looked down their noses at Romans; and Jews, with their exalted history and highly developed religion, felt superior to other cultures.

The Galatians' insistence on strict Jewish rules would bring side effects. Subtle distinctions between Christians would inevitably creep in: *Faith in Christ is fine, but a circumcised person who keeps the Jewish law . . . that's far better.* Already, such thoughts had infected two esteemed apostles, Peter and Barnabas. Circumcised Christians were snubbing uncircumcised ones as second-class citizens.

The letter to the Galatians, then, is protesting against treason. It lashes out against subtle dangers that can ultimately pervert the gospel and divide the church. Paul insists that Jesus Christ came to tear down walls between people, not to build them up. In him there is neither Jew nor Greek, slave nor free, male nor female (3:28). Faith in him, not anyone's set of laws (2:16), opens the door to acceptance by God.

How to Read Galatians

Galatians reads like a dramatic court trial. On one side of the courtroom stand Paul's accusers. Persuasive and powerful, these "Judaizers" have followed Paul from town to town, spreading rumors and contradicting his version of the Christian faith.

On the other side sits the jury, the Galatian Christians. They have enjoyed warm friendship with Paul in the past, but some of the charges against him are serious. Did he invent parts of the gospel he preached to them? Has God really given him a special insight? Is it true that his message of "freedom" will lead to a weak, immoral church? Should they turn their backs on their Jewish heritage?

Paul, acting in his own self-defense, paces the courtroom. He uses a variety of debating styles: tight logic, historical reviews, and personal outrage. His integrity, and ultimately Jesus Christ's integrity, is at stake.

In topical content, Galatians covers much the same ground as Romans. But in style, it crackles with a fighting spirit. As you read it, try to visualize that courtroom scene, and judge for yourself Paul's effectiveness as a defendant.

3-TRACK READING PLAN

For an explanation and complete listing of the 3-track reading plan, turn to page 7.

TRACK 1:   ***Two-Week Courses on the Bible***
The Track 1 reading program on the Life and Teachings of Paul includes one chapter from Galatians. See page 7 for a complete listing of this course.

TRACK 2:   ***An Overview of Galatians in 1 Day***
☐ Day 1. Read the Introduction to Galatians, then chapter 3. You'll have to concentrate to follow all the arguments. But this chapter gives an essential interpretation of the Old Testament. Study it as a sample of Paul's defense in Galatians.

Now turn to page 9 for your next Track 2 reading project.

TRACK 3:   ***All of Galatians in 5 Days***
After you have read through Galatians, turn to pages 10–14 for your next Track 3 reading project.
☐1   ☐2   ☐3   ☐4   ☐5–6

---

1 Paul, an apostle—sent not from men nor by man, but by Jesus Christ and God the Father, who raised him from the dead— ²and all the brothers with me,

To the churches in Galatia:

³Grace and peace to you from God our Father and the Lord Jesus Christ, ⁴who gave himself for our sins to rescue us from the present evil age, according to the will of our God and Father, ⁵to whom be glory for ever and ever. Amen.

No Other Gospel

⁶I am astonished that you are so quickly deserting the one who called you by the grace of Christ and are turning to a different gospel— ⁷which is really no gospel at all. Evidently some people are throwing you into confusion and are trying to pervert the gospel of Christ. ⁸But even if we or an angel from heaven should preach a gospel other than the one we preached to you, let him be eternally condemned! ⁹As we have already said, so now I say again: If anybody is preaching to you a gospel other than what you accepted, let him be eternally condemned!

¹⁰Am I now trying to win the approval of men, or of God? Or am I trying to please men? If I were still trying to please men, I would not be a servant of Christ.

Paul Called by God

¹¹I want you to know, brothers, that the gospel I preached is not something that man made up. ¹²I did not receive it from any man, nor was I taught it; rather, I received it by revelation from Jesus Christ.

¹³For you have heard of my previous way of life in Judaism, how intensely I persecuted the church of God and tried to destroy it. ¹⁴I was advancing in Judaism beyond many Jews of my own age and was extremely zealous for the traditions of my fathers. ¹⁵But when God, who set me apart from birth*a* and called me by his grace, was pleased ¹⁶to reveal his Son in me so that I might preach him among the Gentiles, I did not consult any man, ¹⁷nor did I go up to Jerusalem to see those who were apostles before I was, but I went immediately into Arabia and later returned to Damascus.

¹⁸Then after three years, I went up to Jerusalem to get acquainted with Peter*b* and stayed with him fifteen days. ¹⁹I saw none of the other apostles—only James, the Lord's brother. ²⁰I assure you before God that what I am writing you is no lie. ²¹Later I went to Syria and Cilicia. ²²I was personally unknown to the churches of Judea that are in Christ. ²³They only heard the report: "The man who formerly persecuted us is now

a15 Or from my mother's womb   *b18 Greek Cephas*

preaching the faith he once tried to destroy." [24]And they praised God because of me.

Paul Accepted by the Apostles

2 Fourteen years later I went up again to Jerusalem, this time with Barnabas. I took Titus along also. [2]I went in response to a revelation and set before them the gospel that I preach among the Gentiles. But I did this privately to those who seemed to be leaders, for fear that I was running or had run my race in vain. [3]Yet not even Titus, who was with me, was compelled to be circumcised, even though he was a Greek. [4]This matter arose⌋ because some false brothers had infiltrated our ranks to spy on the freedom we have in Christ Jesus and to make us slaves. [5]We did not give in to them for a moment, so that the truth of the gospel might remain with you.

[6]As for those who seemed to be important—whatever they were makes no difference to me; God does not judge by external appearance—those men added nothing to my message. [7]On the contrary, they saw that I had been entrusted with the task of preaching the gospel to the Gentiles,[a] just as Peter had been to the Jews.[b] [8]For God, who was at work in the ministry of Peter as an apostle to the Jews, was also at work in my ministry as an apostle to the Gentiles. [9]James, Peter[c] and John, those reputed to be pillars, gave me and Barnabas the right hand of fellowship when they recognized the grace given to me. They agreed that we should go to the Gentiles, and they to the Jews. [10]All they asked was that we should continue to remember the poor, the very thing I was eager to do.

Paul Opposes Peter

[11]When Peter came to Antioch, I opposed him to his face, because he was clearly in the wrong.

2:11 Forcing a Confrontation

Galatians 2 gives a fascinating behind-the-scenes account of how the Jewish/Gentile question was splitting the early church. Peter and James, sympathetic to Jewish Christians, acted hypocritically in their treatment of Gentiles until Paul confronted them publicly. Acts 15 gives a more detailed account of the official disagreements and how they were finally resolved.

[12]Before certain men came from James, he used to eat with the Gentiles. But when they arrived, he began to draw back and separate himself from the Gentiles because he was afraid of those who belonged to the circumcision group. [13]The other Jews joined him in his hypocrisy, so that by their hypocrisy even Barnabas was led astray.

[14]When I saw that they were not acting in line with the truth of the gospel, I said to Peter in front of them all, "You are a Jew, yet you live like a Gentile and not like a Jew. How is it, then, that you force Gentiles to follow Jewish customs?

[15]"We who are Jews by birth and not 'Gentile sinners' [16]know that a man is not justified by observing the law, but by faith in Jesus Christ. So we, too, have put our faith in Christ Jesus that we may be justified by faith in Christ and not by observing the law, because by observing the law no one will be justified.

[17]"If, while we seek to be justified in Christ, it becomes evident that we ourselves are sinners, does that mean that Christ promotes sin? Absolutely not! [18]If I rebuild what I destroyed, I prove that I am a lawbreaker. [19]For through the law I died to the law so that I might live for God. [20]I have been crucified with Christ and I no longer live, but Christ lives in me. The life I live in the body, I live by faith in the Son of God, who loved me and gave himself for me. [21]I do not set aside the grace of God, for if righteousness could be gained through the law, Christ died for nothing!"[d]

Faith or Observance of the Law

3 You foolish Galatians! Who has bewitched you? Before your very eyes Jesus Christ was clearly portrayed as crucified. [2]I would like to learn just one thing from you: Did you receive the Spirit by observing the law, or by believing what you heard? [3]Are you so foolish? After beginning with the Spirit, are you now trying to attain your goal by human effort? [4]Have you suffered so much for nothing—if it really was for nothing? [5]Does God give you his Spirit and work miracles among you because you observe the law, or because you believe what you heard?

[6]Consider Abraham: "He believed God, and it was credited to him as righteousness."[e] [7]Understand, then, that those who believe are children of Abraham. [8]The Scripture foresaw that God would justify the Gentiles by faith, and announced the gospel in advance to Abraham: "All nations will be blessed through you."[f] [9]So those who have faith are blessed along with Abraham, the man of faith.

[10]All who rely on observing the law are under a curse, for it is written: "Cursed is everyone who does not continue to do everything written in the Book of the Law."[g] [11]Clearly no one is justified before God by the law, because, "The righteous will live by faith."[h] [12]The law is not based on

---

[a]7 Greek *uncircumcised*   [b]7 Greek *circumcised*; also in verses 8 and 9   [c]9 Greek *Cephas*; also in verses 11 and 14
[d]21 Some interpreters end the quotation after verse 14.   [e]6 Gen. 15:6   [f]8 Gen. 12:3; 18:18; 22:18
[g]10 Deut. 27:26   [h]11 Hab. 2:4

faith; on the contrary, "The man who does these things will live by them."[a] ¹³Christ redeemed us from the curse of the law by becoming a curse for us, for it is written: "Cursed is everyone who is hung on a tree."[b] ¹⁴He redeemed us in order that the blessing given to Abraham might come to the Gentiles through Christ Jesus, so that by faith we might receive the promise of the Spirit.

The Law and the Promise

¹⁵Brothers, let me take an example from everyday life. Just as no one can set aside or add to a human covenant that has been duly established, so it is in this case. ¹⁶The promises were spoken to Abraham and to his seed. The Scripture does not say "and to seeds," meaning many people, but "and to your seed,"[c] meaning one person, who is Christ. ¹⁷What I mean is this: The law, introduced 430 years later, does not set aside the covenant previously established by God and thus do away with the promise. ¹⁸For if the inheritance depends on the law, then it no longer depends on a promise; but God in his grace gave it to Abraham through a promise.

¹⁹What, then, was the purpose of the law? It was added because of transgressions until the Seed to whom the promise referred had come. The law was put into effect through angels by a mediator. ²⁰A mediator, however, does not represent just one party; but God is one.

²¹Is the law, therefore, opposed to the promises of God? Absolutely not! For if a law had been given that could impart life, then righteousness would certainly have come by the law. ²²But the Scripture declares that the whole world is a prisoner of sin, so that what was promised, being

3:17 The 430-Year Gap

In chapter 3, Paul uses clever arguments to put the entire Old Testament law in a new perspective. The law was never intended to make possible a way to God, he says (verses 11,21). Rather, the law was given to "lead us to Christ" (verse 24) by convincing us of the impossibility of gaining God's acceptance on our own. To prove his point, Paul mentions a 430-year gap between Abraham and Moses. God gave his promises to Abraham, who lived long before Moses ever received the law; therefore, Abraham couldn't possibly have depended on the law. God's promise reached final fulfillment in Jesus, whom Paul calls Abraham's "seed" (verse 16).

---

[a]12 Lev. 18:5   [b]13 Deut. 21:23   [c]16 Gen. 12:7; 13:15; 24:7

Legalism
Can we do anything to make God love us more?

BEFORE HIS CONVERSION, PAUL WAS one of the best legalists who ever lived. A loyal Jew, he tortured Christians who stepped outside Jewish tradition to follow Christ. If a person could reach God by obeying the law, then he, the strict Pharisee, would have done it.

But in Galatians, he blasts the idea that God's love is conditioned by how many rules we obey. Legalism is like a cage: It can only condemn people and lock them behind bars. As Paul points out, no one has kept all of God's laws perfectly, and all who try ultimately fail (3:10–11).

> But now that you know God—or rather are known by God—how is it that you are turning back to those weak and miserable principles? 4:9

No Strings Attached

Chapters 3–4 draw sharp contrasts: a prisoner and a free man, a sheltered child and an adult. Don't act like a slave or a child, Paul says. Act like a privileged son, an heir to a great fortune!

Galatians has been called the "Magna Charta of Christian liberty." "It is for freedom that Christ has set us free," Paul declares (5:1). Galatians teaches that there is nothing we can do to make God love us more—or love us less. We don't have to "earn" God's love by slavishly following rules.

Martin Luther said Galatians was "my own little epistle. I have betrothed myself to it; it is my Katie von Bora [Luther's wife]." This slim book proclaims that God has given his love freely, with no strings attached. We should never get over the awesome implications of that truth, Galatians says. Evidently, Paul didn't.

Life Questions: The early Christians went in two directions. Some, like the people in Galatia, became obsessed with legalism. Others took their Christian freedom too far: They refused to follow anyone's rules. Which is the greater danger in your circle?

given through faith in Jesus Christ, might be given to those who believe.

²³Before this faith came, we were held prisoners by the law, locked up until faith should be revealed. ²⁴So the law was put in charge to lead us to Christ[a] that we might be justified by faith. ²⁵Now that faith has come, we are no longer under the supervision of the law.

Sons of God

²⁶You are all sons of God through faith in Christ Jesus, ²⁷for all of you who were baptized into Christ have clothed yourselves with Christ. ²⁸There is neither Jew nor Greek, slave nor free, male nor female, for you are all one in Christ Jesus. ²⁹If you belong to Christ, then you are Abraham's seed, and heirs according to the promise.

4 What I am saying is that as long as the heir is a child, he is no different from a slave, although he owns the whole estate. ²He is subject to guardians and trustees until the time set by his father. ³So also, when we were children, we were in slavery under the basic principles of the world. ⁴But when the time had fully come, God sent his Son, born of a woman, born under law, ⁵to redeem those under law, that we might receive the full rights of sons. ⁶Because you are sons, God sent the Spirit of his Son into our hearts, the Spirit who calls out, "Abba,[b] Father." ⁷So you are no longer a slave, but a son; and since you are a son, God has made you also an heir.

Paul's Concern for the Galatians

⁸Formerly, when you did not know God, you were slaves to those who by nature are not gods. ⁹But now that you know God—or rather are known by God—how is it that you are turning back to those weak and miserable principles? Do you wish to be enslaved by them all over again? ¹⁰You are observing special days and months and seasons and years! ¹¹I fear for you, that somehow I have wasted my efforts on you.

¹²I plead with you, brothers, become like me, for I became like you. You have done me no wrong. ¹³As you know, it was because of an illness that I first preached the gospel to you. ¹⁴Even though my illness was a trial to you, you did not treat me with contempt or scorn. Instead, you welcomed me as if I were an angel of God, as if I were Christ Jesus himself. ¹⁵What has happened to all your joy? I can testify that, if you could have done so, you would have torn out your eyes and given them to me. ¹⁶Have I now become your enemy by telling you the truth?

¹⁷Those people are zealous to win you over, but for no good. What they want is to alienate you ⌊from us⌋, so that you may be zealous for

them. ¹⁸It is fine to be zealous, provided the purpose is good, and to be so always and not just when I am with you. ¹⁹My dear children, for whom I am again in the pains of childbirth until

4:16 Paul's Anguish

Paul's letter wavers between abstract reasoning and intensely emotional pleading. As this paragraph shows, Paul had once enjoyed intimate closeness with the people of Galatia. He feels anguish and personal rejection because they now seem to be turning their backs on the faith he had carefully taught them. He is in the pains of childbirth, he says, waiting anxiously for them to grow out of their false ideas (verse 19).

Christ is formed in you, ²⁰how I wish I could be with you now and change my tone, because I am perplexed about you!

Hagar and Sarah

²¹Tell me, you who want to be under the law, are you not aware of what the law says? ²²For it is written that Abraham had two sons, one by the slave woman and the other by the free woman. ²³His son by the slave woman was born in the ordinary way; but his son by the free woman was born as the result of a promise.

²⁴These things may be taken figuratively, for the women represent two covenants. One covenant is from Mount Sinai and bears children who are to be slaves: This is Hagar. ²⁵Now Hagar stands for Mount Sinai in Arabia and corresponds to the present city of Jerusalem, because she is in slavery with her children. ²⁶But the Jerusalem that is above is free, and she is our mother. ²⁷For it is written:

"Be glad, O barren woman,
    who bears no children;
break forth and cry aloud,
    you who have no labor pains;
because more are the children of the desolate
    woman
    than of her who has a husband."[c]

²⁸Now you, brothers, like Isaac, are children of promise. ²⁹At that time the son born in the ordinary way persecuted the son born by the power of the Spirit. It is the same now. ³⁰But what does the Scripture say? "Get rid of the slave woman and her son, for the slave woman's son will never share in the inheritance with the free woman's son."[d] ³¹Therefore, brothers, we are not children of the slave woman, but of the free woman.

---

[a]24 Or *charge until Christ came*   [b]6 Aramaic for *Father*   [c]27 Isaiah 54:1   [d]30 Gen. 21:10

Freedom in Christ

5 It is for freedom that Christ has set us free. Stand firm, then, and do not let yourselves be burdened again by a yoke of slavery.

²Mark my words! I, Paul, tell you that if you let yourselves be circumcised, Christ will be of no value to you at all. ³Again I declare to every man who lets himself be circumcised that he is obligated to obey the whole law. ⁴You who are trying to be justified by law have been alienated from Christ; you have fallen away from grace. ⁵But by faith we eagerly await through the Spirit the righteousness for which we hope. ⁶For in Christ Jesus neither circumcision nor uncircumcision has any value. The only thing that counts is faith expressing itself through love.

⁷You were running a good race. Who cut in on you and kept you from obeying the truth? ⁸That kind of persuasion does not come from the one who calls you. ⁹"A little yeast works through the whole batch of dough." ¹⁰I am confident in the Lord that you will take no other view. The one who is throwing you into confusion will pay the penalty, whoever he may be. ¹¹Brothers, if I am still preaching circumcision, why am I still being persecuted? In that case the offense of the cross has been abolished. ¹²As for those agitators, I wish they would go the whole way and emasculate themselves!

¹³You, my brothers, were called to be free. But do not use your freedom to indulge the sinful nature*a*; rather, serve one another in love. ¹⁴The entire law is summed up in a single command: "Love your neighbor as yourself."*b* ¹⁵If you keep on biting and devouring each other, watch out or you will be destroyed by each other.

Life by the Spirit

¹⁶So I say, live by the Spirit, and you will not gratify the desires of the sinful nature. ¹⁷For the sinful nature desires what is contrary to the Spirit, and the Spirit what is contrary to the sinful nature. They are in conflict with each other, so that you do not do what you want. ¹⁸But if you are led by the Spirit, you are not under law.

¹⁹The acts of the sinful nature are obvious: sexual immorality, impurity and debauchery; ²⁰idolatry and witchcraft; hatred, discord, jealousy, fits of rage, selfish ambition, dissensions, factions ²¹and envy; drunkenness, orgies, and the like. I warn you, as I did before, that those who live like this will not inherit the kingdom of God.

a 13 Or *the flesh*; also in verses 16, 17, 19 and 24   *b 14* Lev. 19:18

Paul Fights Back
When freedom gets dangerous

OVER THE YEARS PAUL CAUGHT on to his opponents' crafty ways of undermining him. Galatians provides a textbook case of his response to critics.

First, Paul answered their personal attacks. Some had questioned his right to be called an apostle. In chapters 1 and 2, Paul insists that he received the gospel directly from God. In addition, he has met every criterion of an apostle.

Chapters 3 and 4 deal with Paul's ideas. Had he strayed too far from Old Testament law and customs? Some hinted that Paul was preaching an incomplete gospel. He answered those objections with a carefully reasoned look at the Old Testament, focusing on Abraham, the father of the Jewish race.

What to Do with Freedom

Then Paul turned to more practical matters. Stressing freedom, not rules, left him open to criticism. Did his strong emphasis on freedom lead to loose morals? To answer this question, he ended Galatians, a letter devoted to Christian liberty, with a warning.

"Why did Christ set us free?" Paul asks. To make possible a life of orgies, drunkenness, and witchcraft? Obviously no. Christ freed us from worrying about whether we are "doing enough" to please God and from uselessly following external forms. But we should use that freedom to serve one another in love and to live a Spirit-filled life.

His arguments and emotions exhausted, Paul concludes, "Neither circumcision nor uncircumcision means anything; what counts is a new creation" (6:15). A released prisoner, a freed slave, the bountiful fruit of a living tree—all the images in Galatians convey *life*, an abundant life in the Spirit of God, readily available to every Christian.

> The only thing that counts is faith expressing itself through love. 5:6

Life Questions: Read over the qualities of life in the Spirit listed in 5:22–23. Do these characterize your life?

²²But the fruit of the Spirit is love, joy, peace, patience, kindness, goodness, faithfulness, ²³gentleness and self-control. Against such things there is no law. ²⁴Those who belong to Christ Jesus have crucified the sinful nature with its passions and desires. ²⁵Since we live by the Spirit, let us keep in step with the Spirit. ²⁶Let us not become conceited, provoking and envying each other.

6:2 Mixing Gentleness with Harshness

Galatians contains some of Paul's harshest language, for he sensed a danger that could destroy the church's faith. But the book also includes some of Paul's most familiar and comforting words. Chapter 6 describes a spirit of tolerance and forgiveness toward those who fail. It also offers encouragement for people who grow tired of doing good when it appears justice is not working out.

Doing Good to All

6 Brothers, if someone is caught in a sin, you who are spiritual should restore him gently. But watch yourself, or you also may be tempted. ²Carry each other's burdens, and in this way you will fulfill the law of Christ. ³If anyone thinks he is something when he is nothing, he deceives himself. ⁴Each one should test his own actions. Then he can take pride in himself, without comparing himself to somebody else, ⁵for each one should carry his own load.

⁶Anyone who receives instruction in the word must share all good things with his instructor.

⁷Do not be deceived: God cannot be mocked. A man reaps what he sows. ⁸The one who sows to please his sinful nature, from that nature[a] will reap destruction; the one who sows to please the Spirit, from the Spirit will reap eternal life. ⁹Let us not become weary in doing good, for at the proper time we will reap a harvest if we do not give up. ¹⁰Therefore, as we have opportunity, let us do good to all people, especially to those who belong to the family of believers.

Not Cirmcision but a New Creation

¹¹See what large letters I use as I write to you with my own hand!

¹²Those who want to make a good impression outwardly are trying to compel you to be circumcised. The only reason they do this is to avoid being persecuted for the cross of Christ. ¹³Not even those who are circumcised obey the law, yet they want you to be circumcised that they may boast about your flesh. ¹⁴May I never boast except in the cross of our Lord Jesus Christ, through which[b] the world has been crucified to me, and I to the world. ¹⁵Neither circumcision nor uncircumcision means anything; what counts is a new creation. ¹⁶Peace and mercy to all who follow this rule, even to the Israel of God.

¹⁷Finally, let no one cause me trouble, for I bear on my body the marks of Jesus.

¹⁸The grace of our Lord Jesus Christ be with your spirit, brothers. Amen.

---

a8 Or his flesh, from the flesh   *b14 Or whom*

EPHESIANS

For the Discouraged
Good news for those who feel abandoned and unloved

> *You are no longer foreigners and aliens, but fellow citizens with God's people and members of God's household.*
> *2:19*

IMAGINE YOURSELF A CHILD, ABANDONED on the streets of New York. Your immigrant parents died on the ship on the way to America. You have no money and no relatives. You can't speak English. And you are left to fend for yourself.

As many as 30,000 orphans found themselves in exactly that predicament in 1850. They slept in alleys, huddling for warmth in boxes or metal drums. To survive, the boys mostly stole, caught rats to eat, or rummaged in garbage cans. Girls sometimes worked as "panel thieves" for prostitutes, slipping their tiny hands through camouflaged openings in the walls to lift a watch or wallet from a preoccupied customer.

Immigrants were flooding New York City then, and no one had the time or money to look after the orphans—no one, that is, except Charles Loring Brace, a 26-year-old minister. Horrified by their plight, he organized a unique solution, the Orphan Train. The idea was simple: Pack hundreds of orphans on a train heading west and announce to towns along the way that anyone could claim a new son or daughter when the Orphan Train chugged through.

Adopted into a New Life

By the time the last Orphan Train steamed west in 1929, 100,000 children had found new homes and new lives. Two orphans from such trains became governors, one served as a U.S. congressman, and still another was a U.S. Supreme Court justice.

The Orphan Train provides a vivid parable of the message of Ephesians. To capture Paul's enthusiasm in this book, imagine one more stage in your life as a street urchin in New York.

You have learned to survive and fight off starvation. But one day, someone takes you and puts you on a smoke-belching train jammed with hundreds of other foreign-speaking youngsters. Three days later you are selected by a kindly middle-aged couple in Michigan who introduce themselves as Mr. and Mrs. Henry Ford. You are driven (in an automobile!) to the largest house you have ever seen, and they quietly explain that you are now part of their family. Everything they have is yours to use and enjoy. At long last, by some miracle, you have a family and a home—and what a home!

Welcome to the Family

Paul conveys a feeling something like that in Ephesians, a rich book that expands the message of Jesus' parable of the Lost Son (Luke 15). A big "Welcome Home!" banner is stretched across the lawn, confetti swirls in the air, balloons lunge skyward, and a band plays. Christians have been adopted directly into the family of God. This is a good news book, to put it mildly.

If you feel discouraged or wonder if God really cares or question whether the Christian life is worth the effort, read Ephesians. You will no longer feel like an orphan. Paul describes the "riches of Christ" available to all and points to us, God's adopted children, as his sparkling "Exhibit A" in all the universe (3:10).

Ephesians contains staggering thoughts. Paul wants his readers to grasp "how wide and long and high and deep is the love of Christ" (3:18). He cranks up the volume to express that love, and not one low, mournful note sneaks in.

How to Read Ephesians

In many ways, Ephesians is Paul's "summing-up" book. The same subjects appear in greater detail in books like Romans, 1 Corinthians and 1 Thessalonians. But in Ephesians, Paul gives an overall view of the grand scheme of the gospel. Only now, Paul says, has God's hidden plan for all of history come to light.

Because it compresses such large thoughts into such a short space, Ephesians deserves very careful study. Read the first three chapters slowly, digesting one paragraph at a time. Such study will prove rewarding: Ephesians gives exuberant good news about the nature of the universe and God's plan for believers.

Like other letters from Paul, Ephesians divides fairly neatly between doctrine (chapters 1–3) and practical advice (4–6). The last half details how our lives should change as a result of the great things described in the first part.

3-TRACK READING PLAN

For an explanation and complete listing of the 3-track reading plan, turn to page 7.

TRACK 1: **Two-Week Courses on the Bible**
The Track 1 reading program on the Life and Teachings of Paul includes one chapter from Ephesians. See page 7 for a complete listing of this course.

TRACK 2: **An Overview of Ephesians in 2 Days**
☐ Day 1. Read the Introduction to Ephesians, then chapter 2.
☐ Day 2. Read chapter 3. You may also want to look at the famous "armor" passage (6:10–18).
Now turn to page 9 for your next Track 2 reading project.

TRACK 3: **All of Ephesians in 6 Days**
After you have read through Ephesians, turn to pages 10–14 for your next Track 3 reading project.
☐1 ☐2 ☐3 ☐4 ☐5 ☐6

---

1 Paul, an apostle of Christ Jesus by the will of God,

To the saints in Ephesus,ᵃ the faithfulᵇ in Christ Jesus:

²Grace and peace to you from God our Father and the Lord Jesus Christ.

Spiritual Blessings in Christ

³Praise be to the God and Father of our Lord Jesus Christ, who has blessed us in the heavenly realms with every spiritual blessing in Christ. ⁴For he chose us in him before the creation of the world to be holy and blameless in his sight. In love ⁵heᶜ predestined us to be adopted as his sons through Jesus Christ, in accordance with his pleasure and will— ⁶to the praise of his glorious grace, which he has freely given us in the One he loves. ⁷In him we have redemption through his blood, the forgiveness of sins, in accordance with the riches of God's grace ⁸that he lavished on us with all wisdom and understanding. ⁹And heᵈ

made known to us the mystery of his will according to his good pleasure, which he purposed in Christ, ¹⁰to be put into effect when the times will have reached their fulfillment—to bring all things in heaven and on earth together under one head, even Christ.

¹¹In him we were also chosen,ᵉ having been predestined according to the plan of him who works out everything in conformity with the purpose of his will, ¹²in order that we, who were the first to hope in Christ, might be for the praise of

1:13 Branded

Cattle ranchers brand their cattle, loggers carve a symbol on a tree, dignitaries seal their important papers with wax—all these are marks of ownership. According to Paul, the Holy Spirit is God's proof of ownership for Christians. More, he is a "deposit" guaranteeing a great inheritance.

ᵃ1 Some early manuscripts do not have *in Ephesus.*   ᵇ1 Or *believers who are*   ᶜ4,5 Or *sight in love.* ⁵*He*
ᵈ8,9 Or *us. With all wisdom and understanding,* ⁹*he*   ᵉ11 Or *were made heirs*

his glory. [13]And you also were included in Christ when you heard the word of truth, the gospel of your salvation. Having believed, you were marked in him with a seal, the promised Holy Spirit, [14]who is a deposit guaranteeing our inheritance until the redemption of those who are God's possession—to the praise of his glory.

Thanksgiving and Prayer

[15]For this reason, ever since I heard about your faith in the Lord Jesus and your love for all the saints, [16]I have not stopped giving thanks for you, remembering you in my prayers. [17]I keep asking that the God of our Lord Jesus Christ, the glorious Father, may give you the Spirit[a] of wisdom and revelation, so that you may know him better. [18]I pray also that the eyes of your heart may be enlightened in order that you may know the hope to which he has called you, the riches of his glorious inheritance in the saints, [19]and his incomparably great power for us who believe. That power is like the working of his mighty

1:19 Proven Power

Throughout the Old Testament, God cites the liberation of slaves from Egypt as evidence of his power (over the most powerful nation of the time). "I am the God who brought you out of Egypt," he says. The New Testament holds up an even greater proof: God's ability to give life to the dead. That same life-giving power is available to the individual believer, Paul proclaims.

strength, [20]which he exerted in Christ when he raised him from the dead and seated him at his right hand in the heavenly realms, [21]far above all rule and authority, power and dominion, and every title that can be given, not only in the present age but also in the one to come. [22]And God placed all things under his feet and appointed him to be head over everything for the church, [23]which is his body, the fullness of him who fills everything in every way.

Made Alive in Christ

2 As for you, you were dead in your transgressions and sins, [2]in which you used to live when you followed the ways of this world and of the ruler of the kingdom of the air, the spirit who is now at work in those who are disobedient. [3]All of us also lived among them at one time, gratifying the cravings of our sinful nature[b] and following its desires and thoughts. Like the rest, we were by nature objects of wrath. [4]But because of

his great love for us, God, who is rich in mercy, [5]made us alive with Christ even when we were dead in transgressions—it is by grace you have been saved. [6]And God raised us up with Christ and seated us with him in the heavenly realms in Christ Jesus, [7]in order that in the coming ages he might show the incomparable riches of his grace, expressed in his kindness to us in Christ Jesus. [8]For it is by grace you have been saved, through faith—and this not from yourselves, it is the gift

2:8 Given, Not Earned

As a converted legalist, Paul insisted on one fact of the gospel: Eternal life comes not by any ritual of rule-keeping (which he calls "works"), but by the grace of God. Yet in this paragraph he notes that God intends for us to "do good works." Paul makes a clear distinction: Good works do nothing to help us obtain God's favor, but they follow naturally as we experience the love of Christ.

of God— [9]not by works, so that no one can boast. [10]For we are God's workmanship, created in Christ Jesus to do good works, which God prepared in advance for us to do.

One in Christ

[11]Therefore, remember that formerly you who are Gentiles by birth and called "uncircumcised" by those who call themselves "the circumcision" (that done in the body by the hands of men)— [12]remember that at that time you were separate from Christ, excluded from citizenship in Israel and foreigners to the covenants of the promise, without hope and without God in the world. [13]But now in Christ Jesus you who once were far away have been brought near through the blood of Christ.

[14]For he himself is our peace, who has made the two one and has destroyed the barrier, the dividing wall of hostility, [15]by abolishing in his flesh the law with its commandments and regulations. His purpose was to create in himself one new man out of the two, thus making peace, [16]and in this one body to reconcile both of them to God through the cross, by which he put to death their hostility. [17]He came and preached peace to you who were far away and peace to those who were near. [18]For through him we both have access to the Father by one Spirit.

[19]Consequently, you are no longer foreigners and aliens, but fellow citizens with God's people and members of God's household, [20]built on the foundation of the apostles and prophets, with Christ Jesus himself as the chief cornerstone. [21]In

---

[a]17 Or *a spirit*   [b]3 Or *our flesh*

him the whole building is joined together and rises to become a holy temple in the Lord. ²²And in him you too are being built together to become a dwelling in which God lives by his Spirit.

2:14 Destroying the Barriers

A Jewish missionary to the Gentiles, Paul wrote and talked constantly about tearing down the barriers between Jews and Gentiles. Jews kept themselves separate from Gentiles by many cultural and religious barriers. Perhaps the most vivid symbol of separation was an actual wall in the temple. Non-Jews could never enter the temple courts beyond that wall, and a further wall separated Jewish men from Jewish women. Here Paul describes how Christ utterly destroyed the "wall of hostility." (See also Galatians 3:28.)

Paul the Preacher to the Gentiles

3 For this reason I, Paul, the prisoner of Christ Jesus for the sake of you Gentiles—

²Surely you have heard about the administration of God's grace that was given to me for you, ³that is, the mystery made known to me by revelation, as I have already written briefly. ⁴In reading this, then, you will be able to understand my insight into the mystery of Christ, ⁵which was not made known to men in other generations as it has now been revealed by the Spirit to God's holy apostles and prophets. ⁶This mystery is that through the gospel the Gentiles are heirs together with Israel, members together of one body, and sharers together in the promise in Christ Jesus.

⁷I became a servant of this gospel by the gift of God's grace given me through the working of his power. ⁸Although I am less than the least of all God's people, this grace was given me: to preach to the Gentiles the unsearchable riches of Christ, ⁹and to make plain to everyone the administration of this mystery, which for ages past was kept hidden in God, who created all things. ¹⁰His intent was that now, through the church, the manifold wisdom of God should be made known to the rulers and authorities in the heavenly realms, ¹¹according to his eternal purpose which he accomplished in Christ Jesus our Lord. ¹²In him and through faith in him we may approach God with freedom and confidence. ¹³I ask you, therefore, not to be discouraged because of my sufferings for you, which are your glory.

A Prayer for the Ephesians

¹⁴For this reason I kneel before the Father, ¹⁵from whom his whole family[a] in heaven and on earth derives its name. ¹⁶I pray that out of his

glorious riches he may strengthen you with power through his Spirit in your inner being, ¹⁷so that Christ may dwell in your hearts through faith. And I pray that you, being rooted and established in love, ¹⁸may have power, together with all the saints, to grasp how wide and long and high and deep is the love of Christ, ¹⁹and to know this love that surpasses knowledge—that you may be filled to the measure of all the fullness of God.

²⁰Now to him who is able to do immeasurably more than all we ask or imagine, according to his power that is at work within us, ²¹to him be glory in the church and in Christ Jesus throughout all generations, for ever and ever! Amen.

3:16 Reading Between Lines

Paul's prayers often give some of the best insights into the local situation. This prayer (verses 14–21) and the one in chapter 1 (verses 15–23) indicate the church at Ephesus was well-grounded. In Ephesians Paul does not dwell on any urgent problems; instead, he tries to raise the sights of young Christians who have not fully grasped the extent of God's love and grace.

Unity in the Body of Christ

4 As a prisoner for the Lord, then, I urge you to live a life worthy of the calling you have received. ²Be completely humble and gentle; be patient, bearing with one another in love. ³Make every effort to keep the unity of the Spirit through the bond of peace. ⁴There is one body and one Spirit— just as you were called to one hope when you were called— ⁵one Lord, one faith, one baptism; ⁶one God and Father of all, who is over all and through all and in all.

⁷But to each one of us grace has been given as Christ apportioned it. ⁸This is why it[b] says:

"When he ascended on high,
he led captives in his train
and gave gifts to men."[c]

⁹(What does "he ascended" mean except that he also descended to the lower, earthly regions[d]? ¹⁰He who descended is the very one who ascended higher than all the heavens, in order to fill the whole universe.) ¹¹It was he who gave some to be apostles, some to be prophets, some to be evangelists, and some to be pastors and teachers, ¹²to prepare God's people for works of service, so that the body of Christ may be built up ¹³until we all reach unity in the faith and in the knowledge of

---

a15 Or whom all fatherhood   *b8 Or God*   *c8 Psalm 68:18*   *d9 Or the depths of the earth*

the Son of God and become mature, attaining to the whole measure of the fullness of Christ.

¹⁴Then we will no longer be infants, tossed back and forth by the waves, and blown here and there by every wind of teaching and by the cunning and craftiness of men in their deceitful scheming. ¹⁵Instead, speaking the truth in love, we will in all things grow up into him who is the Head, that is, Christ. ¹⁶From him the whole body, joined and held together by every supporting ligament, grows and builds itself up in love, as each part does its work.

Living as Children of Light

¹⁷So I tell you this, and insist on it in the Lord, that you must no longer live as the Gentiles do, in the futility of their thinking. ¹⁸They are darkened in their understanding and separated from the life of God because of the ignorance that is in them due to the hardening of their hearts. ¹⁹Hav-

ing lost all sensitivity, they have given themselves over to sensuality so as to indulge in every kind of impurity, with a continual lust for more.

²⁰You, however, did not come to know Christ

4:19 Loss of Sensitivity

Medical conditions that destroy nerves—leprosy, spinal cord injury, diabetes—are among the most difficult to treat. Without a sense of touch or pain, the patient can get a bedsore by lying in the same position too long, or a footsore by wearing too-tight shoes. The body no longer warns of danger. According to Paul, people can also develop a kind of moral insensitivity, silencing their consciences and hardening their hearts. That condition can prove fatal.

Letters from Prison
Time at last to tackle the grandest question of all

TO STIMULATE CREATIVITY, MANY AUTHORS seek out a scenic setting. Yet some of the world's most famous literature originated in, of all places, a prison cell. John Bunyan wrote his *Pilgrim's Progress* there. Russian novelist Alexander Solzhenitsyn's vast output had its conception behind barbed wire, as did his compatriot Dostoevski's.

Parts of the Bible were written in prison as well. Ephesians represents one of Paul's "prison letters" (along with Philippians, Colossians, and Philemon).

I am an ambassador in chains. Pray that I may declare it [the gospel] fearlessly, as I should. 6:20

Time on His Hands

Prison offers authors one precious commodity: time to think and reflect. When Paul wrote his prison letters, he was no longer journeying from town to town, stamping out fires set by his enemies. Settled into passably comfortable surroundings (probably confined to a house), he could slip off his sandals and devote attention to lofty concepts.

Unlike Paul's other letters, Ephesians does not address any urgent problems. With a sigh of relief, the apostle turned to the grandest question of all: "What is God's overall purpose for this world?" Paul answers the question this way: "To bring all things in heaven and on earth together under one head, even Christ" (1:10).

A Positive Approach

The apostle Paul often borrowed from the language of athletics to press home a crucial point, and Ephesians ends with a well-composed pep talk. In keeping with this letter's uplifting style, Paul does not scold or warn; rather, he begins, "I urge you to live a life worthy of the calling you have received" (4:1).

Already Paul has taught that Christ lives in each Christian—we are his body. Now he exhorts his readers to think through what it means to represent Christ in the world. When people look at Christians, do they see the qualities of Christ on display?

The last half of Ephesians spells out practical steps toward Christian maturity. Paul blends each new thought into his overall theme, urging us to love *as Christ loved*, to forgive *as Christ forgave*, to submit *as you would to Christ* (5:2; 4:32; 5:21).

Ironically, it took a stint in prison to free up Paul for this endeavor. The book of Ephesians can hardly introduce a new thought without bursting into a song or a prayer. It is no wonder the English poet Samuel Taylor Coleridge called the book "the divinest composition of man."

Life Questions: Suppose you were put in prison. What kind of letters would you write?

that way. ²¹Surely you heard of him and were taught in him in accordance with the truth that is in Jesus. ²²You were taught, with regard to your former way of life, to put off your old self, which is being corrupted by its deceitful desires; ²³to be made new in the attitude of your minds; ²⁴and to put on the new self, created to be like God in true righteousness and holiness.

²⁵Therefore each of you must put off falsehood and speak truthfully to his neighbor, for we are all members of one body. ²⁶"In your anger do not sin"ᵃ: Do not let the sun go down while you are still angry, ²⁷and do not give the devil a foothold. ²⁸He who has been stealing must steal no longer, but must work, doing something useful with his own hands, that he may have something to share with those in need.

²⁹Do not let any unwholesome talk come out of your mouths, but only what is helpful for building others up according to their needs, that it may benefit those who listen. ³⁰And do not grieve the Holy Spirit of God, with whom you were sealed for the day of redemption. ³¹Get rid of all bitterness, rage and anger, brawling and slander, along with every form of malice. ³²Be kind and compassionate to one another, forgiving each other, just as in Christ God forgave you.

5 Be imitators of God, therefore, as dearly loved children ²and live a life of love, just as Christ loved us and gave himself up for us as a fragrant offering and sacrifice to God.

³But among you there must not be even a hint of sexual immorality, or of any kind of impurity, or of greed, because these are improper for God's holy people. ⁴Nor should there be obscenity, foolish talk or coarse joking, which are out of place, but rather thanksgiving. ⁵For of this you can be sure: No immoral, impure or greedy person—such a man is an idolater—has any inheritance in the kingdom of Christ and of God.ᵇ ⁶Let no one deceive you with empty words, for because of such things God's wrath comes on those who are disobedient. ⁷Therefore do not be partners with them.

⁸For you were once darkness, but now you are light in the Lord. Live as children of light ⁹(for the fruit of the light consists in all goodness, righteousness and truth) ¹⁰and find out what pleases the Lord. ¹¹Have nothing to do with the fruitless deeds of darkness, but rather expose them. ¹²For it is shameful even to mention what the disobedient do in secret. ¹³But everything exposed by the light becomes visible, ¹⁴for it is light that makes everything visible. This is why it is said:

"Wake up, O sleeper,
    rise from the dead,
and Christ will shine on you."

¹⁵Be very careful, then, how you live—not as unwise but as wise, ¹⁶making the most of every opportunity, because the days are evil. ¹⁷Therefore do not be foolish, but understand what the Lord's will is. ¹⁸Do not get drunk on wine, which leads to debauchery. Instead, be filled with the Spirit. ¹⁹Speak to one another with psalms, hymns and spiritual songs. Sing and make music in your heart to the Lord, ²⁰always giving thanks to God the Father for everything, in the name of our Lord Jesus Christ.

²¹Submit to one another out of reverence for Christ.

5:21 The Key to Submission

Many readers have struggled with the advice Paul gives in the next few paragraphs. This simple sentence sets the tone for all that follows: We are to submit to others because of our reverence for Christ. In other words, in any human relationship—husband and wife, child and parent, slave and master—a third party is involved, Christ himself. Paul urges us to conduct those relationships in light of Christ's own spirit.

Wives and Husbands

²²Wives, submit to your husbands as to the Lord. ²³For the husband is the head of the wife as Christ is the head of the church, his body, of which he is the Savior. ²⁴Now as the church submits to Christ, so also wives should submit to their husbands in everything.

²⁵Husbands, love your wives, just as Christ loved the church and gave himself up for her ²⁶to make her holy, cleansingᶜ her by the washing with water through the word, ²⁷and to present her to himself as a radiant church, without stain or wrinkle or any other blemish, but holy and blameless. ²⁸In this same way, husbands ought to love their wives as their own bodies. He who loves his wife loves himself. ²⁹After all, no one ever hated his own body, but he feeds and cares for it, just as Christ does the church— ³⁰for we are members of his body. ³¹"For this reason a man will leave his father and mother and be united to his wife, and the two will become one flesh."ᵈ ³²This is a profound mystery—but I am talking about Christ and the church. ³³However, each one of you also must love his wife as he loves himself, and the wife must respect her husband.

Children and Parents

6 Children, obey your parents in the Lord, for this is right. ²"Honor your father and moth-

ᵃ26 Psalm 4:4   ᵇ5 Or *kingdom of the Christ and God*   ᶜ26 Or *having cleansed*   ᵈ31 Gen. 2:24

er"—which is the first commandment with a promise— [3]"that it may go well with you and that you may enjoy long life on the earth."[a]

[4]Fathers, do not exasperate your children; instead, bring them up in the training and instruction of the Lord.

Slaves and Masters

[5]Slaves, obey your earthly masters with respect and fear, and with sincerity of heart, just as you would obey Christ. [6]Obey them not only to win their favor when their eye is on you, but like slaves of Christ, doing the will of God from your heart. [7]Serve wholeheartedly, as if you were serving the Lord, not men, [8]because you know that the Lord will reward everyone for whatever good he does, whether he is slave or free.

[9]And masters, treat your slaves in the same way. Do not threaten them, since you know that he who is both their Master and yours is in heaven, and there is no favoritism with him.

The Armor of God

[10]Finally, be strong in the Lord and in his mighty power. [11]Put on the full armor of God so that you can take your stand against the devil's schemes. [12]For our struggle is not against flesh and blood, but against the rulers, against the authorities, against the powers of this dark world and against the spiritual forces of evil in the heavenly realms. [13]Therefore put on the full armor of God, so that when the day of evil comes, you may be able to stand your ground, and after you have done everything, to stand. [14]Stand firm then, with the belt of truth buckled around your waist, with the breastplate of righteousness in place, [15]and with your feet fitted with the readiness that comes from the gospel of peace. [16]In addition to all this, take up the shield of faith, with which you can extinguish all the flaming arrows of the evil

one. [17]Take the helmet of salvation and the sword of the Spirit, which is the word of God. [18]And pray in the Spirit on all occasions with all kinds of prayers and requests. With this in mind, be

6:11 The Armor of God

Ephesians concludes with a concise analogy, perhaps inspired by a glimpse of a Roman soldier, outfitted in armor, patrolling the grounds of Paul's prison. Paul viewed the Christian life as a kind of warfare, and he wanted his readers to prepare for combat with a dangerous opponent. Bible scholars often note two details: (1) Only the "sword of the Spirit" is an offensive weapon; all the rest were used for defense. (2) No armor protects the back and rear; Paul made no provision for running away from a spiritual battle.

alert and always keep on praying for all the saints.

[19]Pray also for me, that whenever I open my mouth, words may be given me so that I will fearlessly make known the mystery of the gospel, [20]for which I am an ambassador in chains. Pray that I may declare it fearlessly, as I should.

Final Greetings

[21]Tychicus, the dear brother and faithful servant in the Lord, will tell you everything, so that you also may know how I am and what I am doing. [22]I am sending him to you for this very purpose, that you may know how we are, and that he may encourage you.

[23]Peace to the brothers, and love with faith from God the Father and the Lord Jesus Christ. [24]Grace to all who love our Lord Jesus Christ with an undying love.

[a]3 Deut. 5:16

PHILIPPIANS

Cheerful Sounds from a Jail Cell
Joy when it's least expected

> *Finally, my brothers,*
> *rejoice in the Lord!*
> *3:1*

OY. THE WORD HAS A quick, poignant ring to it. Yet it, like other words, has been drained of meaning over the years, even tapped as a name for a dishwashing detergent. Nowadays *joy* is used most commonly for a sensation like *thrill*.

We think of joy as something you save up for months to experience and then splurge on in a moment of exhilaration: a trip to Disney World, a free-fall dive, a heart-stopping ride on the world's meanest roller coaster, a hot-air balloon trip. Paul had a different understanding of the word, as this letter reveals.

When You Feel Like Despairing

Philippians uses the word *joy* or *rejoice* every few paragraphs, but the joy it describes doesn't vanish after your heart starts beating normally again. Rejoice, says Paul, when someone selfishly tries to steal the limelight from you. And when you meet persecution for your faith. And when you are facing death.

In fact, the most joyous book in the Bible comes from the pen of an author chained to a Roman guard. Many scholars believe Paul wrote Philippians in Rome just about the time Nero began tossing Christians to ravenous lions and burning them as torches to illuminate his banquets. How could a rational man devote a letter to the topic of joy while his survival was in serious jeopardy? In such an environment, how could joy possibly thrive?

Turning Evil into Good

Paul hints at an answer in a burst of eloquence in chapter 2 (verses 5–11). This pithy, metrical paragraph may have been a hymn familiar to the early church. In it, Paul discusses Christ's perspective in coming to earth.

During the Christmas season we celebrate the grand night God visited earth as a baby. But to the rest of the universe the event looked like an astounding humiliation. God, the Creator of all, took on the unimpressive body of a human being to endure a confining life and grisly death on planet Earth.

Paul points to this death to show that God can take even the darkest moment in history and turn it into good. The cross, and Jesus' not staying dead, proves that nothing is powerful enough to stamp out a reason for joy—joy "in the Lord," as Paul says.

Victory in Jail

Thus even the normally depressing state of imprisonment didn't bother Paul. As he wrote Philippians, he must have recalled his first visit to Philippi. Then, a most unusual jailbreak occurred: The jail broke, but the prisoners didn't (Acts 16:22–28).

Even when Paul stayed in jail for long periods, God used the experience to advance the gospel. As he wrote Philippians, conversions were occurring among the Roman palace soldiers, forced by guard duty to overhear Paul's daily ministry.

Paul summarized his life philosophy in a famous "to be or not to be" soliloquy, concluding that "to live is Christ and to die is gain" (1:21). God is even stronger than death, and that makes a Christian's joy indestructible.

How to Read Philippians

Philippians is simple and straightforward. It's not a formal treatise, but a warm letter to friends. Read it like you would read any personal letter. From the clues Paul gives, try to imagine the relationship between him and the Philippians. What did he like about them? Why were they so important to him?

The Introduction refers to the common use of the words *joy* and *rejoice.* Check out each of these, noticing how Paul can find joy in any circumstances. Use Philippians like a devotional book, first reflecting on what it says, then applying it to your own life.

3-TRACK READING PLAN

For an explanation and complete listing of the 3-track reading plan, turn to page 7.

TRACK 1: **Two-Week Courses on the Bible**
The Track 1 reading program on the Life and Teachings of Paul includes one chapter from Philippians. See page 7 for a complete listing of this course.

TRACK 2: **An Overview of Philippians in 1 Day**
☐ Day 1. Read the Introduction to Philippians, then chapter 2, noticing especially the central passage set off in poetic form (verses 5–11).
Now turn to page 9 for your next Track 2 reading project.

TRACK 3: **All of Philippians in 4 Days**
After you have read through Philippians, turn to pages 10–14 for your next Track 3 reading project.
☐1   ☐2   ☐3   ☐4

---

1 Paul and Timothy, servants of Christ Jesus,

To all the saints in Christ Jesus at Philippi, together with the overseers*a* and deacons:

²Grace and peace to you from God our Father and the Lord Jesus Christ.

Thanksgiving and Prayer

³I thank my God every time I remember you. ⁴In all my prayers for all of you, I always pray with joy ⁵because of your partnership in the gospel from the first day until now, ⁶being confident of this, that he who began a good work in you will carry it on to completion until the day of Christ Jesus.

⁷It is right for me to feel this way about all of you, since I have you in my heart; for whether I am in chains or defending and confirming the gospel, all of you share in God's grace with me. ⁸God can testify how I long for all of you with the affection of Christ Jesus.

⁹And this is my prayer: that your love may abound more and more in knowledge and depth of insight, ¹⁰so that you may be able to discern what is best and may be pure and blameless until the day of Christ, ¹¹filled with the fruit of righ-

teousness that comes through Jesus Christ—to the glory and praise of God.

Paul's Chains Advance the Gospel

¹²Now I want you to know, brothers, that what has happened to me has really served to advance the gospel. ¹³As a result, it has become clear

1:7 Paul's Partners

Strong-minded though he was, Paul never worked alone. The warmth in this book comes partly from his confidence that the Philippian Christians were his partners (verse 5), sharing in God's grace. He counted on their prayers (verse 19). At the end of this letter, Paul returns to this theme of partnership, rejoicing in the Philippians' love and thoughtfulness (4:10–19).

throughout the whole palace guard*b* and to everyone else that I am in chains for Christ. ¹⁴Because of my chains, most of the brothers in the Lord have been encouraged to speak the word of God more courageously and fearlessly.

¹⁵It is true that some preach Christ out of envy and rivalry, but others out of goodwill. ¹⁶The

---

a1 Traditionally *bishops*   *b13* Or *whole palace*

latter do so in love, knowing that I am put here for the defense of the gospel. [17]The former preach Christ out of selfish ambition, not sincerely, supposing that they can stir up trouble for me while I am in chains.[a] [18]But what does it matter? The important thing is that in every way, whether from false motives or true, Christ is preached. And because of this I rejoice.

Yes, and I will continue to rejoice, [19]for I know that through your prayers and the help given by the Spirit of Jesus Christ, what has happened to me will turn out for my deliverance.[b] [20]I eagerly expect and hope that I will in no way be ashamed, but will have sufficient courage so that now as always Christ will be exalted in my body, whether by life or by death. [21]For to me, to live is Christ and to die is gain. [22]If I am to go on living in the body, this will mean fruitful labor for me. Yet what shall I choose? I do not know! [23]I am torn between the two: I desire to depart and be with Christ, which is better by far; [24]but it is more necessary for you that I remain in the body. [25]Convinced of this, I know that I will remain,

and I will continue with all of you for your progress and joy in the faith, [26]so that through my being with you again your joy in Christ Jesus will overflow on account of me.

[27]Whatever happens, conduct yourselves in a manner worthy of the gospel of Christ. Then, whether I come and see you or only hear about you in my absence, I will know that you stand firm in one spirit, contending as one man for the faith of the gospel [28]without being frightened in any way by those who oppose you. This is a sign to them that they will be destroyed, but that you will be saved—and that by God. [29]For it has been granted to you on behalf of Christ not only to believe on him, but also to suffer for him, [30]since you are going through the same struggle you saw I had, and now hear that I still have.

Imitating Christ's Humility

2 If you have any encouragement from being united with Christ, if any comfort from his love, if any fellowship with the Spirit, if any tenderness and compassion, [2]then make my joy

---

[a] 16,17 Some late manuscripts have verses 16 and 17 in reverse order. [b] 19 Or *salvation*

Paul's Favorite Church
When others failed, these friends didn't

> I thank my God every time I remember you. 1:3

THE CHRISTIAN CHURCH HASN'T HAD a perfect record throughout history. If you take a random sample of adjectives people use to describe the church, the list will likely include such labels as *racist, judgmental, narrow, divided, pompous.*

The church of Jesus Christ has fallen far short of the ideals he entrusted to it—so far short that we may sometimes forget what the church is supposed to look like. Problems existed from the beginning: Paul's letters to Galatia, Corinth, and Colosse flame with indignation against defects in the early church.

Occasionally, however, a church came along that worked, against all odds. Philippi was one of those rare congregations.

Loyal Friends

From its birth, the church in Philippi had two strikes against it. Its first recorded converts were an Asiatic Jewish merchant, a Greek slave girl employed as a sideshow fortune-teller, and a gruff Roman jailer (Acts 16). Yet more than a decade later, when Paul wrote the church, he could hardly find words warm enough to express his pride and affection.

Paul turned down money gifts from other churches, out of fear that his enemies might twist the facts and accuse him of being a crook. But he trusted the Philippians. At least four separate times they sacrificed to meet his needs. And they also sent Epaphroditus on an arduous journey to care for Paul in prison.

Paul wrote Philippians, in fact, mainly as a thank-you for all that his friends had done. Its bright, happy tone reflects the fondness he felt for his favorite church.

Nevertheless, Paul couldn't resist an opportunity to give some fatherly advice. In a fireside-chat tone, he warned of encroaching dangers: divisions, a strain of perfectionism, and inroads by those who wished to turn Christians back to the Jewish faith. Always, though, he returned to his underlying theme of joy, an emotion that seemed to come easily when Paul remembered the Philippians.

Life Questions: What does Paul single out for praise in the Philippian church? How are those qualities present in your church?

complete by being like-minded, having the same love, being one in spirit and purpose. ³Do nothing out of selfish ambition or vain conceit, but in humility consider others better than yourselves. ⁴Each of you should look not only to your own interests, but also to the interests of others.

⁵Your attitude should be the same as that of Christ Jesus:

⁶Who, being in very nature*a* God,
did not consider equality with God
something to be grasped,
⁷but made himself nothing,
taking the very nature*b* of a servant,
being made in human likeness.
⁸And being found in appearance as a man,
he humbled himself
and became obedient to death—
even death on a cross!
⁹Therefore God exalted him to the highest
place
and gave him the name that is above
every name,
¹⁰that at the name of Jesus every knee should
bow,
in heaven and on earth and under the
earth,
¹¹and every tongue confess that Jesus Christ is
Lord,
to the glory of God the Father.

Shining as Stars

¹²Therefore, my dear friends, as you have always obeyed—not only in my presence, but now much more in my absence—continue to work

2:12–13 Working with God

Philippians, a practical book, presents theology simply and without elaboration. These verses describe both the human and divine element in our faith: We "work out" our salvation, and yet God "works" in us to accomplish it. Philippians 3:16 expresses a similar paradox: Paul urges that we "live up to what we have already attained."

out your salvation with fear and trembling, ¹³for it is God who works in you to will and to act according to his good purpose.

¹⁴Do everything without complaining or arguing, ¹⁵so that you may become blameless and pure, children of God without fault in a crooked and depraved generation, in which you shine like stars in the universe ¹⁶as you hold out*c* the word of life—in order that I may boast on the day of Christ that I did not run or labor for nothing. ¹⁷But even if I am being poured out like a drink

offering on the sacrifice and service coming from your faith, I am glad and rejoice with all of you. ¹⁸So you too should be glad and rejoice with me.

Timothy and Epaphroditus

¹⁹I hope in the Lord Jesus to send Timothy to you soon, that I also may be cheered when I receive news about you. ²⁰I have no one else like him, who takes a genuine interest in your welfare. ²¹For everyone looks out for his own interests, not those of Jesus Christ. ²²But you know that Timothy has proved himself, because as a son with his father he has served with me in the work of the gospel. ²³I hope, therefore, to send him as soon as I see how things go with me. ²⁴And I am confident in the Lord that I myself will come soon.

²⁵But I think it is necessary to send back to you Epaphroditus, my brother, fellow worker and fellow soldier, who is also your messenger,

2:25 A Helper for Paul

The paragraph on Epaphroditus reveals the warm feelings between Paul and the church at Philippi. If Paul was imprisoned at Rome, as many scholars believe, then Epaphroditus traveled more than 700 miles to be with him. He fell sick while visiting Paul and was now returning to Philippi, probably carrying this letter to hand-deliver.

whom you sent to take care of my needs. ²⁶For he longs for all of you and is distressed because you heard he was ill. ²⁷Indeed he was ill, and almost died. But God had mercy on him, and not on him only but also on me, to spare me sorrow upon sorrow. ²⁸Therefore I am all the more eager to send him, so that when you see him again you may be glad and I may have less anxiety. ²⁹Welcome him in the Lord with great joy, and honor men like him, ³⁰because he almost died for the work of Christ, risking his life to make up for the help you could not give me.

No Confidence in the Flesh

3 Finally, my brothers, rejoice in the Lord! It is no trouble for me to write the same things to you again, and it is a safeguard for you.

²Watch out for those dogs, those men who do evil, those mutilators of the flesh. ³For it is we who are the circumcision, we who worship by the Spirit of God, who glory in Christ Jesus, and who put no confidence in the flesh— ⁴though I myself have reasons for such confidence.

If anyone else thinks he has reasons to put

---

a6 Or *in the form of*   *b7* Or *the form*   *c16* Or *hold on to* confidence in the flesh, I have more: [5]circumcised on the eighth day, of the people of Israel, of the tribe of Benjamin, a Hebrew of Hebrews; in regard to the law, a Pharisee; [6]as for zeal, persecuting the church; as for legalistic righteousness, faultless.

[7]But whatever was to my profit I now consider loss for the sake of Christ. [8]What is more, I consider everything a loss compared to the surpassing greatness of knowing Christ Jesus my Lord, for whose sake I have lost all things. I consider them rubbish, that I may gain Christ [9]and be found in him, not having a righteousness of my own that comes from the law, but that which is through faith in Christ—the righteousness that comes from God and is by faith. [10]I want to know Christ and the power of his resurrection and the fellowship of sharing in his sufferings, becoming like him in his death, [11]and so, somehow, to attain to the resurrection from the dead.

Pressing on Toward the Goal

[12]Not that I have already obtained all this, or have already been made perfect, but I press on to take hold of that for which Christ Jesus took hold of me. [13]Brothers, I do not consider myself yet to have taken hold of it. But one thing I do: Forgetting what is behind and straining toward what is ahead, [14]I press on toward the goal to win the prize for which God has called me heavenward in Christ Jesus.

[15]All of us who are mature should take such a view of things. And if on some point you think differently, that too God will make clear to you. [16]Only let us live up to what we have already attained.

[17]Join with others in following my example, brothers, and take note of those who live according to the pattern we gave you. [18]For, as I have often told you before and now say again even with tears, many live as enemies of the cross of Christ. [19]Their destiny is destruction, their god is their stomach, and their glory is in their shame. Their mind is on earthly things. [20]But our citizenship is in heaven. And we eagerly await a Savior from there, the Lord Jesus Christ, [21]who, by the power that enables him to bring everything under his control, will transform our lowly bodies so that they will be like his glorious body.

4 Therefore, my brothers, you whom I love and long for, my joy and crown, that is how you should stand firm in the Lord, dear friends!

Exhortations

[2]I plead with Euodia and I plead with Syntyche to agree with each other in the Lord. [3]Yes, and I ask you, loyal yokefellow,[a] help these women who have contended at my side in the cause of the gospel, along with Clement and the rest of my fellow workers, whose names are in the book of life.

[4]Rejoice in the Lord always. I will say it again: Rejoice! [5]Let your gentleness be evident to all.

4:2 Women in the Church

Although these two women were stirring up trouble in Philippi, women played a positive role in that church. In fact, Paul's first convert in Europe was Lydia, a businesswoman. Paul met with her and a group of women by a river, and later stayed in her house (see Acts 16).

The Lord is near. [6]Do not be anxious about anything, but in everything, by prayer and petition, with thanksgiving, present your requests to God. [7]And the peace of God, which transcends all understanding, will guard your hearts and your minds in Christ Jesus.

[8]Finally, brothers, whatever is true, whatever is noble, whatever is right, whatever is pure, whatever is lovely, whatever is admirable—if anything is excellent or praiseworthy—think about such things. [9]Whatever you have learned or received or heard from me, or seen in me—put it into practice. And the God of peace will be with you.

Thanks for Their Gifts

[10]I rejoice greatly in the Lord that at last you have renewed your concern for me. Indeed, you have been concerned, but you had no opportunity to show it. [11]I am not saying this because I am in need, for I have learned to be content whatever the circumstances. [12]I know what it is to be in need, and I know what it is to have plenty. I have learned the secret of being content in any and every situation, whether well fed or hungry, whether living in plenty or in want. [13]I can do everything through him who gives me strength.

[14]Yet it was good of you to share in my troubles. [15]Moreover, as you Philippians know, in the

4:13 Paul's Secret

Shipwrecked, beaten, imprisoned, Paul had seen the down side of life. He had also known prosperity. Both, he suggests, offer temptations. But Paul had discovered a secret for contentment in all situations: his deeply personal sense of living in Christ. In this he found strength to handle anything.

---

[a] 3 Or loyal Syzygus

early days of your acquaintance with the gospel, when I set out from Macedonia, not one church shared with me in the matter of giving and receiving, except you only; [16]for even when I was in Thessalonica, you sent me aid again and again when I was in need. [17]Not that I am looking for a gift, but I am looking for what may be credited to your account. [18]I have received full payment and even more; I am amply supplied, now that I have received from Epaphroditus the gifts you sent. They are a fragrant offering, an acceptable sacrifice, pleasing to God. [19]And my God will meet all your needs according to his glorious riches in Christ Jesus.

[20]To our God and Father be glory for ever and ever. Amen.

Final Greetings

[21]Greet all the saints in Christ Jesus. The brothers who are with me send greetings. [22]All the saints send you greetings, especially those who belong to Caesar's household.

[23]The grace of the Lord Jesus Christ be with your spirit. Amen.[a]

---

[a]23 Some manuscripts do not have *Amen*.

COLOSSIANS

Battling the Cults
For everything worthwhile, there exists a counterfeit

See to it that no one takes you captive through hollow and deceptive philosophy. 2:8

YOU SEE THEM IN STRANGE outfits on street corners, chanting phrases with too many vowels and punctuating the chants with a noisy tambourine. Or in airports, thrusting books or flowers into your face. Or in California, all over California. You think of them as crazy cults, populated by misfits. Then one day you hear about a friend of yours.

She seemed normal until suddenly, without warning, she snapped. Her parents searched desperately, even hiring private detectives to help get her back. They found her surrounded by allies, with a new name, a new hairstyle, and, so it seemed, a new brain. She stared at them with clear eyes and told them they were missing out on the most wonderful experience of life. She had joined a cult.

A Breeding Ground

Cults come in all varieties, some recent spin-offs from the New Age movement, others sporting exotic names like Hare Krishna or the Church of Scientology. They demand much from their members: a lifetime of discipline and absolute loyalty. And they also promise much in return: the pathway to a secret, hidden knowledge available only to those who follow them.

The first-century town of Colosse was a perfect breeding ground for cults. Situated on a major trade route from the East, Colosse entertained a steady stream of Oriental traders with mysterious religious ideas. Even Jews in that area worshiped angels and river spirits.

Early Christian converts soon confronted new variations of the gospel. Then, as now, many cults didn't reject Jesus Christ outright; they merely worked him into a more elaborate scheme. Christ and simple forms of worship, they taught, were fine for beginners, but for the "deep things of God," well, some further steps would be required.

The Best Defense

Paul doesn't give a complete glossary of the "hollow and deceptive philosophy" the Colossians were sorting through. From his arguments, we can gather that the philosophy must have included strains of Jewish legalism mixed in with angel worship, Greek philosophy, and strict self-denial.

The best defense is a good offense. Rather than attacking each peculiar belief point by point, Paul countered with a positive theology. The principles he outlines in this book can be used today to judge new cults.

"Christ is enough," Paul declares. He is God, the fullness of God, the One who made the world, the reason that everything exists. All the mystery and treasure and wisdom you could ask for are found in the person of Jesus Christ; there is no need to look elsewhere.

Approach God Directly

Because Jesus bridged the chasm between God and us, we don't have to approach God indirectly, through a ladder of angels or other gods. We have no need to prove our worth through superior behavior. We can come to God directly and boldly because of Christ.

As for Jewish practices, they were mere shadows, made obsolete by Christ's coming. Why not concentrate on the actual image that God sent to earth?

Before Christ, Paul grants, a mystery was kept hidden for many centuries (1:26). But with Christ, everything broke out into the open. The fullness of God lived, died, and came back from death in broad daylight. Why settle for counterfeits?

How to Read Colossians

Although this letter was written to counter specific problems in the church at Colosse, it includes some of Paul's most eloquent writing about Jesus Christ. Chapter 1 contains a soaring paragraph (1:15–20) that may have been used as a hymn by the early church. Note in this book how Paul concludes all his arguments by referring to Christ.

Chapters 2 and 3 deal with dangerous tendencies in Colosse. Paul argues against a "mystery" religion by firmly asserting that Christ is the complete expression of the mystery of God. As you read these two chapters, try to imagine what kind of behavior at Colosse troubled Paul.

3-TRACK READING PLAN

For an explanation and complete listing of the 3-track reading plan, turn to page 7.

TRACK 1: **_Two-Week Courses on the Bible_**
See page 7 for information on these courses.

TRACK 2: **_An Overview of Colossians in 1 Day_**
☐ Day 1. Read the Introduction to Colossians, then chapter 1, noting especially Paul's prayer, which precedes the hymnlike paragraph (verses 15–20).

Now turn to page 9 for your next Track 2 reading project.

TRACK 3: **_All of Colossians in 4 Days_**
After you have read through Colossians, turn to pages 10–14 for your next Track 3 reading project.
☐1   ☐2   ☐3   ☐4

1 Paul, an apostle of Christ Jesus by the will of God, and Timothy our brother,

²To the holy and faithful*a* brothers in Christ at Colosse:

Grace and peace to you from God our Father.*b*

Thanksgiving and Prayer

³We always thank God, the Father of our Lord Jesus Christ, when we pray for you, ⁴because we have heard of your faith in Christ Jesus and of the love you have for all the saints— ⁵the faith and love that spring from the hope that is stored up for you in heaven and that you have already heard about in the word of truth, the gospel ⁶that has come to you. All over the world this gospel is bearing fruit and growing, just as it has been doing among you since the day you heard it and understood God's grace in all its truth. ⁷You learned it from Epaphras, our dear fellow servant, who is a faithful minister of Christ on our*c* behalf, ⁸and who also told us of your love in the Spirit.

⁹For this reason, since the day we heard about you, we have not stopped praying for you and asking God to fill you with the knowledge of his will through all spiritual wisdom and understanding. ¹⁰And we pray this in order that you may live a life worthy of the Lord and may please him in every way: bearing fruit in every good work, growing in the knowledge of God, ¹¹being strengthened with all power according to his glorious might so that you may have great endurance and patience, and joyfully ¹²giving thanks to the Father, who has qualified you*d* to share in the inheritance of the saints in the kingdom of light. ¹³For he has rescued us from the dominion of darkness and brought us into the kingdom of the Son he loves, ¹⁴in whom we have redemption,*e* the forgiveness of sins.

The Supremacy of Christ

¹⁵He is the image of the invisible God, the firstborn over all creation. ¹⁶For by him all things were created: things in heaven and on earth, visible and invisible, whether thrones or powers or rulers or authorities; all things were created by him and for him. ¹⁷He is before all things, and in him all things hold together. ¹⁸And he is the head of the body, the church; he is the beginning and the firstborn from among the dead, so that in everything he might have the supremacy. ¹⁹For God was pleased to have all his fullness dwell in

*a*2 Or *believing*   *b*2 Some manuscripts *Father and the Lord Jesus Christ*   *c*7 Some manuscripts *your*
*d*12 Some manuscripts *us*   *e*14 A few late manuscripts *redemption through his blood*

him, 20and through him to reconcile to himself all things, whether things on earth or things in heaven, by making peace through his blood, shed on the cross.

21Once you were alienated from God and were enemies in your minds because of*a* your evil

> ### 1:21 Getting Practical
>
> *Although Paul's letters often launch out into theological deep water, they always lead back to practical issues: What difference does theology make to daily life? The preceding paragraph (verses 15–20) contains a compressed summary of the absolute supremacy of Christ. Now Paul turns to the practical: Christ's supreme power does not distance us from but rather brings us closer to God. He alone has the ability to span the vast gap between God and humanity.*

behavior. 22But now he has reconciled you by Christ's physical body through death to present you holy in his sight, without blemish and free from accusation— 23if you continue in your faith, established and firm, not moved from the hope held out in the gospel. This is the gospel that you heard and that has been proclaimed to every creature under heaven, and of which I, Paul, have become a servant.

Paul's Labor for the Church

24Now I rejoice in what was suffered for you, and I fill up in my flesh what is still lacking in regard to Christ's afflictions, for the sake of his body, which is the church. 25I have become its servant by the commission God gave me to present to you the word of God in its fullness— 26the mystery that has been kept hidden for ages and generations, but is now disclosed to the saints. 27To them God has chosen to make known among the Gentiles the glorious riches of this mystery, which is Christ in you, the hope of glory.

28We proclaim him, admonishing and teaching everyone with all wisdom, so that we may present everyone perfect in Christ. 29To this end I labor, struggling with all his energy, which so powerfully works in me. 2 I want you to know how much I am struggling for you and for those at Laodicea, and for all who have not met me personally. 2My purpose is that they may be encouraged in heart and united in love, so that they may have the full riches of complete understanding, in order that they may know the mystery of God, namely,

Christ, 3in whom are hidden all the treasures of wisdom and knowledge. 4I tell you this so that no one may deceive you by fine-sounding arguments. 5For though I am absent from you in body, I am present with you in spirit and delight to see how orderly you are and how firm your faith in Christ is.

Freedom From Human Regulations Through Life With Christ

6So then, just as you received Christ Jesus as Lord, continue to live in him, 7rooted and built up in him, strengthened in the faith as you were taught, and overflowing with thankfulness.

8See to it that no one takes you captive through hollow and deceptive philosophy, which depends on human tradition and the basic principles of this world rather than on Christ.

9For in Christ all the fullness of the Deity lives in bodily form, 10and you have been given fullness in Christ, who is the head over every power and authority. 11In him you were also circumcised, in the putting off of the sinful nature,*b* not with a circumcision done by the hands of men but with the circumcision done by Christ, 12having been buried with him in baptism and raised with him through your faith in the power of God, who raised him from the dead.

13When you were dead in your sins and in the uncircumcision of your sinful nature,*c* God made you*d* alive with Christ. He forgave us all our sins, 14having canceled the written code, with its regulations, that was against us and that stood opposed to us; he took it away, nailing it to the cross. 15And having disarmed the powers and authorities, he made a public spectacle of them, triumphing over them by the cross.*e*

16Therefore do not let anyone judge you by what you eat or drink, or with regard to a religious festival, a New Moon celebration or a Sab-

> ### 2:16 The Search for Wholeness
>
> *Legalism in Paul's day concerned such issues as diet, festival days, and religious ceremony. In these two paragraphs, Paul tells why such rules that appear "spiritual" can actually lead a person away from God. Then, in chapter 3, he details what holy living should look like.*
>
> *In his letter, Paul portrays the Christian life very optimistically. The Christians in Colosse were searching for "fullness" in the same way modern people work to become "holistic" or "self-actualized." After first affirming that Jesus contains all the fullness of God, Paul asserts that true fullness is found only in Christ (verse 10).*

---

a21 Or minds, as shown by in him   *b11 Or the flesh*   *c13 Or your flesh*   *d13 Some manuscripts us*   *e15 Or them*

bath day. [17]These are a shadow of the things that were to come; the reality, however, is found in Christ. [18]Do not let anyone who delights in false humility and the worship of angels disqualify you for the prize. Such a person goes into great detail about what he has seen, and his unspiritual mind puffs him up with idle notions. [19]He has lost connection with the Head, from whom the whole body, supported and held together by its ligaments and sinews, grows as God causes it to grow.

[20]Since you died with Christ to the basic principles of this world, why, as though you still belonged to it, do you submit to its rules: [21]"Do not handle! Do not taste! Do not touch!"? [22]These are all destined to perish with use, because they are based on human commands and teachings. [23]Such regulations indeed have an appearance of wisdom, with their self-imposed worship, their false humility and their harsh treatment of the body, but they lack any value in restraining sensual indulgence.

Rules for Holy Living

3 Since, then, you have been raised with Christ, set your hearts on things above, where Christ

3:1 Familiar Words

If Colossians strikes you as vaguely familiar, don't be surprised. Paul's letters tend to follow a pattern: a greeting, a prayer, some doctrine, and a practical application of how we should live. Colossians sounds especially familiar because many of its verses have close parallels in Ephesians. In fact, of Ephesians's 155 verses, 78 appear in some form in Colossians.

is seated at the right hand of God. [2]Set your minds on things above, not on earthly things. [3]For you died, and your life is now hidden with Christ in God. [4]When Christ, who is your[a] life, appears, then you also will appear with him in glory.

[5]Put to death, therefore, whatever belongs to your earthly nature: sexual immorality, impurity, lust, evil desires and greed, which is idolatry. [6]Because of these, the wrath of God is coming.[b] [7]You used to walk in these ways, in the life you once lived. [8]But now you must rid yourselves of all such things as these: anger, rage, malice, slander, and filthy language from your lips. [9]Do not lie to each other, since you have taken off your old self with its practices [10]and have put on the new self, which is being renewed in knowledge in the image of its Creator. [11]Here there is no Greek or Jew, circumcised or uncircumcised, barbarian, Scythian, slave or free, but Christ is all, and is in all.

[12]Therefore, as God's chosen people, holy and dearly loved, clothe yourselves with compassion,

3:11 The Original Barbarians

The word "barbarians" meant those who did not speak Greek. To civilized people of that day, their languages sounded like a stammering repetition of the same syllables— barbarbarbar—hence the word barbarian. Scythians were likewise considered uncivilized and brutish. By mentioning such people, Paul was underscoring the all-encompassing breadth of God's grace.

kindness, humility, gentleness and patience. [13]Bear with each other and forgive whatever grievances you may have against one another. Forgive as the Lord forgave you. [14]And over all these virtues put on love, which binds them all together in perfect unity.

[15]Let the peace of Christ rule in your hearts, since as members of one body you were called to peace. And be thankful. [16]Let the word of Christ dwell in you richly as you teach and admonish one another with all wisdom, and as you sing psalms, hymns and spiritual songs with gratitude in your hearts to God. [17]And whatever you do, whether in word or deed, do it all in the name of the Lord Jesus, giving thanks to God the Father through him.

Rules for Christian Households

[18]Wives, submit to your husbands, as is fitting in the Lord.

[19]Husbands, love your wives and do not be harsh with them.

[20]Children, obey your parents in everything, for this pleases the Lord.

[21]Fathers, do not embitter your children, or they will become discouraged.

[22]Slaves, obey your earthly masters in everything; and do it, not only when their eye is on you and to win their favor, but with sincerity of heart and reverence for the Lord. [23]Whatever you do, work at it with all your heart, as working for the Lord, not for men, [24]since you know that you will receive an inheritance from the Lord as a reward. It is the Lord Christ you are serving. [25]Anyone who does wrong will be repaid for his wrong, and there is no favoritism.

4 Masters, provide your slaves with what is right and fair, because you know that you also have a Master in heaven.

---

[a]4 Some manuscripts *our* [b]6 Some early manuscripts *coming on those who are disobedient*

Further Instructions

²Devote yourselves to prayer, being watchful and thankful. ³And pray for us, too, that God may open a door for our message, so that we may proclaim the mystery of Christ, for which I am in chains. ⁴Pray that I may proclaim it clearly, as I should. ⁵Be wise in the way you act toward outsiders; make the most of every opportunity. ⁶Let your conversation be always full of grace, seasoned with salt, so that you may know how to answer everyone.

Final Greetings

⁷Tychicus will tell you all the news about me. He is a dear brother, a faithful minister and fellow servant in the Lord. ⁸I am sending him to you for the express purpose that you may know about our*a* circumstances and that he may encourage your hearts. ⁹He is coming with Onesimus, our faithful and dear brother, who is one of you. They will tell you everything that is happening here.

¹⁰My fellow prisoner Aristarchus sends you his greetings, as does Mark, the cousin of Barnabas. (You have received instructions about him; if he comes to you, welcome him.) ¹¹Jesus, who is called Justus, also sends greetings. These are the only Jews among my fellow workers for the kingdom of God, and they have proved a comfort to me. ¹²Epaphras, who is one of you and a servant of Christ Jesus, sends greetings. He is always wrestling in prayer for you, that you may stand firm in all the will of God, mature and fully

4:12 Prominent Names

Characteristically, Paul ended his letters with personal messages. Epaphras, who is mentioned twice in Colossians (1:7; 4:12), served with Paul and may have founded the church there. The short book of Philemon (verse 23) mentions him as a fellow prisoner with Paul. The main characters in that book, Philemon and his slave Onesimus, also came from Colosse, and Paul refers to a hoped-for visit to Colosse in his letter to Philemon (verse 22).

assured. ¹³I vouch for him that he is working hard for you and for those at Laodicea and Hierapolis. ¹⁴Our dear friend Luke, the doctor, and Demas send greetings. ¹⁵Give my greetings to the brothers at Laodicea, and to Nympha and the church in her house.

¹⁶After this letter has been read to you, see that it is also read in the church of the Laodiceans and that you in turn read the letter from Laodicea.

¹⁷Tell Archippus: "See to it that you complete the work you have received in the Lord."

¹⁸I, Paul, write this greeting in my own hand. Remember my chains. Grace be with you.

---

*a*8 Some manuscripts *that he may know about your*

1 THESSALONIANS

What Made Paul Successful?

The apostle fusses over the city that once chased him away

A MODERN-DAY EVANGELIST LAMENTED, "WHENEVER THE apostle Paul visited a city, the residents started a riot; when I visit one, they serve tea." The church in Thessalonica, like many of Paul's churches, was born amid violent upheaval. An angry mob took offense at Paul's work and chased him out of town, accusing him of causing "trouble all over the world" (Acts 17:6).

Generally, people do not start riots without a good reason, and in Paul's case they had one. Almost everywhere he visited, an enthusiastic church came to life, provoking the jealousy of the Jewish and Roman establishments.

> *How can we thank God enough for you in return for all the joy we have in the presence of our God because of you? 3:9*

A Concerned Parent

This letter, 1 Thessalonians, gives important clues into what made Paul so effective at founding churches. Accepted as one of the earliest of Paul's letters, it probably dates from A.D. 50 or 51 and provides a firsthand account of Paul's relationship with a missionary church barely 20 years after Jesus' departure.

Someone once asked John and Charles Wesley's mother which of her ten surviving children she loved the most. She replied, "The one who is sick until he's well, and the one who's away from home until he's back." If someone had asked Paul which church concerned him most, he probably would have answered, "The one with the most problems until it's healthy, the one I've been separated from longest until I return."

When Paul lived with the Thessalonians, he was gentle and loving, "like a mother caring for her little children" (2:7). Later, absent from them, he wrote as if he had only them on his mind all day. In 1 Thessalonians, he praised their strengths, fussed over reports of their weaknesses, and continually thanked God for their spiritual progress.

Questioning Paul's Motives

Some people in the church had questioned Paul's motives, so he opened the letter with a careful review of his work among them. In those days free-lance teachers of religion and philosophy sought a profit; Paul reminded the Thessalonians that he had worked night and day to avoid becoming a financial burden. He also painstakingly explained his unavoidable absence from them.

First Thessalonians stands out from the four books that precede it because, unlike them, this letter doesn't major in theology. Rather, it reveals the gratitude, disappointment, and joy of a beloved missionary who can't stop thinking about the church he left behind. Surely one reason for Paul's success centers on his churches' having made as big an impression on Paul as he made on them.

How to Read 1 Thessalonians

This book provides a touching glimpse of Paul as a pastor. Paul visited Thessalonica at a troubled time in his ministry, while enemies were tailing him from town to town (see Acts 16–17). After he left, the church continued to meet hostility.

First Thessalonians is our earliest record of the life of a Christian community. Paul wrote this letter after receiving a mostly positive report (from Timothy) on the Thessalonians' spiritual health. He rejoiced at the good news, but also showed concern over the church's problems.

As you read 1 Thessalonians, notice the issues that Paul addresses: Christians were raising questions about Jesus' return to earth and were disagreeing on matters of morality. But mainly, look for signs of Paul's relationship to the church at Thessalonica.

3-TRACK READING PLAN

For an explanation and complete listing of the 3-track reading plan, turn to page 7.

TRACK 1: ***Two-Week Courses on the Bible***
See page 7 for information on these courses.

TRACK 2: ***An Overview of 1 Thessalonians in 1 Day***
☐ Day 1. Read the Introduction to 1 Thessalonians, then chapters 3 and 4. The chapters are very short, so you can easily read two together.

Now turn to page 9 for your next Track 2 reading project.

TRACK 3: ***All of 1 Thessalonians in 3 Days***
After you have read through 1 Thessalonians, turn to pages 10–14 for your next Track 3 reading project.
☐1–2 ☐3–4 ☐5

1 Paul, Silas^a and Timothy,

To the church of the Thessalonians in God the Father and the Lord Jesus Christ:

Grace and peace to you.^b

Thanksgiving for the Thessalonians' Faith

²We always thank God for all of you, mentioning you in our prayers. ³We continually remember before our God and Father your work produced by faith, your labor prompted by love, and your endurance inspired by hope in our Lord Jesus Christ.

⁴For we know, brothers loved by God, that he has chosen you, ⁵because our gospel came to you not simply with words, but also with power, with the Holy Spirit and with deep conviction. You know how we lived among you for your sake. ⁶You became imitators of us and of the Lord; in spite of severe suffering, you welcomed the message with the joy given by the Holy Spirit. ⁷And so you became a model to all the believers in Macedonia and Achaia. ⁸The Lord's message rang out from you not only in Macedonia and Achaia—your faith in God has become known everywhere. Therefore we do not need to say anything about it, ⁹for they themselves report what kind of reception you gave us. They tell how you turned to God from idols to serve the living and true God, ¹⁰and to wait for his Son from heaven, whom he raised from the dead—Jesus, who rescues us from the coming wrath.

Paul's Ministry in Thessalonica

2 You know, brothers, that our visit to you was not a failure. ²We had previously suffered and been insulted in Philippi, as you know, but with the help of our God we dared to tell you his gospel in spite of strong opposition. ³For the appeal we make does not spring from error or impure motives, nor are we trying to trick you. ⁴On the contrary, we speak as men approved by God to be entrusted with the gospel. We are not trying to please men but God, who tests our hearts. ⁵You know we never used flattery, nor did we put on a mask to cover up greed—God is our witness. ⁶We were not looking for praise from men, not from you or anyone else.

As apostles of Christ we could have been a burden to you, ⁷but we were gentle among you, like a mother caring for her little children. ⁸We loved you so much that we were delighted to share with you not only the gospel of God but our lives as well, because you had become so dear to us. ⁹Surely you remember, brothers, our toil and hardship; we worked night and day in order not to be a burden to anyone while we preached the gospel of God to you.

¹⁰You are witnesses, and so is God, of how holy, righteous and blameless we were among you who believed. ¹¹For you know that we dealt with each of you as a father deals with his own children, ¹²encouraging, comforting and urging you to live lives worthy of God, who calls you into his kingdom and glory.

---

^a1 Greek *Silvanus*, a variant of *Silas*   ^b1 Some early manuscripts *you from God our Father and the Lord Jesus Christ*

God's Promises When You...

Feel Guilty: "Therefore, there is now no condemnation for those who are in Christ Jesus, because through Christ Jesus the law of the Spirit of life set me free from the law of sin and death." Romans 8:1–2 (See also 1 Corinthians 6:11; Ephesians 3:12; Hebrews 10:22–23)

Feel Dejected: "'Come to me, all you who are weary and burdened, and I will give you rest... Learn from me, for I am gentle and humble in heart, and you will find rest for your souls.'" Matthew 11:28–30 (See also Romans 8:26–27; Hebrews 4:16; James 4:8, 10)

Feel Unloved: "This is how God showed his love among us: He sent his one and only Son into the world that we might live through him. This is love: not that we loved God, but that he loved us and sent his Son as an atoning sacrifice for our sins." 1 John 4:9 (See also Matthew 10:30–31; John 3:16; John 15:9, 13)

Are Disappointed: "'If you remain in me and my words remain in you, ask whatever you wish, and it will be given you. This is to my Father's glory, that you bear much fruit, showing yourselves to be my disciples.'" John 15:7 (See also Mark 9:21–24; John 15:7; Ephesians 3:20)

Are Anxious: "Do not be anxious about anything, but in everything, by prayer and petition, with thanksgiving, present your requests to God. And the peace of God, which transcends all understanding, will guard your hearts and your minds in Christ Jesus." Philippians 4:6–7 (See also Matthew 6:25; Matthew 11:28–29; 1 Peter 5:7)

Are Confused: "If any of you lacks wisdom, he should ask God, who gives generously to all without finding fault, and it will be given to him." James 1:5 (See also John 8:12; John 14:27; 1 Corinthians 2:15–16)

Are Tempted: "For we do not have a high priest who is unable to sympathize with our weaknesses, but we have one who has been tempted in every way, just as we are—yet was without sin. Let us then approach the throne of grace with confidence, so that we may receive mercy and find grace to help us in our time of need." Hebrews 4:15–16 (See also 1 Corinthians 10:13; Hebrews 2:18; 1 Peter 5:8–10)

Need Forgiveness: "If we confess our sins, he is faithful and just and will forgive us our sins and purify us from all unrighteousness." 1 John 1:9 (See also Luke 15:3–7; Acts 10:43; Ephesians 1:7)

Fail: "For all have sinned and fall short of the glory of God, and are justified freely by his grace through the redemption that came by Christ Jesus." Romans 8:23–24 (See also Romans 5:8; Hebrews 10:36; 1 John 1:8–9)

Doubt: "If anyone acknowledges that Jesus is the Son of God, God lives in him and he in God. And so we know and rely on the love God has for us." 1 John 4:15–16 (See also John 3:18; John 11:25–26; Romans 4:5)

Are Looking for Peace: "Peace I leave with you; my peace I give you. I do not give to you as the world gives. Do not let your hearts be troubled and do not be afraid." John 14:21 (See also John 14:27, Romans 5:1–2, Ephesians 2:14, 2 Thessalonians 3:16)

God's Promises

W⦿W
1997

God's Plan for You

In the pages of this Bible you'll find God's words of love, written specifically for you. You'll also find God's great plan for your life here on earth, and for eternity.

God loves you and wants to have a relationship with you. That's the basis of his plan for your life. John 3:16 (page 1103) says, "For God so loved the world that he gave his one and only Son, that whoever believes in him shall not perish but have eternal life."

God's love is available to you today if you open your heart to receive it. Take a moment to write your name into the spaces provided below to see how much God loves you:

"For God so loved _____ that he gave his one and only son, that if _____ believes in him _____ shall not perish but have eternal life."

If you'd like to invite Jesus Christ into your life or if you'd like to renew your relationship with him, say the following prayer:

Jesus, I want you to live in my heart and lead my life.
I need you to show me how to develop a deep and meaningful relationship with you.
I know I have done things that are wrong in your eyes, and I'm sorry.
Help me to do the things that bring joy to your heart and help me to stop doing the things that break your heart.

Give me your wisdom so I can know what is right and wrong.
When I read the Bible, send your Holy Spirit to teach me.
Help me to learn to talk with you every day through prayer.
I want to be in a living relationship with you;
help me to grow more in love with you every day.

Thank you, Lord, for loving me.
Thank you for your forgiveness.
Thank you for a new beginning!
Amen.

Now take a moment to read these promises that God has made for you:

"If we confess our sins, [God] is faithful and just and will forgive us our sins and purify us from all unrighteousness" (1 John 1:9, page 1305)

"For I am convinced that neither death nor life, neither angels nor demons, neither the present nor the future, nor any powers, neither height nor depth, nor anything else in all creation, will be able to separate us from the love of God that is in Christ Jesus our Lord" (Romans 8:38-39, page 1184).

"I give them eternal life, and they shall never perish; no one can snatch them out of my hand." (Jesus, speaking in John 10:28, page 1115).

That's God's plan for your life. He wants to help you direct your thoughts, actions and activities in a way that pleases him.

God's Plan

WOW
1997

[13]And we also thank God continually because, when you received the word of God, which you heard from us, you accepted it not as the word of men, but as it actually is, the word of God, which

is at work in you who believe. [14]For you, brothers, became imitators of God's churches in Judea, which are in Christ Jesus: You suffered from your own countrymen the same things those churches suffered from the Jews, [15]who killed the Lord Jesus and the prophets and also drove us out. They displease God and are hostile to all men [16]in their effort to keep us from speaking to the Gentiles so that they may be saved. In this way they always heap up their sins to the limit. The wrath of God has come upon them at last.[a]

Paul's Longing to See the Thessalonians

[17]But, brothers, when we were torn away from you for a short time (in person, not in thought), out of our intense longing we made every effort to see you. [18]For we wanted to come to you—certainly I, Paul, did, again and again—but Satan stopped us. [19]For what is our hope, our joy, or the crown in which we will glory in the presence of our Lord Jesus when he comes? Is it not you? [20]Indeed, you are our glory and joy.

3 So when we could stand it no longer, we thought it best to be left by ourselves in Athens. [2]We sent Timothy, who is our brother and God's fellow worker[b] in spreading the gospel of Christ, to strengthen and encourage you in your faith, [3]so that no one would be unsettled by these trials. You know quite well that we were destined for them. [4]In fact, when we were with you, we kept telling you that we would be persecuted. And it turned out that way, as you well know. [5]For this reason, when I could stand it no longer, I sent to find out about your faith. I was afraid that in some way the tempter might have tempted you and our efforts might have been useless.

Timothy's Encouraging Report

[6]But Timothy has just now come to us from you and has brought good news about your faith

and love. He has told us that you always have pleasant memories of us and that you long to see us, just as we also long to see you. [7]Therefore, brothers, in all our distress and persecution we were encouraged about you because of your faith. [8]For now we really live, since you are standing firm in the Lord. [9]How can we thank God enough for you in return for all the joy we have in the presence of our God because of you? [10]Night and day we pray most earnestly that we may see you again and supply what is lacking in your faith.

[11]Now may our God and Father himself and our Lord Jesus clear the way for us to come to you. [12]May the Lord make your love increase and overflow for each other and for everyone else, just as ours does for you. [13]May he strengthen your hearts so that you will be blameless and holy in the presence of our God and Father when our Lord Jesus comes with all his holy ones.

Living to Please God

4 Finally, brothers, we instructed you how to live in order to please God, as in fact you are living. Now we ask you and urge you in the Lord Jesus to do this more and more. [2]For you know what instructions we gave you by the authority of the Lord Jesus.

[3]It is God's will that you should be sanctified: that you should avoid sexual immorality; [4]that each of you should learn to control his own body[c] in a way that is holy and honorable, [5]not in passionate lust like the heathen, who do not know God; [6]and that in this matter no one should wrong his brother or take advantage of him. The Lord will punish men for all such sins, as we have already told you and warned you. [7]For God did not call us to be impure, but to live a holy life. [8]Therefore, he who rejects this instruction does not reject man but God, who gives you his Holy Spirit.

[9]Now about brotherly love we do not need to write to you, for you yourselves have been taught by God to love each other. [10]And in fact, you do

---

[a]16 Or *them fully*   [b]2 Some manuscripts *brother and fellow worker*; other manuscripts *brother and God's servant*
[c]4 Or *learn to live with his own wife*; or *learn to acquire a wife*

love all the brothers throughout Macedonia. Yet we urge you, brothers, to do so more and more. ¹¹Make it your ambition to lead a quiet life, to mind your own business and to work with your hands, just as we told you, ¹²so that your daily life may win the respect of outsiders and so that you will not be dependent on anybody.

The Coming of the Lord

¹³Brothers, we do not want you to be ignorant about those who fall asleep, or to grieve like the rest of men, who have no hope. ¹⁴We believe that Jesus died and rose again and so we believe that God will bring with Jesus those who have fallen asleep in him. ¹⁵According to the Lord's own word, we tell you that we who are still alive, who are left till the coming of the Lord, will certainly not precede those who have fallen asleep. ¹⁶For

the Lord himself will come down from heaven, with a loud command, with the voice of the archangel and with the trumpet call of God, and the dead in Christ will rise first. ¹⁷After that, we who are still alive and are left will be caught up together with them in the clouds to meet the Lord in the air. And so we will be with the Lord forever. ¹⁸Therefore encourage each other with these words.

5 Now, brothers, about times and dates we do not need to write to you, ²for you know very well that the day of the Lord will come like a thief in the night. ³While people are saying, "Peace and safety," destruction will come on them suddenly, as labor pains on a pregnant woman, and they will not escape.

⁴But you, brothers, are not in darkness so that this day should surprise you like a thief. ⁵You are

Preparing for the End
Obsessed with Jesus' second coming

YOU SEE THEM OCCASIONALLY ON the street corners of modern cities: strange-looking people with hand-lettered wooden signs draped over their bodies. "Jesus is coming again!" they proclaim. "Prepare to meet thy doom!" Similar messages are scrawled on rocks or on highway overpasses. And every few years a new prophet comes along suggesting a new, revised date for Jesus' return.

> Now, brothers, about times and dates we do not need to write to you. 5:1

Archaeologists have yet to unearth Thessalonican graffiti, but this letter makes clear that 19 centuries ago people were already awaiting Jesus' promised return to earth. In fact, they were worried. What about people who died before Jesus returned? they wondered. Would they somehow miss out on life after death? Paul gives a direct and encouraging answer.

A Mixture of Fear and Hope

The Thessalonians had good reason to concern themselves with the future: They lived in constant danger of persecution by the authorities. On any night a knock on the door or the scrape of footsteps outside could mean imprisonment or death. Understandably, the young church looked to Jesus' second coming with longing and hope.

Paul assured them that hope in the future was well-founded, whether or not they lived to see Jesus' return. But he warned against an undue fixation on the future. He urged the Thessalonians to get back to work, indicating that some enthusiasts had quit their jobs to prepare for Jesus' return. Lead a quiet life and mind your own business, Paul advised (4:11).

Waiting for Jesus' Return

The Thessalonians were merely the first in a long line of Christians obsessed with future events. Whole generations since have been caught up in frenzied speculations on the exact time and place of the second coming, only to watch their predictions misfire. Paul shrugs off such speculation (5:1–2). He presents the right way and the wrong way to prepare for Jesus' return.

Paul does not show undue alarm. The mild tone of his rebukes indicates his confidence in the Thessalonians. He asks that they follow God "more and more," as in fact they are already doing (4:1,10; 5:11).

History records that the first readers of this letter responded well. Despite lurking problems (4:3–12), the church in Thessalonica continued to show vigor and health for many years. Christians there stayed so faithful throughout persecutions that their city became known as "The City of Orthodoxy."

Life Questions: How should Jesus' second coming affect us and how can we prepare for it? What extremes does Paul warn against?

all sons of the light and sons of the day. We do not belong to the night or to the darkness. ⁶So then, let us not be like others, who are asleep, but let us be alert and self-controlled. ⁷For those who

4:13 The Sleep of Death

The Bible sometimes uses the word asleep *to describe people who have died. In this context, Paul was answering a question the Thessalonians had asked. What of people who died before Christ's second coming—would they be left behind? Paul assures them that all people in Christ would have an afterlife with him—not just those still alive when he returned.*

sleep, sleep at night, and those who get drunk, get drunk at night. ⁸But since we belong to the day, let us be self-controlled, putting on faith and love as a breastplate, and the hope of salvation as a helmet. ⁹For God did not appoint us to suffer wrath but to receive salvation through our Lord Jesus Christ. ¹⁰He died for us so that, whether we are awake or asleep, we may live together with him. ¹¹Therefore encourage one another and build each other up, just as in fact you are doing.

Final Instructions

¹²Now we ask you, brothers, to respect those who work hard among you, who are over you in the Lord and who admonish you. ¹³Hold them in the highest regard in love because of their work. Live in peace with each other. ¹⁴And we urge you, brothers, warn those who are idle, encourage the timid, help the weak, be patient with everyone. ¹⁵Make sure that nobody pays back wrong for wrong, but always try to be kind to each other and to everyone else.

¹⁶Be joyful always; ¹⁷pray continually; ¹⁸give thanks in all circumstances, for this is God's will for you in Christ Jesus.

¹⁹Do not put out the Spirit's fire; ²⁰do not treat prophecies with contempt. ²¹Test everything. Hold on to the good. ²²Avoid every kind of evil.

²³May God himself, the God of peace, sanctify you through and through. May your whole spirit, soul and body be kept blameless at the coming of our Lord Jesus Christ. ²⁴The one who calls you is faithful and he will do it.

²⁵Brothers, pray for us. ²⁶Greet all the brothers with a holy kiss. ²⁷I charge you before the Lord to have this letter read to all the brothers.

²⁸The grace of our Lord Jesus Christ be with you.

2 THESSALONIANS

A Patient Who Didn't Follow Orders
When good advice goes ignored

And as for you, brothers, never tire of doing what is right. 3:13

HIS LIGHT HUMOR AND CASUAL manner are gone now. When he was setting the bone, the doctor joked about the benefits of your wearing your arm in a sling every day: instant sympathy from your friends, an opportunity for wild stories on how you got hurt, an easy alibi to avoid heavy work.

But now, three weeks later, lines of concern crease his forehead as he studies the X-rays and notes the slow progress of healing. "I told you to take it easy! Are you giving that arm any rest at all? You can't expect new bone to grow overnight, you know."

When you describe the throbbing pain of the last few days, he grimaces, shakes his head, and scribbles something on a prescription pad. "You shouldn't be feeling pain at this stage," he grumbles. "If you had followed my advice from the beginning you wouldn't need these pills." He then repeats all the instructions he gave you on the first visit, using stronger, less friendly words.

Same Advice, Sterner Words

The book of 2 Thessalonians resembles such a follow-up visit to a family doctor. If you list the topics Paul covers, you will find an uncanny similarity to the subjects of his first letter: Jesus' second coming, spiritual growth, idleness among certain nonworkers. However, a sterner, more formal approach replaces the warm tenderness of the first letter.

Obviously, the Thessalonians failed to listen well the first time. Paul wrote this second letter just a few months later, summarizing his message this way: "So then, brothers, stand firm and hold to the teachings we passed on to you, whether by word of mouth or by letter" (2:15). Instead of coaxing, Paul now commands.

Squelching a Rumor

One topic, Jesus' return, dominates 2 Thessalonians more than any other. Church members were stirred up by a false report, allegedly from Paul, claiming the last days had already arrived (2:2). Paul denies the report and outlines several events that must occur before the day of the Lord arrives.

Here, as elsewhere, the Bible does not focus on the last days in an abstract, theoretical way. Rather, it draws a practical application to how we should live. Paul cautions his readers to be patient and steady. He asks them to trust that Jesus' return will finally bring justice to the earth, urges them to live worthily for that day, and commands them not to tolerate idleness—a prescription for health that has equal potency today.

How to Read 2 Thessalonians

SECOND Thessalonians has many parallels to its companion letter. The Christians in Thessalonica were still struggling with major problems, and each of the three chapters of this book concerns one of them.

Chapter 1 gives encouragement to Christians who were undergoing persecution for their faith. Chapter 2 attacks head-on the false teaching about the day of the Lord. Rumors about the day of the Lord had caused great excitement and speculation, leading to the practical errors Paul addresses in chapter 3.

Paul's specific words about what must happen before the day of the Lord make this letter a key part of New Testament prophecy. The prophecy passages aren't self-explanatory, and may require a Bible reference book for understanding.

Although 2 Thessalonians is Paul's shortest letter to a church, it contains four of his prayers. Note especially his concern for the Thessalonians as expressed in the prayers.

3-TRACK READING PLAN

For an explanation and complete listing of the 3-track reading plan, turn to page 7.

TRACK 1: **_Two-Week Courses on the Bible_**
See page 7 for information on these courses.

TRACK 2: **_An Overview of 2 Thessalonians in 1 Day_**
☐ Day 1. Read the Introduction to 2 Thessalonians, then chapter 2, the key chapter predicting what events will precede Jesus' return.

Now turn to page 9 for your next Track 2 reading project.

TRACK 3: **_All of 2 Thessalonians in 2 Days_**
After you have read through 2 Thessalonians, turn to pages 10–14 for your next Track 3 reading project.
☐1–2   ☐3

---

1 Paul, Silas[a] and Timothy,

To the church of the Thessalonians in God our Father and the Lord Jesus Christ:

²Grace and peace to you from God the Father and the Lord Jesus Christ.

Thanksgiving and Prayer

³We ought always to thank God for you, brothers, and rightly so, because your faith is growing more and more, and the love every one of you has for each other is increasing. ⁴Therefore, among God's churches we boast about your perseverance and faith in all the persecutions and trials you are enduring.

⁵All this is evidence that God's judgment is right, and as a result you will be counted worthy of the kingdom of God, for which you are suffering. ⁶God is just: He will pay back trouble to

those who trouble you ⁷and give relief to you who are troubled, and to us as well. This will happen when the Lord Jesus is revealed from heaven in blazing fire with his powerful angels. ⁸He will punish those who do not know God and do not obey the gospel of our Lord Jesus. ⁹They will be punished with everlasting destruction and shut out from the presence of the Lord and from the majesty of his power ¹⁰on the day he comes to be glorified in his holy people and to be marveled at among all those who have believed. This includes you, because you believed our testimony to you.

¹¹With this in mind, we constantly pray for you, that our God may count you worthy of his calling, and that by his power he may fulfill every good purpose of yours and every act prompted by your faith. ¹²We pray this so that the name of our Lord Jesus may be glorified in you, and you in him, according to the grace of our God and the Lord Jesus Christ.[b]

The Man of Lawlessness

2 Concerning the coming of our Lord Jesus Christ and our being gathered to him, we ask you, brothers, ²not to become easily unsettled or alarmed by some prophecy, report or letter supposed to have come from us, saying that the day of the Lord has already come. ³Don't let anyone deceive you in any way, for ⌞that day will not come⌟ until the rebellion occurs and the man of lawlessness[c] is revealed, the man doomed to de-

1:6 Is Life Unfair?

This question bothers nearly everyone who gets persecuted or who sees someone profit from wrongdoing. Paul's answer would likely be, "Yes, but only temporarily." He had the firm conviction that one day God would indeed turn the tables on the unfairness of life.

_a1_ Greek _Silvanus_, a variant of _Silas_   _b12_ Or _God and Lord, Jesus Christ_   _c3_ Some manuscripts _sin_

struction. ⁴He will oppose and will exalt himself over everything that is called God or is worshiped, so that he sets himself up in God's temple, proclaiming himself to be God.

⁵Don't you remember that when I was with you I used to tell you these things? ⁶And now you know what is holding him back, so that he may be revealed at the proper time. ⁷For the secret power of lawlessness is already at work; but the one who now holds it back will continue to do

---

2:7 Exactly What Will Happen?

Nearly every age has come up with a different interpretation of this passage. No one is certain about the "secret power of lawlessness" or "the one who now holds it back." A British writer, Tom Davies, quite sincerely, proposes television as the lawless one, since it has made violence so popular. This passage is obscure because Paul refers to further information he had taught the Thessalonians in person. (Even another New Testament author admitted that Paul's letters contain "some things that are hard to understand" [2 Peter 3:16].)

---

so till he is taken out of the way. ⁸And then the lawless one will be revealed, whom the Lord Jesus will overthrow with the breath of his mouth and destroy by the splendor of his coming. ⁹The coming of the lawless one will be in accordance with the work of Satan displayed in all kinds of counterfeit miracles, signs and wonders, ¹⁰and in every sort of evil that deceives those who are perishing. They perish because they refused to love the truth and so be saved. ¹¹For this reason God sends them a powerful delusion so that they will believe the lie ¹²and so that all will be condemned who have not believed the truth but have delighted in wickedness.

Stand Firm

¹³But we ought always to thank God for you, brothers loved by the Lord, because from the beginning God chose you[a] to be saved through the sanctifying work of the Spirit and through belief in the truth. ¹⁴He called you to this through our gospel, that you might share in the glory of our Lord Jesus Christ. ¹⁵So then, brothers, stand firm and hold to the teachings[b] we passed on to you, whether by word of mouth or by letter.

¹⁶May our Lord Jesus Christ himself and God our Father, who loved us and by his grace gave us eternal encouragement and good hope, ¹⁷encour-

age your hearts and strengthen you in every good deed and word.

Request for Prayer

3 Finally, brothers, pray for us that the message of the Lord may spread rapidly and be honored, just as it was with you. ²And pray that we may be delivered from wicked and evil men, for not everyone has faith. ³But the Lord is faithful, and he will strengthen and protect you from the evil one. ⁴We have confidence in the Lord that you are doing and will continue to do the things we command. ⁵May the Lord direct your hearts into God's love and Christ's perseverance.

Warning Against Idleness

⁶In the name of the Lord Jesus Christ, we command you, brothers, to keep away from every brother who is idle and does not live according to the teaching[c] you received from us. ⁷For you yourselves know how you ought to follow our example. We were not idle when we were with you, ⁸nor did we eat anyone's food without paying for it. On the contrary, we worked night and day, laboring and toiling so that we would not be a burden to any of you. ⁹We did this, not because we do not have the right to such help, but in order to make ourselves a model for you to follow. ¹⁰For even when we were with you, we gave you this rule: "If a man will not work, he shall not eat."

3:10 No Work, No Eat

Paul's first letter to the Thessalonians had affirmed that Jesus could return at any time, unexpectedly. Evidently, this anticipation had prompted some to quit their jobs and do nothing but wait for the second coming. (Dozens of times religious sects have followed the same pattern in the United States by heading for remote areas to await Christ's return.) To correct the imbalance, in this second letter Paul stresses that certain events must happen before Christ's return. He also strongly warns against idleness.

---

¹¹We hear that some among you are idle. They are not busy; they are busybodies. ¹²Such people we command and urge in the Lord Jesus Christ to settle down and earn the bread they eat. ¹³And as for you, brothers, never tire of doing what is right.

¹⁴If anyone does not obey our instruction in

---

[a] 13 Some manuscripts *because God chose you as his firstfruits*   [b] 15 Or *traditions*   [c] 6 Or *tradition*

this letter, take special note of him. Do not associate with him, in order that he may feel ashamed. **15**Yet do not regard him as an enemy, but warn him as a brother.

Final Greetings

16Now may the Lord of peace himself give you peace at all times and in every way. The Lord be with all of you.

17I, Paul, write this greeting in my own hand, which is the distinguishing mark in all my letters. This is how I write.

18The grace of our Lord Jesus Christ be with you all.

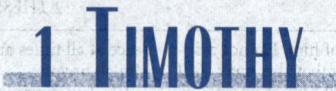

1 TIMOTHY

The Hardest Job
Timothy steps into a hornet's nest

> *Don't let anyone look down on you because you are young, but set an example for the believers. 4:12*

WHO HAS THE MOST DIFFICULT job? A brain surgeon? A trapeze artist who risks death with every leap? A nuclear engineer? Or perhaps an air traffic controller, who determines the safety of thousands of passengers. A number of professions might be nominated as the most difficult of all.

But if the apostle Paul were alive today, to that question he would very likely reply, "Without doubt—a pastor's job is hardest." In contrast to professionals who specialize, a pastor must call upon wide-ranging skills. In a given week a pastor may act as a psychologist, priest, social worker, hospital chaplain, administrator, personnel supervisor, philosopher, and communicator.

Paul was acutely aware of the vital nature of such a job. Churches sprouted up wherever he visited, but whether they survived or failed depended largely on what kind of local leadership developed.

Final Words to a Young Friend

To assure that his work would continue, Paul turned more and more to a few loyal friends, especially Timothy and Titus. He wrote them explicit instructions in the three letters that follow, known collectively as "The Pastoral Letters."

Paul wrote 1 Timothy near the end of his life. Rugged years of ministry had passed, years marked by stonings, beatings, jailings, and riots. Paul knew that his age, his enemies, or the increasingly brutal Roman empire would soon catch up with him.

Timothy, a young man, ranked high in Paul's esteem. Converted during Paul's first missionary journey, he had over the years gained the apostle's complete trust. When a volcano of discontent rumbled in some distant church like Corinth or Thessalonica, Paul quickly dispatched Timothy to try and prevent an eruption.

"I have no one else like him," Paul once wrote of Timothy. "As a son with his father he has served with me in the work of the gospel" (Philippians 2:20,22). Through a swarm of controversies, into prison, on the road—wherever Paul went—Timothy loyally followed. Six of Paul's letters begin with the news that Timothy is at his side.

Timothy Becomes a Pastor

Timothy took on, at Paul's request, that difficult job of heading a local church. The congregation at Ephesus, loose and informal, needed order and a more defined structure. To muddle the scene further, certain members of the church had embraced false doctrines. In this letter, Paul advises his understudy on such matters as worship procedures, the control of unruly women, leadership standards, and policies regarding widows, slaves, and rich people.

Although this book addresses a historical situation from the first century, many problems in the early church—underpaid staff members, a generation gap, an integrity shortage, abuse of social aid, love of money—persist today. A pastor's job description hasn't changed much, or grown any easier, over the centuries.

How to Read 1 Timothy

Despite a weak stomach and timid disposition, Timothy had proved his mettle to Paul in many ways, and Paul wrote this letter to challenge him to a difficult task.

Paul doesn't give many details on the false doctrines Timothy had to combat. These letters, however, include vague hints about super-spiritual living, Jewish genealogies, myths, and fables. Look for the problems Paul alludes to and ask yourself whether they have any modern equivalents.

In his instructions, Paul counseled Timothy to combat heresy not by being forceful and argumentative, but by living an exemplary life and by bringing order to the church. Paul's challenge to live a model life applies directly to us; it remains a powerful prescription for the Christian life.

PEOPLE YOU'LL MEET IN 1 TIMOTHY

TIMOTHY *(p. 1256)*

3-TRACK READING PLAN

For an explanation and complete listing of the 3-track reading plan, turn to page 7.

TRACK 1: *Two-Week Courses on the Bible*
See page 7 for information on these courses.

TRACK 2: *An Overview of 1 Timothy in 1 Day*
☐ Day 1. Read the Introduction to 1 Timothy, then chapter 1, which serves as a good introduction to Paul's "Pastoral Letters."
Now turn to page 9 for your next Track 2 reading project.

TRACK 3: *All of 1 Timothy in 4 Days*
After you have read through 1 Timothy, turn to pages 10–14 for your next Track 3 reading project.
☐1–2 ☐3–4 ☐5 ☐6

---

1 Paul, an apostle of Christ Jesus by the command of God our Savior and of Christ Jesus our hope,

²To Timothy my true son in the faith:

Grace, mercy and peace from God the Father and Christ Jesus our Lord.

Warning Against False Teachers of the Law

³As I urged you when I went into Macedonia, stay there in Ephesus so that you may command certain men not to teach false doctrines any longer ⁴nor to devote themselves to myths and endless genealogies. These promote controversies rather than God's work—which is by faith. ⁵The goal of this command is love, which comes from a pure heart and a good conscience and a sincere faith. ⁶Some have wandered away from these and turned to meaningless talk. ⁷They want to be teachers of the law, but they do not know what they are talking about or what they so confidently affirm.

⁸We know that the law is good if one uses it properly. ⁹We also know that law*ª* is made not for the righteous but for lawbreakers and rebels, the ungodly and sinful, the unholy and irreligious; for those who kill their fathers or mothers, for murderers, ¹⁰for adulterers and perverts, for slave traders and liars and perjurers—and for whatever else is contrary to the sound doctrine ¹¹that conforms to the glorious gospel of the blessed God, which he entrusted to me.

The Lord's Grace to Paul

¹²I thank Christ Jesus our Lord, who has given

ª9 Or that the law

me strength, that he considered me faithful, appointing me to his service. [13]Even though I was once a blasphemer and a persecutor and a violent man, I was shown mercy because I acted in ignorance and unbelief. [14]The grace of our Lord was poured out on me abundantly, along with the faith and love that are in Christ Jesus.

1:3 Strategic Place

The city of Ephesus crops up throughout the New Testament, which indicates its strategic importance as gateway to Asia. Paul's first visit there resulted in a major riot (Acts 19). He nevertheless stayed on three years, instructing believers and establishing a powerful church. As this letter was written, Paul's trusted associate Timothy was serving as pastor in Ephesus. Revelation 2 indicates that Timothy had mixed success in combating the problems identified in this letter.

---

[15]Here is a trustworthy saying that deserves full acceptance: Christ Jesus came into the world to save sinners—of whom I am the worst. [16]But for that very reason I was shown mercy so that in me, the worst of sinners, Christ Jesus might display his unlimited patience as an example for those who would believe on him and receive eternal life. [17]Now to the King eternal, immortal, invisible, the only God, be honor and glory for ever and ever. Amen.

[18]Timothy, my son, I give you this instruction in keeping with the prophecies once made about you, so that by following them you may fight the

---

1:18 Timothy's Calling

In three separate places in his letters to Timothy, Paul refers to his associate's special calling to the ministry. This passage alludes to prophecies made about him. 1 Timothy 4:14 mentions a special ceremony when the church elders "laid their hands" on him. And in 2 Timothy (1:6) Paul specifies that he, too, had been part of such a ceremony. Timothy came from a Christian household; both his grandmother and mother were believers (2 Timothy 1:5).

---

good fight, [19]holding on to faith and a good conscience. Some have rejected these and so have shipwrecked their faith. [20]Among them are Hymenaeus and Alexander, whom I have handed over to Satan to be taught not to blaspheme.

Instructions on Worship

2 I urge, then, first of all, that requests, prayers, intercession and thanksgiving be made for everyone— [2]for kings and all those in authority, that we may live peaceful and quiet lives in all godliness and holiness. [3]This is good, and pleases God our Savior, [4]who wants all men to be saved and to come to a knowledge of the truth. [5]For there is one God and one mediator between God and men, the man Christ Jesus, [6]who gave himself as a ransom for all men—the testimony given in its proper time. [7]And for this purpose I was appointed a herald and an apostle—I am telling the truth, I am not lying—and a teacher of the true faith to the Gentiles.

[8]I want men everywhere to lift up holy hands in prayer, without anger or disputing.

[9]I also want women to dress modestly, with decency and propriety, not with braided hair or gold or pearls or expensive clothes, [10]but with good deeds, appropriate for women who profess to worship God.

[11]A woman should learn in quietness and full submission. [12]I do not permit a woman to teach or to have authority over a man; she must be silent. [13]For Adam was formed first, then Eve. [14]And Adam was not the one deceived; it was the woman who was deceived and became a sinner. [15]But women[a] will be saved[b] through childbearing—if they continue in faith, love and holiness with propriety.

Overseers and Deacons

3 Here is a trustworthy saying: If anyone sets his heart on being an overseer,[c] he desires a noble task. [2]Now the overseer must be above reproach, the husband of but one wife, temperate, self-controlled, respectable, hospitable, able to teach, [3]not given to drunkenness, not violent but gentle, not quarrelsome, not a lover of money. [4]He must manage his own family well and see that his children obey him with proper respect. [5](If anyone does not know how to manage his own family, how can he take care of God's church?) [6]He must not be a recent convert, or he

---

3:1 Time to Get Organized

Chapters 2 and 3 give detailed instructions concerning worship and church organization. When Paul wrote this letter, near the end of his life, churches such as Ephesus had been established for many years. The time had come for a more formal organization and for instructions governing appropriate and inappropriate behavior in church.

---

a 15 Greek *she*   *b 15* Or *restored*   *c 1* Traditionally *bishop*; also in verse 2

may become conceited and fall under the same judgment as the devil. ⁷He must also have a good reputation with outsiders, so that he will not fall into disgrace and into the devil's trap.

⁸Deacons, likewise, are to be men worthy of respect, sincere, not indulging in much wine, and not pursuing dishonest gain. ⁹They must keep hold of the deep truths of the faith with a clear conscience. ¹⁰They must first be tested; and then if there is nothing against them, let them serve as deacons.

3:10 Too Young for the Job?

Few people succeed in athletics or professional careers without practice, time, and effort. Paul looked for some of those same qualities in choosing experienced leaders for churches. Ironically, however, Timothy himself was only in his thirties. His upbringing had prepared him early for spiritual leadership, and in his case Paul urged boldness and confidence (4:12).

¹¹In the same way, their wives*a* are to be women worthy of respect, not malicious talkers but temperate and trustworthy in everything.

¹²A deacon must be the husband of but one wife and must manage his children and his household well. ¹³Those who have served well gain an excellent standing and great assurance in their faith in Christ Jesus.

¹⁴Although I hope to come to you soon, I am writing you these instructions so that, ¹⁵if I am delayed, you will know how people ought to conduct themselves in God's household, which is the church of the living God, the pillar and foundation of the truth. ¹⁶Beyond all question, the mystery of godliness is great:

He*b* appeared in a body,*c*
    was vindicated by the Spirit,
was seen by angels,
    was preached among the nations,
was believed on in the world,
    was taken up in glory.

Instructions to Timothy

4 The Spirit clearly says that in later times some will abandon the faith and follow deceiving spirits and things taught by demons. ²Such teachings come through hypocritical liars, whose consciences have been seared as with a hot iron. ³They forbid people to marry and order them to abstain from certain foods, which God created to be received with thanksgiving by those who believe and who know the truth. ⁴For everything God created is good, and nothing is to be rejected if it is received with thanksgiving, ⁵be-

cause it is consecrated by the word of God and prayer.

⁶If you point these things out to the brothers, you will be a good minister of Christ Jesus, brought up in the truths of the faith and of the good teaching that you have followed. ⁷Have nothing to do with godless myths and old wives' tales; rather, train yourself to be godly. ⁸For physical training is of some value, but godliness has value for all things, holding promise for both the present life and the life to come.

⁹This is a trustworthy saying that deserves full acceptance ¹⁰(and for this we labor and strive), that we have put our hope in the living God, who is the Savior of all men, and especially of those who believe.

¹¹Command and teach these things. ¹²Don't let anyone look down on you because you are young, but set an example for the believers in speech, in life, in love, in faith and in purity. ¹³Until I come, devote yourself to the public reading of Scripture, to preaching and to teaching. ¹⁴Do not neglect your gift, which was given you through a prophetic message when the body of elders laid their hands on you.

¹⁵Be diligent in these matters; give yourself wholly to them, so that everyone may see your progress. ¹⁶Watch your life and doctrine closely. Persevere in them, because if you do, you will save both yourself and your hearers.

Advice About Widows, Elders and Slaves

5 Do not rebuke an older man harshly, but exhort him as if he were your father. Treat younger men as brothers, ²older women as mothers, and younger women as sisters, with absolute purity.

³Give proper recognition to those widows who are really in need. ⁴But if a widow has children or grandchildren, these should learn first of all to put their religion into practice by caring for their own family and so repaying their parents and grandparents, for this is pleasing to God. ⁵The widow who is really in need and left all alone puts her hope in God and continues night and day to pray and to ask God for help. ⁶But the widow who lives for pleasure is dead even while she lives. ⁷Give the people these instructions, too, so that no one may be open to blame. ⁸If anyone does not provide for his relatives, and especially for his immediate family, he has denied the faith and is worse than an unbeliever.

⁹No widow may be put on the list of widows unless she is over sixty, has been faithful to her husband,*d* ¹⁰and is well known for her good deeds, such as bringing up children, showing hospitality, washing the feet of the saints, helping

---

a 11 Or *way, deaconesses*   *b 16* Some manuscripts *God*   *c 16* Or *in the flesh*   *d 9* Or *has had but one husband*

those in trouble and devoting herself to all kinds of good deeds.

[11]As for younger widows, do not put them on such a list. For when their sensual desires overcome their dedication to Christ, they want to marry. [12]Thus they bring judgment on themselves, because they have broken their first pledge. [13]Besides, they get into the habit of being idle and going about from house to house. And not only do they become idlers, but also gossips and busybodies, saying things they ought not to. [14]So I counsel younger widows to marry, to have children, to manage their homes and to give the enemy no opportunity for slander. [15]Some have in fact already turned away to follow Satan.

[16]If any woman who is a believer has widows

Athlete in Training
Overcoming personal disabilities

BRAD LAUWERS WAS IN THE locker room, showering after a grueling football workout, when he first noticed the lump. He bent down and rubbed his ankle gently, cupping his hand around the swelling. He felt no pain or stiffness. *Probably just some fluid*, he thought. *It will disappear in a few days.*

The swelling didn't disappear, and a month later Brad lay in a hospital bed awaiting amputation of his left leg. The lump turned out to be a malignant tumor that was sending runners out in several directions in Brad's foot. The next day a surgeon removed Brad's leg just inches below the knee.

Of all the adjustments to his new life—including "one-legged" jokes, the awkward reactions of friends, and learning to walk on an artificial leg—Brad most feared the loss of athletics, his main love in life. He had been a standout on his high school basketball and football teams in Alaska, a sports-crazy state. His doctor, also an amputee (from a war injury), tried to be encouraging: "Remember, Brad, there's *nothing* you cannot do."

> *Train yourself to be godly. For physical training is of some value, but godliness has value for all things, holding promise for both the present life and the life to come.*
> *4:7–8*

Against All Odds

Four months later, Brad visited the campus of UCLA for a prosthetic leg fitting. Even before fully learning to walk on his artificial leg, he sought out a basketball backboard and began tossing up reverse lay-ups. The designers had warned him against subjecting the leg to the jarring stops and turns of basketball and had vetoed football outright, suggesting he take up swimming or water-skiing instead. But Brad never gave up his dream of returning to his two favorite sports.

As he trained, his artificial limb rubbed his leg stump raw and covered it with blisters. Undaunted, he ran until the blisters hardened into calluses. Then he began working on jumps and pivots.

Incredibly, in August, less than one year after the amputation, Brad played his first game as a one-legged quarterback for Dimond High School. Some thought his appearance was a mere sentimental gesture. They were wrong: Brad ended the year leading the state in passing! He completed 58 percent of his passes and racked up 662 yards in seven games as a part-time quarterback on the state championship squad. After football season, he started on Dimond's basketball team. From there, he went on to major in physical education at Washington State University.

When asked about his exploits, Brad shrugs and mentions two factors in his extraordinary achievement: gritty determination and long hours of often painful training.

A Lesson from Athletics

Paul uses the analogy of physical training in his letter to Timothy, urging him to train himself for godliness the same way disciplined athletes train for competition. Brad Lauwers had to overcome physical barriers; Timothy faced personality barriers. Several times Paul refers to Timothy's reserved, timid disposition, which probably contributed to his chronic stomach trouble.

Given his shyness and his half-Jewish, half-Gentile ancestry, Timothy did not seem the ideal choice for a heresy fighter in a turbulent church. But Paul was convinced he could do the job. He encouraged Timothy with such motivational phrases as "I charge you" and "I urge you." He also reminded Timothy of his ordination, a commitment he had made long before.

Harassed Christians need a model, an example of how they should live, perhaps even more than they need words of wisdom. In 1 Timothy, Paul urges his loyal friend to become that model by accepting the discipline and hard work required.

Life Questions: Do you have any personality traits that make Christian service seem difficult? What specific "training instructions" did Paul give Timothy that might also apply to you?

in her family, she should help them and not let the church be burdened with them, so that the church can help those widows who are really in need.

5:9 Welfare Mentality

Chapter 5 gives fascinating insight into early church problems that have parallels in today's social programs. Evidently, some members of the Ephesus congregation had been taking advantage of others' charity. Young widows were using the church's resources when they should have been looking for other means of support. Paul outlines a form of "enrollment" to establish who was truly needy.

[17]The elders who direct the affairs of the church well are worthy of double honor, especially those whose work is preaching and teaching. [18]For the Scripture says, "Do not muzzle the ox while it is treading out the grain,"[a] and "The worker deserves his wages."[b] [19]Do not entertain an accusation against an elder unless it is brought by two or three witnesses. [20]Those who sin are to be rebuked publicly, so that the others may take warning.

[21]I charge you, in the sight of God and Christ Jesus and the elect angels, to keep these instructions without partiality, and to do nothing out of favoritism.

[22]Do not be hasty in the laying on of hands, and do not share in the sins of others. Keep yourself pure.

[23]Stop drinking only water, and use a little wine because of your stomach and your frequent illnesses.

[24]The sins of some men are obvious, reaching the place of judgment ahead of them; the sins of others trail behind them. [25]In the same way, good deeds are obvious, and even those that are not cannot be hidden.

6 All who are under the yoke of slavery should consider their masters worthy of full respect, so that God's name and our teaching may not be slandered. [2]Those who have believing masters are not to show less respect for them because they are brothers. Instead, they are to serve them even better, because those who benefit from their service are believers, and dear to them. These are the things you are to teach and urge on them.

Love of Money

[3]If anyone teaches false doctrines and does not agree to the sound instruction of our Lord Jesus Christ and to godly teaching, [4]he is conceited and understands nothing. He has an unhealthy interest in controversies and quarrels about words that result in envy, strife, malicious talk, evil suspicions [5]and constant friction between men of corrupt mind, who have been robbed of the truth and who think that godliness is a means to financial gain.

[6]But godliness with contentment is great gain. [7]For we brought nothing into the world, and we

6:7 Two Familiar Quotes

Paul's parting advice to Timothy includes two sayings that have become familiar quotations. Verse 7 is usually quoted accurately. But verse 10, also familiar, is often misquoted as "money is the root of all evil." An established church had already developed a professional class of Christian workers, and Paul warned against the motive of profit-seeking.

can take nothing out of it. [8]But if we have food and clothing, we will be content with that. [9]People who want to get rich fall into temptation and a trap and into many foolish and harmful desires that plunge men into ruin and destruction. [10]For the love of money is a root of all kinds of evil. Some people, eager for money, have wandered from the faith and pierced themselves with many griefs.

Paul's Charge to Timothy

[11]But you, man of God, flee from all this, and pursue righteousness, godliness, faith, love, endurance and gentleness. [12]Fight the good fight of the faith. Take hold of the eternal life to which you were called when you made your good confession in the presence of many witnesses. [13]In the sight of God, who gives life to everything, and of Christ Jesus, who while testifying before Pontius Pilate made the good confession, I charge you [14]to keep this command without spot or blame until the appearing of our Lord Jesus Christ, [15]which God will bring about in his own time—God, the blessed and only Ruler, the King of kings and Lord of lords, [16]who alone is immortal and who lives in unapproachable light, whom no one has seen or can see. To him be honor and might forever. Amen.

[17]Command those who are rich in this present world not to be arrogant nor to put their hope in wealth, which is so uncertain, but to put their hope in God, who richly provides us with everything for our enjoyment. [18]Command them to do good, to be rich in good deeds, and to be gener-

---

a18 Deut. 25:4　　*b18* Luke 10:7

ous and willing to share. **19**In this way they will lay up treasure for themselves as a firm foundation for the coming age, so that they may take hold of the life that is truly life.

20Timothy, guard what has been entrusted

to your care. Turn away from godless chatter and the opposing ideas of what is falsely called knowledge, **21**which some have professed and in so doing have wandered from the faith.

Grace be with you.

2 TIMOTHY

Passing the Torch
The apostle Paul's last known words

E VERY FOUR YEARS THE WORLD watches an ancient ritual unfold: the passing of the Olympic torch. The spectacular pageantry of the opening ceremonies cannot begin until the final carrier of the torch arrives in the stadium. The torch symbolically links the modern Olympic Games to their 2,700-year history.

"Passing the torch" has become a familiar phrase, used when the president of a corporation such as General Motors introduces his successor to the public, or when an esteemed orchestra conductor hands over his baton, or a great sports figure tutors her replacement. Often the retiring person delivers an emotional farewell speech. He or she has finished the work; the time has come to pass the torch to another.

> And the things you have heard me say in the presence of many witnesses entrust to reliable men who will also be qualified to teach others. 2:2

Choosing Timothy

As the weary apostle Paul neared certain death, with imprisonment preventing him from traveling, he, too, began to think of a successor. It was time to pass the torch, and he decided on the young man Timothy.

At first glance, shy Timothy hardly seemed an adequate replacement, but Paul had few options. "Everyone in the province of Asia has deserted me," he lamented (1:15). This letter, 2 Timothy, reveals his deep reliance on Timothy's loyal friendship. Life was closing in on the apostle, and he felt a somber sense of abandonment.

At times in this letter, Paul lectures Timothy like a master sergeant, calling on him to stand firm, overcome shame, and hold to the faith. Elsewhere, his tone softens into the fond affirmation of a grateful father. Throughout, the bonds of deep friendship are evident: from Paul recalling Timothy's family heritage (1:5) to his urging Timothy to bring him a heavy coat before winter (4:13,21).

An Emotional Moment

Paul's moods alternate between sadness and confidence, nostalgia and grave concern. As he wrote this letter, he contemplated the disquieting months ahead and the prospect of young, divided churches left without his guidance. In these, his last known written words, he sought to prepare Timothy for the inevitable day when the message of God would depend on him and other reliable workers (2:2).

Despite his circumstances, Paul's farewell message from behind bars is gracious, even triumphant. The spreading of the gospel is far too big a task to be limited to any one man. "I am . . . chained like a criminal," Paul declares, "but God's word is not chained" (2:9).

How to Read 2 Timothy

S econd Timothy has proved encouraging to Christian workers throughout history. Paul, facing death, did not wallow in self-pity, but instead used this last communication to inspire and challenge his associate Timothy.

This letter reveals much about Paul's emotional state and physical circumstances. As you read it, look for glimpses into Paul's loneliness and suffering. The apostle tells where he turned for strength when he faced personal trials.

In addition, 2 Timothy gives much valuable counsel to those of us who, like Timothy, have inherited the task of representing Christ on earth. Paul stresses the importance of relying on Scripture and of living a life of discipline. As you read this letter, put yourself in Timothy's place; imagine receiving one last personal letter from your great mentor. What final words of advice does he give?

3-TRACK READING PLAN

For an explanation and complete listing of the 3-track reading plan, turn to page 7.

TRACK 1: **Two-Week Courses on the Bible**
See page 7 for information on these courses.

TRACK 2: **An Overview of 2 Timothy in 1 Day**
☐ Day 1. Read the introduction to 2 Timothy and then chapter 2, which contains a summary of Paul's challenge to Timothy.

Now turn to page 9 for your next Track 2 reading project.

TRACK 3: **All of 2 Timothy in 4 Days**
After you have read through 2 Timothy, turn to pages 10–14 for your next Track 3 reading project.

☐1   ☐2   ☐3   ☐4

---

1 Paul, an apostle of Christ Jesus by the will of God, according to the promise of life that is in Christ Jesus,

²To Timothy, my dear son:

Grace, mercy and peace from God the Father and Christ Jesus our Lord.

Encouragement to Be Faithful

³I thank God, whom I serve, as my forefathers did, with a clear conscience, as night and day I constantly remember you in my prayers. ⁴Recalling your tears, I long to see you, so that I may be filled with joy. ⁵I have been reminded of your sincere faith, which first lived in your grandmother Lois and in your mother Eunice and, I am persuaded, now lives in you also. ⁶For this reason I remind you to fan into flame the gift of God, which is in you through the laying on of my hands. ⁷For God did not give us a spirit of timidity, but a spirit of power, of love and of self-discipline.

⁸So do not be ashamed to testify about our Lord, or ashamed of me his prisoner. But join with me in suffering for the gospel, by the power of God, ⁹who has saved us and called us to a holy life—not because of anything we have done but because of his own purpose and grace. This grace was given us in Christ Jesus before the beginning of time, ¹⁰but it has now been revealed through the appearing of our Savior, Christ Jesus, who has destroyed death and has brought life and immortality to light through the gospel. ¹¹And of this gospel I was appointed a herald and an apostle and a teacher. ¹²That is why I am suffering as

I am. Yet I am not ashamed, because I know whom I have believed, and am convinced that he is able to guard what I have entrusted to him for that day.

¹³What you heard from me, keep as the pattern of sound teaching, with faith and love in Christ Jesus. ¹⁴Guard the good deposit that was entrusted to you—guard it with the help of the Holy Spirit who lives in us.

¹⁵You know that everyone in the province of Asia has deserted me, including Phygelus and Hermogenes.

¹⁶May the Lord show mercy to the household of Onesiphorus, because he often refreshed me and was not ashamed of my chains. ¹⁷On the contrary, when he was in Rome, he searched hard for me until he found me. ¹⁸May the Lord grant that he will find mercy from the Lord on that day! You know very well in how many ways he helped me in Ephesus.

2 You then, my son, be strong in the grace that is in Christ Jesus. ²And the things you have heard me say in the presence of many witnesses entrust to reliable men who will also be qualified to teach others. ³Endure hardship with us like a good soldier of Christ Jesus. ⁴No one serving as a soldier gets involved in civilian affairs—he wants to please his commanding officer. ⁵Similarly, if anyone competes as an athlete, he does not receive the victor's crown unless he competes according to the rules. ⁶The hardworking farmer should be the first to receive a share of the crops. ⁷Reflect on what I am saying, for the Lord will give you insight into all this.

⁸Remember Jesus Christ, raised from the

dead, descended from David. This is my gospel, [9]for which I am suffering even to the point of being chained like a criminal. But God's word is not chained. [10]Therefore I endure everything for

2:4 Soldier, Athlete, Farmer

Writing to a friend who knew him well, Paul saw no need to expand on the three analogies in this paragraph; he simply mentions them and tells Timothy to reflect on them. Paul was fully conscious of the threats and dangers facing his own life, and he wanted Timothy to train himself in preparation for any hardships that he might have to face.

the sake of the elect, that they too may obtain the salvation that is in Christ Jesus, with eternal glory.

[11]Here is a trustworthy saying:

If we died with him,
    we will also live with him;
[12]if we endure,
    we will also reign with him.
If we disown him,
    he will also disown us;
[13]if we are faithless,
    he will remain faithful,
    for he cannot disown himself.

A Workman Approved by God

[14]Keep reminding them of these things. Warn them before God against quarreling about words; it is of no value, and only ruins those who listen. [15]Do your best to present yourself to God as one approved, a workman who does not need to be ashamed and who correctly handles the word of truth. [16]Avoid godless chatter, because those who indulge in it will become more and more ungodly. [17]Their teaching will spread like gangrene. Among them are Hymenaeus and Philetus, [18]who have wandered away from the truth. They say that the resurrection has already taken place, and they destroy the faith of some. [19]Nevertheless, God's solid foundation stands firm, sealed with this inscription: "The Lord knows those who are his,"[a] and, "Everyone who confesses the name of the Lord must turn away from wickedness."

[20]In a large house there are articles not only of gold and silver, but also of wood and clay; some are for noble purposes and some for ignoble. [21]If a man cleanses himself from the latter, he will be an instrument for noble purposes, made holy, useful to the Master and prepared to do any good work.

[22]Flee the evil desires of youth, and pursue

righteousness, faith, love and peace, along with those who call on the Lord out of a pure heart. [23]Don't have anything to do with foolish and stupid arguments, because you know they produce quarrels. [24]And the Lord's servant must not quarrel; instead, he must be kind to everyone, able to teach, not resentful. [25]Those who oppose him he must gently instruct, in the hope that God will grant them repentance leading them to a knowledge of the truth, [26]and that they will come to their senses and escape from the trap of the devil, who has taken them captive to do his will.

Godlessness in the Last Days

3 But mark this: There will be terrible times in the last days. [2]People will be lovers of themselves, lovers of money, boastful, proud, abusive, disobedient to their parents, ungrateful, unholy, [3]without love, unforgiving, slanderous, without self-control, brutal, not lovers of the good, [4]treacherous, rash, conceited, lovers of pleasure rather than lovers of God— [5]having a form of godliness but denying its power. Have nothing to do with them.

[6]They are the kind who worm their way into homes and gain control over weak-willed women, who are loaded down with sins and are swayed by all kinds of evil desires, [7]always learning but never able to acknowledge the truth. [8]Just as Jannes and Jambres opposed Moses, so also these men oppose the truth—men of depraved minds, who, as far as the faith is concerned, are

3:8 Who Were Jannes and Jambres?

These names, not mentioned in the Old Testament, were handed down in Jewish tradition as the names of the Egyptian magicians who opposed Moses during the ten plagues against Egypt (Exodus 7:11; 9:11).

rejected. [9]But they will not get very far because, as in the case of those men, their folly will be clear to everyone.

Paul's Charge to Timothy

[10]You, however, know all about my teaching, my way of life, my purpose, faith, patience, love, endurance, [11] persecutions, sufferings —what kinds of things happened to me in Antioch, Iconium and Lystra, the persecutions I endured. Yet the Lord rescued me from all of them. [12]In fact, everyone who wants to live a godly life in Christ Jesus will be persecuted, [13]while evil men and impostors will go from bad to worse, deceiving and being deceived. [14]But as for you, continue in what you have learned and have become con-

---

[a] 19 Num. 16:5 (see Septuagint)

vinced of, because you know those from whom you learned it, [15]and how from infancy you have known the holy Scriptures, which are able to make you wise for salvation through faith in Christ Jesus. [16]All Scripture is God-breathed and is useful for teaching, rebuking, correcting and

3:16 Scripture Is God-breathed

This important verse gives the origin of the term inspiration, *which literally means "God-breathed." Although the Bible doesn't spell out the mechanics of how God inspired the writers, it makes clear the ultimate source was God himself.*

training in righteousness, [17]so that the man of God may be thoroughly equipped for every good work.

4 In the presence of God and of Christ Jesus, who will judge the living and the dead, and in view of his appearing and his kingdom, I give you this charge: [2]Preach the Word; be prepared in season and out of season; correct, rebuke and encourage—with great patience and careful instruction. [3]For the time will come when men will not put up with sound doctrine. Instead, to suit their own desires, they will gather around them a great number of teachers to say what their itching ears want to hear. [4]They will turn their ears away from the truth and turn aside to myths. [5]But you, keep your head in all situations, endure hardship, do the work of an evangelist, discharge all the duties of your ministry.

[6]For I am already being poured out like a drink offering, and the time has come for my departure. [7]I have fought the good fight, I have finished the race, I have kept the faith. [8]Now there is in store for me the crown of righteousness, which the Lord, the righteous Judge, will award to me on that day—and not only to me, but also to all who have longed for his appearing.

Personal Remarks

[9]Do your best to come to me quickly, [10]for Demas, because he loved this world, has deserted me and has gone to Thessalonica. Crescens has gone to Galatia, and Titus to Dalmatia. [11]Only

A Letter from Death Row
Paul sees the end

OCCASIONALLY, WRITINGS SURFACE FROM DEATH row, the earnest scratchings of prisoners who know each word may be their last. Whole books, for example, were discovered amid the ruins of Nazi death camps. Understandably, these writings don't usually dwell on abstract, philosophical themes. They chronicle the day-to-day reality of the struggle to survive.

I am already being poured out like a drink offering, and the time has come for my departure. 4:6

Quite naturally, Paul did not devote much space to doctrine in his death row letter. He stuck to personal advice on vital issues such as courage and personal integrity.

Paul's Grim Future

Although Paul does not elaborate on his present circumstances in 2 Timothy, he mentions that at his first trial not a single witness came forward to defend him (4:16). Through supernatural strength he successfully defended himself, but his prospects in a new trial appeared grim (4:6).

Paul's arrest probably occurred in the wave of anti-Christian persecutions begun by Nero in A.D. 64. That crazed emperor tortured Christians by crucifying them, by wrapping them in animal skins and turning his hunting dogs loose on them, and by burning them alive, as human torches, to illuminate the games in his garden. Is it any wonder that Paul, imprisoned in that era, exhorted Timothy on the need for boldness and the likelihood of suffering for Christ?

The Coming Conflict

Toward the end of his life, Paul viewed the future as a growing struggle. Immorality and false teaching would "spread like gangrene" (2:17); he urged Christians to counteract those forces with personal purity. The battle between good and evil would only intensify, he said.

After making some predictions about "the last days," Paul composed a formal charge to Timothy—a will and testament to his spiritual son (4:1–8). He concluded, "I have fought the good fight, I have finished the race, I have kept the faith" (4:7). Tradition teaches that Paul was killed by Rome for his faith. But because of his life and the legacy he passed on, the world would never be the same.

Life Questions: If you drafted a spiritual "last will and testament" for your friends, what would you say?

Luke is with me. Get Mark and bring him with you, because he is helpful to me in my ministry. [12]I sent Tychicus to Ephesus. [13]When you come, bring the cloak that I left with Carpus at Troas, and my scrolls, especially the parchments.

[14]Alexander the metalworker did me a great deal of harm. The Lord will repay him for what he has done. [15]You too should be on your guard

4:17 Second Imprisonment in Rome

Acts 28 describes a period when Paul was held under house arrest in Rome, but the conditions hinted at in this letter are quite different. Paul wrote 2 Timothy much later, after the Roman empire had turned against Christians, and the tone of this letter (verses 6–9) implies that he had little hope of freedom. His request for a cloak and parchments (verse 13) indicates he was arrested suddenly, without warning.

against him, because he strongly opposed our message.

[16]At my first defense, no one came to my support, but everyone deserted me. May it not be held against them. [17]But the Lord stood at my side and gave me strength, so that through me the message might be fully proclaimed and all the Gentiles might hear it. And I was delivered from the lion's mouth. [18]The Lord will rescue me from every evil attack and will bring me safely to his heavenly kingdom. To him be glory for ever and ever. Amen.

Final Greetings

[19]Greet Priscilla[a] and Aquila and the household of Onesiphorus. [20]Erastus stayed in Corinth, and I left Trophimus sick in Miletus. [21]Do your best to get here before winter. Eubulus greets you, and so do Pudens, Linus, Claudia and all the brothers.

[22]The Lord be with your spirit. Grace be with you.

---

[a]19 Greek *Prisca*, a variant of *Priscilla*

TITUS

Diverse People, Diverse Problems
An island of liars, brutes, and gluttons

> *These, then, are the things you should teach. 2:15*

MODERN PEOPLE READING ABOUT THE past can blur people together into a uniform, faceless crowd of strangers. It's hard to visualize individual people you read about.

Actually, the people Paul addressed were as diverse as those you might meet on the streets of Los Angeles or New York City today. Consider Crete, an island populated by five fiercely independent ethnic groups. Its main knowledge of the outside world came through pirates and coarse sailors. Add to that mix a large community of straight-laced Jews, and you can see why the Cretan church was born amid conflict.

Titus the Troubleshooter

When problems erupted in this stormy congregation, Paul dispatched Titus, his trusted associate of 15 years. The book of Galatians (2:1–5) introduced Titus as proof that a non-Jew could become a fully acceptable Christian.

When Titus's name occurs in the New Testament, he is usually seen serving as Paul's troubleshooter, the one called on to deal with local crises. Twice he was sent on a diplomatic mission to the rowdy church at Corinth. This letter indicates he faced an equally challenging task on Crete. Paul wrote the book of Titus as a set of personal instructions on how to handle a difficult assignment.

Because he was writing to people who knew the local circumstances well, Paul rarely bothered to give background for us years-later "over-the-shoulder" readers. But we can gain insights into the conditions by reading between the lines. For example, when Paul tells Titus to search for a leader "not quick-tempered, not given to drunkenness, not violent, not pursuing dishonest gain" (1:7), that description implies something about the average Cretan. One of the island's own poets described Cretans as "always liars, evil brutes, lazy gluttons" (1:12), and the Greeks had even coined a special verb for lying: "to Cretize."

Practical Theology

Titus 2 lists some of the diverse groups in the church: older men, older women, younger women, young men, slaves. Each presented a set of problems that needed attention, and Paul gave Titus specific counsel on each group. Although he was mainly emphasizing the need for good living, Paul also dropped in a few concise restatements of the gospel message. His theology was never distantly theoretical; he applied it to real-life human problems.

Taken as a group, the three pastoral letters (1 and 2 Timothy plus Titus) show Paul, an old man now, learning to rely more and more on capable assistants to carry on his work. The Cretans needed a hard-hitting, practical reminder of "sound doctrine" based on a God "who does not lie" (1:2). The instructions in Titus give the man for whom the book was named—and us—the needed jolt.

How to Read Titus

Like 1 and 2 Timothy, Titus was written to an individual, not a church. This letter has similarities to 1 Timothy, but is less personal and more official. The book of Acts doesn't mention Titus, but 14 references to him in Paul's letters indicate that he was one of Paul's most trusted helpers.

In some letters, such as Galatians, Paul fought valiantly against legalism. But the church on Crete, full of immature Christians, needed basic lessons in morality, and Paul spelled them out for Titus. Using a very straightforward style, he told his associate what he would prescribe in such circumstances.

Because it is written in such a direct style—almost like a training manual—Titus needs little explanation. Paul's meaning comes through clearly. Note particularly how Paul adapts his overall principles to specific groups in chapter 2. And give careful study to the "nuggets" of theology in these passages: 1:1–4, 2:11–14, and 3:4–7.

PEOPLE YOU'LL MEET IN TITUS

TITUS (p. 1268)

3-TRACK READING PLAN

For an explanation and complete listing of the 3-track reading plan, turn to page 7.

TRACK 1: *Two-Week Courses on the Bible*
See page 7 for information on these courses.

TRACK 2: *An Overview of Titus in 1 Day*
☐ Day 1. Read the Introduction to Titus, then chapter 2, which contains Paul's practical advice for the diverse groups in the Cretan church.

Now turn to page 9 for your next Track 2 reading project.

TRACK 3: *All of Titus in 2 Days*
After you have read through Titus, turn to pages 10–14 for your next Track 3 reading project.
☐ 1   ☐ 2–3

1 Paul, a servant of God and an apostle of Jesus Christ for the faith of God's elect and the knowledge of the truth that leads to godliness— ²a faith and knowledge resting on the hope of eternal life, which God, who does not lie, promised before the beginning of time, ³and at his appointed season he brought his word to light through the preaching entrusted to me by the command of God our Savior,

⁴To Titus, my true son in our common faith:

1:2 No Lies

Right away Paul characterizes God as the One who does not lie. God's truthfulness made a sharp contrast to the Cretans themselves (verse 12) as well as to many gods of that era. The Romans exalted their emperors, worshiping them as divine despite the flaws and weaknesses that everyone knew about. Paul contrasts the message about Jesus as the eternal "word" of truth.

Grace and peace from God the Father and Christ Jesus our Savior.

Titus' Task on Crete

⁵The reason I left you in Crete was that you might straighten out what was left unfinished and appoint*ᵃ* elders in every town, as I directed you. ⁶An elder must be blameless, the husband of but one wife, a man whose children believe and are not open to the charge of being wild and disobedient. ⁷Since an overseer*ᵇ* is entrusted with God's work, he must be blameless—not overbearing, not quick-tempered, not given to drunkenness, not violent, not pursuing dishonest gain. ⁸Rather he must be hospitable, one who loves what is good, who is self-controlled, upright, holy and disciplined. ⁹He must hold firmly to the trustworthy message as it has been taught, so that he can encourage others by sound doctrine and refute those who oppose it.

¹⁰For there are many rebellious people, mere talkers and deceivers, especially those of the circumcision group. ¹¹They must be silenced, because they are ruining whole households by

ᵃ5 Or ordain   ᵇ7 Traditionally bishop

teaching things they ought not to teach—and that for the sake of dishonest gain. 12Even one of their own prophets has said, "Cretans are always liars, evil brutes, lazy gluttons." 13This testimony is true. Therefore, rebuke them sharply, so that they will be sound in the faith 14and will pay no attention to Jewish myths or to the commands of those who reject the truth. 15To the pure, all things are pure, but to those who are corrupted and do not believe, nothing is pure. In fact, both their minds and consciences are corrupted. 16They claim to know God, but by their actions they deny him. They are detestable, disobedient and unfit for doing anything good.

What Must Be Taught to Various Groups

2 You must teach what is in accord with sound doctrine. 2Teach the older men to be temperate, worthy of respect, self-controlled, and sound in faith, in love and in endurance.

3Likewise, teach the older women to be reverent in the way they live, not to be slanderers or addicted to much wine, but to teach what is good. 4Then they can train the younger women to love their husbands and children, 5to be self-controlled and pure, to be busy at home, to be kind, and to be subject to their husbands, so that no one will malign the word of God.

6Similarly, encourage the young men to be self-controlled. 7In everything set them an example by doing what is good. In your teaching show integrity, seriousness 8and soundness of speech that cannot be condemned, so that those who oppose you may be ashamed because they have nothing bad to say about us.

9Teach slaves to be subject to their masters in everything, to try to please them, not to talk back to them, 10and not to steal from them, but to show that they can be fully trusted, so that in every way they will make the teaching about God our Savior attractive.

11For the grace of God that brings salvation has appeared to all men. 12It teaches us to say "No" to ungodliness and worldly passions, and

2:15 Foolish Questions

In addition to the problems hinted at in chapter 2, the Cretan church struggled with issues its Jewish members introduced. These trends toward myths and "foolish controversies and genealogies and arguments and quarrels about the law" (3:9) resemble the heresies Paul had warned against in the book of Colossians. Titus had to be prepared to deal with problems both of doctrine and of righteous living.

to live self-controlled, upright and godly lives in this present age, 13while we wait for the blessed hope—the glorious appearing of our great God and Savior, Jesus Christ, 14who gave himself for us to redeem us from all wickedness and to purify for himself a people that are his very own, eager to do what is good.

15These, then, are the things you should teach. Encourage and rebuke with all authority. Do not let anyone despise you.

Doing What Is Good

3 Remind the people to be subject to rulers and authorities, to be obedient, to be ready to do whatever is good, 2to slander no one, to be peaceable and considerate, and to show true humility toward all men.

3At one time we too were foolish, disobedient, deceived and enslaved by all kinds of passions and pleasures. We lived in malice and envy, being hated and hating one another. 4But when the kindness and love of God our Savior appeared, 5he saved us, not because of righteous things we had done, but because of his mercy. He saved us through the washing of rebirth and renewal by the Holy Spirit, 6whom he poured out on us generously through Jesus Christ our Savior, 7so that, having been justified by his grace, we might become heirs having the hope of eternal life.

3:5 Nuggets of Theology

Despite its practical, instructive tone, Titus contains three outstanding passages of Paul's theology. They appear in 1:1–4, 2:11–14, and 3:4–7. This last passage balances off Paul's stress on clean living in Titus. Verse 5 makes clear that "righteous things" do not earn us acceptance by God. Rather, they are a natural response from people who have experienced God's forgiveness and love.

8This is a trustworthy saying. And I want you to stress these things, so that those who have trusted in God may be careful to devote themselves to doing what is good. These things are excellent and profitable for everyone.

9But avoid foolish controversies and genealogies and arguments and quarrels about the law, because these are unprofitable and useless. 10Warn a divisive person once, and then warn him a second time. After that, have nothing to do with him. 11You may be sure that such a man is warped and sinful; he is self-condemned.

Final Remarks

12As soon as I send Artemas or Tychicus to you, do your best to come to me at Nicopolis,

3:12 Mail Carriers

In Roman times, the most reliable postal system was to give a letter to a trusted friend. Paul used Tychicus to carry letters both to Ephesus and to Colosse. Tychicus also accompanied Paul on his trip to distribute gifts to the poor of Jerusalem (Acts 20:4).

because I have decided to winter there. ¹³Do everything you can to help Zenas the lawyer and Apollos on their way and see that they have everything they need. ¹⁴Our people must learn to devote themselves to doing what is good, in order that they may provide for daily necessities and not live unproductive lives.

¹⁵Everyone with me sends you greetings. Greet those who love us in the faith.

Grace be with you all.

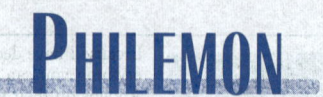

PHILEMON

Letter to a Slave Owner
A slave's life hangs in the balance

> *Although in Christ I could be bold and order you to do what you ought to do, yet I appeal to you on the basis of love. 8–9*

ONESIMUS WAS A RUNAWAY SLAVE, a hunted fugitive whose life was in constant danger. He had two options. He could spend his days hiding in the dark, grimy alleys of a Roman city, dodging soldiers and bounty hunters. Or, he could do the unthinkable and return to his master.

The laws of the empire were harsh. If Onesimus did return, his master Philemon had the legal power to sentence him to immediate execution. If Philemon mercifully decided to let him live, Onesimus would have the letter *F* (for *Fugitivus*) seared on his forehead with a branding iron, marking him for life.

Paul Defends a Runaway

His conversion to Christ through Paul's ministry greatly complicated the decision of the runaway slave. Onesimus knew he couldn't keep running all his life. He had wronged his legal owner, and, painful as it seemed, he needed to make amends.

The apostle Paul, sympathetic to the slave's cause, agreed to use his full influence on Philemon. Onesimus's life hung in the balance. This 468-word letter to the slave owner masterfully brings together Paul's skills of persuasion and diplomacy.

Every phrase in Philemon is crafted to produce the best possible effect. Paul appeals to Philemon's friendship, his status as a Christian leader, his sense of love and compassion. He doesn't outright order Philemon to consent, yet he applies blatant pressure, reminding Philemon that "you owe me your very self" (verse 19). Addressing the letter to Philemon's church (verse 2) increases the pressure, as does Paul's promise of a personal visit (verse 22).

Christianity and Slavery

Slavery existed for 1,800 years after this letter was written, and it took the full moral force of Christianity to ban it from the globe. But the tiny book of Philemon shows that the faith had a profound impact on slavery long before abolition.

Christ can revolutionize any social relationship. Onesimus, a runaway, decided to turn himself in. In Philemon, Paul asks for a second miracle. He pleads with the owner to "welcome him as you would welcome me" (verse 17). Such an attitude, in that culture, was social dynamite.

How to Read Philemon

Obviously, Paul had a close relationship with both the slave Onesimus and his owner Philemon. Some scholars believe that Onesimus first heard about Christ when he shared a jail cell with the apostle (see verses 9–10). As you read Philemon, look for clues into Paul's relationship with each person.

Philemon gives us a model of Christian diplomacy. As you read it, think of awkward social situations you know about: two estranged friends or a parent-child conflict, for example. Notice the kind of persuasion used by Paul, and try to apply it to your own circumstances.

3-TRACK READING PLAN

For an explanation and complete listing of the 3-track reading plan, turn to page 7.

TRACK 1: ***Two-Week Courses on the Bible***
See page 7 for information on these courses.

TRACK 2: ***Philemon in 1 Day***
☐ Day 1. Just one chapter long, Philemon will take only a few minutes to read.
Now turn to page 9 for your next Track 2 reading project.

TRACK 3: ***All of Philemon in 1 Day***
After you have read through Philemon, turn to pages 10–14 for your next Track 3 reading project.
☐Philemon

---

¹Paul, a prisoner of Christ Jesus, and Timothy our brother,

To Philemon our dear friend and fellow worker, ²to Apphia our sister, to Archippus our fellow soldier and to the church that meets in your home:

³Grace to you and peace from God our Father and the Lord Jesus Christ.

Thanksgiving and Prayer

⁴I always thank my God as I remember you in my prayers, ⁵because I hear about your faith in the Lord Jesus and your love for all the saints. ⁶I pray that you may be active in sharing your faith, so that you will have a full understanding of every good thing we have in Christ. ⁷Your love has given me great joy and encouragement, because you, brother, have refreshed the hearts of the saints.

Paul's Plea for Onesimus

⁸Therefore, although in Christ I could be bold and order you to do what you ought to do, ⁹yet I appeal to you on the basis of love. I then, as Paul—an old man and now also a prisoner of Christ Jesus— ¹⁰I appeal to you for my son Onesimus,ᵃ who became my son while I was in chains. ¹¹Formerly he was useless to you, but now he has become useful both to you and to me.

¹²I am sending him—who is my very heart—back to you. ¹³I would have liked to keep him with me so that he could take your place in helping me while I am in chains for the gospel. ¹⁴But I did not want to do anything without your consent, so that any favor you do will be spontaneous and not forced. ¹⁵Perhaps the reason he was separated from you for a little while was that you might have him back for good— ¹⁶no longer as a slave, but better than a slave, as a dear brother. He is very dear to me but even dearer to you, both as a man and as a brother in the Lord.

¹⁷So if you consider me a partner, welcome him as you would welcome me. ¹⁸If he has done you any wrong or owes you anything, charge it to me. ¹⁹I, Paul, am writing this with my own hand.

> ### 11 No Longer Useless
>
> **Onesimus *in Greek means "useful," and Paul playfully makes a pun from the name. A runaway slave was useless; a converted former slave can prove very useful—provided Philemon receives him in the right spirit. Accept him back, urges Paul, "no longer as a slave, but . . . as a dear brother" (verse 16).***

I will pay it back—not to mention that you owe me your very self. ²⁰I do wish, brother, that I may have some benefit from you in the Lord; refresh my heart in Christ. ²¹Confident of your obedience, I write to you, knowing that you will do even more than I ask.

²²And one thing more: Prepare a guest room for me, because I hope to be restored to you in answer to your prayers.

²³Epaphras, my fellow prisoner in Christ Jesus, sends you greetings. ²⁴And so do Mark, Aristarchus, Demas and Luke, my fellow workers.

²⁵The grace of the Lord Jesus Christ be with your spirit.

ᵃ10 *Onesimus* means *useful.*

HEBREWS

Time to Decide
Does it matter what you believe as long as you're sincere?

How shall we escape if we ignore such a great salvation? 2:3

YOU CAN GO THROUGH MUCH of life deliberately avoiding hard decisions. But sometimes you have no choice; the situation forces you to make a decision. Consider an example from the sport of rock-climbing. Sooner or later, every rock-climber faces a dreaded section of slick granite that offers no ledges or cracks to grasp. When you come to such a wall, you can abandon the climb. Or, you can risk a move like "the pendulum."

The Pendulum
The pendulum works the way it sounds: as high above you as you can reach, you fasten a loop with a metal nut and slide the rope through the loop. Then you climb down a few feet, dangle on the end of the rope, and try to swing across the sheer section. It takes nerve. You must lean out against the rope into empty space and, with a well-timed push, vault across the face of the cliff. If your lunge toward a safer spot fails, you swing helplessly back and try again.

After your entire party has swung the pendulum, you pull the rope all the way through the loop. From then on, there's no turning back. You have crossed a section of cliff that requires a rope to swing on and a loop to attach it to. The loop is now out of your reach, and the rope coiled at your feet. There is only one way to go: up.

Worth the Risk?
The author of Hebrews wrote to people who faced just such a climactic, can't-turn-back decision. It involved not a rock climb, but their entire future. Should they stick with the familiar routine of the Jewish religion? After all, it enjoyed Rome's official protection and had traditions going back thousands of years. Or should they take a risk and join the growing body of people who called themselves Christians? Those readers needed some compelling reasons to choose Christianity. At that time new converts were being thrown out of Jewish temples, tossed into jail, and even tortured. Was faith in Christ worth the risk?

The tug of the old and the fear of the new kept many interested people, especially Jews, teetering on the edge of Christianity. And the book of Hebrews seems designed to push such people toward a decisive commitment, in one direction or the other. Point by point, the author shows how Christ improved on the Jewish way. Hebrews is a no-holds-barred argument on why Christianity is *better* (a key word in Hebrews) than Judaism. The new faith is worth any risk.

Drawing on the Old Testament
For the sake of Jewish readers, the author painstakingly cites Old Testament passages, more than 80 times in all. He develops the case for Christ like a lawyer, but with the charged emotions befitting the life-and-death issues involved.

Although Hebrews mainly focuses on the Jewish religion, comparing it to Christianity, the book also speaks to our time. Today people ask, 'Are religions all that different? Isn't the most important thing to be sincere?' Hebrews insists there are decisive reasons to choose Christ. The author urges his readers to leap forward to a new experience with God through Jesus.

How to Read Hebrews

Who wrote Hebrews? Did the author have a particular group of readers in mind? Scholars have debated these questions for centuries without reaching agreement. The truth is, no one knows for certain either the author or the intended audience of Hebrews.

Nevertheless, the book does give some information about its first readers. They had heard the gospel through contemporaries of Jesus (2:3), and their conversion had brought on physical persecution (10:32–34). One fact leaps out: Their spiritual state greatly distressed the unidentified author. Five times in the book of Hebrews he interrupts a careful line of reasoning to fire off a warning (2:1; 3:7; 5:11; 10:26; 12:25).

Hebrews is actually a commentary on the Old Testament. It examines many Jewish customs and shows how Jesus brought about a "better covenant" to replace many of those laws. (*Covenant* means the same thing as *Testament:* a firm agreement between God and humanity.) Therefore, to fully appreciate Hebrews, you should have some familiarity with such books as Exodus, Leviticus, and Numbers.

As you read, look at the bottom of each page for NIV footnotes referring to the Old Testament. If you can't figure out what a text in Hebrews means, try looking back to the original passage.

To follow the logic in Hebrews, note each use of the word *better* and *superior*. The author compares Jesus Christ to the angels, to Moses, to the priests Aaron and Melchizedek, and to Abraham.

3-TRACK READING PLAN

For an explanation and complete listing of the 3-track reading plan, turn to page 7.

TRACK 1: *Two-Week Courses on the Bible*
See page 7 for information on these courses.

TRACK 2: *An Overview of Hebrews in 3 Days*
☐ Day 1. Read the Introduction to Hebrews, then chapter 2. There you will learn about God's decision to send his Son to earth and why it was so important that Jesus come as a fully human being, not as some kind of alien.
☐ Day 2. Hebrews 11 lists many Old Testament heroes, with a capsule description of how each one demonstrated faith. Read this famous chapter.
☐ Day 3. Read Hebrews 12, which combines a pep talk with a brief summary of the entire book.

Now turn to page 9 for your next Track 2 reading project.

TRACK 3: *All of Hebrews in 11 Days*
After you have read through Hebrews, turn to pages 10–14 for your next Track 3 reading project.
☐1 ☐2 ☐3–4 ☐5–6 ☐7 ☐8 ☐9 ☐10
☐11 ☐12 ☐13

The Son Superior to Angels

1 In the past God spoke to our forefathers through the prophets at many times and in various ways, ²but in these last days he has spoken to us by his Son, whom he appointed heir of all things, and through whom he made the universe. ³The Son is the radiance of God's glory and the exact representation of his being, sustaining all things by his powerful word. After he had provided purification for sins, he sat down at the right hand of the Majesty in heaven. ⁴So he became as much superior to the angels as the name he has inherited is superior to theirs.

⁵For to which of the angels did God ever say,

"You are my Son;
today I have become your Father*ᵃ*"*ᵇ*?

Or again,

"I will be his Father,
and he will be my Son"*ᶜ*?

---

*ᵃ*5 Or *have begotten you*   *ᵇ*5 Psalm 2:7   *ᶜ*5 2 Samuel 7:14; 1 Chron. 17:13

⁶And again, when God brings his firstborn into the world, he says,

"Let all God's angels worship him."ᵃ

⁷In speaking of the angels he says,

"He makes his angels winds,
  his servants flames of fire."ᵇ

⁸But about the Son he says,

"Your throne, O God, will last for ever and
    ever,
  and righteousness will be the scepter of
    your kingdom.
⁹You have loved righteousness and hated
    wickedness;
  therefore God, your God, has set you
    above your companions
  by anointing you with the oil of joy."ᶜ

¹⁰He also says,

"In the beginning, O Lord, you laid the
    foundations of the earth,
  and the heavens are the work of your
    hands.

1:10 Not by Chance

Quotations from the Old Testament fill the book of Hebrews from the second paragraph onwards. The author is making the point that God's plan, unfolding from the beginning of time, has now culminated in the visit of the Son to earth.

¹¹They will perish, but you remain;
  they will all wear out like a garment.
¹²You will roll them up like a robe;
  like a garment they will be changed.
But you remain the same,
  and your years will never end."ᵈ

¹³To which of the angels did God ever say,

"Sit at my right hand
until I make your enemies
  a footstool for your feet"ᵉ?

¹⁴Are not all angels ministering spirits sent to serve those who will inherit salvation?

Warning to Pay Attention

2 We must pay more careful attention, therefore, to what we have heard, so that we do not drift away. ²For if the message spoken by angels was binding, and every violation and dis-

obedience received its just punishment, ³how shall we escape if we ignore such a great salvation? This salvation, which was first announced by the Lord, was confirmed to us by those who heard him. ⁴God also testified to it by signs, wonders and various miracles, and gifts of the Holy Spirit distributed according to his will.

1:14 Respect for Angels

In earlier times, people freely accepted the existence of angels and accorded them honor and respect. Jewish people retold stories of how angels had assisted Abraham, Moses, Elijah, Balaam, and Daniel. (In fact, several New Testament letters warn Jewish Christians against the common practice of worshiping angels.) To prove its argument about Christ being superior, Hebrews must show that angels served his purposes, not vice versa.

Jesus Made Like His Brothers

⁵It is not to angels that he has subjected the world to come, about which we are speaking. ⁶But there is a place where someone has testified:

"What is man that you are mindful of him,
  the son of man that you care for him?
⁷You made him a littleᶠ lower than the
    angels;
  you crowned him with glory and honor
⁸ and put everything under his feet."ᵍ

In putting everything under him, God left nothing that is not subject to him. Yet at present we do not see everything subject to him. ⁹But we see Jesus, who was made a little lower than the angels, now crowned with glory and honor because he suffered death, so that by the grace of God he might taste death for everyone.

¹⁰In bringing many sons to glory, it was fitting that God, for whom and through whom everything exists, should make the author of their salvation perfect through suffering. ¹¹Both the one who makes men holy and those who are made holy are of the same family. So Jesus is not ashamed to call them brothers. ¹²He says,

"I will declare your name to my brothers;
  in the presence of the congregation I will
    sing your praises."ʰ

¹³And again,

"I will put my trust in him."ⁱ

And again he says,

ᵃ6 Deut. 32:43 (see Dead Sea Scrolls and Septuagint)   ᵇ7 Psalm 104:4   ᶜ9 Psalm 45:6,7   ᵈ12 Psalm 102:25-27
ᵉ13 Psalm 110:1   ᶠ7 Or *him for a little while*; also in verse 9   ᵍ8 Psalm 8:4-6   ʰ12 Psalm 22:22
ⁱ13 Isaiah 8:17

"Here am I, and the children God has given me."[a]

[14]Since the children have flesh and blood, he too shared in their humanity so that by his death he might destroy him who holds the power of death—that is, the devil—[15]and free those who all their lives were held in slavery by their fear of death. [16]For surely it is not angels he helps, but Abraham's descendants. [17]For this reason he had to be made like his brothers in every way, in order that he might become a merciful and faithful high priest in service to God, and that he might make atonement for[b] the sins of the people. [18]Because he himself suffered when he was tempted, he is able to help those who are being tempted.

Jesus Greater Than Moses

3 Therefore, holy brothers, who share in the heavenly calling, fix your thoughts on Jesus, the apostle and high priest whom we confess. [2]He was faithful to the one who appointed him, just as Moses was faithful in all God's house. [3]Jesus has been found worthy of greater honor than Moses, just as the builder of a house has greater honor than the house itself. [4]For every house is built by someone, but God is the builder of everything. [5]Moses was faithful as a servant in all

---

2:17 Like Us in Every Way

Hebrews goes further than any other New Testament book in explaining Jesus' human nature. Why was it so important that Jesus share our humanity? Hebrews stresses three reasons: (1) so that, in dying, he could free us from the power of death (verses 14–15); (2) so that, by becoming the final sacrifice for sin, he could reconcile us to God (5:8–9); and (3) so that, in experiencing temptation, he can better help us with our own temptations (verse 18).

---

[a]13 Isaiah 8:18   [b]17 Or *and that he might turn aside God's wrath, taking away*

Is Christ Better?
The uniqueness of Jesus

IN TIME, A WORK OF art by a great artist gains enormous value because of its creator's reputation. Even a musty notebook full of scratchings, if found to be Leonardo da Vinci's, would suddenly be worth millions of dollars. Similarly, every house designed by American architect Frank Lloyd Wright retains high value simply because of his name.

To dramatize his argument that Christ is superior to any religious system, the author of Hebrews uses an analogy: Which has greater honor, the builder of a house or the house itself? Obviously, the builder has more honor; the house is just one expression of his genius.

> Jesus has been found worthy of greater honor than Moses, just as the builder of a house has greater honor than the house itself. 3:3

In a Category by Himself

Likewise, Hebrews says, Christ has more honor than anyone else on earth. As Creator of the universe, he actually designed and made all people (1:2). That puts him in a different category of greatness, far above Moses, Aaron, and other Jewish heroes.

"Therefore," Hebrews urges, "fix your thoughts on Jesus" (3:1). He deserves all respect and allegiance. By becoming human, Jesus learned firsthand the temptations and sufferings that people undergo, so that he can now represent us sympathetically to God (4:14–15). The author goes on to prove that Jesus fulfilled all the Old Testament requirements. He was the one priest who could permanently bring together God and the human race (7:23–27). And, as God, he had the power through his death to remove the final barrier of sin between God and humankind (9:11–15).

Free Access to God

Over time, the author argues, God chose various ways to reveal himself: creation, the prophets, and the Old Testament Scriptures. But the final, complete self-expression culminated in his Son. Jesus is the one worthy of honor.

Because of Jesus, we no longer have to approach God through a priest, as the Israelites did. Christ's work makes God available to all who have faith in him. And God no longer dwells in an elaborately designed temple; *we* have become his house (3:6), his work of art.

Life Questions: People sometimes say about Jesus, "I don't believe he was God, but he was a very fine man—like Gandhi or Buddha." What arguments does the author of Hebrews use to contradict this?

God's house, testifying to what would be said in the future. [6]But Christ is faithful as a son over God's house. And we are his house, if we hold on to our courage and the hope of which we boast.

Warning Against Unbelief

[7]So, as the Holy Spirit says:

"Today, if you hear his voice,
[8] do not harden your hearts
as you did in the rebellion,
during the time of testing in the desert,
[9]where your fathers tested and tried me
and for forty years saw what I did.
[10]That is why I was angry with that generation,
and I said, 'Their hearts are always going
astray,
and they have not known my ways.'
[11]So I declared on oath in my anger,
'They shall never enter my rest.' "[a]

[12]See to it, brothers, that none of you has a sinful, unbelieving heart that turns away from the living God. [13]But encourage one another daily, as long as it is called Today, so that none of you may be hardened by sin's deceitfulness. [14]We have come to share in Christ if we hold firmly till the end the confidence we had at first. [15]As has just been said:

"Today, if you hear his voice,
do not harden your hearts
as you did in the rebellion."[b]

[16]Who were they who heard and rebelled? Were they not all those Moses led out of Egypt? [17]And with whom was he angry for forty years? Was it not with those who sinned, whose bodies fell in the desert? [18]And to whom did God swear that they would never enter his rest if not to those who disobeyed[c]? [19]So we see that they were not able to enter, because of their unbelief.

A Sabbath-Rest for the People of God

4 Therefore, since the promise of entering his rest still stands, let us be careful that none of you be found to have fallen short of it. [2]For we also have had the gospel preached to us, just as they did; but the message they heard was of no value to them, because those who heard did not combine it with faith.[d] [3]Now we who have believed enter that rest, just as God has said,

"So I declared on oath in my anger,
'They shall never enter my rest.' "[e]

And yet his work has been finished since the creation of the world. [4]For somewhere he has spoken about the seventh day in these words: "And on the seventh day God rested from all his work."[f] [5]And again in the passage above he says, "They shall never enter my rest."

[6]It still remains that some will enter that rest, and those who formerly had the gospel preached to them did not go in, because of their disobedience. [7]Therefore God again set a certain day, calling it Today, when a long time later he spoke through David, as was said before:

"Today, if you hear his voice,
do not harden your hearts."[b]

[8]For if Joshua had given them rest, God would not have spoken later about another day. [9]There remains, then, a Sabbath-rest for the people of God; [10]for anyone who enters God's rest also rests from his own work, just as God did from his. [11]Let us, therefore, make every effort to enter that rest, so that no one will fall by following their example of disobedience.

[12]For the word of God is living and active. Sharper than any double-edged sword, it penetrates even to dividing soul and spirit, joints and marrow; it judges the thoughts and attitudes of the heart. [13]Nothing in all creation is hidden from God's sight. Everything is uncovered and laid bare before the eyes of him to whom we must give account.

4:13 Mind Reader

Advances in technology—MRI tests, x-ray machines, CAT scans—make it possible for doctors to peer inside the human body and judge what goes on there. But no one has yet devised a machine that can peer inside the brain to detect thoughts and attitudes. God has such ability; why try to hide?

Jesus the Great High Priest

[14]Therefore, since we have a great high priest who has gone through the heavens,[g] Jesus the Son of God, let us hold firmly to the faith we profess. [15]For we do not have a high priest who is unable to sympathize with our weaknesses, but we have one who has been tempted in every way, just as we are—yet was without sin. [16]Let us then approach the throne of grace with confidence, so that we may receive mercy and find grace to help us in our time of need.

5 Every high priest is selected from among men and is appointed to represent them in matters related to God, to offer gifts and sacrifices for sins. [2]He is able to deal gently with those who are ignorant and are going astray, since he himself is subject to weakness. [3]This is why he

---

[a]11 Psalm 95:7-11   [b]15,7 Psalm 95:7,8   [c]18 Or *disbelieved*
the faith of those who obeyed   [e]3 Psalm 95:11; also in verse 5   [d]2 Many manuscripts *because they did not share in*
[f]4 Gen. 2:2   [g]14 Or *gone into heaven*

has to offer sacrifices for his own sins, as well as for the sins of the people.

[4]No one takes this honor upon himself; he must be called by God, just as Aaron was. [5]So Christ also did not take upon himself the glory of becoming a high priest. But God said to him,

"You are my Son;
today I have become your Father."[a]"[b]

[6]And he says in another place,

"You are a priest forever,
in the order of Melchizedek."[c]

[7]During the days of Jesus' life on earth, he offered up prayers and petitions with loud cries and tears to the one who could save him from death, and he was heard because of his reverent submission. [8]Although he was a son, he learned obedience from what he suffered [9]and, once made perfect, he became the source of eternal salvation for all who obey him [10]and was designated by God to be high priest in the order of Melchizedek.

Warning Against Falling Away

[11]We have much to say about this, but it is hard to explain because you are slow to learn. [12]In fact, though by this time you ought to be teachers, you need someone to teach you the elementary truths of God's word all over again. You need milk, not solid food! [13]Anyone who lives on milk, being still an infant, is not acquainted with the teaching about righteousness. [14]But solid food is for the mature, who by constant use have trained themselves to distinguish good from evil.

6 Therefore let us leave the elementary teachings about Christ and go on to maturity, not laying again the foundation of repentance from acts that lead to death,[d] and of faith in God, [2]instruction about baptisms, the laying on of hands, the resurrection of the dead, and eternal judgment. [3]And God permitting, we will do so.

[4]It is impossible for those who have once been enlightened, who have tasted the heavenly gift, who have shared in the Holy Spirit, [5]who have tasted the goodness of the word of God and the powers of the coming age, [6]if they fall away, to be brought back to repentance, because[e] to their loss they are crucifying the Son of God all over again and subjecting him to public disgrace.

[7]Land that drinks in the rain often falling on it and that produces a crop useful to those for whom it is farmed receives the blessing of God. [8]But land that produces thorns and thistles is worthless and is in danger of being cursed. In the end it will be burned.

[9]Even though we speak like this, dear friends, we are confident of better things in your case—things that accompany salvation. [10]God is not unjust; he will not forget your work and the love

6:4 Can a Believer Fall Away?

This passage has caused interpreters great difficulty. People who don't believe in "eternal security" think the passage refers to Christians who fall away from the faith. Others, such as John Calvin, insist that the author of Hebrews must be referring to people who never fully became Christians, because other verses seem to teach the eternal security of those in Christ (see John 5:24; 6:37; Romans 8:1; Hebrews 8:12). Regardless, the author is writing about a hypothetical situation. He is not describing what happened, but only what could happen: if such a falling away ever did occur, it would be impossible to rescue such people again. A somewhat similar argument appears at the end of chapter 10.

you have shown him as you have helped his people and continue to help them. [11]We want each of you to show this same diligence to the very end, in order to make your hope sure. [12]We do not want you to become lazy, but to imitate those who through faith and patience inherit what has been promised.

The Certainty of God's Promise

[13]When God made his promise to Abraham, since there was no one greater for him to swear by, he swore by himself, [14]saying, "I will surely bless you and give you many descendants."[f] [15]And so after waiting patiently, Abraham received what was promised.

[16]Men swear by someone greater than themselves, and the oath confirms what is said and puts an end to all argument. [17]Because God wanted to make the unchanging nature of his purpose very clear to the heirs of what was promised, he confirmed it with an oath. [18]God did this so that, by two unchangeable things in which it is impossible for God to lie, we who have fled to take hold of the hope offered to us may be greatly encouraged. [19]We have this hope as an anchor for the soul, firm and secure. It enters the inner sanctuary behind the curtain, [20]where Jesus, who went before us, has entered on our behalf. He has become a high priest forever, in the order of Melchizedek.

---

[a]5 Or *have begotten you while*   [b]5 Psalm 2:7   [c]6 Psalm 110:4   [d]1 Or *from useless rituals*   [e]6 Or *repentance*   [f]14 Gen. 22:17

Melchizedek the Priest

7 This Melchizedek was king of Salem and priest of God Most High. He met Abraham returning from the defeat of the kings and

blessed him, ²and Abraham gave him a tenth of everything. First, his name means "king of righteousness"; then also, "king of Salem" means "king of peace." ³Without father or mother, without genealogy, without beginning of days or end of life, like the Son of God he remains a priest forever.

⁴Just think how great he was: Even the patriarch Abraham gave him a tenth of the plunder! ⁵Now the law requires the descendants of Levi who become priests to collect a tenth from the people—that is, their brothers—even though their brothers are descended from Abraham. ⁶This man, however, did not trace his descent from Levi, yet he collected a tenth from Abraham and blessed him who had the promises. ⁷And without doubt the lesser person is blessed by the greater. ⁸In the one case, the tenth is collected by men who die; but in the other case, by him who is declared to be living. ⁹One might even say that Levi, who collects the tenth, paid the tenth through Abraham, ¹⁰because when Melchizedek met Abraham, Levi was still in the body of his ancestor.

Jesus Like Melchizedek

¹¹If perfection could have been attained through the Levitical priesthood (for on the basis of it the law was given to the people), why was there still need for another priest to come—one in the order of Melchizedek, not in the order of Aaron? ¹²For when there is a change of the priesthood, there must also be a change of the law. ¹³He of whom these things are said belonged to a different tribe, and no one from that tribe has ever served at the altar. ¹⁴For it is clear that our

Lord descended from Judah, and in regard to that tribe Moses said nothing about priests. ¹⁵And what we have said is even more clear if another priest like Melchizedek appears, ¹⁶one who has become a priest not on the basis of a regulation as to his ancestry but on the basis of the power of an indestructible life. ¹⁷For it is declared:

"You are a priest forever,
  in the order of Melchizedek."ᵃ

¹⁸The former regulation is set aside because it was weak and useless ¹⁹(for the law made nothing perfect), and a better hope is introduced, by which we draw near to God.

²⁰And it was not without an oath! Others became priests without any oath, ²¹but he became a priest with an oath when God said to him:

"The Lord has sworn
  and will not change his mind:
'You are a priest forever.'"ᵃ

²²Because of this oath, Jesus has become the guarantee of a better covenant.

²³Now there have been many of those priests, since death prevented them from continuing in office; ²⁴but because Jesus lives forever, he has a permanent priesthood. ²⁵Therefore he is able to save completelyᵇ those who come to God through him, because he always lives to intercede for them.

²⁶Such a high priest meets our need—one who is holy, blameless, pure, set apart from sinners, exalted above the heavens. ²⁷Unlike the other high priests, he does not need to offer sacrifices day after day, first for his own sins, and then for the sins of the people. He sacrificed for their sins once for all when he offered himself. ²⁸For the law appoints as high priests men who are weak; but the oath, which came after the law, appointed the Son, who has been made perfect forever.

ᵃ17,21 Psalm 110:4   *ᵇ25* Or *forever*

The High Priest of a New Covenant

8 The point of what we are saying is this: We do have such a high priest, who sat down at the right hand of the throne of the Majesty in heaven, ²and who serves in the sanctuary, the true tabernacle set up by the Lord, not by man.

³Every high priest is appointed to offer both gifts and sacrifices, and so it was necessary for this one also to have something to offer. ⁴If he were on earth, he would not be a priest, for there are already men who offer the gifts prescribed by the law. ⁵They serve at a sanctuary that is a copy and shadow of what is in heaven. This is why Moses was warned when he was about to build the tabernacle: "See to it that you make everything according to the pattern shown you on the mountain."[a] ⁶But the ministry Jesus has received is as superior to theirs as the covenant of which he is mediator is superior to the old one, and it is founded on better promises.

⁷For if there had been nothing wrong with that first covenant, no place would have been sought for another. ⁸But God found fault with the people and said[b]:

---

[a]5 Exodus 25:40   [b]8 Some manuscripts may be translated *fault and said to the people.*

New Light on the Old Testament
The advantages of living now

TO UNDERSTAND THE DIFFERENCE BETWEEN an original and a copy, consider trying to photograph the largest animal, a whale. Roy Chapman Andrews describes it:

"Once in Alaska we raised a humpback's spout and ran up close before the animal submerged. Ten minutes later, without warning, the floor of the ocean seemed to rise and a mountainous black body, dripping with foam, heaved upward, almost over our heads. It paused an instant, then fell sidewise to be swallowed up by a vortex of green water. With the camera ready in my hands I stared at the thing. The whale had dropped back scarcely twenty feet away; if it had fallen the other way, the vessel would have been crushed beneath its forty tons."

> For if there had been nothing wrong with that first covenant, no place would have been sought for another. 8:7

How can you adequately communicate the impact of something that immense? Photographers have recorded humpback whales bursting from the water, or "lobtailing" (standing on their heads and waving their mighty flukes high in the air). But no photograph can capture the sheer bigness of such an animal. A baby blue whale gains a ton of weight a month. An adult blue whale's heart weighs 1,000 pounds. How can any two-dimensional photograph convey such gargantuan size?

Comparing the Copy to the Original

Even the best photograph is just a copy, a representation of its subject's reality. No 8x10 rectangle can contain a whale. No photo sequence of the Grand Canyon is as grand as the canyon itself. The photograph preserves a mere two-dimensional copy of reality.

Hebrews uses that word *copy* to describe the images and rituals of the Old Testament: Passover feasts, sacrifices, and other priestly duties. They were mere shadows, expressing the reality to come in Jesus Christ. No ceremony alone, however elaborate, can adequately express the experience of God himself, any more than a photograph of a whale or a mountain can adequately represent a whale or a mountain.

According to Hebrews, the Old Testament rituals were a copy, but Christ is the original. The author pulls up time-hallowed images from the Jewish tradition—sacrifices, laws, blood, the tabernacle, the priest, the Day of Atonement—and explains how Christ revealed once and for all the meaning these images only hinted at. The incomplete, shadowy copy contrasts with the perfect, genuine reality.

Which Is Better?

As always, Hebrews stresses the advantages of living now, rather than in the Old Testament ("the first covenant"). Because of Christ, sacrifices are no longer necessary (10:11–12), and God's laws are now written in our minds and on our hearts, not in a formal code (8:10). "It is finished," Christ cried out from the cross (John 19:30); the author of Hebrews describes how.

Copies have some value. A photograph of a whale, for example, conveys much to those who will never encounter one. But, as the author of Hebrews asks, who would prefer a copy to the real thing?

Life Questions: What practical help does Hebrews give on how to read the Old Testament? Of what value are the Old Testament laws and religious rituals?

"The time is coming, declares the Lord,
    when I will make a new covenant
with the house of Israel
    and with the house of Judah.
⁹It will not be like the covenant
    I made with their forefathers
when I took them by the hand
    to lead them out of Egypt,
because they did not remain faithful to my
        covenant,
    and I turned away from them,
                        declares the Lord.
¹⁰This is the covenant I will make with the
        house of Israel
    after that time, declares the Lord.
I will put my laws in their minds
    and write them on their hearts.
I will be their God,
    and they will be my people.
¹¹No longer will a man teach his neighbor,
    or a man his brother, saying, 'Know the
        Lord,'
because they will all know me,
    from the least of them to the greatest.
¹²For I will forgive their wickedness
    and will remember their sins no more."ᵃ

¹³By calling this covenant "new," he has made
the first one obsolete; and what is obsolete and
aging will soon disappear.

Worship in the Earthly Tabernacle

9 Now the first covenant had regulations for
worship and also an earthly sanctuary. ²A
tabernacle was set up. In its first room were the
lampstand, the table and the consecrated bread;
this was called the Holy Place. ³Behind the second curtain was a room called the Most Holy
Place, ⁴which had the golden altar of incense and
the gold-covered ark of the covenant. This ark
contained the gold jar of manna, Aaron's staff
that had budded, and the stone tablets of the
covenant. ⁵Above the ark were the cherubim of
the Glory, overshadowing the atonement cov-
er.ᵇ But we cannot discuss these things in detail
now.

⁶When everything had been arranged like this,
the priests entered regularly into the outer room
to carry on their ministry. ⁷But only the high
priest entered the inner room, and that only once
a year, and never without blood, which he offered
for himself and for the sins the people had committed in ignorance. ⁸The Holy Spirit was showing by this that the way into the Most Holy Place
had not yet been disclosed as long as the first
tabernacle was still standing. ⁹This is an illustration for the present time, indicating that the gifts
and sacrifices being offered were not able to clear

the conscience of the worshiper. ¹⁰They are only
a matter of food and drink and various ceremonial washings—external regulations applying
until the time of the new order.

The Blood of Christ

¹¹When Christ came as high priest of the good
things that are already here,ᶜ he went through
the greater and more perfect tabernacle that is
not man-made, that is to say, not a part of this

> ### 9:11 More Perfect
>
> *Descriptions of the tabernacle and offerings
> take up much of Exodus, Leviticus, Numbers,
> and Deuteronomy, leading some scholars to
> judge it the largest single subject covered in the
> Bible. Yet Hebrews, concerned to prove the
> superiority of a new covenant, devotes a mere
> 10 verses to the tabernacle (verses 1–10). The
> great high priest, Christ himself, has made the
> old system obsolete.*

creation. ¹²He did not enter by means of the
blood of goats and calves; but he entered the
Most Holy Place once for all by his own blood,
having obtained eternal redemption. ¹³The blood
of goats and bulls and the ashes of a heifer sprinkled on those who are ceremonially unclean
sanctify them so that they are outwardly clean.
¹⁴How much more, then, will the blood of Christ,
who through the eternal Spirit offered himself
unblemished to God, cleanse our consciences
from acts that lead to death,ᵈ so that we may
serve the living God!

¹⁵For this reason Christ is the mediator of a
new covenant, that those who are called may receive the promised eternal inheritance—now
that he has died as a ransom to set them free
from the sins committed under the first covenant.

¹⁶In the case of a will,ᵉ it is necessary to prove
the death of the one who made it, ¹⁷because a will
is in force only when somebody has died; it never
takes effect while the one who made it is living.
¹⁸This is why even the first covenant was not put
into effect without blood. ¹⁹When Moses had
proclaimed every commandment of the law to all
the people, he took the blood of calves, together
with water, scarlet wool and branches of hyssop,
and sprinkled the scroll and all the people. ²⁰He
said, "This is the blood of the covenant, which
God has commanded you to keep."ᶠ ²¹In the
same way, he sprinkled with the blood both the
tabernacle and everything used in its ceremonies.
²²In fact, the law requires that nearly everything

ᵃ*12* Jer. 31:31-34   ᵇ*5* Traditionally *the mercy seat*   ᶜ*11* Some early manuscripts *are to come*   ᵈ*14* Or *from
useless rituals*   ᵉ*16* Same Greek word as *covenant;* also in verse 17   ᶠ*20* Exodus 24:8

be cleansed with blood, and without the shedding of blood there is no forgiveness.

²³It was necessary, then, for the copies of the heavenly things to be purified with these sacrifices, but the heavenly things themselves with better sacrifices than these. ²⁴For Christ did not enter a man-made sanctuary that was only a copy of the true one; he entered heaven itself, now to appear for us in God's presence. ²⁵Nor did he enter heaven to offer himself again and again, the way the high priest enters the Most Holy Place every year with blood that is not his own. ²⁶Then Christ would have had to suffer many times since the creation of the world. But now he has appeared once for all at the end of the ages to do away with sin by the sacrifice of himself. ²⁷Just as man is destined to die once, and after that to face judgment, ²⁸so Christ was sacrificed once to take away the sins of many people; and he will appear a second time, not to bear sin, but to bring salvation to those who are waiting for him.

9:26 A Once-for-all Sacrifice

Jewish readers of Hebrews were very familiar with the religious rituals described in this chapter (see Leviticus 9 and 16 for the original instructions). Step by step, the author shows how Christ's new covenant improves on the old one. Instead of many sacrifices, he made only one, himself, thus gaining free and complete forgiveness for us. The chapter uses an analogy to explain why Christ's death was necessary (verse 17). It compares God's grace to a will. Wealth is only passed down when a death occurs; Christ's death freed the inheritance for us.

Christ's Sacrifice Once for All

10 The law is only a shadow of the good things that are coming—not the realities themselves. For this reason it can never, by the same sacrifices repeated endlessly year after year, make perfect those who draw near to worship. ²If it could, would they not have stopped being offered? For the worshipers would have been cleansed once for all, and would no longer have felt guilty for their sins. ³But those sacrifices are an annual reminder of sins, ⁴because it is impossible for the blood of bulls and goats to take away sins.

⁵Therefore, when Christ came into the world, he said:

"Sacrifice and offering you did not desire,
  but a body you prepared for me;

⁶with burnt offerings and sin offerings
  you were not pleased.
⁷Then I said, 'Here I am—it is written about
    me in the scroll—
  I have come to do your will, O God.'"ᵃ

⁸First he said, "Sacrifices and offerings, burnt offerings and sin offerings you did not desire, nor were you pleased with them" (although the law required them to be made). ⁹Then he said, "Here I am, I have come to do your will." He sets aside the first to establish the second. ¹⁰And by that will, we have been made holy through the sacrifice of the body of Jesus Christ once for all.

¹¹Day after day every priest stands and performs his religious duties; again and again he offers the same sacrifices, which can never take away sins. ¹²But when this priest had offered for all time one sacrifice for sins, he sat down at the

10:12 Why Christ Sat Down

Hebrews makes special mention that Christ "sat down" after finishing his priestly duties. Jewish priests never sat down; the tabernacle and the temple did not have seats. They did their work standing up as a symbol that it was never finished. Having finished the work of a priest once for all, Christ "sat down."

right hand of God. ¹³Since that time he waits for his enemies to be made his footstool, ¹⁴because by one sacrifice he has made perfect forever those who are being made holy.

¹⁵The Holy Spirit also testifies to us about this. First he says:

¹⁶"This is the covenant I will make with them
    after that time, says the Lord.
  I will put my laws in their hearts,
    and I will write them on their minds."ᵇ

¹⁷Then he adds:

  "Their sins and lawless acts
    I will remember no more."ᶜ

¹⁸And where these have been forgiven, there is no longer any sacrifice for sin.

A Call to Persevere

¹⁹Therefore, brothers, since we have confidence to enter the Most Holy Place by the blood of Jesus, ²⁰by a new and living way opened for us through the curtain, that is, his body, ²¹and since we have a great priest over the house of God, ²²let us draw near to God with a sincere heart in full assurance of faith, having our hearts sprinkled to cleanse us from a guilty conscience and having

---

ᵃ7 Psalm 40:6-8 (see Septuagint)   ᵇ16 Jer. 31:33   ᶜ17 Jer. 31:34

our bodies washed with pure water. [23]Let us hold unswervingly to the hope we profess, for he who promised is faithful. [24]And let us consider how we may spur one another on toward love and good deeds. [25]Let us not give up meeting together, as some are in the habit of doing, but let us encourage one another—and all the more as you see the Day approaching.

[26]If we deliberately keep on sinning after we have received the knowledge of the truth, no sacrifice for sins is left, [27]but only a fearful expectation of judgment and of raging fire that will consume the enemies of God. [28]Anyone who rejected the law of Moses died without mercy on the testimony of two or three witnesses. [29]How much more severely do you think a man deserves to be punished who has trampled the Son of God under foot, who has treated as an unholy thing the blood of the covenant that sanctified him, and who has insulted the Spirit of grace? [30]For we know him who said, "It is mine to avenge; I will repay,"[a] and again, "The Lord will judge his people."[b] [31]It is a dreadful thing to fall into the hands of the living God.

[32]Remember those earlier days after you had received the light, when you stood your ground in a great contest in the face of suffering. [33]Sometimes you were publicly exposed to insult and persecution; at other times you stood side by side with those who were so treated. [34]You sympathized with those in prison and joyfully accepted the confiscation of your property, because you knew that you yourselves had better and lasting possessions.

[35]So do not throw away your confidence; it will be richly rewarded. [36]You need to persevere so that when you have done the will of God, you will receive what he has promised. [37]For in just a very little while,

"He who is coming will come and will not delay.
[38]   But my righteous one[c] will live by faith.
    And if he shrinks back,
    I will not be pleased with him."[d]

[39]But we are not of those who shrink back and are destroyed, but of those who believe and are saved.

By Faith

11 Now faith is being sure of what we hope for and certain of what we do not see. [2]This is what the ancients were commended for.

[3]By faith we understand that the universe was formed at God's command, so that what is seen was not made out of what is visible.

[4]By faith Abel offered God a better sacrifice than Cain did. By faith he was commended as a righteous man, when God spoke well of his offerings. And by faith he still speaks, even though he is dead.

[5]By faith Enoch was taken from this life, so that he did not experience death; he could not be found, because God had taken him away. For before he was taken, he was commended as one who pleased God. [6]And without faith it is impossible to please God, because anyone who comes to him must believe that he exists and that he rewards those who earnestly seek him.

[7]By faith Noah, when warned about things not yet seen, in holy fear built an ark to save his family. By his faith he condemned the world and became heir of the righteousness that comes by faith.

[8]By faith Abraham, when called to go to a place he would later receive as his inheritance, obeyed and went, even though he did not know where he was going. [9]By faith he made his home in the promised land like a stranger in a foreign country; he lived in tents, as did Isaac and Jacob, who were heirs with him of the same promise. [10]For he was looking forward to the city with foundations, whose architect and builder is God.

[11]By faith Abraham, even though he was past age—and Sarah herself was barren—was enabled to become a father because he[e] considered him faithful who had made the promise. [12]And so from this one man, and he as good as dead, came descendants as numerous as the stars in the sky and as countless as the sand on the seashore.

[13]All these people were still living by faith when they died. They did not receive the things promised; they only saw them and welcomed them from a distance. And they admitted that they were aliens and strangers on earth. [14]People who say such things show that they are looking for a country of their own. [15]If they had been thinking of the country they had left, they would have had opportunity to return. [16]Instead, they were longing for a better country—a heavenly one. Therefore God is not ashamed to be called their God, for he has prepared a city for them.

11:16 Not Ashamed

The list of God's favorites in Hebrews 11 includes blemished characters such as Samson and Rahab, triumphant winners such as David and Barak, and then a whole list of anonymous "failures" who faced torture and persecution. Yet at some point all of these displayed the kind of faith that pleases God.

---

[a]30 Deut. 32:35   [b]30 Deut. 32:36; Psalm 135:14   [c]38 One early manuscript *But the righteous*   [d]38 Hab. 2:3,4
[e]11 Or *By faith even Sarah, who was past age, was enabled to bear children because she*

[17]By faith Abraham, when God tested him, offered Isaac as a sacrifice. He who had received the promises was about to sacrifice his one and only son, [18]even though God had said to him, "It is through Isaac that your offspring[a] will be reckoned."[b] [19]Abraham reasoned that God could raise the dead, and figuratively speaking, he did receive Isaac back from death.

[20]By faith Isaac blessed Jacob and Esau in regard to their future.

[21]By faith Jacob, when he was dying, blessed each of Joseph's sons, and worshiped as he leaned on the top of his staff.

[22]By faith Joseph, when his end was near, spoke about the exodus of the Israelites from Egypt and gave instructions about his bones.

[23]By faith Moses' parents hid him for three months after he was born, because they saw he was no ordinary child, and they were not afraid of the king's edict.

[24]By faith Moses, when he had grown up, refused to be known as the son of Pharaoh's daughter. [25]He chose to be mistreated along with the people of God rather than to enjoy the pleasures of sin for a short time. [26]He regarded disgrace for the sake of Christ as of greater value than the treasures of Egypt, because he was looking ahead to his reward. [27]By faith he left Egypt, not fearing the king's anger; he persevered because he saw him who is invisible. [28]By faith he kept the Passover and the sprinkling of blood, so that the destroyer of the firstborn would not touch the firstborn of Israel.

[29]By faith the people passed through the Red Sea[c] as on dry land; but when the Egyptians tried to do so, they were drowned.

[30]By faith the walls of Jericho fell, after the people had marched around them for seven days.

[31]By faith the prostitute Rahab, because she welcomed the spies, was not killed with those who were disobedient.[d]

[32]And what more shall I say? I do not have

---

[a]18 Greek seed   [b]18 Gen. 21:12   [c]29 That is, Sea of Reeds   [d]31 Or unbelieving

---

What Is True Faith?
Not even giants of faith get exactly what they want

> These were all commended for their faith, yet none of them received what had been promised.
> 11:39

WHAT IS FAITH? AND HOW can you be sure you've got it? Some Christians think of faith as an almost magical force: If you muster up enough of it, you'll get rich, stay healthy, and live a contented life, they say. Yet how does one "muster up" faith? What are signs of true faith?

The author of Hebrews launches into a detailed description of faith, complete with references to several dozen biographical models. (Some have dubbed Hebrews 11 the "Faith Hall of Fame.") "Without faith," Hebrews says bluntly, "it is impossible to please God" (11:6).

Not What You'd Expect

But the picture of faith emerging from these chapters contains some surprises. The author uses words and phrases like "persevere," "endure," "do not lose heart." In many instances, the heroes cited did not receive the promise they hoped for; some ended up flogged and destitute, hiding out in goatskins (11:36–38). Many died horrible deaths.

Faith, concludes the author, most resembles a difficult race. The runner has his or her eyes on the winner's prize, and, despite nagging temptations to slacken the pace, refuses to let up until he or she crosses the finish line. "Throw off everything that hinders," Hebrews coaches (12:1). "Strengthen your feeble arms and weak knees" (12:12).

Is It Worth the Struggle?

Why do people punish their bodies to run a grueling marathon race? Most runners name two reasons: the sense of personal reward they get and the physical benefits of the exercise. The same two rewards apply in the spiritual realm: Great prizes await those who persevere, and the very process of living by faith builds strong character. In this race, no one loses. If you finish, you get the reward.

Here, as elsewhere, Hebrews holds up Jesus, who endured great suffering for our sakes (12:2–3), as the ultimate example. The faith described in Hebrews is not sugarcoated; God does not guarantee a life of luxury and ease. It is tough faith: a constant commitment to hang on and believe God against all odds, no matter what.

Life Questions: Hebrews 11 mentions some people who prospered and some who suffered, yet all had faith. Taking into account what this passage says, try to come up with your own definition of faith.

time to tell about Gideon, Barak, Samson, Jephthah, David, Samuel and the prophets, ³³who through faith conquered kingdoms, administered justice, and gained what was promised; who shut the mouths of lions, ³⁴quenched the fury of the flames, and escaped the edge of the sword; whose weakness was turned to strength; and who became powerful in battle and routed foreign armies. ³⁵Women received back their dead, raised to life again. Others were tortured and refused to be released, so that they might gain a better resurrection. ³⁶Some faced jeers and flogging, while still others were chained and put in prison. ³⁷They were stoned[a]; they were sawed in two; they were put to death by the sword. They went about in sheepskins and goatskins, destitute, persecuted and mistreated— ³⁸the world was not worthy of them. They wandered in deserts and mountains, and in caves and holes in the ground.

³⁹These were all commended for their faith, yet none of them received what had been promised. ⁴⁰God had planned something better for us so that only together with us would they be made perfect.

God Disciplines His Sons

12 Therefore, since we are surrounded by such a great cloud of witnesses, let us throw off everything that hinders and the sin that so easily entangles, and let us run with perseverance

12:1 Pep Talk

Chapter 12 makes clear why Hebrews 11 devoted such attention to martyrs from the past. The early Christians who first read this book were facing persecution, and their faith was bending under the pressure. Think of the "great cloud of witnesses" who have gone before, Hebrews urges, and fix your eyes on Jesus, who volunteered to die on your behalf. With its imagery borrowed from athletics, this portion of Hebrews sounds like a coach's halftime speech delivered to competitors in danger of giving up.

the race marked out for us. ²Let us fix our eyes on Jesus, the author and perfecter of our faith, who for the joy set before him endured the cross, scorning its shame, and sat down at the right hand of the throne of God. ³Consider him who endured such opposition from sinful men, so that you will not grow weary and lose heart.

⁴In your struggle against sin, you have not yet resisted to the point of shedding your blood. ⁵And you have forgotten that word of encouragement that addresses you as sons:

"My son, do not make light of the Lord's
    discipline,
  and do not lose heart when he rebukes
    you,
⁶because the Lord disciplines those he loves,
  and he punishes everyone he accepts as a
    son."[b]

⁷Endure hardship as discipline; God is treating you as sons. For what son is not disciplined by his father? ⁸If you are not disciplined (and everyone undergoes discipline), then you are illegitimate children and not true sons. ⁹Moreover, we have all had human fathers who disciplined us and we respected them for it. How much more should we submit to the Father of our spirits and live! ¹⁰Our fathers disciplined us for a little while as they thought best; but God disciplines us for our good, that we may share in his holiness. ¹¹No discipline seems pleasant at the time, but painful. Later on, however, it produces a harvest of righteousness and peace for those who have been trained by it.

¹²Therefore, strengthen your feeble arms and weak knees. ¹³"Make level paths for your feet,"[c] so that the lame may not be disabled, but rather healed.

Warning Against Refusing God

¹⁴Make every effort to live in peace with all men and to be holy; without holiness no one will see the Lord. ¹⁵See to it that no one misses the grace of God and that no bitter root grows up to cause trouble and defile many. ¹⁶See that no one is sexually immoral, or is godless like Esau, who for a single meal sold his inheritance rights as the oldest son. ¹⁷Afterward, as you know, when he wanted to inherit this blessing, he was rejected. He could bring about no change of mind, though he sought the blessing with tears.

¹⁸You have not come to a mountain that can

12:18 A Vivid Contrast

The author of Hebrews has been arguing that Christ's new covenant is far better than the old one between God and the Jews. This one section (verses 18–28) uses powerful images to summarize the great difference between encountering God in the way Moses did in the Old Testament and encountering him through Jesus. It also predicts that even greater things are in store: a new kingdom and new creation.

be touched and that is burning with fire; to darkness, gloom and storm; ¹⁹to a trumpet blast or to such a voice speaking words that those who heard it begged that no further word be spoken

---

[a]37 Some early manuscripts *stoned; they were put to the test;* [b]6 Prov. 3:11,12 [c]13 Prov. 4:26

to them, [20]because they could not bear what was commanded: "If even an animal touches the mountain, it must be stoned."[a] [21]The sight was so terrifying that Moses said, "I am trembling with fear."[b]

[22]But you have come to Mount Zion, to the heavenly Jerusalem, the city of the living God. You have come to thousands upon thousands of angels in joyful assembly, [23]to the church of the firstborn, whose names are written in heaven. You have come to God, the judge of all men, to the spirits of righteous men made perfect, [24]to Jesus the mediator of a new covenant, and to the sprinkled blood that speaks a better word than the blood of Abel.

[25]See to it that you do not refuse him who speaks. If they did not escape when they refused him who warned them on earth, how much less will we, if we turn away from him who warns us from heaven? [26]At that time his voice shook the earth, but now he has promised, "Once more I will shake not only the earth but also the heavens."[c] [27]The words "once more" indicate the removing of what can be shaken—that is, created things—so that what cannot be shaken may remain.

[28]Therefore, since we are receiving a kingdom that cannot be shaken, let us be thankful, and so worship God acceptably with reverence and awe, [29]for our "God is a consuming fire."[d]

Concluding Exhortations

13 Keep on loving each other as brothers. [2]Do not forget to entertain strangers, for by so doing some people have entertained angels without knowing it. [3]Remember those in prison as if you were their fellow prisoners, and those who are mistreated as if you yourselves were suffering.

[4]Marriage should be honored by all, and the marriage bed kept pure, for God will judge the adulterer and all the sexually immoral. [5]Keep your lives free from the love of money and be content with what you have, because God has said,

"Never will I leave you;
never will I forsake you."[e]

[6]So we say with confidence,

"The Lord is my helper; I will not be afraid.
What can man do to me?"[f]

[7]Remember your leaders, who spoke the word of God to you. Consider the outcome of their way of life and imitate their faith. [8]Jesus Christ is the same yesterday and today and forever. [9]Do not be carried away by all kinds of strange teachings. It is good for our hearts to be strength-ened by grace, not by ceremonial foods, which are of no value to those who eat them. [10]We have an altar from which those who minister at the tabernacle have no right to eat.

[11]The high priest carries the blood of animals into the Most Holy Place as a sin offering, but the bodies are burned outside the camp. [12]And so Jesus also suffered outside the city gate to make the people holy through his own blood. [13]Let us, then, go to him outside the camp, bearing the disgrace he bore. [14]For here we do not have an enduring city, but we are looking for the city that is to come.

[15]Through Jesus, therefore, let us continually offer to God a sacrifice of praise—the fruit of lips that confess his name. [16]And do not forget to do good and to share with others, for with such sacrifices God is pleased.

13:15 Sacrifice of Praise

In form, Hebrews is more theological than practical. But in the last chapter the author adds a list of specific commands and suggestions. Even here, however, he makes one last reference to sacrifice. Now, we have only a "sacrifice of praise" to offer, because Christ accomplished all that was needed.

[17]Obey your leaders and submit to their authority. They keep watch over you as men who must give an account. Obey them so that their work will be a joy, not a burden, for that would be of no advantage to you.

[18]Pray for us. We are sure that we have a clear conscience and desire to live honorably in every way. [19]I particularly urge you to pray so that I may be restored to you soon.

[20]May the God of peace, who through the blood of the eternal covenant brought back from the dead our Lord Jesus, that great Shepherd of the sheep, [21]equip you with everything good for doing his will, and may he work in us what is pleasing to him, through Jesus Christ, to whom be glory for ever and ever. Amen.

[22]Brothers, I urge you to bear with my word of exhortation, for I have written you only a short letter.

[23]I want you to know that our brother Timothy has been released. If he arrives soon, I will come with him to see you.

[24]Greet all your leaders and all God's people. Those from Italy send you their greetings.

[25]Grace be with you all.

---

[a]20 Exodus 19:12,13 [b]21 Deut. 9:19 [c]26 Haggai 2:6 [d]29 Deut. 4:24 [e]5 Deut. 31:6 [f]6 Psalm 118:6,7

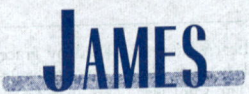

JAMES

Words Are Not Enough
You can believe all the right things, yet still be dead wrong

> Do not merely listen to the word, and so deceive yourselves. Do what it says.
> 1:22

WHERE THERE IS LIFE, THERE is motion. Some antelopes, as well as the cheetah, can sprint faster than some cars on the highway. Bighorn sheep, charging one another headfirst, collide with such force that the sound echoes like a gunshot through mountain ranges. Canada geese, fanned out across the sky in an orderly V, battle winds for 1,000 miles, nonstop, before dropping back to earth.

Sometimes we keep relics of life: an elkhead hanging above a fireplace, a fragile, perfect seashell, an exotic butterfly mounted on a pin. But these are mere mementos: life has gone from them, and with it motion.

A Sure Sign of Life

Authors of the Bible often look to nature for analogies to express spiritual truth. And the book of James, controversial because of its emphasis on "good works," is perhaps best understood through the analogy of motion. In the spiritual realm also, where there's life there will be motion.

When a person becomes a Christian, new life begins, and inevitably that life must express itself through "spiritual motion," or good deeds. In James's words, "What good is it ... if a man claims to have faith but has no deeds?" (2:14).

Movement does not cause life, but it does invariably follow life. It's a sure sign that life is present. Similarly, genuine faith in Christ should always result in actions that demonstrate faith.

Does James Contradict Paul?

James is not writing about how to become a Christian, but rather how to act like one. Having all the correct beliefs about God will hardly suffice: Even demons believe in God. Real, life-giving faith should produce motion, and James minces no words in describing the specific spiritual actions expected of Christians.

Christian thinkers, notably Martin Luther, have struggled to reconcile the message of James with that of Paul, who so firmly warned against slavish legalism. But Paul never belittled holy living. When he wrote to carousers, such as in his letters to the Corinthians, he railed against immorality as strongly as James.

Evidently, James's readers were not even flirting with legalism. They lived at the other extreme, ignoring those laws God had clearly revealed. James had a simple remedy: "Do not merely listen to the word.... Do what it says" (1:22).

Straight to the Point

Unlike the apostle Paul, James was no urbane man of letters. He was a simple, homespun preacher, perturbed at people who were not living right. His letter covers a wide range of topics, applying the Christian faith to specific problems and commanding readers to live out their beliefs.

Be humble! James orders. *Submit to God! Stop sinning!* James is as forthright as an Old Testament prophet; it's hard to miss his point.

Modern readers of James face the same dilemma as the first recipients of this unsettling letter. His words are easy enough to understand, but are we doing what he says? What kind of motion characterizes our spiritual lives? As Luther himself said, "You are saved by faith alone, but if faith is alone it is not faith."

How to Read James

Few New Testament writers achieve the clarity or the "punch" of James. He doesn't spend time expanding subpoints or worrying about literary structure. As a result, the book of James reads like a collection of pithy proverbs. (It's sometimes called the "Proverbs of the New Testament.") In your study, it may help to group the material by subject; James tends to return to themes repeatedly.

As leader of the headquarters church in Jerusalem, James knew how to speak with authority. You don't have to look for hidden meanings in this book. James tells you clearly how you should act, in 54 direct commands. Note that many of these have parallels to Jesus' Sermon on the Mount. As you read, keep in mind the diverse audience he was addressing, which included the rich and the poor. Note his "asides" to specific groups.

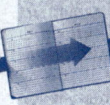

3-TRACK READING PLAN

For an explanation and complete listing of the 3-track reading plan, turn to page 7.

TRACK 1:   **Two-Week Courses on the Bible**
See page 7 for information on these courses.

TRACK 2:   **An Overview of James in 1 Day**
☐ Day 1. Read the Introduction to James, then chapter 1, on how the Christian should respond to tough times, or "trials."
Now turn to page 9 for your next Track 2 reading project.

TRACK 3:   **All of James in 4 Days**
After you have read through James, turn to pages 10–14 for your next Track 3 reading project.
☐1   ☐2   ☐3–4   ☐5

---

1 James, a servant of God and of the Lord Jesus Christ,

To the twelve tribes scattered among the nations:

Greetings.

Trials and Temptations

²Consider it pure joy, my brothers, whenever you face trials of many kinds, ³because you know that the testing of your faith develops perseverance. ⁴Perseverance must finish its work so that you may be mature and complete, not lacking anything. ⁵If any of you lacks wisdom, he should ask God, who gives generously to all without finding fault, and it will be given to him. ⁶But when he asks, he must believe and not doubt, because he who doubts is like a wave of the sea, blown and tossed by the wind. ⁷That man should not think he will receive anything from the Lord; ⁸he is a double-minded man, unstable in all he does.

⁹The brother in humble circumstances ought to take pride in his high position. ¹⁰But the one who is rich should take pride in his low position, because he will pass away like a wild flower. ¹¹For the sun rises with scorching heat and withers the plant; its blossom falls and its beauty is destroyed. In the same way, the rich man will fade away even while he goes about his business.

¹²Blessed is the man who perseveres under trial, because when he has stood the test, he will receive the crown of life that God has promised to those who love him.

¹³When tempted, no one should say, "God is tempting me." For God cannot be tempted by evil, nor does he tempt anyone; ¹⁴but each one is tempted when, by his own evil desire, he is dragged away and enticed. ¹⁵Then, after desire has conceived, it gives birth to sin; and sin, when it is full-grown, gives birth to death.

1:3 Productive Pain

James's call for joy in the face of trials may seem shocking or even insensitive at first. A close reading, though, makes clear that James finds joy in the results of the trials, not in the trials themselves. Even difficult times can produce good qualities, such as perseverance. This positive, or "redemptive," approach to suffering surfaces throughout the New Testament (see Romans 5:1–5; 1 Peter 1:3–9).

16Don't be deceived, my dear brothers. 17Every good and perfect gift is from above, coming down from the Father of the heavenly lights, who does not change like shifting shadows. 18He chose to give us birth through the word of truth, that we might be a kind of firstfruits of all he created.

Listening and Doing

19My dear brothers, take note of this: Everyone should be quick to listen, slow to speak and slow to become angry, 20for man's anger does not bring about the righteous life that God desires. 21Therefore, get rid of all moral filth and the evil that is so prevalent and humbly accept the word planted in you, which can save you.

22Do not merely listen to the word, and so deceive yourselves. Do what it says. 23Anyone who listens to the word but does not do what it says is like a man who looks at his face in a mirror 24and, after looking at himself, goes away and immediately forgets what he looks like. 25But the man who looks intently into the perfect law that gives freedom, and continues to do this, not forgetting what he has heard, but doing it—he will be blessed in what he does.

26If anyone considers himself religious and yet does not keep a tight rein on his tongue, he deceives himself and his religion is worthless. 27Religion that God our Father accepts as pure and faultless is this: to look after orphans and widows in their distress and to keep oneself from being polluted by the world.

Favoritism Forbidden

2 My brothers, as believers in our glorious Lord Jesus Christ, don't show favoritism.

2:1 Play No Favorites

James 1 tells Christians to act out their faith. James 2 gives a very pointed example of church members deferring to the wealthy and powerful. This direct application, hitting close to home, characterizes James. He leaves no room for ambiguity.

2Suppose a man comes into your meeting wearing a gold ring and fine clothes, and a poor man in shabby clothes also comes in. 3If you show special attention to the man wearing fine clothes and say, "Here's a good seat for you," but say to the poor man, "You stand there" or "Sit on the floor by my feet," 4have you not discriminated among yourselves and become judges with evil thoughts?

5Listen, my dear brothers: Has not God chosen those who are poor in the eyes of the world to be rich in faith and to inherit the kingdom he promised those who love him? 6But you have insulted the poor. Is it not the rich who are exploiting you? Are they not the ones who are dragging you into court? 7Are they not the ones who are slandering the noble name of him to whom you belong?

8If you really keep the royal law found in Scripture, "Love your neighbor as yourself,"a you are doing right. 9But if you show favoritism, you sin and are convicted by the law as lawbreakers. 10For whoever keeps the whole law and yet stumbles at just one point is guilty of breaking all of it. 11For he who said, "Do not commit adultery,"b also said, "Do not murder."c If you do not commit adultery but do commit murder, you have become a lawbreaker.

12Speak and act as those who are going to be judged by the law that gives freedom, 13because judgment without mercy will be shown to anyone who has not been merciful. Mercy triumphs over judgment!

Faith and Deeds

14What good is it, my brothers, if a man claims to have faith but has no deeds? Can such faith save him? 15Suppose a brother or sister is without clothes and daily food. 16If one of you says to him, "Go, I wish you well; keep warm and well fed," but does nothing about his physical needs, what good is it? 17In the same way, faith by itself, if it is not accompanied by action, is dead.

18But someone will say, "You have faith; I have deeds."

Show me your faith without deeds, and I will show you my faith by what I do. 19You believe that there is one God. Good! Even the demons believe that—and shudder.

20You foolish man, do you want evidence that faith without deeds is uselessd? 21Was not our ancestor Abraham considered righteous for what he did when he offered his son Isaac on the altar? 22You see that his faith and his actions were working together, and his faith was made complete by what he did. 23And the scripture was fulfilled that says, "Abraham believed God, and it was credited to him as righteousness,"e and he was called God's friend. 24You see that a person is justified by what he does and not by faith alone.

25In the same way, was not even Rahab the prostitute considered righteous for what she did when she gave lodging to the spies and sent them off in a different direction? 26As the body without the spirit is dead, so faith without deeds is dead.

a8 Lev. 19:18   b11 Exodus 20:14; Deut. 5:18   c11 Exodus 20:13; Deut. 5:17   d20 Some early manuscripts dead
e23 Gen. 15:6

Taming the Tongue

3 Not many of you should presume to be teachers, my brothers, because you know that we who teach will be judged more strictly. ²We all stumble in many ways. If anyone is never at fault in what he says, he is a perfect man, able to keep his whole body in check.

³When we put bits into the mouths of horses to make them obey us, we can turn the whole animal. ⁴Or take ships as an example. Although they are so large and are driven by strong winds, they are steered by a very small rudder wherever the pilot wants to go. ⁵Likewise the tongue is a small part of the body, but it makes great boasts. Consider what a great forest is set on fire by a small spark. ⁶The tongue also is a fire, a world of evil among the parts of the body. It corrupts the whole person, sets the whole course of his life on fire, and is itself set on fire by hell.

⁷All kinds of animals, birds, reptiles and creatures of the sea are being tamed and have been tamed by man, ⁸but no man can tame the tongue. It is a restless evil, full of deadly poison.

⁹With the tongue we praise our Lord and Father, and with it we curse men, who have been made in God's likeness. ¹⁰Out of the same mouth come praise and cursing. My brothers, this should not be. ¹¹Can both fresh water and salt*a* water flow from the same spring? ¹²My brothers, can a fig tree bear olives, or a grapevine bear figs? Neither can a salt spring produce fresh water.

3:3 Colorful Language

Vivid, homey pictures from nature give a visual character to James's words, almost as if each thought were a photograph. He refers to sea froth, wilted flowers, a forest fire, a horse's bit, the morning mist, a hungry moth, the farmer's spring rains, a giant ship, and a saltwater spring. Paul, a more educated writer, alluded to culture and athletics and human relationships. But James felt most comfortable borrowing simple images from nature.

Two Kinds of Wisdom

¹³Who is wise and understanding among you? Let him show it by his good life, by deeds done in the humility that comes from wisdom. ¹⁴But if you harbor bitter envy and selfish ambition in your hearts, do not boast about it or deny the truth. ¹⁵Such "wisdom" does not come down from heaven but is earthly, unspiritual, of the devil. ¹⁶For where you have envy and selfish ambition, there you find disorder and every evil practice.

¹⁷But the wisdom that comes from heaven is first of all pure; then peace-loving, considerate, submissive, full of mercy and good fruit, impartial and sincere. ¹⁸Peacemakers who sow in peace raise a harvest of righteousness.

Submit Yourselves to God

4 What causes fights and quarrels among you? Don't they come from your desires that battle within you? ²You want something but don't

4:1 The Need for Self-Control

If you had to distill the message of James into one word, it might be self-control. Chapters 4 and 5, which contain some of James's most striking imagery, show how simple greed and desire can corrode the church and destroy unity. And, indeed, many of the Jewish Christians he was writing to soon experienced an abrupt turn of fortune. They lost their wealth and suffered severe persecution.

get it. You kill and covet, but you cannot have what you want. You quarrel and fight. You do not have, because you do not ask God. ³When you ask, you do not receive, because you ask with wrong motives, that you may spend what you get on your pleasures.

⁴You adulterous people, don't you know that friendship with the world is hatred toward God? Anyone who chooses to be a friend of the world becomes an enemy of God. ⁵Or do you think Scripture says without reason that the spirit he caused to live in us envies intensely?*b* ⁶But he gives us more grace. That is why Scripture says:

> "God opposes the proud
> but gives grace to the humble."*c*

⁷Submit yourselves, then, to God. Resist the devil, and he will flee from you. ⁸Come near to God and he will come near to you. Wash your hands, you sinners, and purify your hearts, you double-minded. ⁹Grieve, mourn and wail. Change your laughter to mourning and your joy to gloom. ¹⁰Humble yourselves before the Lord, and he will lift you up.

¹¹Brothers, do not slander one another. Anyone who speaks against his brother or judges him speaks against the law and judges it. When you judge the law, you are not keeping it, but sitting in judgment on it. ¹²There is only one Lawgiver and Judge, the one who is able to save and de-

---

a 11 Greek bitter (see also verse 14)   b 5 Or that God jealously longs for the spirit that he made to live in us; or that the Spirit he caused to live in us longs jealously   c 6 Prov. 3:34

stroy. But you—who are you to judge your neighbor?

Boasting About Tomorrow

¹³Now listen, you who say, "Today or tomorrow we will go to this or that city, spend a year there, carry on business and make money." ¹⁴Why, you do not even know what will happen tomorrow. What is your life? You are a mist that appears for a little while and then vanishes. ¹⁵Instead, you ought to say, "If it is the Lord's will, we will live and do this or that." ¹⁶As it is, you boast and brag. All such boasting is evil. ¹⁷Anyone, then, who knows the good he ought to do and doesn't do it, sins.

Warning to Rich Oppressors

5 Now listen, you rich people, weep and wail because of the misery that is coming upon you. ²Your wealth has rotted, and moths have eaten your clothes. ³Your gold and silver are corroded. Their corrosion will testify against you and eat your flesh like fire. You have hoarded

ᵃ5 Or *yourselves as in a day of feasting*

wealth in the last days. ⁴Look! The wages you failed to pay the workmen who mowed your fields are crying out against you. The cries of the harvesters have reached the ears of the Lord Almighty. ⁵You have lived on earth in luxury and self-indulgence. You have fattened yourselves in the day of slaughter.ᵃ ⁶You have condemned and murdered innocent men, who were not opposing you.

Patience in Suffering

⁷Be patient, then, brothers, until the Lord's coming. See how the farmer waits for the land to yield its valuable crop and how patient he is for the autumn and spring rains. ⁸You too, be patient and stand firm, because the Lord's coming is near. ⁹Don't grumble against each other, brothers, or you will be judged. The Judge is standing at the door!

¹⁰Brothers, as an example of patience in the face of suffering, take the prophets who spoke in the name of the Lord. ¹¹As you know, we consider blessed those who have persevered. You have

---

Conflicts of Rich and Poor
A different kind of class struggle

> "God opposes the proud but gives grace to the humble." 4:6

OUR SOCIETY TENDS TO DIVIDE the rich and the poor. The two groups have little daily contact, and you would have a very hard time communicating a unified message to both the very rich and the very poor.

Yet it seems James's original readers included both those groups. In one paragraph James addresses the haughty, privileged people of wealth, and in the next paragraph he turns to poor people undergoing severe trials. (Note the shift between 5:1 and 5:7.)

The two groups had different problems. The wealthy were selfish. They showed insensitivity and snobbishness to the poor. For their part, the poor responded with envy and grumbling. They blamed God for their poverty.

Who Is Double-minded?

James gave advice on the specific problems of each group, but he also implied they have much in common. For both rich and poor the most important struggle is not outside—the conditions we live in—but rather inside. All of us experience the inner conflict of being pulled by powerful, contrary forces. Will we move toward Christ and the life he taught, or in the opposite direction? Will we trust God or reject him?

James coined a new word to describe this inner conflict: he called it being "double-minded" (4:8). For rich and poor, this conflict may express itself in different ways, as James went on to explain. But double-mindedness is a tug-of-war between divided loyalties. The essential struggle to obey God is no different for either group.

As he discussed the rich and the poor, James relied on many of the actual phrases Jesus had used, especially in the Sermon on the Mount. (This is quite understandable if the author was James the brother of Jesus, as many scholars believe.) He applied what Jesus taught in a fresh, new way, calling on all of us—rich and poor—to be single-minded in our commitment to follow that way.

Life Questions: James 2 warns against favoritism based on social class. Does such favoritism happen among Christians today? Is there any difference between the way rich and poor people think about following Jesus?

heard of Job's perseverance and have seen what the Lord finally brought about. The Lord is full of compassion and mercy.

¹²Above all, my brothers, do not swear—not

5:10 Waiting It Out

In this section, James expands on the idea (1:2–4) that God can use suffering for our benefit. He realistically concedes that rejoicing in the face of trials may not come right away. To develop such an attitude will take patience and perseverance. James mentions two sources of support for someone trying to cope with suffering: (1) the past example of people like the prophets and Job; (2) the church's ministry of healing and prayer.

by heaven or by earth or by anything else. Let your "Yes" be yes, and your "No," no, or you will be condemned.

The Prayer of Faith

¹³Is any one of you in trouble? He should pray. Is anyone happy? Let him sing songs of praise. ¹⁴Is any one of you sick? He should call the elders of the church to pray over him and anoint him with oil in the name of the Lord. ¹⁵And the prayer offered in faith will make the sick person well; the Lord will raise him up. If he has sinned, he will be forgiven. ¹⁶Therefore confess your sins to each other and pray for each other so that you may be healed. The prayer of a righteous man is powerful and effective.

¹⁷Elijah was a man just like us. He prayed earnestly that it would not rain, and it did not rain on the land for three and a half years. ¹⁸Again he prayed, and the heavens gave rain, and the earth produced its crops.

¹⁹My brothers, if one of you should wander from the truth and someone should bring him back, ²⁰remember this: Whoever turns a sinner from the error of his way will save him from death and cover over a multitude of sins.

1 PETER

A Word to the Suffering
What to do when trouble comes

> *Dear friends, do not be surprised at the painful trial you are suffering, as though something strange were happening to you. 4:12*

A DISTANT, SWIRLING CLOUD OF DUST signaled the approach of Turkish death squads. But who could escape? The villages of Armenia sat exposed and defenseless on a rocky plain. Doomed Christians clung together on the floors of their homes, praying, singing, and shivering with fear.

This scene was repeated often during World War I, and it usually ended in a massacre. The Turkish assault against Armenian Christians was one of history's worst religion-inspired bloodbaths: Over one million people died. But, sadly, the Armenian tragedy was but one of many attacks against 20th-century Christians.

More people have died for their religious faith in this century than in all the rest of history combined. Thousands of Christians died in East Africa, first in the Mau Mau uprising and then during Ugandan dictator Idi Amin's reign of terror. Millions more suffered under Soviet and Chinese governments. And the oppression goes on: Even today some countries imprison and torture converts to Christianity. This fact alone makes the book of 1 Peter starkly relevant for modern readers.

How to Respond to Persecution

What advice would you give Christians about to undergo persecution? The apostle Peter took up that challenge just as ominous rumblings from Rome were striking fear in every Christian community. Half-crazed Nero had seized on believers as scapegoats for the ills of his empire.

Should the persecuted Christians flee or resist? Should they tone down their outward signs of faith? Give up? Peter's readers, their lives in danger, needed clear advice on suffering.

They also wanted explanations of the meaning of suffering. Why does God allow it? Can good result? Does God care? In short, they were asking the questions that occur to any Christian who goes through great trial.

According to Peter, suffering should not catch a Christian off guard. We are "strangers" (1:17) in a hostile world, and where Christians thrive, storm clouds may gather. Suffering is an expected part of a life of sincere faith.

Peter's Own Experience

On the subject of suffering, Peter makes an ideal counselor for readers then and now. He had been flogged and imprisoned for his own faith, once even expecting execution (Acts 12). Also, Peter had personally watched Jesus endure suffering, and in this letter he points to him as an example of how to respond.

Peter encourages his readers to "live such good lives among the pagans that, though they accuse you of doing wrong, they may see your good deeds and glorify God" (2:12). Suffering can refine believers and give us an opportunity to prove our faith, the result thus working out for our benefit.

This book emphasizes a further point also: Suffering is temporary, to be endured only for "a little while" (1:6; 5:10). Those who suffer with Christ will also glory with him in a life forever free of pain. Skeptics have criticized the church for stressing a future life rather than working to improve this one. "You promise pie in the sky by and by," they taunt. But to Peter's readers—wary of enemies on the prowl, unsure of surviving another day—that message was as tangible and nourishing as food.

According to 1 Peter, our hope that suffering will one day cease is not a mirage but a "living hope" (1:3) in the One who has conquered death.

How to Read 1 Peter

At first Christianity enjoyed official toleration by the Roman empire, but gradually the government turned against it. Rome resented the Christians' talk about another kingdom and their objections to idolatry and decadence.

Although 1 Peter was originally written to people in severe danger, its lessons apply to all of us, for we all experience pain of some kind. Why don't things work out the way we want? Is God trying to tell us something? Peter gives authoritative answers. As you read, try to apply what he says to your own situation.

Peter's writing style reveals his simple fisherman background: He uses pithy peasant expressions and awkwardly shifts back and forth between doctrine and advice. Chapter 2 (verses 18–25) shows an excellent example. Peter gives a deep insight into what it meant for Christ to suffer on our behalf, but he includes it in a practical section on slaves and governments. Thus, he blends doctrine (what to believe) with practice (how to behave).

More a preacher than a writer, Peter structured his book like a rambling sermon. Look for the 34 direct commands included. Peter's reliance on common figures of speech—a cornerstone, a lamb, a shepherd—makes the book very quotable.

But Peter was not simply giving homespun advice; he was well-grounded in the teachings of Jesus and the prophets. Proportionately, he quotes from the Old Testament more than any other New Testament author.

PEOPLE YOU'LL MEET IN 1 PETER

PETER (p. 1298)

3-TRACK READING PLAN

For an explanation and complete listing of the 3-track reading plan, turn to page 7.

TRACK 1:　*Two-Week Courses on the Bible*
See page 7 for information on these courses.

TRACK 2:　*An Overview of 1 Peter in 1 Day*
☐ Day 1. Read the Introduction to 1 Peter, then chapter 1 for a capsule summary of the letter's style and message.
Now turn to page 9 for your next Track 2 reading project.

TRACK 3:　*All of 1 Peter in 4 Days*
After you have read through 1 Peter, turn to pages 10–14 for your next Track 3 reading project.
☐1　　☐2　　☐3　　☐4–5

---

1 Peter, an apostle of Jesus Christ,

To God's elect, strangers in the world, scattered throughout Pontus, Galatia, Cappadocia, Asia and Bithynia, [2]who have been chosen according to the foreknowledge of God the Father, through the sanctifying work of the Spirit, for obedience to Jesus Christ and sprinkling by his blood:

Grace and peace be yours in abundance.

Praise to God for a Living Hope

[3]Praise be to the God and Father of our Lord Jesus Christ! In his great mercy he has given us new birth into a living hope through the resurrection of Jesus Christ from the dead, [4]and into an inheritance that can never perish, spoil or fade—kept in heaven for you, [5]who through faith are shielded by God's power until the coming of the salvation that is ready to be revealed in the last time. [6]In this you greatly rejoice, though now for a little while you may have had to suffer grief in all kinds of trials. [7]These have come so that your faith—of greater worth than gold, which perishes even though refined by fire—may be proved genuine and may result in praise, glory and honor when Jesus Christ is revealed. [8]Though you have not seen him, you love him;

and even though you do not see him now, you believe in him and are filled with an inexpressible and glorious joy, ⁹for you are receiving the goal of your faith, the salvation of your souls.

¹⁰Concerning this salvation, the prophets, who spoke of the grace that was to come to you, searched intently and with the greatest care, ¹¹trying to find out the time and circumstances to which the Spirit of Christ in them was pointing when he predicted the sufferings of Christ and the glories that would follow. ¹²It was revealed to them that they were not serving themselves but you, when they spoke of the things that have now been told you by those who have preached the gospel to you by the Holy Spirit sent from heaven. Even angels long to look into these things.

Be Holy

¹³Therefore, prepare your minds for action; be self-controlled; set your hope fully on the grace to be given you when Jesus Christ is revealed. ¹⁴As obedient children, do not conform to the evil desires you had when you lived in ignorance. ¹⁵But just as he who called you is holy, so be holy in all you do; ¹⁶for it is written: "Be holy, because I am holy."ᵃ

¹⁷Since you call on a Father who judges each man's work impartially, live your lives as strangers here in reverent fear. ¹⁸For you know that it was not with perishable things such as silver or gold that you were redeemed from the empty way of life handed down to you from your forefathers, ¹⁹but with the precious blood of Christ, a lamb without blemish or defect. ²⁰He was chosen before the creation of the world, but was revealed in these last times for your sake. ²¹Through him you believe in God, who raised him from the dead and glorified him, and so your faith and hope are in God.

²²Now that you have purified yourselves by obeying the truth so that you have sincere love for your brothers, love one another deeply, from the heart.ᵇ ²³For you have been born again, not of perishable seed, but of imperishable, through the living and enduring word of God. ²⁴For,

"All men are like grass,
    and all their glory is like the flowers of the
        field;
the grass withers and the flowers fall,
²⁵   but the word of the Lord stands forever."ᶜ

And this is the word that was preached to you.

2 Therefore, rid yourselves of all malice and all deceit, hypocrisy, envy, and slander of every kind. ²Like newborn babies, crave pure spiritual milk, so that by it you may grow up in your salvation, ³now that you have tasted that the Lord is good.

The Living Stone and a Chosen People

⁴As you come to him, the living Stone—rejected by men but chosen by God and precious to

him— ⁵you also, like living stones, are being built into a spiritual house to be a holy priesthood, offering spiritual sacrifices acceptable to God through Jesus Christ. ⁶For in Scripture it says:

"See, I lay a stone in Zion,
    a chosen and precious cornerstone,
and the one who trusts in him
    will never be put to shame."ᵈ

⁷Now to you who believe, this stone is precious. But to those who do not believe,

"The stone the builders rejected
    has become the capstone,ᵉ"ᶠ

⁸and,

"A stone that causes men to stumble
    and a rock that makes them fall."ᵍ

They stumble because they disobey the message—which is also what they were destined for.

⁹But you are a chosen people, a royal priesthood, a holy nation, a people belonging to God, that you may declare the praises of him who

---

*16 Lev. 11:44,45; 19:2; 20:7   ᵇ22 Some early manuscripts *from a pure heart*   ᶜ25 Isaiah 40:6-8   ᵈ6 Isaiah 28:16
ᵉ7 Or *cornerstone*   ᶠ7 Psalm 118:22   ᵍ8 Isaiah 8:14

called you out of darkness into his wonderful light. [10]Once you were not a people, but now you are the people of God; once you had not received mercy, but now you have received mercy.

[11]Dear friends, I urge you, as aliens and strangers in the world, to abstain from sinful desires, which war against your soul. [12]Live such

2:11 Endangered Strangers

At first Christians had enjoyed the official protection of the Roman empire. Under Nero (A.D. 54–68) all that changed, and the apostles Peter and Paul were probably martyred during Nero's regime. Peter addressed this letter to "strangers in the world" (1:1), an indication that Christians were now viewed as a separate, persecuted minority without legal rights.

good lives among the pagans that, though they accuse you of doing wrong, they may see your good deeds and glorify God on the day he visits us.

Submission to Rulers and Masters

[13]Submit yourselves for the Lord's sake to every authority instituted among men: whether to the king, as the supreme authority, [14]or to governors, who are sent by him to punish those who do wrong and to commend those who do right. [15]For it is God's will that by doing good you should silence the ignorant talk of foolish men. [16]Live as free men, but do not use your freedom as a cover-up for evil; live as servants of God. [17]Show proper respect to everyone: Love the brotherhood of believers, fear God, honor the king.

[18]Slaves, submit yourselves to your masters with all respect, not only to those who are good and considerate, but also to those who are harsh. [19]For it is commendable if a man bears up under the pain of unjust suffering because he is conscious of God. [20]But how is it to your credit if you receive a beating for doing wrong and endure it? But if you suffer for doing good and you endure it, this is commendable before God. [21]To this you were called, because Christ suffered for you, leaving you an example, that you should follow in his steps.

[22]"He committed no sin,
    and no deceit was found in his mouth."[a]

[23]When they hurled their insults at him, he did not retaliate; when he suffered, he made no threats. Instead, he entrusted himself to him who judges justly. [24]He himself bore our sins in his body on the tree, so that we might die to sins and live for righteousness; by his wounds you have

been healed. [25]For you were like sheep going astray, but now you have returned to the Shepherd and Overseer of your souls.

Wives and Husbands

3 Wives, in the same way be submissive to your husbands so that, if any of them do not believe the word, they may be won over without words by the behavior of their wives, [2]when they see the purity and reverence of your lives. [3]Your beauty should not come from outward adornment, such as braided hair and the wearing of gold jewelry and fine clothes. [4]Instead, it should be that of your inner self, the unfading beauty of a gentle and quiet spirit, which is of great worth in God's sight. [5]For this is the way the holy women of the past who put their hope in God used to make themselves beautiful. They were submissive to their own husbands, [6]like Sarah, who obeyed Abraham and called him her master. You are her daughters if you do what is right and do not give way to fear.

[7]Husbands, in the same way be considerate as you live with your wives, and treat them with respect as the weaker partner and as heirs with you of the gracious gift of life, so that nothing will hinder your prayers.

Suffering for Doing Good

[8]Finally, all of you, live in harmony with one another; be sympathetic, love as brothers, be compassionate and humble. [9]Do not repay evil with evil or insult with insult, but with blessing, because to this you were called so that you may inherit a blessing. [10]For,

"Whoever would love life
    and see good days
must keep his tongue from evil
    and his lips from deceitful speech.
[11]He must turn from evil and do good;
    he must seek peace and pursue it.
[12]For the eyes of the Lord are on the righteous
    and his ears are attentive to their prayer,
but the face of the Lord is against those who
    do evil."[b]

[13]Who is going to harm you if you are eager to do good? [14]But even if you should suffer for what is right, you are blessed. "Do not fear what they fear[c]; do not be frightened."[d] [15]But in your hearts set apart Christ as Lord. Always be prepared to give an answer to everyone who asks you to give the reason for the hope that you have. But do this with gentleness and respect, [16]keeping a clear conscience, so that those who speak maliciously against your good behavior in Christ may be ashamed of their slander. [17]It is better, if it is God's will, to suffer for doing good than for do-

---

[a]*22* Isaiah 53:9   [b]*12* Psalm 34:12-16   [c]*14* Or *not fear their threats*   [d]*14* Isaiah 8:12

ing evil. ¹⁸For Christ died for sins once for all, the righteous for the unrighteous, to bring you to God. He was put to death in the body but made alive by the Spirit, ¹⁹through whom*a* also he went and preached to the spirits in prison ²⁰who disobeyed long ago when God waited patiently in the days of Noah while the ark was being built. In it only a few people, eight in all, were saved through water, ²¹and this water symbolizes baptism that now saves you also—not the removal of dirt from the body but the pledge*b* of a good conscience toward God. It saves you by the resurrection of Jesus Christ, ²²who has gone into heaven and is at God's right hand—

with angels, authorities and powers in submission to him.

Living for God

4 Therefore, since Christ suffered in his body, arm yourselves also with the same attitude, because he who has suffered in his body is done with sin. ²As a result, he does not live the rest of his earthly life for evil human desires, but rather for the will of God. ³For you have spent enough time in the past doing what pagans choose to do—living in debauchery, lust, drunkenness, orgies, carousing and detestable idolatry. ⁴They think it strange that you do not plunge with them

a 18,19 Or alive in the spirit, ¹⁹through which   b21 Or response

---

A Man Named "The Rock"
Peter slowly learned how to live up to his nickname

> Humble yourselves, therefore, under God's mighty hand, that he may lift you up in due time. 5:6

YOU CAN'T MISS PETER IN the four Gospels. He stands out like a bumpkin, pushing to the head of the line and coming out with loud, outrageous assertions. Every list of the disciples names him first, and Peter is often seen elbowing his way to center stage.

He was likable enough, with a big heart and unlimited enthusiasm. He just had too many rough edges. He swung like a pendulum, bold and courageous at one moment, yet cowardly when it really counted.

Signs of Mellowing

But by the time Peter sat down to write this letter, late in his life, a lot had changed. You can sense the change in the very words he chooses: words like *humble* and *submit*. This book contains nothing of the brash, aggressive style evident in the Gospels. He is heeding Jesus' last command to him: "Feed my sheep" (John 21:17). Gruff Peter has become a tender shepherd.

To get the full impact of Peter's transformation, you must read about him in the Gospels (especially in Mark), and then turn directly to this letter. Blustery, loudmouthed Peter now counsels wives to have "the unfading beauty of a gentle and quiet spirit" (3:4) and husbands to treat their wives with consideration and respect (3:7). The man who sliced off an ear in Jesus' defense (John 18:10) now advises submission to every government authority (2:13). Peter once vigorously protested Jesus' prediction of death (Mark 8:32); now he solemnly commends Christ's suffering as an ideal (2:21–24).

It's easy to believe Peter is describing himself when he writes such statements as "Once you were not a people, but now you are the people of God" (2:10) and "You were like sheep going astray, but now you have returned to the Shepherd and Overseer of your souls" (2:25). Over time the shifting sand of Peter's personality solidified into granite.

Never Too Late

Peter finally earned the nickname that Jesus gave him long before: the "rock" (Matthew 16:18). And when he instructs his readers to stand fast in the true grace of God (5:12), you get the feeling Peter has learned through hard experience the lessons he is now passing on to others.

If Paul is the apostle of faith, Peter is the apostle of hope. God does not give up on people, as Peter's life amply demonstrates. We have reason to hope, whatever our circumstances—even when facing suffering or death.

Tradition reports that Peter was crucified head downward on a Roman cross; he thought himself unworthy to die right side up like Jesus. Peter died still believing his promise of a happy ending: "And the God of all grace, who called you to his eternal glory in Christ, after you have suffered a little while, will himself restore you and make you strong, firm and steadfast" (5:10). He wrote like a man who knew.

Life Questions: If Jesus were to give you a nickname, what would it be? Has your personality undergone major changes? What still needs work?

into the same flood of dissipation, and they heap abuse on you. [5]But they will have to give account to him who is ready to judge the living and the dead. [6]For this is the reason the gospel was preached even to those who are now dead, so that they might be judged according to men in regard to the body, but live according to God in regard to the spirit.

3:19 The Spirits in Prison

At least 18 major theories have been proposed to explain Peter's meaning in verses 18–22. Primarily, scholars differ over what the phrase "spirits in prison" refers to. Were "the spirits" people in some intermediate state of death, or the fallen angels alluded to in Genesis 6:1–4? No one knows for sure. Peter uses the obscure reference to make a point about the ultimate good that came from the suffering Jesus endured.

[7]The end of all things is near. Therefore be clear minded and self-controlled so that you can pray. [8]Above all, love each other deeply, because love covers over a multitude of sins. [9]Offer hospitality to one another without grumbling. [10]Each one should use whatever gift he has received to serve others, faithfully administering God's grace in its various forms. [11]If anyone speaks, he should do it as one speaking the very words of God. If anyone serves, he should do it with the strength God provides, so that in all things God may be praised through Jesus Christ. To him be the glory and the power for ever and ever. Amen.

Suffering for Being a Christian

[12]Dear friends, do not be surprised at the painful trial you are suffering, as though something strange were happening to you. [13]But rejoice that you participate in the sufferings of Christ, so that you may be overjoyed when his glory is revealed. [14]If you are insulted because of the name of Christ, you are blessed, for the Spirit of glory and of God rests on you. [15]If you suffer, it should not be as a murderer or thief or any

other kind of criminal, or even as a meddler. [16]However, if you suffer as a Christian, do not be ashamed, but praise God that you bear that name. [17]For it is time for judgment to begin with the family of God; and if it begins with us, what will the outcome be for those who do not obey the gospel of God? [18]And,

> "If it is hard for the righteous to be saved,
>   what will become of the ungodly and the
>   sinner?"[a]

[19]So then, those who suffer according to God's will should commit themselves to their faithful Creator and continue to do good.

To Elders and Young Men

5 To the elders among you, I appeal as a fellow elder, a witness of Christ's sufferings and one who also will share in the glory to be revealed: [2]Be shepherds of God's flock that is under your care, serving as overseers—not because you must, but because you are willing, as God wants you to be; not greedy for money, but eager to serve; [3]not lording it over those entrusted to you, but being examples to the flock. [4]And when the Chief Shepherd appears, you will receive the crown of glory that will never fade away.

[5]Young men, in the same way be submissive to those who are older. All of you, clothe yourselves with humility toward one another, because,

> "God opposes the proud
>   but gives grace to the humble."[b]

[6]Humble yourselves, therefore, under God's mighty hand, that he may lift you up in due time. [7]Cast all your anxiety on him because he cares for you.

[8]Be self-controlled and alert. Your enemy the devil prowls around like a roaring lion looking for someone to devour. [9]Resist him, standing firm in the faith, because you know that your brothers throughout the world are undergoing the same kind of sufferings.

[10]And the God of all grace, who called you to his eternal glory in Christ, after you have suffered a little while, will himself restore you and make you strong, firm and steadfast. [11]To him be the power for ever and ever. Amen.

Final Greetings

[12]With the help of Silas,[c] whom I regard as a faithful brother, I have written to you briefly, encouraging you and testifying that this is the true grace of God. Stand fast in it.

[13]She who is in Babylon, chosen together with you, sends you her greetings, and so does my son Mark. [14]Greet one another with a kiss of love.

Peace to all of you who are in Christ.

4:13 Radical Shift

This one verse, above all others, shows how much Peter had changed. He received Jesus' strongest rebuke (Mark 8:33) for objecting to the suggestion that Jesus would suffer. But now he presents suffering for Christ as a privilege, a way to participate in Christ's glory.

[a]18 Prov. 11:31   [b]5 Prov. 3:34   [c]12 Greek *Silvanus*, a variant of *Silas*

2 PETER

A Threat from Within
The worst dangers aren't always well marked

FIRST-CENTURY APOSTLES MUST HAVE FELT like pioneers in a mosquito-infested swamp. A pest attacked them. *Slap!* They'd kill it, and instantly another would land. Wherever they went new dangers swarmed up. One group denied Jesus was God; then another declared him God but not fully man. The apostles denounced legalism, only to encounter free-swingers who assumed "anything goes." Members of one church quit work and huddled together to await Jesus' return; those of another gave up on his returning at all.

Second Peter was written in response to a young church's jumpy tendencies. Whereas 1 Peter centered on fearsome dangers from outside, this letter speaks to dangers from within. False teachers were stirring up dissent, questioning basic doctrines, and leading Christians into immorality.

> *Dear friends, this is now my second letter to you. I have written both of them as reminders to stimulate you to wholesome thinking. 3:1*

Warning Signs

In its advice to the various squabbling groups, 2 Peter calls for a return to the true gospel. "I will always remind you of these things," the author says (1:12) and proceeds to go over some basic facts of how Christians should believe and behave. The book doesn't introduce many new insights; rather, it erects a giant warning sign against common pitfalls that endanger the church.

A key word, *knowledge*, echoes throughout this letter: 2 Peter refreshes readers' memories regarding the proper knowledge that makes possible "everything we need for life and godliness" (1:3). The author carefully grounds his knowledge in Old Testament prophets and eyewitness accounts of Jesus' life, not in "cleverly invented stories" (1:16). And he urges his readers to resist dangers by living blamelessly.

The answer to false knowledge, the author bluntly insists, is true knowledge; the answer to immoral living is moral living. As he prepares to die (1:14), the author of 2 Peter gets in one last appeal for truth.

How to Read 2 Peter

Although 1 and 2 Peter claim the same author, they have large differences in style and approach. Second Peter is unrefined in writing style, more shrill and less gentle than the first letter. (Many scholars question whether the apostle Peter actually wrote the whole letter, but the letter does claim his authorship and shows some signs of his influence.)

Perhaps the difference in audiences explains the two approaches. The Bible views suffering—persecution from outside—as a purifying influence that often results in an even stronger church. Thus 1 Peter has an encouraging and devotional tone. But the real danger to a church comes from the inside, from immoral behavior and false teaching. Second Peter, in strong words, addresses those "inside" dangers.

As you read it, try to put yourself in the place of the original audience. What dangers does the author warn against? Are there parallels today? Chapters 1 and 3 can be universally applied. Chapter 2 concerns itself more directly with the particular false teachers plaguing the first-century church.

In tone and actual content, 2 Peter resembles the tiny book of Jude. Both deal with the same problems and propose the same solutions.

When reading 2 Peter, look for the key word *knowledge*, and related words like *thinking*, *reminders/remind*, and *remember*. The author appeals to true knowledge that can correct many of the young church's errors.

3-TRACK READING PLAN

For an explanation and complete listing of the 3-track reading plan, turn to page 7.

TRACK 1: *Two-Week Courses on the Bible*
See page 7 for information on these courses.

TRACK 2: *An Overview of 2 Peter in 1 Day*
☐ Day 1. Read the Introduction to 2 Peter, then chapter 1.
Now turn to page 9 for your next Track 2 reading project.

TRACK 3: *All of 2 Peter in 3 Days*
After you have read through 2 Peter, turn to pages 10–14 for your next Track 3 reading project.
☐1   ☐2   ☐3

1 Simon Peter, a servant and apostle of Jesus Christ,

To those who through the righteousness of our God and Savior Jesus Christ have received a faith as precious as ours:

²Grace and peace be yours in abundance through the knowledge of God and of Jesus our Lord.

Making One's Calling and Election Sure

³His divine power has given us everything we need for life and godliness through our knowledge of him who called us by his own glory and goodness. ⁴Through these he has given us his very great and precious promises, so that through them you may participate in the divine nature and escape the corruption in the world caused by evil desires.

⁵For this very reason, make every effort to add to your faith goodness; and to goodness, knowledge; ⁶and to knowledge, self-control; and to self-control, perseverance; and to perseverance, godliness; ⁷and to godliness, brotherly kindness; and to brotherly kindness, love. ⁸For if you possess these qualities in increasing measure, they will keep you from being ineffective and unproductive in your knowledge of our Lord Jesus Christ. ⁹But if anyone does not have them, he is nearsighted and blind, and has forgotten that he has been cleansed from his past sins.

¹⁰Therefore, my brothers, be all the more eager to make your calling and election sure. For if you do these things, you will never fall, ¹¹and you will receive a rich welcome into the eternal kingdom of our Lord and Savior Jesus Christ.

Prophecy of Scripture

¹²So I will always remind you of these things, even though you know them and are firmly established in the truth you now have. ¹³I think it is right to refresh your memory as long as I live in the tent of this body, ¹⁴because I know that I will soon put it aside, as our Lord Jesus Christ has

1:14 Approaching Death

The person writing these words was nearing death, a fact that may partially explain the book's forceful tone. An eyewitness (verse 16) of Jesus on earth was watching a young church stray from Christ's clear teaching. This letter may offer the last chance to oppose the deterioration.

made clear to me. ¹⁵And I will make every effort to see that after my departure you will always be able to remember these things.

¹⁶We did not follow cleverly invented stories when we told you about the power and coming of our Lord Jesus Christ, but we were eyewitnesses of his majesty. ¹⁷For he received honor and glory from God the Father when the voice came to him from the Majestic Glory, saying, "This is my Son, whom I love; with him I am well pleased."ᵃ ¹⁸We ourselves heard this voice that came from heaven when we were with him on the sacred mountain.

¹⁹And we have the word of the prophets made more certain, and you will do well to pay attention to it, as to a light shining in a dark place,

ᵃ17 Matt. 17:5; Mark 9:7; Luke 9:35

until the day dawns and the morning star rises in your hearts. ²⁰Above all, you must understand that no prophecy of Scripture came about by the prophet's own interpretation. ²¹For prophecy never had its origin in the will of man, but men spoke from God as they were carried along by the Holy Spirit.

False Teachers and Their Destruction

2 But there were also false prophets among the people, just as there will be false teachers among you. They will secretly introduce destructive heresies, even denying the sovereign Lord who bought them—bringing swift destruction on themselves. ²Many will follow their shameful ways and will bring the way of truth into disrepute. ³In their greed these teachers will exploit you with stories they have made up. Their condemnation has long been hanging over them, and their destruction has not been sleeping.

⁴For if God did not spare angels when they sinned, but sent them to hell,ᵃ putting them into gloomy dungeonsᵇ to be held for judgment; ⁵if he did not spare the ancient world when he brought the flood on its ungodly people, but protected Noah, a preacher of righteousness, and

2:5 Three Worlds

Second Peter refers to three great ages of the earth. The first, the ancient world, was destroyed by the flood in Noah's day. The present time, in which we are now living, will be destroyed by fire (3:10). But the author points with hope to an age that has not yet come: a new heaven and a new earth (3:13).

seven others; ⁶if he condemned the cities of Sodom and Gomorrah by burning them to ashes, and made them an example of what is going to happen to the ungodly; ⁷and if he rescued Lot, a righteous man, who was distressed by the filthy lives of lawless men ⁸(for that righteous man, living among them day after day, was tormented in his righteous soul by the lawless deeds he saw and heard)— ⁹if this is so, then the Lord knows how to rescue godly men from trials and to hold the unrighteous for the day of judgment, while continuing their punishment.ᶜ ¹⁰This is especially true of those who follow the corrupt desire of the sinful natureᵈ and despise authority.

Bold and arrogant, these men are not afraid to slander celestial beings; ¹¹yet even angels, although they are stronger and more powerful, do not bring slanderous accusations against such beings in the presence of the Lord. ¹²But these

men blaspheme in matters they do not understand. They are like brute beasts, creatures of instinct, born only to be caught and destroyed, and like beasts they too will perish.

¹³They will be paid back with harm for the harm they have done. Their idea of pleasure is to carouse in broad daylight. They are blots and blemishes, reveling in their pleasures while they feast with you.ᵉ ¹⁴With eyes full of adultery, they never stop sinning; they seduce the unstable; they are experts in greed—an accursed brood! ¹⁵They have left the straight way and wandered off to follow the way of Balaam son of Beor, who loved the wages of wickedness. ¹⁶But he was rebuked for his wrongdoing by a donkey—a beast without speech—who spoke with a man's voice and restrained the prophet's madness.

¹⁷These men are springs without water and mists driven by a storm. Blackest darkness is reserved for them. ¹⁸For they mouth empty, boastful words and, by appealing to the lustful desires of sinful human nature, they entice people who are just escaping from those who live in error. ¹⁹They promise them freedom, while they themselves are slaves of depravity—for a man is a slave to whatever has mastered him. ²⁰If they have escaped the corruption of the world by knowing our Lord and Savior Jesus Christ and are again entangled in it and overcome, they are worse off at the end than they were at the beginning. ²¹It would have been better for them not to have known the way of righteousness, than to have known it and then to turn their backs on the sacred command that was passed on to them. ²²Of them the proverbs are true: "A dog returns to its vomit,"ᶠ and, "A sow that is washed goes back to her wallowing in the mud."

The Day of the Lord

3 Dear friends, this is now my second letter to you. I have written both of them as reminders to stimulate you to wholesome thinking. ²I want you to recall the words spoken in the past by the holy prophets and the command given by our Lord and Savior through your apostles.

³First of all, you must understand that in the last days scoffers will come, scoffing and following their own evil desires. ⁴They will say, "Where is this 'coming' he promised? Ever since our fathers died, everything goes on as it has since the beginning of creation." ⁵But they deliberately forget that long ago by God's word the heavens existed and the earth was formed out of water and by water. ⁶By these waters also the world of that time was deluged and destroyed. ⁷By the same word the present heavens and earth are reserved for fire, being kept for the day of judgment and destruction of ungodly men.

ᵃ4 Greek *Tartarus*   ᵇ4 Some manuscripts *into chains of darkness*   ᶜ9 Or *unrighteous for punishment until the day of judgment*   ᵈ10 Or *the flesh*   ᵉ13 Some manuscripts *in their love feasts*   ᶠ22 Prov. 26:11

[8]But do not forget this one thing, dear friends: With the Lord a day is like a thousand years, and a thousand years are like a day. [9]The Lord is not slow in keeping his promise, as some understand slowness. He is patient with you, not wanting anyone to perish, but everyone to come to repentance.

[10]But the day of the Lord will come like a thief. The heavens will disappear with a roar; the elements will be destroyed by fire, and the earth and everything in it will be laid bare.[a]

3:10 The Fate of the Earth

The time of global destruction described here was a common theme in letters to the early churches. Talk of a coming judgment and the overthrow of the existing world threatened and alarmed Rome, the chief power in the existing world then. Such doomsday prophecies aroused Roman hostility against Christians.

[11]Since everything will be destroyed in this way, what kind of people ought you to be? You ought to live holy and godly lives [12]as you look forward to the day of God and speed its coming.[b] That day will bring about the destruction of the heavens by fire, and the elements will melt in the heat. [13]But in keeping with his promise we are looking forward to a new heaven and a new earth, the home of righteousness.

[14]So then, dear friends, since you are looking forward to this, make every effort to be found spotless, blameless and at peace with him. [15]Bear in mind that our Lord's patience means salvation, just as our dear brother Paul also wrote you

3:15 A Fellow Author

This comment is one of the rare instances in which a New Testament author refers directly to another New Testament book. Evidently, 2 Peter was written late enough that a group of Paul's letters already existed. Scholars use clues like this one to date books of the Bible.

with the wisdom that God gave him. [16]He writes the same way in all his letters, speaking in them of these matters. His letters contain some things that are hard to understand, which ignorant and unstable people distort, as they do the other Scriptures, to their own destruction.

[17]Therefore, dear friends, since you already know this, be on your guard so that you may not be carried away by the error of lawless men and fall from your secure position. [18]But grow in the grace and knowledge of our Lord and Savior Jesus Christ. To him be glory both now and forever! Amen.

---

[a] 10 Some manuscripts *be burned up*   [b] 12 Or *as you wait eagerly for the day of God to come*

1 JOHN

Words That Get Polluted
A problem with the new generation

> *Let us not love with words or tongue but with actions and in truth. 3:18*

OVER TIME, COMMON PHRASES CAN be stripped of meaning and applied to something else entirely. Take "born again," for example. First coined by Jesus, this phrase was resurrected in the sixties during the Jesus Movement. Soon it was snatched up as an advertising slogan to describe such things as a used car and even a comeback football player.

Christianity has been around so long that people borrow its words for quite different meanings. *Jesus*, the center of our faith, is also a common curse word.

Same Words, Different Meanings

This tendency to pollute language is not new. Even at the close of the first century, words were being twisted and drained of their original meanings. When the apostle John wrote his letters, the Christian faith was perhaps 50 or 60 years old. A generation had grown up in Christian homes, and a distinct subculture was already developing.

Some people were using familiar phrases such as "knowing God," "walk in the light," and "born of God," but with new, distorted meanings. The apostle responded with fire. He knew that a confused, subtle distortion of truth is harder to resist than an outright denial.

In this book, John chooses key words (*light, sin, Christ, love, faith*, etc.), "disinfects" them, and then restores their original meanings. He points back to the truths behind the words. Repeatedly, he begins with the phrase "If we claim . . . " and proceeds to show what actions must result if we claim to live in the true light and to know God.

A Step Further

John wrote his Gospel account of Jesus' life in order to bring readers to a belief in Christ (John 20:31). He directed this letter to people who were already Christians, outlining how that faith should affect a person's life. God is light, he says; so walk in the light. He is spirit; so worship him in the proper spirit. He is love; so demonstrate that love to others.

At times John shows the tender concern of a pastor, calling his readers "my dear children" (2:1) and urging them to "love one another" (3:11). But in other places his stern language hints at why he once wore the nickname "Son of Thunder."

John was probably the last surviving apostle when he wrote this book. He lived almost to the end of the first century. But he was not too old to fight vigorously against whatever might corrupt the faith that had inspired him for so many years.

How to Read 1 John

First John is constructed like a piece of music. Its author states a few simple themes—light, truth, life, love—then builds variations on them. Relying on simple words and a rhythmic style, John writes in universal terms that apply to any time period.

Yet the book is understood far better if you know something about the environment in which John was writing. Therefore, begin your reading with "Who Were the Gnostics?" on page 1309.

As you read John, note the pattern. He defines a word, such as *light*, discusses its opposite, *darkness,* and then describes what a life in the light should look like. In every case, he shows God as the source of power in the Christian life.

3-TRACK READING PLAN

For an explanation and complete listing of the 3-track reading plan, turn to page 7.

TRACK 1: ***Two-Week Courses on the Bible***
See page 7 for information on these courses.

TRACK 2: ***An Overview of 1 John in 1 Day***
☐ Day 1. Read the Introduction to 1 John, then chapter 3, a great summary of the love of God and how it should affect our lives.
Now turn to page 9 for your next Track 2 reading project.

TRACK 3: ***All of 1 John in 4 Days***
After you have read through 1 John, turn to pages 10–14 for your next Track 3 reading project.
☐1–2   ☐3   ☐4   ☐5

The Word of Life

1 That which was from the beginning, which we have heard, which we have seen with our eyes, which we have looked at and our hands have touched—this we proclaim concerning the Word of life. ²The life appeared; we have seen it and testify to it, and we proclaim to you the eternal life, which was with the Father and has appeared to us. ³We proclaim to you what we have seen and heard, so that you also may have fellowship with us. And our fellowship is with the

1:3–4 Eyewitness

In contrast to most New Testament letters, this one does not identify its author. Certain hints and distinctive patterns of style, though, make it very likely that the apostle John wrote it in advanced age. Simply compare the first paragraph of this letter with the first few paragraphs of the Gospel of John to see the similarities. The author also emphasizes that he was a close eyewitness of Jesus' life, a fact consistent with the "disciple whom Jesus loved."

Father and with his Son, Jesus Christ. ⁴We write this to make our*ᵃ* joy complete.

Walking in the Light

⁵This is the message we have heard from him and declare to you: God is light; in him there is no darkness at all. ⁶If we claim to have fellowship with him yet walk in the darkness, we lie and do not live by the truth. ⁷But if we walk in the light, as he is in the light, we have fellowship with one another, and the blood of Jesus, his Son, purifies us from all*ᵇ* sin.

⁸If we claim to be without sin, we deceive ourselves and the truth is not in us. ⁹If we confess our sins, he is faithful and just and will forgive us our sins and purify us from all unrighteousness. ¹⁰If we claim we have not sinned, we make him out to be a liar and his word has no place in our lives.

2 My dear children, I write this to you so that you will not sin. But if anybody does sin, we have one who speaks to the Father in our defense—Jesus Christ, the Righteous One. ²He is the atoning sacrifice for our sins, and not only for ours but also for*ᶜ* the sins of the whole world.

³We know that we have come to know him if we obey his commands. ⁴The man who says, "I know him," but does not do what he commands is a liar, and the truth is not in him. ⁵But if anyone obeys his word, God's love*ᵈ* is truly made complete in him. This is how we know we are in him: ⁶Whoever claims to live in him must walk as Jesus did.

⁷Dear friends, I am not writing you a new command but an old one, which you have had since the beginning. This old command is the message you have heard. ⁸Yet I am writing you a new command; its truth is seen in him and you, because the darkness is passing and the true light is already shining.

⁹Anyone who claims to be in the light but hates his brother is still in the darkness. ¹⁰Who-

---

ᵃ4 Some manuscripts *your and not only ours but also*   *ᵇ7* Or *every*   *ᶜ2* Or *He is the one who turns aside God's wrath, taking away our sins,*   *ᵈ5* Or *word, love for God*

ever loves his brother lives in the light, and there is nothing in him[a] to make him stumble. [11]But whoever hates his brother is in the darkness and walks around in the darkness; he does not know where he is going, because the darkness has blinded him.

[12]I write to you, dear children,
  because your sins have been forgiven on
    account of his name.
[13]I write to you, fathers,
  because you have known him who is from
    the beginning.
I write to you, young men,
  because you have overcome the evil one.
I write to you, dear children,
  because you have known the Father.
[14]I write to you, fathers,
  because you have known him who is from
    the beginning.
I write to you, young men,
  because you are strong,
  and the word of God lives in you,
  and you have overcome the evil one.

2:12 A Friendly Interruption

John begins his book with a stern warning against false ideas. But this lyrical section interrupts the flow with a warm greeting to true believers in the church. Many commentators believe that John intended the three categories (dear children, young men, fathers) to represent three different stages in his readers' spiritual lives.

Do Not Love the World

[15]Do not love the world or anything in the world. If anyone loves the world, the love of the Father is not in him. [16]For everything in the world—the cravings of sinful man, the lust of his eyes and the boasting of what he has and does—comes not from the Father but from the world. [17]The world and its desires pass away, but the man who does the will of God lives forever.

Warning Against Antichrists

[18]Dear children, this is the last hour; and as you have heard that the antichrist is coming, even now many antichrists have come. This is how we know it is the last hour. [19]They went out from us, but they did not really belong to us. For if they had belonged to us, they would have remained with us; but their going showed that none of them belonged to us. [20]But you have an anointing from the Holy One, and all of you know the truth.[b] [21]I do not

write to you because you do not know the truth, but because you do know it and because no lie comes from the truth. [22]Who is the liar? It is the man who denies that Jesus is the Christ. Such a man is the antichrist—he denies the Father and

2:22 Tough Love

John had two nicknames. "The apostle of love" uses the word love 35 times in this brief letter alone. But the letter also hints why he earned his original nickname, "Son of Thunder" (Mark 3:17). As one of Jesus' disciples, John had wanted to call fire down from heaven on unresponsive villages (Luke 9:54). Jesus rebuked such a notion, and John mellowed considerably over the years. Still, he reserves some choice words for enemies of the gospel: He brands them antichrists (2:18), liars (2:22), and children of the devil (3:10).

the Son. [23]No one who denies the Son has the Father; whoever acknowledges the Son has the Father also.

[24]See that what you have heard from the beginning remains in you. If it does, you also will remain in the Son and in the Father. [25]And this is what he promised us—even eternal life.

[26]I am writing these things to you about those who are trying to lead you astray. [27]As for you, the anointing you received from him remains in you, and you do not need anyone to teach you. But as his anointing teaches you about all things and as that anointing is real, not counterfeit—just as it has taught you, remain in him.

Children of God

[28]And now, dear children, continue in him, so that when he appears we may be confident and unashamed before him at his coming.

[29]If you know that he is righteous, you know that everyone who does what is right has been born of him.

3 How great is the love the Father has lavished on us, that we should be called children of God! And that is what we are! The reason the world does not know us is that it did not know him. [2]Dear friends, now we are children of God, and what we will be has not yet been made known. But we know that when he appears,[c] we shall be like him, for we shall see him as he is. [3]Everyone who has this hope in him purifies himself, just as he is pure.

[4]Everyone who sins breaks the law; in fact, sin is lawlessness. [5]But you know that he appeared so that he might take away our sins. And in him is no sin. [6]No one who lives in him keeps on sin-

---

[a]10 Or it   [b]20 Some manuscripts *and you know all things*   [c]2 Or *when it is made known*

ning. No one who continues to sin has either seen him or known him.

[7]Dear children, do not let anyone lead you astray. He who does what is right is righteous, just as he is righteous. [8]He who does what is sinful is of the devil, because the devil has been sinning from the beginning. The reason the Son of God appeared was to destroy the devil's work. [9]No one who is born of God will continue to sin, because God's seed remains in him; he cannot go on sinning, because he has been born of God. [10]This is how we know who the children of God are and who the children of the devil are: Anyone who does not do what is right is not a child of God; nor is anyone who does not love his brother.

Love One Another

[11]This is the message you heard from the beginning: We should love one another. [12]Do not

---

3:11 Love Versus Hate

Very often John defines words in relation to their opposites: light versus darkness, truth versus falsehood, life versus death. In this paragraph, he begins with a command to "love one another," then goes on to illustrate the life of hate before coming back to define love. Many of 1 John's themes are developed in this "circular" method.

---

be like Cain, who belonged to the evil one and murdered his brother. And why did he murder him? Because his own actions were evil and his brother's were righteous. [13]Do not be surprised, my brothers, if the world hates you. [14]We know that we have passed from death to life, because we love our brothers. Anyone who does not love remains in death. [15]Anyone who hates his brother is a murderer, and you know that no murderer has eternal life in him.

[16]This is how we know what love is: Jesus Christ laid down his life for us. And we ought to lay down our lives for our brothers. [17]If anyone has material possessions and sees his brother in need but has no pity on him, how can the love of God be in him? [18]Dear children, let us not love with words or tongue but with actions and in truth. [19]This then is how we know that we belong to the truth, and how we set our hearts at rest in his presence [20]whenever our hearts condemn us. For God is greater than our hearts, and he knows everything.

[21]Dear friends, if our hearts do not condemn us, we have confidence before God [22]and receive from him anything we ask, because we obey his commands and do what pleases him. [23]And this is his command: to believe in the name of his Son, Jesus Christ, and to love one another as he commanded us. [24]Those who obey his commands live in him, and he in them. And this is how we know that he lives in us: We know it by the Spirit he gave us.

Test the Spirits

4 Dear friends, do not believe every spirit, but test the spirits to see whether they are from God, because many false prophets have gone out into the world. [2]This is how you can recognize the Spirit of God: Every spirit that acknowledges that Jesus Christ has come in the flesh is from God, [3]but every spirit that does not acknowledge Jesus is not from God. This is the spirit of the antichrist, which you have heard is coming and even now is already in the world.

[4]You, dear children, are from God and have overcome them, because the one who is in you is greater than the one who is in the world. [5]They are from the world and therefore speak from the viewpoint of the world, and the world listens to them. [6]We are from God, and whoever knows God listens to us; but whoever is not from God does not listen to us. This is how we recognize the Spirit[a] of truth and the spirit of falsehood.

God's Love and Ours

[7]Dear friends, let us love one another, for love comes from God. Everyone who loves has been born of God and knows God. [8]Whoever does not love does not know God, because God is love. [9]This is how God showed his love among us: He sent his one and only Son[b] into the world that we might live through him. [10]This is love: not that we loved God, but that he loved us and sent his Son as an atoning sacrifice for[c] our sins. [11]Dear friends, since God so loved us, we also ought to love one another. [12]No one has ever seen God; but if we love one another, God lives in us and his love is made complete in us.

[13]We know that we live in him and he in us, because he has given us of his Spirit. [14]And we have seen and testify that the Father has sent his Son to be the Savior of the world. [15]If anyone acknowledges that Jesus is the Son of God, God lives in him and he in God. [16]And so we know and rely on the love God has for us.

God is love. Whoever lives in love lives in God, and God in him. [17]In this way, love is made complete among us so that we will have confidence on the day of judgment, because in this world we are like him. [18]There is no fear in love. But perfect love drives out fear, because fear has to do with punishment. The one who fears is not made perfect in love.

---

[a]6 Or *spirit*　　[b]9 Or *his only begotten Son*　　[c]10 Or *as the one who would turn aside his wrath, taking away*

[19]We love because he first loved us. [20]If anyone says, "I love God," yet hates his brother, is a liar. For anyone who does not love his brother, whom he has seen, cannot love God, whom he has not seen. [21]And he has given us this command: Whoever loves God must also love his brother.

Faith in the Son of God

5 Everyone who believes that Jesus is the Christ is born of God, and everyone who loves the father loves his child as well. [2]This is how we know that we love the children of God: by loving God and carrying out his commands. [3]This is love for God: to obey his commands. And his commands are not burdensome, [4]for everyone born of God overcomes the world. This is the victory that has overcome the world, even our faith. [5]Who is it that overcomes the world? Only he who believes that Jesus is the Son of God.

[6]This is the one who came by water and blood—Jesus Christ. He did not come by water only, but by water and blood. And it is the Spirit who testifies, because the Spirit is the truth. [7]For there are three that testify: [8]the[a] Spirit, the water and the blood; and the three are in agreement. [9]We accept man's testimony, but God's testimony is greater because it is the testimony of God, which he has given about his Son. [10]Anyone who believes in the Son of God has this testimony in his heart. Anyone who does not believe God has made him out to be a liar, because he has not

---

[a]7,8 Late manuscripts of the Vulgate *testify in heaven: the Father, the Word and the Holy Spirit, and these three are one.* [8]*And there are three that testify on earth: the* (not found in any Greek manuscript before the sixteenth century)

Who Were the Gnostics?
A dangerous cult that proved fatally attractive

AS CHRISTIANITY SPREAD ACROSS THE Mediterranean, it came into contact with other religions. Greeks and Romans tried to absorb the faith into their own philosophies, just as some Jews had initially.

Intellectual centers of the Mediterranean raised questions about Jesus: Who was he? If he was God, how could he die? And a popular new cult called Gnosticism (from the Greek word for knowledge, *gnosis*) gained ground in an attempt to explain these things. The cult thrived, especially among the intellectual elite.

> *This is how you can recognize the Spirit of God: Every spirit that acknowledges that Jesus Christ has come in the flesh is from God. 4:2*

Could God Have a Body?

Gnostics balked at the Christian concept of God's becoming human. Because they believed a physical body was intrinsically evil, they denied that a pure God could take on a body. Some dealt with the problem by claiming that Jesus was never a real human being, but a phantom, a temporary appearance of God who only looked human. Others proposed that God had "descended" on Jesus at his baptism, but left him before his death.

The apostle John debated in person with Gnostics of his day, and he had Gnostic thinking in mind when he wrote this letter. The very first sentence expressly states that the author has seen, heard, and touched Jesus—implying he could not have been a phantom, or pure spirit. Throughout the letter, and especially in 4:2–3, the author lambastes those who deny that Jesus came in the flesh.

Live As You Please

To Gnostics, all matter was evil. Only the spirit was pure, and Gnostics sought to rise to a higher, more spiritual plane. This teaching often produced a side effect: People who strove to rise above matter didn't care about personal ethics. Their pure spirits could not be tainted by "earthly" sin. Thus, they could act any way they wanted.

Aging John roared out against the twin dangers of Gnosticism: immoral living and doubts that Christ became a man. Beliefs must be judged by the actions they produce, and John stresses the theme of brotherly love. He primarily refutes errors by presenting a wholesome picture of the Christian life as it is supposed to be lived.

True fellowship is not a secret initiation into a New Age-type elite, but a relationship with the Father through Christ. And that also entails responsibilities to others in God's family.

Life Questions: Gnosticism showed itself in several ways: the belief that matter was evil, a desire for "super-spirituality," a tendency toward loose morals. How can we counter those same trends among Christians today?

believed the testimony God has given about his Son. [11]And this is the testimony: God has given us eternal life, and this life is in his Son. [12]He who has the Son has life; he who does not have the Son of God does not have life.

5:8 Water, Blood, and Spirit

The apostle John relied heavily on symbolic language in his Gospel account of Jesus' life. Here, too, he uses symbols in giving proofs of Jesus. Water may refer to Jesus' baptism, blood to his death on the cross, and the Spirit to the Holy Spirit who descended on Jesus. John refers to these three as a "testimony" from God about his Son.

Concluding Remarks

[13]I write these things to you who believe in the name of the Son of God so that you may know that you have eternal life. [14]This is the confidence we have in approaching God: that if we ask anything according to his will, he hears us. [15]And if we know that he hears us—whatever we ask— we know that we have what we asked of him.

[16]If anyone sees his brother commit a sin that does not lead to death, he should pray and God will give him life. I refer to those whose sin does not lead to death. There is a sin that leads to death. I am not saying that he should pray about that. [17]All wrongdoing is sin, and there is sin that does not lead to death.

[18]We know that anyone born of God does not continue to sin; the one who was born of God keeps him safe, and the evil one cannot harm him. [19]We know that we are children of God, and that the whole world is under the control of the evil one. [20]We know also that the Son of God has come and has given us understanding, so that we may know him who is true. And we are in him who is true—even in his Son Jesus Christ. He is the true God and eternal life.

[21]Dear children, keep yourselves from idols.

2 JOHN

Undesirable Guests
When a "Welcome" sign is inappropriate

> Watch out that you do not lose what you have worked for. 8

ROMAN ROADS MADE FIRST-CENTURY TRAVEL safer and easier than ever before, but Holiday Inns were still centuries away. Therefore, when teachers of the Christian faith traveled the empire, they relied on local Christians for food and lodging.

Before long, false teachers (such as Gnostics) also hit the circuit, joined by religious racketeers attracted primarily to the free food and lodging. The two letters, 2 John and 3 John, the shortest books in the entire Bible, concern themselves with the mounting problems of hospitality for the "circuit-rider" teachers.

Show Discretion, But Also Love

Heresies had already sprung up in many local churches, and 2 John urges true Christians to use discretion in testing a visitor's message and motive. The author cautions against entertaining visitors who do not teach the truth about Christ.

True to his nickname, the apostle of love repeats his motto, "Love one another," even in this letter of warning. The ancient writer Jerome (A.D. 374–419) tells of the frail apostle John, in extreme old age, being carried into his congregation mumbling only, "Love one another." When asked why he talked of nothing else, John replied, "Because it is the Lord's command, and if this only is done, it is enough."

How to Read 2 and 3 John

These two books are best read together, since each gives one side of a problem facing a young church. Try to imagine the setting back then, when Christianity was still new and many teachers came along claiming special insights. Do you see any parallels among Christians today? Look for the specific advice John gave in those circumstances.

3-TRACK READING PLAN

For an explanation and complete listing of the 3-track reading plan, turn to page 7.

TRACK 1: *Two-Week Courses on the Bible*
See page 7 for information on these courses.

TRACK 2: *Read 2 and 3 John Together in 1 Day*
☐ Day 1. These books are only one short chapter each, so you can easily read the two together.
Now turn to page 9 for your next Track 2 reading project.

TRACK 3: *All of 2 and 3 John in 1 Day*
Read both books in one day. After you have finished, turn to pages 10–14 for your next Track 3 reading project.
☐2 John, 3 John

¹The elder,

To the chosen lady and her children, whom I love in the truth—and not I only, but also all who know the truth— ²because of the truth, which lives in us and will be with us forever:

³Grace, mercy and peace from God the Father and from Jesus Christ, the Father's Son, will be with us in truth and love.

⁴It has given me great joy to find some of your children walking in the truth, just as the Father commanded us. ⁵And now, dear lady, I am not writing you a new command but one we have had from the beginning. I ask that we love one another. ⁶And this is love: that we walk in obedience to his commands. As you have heard from the beginning, his command is that you walk in love.

⁷Many deceivers, who do not acknowledge Jesus Christ as coming in the flesh, have gone out into the world. Any such person is the deceiver and the antichrist. ⁸Watch out that you do not lose what you have worked for, but that you may be rewarded fully. ⁹Anyone who runs ahead and does not continue in the teaching of Christ does not have God; whoever continues in the teaching has both the Father and the Son. ¹⁰If anyone comes to you and does not bring this teaching, do not take him into your house or welcome him. ¹¹Anyone who welcomes him shares in his wicked work.

7 Pesky Deceivers

This paragraph shows that the enemies warned about in 1 John were still roaming about, stirring up trouble in the churches. The description of their beliefs—"who do not acknowledge Jesus Christ as coming in the flesh"—brings to mind the teaching of the Gnostics (see "Who Were the Gnostics?" page 1309), one of the main targets of that first letter.

¹²I have much to write to you, but I do not want to use paper and ink. Instead, I hope to visit you and talk with you face to face, so that our joy may be complete.

¹³The children of your chosen sister send their greetings.

3 JOHN

Guidelines for Hospitality
The same questions crop up in every age, in every place

TAKEN TOGETHER, THIS LETTER AND its companion give a balanced view of proper Christian hospitality. Second John warned against entertaining false teachers. But 3 John praises a man named Gaius for warmly welcoming genuine Christian teachers. His actions had been opposed by Diotrephes, a cantankerous church dictator, who was also gossiping against John.

In a very condensed form, John's two letters deal with heresy and church splits, two problems that have plagued the church in every age, in every place. To defend against those dangers, John urges love and discernment. Believers must know whom to accept and support, and whom to resist.

> *I have no greater joy than to hear that my children are walking in the truth. 4*

How to Read 3 John

See How to Read 2 and 3 John, page 1310.

¹The elder,

To my dear friend Gaius, whom I love in the truth.

²Dear friend, I pray that you may enjoy good health and that all may go well with you, even as your soul is getting along well. ³It gave me great joy to have some brothers come and tell about your faithfulness to the truth and how you continue to walk in the truth. ⁴I have no greater joy than to hear that my children are walking in the truth.

⁵Dear friend, you are faithful in what you are doing for the brothers, even though they are strangers to you. ⁶They have told the church about your love. You will do well to send them on their way in a manner worthy of God. ⁷It was for the sake of the Name that they went out, receiving no help from the pagans. ⁸We ought therefore to show hospitality to such men so that we may work together for the truth.

⁹I wrote to the church, but Diotrephes, who loves to be first, will have nothing to do with us. ¹⁰So if I come, I will call attention to what he is doing, gossiping maliciously about us. Not satisfied with that, he refuses to welcome the brothers. He also stops those who want to do so and puts them out of the church.

¹¹Dear friend, do not imitate what is evil but what is good. Anyone who does what is good is from God. Anyone who does what is evil has not seen God. ¹²Demetrius is well spoken of by everyone—and even by the truth itself. We also speak well of him, and you know that our testimony is true.

¹³I have much to write you, but I do not want to do so with pen and ink. ¹⁴I hope to see you soon, and we will talk face to face.

Peace to you. The friends here send their greetings. Greet the friends there by name.

4 No Greater Joy

Scholars estimate that the apostle John was between 80 and 90 years old when he wrote the letters bearing his name. He identifies himself as "the elder" (which may also refer to his office in a local church) and writes fondly of "my children." The letters carry the tone of an old man dispensing his last words of advice and taking grandfatherly pride in the progress of his spiritual heirs.

JUDE

Watch Out!
Sounding an alarm

I felt I had to write and urge you to contend for the faith. 3

IF YOU SIGN UP FOR a driver's training course, you'll begin with several hours of classroom lectures on "Rules of the Road." The instructor will drill you on the shapes and colors of warning signs—signs that announce danger on the highways.

Driving seems all very academic, until you slide behind the wheel. There, a missed stop sign won't just lower a test score; it could cost you your life. Your instructor, rather than calmly correcting you, will shout, "Look out!"

Jude writes in the style of a teacher who is watching a freight train bear down on his student driver. Bells ring out, crossing gates go down, red lights flash. He admits this kind of letter isn't his preference; he intended a more high-minded treatise on salvation (verse 3). But the church was facing mortal dangers, and so Jude dashed off a vehement warning.

Who Were the Troublemakers?

Jude doesn't elaborate on what the troublemakers (verse 4) were teaching—perhaps he didn't want to honor their ideas by discussing them. Their behavior, however, is fair game: He fires away at their hypocrisy, divisiveness, and loose morals. He calls them spies and urges believers to fight for the true faith. At his poetic best, he borrows vivid images from nature to describe these people (12–13).

Short and vigorous, the book of Jude brings to mind a message from one of the fiery Old Testament prophets. Yet Jude holds out hope for his readers. Sincere believers can keep themselves in God's love, and some wavering souls can still be snatched "from the fire" (21–23). (Even when battling heretics, Jude does not hint at persecuting the offenders—no burnings at the stake here.)

Jude closes with a familiar and joy-filled doxology, the one part of his letter still quoted widely in modern churches.

How to Read Jude

In tone, Jude reads a lot like James and 2 Peter: It is simple, hard-hitting, and stern. In fact, it seems to copy entire sections of 2 Peter.

You can read through Jude in a few minutes, to get the force of his argument. But to truly appreciate his letter, you should reflect on (and look up) his various Old Testament references. Jude supports his arguments with extensive illustrations from history, and he even quotes from two Jewish books not accepted as part of the Bible, *The Assumption of Moses* (verse 9) and the book of *Enoch* (verse 14).

All these citations support Jude's main thrust, which he summarizes eloquently in the last few paragraphs.

3-TRACK READING PLAN

For an explanation and complete listing of the 3-track reading plan, turn to page 7.

TRACK 1: **Two-Week Courses on the Bible**
See page 7 for information on these courses.

TRACK 2: **Read Jude in 1 Day**
☐ Day 1. Just one chapter long, Jude will take only a few minutes to read.
Now turn to page 9 for your next Track 2 reading project.

TRACK 3: **All of Jude in 1 Day**
After you have read Jude, turn to pages 10–14 for your next Track 3 reading project.
☐ Jude

¹Jude, a servant of Jesus Christ and a brother of James,

To those who have been called, who are loved by God the Father and kept by*ᵃ* Jesus Christ:

²Mercy, peace and love be yours in abundance.

The Sin and Doom of Godless Men

³Dear friends, although I was very eager to write to you about the salvation we share, I felt I had to write and urge you to contend for the faith that was once for all entrusted to the saints. ⁴For certain men whose condemnation was written about*ᵇ* long ago have secretly slipped in among you. They are godless men, who change the grace of our God into a license for immorality and deny Jesus Christ our only Sovereign and Lord.

⁵Though you already know all this, I want to remind you that the Lord*ᶜ* delivered his people out of Egypt, but later destroyed those who did not believe. ⁶And the angels who did not keep their positions of authority but abandoned their own home—these he has kept in darkness, bound with everlasting chains for judgment on the great Day. ⁷In a similar way, Sodom and Gomorrah and the surrounding towns gave themselves up to sexual immorality and perversion. They serve as an example of those who suffer the punishment of eternal fire.

⁸In the very same way, these dreamers pollute their own bodies, reject authority and slander celestial beings. ⁹But even the archangel Michael, when he was disputing with the devil about the body of Moses, did not dare to bring a slanderous accusation against him, but said, "The Lord rebuke you!" ¹⁰Yet these men speak abusively against whatever they do not understand; and what things they do understand by instinct, like unreasoning animals—these are the very things that destroy them.

¹¹Woe to them! They have taken the way of Cain; they have rushed for profit into Balaam's error; they have been destroyed in Korah's rebellion.

¹²These men are blemishes at your love feasts, eating with you without the slightest qualm—shepherds who feed only themselves. They are clouds without rain, blown along by the wind; autumn trees, without fruit and uprooted—twice dead. ¹³They are wild waves of the sea, foaming up their shame; wandering stars, for whom blackest darkness has been reserved forever.

11 Bad Models

Jude mentions three Old Testament characters as powerful illustrations of qualities to avoid: the selfishness of Cain, the greed of Balaam, the rebelliousness of Korah. (Their stories can be found in Genesis 4, Numbers 22, and Numbers 16.) After filling his letter with such negative examples, however, Jude concludes triumphantly that God "is able to keep you from falling" (verse 24).

¹⁴Enoch, the seventh from Adam, prophesied about these men: "See, the Lord is coming with thousands upon thousands of his holy ones ¹⁵to judge everyone, and to convict all the ungodly of all the ungodly acts they have done in the ungodly way, and of all the harsh words ungodly sinners have spoken against him." ¹⁶These men are grumblers and faultfinders; they follow their own evil desires; they boast about themselves and flatter others for their own advantage.

A Call to Persevere

¹⁷But, dear friends, remember what the apostles of our Lord Jesus Christ foretold. ¹⁸They said to you, "In the last times there will be scoffers who will follow their own ungodly desires." ¹⁹These are the men who divide you, who follow mere natural instincts and do not have the Spirit.

²⁰But you, dear friends, build yourselves up in your most holy faith and pray in the Holy Spirit.

---

*ᵃ*1 Or *for;* or *in*   *ᵇ*4 Or *men who were marked out for condemnation*   *ᶜ*5 Some early manuscripts *Jesus*

²¹Keep yourselves in God's love as you wait for the mercy of our Lord Jesus Christ to bring you to eternal life.

²²Be merciful to those who doubt; ²³snatch others from the fire and save them; to others show mercy, mixed with fear—hating even the clothing stained by corrupted flesh.

Doxology

²⁴To him who is able to keep you from falling and to present you before his glorious presence without fault and with great joy— ²⁵to the only God our Savior be glory, majesty, power and authority, through Jesus Christ our Lord, before all ages, now and forevermore! Amen.

REVELATION

A Book Full of Mysteries
Why Revelation is hard to understand

T HE ROMAN EMPIRE HAD ITS own version of Alcatraz: a rocky island called Patmos. Prisoners banished to that hard-labor colony usually wasted away and died. In that desolate setting a man named John had a series of visions he wrote down as Revelation, the strangest book in the New Testament.

John probably wrote this book about 60 years after Jesus left the earth. Questions were troubling the church. Was Jesus coming back as he had promised? Where did he go? To do what? Why didn't he return immediately? Revelation addresses those issues.

> *Blessed is the one who reads the words of this prophecy, and blessed are those who hear it and take to heart what is written in it, because the time is near. 1:3*

Writing in Code

No other New Testament book resembles Revelation in style. Yet during its time similar Jewish "apocalyptic" books (books that symbolically picture the ultimate destruction of evil and the triumph of good) flourished. Authors, writing to persecuted Christians anxious about their future, predicted what would take place. Often, they used coded language to protect theselves; for example, they substituted a word like *Babylon* when criticizing Rome, just in case their writings fell into the wrong hands.

The codes in Revelation are effective—so effective that few people today agree on exactly what they mean. Some people think many of the predictions in Revelation have not yet been fulfilled; perhaps John was writing about events that will come to pass in our own generation, they say. A best-selling book, Hal Lindsey's *The Late Great Planet Earth,* interprets Revelation that way.

Others explain Revelation in terms of the first century, concluding that many of the events prophesied in code took place during the Roman empire. Still others find clues to John's meaning spread out over 2,000 years of church history, or surmise that he employed symbols merely to describe an idealized battle of good and evil.

Two Dangers

Because of all the conflicting theories about Revelation, readers are tempted to respond in one of two ways. Some judge the book so perplexingly weird that they can find no reason to read it at all. How can anyone be sure of its meaning?

Others fall prey to the opposite danger. They pore over Revelation and conclude they have discovered the secret explanation of each obscure detail. To the latter group, it may be humbling to learn that every generation since the first century has come up with different interpretations of the prophecies.

Why Read Revelation?

Why read this strange book? John gives a good clue in the first phrase, which introduces this book as "the revelation of Jesus Christ." Revelation gives a unique picture of Jesus Christ, and the New Testament would be incomplete without it. The Gospels describe Jesus' life on earth from four different viewpoints. The letters discuss the deep significance of the resurrected Christ and what he accomplished. But Revelation shows Jesus Christ from a new perspective: as the mighty ruler of the cosmic forces of good. When John saw him in this exalted state, he fell at Jesus' feet as though dead (1:17).

Although Revelation does not remove the mystery surrounding Jesus' return and the end of the world, it does throw light on those events. It cannot be reduced to a mere timetable of events; it speaks lasting truths to every generation of readers. Revelation tells of Christ's future triumph over all the evil in the universe. This crucial message of final hope was needed by its original readers in the first century and is still needed by us today.

How to Read Revelation

Revelation is probably the most intimidating book in the Bible. It packs in so many symbols and obscure details that most readers find themselves plagued by the sensation that they are missing something.

All new forms of writing seem intimidating at first: for example, consider your very first science fiction book, filled with weird names and unearthly creatures, and governed by its own rules of writing. Science fiction seems very strange until you learn the techniques used by virtually all science fiction writers. Once you understand the form, it makes more sense. The same applies to Revelation. It will likely seem strange at first, because it uses techniques of symbolism and visions not commonly used elsewhere in the New Testament.

It is best to read Revelation one vision at a time, rather than all at once. The seven main visions give a view of similar events from different angles.

1. The church on earth (1—3)
2. The Lamb and the seven seals (4—7)
3. Seven angels with trumpets (8—11)
4. The church persecuted by Satan and the beast (12—14)
5. The seven bowls of God's wrath (15—16)
6. Judgment of Babylon (17—19:10).
7. Final judgment and final victory (19:11 to end).

Try to read completely through a vision, following the boldface sectional headings marked in the Bible text.

As you read, look behind the visual symbols for the meaning they point to. Ask yourself, What does this tell me about Christ, about God, about the real meaning of history? Don't try to analyze details at first; just follow the main flow of thought.

Keep in mind also the condition of the persecuted Christians who first received this book. They needed not a precise calendar of future events, but rather a word of encouragement and hope. They needed faith that, no matter how things looked, God was in charge of history and good would ultimately triumph. Revelation provides this hope, for them and for us.

Finally, a good Bible dictionary or commentary will clear up much of the confusion about Revelation.

3-TRACK READING PLAN

For an explanation and complete listing of the 3-track reading plan, turn to page 7.

TRACK 1: *Two-Week Courses on the Bible*
See page 7 for information on these courses.

TRACK 2: *An Overview of Revelation in 3 Days*
☐ Day 1. Read the Introduction to Revelation, then chapter 1, to see how John introduces this book.
☐ Day 2. Read chapter 12 as a sample of the writing contained in this book of visions.
☐ Day 3. Read chapter 21 for a glimpse of the final end of the universe.

Now turn to page 9 for your next Track 2 reading project.

TRACK 3: *All of Revelation in 19 Days*
After you have read through Revelation, turn to pages 10—14 for your next Track 3 reading project.

☐1 ☐2 ☐3 ☐4—5 ☐6 ☐7 ☐8 ☐9
☐10—11 ☐12 ☐13 ☐14 ☐15—16 ☐17 ☐18 ☐19
☐20 ☐21 ☐22

Prologue

1 The revelation of Jesus Christ, which God gave him to show his servants what must soon take place. He made it known by sending his angel to his servant John, [2]who testifies to everything he saw—that is, the word of God and the testimony of Jesus Christ. [3]Blessed is the one who reads the words of this prophecy, and blessed are those who hear it and take to heart what is written in it, because the time is near.

Greetings and Doxology

[4]John,

To the seven churches in the province of Asia:

Grace and peace to you from him who is, and who was, and who is to come, and from the seven spirits[a] before his throne, [5]and from Jesus Christ, who is the faithful witness, the firstborn from the dead, and the ruler of the kings of the earth.

To him who loves us and has freed us from our sins by his blood, [6]and has made us to be a kingdom and priests to serve his God and Father—to him be glory and power for ever and ever! Amen.

[7]Look, he is coming with the clouds,
and every eye will see him,
even those who pierced him;
and all the peoples of the earth will
mourn because of him.
So shall it be! Amen.

[8]"I am the Alpha and the Omega," says the Lord God, "who is, and who was, and who is to come, the Almighty."

One Like a Son of Man

[9]I, John, your brother and companion in the suffering and kingdom and patient endurance that are ours in Jesus, was on the island of Patmos because of the word of God and the testimony of Jesus. [10]On the Lord's Day I was in the Spirit, and I heard behind me a loud voice like a trumpet, [11]which said: "Write on a scroll what you see and send it to the seven churches: to Ephesus, Smyrna, Pergamum, Thyatira, Sardis, Philadelphia and Laodicea."

[12]I turned around to see the voice that was speaking to me. And when I turned I saw seven golden lampstands, [13]and among the lampstands was someone "like a son of man,"[b] dressed in a robe reaching down to his feet and with a golden sash around his chest. [14]His head and hair were white like wool, as white as snow, and his eyes were like blazing fire. [15]His feet were like bronze glowing in a furnace, and his voice was like the sound of rushing waters. [16]In his right hand he held seven stars, and out of his mouth came a sharp double-edged sword. His face was like the sun shining in all its brilliance.

1:13 Familiar Title

Revelation's original readers would have recognized this description immediately, for Jesus used the title "Son of Man" about 90 times in the Gospels. The phrase first appears in Daniel 7:13, introducing the Messiah who would rule all history.

[17]When I saw him, I fell at his feet as though dead. Then he placed his right hand on me and said: "Do not be afraid. I am the First and the Last. [18]I am the Living One; I was dead, and behold I am alive for ever and ever! And I hold the keys of death and Hades.

[19]"Write, therefore, what you have seen, what is now and what will take place later. [20]The mystery of the seven stars that you saw in my right hand and of the seven golden lampstands is this: The seven stars are the angels[c] of the seven churches, and the seven lampstands are the seven churches.

To the Church in Ephesus

2 "To the angel[d] of the church in Ephesus write:

These are the words of him who holds the seven stars in his right hand and walks among the seven golden lampstands: [2]I know your deeds, your hard work and your perseverance. I know that you cannot tolerate wicked men, that you have tested those who claim to be apostles but are not, and have found them false. [3]You have persevered and have endured hardships for my name, and have not grown weary.

[4]Yet I hold this against you: You have forsaken your first love. [5]Remember the height from which you have fallen! Repent and do the things you did at first. If you do not repent, I will come to you and remove your lampstand from its place. [6]But you have this in your favor: You hate the practices of the Nicolaitans, which I also hate.

[7]He who has an ear, let him hear what the Spirit says to the churches. To him who overcomes, I will give the right to eat from the tree of life, which is in the paradise of God.

---

a4 Or *the sevenfold Spirit*   *b13* Daniel 7:13   *c20* Or *messengers*   *d1* Or *messenger*; also in verses 8, 12 and 18

To the Church in Smyrna

[8]"To the angel of the church in Smyrna write:

These are the words of him who is the First and the Last, who died and came to life again. [9]I know your afflictions and your poverty—yet you are rich! I know the slander of those who say they are Jews and are not, but are a synagogue of Satan. [10]Do not be afraid of what you are about to suffer. I tell you, the devil will put some of you in prison to test you, and you will suffer persecution for ten days. Be faithful, even to the point of death, and I will give you the crown of life.

[11]He who has an ear, let him hear what the Spirit says to the churches. He who overcomes will not be hurt at all by the second death.

To the Church in Pergamum

[12]"To the angel of the church in Pergamum write:

These are the words of him who has the sharp, double-edged sword. [13]I know where you live—where Satan has his throne. Yet you remain true to my name. You did not renounce your faith in me, even in the days of Antipas, my faithful witness, who was put to death in your city—where Satan lives.

2:13 Satan's Throne

When John wrote Revelation, the first century was drawing to a close. Now clearly separate from Judaism, the Christian church had lost its semi-official protection, and Roman emperors such as Nero had directed bloody persecutions. Antipas, mentioned here, was the first martyr of western Asia. The city of Pergamum served as headquarters for several pagan cults, and the practice of emperor worship spread from here throughout the region—possibly the meaning behind the phrase "where Satan has his throne."

---

[14]Nevertheless, I have a few things against you: You have people there who hold to the teaching of Balaam, who taught Balak to entice the Israelites to sin by eating food sacrificed to idols and by committing sexual immorality. [15]Likewise you also have those who hold to the teaching of the Nicolaitans. [16]Repent therefore! Otherwise, I will soon come to you and will fight against them with the sword of my mouth.

[17]He who has an ear, let him hear what the Spirit says to the churches. To him who overcomes, I will give some of the hidden manna. I will also give him a white stone with a new name written on it, known only to him who receives it.

To the Church in Thyatira

[18]"To the angel of the church in Thyatira write:

These are the words of the Son of God, whose eyes are like blazing fire and whose feet are like burnished bronze. [19]I know your deeds, your love and faith, your service and perseverance, and that you are now doing more than you did at first.

[20]Nevertheless, I have this against you: You tolerate that woman Jezebel, who calls herself a prophetess. By her teaching she misleads my servants into sexual immorality and the eating of food sacrificed to idols. [21]I have given her time to repent of her immorality, but she is unwilling. [22]So I will cast her on a bed of suffering, and I will make those who commit adultery with her suffer intensely, unless they repent of her ways. [23]I will strike her children dead. Then all the churches will know that I am he who searches hearts and minds, and I will repay each of you according to your deeds. [24]Now I say to the rest of you in Thyatira, to you who do not hold to her teaching and have not learned Satan's so-called deep secrets (I will not impose any other burden on you): [25]Only hold on to what you have until I come.

[26]To him who overcomes and does my will to the end, I will give authority over the nations—

[27]"He will rule them with an iron scepter;
    he will dash them to pieces like
        pottery'[a]—

just as I have received authority from my Father. [28]I will also give him the morning star. [29]He who has an ear, let him hear what the Spirit says to the churches.

To the Church in Sardis

3 "To the angel[b] of the church in Sardis write:

These are the words of him who holds the seven spirits[c] of God and the seven stars. I know your deeds; you have a reputation of being alive, but you are dead. [2]Wake up! Strengthen what remains and is about to die, for I have not found your deeds complete in the sight of my God. [3]Remember, therefore, what you have received and heard; obey it, and repent. But

---

[a]27 Psalm 2:9   [b]1 Or *messenger*; also in verses 7 and 14   [c]1 Or *the sevenfold Spirit*

if you do not wake up, I will come like a thief, and you will not know at what time I will come to you.

⁴Yet you have a few people in Sardis who have not soiled their clothes. They will walk with me, dressed in white, for they are worthy. ⁵He who overcomes will, like them, be dressed in white. I will never blot out his name from the book of life, but will acknowledge his name before my Father and his angels. ⁶He who has an ear, let him hear what the Spirit says to the churches.

3:1 Cities on a Mail Route

The cities mentioned in chapters 2 and 3 were actual cities in the ancient world where a church existed. John listed them in the order in which a messenger on the road would have found them, starting with the chief city of Ephesus and then circling back clockwise. The cities lie in what is now part of modern Turkey. Religious wars took their toll: None of the churches in these cities survived.

To the Church in Philadelphia

⁷"To the angel of the church in Philadelphia write:

These are the words of him who is holy and true, who holds the key of David. What he opens no one can shut, and what he shuts no one can open. ⁸I know your deeds. See, I have placed before you an open door that no one can shut. I know that you have little strength, yet you have kept my word and have not denied my name. ⁹I will make those who are of the synagogue of Satan, who claim to be Jews though they are not, but are liars—I will make them come and fall down at your feet and acknowledge that I have loved you. ¹⁰Since you have kept my command to endure patiently, I will also keep you from the hour of trial that is going to come upon the whole world to test those who live on the earth.

¹¹I am coming soon. Hold on to what you have, so that no one will take your crown. ¹²Him who overcomes I will make a pillar in the temple of my God. Never again will he leave it. I will write on him the name of my God and the name of the city of my God, the new Jerusalem, which is coming down out of heaven from my God; and I will also write on him my new name. ¹³He who has an ear, let him hear what the Spirit says to the churches.

To the Church in Laodicea

¹⁴"To the angel of the church in Laodicea write:

These are the words of the Amen, the faithful and true witness, the ruler of God's creation. ¹⁵I know your deeds, that you are neither cold nor hot. I wish you were either one or the other! ¹⁶So, because you are lukewarm—neither hot nor cold—I am about to spit you out of my mouth. ¹⁷You say, 'I am rich; I have acquired wealth and do not need a thing.' But you do not realize that you are wretched, pitiful, poor, blind and naked. ¹⁸I counsel you to buy from me gold refined in the fire, so you can become rich; and white clothes to wear, so you can cover your shameful nakedness; and salve to put on your eyes, so you can see.

¹⁹Those whom I love I rebuke and discipline. So be earnest, and repent. ²⁰Here I am! I stand at the door and knock. If anyone hears my voice and opens the door, I will come in and eat with him, and he with me.

²¹To him who overcomes, I will give the right to sit with me on my throne, just as I overcame and sat down with my Father on his throne. ²²He who has an ear, let him hear what the Spirit says to the churches."

The Throne in Heaven

4 After this I looked, and there before me was a door standing open in heaven. And the voice I had first heard speaking to me like a trumpet said, "Come up here, and I will show you what must take place after this." ²At once I was in the Spirit, and there before me was a throne in heaven with someone sitting on it. ³And the one who sat there had the appearance of jasper and carnelian. A rainbow, resembling an emerald, encircled the throne. ⁴Surrounding the throne were twenty-four other thrones, and seated on them were twenty-four elders. They were dressed in white and had crowns of gold on their heads. ⁵From the throne came flashes of lightning, rumblings and peals of thunder. Before the throne, seven lamps were blazing. These are the seven spirits*a* of God. ⁶Also before the throne there was what looked like a sea of glass, clear as crystal.

In the center, around the throne, were four living creatures, and they were covered with eyes, in front and in back. ⁷The first living creature was like a lion, the second was like an ox, the third had a face like a man, the fourth was like a flying eagle. ⁸Each of the four living creatures had six

---

a5 Or the sevenfold Spirit

wings and was covered with eyes all around, even under his wings. Day and night they never stop saying:

"Holy, holy, holy
is the Lord God Almighty,
who was, and is, and is to come."

⁹Whenever the living creatures give glory, honor and thanks to him who sits on the throne and who lives for ever and ever, ¹⁰the twenty-four elders fall down before him who sits on the throne, and worship him who lives for ever and ever. They lay their crowns before the throne and say:

¹¹"You are worthy, our Lord and God,
to receive glory and honor and power,
for you created all things,
and by your will they were created
and have their being."

4:7 Strange Creatures

The Old Testament prophet Ezekiel had a somewhat similar vision (Ezekiel 1:9–10). In his version, however, each individual creature had four faces: human, lion, ox, and eagle. These symbols held special meaning for people of that day, much as the American eagle or British lion does today. For more information see "A Startling Image of Jesus," below.

The Scroll and the Lamb

5 Then I saw in the right hand of him who sat on the throne a scroll with writing on both sides and sealed with seven seals. ²And I saw a mighty angel proclaiming in a loud voice, "Who is worthy to break the seals and open the scroll?" ³But no one in heaven or on earth or under the earth could open the scroll or even look inside it. ⁴I wept and wept because no one was found who

A Startling Image of Jesus
A helpless lamb—the mightiest of all creatures

IMAGES OF JESUS ABOUND IN Revelation, and one way to study the book is to follow a single image through the entire book. After his luminous appearance in the first chapter, Jesus is presented as a king, a child, a warrior on a horse, the Lord of the whole earth, the husband of a bride. Of all the images, however, none is so startling and unlikely as the one in John's second vision. Yet it takes hold and appears repeatedly throughout the book.

> I wept and wept because no one was found who was worthy to open the scroll or look inside.
> 5:4

To set the stage for this vision, the book of Revelation uses more visual drama than a science fiction movie. Lightning flashes, the sky growls, and awesome creatures encircle a lofty throne. Four of the creatures (4:6) seem to symbolize the most impressive examples of all creation, for a common saying in those days went,

> The mightiest among the birds is the eagle.
> The mightiest among the domestic animals is the bull.
> The mightiest among the wild beasts is the lion.
> And the mightiest of all is man.

Only One Worthy

A question resounds in the heavens, "Who is worthy to break the seals and open the scroll?" (5:2). In other words, who is worthy to introduce the next phase of history? No one can answer, much to John's dismay. Not one of the four impressive creatures qualifies.

But suddenly John sees another creature, a "Lamb, looking as if it had been slain" (5:6). The image contains a great paradox. None of the majestic angels or elders or living creatures has the right to break the seals. Only a Lamb does—a helpless, slaughtered Lamb.

John records a song of celebration ("You are worthy to take the scroll and to open its seals, because you were slain, and with your blood you purchased men for God" [5:9]), a song later set to earthly music in Handel's *Messiah*. And elsewhere in Revelation true believers are identified as being recorded in the "Lamb's book of life" (21:27).

This powerful image resurfaces often in Revelation, a book of warfare between good and evil. Christ the King is also the Lamb, the one who died for us. His death on the cross, seemingly a great defeat, actually ushered in a decisive victory, for him and for us. Good was not destroyed; it triumphed.

Life Questions: What meaning does the image of Jesus as a slain Lamb have for you? What are your favorite "pictures" or images of Jesus?

was worthy to open the scroll or look inside. ⁵Then one of the elders said to me, "Do not weep! See, the Lion of the tribe of Judah, the Root of David, has triumphed. He is able to open the scroll and its seven seals."

5:1 Seals and Scrolls

Certain words and phrases used in Revelation had a clearer meaning to ancient readers familiar with the objects. For example, important documents were sent written on a papyrus scroll sealed with several wax seals. Only the proper person, in the presence of witnesses, could open the document. Thus in this vision, only the "worthy" creature is able to break the seal.

⁶Then I saw a Lamb, looking as if it had been slain, standing in the center of the throne, encircled by the four living creatures and the elders. He had seven horns and seven eyes, which are the seven spirits*a* of God sent out into all the earth. ⁷He came and took the scroll from the right hand of him who sat on the throne. ⁸And when he had taken it, the four living creatures and the twenty-four elders fell down before the Lamb. Each one had a harp and they were holding golden bowls full of incense, which are the prayers of the saints. ⁹And they sang a new song:

"You are worthy to take the scroll
   and to open its seals,
because you were slain,
   and with your blood you purchased men
      for God
   from every tribe and language and people
      and nation.
¹⁰You have made them to be a kingdom and
      priests to serve our God,
   and they will reign on the earth."

¹¹Then I looked and heard the voice of many angels, numbering thousands upon thousands, and ten thousand times ten thousand. They encircled the throne and the living creatures and the elders. ¹²In a loud voice they sang:

"Worthy is the Lamb, who was slain,
   to receive power and wealth and wisdom and
      strength
and honor and glory and praise!"

¹³Then I heard every creature in heaven and on earth and under the earth and on the sea, and all that is in them, singing:

"To him who sits on the throne and to the
      Lamb

be praise and honor and glory and power,
   for ever and ever!"

¹⁴The four living creatures said, "Amen," and the elders fell down and worshiped.

The Seals

6 I watched as the Lamb opened the first of the seven seals. Then I heard one of the four living creatures say in a voice like thunder, "Come!" ²I looked, and there before me was a white horse! Its rider held a bow, and he was given a crown, and he rode out as a conqueror bent on conquest.

³When the Lamb opened the second seal, I heard the second living creature say, "Come!" ⁴Then another horse came out, a fiery red one. Its rider was given power to take peace from the earth and to make men slay each other. To him was given a large sword.

⁵When the Lamb opened the third seal, I heard the third living creature say, "Come!" I looked, and there before me was a black horse! Its rider was holding a pair of scales in his hand. ⁶Then I heard what sounded like a voice among the four living creatures, saying, "A quart*b* of wheat for a day's wages,*c* and three quarts of barley for a day's wages,*c* and do not damage the oil and the wine!"

⁷When the Lamb opened the fourth seal, I heard the voice of the fourth living creature say, "Come!" ⁸I looked, and there before me was a pale horse! Its rider was named Death, and Hades was following close behind him. They were given power over a fourth of the earth to kill by sword, famine and plague, and by the wild beasts of the earth.

⁹When he opened the fifth seal, I saw under the altar the souls of those who had been slain because of the word of God and the testimony they had maintained. ¹⁰They called out in a loud voice, "How long, Sovereign Lord, holy and true, until you judge the inhabitants of the earth and avenge our blood?" ¹¹Then each of them was given a white robe, and they were told to wait a little longer, until the number of their fellow servants and brothers who were to be killed as they had been was completed.

¹²I watched as he opened the sixth seal. There was a great earthquake. The sun turned black like sackcloth made of goat hair, the whole moon turned blood red, ¹³and the stars in the sky fell to earth, as late figs drop from a fig tree when shaken by a strong wind. ¹⁴The sky receded like a scroll, rolling up, and every mountain and island was removed from its place.

¹⁵Then the kings of the earth, the princes, the generals, the rich, the mighty, and every slave and every free man hid in caves and among

---

a6 Or the sevenfold Spirit   *b6 Greek a choinix (probably about a liter)*   *c6 Greek a denarius* the rocks of the mountains. ¹⁶They called to the mountains and the rocks, "Fall on us and hide us from the face of him who sits on the throne and from the wrath of the Lamb! ¹⁷For the great day of their wrath has come, and who can stand?"

144,000 Sealed

7 After this I saw four angels standing at the four corners of the earth, holding back the four winds of the earth to prevent any wind from blowing on the land or on the sea or on any tree.

7:1 Significant Numbers

Numbers had a great symbolic significance in the Bible, and especially to the writer of Revelation. This concept is foreign to most modern readers; a rough parallel might be the "unlucky" significance some attach to the number 13. The most obviously symbolic numbers in Revelation are 4, 7, 12, and their multiples.

The number 4 seems to stand for the created universe (four points of the compass, four winds of the earth), and thus the four living creatures (4:6) represent all creation. In the Bible, the number 7 denotes perfection or completion, probably because the Genesis creation account covers seven days. The 12 tribes of Israel in the Old Testament and 12 apostles in the New Testament indicate that the number 12 stands for the church, or God's redeemed people from both covenants.

A number multiplied by 10s, such as 144,000 (12x12x10x10x10), suggests an indefinite but very large figure. Therefore, 144,000 may stand for the entire church throughout history.

²Then I saw another angel coming up from the east, having the seal of the living God. He called out in a loud voice to the four angels who had been given power to harm the land and the sea: ³"Do not harm the land or the sea or the trees until we put a seal on the foreheads of the servants of our God." ⁴Then I heard the number of those who were sealed: 144,000 from all the tribes of Israel.

⁵From the tribe of Judah 12,000 were sealed,
from the tribe of Reuben 12,000,
from the tribe of Gad 12,000,
⁶from the tribe of Asher 12,000,
from the tribe of Naphtali 12,000,
from the tribe of Manasseh 12,000,
⁷from the tribe of Simeon 12,000,
from the tribe of Levi 12,000,
from the tribe of Issachar 12,000,
⁸from the tribe of Zebulun 12,000,

from the tribe of Joseph 12,000,
from the tribe of Benjamin 12,000.

The Great Multitude in White Robes

⁹After this I looked and there before me was a great multitude that no one could count, from every nation, tribe, people and language, standing before the throne and in front of the Lamb. They were wearing white robes and were holding palm branches in their hands. ¹⁰And they cried out in a loud voice:

"Salvation belongs to our God,
who sits on the throne,
and to the Lamb."

¹¹All the angels were standing around the throne and around the elders and the four living creatures. They fell down on their faces before the throne and worshiped God, ¹²saying:

"Amen!
Praise and glory
and wisdom and thanks and honor
and power and strength
be to our God for ever and ever.
Amen!"

¹³Then one of the elders asked me, "These in white robes—who are they, and where did they come from?"

¹⁴I answered, "Sir, you know."

And he said, "These are they who have come out of the great tribulation; they have washed their robes and made them white in the blood of the Lamb. ¹⁵Therefore,

"they are before the throne of God
and serve him day and night in his
temple;
and he who sits on the throne will spread his
tent over them.
¹⁶Never again will they hunger;
never again will they thirst.
The sun will not beat upon them,

7:14 The Great Tribulation

Bible interpreters have proposed many theories to explain "the great tribulation," a time of intense persecution for Christians. Some believe it will occur in the future, around the time of Christ's return. (For more detail, see "Forty-two Months of Trials," page 1328.) Others believe John was referring to persecutions against the church occurring in his own day. Regardless, John stresses the overarching promise that the time of tribulation does not last forever. One day the faithful will no longer hunger or thirst and will never again have reason to cry (verses 16–17).

nor any scorching heat.
¹⁷For the Lamb at the center of the throne will
be their shepherd;
he will lead them to springs of living
water.
And God will wipe away every tear from
their eyes."

The Seventh Seal and the Golden Censer

8 When he opened the seventh seal, there was
silence in heaven for about half an hour.

8:1 Dramatic Structure

*Revelation unfolds with a sense of ever-
increasing drama, hinged on the symbolic
number 7. Here, heaven itself pauses in silence
before the opening of the seventh seal. Chapter
11 includes a long pause before the seventh
trumpet sounds its judgment. Finally, in
chapter 16 the seventh bowl introduces the
greatest calamity of all, the battle of
Armageddon.*

²And I saw the seven angels who stand before
God, and to them were given seven trumpets.
³Another angel, who had a golden censer,
came and stood at the altar. He was given much
incense to offer, with the prayers of all the saints,
on the golden altar before the throne. ⁴The
smoke of the incense, together with the prayers
of the saints, went up before God from the angel's hand. ⁵Then the angel took the censer, filled
it with fire from the altar, and hurled it on the
earth; and there came peals of thunder, rumblings, flashes of lightning and an earthquake.

The Trumpets

⁶Then the seven angels who had the seven
trumpets prepared to sound them.
⁷The first angel sounded his trumpet, and
there came hail and fire mixed with blood, and
it was hurled down upon the earth. A third of
the earth was burned up, a third of the trees
were burned up, and all the green grass was
burned up.
⁸The second angel sounded his trumpet, and
something like a huge mountain, all ablaze, was
thrown into the sea. A third of the sea turned into
blood, ⁹a third of the living creatures in the sea
died, and a third of the ships were destroyed.
¹⁰The third angel sounded his trumpet, and a
great star, blazing like a torch, fell from the sky
on a third of the rivers and on the springs of
water— ¹¹the name of the star is Wormwood.ᵃ
A third of the waters turned bitter, and many

people died from the waters that had become
bitter.
¹²The fourth angel sounded his trumpet, and
a third of the sun was struck, a third of the moon,
and a third of the stars, so that a third of them
turned dark. A third of the day was without light,
and also a third of the night.
¹³As I watched, I heard an eagle that was flying
in midair call out in a loud voice: "Woe! Woe!
Woe to the inhabitants of the earth, because of
the trumpet blasts about to be sounded by the
other three angels!"

9 The fifth angel sounded his trumpet, and I
saw a star that had fallen from the sky to
earth. The star was given the key to the shaft of
the Abyss. ²When he opened the Abyss, smoke
rose from it like the smoke from a gigantic furnace. The sun and sky were darkened by the
smoke from the Abyss. ³And out of the smoke
locusts came down upon the earth and were giv-
en power like that of scorpions of the earth.
⁴They were told not to harm the grass of the earth
or any plant or tree, but only those people who
did not have the seal of God on their foreheads.
⁵They were not given power to kill them, but only
to torture them for five months. And the agony
they suffered was like that of the sting of a scorpion when it strikes a man. ⁶During those days
men will seek death, but will not find it; they will
long to die, but death will elude them.
⁷The locusts looked like horses prepared for
battle. On their heads they wore something like
crowns of gold, and their faces resembled human
faces. ⁸Their hair was like women's hair, and
their teeth were like lions' teeth. ⁹They had
breastplates like breastplates of iron, and the
sound of their wings was like the thundering of
many horses and chariots rushing into battle.
¹⁰They had tails and stings like scorpions, and in
their tails they had power to torment people for
five months. ¹¹They had as king over them the
angel of the Abyss, whose name in Hebrew is
Abaddon, and in Greek, Apollyon.ᵇ
¹²The first woe is past; two other woes are yet
to come.
¹³The sixth angel sounded his trumpet, and
I heard a voice coming from the hornsᶜ of the
golden altar that is before God. ¹⁴It said to the
sixth angel who had the trumpet, "Release the
four angels who are bound at the great river
Euphrates." ¹⁵And the four angels who had been
kept ready for this very hour and day and month
and year were released to kill a third of mankind.
¹⁶The number of the mounted troops was two
hundred million. I heard their number.
¹⁷The horses and riders I saw in my vision
looked like this: Their breastplates were fiery red,
dark blue, and yellow as sulfur. The heads of the

ᵃ11 That is, Bitterness   ᵇ11 *Abaddon* and *Apollyon* mean *Destroyer.*   ᶜ13 That is, projections

horses resembled the heads of lions, and out of their mouths came fire, smoke and sulfur. ¹⁸A third of mankind was killed by the three plagues of fire, smoke and sulfur that came out of their mouths. ¹⁹The power of the horses was in their mouths and in their tails; for their tails were like snakes, having heads with which they inflict injury.

²⁰The rest of mankind that were not killed by these plagues still did not repent of the work of their hands; they did not stop worshiping demons, and idols of gold, silver, bronze, stone and wood—idols that cannot see or hear or walk. ²¹Nor did they repent of their murders, their magic arts, their sexual immorality or their thefts.

Revelation's Use of Symbols
Why are there so many theories explaining Revelation?

"THERE NEVER HAS BEEN A book provoking more delirium, foolishness, and irrational movements, without any relationship to Jesus Christ," concluded Jacques Ellul, author of a commentary on Revelation. Readers tend to fixate wildly on details, mainly because John relied so heavily on symbols to express his meaning in this book.

Creatures covered with eyes and sprouting horns, eagles wheeling in the sky, molten mountains hurtling into the ocean—such rich imagery excites frenzied attempts to explain every word. John interprets some symbols for us—"The seven stars are the angels of the seven churches" (1:20)—and hints broadly at the meaning of others, such as the four horsemen in chapter 6. But many questions remain unanswered. For example, do the major visions describe consecutive periods of history, or do they foretell the same events from different angles?

> *The locusts looked like horses prepared for battle. On their heads they wore something like crowns of gold, and their faces resembled human faces.*
> *9:7*

Look at the Broad Picture

Artists find that symbols communicate with special power. When Spanish artist Pablo Picasso painted his massive *Guernica*, he attempted to express what had happened in war-ravaged Spain on April 28, 1937. He created a work of art, not a photographic record. The painting does communicate the tragedy at Guernica, but artfully, symbolically.

In a similar way, John poetically renders human events so strange and climactic as to be otherwise inexpressible. If he had wanted to, God could have revealed a precise timetable of future events, but instead Jesus warned specifically against such speculation about the future. In keeping with that approach, Revelation does not so much outline future events as hint at the cosmic significance that goes on *behind* history.

Readers new to Revelation should start by viewing scenes as a whole, looking for an overall meaning. The visions are like Jesus' parables: Each has a main thrust, and some of the details may serve merely to dramatize or add literary fullness to the scene. No one can find the precise meaning behind every detail in John's visions. Those who seek to explain each symbol too quickly may easily miss the meaning of the symbol as well as the grand emotional sweep of the book.

Searching for a System

Revelation will always attract scholars who search for the meaning behind each symbol. It is no easy undertaking: Over 300 allusions to the Old Testament and an elaborate system of symbolic numbers must be factored into any explanation. History has proved thousands of explainers wrong. People from every generation—especially in the hectic days around A.D. 1000 and in the 14th and 19th centuries, as well as in contemporary times dominated by Middle East tensions—have insisted the end of the world was just around the corner.

Today, some believe that Revelation's symbols—statues that talk, fire coming from heaven, totalitarian economic control, massive changes in the earth and sea—come hauntingly close to 20th-century phenomena. The wholesale devastation of earth prophesied in the middle chapters seems eerily up-to-date.

Yet, calamities merely provide a backdrop to John's main thrust: Followers of Christ will be made safe at last. "God will wipe away every tear from their eyes," he says (7:17). Much of Revelation remains shrouded in mystery, but the final results shine out clearly.

Life Questions: Two potential dangers in reading Revelation (see Introduction) are avoiding it entirely or getting obsessed with its details. Which danger are you most familiar with? Why do we need the message of Revelation today?

The Angel and the Little Scroll

10 Then I saw another mighty angel coming down from heaven. He was robed in a cloud, with a rainbow above his head; his face

was like the sun, and his legs were like fiery pillars. ²He was holding a little scroll, which lay open in his hand. He planted his right foot on the sea and his left foot on the land, ³and he gave a loud shout like the roar of a lion. When he shouted, the voices of the seven thunders spoke. ⁴And when the seven thunders spoke, I was about to write; but I heard a voice from heaven say, "Seal up what the seven thunders have said and do not write it down."

⁵Then the angel I had seen standing on the sea and on the land raised his right hand to heaven. ⁶And he swore by him who lives for ever and ever, who created the heavens and all that is in them, the earth and all that is in it, and the sea and all that is in it, and said, "There will be no more delay! ⁷But in the days when the seventh angel is about to sound his trumpet, the mystery of God will be accomplished, just as he announced to his servants the prophets."

⁸Then the voice that I had heard from heaven spoke to me once more: "Go, take the scroll that lies open in the hand of the angel who is standing on the sea and on the land."

⁹So I went to the angel and asked him to give me the little scroll. He said to me, "Take it and eat it. It will turn your stomach sour, but in your mouth it will be as sweet as honey." ¹⁰I took the little scroll from the angel's hand and ate it. It tasted as sweet as honey in my mouth, but when I had eaten it, my stomach turned sour. ¹¹Then I was told, "You must prophesy again about many peoples, nations, languages and kings."

The Two Witnesses

11 I was given a reed like a measuring rod and was told, "Go and measure the temple of God and the altar, and count the worshipers there. ²But exclude the outer court; do not measure it, because it has been given to the Gentiles. They will trample on the holy city for 42 months.

³And I will give power to my two witnesses, and they will prophesy for 1,260 days, clothed in sackcloth." ⁴These are the two olive trees and the two lampstands that stand before the Lord of the earth. ⁵If anyone tries to harm them, fire comes from their mouths and devours their enemies. This is how anyone who wants to harm them must die. ⁶These men have power to shut up the sky so that it will not rain during the time they are prophesying; and they have power to turn the waters into blood and to strike the earth with every kind of plague as often as they want.

⁷Now when they have finished their testimony, the beast that comes up from the Abyss will attack them, and overpower and kill them. ⁸Their bodies will lie in the street of the great city, which is figuratively called Sodom and Egypt, where also their Lord was crucified. ⁹For three and a half days men from every people, tribe, language and nation will gaze on their bodies and refuse them burial. ¹⁰The inhabitants of the earth will gloat over them and will celebrate by sending each other gifts, because these two prophets had tormented those who live on the earth.

¹¹But after the three and a half days a breath of life from God entered them, and they stood on their feet, and terror struck those who saw them. ¹²Then they heard a loud voice from heaven saying to them, "Come up here." And they went up to heaven in a cloud, while their enemies looked on.

¹³At that very hour there was a severe earthquake and a tenth of the city collapsed. Seven thousand people were killed in the earthquake, and the survivors were terrified and gave glory to the God of heaven.

¹⁴The second woe has passed; the third woe is coming soon.

The Seventh Trumpet

¹⁵The seventh angel sounded his trumpet, and there were loud voices in heaven, which said:

"The kingdom of the world has become the
        kingdom of our Lord and of his
        Christ,
    and he will reign for ever and ever."

¹⁶And the twenty-four elders, who were seated on their thrones before God, fell on their faces and worshiped God, ¹⁷saying:

"We give thanks to you, Lord God Almighty,
    the One who is and who was,
because you have taken your great power
    and have begun to reign.
¹⁸The nations were angry;
    and your wrath has come.
The time has come for judging the dead,
    and for rewarding your servants the
        prophets
and your saints and those who reverence
    your name,
    both small and great—
and for destroying those who destroy the
    earth."

¹⁹Then God's temple in heaven was opened, and within his temple was seen the ark of his covenant. And there came flashes of lightning, rumblings, peals of thunder, an earthquake and a great hailstorm.

The Woman and the Dragon

12 A great and wondrous sign appeared in heaven: a woman clothed with the sun, with the moon under her feet and a crown of twelve stars on her head. ²She was pregnant and cried out in pain as she was about to give birth. ³Then another sign appeared in heaven: an enormous red dragon with seven heads and ten horns and seven crowns on his heads. ⁴His tail swept a third of the stars out of the sky and flung them to the earth. The dragon stood in front of the woman who was about to give birth, so that he

A Look Behind the Scenes
Christmas from heaven's perspective

CHRISTMAS DAY. WE CELEBRATE IT with a sudden splurge of money and gifts and an attempt to rediscover the joy of the first Christmas. Manger displays in town squares recreate the scene in Bethlehem on that day long ago.

As many interpret it, chapter 12 describes Christmas day also, but its point of view differs radically from that of the Gospels. Revelation does not tell of shepherds, a crazed king bent on infanticide, and a stable; rather, it pictures a murderous dragon leading a ferocious struggle in heaven. His attack when Christ was born launches a series of bloody rebellions against the forces of good.

> The dragon stood in front of the woman who was about to give birth, so that he might devour her child the moment it was born. 12:4

Two Histories at Once

The view of Christ's birth in Revelation 12 gives a glimpse into the pattern of the entire book. John is fusing things seen with things normally not seen. In daily life, two parallel histories occur simultaneously: one on earth and one in heaven. Revelation, however, views them together. It parts the curtain, allowing a quick look behind the scenes at the cosmic impact of what happens on earth.

Every inch of this planet is claimed by God and counterclaimed by Satan. We normally experience only the visible, everyday effects of this struggle. We feel it, for example, when we make a choice between what we know is wrong and what is right. But, as we are living out our lives on earth, the supernatural universe is simultaneously at war. Revelation draws the contrasts sharply: good versus evil, the Lamb versus the dragon, Jerusalem versus Babylon, the bride versus the prostitute.

Is God in Control of History?

Sometimes the "war in heaven" can break out into actual violence on earth, as it did when Jesus came. Revelation was originally written to people who were facing extreme persecution from the Roman empire. Revelation establishes that a war is being waged on this planet between good and evil, a war that reflects a larger struggle in the whole universe. But, no matter how it looks, God is in firm control of history. To first-century Christians, Rome was the arch-villain, and allusions to that empire crop up in these chapters. John asserts that Jesus Christ, and not an emperor, determines the flow of history.

Events are marching onward to a definite climax; history has meaning. Ultimately, even the despots of history will end up fulfilling the plan mapped out for them by God. Pontius Pilate and his Roman soldiers demonstrated that truth starkly. They thought they were getting rid of Jesus by crucifying him. Instead, they made possible the salvation of the world.

Life Questions: As Revelation tells it, events that appear tragic can work great good. Have you ever experienced that in your life?

might devour her child the moment it was born. ⁵She gave birth to a son, a male child, who will rule all the nations with an iron scepter. And her child was snatched up to God and to his throne. ⁶The woman fled into the desert to a place prepared for her by God, where she might be taken care of for 1,260 days.

⁷And there was war in heaven. Michael and his angels fought against the dragon, and the dragon and his angels fought back. ⁸But he was not strong enough, and they lost their place in heaven. ⁹The great dragon was hurled down—that ancient serpent called the devil, or Satan, who leads the whole world astray. He was hurled to the earth, and his angels with him.

¹⁰Then I heard a loud voice in heaven say:

"Now have come the salvation and the
          power and the kingdom of our God,
    and the authority of his Christ.
For the accuser of our brothers,
    who accuses them before our God day
          and night,
    has been hurled down.
¹¹They overcame him
    by the blood of the Lamb
    and by the word of their testimony;
they did not love their lives so much
    as to shrink from death.
¹²Therefore rejoice, you heavens
    and you who dwell in them!
But woe to the earth and the sea,
    because the devil has gone down to you!
He is filled with fury,
    because he knows that his time is short."

¹³When the dragon saw that he had been hurled to the earth, he pursued the woman who had given birth to the male child. ¹⁴The woman was given the two wings of a great eagle, so that she might fly to the place prepared for her in the desert, where she would be taken care of for a time, times and half a time, out of the serpent's reach. ¹⁵Then from his mouth the serpent spewed water like a river, to overtake the woman and sweep her away with the torrent. ¹⁶But the earth helped the woman by opening its mouth and swallowing the river that the dragon had spewed out of his mouth. ¹⁷Then the dragon was enraged at the woman and went off to make war against the rest of her offspring—those who obey God's commandments and hold to the testimony of Jesus. ¹And the dragon[a] stood on the shore of the sea.

The Beast out of the Sea

And I saw a beast coming out of the sea. He had ten horns and seven heads, with ten crowns on his horns, and on each head a blasphemous name. ²The beast I saw resembled a leopard, but had feet like those of a bear and a mouth like that of a lion. The dragon gave the beast his power and his throne and great authority. ³One of the heads of the beast seemed to have had a fatal wound, but the fatal wound had been healed. The whole world was astonished and followed the beast. ⁴Men worshiped the dragon because he had given authority to the beast, and they also worshiped the beast and asked, "Who is like the beast? Who can make war against him?"

⁵The beast was given a mouth to utter proud words and blasphemies and to exercise his authority for forty-two months. ⁶He opened his

13:5 Forty-two Months of Trials

This mysterious number has prompted much speculation. Literally it means "a time, times and half a time" (see 12:14), that is, one year plus two years plus half a year, or three and a half years. It occurs several places in Revelation. Could it simply be half the perfect number 7, thus representing the age of the new covenant (the time between the first and second coming of Christ)? Or does it refer to literal months: a brief but intense three-and-one-half year period of great persecution against the church? If so, did these 42 months already take place during the Roman persecutions of Christians? Or are they still in the future?

Those who believe the 42 months are in the future frequently speak of the period as "the great tribulation" and call the beast the antichrist, a name used elsewhere in the Bible. Several schools of thought have developed around the tribulation. Pre-tribulationists believe that Jesus will come to remove the church from earth just before the great tribulation. Post-tribulationists believe the church will go through a time of trials before Jesus returns. Mid-tribulationists believe the church will be taken away during the tribulation.

mouth to blaspheme God, and to slander his name and his dwelling place and those who live in heaven. ⁷He was given power to make war against the saints and to conquer them. And he was given authority over every tribe, people, language and nation. ⁸All inhabitants of the earth will worship the beast—all whose names have not been written in the book of life belonging to the Lamb that was slain from the creation of the world.[b]

⁹He who has an ear, let him hear.

---

[a]1 Some late manuscripts *And I that was slain*   [b]8 Or *written from the creation of the world in the book of life belonging to the Lamb*

[10]If anyone is to go into captivity,
   into captivity he will go.
If anyone is to be killed[a] with the sword,
   with the sword he will be killed.

This calls for patient endurance and faithfulness on the part of the saints.

The Beast out of the Earth

[11]Then I saw another beast, coming out of the earth. He had two horns like a lamb, but he spoke like a dragon. [12]He exercised all the authority of the first beast on his behalf, and made the earth and its inhabitants worship the first beast, whose fatal wound had been healed. [13]And he performed great and miraculous signs, even causing fire to come down from heaven to earth in full view of men. [14]Because of the signs he was given power to do on behalf of the first beast, he deceived the inhabitants of the earth. He ordered them to set up an image in honor of the beast who was wounded by the sword and yet lived. [15]He was given power to give breath to the image of the first beast, so that it could speak and cause all who refused to worship the image to be killed. [16]He also forced everyone, small and great, rich and poor, free and slave, to receive a mark on his right hand or on his forehead, [17]so that no one could buy or sell unless he had the mark, which is the name of the beast or the number of his name.

[18]This calls for wisdom. If anyone has insight, let him calculate the number of the beast, for it is man's number. His number is 666.

The Lamb and the 144,000

14 Then I looked, and there before me was the Lamb, standing on Mount Zion, and with him 144,000 who had his name and his Father's name written on their foreheads. [2]And I heard a sound from heaven like the roar of rushing waters and like a loud peal of thunder. The sound I heard was like that of harpists playing their harps. [3]And they sang a new song before the throne and before the four living creatures and the elders. No one could learn the song except the 144,000 who had been redeemed from the earth. [4]These are those who did not defile themselves with women, for they kept themselves pure. They follow the Lamb wherever he goes. They were purchased from among men and offered as firstfruits to God and the Lamb. [5]No lie was found in their mouths; they are blameless.

The Three Angels

[6]Then I saw another angel flying in midair, and he had the eternal gospel to proclaim to those who live on the earth—to every nation, tribe, language and people. [7]He said in a loud voice, "Fear God and give him glory, because the hour of his judgment has come. Worship him who made the heavens, the earth, the sea and the springs of water."

14:1 Good News with Bad

According to Revelation, human history will end not with a whimper but with a series of loud bangs. And yet John frequently reminds his readers that the spasms of violence will lead to a time of eternal peace, with God ruling over a restored heaven and earth. The peaceful scene of a heavenly choir in this chapter is sandwiched between two accounts of tribulation and judgment. John drops in such scenes like orchestral interludes in the midst of a tumultuous opera: They reassure us of a future in which all creation performs together in harmony.

[8]A second angel followed and said, "Fallen! Fallen is Babylon the Great, which made all the nations drink the maddening wine of her adulteries."

[9]A third angel followed them and said in a loud voice: "If anyone worships the beast and his image and receives his mark on the forehead or on the hand, [10]he, too, will drink of the wine of God's fury, which has been poured full strength into the cup of his wrath. He will be tormented with burning sulfur in the presence of the holy angels and of the Lamb. [11]And the smoke of their torment rises for ever and ever. There is no rest day or night for those who worship the beast and his image, or for anyone who receives the mark of his name." [12]This calls for patient endurance on the part of the saints who obey God's commandments and remain faithful to Jesus.

[13]Then I heard a voice from heaven say, "Write: Blessed are the dead who die in the Lord from now on."

"Yes," says the Spirit, "they will rest from their labor, for their deeds will follow them."

The Harvest of the Earth

[14]I looked, and there before me was a white cloud, and seated on the cloud was one "like a son of man"[b] with a crown of gold on his head and a sharp sickle in his hand. [15]Then another angel came out of the temple and called in a loud voice to him who was sitting on the cloud, "Take your sickle and reap, because the time to reap has come, for the harvest of the earth is ripe." [16]So he who was seated on the cloud swung his sickle over the earth, and the earth was harvested.

[17]Another angel came out of the temple in

---

[a]10 Some manuscripts *anyone kills*   [b]14 Daniel 7:13

heaven, and he too had a sharp sickle. [18]Still another angel, who had charge of the fire, came from the altar and called in a loud voice to him who had the sharp sickle, "Take your sharp sickle and gather the clusters of grapes from the earth's vine, because its grapes are ripe." [19]The angel swung his sickle on the earth, gathered its grapes and threw them into the great winepress of God's wrath. [20]They were trampled in the winepress outside the city, and blood flowed out of the press, rising as high as the horses' bridles for a distance of 1,600 stadia.[a]

Seven Angels With Seven Plagues

15 I saw in heaven another great and marvelous sign: seven angels with the seven last plagues—last, because with them God's wrath is completed. [2]And I saw what looked like a sea of glass mixed with fire and, standing beside the sea, those who had been victorious over the beast and his image and over the number of his name. They held harps given them by God [3]and sang the song of Moses the servant of God and the song of the Lamb:

"Great and marvelous are your deeds,
　　Lord God Almighty.
Just and true are your ways,
　　King of the ages.
[4]Who will not fear you, O Lord,
　　and bring glory to your name?
For you alone are holy.
All nations will come
　　and worship before you,
for your righteous acts have been revealed."

[5]After this I looked and in heaven the temple, that is, the tabernacle of the Testimony, was opened. [6]Out of the temple came the seven angels with the seven plagues. They were dressed in clean, shining linen and wore golden sashes around their chests. [7]Then one of the four living creatures gave to the seven angels seven golden bowls filled with the wrath of God, who lives for ever and ever. [8]And the temple was filled with smoke from the glory of God and from his power, and no one could enter the temple until the seven plagues of the seven angels were completed.

The Seven Bowls of God's Wrath

16 Then I heard a loud voice from the temple saying to the seven angels, "Go, pour out the seven bowls of God's wrath on the earth."

[2]The first angel went and poured out his bowl on the land, and ugly and painful sores broke out on the people who had the mark of the beast and worshiped his image.

[3]The second angel poured out his bowl on the sea, and it turned into blood like that of a dead man, and every living thing in the sea died.

[4]The third angel poured out his bowl on the rivers and springs of water, and they became blood. [5]Then I heard the angel in charge of the waters say:

"You are just in these judgments,
　　you who are and who were, the Holy
　　　　One,
　　because you have so judged;
[6]for they have shed the blood of your saints
　　　　and prophets,
　　and you have given them blood to drink
　　　　as they deserve."

[7]And I heard the altar respond:

"Yes, Lord God Almighty,
　　true and just are your judgments."

[8]The fourth angel poured out his bowl on the sun, and the sun was given power to scorch people with fire. [9]They were seared by the intense heat and they cursed the name of God, who had control over these plagues, but they refused to repent and glorify him.

[10]The fifth angel poured out his bowl on the throne of the beast, and his kingdom was plunged into darkness. Men gnawed their tongues in agony [11]and cursed the God of heaven because of their pains and their sores, but they refused to repent of what they had done.

[12]The sixth angel poured out his bowl on the great river Euphrates, and its water was dried up to prepare the way for the kings from the East. [13]Then I saw three evil[b] spirits that looked like frogs; they came out of the mouth of the dragon, out of the mouth of the beast and out of the mouth of the false prophet. [14]They are spirits of demons performing miraculous signs, and they go out to the kings of the whole world, to gather them for the battle on the great day of God Almighty.

[15]"Behold, I come like a thief! Blessed is he who stays awake and keeps his clothes with him, so that he may not go naked and be shamefully exposed."

[16]Then they gathered the kings together to the place that in Hebrew is called Armageddon.

16:16 The Battle of Armageddon

Armageddon has been the site of many military struggles in Israel's history. Some historians estimate more wars have been fought here than any other location in the world. It is an appropriate setting (or symbol) for the final struggle between good and evil.

---

[a]20 That is, about 180 miles (about 300 kilometers)　[b]13 Greek *unclean*

¹⁷The seventh angel poured out his bowl into the air, and out of the temple came a loud voice from the throne, saying, "It is done!" ¹⁸Then there came flashes of lightning, rumblings, peals of thunder and a severe earthquake. No earthquake like it has ever occurred since man has been on earth, so tremendous was the quake. ¹⁹The great city split into three parts, and the cities of the nations collapsed. God remembered Babylon the Great and gave her the cup filled with the wine of the fury of his wrath. ²⁰Every island fled away and the mountains could not be found. ²¹From the sky huge hailstones of about a hundred pounds each fell upon men. And they cursed God on account of the plague of hail, because the plague was so terrible.

The Woman on the Beast

17 One of the seven angels who had the seven bowls came and said to me, "Come, I will show you the punishment of the great prostitute, who sits on many waters. ²With her the kings of the earth committed adultery and the inhabitants of the earth were intoxicated with the wine of her adulteries."

³Then the angel carried me away in the Spirit into a desert. There I saw a woman sitting on a scarlet beast that was covered with blasphemous names and had seven heads and ten horns. ⁴The woman was dressed in purple and scarlet, and was glittering with gold, precious stones and pearls. She held a golden cup in her hand, filled with abominable things and the filth of her adulteries. ⁵This title was written on her forehead:

MYSTERY
BABYLON THE GREAT
THE MOTHER OF PROSTITUTES
AND OF THE ABOMINATIONS OF THE EARTH.

⁶I saw that the woman was drunk with the blood of the saints, the blood of those who bore testimony to Jesus.

When I saw her, I was greatly astonished. ⁷Then the angel said to me: "Why are you astonished? I will explain to you the mystery of the woman and of the beast she rides, which has the seven heads and ten horns. ⁸The beast, which you saw, once was, now is not, and will come up out of the Abyss and go to his destruction. The inhabitants of the earth whose names have not been written in the book of life from the creation of the world will be astonished when they see the beast, because he once was, now is not, and yet will come.

⁹"This calls for a mind with wisdom. The seven heads are seven hills on which the woman sits. ¹⁰They are also seven kings. Five have fallen, one is, the other has not yet come; but when he does come, he must remain for a little while. ¹¹The beast who once was, and now is not, is an eighth king. He belongs to the seven and is going to his destruction.

¹²"The ten horns you saw are ten kings who have not yet received a kingdom, but who for one hour will receive authority as kings along with the beast. ¹³They have one purpose and will give their power and authority to the beast. ¹⁴They will make war against the Lamb, but the Lamb will overcome them because he is Lord of lords and King of kings—and with him will be his called, chosen and faithful followers."

¹⁵Then the angel said to me, "The waters you saw, where the prostitute sits, are peoples, multitudes, nations and languages. ¹⁶The beast and the ten horns you saw will hate the prostitute. They will bring her to ruin and leave her naked; they will eat her flesh and burn her with fire. ¹⁷For God has put it into their hearts to accomplish his purpose by agreeing to give the beast their power to rule, until God's words are fulfilled. ¹⁸The woman you saw is the great city that rules over the kings of the earth."

The Fall of Babylon

18 After this I saw another angel coming down from heaven. He had great authority, and the earth was illuminated by his splendor. ²With a mighty voice he shouted:

"Fallen! Fallen is Babylon the Great!
    She has become a home for demons
and a haunt for every evilᵃ spirit,
    a haunt for every unclean and detestable
        bird.
³For all the nations have drunk
    the maddening wine of her adulteries.

18:2 What Is Babylon?

Many people believe Babylon was a coded substitute for Rome, the city set on seven hills (17:9). Revelation was almost surely written to Christians undergoing great persecution from harsh Roman emperors. Scholars who see Babylon as Rome sometimes try to identify the kings mentioned here as specific Roman rulers.

However, not all interpreters agree. Some suggest that Babylon stands for Jerusalem, and others believe we cannot clearly identify Babylon. Rather, they say, it can represent all powerful world systems that kill faithful Christians and seduce people away from God. Regardless, chapter 18 reveals that the great enemy, Babylon, will disappear forever (verse 21).

ᵃ2 Greek *unclean*

The kings of the earth committed adultery
    with her,
  and the merchants of the earth grew rich
    from her excessive luxuries."

[4]Then I heard another voice from heaven say:

"Come out of her, my people,
  so that you will not share in her sins,
  so that you will not receive any of her
    plagues;
[5]for her sins are piled up to heaven,
  and God has remembered her crimes.
[6]Give back to her as she has given;
  pay her back double for what she has
    done.
  Mix her a double portion from her own
    cup.
[7]Give her as much torture and grief
  as the glory and luxury she gave herself.
In her heart she boasts,
  'I sit as queen; I am not a widow,
  and I will never mourn.'
[8]Therefore in one day her plagues will
    overtake her:
  death, mourning and famine.
She will be consumed by fire,
  for mighty is the Lord God who judges
    her.

[9]"When the kings of the earth who committed adultery with her and shared her luxury see the smoke of her burning, they will weep and mourn over her. [10]Terrified at her torment, they will stand far off and cry:

"'Woe! Woe, O great city,
  O Babylon, city of power!
In one hour your doom has come!'

[11]"The merchants of the earth will weep and mourn over her because no one buys their cargoes any more— [12]cargoes of gold, silver, precious stones and pearls; fine linen, purple, silk and scarlet cloth; every sort of citron wood, and articles of every kind made of ivory, costly wood, bronze, iron and marble; [13]cargoes of cinnamon and spice, of incense, myrrh and frankincense, of wine and olive oil, of fine flour and wheat; cattle and sheep; horses and carriages; and bodies and souls of men.
[14]"They will say, 'The fruit you longed for is gone from you. All your riches and splendor have vanished, never to be recovered.' [15]The merchants who sold these things and gained their wealth from her will stand far off, terrified at her torment. They will weep and mourn [16]and cry out:

"'Woe! Woe, O great city,
  dressed in fine linen, purple and scarlet,
  and glittering with gold, precious stones
    and pearls!

[17]In one hour such great wealth has been
    brought to ruin!'

"Every sea captain, and all who travel by ship, the sailors, and all who earn their living from the sea, will stand far off. [18]When they see the smoke of her burning, they will exclaim, 'Was there ever a city like this great city?' [19]They will throw dust on their heads, and with weeping and mourning cry out:

"'Woe! Woe, O great city,
  where all who had ships on the sea
    became rich through her wealth!
In one hour she has been brought to ruin!
[20]Rejoice over her, O heaven!
  Rejoice, saints and apostles and prophets!
God has judged her for the way she treated
    you.'"

[21]Then a mighty angel picked up a boulder the size of a large millstone and threw it into the sea, and said:

"With such violence
  the great city of Babylon will be thrown
    down,
  never to be found again.

18:21 Newspaper Prophecy

The fact that Baghdad, Iraq, sits just 50 miles from the historical site of Babylon led some commentators to predict that the Gulf War of 1991 would escalate into the battle of Armageddon. Instead, the "mother of all battles" on the ground lasted just 100 hours.

Revelation has defied many such prognosticators. A man who claimed to have cracked the biblical code wrote the best-selling book 88 Reasons Why the Rapture Will Be in 1988. And not long before that a well-known television evangelist predicted the Soviet Union would invade Israel in 1982. Revelation contains a code intriguing enough to hold the interest of every generation, but obscure enough to have kept the best scholars guessing for almost 2,000 years. That may have been John's intent: to have each new wave of readers grapple with its meaning in their own historical context.

[22]The music of harpists and musicians, flute
    players and trumpeters,
  will never be heard in you again.
No workman of any trade
  will ever be found in you again.
The sound of a millstone
  will never be heard in you again.
[23]The light of a lamp
  will never shine in you again.
The voice of bridegroom and bride

will never be heard in you again.
Your merchants were the world's great men.
By your magic spell all the nations were
    led astray.
24In her was found the blood of prophets and
        of the saints,
    and of all who have been killed on the
        earth."

Hallelujah!

19 After this I heard what sounded like the roar of a great multitude in heaven shouting:

"Hallelujah!
Salvation and glory and power belong to our
    God,
2   for true and just are his judgments.
He has condemned the great prostitute
    who corrupted the earth by her adulteries.
He has avenged on her the blood of his
        servants."

3And again they shouted:

"Hallelujah!
The smoke from her goes up for ever and
    ever."

4The twenty-four elders and the four living creatures fell down and worshiped God, who was seated on the throne. And they cried:

"Amen, Hallelujah!"

5Then a voice came from the throne, saying:

"Praise our God,
    all you his servants,
you who fear him,
    both small and great!"

6Then I heard what sounded like a great multitude, like the roar of rushing waters and like loud peals of thunder, shouting:

"Hallelujah!
    For our Lord God Almighty reigns.
7Let us rejoice and be glad
    and give him glory!
For the wedding of the Lamb has come,
    and his bride has made herself ready.
8Fine linen, bright and clean,
    was given her to wear."
(Fine linen stands for the righteous acts of the saints.)

9Then the angel said to me, "Write: 'Blessed are those who are invited to the wedding supper of the Lamb!'" And he added, "These are the true words of God."

10At this I fell at his feet to worship him. But he said to me, "Do not do it! I am a fellow servant with you and with your brothers who hold to the testimony of Jesus. Worship God! For the testimony of Jesus is the spirit of prophecy."

A Happy Ending after All
The last word is the best news of all

> Then I saw a new heaven and a new earth. 21:1

WE SENSE IT AT RARE moments. The first real day of spring, when the air is heavy with the scent of blooms and new life sprouts everywhere. Or even in winter, when an unexpected snowstorm clothes a gray, dingy city in pure white. Or when we watch a baby animal at play in the zoo. Or remember the first sudden twinge of romantic love.

This world may be full of pollution, war, crime, and hate. But inside us, all of us, linger remnants that remind us of what the world could be like—of what we could be like. The Old Testament prophets dreamed of "that day" when creation would be made new. And those sensations, following a dismal monotone of predicted catastrophes, burst out of the last few chapters of Revelation. That perfect world is not merely a dream; it will come true.

A New World at Last

There will be no more tears then, nor pain. Wild animals will frolic, not kill. Once again creation will work the way God intended. Peace will reign not only between God and individuals, but between him and all creation. The kingdom comes out into the open. The City of God flings wide its gates.

Revelation ends on a note of great triumph. Somehow, out of all the bad news augured here, good news emerges—spectacular Good News. To those who believe, Revelation becomes a book not of fear, but of hope. God will prevail. All will be made new.

The Bible began, back in Genesis, with a tragic defeat when humanity, made in the image of God, rebelled. It ends with a reunion—a marriage, Revelation calls it. There is a happy ending after all.

Life Questions: If you could design a perfect world, what would it look like?

The Rider on the White Horse

11I saw heaven standing open and there before me was a white horse, whose rider is called Faithful and True. With justice he judges and makes war. **12**His eyes are like blazing fire, and on his head are many crowns. He has a name written on him that no one knows but he himself. **13**He is dressed in a robe dipped in blood, and his name is the Word of God. **14**The armies of heaven were following him, riding on white horses and dressed in fine linen, white and clean. **15**Out of his mouth comes a sharp sword with which to strike down the nations. "He will rule them with an iron scepter."*a* He treads the winepress of the fury of the wrath of God Almighty. **16**On his robe and on his thigh he has this name written:

KING OF KINGS AND LORD OF LORDS.

17And I saw an angel standing in the sun, who cried in a loud voice to all the birds flying in midair, "Come, gather together for the great supper of God, **18**so that you may eat the flesh of kings, generals, and mighty men, of horses and their riders, and the flesh of all people, free and slave, small and great."

19Then I saw the beast and the kings of the earth and their armies gathered together to make war against the rider on the horse and his army. **20**But the beast was captured, and with him the false prophet who had performed the miraculous signs on his behalf. With these signs he had deluded those who had received the mark of the beast and worshiped his image. The two of them were thrown alive into the fiery lake of burning sulfur. **21**The rest of them were killed with the sword that came out of the mouth of the rider on the horse, and all the birds gorged themselves on their flesh.

The Thousand Years

20 And I saw an angel coming down out of heaven, having the key to the Abyss and holding in his hand a great chain. **2**He seized the dragon, that ancient serpent, who is the devil, or Satan, and bound him for a thousand years. **3**He threw him into the Abyss, and locked and sealed it over him, to keep him from deceiving the nations anymore until the thousand years were ended. After that, he must be set free for a short time.

4I saw thrones on which were seated those who had been given authority to judge. And I saw the souls of those who had been beheaded because of their testimony for Jesus and because of the word of God. They had not worshiped the beast or his image and had not received his mark on their foreheads or their hands. They came to life and reigned with Christ a thousand years.

5(The rest of the dead did not come to life until the thousand years were ended.) This is the first resurrection. **6**Blessed and holy are those who have part in the first resurrection. The second

20:3 The Millennium

Christians interpret the thousand-year reign referred to here in a variety of ways:

1. Postmillennialism believes that the church itself will, through its expanding influence, bring about a time of peace and prosperity in preparation for the return of Christ. This view was far more popular in the 19th century, when people were optimistic about progress and the future.

2. Premillennialism believes that Christ will return to earth and reign here in person, ushering in a period of great peace. During this period, Satan will be bound up, but will lead a final revolt at the end of the thousand years.

3. Amillennialism interprets this passage much less literally. Some amillennialists hold that the millennium has already been going on, but the reign of Christ is taking place in heaven, not on earth. Others believe the church is establishing the kingdom of Christ now, between Jesus' first and second coming.

Because so little information is given on the millennium, no one can be completely sure. The "thousand year" period itself may be symbolic, standing for a very long period of time. Regardless, all positions agree that ultimately this world will end with Jesus' establishment of an eternal kingdom.

death has no power over them, but they will be priests of God and of Christ and will reign with him for a thousand years.

Satan's Doom

7When the thousand years are over, Satan will be released from his prison **8**and will go out to deceive the nations in the four corners of the earth—Gog and Magog—to gather them for battle. In number they are like the sand on the seashore. **9**They marched across the breadth of the earth and surrounded the camp of God's people, the city he loves. But fire came down from heaven and devoured them. **10**And the devil, who deceived them, was thrown into the lake of burning sulfur, where the beast and the false prophet had been thrown. They will be tormented day and night for ever and ever.

The Dead Are Judged

11Then I saw a great white throne and him who was seated on it. Earth and sky fled from his presence, and there was no place for them. **12**And

a 15 Psalm 2:9

I saw the dead, great and small, standing before the throne, and books were opened. Another book was opened, which is the book of life. The dead were judged according to what they had done as recorded in the books. [13]The sea gave up the dead that were in it, and death and Hades gave up the dead that were in them, and each person was judged according to what he had done. [14]Then death and Hades were thrown into the lake of fire. The lake of fire is the second death. [15]If anyone's name was not found written in the book of life, he was thrown into the lake of fire.

The New Jerusalem

21 Then I saw a new heaven and a new earth, for the first heaven and the first earth had passed away, and there was no longer any sea. [2]I saw the Holy City, the new Jerusalem, coming down out of heaven from God, prepared as a bride beautifully dressed for her husband. [3]And I heard a loud voice from the throne saying, "Now the dwelling of God is with men, and he will live with them. They will be his people, and God himself will be with them and be their God. [4]He will wipe every tear from their eyes. There will be no more death or mourning or crying or pain, for the old order of things has passed away."

[5]He who was seated on the throne said, "I am making everything new!" Then he said, "Write this down, for these words are trustworthy and true."

[6]He said to me: "It is done. I am the Alpha and the Omega, the Beginning and the End. To him who is thirsty I will give to drink without cost from the spring of the water of life. [7]He who overcomes will inherit all this, and I will be his God and he will be my son. [8]But the cowardly, the unbelieving, the vile, the murderers, the sexually immoral, those who practice magic arts, the idolaters and all liars—their place will be in the fiery lake of burning sulfur. This is the second death."

[9]One of the seven angels who had the seven bowls full of the seven last plagues came and said to me, "Come, I will show you the bride, the wife of the Lamb." [10]And he carried me away in the Spirit to a mountain great and high, and showed me the Holy City, Jerusalem, coming down out of heaven from God. [11]It shone with the glory of God, and its brilliance was like that of a very precious jewel, like a jasper, clear as crystal. [12]It had a great, high wall with twelve gates, and with twelve angels at the gates. On the gates were written the names of the twelve tribes of Israel. [13]There were three gates on the east, three on the north, three on the south and three on the west. [14]The wall of the city had twelve foundations, and on them were the names of the twelve apostles of the Lamb.

[15]The angel who talked with me had a measuring rod of gold to measure the city, its gates and its walls. [16]The city was laid out like a square, as long as it was wide. He measured the city with the rod and found it to be 12,000 stadia[a] in length, and as wide and high as it is long. [17]He measured its wall and it was 144 cubits[b] thick,[c] by man's measurement, which the angel was using. [18]The wall was made of jasper, and the city of pure gold, as pure as glass. [19]The foundations of the city walls were decorated with every kind of precious stone. The first foundation was jasper, the second sapphire, the third chalcedony, the fourth emerald, [20]the fifth sardonyx, the sixth carnelian, the seventh chrysolite, the eighth beryl, the ninth topaz, the tenth chrysoprase, the eleventh jacinth, and the twelfth amethyst.[d] [21]The twelve gates were twelve pearls, each gate made of a single pearl. The great street of the city was of pure gold, like transparent glass.

[22]I did not see a temple in the city, because the Lord God Almighty and the Lamb are its temple. [23]The city does not need the sun or the moon to shine on it, for the glory of God gives it light, and the Lamb is its lamp. [24]The nations will walk by its light, and the kings of the earth will bring their splendor into it. [25]On no day will its gates ever be shut, for there will be no night there. [26]The glory and honor of the nations will be brought into it. [27]Nothing impure will ever enter it, nor will anyone who does what is shameful or deceitful, but only those whose names are written in the Lamb's book of life.

The River of Life

22 Then the angel showed me the river of the water of life, as clear as crystal, flowing from the throne of God and of the Lamb [2]down the middle of the great street of the city. On each side of the river stood the tree of life, bearing twelve crops of fruit, yielding its fruit every month. And the leaves of the tree are for the healing of the nations. [3]No longer will there be any curse. The throne of God and of the Lamb will be in the city, and his servants will serve him. [4]They will see his face, and his name will be on their foreheads. [5]There will be no more night. They will not need the light of a lamp or the light of the sun, for the Lord God will give them light. And they will reign for ever and ever.

[6]The angel said to me, "These words are trustworthy and true. The Lord, the God of the spirits

---

[a]16 That is, about 1,400 miles (about 2,200 kilometers)   [b]17 That is, about 200 feet (about 65 meters)   [c]17 Or *high*   [d]20 The precise identification of some of these precious stones is uncertain.

of the prophets, sent his angel to show his servants the things that must soon take place."

Jesus Is Coming

[7]"Behold, I am coming soon! Blessed is he who keeps the words of the prophecy in this book."

22:1 Eden Regained

The last two chapters of Revelation contain numerous parallels to the description of the Garden of Eden in the first three chapters of Genesis. Revelation describes a new creation that excludes all the things that spoiled Eden. There will be no night and no death. Satan will disappear forever, and nothing impure will enter the new city. People will walk with God again, just as they did in Eden. There will be no crying or pain. Once again humankind will rule over creation, this time with open access to the tree of life. Everything put wrong by human rebellion in Eden will be set right. In Eden, Adam and Eve were driven from the garden; in the new earth, they will see God's face.

[8]I, John, am the one who heard and saw these things. And when I had heard and seen them, I fell down to worship at the feet of the angel who had been showing them to me. [9]But he said to me, "Do not do it! I am a fellow servant with you and with your brothers the prophets and of all who keep the words of this book. Worship God!"

[10]Then he told me, "Do not seal up the words of the prophecy of this book, because the time is near. [11]Let him who does wrong continue to do wrong; let him who is vile continue to be vile; let him who does right continue to do right; and let him who is holy continue to be holy."

[12]"Behold, I am coming soon! My reward is with me, and I will give to everyone according to what he has done. [13]I am the Alpha and the Omega, the First and the Last, the Beginning and the End.

[14]"Blessed are those who wash their robes, that they may have the right to the tree of life and may go through the gates into the city. [15]Outside are the dogs, those who practice magic arts, the sexually immoral, the murderers, the idolaters and everyone who loves and practices falsehood.

[16]"I, Jesus, have sent my angel to give you[a] this testimony for the churches. I am the Root and the Offspring of David, and the bright Morning Star."

[17]The Spirit and the bride say, "Come!" And let him who hears say, "Come!" Whoever is thirsty, let him come; and whoever wishes, let him take the free gift of the water of life.

[18]I warn everyone who hears the words of the prophecy of this book: If anyone adds anything to them, God will add to him the plagues described in this book. [19]And if anyone takes words away from this book of prophecy, God will take away from him his share in the tree of life and in the holy city, which are described in this book.

[20]He who testifies to these things says, "Yes, I am coming soon."

Amen. Come, Lord Jesus.

[21]The grace of the Lord Jesus be with God's people. Amen.

---

[a] 16 The Greek is plural.

Weights & Measures

The figures of the table are calculated on the basis of a shekel equaling 11.5 grams, a cubit equaling 18 inches and an ephah equaling 22 liters. The quart referred to is either a dry quart (slightly larger than a liter) or a liquid quart (slightly smaller than a liter), whichever is applicable. The ton referred to in the footnotes in the American ton of 2,000 pounds.

This table is based upon the best available information, but it is not intended to be mathematically precise; like the measurement equivalents in the footnotes, it merely gives the approximate amounts and distances. Weights and measures differed somewhat at various times and places in the ancient world. There is uncertainty particularly about the ephah and the bath; further discoveries may give more light on these units of capacity.

	BIBLICAL UNIT		APPROXIMATE AMERICAN EQUIVALENT	APPROXIMATE METRIC EQUIVALENT
WEIGHTS	talent	*(60 minas)*	75 pounds	34 kilograms
	mina	*(50 shekels)*	1¼ pounds	0.6 kilogram
	shekel	*(2 bekas)*	⅖ ounce	11.5 grams
	pim	*(⅔ shekel)*	⅓ ounce	7.6 grams
	beka	*(10 gerahs)*	⅕ ounce	5.5 grams
	gerah		¹⁄₅₀ ounce	0.6 gram
LENGTH	cubit		18 inches	0.5 meter
	span		9 inches	23 centimeters
	handbreadth		3 inches	8 centimeters
CAPACITY				
Dry Measure	cor [homer]	*(10 ephahs)*	6 bushels	220 liters
	lethek	*(5 ephahs)*	3 bushels	110 liters
	ephah	*(10 omers)*	⅗ bushel	22 liters
	seah	*(⅓ ephah)*	7 quarts	7.3 liters
	omer	*(¹⁄₁₀ ephah)*	2 quarts	2 liters
	cab	*(¹⁄₁₈ ephah)*	1 quart	1 liter
Liquid Measure	bath	*(1 ephah)*	6 gallons	22 liters
	hin	*(⅙ bath)*	4 quarts	4 liters
	log	*(¹⁄₇₂ bath)*	⅓ quart	0.3 liter

Acknowledgments

Philip Yancey, General Editor of *The Student Bible,* came up with the original concept while serving as Editor of *Campus Life* magazine. He now divides his time between free-lance writing and his responsibilities as Editor at Large for *Christianity Today.* He has authored thirteen books, including *Where Is God When It Hurts?, Disappointment with God,* and *The Jesus I Never Knew.*

Tim Stafford wrote many of the notes for *The Student Bible,* especially in the Old Testament portions. He too divides his time between free-lance writing and editorial responsibilities at *Christianity Today.* His books include *That's Not What I Meant, Sexual Chaos,* and *Knowing the Face of God.*

Not long after its publication in 1986, *The Student Bible* became the best-selling edition of the Bible in the United States, and since then has attracted over three million readers. Many of these readers wrote to say that the combination of scholarship and simplicity opened up the Bible for them in a new way. Partly in response to those letters, *The Student Bible* has undergone substantial revisions.

In 1992 a new edition updated existing material and added many new features, including 400 new Highlights and a greatly expanded Subject Guide. This edition also included a "parallel passages" feature under many boldface sectional headings in Matthew, Mark, Luke and John, sending you to other places where the same event or teaching is recorded. Note also the Glossary of Nonbiblical People and Places beginning on page 1349, where you will find a brief description of names used in Introductions, Insights and Highlights. Hunter and Edith Norwood and Chase and Harriet Stafford did much of the research and initial writing of the added Highlights, and Connie Van Dyke prepared additional material for the Subject Guide.

Now, in this ten-year (1996) edition, *The Student Bible* has undergone further revision. Tim Stafford wrote the profiles of "100 People You Should Know." Sharon Wright redesigned the entire Bible, creatively combining new graphic elements and typefaces with a second color. And many changes were made to the "Where to Find It" section in the back, making it a more useful and convenient reference resource.

Any Bible publishing project relies on many people, and the following are a few of those who helped with *The Student Bible:*

Nathan Young designed the original *Student Bible* and was invaluably cheerful, flexible and skilled.

Dirk Buursma, Michael Vander Klipp, Doris Rikkers and Sandra Vander Zicht, editors at Zondervan, helped refine both words and design. In addition, they watched over the many complicated details of typesetting and production.

Virginia Vagt, through her research and common sense, turned the original concept for *The Student Bible* in new directions.

Scott Bolinder and Harold Myra helped greatly in improving, encouraging, and aiding the work.

Dr. Kenneth Kantzer made careful suggestions about questions of scholarship and theology.

Lenora Rand, Connie Van Dyke and Verlyn Verbrugge did much of the painstaking work for the Subject Guide.

In the process of developing *The Student Bible,* many helpful people and organizations contributed their insights, especially these: Association of Christian Schools International, Billy Graham Evangelistic Association, Campus Crusade for Christ, Dr. Jim Engel, Focus on the Family, Fuller Theological Seminary, the International Bible Society, InterVarsity Christian Fellowship, Josh McDowell, National Network of Youth Ministries, the Navigators, Search Institute, Student Venture, Chuck Swindoll, Dr. Mel White, Young Life, Youth for Christ and Youth Specialties.

THE NEW INTERNATIONAL VERSION is a completely new translation of the Holy Bible made by over a hundred scholars working directly from the best available Hebrew, Aramaic and Greek texts. It had its beginning in 1965 when, after several years of exploratory study by committees from the Christian Reformed Church and the National Association of Evangelicals, a group of scholars met at Palos Heights, Illinois, and concurred in the need for a new translation of the Bible in contemporary English. This group, though not made up of official church representatives, was trans-denominational. Its conclusion was endorsed by a large number of leaders from many denominations who met in Chicago in 1966.

Responsibility for the new version was delegated by the Palos Heights group to a self-governing body of fifteen, the Committee on Bible Translation, composed for the most part of biblical scholars from colleges, universities and seminaries. In 1967 the New York Bible Society (now the International Bible Society) generously undertook the financial sponsorship of the project—a sponsorship that made it possible to enlist the help of many distinguished scholars. The fact that participants from the United States, Great Britain, Canada, Australia and New Zealand worked together gave the project its international scope. That they were from many denominations—including Anglican, Assemblies of God, Baptist, Brethren, Christian Reformed, Church of Christ, Evangelical Free, Lutheran, Mennonite, Methodist, Nazarene, Presbyterian, Wesleyan and other churches—helped to safeguard the translation from sectarian bias.

How it was made helps to give the New International Version its distinctiveness. The translation of each book was assigned to a team of scholars. Next, one of the Intermediate Editorial Committees revised the initial translation, with constant reference to the Hebrew, Aramaic or Greek. Their work then went to one of the General Editorial Committees, which checked it in detail and made another thorough revision. This revision in turn was carefully reviewed by the Committee on Bible Translation, which made further changes and then released the final version for publication. In this way the entire Bible underwent three revisions, during each of which the translation was examined for its faithfulness to the original languages and for its English style.

All this involved many thousands of hours of research and discussion regarding the meaning of the texts and the precise way of putting them into English. It may well be that no other translation has been made by a more thorough process of review and revision from committee to committee than this one.

From the beginning of the project, the Committee on Bible Translation held to certain goals for the New International Version: that it would be an accurate translation and one that would have clarity and literary quality and so prove suitable for public and private reading, teaching, preaching, memorizing and liturgical use. The Committee also sought to preserve some measure of continuity with the long tradition of translating the Scriptures into English.

In working toward these goals, the translators were united in their commitment to the authority and infallibility of the Bible as God's Word in written form. They believe that it contains the divine answer to the deepest needs of humanity, that it sheds unique light on our path in a dark world, and that it sets forth the way to our eternal well-being.

The first concern of the translators has been the accuracy of the translation and its fidelity to the thought of the biblical writers. They have weighed the significance of the lexical and grammatical details of the Hebrew, Aramaic and Greek texts. At the same time, they have striven for more than a word-for-word translation. Because thought patterns and syntax differ from language to language, faithful communication of the meaning of the writers of the Bible demands frequent modifications in sentence structure and constant regard for the contextual meanings of words.

A sensitive feeling for style does not always accompany scholarship. Accordingly the Committee on Bible Translation submitted the developing version to a number of stylistic consultants. Two of them read every book of both Old and New Testaments twice—once before and once after the last major revision—and made invaluable suggestions. Samples of the translation were tested for clarity and ease of reading by various kinds of people—young and old, highly educated and less well educated, ministers and laymen.

Concern for clear and natural English—that the New International Version should be idiomatic but not idiosyncratic, contemporary but not dated—motivated the translators and consultants. At the same time, they tried to reflect the differing styles of the biblical writers. In view of the international use of English, the translators sought to avoid obvious Americanisms on the one hand and obvious Anglicisms on the other. A British edition reflects the comparatively few differences of significant idiom and of spelling.

As for the traditional pronouns "thou," "thee" and "thine" in reference to the Deity, the translators judged that to use these archaisms (along with the old verb forms such as "doest," "wouldest" and "hadst") would violate accuracy in translation. Neither Hebrew, Aramaic nor Greek uses special pronouns for the persons of the Godhead. A present-day translation is not enhanced by forms that in the time of the King James Version were used in everyday speech, whether referring to God or man.

For the Old Testament the standard Hebrew text, the Masoretic Text as published in the latest editions of *Biblia Hebraica,* was used throughout. The Dead Sea Scrolls contain material bearing on an earlier stage of the Hebrew text. They were consulted, as were the Samaritan Pentateuch and the ancient scribal traditions relating to textual changes. Sometimes a variant Hebrew reading in the margin of the Masoretic Text was followed instead of the text itself. Such instances, being variants within the Masoretic tradition, are not specified by footnotes. In rare cases, words in the consonantal text were divided differently from the way they appear in the Masoretic Text. Footnotes indicate this. The translators also consulted the more important early versions—the Septuagint; Aquila, Symmachus and Theodotion; the Vulgate; the Syriac Peshitta; the Targums; and for the Psalms the *Juxta Hebraica* of Jerome. Readings from these versions were occasionally followed where the Masoretic Text seemed doubtful and where accepted principles of textual criticism showed that one or more of these textual witnesses appeared to provide the correct reading. Such instances are footnoted. Sometimes vowel letters and vowel signs did not, in the judgment of the translators, represent the correct vowels for the original consonantal text. Accordingly some words were read with a different set of vowels. These instances are usually not indicated by footnotes.

The Greek text used in translating the New Testament was an eclectic one. No other piece of ancient literature has such an abundance of manuscript witnesses as does the New Testament. Where existing manuscripts differ, the translators made their choice of readings according to accepted principles of New Testament textual criticism. Footnotes call attention to places where there was uncertainty about what the original text was. The best current printed texts of the Greek New Testament were used.

There is a sense in which the work of translation is never wholly finished. This applies to all great literature and uniquely so to the Bible. In 1973 the New Testament in the New International Version was published. Since then, suggestions for corrections and revisions have been received from various sources. The Committee on Bible Translation carefully considered the suggestions and adopted a number of them. These were incorporated in the first printing of the entire Bible in 1978. Additional revisions were made by the Committee on Bible Translation in 1983 and appear in printings after that date.

As in other ancient documents, the precise meaning of the biblical texts is sometimes uncertain. This is more often the case with the Hebrew and Aramaic texts than with the Greek text. Although archaeological and linguistic discoveries in this century aid in understanding difficult passages, some uncertainties remain. The more significant of these have been called to the reader's attention in the footnotes.

In regard to the divine name *YHWH,* commonly referred to as the *Tetragrammaton,* the translators adopted the device used in most English versions of rendering that name as "Lord" in capital letters to distinguish it from *Adonai,* another Hebrew word rendered "Lord," for which small letters are used. Wherever the two names stand together in the Old Testament as a compound name of God, they are rendered "Sovereign Lord."

Because for most readers today the phrases "the Lord of hosts" and "God of hosts" have little meaning, this version renders them "the Lord Almighty" and "God Almighty." These renderings convey the sense of the Hebrew, namely, "he who is sovereign over all the 'hosts' (powers) in heaven and on earth, especially over the 'hosts' (armies) of Israel." For readers unacquainted with Hebrew this does not make clear the distinction between *Sabaoth* ("hosts" or "Almighty") and *Shaddai* (which can also be translated "Almighty"), but the latter occurs infrequently and is always footnoted. When *Adonai* and *YHWH Sabaoth* occur together, they are rendered "the Lord, the Lord Almighty."

As for other proper nouns, the familiar spellings of the King James Version are generally retained. Names traditionally spelled with "ch," except where it is final, are usually spelled in this translation with "k" or "c," since the biblical languages do not have the sound that "ch" frequently indicates in English—for example, in *chant.* For well-known names such as Zechariah, however, the traditional spelling has been retained. Variation in the spelling of names in the original languages has usually not been indicated. Where a person or place has two or more different names in the Hebrew, Aramaic or Greek texts, the more familiar one has generally been used, with footnotes where needed.

To achieve clarity the translators sometimes supplied words not in the original texts but required by the context. If there was uncertainty about such words, it is enclosed in brackets. Also for the sake of clarity or style, nouns, including some proper nouns, are sometimes substituted for pronouns, and vice versa. And though the Hebrew writers often shifted back and forth between first, second and third personal pronouns without change of antecedent, this translation often makes them uniform, in accordance with English style and without the use of footnotes.

Poetical passages are printed as poetry, that is, with indentation of lines with separate stanzas. These are generally designed to reflect the structure of Hebrew poetry. This poetry is normally characterized by parallelism in balanced lines. Most of the poetry in the Bible is in the Old Testament, and scholars differ regarding the scansion of Hebrew lines. The translators determined the stanza divisions for the most part by analysis of the subject matter. The stanzas therefore serve as poetic paragraphs.

As an aid to the reader, italicized sectional headings are inserted in most of the books. They are not to be regarded as part of the NIV text, are not for oral reading, and are not intended to dictate the interpretation of the sections they head.

The footnotes in this version are of several kinds, most of which need no explanation. Those giving alternative translations begin with "Or" and generally introduce the alternative with the last word preceding it in the text, except when it is a single-word alternative; in poetry quoted in a footnote a slant mark indicates a line division. Footnotes introduced by "Or" do not have uniform significance. In some cases two possible translations were considered to have about equal validity. In other cases, though the translators were convinced that the translation in the text was correct, they judged that another interpretation was possible and of sufficient importance to be represented in a footnote.

In the New Testament, footnotes that refer to uncertainty regarding the original text are introduced by "Some manuscripts" or similar expressions. In the Old Testament, evidence for the reading chosen is given first and evidence for the alternative is added after a semicolon (for example: Septuagint; Hebrew *father*). In such notes the term "Hebrew" refers to the Masoretic Text.

It should be noted that minerals, flora and fauna, architectural details, articles of clothing and jewelry, musical instruments and other articles cannot always be identified with precision. Also measures of capacity in the biblical period are particularly uncertain (see the table of weights and measures following the text).

Like all translations of the Bible, made as they are by imperfect man, this one undoubtedly falls short of its goals. Yet we are grateful to God for the extent to which he has enabled us to realize these goals and for the strength he has given us and our colleagues to complete our task. We offer this version of the Bible to him in whose name and for whose glory it has been made. We pray that it will lead many into a better understanding of the Holy Scriptures and a fuller knowledge of Jesus Christ the incarnate Word, of whom the Scriptures so faithfully testify.

The Committee on Bible Translation

June 1978
(Revised August 1983)

Names of the translators and editors may be secured
from the International Bible Society,
translation sponsors of the New International Version,
1820 Jet Stream Drive, Colorado Springs, Colorado
80921-3696 U.S.A.

WHERE
TO FIND IT

100 People
YOU SHOULD KNOW

Glossary
OF NONBIBLICAL PEOPLE AND PLACES

This glossary lists the names and gives brief descriptions of most of the nonbiblical people and places cited in Introductions, Insights, and Highlights. We have made every effort to be accurate and comprehensive, while acknowledging the limitations of such a list.

Alcatraz an island in the San Francisco Bay, former site of a famous U.S. prison (reference can be found on page 1316).

Idi Amin (1925–) at one time the cruel dictator of the East African nation of Uganda, known for his persecution of Christians (references can be found on pages 912 and 1294).

Roy Chapman Andrews (1884–1960) U.S. naturalist and explorer, best known for books on his central Asiatic field trips (reference can be found on page 1281).

Armenia a region and ancient kingdom in southwestern Asia, now divided between Russia, Turkey and Iran (reference can be found on page 1294).

Augustine (354–430) bishop of Hippo in Roman Africa who was in his day the dominant personality of the Western church (reference can be found on page 1174).

Joseph Bayly American author, educator, and longtime columnist for *Eternity* magazine, known for books such as *The View From a Hearse* and *Psalms of My Life* (reference can be found on page 547).

Bernard of Clairvaux (1090–1153) the abbot of Clairvaux in France, a mystic and reformer known as a writer of sermons and treatises (reference can be found on page 704).

William Booth (1829–1912) founder of the Salvation Army, deeply committed to evangelistic and social justice activities (reference can be found on page 592).

Dietrich Bonhoeffer (1906–1945) German theologian who resisted the Nazi regime and was executed for treason; known for such books as *The Cost of Discipleship* (reference can be found on page 691).

Charles Loring Brace (1826–1890) U.S. reformer and pioneer social welfare worker, founder and director of the Children's Aid Society of New York City (reference can be found on page 1229).

Buddha (563–483 B.C.) Indian philosopher, founder of Buddhism (reference can be found on page 1277).

Frederick Buechner (1926–) ordained Presbyterian minister, called by the *New York Times* the leading clergyman/writer in the U.S., the widely read author of many novels and works of nonfiction (reference can be found on page 569).

John Bunyan (1628–1688) English Puritan minister, considered to be the greatest literary genius to come out of the Puritan movement (reference can be found on page 1233).

John Calvin (1509–1564) French-born Genevan theologian and reformer, a leader in the Protestant Reformation of the 16th century (reference can be found on page 1279).

Rachel Carson (1907–1964) U.S. scientist and writer, a pioneer in the environmentalist movement, especially in her warnings about the effects of pesticides on the environment (reference can be found on page 634).

Chartres a city in northwestern France, site of the great cathedral of Notre Dame (reference can be found on page 120).

G.K. Chesterton (1874–1936) English journalist and author, outstanding as critic, polemicist, and rhetorical poet (reference can be found on page 1174).

Winston Churchill (1874–1965) British statesman and orator, the great national leader during World War II (references can be found on pages 777 and 971).

Samuel Taylor Coleridge (1772–1834) English poet, lecturer, journalist, and critic of literature, theology, philosophy, and society (reference can be found on page 1233).

Charles Colson U.S. government official during Richard Nixon's presidency, convicted for his role in the Watergate scandal; now active as an evangelical Christian author and the founder and leader of a prison ministry (reference can be found on page 1151).

Leonardo da Vinci (1452–1519) Florentine artist and scientist, known for such works as *The Last Supper* and the *Mona Lisa* (references can be found on pages 1123 and 1277).

Fedor Mikhailovich Dostoevski (1821–1881) Russian novelist of international reputation, generally acknowledged as one of the profoundest creative artists of the 19th century, known for such works as *The Brothers Karamazov* (reference can be found on page 1233).

Albert Einstein (1879–1955) German-born physicist, who emigrated to the United States; creator of the theory of relativity (reference can be found on page 569).

Jacques Ellul (1912–1994) French historian and sociologist known for works such as *The Meaning of the City* and *The Technological Society* (reference can be found on page 1325).

Henry Ford (1863–1947) U.S. industrialist known as the creator of modern mass production, most notably in the assembly-line method of automobile production (reference can be found on page 1229).

Robert Frost (1874–1963) American poet who used symbols from common life to express the values of rural New England, four-time winner of the Pulitzer Prize (reference can be found on page 948).

Mohandas Karamchand Gandhi (1869–1948) architect of India's freedom through a nonviolent revolution (references can be found on pages 83 and 1277).

Grand Canyon an immense gorge cut by the Colorado River into the high plateaus of the northern part of Arizona (reference can be found on page 1281).

Alex Haley (1923–1992) African-American author best known for his book *Roots*, the basis of a made-for-television mini-series (reference can be found on page 995).

Georg Friedrich Handel (1685–1759) German-born composer who spent the majority of his life in England; the greatest English composer of the late baroque era, known best for his oratorio *The Messiah* (reference can be found on page 1321).

Hare Krishna a religious sect of Hindu character, founded by an Indian holy man; its followers are characterized by rhythmic chanting of the 'Hare Krsna' (reference can be found on page 1242).

Paul Harvey (1918–) an American radio newscaster known for his unique intonation and special interest stories (reference can be found on page 1039).

Herodotus (5th century B.C.) Greek author of a history of the Persian Wars (references can be found on pages 421, 530, 532).

Hindus adherents of Hinduism, a religious system whose precepts govern a vast range of human activity outside the scope of most modern religions; the Republic of India is home to more than 95 percent of all Hindus (reference can be found on page 417).

Hiroshima a seaport city in southwestern Japan, the first city on which the U.S. air force dropped an atomic bomb in 1945 (reference can be found on page 839).

Adolf Hitler (1889–1945) Austrian-born politician, leader of the Nazi party, who became dictator of Germany in 1933 and led the nation into World War II (references can be found on pages 85, 396, 528, 912).

Homer Greek epic poet, regarded as the author of many narrative poems, and according to later tradition, author of the *Iliad* and *Odyssey* (reference can be found on page 711).

Howard Hughes (1905–1976) an eccentric American businessman who amassed a fortune but died a miserable recluse (reference can be found on page 693).

Samuel Huntington (1731–1796) signer of the Declaration of Independence, president of the continental congress (1779-81) and governor of Connecticut (reference can be found on page 308).

Saddam Hussein (1937–) the cruel president of Iraq, who led his nation into the Persian Gulf War (1991) as a result of Iraq's invasion of Kuwait (references can be found on pages 85, 912, 945).

Kali Hindu goddess, usually represented as black with bloody hands, eyes, teeth, and tongue, whose worship appears to be an extension of the widespread mother-goddess cult (reference can be found on page 417).

John F. Kennedy (1917–1963) 35th president of the U.S., the youngest man and first Roman Catholic to be elected to that office; fourth U.S. president in history to die by an assassin's bullet (reference can be found on page 480).

Ruholla Mussavi Khomeini (1900–1989) one-time religious leader of Iran, served as the leader of the Shi'ite Muslims, who comprise about 90 percent of Iran's population (reference can be found on page 912).

Derek Kidner former warden of Tyndale House, Cambridge, and author of numerous Old Testament commentaries and expositions (reference can be found on page 55).

Martin Luther King (1929–1968) U.S. African-American clergyman who received the 1964 Nobel Peace Prize for his leadership in the nonviolent struggle for racial equality in the U.S. (reference can be found on page 971).

Ku Klux Klan a secret, masked organization that, after the American Civil War, became the chief instrument of the white underground resistance movement in the south against northerners and African-Americans (reference can be found on page 945).

Ann Landers (1918–) born Esther Pauline Friedman, is best known as 'Ann Landers,' syndicated advice-column writer for newspapers around the U.S. (reference can be found on page 68).

C.S. Lewis (1898–1963) Irish-born author who achieved worldwide fame for books on Christian apologetics and other subjects; known for books such as *The Screwtape Letters, Mere Christianity*, and *The Chronicles of Narnia* (reference can be found on page 1120).

Abraham Lincoln (1809–1865) 16th president of the U.S., led the nation during the Civil War; the issuer of the Emancipation Proclamation, which directly or indirectly led to freedom for hundreds of thousands of slaves (references can be found on pages 83, 604, 1080, 1120, 1180).

Martin Luther (1483–1546) German religious leader who began the Protestant Reformation (references can be found on pages 963, 1174, 1176, 1225, 1288).

Douglas MacArthur (1880–1964) American general who gained fame for his military leadership in World War II (reference can be found on page 336).

Mao Tse Tung (1893–1976) Chinese revolutionist and statesman, Communist Party leader and founder of the Chinese communist state (reference can be found on page 912).

Mau Mau a nativistic cult among the Kikuya tribe in Kenya responsible for a 1950 rebellion directed against the presence of Europeans in Kenya and their ownership of land (reference can be found on page 1294).

Michelangelo (1475–1564) a native Italian, he is considered to be the greatest painter of the Renaissance and the most famous of all sculptors since the time of the Greeks, best known for his statue of "David" and his four-year painting project in the Sistine Chapel in Rome (reference can be found on page 23).

Bill Miner (1847–1913) notorious outlaw who terrorized stagecoach runs in the western U.S. (reference can be found on page 230).

Nazis followers of the National Socialist party in Germany, a party headed by Adolf Hitler, who took control of the country in 1933 (reference can be found on page 945).

John Newton (1725–1807) one of the leaders of the Evangelical revival in England, a former seafarer who after his conversion to Christianity wrote hymns (most notably *Amazing Grace*) and devotional letters (reference can be found on page 540).

Blaise Pascal (1623–1662) French mathematician and philosopher, author of a comprehensive treatise on Christian apologetics (reference can be found on page 703).

Louis Pasteur (1822–1895) French chemist and microbiologist who developed a vaccine for rabies and the method of heat pasteurization for liquid foods and beverages (reference can be found on page 138).

J.B. Phillips British pastor who devoted much of his life to writing a fresh translation of the New Testament, publishing the entire New Testament in 1958 and revising it in 1972 (reference can be found on page 1139).

Pablo Picasso (1881–1973) Spanish painter, sculptor, and engraver, the most influential independent artist of the 20th century (reference can be found on page 1325).

Grigori Efimovich Rasputin (1872–1916) Russian peasant and mystic notorious for his phenomenal sexual appetite and his impact as the voice of the peasantry (reference can be found on page 1181).

John D. Rockefeller (1874–1960) American oil magnate and philanthropist (reference can be found on page 698).

Franklin Delano Roosevelt (1882–1945) the U.S.'s 32nd president and only president to be reelected three times, he served during the New Deal era and World War II (reference can be found on page 201).

Dorothy Sayers (1893–1957) noted English writer of mystery novels, featuring the sleuth Lord Peter Wimsey (reference can be found on page 1057).

Scientology, Church of a quasi-scientific and religious discipline founded by American Ron Hubbard, it formally became the Church of Scientology in 1955 (reference can be found on page 1242).

Ignaz Philipp Semmelweis (1818–1865) Hungarian physician who had a dramatic influence on the development of knowledge and control of infection, notably through his work in the control of puerperal (childbirth) fever (reference can be found on page 138).

William Shakespeare (1564–1616) Elizabethan Englishman generally acknowledged as not only England's, but the world's, greatest poet and playwright (references can be found on pages 644 and 711).

Sistine Chapel the pope's private chapel, built under commission from Sixtus IV; Julius II commissioned Michelangelo to paint its ceiling (reference can be found on page 23).

Aleksandr Solzhenitsyn (1918–) noted Russian author known for such works as *One Day in the Life of Ivan Denisovich* and *The Gulag Archipelago* (references can be found on pages 548, 1151, 1233).

Josef Stalin (1879–1953) leader of the Communist party of the Soviet Union, generalissimo and dictator of the USSR and one of the most powerful, complex, and controversial figures in world history (reference can be found on page 912).

J.R.R. Tolkien (1892–1973) English author best known for his imaginative works such as *Lord of the Rings* (reference can be found on page 388).

Harry Truman (1884–1972) 33rd president of the U.S., serving from 1945–1953 (reference can be found on page 336).

Abigail Van Buren (1918–) born Pauline Esther Friedman, she is best known for her work as writer of the advice column "Dear Abby" for U.S. newspapers (reference can be found on page 68).

Katie von Bora (1499–1552) a former nun, she married Protestant Reformer Martin Luther in 1525 (reference can be found on page 1225).

Lech Walesa champion of the working class in Poland who rallied the nation to independence from Russian influence (reference can be found on page 83).

George Washington (1732–1799) commander in chief, statesman, and first president of the U.S. (references can be found on pages 83, 308, 324, 462, 1180).

Charles Wesley (1707–1788) English clergyman, poet, and hymnwriter who, together with his brother John, started the Methodist movement in the Church of England (reference can be found on page 1247).

John Wesley (1703–1791) English clergyman and founder of Methodism (references can be found on pages 1174 and 1247).

Oscar Wilde (1854–1900) Irish poet and dramatist, author of such works as *The Importance of Being Earnest* and *The Picture of Dorian Gray* (reference can be found on page 693).

Thomas Wolfe (1900–1938) American novelist, known for such works as *Look Homeward, Angel* (reference can be found on page 694).

Frank Lloyd Wright (1867–1959) U.S. architect who became world famous as creator and expounder of 'organic architecture,' designing buildings that harmonize with users and the environment (reference can be found on page 1277).

Well-known Biblical Events

OVERVIEW OF BIBLICAL EVENTS

(in approximate order of occurrence)

Creation: *Genesis 1–2*
The first sin, or fall: *Genesis 3*
Cain kills Abel: *Genesis 4*
Noah and the ark: *Genesis 6–9*
Sodom and Gomorrah: *Genesis 18–19*
Abraham sacrifices Isaac: *Genesis 22*
Jacob's ladder: *Genesis 28:10–22*
Joseph and the coat of many colors: *Genesis 37*
Moses' birth: *Exodus 2*
Moses and the burning bush: *Exodus 3*
Plagues on Egypt: *Exodus 7–11*
The exodus: *Exodus 12–13*
The Ten Commandments: *Exodus 20*
The battle of Jericho: *Joshua 6*
Gideon and the fleece: *Judges 6–7*
Samson and Delilah: *Judges 13–16*
God calls young Samuel: *1 Samuel 1–3*
David and Goliath: *1 Samuel 17*
David and Bathsheba: *2 Samuel 11*
Elijah versus the priests of Baal: *1 Kings 18*
The miracles of Elisha: *2 Kings 4–5*
Ezekiel and the dry bones: *Ezekiel 37*
Daniel in the lions' den: *Daniel 6*
Jonah and the fish: *Jonah 1*
Hosea and his adulterous wife: *Hosea 1–3*
Jesus' birth: *Luke 1–2*
Jesus' baptism: *Mark 1:9–11*
Temptation of Jesus: *Luke 4:1–13*
Jesus clears the temple: *John 2:12–25*
The transfiguration of Jesus: *Matthew 17:1–13*
Jesus raises Lazarus from the dead: *John 11:1–46*
Jesus' triumphal entry into Jerusalem: *Mark 11:1–11*
Jesus and the widow's offering: *Mark 12:41–44*
The Last Supper: *Luke 22:7–38*
Jesus washes his disciples' feet: *John 13:1–17*
Jesus at Gethsemane: *Matthew 26:36–56*
Judas betrays Jesus: *Luke 22:1–53*

Peter denies Christ: *Luke 22:54–62*
Jesus' crucifixion: *Matthew 26:57–27:66*
Jesus' resurrection and ascension: *Luke 24*
Holy Spirit at Pentecost: *Acts 2*
Stephen martyred: *Acts 6–7*
Paul's conversion: *Acts 9:1–31*
Peter's escape from prison: *Acts 12:1–19*
Paul and Silas in prison: *Acts 16:16–40*

MINISTRY OF JESUS

(in Biblical order)

Jesus baptized: *Matthew 3:13–17; Mark 1:9–11; Luke 3:21–22; John 1:29–34*
Jesus tempted by Satan: *Matthew 4:1–11; Mark 1:12–13; Luke 4:1–13*
Jesus' first miracle: *John 2:1–11*
Jesus and Nicodemus: *John 3:1–21*
Jesus talks to a Samaritan woman: *John 4:5–42*
Jesus heals an official's son: *John 4:46–54*
People of Nazareth try to kill Jesus: *Luke 4:16–30*
Jesus calls four fishermen: *Matthew 4:18–22; Mark 1:16–20; Luke 5:1–11*
Jesus heals Peter's mother-in-law: *Matthew 8:14–15; Mark 1:29–31; Luke 4:38–39*
Jesus begins preaching in Galilee: *Matthew 4:23–25; Mark 1:35–39; Luke 4:42–44*
Matthew decides to follow Jesus: *Matthew 9:9–13; Mark 2:13–17; Luke 5:27–32*
Jesus chooses twelve disciples: *Matthew 10:2–4; Mark 3:13–19; Luke 6:12–15*
Jesus preaches the Sermon on the Mount: *Matthew 5:1–7:29; Luke 6:20–49*
A sinful woman anoints Jesus: *Luke 7:36–50*
Jesus travels again through Galilee: *Luke 8:1–3*
Jesus tells kingdom parables: *Matthew 13:1–52; Mark 4:1–34; Luke 8:4–18*
Jesus quiets the storm: *Matthew 8:23–27; Mark 4:35–41; Luke 8:22–25*
Jairus's daughter raised to life: *Matthew 9:18–26; Mark 5:21–23; Luke 8:40–56*
Jesus sends out the twelve: *Matthew 9:35–11:1; Mark 6:6–13; Luke 9:1–6*
John the Baptist killed by Herod: *Matthew 14:1–12; Mark 6:14–29; Luke 9:7–9*
Jesus feeds the 5,000: *Matthew 14:13–21; Mark 6:30–44; Luke 9:10–17; John 6:1–14*
Jesus walks on water: *Matthew 14:22–32; Mark 6:47–52; John 6:16–21*
Jesus feeds the 4,000: *Matthew 15:32–39; Mark 8:1–10*
Peter confesses Jesus as the Son of God: *Matthew 16:13–20; Mark 8:27–30; Luke 9:18–21*
Jesus predicts his death: *Matthew 16:21–26; Mark 8:31–37; Luke 9:22–25*
Jesus is transfigured: *Matthew 17:1–13; Mark 9:2–13; Luke 9:28–36*
Jesus pays his temple taxes: *Matthew 17:24–27*
Jesus attends the Feast of Tabernacles: *John 7:10–52*
Jesus heals a man born blind: *John 9:1–41*
Jesus visits Mary and Martha: *Luke 10:38–42*
Jesus raises Lazarus from the dead: *John 11:1–44*
Jesus begins his last trip to Jerusalem: *Luke 17:11*
Jesus blesses the little children: *Matthew 19:13–15; Mark 10:13–16; Luke 18:15–17*

Jesus talks to the rich young man: *Matthew 19:16–30; Mark 10:17–31; Luke 18:18–30*
Jesus again predicts his death: *Matthew 20:17–19; Mark 10:32–34; Luke 18:31–34*
Jesus heals blind Bartimaeus: *Matthew 20:29–34; Mark 10:46–52; Luke 18:35–43*
Jesus talks to Zacchaeus: *Luke 19:1–10*
Jesus visits Mary and Martha again: *John 12:1–11*

MIRACLES OF JESUS

(in Biblical order)

HEALING OF INDIVIDUALS

Man with leprosy: *Matthew 8:1–4; Mark 1:40–44; Luke 5:12–14*
Roman centurion's servant: *Matthew 8:5–13; Luke 7:1–10*
Peter's mother-in-law: *Matthew 8:14–15; Mark 1:30–31; Luke 4:38–39*
Two demon-possessed men from Gadara: *Matthew 8:28–34; Mark 5:1–15; Luke 8:27–39*
Paralyzed man: *Matthew 9:2–7; Mark 2:3–12; Luke 5:18–26*
Woman with bleeding: *Matthew 9:20–22; Mark 5:25–34; Luke 8:43–48*
Two blind men: *Matthew 9:27–31*
Mute, demon-possessed man: *Matthew 9:32–33*
Man with a shriveled hand: *Matthew 12:10–13; Mark 3:1–5; Luke 6:6–11*
Blind, mute and demon-possessed man: *Matthew 12:22–23; Luke 11:14*
Canaanite woman's daughter: *Matthew 15:21–28; Mark 7:24–30*
Boy with epilepsy: *Matthew 17:14–21; Mark 9:17–29; Luke 9:38–43*
Two blind men (including Bartimaeus): *Matthew 20:29–34; Mark 10:46–52; Luke 18:35–43*
Demon-possessed man in synagogue: *Mark 1:21–28; Luke 4:31–37*
Blind man at Bethsaida: *Mark 8:22–26*
Crippled woman: *Luke 13:10–17*
Man with dropsy: *Luke 14:1–4*
Ten men with leprosy: *Luke 17:11–19*
The high priest's servant: *Luke 22:50–51*
Official's son at Capernaum: *John 4:46–54*
Sick man at the pool of Bethesda: *John 5:1–15*
Man born blind: *John 9:1–41*

CONTROL OF NATURE

Calming the storm: *Matthew 8:23–27; Mark 4:37–41; Luke 8:22–25*
Feeding of 5,000: *Matthew 14:1–21; Mark 6:30–44; Luke 9:10–17; John 6:1–14*
Walking on water: *Matthew 14:22–32; Mark 6:47–52; John 6:16–21*
Feeding of 4,000: *Matthew 15:32–39; Mark 8:1–9*
Fish with coin: *Matthew 17:24–27*
Fig tree withers: *Matthew 21:18–22; Mark 11:12–14, 20–25*
Huge catch of fish: *Luke 5:4–11; John 21:1–11*
Water into wine: *John 2:1–11*

RAISING THE DEAD

Jairus's daughter: *Matthew 9:18–26; Mark 5:21–43; Luke 8:40–56*
Widow at Nain's son: *Luke 7:11–17*
Lazarus: *John 11:1–44*

PARABLES OF JESUS

(in alphabetical order)

Canceled debts: *Luke 7:41–43*

Cost of discipleship: *Luke 14:28–33*

Faithful and wise servant: *Matthew 24:45–51; Luke 12:42–48*

Fig tree: *Matthew 24:32–35; Mark 13:28–31; Luke 21:29–33*

Good Samaritan: *Luke 10:30–37*

The great banquet: *Luke 14:16–24*

Growing seed: *Mark 4:26–29*

Hidden treasure and pearl: *Matthew 13:44–46*

Honor at a banquet: *Luke 14:7–14*

Lamp under a bowl: *Matthew 5:14–16; Mark 4:21–22; Luke 8:16; 11:33–36*

Lost coin: *Luke 15:8–10*

Lost sheep: *Matthew 18:12–14; Luke 15:4–7*

Mustard seed: *Matthew 13:31–32; Mark 4:30–32; Luke 13:18–19*

New cloth on an old garment: *Matthew 9:16; Mark 12:21; Luke 5:36*

New wine in old wineskins: *Matthew 9:17; Mark 2:22; Luke 5:37–39*

Net: *Matthew 13:47–50*

Obedient servants: *Luke 17:7–10*

Owner of a house: *Matthew 13:52*

Persistent friend: *Luke 11:5–8*

Persistent widow: *Luke 18:2–8*

Pharisee and the tax collector: *Luke 18:10–14*

Prodigal (lost) son: *Luke 15:11–32*

Rich fool: *Luke 12:16–21*

Rich man and Lazarus: *Luke 16:19–31*

Sheep and goats: *Matthew 25:31–46*

Shrewd manager: *Luke 16:1–8*

Sower: *Matthew 13:1–8, 18–23; Mark 4:3–8, 14–20; Luke 8:5–8, 11–15*

Talents: *Matthew 25:14–30*

Tenants: *Matthew 21:33–34; Mark 12:1–11; Luke 20:9–18*

Ten minas: *Luke 19:12–27*

Ten virgins: *Matthew 25:1–13*

Two sons: *Matthew 21:28–32*

Unfruitful fig tree: *Luke 13:6–9*

Unmerciful servant: *Matthew 18:23–35*

Watchful servants: *Mark 13:34–37; Luke 12:35–40*

Wedding banquet: *Matthew 22:2–14*

Weeds: *Matthew 13:24–30, 36–43*

Wise and foolish builders: *Matthew 7:24–27; Luke 6:47–49*

Workers in the vineyard: *Matthew 20:1–16*

Yeast: *Matthew 13:33; Luke 13:20–21*

TEACHINGS OF JESUS

(in alphabetical order)

Beatitudes: *Matthew 5:1–12*
Bread of life: *John 6:25–59*
Born again: *John 3:1–21*
Discipleship: *Luke 14:25–35*
Give to Caesar: *Mark 12:13–17*
Good shepherd: *John 10:1–21*
Golden Rule: *Luke 6:31*
Greatest commandment: *Matthew 22:34–40*
Living water: *John 4:1–26*
Lord's prayer: *Matthew 6:5–15*
Sending out the Twelve: *Matthew 10*
Sermon on the Mount: *Matthew 5–7*
Vine and branches: *John 15:1–17*
The way and the truth and the life: *John 14:5–14*
Wealth: *Matthew 19:16–30*
Worry: *Luke 12:22–34*

JESUS' LAST WEEK

(in Biblical order)

The triumphal entry: *Matthew 21:1–11; Mark 11:1–11; Luke 19:29–44; John 12:12–19*
Jesus curses the fig tree: *Matthew 21:18–22; Mark 11:12–14*
Jesus clears the temple: *Matthew 21:12–13; Mark 11:15–18; Luke 19:45–48*
Jesus' authority questioned: *Matthew 21:23–27; Mark 11:27–33; Luke 20:1–8*
Jesus teaches in the temple: *Matthew 21:28–23:39; Mark 12:1–44; Luke 20:9–21:4*
Jesus' feet anointed: *Matthew 26:6–13; Mark 14:3–9; John 12:2–11*
The plot against Jesus: *Matthew 26:14–16; Mark 14:10–11; Luke 22:3–6*
The Last Supper: *Matthew 26:17–29; Mark 14:12–25; Luke 22:7–38; John 13:1–38*
Jesus comforts his disciples: *John 14:1–16:33*
Jesus' high priestly prayer: *John 17:1–26*
Gethsemane: *Matthew 26:36–46; Mark 14:32–42; Luke 22:40–46*
Jesus' arrest and trial: *Matthew 26:47–27:26; Mark 14:43–15:15; Luke 22:47–23:25; John 18:2–19:16*
Jesus' crucifixion and death: *Matthew 27:27–56; Mark 15:16–41; Luke 23:26–49; John 19:17–37*
Jesus' burial: *Matthew 27:57–66; Mark 15:42–47; Luke 23:50–56; John 19:38–42*

JESUS' RESURRECTION APPEARANCES
(in Biblical order)

The empty tomb : *Matthew 28:1–8; Mark 16:1–8; Luke 24:1–12; John 20:1–10*
To Mary Magdalene in the garden: *Mark 16:9–11; John 20:11–18*
To other women: *Matthew 28:9–10*

To two people going to Emmaus: *Mark 16:12–13; Luke 24:13–32*

To Peter: *Luke 24:34; 1 Corinthians 15:5*

To the ten disciples in the upper room: *Luke 24:36–43; John 20:19–25*

To the eleven disciples in the upper room: *Mark 16:14; John 20:26–31; 1 Corinthians 15:5*

To seven disciples fishing: *John 21:1–14*

To the eleven disciples on a mountain: *Matthew 28:16–20; Mark 16:15–18*

To more than 500 people: *1 Corinthians 15:6*

To James: *1 Corinthians 15:7*

To his disciples at his ascension: *Luke 24:36–51; Acts 1:3–9; 1 Corinthians 15:7*

To Paul: *Acts 9:1–19; 22:3–16; 26:9–18; 1 Corinthians 9:1*

Some Notable Psalms

A Lineup of Rulers

The two-part book of Kings can be confusing. First, there's one nation to keep track of, then two, then one again. In all, 39 rulers are profiled. Little wonder it takes a Biblical scholar to keep all the details straight.

The following list of 38 kings and one queen should help clarify the history of Israel in the North and Judah in the South. As you come across the name of a ruler in one of the history books or in a book of the prophets, simply refer to the capsule description below for a brief summary of life during the time of that ruler or prophet.

In all, the kingdoms of Israel and Judah were united for 120 years and divided for just over 200 years. Then Israel disappeared and Judah lasted alone another 135 years. After that, no independent Jewish nation existed until the 20th century.

The timeline on the bottom of pages 1363–1369 places the major prophets in the appropriate time period, along with the rulers of their era. Prophets whose names appear in gray boxes spoke to Israel; those listed against a blue background spoke to Judah. (Dating of some rulers is inexact because of overlapping reigns.)

UNITED KINGDOM

SAUL
DAVID
SOLOMON

These first three kings of Israel each ruled approximately 40 years, and so for 120 years, Israel was one nation. The books of Samuel and Chronicles, along with 1 Kings, describe their reigns in great detail. Later, Jews would look back on this time as the Golden Age of Israel.

DIVIDED KINGDOM

ISRAEL

JEROBOAM I   22 Years

He was handpicked by God to lead a reform, but this first king of the Northern Kingdom proved to be one of Israel's worst. For years afterward, evil kings were described as "walking in the ways of Jeroboam." It was he who firmly established the split-off nation of Israel, uniting 10 rebel tribes. To prevent his people from worshiping in Jerusalem (now enemy territory), he built a new capital city and set up the notorious "high places" as alternative worship sites. The high places and calf worship plagued Israel throughout its entire history. First Kings records that God decided to abandon Israel during the reign of Jeroboam, the Northern Kingdom's very first ruler. (1 Kings 11:26–15:25; 2 Chronicles 10:2–13:20)

JUDAH

REHOBOAM   17 Years

Judah's first king had a checkered career. Sometimes he obeyed God and listened to the prophets; sometimes he did not. At first, the Jewish religion gained strength when all priests and Levites came over to Judah. But, before long, idolatry found its way into Judah as well as into Israel, and Judah suffered humiliating punishment from the armies of Egypt. Thus Judah's first king set an unfortunate pattern for his successors. (1 Kings 11:43–14:31; 2 Chronicles 10–12)

ABIJAH   3 Years

War with Israel in the North dragged on throughout Abijah's three-year reign. The two splinter nations were still adjusting to each other's independence. Abijah offered no improvement on his father Rehoboam's immoral ways. (1 Kings 15:1-8; 2 Chronicles 13:1–14:1)

ISRAEL

JEROBOAM I (CONTINUED)

NADAB   2 Years

Jeroboam's son followed the errors of his father in every way, and his reign merits only eight verses. Israel's first dynasty ended abruptly when Nadab fell victim to a murder plot launched by Baasha. (1 Kings 15:25-32)

BAASHA   24 Years

After gaining the throne in a violent manner, Baasha lasted 24 years. He showed no inclination to reverse the evil practice begun by Jeroboam. The prophet Jehu predicted his death. (1 Kings 15:33—16:7; 2 Chronicles 16)

ELAH   2 years

The Bible records only one incident from Elah's reign: His chariot commander staged a military coup while Elah was off getting drunk. Elah was killed, along with all other descendants of his father, Baasha. Israel's second dynasty, therefore, only lasted 26 years, and another family took the throne. (1 Kings 16:8-14)

ZIMRI   7 Days

Evidently, mutinous chariot commander Zimri acted without his army's support. The army revolted against him, and his "reign" ended seven days after it had begun, in a suicidal fire set in his palace. (1 Kings 16:15-20)

JUDAH

ASA   41 Years

Asa and his son Jehoshaphat were the only kings mentioned in 1 Kings who did "what was right in the eyes of the Lord." Second Chronicles gives a much fuller account of Asa's 41 years. He began religious reforms that turned into a kind of wildfire revival. He drove heathen cults out of the land—even removing his own grandmother as queen mother because of her idolatry. Asa also welcomed to Judah many refugees from Israel. Late in his reign he backslid and got bogged down in foreign wars, making an alliance with neighboring Aram to hold Israel at bay. (1 Kings 15:9-24; 2 Chronicles 14—16)

ISRAEL

OMRI   12 Years

Secular historians rate Omri as one of Israel's most powerful and capable political rulers. In fact, Assyrian records call Israel "the land of Omri." He outlasted a rival to the throne, expanded Israel's lands, and founded the city of Samaria, which would remain Israel's capital for 150 years. But he gets scant mention in the Bible; it dismisses him for sinning "more than all those before him." (1 Kings 16:21-28)

AHAB   22 Years

In a competition for all-time worst king of Israel, Ahab would win hands down. He married the notorious Jezebel, a pagan priestess who promptly installed Baal worship as Israel's official religion. First Kings departs from its usually brief style to give a detailed treatment of Ahab's life and the great spiritual crisis then. During that time, Elijah appeared on the scene to represent the true God against Queen Jezebel's religion. God gave Ahab plenty of opportunities to reform. Ahab humbled himself at least once, postponing disaster, but a nasty incident over Naboth's vineyard sealed his fate. Politically, Ahab forged a successful alliance with Israel's neighbor, Judah, and the divided kingdoms lived at peace for the first time since Jeroboam. Ultimately, however, his evil practices would spread into Judah. (1 Kings 16:29–22:40; 2 Chronicles 18)

AHAZIAH   2 years

Like his father, Ahab, and mother, Jezebel, Ahaziah continued to worship Baal and to fight against Elijah. He was no match. His reign lasted only part of two years, and the descriptions of him reveal a weak, vengeful ruler. (1 Kings 22:40–2 Kings 1:18)

JORAM   12 Years

JUDAH

ASA (CONTINUED)

JEHOSHAPHAT   25 Years

Judah enjoyed the rare blessing of two good kings back to back. Jehoshaphat continued the spirit of Asa's rule, and found ways to further it. He sent out princes to teach from the Book of the Law in the cities of Judah and established courts of justice throughout the country. With a large army and well-fortified cities, he attained a level of peace and prosperity rare in Judah's history. His one serious mistake was in linking himself to Israel's wicked king Ahab through marriage and military alliance. (1 Kings 22:41-50; 2 Chronicles 17–20)

	AHAB		AHAZIAH	JORAM
885 B.C. PROPHETS		ELIJAH		850 B.C.
ASA		JEHOSHAPHAT		

ISRAEL

JORAM (CONTINUED)

Although an improvement over his father and mother (Ahab and Jezebel), Joram ultimately failed to do right. He modified some of the worship of Baal, and at times had a respectful relationship with the prophet Elisha. But Joram lived in treacherous times. The nation of Aram was attacking from the east, and God had set in motion an internal plot, led by Jehu, against Ahab's heirs. Finally Joram fell victim to Jehu's arrow, ending the evil dynasty founded by Omri. (2 Kings 3:1—9:26)

JEHU   28 years

Not to be confused with the prophet of the same name, this Jehu was a fast-driving, impetuous military man. He began a holy mission to purge Ahab's influence out of Israel and Judah, but considerably overstepped his bounds. He killed Joram, had Jezebel thrown from a window, and slew 70 princes, piling their heads in two heaps by a gate. Then he slew all the priests and prophets of Baal and tricked the worshipers of Baal into a trap that led to a mass slaughter. Unfortunately, Jehu's zeal for violence did not translate into zeal for justice. His actions tore Israel apart for generations, and he did little to attend to the nation's spiritual health. Israel also began to lose political strength. (2 Kings 9—10)

JUDAH

JEHORAM   8 Years

After 60 good years under Asa and Jehoshaphat, Judah experienced a terrible regression under Jehoram. He began by killing his brothers and then marrying Athaliah, daughter of Israel's Ahab and Jezebel. She promptly led him into Baal worship. Elijah, who mostly prophesied to Israel, sent Judah's king Jehoram a letter predicting the severe bowel disease that would lead to his death. Second Chronicles reports that "he passed away, to no one's regret." (2 Kings 8:16-24; 2 Chronicles 21)

AHAZIAH   1 Year

In effect Ahaziah served as a mere puppet representative of the notorious queen Athaliah, daughter of Ahab and Jezebel. He fell victim to the bloody purge of Jehu. (2 Kings 8:25-29; 2 Chronicles 22:1-9)

ATHALIAH   7 Years

Queen Athaliah first corrupted her husband Jehoram and dominated her son Ahaziah. Then, after Ahaziah's death, she killed off her infant grandchildren to remove rivals to the throne. She ruled Judah for seven years, leading the kingdom into a dark time of Baal worship and evil. Providentially, however, one heir escaped her reach. The young Joash, hidden away by a relative, emerged at the age of seven. This led to a popular revolt against Athaliah. Athaliah, the only woman to rule either of the two kingdoms, was the last of Ahab's family to die. She had come within one baby of wiping out King David's royal line. (2 Kings 11; 2 Chronicles 22:10—23:21)

JOASH   40 Years

850 B.C.			820 B.C.
	JEHU		
	ELISHA		▶

JEHORAM   AHAZIAH   ATHALIAH   JOASH

ISRAEL	JUDAH

JEHU (CONTINUED)

JOASH (CONTINUED)

He swept into power at the crest of a revolt against his wicked grandmother Athaliah. And as long as Joash followed the advice of Jehoiada the priest, he did well. Most notably, he organized massive projects to repair the temple. After Jehoiada died, however, Joash allowed idolatry to prosper once more. He strayed so far from the ideals of his youth that he ordered the prophet Zechariah to be stoned—the same Zechariah whose father, Jehoiada, had saved his life. Punishment came swiftly, at the hands of a plundering army. Finally, Joash's own servants turned against him and avenged Zechariah's murder. (2 Kings 12; 2 Chronicles 24)

JEHOAHAZ   17 Years

After all his father Jehu had done to exterminate Baal worship, Jehoahaz immediately reinstated it. He ruled 17 years, marked by a series of embarrassing military defeats at the hands of neighboring Aram. He did turn to God in desperation at least once, and Israel got some reprieve. (2 Kings 13:1-9)

JEHOASH   16 Years

Although Jehoash did not break the evil pattern of Israel's kings, he showed some bright spots. He honored the prophet Elisha, and God allowed him to recover much of the territory that Aram had taken from Israel. (Note that Judah also had a king named Joash, the shortened version of Jehoash.) (2 Kings 13:10–14:16)

AMAZIAH   29 Years

Second Kings concludes that Amaziah "did what was right in the eyes of the LORD, but not as his father David had done." Yet the author mostly comments on Amaziah's failures. He began his rule by executing those who had killed his father. Then he ignored a prophet's advice and attacked Edom, bringing back idols from there. Flush with military success, he launched a foolhardy campaign against Israel. The trouncing that resulted discredited his leadership, and he spent his last 12 years in exile. (2 Kings 14:1-22; 2 Chronicles 25)

JEROBOAM II   41 Years

It seems that God gave Israel one last chance under King Jeroboam II. This king ruled a strong and prosperous nation. The Bible gives scant mention of his reign, but it lasted 41 years, during which Israel recovered nearly all its former territory. The prophet Jonah lived then, possibly assisting the king in his frontier defense against Assyria. In addition, Amos and Hosea were active, railing against the terrible social and religious corruption of those affluent times. In a remarkable turn of events, Israel survived as a nation for only a few decades after this stable period. (2 Kings 14:23-29)

AZARIAH   52 Years

Called Uzziah in Chronicles, this king reigned some 50 years, the longest of Judah's kings. As a young man, he took advice from a prophet named Zechariah. He built up the army of Judah and worked on its agriculture and water supplies. Until Azariah, Judah had been a struggling kingdom, with enemy fortifications just five miles from Jerusalem. Under him, the nation achieved true strength. Even so, Azariah gets a short review in the Bible because of his spiritual failings. He did not remove the high places, and he violated the Law of Moses by taking on the work of priests himself. (2 Kings 15:1-17; 2 Chronicles 26)

ZECHARIAH   6 Months
SHALLUM   1 Month

After Jeroboam II, the nation splintered into rival factions. The first king (Zechariah) ruled for six months, the second (Shallum) only one month. Both died violently. (2 Kings 15:8-16)

820 B.C.						750 B.C.
JEHU	JEHOAHAZ	JEHOASH	JEROBOAM II			
ELISHA (CONTINUED)			JONAH			AMOS
JOASH		AMAZIAH		AZARIAH		

ISRAEL	JUDAH

MENAHEM 10 Years

Menahem lasted for ten turbulent years. He gained the throne by murder, and his reign showed a similar ruthlessness. The first of Assyria's three invasions—Israel's "World War I" (see Introduction to 2 Kings)—occurred during Menahem's years, and he frantically tried to buy off the invaders. (2 Kings 15:14-22)

AZARIAH (CONTINUED)

PEKAHIAH 2 Years

Israel was quickly sliding toward anarchy and extermination. Pekahiah survived only two years before a military coup overthrew him. (2 Kings 15:23-26)

PEKAH 20 Years

Pekah turned to international intrigue and conspiracy. He attempted to dethrone the king of Judah in the South. But Judah bought help from Assyria, which promptly invaded Israel for the second time. After occupying all major cities in Israel except the capital Samaria, Assyria began deporting thousands of conquered Israelites to other lands. (2 Kings 15:27-31)

JOTHAM 16 Years

After serving as Azariah's proxy king for 15 years (while Azariah was quarantined with leprosy), Jotham took over and continued the practices of his father. He expanded Judah's economic and military strength, but did not pursue religious reforms as fully as he should have. (2 Kings 15:32-38; 2 Chronicles 27)

AHAZ 16 Years

At the very moment Ahaz was being crowned, armies from the North led by King Pekah of Israel were marching into Judah. Ahaz ignored the prophet Isaiah's advice to put his trust in God rather than military alliances. Turning to the mighty empire of Assyria, he purchased aid with treasures from the temple and the king's palace. The strategy worked temporarily: Israel's armies withdrew to defend themselves. But Ahaz opened the doors for later Assyrian invasions of Judah itself. Worse, he made copies of foreign gods and set them up in Jerusalem. Under him, religion in Judah took a precipitous drop. He went so far as to sacrifice his sons in the fire, following the detestable ways of foreign nations. (2 Kings 16; 2 Chronicles 28)

HOSHEA 9 Years

The Bible judges Hoshea as less wicked than some of his predecessors. Nevertheless, Israel's death was certain. Hoshea angered Assyria by turning south to Egypt for aid. The Assyrians attacked, and after a terrible three-year siege, the last stronghold, Samaria, fell to the conquerors. Assyria deported the vast majority of Israel's population, who became the "ten lost tribes of Israel." (2 Kings 17)

ASSYRIAN INVASION

MENAHEM		PEKAHIAH	PEKAH				HOSHEA	
				HOSEA				
					ISAIAH			▶
					MICAH			▶
	JOTHAM						AHAZ	

750 B.C.   715 B.C.

ONLY JUDAH SURVIVES

HEZEKIAH   29 Years

King Hezekiah gets full treatment in both Kings and Chronicles. The first book stresses the political side of his reign while the second reports on his religious reforms. Both were impressive; Hezekiah was one of the best and most important kings of Judah. He immediately stopped idolatry by reopening and cleansing the temple and calling for a period of national repentance. He resurrected the Passover celebration, and worship in Israel reached a peak that had not been seen since the time of David and Solomon. In all this, he listened carefully to advice from the prophet Isaiah. Yet Hezekiah hardly lived in a peaceful era. He faced imminent danger from Assyria and barely survived an invasion and siege. God honored his faithfulness with a miraculous military intervention. In an unprecedented act, he also added 15 years to Hezekiah's life. (2 Kings 18–20; 2 Chronicles 29–32; Isaiah 36–39)

MANASSEH   55 Years

Whatever good Hezekiah had accomplished in his exemplary reign, his son Manasseh undid in 55 years of the worst rule in Judah's history. He reversed Hezekiah's reforms, bringing in all forms of idolatry, including the occult and witchcraft. He killed off prophets, erected idols in God's temple, and sacrificed his own sons on the altar of a heathen god. The Assyrian empire took Manasseh prisoner, leading him away with a hook through his nose. Later he repented, but great damage had been done. After Manasseh, God pronounced a final judgment on the future of Judah. (2 Kings 21:1-18; 2 Chronicles 33:1-20)

715 B.C.

ISAIAH (CONTINUED)

MICAH (CONTINUED)

HEZEKIAH

MANASSEH

640 B.C.

AMON 2 Years

Amon merely continued the practices of his father. He died at the hands of his servants. (2 Kings 21:19-26; 2 Chronicles 33:21-25)

JOSIAH 31 Years

Judah's slide to destruction was interrupted by the amazing rule of its all-time best king. Josiah came to the throne at age eight, but received good counsel from the high priests. In 31 years he carried out the most extensive religious reforms Judah had ever seen. He removed and destroyed the altars, idols, and symbols of ungodly worship from the temple, and destroyed pagan centers throughout the land. In a thrilling sequence of events, he oversaw the rediscovery of the Law of Moses and acted immediately on what it taught. No king equals Josiah for his sincere and devout practices. He even extended his reforms into the decimated regions of Israel in the North.

Josiah had a time of military peace, for during his reign the Assyrian empire was disintegrating. But he unwisely thrust himself into international politics by marching against Egypt. (The prophet Jeremiah had urged against the Egyptian campaign.) Judah would never recover from this fatal mistake, for Josiah died suddenly in battle. His death shocked the nation. After Josiah's death, Egypt installed a puppet king, and no one after him had the ability to rally Judah's religious or political strength. (2 Kings 22:1—23:30; 2 Chronicles 34—35)

JEHOAHAZ 3 Months

The third son of Josiah lasted only three months before being sacked by a pharaoh and carried off in chains. (2 Kings 23:30-34; 2 Chronicles 36:1-4)

640 B.C.			600 B.C.
	ZEPHANIAH		
		JEREMIAH	
	NAHUM		HABAKKUK
AMON		JEHOAHAZ	

JUDAH

JEHOIAKIM   11 Years

Installed by an Egyptian pharaoh, Jehoiakim found himself trapped when Egypt was defeated by a surging Babylon. He quickly shifted allegiance to Nebuchadnezzar of Babylon. One of Judah's worst kings, he stubbornly tried to have the prophet Jeremiah put to death. (Numerous passages in Jeremiah's book make plain his scorn for Jehoiakim.) Finally, after an ill-advised revolt against Nebuchadnezzar, Jehoiakim was captured and killed. (2 Kings 23:36—24:6; 2 Chronicles 36:5-8)

JEHOIACHIN   3 Months

The struggles with Babylon were the "World War II" in Israel's history (see Introduction to 2 Kings). After holding out for three months against Nebuchadnezzar's armies, Jehoiachin surrendered, and was carried away with many other captives, including the prophet Ezekiel. He lived in a Babylonian prison for 40 years. (2 Kings 24:6-17; 25:27-30; 2 Chronicles 36:8-10)

ZEDEKIAH   11 Years

Zedekiah ruled over Judah during the last 11 years of its existence as an independent state. A weak king, he took bad advice from princes and advisers and often made unwise decisions. He ignored Jeremiah's advice to remain loyal to Babylon and joined an alliance against that empire. As a result, Nebuchadnezzar laid siege to Jerusalem for almost two years, bringing the city to the verge of starvation. At last the Babylonians made a breach in the wall and overran the city. They burned Solomon's temple, the king's palace, and other buildings, and destroyed the walls around Jerusalem. Finally, they took everything of value from the temple. The city was utterly looted. (2 Kings 24:17—25:7; 2 Chronicles 26:11-20)

BABYLONIAN INVASION

Zechariah, Haggai, and Malachi prophesied later, to the Jewish refugees who had returned from Babylon.

586 B.C. BABYLONIAN INVASION

640 B.C.				525 B.C.
	DANIEL			
JEREMIAH (CONTINUED)				
	EZEKIEL			
JEHOIAKIM	ZEDEKIAH			

Subject Guide

The Subject Guide is not a "concordance" that shows where the Bible uses a certain word. Rather, it lists major subjects that may be of interest, along with the Bible passages (not single verses, usually) that speak to these subjects. Topics of pressing interest or major significance have been highlighted within the list. Although we have tried to be comprehensive, any list of subjects must necessarily be restrictive. The italicized titles in quotes refer to Highlights, Insights, or Introductions on the subject. Page numbers are given in boldface type.

A

AARON — brother of and spokesman for Moses; became the first high priest
  character profile, *"Working Together . . . and Apart"*—**p. 176**
  with Moses, Exodus 4:10–12:50—**p. 87**
  made priest, Exodus 28–29 **p. 112**; *"The First High Priest"*—**p. 134**
  his role with golden calf, Exodus 32—**p. 116**
  budding of his staff, Numbers 17—**p. 180**
  his death, Numbers 20:23–29—**p. 184**

ABEL — Adam's second son; murdered by his brother Cain
  character profile, *"Blood Brothers"*—**p. 30**
  his life, Genesis 4:1–9—**p. 29**
  example of faith, Hebrews 11:1–4—**p. 1284**
  relationship to Christ, Hebrews 12:22–24—**p. 1287**

ABIATHAR — high priest in the days of Saul and David
  character profile, *"Outlaw Priest"*—**p. 367**

ABIGAIL — wife of Nabal, became David's wife after Nabal's death
  character profile, *"Beauty and Brains"*—**p. 325**

ABISHAI — nephew of David and one of his chief warriors
  character profile, *"Bloody Brothers"*—**p. 443**

ABNER — cousin of Saul and commander of his army
  character profile, *"On the Wrong Side"*—**p. 335**

ABORTION — death of a fetus through a medical procedure
  penalty for harming fetus, Exodus 21:22–25—**p. 106**
  unborn life important to God, Psalm 139—**p. 653**

ABRAHAM — founder of the Jewish nation
  called by God, Genesis 11:26–12:20—**p. 35**
  character profile, *"Abraham"*—**p. 36**
  his life, Genesis 11:26–25:11—**p. 35**
  and Melchizedek, Genesis 14:18–24—**p. 38**
  covenant with, Genesis 15;17—**p. 39**
  and Hagar, Genesis 16—**p. 39**
  prayed for Sodom and Gomorrah, Genesis 18:16–33—**p. 41**
  asked to sacrifice his son, Genesis 22—**p. 46**
  his death, Genesis 25:1–11—**p. 50**
  his true offspring are believers, Romans 4—**p. 1179**; Galatians 3:6–29—**p. 1224**
  faith demonstrated by deeds, James 2:20–24—**p. 1290**

ABSALOM — third son of David, by Maacah
  character profile, *"All That Glitters"*—**p. 348**
  his revenge on Amnon, 2 Samuel 13–14—**p. 345**
  in hiding, *"A Refuge with His Family"*—**p. 346**
  rebellion against David, 2 Samuel 15:1–19:8—**p. 348**; *"No Way Back"*—**p. 350**

ADAM — the first man
  character profile, *"First in Everything"*—**p. 26**
  his creation and life, Genesis 1:26–5:5—**p. 25**
  his fall into sin, Genesis 3—**p. 27**
  Jesus and the line of Adam, Luke 3:23–38—**p. 1066**
  Jesus as second Adam, Romans 5:12–21—**p. 1181**; 1 Corinthians 15:21–22,42–57—**p. 1207**

ADOPTION — becoming a child of one who is not your biological parent
  Abraham and adoption of an heir, Genesis 15:1–6—**p. 39**; Genesis 16—**p. 39**
  Israel as God's adopted son, Exodus 4:21–23—**p. 87**; Jeremiah 31:9, 16–20—**p. 99**
  Believers as God's adopted children, John 1:12–13—**p. 1100**; Romans 8:12–25—**p. 1184**; Galatians 3:26–4:7—**p. 1226**; Ephesians 1:3–8—**p. 1230**

ADULTERY — sexual unfaithfulness of a married person
  laws against, Numbers 5:12–31—**p. 166**
  David and Bathsheba, 2 Samuel 11–12—**p. 342**
  warnings against, Proverbs 5—**p. 665**; Proverbs 6:20–35—**p. 666**
  avoiding, *"A Safeguard Against Lust"*—**p. 179**
  Jesus' views on, Matthew 5:27–32—**p. 1001**
  effect on the church, 1 Corinthians 5—**p. 1198**

AFTERLIFE — *see* ETERNAL LIFE, HEAVEN, HELL, RESURRECTION

AGRIPPA descendent of Herod; king before whom Paul pled his case
  character profile, *"Roman Heart"*—**p. 1169**

AHAB — Israel's most wicked king
  character profile, *"Worst King Yet"*—**p. 393**
  ascended throne, 1 Kings 16:29–33—**p. 386**
  contest with Elijah, 1 Kings 18—**p. 387**
  and Naboth's vineyard, 1 Kings 21—**p. 392**
  his death, 1 Kings 22:34–38—**p. 394**

ALCOHOL — *see* DRINKING ALCOHOL, WINE

Ambition
—strong desire for success, honor, or power (*see also* PRIDE, SERVANTHOOD)
  competing with God, *"Human Ambition"*—**p. 35**
  at the tower of Babel, Genesis 11:1–11—**p. 35**
  results of, Matthew 16:21–27—**p. 1016**
  of disciples, Mark 9:33–37—**p. 1048**; 10:35–45—**p. 1048**
  the antichrist, 2 Thessalonians 2:1–4—**p. 1253**

ANDREW — apostle; brother of Simon Peter
  character profile, *"Out of the Spotlight"*—**p. 1107**

ANGELS — heavenly beings created by God
assist people, Genesis 24–**p. 49**
protect people, Psalm 91:11–13–**p. 627**
execute judgment, Matthew 13:24–50–**p. 1012**;
Revelation 14:17–16:21–**p. 1329**
deliver messages, *"A Message from God"*–**p. 717**; Luke
1:26–38–**p. 1063**; 2:8–15–**p. 1064**
purpose of, *"Respect for Angels"*–**p. 1276**
Christ greater than, Hebrews 1:5–14–**p. 1275**
serve in heaven, Revelation 8–9–**p. 1324**
spiritual warriors, Revelation 12:7–12–**p. 1328**

ANGER
of God:
toward sin, Numbers 11:1–35–**p. 173**; *"God Is Slow to
Anger"*–**p. 958**; Romans 1:18–32–**p. 1176**
tempered with mercy, Psalm 103–**p. 632**; Hosea
11:8–11–**p. 923**
averted through Christ, Romans 5–**p. 1179**
of human beings:
Cain's, *"Improper Offerings"*–**p. 29**
Moses', Exodus 32:15–35–**p. 117**
Abigail's, *"Beauty and Brains"*–**p. 325**
Jonah's, Jonah 3–4–**p. 947**
dealing with, *"Angry Inside"*–**p. 576**
'In your anger do not sin', Ephesians 4:26–**p. 1234**
be slow to anger, James 1:19–20–**p. 1290**

ANIMALS
purpose of, *"Just for Fun"*–**p. 633**
God's love for, *"The Wildness of Animals"*–**p. 570**
showing God's power, *"Behemoth and Leviathan?"*–
p. 571

ANNAS — high priest at the time of John the Baptist;
Jesus stood trial before him in an unofficial
capacity
character profile, *"Collaborators"*–**p. 1117**

ANTICHRIST — an evil person or power; a false Christ,
expected in the end times
prophesied by Daniel, Daniel 11:36–45–**p. 913**
Jesus' teaching on, Mark 13:1–37–**p. 1053**
will be destroyed, 2 Thessalonians 2:1–12–**p. 1253**
qualities of, 1 John 2:18–23–**p. 1306**; 4:1–6–**p. 1307**
visions of, Revelation 11–13–**p. 1326**
destruction of, Revelation 19:19–21–**p. 1334**

ANXIETY
overcome by trust in God, Matthew 6:25–34–**p. 1003**;
Luke 12:22–34–**p. 1082**
subdued through prayer, Philippians 4:4–9–**p. 1240**

APOLLOS — an Alexandrian Jew who preached in
Corinth
character profile, *"Brimming with Confidence"*–**p. 1198**
with Priscilla and Aquila, Acts 18:24–28–**p. 1160**
followers of, 1 Corinthians 3:1–9–**p. 1196**
partners with Paul, 1 Corinthians 4:1–7–**p. 1197**

APOSTLES — title given to the followers of Christ who
founded the early church, especially the 12
disciples and Paul
commissioned, Matthew 28:16–20–**p. 1033**
disciples called, Luke 5:1–11–**p. 1068**; 6:12–16–**p. 1070**
replacement for Judas, Acts 1:12–26–**p. 1134**
received Holy Spirit, Acts 2–**p. 1134**
Paul as, 1 Corinthians 9–**p. 1201**; Galatians 1:1–2:10–
p. 1223
foundation of the church, Ephesians 2:19–22–**p. 1231**;
Revelation 21:14–**p. 1335**

AQUILA — husband of Priscilla; co-worker with Paul
and instructor of Apollos
character profile, *"Power Couple"*–**p. 1160**

ARK OF THE COVENANT — the Israelites' sacred chest
containing the tablets of the law
description of, Exodus 25:10–22–**p. 110**
and crossing the Jordan, Joshua 3–**p. 241**
contents of, *"What's In the Ark"*–**p. 181**
represented God's power, 1 Samuel 4–5–**p. 301**
David returns it to Jerusalem, 2 Samuel 6:1–15–**p. 338**;
1 Chronicles 13:1–14–**p. 446**; 15:1–16:6–**p. 447**
reverence for, *"Why Did Uzzah Die?"*–**p. 446**
lost, *"Proof of the Covenant"*–**p. 467**

ARMAGEDDON
in the valley of Megiddo, *"A Bloody Battlefield"*–**p. 496**
final role, *"The Battle of Armageddon"*–**p. 1330**

ART — creative expression such as music, dance,
painting, sculpture, writing, architecture
ordained by God, Exodus 31:1–11–**p. 116**; 35:30–36:2–
p. 121
excellence needed, Psalm 33:1–3–**p. 591**

ARTAXERXES — King of Persia; allowed Ezra to rebuild
Jerusalem temple
character profile, *"Friendly Foreigner"*–**p. 505**

ASAHEL — nephew of David and one of his warriors
character profile, *"Bloody Brothers"*–**p. 443**

ASCENSION — Christ's rising into heaven after the
resurrection
prophesied, Psalm 27–**p. 588**
described, Luke 24:36–53–**p. 1098**; Acts 1:1–11–
p. 1134
related to Pentecost, John 16:5–16–**p. 1122**; Ephesians
4:7–13–**p. 1232**

Assurance of Salvation
—certainty of God's forgiveness and love

built on trust, Psalm 37–**p. 594**
through Christ, Romans 8–**p. 1183**
produced by faith, 2 Timothy 1:8–12–**p. 1264**
achieved by obeying God, 1 John 2:28–3:24–
p. 1306
achieved by believing God's word, 1 John 5:9–13–
p. 1308

ASTROLOGY — seeking information about human
events from the stars (see also WITCHCRAFT)
powerless, Isaiah 47:12–15–**p. 758**
Daniel discredits, Daniel 2–**p. 899**

ATHALIAH — after her son Ahaziah died, she made
herself queen and killed all challengers to the
throne
character profile, *"Live by the Sword . . ."*–**p. 482**

ATHENS
Paul preaching in, *"Flexible Approach"*–**p. 1158**

ATHLETICS
Christianity compared to running, 1 Corinthians
9:24–27–**p. 1202**; Hebrews 12:1–2–**p. 1286**
Christianity compared to wrestling, Ephesians 6:10–18–
p. 1235
competing according to rules, 2 Timothy 2:5–**p. 1264**
training for, *"Athlete in Training"*–**p. 1260**; *"Soldier, Athlete,
Farmer"*–**p. 1265**
in Ephesus, *"Sports and Education"*–**p. 1161**

ATONEMENT — payment for sin; associated with the
Israelites' Day of Atonement, when a blood
sacrifice was made for the sins of the nation (see
also JUSTIFICATION, SALVATION)
by sacrifice, *"The Reason for Sacrifice"*–**p. 132**
Hebrew ritual of, Leviticus 16–**p. 144**

Christ as our, Romans 3:21–26–**p. 1178**; 2 Corinthians 5:14–21–**p. 1215**; Hebrews 9–**p. 1282**; 1 Peter 2:22–25–**p. 1297**; 1 John 1:8–2:2–**p. 1305**

B

BAAL– god of the Phoenicians and Canaanites
worshiped in Israel, 1 Kings 16:29–34–**p. 386**; 2 Kings 17:7–23–**p. 416**; 21:1–9–**p. 422**
defeated by Elijah, 1 Kings 18–**p. 387**; *"Elijah Rubs It In"*– **p. 389**

BABYLON
as symbol of evil, *"An Evil Queen"*–**p. 758**; *"Apocalyptic Arrogance"*–**p. 837**; *"What Is Babylon?"*–**p. 1331**
and archaeology, *"The Throne Room"*–**p. 904**
fall of, *"Sneak Attack"*–**p. 905**
cruelty of, *"Gambling Prizes"*–**p. 930**
prophecies against, Isaiah 13:1–14:23–**p. 723**; 21:1–10–**p. 730**; 47:1–15–**p. 757**; Jeremiah 50:1–51:58–**p. 832**

BACKSLIDING– departure from a life of faith in and obedience to God
displeases God, Psalm 78–**p. 618**
a serious sin, Hebrews 6:4–6–**p. 1279**; 10:26–31– **p. 1284**
forgiveness for, Revelation 2:4–5–**p. 1318**; 3:2–3,15–21–**p. 1319**
examples of:
Israel at Mount Sinai, Exodus 32–**p. 116**
Solomon, 1 Kings 11–**p. 377**
Hymenaeus and Alexander, 1 Timothy 1:19–20– **p. 1258**
in the end times, 2 Timothy 3:1–10–**p. 1265**

BALAAM– man employed by the Moabites to curse the Israelites
character profile, *"Whose Side Is Balaam On?"*–**p. 187**
his loyalty, *"Whose Side Is Balaam On?"*–**p. 187**
stopped by God, Numbers 22–24–**p. 185**
prophecy fulfilled, *"Balaam's Prophecy"*–**p. 189**
death of, Numbers 31:1–24–**p. 195**

BAPTISM– a water ritual, used as a spiritual symbol (*see also* HOLY SPIRIT, JOHN THE BAPTIST)
Jesus' baptism, Matthew 3:13–15–**p. 999**
as sign of repentance, Matthew 3:1–12–**p. 999**
as sign of conversion, Matthew 28:16–20–**p. 1033**
in the early church, Acts 2:37–41–**p. 1135**; 8:26–39– **p. 1145**
and the believer's death and resurrection in Christ, Romans 6–**p. 1181**; Colossians 2:11–12–**p. 1244**
of the Holy Spirit, Acts 1:1–8–**p. 1134**; 1 Corinthians 12:12–13–**p. 1204**

BARABBAS– criminal released by Pilate instead of Jesus
set free, Matthew 27:11–26–**p. 1030**

BARGAINING
in the middle East, *"Let's Make a Deal"*–**p. 48**; *"Oriental Bargaining"*–**p. 92**

BARNABAS– disciple; name changed from Joseph to one that means "son of encouragement"
character profile, *"The Encourager"*–**p. 1152**

BATHSHEBA– committed adultery with David and later married him (*see also* DAVID, SOLOMON)
character profile, *"Only Following Orders"*–**p. 342**
life of, 2 Samuel 11:1–12:25–**p. 342**
helped Solomon become king, 1 Kings 1:11–31–**p. 364**

BEAUTY
inner, 1 Samuel 16:1–13–**p. 315**; *"Skin-Deep Beauty"*– **p. 671**; 1 Timothy 2:9–**p. 1258**; 1 Peter 3:1–7– **p. 1297**
of Bathsheba, 2 Samuel 11–**p. 342**
of Esther, Esther 2:1–18–**p. 530**
changing standards of, *"Tan Lines"*–**p. 706**

BEGGARS– *see* POOR

BETRAYAL
by a friend, *"Betrayed by a Friend"*–**p. 606**
of Jesus by Judas, Matthew 26:14–16,47–49–**p. 1028**

BIBLE
as history, *"Selective History"*–**p. 85**; *"Three Kinds of Bricks"*–**p. 88**; *"Unfair Credit?"*–**p. 414**; *"The Ring of Truth"*–**p. 504**; *"Off at War"*–**p. 531**; *"Is Esther Accurate?"*–**p. 537**; *"Bridge Chapters"*–**p. 744**; *"Dating by Emperors"*–**p. 1064**; *"The Linking Book"*–**p. 1132**; *"During the Reign of . . ."*–**p. 1149**; *"Sailing Log"*–**p. 1171**
compilation of, *"Out of Print"*–**p. 185**; *"Using Other Sources"*–**p. 379**; *"The Five Books"*–**p. 615**; *"Belong in the Bible?"*–**p. 1111**; *"Sound Familiar?"*–**p. 605**
in praise of, Psalm 19:7–11–**p. 584**; 119:1–176–**p. 643**
used by Satan, *"Satan and the Bible"*–**p. 627**
languages, *"A Change in Language"*–**p. 899**
literary devices in, *"Well-Turned Phrase"*–**p. 830**; *"Structured Passion"*–**p. 840**; *"A Passion for Punning"*– **p. 951**
translation of, *"Lost in Translation"*–**p. 1045**
importance of, 2 Timothy 3:14–17–**p. 1265**
inspired by God, *"Scripture is God-Breathed"*–**p. 1266**; 2 Peter 1:19–21–**p. 1301**
act on, James 1:19–27–**p. 1290**
interpreting, *"A Book Full of Mysteries"*–**p. 1316**; *"Seals and Scrolls"*–**p. 1322**; *"Old Testament Echoes"*–**p. 1326**

BITTERNESS– lingering resentment or anger
avoid, Ephesians 4:29–32–**p. 1234**
as sin, James 3:13–18–**p. 1291**

BLASPHEMY– bringing reproach against God and his name
a sin against God, Exodus 20:7–**p. 104**; Leviticus 24:13–23–**p. 153**
Jesus charged with, Matthew 9:1–8–**p. 1005**; Matthew 26:57–67–**p. 1029**
against the Holy Spirit, Mark 3:20–30–**p. 1038**

BLESSINGS
material blessings, Deuteronomy 7:12–16–**p. 210**; Psalm 67–**p. 610**
spiritual blessings, Psalm 32–**p. 591**; John 1:14–17– **p. 1100**; Ephesians 1:3–14–**p. 1230**
showers of blessings, Ezekiel 34:26–30–**p. 882**
the Beatitudes, Matthew 5:1–11–**p. 1000**; Luke 6:20–22–**p. 1071**

BLOOD– used to represent the life of a creature, often in sacrifices or rituals of cleansing
instructions to Noah about shedding, Genesis 9:1–6– **p. 33**
role in the covenant, *"Covenant Blood"*–**p. 110**
for purification of priests, Exodus 29–**p. 113**
in offerings to God, especially for sin, Leviticus 1,3,4– **p. 128**
the Day of Atonement, Leviticus 16–**p. 144**

BLOOD OF CHRIST– shed on the cross as Jesus died
wine as sign of, in the Lord's Supper, Matthew 26:27–29–**p. 1028**; 1 Corinthians 11:23–32–**p. 1203**
as payment for sin, Hebrews 9:11–28–**p. 1282**
redemption through, Ephesians 1:7–8–**p. 1230**; 1 Peter 1:18–19–**p. 1296**
reconciliation through, Ephesians 2:11–18–**p. 1231**
cleansing through, 1 John 1:7–10–**p. 1305**

C

Christians — name given to followers of Christ

CULTS – *see* FALSE TEACHERS

CULTURE
skills learned from Egypt, *"The Skills of Civilization"*–**p. 110**

CURSING – *see* PROFANITY

CYRUS – Persian king; allowed exiles to return to Jerusalem to rebuild the temple
character profile, *"Good Shepherd"*–**p. 755**

D

DANCING
David before the ark, 2 Samuel 6:12–23–**p. 338**
in worship, Exodus 15–**p. 98**; Psalm 150–**p. 659**
in celebration, Luke 15:22–27–**p. 1085**
provocative, Matthew 14:1–12–**p. 1013**

DANIEL
character profile, see *"Introduction to Daniel"*–**p. 897**
interpreted dreams, Daniel 2–**p. 899**; Daniel 4–**p. 902**
in the lions' den, Daniel 6–**p. 905**
not Ezekiel's fellow exile, *"Different Daniel"*–**p. 874**
visions of, *"Long Delay"*–**p. 909**

DARKNESS
dispelled by God, Genesis 1:1–5–**p. 25**
picture of God's judgment, Joel 2:1–2–**p. 928**; Jude 8–13–**p. 1314**
Jesus came to dispel, John 1:1–9–**p. 1100**
symbol of evil, Romans 13:11–14–**p. 1189**; Ephesians 5:1–14–**p. 1234**; 1 Thessalonians 5:1–10–**p. 1250**
not in heaven, Revelation 22:1–5–**p. 1335**

DAVID – Israel's greatest king; associated with many of the psalms (*see also* JONATHAN, SAUL)
character profile, see *"Introduction to 2 Samuel"*–**p. 331**
chosen king, 1 Samuel 16–**p. 315**
and Goliath, 1 Samuel 17–**p. 315**
conflict with Saul, *"A Sense of God's Timing"*–**p. 324**
as a mercenary, *"Faking It"*–**p. 315**
as king, *"The Life of King David"*–**p. 331**; *"A Family Record"*–**p. 429**
and Joab, *"Easy on Joab"*–**p. 336**
God's promise to, 2 Samuel 7–**p. 338**; *"The Royal Line"*–**p. 434**; *"Conditional Promise"*–**p. 459**; *"The Imprint of the Master"*–**p. 973**
and Saul's family, *"Saul's Lame Grandson"*–**p. 341**
his love for God, *"What God Values"*–**p. 315**; *"Seeking Guidance"*–**p. 338**; *"David's Great Prayer"*–**p. 460**
and Bathsheba, 2 Samuel 11–12–**p. 342**; *"Adultery and Murder"*–**p. 344**
results of his sin, *"Sin As a Cancer"*–**p. 352**
and Absalom, *"Absalom, Absalom!"*–**p. 353**
confession of sin, Psalm 51–**p. 603**; *"David's Finest Moment"*–**p. 345**; *"David Caught in the Act"*–**p. 604**
last words of, *"Final Words"*–**p. 359**
Jesus as son of, Matthew 1:1–18–**p. 997**; Luke 1:26–38–**p. 1063**
Jesus as Lord of, Matthew 21:41–45–**p. 1023**

DAY OF ATONEMENT (Yom Kippur)
described and reinterpreted, Leviticus 16–**p. 144**; *"Jewish Holy Days"*–**p. 115**

DAY OF THE LORD – a common Old Testament phrase for God's final victory over evil
as punishment for Israelites, Zephaniah 1:14–2:7–**p. 968**; *"The Day of the Lord"*–**p. 937**
as cleansing the world, Isaiah 24–**p. 733**; *"Beyond Darkness"*–**p. 966**

DEACON – an official in the early church who served the needs of people
established, Acts 6:1–4–**p. 1140**
requirements for, 1 Timothy 3:8–13–**p. 1259**

DEATH
physical:
result of sin, Genesis 3–**p. 27**; Romans 5:12–21–**p. 1181**
God cares about, *"Precious Death"*–**p. 642**
what happens at, *"Life after Death"*–**p. 581**; *"The Afterlife"*–**p. 878**
being unprepared for, Luke 12:13–21–**p. 1081**
victory over, 1 Corinthians 15–**p. 1206**
of Christians, *"The Sleep of Death"*–**p. 1251**
spiritual:
by nature true of everyone, Ephesians 2:1–10–**p. 1231**
to self, John 12:23–26–**p. 1118**
because of sin, *"A Matter of Life and Death"*–**p. 673**; *"Need for a Cure"*–**p. 1178**
to sin, Romans 6:1–23–**p. 1181**
of Lazarus, *"If Only . . ."*–**p. 1116**
of Jesus (*see* BLOOD OF CHRIST, CROSS)
of Stephen, Acts 7–**p. 1141**

DEBORAH – one of Israel's greatest judges and a prophetess
character profile, *"Multi-talented Woman"*–**p. 270**
delivers Israel, Judges 4–**p. 269**
song of, Judges 5–**p. 271**

DEBTS (*see also* FORGIVENESS, LORD'S PRAYER)
compassion to debtors, Exodus 22:25–27–**p. 107**; *"Ruthless Bill Collectors"*–**p. 934**
warning against, *"Danger in Debt"*–**p. 665**
pay promptly, Romans 13:8–10–**p. 1189**

DEEDS – actions or accomplishments, often in the sense of attempts to please God through moral living (*see also* FAITH)
do not gain salvation, Ephesians 2:1–10–**p. 1231**
outgrowth of faith, *"Given, Not Earned"*–**p. 1231**; James 2:14–26–**p. 1290**; *"Words Are Not Enough"*–**p. 1288**

DELILAH – *see* SAMSON

DELIVERANCE
of Joseph, *"A Forgotten Man"*–**p. 71**
of Israelites, *"Free at Last"*–**p. 646**; *"Day of the Locusts"*–**p. 90**; *"Independence Day"*–**p. 95**
from any problem, *"Worst Case"*–**p. 637**

DEMONS – powerful evil spirits that can possess a person (*see also* EVIL)
driven out, Matthew 8:28–34–**p. 1005**; Mark 5:1–10–**p. 1041**; Acts 16:16–19–**p. 1156**; *"Homeless"*–**p. 1074**
ignore teaching of, 1 Timothy 4:1–10–**p. 1259**

DESERT
of Sinai, *"Change of Scenery"*–**p. 101**

DEVIL – *see* SATAN

DISABILITIES
barriers to those with, *"Barriers to the Disabled"*–**p. 1037**

DISCIPLES
of John the Baptist, *"New Recruits"*–**p. 1043**
calling of, *"Gradual Disciples"*–**p. 1101**
training of, *"Training the 12 Disciples"*–**p. 1047**; *"Baffling Thoughts"*–**p. 1048**
doubting the Resurrection, *"Doubting Thomas"*–**p. 1130**
replacing Judas Iscariot, *"Inner Circle"*–**p. 1050**
transforming of, *"A Change of Heart and Mind"*–**p. 1129**; *"A Man Named 'The Rock' "*–**p. 1298**
make them of all nations, Matthew 28:6–20–**p. 1032**
called Christians, Acts 11:26–**p. 1149**

DISCIPLESHIP – the act of following and learning from a teacher, especially Jesus
not waiting, *"Burying His Father"*–**p. 1076**
cost of, Luke 14:25–34–**p. 1084**
evidence of, John 15:1–17–**p. 1122**
result of love, John 21:15–19–**p. 1130**

DISCIPLINE — training that molds, instructs, corrects
by parents, Proverbs 23:13–23—**p. 683**; *"How to Raise Children"*—**p. 682**
by God, *"Like Everybody Else"*—**p. 865**; Hebrews 12:1–13—**p. 1286**
by the church, 1 Corinthians 5—**p. 1198**
by God's Word, 2 Timothy 3:14–17—**p. 1265**

DISCOURAGEMENT (*see also* COMFORT)
overcoming, Joshua 1:1–9—**p. 240**; Psalm 42—**p. 598**; Psalm 77:1–15—**p. 617**; John 14:1–27—**p. 1121**; 2 Corinthians 4:7–12,16–18—**p. 1214**; *"For the Discouraged"*—**p. 1229**
of Job, *"Why Keep on Living?"*—**p. 543**
in life, *"Companion Book"*—**p. 699**

DISCRIMINATION (*see also* RACISM)
against the Israelites, *"New Tyrant in Town"*—**p. 85**
on basis of wealth, *"Play No Favorites"*—**p. 1290**
eliminated in Christ, *"The Original Barbarians"*—**p. 1245**; Ephesians 2:11–18—**p. 1231**

DISEASE (*see also* HEALING)
cleansing from, *"A Bird Set Free"*—**p. 142**
treatment of, *"Bad Medical Advice"*—**p. 476**

DISOBEDIENCE (*see also* OBEDIENCE)
Israel's in entering Canaan, *"Imperfect Timing"*—**p. 178**
warnings against, *"Final Warnings"*—**p. 198**; *"A Scent of Doom"*—**p. 231**

DIVORCE
Mosaic law on, Deuteronomy 24:1–4—**p. 225**
God's view of, *"I Hate Divorce"*—**p. 987**
Jesus' teaching on, Matthew 19:1–12—**p. 1019**; Mark 10:2–12—**p. 1048**; *"Teaching on Divorce"*—**p. 1049**
a pardonable sin, John 4:4–42—**p. 1104**
Paul's teaching on, 1 Corinthians 7:10–16—**p. 1199**

Doubt (*see also* FAITH)
of Abraham, Genesis 12:10–20—**p. 36**
of Sarah, Genesis 18:1–15—**p. 41**
of Moses, Exodus 4:1–17—**p. 87**
of Gideon, Judges 6—**p. 272**
of Peter, Matthew 14:22–32—**p. 1014**
overcoming, Mark 9:14–29—**p. 1047**; 11:22–25—**p. 1051**; James 1:2–7—**p. 1289**
of John the Baptist, Luke 7:18–23—**p. 1072**
of Thomas, John 20:24–31—**p. 1129**

DREAMS (*see also* VISIONS)
of Jacob, Genesis 28:10–22—**p. 56**
interpreted by Joseph, Genesis 37—**p. 66**; 41—**p. 71**
meaning of, *"A Nightmare"*—**p. 708**; *"A Nation of Dreamers"*—**p. 90**
false prophecy through, Jeremiah 23:25–32—**p. 804**; Ezekiel 13:1–9—**p. 857**
interpreted by Daniel, Daniel 2—**p. 899**; 4—**p. 902**
at the birth of Jesus, Matthew 2—**p. 998**
of Pilate's wife, Matthew 27:19—**p. 1030**
in the last days, Acts 2:14–21—**p. 1135**

Drinking Alcohol (*see also* WINE)
warnings about, Proverbs 20:1—**p. 679**; 23:29–35—**p. 683**; Isaiah 5:11–12—**p. 716**; *"The Dangers of Wine"*—**p. 684**; Ephesians 5:18—**p. 1234**
vow against, *"Teetotalers"*—**p. 819**
examples of overindulgence
of Noah, Genesis 9:20—**p. 34**
of Lot, Genesis 19:32–35—**p. 44**
of Xerxes, Esther 1:10—**p. 529**
at the Lord's Supper, 1 Corinthians 11:21—**p. 1203**

E

EARTH (*see also* ECOLOGY)
created by God, Genesis 1:1–25—**p. 25**; *"Ecology Plus"*—**p. 633**
care for, Genesis 1:26–31—**p. 25**
exhibits God's love, Psalm 33:1–11—**p. 591**
not eternal, *"Outlasting the Universe"*—**p. 631**
ages of, *"Three Worlds"*—**p. 1302**
waits for redemption, Romans 8:18–25—**p. 1184**
destruction of, *"The Fate of the Earth"*—**p. 1303**
new, *"New Earth"*—**p. 775**; 2 Peter 3:3–13—**p. 1302**; Revelation 21:1–22:5—**p. 1335**; *"Eden Regained"*—**p. 1336**

ECOLOGY — keeping a proper balance in nature
God's concern for, *"Respect for Nature"*—**p. 223**
appreciation of, *"Ecology Plus"*—**p. 633**

EDOM — *see* Esau

EGYPT
Joseph taken there, Genesis 37—**p. 66**
Israelites moved there, Genesis 39–50—**p. 69**
exodus from, Exodus 1–13—**p. 85**
judgment of, Isaiah 19—**p. 728**; Jeremiah 42—**p. 824**; Ezekiel 29–30—**p. 875**
Jesus taken there, Matthew 2:13–20—**p. 998**

ELDER — a designated leader of the Jewish people and of the church
leaders of the Jewish council, Acts 5:17–42—**p. 1139**
leaders appointed in churches, Acts 14:21–25—**p. 1154**; Titus 1:5–9—**p. 1269**
Paul's farewell speech to, Acts 20:13–38—**p. 1162**
qualifications for, 1 Timothy 3:1–7—**p. 1258**

ELECTION — God's choosing a people for himself
of Abraham, Genesis 12:1–9—**p. 35**
of Israel, Exodus 19:1–6—**p. 102**; Deuteronomy 10:12–22—**p. 213**; Isaiah 41:8–16—**p. 750**
of Jesus' disciples, John 15:9–17—**p. 1122**
of Jacob, Romans 9:6–13—**p. 1185**
of the church, Ephesians 1:3–14—**p. 1230**; 1 Peter 2:1–10—**p. 1296**
make it sure, 2 Peter 1:3–10—**p. 1301**

ELI — a priest and judge of Israel
character profile, *"An End and a Beginning"*—**p. 301**
life of, 1 Samuel 1–4—**p. 298**

ELIJAH — Israelite prophet well known for his confrontation with the priests of Baal (*see also* BAAL, ELISHA)
character profile, *"Miracle Worker"*—**p. 386**
life of, 1 Kings 17–19—**p. 386**; 21—**p. 392**
and Baal, 1 Kings 18:16–46—**p. 387**; *"The Contest"*—**p. 388**
death of, 2 Kings 2—**p. 398**; *"An Obscure Compliment"*—**p. 399**
second coming, *"The Second Elijah"*—**p. 989**
at transfiguration, Luke 9:28–36—**p. 1075**

ELISHA — prophet who succeeded Elijah
character profile, *"Replacing a Legend"*—**p. 400**
chosen by Elijah, 1 Kings 19:16–21—**p. 390**
life of, 2 Kings 2–13—**p. 398**; *"Replacing a Legend"*—**p. 400**
mocked, *"Background on the Bears"*—**p. 399**
heals Naaman, 2 Kings 5:1–27—**p. 403**; *"Harder on the Rich"*—**p. 403**

ELIZABETH — mother of John the Baptist
character profile, *"End of an Era"*—**p. 1062**

ENEMY
cursing, *"What about Curses?"*—**p. 655**; *"Tough Love"*—**p. 1306**
treat with kindness, Proverbs 25:21–22—**p. 686**; Romans 12:19–21—**p. 1189**
love for, *"Good News for the Enemy?"*—**p. 945**; Luke 6:27–36—**p. 1071**

ENOCH
his faith, *"The Man Who Did Not Die"*—**p. 30**

ENVY (*see also* JEALOUSY, GREED)
of Joseph by brothers, Genesis 37—**p. 66**
comes from inside, Mark 7:20–23—**p. 1045**
trouble from, James 3:13–4:10—**p. 1291**

EPHESUS
religion in, *"Commercialized Religion"*—**p. 1161**
Paul preaching in, *"Sports and Education"*—**p. 1161**
Paul's farewell to, Acts 20:13–38—**p. 1162**
church in, *"Strategic Place"*—**p. 1258**

ESAU — son of Isaac and Rebekah; older brother of Jacob
character profile, *"Surprising Choice"*—**p. 63**
despised his birthright, *"No Sympathy for Esau"*—**p. 51**
cheated by Jacob, Genesis 25:19–34—**p. 51**; Genesis 27:1–28:9—**p. 52**
forgives Jacob, Genesis 33—**p. 62**
descendants of, *"Blood Feud"*—**p. 184**; *"Bad Blood"*—**p. 883**; *"Poetic Justice"*—**p. 942**

ESTHER
character profile, see *"Introduction to Esther"*—**p. 528**
made queen, Esther 2—**p. 530**
her wisdom, *"Subtle Approach"*—**p. 534**

Eternal Life — life everlasting with God, which begins at conversion (*see also* BORN AGAIN, CONVERSION, SALVATION, HEAVEN)

in Psalms, *"Life after Death"*—**p. 581**
hints of in Old Testament, *"Is There an Afterlife?"*—**p. 697**
to inherit, Matthew 19:16–30—**p. 1019**
through rebirth, John 3:1–21—**p. 1102**
gift of God, Romans 6:15–23—**p. 1182**
assurance of, 1 John 5:1–15—**p. 1308**

EVANGELISM — telling and living the good news of Christ's salvation (*see also* MISSIONS)
by lifestyle, *"Old Testament Evangelism"*—**p. 206**
call to, Matthew 28:16–20—**p. 1033**; Luke 24:45–52—**p. 1098**; Acts 1:1–11—**p. 1134**
gift of, Ephesians 4:1–16—**p. 1232**; 2 Timothy 4:1–5—**p. 1266**

EVE — the first woman
character profile, *"First in Everything"*—**p. 26**
life of, Genesis 1:26–5:2—**p. 25**
temptation of, Genesis 3—**p. 27**
mentioned in the New Testament, 1 Corinthians 11:2–16—**p. 1203**; 1 Timothy 2:8–15—**p. 1258**

EVIL (*see also* SATAN, SIN)
introduction of, Genesis 3:1–24—**p. 27**
used by God, *"You Intended Evil"*—**p. 81**; *"Evil Spirit"*—**p. 277**
people, *"Blowing in the Wind"*—**p. 575**
repent of, Jeremiah 18:1–12—**p. 798**
problem of, Job 1–42—**p. 540**; *"The Song of the Cross"*—**p. 540**; *"God's Fault?"*—**p. 700**; *"The Problem of Evil"*—**p. 961**
spreads, *"One-way Contamination"*—**p. 973**; *"Evil Everywhere"*—**p. 577**
battle with good, *"A Look Behind the Scenes"*—**p. 1327**

EVOLUTION — theory of the development of species (*see also* CREATION)
controversy over, *"Where We Came From"*—**p. 28**

EXCOMMUNICATION
for purpose of teaching, *"Handed Over to Satan"*—**p. 1198**; 1 Corinthians 5—**p. 1198**; 1 Timothy 1:20—**p. 1258**

EXAMPLE
Christ as, John 13:1–17—**p. 1119**; Philippians 2:1–11—**p. 1238**
Old Testament stories as, 1 Corinthians 10:1–13—**p. 1202**; Hebrews 11:4–40—**p. 1284**
Christians as, Philippians 2:14–15—**p. 1239**; 1 Thessalonians 1—**p. 1248**; 1 Peter 2:11–12—**p. 1297**
Job, of patience, James 5:10–11—**p. 1292**
Elijah, of prayer, James 5:16–18—**p. 1293**

EXILE
northern kingdom to Assyria, 2 Kings 17—**p. 416**
southern kingdom to Babylon, 2 Kings 25—**p. 427**; 2 Chronicles 36—**p. 496**
return from, *"After the Exile"*—**p. 441**; *"Beginning Again"*—**p. 498**; *"Starting Over"*—**p. 32**
Jews' enemies after, *"A Flash Forward"*—**p. 502**; *"Powerful Opponents"*—**p. 513**
won't last forever, *"Gone, But Not Forever"*—**p. 806**

EYEWITNESSES
of Jesus' ministry, *"Eyewitness Reports"*—**p. 1042**; *"Like a Joy-filled Musical"*—**p. 1060**; *"Eyewitness Details"*—**p. 1102**; *"Eyewitness"*—**p. 1305**
of Jesus' resurrection, *"Coverup"*—**p. 1033**; *"More than a Ghost"*—**p. 1136**; *"Basic Christianity"*—**p. 1206**
of Paul's ministry, *"Firsthand Report"*—**p. 1156**

EZEKIEL
character profile, *"Radical Priest"*—**p. 851**
life of, *"Seeing the Unseen God"*—**p. 847**
burden of, *"The Sad Truth"*—**p. 882**
proof of his message, *"Prophet's Proof"*—**p. 869**
as a watchman, *"Watch Out"*—**p. 880**

EZRA — a leader of the Jews who returned from exile
character profile, *"Ezra, a Man of the Heart"*—**p. 506**
life of, Ezra 7–10—**p. 505**; Nehemiah 8—**p. 519**; 12—**p. 524**
concern about intermarriage, *"Ezra, a Man of the Heart"*—**p. 506**

F

Faith — trust in and reliance on God

of Abraham, *"Abraham"*—**p. 36**; Genesis 15:6—**p. 39**
Abraham's lack of, *"A Substitute Wife"*—**p. 39**
simple, *"Keep It Simple"*—**p. 232**
shown by widow of Zarephath, *"Down to the Last Meal"*—**p. 387**
shown by Ezra, *"Risk of Faith"*—**p. 508**
during suffering, *"When Bad Things Happened to a Good Person"*—**p. 538**; *"Seeing in the Dark"*—**p. 572**; *"Refiner's Fire"*—**p. 1296**
living by, *"Beyond Understanding"*—**p. 702**; *"Whom to Trust?"*—**p. 797**; Matthew 6:25–34—**p. 1003**; *"Time to Decide"*—**p. 1274**
during crisis, *"A Time of Crisis"*—**p. 741**
lukewarm, *"When Faith Grows Weary"*—**p. 985**
necessary for salvation, Romans 3:21–5:11—**p. 1178**; Galatians 2–3—**p. 1224**; Ephesians 2:1–10—**p. 1231**
our part in, *"Working with God"*—**p. 1239**
heroes of, Hebrews 11—**p. 1284**; *"What Is True Faith?"*—**p. 1285**
shown by deeds, *"Bargain Hunting"*—**p. 814**; James 2:14–26—**p. 1290**; *"Words Are Not Enough"*—**p. 1288**

FAITHFULNESS
of God, Psalm 78—**p. 618**; Psalm 111—**p. 640**;
Lamentations 3:22–32—**p. 844**
an aspect of the Spirit's fruit, Galatians 5:16–26—**p. 1227**
of Moses, Hebrews 3—**p. 1277**
expected of Christians, Revelation 2:8–11—**p. 1319**

FALSE PROPHETS
used by God, "Whose Side Is Balaam On?"—**p. 187**
tests for, "Testing Prophets"—**p. 217**
denounced, "Doglike Prophets"—**p. 767**
predicting good, "Greedy Doctors"—**p. 786**; "Whitewash"—
p. 858; "Plenty of Beer"—**p. 952**
use of dreams, "Questionable Dreams"—**p. 804**

FALSE TEACHERS
avoiding, "Unequal Yokes"—**p. 1215**
recognizing, "Battling the Cults"—**p. 1242**; "Foolish
Questions"—**p. 1270**; "A Threat from Within"—**p. 1300**;
"Who Were the Gnostics?"—**p. 1308**; "Undesirable
Guests"—**p. 1310**; "Watch Out"—**p. 880**
distorting the truth, "Words That Get Polluted"—**p. 1304**
Gnostics, "Pesky Deceivers"—**p. 1311**
emperor worship, "Satan's Throne"—**p. 1319**

FAME
transience of, Isaiah 14:9–20—**p. 724**
unreliability of, Ezekiel 33:30–32—**p. 881**
unimportant, 1 Corinthians 3:1–23—**p. 1196**

Family

established in Garden of Eden, Genesis 2:18–24—
p. 27
obligations to, "A Brother's Duty"—**p. 67**
quarrels within, "Family Battles"—**p. 69**; "Family
Jealousy"—**p. 175**
built by God, Psalm 127–128—**p. 649**
of God, "For the Discouraged"—**p. 1229**; Ephesians
2:19–22—**p. 1231**
family relations, Ephesians 5:21–6:4—**p. 1234**;
Colossians 3:18–21—**p. 1245**

FAMINE
in Egypt and Palestine, "An Unusual Famine"—**p. 72**
in Israel, Ruth 1:1—**p. 292**; 1 Kings 17—**p. 386**; 2 Kings
6:25–8:2—**p. 405**

FASTING— abstinence from food or drink for a period
of time, especially for spiritual reasons
at a time of national crisis, 2 Chronicles 20:1–13—
p. 478; Esther 4—**p. 532**; Joel 2:15–17—**p. 929**
true, Isaiah 58—**p. 768**
proper time for, "Repent for How Long?"—**p. 978**
Jesus' teaching on, Matthew 6:16–18—**p. 1003**
disciples', Acts 13:1–3—**p. 1150**; 14:23—**p. 1154**

FEAR— reverence and awe for God
commanded, Deuteronomy 6:10–25—**p. 209**;
Ecclesiastes 12:8–14—**p. 703**
good, Psalm 33—**p. 591**
guide to living, "The Fear of the Lord"—**p. 668**
the beginning of wisdom, Proverbs 9:10–12—**p. 668**

FEAR— fright or alarm
combating, Psalm 23—**p. 587**; 56—**p. 606**; 91—**p. 627**;
Jeremiah 1:4–19—**p. 779**; Luke 12:4–12—**p. 1081**
comfort in, John 14—**p. 1121**

FELLOWSHIP
expressed in sharing, Acts 2:42–47—**p. 1136**; 4:24–35—
p. 1138
with the Holy Spirit, 2 Corinthians 13:14—**p. 1221**
in church, Ephesians 4:17–5:21—**p. 1233**
with God, 1 John 1—**p. 1305**

FESTIVALS— see JEWISH HOLY DAYS

FLATTERY
deceives, "Flattering Advice"—**p. 350**; "Dangerous
Flattery"—**p. 689**
displeases God, Psalm 12—**p. 579**

FOOD
provided by God, "No More Free Lunch"—**p. 243**
provided by Christ, Matthew 14:13–21—**p. 1013**; John 6—
p. 1107
glorify God through, 1 Corinthians 10:23–11:1—**p. 1202**
as god, Philippians 3:19—**p. 1240**

FOOL (see also WISDOM)
in biblical terms, "The Making of a Fool"—**p. 686**

FOREIGN NATIONS
opposing Judah and Israel, "Troublesome Neighbors"—
p. 413
Israel's alliances with, "Ahaz's Fateful Decisions"—**p. 415**;
"The Siege Lifted"—**p. 820**; "False Hope"—**p. 846**; "The
Runaways"—**p. 868**; "Unreliable Egypt"—**p. 875**
praising God, "Who are God's People?"—**p. 601**; "House of
Prayer"—**p. 767**
loved by God, "God Reaches Out"—**p. 610**
loss of power of, "The Decline of Tyre"—**p. 732**
used by God, "Good Shepherd"—**p. 755**
cruelty of, "Most Ruthless"—**p. 876**
preaching gospel to, "To All Nations"—**p. 1053**
entering the church, "Earthshaking Change"—**p. 1149**
salvation of, "Hope for the Gentiles"—**p. 793**; "The Wise
Men"—**p. 998**
judged by God, "Just What They Deserved"—**p. 871**

Forgiveness

human, Genesis 33—**p. 62**; 50:15–21—**p. 81**; Luke
15:17–24—**p. 1085**; Acts 7:60—**p. 1144**
God's, Exodus 34:4–7—**p. 118**; Psalm 103:8–12—
p. 632; Micah 7:18–20—**p. 956**; "Nobody Like
God"—**p. 956**
absolute, "An End to Guilt"—**p. 833**
for sins, Psalm 130—**p. 650**
how often, Matthew 18:21–35—**p. 1018**
through Christ, Mark 2:1–11—**p. 1037**; Colossians
2:6–15—**p. 1244**; "A Modern Peace Child"—
p. 1180
in the church, 2 Corinthians 2:5–11—**p. 1212**

FREE WILL
Pharaoh's, "Pharaoh's Hard Heart"—**p. 91**
Israel's, "Free Choice"—**p. 262**
David's, "Satan or the Lord?"—**p. 360**

FREEDOM
through obeying, "Free At Last"—**p. 646**
in Christ, John 8:31–36—**p. 1112**; Galatians 4:21–5:26—
p. 1226; "Legalism"—**p. 1225**; "Paul Fights Back"—
p. 1227
from sin and our human nature, Romans 6—**p. 1181**
from law, Romans 8:1–17—**p. 1183**; Galatians 3:8–25—
p. 1224

FRIENDSHIP
acts of, "Loyal Friends in Death"—**p. 330**; "How to be a
Good Friend"—**p. 678**
faithfulness in, Proverbs 27:6,10,17—**p. 687**
giving advice in, "A Mixture of True and False"—**p. 545**;
"What Not to Say to a Hurting Person"—**p. 544**;
"A Wrong Time for Cheer"—**p. 552**; "Battle of Words"—
p. 552; "A Silent Friend Decides to Speak Up"—**p. 562**;
"Kinder, Gentler Friend"—**p. 563**
importance of, Ecclesiastes 4:7–12—**p. 697**
of David and Jonathan, 1 Samuel 20—**p. 319**; "Final
Farewell"—**p. 323**; "The Survival of a Family"—**p. 325**

of Jesus with Mary, Martha, and Lazarus, John
11:1–44–**p. 1115**

of Ruth and Naomi, *"A Rare Bond of Love"*–**p. 291**

with the world, James 4–**p. 1291**

with the wrong people, *"Unholy Alliance"*–**p. 394**

FRUIT OF THE SPIRIT
described, Galatians 5:16–26–**p. 1227**

FUTURE (*see also* SECOND COMING)
seeking omens of, *"The Witch of Endor"*–**p. 328**; *"Liver-
Gazing"*–**p. 866**

revealed by God, *"Foretelling the Future"*–**p. 757**; *"A
Glimpse of Things to Come"*–**p. 772**

of the earth, *"Catastrophes to Come?"*–**p. 983**

preoccupation with, Matthew 6:25–34–**p. 1003**; Luke
12:13–48–**p. 1081**; *"Preparing for the End"*–**p. 1250**

Jesus' statements about, *"When Will Jesus Return?"*–
p. 1026

uncertain, James 4:13–17–**p. 1292**

of God's kingdom, *"A Happy Ending after All"*–**p. 1333**

G

GABRIEL– an angel who carried messages from God
with Daniel, Daniel 8, 9–**p. 1293**

with Zechariah, Luke 1:5–25–**p. 1061**

with Mary, Luke 1:26–38–**p. 1063**

GALILEE– region in northern Palestine
towns given to Hiram, *"Good-for-nothing Towns"*–**p. 376**

Jesus' ministry there predicted, Isaiah 9:1–7–**p. 720**;
Matthew 4:12–17–**p. 1000**

Jesus' ministry in, *"Into the Countryside"*–**p. 1036**

home of Mary and Joseph, Luke 1:26–**p. 1063**; Luke
2:39–**p. 1065**

GARDEN OF EDEN
God created, Genesis 2:8–17–**p. 26**

expulsion from, Genesis 3–**p. 27**

GENEALOGY
shows God's care, *"Compressed History"*–**p. 431**

importance to the Israelites, *"A Family Record"*–**p. 429**;
"Key People"–**p. 436**; *"The Source of Genealogies"*–
p. 441; *"A People Preserved"*–**p. 500**; *"Remembering our
Past"*–**p. 517**

of Jesus, *"A Bridge from Old to New"*–**p. 995**; *"A Gospel for
the Gentiles"*–**p. 1067**

GENTILES– see FOREIGN NATIONS

GIDEON– a warrior and leader of Israel
character profile, *"Unlikely Leaders"*–**p. 272**

life of, Judges 6–8–**p. 272**

prepared by God, *"Unlikely Leaders"*–**p. 272**

GIFTS– special abilities given to believers through the
grace of God
stewardship of, Matthew 25:14–30–**p. 1027**; *"Original
Talent"*–**p. 1027**

use of, Romans 12:3–8–**p. 1188**; 1 Peter 4:10–11–
p. 1299

desire for, 1 Corinthians 12–14–**p. 1203**; *"Speaking in
Tongues"*–**p. 1205**

God distributes, Ephesians 4:7–13–**p. 1232**

GIVING
appropriate, *"The Perfect Gift"*–**p. 74**

for the tabernacle, *"Enthusiastic Givers"*–**p. 121**

to God, *"Does God Need Our Gifts?"*–**p. 603**; Malachi
3:6–12–**p. 988**

in secret, Matthew 6:1–4–**p. 1002**

generous, *"Any Poor People?"*–**p. 219**; 1 Corinthians
16:1–4–**p. 1208**; 2 Corinthians 8–9–**p. 1216**; *"Don't
Forget the Poor"*–**p. 1216**; *"Bonuses of Giving"*–**p. 1217**

GLORY– the grandeur and majesty of God
revealed, Exodus 40:34–38–**p. 125**; 2 Chronicles
7:1–4–**p. 469**

of God, Psalm 29–**p. 589**; 93–**p. 628**; 96–**p. 629**

manifested in Jesus, John 1:14–18–**p. 1100**; 12:20–33–
p. 1118; 2 Corinthians 3–**p. 1212**

believers fall short of, Romans 3:10–23–**p. 1178**

GOD
his creativity, Genesis 1–2–**p. 25**

encounters with, *"Wrestling with God"*–**p. 596**; *"God
Speaks to Job"*–**p. 569**; *"A Love Poem to God's Law"*–
p. 644; *"Seeing the Unseen God"*–**p. 847**; *"Drawing
Near"*–**p. 1280**

his name, Exodus 3–**p. 86**

self-description, *"Capsule Description"*–**p. 118**

his holiness, *"A Portable Cathedral"*–**p. 120**; *"Living with
Fire"*–**p. 127**; *"The Glory of the Lord"*–**p. 136**; *"A High-
Water Mark"*–Isaiah 40–**p. 748**

his love for his people, *"Freedom Fighters"*–**p. 265**; *"The New
Sodom"*–**p. 713**; *"The People Who Refuse to Die"*–**p. 811**

apparent absence of, *"Arms Too Short"*–**p. 546**; *"Where Is
God?"*–**p. 557**; *"Is God Really Listening?"*–**p. 565**; *"The
Song of the Cross"*–**p. 586**; *"Wrestling with God"*–
p. 596; *"No Happy Ending"*–**p. 599**

as a shepherd, Psalm 23–**p. 587**; *"The Good Shepherd"*–
p. 881

knowledge of, *"The Face of God"*–**p. 582**; *"Walking with
God"*–**p. 663**; *"How to Understand God"*–**p. 750**;
"Handling Tough Questions"–**p. 786**

always near, *"Near and Nearer"*–**p. 647**

preparing for, *"Voice in the Wilderness"*–**p. 748**

arguing with, *"Quarrels with God"*–**p. 756**

appearing in foreign lands, *"Foreign Appearance"*–**p. 849**

his justice, *"God Is Unfair?"*–**p. 863**; *"Atrocities"*–**p. 934**;
"The Problem of Evil"–**p. 961**

hiding from, *"An Inescapable God"*–**p. 940**; *"Mind
Reader"*–**p. 1278**

his plan revealed, *"Not by Chance"*–**p. 1276**

GOLDEN RULE
stated by Jesus, *"Golden Rule"*–**p. 1004**; Luke 6:27–36–
p. 1071

GOLGOTHA– a place outside Jerusalem where
executions occurred
Jesus crucified at, Mark 15:21–32–**p. 1058**; Luke
23:26–43–**p. 1096**

GOSPEL– the "good news"; the message of Christianity
told to Abraham, *"The Gospel to Abraham"*–**p. 42**

written for non-Jews, *"The Fast-paced Gospel"*–**p. 1034**

preaching it, Acts 8:1–4–**p. 1144**; Romans 15:14–16–
p. 1191

summarized, *"The Gospel in a Nutshell"*–**p. 1103**; *"What It's
There For"*–**p. 1181**; Ephesians 2:1–10–**p. 1231**;
Colossians 1:3–23–**p. 1243**

not ashamed of, Romans 1:16–17–**p. 1176**

only one, Galatians 1:6–9–**p. 1223**

GOSSIP
as a sin, Romans 1:29–**p. 1176**; 2 Corinthians 12:20–
p. 1220

power of, *"Verbal Dynamite"*–**p. 676**

GOVERNMENT
confronting, Exodus 5–14–**p. 88**; 2 Samuel 12:1–14–
p. 343; 1 Kings 21–**p. 392**

of Israel by judges, *"Freedom Fighters"*–**p. 265**

Israel's form of, *"Why Not a King?"*–**p. 305**

of Israel by theocracy, *"Church and State"*–**p. 456**

David's goals for, *"The Company You Keep"*–**p. 631**

qualities needed for, *"Good Government"*–**p. 685**

Judah lacking, *"Total Anarchy"*–**p. 715**

under tyrants, *"In the Hands of Tyrants"*–**p. 912**

disobedience toward, Acts 5:17–42–**p. 1139**

of Israel by Romans, *"Two Rulers"*–**p. 1168**

duty to, Romans 13:1–7–**p. 1189**; Titus 3:1–2–**p. 1270**;
1 Peter 2:13–17–**p. 1297**

GRACE – the undeserved love and salvation God gives
to Jacob, *"A Stairway to Heaven"*–**p. 56**
to Israel, *"Why the Israelites?"*–**p. 210**; *"The Turning Point"*–
p. 879
parables of, *"Unfair Pay"*–**p. 1020**; Luke 15:11–31–
p. 1085
through Christ, Romans 5–**p. 1179**
for salvation, Ephesians 2–**p. 1231**

GREED
defined, *"Never Enough"*–**p. 698**
futility of, Ecclesiastes 5:8–6:12–**p. 698**
as motive in preaching the gospel, *"Gospel Greed"*–
p. 1145
evil of, Luke 12:13–34–**p. 1081**; 1 Timothy 6:3–10–
p. 1261; James 5:1–6–**p. 1292**

GRIEF – *see* COMFORT, DISCOURAGEMENT, SORROW

GUIDANCE
of the Israelites, *"Unmistakable Guidance"*–**p. 172**
sought by Gideon, *"Putting Out a Fleece"*–**p. 274**
from God's Word, Psalm 119–**p. 643**; 2 Timothy
3:14–17–**p. 1265**
practical, *"Uncommon Sense"*–**p. 660**
from the law, *"Whom to Believe?"*–**p. 719**
from Holy Spirit, John 16:5–16–**p. 1122**

Guilt *(see also* CONFESSION, BACKSLIDING, FORGIVENESS)
Old Testament guilt offering, Leviticus 5:14–6:7–
p. 131
overwhelmed by, Psalm 38–**p. 595**
all guilty before God, Romans 3:10–23–**p. 1178**
acknowledging, Ezra 9–**p. 508**; Psalm 32–**p. 591**;
51–**p. 603**; 1 John 1:7–10–**p. 1305**
relief from, 1 John 1:5–2:2–**p. 1305**

H

HANNAH – mother of Samuel
character profile, *"Deepest Longing"*–**p. 299**
her life, 1 Samuel 1–2–**p. 298**
her prayer for a child, *"Sad, Not Drunk"*–**p. 298**
her life a picture of Israel, *"What Leadership Requires"*–
p. 296

HAPPINESS – *see* JOY

HEALING
prayers for, 2 Samuel 12:15–25–**p. 344**; 1 Kings
17:7–24–**p. 386**; 2 Kings 5–**p. 403**; 2 Corinthians
12:7–10–**p. 1220**
by Jesus' wounds, *"Healing Wounds"*–**p. 763**
by Jesus, Matthew 8:1–17–**p. 1004**; Mark 5–**p. 1041**;
Luke 4:38–41–**p. 1068**
by disciples, Acts 3:1–10–**p. 1136**; 5:12–16–**p. 1139**;
14:8–10–**p. 1154**; 28:7–10–**p. 1172**
encouraged, James 5:13–18–**p. 1293**

HEART – figuratively, the center of a person; that
which gives direction to a person
obeying with your, *"Law of the Heart"*–**p. 226**
God knows, 1 Samuel 16:1–13–**p. 315**
cleansing of, Psalm 51–**p. 603**
undivided, *"Heart Surgery"*–**p. 624**
life flows from, Proverbs 4:23–**p. 665**
deceitful, Jeremiah 17:9–10–**p. 797**
leads to action, Matthew 12:33–37–**p. 1010**

Heaven – a place of perfect happiness and eternal communion with God
hints of in Old Testament, *"Life after Death"*–**p. 581**
God rules from, Psalm 99–**p. 630**; Isaiah 66:1–2–
p. 775
new, Isaiah 65:17–25–**p. 775**; Revelation 21–22–
p. 1335
treasures in, Matthew 6:19–24–**p. 1003**
for righteous, Matthew 25:31–46–**p. 1027**
citizenship in, Philippians 3:12–4:1–**p. 1240**
inhabitants of, Hebrews 11–**p. 1284**
visions of, Revelation 4–5–**p. 1320**; Revelation 7–
p. 1323

HELL – a place of eternal punishment and sorrow
hints of in Old Testament, Job 24:21–26–**p. 557**; Psalm
49:10–15–**p. 602**; Daniel 12–**p. 913**
to avoid, Matthew 5:21–30–**p. 1001**; Romans 8:1–16–
p. 1183
for evildoers, Matthew 13:24–30,36–43–**p. 1012**
punishment in, 2 Thessalonians 1:3–12–**p. 1253**; Jude
5–13–**p. 1314**; Revelation 20:11–14–**p. 1334**
keep others from, Jude 17–23–**p. 1314**

HERESIES – *see* FALSE TEACHERS

HEROD – name of a line of rulers of Palestine
character profile, the Herods: *"Lower Authority"*–**p. 1014**
the Great, Matthew 2–**p. 998**
Antipas, Matthew 14:1–12–**p. 1013**; *"Guards Without
Allies"*–**p. 1150**
Agrippa I, Acts 12:1–23–**p. 1150**

HEZEKIAH – king of Judah for 29 years; reopened the
temple his father had closed
character profile, *"Cleaning House"*–**p. 488**
life of, 2 Kings 18–20–**p. 419**; *"King of Contradictions"*–
p. 419
restores worship, 2 Chronicles 29–31–**p. 487**
crisis with Isaiah, Isaiah 36–39–**p. 744**

HISTORY
God working in, *"God's Hand in History"*–**p. 721**;
"Catastrophes Through God's Eyes"–**p. 730**; *"Like a Wise
Farmer"*–**p. 737**; *"A New Song"*–**p. 749**; *"Ransom for
the Captives"*–**p. 753**; *"World at War"*–**p. 827**;
"Kidnapped"–**p. 897**; *"In the Hands of Tyrants"*–**p. 912**;
"The Meaning of a Natural Disaster"–**p. 926**; *"Light in a
Dark Time"*–**p. 949**; *"A Look Behind the Scenes"*–
p. 1327
as encouragement, *"Why the Cleanup?"*–**p. 433**
interpreting, *"Moral of the Story"*–**p. 442**
prophesied, *"A Prophecy for the World"*–**p. 735**;
"Foretelling the Future"–**p. 757**; *"New King, New
Kingdom"*–**p. 980**

HOLOCAUST
original meaning of, *"Original Holocaust"*–**p. 129**

HOLY – separated or set apart for God
called to be, Exodus 19:1–5–**p. 102**; Leviticus
11:44–45–**p. 138**; 1 Peter 1:13–16–**p. 1296**; 2:9–10–
p. 1296
lifestyle, *"National Reminders"*–**p. 171**
God's character, Psalm 99–**p. 630**; Isaiah 6–**p. 717**
One of Israel, *"A Key Phrase"*–**p. 723**
all things becoming, *"No More Separation"*–**p. 983**
imitate God's holiness, Ephesians 4:17–5:21–**p. 1233**

Holy Spirit — the third person of the Trinity; also known as the Counselor who is active in the lives of believers (*see also* FRUIT OF THE SPIRIT)

in the Old Testament, *"The Spirit and Samson"*—
p. 283; Psalm 51:11—p. 603; Isaiah 11:1–5—
p. 722; 61:1–3—p. 770
his coming prophesied, *"A New Spirit"*—p. 884; *"The Spirit Poured Out"*—p. 930
anointed Jesus, Luke 3:21–22—p. 1066; 4:1–27—p. 1067
comfort from, John 14:15–31—p. 1121
work of, John 16:5–16—p. 1122; *"Branded"*—p. 1230
coming to the disciples, Acts 2—p. 1134
in the early church, *"The Secret to the Early Church"*—p. 1139
directs the church, Acts 13:1–4—p. 1150; 16:6–7—p. 1156
filled with, Acts 19:1–7—p. 1161; Ephesians 5:18—p. 1234
life through, Romans 8:1–17—p. 1183
in Christians, 1 Corinthians 2:6–16—p. 1195; 3:16–17—p. 1197

HOMOSEXUALITY
result of sin, Romans 1:18–32—p. 1176
listed as sin, 1 Corinthians 6:9–11—p. 1199; 1 Timothy 1:9–11—p. 1257

HONESTY
Samuel's, *"Accuse Me!"*—p. 309
God desires, Psalm 15—p. 580

HOPE
for the Israelites, *"Hope in a Time of Sorrow"*—p. 449; *"Free Again"*—p. 810; *"The Turning Point"*—p. 879; *"New Hope"*—p. 925
in the Lord, Psalm 42–43—p. 598; 1 Timothy 6:17–19—p. 1261
while waiting for God, *"A Desperate Hope"*—p. 549; *"An Outburst of Hope"*—p. 553; *"A New Song"*—p. 749; *"Hope for the Grieving"*—p. 844
because of the past, *"A Time for Hope"*—p. 462; *"Remembering Back"*—p. 618
for total redemption, *"A Glimpse of Things to Come"*—p. 772; *"A Happy Ending after All"*—p. 1333
does not disappoint, Romans 5:1–11—p. 1179
for resurrection, 1 Corinthians 15—p. 1206
in Christ, Colossians 1:3–27—p. 1243; 1 Peter 1:13–16—p. 1296

HOSPITALITY
expected, *"A Breach of Hospitality"*—p. 287
Jesus' words on, Luke 14:12–14—p. 1084
responsibility of, Romans 12:13—p. 1189; 1 Peter 4:9—p. 1299; *"Guidelines for Hospitality"*—p. 1312
entertaining angels, Hebrews 13:1–3—p. 1287
when not to extend, *"Undesirable Guests"*—p. 1310

HUMAN BEINGS
created in God's image, Genesis 1:26–31—p. 25
made by God, *"Where We Came From"*—p. 28
glory of, Psalm 8—p. 578
intricately made, Psalm 139:13–16—p. 653
apart from God, *"Three Problem People"*—p. 662; *"Outside the Palace"*—p. 695

HUMILITY
of David, *"Rare Trait"*—p. 450
living in, Micah 6:6–8—p. 955; Colossians 3:12–17—p. 1245; 1 Peter 5:5–7—p. 1299
like children, Matthew 18:1–4—p. 1017
encouraged, *"Luke and the Underdog"*—p. 1087; *"The Role of a Servant"*—p. 1119; Romans 12:1–21—p. 1188; 1 Peter 5:5–7—p. 1299

of Christ, 2 Corinthians 8:8–9—p. 1217; Philippians 2:1–11—p. 1238

HUSBAND
duty to wife, 1 Corinthians 7:1–5—p. 1199
love for wife, Ephesians 5:25–33—p. 1234; Colossians 3:19—p. 1245

HYPOCRISY
in worshiping God, *"Hypocrites"*—p. 738; *"Letting the Inside Match the Outside"*—p. 1002
avoid, Matthew 6:1–24—p. 1002
described, Matthew 23—p. 1024
condemned, James 1:19–2:13—p. 1290; 1 John 3:17–19—p. 1307

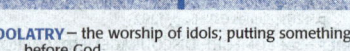

IDOLATRY — the worship of idols; putting something before God
commandment against, Exodus 20:3–6—p. 104
Canaanite, *"Detestable Ways"*—p. 221
during time of the judges, *"Sad Commentary"*—p. 286
attraction of, *"Why All the Fuss about Idols"*—p. 400
Judah's lust for, *"Provoking God"*—p. 774
Israel's lust for, *"Smoldering Passion"*—p. 920
as adultery, *"Ritual Sex"*—p. 781; *"A Lover's Quarrel"*—p. 782; *"Worse than a Whore"*—p. 860; *"The Runaways"*—p. 868; *"Tearing God's Heart"*—p. 915
emptiness of, *"Idolatry"*—p. 800; Isaiah 44:6–23—p. 754
greed is, Colossians 3:5—p. 1245

IDOLS
of Laban, *"Household Gods"*—p. 61
of Egypt, *"Attack on False Gods"*—p. 94
golden calf, *"Recent Discovery"*—p. 116
Israel defending its, *"Topsy-turvy"*—p. 273
of Judah, *"Notorious Asherah Poles"*—p. 382; *"Queen of Heaven"*—p. 826
worthless, *"An Exiled God"*—p. 829; *"A Dim View of Idolatry"*—p. 853

IMAGE OF GOD — (*see* HUMAN BEING)

INCARNATION — God taking human flesh; birth of Jesus
taught, Matthew 1:18–25—p. 997; Luke 1–2—p. 1061; John 1:1–18—p. 1100
reason for, *"Contempt, not Sympathy"*—p. 548; *"Why Come to Earth?"*—p. 1039
heresies denying, *"Who Were the Gnostics?"*—p. 1308

INCEST — sexual relations with a family member
Lot and his daughters, *"Family Quarrels"*—p. 44
Reuben's, *"A Sin that Lies Sleeping"*—p. 65
forbidden, Leviticus 18:1–18—p. 146

INFERTILITY
Sarah's, Genesis 18:1–15—p. 41
Hannah's prayer concerning, 1 Samuel 1:1–2:11—p. 298
Elizabeth's, Luke 1:7–25—p. 1062

INSPIRATION — the Bible as inspired by the Holy Spirit (*see* BIBLE)

INTERCESSION — the prayer of one person for another
examples of, Genesis 18:23–32—p. 42; 1 Kings 8:33–51—p. 374; Ezra 9:5–15—p. 508; Daniel 9:3–19—p. 909
of Jesus for us, John 17—p. 1124; Romans 8:31–34—p. 1184; Hebrews 7:24–25—p. 1280; 1 John 2:1—p. 1305
of the Holy Spirit, Romans 8:26–27—p. 1184
commanded, 1 Timothy 2:1–2—p. 1258; James 5:16—p. 1293

J

LAZARUS – brother of Mary and Martha; close friend of Jesus
Jesus raises from the dead, John 11:1–44–**p. 1115**

LAZARUS – character in story Jesus told
carried to Abraham's side, Luke 16:19–31–**p. 1086**

LAZINESS
results of, *'The Problem with Laziness'*–**p. 684**; *'The Excuses of a Lazy Man'*–**p. 687**
warnings against, 2 Thessalonians 3:6–15–**p. 1254**

LEADERSHIP
God's help for, *'Who, Me?'*–**p. 86**; *'Unlikely Leaders'*–**p. 272**; *'A Donkey Hunt'*–**p. 305**
rivalry in, *'Burdens of Leadership'*–**p. 174**; *'A Sense of God's Timing'*–**p. 324**; *'Potential Rivals'*–**p. 334**
Joshua's, *'Filling Moses' Shoes'*–**p. 263**
Israel's need for, *'What Leadership Requires'*–**p. 296**
failures of, *'Why Saul Was Rejected'*–**p. 313**; *'The Man Who Had Everything'*–**p. 362**
by David, *'The Life of King David'*–**p. 331**
by Ezra, *'Ezra, a Man of the Heart'*–**p. 506**
by Nehemiah, *'A Man of Action'*–**p. 511**
through suffering, *'New King, New Kingdom'*–**p. 980**
Jesus', *'What Should a Leader Look Like?'*–**p. 1011**; *'Good Shepherd'*–**p. 1115**
following, Hebrews 13:7–17 –**p. 1287**
qualities of, 1 Timothy 3:1–10–**p. 1258**

LEGALISM – *see* LAW

LEPROSY (*see also* DISEASE)
wrong diagnosis of, *'Misidentification'*–**p. 140**

LEVITE – a descendant of Levi who served God and worked in the temple. (Priests were Levites, but not all Levites were priests; some had lesser duties.)
as representatives, *'Designated Firstborn'*–**p. 164**
duties established for, Numbers 3–**p. 163**; 1 Chronicles 23–24–**p. 454**; *'Keeping the Temple'*–**p. 454**
received cities, Numbers 35–**p. 199**
support of, *'No Land for Levites'*–**p. 182**

LIFE (*see also* ETERNAL LIFE)
shortness of, Psalm 39–**p. 596**
a wise, *'God and 'How-to-Succeed' '*–**p. 667**; *'A Matter of Life and Death'*–**p. 673**
purpose of, *'When Life Seems Senseless'*–**p. 693**
cycles in, *'Change or No Change?'*–**p. 698**
good things in, *'Good for Something'*–**p. 698**
making sense of, *'The Gamble'*–**p. 703**
unfairness of, *'Life Is Unfair'*–**p. 701**; *'Is Life Unfair?'*–**p. 1253**
saving your, Matthew 16:24–28–**p. 1017**
eternal, John 3:16–21–**p. 1103**; John 6:25–69–**p. 1108**; *'The Worst Danger of All'*–**p. 1207**; Colossians 3:1–4–**p. 1245**
living water, John 4:1–26–**p. 1104**
sacrifice of, *'A Modern Shepherd'*–**p. 1114**
Jesus brings it to the full, John 10:1–18–**p. 1114**
a gift of God, Acts 17:24–28–**p. 1158**

LIGHT
created first by God, Genesis 1:1–5–**p. 25**
seeing by God's, *'Light Makes Light'*–**p. 594**
God's Word as, Psalm 119:105–**p. 646**
of the world, Matthew 5:14–16–**p. 1001**
Jesus as, John 1:1–18–**p. 1100**; 8:12–**p. 1111**
believers as children of, Ephesians 5:8–14–**p. 1234**; 1 John 1–**p. 1305**

LION
killed by Samson, Judges 14–**p. 282**
killed by David, 1 Samuel 17:34–35–**p. 316**
and lamb together, Isaiah 11:6–9–**p. 722**; 65:25–**p. 775**

Daniel in den of, Daniel 6–**p. 905**
Christ as, Revelation 5:1–5–**p. 1321**

LISTENING
becoming wise by, *'The Supreme Gift of Wisdom'*–**p. 671**

LITERACY – ability to read and write
Moses', *'First Writing'*–**p. 101**
in ancient times, *'Early Literacy'*–**p. 275**

LONELINESS
cry of, Psalm 22–**p. 585**
Jesus', Matthew 26:36–46–**p. 1029**
Paul's, 2 Timothy 4:16–18–**p. 1267**

LORD
revealed to Moses, Exodus 3–**p. 86**
of lords, Deuteronomy 10:17–**p. 213**; 1 Timothy 6:13–16–**p. 1261**; Revelation 19:13–16–**p. 1334**
Jesus as, Acts 2:14–36–**p. 1186**; Romans 10:9–10–**p. 1186**; Philippians 2:5–11–**p. 1239**

LORD'S PRAYER
taught, Matthew 6:5–15–**p. 1003**

LORD'S SUPPER – a ritual sharing bread and wine; also called Communion and Eucharist
Jesus began, *'Original Lord's Supper'*–**p. 1055**; Luke 22:7–23–**p. 1093**
instructions concerning, 1 Corinthians 11:17–34–**p. 1203**

LOT – nephew of Abraham who settled in the land near Sodom
character profile, *'Different Pathways'*–**p. 38**
separates from Abram, Genesis 13–**p. 37**
in Sodom, Genesis 18:16–19:38–**p. 41**

Love

shown to an enemy, *'A Captive's Compassion'*–**p. 403**; Romans 12:18–21–**p. 1189**
responding to God's, *'God's Great Concern'*–**p. 658**; *'Spurned'*–**p. 986**
between man and woman, *'Whom Should You Marry?'*–**p. 680**; *'An Intoxicating Love'*–**p. 704**; *'Let Love Sleep'*–**p. 707**
proverbs about, *'Love is the Greatest'*–**p. 670**
symbols of, *'His Banner over Me'*–**p. 706**; *'Parable of Love'*–**p. 918**
power of, *'Love and Death'*–**p. 710**
expressions of, *'A Brotherly Kiss'*–**p. 710**
of God for his people, *'Does God Care?'*–**p. 752**; *'A Lover's Quarrel'*–**p. 782**; Jeremiah 31:1–6–**p. 812**
of God for non-Jews, *'Good News for the Enemy?'*–**p. 945**
commanded, Mark 12:28–34–**p. 1052**; *'More Than a Feeling'*–**p. 214**; John 13:34–35–**p. 1120**; Romans 12:9–21–**p. 1189**
described, 1 Corinthians 13–**p. 1205**
an aspect of the Spirit's fruit, Galatians 5:13–26–**p. 1227**
of the world, 1 John 2:15–17–**p. 1306**
God is, 1 John 4:7–21–**p. 1307**

LUKE – author of the third Gospel; physician who traveled with Paul
sources, *'Luke the Historian'*–**p. 1062**; *'Jesus' Childhood'*–**p. 1065**
emphasis of, *'A Physician Looks at the Poor'*–**p. 1069**; *'Severe and Gentle Stories'*–**p. 1085**
travel companion of Paul, Acts 16:10–17–**p. 1156**; 20:5–21:18–**p. 1162**; 27:1–28:16–**p. 1170**

LUST — intense desire (*see* SEX)

LYING
by Abraham, *"Abraham's Half-Truth"*—**p. 37**
law against, Exodus 20:16—**p. 105**
penalty for, Leviticus 6:1–7—**p. 131**
by the Gibeonites, *"Tricked!"*—**p. 247**
by David, *"Disobeying the Law"*—**p. 321**; *"David's Double Game"*—**p. 327**
to David, *"The Traitors' Story"*—**p. 354**
by Peter, Matthew 26:69–74—**p. 1030**
Satan the father of, John 8:44—**p. 1112**
by Ananias and Sapphira, *"Deadly Deceit"*—**p. 1138**
mark of old nature, Ephesians 4:17–5:21—**p. 1233**

M

MAGIC — *see* ASTROLOGY, WITCHCRAFT

MARK — author of the second Gospel and missionary helper to Paul and Barnabas
character profile, *"Slow Starter"*—**p. 1155**
as author, *"The Anonymous Author"*—**p. 1056**

MARRIAGE (see also DIVORCE, HUSBAND, LOVE, WIFE)
God ordained, Genesis 2:18–25—**p. 27**; *"The First Marriage"*—**p. 27**
with unbelievers, *"Marrying Foreigners"*—**p. 49**; *"Intermarriage"*—**p. 269**; *"The First Sign of Trouble"*—**p. 282**; *"Inconsistent Ethics"*—**p. 470**; *"Corrupt Leaders"*—**p. 510**
for political marriages, *"Political Marriages"*—**p. 407**
importance of, *"Whom Should You Marry?"*—**p. 680**; Matthew 19:1–12—**p. 1019**
joys of, *"An Intoxicating Love"*—**p. 704**
Jewish customs about, *"More Than Engaged"*—**p. 998**
Jesus' teaching on, *"No-Fault Divorce?"*—**p. 1019**
relationship, Ephesians 5:22–33—**p. 1234**; Colossians 3:18–19—**p. 1245**; 1 Peter 3:1–7—**p. 1297**
Paul's advice on, 1 Corinthians 7—**p. 1199**

MARTHA AND MARY — sisters of Lazarus; friends of Jesus
character profile, *"Doer and Seeker"*—**p. 1079**
Jesus at home of, Luke 10:38–42—**p. 1079**
at Lazarus's death, John 11—**p. 1115**
washed Jesus' feet, John 12:1–8—**p. 1117**

MARTYR — one who gives up life for the faith
Stephen as, Acts 7—**p. 1141**
Paul as, *"A Hint of Trials to Come"*—**p. 1197**; *"A Letter from Death Row"*—**p. 1266**
by Nero, *"Endangered Strangers"*—**p. 1297**
many examples of, Hebrews 11:35–40—**p. 1286**; Revelation 6:9–11—**p. 1322**

MARY — mother of Jesus; wife of Joseph
character profile, *"Saying Yes to God"*—**p. 1064**
Jesus born to, Matthew 1:18–2:23—**p. 997**; Luke 1:26–56—**p. 1063**; Luke 2—**p. 1064**
concerned for Jesus, Mark 3:20–35—**p. 1038**; Luke 2:41–52—**p. 1065**
requests Jesus' first miracle, John 2:1–11—**p. 1102**
at crucifixion, John 19:16–27—**p. 1127**

MARY MAGDALENE — a close friend of Jesus
character profile, *"First to See"*—**p. 1128**
present at crucifixion, Mark 15:33–41—**p. 1058**
had been demon-possessed, Luke 8:1–3—**p. 1073**
first one at empty tomb, John 20:1–18—**p. 1128**

MATTHEW — author of the first Gospel; left his work to follow Jesus; also called Levi
transformed, *"Unpopular Profession"*—**p. 1006**
hosted a dinner for Jesus, Mark 2:13–17—**p. 1037**

MEDIATOR — someone who helps bring harmony between two parties
Jesus as, 1 Timothy 2:1–6—**p. 1258**; Hebrews 9:11–28—**p. 1282**

MEDITATION — *see* QUIET TIME

MELCHIZEDEK — priest and king
character profile, *"The Twelfth Man"*—**p. 639**
blessed Abram, Genesis 14:17–20—**p. 38**
pointed to Christ, Psalm 110—**p. 638**; Hebrews 5:1–10—**p. 1278**; Hebrews 7—**p. 1280**; *"Who is Melchizedek?"*—**p. 1280**
as example of leader, *"The Twelfth Man"*—**p. 639**

MEMORIALS
created for future generations, *"Monuments"*—**p. 264**

MEMORIES
giving hope, *"Fond Memories"*—**p. 547**; *"Remembering Back"*—**p. 618**; *"The Good Old Days"*—**p. 722**

Mercy

pleading for, Psalm 4—**p. 576**; Luke 18:9–14—**p. 1087**
of God, Psalm 108:8–12—**p. 637**; Psalm 123—**p. 648**; *"Too Merciful a God?"*—**p. 572**; Luke 1:46–79—**p. 1063**; Romans 9:15–18—**p. 1185**
for the merciful, *"A Key Characteristic"*—**p. 597**; James 2:12–13—**p. 1290**

MESSENGERS
in Persia, *"Pony Express"*—**p. 532**
of good news, *"Beautiful Feet"*—**p. 763**
Paul's, *"Mail Carriers"*—**p. 1271**

MESSIAH — a king and deliverer expected by the Jewish people; Christ
precedent for, *"Mystery Man"*—**p. 38**
promised by God, *"God's Great Promise"*—**p. 340**; *"Promise to David"*—**p. 651**
meaning of, *"The Messiah in the Psalms"*—**p. 575**
prophecies concerning, Psalm 2—**p. 575**; 110—**p. 638**; *"The Song of the Cross"*—**p. 586**; *"A Wedding Fit for a King"*—**p. 600**; *"Suffering Servant"*—**p. 764**; Isaiah 9:1–7—**p. 720**; 11:1–12—**p. 722**; 53:1–12—**p. 763**; 61:1–3—**p. 770**; Daniel 7:13–14—**p. 908**; *"Jesus Asks a Question"*—**p. 1092**
as a leader, *"The Twelfth Man"*—**p. 639**
David's son as, *"A Bridge from Old to New"*—**p. 995**
Jesus as, Matthew 11:1–6—**p. 1007**; *"The Killing of a King"*—**p. 1031**; *"Short-lived Acceptance"*—**p. 1051**; *"The Day of Execution"*—**p. 1057**; Luke 4:14–21—**p. 1067**

MICHAEL — the archangel appointed to guard the Jewish people
with Daniel, Daniel 10—**p. 910**; 12:1–13—**p. 913**
and war in heaven, Revelation 12—**p. 1327**

MILITARY (*see also* WAR)
serving in, *"Uncommon Military Rules"*—**p. 222**
trusting in, *"Lessons from the Battlefield"*—**p. 492**; *"Faith in God or the Military?"*—**p. 726**; *"Worshiping the Military"*—**p. 963**

MILLENNIUM — Latin word for "thousand years"; used in connection with a period in the last days
described, Revelation 20:1–15—**p. 1334**
views of, *"The Millennium"*—**p. 1334**

MINISTER — *see* PASTOR

MINISTRY
Paul's style of, *"A Human Letter"*—**p. 1212**
self-supporting, *"Working for a Living"*—**p. 1249**

MIRACLES — extraordinary events done through God's power
ten plagues, *"Day of the Locusts"*—**p. 90**
limited effect of, *"When God Was Obvious"*—**p. 109**; *"Miracles Aren't Enough"*—**p. 1009**; *"Don't Tell"*—**p. 1042**; *"Sensation-Seekers"*—**p. 1080**
of Elisha, *"Elisha's Miracles"*—**p. 402**
after Sermon on the Mount, *"Actions Follow Words"*—**p. 1005**
feeding crowds, *"Two Feedings"*—**p. 1015**; *"Better Bread"*—**p. 1108**
not done in Nazareth, *"No Respect at Home"*—**p. 1013**
done at a distance, *"A Long-distance Miracle"*—**p. 1106**
lead to belief, John 4:43–54—**p. 1106**; 20:30–31—**p. 1129**; *"John's Reason for Writing"*—**p. 1120**
done to glorify God, John 11:1–44—**p. 1115**

MIRIAM — prophetess, sister of Moses and Aaron
character profile, *"Jealous Sister"*—**p. 175**
led singing/dancing, Exodus 15:19–21—**p. 99**
disagreed with Moses, Numbers 12—**p. 174**

MISSIONS (*see also* EVANGELISM)
Israel's role in, *"Catastrophes Through God's Eyes"*—**p. 730**; *"Israel's Final Destiny"*—**p. 760**
highly praised, Isaiah 52:7–10—**p. 763**; Romans 10:14–15—**p. 1186**
command to, Matthew 28:16–20—**p. 1033**; Luke 24:45–52—**p. 1098**; Acts 1:1–11—**p. 1134**
responsibility of every Christian, Acts 8:1–6—**p. 1144**; 1 Peter 3:15–16—**p. 1297**
Barnabas and Saul (Paul) sent, Acts 13:1–3—**p. 1150**
Paul's journeys, Acts 13–28—**p. 1150**

Money

God owns everything, Deuteronomy 8—**p. 210**; Psalm 24—**p. 587**
rules about loans, *"Respect People, Not Money"*—**p. 225**
serving, Matthew 6:19–34—**p. 1003**
stories about, *"Matthew and Money"*—**p. 1018**
trusting, *"When Money is Useless"*—**p. 1081**; Psalm 62:10—**p. 609**
love of, 1 Timothy 6:3–19—**p. 1261**; *"Two Familiar Quotes"*—**p. 1261**; James 5:1–5—**p. 1292**

MORDECAI — Benjamite exile who raised Esther, queen of Persia
character profile, *"Standing Tall"*—**p. 532**

MOSES — used by God to deliver Israelites from slavery in Egypt; God gave him the Ten Commandments
character profile, see *"Introduction to Exodus"*—**p. 83**
life of, Exodus 2–40—**p. 85**; Numbers 1–36—**p. 161**; Deuteronomy 1–34—**p. 203**
birth of, Exodus 2—**p. 85**
called by God, Exodus 3–4—**p. 86**
leads Israelites out of Egypt, Exodus 5–15—**p. 88**; *"Free at Last"*—**p. 646**
received law, Exodus 19–31—**p. 102**
wilderness wanderings, Numbers 13–36—**p. 175**
his communication with God, *"The Lord said to Moses . . ."*—**p. 170**
punished by God, *"Moses' Sin"*—**p. 183**; *"Moses Stayed Out"*—**p. 192**
final message to Israel, *"A Personal Plea"*—**p. 201**; *"Dying Words"*—**p. 235**
blames Israelites, *"Distributing Blame"*—**p. 204**
foresees Israel's future, *"A Scent of Doom"*—**p. 231**; *"Moses Gets a Preview"*—**p. 237**
death of, Deuteronomy 34—**p. 237**
appears at Jesus' transfiguration, Matthew 17:1–13—**p. 1017**

MOTHER
Eve, mother of all living, Genesis 3:20–4:25—**p. 29**
barren women blessed with children, Genesis 21—**p. 45**; 25:21–26—**p. 51**; 29–30—**p. 56**; 1 Samuel 1—**p. 298**; Luke 1—**p. 1061**
a gift of God, Psalm 127–128—**p. 649**
responsibilities of, Proverbs 31—**p. 691**; 2 Timothy 1:1–7—**p. 1264**
God compared to, Isaiah 49:15—**p. 760**; 66:10–13—**p. 776**

MURDER
of Abel by Cain, Genesis 4—**p. 29**; 1 John 3:11–15—**p. 1307**
law concerning, Genesis 9:5–6—**p. 33**; *"Reverence for Life"*—**p. 33**; Exodus 20:13—**p. 105**; Numbers 35:16–34—**p. 199**
of rivals, *"Married Despots"*—**p. 481**
Jesus' teaching on, Matthew 5:21–26—**p. 1001**

MUSIC
used by the prophets, *"Musical Prophets"*—**p. 306**
organized by David, 1 Chronicles 25—**p. 456**
encouraging a new song, Psalm 98—**p. 629**
used in worship, *"Call and Response"*—**p. 652**
in praise, *"Lyrics for the Living God"*—**p. 592**; Psalm 150—**p. 659**
in heaven, Revelation 5—**p. 1321**; 7—**p. 1323**; 19—**p. 1333**

MYSTERY — something formerly hidden but now revealed in the gospel
of Christ's return, 1 Corinthians 15:50–58—**p. 1208**
of God, Ephesians 3—**p. 1232**; Colossians 1:24–2:5—**p. 1244**
of basic truths about Jesus, 1 Timothy 3:16—**p. 1259**

NAMES
symbolic, *"The Name of a God"*—**p. 903**; *"Children's Strange Names"*—**p. 917**; *"Names with Meaning"*—**p. 955**
importance of, *"The Power of a Name"*—**p. 1077**

NATHAN prophet to David; chronicler of Israel's history
character profile, *"The King's Conscience"*—**p. 339**

NATURE (*see also* CREATION)
declares God's glory, Psalm 19:1–6—**p. 584**
as proof of God's existence, *"A Faint Whisper of God"*—**p. 558**; Romans 1:18–20—**p. 1176**
praising God, *"Ecological Choir"*—**p. 630**
images from, *"The Message of a Blizzard"*—**p. 567**; *"Deeper and Deeper"*—**p. 649**; *"As Reliable as the Wind"*—**p. 924**; *"Colorful Language"*—**p. 1291**; *"Unnatural Botany"*—**p. 1187**
disasters in, *"The Meaning of a Natural Disaster"*—**p. 926**
power of, *"Doomsday"*—**p. 927**

NAZIRITE — Israelite consecrated to God for special service
examples of, *"Well-known Nazirites"*—**p. 168**
described, Numbers 6:1–21—**p. 167**; *"National Reminders"*—**p. 171**

NEBUCHADNEZZAR — ruler of Babylonian empire who destroyed Jerusalem and took Jews into captivity
character profile, *"Power and Pride"*—**p. 902**
takes Jerusalem, 2 Kings 25:1–26—**p. 427**; 2 Chronicles 36—**p. 496**; Jeremiah 39—**p. 822**
with Daniel, Daniel 1–4—**p. 899**

NEHEMIAH– a leader of the Jews who returned from exile
character profile, see *"Introduction to Nehemiah"*–**p. 511**
life of, *"A Man of Action"*–**p. 511**
his character, *"Politician Without Greed"*–**p. 516**; *"Never-ending Task"*–**p. 526**

NEIGHBOR
love as yourself, Leviticus 19:18–**p. 147**; Matthew 22:37–40–**p. 1024**; Romans 13:8–10–**p. 1189**
identification of, Luke 10:25–37–**p. 1078**

NICODEMUS– important Pharisee attracted to Jesus
character profile, *"A Reputation at Stake"*–**p. 1103**
talks to Jesus, John 3:1–21–**p. 1102**; *"A Reputation at Stake"*–**p. 1103**
argues for fair treatment of Jesus, John 7:50–52–**p. 1111**
helps in Jesus' burial, John 19:38–42–**p. 1128**

NINEVEH– important city in Assyria
repentance of, Jonah 3–4–**p. 947**
and archaeology, *"How Big a City"*–**p. 947**
its defense, *"Battle Tactics"*–**p. 959**
destruction predicted, Nahum 1–3–**p. 958**; Zephaniah 2:13–15–**p. 968**

NOAH
character profile, *"Starting Over"*–**p. 32**
ark and flood, Genesis 6–8–**p. 31**
covenant with, Genesis 9–**p. 33**

NUMBERS
as symbols, *"Significant Numbers"*–**p. 1323**
use of "7", *"Dramatic Structure"*–**p. 1324**

OATHS– see SWEARING

OBEDIENCE
reasons for, *"Who Needs Laws?"*–**p. 216**
understanding not necessary for, *"God's Secrets"*–**p. 232**
Israel's entering Canaan, *"The Difference 40 Years Can Make"*–**p. 238**
Israel's, after exile, *"A People of the Book"*–**p. 520**; *"The Prophet Who Got Results"*–**p. 971**
essential for Christians, Luke 6:46–49–**p. 1071**
Paul's, *"Paul's Legal Battles"*–**p. 1163**
to governing authorities, Romans 13:1–7–**p. 1189**
children's, Ephesians 6:1–4–**p. 1234**
in love, 1 John 3:11–24–**p. 1307**

OCCULT(*see also* WITCHCRAFT)
avoid, Leviticus 19:26–31–**p. 147**

OFFERING
for the needy in Jerusalem, *"No Cheating"*–**p. 1162**; Acts 11:27–30–**p. 1149**; Romans 15:23–29–**p. 1191**; 1 Corinthians 16:1–4–**p. 1208**; 2 Corinthians 8–9–**p. 1216**

OLD AGE
God's concern for those of, Psalm 71–**p. 613**
value in, Proverbs 16:31–**p. 677**; Proverbs 20:29–**p. 680**

ONESIMUS– slave who ran away, became a Christian, and returned to his master
Paul's love for, *"Letter to a Slave Owner"*–**p. 1272**
pun on name, *"No Longer Useless"*–**p. 1273**

OPPOSITION
to the returning exiles, *"How to Stop God's Work"*–**p. 502**
to Nehemiah, *"Psychological Warfare"*–**p. 517**

ORPHAN
care for, James 1:19–27–**p. 1290**

PAIN
reason for, *"Pain as a Warning"*–**p. 564**; *"Pain with a Purpose"*–**p. 776**; *"What Suffering Produces"*–**p. 1216**
questioning, Job 1–42–**p. 540**; Jeremiah 15:15–21–**p. 796**; Habakkuk 1–3–**p. 962**
not always punishment, *"Pain as Punishment"*–**p. 543**
God works in it for good, Romans 8:28–39–**p. 1184**
producing perseverance, *"Productive Pain"*–**p. 1289**; Romans 5:1–5–**p. 1179**
wiped away, Revelation 21:1–4–**p. 1335**

PALESTINE(*see also* CANAAN)
conquered by Israel, *"Seven-Year Fight"*–**p. 254**

PARABLE– a story told to illustrate an idea
use by Jesus foretold, *"Speaking in Parables"*–**p. 619**
of God's vineyard, *"Grapevines"*–**p. 621**; *"What Can God Do?"*–**p. 716**
Jeremiah's, *"Living Parables"*–**p. 818**
purpose of, *"Stories to Remember"*–**p. 1012**; Matthew 13:10–17–**p. 1011**; *"Handling Tough Questions"*–**p. 1089**
lack of in Mark, *"Scarce Parables"*–**p. 1040**
of the lost son, *"Two Lost Brothers?"*–**p. 1085**
list of, *"Parables of Jesus"*–**p. 1382**

PARENTS
honor, Exodus 20:12–**p. 105**
caring for, *"Long-lost Relatives"*–**p. 321**
lacking discipline, *"Bad News for Eli"*–**p. 300**; *"Vicious Children"*–**p. 346**
as teachers, Proverbs 1:8–9–**p. 662**; Proverbs 4–**p. 664**; *"How to Raise Children"*–**p. 682**
influence on children, *"Good Parenting"*–**p. 682**; *"Playing Favorites"*–**p. 58**
should be obeyed, Ephesians 6:1–4–**p. 1234**; Colossians 3:20–21–**p. 1245**

PASSOVER
reason for its menu, *"Fast Food"*–**p. 96**
instituted, Exodus 12:1–27–**p. 94**; *"Independence Day"*–**p. 95**
celebrated by Hezekiah, *"Delayed Passover"*–**p. 489**
celebrated by Josiah, 2 Chronicles 35–**p. 495**
at time of Jesus' death, *"Festival Time in Jerusalem"*–**p. 1054**

PASTOR– one who serves the church in the ministry of preaching, teaching, and pastoral care
judged by message, *"Style or Substance?"*–**p. 1219**
gift of, Ephesians 4:1–16–**p. 1232**
lifestyle of, 1 Timothy 3–4–**p. 1258**
instructions for, 2 Timothy 1:8–4:8–**p. 1264**; Titus 1–3–**p. 1269**

PATIENCE
of God, Exodus 34:6–**p. 118**; 2 Peter 3:1–9–**p. 1302**
of David, *"A Child with Its Mother"*–**p. 650**
an aspect of the Spirit's fruit, Galatians 5:16–26–**p. 1227**
commanded of Christians, Hebrews 12:1–13–**p. 1286**; James 5:7–8–**p. 1292**

PAUL– apostle converted after Jesus' resurrection who had a special mission of bringing the gospel to the Gentiles; author of many New Testament letters to new churches (*see also* SAUL)
character profile, *"Turnaround"*–**p. 1177**
teacher of, *"Questions, Anyone?"*–**p. 1186**
converted, Acts 9:1–31–**p. 1146**; *"Recruiting from the Opposition"*–**p. 1151**; *"Three Versions"*–**p. 1165**
as preacher, *"Visiting Speaker"*–**p. 1152**
first missionary journey, Acts 13:1–14:28–**p. 1150**

Peace

PENTECOST — Jewish holiday, also called the Feast of Weeks

PERSECUTION

PERSEVERANCE — standing firm in the faith (*see also* BACKSLIDING)

PETER — originally named Simon; one of the disciples closest to Jesus (and the one most frequently mentioned in the Gospels); a strong leader in the early church

PHARAOH — title of ancient Egyptian rulers

PHARISEES — a strict Jewish sect; careful observers of the law, known for their piety

PHILIP — an evangelist of the early church

PHILIPPI

PHILISTINES — people who migrated to and lived in an area of Canaan during Old Testament times; they frequently warred with the Israelites

PILATE – a Roman ruler in Palestine during Jesus' lifetime
character profile, *"Governor Cynic"*–**p. 1126**
authorized Jesus' crucifixion, Matthew 27:11–26–**p. 1030**
with Jesus, John 18:28–19:22–**p. 1126**

PLAGUES
sent by God, *"Day of the Locusts"*–**p. 90**
ten, Exodus 7:14–12:29–**p. 90**

PLEASURE
eternal, Psalm 16–**p. 580**
God's, Psalm 147:10–11–**p. 658**
earthly, Ecclesiastes 2:1–16–**p. 695**

POETRY
in the Psalms, *"The Right Words"*–**p. 650**
in Proverbs, *"Hebrew Poetry"*–**p. 669**

POLITICS – *see* GOVERNMENT

POOR
God's care for, Deuteronomy 10:17–19–**p. 213**; 24:19–22–**p. 225**; Luke 1:39–56–**p. 1063**
responsibility to, Deuteronomy 15:1–11–**p. 218**; 24:10–22–**p. 225**
reasons for being, *"What Makes People Poor?"*–**p. 669**
oppression of, *"Justice, Not Religion"*–**p. 714**; *"Justice for the Poor"*–**p. 655**; *"Lucky Rich"*–**p. 674**; Amos 2:6–16–**p. 934**
punishment for oppressing, *"Prize Cows"*–**p. 936**
Jesus' identification with, Matthew 25:31–46–**p. 1027**
Luke's identification with, *"A Physician Looks at the Poor"*–**p. 1069**
Paul's concern for, *"Remembering the Poor"*–**p. 1208**; *"Don't Forget the Poor"*–**p. 1216**
equal treatment of, James 2:1–13–**p. 1290**

POPULARITY
not to be sought, Philippians 2:1–11–**p. 1238**
judging by, James 2:1–13–**p. 1290**

Power *(see also MIRACLES)*
of kings, *"Adultery and Murder"*–**p. 344**
of God, 1 Chronicles 29:10–13–**p. 460**; *"Chariots of Fire"*–**p. 404**; *"God Pulls Out the Stops"*–**p. 568**; *"God's Answer to Injustice"*–**p. 957**
temporary, *"Another Powerful City"*–**p. 960**
symbols of, *"Brute Power"*–**p. 976**
Jesus' perspective on, *"Taste of Power"*–**p. 1078**
in this world, *"Who Had Real Power?"*–**p. 1083**
of the gospel, Romans 1:16–17–**p. 1176**
not to be sought, Philippians 2:1–11–**p. 1238**

PRAISE
God worthy of, Psalm 18–**p. 582**; Revelation 4–5–**p. 1320**
commanded, Psalm 145–150–**p. 657**
public, *"Going Public"*–**p. 583**
for Christ and salvation, Ephesians 1:3–14–**p. 1230**

PRAYER – communication with God *(see also INTERCESSION)*
of Moses, *"Famous Prayers"*–**p. 173**
of Jehoshaphat, *"A Model Prayer"*–**p. 478**
toward Jerusalem, *"Where God Dwells"*–**p. 374**; *"A Jewish Orientation"*–**p. 906**
of Nehemiah, *"The Arrow Prayer"*–**p. 513**
and action, *"Praise the Lord and Fight"*–**p. 515**
recalling God's providence, *"Stained-Glass Prayer"*–**p. 521**
answered, Psalm 34–**p. 592**
for healing, *"Fifteen More Years"*–**p. 747**
answered negatively, *"God's Answer: No!"*–**p. 802**; *"Don't Ask God"*–**p. 864**

of Daniel, *"Revealing Prayer"*–**p. 900**
waiting for answers to, *"Slow to Answer Prayer"*–**p. 911**
for enemies, *"Praying for Persecutors"*–**p. 1003**
Jesus' teaching on, Matthew 6:5–15–**p. 1003**; 7:7–12–**p. 1004**; Luke 18:1–14–**p. 1087**
submission in, Matthew 26:36–46–**p. 1029**
Jesus' habit of, *"Seeking Privacy"*–**p. 1055**
confidence in, John 15:1–8–**p. 1122**
Jesus', for his disciples, John 17–**p. 1124**; *"Jesus' Longest Prayer"*–**p. 1125**
Paul's, Romans 1:8–12–**p. 1175**; Ephesians 1:15–19–**p. 1231**; 3:14–18–**p. 1232**; Colossians 1:9–14–**p. 1243**
when suffering, Romans 8:18–27–**p. 1184**
when answer differs from request, 2 Corinthians 12:7–10–**p. 1220**
for wisdom, James 1:5–7–**p. 1289**

PREDESTINATION – doctrine that God has predetermined that all believers are saved through Christ *(see also* ELECTION, FREE WILL*)*
Jacob chosen, *"Con Man in God's Family?"*–**p. 53**
Jews chosen, *"Why the Israelites?"*–**p. 210**
Eli's sons rejected, *"God in Charge"*–**p. 300**
God's foreknowledge, Romans 8:28–30–**p. 1184**
in love, Ephesians 1:3–14–**p. 1230**

PRIDE *(see also* HUMILITY*)*
of Joseph, *"Big Mouth"*–**p. 66**
warnings against, Proverbs 8:13–**p. 668**; 16:5,14–**p. 676**; 21:4,24–**p. 680**
God humbles, Isaiah 2:10–22–**p. 714**
of Jews in Jerusalem, *"Smiles Instead of Tears"*–**p. 731**
of Antiochus, *"Exalted Above the Gods"*–**p. 913**
of the complacent, *"Unbelievable!"*–**p. 962**
avoid, Romans 12–**p. 1188**
God opposes, James 4:4–6–**p. 1291**

PRIEST – one designated to perform sacred rites and act as an intermediary between people and God *(see also* AARON, MELCHIZEDEK*)*
Old Testament, Exodus 28–29–**p. 112**; 39:1–31–**p. 124**; Leviticus 8–10–**p. 134**
purification for, *"The Whole Body"*–**p. 114**
regulations for, *"Priestly Privileges"*–**p. 134**
punished for disobedience, *"Fatal Error"*–**p. 136**
in politics, *"The Priests Take Up Arms"*–**p. 483**
false, *"Poor Trade"*–**p. 918**
Jesus as, Hebrews 4:14–5:10–**p. 1278**; Hebrews 7:1–10:18–**p. 1280**
Christians as, 1 Peter 2:4–12–**p. 1296**; Revelation 1:6–**p. 1318**

PRISCILLA – wife of Aquila; co-worker with Paul and instructor of Apollos
character profile, *"Power Couple"*–**p. 1160**

PRISON
Joseph in, Genesis 39–40–**p. 69**
visit those in, Matthew 25:31–46–**p. 1027**
Peter's release from, Acts 12:1–19–**p. 1150**
Paul in, Acts 16:16–40–**p. 1156**; 21:27–28:31–**p. 1164**; *"Letters from Prison"*–**p. 1233**; *"A Letter from Death Row"*–**p. 1266**

PROFANITY
command against, Exodus 20:7–**p. 104**; Matthew 5:21–22–**p. 1001**; Ephesians 4:29–32–**p. 1234**
dangerous effects of, James 3:1–12–**p. 1291**

PROMISE *(see also* COVENANT*)*
God's to Abraham, *"Promises, Promises"*–**p. 47**
waiting for God's, *"Shame Forever?"*–**p. 626**
Christ's, John 14–**p. 1121**
believing, Romans 4:13–25–**p. 1179**
God's, *"Unchanged Promises"*–**p. 816**; Hebrews 6:13–20–**p. 1279**; Hebrews 7:18–8:13–**p. 1280**

PROPHECY – an inspired revelation about future events (*see also* MESSIAH, MILLENNIUM, SECOND COMING)

fulfillment of, *"Prediction Fulfilled"*–**p. 500**; *"Out Through the Hole"*–**p. 857**; *"Alexander the Great"*–**p. 872**; *"Stones Overturned"*–**p. 1025**; *"Wailing Wall"*–**p. 1090**; *"Speeding Up Death"*–**p. 1127**

about Jesus, *"Foreshadowing Jesus"*–**p. 612**; *"A Child Is Born"*–**p. 720**; *"Suffering Servant"*–**p. 764**; *"Jesus Began Here"*–**p. 771**; *"Messiah's Birthplace"*–**p. 953**; *"Donkey of Peace"*–**p. 980**; *"A Prophecy of Jesus"*–**p. 982**; *"Old Testament 101"*–**p. 1098**

double meanings, *"A Famous Sign"*–**p. 718**; *"Who Are the Shepherds?"*–**p. 981**

illustrated, *"A Dramatic Object Lesson"*–**p. 729**; *"Living Parables"*–**p. 818**; *"Seeing the Unseen God"*–**p. 847**

time sequence in, *"Shifting Stance in Time"*–**p. 740**; *"Seeing in Two Dimensions"*–**p. 954**

change in tone of, *"End of the Silence"*–**p. 880**

purpose of, *"Prophetic Entertainment"*–**p. 881**

interpretation of, *"Newspaper Prophecy"*–**p. 1332**

source is God, 2 Peter 1:19–21–**p. 1301**

PROPHETS (*see also* FALSE PROPHETS)

Moses as, Deuteronomy 18:14–21–**p. 221**

and kings, *"Standing Up to the King"*–**p. 381**; *"The Prophet and Politics"*–**p. 405**; *"A True or False Prophet?"*–**p. 477**

used by God, *"The Contest"*–**p. 388**

powerful, *"Replacing a Legend"*–**p. 400**

pain felt by, *"God's Reluctant Messenger"*–**p. 777**; *"A Fountain of Tears"*–**p. 789**; *"The Sad Truth"*–**p. 882**

plots against, *"Hometown Enemies"*–**p. 792**

relationships between, *"Favored by God and Kings"*–**p. 909**; *"Bad News, Good News"*–**p. 976**

rescue of, *"Scripture Saves a Life"*–**p. 807**; *"Close to Death"*–**p. 821**

sustained by God, *"Eat the Scroll"*–**p. 850**

parallels in, *"Writing to Ezekiel"*–**p. 809**; *"Jeremiah and Ezekiel"*–**p. 862**; *"Parallel with Isaiah"*–**p. 953**

background of, *"Royal Blood"*–**p. 967**

Jesus as the final, John 6:14–15–**p. 1108**; Acts 3:21–23–**p. 1137**

PROSTITUTION – sexual intercourse engaged in for money

condemned, Leviticus 19:29–**p. 147**

warning against, Proverbs 6:20–35–**p. 666**; 1 Corinthians 6:12–20–**p. 1199**

PROVIDENCE OF GOD

for Joseph, *"Important Officials"*–**p. 70**

for Israelites, *"Food Supply"*–**p. 100**; *"Miracles in the Desert"*–**p. 231**

in saving Joash, *"Preserving the Royal Line"*–**p. 410**

in saving the Jews, *"A Profile of Courage"*–**p. 528**

working through people, *"One Safe Jew?"*–**p. 533**

in nature, Psalm 104–**p. 632**; Matthew 10:29–30–**p. 1007**; Acts 14:14–17–**p. 1154**

throughout life, *"Love Before Birth"*–**p. 653**; *"I Carried You"*–**p. 757**

in protecting Christianity, *"A Secular View"*–**p. 1160**

PUNISHMENT (*see also* HELL)

of Lot's wife, *"Don't Look Back"*–**p. 44**

of God for sin, *"A Catastrophe Sent From God"*–**p. 43**; *"The End of Shiloh"*–**p. 302**; *"An End to Punishment"*–**p. 739**; *"A City in Ruins"*–**p. 839**

appropriate, *"Punishment by Restitution"*–**p. 107**; *"An Eye for an Eye"*–**p. 154**; *"Needless Deaths"*–**p. 356**

eternal, Matthew 25:31–46,–**p. 1027**; Revelation 20:11–15,–**p. 1334**

Q

QUIET TIME – a period set aside for prayer, meditation, and Bible study

for renewal, Psalm 1–**p. 575**; Psalm 119:9–48–**p. 643**

practiced by Jesus, *"The Need to Get Away"*–**p. 1043**; Matthew 14:22–23–**p. 1014**; Luke 5:15–16–**p. 1069**; 6:12–13–**p. 1070**

to overcome temptation, Mark 14:32–38–**p. 1055**

for strength, Ephesians 6:10–20–**p. 1235**

for a sense of peace, Philippians 4:6–9–**p. 1240**

R

RACHEL – favored wife of Jacob; mother of Joseph and Benjamin

character profile, *"Love and Grief"*–**p. 60**

life of, Genesis 29:14–31:55–**p. 57**; *"The Women of Genesis"*–**p. 55**

death of, Genesis 35:16–20–**p. 64**

RACISM – belief that one race is superior to others

in Egypt, *"Prejudice"*–**p. 75**

abolished in Christ, *"Forcing a Confrontation"*–**p. 1224**; Galatians 3:26–4:7–**p. 1226**; *"Destroying the Barriers"*–**p. 1232**

RAHAB – a prostitute who helped the Israelites capture Jericho

character profile, *"A Prostitute's Faith"*–**p. 244**

took in spies, Joshua 2:1–21–**p. 240**; 6:15–25–**p. 243**

ancestor of Christ, *"Rahab's Future"*–**p. 241**

example of faith, James 2:25–26–**p. 1290**

RAHAB – sea monster in mythology

symbol for Egypt, *"Rahab the Monster"*–**p. 762**

RAINBOW

sign of covenant with Noah, Genesis 9:12–16–**p. 33**; *"The Reason for Rainbows"*–**p. 33**

RAPE – sexual intercourse forced on one person by another

at Sodom, Genesis 19:1–8–**p. 42**

of Dinah, Genesis 34–**p. 63**

penalty for, Deuteronomy 22:25–29–**p. 224**

at Gibeah, Judges 19:16–28–**p. 287**

of Tamar, 2 Samuel 13–**p. 345**

REBEKAH – wife of Isaac; mother of Esau and Jacob

character profile, *"Forceful Woman"*–**p. 48**

marries Isaac, Genesis 24–**p. 49**; *"The Women of Genesis"*–**p. 55**

helps Jacob, Genesis 25:19–34–**p. 51**; 27:1–28:9–**p. 52**

REBELLION

against God, *"When God Was Obvious"*–**p. 109**; *"Forty Years of Misery"*–**p. 159**; *"The Worst Rebellion"*–**p. 177**; *"Children of the Desert"*–**p. 204**

at end of the present age, Matthew 24:4–25–**p. 1025**; 2 Thessalonians 2–**p. 1253**; Revelation 13–14–**p. 1328**

RECONCILIATION – to settle differences; to be in harmony again

of Jacob and Esau, *"Surface Reconciliation"*–**p. 63**

of Joseph and his brothers, *"Family Battles"*–**p. 69**

between people, Matthew 5:23–26–**p. 1001**; Philippians 4:2–3–**p. 1240**

to God, *"Looking for an Arbitrator"*–**p. 547**; 2 Corinthians 5:11–6:2–**p. 1214**; Ephesians 2:11–22–**p. 1231**; Colossians 1:15–23–**p. 1243**

REDEEMER — one who frees or rescues another, especially from sin
Boaz as, *"Expensive Bride"*—**p. 295**
God as, Isaiah 54:1–8—**p. 765**; Luke 1:67–69—**p. 1063**
Christ as, Galatians 3:6–14—**p. 1224**; Colossians 1:13–14—**p. 1243**; Hebrews 9:11–14—**p. 1282**; *"A Modern Peace Child"*—**p. 1180**; 1 Peter 1:17–21—**p. 1296**

REHOBOAM — son of Solomon; first king of Judah
character profile, *"A Fool's Answer"*—**p. 472**
life of, 1 Kings 12—**p. 379**; 1 Kings 14—**p. 382**

RELIGION
true, *"Religion at Its Best"*—**p. 768**; *"What God Wants"*—**p. 955**; *"Which One Showed Love?"*—**p. 1078**
mixed, *"How to Be Religious Without Pleasing God"*—**p. 921**; *"The New Golden Calf"*—**p. 922**
Paul on Greek religion, Acts 17:22–31—**p. 1158**
combating false, *"Battling the Cults"*—**p. 1242**
pure, James 1:26–27—**p. 1290**

Repentance — to feel sorry for and turn from sins; a common theme of Old Testament prophets
by Israel's kings, *"A Tardy Change of Mind"*—**p. 493**; *"Turnaround"*—**p. 1177**
of the exiles, *"Beginning Again"*—**p. 498**; *"Unprecedented Response"*—**p. 509**
of David, *"David Caught in the Act"*—**p. 604**
temporary, *"A Superficial Change"*—**p. 781**
call to, *"Before It's Too Late"*—**p. 936**
preached by Jesus, Matthew 4:12–17—**p. 1000**; Luke 13:1–5—**p. 1082**
parable concerning, Luke 18:9–14—**p. 1087**
preached by Peter, Acts 2:38–41—**p. 1135**
preached by Paul, Acts 17:22–31—**p. 1158**
described by Paul, 2 Corinthians 7:9–10—**p. 1216**

RESPONSIBILITY
for sin, Ezekiel 18—**p. 862**
accepting, *"No Excuses"*—**p. 1176**
to love others, 1 John 3:11–24—**p. 1307**

REST
day of, Genesis 2:1–3—**p. 26**; Exodus 20:8—**p. 104**
for the land, *"Revenge of the Land"*—**p. 156**
year of, *"A Year of Freedom"*—**p. 522**
in God, Psalm 23—**p. 587**; 62—**p. 608**
for weary, Matthew 11:25–30—**p. 1009**

RESURRECTION
hinted in Old Testament, *"A Promise of Eternal Life"*—**p. 734**; *"Resurrection?"*—**p. 913**; Job 19:23–27—**p. 553**; Ezekiel 37:1–14—**p. 884**; Daniel 12:1–2—**p. 913**
foretold, *"Resurrection!"*—**p. 581**; *"Stubbornly Unconvinced"*—**p. 1086**
of Jesus, Matthew 27:57–28:20—**p. 1032**; *"Final Glimpses of Jesus"*—**p. 1095**; *"More Than a Ghost"*—**p. 1136**
Jesus predicts his own, Mark 8:31—**p. 1046**; 9:31—**p. 1048**; 10:33–34—**p. 1049**
of the dead, 1 Corinthians 15—**p. 1206**; *"The Worst Danger of All"*—**p. 1207**; 1 Thessalonians 4:13–18—**p. 1250**
of the body, *"The Body as a Tent"*—**p. 1214**
as proof of God's power, *"Proven Power"*—**p. 1231**; Ephesians 1:15–23—**p. 1231**
spiritual in Christ, Romans 6:1–14—**p. 1181**; Colossians 2:9–15—**p. 1244**; 3:1–17—**p. 1245**

REVENGE (*see also* CITIES OF REFUGE)
Joseph not taking, *"Weeping and Terror"*—**p. 76**
of David, *"Paying Back Joab"*—**p. 365**

belongs to God, *"God's Vengeance"*—**p. 235**
on enemies, *"Jehu's Slaughters"*—**p. 410**; do not take, Matthew 5:38–47—**p. 1001**; Romans 12:17–21—**p. 1189**

REVERENCE (*see also* FEAR)
for God, *"Living With Fire"*—**p. 127**; *"Touch and Die"*—**p. 165**; *"Is God Frightening?"*—**p. 593**

REVELATION — God's disclosure of himself and his truth
in nature, Psalm 19:1–6—**p. 584**; Acts 14:14–17—**p. 1154**; Romans 1:18–23—**p. 1176**
in Jesus Christ, John 1:1–18—**p. 1100**; Hebrews 1—**p. 1275**
in the Bible, 2 Timothy 3:14–17—**p. 1265**; 2 Peter 1:19–21—**p. 1301**

REWARD
everyone according to deeds, Leviticus 26—**p. 155**; Psalm 62:11–12—**p. 609**; Jeremiah 17:10—**p. 798**; 2 Corinthians 5:1–10—**p. 1214**
for evil, *"Short-Run Rewards"*—**p. 615**
for serving God, *"Why Serve God?"*—**p. 988**
in heaven, Matthew 5:3–12—**p. 1000**; Mark 10:29–31—**p. 1049**; 1 Corinthians 3:10–15—**p. 1197**

RICHES — *see* MONEY, POOR, WEALTH

RIGHTEOUSNESS — the state of being perfect, without sin
attribute of God, Psalm 7—**p. 577**; Jeremiah 23:1–6—**p. 803**
rewarded by God, *"Never Abandoned"*—**p. 595**
from God, *"Luther's Gateway"*—**p. 1176**
by faith, *"What God Looks For"*—**p. 39**; *"The Benefits of Faith"*—**p. 591**; *"Righteous by Faith"*—**p. 963**; Romans 4:6–8—**p. 1179**; Galatians 2:15–21—**p. 1224**; Philippians 3:7–11—**p. 1240**
goal of Christian life, Matthew 6:25–34—**p. 1003**; 1 Timothy 6:11–16—**p. 1261**; 1 Peter 2:24–25—**p. 1297**

ROCK
God as, Deuteronomy 32:1–4—**p. 233**; Psalm 18—**p. 582**; Isaiah 26—**p. 734**
Peter as, Matthew 16:16–20—**p. 1016**; John 1:35–42—**p. 1101**
Christ as, 1 Corinthians 10:1–4—**p. 1202**; 1 Peter 2:1–10—**p. 1296**

ROME — capital of the Roman empire; ruled Palestine during the time of Christ; a church was started here
Paul travels to, *"Rome at Last"*—**p. 1171**; Acts 27:1–28:31—**p. 1170**
letter (Romans) to church in, *"A Most Demanding Audience"*—**p. 1174**
treatment of Christians in, *"Christians and the Empire"*—**p. 1189**

RUTH — Moabite woman who married Boaz and became an ancestor of Jesus
character profile, *"Character Counts"*—**p. 294**
ethnic background, *"The Worst of Times"*—**p. 293**
friendship with her mother-in-law, *"A Rare Bond of Love"*—**p. 291**
in Jesus' genealogy, Matthew 1:5—**p. 997**

S

SABBATH — a day of worship and rest; traditionally Saturday for Jews
to be kept holy, Exodus 20:8–11—**p. 104**; Ezekiel 20:1–29—**p. 864**
laws concerning, Exodus 31:14–15—**p. 116**; Leviticus 23:1–3—**p. 151**
made for people, Mark 2:23–3:6—**p. 1038**
symbol of eternal rest, Hebrews 4:1–11—**p. 1278**

SACRIFICE — offering of something valuable to God
Cain's and Abel's, Genesis 4:1–5—**p. 29**
Noah's, Genesis 8:20–22—**p. 33**
Abraham's, Genesis 12:1–11—**p. 35**; 22:1–19—**p. 46**
prescribed, Leviticus 1–7—**p. 128**
offered as representative, *"The One for the Many"*—**p. 130**
types of, *"The Reason for Sacrifice"*—**p. 132**
choice of, *"The Very Best for God"*—**p. 151**
Christ as, Isaiah 53—**p. 763**; Hebrews 10—**p. 1283**
our lives as, Romans 12:1–2—**p. 1188**; *"A Better Sacrifice"*—**p. 597**
of praise, *"Sacrifice of Praise"*—**p. 1287**

SADDUCEES — a small but powerful Jewish sect in Christ's time; denied life after death
Jesus warns against, Matthew 16:1–12—**p. 1016**
Jesus confronts, Mark 12:18–23—**p. 1052**
opposed early church, Acts 4:1–22—**p. 1137**; Acts 5:17–42—**p. 1139**
opposed Paul, Acts 23:1–11—**p. 1166**

Salvation — deliverance from danger or evil; especially deliverance from all that separates people from God (*see also* **CONVERSION, JUSTIFICATION, REPENTANCE**)

available to all, *"Who Can Be Saved?"*—**p. 766**; Romans 10:1–13—**p. 1186**
marked for, *"The Saving Mark"*—**p. 855**
Jesus' mission of, Luke 19:1–10—**p. 1088**
through faith, Acts 16:16–34—**p. 1156**
to be completed at end of time, Romans 5:6–11—**p. 1181**
by grace, Ephesians 2:1–10—**p. 1231**; Titus 3:3–8—**p. 1270**

SAMARITAN — an inhabitant of Samaria; a people held in contempt by the Jews
origin of, *"Scorched-Earth Policy"*—**p. 418**
conflict with returned exiles, Ezra 4–5—**p. 502**; Nehemiah 4–6—**p. 515**
parable of the good, Luke 10:25–37 —**p. 1078**
and the Jews, *"Bridging Differences"*—**p. 1105**
woman with Jesus, John 4:1–42—**p. 1104**

SAMSON — one of the last judges of Israel; a Nazirite known for his physical strength
character profile, *"Samson: A Weakness for Women"*—**p. 281**
life of, Judges 13–16—**p. 280**
and Delilah, Judges 16—**p. 283**; *"Samson: A Weakness for Women"*—**p. 281**
death of, *"Bring the House Down"*—**p. 284**

SAMUEL — last of the judges of Israel
character profile, *"Faithful Leadership"*—**p. 304**
his early years, 1 Samuel 1:1–3:21—**p. 298**
as a prophet, *"Still a Boy"*—**p. 301**
leads Israel, 1 Samuel 5:1–8:22—**p. 302**
with Saul, 1 Samuel 9:1–15:35—**p. 305**
anoints David, 1 Samuel 16:1–13—**p. 315**
his death, 1 Samuel 25:1—**p. 324**
man of faith, Hebrews 11:32—**p. 1285**

SANCTIFICATION — act of God by which a believer conforms more and more to the image of Christ (*see also* **HOLY**)
Jesus' prayer for, John 17:17–19—**p. 1124**
possible only in Christ, 1 Corinthians 1:1–2—**p. 1195**; 1 Thessalonians 5:16–24—**p. 1251**
by pressing on, Philippians 3:12–4:1—**p. 1240**
Christ's power in, 2 Peter 1:3–11—**p. 1301**

SANHEDRIN — highest Jewish court during Roman times
limits to power, *"Appeal for a Death Penalty"*—**p. 1056**
Jesus before, Matthew 26:57–68—**p. 1029**; John 18—**p. 1125**
apostles before, Acts 4:1–22—**p. 1137**; Acts 5:17–42—**p. 1139**
Paul before, Acts 23:1–11—**p. 1166**

SARAH — wife of Abraham; gave birth to Isaac in her 90s
character profile, *"Who's Laughing?"*—**p. 42**
life of, Genesis 11:29–12:20—**p. 35**; 16:1–18:15—**p. 39**; 21:1–21—**p. 45**; *"The Women of Genesis"*—**p. 55**
death and burial of, Genesis 23:1–20—**p. 48**

SATAN — the enemy of God; also called the devil, Beelzebub
tempts Eve, Genesis 3—**p. 27**
restrained by God, *"The Extent of Satan's Power"*—**p. 540**
torments Job, Job 1–2—**p. 540**
metaphor for, *"Fall of the Morning Star"*—**p. 725**
our accuser, Zechariah 3—**p. 976**
tempts Jesus, Matthew 4:1–11—**p. 999**
father of lies, John 8:42–47—**p. 1112**
resist, *"The Armor of God"*—**p. 1235**; 1 Peter 5:8–11—**p. 1299**
children of, 1 John 2:28–3:10—**p. 1306**
war against Christ and the church, Revelation 12—**p. 1327**
final victory over, Revelation 20—**p. 1334**

SAUL — the first king of Israel; became extremely jealous of David
character profile, *"Why Saul Was Rejected"*—**p. 313**
early days as king, 1 Samuel 9–15—**p. 305**
and David, 1 Samuel 16:1–30:31—**p. 315**
failures of, *"Big Ego"*—**p. 311**; *"Why Saul Was Rejected"*—**p. 313**
as a prophet, *"Out of Control"*—**p. 319**
death of, 1 Samuel 31:1–13—**p. 330**

SAUL — persecutor of Christians who later was converted and became Paul the missionary (*see also* **PAUL**)
persecution and conversion of, Acts 9:1–30—**p. 1146**
name changed to Paul, Acts 13:9—**p. 1152**

SAVIOR — one who rescues from danger or saves; used in connection with Christ (*see also* **SALVATION**)
prophecy concerning, Isaiah 59:15–21—**p. 769**
Jesus as, Acts 4:1–12—**p. 1137**; 13:13–52—**p. 1152**

SCAPEGOAT
taking the blame, *"Scapegoat"*—**p. 145**

SECOND COMING — the time when Christ will come again as King
Jesus' teaching on, Matthew 24–25—**p. 1025**; John 14:1–4—**p. 1121**; Acts 1:6–8—**p. 1134**
with resurrection, 1 Corinthians 15:12–28—**p. 1207**
unexpected, 1 Thessalonians 4:13–5:11—**p. 1250**
preceded by antichrist, 2 Thessalonians 2—**p. 1253**
reason for delay of, 2 Peter 3—**p. 1302**
preoccupation with, *"Preparing for the End"*—**p. 1250**; *"A Patient Who Didn't Follow Orders"*—**p. 1252**; *"A Book Full of Mysteries"*—**p. 1316**
vision of, Revelation 19–20—**p. 1333**

SECURITY
place of, *"The Hideout"*—**p. 609**
finding, *"Meek Will Inherit"*—**p. 969**; *"Safe Streets"*—**p. 979**
in God, Psalm 91—**p. 627**

SELF-CONTROL
necessary, *"Five Dangerous Responses"*—**p. 689**
an aspect of the Spirit's fruit, Galatians 5:16–26—**p. 1227**
achieving, *"Athlete in Training"*—**p. 1260**
importance of, *"The Need for Self-Control"*—**p. 1291**

SORROW– (*see also* COMFORT, DISCOURAGEMENT, GRIEF)
God responds to, Exodus 3:1–9–**p. 86**
symbol of, *"Torn Hearts"*–**p. 929**
Jesus experiences, Matthew 26:36–46–**p. 1029**

SOUL– the nonphysical element in humans (sometimes called "spirit")
in context of death, Ecclesiastes 12:7–**p. 703**; Revelation 6:9–10–**p. 1322**
distinguished from spirit, 1 Thessalonians 5:23–**p. 1251**; Hebrews 4:12–**p. 1278**
activities of, Deuteronomy 6:1–5–**p. 209**; Psalm 42–**p. 598**; 103–**p. 632**; 130–**p. 650**

SPEECH
power of, *"Who Owns Your Lips?"*–**p. 579**; *"Verbal Dynamite"*–**p. 676**
control of, James 3:1–12–**p. 1291**

SPIRIT– *see* DEMONS, FRUIT OF THE SPIRIT, HOLY SPIRIT

STARVATION
in Jerusalem, *"Starving to Death"*–**p. 845**

STEALING
command against, Exodus 20:15–**p. 105**; Ephesians 4:28–**p. 1234**
laws about, Exodus 22:1–15–**p. 107**; Leviticus 19:11–13–**p. 147**
robbing God, Malachi 3:8–10–**p. 988**

STEPHEN– the first Christian martyr
character profile, *"Dying to Live"*–**p. 1141**
chosen as deacon, Acts 6:1–7–**p. 1140**
tried and executed, Acts 6:8–8:3–**p. 1141**

STEWARDSHIP– management and accountability for something that belongs to someone else; especially human stewardship of God's gifts
parable concerning, Matthew 25:14–30–**p. 1027**
faithful, Luke 12:35–48–**p. 1082**; 16:10–12–**p. 1086**
of time, Ephesians 5:15–16–**p. 1234**

SUBMISSION
because of love for Christ, *"The Key to Submission"*–**p. 1234**
of Christians to each other, Ephesians 5:21–**p. 1234**
to government, Romans 13:1–7–**p. 1189**; 1 Peter 2:13–17–**p. 1297**

Success

Lot's in Sodom, *"A Man of Substance"*–**p. 43**
basis for real, *"Secret of Success"*–**p. 240**
from God, Proverbs 3–**p. 663**
true, Matthew 5:1–12–**p. 1000**; *"God and 'How-to-Succeed'"*–**p. 667**
parable concerning, Luke 12:13–21–**p. 1081**
without love, 1 Corinthians 13–**p. 1205**
from God's perspective, *"Not Ashamed"*–**p. 1284**

SUFFERING– to endure physical or emotional loss and pain (see also COMFORT, DISCOURAGEMENT, PAIN)
the problem of, Job 1–42–**p. 540**; *"When Bad Things Happened to a Good Person"*–**p. 538**; *"What Not to Say to a Hurting Person"*–**p. 544**; *"When God Seems Angry"*–**p. 551**; *"What Job Teaches about Suffering"*–**p. 567**; *"A Silent Friend Decides to Speak Up"*–**p. 562**; *"Suffering and Sin"*–**p. 1113**
God knows our, Psalm 69–**p. 612**
God's presence in, Psalm 73–**p. 615**; *"Pain in Redemption"*–**p. 813**; *"Only Good Things?"*–**p. 1184**
without God, *"Total Devastation"*–**p. 928**

with Christ, Romans 8:12–17–**p. 1184**; 2 Corinthians 1:5–**p. 1211**; 1 Peter 4:12–19–**p. 1299**
compared to eternal glory, *"Worth the Struggle"*–**p. 1184**; 2 Corinthians 4:16–18 –**p. 1214**
for Christ, Colossians 1:24–**p. 1244**; Hebrews 10:32–39–**p. 1284**; Revelation 1–**p. 1318**
benefits of, *"Waiting It Out"*–**p. 1293**; *"A Word to the Suffering"*–**p. 1294**; *"Radical Shift"*–**p. 1299**
Christ's, 1 Peter 2:13–25–**p. 1297**; *"The Spirits in Prison"*–**p. 1299**
for doing right, 1 Peter 3:8–22–**p. 1297**; 4:12–19–**p. 1299**

SUICIDE (*see also* JUDAS ISCARIOT, SAUL)
jailer saved from, Acts 16:22–36–**p. 1156**

SWEARING– taking an oath, making a solemn promise (*see also* PROFANITY)
Jesus' teaching on, Matthew 5:33–37–**p. 1001**
of God by himself, Hebrews 6:13–15–**p. 1279**
James's teaching on, James 5:12–**p. 1293**

SYMBOL
of peace, *"Peace Symbol"*–**p. 32**
of Christ, *"Bronze Snake"*–**p. 184**; *"Last-place Winner"*–**p. 642**; *"Jesus as the Vine"*–**p. 1122**; *"Water, Blood, and Spirit"*–**p. 1309**
of victory, *"Scalps"*–**p. 318**
of humiliation, *"Act of Humiliation"*–**p. 250**; *"Thumbs and Big Toes"*–**p. 267**; *"David's Bad Conscience"*–**p. 323**
of importance, *"The Apple of Your Eye"*–**p. 666**
of evil, *"Gog and Magog"*–**p. 886**
of ineffectiveness, *"Kicking the Oxgoads"*–**p. 1170**
vine and kingdom of God, Psalm 80:8–18–**p. 621**; Isaiah 5:1–7–**p. 716**; John 15:1–17–**p. 1122**
of believers, *"A Play on Words"*–**p. 1296**
in Revelation, *"Strange Creatures"*–**p. 1321**; *"Revelation's Use of Symbols"*–**p. 1325**

T

TABERNACLE– place of worship for Israelites from the time of the desert experience to the completion of the temple when Solomon was king
building instructions, Exodus 25–26–**p. 110**; *"Following Orders"*–**p. 125**
where God dwells, *"A Portable Cathedral"*–**p. 120**
furnishings of, *"Sacred Furniture"*–**p. 122**
during David's reign, *"Two Tabernacles"*–**p. 448**
spiritual, Hebrews 9–**p. 1282**

TALENTS– *see* GIFTS, STEWARDSHIP

TAXES
Jesus' response to, Matthew 22:15–22–**p. 1023**
Paul's words on, Romans 13:1–7–**p. 1189**

TEMPLE– the Israelite place of worship; the first and most magnificent was built by Solomon
curtain in, *"A Torn Curtain"*–**p. 112**; *"A Temporary Separation"*–**p. 465**; *"A Curtain is Torn"*–**p. 1032**
through many years, *"History of the Temple"*–**p. 370**; *"Between the Temples"*–**p. 497**
limited access, *"Off-limits for People"*–**p. 373**; *"The Temple Destroyed"*–**p. 841**
Solomon's, 1 Kings 5–8–**p. 369**; *"A Man of Blood"*–**p. 453**
God's home, *"Homecoming"*–**p. 623**
opposition to rebuilding, *"Ironic Outcome"*–**p. 505**
rebuilt, Ezra 1–6–**p. 500**; *"The Prophet Who Got Results"*–**p. 971**; *"Starting Over"*–**p. 32**; *"Change of Tone"*–**p. 972**
abuse of, *"A Den of Robbers"*–**p. 787**; *"Detestable Things"*–**p. 854**; *"Drastic Action"*–**p. 1022**; *"Big Business"*–**p. 1051**; John 2:12–25–**p. 1102**
abandoned by God, *"Good-bye, God"*–**p. 855**

Temptation – something that tests a person's righteousness and strength of character

TEN COMMANDMENTS – the moral laws given to Moses by God

THANKFULNESS

THESSALONICA

THOMAS – one of the 12 disciples, often called "Doubting Thomas"

TIME

TIMOTHY – Paul's helper on missionary journeys; while still a young man he took on the responsibilities of guiding the church in Ephesus

TITHE – a tenth of one's income that is given to God

TITUS

TONGUE – see SPEECH

TONGUES – God-given gift of praise in other languages

TRADITION – teachings and religious observances passed down from generation to generation

TRANSFIGURATION

TRIALS – tests or ordeals that people go through to teach obedience, Deuteronomy 8:1–5–**p. 210**

TRIBULATION – trouble in one's life; often associated with the Great Tribulation, a period of suffering sent by God in the end times

TRINITY – the Christian doctrine of God as Father, Son, and Holy Spirit, three-in-one

TRUST – see FAITH

TRUTH

U

UNBELIEF (see also FAITH)

UNCLEANNESS

Unity

Israel's need for, *"Hanging by a Thread"*—p. 285;
"The First King"—p. 308; *"Accent on Unity"*—
p. 445
goodness of, Psalm 133—p. 651
Jesus' prayer for, John 17—p. 1124
of early church, Acts 2:42—47—p. 1136; *"Paul the
Fund-raiser"*—p. 1191; *"Personality Cults"*—
p. 1197; *"Lessons from the Human Body"*—
p. 1204; *"No Second-Class Christians"*—p. 1222
absent in Corinth, 1 Corinthians 1—4—p. 1195
symbolized in Lord's Supper, 1 Corinthians
10:16—17—p. 1202; 11:17—34—p. 1203
in Christ, Galatians 3:26—28—p. 1226; Ephesians
4:1—16—p. 1232

URIM AND THUMMIM
God's instruction concerning, Exodus 28:30—p. 113
given to Aaron and descendants, Leviticus 8:8—p. 134;
Deuteronomy 33:8—11—p. 236
after the exile, *"The Need for Guidance"*—p. 501

VIRGIN BIRTH — the birth of Jesus Christ while his
mother Mary was a virgin
predicted, Isaiah 7:1—14—p. 718
described, Matthew 1:18—25—p. 997; Luke 1:26—38—
p. 1063

VISIONS — revelations; things seen through something
other than ordinary sight
as guidance, *"Appealing to a Vision"*—p. 542
Isaiah's, Isaiah 6—p. 717
Ezekiel's, Ezekiel 1—3—p. 849; 37:1—14—p. 884; *"Dry
Bones"*—p. 885
Daniel's, *"Kidnapped"*—p. 897; *"Symbols of Power"*—p. 907
in last days, Joel 2:28—32—p. 930
Peter's, Acts 10:1—11:18—p. 1147
Paul's, Acts 18:9—10—p. 1159; 2 Corinthians 12:1—10—
p. 1220
John's, Revelation 1—22—p. 1318

WAR (see also PEACE)
reasons for, *"Acts of War"*—p. 195; *"Reasons for Warfare"*—
p. 211; *"Is a War Ever Holy?"*—p. 249; *"Old Enemies"*—
p. 314; *"Comedy of Errors"*—p. 451
strategy in, *"War Strategy"*—p. 245; *"Battle Strategy"*—p. 328
methods of, *"Camel Power"*—p. 273; *"Military Setbacks"*—
p. 267; *"Everyone Watched Goliath"*—p. 316; *"Not Ready
for Chariots"*—p. 340
weapons for, *"Advanced Weaponry"*—p. 251; *"Deadly
Rocks"*—p. 317
preparing for, *"A Military Hero"*—p. 343
hired soldiers in, *"Mercenaries"*—p. 349
necessary limits of, *"Limits of a Just War"*—p. 487
God's hand in, Psalm 79—p. 620; *"World at War"*—p. 827
will end, Isaiah 2:1—5—p. 714
images from, *"Victory Party"*—p. 1212
spiritual, Ephesians 6:10—20—p. 1235; Revelation 12—p. 1327

WARNINGS
to Judah, *"Prophet, Poet, and Politician"*—p. 711; *"Isaiah in
His Prime"*—p. 738
to Christians, *"Like an Angry Letter from Home"*—p. 1196;
"Watch Out"—p. 880

WATER
as symbol, *"An Astounding Trade"*—p. 780; *"River from the
Temple"*—p. 895; John 4:10—14—p. 1105; John
7:37—38—p. 1111; Revelation 22:1—2—p. 1335
importance of, *"Waters of Babylon"*—p. 835

WEALTH (see also MONEY, POOR)
distribution of, *"Property Rights"*—p. 155
God's hand in, 1 Samuel 2:1—10—p. 298
Solomon's, *"The Man Who Had Everything"*—p. 362
of the wicked, *"Wicked People Prosper"*—p. 554; *"Money
Can't Buy Life"*—p. 602
arrogance in, Amos 6:1—7—p. 937; 1 Timothy 6:3—19 —
p. 1261
Jesus' teaching on, Matthew 19:16—30—p. 1019; *"The
Wealth Barrier"*—p. 1049
no favoritism toward those with, James 2:1—13—p. 1290
because of obedience, *"Healthier, Wealthier, and Wiser"*—
p. 213
reasons for, *"What Makes People Poor?"*—p. 669
doesn't bring happiness, *"When Life Seems Senseless"*—p. 693

WEAPONS — see WAR

WEEPING
of Joseph, *"Joseph in Tears"*—p. 73
of David, 2 Samuel 1—p. 333; 18:19—19:8—p. 353
doesn't last, *"One-night Guest"*—p. 590
of a woman with Jesus, Luke 7:36—50—p. 1072
of Jesus, Luke 19:41—44—p. 1090; John 11:1—43—p. 1115

WELFARE (see also POOR)
God's programs of, *"A Form of Welfare"*—p. 147; *"Tithe to
the Poor"*—p. 218; *"Don't Forget the Poor"*—p. 1216;
"Caring for the Poor"—p. 293
in the early church, *"Welfare Mentality"*—p. 1261

WIDOW — a woman whose husband is dead; in
ancient Israel a husband's death usually brought
poverty and powerlessness
special to God, Exodus 22:22—24—p. 107; Deuteronomy
24:17—22—p. 225; *"Poor and Helpless"*—p. 675
praised by Jesus, *"Exploiting Widows"*—p. 1053
in the church, 1 Corinthians 7:8—9—p. 1199; 1 Timothy
5:3—16;—p. 1259

WIFE (see also HUSBAND, MARRIAGE)
virtuous, Proverbs 31:10—31—p. 691
relationship to husband, Ephesians 5:21—33—p. 1234;
Colossians 3:18—19—p. 1245; 1 Peter 3:1—7—p. 1297

WILDERNESS — see DESERT

Will of God

in suffering, *"What Job Teaches about Suffering"*—
p. 567; 1 Peter 4:12—19—p. 1299
submission to, *"The Potter and the Clay"*—p. 798;
"Counseling Surrender"—p. 808; Matthew
26:36—46—p. 1029; James 4:13—15—p. 1292
Jesus came to do, John 4:34—p. 1105; 6:38—p. 1108;
Philippians 2:5—11—p. 1239
discovering, Romans 12:1—8—p. 1188;
1 Thessalonians 4:1—8—p. 1249
everything done in accordance with, Ephesians
1:3—14—p. 1230

WINE (see also DRINKING ALCOHOL)
used in Persia, *"The Influence of Wine"*—p. 530
drunkenness from, Proverbs 23:29—35—p. 683
in the Lord's Supper, Matthew 26:17—30—p. 1028
water into, John 2:1—11—p. 1102
for health, 1 Timothy 5:23—p. 1261

Z

The Student Bible, NIV

Notes written and edited by *Philip Yancey and Tim Stafford*

Project management and editorial by *Doris Rikkers and Sandra Vander Zicht (1986),
Dirk Buursma (1992), Michael Vander Klipp (1996)*

Interior design by *Sharon Wright, Belmont, MI*

Cover design by *Steve Allen, Snellville, GA*

Interior proofreading by *Peachtree Editorial and Proofreading Service, Peachtree City, GA*

Interior typesetting by *Auto-Graphics, Inc., Pomona, CA*

Printing and binding by *Quebecor Printing Kingsport, Kingsport, TN*

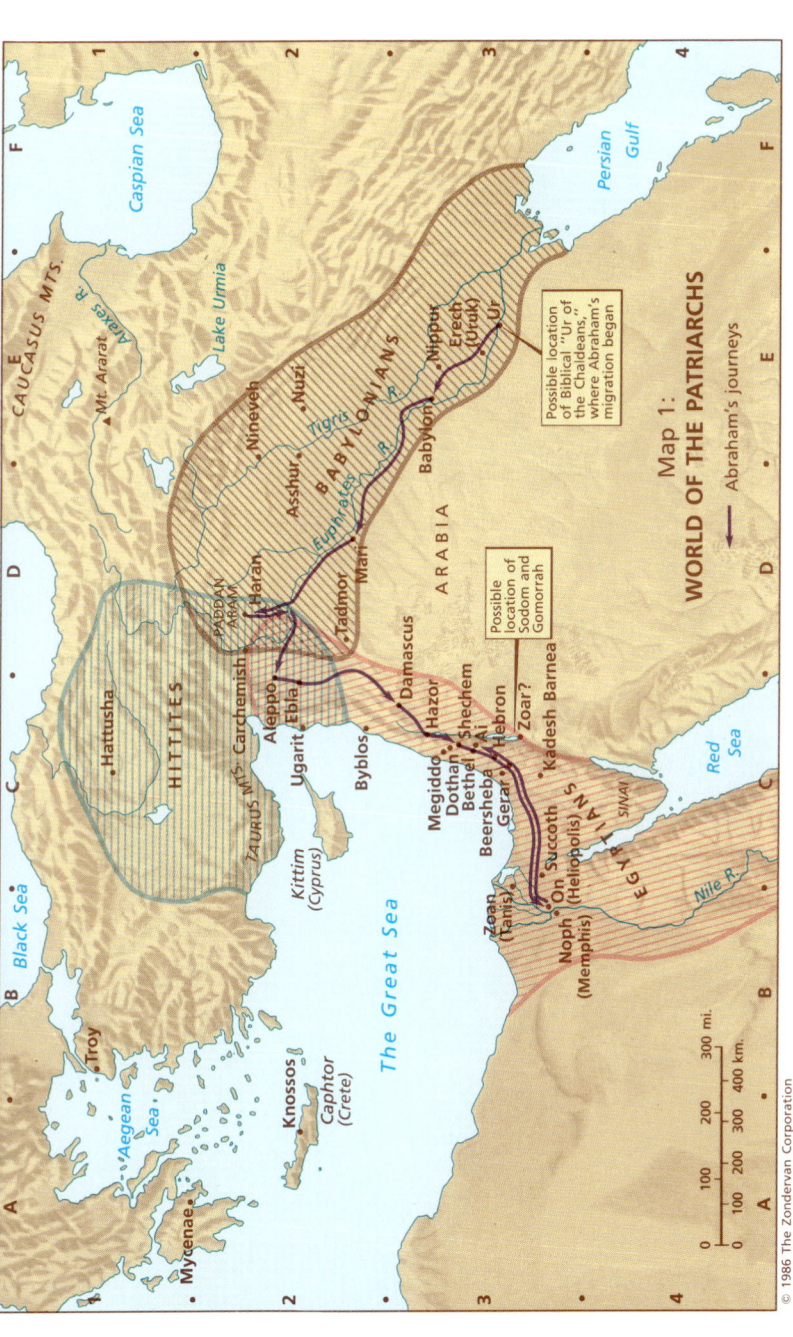

Map 1:
WORLD OF THE PATRIARCHS

→ Abraham's journeys

Possible location
of Biblical "Ur of
the Chaldeans,"
where Abraham's
migration began

Possible location
of Sodom and
Gomorrah

Caspian Sea

Black Sea

Persian Gulf

CAUCASUS MTS.

Mt. Ararat
Araxes R.
Lake Urmia

Nineveh
Asshur
Nuzi

Tigris R.
Euphrates R.

BABYLONIANS

Nippur
Erech
(Uruk)
Babylon
Ur

ARABIA

Haran
PADDAN ARAM
Tadmor
Mari

HITTITES
Hattusha
TAURUS MTS. Carchemish
Aleppo Ebla
Ugarit
Damascus
Hazor
Byblos
Megiddo Shechem
Dothan Ai
Bethel
Beersheba
Gerar Hebron Zoar?
Kadesh Barnea

EGYPTIANS
Succoth
On (Heliopolis)
Zoan (Tanis)
Noph (Memphis)
SINAI
Nile R.

Kittim (Cyprus)

The Great Sea

Red Sea

Troy
Mycenae
Aegean Sea
Knossos
Caphtor (Crete)

300 mi.
400 km.
0   100   200
0   100   200

© 1986 The Zondervan Corporation

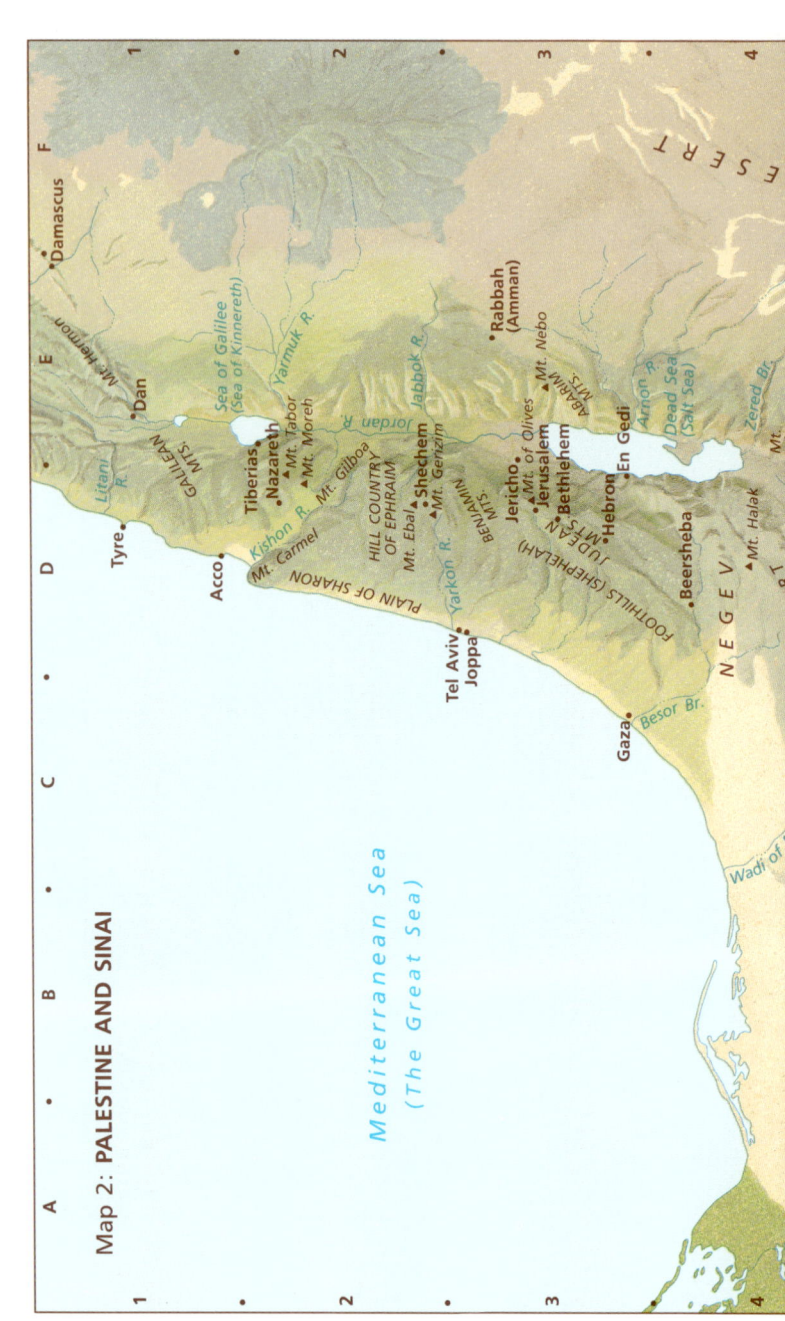

Map 2: **PALESTINE AND SINAI**

Mediterranean Sea
(The Great Sea)

Damascus

Mt. Hermon

Dan

GALILEE MTS.

Litani R.

Sea of Galilee
(Sea of Kinnereth)

Yarmuk R.

Tyre

Tiberias

Nazareth
Mt. Tabor
Mt. Moreh

Jordan R.

Rabbah
(Amman)

Mt. Nebo

Jabbok R.

Acco

Mt. Carmel

Kishon R.

Mt. Gilboa

HILL COUNTRY
OF EPHRAIM

Mt. Ebal
Shechem
Mt. Gerizim

ABARIM MTS.

En Gedi

Dead Sea
(Salt Sea)

Zered Br.

Arnon R.

Mt.

PLAIN OF SHARON

Yarkon R.

BENJAMIN MTS.

Jericho
Mt. of Olives
Jerusalem
Bethlehem

JUDEAN MTS.

Hebron

Tel Aviv
Joppa

FOOTHILLS (SHEPHELAH)

Beersheba

Mt. Halak

Gaza

Besor Br.

NEGEV

Wadi of E

DESERT

Little
Bitter
Lake

Lake

DESERT
OF
PARAN

S I N A I

DESERT
OF
SIN

DESERT
OF
SINAI

▲Mt. Sinai
(Mt. Horeb)

Ezion Geber

ARAB

EDO
DESER

E A S T E R

Red Sea

0   10   20   30   40 mi.

0 10 20 30 40 50 60 km.

A   B   C   D   E   F

5   6   7   8

© 1986 The Zondervan Corporation

Map 3: **EXODUS AND CONQUEST OF CANAAN**

Area controlled by ancient Israel
Probable route of wandering in the Sinai
Entry into and conquest of Canaan
✕ Battle

The Great Sea

Kedesh
Hazor
BASHAN
Merom
Sea of Kinnereth
Mt. Tabor
Edrei
Mt. Gilboa
Shechem
Shiloh
Bethel
Gilgal?
Abel Shittim
Gibeon
AMMON
Beth Horon
Ai
Jericho
Heshbon
Jarmuth
Jerusalem
Mt. Nebo
Azekah
Libnah?
Lachish?
Hebron
Jahaz?
Eglon?
Makkedah?
Dibon
Debir?
Arnon R.
Beersheba
Iye Abarim?
Salt Sea
Zered Br.

EGYPT
Rameses
GOSHEN
Pithom?
Succoth
Lake Menzaleh
DESERT OF SHUR
Wadi of Egypt
DESERT OF ZIN
Oboth?
Punon
On (Heliopolis)
Great Bitter Lake
Kadesh Barnea
Noph (Memphis)
Besor Br.
PHILISTIA
MOAB
EDOM
Nile River
Marah?
SINAI
Elim?
DESERT OF PARAN
Ezion Geber
Dophkah?
Hazeroth?
DESERT OF SIN
MIDIAN
Rephidim?
Mt. Sinai (traditional location)
Red Sea

0   25   50   75 mi.
0   25   50   75   100 km.

© 1986 The Zondervan Corporation

Map 4:
LAND OF THE TWELVE TRIBES

⊙ Cities of refuge
• Other cities

© 1986 The Zondervan Corporation

Map 5:
KINGDOM OF DAVID AND SOLOMON

Saul's kingdom
David and Solomon's kingdom
Territory under Solomon's control

© 1986 The Zondervan Corporation

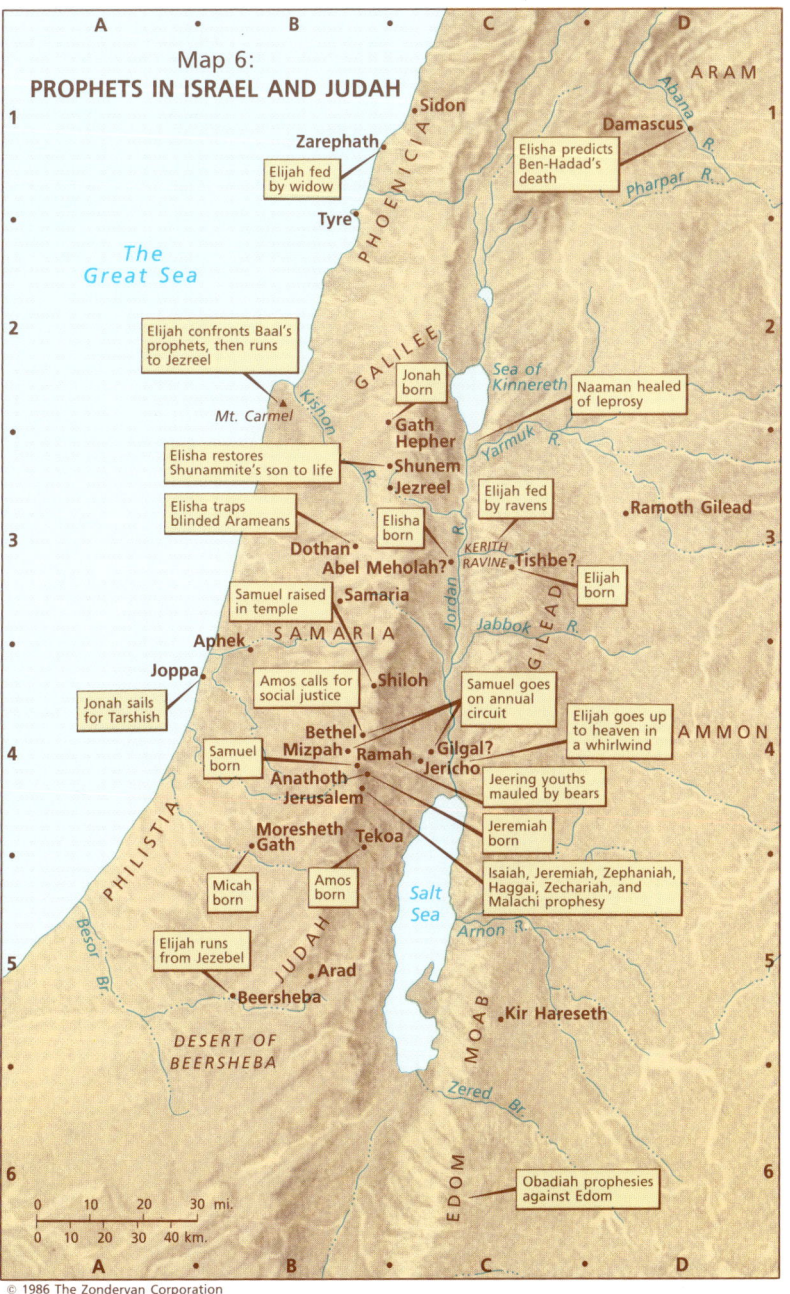

Map 6:
PROPHETS IN ISRAEL AND JUDAH

ARAM

A · B · C · D

The Great Sea

1 Sidon
Zarephath
Elijah fed by widow
Tyre

Damascus
Elisha predicts Ben-Hadad's death

Abana R.
Pharpar R.

PHOENICIA

2 Elijah confronts Baal's prophets, then runs to Jezreel

GALILEE

Mt. Carmel
Kishon

Jonah born
Gath Hepher

Sea of Kinnereth

Naaman healed of leprosy

Yarmuk R.

Elisha restores Shunammite's son to life
Shunem
Jezreel

Elijah fed by ravens

Ramoth Gilead

3 Elisha traps blinded Arameans

Dothan
Abel Meholah?

Elisha born

KERITH RAVINE
Tishbe?

Elijah born

Jordan R.
Jabbok R.

GILEAD

Samuel raised in temple
Samaria

SAMARIA

Aphek

Joppa

Amos calls for social justice
Shiloh

Jonah sails for Tarshish

Samuel goes on annual circuit

Elijah goes up to heaven in a whirlwind

AMMON

4 Samuel born

Bethel
Mizpah
Ramah
Gilgal?
Jericho

Jeering youths mauled by bears

Anathoth
Jerusalem

Jeremiah born

PHILISTIA

Moresheth Gath
Tekoa

Isaiah, Jeremiah, Zephaniah, Haggai, Zechariah, and Malachi prophesy

Micah born
Amos born

Salt Sea

Arnon R.

5 Elijah runs from Jezebel
Arad

Beersheba

JUDAH

MOAB

Kir Hareseth

DESERT OF BEERSHEBA

Besor Br.

Zered Br.

EDOM

6 Obadiah prophesies against Edom

0   10   20   30 mi.
0 10 20 30 40 km.

© 1986 The Zondervan Corporation

Map 7a:
ASSYRIAN EMPIRE (c. 700 B.C.)

— Exiles from Israel into
  Assyrian captivity (722 B.C.)

0   100   200   300 mi.
0 100 200 300 400 km.

Map 7b: BABYLONIAN EMPIRE (c. 600 B.C.)

— Exiles from Judah into Babylonian captivity (605, 597, 586 B.C.)
— Return of exiles under Sheshbazzar and Zerubbabel (537 B.C.)
— Return of exiles under Ezra (458 B.C.) and Nehemiah (445 B.C.)

0   100   200   300 mi.
0 100 200 300 400 km.

© 1986 The Zondervan Corporation

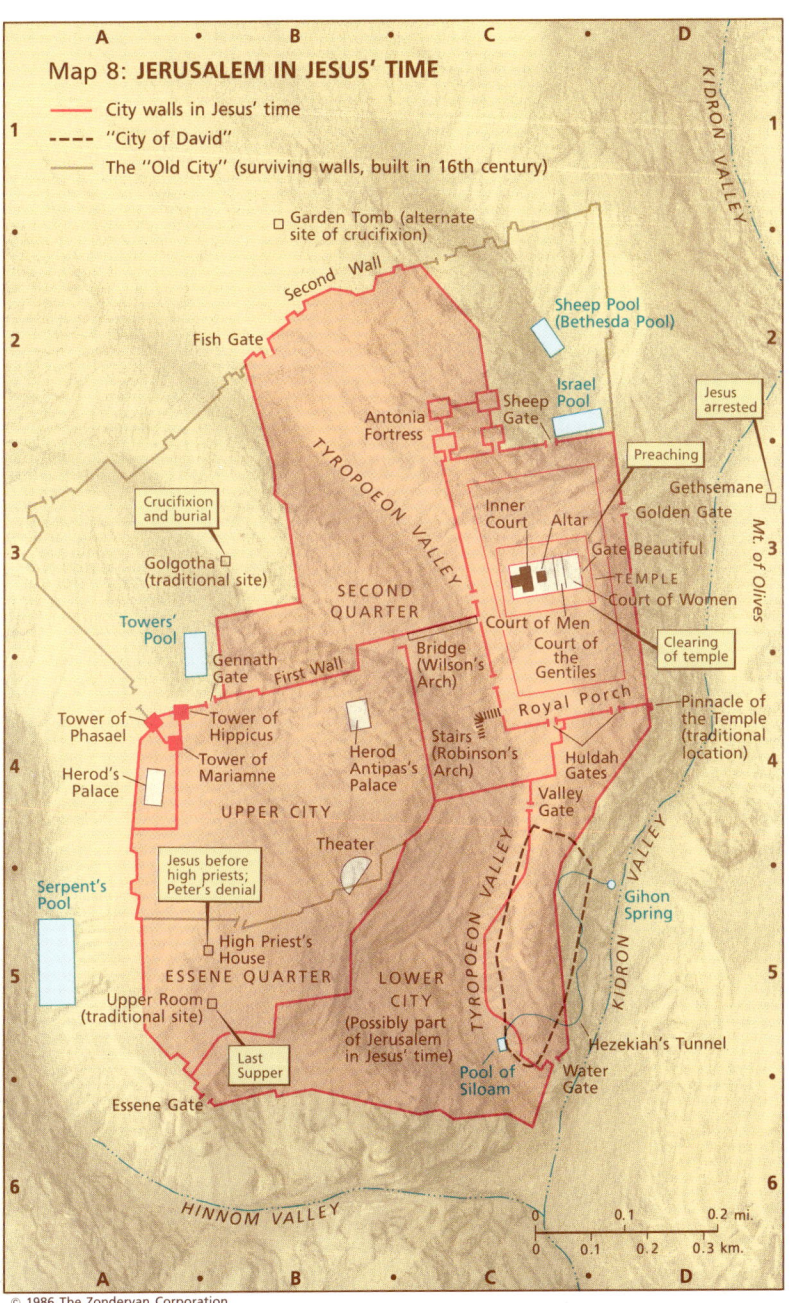

Map 8: JERUSALEM IN JESUS' TIME

— City walls in Jesus' time
- - - "City of David"
— The "Old City" (surviving walls, built in 16th century)

KIDRON VALLEY

Garden Tomb (alternate site of crucifixion)

Second Wall

Sheep Pool (Bethesda Pool)

Fish Gate

Israel Pool

Jesus arrested

Antonia Fortress

Sheep Gate

Preaching

Crucifixion and burial

Inner Court

Altar

Gethsemane

Golden Gate

Gate Beautiful

TEMPLE

Golgotha (traditional site)

SECOND QUARTER

Court of Women

Mt. of Olives

TYROPOEON VALLEY

Towers' Pool

Court of Men

Court of the Gentiles

Clearing of temple

Gennath Gate

First Wall

Bridge (Wilson's Arch)

Royal Porch

Tower of Phasael

Tower of Hippicus

Stairs (Robinson's Arch)

Pinnacle of the Temple (traditional location)

Herod's Palace

Tower of Mariamne

Herod Antipas's Palace

Huldah Gates

UPPER CITY

Theater

Valley Gate

Jesus before high priests; Peter's denial

Serpent's Pool

High Priest's House

ESSENE QUARTER

LOWER CITY

TYROPOEON VALLEY

KIDRON VALLEY

Gihon Spring

Upper Room (traditional site)

(Possibly part of Jerusalem in Jesus' time)

Last Supper

Hezekiah's Tunnel

Essene Gate

Pool of Siloam

Water Gate

HINNOM VALLEY

0   0.1   0.2 mi.
0   0.1   0.2   0.3 km.

© 1986 The Zondervan Corporation

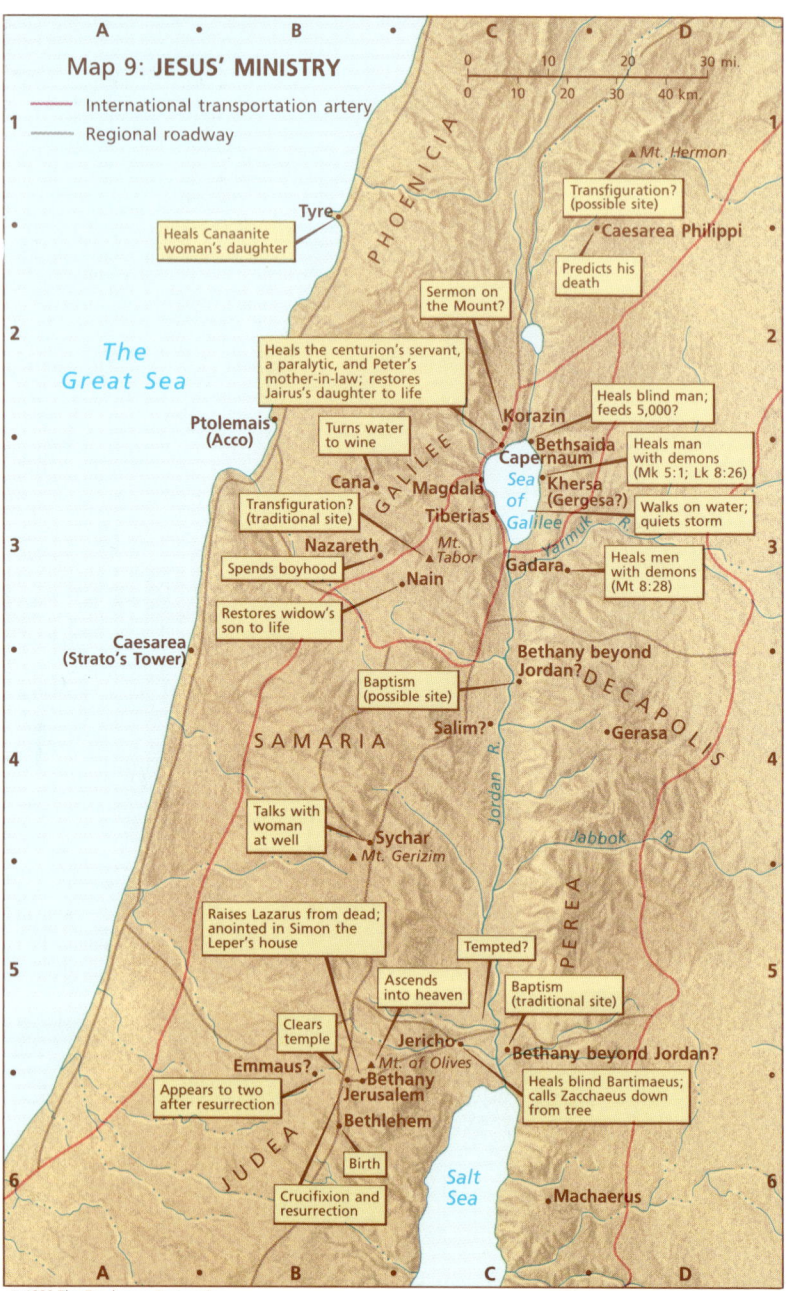

Map 9: JESUS' MINISTRY

International transportation artery
Regional roadway

A   B   C   D

1

PHOENICIA

▲ Mt. Hermon

Transfiguration?
(possible site)

● Caesarea Philippi

Predicts his
death

Tyre ●

Heals Canaanite
woman's daughter

The
Great Sea

2

Sermon on
the Mount?

Heals the centurion's servant,
a paralytic, and Peter's
mother-in-law; restores
Jairus's daughter to life

Korazin ●

Heals blind man;
feeds 5,000?

Ptolemais
(Acco) ●

Turns water
to wine

Bethsaida

GALILEE

Capernaum

Heals man
with demons
(Mk 5:1; Lk 8:26)

Cana ●

Magdala ●

Sea
of
Galilee

Khersa
(Gergesa?)

Walks on water;
quiets storm

Transfiguration?
(traditional site)

Tiberias ●

Nazareth ●

▲ Mt.
Tabor

Yarmuk R.

3

Spends boyhood

Gadara ●

Heals men
with demons
(Mt 8:28)

● Nain

Restores widow's
son to life

Caesarea
(Strato's Tower) ●

Bethany beyond
Jordan?

DECAPOLIS

Baptism
(possible site)

Salim? ●

4

SAMARIA

Jordan R.

● Gerasa

Talks with
woman
at well

Sychar ●
▲ Mt. Gerizim

Jabbok R.

PEREA

Raises Lazarus from dead;
anointed in Simon the
Leper's house

Tempted?

5

Ascends
into heaven

Baptism
(traditional site)

Clears
temple

Jericho ●

▲ Mt. of Olives

Bethany beyond Jordan?

Emmaus? ●

● Bethany
Jerusalem ●

Heals blind Bartimaeus;
calls Zacchaeus down
from tree

Appears to two
after resurrection

Bethlehem ●

JUDEA

Birth

Salt
Sea

6

Crucifixion and
resurrection

● Machaerus

0   10   20   30 mi.
0   10   20   30   40 km.

© 1986 The Zondervan Corporation

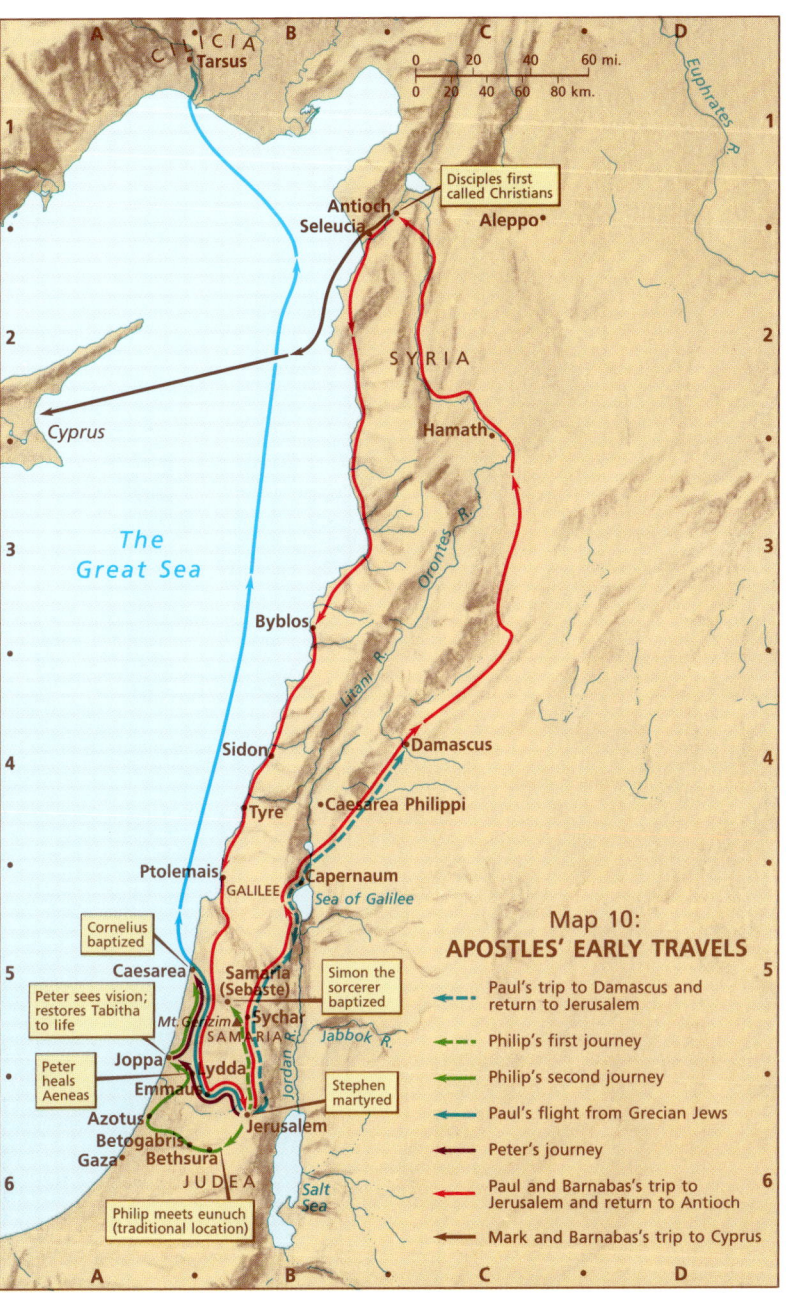

Map 10:
APOSTLES' EARLY TRAVELS

- - - ▶ Paul's trip to Damascus and return to Jerusalem
- - - ▶ Philip's first journey
───▶ Philip's second journey
───▶ Paul's flight from Grecian Jews
───▶ Peter's journey
───▶ Paul and Barnabas's trip to Jerusalem and return to Antioch
───▶ Mark and Barnabas's trip to Cyprus

Disciples first called Christians

Cornelius baptized

Peter sees vision; restores Tabitha to life

Peter heals Aeneas

Simon the sorcerer baptized

Stephen martyred

Philip meets eunuch (traditional location)

CILICIA
Tarsus
Antioch
Seleucia
Aleppo

S Y R I A

Hamath

The Great Sea

Byblos

Orontes R.

Litani R.

Sidon
Damascus

Tyre
Caesarea Philippi

Ptolemais
Capernaum
GALILEE
Sea of Galilee

Caesarea
Samaria (Sebaste)
Sychar
Mt. Gerizim
SAMARIA
Jabbok R.
Joppa
Lydda
Emmaus
Jerusalem
Azotus
Betogabris
Gaza
Bethsura
J U D E A
Salt Sea

Jordan R.

Cyprus

Euphrates R.

© 1986 The Zondervan Corporation

Map 11:
PAUL'S MISSIONARY JOURNEYS

— First Missionary Journey (A.D. 46–48)
— Second Missionary Journey (A.D. 49–52)
— Third Missionary Journey (A.D. 53–57)
— Trip to Rome (A.D. 59–60)

© 1986 The Zondervan Corporation

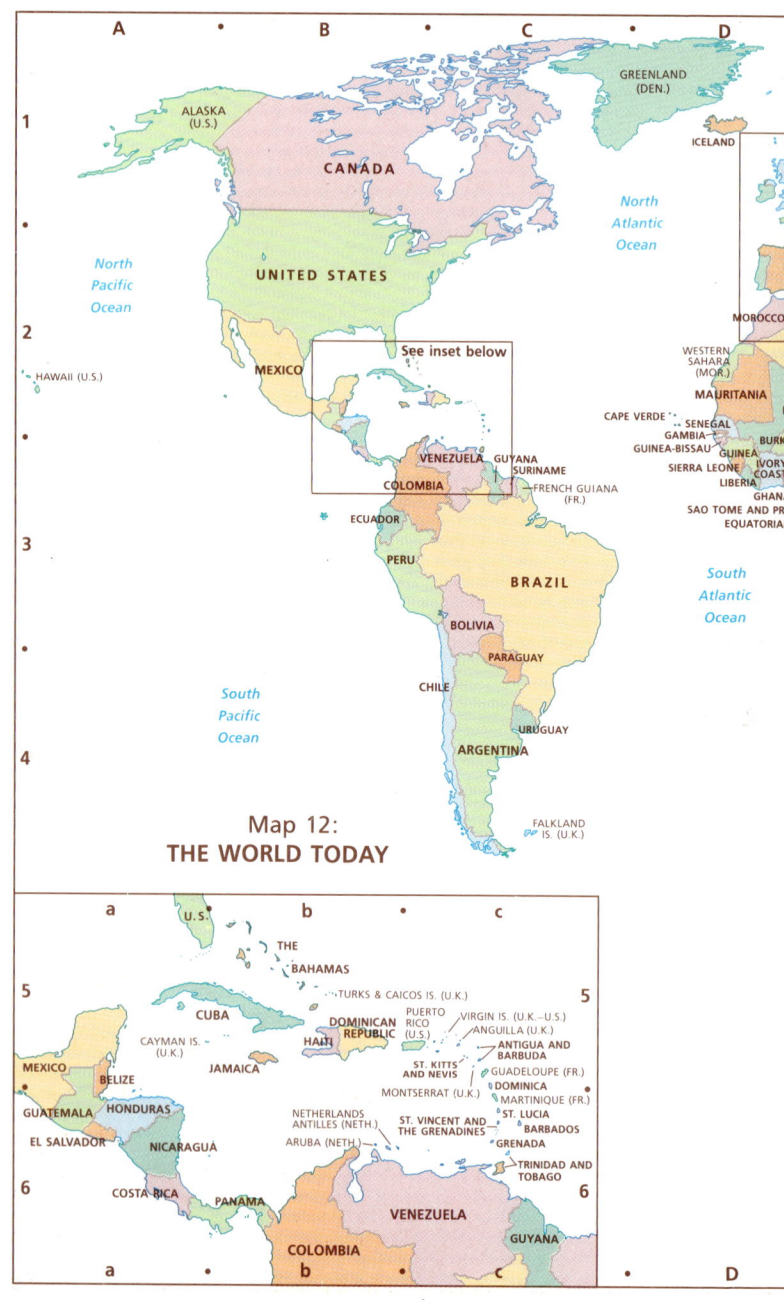

Map 12:
THE WORLD TODAY

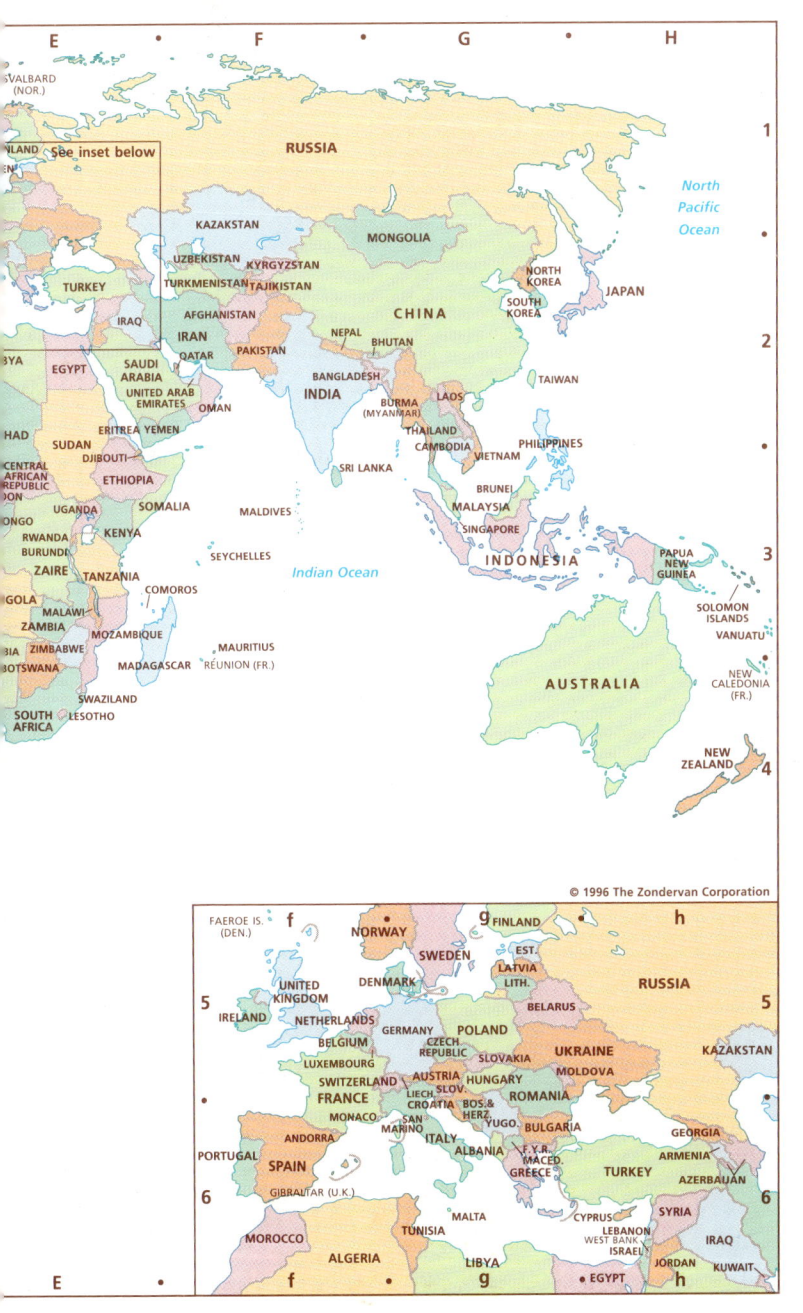

E   F   G   H

SVALBARD
(NOR.)

RUSSIA

1

NLAND

EN

See inset below

North
Pacific
Ocean

KAZAKSTAN

MONGOLIA

UZBEKISTAN KYRGYZSTAN

NORTH
KOREA

JAPAN

TURKEY

TURKMENISTAN TAJIKISTAN

CHINA

SOUTH
KOREA

IRAQ

AFGHANISTAN

IRAN

NEPAL

BHUTAN

2

YA

EGYPT

SAUDI
ARABIA

PAKISTAN

QATAR

BANGLADESH

TAIWAN

UNITED ARAB
EMIRATES

INDIA

BURMA
(MYANMAR)

LAOS

OMAN

YEMEN

THAILAND

HAD

SUDAN

ERITREA

DJIBOUTI

CAMBODIA

VIETNAM

PHILIPPINES

CENTRAL
AFRICAN
REPUBLIC
OON

ETHIOPIA

SRI LANKA

BRUNEI

UGANDA

SOMALIA

MALDIVES

MALAYSIA

ONGO

RWANDA

KENYA

SINGAPORE

BURUNDI

ZAIRE

TANZANIA

SEYCHELLES

Indian Ocean

INDONESIA

3

PAPUA
NEW
GUINEA

IGOLA

MALAWI

COMOROS

ZAMBIA

SOLOMON
ISLANDS

BIA

ZIMBABWE

MOZAMBIQUE

MAURITIUS

VANUATU

BOTSWANA

MADAGASCAR

RÉUNION (FR.)

AUSTRALIA

NEW
CALEDONIA
(FR.)

SWAZILAND

SOUTH
AFRICA

LESOTHO

NEW
ZEALAND

4

© 1996 The Zondervan Corporation

FAEROE IS.
(DEN.)

f

NORWAY

g

FINLAND

h

SWEDEN

EST.

LATVIA

RUSSIA

UNITED
KINGDOM

DENMARK

LITH.

5

IRELAND

NETHERLANDS

BELARUS

5

BELGIUM

GERMANY

POLAND

KAZAKSTAN

LUXEMBOURG

CZECH
REPUBLIC

SLOVAKIA

UKRAINE

SWITZERLAND

AUSTRIA

HUNGARY

MOLDOVA

FRANCE

LIECH. SLOV.

MONACO

CROATIA

ROMANIA

SAN
MARINO

BOS.&
HERZ.

YUGO.

GEORGIA

ANDORRA

ITALY

BULGARIA

PORTUGAL

SPAIN

ALBANIA

F.Y.R.
MACED.

TURKEY

ARMENIA

AZERBAIJAN

GIBRALTAR (U.K.)

GREECE

6

MALTA

CYPRUS

SYRIA

6

TUNISIA

LEBANON

WEST BANK

IRAQ

MOROCCO

ALGERIA

LIBYA

ISRAEL

JORDAN

KUWAIT

EGYPT

E   f   g   h

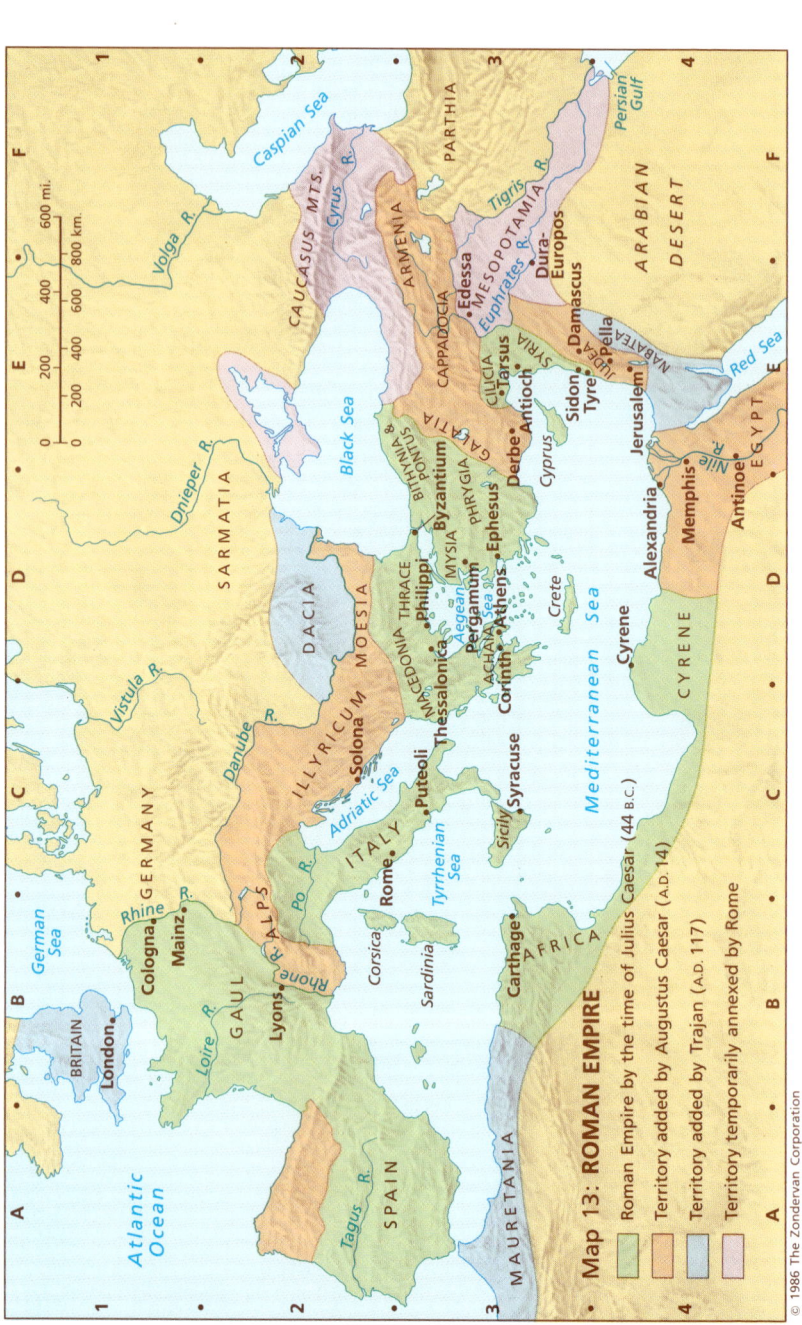

Map 13: **ROMAN EMPIRE**

Roman Empire by the time of Julius Caesar (44 B.C.)

Territory added by Augustus Caesar (A.D. 14)

Territory added by Trajan (A.D. 117)

Territory temporarily annexed by Rome

© 1986 The Zondervan Corporation